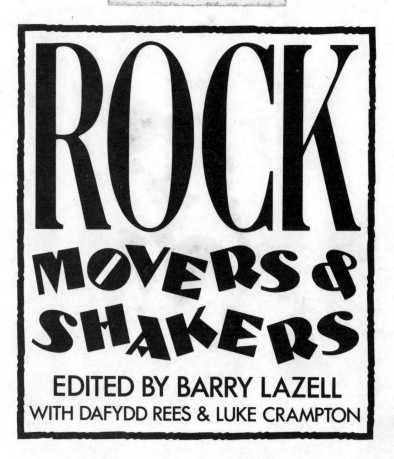

ROCK MOVERS & SHAKERS

EDITED BY BARRY LAZELL
WITH DAFYDD REES & LUKE CRAMPTON

BILLBOARD PUBLICATIONS, INC./NEW YORK

A Banson Production

Compiled by Luke Crampton, Barry Lazell & Dafydd Rees

Edited by Reet Nelis, Anne Tauté
Ben Barkow, Charlotte Pettifar

Designed by Jim Wire Graphic Design

Typeset by System Graphics Ltd.

Origination by Brian Fretwell Associates Ltd.

Printed by Snoeck Ducaju & Zoon N.V., Belgium

First published 1989 in the United States and Canada by Billboard Publications, Inc., 1515 Broadway, New York, N.Y. 10036.

Library of Congress Cataloging-in-Publication Data

Rock movers and shakers.

1. Rock musicians--Biography. I. Lazell, Barry.
ML385.R736 1988 784.5′4′00922 [B] 88-19260
ISBN 0-8230-7608-3

Simultaneously published in the United Kingdom by Guinness Books.

First Printing, 1989

1 2 3 4 5 6 7 8 9/94 93 92 91 90 89

Front cover illustrations (from left to right):
Frankie Avalon, Chuck Berry, Elvis Costello, Bob Dylan, The Everly Brothers, Connie Francis, Marvyn Gaye, Whitney Houston, Billy Idol, Michael Jackson, Kiss, Cyndi Lauper.
Back cover: Madonna, Willie Nelson, Roy Orbison, Prince, Suzi Quatro, David Lee Roth (Van Halen), Bruce Springsteen, Tina Turner, U2, Ritchie Valens, Tom Waits, XTC, Neil Young, Frank Zappa.

Photographs:
John Beecher pp 105, 142, 149, 173, 234, 299; Live Aid 403;
Philip Parr 370; Rex Features 5, 10, 15, 24, 26, 72, 115, 118, 141, 144, 152, 191, 195, 292, 310, 334, 338, 340, 375, 384, 408, 427, 448. All others courtesy of MRIB, Luke Crampton, Barry Lazell, Dafydd Rees.

INTRODUCTION

This book has been compiled as an entertaining reference work with the primary objective of identifying the major acts which have been influential in the development of rock music over the past 30 years, and chronologically documenting their careers.

Most readers will have their own particular favorites, but the choice of entries was limited by space. It was necessary to maintain a balance between acts important in US and UK and to present, without opinion, acts which have a fascinating history but little chart impact, and others with an endless chart career but limited biography.

In assembling this chronology, it was not possible to update all entries as the cut-off date varied between April and December 1988. Subsequent editions of the book will allow updates and may exclude artists currently important to pop culture if their careers fail to develop.

For group entries, the line-up (with instrument played) is either the original one or the best-known. The chronological information is as complete as possible with the year, month and exact day, if available, but research revealed many conflicting dates. Entries include all US and UK peak chart positions for each act and records are singles unless LP or EP is stated. A degree sign after an artist's or group's name denotes a separate entry in the book for that act.

Source material includes *Billboard*, Joel Whitburn's *Top Pop Singles* and *Albums*, Fred Bronson's *Book of Number One Hits*, Guinness *Hit Singles* and *Albums*, *Radio & Records*, *Rolling Stone*, *Record Collector*, miscellaneous US and UK rock magazines and books, three record company biographies and numerous LP sleeve notes.

Special thanks to Pete, Karen, Lea, Frances, Jam and Lewis, and all at MRIB; and to contributors Pete Frame, Peter Compton, Chris May, John Tracy and Adam Douglas.

Dedications and apologies to Linda, Elaine and Marilyn.

ABBA

Benny Andersson (keyboard, synthesizer and vocals)
Bjorn Ulvaeus (guitar and vocals)
Agnetha Faltskog (vocals)
Frida (Anni-Frid) Lyngstad (vocals)

1970 Nov Andersson (b. Dec.16, 1946, Stockholm, Sweden), Ulvaeus (b. Apr.25, 1945, Gothenberg, Sweden), Faltskog (b. Apr.5, 1950, Jonkopping, Sweden) and Lyngstad (b. Nov.15, 1945, Narvik, Norway) first perform together in public, at a Gothenberg restaurant. All are already Swedish recording acts: the girls as solo performers; the men as a duo (songwriting and performing) and as former members of groups like The Hep Stars and Hootenanny Singers. Andersson and Lyngstad are engaged, as are Ulvaeus and Faltskog.

1971 July [7] Ulvaeus and Faltskog marry in Verum, Sweden.

Oct Andersson and Ulvaeus become producer partners at Polar Music, owned by Stig Anderson.

1972 June *People Need Love* is released in Sweden under the name "Bjorn, Benny, Agnetha & Frida", and hits #2. Issued in US, it makes US #115.

1973 Jan Andersson, Ulvaeus and manager Stig Anderson are asked to submit a song for the Swedish heat of the Eurovision Song Contest. They produce *Ring Ring*, which the quartet records and agrees to perform.

Feb *Ring Ring* fails to be chosen as Swedish Eurovision entry but is recorded in Swedish, German, Spanish and English (lyrics for the latter provided by Neil Sedaka° and Phil Cody) for a single on which their names are first shortened to Abba (from the four initials).

Feb [23] Linda Ulvaeus, daughter of Bjorn and Agnetha, is born in Stockholm.

Apr/June *Ring Ring*, in Swedish, tops all the Scandinavian charts, and an English version is #1 in Austria, Holland, Belgium and South Africa.

Oct *Ring Ring* is released in UK, unsuccessfully.

1974 Feb A new Andersson/Ulvaeus/Anderson song *Waterloo*, in English, is accepted as Sweden's Eurovision entry.

Apr *Waterloo* wins the Eurovision Song Contest held in Brighton, UK, and charts immediately in UK, hitting #1.

June *Waterloo* charts in US, at #6. Abba makes first US trip to promote it, appearing on TV's "Mike Douglas Show".

July *Ring Ring* is reissued in UK, but only achieves #32.

Sept *Honey Honey* is US follow-up, and reaches #27.

Nov First major European tour, covers Denmark, West Germany, Austria and Switzerland. *So Long* is issued as a UK single, but flops.

1975 July *I Do, I Do, I Do, I Do, I Do* charts in UK after 3 months on issue, reaching #38.

Aug *S.O.S.* is released in US, eventually reaching #15, and Abba visits US for a promotional tour.

Sept *S.O.S.* is released in UK where it restores them to the top 10 at #6.

1976 Jan *Mamma Mia* is second UK #1 hit, ending the 9-week reign of *Bohemian Rhapsody* by Queen°.

Apr *Fernando* hits UK #1, while *I Do, I Do, I Do, I Do, I Do* marks US top 20 return at #15. LP Greatest Hits is the first of their eight consecutive #1 UK LPs, while in Australia they also have *Fernando* at #1, plus four other singles in the same top 30.

June [18] Royal performance in Stockholm for Sweden's King and his Queen-to-be, the day before the royal wedding.

July *Mamma Mia* reaches only #32 in US.

Aug *Dancing Queen* becomes their third consecutive UK #1, and sells over 850,000 copies.

Oct *Fernando* makes #13 in US, and Abba visits for extensive network TV appearances.

Nov LP *Arrival* is released in 34 countries simultaneously, and will reach #1 in UK and #20 in US.

Dec *Money Money Money*, taken from the LP, climbs to UK #3. Tickets go on sale for Abba's forthcoming show at London's Royal Albert Hall, and 3½ million applications arrive for only 11,000 seats.

1977 Feb First UK live dates, including [14] two Royal Albert Hall performances. *Knowing Me, Knowing You* is issued in UK, and goes to #1.

Mar *Abba – The Movie* is filmed at the end of a world tour in Australia.

Apr *Dancing Queen* hits US #1, having climbed the chart since Dec. It is Abba's biggest US seller and only chart-topper.

July *Knowing Me, Knowing You* reaches #14 in US.

ABBA *cont.*

Oct *The Name Of The Game* hits UK #1.
Nov *Money Money Money*, belatedly issued in US, is only a minor hit, climbing to #56.
Dec [4] Peter Ulvaeus, son of Bjorn and Agnetha, is born in Stockholm.
1978 Jan *Abba – The Album* is released, entering UK LP chart at #1.
Feb [16] *Abba – The Movie* has a UK première in London.
Feb *Take A Chance On Me* tops UK chart, completing a second consecutive #1 hat-trick.
Apr *Take A Chance On Me* charts in US, climbing to #3 and earning a gold disk for one million sales.
May Abba's Polar Studio in Stockholm, one of the most advanced in the world, is completed.
June [12] *Abba – The Album* sells its millionth copy in UK.
Sept *Summer Night City* charts in UK, reaching #5.
Oct [6] Andersson and Lyngstad marry in Sweden, with no publicity.
Dec [24] Ulvaeus and Faltskog separate and announce they are filing for divorce.
1979 Jan [8] In New York, Abba participates in UNICEF gala for The Year of the Child, along with acts like Donna Summer°, Rod Stewart°, The Bee Gees°, and Earth, Wind & Fire°. They sing *Chiquitita*, donating all subsequent royalties from it to UNICEF.
Feb *Chiquitita* charts in UK, reaching #2.
May *Does Your Mother Know?* and LP *Voulez Vous* are released. The LP is a UK #1 and sells a million in 5 weeks; the single charts at UK #4 and US #19.
July Double A-side *Angeleyes/Voulez Vous* is released in UK, hitting #3.
Sept [13] First-ever North American tour opens in Edmonton, Canada.
Sept *Angeleyes/Voulez Vous* is issued in US, but charts disappointingly at #64.
Oct *Gimme Gimme Gimme (A Man After Midnight)* is released in UK, and hits #3.
Oct [19] A tour begins of nine European countries, ending in UK.
Nov LP *Greatest Hits Vol.2* is released in UK to coincide with six sold-out Wembley Arena concerts.
Dec *I Have A Dream* charts in UK, climbing to #2. *Chiquitita* charts in US and reaches #29.
1980 Aug *The Winner Takes It All* is first Abba UK #1 hit for 2½ years.
Nov Single and LP *Super Trouper* are released in UK; both are instant chart-toppers.
1981 Jan Ulvaeus marries Lena Kallessjo, in Stockholm.
Feb Andersson and Lyngstad decide to divorce.
Mar *The Winner Takes It All* reaches US #8, their first US top 10 hit for 2½ years.
May *Super Trouper* reaches US #45.
July Disco-styled *Lay All Your Love On Me* is released in UK as a 12" single only, aimed at the disco market. It hits #7.
Dec *One Of Us* and LP *The Visitors* are released in UK. The single hits #3 and is Abba's last UK top 10 single; the LP is another #1.
1982 Jan [3] A daughter, Emma Ulvaeus is born to Bjorn and Lena.
Jan [10] Ludvig Andersson is born, son of Benny and his new fiancée.
Feb *Head Over Heels* reaches UK #25.
Mar *When All Is Said And Done* is their final US hit, reaching #27.
Aug First concrete sign that Abba members are going their separate ways in music as well as their personal lives: Lyngstad releases solo LP *Something's Going On* and *I Know There's Something Going On*, which hit UK #18 and #43 respectively. The single will reach US #13 in 1983.
Oct *The Day Before You Came* reaches #32 in UK.
Nov Double LP anthology *The Singles: The First Ten Years* completes the group's run of UK #1 LPs, and is a huge Christmas seller.
Dec *Under Attack* charts at UK #26. Also included on *The Singles*, this is the final Abba recording.
1983 May Faltskog begins a solo hit-making career with *The Heat Is On*, which charts at UK #35. No official notice that Abba is over comes from the four members (but from now on both female vocalists will pursue solo work, while Andersson and Ulvaeus, still writing and producing at Polar Studios, will begin a collaboration with UK lyricist Tim Rice that results in the musical *Chess*, in 1985).
Nov Abba's last UK hit single is appropriate: *Thank You For The Music*, the old airplay and stage favorite from *Abba – The Album* in 1978. It reaches #33, leaving Abba only 4 months short of a decade of entries on the UK charts.

ABC

Martin Fry (vocals)
Mark White (guitar)
Stephen Singleton (saxophone)
Mark Lickley (bass)
David Palmer (drums)

1980 The band is formed in Sheffield, UK, when Fry joins White and Singleton after interviewing them for his fanzine *Modern Drugs* in their former group Vice Versa.
Dec First live performance as ABC, in Sheffield. The name is because "the first 3 letters of the alphabet are known the world over".
1981 They sign to Phonogram Records, for releases on their own Neutron label in UK and Mercury in US.
Nov Debut single *Tears Are Not Enough* charts in UK, reaching #19.
1982 Mar *Poison Arrow* is first UK top 10 hit, climbing to #6.
June *The Look Of Love* hits UK #4.
July LP *The Lexicon Of Love*, produced by Trevor Horn (ex-Yes°), enters UK LP chart at #1. ABC tours UK, then begins a world tour.
Sept *All Of My Heart* hits UK #5.
Dec *The Look Of Love*, their US chart debut, reaches #18, aided by MTV video promotion. LP *The Lexicon Of Love* climbs to US #30. World tour reaches the US and boosts sales.
1983 Mar *Poison Arrow* reaches US #25.
May Drummer David Palmer leaves.
Nov *That Was Then But This Is Now* makes #18 in UK, but only #89 in US. LP *Beauty Stab*, produced this time by ABC, reaches UK #12.
1984 Feb *S.O.S.* reaches UK #39, and LP *Beauty Stab* climbs to US #69.
Nov *(How To Be A) Millionaire* reaches UK #49. It is produced by Fry and White, now the only full band members, as Singleton and Lickley have left and been replaced by session players for recordings.
1985 Apr *Be Near Me* climbs to UK #26.
Oct LP *How To Be A Zillionaire* reaches UK #28 and US #30.
Nov *Be Near Me* belatedly gives ABC their first US top 10 hit, at #9. A disco remix of it is a huge US club favorite, and a dance chart #1.

1986 Jan *Ocean Blue* reaches UK #51.
Mar *(How To Be A) Millionaire* reaches US #20.
1987 After Fry has been seriously ill and recuperated, he and White start writing and recording again.
June *When Smokey Sings*, a tribute to Smokey Robinson°, first release from sessions with US producer Bernard Edwards, reaches UK #11.
Sept *When Smokey Sings* hits US #5.

Oct *The Night You Murdered Love* climbs to #31, and LP *Alphabet City* makes UK #7.
Dec *King Without A Crown* reaches UK #44.

AC/DC

Angus Young (guitar)
Malcolm Young (guitar)
Bon (Ronald) Scott (vocals)
Brian Johnson (vocals)
Mark Evans (bass)
Cliff Williams (bass)
Phillip Rudd (drums)
Simon Wright (drums)

1973 Dec Angus Young (b. Mar.31, 1959, Glasgow, Scotland, UK) and brother Malcolm (b. Jan.6, 1953, Glasgow), debut the group in a bar in Sydney, Australia, to which the family emigrated in 1963. Other original members are local playing friends, none permanent.
1974 Mar Fellow immigrant Bon Scott (b. July 9, 1946, Kirriemuir, Scotland) joins as vocalist, and the band moves to Melbourne, where Rudd (b. May 19, 1946, Melbourne, Aus.) and Evans (b. Melbourne) join.
Apr/Dec AC/DC tours Australia, building a live following for an exuberant hard rock style. They sign to Albert Productions label, run by producers Harry Vanda and George Young (both ex-Easybeats°; Young is also older brother of Angus and Malcolm). Debut LP *High Voltage* is released in Australia only.
1975 Jan/Dec They tour Australia, where their second Australia-only LP *TNT* is released.
1976 Jan Upon signing to Atlantic Records, the band moves base to UK, where early dates are at the Marquee and other London clubs.
Apr The release of first UK single *It's A Long Way To The Top* is accompanied by a national tour supporting Back Street Crawler.
May UK LP *High Voltage* is released, with tracks from earlier Australian LPs.
June First headlining UK tour, billed as the *"Lock Up Your Daughters"* tour. Their visual image, with Angus Young as a short-trousered, naughty schoolboy, helps build their following.
July European tour, supporting Rainbow°.
Aug Second UK tour and appearance at Reading Rock Festival accompany the release of *Jailbreak*.
Oct First US visit, playing clubs.
Dec LP *Dirty Deeds Done Dirt Cheap* is released in UK, but does not chart. The band returns to Australia for a 26-date year-end tour, and stays for the recording of next LP in Sydney with Vanda and Young.
1977 Feb/May UK tour, playing material just recorded and as yet unheard on LP. Second European tour, supporting Black Sabbath°.
June Evans leaves and Cliff Williams (b. Dec.14, 1949, Romford, UK), replaces him on bass.
July AC/DC tours US to build a following.
Oct LP *Let There Be Rock* is their first UK chartmaker, at #17, and reaches US #154.
1978 Jan New LP recordings are made at Albert Studios in Sydney.
May LP *Powerage* charts at UK #26, and US #133.
June *Rock'n'Roll Damnation* is first UK hit single, reaching #24.
July/Oct *Powerage* tour in UK is broken by sessions for next LP. LP *If You Want Blood, You've Got It* reaches UK #13, but single, *Whole Lotta Rosie*, is unsuccessful.
1979 Jan/May LP *Highway To Hell* is recorded with new producer, Mutt Lange.
July *Highway To Hell* tour of US and UK heralds LP of the same title, which hits UK #8 and US #17, where it is also the band's first million-seller.
Aug AC/DC supports The Who° at Wembley Stadium, UK.
1980 Jan *Touch Too Much* reaches UK #29.
Feb [21] Bon Scott dies by choking on his own vomit while unconscious in a friend's car after an all-night drinking bout in London.
Apr The band announces that Brian Johnson (former lead singer of UK band, Geordie) will replace Scott.
Apr/May The band records LP *Back In Black* in the Bahamas.
July Start (in US) of *Back In Black* world tour, which includes Europe, Australia and Japan.
Aug LP *Back In Black* is issued, and hits UK #1 and US #4.
Sept *You Shook Me All Night Long* rises to #38 in UK and #35 in US – their first US top 40 hit single.
Dec *Rock'n'Roll Ain't Noise Pollution* reaches UK #15.
1981 Apr LP *Dirty Deeds Done Dirt Cheap*, issued belatedly in US, hits #3.
Aug A headlining appearance at Masters of Rock festival at Castle Donington, UK.

Dec LP *For Those About To Rock (We Salute You)* is released, hits UK #3 and US #1, and tops one million sales.
1982 Feb *Let's Get It Up* is their highest-placed UK single, at #13. It reaches US #44.
July *For Those About To Rock* is released as a UK single and climbs to #15.
1983 Aug Rudd leaves and is replaced on drums by Simon Wright (b. 1963). LP *Flick Of The Switch* is issued, and hits UK #4 and US #15.
Oct *Guns For Hire* reaches UK #37 and US #84.
1984 Aug AC/DC returns to Castle Donington rock festival as headliners, and *Nervous Shakedown* hits UK #35.
1985 Jan A headlining appearance at Rock in Rio festival in Brazil.
July LP *Fly On The Wall* is released, with the band touring US to promote it. LP reaches US #32 and UK #7.
1986 Jan UK and European tour to promote *Shake Your Foundations*, which climbs to UK #24.
May Release of LP *Who Made Who*, containing old and new AC/DC songs used on the soundtrack of Stephen King movie *Maximum Overdrive*. It makes UK #11 and US #33. *Who Made Who* is also a UK single, reaching #16.
1987 Dec After a lengthy silence, AC/DC completes new recordings with producers Vanda and Young for LP *Blow Up Your Video*.
1988 Jan *Heatseeker*, from the LP, reaches UK #12.
Feb LP *Blow Up Your Video* hits UK #2 and US #12.
Apr *That's The Way I Want To Rock'n'Roll* reaches UK #22.

ACE

Paul Carrack (keyboards and vocals)
Alan King (guitar and vocals)
Phil Harris (guitar)
Terry Comer (bass)
Fran Byrne (drums)

1972 Dec Carrack (b. Apr. 1951, UK), King (b. Sept. 1946, UK), Harris (b. July 1948, UK) and Comer (b. Feb. 1949, UK) team up from former bands Mighty Baby and Dust.
1973 Jan Ace breaks into the flourishing 1970s UK pub rock circuit, and gains a solid following.
1974 Sept Fran Byrne (b. Mar. 1948, UK) replaces original drummer, Steve Witherington, and the band signs to UK Anchor label.
Nov UK debut *How Long* gets instant airplay, and climbs to #20.
Dec First LP *Five A Side* is issued in UK, but is not a major seller.
1975 Mar *How Long* charts in US, eventually hitting #3. LP *Five A Side* climbs to US #11.
Aug *Rock & Roll Runaway* is their only other (mildly) successful single, reaching US #71.
Dec Second LP *Time For Another* fails to become a major seller.

ACE *cont.*

1976 Mar Phil Harris leaves the band.

1977 Jan Third LP *No Strings*, made with new guitarist Jon Woodhead, fails to sell.

May A projected UK tour is called off, with only one final gig played [8] at The Roundhouse, London.

July Ace relocates to California, and almost immediately breaks up, with Carrack, Comer and Byrne moving to Frankie Miller's band.

1987 Carrack launches a solo career with Chrysalis, which proves successful only in the US.

JOHNNY ACE

1949 June Following wartime service in the US Navy, John Alexander, Jr. (b. June 29, 1929, Memphis, Tenn., US) returns to Memphis and joins R&B/blues band run by Adolph Duncan, as a pianist.

1952 He signs to record as a vocalist with Duke Records, based in Houston.

1953 First single for Duke, *My Song*, tops US R&B charts. It sets a style followed by subsequent releases: sensitive baritone vocal with subdued jazz small-group backing, highly popular with black US audiences of the time.

1954 Dec He is named Most Programmed Artist of 1954 following a national DJ poll organized by US music trade weekly, *Cash Box*.

Dec [24] While playing Russian roulette backstage at a concert at the City Auditorium in Houston, Ace accidentally shoots himself through the head and dies.

1955 Feb The posthumously released *Pledging My Love* is his biggest-ever success, topping US R&B chart for 9 weeks. It becomes a standard rock ballad. (Ironically, Elvis Presley's° version is on the B-side of his current single at the time of his death, nearly 23 years later. The original *Pledging My Love* will have a further lease of life in the mid-1980s film *Christine*.)

ADAM AND THE ANTS

1977 Apr Adam (b. Stuart Goddard, Nov.3, 1954, London, UK) forms an early version of The Ants after leaving Hornsey Art College, London, where he has previously played in B-Sides and Bazooka Joe with some of the band, who are: Andy Warren (bass and vocals), Lester Square (guitar – replaced by Mark Gaumont) and Paul Flanagan (drums – replaced by Dave Barbe). Jordan, a girl acquaintance of Sex Pistols'° manager Malcolm McLaren, also joins for a while on additional vocals.

July Becoming popular on London's live punk circuit, they are first act to play the Vortex club [11], and they film an appearance in the Derek Jarman movie, *Jubilee*.

1978 Jan First radio session, on BBC "John Peel Show", but no luck with a record deal yet, apart from *Deutscher Girls* and *Plastic Surgery* on LP soundtrack, *Jubilee*.

Oct Without Jordan, and with new guitarist Matthew Ashman, Ant signs to Decca Records and tours Belgium, Italy and West Germany.

1979 Jan Decca single *Young Parisians* fails to chart, and the band leaves to sign to Do It Records and plays first headlining UK tour.

July Do It debut *Zerox* is released, but does not chart immediately.

Oct Leigh Gorman replaces Warren on bass and Malcolm McLaren becomes their manager. LP *Dirk Wears White Sox* is released in UK.

1980 Jan [28] Supported by McLaren, The Ants split from Adam to become "more autonomous". McLaren will quickly pair Ashman, Gorman and Barbe with girl singer Annabella Lwin as new act Bow Wow Wow.

Jan [14] Independent labels chart is launched in UK, and has *Dirk Wears White Sox* as first #1 LP.

Feb Adam forms new Ants with Marco Pirroni (guitar), Kevin Mooney (bass – replaced after a while by Gary Tibbs), and two drummers, Merrick and Terry Lee Miall.

May They tour UK promoting new flamboyant visual image and a drum/percussion oriented sound. *Car Trouble* completes Do It contract.

July They sign to CBS Records.

Aug CBS debut *Kings Of The Wild Frontier* reaches UK #48.

Nov *Dog Eat Dog* is first major hit, climbing to UK #4.

1981 Jan *Antmusic* hits UK #2. Decca reissues *Young Parisians*, and this time it makes UK #9. LP *Kings Of The Wild Frontier* hits #1.

Feb Having already been independent chart-toppers, Do It singles *Car Trouble* and *Zerox* now peak on UK national chart at #33 and #45. LP *Dirk Wears White Sox* makes #16.

Mar *Kings Of The Wild Frontier* is reissued, and this time hits UK #2.

May *Stand And Deliver*, with hugely popular "Dandy Highwayman" video, enters UK chart at #1 in its first week.

Sept *Prince Charming* hits UK #1.

Nov LP *Prince Charming* hits UK #2. The group appears before HM The Queen in the annual Royal Variety Performance alongside Alvin Stardust, The Searchers° and Cliff Richard°.

1982 Jan *Ant Rap* hits UK #3. Tibbs and Miall decide to leave, and are not replaced.

Mar Polydor label reissues old track *Deutscher Girls* from *Jubilee* film soundtrack; it reaches UK #13. *Antmusic* EP, of old Do It tracks, climbs to #46.

Apr Rather than replace Tibbs and Miall, Adam breaks up The Ants but retains Pirroni as partner.

June First release as Adam Ant, *Goody Two-Shoes*, tops UK chart.

Sept *Friend Or Foe* reaches UK #9.

Oct LP *Friend Or Foe* hits UK #5.

Dec *Desperate But Not Serious* breaks the run of UK top 10 hits by only reaching #33.

1983 Feb *Goody Two-Shoes* provides long-awaited US hit, reaching #12.

Mar *Desperate But Not Serious* is a minor US follow-up success, at #66. LP *Friend Or Foe* reaches US #16.

May [16] Ant appears on US TV as special guest in "Motown 25" anniversary, alongside many Motown legends.

Nov *Puss'n Boots* hits UK #5, and LP *Strip* makes #20.

Dec *Strip* reaches only UK #41, while LP *Strip* makes US #65.

1980 Feb *Lost In Love* is debut US/UK single, but UK sales are shared with the Demis Roussos version, and neither charts.
May *Lost In Love* hits US #3, and establishes their rich harmonic sound, much more in line with US than UK radio and audience taste.
Sept *All Out Of Love* hits US #2 and is a million-seller. It also charts in UK, reaching #11. LP *Lost In Love* climbs to US #25.
1981 Jan *Every Woman In The World* reaches #5 in US.
July *The One That You Love* tops US chart and is another million-seller. LP *The One That You Love* climbs to US #10.
Nov *Here I Am (Just When I Thought I Was Over You)* makes US #5.
1982 Mar *Sweet Dreams* climbs to #5 in US.
Aug LP *Now And Forever* reaches US #25.
Sept *Even The Nights Are Better* reaches US #5 – their fourth of five hits to attain this chart position, and their second (and last) UK chart hit, reaching #44.
Oct *Young Love* breaks their major hit run by only climbing to US #38.
1983 Jan *Two Less Lonely People In The World* also reaches US #38.
Oct *Making Love Out Of Nothing At All* recaptures lost US chart ground: a #2 and another million-seller.
Nov LP *Greatest Hits* reaches #7 in US.
1985 July After a lengthy chart absence, *Just As I Am* reaches US #19.
Aug *The Power Of Love (You Are My Lady)* reaches US #68, but is a much bigger hit worldwide for Jennifer Rush, who has a UK million-seller with the song. LP *Air Supply* climbs to US #26.
1986 Sept *Lonely Is The Night* makes US #76.
Oct LP *Hearts In Motion* has ex-Chic° member Bernard Edwards producing, but fails to find wide commercial appeal in US, and does not spin off hit singles as earlier LPs did. Air Supply (now back to only Hitchcock and Russell) seeks new impetus.
1988 Hitchcock completes first (unsuccessful) solo LP as group inactivity continues.

THE ALARM

Mike Peters (guitar and vocals)
Dave Sharp (guitar)
Eddie MacDonald (bass)
Nigel Twist (drums)

1981 After playing together for 4 years in Rhyl, Wales, UK, first as punk band, The Toilets, and then as mod group, 17, the quartet makes a fresh start as The Alarm when the success of U2 inspires them to embrace a similar "emotionally honest" new attitude to their own material.
Sept The group records *Unsafe Buildings* in a Manchester studio for their own White Cross label, pressing 2000 copies to sell at gigs and to use as demos for audition.
Oct They move to London in search of a deal and live work.
1982 Aug After supporting The Jam°, U2° and The Beat° and gaining music press support and industry interest, Alarm signs to IRS Records.
Oct *Marching On* is their first IRS single; good reviews but no hit.
1983 Sept *68 Guns* is released and provides chart debut, reaching #17 in UK. The group makes major TV debut playing it on "Top of the Pops".
1984 Feb *Where Were You Hiding When The Storm Broke* repeats success, climbing to UK #22. UK debut LP *Declaration* is issued.
Apr *The Deceiver* peaks at UK #51.
Nov *The Chant Has Just Begun* is another minor UK hit at #48.
1985 Mar *Absolute Reality* reaches UK #35.
Oct LP *Strength* is released, with the title track also on a single which makes UK #40.
1986 Feb *Spirit Of '76*, an affectionate time-warp hymn to punk music, hits UK #22.
May *Knife Edge* reaches UK #43.
July [11-12] Alarm supports Queen° during two nights' shows at Wembley Stadium, London.
1987 Oct After a long period of silence, during which the band has been touring and writing new material, *Rain In The Summertime* makes UK #18.
Nov LP *Eye Of The Hurricane* reaches UK #23 and a modest US #77.
Dec *Rescue Me*, taken from the LP, charts fleetingly at UK #48, and Alarm looks for a stronger song to re-establish its name.
1988 Apr *Presence Of Love* makes US #77.

ALL ABOUT EVE

Julianne Reagan (vocals)
Tim Bricheno (guitar)
Andy Cousin (bass)
Mark Price (drums)

1985 The band forms in London, UK, around the existing long-term partnership of Reagan and Bricheno, and launches its own independent record label Eden, through which a succession of increasingly popular UK singles, including *D For Desire* and the anthemic *In The Clouds*, will be released. (The group will gig locally for the next 18 months, all the time closely refining its "80s hippie" image.)
1986 Oct Close links are established with goth-rock band The Mission°; Julianne adds vocals to the latter's LP *God's Own Medicine*, while The Mission's Wayne Hussey produces All About Eve's *Our Summer*. This relationship is made cozier still when the group plays support on The Mission's major UK tour.
1987 May Price joins on drums, and *Our Summer* reaches #3 in the UK independent chart.
Aug *Flowers In Our Hair*, also reaches UK independent chart #3, but by now they are signed to Phonogram Records, which has become aware of a burgeoning cult following.
Nov *In The Clouds* is re-released by the major label, and reaches UK #47.
1988 Feb Debut LP *All About Eve* reaches UK #7, while *Wild Hearted Woman*, taken from it, makes #33. The LP success coincides with their first large-venue sell-out date, at London's Hammersmith Odeon.
Apr *Every Angel*, another single from the LP, climbs to UK #30.

THE ALLMAN BROTHERS BAND

Duane Allman (guitar)
Gregg Allman (keyboards, guitar and vocals)
Dickey Betts (guitar and vocals)
Berry Oakley (bass)
Butch Trucks (drums)
Jaimoe Johanson (drums)

1967 Having been The House Rockers and Allman Joys in Florida, US, (where they have lived since childhood), brothers Duane Allman (b. Nov.20, 1946, Nashville, Tenn.) and Gregg (b. Dec.8, 1947, Nashville) form Hourglass in LA. They sign to Liberty Records and release LPs *Hourglass* and *Power Of Love*, without chart success.
1968 Apr Third projected Hourglass LP is recorded at Rick Hall's Fame studio in Muscle Shoals, Ala., but is rejected by Liberty, and the band splits up.
June The brothers return to Jacksonville, Fla., playing informally with 31st of February, a band run by Butch Trucks, and record some demos with them (later issued as LP *Duane And Gregg* in 1973).
Sept Rick Hall, impressed by Duane's guitar playing, invites him back to Fame as a salaried session man. His subsequent contributions to tracks by Wilson Pickett°, King Curtis and Clarence Carter for Atlantic prompt the label's Jerry Wexler to have him back Aretha Franklin° and record material of his own for a projected solo LP.
1969 Encouraged by Phil Walden, about to form Atlantic-distributed Capricorn Records, Allman decides to form a band. He hires Muscle Shoals drummer Johanson, calls in Gregg and Trucks from now-aborted 31st of February, and after playing in Florida with Second Coming, in which are old friends Oakley and Betts, invites them to join, too. They move to Macon, Ga., to rehearse, then record for Atlantic in New York.
1970 Feb Debut LP *Allman Brothers Band*, on Atlantic's Atco label, reaches only #188 in US, but is bigger in the South, where the band starts extensive touring. Duane continues session work between bookings.
May Eric Clapton° sees the band play in Miami while recording there, and invites Duane to join sessions for what will become Derek and The Dominoes' LP *Layla*. He later says Allman was "the catalyst" of this whole project, and Allman's guitar duetting with Clapton on the title track will become his most famous work outside the brothers' band.
July [3] The band plays at Atlanta Pop Festival, alongside Jimi Hendrix°, Jethro Tull°, B.B. King° and others.
Dec LP *Idlewild South*, recorded in Macon, makes US #38.
1971 Jan First charting single is *Revival (Love Is Everywhere)*, at US #92.

THE ALLMAN BROTHERS BAND *cont.*

Mar [12/13] Double live LP is recorded at Fillmore East in New York.
Mar [22] The entire band is arrested in Jackson, Ala., for drug possession.
Sept They move to Phil Walden's new Capricorn label for LP *At Fillmore East*, which reaches US #13.
Oct [29] Duane Allman is killed when he crashes his motorbike avoiding a lorry, in Macon.
Nov [1] The band plays at Duane's funeral, and decides not to replace him.

1972 May LP *Eat A Peach*, which includes the last three tracks recorded by Duane, hits US #4. *Ain't Wastin' Time No More* makes US #77.
Nov [11] Oakley is killed in a motorbike crash in Macon, only three blocks from the site of Allman's death a year before.
Nov Chuck Leavell joins on keyboards.

1973 Jan Lamar Williams joins to replace Oakley on bass.
Apr First two LPs are repackaged together as *Beginnings*, which makes US #25.
July [28] Largest-ever rock festival audience (600,000) sees The Allman Brothers Band, Grateful Dead°, and The Band° at Watkins Glen Raceway, N.Y.
Aug [25] Butch Trucks crashes his car in Macon, but escapes with a broken leg.
Sept LP *Brothers And Sisters*, dedicated to Oakley, is US #1 for 5 weeks, and a UK chart debut at #42.
Oct *Ramblin' Man* is their biggest-ever single, reaching US #2.
Nov Gregg Allman makes solo LP *Laid Back*, which climbs to US #13.

1974 Feb Instrumental *Jessica* reaches US #65, highlighting the playing of Betts, who begins to guide the band's direction. Gregg Allman's solo single *Midnight Rider* reaches US #19.
Aug Betts makes solo LP *Highway Call* as Richard Betts, reaching US #19.
Dec Gregg Allman's LP *The Greg Allman Tour* makes US #50, having been recorded live by the spin-off Gregg Allman Band, which features most of Brothers Band (but not Betts).

1975 June [30] Allman marries Cher°, 4 days after her divorce from Sonny Bono. They will separate acrimoniously after only 10 days, followed by a 3½-year on-off-on-off marriage.
Oct LP *Win, Lose Or Draw* reaches US #5.

1976 Jan Double LP *The Road Goes On Forever*, a compilation of best work to date, reaches US #43 and UK #54. Allman testifies against his former road manager Scooter Herring, on trial for drug trafficking. Herring is sentenced to 75 years in jail, and Allman is ostracized by other band members, who claim he has betrayed their former fraternal loyalty, and vow not to work with him again.
July [16] The band splits to go separate ways: Allman recording with Cher (LP Allman And Woman) and then forming Gregg Allman Band; Betts forming Great Southern; Trucks studying music at college, and the others forming the band Sea Level.
Dec LP *Wipe The Windows, Check The Oil, Dollar Gas*, compiling previously unreleased live recordings, reaches US #75.

1977 July LP *Playin' Up A Storm* by Gregg Allman Band reaches US #42.

1978 The band reforms with rifts healed after Allman, Trucks and Johanson join Great Southern on stage at a Central Park, New York, concert. Great Southern's Dan Toler (guitar) and Rook Goldflies (bass) join the new line-up, which debuts at Capricorn Annual Barbecue in Macon.

1979 Jan [16] Allman and Cher are divorced.
Apr Reunion LP *Enlightened Rogues* makes #9 in US, and single *Crazy Love* reaches #29.

1980 Jan [18] Capricorn Records announces bankruptcy, leaving the band without a label.
July They sign to Arista Records.
Sept First Arista LP *Reach For The Sky* climbs to US #29.

1981 Sept *Straight From The Heart* reaches US #39, but LP *Brothers Of The Road*, from which it is taken, sells disappointingly at #72, and garners poor reviews. Chuck Leavell rejoins them shortly after, but with their style well out of fashion among emerging 1980s trends, the band has little more to offer collectively, and splits once again.

1983 Jan [25] The band's ex-bassist, Lamar Williams, dies of cancer in Los Angeles.

1987 May After a 4-year break, Greg Allman returns, signed to Epic Records, with a solo LP *I'm No Angel* which reaches US #30.

HERB ALPERT

1958 After US Army service, Alpert (b. Mar.31, 1937, Los Angeles, US), starts in the record industry as a writer and producer in partnership with Lou Adler. With Sam Cooke°, they write four consecutive Cooke hits, *Love You Most Of All*, *Everybody Likes To Cha Cha Cha*, *Only Sixteen* and *Wonderful World*, under the collective pseudonym Barbara Campbell.

1959 Alpert and Adler become producers for Dore Records, which has top 10 US hit with Jan and Dean's° *Baby Talk*. Alpert also records as a vocalist without success for RCA as Dore Alpert, and tries for bit parts in Hollywood films.

1962 Mar Alpert splits with Adler, joining Jerry Moss, who produced him for RCA, to form Carnival Records, which they swiftly change to A&M (based on their surnames). The label initially operates from Alpert's garage at home.
Oct A trumpet player since age 8, he records Mexican-style trumpet instrumental *The Lonely Bull*, and releases it on A&M under the name of The Tijuana Brass.
Dec *The Lonely Bull* reaches #6 in US, establishing both Alpert and A&M.

1963 Jan LP *The Lonely Bull* is released, reaching US #24. Alpert puts together a live touring version of The Tijuana Brass which will grow into one of the top-grossing live attractions in the US in mid-60s. *The Lonely Bull* reaches UK #22.

1964 Feb LP *Tijuana Brass Vol.2* reaches #17 in US.

1965 Feb LP *South Of The Border* reaches US #6.
May *Whipped Cream* reaches #68 in US.
Nov Already on chart for 6 months, LP *Whipped Cream And Other Delights* hits US #1. *A Taste Of Honey*, his first US top 10 single for 3 years, hits #7.

1966 Jan UK single is *Spanish Flea*, which climbs to #3 and re-establishes Alpert in the UK.
Feb Both sides of *Zorba The Greek/Tijuana Taxi* reach US top 40, at #11 and #38.
Mar [15] Alpert wins US Grammy Award for *A Taste Of Honey*, which is voted Record of the Year for 1965, and Best Non-Jazz Instrumental.
Mar LP *Going Places* tops US chart for 6 weeks, and hits UK #4.
Apr Both sides of *What Now My Love/Spanish Flea* reach US top 30, at #24 and #27. *Tijuana Taxi* makes UK #37.
May LP *What Now My Love* tops US chart for 9 weeks, and *Whipped Cream And Other Delights* hits UK #2.
June LP *What Now My Love* reaches UK #18.
July *The Work Song* reaches #18 in US.
Oct *Flamingo* makes #28 in US.
Dec *Mame* climbs to #19 in US.

1967 Jan LP *S.R.O.* climbs to US #2 and UK #5.
Mar [2] *What Now My Love* wins US Grammy Award for Best Non-Jazz Instrumental of 1966.
Apr *Wade In The Water* reaches US #37.
May Alpert records the theme tune for spoof James Bond movie, *Casino Royale*, which reaches #27 in both US and UK.
June LP *Sounds Like* hits US #1, then climbs to UK #21.
Aug An instrumental version of film theme *The Happening* follows 3 months after US #1 vocal version by The Supremes°, but still makes US #32.
Oct *A Banda* reaches #35 in US.

1968 Jan LP *Herb Alpert's 9th* hits US #4, then makes UK #26.
June *This Guy's In Love With You* tops US chart for 4 weeks: his first vocal hit and first million-seller and #1 single. Oddly, it is his last US top 40 single for many years.
July LP *The Beat Of The Brass* hits US #1 and UK #4.
Aug *This Guy's In Love* With You hits #3 in UK.
Sept *To Wait For Love* is his second vocal hit, but much less successful, reaching US #51.

1969 June A vocal version of the Nilsson° song *Without Her* reaches only US #63 and UK #36. Subsequent releases will revert to trumpet-led instrumentals.
Aug LP *Warm* reaches US #28 and UK #30.

1970 Jan While on sabbatical from live performing and helping with A&M administration, Alpert is impressed by demo tapes from a brother/sister act, The Carpenters°, whom he signs to the label. They will score 12 million-selling singles for A&M over next 5 years.
June LP *Greatest Hits* reaches UK #8.

1971 Jan *Jerusalem* climbs to #42 in UK.

1979 Oct He scores a comeback US #1 hit with *Rise*, featuring contemporary disco rhythm and none of the old Mexican feel. It is a million-plus-selling single.
Nov *Rise* climbs to #13 in UK.
Dec LP *Rise* reaches US #6 and UK #37.
1980 Jan *Rotation* hits US #30 and UK #46.
Feb [27] *Rise* wins US Grammy Award as Best Pop Instrumental Performance of 1979.
1982 Aug *Route 101* reaches #37 in US.
1987 Jan Alpert plays cameo trumpet on UB40's UK hit *Rat In Mi Kitchen*.
Apr After a quiet period, LP *Keep Your Eye On Me*, partly made with dance producers Jimmy Jam and Terry Lewis, signals another commercial return. It reaches US #18 and UK #79. The title track on single reaches UK #19.
June Dance-styled *Diamonds*, also from the LP and featuring Janet Jackson° on vocals, hits US #5 and UK #27.
Sept *Making Love In The Rain*, from the LP, peaks at US #35. Alpert meanwhile continues to co-run A&M, now just past its 25th birthday, and grown over that period into one of the biggest and most successful independent labels in the world.

ALTERED IMAGES

Clare Grogan (vocals)
Tony McDaid (guitar)
Jim McIven (guitar and keyboards)
John McElhone (bass)
Michael "Tich" Anderson (drums)

1979 Mar School friends McDaid, McElhone, and Anderson form the band in Glasgow, Scotland, UK. McIven and Grogan are invited in during early rehearsals.
Aug First live gig at Glasgow pub, The Countdown, is followed by others which build a strong local following.
Nov Grogan begins 6 weeks filming *Gregory's Girl* with Bill Forsyth.
1980 June A demo tape sent to Siouxsie & The Banshees° leads to a supporting slot on Banshees' Glasgow date, and then on a full UK tour.
Sept The band plays Futurama Festival in Leeds, UK, impressing BBC DJ John Peel, and also CBS Records, which offers a recording contract.
1981 Feb First single, *Dead Pop Stars*, produced by Banshees' bassist Steve Severin, causes some controversy because of John Lennon's° death (though recorded prior to that event). It gives them a UK chart debut, reaching #67.
Sept After a failed second release, new producer Martin Rushent is brought in for *Happy Birthday*. It climbs to #2 after successful "Top of the Pops" TV slot.
Oct First LP *Happy Birthday* reaches #26 in UK.
Dec *I Could Be Happy* peaks at UK #7.
1982 Mar Third UK top 20 hit *See Those Eyes* makes #11.
May LP *Pinky Blue* reaches UK #12, and extracted title track, *Pinky Blue* makes #11.
July McIven and Anderson leave. Stephen Lironi joins on guitar but the band does not recruit another drummer, using session players instead.
1983 Mar Mike Chapman is made producer and *Don't Talk To Me About Love* is issued, and hits UK #7.
June LP *Bite*, produced by Chapman and Tony Visconti, charts at UK #16. *Bring Me Closer* is extracted and gives last top 30 entry at #29.
Aug *Love To Stay* proves to be an inappropriate title, reaching UK #46. The band's fashionable, eager teen image of 1981 is now passé, and reception of *Bite's* more mature style disappoints them. (Their eventual split leaves main personality, Grogan, pursuing a solo acting and recording career.)

AMEN CORNER

Andy Fairweather-Low (vocals and guitar)
Blue Weaver (organ)
Neil Jones (guitar)
Clive Taylor (bass)
Mike Smith (tenor sax)
Allan Jones (baritone sax)
Dennis Byron (drums)

1966 The group forms in Cardiff, Wales, UK, gaining a reputation as a strong live R&B band, the twin saxes giving a "fatter", more American sound than most UK beat groups of the time.
1967 May They sign to Deram label, part of UK Decca, as a recording act.
July First single, the slow and bluesy *Gin House*, charts immediately in UK, reaching #12.
Oct *World Of Broken Hearts* shows a more commercial pop sound, and peaks at UK #26.
1968 Jan The group covers American Breed's major US hit *Bend Me, Shape Me* in brasher form, and hits UK #3.
Mar First LP *Round Amen Corner* is released in UK, reaching #26.
Aug *High In The Sky*, another brash dance single, hits UK #6.
1969 Jan A new recording deal is signed with UK Immediate Records. *(If Paradise Is) Half As Nice* streaks to #1 within 2 weeks of issue.
July *Hello Suzie*, their last UK hit, peaks at #4.
1970 Immediate Records closes down with financial problems and the group's last single *Get Back* is left with no promotion. Rather than find another deal, they split up. Fairweather-Low, Weaver, Byron, Taylor and Neil Jones regroup as Fair Weather; the saxists form the nucleus of a band, Judas Jump.
July *Natural Sinner*, recorded as a UK single by Fair Weather, reaches #6 on the chart, but members rapidly become disillusioned. They split again to do session and solo work.

AMERICA

Dewey Bunnell (vocals and guitar)
Gerry Beckley (vocals and guitar)
Dan Peek (vocals and guitar)

1967 Bunnell (b. Jan.19, 1952, Yorks., UK), Beckley (b. Sept.12, 1952, US) and Peek (b. 1950, US) meet at school in UK; all sons of US servicemen stationed on UK bases.
1971 Completing school they form an acoustic folk-rock trio in London, and sign to Warner Bros. Records UK.
1972 Jan First release *Horse With No Name* is instant UK hit, reaching #2.
Mar Released in US on the strength of UK success, *Horse With No Name* shoots to US #1. America goes "home" (a place they hardly know) to build on their success. Debut LP *America* hits #1 in US as well.
May *I Need You* climbs to US #9, but fails in UK.
Dec *Ventura Highway* is a third US top 10 hit (#9) and a minor UK success (#43), after which the UK market forgets them for a decade, and the trio works wholly in the US.

AMERICA *cont.*

1973 Jan Aptly titled LP *Homecoming*, hits US #9.
1974 July After a less successful 1973, George Martin becomes their producer. LP *Holiday* hits US #3.
Oct Martin-produced *Tin Man* returns them to US singles top 10 (#4).
1975 Feb *Lonely People* is US smash (#5).
June *Sister Golden Hair* (from LP *Hearts*, charted #4) is US #1.
Sept *Daisy Jane* breaks US top 10 hits run, peaking at #20.
Dec LP *History: America's Greatest Hits* hits US #3.
1976 June LP *Hideaway* reaches US #11.
1977 May Peek leaves (later to become a born-again Christian and record solo religious material).
1981 Nov Less successful as a twosome, America is much criticized when they tour South Africa in defiance of UN cultural boycott.

1982 Sept Following a new record deal with Capitol, the duo makes a brief chart comeback with *You Can Do Magic* (US #8, UK #59), and follows with well-received LP *View From The Ground*, produced by UK's Russ Ballard.
1983 Jan *Right Before Your Eyes* reaches US #45.
Aug *The Border* reaches US #33, after which America's chart comeback ceases.

LAURIE ANDERSON

1973 Jan After years studying violin, and graduating in and teaching art history, multi-media artist Anderson (b. 1947, Chicago, Ill., US), begins giving public performances of her work, combining music with mime, speech, graphics, film, sculpture and slides.
1976 She reaches international audiences via museum, festival and concert performances in Europe.
1981 May/June She records 8-minute *O Superman* in a limited edition of 5000 copies for New York independent label, One Ten.
Aug *O Superman* (an extract from 7-hour work United States) is picked up by Warner Bros, which then signs her to LP contract.
Oct Despite *O Superman's* length, its odd electronically-treated vocal and atmospheric style gets it UK airplay and it quickly charts, climbing to #2. Similar success follows around Europe, though US radio cold-shoulders it.
1982 May LP *Big Science* is released, charting at #29 in UK, but she does not pursue her success.
1983 Feb *America*, 7 hours long and in four parts, premières in US. (Anderson continues with her avant-garde work, but is not to surface again in the mainstream rock scene.)

THE ANIMALS

Eric Burdon (vocals)
Alan Price (keyboards)
Hilton Valentine (guitar)
Chas Chandler (bass)
John Steel (drums)

1962 Eric Burdon (b. May 11, 1941, Walker, Tyneside, UK) joins The Alan Price Combo, Newcastle-based group playing R&B and rock'n'roll. Existing members are Alan Price (b. Apr.19, 1941, Fairfield, Co. Durham, UK), Valentine (b. May 21, 1943, N. Shields, UK), Chandler (b. Dec.18, 1938, Heaton, Tyneside) and Steel (b. Feb.4, 1941, Gateshead, Co. Durham). They gain a regular slot at Newcastle's Downbeat Club, and are referred to by local fans as "the animals" because of their notoriously wild stage act.
1963 The group, renamed The Animals, moves to the Club A-Go-Go, a larger Newcastle City Centre club.
Dec A demo EP made for fans is heard in London, and leads to plentiful work offers.
Dec [27] First radio broadcast is on BBC show "Saturday Club".
1964 Jan The group moves to London, and signs with emerging record producer Mickie Most, who interests EMI Records in them.
Apr First single *Baby Let Me Take You Home*, an R&B adaptation of Bob Dylan's° *Baby Let Me Follow You Down*, is released in UK on EMI's Columbia label, and climbs to #19. First UK tour, supporting Chuck Berry°.
June *House Of The Rising Sun*, a Price rearrangement of a traditional folk-blues, is almost not issued when EMI argues that its length (4½ mins) will prevent radio play, but Most and the group prevail. It enters UK chart at #15 and moves to #1 the next week.
Aug *House Of The Rising Sun* is issued (in shortened form) in US by MGM Records, and shoots to #1, selling over a million copies.
Sept *Baby Let Me Take You Home*, previously unsuccessful in US, is reissued on the back of Rising Sun's success, but it is the B-side, *Gonna Send You Back To Walker* which becomes a US chart entry, peaking at #57.
Oct *I'm Crying*, the only single penned by the group themselves, hits UK #6 and US #19.
Nov Debut LP *The Animals* hits UK #6 and US #7.
1965 Jan Released in the US as a single, a revival of John Lee Hooker's° *Boom Boom* reaches #43.
Feb The group angers Nina Simone° by covering her *Don't Let Me Be Misunderstood*. It hits UK #4, and US #15.
Apr A cover of Sam Cooke's° *Bring It On Home To Me* climbs to UK #4, while in US it makes #32, and the US-only LP *The Animals On Tour* reaches #99.
June LP *Animal Tracks* reaches #6 in UK.
July *We've Gotta Get Out Of This Place*, an original Barry Mann/Cynthia Weill song, peaks at UK #3 and US #13.
Oct LP *Animal Tracks* peaks at #57 in US.
Nov *It's My Life* makes UK #7 and US #23, after which (due to growing musical disagreement with Burdon, and his dislike of flying which has made US tours anathema to him), Price leaves for what will become a distinguished solo career. He is replaced by ex-Mike Cotton Sound pianist Dave Rowberry (b. Dec.27 1943, Newcastle, UK).
1966 Jan Burdon refuses to re-sign the group's contract with Mickie Most and EMI because of unhappiness over the material on offer. The group switches to new producer Tom Wilson, and Decca Records. The US agreement with MGM is unaffected.
Feb Decca debut *Inside Looking Out* continues UK top 10 run at #7, but peaks at US #34. Steel leaves and is replaced by Barry Jenkins (b. Dec.22, 1944, Leicester, UK) from The Nashville Teens.
Mar Compilation LP *The Best Of The Animals* hits US #6, the group's best-selling US LP, remaining charted for 113 weeks.
May Compilation LP *The Most Of The Animals* is released in UK by EMI, anthologizing the Mickie Most-produced singles up to *It's My Life*. It hits #4.
June The Gerry Goffin/Carole King° song *Don't Bring Me Down* revives US chart fortunes at #12, and is another UK top tenner at #6. In UK, LP *Animalisms* hits #4.
Sept A widening split between Burdon and the others (he is getting heavily involved with LSD, they are not) prompts the group to split at the end of a US tour. Jenkins remains with Burdon to form the nucleus of a new group, while the others go their separate ways.

Oct The last single by the original group, *See See Rider*, is only issued in the US, and ironically is one of their biggest hits, making #10. LP *Animalization* (also not issued in UK) reaches US #12.

Nov *Help Me Girl*, credited to Eric Burdon & The Animals (though it is actually recorded by Burdon in New York with session players, led by jazzman Benny Golson), reaches UK #14 and US #29.

1967 Jan The original group's final LP *Animalism*, partly recorded on the last US tour, (and mostly featuring blues and R&B standards) is belatedly released in US and reaches #33. Meanwhile, Burdon relocates to California and forms Eric Burdon & The Animals, which has himself and Jenkins, plus John Weider (b. Apr.21, 1947, London, UK) and Vic Briggs (b. Feb.14, 1945, Twickenham, UK) on guitars and Danny McCulloch (b. July 18, 1945, London, UK) on bass. This group is signed to MGM for the UK and US.

Apr A Burdon solo LP, *Eric Is Here*, recorded at the same time as *Help Me Girl*, is issued in the US, and reaches #121.

May First release by the new group is *When I Was Young*, which eschews the traditional Animals R&B sound in favor of psychedelic-flavored hard rock, showing the influence on Burdon of the burgeoning US West Coast scene. It reaches US #15 and UK #45.

July Compilation LP *The Best Of Eric Burdon & The Animals, Vol. 2* reaches US #71.

Sept *San Franciscan Nights*, celebrating Burdon's new lifestyle, reaches US #9, while *Good Times*, which berates his hard-drinking past, makes UK #20.

Nov *San Franciscan Nights* climbs to UK #7, while LP *Winds Of Change*, a showcase of the new progressive group style, makes US #42, but fails to chart in UK.

1968 Jan *Monterey*, a tribute to the 1967 Monterey Pop Festival, peaks at US #15.

Feb Two-part single *Sky Pilot*, a controversial attack on the complacency of religion in the face of war (and on which Weider experiments with electric violin), reaches UK #40.

May LP *The Twain Shall Meet* makes US #79 without charting in the UK.

June Briggs and McCulloch leave, replaced by ex-Big Roll Band and Dantalian's Chariot members, Zoot Money (keyboards) and Andy Summers (guitar). The band becomes Eric Burdon & The New Animals.

July *Sky Pilot* peaks at #14 in US.

Sept LP *Every One Of Us* reaches US #152.

Dec *White Houses* is the band's final US hit single, as Burdon announces, at the end of US and Japanese tours, that they will disband after a Christmas concert in his home city of Newcastle.

1969 Jan As it ends, a revival of Johnny Cash's *Ring Of Fire* gives the group one further UK chart entry, at #35.

Feb Double LP set *Love Is* peaks at US #123 after the group has split.

Apr Compilation LP *The Greatest Hits Of Eric Burdon & The Animals* makes US #153.

1970 Jan Now in LA, with more interest in looking for movie parts than forming another band, Burdon (at producer Jerry Goldstein's suggestion), teams up with Night Shift, a heavy funk band from Long Beach, Cal., which changes its name to War°. They record together, and Burdon tours in US backed by War.

Aug *Spill The Wine*, credited to Eric Burdon & War, hits US #3 and tops a million sales. LP *Eric Burdon Declares War* peaks at US #18.

Oct Following a UK tour by Burdon and the group, LP *Eric Burdon Declares War* reaches #50.

THE ANIMALS *cont.*

1971 Jan *They Can't Take Away Our Music* and double LP set *The Black Man's Burdon* by Eric Burdon and War° reach US #50 and #82 respectively, after which the band begins a European tour, only to have Burdon, suffering from exhaustion, quit midway through and return to the US. War continues the tour without him (and will quickly develop into one of the most successful US funk bands of the 1970s). When he recovers, Burdon devotes his energy to fulfilling an ambition, and records LP *Guilty* with blues singer Jimmy Witherspoon. A one-off project, this does not chart.

Oct Retrospective budget LP *Most Of The Animals* reaches UK #18.

1972 Oct *House Of The Rising Sun* is reissued in the UK and is a best-seller again, reaching #25.

1973 Aug [23] Burdon performs at Reading Festival, UK, with a new backup trio comprising Aaron Butler (guitar), Randy Rice (bass) and Alvin Taylor (drums).

1974 Oct Still living in California, Burdon and wife Rose have a daughter, Mirage, born in Palm Springs.

1975 Jan Signed to Capitol Records with his recent live group as The Eric Burdon Band, LP *Sun Secrets* reaches US #51.

Aug Second Eric Burdon Band LP *Stop* (with a different line-up) sells less well, peaking at US #171, and the band splits.

1976 Jan The original five Animals get together to play for fun at Chandler's house, and their rapport is such that they hire a mobile studio to cut an LP.

1977 Mar Chas Chandler produces Burdon solo LP *Survivor*, mostly co-written by the singer and ex-New Animals keyboard player Zoot Money, for Polydor in West Germany. Released in UK the next year, it will not chart.

Aug LP *Before We Were So Rudely Interrupted...*, credited to The Original Animals, and taken from the previous year's reunion session, is issued on Chandler's Barn label. It does not chart in UK, but climbs to US #70.

1982 Oct *House Of The Rising Sun* has its second, and still more successful, reissue in UK, at #11.

1983 July The original quintet regroups again for LP *Ark* on IRS Records. It does not chart in UK.

Aug Lucrative US and worldwide tour. The liaison is not intended as a permanent arrangement, but as a series of reunions because of proven popular appeal.

Sept *The Night*, from the LP *Ark*, reaches US #48, while LP climbs to #66.

Dec [31] LP *Rip It To Shreds: Greatest Hits Live* is recorded at Wembley Arena, UK, by the reunited line-up, but does not chart in UK, and only reaches US #193. The Animals split again after this (though will reunite sporadically for specific live commitments, particularly in the US.)

PAUL ANKA

1956 July Already an experienced part-time entertainer and budding songwriter while still at high school, Anka (b. July 30, 1941, Ottawa, Canada), spends the summer vacation away from his family's restaurant, staying with an uncle in Los Angeles, in an attempt to break into show business.

Sept He records *I Confess* as a one-off for Modern Records, backed by R&B group The Cadets.

Oct Back in school (Fisher Park High, Ottawa), he begins work on *Diana*, a song inspired by a crush on the Anka family's baby-sitter Diana Ayoub, who is 18 and therefore out of reach.

1957 Apr He wins an Easter trip to New York, and uses the 10 days to knock on record company doors. Don Costa at ABC Records signs him, impressed by his (then rare) singer/ songwriter abilities.

July *Diana* is released and enters US singles chart.

Aug *Diana* is an immediate UK hit, reaching #1 within a month, and staying at #1 for 9 weeks. *Diana* also hits US #1. Worldwide sales will eventually top 9 million.

Nov *I Love You Baby* fails as US follow-up, but is a UK smash (#3), helped by a successful "Sunday Night at The London Palladium" TV spot, and a UK, Europe and Australia tour.

1958 Feb *You Are My Destiny* returns him to US top 10 at #7, and is #5 in UK.

Apr *Crazy Love* reaches US #19.

Oct Anka gives *It Doesn't Matter Anymore* to Buddy Holly°, who has expressed interest in recording an Anka song. It will become a 1959 posthumous UK #l and US #14 for Holly.

Dec Old standard *(All Of A Sudden) My Heart Sings*, chosen as a contrast from his own songs, is a US #15 and UK #10 hit.

1959 Mar He makes his first Hollywood movie, *Girls' Town*, with Mamie Van Doren.

July Self-penned *Lonely Boy* is second US #1 hit, and reaches UK #3.

Aug First nightclub appearance, at Sahara Hotel, Las Vegas.

Sept *Put Your Head On My Shoulder* is a million-seller, hitting #2 in US and #5 in UK.

Dec *It's Time To Cry* hits US #4, but only makes UK #30.

1960 Mar *Puppy Love* is a US smash (#2) and a minor UK hit (#33).

June He becomes the youngest performer to star at New York's Copacabana nightclub.

July *My Home Town* is US #8.

Oct *Summer's Gone* reaches #11, and is followed by three more US top 20 hits in 8 months: *The Story Of My Love* (#16), *Tonight My Love, Tonight* (#13), and *Dance On Little Girl* (#10). None of these are UK hits. During their US chart run, Anka acts in war movie *The Longest Day*, and writes its theme song.

1961 Dec He leaves ABC Records to sign a million-dollar contract with RCA.

1962 Mar First RCA release *Love Me Warm And Tender* restores Anka to UK chart at #17, and reaches US #12.

Dec The Bossa Nova craze is briefly acknowledged with latin-tempoed *Eso Beso*, a US #19.

1963 Feb [16] Anka marries Marie-Ann DeZogheb, in Paris, France.

Apr He writes *Remember Diana*, sequel to his first hit, but it is not as successful, peaking at US #39.

1969 Feb *Goodnight My Love* makes US #27.

Apr He writes the English lyrics to a French song *My Way*, which is recorded by Frank Sinatra, hits US #27 and UK #4, and becomes Sinatra's new signature tune.

1971 Anka's *She's A Lady* is a #12 UK hit for Tom Jones°, and becomes #2 in US where it sells a million.

1974 July Anka releases a duet with protégée Odia Coates, *You're Having My Baby*, which climbs to US #l, and is a million-seller. UK #5.

1975 Jan His duet with Coates *One Man Woman/One Woman Man*, hits #7 in US but fails to chart in UK.

Apr *I Don't Like To Sleep Alone* is a solo US top tenner (#8).

July Duet *(I Believe) There's Nothing Stronger Than Our Love* is US #15.

1976 Jan Solo *Times Of Your Life* hits US #7, and is Anka's final top 10 hit. (He will continue to score minor chart successes, while based in Las Vegas with his wife and four daughters, and playing cabaret dates there and at Lake Tahoe.)

1983 June Signing to CBS Records brings Anka a latter-day US success with *Hold Me 'Til The Mornin' Comes* (#40), from LP *Walk A Fine Line*.

ANTHRAX

Joey Belladonna (vocals)
Dan Spitz (guitar)
Ian "Not" Scott (guitar)
Frank Bello (bass)
Charlie Bonante (drums)

1981 July The band is initially formed in New York with Dan Lilker on bass and Neil Turbin handling vocals. The members are drawn together by their mutual interest in hardcore thrash heavy metal music, comics and skateboarding.

1982 Hectic small-town touring throughout the US occupies most of the year.

1983 May The band meets Johnny Z., who signs them to his Megaforce label and releases *Soldiers Of Metal*. They tour further, supporting Manowar and Metallica°.

1984 Feb LP *Fistful Of Metal* is released on Megaforce in US, and licensed to Music for Nations in Europe. The LP is notable for some of the fastest metal riff music ever heard, but is not successful. As they tour continuously in the US, Scott forms the concurrent splinter group Stormtroopers of Death (SOD), to play even faster thrash. SOD's LP *Speak English Or Die* is released. Lilker leaves to join Nuclear Assault, and former Anthrax roadie Frank Bello becomes their permanent bassist.

June Turbin relinquishes vocal duties. He is temporarily replaced by Matt Falklon, but ultimately Joey Belladonna steps in, and his range and power gives a new polished focus to their recordings.

1985 Feb *Armed And Dangerous*, a five-track mini-LP recorded in New York, includes a revival of The Sex Pistols'° *God Save The Queen*, and inspires interest from Island Records' US division, which signs the band to record its second LP, with producer Carl Canedy, again in New York.

1986 Feb LP *Spreading The Disease* is released, with Music for Nations again picking up the European license. *Madhouse*, taken from it, is reissued several times in the ensuing months.

June The band makes its UK debut live at London's Hammersmith Palais, followed by a European tour supporting Metallica°. The latter part of the year and early 1987 is spent in Miami and the Bahamas recording a third LP with producer Eddie Kramer.

1987 Mar *I Am The Law* is the first release from the new LP, and is their UK chart debut at #32.

May LP *Among The Living* receives critical acclaim and charts in UK at #18. It will spawn further popular tracks, *Indians* and *I'm The Man*.

Nov Two sold-out dates at London's Hammersmith Odeon confirm Anthrax as a serious international force in heavy metal rock.

THE ARCHIES

1968 Aug The Archies, based on characters in US Archie cartoons and comics, are launched by producer/publisher Don Kirshner, previously initiator of The Monkees°.

Sept Studio musicians and session singers are hired to record the first "Archies" song, *Bang-Shang-A-Lang*. Main vocalist is Ron Dante (b. Aug.22, 1945), whose voice becomes identified as The Archies' sound, even though he is never actually seen performing.

Oct *Bang-Shang-A-Lang* charts in US, reaching #22.

1969 July *Sugar Sugar* is released as a US single. This will become the biggest worldwide seller of 1969, with over 6 million copies sold.

Sept *Sugar Sugar* is US #1 for 4 weeks.

Oct Despite Archie cartoons not being known in UK, *Sugar Sugar* is released and tops the chart for 8 weeks, selling over 900,000 copies in UK alone.

Dec Follow-up *Jingle Jangle*, a duet between Dante and session singer Toni Wine, reaches #10 in US and is another million-seller, but fails to chart in UK.

1970 Mar *Who's Your Baby* is The Archies' final US hit, (#40). Records cease to be released once the gimmick appeal is gone: it cannot break up, having never really existed. (Dante will continue session work, and become Barry Manilow's producer in the 1970s.)

1987 Aug *Sugar Sugar* is rediscovered as a dance novelty by UK clubs and re-charts at #91. It will remain a popular oldie.

ARGENT

Rod Argent (keyboards and vocals)
Russ Ballard (vocals and guitar)
Jim Rodford (bass)
Bob Henrit (drums)

1969 Argent (b. June 14, 1945) forms a new UK band following the breakup of The Zombies°, of whom he was leader. He recruits his cousin Rodford (b. July 7, 1945) and former Roulettes' members Ballard (b. Oct.31, 1947) and Henrit (b. May 2, 1945).

1970 Jan First LP *Argent* released by CBS is not a chart success, but one song *Liar*, is covered in US by Three Dog Night° and is a hit.

Jan/Feb Argent builds an immediate live reputation in US with a tour taking in major LA and New York rock venues.

1971 Feb Second LP *Ring Of Hands* shows a heavier sound, less related to the old Zombies'° style.

1972 Mar *Hold Your Head Up* is their first UK chart entry, climbing to #5.

May LP *All Together Now* is UK #13.

June *Hold Your head Up* charts in US, reaching #5. The LP follows it, peaking at US #23. *Tragedy* is a smaller UK single hit, at #34.

1973 Mar New LP *In Deep* and single *God Gave Rock'n'Roll To You* are their final UK hits (#49 and #18).

1974 May Ballard leaves to follow a solo career, replaced by guitarists John Verity and John Grimaldi.

1975 Apr Unsuccessful LP *Circus* is released.

Oct Switch of label to RCA brings further LP *Counterpoint*, but no renewed commercial success.

1976 June Grimaldi resigns and, rather than replace him, the band decides to split. Rodford, Henrit and Verity form Phoenix; Argent moves into solo production and performance. (He will have a solo instrumental UK hit (#14) in June 1978 with *Argentine Melody*, the TV theme for the Argentine World Cup.)

JOAN ARMATRADING

1958 Immigrant Armatrading family settles in Birmingham, UK.

1965 Having taught herself to play piano and guitar as a child, Joan (b. Dec.9, 1950, St. Kitts, Caribbean) writes her first song aged 14, but intends to follow a career in law.

1972 She begins her professional career with Pam Nestor (b. Apr.28, 1948, Guyana) as a songwriting and performing partnership, and they move to London, UK.

1974 A deal with Cube Records produces LP *Whatever's For Us*, but Nestor leaves, unhappy with her part in the arrangement.

1975 Armatrading signs solo to A&M Records, and begins to write her own lyrics, previously supplied by Nestor.

Apr LP *Back To The Night* is issued, but is not a success.

1976 Aug Teaming with producer Glyn Johns results in LP *Joan Armatrading*, which reaches #12 in UK, and #67 in US, and includes *Love And Affection*, a #9 UK hit.

1977 Oct LP *Show Some Emotion* is UK #6 hit, and US #52.

1978 Oct LP *To The Limit* makes UK #13, and introduces a harder, rockier style.

1980 May *Me, Myself, I* reaches UK #21, and LP of the same title hits #5.

1981 Sept LP *Walk Under Ladders* is another big UK seller (#6), and yields *I'm Lucky* (#46) and *No Love* (#50).

1983 Apr LP *The Key* is major UK (#10) and US (#32) hit. Taken from it, *Drop The Pilot* reaches UK #11, and is a belated US success at #78.

1985 Feb LP *Secret Secrets* (UK #14, US #73) brings her back to the charts after a lengthy recording absence filled only by a compilation LP of old material.

1986 May LP *Sleight Of Hand* charts at UK #34, which confirms her still-existing UK following.

1988 Armatrading returns to the studio to record new LP *The Shouting Stage* for release in July.

THE ART OF NOISE

Anne Dudley (keyboards)
J.J. Jeczalik (keyboards and programmer)
Gary Langan (engineer)

1984 Jan Having met through their individual work as part of Trevor Horn's early 1980s production team (creators of hits for ABC°, Dollar, Frankie Goes To Hollywood° and Malcolm McLaren), the original three members, all noted arrangers and producers in their own right, first get together after working on a strenuous session with Yes°. The initial idea (consistently adhered to), is to release original sound, normally instrumental-only, in a faceless, almost group-less guise. The name, coined by ZTT Records' Paul Morley, comes from an Italian futurist manifesto.

THE ART OF NOISE *cont.*

Apr First release *Beat Box* reaches US #101, but is a US dancefloor favorite, and released on Island, climbs to #10 on R&B chart.

Aug *Close (To The Edit)* stalls at US #102, but again does well on the R&B chart (#23), and climbs to US #4 on the dance chart.

Nov LP *(Who's Afraid Of) The Art Of Noise*, released on Horne's ZTT label, reaches UK #27.

1985 Jan First UK hit single is *Close (To The Edit)*, an original, quirky non-vocal, which makes #8.

Apr *Moments In Love/Beat Box* reaches UK #51 (the former later used by Madonna° at her wedding to Sean Penn).

Aug LP *(Who's Afraid Of) The Art Of Noise* makes US #85.

Nov *Legs*, on the new China label in UK, makes #69.

1986 Mar A collaboration with Duane Eddy°, on an update of his 1959 classic *Peter Gunn*, puts them back in the UK top 10 at #8.

June *Peter Gunn* reaches US #50. (It will later win a Grammy award as Best Rock Instrumental of 1986.) LP *In Visible Silence*, reaches UK #78, and includes offbeat collaboration with TV character Max Headroom on *Paranoimia*. Extracted as a single, it makes UK #12. (Its success leads to the group's creation of the theme for Headroom's second UK TV series, and then to involvement with UK TV theme work ("Krypton Factor 2" and "The Return of Sherlock Holmes") and commercials for lager, aftershave and hair cream.

July The band's first-ever live concerts take place in Japan, US and (one date) UK. All are sold out.

1987 Jan *Legacy* is released in UK, without charting.

July ZTT Records issues a compilation LP of early material, entitled *Daft*, which fails to chart.

Oct Third LP *In No Sense? Nonsense!* reaches UK #55 (without Langan, who subsequently becomes a floating group member).

Nov The band completes work on theme music for Dan Aykroyd's film *Dragnet*, to be included on the soundtrack LP and released as a UK and US single.

1988 Feb Work is completed on a soundtrack contribution to the Fat Boys' film *Disorderlies*.

Mar *Dragnet '88* reaches UK #94, issued to coincide with the movie's UK release. (Individually, the band members' careers also blossom. Dudley's successes as producer/writer/arranger/player include hits by Lloyd Cole°, Rush°, Boy George, K.D. Lang, McCartney°, A-Ha°, New Edition and Five Star°; Jeczalik's production and mixing credits include The Pet Shop Boys°, Godley & Creme° and McCartney°; Langan's talents are on hand for Spandau Ballet°, ABC°, Billy Idol°, Public Image Ltd°, and many others.)

ASHFORD AND SIMPSON

Nickolas Ashford (vocals)
Valerie Simpson (vocals)

1964 Ashford (b. May 4, 1943, Fairfield, S.C., US) meets Simpson (b. Aug.26, 1948, Bronx, New York) at Harlem's White Rock Baptist Church. He is a college dropout, she a music student. Shared musical interest leads them to write songs. They sell their first job lot to a publisher for $75, and make a few unsuccessful singles as Valerie & Nick.

1966 June The duo's first hit composition *Let's Go Get Stoned* is recorded by Ray Charles° and makes US #31. Chart success gains them a writing contract with Motown.

1967 June First hit for Motown is *Ain't No Mountain High Enough*, the first duet hit by Marvin Gaye° and Tammi Terrell, which charts at US #19.

1968 May First hit both written and produced by the duo, *Ain't Nothing Like The Real Thing*, sung by Gaye° and Terrell, hits US #8 and UK #34.

1970 Apr They take on role of writers and producers for Diana Ross° when she leaves The Supremes°. First Ross solo is *Reach Out And Touch (Somebody's Hand)*, which makes US #20 and UK #35.

Aug They rearrange *Ain't No Mountain High Enough* for Ross°. It becomes their first US #1 hit (UK #6).

1971 July Simpson releases solo LP *Exposed* on Motown, featuring the duo's songs and production.

1972 Aug Second solo LP *Valerie Simpson* is released in US.

1973 Nov Discouraged by Motown from singing themselves, the duo signs a new deal with Warner Bros., and releases Ashford and Simpson LP *Gimme Something Real*, a minor US hit (#156).

1974 Jan First (minor) US hit single as Ashford and Simpson is *(I'd Know You) Anywhere* (#88). The two are married, and daughter Nicole is born.

1978 Nov *It Seems To Hang On* is their first UK hit single (#48).

Dec *I'm Every Woman* is a major hit for Chaka Khan° (US #21, UK #11).

1979 Oct *Found A Cure* is their own first US top 40 hit, peaking at #36.

1982 A new recording deal is signed with Capitol Records.

1985 Feb *Solid* finally gives them a major hit as performers, reaching US #12 and UK #3. LP *Solid* quickly follows, charting at US #29 and UK #42. (These successes are not followed up on a similar scale, but Ashford and Simpson continue to be active in performance, production and songwriting.)

1986 Sept *Count Your Blessings* reaches only US #84.

1988 June They perform as part of the soul set at the Nelson Mandela 70th Birthday Party in London.

ASIA

John Wetton (vocals and bass)
Steve Howe (guitar)
Geoff Downes (keyboards)
Carl Palmer (drums)

1981 Jan Having folded UK, Wetton (b. July 12, 1949, Derby, UK), talks to Steve Howe (b. Apr.8, 1947, London, UK), who has just left Yes°, about forming a new band, since Geffen Records in the US is keen to sign such a new project. They approach former Emerson, Lake & Palmer° drummer Carl Palmer (b. Mar.20, 1947, Birmingham, UK), and Yes°/Buggles° keyboards player Geoff Downes, and form Asia.

1982 Mar After much preparation, debut LP *Asia* is lambasted by UK critics as staid and stale, though it is received more kindly elsewhere.

May LP *Asia* hits #1 in US, where it reigns for 2 months, but stalls by comparison in UK, at #14.

June *Heat Of The Moment*, taken from the LP, becomes a major US hit (#4). It is only a moderate UK seller (#46). The band begins stadium-filling, live work in US and around the world.

Sept Second single *Only Time Will Tell* reaches US #17 and UK #54.

1983 Aug Second LP *Alpha*, released at end of world tour, hits UK #5 and US #6.

Sept *Don't Cry*, taken from the LP, climbs to US #10 and UK #33. Wetton leaves, and is replaced by Greg Lake (b. Nov.10, 1948, Bournemouth, UK), Palmer's earlier partner in ELP.

Dec Second US extract from LP *Alpha* is *The Smile Has Left Your Eyes* (#34). It is not a UK hit.

Dec [6] "*Asia In Asia*", a live TV concert from Budokan Theatre, Tokyo, has an audience of over 20 million in the US (via MTV), and is also heard on 285 US radio stations. It is Lake's first appearance with the band and proves the peak of its career.

1985 Dec Wetton rejoins Asia for much less successful third LP *Astra*, which peaks at US #67 and UK #68. *Go* is a minor US seller (#46). Asia eventually disbands as the members follow other projects.

THE ASSOCIATES

Billy Mackenzie (vocals)
Alan Rankine (keyboards)

1976 Mackenzie (b. Mar.27, 1957) and Rankine first perform together as a cabaret combo called The Absorbic Ones in their native Dundee, Scotland, UK.

1979 After forming a succession of ad-hoc bands, the two emerge as The Associates on their own Double Hip label, with a version of David Bowie's° *Boys Keep Swinging*, looking set to become part of the energetic Scottish new wave of the early 80s.

1980 Aug Signed to ex-Polydor A&R man Chris Parry's independent Fiction label, they release debut LP *The Affectionate Punch*, recorded with the help of Australian drummer John Murphy.

1981 Growing enthusiasm generated by live appearances results in a five-single deal with Beggars Banquet Records' subsidiary label Situation Two. All achieve top 10 success in the UK independent singles chart during the year.

Oct Mini-LP *Fourth Drawer Down*, an anthology of *Situation 2* singles, tops the independent chart.

1982 Feb They establish their own Associates label, distributed by WEA, which takes them out of the independent arena and into the mainstream.

Mar *Party Fears Two*, their most successful single, hits UK #9.
May *Club Country* reaches UK #13. It is taken from LP *Sulk*, which climbs to UK #10.
Aug Following their first major UK tour, double A-side coupling *18 Carat Love Affair* and a revival of Diana Ross's° *Love Hangover*, reaches UK #21.
1984 June After an 18 month lay-off to write new material, the band returns, now signed direct to WEA, with *Those First Impressions*, which makes UK #43.
Sept *Waiting For The Love Boat* reaches UK #53.
1985 Jan *Breakfast* peaks at #49 in UK.
Feb LP *Perhaps* only reaches UK #23 and fades quickly. Disillusioned by this relative failure, the two central members decide to pursue solo activities. (This will result in Rankine solo LP, *She Loves Me Not*, on Virgin in 1987, and cameo collaborations with favored artists by Mackenzie, including Yello's *The Rhythm Divine* in Aug. 1987. Mackenzie's determination to keep The Associates' name alive will spur the recording of new material for WEA in the first half of 1988, for release in the fall.)

THE ASSOCIATION

Terry Kirkman (vocals and keyboards)
Jim Yester (vocals and guitar)
Gary "Jules" Alexander (vocals and guitar)
Russ Giguere (vocals and guitar)
Larry Ramos, Jr. (vocals and guitar)
Brian Cole (vocals and bass)
Ted Bluechel, Jr. (vocals and drums)

1965 Nov Recruited by Kirkman, and after 6 months rehearsing, the California group (minus Ramos) has its stage debut at Pasadena's Ice House. *Babe I'm Gonna Love You* is recorded for Jubilee label as a one-off deal, but does not chart.
1966 May *Along Comes Mary* gets US radio play despite some interpretations as a drug hymn, and becomes US chart debut, climbing to #7.
June LP sessions held at Columbia and GSP studios in Hollywood.
Aug *Cherish*, a soft ballad in contrast to *Mary*, is released with debut LP *And Then...Along Comes The Association*. The LP reaches US #5, and *Cherish* is their first #1 hit.
1967 Jan LP *Renaissance* is less successful, reaching US #34, while *Pandora's Golden Heebie Jeebies* is in stark contrast to *Cherish* and very experimental. It disorients US radio, and only reaches #35.
Apr Warner Bros. buys Valiant Records, and with it the group's recording contract. Alexander leaves, and is replaced by Ramos.
June *Windy*, their biggest seller, is released and hits US #1.
July LP *Insight Out* is issued, and climbs to US #8.
Sept *Never My Love* returns to the soft style of *Cherish*, and hits US #2.
Nov Association is voted #1 Group of the Year in US by Bill Gavin Radio-Record Congress, displacing The Beatles° after 3 years.
1968 Feb *Everything That Touches You* is their final US top 10 hit, peaking at #10.
May *Time For Livin'* reaches #39 in US, and LP *Birthday*, #23. The group visits UK to promote *Time For Livin'*, and it becomes their only UK top 50 hit, peaking at #21. They appear on UK TV "Top of the Pops" and at NME Poll Winners Concert, Wembley.
Sept *Six Man Band*, an uncharacteristic (and autobiographical) heavy rock track, is their last US top 50 single, peaking at #47. Soon after, Alexander rejoins and they become a seven-man band.
1969 Jan LP *Greatest Hits* hits US #4, and is their third and last gold LP (*Along Comes* and *Insight Out* are the others).
Mar The group's new songs feature in the movie *Goodbye Columbus*. The title track charts at US #80, and soundtrack LP at #99.
Oct LP *The Association* regains sales ground at US #32, but there is no hit single.
1970 July Giguere leaves to record solo LP *Hexagram 16*, and is replaced by Richard Thompson on keyboards for LP *The Association Live*, which charts at US #79.
1972 May A new recording deal with Columbia Records in US produces LP *Waterbeds In Trinidad*, but is not a commercial success.
Aug [2] Brian Cole dies in Los Angeles from an apparent heroin overdose. (Little more is heard of the group which moves into the cabaret circuit and then disbands. Reunions will occur during 1980s, notably US HBO TV special on Sept.26, 1980, and *Dreamer*, for Elektra Records, which will chart them again in US (#66) in Feb. 1981.)

RICK ASTLEY

1983 Brought up in Newton-le-Willows, Merseyside, UK, where his early interests include choir singing and playing piano and drums, Astley (b. Feb.6, 1966, Warrington, UK), joins his first band, Give Way, as a drummer.
1984 He joins FBI as lead singer, a new band whose numbers are increasingly influenced by music heard on visits to Wigan's legendary soul music club, The Pier Casino.
1985 Feb Astley is spotted at the Monks Sports and Social club, Warrington, by Pete Waterman, of the Stock/Aitken/Waterman writing and production hit factory, who offers him solo work in London.
1987 July Following 18 months of rehearsal, grooming and styling with the SAW team at PWL studios in London, while also employed as a tape operator, Astley is launched in the UK.
Aug Debut single *Never Gonna Give You Up* tops UK chart for 5 weeks, and becomes UK's biggest-selling single of the year, before moving on to repeat its chart-topping status throughout Europe.
Nov *Whenever You Need Somebody* hits UK #2, and marks the start of a 6-month non-stop worldwide promotion trek, while debut LP of the same title enters the UK LP chart at #1, and will sell in excess of a million copies in 6 months in the UK.
Dec *When I Fall In Love*, a faithfully-styled revival of Nat King Cole's 1957 classic ballad, hits UK #2. The reissue of Cole's original halts its progress to the top, so the single is flipped to give joint promotion (and additional sales) to double A-side coupling, *Back In Your Arms Again*.
1988 Feb [22] Astley wins the British Phonographic Industry award for Best British Single of 1987, with *Never Gonna Give You Up*.
Mar After a 3-month climb, *Never Gonna Give You Up* tops US chart for 2 weeks. *Together Forever*, from debut LP, hits UK #2.
May LP *Whenever You Need Somebody* climbs to US #19.
June *Together Forever* becomes Astley's second US chart-topper.

ASWAD

Brinsley Forde (vocals)
Tony Gad (guitar)
Angus "Drummie" Zeb (drums)

1975 The band forms in UK with Forde (former child star of 1971 UK BBC TV children's series "Here Come the Double Deckers"), and Zeb, plus Donald Benjamin (guitar), Courtney Hemmings (keyboards) and Ras George Levi (bass).
1976 They sign to Island Records, the first UK reggae act to secure a major deal, and release *Back To Africa*, which tops the UK reggae chart, and LP *Aswad*, equally popular in specialist reggae circles.
1978 The group moves to independent label, Grove Muzic, and supports the popular Rock Against Racism cause.
1979 Grove licenses its *Aswad* releases to Island, including second LP *Hulet*.
1980 They contribute music to UK film *Babylon*, which deals with the pressures of young black life in contemporary London, and in which Forde has a star acting role. *Soundtrack* LP, containing their tracks, is released by Chrysalis Records. Meanwhile Aswad signs to CBS Records.
1982 July LP *Not Satisfied*, for CBS, is their first UK chart success, reaching #50.
1983 Dec Aswad re-signs to Island, and LP *Live And Direct* charts at UK #57.
1984 Mar *Chasing For The Breeze*, recorded in Jamaica, becomes their first UK chart single, reaching #51.
Oct *54-46 (Was My Number)* reaches #70 in UK.
Nov Aswad tours the UK, promoting LP *Rebel Souls*, which makes UK #48.
1985 They tour on and off for the next 2 years, their popularity now confirmed as Britain's premier reggae act. Three UK singles and LP *Going To The Top*, on their own independent label, Simba Records, are released.
1986 With a change of management and a reduction of the group to three, they re-sign to Island via the Mango label.
1987 The band tours, rehearses and records new material for 1988 release.
1988 Mar *Don't Turn Around*, a reggae re-styling of an Albert Hammond/Diane Warren song first recorded by Tina Turner°, tops UK chart for 2 weeks.
Apr LP *Distant Thunder* reaches UK #10.
June *Give A Little Love* peaks at UK #11.

ATLANTA RHYTHM SECTION

Ronnie Hammond (vocals)
Barry Bailey (guitar)
J.R. Cobb (guitar)
Dean Daughtry (keyboards)
Paul Goddard (bass)
Robert Nix (drums)

1970 After working together on a Roy Orbison° session, the members (all studio musicians around Atlanta, Ga., US) team up. Cobb (b. Feb.5, 1944, Birmingham, Ala.) and Daughtry (b. Sept.8, 1946, Kingston, Ala.) have previously been together in The Classics IV°, along with ARS producer Buddy Buie. Former studio engineer Hammond becomes lead vocalist.

1974 Sept After two LPs for MCA, the band signs to Polydor Records and releases first charting LP *Third Annual Pipe Dream* (#74 in US).

Oct *Doraville*, a song about the band's Georgia hometown, is their first hit single, reaching US #35.

1977 Mar *So In To You* reaches US #7. First major hit LP *A Rock And Roll Alternative*, reaches US #11.

1978 Apr *Imaginary Lover* hits #7. Nix leaves, replaced by Roy Yeager (b. Feb.4, 1946, Greenwood, Miss., US). LP *Champagne Jam* is their biggest seller yet, reaching US top 10 and being certified platinum.

July *I'm Not Gonna Let It Bother Me Tonight* climbs to #14 in US.

1979 June *Do It Or Die* from LP *Underdog* reaches US #19.

Aug LP *Underdog* reaches US #26.

Oct ARS revives *Spooky*, originally a #3 hit in 1968 for some members when in Classics IV°. This time, it reaches US #17.

1981 Sept A change of label to CBS brings one more US hit single, *Alien*, which reaches #29. But parent LP *Quinella* struggles at #84 as Atlanta loses its hit impetus. (Further releases and touring keeps the group busy a while longer, but it fades from the commercial scene.)

PATTI AUSTIN

1981 Having performed professionally from age 5, Austin (b. Aug.10, 1948, New York, N.Y., US) is signed to Quincy Jones' Quest Records. A childhood protégée of Dinah Washington and Sammy Davis Jr., she has sung commercial jingles regularly since age 19, and LP backup vocals for Michael Jackson°, Billy Joel°, Paul Simon° and others, as well as jazz/funk ballad LPs for CTI and CBS Records.

Apr She sings female vocal parts on Quincy Jones' LP *The Dude*, which reaches US #13 and UK #19.

1982 Jan Her own US chart debut is *Every Home Should Have One*, which reaches #62. LP of the same title makes US #66 and UK #99.

May *Baby Come To Me*, a ballad duet with James Ingram°, peaks at US #73.

1983 Feb After featuring in the top-rated US TV soap drama "General Hospital", *Baby Come To Me* is reissued due to public demand, and tops US chart for 2 weeks.

Mar *Baby Come To Me* reaches UK #11, her only UK chart entry.

Apr *Every Home Should Have One* is reissued, this time peaking at US #69.

July Another duet with Ingram, *How Do You Keep The Music Playing* (theme from the movie *Best Friends*), reaches US #45.

1984 Feb *It's Gonna Be Special* (from the film *Two of a Kind*) peaks at US #82.

May LP *Patti Austin* reaches US #87.

1985 Mar She duets with Narada Michael Walden on *Gimme Gimme Gimme*, which reaches #39 on R&B chart only.

Nov LP *Gettin' Away With Murder* sells less well than her two previous sets, peaking at US #182. The single from it, *Honey From The Bees*, fails to become a pop hit, but is a huge disco favorite in US, reaching #6 on the dance/disco (12" single) chart, as well as R&B #24.

1986 May *The Heat Of Heat* returns her to the US pop chart, climbing to #55. (After this, things will be quieter on record, but she is a consistently popular live and TV singer, recognized as one of the most stylish female voices in black music.)

June LP *The Real Me* is released once again on Quincy Jones' Quest label, produced by David Pack.

FRANKIE AVALON

1957 Francis Avallone (b. Sept.18, 1939, Philadelphia, US) a trumpet-playing prodigy and local TV celebrity in his pre-teen years, comes under the guidance of local businessmen Bob Marcucci and Peter De Angelis, opens a teenage dance club with them, and joins the Philadelphia rock group Roçco & The Saints. The group, with Avalon, has a brief slot singing *Teacher's Pet* in the film *Disc Jockey Jamboree*.

June Avalon signs to Marcucci and De Angelis' new locally-based Chancellor label as a solo singer.

1958 Jan First hit *Dede Dinah* charts in US, climbing to #7.

July *Ginger Bread* is his second US top 10 hit, reaching #9.

1959 Mar *Venus* reaches US #1, and is his first million-selling single.

Apr *Venus* charts in UK, reaching #16.

May Double A-side *Bobby Sox To Stockings/A Boy Without A Girl* indicates his US teen audience popularity when both sides make top 10 (#8 and #10).

Dec *Why* is a second US million-selling single, and his second #1.

1960 Jan *Why* is covered in UK by Anthony Newley, who has a #1 hit. Avalon's version is his second and last UK hit, reaching #20. As US record sales dip sharply through the rest of year, he makes a sideways move into films, becoming the token teen attraction in *The Alamo*.

1961 Avalon makes many lesser movies mostly in beach party-type films co-starring Annette Funicello.

1962 May *You Are Mine* is his final US top 30 entry, peaking at #26.

1976 Mar After a long but eventually unspectacular Hollywood and TV career, Avalon has surprise US hit (#46) with a remake of his own *Venus* dressed up in topical disco arrangement. It is not to launch a prolonged comeback on record, and he remains mainly an actor and (in live work) a trumpeter.

AVERAGE WHITE BAND

Hamish Stuart (vocals and guitar)
Alan Gorrie (vocals and bass)
Onnie McIntyre (guitar)
Roger Ball (alto and baritone sax)
Malcolm "Molly" Duncan (tenor/soprano sax)
Robbie McIntosh (drums)

1972 The band is founded by Gorrie (b. July 19, 1946, Perth, Scotland, UK) with musician friends who have helped him on solo recordings the year before. McIntosh (b. 1950, Scotland) has earlier been with Oblivion Express, while Stuart (b. Oct.8, 1949, Glasgow), Ball (b. June 4, 1944, Dundee), Duncan (b. Aug.24, 1945, Montrose) and McIntyre (b. Sept.25, 1945, Lennox Town) have played with various Scots bands since the mid-60s.

July They make their first appearance together at the Lincoln Festival, UK.

1973 Jan [13] They support Eric Clapton° at his comeback concert at the Rainbow Theatre, London. The band's blue-eyed R&B/funk style interests MCA Records, which signs them for LP *Show Your Hand*.
1974 July Second LP *Average White Band* switches labels to Atlantic, and is produced in US by Arif Mardin.
Sept [23] McIntosh dies at a Los Angeles party from a heroin overdose when he believes he is snorting cocaine. He is immediately replaced by black UK drummer Steve Ferrone (b. Apr.25, 1950, Brighton, UK).
1975 Feb LP and the single taken from it, *Pick Up The Pieces*, hit US #1 in the same week. The single moves to UK #5, and the LP to UK #6.
Apr Original MCA LP is reissued in US as *Put It Where You Want It*, and charts at #39.
May *Cut The Cake* is US smash (#10), and reaches #37 in UK.
July LP *Cut The Cake*, dedicated to McIntosh, climbs to US #4 and UK #28.
Sept *If I Ever Lose This Heaven* reaches #39 in US, where the band is now based. *School Boy Crush* follows and reaches #33.
1976 Sept LP *Soul Searching* reaches US #8. *Queen Of My Soul*, taken from it, makes US #40 and UK #22.
1977 Mar LP *Person To Person* reaches #28 in US, but fails to sell in UK.
July The band releases LP *Benny And Us* with most lead vocals taken by soul singer Ben E. King°. It is successful (US #33), and foreshadows later work as recording sidemen with black artists like Chaka Khan°.
1978 They change UK record label to RCA, after which most releases will be bigger sellers in UK than US. RCA LP *Warmer Communications* is their last with Arif Mardin.
1979 Mar LP *Feel No Fret* charts at UK #15, where it is their best-selling LP since *Average White Band*. It yields *Walk On By*, a #46 UK hit.
1980 May Disco-styled *Let's Go Round Again* is not big US seller, but reaches UK #12. It is taken from LP *Shine* (UK #14), which is Average White Band's final big-selling album.

KEVIN AYERS

1968 Dec Ayers (b. Aug.16, 1945, Herne Bay, Kent, UK) resigns as Soft Machine vocalist/bassist in exhausted disillusionment, for 6 months' rest, recuperation, and songwriting in Ibiza.
1969 Nov Back in UK, he signs to Harvest (EMI) as a solo artist, and releases LP *Joy Of A Toy*, a minor seller.
1970 Mar He forms backing band The Whole World, including Mike Oldfield° (bass) and David Bedford (piano). LP *Shooting At The Moon* is issued in UK. It is not a chart success, but (like its predecessor and successors) popular with critics.
1971 Aug The Whole World splits up, with Oldfield° starting a solo career.
1972 Jan Ayers releases LP *Whatever She Brings We Sing*, then forms quartet Kevin Ayers and Archibald, with Steve Hillage on guitar.
Dec The band changes name to Kevin Ayers and Decadence, tours France, then breaks up.
1973 May Ayers records LP *Bananamour*, and forms a sextet called 747 to tour and promote it.
Sept A new recording deal is signed with UK Island Records, but 747 splits after a disastrous Edinburgh Festival appearance.
1974 May LP *The Confessions Of Dr. Dream* is released in UK. New backing band, The Soporifics, forms to promote and tour.
June [1] Ayers records one-off live LP *June 1, 1974* with John Cale°, Nico and Brian Eno°.
1975 Mar LP *Sweet Deceiver* is recorded with The Soporifics, which tours Europe, then breaks up. Ayers has a second 6-month recuperative retirement.
1976 Jan He returns to re-sign with his old record label, Harvest.
July LP *Yes We Have No Mañanas* is issued in UK, and Ayers forms a new band to play it live. The Kevin Ayers Band includes Andy Summers (later with Police°) on guitar, and Zoot Money on keyboards, but they only last the duration of the tour.
1977 May After a further UK tour with new musicians, Ayers "retires" to the south of France.
1978 Apr He returns to record and release LP *Rainbow Takeaway* in UK.
1980 Feb Final Harvest LP *That's What You Get Babe* is released in UK. Ayers follows with a tour and plays some live promotional dates in US, but no US breakthrough occurs. (He does not seek a major label deal again, but buys a home on Majorca in the Mediterranean, and is content to work quietly from there.)
1988 LP *Falling Up* released by Virgin in UK fails to rekindle his career.

AZTEC CAMERA

Roddy Frame (vocals and guitar)
Eddie Kulak (keyboards)
Gary Sanford (guitar)
Paul Powell (bass)
Dave Ruffy (drums)

1980 Jan Frame (b. Jan.29, 1964, East Kilbride, Scotland) forms the band – which will always revolve around his visions and songwriting – with Dave Mulholland (drums) and Campbell Owens (bass).
Dec After playing their innovative brand of melodic rock in Scottish towns, they sign to Glasgow independent label Postcard Records.
1981 Apr Debut single *Just Like Gold* is an immediate hit on the UK independent chart, where it reaches #10.
Aug *Mattress Of Wire* also hits UK independent chart, at #8. The rest of the year will be spent touring England for the first time.
1982 June A new independent label deal is signed with Rough Trade Records in London. Dave Ruffy is the band's fifth temporary drummer, and likes it so much he decides to stay. Bernie Clarke also joins (temporarily) on keyboards.
Oct *Pillar To Post* is another UK independent chart hit, at #4.
1983 Mar *Oblivious* becomes their first chart entry outside the independent field, at UK #47.
May Highly-rated debut LP *High Land, Hard Rain* reaches UK #22. The band is signed via a US deal to Sire Records, and the LP reaches US #129.
June *Walk Out To Winter* peaks at UK #64.
Aug The band begins a 3-month tour of major US venues as support for Elvis Costello°. Frame, only 19 years old, has to lie about his age in several US states.
Oct In mid-tour, they sign a new UK record deal with WEA Records.
Nov WEA reissues *Oblivious*, which is the band's first top 20 hit, at UK #18. Resisting the temptation to re-release more old material, Frame prepares songs for a new LP.
1984 Sept *All I Need Is Everything* (with an acoustic version of Van Halen's° *Jump* on the B-side) reaches UK #34.
Oct LP *Knife* reaches UK #14 and US #175, and the band begins an extensive world tour to promote it.
Nov *Still On Fire* fails, and after the tour Frame retreats to write new songs for a third LP.
1985 Apr 10" LP *Aztec Camera*, including live tracks recorded at The Dominion, London, in October 1984, reaches US #181.
1986 Sept With session help from Marcus Miller, Steve Jordan, and System's keyboardist David Frank, the band records Frame's latest songs in New York and Boston.
1987 Oct *Deep Wide And Tall*, from the simultaneously-released LP *Love*, fails to chart, while the LP initially peaks at UK #49.
Nov The band tours in US to promote LP *Love*.
1988 Jan They return to UK for more live dates, before leaving to tour Australia.
Mar Aztec's hard work and quality product begin to pay off, as *How Men Are* becomes a surprise UK hit, reaching #25.
June *Somewhere In My Heart* hits UK #3, their biggest hit to date. It revives UK sales interest in the LP *Love*, which now peaks at #10. A major UK tour culminates in two sold-out dates at London's Royal Albert Hall.

THE B52'S

Cindy Wilson (guitar and vocals)
Kate Pierson (organ and vocals)
Ricky Wilson (guitar)
Fred Schneider (keyboards and vocals)
Keith Strickland (drums)

1976 Oct The group forms in Athens, Ga., US, taking its name from the Southern US nickname for a kind of bouffant hairstyle adopted by its two female members. Pierson (b. Apr.27, 1948, Weehawken, N.J.), Schneider (b. July 1, 1951, Newark, Ga.) and Strickland (b. Oct.26, 1953, Athens) have had part-time experience in local groups, while Ricky Wilson (b. Mar.19, 1953, Athens) and sister Cindy (b. Feb.28, 1957, Athens) are novices.
1977 Feb [14] First live performance, at a Valentine party in Athens. Quickly developing a highly visual stage act featuring boots, mini-skirts and the girls' B52 hairdos, they go to New York, and through a series of gigs at Max's Kansas City club, become cult favorites.
1978 Aug Two songs, *Rock Lobster* and *52 Girls*, are recorded for a privately-pressed record which fast sells out its 2000 copies, and brings them to the attention of Island Records' boss, Chris Blackwell.

THE B52'S *cont.*

1979 June They visit Nassau to record their debut LP for Island, and sign to Warner Bros. for US.

July They visit UK to tour and promote their first releases. Despite UK critics' scepticism of their frivolous image, audiences love them.

Aug LP *The B52's* reaches UK #22, while *Rock Lobster* (the band's self-financed original reissued by Island) makes #37.

1980 May *Rock Lobster* is a belated US success, at #56.

Aug *Give Me Back My Man* climbs to UK #51.

Sept LP *Wild Planet* reaches #18 in UK.

Nov *Private Idaho* peaks at US #74.

1981 July Mini-LP *The Party Mix Album*, featuring dance-oriented remixes of familiar songs, makes UK #36 and US #62.

1982 Mar Mini-LP *Mesapotamia*, produced by David Byrne of Talking Heads°, reaches UK #18 and US #35.

1983 May *Future Generation* peaks at #63 in UK, while LP *Whammy!* reaches #33.

July *Legal Tender* reaches US #81, and LP *Whammy!* makes #29.

1986 May Double A-side reissue of *Rock Lobster* with another early favorite *Planet Claire*, produces their biggest-ever hit, reaching UK #12. (But it proves to be an isolated revival as there will be no renewed activity from the group.)

THE BABYS

John Waite (vocals and bass)
Wally Stocker (vocals and guitar)
Mike Corby (vocals and keyboards)
Tony Brock (drums)

1976 Waite (b. July 4, 1954, UK), Corby (b. July 3, 1955, UK), Stocker (b. Mar.17, 1954, UK) and Brock (b. Mar.31, 1954, UK) come together in London with UK rock TV producer Mike Mansfield, who directs a promo video for them demonstrating visual appeal as well as sound. This impresses Chrysalis Records, which signs them.

1977 Mar Debut LP *The Babys* is not a strong seller, but *If You've Got The Time*, taken from it, reaches #88 in US chart – sufficient to move the quartet to US to promote themselves further.

Dec After much US TV exposure, *Isn't It Time* reaches #13 in US, and LP *Broken Heart* is a US hit (#34). Corby leaves, and is replaced on keyboards by Jonathan Cain.

1978 Jan *Isn't It Time* is a minor UK hit (#45).

1979 Mar *Every Time I Think Of You*, from LP *Head First*, reaches US #13. By now, Ricky Phillips has joined as bassist, with Waite concentrating on vocals.

1980 Mar LP *Union Jacks* yields *Back On My Feet Again*, which reaches US #33.

1981 Jan Cain leaves to join Journey°.

Nov The remaining quartet records LP *On The Edge*, and from this comes final US hit *Turn And Walk Away*, which peaks at #51. After this The Babys disbands, and Waite is retained by Chrysalis as a soloist.

1982 July Waite releases first solo LP *Ignition* which reaches US #68. Singles from it fail to chart.

1984 July LP *No Brakes* makes UK #10.

Sept He makes a spectacular chart return with *Missing You* which becomes one of the year's biggest hits reaching US #1, and UK #9 in Oct. He is then cast as a hairdresser in US soap, "Paper Dolls".

1985 Oct *Every Step Of The Way*, from new LP *Mask Of Smiles*, makes US #26.

1987 Sept LP *Rovers Return* reaches US #77.

BACHMAN-TURNER OVERDRIVE

Randy Bachman (guitar and vocals)
Tim Bachman (guitar)
C.F. (Fred) Turner (bass and vocals)
Robbie Bachman (drums)

1972 The band evolves in Vancouver, Canada, out of Brave Belt, in which Randy (b. Sept.27, 1943, Winnipeg) and Robbie (b. Feb.18, 1953, Winnipeg) Bachman have played for 2 years unsuccessfully with Chad Allan (both Randy Bachman and Allan also being former members of Guess Who°, Canada's most successful band of the 1960s). The new name partly comes from the trucking industry magazine Overdrive, and appropriately the band will develop a blue-collar image and lyrical inclination.

1973 Aug After 24 record company rejections of their no-frills, solid-rock approach, the band signs to Mercury Records, which releases LP *Bachman-Turner Overdrive*. Promoted by regular US touring (the band's hallmark), it climbs to US #70, but Tim Bachman leaves shortly afterwards, replaced on guitar by Blair Thornton.

Dec First US hit single is *Blue Collar*, which peaks at #68.

1974 Apr *Let It Ride* reaches #23 in US.

July LP *Bachman-Turner Overdrive 2* hits US #4.

Aug *Takin' Care Of Business* is their first top 20 single, reaching US #12.

Oct LP *Not Fragile* tops the US chart.

Nov *You Ain't Seen Nothing Yet*, a song only included on LP *Not Fragile* as an afterthought, and sung jokily by Randy with a stutter, also hits US #1, and is a million-plus seller.

Dec *You Ain't Seen Nothing Yet* is the band's UK chart debut, and hits #2, while LP *Not Fragile* peaks at #12.

1975 Feb *Roll On Down The Highway* makes US #14 and UK #22. It is their last UK chartmaker.

Mar A former Brave Belt LP is reissued by Reprise Records as *Bachman-Turner Overdrive As Brave Belt*, but its appeal is mostly esoteric, and it reaches only US #180.

July *Hey You* makes US #21, while LP *Four-Wheel Drive* hits US #5.

1976 Jan *Down To The Line* reaches US #43.

Feb LP *Head On* peaks at #23 in US, while *Take It Like A Man*, extracted from it, makes #33.

May *Lookin' Out For #1* peaks at US #65, the band's smallest US hit since its debut.

Sept Compilation LP *The Best Of BTO (So Far)* reaches US #19.

Oct *Gimme Your Money Please* reaches only US #70.

1977 Apr Randy Bachman leaves to go solo, and is placed by Jim Clench on the LP *Freeways*, which climbs to US #70.

1978 Mar LP *Street Action*, on which the band's name is shortened to BTO, reaches only US #130.

1979 Apr LP *Rock'n'Roll Nights*, also as BTO, is another disappointing seller at US #165, while *Heartaches*, taken from it, peaks at #60 and is the band's final US hit single.

May Randy Bachman re-emerges with new band Ironhorse, which signs to Scotti Brothers and has a minor US seller with LP *Ironhorse*, reaching #153. More successful is *Sweet Lui-Louise*, which climbs to US #36 and UK #60.

1980 May Ironhorse has another US hit (#89) with *What's Your Hurry Darlin'*, from unsuccessful second LP *Everything Is Grey*. (After this, the band will break up, and Randy Bachman will work solo again for a while, before re-forming BTO in 1984 with Turner and Tim Bachman.)

1984 Sept A hoped-for comeback LP, on the Compleat label, simply titled *Bachman-Turner Overdrive*, stalls at US #191. (The reunion holds, however, and the trio works as a touring attraction in US and Canada, much as in the early 1970s, but there will be no more hit records.)

BAD COMPANY

Paul Rodgers (vocals)
Mick Ralphs (guitar)
Boz Burrell (bass)
Simon Kirke (drums)

1973 Aug Left without a band after the breakup of Free°, Kirke (b. July 28, 1949, Wales, UK) and Rodgers (b. Dec.17, 1949, Middlesborough) join up with Ralphs (b. Mar. 31, 1948, Hereford), who has just left Mott The Hoople°. The band's name is taken from title of a 1972 film starring Jeff Bridges.
Nov Former King Crimson° bassist Boz Burrell (b. Raymond Burrell, 1946, Lincoln) joins after the others have spent 2 months in rehearsal.
1974 Mar [8] First live appearance, at City Hall, Newcastle-upon-Tyne.
Apr They sign to Island Records in UK, and to Led Zeppelin°-owned Swan Song in US, and record LP *Bad Company* in 10 days in Ronnie Lane's mobile studio.
June LP *Bad Company* hits UK #3, and *Can't Get Enough*, taken from it, climbs to #15.
Sept LP *Bad Company* tops US chart.
Nov *Can't Get Enough* climbs to US #5.
1975 Feb *Movin' On* hits US #19, though it is not released as a single in UK.
Apr LP *Straight Shooter* is released and hits #3 in both UK and US.
May *Good Lovin' Gone Bad* reaches UK #31 and US #36.
Sept *Feels Like Makin' Love* climbs to UK #20 (where it is their last charting single), and to US #10.
1976 Feb LP *Run With The Pack* hits UK #4 and US #5.
May *Young Blood* reaches #20 in US.
Aug *Honey Child* makes #59 in US.
1977 Apr LP *Burnin' Sky* is their first not to reach top 10, climbing to UK #17 and US #15.
June Title track from *Burnin' Sky* is issued as a US single, hitting #78.
1979 Apr LP *Desolation Angels* updates basic four-piece rock sound with synthesizer and strings, and is released amid (unfounded) rumors about the band splitting up. It hits UK #10 and US #3, a month later.
June *Rock'n'Roll Fantasy* is last major US hit single, reaching #13.
Aug *Gone, Gone, Gone* reaches #56 in US.
1982 Aug After a 3-year silence, the band returns with LP *Rough Diamond* and shows unabated popularity by taking it to UK #15.
Oct LP *Rough Diamonds* reaches #26 in US, but single *Electricland* is less successful, climbing only to #74.
1983 July After several months of inactivity, apart from hints that both Kirke and Burrell are putting together their own new bands, Bad Company officially announces its break-up.
Dec [8] Rodgers plays alongside Eric Clapton°, Jimmy Page and many other contemporaries in the Ronnie Lane ARMS Appeal concert at New York's Madison Square Garden.

BADFINGER

Pete Ham (guitar, piano and vocals)
Joey Molland (guitar, keyboards and vocals)
Tom Evans (bass and vocals)
Mike Gibbins (drums)

1968 July Ham (b. Apr.27, 1947, Swansea, Wales, UK), Evans (b. 1947, Liverpool) and Gibbins (b. 1949, Swansea) have been playing for 2 years as backing group for UK vocalist David Garrick, along with guitarist Ron Griffiths, when Paul McCartney° accepts their demo tape and they sign to Apple Records, calling themselves The Iveys.
Nov Apple issues The Iveys' *Maybe Tomorrow* in UK; it fails to sell.
Dec Griffiths leaves and is replaced by Molland (b. June 21, 1948, Liverpool).
1969 Feb *Maybe Tomorrow* is released in US and reaches #67.
July Proposed LP *Maybe Tomorrow* is withdrawn from UK and US release schedule, while *No Escaping Your Love* is a Europe-only release.
Sept The group records McCartney° song *Come And Get It* in a session produced by McCartney.
Dec The group changes name to Badfinger for UK release of *Come And Get It*. It is heard in the film *The Magic Christian* with Peter Sellers/Ringo Starr°, which premières in London.
1970 Jan *Come And Get It* hits UK #4. LP *Magic Christian Music* is issued in UK but does not chart.
Feb *Come And Get It* charts in US, reaching #7.
Apr LP *Magic Christian Music* charts in US, reaching #55.
Oct The group begins an 8-week US tour, and *No Matter What* is released in US.
Nov *No Matter What* reaches US #8. LP *No Dice* is issued, failing to chart in UK, but making US #28.
1971 Jan *No Matter What*, released in UK, hits #5.
Aug [1] Badfinger plays in George Harrison's° benefit concert for Bangladesh at Madison Square Garden, New York.
Dec *Day After Day* and LP *Straight Up* are released in US, charting at #4 and #31 respectively. The single is a US million-seller.
1972 Jan Single and LP are issued in UK; *Day After Day* reaches #10, but *Straight Up* does not sell.
Feb Harry Nilsson° tops US chart with *Without You*, written by Badfinger's Ham and Evans.
Mar Nilsson's° *Without You* hits UK #1, for 5 weeks.
Apr *Baby Blue* is US hit, reaching #14.
1973 Dec After a quiet spell, LP *Ass* is the group's last Apple release, but sells poorly. A new recording deal is signed with Warner Bros.
1974 Mar First Warner LP *Badfinger* reaches only US #161.
Nov LP *Wish You Were Here*, released in US while the group is touring there, still only crawls to #148 on US chart. Because of frustration over this and management and financial problems, Molland leaves at end of tour, and Ham becomes deeply depressed.
1975 Apr [23] Also plagued by personal problems, Ham commits suicide, hanging himself in his London garage. Other members drift into minor groups.
1978 Molland and Evans reform Badfinger with new men Tony Kaye (keyboards) and Peter Clarke (drums), signing to Elektra Records and recording LP *Airwaves*, but this does not restore erstwhile chart glory.
1981 Mar Almost forgotten but still together, the group records LP *Say No More* for US Radio label – not itself a hit, but yielding *Hold On*, a minor US chartmaker at #56. The pace is not maintained, and Badfinger fades from the scene.
1983 Evans, depressed by the continuing battle to receive a fair royalty for the million-selling *Without You*, also ends his life.

JOAN BAEZ

1960 After an acclaimed debut at the 1959 Newport Folk Festival, Baez (b. Jan.9, 1941, Staten Island, New York, US) signs to Vanguard Records as a folk singer, and releases her eponymous debut LP, which will chart at US #15 in 1962, and at UK #9 in 1965.
1961 Oct LP *Joan Baez, Vol.2* is released, becoming her first chart entry at US #13.
1962 Oct LP *Joan Baez In Concert* is released, and climbs to US #10.
1963 May [17] She headlines the first-ever Monterey Folk Festival, alongside protégé Bob Dylan°.
July Baez appears at Newport Folk Festival (the first to be held since she debuted there), and also introduces Bob Dylan°.
Nov Her first hit single is protesters' anthem *We Shall Overcome*, recorded live at Miles College in Birmingham, Ala., which reaches US #90.
Dec Early recordings made at the 1959 Newport Folk Festival, with Bill Wood and Ted Alevizos, are released on LP *The Best Of Joan Baez*, for Squire Records, which reaches US #45. Live LP *Joan Baez In Concert, Part 2* is released. It will chart at US #7 in early 1964, and 6 months later become her UK chart debut at #8.
1964 Nov LP *Joan Baez 5* is released. It will reach US #12 in the New Year, and will be her biggest UK hit (#3) in mid-1965.
1965 June She founds the Institute for the Study of Non-Violence, in Carmel, Cal., as *We Shall Overcome* becomes her first UK hit single, reaching #26.
Aug *There But For Fortune* climbs to #8 in UK.
Sept Bob Dylan's° song *It's All Over Now Baby Blue* takes her to UK #22.
Oct *There But For Fortune* reaches US #50.
Dec Another Dylan° song, *Farewell Angelina*, makes UK #35.
1966 Jan LP *Farewell Angelina* hits US #10 and UK #5.
July *Pack Up Your Sorrows*, written by Baez' brother-in-law Richard Farina, who died in a motorcycle crash 2 months earlier, reaches UK #50.
Aug Because of her strident opposition to the Vietnam War, the Daughters of the American Revolution refuse to allow Baez to perform live at Constitution Hall, Washington, D.C.

JOAN BAEZ *cont.*

Oct [16] Baez is one of 124 anti-draft demonstrators arrested for blocking the entrance to the armed forces' induction centre at Oakland, Cal., and jailed for 10 days. Meanwhile, LP *Joan* reaches US #38.

1968 She marries student protest leader David Harris (and will campaign continuously on his behalf when he is jailed for draft evasion some months later).

1969 Jan LP *Any Day Now*, consisting wholly of Bob Dylan° songs, is released and will reach US #30.

May *Love Is Just A Four-Letter Word* climbs to US #86.

June She releases LP *David's Album*, a collection of songs dedicated to her imprisoned husband; it reaches US #36.

July Compilation LP *Joan Baez On Vanguard* peaks at UK #15.

Aug [17] She performs at the Woodstock Festival.

1970 May LP *One Day At A Time* reaches US #80.

Aug [30] She plays at the Isle of Wight Pop Festival, UK, at which Jimi Hendrix° makes his last appearance.

1971 Jan Compilation LP *The First 10 Years* reaches US #73 and UK #41. It is her last LP to chart in the UK.

Oct A cover version of The Band's° Civil War story-song *The Night They Drove Old Dixie Down*, hits US #3 and UK #6, and is a million-seller. It is taken from LP *Blessed Are*, which returns her to US top 20 at #11.

Dec A revival of The Beatles'° *Let It Be* reaches US #49.

1972 May After more than a decade with Vanguard, Baez signs to A&M Records and releases LP *Come From The Shadows*, reaching US #48.

Aug *In The Quiet Morning*, a song written by her sister Mimi Farina in tribute to Janis Joplin°, reaches US #69.

1973 May Indicating that her political stance has not relaxed, Baez devotes one side of LP *Where Are You Now, My Son?* to a sound documentary of US bombing in Vietnam. The LP is a moderate seller, reaching US #138.

1975 July *Blue Sky* peaks at US #57, while LP *Diamonds And Rust* is her biggest-seller for 4 years, reaching US #11.

Nov Title track from *Diamonds And Rust*, an autobiographical song concerned with Baez' early involvement with Bob Dylan° (whom she has recently reacquainted), is her last US hit single, reaching #35.

Oct [29] Baez joins Dylan° as part of his Rolling Thunder Revue tour of the US, which launches in Plymouth, Mass.

1976 Apr Live LP *From Every Stage* reaches US #34.

Dec LP *Gulf Winds* reaches #62 in US.

1977 Aug LP *Blowin' Away* is the first result of signing to Portrait Records; it reaches US #54.

1978 Jan Compilation LP *The Best Of Joan C. Baez*, on A&M, peaks at US #121.

Feb She appears opposite Bob Dylan° in his autobiographical film, *Renaldo and Clara*.

1979 Aug LP *Honest Lullaby*, on Portrait, reaches US #113, and is Baez' last chartmaking LP.

1981 Aug On tour in South America, she is greeted with bomb threats and general harassment, having been vocal in opposition to the right-wing coup in Chile.

1982 June Still a tireless campaigner in peace causes, Baez (with Jackson Browne°, Linda Ronstadt° and others) performs for one million people in Central Park, New York, at the culmination of a Peace rally.

1987 Her autobiography *And A Voice To Sing With* is published.

1988 She signs to LA label Cypress and releases (unsuccessful) LP *Recently*.

ANITA BAKER

1980 As lead singer of Chapter 8, Baker (b. Detroit, Mich., US) records *I Just Want To Be Your Girl* which collects strong R&B airplay, but neither it nor LP *Chapter 8* achieve chart success. The group breaks up, and Baker settles into an office job in Detroit.

1983 Jan She is offered a solo recording contract by US independent black music label, Beverly Glen Records.

June First solo release is double-A-sided *No More Tears/Will You Be Mine*, which makes #49 in US R&B music chart.

Oct *Angel* hits R&B #5, but despite its sales, fails to cross over to the US pop chart.

Nov LP *The Songstress*, which contains the singles, is her first across-the-board (minor) US success, reaching #139. It has already made #12 on R&B LP chart.

1984 Feb *You're The Best Thing Yet* is another R&B chartmaker (#28). Baker now falls out with Beverly Glen, and will spend time in legal efforts to get out of her contract.

1985 Free to move elsewhere, Baker signs to Elektra Records, and teams with producer Michael Powell to record a series of songs (her own and some covers) over which she has total creative control. She regards the labor-of-love project as her personal exorcism of earlier manipulations.

1986 Apr LP *Rapture* results from the 1985 sessions, and hits first in UK, eventually making #13.

July [26/27] Following UK acclaim for the LP, Baker visits London and plays two sold-out shows at Hammersmith Odeon, to unanimous critical euphoria.

Nov *Sweet Love* finally gives her a major US hit single, reaching #8.

Dec *Sweet Love* peaks at UK #13, while LP *Rapture* reaches US #12.

1987 Feb A remix of *Caught Up In The Rapture* (originally from the LP) reaches US #37 and UK #51.

Apr Baker's success of the previous 12 months culminates in a newcomer Grammy Award. (A long recording silence will follow while she applies herself to a further LP project, yet to come.)

1988 Oct Once again produced and co-written by Michael Powell, third LP *Giving You The Best That I Got* hits US#2 and UK#9. Title cut makes US#6 and UK#55.

Nov Baker begins major tour to promote LP.

LONG JOHN BALDRY

1957 After leaving school, Baldry (b. Jan. 12, 1941, London, UK), starts singing folk, jazz and R&B in London clubs and coffee bars. His "Long" name comes from his 6'7" height.

1958/9 He sings regularly with Alexis Korner's and Cyril Davies' R&B groups in UK, and tours Europe with blues singer Ramblin' Jack Elliott.

1961 Baldry joins Alexis Korner's Blues Inc.

1962 After appearing on UK LP *R&B From The Marquee* with Korner, he travels to Germany and works with Horace Silver Quintet when they tour USAF bases there.

Nov Back in UK, he joins Cyril Davies R&B All-Stars.

1963 Apr All-Stars sign to Pye records and release *Country Line Special*.

Sept Second Davies All-Star single is *Preachin' The Blues*.

1964 Jan [7] Davies dies of leukemia and Baldry forms Hoochie Coochie Men from All-Stars members.

July They sign to United Artists Records and release solo single *Up Above My Head*, which sells poorly.

Dec Debut LP *Long John's Blues* is issued in UK.

1965 Oct After a steady career on the UK R&B club circuit, Hoochie Coochie Men break up. Baldry joins Rod Stewart°, Brian Auger and Julie Driscoll in The Steampacket.

1966 Sept The Steampacket splits, and Baldry goes to Bluesology, with Reg Dwight (later Elton John°) on piano.

1967 May *Cuckoo* is sixth and last of unsuccessful singles for United Artists, and Baldry leaves.

Oct He signs to Pye Records, and records an uncharacteristic ballad *Let The Heartaches Begin*.

Nov *Let The Heartaches Begin* tops UK chart for 2 weeks, bringing Baldry widespread UK TV exposure.

1968 Jan *Let The Heartaches Begin* charts in US at #88.

Sept Ballad *When The Sun Comes Shinin' Through* reaches UK #29.

Nov Mexico, a Latin-style theme to BBC TV coverage of Mexico Olympics, reaches UK #15.

1969 Feb *It's Too Late Now* is last UK hit at #21.

1971 June Baldry signs to Warner Bros. Records and records LP *It Ain't Easy*, produced by ex-colleagues Rod Stewart° and Elton John°. No UK chart success, but it makes #83 in US, and he makes first US tour to promote it.

Sept *Don't Try To Lay No Boogie-Woogie On The King Of Rock And Roll* hits US #73.

1972 May LP *Everything Stops For Tea* is issued in US, and reaches #180.

1976 He signs to Casablanca Records in US for two LPs, but no chart success.

1979 July LP *Baldry's Out!*, for new label EMI America, is released. The title is a reference to some months spent in a mental institution.

1980 After regular touring around the US and Canada, Baldry decides to make Canada a permanent base and becomes a Canadian citizen. (He continues to live and perform there, away from the international stage, through the 1980s.)

HANK BALLARD

1953 May Ballard (b. Henry Ballard, Nov.18, 1936, Detroit, US) leaves Ford car factory to join the Detroit-based Royals, a doo-wop group signed to Federal Records, as lead singer. Later the name is changed to The Midnighters to avoid confusion with label-mates The Five Royales.

1954 Mar First single under new name is *Work With Me Annie*, written by Ballard. Ripe with sexual innuendo and widely radio-banned, it still becomes a #1 US R&B chart hit.

July *Sexy Ways* continues the Annie saga, reaching #3 in US R&B chart.

1955 The theme continues with *Annie Had A Baby* and *Annie's Aunt Fanny* during the year, also prompting answer records like Etta James' *Roll With Me Henry*.

1959 Jan After a lengthy spell without hits, the group switches to the King label (Federal's parent), with the name amended to Hank Ballard & The Midnighters.

Mar *Teardrops On Your Letter* is an R&B chart smash (#4), and also enters US pop chart at #87. The B-side is Ballard composition *The Twist*.

May *Kansas City* reaches US #72, though eclipsed by Wilbert Harrison's° #1 version.

July *The Twist* is reissued because of Chubby Checker° cover version.

Sept Checker's° record has massive national TV promotion and goes to US #1. Ballard's sells well in Checker's wake, reaching US #28.

1960 Aug *Finger Poppin' Time*, a Ballard song about a dance, is the long-awaited pop chart triumph, climbing to US #7 and selling over a million copies.

Nov Follow-up million-seller *Let's Go, Let's Go, Let's Go*, hits US #6.

1961 Jan *The Hoochi-Coochie-Coo*, another dance, reaches #23 in US.

Mar *Let's Go Again (Where We Went Last Night)* climbs to US #39.

May *The Continental Walk* uses another new dance fad, and reaches US #33.

July *The Switch-A-Roo*, also a dance, climbs to US #26.

Sept *Nothing But Good* hits US #49. The B-side *Keep On Dancing* hits #66, but the dance gimmick is about to run out of momentum.

1962 Feb Chubby Checker° tops US chart again with *The Twist* during the dance's worldwide revival, and Ballard counters with *Do You Know How To Twist?* It reaches US #87, but is his last hit. The Midnighters splits soon after; Ballard stays on King label as a soloist, and begins to work with James Brown° band.

1968 After a long period with few releases, Ballard becomes a full-time member of the James Brown° tour revue.

1970 He moves to Silver Fox Records, the first of several label switches which will bring no hits and increasing obscurity.

1972 Nov He returns to work with James Brown° for a period. His recitation on a Brown LP *Get On The Good Foot* praises Brown for rescuing him from a self-destructive spiral.

1974 He tries a novelty revival of his *Let's Go* hit as topical *Let's Go Streaking*, but finds no success despite the return to his risqué roots.

1986 Dec After years playing US soul club circuit with his old hits, he visits UK to perform London Christmas show organized by Charly Records, licensee of his King hits in UK. The show is recorded for a UK live LP which gains critical favor, and Ballard belatedly earns R&B legend status in the UK, where he never had a hit.

AFRIKA BAMBAATAA

1976 After 2 years as a teenage lieutenant in a Bronx, New York, street gang called The Black Spades, Bambaataa turns his talent to the formation of Zulu Nation, a Bronx-based grouping of cultural/political street people. The music of turntable DJs and rappers at block parties and in clubs, is central to the group from its inception, but political activities are gradually phased out as Bambaataa's reputation as a DJ and Emcee grows, and the momentum of the rap/electro/hip-hop genre he is helping to pioneer develops.

1980 Bambaataa makes his first venture into recorded hip-hop for producer Paul Winley, with different versions of *Zulu Nation Throwdown* by two rap groups in his collective, Cosmic Force and Soulsonic Force. Unhappy with Winley's control, Bambaataa looks for a more congenial base, finding it at Tommy Boy, the fledgling NY street dance label run by Tom Silverman.

1982 Feb Debut Tommy Boy release is *Jazzy Sensation* (based on Gwen Guthrie's *Funky Sensation*) by another Zulu Nation rap group, The Jazzy Five, co-produced by Bambaataa and Arthur Baker.

Sept *Planet Rock*, credited to Afrika Bambaataa And Soul Sonic Force (Emcee G.L.O.B.E., Mr. Biggs and Pow Wow), and fusing rap with the electronic music of European groups like Tangerine Dream and Kraftwerk° (whose *Trans-Europe Express* is a primary inspiration for the track), is a huge street-level, 12" single hit in New York and other US inner-city areas. Lack of airplay restricts it to US #48, but it still gets a gold disk for a million-plus sales. In UK it reaches #53. (It will have a huge dance record influence on both sides of the Atlantic with its bass line used on at least 70 American releases in 1983.)

AFRIKA BAMBAATAA *cont.*

1983 Mar Bambaataa, Baker and Soul Sonic Force follow up with *Looking For The Perfect Beat*, a US and UK dance and soul chart smash, though not a pop hit.

1984 Mar *Renegades Of Funk*, Bambaataa's last Tommy Boy release, cements his position as the most influential producer/arranger/catalyst in the new musical style, and is a pop crossover in UK, reaching #30.

June Moving to New York label Celluloid, Bambaataa releases his first LP *Shango Funk Theology*, co-produced with bassist Bill Laswell and featuring a studio line-up of rappers and funk musicians known as Shango.

Sept Tom Silverman teams Bambaataa with soul veteran James Brown° on *Unity*, which charts at UK #49.

1985 Feb The liaison with Laswell continues on *World Destruction by Time Zone*, which pairs Bambaataa and Public Image Ltd° (and ex-Sex Pistols°) singer John Lydon. It reaches UK #44.

1986 He severs connection with Soul Sonic Force, following the prosecution of two of its members for armed robbery in the late 1970s.

1987 Signed to The Family, he releases Bambaataa's Theme and LP *Beware (The Funk Is Everywhere)*.

1988 He records LP *The Light With The Family*, with Bill Laswell returning to co-produce some tracks.

BANANARAMA

Sarah Dallin (vocals)
Keren Woodward (vocals)
Siobhan Fahey (vocals)

1981 Jan Dallin, Woodward and Fahey are flat mates in Covent Garden, London, UK, when they leave day jobs at the BBC and Decca Records press office to perform as an unaccompanied vocal trio in pubs and clubs.

June Gary Crowley, a DJ (and Fahey's former Decca colleague), helps them make some demos, leading to a one-off deal with Demon Records.

Sept First recording *Ai A Mwana*, with production by ex-Sex Pistol° Paul Cook, appears in UK on Demon and enters the independent charts, attracting London Records which signs the trio and reissues *Ai A Mwana*.

Oct Fun Boy Three asks the trio to back them vocally on a new single.

1982 Mar *It Ain't What You Do, It's The Way That You Do It* by Fun Boy Three With Bananarama, hits UK #4.

Apr The trio revives Velvelettes' oldie *He Was Really Sayin' Somethin'* with Fun Boy Three backing up, and takes it to UK #5.

July First link with producers Tony Swain and Steve Jolley on *Shy Boy* which reaches UK #4.

Dec *Cheers Then*, a ballad which departs from the now-familiar jaunty trio sound, is a comparative UK flop, only reaching #45.

1983 Mar The revival *Na Na Hey Hey Kiss Him Goodbye*, climbs to UK #5. First LP *Deep Sea Skiving* hits UK #7.

July *Shy Boy* provides US chart debut peaking at #83. LP *Deep Sea Skiving* climbs to US #63.

Aug *Cruel Summer* reaches UK #8.

1984 Mar *Robert De Niro's Waiting* is their biggest UK hit single, reaching #3.

Apr LP *Bananarama* is issued in UK reaching #16.

May *Robert De Niro* hits only #95 in US, but the actor himself loves the song, and calls to tell them.

June *Rough Justice* peaks at UK #23.

July *Cruel Summer* is released in US after being heard in the movie *The Karate Kid*. It becomes their first major US hit, reaching #9. LP *Bananarama* also charts in US, reaching #30.

Nov Though not issued in UK, *The Wild Life*, from the film of the same title, becomes a US single, making only #70.

Dec UK release *Hotline To Heaven* also disappoints commercially, peaking at #58. The trio appears as part of the all-star chorus for Band Aid°.

1985 Aug *Do Not Disturb*, their only release of 1985, peaks at UK #31.

1986 May First link with the production team Stock/ Aitken/Waterman results in a revival of Shocking Blue's 1970 hit *Venus*.

July *Venus* reaches #8 in UK, but in US goes all the way, to give them the chart-topper never achieved at home. LP *True Confessions* follows, but peaks at UK #46 and sells disappointingly.

Aug *More Than Physical* reaches UK #41.

Sept LP *True Confessions* does well in US, where it reaches #15.

Dec [30] Keren Woodward and her husband David have a son, Thomas.

1987 Feb BBC TV's "In At The Deep End" shows the making of an amateur promo video for new Bananarama single *A Trick Of The Night*. This is shown on "Top of the Pops" when the single peaks at UK #32.

Apr Bananarama is in the line-up of Stock/ Aitken/Waterman's *Let It Be* single by Ferry Aid, a benefit record for the Zeebrugge Disaster Fund. This enters UK chart at #1, while *Love In The First Degree* reaches US #48.

July *I Heard A Rumour* reaches UK #14.

Aug Siobhan Fahey marries Dave Stewart of Eurythmics°.

Sept LP *Wow!* sells disappointingly in UK, only reaching #59, but peaks in US at #44.

Oct *I Heard A Rumour* hits US #4. *Love In The First Degree* peaks at UK #3, its B-side, *Mr. Sleeze*, contributing strongly to its sales.

Dec Fahey retires from the group to enjoy married life in California. A friend, Jacquie Sullivan is the new recruit.

1988 Jan *I Can't Help It* reaches US #47.

Apr *I Want You Back* hits UK #5.

July LP *Greatest Hits* is released.

THE BAND

Jaime "Robbie" Robertson (guitar and vocals)
Richard Manuel (piano and vocals)
Garth Hudson (organ)
Rick Danko (bass and vocals)
Levon Helm (drums and vocals)

1965/66 Robertson (b. July 5, 1944, Toronto, Canada), Manuel (b. Apr.3, 1945, Stratford, Canada), Hudson (b. Aug.2, 1937, London, Canada), Danko (b. Dec.9, 1943, Simcoe, Canada) and Helm (b. May 26, 1942, Marvell, Ark., US) having all worked in Canada as members of The Hawks (backing band of Ronnie Hawkins°) accompany Bob Dylan° on a world tour.

1967 Dylan° moves to Woodstock, N.Y., and the ex-Hawks take a house nearby. Dylan and the group record extensively in this large, pink-colored house, the results first becoming the celebrated original rock bootleg *Great White Wonder*, released officially by CBS in 1975 as *The Basement Tapes*.

1968 Aug The Band's debut LP *Music From Big Pink* (named after the house), using some Dylan° songs *(Tears of Rage, This Wheel's On Fire and I Shall Be Released)* plus their own originals, reaches US #30.

Sept *The Weight* makes UK #21 and US #63, though versions by Aretha Franklin°, Supremes/Temptations° and Jackie DeShannon all go higher in US chart than The Band's original.

1969 Oct LP *The Band* hits US #9 and UK #25. It includes biggest US hit single *Up On Cripple Creek* (US #25), and biggest UK hit single *Rag Mama Rag* (UK #16 and US #57), plus *The Night They Drove Old Dixie Down*, a big hit for Joan Baez° (US #3/UK #6).

1970 Sept LP *Stage Fright* (apparently inspired by working on the road), reaches US #5 and UK #15, and includes a minor US hit single *Time To Kill*.

1971 Oct LP *Cahoots* makes #21 in US and UK #41, and includes *Life Is A Carnival* (US #72) on which Allen Toussaint guests, and *4% Pantomime* on which Van Morrison° (who co-wrote it with Robertson) guests.

1972 Sept Double live LP *Rock Of Ages* reaches US #6, and extract *Don't Do It* reaches US #34.

1973 Dec *Ain't Got No Home*, originally by Clarence "Frogman" Henry, reaches US #73.

1974 Feb The Band reunites with Dylan°, works on his LP *Planet Waves*, and releases its own LP *Moondog Matinée*, a collection of cover versions of its favorites, which reaches US #28.

July The Band tours with Dylan°, and a live double LP *Before The Flood*, results.

1976 Jan LP *Northern Lights-Southern Cross* reaches US #26.

Oct The Band decides to split up, possibly because Robertson, the most prolific songwriter, has moved into other areas, like producing Neil Diamond's° LP *Beautiful Noise*.

Nov [25] Their remarkable final concert at San Francisco's Winterland auditorium has star guests Dylan°, Diamond°, Neil Young°, Ringo Starr°, Van Morrison°, Toussaint, Joni Mitchell°, Muddy Waters° and Eric Clapton°, among others. The event is recorded and filmed by Martin Scorsese.

1977 Apr LP *Islands*, recorded before the split, is released and reaches US #64.

1978 May The film (often cited as the finest rock movie ever made), and triple LP *The Last Waltz* from their farewell concert, are released. The LP, on Warner Bros., reaches US #16 and UK #39. (Each member of the group continues in music; Danko and Helm make solo LPs, as does Robertson (in 1987), though Hudson and Manuel are rarely heard.)

1986 The band reconvenes for live work, with James Wieder replacing Robertson on guitar.

Mar [6] Manuel, apparently in a fit of depression, hangs himself.

BAND AID

1984 Nov Bob Geldof of Boomtown Rats° sees a BBC TV report on famine in Ethiopia, and determines to raise funds. He, and Midge Ure of Ultravox°, write a song and devise the idea of an all-star record for which nobody (from artists to manufacturer to record shops) takes any profit. Intensive calls around UK record industry set up the project.

Nov [25] 36 artists gather in a London studio to record *Do They Know It's Christmas?*, including Geldof and Ure with the members of their bands, plus: Bananarama°, Phil Collins°, Culture Club° (Boy George and John Moss), Duran Duran°, Heaven 17° (Glenn Gregory and Martin Ware), Kool & The Gang° (Robert Bell, James Taylor, and Dennis Thomas), Marilyn, George Michael°, Spandau Ballet°, Status Quo° (Rick Parfitt and Francis Rossi), Sting°, U2° (Bono and Adam Clayton), Jody Watley, Paul Weller, and Paul Young°.

Dec [7] The record is launched with an Ethiopia Benefit concert at Royal Albert Hall, London, organized by the Save the Children Fund.

Dec [15] *Do They Know It's Christmas?* enters UK chart at #1. It stays at #1 for 5 weeks, selling over 3 million copies to become the biggest-selling single ever in the UK.

1985 Jan It peaks at #13 in US chart, but also sells over a million copies.

Mar First shipment of relief supplies paid by Band Aid reaches Ethiopia.

July Live Aid concert is televised worldwide from Wembley Stadium, London, and JFK Stadium in Philadelphia, featuring most of the world's biggest rock stars, and raising over £50/$69 million.

Dec *Do They Know It's Christmas?* re-charts in the UK, peaking at #3 (and will continue to be re-issued every Christmas from now on as a perennial reminder).

THE BANGLES

Susanna Hoffs (guitar and vocals)
Vicki Peterson (guitar and vocals)
Michael Steele (bass and vocals)
Debbi Peterson (drums and vocals)

1981 Dec After playing in Los Angeles as The Colours, Vicki (b. Jan.11), and Debbi Peterson (b. Aug.), and Susannah Hoffs (b. Jan.) become The Bangs. (Members of the group do not want their exact birth dates known.) With bassist Annette Zilinskas, they release *Getting Out Of Hand* on their own independent label, Down Kiddie, with minimal sales.

1982 Jan They are forced to alter their name to The Bangles because of a New Jersey group already recording as The Bangs.

June Five-song mini-LP *The Bangles* is issued on US IRS label. Zilinskas leaves to join Blood On The Saddle and is replaced by Michael Steele (b. June 2).

1983 The group signs to CBS Records.

1984 Sept *Hero Takes A Fall* is released in US and UK, but does not chart.

1985 Mar *Going Down To Liverpool* and LP *All Over The Place* are released, again without significant sales.

1986 Jan *Manic Monday*, written by Prince° under the pseudonym Christopher, marks the group's chart debut, hitting #2 in both US and UK.

Mar LP *Different Light* is released. It will reach US #2 and UK #3 in Jan. 1987 after many months on chart.

Apr *If She Knew What She Wants* reaches US #29 and UK #31.

July *Going Down To Liverpool*, reissued in UK, makes the chart at #56.

Nov *Walk Like An Egyptian*, taken from the LP *Different Light*, climbs to UK #3.

Dec *Walk Like An Egyptian* is the group's biggest US hit, topping the chart for 4 weeks.

1987 Jan *Walking Down Your Street*, the fourth single from *Different Light*, makes US #11 and UK #16.

Nov Bangles' revival of Simon and Garfunkel's° 1966 hit *A Hazy Shade Of Winter*, used on the soundtrack of movie *Less Than Zero*, and issued as a US single on the Def Jam label, hits #2.

BARCLAY JAMES HARVEST

John Lees (guitar and vocals)
Woolly (Stewart) Wolstenholme (keyboards and vocals)
Les Holroyd (bass and vocals)
Mel Pritchard (drums)

1966 Sept The band forms in Oldham, UK, where Lees (b. Jan.13, 1947, Oldham) and Wolstenholme (b. Apr.15, 1947) are at art school together, and have been playing in blues band The Blues Keepers. They recruit two members of another local blues group, Heart And Soul And The Wickeds: Holroyd (b. Mar.12, 1948, Oldham) and Pritchard (b. Jan.8, 1948, Oldham).

1967 The band turns fully professional with the backing of local businessman John Crowther, and extensive live work follows around north-west England.

1968 May Signed to EMI's Parlophone label, they release debut single *Early Morning*, which sets the tone of the band's future folk and classical-tinged "art-rock" style.

1969 June EMI launches its "progressive music" label Harvest, tagged after the band. Second single *Brother Thrush* appears on Harvest, but like all their EMI output, fails to chart.

1970 June First LP *Barclay James Harvest* is released, promoted by a UK tour on which the band is accompanied by an orchestra of classical musicians from The New Symphonia, conducted by Robert Godfrey. Though considered a pioneering artistic effort, it is a disaster. The LP also is not a hit.

1971 Aug After the release of two more LPs, the band is a live success performing with orchestra at Weeley Festival, Essex, UK.

1973 May *Rock And Roll Woman* is the band's last Harvest release; problems with EMI and with its original management dog progress the rest of the year until a complete break is made, new management found, and the band signs to Polydor Records.

1974 June First Polydor releases *Poor Boy Blues* and LP *Everyone Is Everybody Else* fail to chart.

Dec Double LP *Barclay James Harvest Live*, featuring stage versions of much of their best-known repertoire, is the band's first chart entry in the UK, reaching #40.

1975 Oct LP *Time Honoured Ghosts*, recorded in San Francisco with producer Elliot Mazer, reaches UK #32.

1976 Oct LP *Octoberon*, produced by the band itself at 10cc's° Strawberry Studios in Stockport, UK, reaches UK #19, their first top 20 entry.

1977 Feb LP *Octoberon*, their only US chart entry, peaks at #174.

Apr First single to chart in UK is actually an EP: *Barclay James Harvest Live* (containing *Rock'n'Roll Star* and *Medicine Man*) reaches UK #49.

July Lees releases solo LP *A Major Fancy*, for Harvest, which is not a major seller.

BARCLAY JAMES HARVEST *cont.*

Oct LP *Gone To Earth* reaches UK #30, but becomes a far bigger hit in Europe, particularly West Germany, where it sells over 100,000 copies and elevates the band to superstar status (which they will maintain in Germany and other countries through into the late 1980s).

1978 Oct The band's twelfth LP, *Barclay James Harvest XII*, peaks at UK #31.

1980 Feb *Love On The Line*, taken from unsuccesful LP *Eyes Of The Universe*, reaches UK #63.

Nov *Life Is For Living* makes UK #61.

1981 May LP *Turn Of The Tide* reaches UK #55.

1982 Aug Live LP *Concert For The People*, recorded in Berlin during one of their sell-out German tours, is their highest-placed UK chart LP, at #15.

1983 May *Just A Day Away*, taken from forthcoming LP *Ring Of Changes*, is their last UK singles chart entry, at #68.

June LP *Ring Of Changes* peaks at #36 in UK.

1984 Apr LP *Victims Of Circumstance* reaches UK #33.

1987 Feb LP *Face To Face* reaches UK #65. (By now, the band is playing mainly to a devoted core audience in the UK, but most of its time is spent on tour in Europe, where superstar status and huge record sales are still the band's reward.)

SYD BARRETT

1968 Apr Barrett (b. Jan.6, 1946, Cambridge, UK) is asked to leave Pink Floyd° due to increasing LSD-related personality problems and onstage unreliability. He goes into immediate seclusion in Cambridge.

1969 Dec He is retained as a solo act by EMI's Harvest label, and *Octopus* is released as a first sample of his new material, but it is unsuccessful.

1970 Jan LP wryly titled *The Madcap Laughs*, is released in UK, and peaks at #40.

Nov LP *Barrett* is released in UK, but does not chart. Barrett does no promotion for the LP, staying in seclusion except when in the recording studio.

1972 Feb He makes a brief reappearance in Stars, a Cambridge-based trio featuring Jack Monk (bass) and Twink (drums), but after three local appearances they split without recording, and Barrett becomes a recluse again. Renewed critical interest in him prompts EMI to reissue Barrett's two earlier LPs as a double pack.

1975 Sept Pink Floyd° includes *Shine On You Crazy Diamond*, a song about and dedicated to Barrett, on the LP *Wish You Were Here*. Barrett visits the band in the studio while the LP is made, but he is never again tempted from his self-induced seclusion into any active part in music.

LEN BARRY

1964 After several years as lead singer, Barry (b. Len Borisoff, June 12, 1942, Philadelphia, US) leaves The Dovells.

1965 May First solo release after signing to US Decca is *Lip Sync*, an R&B-styled, uptempo track sung in a high tenor, which sets the style for all hits that follow. It peaks at US #84.

Oct *1-2-3* duplicates previous arrangement, but is much stronger, becoming an instant dance floor sensation (as it will remain for many years) and climbing to US #2.

Nov *1-2-3* is instant UK success, hitting #2.

Nov/Dec On the strength of his hits, he begins live work with a stage act which will become noted for its wildness and overt James Brown° influences. He becomes unpopular with other acts because of readily-quoted intolerance of long hair and casual dress, particularly in UK acts.

1966 Jan *Like A Baby* hits US #20, and climbs to UK #12 following his UK visit.

Mar *Somewhere* (from *West Side Story*) is rearranged in the style of *1-2-3* and reaches US #26. It brushes UK chart at #47 and is Barry's final UK seller.

June *It's That Time Of The Year* reaches US #91.

Sept With musical formula now wearing thin, *I Struck It Rich* only crawls to US #98, ending a 12-month hit career.

1969 Aug Having recorded unsuccessfully for RCA and shifting his toned-down stage act to the cabaret circuit, Barry hits in US as a producer and writer (and possibly instrumentalist) with *Keem-O-Sabe* by Electric Indian, which reaches #16. (After this, his career will settle into songwriting and production for other, mainly black or dance-oriented, acts.)

BAUHAUS

Peter Murphy (vocals)
Daniel Ash (guitar and vocals))
David Jay (Haskins) (bass and vocals)
Kevin Haskins (drums)

1978 The band forms in Northampton, UK, after the Haskins brothers have played in punk group The Submerged Tenth, and the trio without Murphy has played as The Craze. The quartet's first name is Bauhaus 1919 (taken from the German art movement which began that year).

Dec [31] First public gig as Bauhaus, at a Wellingborough, UK, pub.

1979 Aug A one-off deal with Small Wonder Records in London produces 12" single *Bela Lugosi's Dead*, which does not chart but will sell consistently in UK for years.

Nov After a concert at London's Rock Garden, and a session for John Peel's BBC Radio show, Bauhaus has a large cult following. Beggars Banquet Records signs them to 4AD, its independently-distributed subsidiary label.

1980 Jan *Dark Entries*, a remake of the B-side of *Bela Lugosi*, is released, reinforcing their brooding, sonorous style.

Apr First European tour, of Germany, Holland and Belgium.

June *Terror Couple Kill Colonel* (inspired by a newspaper headline) is released, entering the UK independent charts.

Sept First tour of US.

Oct A revival of T.Rex's *Telegram Sam* is again a UK independent chart hit.

Nov Debut LP *In The Flat Field* tops UK independent LP chart for 2 weeks.

1981 Mar *Kick In The Eye* appears on main Beggars Banquet label. First UK national chart hit, at #59.

July *The Passions Of Lovers*, written and recorded within a day, reaches #56 in UK.

Oct LP *Mask* is a major success, reaching UK #30.

Nov David Jay teams with poet/painter René Halkett (student of original Bauhaus movement) on *Nothing*. Peter Murphy appears in a highly-rated UK TV ad for Maxell Tapes.

1982 Jan First UK TV appearance, on BBC's "Riverside". The band films a scene for David Bowie°/Catherine Deneuve film *The Hunger*, performing *Bela Lugosi's Dead* at Heaven nightclub, London.

Mar EP *Searching For Satori* (which includes a remixed version of *Kick In The Eye*), hits UK #45.

July *Spirit* reaches UK #42, though Bauhaus are publicly unhappy about its arrangement and production.

Oct UK tour in preparation for new LP, supported by Southern Death Cult. Bauhaus' biggest hit comes with the revival of David Bowie's° *Ziggy Stardust*, a tongue-in-cheek issue after a BBC radio session including their version, creates interest. It reaches UK #15, and they perform it on UK TV's "Top of the Pops".

Nov LP *The Sky's Gone Out* receives a huge boost from the hit and is itself a smash, reaching UK #4.

1983 Jan *Lagartija Nick* reaches UK #44.

Feb Murphy contracts viral pneumonia, and misses much of recording the LP *Burning From The Inside*.

Apr *She's In Parties* is last UK hit single, reaching #26.

May The band tours Japan.

June UK tour begins to promote imminent LP release.

July LP *Burning From The Inside* is issued. A compilation of individual rather than band work, it suggests the members feel a need to go their own ways.

July [5] Final UK tour date in London ends with lengthy encores and "farewell" from the band, and a later press release confirms their dissolution. (Murphy will pursue a solo career; Ash and Haskins will work as Tones on Tail then regroup with Jay as Love and Rockets.)

THE BAY CITY ROLLERS

Eric Faulkner (guitar)
Stuart "Woody" Wood (guitar)
Leslie McKeown (vocals)
Alan Longmuir (bass)
Derek Longmuir (drums)

1967 The group is formed at Tynecastle School, Edinburgh, Scotland, by Alan (b. June 20, 1953, Edinburgh) and Derek (b. Mar.19, 1955, Edinburgh) Longmuir, plus four friends. Tam Paton, resident bandleader at the Edinburgh Palais, gives up his job to manage them. He picks the group name by sticking a pin in a map of the US, and finding it in Bay City, Utah.

1969 The group begins a 12-month Saturday residency at the Top Storey Club, Edinburgh.

1971 June They sign to Bell Records in UK and release first single, a revival of Gentrys' 1965 US hit *Keep On Dancing*, produced by Jonathan King°.

Sept *Keep On Dancing* charts in UK, reaching #9.

1972 Mar Next single, *We Can Make Music*, fails to sell.

June Faulkner (b. Oct.21, 1955, Edinburgh) joins for third (also unsuccessful) single *Mañana*. The song wins Radio Luxembourg Grand Prix Song Contest.

1973 Jan *Saturday Night* fails in UK. Early members John Devine and Nobby Clarke leave, replaced by Wood (b. Feb.25, 1957, Edinburgh) and McKeown (b. Nov.12, 1955).

1974 Feb *Remember (Sha La La)* restores UK success, peaking at #6.

May *Shang-A-Lang* climbs to UK #2 after strong TV exposure.

Aug *Summerlove Sensation* hits #3 in UK.

Oct First LP *Rollin'* is issued, going to UK #1. *All Of Me Loves All Of You* is released and hits UK #4. A 26-date UK tour with scenes of teenage girl fan mania everywhere; national UK press coins "Rollermania" for the craze, and picks up on the group's tartan stage uniforms as a clothing fad.

1975 Mar *Bye Bye Baby*, reviving an old Four Seasons'° song, becomes their biggest UK hit, reaching #1 for 6 weeks.

May LP *Once Upon A Star* is an immediate smash, entering UK LP chart at #1.

July *Give A Little Love* is their second UK #1 single.

Sept [20] The group is launched in the US via a live appearance on Howard Cosell's "Saturday Night Variety Show" on ABC TV, appropriately singing *Saturday Night*.

Oct Success finally spreads to the US when *Saturday Night*, an early failed UK single, enters US chart. LP *Bay City Rollers* also charts in US, reaching #20.

Nov *Money Honey* climbs to UK #3.

Dec LP *Wouldn't You Like It* hits #3 in UK.

1976 Jan *Saturday Night* is #1 on the first US chart of the year.

Feb *Money Honey* charts at US #9.

Apr *Love Me Like I Love You* makes UK #4.

Apr [14] Eric Faulkner almost dies after taking a drug overdose at Tam Paton's house, while in a state of exhaustion.

June Unreleased in UK, *Rock And Roll Love Letter* reaches US #28. LP of the same title reaches US #31. It is not UK-released. Alan Longmuir leaves, and is replaced by guitarist Ian Mitchell (b. Aug.22, 1958, Scotland), with Stuart Wood switching to bass.

Sept LP *Dedication* reaches UK #4 and US #26. The group revives Dusty Springfield's° *I Only Want To Be With You* as a single, and take it to UK #4 and US #12.

1977 May *It's A Game* reaches #16 in UK.

July *You Made Me Believe In Magic* is final Rollers' single to chart in UK, and only reaches #34. It sells better in the US, making #10.

Aug *It's A Game* is the Rollers' last charting LP, reaching UK #18 and US #23.

Nov *The Way I Feel Tonight* fails to sell in UK, but provides a final US top 30 hit at #24. Ian Mitchell leaves to form the Ian Mitchell Band, replaced by guitarist Pat McGlynn (b. Mar.31, 1958, Edinburgh).

1978 LP *Strangers In The Wild* is unsuccessful; it is clear that the Rollers have gone out of fashion. Eric Faulkner leaves to go solo and will have success in Japan. (The group will prevail into the 1980s pushing the nostalgia aspect of its hits and costumes in minor UK and US venues and clubs.)

1982 May [6] The group's former manager, Tam Paton, is convicted of a gross indecency charge and sentenced to 3 years in jail.

THE BEACH BOYS

Brian Wilson (bass, keyboards and vocals)
Mike Love (percussion and vocals)
Carl Wilson (guitar and vocals)
Al Jardine (guitar and vocals)
Dennis Wilson (drums and vocals)

1961 The group forms in the Los Angeles suburb of Hawthorne, Cal., US, around the Wilson brothers: Brian (b. June 20, 1942, Inglewood, Cal.), Dennis (b. Dec.4, 1944, Hawthorne, Cal.) and Carl (b. Dec.21, 1946, Hawthorne,). They are joined by cousin Mike Love (b. Mar.15, 1944, Baldwin Hills, Cal.), and Al Jardine (b. Sept.3, 1942, Lima, Oh.), a classmate of Brian's at El Camino Junior College. Especially keen on the harmony elements of pop, Brian regularly coaches the others in the close-harmony vocal style of The Four Freshmen. They play some early live dates as The Pendletones and Carl and The Passions.

Oct At the prompting of Dennis, who is becoming engrossed in surfing, Love and Brian Wilson write *Surfin'*. The Wilsons' sometime songwriter father, Murry, arranges with an acquaintance, song publisher Hite Morgan, to have the group record it at locally-based Keen Recording Studio. Intended purely as a demo, the record does not feature Dennis Wilson, but has Brian playing drums, Carl on guitar, Jardine on stand-up bass, and Love on lead vocal.

Dec [8] Morgan interests local label Candix in both song and group, and Candix signs them, releasing *Surfin'* under the name The Beach Boys, a name coined by record distributor Russ Regan. (The group wants to be called The Pendletones, which the label does not like, and Candix wants to dub them The Surfers, a name already used by another group, as pointed out by Regan.)

Dec [31] The Beach Boys debut under their new name on the bill of Ritchie Valens'° Memorial Concert at Municipal Auditorium, Long Beach, a date for which they earn $300.

1962 Feb Jardine leaves to study dentistry, and a schoolfriend of the group, David Marks, comes in on rhythm guitar, with Brian Wilson switching to bass. Dennis Wilson, originally only marginally involved, is now settled as drummer.

Mar *Surfin'* reaches #75 in US.

May The under-funded Candix label folds. Murry Wilson, who has assumed the role of manager, takes their demos to Dot, Decca and Liberty Records in search of a new deal, finally interesting Capitol Records' producer Nick Venet with demo *Surfin' Safari*.

June The group is signed to Capitol Records.

Oct Debut release *Surfin' Safari* climbs to US #14, while the B-side *409*, a hot rod song, reaches #76.

Nov LP *Surfin' Safari*, a mixture of oldies and Brian Wilson songs (mainly written with a neighbor, Gary Usher) is released, peaking at US #32.

1963 Jan *Ten Little Indians*, from the LP, stalls at US #49. Meanwhile, Al Jardine returns after a year of trying to study seriously, and David Marks (whose relationship with the Wilsons has become stormy) leaves.

May *Surfin' USA* returning to the surf theme, is their first top 10 hit, peaking at #3. It is Brian Wilson's adaptation of the lyrics of Chuck Berry's° *Sweet Little Sixteen*, and is the first single to highlight the vocal harmonies that become the group's trademark.

June *Shut Down*, a song about hot rodding, on the B-side of *Surfin' USA*, makes US #23 in its own right.

July LP *Surfin' USA* hits US #2. Meanwhile, Jan And Dean° top US chart with *Surf City*, a song written for them by Brian Wilson.

Aug *Surfin' USA* is their UK chart debut, reaching #32.

Sept *Surfer Girl*, while still on a surf theme, is a slow harmony ballad, and reaches US #7. The B-side *Little Deuce Coupe*, by now predictably a car/hot rod song, is again a US hit in its own right, reaching #15.

Oct LPs *Surfer Girl* and *Little Deuce Coupé* are released within 4 weeks of each other, the former showcasing surf numbers, and the latter hot rod and car songs. They are the first Beach Boys LPs produced by Brian Wilson. Despite the near-simultaneous release, both are major sellers: *Surfer Girl* peaks at US #7, and *Little Deuce Coupé* at #4.

Dec *Be True To Your School*, from LP *Little Deuce Coupé*, hits US #6, while B-side ballad *In My Room* reaches #23

1964 Mar *Fun Fun Fun* hits #5 in US.

May LP *Shut Down Vol. 2* reaches US #13.

THE BEACH BOYS *cont.*

July *I Get Around* is the group's first US #1, topping the chart for 2 weeks and selling over a million. The B-side *Don't Worry Baby* peaks at US #24.

Aug LP *All Summer Long* hits US #4, while in UK *I Get Around* is their second chart entry and climbs to #8.

Oct *When I Grow Up (To Be A Man)* reaches US #9.

Nov The group makes its first promotional visit to UK, performing *I Get Around, When I Grow Up (To Be A Man)* and *Dance Dance Dance* live on TV's "Ready Steady Go". Two tracks from EP *Four By The Beach Boys, Wendy* and *Little Honda*, reach #44 and #65 in US respectively, while in UK *When I Grow Up (To Be A Man)* reaches #28.

Dec LP *The Beach Boys Concert*, recorded live, is their first #1 LP, topping US chart for 4 weeks, while single *Dance Dance Dance* makes US #8. LP *The Beach Boys Christmas Album* is released for the Christmas market.

Dec [23] Brian Wilson suffers a nervous breakdown on a flight from LA to Houston. Suffering also from partial deafness in one ear, he quickly makes the decision to retire from live performance with the group, and concentrate on writing and producing the records.

1965 Jan Glen Campbell° steps in as temporary replacement for Brian Wilson on live gigs. *Dance Dance Dance* reaches UK #24.

Apr Bruce Johnston (b. June 27, 1944, Peoria, Ill., US), former member of Bruce and Terry, and The Rip Chords, replaces Campbell to become a full-time Beach Boy. Neither is heard on the group's revival of Bobby Freeman's *Do You Wanna Dance*, which makes US #12, or its B-side *Please Let Me Wonder*, which peaks at #52.

May *Help Me Rhonda* hits US #1 for 2 weeks, while LP *The Beach Boys Today!* makes US #4.

June *Help Me Rhonda* reaches #27 in UK.

Aug *California Girls*, on which Brian Wilson borrows some Phil Spector production stylings to broaden the group's sound, hits US #3, and LP *Summer Days (And Summer Nights!!)* reaches #2.

Sept *California Girls* peaks at #26 in UK.

Oct LP *Surfin' USA* is the first Beach Boys LP to chart in UK (many of them not having been UK-released), reaching #17.

Dec *The Little Girl I Once Knew*, another more complex production, reaches US #20. By contrast, LP *Beach Boys Party* is the raw result of impromptu "live in the studio" sessions with friends, and climbs to US #6.

1966 Jan *Barbara Ann*, a revival of The Regents', 1961 hit and taken from LP *Party*, with guest lead vocal by Dean Torrence (of Jan And Dean°), hits US #2. The Beach Boys tour Japan and Brian Wilson begins work on what will be LP *Pet Sounds*.

Mar *Barbara Ann* peaks at #4 in UK, and LP *Beach Boys Party* makes #3.

Apr Brian Wilson releases *Caroline No*, the first solo single by a Beach Boys member; it reaches US #32.

May *Sloop John B*, the revival of a traditional song, hits US #3 and UK #2, and sells over a million. Belatedly released in UK, LP *The Beach Boys Today!* makes #6. Painstakingly produced and richly-textured LP *Pet Sounds*, the result of many months of Brian Wilson's work, sets new standards for the group, and is critically acclaimed as its best work yet. It reaches US #10, which is a disappointment, but hits UK #2, behind The Beatles'° LP *Revolver*.

Aug Released in UK a year after its US success, LP *Summer Days (And Summer Nights!!)* peaks at #4 while *Pet Sounds* rests two places above it.

Sept A double A-side coupling *Wouldn't It Be Nice* and *God Only Knows* is taken from LP *Pet Sounds*. The former reaches US #8, and the latter #39, while in UK *God Only Knows* is made sole A-side and climbs to #2. Compilation LP *Best Of The Beach Boys* makes US #8.

Nov *Good Vibrations*, a track which Brian Wilson has been working on for 6 months, using 17 sessions at four different studios, tops both US and UK charts and is a US million-seller. It will be critically rated the group's best-ever recording. The group tours UK to ecstatic audiences, and displaces The Beatles° as World Best Group in the annual NME poll, while LP *Best Of The Beach Boys* (a different compilation from the earlier US release) hits #2, and will remain charted in UK for 142 weeks.

1967 Jan Brian Wilson begins working on sessions for an LP to develop the sounds created on *Pet Sounds*. First working title for the LP is *Dumb Angel*, later changed to *Smile*. Stresses begin to tell on the group, and on Brian Wilson in particular, while this work is in progress. There is heavy drug use, while Brian's ideas and modes of work (such as standing a grand piano in a huge sandbox) become increasingly eccentric as his stability deteriorates.

Jan [3] Carl Wilson, having received a US Army Draft notice refuses to be sworn in, saying he is a conscientious objector. (He will be arraigned for trial in June 1967, but the case will drag on for years until community service in lieu is settled.)

Apr LP *Surfer Girl*, never previously released in UK, appears instead of a new LP, and reaches UK #13.

May [2] The *Smile* sessions finally cease in disarray.

June Lacking new material, Capitol Records in UK extracts the cover version of The Crystals'° *Then He Kissed Me* (retitled *Then I Kissed Her*) from LP *Summer Days (And Summer Nights!!)*, and it hits UK #4.

Aug The group creates its own label, Brother Records, distributed by Capitol (though the cause of much rancor between the two camps) for the release of *Heroes And Villains*, a track created in similar fashion to *Good Vibrations*. It proves less successful, peaking at US #12 and UK #8.

Sept Compilation LP *Best Of The Beach Boys, Vol.2* peaks at US #50. (A slightly different version will hit UK #3 in Nov.)

Nov LP *Smiley Smile* peaks disappointingly for the band at US #41, while reaching UK #9. It contains parts of the abandoned LP *Smile*, plus some lightweight later material, and is carried by the already familiar *Good Vibrations* and *Heroes And Villains*. *Wild Honey*, a return to a simpler R&B/rock sound, reaches US #31 and UK #29.

Dec The Beach Boys play a UNICEF concert in Paris, France, and there meet Maharishi Mahesh Yogi and are introduced to transcendental meditation.

1968 Jan R&B-flavored LP *Wild Honey*, reaches US #24 and UK #7, while the extracted *Darlin'* returns the group to both US and UK top 20, at #19 and #12 respectively.

May The group tours with the Maharishi, but the concerts are poorly attended. Their live show, based around an old-fashioned greatest hits presentation, is an increasing anachronism in an era of progressive rock concerts. *Friends*, a song inspired by their transcendental meditation conversion, peaks at US #47 and UK #25.

July LP *Friends*, again heavily influenced by T.M., is their poorest-selling US LP yet, peaking at #126.

Aug *Do It Again*, a celebratory return to the group's early sound, hits US #20, and is UK #1 for a week.

Oct LP *Friends* fares better in UK, reaching #13, while compilation LP *Best Of The Beach Boys, Vol.3* makes UK #9 after stalling at US #153.

Dec The group tours UK and plays the London Palladium, [1], where onstage recordings are made which will later appear as a live LP. *Bluebirds Over The Mountain*, a revival of an obscure oldie by Ersel Hickey, is a moderate success at US #61 and UK #33.

1969 Apr [1] The group sues Capitol Records for over $2 million, claiming unpaid royalties and production fees, plus other losses incurred through general mismanagement on Capitol's part. LP *20/20* climbs to US #68 and a healthy UK #3. Taken from it, *I Can Hear Music*, another of the group's revivals (originally by The Ronettes°), makes US #24 and UK #10.

May The group holds a press conference to announce the impending end of its Capitol contract, a poor financial situation, and a quest for a new and better label deal.

June *Break Away*, the last single recorded for Capitol, makes US #63, but climbs to UK #6.

Aug [3] Carl Wilson is indicted in LA for failing to appear for community service work (as an orderly in a hospital) in lieu of the military. (These problems originating from his refusal to be drafted continue to drag on until a mutually acceptable form of community service is found – which means free Beach Boys' concerts at hospitals, prisons, and so on.)

1970 Jan The group resurrects its Brother Records label as part of a new deal with Warner/Reprise Records.

Mar *Add Some Music To Your Day* reaches US #64, but is not released in UK.

June Capitol in UK remixes *Cottonfields*, from LP *20/20*, and the resulting stronger track hits UK #3. It is not released in US.

Oct LP *Sunflower*, first LP on Brother/Reprise, peaks at US #151. In UK, the LP remains with EMI (owner of US Capitol) on the Stateside label, and reaches #29, while UK-only compilation LP *Greatest Hits* on Capitol hits UK #5. In US the group's live shows take on a new lease of life as the hip rock crowd discovers them in an event-stealing appearance at the Big Sur festival in California.

Nov Brian Wilson returns to the stage for shows at LA's Whiskey A-Go-Go club, where the group is rapturously received. A recurring ear problem forces him to make this live stint temporary.

Dec Dennis Wilson records a solo single, *Sound Of Free*, under the name Dennis Wilson and Rumbo, released only in UK. Shrouded in obscurity, it does not chart.

1971 Jan Former journalist and radio DJ Jack Rieley takes over the group's management, encouraging it to finish *Surf's Up*, a Brian Wilson song from the abandoned *Smile* sessions, of which Brian himself has recently performed a solo version on a Leonard Bernstein TV show.

Feb The group plays a sell-out concert at New York's Carnegie Hall, to rave reviews. Rieley has prompted a long overdue update of the group's live image, dropping its stage uniforms and lengthening the song sets.

Apr The Beach Boys play a joint concert with The Grateful Dead° at the Fillmore East, New York, cementing new-found favor with the progressive rock audience.

June [11] Dennis Wilson accidentally puts his right hand through a window pane and severs some nerves. He is replaced for live work by Ricky Fataar, former drummer with South African group Flame, which The Beach Boys have earlier signed to Brother Records and used for some time as a support band.

Oct An LP originally to be titled *Landlocked* because of its ecological concerns, but renamed *Surf's Up* after the addition of that track, reaches US #29 and UK #15. *Long Promised Road*, extracted as a single, reaches US #89.

1972 Jan Bruce Johnston leaves for a solo career, due to personality clashes with Rieley. His place is taken by Ricky Fataar's former Flame colleague, Blondie Chaplin.

Feb The group makes a TV special in Amsterdam, Holland, and plans to record in that country.

May The group plays UK, appearing at Lincoln Festival, London's Royal Festival Hall, and Crystal Palace at which they are joined onstage by Elton John° and The Who's° Keith Moon.

June LP *Carl And The Passions/So Tough*, with the title evoking one of the group's pre-Beach Boys names, reaches US #50 and UK #25. In the US, the LP is jointly packaged with a reissue of *Pet Sounds*, US rights to which have reverted to the group from Capitol. After its release, the group has a demountable recording studio transported from LA to Baambrugge, Holland, at considerable expense, and members take up temporary Dutch residence while the next LP is planned.

1973 Mar LP Holland, the result of sessions in that country (costing an estimated $250,000), plus additional LA-recorded track *Sail On Sailor* (added at the insistence of Reprise Records executives, who feel the LP lacks commerciality without it), reaches US #36 and UK #20. The LP contains a free EP, *Mount Vernon And Fairway*, which has a musical fairy tale written by Brian Wilson. *Sail On Sailor* is extracted as a US single and reaches #79, while the UK has *California Saga (On My Way To Sunny Californ-i-a)*, which peaks at #37. Shortly after the LP's release, Rieley is fired as manager, and replaced by Mike Love's brother, Steve.

June [4] Murry Wilson, father of Brian, Carl and Dennis, and their original manager, dies.

1974 Jan Double live LP *The Beach Boys In Concert* reaches US #25, though fails to chart in UK. After its release, Chaplin and Fataar leave, and a recovered Dennis Wilson, who had considered staying out of the group to try solo projects, returns on drums. James William Guercio, producer of Chicago° and Blood, Sweat & Tears° and owner of Caribou Studios, Colorado, but a long-time fan of the group, joins on bass and takes over some management duties.

Sept Double LP re-package of *Wild Honey* and *20/20* reaches US #50.

THE BEACH BOYS *cont.*

Oct Double compilation LP *Endless Summer*, put together by Capitol to satisfy nostalgia for the group's 1960s classics, tops the US chart for a week (only the second #1 LP of the group's career), and will stay on chart in US for 155 weeks. *Surfin' USA* is extracted and becomes a US hit again, at #36. The Beach Boys sing guest vocals on a single by Chicago°, *Wishing You Were Here*, which reaches US #11. The teaming is made by Guercio, who also pairs the two groups on a hugely successful 12-city US tour which grosses $7 million.

Nov Double LP re-package of *Friends* and *Smiley Smile* reaches US #125.

1975 May *Sail On Sailor* is reissued in US, 2 years after first charting, and peaks at #49.

June [21] The group plays London's Wembley Stadium to a rousing reception from 72,000 people, second on the bill to Elton John°, who finds it impossible to follow the group successfully on stage. In US, Capitol's second double LP nostalgia compilation *Spirit Of America* peaks at #8.

Sept Compilation LP, *Good Vibrations – Best Of The Beach Boys* (of later tracks on Brother/Reprise), reaches US #25.

1976 July Having not promoted either *Endless Summer* or *Spirit Of America*, Capitol/EMI in the UK puts together its own Beach Boys compilation LP, *20 Golden Greats*, with a TV ad campaign behind it. The result tops the UK chart for 10 weeks. *Good Vibrations* is reissued as a UK single, and hits again at #18.

Aug Having dropped out of a largely non-productive deal to work with Bruce Johnston and Terry Melcher's Equinox Records, Brian Wilson returns to produce LP *15 Big Ones*, a title which refers to the group's 15th birthday and the number of tracks on the LP (which mostly contains revivals of other acts' nostalgic oldies). The LP hits US #8, and extracted single, a revival of Chuck Berry's° *Rock And Roll Music* becomes the group's first US top 10 hit since *Good Vibrations* 10 years earlier, peaking at #5. Brian Wilson rejoins the stage line-up at a concert in Oakland, Cal. In UK, the LP and single are overshadowed by the concurrent success of Capitol reissues, and only reach #31 and #36 respectively.

Aug [5] NBC TV in US ties into the LP success with a 15th anniversary special: *"The Beach Boys: It's OK"*.

Sept [18] Brian Wilson is nominated to the Rock Hall of Fame, along with The Beatles°, Elvis Presley° and Bob Dylan°, on a US TV show devoted to the event.

Oct *It's OK*, also taken from *15 Big Ones*, reaches US #29.

Dec [31] The group, with Brian Wilson again in the line-up, plays a show to commemorate the 15th anniversary of their first gig, at LA Forum.

1977 Jan The live tracks recorded at the London Palladium in Dec. 1968 are released by Capitol in US as LP *Beach Boys '69: Live In London*, charting at #75.

Apr [1] The group signs to Caribou Records, having just completed an LP for Reprise, and owing the label one more.

May LP *The Beach Boys Love You*, produced by Brian Wilson, reaches US #53 and UK #28.

July [30] The group plays an exclusive gig for UK CBS Records' (distributors of Caribou Records) annual sales conference in London, having abandoned plans to do a UK Wembley concert.

Sept Dennis Wilson is the first Beach Boy to release a solo LP, *Pacific Ocean Blue* on Caribou Records, which climbs to US #96.

1978 June Title song from the film *Almost Summer*, written by Love, Jardine and Brian Wilson, and performed by Celebration, featuring Mike Love, reaches US #28.

Oct *M.I.U. Album* (the initials standing for Maharishi International University) is released to fulfill the Reprise contract, but is universally panned. It makes US #151, but fails to chart in UK. *Peggy Sue*, from the LP, reaches US #59.

1979 Jan [23] Brian Wilson is divorced from Marilyn Rovell, after 15 years.

Apr *Here Comes The Night*, with a strong disco flavor, is first release by the group on Caribou, and reaches US #44 and UK #37.

May LP *L.A. (Light Album)* peaks at US #100 and UK #32. Johnston returns to the group both as its producer and as a performer.

June *Good Timin'*, taken from the LP, makes US #40.

July *Lady Lynda*, written by Al Jardine about his wife, also from *L.A. (Light Album)*, is The Beach Boys' first UK Top 10 hit since 1970, reaching #6.

Oct *Sumahama*, from the LP, reaches US #45.

1980 Jan [13] The group plays a Los Angeles benefit concert for the people of Kampuchea, along with Starship and The Grateful Dead°.

Apr LP *Keepin' The Summer Alive* reaches US #75 and UK #54.

June In UK, the group plays two concerts at Wembley Arena [6-7], and tops the bill of Knebworth Festival [20].

July [4] The group gives a free performance to half a million people in Washington, D.C., on US Independence Day. The July 4 concert will become a regular feature of The Beach Boys' calendar in the 1980s.

1981 May Carl Wilson reaches US #185 with his solo LP Carl Wilson, and leaves (to tour with his own Carl Wilson Band). Englishman Adrian Baker, a long-time admirer and professional emulator of The Beach Boys' sound, is called in to fill out group harmonies on live work.

Sept Following the medley craze sparked on both sides of the Atlantic by the Star Sound hit *Stars On 45*, Capitol puts together *The Beach Boys Medley* which links excerpts from their 1960s classics. It peaks at UK #47, but climbs to US #12, the group's first US top 20 hit for 5 years.

Oct Mike Love's solo LP *Looking Back With Love* is released, but does not chart. Two other solo LPs of his remain unreleased. He tours with own group, The Endless Summer Beach Band.

1982 Jan Double compilation LP *Ten Years Of Harmony (1970-1980)* reaches only US #156, but taken from it, *Come Go With Me*, a revival of The Del Vikings' oldie, makes US #18.

Feb Love records in UK with Adrian Baker, who remains close to the group.

Apr Carl Wilson returns to The Beach Boys, and his own manager Jerry Schilling becomes the group's manager.

1983 Sept Double compilation LP *The Very Best Of The Beach Boys*, released in UK by Capitol, benefits from TV advertising and goes to UK #1.

Dec [28] Dennis Wilson drowns while swimming from his boat in the harbor at Marina Del Ray, Cal. Special dispensation is granted (with the help of President Reagan, who sends his condolences to the Wilson family) for a burial at sea – normally reserved for Naval personnel – of the only genuine surfer in The Beach Boys.

1984 The Beach Boys make a one-off recording with Frankie Valli and The Four Seasons°, *East Meets West*, written by Bob Crewe and Bob Gaudio. The single is released on The Seasons' own FBI label in US, but does not chart.

1985 June LP *The Beach Boys*, produced by Steve Levine, reaches US #52 and UK #60, while *Getcha Back*, taken from it, makes US #26 without charting in UK.

July The group plays at the Live Aid concert in Philadelphia, US.

Aug *It's Gettin' Late*, also from the LP, makes US #82.

1986 July *Rock'n'Roll To The Rescue*, written by Mike Love and Terry Melcher, reaches US #68. It trailers double compilation LP *Made In The USA*, released by Capitol in celebration of the group's 25th anniversary, which contains 20 1962-1968 Capitol tracks; plus later hits *Rock And Roll Music*, *Come Go With Me* and *Getcha Back*, and two new Beach Boys' recordings produced by Terry Melcher, including the single.

Oct Also from the LP, a revival of The Mamas and The Papas'° *California Dreamin'*, with electric 12-string guitar played by Roger McGuinn of The Byrds°, makes US #57.

1987 Sept The group is invited to co-perform on a remake of *Wipe Out* by rap act The Fat Boys, which hits UK #2 and US #12.

1988 Brian Wilson is reported working on a re-mastered and extended version of *Pet Sounds*, for release on CD, and to be investigating release of the never-issued *Smile* tapes. He also records his first solo LP *Brian Wilson* for release on the reactivated Reprise label.

THE BEASTIE BOYS

King Ad-Rock (Adam Horovitz) (vocals)
MCA (Adam Yauch) (vocals)
Mike D (Michael Diamond) (vocals)

1981 Horovitz (b. Oct.31, 1966, Manhattan, New York, US), Yauch (b. Aug.15, 1967, Brooklyn, New York) and Diamond (b. Nov.20, 1965, New York) team up as a hardcore rock band. For NY independent label, Rat Cage Records, they record an 8-song EP *Polly Wog Stew*.

1983 Aug *Cookie Puss*, more a harangue than a song, is backed by *Beastie Revolution*, a snatch of which is used on a British Airways commercial, resulting in the group getting a $40,000 pay-off from the airline.

Oct They begin to rap as part of their stage act, notably on *Cookie Puss*, which is otherwise difficult to "perform" live. As the rap portion of their show expands and the hard rock portion shrinks, they add DJ Double RR (Rick Rubin) to scratch on turntables behind them.

1984 Oct The group signs to Rubin's new Def Jam label (in association with CBS), and releases its first full rap single *Rock Hard*.

Nov They perform *She's On It* in the rap movie *Krush Groove*, alongside L.L. Cool J.°, Kurtis Blow°, The Fat Boys and other rising stars of the genre.

1985 The trio supports Madonna° on a US tour.

1986 Sept On a UK visit as part of the Raisin' Hell tour, their outrageous stage act and apparently similar behavior offstage begins a love/hate relationship with the UK press.

1987 Mar The group's debut LP *Licensed To Ill* is the first rap LP to top the US chart, holding at #1 for 7 weeks, while the single *(You Gotta) Fight For Your Right (To Party)* is a US hit at #7.

Apr *(You Gotta) Fight For Your Right (To Party)* is their first UK hit, reaching #11.

May [30] On tour in the UK, Horovitz is arrested in Liverpool on a charge of Actual Bodily Harm, when he allegedly hits a girl fan during a riot that follows their Royal Court concert. (He will be acquitted in Nov. when the case goes to court.) The tabloid press wastes no chance to invent lurid stories about their supposed anti-social behavior, such as the one about them laughing at mentally handicapped children. The Volkswagen medallions worn by the trio also bring trouble as throughout the UK fans try to emulate the style by stealing VW emblems from cars.

June *No Sleep Till Brooklyn* makes #14 in UK, and LP *Licensed To Ill* hits #7.

Aug *She's On It* reaches UK #10.

1988 While members consider their future as The Beastie Boys, Horovitz follows a cameo performance in TV series "The Equalizer" with his first major role in the movie *Santa Ana Project*.

THE BEAT

Dave Wakeling (vocals and guitar)
Andy Cox (guitar)
David Steele (bass)
Everett Morton (drums)

1978 Sept Wakeling (b. Feb.19, 1956), Cox (b. Jan.25, 1956) and Steele (b. Sept.8, 1960) begin playing ska-influenced rock in their Birmingham, UK, home area, being joined later in the year by West Indian drummer Morton (b. Apr.5, 1951), formerly of Joan Armatrading's° band.

1979 Mar They play their first professional gig, at a Birmingham club.

May Ranking Roger (b. Feb.21, 1961), drummer for Birmingham punk band The Dum Dum Boys, joins as second vocalist and reggae toaster.

Oct Jerry Dammers of The Specials° meets The Beat and offers to cut and release a single on their 2-Tone label.

Nov The band recruits Jamaican sax player Saxa (b. 1930) for their recording session, and he decides to stay as a permanent member. *Tears Of A Clown/Ranking Full Stop* is released as a double A-side single, and climbs to UK #6 in Dec.

1980 Jan Success brings an offer from Arista Records. The Beat sets up own label Go-Feet (based on the 2-Tone model), under Arista's wing.

Feb First Go-Feet single *Hands Off – She's Mine* is released in UK, and reaches #9.

May *Mirror In The Bathroom* hits UK #4. First LP *Just Can't Stop It* is released in UK, hits #3 and remains charted for 32 weeks.

Aug Double A-side *Best Friend/Stand Down Margaret* charts at UK #22, the latter title being a pointed statement at UK Prime Minister Margaret Thatcher.

Oct First US tour (renamed The English Beat to avoid confusion with the US band) supporting The Pretenders° and Talking Heads°.

Dec *Too Nice To Talk To* puts them back in UK top 10, peaking at #7.

1981 Apr Double A-side *Drowning/All Out To Get You* reaches UK #22.

May Second LP *Wha'ppen* is issued in UK, and hits #3.

June *Doors Of Your Heart* is last Beat single to reach UK top 40, prior to a 2-year run of minor successes.

1982 Oct LP *Special Beat Service* is released in UK, but reflects Beat's now lower commercial profile by only reaching #21.

Nov Saxa announces that due to poor health he will no longer play live with the band, but will continue in the studio. Onstage replacement is Wesley Magoogan, while former tour manager David "Blockhead" Wright joins on keyboards.

1983 May *Can't Get Used To Losing You*, a revival of the old Andy Williams hit, is released in UK by Arista just as the band thinks of quitting. It climbs to #3, making it their highest-placed single of all. The Beat appears on UK TV to promote it, but it proves to be a coda to the band's success.

July Focal founder member Wakeling announces he is to leave. *Ackee 1-2-3* makes UK #54, but it is The Beat's last hit single and, without replacing Wakeling, it splits up. (Wakeling will form General Public with Ranking Roger, while Cox and Steele will help found Fine Young Cannibals.)

THE BEATLES

John Winston Lennon (vocals and guitar)
James Paul McCartney (vocals and guitar)
George Harrison (vocals and guitar)
Ringo Starr (vocals and drums)

1957 June Lennon° (b. Oct.9, 1940, Liverpool, UK) meets McCartney° (b. June 18, 1942, Liverpool); both become members of The Quarrymen and their writing partnership begins.

1958 July Lennon's mother, Julia, dies in a road accident in Liverpool.

Aug Harrison° (b. Feb.25, 1943, Liverpool) joins The Quarrymen as guitarist.

1959 Nov The Quarrymen disbands.

1960 Apr John, Paul, and George re-group with Pete Best (b. 1941, Liverpool) on drums and John's art school friend, Stuart Sutcliffe, on guitar. They name the band Long John & The Silver Beatles. The "Long John" goes almost immediately, and "Silver" follows, leaving The Beatles.

May Alan Williams becomes The Beatles' manager, and secures them Liverpool club bookings.

Aug First working trip to Hamburg, West Germany, lasts 4 months. The group plays the Indra, Kaiserkeller and Top Ten clubs.

Dec George is deported from West Germany when it is discovered he is under age for a work permit, so the group returns to Liverpool.

1961 Mar [21] The group debuts at the Cavern Club as guests of The Bluegenes.

Apr Second Hamburg trip, which will last for 3 months.

May First recording session, backing Tony Sheridan for Polydor in Germany, and cutting two tracks – *Ain't She Sweet* and *Cry For A Shadow* – without Sheridan.

June Sutcliffe marries and leaves the group to study art in Hamburg.

Dec Brian Epstein becomes The Beatles' manager.

1962 Jan [1] The group fails an audition in London for a recording contract with Decca Records.

Apr [10] Stuart Sutcliffe dies of a brain hemorrhage, in Hamburg.

Apr [11] The group flies from Manchester on their third Hamburg trip, to play 7 weeks at the Star Club.

June [6] The group auditions for George Martin at EMI Records in London.

July The Beatles are signed to EMI's Parlophone label by George Martin.

Aug [18] Ringo Starr° (b. Richard Starkey, July 7, 1940, Liverpool) joins as drummer at Lennon, McCartney and Harrison's request; Pete Best is fired.

Aug [23] John marries Cynthia Powell, with Paul as best man.

Sept [11] *Love Me Do* and *P.S. I Love You* are recorded at Abbey Road studios.

Oct *Love Me Do* is released in UK and charts at the lower end of the top 50 after a week on sale.

Nov [26] *Please Please Me* is recorded.

Dec *Love Me Do* peaks at #17.

Dec [18] Final Hamburg trip, playing the Star Club for 2 weeks.

1963 Jan *Please Please Me* is second UK single, and charts immediately.

Feb *Please Please Me* hits #1 on three of the four published UK charts.

Feb [11] First LP recording sessions at Abbey Road.

Mar First LP *Please Please Me*, is issued in UK. The group plays support on a nationwide UK tour headed by Chris Montez and Tommy Roe°.

Apr [8] Julian Lennon is born to John and Cynthia in Liverpool.

Apr LP *Please Please Me* tops UK chart, holding #1 until November. Third UK single *From Me To You* is released and hits #1 after 2 weeks.

May/June First headlining tour of UK, supported by Roy Orbison° and Gerry & The Pacemakers°.

July EP *Twist And Shout* is released in UK, climbing to #2.

Aug [3] Final Beatles' appearance at Liverpool's Cavern Club.

Aug Fourth UK single *She Loves You* is released, and hits #1 in its second chart week.

Oct *She Loves You* tops a million UK sales. It is to remain the all-time biggest selling single in Britain for over 14 years.

Nov [4] The group appears in UK Royal Variety Show, watched by the Queen Mother.

Nov Second UK LP *With The Beatles* is released, with advance orders of 300,000. It replaces *Please Please Me* at #1. *She Loves You* returns to UK #1.

Dec Fifth UK single *I Want To Hold Your Hand* is released, enters UK chart at #1 and dethrones *She Loves You*. The group also has three EPs in the top 20. *I Want To Hold Your Hand* is rush released in US immediately after Christmas amidst a major publicity campaign designed by Capitol Records to break the group to US audience.

1964 Jan *I Want To Hold Your Hand* charts in US and hits #1 in 3 weeks. It sells a half million copies in 10 days. *She Loves You* and *Please Please Me* are released in US and both chart instantly. Two LPs, *Meet The Beatles* and *Introducing The Beatles* soar to US #1 and #2 respectively.

Feb [7] The group flies to New York for first US visit.

Feb [9] They are launched to US public via an appearance on TV's "Ed Sullivan Show".

Mar Filming begins on *A Hard Day's Night* at Twickenham, UK. *She Loves You* replaces *I Want To Hold Your Hand* as US #1.

Apr *Can't Buy Me Love* is issued in UK and US simultaneously. It enters UK chart at #1.

Apr [4] The Beatles hold all top five places in US singles chart with *Can't Buy Me Love, Twist And Shout, She Loves You, I Want To Hold Your Hand*, and *Please Please Me*.

Apr LP *The Beatles Second Album* (actually their third) is released in US and replaces *Meet The Beatles* at #1. John's first book, *In His Own Write*, is published.

May *Do You Want To Know A Secret*, issued as a US single, hits #2. *Love Me Do* is issued belatedly as a US single and hits #1.

June [4-14] Jimmy Nicol becomes The Beatles' temporary drummer when Ringo collapses in Denmark before the start of a world tour.

July World première of film *A Hard Day's Night* in London. Single and LP of *A Hard Day's Night* are released; both enter UK charts at #1 and quickly go to #1 in US too, which gives the group a rare transatlantic four-chart scoop with the same title. Additional LP *Something New* is issued in US and hits #2 behind *A Hard Day's Night*.
Aug The film *A Hard Day's Night* is released worldwide.
Aug [19] First tour of US opens at the Cow Palace, San Francisco.
Sept *Matchbox* is released as a US single, reaching #18.
Sept [20] US tour ends in New York with a charity concert.
Oct [25] The Beatles win five UK Ivor Novello Awards; 1963's Most-Broadcast Song and Top-Selling Single *She Loves You*, Second-Best-Selling Single *I Want To Hold Your Hand*, Second Most Outstanding Song *All My Loving*, and Most Outstanding Contribution to Music.
Nov *I Feel Fine* is released in UK and US, and hits #1 in both. The B-side *She's A Woman* reaches US #4.

Dec Fourth UK LP *Beatles For Sale* is issued and instantly replaces *A Hard Day's Night* at #1. LP Beatles '65 is released in US and hits #1 in its second chart week.
1965 Feb [11] Ringo marries Maureen Cox.
Feb *Eight Days A Week* is released in US and hits #1.
Feb [25] Filming begins on *Help!* in the Bahamas.
Apr *Ticket To Ride* is released in UK and US and hits #1 in both.
May Filming of *Help!* is completed.
June [12] All four Beatles are awarded the MBE in HM The Queen's Birthday Honours List.
June LP *Beatles VI* is released in US and hits #1. John's second book *A Spaniard In The Works* is published.
July *Help!* is released worldwide and hits #1 in UK and US.
Aug The movie *Help!* is released worldwide. The *Help!* soundtrack LP is released and hits #1 in UK and US.
Aug [13] The group flies to New York for another US tour.
Aug [15] A concert at New York's Shea Stadium draws 56,000, a new outdoor audience record.
Aug [27] Resting during US tour, the group spends a private evening with Elvis Presley° at his Bel Air, Cal., home.
Sept *Yesterday* is released as a US single and hits #1.
Sept [13] Zak Starkey is born to Ringo and wife Maureen in London.
Oct [26] HM The Queen presents the Beatles with their MBEs at Buckingham Palace, London.
Dec *We Can Work It Out/Day Tripper*, the first double A-side Beatles' single, hits #1 in UK and US. LP *Rubber Soul* appears and hits UK and US #1.
1966 Jan [21] George marries Patti Boyd at Epsom, UK.
Feb *Nowhere Man* is released as an additional single in US, and hits #3.
Mar [4] John Lennon, interviewed by Maureen Cleave in *London Evening Standard*, contends that "The Beatles are probably bigger than Jesus right now."
June *Paperback Writer* is released and hits #1 in UK and US. LP *Yesterday And Today* is released in US. Its original, controversial "butcher" cover is quickly withdrawn, and it hits US #1.
June [23] The Beatles fly to Germany for the first leg of what will be their last world tour.
July Savage reaction in much of the US to John's reported remarks about The Beatles being "bigger than Jesus".
Aug [12] They arrive in Chicago for final US tour, where, at a news conference, John publicly apologizes for his controversial remarks.
Aug LP *Revolver* is released worldwide and hits UK and US #1. *Yellow Submarine/Eleanor Rigby* is released as their second double A-side single, and hits UK and US #1.
Aug [23] The group plays New York's Shea Stadium.
Aug [29] Last Beatles' concert takes place at Candlestick Park, San Francisco.
Sept John films a role in movie *How I Won The War* in Germany and Spain.
Nov Rumors circulate the world that Paul has been killed in a car crash.
Dec Compilation LP *A Collection of Beatles Oldies* is released in UK and hits #4.
1967 Feb Double A-side *Penny Lane/Strawberry Fields Forever* is issued, and hits UK #2 and US #1.
Mar [11] The group wins three US Grammy awards for *Michelle*, *Eleanor Rigby* and LP *Revolver*.
Mar [25] Two UK Ivor Novello awards are won, for 1966's Top-Selling Single *Yellow Submarine*, and Most-Performed Work, *Michelle*.
Apr [2] Recording is completed for LP *Sergeant Pepper's Lonely Hearts Club Band*.
Apr [19] The Beatles & Co. partnership is formed.
May Paul publicly admits to having taken LSD. EMI announces that total world sales of Beatles' records have topped 200 million. John announces that The Beatles will do no more touring.
June LP *Sergeant Pepper's Lonely Hearts Club Band* is released worldwide and hits UK #1 in its first week and US #1 in its second.
June [25] *All You Need Is Love* is recorded at Abbey Road, the final session shown live on TV worldwide as part of the first-ever global TV link-up "Our World".
July *All You Need Is Love* is issued, hitting UK and US #1.
Aug [19] Jason Starkey is born to Ringo and wife Maureen, in London.

THE BEATLES *cont.*

Aug [25] The Beatles and friends go to Bangor, Wales, to study transcendental meditation with Maharishi Mahesh Yogi.

Aug [27] Brian Epstein dies of a drug overdose after deep depression.

Aug [31] The Beatles announce they will assume management of their own affairs following Epstein's death.

Sept *Magical Mystery Tour* TV film is made on location around the UK.

Oct [18] The movie *How I Won The War* is premièred in London.

Nov *Hello Goodbye* is released and hits UK and US #1.

Dec Ringo films a cameo role in *Candy*. LP *Magical Mystery Tour* is released in US, and as a double EP set in UK. The US LP hits #1 and UK EP set replaces *Hello Goodbye* at #1.

Dec [7] The Apple Boutique opens in London.

Dec [25] Paul announces his engagement to long-time girlfriend, actress Jane Asher.

Dec [26] *Magical Mystery Tour* is shown on UK TV.

1968 Feb [16] The Beatles fly to India to study with Maharishi Mahesh Yogi.

Mar [9] Four Grammy awards are won by the LP *Sergeant Pepper.*

Mar *Lady Madonna* is released, and hits UK #1 and US #4.

Apr Apple Corps Ltd. and Apple Publicity begin operations in London.

May The group undertakes a major worldwide publicity initiative to promote the Apple organization. John begins his liaison with Yoko Ono after meeting her at an art exhibition.

June John and Yoko have an "Acorn Event" at Coventry Cathedral's National Sculpture Exhibition. Paul meets Linda Eastman while on a US business trip. The Beatles announce that all future recordings will be on their soon-to-be-formed Apple label.

July [17] The full-length cartoon film *Yellow Submarine* is premièred in London.

July [20] Jane Asher announces that Paul has broken off their engagement.

July [30] The Apple Boutique is closed down after heavy money losses.

July [31] *Hey Jude* is recorded.

Aug [22] Cynthia Lennon sues John for divorce, citing Yoko Ono.

Aug *Hey Jude* is released worldwide, along with Mary Hopkin's° *Those Were The Days*, among the first batch of Apple label records. It hits UK and US #1.

Sept [8] The group appears on David Frost's UK TV show "Frost On Sunday", playing *Hey Jude*.

Oct [31] Linda Eastman moves to the UK to live with Paul.

Nov [8] John and Cynthia are divorced.

Nov Double LP *The Beatles* ("the white album") is released and hits UK and US #1; their first LP on Apple.

1969 Jan The group rehearses for forthcoming tour and LP projects at Twickenham Film Studios, UK, and is filmed while doing so for a planned documentary. *Yellow Submarine* soundtrack LP is issued, featuring one side of Beatles' recordings. It hits UK #4 and US #2.

Jan [30] The Beatles, with Billy Preston guesting on organ, perform four songs on the roof of the Apple building in Saville Row, filmed for the movie *Let It Be*.

Feb [3] Allen Klein becomes The Beatles' business manager, and Eastman & Eastman their legal consultants.

Feb [8] George has his tonsils removed at a London hospital.

Mar Ringo begins filming movie *The Magic Christian* with Peter Sellers.

Mar [12] Paul marries Linda Eastman at Marylebone Registry Office, London.

Mar [20] John marries Yoko Ono in Gibraltar.
Mar [26] John and Yoko begin a "bed-in" at the Amsterdam Hilton.
Mar [31] George and Patti Harrison are fined £250 for marijuana possession.
Apr *Get Back* is released and hits UK and US #1.
Apr [22] John changes his middle name from Winston to Ono by deed poll.
May *The Ballad Of John And Yoko* is released and hits #1 in UK, but finds some airplay problems in US (because Christ is mentioned in the lyrics), and only reaches #8.
May [19] The group receives an Ivor Novello Award for *Hey Jude*, as the UK Top-Selling Single of 1968.
June John and Yoko hold a "bed-in" in Montreal, and record *Give Peace A Chance* in their hotel room.
July [1] John and Yoko are hospitalized briefly after a car crash in Scotland.
July The group's relationship with NEMS, Epstein's former company, ends. *Give Peace A Chance* is released on a single credited to The Plastic Ono Band and makes UK #2 and US #14.
1969 Aug [8] Photo for the *Abbey Road* LP sleeve is taken at 10 a.m.
Aug [28] Mary McCartney is born to Paul and Linda, in London.
Sept John performs at Toronto Peace Festival with an impromptu Plastic Ono Band, including Eric Clapton°. LP *Abbey Road* is released, hitting UK and US #1.
Oct *Something/Come Together* is extracted from LP *Abbey Road* as a double A-side single and hits US #1 and UK #4. *Cold Turkey* is released by John with The Plastic Ono Band, and reaches UK #14 and US #30.
Dec First appearance of a previously unreleased Beatles' track *Across The Universe*, on the World Wildlife Fund compilation LP *No One's Gonna Change Our World*.
1970 Jan [16] The police shut down an exhibition of John Lennon's erotic lithographs at a London gallery, for alleged obscenity.
Feb *Instant Karma* is released by John and hits UK #4 and US #3. The compilation LP, *Hey Jude*, is released in US and hits #2. (It remains unissued in UK for many years.)
Mar *Let It Be* is released and hits UK #2 and US #1.
Mar [21] *Let It Be* sets a never-beaten record for highest first-time entry on US singles chart, debuting at #6.
Apr Paul officially parts from The Beatles as his solo LP *McCartney* hits UK #2 and US #1. Ringo's solo LP *Sentimental Journey* is released and reaches UK #20 and US #22.
May LP *Let It Be* is released and hits UK and US #1. *The Long And Winding Road* is issued in US to accompany LP *Let It Be*, and also hits #1. The movie *Let It Be* is premièred and released worldwide. It is widely viewed as a documentary of The Beatles' break-up.
Aug Paul suggests in writing to John the dissolution of The Beatles' legal partnership.
Oct Three Beatles are busy working on solo LPs while Ringo already has his second solo LP, *Beaucoups of Blues* released.
Nov [11] Ringo's daughter Lee Starkey is born.
Dec Paul files suit against Beatles & Co to have Beatles' partnership dissolved and end its links with Allen Klein. There will be no more Beatles' music as a group and all four members will pursue solo careers throughout the 1970s.
1973 Apr Two double LP compilations of Beatles' classics, *The Beatles 1962-1966* and *The Beatles 1967-1970* are released. They reach the top two positions in US LP chart and #2 and #3 in UK.
1976 Mar *Yesterday* is finally released as a UK single, 11 years after its US release. It makes UK #8 and is joined by other chart sellers from a re-promotion of back catalog singles: *Hey Jude* (#12), *Paperback Writer* (#23), *Get Back* (#28), *Strawberry Fields Forever* (#32) and *Help!* (#37).
June Rock tracks by The Beatles are compiled on double LP *Rock'n'Roll Music* and reach top 20 in UK and US. Former LP track *Got To Get You Into My Life* is issued as a US single and reaches #19.
1977 May *The Beatles At The Hollywood Bowl*, a live LP taped in 1965 but never issued, is released worldwide with a TV campaign in UK, and tops UK and US charts.
1982 Apr *The Beatles Movie Medley* is released as a single and reaches UK #10 and US #12.
Oct *Love Me Do* is reissued as a UK single on its own 20th anniversary and becomes a major hit, reaching UK #4. The story comes full circle with the subsequent release of all Beatles' singles on their relevant double-decade anniversaries.
1987 The Beatles' timeless popularity is reiterated as each original UK LP is issued on CD, to re-enter the charts in both UK and US throughout the year.
1988 The remaining Beatles successfully sue Capitol Records in US for unpaid royalties.

THE BEAU BRUMMELS

Ron Elliott (vocals and guitar)
Sal Valentino (vocals)
Ron Meagher (bass)
John Peterson (drums)

1964 June After graduating from high school in the Bay area of San Francisco, Elliott (b. Oct.21, 1943), Valentino (b. Sep.8, 1942), Meagher (b. Oct.2, 1941) and Peterson (b. Jan.8, 1942) get together as a group, along with Irishman Declan Mulligan.
Nov Tom Donahue, prominent San Francisco DJ, is impressed by their Searchers°-like "English" sound, driven by 12-string guitar and vocal harmonies. He signs them to his Autumn Records label, but Mulligan quits before the group records.
Dec *Laugh Laugh*, produced by Sly Stone, is released as their first US single.
1965 Jan *Laugh Laugh* climbs to #15. Because of their sound, The Beau Brummels is dubbed "America's Answer to the British Invasion", which gets it much US TV exposure.
Apr *Just A Little* charts in US, and reaches #9, the group's only top-tenner.
May Debut LP *Introducing The Beau Brummels* is released, and reaches US #24.
July Third and last US top 40 hit, *You Tell Me Why*, enters the chart to peak at #38.
Oct Fourth hit single *Don't Talk To Strangers* only charts at US #52 now that The Byrds° have started to make a much bigger chart impact with a similar sound.
Dec *Good Time Music* is their last single on Autumn, which closes down, bankrupt, at the end of the year. With the label having too many problems to distribute or promote properly, it only scrapes into US top 100 at #97.
1966 Jan Among Autumn Records assets, The Beau Brummels' contract is bought by Warner Bros. Records.

THE BEAU BRUMMELS *cont.*

May Warner releases a version of Bob Dylan's° *One Too Many Mornings* by the group as a single but it gains only minor attention, reaching #95 in a 3-week US chart stay. It is the final Brummels' hit single.

1967 July After Peterson and Meagher leave (the former to join Harper's Bizarre°), Elliott and Valentino record a progressive rock LP, *Triangle*, for Warner Bros.

Oct *Triangle* makes a minor chart showing at US #197 – their second and final chartmaking LP.

1968 Dec Beau Brummels' name is officially retired with Elliott and Valentino splitting to work (mostly obscurely) as soloists and with groups like Pan and Stoneground.

1974 Dec Beau Brummels' hitmaking line-up, augmented by additional guitarist Dan Levitt, re-forms.

1975 Apr LP *The Beau Brummels* is released for Warner Bros.

July LP has a 3-week US chart run, but only makes #180, and the group decides to disband for good.

JEFF BECK

1967 Mar After leaving The Yardbirds°, Beck (b. June 24, 1944) launches a solo career with *Hi-Ho Silver Lining*, which features him on lead guitar, and as lead vocalist, a role he will rarely undertake again. Rod Stewart° sings lead on the B-side. It peaks at UK #14.

Aug Follow up, *Tallyman*, written by Graham Gouldman (of Wax and later of 10cc°) reaches UK #30. Stewart° is not allowed by producer Mickie Most to sing lead vocal.

1968 Feb Third single, *Love Is Blue*, an instrumental version of a song from the Eurovision Song Contest, is recorded at Mickie Most's behest (Beck will later claim he was forced to cut it against his better judgement) and reaches UK #23.

July Beck guests on *Barabajagal* by Donovan° which reaches UK #12 and US #36. Plans for Beck and Stewart° to form a group with Tim Bogert (bass) of Vanilla Fudge°, and Carmine Appice (drums), are dropped after Beck is hospitalized following a car accident.

Aug The Jeff Beck Group – Beck, Stewart°, Ron Wood (bass) and Mickey Waller (drums) – releases debut LP, *Truth*, which reaches #15 in US but fails to register in UK. Waller is replaced by Tony Newman, and Nicky Hopkins joins on keyboards.

1969 Aug The group releases LP *Beck-Ola*, which makes US #15 and UK #39. Rod Stewart° and Ron Wood leave to join The Faces°.

1970 Beck forms a new group, with Cozy Powell (drums), Clive Chaman (bass), Max Middleton (keyboards) and Bobby Tench (vocals).

1971 Nov LP *Rough And Ready* is released and reaches US #46.

1972 May LP *Jeff Beck Group* (often known as the "orange" album since it pictures one on the sleeve), produced by Steve Cropper of Booker T. and The MG's°, reaches US #19.

1973 Jan Bogert and Appice resurrect the idea of forming a group with Beck and "supergroup" Beck, Bogert and Appice is born.

Apr LP *Beck, Bogert & Appice* reaches US #12 and UK #28. It includes Stevie Wonder's° *Superstition*. During a world tour, they cut a live double LP in Japan, the only country where it is released.

May *I've Been Drinking*, originally the B-side of *Love Is Blue* from 1968, is re-issued, credited to Jeff Beck and Rod Stewart°, and reaches UK #27.

1975 Apr Declaring himself tired of working with vocalists, Beck forms a totally instrumental group of himself, Max Middleton, Philip Chen (bass) and Richard Bailey (drums). This line-up plays on LP *Blow By Blow*, produced by George Martin, which hits US #4.

1976 June Using Middleton, Bailey, Jan Hammer (ex-Mahavishnu Orchestra, drums/synthesizer), Wilbur Bascomb (bass), and Narada Michael Walden (drums/keyboards), and with George Martin producing, Beck releases LP *Wired*, which reaches US #16 and UK #38.

1977 Jan Beck is invited to join The Jan Hammer Group for a year-long world tour.

Apr LP *Jeff Beck With The Jan Hammer Group Live* peaks at US #23.

1980 July After a long rest period and search for new collaborators, Beck records LP *There And Back*, assisted on some tracks by Simon Phillips (drums), Mo Foster (bass), Tony Hymas (keyboards) and Jan Hammer. It reaches US #21 and UK #38.

1981 Beck appears at the Amnesty International Benefit Concert, and contributes to the resulting LP, *The Secret Policeman's Other Ball*, along with Sting°, Eric Clapton°, Phil Collins° and Bob Geldof.

Dec LP *The Secret Policeman's Other Ball* reaches UK #69.

1983/4 Beck spends months contributing his talents to ARMS, the multiple sclerosis charity, along with Eric Clapton°, Jimmy Page, Steve Winwood°, Bill Wyman, Charlie Watts and others.

1985 July After a brief tour with Rod Stewart°, and collaboration on single reviving Curtis Mayfield's° *People Get Ready* (US #48), Beck releases his second LP of the 1980s, *Flash*. Credited producers include Nile Rodgers (of Chic°) and Arthur Baker, and performers include Rod Stewart°, Jan Hammer, Carmine Appice, Tony Hymas, and vocalist Jimmy Hall. *Flash* briefly charts at UK #83. Beck works on Mick Jagger's solo LP, *She's The Boss*.

1986 Beck releases his version of The Troggs'° *Wild Thing*.

1987 Beck works on Mick Jagger's second solo album, *Primitive Cool*. A reported collaboration with ex-Sex Pistols'° manager, Malcolm McLaren, has yet to produce commercial results.

THE BEE GEES

Barry Gibb (vocals and guitar)
Maurice Gibb (vocals and bass)
Robin Gibb (vocals)
Vince Melouney (guitar)
Colin Peterson (drums)

1958 Barry Gibb (b. Sept.1, 1947, Manchester, UK) and his twin brothers Maurice and Robin (b. Dec.22, 1949, Isle of Man, UK) emigrate to Australia with their parents.

1967 Feb [2] Having tried with little success to take their unusual sibling harmonies into the Australian market, they begin the trip back to Britain, and hear that they have finally topped the Australian chart with *Spicks & Specks*.

Feb [24] They sign to Robert Stigwood (who is in partnership with Brian Epstein).

Mar Australians Melouney (b. Aug.19, 1945), and Peterson (b. Mar.24, 1946), are recruited.

May Immediate success comes with the group's first British-made single *New York Mining Disaster 1941* which hits UK #12 and US #14, and is a global million-seller.

July *To Love Somebody* reaches UK #41 and US #17.

Aug LP *Bee Gees 1st* makes UK #8 and US #7.

Oct *Massachusetts* hits UK #1 and US #11.

Nov *Holiday* reaches US #16.

Dec *World* reaches UK #9.

1968 Feb *Words* reaches UK #8 and US #15. LP *Horizontal* makes UK #16 and US #12.

Apr *Jumbo* reaches UK #25 and US #57.

Aug *I've Gotta Get A Message To You* hits UK #1 and US #8.

Sept LP *Idea* hits UK #4 and US #17.

Dec LP *Rare, Precious & Beautiful*, a compilation of tracks cut pre-fame in Australia, reaches US #99.

1969 Mar Despite immense fame, the group is prone to internal strife. *First Of May* (UK #6 and US #37) and *I Started A Joke* (US #6) are the last Bee Gees' hits on which Melouney and Peterson appear, while Robin Gibb leaves his brothers for a solo career.

Apr Double LP *Odessa*, in a suede sleeve, makes UK #10 and US #20.
June Barry and Maurice continue as The Bee Gees, charting with *Tomorrow Tomorrow* (UK #2 and US #73).
July Robin, solo, hits UK #2 with *Saved By The Bell*. Barry and Maurice star in the movie *Cucumber Castle*.
Sept *Best Of The Bee Gees* makes UK #7 and US #9.
1970 Feb Still solo, Robin takes *August October* to UK #45.
Apr Barry and Maurice score a minor hit with *I.O.I.O.* (UK #49 and US #94). Second volume of Australian material, *Rare, Precious & Beautiful Vol.2* reaches US #100.
May LP *Cucumber Castle* reaches UK #57 and US #94.
Dec The brothers settle their differences, but have lost much of their UK popularity, evidenced by *Lonely Days* only reaching UK #33.
1971 Jan US popularity is less affected by squabbles, and *Lonely Days* hits US #3, while LPs *2 Years On* and *Trafalgar* chart at #32 and #34, but fail to chart in UK.
Aug *How Can You Mend A Broken Heart* hits US #1 and is a million-seller, but fails to reach the UK chart.
Nov *Don't Wanna Live Inside Myself* makes US #53.
1972 Feb *My World* reaches UK #16 and US #16.
Aug *Run To Me* (UK #9 and US #16) continues their comparative comeback, but *Alive* (US #34) fails to register in UK.
Dec LP *To Whom It May Concern* reaches US #35.
1973 Apr No chart action in UK, but *Saw A New Morning* reaches US #94.
Mar/Aug LPs *Life In A Tin Can* and *Best Of The Bee Gees Vol. 2* chart in US (at #69 and #98).
1974 New LP *A Kick In The Pants* is rejected by RSO Records (to which the group is now signed in UK after previous releases on Polydor) and Atco (RSO's US distributor and previous Bee Gees' US label), but the group starts to use Arif Mardin as producer, and LP *Mr. Natural* is a first faltering step back (US #178), as is the extract *Mr. Natural* (US #93).
1975 Apr Still with Mardin, The Bee Gees assemble a regular backup group of Alan Kendall (guitar), Dennis Bryon (drums) and Blue Weaver (keyboards), and record LP *Main Course*, which reaches US #14.
Aug *Jive Talkin'*, from LP *Main Course*, climbs to UK #5 and hits US #1.
Dec *Nights On Broadway*, also from the LP, hits US #7.
1976 Mar *Fanny (Be Tender With My Love)* makes US #12.
Sept *You Should Be Dancing*, tops US chart and hits UK #5.
Nov *Love So Right* reaches US #3 and UK #41.
LP *Children Of The World* climbs to US #8.
Dec Compilation LP *Bee Gees Gold Volume One*, reaches US #50.
1977 Robert Stigwood, owner of RSO Records and manager of The Bee Gees, makes the disco music film *Saturday Night Fever*, and constructs the score around songs written and sung by The Bee Gees (*Stayin' Alive, How Deep Is Your Love, Night Fever, More Than A Woman, Jive Talkin'* and *You Should Be Dancing*), and songs written by them for others (*If I Can't Have You* by Yvonne Elliman, and *More Than A Woman* by Tavares).
July Double LP *Here At Last . . . Bee Gees Live* hits US #8.
Dec *How Deep Is Your Love* hits US #1 and UK #3. Soundtrack double LP *Saturday Night Fever* tops both US and UK LP charts when the movie is released in 1978. It will eventually sell over 30 million copies worldwide.
1978 Feb *Stayin' Alive* tops US chart and reaches UK #4. *Night Fever* tops both US and UK chart.
May Yvonne Elliman's *If I Can't Have You* tops US chart and hits UK #4. Tavares' *More Than A Woman* reaches UK #7 and US #32.
Aug The group acts and sings in flop film, *Sergeant Pepper's Lonely Hearts Club Band* (based on the celebrated Beatles'° LP), the soundtrack of which reaches US #5 and UK #38. Barry Gibb's contribution to movie *Grease* is more successful; his title song, recorded by Frankie Valli, tops US chart and hits UK #3.
Oct *Oh Darlin'* by Robin Gibb is released and reaches US #15.
Dec *Too Much Heaven* hits UK #3.
1979 Jan *Too Much Heaven* tops the US chart.
Mar Disco-mold LP *Spirits (Having Flown)* tops both US and UK charts. *Tragedy* tops US and UK charts.
June *Love You Inside Out* hits US #1, but only reaches UK #13.
Dec Compilation LP *Bee Gees Greatest* tops US chart and reaches UK #6.
1980 Jan The title track of LP *Spirits* makes UK #16.
Dec Barry Gibb collaborates with Barbra Streisand°, producing her US #1 LP *Guilty*, and duetting with her on the title track (his composition), which reaches US #3 and UK #34.
1981 *What Kind Of Fool*, a duet by Barry and Streisand°, reaches US #10.
Oct *He's A Liar* reaches US #30.
Nov LP *Living Eyes* reaches US #41 and UK #73.
Dec *Living Eyes* single reaches US #45.
1982 Oct Barry produces LP *Heartbreaker* for Dionne Warwick°, which contains hit singles *Heartbreaker* and *All The Love In The World*.
1983 Jan The Bee Gees contribute songs to the soundtrack of movie *Stayin' Alive*, a sequel to *Saturday Night Fever*.
Feb *The Woman In You*, from the LP *Stayin' Alive*, reaches US #24. Robin releases second solo LP *How Old Are You?*, and extract, *Another Lonely Night In New York*, peaks at UK #71.
Aug LP *Stayin' Alive*, from the film soundtrack, reaches UK #14 and US #6.
Sept *Someone Belonging To Someone*, from the LP, reaches US and UK #49.
Oct Barry works with C&W singer Kenny Rogers° on LP *Eyes That See In The Dark* as producer, and contributes several songs; *Islands In The Stream*, Rogers' duet with Dolly Parton°, makes UK #7 and US #1.
1984 July Robin releases his third solo LP *Secret Agent*. Extract, *Boys (Do Fall in Love)*, reaches US #37.
Oct Barry releases his first solo LP *Now Voyager*. *Shine Shine*, taken from it, reaches US #37.
1985 Jan Barry, with Karl Richardson and Albhy Galuten, produces LP *Eaten Alive* for Diana Ross°.
Feb Diana Ross'° *Chain Reaction*, written by the Gibb brothers, hits UK #1, but only climbs to US #66. Robin releases solo LP *Walls Have Eyes* which fails to chart in UK or US.
1986 A quiet year, but Barry releases *We Are The Bunburys* under the alias of The Bunburys, supposedly cricket-playing rabbits.
1987 Oct The Bee Gees triumphantly return to UK chart, hitting #1 with *You Win Again*, and #5 with LP *E.S.P.*
Nov Their US comeback is more muted: *You Win Again* reaches #75 and LP *E.S.P.* makes #96.
1988 Apr The Bee Gees win an Ivor Novello Award for Outstanding Contribution to British Music. They are unable to attend the ceremony, mourning the death of younger brother, Andy.
June They return to public view with a live appearance at Nelson Mandela's 70th Birthday Party.

HARRY BELAFONTE

1955 Having been a messenger for a garments firm, a pop/jazz vocalist during club residencies in New York and Miami, an actor on stage in New York and in movies *Bright Road* (1953) and *Carmen Jones* (1954) in Hollywood, and a restaurateur in Greenwich Village, where he has acquired his folk leanings and repertoire, Belafonte (b. Mar.1, 1927, Harlem, New York, US) signs to RCA Records as a folk singer.
1956 Jan LP *Mark Twain And Other Folk Favorites* hits US #3.
Mar LP *Belafonte* tops US chart for 6 weeks.
Aug LP *Calypso* hits US #1, where it stays for all but 7 of the next 38 weeks. It will sell a half million copies by mid-1957, and a million by the end of the decade – staggering LP sales for the 1950s. The West Indian calypso style, which Belafonte first assimilated while living in Jamaica from age 9 to 13, rapidly becomes his forte.
Dec *Jamaica Farewell*, taken from LP *Calypso*, reaches US #17, and seasonal *Mary's Boy Child* makes US #15.
1957 Feb *Banana Boat Song (Day-O)* hits US #5, and is a million-seller despite competition from US top 30 versions by The Tarriers, The Fontane Sisters, Steve Lawrence and Sarah Vaughan. (It will be the subject of a popular parody by Stan Freberg, 2 months later.)
Apr *Mama Look At Bubu* reaches US #13, while *Banana Boat Song (Day-O)* is his first UK hit at #2, after seeing off a UK cover version (#8) by Shirley Bassey.
May LP *An Evening With Harry Belafonte* hits US #2.
July Double A-side *Island In The Sun/Cocoanut Woman* chart in US at #25 and #48 respectively. Strangely, Belafonte will never have another US chart single.
Aug *Island In The Sun* is a much bigger success in UK, hitting #3 and staying in the top 30 for 25 weeks. Belafonte also stars in a UK-made film of this title, alongside James Mason and Joan Fontaine.
Sept *Scarlet Ribbons* reaches UK #19.
Oct LP *Belafonte Sings Of The Caribbean* hits US #3.

HARRY BELAFONTE *cont.*

Nov *Mary's Boy Child* is released belatedly in UK and becomes a gigantic hit. It tops the chart for 6 weeks, and sells a million copies after 8 weeks – only the second record (after Bill Haley's° *Rock Around The Clock*) to achieve this UK total.

1958 Sept *Little Bernadette* peaks at UK #16.

Nov LP *Belafonte Sings The Blues* reaches US #16.

Dec *Mary's Boy Child* charts in UK for a second Christmas, reaching #11, and is joined by *The Son Of Mary* (sung to the traditional tune *Greensleeves*), which climbs to #18.

1959 June LP *Love Is A Gentle Thing* reaches US #18.

Aug LP *Porgy And Bess* with Lena Horne reaches US #13.

Nov Double-LP live set *Belafonte At Carnegie Hall*, his most enduring LP, is released, hits US #3, and will remain charted for 168 weeks.

Dec *Mary's Boy Child* charts in UK for the third Christmas running, at #30.

1961 Feb Live LP *Belafonte Returns To Carnegie Hall* hits US #3.

Sept A duet with folk singer Odetta on novelty number *Hole In The Bucket* reaches UK #32.

Oct LP *Jump Up Calypso* hits US #3.

1962 June LP *The Midnight Special* makes US #8, his last US top 10 LP (though he will continue to chart LPs through most of the 1960s, the last being *Homeward Bound* (#192) in 1970. Most of these retain his folk or calypso roots, but his 1960s career impinges little on mainstream pop and rock).

1985 Jan Belafonte is the original mover in organizing the USA for Africa project to record the charity single *We Are The World*, (in which he joins the chorus), his initial idea being a black artists' charity concert.

1987 He replaces Danny Kaye as the international Goodwill Ambassador for UNICEF.

1988 May Signed to EMI/Manhattan, he releases his first LP for 15 years, *Paradise In Gazankulu*, an ethnic blend with backing tracks recorded by South African musicians in Johannesburg, on which he sings a duet with Jennifer Warnes°.

June [11] He performs at the Nelson Mandela 70th Birthday concert at Wembley, London, UK, along with Dire Straits°, Stevie Wonder°, Simple Minds° and many others.

ARCHIE BELL AND THE DRELLS

Archie Bell
Lee Bell
James Wise
Willie Pernell

1965 The group comes together at Phillis Wheatley Senior High School in Houston, Texas.

1967 Local talent scout Skipper Lee Frazier becomes their manager after they win one of his talent shows, and gets them signed to Atlantic.

1968 Jan Bell is called up for US Army service when first single *Dog Eat Dog* is released.

Mar US DJs turn over the single and play catchy dance number B-side *Tighten Up* instead, which begins to sell the record.

May *Tighten Up* is US #1 for 2 weeks. The group (minus Bell, who is still in the Army) receives a gold disk for million-plus sales.

Aug *I Can't Stop Dancing* reaches US #9. The group is now teamed with writer/producer team Kenny Gamble and Leon Huff, who will guide the rest of its career.

Oct *Do The Choo Choo*, based on another dance craze, climbs to US #44.

1969 Jan *There's Gonna Be A Showdown* peaks at #21 in US and is their last US top 50 hit, but with Bell's return from the Army, they will also place six further singles in lower chart slots during 1969 and 1970.

1972 Nov *Here I Go Again*, not a hit in US, becomes a belated UK breakthrough due to dance floor play, and hits #16.

1973 Feb *There's Gonna Be A Showdown* also belatedly hits in UK at #35.

May The group switches to Glades label for one-off hit *Dancing To Your Music*, which makes US #61.

1976 Jan They sign to Philadelphia International Records, owned by Gamble and Huff, and release LP *Dance Your Troubles Away*, which reaches US #95.

June *Soul City Walk*, from the LP, reaches UK #13 without US pop success.

1977 June *Everybody Have A Good Time* hits UK #43, again without charting in US.

Aug Bell joins The O'Jays°, Billy Paul, Lou Rawls, Teddy Pendergrass° and Dee Dee Sharp Gamble as The Philadelphia International All-Stars on *Let's Clean Up The Ghetto*, which reaches US #91 and UK #34.

1981 Bell goes solo, signs to Beckett Records, and issues LP *I Never Had It So Good*, which is not a big seller.

1982 He moves to WMOT Records and releases solo single *Touching You*. It is not a hit, and Bell's record career comes to a stop, though he will continue performing live in US through the 1980s.

1986 July 1976 track *Don't Let Love Get You Down* is reissued in UK, charts at #49, and brings the name Archie Bell and The Drells back to brief limelight again.

PAT BENATAR

1970s Having studied classical singing in New York, Benatar (b. Pat Andrzejewski, Jan.10, 1953, Brooklyn, New York, US) marries her high school sweetheart Dennis Benatar and moves for a while to Virginia.

1979 Singing in a cabaret at New York's Catch a Rising Star, she impresses its owner Rick Newman, who thereafter manages her. She signs to Chrysalis Records (keeping her husband's name although they divorce later this year).

June She records debut LP *In The Heat Of The Night* with UK producer Mike Chapman.

1980 Mar LP *In The Heat Of The Night* peaks at US #12, as simultaneously *Heartbreaker*, which is taken from it, reaches US #23.

June *We Live For Love* reaches US #27.

Aug *You Better Run*, a revival of a mid-60s Young Rascals'° hit, reaches US #42, and her second LP *Crimes Of Passion*, produced this time by Keith Olsen, is released.

Dec *Hit Me With Your Best Shot* hits US #9, and is a million-seller.

1981 Jan LP *Crimes Of Passion* hits #2 in US.

Feb LP *Crimes Of Passion* wins a Grammy Award as Best Female LP Rock Vocal Performance of 1980.

Mar *Treat Me Right* reaches #18 in US.

Aug LP *Precious Time* tops US chart for a week, and reaches #30 in UK.

Sept *Fire And Ice* climbs to US #17.

Oct *Promises In The Dark* peaks at US #38.

1982 Feb Benatar marries her guitarist/producer Neil Geraldo, on the island of Maui in Hawaii.

Feb [24] She wins a Grammy Award for Best Female Rock Performance of 1981, with *Fire And Ice*.

Dec *Shadows Of The Night* climbs to US #13.

1983 Jan LP *Get Nervous* hits US #4, and briefly charts in UK at #90.

Feb [25] *Shadows Of The Night* wins her another Grammy Award, as Best Female Rock Performance of 1982.

Mar *Little Too Late* peaks at US #20.

May *Looking For A Stranger* reaches US #39.

Dec *Love Is A Battlefield* takes her back into US top 10, reaching #5, while LP *Live From Earth* makes US #13.

1984 Feb Benatar wins her fourth Grammy, again for Best Female Rock Performance, with *Love Is A Battlefield*, which also becomes her first UK hit single, at #49.

1985 Jan *We Belong* hits US #5 and UK #22. It is taken from LP *Tropico* which reaches US #14 and UK #34.

Feb *Ooh Ooh Song* follows up less strongly, reaching US #36.

Apr *Love Is A Battlefield* is reissued in UK, this time making #17.

June *Shadows Of The Night*, not previously a UK hit, is reissued and reaches #50.

Sept *Invincible*, the theme from the film *Legend of Billie Jean*, reaches US #10 and UK #53.

Dec LP *Seven The Hard Way* climbs to US #26 and UK #69.

1986 Jan *Sex As A Weapon* makes US #28 and UK #67.

Mar *Le Bel Age* climbs to US #54.

1987 Nov In the absence of new material from Benatar (who is now mother of a small child), compilation LP *Best Shots* featuring her hit single tracks is released in UK. It becomes her biggest UK success, peaking at #6.

1988 June *All Fired Up* charts in UK at #35.

July LP *Wide Awake In Dreamland* is released.

CLIFF BENNETT

1959 Bennett (b. June 4, 1940, Slough, UK) forms The Rebel Rousers as a part-time group playing dancehall cover versions of rock hits, in West Drayton, UK. A sextet, they are unusual for the time in having piano and sax in the line-up. The name is taken from the 1958 Duane Eddy° hit, *Rebel Rouser.*

1961 June First professional line-up of the group is: Bennett (vocals), Sid Phillips (sax and piano), Mick King (guitar), Moss Groves (sax), Frank Allen (bass) and Mick Burt (drums). Signed to EMI Records' Parlophone label, they link with producer Joe Meek for debut *You Got What I Like.* It is not a hit.

Oct Second single *That's What I Said* is not a hit, but the group is becoming a big attraction in the UK with its full, US-style R&B sound.

1962 May A contract is won to play the Star Club in Hamburg, West Germany, for 6 months. King is unwilling to go, and is replaced on guitar by Bernie Watson from The Savages.

Nov Watson, often musically at odds with the others, is asked to leave, and replaced by Dave Wendells from The Crescents.

1963 Nov Roy Young, former leader of Star Club house band, joins on piano and as second vocalist.

1964 They sign to a management contract with Brian Epstein's NEMS Enterprises.

July Allen leaves to replace Tony Jackson in The Searchers°, and is replaced by Bobby Thompson from Kingsize Taylor's Band.

Nov A revival of The Drifters'° *One Way Love* is their breakthrough UK single hit (#9).

1965 Feb Another Drifters° cover, *I'll Take You Home*, reaches UK #42.

June Wendells is fired and Thompson departs to The Rockin' Berries.

July Chas Hodges joins on bass.

1966 July Paul McCartney° produces Bennett's version of *Got To Get You Into My Life*, a cover of a song on The Beatles' LP *Revolver.*

Sept *Got To Get You Into My Life* is the group's biggest but also final UK hit, reaching #6.

Oct Budget-priced LP *Drivin' You Wild* makes UK #25.

1968 June Bennett splits from The Rebel Rousers, which then continues as The Roy Young Band. Bennett forms The Cliff Bennett Band with Mick Green (guitar), Robin MacDonald (bass) and Frank Farley (drums), plus a four-piece brass section.

Sept A cover of Marvin Gaye's *One More Heartache* is unsuccessful; the brass players are dropped.

Dec A cover of The Beatles'° *Back In The USSR* is unsuccessful.

1969 Mar Green and MacDonald leave to join Engelbert Humperdinck, and are replaced by Ken Hensley and Paul Bass.

June The group releases *Memphis Streets* (not a hit), then Farley leaves to get married, and the members split.

July Bennett forms Toe Fat, which makes two EMI LPs and stays together for 18 months. They tour the US, where the LPs are issued on Motown's Rare Earth label, but find no lasting success.

1971 Bennett signs a new recording deal with CBS, and emerges with a band and LP titled *Rebellion.*

1975 July After a period of obscurity, Bennett forms Shanghai with his former guitarist Mick Green, plus Brian Alterman (guitar), Speedy Keen (bass) and Pete Kircher (drums). They are a solid R&B/rock band, an update of The Rebel Rousers, but LP *Fallen Heroes* sells minimally.

1976 Dec Unfashionably polished for the dawn of the UK punk era, Shanghai is clearly passé, and splits. (Bennett sees no future in a new band and apart from occasional one-off recordings and appearances, will retire from the full-time music scene.)

GEORGE BENSON

1963 Having played guitar since age 8, sung with R&B bands in Pittsburgh since leaving school, then graduated to guitar session work and some small-label recording, Benson (b. Mar.22, 1943, Pittsburgh, Pa., US) moves to New York and joins jazz organist Brother Jack McDuff's group, recording for Prestige Records.

1966 He signs to Columbia Records as a jazz soloist, making first LPs under his own name.

1969 Aug Now signed to A&M Records, his first US success is LP *Tell It Like It Is*, with guitarwork influenced by the style of labelmate Wes Montgomery, who took a jazz guitar LP into the US top 20 in 1967 with *A Day In The Life.* Benson's LP peaks at US #145.

1970 He joins veteran jazz producer Creed Taylor's CTI label, whose workshop approach has resident virtuoso players backing each other on "solo" efforts. First CTI LP is *Beyond The Blue Horizon*, which does not chart.

1974 Feb As a staff musician at CTI Records, he plays guitar on the LP sessions of almost every act on the label, but scores in his own right with LP *Bad Benson*, which makes US #78.

1975 Nov First hit single (and only one for CTI) is *Supership*, on which he is credited as George "Bad" Benson. It reaches UK #30.

1976 Aug Signed to Warner Bros. Records, he shoots spectacularly to US #1 with LP *Breezin'*, while *This Masquerade* is his first US hit single, at #10. The LP sells over a million, and it starts a permanent shift of emphasis in Benson's records: LPs have showcased chiefly his guitar playing, but now his Warner Bros. output with producer Tommy LiPuma focuses on his vocals.

Sept Earlier-recorded LPs *Good King Bad* on CTI and *The Other Side Of Abbey Road* on A&M collect spin-off success from *Breezin'*, reaching US #51 and #125 respectively. The latter, originally from 1969, is a jazz guitar version of the entire Beatles° *Abbey Road* LP.

Nov Guitar instrumental title track from *Breezin'* peaks at US #63, while CTI LP *Benson And Farrell* (a collaboration with jazz flautist Joe Farrell) makes #100.

1977 Feb Benson wins four Grammy awards. *This Masquerade* is Record of the Year for 1976, *Theme From Good King Bad* is Best R&B Instrumental and LP *Breezin'* is Best Pop Instrumental Performance and Best-Engineered Non-Classical Recording.

Mar Warner LP, *In Flight*, is another million-seller, peaking at US #9, while CTI LP *George Benson In Concert: Carnegie Hall*, recorded live in 1975, reaches #122.

June A revival of Nat King Cole/Bobby Darin° hit *Nature Boy* makes UK #26, and LP *In Flight* peaks at 19 – his first UK charted LP.

July *Gonna Love You More* reaches US #71.

Oct *The Greatest Love Of All*, theme from the Muhammed Ali biopic movie *The Greatest*, and released as a one-off by Arista Records (which has soundtrack rights), reaches US #24 and UK #27. The song will be revived as a US #1 in 1986 by Whitney Houston°.

1978 Apr Third million-selling LP is the double set *Weekend In L.A.*, which hits US #5. It fares less well in UK, stalling at #47.

June A revival of The Drifters'° *On Broadway*, taken from *Weekend In L.A.*, hits US #7.

1979 Apr *Love Ballad* peaks at US #18 and UK #29, while double LP, *Livin' Inside Your Love*, makes US #7 and UK #24.

1980 Sept *Give Me The Night* is Benson's biggest US hit single in both US (#4) and UK (#7), and LP of the same title – a further US million-seller – hits #3 in both countries.

Nov *Love X Love* reaches US #61, but is more popular in the UK, where it hits #10.

1981 Feb *What's On Your Mind* reaches UK #45.

Sept He duets with Aretha Franklin° on *Love All The Hurt Away*, which reaches US #46.

Dec Double compilation LP *The George Benson Collection* makes US #14 and UK #19.

1982 Feb *Turn Your Love Around* restores him to the US top 10 at #5, having just peaked at UK #29.

Mar *Never Give Up On A Good Thing* reaches US #52, but makes UK #14.

1983 June *Lady Love Me (One More Time)* reaches UK #11, while *Inside Love (So Personal)* makes US #43. Both are taken from new LP *In Your Eyes*, which makes US #27, and is one of his most successful UK LPs, hitting #3 and staying on chart for 53 weeks.

Aug *Feel Like Makin' Love* reaches UK #28.

Sept *Lady Love Me (One More Time)* reaches US #30.

Oct Title track from *In Your Eyes* hits UK #7 – his last top 10 single.

Dec *Inside Love (So Personal)* is belatedly issued in UK, though makes only #57.

1985 Jan *20/20* reaches US #48 and UK #29. It is taken from LP of the same title, which climbs to US #45 and UK #9.

Apr A revival of Bobby Darin° hit, *Beyond The Sea*, climbs to UK #60.

Nov UK-compiled TV-advertised *LP The Love Songs*, featuring all his major hit singles, tops UK chart for 2 weeks.

1986 Aug *Kisses In The Moonlight* makes UK #60.

Sept LP *While The City Sleeps...* reaches UK #13.

Dec *Shiver* is Benson's biggest UK hit single for over 3 years, peaking at #19.

1987 Feb *Teaser* reaches UK #45.

BROOK BENTON

1957 After singing with gospel quartets and recording unsuccessfully as a soloist on Epic, Benton (b. Ben Franklin Peay, Sept.19, 1931, Camden, S.C., US) is working as a truck driver in New York when he meets music publisher Clyde Otis and joins him as a studio demo singer, also forming a songwriting team with Otis and arranger Belford Hendricks.

1958 Mar He has his first minor US hit (#82) with *A Million Miles From Nowhere*, while signed to RCA subsidiary Vik Records.

May Nat King Cole has a US hit with Benton's composition *Looking Back*, reaching #6.

Dec Clyde McPhatter has US hit with Benton's song *A Lover's Question*, reaching #6.

1959 Jan Otis persuades Mercury Records to sign Benton as a vocalist, with himself and Hendricks producing and arranging his recordings.

Apr First Mercury release *It's Just A Matter Of Time*, written by all three, hits US #3, tops US R&B chart for 10 weeks, and is a million-seller. A lush, deep-voiced ballad, it also sets the style for Benton's hit career.

June *Endlessly* reaches US #12 and its B-side *So Close* climbs to #38.

July *Endlessly* is his UK chart debut, reaching #28.

Aug *Thank You Pretty Baby* makes US #16 and tops the R&B chart for 4 weeks.

Nov *So Many Ways* hits #6 in US, also topping the R&B chart for 3 weeks.

1960 Mar *Baby (You Got What It Takes)*, a duet with Dinah Washington, reaches US #5, tops the R&B chart for 8 weeks, and is a million-seller.

May *The Ties That Bind* makes #37 in US.

June Second duet with Washington, *A Rockin' Good Way (To Mess Around And Fall In Love)*, reaches US #7, also topping the R&B chart for 5 weeks.

Sept *Kiddio* reaches #7 in US and is also R&B chart #1 for 9 weeks. Its B-side *The Same One* hits US #16 in its own right.

Nov *Kiddio* reaches #29 in UK.

Dec *Fools Rush In* reaches #24 in US.

1961 Feb *Fools Rush In* reaches #50 in UK.

Apr *Think Twice* reaches US #11, and its B-side *For My Baby* makes #28.

June His first LP to chart in US is the compilation *Brook Benton Golden Hits*, which reaches #82.

July A revival of the traditional *The Boll Weevil Song* is another million-seller, and is Benton's highest chart-placed US single at #2, while peaking at #30 in UK – his final UK chart entry.

Sept Another traditional song *Frankie And Johnny* reaches US #20.

Oct LP *The Boll Weevil Song & 11 Other Great Hits* climbs to US #70.

1962 Jan *Revenge* reaches #15 in US.

Feb *Shadrack* climbs to US #19.

Mar *Walk On The Wild Side* makes US #43.

June *Hit Record* is ironically his lowest chart-placed record since his first, climbing to US #45. Benton quickly eschews its gimmick-laden style and goes back to blues-ballads.

Oct *Lie To Me*, in more familiar style, reaches US #13.

Dec LP *Singin' The Blues* makes US #40.

1963 Jan *Hotel Happiness* is his biggest seller for nearly 2 years, reaching #3 in US – but will be his last US top 10 entry for 7 years.

Apr *I Got What I Wanted* makes US #28.

July *My True Confession* reaches US #22.

Oct *Two Tickets To Paradise* reaches #32 in US.

1964 Feb *Going Going Gone* climbs to US #35.

June *Too Late To Turn Back Now/Another Cup Of Coffee* is his last Mercury single to make US top 50 – the two almost equally popular sides make #43 and #47 respectively.

Aug *A House Is Not A Home* reaches only US #75, its sales split with those of Dionne Warwick's° version which hits US #71 in the same week.

Oct *Lumberjack* is his last Mercury hit of any consequence, making US #53.

1965 July Benton leaves Mercury as his last release achieves only US #100, and signs to RCA Records.

Dec *Mother Nature, Father Time* reaches US #53, but is his only RCA release to chart.

1967 Sept After 2 barren years and another label change, he has one US chart success on Frank Sinatra's Reprise Records: *Laura (Tell Me What He's Got That I Ain't Got)* makes US #78. Benton regards it as one of his own favorite recordings.

1968 Oct He signs to Atlantic subsidiary label Cotillion, where he records in a laid-back soul idiom which updates his earlier style, beginning with *Do Your Own Thing*, a minor return to US chart at #99.

1969 Aug *Nothing Can Take The Place Of You* reaches US #74.

1970 Feb LP *Brook Benton Today* is released and reaches US #27.

Mar Benton has his first million-seller for almost a decade with what becomes widely regarded as the definitive version of Tony Joe White's soul ballad *Rainy Night In Georgia*. It hits US #4 (and R&B #1), though does not sell in the UK through poor promotion.

May A version of Frank Sinatra's *My Way* proves an inappropriate follow-up, reaching only US #72.

June His strong interpretation of Joe South's *Don't It Make You Want To Go Home* makes US #45.

1971 Jan He duets with The Dixie Flyers on *Shoes*, which makes US #67, but is his last hit for Cotillion and also proves his US chart swansong. (His move to MGM, Stax and All Platinum later in the 1970s, plus a brief tie-up with the Brut perfume company when it tries to get into music, bring some well-reviewed records but little sales action. For the next 17 years of his life he will achieve little as a record seller, but because his relaxed style and wide repertoire of past hits have enduring appeal, he will remain in demand on the US club circuit as a ballad singer.

1988 Apr [9] Benton dies in hospital in New York, aged 56, following an illness.

CHUCK BERRY

1952 Berry (b. Charles Berry, Oct.18, 1926, San Jose, Cal., US) forms a club trio in St. Louis, Mo., with himself on guitar, Johnnie Johnson on piano and Ebby Harding on drums; they play evening gigs while Berry works by day as a hairdresser and beautician.

1955 May Playing in Chicago, he meets Muddy Waters°, who puts him in touch with Chess Records, which takes interest in Berry's demos of his own songs, and signs him to a record deal.

July First release is the self-penned *Maybelline*, which lays down Berry's basic style: uptempo blues-based with a country rockabilly infusion, driven by a guitar rhythm – a style which will inspire thousands of artists over the following 30 years.

Aug *Maybelline* reaches US #5, also topping the R&B chart for 9 weeks. It is not issued as a single in UK.

Nov [12] Berry is named Most Promising R&B Artist in Billboard's Annual DJ Poll in US.

1956 June After two unsuccessful singles, *Roll Over Beethoven* is his second US hit, reaching #29.

Dec He appears in the film *Rock Rock Rock*, singing *You Can't Catch Me*.

1957 May *School Day* reaches US #3 and is a million-seller, also hitting R&B chart #1.

June *School Day* is his UK chart debut, at #21.

Aug *Oh Baby Doll* makes US #57.

Sept He appears in the film *Mr. Rock And Roll*, which stars pioneer rock DJ, Alan Freed.

Dec *Rock And Roll Music* reaches #8 in US.

1958 Mar *Sweet Little Sixteen* hits US #2 and tops the R&B chart for 3 weeks; another million-seller and his biggest early hit.

May *Sweet Little Sixteen* reaches UK #13.

June *Johnny B Goode*, his song later most covered by other artists, reaches US #8 and UK #27. It will be his last UK hit for 5 years.

July Berry appears at the Newport Jazz Festival; his performance of *Sweet Little Sixteen* will be seen some months later in *Jazz On A Summer's Day*, the documentary film of the event made by Bert Stern.

Aug *Beautiful Delilah* sells disappointingly and only makes US #81.

Sept *Carol* puts Berry back in US top 20 at #18.

Dec *Sweet Little Rock And Roller* reaches US #47. Both sides of a special seasonal single make US chart – *Run Rudolph Run* at #69 and *Merry Christmas Baby* at #71.

1959 Mar *Anthony Boy* reaches #60 in US.

May *Almost Grown* hits US #32. Its B-side *Little Queenie* (which itself makes #80) is from the film *Go Johnny Go*, in which Berry also sings *Memphis Tennessee* and has a small acting role.

July *Back In The USA* reaches US #37. Soon after, Berry has reason for dissatisfaction with the USA, whose consumer lifestyle his songs generally celebrate – he is arrested and charged with violating the Mann Act, by transporting a minor across a State Line for immoral purposes. He has brought an American Indian girl from Texas to work as hat-check in the nightclub he owns in St. Louis, but fires her when she is suspected of working as a prostitute. In revenge, she goes to the police and confesses to being only 14, so putting Berry technically in the wrong. An initial trial is quashed from above for racist overtones, but prosecutors will continue to pursue Berry with the affair.

1960 Mar *Too Pooped To Pop* reaches #42 in US, with the B-side *Let It Rock* climbing to #64.

1961 May Berry opens Berry Park, a 30-acre amusement park in Wentzville, Mo., into which he has invested much of his money, and which will remain his major business interest.

1962 Feb Berry is finally convicted on the Mann Act charge, and begins a 2-year sentence in an Indiana Federal prison.

1963 June New interest in Berry's music hits the UK as the R&B boom takes hold, with hundreds of groups across the country using his songs as basic repertoire. A compilation LP of oldies, simply titled *Chuck Berry*, is issued to capitalize on this boom, and climbs to UK #12.

July *Go Go Go*, an earlier failed US single, is released in UK and reaches #38. The Rolling Stones° also enter UK chart with their first single, a revival of Berry's *Come On*, which will climb to #21.

Aug Renewed interest hits the US, where The Beach Boys° and Lonnie Mack have just had top 5 hits with revivals of *Sweet Little Sixteen* (re-written as *Surfin' USA*) and *Memphis Tennessee* (instrumentally, as *Memphis*). With Berry still in jail, Chess Records puts his versions of these songs, plus others, on an LP which has audience noise dubbed on and is released as *Chuck Berry On Stage*.

Oct LP *Chuck Berry On Stage* reaches US #29 (his first charted LP), and UK #6.

Nov Another reissued oldie, *Memphis Tennessee*, eclipses a cover version by Dave Berry° to become Berry's first-ever UK top 10 hit, peaking at #6.

Dec *Run Rudolph Run* is a UK Christmas release, climbing to #36. Compilation LP *More Chuck Berry* makes UK #9.

1964 Jan Out of prison and in demand (as another boost, The Beatles° have just included *Roll Over Beethoven* on their second LP), Berry returns to Chess Records' Chicago studio to record some new songs.

Mar Newly-recorded *Nadine (Is It You?)* reaches US #23 and UK #27.

May [9] He begins his first tour of the UK at Finsbury Park Astoria, London, supported by The Animals°, Carl Perkins° and The Nashville Teens.

June *No Particular Place To Go*, which updates *School Day's* melody with new car-cruising lyrics, reaches US #10 and UK #3. LP *The Latest And The Greatest* makes UK #8. LP *Chuck Berry's Greatest Hits* is released in US, and climbs to #34.

Sept *You Never Can Tell* reaches US #14 and UK #23.

Oct LP *You Never Can Tell*, issued only in UK, reaches #18.

Nov *Little Marie*, a lyrical sequel to Memphis Tennessee, reaches US #54.

1965 Jan LP *St Louis To Liverpool*, released only in US, climbs to #124. Berry records in London with UK group The Five Dimensions. These songs will be released on the LP *Chuck Berry In London;* it is not a hit.

1966 June He leaves Chess to sign to Mercury Records for a $50,000 advance, but his time with this label will produce no hits.

1969 Sept [13] He appears at the Toronto Rock'n'Roll Revival Concert in Canada, along with Little Richard°, Gene Vincent°, Jerry Lee Lewis°, Bo Diddley°, The Doors°, Alice Cooper° and John Lennon's° Plastic Ono Band.

1970 Feb Berry re-signs to Chess and records the LP *Back Home*, which includes Tulane, later a UK hit for The Steve Gibbons Band.

1972 June Tracks made in a London studio with members of The Faces° backing him, together with a live show recorded at the Lanchester Arts Festival while on UK tour, are packaged as LP *The London Chuck Berry Sessions*. It will eventually climb to US #8, and is his biggest-selling LP.

Oct The double-entendre audience participation novelty number *My Ding-A-Ling*, taken from the live portion of the LP, tops US chart for 2 weeks, becoming a million-plus seller and Berry's most successful single ever.

Nov *My Ding-A-Ling* is #1 in UK for 4 weeks, in spite of efforts by public morals campaigner, Mary Whitehouse, to have it banned. Double compilation LP *Chuck Berry's Golden Decade*, originally issued in 1967, has sales reactivated by the success of *My Ding-A-Ling*, and climbs to US #72.

1973 Feb *Reelin' And Rockin'*, also a live LP extract, reaches #27 in US and #18 in UK, but will be Berry's last hit single in either country.

Sept LP *Bio*, blues-based like most of his 1970s Chess recordings, sells disappointingly, only reaching US #175.

1975 Mar LP *Chuck Berry '75*, on which he duets for the first time on some tracks with his daughter, Ingrid Berry Gibson, is released.

1977 Feb A compilation LP of hits *Motorvatin'*, aided by TV advertising, reaches UK #7.

1978 Mar Berry plays himself in the film *American Hot Wax*, which tells the story of DJ Alan Freed.

1979 June [7] He performs at the White House by special request of President Jimmy Carter.

July [10] Berry is sentenced to 4 months in jail, for income tax evasion in 1973.

Oct LP *Rockit* is released, the only fruit of a new recording deal with Atlantic Records.

Nov [19] He is released from jail after serving his sentence in Lompoc Prison Farm, Cal.

1986 Oct [16] A special concert at the Fox Theater in St. Louis, organized by The Rolling Stones'° Keith Richards (who leads the backing band), is held to celebrate Berry's 60th birthday and to form the basis of a documentary film.

1988 Jan *Chuck Berry: The Autobiography* is published, a revealing record of his personal and musical life, mostly written during his 1979 incarceration.

Feb Taylor Hackford's film *Hail! Hail! Rock'n'Roll* is released, documenting the 1986 Birthday Concert. Among Richards' hand-picked band sharing stage and screen is Berry's original pianist, Johnnie Johnson.

Mar In UK to promote both book and film, Berry plays a London concert at Hammersmith Odeon, sings *Memphis Tennessee* on a TV chat show, and tells a magazine interviewer he may retire "soon".

DAVE BERRY

1961 Berry (b. David Grundy, 1941, Sheffield, UK) – forms Dave Berry and The Cruisers, an R&B group inspired by his hero Chuck Berry°, from whom his stage name is taken. They become a popular attraction in Sheffield via a residency at the Esquire Club, and play other club dates in northern England.

1963 Aug Spotted by a Decca A&R man at a Doncaster, UK, dancehall date, Berry and group sign to the label.

Sept Debut single (and the only one on which The Cruisers provide backup; they subsequently back him only on stage) revives Chuck Berry's° *Memphis Tennessee*, which charts immediately and brings about the reissue of Berry's original in UK.

Nov Chuck Berry's° *Memphis Tennessee* wins UK chart battle, reaching the top 10, but Dave Berry's version establishes him at #19.

Dec A remark by George Harrison° on UK TV that Elvis Presley's° *My Baby Left Me* should be reissued prompts Berry to record it as follow-up, using top studio players like Big Jim Sullivan and later members of Led Zeppelin°, Jimmy Page and John Paul Jones.

1964 Feb *My Baby Left Me* reaches UK #37.

May He covers The Shirelles'° *Baby It's You* as a single when The Beatles° revive it on their debut LP. It makes #24 in UK.

Aug *The Crying Game*, featuring a distinctive guitar part by Jimmy Page, is the first UK top tenner, reaching #5. Well-exposed on TV, it also crystalizes the public's image of Berry in performance: black-dressed, slinky, theatrical and mysterious. He will maintain this performing style throughout his career, into the 1980s.

Nov *One Heart Between Two* reaches #41 in UK.

Dec LP *Dave Berry* is issued in UK, but is not a hit (none of his LPs are).

1965 He enters Knokke Song Festival in Belgium and wins the Press Prize, so gaining a sudden high profile in Europe.

Apr *Little Things*, a cover of a US hit by Bobby Goldsboro is Berry's second UK top ten hit, reaching #5.

July *This Strange Effect*, written by Ray Davies of The Kinks°, reaches only #37 in UK, but is a #1 hit in Holland and Belgium, confirming Berry's continental star status.

1966 July After two flop UK singles but huge onstage and TV success in Europe, he returns to UK chart with *Mama*, a cover of a US hit by B.J. Thomas. It reaches #5, but will be his last UK chart record.

1970 *Chaplin House* is his final Decca release, after which he signs to CBS, though there is to be no change in his chart fortunes. (Berry will go on performing in UK clubs and eventually on 60s revival tours. He will also consistently tour Europe, Canada and South Africa throughout the 1970s and 1980s.)

BIG AUDIO DYNAMITE

Mick Jones (guitar and lead vocals)
Don Letts (effects and vocals)
Don Donovan (keyboards)
Leo Williams (bass)
Greg Roberts (drums)

1984 The day after he leaves The Clash°, Jones begins recruiting members for his new musical project, Big Audio Dynamite. Still signed to CBS in the UK, he negotiates a new CBS contract in the US.

1985 Sept After 18 months of recruitment, writing and recording, first single *The Bottom Line* is released, but fails to chart.

Nov LP *This Is Big Audio Dynamite* is a minor UK seller, reaching #100.

1986 Apr After extensive UK touring, their first hit single (and the first hit to feature a sampling technique) *E=MC2* climbs to UK #11, and revives sales of the debut LP, which now makes UK #27.

June *Medicine Show* reaches UK #29.

July During the recording of a second LP in Soho, London, ex-Clash° co-founder Joe Strummer wanders into the studio, resulting in him co-producing and co-writing many of the band's new tracks – a reunion which receives considerable press interest.

Nov LP *No 10 Upping St* makes UK #11, and *C'mon Every Beatbox*, taken from it, peaks at UK #51.

1987 Feb *V13* reaches UK #49. (The rest of the year will be spent touring UK, Europe and the US, where their live achievements will include a record 5 sold-out nights at LA's The Roxy, and 9 at New York's Irving Plaza.)

June The band supports U2° on a major European stadium tour. *Planet Bad*, a "nightclub" hosted by group members, becomes a feature in some of the cities where they play.

Aug First live venture to South America is 7 nights in Brazil.

1988 Jan The band spends time writing and recording new songs at its Notting Hill, London, base.

June *Just Play Music*, which hits out at the over-sampling on current singles (a trend the band helped launch), reaches UK #51. LP *Tighten Up, Volume 88* (featuring a cover painting by ex-Clash° colleague Paul Simonon), is released.

THE BIG BOPPER

1956 As a DJ on KTRM radio in Beaumont, Tex., US, massive J.P. Richardson (b. Oct.29, 1932, Sabine Pass, Tex.) nicknames himself The Big Bopper.

1957 A prolific spare-time songwriter, he sends some songs to "Pappy" Dailey, Mercury Records' Houston representative, which results in a contract to record C&W. Two hillbilly-style C&W singles appear in US under his real name, but neither sells.

1958 June He writes a novelty rock song *The Purple People Eater Meets The Witch Doctor*, parodying the current hits by Sheb Wooley and David Seville. Initially on Bopper's own Texas-based D label, this is quickly taken up by Mercury when the B-side, *Chantilly Lace*, gets airplay.

Aug *Chantilly Lace* charts in US, eventually reaching #6, selling over a million, and remaining on chart for 6 months.

Dec Both sides of next single *The Big Bopper's Wedding/Little Red Riding Hood* chart in US, at #38 and #72 respectively.

1959 Jan *Chantilly Lace* charts in UK, climbing to #14. Bopper, who has put together a stage act based on his hits and comic radio persona, joins The Winter Dance Party, a multi-artist rock one-nighter tour of Minnesota, Wisconsin and Iowa cities.

Feb [2] After a tour date at Clear Lake, Iowa, Bopper persuades Waylon Jennings to give him his seat on a light aircraft being chartered by Buddy Holly° to the next venue, since his bulk makes sleeping on a tour coach uncomfortable, and he has developed a heavy cold.

Feb [3] Just before 1 a.m. the plane leaves nearby Mason City Airport in falling snow, then crashes within minutes, killing the pilot and its passengers The Big Bopper, Holly°, and Ritchie Valens°.

1960 Jan Posthumous success as a songwriter comes when *Running Bear*, written by Bopper for fellow Texan Johnny Preston, is a US and UK #1 hit.

BIG COUNTRY

Stuart Adamson (guitar, synthesizer and vocals)
Bruce Watson (guitar)
Tony Butler (bass)
Mark Brzezicji (drums)

1981 June Stuart Adamson (b. Apr.11, 1958, Manchester, UK) leaves The Skids and returns home to Dunfirmline, Scotland, to plan a new band.

1982 Adamson recruits Watson (b. Mar.11, 1961, Ontario, Canada), Butler (b. Feb.13,1947, London , UK) and Brzezicji (b. June 21, 1957, Slough, UK). Butler has temporarily played bass with The Pretenders°. They sign to Mercury Records, UK, and debut with *Harvest Home*, which fails to chart but introduces the band's unique twin guitar-based sound and gains them notice.

1983 Apr *Fields Of Fire (400 Miles)* is their UK chart debut, reaching #10.

June *In A Big Country* reaches #17 in UK.

Sept *Chance* climbs to UK #9, while their first LP *The Crossing*, which includes all singles to date, hits UK #3 in an extended chart run.

Nov LP *The Crossing* is their US chart debut, peaking at #18.

Dec *In A Big Country* takes them into US singles chart, reaching #17.

1984 Feb *Wonderland* reaches UK #8, and *Fields Of Fire (400 Miles)* makes US #52.

June *Wonderland* reaches #86 in US.

Oct *East Of Eden* reaches #17 in UK. LP *Steeltown* enters UK chart at #1.

Dec [13/14] The band sells out Wembley Arena, London, for 2 nights.

Dec *Where The Rose Is Sown* hits UK #29, while LP *Steeltown* makes US #70.

1985 Jan *Just A Shadow* peaks at #25 in UK.

1986 May After a lengthy chart absence during which they have been recording a new LP, *Look Away* is their biggest UK hit single, reaching #7. It fails to restore them to US chart favor.

July *The Teacher* reaches #28 and LP *The Seer* hits #2 in UK.
Oct *One Great Thing* climbs to UK #19.
Dec *Hold The Heart* peaks at UK #55. After this, Big Country falls silent for another extended period.

THE BIG THREE

Brian Griffiths (vocals and guitar)
Johnny Gustafson (vocals and bass)
Johnny Hutchinson (drums)

1961 Jan Having played as a quartet, Cass & The Casanovas, with vocalist Brian Casser, the trio forms in Liverpool, UK. Original guitarist is Adrian Barber, who has a talent for electronics and constructs the sound equipment. They rapidly gain a reputation as one of the city's best R&B/rock groups.
1962 July Griffiths joins when the band departs for a month to play the Star Club in Hamburg, West Germany, and feels the need of an extra guitarist to ensure the level of stage activity which the German audience demands.
Aug Barber, attracted to Hamburg, remains there, and The Big Three returns home a trio again.
Nov They sign to management by Brian Epstein, who has The Beatles° and Gerry & The Pacemakers°.
1963 Jan They sign to a recording contract with UK Decca.
Mar First single is a Ritchie Barrett R&B song *Some Other Guy*, a staple of most Mersey bands' stage acts. It reaches #29, making them the third Liverpool group to hit UK charts after The Beatles° and Gerry & The Pacemakers°.
Aug *By The Way* climbs to UK #23.
Nov *I'm With You* stalls at #53. Much stronger is EP *The Big Three Live At The Cavern*, later recognized as their best record. Gustafson and Griffiths are disillusioned, and leave to form The Seniors, from whence Gustafson will join The Merseybeats. Paddy Chambers (guitar) and Faron (vocals and bass) join to keep the group name alive.
1964 Apr Chambers leaves, replaced by Paul Pilnick.
June *Bring It On Home To Me* fails to sell in UK, and the Decca contract is terminated.
Oct The band breaks up, with Hutchinson, disillusioned, leaving the music business.
1973 A brief revival of The Big Three, featuring Brian Griffiths, Johnny Gustafson and Nigel Olsson (drums) lasts only as long as the release of unnoticed LP *Resurrection*.

BLACK

Colin Vearncombe (vocals, guitar and keyboards)

1981 Jan [1] Black begins as a trio at its debut concert in Liverpool, UK, after which it will revolve solely around Vearncombe (b. May 26, 1951, Liverpool).
1981/2 Vearncombe plays locally, recording demos, and releasing the group's first (unsuccessful) single, *Human Features*.
1982 June Vearncombe meets Pete Fulwell, manager of Pete Wylie of Wah!, who owns the Eternal studio and label in Liverpool. Fulwell in turn introduces him to keyboard player and engineer Dave Dickie, and this duo becomes the new Black line-up, writing songs and recording demos at Eternal.
Dec Black supports The Thompson Twins° on a major UK tour, and receives positive reviews and record company attention.
1983 Apr They sign to WEA Records, and will release just two singles (both unsuccessful) over the next 2 years: *Hey Presto* (1984) and *More Than The Sun* (1985).
1985 June They play a mini-tour supporting the Scots band Orange Juice.
Dec WEA's contract is severed and the disillusioned Dickie turns to production. Though no longer a Black member, he will engineer and produce all future recordings by Vearncombe.
1986 Sept Black returns to independent status, and *Wonderful Life* is released on the Ugly Man label, charting at UK #72, as well as being a big independent chart hit.
Dec Vearncombe signs as Black to A&M Records, and releases *Everything's Coming Up Roses*, which does not chart.
1987 June The atmospheric ballad *Sweetest Smile* is Black's first major hit, reaching UK #8, and launching its name in Europe.
Sept A&M reissues *Wonderful Life*, which climbs to UK #8, and LP *Wonderful Life* is released and hits UK #3.
Nov WEA releases mini-LP *Black*, a retrospective of 1984/1985 recordings.
Dec After a sell-out UK tour, *Paradise* reaches UK #38.

CILLA BLACK

1963 Jan [25] After working as a cloakroom attendant and occasionally guesting with groups (notably Kingsize Taylor and The Dominoes, and The Beatles°), usually billed as "Swinging Cilla", Black (b. Priscilla White, May 27, 1943, Liverpool, UK) makes her debut as a vocalist at Liverpool's Cavern club.
Aug She is signed to Beatles'° manager Brian Epstein, and to a recording contract with EMI (whose George Martin has spotted her while checking out Gerry & The Pacemakers° in Liverpool).
Sept [27] Her debut *Love Of The Loved*, an unrecorded song donated by Lennon° and McCartney°, is launched with an appearance on UK TV's *"Ready Steady Go"*.
Oct *Love Of The Loved*, released on EMI's Parlophone label, reaches UK #35.
Dec She performs in The Beatles'° Christmas show on stage at Finsbury Park Astoria, London, UK.
1964 Feb A cover of Dionne Warwick's° US hit *Anyone Who Had A Heart*, tops UK chart for 4 weeks, selling over 900,000 copies in the UK – one of the all-time UK best-selling singles by a female singer.
May *You're My World*, adapted from the Italian ballad *Il Mondo*, is a second UK #1, topping the chart for 3 weeks.
Aug *It's For You*, another Lennon°/McCartney° song unrecorded by The Beatles°, hits UK #6, while *You're My World* is her US chart debut and biggest hit, reaching #26.
Oct *It's For You* peaks at #79 in US.
Dec She has a cameo role in Gerry & The Pacemakers'° film *Ferry Cross The Mersey*, singing *Is It Love?*
1965 Jan A cover of The Righteous Brothers'° *You've Lost That Lovin' Feelin'*, hits UK #5 outselling the original for its first 2 weeks, until the Brothers visit UK for TV promotion and leap to #1.
Mar First LP *Cilla* hits UK #5.
May *I've Been Wrong Before* peaks at UK #17.
1966 Feb *Love's Just A Broken Heart* hits UK #5.
Apr *Alfie*, theme to the film of the same name starring Michael Caine, makes UK #9.
June *Don't Answer Me* reaches UK #6, while LP *Cilla Sings A Rainbow* hits #4.
Sept *Alfie* peaks at US #95, in competition with a #32 cover version by Cher°. It is her last US chart entry.
Nov *A Fool Am I* reaches UK #13.
Dec She stars in pantomime for the first time, in *Little Red Riding Hood*.
1967 June *What Good Am I* peaks at UK #24. Shortly afterwards, claiming inattention to her career, Black splits from Epstein's management agency. The disagreements resolved, she returns to Epstein, and is reportedly devastated by his death 2 months later.
Dec *I Only Live To Love You* reaches UK #26.
1968 Jan [30] Her UK BBC television series is launched, with new McCartney° song, *Step Inside Love*, as the theme tune.
Feb Ringo Starr° guests on the TV show, duetting with Black on *Act Naturally*.
Apr *Step Inside Love* is released as a single and peaks at UK #8, her first top 10 hit for nearly 2 years.
May LP *Sher-oo* reaches #7 in UK.
June *Where Is Tomorrow* sells disappointingly, reaching UK #39.
Dec Compilation LP *The Best Of Cilla Black*, with all her A-side hits to date, reaches UK #21.
1969 Mar *Surround Yourself With Sorrow* makes UK #3, her biggest hit since *You're My World*. Black marries her personal manager, Bobby Willis (a marriage still going strong in the late 1980s).
Aug *Conversations* peaks at UK #7.
1970 Jan *If I Thought You'd Ever Change Your Mind* reaches UK #20.
Aug LP *Sweet Inspiration* reaches #42 in UK.
1971 Dec *Something Tells Me (Something's Gonna Happen Tonight)*, theme from her new UK TV series, hits UK #3.
1974 Feb *Baby We Can't Go Wrong*, the theme from her third UK TV series, peaks at only #36, and unexpectedly proves to be her final UK hit single. Having already moved sideways to a "family entertainer" role (the perfect vehicle for her engaging and gregarious Liverpool personality), she will henceforth concentrate on cabaret and TV work quite divorced from the rock field.
1983 Feb TV-advertised retrospective LP *The Very Best Of Cilla Black* returns her to the UK chart after almost a decade, reaching #20. She has let her career wane during the late 1970s and early 80s while raising her family, but she now returns to UK public view with a vengeance via TV, occasionally still singing, but mainly hosting top-rated shows "Surprise Surprise" and "Blind Date".

BLACK OAK ARKANSAS

Jim Dandy Mangrum (vocals)
Ricky Reynolds (guitar)
Jimmy Henderson (guitar)
Stan Knight (guitar)
Pat Daugherty (bass)
Wayne Evans (drums)

1971 July After moving to Los Angeles from rural Arkansas, where they were first a teenage gang and then a group called The Knowbody Else, Black Oak releases eponymous LP for Atco. The name comes from former home and birthplace of leader Mangrum (b. Mar.30, 1948, Black Oak, Ark., US), whose "Jim Dandy" tag comes from a 1950s hit record.

Sept LP *Black Oak Arkansas* makes minor US chart showing at #127. The group begins a constant tour schedule, which brings a large teen following in tune with their unfrilled macho boogie act.

1972 Mar LP *Keep The Faith* reaches US #103.

July Third LP with the mammoth title *If An Angel Came To See You, Would You Make Her Feel At Home?* reaches #93.

1973 Dec *Jim Dandy* is released as US single and reaches #25. *High On The Hog* is their most successful Atco LP, only reaching US #52, but selling 500,000 and staying on chart for 22 weeks.

1974 Aug LP *Street Party* hits US #52.

1975 Oct With much-changed personnel around figurehead Jim Dandy, the group signs to MCA and releases LP *X-Rated*, which charts at US #99.

1976 Jan *Strong Enough To Be Gentle* is a minor US hit single at #89.

1977 Jan With Mangrum the only remaining member of the original group, they switch labels again to Capricorn, but LP *Race With The Devil* is not a success, and they fade from the public eye.

BLACK SABBATH

Tony Iommi (guitar)
Geezer (Terry) Butler (bass)
Ozzy Osbourne (vocals)
Bill Ward (drums)

1967 Schoolmates Iommi (b. Feb.19, 1948, Birmingham, UK), Ward (b. May 5, 1948, Birmingham), Butler (b. July 17, 1949, Birmingham) and Osbourne (b. Dec.3, 1948, Birmingham), form a blues band, first named Polka Tulk but soon changed to Earth.

1968 Playing a jazz-blues fusion, they tour exhaustively in UK then to Europe, and break The Beatles'° long-held house record at the Star Club, Hamburg, West Germany.

1969 Prompted by manager Jim Simpson, the band switches name to Black Sabbath (the title of an early song originated by Butler's abiding interest in popular black magic novelist Dennis Wheatley) and changes to a suitably matching macabre image.

Dec After a year's constant touring to build a huge live following, the group signs to Philips Records' subsidiary, Fontana.

1970 Jan Debut release is *Evil Woman (Don't Play Your Games With Me)*, a cover of a US hit by Crow, but it fails to chart.

Apr *Evil Woman* is reissued (again without success) on Philips' new "progressive rock" label Vertigo, alongside their first LP *Black Sabbath*, recorded in 2 days on a $1200 budget. Filled with occult imagery, it climbs to UK #9, staying on chart for 5 months.

Oct Second LP *Paranoid*, which features many of their early stage favorites like *War Pigs*, tops UK chart for 2 weeks, and the title track hits #4. Both will become their most enduring records, and be regarded as classics of early heavy metal rock.

Dec Following a US college tour, LP *Black Sabbath*, released in US on Warner Bros., climbs to #23 (eventually staying on chart for 65 weeks), while *Paranoid* reaches US #61.

1971 Mar LP *Paranoid* is issued in US, hits #12 and also spends 65 weeks on chart. Their US and UK popularity thus cemented, they become a watchword for "hard rock lifestyle": a mixture of drink, drugs, groupies and exhausting schedules.

Sept LP *Master Of Reality* hits UK #5 and US #8.

1972 Mar *Iron Man*, belatedly taken from LP *Paranoid* in US, charts at #52.

Oct LP *Black Sabbath Vol. 4* hits UK #8 and US #13. The band changes management, replacing Simpson (to his displeasure) with Patrick Meehan, and releases *Tomorrow's Dream*, its first UK single since *Paranoid* – which surprisingly fails to chart.

1974 Jan LP *Sabbath Bloody Sabbath* further defines the group's simple, bone-crushing sound, and hits UK #4 and US #11, while Meehan is replaced as manager by agent Don Arden. The disgruntled Simpson takes action over what he considers a broken contract with the band and Osbourne is handed a subpoena as he walks onstage at a US tour date, precipitating an almost 2-year enforced hiatus for Sabbath, as legal battles over management rage. Osbourne begins to drift away from the others because of his hard-drinking lifestyle and unwillingness to move away from Sabbath's established musical formula.

1975 Sept With legal matters finally resolved and their UK contract (and back-catalog) shifted to NEMS Records, they return with a major UK tour.

Oct LP *Sabotage* makes #7 in UK and #28 in US.

1976 Feb Double compilation LP *We Sold Our Souls For Rock'n'Roll* reaches UK #35 and US #48.

Nov They return to Vertigo Records for LP *Technical Ecstasy*, which appears after crises in its recording, mainly due to Iommi wishing to experiment with more complex arrangements, overdubs and even a horn section, all against Osbourne's will. It charts at UK #13 and US #51.

1977 Nov Osbourne leaves, unhappy with much of the band's direction. He is replaced on some live dates by ex-Savoy Brown singer, Dave Walker.

1978 Jan Osbourne rejoins, but relations with the rest of the band are strained.

June First UK hit single since *Paranoid* is *Never Say Die*, a taster of the forthcoming LP; it reaches UK #21.

Oct LP *Never Say Die* reaches UK #12, while *Hard Road*, taken from it, climbs to #33.

Dec LP *Never Say Die* peaks at #78 in US.

1979 Jan The basic conflicts between Osbourne and the band still unresolved, he departs to form Blizzard of Oz and a successful solo career.

Mar Sabbath attempts to shed business and legal problems by signing a new management deal with Don Arden. Former Rainbow° vocalist Ronnie James Dio is recruited in Osbourne's place as lead singer.

July Butler leaves, replaced on live work by Geoff Nicols from Quartz, but he decides to return in time for the next LP recording sessions.

1980 May LP *Heaven & Hell*, which sees Dio exerting his myth-oriented lyrics on the group, reaches UK #9.

July *Neon Nights* is their third consecutive UK hit single at #22, while LP *Heaven And Hell* reaches US #28. LP *Sabbath: Live At Last*, a previously unheard onstage recording made in 1975 by the original line-up, is released by NEMS. Though the band disowns it, the LP climbs to UK #5.

Sept Encouraged by LP success, NEMS reissues *Paranoid*, which re-charts in UK at #14 almost 10 years after its original success. It also tops the UK indepedent chart, sitting oddly among current new wave records.

Nov Following a successful US tour, Bill Ward leaves, his departure forced by recurring bad health, and is replaced on drums by Vinnie Appice, younger brother of Carmine Appice of Vanilla Fudge° fame.

Dec *Die Young* reaches #41 in UK.

1981 Nov LP *Mob Rules* peaks at UK #12 and US #31, while the extracted title song reaches UK #46. Sabbath experiences more clashes as Iommi voices his resentment of Dio's influence on the LP.

1982 Feb *Turn Up The Night* makes #37, and is their last UK hit single.

Nov Dio quits after Iommi accuses him of tampering with the mix of the band's forthcoming live LP in order to bring his vocals up. He takes Appice with him to form his own group, Dio.

1983 Jan Double live LP *Live Evil* reaches UK #13 and US #37, though when it appears minus both vocalist and drummer, the band seems about to fold.

June Personnel problems are solved when Ward returns, and Ian Gillan, former vocalist with Deep Purple° and his own band Gillan, is persuaded to join.

Aug The band headlines the Reading Festival, UK, with its new line-up. Bev Bevan of ELO° plays drums when Ward is forced by illness to withdraw again.

Oct LP *Born Again* hits #4 in UK and #39 in US.

1984 Mar [10] Gillan leaves to join the imminent reformation of Deep Purple°.

1985 July [13] The original Black Sabbath line-up, including Osbourne, reforms just to play at the Live Aid concert. Philadelphia.

1986 Mar LP *Seventh Star*, credited to "Black Sabbath with Tony Iommi" (he being the only remaining member of the old band, playing with newly-recruited musicians) reaches UK #27, but the incarnation shows little sign of maintaining the fan following or success which Black Sabbath achieved in earlier years.

BLIND FAITH

Eric Clapton (vocals and guitar)
Steve Winwood (vocals and keyboards)
Rick Grech (bass)
Ginger Baker (drums)

1969 Feb Eric Clapton° and Ginger Baker, remaining together after the demise of Cream° in Nov. 1968, join with Steve Winwood° who has just quit Traffic°. Rick Grech is invited to complete the band, and he leaves Family° during a US tour to do so. The music press dubs the line-up an "instant supergroup"; their name is apparently an anticipatory response to this.

June [7] After recording an LP, the band makes live debut in Hyde Park, London. 150,000 people watch for free.

July [12] US live debut at Madison Square Garden, New York, is the start of a sell-out US stadium tour which earns a fortune, yet convinces band members that Blind Faith is musically unsatisfying, and that they will split when the tour is complete.

Aug LP *Blind Faith* is released, and tops both US and UK charts for 2 weeks. The original UK sleeve with a picture of a nude ll-year-old girl holding a "phallic" model airplane is considered too controversial for use in US. No single is released from the LP.

Sept The band completes US tour; Clapton° has already lost interest, and carries on touring with Delaney and Bonnie°. Blind Faith does not play together again. (Grech will stay with Baker in Airforce at the end of 1969, while Winwood° will work solo before reforming Traffic° early in 1970.)

BLONDIE

Deborah Harry (vocals)
Chris Stein (guitar)
Jimmy Destri (keyboards)
Gary Valentine (bass)
Clem Burke (drums)

1974 Aug The group forms in New York, the original line-up pairing Harry (b. July 1, 1945, Miami, Fla., US) with the backing musicians from her previous girl vocal group The Stilettos. Previously, Harry has recorded as a member of folk-rock band Wind In The Willows (who had an eponymous LP on Capitol in July 1968) but other original members Stein (b. Jan.5, 1950, Brooklyn, New York) bassist Fred Smith and drummer Billy O'Connor have only played in local bands. With two girl backup singers, and a repertoire based on the girl group sounds of the 1960s, the group begins to play at noted New York punk birthplace, CBGBs.

Oct Czechoslovakian refugee Ivan Kral joins on guitar, and Tish and Snookie replace Julie and Jackie as backup singers.

1975 Jan Kral, bored, leaves tc join the Patti Smith° group.

May Ex-Sweet Revenge drummer Clem Burke (b. Nov.24, 1955, NY, US) replaces O'Connor when the latter goes to law school.

Aug Smith leaves to join Television°, and is replaced by Gary Valentine, a friend of Burke's.

Oct Ex-Knickers member Jimmy Destri joins on keyboards.

1976 The group signs to small Private Stock label, and makes debut single *X-Offender* and LP *Blondie* with producer Richard Gottehrer (once a member of The Strangeloves).

1977 Jan They make their US West Coast debut at the Whisky A-Go Go in LA, then tour nationally supporting Iggy Pop°.

Feb LP *Blondie* is released in UK, where it attracts attention as being more accessible than other punk groups such as New York Dolls and Sex Pistols°. Shortly after, the band visits UK as support to Television°.

July Valentine leaves to form his own group, The Know. He is temporarily replaced on bass by Frank Infante (ex-World War III) for the recording of second LP *Plastic Letters*, again produced by Gottehrer.

Aug Chrysalis Records buys Blondie's contract from Private Stock, also acquiring previously-recorded material.

Oct LP *Plastic Letters* is released by Chrysalis, who also reissues the debut LP.

Nov Infante moves to rhythm guitar, and UK bass player Nigel Harrison (ex Silverhead) joins.

1978 Mar Blondie breaks through in UK with *Denis*, a remake of Randy & The Rainbows' *Denise* (a US #10 in 1963). It hits UK #2, while LP *Plastic Letters* climbs to UK #10 and US #72.

May *I'm Always Touched By Your Presence Dear*, also from the LP, hits UK #10. The group records a third LP, switching producer to Mike Chapman (who as half of the Chinnichap production team has made numerous UK hits for Mud°, The Sweet°, Smokie and others.)

Sept *Picture This*, first single from next LP, reaches UK #12. LP *Parallel Lines* is released. In early 1979 it will hit #6 and top the UK chart for 4 weeks, staying charted in both countries for over 100 weeks.

Nov *Hanging On The Telephone*, second single from LP *Parallel Lines*, hits UK #5.

1979 Feb *Heart Of Glass*, a disco-flavored third single from *Parallel Lines*, tops UK chart for 4 weeks, and sells over a million copies in UK alone, making it Blondie's biggest UK success.

Apr The group finally has a US chart hit (where it also goes to #1) with *Heart Of Glass*.

May *Sunday Girl* also from *Parallel Lines* tops UK chart for 3 weeks.

Aug *One Way Or Another*, from the same LP, reaches US #24.

BLONDIE *cont.*

Sept Bomp Records in US and London Records in UK release *Little GTO*, by "The New York Blondes featuring Madame X". The latter is actually Harry, who is clearly heard on vocals. Chrysalis threatens legal action, and the single is withdrawn.

Oct *Dreaming* from fourth LP *Eat To The Beat*, produced by Chapman, hits UK #2. LP *Eat To The Beat* hits UK #1, and will remain charted for 9 months.

Dec *Dreaming* reaches US #27 and LP *Eat To The Beat* #17, while in UK *Union City Blue*, a song connected with the feature film *Union City* in which Harry makes an appearance, peaks at #13.

1980 Mar *Atomic*, from *Eat To The Beat*, tops UK chart for 2 weeks. The group is produced by Giorgio Moroder on *Call Me*, from the soundtrack of Richard Gere movie *American Gigolo*. Harry writes the song's lyrics to fit Moroder's existing backing track. As a single, it tops UK chart for a week, and 6 weeks in the US, where it is a million-seller.

June Harry stars with Meat Loaf in the film *Roadie*. The soundtrack includes Blondie's version of Johnny Cash's *Ring Of Fire*.

July *Atomic* reaches #39 in US.

Nov *The Tide Is High*, a reggae number written by John Holt and previously recorded by The Paragons, hits UK #1 for 2 weeks, while LP *Autoamerican*, which returns to Chapman's production, hits #3.

1981 Jan *The Tide Is High* also tops US chart for a week (selling over a million), and LP *Autoamerican* reaches #7.

Feb Also excerpted from *Autoamerican* is *Rapture* (a Stein/Harry number in New York "rap" vein), which strongly features guest saxophonist Tom Scott. It hits UK #5 and tops the chart for 2 weeks, becoming another million-seller. Harry announces that she is to record a solo LP, produced by Nile Rodgers and Bernard Edwards of Chic°.

Aug Harry solo single *Backfired* reaches UK #32 and US #43, while her LP *Koo Koo* makes UK #6 and US #25.

Nov Compilation LP *The Best Of Blondie* reaches US #30 and UK #4, and second Harry solo single *The Jam Was Moving* misses UK chart, but makes US #82.

1982 Jan Infante sues the band, claiming he is being excluded from taking part in group activities. Following an out-of-court settlement, he remains a member.

June *Island Of Lost Souls*, a foretaste of Blondie's final LP, reaches UK #11 and US #37. It is the group's last US hit single.

July LP *The Hunter*, again a Mike Chapman production, reaches UK #9 and US #33.

Aug *War Child*, taken from *The Hunter*, is their final UK hit, reaching #39. A projected UK tour is cancelled due to insufficient advance audience interest.

Oct The group splits up. (Subsequently, Stein will launch his own label, Animal Records, through Chrysalis, before becoming seriously ill. Harry will nurse him back to health and take occasional film acting roles (notably *Videodrome* with James Woods) before eventually relaunching her own solo singing career. The duo will also write a book, *Making Tracks: The Rise of Blondie*. The others will mainly move into production or work with new groups: Burke eventually drums with The Eurythmics°.)

1986 Dec Harry returns to UK chart with *French Kissin' (In The USA)*, which makes #8, and LP *Rockbird*, which peaks at #31.

1987 Jan *French Kissin' (In The USA)* makes a less strong US chart impression, at #57.

Mar Another Harry solo, *Free To Fall*, peaks at UK #46.

May *In Love With Love*, third single from *Rockbird*, reaches UK #45.

BLOOD, SWEAT & TEARS

Al Kooper (keyboards and vocals)
Steve Katz (guitar and vocals)
Fred Lipsius (piano and alto sax)
Dick Halligan (keyboards, trombone and flute)
Randy Brecker (trumpet and flugelhorn)
Jerry Weiss (trumpet and flugelhorn)
Jim Fielder (bass)
Bobby Colomby (drums)

1968 June Formed by Kooper (b. Feb.5, 1944, New York, N.Y., US) and Katz (b. May.9, 1945, New York) as an experimental rock group accommodating jazz and serious music forms and players, the band debuts with LP on Columbia Records, *The Child Is Father To The Man*, which wraps Kooper's songs and some pop cover versions in tight brass and string arrangements. It reaches US #47 and UK #40, but Kooper, Brecker and Weiss leave.

1969 Mar A new line-up fronted by David Clayton-Thomas (b. David Thomsett, Sept.13, 1941, Surrey, UK) produces LP *Blood, Sweat And Tears*, which tops US chart for 7 weeks and sells over 2 million copies by the end of the year (also winning a Grammy as Album of the Year), while laying the ground rules for most of the 1970s rock/jazz fusion boom. Also new to the band on this LP are horn players Chuck Winfield, Lew Soloff and Jerry Hyman.

Apr A revival of old Motown ballad *You've Made Me So Very Happy* hits US #2, the first of three million-sellers from the LP.

May *You've Made Me So Very Happy* reaches UK #35 (the band's only UK hit single), while LP *Blood, Sweat And Tears* makes #15.

July *Spinning Wheel*, written by Clayton-Thomas, hits US #2.

July [5] The band plays at Atlanta Pop Festival to 140,000 people.

Nov Laura Nyro-penned *And When I Die* hits US #2.

1970 June They embark on a US State Department-sponsored tour of East Europe, taking in Romania, Poland and Yugoslavia.

Aug LP *Blood, Sweat And Tears 3* tops US chart for 2 weeks, while *Hi-De-Ho*, taken from it, makes #14.

Sept LP *Blood, Sweat And Tears 3* reaches UK #14.

Nov *Lucretia MacEvil* peaks at US #29.

1971 Feb The band scores and plays music for the film *The Owl And The Pussycat*, the soundtrack LP of which reaches US #186.

Aug LP *BS&T 4*, made without Hyman but with additional horn player Dave Bargeron, reaches US #10, while the extracted *Go Down Gamblin'* makes #32.

Nov *Lisa, Listen To Me* is a minor US hit at #73.

1972 Apr Compilation LP *Greatest Hits* reaches US #19.

Nov *So Long Dixie* reaches #44 in US, and LP *New Blood* peaks at #32. By this time, Clayton-Thomas has left to go solo, while original members Lipsius and Halligan have also departed. Among the extensive "new blood" in the band is Jerry Fisher, who takes over vocals. Shortly after, founder Steve Katz also leaves.

1973 Sept LP *No Sweat* peaks at US #72. By now, the band's personnel is extremely fluid, varying from concert to concert, and Jerry LaCroix takes over vocal/harmonica duties briefly.

1974 July *Tell Me That I'm Wrong*, with Clayton-Thomas back on vocals, is a minor US hit at #83.

Sept LP *Mirror Image* sells comparatively poorly, only reaching US #149.

1975 July LP *New City* makes US #47, while a revival of The Beatles'° *Got To Get You Into My Life*, from it, reaches #62.

1976 Aug LP *More Than Ever* is another disappointing seller (US #165), after which the band is dropped by Columbia. Drummer Colomby, the sole remaining original member, leaves.

1977 Nov Signed to ABC records with a line-up now comprising Clayton-Thomas (vocals), Dave Bargeron (trombone), Randy Bernson (guitar), Larry Willis (keyboards), Tony Klatka (trumpet), Chris Albert (trumpet), Gregory Herbert (saxophone), Neil Stubenhaus (bass) and Bobby Economo (drums), they record LP *Brand New Day*, produced by Bobby Colomby, but it is not a major seller.

1980 Mar LP *Nuclear Blues* is their second and last ABC release, again not a hit. (After this, the band fades from view for most of the next 8 years, although Clayton-Thomas and Colomby (who jointly own the name Blood, Sweat & Tears), occasionally put together an aggregation for live work.)

1988 July Clayton-Thomas and a re-formed Blood, Sweat & Tears play live dates in the US.

MIKE BLOOMFIELD

1967 Apr After leaving The Paul Butterfield° Blues Band, Bloomfield (b. July 28, 1944, Chicago, US), who learned blues guitar as a teenager from Chicago giants like Muddy Waters°, and also played live and on LP with Bob Dylan° in 1965, forms Electric Flag. The band has Bloomfield on guitar, Barry Goldberg (keyboards), Buddy Miles (drums), Nick Gravenites (vocals) Harvey Brooks (bass), Marcus Doubleday (trumpet), and Peter Strazza and Herbie Rich (saxes). Bloomfield intends to combine blues with varied musical elements from the others' backgrounds.

June [16] Electric Flag debuts live at Monterey Pop Festival, California. LP debut is *The Trip*, soundtrack to an underground Peter Fonda film, which is a cult but not a chart hit.

1968 Apr First official Electric Flag LP is *A Long Time Comin'*, which reaches US #31. Bloomfield leaves the internal-conflict-ridden

band while the LP is on chart, leaving Miles to organize one more Electric Flag LP *The Electric Flag*, which reaches US #76 in Feb. 1969 before they all drift apart.
Bloomfield joins Al Kooper and Steve Stills on LP *Super Session*, which reaches US #12.

1969 Feb First joint project success prompts an onstage recording of double LP *The Live Adventures Of Mike Bloomfield And Al Kooper* at The Fillmore, San Francisco. It hits US #18.

Apr He plays live in Chicago with original idol Muddy Waters°, the results being released on LP *Fathers And Sons*.

Nov Bloomfield solo LP *It's Not Killing Me* is less successful, making US #127.

1973 June He collaborates on LP *Triumvirate* with John Hammond Jr. and Dr. John°. It reaches US #105.

1974 Bloomfield reunites with Miles, Goldberg and Gravenites with Roger Troy (bass), as Electric Flag for Atlantic label. LP *The Band Kept Playing* does not sell, and the group splits again.

1976 June He plays on *KGB*, debut LP by KGB, which also includes Goldberg (keyboards), Ray Kennedy (vocals), Rick Grech (bass) and Carmine Appice (drums). LP struggles to US #124, and Bloomfield leaves before the second (and last) KGB LP *Motion*, never to play as a member of a band again.

1977 LP *If You Love These Blues, Play 'Em As You Please* is released in association with magazine *Guitar Player* as a virtuoso primer for blues guitarists, and is nominated for a Grammy Award. He signs to small Takoma label, and records a series of uncommercial blues/roots LPs over the next 4 years, including *Analine, Between The Hard Place And The Ground* and *Michael Bloomfield*.

1981 Feb [15] Bloomfield dies in San Francisco of an apparently accidental drug overdose, just after the release of final LP, ironically titled *Living In The Fast Lane*.

KURTIS BLOW

1976 After studying voice at the High School of Music and Art, and communications at New York City College, Blow (b. Kurt Walker, Aug.9, 1959, New York, N.Y., US) begins rapping as a DJ in Harlem, New York, clubs. He will hone his art over 3 years at New York venues like Small's Paradise, working with Grandmaster Flash°, among others.

1979 Nov He signs to Mercury Records just as Sugarhill Gang's° *Rapper's Delight* is becoming the first international rapping pop hit.

Dec Debut release is the seasonal *Christmas Rappin'*, which does not chart in US, but reaches #30 in UK.

1980 Sept *The Breaks* only reaches US #87, but with huge specialist-market sales, particularly in New York, is a certified million-seller, and hits #4 on the R&B chart. It marks Blow's record debut with partner Davy D. on backing tracks. It reaches UK #47.

1981 After finding wider performing success around US with Davy D. accompanying him at the turntables, he tours Europe and UK.

Aug LP *Deuce* reaches US #90.

1985 Mar *Party Time* reaches UK #67.

Apr Novelty rap *Basketball* hits US #71.

1986 Feb *If I Ruled The World* is his biggest hit single, reaching UK #24. *I'm Chillin'* makes UK #64, after which Blow's profile drops as his flow of recordings stops.

THE BLUEBELLS

Robert (Bobby Bluebell) Hodgens (rhythm guitar)
Kenneth McCluskey (lead vocals)
Dave McCluskey (drums)
Russell Irvin (lead guitar)
Lawrence Donegan (bass)

1979 The band is formed in the members' native Glasgow, Scotland UK, by Hodgens, who initially asks Dave McCluskey to join him while they are both at a U2° gig. They then play local gigs and record demos for 18 months.

1981 June Liking a demo tape he has received, Nick Heyward of Haircut 100° asks the group to play support on a forthcoming major UK tour.

1982 Jan With some industry A&R excitement about the band after the tour, they sign to London Records.

Oct First single *Forever More* is released, unsuccessfully. Donegan leaves to join Lloyd Cole°, while Irvin simply quits. They are replaced by Neil Baldwin on bass and Craig Gennon on lead guitar.

1983 Mar *Cath* reaches UK #62. After it, Elvis Costello° joins them in the studio to help produce tracks for their first LP, and invites them to play support on his forthcoming UK tour.

July *Sugar Bridge (It Will Stand)* reaches UK #72.

1984 Apr *I'm Falling* finally gives the band a major chart record, reaching UK #11.

June *Young At Heart* becomes their biggest hit and only UK top 10 single, at #8.

Aug The band's only LP *Sisters* is released and climbs to UK #22.

Sept *Cath* is reissued with the Costello-produced *Will She Always Be Waiting* as a double A-side, and peaks at UK #38.

Dec The band tours the US club circuit.

1985 Feb *All I Am (Is Loving You)* is their last single, peaking at UK #58.

June Gennon leaves to join The Smiths°, replaced by former Hipsway guitarist Alistair McLeod.

1987 Jan Having tried for 18 months to work with numerous producers, the band decides to call it a day. (Hodgens opts to develop a new band, while the brothers McCluskey form their own outfit, The McCluskey Brothers, and release an independent folk-oriented LP in Oct.1987.)

BLUE CHEER

Dick Peterson (bass and vocals)
Randy Holden (guitar)
Paul Whaley (drums)

1967 The band forms in San Francisco in response to the US success of UK power trio Cream°, playing similar blues-based high-volume rock. The name comes from a strain of the drug LSD.

1968 Mar *Summertime Blues* and LP *Vincebus Eruptum* are released in US, following a recording deal with Philips. The single (a distorted revival of the 1959 Eddie Cochran° hit) reaches US #14, and LP makes #11.

Sept Leigh Stephens replaces Holden on guitar for second LP *Outside Inside*, better received by critics than their debut, but not by the public: it stalls at US #90.

1969 Apr Whaley and Stephens leave, to be replaced on LP *New! Improved!* by Bruce Stephens (guitar and vocals), Norman Mayell (drums) and Ralph Burns Kellogg (keyboards). The LP charts at US #84.

1970 Nov *The Original Human Being* is final US charting LP, reaching #188. By this time, their original national US breakthrough has evaporated, and they are a local San Francisco cult group again, until they break up early in 1971. (A brief, but unsuccessful, reunion will occur in 1979.)

BLUE ÖYSTER CULT

Eric Bloom ("stun guitar" and vocals)
Donald "Buck Dharma" Roeser (lead guitar)
Joe Bouchard (bass and vocals)
Allen Lanier (rhythm guitar and keyboards)
Albert Bouchard (drums and vocals)

1970 The band forms in Long Island, N.Y., US, out of The Stalk-Forrest Group, which itself has developed from Soft White Underbelly, a band launched at Stony Brook University by Roeser, Lanier, and Al Bouchard, along with *Crawdaddy* magazine writer Sandy Pearlman and Richard Meltzer. From its early beginings, Pearlman has had a major influence on band, and as its producer/manager, he is tagged as a Svengali figure.

1971 Dec After Elektra has rejected two LPs from the group (first as Soft White Underbelly, then as The Stalk-Forrest Group), they sign as Blue Oyster Cult to Columbia Records.

1972 June Debut LP *Blue Oyster Cult* encapsulates their trademark sound: fast, loud and heavy. It is a fair seller in the US, reaching #172, and the band begins touring extensively in the US as regular support act to Alice Cooper°.

1973 Apr LP *Tyranny & Mutation*, similar hard and heavy rock, climbs to US #122. Like the first LP, it features some lyrics by non-member rock writer Richard Meltzer.

1974 June LP *Secret Treaties*, which reaches US #53, includes some songs written by Patti Smith°, who becomes Lanier's girlfriend. It is the most critically praised of their LPs.

1975 Apr Live LP *On Your Feet Or On Your Knees* achieves the band's highest US LP chart placing, at #22.

1976 Aug LP *Agents of Fortune* contains the band's only sizeable hit single, the uncharacteristically mellow and Byrds°-influenced *(Don't Fear) The Reaper*. This reaches US #12, while the LP peaks at US #29 and UK #26, and is eventually awarded a platinum disk for a million-plus sales.

BLUE OYSTER CULT *cont.*

1977 Dec LP *Spectres* reaches #43 in US.

1978 Feb LP *Spectres* peaks at UK #60, while in the US the band embarks on a massive 250-date tour, promoting the previous LP and recording for a planned live release.

June Two years after its US success, *(Don't Fear) The Reaper* becomes the band's only UK hit single, climbing to #12.

Oct Live LP, *Some Enchanted Evening*, peaks at US #44 and UK #18.

1979 Aug LP *Mirrors* climbs to US #44 and UK #46.

Sept *In Thee*, taken from Mirrors, reaches US #74.

1980 Aug LP *Cultosaurus Erectus* peaks at US #34 and UK #12, where it is their highest chart-placed LP. Fantasy novelist Michael Moorcock co-writes one of its tracks, *Black Blade*.

1981 Aug LP *Fire Of Unknown Origin* reaches US #24 and UK #29. Again, Moorcock co-writes one track, while the band's previously most prolific songwriter, Al Bouchard, leaves after the culmination of a UK tour at the Castle Donington "Monsters of Rock" festival. He is replaced on drums by Rick Downey.

Oct *Burnin' For You*, extracted from LP *Fire Of Unknown Origin*, makes US #40.

1982 June Third live LP *ETL (Extra-Terrestrial Live)* reaches US #29 and UK #39.

Oct Roeser releases solo LP *Flat Out*, for Portrait Records, as Buck Dharma. It does not chart in US or UK.

1983 Dec LP *The Revolution By Night* reaches US #93 and UK #95.

1984 Feb *Shooting Shark*, taken from the LP, reaches US #83. (A hiatus on record follows for the band, although they continue to tour extensively and successfully. Pearlman sees their career in terms of phases of development, the end of each phase being signalled by one of their live LPs, which encapsulates the repertoire at that point. This being so, phase four is still in seed in the late 1980s.)

1987 Following a long period of inactivity the band re-groups to release LP *Spectres*, to little commercial success.

THE BLUES PROJECT

Tommy Flanders (vocals)
Steve Katz (guitar and vocals)
Danny Kalb (guitar)
Al Kooper (organ and vocals)
Andy Kulberg (bass and flute)
Roy Blumenfeld (drums)

1965 June The group is formed in New York by Kalb and Blumenfeld as an experiment in playing urban and country blues on electric instruments, using an assortment of folk, jazz, and rock session musicians from around Greenwich Village, where they make a live debut at the Café Au Go Go.

1966 Mar They venture outside New York to play in San Francisco and across the US at college campus gigs.

May They sign to Verve Folkways Records and release LP *Live At The Café Au Go Go*, recorded at their Bleecker St. home base, which reaches US #77.

Dec Flanders leaves, and Katz and Kooper take vocals on second LP *Projections*, which makes US #52.

1967 Apr *No Time Like The Right Time* is their only hit single (US #96).

June [16] They play at Monterey Pop Festival in California.

Oct LP *Live At Town Hall* reaches US #71, after which Kooper leaves following disagreements, and Kalb becomes ill and drops out. Katz then joins Kooper in Blood, Sweat & Tears°, and Blues Project fragments, with Blumenfeld and Kulberg recruiting other musicians to continue as Sea Train.

1968 LP *Planned Obsolescence* is put together from the last recordings of the quintet.

1971 Kalb forms a new version of group with Blumenfeld and bassist/sax player Don Kretmar. They sign to Capitol, and record LP *Lazarus*.

1972 The group becomes a sextet with the return of Flanders and addition of David Cohen (piano) and Bill Lussenden. It records a second Capitol LP, *Blues Project*, then disbands.

1973 June [24] The original line-up, minus Flanders, reunites for a concert in Central Park, New York, recorded for MCA as LP *Reunion In Central Park*.

1981 Mar [17] The original line-up, again minus Flanders, reunites once more for a single concert at Bonds, New York.

COLIN BLUNSTONE

1967 Dec After The Zombies° break up, former lead singer Blunstone (b. June 24, 1945, Hatfield, UK) leaves music for an insurance office job, but will decide to return as a soloist within the year.

1969 Jan He signs to Deram and records a new version of original Zombies'° hit *She's Not There* with baroque string arrangement, under the pseudonym Neil MacArthur. It charts in UK at #34.

Dec Second Neil MacArthur single *It's Not Easy* fails to chart.

1971 Jan Blunstone signs a new solo deal with Epic, this time under his real name.

Mar Epic debut *Mary Won't You Warm My Bed* does not chart.

Nov First solo LP *One Year* is released.

1972 Mar A revival of Denny Laine's *Say You Don't Mind* reaches UK #15.

Nov *I Don't Believe In Miracles* makes UK #31. LP *Ennismore* is released, to excellent reviews but no chart placing. All Blunstone's LPs will be highly-rated in print but sell less well – the same fate that befalls The Zombies°.

1973 Feb *How Could We Dare To Be Wrong* completes UK hit hat-trick, hitting #45. (But eight further Epic singles over the next 5 years, will fail to chart.)

1981 Mar He sings guest lead vocal on a revival by Dave Stewart of Motown oldie *What Becomes Of The Brokenhearted*, which climbs to UK #13.

Sept He leaves Epic for the Panache label, but sole release *Miles Away* does not sell.

1982 May He changes labels again to PRT, and scores a final hit with another Motown revival, Smokey Robinson's° *The Tracks Of My Tears*, reaching UK #60. (After this, Blunstone will drift again out of the public eye, and scarcely be heard of during the 1980s.)

MARC BOLAN AND T.REX

1965 Nov After a teenage career as a male model, among other things, Bolan (b. Marc Feld, Sept.30, 1947, London, UK) changes his performing name from Toby Tyler to Marc Bolan, and releases first UK single *The Wizard*, on Decca. He performs it on TV's "Ready Steady Go", but it does not sell.

1966 June *The Third Degree* is another flop single.

Nov Bolan links with new producer Simon Napier-Bell (also The Yardbirds'° manager), and records third single *Hippy Gumbo* for EMI (another failure), plus many other tracks which will only emerge in 1974 after he achieves fame.

1967 May He signs to Track Records and joins south London psychedelic group John's Children as guitarist/harmony vocalist, along with Andy Ellison (vocals), John Hewlett (bass) and Chris Townson (drums).

Sept John's Children breaks up after three unsuccessful singles, and Bolan forms the acoustic duo Tyrannosaurus Rex, with percussionist Steve Peregrine Took.

1968 Feb The duo signs new recording deal with producer Tony Visconti, for release on EMI's Regal Zonophone label.

May Debut Tyrannosaurus Rex single *Debora* reaches UK #34.

July LP *My People Were Fair And Had Sky In Their Hair, But Now They're Content To Wear Stars On Their Brow* makes UK #15.

Sept *One Inch Rock* peaks at #28 in UK.

Nov LP *Prophets, Seers And Sages, The Angels Of The Ages* is issued in UK but fails to chart.

1969 Jan *Pewter Suitor* is issued, but does not chart.

June Third LP *Unicorn* reaches UK #12.

Aug *King Of The Rumbling Spires*, spends one week at UK #44, and is the group's first record to feature Bolan playing electric guitar.

Oct Following a poorly received US tour, Steve Took leaves and is replaced by Mickey Finn.

1970 Jan *By The Light Of The Magical Moon* is released by the new duo in UK, but does not chart.

Mar LP *A Beard Of Stars* peaks at #21 in UK.

Aug Bolan, Visconti, David Bowie° and Rick Wakeman release an impromptu UK single *Oh Baby*, under the name Dib Cochran and The Earwigs. It does not sell, but will later become an in-demand collectors' rarity.

Oct Tony Visconti shifts label outlet for his productions from Regal Zonophone to Fly Records in UK. After much urging from his producer, Bolan abbreviates his group name to T.Rex, and releases *Ride A White Swan*, which climbs steadily to peak at UK #2 at the end of the year.

Dec T.Rex expands to a quartet with the addition of Steve Curry on

bass, and Bill Legend on drums (in fact Bill Fifield, but known to Bolan as Legend because he was recruited from the Mickey Jubbled group, Legend.) LP *T.Rex* peaks at UK #13, in a chart residency lasting 6 months.

1971 Feb *Ride A White Swan* is US chart debut at #76.

Mar *Hot Love* tops UK chart for 6 weeks.

June *Hot Love* peaks at #72 in US, while LP *T.Rex* edges in at #188.

July *Get It On* tops UK chart for 4 weeks, and will become Bolan and T.Rex's biggest international hit.

Aug Compilation LP *The Best Of T.Rex*, largely composed of tracks by Tyrannosaurus Rex, reaches UK #21.

Oct *Electric Warrior*, first LP by the four-piece group, is released.

Nov As Bolan decides to leave Fly Records for a new deal, the label issues LP track *Jeepster* (never intended by Bolan for single release) in UK, and it leaps to #2.

Dec LP *Electric Warrior* tops UK chart for 6 weeks, and reaches US #32.

1972 Jan [1] Bolan signs new deal with EMI, to release records in UK on his own T.Rex Wax Co. label.

Feb *Telegram Sam*, the first new label release, tops UK chart for 2 weeks.

Mar *Bang A Gong (Get It On)* is Bolan's biggest US hit, peaking at #10. The title amendment has been necessary in the US because the group Chase has had a top 30 hit with a different song titled Get It On in mid-1971. T.Rex plays two sold-out concerts at Wembley Empire Pool, London, to audiences of 100,000, while being filmed by Ringo Starr° for Apple documentary film on the group's success, *Born To Boogie*. Double LP reissue coupling together *My People Were Fair... and Prophets, Seers And Sages* by Tyrannosaurus Rex tops UK chart for a week, while a single reissue twinning *Debora* and *One Inch Rock* hits UK #7.

May *Metal Guru* ("It's about a car," says Bolan) tops UK chart for 4 weeks as the country is afflicted by "T.Rextasy". In US, *Telegram Sam* reaches #67. LP *Bolan Boogie*, on Fly, compiling the hits up to *Jeepster*, tops UK chart for 3 weeks.

July Newly-recorded LP *The Slider* hits #4 in UK (reputedly selling 100,000 copies in 4 days), and also becomes the group's most successful US LP, peaking at #17.

Sept *Children Of The Revolution* hits UK #2.

Dec The movie *Born To Boogie*, featuring T.Rex, is premièred in London. *Solid Gold Easy Action* peaks at UK #3, while another double reissue LP coupling *Unicorn* and *A Beard Of Stars* charts briefly at #44.

1973 Mar *Twentieth Century Boy* hits UK #3, while LP *Tanx* makes #4, and also reaches US #102.

June *The Groover* reaches UK #4 – T.Rex's tenth and final UK top 5 hit.

July Jack Green joins the group on additional guitar, and three girl backup vocalists are recruited, including US soul singer Gloria Jones, who will become Bolan's girlfriend.

Aug *Blackjack* is issued in UK under the name Marc Bolan With Big Carrot, but does not chart.

Nov Compilation LP *Great Hits* (an anthology from *Telegram Sam* onwards) peaks at UK #32.

Dec *Truck On (Tyke)* reaches UK #12.

1974 Jan Davy Lutton replaces Legend on drums and Gloria Jones starts to play keyboards on stage, as T.Rex plays its first major UK tour in 2 years.

Feb *Teenage Dream* reaches UK #13. This is the first release on which the group's name is amended to Marc Bolan and T.Rex.

Mar LP *Zinc Alloy And The Hidden Riders Of Tomorrow* reaches UK #12 as Bolan parts company with his long-time producer Visconti.

Apr Bolan leaves the UK to live in tax exile for several months in Monte Carlo.

June Tracks recorded as demos in 1966 with Simon Napier-Bell finally gain commercial release in UK via Track Records, as LP *The Beginning Of Doves* and maxi-single *Jasper C. Debussy*. Neither charts.

July *Light Of Love* reaches #22 in UK.

Nov *Zip Gun Boogie* peaks at #41 in UK.

Dec Mickey Finn and Jack Green leave the group, while Dino Dines joins on keyboards.

1975 Feb LP *Bolan's Zip Gun* is released in UK, sells poorly and fails to chart.

July *New York City* restores Bolan to UK top 20, peaking at #15.

Sept Rolan, son of Bolan and Gloria Jones, is born in London.

Oct *Dreamy Lady* (credited to T.Rex Disco Party) reaches UK #30.

1976 Mar LP *Futuristic Dragon* and single *London Boys* are released in UK, charting at #50 and #40 respectively.

July *I Love To Boogie* becomes Bolan's last UK top 20 hit, peaking at #13.

Oct *Laser Love* reaches UK #41. It features Bolan with a T.Rex made up of session men like Miller Anderson (guitar) and Herbie Flowers (bass), the last group survivor from the major hit years, bassist Steve Curry having now also left.

Nov The session players also make up the final touring line-up of T.Rex, accompanying Bolan on a charity date at London's Drury Lane Theatre Royal, followed by a UK tour which has punk band The Damned° as support act.

1977 Jan Bolan and Gloria Jones issue duet revival of The Teddy Bears' *To Know Him Is To Love Him* in UK, but it does not chart and later becomes another collectors' item.

Mar [20] The final live T.Rex gig takes place at The Locarno in Portsmouth, UK.

Apr *The Soul Of My Suit* reaches UK #42, while LP *Dandy In The Underworld*, Bolan's final LP to be issued in his lifetime, peaks at #26. (The LP title track will be issued as a quick UK follow-up single and flop completely.)

Aug *Celebrate Summer* fails to chart in UK, making it Bolan's second consecutive miss. Meanwhile, he begins a stint as a guest pop journalist, writing a weekly column in UK magazine *Record Mirror*, and also hosts a series of six weekly Wednesday late-afternoon UK TV shows, called "Marc". Guests include David Bowie°, who sings a live duet with Bolan on one show.

Sept [16] After a long night out at a London club, Bolan and Gloria Jones are on their way home when, at 5 a.m., their car (driven by Jones) leaves the road at a bend on Barnes Common, London, and crashes into a tree. Jones is badly injured, and Bolan is killed.

1978 Apr *Crimson Moon* is the first posthumous Bolan release and, though it does not chart, begins a sequence of reissues and releases comprising previously unheard material which will still be in full flood a decade after his death. (In all, four singles will chart in UK posthumously – the EP *Return Of The Electric Warrior* (#50 in 1981), *You Scare Me To Death* (#51 in 1981), a reissue of *Telegram Sam* (#69 in 1982) and a medley of hit extracts titled *Megarex* (#72 in 1985). Five LPs – *Solid Gold, T.Rex In Concert, You Scare Me To Death, Dance In The Midnight* and *Best Of The 20th Century Boy* – will also be posthumous UK chart entries.)

1980 Oct [27] Bolan's first performing partner Steve Peregrine Took dies from asphyxiation.

BON JOVI

Jon Bon Jovi (vocals)
Richie Sambora (guitar)
David Bryan (keyboards)
Alec John Such (bass)
Tico Torres (drums)

1983 Mar The band is formed in Sayreville, N.J., US, by Bon Jovi (b. John Bongiovi, Mar.2, 1962, N.J.) and Bryan (b. Feb.7, 1962, N.J.) who have played together in high school and later in local cover version bands. They recruit Sambora (b. July 11, 1959), Such (b. Nov.14, 1956) and Torres (b. Oct.7, 1953) – all local musicians.

1984 Jan After signing to Mercury label, debut LP *Bon Jovi* is released in US. While recording it the band also builds its live reputation as an exciting heavy rock act with extensive US touring.

Apr *Runaway*, a track first recorded by Jovi as a solo effort before the band was formed, is first hit single, climbing to US #39. LP *Bon Jovi* reaches US #43 and UK #71.

July *She Don't Know Me* reaches US #48.

Oct First UK tour, including a concert, is broadcast on BBC Radio 1.

1985 May *Only Lonely* reaches #54 in US. LP *7800 Degrees Fahrenheit* reaches US #37 and UK #28. It is their first gold LP for a half million sales.

Aug *In And Out Of Love* hits US #69.

1986 Sept *You Give Love A Bad Name* is first UK hit single, reaching #14.

Oct LP *Slippery When Wet* hits US #1 and UK #6, becoming an 8 million-selling LP in US by the end of 1987.

Nov *You Give Love A Bad Name* hits US #1, their first million-selling single worldwide.

Dec *Livin' On A Prayer* hits UK #4.

1987 Jan LP *Slippery When Wet* returns to US #1 for a further 7 weeks.

Feb *Livin' On A Prayer* hits US #1 for 3 weeks.

Apr *Wanted Dead Or Alive* reaches UK #13.

June *Wanted Dead Or Alive* hits US #7.

Aug [22] Bon Jovi tops the bill of annual Monsters of Rock festival at Castle Donington, UK, climaxing a year in which it has become the most popular heavy rock band in the world.

1988 Apr As the group enjoys a rest, its manager, Doc McGee is convicted of drug offences and sentenced to extensive community service.

GRAHAM BOND

1962 Nov After playing jazz as an alto sax semi-pro for some years in Don Randell's band, Bond joins Alexis Korner's Blues Incorporated on saxophone.

1963 Feb Having become hooked on the use of the electric organ in an R&B/blues context, he switches to that instrument and leaves Korner, to form the Graham Bond Organization with Jack Bruce (bass) and Ginger Baker (drums), later joined by John McLaughlin (guitar).

Oct McLaughlin leaves and is replaced by Dick Heckstall-Smith on sax.

1964 June Bond's first single is one-off *Long Tall Shorty*, on Decca.

1965 Jan He signs to EMI's Columbia label and releases *Wade In The Water*, the first of four non-hit singles for EMI between this time and early 1966.

Mar First LP *The Sound Of '65* is released in UK, but is not a chartmaker.

Oct Bruce leaves to join John Mayall°.

Nov LP *There's A Bond Between Us* is released in UK.

1966 July Baker leaves to join Cream°, and is replaced on drums by Jon Hiseman.

1967 Feb *You've Gotta Have Love, Baby* is released on UK Page One label.

Sept Heckstall-Smith leaves to join John Mayall°, followed by Hiseman to the same band. Bond splits Organization shortly after and goes to the US where he is inactive for a while.

1969 Dec Returning to UK to join Baker in Airforce, Bond also signs to Warner Bros. as a soloist.

1970 May LP *Solid Bond* is released, which features the playing of old colleagues, Bruce, Baker, Hiseman, McLaughlin and Heckstall-Smith. It is his only hit, reaching UK #40.

1971 Feb He forms Magick with UK singer Diane Stewart, whom he has met through their shared interest in the occult, and married. LP *Holy Magick* is released on Vertigo.

1972 Nov After Magick (and his marriage) break up, Bond collaborates with poet and lyricist Pete Brown on LP *Two Heads Are Better Than One* for Chapter One Records.

1973 He forms Magus with UK folk singer Carolanne Pegg, but they are not stable financially or musically and soon founder, leaving Bond with a nervous breakdown which is aggravated by drugs.

1974 May [8] Bond is found dead under a London tube train at Finsbury Park station. It is unclear whether he has fallen, been pushed, or committed suicide while in depression after drying out from heroin and being hospitalized for his breakdown.

GARY U.S. BONDS

1959 Bonds (b. Gary Anderson, June 6, 1939, Jacksonville, Fla., US) has been performing in Norfolk, Va., with his group The Turks when he signs to Frank Guida's local LeGrand Records as a soloist. The studio is a poorly-equipped room behind Guida's record shop, Frankie's Birdland, but the odd acoustics and makeshift effects combine to create a unique "outdoor" sound.

1960 Sept First single *New Orleans* is issued nationally after local interest. Guida renames Anderson as U.S. Bonds because "buy U.S. Bonds" proves an effective promotional tag. Anderson is not aware of his new identity until he hears it on the radio.

Nov *New Orleans* hits US #6, but quickly-released follow-up *Not Me* will flop completely.

1961 Feb *New Orleans* reaches #16 in UK.

June *Quarter To Three*, a manic R&B party record which Bonds later recalls making while he and the band were drunk, tops US chart for 2 weeks and is a million-seller.

Aug *Quarter To Three* reaches #7 in UK. The song will become involved in a lawsuit in 1962, because of Chubby Checker's° alleged plagiarism of it on his hit *Dancin' Party*.

Sept *School Is Out* hits US #5, but fails to reach UK chart, as will the balance of Bonds' LeGrand label US hits. From this record on, his billing is adapted to Gary U.S. Bonds, at the request of both himself and the United States Bonds authorities.

Oct LP *Dance Till Quarter To Three* reaches #6 on US LP chart.

Nov *School Is In* is an answerback part 2 of the previous release, but still makes US #28.

1962 Feb *Dear Lady Twist* cashes in on the year's big dance craze, and hits US #9.

May Same craze-oriented *Twist, Twist Señora* also reaches US #9.

July *Seven Day Weekend* reaches US #27.

Sept Unique sound formula proves to have worn thin on *Copy Cat*, which only makes US #92.

1962/75 His hit run stops, though he continues recording for LeGrand for 4 or 5 more years – in 1963 turning down *If You Wanna Be Happy*, with which label-mate Jimmy Soul has US #1 instead. He will continue to play live dates across US through 1960s and 1970s, but spend more time songwriting with Jerry "Swamp Dogg" Williams than recording.

1975 Mar He records *Grandma's Washboard Band* for Prodigal Records, but it arouses no interest.

1980 He meets Bruce Springsteen°, a long-time fan who has long performed *Quarter To Three* on stage. Springsteen suggests Bond works with him and his guitarist Miami Steve Van Zant on a comeback LP, *Dedication*, as a shared production.

1981 Apr LP *Dedication* is released by EMI America Records. It climbs to #34 in US, then to #43 in UK in August.

June *This Little Girl* from the LP, written by Springsteen°, reaches US #11 and UK #43.

Aug A revival of oldie *Jole Blon* reaches US #65 and UK #51.

Nov The Lennon°/McCartney° song *It's Only Love* is an additional UK release, reaching #43.

1982 July LP *On The Line*, again produced by Springsteen° and Van Zant, reaches US #52 and UK #55. A revival of The Box Tops'° *Soul Deep* makes UK #59.

Aug Springsteen°-written *Out Of Work* reaches US #21.

1984 Aug Bonds puts together new backing group, The American Men, and signs to Phoenix Records, releasing LP *Standing In The Line Of Fire*. (After this, his chart success will wane again, but the comeback generated by the Springsteen° association and its hits will maintain his high profile as a live performer.)

BONEY M

Marcia Barrett (vocals)
Liz Mitchell (vocals)
Maizie Williams (vocals)
Bobby Farrell (vocals)

1976 Although all its members are of West Indian origin, the quartet is put together in West Germany, where they have been working as studio session singers, by writer/producer Frank Farian. Their role is to sing vocals on Farian's electronic disco-style productions, and also to provide a focus for live and TV performances of the records. Even when the major hits come, the group will remain essentially the puppets of Farian, never really rising out of their session singer roles.

1977 Feb *Daddy Cool*, with electronic dance beat and stylized female/bass male vocals, sets the basic style and sound of the group. It reaches UK #6 and US #65.

Apr A revival of Bobby Hebb's 1966 hit *Sunny* hits UK #3. LP *Take The Heat Off Me* is issued, climbing to UK #40.

July *Ma Baker* hits UK #2, but only creeps to US #96.

Dec *Belfast*, with a "socially aware" lyric, climbs to UK #11.

1978 May An adaptation of reggae oldie, *Rivers Of Babylon*, shoots to #1 in UK and stays at the top for 5 weeks.

Aug *Rivers Of Babylon* reaches US #30, and is their biggest US hit.

Sept When *Rivers Of Babylon* finally fades, UK radio starts playing the B-side, *Brown Girl In The Ring*, and the single takes off again with this as the featured side, now climbing to UK #2. Total UK sales are eventually just short of 2 million, making it the country's #2 all-time best-selling single (behind only Wings' *Mull Of Kintyre*). LP *Night Flight To Venus*, containing both sides of the mega-single, hits UK #1 for 4 weeks, staying on chart for 65 weeks.

Oct *Rasputin*, taken from the LP, and with a disco arrangement grossly parodying Cossack dance music, hits UK #2.

Dec A revival of Harry Belafonte's° 1957 Yule hit *Mary's Boy Child* is released for Christmas, arranged by Farian in a medley with his own *Oh My Lord* (which ensures him half the writing/publishing royalties). It rapidly tops UK chart, staying for 4 weeks and selling over 1½ million copies, putting it in the UK all-time top 5 singles sellers. In US it reaches #85, and is their last US chart entry.

1979 Mar A revival of *Painter Man*, originally by the mid-60s UK band Creation, reaches UK #10.

May Calypso-styled *Hooray! Hooray! It's A Holi-Holiday* hits UK #3.

Sept *Gotta Go Home* climbs to UK #12. LP *Oceans Of Fantasy* tops UK chart.

1980 Jan *I'm Born Again* is their first single not to make the UK top 30, peaking at #35.

May Another revival, The Smoke's 1967 UK hit *My Friend Jack*, reaches UK #57. Hits compilation LP *The Magic Of Boney M* tops UK chart for 2 weeks. It is their last LP to chart in UK.

1981 Feb *Children Of Paradise* reaches UK #66.

Dec *We Kill The World (Don't Kill The World)*, with an ecological message lyric, revives UK chart fortunes by climbing to #39, but it will be their final hit record. Always a fairly faceless group, kept in the public eye purely by their successes, Boney M will disappear from the scene quickly and totally. (Producer Farian will still be around, however, and becomes hit-active later in the 1980s with Far Corporation, among others.)

THE BONZO DOG DOO-DAH BAND

Vivian Stanshall (vocals and trumpet)
Neil Innes (vocals and piano)
Rodney Slater (sax and trumpet)
Roger Ruskin Spear (sax, kazoo and mechanical objects)
Vernon Dudley Bowhay-Nowell (guitar and banjo)
Sam Spoons (Martin Stafford) (percussion).
"Legs" Larry Smith (drums)

1965 The group is formed by a group of art students at Goldsmith's College, London, UK, as a whimsical, 1920s-inspired outfit (originally the Bonzo Dog Dada Band). Led by Slater and Spear but with an otherwise fluid personnel of up to thirty, the number is reduced to a stable seven when they start playing London pub gigs.

1966 Apr They move to the club and cabaret circuit, where Spear's job is mainly to manage the considerable number of props and gadgets involved in their stage act. They also sign to EMI's Parlophone label, releasing *My Brother Makes The Noises For The Talkies*, which does not chart.

Sept They revive The Hollywood Argyles' *Alley Oop*, again without success.

1967 Oct Moving to Liberty Records, the group shows its increasingly diversified musical approach, and skills at parody, on debut LP *Gorilla*, but this and the extracted *Equestrian Statue* still fail to chart.

Dec They appear in The Beatles'° TV musical film *Magical Mystery Tour*, performing *Death Cab For Cutie*.

1968 Jan They begin a residency on the UK TV satirical comedy series *"Do Not Adjust Your Set"*, indulging their musical and comic talents through 13 weekly shows.

Apr When the TV series ends, Spoons and Bohay-Nowell leave, and Dennis Cowan joins on bass in preparation for LP recording sessions.

Dec *I'm The Urban Spaceman*, an Innes song produced by Apollo C. Vermouth (Paul McCartney°), hits UK #5.

1969 Jan LP *The Doughnut In Granny's Greenhouse* makes UK #40.

Mar *Mr. Apollo* is released but does not chart.

Aug LP *Tadpoles* reaches #36 in UK.

Nov LP *Keynsham* (named after the district of Bristol, UK, plugged incessantly on Radio Luxembourg by football pools' entrepreneur Horace Bachelor) does not chart; nor do *I Want To Be With You* and *You Done My Brain In*, extracted from it in quick succession.

1970 Jan The group breaks up, victims of sporadic chart success despite being a consistently popular club and touring attraction.

Aug Compilation LP *The Best Of The Bonzo Dog Doo-Dah Band* is released in UK, without charting. Meanwhile, most of the individual members pursue solo projects. (Stanshall and Innes will keep the highest profiles through into the 1980s: the former as a TV and radio personality, creator of "Sir Henry At Rawlinson End" and narrator of Mike Oldfield's° *Tubular Bells;* the latter as a composer, songwriter, TV performer, ad jingle singer, and collaborator with Eric Idle on "Rutland Weekend Television" and The Beatles'° spoof, The Rutles°).

1972 Mar Stanshall, Innes and Cowen revive the Bonzo Dog name, with some help from other former members, to make LP *Let's Make Up And Be Friendly*, though it is not a strong seller.

1974 June Double compilation LP *The History Of The Bonzos* climbs to UK #41.

BOOKER T. AND THE MG'S

Booker T. Jones (keyboards)
Steve Cropper (guitar)
Lewis Steinberg (bass)
Donald "Duck" Dunn (bass)
Al Jackson Jr. (drums)

1962 May Jones (b. Dec.11, 1944, Memphis, Tenn., US), Cropper (b. Oct.21, 1941, Willow Springs, Mo.), Jackson (b. Nov.27, 1935, Memphis) and Steinberg are all working as regular session musicians in Stax Records' Memphi studio (as well as recording as part of the Mar-Keys) when they record two impromptu tracks at the end of a session backing Billy Lee Riley. Stax owner, Jim Stewart, likes the bluesy instrumental *Behave Yourself*, and releases it in US on subsidiary label Volt Records.

July After radio DJs begin playing the B-side, *Green Onions*, a rhythmic organ/guitar instrumental, this is reissued on Stax as the A-side.

Sept *Green Onions* hits US #3 and is certified as a million-seller. It is not a hit in UK at this time, but begins a UK cult following.

Dec LP *Green Onions* reaches US #33.

1963 Jan *Jellybread* is a disappointing second single, reaching only US #82.

Sept *Chinese Checkers* reaches #78 in US.

1964 Mar Steinberg is asked to leave because of unpunctuality for studio sessions, and is replaced by Dunn (b. Nov.24, 1941, Memphis), also a former Mar-Keys member.

Aug LP *Green Onions* is belatedly released in UK and is their first UK success, reaching #11.

1965 July After some lesser-selling records (during which time they also provide backing on hits by most other Stax acts), *Boot-Leg* gives them another medium-sized US hit, reaching #58 and spending 10 weeks on chart.

1967 June *Hip Hug-Her* brings them back to US top 40 success, peaking at #37.

June [16] The group plays Monterey Pop Festival in California, also backing Otis Redding° at the event.

BOOKER T. AND THE MG'S *cont.*

Aug LP *Hip Hug-Her* reaches #35 in US.

Sept An instrumental cover of The Young Rascals'° vocal hit *Groovin'* reaches US #21, while the B-side *Slim Jenkins' Place* (originally titled *Slim Jenkins' Joint*, but changed to avoid possible controversy) climbs to US #70.

1968 Aug *Soul Limbo* reaches #17 in US.

1969 Jan *Soul Limbo* is their first UK singles chart entry, peaking at #30. The Caribbean-flavored tune will be more widely known in later years in UK as the theme to BBC TV's Cricket coverage.

Feb *Hang 'Em High*, theme from the Clint Eastwood movie, returns them to US top 10, at #9.

May *Time Is Tight*, from Booker T.'s own score for the film *Up Tight*, hits US #6. The group's soundtrack LP from the movie climbs to US #98.

June *Time Is Tight* makes #4 in UK, where it is their biggest hit.

July An instrumental revival of Simon and Garfunkel's° *Mrs. Robinson* reaches US #37.

Aug LP *The Booker T. Set* reaches US #53.

Sept UK prefers *Mrs. Robinson's* B-side *Soul Clap '69*, which reaches #35.

1970 June LP *McLemore Avenue* reaches US #76. The LP contains instrumental covers of all songs on The Beatles'° LP *Abbey Road*, and the sleeve photo is also similar, showing the MG's walking across the street outside their studio.

Aug *Something*, from LP *McLemore Avenue*, reaches US #76.

1971 Apr LP *Melting Pot* reaches #43 in US.

May *Melting Pot* is their last US hit single, reaching #45 and on chart for 4 months. Tired of the strain of working with the band and a punishing session schedule at the Stax studios, Jones quits soon afterwards, leaves Memphis, and goes to live and work in LA. (He will marry singer Priscilla Coolidge, sign to A&M Records, and begin a solo career as songwriter and soul vocalist.)

Aug Cropper also leaves Stax to open his own TMI recording studio and label in Memphis and work as a producer and session player, free from previous pressures.

1973 Dunn and Jackson make LP *The MG's* for Stax, with Bobby Manuel (guitar) and Carson Whitsett (keyboards) taking up the two vacant roles, but it raises little interest.

1975 Oct [1] Al Jackson is shot dead when he disturbs an intruder at his Memphis home.

1976 LP *Union Extended*, consisting of previously unreleased Booker T. & The MG's tracks, is released in UK only.

1977 Feb [4] Jones, Cropper and Dunn reunite as part of an all-star band to play on the 25th Birthday show of US TV's "American Bandstand". The trio stays together, adding drummer Willie Hall, to record LP *Universal Language* for Asylum Records which has poor reviews and sales, and it splits again.

1980 Jan Due to its inclusion on soundtrack of the film *Quadrophenia*, *Green Onions* becomes popular again in UK, and finally charts 17½ years after its US top 10 success, hitting #7.

June Cropper and Dunn feature in movie *The Blues Brothers*, as members of the starring duo's backing band. (They will continue into the 1980s as respected freelance players and producers, working with many other acts. Jones continues to have a mildly successful career as a soul vocalist, but is heard of progressively less as the 80s pass.)

THE BOOMTOWN RATS

Bob Geldof (vocals)
Johnnie Fingers (keyboards and vocals)
Gerry Cott (guitar)
Pete Briquette (bass and vocals),
Gerry Roberts (guitar and vocals),
Simon Crowe (drums and vocals)

1975 Having interviewed the likes of Elton John° and Little Richard° for *NME* and other papers as a music journalist, Geldof (b. Oct.5, 1954, Dublin, Ireland) forms the group (originally named The Nightlife Thugs) in Dun Laoghaire, Ireland.

1976 Oct They move to England and are signed to Ensign Records because of their robust new wave sound which is fuller and more disciplined than that of most aspiring UK punk groups.

1977 Sept *Looking After No.1* is issued after weeks of touring the UK, including support dates with Tom Petty°. It reaches UK #11, and LP debut *The Boomtown Rats* climbs to UK #18.

Dec *Mary Of The Fourth Form* makes UK #15.

1978 May *She's So Modern* reaches UK #12.

July *Like Clockwork* is their first top 10 hit, peaking at UK #6, while

second LP *A Tonic For the Troops* hits UK #8 and remains charted for 44 weeks.

Nov *Rat Trap* tops UK chart for 2 weeks.

1979 Jan [29] San Diego, Cal., schoolgirl Brenda Spencer shoots and kills several of her schoolmates. Pressed for a reason, she says: "I don't like Mondays", which inspires Geldof to write a song.

Apr [7] Their first American tour includes the California Music Festival, alongside Ted Nugent°, Aerosmith°, Cheap Trick° and Van Halen°.

May US tour ends at the New York Palladium.

July *I Don't Like Mondays* hits UK #1 in its second week on chart, and remains top for 4 weeks, and (aided by a striking promo video), becomes the Rats' biggest-selling single. It is also their most controversial, as Spencer's parents attempt to have the song banned in the US, and many US radio stations refuse to program it. Despite this, it will become their sole US hit, making #73 in Mar.1980.

Nov LP *The Fine Art of Surfacing*, chiefly the work of Geldof and Fingers, reaches UK #7.

Dec *Diamond Smiles* peaks at #13 in UK.

1980 Feb *Someone's Looking At You* hits UK #4. After promoting it, the band sets off on a lengthy world tour which covers Europe, US, Japan and Australia.

Dec A switch to Mercury Records sees release of *Banana Republic*, which hits UK #3.

1981 Feb LP *Mondo Bongo* reaches UK #6, while *The Elephants' Graveyard (Guilty)*, taken from it, peaks at #26. Gerry Cott leaves soon after, and the band continues as a quintet.

Dec *Never In A Million Years* peaks at UK #62, their first disappointing single placing.

1982 Apr *House On Fire*, with an offbeat arrangement, rekindles interest and peaks at UK #24. LP *V Deep* reaches only UK #64.

June *Charmed Lives* is their first single to fail to chart in UK.

Aug Geldof has a starring role in *The Wall*, a movie based on the 1979 Pink Floyd° LP of the same title.

1984 Feb *Tonight* shows briefly in UK chart at #73.

May *Drag Me Down* reaches UK #50, and is the last Boomtown Rats UK hit single.

Nov Geldof, with Midge Ure, writes and organizes the recording of Band Aid's° *Do They Know It's Christmas?*, which becomes the biggest-selling record ever in the UK. The other Boomtown Rats are also in the Band Aid° personnel. Geldof now throws himself full time into humanitarian concerns, becoming the conscience of the UK (and later, the Western World) with regard to Third World starvation. He sets aside his musical career, and The Boomtown Rats effectively ceases to be.

1985 Jan [28] Geldof participates in the making of the US equivalent of the Band Aid° record, USA For Africa's *We Are The World*.

Jul [13] The band is together to play at Wembley in the UK leg of the Live Aid concert, also organized by Geldof.

1986 Jun Geldof receives an honorary knighthood from HM The Queen, in recognition of his humanitarian activities, and is henceforth Bob Geldof KBE.

Aug Geldof marries his long-time girlfriend, UK TV presenter and writer, Paula Yates.

Nov Geldof launches a solo recording career on Mercury Records with *This Is The World Calling*, which reaches UK #25. Solo LP *Deep In The Heart Of Nowhere*, however, fails to chart. (He will continue his work effort for the Band Aid° charity, while in 1987 becoming a star of UK TV commercials for milk.)

PAT BOONE

1955 Jan After winning on the "Ted Mack" and "Arthur Godfrey" US TV talent shows, Boone (b. Charles Boone, June 1, 1934, Jacksonville, Fla., US, and the great-great-great-great grandson of western pioneer Daniel Boone) signs to Dot Records. Married to Shirley Foley (daughter of country singer Red Foley), he has previously made some C&W records for the Republic label, but is also a student of Speech and English at Columbia University.

Apr First Dot release covers Otis Williams and The Charms' R&B song *Two Hearts, Two Kisses*, and reaches US #16. Covers of R&B originals will become a Boone forte in his early career.

Sept *Ain't That A Shame*, a rock-styled cover of a Fats Domino° song, hits #2 in US and is his first million-seller (Domino's original makes US #10 at the same time). Boone will always introduce the song on stage as *Isn't That A Shame*, since the English student in him finds the title ungrammatical.

Nov A cover of The El Dorados' R&B rocker *At My Front Door (Crazy Little Mama)* reaches US #7, while the ballad B-side *No Arms Can Ever Hold You* makes #26 in its own right.

Dec *Ain't That A Shame* is his UK chart debut, reaching #5.

1956 Jan *Gee Whittakers!* makes US #19.

Mar Contrasting coupling of ballad *I'll Be Home*, covered from The Moonglows, and rocker *Tutti Frutti* from Little Richard°, is his first double-sided US top 20 hit, as the songs peak at #5 and #12 respectively to make his second million-seller.

June Another Little Richard° cover *Long Tall Sally* makes US #8, while *I'll Be Home* is his second, and all-time biggest, UK hit, topping the chart for 6 weeks. Because of its lyrics, the song will be a regularly-requested item on armed forces radio shows in UK for the next 10 years.

Aug A cover of Ivory Joe Hunter's *I Almost Lost My Mind* hits US #1; his third million-seller. The B-side *I'm In Love With You* reaches #57.

Sept *I Almost Lost My Mind* reaches #8 in UK, with *Long Tall Sally* simultaneously making #18.

Oct A further million-seller is film theme *Friendly Persuasion*, which makes US #8 while its B-side *Chains Of Love* peaks at #20.

Nov LP *Howdy!* reaches US #14.

1957 Feb *Don't Forbid Me*, a ballad rejected by Elvis Presley° and recorded in 15 minutes by Boone at the end of a session, hits US #1 and is his fifth million-seller. The B-side *Anastasia* reaches #37. In UK, *Friendly Persuasion* peaks at #3.

Mar *Don't Forbid Me* stays at UK #2 for 5 weeks, kept from the chart top by Dot label-mate Tab Hunter with *Young Love*.

Apr Rocker *Why Baby Why* hits US #6. Ballad B-side *I'm Waiting Just For You* reaches #27, and is another US million-seller.

May *Why Baby Why* reaches #17 in UK.

June *Love Letters In The Sand* tops US chart for 5 weeks, and is his biggest-selling record (3½ million copies). It is sung in the film *Bernadine*, in which which he makes his starring movie debut opposite Terry Moore, after successfully screen-testing for 20th Century Fox. Title song *Bernadine*, on the B-side, reaches #23, and the two hits stay on US chart for 34 and 26 weeks respectively. On US LP chart, inspirational EP *A Closer Walk With Thee* reaches #13.

Aug *Love Letters In The Sand* is another long-staying UK #2, holding the position for 8 weeks behind Paul Anka's° *Diana*.

Sept *Remember You're Mine* reaches UK #10, while B-side *There's A Gold Mine In The Sky* makes #28; Boone's eighth million-seller. LP *Pat* peaks at US #20.

Oct [3] "The Pat Boone Chevy Showroom", a weekly musical series, begins on ABC TV in US (and will run until mid-1960).

Nov *Remember You're Mine* hits #5 in UK.

Dec *April Love* is taken from film of the same title, his second starring role (opposite Shirley Jones, later of The Partridge Family), and tops US chart for 2 weeks, becoming another million-seller. The song is nominated for an Oscar in 1958. Compilation LP *Pat's Great Hits* hits US #3, while his inspirational LP *Hymns We Love* climbs to #21, and soundtrack LP from *April Love* peaks at #12. In UK, seasonal *White Christmas* reaches #30.

1958 Feb *April Love* reaches #7 in UK.

PAT BOONE *cont.*

Mar Gospel rocker *A Wonderful Time Up There* (an oldie originally titled Gospel Boogie) hits US #10, and B-side ballad *It's Too Soon To Know* makes #14. This is his tenth million- seller.

May *A Wonderful Time Up There* hits UK #2, while *It's Too Soon To Know* reaches #8.

June *Sugar Moon* climbs to US #5, peaking just as Boone graduates from Columbia University with a degree in Speech and English. His eleventh million-seller, this also ends a run of nine consecutive singles which have topped a million apiece in US sales.

July *If Dreams Came True* reaches US #7, and B-side *That's How Much I Love You* makes #39. In UK, *Sugar Moon* climbs to #6.

Sept LP *Stardust* hits US #2 and UK #10.

Oct *For My Good Fortune* makes US #31, and B-side *Gee But It's Lonely* (written for Boone by Phil Everly of The Everly Brothers°) climbs to #31. In UK, *If Dreams Came True* makes #13.

Dec Boone stars in film musical *Mardi Gras*, from which *I'll Remember Tonight* makes US #34. In UK, *Gee But It's Lonely* reaches #30.

1959 Feb *With The Wind And The Rain In Your Hair* reaches US #21. The B-side revives an early Elvis Presley° hit, *Good Rockin' Tonight*, and climbs to US #49. Meanwhile, *I'll Remember Tonight* reaches UK #17.

Apr *For A Penny* reaches US #23, and *With The Wind And The Rain In Your Hair* peaks at UK #21.

July *Twixt Twelve And Twenty* peaks at US #17. The title is taken from a book written by Boone, giving advice to teenagers on the conduct of their lives and loves, which adds greatly to his "do-gooder" clean-cut image. In UK, *For A Penny* reaches #19.

Aug LP *Tenderly* reaches US #17, and *Twixt Twelve And Twenty* makes UK #16.

Oct *Fool's Hall Of Fame* reaches US #29.

Dec *Beyond The Sunset* peaks at US #71, Boone's poorest-selling single to date.

1960 Mar *(Welcome) New Lovers* puts him back in US top 20 at #18.

May Inspirational LP *He Leadeth Me* reaches #12 in UK, while not having charted in US.

June *Walking The Floor Over You* reaches US #44, with B-side *Spring Rain* pacing it at #50, while LP *Moonglow* peaks at #26. In UK, 1957 LP *Hymns We Love* belatedly charts at #14, to follow the UK success of his other LP of hymns.

July *Walking The Floor Over You* makes #28 in UK.

Aug *Delia Gone* reaches #66 in US.

Nov More split popularity for *Dear John*, which makes US #44, and B-side *Alabam*, almost matching it at #47.

1961 Feb *The Exodus Song*, which adds Boone's own lyrics to the film theme, reaches US #64.

June Sale fortunes revive dramatically with *Moody River*, a deceptively jaunty song with a lyric about suicide, which hits US #1 for a week and sells over a million.

July *Moody River* reaches UK #14.

Sept *Big Cold Wind* climbs to US #19, and LP *Moody River* reaches US #29.

Dec Seasonal LP *White Christmas* reaches US #39.

1962 Jan *Johnny Will* peaks at US #35 and hits UK #4.

Mar *I'll See You In My Dreams* climbs to US #32 and UK #17.

Apr He stars in the musical film *State Fair*, with Bobby Darin° and Ann-Margret. The soundtrack LP climbs to #12 in US.

May *Quando Quando Quando* charts briefly in US at #95, and slightly better in UK at #41.

July Boone's last major hit is *Speedy Gonzales*, a novelty rock disk featuring the voice of the cartoon character. It hits US #6 and UK #2 (where it stays for 5 weeks behind Frank Ifield's *I Remember You*), and is a chart-topper in many other countries, selling over 2 million copies worldwide.

Oct *Ten Lonely Guys* peaks at #45 in US, while compilation LP *Pat Boone's Golden Hits* makes US #66.

Dec He stars in movie *The Main Attraction* with Mai Zetterling, from which the title song is released in UK and reaches #12. This is Boone's last UK chart single.

1963 Mar Bossa nova-styled *Meditation* reaches US #91.

June He stars in British-made romantic comedy film *Never Put It In Writing*.

1964 Oct *Beach Girl*, in a contemporary surf music arrangement, makes US #72.

1966 Dec Humorously-styled *Wish You Were Here, Buddy* makes US #49. This is his last chart success on Dot Records, which he leaves shortly after, to move briefly to Capitol, and then to Bill Cosby's Tetragrammaton label.

1969 Apr His last US hit (and only one for the short-lived Tetragrammaton) is a cover of John Stewart's *July, You're A Woman*, which spends 2 weeks at #100.

1970s With the hits dried up, his recording career takes a back seat to his TV, cabaret and Christian activities from here on. His style becomes country-oriented via recordings for MGM and for Motown's Melodyland country label, and he will also record with his four (now grown) daughters.

1976 May Compilation double LP *Pat Boone Originals*, featuring forty 1955-62 Dot label hits, climbs to UK #16, aided by TV advertising.

1977 Oct Boone's third daughter, Debby Boone, makes solo record *You Light Up My Life*, theme song from the film of the same title, and it becomes the year's biggest hit in the US, topping the chart for 10 consecutive weeks, and selling over 2 million copies, thus surpassing the achievements of most of her father's records. (Boone himself will never attempt a serious musical comeback in later years, but remains a frequently seen US TV personality.)

BOSTON

Tom Scholz (guitar and keyboards)
Brad Delp (guitar and vocals)
Barry Goudreau (guitar)
Fran Sheehan (bass)
Sib Hashian (drums)

1975 While a product designer for Polaroid, Scholz (b. Mar.10, 1947, Toledo, Ohio, US), makes sophisticated rock demos with musician friends in his spare time, using a self- constructed basement studio in Boston, Mass., US.

1976 His demos sufficiently impress US Epic label to gain a recording contract for him and his friends Delp (b. June 12, 1951, Boston), Goudreau (b. Nov.29, 1951, Boston), Sheehan (b. Mar.26, 1949, Boston) and Hashian (b. Aug.17, 1949, Boston). They are named Boston after their home base. Their debut LP, mostly featuring Scholz's basement originals, is completed in LA studio sessions with producer John Boylan.

Sept LP *Boston* is released in US. It hits #3 and eventually sells over 6 million copies.

Dec *More Than A Feeling* reaches US #5.

1977 Jan *More Than A Feeling* charts in UK, at #12.

Feb *Long Time* climbs to US #22. LP *Boston* makes UK #11.

June *Peace Of Mind* reaches US #38.

Sept LP *Don't Look Back* hits UK #9.

Oct *Don't Look Back* reaches US #4 and UK #43.

1978 Nov [4,5] The band plays live in Boston itself for the first time; two sold-out shows at Boston Garden.

1979 Jan *A Man I'll Never Be* makes US #31.

1986 Oct After a 7-year absence during which Boston has been all but forgotten, the band resurfaces on MCA Records with LP *Third Stage*, which hits US #1 and reaches UK #37. Extract *Amanda* climbs to US #1, but fails to chart in UK.

1987 Feb *We're Ready* reaches US #9, with no UK interest, but US renaissance is enough to restore Boston to the large-venue US live circuit they attained so effortlessly in the 1970s.

DAVID BOWIE

1964 Jan Bowie (b. David Jones, Jan.8, 1947, Brixton, London, UK) forms The King Bees with school friend George Underwood, while working at an advertising agency.

June The group releases a one-off UK single *Liza Jane*, on Decca's Vocalion label, with little success.

Dec Bowie moves to new London-based group The Manish Boys.

1965 Mar The Manish Boys sign to Parlophone label at EMI, and release *I Pity The Fool*, another non-seller.

Mar [8] First TV appearance is on "Gadzooks! It's All Happening" with The Manish Boys, who are almost barred from playing because of the length of Bowie's hair.

June The Manish Boys disbands. Bowie forms The Lower Third, playing summer gigs in seaside towns.

Aug The Lower Third records *You've Got A Habit Of Leaving* for Parlophone. It is attributed to Davy Jones.

Sept After seeing The Lower Third at London's Marquee club, Ken Pitt becomes Bowie's manager.

1966 Jan The Lower Third signs to Pye Records, and Bowie adopts his professional surname for the first time after Pitt learns that another Davy Jones has been signed for new US TV group The Monkees°. *Can't Help Thinking About Me*, by David Bowie & The Lower Third, is released in UK by Pye. Much airplay on major pirate station Radio London makes it his best seller yet, but still no hit.

Feb The Lower Third splits up, and Bowie continues as a soloist.

Apr First solo single is *Do Anything You Say*, again not a hit.

Aug He plays "The Bowie Showboat", a regular Sunday afternoon slot at Marquee club, London, backed by The Buzz and broadcast by sponsor Radio London. *I Dig Everything* is released unsuccessfully by Pye, which then drops Bowie's contract.

Sept Pitt persuades Denny Cordell at Decca Records' new "progressive" Deram label to sign Bowie.

Dec *Rubber Band* is first Deram single, again unsuccessful.

1967 Apr *The Laughing Gnome*, a novelty song in Anthony Newley style, is released, but is not a success at this time.

June First LP *David Bowie* is released by Deram, garnering good reviews but unimpressive sales.

July *Love You Till Tuesday*, from the LP, is released in UK.

Aug Bowie meets fringe theatrical Lindsay Kemp and takes mime and dance lessons from him.

Dec He works on tracks for BBC "Top Gear" radio show with producer Tony Visconti, the beginning of a long working partnership. He appears in Kemp's mime production *Pierrot In Turquoise*, in Oxford.

1968 July He forms a trio named Feathers, with his girlfriend Hermione Farthingale and bassist John Hutchinson; they record privately but never professionally, and play live at London's Middle Earth and some other clubs and colleges.

1969 Feb Feathers disbands, and Bowie and Pitt make a 30-minute film intended for TV, based around songs from the first LP and a new number, *Space Oddity*.

May Bowie co-founds the Beckenham Arts Lab, a performance club in a pub back room in south London suburbs where he regularly tries out new material.

June He meets Angela (Angie) Barnet (whom he will later marry) at a reception at The Speakeasy Club, London, for King Crimson°. Calvin Lee of UK Mercury label at Philips Records has heard *Space Oddity*, and convinced it will hit, offers a new record deal.

June [20] Bowie signs to Philips and the same day is in Trident Studio, London, re-recording *Space Oddity* with producer Gus Dudgeon.

July [11] *Space Oddity* is released in UK.

Aug [5] Bowie's father dies.

Aug He wins song festivals in Malta and Italy with *When I Live My Dream*. He organizes and plays in The Beckenham Free Festival, which 5000 attend at a recreation ground; it is later commemorated in his song *Memory Of A Free Festival*.

Sept Following strong airplay helped by general space fervor after the US moon landing, *Space Oddity* is his first UK chart entry, reaching #5.

Oct As an acoustic solo act, he supports Humble Pie° on a UK tour.

Nov Bowie and Angie Barnet move into a flat in Haddon Hall, Beckenham, Kent. LP *David Bowie*, produced by now close friend Tony Visconti, is released in UK on Philips, and in US as *Man Of Words, Man Of Music* on Mercury. Bowie receives Ivor Novello Award from UK Songwriters Guild for *Space Oddity*, recognizing outstanding originality.

1970 Feb He forms new backing band, Hype, with Visconti on bass, John Cambridge on drums, and Mick Ronson on guitar.

Mar *The Prettiest Star*, written for Angie, is issued as a UK single.

Mar [20] Bowie and Angie Barnet are married at Bromley Registry Office.

June *Memory Of A Free Festival* is issued as a UK single, re-recorded with new backing by Hype, who now has Mick "Woody" Woodmansey on drums.

Aug Bowie and Pitt part amicably. Tony DeFries, originally brought in to handle financial affairs, becomes his new manager.

Nov LP *The Man Who Sold The World* is released in US before UK, but makes no impression. US Mercury Records arranges a promotional trip there to push the LP to DJs and media.

1971 Jan Single *Holy Holy* is released.

Jan [27] Bowie arrives in US for his first visit. He does not perform live because of work permit problems, but gets plenty of publicity when he wears dresses in Texas and LA.

Mar Bowie works with Arnold Corns, a group based around his protégé dress designer Freddi Burretti (renamed Rudi Valentino). He plays and sings on single *Moonage Daydream*. After this fails to sell, Arnold Corns disbands.

Apr LP *The Man Who Sold The World* is released in UK, but with a different sleeve showing Bowie in a dress. This is later withdrawn and copies of the original, which does not sell well, will become very high-priced collectors' items. Demo recordings are made for what will become the LP *Hunky Dory*. Visconti is no longer available to play bass, and Trevor Bolder is recruited.

May [28] Duncan Zowie Haywood is born in Bromley Hospital, Kent, son of David and Angie Bowie.

June Peter Noone (of Herman's Hermits°) charts in UK with Bowie song *Oh You Pretty Things*, reaching #12. Tony DeFries negotiates the signing of Bowie to RCA Records worldwide, on the strength of the *Hunky Dory* demo tapes and commercial success of *Oh You Pretty Things* in UK.

June [20] He plays solo acoustic set at Glastonbury Fayre, a hippy-slanted UK festival.

July Tracks for what will become the LP *Ziggy Stardust* are recorded.

Dec LP *Hunky Dory* is released, with no immediate success.

1972 Jan *Changes* is first RCA Bowie single. It has no UK chart success but gives him a US chart debut at #66. Bowie declares his bisexuality in an interview in *Melody Maker*.

Feb Lengthy UK tour starts with a slot in the Lancaster Arts Festival. On tour the band acquires the name The Spiders, from the next LP title.

Apr LP *Hunky Dory* makes a belated US chart showing at #176, the first Bowie LP chart entry anywhere. *Starman* is released as a single.

June LP *The Rise And Fall Of Ziggy Stardust And The Spiders From Mars* is released and proves UK LP chart breakthrough, climbing to #5. It reaches US #75.

July *Starman* charts, reaching UK #10 and US #65.

July [8] Lou Reed° joins Bowie and band live on stage at London's Royal Festival Hall, at a concert to benefit Save the Whale campaign.

Sept [7] Long UK tour finally ends in Hanley, Stoke-on-Trent.

Sept *John I'm Only Dancing* is released in UK, and reaches #12. LP *Hunky Dory* charts in the wake of *Ziggy Stardust*, hitting UK #3.

Sept [22] Debut US tour by Bowie and The Spiders begins in Cleveland.

Sept [28] Bowie sells out first-ever New York show at Carnegie Hall.

Nov RCA reissues LP *The Man Who Sold The World* and the first Philips/Mercury LP, now retitled *Space Oddity*, in both UK and US. They now chart at UK #26, US #105, and at UK #17, US #16 respectively. *The Jean Genie*, written on the road in US and recorded in New York, is released as a single, climbing to UK #2 but only US #71.

Dec Bowie returns by sea at the end of US tour, and plays a Christmas Eve concert at The Rainbow, London.

1973 Jan *Space Oddity* single is reissued by RCA in the US, this time charting at #15 – his first US top 20 hit.

DAVID BOWIE *cont.*

Jan [25] He departs aboard the QE2 on a 100-day world tour, opening in US.
Apr [8] Japanese leg of tour opens in Tokyo. He also plays at Hiroshima.
Apr LP *Aladdin Sane*, with songs written on first US tour, is released, and hits UK #1 and US #12. *Drive-In Saturday* hits UK #3.
May [12] A week after completing the world tour, he plays to 18,000 fans at Earls Court, London.
May [16] UK tour opens in Aberdeen.
June Prompted by onstage popularity, *Life On Mars* is issued as a UK single, hitting #3.
July UK tour closes at Hammersmith Odeon, London, where Bowie announces on stage that he is to retire from live performing. Although he is tired and genuinely wants several years' rest, it eventually transpires that the *Ziggy Stardust* fantasy stage persona is being retired, not Bowie.
Sept Deram reissues *The Laughing Gnome*, which this time charts at UK #6.
Oct LP *Pin-Ups*, containing revivals of Bowie's favorites by other acts from the 1960s, is released, tops UK LP chart and makes US #23. A revival of The Merseys' *Sorrow*, from the LP, hits UK #3.
Oct [18] Bowie films US TV show "The Midnight Special" at the Marquee, London, with guests The Troggs° and Marianne Faithfull°.
Dec RCA announces that Bowie has sold 1,056,400 LPs and 1,024,068 singles in UK alone since it signed him.

1974 Feb Lulu° revives *The Man Who Sold The World* and it climbs to UK #3. Bowie produces and sings backing vocals on the single.
Mar *Rebel Rebel* hits UK #5.
Apr He travels to US, where he will live and work for almost 2 years.
May *Rock And Roll Suicide* makes UK #22.
June [14] "Diamond Dogs" tour, a highly choreographed and theatrical stage performance drawing on concepts from the LP, opens in Montreal, Canada.
June LP *Diamond Dogs* is released, with a controversial sleeve painting by Belgian artist Guy Peellaert. It hits UK #1 and US #5. *Rebel Rebel* is released as a US single, and reaches #64.
July *Diamond Dogs* single reaches UK #21, but fails to chart in US.
July [20] Tour closes at Madison Square Garden, New York. Plans to take it to London prove financially unsound.
Oct A revival of Eddie Floyd's° *Knock On Wood* climbs to UK #10.
Nov LP *David Live*, recorded at The Tower, Philadelphia on the "Diamond Dogs" tour, hits UK #2 and US #8.
Dec *Changes*, a belated US single release, reaches #41.

1975 Jan Bowie initiates legal action to break from manager DeFries.
Jan [26] BBC TV "Omnibus" program shows a documentary film on Bowie, *Cracked Actor*.
Feb Nicolas Roeg signs him to star in the movie *The Man Who Fell To Earth*.
Mar *Young Americans* reaches UK #18 and US #28.
Apr LP *Young Americans*, highlighting new soul-based style, hits UK #2 and US #9. John Lennon° plays on two tracks.
July Bowie begins filming *The Man Who Fell To Earth*.
Aug/Sept *Fame*, co-written with Lennon°, is extracted from LP. Reaches UK #17, but is his most successful US single ever, making #1 for 2 weeks.
Oct *Space Oddity* is reissued in UK on a 3-track single with *Changes* and the previously unissued *Velvet Goldmine*. It tops UK chart for 2 weeks.

1976 Jan *Golden Years*, from the new LP, reaches UK #8 and US #10.
Feb [2] World tour opens in Vancouver, Canada.
Feb LP *Station To Station* hits UK #5 and US #3. Bowie sues manager Michael Lippman after firing him.
Mar [18] Première of *The Man Who Fell To Earth* in London is not attended by Bowie, who is on tour in US.
Mar [21] Bowie is arrested with Iggy Pop° and others at a Massachusetts hotel on suspicion of marijuana possession, and bailed for $2,000. The case is adjourned and dropped a year later.
Mar [26] The US portion of the world tour ends in New York. He sails for Europe.
Apr [27] After a trip to Moscow, Bowie is detained for hours on a train at the Russian/Polish border by customs officers who take exception to Nazi books and mementoes found in his luggage. It is research material for a film on Goebbels.
May [3-8] He plays 6 shows at Wembley, London, his first UK gigs for almost 3 years.
June *TVC 15* is only a moderate single success – UK #33 and US #64. LP *Changesonebowie*, a compilation of past hits selected by Bowie, reaches UK #2 and US #10.
Oct He moves to West Berlin to live semi-reclusively for a while.

1977 Jan LP *Low* is released, introducing synthesized "European" sound, and hits UK #2 and US #11.
Mar *Sound And Vision*, from the LP, hits UK #3 but stalls in US at #69.
Sept [9] He appears on Marc Bolan's° UK TV show, "Marc", singing *Heroes* and a duet with Bolan titled *Standing Next To You*. Afterwards they tape demos, but Bolan's death only days later [16], ends the possibility of further work together.
Sept [11] Bowie records guest appearance on a Christmas TV show being made by Bing Crosby, duetting with Crosby on *The Little Drummer Boy*. (Crosby will die a month later, before the show is screened, but the duet will be a UK hit 5 years later.)
Oct *Heroes* single reaches UK #24. French and German-language versions are released in those countries.
Nov LP *Heroes* is released, reaching UK #3 and US #35.

1978 Jan *Beauty And The Beast*, from LP *Heroes*, is a minor UK hit at #39. Bowie and wife Angie agree to split. He begins filming *Just A Gigolo* in Berlin, with Sydne Rome and Marlene Dietrich, directed by David Hemmings.
Mar He speaks the narration on a new version of Prokofiev's *Peter And The Wolf*, issued on LP by RCA, with Eugene Ormandy conducting The Philadelphia Orchestra.
Mar [29] 1978 world tour starts in San Diego, California.
May [9] US part of the tour ends at Madison Square Garden, NY.
May [14] First European tour date, in Hamburg, West Germany.
June [14] First UK date, in Newcastle.
July [1] First leg of tour closes at Earls Court, London.
Sept 1964 King Bees' single *Liza Jane* is reissued in UK, without success.
Oct Double live LP *Stage* hits UK #5.
Nov [11] World tour recommences in Adelaide, Australia.
Nov [16] World première of *Just A Gigolo*, in West Berlin.
Dec [6] First Japanese tour date, in Osaka.
Dec [12] World tour ends in Tokyo, and Bowie and son Zowie stay for Christmas in Japan.

1979 May *Boys Keep Swinging* reaches UK #7. LP *Lodger* is released, and hits UK #4.
Aug *DJ* reaches UK #29.
Dec Unissued 1975 version of *John I'm Only Dancing* appears as a single, reaching UK #12.
Dec [31] He sings new acoustic version of *Space Oddity* on UK TV's "Kenny Everett New Year TV Show".

1980 Feb [8] Divorce becomes final between Bowie and Angie. He gains the custody of son Zowie, now known as Joe. Angie gets £30,000 settlement.
Mar Brecht/Weill's *Alabama Song* is revived on a UK single, coupled with the acoustic *Space Oddity*. It climbs to #23, with little exposure.
June Bowie researches the history of John Merrick, the Elephant Man, in London, prior to portraying him on stage in the US.
July [29] He opens on stage in Denver, in the title role of *The Elephant Man*, breaking the venue's box office record and pleasing the critics.
Aug *Ashes To Ashes*, a continuation of the *Major Tom* saga, from *Space Oddity*, is Bowie's second UK #1 single.
Aug [5] *The Elephant Man* moves from Denver to Chicago for 3 weeks.
Sept LP *Scary Monsters And Super Creeps* is released, and hits UK #1.
Sept [23] *The Elephant Man* opens on Broadway, New York, with Bowie.
Oct He films a cameo appearance for German movie, *Christiane F.*
Nov *Fashion* hits UK #5 and restores him to US singles chart at #70.

1981 Jan [3] Final night in *The Elephant Man* on Broadway.
Jan TV-advertised LP *The Very Best Of David Bowie* hits UK #3. *Scary Monsters* single makes UK #20.
Feb [24] He receives #1 Male Singer award in the annual UK Rock & Pop Awards.
Apr *Up The Hill Backwards* reaches #32 in UK.
July At Montreux, Switzerland, Bowie records vocal for Giorgio Moroder's theme for the film *Cat People*, and also joins Queen° in the studio, where they record *Under Pressure*.

Aug He takes the title role in Berthold Brecht's *Baal*, in a production being filmed for TV by the BBC.

Nov *Under Pressure* by Queen° and David Bowie hits UK #1 and will climb to US #29.

Dec *Wild Is The Wind* reaches UK #24. Compilation LP *Changestwobowie* is issued, reaching UK #24 and US #68.

1982 Feb *Christiane F*, a huge box office hit in Germany, is shown in US, having premièred in UK in Dec.

Mar [2] *Baal* is shown on BBC TV. A 5-song EP of songs from the play reaches #29.

Mar He starts filming *The Hunger*, a fantasy about vampirism co-starring Catherine Deneuve.

Apr *Cat People (Putting Out Fire)*, the movie theme with Bowie vocal, is issued on single, reaching UK #26 and US #67.

July Bowie completes filming *The Hunger*.

Sept He begins filming *Merry Christmas Mr. Lawrence* in the Pacific, with co-stars Tom Conti and Riuichi Sakamoto.

Nov Work ends on *Merry Christmas Mr. Lawrence* and he flies to New York for LP recording sessions.

Dec His 1977 duet with Bing Crosby, *Peace On Earth-Little Drummer Boy*, issued as a UK single, hits #3.

1983 Jan [27] He signs a new 5-year recording contract in New York with EMI America Records, reportedly worth $10 million.

Apr First EMI single *Let's Dance* hits UK #1 and stays there for 3 weeks. It tops US chart in May, to become the first Bowie single to be a #1 in both US and UK. It is also his first million-selling single since *Fame*. LP *Let's Dance* is released, and hits UK #1 and US #4.

May [30] Prior to touring, he tops the bill of US '83 Festival in San Bernardino, Cal., being paid a record fee of $1½ million.

June [2] "Serious Moonlight '83" UK tour opens at Wembley Arena, London. Each show is sold out within the day of announcement.

June *China Girl* hits UK #2 despite a BBC ban on its video (which has a brief nude sex scene. It reaches US #10.

July [12] "Serious Moonlight '83" North American tour opens in Montreal, Canada.

Oct *Modern Love* hits UK #2 and US #14.

Nov [24] Pacific leg of the tour opens in New Zealand.

Dec [12] Final date of "Serious Moonlight '83", in Bangkok, Thailand.

1984 Sept LP *Tonight* is released, to generally disappointing critical reaction.

Oct *Blue Jean* reaches UK #6 and US #8.

Dec *Tonight* charts at the same low spot (#53) in both UK and US.

1985 Feb Bowie links with highly-rated jazz group, The Pat Metheny Band, on *This Is Not America*, theme for the movie *The Falcon And The Snowman* (in which he does not appear). It reaches UK #14 and US #32.

June *Loving The Alien* reaches UK #19.

July [13] He appears in the Live Aid concert at Wembley, UK, shown worldwide on TV, and also records a revival of Martha & The Vandellas'° *Dancing In The Street* with Mick Jagger, introduced via video at Live Aid, with the promise that all its royalties will go to the appeal.

Sept *Dancing In The Street* is released, entering UK chart at #1 and holding top slot for a month. It makes US #7.

1986 Mar The theme from movie *Absolute Beginners*, in which Bowie has a character part, hits UK #2, but only #53 in US.

Apr *Absolute Beginners* opens in the UK, to mixed reception.

July *Underground*, the theme from *Labyrinth*, a spectacular children's fantasy film in which Bowie plays the Goblin King, reaches UK #21.

Nov He sings the theme for full-length cartoon film *When The Wind Blows*, which deals with nuclear holocaust. It reaches UK #44 as a single.

1987 Apr *Day In-Day Out* reaches UK #17. UK BBC TV bans the promo video claiming it "contains disturbing images". Meanwhile, Bowie flies round the world with his new live band (including one-time schoolfriend Peter Frampton° on guitar), holding a series of press conferences/performances to announce dates and venues of his forthcoming world tour (to cover Europe, UK, US, Australia and Japan, and to be named after *Glass Spiders*, a track on his imminent LP).

May LP *Never Let Me Down* reaches UK #6 and US #34, while the 'Glass Spider" 1987 world tour, featuring Peter Frampton as lead guitarist, begins in Rotterdam, Holland.

June Guest acts on individual "Glass Spider" tour dates in UK cities include Alison Moyet°, Big Country°, and Terence Trent D'Arby°.

July *Time Will Crawl*, taken from the LP, peaks at UK #33.

Oct A woman in Dallas, Tex., US, alleges being sexually attacked by Bowie "in a Dracula-like fashion" in a hotel room after a US "Glass Spider" tour concert. Bowie dismisses her as a sensation-seeker, and the charges are eventually thrown out of court.

THE BOX TOPS/BIG STAR

Alex Chilton (guitar and vocals)
Gary Talley (guitar)
John Evans (organ)
Bill Cunningham (bass and piano)
Danny Smythe (drums)

1967 After high school, Chilton (b. Dec.20, 1950, Memphis, Tenn., US), Talley (b. Aug.17, 1947, Memphis), Cunningham (b. Jan.23, 1950, Memphis), Evans and Smythe form as a white soul group in Memphis, and come to the attention of producer/writer Dan Penn, who works with them at the city's American Recording Studios.

July The group is signed to Bell Records' Mala label, debuting with *The Letter*, produced by Penn.

Sept *The Letter* tops US chart and sells over a million copies.

Oct *The Letter* hits #5 in UK.

Dec *Neon Rainbow* reaches #24 in US.

1968 Apr *Cry Like A Baby*, featuring a distinctive electric sitar sound, reaches US #2 and UK #15, and is their second million-seller. Evans and Smythe leave the group to go back to college and are replaced by Rick Allen on organ and bass, and Tom Boggs on drums.

June *Choo Choo Train* reaches #26 in US.

Oct Gospel-flavored, *I Met Her In Church*, climbs to US #37.

1969 Feb *Sweet Cream Ladies, Forward March* reaches US #28.

May Bob Dylan° song *I Shall Be Released* reaches US #67. Jerry Riley joins on guitar, replacing Gary Talley.

Aug The group returns to US top 20 with *Soul Deep* (#18); it is also their third and last hit at UK #22.

Nov *Turn On A Dream* reaches US #58.

1970 Mar They move to Bell label for final chart hit *You Keep Tightening Up On Me* (US #92). The line-up changes: Cunningham leaves, and Swain Scharfer (piano) and Harold Cloud (bass) join.

1972 The group having lost impetus, Chilton leaves to form Big Star. He and songwriting partner, guitarist Chris Bell (b. Jan.12, 1951, Memphis), recruit bassist Andy Hummel (b. Jan.26, 1951, Memphis) and drummer Jody Stephens (b. Oct.4, 1952) and work on combining Beatle°-style harmonies and punch guitars, later identified as "power pop".

Apr They sign to Terry Manning's Memphis-based Ardent label, associated with Stax, and make LP *#1 Record*. Stax, oriented to black music, finds the LP hard to promote, and it does not sell.

1973 After heavy studio disagreements with Chilton, Bell leaves to continue songwriting in Memphis (then to pursue a minor solo acoustic career that will take him to the UK in 1975).

1974 Feb LP *Radio City* is released, to critical approval but few sales. Meanwhile, Tommy Cogbill, who produced later Box Tops' Mala hits, revives the group one last time with *Willobee And Dale* on Stax. However, its name means little commercially now and the single and The Box Tops disappear.

1975 After recording third LP with the aid of guitarist Steve Cropper and other session men, Big Star breaks up with the LP unreleased, and Chilton goes to New York for a solo career which will regularly find critical interest and a cult following, but no chart success.

1978 July LP *#1 Record/Radio City* is released in UK for the first time, as a double package. The previously unheard *Third Album* also belatedly appears, on UK Aura label.

Dec [27] Bell is killed in a car crash in Memphis.

BILLY BRAGG

1977 Following 4 years of dead-end jobs after leaving school, Bragg (b. Dec.20, 1957, Barking, London, UK) forms punk/R&B band Riff Raff. They record the EP *I Wanna Be A Cosmonaut* for Chiswick Records, but manage few sales.

1981 Riff Raff splits, and unemployed Bragg signs up for the British Army. Posted to a tank division, he finds he cannot stand army life and buys himself out after 90 days.

1982 He begins to tour the UK as a solo singer/songwriter, keeping on the road via bus and train.

BILLY BRAGG *cont.*

1983 He is given 3 afternoons of studio time to record demos of his songs for music publisher Chappell.

July The song demos are collected as mini-LP *Life's A Riot With Spy Vs Spy*, released on Utility, a subsidiary of Charisma Records, and are well reviewed.

July [27] First radio session, for BBC Radio 1's "John Peel Show" in UK.

Oct Bragg signs to Go! Discs Records, which takes over the LP from Charisma.

1984 Jan LP *Life's A Riot With Spy Vs Spy* reaches UK #32, and tops the UK independent chart for 2 months. He follows the success with more touring, including dates throughout Europe.

Aug First tour of US, where he is well received.

Sept He emphasizes his political colors in UK by playing Food for the Miners benefit shows.

Oct [19] He is arrested with others during an anti-apartheid sit-down outside South Africa House, in London.

Oct LP *Brewing Up With Billy Bragg* reaches #16 in UK.

1985 Feb Kirsty McColl's version of Bragg's song *A New England* reaches UK #7.

Mar EP *Between The Wars* is his own UK singles chart debut, making #15.

1986 Jan *Days Like These* reaches UK #43. He plays on the Red Wedge Tour of UK in support of the Labour Party, with The Style Council° and The Communards°.

July *Levi Stubbs Tears* reaches UK #43.

Oct LP *Talking With The Taxman About Poetry* reaches UK #8.

Nov [2] He is arrested and charged with criminal damage after cutting an air base fence in Norfolk, UK, in an anti-nuclear demonstration.

Nov *Greetings To The New Brunette* makes UK #58.

1987 June Double LP *Back To Basics* climbs to UK #37.

1988 May With a cover version of The Beatles'° *She's Leaving Home* Bragg enjoys a surprise chart-topper as one side of a double-A side charity record UK #1 along with Wet Wet Wet's° version of *With A Little Help From My Friends*. Both songs are featured on the compilation LP *Sergeant Pepper Knew My Father*.

BREAD

David Gates (keyboards and vocals)
James Griffin (guitar and vocals)
Rob Royer (guitar and vocals)
Mike Botts (drums)
Larry Knechtel (drums and vocals)

1969 Gates (b. Dec.11, 1940, Tulsa, Okla., US) a songwriter/producer/session musician, meets Royer and Griffin, who are involved with the group Pleasure Faire, Griffin as a songwriter. Gates produces Pleasure Faire, and though the resulting LP is not a major success, the trio get on well and join forces. They take their demos to Elektra Records, a folk label which has moved into rock with acts like The Doors°, but which has not previously signed a pure pop band.

Oct The group, now named Bread, releases debut LP *Bread*, which reaches US #127, but fails to chart in UK, despite critical acclaim. Session man Jim Gordon plays drums on the LP.

1970 Aug *Make It With You*, from second LP *On The Waters*, tops the US chart and becomes the group's only UK top 5 hit. The LP reaches US #12 and UK #34.

Nov *It Don't Matter To Me*, from LP *Bread*, is reissued and reaches US #10.

1971 Feb *Let Your Love Go*, from third LP *Manna*, makes US #28.

Mar LP *Manna* reaches US #21, but fails to chart in UK. Griffin and Royer's lyrics to the song *For All We Know* from movie *Lovers And Other Strangers* wins them an Oscar for Best Film Song of 1970, with Griffin using the alias Arthur James and Royer being credited as Robb Wilson.

May *If*, from LP *Manna*, hits US #4. Royer leaves and is replaced by Larry Knechtel, multi-instrumentalist but primarily a guitarist (and former member of Duane Eddy's° Rebels, and pianist on *Bridge Over Troubled Water* by Simon° and Garfunkel°).

Aug *Mother Freedom*, the first release to include Knechtel, reaches US #37.

Nov The title track from the still unissued LP *Baby I'm-A Want You* is released and hits US #4 and UK #14.

1972 Mar LP *Baby I'm-A Want You* is finally released and hits US #3 and UK #9, while the single from it, *Everything I Own*, reaches US #5 and UK #32.

June *Diary*, also from the LP, makes US #15.

Sept The title track, from their fifth LP *Guitar Man*, reaches US #11 and UK #16, the guitar solo played by Knechtel.

Oct LP *Best Of Bread* is released in UK, and hits #7.

Nov LP *Guitar Man* reaches #18 in US.

Dec *Sweet Surrender*, from LP *Guitar Man*, reaches US #15.

1973 Mar *Aubrey*, third single from LP *Guitar Man*, reaches US #11. The group disbands amid rumors of disagreement between Gates and Griffin over whose songs should be released as singles. (Gates has composed the majority of Bread's hits.)

May Compilation LP *Best Of Bread* hits US #2 and has a 2-year chart residency. Gates and Griffin embark on solo careers, Botts works with Linda Ronstadt° and Knechtel returns to sessions.

1974 July Compilation LP *Best Of Bread Vol. 2* reaches US #32 and UK #48.

1977 Jan/Feb After relatively unsuccessful solo careers Gates and Griffin bury the hatchet, and Bread reforms with the same line-up as before. LP *Lost Without Your Love* reaches US #26 and UK #17, while the title track reaches US #9 and UK #27.

May *Hooked On You*, from the LP, reaches UK #60.

Nov TV advertised 20-track compilation LP, *The Sound Of Bread*, sells prodigiously in UK, achieving double platinum status and topping the chart for 3 weeks. A similar US compilation fails to chart. The group drifts apart again into solo work. (Griffin later records an LP with Terry Sylvester of The Hollies°, but Gates is the most successful with his songwriting, topping the UK chart in 1974-5 with covers of *If* (by actor Telly Savalas) and *Everything I Own* (by Ken Boothe), which is also revived in 1987 by Boy George, hits UK #1 and sells over a million worldwide.)

BRINSLEY SCHWARZ

Nick Lowe (bass and vocals)
Brinsley Schwarz (guitar and vocals)
Bob Andrews (keyboards and vocals)
Billy Rankin (drums)

1969 Oct Schwarz and Lowe° have been working together for 4 years in the UK, first in school bands and then the Tunbridge Wells-based, Kippington Lodge, when they and Andrews recruit new drummer Rankin, and change name and musical style.

1970 Feb They sign to management company Famepushers, which helps them to a recording contract with United Artists Records.

Apr [3] Famepushers tries to launch them by flying a planeload of UK rock writers to New York to see the group play support to Van Morrison° at the Fillmore East, at a cost of £120,000. A good idea turns into a near disaster: the trip suffers delays and hassles; the maltreated journalists do not find Brinsley Schwarz' set ample compensation, and few subsequently take the band seriously enough to listen fairly to its records.

Apr LP *Brinsley Schwarz* is released, containing six of Lowe's songs and a seventh written by him with the others. It does not chart.

Sept The original quartet completes recordings for next LP, *Despite It All*, after which additional singer/guitarist Ian Gomm is recruited.

Nov LP *Despite It All*, with seven Lowe songs and one by Andrews, also fails to chart.

1972 Feb LP *Silver Pistol* (mainly composed of songs by Lowe and Gomm, and recorded in their own house, which is pictured on the sleeve) is released, but the shadow of the ill-starred US launch remains, and it fails to chart.

Sept By now, Brinsley Schwarz has become one of the first UK "pub-rock" groups, and a substantial live attraction even without selling records.

1973 Oct Fifth LP *Please Don't Ever Change* fares no better than its predecessors, although a measure of the group's status within the music industry is that they appear on two of the most collectable compilation LPs of the year, *Greasy Truckers Party* and *Glastonbury Fayre*.

1974 Mar Budget-priced compilation LP *Original Golden Greats* includes a track earlier issued incognito (as "*The Hitlers*") on single, and two previously unreleased items, one of which (*Run Rudolf Run*) is a live recording from a tour on which the band played as support to Paul McCartney° and Wings.

July LP *The New Favourites Of Brinsley Schwarz*, produced by Dave Edmunds°, is released but (by now unsurprisingly) fails to chart. It incudes Nick Lowe's *(What's So Funny 'bout) Peace, Love And Understanding,* which will later be recorded by Elvis Costello° (whose early recordings will be produced by Lowe).

Nov The group appears with Dave Edmunds° as "The Electricians" in feature film *Stardust,* starring David Essex°.

1975 Mar The group gives up the unequal struggle and disbands, having never been able to live down the circumstances of its launch. Schwarz and Rankin briefly join another "pub rock" band, Ducks DeLuxe. (Schwarz and Andrews will then join The Rumour, which becomes Graham Parker's° backing band; Rankin will rarely be heard, while Gomm will launch a solo career, scoring a US top 20 hit in 1979 with *Hold On.* Lowe will move into production, with successes for Elvis Costello°, Graham Parker° and others, and will score several solo UK hits himself from 1978, before joining Rockpile with Edmunds, Terry Williams (ex-Man, later in Dire Straits°) and Billy Bremner.)

1978 July Retrospective LP *Fifteen Thoughts Of Brinsley Schwarz* is released.

ELKIE BROOKS

1964 Aug Having sung professionally since age 15, Brooks (b. Elaine Bookbinder, Feb.25, 1945, Manchester, UK) makes her recording debut with a revival of Etta James' *Something's Got A Hold On Me,* on Decca. Like all her releases during the 1960s, it fails to chart.

1965 June After two more Decca singles, she moves to EMI's HMV label for *He's Gotta Love Me,* the first of three releases through this outlet.

1966/68 Brooks spends 3 years without recording but doing extensive studio and stage vocal backup work, as well as being a featured singer with Eric Delaney's and Humphrey Lyttleton's bands.

1969 Apr She records a one-off, *Come September,* for NEMS Records. Again, it does not sell.

1970 Brooks joins Dada, a large UK jazz-rock fusion band, sharing lead vocals with Paul Korda on their only LP *Dada,* recorded for Atco.

1972 Apr Dada fragments, and several of its members including Brooks and Korda's replacement Robert Palmer°, regroup as Vinegar Joe, with an eponymous LP for Island Records on which Brooks and Palmer are joint vocalists.

1974 Feb After much live acclaim, particularly in Europe, but poor sales for two LPs *Rock And Roll Gypsies* and *Six-Star General,* Vinegar Joe breaks up.
Brooks releases a solo single, *Rescue Me,* on Island, but it too fails to chart. At the invitation of southern boogie band Wet Willie, she moves to Macon, Ga. to spend a year singing backup vocals for them on tour.

1975 Oct Back in the UK, she signs to A&M Records as a soloist, releasing LP *Rich Man's Woman,* not a hit, but highly rated by critics as a mature vocal set.

1977 May *Pearl's A Singer,* produced and part-written by veteran duo Jerry Leiber and Mike Stoller, finally provides her breakthrough, hitting UK #8.

Sept LP *Two Days Away,* also produced by Leiber and Stoller, reaches UK #18.

Oct *Sunshine After The Rain* is her second hit from the LP, making UK #10.

1978 Mar *Lilac Wine* reaches #16 in UK.

June LP *Shooting Star* peaks at UK #20, while a revival of Neil Young's° *Only Love Can Break Your Heart* reaches #43.

Dec *Don't Cry Out Loud* climbs to UK #12.

1979 May *The Runaway* reaches UK #50 (and is her last hit single for almost 3 years, as her next six releases will fail to chart).

Oct LP *Live And Learn,* another Leiber/Stoller production, reaches UK #34.

Dec [21] Having married her sound engineer Trevor Jordan a year previously, she gives birth to a son, Jermaine Jordan.

1982 Feb Compilation LP *Pearls,* including her hit singles plus new material, is Brooks' biggest UK seller, reaching #2.

May *Our Love* restores her to the UK singles chart at #43.

Aug A revival of The Moody Blues'° *Nights In White Satin* reaches UK #33.

Dec LP *Pearls 2* hits #5 in UK.

1983 Feb A revival of Rod Stewart's° *Gasoline Alley* peaks at UK #52.

1984 July LP *Minutes,* her last for A&M, makes UK #35.

1985 Jan LP *Screen Gems,* a collection of movie standards recorded for EMI, reaches UK #35.

1987 Jan A move to new label Legend Records brings about a major UK chart revival, as *No More The Fool* (written by Russ Ballard) hits #5.

Feb LP *No More The Fool,* produced by Ballard, hits UK #5, while a TV-advertised compilation LP, *The Very Best Of Elkie Brooks,* containing her A&M hits, reaches #10.

Apr *Break The Chain* reaches UK #55.

1988 June LP *Bookbinder's Kid* is released and reaches UK #57.

BROS

Matt Goss (vocals)
Luke Goss (drums)
Craig Logan (bass)

1980 Having participated in two school groups, the Goss twins, (b. Sept.29, 1968, Lewisham, London, UK, two months premature) form, at age 12, Caviar, their most serious venture to date. They meet Logan (b. Apr.22, 1969, Kirkcaldy, Fife, Scotland) in the dinner queue-line, borrow 50p and ask him to join the band. (They will continue writing and practising throughout their school careers, convinced that they will become major teen stars.)

1984 Leaving school, they start to gig, originally under the name Gloss, in working men's clubs and similar venues around south London.

1985 Having written over 20 original songs they team up with their subsequent producer and publisher Nicky Graham, who introduces them to Thomas Watkins, manager of The Pet Shop Boys°.

1987 Apr The trio signs a worldwide deal with CBS Records, which nurtures the potential new teen hero act for an autumn launch.

Aug First single *I Owe You Nothing* is released in UK, but flops.

1988 Feb *When Will I Be Famous* is their first hit, reaching UK #2 after taking 4 months to peak. It causes controversy over the extent of vocal involvement by backing singer Dee Lewis.

Mar *Drop The Boy* hits UK #2, as the trio starts to dominate teen mags and youth TV programs in the UK, in true teenage idol tradition.

BROS *cont.*

Their faces adorn a horde of cash-in fan publications, and their UK fan club receives applications for membership at the rate of 3000 a week.

Apr LP *Push*, produced by Nicky Graham and augmented by Andy Richards on keyboards, hits UK #2. All songs on it are credited to "The Brothers", though actually written by manager Watkins and producer Graham.

May The trio appears at Montreux Rock Festival in Switzerland, televized around the world. The Bros' segment is the most often repeat-screened during UK TV coverage.

June *I Owe You Nothing*, astutely reissued with a face-lift remix, gives Bros its first UK chart-topper within 2 weeks of re-release. It coincides with their first headlining UK tour (sponsored by Pepsi Cola for £250,000), which starts on June 23 and runs for 11 sold-out dates.

JAMES BROWN

1954 After some delinquent teenage years in Augusta, Ga., US, doing a stretch in a state industrial school corrective institution, and subsequently singing on tour with gospel groups and learning to play drums and organ, Brown (b. May 3, 1933, Augusta) forms an R&B vocal group, The Famous Flames, in Macon, Ga., and begins to play live gigs around Georgia, in a style which blends gospel with raucous jump blues-based R&B.

1956 Jan With The Famous Flames, Brown is signed by Ralph Bass to Federal, a subsidiary label of King Records, Cincinnati, Oh.

Feb [4] He records *Please, Please, Please*, (originally cut as a demo single for Bass the previous Nov., at radio station WIBB in Macon).

Apr *Please, Please, Please* creeps into the R&B chart, mainly on regional sales from Georgia and bordering states, where it benefits from the group's rapidly-growing touring popularity. (It will continue to sell steadily for the next 2 years, wherever Brown takes his live show, but never cross to the US top 100.)

1959 Jan After further regional hits in the Southeastern states, *Try Me*, a song from Brown's gospel roots, is his first national hit, reaching #48 and topping the R&B chart for a week. He signs to Universal Attractions booking agency and its owner Ben Bart takes a special interest in the young star. With Bart's guidance, not least on the business side, Brown takes a unique and unprecedented show on the road, mixing calculated hysteria with absolute musical precision. (This will break box office records in all the major R&B venues around the US between 1959 and 1962.)

1960 June *Think*, his second US crossover hit, reaches #33.

1960/62 Brown begins to put out singles at a rate of one every 2 or 3 months – a practice he will follow for the next 10 years, and which satisfies the demand constantly fuelled by continuous touring. Most of them are medium-sized pop hits, and in this 2-year period include: *This Old Heart* (#79 – his last for Federal), *The Bells* (#68 – his first hit on parent King label), *Bewildered* (#40), *I Don't Mind* (#47), *Baby You're Right* (#47) and *Lost Someone* (#48). Though none are UK hits, many of them pass into the repertoires of groups spearheading the UK beat boom in the mid-60s.

1962 May *Night Train*, a personalization of the old Jimmy Forrest hit on which Brown name-checks his regular tour venues, hits US #35. Follow-up chartmakers in 1962 are *Shout And Shimmy* (#61), *Mashed Potatoes USA* (#82) and *Three Hearts In A Tangle* (#93).

Oct [24] The legendary stage act at Harlem's Apollo Theater, New York, is taped for a live LP.

1963 June First US top 20 is the schmaltzy but intense ballad *Prisoner of Love*, which makes #18. LP *Live At The Apollo*, recorded the previous Oct., is released and sells quite unprecedentedly for an R&B LP, (over a million within the year) peaking at US #2.

Aug *These Foolish Things*, another old standard updated with gospel fervor, makes US #55.

Oct LP *Prisoner Of Love* makes US #73.

Dec *Signed, Sealed And Delivered* reaches US #77.

1964 Mar *Oh Baby Don't You Weep*, a major seller, reaches US #23.

Apr Restricted by arrangements at King, and determined to build upon the huge audience crossover success of such hits as LP *Live At The Apollo*, Brown and Bart form their own production company, Fair Deal, and, ignoring King, send a set of new recordings to Mercury subsidiary Smash. King issues live LP *Pure Dynamite! Live At The Royal* (recorded at the Royal Theater, Baltimore), which hits US #10.

May/Sept The first two releases on Smash, *Caldonia* and *The Things That I Used To Do*, only reach US #95 and #99 respectively, but third live LP *Showtime* makes #61. Third single *Out Of Sight* climbs to #24, pioneering a whole new Brown style, with hard, rhythmic, dance-funk base and stripped-down phrase-shouting song structure. Brown quickly develops this "funk" sound into a blend which will revolutionize the whole R&B idiom, and power his own next few hits.

Dec After the success of *Out Of Sight*, King Records accedes to Brown's demands for greater creative and marketing freedom and he returns to the label, with *Have Mercy Baby* which reaches US #92. The new deal also allows him to continue sending productions to Smash (but only instrumentals, normally with Brown at the organ).

Dec [18] Brown tries to attend the funeral of Sam Cooke° in Chicago but fans rush his car and the limousine drives away rather than cause further disruption.

1965 May Instrumental LP *Grits And Soul* on Smash reaches US #124.

Sept Teamed with new band leader Nat Jones, Brown develops his *Out Of Sight* rhythm pattern with *Papa's Got A Brand New Bag*. It gives him his first US top 10 at #8, tops the R&B chart for 8 weeks, and is a million-seller. It is also his UK chart debut, reaching #25, and will win a Grammy award as the Best R&B Recording of 1965.

Oct LP *Papa's Got A Brand New Bag* reaches US #26.

Dec *I Got You (I Feel Good)* hits US #3 and spends 6 weeks as R&B #1, selling over a million. An instrumental version of *Try Me* reaches #63; it comes from Smash label instrumental LP *James Brown Plays James Brown Yesterday And Today*. It also has a non-vocal version of *Papa's Got A Brand New Bag*, which makes US #42.

1966 Mar *I Got You (I Feel Good)* reaches UK #29, while LP of the same title makes US #36.

Apr *Ain't That A Groove* reaches US #42.

May The slow, intense, orchestra-backed ballad *It's A Man's Man's Man's World* hits US #8, and R&B #1 for 2 weeks and is another million-seller. Instrumental LP *James Brown Plays New Breed* makes US #101.

July *It's A Man's Man's Man's World* reaches UK #13.

Aug *Money Won't Change You* peaks at US #53.

Oct LP *It's A Man's Man's Man's World* reaches US #90.

Nov *Don't Be A Drop-Out* recorded to support the US "Stay in School" campaign reaches US #50.

1967 Feb *Bring It Up* reaches US #29.

Mar A revival of Wilbert Harrison's° *Kansas City* makes US #55.

Apr *Think*, a duet with backing singer Vicki Anderson, revives Brown's own 1960 hit and just makes the US chart at #100. (Brown will later return to this song as a soloist.)

May LP *Raw Soul* peaks at US #88, while *Let Yourself Go* reaches US #46.

July LP *Live At The Garden* reaches US #41.

Aug Alfred Ellis replaces Jones as The Famous Flames' leader and Brown's chief musical collaborator. The two define their musical path in a new direction unrelated to any other R&B or pop trend, building a funk sub-genre with the rhythm section (usually highlighting "funky drummer" Clyde Stubblefield and guitarist Jimmy Nolan), with vocals and lyrics used as rhythmic addenda rather than the focal point of the recordings. The first example, *Cold Sweat*, hits US #7, with 3 weeks at R&B #1 and tops a million.

Oct LP *Cold Sweat* reaches US #35.

Nov *Get It Together* reaches US #40.

1968 Jan *I Can't Stand Myself (When You Touch Me)* reaches US #28.

Feb B-side *There Was A Time* charts in its own right, reaching US #36.

Apr [4] After the assassination of Martin Luther King and riots in 30 US cities, Brown makes a national TV appeal urging restraint and more constructive channelling of justified anger. Its calming effect results in an official commendation from Vice President Hubert Humphrey. *I Got The Feelin'*, another million-seller, peaks at US #6 and tops the R&B chart for 2 weeks.

May LP *I Can't Stand Myself* climbs to US #17.

June *Licking Stick, Licking Stick*, the epitome of funk minimalism combined with mesmeric appeal, reaches US #14. Released at the same time (and reaching US #52) is the contrasting *America Is My Home*, another spoken narration which affirms Brown's social conscience and patriotism. (Much of US black youth is now looking to him as an important figurehead: a deprived individual who has fulfilled the classic American dream via his talent.)

July LP *I Got The Feelin'* reaches US #135.

Aug *I Guess I'll Have To Cry, Cry, Cry*, the last hit to be credited to James Brown & The Famous Flames, peaks at US #55. Hereafter Brown is listed alone though the original band still remains intact and busy on the road.

Oct *Say It Loud – I'm Black And I'm Proud*, provides another million-seller, reaching US #10 and tops R&B chart for 6 weeks. LP *Live At The Apollo, Vol.2* makes US #32 and stays charted for 9 months.

Dec *Goodbye My Love* reaches US #31.

1969 Mar *Give It Up Or Turnit A Loose* climbs to US #15, and spends 2 weeks at R&B #1.

May *I Don't Want Nobody To Give Me Nothin' (Open Up The Door, I'll Get It Myself)* reaches US #20, while LP *Say It Loud – I'm Black And I'm Proud* peaks at #53.

July [3] Brown plays the Newport Jazz Festival, alongside several rock and blues acts like Blood, Sweat & Tears° and Johnny Winter°.

July [23] Los Angeles declares James Brown Day, in honor of his sold-out concert at the LA Forum. Mayor Sam Yorty is late to hand Brown the proclamation, so the singer walks out (though the concert goes ahead).

July LP *Gettin' Down To It* peaks at US #99.

Aug Brown inaugurates a dance, The Popcorn. *Mother Popcorn (You Got To Have A Mother For Me)* is a million-seller, reaching US #11 and R&B #1 for 2 weeks, while wholly instrumental *The Popcorn* makes #30.

Sept [6] At the end of a Memphis, Tenn., concert Brown announces his intention to retire from the road after next Independence Day. (In fact, he cuts down touring in 1975, but never gives it up completely.) The instrumental *Lowdown Popcorn* reaches US #41, and (also instrumental) LP *James Brown Plays And Directs The Popcorn* makes US #40.

Oct *World* reaches US #37 and LP *It's A Mother* peaks at #26.

Nov *Let A Man Come In And Do The Popcorn (Part 1)* climbs to US #21.

Dec Largely instrumental *Ain't It Funky Now* reaches US #24.

1970 Jan *Let A Man Come In And Do The Popcorn (Part 2)* reaches US #40.

Mar *It's A New Day* reaches US #32.

Apr *Funky Drummer* makes US #51, while instrumental LP *Ain't It Funky* reaches #43.

May *Brother Rapp* reaches US #32.

June LP *Soul On Top*, recorded by Brown with the Louie Bellson Orchestra, climbs to US #125. The Famous Flames breaks up and Brown reorganizes his band, The JB's, incorporating many younger musicians, like Bootsy Collins, and more experienced players, like Fred Wesley and Alfred Ellis.

July LP *It's A New Day So Let A Man Come In* peaks at US #121.

Aug *Get Up, I Feel Like Being A Sex Machine*, one of his most distinctive and enduringly influential releases, reaches US #15 and is Brown's first million-seller of the decade.

Oct *Get Up, I Feel Like Being A Sex Machine* restores him to the UK chart after 4 years, reaching #32.

Nov *Super Bad*, another million-seller, reaches US #13 and tops the R&B chart for 2 weeks. Live LP *Sex Machine* reaches US #29.

Nov [19] Brown marries Deirdre Jenkins at her home in Barnwell, S.C.

1971 Jan *Get Up, Get Into It, Get Involved* reaches US #34.

Mar *Soul Power* climbs to US #29, while instrumental *Spinning Wheel* makes #90, and live LP *Super Bad* #61.

May *I Cried* reaches US #50.

July *Escape-ism*, a spoken monologue by Brown over The JB's rhythm track, peaks at US #35. The first release on his own People label, following a decision to split from King, it fills the gap while negotiations over a worldwide deal proceed with Polydor.

Aug Brown turns the summer's fashion craze into dancefloor number *Hot Pants (She Got To Use What She Got To Get What She Wants)*, on People. It reaches US #15, tops the R&B chart, and is another million-seller. After this, he signs to Polydor with full creative control, bringing to the label his entire back-catalog of recordings from the previous two decades. He also parts from many of The JB's, including Ellis who is replaced by Wesley as leader, and Collins, who moves with other JB members to George Clinton's° Parliament/Funkadelic group.

Sept His Polydor debut *Make It Funky* reaches US #22 and tops the R&B chart for 2 weeks.

Oct LP *Hot Pants* reaches US #22.

Nov *My Part: Make It Funky Part 3*, a variation on the previous single, peaks at US #68.

Dec *I'm A Greedy Man* reaches US #35 while seasonal *Hey America* reaches UK #47.

1972 Feb Double live LP *Revolution Of The Mind – Live At The Apollo, Vol.3* reaches US #39. The JB's hit single in their own right, *Gimme Some More* reaches US #67. Written and produced by Brown (possibly featuring him on keyboards), it is released on People.

Mar *Talking Loud And Saying Nothing* reaches US #27 and spends a week on the R&B chart at #1, while *King Heroin*, a harrowing anti-drug message narrated by Brown, peaks at US #40.

June *There It Is* makes US #43, while *Pass The Peas* by The JB's (featuring Brown uncredited) creeps to #95.

July Brown's revival of Bill Doggett's 1956 million-seller *Honky Tonk* climbs to US #44.

Aug LP *James Brown Soul Classics*, a compilation of previous hits, reaches US #83 and LP *There It Is*, with new material, reaches #60.

Sept *Get On The Good Foot* puts him back in the US top 20 at #18, and is R&B chart #1 for 4 weeks, his first million-seller for over a year.

Dec [11] After a concert in Knoxville, Tenn., Brown is arrested while talking to fans about drug abuse and charged with "Disorderly Conduct", when an informant tells police that he is trying to incite a riot. Brown threatens Knoxville with a million-dollar lawsuit, and the incident is hastily written off as a "misunderstanding".

Dec *I Got A Bag Of My Own* reaches US #44.

1973 Jan Brown duets with his new protégée Lyn Collins on *What My Baby Needs Now Is A Little More Lovin'*, which climbs to US #56.

Feb *I Got Ants In My Pants (And I Want To Dance)* reaches US #27, while double LP *Get On The Good Foot* makes #68.

Mar Brown and Wesley of The JB's score the movie *Black Caesar*, starring Fred Williamson. Soundtrack LP by Brown (now billed on LP sleeves as "The Godfather of Soul") reaches US #31, while *Down And Out In New York City*, extracted from it, makes #50.

June *Think*, a revival of his 1960 hit, also a duet with Vicki Anderson in 1967, reaches US #77.

July *Doing It To Death*, credited to Wesley & The JB's, but written and produced by Brown (playing incognito), reaches US #22 and tops the R&B chart for 2 weeks, selling over a million.

Aug In another marketing move that only Brown would contemplate, he releases yet another (different) recording of *Think*, which peaks at US #92.

Sept Brown and Wesley's score for a second movie, *Slaughter's Big Rip-Off* (starring Jim Brown – no relation) is released on LP and makes US #92, while extract *Sexy, Sexy, Sexy* climbs to #50.

1974 Jan *Stoned To The Bone* reaches US #58.

May *The Payback* reaches US #26, spending 3 months on chart, and hits R&B #1 for 2 weeks. It sells over a million, while double LP of the same title reaches US #34, and is also a gold disk winner (for a half-million sales).

Aug *My Thang* climbs to US #29, and tops the R&B chart for 2 weeks.

Sept Double LP *Hell* reaches US #35.

Oct *Papa Don't Take No Mess* reaches US #31, and spends a week at R&B chart #1.

Dec Double A-side *Funky President (People It's Bad)/Coldblooded* peaks at US #44.

1975 Mar *Reality* reaches US #80, while LP of the same title makes #56. Brown's billing is now "Minister of New New Super Heavy Funk".

May *Sex Machine, Part 1* (an updated re-recording of *Get Up I Feel Like Being A Sex Machine*) makes US #61.

June LP *Sex Machine Today* reaches US #103.

Oct LP *Everybody's Doing The Hustle And Dead On The Double Bump* limps to US #193.

1976 Sept *Get Up Offa That Thing* reaches US #45 and UK #22 (his first UK hit for almost 5 years), while LP of the same title makes US #147.

1977 Feb *Body Heat* makes US #88 and UK #36. This will be his last US top 100 entry for nearly 9 years. LP of the same title reaches US #126.

Sept [29] The JB's, frequently rumored to be at odds with Brown over peremptory treatment and disputed wages, walk out in mid-tour in Hallendale, Fla., complaining of underpayment. (Most will later return.)

1978 June LP *Jam/1980s* reaches only US #121 but remains charted for 22 weeks.

1979 Aug LP *The Original Disco Man* (the title a jibe at the style which has supplanted his own sound as the US dancefloor mainstay) makes US #152.

1980 June Brown makes a cameo appearance in the film *The Blues Brothers*, playing a manic singing and dancing preacher.

Aug A double live LP *James Brown . . . Live/Hot On The One*, recorded in Tokyo, Japan, reaches US #170.

1981 Jan He returns to the UK chart with *Rapp Payback (Where Iz Moses?)*, recorded for Florida's TK Records, and leased in UK to RCA. It is hugely popular on UK dancefloors and reaches UK #39.

1983 July *Bring It On . . . Bring It On*, another independent production, for Augustasounds in his native Georgia, is a UK hit, reaching #45.

Dec [18] Jimmy Nolan, Brown's former lead guitarist, dies in Atlanta from a heart attack, aged 47.

1984 Sept New York's Tommy Boy label teams Brown on a one-off recording project with electro-rapper Afrika Bambaataa°. *Unity (The Third Coming)* reaches UK #49.

1985 May With Brown's old hits starting to become cult favorites in UK clubs, Polydor in UK commissions from top club DJ Froggy a spliced medley of snatches from 12 of them. *Froggy Mix* reaches UK #50 and is unique in being entirely by Brown, but one he has not actually recorded.

June *Get Up, I Feel Like Being A Sex Machine* is reissued in UK after 15 years and reaches #47.

1986 Feb *Living In America*, written and produced by Dan Hartman, is the theme from film *Rocky 4*, recorded by Brown at the specific request of Sylvester Stallone. It is his first million-seller in 13 years, hitting US #4 and UK #5.

Mar *Get Up, I Feel Like Being A Sex Machine* re-enters UK chart, this time peaking at #46.

Oct *Gravity* reaches US #93 and UK #65, while LP of the same title makes US #156 and UK #85.

1987 Oct TV-advertised hits compilation LP *The Best Of James Brown – Godfather Of Soul* reaches UK #17 – his first LP to chart in the UK.

1988 Jan *She's The One*, recorded in the early 1970s but not issued at the time, is released by Polydor to satisfy UK demand for new Brown material. Remixed by Tim Rogers, it reaches UK #45.

Mar [7] Brown visits UK to be presented with a special award for 20 years of innovation in dance music, by the assembled delegates to the World DJ Convention at London's Royal Albert Hall. His unannounced presence and dramatic stage entrance to accept the award causes a 5-minute standing ovation.

May *The Payback Mix*, a sampled medley (by mixing team Coldcut) of snippets from Brown oldies and some by former associates like The JB's and Bobby Byrd, reaches UK #12.

June *I'm Real*, recorded by Brown with production team Full Force, reaches UK #31. It fails to make US top 100 but achieves #2 on US R&B chart. LP of the same title, containing brand-new material, makes UK #27 but only US #96.

JACKSON BROWNE

1966 Apr Browne (b. Oct.9, 1948, Heidelberg, West Germany) who has lived in Orange County, Cal., US, since childhood, when his parents returned from Europe after US Army service, and has become an active folk-oriented singer, songwriter, proficient pianist and guitarist after being encouraged at an early age to study music, becomes an active member of the folk-rock fraternity at LA's Paradise club, and is invited to join the Nitty Gritty Dirt Band. He does not stay for long, but leaves two of his songs, *Melissa* and *Holding* for eventual inclusion on the band's 1967 debut LP.

1967 Jan Signed as a songwriter to Elektra Records' publishing arm, Nina Music, he goes to New York, where he picks up a number of gigs on the club circuit (including playing guitar in Nico's backing band), but it is as a songwriter that he makes headway, when Nico takes three of his compositions for her in-progress LP *Chelsea Girl*. Songs cut as demos for his publishers will later appear illicitly on bootleg LPs.

1968 He returns to LA when Elektra signs him as a recording artist, but his attempts to record an LP at the rural Paxton Lodge ranch studio in California prove ultimately abortive, and the results are never issued. The label lets him go and signs in preference his frequent collaborator from the Paradise club days, Steve Noonan, to whose debut LP *Browne* contributes five songs. Meanwhile, his songs are also being picked up and recorded by acts like Tom Rush, who cuts *Shadow Dream Song* on his LP *The Circle Game* for Elektra.

1971 Oct His reputation as a songwriter finally leads to a deal with David Geffen's newly-launched Asylum Records (although Geffen initially fails to recognize Browne's name at first contact, and throws out his demo tape unheard).

1972 Mar Debut LP *Jackson Browne* (sometimes called *Saturate Before Using* – a legend printed on the sleeve) is recorded with assistance from Russ Kunkel (drums), Leland Sklar (bass) and Craig Doerge (keyboards) along with David Crosby (harmony vocals) and The Byrds'° Clarence White (guitar). It peaks at US #53.

May Debut single *Doctor My Eyes*, from the LP, reaches US #8. (It is not a UK hit, but a cover version by the Jackson 5° will reach UK #9 in 1973). A US tour supporting Joni Mitchell° brings Browne the singer before audiences for the first time, and he accompanies Mitchell on some European dates.

Sept As Browne tours US with The Eagles°, his second single, *Rock Me On the Water*, peaks at US #48. *Take It Easy*, a song co-written by Browne with member Glenn Frey, reaches US #12. His own version will appear on Browne's second LP.

1973 Nov LP *For Everyman* features largely personnel as before, with the significant addition of multi-instrumentalist David Lindley. It reaches US #43, while the excerpted *Redneck Friend* (said to concern masturbation), peaks at #85. Browne appears on the sleeve of second Eagles° LP, *Desperado*, for which he co-writes *Doolin' Dalton*.

1974 Jan A second single from the LP, coupling *Ready Or Not* and *Take It Easy* is not a hit. Browne co-writes *James Dean* for third Eagles° LP *On The Border*.

Dec Third LP *Late For The Sky*, with a sleeve done in the style of French painter Magritte, reaches US #14. It features his friend David Lindley (guitar and violin), plus Jai Winding (keyboards), Doug Haywood (bass and vocals) and Larry Zack (drums). Neither *Walking Slow* nor *Fountain Of Sorrow*, both extracted as US singles, reach the chart.

1976 Mar [25] Browne's wife Phyllis commits suicide.

Dec LP *The Pretender*, a set of personal songs which clearly relate to his recently-shattered private life, hits US #5 and is a million-selling LP. It also marks his UK chart debut, reaching #26.

1977 Mar *Here Come Those Tears Again*, taken from the LP, makes US #23.

June Title track from *The Pretender* reaches US #58.

1978 Feb The unique live "road" LP *Running On Empty*, recorded not just on stage but also in hotel rooms, dressing rooms, and (in one case) on the tour bus, is a second US million-selling LP, reaching #5. In UK, it peaks at #28.

Apr Title track from *Running On Empty* reaches US #11.
Aug *Stay*, taken from *Running On Empty*, and a revival of the 1960 Maurice Williams & The Zodiacs hit, reaches US #11, and climbs to UK #12 – his first (and only major) UK hit single.
1980 Jan 3-LP set *No Nukes*, a various arts live compilation, reaches US #19. Produced by Browne, John Hall and Bonnie Raitt, it features a host of US stars like James Taylor°, The Doobie Brothers° and Tom Petty°, and has three of Browne's tracks: one with his own band, and the others duets with Graham Nash and Bruce Springsteen° (another version of *Stay*). The set comes from a Madison Square Garden concert organized by MUSE (Musicians United For Safe Energy), of which Browne is an enthusiastic supporter.
Sept LP *Hold Out* tops the US chart for a week, and is another million-seller, while also making UK #44. *Boulevard*, taken from it, reaches US #19.
Nov *That Girl Could Sing*, extracted from *Hold Out*, reaches US #22.
1982 Oct *Somebody's Baby*, from the soundtrack of movie *Fast Times At Ridgemont High*, becomes Brown's biggest US hit single to date, at #7.
1983 Sept Now without Lindley (replaced by Rick Vito, later with Fleetwood Mac°), but still retaining a long-standing band including Russ Kunkel, Craig Doerge, Bob Glaub and Doug Haywood, Browne hits US #8 with LP *Lawyers In Love*, his first for 3 years. It makes UK #37, and the title track is a single hit in US, peaking at #13.
Nov *Tender Is The Night*, also from the LP, reaches US #25.
1984 Feb *For A Rocker*, a third single from LP *Lawyers In Love*, peaks at US #45.
1986 Jan He duets with Clarence Clemons, Bruce Springsteen's° sax player, on his single *You're A Friend Of Mine* (with additional vocals by actress Daryl Hannah, Browne's girlfriend), which reaches US #18.
Apr Having become an outspoken critic of US foreign policy, and strong supporter of Amnesty International, Browne bares his conscience on these matters after another 3-year hiatus with LP *Lives In The Balance*, which reaches US #23, while the extracted single *For America* peaks at #30.
July *In The Shape Of A Heart*, from the LP, peaks at US #70.
Oct *In The Shape Of A Heart* reaches UK #66 – the first-ever instance of a record by Browne scoring better in UK than US, boosted by his well-received "Lives In The Balance" UK tour.
1988 June [11] Browne appears in the Nelson Mandela 70th Birthday Party at Wembley, UK (an event shown on TV throughout the world), leading a star band on a song specially written for the occasion.

PEABO BRYSON

1976 After 5 years with R&B touring group Moses Dillard & The Tex-Town Display and a period of minor soul chart success as vocalist/producer with Bang Records, Bryson (b. Robert Peabo Bryson, Apr.13, 1951, Greenville, S.C., US) achieves a US #94 hit as a singer on The Michael Zager Band's *Do It With Feeling*.
1977 He signs to Capitol Records in US.
1978 May LP *Reaching For The Sky* sets his style as a romantic soul ballad singer, and makes US #49. Taken from it, *Feel The Fire* and the title track, sell only in the soul field (US R&B #13 and #6 respectively).
1979 Mar LP *Crosswinds* reaches US #35, while *I'm So Into You*, taken from it, hits R&B chart #2 but fails to cross over to US pop chart.
1980 Mar He tours US with Natalie Cole°, and they collaborate on LP *We're The Best Of Friends*, which reaches US #44.
June LP *Paradise* reaches US #79.
1981 Feb After guesting on tour with Roberta Flack°, Bryson features with her on double live LP *Live And More*, which makes US #52.
Apr LP *Turn The Hands Of Time* peaks at US #82, and Melissa Manchester's *Lovers After All*, on which he guests, reaches US #54.
1982 Feb LP *I Am Love* reaches US #40, and spins off his first solo US pop hit single, *Let The Feeling Flow*, which makes #42.
1983 Jan LP *Don't Play With Fire* reaches #55 in US.
Sept A ballad duet with Roberta Flack°, *Tonight I Celebrate My Love For You*, from the duo's LP of duets *Born To Love*, is Bryson's only UK hit – a massive one, at #2.
Oct Bryson/Flack LP *Born To Love* climbs to US #25 and UK #15.
Nov After slowly climbing the US chart since July, *Tonight I Celebrate My Love* peaks at #16. It stays on the US chart for 29 weeks.
1984 Jan Another duet with Flack, *You're Looking Like Love To Me*, reaches US #58.
Aug Changing to Elektra records, he reaches #44 with LP *Straight From The Heart*, while taken from it, *If Ever You're In My Arms Again*, provides his all-time biggest US single, peaking at #10.
Oct *Slow Dancin'* proves a disappointing follow-up, only making US #82.
1985 July *Take No Prisoners (In The Game Of Love)* reaches US #78.
Aug LP *Take No Prisoners* peaks at US #102. (After this Bryson will be quieter due in part to the fact that others in his field, like Freddie Jackson°, Jeffrey Osborne° and James Ingram°, are now also scoring major hits with strong soul ballads, breaking his former near-monopoly.)
1988 Feb A duet with Regina Belle on *Without You*, taken from both Bill Cosby film soundtrack, *Leonard Part XI*, and from Bryson's LP *Positive*, is released by Elektra and reaches US #89.

TIM BUCKLEY

1966 After performing with California C&W bands and as a solo singer/guitarist in LA folk clubs, and being spotted by Frank Zappa's° manager, Herb Cohen, Buckley (b. Feb.14 1947, Washington, D.C., US) is signed to Elektra Records.
Oct His debut LP *Tim Buckley*, introduces an individual folk/rock style which garners good reviews, though it does not chart.
1967 Nov After a spell in New York playing with ex-Velvet Underground° singer Nico and others, he releases LP *Goodbye And Hello*, produced by Jerry Yester of The Lovin' Spoonful°. This contains his best-known and most-covered (notably by Blood, Sweat & Tears°) song *Morning Glory*, but it sells disappointingly, reaching only US #171.
1968 Mar [8] Buckley plays on the opening night bill of The Fillmore East in New York, with Albert King and Big Brother & The Holding Company.
Oct He tours UK, appearing on several TV shows and recording a six-song session for BBC Radio 1's "Top Gear" show.
1969 May LP *Happy Sad*, more jazz-oriented, and produced by both Yester and Zal Yanovsky of The Lovin' Spoonful°, reaches US #81.
1970 Feb He moves to Cohen and Zappa's° Straight Records for LP *Blue Afternoon*, which is a minor US chartmaker at #192.
Oct LP *Lorca* is recorded for Elektra to fulfill contractual obligations, and has some material in an experimental free-form jazz style, rendering it wholly uncommercial.
1971 Jan LP *Starsailor* further develops Buckley's jazzy, avant-garde experimentations. It fails to sell at all, but does introduce his second best-known number *Song To The Siren*, later revived in UK by *This Mortal Coil*. However, disillusioned by its non-acceptance, he drops out of writing, playing and recording for over a year.
1972 Oct After working as a chauffeur and a taxi driver for a while, he records LP *Greetings From L.A.* for Warner Bros. in unaccustomed funk-rock style, produced by Jerry Goldstein (ex-Strangeloves). More accessible than his previous two LPs, and well reviewed, it still does not chart.
1973 Dec LP *Sefronia*, on Frank Zappa° and Herb Cohen's new label Discreet Records, combines new songs with revivals of oldies like the 1963 Jaynettes' hit *Sally Go Round The Roses*.
1974 Aug He tours Europe, playing at Knebworth Festival in UK and on BBC TV's "Old Grey Whistle Test".
Nov LP *Look At The Fool* is another funk-based set, though less well received.
1975 Apr Buckley returns to live work in US, touring Texas and California, and begins planning a retrospective double LP set of his work, to be recorded live on stage.
June [29] He dies in hospital in Santa Monica, Cal., of an overdose of heroin and morphine, having taken the drug mix at a friend's house, believing it to be cocaine.

BUCKS FIZZ

Cheryl Baker (vocals)
Jay Aston (vocals)
Mike Nolan (vocals)
Bobby Gubby (vocals)

1981 Mar The group is formed from experienced session singers in London, UK, expressly to represent UK in the Eurovision Song Contest with the purpose-written song *Making Your Mind Up*. Baker (b. Mar.8, 1954, London) has entered in 1978 with Co-Co, which lost

BUCKS FIZZ *cont.*

the contest, but had a #13 UK hit with its entry *Bad Old Days*. Aston (b. May 4, 1961, London), Nolan (b. Dec.7, 1954, London) and Gubby (b. Aug.23, 1961, London) have no previous chart pedigree. The group signs to RCA Records.

Apr [4] The group wins Eurovision, and *Making Your Mind Up* shoots to #1 in UK, where it stays for 3 weeks. This success ensures the group will stay together, rather than return to session work.

June *Piece Of The Action* reaches #12 in UK.

Sept *One Of Those Nights* is a slower, smoother sound but less popular, reaching UK #20. Debut LP *Bucks Fizz*, makes UK #14.

1982 Jan Uptempo *The Land Of Make Believe* takes them back to UK #1, peaking for 2 weeks.

Apr *My Camera Never Lies* also hits UK #1: the group's third and last chart-topper.

May Second LP *Are You Ready?* reaches UK #10.

July *Now Those Days Are Gone*, highlighting their close-harmony talent, hits UK #8.

1983 Jan *If You Can't Stand The Heat* makes UK #10.

Mar *Run For Your Life* peaks at UK #14.

Apr LP *Hand Cut* reaches UK #17.

June *When We Were Young*, a richly-produced Abba° pastiche, hits UK #10.

Oct *London Town* breaks the group's run of UK top 20 successes, peaking at #34.

Dec Compilation LP *Greatest Hits*, including the singles to date, reaches UK #25.

1984 Jan *Rules Of The Game* reaches only UK #57.

Sept *Talking In Your Sleep*, a cover of a 1983 US #3 hit by Detroit group The Romantics, makes #47.

Nov *Golden Days* peaks at UK #54, while LP *I Hear Talk* reaches UK #66.

Dec Gubby, as Bobby G., reaches UK #65 with self-penned theme song for UK TV series "Big Deal", issued on the BBC's own label. Shortly after leaving a gig at Newcastle-upon-Tyne, the Bucks Fizz tour bus crashes in icy conditions and the group and its entourage suffer various degrees of injury. Most serious is Nolan, who is taken comatose to hospital and believed brain-damaged. (He will, however, regain consciousness and fight his way back to recovery and an eventual return to performing.)

1985 Jan Title track from *I Hear Talk* reaches UK #34.

July *You And Your Heart So Blue* makes #43 in UK.

Sept *Magical* reaches #57.

Nov Bobby G.'s *Big Deal* theme is reactivated (again on BBC Records) due to a new series on TV, and climbs higher than before, peaking at #46.

1986 July A label switch from RCA to Polydor is followed by the euphoric, tribal-sounding *New Beginning (Mamba Seyra)*, sung partly in Swahili, which reaches #8: the group's first top 10 hit for 3 years.

Sept A brisk revival of Stephen Stills' *Love The One You're With* peaks at #47.

Nov *Keep Each Other Warm* makes UK #45, their last recording for Polydor.

THE BUCKINGHAMS

Dennis Tufano (guitar and lead vocals)
Dennis Miccoli (keyboards)
Carl Giammarese (guitar)
Nick Fortuna (bass)
Jon Poulos (drums)

1965 The group forms in Chicago, Ill., US, as The Pulsations, then records for local Alley Cat and Spectra-Sound label as The Falling Pebbles and The Centuries. Renaming themselves after Chicago's Buckingham Fountain, they revive The Drifters°/ Searchers'° hit *Sweets For My Sweet* on Spectra-Sound as The Buckinghams, before signing to larger Chicago label, USA Records.

1966 Dec After three singles – *I'll Go Crazy, I Call Your Name* and *I've Been Wrong* – have failed to sell, *Kind Of A Drag* captures radio attention around US and charts nationally.

1967 Feb *Kind Of A Drag* tops US chart for 2 weeks, and becomes a million-seller. It is written by Jim Holvay, of Chicago group The Mob. The group's contract is bought from USA by CBS Records, which teams them with producer Jim Guercio.

Mar Miccoli leaves; replaced on keyboards by Martin Grebb.

Apr LP *Kind Of A Drag*, compiled by USA from earlier recordings, reaches US #109. USA releases *Laudy Miss Claudy* to compete with the CBS debut, but it only makes US #41.

May *Don't You Care* on CBS, adds a fuller, brassier sound to the smooth vocal/keyboard blend introduced on *Kind Of A Drag*, and climbs to US #6. It is again written by Holvay, along with fellow Mob player Gary Beisber, and producer Guercio.

Aug LP *Time And Changes* reaches US #58. Taken from it, *Mercy Mercy Mercy*, a brass-backed vocal version of an early 1967 US top 20 instrumental hit by jazzman Cannonball Adderley, hits US #5.

Oct *Hey Baby (They're Playing Our Song)* peaks at US #12.

1968 Jan *Susan*, with topical "freak out" psychedelic arrangement, makes US #11.

Mar LP *Portraits* reaches #53 in US.

June *Back In Love Again* stalls at US #57, and is their final hit single, with the group rapidly fading from sight after an en masse drug arrest. They remain together for 2 more years, but split with Guercio, who then develops their brass-rock sound (with even greater success) on subsequent work with fellow CBS acts Chicago° and Blood, Sweat & Tears°.

Oct Appropriately-titled LP *In One Ear And Gone Tomorrow* reaches US #161.

1969 June Compilation LP *Greatest Hits* is their US chart swan song, at #73.

1973 June Tufano and Giammarese, having signed to A&M Records as a duo under that name following The Buckinghams' break-up, return to US chart with *Music Everywhere*, which reaches #68. Poulos manages them and other acts, while Fortuna is a session bassist and Grebb has joined The Fabulous Rhinestones.

1980 Mar [26] Poulos dies of drug-related causes.

1981 The Buckinghams (Tufano, Giammarese, Fortuna and a new keyboard player and drummer) reunite for a live performance in Chicago, as part of the annual Chicago Fest.

BUFFALO SPRINGFIELD

Stephen Stills (vocals and guitar)
Neil Young (vocals and guitar)
Richie Furay (vocals and guitar)
Bruce Palmer (bass)
Dewey Martin (vocals and drums)

1966 Mar The group forms with members who have been variously linked in other projects: Stills (b. Jan.3, 1945, Dallas, Tex., US) and Furay (b. May 9, 1944, Dayton, Oh.) in New York folk group The Au Go Go Singers (an East Coast answer to The New Christy Minstrels); Young° (b. Nov.12, 1945, Toronto, Canada) and Palmer (b. 1946, Liverpool, Canada) in The Mynah Birds. Prime mover Stills invites them all to LA to investigate teaming up, where they are joined by ex-Dillards' drummer Martin (b. Sept.30, 1942, Chesterville, Canada) and (briefly) by bass player Ken Koblun, a former colleague of Young's in The Squires, who returns to Canada.

1967 Jan Signed to Atco Records, and adopting a name seen on a steamroller during local road repairs, Buffalo Springfield releases its eponymously-titled debut LP, which includes seven songs written by Stills and five by Young°. Initial sales are slight.

Mar Stills is inspired to write a song about unrest among LA youth, who have been subjected to police oppression in the name of law and order. This song, *For What It's Worth*, will become an anthem of the era, and is the group's only major hit, reaching US #7. The LP, which does not include the hit, starts to sell on the back of it, eventually peaking at US #80. In UK (where *For What It's Worth* does not chart), the LP sleeve and label both suggest the hit is included. In fact the LP omits it and instead features Stills' *Baby Don't Scold Me* (later something of a collector's item as it is replaced by *For What It's Worth* on all subsequent pressings).

May Palmer, a Canadian, is deported from the US for visa infringement, but will rejoin the group at intervals, his bass slot on stage otherwise being filled by Koblun or Jim Fielder (later in Blood, Sweat & Tears°). Second LP *Stampede* is recorded but never released (although it appears as a bootleg). It includes Koblun, Fielder and guitarist Doug Hastings, who is recruited for a short period when Young° (who rarely sees eye-to-eye with Stills) leaves the group.

June [16] Without Young° and Palmer, but with Hastings on guitar and additional guest vocalist David Crosby from The Byrds°, the band plays at the Monterey Pop Festival.

Aug *Bluebird*, written by Stills, reaches US #58. This includes participation from Bob West on bass and Charlie Chin (later in Cat Mother and The All Night Newsboys) on banjo.

Sept Young° rejoins to work on a new LP (though he will in-out more than once again), and the group's recording engineer Jim Messina takes over as a more permanent bass player.

Oct *Rock'n'Roll Woman*, another Stills' song, peaks at US #44.

Dec LP *Buffalo Springfield Again* reaches US #44. Its sleeve features a list of people who have inspired or influenced the group, including Hank B. Marvin of The Shadows° (the inspiration for Young's° early guitar playing).

1968 Jan From the LP, Young's° song *Expecting To Fly* reaches US #98, but the group is rapidly de-stabilizing as it attempts to record a third LP with Young and Palmer as often missing as present.

May [5] The group finally implodes after a last gig in LA, and the members quickly fan out to launch other projects: Stills to form Crosby, Stills & Nash° (after assisting Al Kooper to complete the LP *Super Session*), Young° and Palmer to solo careers (the latter briefly before fading, the former with major success after signing to Reprise Records); and Furay to plan the formation of Poco°. Martin will attempt to form a new Buffalo Springfield 6 months later, but is prevented from using the name, and drops out of sight soon after.

Sept Third Buffalo Springfield LP *Last Time Around*, assembled posthumously by Messina from the later sessions, reaches US #42.

Oct *On The Way Home*, taken from the LP, reaches US #82, by which time Messina has joined Furay in the newly-launched Poco°.

1969 Apr Compilation LP *Retrospective/The Best Of Buffalo Springfield*, which includes their chart singles, equals their highest US LP chart placing by peaking at #42.

1973 Dec Double compilation LP *Buffalo Springfield* reaches US #104 in the wake of the success achieved by Stills, Young, Furay and Messina in their various post-Springfield projects.

JIMMY BUFFETT

1969 Having majored in history and journalism at the University of Southern Mississippi and become a freelance journalist for a while (including a stint at *Billboard* magazine), Buffett (b. Dec.25, 1946, Mobile, Ala., US) moves to Nashville to attempt to secure a deal as a country singer.

1970 Sept Signed to Andy Williams' Barnaby label, he releases debut LP *Down To Earth*, which reputedly sells only 324 copies.

1971 The tapes of Buffett's second LP are misplaced by Barnaby, delaying its release indefinitely. He leaves the label and Nashville shortly afterwards.

1972 Buffett settles in Key West, Fla., where he buys a 50-foot ketch as his home and begins the lifestyle for which he will later become famous and which will influence much of his songwriting. By night, he plays at local bars The Green Parrot and Ernest Hemingway's old haunt Sloppy Joe's.

1973 He signs to ABC/Dunhill Records. LP *A White Sport Coat And A Pink Crustacean* (a play on the title of an old Marty Robbins hit) does not chart but introduces the wryly humorous and buccaneering style which will permeate subsequent hits.

1974 Apr LP *Living And Dying In 3/4 Time* reaches US #176. He appears in the movie *Rancho Deluxe*, for which he writes the music (and has 6 tracks on the non-charting soundtrack LP, on United Artists).

July *Come Monday* is his first US hit single, peaking at #30.

1975 Buffett forms his Coral Reefer Band with Roger Bartlett (guitar), Greg Taylor (harmonica), Harry Dailey (bass) and Phillip Fajardo (drums).

Apr LP *A1A* (the designation of a beach access road off US Route #1 in Florida) makes US #25.

1976 Apr LP *Havana Daydreamin'*, on ABC Records, reaches US #65. Following this success, the previously unissued second Barnaby LP is released, under the title *High Cumberland Jubilee*, but fails to chart.

1977 July LP *Changes In Latitudes, Changes In Attitudes* climbs to US #12 and earns a platinum disk as Buffett's first million-seller. Extracted single *Margaritaville* hits US #8.

Oct Title track from *Changes In Latitudes, Changes In Attitudes* makes US #37.

1978 May He makes a cameo appearance in the film *FM*, singing *Livingston Saturday Night*, which is included on the soundtrack LP and hits US #5 and UK #37.

1979 May LP *Son Of A Son Of A Sailor* hits US #10, a second million-seller, while *Cheeseburger In Paradise*, taken from it, makes US #32. Jay Spell joins the Coral Reefer Band on keyboards.

Sept *Livingston Saturday Night* reaches US #52.

Oct LP *Volcano*, recorded in Monserrat, is his first for MCA after ABC label has been phased out. It sells a half-million copies and reaches US #14, while *Fins* makes US #35.

Dec *Manana* peaks at US #84, while live double LP *You Had To Be There* makes #72.

1980 Jan Title track from *Volcano* makes only US #66.

Mar *Survive* climbs to US #77.

1981 Mar *It's My Job* reaches US #57 (and is Buffett's last hit single), while LP *Coconut Telegraph* makes US #30. By now, his touring has become less frequent as he spends much time at sea in the Caribbean on his ketch, Euphoria II.

1982 Feb LP *Somewhere Over China* reaches US #31. Buffett opens a store in Key West, named Margaritaville, in which he sells the tropical shirts which have become an essential part of his image. He launches *The Coconut Telegraph*, a regular newsletter for his fans which mails out a consistent 4000 copies.

1983 Nov LP *One Particular Harbor* makes US #59.

1984 Oct LP *Riddles In The Sand* reaches US #87. His range of "Caribbean Soul" tropical shirts is put into retail outlets across US.

1985 Aug LP *Last Mango In Paris* makes US #53. A competition accompanies its release, offering a trip on Buffett's ketch as the prize. 100,000 people enter and five winners receive a free cruise. Meanwhile, Buffett's song *Turning Around* is used on the soundtrack of the film *Summer Rentals*.

Dec Compilation LP *Songs You Know By Heart – Jimmy Buffett's Greatest Hit(s)*, with chart singles and favorite LP tracks, peaks at US #100. A video is made for *Who's The Blonde Stranger*, in which Florida Governor Bob Graham makes a guest appearance. Buffett completes the script for a projected movie to be titled *Margaritaville*.

1986 July LP *Floridays*, recorded variously in Memphis, Fort Lauderdale and LA, and co-produced by Buffett with Mike Utley, reaches US #67.

1987 He divides his time between music and other pursuits: writing a children's book *The Jolly Man* with 8-year-old daughter Savannah Jane (who also plays mini-conga on *Floridays*), editing *The Coconut Telegraph* and running the "Margaritaville" restaurant and clothing stores. He becomes chairman of the Save the Manatee committee, dedicated to the protection of the endangered marine animal.

1988 July LP *Hot Water*, recorded at Buffett's own Shrimpboat Sound Studios in Key West, is released to coincide with a major 31-city US tour from late June to mid-Aug. It peaks at US #46. *Homemade Music* is extracted and promoted via an offbeat "outrageous" video.

BUGGLES

Trevor Horn (vocals and bass)
Geoff Downes (keyboards)

1979 Jan Having played together in a backing band of UK vocalist Tina Charles, Horn and Downes form Buggles as a non-performing record-making unit.

Sept Signed to Island Records in the UK, the duo releases *Video Killed The Radio Star*, which shoots to #1 within a month of issue, helped by an innovative promo video.

Nov *Video Killed The Radio Star* charts in US, reaching #40.

1980 Feb *The Plastic Age* reaches #16 in UK, and similarly named LP *The Age Of Plastic* hits #27.

Mar The duo joins Yes° in the studio to assist in the production of LP, *Drama*.

Apr *Clean Clean* reaches UK #38.

Aug By the time Buggles-assisted Yes° LP *Drama* is complete, the duo has accepted Chris Squire's idea that they fully join Yes°, in place of departed keyboardist Rick Wakeman and vocalist Jon Anderson. The new combination begins a lengthy US tour.

Nov *Elstree* is released in UK after Buggles' demise, but still reaches #55.

Dec The combined Buggles/Yes° group breaks up completely at the tour's conclusion. (Downes and Yes' Steve Howe will form Asia°, while Horn will become an influential producer.)

1981 Aug [1] MTV music cable channel opens in US, with Buggles' *Video Killed The Radio Star* the very first item screened.

SOLOMON BURKE

1955 Dec A former boy preacher, Burke (b. 1936, Philadelphia, Pa., US), broadcaster on "Solomon's Temple", and soloist in his family's own Philadelphia church, The House of God for All People, signs to Apollo Records in New York and makes his first recording, *Christmas Presents From Heaven*. (This and subsequent singles on Apollo and Singular Records from 1956-1959 will feature him trying to mold a distinctive secular style from his gospel roots, and will not sell.)

1960 Dec He signs to Atlantic Records.

1961 Nov Second Atlantic release, the C&W song *Just Out Of Reach (Of My Two Empty Arms)* climbs to US #24 – one of the first country/R&B hybrids, and one of the first definable hits in the 1960s soul genre in which Atlantic is to be a prime mover.

1962 Mar *Cry To Me*, written by Burke's new producer Bert Berns, reaches US #44, and will be covered by The Rolling Stones° and others.

July Double A-sided *Down In The Valley/I'm Hanging Up My Heart For You* charts in US at #71 and #85.

Sept Another country song, *I Really Don't Want To Know*, peaks at US #93.

1963 June *If You Need Me* is a song given to Burke while on tour, by its co-writer and fellow R&B singer, Wilson Pickett°. In US chart competition with Pickett's own version, Burke's single reaches #37 against Pickett's #64. It also hits R&B #2.

Aug *Can't Nobody Love You* makes US #66.

Dec *You're Good For Me* reaches US #49.

1964 Feb Another C&W oldie, *He'll Have To Go*, climbs to US #51.

June *Goodbye Baby (Baby Goodbye)* reaches US #33.

Aug The gospel-like *Everybody Needs Somebody To Love* (later used by Burke as a fund-raiser march in his church) peaks at US #58.

Dec *The Price*, which Burke writes about his own disintegrating marriage, makes US #57.

1965 Apr His biggest US hit is *Got To Get You Off My Mind*, reaching #22 and also spending 4 weeks at #1 on the R&B chart.

July *Tonight's The Night* (coupled with a cover of Bob Dylan's° *Maggie's Farm*) is his last US top 30 entry, reaching #28 (and R&B #2).

Aug Compilation LP *The Best Of Solomon Burke* is one of only two LPs during his entire career to make the US chart, reaching #141.

Sept With the rise to chart status of other solo soul singers with styles approximating his own (many also on Atlantic), Burke's sales reduce, as *Someone Is Watching* peaks at only US #89. (His next three singles, *Only Love (Can Save Me Now)*, *Baby Come On Home* and *I Feel A Sin Coming On*, will only reach #94, #96 and #97 respectively, through 1965/1966.)

1967 Feb *Keep A Light In The Window Till I Come Home* is his best seller for 2 years, reaching US #64.

July *Take Me (Just As I Am)*, recorded at Stax in Memphis, continues his resurgence, making US #49.

1968 June Burke makes US #68 with *I Wish I Knew (How It Would Feel To Be Free)*. He soon finds out, for Atlantic lets him go.

1969 June Signing a new recording deal with Bell Records, he covers Creedence Clearwater Revival's° *Proud Mary*, only 3 months after the original has been a million-seller, but it climbs to US #45. It is, however, his only hit for Bell, and he finds it hard to maintain with other labels the consistency he managed at Atlantic.

July LP *Proud Mary* tops his only other LP chart entry by one place, reaching #140.

1971 May Signed now to MGM Records, he re-charts in US after 2 years' absence, with *The Electronic Magnetism (That's Heavy, Baby)*, which climbs to #96.

1972 Apr Also on MGM (where his releases vary greatly in quality, much of the material offered him being sub-standard), *Love's Street And Fool's Road*, a song from movie *Cool Breeze*, reaches US #89.

1975 Mar After 3 years and a brief spell on the Dunhill label, Burke has switched labels again to Chess Records when he returns with Barry White°-styled *You And Your Baby Blues*, reaching #96. Shortly after this, he semi-retires from secular performing and recording to concentrate on his religious duties as Bishop of his church. (This will remain his foremost activity through into the late 1980s, with most LP releases being gospel or inspirational material, though he will make occasional US tours as part of "The Soul Clan", an aggregation of soul soloists who first made their names on the Atlantic labels during the 1960s, which also includes Eddie Floyd°, Joe Tex, Ben E. King° and Wilson Pickett°.)

DORSEY BURNETTE

1957 Sept After the breakup of the Johnny Burnette Rock'n'Roll Trio°, Burnette (b. Dec.28, 1932, Memphis, Tenn., US) moves with brother Johnny to LA to pursue a joint songwriting career and individual recording projects.

Dec First songwriting success (with Johnny), *Waiting In School*, for Ricky Nelson° on Imperial Records, reaches US #18. He will write several more of Nelson's hits like *Believe What You Say*, *It's Late* and *A Long Vacation*.

1958 He records *My Honey* for Imperial with Johnny as The Burnette Brothers, but it fails to chart.

1959 Dec He signs to Era Records as a soloist.

1960 Mar *Tall Oak Tree*, an ecology-slanted song written for Ricky Nelson° but turned down, reaches US #23 in Burnette's own version on Era.

Aug *Hey Little One* reaches US #48.

1961 He moves to US Dot label and switches style towards country music.

1962 He changes labels again to Frank Sinatra's Reprise Records.

1968 He signs to Liberty Records (on which Johnny Burnette° had solo hits) as a country singer.

1969 Feb *The Greatest Love* returns him to US pop chart at #67.

1972 He signs to Capitol Records and begins a 4-year spell of country hits, with ten C&W chart singles and the LPs *Here And Now* and *Dorsey Burnette*.

1973 He is voted Year's Most Promising Newcomer by Academy of Country Music, despite a 20-year career.

1975 He joins Motown's country label Melodyland, and has a C&W hit with *Molly (I Ain't Gettin' Any Younger)*.

1977 He signs to the Calliope label for country LP *Things I Treasure*.

1979 Aug [19] He dies of a heart attack at Canoga Park, California.

JOHNNY BURNETTE AND THE ROCK'N'ROLL TRIO

1952 After attending high school with Elvis Presley°, Burnette (b. Mar.28, 1934, Memphis, Tenn., US) works for a while as a Mississippi bargeman and attempts to earn additional living as a boxer and a singer. He persuades older brother Dorsey Burnette° and neighbor Paul Burlison (b. Feb.4, 1929, Brownsville, Tenn.), a member of local band The Memphis Four, to form a trio.

1953 With Burnette on guitar and lead vocals, his brother on stand-up bass and Burlison on lead guitar, they begin to play Memphis dates and become regulars at The Hideaway Club. First single *You're Undecided* for Von Records in Boonsville, Miss., is not a hit.

1955 When friend Elvis Presley° becomes successful on local Sun label, the trio auditions there for Sam Phillips, but he finds their sound too Elvis-like and rejects them.

1969 Oct Signed to Straight Records, and now assuming artistic control over recording, he produces the double LP *Trout Mask Replica*, which marks his chart debut in UK at #21, fails in US, but is destined for cultural landmark status. It features the first assemblage of the definitive Magic Band, including Zoot Horn Rollo (Bill Harkleroad) on guitar, Rockette Morton (Mark Boston) on guitar and bass, and The Mascara Snake on clarinet.

1971 Jan LP *Lick My Decals Off, Baby* is another UK chartmaker, at #20.

Feb Beefheart and The Magic Band make their New York live debut at Ungano's.

May LP *Mirror Man* appears, featuring the remaining material recorded but not released for Buddah in 1968, much to Beefheart's displeasure. It makes UK #49.

1972 Feb He falls out with Zappa°, and LP *The Spotlight Kid* appears on Reprise. It is Beefheart's US chart debut, reaching #131, and makes UK #44.

Dec LP *Clear Spot* reaches only US #191, and fails to chart in the UK.

1973 Mar *Too Much Time*, from LP *Clear Spot* is released in UK, with no success.

1974 May LP *Unconditionally Guaranteed*, charts at US #192 and is Beefheart's last LP with the existing Magic Band as Rollo and Morton leave to form their own group, Mallard. A new deal is signed with Virgin Records in UK, and with Mercury in US.

Nov LP *Blue Jeans and Moonbeams*, is poorly received despite new line-up.

1975 July He supports Pink Floyd° at Knebworth Festival, UK.

Nov Back with Zappa°, singing with The Mothers of Invention, he tours and contributes to LP *Bongo Fury*. Afterwards, Beefheart temporarily retires, returning to the Mojave Desert, Cal. to paint.

1978 Nov LP *Shiny Beast (Bat Chain Puller)*, released by Warner Bros. in US, breaking a long silence, has no chart success. UK release is delayed until Virgin wins a suit to enforce its own rights to Beefheart material.

1980 Sept LP *Doc At The Radar Station* is released internationally on Virgin, coinciding with a successful tour of the US and Europe by Beefheart, and unprecedented US TV appearance on "Saturday Night Live".

1982 Sept LP *Ice Cream For Crow* returns him to UK chart, at #90. Issued via Epic Records in US, it fails to chart.

1986 After a long silence, and an eventual announcement that he is leaving music to concentrate entirely on painting, Beefheart exhibits his work in London.

CARAVAN

Pye Hastings (vocals and guitar)
David Sinclair (keyboards)
Richard Sinclair (bass and vocals)
Richard Coughlan (drums)

1968 Jan The Canterbury-based UK band re-emerges as Caravan, with Hastings, David and Richard Sinclair and Coughlan, after touring as The Wilde Flowers with Kevin Ayers°, Robert Wyatt and Hugh Hopper (who leave to form Soft Machine).

Oct LP *Caravan* appears on MGM's Verve label. Its gentle eccentricity establishes it as a classic English underground band.

1970 Sept The band moves to Decca for LP *If I Could Do It All Again, I'd Do It All Over You*.

1971 May LP *In The Land Of Grey And Pink* is released on Decca's "progressive" Deram label.

Nov David Sinclair leaves to join Robert Wyatt's Matching Mole and is replaced by Steve Miller (ex-Delivery).

1972 May LP *Waterloo Lily* is released, the band's fourth to receive critical approval, yet still unsuccessful beyond a devoted following.

July Geoff Richardson joins the line-up on electric violin, while Stuart Evans (bass) and Derek Austin (keyboards) join briefly for a tour of Australia.

Nov Richard Sinclair leaves to form Hatfield & The North, taking Miller with him. Interim replacement is John Perry.

1973 Oct David Sinclair rejoins Caravan for LP *For Girls Who Grow Plump In The Night*, which has brass and orchestral arrangements. The planned LP sleeve, depicting a naked, pregnant woman, is vetoed by Decca, but a compromise is reached on the released version: the woman, still clearly pregnant, wears flimsy nightwear.

1974 Apr Live LP *Caravan And The New Symphonia* is released, recorded 6 months earlier with the New Symphonia Orchestra conducted by Martyn Ford at London's Drury Lane Theatre Royal. The LP features much earlier material reworked for the orchestral arrangements.

July Mike Wedgwood (ex-Kiki Dee and Curved Air) replaces Perry in the band.

1975 Aug LP *Cunning Stunts* reaches US #124 and is the band's only international success. It charts at UK #50 after the band plays Reading Festival. Jan Schelhaas, ex-The National Head Band and Gary Moore's band, joins on keyboards and Dek Messecar replaces Wedgwood, who leaves for a solo career in US.

1976 May LP *Blind Dog At St. Dunstan's* reaches UK #53.

Nov Decca issues compilation LP *The Canterbury Tales*, to coincide with a UK tour.

1977 Aug LP *Better By Far*, produced by Tony Visconti, is released on Arista but with no success. The band retires from live work for a year, as both Sinclairs and Schelhaas work with Camel for an extended period.

1980 Nov LP *The Album*, is released on manager Terry King's Kingdom label, with David Sinclair back in the line-up.

1982 June The four original members (the Sinclairs, Hastings and Coughlan) re-form for the first time in 11 years, with Mel Collins joining on saxophone, for LP *Back To Front* on Kingdom. It is not a success. (Apart from further repackages and compilations, there will be no further new recordings or appearances from Caravan.)

BELINDA CARLISLE

1985 May After three successful LPs with all-American rock group The Go-Gos, including the multi-platinum *Beauty And The Beat* and seven US hit singles, including the million-seller *We Got The Beat*, founder member Carlisle (b. Aug.17, 1958) remains signed to IRS Records, and prepares a solo career and LP with the assistance of former Go-Go colleague Charlotte Caffey.

1986 Aug Debut solo LP *Belinda* reaches US #13, while *Mad About You*, taken from it, hits #3. Both fail to cross to the UK.

Oct *I Feel The Magic*, also from the LP, reaches US #82. Carlisle tours in US as support to Robert Palmer°, followed by a 3-month club tour of her own.

1987 Oct Second LP *Heaven On Earth* is released. Although now signed to MCA in the US, Virgin Records picks up release rights for the UK. Collaborators on this follow-up project include Thomas Dolby°, Charlotte Caffey, Ellen Shipley, and Michelle Phillips, one-time member of The Mamas And The Papas°.

Dec *Heaven Is A Place On Earth*, taken from the LP, tops US chart for a week. Its success is aided by the impact of a promo video directed by actress Diane Keaton.

1988 Jan *Heaven Is A Place On Earth* tops UK chart for two weeks, while LP *Heaven On Earth* makes US #13 and hits UK #4, attaining platinum status in both countries.

Mar *I Get Weak*, second single from the LP, hits US #2 and UK #10.

May Carlisle sets out on her first major solo headlining tour, starting in US and Canada.

June She visits Japan, while *Circle In The Sand*, from LP *Heaven On Earth*, hits US #7 and UK #4.

Aug Debut US release *Mad About You* is re-issued by IRS in UK and climbs to #67.

Sept She plays her first UK tour, including three sold-out dates at London's Hammersmith Odeon. *World Without You* is released to tie in with the tour.

ERIC CARMEN

1970 Carmen (b. Aug.11, 1949, Cleveland, Oh., US), classically trained at Cleveland Institute of Music and ex-Cyrus Erie and The Quick, joins as lead singer of the 1968 *It's Cold Outside* chart makers The Choir, formed by Wally Bryson and Dave Smalley on guitar and Jim Bonfanti on drums, out of previous group The Outsiders.

1972 The group becomes The Raspberries and signs to Capitol Records.

May *Don't Want To Say Goodbye* makes US #86. Debut LP *The Raspberries* climbs to US #51.

Oct *Go All The Way* hits US #5.

Dec LP *Fresh* peaks at US #36.

1973 Jan *I Wanna Be With You* reaches US #16.

June *Let's Pretend* climbs to US #35.

Sept *Tonight* makes US #69.

Nov LP *Side 3* reaches US #128. Smalley and Bonfanti leave to form Dynamite and are replaced by Mike McBride, ex-Cyrus Erie on drums, and bassist Scott McCarl.

Dec *I'm A Rocker* makes US #94.

ERIC CARMEN *cont.*

1974 Nov *Overnight Sensation (Hit Record)*, like all previous chart singles penned by Carmen, reaches US #18. LP *Starting Over* includes new line-up with McBride and McCarl.

1975 Apr The Raspberries split after poor sales of their LP *Starting Over* and Carmen moves to a solo career, signing to Arista Records.

Nov First solo LP *Eric Carmen* is issued and climbs to US #21.

1976 Mar *All By Myself*, based on a Rachmaninoff melody, hits US #2 and is a million-seller.

May *All By Myself* reaches UK #12. Carmen visits UK for TV and radio promotion. LP *Eric Carmen* spends 1 week on UK chart at #58.

June LP *Raspberries' Best Featuring Eric Carmen* makes US #138.

July *Never Gonna Fall In Love Again* makes US #11. (Irish singer Dana has already charted with the song in March, reaching UK #31.)

Sept *Sunrise* makes US #34.

Oct He begins recording second LP in London, UK, with producer Gus Dudgeon.

1977 Feb Disagreements lead Dudgeon to quit and Carmen completes the LP alone.

Oct LP *Boats Against The Current* climbs to US #45.

Nov *She Did It* peaks at US #23.

Dec *Boats Against The Current* reaches US #88.

1978 Dec *Change Of Heart* makes US #19, but LP of the same name reaches only US #137.

1979 Feb Carmen's remake of The Four Tops'° 1964 smash *Baby I Need Your Lovin'* makes US #62.

1980 July *It Hurts Too Much* reaches US #75 and the LP from which it is taken, *Tonight You're Mine*, makes US #160.

1985 Mar After a 5-year absence, he signs to Geffen records. *I Wanna Hear It From Your Lips* reaches US #35. Second LP titled *Eric Carmen* makes US #128.

Apr *I'm Through With Love* reaches US #87.

1987 Nov *Hungry Eyes*, from the movie soundtrack *Dirty Dancing*, is released.

1988 Feb *Hungry Eyes* hits US #4, but fails to reach UK top 75.

June Carmen joins others on "Dirty Dancing" package tour, as Arista Records releases compilation LP *The Best Of Eric Carmen* which rises to US #69.

Aug *Make Me Lose Control* hits US #3, taking his record sales to over 15 million worldwide.

Sept Carmen releases new single *Reason To Try*, taken from the official summer Olympics LP *One Moment In Time*.

KIM CARNES

1960s After working as a demo session and jingle singer in LA, Carnes (b. July 20, 1946, Pasadena, Cal., US), meets her future husband Dave Ellingson when both are members of The New Christy Minstrels.

1971 They leave The Minstrels and, as Kim and Dave, record *Nobody Knows*, the theme from movie *Vanishing Point* for Jimmy Bowen's Amos label in LA. Bowen signs them to a publishing deal and they work as staff writers alongside Glenn Frey and J.D. Souther.

1974 First Carnes solo LP for Amos, *Rest On Me*, features backup players including James Burton and ex-Cricket, Glen D. Hardin.

1975 She signs to A&M Records and LP *Kim Carnes* is issued, to muted interest.

1977 Kim and Dave composition *Love Comes From Unexpected Places* wins the Tokyo Song Festival. LP *Sailin'* is released, produced by Jerry Wexler.

1978 July A duet with Gene Cotton on self-written *You're A Part Of Me* reaches US #36.

1979 Mar Carnes is the first artist signed to new EMI America label and reaches US #56 with *It Hurts So Bad*. Carnes and Ellingson write all the songs for Kenny Rogers'° LP *Gideon*, which makes US #12.

1980 May A duet with Rogers° on *Don't Fall In Love With A Dreamer* hits US #4.

July A revival of Miracles' *More Love* hits US #10. LP *Romance Dance* reaches US #57.

Oct A remake of The Box Tops'° 1968 hit *Cry Like A Baby* makes US #44.

1981 May *Bette Davis Eyes*, a revival of 1974 Jackie DeShannon song, tops the US chart for 9 weeks, displacing EMI America label-mate Sheena Easton's° *Morning Train*, and hits UK #10.

June LP *Mistaken Identity* tops the US chart for 4 weeks and reaches UK #26.

Sept *Draw Of The Cards* makes US #28 and UK #49.

Nov *Mistaken Identity* reaches US #60.

Dec [18] Carnes and Tina Turner° are featured at Rod Stewart's° LA Forum concert, broadcast live to an estimated 35 million people.

1982 Feb [24] At US Grammy Awards, *Bette Davis Eyes* wins both Record of the Year and Song of the Year awards.

Aug *Voyeur* reaches US #29, while LP of the same name makes US #49.

Oct *Voyeur* makes UK #68.

1983 Jan *Does It Make You Remember* reaches US #36.

Nov *Invisible Hands* reaches US #40. LP *Café Racers* reaches US #97.

1984 Feb *You Make My Heart Beat Faster (And That's All That Matters* peaks at US #54.

June *I Pretend* reaches US #74.

Nov *What About Me?*, sung with Kenny Rogers° and James Ingram°, makes US #15.

1985 Jan A duet with Barbra Streisand°, *Make No Mistake, He's Mine*, reaches US #51. (Co-written by Carnes, it will become a 1987 country chart-topper for Ronnie Milsap and Kenny Rogers°.) *Invitation To Dance*, a solo from film *That's Dancing!*, charts at US #68. Carnes becomes the only artist ever to hold simultaneous positions on US chart as a soloist, in a duet and as one of a trio.

Jan [28] Carnes joins 44 other artists at A&M's Hollywood Studios to record *We Are The World* under the collective name USA For Africa.

June *Crazy In The Night (Barking At Airplanes)* reaches US #15.

Aug *Abadabadango* makes US #67.

1986 June *Divided Hearts* climbs to US #67. Carnes leaves EMI America.

1988 July Country-oriented LP *View From The House*, produced by former label boss Bowen, is released on MCA, who sign her for a long-term contract.

THE CARPENTERS

Karen Carpenter (vocals and drums)
Richard Carpenter (keyboards and vocals)

1965/67 Richard Carpenter (b. Oct.15, 1946, New Haven, Conn., US) and sister Karen (b. Mar.2, 1950, New Haven), having relocated from New Haven to Downey, Cal., form a jazz trio with tuba/bass player Wes Jacobs. They release two singles for local Magic Lamp label, before entering and winning a Battle of the Bands contest at the Hollywood Bowl. They perform *The Girl From Ipanema* and *Iced Tea* and are spotted by RCA A&R chief Neely Plumb who signs them to the label as The Richard Carpenter Trio. They cut four tracks which are never released.

1968 When Jacobs leaves to study music, Karen and Richard form Spectrum with John Bettis, a friend of Richard's from California State College. Despite support gigs at Disneyland, The Troubadour and The Whiskey A-Go Go, the band is short-lived, but the duo perseveres and records some tracks in the home of top LA session bassist Joe Osborn, which reach A&M label boss Herb Alpert°.

1969 Apr [22] The Carpenters sign with A&M Records.

Nov Debut LP *Offering* is released, but fails to chart.

1970 May Debut single, a version of The Beatles'° *Ticket To Ride*, charts at US #54.

July *(They Long To Be) Close To You*, an unknown Bacharach/David song recorded by Dionne Warwick° 7 years previously, tops the US chart for 4 weeks.

Sept LP *Close To You* enters the US chart for an 87-week run and will hit #2.

Oct Helped by a TV commercial for a bank targeting its audience at newlyweds, *(They Long To Be) Close To You* hits UK #6. The Paul Williams/Roger Nichols-penned *We've Only Just Begun* hits US #2.

1971 Jan *We've Only Just Begun* makes UK #28. LP *Close To You* reaches UK #23.

Mar *For All We Know*, from film *Lovers And Other Strangers* hits US #3. (It will subsequently win an Oscar for Best Song of the Year.) Debut LP *Offering*, retitled *Ticket To Ride*, reaches US #150.

Mar [16] The duo wins Grammys as Best New Artist and Best Contemporary Vocal Performance by a Group for *Close To You*.

June *Rainy Days And Mondays* hits US #2. LP *Carpenters* enters the US chart and will hit #2.

July Having spent the first half of the year touring the world, The Carpenters launch their own US NBC-TV series "Make Your Own Kind of Music". The show features regulars Al Hirt and Mark

Lindsay (ex-Paul Revere & The Raiders°) and will run until September.

Oct *Superstar/Bless The Beasts And Children*, (the latter from film of same name), hits US #2 and #67. *Superstar*, written by Keon Russell, backed with *For All We Know*, makes UK #18.

Nov LP *The Carpenters* reaches UK #12.

1972 Jan *Merry Christmas Darling* makes UK #45.

Feb Originally recorded by Akron, Oh.'s Ruby & The Romantics, *Hurting Each Other* hits US #2.

Mar The Carpenters win their third Grammy as Best Pop Vocal Performance by a Group for the LP *Carpenters*.

Apr LP *Ticket To Ride* reaches UK #20.

June *It's Going To Take Some Time* reaches US #12.

July LP *A Song For You* enters the US chart, hitting #4.

Aug *Goodbye To Love* hits US #7.

Sept The Carpenters tour UK.

Oct *Goodbye To Love* is double A-sided with *I Won't Last A Day Without You* in UK where it hits #9. LP *A Song For You* makes UK #13.

1973 Apr *Sing* hits US #3.

June LP *Now And Then* is released and features the novel idea of one side comprising eight segued pop classics. It hits #2 in both US and UK.

July *Yesterday Once More* also hits US and UK #2.

Dec The Carpenter-Bettis penned *Top Of The World* tops the US chart and hits UK #5. LP *The Singles 1969-1973*, featuring twelve of their hits, is released (and will eventually top both US and UK charts).

1974 Mar *Jambalaya (On The Bayou)*, backed with *Mr Guder* reaches UK #12.

May [1] The duo performs, at the request of President Nixon, at a White House state dinner honoring West German Chancellor Willy Brandt.

May *I Won't Last A Day Without You*, also penned by Williams and Nichols, reaches US #11. The track is reissued in UK and makes #32.

1975 Jan *Please Mr Postman*, a cover of The Marvelettes 1961 chart-topper, hits US #1 and UK #2.

May *Only Yesterday* hits US #4 and UK #7.

June LP *Horizon* reaches US #13.

July LP *Horizon* tops the UK chart.

Sept *Solitaire* reaches US #17 and UK #32.

Dec Following 5 years of constant recording and touring, Karen, now weighing only 90 pounds, takes 2 months off to recuperate. She sends Christmas greetings to her UK fans in the form of *Santa Claus Is Comin' To Town* which makes UK #37.

1976 Apr A cover of Herman's Hermits'° 1967 smash, *There's A Kind Of Hush (All Over The World)* makes US #12 and UK #22.

July *I Need To Be In Love* reaches US #25 and UK #36. LP *A Kind Of Hush* makes US #33 and hits UK #3.

Sept Originally a hit for Wayne King in 1931, *Goofus* makes only US #56, breaking a run of seventeen consecutive top 30 hits.

1977 Jan LP *Live At The Palladium* makes UK #28.

July *All You Get From Love Is A Love Song* peaks at US #35.

Oct LP *Passage* makes only US #49 but reaches UK #12.

Nov *Calling Occupants Of Interplanetary Craft (The Recognized Anthem Of World Contact Day)* reaches US #32 but hits UK #9.

1978 Apr *Sweet Sweet Smile* makes US #44 and UK #40.

Dec *I Believe You* reaches US #68. LP *The Singles 1974-78*, a UK-only release, hits #2. LP *Christmas Portrait* makes US #145.

1979 Karen, having taken a rest from The Carpenters, records a solo LP with Phil Ramone. The LP is not finished as she rejoins Richard to commence work on a new LP titled *Made In America*.

1981 Aug *Touch Me When We're Dancing* returns the duo to the US top 20, climbing to #16. LP *Made In America* makes US #52 and UK #12.

Oct *(Want You) Back In My Life Again* reaches US #72.

1982 Jan *Those Good Old Dreams* peaks at US #63.

May *Beechwood 4-5789*, a remake of another Marvelettes smash, makes only US #74. (It will be the duo's last US chart entry.)

1983 Feb [4] Found unconscious at her parents' home in Downey, Karen is rushed to Downey Community Hospital where she dies, aged 32, of cardiac arrest at 9.51 a.m. Pacific Standard Time. The LA coroner gives the cause of death as "heartbeat irregularities brought on by chemical imbalances associated with anorexia nervosa".

June [25] Karen Carpenter is remembered in a tribute at The First Congregational Church of Long Beach.

Oct *Make Believe It's Your First Time* reaches UK #60.

Nov LP *Voice Of The Heart* makes US #46 and UK #6.

1984 Oct LP *Yesterday Once More*, a UK-only TV-advertised album, hits UK #10.

1985 Jan LP *An Old-Fashioned Christmas* makes US #190 for 1 week.

June [26] Richard commences work on solo LP *Time*. (He will sing lead vocals on the majority of the tracks. Dusty Springfield° will guest on *Something In Your Eyes* and Dionne Warwick° on *In Love Alone*.)

1987 Oct LP *Time* is released, but fails to chart in both US and UK.

THE CARS

Ric Ocasek (vocals and guitar)
Benjamin Orr (vocals and bass guitar)
Elliot Easton (guitar)
Greg Hawkes (keyboards)
David Robinson (drums)

1976 Ocasek, Orr, Easton and Hawkes are playing together in Boston, Mass., US, as Cap'n Swing when Robinson joins and suggests a new name, The Cars.

Dec [31] The group makes its live debut at a New Year's Eve show at Pease Air Force Base, Portsmouth, N.H., US.

1977 Feb They begin playing regularly at Boston club, The Rat, and are noted by Fred Lewis, who becomes their manager.

Mar Lewis arranges a spot opening Bob Seger's° concert at Boston's Music Hall, and a demo tape of *Just What I Needed* becomes Boston's WCOZ-FM radio station's #1 request.

Nov They sign to Elektra Records after being seen at Holy Cross College, Boston.

1978 First LP *The Cars* is recorded in just 2 weeks, with producer Roy Thomas Baker, in England.

Sept Debut single *Just What I Needed* reaches US #27.

Nov The group makes a mini-tour of UK, Belgium, France and West Germany. *My Best Friend's Girl*, the first picture disk single available commercially in UK, hits #3.

Dec *My Best Friend's Girl* peaks at US #35.

THE CARS *cont.*

Dec [27] LP *The Cars*, reaching US #18, is a US million-seller and turns platinum. It also makes UK #29.
1979 Jan The Cars is voted Best New Band of the Year in US *Rolling Stone* magazine.
Mar *Just What I Needed* is released in UK and reaches #17.
Aug LP *Candy-O* hits US #3 and UK #30. The band plays to an audience of 500,000 in Central Park, New York.
Sept *Let's Go* reaches US #14.
1980 Oct *Touch And Go* reaches US #37. LP *Panorama* hits US #5.
1981 The band buys Intermedia Studio, Boston, and relaunches it as Synchro Sound, recording there itself.
1982 Jan LP *Shake It Up* hits US #9.
Feb *Shake It Up* hits US #4.
May *Since You're Gone* reaches only US #41, but brings the band back to UK chart at #37.
1983 Mar Ocasek releases solo LP, *Beatitude* on Geffen Records, which reaches US #28. *Something To Grab For* peaks at US #47.
1984 Apr *You Might Think* hits US #7, with considerable help of a ground-breaking special effects video (which will later win several creative awards). LP *Heartbeat City* hits US #3.
July *Magic* reaches US #12.
Sept The ballad *Drive*, featuring Orr on lead vocals, is The Cars' most successful US single at #3. It becomes a million-seller.
Oct *Drive* hits UK #5, its first UK top 10 hit for 6 years. LP *Heartbeat City* reaches UK #25.
1985 Mar *Why Can't I Have You?* reaches US #33.
Apr Guitarist Easton releases solo LP *Change No Change*, which reaches US #99.
Aug *Drive* is repromoted in UK after its use during Live Aid program showing famine in Ethiopia. It re-charts and hits UK #4. Royalties go to the Band Aid Trust.
Nov Compilation LP *The Cars' Greatest Hits* reaches UK #27.
1986 Jan *Tonight She Comes* hits US #7.
Mar *I'm Not The One* reaches US #32.
Nov Ocasek's solo *Emotion in Motion* reaches US #15. His second solo LP, *This Side Of Paradise* on Geffen, makes US #31.
Dec Orr's solo LP, *The Lace*, reaches US #92.
1987 Jan Ocasek's *True To You* reaches US #75, while Orr's first solo single, *Stay The Night*, makes US #24.
Sept LP *Door To Door* reaches US #26 and UK #72.
Oct *You Are The Girl* reaches US #17.
Nov *Strap Me In* makes only US #85. Rumors, which have occurred many times before, abound that the band is splitting.

THE CASCADES

John Gummoe (guitar and lead vocals)
Eddie Snyder (piano and vocals)
Dave Stevens (bass and vocals)
Dave Wilson (sax and vocals)
Dave Zabo (drums and vocals)

1962 The group is formed by Gummoe in San Diego, Cal., US, while Stevens and Zabo are still at high school. They build a live reputation playing clubs across California, and eventually sign to Valiant Records in LA.
1963 Mar Debut release *Rhythm Of The Rain* hits #3 in US, and is a million-seller, its sound anticipating the soft-rock close-harmony US West Coast group style of the mid-60s.
Apr *Rhythm Of The Rain* hits #4 in UK.
May LP *Rhythm Of The Rain* is a moderate US seller at #111. Follow-up *Shy Girl* stalls at US #91, prompting Valiant to switch promotion to the other side of the record, which many radio DJs are playing instead.
June *Shy Girl*'s B-side, *The Last Leaf*, fares somewhat better, peaking at US #60. *Shy Girl* competes in UK with domestic cover version by Mark Wynter. Both chart, but Wynter reaches #24 while The Cascades peak at #32. This is their last UK chart success.
Dec Having left Valiant, the group signs to RCA Records.
1964 Jan *For Your Sweet Love* makes only US #86, and will be The Cascades sole RCA hit. It is followed by a 5-year period of silence.
1969 Sept The group resurfaces on Uni Records, still in its remembered close-harmony style, and makes US #61 with *Maybe The Rain Will Fall*. This is its chart swan song, but its place in pop history is assured by *Rhythm Of The Rain*, which will remain a favorite staple of oldies radio hereafter.

JOHNNY CASH

1950 An avid country music fan since childhood, having written his first song at age 12, Cash (b. Feb.26, 1932, Kingsland, Ark., US), joins the US Air Force after graduating from high school and is stationed in West Germany, where he learns to play guitar and write songs for it, and forms a group called The Landsberg Barbarians, with five other servicemen who have backgrounds in country music.
1953 Cash's first published song is *Hey Porter*, printed in the service newspaper *Stars and Stripes*.
1954 July [3] He leaves the US Air Force and moves to Memphis, Tenn., US.
Aug [7] Cash marries Vivian Liberto, whom he met 3 weeks before entering the service and with whom he corresponded daily through his German posting.
Aug Working around Memphis as a door-to-door salesman, and enrolled in a radio announcers' course part-time, Cash meets The Tennessee Three, a trio of part-time musicians who work as mechanics at the same garage as Cash's brother. He begins to rehearse and play small local gigs with the trio: Marshall Grant (guitar), Luther Perkins (guitar) and Red Kernodle (steel guitar).
1955 Encouraged by Elvis Presley's° success at Sam Phillips' Sun Records, Cash and the trio try to audition for Phillips as a gospel act. Phillips insists they can only succeed commercially singing country. Grant moves to playing bass, Perkins switches from acoustic to electric guitar and Kernodle leaves, deciding that showbiz is not for him. Sun signs the remaining trio, largely on the strength of Cash's voice and his songs *Hey Porter* and *Cry Cry Cry*.
May [24] Daughter Rosanne is born. (During the 1980s, she will become a major country artist in her own right, having done back-up singing and solo spots in her father's stage show during the 1970s.)
June [21] First single, *Cry Cry Cry*, is released.
Sept *Cry Cry Cry* hits #1 in Memphis, and the group supports Elvis Presley° on local gigs and features in a 15-minute radio show on KWEM, Memphis (sponsored by Cash's employer).
Nov *Cry Cry Cry* makes a 1 week entry in the US national country chart at #14.
Dec Cash plays a guest slot on the "Louisiana Hayride" show in Shreveport, La. (becoming a weekly regular the following month), and plays live gigs around the mid-south with Carl Perkins°, supporting Elvis Presley°, George Jones and others.
1956 Jan Cash leaves his day job to concentrate on performing.
Mar Double-sided *So Doggone Lonesome/Folsom Prison Blues* hits #5 on the country chart. Bob Neal, ex-manager of Elvis Presley°, becomes Cash's manager.
May *I Walk The Line* is released. Written by Cash and originally performed on "Louisiana Hayride" as a slow ballad, Phillips insists on speeding up the tempo and it becomes Cash's first pop crossover success.
July [7] He appears on the "Grand Ole Opry" in Nashville, Tenn.
Nov *I Walk The Line* peaks at US #17, having hit #2 on the country chart for several weeks.
1957 Jan *There You Go* hits #2 on the country chart. Cash is in demand for live appearances all over the US, having toured Florida, Colorado, California, and even some dates in Ontario, Canada.
Jan [19] He appears on US network TV, in CBS' "Jackie Gleason Show".
July *Next In Line* makes US #99 and #9 on the country chart.
Sept Cash undergoes throat surgery in a Memphis hospital and is ordered not to sing for a month.
Oct *Home Of The Blues* reaches US #88 and #5 on the country chart. LP *Johnny Cash With His Hot & Blue Guitar*, the only LP released by Sun while Cash is with the label (there will be six more after he leaves), does not chart.
1958 Mar Pop-oriented *Ballad Of A Teenage Queen* reaches US #14 and tops the country chart. Produced and written by Jack Clement to widen Cash's appeal to a teenage audience, the original trio recording has dubbed male and female backup voices added to give the pop/rock feel.
July *Guess Things Happen That Way* reaches US #11 and tops the country chart. B-side *Come In Stranger* charts independently at US #66.
Aug [1] Cash's Sun contract expires, and he and The Tennessee Two sign to CBS/Columbia Records. He ends his residency on the

"Grand Ole Opry" and moves with family, band and manager Bob Neal from Memphis to LA.

Sept *The Ways Of A Woman In Love*, released by Sun upon Cash's departure, reaches US #24.

Nov Both sides of his first CBS/Columbia single, *All Over Again/What Do I Care?*, chart at #38 and #52 respectively.

1959 Jan Debut CBS/Columbia LP *The Fabulous Johnny Cash* is his first US LP chart entry, reaching #19. *It's Just About Time* (on Sun) makes US #47.

Feb *Don't Take Your Guns To Town* reaches US #32.

June *Frankie's Man Johnny* peaks at US #57.

Aug *Katy Too* (on Sun) makes US #66.

Sept Double A-sides *I Got Stripes* and *Five Feet High And Rising* reach US #43 and #76 respectively.

Dec Christmas record *The Little Drummer Boy* makes US #63.

1960 Mar *Straight A's In Love* (on Sun) peaks at US #84.

July *Second Honeymoon* reaches US #79 and *Down The Street To 301* (on Sun) makes US #85.

1961 Constantly on the road, and beginning to rely heavily on drink and pills, Cash becomes estranged from his family, which by now includes four daughters. He spends time with the bohemian folk scene in New York's Greenwich Village.

Dec *Tennessee Flat-Top Box* makes US #84.

1963 Cash is arrested crossing the Mexican border with a guitar case full of amphetamine tablets and spends a night in jail.

May LP *Blood, Sweat And Tears* reaches US #80, his second chart album in almost 5 years.

July *Ring Of Fire*, a brass-flavored Mexican/western arrangement, climbs to US #17. The song is co-written by Merle Haggard and June Carter, who is an established country performer. Carter and Cash begin playing as a duo.

Sept LP *Ring Of Fire – The Best Of Johnny Cash* reaches US #26.

Nov *The Matador*, styled similarly to *Ring Of Fire*, makes US #44.

1964 Mar *Understand Your Man* reaches US #35. Cash becomes an erratic and unreliable performer and he and his band start to miss gigs.

Aug LP *I Walk The Line*, featuring six newly-recorded versions of his old Sun hits, reaches US #53.

Nov A version of Bob Dylan's° *It Ain't Me Babe* reaches US #58.

Dec LP *Bitter Tears (Ballads Of The American Indian)* reaches US #47.

1965 Apr *Orange Blossom Special* reaches US #80 and LP of the same title makes US #49.

June *It Ain't Me Babe* is Cash's first UK chart entry, reaching #28.

1966 Mar *The One On The Right Is On The Left*, a tongue-twisting novelty, makes US #46.

July LP *Everybody Loves A Nut* makes UK #28 and reaches US #88, with the title track making US #96 as a single.

1967 Cash is found one night near death in a small Georgia town and a policeman has to revive him. Vivian divorces him.

Aug Compilation LP *Johnny Cash's Greatest Hits, Volume 1* reaches US #82 and will stay on chart for 71 weeks.

1968 Feb *Rosanna's Going Wild* peaks at US #91.

Mar Cash marries June Carter.

May LP *From Sea To Shining Sea* reaches UK #40.

July A new version of *Folsom Prison Blues*, originally recorded in the mid-1950s for Sun, is issued to trailer LP *Johnny Cash at Folsom Prison* and climbs to US #32. LP *Old Golden Throat* makes UK #37.

Aug Live LP *Johnny Cash at Folsom Prison*, a recording of a concert in the jail, is a major crossover success for Cash. It reaches US #13 (spending 122 weeks on chart) and UK #8 (53 weeks on chart). Cash is booked for frequent US TV appearances.

1969 Feb *Daddy Sang Bass* peaks at US #42.

Feb [17] Cash records a session in Nashville with Bob Dylan°. *Girl From The North Country*, included on Dylan's LP *Nashville Skyline*, is the only duet released from the session.

JOHNNY CASH *cont.*

Apr LP *Then Holy Land*, gospel music with a narration, reaches US #54.

June [7] Cash begins his own US ABC TV series, "The Johnny Cash Show".

Aug Live LP *Johnny Cash At San Quentin*, the soundtrack to UK Granada TV documentary of the same title, focusing on a Cash concert in the prison, tops the US LP chart for 4 weeks and is later a million-seller. Extracted *A Boy Named Sue*, a tongue-in-cheek narrative song, hits US #2 and is also a million-seller.

Oct *A Boy Named Sue* hits UK #4. LP *Johnny Cash At San Quentin* hits UK #2 (and will stay charted in UK for 114 weeks).

Nov Double A-sided *Blistered/See Ruby Fall* reaches US #50. LP *Greatest Hits, Volume 1* makes UK #23 and stays on chart for 6 months.

Dec *Get Rhythm*, the original 1956 B-side of *I Walk The Line*, is reissued by Sun, climbing to US #60.

1970 Feb A version of Tim Hardin's *If I Were A Carpenter*, duetted with June Carter, reaches US #36.

Mar LP *Hello, I'm Johnny Cash* hits both US and UK #6.

Apr [17] Cash plays at the White House at the invitation of President Nixon (who makes a special request for *A Boy Named Sue*).

May *What Is Truth?* reaches US #19 and UK #21.

July LP *The World Of Johnny Cash* climbs to US #54 and hits UK #5.

Sept *Sunday Morning Coming Down* makes US #46.

Dec *Flesh And Blood*, from the *I Walk The Line* soundtrack, makes US #54.

1971 Apr *The Man In Black*, an archetypal Cash narrative song, reaches US #58.

May "The Johnny Cash Show" on US TV closes after 2 years. The Cashes travel to Israel to film *Gospel Road*, about Christianity and modern-day life in the Holy Land.

June *Kate* climbs to US #75.

Aug LP *Man In Black* reaches US #56.

Sept LP *Man In Black* climbs to UK #18.

Nov LP *The Johnny Cash Collection (His Greatest Hits, Volume II)* reaches US #94.

1972 He appears with Kirk Douglas in western movie *A Gunfight*, and guest-stars on US TV's "Columbo".

May *A Thing Called Love* hits UK #4, while LP of the same title reaches US #112 and UK #8.

Oct Compilation LP *Star Portrait* reaches UK #16. LP *Johnny Cash: America (A 200-Year Salute In Story And Song)* reaches US #176.

1973 Mar LP *Any Old Wind That Blows* reaches US #188. Cash joins evangelist Billy Graham on stage and sings a duet with Cliff Richard° at Wembley Stadium, London.

1976 May [10] Novelty song *One Piece At A Time* reaches US #29.

July *One Piece At A Time* makes UK #32. LP of the same title makes US #185 and UK #49. (It will be his last US chart entry.)

Aug Cash starts a new 4-week summer series, "The Johnny Cash Show", on US CBS TV, originating from "Grand Ole Opry" in Nashville, and with country music guest stars.

Oct Compilation LP *The Best Of Johnny Cash* makes UK #48.

1978 Sept LP *Itchy Feet* is Cash's last chart LP, reaching UK #36.

1981 Apr [23] Cash records a joint session in Stuttgart, West Germany, with Carl Perkins° and Jerry Lee Lewis°, released as LP *The Survivors*.

1985 Aug Cash teams with Waylon Jennings, Willie Nelson° and Kris Kristofferson° for LP *The Highwayman* which tops US country chart.

1986 July Cash joins Jerry Lee Lewis°, Carl Perkins° and Roy Orbison° for LP *Class Of '55* which reaches #16 on US country chart.

1987 Mar Compilation LP *1958-1986: The CBS Years* anthologizes a selection of hits.

May Cash debuts for Mercury with LP *Johnny Cash Is Coming To Town*.

1988 Sept LP *Water From The Wells Of Home* features a cast including Paul McCartney°, The Everly Brothers°, Waylon Jennings, Emmylou Harris , daughter Rosanne Cash, and son John Carter Cash. He also begins work on LP *Classic Cash* for pre-Christmas release, re-recording versions of several of his best-known hits.

DAVID CASSIDY

1970 Sept [25] Cassidy (b. Apr.12, 1950, New York, N.Y.,US), son of actor Jack Cassidy, having gone from high school into a Broadway part in *Fig Leaves Are Falling*, and then into small TV drama roles, launches in NBC-TV's "The Partridge Family", a musical sitcom based on real life family group The Cowsills°. Co-starring with step-mother Shirley Jones, Cassidy plays Keith, the group's lead singer. In the first episode, the Partridges record *I Think I Love You* in their garage and become stars when the single hits #1.

Oct The Partridge Family is signed to Bell Records (with only Cassidy and Jones actually recording) and records *I Think I Love You* in real life, with Cassidy on lead vocal.

Nov *I Think I Love You* tops the US chart for 3 weeks, ultimately selling over 5 million copies. LP *The Partridge Family Album* hits US #4.

1971 Mar *Doesn't Somebody Want To Be Wanted* hits US #6 and is another million-seller. With the TV show not yet airing in UK, *I Think I Love You* peaks at #18.

May LP *The Partridge Family Up To Date* hits US #3.

June *I'll Meet You Halfway* hits US #9.

Sept *I Woke Up In Love This Morning* reaches US #13. Third LP, *The Partridge Family Sound Magazine*, climbs to US #9.

Sept [17] BBC TV airs "The Partridge Family" for the first time.

Oct Cassidy is launched as a solo recording artist following his ascent to TV teen idol status, with a revival of The Association's° US #1 hit *Cherish*.

Dec *Cherish* hits US #9 and becomes a million-seller.

1972 Jan Family single *It's One Of Those Nights (Yes Love)* reaches US #20.

Mar Cassidy solo LP *Cherish* peaks at US #15 while The Family's *It's One Of Those Nights (Yes Love)* climbs to UK #11. Cassidy attempts to counter his whiter-than-white image, and appears in semi-nude photos in *Rolling Stone* magazine, accompanying an interview in which he voices his disaffection with the teenybop pigeonhole. The resulting controversy rebounds badly on his US solo career.

Apr Cassidy's second solo *Could It Be Forever* peaks at US #37, while The Family LP *The Partridge Family Shopping Bag* is its first to miss the US top 10, peaking at #18.

May Cassidy is launched as a soloist in UK with *Could It Be Forever*, using *Cherish* as the B-side, and hits #2.

June Solo LP *Cherish* hits UK #2. Family LP *Sound Magazine* peaks at UK #14.

Aug The Family's revival of Neil Sedaka's° *Breaking Up Is Hard To Do* hits UK #3 and makes US #28.

Sept Cassidy's solo revival of The Young Rascals'° *How Can I Be Sure* hits UK #1 for 2 weeks, having only reached US #25. Huge media coverage confirms him as a major teenage idol in UK.

Oct R&B-flavored solo *Rock Me Baby*, a deliberate attempt to harden his teenybop musical image, makes US #38 (his last US hit single) and UK #11. LP *The Partridge Family At Home With Their Greatest Hits* reaches US #21.

Oct [21] UK's ITV, having picked up the series after BBC dropped it, airs "The Partridge Family".

1973 Feb The Family revives Gene Pitney's° oldie *Looking Thru The Eyes Of Love*, which makes US #39 and hits UK #9. Solo LP *Rock Me Baby* hits UK #2 after peaking at US #41.

Apr Cassidy now concentrates his solo recording career in UK, where his fan following is strongest. *I Am A Clown* hits UK #3. The Partridge Family US singles chart swan song is *Friend And Lover* at #99.

June The Family revives The Ronettes'° *Walking In The Rain*, which hits UK #10 but is its final UK chartmaker.

July Last US chartmaking Family LP, *Crossword Puzzle*, makes US #167.

Oct Double A-side *Daydreamer/The Puppy Song* tops the UK chart for 3 weeks, after being spectacularly introduced on TV (on the gala 500th edition of "Top of the Pops") by an apparently live clip (though in reality pre-taped) showing Cassidy arriving in UK by plane and alighting to perform both the songs on the airport tarmac.

Dec LP *Dreams Are Nothin' More Than Wishes* is Cassidy's most successful UK solo LP, hitting #1 for a week.

1974 May [26] Tragedy occurs during a UK concert at White City, London, when among a frenzied crowd, over 1000 people need medical treatment. Six girls are taken to hospital, and 14-year-old Bernadette Whelan dies 4 days later from heart failure.

June *If I Didn't Care* hits UK #9.

Aug A revival of Lennon°/McCartney's° *Please Please Me* climbs to UK #16. ("The Beatles° wrote the soundtrack to my youth" is Cassidy's most famous quote of the time.) His solo LP *Cassidy Live* hits UK #9.

Aug [31] "The Partridge Family" ends its run on US TV, leaving Cassidy free to pursue a full-time solo career.

1975 Feb He signs worldwide to RCA (but this will bring no US chart success).

July First RCA single *I Write The Songs*, written by Beach Boy° Bruce Johnston and having been turned down by Leon Russell°, reaches UK #11. (Barry Manilow° will take it to US #1 at the end of the year.)

Aug LP *The Higher They Climb*, featuring assistance from members of The Beach Boys°, The Turtles° and America°, reaches UK #22.

Nov A revival of The Beach Boys'° *Darlin'* makes UK #16.

1978 Cassidy stars in a production of *Voice of the Turtle* at West Point, N.Y., US. He wins an Emmy as Best Actor in a TV drama for his role in "A Chance To Live".

1983 May [2] Cassidy plays George M. Cohan in a benefit performance "Parade of Stars Playing The Palace" for the Actors' Fund of America. He takes the lead role in the Broadway production of Tim Rice and Andrew Lloyd Webber's *Joseph and the Amazing Technicolor Dream Coat*.

1985 Mar A new recording deal with MLM/Arista Records produces a comeback single, the self-penned *The Last Kiss*, which hits UK #6, but makes no impression in US. It is notable for the back-up vocal assistance from George Michael°, who admits that Cassidy was one of his teen idols.

May *Romance (Let Your Heart Go)* climbs to UK #54. LP *Romance* reaches UK #20, as a UK tour sells out.

1987 He takes over the lead role as the Rock star from Cliff Richard° in the London West End production of Dave Clark's° musical *Time*.

CHAD AND JEREMY

Chad Stuart (vocals and guitar)
Jeremy Clyde (vocals and guitar)

1963 Stuart (b. Dec.10, 1943, UK) and Clyde (b. Mar.22, 1944, UK) meet at the Central School of Drama in London. They both play guitar and decide to form an acoustic folk-pop duo, with Stuart handling the musical side of their songs and Clyde the lyrics.

Dec The duo signs to UK independent label Ember Records and, after appearing on UK TV's "Ready Steady Go", releases *Yesterday's Gone*, part-written by Stuart, which reaches UK #37. It is the duo's only UK success.

1964 July In the euphoria for UK acts following The Beatles° in US, *Yesterday's Gone*, licensed by World Artists Records, climbs to US #21, beating a UK cover by The Overlanders.

Oct *A Summer Song* hits US #7 after failing in UK. (When previewed on BBC TV's "Juke Box Jury" it had been voted a miss, but panellist Ringo Starr° predicted that "it will do well in the States".) Chad and Jeremy move to Hollywood, realizing their audience and best chance of success probably lies in the US.

Nov Debut LP *Yesterday's Gone*, containing both hits, reaches US #22.

1965 Jan Standard revival *Willow, Weep For Me* makes US #15, after well-received appearances on US TV shows like "Hullabaloo".

Apr LP *Chad & Jeremy Sing For You* reaches US #69. Another standard revival, *If I Loved You*, from the musical *Carousel*, makes US #23.

May *What Do You Want With Me* peaks at US #51 and the duo signs to CBS/Columbia Records.

June *Before And After*, written by Van McCoy, makes US #17.

July The duo's version of Lennon°/McCartney's° *From A Window*, issued by World Artists, peaks at US #97 while Billy J. Kramer's° version makes US #23.

Aug Columbia follow-up, *I Don't Wanna Lose You Baby*, reaches US #35. First Columbia LP, *Before And After*, makes #37.

Nov Another standard ballad, *I Have Dreamed*, from musical *The King And I*, makes US #91.

Dec LP *I Don't Wanna Lose You Baby* reaches US #77.

1966 May LPs *The Best Of Chad & Jeremy* and *More Chad & Jeremy*, compiling their early Ember/World Artists tracks, are issued in US on Capitol, and chart at US #49 and #144 respectively. *Distant Shores* makes US #30.

Oct LP *Distant Shores* climbs to US #61. *You Are She* makes #87 and is their final US chart entry. The duo splits when Clyde joins the London stage musical, *The Passion Flower Hotel*. Although the split causes some bad feeling, they re-form after Clyde's stage work is over.

Dec Chad and Jeremy appear in an episode of "Batman". Catwoman steals their voices and threatens to use her voice eraser machine unless her demands of $22.5 million for their return are met.

1967 Nov LP *Of Cabbages And Kings*, which makes US #186, is a five-movement piece scored and arranged by Stuart. The critics praise it but Chad and Jeremy announce a final split. (Stuart begins to write musicals and Clyde immerses himself in acting, his most prominent early stage role is in *Conduct Unbecoming* in London's West End. He will continue to be seen in UK TV roles throughout the 1970s and 1980s.)

THE CHAMBERS BROTHERS

George Chambers (bass and vocals)
Willie Chambers (guitar and vocals)
Lester Chambers (harmonica and vocals)
Joe Chambers (guitar and vocals)
Brian Keenan (drums)

1954/60 The Chambers family moves from Mississippi to LA, where George Chambers (b. Sept.26, 1931, Flora, Miss., US), home after a tour of US Army duty in Korea, organizes brothers Willie (b. Mar.3, 1938, Flora), Lester (b. Apr.13, 1940, Flora) and Joe (b. Aug.24, 1942, Scott County, Miss.) into a gospel group. George has sung professionally but the brothers play almost exclusively to church congregations for several years.

1961/64 George meets Ed Pearl, owner of LA's famous Ash Grove coffee house where, after a successful audition, the group makes its club debut. The brothers become increasingly influenced by the coffee house folk scene, adding folk numbers to their gospel set.

1965 July They receive an ecstatic reception at the Newport Folk Festival and develop wider musical styles, picking up rock and blues influences. Lester learns harmonica with the help of blues legend Sonny Terry.

Aug They sign to Vault Records in LA and record LP *People Get Ready*, a set of rough soul-blues numbers, highlighted by the title track and *Your Old Lady*.

1966 LP *The Chambers Brothers Now* is issued, featuring new recruit ex-Manfred Mann° drummer Keenan (b. Jan.28, 1944, New York).

1967 Oct CBS/Columbia Records signs the group.

Dec Debut LP, *The Time Has Come*, is issued in US. It gains significant rock and "progressive" FM airplay (and will eventually hit US #4 and earn a gold disk by Dec. 1968).

1968 Now selling out clubs and auditoriums around the country, they perform in a network TV showcase for new artists, and are invited back.

Aug [4-5] They appear at Newport Pop Festival in Costa Mesa, Cal., with The Byrds°, Jefferson Airplane°, Steppenwolf° and others.

Sept *The Time Has Come Today*, from LP of the same title, reaches US #11.

THE CHAMBERS BROTHERS *cont.*

Dec LP *A New Time – A New Day* climbs to US #16. Taken from it, a revival of Otis Redding's° *I Can't Turn You Loose* makes US #37.

1969 Jan Vault Records issues an older cut, the group's revival of The Isley Brothers'° *Shout*, which reaches US #83.

July *Wake Up*, used on the soundtrack of movie *The April Fools*, reaches US #92.

Feb Double LP *Love, Peace And Happiness*, one of which was recorded live at New York's Fillmore East, peaks at US #58. The title track is their last US hit single, making a brief entry at #96.

Dec Double compilation LP of material recorded during 1965-66, *The Chambers Brothers' Greatest Hits*, is released by Vault and charts at US #193.

1971 Mar LP *New Generation* reaches US #145.

Dec Columbia issues its own version of LP *The Chambers Brothers' Greatest Hits*, which makes US #166.

1972 Mar The group has broken up when LP *Oh My God!* is released. Drummer Keenan joins Genya Ravan's band.

1974 The Brothers reassemble to record LP *Unbonded* in a new deal with Avco Records.

1975 LP *Right Move* is released, though by now the chartmaking sales are behind them, and they will dissolve and re-form more than once in the coming years.

THE CHAMPS

Danny Flores (Chuck Rio) (tenor saxophone)
Dave Burgess (rhythm guitar)
Buddy Bruce (lead guitar)
Cliff Hils (bass)
Gene Alden (drums)

1957 Nov Burgess, an A&R man at Challenge Records in LA, deciding his instrumental *Train To Nowhere* has hit potential, records it while working with a studio group for singer Jerry Wallace. A B-side is needed and Flores suggests his latin-flavored *Tequila*, written while on a trip to Tijuana.

Dec [26] The record is released on Gene Autry's Challenge label. (Burgess shortened the name of Autry's horse, Champion, to come up with a name for the group.)

1958 Jan US radio DJs dismiss the A-side and play flip-side *Tequila*.

Mar *Tequila* tops US chart for 5 weeks, having hit #1 only 2 weeks after entering. It reaches the million sales mark in US and is R&B #1 for 4 weeks.

Apr *Tequila* hits UK #4. The Champs needs to tour to capitalize on its success. Hils and Bruce do not want to work live and are replaced by Dave Norris on guitar and Joe Burnas on bass.

June Follow-up *El Rancho Rock* climbs to US #30. Burnas leaves and Van Norman takes his place.

Aug *Midnighter*, B-side of *El Rancho Rock*, makes US #94. Flores and Alden leave to make way for Jimmy Seals on sax and Dash Crofts on drums, and Dean Beard joins on piano.

Sept *Chariot Rock* climbs to US #59.

1959 May [4] At the first-ever Grammy Awards ceremony, *Tequila* wins Best R&B Performance of 1958.

1960 Feb Confounding ideas that The Champs is a spent force, it rearranges the original hit formula to come up with *Too Much Tequila*, which reaches US #30. Other 1960 releases fail to make the grade. The Champs continues with interruptions: Beard leaves and is not replaced; Norman dies in a car crash, his place being taken by Bobby Morris; Burgess decides that playing live is keeping him out of Challenge studio too much, so brings in session guitarist Glen Campbell° to replace him.

Mar *Too Much Tequila* reaches UK #49.

1962 Feb The group adapts its original hit to cash in on a huge dance craze with *Tequila Twist*, but the record stalls at US #99.

July Radio DJs once again flip A-side *Tequila Twist* and play catchy B-side latin dance number *Limbo Rock*, which climbs to US #40. (When revived with added lyrics by Chubby Checker° a few months later, it will hit US #1 and spur a big new limbo dance craze.)

Oct The band cashes in on the new craze it helped launch, but *Limbo Dance* only manages a 1-week US chart appearance at #97.

1965 After several more switches in the line-up and more unsuccessful singles, Burgess decides to fold the band. (None of the original members will have distinguished hit careers elsewhere, but Glen Campbell° becomes a country/pop superstar and Seals and Crofts° form a soft-rock duo which will have a string of US top 20 hits from 1972-78.)

1987 *Tequila* has a brief return to the limelight when featured in the Pee Wee Herman movie *Pee Wee's Big Adventure*.

GENE CHANDLER

1959 After 2 years US Army service in Germany, Chandler (b. Eugene Dixon, July 6, 1937, Chicago, Ill., US), who had led The Gaytones vocal group at Englewood High School, rejoins R&B vocal quintet The Dukays (originally formed in 1957) in Chicago.

1961 July The group, signed to Nat Records, charts with *The Girl's A Devil*, reaching US #64.

Nov Nat sells gimmicky *Duke Of Earl*, intended as the follow-up, to Vee Jay Records (which already owns the publishing), where A&R man Calvin Carter is convinced it will be a hit. Vee Jay signs him as a soloist but he remains a member of The Dukays for Nat. He also becomes Gene Chandler, borrowing the name from his favorite actor, Jeff Chandler.

1962 Feb *Nite Owl*, the official Dukays follow-up, reaches US #73, but *Duke Of Earl*, credited to Gene Chandler, tops the US chart for 3 weeks and is a million-seller. Chandler changes his name to "The Duke of Earl" and appears on stage in top hat, cape and monocle. He has a cameo role in the movie *Don't Knock The Twist*.

Apr LP *The Duke Of Earl* and single *Walk On With The Duke*, both credited to "The Duke", are not hits. The LP reaching US #69 and the single only #91, prompts a name change back to Gene Chandler.

Dec *You Threw A Lucky Punch* (an "answer" disk to Mary Wells' US hit *You Beat Me To The Punch*) reaches US #49.

1963 May *Rainbow*, B-side of *Lucky Punch* climbs to US #47.

Sept *Man's Temptation* reaches US #71 and is Chandler's final hit for Vee Jay.

1964 May He moves to Ewart Abner's newly-formed Constellation Records. Debuts with *Soul Hootenanny (Pt.1)*, which peaks at US #92, and follows with a rush of US chart singles.

Aug *Just Be True* hits US #19.

Nov *Bless Our Love* reaches US #39.

1965 Jan *What Now* makes US #40.

June *Nothing Can Stop Me* hits US #18.

Aug *Good Times* reaches only US #92.

1966 Jan LP *Gene Chandler – Live On Stage In '65* reaches US #124, but extracted *Rainbow '65* (a live treatment of his 1962 hit) makes #69.

Mar *(I'm Just A) Fool For You* charts at US #88 and Chandler leaves Constellation.

1967 Jan *I Fooled You This Time*, recorded for Checker in Chicago, makes US #45, but Chandler signs a long-term deal with Brunswick Records and three chart singles follow.

Apr *Girl Don't Care* makes US #66.

June *To Be A Lover* reaches US #94.

Sept *There Goes The Lover* reaches US #98.

1968 June *Nothing Can Stop Me*, reissued in UK by Soul City label, gives him a UK chart entry at #41.

Sept *There Was A Time* makes US #82.

Nov A duet with Barbara Acklin, *From The Teacher To The Preacher*, reaches US #57.

1969 Dec Chandler moves into label management with Bamboo Records, signing Mel and Tim, and producing their *Backfield In Motion*, which hits US #10 and sells over a million. He also launches Mr. Chand Records to showcase his own productions, but less successfully.

1970 Sept He recaptures his initial chart form with *Groovy Situation*, for Mercury. It reaches US #11, his second million-seller.

Nov *Simply Call It Love* makes US #75, while LP *The Gene Chandler Situation* reaches only US #178.

1971 Jan Chandler teams with Jerry Butler° for *You Just Can't Win (By Making The Same Mistake)* which reaches US #94, his last chart single for 8 years.

Apr Duetted LP *Gene & Jerry – One & One* reaches US #143.

1979 Now a vice-president of Chi-Sound Records, he records LP *Get Down* for the label. The LP spends nearly 6 months on US chart peaking at #47. The title track from it reaches US #53.

Mar *Get Down* becomes a huge UK dance floor hit at UK #11.

Oct *When You're #1* stops ninety-eight positions short at US #99, while LP of the same title reaches US #153. The single fares better in UK, making #43.

1980 July *Does She Have A Friend For Me* fails to chart in US, but will later reach UK #28.

Aug LP *Gene Chandler '80* spends 5 months on chart but climbs to only US #87. (Chandler will continue as an executive of Chi-Sound and does not give up recording even when hits cease. LPs such as *Here's To Love* (1981) and *I'll Make The Living (If You'll Make The Loving Worthwhile)* (1982) will continue to keep his name alive in the US R&B market of the 80s.)

THE CHANTAYS

Bob Spickard (guitar)
Brian Carman (guitar)
Rob Marshall (piano)
Warren Waters (bass)
Bob Welch (drums)

1961 Sept While still at high school in Santa Ana, Cal., US, Spickard and Waters decide to form a group having been inspired by The Rhythm Rockers, the most popular local surf band. Spickard learns electric guitar and Waters bass. They recruit class-mate Marshall, who plays classical piano, Carman, who tries sax but soon abandons it for guitar, and Welch on drums. Spickard coins their name, based on the French "chanter" (to sing), although they plan to be an instrumental group.

Dec [15] First live gig is self-promoted at the Tustin Youth Center, Santa Ana. Playing with borrowed amplifiers, they make $95 profit.

1962 July They are spotted by DJ Jack Sands while playing at Lake Arrowhead, Cal. Sands is impressed by their sound and audience popularity and becomes their manager. He arranges for them to record two Spickard/ Carman compositions, *Move It* and *Pipeline* at Pal studios in Cucamonga, Cal.

Sept Signed to Downey Records on the strength of its demos, the group re-records *Move It* and *Pipeline* for commercial release.

1963 Jan After limited reaction to *Move It*, California DJs discover the unusual instrumental *Pipeline* on the B-side. Originally titled *Liberty's Whip*, the tune has become surfing term "pipeline" after Spickard and Carman became inspired watching a film about Hawaiian surfers.

Feb With the record a big California hit, it is picked up from Downey by bigger Dot label for national distribution and enters US chart.

May *Pipeline* hits US #4. LP *Pipeline* climbs to US #26.

June *Tragic Wind* fails to cross from early California sales to national success. *Pipeline* reaches UK #15.

Dec *Pipeline* receives Record of the Year award from Australia, where it has hit #1.

1964 July The group plays a 3-month tour of Hawaii. Welch has left for university in Europe and is replaced on drums by Steve Khan. At the end of the tour Waters leaves to go to college and Carman to work for Rickenbacker Guitars.

1965 Nov *Fear Of The Rain* is released on Reprise Records, with the group playing under the pseudonym The Ill Winds, but it fails to sell.

Dec Spickard is invited to take the group to Japan for a 3-week tour. With guitar instrumental music hugely popular in Japan, *Pipeline* is revered as a classic. Most original members are unable to take time off from study or day jobs, so Spickard and Marshall invite drummer Tommy Hannigan and ex-The Rhythm Rockers guitarist John Longstreth. Road manager Mark Howlett learns and plays bass as they tour. The group receives superstar treatment and mass fan adoration, playing one gig to a 24,000 audience.

1966 July The original line-up, as Ill Winds, records *A Letter* but with no success and The Chantays splits up. (The members move into business careers in California and will stay in touch with each other, eventually staging a one-off live Chantays reunion in 1979. In 1980, Spickard will form a part-time group, The California Good Time Band, including Carman and Welch.)

1977 Sept Ex-Beach Boys° Bruce Johnston revives *Pipeline*, which reaches UK #33.

HARRY CHAPIN

1971 June A member of the Brooklyn Heights Boys Choir and a musical act before college with his brothers, Chapin (b. Dec.7, 1942, Greenwich Village, New York, N.Y., US, son of a big band drummer), after several years making film documentaries (including 1969 Oscar-nominated *Legendary Champions*), advertises in *Village Voice* for help to perform the narrative songs he has been writing. He is joined by John Wallace (an old Brooklyn choirboy friend) on bass, Ron Palmer on acoustic guitar, and Tim Scott adding an unusual blend on cello.

June [29] The group, having rehearsed for a week, rents the Village Club for 13 weeks, and establishes a live reputation performing Chapin's "story songs".

Dec After interest from several record companies, Chapin signs to Elektra.

1972 June Debut LP *Heads And Tales* reaches US #60, staying charted for 6 months, while *Taxi*, extracted as a single despite its near 7-minute length, makes US #24.

Nov *Sunday Morning Sunshine* and second LP *Sniper And Other Love Songs* reach US #75 and #160 respectively.

1974 Mar *W-O-L-D*, the story of a radio station DJ, climbs to US #36, while Chapin's third LP *Short Stories* peaks at #61.

May *W-O-L-D*, his only UK chart success, makes #34.

Dec *Cat's In The Cradle*, based on a poem by his wife about a neglectful father, tops US chart and is a million-seller but fails to chart in UK.

1975 Jan Boosted by its success, LP *Verities And Balderdash* hits US #4 and earns a gold disk. Chapin turns his talents to writing musical revue *The Night That Made America Famous* and also performs in its 7-week Broadway run.

Mar *I Wanna Learn A Love Song* reaches US #44. Chapin wins an Emmy Award for his music on the US ABC-TV children's series "Make A Wish", hosted by his brother Tom. He co-founds WHY (World Hunger Year), raising funds to combat international famine. It will receive over $350,000 from benefit concerts in its first year.

Oct LP *Portrait Gallery* reaches US #53.

1976 May Double live LP *Greatest Stories – Live* is Chapin's second gold LP and climbs to US #48.

July *Better Place To Be (Parts 1 & 2)* reaches US #86. Increasingly politically active, he is a delegate at the Democratic Convention.

Nov LP *On The Road To Kingdom Come* reaches US #87.

1977 Oct Double LP *Dance Band On The Titanic*, produced by his brother Steve, reaches US #58.

1978 July LP *Living Room Suite* reaches US #133.

1979 Nov Double live LP *Legends Of The Lost And Found – New Greatest Stories Live* reaches US #163.

1980 Dec Chapin signs to Boardwalk Records, and LP *Sequel*, his only one for the label, peaks at US #58. The 6½-minute title track from it (a sequel to the story *Taxi*) climbs to US #23.

1981 July [16] Chapin dies in a road accident in Jericho, New York, when a truck runs into the back of his car while he is driving to a benefit performance. At a memorial service held in Brooklyn, New York, the Harry Chapin Memorial Fund is announced, launched with a $10,000 donation from Elektra Records.

Aug [17] A benefit concert for the fund is held at Nassau Coliseum, Long Island, headlined by Kenny Rogers°. It is estimated that during his career Chapin has raised over $5 million from benefit performances for the causes to which he was committed.

TRACY CHAPMAN

1982 Having started writing songs at age 8, Chapman, (b. 1964, Cleveland, Oh., US) graduates from Wooster School, Conn. and goes to Tufts University, Medford, Mass., where she majors in anthropology and African studies. (During her sophomore year at Wooster, the school chaplain The Reverend Robert Tate takes a collection to buy Chapman a new guitar – he will receive a thank you credit on the liner notes of Chapman's debut LP.)

1986 Chapman joins an African drum ensemble at college, but develops her own folk guitar playing and performs self-written acoustic songs on the Boston folk circuit. Schoolmate Brian Koppelman's father, Charles, president of SBK Publishing, introduces her to producer David Kershenbaum and also to Elektra Records where she links up with ex-Bob Dylan° manager, Elliott Roberts.

1987 She records her debut LP with Kershenbaum producing.

Mar Chapman visits London, playing three nights at The Donmar Warehouse, with Natalie Merchant from 10,000 Maniacs.

May She plays two nights at The Bitter End club in New York City.

1988 Apr LP *Tracy Chapman* immediately attracts critical favor and rapid success, particularly in the UK. Chapman tours US and plays some selected UK dates supporting her label-mates, 10,000 Maniacs.

July She appears at Nelson Mandela's televised 70th Birthday Party and is called back after her initial slot to fill in for Stevie Wonder°

TRACY CHAPMAN *cont.*

who is unable to go on after a computer program of his is stolen. Her appearance results in LP *Tracy Chapman* selling 12,000 copies 2 days later. It tops the UK chart and *Fast Car*, extracted from it, hits UK #7. The LP hits US #6 and *Fast Car* climbs to US #20.

Sept *Talkin' 'Bout A Revolution* is released.

RAY CHARLES

1946 Charles (b. Ray Charles Robinson, Sept.23, 1930, Albany, Ga., US), who has lived in Greenville, Fla., since age 2, and been blind since suffering from glaucoma at age 7, having studied music (classical piano and clarinet) at Florida's State School for Deaf and Blind, begins playing for his living with various bands around Jacksonville, Fla., including Henry Washington's Big Band and Joe Anderson's band.

1948 Moving to Seattle, Wash., after being orphaned a year earlier, 17-year-old R.C. Robinson (as he is billed) forms The Maxim Trio with G.D. McGhee on guitar and Milton Garred on bass, to play light jazz and blues modelled on the Nat "King" Cole Trio style.

1949 The trio signs to Downbeat Records and releases Charles' own composition *Confession Blues*. He alters his billing to his two forenames to avoid confusion with boxer/singer Sugar Ray Robinson. Downbeat becomes Swingtime Records and releases a string of singles by Charles, including *See See Rider* and *I Wonder Who's Kissing Her Now?* (used 38 years later as soundtrack for a UK TV Volkswagen car ad).

1951 Jan First US R&B chart entry is *Baby Let Me Hold Your Hand*, followed by *Kiss-A-Me Baby*.

1952 June Atlantic Records buys Charles' contract from Swingtime for $2,500, releasing *Roll With My Baby*.

1953 *Mess Around*, later an R&B standard, is written for Charles by Atlantic owner Ahmet Ertegun, and is one of the first uptempo numbers in his previously jazz-ballad repertoire.

1954 Mar *It Should Have Been Me*, his first major seller for Atlantic, hits US R&B #7. (Over the next 3 years R&B chart successes follow: *Don't You Know*, *I've Got A Woman* (R&B #2), *This Little Girl Of Mine* (R&B #2), *Drown In My Own Tears* and *Hallelujah I Love Her So*.)

1957 July His first LP *Ray Charles* is released.

Nov Charles' first crossover success is *Swanee River Rock (Talkin' 'Bout That River)*, which makes US #34.

1958 July [5] Charles appears at the Newport Jazz Festival, his performance is recorded by Atlantic for a live LP.

Dec *Rockhouse* peaks at US #79. LP *Ray Charles At Newport*, from the summer's festival, is released.

1959 Feb *(Night Time Is) The Right Time* reaches US #95. LP *Soul Brothers*, recorded with jazz vibist Milt Jackson, is released.

May Charles plays an outdoor festival at Herndon Stadium in Atlanta, Ga., with B.B. King°, Ruth Brown, The Drifters°, Jimmy Reed° and other major R&B names. His performance is recorded by Atlantic for future LP release.

Aug Self-penned gospel-style rocker *What'd I Say* tops US R&B chart for 2 weeks and hits US #6, his first million-seller. (Jerry Lee Lewis°, Bobby Darin° and Elvis Presley° will all have 1960s hits with revivals of the song.)

Nov Charles signs to ABC Paramount Records on a 3-year contract. (Atlantic is unable to match the offer of a large advance and ownership of his own material.)

Dec *I'm Movin' On* (a cover of Hank Snow's C&W number), on Atlantic, reaches US #40.

1960 Jan Double A-side *Let The Good Times Roll/Don't Let The Sun Catch You Cryin'*, on Atlantic, makes US #78 and #95 respectively.

Mar LP *The Genius Of Ray Charles*, on Atlantic, makes US #17, his first US chart LP.

Aug ABC debut *Sticks And Stones* reaches US #40, while Atlantic LP *Ray Charles In Person*, recorded at Herndon stadium in May 1959, reaches US #13.

Nov A revival of Hoagy Carmichael's *Georgia On My Mind*, recorded after Charles' chauffeur constantly sang it on trips, tops the US chart and is his second million-seller. Similarly-styled *Come Rain Or Come Shine*, a 1959 recording issued by Atlantic, makes US #83. Debut ABC LP, *The Genius Hits The Road*, from which *Georgia* is taken and which has US place names as the themes of its songs, hits US #9, his first top 10 LP.

Dec *Georgia On My Mind* is his UK chart debut, at #24. *Ruby* makes US #28 and B-side *Hard-Hearted Hannah* reaches US #55.

1961 Feb *Them That Got* makes US #58.

Apr [12] Charles wins four 1960 Grammy awards: Best Male Vocal Performance and Best Performance by a Pop Single Artist for *Georgia On My Mind*, Best Male Vocal Album Performance for LP *The Genius Of Ray Charles* and Best R&B Performance for *Let The Good Times Roll*.

Apr LP *Dedicated To You* reaches US #11.

May Instrumental *One Mint Julep*, released on ABC's subsidiary jazz label Impulse, hits US #8. It is taken from Charles' largely instrumental big band LP *Genius+ Soul = Jazz* which includes a guest line-up of jazzmen. The LP hits US #4.

June *I've Got News For You* makes US #66 and B-side *I'm Gonna Move To The Outskirts Of Town* reaches US #84.

Sept LP *What'd I Say*, of earlier Atlantic material, makes US #20, while on the same label, relaxed instrumental LP *The Genius After Hours* reaches US #49.

Oct *Hit The Road Jack*, written by Charles' friend, R&B singer Percy Mayfield, tops the US chart for 2 weeks, becoming his third million-seller. An LP of duets, *Ray Charles And Betty Carter*, climbs to US #52.

Nov *Hit The Road Jack* hits UK #6.

Dec Atlantic LP *The Genius Sings The Blues* reaches US #73.

Dec [5] Charles is charged with possession of narcotics.

1962 Jan *Unchain My Heart* hits US #9. B-side *But On The Other Hand, Baby* makes US #72. Atlantic issues LP *Do The Twist!* (which has nothing to do with the current dance craze, but is a compilation of early material with tempos to suit twisting). It makes US #11, his highest-placed Atlantic LP.

Mar A duet between Charles and Betty Carter, *Baby, It's Cold Outside*, peaks at US #91. Charles launches his own label, Tangerine Records.

May *Hide Nor Hair* reaches US #20, with B-side *At The Club* making US #44.

June Charles records outstanding country music songs in his own style for LP *Modern Sounds In Country And Western Music*. It tops the

US chart for 14 weeks and is his only million-selling LP. Taken from it, a revival of Don Gibson's *I Can't Stop Loving You* sells over 2 million copies and tops the US chart for 5 weeks. B-side *Born To Lose* makes US #41.

July *I Can't Stop Loving You* tops the UK chart.

Aug LP *Modern Sounds In Country And Western Music* hits UK #6, his first UK chart LP.

Sept Second single from the country LP, *You Don't Know Me*, hits US #2 and is another million-seller. B-side *Careless Love* peaks at US #60. Double LP *The Ray Charles Story* an Atlantic compilation of his 1950s work, reaches US #14, while ABC compilation LP *Ray Charles' Greatest Hits*, containing the more recent hits prior to *I Can't Stop Loving You*, hits US #5.

Oct *You Don't Know Me* hits UK #9.

Dec Charles follows up his successful country experiment and LP *Modern Sounds In Country And Western Music, Vol.2* hits US #2. From it, *You Are My Sunshine* hits US #7. B-side *Your Cheating Heart* reaches US #29 and UK #13 (as UK A-side).

1963 Mar LP *Modern Sounds In Country And Western Music Vol.2* reaches UK #15. Charles opens his own studios and offices in LA. *Don't Set Me Free* makes US #20 and UK #37. B-side *The Brightest Smile In Town* charts briefly at US #92.

May [16] Charles wins a Grammy award for *I Can't Stop Loving You* as Best R&B Recording of 1962.

May Similarly-styled *Take These Chains From My Heart*, extracted from the second country LP, hits US #8.

June *Take These Chains From My Heart* hits UK #5 (his fourth and last in UK top 10).

July Double A-side *No One/Without Love (There Is Nothing)* makes US #21 and #29.

Aug Compilation LP *Ray Charles' Greatest Hits* reaches UK #16.

Oct *Busted*, a return to bluesy big band style, hits US #4 and is another million-seller. Taken from the LP, *Ingredients In A Recipe For Soul* his US #2, while *No One* reaches UK #35.

Nov *Busted* makes UK #21.

1964 Jan A revival of *That Lucky Old Sun* reaches US #20. The song is featured (with eight other Charles numbers) in film *Ballad In Blue*, in which he stars with Dawn Addams and Tom Bell.

Mar Double A-side *My Heart Cries For You/Baby Don't You Cry* makes US #38 and #39 respectively.

Apr LP *Sweet And Sour Tears* hits US #9.

May [12] Charles wins a Grammy award for *Busted*, as Best R&B Recording of 1963.

June *My Baby Don't Dig Me* reaches US #51.

Aug Double A-side *No One To Cry To/A Tear Fell*, makes US #55 and #50 respectively.

Oct *No One To Cry To* reaches UK #38, while *Smack Dab In The Middle* makes US #52. They are taken from LP *Have A Smile With Me*, which peaks at US #36.

1965 Feb A revival of *Makin' Whoopee* peaks at US #46 and UK #42.

Mar Another revival, of Johnnie Ray's *Cry*, reaches US #58. LP *Ray Charles Live In Concert* makes US #80.

Apr Taken from the LP, a live revival of his own *I Got A Woman* peaks at US #79.

July A version of Joe Barry's *I'm A Fool To Care* makes US #84.

Sept LP *Country And Western Meets Rhythm And Blues* peaks at US #116.

1966 Feb After a string of middling hits, *Crying Time* hits US #6, and charts briefly in UK at #50.

Apr Charles' revival of Buck Owens' country ballad *Together Again* reaches US #19 and UK #48 (for 1 week). LP *Crying Time* makes US #15.

July Bluesy *Let's Go Get Stoned* reaches US #31. It is the first single to give a full co-credit to Charles' own Tangerine Records with ABC.

Oct *I Chose To Sing The Blues* peaks at US #32, while LP *Ray's Moods* makes US #52.

Dec Double A-side *Please Say You're Fooling/I Don't Need No Doctor* makes US #64 and #72 respectively.

Dec [3] Charles is convicted on charges of possessing heroin and marijuana. He is given a 5-year suspended prison sentence, a $10,000 fine, and put on probation for 4 years. Medical tests showing that he has refrained from drug use since his original arrest, keep him out of jail.

1967 Mar *I Want To Talk About You* makes US #98.

Mar [2] Charles wins two Grammy awards for *Crying Time* as Best R&B Recording and Best R&B Solo Vocal Performance of 1966.

Apr Double compilation LP *A Man And His Soul* reaches US #77 and stays on chart for 62 weeks, eventually earning a gold disk for a half million sales.

July *Here We Go Again*, a return to country soul, makes US #15 and UK #38.

Aug LP *Ray Charles Invites You To Listen*, the first LP to carry the ABC-Tangerine Records dual logo, reaches US #76.

Sept Charles' dramatic deep soul theme song, written by Quincy Jones, from Rod Steiger/Sidney Poitier movie *In The Heat Of The Night* makes US #33.

Dec His individual re-working of The Beatles'° *Yesterday* makes US #25 and UK #44.

1968 Jan Atlantic reissues his 1959 recording *Come Rain Or Come Shine*, which peaks at US #98.

Mar *That's A Lie* makes US #64.

May *A Portrait Of Ray* reaches US #51.

July Another Lennon°/McCartney° cover, *Eleanor Rigby*, climbs to US #35, while B-side *Understanding* makes #46.

Aug *Eleanor Rigby* reaches UK #36.

Sept *Sweet Young Thing Like You* peaks at US #83.

Oct LP *Ray Charles' Greatest Hits, Vol.2*, compiled for UK, makes UK #24.

1969 Jan Charles duets with Jimmy Lewis on *If It Wasn't For Bad Luck*, which reaches US #77.

Apr LP *I'm All Yours – Baby!* peaks at US #167.

May *Let Me Love You* makes US #94.

June [13] He appears with Aretha Franklin°, Sam and Dave°, The Staple Singers° and many more, at Soul Bowl '69 at Houston Astrodome, Tex., promoted as the biggest-ever soul music festival.

Aug LP *Doing His Thing* peaks at US #172.

1970 Mar *Laughin' And Clownin'* stalls at US #98.

July Instrumental LP *My Kind Of Jazz*, on Tangerine, reaches US #155.

Aug LP *Love Country Style* peaks at US #192.

Dec *If You Were Mine* makes US #41 and stays on chart for 18 weeks.

1971 Apr *Don't Change On Me* reaches US #36.

May *Booty Butt*, an R&B instrumental credited to The Ray Charles Orchestra (allowing it to be issued on Tangerine, independent of ABC), makes US #36.

July LP *Volcanic Action Of My Soul* reaches US #52, his biggest-selling LP for over 3 years.

Oct *Feel So Bad* makes US #68.

Dec Double LP *A 25th Anniversary In Show Business Salute To Ray Charles* is a collaboration between ABC and Atlantic with an LP of Charles' hits on each label. It is released on Atlantic around the world, and on ABC in US, where it reaches #152.

1972 Jan A revival of Chuck Willis' *What Am I Living For?* reaches US #54.

June LP *A Message From The People* climbs to US #52.

July A cover of Melanie's° *Look What They've Done To My Song, Ma* reaches US #65.

Dec His last ABC LP, *Through The Eyes Of Love*, peaks at US #186.

1973 Charles leaves ABC, taking his Tangerine Records operation and the rights to all his ABC releases. Tangerine becomes new label Crossover Records, which will release both Charles' new recordings and reissues.

June Atlantic double LP *Ray Charles Live*, comprising the two earlier live LPs from Newport in 1958 and Herndon Stadium in 1959, makes US #182. Charles' last ABC single, *I Can Make It Thru The Days (But Oh Those Lonely Nights)*, reaches US #84.

Sept [7] Charles headlines the second Ann Arbor Jazz and Blues Festival, Mich.

Dec His first Crossover single is *Come Live With Me*, peaking at US #82.

1974 First Crossover LP *Come Live With Me* is released but fails to chart.

1975 July Second Crossover LP *Renaissance* peaks at US #175.

Sept A cover of Stevie Wonder's° *Living For The City*, taken from LP *Renaissance*, makes US #91.

1976 Dec Charles and Cleo Laine record a double LP of Gershwin's *Porgy And Bess*, released by RCA, which makes US #138.

1977 Feb [28] He is attacked, while performing, by a man who rushes on stage with a rope and tries to strangle him.

Dec LP *True To Life*, a one-off return to Atlantic with a Crossover Records production, climbs to US #78.

1978 Feb [24] Charles guests on US TV's "The Second Barry Manilow° Special".

RAY CHARLES *cont.*

1980 June Charles appears as the streetwise owner of a musical instrument store in movie *The Blues Brothers*.

Aug TV-advertised compilation LP of Charles oldies, *Heart To Heart – 20 Hot Hits*, reaches UK #29.

Oct Charles teams with Clint Eastwood to release *Beers To You*, from Eastwood-starring film *Any Which Way You Can*.

1983 He signs to CBS/Columbia's Nashville division to concentrate on country-based music. First CBS/Columbia LP *Wish You Were Here Tonight* is a US country chart success, but does not cross over.

June He appears in the 30th annual Kool Jazz Festival in New York, co-headlining with Miles Davis° and B.B. King°.

1985 Jan [28] Charles takes a major role in the recording of USA For Africa's° *We Are The World*, leading the gospel-like climax.

Mar LP *Friendship*, featuring Charles in ten duets with major country music stars like Willie Nelson°, Mickey Gilley and Hank Williams Jr., makes US #75, his first US LP chart entry since 1977. Extracted *Seven Spanish Angels* with Nelson, tops the US country chart.

Apr *We Are The World* tops both US and UK charts.

Dec Charles produces country soul-styled seasonal LP *The Spirit Of Christmas*.

1986 Dec [26] Charles is honored at the ninth annual Kennedy Center ceremony in Washington, D.C.

1987 Apr Charles guests with Billy Joel° on his *Baby Grand*, which makes US #75. (Charles will remain quiet on the recording scene but will continue to play live throughout the world, more often than not in a big band. He will act, guesting in TV series "Moonlighting", "St. Elsewhere" and "Who's The Boss", in which he sings *Always A Friend*.)

CHEAP TRICK

Robin Zander (vocals and guitar)
Rick Nielsen (vocals and guitar)
Tom Petersson (vocals and bass)
Bun E. Carlos (drums)

1961 Nielsen (b. Dec.22, 1946, Rockford, Ill., US) begins playing in several bands (which will include The Phaetons, Boyz and The Grim Reapers) in his hometown of Rockford. (He also begins collecting rare and bizarre guitars which will number over 100 within 20 years.)

1969 He forms a new band Fuse with Petersson (b. 1950, Rockford) and Carlos (b. Brad Carlson, June 12, 1953, Rockford) and they release an unsuccessful LP on Epic.

1971 The band moves to Philadelphia and changes name to Sick Man of Europe.

1973/76 After a European tour, they return to Rockford where they form new combo Cheap Trick, with folk vocalist Zander (b. Jan.23, 1953, Rockford). The group gigs incessantly, completing more than 200 concerts a year, including support slots for The Kinks°, Santana°, Kiss°, Boston° and many others.

1977 Jan Debut LP *Cheap Trick* is released on Epic. It sells 150,000 copies in US but fails to chart. Its release in Japan is immediately popular, where it goes gold.

Oct Second LP *In Color* climbs to US #73 on the strength of continued touring. Once again it goes gold in Japan.

1978 Feb First major visit to Tokyo sees unexpected "Trickmania". Their dates at the Budokan arena sell out within 2 hours. A live recording of the gigs is made, which captures both their live expertise and the fanatical Japanese reaction.

Sept First US chart single is *Surrender* at #62.

Nov Third LP *Heaven Tonight* reaches US #48 and achieves platinum status in Japan.

1979 Feb LP *Cheap Trick At Budokan* begins a 1-year stay on the US chart, where it will hit #4 and become the group's first US platinum selling LP. Released simultaneously in UK, it makes #29.

Apr [7-8] Cheap Trick plays the California Music Festival in LA's Memorial Coliseum, with Van Halen°, Aerosmith° and Ted Nugent°.

July From the live project, single *I Want You To Want Me* hits US #7 and UK #29. In Japan, the LP achieves triple platinum.

Sept Follow-up *Ain't That A Shame*, a live cover of the Fats Domino° standard, reaches US #35.

Nov Studio LP *Dream Police* hits US #6 and reaches UK #41. The title track makes US #26.

1980 Feb *Voices* climbs to US #32. UK-released only *Way Of The World* peaks at #73. Nielsen, Zander and Carlos contribute to John Lennon's° *Double Fantasy* LP sessions in New York.

May A 10" mini-LP, *Found All The Parts*, featuring songs recorded from 1976-79, makes US #39.

June The band contributes its recent single to new Debbie Harry/Meatloaf movie *Roadie*.

July *Everything Works If You Let It* makes US #44.

Aug [26] Petersson leaves to form a group with his wife Dagmar. He is replaced first by Pete Comita and then by Jon Brant (b. Feb.20, 1954).

Nov LP *All Shook Up* (Petersson's last) peaks at US #24. Produced by Englishman George Martin, it includes single *Stop This Game* which makes US #48.

1981 Epic rejects an entire LP as the band returns to the studio to record further. (The label also rejects an LP from Petersson in 1982.)

1982 June LP *One On One* is released by Epic, climbs to US #39 and makes UK #95 for 1 week. Taken from it, *If You Want My Love* peaks at US #45 and UK #57. (In Japan, all eight LPs have topped the chart.)

Oct *She's Tight* reaches US #65.

1983 Oct LP *Next Position Please* makes US #61.

1985 Oct *Tonight It's You* reaches US #44. LP *Standing On The Edge* makes US #35.

1987 Nov LP *The Doctor* reaches only US #86.

1988 Mar With the group using outside writers and Petersson rejoining the line-up, LP *Lap Of Luxury* is a return to form, and Richie Zito-produced ballad *The Flame* begins a 14-week rise to the top of the US chart, but does not reach UK top 75.

Apr The band travels to Switzerland to take part in the Montreux Rock Festival.

July [9] A tour commences in Louisville, Ky. as Robert Plant's° special guests, while *The Flame* is at US #1.

Aug The single's success spurs sales of LP *Lap Of Luxury*, which climbs to US #18.

Sept Cheap Trick's version of *Don't Be Cruel* becomes the first cover of an Elvis Presley° hit to make the US top 10 since his death.

CHUBBY CHECKER

1958 Dec Checker (b. Ernest Evans, Oct.3, 1941, S.C., US), signed under his real name to Cameo-Parkway Records in Philadelphia, Pa., after Henry Colt, his boss at a chicken market, impressed by his singing, brought him to the attention of Cameo's Kal Mann, impresses Dick Clark ("American Bandstand") and his wife Bobbie with his ability to imitate other acts' styles while the Clarks visit Cameo to commission a novelty recording as a Christmas greeting. He records *The Class*, written by Mann, and Cameo changes his name after Bobbie Clark comments on his resemblance to a teenage Fats Domino (Fats = Chubby; Domino = Checker). The Clarks send it out as their Christmas card.

1959 June Cameo releases *The Class* on Parkway label and it climbs to US #38. It features Checker imitating Fats Domino°, The Coasters°, Elvis Presley° and The Chipmunks.

July Dick Clark on "American Bandstand" is bombarded with requests for *The Twist*, a Hank Ballard° & The Midnighters' 18-month-old B-side, because of nationwide teen enthusiasm for the dance. He suggests Philadelphia act Danny & The Juniors° cover it but they decline, so Clark phones Cameo and suggests the song for Checker, who records it with vocal group The Dreamlovers, in a 35-minute session.

1960 Sept Checker's cover enters US chart 2 weeks after Ballard's° original which peaks at US #28, but the exposure given to Checker's cover by "American Bandstand" takes it to the top of the US chart for a week. It sells over a million copies and reaches UK #44.

Nov *The Hucklebuck*, reviving a 1949 Tommy Dorsey dance hit, in new musical idiom, reaches US #14. The B-side, reviving Jerry Lee Lewis'° *Whole Lotta Shakin' Goin' On*, makes US #42 in its own right.

Dec LP *Twist With Chubby Checker* hits US #3. He stars in Clay Cole's "Christmas Rock'n'Roll Show" at the Paramount Theater, Brooklyn, N.Y., with Neil Sedaka°, Bobby Vee°, The Drifters°, Dion°, Bo Diddley° and others.

1961 The New York State Safety Council announces that of 54 cases of back trouble reported in a single week, 49 were due to too much twisting.

Feb Pony Time hits US #1 for 3 weeks and is Checker's second million-seller, setting off a new dance craze for The Pony. The song is a re-write of *Boogie Woogie*, written and recorded by Clarence "Pinetop" Smith in 1928, but the record is a cover of Don Covay & The Goodtimers' original (which peaks at US #60).

Apr *Pony Time* reaches UK #27.

May *Dance The Mess Around* peaks at US #24 and is a minor dance craze. B-side *Good Good Lovin'* makes US #43.

June LP *It's Pony Time* peaks at US #110.

July He features in "The Dick Clark Caravan of Stars", a summer rock stage show in Atlantic City, N.J., with Duane Eddy°, Fabian°, Freddy Cannon, Bobby Rydell° and others.

Aug On the first anniversary of *The Twist*, *Let's Twist Again* is released to catch the beginning of a new wave of interest in the dance, spreading from teen hops to adult clubs and from US to other countries. It hits US #8 and reaches UK #37, earning Checker a third gold disk. (It will also win a Grammy as Best Rock'n'Roll Record of 1961.)

Oct [22] As the twist reaches fashionable nightspots like New York's Peppermint Lounge, Checker appears on US TV's "Ed Sullivan Show" singing *The Twist* and demand for it is sparked again. LP *Let's Twist Again* reaches US #11.

Nov *The Fly*, a twist variation with arm movements to approximate a buzzing fly, hits US #7.

Dec Checker's revival of Bobby Helms' seasonal hit *Jingle Bell Rock*, as a duet with label-mate Bobby Rydell° makes US #21. He features in film *Twist Around The Clock*, which revolves around New York DJ Clay Cole.

1962 Jan *The Twist* is re-released in US and tops the chart again for 2 weeks – the only single ever to hit US #1 on two separate occasions. Its total top 100 residence lasts for 38 weeks. LP *For Twisters Only* hits US #8. Compilation LP (of tracks from his previous four LPs), *Your Twist Party*, hits US #2.

Feb *The Twist* and *Let's Twist Again* are reissued in UK as the dance craze hits the country for the first time. Checker makes a UK promotion visit, demonstrating the dance movements on TV. *The Twist* reaches #14 but *Let's Twist Again* becomes the UK's twist anthem, hitting #2, and spends 31 weeks on chart during the year. LP *Twist With Chubby Checker* reaches UK #13. LP *Bobby Rydell/Chubby Checker*, a collection of duets, hits US #7.

Mar LP *For Twisters Only* makes UK #17.

Apr *Slow Twistin'*, a duet with (uncredited) label-mate Dee Dee Sharp, hits US #3 and UK #23. Another duet with Bobby Rydell°, *Teach Me To Twist*, makes UK #45.

May LP *For Teen Twisters Only*, which includes the hits *The Fly* and *Slow Twistin'*, climbs to US #17.

June LP *Twistin' Round The World* peaks at US #54. Checker features in movie *Don't Knock The Twist* and sings six songs. They appear on soundtrack LP *Don't Knock The Twist* which makes US #29.

July *Dancin' Party* reaches US #12. Sounding much like Gary U.S. Bonds'° 1961 hit *Quarter To Three*, it prompts Bonds to sue for plagiarism for £100,000. (The case is settled out of court.)

Sept *Dancin' Party* reaches UK #19.

Nov Double A-side *Limbo Rock* and *Popeye (The Hitchhiker)*, each side promoting a different current dance craze, becomes Checker's biggest two-sided US chart success. *Popeye* peaks first, hitting #10.

Dec *Limbo Rock* (a Champs° instrumental US chart hit earlier in the year) hits US #2. It stays in the top 100 for 23 weeks and charts in UK at #32. The Checker-Rydell duet *Jingle Bell Rock* makes UK #40 and US chart again at #92. LP *All The Hits (For Your Dancin' Party)*, which includes *Limbo Rock*, reaches US #23 and LP *Down To Earth*, a selection of duets with Dee Dee Sharp, makes US #117.

1963 Feb LP *Limbo Party* peaks at US #11 and compilation LP *Chubby Checker's Biggest Hits* makes US #27.

Mar [2] Checker hosts "The Limbo Party", a stage show at the Cow Palace, San Francisco, with guests including Marvin Gaye°, The Crystals°, Lou Christie° and The Four Seasons°.

Mar *Let's Limbo Some More* peaks at US #20.

Apr B-side of *Let's Limbo*, *Twenty Miles*, becomes a bigger US hit than its A-side, at #15. LP *Let's Limbo Some More* makes US #87.

June *Birdland*, plugging yet another dance craze, the Bird, climbs to US #12.

Aug Checker moves in on The Beach Boys°/Jan and Dean°-led surfing fad with *Surf Party* but it makes only US #55 and is overtaken by back-to-1962 *Twist It Up*, which reaches US #25, at a time when twist songs are thought to be dead. LP *Beach Party* makes US #90.

Oct Live LP *Chubby Checker In Person* reaches US #104.

Nov *What Do Ya Say*, recorded in London with producer Tony Hatch, reaches UK #37 after Checker's UK promotional visit and TV slots, but it will be his last UK hit for 12 years.

Dec *Loddy Lo* climbs to US #12.

1964 Feb *Hooka Tooka*, B-side of *Loddy Lo*, is another double-sided US hit for Checker when it replaces its A-side in the top 20 to peak at #17.

Apr *Hey, Bobba Needle* reaches US #23.

July *Lazy Elsie Molly* makes US #40.

Sept *She Wants T'Swim*, following Bobby Freeman's° US top 5 hit *C'mon And Swim*, peaks at US #50 but the Swim is a short-lived dance craze. (Checker now has other interests, having married Dutch beauty queen Catharina Lodders (Miss World 1962), with whom he will have a long marriage and three children.)

1965 Jan *Lovely, Lovely* peaks at US #70.

May *Let's Do The Freddie*, a cash-in on Freddie & The Dreamers'° stage act "dance" which becomes a US craze, makes US #40, but is outsold by the group's own (different) song *Do The Freddie*.

1966 July *Hey You! Little Boo-Ga-Loo* is his final hit single on Parkway, reaching US #76.

1969 Apr Signed to Buddah Records, Checker makes a minor US chart comeback with a cover of The Beatles'° *White Album* LP track *Back In The U.S.S.R.*

1970 June [23] Checker is arrested with three others in Niagara Falls, after police discover marijuana and other drugs in their car.

1973 Jan Double compilation LP of his chart singles *Chubby Checker's Greatest Hits* makes US #152, his first US LP chart entry since 1963.

Apr [29] An oldies edition of US TV's "Midnight Special", hosted by Jerry Lee Lewis°, features Checker among the guest performers.

1975 Dec Capitalizing on an unexpected revival of the twist in UK discotheques (and an opportunistic UK revival of *Let's Twist Again* by John Asher which makes #14), a double A-side reissue of *Let's Twist Again* with *The Twist* hits UK #5.

1982 Mar Signed to MCA Records, Checker returns to the US top 100 for the first time in 13 years, at #91, with *Running* which also makes the top 40 dance chart. LP *The Change Has Come* reaches US #186.

CHUBBY CHECKER *cont.*

1988 May The Fat Boys team with Checker to record a new version of his most famous hit, this time titled *The Twist (Yo' Twist)*.

June [11] Checker and the group perform the song at The Nelson Mandela 70th Birthday Concert at London's Wembley Stadium. The record takes off in the UK 3 weeks later, hitting #2.

Aug *The Twist (Yo' Twist)* peaks at US #16.

CHER

1963 Cher (b. Cherilyn Sarkasian La Pier, May 20, 1946, El Centro, Cal., US), having moved to LA to attend acting classes, meets Sonny Bono, who is working for Phil Spector, and through him begins doing back-up vocals for Spector on singles by The Ronettes° and others.

1964 Sonny and Cher marry in Tijuana. Spector uses Cher as the soloist on novelty single *Ringo I Love You*, released on Spector's minor label, Annette, to cash in on Beatlemania, and credited to "Bonnie Jo Mason".

1965 While Sonny & Cher° are experimenting with early duo recordings, Sonny interests Imperial Records in signing Cher as a soloist. First release, *Dream Baby*, under her full name Cherilyn, fails to sell.

Aug With Sonny & Cher° signed to Atco as a duo, Imperial changes the billing to Cher on her solo material. Sharing in the publicity generated as the duo's *I Got You Babe* tops the US chart, her cover of Bob Dylan's° *All I Really Want To Do* reaches US #15. (The Byrds'° version makes US #40.)

Sept The duo's *I Got You Babe* tops the UK chart while *All I Really Want To Do* hits UK #9. (The Byrds'° version hits UK #4.)

Oct Debut solo LP *All I Really Want To Do*, with folk rock sound, produced by Sonny from Spector experience, reaches US #16 and hits UK #7.

Nov *Where Do You Go*, written and produced by Sonny in a style similar to debut LP, makes US #25 but fails to chart in UK.

1966 Apr *Bang Bang (My Baby Shot Me Down)*, Cher's first solo million-seller, hits US #2 and UK #3. Produced by Sonny, it combines stark melodrama, racing gypsy violins and arresting tempo changes.

June LP *The Sonny Side Of Cher* reaches US #26 and UK #11.

Aug Cher covers Cilla Black's° movie title track *Alfie*, starring Michael Caine. When the film opens in US, Cher's version is added over the credits and reaches US #32. Cilla Black's makes only US #95 (but was a top 10 hit in UK, where Cher's is not released). *I Feel Something In The Air*, a slightly controversial Sonny song about unmarried pregnancy, reaches UK #43. (Released in US as *Magic In The Air*, it failed to chart.)

Oct Cher's cover of Bobby Hebb's (US #2 and UK #12) hit *Sunny* – in her case, sung with an implied "o" in the word rather than "u" – is released only in UK and makes #32. (Georgie Fame's° cover makes UK #13.)

Nov LP *Cher* reaches US #66. *Behind The Door* charts briefly at US #97. Its B-side, another slightly controversial lyric, *Mama (When My Dollies Have Babies)*, is promoted in UK, but gets no airplay and fails to chart.

1967 Sept After a recording gap with Sonny & Cher° engaged on film *Good Times*, Cher's *Hey Joe* makes US #94.

Dec *You Better Sit Down Kids*, written by Sonny about family break-up, hits US #9. LP *With Love – Cher* makes US #47. Both fail to hit in UK, despite good airplay for the single, and mark the end of Cher's Imperial recording contract.

1968 She signs to Atco (to which Sonny & Cher° are still contracted). Her first solo on Atco, *Yours Until Tomorrow*, flops in US and is not released in UK.

1969 Aug LP *3614 Jackson Highway* (named after Muscle Shoals Sound Studio address, where it is recorded with producers Jerry Wexler, Tom Dowd and Arif Mardin) makes US #160. Other Atco singles released in US and UK fail to chart. Cher has an acting role in film *Chastity*, produced, written and scored by Sonny. She also sings the theme song, *Band Of Thieves*. (Chastity, non-coincidentally, is also the name of the Bonos' daughter.)

1971 May Both the duo and Cher as a soloist are signed to a new recording deal with Kapp Records, but Cher's first single *Put It On Me* flops.

Aug [1] Sonny & Cher° start "The Sonny and Cher Comedy Hour" on prime time CBS TV (which will follow a successful short summer run with three long, high-rating series). The routines, in a variety of characterizations, serve to hone Cher's acting skills for later film work.

Nov *Gypsies, Tramps And Thieves*, produced by Snuff Garrett (the Bonos' next-door neighbor in Bel Air, Cal.), a dramatic story-song written for her by Bob Stone, hits US #1 for 2 weeks and UK #4. It is her second solo million-seller. LP of the same title reaches US #16.

1972 Feb Double compilation LP *Cher Superpak*, anthologizing Imperial tracks, makes US #92.

Mar *The Way Of Love*, a ballad taken from LP *Gypsies, Tramps And Thieves*, hits US #7 but fails to chart in UK.

June *Living In A House Divided* reaches US #22 but fails in UK. The Bonos' marriage is starting to shake despite their successful professional relationship.

Sept LP *Foxy Lady* reaches US #43.

Oct *Don't Hide Your Love* reaches US #46.

1973 Jan Garrett stops working with the Bonos after selecting *The Night The Lights Went Out In Georgia*, a Bobby Russell story-song of jealousy and murder, for a Cher single, which Sonny vetoes unknown to Cher at the time. (The song hits US #1 by Vicki Lawrence 3 months later.)

May LP *Bittersweet White Light* reaches US #140.

Oct *Half Breed*, written specifically for Cher by Mary Dean and Al Capps, and produced by Garrett who knows it to be a smash, is Cher's first release for MCA. It tops the US chart for 2 weeks and sells over a million, but makes no chart impression in UK. LP of the same title peaks at US #28.

1974 Mar *Dark Lady*, written by The Ventures° keyboards player Johnny Durrill, hits US #1 and becomes Cher's fourth solo million-seller. It reaches #36 in UK (where it will be her last chart entry for over a decade). The Bonos announce their marital break-up.

May Sonny & Cher's° US TV series finishes.

June *Train Of Thought* reaches US #27.

June [26] Cher is divorced from Sonny Bono, at Santa Monica Supreme Court, Cal.

June [30] She marries Gregg Allman of The Allman Brothers° band, in Los Angeles. (It will be a stormy liaison and 9 days later she will announce that she wants another divorce.)

July LP *Dark Lady* peaks at US #69.

Sept *I Saw A Man And He Danced With His Wife* peaks at US #42.

Dec Compilation LP *Greatest Hits* reaches US #152, and marks the end of Cher's MCA recording deal. She signs to Warner Bros., and is reunited with her first producer, Phil Spector.

1975 Feb [16] US TV series "Cher" begins on CBS: a weekly hour of music and comedy. Spector produces a highly-rated single, coupling *A Woman's Story* (later revived by Marc Almond) and *Baby I Love You*. The first release on the Warner-Spector label, it fails to chart.

Apr A Spector-produced duet with Harry Nilsson° of revival *A Love Like Yours* also flops. Cher does not continue working with Spector.

May LP *Stars*, produced by Jimmy Webb, is Cher's only Warner Bros. LP to chart, reaching #153.

1976 Jan [4] Cher's TV series is cancelled by the network and has its last show. (It will be replaced for a while by less successful "Sonny and Cher" series. The Bono reunion is purely professional; Cher, meanwhile, is frequently parted from Gregg Allman.)

Oct LP *I'd Rather Believe In You* teams her with producers Steve Barri and Michael Omartian, but raises little interest.

1977 Nov LP *Allman And Woman: Two The Hard Way* is recorded with husband Gregg Allman but does not chart.

1979 Apr Signed to predominantly disco-oriented Casablanca Records, Cher hits US #8 with *Take Me Home*. It is another US million-seller but fails in UK. LP of the same title makes US #25 and earns a gold disk. (She is now making the gossip columns as "constant companion" of another Casablanca artist, Gene Simmons of Kiss°, but the relationship will not be long-lived.)

June *Wasn't It Good* reaches US #49.

Sept *Hell On Wheels*, her last hit for Casablanca, makes US #59 and is her final US chart entry for several years.

1980 Aug [30] She makes an unannounced appearance as vocalist with Black Rose, a band formed by current boyfriend Les Dudek, in New York's Central Park.

Nov LP *Black Rose* is released, with Cher on vocals, but does not sell.

1982 Feb Cher duets (uncredited) with Meatloaf on *Dead Ringer For Love* (which hits UK #5, but fails to chart in US), and appears with him in mini-movie promo video.

Mar She signs to CBS/Columbia Records. Debut *Rudy* is universally ignored.

Nov After her Broadway acting debut in *Come Back To The Five And Dime, Jimmy Dean, Jimmy Dean*, directed by Robert Altman who films it with Cher keeping her leading role, she releases LP *I Paralyze* on CBS/Columbia, but it does not sell.

1984 Mar She is nominated for an Oscar as Best Supporting Actress in movie *Silkwood*, which stars Meryl Streep.

1985 Mar Cher has another critically-rated performance, in a leading role in Peter Bogdanovich's film *Mask*.

1987 She co-stars with Jack Nicholson in *The Witches Of Eastwick* and later in the year appears in comedy *Moonstruck*.

Oct *I Found Someone*, produced by Michael Bolton, on Geffen Records, hits UK #5 after a 14-year chart absence. LP *Cher*, made with several producers, makes UK #26.

1988 Mar *I Found Someone* hits US #10.

Apr Cher wins an Academy Award as Best Actress for her work in *Moonstruck*. Second single from LP *Cher*, *We All Sleep Alone*, co-written and co-produced by Bon Jovi°, reaches UK #47.

May LP *Cher* makes US #32, earning a gold disk.

June *We All Sleep Alone* reaches US #14.

Sept *Skin Deep*, third single from LP *Cher*, is released.

CHIC

Nile Rodgers (guitar)
Bernard Edwards (bass)
Tony Thompson (drums)
Alfa Anderson (vocals)
Luci Martin (vocals)

1972 After playing together in various New York clubs since meeting in 1970, Edwards (b. Oct.31, 1952, Greenville, N.C., US) and Rodgers (b. Sept.19, 1952, New York, N.Y., US) team with Thompson to form The Big Apple Band, a rock-fusion trio.

1973/76 The trio feels it is going nowhere with steady club work and tours, backing New York City and Carol Douglas, and switches from rock to the newly-emerging disco genre. It adds Norma Jean Wright (for whom it produces and writes an early LP on the Bearsville label) as female lead voice.

1977 June The group adopts the name Chic, and self-produces several dance-oriented tracks in an unsuccessful attempt to win a recording deal. Tom Cossie and Mark Kreiner buy Chic's masters of the already-recorded tracks, and form M.K. Productions.

Sept The group signs to Atlantic Records (which earlier turned it down) after the personal intervention of company president Jerry Greenberg.

1978 Jan Debut release *Dance Dance Dance (Yowsah Yowsah Yowsah)* hits #6 in both US and UK and is a US million-seller. LP *Chic* reaches US #27. Wright leaves and Martin and Anderson are recruited as joint lead vocalists.

May *Everybody Dance* reaches only US #38, but in UK hits #9.

Dec *Le Freak* hits US #1 for 6 weeks. One of the biggest-selling singles of the decade, it tops 4 million in the US. In UK it hits #7.

1979 Jan LP *C'Est Chic*, containing *Le Freak*, hits US #4 and is a million-seller in its own right.

Apr *I Want Your Love* hits US #7, another million-seller, and UK #4. LP *C'Est Chic* peaks at UK #2. A Rodgers/Edwards production for Sister Sledge's *He's The Greatest Dancer* hits US #9 and UK #6. (Sister Sledge's LP and single *We Are Family* will follow, with further singles and a second LP, all successfully guided by Chic organization.)

Aug *Good Times*, a second US #1 and further million-seller, hits UK #5. Built around a distinctive bass line, the record is one of the most imitated in popular music in succeeding years. (The Sugarhill Gang's° *Rapper's Delight* will be found guilty of plagiarizing the arrangement and give joint composer credits to Rodgers and Edwards.)

Sept LP *Risqué* hits US #5 and peaks at UK #29.

Nov *My Forbidden Lover* reaches US #43 and UK #15.

1980 Jan *My Feet Keep Dancing* (featuring a unique tap dance solo) reaches UK #21, while compilation LP *Les Plus Grands Succès De Chic: Chic's Greatest Hits* makes US #88 and UK #30. Rodgers/Edwards' production of *Spacer* by Sheila B. Devotion makes UK #18.

Sept *Rebels Are We* peaks at US #61, and LP *Real People* at #30. Diana Ross'° *Upside Down*, produced by Rodgers/Edwards, hits US #1 and UK #2; it is taken from LP *Diana*, also produced by the duo, though remixed by Ross without their cooperation because she feels her vocals have been sublimated to their production.

Nov Double A-side *Real People/Chip Off The Old Block* reaches only US #79.

1981 Aug Rodgers and Edwards produce *Koo Koo*, solo LP by Debbie Harry of Blondie°, which reaches US #25 and hits UK #6.

1982 Jan LP *Take It Off* makes US #124, but fails to chart in UK.

June *Soup For One*, theme from the film of the same title with score by Rodgers and Edwards, is Chic's last US hit single, at #80.

Dec LP *Tongue In Chic* peaks at US #173 and makes no UK chart showing.

1983 Mar *Hangin'* is Chic's last UK chart appearance, peaking at #64. (As the group fades, Rodgers and Edwards branch out in new directions. Rodgers will produce David Bowie's° *Let's Dance* LP and single (1983) and make his own LP *Adventures In The Land Of The Good Groove*. He will produce Madonna's° breakthrough LP *Like A Virgin*, among other projects, and briefly join The Honeydrippers with Robert Plant°, Jimmy Page and Jeff Beck°. In 1985, both Edwards and Chic's Tony Thompson will join Power Station, with Robert Palmer° and members of Duran Duran°. This will lead Edwards into successful production of Palmer's° solo LPs. In 1987 Rodgers will team up with Phillipe Saisse and Felicia Collins to form the trio Outloud.)

CHICAGO

Peter Cetera (vocals and bass)
Robert Lamm (vocals and keyboards)
Terry Kath (guitar)
Danny Seraphine (drums)
James Pankow (trombone)
Lee Loughnane (trumpet)
Walter Parazaider (saxophone)
Laudir de Oliveira (percussion)

1966 A band, called The Missing Links, name-changing to The Big Thing, forms around friends Kath and Parazaider at university in Chicago, US. Under the guidance of another friend, James William Guercio, the group plays small clubs and Guercio offers to manage it full time if the members change name to Chicago Transit Authority.

1967 Guercio moves them to LA, where he pays their rent and finds them occasional work, including a stint at the Whisky A Go-Go club.

1969 Jan Through Guercio's influence at CBS/Columbia Records (he is currently working with Blood Sweat & Tears° and has guided The Buckinghams°), the group signs a worldwide contract. (Guercio will produce all the material.)

May Debut LP *Chicago Transit Authority* begins a 3-year stay on the US chart. Unusually for a first effort, it is a double LP. Containing a popular fusion of jazz pop ballads and rock (and protest chants from 1969 Democratic Convention) it will peak at US #17 and hit UK #9. Touring to promote the LP, the group supports Janis Joplin° and Jimi Hendrix°.

July After legal threats from the Chicago Transit Authority, Guercio persuades the band to shorten its name to Chicago.

Aug First single *Questions 67 And 68* reaches US #71.

Sept [13] Chicago performs at the "Rock'n'Revival Concert" in Toronto, Canada, on a bill which includes Chuck Berry°, Jerry Lee Lewis°, Alice Cooper° and The Plastic Ono Band making its live debut.

1970 Feb A cover of Spencer Davis Group's° *I'm A Man* hits UK #8. Follow-up double LP *Chicago II* begins a 134-week US chart stay, eventually hitting #4 and UK #6.

June *Make Me Smile* hits US #9.

Sept *25 Or 6 To 4* becomes a worldwide smash, hitting US #4 and UK #7.

1971 Jan Re-released from the debut LP, *Does Anybody Really Know What Time It Is?* hits US #7. Third consecutive double LP, *Chicago III* hits US #2.

Apr *Free* makes US #20. While LP *Chicago III* reaches UK #31 for 1 week, Chicago becomes the first rock group to play New York's Carnegie Hall. All the songs performed are taped for possible release.

May [20] Cetera, attending a baseball game, is beaten up by a gang and undergoes hours of emergency surgery.

June *Lowdown* makes US #35.

Aug Double A-side, *Beginnings/Color My World* from the first LP, hits US #7.

CHICAGO *cont.*

Nov Another re-issue, the previously charted *Questions 67 And 68* coupled with previous UK hit *I'm A Man*, makes US #24. LP *Chicago At Carnegie Hall* is released as a four-album box set. An argument between some band members and Guercio precedes its release. Guercio insists it should be released but Chicago feels the recordings are of a poor quality. The set hits US #3, becoming the highest charting four-LP box set (it fails to chart in UK).

1972 Feb Chicago undertakes successful tours of Japan and Australia, beginning a world tour which will include dates in Yugoslavia, Poland and Czechoslovakia.

July New studio LP, and their first one-disk set, *Chicago V* hits US #1. It includes the US #3 hit, *Saturday In The Park*. In UK, the LP climbs to #24. Guercio writes and directs film *Electra Glide In Blue*, which features performances from four Chicago members.

Dec *Dialogue (Part I & II)* reaches US #24.

1973 Feb Chicago records at Guercio's newly-built studio, Caribou.

Aug *Feelin' Stronger Every Day* hits US #10. A Japan-only release, LP *Chicago Live In Japan* sells over 1 million copies in the Far East. LP *Chicago VI* hits US #1 for 5 weeks, but fails to make the UK chart.

Dec *Just You 'N' Me* hits US #4.

1974 Mar Another double LP, *Chicago VIII*, climbs to US #1. It includes *(I've Been) Searchin' So Long* which hits US #90.

June Second single from the LP, *Call On Me*, hits US #6. Keyboardist Lamm releases solo LP *Skinny Boy*, which fails to chart.

Nov Taken from seventh LP, *Wishin' You Were Here*, featuring backing vocals from three of The Beach Boys°, whom Guercio is managing, peaks at US #11.

1975 Apr *Harry Truman* climbs to US #13.

June *Old Days* hits US #5, while the LP from which it comes, *Chicago VIII*, tops the US chart. The group embarks on a major US tour with The Beach Boys°.

Sept *Brand New Love Affair (Part I & II)* makes only US #61.

Nov LP *Chicago IX – Chicago's Greatest Hits* hits US #1 for 5 weeks.

1976 May Chicago's Mayor Richard Daley awards the group with the city's "Medal of Merit".

July LP *Chicago X* begins a 44-week chart run, eventually hitting US #3.

Aug *Another Rainy Day In New York City* peaks at US #32.

Oct Ballad *If You Leave Me Now*, featuring a distinctive Jimmie Haskell arrangement, becomes Chicago's biggest worldwide smash hitting both US and UK #1. LP *Chicago X* reaches UK #21.

1977 Jan Chicago undertakes another world tour beginning with sold-out dates in UK and Europe.

Feb [19] LP *Chicago X* wins a Grammy for Best Album of the Year.

Apr *You Are On My Mind* reaches US #49.

June Guercio, increasingly involved in other projects, stops managing Chicago. The band appears at a Geraldo Rivera "One to One" benefit show.

Nov LP *Chicago XI* hits US #6, but fails in UK.

Dec *Baby, What A Big Surprise* hits US #4 and makes UK #41.

1978 Jan [23] Founder and lead guitarist Kath, who has been buying guns for 6 years, accidentally shoots himself in the head believing the barrel to be empty. US TV bandleader Doc Severinsen visits the group after Kath's funeral and persuades it to continue as Chicago.

Apr *Little One* makes US #44.

June *Take Me Back To Chicago*, the final single produced by Guercio, reaches US #63.

Aug The group signs a management deal with Jeff Wald.

Nov LP *Hot Streets* reaches US #12 and is supported by a "comeback" US tour.

Dec *Alive Again*, with Donnie Dacus (ex-Stephen Stills Band) replacing Kath, makes US #14.

1979 Mar *No Tell Lover* makes US #14.

Apr *Gone Long Gone* reaches US #73.

Sept LP *Chicago 13*, breaking the roman numeral sequence, peaks at US #21. *Must Have Been Crazy* makes US #83.

Dec [21-22] Chicago joins The Eagles° and Linda Ronstadt° for two benefit concerts at San Diego's Sports Arena and LA's Aladdin Theater, which raise almost $500,000 for the presidential campaign of California governor Jerry Brown, .

1980 Aug LP *Chicago XIV* makes only US #71. *Thunder And Lightning* reaches US #56. The band begins its longest period of silence as careers are re-assessed.

1981 CBS/Columbia drops Chicago, releasing an end of year LP *Chicago – Greatest Hits, Volume II*, which makes US #171. Cetera releases solo LP *Peter Cetera* on Full Moon label, which makes US #143. Chicago signs to Full Moon and Bill Champlin (ex-Sons Of Champlin) joins as additional vocalist.

1982 July Produced by Canadian David Foster, *Hard To Say I'm Sorry*, also used in Daryl Hannah-starring movie *Summer Lovers*, features Champlin on vocals. It hits US #1.

Aug Foster-produced LP *Chicago 16* hits US #9, the group's first top 10 LP in 5 years.

Sept *Hard To Say I'm Sorry* hits UK #4, and supporting LP *Chicago 16* makes UK #44.

Dec *Love Me Tomorrow* reaches US #22. UK-only compilation LP *Love Songs* makes UK #42.

1983 Jan *What You're Missing* reaches US #81.

1984 June *Stay The Night* climbs to US #16. It is taken from new LP *Chicago 17*, released on Full Moon, which will hit US #4.

Oct *Hard Habit To Break*, another collaboration with Foster, enters the chart and will hit US #3 and UK #8.

1985 Jan LP *Chicago 17* peaks at UK #24, while follow-up single *You're The Inspiration* hits US #3 and makes UK #14. Cetera leaves to pursue a solo career. He is replaced by Jason Scheff, son of Jerry Scheff, Elvis Presley's° bass player for many years.

Apr *Along Comes A Woman* reaches US #14.

1986 Aug Cetera's theme from film *The Karate Kid II, The Glory Of Love* tops the US chart. His second solo LP *Solitude/Solitaire* reaches US #23.

Oct Chicago's re-recording of its 1970 hit *25 Or 6 To 4* peaks at US #48 but fails in UK.

Dec Cetera teams with gospel singer Amy Grant for *The Next Time I Fall* which hits US #1. LP *Chicago 18*, produced by Foster, reaches US #43.

1987 Feb *Will You Still Love Me?* hits US #3 during a 23-week run. Cetera co-writes and produces former Abba° star Agnetha Faltskog's LP *I Stand Alone* and duets with her on the title track.

1988 Aug LP *Chicago 19*, produced by Bill Nevison, makes US #43.

Sept Third Cetera LP *One More Story* begins a US chart climb, together with single *One Good Woman*, which hits the US top 10. It is produced by Madonna's° musical director, Patrick Leonard and includes one cut co-written with Foster.

Oct Lamm announces a solo project with co-producer Randy Goodrum, as the group reveals plans to take part in Amnesty International's 25th anniversary.

THE CHIFFONS

Judy Craig (lead vocals)
Barbara Lee (vocals)
Patricia Bennett (vocals)
Sylvia Peterson (vocals)

1960 The group, all from New York, N.Y., US, forms while still at high school, singing during lunchbreaks and in the neighborhood after school. Ronnie Mack, a local songwriter and pianist, drafts them to rehearse and perform some of his songs for a demo tape.

Sept Mack sells *Tonight's The Night*, featuring guitar work by Butch Mann (later of The Drifters°) to local label Big Deal, resulting in a minor US hit which reaches #76.

1962 After making the industry rounds with his demos, Mack interests Brooklyn quintet The Tokens° (of *The Lion Sleeps Tonight* 1961 US #1 fame), now producing under the name Bright Tunes, who sign Mack and The Chiffons.

Dec *He's So Fine* is recorded (with The Tokens playing the backup instruments) at Mirror Sound Studios, Manhattan, where the session engineer, impressed by the "doo-lang" chant with which the group accompanies the song, suggests that it should form the introduction.

1963 Jan Capitol Records, with which The Tokens have a first-refusal deal, turn down *He's So Fine*, but smaller label Laurie buys it.

Mar *He's So Fine* tops US chart for 4 weeks, selling over a million.

May Ronnie Mack collapses in the street, and is hospitalized in New York with Hodgkins' Disease. At his hospital bed, he is presented with a gold disk for his #1 song by The Tokens, but dies shortly afterwards. *He's So Fine* charts in the UK, reaching #16.

June LP *He's So Fine* peaks at US #97.

July The follow-up, *One Fine Day*, hits US #5. Composers Goffin and King°, having originally recorded this song with Little Eva° on lead vocal for The Tokens, take it to The Chiffons' producers, who buy the whole production and erase Little Eva's voice track, substituting The Chiffons'. The Tokens also record The Chiffons under the pseudonym The Four Pennies on *My Block*. Released on Laurie subsidiary label Rust, it reaches US #67.

Aug *One Fine Day* reaches #29 in UK.

Oct *A Love So Fine*, the third consecutive Chiffons release with the word "fine" in the title, peaks at US #40, but fails in UK (as will their next few singles).

Nov *When The Boy's Happy (The Girl's Happy Too)* by The Four Pennies is released. It charts briefly at US #95, but the pseudonym is abandoned after this.

1964 Jan *I Have A Boyfriend* reaches US #36.

June The group supports The Rolling Stones° on first US tour.

Aug *Sailor Boy* peaks at only US #81. The group sues to extricate itself from the contract with Bright Tunes – a deal from which they earned little money, since the producers financed all their studio time by deductions from The Chiffons' royalties. A court eventually frees them on grounds of their having been minors when signing the original agreement. Other labels are now wary of them, so they return to Laurie and sign a direct deal.

1965 *Nobody Knows What's Going On* reaches US #49.

1966 June *Sweet Talkin' Guy* restores them to US top 10 after 3 years, hitting #10. It also makes the UK chart, climbing to #31.

Aug *Out Of This World*, a near-identical clone of *Sweet Talkin' Guy*, peaks at US #67.

Oct *Stop, Look and Listen* stalls at US #85, and is the group's last US hit.

1969 Craig quits the group, which, despite hitless years, is still performing in New York and touring the US on a regular basis.

1972 Apr *Sweet Talkin' Guy* is reissued in UK, and becomes a surprise smash hit, at #3.

1976 Aug [31] US district court judge Richard Owen finds George Harrison° guilty of "subconscious plagiarism" of Ronnie Mack's song *He's So Fine* when writing his 1970 million-seller *My Sweet Lord*. Earnings from the song, frozen since the suit was filed in 1971, go partly to the inheritors of Mack's estate. Taking advantage of the publicity surrounding the trial and verdict, The Chiffons record their own version of *My Sweet Lord*, but it fails to sell.

THE CHI-LITES

Eugene Record (lead vocals)
Marshall Thompson (drums)
Robert "Squirrel" Lester (vocals)
Creadel Jones (vocals)
Clarence Johnson (vocals)

1960 The group forms in Chicago, Ill., US, as an R&B quintet, The Hi-Lites, initially led by Thompson, who backed R&B acts at Chicago's Regal Theater and, with Jones, is ex-The Desideros; Record, Johnson and Lester are ex-The Chantours. A rival band also called The Hi-Lites claims original title use, so they become Marshall & The Chi-Lites. (Marshall being Thompson's forename and C added as a location identify of their home town Chicago.) They sign to Mercury and release *Pots And Pans*, which fails.

1967 After passing through several R&B labels including Blue Rock, Daran and Ja Wes labels and gaining local success, Marshall & The Chi-Lites sign to Dakar label, through MCA.

1969 Mar Now known as The Chi-Lites and signed to another MCA subsidiary, Brunswick, the group's *Give It Away* reaches US #88. It is written by Record, who is establishing himself as a successful songwriter (particularly for fellow Brunswick artiste Barbara Acklin, whom he also marries).

Aug *Let Me Be The Man My Daddy Was* peaks at US #94.

Sept LP *Give It Away* spends 3 weeks on chart, peaking at US #180.

1970 Aug *I Like Your Lovin' (Do You Like Mine)* tops US R&B chart and makes US #72.

1971 Jan *Are You My Woman? (Tell Me So)* also reaches US #72.

Apr With Record now singer/writer/producer, his *(For God's Sake) Give More Power To The People* makes US #26 and UK #32. LP of the same title will later climb to US #12.

July *We Are Neighbors* peaks at US #70.

1972 Jan During a 14-week chart stay, Record ballad *Have You Seen Her* hits both US and UK #3, while *I Want To Pay You Back (For Loving Me)* peaks at US #95.

May The group is now at the height of pop and R&B success. Harmonica-laden *Oh Girl* hits US #1, breaking a 6-week top spot residence by Roberta Flack's° *The First Time Ever I Saw Your Face*. It also reaches UK #14. LP *A Lonely Man* hits US #5 and goes gold (no LP will make the UK chart).

Aug *The Coldest Days Of My Life* climbs to US #47.

Oct LP *The Chi-Lites Greatest Hits* begins a 6-month US chart stay while *A Lonely Man/The Man And The Woman (The Boy And The Girl)* makes US #57.

Dec *We Need Each Other* reaches US #61 as the group completes its most successful year.

1973 Mar *A Letter To Myself* climbs to US #33. LP of the same title makes US #50. Record is made a senior executive at Brunswick.

Sept LP *Chi-Lites* peaks at US #89. Taken from it, *My Heart Just Keeps On Breakin'* reaches US #92. *Stoned Out Of My Mind* makes US #30 and is another R&B chart-topper.

Dec *I Found Sunshine* peaks at US #47.

1974 Mar *Homely Girl* makes US #54 and hits UK #5. A UK tour follows.

July *There Will Never Be Any Peace (Until God Is Seated At The Conference Table)* proves unpopular with impatient US DJs and makes only US #63. *I Found Sunshine* makes UK #35. LP *Toby* peaks at US #181, (their lowest LP showing in 5 years, and their last for 6 more.)

Nov *Too Good To Be Forgotten* hits UK #10 while *You Got To Be The One* peaks at US #83.

1975 Mar *Toby/That's How Long* reaches US #78. Rumors persist of Record's dissatisfaction with their current form.

June Re-released double A-side *Have You Seen Her/Oh Girl* hits UK #5.

Sept Another Record pop/soul ballad, *It's Time For Love*, hits UK #5 but makes only US #94 (and is the final group US chart single).

Nov Record announces his decision to leave The Chi-Lites and pursue a solo career, as LP *Half A Love* fails to sell.

1976 July *You Don't Have To Go* hits UK #3. The remaining members sign a new deal with Mercury, who will release their unsuccessful LP *Happy Being Lonely*. Two compilation LPs are also released: *Very Best Of The Chi-Lites* (Brunswick) and *Chilitime* (London).

1977 Without Record, The Chi-Lites release LP *The Fantastic Chi-Lites*, on Mercury, which fails to chart. Still a Brunswick executive, Record issues *Greatest Hits Volume 2* in US only.

1979 Aug With other Chi-Lites now inactive, Record signs to Warner Bros. as a solo and releases *Magnetism* and LP *Welcome To My Fantasy*. Both fail beyond the disco market in US and UK.

1980 Nov Record reunites The Chi-Lites and establishes the label Chi-Sound. LP *Heavenly Body* makes US #179 but has no hit singles.

1982 Apr Another Chi-Sound LP *Me And You* makes US #162.

1983 Aug Now established on US label Larc and licensed in UK through specialist dance label Red Bus, LP *Bottom's Up*, led by Record, climbs to US #98. Taken from it, *Changing For You* reaches UK #61. (The Chi-Lites will remain popular on the soul cabaret circuit, particularly in UK where compilation LPs will periodically appear including *The Chi-Lites Classic* (1984) and *20 Golden Pieces Of The Chi-Lites* (1985).)

CHINA CRISIS

Gary Daly (vocals)
Eddie Lundon (guitar)
Brian MacNeil (keyboards)
Gazza Johnson (bass)
Kevin Wilkinson (drums)

1979 After leaving school at age 17, Daly and Lundon join forces in Kirkby, Merseyside, UK, and become (and will remain) the core of China Crisis. The band plays locally and develops a following as an integral part of the early 1980s Mersey music scene.

1982 Aug Signed to Liverpool independent label, Inevitable, the group releases *African And White*. Picked up by Virgin Records, it climbs to UK #45, and the band signs a long-term contract with Virgin.

Dec Debut LP *Difficult Shapes And Passive Rhythms* reaches UK #21.

1983 Feb *Christian* climbs to UK #12. The band begins a European tour supporting Simple Minds°.

June *Tragedy And Mystery* peaks at UK #46.

Oct *Working With Fire And Steel* reaches UK #48.

Nov LP *Working With Fire And Steel – Possible Pop Songs Vol.2* makes UK #20.

1984 Feb Taken from the LP, *Wishful Thinking* hits UK #9.

Mar *Hanna Hanna* peaks at UK #44.

1985 Jan The group's car turns over on an icy road in the UK during an early morning journey home from the recording studio. Daly has a

CHINA CRISIS *cont.*

broken arm and Johnson a broken upper jaw but the others escape without serious injury.

Apr The Steely Dan°-influenced *Black Man Ray*, recorded at sessions with ex-Steely Dan Walter Becker producing, climbs to UK #14.

May Becker-produced LP *Flaunt The Imperfection* hits UK #9. The band tours UK and Ireland.

June Extracted from the LP, *King In A Catholic Style (Wake Up)* reaches UK #19. The band tours US, with limited success.

Sept *You Did Cut Me* peaks at UK #54.

1986 Jan China Crisis becomes the first major rock band to play in Gibraltar.

July The group teams with producers Clive Langer and Alan Winstanley to record a new LP.

Sept Lundon and Daly play a few UK pub dates under the name Kirk Douglas & The Long Coats From Hell.

Nov *Arizona Sky*, taken from their forthcoming LP, peaks at UK #47.

Dec Fourth LP *What Price Paradise?* charts for only 2 weeks, peaking at UK #63.

1987 Feb *Best-Kept Secret*, also from the LP, reaches UK #36.

THE CHORDETTES

Dorothy Schwartz (lead vocals)
Janet Ertel (bass vocals)
Carol Bushman (baritone vocals)
Jinny Osborn (tenor vocals)

1949 After perfecting their harmonies on local engagements around hometown of Sheboygan, Wis., US, the vocal quartet attracts national attention by winning and subsequently becoming regular performers on Arthur Godfrey's US TV talent show.

1953 Jan Dorothy Schwartz is replaced by Lynn Evans.

June Jinny Osborn is replaced by Margie Needham.

1954 Godfrey's musical director Archie Bleyer leaves the show to run his recently launched Cadence label, and signs The Chordettes. Bleyer's relationship with the group extends beyond business. He is married to Janet Ertel. The group, earlier an adult-oriented act in the 1940s showbiz tradition, quickly modifies to meet changing tastes.

Nov After several failures, *Mr. Sandman* hits US #1 for 7 consecutive weeks, and sells over a million.

1955 Jan *Mr. Sandman* reaches UK #11 despite top 20 competition from Max Bygraves and Dickie Valentine.

Dec *The Wedding* makes US #91.

1956 Mar *Eddie My Love* reaches US #17. A cover of the Teen Queens' (US #14) R&B original, it shows their continued interest in the growing teen market. (Another cover by the Fontane Sisters outsells both, reaching US #11.)

July *Born To Be With You* hits US #5. (The song will be successfully reprised by Dave Edmunds° in 1973.)

Sept *Born To Be With You* is their first UK top 10 hit at #8.

Nov The soldier-boy love anthem *Lay Down Your Arms* reaches US #16, and the B-side *Teen Age Goodnight* makes #45. (In UK, a cover of *Lay Down Your Arms* by Anne Shelton hits #1 and becomes an enduring "forces favorite".)

1957 Aug [5] The group guests on the first edition of Dick Clark's "American Bandstand" to be nationally aired in the US on ABC-TV.

Oct A second double-sided US hit sees *Just Between You And Me* rise to #15, and *Soft Sands* to #73.

1958 Mar The group's second million-seller is the teen novelty *Lollipop*, which hits US #2. The original version by Ronald & Ruby (Ruby being a pseudonym for writer Beverly Ross) stalls at US #39.

May *Lollipop* hits UK #6, although a cover by The Mudlarks attracts more UK airplay to hit #2.

June Theme from Walt Disney US TV series "Zorro" climbs to US #17.

1959 Apr *No Other Arms, No Other Lips* reaches US #27.

Aug *A Girl's Work Is Never Done* is a minor US hit at #89.

1961 Aug The group's version of movie theme song *Never On Sunday* becomes their last US top 20 hit, reaching #13, while the B-side *Faraway Star* appears for a week at #90. It proves to be their chart swan song. (Their cabaret career will continue into the 1960s, while compilation LPs of their material will remain among Cadence's most consistent sellers, until Bleyer folds the company in Sept. 1964.)

1963 Jan [12] Janet Ertel becomes mother-in-law to half of another former Cadence act, when Phil Everly of The Everly Brothers° marries her daughter (and Bleyer's stepdaughter) Jackie Ertel.

THE CHRISTIANS

Garry Christian (vocals)
Russell Christian (vocals)
Henry Priestman (vocals)
Roger Christian (vocals)

1984 Having flirted musically with The Yachts in the late 1970s and It's Immaterial in the early 80s, Henry Priestman, main songwriting and creative force in the band, meets the three Christian brothers (part of a brood of eleven Christian offspring) in Pete Wylie's Liverpool, UK, studio. As a soul acappella trio, they have previously called themselves Equal Temperament, The Gems and even Natural High – the name used for their appearance in 1974 on UK TV talent show "Opportunity Knocks".

1985 The Christian brothers begin to concentrate on Priestman's material – songs that will become the core of the band's career. They play one live concert The Liver Aid Ethiopian Famine benefit in Liverpool. The rest of the time they spend in Priestman's 8-track studio, recording a demo tape of what will later become their first three UK singles.

1986 Mar A day before signing to independent label Demon, the band is snapped up by Island Records on the strength of its demo. First recording efforts, with Clive Langer producing, are fruitless, but a later link-up with Laurie Latham suits both group and record company.

Sept *Forgotten Town*, *Hooverville* and *When The Fingers Point* are cut with Latham, but as the group embarks on a UK mini-tour Roger Christian becomes irritated by the attentions being focused on the more photogenic Garry, and also strongly objects to touring.

Nov/Dec Relations become strained and Priestman himself threatens to leave on three occasions if the family bickering doesn't stop.

1987 Feb The band makes its debut as a trio without Roger on UK Channel 4 TV's "Saturday Live."

Mar Debut single *Forgotten Town* climbs to UK #22.

Apr They tour UK and complete work on their first LP.

July *Hooverville* is released, peaking at UK #21.

Oct *When The Fingers Point* reaches UK #34. LP *The Christians* enters UK chart at #2, then rises to #1, becoming Island's biggest-selling LP by a debuting group.

1988 Jan *Ideal World* reaches UK #14. The group undertakes an extensive European tour establishing itself as a major UK act.

May *Born Again* is the fifth hit single to be extracted from the debut LP, and reaches UK #25.

June The group opens for Fleetwood Mac° on selected UK dates.

Aug A cover of Isley Brothers'° classic *Harvest For The World* is released.

LOU CHRISTIE

1962 Oct Having sung on unsuccessful releases by The Classics (1960) and Lugee & The Lions (1961), Christie (b. Lugee Sacco, Feb.19, 1943, Glen Willard, Pa., US) records his first solo *The Gypsy Cried*, highlighting his trademark falsetto, for C&C Records in Pittsburgh. It is his first recorded composition with Twyla Herbert, a clairvoyant 15 years older than himself, with whom he has written since 1958.

1963 Mar *The Gypsy Cried* is picked up by Roulette and climbs to US #24.

June The Four Seasons°-like *Two Faces Have I*, his first US top 10 hit, reaches #6.

Aug *How Many Teardrops* peaks at US #46.

Sept LP *Lou Christie* climbs to US #124.

1964 After touring the US with Dick Clark's "Caravan of Stars" package, Christie is called up for US Army Reserve duty and spends 6 months stationed at Fort Knox.

1965 Out of the army, he signs a management deal with Bob Marcucci (former mentor of Fabian° and Frankie Avalon°), and a recording deal with MGM. Christie and Herbert write *Lightnin' Strikes*, which MGM hates but is pressured into releasing.

1966 Feb *Lightnin' Strikes* tops the US chart and becomes a million-seller.

Mar *Lightnin' Strikes* is Christie's UK chart debut, reaching #11. In US its success prompts labels owning earlier recordings to release them: *Big Time* on Colpix charts at only #95, while *Outside The Gates Of Heaven* on C&E reaches #45.

Apr Official follow-up to *Lightnin' Strikes* is the similarly-arranged *Rhapsody In The Rain*, which is banned by many US radio stations for suggestive lyrics. Despite this, it climbs to US #16 and makes UK #37. LP *Lightnin' Strikes* peaks at US #103.

July *Painter* reaches US #81, but LP *Painter Of Hits* does not chart.
1967 May He moves to Columbia/CBS Records. *Shake Hands And Walk Away Cryin'* reaches only US #95.
1969 Oct After 2 quiet years, Christie signs to Buddah Records for *I'm Gonna Make You Mine*, which provides a major chart comeback. It hits US #10 and UK #2. He tours UK for promotion and appears on BBC TV's "Top of the Pops". (He will also be resident in the UK for some years during the 1970s, having married an English girl, former beauty queen, Francesca Winfield.)
1970 Jan *She Sold Me Magic*, his last UK hit, reaches #25. *Are You Getting Any Sunshine?* peaks at US #74.
1974 Mar Christie's last US hit at #80 is a revival of 1930s standard *Beyond The Blue Horizon*, for the independent Three Brothers label. (He will undertake unsuccessful recording spells with Midsong International and Lifesong and rely increasingly on oldies revival tours and club engagements for the remainder of his career.)

CLANNAD

Maire Ni Bhraonain (lead vocals and harp)
Pol O. Braonain (guitar, keyboards and vocals)
Ciaran O. Braonain (bass, synthesizers and vocals)
Noel O. Dugain (guitar and vocals)
Padraig O. Dugain (mandola, guitar and vocals)

1976 The daughter and sons of Irish band leader Lee O. Braonain and their uncles form Clannad (Gaelic for "family") with the main intention of entering local Irish folk festivals.
1979 Clannad sells out five nights at New York's Bottom Line, supported strongly by the local Irish community.
1980 Sister Enya Ni Bhraonain joins the band on vocals and keyboards. (She will play on two Clannad's LPs and leave in 1982, before finding success in 1988 as Enya with UK hit *Orinoco Flow*.)
1982 After 6 popular Irish tours and some local releases, Clannad is commissioned to score the music for "Harry's Game", a UK Yorkshire TV drama series about the troubles in Northern Ireland.
Nov *Theme From Harry's Game*, released on RCA Records, hits UK #5. Its haunting melodic style attracts critical praise in the TV industry.
1983 Apr The group wins UK Ivor Novello Songwriting Award for Best Television Film Theme for *Theme From Harry's Game*. Debut UK LP *Magical Ring* reaches UK #26, going gold after a 21-week run.
July *New Grange* peaks at UK #65.
Sept Clannad sets off on a lengthy European tour.
1984 Jan The group begins work composing and recording everything for a 26-part UK TV series "Robin of Sherwood".
May Selected excerpts from the score are released on LP *Legend*, which reaches UK #15 during a 40-week chart stay. From it, the main theme *Robin (The Hooded Man)* makes UK #42.
June LP *Magical Ring* is reissued and charts for 1-week at UK #91.
1985 Feb Clannad receives a British Academy Award for Best Soundtrack of the Year for the Robin Hood project, the first Irish group to achieve this. Meanwhile U2° begins using *Theme From Harry's Game* to close every concert, giving Clannad's music worldwide exposure.
Mar The group spends 6 months recording new non-theme songs in Dublin, London and Switzerland.
Nov Subsequent LP *Macalla* makes UK #33.
1986 Jan An uncredited duet from the LP featuring U2's° Bono and Maire, *In A Lifetime*, reaches UK #20. Clannad begins a 23-date sell-out UK tour.
1987 Feb The band, writing and recording a new LP in Wales, aims for a more commercial outlook and enlists production help from Russ Kunkel and Greg Ladanyi, who in turn invite contributions from Bruce Hornsby°, Steve Perry and J.D. Souther.
Nov LP *Sirius* peaks at UK #34.
1988 Feb Following a 2-year hiatus, Clannad begins a world tour, which will take in UK, Europe, Australia, US and Canada with all dates sold-out. It includes seven sell-out concerts in native Dublin to celebrate the city's millennium.
Mar During US dates, LP *Sirius* makes US #183.
July Clannad returns to Ireland to work in a studio on new BBC TV three-part series, "The Atlantic Realm".

ERIC CLAPTON

1962 Educated at Ripley primary school and St. Bede's secondary modern, Clapton (b. Mar.30, 1945, Ripley, Surrey, UK), is given his first guitar by his grandparents, who raised him after his parents separated. After 2 years of mild interest in blues, R&B and rock'n'roll, he learns guitar licks from the records of old blues masters like Blind Lemon Jefferson and Son House. While studying stained glass design at Kingston College of Art, he makes his first public performance as a busker. Later in the year he works on a building site by day and plays with local amateur bands by night.

1963 Jan Clapton joins The Roosters, a London R&B band which includes Tom McGuinness (later of Manfred Mann° and McGuinness Flint).
Aug Clapton and McGuinness leave The Roosters to join Merseybeat-style band Casey Jones & The Engineers.
Oct Clapton is asked to replace lead guitarist "Top" Topham in R&B group The Yardbirds°, who have just taken over The Rolling Stones'° residency at the Crawdaddy Club in Richmond. He becomes the group's focal point with his playing ability and his suitably sharp dressing. The group's manager, Giorgio Gomelsky, gives him the nickname "Slowhand".
1965 Mar Opposing the group's shift from R&B to mainstream pop, Clapton leaves. (2 weeks later, The Yardbirds° hit UK #4 with *For Your Love*.) John Mayall° invites him to join his Bluesbreakers.
Aug After a brief spell with The Bluesbreakers, Clapton sets off in a large American car with a group of musicians known variously as The Glands and The Greek Loon Band. The intention is to play their way around the world, but at Athens some members have to return to UK. The remaining musicians step in for a Greek club band and the club owner tries to blackmail Clapton into staying. He is forced to flee minus his clothes and new Marshall amplifier.
Nov Clapton rejoins The Bluesbreakers. His first recording with the band, *I'm Your Witchdoctor* (produced by Yardbird° Jimmy Page), is issued on Immediate label. Clapton earns his first session fee on

Champion Jack Dupree's *From New Orleans To Chicago*. Producer Mike Vernon invites Clapton and Mayall° to record for his Purdah label, resulting in *Lonely Years*, an authentic-sounding set of Chicago blues. Vernon is invited to produce The Bluesbreakers eponymous LP, which features Clapton's first recorded lead vocal on Robert Johnson's *Ramblin' On My Mind*.

1966 Clapton and fellow musicians Jack Bruce, Paul Jones, Peter York and Steve Winwood° cut three tracks for Elektra Records as The Powerhouse. They are included on compilation *What's Shakin'*, which sells poorly.

June Drummer Ginger Baker sits in on a Bluesbreakers' performance in Oxford and later suggests to Clapton that they form a group. Clapton proposes Bruce as bass player/singer. (Bruce had joined and left The Bluesbreakers to join Manfred Mann°.) The three begin secret rehearsals, but UK music paper *Melody Maker* runs a speculative scoop.

July Clapton plays his last Bluesbreakers gig at the Marquee before Mayall° fires him in favor of Peter Green, later of Fleetwood Mac°. Meanwhile Clapton's new group, Cream°, is already signed to Robert Stigwood's Reaction label. As the group's popularity soars, "Clapton Is God" graffiti appear on buildings in London. On the first US tour Clapton plays guitar on Frank Zappa° and The Mothers of Invention's LP *We're Only In It For The Money*.

July [25] Clapton plays lead guitar for George Harrison's° *While My Guitar Gently Weeps* on LP *The Beatles (aka The White Album)*. He also plays on Harrison's solo LP, *Wonderwall Music*.

1968 Nov Cream° disbands after two sold-out London concerts.

1969 Feb Clapton and Baker, with Steve Winwood°, form a new group, eventually named Blind Faith°.

May Rick Grech, bass player and violinist with Family°, joins the line-up.

June Blind Faith° makes its debut in a free concert in London's Hyde Park before an audience of 36,000. When the group announces its first US tour, advance promotion bills them as "The Ultimate Supergroup".

Aug The group's first, and only LP, *Blind Faith*, is released amid controversy over a naked 11-year-old girl pictured on the album sleeve. Clapton spends hours jamming with Blind Faith's° US support act, Delaney and Bonnie.°

Sept Clapton, after rehearsing on the plane trip, appears with John Lennon's° Plastic Ono Band in a concert in Toronto, which is recorded for Lennon's LP *Live Peace In Toronto*. A few weeks later in UK, Clapton plays on Lennon's *Cold Turkey*.

Dec Clapton appears with Lennon° as part of the Plastic Ono Supergroup in a UNICEF benefit concert at the London Lyceum.

1970 Jan Blind Faith° splits and Clapton joins (and helps finance) the "Delaney and Bonnie and Friends" US tour. As well as The Bramletts, the tour band includes George Harrison°, Rita Coolidge, Dave Mason, Bobby Keyes and others. An LP of the tour, *Delaney And Bonnie On Tour*, is released on Atlantic.

Mar Clapton records his first solo LP, *Eric Clapton*, in LA with members of the touring band and Leon Russell°.

June He plays a charity concert for Dr. Benjamin Spock's civil liberties fund. His band, borrowed from the Delaney and Bonnie° tour, is Carl Radle (bass), Bobby Whitlock (keyboards), Jim Gordon (drums) and Dave Mason of Traffic° on guitar. Mason plays only one concert, but the others stay with Clapton to become Derek & The Dominoes. They set out on a summer club tour in UK before embarking on a US tour.

July LP *Eric Clapton* reaches US #30 and UK #17. Derek & The Dominoes play on George Harrison's° LP *All Things Must Pass*, with producer Phil Spector. Spector also cuts a Derek & The Dominoes single, *Tell The Truth*, which is withdrawn soon after release. The band invites Duane Allman to join its recording in Miami after Clapton sees him play with The Allman Brothers°. A double LP is finished in less than 10 days. (Clapton's own sessions for the year include work on Leon Russell's° debut LP, Vivian Stanshall and Neil Innes' *Labio-Dental Fricative* and as a member of an all-star band for gospel singer Doris Troy's Apple Records LP.)

Oct Clapton's version of J.J. Cale's° *After Midnight*, from his first LP, reaches US #18.

Nov Derek & The Dominoes' LP *Layla And Other Assorted Love Songs* is released. Clapton's refuses to have his name printed on the sleeve in an attempt to escape his guitar-hero image. The LP fails to chart in UK but makes US #16.

1971 Clapton retires to his Surrey home in an attempt to overcome his drug addiction.

Aug George Harrison° persuades Clapton to play in his group for the "Concert for Bangla Desh", which includes Leon Russell°, Billy Preston, Ringo Starr°, Klaus Voorman and others. (Later in the year Clapton plays some tour dates with The Dominoes and works on sessions for Harrison, Dr. John°, a reunited Bluesbreakers and as part of the all-star band on Howlin' Wolf's° LP *The London Sessions*.)

Dec He guests in Leon Russell's° concert at London's Rainbow Theatre.

1972 Apr With Clapton inactive, compilation LP *History Of Eric Clapton* peaks at US #6 during its 42-week chart run. It features his work with The Yardbirds°, The Bluesbreakers, Cream°, Blind Faith°, Derek & The Dominoes and Delaney and Bonnie°.

Aug *Layla* hits UK #7 as LP *History Of Eric Clapton* peaks at UK #20.

Oct Polydor releases LP *Eric Clapton At His Best*, a collection of songs from LPs *Eric Clapton* and *Layla*, which reaches US #87. *Let It Rain* makes US #48.

1973 Jan [13] The Who's° Pete Townshend gets Clapton back on a stage, organizing an all-star comeback concert for him at London's Rainbow Theatre. Townshend also recruits Ron Wood, Steve Winwood°, Jim Capaldi and others. The concert is recorded and released as *Eric Clapton's Rainbow Concert*. Despite these efforts, Clapton retreats once again.

Feb Polydor's second retrospective LP, *Clapton*, reaches US #67. *Bell Bottom Blues* makes US #78.

Mar RSO Records releases LP *Derek & The Dominoes In Concert* which reaches US #20 and UK #36.

Sept LP *Eric Clapton's Rainbow Concert* enters UK and US charts, reaching #19 and #18 respectively.

Nov Clapton begins electro-acupuncture treatment for his addiction. He follows 2 months' treatment with a period of convalescence on a friend's farm in Wales.

1974 Apr When Clapton informs label boss Stigwood that he is ready to return, Stigwood throws a party at a Chinese restaurant in London's Soho district and invites producer Tom Dowd to oversee forthcoming project. Clapton goes to Miami to record. He has only two songs in mind: Charles Scott Boyer's *Please Be With Me* and his own *Give Me Strength*. The band assembled is Radle, Jamie Oldaker (drums), Dick Sims (keyboards), George Terry (guitar) and Yvonne Elliman (vocals). (They will form the basis of the line-up for his next four LPs.)

July First product of the comeback sessions is a version of Bob Marley's° *I Shot The Sheriff*, which tops the US chart and hits UK #9 as Clapton tours US.

Aug LP *461 Ocean Boulevard*, named after the Miami studio address, tops the US chart for 4 weeks and hits UK #3.

Nov *Willie And The Hand Jive* makes US #26 as Clapton tours Japan.

1975 Apr LP *There's One In Every Crowd* is released, reaching US #21 and UK #15. Clapton contributes a track to Dylan's° LP *Desire*.

May His interpretation of the spiritual *Swing Low Sweet Chariot* reaches UK #19. Clapton tours Australia and Hawaii before touring US.

Aug *Knockin' On Heaven's Door* reaches UK #38, as live LP *E.C. Was Here* is released and makes UK #14 and US #20. With Clapton still the reluctant guitar player, George Terry handles most of the lead guitar work.

1976 Apr LP *No Reason To Cry*, with guest appearances from Bob Dylan° and The Band°, hits UK #8 and US #15.

Oct *Hello Old Friend* reaches US #24. Clapton's live band now includes South American percussionist Sergio Pastora.

Nov Clapton performs *Further On Up The Road* at The Band's° "The Last Waltz" farewell concert on Thanksgiving Day. (Session appearances include Joe Cocker's° LP *Stingray*, Stephen Bishop's LP *Careless* and Ringo Starr's° LP *Rotogravure*.)

1977 June Pastora leaves the group to return to South America.

Aug Clapton and the band play Ibiza bullring. During the year Clapton also contributes to Ronnie Lane and Pete Townshend's LP *Rough Mix* and Roger Daltrey's LP *One Of The Boys* . LP *Slowhand* reaches UK #23.

1978 Jan *Lay Down Sally* makes UK #39.

Apr *Lay Down Sally* hits US #3.

May Clapton's *Wonderful Tonight*, written for his wife Patti, peaks at UK #16.

Oct Promises hits US #9 and reaches UK #37.
Nov Clapton embarks on a 2-month European tour with Radle, Oldaker and Sims.
Dec LP *Backless* reaches UK #18.
1979 Mar Clapton begins a world tour with an all-new UK band, featuring Albert Lee (guitar), Chris Stainton (keyboards), Dave Markee (bass) and Henry Spinetti (drums). In Japan, a live LP is recorded at the Budokan. *Watch Out For Lucy*, original B-side of *Promises*, makes US #40.
1980 May The live Budokan LP, *Just Another Night*, is released. It hits UK #3 and spends 6 weeks at US #2.
June *Tulsa Time*, backed with J.J. Cale's° *Cocaine* reaches US #30.
Nov *Blues Power* reaches US #76.
1981 Feb *I Can't Stand It* hits US #10.
Mar For LP *Another Ticket* ex-Procol Harum° pianist Gary Brooker joins the band. It hits US #7 and UK #18.
May Clapton plays on Phil Collins'° debut LP.
June *Another Ticket* reaches US #78.
Sept Clapton leaves RSO to set up his own WEA-distributed label, Duck Records. He plays a set with Jeff Beck° at "The Secret Policeman's Other Ball" in London, in aid of Amnesty International. (The two will be featured on the concert LP.)
1982 Apr A history of Clapton's solo career LP *Time Pieces – The Best Of Eric Clapton* reaches UK #20 and US #101.
June *I Shot The Sheriff* re-enters the UK chart at #64.
1983 Jan Clapton's first Duck Records release, *I've Got A Rock'n'Roll Heart*, reaches US #18.
Feb LP *Money And Cigarettes* makes US #16 and UK #13.
Apr *The Shape You're In* peaks at UK #75.
Sept [20] Clapton participates in the "A.R.M.S." charity concert at London's Royal Albert Hall.
1984 June Compilation LP *Backtrackin'* peaks at UK #29.
July Clapton joins Bob Dylan° on stage at his Wembley Arena concert in London.
1985 Mar LP *Behind The Sun* hits UK #8 and US #34. *Forever Man* reaches UK #51 and US #26.
June *See What Love Can Do* peaks at US #89.
1986 Jan Clapton and Michael Kamen write the score for UK BBC TV nuclear thriller "Edge of Darkness". The theme reaches UK #65.
Apr Clapton makes a cameo appearance in Michael Caine-starring film *Water*.
Dec LP *August*, produced by, and featuring, Phil Collins°, hits UK #3.
1987 Clapton receives a special award at BPI annual ceremony in London.
Feb Yellow Magic Orchestra original *Behind The Mask*, co-written by Greg Phillinganes, who joins Clapton's band, makes UK #15.
Mar LP *August* makes US #37. He teams with Kamen again to write the score for Mel Gibson movie *Lethal Weapon*.
July Clapton and Tina Turner's° *Tearing Us Apart* reaches UK #50.
Sept LP *Cream – The Best Of Eric Clapton* begins a lengthy UK chart run, hitting UK #3.
1988 Apr Box set *Crossroads*, a major career retrospective, fails to chart in UK, but makes US #34.
June [11] Clapton joins Dire Straits° on stage at the Nelson Mandela 70th Birthday Party concert at London's Wembley Stadium.

THE DAVE CLARK FIVE

Mike Smith (vocals and keyboards)
Dave Clark (drums)
Lenny Davidson (guitar)
Denis Payton (saxophone)
Rick Huxley (guitar)

1958 Clark (b. Dec.15, 1942, Tottenham, London, UK) and bassist Chris Walls advertise in *Melody Maker* for musicians to form a band. They are joined by Huxley (b. Aug.5, 1942, Dartford, Kent, UK) on rhythm guitar, Stan Saxon as singer and sax player and Mick Ryan on lead guitar. The Dave Clark Five featuring Stan Saxon makes its debut at South Grove Youth Club, Tottenham.
1961 After several personnel changes and experience gained on the live circuit, the band, still semi-professional, signs a long-term contract with the Mecca ballroom chain. The line-up is Clark, a film stuntman, on drums, Huxley, a lighting engineer, switched to bass, Davidson (b. May 30, 1944, Enfield, London), a progress clerk, on guitar and backing vocals and Payton (b. Aug.8, 1943, Walthamstow, London), an electrical engineer, replacing tenor saxophonist Jim Spencer. The new focal point of the group is Smith (b. Dec.12, 1943, Edmonton, London), a classically-trained pianist, who takes over vocals permanently when Saxon fails to turn up for a gig one night, having stood-in before when Saxon's voice has given way.
1962 Clark, who controls the group's recordings, sells the master of *Chaquita*, an instrumental modelled on The Champs'° *Tequila*, to Ember Records.
June Pye Records signs the group to its Piccadilly label and releases first vocal record, *I Knew It All The Time*. *Chaquita* is issued on Ember 8 weeks later, but neither sells.
Dec The Piccadilly deal is wound up with release of *First Love*, another instrumental, which again fails to chart.
1963 Jan The band is playing its home venue, the Tottenham Royal, when an A&R man from EMI's Columbia label sees and later signs it.
Mar A rock version of nursery rhyme *The Mulberry Bush* is the group's Columbia debut, but does not chart.
Oct The band covers The Contours' *Do You Love Me*, which (helped by a publicity stunt involving the Duke of Edinburgh's supposed criticism of the lyrics) makes UK #30. Brian Poole & The Tremeloes'° simultaneous version tops the UK chart.
Dec The group wins the Mecca Gold Cup as the ballroom circuit's best band of 1963.
1964 Jan *Glad All Over*, written by Smith and Clark (as will be most of the group's major hits) tops the UK chart, replacing The Beatles'° *I Want To Hold Your Hand* and prompting "London Topples Liverpool"-type stories in UK tabloid press. Its eventual UK sales are over 870,000. 4-track EP *The Dave Clark Five*, featuring *Do You Love Me*, makes UK #28.
Mar *Bits And Pieces* hits UK #2, selling 590,000 copies in UK. It is banned by many ballroom managers who fear damage to wooden dancefloors since its "stomping" break encourages dancers to stamp their feet in time with it. The group turns professional and signs to the Harold Davidson Organization in a deal which guarantees it £50,000 a year for live performances.
Apr *Glad All Over* hits US #6.
Apr [26] The group appears in the New Musical Express Poll Winners concert at Wembley, UK, with The Beatles° and others.
May LP *A Session With The Dave Clark Five* hits UK #3. *Bits And Pieces* hits US #4 and LP *Glad All Over* (first of a long series of US LPs unissued in UK) hits US #3.
May [30] The group plays New York's Carnegie Hall.
May [31] The group appears on US TV's "Ed Sullivan Show". (The group's first US tour is a huge success, but Huxley suffers minor injuries when the Five are mobbed by fans in Washington, D.C. Over the next 3 years, the Five will visit the US constantly, maintaining a high chart profile by ready availability for live and TV work.)
June *Can't You See That She's Mine* hits UK #10. *Do You Love Me* makes US #11 and *I Knew It All The Time* on Congress Records (licensed from UK Piccadilly 2 years earlier) reaches US #53.
July *Can't You See That She's Mine* hits US #4 and LP *The Dave Clark Five Return!* hits US #5.
Aug *Thinking Of You Baby* reaches only UK #26. MGM signs the group to make a feature film.
Sept *Because*, the group's first ballad written by Clark and Smith, hits US #3.
Oct LP *American Tour* climbs to US #11.
Nov *Any Way You Want It* reaches UK #25, while *Everybody Knows* makes US #14.
1965 Jan *Any Way You Want It* reaches US #14 and *Everybody Knows* makes UK #37.
Feb LP *Coast To Coast* hits US #6.
Mar A revival of Chuck Berry's° *Reelin' And Rockin'* peaks at UK #24 and ballad *Come Home* makes US #14.
May *Reelin' And Rockin'* reaches US #23 and LP *Weekend In London* makes US #24.
June *Come Home* reaches UK #16.
Aug The group's film *Catch Us If You Can*, directed by John Boorman, is released in UK and is a success. The title track hits UK #5 while soundtrack LP hits UK #8. A revival of Chris Kenner's *I Like It Like That* hits US #7.
Aug [16] Smith suffers two broken ribs when he is pulled off stage by fans at a show in Chicago during US tour.
Sept Movie *Catch Us If You Can* is released in US as *Having A Wild Weekend*, but hit single is *Catch Us If You Can*, at US #4. Soundtrack LP (as *Having A Wild Weekend*) climbs to US #15.

THE DAVE CLARK FIVE *cont.*

Nov The band appears in London's "Royal Variety Show" performing a version of Jim Reeves' *Welcome To My World*. A revival of Bobby Day's° *Over And Over* peaks at UK #45.

Dec *Over And Over* hits US #1 and is a million-seller.

1966 Jan LP *I Like It Like That* reaches US #32.

Mar *At The Scene*, unreleased in UK, reaches US #18.

Apr Compilation LP *The Dave Clark Five's Greatest Hits* hits US #9.

May R&B-flavored *Try Too Hard* climbs to US #12, while *Look Before You Leap* charts briefly in UK at #50.

June [12] The group makes its twelfth appearance on US TV's "Ed Sullivan Show" – a record for any UK act.

July *Please Tell Me Why* reaches US #28 and LP *Try Too Hard* makes US #77.

Sept *Satisfied With You* reaches US #50.

Oct LP *Satisfied With You* makes US #127.

Nov *Nineteen Days* peaks at UK #48.

Dec Compilation LP *The Dave Clark Five: More Greatest Hits* peaks at US #103.

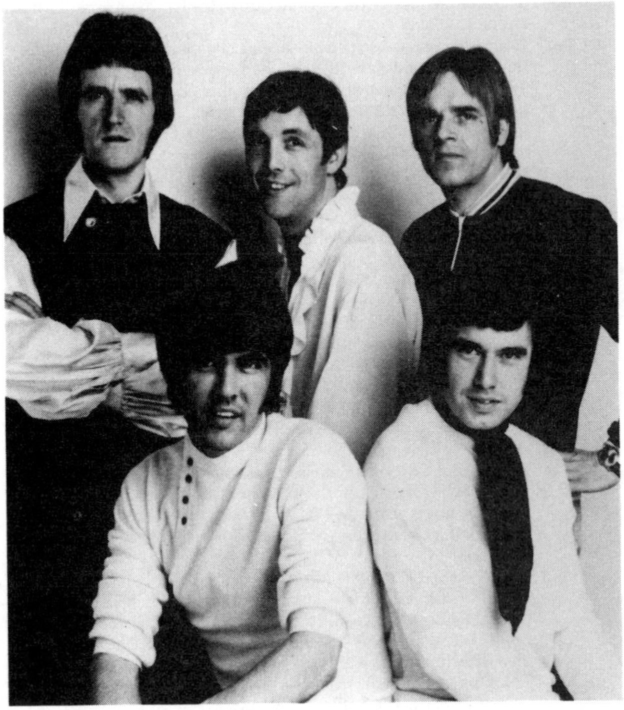

1967 Jan The group forms its own film company, Big Five Films, to make "low-budget features and documentaries". (The first documentary, a profile of The Dave Clark Five itself, will be sold to US TV.)

Feb *I've Got To Have A Reason* climbs to US #48.

Apr LP *5 By 5* reaches US #119. A revival of Marv Johnson's *You Got What It Takes* makes UK #28.

May *You Got What It Takes* hits US #7.

July A rocked-up revival of oldie *You Must Have Been A Beautiful Baby* reaches US #35.

Aug *A Little Bit Now* peaks at US #67 and LP *You Got What It Takes* reaches US #149. (The Five's last LP to chart in US.)

Nov *Red And Blue* reaches US #89.

Dec *Everybody Knows* (not the Five's 1964 hit but a ballad written by Les Reed and Barry Mason, with Lenny Davidson on lead vocal) hits UK #2 behind The Beatles'° *Hello Goodbye*.

1968 Jan *Everybody Knows* peaks at US #43 and is the band's final US chart entry.

Mar Ballad *No One Can Break A Heart Like You* makes UK #28.

Oct A cover of Raymond Froggatt's *Red Balloon* hits UK #7.

Dec The football chant-styled *Live In The Sky* peaks at UK #39.

1969 Nov The group begins a series of successful oldie revivals with Jackie DeShannon's *Put A Little Love In Your Heart*, which makes UK #31.

1970 Jan Medley *Good Old Rock'n'Roll*, a cover of US hit by Cat Mother & The All-Night Newsboys (and featuring rock oldies like *Long Tall Sally*, *Lucille* and *Blue Suede Shoes*) hits UK #7.

Apr *Everybody Get Together*, a cover of The Youngbloods'° US hit *Get Together*, hits UK #8.

July Another revived oldie, Jerry Keller's *Here Comes Summer*, peaks at UK #44.

Aug The group announces its break-up.

Nov *More Good Old Rock'n'Roll*, a medley made by just Clark and Smith on the lines of the earlier hit, reaches UK #34 and is the group's final UK chart single.

1971 *Southern Man* and *Won't You Be My Lady* are released, without success. (Clark and Smith will release singles under the name Dave Clark and Friends until 1973 – mostly covers of US hits like Tommy James'° *Draggin' The Line* and The Stampeders' *Sweet City Woman*. None will chart. Smith will move to commercial jingle writing and promotion. Clark will concentrate on business activities, including music publishing and showbiz involvement with protegés like John Christie. Davidson will move to antique dealing, Payton to property sales and Huxley to musical equipment retailing.)

1978 Mar LP *25 Thumping Great Hits*, compiled by Clark from original group recordings (all of which have remained his property) and licensed to Polydor, hits UK #7.

1985 June Several compilation editions of 1960s UK program "Ready Steady Go" are shown on UK's Channel 4 TV, leased by Clark who purchased the tapes and rights to the series following its demise. The new compilations are by Clark and feature his former group frequently (including some US concert footage not from the programs).

1986 Apr [9] The musical *Time*, devised, co-written and produced by Clark, premieres at the Dominion Theatre in London with Cliff Richard° in the leading role. (It will have a long and successful run and David Cassidy° will take over the lead.)

May LP *Dave Clark's Time – The Album*, an all-star package of songs from the musical, reaches UK #21. It features Cliff Richard°, Freddie Mercury, Dionne Warwick°, Leo Sayer°, Ashford and Simpson° and Stevie Wonder°. Most of the material is new but *Because*, sung on the LP by Julian Lennon, is a revival of The Dave Clark Five's 1964 hit.

PETULA CLARK

1942/43 Encouraged by her father into a showbiz career, Clark (b. Nov.15, 1932, West Ewell, Surrey, UK) is launched into wartime entertainment in UK as a child performer, finding radio stardom on "It's All Yours" and playing over 150 shows in her first 2 years on the stage.

1944 She appears in her first movie, *A Medal For The General*, at age 11. (She will make over 20 more UK films through her teens and into the mid-1950s, including Peter Ustinov's *Vice Versa* in 1948, and *The Card* with Alec Guinness in 1952.)

1949 Her first record, *Put Your Shoes On Lucy*, is released on EMI's Columbia label.

1950 She signs to the newly-formed Polygon label in UK (and will stay with the label until 1971, seeing it change name to Nixa and then Pye Records in the 50s). *You Are My True Love* is released. She wins an award as Most Outstanding Artist on UK TV, partly for her popular Sunday afternoon show "Pet's Parlour".

1952 Dec Seasonal children's novelty *Where Did My Snowman Go?* just misses the UK published (top 12) chart.

1954 July Another children's song, *The Little Shoemaker* (recorded while she is still partially in shock following a car accident on the way to the studio) hits UK #7.

1955 Mar *Majorca* makes UK #12.

Dec Her version of much-covered ballad *Suddenly There's A Valley* hits UK #7.

1957 Sept Clark's cover of Jodi Sands' US hit *With All My Heart*, hits UK #4.

Dec Her cover of *Alone* hits UK #8, ahead of The Shepherd Sisters' original US version at UK #14 and The Southlanders' at UK #17.

1958 Mar *Baby Lover* makes UK #12 (her last UK success for 3 years).

1959 The Vogue label, to which she is signed in France, suggests that she records in French to avoid the cover versions which have afflicted *With All My Heart* and *Alone* in the French-speaking market. In Paris for recording (initially phonetic, as she does not speak the language), she meets Vogue promotion man Claude Wolff, and the two become romantically attached.

1961 Feb Soon after marrying Wolff and settling in France, Clark's *Sailor*, Norman Newell's English adaptation of Lolita's German hit *Seeman*, hits UK #1 for a week despite a competing top 10 version by Anne Shelton.

Apr *Something Missing* makes only UK #44.

Aug *Romeo* hits UK #3. It is a huge hit in Europe and tops a million sales internationally.

Dec *My Friend The Sea* hits UK #7.

1962 Feb *I'm Counting On You* reaches UK #42.

July *Ya Ya Twist*, a rocking adaptation of Lee Dorsey's° US R&B hit, sung in French and intended for the Continental market, reaches UK #14. Another period without major UK hits follows but *Monsieur* and *Chariot*, sung in French, and *Casanova*, in German, are all Continental million-sellers.

1963 May *Casanova/Chariot*, a UK double A-side featuring the original foreign language versions, makes UK #39.

1964 Dec Tony Hatch, who has been producing French sessions for Clark, interests her in his song *Downtown*, originally written with The Drifters° in mind. Completed in only its second studio take, it hits UK #2 behind The Beatles'° *I Feel Fine*.

1965 Jan *I Feel Fine* fails to hold off *Downtown* in US, which hits #1 for 2 weeks and sells over a million. She becomes the first UK female to top the US charts since Vera Lynn in 1952. (*Downtown* will win a US Grammy Award as Best Rock and Roll Recording of 1965.)

Mar LP *Downtown* reaches US #21.

Apr *I Know A Place* makes UK #17.

May *I Know A Place* hits US #3 and Clark becomes the only female vocalist to have her first two chart singles make the US top three. (This achievement will stand until Cyndi Lauper° does the same in 1984.)

June LP *I Know A Place* peaks at US #42.

Aug *You'd Better Come Home* makes UK #44 and US #22.

Oct *Round Every Corner* reaches UK #43 and US #21.

Nov The Clark co-penned *You're The One* makes UK #23 but is not released as a single in US. (The Vogues' cover of it makes US #4.) LP *Petula Clark Sings The World's Greatest International Hits* makes US #129. Clark is offered the chance to co-star in an Elvis Presley° movie, but declines.

1966 Feb *My Love*, a recording Clark dislikes and tries not to have released, tops the US chart for 2 weeks and is her second US million-seller. It hits UK #4.

Mar [15] Clark wins her second Grammy, this time as Best Contemporary Vocal Performance (Female) for *I Know A Place*.

Apr *A Sign Of The Times* reaches UK #49 and US #11.

May LP *My Love* reaches US #68.

July *I Couldn't Live Without Your Love* hits UK #6 and US #9, while LP of the same title reaches UK #11.

Oct LP *I Couldn't Live Without Your Love* makes US #43.

Nov *Who Am I* climbs to US #21, but fails to chart in UK.

1967 Jan *Color My World* makes US #16, again failing in UK.

Feb Clark's version of Charlie Chaplin-penned *This Is My Song* (from his movie *Countess From Hong Kong* starring Sophia Loren) tops the UK chart for 2 weeks, selling over 500,000 copies, and beating a rival version by Harry Secombe which hits #2. Clark's recording is produced by Claude Wolff with Ernie Freeman arranging. Compilation LP *Petula Clark's Hit Parade* reaches UK #18 and LP *Colour My World* hits UK #1.

Mar LP *Color My World/Who Am I* makes US #49.

Apr *This Is My Song* hits US #3.

July *Don't Sleep In The Subway*, a song created by Tony Hatch from unfinished segments of three others, reaches UK #12 and hits US #5.

Sept *The Cat In The Window (The Bird In The Sky)*, fails in UK but makes US #26.

Oct LP *These Are My Songs* reaches UK #38 and US #27.

1968 Jan *The Other Man's Grass (Is Always Greener)* makes UK #20 and US #31.

Mar *Kiss Me Goodbye* peaks at UK #50 and US #15.

Apr LP *The Other Man's Grass Is Always Greener* reaches UK #37 and US #93.

Aug *Don't Give Up* peaks at US #37.

Oct She co-stars in movie musical *Finian's Rainbow* with Fred Astaire and Tommy Steele°. The soundtrack LP reaches US #90, while Clark's own LP *Petula* peaks at US #51.

1969 Jan Compilation LP *Petula Clark's Greatest Hits, Vol.1* makes US #57.

June LP *Portrait Of Petula* reaches US #37.

Dec She co-stars with Peter O'Toole in film *Goodbye Mr Chips*. The soundtrack LP charts at US #164.

1970 Jan LP *Just Pet* peaks at US #176.

Aug LP *Memphis* makes US #198.

1971 Mar *The Song Of My Life* reaches UK #32.

Apr LP *Warm And Tender* peaks at US #178 (her last US chart LP).

1972 Jan Clark's version of Rice/Lloyd Webber's *I Don't Know How To Love Him* from *Jesus Christ Superstar* makes UK #47. She leaves Pye and signs to Polydor (but no big sellers will emerge from this deal, though five Polydor LPs are released over 4 years).

1977 Feb TV-advertised compilation LP *20 All-Time Greatest* reaches UK #18. This comes between a short recording return to Pye (which produces a disco version of *Downtown*) and a signing to CBS, neither being very productive in commercial terms.

1979 She co-stars with Paul Jones in UK TV musical drama "Traces of Love".

1981 After initial unwillingness to follow in Julie Andrews' footsteps, Clark stars as Maria in a stage revival of *The Sound of Music* at London's Apollo Victoria theater, which runs successfully for 14 months.

1983 After making feature film *Never Never Land*, she takes a stage role (non-singing) in a short run of George Bernard Shaw's *Candida*, as well as playing a concert with the London Philharmonic Orchestra at London's Royal Albert Hall (recorded as a live double LP).

1985 Clark starts work on a self-penned musical about the US Civil War, a long-term project in which she hopes one day to star herself on stage or screen.

THE CLASH

Joe Strummer (vocals and guitar)
Mick Jones (guitar)
Paul Simonon (bass)
Nicky "Topper" Headon (drums)

1976 June After 9 abortive months with seminal punk outfit London SS, Jones (b. June 26, 1955, Brixton, London, UK) forms The Clash in Shepherds Bush, London, with Simonon (b. Dec.15, 1955, Brixton) who has never played before, but learns bass guitar. Bernie Rhodes from Malcolm McLaren's London Sex boutique becomes their manager. Guitarist Keith Levene (later of Public Image Ltd°) and drummer Terry Chimes join, and Strummer (b. Jan.25, 1955, London) is persuaded to leave R&B group the 101ers.

Aug [29] First gig (after an unannounced support slot behind The Sex Pistols° in Sheffield) is at Screen on the Green, Islington, London.

Sept [20] The band plays at the 100 Club Punk Festival, London, but club owners are wary of potential punk violence and gigs generally prove hard to find. Levene leaves after only 5 shows.

Dec [6] The band lands a spot on The Sex Pistols'° highly controversial "Anarchy in the UK" tour (the first three gigs have been cancelled because of venue bans).

1977 Jan [1] Debut at Covent Garden's Roxy, a club which is becoming a center of the London punk movement.

Jan Record companies now show interest in the genre, and Rhodes signs The Clash to CBS worldwide. The debut LP is recorded over 3 weekends. Chimes leaves and is replaced by "Topper" Headon (b. May 30, 1955, Bromley, Kent, UK).

Apr Debut single *White Riot* reaches UK #38.

May [1] The "White Riot" UK tour starts at the Roxy, with The Jam° and The Buzzcocks° as support bands (The Jam will pull out on May 29). LP *The Clash* reaches UK #12. *Remote Control* is released, but does not chart.

June [10] Strummer and Headon are each fined £5 in London for spray-painting "Clash" on a wall.

June [11] The duo is detained overnight in Newcastle prison, having failed to appear at Morpeth magistrates court on May 21 to answer a robbery charge relating to the theft of a Holiday Inn pillowcase. They are fined £100. The tour which starts a few days later is wryly named "Out on Parole".

Sept *Complete Control*, recorded with reggae producer Lee "Scratch" Perry, makes UK #28.

1978 Feb Strummer is hospitalized for 11 days with hepatitis.

Mar *Clash City Rockers* reaches UK #35. The band is involved in a feature film with Ray Gange. Debut LP, still not released in US (CBS deem it unsuitable for radio play) but it sells more than

THE CLASH *cont.*

100,000 on import, making it the biggest-selling imported LP ever in the US. [30] Simonon and Headon are arrested in Camden Town, London, for criminal damage, after shooting down racing pigeons with air guns. Fines this time total £800.

Apr [30] The band headlines the Anti-Nazi League Carnival in London, organized by Rock Against Racism.

July *(White Man) In Hammersmith Palais* peaks at UK #32. With some work already done for a second LP, they meet Blue Oyster Cult° producer Sandy Pearlman, and complete the LP with him.

July [8] Strummer and Simonon are arrested and fined (£25 and £50) for being "drunk and disorderly" after a show at the Apollo in Glasgow, Scotland.

Oct [21] Rhodes is fired as manager after both band and CBS find him increasingly hard to deal with. He is replaced by one of the Clash's early champions, *Melody Maker* writer Caroline Coon.

Nov [1] Rhodes, who has a contract giving him 20% of the band's income, is granted a court order stating that all Clash earnings are to be paid directly to him.

Nov The second LP *Give 'Em Enough Rope* hits UK #2 in its first week.

Dec The band plays "Sort It Out" UK tour. *Tommy Gun* is their biggest-selling single yet in the US, at #19.

1979 Feb [17] First US tour, dubbed "Pearl Harbor '79", opens at New York Palladium, with Bo Diddley° as support, and is well received.

Mar LP *Give 'Em Enough Rope* makes only US #128, while *English Civil War (Johnny Comes Marching Home)* reaches UK #25.

June Four-track EP *The Cost Of Living*, headed by a revival of Bobby Fuller's° *I Fought The Law*, reaches UK #22. Coon is fired as manager.

Aug The group records 12 songs in 3 days with veteran producer Guy Stevens.

Sept Second US tour, with The Undertones° supporting, is dubbed "The Clash Take the Fifth" (a reference to temporary fifth member Mickey Gallagher, of Ian Dury's° Blockheads, on keyboards). US support acts include R&B stalwarts Sam and Dave°, Screamin' Jay Hawkins° and Lee Dorsey°, plus "new wave" country-rocker Joe Ely, and psychobilly band The Cramps. The trek coincides with the belated US release of LP *The Clash* which makes US #126.

Nov A new LP, completed with Stevens, is announced as a double set retailing at single LP price.

Dec Double LP *London Calling* (originally to have been *The New Testament*) hits UK #9.

Dec [27] The group co-headlines (with Ian Dury°) the second of four benefit concerts for the people of Kampuchea, at Hammersmith Odeon, London.

1980 Jan Title track from *London Calling* makes UK #11. In need of management, the band signs to Blackhill, run by Peter Jenner and Andrew King (former Pink Floyd° and currently Ian Dury° managers).

Mar LP *London Calling* reaches US #27.

Mar [15] *Rude Boy*, a fictionalized documentary film of a Clash roadie (played by Ray Gange) made by Jack Hazan and David Mingay, opens in London. Much of it has been filmed behind the scenes on the road with the band over the previous 18 months.

May *Train In Vain (Stand By Me)*, the band's first US chart single, reaches #23.

May [21] Strummer is arrested at a much-troubled gig in Hamburg, West Germany, after smashing his guitar over the head of a violently demonstrative member of the audience. He is released after an alcohol test proves negative.

June The band tours in US and Europe. Jamaican DJ Mikey Dread plays on some European dates, and they record *Bankrobber* with him.

Aug They start recordings for self-produced LP at Electric Ladyland studios, New York, with tensions between Jones and the others affecting some sessions. Jones also produces an LP by US singer Ellen Foley, his current girlfriend.

Sept After a flood of Dutch imports of *Bankrobber*, CBS releases it in UK and it climbs to #12.

Nov 10" mini-LP *Black Market Clash*, specially compiled for the US market, reaches US #74.

Dec *The Call Up*, an anti-draft song, peaks at UK #40, while triple LP set *Sandinista!* (issued at the band's insistence at double LP price) has mixed reactions due to its sprawling contents. The Clash's lowest-charting UK LP yet, it reaches #19.

1981 Jan Strummer, dissatisfied with recent temporary management arrangements, meets Bernie Rhodes by chance in London and within 2 months Rhodes is back as manager.

Feb *Hitsville UK* makes UK #56.

Mar LP *Sandinista!* reaches US #24.

May The dance-oriented *The Magnificent Seven* stalls at UK #34.

Dec *This Is Radio Clash* reaches UK #47, and work begins on another LP.

1982 Jan With the LP unfinished, The Clash makes its first tour of the East, taking in Japan, New Zealand, Australia, Hong Kong and Thailand.

Mar The group returns to the UK and finishes recording, with Glyn Johns completing the final mixing.

Apr [26] On the eve of the UK "Know Your Rights" tour, Strummer disappears, and the dates are postponed. (It is later revealed to be a Rhodes publicity stunt.)

May *Know Your Rights* reaches UK #43, while LP *Combat Rock* hits UK #2, and will remain charted for 23 weeks.

May [24] Strummer returns to the band on the same day that Headon leaves (officially because of "a difference of political direction"). Chimes returns temporarily to play drums on the band's US tour, its most extensive yet. This exposure will lead to record US sales.

July [2] Headon is remanded on bail in London, charged with stealing a bus stop and receiving stolen property.

Aug *Rock The Casbah* reaches UK #30.

Sept [22] After its own US tour, the band accepts an invitation to support The Who° on their farewell US tour: eight major stadium shows, including two at Shea Stadium, New York.

Sept *Should I Stay Or Should I Go?* reaches UK #17 and US #45.

Dec The band appears at the Jamaican World Music Festival.

1983 Jan LP *Combat Rock* becomes their biggest US LP, hitting #7 and selling over a million, while *Rock The Casbah* hits US #8.

Feb Chimes leaves.

Apr *Should I Stay Or Should I Go?* is reissued in US, and re-enters the chart, reaching #50.

May Pete Howard joins on drums.

Sept A CBS "Clash Communiqué" reads: "Joe Strummer and Paul Simonon have decided that Mick Jones should leave the group. It is felt that Jones has drifted apart from the original idea of The Clash." Jones departs (and will re-emerge with hitmaking band Big Audio Dynamite°).

1984 Jan Guitarists Vince White and Nick Sheppard are added, and Strummer declares in interviews that "a whole new Clash era is underway".

1985 Nov LP *Cut The Crap* reaches UK #16 after being savaged by the critics, while extracted *This Is England* makes #24. A "Busking Tour" of the UK does not impart the new credibility that Strummer claims for the band, and he and Simonon call it a day.

1986 Jan LP *Cut The Crap* reaches US #171, by which time the band has broken up. (Simonon will fade from view and Strummer will devote most of the next 2 years to acting in films made by Alex Cox – notably *Straight To Hell*. Headon will sign as a soloist to Mercury Records, but his career will fall apart in Nov. 1987 when he is jailed on heroin offences.)

1988 Mar Reissued in UK as a single to trail the forthcoming LP, *I Fought The Law* climbs to #29.

Apr Retrospective double compilation LP *The Story Of The Clash Volume 1* hits UK #7.

May Another spin-off from the compilation, the reissued *London Calling*, makes UK #46.
June After two movie soundtracks, *Walker* and *Permanent Record*, Strummer embarks on "Rock Against the Rich" UK tour.

THE CLASSICS IV

Dennis Yost (vocals)
James R. Cobb (guitar)
Wally Eaton (guitar)
Joe Wilson (bass)
Kim Venable (drums)

1967 The group, formed in Jacksonville, Fla., US in 1966, moves to Atlanta, Ga., under the wing of producer/publisher Bill Lowery and works as session men on records by The Tams, Tommy Roe° and Billy Joe Royal.
1968 Feb Teamed with producer Buddy Buie (who will write most of the group's songs with Cobb) and signed to Imperial Records, the group releases *Spooky*. It hits US #3, selling over a million copies, and establishes The Classics IV soft-rock ballad sound. *Spooky* is its only UK chart entry at #46.
Mar LP *Spooky* reaches US #140.
May *Soul Train* reaches only US #90.
Dec *Stormy* hits US #5 and is its second million-seller. The group's billing is changed for this and next two hits to "Classics IV featuring Dennis Yost".
1969 Mar *Traces* hits US #2 and is a million-seller.
June *Everyday With You Girl* makes US #19. LP *Traces* climbs to US #45.
Sept *Change Of Heart*, with group billing changed to "Dennis Yost & The Classics IV", peaks at US #49. The group has undergone extensive personnel changes, with Yost, Cobb and writer/producer Buie, the stable elements. Lowery is keen to promote Yost as a solo name but he does not become a solo star, largely because The Classics IV's impact has been made through its songs, rather than group personalities.
Dec *Midnight* reaches US #58.
1970 Jan Compilation LP *Golden Greats* makes US #50.
Apr *The Funniest Thing* climbs to US #59.
Dec With Imperial phased out by parent company Liberty, the group is switched to Liberty for *Where Did All The Good Times Go?*, which makes US #69.
1972 Dec Signed to MGM South, the group returns to US chart after a 2-year absence with *What Am I Crying For?*, which climbs to #39.
1973 Mar *Rosanna* reaches US #95.
1974 Cobb and Buie, having left the group, become established in Atlanta Rhythm Section° with *Doraville*, which makes US #35 (and will revive original Classics IV chartmaker *Spooky* in 1979).
1975 Apr *My First Day Without Her* reaches US #94 and is the group's US chart swan song.

JIMMY CLIFF

1962 Cliff (b. James Chambers, 1948, St. Catherine, Jamaica) having quit college and moved to Kingston, Jamaica, to pursue a musical career, teams up with local Chinese/Jamaican musician and producer Leslie Kong and has a #1 local hit in Jamaica with *Hurricane Hattie*, inspired by the storm which swept across the Caribbean.
1965 On a US tour organized by the Jamaican government, with Prince Buster and Byron Lee's Dragonaires, he meets Chris Blackwell of Island Records, who persuades him to sign to the label and move to UK, where he initially works as a backup singer before recording in his own right and performing live (a mixture of ska and R&B) in UK and Europe.
1967 July *Give And Take* receives radio interest but just fails to chart.
1968 He represents Jamaica in an international music festival in Brazil with his own song *Waterfall*. It is a prize-winning entry and a hit in South America.
1969 Nov After five Island singles, *Wonderful World, Beautiful People*, his debut for Trojan Records, hits UK #6 as reggae music becomes popular in UK.
1970 Jan *Wonderful World, Beautiful People* reaches US #25.
Feb *Vietnam*, a self-penned reggae protest song, makes UK #46.
Mar *Come Into My Life* makes US #89.
Sept Cliff writes *You Can Get It If You Really Want*, a UK #2 hit for Desmond Dekker°. *Wild World*, a reggae adaptation of a Cat Stevens° song from Stevens' LP *Tea For The Tillerman*, hits UK #8. (It is not released in US, where the original version is a top 20 hit.)
1971 Cliff records LP *Another Cycle* at Muscle Shoals studio in Alabama, US. It consists entirely of R&B/soul material.
Sept The Pioneers hits UK #5 with the Cliff-penned *Let Your Yeah Yeah Be Yeah*.
1972 He stars in the semi-autobiographical lead role in Perry Henzell's Jamaican-made film *The Harder They Come*, which receives critical acclaim. Cliff has four self-penned songs on the soundtrack LP.
1973 He signs to EMI in UK and Warner/Reprise in US (but will have no further UK chart success). He has a conversion of faith to Islam after meeting Black Muslims in Chicago while on a US visit. It has a profound effect on his songwriting and prompts him to visit Africa, a trip which is mostly concerned with his roots and the lifestyle of his ancestors.
1974 He makes his first full US tour, premiering at New York's Carnegie Hall. LP *Struggling Man* is well reviewed but not a strong seller.
1975 Mar Soundtrack LP from *The Harder They Come* reaches US #140, following the cult movie's belated US release.
Nov LP *Follow My Mind* makes US #195.
1978 LP *Give Thankx* fails to chart, though Cliff rates it as his strongest effort yet.

1980 Cliff signs a new deal with MCA Records, though neither of the two resulting LPs, *I Am The Living* or *Give The People What They Want*, are notably successful. He plays a concert in Soweto, South Africa, to a racially-mixed audience of 75,000 – his condition for the show. He is now a much-toured artist around the African continent, having played in Nigeria, Senegal, The Cameroons, Zambia and South Africa.
1982 July He signs to CBS/Columbia Records for LP *Special*, produced in Jamaica by Chris Kimsey, which peaks at US #186. He follows it with a 6-week US tour, accompanied by his new band Oneness and sharing the bill with Peter Tosh. It closes with two sold out dates at New York's Felt Forum.
Oct Cliff co-headlines the World Music Festival at the Bob Marley Center in Montego Bay, Jamaica.
1983 Aug Cliff returns to Africa for a month-long tour, playing concerts in Lesotho and Zimbabwe.
Oct LP *The Power And The Glory*, mostly recorded with Oneness in Jamaica, includes two tracks cut with Kool & The Gang° in their New Jersey, US, studio.

JIMMY CLIFF *cont.*

1984 Cliff receives a Grammy nomination, on the first occasion that a reggae category is instituted in the awards, for *Reggae Night* (written by LaToya Jackson and Kool's° Amir Bayyan) – one of the tracks recorded the previous year with Kool & The Gang.

1985 May Cliff's composition *Trapped* is recorded by Bruce Springsteen° as his contribution to the USA For Africa LP *We Are The World*. Springsteen has also been playing it live for several months, having been said to have first heard Cliff's original version over an airport P.A. system in Europe.

Aug LP *Cliff Hanger*, much of which is recorded with Kool & The Gang° again, is another critical, if not chart, success.

1986 Feb Cliff wins a Grammy award for Best Reggae Recording of 1985 with LP *Cliff Hanger*.

July Cliff stars in the movie *Club Paradise* with Robin Williams, Peter O'Toole and a host of US comedy talent. He has 7 tracks on the soundtrack LP, including a duet with Elvis Costello°, *Seven Day Weekend*, which is released as a single.

Aug He embarks on a worldwide tour with Oneness, as support to Steve Winwood°.

1988 Mar LP *Hanging Fire*, produced by Kool & The Gang's° Khalis "Ronald Bell" Bayyan, is released.

CLIMIE FISHER

Simon Climie (vocals and keyboards)
Rob Fisher (keyboards)

1981 Having left school with one exam pass (in music), Climie (b. Apr.7, 1960, Fulham, London, UK), determines to write songs and signs a worldwide publishing deal with Chrysalis Music. (Hereafter, his songs will be successfully recorded by artists including Roger Daltrey, Leo Sayer°, Jeff Beck° and Pat Benatar°.)

1982 Fisher (b. Nov.5, 1959, Cheltenham, UK), after studying at Bath University where he has met local musician Pete Byrne, links with Byrne to form Naked Eyes. The duo records and releases a single on their own independent label, and then re-groups as Neon, completing live work with Curt Smith and Roland Orzabal before the latter two form Tears For Fears°.

May Fisher and Byrne revert to their Naked Eyes format, and sign to EMI Records.

1983 June Although they will achieve little on home territory, Naked Eyes makes a major impact in the US with a revival of *Always Something There To Remind Me*, which hits #8.

July LP *Naked Eyes* reaches US #32, while *Always Something There To Remind Me* makes UK #59.

Oct *Promises, Promises* is another major US hit, peaking at #11.

Dec *When The Lights Go Out* reaches US #37 for Naked Eyes.

1984 Sept *(What) In The Name Of Love* is the final Naked Eyes US hit, reaching #39, while their second LP *Fuel For The Fire* makes #83.

Dec Naked Eyes splits up, with Byrne staying in US, to live in LA.

1985 Climie meets Fisher at Abbey Road studios in London while both are involved in the recording of Scritti Politti's° LP *Cupid Psyche '85*.

1986 Mar While Climie continues his songwriting career (most notably penning with Dennis Morgan the 1987 smash *I Knew You Were Waiting (For Me)* for George Michael° and Aretha Franklin°), he now concentrates on writing and recording songs with Fisher. As Climie Fisher, they sign to EMI.

Aug Debut single *This Is Me* is released but fails to chart.

1987 Mar Follow-up *Keeping The Mystery Alive* fares no better than the first release.

Aug *Love Changes (Everything)* completes a hat trick of chart failures.

1988 Jan *Rise To The Occasion*, a ballad single (aided by an unusual uptempo hip-hop version on 12" which finds dancefloor favor), finally gives the duo its debut hit at UK #10.

Apr LP *Everything*, produced by Stephen Hague and Steve Lillywhite, reaches UK #14. *Love Changes (Everything)* is re-released as a UK single, and this time hits #2.

May *This Is Me* is also re-released, climbing to UK #22.

June *Love Changes (Everything)* puts Climie Fisher into the US chart for the first time (#23), with LP *Everything* peaking at #126.

Aug *I Won't Bleed For You* continues the run of UK chart success.

PATSY CLINE

1954 Sept Starry-eyed C&W aspirant, Cline (b. Virginia Patterson Hensley, Sept.8, 1932, Winchester, Va., US), after an apprenticeship served in local beerjoints and taverns, signs with Four Star Records of Pasadena, Cal.

1955 June She makes her debut on prestigious Nashville stage/radio show "Grand Ole Opry" singing *A Church A Courtroom And Then Goodbye*. An appropriate choice: her sexual notoriety soon causes as many ripples in the C&W fraternity as her music. The wife of her manager Bill Peer cites Cline as co-respondent in their divorce, and Cline's own marriage to Gerald Cline dissolves when she meets Charlie Dick, who becomes her second husband. She becomes a regular on Jimmy Dean's weekly "Town And Country Jamboree" appearing in fringed dude-cowboy regalia.

1956 Nov *Walkin' After Midnight*, rejected by Kay Starr years earlier, is foisted on Cline. With other songs, she cuts it with Nashville producer Owen Bradley.

1957 Jan Cline in New York for the first time, appears on the nationally networked CBS television show "Arthur Godfrey's Talent Scouts". She sings *Walkin' After Midnight* and wins. Decca, now marketing her records after a deal with Four Star, rush-releases the song as her fifth single.

Feb *Walkin' After Midnight* crosses from the C&W chart to peak at #12 on US national pop list. She makes her second "Grand Ole Opry" appearance, this time as guest star, and on Alan Freed's stage show she successfully confronts a rock'n'roll audience.

1957/60 Despite nine releases, Decca's failure to find an equally incisive follow-up restricts her to the country scene, where her elevation to superstardom is swift and sure.

1961 May Establishing Bradley's lavish settings and Cline's sophisticated weepie style, both at variance with current Nashville tradition, *I Fall To Pieces* restores her to the pop chart at US #12.

June [14] Cline sustains a fractured hip and near-fatal head injuries when thrown through the windshield in an automobile collision in Madison, Tenn.

Oct The distinctive Willie Nelson° ballad *Crazy*, recorded with Cline on crutches, becomes her biggest seller, hitting US #9. The B-side *Who Can I Count On* makes only US #99.

1962 Jan Double-sided *She's Got You/Strange* reaches US #14 and #97 respectively.

Mar LP *The Patsy Cline Showcase* climbs to US #73.

Apr *She's Got You* reaches UK #43.

May Another double-sided hit, *When I Get Thru With You/Imagine That*, makes US #53 and #90.

Aug *So Wrong* peaks at US #85.

Oct *Heartaches* climbs to US #73 and gives Cline her second UK chart success, reaching #31.

1963 Jan An established "Grand Ole Opry" headliner and America's highest-ranked female country star, 30-year old Cline continues to make the transition from C&W to pop chart, with *Leaving On Your Mind* reaching US #83.

Mar [5] Returning from a Kansas City benefit concert for the widow of disk jockey Cactus Jack Call, who had died in a road accident, the single-engined Piper Commanche carrying Cline and fellow stars Hawkshaw Hawkins and Cowboy Copas crashes near Camden, Tenn., killing all three and the pilot (also her manager) Randy Hughes.

Apr Cline's version of Don Gibson's *Sweet Dreams* becomes a posthumous hit, reaching US #44.

Aug For the last time, Cline's name appears on the pop chart as *Faded Love* climbs to US #96 and her LP *The Patsy Cline Story* makes #74.

1964/69 Regular releases, like *When You Need A Laugh, He Called Me Baby* and *Anytime* reach the C&W chart and sustain Cline's following.

1973 Oct Cline becomes the first female solo performer to be elected to the Country Music Hall of Fame.

1977 Loretta Lynn releases a tribute LP, while a new generation of Nashville stars acknowledges Cline's influence.

1981 Tapes of Cline and Jim Reeves, re-arranged and mixed to simulate duet performances, are released as LP *Greatest Hits*. Issued as singles, *Have You Ever Been Lonely* and *I Fall To Pieces* become C&W hits.

1985 *Sweet Dreams*, a Hollywood movie based on Ellis Nassour's biography with Jessica Lange in the title role, revives interest in the Cline legend. Compilation LPs continue to sell consistently.

GEORGE CLINTON

1955 Clinton (b. July 22, 1940, Plainfield, N.J., US) forms The Parliaments, one of thousands of doo-wop harmonizing groups organized on street corners throughout urban black America.

1956 The group releases its debut single, *Poor Willie*, on ABC.

1958 Second single, *Lonely Island*, is released on New.

1959 Clinton relocates The Parliaments to Detroit, Mich., where for 4 years the group will record a number of tracks for Motown label, none of which is released. The Parliaments make a living playing clubs and bars in Michigan and surrounding states.

1965 Failing to secure a contract with Motown, The Parliaments release *My Girl* on Golden World. It flops.

1966 Dissatisfied and disillusioned with the record business, The Parliaments decide to shed their conventional, mohair-suited, image and adopt a more casual, street-oriented appearance. The line-up is now vocalists Clinton, Raymond Davis, Calvin Simon, Clarence Hoskins and Grady Thomas with Eddie Hazel (guitar), Tawl Ross (guitar), Billy Nelson (bass), Mickey Atkins (organ) and Tiki Fulwood (drums).

1967 July *(I Wanna) Testify*, on Revilot, tops US R&B chart and makes US #20. Four singles, released on Revilot in 18 months, fail to chart.

1969 Clinton, temporarily, loses the rights to the name The Parliaments, in a legal wrangle said to involve Motown, songwriters Holland, Dozier and Holland and Invictus label. To remain active, Clinton signs a new group, Funkadelic, (in fact The Parliaments under a new name) to Westbound.

Oct Funkadelic's *I'll Bet You* makes US #68.

1970 Mar *I Got A Thing, You Got A Thing, Everybody's Got A Thing* peaks at US #90.

Aug Clinton relaunches The Parliaments as Parliament, on Invictus, with LP *Osmium*. Funkadelic continues to record for Westbound. Keyboardist Bernie Worrell joins the Parliament-Funkadelic (P. Funk) family. Funkadelic's *I Wanna Know If It's Good To You?* peaks at US #81.

1971 Apr *You And Your Folks, Me And My Folks* reaches US #91.

Sept *Can You Get To That* peaks at US #93.

1972 Bassist Bootsy Collins, ex-James Brown's° backing band The JBs, joins in time for Funkadelic LP *America Eats Its Young*.

1973 Guitarist Gary Shider joins in time for Funkadelic LP, *Cosmic Slop*.

1974 Funkadelic LP *Standing On The Verge Of Getting It On* is released. Following the collapse of Invictus, Clinton signs Parliament to Casablanca, despite interest from Westbound. Westbound releases LP *Funkadelic's Greatest Hits*.

Aug Parliament's *Up For The Down Stroke* makes US #63.

1975 May LP *Chocolate City* peaks at US #91.

June *Chocolate City* stalls at US #94.

Nov Funkadelic's *Better By The Pound* reaches US #99.

1976 Feb Parliament's LP *Mothership Connection* climbs to US #13.

May *Tear The Roof Off The Sucker (Give Up The Funk)* reaches US #15. Bootsy Collins releases LP *Stretchin' Out*, made with members of Parliament/Funkadelic. (Other in-house projects released in the next 2 years are The Horny Horns (P. Funk horn section Fred Wesley, Maceo Parker, Rick Gardner and Richard Griffith; Wesley and Parker, like Collins. having come to Clinton via James Brown's° JBs), Parlet (P. Funk vocalists Mallia Franklin, Jeanette Washington and Shirley Hayden) and The Brides of Dr. Funkenstein (P. Funk vocalists Lynn Mabry and Dawn Silva).)

Oct Parliament's LP *The Clones Of Dr. Funkenstein* climbs to US #20.

1977 Jan [19] Parliament/Funkadelic/Bootsy play LA's Forum to an audience of more than 18,000.

May LP *Parliament Live/P. Funk Earth Tour* makes US #29. Bootsy Collins releases LP *Ahh . . . The Name Is Bootsy Baby*. The Horny Horns release LP *A Blow For Me, A Toot For You*.

Dec Parliament's LP *Funkentelechy Vs. The Placebo Syndrome* reaches US #13. P. Funk has reached the peak of its commercial acceptance. Clinton now tours with some forty musicians. His stage show incorporates separate sets from Parliament/Funkadelic, Parlet, Bootsy's Rubber Band, The Brides of Dr. Funkenstein and The Horny Horns.

1978 Feb Parliament's *Flash Light* makes US #16. Parlet releases LP *The Pleasure Principle*. The Brides of Dr. Funkenstein release LP *Funk Or Walk*.

July [21] At a dinner sponsored by The Rod McGrew Scholarship Fund, Inc. Communicators with a conscience, Clinton and Collins are challenged to do something more ambitious and less superficial with their music. (Clinton pledges to donate 50 cents for every ticket sold for his Aug. and Sept. concerts to the United Negro College Fund.)

Sept Funkadelic's *One Nation Under A Groove* reaches US #28. The group signs to Warner Bros.

Dec P. Funk plays rapturously-received concerts in London, UK. The adventurous stage show includes a lifesize flying saucer. Clinton's *One Nation Under A Groove* hits UK #9 and eponymous LP reaches UK #56 (his first UK chart successes). Parliament's LP *Motor Booty Affair* makes US #23.

1979 Feb Parliament's *Aqua Boogie (A Psychoalphadisco-betabioaquadoloop)* peaks at US #89.

Oct Funkadelic's *(Not Just) Knee Deep* climbs to US #77.

Dec Parliament's LP *Gloryhallastoopid (Pin The Tale On The Funky)* makes US #77.

1980 Clinton's release schedule is halted by protracted legal disputes with a number of record companies. Issues include disputed royalty payments and usage of the names Parliament and Funkadelic.

1981 Jan A breakaway trio of P. Funk musicians, using the name Funkadelic, releases LP *Connections And Disconnections*, which peaks at US #151.

Feb The official Funkadelic releases LP *The Electric Spanking Of War Babies*, featuring Sly Stone.

1982 Clinton signs as a solo artist to Capitol. (He will record for the label with the P. Funk family, but will not use the names Parliament or Funkadelic.)

Dec LP *Computer Games* makes US #40 as *Loopzilla* reaches UK #57.

1983 *Atomic Dog* tops US R&B chart. Its accompanying video clip wins a *Billboard* award for video animation.

1984 Jan LP *You Shouldn't Nuf Bit, Fish!* peaks at US #102.

Apr *Do Fries Go With That Shake* makes UK #57.

1985 June LP *Some Of My Best Friends Are Jokes* is released. One track is written with Thomas Dolby°, with whom Clinton will collaborate on *May The Cube Be With You*.

THE COASTERS

Carl Gardner (lead tenor)
Leon Hughes (tenor)
Billy Guy (baritone)
Bobby Nunn (bass)

1955 Oct Gardner and Nunn leave The Robins, an R&B vocal group whose most celebrated recording was *Smokey Joe's Café*, made under the direction of songwriters/producers Leiber and Stoller, to start The

THE COASTERS *cont.*

Coasters (the name reflecting their West Coast roots) with Hughes and Guy.

Nov Leiber and Stoller sign a deal whereby their masters will be released on Atlantic subsidiary, Atco. One of their acts is the newly constituted black vocal quartet, The Coasters, the perfect vehicle for Leiber and Stoller's studio genius.

1956 Jan The group cuts four tracks at Hollywood Recorders in LA: *Brazil, Down In Mexico, One Kiss Led To Another* and *Turtle Dovin'*.

Mar Debut *Down In Mexico* enters US R&B chart and hits #9.

Sept *One Kiss Led To Another*, their first entry into pop chart, reaches US #73.

1957 Feb Hughes is replaced by Young Jessie, ex-The Flairs.

May Cranky, funky *Searchin'* hits US #5/R&B #1 and UK #30. Their first million-seller, it establishes The Coasters as one of the most amusing, innovative and influential vocal groups of the rock'n'roll era. Particularly revered by British fans, their songs will soon be revived by The Beatles°, The Stones° and almost every UK beat group of the early 1960s. B-side *Young Blood* also makes the top ten, hitting US #8.

Oct Of six titles recorded, only *Idol With The Golden Head* reaches the chart, peaking at #64.

1958 Mar The Coasters, and Leiber and Stoller, move to New York. Jessie and Nunn, loath to travel, are replaced by Cornel Gunter (second tenor) and Will "Dub" Jones (bass). Legendary "fifth Coaster" King Curtis, whose sax playing will add piquancy to their work, also joins.

May *Yakety Yak* rockets up the chart to hit US #1 and becomes their second UK hit, reaching #12. It epitomizes Leiber and Stoller's "Coaster style", which takes the form of "a white kid's view (Lieber's) of a black person's conception of white society".

1959 Feb *The Shadow Knows* does not chart. The uproarious exploits of incorrigible schoolkid *Charlie Brown* hits US #2 and UK #6, and is a million-seller. It contains speeded-up voices on one line as a sardonic nod to *The Chipmunk Song* which is heading towards US #1.

May Conceived as 3-minute comic operas, and scripted like radio plays, Coasters' records are hailed as pop masterpieces. *Along Came Jones*, mocking the clichés of television westerns, hits US #9.

Aug *Poison Ivy* reaches US #7 and UK #15 and is the group's fourth and last million-seller. The Rolling Stones° cut the most famous of some 20 cover versions. B-side *I'm A Hog For You* reaches US #38.

Dec Double-sided *Run Red Run/What About Us* peaks at US #36 and #47 respectively.

1960 May A revival of *Besame Mucho*, a million-seller for Jimmy Dorsey in the early 1940s, reaches only US #70.

June *Wake Me Shake Me*, written by Guy, recounting the miseries of a recalcitrant garbage man, fails to climb beyond US #51.

Oct Adapted from the half-remembered *Clothesline* by Kent Harris, *Shopping For Clothes* stalls at #83.

1961 Feb Atco attempts to reverse The Coasters' slide with *Wait A Minute*, by Bobby Darin°/Don Kirshner. Cut and shelved over 3 years earlier, it makes US #37.

Apr *Little Egypt*, about a tattooed burlesque dancer who ends up marrying the singer, lifts them to US #23.

Aug *Girls Girls Girls* rises no higher than US #96. As Leiber and Stoller's Atlantic workload increases (The Drifters°, Ben E. King, Ruth Brown, LaVern Baker, The Isley Brothers°), they are able to devote less time to The Coasters.

1964 Mar After a long chart absence, *T'Aint Nothing To Me* reaches US #64. The group continues recording for Atco, without success, until 1966.

1967 CBS subsidiary Date signs The Coasters. Former Cadillacs frontman Earl Carroll replaces Gunter and a reunion with Leiber and Stoller yields *Down Home Girl* (covered by The Stones°), *D.W. Washburn* (covered by The Monkees°) and a revival of the Clovers' hit *Love Potion Number Nine*, which (when leased to King Records) creeps into the chart 4 years later, reaching US #76.

1968/88 Various line-ups take the stage as The Coasters and compilation LPs continue to sell worldwide.

1988 May Among the acts participating in Atlantic's 40th birthday concert at New York's Madison Square Garden are The Coasters, still containing founder members Gardner and Guy, with stalwarts Jones and Gunter, and Tom Palmer.

EDDIE COCHRAN

1954 Having lived in Bell Gardens suburb of LA since age 10 and become a proficient guitarist in his early teens, Cochran (b. Edward Cochrane, Oct.3, 1938, Oklahoma City, Okla., US), makes his first live appearances with (unrelated) Hank Cochran as the C&W-styled Cochran Brothers.

1955 The duo records two hillbilly singles for Ekko Records in LA, then see Elvis Presley° live on stage in Dallas and switch to a harder rock style. *Tired And Sleepy* follows, but none of these early singles sell.

1956 Sept After splitting from Hank, Cochran teams with songwriter Jerry Capehart. They co-write *Skinny Jim* which, via Capehart's contacts at American Music, is recorded by Cochran for associated label, Crest Records. It does not sell, but Cochran and Capehart use it as a demo and try to interest larger record companies.

Oct Cochran has a musical cameo role in the Jayne Mansfield rock'n'roll movie *The Girl Can't Help It*, singing *20 Flight Rock*.

1957 Apr Signed to Liberty on the strength of *Skinny Jim* and his movie appearance, Cochran makes US chart debut with a cover version of Johnny Dee's (actually John D. Loudermilk of later songwriting fame) *Sittin' In The Balcony*, which reaches US #18 and outsells the original version (US #38). A promotional tour of the US follows.

July He appears in film *Untamed Youth* with Mamie Van Doren, in which he performs *Cotton Picker*.

Oct *Drive-In Show* reaches US #82.

1958 Mar *Jeannie Jeannie Jeannie* makes a one-week US chart entry at #94, while Cochran helps with backing vocals on some Gene Vincent° studio sessions.

Sept *Summertime Blues*, co-written with Capehart, is his breakthrough hit and only US top 10 entry, hitting #8 and gaining a gold disk for a million-plus sales.

Nov *Summertime Blues* is Cochran's UK chart debut, reaching #18.

Dec He features in Alan Freed's 10-day New York "Christmas Rock'n'Roll Spectacular" together with The Everly Brothers°, Chuck Berry°, Jackie Wilson°, Bo Diddley° and others.

1959 Jan *C'mon Everybody* reaches US #35. Cochran performs in Alan Freed rock film *Go Johnny Go*. This work forces him to withdraw from the "Winter Dance Party Tour" of Northwestern US states, alongside close friend Buddy Holly°.

Feb He is deeply affected by the deaths of Holly, Valens° and The Big Bopper° and records a version of the tribute song *Three Stars* (which will not be released until several years after his own death). He tries to avoid all flying but begins US tour which will last much of the year, punctuated by returns to LA for recording sessions. The Kelly Four (from Cochran's Irish ancestry) is formed to back him on the road, including long-time friend and studio sideman Connie "Guybo" Smith on bass, and Gene Ridgio on drums.

Mar *Teenage Heaven* makes US #99 for a week.

Apr *C'mon Everybody* hits UK #6. Film *Go Johnny Go* premieres in US, featuring Cochran performing *Teenage Heaven*.

Oct *Somethin' Else* makes US #58 (his last US hit) and UK #22. Its writer, Sharon Sheeley, becomes Cochran's fiancée soon afterwards.

1960 Jan [9] He flies to UK at the invitation of impresario Larry Parnes to co-headline (with Gene Vincent°) a 10-week rock package tour which includes Billy Fury°, Joe Brown and Georgie Fame°. The tour is a huge success, with ecstatic fan fervor, creating newspaper headlines.

Jan [16] Cochran's UK TV debut with the package tour stars is on Jack Good's live rock show "Boy Meets Girls".

Feb A revival of Ray Charles'° *Hallelujah I Love Her So* makes UK #22.

Mar Cochran invites Sharon Sheeley to UK for the tour's last month.

Mar [5] His only live radio broadcast in UK is on BBC Radio Show "Saturday Club", where he sings *What'd I Say, Milk Cow Blues*, his current release *Hallelujah I Love Her So*, and *C'mon Everybody*. On the same day he appears at the New Musical Express Poll Winners concert at the Empire Pool, Wembley.

Apr The tour has proved so successful, Cochran and Vincent° are offered a second UK trek from the end of Apr. They accept but return to US for the intervening 2 weeks, Cochran specifically to do some LP recording.

Apr [16] An additional final tour date is added at the Hippodrome,

Bristol, on the eve of Easter Sunday. Arrangements are made for the two to catch a late train to London after the show for their US flight next morning, but Cochran, Vincent and Sheeley hire a taxi instead.

Apr [17] En route to London on the A4, near Chippenham, Wilts., a tire bursts, causing it to skid into a roadside lamp post. Gene Vincent, Sharon Sheeley and the driver Pat Thompkins are injured, but Cochran is thrown through the windshield with multiple head injuries. Rushed to Bath hospital, he dies within hours without regaining consciousness. One of the local policemen called to the accident is 16-year-old police cadet David Harman (later Dave Dee of Dave Dee, Dozy, Beaky, Mick & Tich°); he salvages Cochran's hardly-damaged Gretsch guitar from the road, and will occasionally play it at the police station before it is returned to Cochran's mother 2 months later.

June Ironically-titled, *Three Steps To Heaven* tops the UK chart and is his biggest UK seller. It fails to chart in US.

July His first LP chart success also comes posthumously, when LP *Singing To My Baby* reaches UK #19.

Oct Double A-side *Lonely/Sweetie Pie* peaks at UK #27, while commemorative LP *The Eddie Cochran Memorial Album* hits UK #9.

1961 July *Weekend* reaches UK #15 on a 4-month chart run.

Dec *Jeannie Jeannie Jeannie* makes UK #31.

1963 Jan LP *Cherished Memories* climbs to UK #15.

May A reissue of the LP *The Eddie Cochran Memorial Album* reaches UK #11 and stays charted for over 5 months. Previously unissued *My Way* climbs to UK #23.

Oct A reissue of Cochran's first LP *Singing To My Baby* makes UK #20.

1964 Aug LP *My Way*, with further previously unissued material, is released in UK, but does not chart.

1968 May A UK revival fad for 1950s rock'n'roll sees the reissue of *Summertime Blues*, alongside re-releases of Buddy Holly's° *Peggy Sue* and Bill Haley's° *Rock Around The Clock*. It climbs to UK #34.

1970 May Compilation LP *The Very Best Of Eddie Cochran* charts at UK #34.

1979 Aug Compilation LP *The Eddie Cochran Singles Album* makes UK #39.

1980 Mar The 20th anniversary of his death is marked in UK by the release of a limited-edition boxed LP set, *20th Anniversary Album*.

1988 Mar *C'mon Everybody* is used as the soundtrack to a UK TV ad for Levi's 501 jeans (the ad theme based on Sharon Sheeley's story of how she wore her Levi's to the party at which she first met Cochran. Sheeley appears uncredited in a party scene in the ad). Reissued and boosted by TV exposure, the single is a UK hit 29 years after its first success, peaking at #14.

Apr Compilation LP *C'mon Everybody*, which makes Cochran's music available on CD, reaches UK #53.

JOE COCKER

1960 Cocker (b. John Robert Cocker, May 20, 1944, Sheffield, Yorks., UK), having left school, buys a cheap drumkit and forms a skiffle group with schoolfriends. He takes a day job as a fitter with the Gas Board and plays in brother Victor's skiffle group The Cavaliers at night.

1963 When The Cavaliers change their name to Vance Arnold & The Avengers, Cocker steps out front and sings. He also sits in with local bands like Dave Berry° & The Cruisers.

1964 After an audition for producer Mike Leander in Manchester, Cocker is offered a contract with Decca Records. He takes leave of absence from the Gas Board and travels to Decca's studio in London. He debuts with a version of Lennon°/McCartney's° *I'll Cry Instead*. Despite a good performance and session backing from guitarist Big Jim Sullivan and the Ivy League on backing vocals, it flops and Cocker reportedly only receives 50p in royalties. He joins his first professional band, The Big Blues, on a brief UK tour with Manfred Mann° and The Hollies° and then tours US army bases in France. When he returns to the UK he no longer has a recording contract, so takes up his Gas Board job again and plays only an occasional local gig. The band splits and Cocker teams with Chris Stainton to write and record *Marjorine* and form The Grease Band.

1965/66 The Grease Band, with Cocker on vocals, Stainton on bass, Tommy Eyre on keyboards, Kenny Slade on drums and Alan Spenner and Henry McCullough both on guitars, plays soul material in clubs and pubs across the north of England. Its first recording, a live version of blues standard *Saved*, is on a free flexidisk with the Sheffield University magazine *Twikker*.

1967 Cocker and Stainton send a demo tape to producer Denny Cordell, who arranges a recording session in London.

1968 May *Marjorine*, credited to a solo Joe Cocker, is issued on EMI's Regal Zonophone label and makes UK #48.

Nov Cocker's distinctive cover of The Beatles° *With A Little Help From My Friends* hits UK #1 for 1 week and reaches US #68. The Beatles, impressed with Cocker's version, send him a congratulatory telegram and place music press ads praising the record. Subsequent TV exposure introduces a wider audience to Cocker's flailing, tortured stage movements. Some find his performance distasteful and when he appears on the "Ed Sullivan Show", he is obscured by dancers as he sings.

1969 May Debut LP *With A Little Help From My Friends* consists mainly of interpretations of other people's songs, but includes several Cocker/Stainton originals. It fails to chart in UK but reaches US #35.

July *Feeling Alright* makes US #69.

Aug Stainton moves to keyboards after Eyre and Slade leave The Grease Band. With Alan Spenner on bass and Bruce Rowlands on drums, the band tours US, highlighted by its performance at the Woodstock Festival, captured on LP and in the film *Woodstock*. Cocker also meets Leon Russell°.

Nov Cocker's recording of Russell's° *Delta Lady* hits UK #10 and reaches US #69. Russell and Cordell set up Shelter Records and supervise the recording of Cocker's next LP at A&M (Cocker's US label) studios in LA. LP *Joe Cocker!*, which reaches US #11, is the last to feature The Grease Band. The group breaks up after Cocker cancels a US tour. (Stainton will stay with Cocker while the others take up session work.)

1970 Feb Another distinctive cover of The Beatles'° *She Came In Through The Bathroom Window* reaches US #30 and earns a gold disk. With no band and a commitment to play US dates, Cocker

JOE COCKER *cont.*

assembles, with the assistance of Cordell and Russell, a disparate collection of 21 musicians who will be known as Mad Dogs and Englishmen. The "Mad Dogs and Englishmen" tour clocks up 65 concerts in 57 days, leaving Cocker so exhausted that he temporarily retires to recuperate in California and then in Sheffield.

May Cocker's cover of The Box Tops'° 1967 hit *The Letter* hits US #7.

July *The Letter* reaches UK #39.

Oct The "Mad Dogs and Englishmen" tour provides the basis for double LP *Mad Dogs And Englishmen* which reaches UK #16 and hits US #2, and a feature film.

Nov *Cry Me A River*, recorded live at the Fillmore East in March 1970, makes US #11.

1971 July Double A-side *High Time We Went/Black-Eyed Blues* reaches US #22. LP *Cocker Happy*, a compilation of his early hits, is released. Cocker joins "Mad Dogs" veteran Rita Coolidge on stage at the Sheffield City Hall as part of a Byrds° package tour.

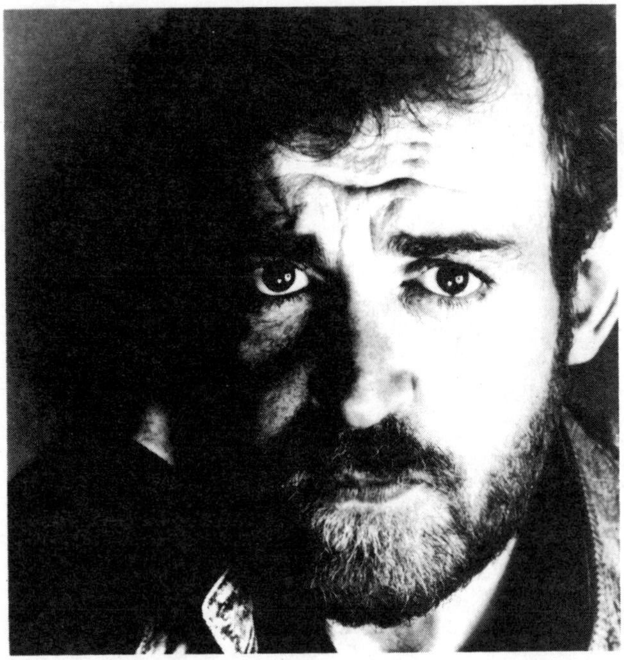

1972 Cocker reunites with Stainton to tour UK as the 12-piece Joe Cocker and The Chris Stainton Band. Cocker is in poor physical shape, sometimes unable to remember his words and in Australia is arrested for possession of marijuana, which prevents him from obtaining a visa to tour US. The group returns to UK and splits.

Feb *Feeling Alright* is reissued and makes US #33.

May A double-pack LP *Joe Cocker/With A Little Help From My Friends* reaches UK #29.

Oct Double A-side *Midnight Rider/Woman To Woman* makes US #27 and #56. The songs are taken from LP *Something To Say*, which consists of studio cuts and live recordings from the year's tour.

Dec LP *Joe Cocker* makes US #30.

1973 Mar *Pardon Me Sir* reaches US #51.

1974 Cocker moves to LA after Stainton joins Tundra.

July *Put Out The Light* makes US #46.

Aug LP *I Can Stand A Little Rain*, produced by Jim Price, climbs to US #11. Released in UK on Cube Records, it fails to chart.

1975 Mar The Billy Preston/Jim Price-penned *You Are So Beautiful* hits US #5.

Aug LP *Jamaica Say You Will*, produced by Price, reaches US #42.

1976 May LP *Stingray*, produced by Rob Fraboni and backed by soul-funk outfit Stuff, makes US #70. With A&M releasing Cocker's records in UK as well, Cube cashes in with LP *Live In LA*.

Oct [2] Cocker appears on NBC-TV's "Saturday Night Live" duetting with John Belushi on Traffic's° *Feelin' Alright*, with the latter doing his famous Cocker impersonation.

1977 Dec LP *Joe Cocker's Greatest Hits* reaches US #114.

1978 Sept LP *Luxury You Can Afford*, Cocker's first on Asylum label, is produced by New Orleans R&B legend Allen Toussaint. It makes US #76.

Dec *Fun Time* reaches US #43.

1981 Oct After another tour, Cocker guests on two tracks, *I'm So Glad I'm Standing Here Today* (US #97, UK #61) and *This Old World's Too Funky For Me* for The Crusaders'° LP *Standing Still*.

1982 Cocker signs to Island Records, who fly him to Compass Point Studios in Nassau, Bahamas, to record LP *Sheffield Steel* with Blackwell producing and Sly and Robbie° providing the rhythm section.

July LP *Sheffield Steel* reaches only US #105 but is critically well received. Cocker's covers of songs by Steve Winwood°, Bob Dylan° and Jimmy Webb are his strongest in years.

Nov Cocker's duet with Jennifer Warnes° on *Up Where We Belong*, from the soundtrack of Taylor Hackford's film *An Officer And A Gentleman*, spends 3 weeks on top of the US chart.

1983 Feb *Up Where We Belong* hits UK #7. Cocker makes an extensive US tour before playing Europe, with a triumphant return to Sheffield on his first major UK concert in more than 10 years.

Apr *Up Where We Belong* wins an Oscar for Best Film Song, having already been awarded a Grammy for the same category.

1984 June Signed to Capitol Records, Cocker's LP *Civilised Man* reaches the anchor position on UK top 100 and makes US #133.

Nov *Edge Of A Dream*, the theme from film *Teachers*, reaches US #69.

1986 Mar *Shelter Me* makes US #91. Cocker performs Randy Newman's° *You Can Leave Your Hat On* in Adrian Lyne's film *9½ Weeks*.

1987 Nov With new production team of Dan Hartman and Charlie Midnight, Cocker releases LP *Unchain My Heart* which reaches US #89. Single *Unchain My Heart*, a cover of the Ray Charles° 1961 smash, reaches UK #46. He contributes *Love Lives On* for film *Harry And The Hendersons* (UK title: *Bigfoot And The Hendersons*).

1988 June UK re-release of *You Don't Love Me Anymore* fails to chart despite tour dates.

THE COCTEAU TWINS

Elizabeth Fraser (vocals)
Robin Guthrie (bass, guitar, drum programing and keyboards)
Simon Raymonde (bass, piano and keyboards)

1981 Nov The original Cocteau Twins – Fraser, Guthrie and Will Heggie – travel from their native Falkirk, Scotland to London, armed with two demo tapes. One is given to BBC Radio 1 DJ John Peel (for whom they will record two radio sessions), the other to Simon Raymonde, a shop assistant (and son of '60s arranger/producer Ivor Raymonde) working in an outlet beneath the 4AD record company office. After listening to it, 4AD label manager Ivo Watts-Russell offers to help.

1982 June First LP, *Garlands*, is released, having cost just £900 to record in 9 days. It is an instant independent chart hit, hitting #2. The Twins resist all offers of management as well as overtures from major record labels, electing always to release material in their own time through 4AD. (For the remainder of 1982 and into 1983, they will support OMD° on a 50-date European tour).

Oct 12" EP *Lullabies* is released, beginning a series of records which are big independent chart successes, but fail to cross to mainstream appeal.

1983 Nov LP *Head Over Heels* finally achieves chart action, reaching UK #51 and remaining on chart for 15 weeks. Fraser and Guthrie appear as part of Watts-Russell's occasional 4AD conglomerate group This Mortal Coil on its debut single, a revival of Tim Buckley's° *Song To The Siren*. This reaches UK #66 (and will remain a permanent fixture on the independent chart for over a year). Heggie leaves and is replaced by Raymonde.

1984 May *Pearly-Dewdrops' Drops* is their first pop crossover hit, reaching UK #29. While this is on chart, they turn down an appearance on BBC TV's "Top Of The Pops".

Nov LP *Treasure* reaches UK #29.

1985 Mar The EP *Aikea Guinea* peaks at UK #41.

Nov Two 12"-only EPs, *Tiny Dynamine* and *Echoes In A Shallow Bay* are released in UK, charting at #52 and #65 respectively.

1986 Jan The Twins release a US CD-only compilation, *The Pink Opaque*.

Apr Fourth LP *Victorialand* hits UK #10.

Oct *Love's Easy Tears* makes UK #53 and is their last single release for almost 2 years.

Nov All the members individually collaborate with 4AD's new signing, pianist Harold Budd, on independent chart LP *The Moon And The Melodies*. They also complete a sold-out tour of the UK.

1988 Sept After a 2½ year hiatus, new studio LP *Blue Bell Knoll* is finally released.

LEONARD COHEN

1951 Cohen (b. Sept.21, 1934, Montreal, Canada) forms a C&W band, The Buckskin Boys, while studying at McGill University and begins attracting attention as a student poet.

1955/56 He publishes two collections: *The Spice Box of Earth* and *Let Us Compare Mythologies* which wins a national poetry prize.

1962 Poetry anthology *Parasites of Heaven* is published. It contains several poems that later become Cohen songs, including *Suzanne* and *Avalanche*.

1963 Cohen publishes his first novel, *The Favorite Game*.

1964 After a brief spell at Columbia University, New York, Cohen publishes a controversial poetry collection, *Flowers of Hitler*.

1966 He has been writing and singing songs for several years when Judy Collins° becomes the first artist to cover one (*Suzanne*), on her LP *In My Life*. Cohen publishes his second novel, *Beautiful Losers*. He performs at The Newport Folk Festival and is signed to CBS/Columbia by talent scout John Hammond.

1967 The Canadian National Film Board produces a documentary film, *Ladies & Gentlemen . . . Mr. Leonard Cohen*. He joins Judy Collins° on stage at her summer concert in New York's Central Park.

1968 Jan Debut LP *The Songs Of Leonard Cohen* is released by CBS/Columbia.

Apr LP *The Songs Of Leonard Cohen* reaches US #83 (but is more successful in UK in the fall, reaching #13 and remaining on chart for 71 weeks). *Suzanne*, extracted from it, does not chart. (Cohen will never have a hit single in US or UK.) He appears in and scores another Canadian NFB film, *The Ernie Game*.

1969 May LP *Songs From A Room* reaches US #63 and UK #2.

1970 Aug [30] Cohen plays the Isle of Wight Festival in UK, where Jimi Hendrix° makes his final live appearance.

1971 May LP *Songs Of Love And Hate* reaches US #145 and hits UK #4. Cohen's songs are used as an integral part of Robert Altman's film *McCabe And Mrs Miller* starring Warren Beatty.

1973 June LP *Live Songs*, recorded on stage in Paris some time earlier, reaches US #156, but is not placed in UK.

1974 Oct LP *New Skin For The Old Ceremony*, with a soft-rock feel, fails to chart in US but makes UK #24.

1977 Dec In a move away from the folky, acoustic feel of earlier LPs, Phil Spector is brought in to produce Cohen. Problems develop when Spector takes to using armed guards in the studio to enforce his will. The end product, LP *Death Of A Ladies' Man*, makes only UK #35.

1979 Sept LP *Recent Songs*, co-produced by Henry Lewy, returns to the spirit of earlier LPs but includes unusual instrumental flourishes, such as the use of a Mariachi band.

1984 *I Am A Hotel*, a half-hour feature film written, scored and directed by Cohen, wins first prize at the Festival International de Télévision de Montreux, Switzerland.

1985 Feb LP *Various Positions* marks a change of direction for Cohen, with its use of modern musical technology and a more upbeat theme, and a change of label to Passport Records. Cohen embarks on a worldwide tour to promote the LP. It reaches UK #52 while *Dance Me To The End Of Love* is released as a single and complemented by a video. Cohen wins a Canadian Juno Award for Best Movie Score for his collaboration with Lewis Furey on the rock-opera *Night Magic*.

1986 Cohen makes a cameo appearance as head of Interpol in NBC-TV's "Miami Vice".

1987 June His long-time backing singer Jennifer Warnes° releases LP *Famous Blue Raincoat*, a collection of Cohen's songs which includes *First, We Take Manhattan*.

1988 Mar Cohen releases *First, We Take Manhattan*, extracted from LP *I'm Your Man*, which is his best-received in years. He performs three nights at London's Royal Albert Hall following its UK release.

July Special UK BBC TV documentary focusing on Cohen excites chart entry for LP *I'm Your Man* at UK #52 and LP *Greatest Hits*, first released in 1975, which enters at UK #99.

LLOYD COLE & THE COMMOTIONS

Lloyd Cole (vocals, guitar)
Neil Clark (guitar)
Lawrence Donegan (bass)
Blair Cowan (keyboards)
Steven Irvine (drums)

1983 July Cole (b. Jan 31, 1956, Scotland) meets Cowan in a hostelry in Glasgow, Scotland, both on their way to a Ramones° concert.

1984 Jan Cole and Cowan team up with Clark, Donegan and Irvine to form Lloyd Cole & The Commotions. Local gigging and demo tapes lead to a record deal with Polydor.

July First single *Perfect Skin* immediately appeals to the rock fraternity and climbs to UK #26.

Oct *Forest Fire* reaches UK #41. LP *Rattlesnakes* is released and makes UK #45. A sell-out European tour follows.

Nov Title track from LP is a disappointing UK #65.

1985 Oct *Brand New Friend*, from forthcoming LP, is a first top 20 hit, making UK #19.

Nov Second LP *Easy Pieces* is released, produced by Clive Langer/Alan Winstanley team, and hits UK #5. It achieves significant sales worldwide, but an increasingly disillusioned Cole gives his gold and platinum award disks to his local café where they are used as tea-trays. *Lost Weekend* reaches UK #17.

1986 June Sandie Shaw° records a cover version of *Are You Ready To Be Heartbroken*, a track from *Rattlesnakes*, which makes only UK #68. Session tapes, produced by Chris Thomas for a new LP, are recorded in between touring but are shelved.

1987 Jan Cole teams with Ian Stanley, ex-collaborator with Tears For Fears° and Peter Gabriel°, and invites him to produce new LP.

Oct First release of this liaison is *My Bag* which reaches only UK #46. Cowan leaves the group, on friendly terms. A UK tour commences and is a sell-out, including two nights at London's Brixton Academy.

Nov The group's breakthrough comes with LP *Mainstream* which hits UK #2.

1988 Jan The tour spreads to Europe.

Apr Back in the UK, the group plays the final tour date at Wembley Arena. *Jennifer She Said* reaches UK #31. A 12" version features covers of Dylan's° *I Don't Believe You* and Presley's° classic *Mystery Train*. While preparing for their first visit to Japan, EP *From The Hip* charts at UK #59.

NATALIE COLE

1962 The second of Nat "King" Cole's five children who all grow up in affluent LA suburb Hancock Park, Cole (b. Feb.6, 1950, Los Angeles, Cal., US) appears on stage for the first time with her father.

1965 Following his death, Cole becomes one of only 200 black students at the 20,000 attendee University of Massachusetts, Amherst, Mass. She becomes politically active as a committed pacifist and a member of the Black Panther Party. She also forms a student band which plays gigs off campus.

1972 Although she feels artistic leanings to follow her father as a vocalist, she collects a degree in child psychology.

1973 Having begun singing in clubs, she tries to hide her background from nostalgic promoters keen to hear her perform her father's work.

Feb Playing at The Executive Inn in Buffalo, N.Y., she meets Canadian promoter Kevin Hunter who becomes her manager and secures bookings on TV and at larger venues.

1974 Dec R&B writer/producers Chuck Jackson and Marvin Yancy invite her to record a debut LP in Curtis Mayfield's° Curtom studio.

1975 June After all the major labels turn her down, she eventually signs to Capitol (the same company for which her father recorded).

July At Yancy's behest, Cole is re-baptized before beginning her first major US tour.

Aug LP *Inseparable* is released and climbs to US #18, earning a gold disk.

Nov Taken from the LP, *This Will Be* hits US #6 and makes UK #32.

1976 Mar *Inseparable* makes US #32.

Apr Cole opens for Bill Cosby at the Las Vegas Hilton. She wins two Grammy awards as Best New Artist and Best Female R&B Vocalist.

May LP *Natalie* is released and climbs to US #13, again earning a gold disk.

NATALIE COLE *cont.*

July [31] Cole secretly marries the Reverend Marvin Yancy in Chicago.
Aug *Sophisticated Lady (She's A Different Lady)* reaches US #25.
Oct *Mr. Melody* peaks at US #49.
1977 Feb [14] She publicly announces, on Valentine's Day, that she was married in 1976 and is now pregnant.
Feb [19] Cole wins Best R&B Female Vocal Performance Grammy for *Sophisticated Lady*.
Mar Third LP *Unpredictable* is released. It hits US #8 and goes platinum.
Apr *I've Got Love On My Mind* hits US #5, and is her first gold single. Cole guests on US TV specials "Sinatra and Friends" and "Paul Anka . . . Music My Way".
Aug *Party Lights* peaks at US #79.
Oct [14] Her son, Robert Adam, is born.
Dec LP *Thankful* is released and becomes her second platinum disk, reaching US #16. Cole is voted Best Female Vocalist by the National Association for the Advancement of Colored People (NAACP).
1978 Jan [14] Cole performs on US TV "Super Bowl" celebration special.
Jan [16] Within 48 hours she is co-hosting the American Music Awards.
Mar [30] Cole begins 4 days of concerts at Long Island's Westbury Music Fair.
Apr *Our Love* hits US #10, having already topped the US soul chart, and is her second gold single.
June Double LP *Natalie . . . Live!*, recorded in N.J. and LA, makes US #31. Cole hosts her own US TV show "The Natalie Cole Special".
1979 Apr LP *I Love You So* peaks at US #52.
1980 Jan Cole duets with Peabo Bryson° on LP *We're The Best Of Friends*, which reaches US #44. From it, *Gimme Some Time* and *What You Won't Do For Love* are both hit soul records.
July LP *Don't Look Back* climbs to US #77.
Sept *Someone That I Used To Love* makes US #21.
1981 Oct LP *Happy Love* peaks at US #132. LP *The Natalie Cole Collection* is her final release on Capitol.
1982 Feb Cole signs worldwide to Epic Records. LP *I'm Ready* reaches US #182.
1983 Sept Cole joins Johnny Mathis on LP *Unforgettable – A Tribute To Nat "King" Cole*.
1985 June Cole signs to Modern Records. *Dangerous* is released and reaches US #57.
July LP *Dangerous* peaks at US #140.
Sept *A Little Bit Of Heaven* reaches US #81.
1986 Sept Cole signs to EMI subsidiary Manhattan.
1987 Aug LP *Everlasting* is released. (On it Cole covers *When I Fall In Love*, which will give her father a posthumous UK #4 at Christmas.)
Oct *Jump Start* makes US #13.
1988 Feb *I Live For Your Love* also makes US #13.
May A re-working of Bruce Springsteen's° *Pink Cadillac* hits US #5 and UK #5. Re-sleeved and re-mastered LP *Everlasting* makes US #42 and peaks at UK #62 (her first UK chart LP).
June [11] She makes a rare live appearance at Nelson Mandela's 70th Birthday Party concert in London's Wembley Stadium, as part of a soul supergroup with Ashford and Simpson° and Al Green° in its line-up.
July *Everlasting* reaches UK #28.
Sept *Jump Start* is reissued in UK and makes #36. Cole begins a US tour.
Dec Cole is featured on the soundtrack of Bill Murray film *Scrooged*.

JUDY COLLINS

1954 Collins (b. May 1, 1939, Seattle, Wash., US), daughter of blind Denver radio personality and musician Chuck Collins, after studying piano in Denver, Col., with acclaimed pianist/conductor Dr. Antonia Brico and making her public debut at age 13 with the Denver Symphony Orchestra, turns to the folk guitar.
1957 She drops out of college in Jacksonville, Ill., and returns to Denver to marry her teacher boyfriend Peter Taylor. They live in a cabin in the Rockies and have a son, Clark.
1959 Collins begins singing professionally with first engagements early in the year in Boulder, Col., and the couple moves to Chicago.
1960 She lands a regular gig at Chicago's Gate of Horn, billed second to poet Lord Buckley.
1961 Collins signs to Elektra Records after owner Jac Holzman hears her performing on the New York folk circuit.
Oct First LP, *A Maid Of Constant Sorrow*, features traditional folk songs and prompts growing reputation on the specialist scene.
1962 July LP *Golden Apples Of The Sun* is released to wide critical approval.
Sept She debuts at New York's Carnegie Hall. The pressures of new-found fame and the break-up of her marriage take their toll. By the end of the year she is seriously ill with tuberculosis and spends 6 months in hospital.
1963 Dec When she returns to the folk scene, it has become more contemporary and her third LP, *Judy Collins #3*, contains overtly political material. (She will later become an active protest marcher.)
1964 Apr LP *Judy Collins #3* reaches US #126.
Oct Live LP *The Judy Collins Concert*, featuring songs by Bob Dylan°, Tom Paxton and Phil Ochs, is released but does not chart.
1965 Nov LP *Fifth Album* climbs to US #69.
1967 Jan *Hard Lovin' Loser* is her first US single chart entry, reaching #97.
Feb LP *In My Life* is recorded in London and includes *Suzanne* and *Dress Rehearsal Rag*, the first recordings of songs by Leonard Cohen°, and some numbers from Peter Weiss' stage production of *The Marat/Sade*, with orchestral backing. It peaks at US #46.
July Collins introduces a visibly nervous Cohen° on stage during a concert in Central Park, New York.
1968 Jan LP *Wildflowers* contains the first of her own songs and broadens her style to interpret songs by Jacques Brel, Brecht/Weill and new writers Joni Mitchell° and Randy Newman°. On chart in the US for nearly 18 months, it will hit #5, earn a gold disk, and become her all-time best-seller.
Jan [20] She appears with Bob Dylan°, The Band° and others in a concert at Carnegie Hall, New York, commemorating folk singer Woody Guthrie, recently deceased.
Dec A version of Joni Mitchell's° *Both Sides Now* taken from LP *Wildflowers* is her biggest hit single, making US #8. It will win a Grammy award for Best Folk Performance of 1968.
1969 Jan LP *Who Knows Where The Time Goes* reaches US #29 and earns a gold disk. Her backing band for this LP includes short-term beau Stephen Stills who is subsequently inspired to write *Suite: Judy Blue Eyes*, recorded by Crosby, Stills & Nash°.
Feb *Someday Soon* reaches US #55 and *Both Sides Now* marks her UK chart debut at #14.
June Collins tries stage acting, with a part in Ibsen's *Peer Gynt* at the New York Shakespeare Festival.
Aug Another Joni Mitchell° song, *Chelsea Morning*, takes her to US #78.
Nov LP *Recollections*, a compilation of early material, reaches US #29.
Dec A revival of The Byrds'° *Turn! Turn! Turn!* peaks at US #69.
1971 Jan LP *Whales And Nightingales* makes US #17 and earns a gold disk. It includes *Farewell To Tarwathie*, a traditional Scottish whaling song arranged around real recordings of the song of the humpback whale.
Feb An arrangement of the traditional *Amazing Grace*, recorded in St. Paul's Chapel at Columbia University and taken from the LP *Whales And Nightingales*, reaches US #15 and hits UK #5. It is her biggest UK hit and one of the longest runs in UK chart history. (Initially on the chart for 32 weeks and continuing via constant re-entries in the lower part, it moves back up to #20 in mid-1972 and finally exits in Jan. 1974.)
Apr *Whales And Nightingales* is her first UK chart LP, reaching #37.
1972 Jan *Open The Door (Song For Judith)* reaches only US #90. LP *Living* makes US #64. Collins takes a year off to write prose and begin work co-directing *Antonia: A Portrait Of The Woman*, a film about her former piano teacher Antonia Brico, (which will later be nominated for an Academy Award).
May She joins other artists in campaigning through benefit concerts for George McGovern's US presidential bid.
July Compilation LP *Colors Of The Day/The Best Of Judy Collins* climbs to US #37.
1973 Mar LP *True Stories & Other Dreams*, notable for its original songs, including *Ché* and *Song For Martin*, peaks at US #27. *Cook With Honey*, taken from it, reaches US #32.
1975 June LP *Judith* climbs to US #17 and becomes her biggest-selling UK LP at #7. *Send In The Clowns*, taken from Stephen Sondheim's musical *A Little Night Music*, hits UK #6 and climbs to US #36.
1976 Oct LP *Bread And Roses* reaches US #25.
1977 Sept Compilation LP *So Early In The Spring: The First 15 Years* peaks at US #42.

Nov *Send In The Clowns* charts again in US, climbing to #19 and completing a total US chart run of 27 weeks.
1979 Mar *Hard Times For Lovers* is her last US hit single, climbing to #66. An LP of the same title follows it, peaking at US #54.
1980 May LP *Running For My Life* makes US #142.
1982 Mar LP *The Times Of Our Lives* peaks disappointingly at US #190.
1985 Dec UK-released TV-advertised compilation LP *Amazing Grace* climbs to UK #34.
1987 After an 18-month break from recording, Collins returns on new label, Gold Castle, with LP *Trust Your Heart*. It includes a new recording of *Amazing Grace*. Collins' book *Trust Your Heart: An Autobiography* is published.
1988 Sept It is announced that a live LP *Grace's Sanity* is to be released shortly.

PHIL COLLINS

1981 Jan Having been a child actor, as the Artful Dodger in London stage production of *Oliver* among other roles, a member of art-rock band Flaming Youth in the early 1970s and later of part-time jazz-rock outfit Brand X, Collins (b. Jan.31, 1951, London, UK), already a major international star as drummer and lead singer of Genesis°, after Peter Gabriel's° 1977 departure, signs to Virgin in UK and Atlantic in US for a parallel solo career, recording LP *Face Value*.
Feb LP *Face Value*, which Collins claims to have been motivated by his divorce from his first wife, enters UK chart at #1, eventually selling over 900,000 copies in UK. *In The Air Tonight*, taken from it, hits UK #2.
Apr *I Missed Again*, also from the LP, makes UK #14.
May *I Missed Again* is his first US solo single, reaching #19. Its B-side features demo versions of the first two hits.
June *If Leaving Me Is Easy* peaks at UK #17.
July LP *Face Value* hits US #7, earning a gold disk for a half million sales.
Aug *In The Air Tonight* reaches US #19.
1982 June He guests on drums for Jethro Tull° at The Prince's Trust concert.
July He plays drums on Robert Plant's° LP *Pictures At Eleven*, which hits UK #2 and US #5.
Sept He produces solo LP *Something's Going On* for former Abba° vocalist Frida, which makes UK #18 and US #41.
Oct *Thru' These Walls* is a minor UK hit, at #56.
Nov Second LP *Hello, I Must Be Going* hits UK #2.
1983 Jan A revival of The Supremes'° 1966 million-seller *You Can't Hurry Love*, taken from the LP, gives Collins his first UK #1 single and tops the chart for 2 weeks.
Feb *You Can't Hurry Love* hits US #10 and LP *Hello, I Must Be Going* hits US #8.
Mar *I Don't Care Anymore* peaks at US #39. *Don't Let Him Steal Your Heart Away* reaches UK #45.
May *I Cannot Believe It's True* makes only US #79.
Dec An unlikely liaison sees Collins produce Adam and The Ants'° *Strip*. It makes UK #41.
1984 Apr Collins is commissioned by Taylor Hackford to write a song for his movie *Against All Odds*. He uses an out-take from *Face Value* titled *How Can You Sit There?*, retitling it *Against All Odds (Take A Look At Me Now)*. It tops the US chart for 3 weeks and is a million-seller, and also hits UK #2. (It will be nominated for an Oscar at the following year's Academy Awards.)
Oct *In The Air Tonight* receives further airplay through exposure on US TV series "Miami Vice", in which Collins has a guest acting role in one episode as game show host Phil The Shill, and in film *Risky Business*. It reaches US #102.
Nov [25] He drums and sings at the recording session for Band Aid's° *Do They Know It's Christmas?*, which will become the UK's all-time best-selling single.
1985 Feb He duets with Philip Bailey on the jointly-credited uptempo dance number *Easy Lover*, which hits US #2 and is another million-seller. *Sussudio*, a taster of his next solo LP, makes UK #12.
Mar *One More Night* spends 2 weeks at US #1 and sells over a million. LP *No Jacket Required*, eventually both a UK and US million-seller, is Collins' first LP to top both UK (for 5 weeks) and US (for 7 weeks) charts. Duet *Easy Lover* with Philip Bailey hits UK #1, topping the chart for 4 weeks.
May *One More Night* hits UK #4.
July *Sussudio* hits US #1 for a week and is another million-seller.
July [13] Uniquely, Collins performs on the same day at Wembley, UK, and Philadelphia, US, both venues of Live Aid, jetting the Atlantic on Concorde between appearances. Amongst his guest slots at the event, he plays drums behind Jimmy Page and Robert Plant° in the reunion of Led Zeppelin°.
Aug *Take Me Home* peaks at UK #19.
Sept *Don't Lose My Number* hits US #4.
Nov Collins' second major duet of the year is with newcomer Marilyn Martin on *Separate Lives*, written by Stephen Bishop and featured as the love theme in film *White Nights*. It hits US #1 and is his fifth US million-seller out of six releases.
1986 Mar Collins produces Howard Jones'° *No One Is To Blame* (UK #16, US #4).
May *Take Me Home* hits US #7.
June He plays in The Prince's Trust charity concert at Wembley Arena, London, with Paul McCartney°, Elton John°, Tina Turner°, Dire Straits'° Mark Knopfler and others.
Nov He joins Greg Phillinganes (keyboards) and Nathan East (bass) to become Eric Clapton's° band for his new LP *August*. Collins will also be part of lengthy world tour to promote the LP.
1987 *12ers*, remixes of previous singles, is released only on CD. In US it is also released as an LP.
1988 June [11] Collins drums in an all-star band put together by Midge Ure for the Nelson Mandela 70th Birthday celebration concert at Wembley, UK.
July A remixed version of debut single *In The Air Tonight*, released through its exposure on a TV commercial for Mercury Communications, hits UK top 10 again at #4.
Sept He stars in the title role of film *Buster* about flower-stall seller and British Great Train Robber Buster Edwards, and compiles the soundtrack LP of 1960s songs, which includes his own version of *A Groovy Kind Of Love*.

THE COMMODORES

Lionel Richie (vocals and keyboards)
William King (trumpet)
Thomas McClary (lead guitar)
Milan Williams (keyboards, trombone, guitar and drums)
Ronald LaPraed (bass and trumpet)
Walter "Clyde" Orange (vocals and drums)

1967 The Mighty Mystics are formed at Tuskegee Institute, Alabama, US, when six students including McClary and Richie combine and enter a talent contest to impress girls. The Mystics later link with another campus group, The Jays, which includes King and Williams. The Commodores name is decided by the toss of a dictionary and a finger-point from King.
1968 Having become local favorites in Montgomery, Ala., The Commodores are sent by the Tuskegee Institute to play a benefit at New York's Town Hall. Local entrepreneur Benny Ashburn handles publicity for the event.
1969 The band members return to their studies at the Institute having aroused popular support on New York's club scene. During the summer, they return to New York and contact Ashburn, who gets them an audition at Small's Paradise, Harlem's best known club.
Sept Orange replaces Andre Callahan as the group's drummer. Bassist Michael Gilbert is drafted and replaced by LaPraed. Ashburn and the band form Commodores Entertainment Corp., using the group's degrees in business majors.
1970 Ashburn, now their full-time mentor and manager, secures The Commodores dates on the European club circuit. They travel on board the S.S. France, and become local favorites in St. Tropez and other French resorts. While on tour, they meet a vacationing Ed Sullivan.
1971 Searching for an exciting opening act for Motown Records biggest stars, The Jackson 5°, Motown's Creative Vice President, Suzanne de Passe, sees the group perform at New York's Turntable and books them for the tour. They sign to the label, having released *Keep On Dancin'* on Atlantic earlier in the year. (It will be 3 years before Motown releases their first LP.) The group begins its first Far East tour.
1974 June Instrumental *Machine Gun*, written by Williams, crosses over from R&B chart to US #22 and UK #20. (It will be played after the National Anthem at closedown on Nigerian TV and radio stations.)
Aug LP *Machine Gun* peaks at US #138. Although it fails in UK, it achieves gold in Japan and Nigeria, where it is the biggest selling international LP.

THE COMMODORES *cont.*

Nov UK follow-up *The Zoo (Human Zoo)* reaches #44. *I Feel Sanctified* peaks at US #75.

1975 Mar Second LP *Caught In The Act* is released. During a 33-week chart stay, it will peak at US #26.

June Taken from the LP, *Slippery When Wet* makes US #19 and wins the Bronze Prize at the Tokyo Music Festival. Following their own headlining tour, The Commodores are invited to support The Rolling Stones° on their world tour.

Dec Richie ballad *Sweet Love* hits US #5. LP *Movin' On* climbs to US #29. Despite international tours and sales, most band members are still completing degree courses, studying while on the road and returning to university for mid-term and final exams.

1976 July During a tour supporting The O'Jays, LP *Hot On The Tracks* peaks at US #12.

Oct Second Richie ballad, *Just To Be Close To You* hits US #7.

1977 Jan Follow-up from the LP, *Fancy Dancer* peaks at US #39.

Feb The Commodores begin their own headlining world tour.

Apr Fifth LP, *Commodores*, is released. It will hit US #3 and spend over a year on chart.

June The band appears with Donna Summer° in disco movie *Thank God It's Friday*, and contribute to its soundtrack.

Aug *Easy* hits US #4 and UK #9. It is written by Richie, as are most of their biggest hits. The Commodores are on a 70-city US tour which will gross $6 million.

Sept *Brickhouse*, a dance anthem, hits US #5.

Oct Released as a double A-side with revived *Sweet Love*, *Brickhouse* climbs to UK #32. During a UK visit, LaPraed's wife dies of cancer. (The next two LPs will be dedicated to her.)

Dec *Too Hot Ta Trot* makes US #24. The Commodores complete their most successful year to date with sell-out US dates. Live double LP *Commodores Live!* hits US #3.

1978 Mar Double A-side *Too Hot Ta Trot/Zoom* makes UK #38.

Apr The group performs in the Congressgebouw, The Hague, Holland at the start of a 21-date European tour.

May LP *Commodores Live!* makes UK #60 and is their UK LP chart debut.

Aug [12] Richie ballad *Three Times A Lady* hits US #1, displacing The Rolling Stones'° *Miss You*. Dedicated to his wife, Richie was inspired to write the song at his parents 37th wedding anniversary. The disk will later go double platinum. (Richie will receive a Country Songwriter award by ASCAP in Nashville.)

Aug [19] *Three Times A Lady* begins a 5-week chart stay at UK #1, becoming Motown's biggest selling single. A worldwide smash, it spurs LP *Natural High* to hit US #3 and UK #8.

Oct *Flying High* makes US #38 and UK #37.

Nov *Just To Be Close To You* reaches UK #62, as the group ends a 4-month US tour in Louisville, Ky.

Dec LP *Greatest Hits* peaks at US #23 and UK #19.

1979 Aug The Commodores participate in the Saarbrucken Festival, at the start of a 19-date European tour.

Oct While new studio LP *Midnight Magic* hits US #3 and UK #15, Richie composed country/soul ballad *Sail On* hits US #4 and UK #8. It focuses on the failing marriage of friend William Smith and is passed on the chart by another Richie ballad, *Still*.

Nov *Still* hits US #1, replacing The Eagles'° *Heartache Tonight*, and hits UK #4.

1980 Jan *Wonderland* makes US #25 and UK #40.

Apr [25] LaPraed marries Jacqueline Echols in Tuskegee, Ala. They will spend their honeymoon on the group's 95-date US tour.

June Spiritually inspired LP *Heroes* is released. It hits US #7 but makes only UK #50. From it, *Old-Fashioned Love* makes US #20.

Oct Title track *Heroes* peaks at US #54. Their current tour is less successful than any in recent years.

1981 Jan The Commodores perform the title theme in movie *Underground Aces*. Richie, thinking of a solo career, duets with Diana Ross° on self-penned *Endless Love*., The group's *Lady (You Bring Me Up* hits US #8 and makes UK #56. Richie's final LP with the group, *In The Pocket*, climbs to US #13 and UK #69.

Nov Final Richie ballad for The Commodores *Oh No* hits US #4 and UK #44.

1982 Feb Last group single featuring Richie vocals, *Why You Wanna Try Me* peaks at US #66. He leaves the group to write and produce for himself and others.

Aug UK K-tel compilation LP *Love Songs* hits UK #5, their most successful UK LP (and not on Motown).

Aug [17] Manager Ashburn dies of a heart attack in N.J., US.

Dec *Painted Picture* peaks at UK #70. Richie's solo *Truly* hits US #1. US compilation LP, on Motown, *All The Greatest Hits* climbs to US #37.

1983 Apr The Commodores record the theme for US TV show "Teachers Only", called *Reach High*. It fails to chart. McClary quits to record solo LP *Thomas McClary* and single *Thin Walls* for Motown, both with limited success.

June Another compilation, *Commodores Anthology* peaks at US #141.

Sept *Only You* makes US #54.

Nov First LP since Richie's departure, *Commodores 13* reaches US #103. (As live interest also wanes, the group will spend the next year re-assessing with no activity. Urgently needing a new vocalist, the members recruit ex-Heatwave° UK singer, J.D. Nicholas (b. Apr.12, 1952), who has recently sung for Diana Ross°.)

1985 Jan Composed by Orange as a tribute to Marvin Gaye° and Jackie Wilson°, *Nightshift* hits both US and UK #3. It features co-lead vocals by Orange and Nicholas and is taken from LP *Nightshift*, which makes US #12 and UK #13.

June *Animal Instinct* reaches US #43 and UK #74.

Sept *Janet* peaks at US #87.

Nov Another UK TV compilation, on Telstar, LP *The Very Best Of The Commodores* makes UK #25. Motown drops The Commodores after 11 years.

1986 Mar *Nightshift* wins a Grammy award and helps them sign a new recording deal with Polydor Records. The band also signs a management deal with Natalie Cole's° manager Dan Cleary.

Nov First Polydor single *Goin' To The Bank* reaches US #65 and UK #43, as the band begins a tour of Belgium, Holland, West Germany and UK.

Dec LP *United* makes US #101, but fails to chart in UK.

1988 Sept Used extensively as the theme to UK Halifax Building Society TV commercial, *Easy* re-enters the UK chart making #15.

Oct LP *Rock Solid* is released together with single *Solitaire*. The Commodores have sold over 40 million records worldwide, with 24 platinum and gold disks.

THE COMMUNARDS

Jimi Somerville (vocals)
Richard Coles (keyboards)

1984 Steve Bronski (b. Feb.7, 1960) and Larry Steinbachek (b. May 6, 1960), who evolve an electronic dance music style on their twin synthesizers, and Somerville (b. June 22, 1961, Glasgow, Scotland, UK), who adds falsetto vocals, form a group called Bronski Beat in London. The trio signs to London Records via its own Forbidden Fruit label.

June Debut *Smalltown Boy* hits UK #3.

Oct *Why?* hits UK #10. LP *The Age Of Consent* hits UK #4.

Dec Somerville announces his intention to leave because of his dislike of the star treatment the band is getting but is persuaded to stay.

1985 Jan A revival of the Gershwin oldie *It Ain't Necessarily So* reaches UK #16.

Feb Somerville is fined £50 at London's Bow Magistrates' Court for gross indecency.

Mar *Smalltown Boy* is Bronski Beat's only US chart single at #48. LP *The Age Of Consent* hits US #36.

May A revival of Donna Summer's° *I Feel Love*, in a medley with Summer's *Love To Love You Baby* and John Leyton's *Johnny Remember Me*, hits UK #3. It jointly credits ex-Soft Cell° singer Marc Almond, who duets with Somerville. Somerville leaves to work with keyboardist Coles (b. June 23, 1962, Northampton, UK), an ex-student of the Royal School Of Church Music who has occasionally played on stage with Bronski Beat. They first name themselves The Committee, then discover the name is already in use and decide upon The Communards. Bronski and Steinbachek recruit John Jon (Foster) as the new Bronski Beat vocalist.

Sept Bronski Beat's mini-LP *Hundreds And Thousands*, consisting mostly of dance remixes of tracks from the first LP, makes UK #24.

Oct The Communards signs to London Records in UK and debuts with *You Are My World*, which establishes their sound, a variation on Bronski Beat's dance-oriented keyboard arrangements, highlighting Somerville's falsetto voice. It reaches UK #30.

1986 Jan They play on the Red Wedge tour of UK, with The Style Council° and Billy Bragg°, in support of UK Labour Party. For this and later stage work, the duo recruits its regular backing band of (mainly female) session players. Bronski Beat's *Hit That Perfect Beat*, featured in film *Letter To Brezhnev*, is the group's first single to feature John Jon's lead vocals. It hits UK #3.

Apr Bronski Beat's *Come On, Come On* reaches UK #20.

May Bronski Beat's LP *Truthdare Doubledare* makes UK #18.

June The Communards' *Disenchanted* peaks at UK #29.

Sept The Communards' dance-styled revival of Thelma Houston and Harold Melvin's hit *Don't Leave Me This Way* tops the UK chart for 4 weeks and is the year's second-biggest UK single, selling 750,000 copies. Somerville duets on it with Sarah-Jayne Morris, who becomes a regular onstage duettist/backup vocalist.

Oct LP *Communards*, containing the hit singles, reaches UK #7.

Nov John Jon leaves Bronski Beat. (The group remains inactive in 1987 and into 1988. Different reports have them splitting from London Records and breaking up altogether.)

Dec The Communards' *So Cold The Night* hits UK #8, helped by a European tour which is followed by major London dates.

1987 Feb A remake of their first single, as *You Are My World '87*, reaches UK #21.

Mar *Don't Leave Me This Way* is the band's first US success, reaching #40.

Sept *Tomorrow*, extracted from forthcoming LP *Red*, peaks at UK #23.

Oct LP *Red* reaches UK #11.

Nov A revival of Gloria Gaynor's hit *Never Can Say Goodbye*, taken from LP *Red* and with similar arrangement to *Don't Leave Me This Way*, hits UK #4.

1988 Mar *For A Friend*, dedicated to Coles and Somerville's friend Mark Ashton, who died of AIDS, reaches UK #28.

June Another pro-gay song *There's More To Love* reaches UK #20.

RY COODER

1969 Having started out as a member of Jackie DeShannon's backing group, played in LA in 1966 with Taj Mahal in blues group The Rising Sons, with Captain Beefheart's° Magic Band in 1967 on LP *Safe As Milk*, and as a studio session guitarist, working with The Everly Brothers°, Paul Revere & The Raiders°, Randy Newman° and a host of others, Cooder (b. Mar.15, 1947, Los Angeles, Cal., US) visits London, UK, with arranger/producer Jack Nitzsche and meets The Rolling Stones°. Tipped to join the band in Brian Jones' place, he does not do so, but plays mandolin on the Stones' LP *Let It Bleed*, works with Nitzsche and Randy Newman on the soundtrack for Mick Jagger/James Fox film *Performance*, playing dulcimer and bottleneck guitar, and works on *Candy* film soundtrack.

1970 Cooder signs to Reprise Records as a soloist.

Dec He plays extensively on Little Feat° debut LP.

1971 Jan Debut LP *Ry Cooder* fails to chart, though is critically well-rated for its authentic folk-blues approach. Plays on Rolling Stones'° LP *Sticky Fingers*.

1972 Mar LP *Into The Purple Valley*, his US chart debut, reaches #113.

Nov LP *Boomer's Story* is released, but does not chart.

1974 June LP *Paradise And Lunch* makes US #167.

1976 Nov LP *Chicken Skin Music* reaches US #177. Cooder tours with "The Chicken Skin Revue", with Hawaiian steel guitarist Gabby Pahinui, Tex-Mex accordionist Flaco Jiminez, and gospel vocal backup trio led by Bobby King, who all played on the LP.

1977 Sept Live LP *Show Time*, recorded at the Great American Music Hall, San Francisco, with "The Chicken Skin Revue", peaks at US #158.

1978 June LP *Jazz* revives late 1940s big band music with sidemen from the era and arrangements by Joseph Byrd. He reunites with Captain Beefheart° to work on *Blue Collar* film soundtrack.

1979 Sept LP *Bop Till You Drop* (the first rock LP to be recorded using digital process) reaches US #62 and marks Cooder's UK chart debut at #36. He performs at Cambridge Folk Festival, UK.

1980 June He scores Walter Hill's movie *The Long Riders*, drawing on US hillbilly-folk styles, and Hill's film *Southern Comfort*, but no soundtrack recording is made available.

Nov LP *Borderline* peaks at US #43 and UK #35.

1982 Feb He scores film *The Border*, starring Jack Nicholson. The soundtrack LP has Sam The Sham and Freddy Fender guesting.

June LP *The Slide Area* reaches US #105 and UK #18, but Cooder, unhappy with the LP and its US sales, backs out of tours and retreats to work at home in Santa Monica, Cal. on movie soundtracks.

1983 June Plays club dates in San Francisco in a small band put together by Duane Eddy°.

Dec [8] Plays with Eric Clapton°, Jeff Beck°, Jimmy Page and others in the Ronnie Lane Benefit Concert for ARMS, at New York's Madison Square Garden.

1985 Jan Cooder scores Wim Wenders' modern-day western movie *Paris, Texas*.

May LP of soundtrack for Louis Malle's *Alamo Bay*, which includes contributions from John Hiatt and Los Lobos°, is released by independent Slash Records, but does not chart.

1987 Film music projects are *Blue City* and the blues movie *Crossroads*, the latter including collaborations with Sonny Terry and The

RY COODER *cont.*

Frank Frost Blues Band from Mississippi.

Dec LP *Get Rhythm*, made with his current band (including Van Dyke Parks on keyboards and Jim Keltner on drums), guest vocalists Larry Blackmon (of Cameo°) and actor Harry Dean Stanton (who starred in *Paris, Texas*) renovates his non-movie recording career.

1988 May *Get Rhythm*, a revival of a Johnny Cash° song, and from LP of the same title, becomes his first chart single at UK #93.

June *Pecos Bill*, with Cooder playing music to Robin Williams' narrative, is released in US on Windham Hill label.

SAM COOKE

1955 Cooke (b. Jan.22, 1935, Chicago, Ill., US), one of the Reverend Charles S. Cooke's eight children, having performed in church with two of his sisters and a brother as the Singing Children and moved to adult gospel singing with R.B. Robertson's Highway QCs and The Pilgrim Travelers in Chicago, becomes lead tenor with star gospel group The Soul Stirrers, quickly developing a distinctive vocal style.

1956 Specialty Records A&R man Bumps Blackwell, sensing pop potential in Cooke's voice, records several non-gospel tracks with him and releases *Loveable*, a reworking of The Soul Stirrers' *Wonderful* with Cooke thinly disguised as "Dale Cook" so as not offend his gospel fans, but the pseudonym is seen through and Specialty boss Art Rupe, safeguarding his label's large stake in the gospel market, refuses to release any more pop records by Cooke.

1957 Blackwell leaves Specialty for Keen Records and signs Cooke. Several gospel-styled but purely secular ballads are cut on Keen, including the lush *(I Love You) For Sentimental Reasons* and the bouncier *You Send Me*, written by brother Charles. Neither charts initially.

Dec [1] Cooke appears on US TV's "Ed Sullivan Show" (Buddy Holly° and The Crickets also debut), singing *You Send Me*, which tops the US chart for 3 weeks and sells almost 2½ million copies.

1958 Jan Specialty releases a 1956 taboo Cooke pop number, *I'll Come Running Back To You*, which reaches US #18. *(I Love You) For Sentimental Reasons*, released by Keen in 1957, makes US #17. *You Send Me* makes US #29 for 1 week.

Mar Cooke's eponymous debut LP reaches US #16 while *Lonely Island You Were Made For Me*, released immediately prior to *You Send Me*, reaches US #39.

Apr [5] Irvin Feld's "Greatest Show of Stars" begins a 40-date tour at Norfolk, Va., with Cooke headlining, alongside The Everly Brothers°, Clyde McPhatter and a host of rock and R&B names.

Oct *Win Your Love For Me* reaches US #33.

Nov [10] Cooke and Lou Rawls, a member of his tour backing group The Pilgrim Travelers Quartet, suffer minor injuries in a car crash in Arkansas, in which Cooke's chauffeur Edward Cunningham is killed.

1959 Jan *Love You Most Of All* peaks at US #26.

Apr *Everybody Likes To Cha Cha Cha*, released to cash in on a novelty dance craze, reaches US #31.

July *Only Sixteen*, written by "Barbara Campbell" (a collective pseudonym for Cooke and friends Lou Adler and Herb Alpert°) makes US #28.

Aug *Only Sixteen* reaches UK #23 but Craig Douglas'° cover version tops the UK chart for 4 weeks.

Nov *There, I've Said It Again* makes US #81.

Nov [9] RCA Records, aware that Cooke's contract with Keen is close to expiry, offers him a $100,000 guarantee.

1960 Jan [22] Cooke signs to RCA, which acquires his Keen back catalog and pairs him with producers Hugo Peretti and Luigi Creatore.

Mar [14] Cooke's first West Indies tour opens in Montego Bay, Jamaica. He is a sell-out sensation in the Caribbean. (This visit and two later ones are significant because Cooke's style will have a major influence on a generation of Jamaican artists-to-be, including Bob Marley° and Jimmy Cliff°.)

Apr RCA debut *Teenage Sonata* reaches US #50.

July Belatedly issued on Keen, *Wonderful World* (a perennial favorite for later cover versions by Herman's Hermits°, Art Garfunkel° and others) climbs to #12. *Wonderful World* reaches UK #27.

Oct Gospel-styled *Chain Gang* hits US #2 and UK #9 and is his second million-seller.

1961 Jan *Sad Mood* climbs to US #29. Cooke launches his own Sar Records, one of the early artist-owned labels. (It will find chart success later in the year with The Simms Twins' *Soothe Me* and in 1962-64 with several singles by The Valentinos, made up of the Womack brothers.)

Apr *That's It, I Quit, I'm Movin' On* reaches US #31.

July *Cupid* reaches US #17.

Sept *Cupid* hits UK #7. (It will bring US and UK chart success later to Johnny Nash, The (Detroit) Spinners and Tony Orlando & Dawn°.)

Oct *Feel It* reaches US #56.

1962 Mar Self-penned *Twistin' The Night Away*, an infectious tribute to the worldwide dance craze, hits US #9, eventually selling a million and a half copies.

Apr *Twistin' The Night Away* hits UK #6.

July Another dance-styled release, *Having A Party*, reaches US #17. LP *Twistin' The Night Away* is Cooke's first US chart LP at #72.

Aug B-side *Bring It On Home To Me*, a mid-tempo ballad gospel-style duet with Lou Rawls, replaces A-side *Party* on radio and US chart, climbing to #13.

Nov *Nothing Can Change This Love* makes US #12 and gospelly B-side *Somebody Have Mercy* reaches US #70. Cooke makes his only UK tour, sharing top billing with Little Richard°.

Dec Compilation LP *The Best Of Sam Cooke*, including most of his biggest successes from *You Send Me* to *Bring It On Home To Me*, reaches US #22.

1963 Feb A revival of Little Richard's° *Send Me Some Loving* reaches US #13.

Apr LP *Mr Soul* climbs to US #92.

May *Another Saturday Night* hits US #10 and reaches UK #23.

July Cooke's son Vincent drowns in their home swimming pool.

Sept *Frankie And Johnny*, a smooth R&B version of an old folk song, reaches US #14 and UK #30.

Oct LP *Night Beat* peaks at US #62.

Dec Cooke's version of Willie Dixon's familiar blues *Little Red Rooster*, recorded in an all-star session with Ray Charles° on piano and Billy Preston on organ, reaches US #11.

1964 Feb [15] Cooke announces he is to revise his live concert schedule, cutting his previous 8 months on the road to 2, to devote more time to developing his record label.

Mar *(Ain't That) Good News* peaks at US #11.

June LP *Ain't That Good News* reaches US #34.

June [24] Cooke begins a 2-week engagement at New York's Copacabana nightclub, with a 70-foot billboard in Times Square announcing it.

July *Good Times* reaches US #11, with B-side *Tennessee Waltz* making #35.

DEEP PURPLE

Ian Gillan (vocals)
Ritchie Blackmore (guitar)
Jon Lord (keyboards)
Roger Glover (bass)
Ian Paice (drums)

1967 Two London businessmen, Tony Edwards, a textile company boss, and John Coletta, an advertising consultant, with no experience in the music world, decide to invest in a pop group. They give carte blanche to Lord (b. June 9, 1941, Leicester, UK), ex-Artwoods and now a session musician, Chris Curtis (b. Aug.26, 1942, Liverpool, UK), ex-The Searchers° drummer, and ex-Outlaws guitarist Blackmore (b. Apr.14, 1945, Weston-Super-Mare, UK), whom they have met, to form a new band. Musicians are auditioned from a *Melody Maker* ad at an old mansion, Deeves Hall, Herts.

1968 Feb The group forms as Roundabout. The line-is Lord, Blackmore, Curtis (vocals), Dave Curtis (bass) and Bobby Woodman (drums).

Mar After unpromising rehearsals, the line-up is changed. Curtis, Curtis and Woodman are replaced by Paice (b. June 29, 1948, Nottingham, UK) and singer Rod Evans (b. Edinburgh, Scotland), both ex-MI5 and ex-Maze, and bassist Nick Simper (b. Southall, London), ex-Johnny Kidd & The Pirates° (who survived the car crash which killed Kidd).

Apr [20] The group makes its live debut in Tastrup, Denmark, and changes its name to Deep Purple, using US group Vanilla Fudge° as its model.

May Deep Purple records an LP (in an 18-hour session) and is signed to EMI in UK and Bill Cosby's Tetragrammaton label in US.

Aug [10] The group's first major UK performance is at the Sunbury festival.

Sept First single, a revival of Joe South°-penned Billy Joe Royal hit *Hush* hits US #4, without charting in UK.

Oct LP *Shades Of Deep Purple* reaches US #24, again without a UK placing. The group tours US.

Dec Another revival, of Neil Diamond's° *Kentucky Woman*, reaches US #38.

1969 Feb LP *The Book Of Taliesyn* reaches US #54. Taken from it, a revival of Ike and Tina Turner's° *River Deep, Mountain High* reaches US #53.

July LP *Deep Purple* reaches US #162. Evans and Simper are fired, and the US Tetragrammaton label folds, leaving Deep Purple with no product outlet.

Aug Glover (b. Nov.30, 1945, Brecon, S.Wales, UK) and Gillan (b. Aug.19, 1945, Hounslow, Middx., UK), join from UK group Episode Six, playing their first gig with the band at London's Speakeasy club.

Sept [15] Deep Purple perform *Concerto For Group And Orchestra*, composed by Lord, with The Royal Philharmonic Orchestra conducted by Malcolm Arnold, at London's Royal Albert Hall.

1970 Jan LP *Concerto For Group And Orchestra*, originally recorded for the BBC at the Royal Albert Hall concert, reaches UK #26 (the group's UK chart debut) and US #149 (on Warner Bros.).

Aug LP *Deep Purple In Rock* hits UK #4 and makes US #143.

Oct *Black Night* is the group's first UK singles hit at #2, behind Freda Payne's *Band Of Gold*.

Oct [27] Gillan plays the role of Jesus in Tim Rice and Andrew Lloyd Webber's *Jesus Christ Superstar*, in a live performance at St Peter's Lutheran Church, New York.

Nov Studio cast recording of LP *Jesus Christ Superstar* is released and hits UK #6 and tops the US chart.

Dec *Black Night* climbs to US #66.

DEEP PURPLE *cont.*

1971 Mar *Strange Kind Of Woman* hits UK #8.

July The group tours US with The Faces°.

Sept LP *Fireball* tops the UK chart for 1 week, and reaches US #32.

Oct The band forms its own Purple label, marketed by EMI.

Dec Extracted title track from LP *Fireball* reaches UK #15.

Dec [3] Deep Purple is recording in Montreux Casino, Switzerland, when it burns down during a set by Frank Zappa's° Mothers of Invention. The group immortalizes the incident in *Smoke On The Water* on its next LP.

1972 Apr LP *Machine Head* tops the UK chart for 3 weeks, aided by a TV advertising campaign. (It will later hit US #7.) *Never Before* reaches UK #35. Lord releases LP *Gemini Suite*, with the London Symphony Orchestra.

June The band performs on the first night at the re-opened Rainbow Theatre, London.

Aug The group tours Japan, where concerts are recorded for LP release.

Oct LP *Purple Passages*, a compilation on Warner of tracks from the group's three Tetragrammaton LPs, reaches US #57. Gillan informs the group he is to leave after existing tour commitments.

Dec The group plays its last gig of the year, having been on the road for 44 weeks during 1972.

1973 Jan Live LP *Made In Japan*, recorded during the group's 1972 summer tour, reaches UK #16.

Mar LP *Who Do We Think We Are* hits UK #4 and US #15.

Apr LP *Made In Japan* hits US #6.

May *Woman From Tokyo*, issued as a US single, peaks at #60.

June [29] Gillan quits after a show in Osaka at the end of a tour of Japan. Glover also leaves, initially to be Purple label's A&R man, and to begin a solo career with the label.

Aug *Smoke On The Water*, from LP *Machine Head* about the Montreux Casino fire, is belatedly released in US and hits #4, selling a million and earning the group its only gold disk for a single.

Sept Vocalist David Coverdale (b. Sept.22, 1949, Saltburn, UK), working in a menswear shop in Redcar, Yorks., UK, answers an ad placed by Purple, as does ex-Trapeze bassist Glenn Hughes (b. Penkridge, UK). Coverdale, asked to supply a photo of himself, sends the only one in his possession – taken as a boy in scout uniform. They join as replacements for Gillan and Glover.

1974 Mar LP *Burn*, featuring the new line-up, hits UK #3 and US #9.

Apr *Might Just Take Your Life* makes US #91.

Nov LP *Stormbringer*, recorded in West Germany, hits UK #6 and reaches US #20.

Nov [13] An imposter posing as Blackmore borrows a Porsche in Iowa City and wrecks it, having already conned food and shelter out of several Deep Purple fans. (Blackmore at the time is in US, but in San Francisco with the band.) The imposter is arrested and charged with misrepresentation.

1975 Apr [7] Blackmore quits to put together his own band Rainbow, and is replaced by ex-James Gang guitarist Tommy Bolin (b. 1951, Sioux City, Ia., US).

July Compilation LP *24 Carat Purple* reaches UK #14.

Oct [16] Glover's *The Butterfly Ball*, released late in 1974, is performed at London's Royal Albert Hall, with Gillan as lead vocalist.

Nov LP *Come Taste The Band*, featuring Bolin on guitar, reaches UK #19 and US #43. The group begins a world tour, taking in the Far East, Australasia, US, Europe and UK. *Guinness Book of Records* lists the group as the "world's loudest band".

1976 July The group splits at the end of the UK tour dates in Liverpool. (Coverdale begins a solo career before forming Whitesnake°, Lord and Paice team with Tony Ashton to form Paice, Ashton and Lord, Hughes rejoins his former band Trapeze, and Bolin returns to US to form The Tommy Bolin Band. He will die on Dec.4, 1976, from a heroin overdose.) Gillan's LP *Child In Time* makes UK #55.

Nov LP *Deep Purple Live* (US title: *Made In Europe*) reaches UK #12 and US #148.

1977 May Belated UK release, *Smoke On The Water* reaches #21.

Nov EP *New Live And Rare*, including an unheard live version of *Black Night*, makes UK #31.

1978 Oct Compilation EP *New Live And Rare II* climbs to UK #45.

1979 Apr LP *The Mark II Purple Singles*, a compilation of A and B-sides made by the Gillan/Lord/Glover/Blackmore/Paice line-up, reaches UK #24.

Oct Gillan's LP *Mr. Universe* reaches UK #11.

1980 A bogus Deep Purple, fronted by Rod Evans, plays a US tour. (Blackmore and Glover will take legal action to prevent Evans from using the name.)

June Gillan's *Sleepin' On The Job* makes UK #55.

Aug TV-advertised hits compilation LP *Deepest Purple* tops the UK chart for a week. To tie in with this, *Black Night* is reissued in UK and reaches #43. Gillan's LP *Glory Road* hits UK #3 and makes US #183.

Oct Gillan's *Trouble* reaches UK #14.

Nov Compilation EP *New Live And Rare III*, including *Smoke On The Water*, makes UK #48. LP *Deepest Purple/The Very Best Of Deep Purple* reaches US #148.

Dec Live LP *In Concert*, featuring tracks recorded between 1970-72, makes UK #30.

1981 Feb Gillan's *Mutually Assured Destruction* peaks at UK #32.

Apr Gillan's LP *Future Shock* hits UK #2.

May Gillan revives Freddy Cannon's 1960 hit *New Orleans*, reaching UK #17.

June Gillan's *No Laughing In Heaven* makes UK #31.

Oct Gillan reaches UK #36 with *Nightmare*.

Nov LP *Double Trouble*, second Gillan album of the year, makes UK #12.

1982 Jan Gillan makes UK #25 with *Restless*.

Sept LP *Deep Purple Live In London*, originally recorded for BBC radio in 1974, reaches UK #23. Gillan's *Living For The City* reaches UK #50.

Oct Gillan's LP *Magic* makes UK #17.

1983 Sept Gillan joins Black Sabbath for LP *Born Again*.

1984 Nov Amid rumors that each member is offered $2 million to re-form, the group begins a world tour with the line-up of Blackmore, Gillan, Glover, Lord and Paice. The band signs to Polydor Records (Mercury in US) and releases LP *Perfect Strangers*, which hits UK #5 and US #17.

1985 Feb Title track from LP *Perfect Strangers* reaches UK #48, while *Knocking At Your Back Door* makes US #61.

June *Knocking At Your Back Door* reaches UK #68, while double compilation LP *The Anthology* makes UK #50.

1987 Feb LP *The House Of Blue Light* hits UK #10 and US #34. The band tours Europe, and causes a storm when Blackmore repeatedly refuses to play *Smoke On The Water*.

1988 June LP *Nobody's Perfect*, recorded live during 1987, reaches UK #38. From it, a re-recording of the band's original hit *Hush* makes UK #62.

July A 2-month "Nobody's Perfect" US tour begins in Saratoga, N.Y.

Aug LP *Nobody's Perfect* peaks at US #105.

DEF LEPPARD

Joe Elliott (vocals)
Phil Collen (guitar)
Steve Clark (guitar)
Rick Savage (bass)
Rick Allen (drums)

1977 The group is formed in Sheffield, UK, when ex-schoolboys Pete Willis and Elliott (b. Aug.1, 1959) leave their own fledgling group to join heavy metal band Atomic Mass led by British Rail apprentice Savage (b. Dec.2, 1960). Elliott abandons his guitar playing ambitions to take lead vocals and Savage switches to bass, allowing Willis to play guitar. The name is changed to Def Leppard (from Elliott's initial suggestion of Deaf Leopard). Clark (b. Apr.23, 1960), a college acquaintance of Willis, joins on second guitar.

1978 July The group's live debut is at Westfield School, Sheffield, for a £5 fee. Small pub gigs follow with a series of drummers (none of whom proves suitable).

Nov The group records a 3-track EP with a stand-in drummer in a small studio in Hull and forms its own Bludgeon Riffola label with a loan from Elliott's father. It recruits Derbyshire drummer Allen (b. Nov.1, 1963), who at 15 is the youngest in a young band (Elliott is the oldest at 19).

1979 Jan The 3-track EP *Getcha Rocks Off* is released in an initial pressing of 1,000. It is picked up first by local Radio Hallam's rock show, for which the band records six songs. A session for BBC Radio 1's prestigious John Peel show follows and the music press identifies the band with the emergent new wave of British heavy metal. The record is picked up and re-pressed by Phonogram Records and sells 24,000 copies. Sheffield record retailer Peter Martin notes the

demand for the record and during the summer he and promoter Frank Stuart Brown become the group's first managers.

Aug Def Leppard signs to Phonogram's Vertigo label and begins recording with producer Tom Allom. An LP is completed in only 18 days.

Nov Vertigo debut *Wasted* reaches UK #61.

1980 Feb The follow-up, *Hello America*, makes UK #45.

Mar Debut LP *On Through The Night* peaks at UK #15. The band supports Sammy Hagar and AC/DC° on UK tours and meets Peter Mensch, an employee of AC/DC's New York-based Leber/Krebs management. He becomes the group's new manager and directs it towards the US market. UK fans react against this new commercialism and with a hail of bottles force the band to leave the stage at the Reading rock festival. US audiences are enthusiastic about the band after a national tour opening for Ted Nugent°.

July LP *On Through The Night* reaches US #51.

1981 The group records with a new producer, Robert "Mutt" Lange, under whose guidance LP *High'n'Dry* takes 3 months to complete and the smoother, tighter result is aimed particularly at US FM rock radio.

July LP *High'n'Dry* enters the UK chart, reaching #26 and makes US #38, with the help of touring. Willis finds himself increasingly out of step with the rest of the band and considers leaving.

Dec By the end of the year the group, exhausted by the demands of constant gigging, slips into a period of inactivity.

1982 The group spends several months in the studio working on an LP, again with Lange producing. During the sessions, Willis' incompatability with the rest of the group comes to a head and he is fired. Collen (b. Dec.8, 1957), ex-metal band Girl, replaces him.

1983 Feb *Photograph* enters the UK chart, reaching #66. LP *Pyromania* begins a 92-week US chart run, during which time it will spend 2weeks at #2, beneath Michael Jackson's° *Thriller*.

Mar LP *Pyromania* enters the UK chart, reaching #18. The group begins a world tour to promote it, starting in UK, then Europe, and by the time it reaches US the LP is in the top 10. With live support, it continues selling and will eventually sell more than six and half million copies in US alone. The US tour is followed by Japanese and Australian dates.

May *Photograph* reaches US #12.

Aug *Rock Of Ages* reaches UK #41 and US #16.

Nov *Foolin'* reaches US #28.

1984 The group members take an 8-month break before teaming up to record with Lange. But pre-production in Dublin indicates that Lange has been overworked and is too tired to work effectively (he had followed *Pyromania* with *Heartbreak City* for The Cars° and Foreigner's° 4).

June A remix of *Bringin' On The Heartbreak* from LP *High'n'Dry* reaches US #61. LP *High And Dry* with a remix of *Bringin' On The Heartbreak* and new track *Me And My Wine* re-charts to make US #72.

Aug Recording begins in Holland with producer/writer Jim Steinman (of Meatloaf and Bonnie Tyler° repute).

Dec Recording is halted for a Christmas break and the group decides to fire Steinman and produce the LP itself.

Dec [31] Driving from Sheffield to Derbyshire, Allen is involved in a serious auto accident. The impact of the crash tears off his left arm and badly damages his right. Surgeons sew the arm back on only to be forced to remove it 3 days later when infection sets in.

1985 Jan [2] The rest of the group returns to Holland to continue recording. Allen affirms by phone that he wants to return to the band.

Apr Allen rejoins the group. Little progress is made in the studio, even with the services of Lange's engineer Nigel Green. It is decided to scrap the tapes and wait until Lange is ready to work. Meanwhile, Allen learns to play in spite of his disability. He works with a Fairlight computer to create drum sounds and uses it to record most of the LP's drum tracks on his own. He has a sophisticated Simmons electronic drumkit custom-built, with an SD57 computer to store sounds and fills. By summer, Lange is ready to record.

1986 Aug Def Leppard plays three "Monsters of Rock" festivals in UK and Europe. Receptions, especially for Allen, are warm and the experience gives them fresh motivation in the studio.

1987 July *Animal*, the first extract from forthcoming LP *Hysteria*, is released, hitting UK #6.

Aug LP *Hysteria*, 3 years in the making, is released. It enters the UK chart at #1. A highly successful UK tour follows.

Sept *Pour Some Sugar On Me* reaches UK #20. *Women* reaches US #80.

Oct The group embarks on a major world tour.

Nov *Hysteria* makes UK #26.

Dec *Animal* reaches US #19.

1988 Mar *Hysteria* hits US #10.

Apr *Armageddon It* peaks at UK #20.

July *Pour Some Sugar On Me* hits US #2. After 49 weeks on the US charts, LP *Hysteria* finally climbs to the top. (Only Fleetwood Mac's° and Whitney Houston's° eponymous LPs have taken longer.) The band becomes the first to have sold more than 5 million copies of two consecutive LPs in US.

July [16] Road crew technician Steve Cayter dies of a brain hemorrhage on stage before a show in Alpine, Wis.

Oct A year-long worldwide tour concludes.

DESMOND DEKKER

1963 Having worked as a welder before joining studio group The Aces, Dekker (b. Desmond Dacris, 1943, Kingston, Jamaica) records his first Jamaican single, *Honour Your Mother And Father*, for Yabba label. (With The Aces, he will have hits in Jamaica with *Generosity* (1964), *Get Up Adinah* (1964), *King Of The Ska* (1965), *007 (Shanty Town)* (1966), *Jezebel* (1966), and *Rock Steady* (1966).)

1966 After a variety of producers, Dekker and The Aces start recording for Leslie Kong (and will continue to be produced exclusively by Kong until his death in 1971).

1967 Aug *007 (Shanty Town)*, a chart-topper in Jamaica, is a celebration of the Kingston "rude boy" lifestyle. It is an underground club hit in the US for 6 months before it reaches #14. Its release in UK on Pyramid achieves #14.

1969 Apr Dekker becomes the first Jamaican artist to hit UK #1 with *The Israelites*, which tops the chart for 3 weeks.

DESMOND DEKKER *cont.*

June *The Israelites* hits US #9.
July *It Miek* hits UK #7 and LP *This Is Desmond Dekker* reaches UK #27.
Sept LP *Israelites* reaches US #153.
1970 Jan *Pickney Gal* climbs to UK #42.
Oct Dekker almost scores a second UK #1 with *You Can Get It If You Really Want*, missing out at #2. Written by Jimmy Cliff°, it is the first non-original song Dekker has recorded.
1971 After his producer Kong dies of a heart attack, Dekker, who has visited the UK regularly since the success of *007 (Shanty Town)*, moves to London. But by this time, the ska phenomenon is being replaced by reggae, with a new generation of Jamaican artists emerging, spearheaded by Bob Marley & The Wailers°. Dekker fails to enjoy further mainstream chart success.
1975 June *The Israelites* is reissued in UK by Cactus reggae label and hits UK #10.
Sept *Sing A Little Song* reaches UK #16.
1980 Dekker performs and records on a sporadic basis from London, recording versions of his old hits on Stiff LP *Black And Dekker*.
1981 LP *Compass Point* is produced by Robert Palmer° but fails to impress.
1985 Jan [6] Dekker performs with fellow reggae artists Dennis Brown, Smiley Culture, Lee Perry and others, at an Ethiopian Benefit Concert at Brixton Academy, London.

DELANEY & BONNIE

Delaney Bramlett
Bonnie Lynn Bramlett

1967 Delaney Bramlett (b. July 1, 1939, Pontotoc Co., Miss., US) and Bonnie Lynn (b. Nov.8, 1944, Acton, Ill., US) meet in Los Angeles on Jack Good's rock TV show "Shindig". He is in resident band The Shindogs, while she is a session singer (formerly with Ike and Tina Turner's° Ikettes). They marry within a week of meeting.
1968 They record LP *Home* with Booker T. and The MG's° for Stax Records in Memphis, but it is not released at this time.
1969 July They sign to Elektra, releasing LP *The Original Delaney And Bonnie – Accept No Substitute*, which makes a minor US chart showing at #175.
Sept Delaney and Bonnie and Friends (the latter a frequently-changing aggregation of session men) are hired as opening act on US tour by Blind Faith°, which leads to immediate friendship with Eric Clapton°, who admires their music and joins in inter-date jam sessions on the tour bus.
Dec [15] Delaney and Bonnie appear as guest musicians with John Lennon's° Plastic Ono Band for the "War Is Over" concert at The Lyceum, London, UK.
1970 Jan After Blind Faith folds, Clapton joins Delaney and Bonnie's Friends as guitarist on a 2-month US tour of their own, which he has agreed to co-finance.
Comin' Home, credited jointly to the group and Clapton, is released by Atco Records, reaching US #84 and UK #16. It is their only UK hit single. The Bonnie-sung ballad *Groupie (Superstar)* on the B-side will become a million-selling song when covered and revised to *Superstar* by The Carpenters° in 1971.
Apr Clapton departs at tour's end to work on his first solo LP, on which the Bramletts will both guest, and many of the Friends (Jim Gordon, Carl Radle, Bobby Keys, Jim Price and Rita Coolidge) also leave to become part of "Mad Dogs and Englishmen" touring group with Joe Cocker°.
June LP *Delaney & Bonnie & Friends On Tour With Eric Clapton* reaches US #29 and UK #39.
Sept *Soul Shake*, the B-side of *Free The People* which stalls at US #75, makes US #43.
Nov LP *To Bonnie From Delaney* reaches US #58.
1971 May LP *Motel Shot* peaks at #65 in US.
July *Never Ending Song Of Love* is their biggest US hit single, reaching #13. It is quickly covered and taken to UK #2 by The New Seekers.
Nov *Only You And I Know* makes US #20.
1972 Feb *Move 'Em Out* climbs to US #59.
Apr *Where There's A Will There's A Way* ends their singles chart career (US #99), before a label switch to CBS/Columbia Records sees LP *D & B Together* climb to US #133, but the title proves ironic, as the couple divorce and split professionally soon afterwards. (Both will record solo through the later 1970s, without great success.)
1979 Mar [16] Bonnie Bramlett makes rock headlines when, singing backup vocals with Stephen Stills in Columbus, Oh., US, she gets into a fierce argument with a less-than-serious Elvis Costello° (staying at the same Holiday Inn) about racial matters relating to music, and punches him in the face.

JOHN DENVER

1965 Denver (b. Henry John Deutschendorf, Dec.31, 1943, Roswell, N.M., US) having studied architecture in Lubbock, Tex. travels to California to pursue his interest in folk music. While working as a draughtsman in LA, he plays the folk scene at night, eventually recording demos, and adopting a performing surname after his favorite city. He joins folk group The Chad Mitchell Trio, replacing Mitchell himself, having auditioned with 250 others.
1967 Denver marries Ann Martell, whom he met at a Trio concert in 1966 at her college, Gustavus Adolphus in Minnesota.
1968 After 3 years in the trio, during which he has been developing his songwriting skills, Denver signs as a solo artist to RCA Records.
1969 Nov His first solo LP *Rhymes And Reasons* reaches US #148. It features his composition *Leaving On A Jet Plane* which is covered by Peter, Paul and Mary° and hits US #1 to become a million-seller.
1970 May LP *Take Me Tomorrow* reaches US #197.
1971 Aug *Take Me Home, Country Roads*, his debut chart single, hits US #2 and becomes a million-seller. It is credited to Denver with Fat City (Bill Danoff and Taffy Nivert, the writers of the song) and taken from LP *Poems, Prayers And Promises*, which makes US #15 and is his first gold LP, selling over a half million copies.
Dec *Friends With You* reaches US #47. LP *Aerie* peaks at US #75.
1972 Mar A revival of Buddy Holly's° *Everyday* reaches US #81.
Aug *Goodbye Again* makes US #88.
Nov LP *Rocky Mountain High* is his first US top 10 LP at #4 and earns another gold disk. It is dedicated to Denver's favorite environment – the Colorado mountains – where he and his wife have settled in Aspen.
1973 Feb Title track from *Rocky Mountain High* hits US #9.
Apr [29] Denver begins a weekly live UK TV special "The John Denver Show" on BBC2, from the company's Shepherds Bush Green studios.
June Denver makes a dual UK chart debut with the LPs *Poems, Prayers And Promises* and *Rhymes And Reasons*, which reach #19 and #21 respectively.
July *I'd Rather Be A Cowboy* reaches US #62.
Sept LP *Farewell Andromeda* reaches US #16 (earning a gold disk), while extracted *Farewell Andromeda (Welcome To My Morning)* makes US #89.
1974 Jan *Please, Daddy* reaches US #69.
Mar Compilation LP *John Denver's Greatest Hits* tops the US chart for 3 weeks (and will sell five million copies). He also hits US #1 with *Sunshine On My Shoulders* (written with Dick Kniss and Mike Taylor). It is used as the theme song to the TV movie of the same title, starring Cliff DeYoung and Elizabeth Cheshire, and also its series sequel "Sunshine".
July *Annie's Song*, a love song for his wife Ann, inspired by a temporary rift in their marriage, tops the US chart for 2 weeks and earns a gold disk for million-plus sales. It was written by Denver in 10 minutes while riding on a ski-lift.
Aug LP *Back Home Again* is his second consecutive US LP chart topper, and another million-seller.
Oct *Annie's Song* tops the UK chart for a week. (It is Denver's only UK solo hit single.) LP *Back Home Again* and compilation LP *The Best Of John Denver* hit UK #3 and #7 at the same time.
Nov Title track from *Back Home Again* hits US #5, becoming Denver's second million-selling single from the LP. Denver is proclaimed as the state's poet laureate by the Governor of Colorado for his promotion of the Rocky Mountains.
1975 Feb *Sweet Surrender*, from Walt Disney film *The Bears And I*, reaches US #13.
Mar Double live LP *An Evening With John Denver*, recorded at Universal City Amphitheater, Cal., on a sold-out US concert tour, hits US #2 (another gold disk) and makes UK #31.
June *Thank God I'm A Country Boy*, written by Denver's long serving back-up guitarist John Summers and originally on live LP *Back Home Again*, is extracted in a new version and hits US #1 (his

third US #1 and fifth million-selling single).
Sept *I'm Sorry* is another US chart-topper and million-seller.
Oct B-side of *I'm Sorry*, a tribute to marine explorer Jacques Cousteau and titled after his ship, *Calypso*, picks up major airplay in its own right and peaks at US #26. LP *Windsong*, from which both sides of the single are taken, hits US #1 for 2 weeks and reaches UK #14. (Denver will shortly launch his own record label, named Windsong after this LP. Its most successful act will be The Starland Vocal Band, including former Fat City members and *Take Me Home, Country Roads* writers Bill and Taffy Danoff, whose *Afternoon Delight* will hit US #1 in 1976.)
Dec Seasonal LP *Rocky Mountain Christmas* reaches US #14 and earns another gold disk, while seasonally-packaged double LP *The John Denver Gift Pack* (comprising both the Christmas LP and *Windsong*) makes US #138.
1976 Jan *Fly Away*, with vocal back-up from Olivia Newton-John° (who had a UK hit with a cover of *Take Me Home, Country Roads* in 1973), reaches US #13.
Mar [29] Denver begins a week at the London Palladium, which is recorded for future release. His band comprises John Sommers and Steve Weisberg (guitars), Dick Kniss (bass), Hal Blaine (drums) and Lee Holdridge (arrangements).
Apr *Looking For Space* makes US #29.
May *It Makes Me Giggle* peaks at US #60.
June UK-only release LP, *Live In London*, recorded earlier in the year, hits UK #2.
July Denver plays a week of concerts in LA (he donates the proceeds to more than thirty different charities).
Sept LP *Spirit* hits US #7, earning a platinum disk, and UK #9. Extracted *Like A Sad Song* reaches US #36.
Dec Seasonal *Christmas For Cowboys* makes US #58. *Newsweek* proclaims Denver "the most popular singer in America", and the Country Music Association (CMA) votes him Entertainer of the Year.

1977 Jan *Baby, You Look Good To Me Tonight* reaches US #65.
Mar A second compilation LP, *John Denver's Greatest Hits, Volume 2* (UK title: *Best Of John Denver Vol.2*), hits US #6, earning another platinum disk, and UK #9.
Mar [22] Johnny Cash°, Glen Campbell° and Roger Miller° join Denver in his US ABC TV special "Thank God I'm A Country Boy".
Apr [21] Denver guests in "Sinatra and Friends" US TV special.
May *My Sweet Lady* (originally B-side of *Thank God I'm A Country Boy*) reaches US #32.
Oct He makes his starring film debut in comedy *Oh, God*, with George Burns.
Nov Denver plays the Blaisdell Arena, Honolulu, Ha.
Dec LP *I Want To Live* reaches US #45.
1978 Jan *How Can I Leave You Again* peaks at US #44.
Feb LP *I Want To Live* makes UK #25.
Feb [23] Denver emcees the 20th annual Grammy awards.
Mar [8] Denver plays a week at South Lake Tahoe, as his annual Pro/Am Ski tournament takes place.
Apr *It Amazes Me* peaks at US #59.
May *I Want To Live* makes US #55.
May [15] Denver's 2-month US tour ends at LA's Forum.
July Irish flautist James Galway hits UK #3 with an instrumental version of *Annie's Song*.
1979 Jan [9] Denver appears in the benefit concert "A Gift of Song – Music for UNICEF", at UN General Assembly in New York, with Abba°, The Bee Gees°, Rod Stewart°, Earth, Wind & Fire°, and others. The show is taped for TV broadcast, and a compilation LP is released. (The performers each pledge royalties from one new song to UNICEF, raising $500,000. Denver is increasingly involved in social and environmental causes including a 2-year commitment to the Presidential Commission on World and Domestic Hunger, and supporting the Wilderness Society Friends of the Earth and the World Wildlife Fund.)
Mar LP *John Denver* reaches US #25 and UK #68.
June [11-21] Denver records LP *Autograph* at Filmways/Heider studios, Hollywood, Cal., with his regular studio and live band – James Burton (guitar), Glen D. Hardin (keyboards), Emory Gordy Jr. (bass), Hal Blaine (drums), Jim Horn (horns), Herb Pedersen (banjo), Denny Brooks (acoustic guitar) and Danny Wheetman (mandolin and harmonica).
Dec LP *A Christmas Together*, recorded with The Muppets, reaches US #26 and is a million-seller. Denver also guests on a Muppets Christmas TV special.
1980 Apr *Autograph* reaches US #52, while LP of same title makes #39.
June *Dancing With The Mountains* peaks at US #97.
1981 Aug *Some Days Are Diamonds (Some Days Are Stone)* reaches US #36, while LP *Some Days Are Diamonds*, recorded at the Sound Emporium, Nashville, Tenn. with producer Larry Butler, peaks at US #32. Denver's performance in Tokyo, Japan, is attended by the Crown Prince of Japan (his first pop concert).
Nov *The Cowboy And The Lady* reaches US #66.
1982 Jan Denver duets with Placido Domingo on *Perhaps Love*. It makes US #59 and UK #46.
May *Shanghai Breezes* reaches US #31. It is taken from LP *Seasons Of The Heart*, which makes US #39. (It is his first self-produced LP, with help from Barney Wyckoff, and his last to earn a gold disk.)
Aug Title track from *Seasons Of The Heart* reaches US #78.
1983 Oct LP *It's About Time*, recorded at Criteria studios, Miami, Fla., with help from The Wailers and The I-Threes, reaches US #61 and UK #90. Shortly after their 15th anniversary, Denver and his wife Ann separate, and later divorce.
1984 Feb He writes and performs *The Gold And Beyond*, the theme song for the 1984 Winter Olympics, singing it for US TV on the slopes of Mount Sarajevo. He opens an exhibition of his photographs (a 15-year legacy of Rocky Mountain landscape and wildlife) at New York's Hammer Gallery.
Sept Denver travels to Africa on a fact-finding trip for The Hunger Project. He records *Africa Sunrise* in Burkina Faso and Mozambique, which will be included on LP *Dreamland Express*.
Nov He plays an informal concert at the US Embassy in Moscow, and teams with French singer Sylvie Vartan for *Love Again*, which makes US #85 (his last US Hot 100 entry).
Dec TV-advertised compilation LP *The John Denver Collection* reaches UK #20.
1985 Aug LP *Dreamland Express*, produced by Roger Nichols, reaches US #90.

JOHN DENVER *cont.*

1986 July [30] RCA Records drops Denver. Industry insiders speculate that RCA's new owner General Electric, a top military contractor, takes exception to his recording *What Are We Making Weapons For?*

1988 Aug *Aviation Week & Space Technology* magazine, under the headline "Ural Mountain High", says that Denver has asked the Soviet Union to launch him to the Mir Space Station. The Soviets are reported to be considering it, with a price tag of $10 million.

Oct LP *Higher Ground*, his first in 3 years on new Windstar label, enters the US country chart.

DEPECHE MODE

Dave Gahan (vocals)
Martin Gore (synthesizer)
Andy Fletcher (bass synthesizer)
Vince Clarke (synthesizer)

1976 Having formed a synth-and-two-guitar trio while still at school in Basildon, Essex, UK, Gore, Fletcher and Clarke are joined by singer Gahan. After leaving school, they replace the guitars with two more synthesizers, naming themselves Depeche Mode after spotting the phrase (meaning "fast fashion") in a French style magazine.

1980 Dec Playing a regular "Futurist" night at the Bridge House in East London, they are spotted by Some Bizzare Records' boss Stevo, who includes their track *Photographic* on his compilation LP *Some Bizzare Album*, but does not sign them.

1981 Feb Demo tapes sent to several labels evoke no response, but they are approached at a London gig by independent Mute label's owner Daniel Miller, whose act Fad Gadget they are supporting. Miller signs the group to Mute, and it remains with him through the 80s in spite of overtures from larger companies.

Apr Debut *Dreaming of Me*, written by Clarke and produced by Miller, reaches UK #57.

July *New Life* climbs to UK #11.

Oct *Just Can't Get Enough* hits UK #8.

Nov Debut LP *Speak And Spell* hits UK #10.

Dec Clarke, the chief songwriter, but a studio addict who is unwilling to tour, leaves the band to form Yazoo° with Alison Moyet°. (After his departure, virtually all the band's material will be written by Gore.)

1982 Jan Clarke is replaced by vocalist and synth player Alan Wilder, ex-The Hitmen, who initially joins for their first US trip, but remains permanently.

Mar *See You*, recorded between Clarke's departure and Wilder's arrival, hits UK #6 while the band is making its US debut at The Ritz Club in New York.

May *The Meaning Of Love* reaches UK #12.

Sept *Leave In Silence* peaks at UK #18.

Oct LP *A Broken Frame* hits UK #8 and the group embarks on its biggest UK tour yet.

1983 Mar *Get The Balance Right* reaches UK #13.

Aug *Everything Counts* hits UK #6 and LP *Construction Time Again* hits UK #6.

Oct *Love In Itself* climbs to UK #21, after seven consecutive top 20 hits.

1984 Apr *People Are People* hits UK #4.

Sept *Master And Servant* hits UK #9.

Oct LP *Some Great Reward* hits UK #5.

Nov Double A-side *Somebody/Blasphemous Rumours* makes UK #16.

1985 June *Shake The Disease* reaches UK #18.

Aug *People Are People*, their US chart debut, peaks at #13 after a 3-month climb. LP *Some Great Reward* makes US #51.

Sept *Master And Servant* reaches only US #87.

Oct *It's Called A Heart* makes UK #18. Compilation LP *The Singles 1981-85*, the gatefold sleeve of which contains a collage of the group's bad reviews, hits UK #6. Released in US as *Catching Up With Depeche Mode*, the LP makes #113.

1986 Jan The group starts work on a new LP at the Hansa Studios in Berlin, West Germany.

Mar Using a guitar for the first time on a single, Depeche Mode climbs to UK #15 with *Stripped*.

Apr LP *Black Celebration* hits UK #4 in its week of entry.

May *A Question Of Lust* reaches UK #28.

Aug The group completes a lengthy tour and begins an 8-month sabbatical, during which they will write material for a new LP.

Sept *A Question Of Time* reaches UK #17.

1987 Feb The group starts work on new LP at The Studio Guillaume Tell, Paris, with engineer/producer Dave Bascombe.

May *Strangelove* climbs to UK #16.

Sept *Never Let Me Down* reaches UK #22.

Oct LP *Music For The Masses* hits UK #10.

Nov LP *Music For The Masses* makes US #35.

1988 Jan *Behind The Wheel* reaches UK #21. The group has had 7 years of consistent UK hits and has become a major hit in Europe, particularly in France and West Germany, through constant tours.

June A sell-out world tour ends in a 70,000 attendance at the Rose Bowl, Pasadena, Cal. as part of UK festival with Orchestral Manoeuvres In The Dark (OMD)°.

Sept [7] Depeche Mode features a re-release of *Strangelove* on the annual MTV awards show in US, as LP *Music For The Masses* tops 2½ million sales worldwide.

DEVO

Bob Mothersbaugh (guitar and vocals)
Mark Mothersbaugh (synthesizers)
Bob Casale (guitar)
Jerry Casale (bass)
Alan Myers (drums)

1974 After early 1970s experimental approach to music while at Kent State University, Oh., US, Casale and Mark Mothersbaugh form a four-piece version of the band in Akron, Oh., comprising Casale, the Mothersbaugh brothers, and their third sibling Jim on drums. The latter leaves, replaced by Myers, Casale brings in his own brother and Mark goes on to play in Jackrabbit (alongside Chrissie Hynde, later of The Pretenders°).

1976 Sept They re-group in Akron as The De-Evolution Band, based on the way they see their music ("the sound of things falling apart"), soon shortening the name to Devo.

Dec Their first release, the double A-side *Jocko Homo/Mongoloid*, recorded in a garage, is issued in US on their own Booji Boy label, named after their supposed "mascot".

1977 Putting together a whole mock philosophy of De-Evolution as a publicity campaign, the band makes its own 16mm movie, *In The Beginning Was The End*, to explain it. This, initially, is shown before each gig.

July *(I Can't Get Me No) Satisfaction*, their fractured version of the 1965 Rolling Stones'° classic, is the second US release on Booji Boy. They make a New York live debut shortly after, introduced on stage by David Bowie°, and befriended and championed by him and Iggy Pop°. This arouses interest from Stiff Records in UK.

1978 Mar Stiff licenses Devo's Booji Boy material for UK, and releases *Jocko Homo/Mongoloid*, which climbs to UK #51.

May *(I Can't Get Me No) Satisfaction* reaches UK #41, while they also make a UK live debut. Their highly non-conformist style of presentation, robot-like in matching one-piece industrial suits, fascinates the UK rock media.

Aug Last UK Stiff hit *Be Stiff* reaches UK #71, by which time the band is signed to Virgin in UK and Warner Bros. in US.

Sept Debut Virgin releases in UK are *Come Back Jonee*, which achieves #60, and LP *Are We Not Men? We Are Devo!*, produced in Germany by Brian Eno°, which makes UK #12.

1979 Jan Mini-LP *Be Stiff*, a compilation of Booji Boy singles, released in UK, does not chart.

July LP *Duty Now For The Future*, produced by Ken Scott, reaches UK #49. They appear in Neil Young's° movie *Rust Never Sleeps*, the title of which is an ad slogan given to Young by Devo.

1980 May LP *Freedom Of Choice*, co-produced by Robert Margouleff, reaches UK #47.

Nov *Whip It* (taken from LP *Freedom Of Choice*, which climbs to US #22 in its wake), is their first US chart entry and their best-selling single, reaching US #14, and earning a gold disk for million-plus US sales. Less successful in UK, it reaches #51.

1981 Devo appears in another Neil Young° film, *Human Highway*.

May Mini-LP *Devo Live* reaches US #49. It is unsuccessful in UK, but becomes a chart-topper in Australia, where the group will play a sell-out tour the following year.

Sept LP *New Traditionalists*, a self-produced set, hosts no hit singles, but makes UK #50 and US #24.

Oct A revival of Lee Dorsey's° *Working In The Coal Mine*, recorded for the National Lampoon movie *Heavy Metal*, reaches US #43.

1982 Dec LP *Oh No, It's Devo!*, produced by Roy Thomas Baker, climbs to US #47.

1983 June They undertake more movie song work with the title song to *Doctor Detroit*, which climbs to US #59. They also make their own semi-spoof documentary home video, *The Men Who Make The Music*.

1984 *Are We Not Men?*, a home video of Devo promo clips from 1977-82, is released.

1985 Oct LP *Shout* is their first on Warner Bros. in UK and includes a version of Jimi Hendrix° song *Are U Experienced*.

1987 Aug *E-Z Listening Disk*, a US-only CD on Ryko-Disk featuring muzak versions of their hits, is a stop-gap release while they prepare a new LP. Meanwhile, Mark Mothersbaugh mounts an exhibition of postcards in LA, and works with a band called The Visiting Kids.

1988 Aug After 2 years' work in their Marina Del Rey Studio, Devo releases LP *Total Devo* on Enigma. David Kendrick takes over from Alan Myers.

DEXY'S MIDNIGHT RUNNERS

Kevin Rowland (vocals and guitar)
Al Archer (guitar)
Pete Williams (bass)
Pete Saunders (organ)
Andy Growcott (drums)
"Big" Jimmy Patterson (trombone)
Steve "Babyface" Spooner (alto sax)
J.B. (tenor sax)

1977 Nov Rowland (b. Aug.17, 1953, Wolverhampton, UK, of Irish parents), having made his playing debut in Lucy and The Lovers, is guitarist in Birmingham UK-based punk band The Killjoys on its only single *Johnny Won't Get To Heaven* on Raw Records. It flops and Rowland and the band's rhythm guitarist Al Archer leave to form their own band in the 1960s soul mold.

1978 July Dexy's Midnight Runners is formed (named after dexedrine, a widely-used pep pill, though the band itself abides by a strict "no drink or drugs" code), with Rowland, Archer, Saunders, Spooner, Patterson, Williams, J.B. and Bobby Junior on drums. They adopt a visual image taken from characters in Robert De Niro movie *Mean Streets*.

1979 Bernie Rhodes, ex-manager of The Clash°, signs the band after seeing it play and negotiates a recording deal with EMI.

1980 Feb *Dance Stance*, a Rowland comment on anti-Irish prejudice, reaches UK #40.

May *Geno*, a tribute to 1960s UK soul singer Geno Washington, tops the UK chart for 2 weeks.

Aug *There There My Dear* hits UK #7. Debut LP *Searching For The Young Soul Rebels* is only released after Rowland seized the master tapes from producer Pete Wingfield and refused to return them until more favorable contract terms were granted. It hits UK #6. Rowland is given a suspended prison sentence after a fight with members of another band during filming of *There There My Dear* promo video.

Oct *Keep It Part Two*, released as a single at Rowland's insistence but against the wishes of the rest of the band and EMI, who protest its uncommerciality, fails to chart and acrimony breaks out in the band's ranks.

Nov [7] The band splits into two: Rowland and Patterson remain as the nucleus of Dexy's Midnight Runners and recruit Micky Billingham (keyboards), Steve Wynne (bass), Billy Adams (guitar), Paul Speare (tenor sax), Brian Maurice (alto sax) and Seb Shelton (drums); the others leave to form The Bureau.

1981 Mar *Plan B*, recorded by the new band but released by EMI unwillingly, during rock-bottom relations between Rowland and the label, peaks at UK #58. The band leaves EMI shortly afterwards.

Aug It signs to Phonogram's Mercury label. *Show Me*, produced by Tony Visconti, reaches UK #16.

Oct Bass player Wynne leaves and is replaced by Giorgio Kilkenny. *Liars A To E*, an eccentric single with string accompaniment, fails to chart.

Nov The band appears live at the Old Vic, London, in "The Projected Passion Review" and gains positive reviews from a press previously alienated by Rowland.

1982 Apr The band takes a new direction with a fusion of its traditional soul style with Irish folk, and adds a three-piece fiddle section (Helen O'Hara, Steve Brennan and Roger MacDuff) which shares billing on records as The Emerald Express. The visual image also changes: the original "Mean Streets" look and the later anoraks and sports gear are discarded for dungarees and gypsy-like accoutrements. *The Celtic Soul Brothers*, resulting from the new collaboration, reaches UK #45.

June Surviving original group member Patterson leaves, followed by the two sax players, who feel their role in the new music is too insignificant.

Aug *Come On Eileen* tops the UK chart for 4 weeks and sells over a million copies in UK. LP *Too-Rye-Ay* hits UK #2.

Oct A revival of Van Morrison's° *Jackie Wilson Said* hits UK #5. The band is billed as Kevin Rowland & Dexy's Midnight Runners, which Rowland explains is a basic nucleus of himself, Adams and Shelton, augmented by hired musicians in various combinations as necessary. When the band appears playing the hit on UK TV's "Top of the Pops", an apparent misunderstanding on the part of the TV production staff leads to the display of a large photo of darts player Jocky Wilson as a studio backdrop, instead of the intended Jackie Wilson picture.

Dec *Let's Get This Straight (From The Start)* reaches UK #17.

1983 Apr A new version of *The Celtic Soul Rebels*, giving Rowland lead billing, reaches UK #20. A tour by the augmented band follows, after which it splits up, and the nucleus musicians retreat into silence for a while. *Come On Eileen* tops the US chart for 1 week, replacing Michael Jackson's° *Billie Jean*, and is itself replaced by Jackson's *Beat It*. LP *Too-Rye-Ay* reaches US #14.

June Follow-up *The Celtic Soul Brothers* peaks at US #86.

1985 Sept After a long silence, LP *Don't Stand Me Down* reaches UK #22. At Rowland's insistence no single is taken from it. The band's associated live shows are not well received and it splits again afterwards.

1986 Dec After 3 years out of the UK singles chart, the band (now basically a solo Rowland) returns with *Because Of You*, the theme tune to UK BBC TV's "Brush Strokes" comedy series, which reaches UK #13.

1988 May Rowland returns as a soloist (though still with Mercury and billed as Kevin Rowland of Dexy's Midnight Runners) with *Walk Away* and LP *The Wanderer*, but neither charts.

NEIL DIAMOND

1955 Dec Diamond (b. Jan.24, 1941, Brooklyn, New York, US) becomes interested in songwriting while still at school, when folk singer Pete Seeger visits his winter holiday group at Surprise Lake camp.

1960 He teams with friend Jack Parker as an Everly Brothers°-style duo, Neil and Jack, cutting two unsuccessful singles, *What Will I Do* and *I'm Afraid* on small New York label Duel Records.

1962 While at New York University on a fencing scholarship, he drops out to become an apprentice songwriter at a small publishing company, Sunbeam Music, earning $50 a week.

1962/64 He has several "production line" songwriting jobs for 2 years, until he sets up on his own in a tiny Manhattan office above a jazz club.

1964 One-off solo single, *Clown Town*, for CBS/Columbia Records, fails to sell. He continues to perform as well as write, mainly in Greenwich Village coffee houses.

1965 Diamond's songs start to earn money with hitmaking acts: Jay & The Americans reach US #18 with *Sunday And Me*; Cliff Richard° records *Just Another Guy* (B-side of his UK #1 hit *The Minute You're Gone*) and further songs are cut by Jimmy Clanton, Bobby Vinton° and The Angels among others. He meets songwriters Jeff Barry and Ellie Greenwich at a demo session and his style and material impress them. He joins their writing and publishing organization.

1966 Barry and Greenwich arrange an audition with Atlantic Records, which recommends Diamond to Bert Berns at Atlantic-distributed New York label Bang Records. He signs to Bang with Barry and Greenwich as his producers.

July Bang debut, the introspective *Solitary Man*, charts at US #55 and just fails to enter UK top 50.

Oct *Cherry Cherry* is his first major hit at US #6.

Nov First LP *The Feel Of Neil Diamond* reaches US #137.

Dec *I Got The Feeling (Oh No No)* makes US #16. The Monkees° follow-up their US chart-topping debut with Diamond's *I'm A Believer* (placed with them by Jeff Barry), which has advance orders of 1,051,280 on the day of release. It tops the US chart for 7 weeks and UK chart for 4, selling an additional 750,000 copies in UK to add to total US sales of over 3 million.

NEIL DIAMOND *cont.*

1967 Mar *You Got To Me* peaks at US #18.

Apr The Monkees° hit US #2 and UK #3 with another Diamond song, *A Little Bit Me, A Little Bit You*, which is another multi-million seller.

May *Girl, You'll Be A Woman Soon* hits US #10. Although Diamond's records are not yet charting in UK, his songs are: Lulu's° cover of one of his B-sides, *The Boat That I Row*, hits UK #6 and Cliff Richard's° double A-side, *I'll Come Running* and *I Got The Feelin' (Oh No No)* reaches UK #26.

Aug Gospel-influenced *Thank The Lord For The Night* makes US #13.

Oct LP *Just For You* reaches US #80.

Nov *Kentucky Woman* reaches US #22.

1968 Jan A revival of Gary "US" Bonds'° *New Orleans*, his first non-original single, peaks at US #51.

Apr *Red Red Wine*, (revived later as an international hit by UB40°) reaches US #62. Diamond leaves Bang, partly through frustration over its refusal to issue *Shilo* as a single, which he considers his best song to date, and signs to MCA Records' new Uni label.

June First Uni release is the autobiographical *Brooklyn Roads*, which makes US #58. LP *Velvet Gloves And Spit* fails to chart. One of its songs, the anti-drug but naive *Pot Smoker's Song*, alienates him from the drug-tolerant rock mainstream of the late 60s (and Uni will remove it from re-pressings of the LP).

Aug *Two-Bit Manchild* peaks at US #66. Diamond moves from New York to LA, Uni Records' base, and makes a guest appearance in Hollywood in TV detective series "Mannix".

Sept Bang label compilation LP *Greatest Hits* reaches US #100.

Oct *Sunday Sun* makes US #68.

1969 Apr *Brother Love's Traveling Salvation Show* peaks at US #22. LP *Brother Love's Traveling Salvation Show*, on Uni, climbs to US #82.

Aug *Sweet Caroline* hits US #4 and is Diamond's first million-plus seller.

Dec *Holly Holy*, his second million-seller, hits US #6.

1970 Jan LP *Touching You, Touching Me* makes US #30.

Mar A cover of Buffy Saint-Marie's *Until It's Time For You To Go*, extracted from the LP, reaches US #53.

Apr Bang Records issues the disputed *Shilo* in competition to Diamond's current material and it climbs to US #24.

May Percussive, African-styled *Soolaimon*, a foretaste of Diamond's *African Trilogy* suite, makes US #30.

Sept Bang reissues *Solitary Man*, which peaks at US #21.

Oct *Cracklin' Rosie* is Diamond's first US chart-topper (for 1 week), and his third million-seller. *Neil Diamond/Gold*, his first live LP, recorded at The Troubadour in Hollywood, hits US #10 while LP *Shilo*, a Bang assemblage of early tracks, makes US #52.

Dec *Cracklin' Rosie* hits UK #3. LP *Tap Root Manuscript*, which includes the experimental *African Trilogy*, reaches US #13. Diamond's early revival of The Hollies'° *He Ain't Heavy He's My Brother* climbs to US #20, and another Bang reissue, *Do It*, originally the B-side of *Solitary Man*, makes US #36.

1971 Mar *Sweet Caroline*, is reissued in UK as follow-up to *Cracklin' Rosie* and hits UK #8. LP *Do It*, another Bang compilation, makes US #100.

Apr LP *Tap Root Manuscript* and LP *Gold* chart simultaneously in UK, making #19 and #23 respectively.

May The autobiographical *I Am . . . I Said*, (which Diamond will later claim to have been his hardest major song to write) hits both US and UK #4 and is another million-seller. Its B-side, *Done Too Soon*, concerning prominent names who died young, charts at US #65.

July Diamond's own version of his song for The Monkees°, *I'm A Believer*, is reissued by Bang and hits US #51.

Dec LP *Stones* peaks at US #11, while the title track reaches US #14.

1972 Jan LP *Stones* reaches UK #18.

June *Song Sung Blue* tops the US chart for a week and is another million-seller. It climbs to UK #14.

Aug LP *Moods* hits US #5 and UK #7.

Aug [24] A concert at LA's Greek Theater is recorded for live LP *Hot August Night*.

Sept Diamond plays 20 nights of sold-out concerts at New York's Winter Garden theater, after which he announces he will take a break from live work to spend time with his family and friends. (This sabbatical will last for almost 3½ years.) Meanwhile, *Play Me* reaches US #11.

Dec *Walk On Water*, taken from LP *Moods*, reaches US #17. It is his last release on Uni, which is absorbed by parent MCA label.

1973 Jan Live double LP *Hot August Night* hits US #5. It will remain charted for 78 weeks and reach UK #32.

Mar Double compilation LP *Double Gold*, another Bang anthology, makes US #36.

May A live version of *Cherry Cherry*, taken from LP *Hot August Night*, reaches US #31.

June His MCA contract expired, Diamond signs to CBS/Columbia Records in a 10-LP deal guaranteeing $5 million.

Nov *Be*, his first CBS/Columbia single, is taken from his soundtrack for movie *Jonathan Livingston Seagull* and makes US #34.

Dec Soundtrack LP *Jonathan Livingston Seagull* hits US #2.

1974 Jan LP *Hot August Night* makes UK #32.

Feb LP *Jonathan Livingston Seagull* reaches UK #35.

Mar [2] Diamond wins a US Grammy award for *Jonathan Livingston Seagull*, as Best Film Soundtrack LP of 1973.

Mar *Skybird*, from the film soundtrack, peaks at US #75.

July Compilation LP *His Twelve Greatest Hits*, on MCA, reaches US #29 and UK #13.

Nov *Longfellow Serenade*, Diamond's first US top 10 single for over 2 years, hits #5.

Dec LP *Serenade* hits US #3 and UK #11.

1975 Feb *I've Been This Way Before* makes US #34.

1976 Jan Diamond tours Australia and New Zealand.

June [30] Diamond has a minor drug bust when police, entering his California home on a search warrant (ostensibly checking a report of intruders), find less than one ounce of marijuana.

July *If You Know What I Mean*, a trailer for his new LP, climbs to US #11.

July [4] Diamond's first US live performance after his layoff opens the new Aladdin Theater For The Performing Arts in Las Vegas.

Aug LP *Beautiful Noise*, produced by friend and near neighbor, Robbie Robertson of The Band°, hits US #4 and UK #10 and is Diamond's first million-selling LP. *If You Know What I Mean* reaches UK #35.

Oct *Don't Think . . . Feel* makes US #43.

Nov The title song from LP *Beautiful Noise*, issued as a UK single, makes #13.

Nov [25] Diamond appears in an all-star guest line-up in The Band's° "Last Waltz" farewell concert at the Winterland, San Francisco, which is also filmed (for later cinema release as *The Last Waltz*) by Martin Scorsese.

1977 Feb [21] Diamond stars in a US NBC TV special about his music, taped at LA's Greek Theater in front of a celebrity-filled audience.

Apr Second live double LP *Love At The Greek*, again recorded at the Greek Theater, hits US #8 and UK #3, and is another million-seller.

1978 Jan *Desiree* reaches US #16 and UK #39. LP *I'm Glad You're Here With Me Tonight*, produced by Bob Gaudio of The Four Seasons°, hits US #6 and UK #16, selling over a million.

Dec A duet with Barbra Streisand°, *You Don't Bring Me Flowers*, tops the US chart for 2 weeks and sells over a million. (It was recorded by the duo and produced by Gaudio after CBS/Columbia heard of the spliced "duet" of their individual versions in the same key played by a Louisville, Ky., radio DJ, which had huge listener response.) Compilation LP *20 Golden Greats*, a UK-originated anthology of Uni/MCA material, hits UK #2 and stays charted for 6 months.

1979 Jan LP *You Don't Bring Me Flowers*, which includes the duet, hits US #4 and UK #15, and sells over a million.

Feb [15] Diamond and Streisand° perform *You Don't Bring Me Flowers*, which collected two nominations, live at the Grammy Awards ceremony.

Mar *Forever In Blue Jeans* makes US #20 and UK #16.

June *Say Maybe* peaks at US #55. Diamond begins work on a remake of the old Al Jolson movie *The Jazz Singer*, taking the lead role opposite Laurence Olivier and providing the soundtrack songs.

1980 Feb LP *September Morn*, another million-seller, hits US #10 and UK #14 while the title track reaches US #17.

Apr *The Good Lord Loves You* makes US #67.

1981 Jan *Love On The Rocks*, from LP *The Jazz Singer*, reaches US #2 and UK #17 and sells over a million.

Feb Soundtrack LP *The Jazz Singer*, released (like its spin-off singles, for contractual reasons) on Capitol, hits US #3 and UK #10 and is a million-seller. (The film is successful, though not a blockbuster:

much of its popularity is as a result of the hit songs and LP.)
Mar *Hello Again*, taken from the movie soundtrack hits US #6 but only UK #51.
June *America*, the third and last extract from *The Jazz Singer*, hits US #8 but fails to chart in UK. With its patriotic immigrant theme, it becomes Diamond's most played and requested song in US.
Nov LP *On The Way To The Sky* makes US #17 and UK #39.
1982 Jan *Yesterday's Songs* reaches US #11. It is taken from LP *On The Way To The Sky*, which peaks at US #17 and is a million-seller.
Mar Title track from *On The Way To The Sky* reaches US #27.
July *Be Mine Tonight* reaches US #35. Compilation LP *His Twelve Greatest Hits, Volume II*, a collection of both CBS/Columbia and Capitol material, makes US #48 and UK #32.
Nov *Heartlight*, inspired by movie *E.T.*, hits US #5 and makes UK #47. LP *Heartlight* hits US #9 and UK #43, and is another million-seller.
1983 Feb *I'm Alive* peaks at US #35.
May *Front Page Story* makes US #65.
1984 Sept *Turn Around* reaches US #62. LP *Primitive* makes US #35.
1986 July *Headed For The Future* makes US #53.
1988 Jan Diamond's third double live LP, *Hot August II*, recorded at LA's Greek Theater again, reaches US #59.

THE DIAMONDS

Dave Somerville (vocals)
Mike Douglas (vocals)
John Felton (vocals)
Evan Fisher (vocals)

1955 The group forms in Toronto, Canada, originally with Somerville and Douglas, joining fellow Canadians Ted Kowalski and Bill Reed.
1956 Jan Signed to Mercury Records in US, and with Californians Felton and Fisher now replacing Reed and Kowalski, they release a cover version of Frankie Lymon & The Teenagers'° *Why Do Fools Fall In Love?*
Apr *Why Do Fools Fall In Love?* reaches US #16, the third most successful of three US top 20 versions.(Lymon hits #7; Gale Storm #15.)
May A cover of The Willows' *Church Bells May Ring*, this time eclipses the original. The Diamonds reach US #20, and The Willows only #62.
July Their cover of The Clovers' *Love Love Love* climbs to the same US chart peak as the original (#30) almost simultaneously.
Sept *Ka-Ding-Dong/Soft Summer Breeze* is a double-sided hit, the titles reaching US #35 and #34 independently. Another cover of *Ka-Ding-Dong* by The Hilltoppers reaches US #38, while original by The G-Clefs peaks at #53. There is a bigger US hit version of *Soft Summer Breeze* by Eddie Heywood (#12).
1957 Apr *Little Darlin'* is their biggest and most enduring hit, selling over a million, hitting US #2 for 8 weeks, and spending 6 months on chart. The original version is by The Gladiolas, and reaches US #41.
July *Little Darlin'* hits UK #3, and proves to be their only UK hit.
Sept *Zip Zip* reaches US #45.
Nov *Silhouettes* hits US #10, while losing out on The Rays' original which hits #3.
1958 Feb *The Stroll* is their second-biggest seller and hits US #5, popularizing the dance of the same name.
May *High Sign*, a rare Diamonds original, reaches US #38.
July Another non-cover, *Kathy-0*, makes US #45.
Nov *Walking Along* reaches #29 in US.
1959 Mar *She Say (Oom Dooby Doom)* is their last US top 20 hit, peaking at #18. Although they are imitators of the 1950s black doo-wop vocal tradition rather than a part of the genre, their records fall from chart success as the vocal group sound rapidly loses commercial favor at the close of the 1950s.
1961 Aug Following several personnel changes, and 2 years playing nightclubs rather than the rock packages with which they toured in l956-8, the group returns with a revival of The Danleers' 1958 hit ballad *One Summer Night*, which reaches US #22. After this, they slide into obscurity and split up.
1973 Apr [27] After a decade apart, the group reunites to appear on US TV in a "Midnight Special" show devoted to oldie hitmakers, alongside Little Richard°, Little Anthony & The Imperials and Jerry Lee Lewis.°

BO DIDDLEY

1951 Diddley (b. Ellas Bates, Dec.30, 1928, McComb, Miss., US, but given the surname McDaniel in infancy on adoption by his mother's cousin Gussie McDaniel) begins playing regularly as an electric blues/R&B act at The 708 club on the south side of Chicago, Ill., where he has lived since age five. He has already been a street corner performer since schooldays, and has gained his professional name from the nickname given him in his teens whilst training as a Golden Gloves boxer.
1955 June Having successfully auditioned for Chess Records in Chicago, Diddley is signed to subsidiary label, Checker, and debuts with double-sided hit *Bo Diddley/I'm A Man*, which hits #2 on US R&B chart but does not cross over to the pop market.
Aug [20] He appears at the Apollo Theater, Harlem, with a band which will play with him regularly through the 1950s: his half-sister "The Duchess" on guitar and back-up vocals, Otis Spann on piano, Billy Boy Arnold on harmonica, Frank Kirkland on drums and Jerome Green on bass, maracas and general onstage banter with Diddley. (Green and "The Duchess" will remain the core of stage back-up through the 1960s.)

Nov [20] He appears on US TV's "Ed Sullivan Show" in a 15-minute segment with other R&B artists, and plays *Bo Diddley*.
1956 June His first UK release is the EP *Rhythm & Blues With Bo Diddley*, which arouses little interest outside esoteric R&B circles.
July *Who Do You Love*, subsequently another of his most-covered numbers, is released in US but does not make the top 100.
1959 July *Crackin' Up* is his first US pop chart entry, peaking at #62.
Oct *Say Man*, a semi-comic jive talk repartee between Diddley and Jerome Green over an archetypal Bo Diddley rhythm track, is his biggest US hit, climbing to #20.
1960 Mar *Road Runner*, another much-covered original, reaches US #75.
1962 Sept *You Can't Judge A Book By The Cover* reaches US #48.
Dec LP *Bo Diddley* reaches US #117 – the only US LP entry of his career.
1963 Sept [29] He begins his first UK tour (with "The Duchess" and Green) jointly supporting The Everly Brothers° with The Rolling Stones° (who are also on their first UK tour, and drop all of Diddley's songs from their own act out of respect).
Oct *Pretty Thing* reaches UK #41, while LP *Bo Diddley* makes #11, both on the strength of tour success.
Nov Two more Diddley LPs chart in UK: *Bo Diddley Is A Gunslinger* (#20) and *Bo Diddley Rides Again* (#19).

BO DIDDLEY *cont.*

1964 Feb LP *Bo Diddley's Beach Party* reaches UK #13.
June *Mona (I Need You Baby)* peaks at UK #42.
Sept He releases the LP *Two Great Guitars*, on which he duets with Chuck Berry on two lengthy guitar jams.
1965 Mar *Hey Good Lookin'* reaches UK #43.
1967 Jan *Ooh Baby* reaches US #88 – his first US hit single for 5 years, but also his final one.
1968 With Muddy Waters° and Little Walter, Diddley records the critically-acclaimed LP *Super Blues Band* (which, however, does not chart).
1969 Sept [13] He performs at the Toronto Rock'n'Roll Revival concert, alongside Chuck Berry°, Jerry Lee Lewis°, Little Richard° and John Lennon° and The Plastic Ono Band, among others. (He will also be seen in D.A. Pennebaker's movie of the event, released in 1970 as *Sweet Toronto* and in revised form in 1972 as *Keep On Rockin'*.)
1971 Oct LP *Another Dimension* attempts to set Diddley within prevailing politically conscious lyricism, but his old fans are unimpressed and the record is not a big seller.
1973 Diddley is featured in the film *Let The Good Times Roll*, along with contemporaries Fats Domino°, Bill Haley°, Little Richard° and others.
July LP *The London Bo Diddley Sessions* is released, including six tracks recorded with UK musicians in London (including Roy Wood of The Move° and Wizzard°).
1976 Apr With the demise of the Checker label, Diddley signs to RCA Records for the LP *The 20th Anniversary Of Rock'n'Roll*. His career as rock'n'roll/R&B elder statesman continues, and he maintains a busy live performance schedule, both as a headliner in his own right and as a support artist.
1979 Feb Never shying from working with younger, emergent acts, he opens for The Clash° on their first US tour.
1980/5 Diddley's tour schedule continues to be busy through the 1980s, though his record releases are now increasingly confined to reissues.
1986 He records the LP *Hey Bo Diddley* live in concert, with Dick Heckstall-Smith's Mainsqueeze as his backing band, during a UK and European tour.
1987 Nov He records with Ronnie Wood at the Ritz, New York, the LP from the show to be released in Aug. 1988.

DION & THE BELMONTS

Dion DiMucci (lead vocals)
Fred Milano (tenor vocals)
Carlo Mastrangelo (bass vocals)
Angelo D'Aleo (tenor vocals)

1957 DiMucci (b. July 18, 1939, Bronx, New York, N.Y., US), Milano (b. Aug.26, 1940, Bronx), Mastrangelo (b. Oct.5, 1939, Bronx) and D'Aleo (b. Feb.3, 1941, Bronx), following equal helpings of school and Bronx street education, first come together as Dion & The Timberlanes, inspired by the many black doo-wop groups harmonizing on their neighborhood corners. Their first recording is *The Chosen Few* for Mohawk Records. Though picked up by the larger Jubilee label, it fails.
1958 The group's name is changed to Dion & The Belmonts, taken from Belmont Avenue which cuts through their corner of the Bronx. *We Went Away* on Mohawk also fails. The group is signed up by the new Laurie label.
June Laurie debut *I Wonder Why*, a doo-wopping upbeater, reaches US #22.
Oct *No One Knows* reaches US #24. It is written by Ernie Maresca, whose name will appear under several Dion hits.
1959 Jan *Don't Pity Me* peaks at US #40, as Dion & The Belmonts begin a rigorous tour of the mid-West, supporting Buddy Holly°, Ritchie Valens° and The Big Bopper° (all three to die tragically in a mid-tour plane crash in early February).
May New York songwriters Doc Pomus and Mort Shuman provide *A Teenager In Love* which hits US #5 and is a million-seller.
June *A Teenager In Love* makes UK #28, despite covers by Marty Wilde° (#2) and Craig Douglas° (#13), which scoop the major UK sales. The group becomes fan-mag pin-ups, discussing in print their penchant for clothes (collegiate sweaters, mostly) and revealing such unlikely interests as skindiving. D'Aleo is conscripted into the US Navy on national service and the group continues as a trio.
Oct *Every Little Thing I Do* reaches US #48, while the Maresca-penned B-side *A Lover's Prayer* makes US #73.
1960 Jan A richly-harmonized, saxophone-propelled reworking of 1937 Rodgers and Hart number, *Where Or When*, hits US #3 and is a second million-seller.
May The group revives a song first heard in the 1940 Walt Disney movie, *Pinocchio, When You Wish Upon A Star*, which peaks at US #30.
Aug A version of Cole Porter's *In The Still Of The Night* reaches only US #38.
Sept The group splits. Dion stays with Laurie as a soloist and The Belmonts sign to the Sabina label.
Dec Returning to teen-oriented material, Dion's solo debut, *Lonely Teenager*, makes US #12, with its B-side *Little Miss Blue* showing briefly at US #96.

1961 Jan *Lonely Teenager* makes UK #47.
Mar Dion's *Havin' Fun* peaks at US #42.
May Dion's *Kissin' Game* peaks at US #82.
July The Belmonts, minus Dion, release *Tell Me Why*, which reaches US #18.
Sept The Belmonts revive *Don't Get Around Much Anymore* which makes US #57.
Oct Dion hits US #1 for 2 weeks with the million-selling *Runaround Sue*, a whooping rocker with an exuberance which belies its tale of woe. Co-written with Maresca, it is derived from Gary "US" Bonds'° recent US chart-topper *Quarter To Three*. (Some 20 years later, the song will become a US hit for Leif Garrett and a UK one for Racey.)
Nov *Runaround Sue* takes Dion to UK #11. He appears in the film *Teenage Millionaire*.
1962 Jan The Belmonts reach US #75 with *I Need Someone*. Dion's LP *Runaround Sue* makes US #11.
Feb Dion's *The Wanderer* hits US #2 and is a million-seller. The B-side, *The Majestic*, makes US #36. He sings both songs in the movie *Twist Around The Clock*.
Mar *The Wanderer* hits UK #10. (It will be his last UK hit until it returns to #16 in 1976. Status Quo° will revive it for a UK top 10 hit in 1984).
May Maresca leaves the demo studio to write a smash of his own: the *Runaround Sue*-inflected *Shout Shout (Knock Yourself Out)* which hits US #6.
June Dion hits US #3 with *Lovers Who Wander*, while B-side *Born To Cry* climbs to US #42.
Aug A Dion original, *Little Diane* (with a prominent kazoo in the backing) hits US #8. His LP *Lovers Who Wander* reaches US #12.
Sept The Belmonts reach US #28 with *Come On Little Angel* (co-written by Maresca).
Dec *Love Came To Me*, self-penned by Dion, hits US #10. He leaves Laurie to sign a major contract with CBS/Columbia. The Belmonts' *Diddle-Dee-Dum (What Happens When Your Love Is Gone)* reaches US #53.
1963 Jan LP *Dion Sings His Greatest Hits*, which has only two solo cuts and 10 with The Belmonts, makes US #29. After years of gruelling package tours, Dion graduates to the live supper club circuit.

Feb Dion's Columbia debut, a revival of Leiber and Stoller's *Ruby Baby* (originally a hit for The Drifters° in 1955), climbs to hit US #2 and sells over a million.

Apr His first Columbia LP, also titled *Ruby Baby*, reaches US #20. Laurie joins the lucky streak with girls' names and issues *Sandy*, which climbs to US #21.

May Dion's *This Little Girl* makes US #21. The Belmonts' own girl-name single, *Ann-Marie*, makes only US #86.

July Dion's revival of The Del Vikings' *Come Go With Me*, his last on Laurie and originally on one of his LPs, reaches US #48. A Laurie compilation LP, *Dion Sings To Sandy (And All His Other Girls!)* makes US #115.

Aug On CBS/Columbia, the offbeat and downbeat *Be Careful Of Stones That You Throw*, a morality tale about not taking people at face value, makes US #31.

Oct Yet another girl song (and yet another by Maresca), Dion's *Donna The Prima Donna* hits US #6.

Nov [2] During a UK tour, Dion appears live on TV's "Ready Steady Go", singing *Donna The Prima Donna*, but becomes irritated by the dancing audience around him and walks out despite being scheduled to perform another song.

Dec Dion hits US #6 with *Drip Drop* (another Leiber/Stoller Drifters° oldie from 1958). It completes a run of 18 Hot 100 hits in 3 years.

1964/65 Apart from a minor hit with Chuck Berry's° *Johnny B Goode* (US #71), the British Invasion and a developing narcotic problem combine to move Dion out of the public eye and he becomes involved in blues. His other singles are pure blues: Muddy Waters'° *I'm Your Hoochie Coochie Man* and Willie Dixon's *Spoonful*. With little US airplay, they fail to chart. Dion experiments with folk and blues material but CBS/Columbia refuses to release much of it.

1966 With folk-rock hitting the charts, CBS/Columbia issues three folk-oriented singles billed as Dion & The Wanderers, but they receive little promotion. By the end of the year, artist and label have parted company.

1967 May Released on ABC Paramount, LP *Together Again*, is a surprise reunion of Dion with all three Belmonts on a collection of material which owes much to their R&B vocal group roots. Two singles, *Berimbau* and *Movin' Man* are extracted, but only collectors show interest.

1968 Dec Dion hits US #4 with Dick Holler's later much-covered martyr memorial song *Abraham Martin And John* and earns another gold disk. On his old label Laurie, with the folky style he has been honing since the passing of his blues passion, it completes what Dion will later describe as a watershed year in his life and career. (He finally kicked his heroin habit in April 1968.)

1969 Jan After an absence of 5 years on the US LP chart, Dion's *Dion* reaches #128.

Feb A folk-styled reworking of Jimi Hendrix's° *Purple Haze* reaches US #63.

Apr Only months after Judy Collins'° version leaves the top 10, Dion's version of Joni Mitchell's° *Both Sides Now* reaches US #91.

1970 June As a singer/songwriter bent over his acoustic guitar, Dion enters another phase of his career and signs to Warner Bros. Records. A candid allusion to his heroin addiction, *Your Own Back Yard* reaches US #75 (to become his last chart single). Two LPs, *Sit Down Old Friend*, featuring just Dion and guitar, and *You're Not Alone*, with a small group accompaniment, fail.

1972 Jan LP *Sanctuary* (which contains live versions of *The Wanderer* and *Ruby Baby* from the Bitter End club, with newer acoustic material) makes US #200 for 2 weeks.

June [2] Dion & The Belmonts reunite again for a one-off show at Madison Square Garden, New York.

Dec LP *Suite For Late Summer*, a concept LP with orchestral accompaniment, reaches US #197.

1973 Mar The Dion & The Belmonts' performance from Madison Square Garden is released as live LP *Reunion*, which reaches US #144.

Apr LP *Dion's Greatest Hits*, collating ten of his hits, reaches US #194 (and will be his last US chart appearance).

1975 Oct Phil Spector produces Dion's LP *Born To Be With You* on his new Phil Spector International label, which is only released in UK.

1976 June *The Wanderer* is reissued in UK, reaching #16.

Aug The production team of Steve Barri and Michael Omartian fails to bring commercial success for Dion with LP *Streetheart* and he leaves Warner Bros.

1978 LP *Return Of The Wanderer*, produced by Terry Cashman and Terry West on Lifesong Records, fails to chart.

1980 Apr Compilation LP *Dion And The Belmonts' 20 Golden Greats*, released on K-tel, reaches UK #31.

1981/87 Dion records LP *Inside Job* for the Christian label Dayspring. Apart from reissues of early material, his releases will consist of inspirational material on this and other Christian labels, as part of his commitment to the born-again faith which has redirected his life.

1988 Dion is reported active again with secular material in New York, in the company of Bruce Springsteen°.

DIRE STRAITS

Mark Knopfler (guitar and vocals)
John Illsley (bass)
Hal Lindes (guitar)
Pick Withers (drums)
Alan Clark (keyboards)

1977 July Knopfler (b. Aug.12, 1949, Glasgow, Scotland, UK), an English graduate part-time teacher and pub-rock player and songwriter, is sharing a flat in Deptford, London, with his social worker and guitarist brother David, and sociology undergraduate Illsley (b. June 24, 1949, Leicester, UK), where they frequently jam and rehearse Knopfler's own material. They are joined by session drummer Withers and a friend of his notes their financial plight and dubs them "Dire Straits". The band scrapes together £120 to record a five-song demo tape at London's Pathway studios.

Aug A copy is given to DJ Charlie Gillett, who features songs from it on his weekly UK BBC Radio London show "Honky Tonk".

Oct Phonogram Records' A&R man John Stainze, one of many impressed by the broadcast demos, tracks the band down and, after strong competition, signs it to Phonogram's Vertigo label.

Dec NEMS agent Ed Bicknell hears the band's tape when Stainze enquires about an agency deal for it and, after seeing the band live at Dingwalls club in London, he asks to manage it and an informal agreement is reached.

1978 Jan [20] Dire Straits begins a 16-date UK tour supporting Talking Heads°.

Feb [14] The group begins recording its first LP at Basing Street Studios, London, UK with producer Muff Winwood. (The LP will cost £12,500 to produce.)

Mar The band gets a short residency at the Marquee, London, and gains strong reviews.

May The band supports The Climax Blues Band on a UK tour and Styx° in Europe (Paris, Hamburg and The Hague). Debut single *Sultans Of Swing* (originally a song on the demo) is released in UK with good reviews but does not chart.

June LP *Dire Straits* reaches UK #37 and the band plays its first UK headlining tour. Bicknell secures a US deal with Warner Bros.

Sept Knopfler visits Muscle Shoals studios in US, meeting producer Jerry Wexler and playing on a Mavis Staples session. A deal is struck with Wexler and Barry Beckett to produce Dire Straits' second LP.

Oct Debut LP *Dire Straits* is released in US and gets heavy airplay. The band plays sell-out tours in Holland, Belgium and West Germany. The LP tops charts in Australia and New Zealand.

Nov The band flies to The Bahamas to record its next LP at Compass Point studios, Nassau, before returning to UK for Christmas.

1979 Feb [23] First tour of US and Canada – 51 sold-out shows over 38 days – opens at The Paradise Club, Boston, Mass.

Mar Bob Dylan° attends an LA concert and invites Knopfler and Withers to play on his next LP.

Apr LP *Dire Straits* hits US #2, while *Sultans Of Swing* hits US #4. After the US success, *Sultans Of Swing* hits UK #8 and the LP UK #5. (The LP will eventually be a million-seller in both countries, and spend 104 weeks on UK chart.)

May [1-12] Knopfler and Withers work with Bob Dylan° in Muscle Shoals on his LP *Slow Train Coming*.

June LP *Communiqué* is released to coincide with another sell-out UK and European tour and hits UK #5.

Aug *Lady Writer* reaches UK #51 and US #45. LP *Communiqué* makes US #11.

Sept The band plays a second US tour.

Dec After major Dublin and Belfast dates, and four London concerts (following a Nov. tour of Scandinavia), the band calls a 6-month work break to recover from the exhaustion of the road and to work on material for a third LP.

DIRE STRAITS *cont.*

1980 July [25] After a month's recording sessions with new producer Jimmy Iovine, David Knopfler quits the band to pursue a solo career.

Sept Following auditions, Lindes (b. June 30, 1953, Monterey, Cal., US) and Clark (b. Mar.5, 1952, Durham, UK) are recruited on guitar and keyboards respectively.

Oct [20] The band begins a 2-week North American tour as LP *Making Movies* is released.

Dec [19-20] A 1-month UK tour is punctuated by two dates in Dortmund, West Germany, with Roxy Music° and Talking Heads°, which are televised across Europe to a multi-million audience.

1981 Jan LP *Making Movies* reaches US #19. *Skateaway*, taken from it, peaks at US #58.

Feb *Romeo And Juliet* hits UK #8, pulling LP *Making Movies* to a belated UK chart peak of #4. The band plays at the San Remo Song Festival in Italy.

Mar [18] First tour of Australia and New Zealand begins. (The concert in Auckland will be the highest-grossing in the band's career to date.)

Apr *Skateaway* reaches UK #37.

May/July Between May 3 and July 6, the band sells out concerts in West Germany, Sweden, Denmark, Norway, Finland, Holland, France, Switzerland, Italy, Belgium and Luxembourg.

Oct *Tunnel Of Love* reaches UK #54.

1982 Feb Knopfler is invited by producer David Puttnam to compose and perform the soundtrack score of movie *Local Hero*.

Mar [1] Recording begins for the band's next LP.

July *Local Hero* soundtrack music is recorded, after Knopfler attends filming in Scotland.

Sept *Private Investigations* hits UK #2, despite its 7-minute length.

Oct LP *Love Over Gold* hits UK #1 for 4 weeks.

Nov LP *Love Over Gold* reaches US #19. Withers leaves and is replaced on drums by Terry Williams, ex-Dave Edmunds'° band Rockpile.

1983 Jan *Industrial Disease* peaks at US #75.

Feb EP *Twisting By The Pool* reaches UK #14.

Mar Knopfler's solo single *Going Home*, the theme from *Local Hero*, makes UK #56.

Apr Marketed in US as a mini-LP, *Twisting By The Pool* reaches US #53.

May Knopfler's *Local Hero* soundtrack LP reaches UK #14.

Nov Knopfler produces Bob Dylan's° LP *Infidels*, and marries Lourdes Salomon at Kensington Register Office, London.

1984 Feb Double A-side *Love Over Gold/Solid Rock* (both live versions) reaches UK #50.

Mar Double LP *Alchemy – Dire Straits Live* hits UK #3.

May LP *Alchemy – Dire Straits Live* makes only US #46.

Oct Knopfler's LP of soundtrack music for film *Cal* reaches UK #65. He writes the score for film *Comfort And Joy*.

1985 Mar Tina Turner° hits US #7 with Knopfler-penned *Private Dancer*.

May *So Far Away* reaches UK #20. It is extracted from LP *Brothers In Arms* which enters UK chart at #1 and holds the top slot for 3 weeks. Shortly after, Lindes leaves the band.

June Dire Straits is awarded the 1985 Silver Clef Award in UK for outstanding services to British music.

July [13] After 10 consecutive nights' concerts at Wembley Arena, London, the band plays at Live Aid at Wembley Stadium. (This will be followed by the 12-month "Brothers in Arms" world tour, ending in Australia in mid-1986. Clark leaves and Guy Fletcher joins on keyboards for the tour.)

Aug LP *Brothers In Arms* tops US chart for 9 weeks, while *Money For Nothing*, from the LP, hits UK #4.

Sept Aided by an innovative animated promo video which gets heavy MTV and other US TV exposure, *Money For Nothing* tops the US chart for 3 weeks, the band's biggest US hit and its first million-selling single. The song is written by Knopfler and Sting°, who also guests on vocals.

Dec Title track from LP *Brothers In Arms* reaches UK #16.

1986 Jan *Walk Of Life* hits US #7.

Feb *Walk Of Life* hits UK #2.

Apr *So Far Away* makes US #19.

May *Your Latest Trick* reaches UK #26.

June [20] Knopfler plays the Prince's Trust concert at Wembley Arena, London, with Paul McCartney°, Elton John°, Tina Turner° and others.

Sept *Money For Nothing* wins as Best Video and Best Group Video at the annual US MTV awards. (The song lyric "I Want My MTV" becomes the cable station's catch-phrase.)

Oct [25] In a celebrity car race before the Australian Grand Prix, Knopfler breaks his collarbone in an accident.

1987 Jan Knopfler guests at Eric Clapton's° concert at London's Royal Albert Hall.

Mar Knopfler plays a duet with one of his original guitar heroes, Chet Atkins, at "The Secret Policeman's Third Ball" in London, in aid of Amnesty International.

Nov LP *Brothers In Arms* sells its 3 millionth copy in UK, becoming the UK's all-time best-selling LP and its second-biggest-selling recording of any kind. (Only Band Aid's° *Do They Know It's Christmas?* has a higher UK sales total.)

Dec Knopfler writes and performs the soundtrack music for Rob Reiner-directed film *The Princess Bride*, also released on LP.

1988 June [11] The band headlines the Nelson Mandela 70th Birthday concert at Wembley Stadium, UK, televised worldwide, with Eric Clapton° guesting as second guitarist. The show helps LP *Brothers In Arms* back into the UK top 20 after 162 weeks on chart.

July Knopfler guests on Joan Armatrading's° LP *The Shouting Stage*.

Sept Knopfler contributes and part produces Randy Newman's° LP *Land Of Dream*.

THE DIXIE CUPS

Barbara Ann Hawkins (vocals)
Rosa Lee Hawkins (vocals)
Joan Johnson (vocals)

1963 Oct Having sung together since grade school in New Orleans, the trio is spotted in a local talent contest by Joe Jones (a new Orleans singer/pianist who had a 1960 #3 US hit with *You Talk Too Much*). He becomes their manager, and takes them to New York to audition for Red Bird Records.

1964 Jan Signed to Red Bird, and provisionally named Little Miss and The Muffets, the girls are placed with songwriter/producers Jeff Barry and Ellie Greenwich, who try them out on *Chapel Of Love*, a song the duo has written with Phil Spector, but which he has failed to record satisfactorily with both The Ronettes° and The Crystals.

June *Chapel Of Love* tops US chart for 3 weeks and is a million seller. It is credited to The Dixie Cups after a last-minute name change just before the record's release.

July *Chapel Of Love* charts in UK, reaching #22.

Aug Follow-up, *People Say*, climbs to US #12.

Sept LP *Chapel Of Love* reaches US #112. (In a practice peculiar to Red Bird, this same LP will reappear twice with the same contents in the next 9 months, the title being changed first to *People Say* and then to *Iko Iko* – to tag the LP after the current hit.)

Nov *You Should Have Seen The Way He Looked At Me* peaks at US #39.

1965 Feb *Little Bell* makes US #51.

May *Iko Iko* a sparce, percussive arrangement of a traditional New Orleans chant, recorded spontaneously at the end of a session, reaches US #20, the group's final US chart entry.

June *Iko Iko* is their second and also final UK hit, peaking at #23.
July *Gee, The Moon Is Shining Bright* fails to chart in US, and Jones, deciding to move his group to a larger label, signs a new deal with ABC-Paramount Records. (The Dixie Cups will have several singles and another LP on RCA in the subsequent 12 months, but all without an inkling of success, lacking the impetus of a hit-sensitive team like Red Bird's Barry and Greenwich behind them. Without moving on further, the group will split.)

DR. FEELGOOD

Lee Brilleaux (vocals and guitar)
Wilko Johnson (guitar)
John B.Sparks (bass)
The Big Figure (drums)

1971 The band is formed on Canvey Island, Essex, UK, to play hard, traditional rock and R&B and electric blues, taking its name from the 1962 US hit *Doctor Feel-Good* by bluesman Piano Red (recorded under the name Dr. Feelgood & The Interns). Johnson (b. John Wilkinson) and The Big Figure (b. Johnny Martin) are both ex-The Roamers, and the others have played in groups in the Essex area. While establishing its own reputation, the band backs 1960s star Heinz. New material, mostly by Johnson, is introduced into the stage act during 3 years of heavy club work.

1974 July [8] Signed to United Artists Records, the band makes its first recording, a medley of rock oldies *Bony Moronie/Tequila*, live at Dingwall's club in London.
Aug [26] Recording sessions for first LP begin with producer Vic Maile at Rockfield studios, Wales.
Nov First single is Johnson-penned *Roxette*, which just fails to make UK top 50.

1975 Jan Debut LP *Down By The Jetty* is released, recorded in mono to reflect the band's raw, basic, R&B sound.
May [23] A live show at City Hall, Sheffield, UK, is recorded for an LP.
Oct Self-produced LP *Malpractice* reaches UK #17. The band tours widely in UK, finding huge support from UK's music press, which champions its hard-edged sound and dynamic live presence as a major rock trend.
Nov [8] A second gig at the Kursaal Ballroom in Southend, Essex (just 8 miles from the band's Canvey Island base) is recorded for a live LP.

1976 Oct Live LP *Stupidity*, compiled from the Sheffield and Southend recordings, tops the UK chart for a week.

1977 Mar Johnson leaves for a solo career after disagreements over the band's material. Henry McCulloch plays as temporary guitarist on one UK tour and is replaced by John "Gypie" Mayo.
June LP *Sneakin' Suspicion*, produced by Bert De Coteaux at Rockfield, Wales (recorded before Johnson's departure), hits UK #10. The title track, written by Johnson, is the band's first hit single, reaching UK #47.
Oct *She's A Wind Up* makes UK #34. Produced by Nick Lowe°, it is taken from LP *Be Seeing You* (the sleeve reflects a current craze within the band for Patrick McGoohan's "The Prisoner" UK TV series) and reaches UK #55.

1978 June [22] The band tops the bill of the fifth anniversary concert at Dingwall's club in London.
Oct *Down At The Doctor's* reaches UK #48. It is extracted from LP *Private Practice*, produced by Richard Gottehrer, which makes UK #41.

1979 Feb The Mayo/Lowe°-penned *Milk And Alcohol*, also from LP *Private Practice*, is the band's biggest-selling single, hitting UK #9. UA gimmick-releases it on white (milk) and brown (alcohol) colored vinyl.
May *As Long As The Price Is Right*, a Larry Wallis song, reaches UK #40.
June Live LP *As It Happens*, recorded at UK gigs at The Pavilion, Hemel Hempstead, Herts. and Crocs in Rayleigh, Essex, reaches UK #42.
Dec *Put Him Out Of Your Mind* reaches UK #73, and is the band's last UK hit single. It is taken from LP *Let It Roll*, produced by Mike Verson, which fails to chart.

1980 Sept LP *A Case Of The Shakes* also fails to chart, and amid some disillusionment within the band, Mayo considers leaving.

1981 Mayo quits, to be replaced Johnny Guitar, ex-The Count Bishops.
Aug LP *On The Job*, the band's third live LP, recorded at Manchester University, UK (and featuring Mayo), also fails to chart.
Nov Compilation LP *Dr. Feelgood's Casebook* is the band's last release on Liberty/UA.

1982 Sparks and Figure leave. Buzz Barwell (drums, ex-Lew Lewis Band) and Pat McMullen (bass, ex-Count Bishops) replace them, leaving Brilleaux the only original member. The band tours UK and Europe despite the personnel upheavals.
Oct LP *Fast Women And Slow Horses* is released on independent UK label Chiswick Records.

1983 Phil Mitchell (bass) replaces McMullen and Gordon Russell replaces Guitar. Brilleaux continues to lead the band through its timeless hard R&B act. (They will work regularly in the small, noisy, club environment which suits them best.)

DR. HOOK

Ray Sawyer (lead vocals and guitar)
Dennis Locorriere (lead vocals and guitar)
George Cummings (steel and lead guitar)
Jance Garfat (bass and vocals)
Bill Francis (keyboards and vocals)
Rik Elswit (guitar and vocals)
John Wolters (drums and vocals)

1968 The group forms in Union City, N.J., US, when Locorriere (b. June 13, 1949, Union City, N.J.) joins Sawyer (b. Feb.1, 1939, Chickasaw, Ala., US), Cummings and Francis, who have been playing together for some years under various short-lived names. They recruit the other members, mostly from the South, and play local bars.

1969 Feb [18] The group has no name until a club owner demands one for his advertising poster and Cummings coins Dr. Hook & The Medicine Show. (Dr. Hook becomes associated with frontman Sawyer who wears an eye patch, after losing his right eye in an auto accident, which gives him a piratical appearance.)

1970 Producer Ron Haffkine hears a Dr. Hook demo tape and asks the group to appear in and perform the music (being written by Shel Silverstein) for the Dustin Hoffman movie *Who Is Harry Kellerman And Why Is He Saying Those Terrible Things About Me?*

1971 June Haffkine signs the band to a recording deal before the movie opens, realizing it will be a success. A deal is completed with CBS/Columbia and the band moves to Haffkine's home in Conn. to spend several months in rehearsal before cutting a debut LP in San Francisco.

1972 June The plaintive and offbeat *Sylvia's Mother*, written by Silverstein, hits US #5, earning a gold disk for a million-plus sales. Debut LP *Dr. Hook & The Medicine Show* (which includes the hit) reaches US #45.
Aug *Sylvia's Mother* hits UK #2.
Sept *Carry Me, Carrie* makes US #71 but fails in UK.

1973 Jan LP *Sloppy Seconds* reaches US #41.
Mar *The Cover Of "Rolling Stone"* hits US #6 and is the group's second million-seller. In UK, the BBC refuses to play it because of the mention of the magazine, a commercial enterprise. The group solves the problem and records a special BBC version titled *The Cover Of "Radio Times"* (the BBC's own weekly magazine). The single still fails to chart in UK.
Mar [29] The group fulfils the ambition inherent in the song by appearing on the cover of *Rolling Stone* magazine.
July *Roland The Roadie And Gertrude The Groupie* makes only US #83.
Oct *Life Ain't Easy* reaches US #68.
Nov LP *Belly Up!* makes only US #141.

1974 Sept Dropped by CBS and virtually bankrupt, the band shortens its name to Dr. Hook.

1975 Feb Capitol Records signs the band to a 1-year option.
July LP *Bankrupt* reaches US #141.
Sept *The Millionaire*, taken from the LP, reaches US #95.

1976 Apr *Only Sixteen*, a revival of Sam Cooke's° 1959 hit taken from LP *Bankrupt*, is halfway up the US top 100 when Capitol's option runs out. The label continues promoting it and the band, and it climbs to hit US #6 and sells over a million copies.
Aug *A Little Bit More*, recorded in Nashville, Tenn., reaches US #11 and UK #2 (held from the top for 4 weeks by Elton John° & Kiki Dee's *Don't Go Breaking My Heart*). The LP of the same title makes US #62 and hits UK #5. The band appears on "Grand Ole Opry" and soon after relocates to Nashville.
Dec *If Not You* reaches US #55 and hits UK #5.

DR. HOOK *cont.*

1977 Jan Sawyer cuts an eponymous solo LP of country songs, backed by Nashville session men.

Aug *Walk Right In*, a remake of The Rooftop Singers' 1963 smash, reaches US #46. LP *Revisited*, compiled of material cut during the band's CBS/Columbia days, is released without charting.

Nov LP *Making Love And Music* reaches UK #39.

1978 Apr *More Like The Movies* reaches UK #14.

1979 Jan LP *Pleasure And Pain* reaches US #66. (It will be the band's only gold LP in US, selling over half a million copies.) *Sharing The Night Together*, after a 4-month chart climb, hits #6 US and earns a gold disk for million-plus sales.

Feb *All The Time In The World* makes US #54.

Aug *When You're In Love With A Beautiful Woman* hits US #6 and is another US million-seller.

Nov *When You're In Love With A Beautiful Woman* tops the UK chart for 3 weeks, while LP *Pleasure And Pain* (from which the hit is taken) reaches UK #47.

1980 Jan *Better Love Next Time* makes US #12 and UK #8.

Apr *Sexy Eyes* hits US #5 (another million-seller) and UK #4. LP *Sometimes You Win*, from which it is extracted, reaches US #71 and UK #14.

Aug *Years From Now* peaks at US #51 and UK #47.

Nov *Sharing The Night Together* reaches UK #43, almost 2 years after its US success. Capitol releases this old track after the band has left the label and signed a new deal with Casablanca Records (released through Mercury in UK).

Dec LP *Rising* on Casablanca/Mercury makes US #175 and UK #44. Extracted from it, *Girls Can Get It* makes US #34 and UK #40.

1981 Jan Compilation LP *Dr. Hook's Greatest Hits* reaches US #142 and hits UK #2.

Apr *That Didn't Hurt Too Bad* reaches US #69.

Nov Live LP *Dr. Hook Live In London* makes UK #90.

1982 Apr *Baby Makes Her Blue Jeans Talk* reaches US #25. LP *Players In The Dark* reaches US #118.

July *Loveline* reaches US #60. (The band will continue to play and tour, despite lack of further recording success, into the mid-80s, eventually splitting when both vocal frontmen Sawyer and Locorriere move to solo careers.)

1988 Sept A new version of Dr. Hook led by Sawyer, but featuring no other former members, tours UK.

DR.JOHN

1957 Rebennack (b. Malcolm John Rebennack, Nov.21, 1941, New Orleans, La., US), playing on countless sessions for New Orleans' Ace, Ebb and Ric R&B labels, begins to establish himself as one of a handful of white musicians working on the New Orleans black music scene.

Sept He records his first release under his own name, *Storm Warning*, for Rex.

1958 Tours with Frankie Ford° and Jerry Byrne (for whom he co-writes the rock'n'roll standard *Lights Out*), and releases his first LP for Ace, followed by others for Rex and the black musicians' co-operative AFO (founded by New Orleans' producer and arranger Harold Battiste).

1962 Leaving New Orleans for LA, Rebennack becomes an in-demand session player, working on numerous records for Sonny Bono (of Sonny and Cher°), Phil Spector, H.B. Barnum and Battiste (who has moved with him).

1963/4 Forming various bands like The Drits and Dray and Zu Zu, Rebennack develops a new identity as Dr. John Creux The Night Tripper, fusing New Orleans R&B with the emergent psychedelia of West Coast rock.

1965 *Zu Zu Man*, for A&M, foreshadows the sound and structures of the first Dr. John LP.

1968 LP *Gris Gris* on Atco, includes the much-covered *Walk On Guilded Splinters*. It is highly rated by critics but fails to chart.

1969 Apr LP *Babylon* also does not chart.

1970 June LP *Remedies* again fails to chart, despite excellent reviews.

1971 Sept He plays organ on Aretha Franklin's° *Spanish Harlem* which hits US #2 and UK #14.

Oct Fourth Atco LP *Dr. John, The Night Tripper (The Sun, Moon And Herbs)*, including contributions from Mick Jagger and Eric Clapton°, reaches US #184.

1972 Apr A revival of The Dixie Cups'° *Iko Iko* is his first US chart entry, reaching US #71.

July LP *Dr. John's Gumbo*, produced by Jerry Wexler, reaches US #112.

1973 June LP *In The Right Place*, his biggest-selling LP, makes US #24. Extracted *Right Place Wrong Time* is his only major US single hit at #9. He tours Europe, accompanied by highly-rated New Orleans band The Meters.

July LP *Triumvirate*, recorded with Mike Bloomfield° and John Paul Hammond, reaches US #105.

Oct *Such A Night* climbs to US #42.

1974 May *(Everybody Wanna Get Rich) Rite Away* reaches US #92 and LP *Desitively Bonnaroo* makes US #105. (Increasingly beset by personal and health problems, these will be his last Atco releases and his last US chart entries; subsequent LPs will tend to be recorded in one-off label deals.)

1975 Nov LP *Hollywood Be Thy Name* is recorded for United Artists. It fails to sell.

1976 Nov LP *Cut Me While I'm Hot* for DJM Records fares similarly. Meanwhile, Dr. John is one of many guest performers on The Band's° farewell concert "The Last Waltz", and later appears on both LP and feature film of the event.

1977 Rebennack joins the short-lived RCO All Stars, the group formed by ex-Band° drummer Levon Helm, and featuring Paul Butterfield° and former MG's Steve Cropper and Donald "Duck" Dunn.

1978 Solo LP *City Lights* is released on A&M.

1981 Moving to New York, Rebennack, unable to secure an attractive US recording contract, concentrates on touring UK and Europe as a solo artist.

1982 He releases the poor-selling but acclaimed LP, *Brightest Smile In Town* for Demon.

1984 Feb Showing that despite his health problems he is still capable of pulling innovatory surprises, he releases the hip-hop-infused *Jet Set*, produced by Ed "The Message" Fletcher on Arthur Baker's New York Streetwise label, which is optioned in UK by Beggars Banquet.

THOMAS DOLBY

1977/79 Dolby (b. Thomas Morgan Robertson, Oct.14, 1958, Cairo, Egypt) plays keyboards with a variety of groups and is a mixer at live gigs for groups including The Members, The Passions and The Fall.

1979 He joins Bruce Woolley and The Camera Club for a few months, continuing his varied musical apprenticeship on a US tour with Lene Lovich, writing and producing her 1980 mini-hit *New Toy* (UK #53).

1981 Mar He releases *Urges/Leipzig* on his own independent label Armageddon. Although unsuccessful, it brings him to the attention of Foreigner°, who enlists his keyboard wizardry on LP 4, and that of Def Leppard°, for its *Pyromania* project.

July He forms his own Venice In Peril label and signs a worldwide license and distribution deal with EMI Records.

Oct First single through EMI, *Europa And The Pirate Twins* makes UK #48.

1982 May LP *The Golden Age Of Wireless* scores a disappointing UK #65, but will be a major US success climbing to US #13. The LP includes two further singles, one of which, *Windpower*, makes UK #31. He promotes the LP touring the UK as a one-man show with computers, keyboards, videos, slides and tape machines and confirms his position as a leading exponent of new techno-rock.

1983 *She Blinded Me With Science*, originally released in Nov. 1982, reaches UK #49 but becomes a US smash, hitting #5. It benefits from an ingenious video featuring eccentric UK TV scientist Magnus Pyke.

Mar LP *Blinded By Science* reaches US #20.

July *Europa And The Pirate Twins* achieves US #67.

1984 Jan *Hyperactive* makes UK #17 and US #62.

Feb LP *The Flat Earth* is Dolby's biggest UK seller, reaching #14. It peaks at US #35. The LP shows greater musical depth and includes an acoustic version of Dan Hicks' *I Scare Myself*, which reaches UK #46. In the previous 12 months Dolby has also completed session and mixing work with acts including Whodini, Adele Bertei and Malcolm McLaren on his LP *Duck Rock*.

1985 Apr He joins Stevie Wonder° and Herbie Hancock in a keyboard medley trio on stage at the American Grammy Awards.

July He plays keyboards for David Bowie's° Live Aid performance at

London's Wembley Stadium. During the next 18 months, Dolby will be involved in many projects, including co-productions of Joni Mitchell's° LP *Dog Eat Dog* and Prefab Sprout's° LP *Steve McQueen* (US title *Two Wheels Burning*), and single collaborations with George Clinton° and Ryuichi Sakamoto.

1986 He scores the soundtracks for Ken Russell's film *Gothic* and George Lucas's *Howard The Duck*.

1987 Jan Dolby settles in LA where he recruits band members to record his first LP in 3 years. During the year he will contribute to Belinda Carlisle's° LP *Heaven On Earth* and produce four new songs for Prefab Sprout's° LP *From Langley Park To Memphis*.

1988 Apr *Airhead*, his first single in 4 years, reaches UK #53 and LP *Aliens Ate My Buick* makes UK #30. In typical quirky Dolby fashion, it includes contributions from George Clinton°, Ed Asner and TV personality Robin Leach.

July Dolby marries "Dynasty" star Kathleen Beller. LP *Aliens Ate My Buick* peaks at US #70.

FATS DOMINO

1949 One of a family of nine, Domino (b. Antoine Domino, Feb.26, 1928, New Orleans, La., US), taught to play piano in his early teens by his brother-in-law, New Orleans musician Harrison Verrett, almost lost his fingers in an accident in the bedmaking factory where he worked but regained their use and his playing ability. Having married his childhood sweetheart Rose Marie a year earlier, he is playing piano in the honky tonks in New Orleans for $3 a week when bandleader/producer Dave Bartholomew, scouting on behalf of Imperial Records, listens to him with Billy Diamond's combo at The Hideaway club, and decides to sign and record him.

Dec Bartholomew helps him rewrite *Junker's Blues* (the first song he heard Domino play) as *The Fat Man*, which is recorded in New Orleans at Domino's first session in Cosimo Matassa's J&M studio.

1950 Apr *The Fat Man*, a useful tie-in with Domino's own "Fats" nickname (and now professional name) from his 5ft 5in, 224lb stature, hits US R&B #6. (By 1953, it will have sold a million, earning Domino his first gold disk.)

Oct After three unsuccessful releases, *Every Night About This Time*, recorded again with Bartholomew's band, makes the R&B chart.

1951 Dec Domino forms his own band and hits US R&B #9 with *Rockin' Chair*. Bartholomew continues to help with arranging and writing (until 1955), but finds Domino's innovative playing (a "creative" approach to keeping time) difficult to work with.

1952 Apr *Goin' Home* tops the US R&B chart and becomes a million-seller.

1953 June *Goin' To The River* hits US R&B #2 and is a third gold disk.

Aug *Please Don't Leave Me* hits US R&B #5.

1954 Mar *You Done Me Wrong* reaches US R&B #10. Domino fails to make the R&B chart again this year, but concentrates on touring US, with visits to New York in the spring, the West Coast and North-West in the summer, and the Mid-West and Chicago in December. His popularity grows steadily.

1955 Jan [28] In New York, Domino begins a 42-date US tour on the "Top Ten R&B Show", with The Clovers, Joe Turner, The Moonglows, Faye Adams and other major R&B acts.

Mar *Don't You Know* makes US R&B #12.

May [22] A show to be headlined by Domino at the Ritz ballroom in Bridgeport, Conn., is cancelled by local police, who justify the action pointing to "a recent near-riot" at New Haven Arena during a rock'n'roll dance.

June *Ain't That A Shame* tops the R&B chart for 11 weeks, and is his first single to cross over and hit US #10. It is a million-seller, but is outsold by Pat Boone's° version, which hits US #2 and UK #7.

Sept *All By Myself* hits US R&B #3, but fails to cross over.

Nov *Poor Me* hits US R&B #3 but again fails to cross over.

Nov [12] In *Billboard*'s annual US DJ poll, Domino is named the country's favorite R&B artist.

1956 Apr *Bo Weevil* makes US #35 (his second to cross over).

June *I'm In Love Again* hits US #3 and tops the R&B chart for 7 weeks, becoming another million-seller. B-side *My Blue Heaven* reaches US #21.

Aug [28] Domino begins a co-headlining (with Frankie Lymon & The Teenagers°) 10 days in Alan Freed's annual rock'n'roll show at the Paramount Theater, Brooklyn, New York.

Sept *When My Dreamboat Comes Home* reaches US #14, with B-side *So-Long* peaking at #44. *I'm In Love Again* marks his UK chart debut, reaching UK #12.

Nov LP *Fats Domino – Rock And Rollin'* is his first chart LP, reaching US #18.

Nov [10] In the annual *Billboard* DJ poll, Domino is again voted Favorite R&B Artist, as well as being the ninth most-played male vocalist (Elvis Presley° being the most-played).

Nov [18] Domino appears on US TV's "Ed Sullivan Show" singing his revival of standard *Blueberry Hill*.

Dec *Blueberry Hill* hits US #3, tops US R&B chart for 8 weeks, and sells over a million. Domino's arrangement of the song becomes the definitive one. He appears in film *Shake, Rattle and Roll*, with R&B singer Joe Turner, and performs *I'm In Love Again*, *Honey Chile* and *Ain't That A Shame*.

1957 Jan *Ain't That A Shame* makes UK #23. Domino appears in Jayne Mansfield-starring movie *The Girl Can't Help It*, singing *Blue Monday*.

Feb *Honey Chile* reaches UK #29, while *Blueberry Hill*, after a lengthy climb, hits UK #6.

Feb [2] Domino appears on "The Perry Como Show" on US TV singing *Blueberry Hill* and *Blue Monday*.

Feb *Blue Monday* hits US #9 (another million seller), and replaces *Blueberry Hill* at US R&B #1, remaining there for 8 weeks. B-side *What's The Reason I'm Not Pleasing You* (originally a pre-war hit for Guy Lombardo) makes US #50.

Feb [15] Domino begins a US tour (lasting until May 5) as part of "The Greatest Show of 1957", a rock'n'roll caravan which also includes Chuck Berry°, Clyde McPhatter, LaVern Baker and others.

Mar LP *This Is Fats Domino!*, which includes both *Blueberry Hill* and *Blue Monday*, reaches US #19. *Blue Monday* reaches UK #23.

Apr LP *Rock And Rollin' With Fats Domino* (his belatedly-charting debut LP, including *Ain't That A Shame*) reaches US #17. *I'm Walkin'* hits US #5, and spends 6 weeks at R&B #1, replacing *Blue Monday*. (By the time *I'm Walking* drops from R&B #1 in April, Domino will have been at the top of the chart for 22 consecutive weeks with three different singles.)

May *I'm Walking* reaches UK #19.

July *Valley Of Tears* hits US #6 and B-side *It's You I Love* reaches US #22. In UK, *Valley Of Tears* makes #25.

Aug *When I See You* reaches US #29. B-side *What Will I Tell My Heart* makes US #64.

Oct *Wait And See* reaches US #23 and B-side *I Still Love You* climbs to US #79.

Nov [12] The rock'n'roll movie *Jamboree* (released in UK as *Disc Jockey Jamboree*) premieres in Hollywood, featuring Domino singing *Wait And See* with a host of rock acts.

Dec *The Big Beat* reaches US #26. It is the title track to movie of the

FATS DOMINO *cont.*

same name, in which Domino performs *I'm Walking*. B-side *I Want You To Know* makes US #48.

1958 Apr *The Big Beat* reaches UK #20.

May *Sick And Tired* reaches US #22. B-side *No No* peaks at US #55.

July *Little Mary* makes US #48, while *Sick And Tired* peaks at UK #26.

Sept *Young School Girl* peaks at US #92.

1959 Jan *Whole Lotta Loving* hits US #6 and is another million-seller.

Mar Both sides of double-A *Telling Lies* and *When The Saints Go Marching In* reach US #50.

June *I'm Ready* reaches US #16. B-side *Margie* makes #51 and UK #19.

Sept *I Want To Walk You Home*, another million-seller, hits US #8. B-side *I'm Gonna Be A Wheel Some Day* reaches US #17.

Oct *I Want To Walk You Home* makes UK #14.

Dec *Be My Guest* hits US #8 and is another million-seller. B-side *I've Been Around* peaks at US #33.

1960 Jan *Be My Guest*, Domino's biggest UK hit single since *Blueberry Hill*, reaches UK #11.

Mar *Country Boy* reaches US #25 and UK #19.

May *Tell Me That You love Me/Before I Grow Too Old* makes US #51 and #84 respectively.

Aug Strings-backed *Walking To New Orleans* hits US #6 and reaches UK #19, with B-side *Don't Come Knockin'* making US #21. This is Domino's last million-selling single.

Oct *Three Nights A Week* reaches US #15, its B-side *Put Your Arms Around Me Honey* peaking at US #58.

Nov *Three Nights A Week* makes UK #45.

Dec *My Girl Josephine* reaches US #14, while B-side *Natural Born Lover* climbs to US #38.

1961 Jan *My Girl Josephine* makes UK #32.

Feb *What A Price* reaches US #22 and B-side *Ain't That Just Like A Woman* peaks at US #33.

Apr [2] Domino begins a wide-ranging tour of US and Canada as part of "The Biggest Show of Stars 1961", with Chubby Checker°, The Drifters°, Bo Diddley°, The Shirelles° and others.

Apr Both sides of *Shu Rah/Fell In Love On Monday* peak separately at US #32.

July *It Keeps Rainin'* reaches US #23 and UK #49.

July [8] Domino completes a 19-day tour of South-Western US states, grossing $83,000.

Sept *Let The Four Winds Blow* reaches US #15.

Dec *What A Party* reaches US #22 and UK #43, with B-side *Rockin' Bicycle* charting briefly at US #83.

1962 Feb A revival of Hank Williams' 1952 country hit *Jambalaya (On The Bayou)* reaches US #30. B-side *I Hear You Knocking* (originally by Domino's New Orleans contemporary Smiley Lewis) makes US #67.

Mar *Jambalaya (On The Bayou)* reaches UK #41.

Apr He records what will be his last session for Imperial in New Orleans. Meanwhile, another Hank Williams revival, *You Win Again* reaches US #22 and B-side *Ida Jane* peaks at US #90.

June His last few Imperial A-sides will fail to make US top 40 as Domino's never-changing sound begins to seem passé alongside the rapidly-developing R&B styles of the early 60s, and the dance disks by Chubby Checker°, Dee Dee Sharp and others. *My Real Name* reaches US #59.

July *Nothing New (Same Old Thing)* and B-side *Dance With Mr. Domino* peak at US #77 and #98 respectively.

Aug Compilation LP *Million Sellers By Fats* reaches US #113.

Oct *Did You Ever See A Dream Walking?*, reviving a pre-war hit by Eddy Duchin, makes US #79. This is his last hit single on Imperial.

1963 Apr [6] Domino's Imperial contract expires and he signs to ABC-Paramount Records, to record in Nashville.

June *There Goes (My Heart Again)*, on ABC, an unmistakably familiar Domino sound despite the substitution of a Nashville recording session for New Orleans, reaches US #59.

Oct LP *Here Comes Fats Domino*, on ABC, makes US #130. Taken from it, a revival of standard *Red Sails In The Sunset*, styled towards Ray Charles'° R&B/country arrangement of *I Can't Stop Loving You*, makes US #35 and UK #34.

1964 Jan *Who Cares* reaches US #63. The LP from which it is taken, *Fats On Fire*, fails to chart.

Mar *Lazy Lady* peaks at US #86.

Sept *Sally Was A Good Old Girl* reaches US #99.

Nov *Heartbreak Hill* is Domino's last ABC hit, also making #99.

1965/66 He signs to Mercury Records for 2 years. Few records are produced, but no hits (two singles, including a version of *I Left My Heart In San Francisco*; LP *Fats Domino '65*, recorded live in Las Vegas, and live LP *Southland USA*, which is recorded but never released).

1967 Mar He makes his first UK visit, playing to a nostalgic audience at London's Saville Theatre.

Dec The Mercury contract has expired and Domino records *The Lady In Black* and a follow-up single on his own Broadmoor label. With poor distribution, they fail to chart.

1968 Sept Domino signs to Reprise Records and his last US chart single, at #100, is a cover of The Beatles'° *Lady Madonna*, deliberately written in Domino style by Paul McCartney° for The Beatles'° original version earlier in the year. (Two similar Beatles' covers, *Lovely Rita* and *Everybody's Got Something To Hide Except Me And My Monkey*, are the follow-ups, but neither will chart.

Oct LP *Fats Is Back*, on Reprise and produced by Richard Perry, makes US #189. This is Domino's final US chart LP.

1970 May Compilation LP *Very Best Of Fats Domino* reaches UK #56 (his only UK chart LP).

1973 He records a live LP for Atlantic Records, in Montreux, Switzerland.

1976 May *Blueberry Hill* is reissued as a UK single, and charts at #41.

1979 May Now recording very rarely, LP *Sleeping On The Job*, made at Sea-Saint studios in New Orleans, is released by Sonet Records. (In the 1980s, Domino will spend much time living at home in New Orleans with his wife and family. He will play regularly in Las Vegas or other venues where his nostalgic style, which is still basically the same as in 1948, will pay top money and draw an appreciative audience, but he will not undertake lengthy tours.)

LONNIE DONEGAN

1952 Donegan (b. Anthony Donegan, Apr.29, 1931, Glasgow, UK), having played professionally in jazz bands since his army service in 1949 and allegedly gaining his stage name when, on the same London bill as US blues guitarist Lonnie Johnson, he is inadvertantly introduced as "Lonnie" Donegan by a confused MC, joins Ken Colyer's Jazzmen as guitar and banjo player. With Colyer, where he is reunited with an army buddy, trombonist Chris Barber, Donegan's blues and folk influences earn him a solo spot in the band's act, leading a small group (Colyer on guitar, Barber on bass, and Bill Colyer on washboard) on US blues and work songs, generically dubbed "skiffle".

1953 Some Donegan "skiffle" numbers are recorded on his first studio session with Colyer's band, but the tracks are not used.

1954 Jan Barber splits from Colyer with many of his musicians, including Donegan, and forms Chris Barber's Jazz Band, signing to Decca.

1955 The band records a 10" LP, *New Orleans Joy*, which contains two tracks, *Rock Island Line* and *John Henry*, credited to the Lonnie Donegan Skiffle Group.

1956 Feb *Rock Island Line* is released, credited to Donegan, and is an unexpected UK hit at #7, spending 25 weeks on chart. (Donegan never receives any royalties from it, having been paid a £50 session fee when it was recorded.) He signs to Pye-Nixa in UK as a soloist.

Apr *Rock Island Line* hits US #8 and takes the cumulative sales over a million.

May [19] He makes his US TV debut on "The Perry Como Show", alongside Ronald Reagan, who is appearing in some comedy sketches.

May Donegan, accompanied by a trio comprising stand-up bass, drums and Denny Wright on electric guitar, tours the US for a month, billed as "The Irish Hillbilly".

June *Lost John*, his first Pye solo release, hits UK #2 and US #58. B-side *Stewball* charts briefly at UK #29.

July *Skiffle Session* reaches UK #26 and is the first EP by a UK artist to chart.

Sept *Bring A Little Water Sylvie* hits UK #8 and B-side *Dead Or Alive* reaches #12. Back from the US, Donegan and group begin a wide UK tour, which will hardly cease over the next 2 years, prompting would-be musicians all over the UK to form easy-to-play-in skiffle groups, many of them the roots of rock'n'roll and British beat careers of the late 50s and 1960s.

Dec 10" LP *Lonnie Donegan Showcase* reaches UK #27 on the singles chart. It is the first LP by a UK artist to chart (UK LP charts do not exist at this time).

1957 Feb *Don't You Rock Me Daddy-O* hits UK #4, beating off a cover from The Vipers Skiffle Group which hits #10.

Apr *Cumberland Gap* enters UK chart at #6 while *Daddy-O* is still in the top 10 and jumps to #1, holding top position for 4 weeks. Again, it defeats a Vipers cover version which hits UK #10.

June He stars in "Skiffle Sensation of 1957" at London's Royal Albert Hall, as double A-side *Putting On The Style/Gamblin' Man* hits UK #1 for 2 weeks. *Putting On The Style*, recorded live, is Donegan's first excursion from folk/blues-based material into novelty/comedy.

Nov *My Dixie Darling* hits UK #10, while Donegan is filming appearances in a movie version of the UK TV pop music show "6.5 Special".

1958 Jan *Jack O' Diamonds* reaches UK #14.

May An adaptation of Woody Guthrie's *Grand Coolie Dam* hits UK #6.

July Double A-side *Sally Don't You Grieve/Betty Betty Betty* hits UK #10.

Sept *Lonesome Traveller* reaches UK #28.

Nov *Lonnie's Skiffle Party* reaches UK #23.

Dec Donegan covers The Kingston Trio's US #1 *Tom Dooley*, adapting the smooth original to his more frenetic style. It hits UK #3 and stays there for 6 weeks while the original climbs to #4 behind it.

1959 Feb *Does Your Chewing Gum Lose Its Flavour (On The Bedpost Overnight?)*, originally a hit in 1924 for Ernest Hare & Billy Jones, hits UK #3.

May *Fort Worth Jail* reaches UK #14.

July A cover of Johnny Horton's US chart-topper *Battle Of New Orleans* spends 4 weeks at UK #2. Donegan is forced to change the lyric and substitute "bloomin'" for "ruddy" which is banned by BBC radio. (This is not his first brush with the BBC censor: in 1956 *Diggin' My Potatoes* was banned for "obscenity" and remained BBC-blacklisted through the 50s.)

Sept *Sal's Got A Sugar Lip* reaches UK #13.

Dec *San Miguel* reaches UK #19.

1960 Jan He records in US with writer/producers Leiber and Stoller. (The tracks will appear in UK as EP *Yankee Doodle Donegan*.)

Mar *My Old Man's A Dustman*, recorded live on stage in Doncaster, UK, is the first single by a UK act to enter the UK chart at #1 (only Elvis Presley° achieved this previously). It stays at the top for 4 weeks.

June *I Wanna Go Home*, a version of the traditional *Wreck Of The John B*, hits UK #5. (It will be revived later by The Beach Boys° as *Sloop John B*.)

Sept *Lorelei* reaches UK #12.

Nov Donegan appears with Cliff Richard° and Adam Faith° in the pop music segment of the Royal Variety Show in London.

Dec *Lively*, a music hall-styled novelty in Donegan's "Dustman" mode, makes UK #14. Issued at the same time, seasonal *Virgin Mary* reaches UK #27.

1961 June *Have A Drink On Me* hits UK #8. (Another diplomatically changed lyric: Huddie Ledbetter's original was titled *Have A Whiff On Me*.)

Sept *Michael Row The Boat*, an uptempo contrast to The Highwaymen's (US and UK #1)gentle version, hits US #6. A belated US release of *Does Your Chewing Gum Lose Its Flavor (On The Bedpost Overnight?)* is his third and last chart entry. It hits US #5, and combined UK/US sales now top the million.

1962 Feb *The Comancheros*, inspired by John Wayne movie, climbs to UK #14.

May An uncharacteristic revival of standard ballad *The Party's Over* hits UK #9.

July Another ballad, the self-composed *I'll Never Fall In Love Again* is only his second UK single not to chart (though the song will be a million-seller for Tom Jones° in the late 60s).

Sept *Pick A Bale Of Cotton* makes UK #11 and is his last hit single. Compilation LP *A Golden Age Of Donegan* is his first entry in the UK LP chart, hitting UK #3 and remaining on chart for 23 weeks.

1963 Feb Compilation LP *A Golden Age Of Donegan Vol. 2* reaches UK #15.

1965 Dec Donegan records the official 1966 Soccer World Cup song, *World Cup Willie*, but it fails to chart even when the England team wins the competition the following summer. By now, much of his live work is in cabaret and he spends half of each year in the US, much of it in Las Vegas.

1966 His publishing company Tyler Music (Tyler being his wife's maiden name), owner of the copyright of most of his hit adaptations of traditional material and well-covered songs like *I'll Never Fall In Love Again*, signs young songwriter Justin Hayward. (Hayward will later join The Moody Blues° and his songs for the group, notably *Nights In White Satin*, will prove to be huge long-term earners for Tyler Music.)

Nov *Auntie Maggie's Remedy* is the last release on Pye. (He will release only eight singles in 11 years. Most are his own independent Tyler Records productions, leased variously to Decca, RCA, Black Lion and Pye for UK release.) He also appears as a regular panelist on the mid-70s UK talent show "New Faces".

1976 Donegan suffers a heart attack and is warned to stop working. He moves to California, US, in semi-retirement, to recuperate.

1978 Mar LP *Putting On The Style*, produced by Adam Faith° on Chrysalis, reaches UK #51, Donegan's first chart entry for 15 years. Playing on it are Ringo Starr°, Elton John°, Brian May of Queen°, and many others who acknowledge Donegan's influence in prompting them to play music in the first place.

1979 May LP *Sundown*, again for Chrysalis, eschews the superstars and offers more country-flavored material, recorded with the help of friend and guitarist Albert Lee.

1981 Nov LP *Jubilee Concert* is a live set of oldies to mark his 25th anniversary. He also records a skiffle EP with Scots group The Shakin' Pyramids.

1985 Donegan undergoes surgery after recurrent heart attacks, from which he recovers sufficiently to work again at a reasonable pace.

1986 Dec He forms a new band, Donegan's Dancing Sunshine Band, with clarinettist Monty Sunshine, a former colleague from the Chris Barber Band 30 years earlier.

1987 Maintaining his musical popularity worldwide via live work with the new band, Donegan, still living in California but spending 3 months each year in the UK, tries some straight acting and appears in BBC TV's police drama "Rockliffe's Babies".

RAL DONNER

1961 May After a single for Scottie Records flopped, Donner (b. Ralph Stuart Donner, Feb.10, 1943, Chicago, Ill., US), a church choir graduate who fronted his first band at 13 and worked clubs between Chicago and New York at 15, sees chart potential in a track from Presley's° LP *Elvis Is Back*, goes to an egg-box studio in Florida and makes a creditable duplication of *The Girl Of My Best Friend*, which reaches US #19. Local studio musicians, The Starfires, become his permanent backing band. The results are leased to George Goldner's Gone label.

Sept Risking eternal image as a Presley clone, Donner records an original song, *You Don't Know What You've Got (Until You Lose It)*, with similar smoldering intensity. It hits US #4 and UK #25 (the first and last time on UK chart).

Nov Assisted by "American Bandstand", on which he appears 4 times, Donner's third single *Please Don't Go* reaches US #39.

1962 Feb *She's Everything (I Wanted You To Be)* returns him to US top 20, peaking at #18.

Apr *(What A Sad Way) To Love Someone* climbs to US #74, making it five in a row for Donner, but his last chart entry.

RAL DONNER *cont.*

1962/80 Donner leaves Gone Records after royalty disputes and continues to make interesting records, with only modest sales, for a wide range of labels including Reprise, Tau, Fontana, Red Bird, Mid-Eagle, Rising Sons, MJ, Sunlight, Chicago-Fire, Starfire, Thunder and Inferno.

1981 Donner is asked to contribute his celebrated Presley impersonation to the soundtrack of Warner Bros. film *This Is Elvis*.

1984 Apr [6] After long hospitalization in Chicago, Donner dies of lung cancer, aged 41.

DONOVAN

1964 Donovan (b. Donovan Phillips Leitch, May 10, 1946, Maryhill, Glasgow, Scotland, UK), having left college after a year, is living in a seaside art studio in St. Ives, Cornwall, writing songs between waiting tables in cafés and frequently traveling around UK to play in folk clubs with kazoo player Gypsy Dave. While performing at another seaside town, Southend, he is spotted by Jeff Stephens and Peter Eden, who offer to manage him.

1965 Jan Demo recordings of some of his own songs, recorded at Stephens and Eden's instigation at a Denmark Street studio in London, interest both Pye Records and Bob Bickford, a production staff member of UK TV show "Ready Steady Go".

Feb Donovan appears on "Ready Steady Go" for 3 consecutive weeks (first act ever to have a mini-"residency" on the show), and is signed by Pye amid the widespread media comments about his apparent similarity in style and appearance (denim cap, racked harmonica, guitar inscribed "this guitar kills", etc.) to newly-emergent folk star Bob Dylan°.

Mar Donovan and Dylan° meet during Dylan's UK tour (documented in D.A. Pennebaker's fly-on-the wall film *Don't Look Back*). Donovan's debut *Catch The Wind* enters the UK chart simultaneously with Dylan's first UK single *The Times They Are A-Changin'*.

Apr *Catch The Wind* hits UK #4 (Dylan's° single peaks at UK #9). Donovan appears at the *New Musical Express* Poll Winners concert at Wembley, London, with The Beatles°, The Rolling Stones°, Tom Jones° and others.

June LP *What's Bin Did And What's Bin Hid*, including six of his own songs, hits UK #3.

July *Colours* hits UK #4. *Catch The Wind* is released in US by country/folk label Hickory Records and makes US #23.

Sept *The Universal Soldier*, written by Buffy Saint-Marie, heads a 4-track EP of the same title devoted to anti-war protest songs (the other three penned by Mick Softley, Bert Jansch and Donovan). It sells in UK as a single and peaks at #13. *Colours* reaches US #61 and LP *Catch The Wind* makes US #30.

Sept [30] Donovan makes his US TV debut on "Shindig".

Oct *The Universal Soldier* reaches US #53. (Glen Campbell's° cover makes US #45.)

Nov *Turquoise* reaches UK #30. LP *Fairy Tale*, mostly self-written, reaches UK #20.

Dec He splits from his managers (remaining with US business manager Allen Klein) and records with producer Mickie Most. Their first recording, a move away from Donovan's folk context to more experimental pop fields, is initially titled *For John And Paul*, then amended to *Sunshine Superman*.

1966 Jan LP *Fairy Tale* peaks at US #85.

Feb To fill the release gap, Pye issues earlier recording *Josie* as a UK single, but it fails to chart.

July As the Donovan/Most production deal is cleared, they sign to Epic Records for US release, continuing to lease productions to Pye in UK.

Sept Released first in US, *Sunshine Superman* hits #1 for a week and earns Donovan a first gold disk for a million-plus sales.

Oct LP *Sunshine Superman* reaches US #11 and LP *The Real Donovan*, a compilation of earlier tracks on Hickory, makes US #96.

Dec *Mellow Yellow*, with "whispering" vocal assistance from Paul McCartney°, hits US #2 and is a second million-seller.

1967 Jan *Sunshine Superman* hits UK #2. Donovan is commissioned by UK's National Theatre to compose incidental music for a new production of Shakespeare's *As You Like It*.

Mar *Mellow Yellow* hits UK #8. *Epistle To Dippy*, never released as a UK single, reaches US #19. LP *Mellow Yellow* (also not issued in UK) makes US #14.

July The UK version of LP *Sunshine Superman* (a compilation of tracks from US LPs *Sunshine Superman* and *Mellow Yellow*), reaches UK #25.

Sept *There Is A Mountain* reaches US #11.

Nov Budget LP *Universal Soldier*, compiled from earlier EP and single tracks, hits UK #5. *There Is A Mountain* hits UK #8.

Dec *Wear Your Love Like Heaven* reaches US #23.

1968 Jan Boxed double LP *A Gift From A Flower To A Garden*, with a set of commercial material (including recent hit single) and another of children's songs, makes US #19. The material is also released as two separate single LPs, *Wear Your Love Like Heaven* and *For Little Ones*, which climb to US #60 and #185 respectively. The double set earns a US gold disk.

Feb [19] Donovan flies to India (in the wake of The Beatles°) to attend a Transcendental Meditation course under Maharishi Mahesh Yogi and becomes his disciple for a while.

Mar *Jennifer Juniper* hits UK #5. The B-side *Poor Cow* is from the film of the same name, to which Donovan contributes several soundtrack songs.

Apr *Jennifer Juniper* peaks at US #26.

May Boxed double LP *A Gift From A Flower To A Garden* reaches UK #13.

July *Hurdy Gurdy Man* hits UK #4 and US #5.

Sept Live LP *Donovan In Concert*, recorded in US at the Anaheim Convention Center, Cal., earlier in the year on tour, makes US #18, but fails to chart in UK.

Oct *Lalena*, unreleased in UK as a single, reaches US #33.

Dec *Atlantis* reaches UK #23. LP *The Hurdy Gurdy Man* (not released in UK) makes US #20.

1969 He contributes songs to movie *If It's Tuesday, This Must Be Belgium*, starring Suzanne Pleshette and Ian McShane.

Mar *To Susan On The West Coast Waiting*, again unissued in UK, reaches US #35.

Apr Compilation LP *Donovan's Greatest Hits* hits US #4. It gains another gold disk but fails to chart in UK.

May *Atlantis*, originally US B-side of *To Susan On The West Coast Waiting*, out-performs its A-side and hits US #7.

Aug *Barabajagal (Love Is Hot)*, recorded with The Jeff Beck° Group and Lesley Duncan and Madeleine Bell on backing vocals, reaches UK #12 and US #36. It is Donovan's last UK hit single.

Oct LP *Barabajagal*, including several former hit singles, reaches US #23, but is not issued in UK.

1970 Donovan splits from Mickie Most, forming his own band Open Road, for live and studio work.

June [28] He appears at UK's Bath Festival of Progressive Music with Led Zeppelin°, Pink Floyd° and others.

Sept LP *Open Road*, described by Donovan as an experiment in "Celtic Rock" reaches US #16 and UK #30. *Riki Tiki Tavi* peaks at US #55.

Dec Double LP *Donovan P. Leitch*, a compilation of material originally released in US by Hickory, appears on Janus Records, peaking at US #128. Open Road breaks up.

1971 Mar *Celia Of The Seals* (on which Open Road bassist Danny Thompson has dual billing) fails to chart in UK but reaches US #84. (He spends some months writing songs and music for, and acting the title role in, Jacques Demy film fantasy *The Pied Piper*. After the filming, he moves to Ireland for an extended period, forced for tax reasons to stay outside the UK.)

July Double LP *HMS Donovan*, including a selection of children's songs, fails to chart in both US and UK, and is his last recording for Pye in UK.

1972 He writes the score for Franco Zefferelli's film *Brother Sun, Sister Moon*. While still living in Ireland, he tours with folk group Planxty.

Sept He reunites with Mickie Most and a new UK deal is signed with Epic Records. (The reunion only lasts through the recording of one LP.)

1973 Mar LP *Cosmic Wheels*, produced by Most and recorded with a star session band including Chris Spedding (guitar), Jim Horn (sax) and Cozy Powell (drums), reaches UK #15 and US #25. (It is Donovan's last LP to make the UK chart.)

May *I Like You*, taken from the LP, is his final US hit single, peaking at #66.

1974 Feb LP *Essence To Essence*, produced by Andrew Oldham with Carole

King° and Peter Frampton° guesting, reaches US #174. After its release, Donovan moves to California.

Dec LP *7-Tease*, produced in Nashville by Norbert Putnam, is a studio concept LP based on the theatrical show with the same title (with dancers, costumes, lighting and visual effects) which Donovan has staged in Cal. during the year. It reaches US #135.

1975 He tours Australia and New Zealand, and spends much of the year resting in Cal. with his family.

1976 June Self-produced, US-recorded LP *Slow Down World* reaches US #174 and is his final US chart entry.

1977 Oct Another reunion with Most, and a recording move to Most's RAK label, produces LP *Donovan*, which does not chart.

1978 Jan *Dare To Be Different* fails to chart.

1980 Aug He performs at the Edinburgh Festival in Scotland and records LP *Neutronica*, released in Europe but unavailable in UK or US.

Dec He appears with Billy Connolly and Ralph McTell on a Christmas benefit show for children's charities at the London Palladium.

1981 Nov He forms a new stage band, with Danny Thompson (bass), Tony Roberts (sax, flute and woodwinds) and John Stephens (drums), who play on unsuccessful single *Lay Down Lassie* and LP *Love Is Only Feeling*. (His career remains quiet through the 80s, with occasional low-key tours and little in the way of recordings.)

THE DOOBIE BROTHERS

Tom Johnston (lead vocals, guitar and keyboards)
Pat Simmons (guitar)
Tiran Porter (bass)
John Hartman (drums)
Keith Knudsen (percussion)
Jeff "Skunk" Baxter (guitar)

1970 Mar The group is formed in San Jose, Cal., US, under the name Pud, playing free Sunday concerts in a local park. It comprises Johnston, who studied graphic design at San Jose State, and was introduced by Moby Grape's° Skip Spence to Hartman (b. Mar.18, 1950, Falls Church, Va., US), recently arrived from West Virginia with the intention of re-forming his favorite band Moby Grape, and bassist Greg Murph (who is soon replaced by Dave Shogren). They begin jamming in a house on Twelfth Street, frequented by members of San Jose's Hells Angels.

Sept Simmons (b. Jan.23, 1950, San Jose), a folk/bluegrass guitarist, joins, and the group becomes The Doobie Brothers ("Doobie" being California slang for a marijuana joint), at the suggestion of room-mate Keith Rosen. They become the house band at the Chateau Liberte, a saloon in the Santa Cruz mountains. A six-track demo is sent by Pacific Recording studios owner Paul Curcio to Lenny Waronker at Warner Bros. Records, which signs them.

1971 Apr LP *The Doobie Brothers*, produced by Ted Templeman (ex-Harper's Bizarre°), fails to chart, despite the extensive Warner Bros.-sponsored "Mother Brothers" US tour to promote it.

Oct Porter, previously with Simmons in a folk trio, replaces Shogren on bass, and Mike Hossack, a second drummer/percussionist, is added to boost the live sound.

1972 Oct LP *Toulouse Street*, the group's US chart debut, reaches #21 and earns a gold disk. Johnston-penned *Listen To The Music*, taken from it, makes US #11.

1973 Feb *Jesus Is Just Alright*, previously recorded by The Byrds°, reaches US #35.

June LP *The Captain And Me* hits US #7 and is another gold disk. Extracted from it, *Long Train Runnin'* hits US #8.

Sept Hossack quits to form his own band Bonaroo, and is replaced on percussion by Knudsen (b. Oct.18, 1952, Ames, Io., US), ex-drummer with Lee Michaels' band.

Oct *China Grove*, the third hit single penned by Johnston, makes US #15.

Dec [24] Johnston is arrested in Visalia, Cal., for marijuana possession.

1974 Jan [26] The group plays The Rainbow, London, the first of four UK dates on its first European tour.

Mar *Listen To The Music* makes UK #29.

Apr LP *What Were Once Vices Are Now Habits* hits US #4, earning another gold disk, and is the band's first UK chart LP, at #19. It includes session guitar contributions from Baxter (b. Dec.13, 1948, Washington, D.C., US), who is with Steely Dan°, but plays live with The Doobie Brothers between Steely Dan commitments.

June *Another Park, Another Sunday* reaches US #32, with the group consistently touring US.

July With the demise of Steely Dan° as a live band, Baxter joins The Doobie Brothers full-time, completing their ambition to field a three-guitar line-up on stage. They return to UK to play the Knebworth festival.

Aug *Eyes Of Silver* reaches US #52.

Nov *Nobody* makes US #58.

1975 Jan [12] The group opens an 18-show, 9-city tour of UK and Europe as part of Warner's "Looney Tunes" package, with Little Feat°, Graham Central Station, Bonaroo, Montrose, and Tower of Power.

Mar Simmons' composition *Black Water*, originally B-side of *Another Park, Another Sunday*, hits US #1 for 1 week and is their first million-selling single.

Apr While on a 7-week US tour, Johnston becomes ill with a stomach disorder and has to drop out. Ex-Steely Dan° vocalist/keyboards player Michael McDonald° (b. 1952, St. Louis, Mo.) is recruited at Baxter's suggestion; after rehearsing for 48 hours in New Orleans he joins the tour, and is quickly accepted as a full-time member.

May Baxter makes a guest appearance on guitar at Elton John's° London concert.

June LP *Stampede*, recorded prior to McDonald's° arrival, hits US #4 and makes UK #14, and is the group's fourth gold LP. From it, a revival of Holland/Dozier/Holland's *Take Me In Your Arms (Rock Me)* (a US hit for Kim Weston) reaches US #11 and UK #29.

June [29] At a concert in Oakland, Cal., Elton John° joins the band to duet on *Listen To The Music*.

Aug *Sweet Maxine* climbs to US #40.

Sept The band plays The Great American Music Fair in Syracuse, N.Y., an event marred by violent conflict between would-be free festival demonstrators and state troopers.

1976 Jan *I Cheat The Hangman* reaches US #60, as Johnston rejoins after his illness.

May LP *Takin' It To The Streets* hits US #8 and peaks at UK #42. It is the band's first LP to be certified platinum for million-plus US sales. Extracted title track, penned by McDonald°, reaches US #13.

July The band backs Carly Simon° on her US #46 hit of McDonald's° *It Keeps You Runnin'*.

Aug *Wheels Of Fortune* peaks at US #87.

Dec LP *Best Of The Doobies*, a compilation of hit singles, hits US #5, earning the group's second platinum LP.

1977 Jan *It Keeps You Runnin'* (included on the compilation LP) reaches US #37. Johnston leaves the band for a solo career.

May [7] The Doobie Brothers participate in Bill Graham's "Day on the Green #1" at Oakland Stadium, Cal. in front of 57,500 fans.

July [1] The band opens a month's US tour at Rushmore Civic Plaza, Rapid City, S.D.

Aug A second Motown revival, of Marvin Gaye's° 1966 hit *Little Darling (I Need You)*, makes US #48.

Aug [28] The band plays UK's Reading Festival, plus four other UK dates, now presenting a tighter, funkier sound (the pervasive influence of McDonald°) than their earlier guitar boogie.

Sept [27] The band plays the "Rock'n'Bowl" at South Bay Bowl, Redondo Beach, Cal., a benefit concert for US Special Olympics.

Oct LP *Living On The Fault Line* hits US #10 (earning a gold disk), and makes UK #25.

Nov *Echoes Of Love* reaches US #66.

1978 July [1] The Doobie Brothers play the Catalyst, Santa Cruz, Cal., in a benefit show for actor Will Geer.

Aug [26] The band plays in Ontario, Canada, at the first Canada Jam festival, to 80,000 people, sharing the bill with The Commodores°, Kansas°, The Village People°, Dave Mason, and Atlanta Rhythm Section°.

1979 Mar With the band's new single and LP climbing up the US chart and showing signs of being their all-time best-sellers, both Baxter and Hartman decide to leave, the former to return to session work and production, the latter to quit music and return to his horse ranch in Sonoma County.

Apr LP *Minute By Minute*, the result of their move into funky soul, tops the US chart for 5 weeks, and is their third US million-selling LP. Taken from it, *What A Fool Believes*, written by McDonald° and Kenny Loggins, is the band's second US #1 (for 1 week) and second million-selling single. It reaches UK #31.

May After extensive auditions, ex-Moby Grape° keyboards and sax player Cornelius Bumpus (b. Jan.13, 1952), experienced session drummer Chet McCracken (b. July 17, 1952, Seattle, Wash., US), and ex-Clover guitarist John McFee (b. Nov.18, 1953, Santa Cruz, Cal.), replace the departed members in time for a summer US tour.

THE DOOBIE BROTHERS *cont.*

July [1] The Doobie Brothers celebrate their tenth anniversary at LA's Friars Club, with Eddie Floyd°, The Jacksons, Kenny Loggins and Sam and Dave° joining the band in an all-star jam of *Soul Man*.

July The title track from *Minute By Minute* makes US #14 and UK #47.

Sept [19] The band plays in the Musicians United For Safe Energy (MUSE) anti-nuclear concerts at New York's Madison Square Garden, alongside Bruce Springsteen°, Jackson Browne°, Carly Simon° and others.

Oct *Dependin' On You* peaks at US #25.

Dec Johnston, signed to Warner Bros. as a soloist, makes US #100 with his LP *Everything You've Heard Is True*.

1980 Jan Johnston's *Savannah Nights* reaches US #34.

Feb [27] The Doobie Brothers sweep the 22nd Grammy awards. *What A Fool Believes* is voted both Song of the Year and Record of the Year and McDonald° receives a Grammy for Best Arrangement Accompanying Vocalists for it. LP *Minute By Minute* wins the award for Best Group Pop Vocal Performance.

July [16] Movie *No Nukes*, documenting the previous year's Madison Square Garden anti-nuclear concerts, including a set by The Doobie Brothers, premieres in New York.

Oct *Real Love* hits US #5. It is taken from LP *One Step Closer*, which hits US #3 (their fourth and last platinum LP) and UK #53.

Nov Porter leaves both the group and the music scene, and session bassist Willie Weeks joins in his place for live work.

1981 Jan Title track from *One Step Closer* makes US #24.

Feb *Wynken, Blynken And Nod* (taken from the various artists LP *In Harmony* on Sesame Street Records which makes US #156 at the same time), reaches US #76.

Mar *Keep This Train A-Rollin'* reaches US #62.

June Johnston's solo LP *Still Feels Good* makes US #158.

Oct After a concert in Hawaii to complete touring for the year, the band decides to split. Simmons and McDonald° are both working on solo LPs, and it is felt there is too much conflict of interest within the group.

Dec Compilation LP *Best Of The Doobies, Volume II* reaches US #39, and earns the band's last gold disk.

1982 Feb *Here To Love You* reaches US #65.

Mar [31] The official break-up of the group is announced, with news of a forthcoming temporary re-formation for a farewell US tour.

Aug McDonald° begins his successful solo career with *I Keep Forgettin' (Every Time You're Near)* and LP *If That's What It Takes*.

Sept The group plays its farewell US tour, with Warner Bros. recording performances for a final live LP.

1983 May *So Wrong*, Simmons' first solo, reaches US #30.

June Simmons' LP *Arcade*, on Elektra, peaks at US #52.

July Simmons' *Don't Make Me Do It* (written by Huey Lewis & The News°) climbs to US #75.

Aug Double live LP *The Doobie Brothers Farewell Tour* reaches US #79, and *You Belong To Me* (previously a hit for Carly Simon°, and a song co-written by McDonald° and Simon° via mail), also peaks at US #79.

1987 June [21] A new line-up of The Doobie Brothers, with Johnston back (but without McDonald°), plays the last of ten reunion concerts, at the Mountain Aire Festival, Cal.

July [4] The band participates in "The July Fourth Disarmament Festival" in the Soviet Union with James Taylor°, Santana°, Bonnie Raitt and several Russian groups.

1988 The group returns to the studio to record a comeback LP for Capitol Records.

THE DOORS

Jim Morrison (vocals)
Ray Manzarek (keyboards)
Robby Kreiger (guitar)
John Densmore (drums)

1964 Feb Morrison (b. Dec.8, 1943, Melbourne, Fla., US), the son of a US Navy admiral, enrols in the Theater Art Department of California's UCLA, where he meets Manzarek (b. Feb 12, 1935, Chicago, Ill., US), a prodigal classical pianist who plays in a blues band with his brothers Rick and Jim on weekends at a Santa Monica, Cal., bar.

1965 July Morrison and Manzarek decide to form a group after Morrison sings his song *Moonlight Drive* to Manzarek, who recruits

Densmore (b. Dec.1, 1945, Los Angeles, Cal.), a physics and psychology major, having met him in a TM course at LA's Third Street Meditation Center.

Sept Morrison, Manzarek and Densmore record a demo of Morrison's songs *Moonlight Drive, Summer's Almost Gone, Break On Through* and *End Of The Night*. They are helped by the other two Manzareks and a female bass player, who all leave immediately afterwards because they dislike the material. Kreiger (b. Jan.8, 1946, Los Angeles), who has earlier played with Densmore in The Psychedelic Rangers band, is recruited on guitar.

1966 Morrison names the group The Doors, inspired by some lines by William Blake in Aldous Huxley's document of a mescaline experience, *The Doors Of Perception*. After rehearsing for 5 months, they play at the London Fog club on Sunset Boulevard but are fired. They find work as back-up band at the Whiskey-A-Go-Go where Elektra's Billy James spots them before they are fired again for performing Morrison's *The End*. Label boss Jac Holzman signs them.

1967 Jan Debut LP *The Doors*, establishes a powerful, theatrical, rock-blues style, and will hit US #2. *Break On Through* does not chart.

July *Light My Fire*, extracted from the LP in a much-abridged version, tops the US chart for 3 weeks, sells over a million, and reaches UK #49.

Sept [17] The band appears on US TV's "Ed Sullivan Show", on which the host requests that Morrison omit the line "girl, we couldn't get much higher" from *Light My Fire*. Morrison agrees, then sings it anyway.

Oct *People Are Strange*, from the forthcoming LP, reaches US #12.

Nov LP *Strange Days* hits US #3.

Dec [9] Morrison is arrested after a concert in New Haven, Conn., during which he has badmouthed the police. He is charged with breach of the peace and resisting arrest.

1968 Jan *Love Me Two Times*, extracted from LP *Strange Days*, makes US #25.

Feb Univeral Pictures offers the band $500,000 to star in a feature film. (It is never made.)

Apr *The Unknown Soldier* reaches US #39. The band makes its own promo film for it which includes Morrison being "shot".

Aug *Hello I Love You*, a relatively jaunty pop song, is The Doors' second US #1 (for 2 weeks) and second million-seller.

Sept LP *Waiting For the Sun*, containing *Hello I Love You*, is the band's only US chart-topping LP, spending 4 weeks at #1. (The sleeve contains the full libretto of Morrison's theatrical poem *Celebration Of The Lizard*, which will not appear on record until the 1970 LP *Absolutely Live*.) The Doors are filling major US rock venues but Morrison's hard-drinking, drug-infused lifestyle and overtly sexual deportment make the band a controversial success. *Hello I Love You* reaches UK #15 as the group visits UK for promotion and concerts.

Oct [6] A film documentary, *The Doors Are Open*, made in London, is shown on UK TV. LP *Waiting For The Sun* makes UK #16, the group's first LP success in UK.

1969 Feb *Touch Me* hits US #3 and is another million-seller.

Mar [1] After a concert in Miami, Fla., Morrison is charged with "lewd and lascivious behavior in public by exposing his private parts and by simulating masturbation and oral copulation", in addition to profanity, drunkenness and other minor offences. The prospect of court appearances makes tour booking impossible for the next 5 months.

Apr [3] Morrison is arrested in LA by the FBI and charged with interstate flight to avoid prosecution on his Miami charges.

Apr *Wishful Sinful* reaches US #44.

June [5] The band premieres its documentary film *Feast Of Friends* at Cinemathique 16 in LA. Local politicians in St. Louis and Hawaii force cancellations of scheduled Doors appearances.

July *Tell All The People* climbs to US #57.

July [25] The band appears at the Seattle Pop Festival in Woodenville, Wash., with Led Zeppelin°, Chuck Berry°, Bo Diddley° and others.

Sept *Runnin' Blue* makes US #64. LP *The Soft Parade* hits US #6.

Sept [13] The band plays the Toronto Rock'n'Roll Revival concert, with John Lennon's° Plastic Ono Band, Chuck Berry° and others.

Nov Morrison is arrested after trying to interfere with an air hostess on a plane from LA to Phoenix, Ariz. The charge is the potentially very serious one of interfering with the flight of an aircraft, as well as public drunkenness. (It will be dropped when the hostess withdraws her evidence.)

1970 Jan [17/18] The Doors play 2 nights at New York's Felt Forum, recorded (as are several later concerts) for a live LP.

Apr LP *Morrison Hotel* hits US #4 and UK #12. One song on it, *Queen Of The Highway*, is dedicated to Morrison's new wife, Pamela. *You Make Me Real/Roadhouse Blues*, taken from the LP, reaches US #50.

Sept [20] In a Miami court, Morrison is found guilty of indecent exposure and profanity, though acquitted on the charge of "lewd and lascivious behavior".

Sept Double LP *Absolutely Live*, recorded in Jan. in New York, which contains a full version of *Celebration Of The Lizard*, hits US #8 and UK #69 at a time when live performances by the group are sporadic.

Oct [30] Morrison is sentenced for the offences of which he was found guilty in September, and receives 8 months' hard labor and a $500 fine. He will remain free while the sentence is appealed against.

Nov [8] On his 27th birthday, Morrison makes the recordings of his poetry (which will later form the basis of *An American Prayer*).

Nov [12] The Doors play their last concert with Morrison in New Orleans. (He will complete recording of another LP which will be released as *L.A. Woman* 6 months later.)

1971 Jan Compilation LP *Doors 13* reaches US #25.

Mar Morrison moves to Paris to concentrate on writing poetry. His first book *The Lords And The New Creatures* goes into paperback after selling an initial 15,000 in hardback. The rest of the band continues to rehearse weekly in the hope that he will decide to return to music.

May *Love Her Madly* is the band's biggest single for over 2 years, peaking at US #11.

June LP *L.A. Woman*, recorded in the last sessions with Morrison, hits US #9.

July [3] Morrison dies in Paris of a heart attack (the suddenness of the death leading to much speculation).

July [9] His family having disowned him, Morrison is buried in the Père Lachaise cemetery in Paris (where his grave will become a graffiti-covered shrine).

Aug *Riders On The Storm* reaches US #14. It is extracted from LP *L.A. Woman* which climbs to UK #28, having just received a gold disk for a half-million sales in US.

Dec *Riders On The Storm* reaches UK #22. The remaining Doors trio releases LP *Other Voices*, which reaches US #31.

1972 Mar Double compilation LP *Weird Scenes Inside The Gold Mine* climbs to US #55 and UK #50. *Tightrope Ride*, a track without Morrison, makes US #71.

Sept The trio releases LP *Full Circle* which reaches US #68. *The Mosquito* reaches US #85.

Dec With inspiration hard to come by, and deprived of its single most important element, the band breaks up. (Manzarek will record two solo LPs and produce many other acts. Kreiger and Densmore will form The Butts Band before moving on into session and solo work.)

1973 Oct Another Doors compilation LP, *Best Of The Doors*, reaches US #158.

1974 Apr [25] Pamela Morrison dies from a suspected heroin overdose.

1976 Apr *Riders On The Storm* is re-released in the UK, reaching #33.

1979 Jan When the 1970 tapes of Morrison reciting his poetry are unearthed, the other three former Doors get together to provide a musical backing for the words and, along with snippets of original live performances, the results are released as LP *An American Prayer – Jim Morrison*. It makes US #54, rekindling interest in the group.

Feb A picture-disk reissue of *Hello I Love You* reaches UK #71.

Aug Morrison's most controversial song from The Doors' first LP, *The End*, is prominently featured on the soundtrack of Francis Ford Coppola's film *Apocalypse Now*.

1980 Nov A new compilation LP, *The Doors' Greatest Hits*, reaches US #17.

1981 July On the 10th anniversay of Morrison's death, Manzarek, Kreiger and Densmore lead fans in a graveside tribute ceremony in Paris.

Sept [18] The compilation LP *The Doors' Greatest Hits* is awarded a platinum disk for US sales of over a million.

1983 Nov *Alive, She Cried*, an LP compiled from live tapes lost for over a decade but discovered in an LA warehouse after the former band members initiate a search for them, reaches US #23 and UK #36.

1984 Jan Extracted from the LP, *Gloria* (recorded at a soundcheck in 1969) reaches US #71.

1987 July LP *Live At The Hollywood Bowl*, the soundtrack of a Doors gig filmed there in the late 1960s (and simultaneously released on home video), reaches US #154 and UK #51. The interest generated also brings the compilation LP *Best Of The Doors* back into the lower reaches of the US chart.

LEE DORSEY

1961 Oct After mixed fortune in the ring (as Kid Chocolate) and the US Navy, Dorsey (b. Irving Lee Dorsey, Dec.4, 1926, New Orleans, La., US), returning to his home town, records nonsensical but catchy, *Ya Ya*, supervised by studio gang boss Harold Battiste, on Bobby Robinson's Fury label. A million-seller, it hits US #7 and enables him to quit his day job in an auto wrecking yard and go on tour, playing prestigious R&B venues in California and Texas. (Among several covers of *Ya Ya* will be one by John Lennon°.)

1962 Feb *Do Re Mi*, equally jaunty and written by local R&B hero Earl King, reaches US #27, but Fury label has problems and Dorsey soon slips from public view. (Later, both Dusty Springfield° and Georgie Fame° cut versions of the song.)

1965 Aug Marshall Sehorn and Allen Toussaint team up to plan a Lee Dorsey revival. *Ride Your Pony*, written by Toussaint and through a lease deal with Bell/Amy Records, restores him to the US chart, at #28. He makes a triumphant stage return at the New York Apollo, after a 3-year hiatus.

1966 Feb *Get Out Of My Life Woman* makes US #44 and launches him in UK, reaching #22. Like all his best material, it is written and produced by Toussaint.

May *Confusion* rises to UK #38 but fails to chart in US.

Sept *Working In The Coal Mine*, ostensibly a song of hapless resignation, is one of the year's hottest international soul/dance hits, making #8 in both US and UK. (The song will be revived by such unlikely people as Devo° and The Judds in the 1980s.) The laid-back Dorsey, described as Mr TNT by some hyperbolic promoters, tours Europe.

Nov *Holy Cow* hits UK #6, becoming his biggest UK hit but paradoxically his last. (The Band° will revive the song on their 1973 LP *Moondog Matinee*; The Shadows° and Chas & Dave will cut UK versions.)

Dec *Holy Cow* peaks at US #23. His only chart LP, *The New Lee Dorsey* rises to US #129 and UK #34.

1967 May *My Old Car* reaches only US #97.

Oct *Go-Go Girl* makes US #62.

1969 June *Everything I Do Gohn Be Funky (From Now On)* peaks at US #95 and is his last chart entry.

1970 LP *Yes We Can* is released. (*Occapella* and *Sneaking Sally Through The Alley*, both taken from the LP, will subsequently be covered by Ringo Starr° and Robert Palmer°. Dorsey will continue to work on and off with Toussaint, but with only localized success, and will devote more time to managing his auto repair shop.)

1980 June The Clash° persuades Dorsey to come out of his semi-retirement and support them on their US tour.

1986 Dec [1] Dorsey dies of emphysema in New Orleans.

CRAIG DOUGLAS

1957 Dec Douglas (b. Terry Perkins, Aug.13, 1941, Newport, Isle of Wight, UK) is working as a milkman when he wins a talent contest on the Isle of Wight singing Harry Belafonte's° *Mary's Boy Child*, and travels to UK mainland to turn professional. Writer/producer Bunny Lewis becomes his manager and renames him Craig Douglas.

1958 Aug UK TV slot of "6.5 Special" leads to a Decca recording contract and a first release coupling covers of Marty Robbins' *Sitting In A Tree House* and Eddie Fontaine's *Nothin' Shakin'*. It is not a hit, and neither is the Oct. follow-up, which covers Jimmie Rodgers' *Are You Really Mine?*

1959 Apr He follows his producer Dick Rowe from Decca to Top Rank Records, and releases *Come Softly To Me*, but only the Fleetwoods' original and a Frankie Vaughan/Kaye Sisters cover version chart in UK.

July UK chart debut with *A Teenager In Love* reaches #12, with Douglas this time coming second in another three-cornered fight: Marty Wilde's° *Teenager* hits #2, and Dion and The Belmonts'° original makes #28. Douglas and Wilde, touring the UK on the same package show, sing it on alternate nights.

Sept *Only Sixteen* is his biggest hit, topping UK chart for 5 weeks and selling over a half million copies. It is a cover of a Sam Cooke° record which itself makes UK #19.

1960 Feb *Pretty Blue Eyes*, covering a Steve Lawrence US hit, hits UK #4.

May *The Heart Of A Teenage Girl*, Douglas' first non-cover hit, hits UK #10.

Aug *Oh What A Day* makes a minor showing at UK #43 and LP *Craig Douglas* reaches #17.

1961 Mar He sings *The Girl Next Door* in a small cameo role in UK film *Climb Up The Wall*, but the song does not chart on record.

May *A Hundred Pounds Of Clay*, a cover of a US hit by Gene McDaniels, runs into problems with BBC radio because of supposed blasphemous lyrics. A re-recorded version with amended lyric by Bunny Lewis replaces the original pressing. The BBC accepts it, and it hits UK #8.

Aug *Time* hits UK #7.

1962 Mar Douglas co-stars with Helen Shapiro° in Richard Lester's UK musical film *It's Trad, Dad!*, which also features a host of pop and trad jazz acts. Soundtrack LP hits UK #3.

Apr He finishes second in another strong UK chart race with Goffin/King song *When My Little Girl Is Smiling*. Douglas' version reaches #12. Jimmy Justice's hits #3 and The Drifters'° original makes #21.

July He switches to Columbia label for *Our Favourite Melodies*, hitting UK #10. The song uses phrases from former hits by Ray Charles°, Del Shannon°, Bobby Vee° and others.

Oct On UK tour, he performs at Liverpool Empire with The Beatles° (just into chart for the first time with *Love Me Do*) as his backing group.

Nov Another label switch returns him to Decca, this time successfully as a revival of Don Gibson's *Oh Lonesome Me* makes UK #14.

1963 Feb Douglas advertises a "video jukebox", but it receives scant attention.

Mar *Town Crier* is his final UK chart entry, reaching #36. (The 1960s see him moving into cabaret, overseas touring and even a brief stint in TV commercial work – a detergent ad – while continuing to record without success for Decca, then Fontana and Pye. By the 1980s, he will still be working clubs and cabaret regularly, updating many of his early hits to a modern idiom.)

THE DRIFTERS

Clyde McPhatter (lead tenor)
Gerhart Thrasher (tenor)
Andrew Thrasher (baritone)
Bill Pinckney (bass)

1953 May Atlantic boss Ahmet Ertegun, having gone to see The Dominoes at Manhattan's Royal Roost and finding that lead singer McPhatter (b. Nov.13, 1933, Durham, N.C., US) has been fired, locates and signs him, suggesting that McPhatter form a new group. The singer rounds up some vocalizing friends (David Baldwin, William Anderson, James Johnson and David Baughan) but the first recording session, co-produced by Ertegun and Jerry Wexler (his first time in the studio), is a disaster and the friends leave McPhatter to find a new group.

June McPhatter rehearses with other friends who form the Thrasher Wonders gospel group, then cuts the first Drifters' song *Gone* with Gerhart Thrasher, his brother Andrew and Willie Ferbee.

Aug Bill Pinckney replaces Ferbee on the second session and this settles down as the initial Drifters line-up. They cut *Money Honey*, written by Jesse Stone and featuring him on piano. McPhatter asks George Treadwell to manage the group.

Nov *Money Honey*, later covered by Elvis Presley° and others, tops the US R&B chart for 11 weeks and becomes a million-seller.

1954 Apr McPhatter's unorthodox, free-ranging tenor voice becomes one of the most popular sounds in US R&B: *Such A Night* (covered by Johnnie Ray in a version banned by some US radio stations and by the BBC, though it tops the UK pop chart) hits #5 and *Lucille* hits #7. McPhatter is drafted, becoming a forces entertainer in Special Services (though he will record occasionally with the group on leave). The similar-voiced David Baughan returns to take lead vocal on stage.

Oct *Honey Love* (written by McPhatter with Atlantic's Wexler) is another US R&B #1.

Dec *Bip Bam* (also recorded by B.B. King°) hits US R&B #7, while a revolutionary arrangement of *White Christmas* (later copied by Presley°) hits #2.

1955 June *Whatcha Gonna Do* hits US R&B #8. McPhatter cuts his first solo sides while on Service leave.

Aug Baughan leaves and Johnny Moore (b. 1934, Selma, Ala., US) becomes lead singer. Andrew Thrasher is fired by Treadwell and replaced by Charlie Hughes.

Sept The Moore-fronted Drifters record in LA with producer Nesuhi Ertegun. Among the songs cut is Leiber and Stoller's *Ruby Baby* (which will make US R&B #13 and become a million-seller for Dion°).

Dec The Drifters hit the US pop chart for the first time as *White Christmas* reaches US #80.

1956 Apr [19] McPhatter is discharged from the Armed Forces. (He does not rejoin the group but begins a successful solo US chart career with *Seven Days*.)

1957 Feb The Drifters reach US #69 with *Fools Fall In Love*, another Leiber/Stoller song.

June After the group reaches US #79 with *Hypnotized*, Moore is drafted and Bobby Hendricks from The Flyers comes in as lead tenor. (The next 2 years will see constant short-term personnel changes, with various members leaving and returning.)

1958 June The latest Drifters line-up (Hendricks, Thrasher, Jimmy Millender and Tommy Evans) has a double-sided hit with oldie *Moonlight Bay* (US #72) and Leiber and Stoller's *Drip Drop* (US #58), but they rile manager Treadwell and he fires them.

July Treadwell, who owns The Drifters name and nominates those who trade under it, hires another vocal group, The Crowns, to become The Drifters.

1959 June Now freelancing for Atlantic, Leiber and Stoller supervise the new group's first session and their elaborate string-backed production transforms *There Goes My Baby* into an eerie, ethereal R&B classic. Co-written by lead singer Ben E. King°, it hits US #2 and earns the group a second gold disk.

Oct *Dance With Me* reaches US #15 and UK #17. The B-side *True Love True Love*, featuring Johnny Lee Williams on lead vocal, makes US #33.

1960 Feb Using their own compositions for The Coasters°, Leiber and Stoller ask Brill Building tunesmiths Pomus and Shuman to write material for The Drifters. After *True Love True Love*, they create *This Magic Moment*, which makes US #16. Ben E. King° is lead singer again, (and will be on the group's next three hits).

May From the same team, *Lonely Winds* reaches US #54.

Sept Pomus/Shuman/Leiber/Stoller writing en masse provide The Drifters with *Save The Last Dance For Me* which tops the US chart for 3 weeks, hits UK #2 and is a million-seller.

Dec Despite colossal record sales and packed houses, The Drifters receive only modest wages. King° complains and, when manager Treadwell invites him to resign, he does. The Pomus/Shuman-penned *I Count The Tears*, King's last with The Drifters, reaches US #17 and UK #28.

1961 Mar With Rudy Lewis (ex-Clara Ward Singers) taking lead, The Drifters cut a Goffin/King song, *Some Kind Of Wonderful*, which makes US #32.

June Co-written by Burt Bacharach, *Please Stay* reaches US #14.

Sept Pomus and Shuman's *Sweets For My Sweet* makes US #16. (The repertoire of every group on Merseyside will include Drifters' material, but only The Searchers° hit UK #1 (Aug. 1963) with a revival of *Sweets For My Sweet*.)

Dec Pomus and Shuman's *Room Full Of Tears* reaches only US #72.

1962 Mar Goffin and King's° *When My Little Girl Is Smiling* reaches US #28 and UK #31.

May A vocal rendering of Acker Bilk's chart topper *Stranger On The Shore* makes only US #73 and *Sometimes I Wonder* misses the chart altogether.

Nov The Drifters hit US #5 with their fourth million-seller, *Up On The Roof*, written by Goffin and King°.

1963 Mar Leiber and Stoller modify a Barry Mann and Cynthia Weil composition and allow Phil Spector to add the attractive guitar frills to *On Broadway*, which hits US #9.

June They also produce *Rat Race*, co-written with Van McCoy, which makes US #71. LP *Up On The Roof*, a compilation of singles, climbs to US #110.

Sept Written by Mann and Weil, *I'll Take You Home* reaches US #25 and UK #37. Leiber and Stoller withdraw from involvement with the group, to concentrate on the launch of their Red Bird label.

1964 Feb New Atlantic staff producer Bert Berns takes over and *Vaya Con Dios*, a huge seller for Les Paul and Mary Ford in 1953, reaches US #43.

May Berns' own song *One Way Love* takes The Drifters to US #56 (but provides UK soul man Cliff Bennett° with his top ten breakthrough at home).

June After Rudy Lewis dies unexpectedly, Johnny Moore returns to take over lead vocals and the group's transition from R&B to smooth soul-pop is apparent in *Under The Boardwalk* which hits US #4 and makes UK #45.

Sept A *Boardwalk* sequel, *I've Got Sand In My Shoes*, reaches US #33.

Nov Mann and Weil's *Saturday Night At The Movies* makes US #18. LP *Under The Boardwalk* (again, a singles compilation) makes US #40.

1965 Jan Goffin and King's° *At The Club* makes US #43 and UK #35.

Feb LP *The Good Life* reaches only US #103.

Apr *Come On Over To My Place*, a double-sider by Mann and Weil, reaches US #60 and UK #40. Atlantic standard *Chains Of Love* reaches US #90.

July *Follow Me* makes US #91.

Aug Written by Jeff Barry and Ellie Greenwich, *I'll Take You Where The Music's Playing* reaches US #51.

1966 Mar A million-seller for Dean Martin in 1955, *Memories Are Made Of This* makes only US #48. The record marks the departure of producer Bert Berns, now running his own Bang and Shout records and at legal loggerheads with Atlantic.

Dec Produced by Bob Gallo and Atlantic engineer Tom Dowd, *Baby What I Mean* peaks at US #62 and reaches UK #49.

1967/70 Atlantic releases one unsuccessful Drifters single per year. LP *Golden Hits* reaches US #122 and UK #27 early in 1968.

1971 With Johnny Moore the only constant factor, The Drifters remain on the clubland circuit. Following the death of George Treadwell, his wife Faye assumes managerial control.

1972 Mar Reissued back to back *At The Club/Saturday Night At The Movies* begins climbing the UK chart, eventually hitting #3.

June A reactivated LP *Golden Hits* reaches UK #26.

June [13] Clyde McPhatter dies of heart, kidney and liver disease following serious alcohol and drug addiction.

Aug A minor hit 7 years earlier, *Come On Over To My Place* hits UK #9.

1973 Aug Still led by Moore, The Drifters sign a deal with the UK office of Bell Records and start a run of hits – all written and produced by permutations of Roger Cook, Roger Greenaway, Geoff Stephens, Barry Mason, Les Reed and Tony Macaulay. The first of these, *Like Brother And Sister* hits UK #7.

1974 July *Kissin' In The Back Row Of The Movies* hits UK #2.

Nov *Down On The Beach Tonight* hits UK #7.

1975 Feb *Love Games* reaches UK #33.

Oct The Drifters, now well-known on the UK club/cabaret/television show circuit, hit UK #3 with *There Goes My First Love*.

Dec *Can I Take You Home Little Girl* hits UK #10. Atlantic takes advantage of their renewed popularity and repackages *24 Original Hits* which hits UK #2 and remains on the LP chart for 34 weeks. Overshadowed by the reissue, the latest Bell LP *Love Games* charts briefly at UK #51.

1976 *Hello Happiness* makes UK #12, *Every Nite's A Saturday Night With You* reaches UK #29 and *You're More Than A Number In My Little Red Book* hits UK #5. None of the group's Bell output makes the US chart.

1977/88 The Drifters continue to play the circuit. *Save The Last Dance For Me/When My Little Girl Is Smiling* returns to the UK chart (#69) as part of a picture disk marketing exercise with other oldies. Johnny Moore drops out but returns, and during the mid-80s Ben E. King° sings alongside him in the group – but only until the reissued *Stand By Me* returns him to the limelight. At least forty people can legitimately claim to have been bona-fide Drifters over the group's 35-year history and most of them have masqueraded in several bogus groups of touring "Drifters".

DURAN DURAN

Simon Le Bon (vocals)
Andy Taylor (guitar)
Nick Rhodes (keyboards)
John Taylor (bass)
Roger Taylor (drums)

1978 The band is formed in Birmingham, UK, by Rhodes (b. Nicholas Bates, June 8, 1962, Birmingham) and John Taylor (b. June 20, 1960, Solihull, UK) on guitar, with bass player and clarinettist Simon Culley, vocalist Stephen Duffy and a drum machine. The group's name is taken from the character played by Milo O'Shea in Jane Fonda science fiction movie *Barbarella* and it plays many early gigs at Barbarella's club in Birmingham.

1979 Colley and Duffy leave and are replaced by vocalist Andy Wickett, ex-TV Eye, and drummer Roger Taylor (b. Apr.26, 1960, Birmingham), ex-local punk group The Scent Organs. John Taylor switches to playing bass, guitarist John Curtis comes and goes, and the band puts an ad in *Melody Maker* for a "live wire guitarist" and recruits Andy Taylor (b. Feb.16, 1961, Cullercoats, Newcastle, UK). Wickett leaves and the band has temporary vocalists for a while.

1980 Jan Brothers Paul and Michael Berrow, owners of Birmingham's newly-opened Rum Runner club, sign the band to a management contract and give it a residency at the club.

Apr Simon Le Bon (b. Oct.27, 1958, Bushey, Herts., UK), who is studying drama at Birmingham University, is recruited after one rehearsal, having been suggested by an ex-girlfriend who is a barmaid at the Rum Runner. (He will become the band's lyricist.)

July After Le Bon completes his term at university, he joins full time and the group plays to great success at the Edinburgh Festival in Scotland.

Nov Duran Duran plays its first major UK tour dates, supporting Hazel O'Connor, and the Berrow brothers negotiate a worldwide recording deal with EMI Records.

1981 Mar First release *Planet Earth*, produced by Colin Thurston, reaches UK #12. The band's musical and visual style fits neatly into the "New Romantic" movement in UK rock music which is rapidly spreading as a backlash against the punk-originated new wave, with similar contemporaries like Spandau Ballet°, Ultravox° and Visage also hitting the chart. (Media coverage is wide and the photogenic line-up, well displayed in several promotional videos, will raise Duran Duran to UK teen sensation status by the end of the year.)

May *Careless Memories* makes UK #37.

June The band begins its first headlining UK tour at Brighton's Dome.

Aug *Girls On Film*, with a risqué promo video directed by Godley & Creme°, hits UK #5.

Sept LP *Duran Duran* hits UK #3.

Dec *My Own Way* climbs to UK #14.

1982 Apr The band starts a world tour which will last through much of the year.

May LP *Rio* hits UK #2 (and will stay charted for the rest of the year).

June *Hungry Like The Wolf*, taken from the LP, with a high-class promo video directed by Russell Mulcahy in Sri Lanka, hits UK #5.

July [29] Andy Taylor marries Tracie Wilson in LA.

Sept *Save A Prayer* hits UK #2.

Nov *Carnival*, a US-only mini-LP release, featuring earlier tracks remixed by the band and David Kershenbaum, climbs to US #98.

Dec Title track from LP *Rio*, with Andy Hamilton guesting on saxophone, hits UK #9.

1983 Feb Aided by US cable music station MTV's use of its promo video (along with those for most of the earlier singles), *Hungry Like The Wolf* climbs to US #3. It hits charts in all major territories around the world and is a million-seller. LP *Rio*, which has been slowly climbing the US chart since June 1982, hits US #6 and becomes a million-seller.

Mar [26] The band attracts 5,000 fans while making an appearance at a video shop in New York and mounted police are deployed to control the crowd. This is the first noted US manifestation of Duran-fever, though such incidents are common in UK.

Mar *Is There Something I Should Know* enters the UK chart at #1. (Only a select company of acts like Elvis Presley°, Cliff Richard°, The Beatles° and a few more have previously achieved this feat in UK.)

May Title track from LP *Rio* reaches US #14.

July [20] The band headlines a charity concert for MENCAP at the Dominion Theatre, London, attended by The Prince and Princess of Wales.

Aug *Is There Something I Should Know* hits US #4 and is a million-seller. It is added to the US version of the band's first LP *Duran Duran*, which climbs to US #10 and is also a million-seller.

Nov The band begins a 5-month, 51-concert world tour, taking in UK, Japan, Australia, Canada and US. *Union Of The Snake*, extracted from the forthcoming LP, hits UK #3.

Dec LP *Seven And The Ragged Tiger*, produced by Alex Sadkin, Ian Little and the band itself, tops the UK chart for 1 week. *Union Of The Snake* hits US #3.

1984 Feb LP *Seven And The Ragged Tiger* hits US #8 and *New Moon On Monday*, taken from the LP, hits UK #9.

Mar *New Moon On Monday* hits US #10.

Apr The band completes its world tour, having played to over 750,000 people and having been recorded and filmed at many venues for live LP and TV/video release.

May *The Reflex*, remixed as a single by Nile Rodgers (ex-Chic°), tops the UK chart for 4 weeks.

June *The Reflex* hits US #1 for 2 weeks and is another worldwide million-seller.

July [27] Roger Taylor marries Giovanna Cantonne in Naples, Italy.

Aug [18] Nick Rhodes marries American model Julie Anne in London.

Nov *The Wild Boys*, produced in London by Rodgers and the band, hits UK #2.

Nov [25] The band takes part in the all-star recording session for Band Aid's° *Do They Know It's Christmas?* at Sarm studios in London, with Le Bon taking one of the lead vocal lines.

Dec *The Wild Boys* hits US #2 and is included on otherwise live LP *Arena* (recorded on stage during the world tour) which hits UK #6 and US #4, and is the band's fourth million-selling LP. Its release ties in with TV showing of *Sing Blue Silver*, a documentary filmed both on stage and behind the scenes during the world tour, directed by Michael Collins and Russell Mulcahy.

1985 Jan While Duran Duran is temporarily inactive, Andy and John Taylor form a recording-only spare-time group with Robert Palmer°, producer Bernard Edwards and fellow ex-Chic° musician Tony Thompson, named Power Station after the New York studio where they are recording.

Feb Power Station makes its performing debut on US TV's "Saturday Night Live".

Mar Duran Duran's *Save A Prayer* peaks at US #16.

Apr Power Station's *Some Like It Hot* reaches UK #14 and US #6. It is a Palmer/Taylor/Taylor composition extracted from LP *The Power Station* which makes UK #12.

May Duran Duran regroups in the studio and records the theme from James Bond film *A View To A Kill*, co-written by the band and composer John Barry, who scored the film. It hits UK #2.

June Power Station's revival of Marc Bolan's° *Get It On*, taken from LP *The Power Station*, reaches UK #22.

July Duran Duran's *A View To A Kill* tops the US chart for 2 weeks and is the band's sixth million-selling single. LP *The Power Station* hits US #6.

July [13] Duran Duran plays the "Live Aid" concert in Philadelphia. Power Station fails to appear as expected, since Palmer° refuses to bring the project out of its one-off studio-bound status.

Aug [10] Le Bon is airlifted from his boat Drum after it overturns while racing.

Aug Power Station's *Get It On* reaches US #9, one place higher than the original 1972 T. Rex version. (The US title is *Bang A Gong*.) Palmer° is replaced in Power Station by ex-Silverhead and Chequered Past singer Michael Des Barres, since the other members are still keen to work live. The new line-up makes a brief guest appearance in a episode of TV's "Miami Vice". Meanwhile, Le Bon, Rhodes and Roger Taylor form their own sideline recording band, Arcadia, and record an LP.

Oct Power Station's *Communication* reaches US #34 and UK #75, after which the group disbands.

Nov Arcadia's first single *Election Day* (featuring a narration by Grace Jones°) hits UK #7 and LP *So Red The Rose* makes UK #30.

Dec Arcadia's *Election Day* hits US #6 and LP *So Red The Rose* climbs to US #23.

1986 Feb Arcadia's *The Promise*, extracted from the LP as a second single, peaks at UK #37.

Mar Arcadia's *Goodbye Is Forever* is the US follow-up from the LP and reaches #33.

Apr Between Power Station winding down and Duran Duran regrouping for LP recordings, John Taylor releases solo single *I Do What I Do*, the theme from movie *9½ Weeks*. It reaches UK #42 and US #23. Roger Taylor announces he is to take a year's sabbatical from Duran Duran and retreats to his country home. (He will not return to Duran Duran.)

May Le Bon takes his yacht Drum to race in Australia.

June Beginning LP sessions as a quartet, Duran Duran completes them as a trio when Andy Taylor leaves to pursue a solo career, having already recorded *Take It Easy* for the soundtrack of film *American Anthem*. (He moves to US, signs to MCA Records and begins work on a solo LP with ex-Sex Pistols° Steve Jones.)

July Arcadia's *The Flame*, remixed from the LP as a third UK single, makes #58. Taylor rejoins Le Bon and Rhodes for a live TV appearance on a pan-European 6-hour version of "The Tube", but this marks the end of Arcadia's activity.

Aug Andy Taylor's solo single *Take It Easy* reaches US #24.

Aug [31] Le Bon is best man at the wedding of Bob Geldof and Paula Yates.

Nov Duran Duran's *Notorious*, the title track from forthcoming LP, hits UK #7, while Andy Taylor's first solo release for MCA, *When The Rain Comes Down* (featured in TV series "Miami Vice"), reaches US #73.

Dec LP *Notorious*, co-produced by Nile Rodgers and the band, showcases the new Duran Duran trio (Andy Taylor is heard on only four tracks, recorded before his departure). It reaches UK #16.

1987 Jan *Notorious* hits US #2 and the LP of the same title peaks at US #12.

Mar *Skin Trade*, extracted from the LP, peaks at UK #22.

Apr Duran Duran appears live at "The Secret Policeman's Third Ball" in London, amid rumors that this might be its last concert.
May *Meet El Presidente*, a further excerpt from LP *Notorious*, peaks at UK #24, while Andy Taylor's debut solo LP *Thunder* makes UK #61, charting for just 1 week.
1988 Jan Le Bon, Rhodes and John Taylor recruit drummer Steve Ferrone and guitarist Warren Cuccurullo to work on a new LP recorded in Paris and produced by Jonathan Elias and Daniel Abraham.
June The LP, still untitled, is mixed and projected for an Oct. 1988 release.

IAN DURY

1970 Nov Dury (b. May 12, 1942, Upminster, Essex, UK), partially crippled since contracting polio at age 7, forms Kilburn & The High Roads while he is a lecturer at Canterbury College of Art, Kent, UK. The group is initially part-time.
1971 Dec Kilburn & The High Roads play their first gigs at Croydon School of Art and Canterbury College.
1973 Jan Dave Robinson (later MD of Stiff Records) introduces the band to regular work on London's pub circuit, where they are spotted by writer/broadcaster Charlie Gillett, who becomes their manager, later to be replaced by Robinson.
May [3] When the band's battered transit van almost falls to pieces, three other pub circuit bands, Ducks Deluxe, Brinsley Schwarz° and Bees Make Honey, play a benefit show at Camden Town Hall to raise money for repair bills.
Oct The group tours the UK as support to The Who°.
1974 Jan Signed to WEA's Raft label, the band records an LP produced by Tony Ashton (ex-Ashton, Gardner & Dyke) which is not issued when the label closes down. WEA lets Kilburn & The High Roads go (but will release the LP in UK in 1978 after Dury's subsequent fame).
July Tommy Roberts becomes the group's new manager and signs it to Pye Records' Dawn label.
Nov Debut release is the single *Rough Kids*, which does not sell.
1975 Feb *Crippled With Nerves* does not chart.
June LP *Handsome* is no more successful than the singles, but will be reissued in Dury's later successful days. The disillusioned group breaks up, forcing cancellation of some projected European live dates. Dury and Rod Melvin will spend the rest of the year writing and planning a new Kilburns.
Nov A six-piece group is formed, Ian Dury & The Kilburns, with Robinson as manager, organizing a regular gig at the Hope & Anchor in Islington, London.
1976 Mar Chaz Jankel joins the band on keyboards, and begins to write with Dury.
June [17] The group splits after a last gig at Walthamstow Town Hall, London, mainly because Dury's doctor orders him off the road for health reasons. (Dury and Jankel stay together and spend a year writing songs for what will become the first solo Ian Dury LP.)
1977 Aug Dury signs to Robinson's Stiff Records. LP *Sex And Drugs And Rock And Roll* is released without chart success.
Sept Ian Dury & The Blockheads is formed for the "Stiff Live Stiffs" UK promotional tour (with Elvis Costello°, Nick Lowe° and others). Dury and Jankel recruit several of the session men they have used in recording LP *New Boots And Panties!*, and the line-up is: Dury (vocals) Jankel (keyboards and guitar), Davey Payne (sax), John Turnbull (guitar), Norman Watt-Roy (bass), Charley Charles (drums) and Mickey Gallagher (keyboards).
Nov Dury's second solo single *Sweet Gene Vincent* is released.
1978 Feb LP *New Boots And Panties!* hits UK #5, staying on the UK chart for 90 weeks.
Mar The band tours the US, supporting Lou Reed°.
May *What A Waste* becomes Dury's first hit single at UK #9. LP *New Boots And Panties!* charts in US, reaching #168. Dury & The Blockheads tour the UK, with comedian Max Wall as support. Wall records a version of Dury's song *England's Glory*, released by Stiff.
June Humphrey Ocean, a former art school friend, covers Dury's *Whoops A Daisy*, also on Stiff.
Oct LP *Wotabunch*, the Kilburn & The High Roads' LP left on the shelf at WEA in 1974, is released.
1979 Jan *Hit Me With Your Rhythm Stick* tops the UK chart for a week, with over 900,000 sales over the 1978 Christmas period in UK alone.
June LP *Do It Yourself*, marketed in a variety of "wallpaper pattern" sleeve designs, hits UK #2.
Aug The R&B/disco-flavored *Reasons To Be Cheerful (Part 3)*, recorded in Rome, hits UK #3 and LP *Do It Yourself* makes US #126.
Dec Dury appears at the People of Kampuchea concert at London's Hammersmith Odeon, along with Paul McCartney°, The Who°, Robert Plant° and many others.
1980 Chaz Jankel leaves for a solo career, signing to A&M. Gallagher rejoins, having left to join The Clash° on tour.
July [5] Wilko Johnson (ex-Dr. Feelgood° and The Solid Senders) joins on guitar.
Sept *I Want To Be Straight*, Dury's first recording to feature Johnson on guitar, reaches UK #22.
Nov *Sueperman's Big Sister* (the incorrect spelling is deliberate, to avoid copyright problems) reaches UK #51.
Dec LP *Laughter* makes UK #48 while Dury & The Blockheads play "Soft as a Baby's Bottom" UK tour.
1981 Feb LP *Laughter* scores US #159.
Aug Dury signs a new worldwide deal with Polydor. He releases *Spasticus Autisticus* in time for the Year of the Disabled, but most UK radio stations refuse to play it. It fails to chart (as will all his Polydor singles) and is deleted the following month, with a Polydor statement: "Just as nobody bans handicapped people – just makes it difficult for them to function as normal people – so *Spasticus Autisticus* was not banned, it was made impossible to function."
Oct LP *Lord Upminster*, recorded at Compass Point studios in Nassau, Bahamas, peaks at UK #53. Sly and Robbie° replace The Blockheads on all but one track and Jankel returns.
Nov LP *Juke Box Duries*, compiled from earlier Stiff singles, does not chart.
1982 Dec Without Dury, The Blockheads releases a revival of *Twist And Shout*, recorded on stage in London. It does not chart.
1983 Nov *Really Glad You Came* is released.
1984 Feb LP *4,000 Weeks Holiday*, credited to Ian Dury & The Music Students, reaches UK #54. Originally scheduled for the previous year, it was withheld by Polydor until *Fuck Off Noddy* and a song about holiday tycoon Billy Butlin were removed. Non-charting single *Very Personal* ends his unproductive spell with Polydor.
1985 Dury reunites with The Blockheads for live work, and acts with Bob Geldof in movie *Number One*.
June Paul Hardcastle's re-mix of *Hit Me With Your Rhythm Stick*, recorded for Stiff with Dury's approval, reaches UK #55. Dury begins to be heard (if not seen) regularly on UK TV, doing voice-overs for holiday and electrical goods advertisements.
Nov *Profoundly In Love With Pandora*, the theme from UK TV series "The Secret Diary of Adrian Mole" reaches UK #45.
1986 In further acting roles, Dury appears in Roman Polanski's movie *Pirates*, and BBC TV series "King of the Ghetto".
1987 Another theme for second "Adrian Mole" series is aired on UK TV. Dury appears in the ill-received Bob Dylan° movie *Hearts Of Fire* and scores the music for UK TV play about truckers, "Night Moves". He will successfully leave behind his flagging recording career and switch his attention to acting, writing music and his first love, painting.

BOB DYLAN

1953 Dylan (b. Robert Allan Zimmerman, May 24, 1941, Duluth, Minn., US) begins to learn guitar.
1954 May [22] He has his bar-mitzvah.
1959 June [5] He leaves Hibbing High School, having played regularly and formed several groups including a rock'n'roll band, noting in the yearbook that he is leaving "to follow Little Richard°". (Though initially he starts a course at the University of Minnesota).
1960 He leaves university to concentrate on playing and singing, and is briefly employed as pianist with Bobby Vee's° backing group. Having adopted a new performing name, courtesy of poet Dylan Thomas, he travels to New York down Highway 61 to visit Woody Guthrie, chief precursor of the current folk boom (and a particular influence on Dylan), but paralyzed with a rare hereditary disease for the past 8 years.
1961 Feb [3] In New York, Dylan makes his first recordings, on some friends' home equipment, playing the standard *San Francisco Bay Blues* and similar numbers.
Apr [11] His first New York live gig is at Gerde's Folk City in Greenwich Village, opening for bluesman John Lee Hooker°.

BOB DYLAN *cont.*

Apr [24] Dylan earns a $50 session fee playing harmonica on recordings for Harry Belafonte's° LP *Midnight Special*.

Sept [30] He joins folk singer Caroline Hester on an LP session for CBS/Columbia, again on harmonica. He impresses producer John Hammond Sr., who noted a glowing *New York Times* review of a performance at Gerde's Folk City. Hammond offers Dylan a recording contract.

Oct [4] As a showcase, he plays New York's Carnegie Chapter Hall – to 53 people.

Oct [20] Dylan records debut LP *Bob Dylan*, which includes raw, authentic versions of traditional songs.

1962 Mar The debut LP is released in US. It does not chart, but causes a major stir on the folk scene. Almost rockabilly-styled *Mixed Up Confusion/Corrina Corrina* is also released, to few sales.

1963 Jan [12] On a brief visit to London, UK, he is given a part as a folk singer in a UK BBC radio play "The Madhouse on Castle Street". In it he sings *Blowin' In The Wind* and *Swan On The River*.

Apr [12] A solo concert at New York's Town Hall draws positive reviews, and is recorded by CBS for a live LP (which does not materialize).

May LP *The Freewheelin' Bob Dylan* is released. With major songs of his own like *A Hard Rain's Gonna Fall*, *Blowin' In The Wind* and *Masters Of War*, it establishes him as a leader in the new folk singer-songwriter and youth protest leagues.

May [12] Dylan is invited to play US TV's "Ed Sullivan Show", but when he is forbidden to sing *Talking John Birch Society Blues*, he refuses to appear.

May [17] He meets Joan Baez° at the Monterey Folk Festival. (The two will become the stars of the year's Newport Folk Festival, at which Baez will introduce Dylan, and will develop a long-term personal and creative union.)

Aug Peter, Paul and Mary's° version of Dylan's *Blowin' In The Wind* hits US #2 and UK #13, and is a million-seller. (The trio will follow it with another hit cover from LP *The Freewheelin' Bob Dylan*, *Don't Think Twice, It's Alright*).

Sept Following Peter, Paul and Mary's° success, interest in *Blowin' In The Wind* and its writer spurs LP *The Freewheelin' Bob Dylan* to US #22 and a gold disk.

1964 Apr LP *The Times They Are A-Changin'*, much of its content on a strong protest theme, reaches US #20.

May With Dylan's name constantly promoted in UK by The Beatles° and others, LP *The Freewheelin' Bob Dylan* makes UK #16. (It will return later in the year to top the chart.)

July LP *The Times They Are A-Changin'* reaches UK #20. (This will also later return with bigger sales.)

Oct LP *Another Side Of Bob Dylan*, less protest-oriented, makes US #43.

Dec LP *Another Side Of Bob Dylan* hits UK #8.

1965 Apr Dylan's UK tour, where he is received as a major celebrity, is documented on film in fly-on-the-wall fashion by D.A. Pennebaker, later released as *Don't Look Back*. The movie reveals that pressure on the young star is steadily more intense as his popularity grows. *The Times They Are A-Changin'* is released as Dylan's first UK single to tie in with the tour, and hits UK #9 following sell-out London concerts. LP of the same title hits UK #4.

May Rock guitar-driven *Subterranean Homesick Blues* makes US #39 (his first US hit single) and hits UK #9. LP *The Freewheelin' Bob Dylan* finally tops the UK chart for 2 weeks after a year on sale (deposing *Beatles For Sale*). It is then swept aside by Dylan's new LP *Bringing It All Back Home*, which is UK #1 for 4 weeks and hits US #6, earning his second gold disk. The LP includes *Subterranean Homesick Blues* on a complete side of electric, rock-oriented material, backed by a group including Al Kooper and Paul Butterfield°. The other side maintains his acoustic folk roots and includes *Mr. Tambourine Man*. His first LP *Bob Dylan* makes UK #13, giving him five simultaneous UK top 20 LP placings.

June The Byrds° hit US #1 with their folk-rock cover of *Mr. Tambourine Man* (and will hit UK #1 a few weeks later). It is the first chart-topping Dylan composition and sparks several pop and folk-rock hit covers of his material by major acts like The Turtles° (*It Ain't Me Babe*), Cher° (*All I Really Want To Do*), Joan Baez° (*It's All Over Now. Baby Blue* and *Farewell Angelina*) and Manfred Mann° (*If You Gotta Go, Go Now*).

July *Maggie's Farm*, taken from LP *Bringing It All Back Home*, reaches UK #22.

July [25] Dylan appears at The Newport Folk Festival and plays a full electric set backed by The Paul Butterfield° Blues Band. The diehard folk "purists" in the audience try to boo him off the stage.

Sept *Like A Rolling Stone*, noted for its revolutionary length (6 mins) as well as its rock backing, hits US #2 and UK #4, becoming Dylan's first million-selling single.

Oct LP *Highway 61 Revisited*, with Dylan's individual lyrics and mainstream rock, hits US #3 and UK #4. *Positively 4th Street*, in similar style to *Like A Rolling Stone*, hits US #7.

Nov *Positively 4th Street* hits UK #8.

Nov [22] Dylan marries Sara Lowndes.

1966 Feb *Can You Please Crawl Out Your Window* reaches US #58 and UK #17.

Apr *(Sooner Or Later) One Of Us Must Know* peaks at UK #33.

May Roisterous *Rainy Day Women #12 & 35* hits US #2, and will become Dylan's second million-selling single.

May [26] Dylan plays London's Royal Albert Hall, on another UK tour, this time backed by an electric band, largely consisting of The Hawks (later to become The Band°). Purists in the audience still consider the folk singer has "sold out" and again make their feelings vocal.

June *Rainy Day Women #12 & 35* hits UK #7.

July [29] Dylan suffers injuries (never fully detailed, but apparently involving broken neck vertebrae) when he crashes his motorcycle near his home in Woodstock, N.Y. His recuperation leads to a period of reclusive inactivity, interpreted by many as an attempt to escape into family life from the extreme pressures of 2 years' success.

Aug Double LP *Blonde On Blonde*, recorded in the first 3 months of the year, hits US #9 and UK #3, and is his fourth gold LP in US with sales over a half million. *I Want You*, a lightweight pop number taken from the LP, reaches US #20 and UK #16.

Oct *Just Like A Woman*, also from the LP, reaches US #33 (but is not issued in UK, where Manfred Mann's° cover hits #10). It is announced that Dylan is spending his recuperative period writing a novel. LP *Blonde On Blonde* hits UK #3.

1967 Feb UK compilation LP *Greatest Hits* hits UK #6.

June US-compiled LP *Greatest Hits* (different from the UK version), hits US #10 and earns another gold disk. *Leopard Skin Pillbox Hat* peaks at US #81. (During almost 18 months of "retirement", Dylan stays in Woodstock and does not appear to be active at all. Tapes later begin to circulate of sessions at Big Pink, a large old house in Woodstock, with The Band°. Several acts, including Manfred Mann° (*The Mighty Quinn*), Peter, Paul and Mary° (*Too Much Of Nothing* and Julie Driscoll & Brian Auger° (*This Wheel's On Fire*) will have hits with songs originating from these sessions. They will also form the basis of *Great White Wonder*, the first big-selling bootleg rock LP.)

Oct Dylan returns to the studio (without The Band°) to record an LP of new material.

1968 Jan [20] Dylan plays with The Band° at a memorial concert for Woody Guthrie (who died, aged 55, on September 3, 1967) at New York's Carnegie Hall – his first public appearance since his motorcycle crash.

Mar LP *John Wesley Harding*, simpler and more country-influenced than his pre-accident recordings, hits US #2 and tops the UK chart for 10 weeks. (No Dylan single is taken from this LP, but Jimi Hendrix° will have a hit with a hard-rock cover of *All Along The Watchtower*.)

1969 May Country-influenced LP *Nashville Skyline*, recorded in Nashville with assistance from Johnny Cash° (they duet on *Girl From The North Country*), hits US #3 and tops the UK chart for 4 weeks. Cash and Dylan also record a TV special at the Grand Ole Opry.

June *I Threw It All Away*, taken from the LP, peaks at US #85 and UK #30.

Aug [31] Dylan and The Band° headline UK's Isle of Wight festival. Some of the set is recorded (for eventual release on LP *Self-Portrait*).

Sept *Lay Lady Lay*, taken from LP *Nashville Skyline* (but originally written, by request, for film *Midnight Cowboy* and rejected), hits US #7 and UK #5. His first top 10 single for 3 years, it will also be his last.

Nov *Tonight I'll Be Staying Here With You*, also from LP *Nashville Skyline*, makes US #50.

1970 June [9] Dylan is awarded an honorary Doctorate in Music from Princeton University.

July Double LP *Self-Portrait*, a scrapbook collection of new songs and familiar covers (including songs by Paul Simon°, Gordon Lightfoot° and The Everly Brothers°), is pasted by critics as a waste of talent. It is Dylan's third successive UK #1 (for 1 week) and hits US #4.

Aug Largely instrumental *Wigwam*, from LP *Self-Portrait*, makes US #41.

Nov [11] Dylan's long-awaited novel, the surreal *Tarantula*, is published, to wide press attention.

Dec LP *New Morning* hits US #7, tops the UK chart and is greeted as a return to form.

1971 Feb Dylan documentary film *Eat The Document*, mostly featuring his 1966 UK tour with The Band°, is premiered at New York's Academy of Music.

Mar [16] He records *Watching The River Flow* and *When I Paint My Masterpiece* in a session with Leon Russell° guesting on piano.

July [31] Dylan and The Band° appear in George Harrison's° "Concert for Bangla Desh" at New York's Madison Square Garden (and perform a side of the triple LP of the event, which hits US #2). This is Dylan's only major live appearance of the year.

Aug *Watching The River Flow* reaches US #41 and UK #24.

1972 Jan Double compilation LP *Bob Dylan's Greatest Hits, Vol.II* (*More Bob Dylan Greatest Hits* in UK) reaches US #14 and UK #12, while specially-recorded protest single *George Jackson*, about the black militant shot dead in a prison fracas, makes US #33. Dylan spends the rest of the year writing the soundtrack to, and appearing as the outlaw Alias in, Sam Peckinpah's movie *Pat Garrett and Billy The Kid*.

1973 Sept Following the film's release, Dylan's soundtrack LP, which includes three tracks with his vocals, is released by CBS/Columbia and reaches US #16 and UK #29. His contract with the label expires and he does not renew it.

Oct The movie soundtrack's highlight, Dylan singing *Knockin' On Heaven's Door*, is released, and becomes his biggest-selling single since *Lay Lady Lay*, reaching US #12 and UK #14.

Nov It becomes clear that Dylan is not re-signing to CBS and it is announced that he will move to David Geffen's Asylum label and is recording an LP with The Band°. Columbia releases LP *Dylan*, a collection of out-takes and rejected covers from LP *Self-Portrait*.

1974 Jan Almost universally decried, LP *Dylan* reaches US #17, while extracted revival of Elvis Presley's° *A Fool Such As I* makes US #55.

Jan [3] Dylan and The Band° open a 39-date US tour (the first in nearly 8 years) in Chicago, to support their first Asylum LP together, cut the previous Nov. (Several dates will be recorded for a live LP.)

Feb Debut Asylum LP *Planet Waves* is Dylan's first US chart-topper (for 4 weeks) and hits UK #7.

Mar *On A Night Like This*, taken from LP *Planet Waves*, reaches US #44.

July Double live LP *Before The Flood*, a compilation of performances from the US tour, with The Band° getting one side to itself, features reworked versions of some of Dylan's 1960s hits. It hits US #3 and UK #8.

Aug Live single from the LP, *Most Likely You Go Your Way (And I'll Go Mine)*, climbs to US #66.

Aug [10] Dylan settles his differences with CBS chief executive Clive Davis and re-signs to the label.

Sept Tracks are recorded for a new CBS/Columbia LP, *Blood On The Tracks*, but after it is scheduled for release, Dylan is unsatisfied with some of the recordings, and the LP is delayed.

1975 Mar After five tracks have been reworked, LP *Blood On The Tracks* is issued. It tops the US chart for 2 weeks and hits UK #4.

Apr *Tangled Up In Blue*, from the LP, climbs to US #31.

Aug Dylan sanctions the official release of double LP *The Basement Tapes*, after years of bootlegs of these 1967 recordings with The Band°. Compiled and remixed by The Band's Robbie Robertson, the LP hits US #7 and UK #8.

Oct [30] An initially low-key and spontaneous US tour, "The Rolling Thunder Revue", starts in Plymouth, Mass. Musical guests joining in along the way include Joni Mitchell°, Joan Baez° and Roger McGuinn.

Dec [8] "The Rolling Thunder Revue" ends its first run at New York's Madison Square Garden with "Night of the Hurricane", a benefit for boxer Rubin "Hurricane" Carter, convicted of murder.

1976 Feb LP *Desire*, including much of the new material sung on the tour, tops the US chart for 5 weeks, earning Dylan's first US platinum disk for million-plus LP sales, and hits UK #3. The track *Hurricane*, which pleads the case for Carter, is issued as a single, reaching US #33 and UK #43.

Apr *Mozambique*, also from LP *Desire*, makes US #54, as "The Rolling Thunder Revue" begins another US tour.

Apr [22] The show at Clearwater, Fla., is taped by NBC for a projected special, but rejected.

Oct LP *Hard Rain*, recorded live from shows at Fort Worth, Tex., and Fort Collins, Col., peaks at US #17 and hits UK #3. (The Fort Collins gig forms the basis of 60-minute TV film *Hard Rain*, replacing the earlier project.)

Nov [25] Dylan joins The Band° at its farewell concert at The Winterland, San Francisco, with a host of other guests.

1977 Mar [1] Dylan's wife Sara files for divorce. Dylan spends most of the year preoccupied with domestic matters and with completing film *Renaldo and Clara*, which is mainly a documentary of "The Rolling Thunder Revue".

1978 Feb [1] *Renaldo and Clara* is premiered in LA.

Mar [1] In the early part of a world tour, Dylan performs at Japan's Budokan concert hall. (The show is recorded for a future LP.)

May Dylan has five tracks on the triple LP of The Band's° final concert, *The Last Waltz*, and appears in Martin Scorsese's documentary film of the event.

May [7] 90,000 tickets for Dylan's UK concerts at Earl's Court, London, are sold out in 8 hours.

June Dylan opens his European tour at Earl's Court, London.

July LP *Street Legal* reaches US #11 and UK #2.

July [15] Dylan plays an open-air festival at Blackbushe Aerodrome, UK, supported by Eric Clapton°.

Aug *Baby Stop Crying*, taken from *Street Legal*, is Dylan's biggest UK hit single for 5 years, interest being spurred by his Wembley concerts. It makes UK #13, though does not chart in US.

Nov *Is Your Love In Vain* reaches UK #56 (and is Dylan's last UK chart single).

Dec [16] A 3-month, 62-date, final US leg of the world tour closes in Miami.

1979 Jan Dylan launches his own label, Accomplice Records; little comes of it.

June Double live LP *Bob Dylan At The Budokan*, recorded in Japan and

BOB DYLAN *cont.*

originally intended only for the Japanese market is released to combat the sale of bootlegs of 1978 tour recordings. It reaches US #13 and hits UK #4.

Sept Rumors persist of Dylan's conversion to born-again Christianity and LP *Slow Train Coming*, with its evangelistic lyrical approach, appears to confirm it. The LP hits US #3 and UK #2, and is his second platinum (million-selling) LP in US. Mark Knopfler of Dire Straits° guests on guitar.

Nov [1] A "Slow Train Coming" US tour opens at the Fox Warfield Theater, San Francisco, where the new religious material is booed.

Nov *Gotta Serve Somebody* reaches US #24 (and wins him a Grammy award 3 months later for Best Male Rock Vocal Performance of 1979).

1980 July LP *Saved* continues the Christian theme, and features a sleeve painted by Dylan himself. It makes US #24 (his first LP since *Another Side Of Bob Dylan* not to enter US top 20) but hits UK #3.

Nov Another US tour reintroduces earlier songs into his stage set, plus some oldies unrecorded by Dylan, like *Fever* and *Abraham, Martin And John*.

1981 June A European tour to preface Dylan's forthcoming LP has a repertoire which balances the newer evangelistic material with versions of familiar oldies.

Sept Religion-inspired LP *Shot Of Love* reaches US #33 and hits UK #6.

Oct Dylan begins a US tour to promote *Shot Of Love* at Milwaukee Auditorium.

1982 Mar Dylan is elected to the Songwriters Hall of Fame.

June He joins Joan Baez° at the "Peace Sunday" concert in Cal., duetting on *Blowin' In The Wind* and *With God On Our Side*.

1983 Dec Dylan, after a period when he is reported to be recording but unhappy with the results, releases LP *Infidels*, co-produced by Mark Knopfler of Dire Straits°. This is his least overtly religious, and best-selling (gold in US) LP for 4 years. It reaches US #20 and hits UK #9.

1984 Jan *Sweetheart Like You*, taken from LP *Infidels*, reaches US #55 (and is Dylan's last US chart single).

Mar Dylan appears live on US TV's "Late Night With David Letterman", playing three songs backed by rock band The Plugz.

Dec Live LP *Real Live*, recorded in London, Dublin and Newcastle while on a European tour in the summer, reaches US #115 and UK #54.

1985 Jan [28] Dylan takes part, with more than thirty other major US acts, in the LA session which produces USA For Africa's° *We Are The World*, to benefit the starving in Africa and elsewhere. The single will top US and UK charts, selling over 7 million worldwide.

July LP *Empire Burlesque* reaches US #33 and UK #11. Dylan is backed on it by members of Tom Petty's° band, The Heartbreakers.

July [13] Dylan performs at Live Aid in Philadelphia, backed by The Rolling Stones'° Keith Richards and Ron Wood on guitars.

Sept Backed by Tom Petty and The Heartbreakers°, he performs at Farm Aid, University of Illinois, Champaign, Ill., US.

1986 Jan Retrospective five-LP box set *Biograph*, a 53-song compilaton of Dylan's recording career from 1962 to 1981, and including 18 unreleased tracks, climbs to US #33.

Jan [20] Dylan performs at the concert, organized by Stevie Wonder°, to celebrate the first Martin Luther King Day in US.

Feb He tours Australasia and Japan, backed by Tom Petty and The Heartbreakers°.

Aug LP *Knocked Out Loaded*, produced in London by Dave Stewart of Eurythmics°, reaches UK #35. Dylan returns to London to film movie *Hearts of Fire* with Richard Marquand. In it, he plays opposite Rupert Everett and Fiona Flanagan as a jaded, middle-aged rock star.

1987 June Dylan tours US with The Grateful Dead°, who back his set as well as playing their own (longer) one.

Oct For a European tour (which opens in Israel), he is backed by Petty's° band, with ex-The Byrds° Roger McGuinn supporting. George Harrison° join Dylan on stage on the final date, at Wembley, UK.

Dec Movie *Hearts of Fire* is released in UK after an almost 6-month delay. Critically panned, it is generally ignored by the public and considered to be one of Dylan's most ill-advised career moves.

1988 June The 33rd Dylan LP, *Down In The Groove*, is a return to form, though much of the material is non-original (it was first intended to be an entire LP of cover versions, like *Self-Portrait*, but its format is twice changed by Dylan during a 6-month delay from original release date). The list of contributing musicians includes Eric Clapton°, hip-hoppers Full Force, Mark Knopfler, Ron Wood, ex-Sex Pistol° Steve Jones and ex-Clash° bassist Paul Simonon. Jerry Garcia, Bob Weir and Brent Mydland of The Grateful Dead° also play on the LP, and two of the new songs, *The Ugliest Girl In The World* and *Silvio*, are co-written with their lyricist Robert Hunter. The six covers range from Wilbert Harrison's° *Let's Stick Together* to the traditional *Shenandoah*. It reaches UK #32.

Oct "Lucky" Dylan joins George "Nelson" Harrison°, Jeff "Otis" Lynne, Roy "Lefty" Orbison° and Tom "Charlie T. Jnr." Petty° as The Traveling Wilburys. Their debut LP *Traveling Wilburys* and single *Handle With Care* are released.

THE EAGLES

Glenn Frey (guitar and vocals)
Bernie Leadon (guitar and vocals)
Randy Meisner (bass and vocals)
Don Henley (drums and vocals)

1971 Aug The group, formed by Frey (b. Nov.6, 1948, Detroit, Mich., US), Leadon (b. July 19, 1947, Minneapolis, Minn., US), Meisner (b. Mar.8, 1947, Scottsbluff, Neb., US) and Henley (b. July 22, 1947, Gilmer, Tex., US) after they played live together in Linda Ronstadt's° backing band, is booked by Asylum Records' boss David Geffen into an Aspen, Col. club to play four sets a night for a month to tighten its act.

1972 Apr Signed to Asylum Records, The Eagles travel to UK to record first LP with producer Glyn Johns at Olympic Studios, Barnes, London.

July *Take It Easy* is their chart debut, reaching US #12.

Oct LP *The Eagles*, including the hit single, climbs to US #22.

Nov *Witchy Woman*, taken from the LP, hits US #9.

Nov [24] The Eagles appear as part of superstar billed , K-ROQ "Woodstock of the West" festival. Only 32,000 show.

1973 Mar *Peaceful Easy Feeling*, also from debut LP, reaches US #22.

June LP *Desperado*, recorded in London with producer Johns (now at Island Studios), reaches US #41. (The title track, although never a single, will be much covered later by Linda Ronstadt°, Bonnie Raitt, The Carpenters° and others.) Movie director Sam Peckinpah plans to turn the LP into a cowboy film, but plans fall through.

July *Tequila Sunrise*, from the LP, reaches US #64.

Oct *Outlaw Man*, also from LP *Desperado*, climbs to US #59.

1974 Jan Don Felder (b. Sept.21, 1947, Topanga, Cal., US) plays slide guitar on *Good Day In Hell* for the next LP sessions at the Record Plant in LA. He so impresses the band that he joins full-time. Producer Bill Szymczyk takes over from Johns in midstream, at the recommendation of Joe Walsh° who toured with the band, to give the group a more rock oriented sound.

Apr [6] The Eagles play the "California Jam" rock festival to an audience of 200,000.

May LP *On The Border* reaches US #17 (later going gold) and is their UK chart debut at #28. Their new producer and an additional player help harden the sound from country into rock.

June *Already Gone* peaks at US #32.

Oct *James Dean* climbs to US #77.

1975 Mar *The Best Of My Love* spends a week at US #1, and is their first million-selling single.

June [21] The Eagles play in Elton John's° concert at London's Wembley Stadium to an audience of 100,000.

July LP *One Of These Nights* tops the US chart for 5 weeks. Track *I Wish You, Peace*, credited to Leadon and Patti Reagan Davis, causes controversy when Davis says in a Las Vegas Sun interview that she enjoys the royalties received from the song. Henley writes to the paper claiming Davis' contribution is negligible.

Aug LPs *One Of These Nights* and *Desperado* hit UK #8 and #39 respectively.

Sept *One Of These Nights* is their first UK chart single, reaching #23.

Nov *Lyin' Eyes* hits US #2 and UK #23. (It will win a Grammy award as 1975's Best Pop Vocal Performance by a Duo, Group or Chorus.)

Dec [20] Leadon leaves having argued over the group's musical direction. (He will re-emerge, still with Asylum Records, with The Bernie Leadon/Michael Georgiades Band in mid-1977.) Successful rock soloist and ex-James Gang member Joe Walsh° (b. Nov.20, 1947, Wichita, Kan., US) joins.

1976 Mar *Take It To The Limit* hits US #4 and UK #12, while compilation LP *Their Greatest Hits, 1971-1975* tops the US chart for 5 weeks (certified platinum) and hits UK #2. The group starts work on a new LP at Criteria Studios in Miami, Fla.

1977 Jan LP *Hotel California* tops the US chart for a week and is certified platinum. (It will return to US #1 for a further week in Feb., and in Mar., then 5 consecutive weeks in Apr./May, when it will also hit UK #2.)

Feb *New Kid In Town*, taken from the LP, hits US #1 and UK #20. It is a US million-seller.

Feb [23] The Eagles win Grammys for *Hotel California* (Best Record of the Year) and *New Kid In Town* (Best Arrangement for Voices).

Mar [5] LP *Their Greatest Hits* is voted Album of the Year by the National Association of Record Merchandisers (NARM).

Mar [14] The group begins a month's US tour at the Civic Center, Springfield, Mass.

Apr [25] The Eagles' European tour begins at Wembley, London. (It will end on May 18 at the Scandinavium, Gothenberg, Sweden.)

May Title track from *Hotel California*, another million-seller, tops the US chart and hits UK #8.

May [28-30] The Eagles join Foreigner°, Heart° and The Steve Miller° Band, playing two concerts at the Oakland Stadium, Cal., in front of 100,000 people.

June [18] A US summer tour begins at The Civic Center, Roanoke, Va.

July *Life In The Fast Lane* reaches US #11, but fails to chart in UK. The Leadon/Georgiades band reaches US #91 with LP *Natural Progressions*.

Sept Following an overseas tour (UK, Scandinavia and Europe) and a summer US tour, Meisner leaves exhausted with life on the road. He will pursue a solo career. (The title track of his debut LP *One More Song*, with Frey and Henley on backing vocals, eulogizes his last days as a member of The Eagles.) He is replaced by Timothy B. Schmit (b. Oct.30, 1947, Sacramento, Cal., US), who also succeeded Meisner in Poco°.

1978 Feb [23] The group wins two Grammy awards: Record of the Year with *Hotel California*, and Best Arrangement for Voices with *New Kid In Town* but refuses to attend the ceremony.

May [7] The Eagles beat *Rolling Stone* magazine 15-8 in a softball game.

May The group is featured on soundtrack LP to rock film *FM*.

July [23] A month's Canadian tour begins in Edmonton.

Dec A revival of Charles Brown's blues standard *Please Come Home For Christmas* reaches US #18 and UK #30.

1979 Nov *Heartache Tonight*, written by Frey and Henley with Bob Seger° and J.D. Souther, hits US #1, selling over a million copies, but makes only UK #40. LP *The Long Run* tops the US chart for 8 weeks and hits UK #4.

Dec Title track from *The Long Run* charts briefly at UK #66 (and will be The Eagles' last UK singles chart entry).

Dec [21] They appear with Chicago° and Linda Ronstadt° at a benefit show for Presidential candidate Jerry Brown.

1980 Feb *The Long Run* title track hits US #8.

Feb [27] *Heartache Tonight* wins a Grammy as 1979's Best Male Rock Vocal Performance by a Duo or Group.

Mar [20] 28-year-old Joseph Riviera holds up Asylum Records office in New York demanding to see either Jackson Browne° or The Eagles, wanting them to finance his trucking operation. He eventually surrenders.

Apr *I Can't Tell You Why* hits US #8.

Nov Meisner's LP *One More Song* makes US #50.

Nov [21] Henley is arrested when a naked 16-year-old girl is found in his LA home suffering from a drug overdose. (He will be fined £2,000, given 2 years' probation, and ordered to attend a drug counselling scheme.)

Dec Double LP *Live* hits US #6 and UK #24. Compiled from onstage recordings, it is released after The Eagles have been inactive throughout 1980, and mutually agreed to split when *The Long Run* was completed. Meisner's solo *Deep Inside My Heart* reaches US #22.

1981 Jan LP *Live* is certified platinum.

Feb *Seven Bridges Road* reaches US #21 and is the group's final US hit single.

Mar Meisner's *Hearts On Fire* reaches US #19.

Oct Felder's *Takin' A Ride*, from cartoon movie *Heavy Metal*, makes US #43.

1982 Jan Henley duets with Fleetwood Mac's° Stevie Nicks on his US #6 *Leather And Lace*.

Aug Frey's solo *I Found Somebody* reaches US #31, while his debut LP *No Fun Aloud*, mostly written with Jack Tempchin (co-writer of *Peaceful Easy Feeling*), peaks at US #32.

Sept Meisner's LP *Randy Meisner* reaches US #94. Extracted from it, *Never Been In Love* makes #28.

Oct Henley's solo *Johnny Can't Read* makes US #42 as his LP *I Can't Stand Still* reaches #24. Schmit peaks at US #59 with his solo revival of The Tymes'° *So Much In Love*, featured in film *Fast Times at Ridgemont High*.

Nov Frey's *The One You Love* climbs to US #15.

Dec Compilation LP *Eagles' Greatest Hits, Vol. 2* reaches US #52. (All members now have solo careers but the most successful will be Frey and Henley.)

1983 Jan Henley's *Dirty Laundry* hits US #3, becoming a million-seller, and makes UK #59, while Frey's *All Those Lies* makes US #41. Felder's LP *Airborne* climbs to US #178.

Feb Henley's *I Can't Stand Still* peaks at US #48.

1984 June Frey's debut LP *The Allnighter* makes US #37.

Aug *Sexy Girl* by Frey reaches US #20.

Nov Schmit's LP *Playin' It Cool*, released on Asylum, peaks at US #160. Frey's *The Allnighter* reaches US #54.

Dec Henley's second LP *Build The Perfect Beast* makes US #13.

1985 Feb Henley's *The Boys Of Summer* hits US #5 and UK #12.

Mar Frey hits US #2 and UK #12 with *The Heat Is On* from film *Beverly Hills Cop*, while Henley's LP *Building The Perfect Beast* reaches UK #14.

Apr *All She Wants To Do Is Dance* by Henley hits US #9.

May Compilation LP *The Best Of The Eagles* hits UK #10.

June Frey's *Smugglers Blues*, from TV series "Miami Vice", reaches US #12 and UK #22. (An episode of the series is based around the song, in which Frey plays a drug smuggler.)

July Frey's LP *The Allnighter* climbs to UK #31, as Henley's *Not Enough Love In The World* reaches US #34.

Oct Henley's *Sunset Grill* makes US #22.

Nov Frey's *You Belong To The City* hits US #2.

1986 Dec [31] At Henley's New Year's Eve party, guests Gary Hart and Donna Rice meet each other.

1987 Dec Schmit's second solo LP *Timothy B.*, on MCA Records, peaks at US #106.

1988 Aug *The Best Of The Eagles* compilation is revived as a UK TV-advertised LP, this time hitting #8, tying in with three-inch CD single release of *Hotel California*.

Sept Frey releases LP *Soul Searchin'*, which makes US #37, as *True Love* peaks at US #13.

Oct More than 250 fans demand their money back after a charity show in Sidcup, Kent, UK, at which local musician Gordon Hurley passed himself off as Don Henley. Meanwhile the real Henley is working on a third LP with help from Bruce Hornsby° and Guns 'N' Roses'° Axl Rose.

EARTH, WIND & FIRE

Maurice White (vocals, drums, percussion and kalimba)
Wade Flemons (vocals)
Don Whitehead (piano, electric piano and vocals)
Sherry Scott (vocals)
Verdine White (bass)
Michael Beal (guitar and harmonica)
Yackov Ben Israel (percussion conga)
Chet Washington (tenor sax)
Alex Thomas (trombone)

1955 White (b. Dec.19, 1944, Memphis, Tenn., US) begins playing drums with Memphis schoolfriend Booker T. Jones (later of Booker T. and The MG's°).

1960 White attends Chicago Conservatory of Music, studying composition and percussion, with the aim of becoming a teacher.

1963 He finds work as a session drummer at Chess Records, working with Billy Stewart, Chuck Berry°, Sonny Stitt, Jackie Wilson°, The Impressions°, The Dells and Etta James.

1966 He joins The Ramsey Lewis Trio and plays on ten of Lewis' LPs. While recording with the Trio, he introduces the kalimba, a small finger piano from Africa.

1969 White forms The Salty Peppers, who have a local Chicago hit with *La La Time* on Capitol Records.

EARTH, WIND & FIRE *cont.*

1970 White changes the group name to Earth, Wind & Fire. They sign to Warner Bros. Records.

1971 Apr Debut LP *Earth, Wind And Fire*, produced by Joe Wissert, reaches US #172 during a 13-week chart stay.

July *Love Is Life* is first US singles chart entry at #93.

1972 Jan LP *The Need Of Love* is released, climbing to US #89. The group leaves Warner Bros. and signs to CBS/Columbia. White dismantles the band and recruits Philip Bailey (vocals, percussion), Jessica Cleaves (vocals), Roland Bautista (guitar), Larry Dunn (piano, organ and clavinet), Ronald Laws (tenor sax and flute) and Ralph Johnson (drums and percussion). The only other remaining member of the original line-up is Maurice's brother Verdine. The new group begins work on its Columbia debut with producer Wissert at Sunset Sound Studios, Hollywood, Cal.

Nov CBS/Columbia debut LP *Last Days And Time*, including selections by Pete Seeger (*Where Have All The Flowers Gone*) and Bread° (*Make It With You*), makes US #87.

1973 June LP *Head To The Sky*, again produced by Wissert, reaches US #27 (later going gold). Al McKay replaces Bautista, Andrew Woolfolk replaces Laws and Johnny Graham is added on guitar.

Sept *Evil* reaches US #50.

1974 Mar LP *Open Our Eyes* climbs to US #15 and goes platinum. White produces Ramsey Lewis' LP *Sun Goddess* (which reaches US #12 at the end of the year). Earth, Wind & Fire opens for Sly & The Family Stone° at New York's Madison Square Garden.

May *Mighty Mighty* reaches US #29.

Aug *Kalimba Story* climbs to US #55.

Sept LP *Another Time*, a reissue of their first two LPs, reaches US #97.

Oct *Devotion* reaches #33 in US.

1975 May LP *That's The Way Of The World* tops the US chart for 3 weeks, eventually selling over 2 million. Earth, Wind & Fire is featured as a rock band in movie *Shining Star*. Film theme, *Shining Star*, hits US #1, gaining a gold disk for a million sales. White's brother, Fred, joins on drums.

Sept *That's The Way Of The World* reaches US #12.

1976 Jan Double LP *Gratitude* tops the US chart for 3 weeks, and again achieves double platinum.

Feb *Sing A Song* hits US #5 and is another million-seller.

Apr *Can't Hide Love* reaches US #39 and wins a Grammy award as Best Vocal Arrangement. *Shining Star* takes a Grammy as Best R&B Single of 1975. White forms his own company, Kalimba Productions.

Oct *Getaway* climbs to US #12. LP *Spirit*, dedicated to White's co-producer Charles Stepney who died earlier in the year, hits US #2. Held off the top by Stevie Wonder's° *Songs In The Key Of Life*, it is still a double platinum seller.

1977 Jan *Saturday Nite* reaches US #21.

Mar *Saturday Nite* is their UK chart debut, reaching #17. Movie *Shining Star* is premiered.

June Backing group girl trio The Emotions, recently on tour with Earth, Wind & Fire, hits US #1 with White-written and produced *Best Of My Love*.

Dec LP *All'n'All* hits US #3, again reaching double platinum.

1978 Jan *Serpentine Fire* makes US #13. *All'n'All* is their first UK LP chart entry, reaching #13.

Mar *Fantasy* climbs to UK #14 and US #32.

May Two minor hits follow in UK: *Jupiter* at #41 and *Magic Mind* at #54.

Sept *Got To Get You Into My Life*, the Lennon°/ McCartney° song which the band performs in film *Sergeant Pepper's Lonely Hearts Club Band*, hits US #9 and UK #33, and is a US million-seller.

Oct [22] Earth, Wind & Fire begins a 75-date sold-out US tour in Louisville, Ky.

Dec Compilation LP *The Best Of Earth Wind & Fire Vol. 1* enters US and UK charts, hitting #6 in both and becoming the group's fourth consecutive US double platinum LP.

1979 Jan *September* hits UK #3 and US #8. Maurice White establishes The American Recording Company (ARC) in LA, with an artist roster including The Emotions, Deniece Williams°, Weather Report° and D.J. Rogers. His production skills are much in demand and he will oversee LPs by artists including Barbra Streisand°, Jennifer Holliday, Ramsey Lewis and Valerie Carter.

Jan [9] Earth, Wind & Fire appears in the benefit concert "A Gift of Song – Music for UNICEF", at UN General Assembly in New York, with Abba°, The Bee Gees°, Rod Stewart°, John Denver° and others. The show is taped for TV and a compilation LP is released, while performers each pledge royalties from one new song to UNICEF, raising $500,000.

Feb [15] LP *All'n'All* wins a Grammy as Best R&B Group Vocal Performance, and the track *Runnin'* is rated Best R&B Instrumental Performance.

June LP *I Am* enters US and UK charts, hitting US #3 and UK #5. *Boogie Wonderland*, featuring The Emotions on guest vocals, hits UK #4 and US #6 and is another gold disk.

Sept *After The Love Has Gone* hits US #2 (another million-seller) and UK #4.

Oct [18] During another sell-out US tour, fifteen youths are arrested at the group's Madison Square Garden concert, charged with mugging audience members.

Nov *Star* reaches UK #16.

Dec *Can't Let Go* and *In The Stone* reach UK #46 and #53 respectively.

1980 Jan *Star* breaks their run of major US hit singles, by reaching only #64.

Feb [27] *After The Love Has Gone* wins a Grammy as Best R&B Group Vocal Performance, while *Boogie Wonderland* takes the Best R&B Instrumental Performance award.

Oct *Let Me Talk* climbs to UK #29 and US #44.

Nov Double LP *Faces* is released, hitting #10 in both US and UK.

1981 Nov LP *Raise* hits US #5 and UK #14. Bautista rejoins the group, replacing Al McKay, who leaves to concentrate on record production.

Dec *Let's Groove* hits #3 in both UK and US, and again goes gold. It also spends 11 week at US R&B #1 – a new record.

1982 Feb *I've Had Enough* reaches UK #29.

1983 Feb [25] Grammy award for Best R&B Group Performance goes to *Wanna Be With You*, a track from LP *Raise*.

Mar *Fall In Love With Me* reaches US #17 and UK #47. LP *Powerlight* makes US #12 and UK #22.

Sept Bailey's debut solo LP *Continuation* makes US #71.

Dec *Magnetic* climbs to US #57. LP *Electric Universe* enters US chart, but climbs only to #40.

1984 Mar *Touch* reaches US R&B #23, but fails to cross over or to sell in UK. White disbands the group, claiming he needs a long rest. (He will spend the next 2 years concentrating on his Kalimba production company.)

Oct Bailey records solo LP *Chinese Wall*.

Nov Bailey's *Easy Lover*, a duet with Phil Collins°, is released as a single in US, and hits #2. He also records spiritual solo LP *The Wonders Of His Love* for US religious label Myrrh. It sells a quarter million in US alone.

1985 Mar *Easy Lover* hits UK #1, while LP *Chinese Wall* reaches US #22.

Apr *Chinese Wall* reaches UK #29, and extract, *Walking On The Chinese Wall*, climbs to US #46.

May *Walking On The Chinese Wall* reaches UK #34. Bailey does not continue his solo career (and rejoins Earth, Wind & Fire when it returns to recording during 1987).

Oct White's solo revival of *Stand By Me* makes US #50. LP *Maurice White* reaches US #61.

1986 May Third pop soul LP by Bailey, *Inside Out*, peaks at US #84 but fails in UK.

Oct White and Bailey meet to discuss re-forming Earth, Wind & Fire.

Nov Second Bailey spiritual LP, *Triumph*, finds only specialist success.

1987 Nov Having achieved six double platinum and two platinum LPs with numerous gold awards, Earth, Wind & Fire reunites with White, Bailey, Verdine White, Andrew Woolfolk and Sheldon Reynolds. LP *Touch The World*, produced by White and Preston Glass, fails in UK, but climbs to US #33.

Dec *System Of Survival* makes US #60 and UK #54.

1988 Oct Following US dates, Earth, Wind & Fire visits UK as part of its "Touch The World" global tour.

SHEENA EASTON

1979 June Easton (b. Apr.27, 1959, Bellshill, Scotland) graduates as a teacher of speech and drama from The Royal Scottish Academy of Music and Drama, a month after successfully auditioning as a singer for EMI Records in London.

1980 Apr Debut release *Modern Girl* reaches #56 in UK.

July [2] She is featured in an edition of UK BBC TV series "The Big Time", which allows people to sample their ambitions. Easton is

seen at her audition, recording her first single, and undergoing the grooming and launch process EMI gives to a new act.

Aug Boosted by the national TV exposure, well-timed second single *9 To 5* shoots to UK #3.

Sept TV has also reactivated demand for *Modern Girl*, which re-charts and this time hits UK #8, giving Easton the rare achievement for a British female singer of two simultaneous UK top 10 hits.

Nov She appears in The Royal Variety Show, London, watched by The Queen Mother. *One Man Woman* reaches UK #14.

1981 Jan LP *Take My Time* reaches UK #17. Single of the same name makes UK #44.

Apr *Morning Train (9 To 5)* hits US #1 for 2 weeks, selling over a million copies. The amended title has been deemed necessary for the US market to avoid confusion with Dolly Parton's° film theme song *9 To 5*, which hit US #1 in Mar.

May LP *Sheena Easton* reaches US #24. *When He Shines* makes UK #12.

July *Modern Girl* reaches US #18.

Aug *For Your Eyes Only* hits UK #8. It is the theme song for a James Bond movie, and Easton becomes the only Bond theme singer to be seen on screen singing the song during the credits.

Sept *Just Another Broken Heart* climbs to UK #33.

Oct *For Your Eyes Only* hits US #4. LP *You Could Have Been With Me* makes UK #33 and US #47..

Dec LP title track *You Could Have Been With Me* makes UK #54.

1982 Feb *You Could Have Been With Me* reaches US #15.

Feb [24] She wins a US Grammy award as Best New Artist of 1981.

Apr LP *You Could Have Been With Me* makes US #47.

June *When He Shines* reaches US #30.

Aug *Machinery* peaks at UK #38, and is her last solo UK hit single.

Sept LP *Madness, Money And Music* makes UK #44. *Machinery* peaks at US #57.

Oct LP *Madness, Money And Music* makes US #85.

Nov *I Wouldn't Beg For Water* reaches US #64.

1983 Mar Easton duets with Kenny Rogers° on a David Foster-produced revival of Bob Seger's° *We've Got Tonight*, which hits US #6. It also tops US country singles chart, and reaches UK #28.

Oct *Telefone (Long Distance Love Affair)* hits US #9. By now she is mostly resident and working in the US, where she stars in her own NBC TV special "Sheena Easton . . . Act One". LP *Best Kept Secret* makes US #33 and UK #99.

1984 Mar *Almost Over You* reaches US #25.

June Easton marries Rob Light.

Nov *Strut* hits US #7.

1985 Feb LP *A Private Heaven* makes US #15, thus becoming her most successful US LP.

Mar *Sugar Walls*, written by Prince°, hits US #9. Mildly erotic symbolism in its lyrics arouses some controversy, but does not deprive it of airplay. Easton becomes the first artist in history to achieve top 5 hits on the pop, R&B, country, dance, and adult contemporary charts in the US.

Nov She sings the theme song *Christmas All Over The World* over the credits of the Dudley Moore film *Santa Claus – The Movie*.

Dec *Do It For Love* reaches US #29. LP *Do You* reaches US #40.

1986 Mar A revival of Martha and The Vandellas'° *Jimmy Mack* climbs to US #65.

July She teams with producer Narada Michael Walden for two-song contribution to Rob Lowe movie *About Last Night*.

Sept *So Far So Good* reaches US #43.

1987 Oct She duets with Prince° on *U Got The Look*, taken from his LP *Sign O' The Times*. The single peaks at US #2, and UK #11. Talk of romantic links between the two is fuelled by provocative duetting on the promotional video for *U Got The Look*. The rumors fade, however, by the end of the year.

1988 July An interview with hostess of original "Big Time" program that launched her career provides interesting viewing on UK BBC-TV.

THE EASYBEATS

"Little" Stevie Wright (vocals)
Harry Vanda (guitar)
George Young (guitar)
Dick Diamonde (bass)
Gordon "Snowy" Fleet (drums)

1963 The group forms in Sydney, Australia. Three of its members – Wright (b. Dec.20, 1948), Young (b. Nov.6, 1947) and Fleet (b. Aug.16, 1945) – are UK-born, while Vanda (b. Harry Wandan, Mar.22, 1947) and Diamonde (b. Dec. 28, 1947) are originally from Holland. All are in Australia due to family emigration, and meet while living at the Villawood Migrant Youth Hostel.

1964 Fleet coins their name, and they become resident group at Sydney's Beatle Village club, where they meet producer Ted Albert, who gets them signed to Australian Parlophone.

1965 Mar First release *For My Woman* fails to score.

July *She's So Fine* hits #1 in Australia, the first of five hits (including chart-toppers *Easy As Can Be*, *Woman* and *Come And See Her*), which rapidly establish them as a major Antipodean teen draw.

1966 June Signed internationally to United Artists, they move to UK to work with producer Shel Talmy. First UK single *Come And See Her* sells moderately.

Dec *Friday On My Mind*, written by Vanda and Young, hits #6 in UK and #1 in Australia.

1967 Mar UK follow-up *Who'll Be The One?* fails to chart while the group returns to Australia to prepare for a US visit. Fleet decides against touring, and is replaced by Tony Cahill.

May *Friday On My Mind* reaches US #16, boosted by the promotional trip. LP of the same name charts at US #180.

June *Heaven And Hell* fails to sell.

1968 May Ballad *Hello, How Are You?*, reaches UK #20 – and proves to be their UK chart swan song.

Sept Final United Artists' release *Good Times* does not chart. A new recording deal is signed with Polydor in UK and Motown subsidiary, Rare Earth, in US.

1969 Nov *St Louis* fails to sell in UK, but scrapes to #100 in US, completing their US chart career. Immediately afterwards, they split up.

1974 Vanda and Young, having moved back to Australia, open a studio complex in Sydney, and soon have success with John Paul Young. They will produce AC/DC° in the mid-1970s, Young's two brothers Angus and Malcolm are group members.

1978 Oct The pair will have varied success as Flash & The Pan, Paintbox and The Marcus Hook Roll Band. As Flash & The Pan they make a UK chart debut (#54) with *And The Band Played On (Down Among The Dead Men)*. Further chart hits will come with *Hey St. Peter* (US #76 in Aug. 1979) and *Waiting For A Train* which hits UK #7 in June 1983.

ECHO & THE BUNNYMEN

Ian McCulloch (vocals)
Will Sergeant (guitar)
Les Pattinson (bass)
Pete de Freitas (drums)

1977 May The Crucial Three is formed by Ian McCulloch (b. May 5, 1959, Liverpool, UK), Pete Wylie (b. Mar.22, 1958, Liverpool, UK) and Julian Cope (b. Oct.21, 1957, Deri, Glamorgan, South Wales), but their rehearsals in Liverpool lead to nothing.

1978 July McCulloch and Cope reunite briefly as members of A Shallow Madness, again with little result.

ECHO AND THE BUNNYMEN *cont.*

Sept McCulloch and restaurant chef Will Sergeant (b. Apr.12, 1958, Liverpool, UK) record demos with the aid of a drum machine which they christen "Echo".

Nov [11] Les Pattinson (b. Apr.18, 1958, Ormskirk, Merseyside, UK) joins on bass 4 days before the band makes its debut at Eric's Club in Liverpool as Echo & The Bunnymen.

1979 Mar The trio signs to local Zoo label and releases *Pictures On My Wall*. B-side *Read It In Books* is an old Crucial Three song, written by McCulloch and Cope, who has left to join The Teardrop Explodes°.

Sept With record companies clamoring, the group signs to small WEA-distributed Korova label. Soon after, and like The Beatles°, one drummer, Echo, is fired and replaced by another, Pete de Freitas (b. Aug.2, 1961, Port of Spain, Trinidad, West Indies).

1980 May The band's second single *Rescue*, and their first distributed through a major label, reaches UK #62.

July Debut LP *Crocodiles* climbs to UK #17.

Sept *The Puppet* is released, but fails to chart.

1981 Apr A five-track 12"-only EP, *Shine So Hard*, with its featured track *Crocodiles*, makes UK #37.

May LP *Heaven Up Here* hits UK #10 and enters the US chart, peaking at #184.

July *A Promise* reaches UK #49.

1982 June *The Back Of Love* is the band's first major hit single, making UK #19.

1983 Feb *The Cutter* is its first UK top 10 hit at #8. LP *Porcupine* hits UK #2 but makes only US #137.

July During a quiet period, Sergeant releases his solo LP *Themes For Grind*.

Aug *Never Stop* reaches UK #15.

1984 Feb *The Killing Moon* hits UK #9. Live mini-LP *Echo & The Bunnymen*, released only in US, reaches #188.

May *Silver* climbs to UK #30. It is taken from LP *Ocean Rain*, which hits UK #4. The publicity for the LP describing it as the "greatest album ever made" apparently has some effect in US, where it becomes the band's only top 100 LP, peaking at #87. Coinciding with the new record releases is "Echo & The Bunnymen Present A Crystal Day", an event in which the band takes its most fervent fans on a day trip around Liverpool culminating in a live show.

July *Seven Seas* reaches UK #16.

Nov McCulloch releases a solo single, a revival of Kurt Weill standard *The September Song*, which makes UK #51.

1985 Nov After a long spell without new material, while the group has been writing and rehearsing, *Bring On The Dancing Horses* reaches UK #21 and compilation LP *Songs To Learn And Sing* hits UK #6.

1986 Feb De Freitas leaves and is replaced by Mark Fox, ex-Haircut 100°.

Sept De Freitas rejoins the band, ousting Fox.

1987 June After another long musical silence, *The Game* charts at UK #28.

July LP *Echo & The Bunnymen*, produced by Laurie Latham, hits UK #4.

Aug A rapidly-released second single from LP *Lips Like Sugar* peaks at UK #36.

1988 Mar *People Are Strange*, taken from movie *The Lost Boys*, is a revival of The Doors'° 1960s hit and is produced by former Doors keyboard player Ray Manzarek, who has also appeared on Echo & The Bunnymen's previous LP. It climbs to UK #29. (It will also feature on the WEA compilation *Under The Covers*.)

Aug Press reports state the band members will split up, despite their denial.

DUANE EDDY

1958 Mar Eddy (b Apr.28, 1938, Corning, N.Y., US), having moved to Tucson, Ariz., then Coolidge, Ariz., in his teens, is a guitarist leading a band called The Rebels when he meets DJ Lee Hazlewood and Lester Sill, who raises the finance to cut four sides by the band, which are leased to a new Philadelphia label, Jamie. The throbbing and reverberating *Movin' 'n' Groovin'* makes US #73 and introduces the "twangy guitar" of Duane Eddy.

July With guitar instrumentals like Bill Justis' *Raunchy* and Link Wray's *Rumble* in the charts, Eddy concocts *Rebel Rouser*, with whooping, handclaps, tremelo effects and abundant echo. It hits US #6 after promotion on Dick Clark's "American Bandstand", where Eddy is revealed to be young, shy and handsome. It is his first million-seller and fans are also roused in UK, where it reaches #19.

Sept Always cut at Audio Recorders in Phoenix, using producer Hazlewood's novel drainpipe echo chamber, Eddy's hits follow the same pattern of catchy tune and rhythm, played on the bass strings of his Gretsch, and composer credits are usually shared by producer and artist. *Ramrod* reaches US #27.

Nov With a title (like most of his hits) suggestive of its mood, *Cannonball* makes US #15 and UK #22. Eddy's studio Rebels comprise Al Casey (guitar/piano), Buddy Wheeler (bass), Donnie Owens and Corky Casey (guitar) and Mike Bermani (drums). Tracks are often taken to Gold Star Studios in Hollywood, where a sax part is added by Plas Johnson or (later) Steve Douglas.

1959 Feb *The Lonely One* reaches US #23. Debut LP *Have Twangy Guitar Will Travel* hits US #5. (It will remain his biggest seller.)

Apr *Yep!* peaks at US #30 and UK #17. B-side, Eddy's pulsating version of Henry Mancini's *Peter Gunn* (recently a US-only smash for Ray Anthony & His Orchestra), hits UK #6.

July *Forty Miles Of Bad Road* hits US #9 and UK #11. The B-side, *The Quiet Three*, reaches US #46. LP *Have Twangy Guitar Will Travel* hits UK #6.

Aug Second LP *Especially For You* reaches US #24.

Oct Fast and furious *Some Kinda Earthquake* makes US #37 and UK #12, and B-side *First Love First Tears* reaches US #59.

Nov LP *Especially For You* hits UK #6.

1960 Jan Third LP *The Twang's The Thang* peaks at US #18. It contains none of his hits and is another mixture of new and old. The ubiquitous "rebel yells" are credited to a Ben Demotto. *Bonnie Came Back* (based on *My Bonnie Lies Over The Ocean*) makes US #26 and UK #12.

Apr In a package with Bobby Darin°, Clyde McPhatter and Emile Ford°, Eddy storms UK with his current Rebels, comprising Larry Knechtel (piano), Jim Horn (sax), Al Casey (bass) and Jimmy Troxel (drums). *Shazam!* (a *Marvel* comics exclamation) reaches US #45 and hits UK #4. LP *The Twang's The Thang* hits UK #2.

July Title theme from film *Because They're Young*, Eddy's biggest international disk, hits US #4 and UK #2 and is his second

million-seller. He also has an acting role in the movie, with James Darren and Tuesday Weld, which stars Dick Clark as a high school teacher.

Aug *Kommotion* reaches US #78 and UK #13.

Nov *Peter Gunn* makes a belated US chart entry, reaching #27.

Dec Folksy LP *Songs Of Our Heritage* climbs to UK #13 but fails to chart in US.

1961 Feb A collection of hits, LP *A Million Dollar's Worth Of Twang*, reaches US #11. It marks the end of Eddy's relationship with the Sill/Hazlewood team. Movie theme *Pepe* reaches US #18 and hits UK #2.

Apr LP *A Million Dollars' Worth Of Twang* hits UK #5. Eddy makes his second movie appearance in *A Thunder Of Drums*. Jamie releases four more Eddy hits: the familiar *Theme From Dixie* (US #39, UK #7), film theme *Ring Of Fire* (US #84, UK #17), the Knechtel/Eddy collaboration *Drivin' Home* (US #87, UK #30) and an old LP track *My Blue Heaven* (US #50).

Aug LP *Girls Girls Girls* reaches US #93. Eddy marries Miriam Johnson.

Oct A one-off single for Parlophone, his version of Duke Ellington's *Caravan*, makes UK #30.

1962 May Eddy signs to RCA Victor. His debut single, a revival of the perennial *Deep In The Heart Of Texas*, reaches US #78 and UK #19. His first RCA LP *Twistin' 'n' Twangin'* reaches US #82.

June LP *A Million Dollar's Worth Of Twang Vol 2* makes UK #18 but fails in US.

Aug The theme from Richard Boone's popular TV western series "Have Gun Will Travel", retitled *The Ballad Of Paladin*, reaches US #33 and hits UK #10. LP *Twistin' 'n' Twangin'* hits UK #8.

Nov Second RCA LP, *Twangy Guitar – Silky Strings*, reaches US #72.

Dec Reunited with Hazlewood, Eddy shuns rock'n'roll for novelty pop, complete with singalong chorus, and releases *Dance With The Guitar Man*, which makes US #12 and hits UK #4 to become his third million-seller. LP *Twangy Guitar – Silky Strings* reaches UK #13.

1963 Jan Third RCA LP, *Dance With The Guitar Man*, reaches US #47.

Mar *Boss Guitar* peaks at US #28 and UK #27.

June *Lonely Boy Lonely Guitar* makes only US #82 and UK #35.

Sept *Your Baby's Gone Surfin'* reaches US #93 and UK #49. *My Baby Plays The Same Old Song On His Guitar All Night Long* fails to chart.

Oct LP *Twangin' Up A Storm* climbs to US #93.

1964 Jan *The Son Of Rebel Rouser* makes US #97.

May LP *Lonely Guitar* becomes Eddy's final charting record at US #144.

1965/71 LPs including *Duane Goes Dylan* and *Duane A Go Go* fail to chart. Eddy appears in movies *The Savage Seven* and *Kona Coast* (1968).

1972 Apr He makes a cameo appearance on B.J. Thomas' US #15 hit *Rock And Roll Lullaby*.

1973 Eddy produces Phil Everly's solo LP *Star Spangled Springer*, adding his twangy trademark to the closing moments.

1975 Mar *Play Me Like You Play Your Guitar*, produced by English writer/producer Tony Macaulay, returns Eddy to the UK chart, hitting #9.

1978 *You Are My Sunshine*, for Elektra Records with help from Waylon Jennings and Willie Nelson°, fails to chart.

1983 May [22] Eddy makes live comeback in US after 15 years' absence at The Baked Potato, LA, with a band comprising Ry Cooder° (guitar), Don Randi (keyboards), Hal Blaine (drums), Steve Douglas (sax) and John Garnache (bass). (The band will later embark on a US tour.)

1986 Mar The Art of Noise° enlists Eddy's aid on its revival of *Peter Gunn*, which hits UK #8 and Eddy twangs his guitar on BBC TV's "Top of the Pops".

June *Peter Gunn* makes US #50.

1987 Sept Eddy cuts LP *Duane Eddy* for Capitol Records, produced by Jeff Lynne, with help from friends Paul McCartney°, George Harrison° and Ry Cooder°.

DAVE EDMUNDS

1966 After learning to play guitar while still at school and forming his first band, The 99ers, Edmunds (b. Apr.15, 1944, Cardiff, Wales, UK), having joined local group The Raiders, moves to London where he joins The Image.

1967 Edmunds and Image drummer Tommy Riley form a new group with bass player John Williams. EMI Records, for whom The Image has recorded on its Parlophone label, names them The Human Beans.

July The Human Beans' first single, issued on EMI's Columbia label, is a cover of Tim Rose's *Morning Dew*.

1968 Feb The group changes its name to Love Sculpture and releases *River To Another Day*, on Parlophone.

July EMI wants a blues LP to cash in on the current UK blues boom so Love Sculpture records and mixes an appropriate LP, *Blues Helping*, in 15 hours with no editing, with producers Kingsley Ward and Malcolm Jones at London's Abbey Road Studios.

Sept *Wang Dang Doodle* (a Willie Dixon song) is released, followed by LP *Blues Helping*, neither of which sells.

Nov Due to the response to a frantic 7-minute version of Khachaturian's *Sabre Dance* recorded for John Peel's "Top Gear" UK radio show, Parlophone releases a new 5-minute version which hits UK #5.

1969 Jan LP *Forms And Feeling* and singles *Farandole* and *In The Land Of The Few* are released but fail to chart. The group begins a 6-week US tour. On its return, the group splits. Edmunds heads for Charles and Kingsley Ward's Rockfield Studios in Monmouthshire, Wales.

1970 Edmunds records Smiley Lewis' *I Hear You Knocking* but is unable to interest EMI in releasing it. Meanwhile he produces an LP for Shakin' Stevens° & The Sunsets.

Nov Manager Gordon Mills chooses *I Hear You Knocking* as the first release on his new MAM label. It tops the UK chart and hits US #4 (and will sell 3 million copies worldwide).

1971 Mar EMI releases *I'm Coming Home*, on its Regal Zonophone. It fails to chart in UK but makes US #75.

July *Blue Monday* is released.

1972 June LP *Rockpile* is released but also fails to chart.

July *Down Down Down* is released. By the end of the year Edmunds is free of any obligation to EMI. Rockfield studio owner Ward signs him to his new RCA-distributed Rockfield label.

1973 Feb First Rockfield release is a cover of The Ronettes'° hit *Baby I Love You*. A tribute to producer Phil Spector, it hits UK #8.

July *Born To Be With You*, originally recorded by The Chordettes°, hits UK #5. Edmunds plays with Welsh group Man.

1974 Feb Edmunds appears in the David Puttnam-produced film *Stardust* and is involved in most of the original soundtrack music. The material is recorded by The Stray Cats (a fictitious band including David Essex° and Keith Moon). Brinsley Schwarz° asks Edmunds to produce its next LP *New Favourites*, and is so doing he strikes up a working relationship with the group's bass player Nick Lowe°.

1975 Apr Edmunds' second LP, *Subtle As A Flying Mallet*, is released but does not chart.

1976 Sept He signs to Led Zeppelin's° SwanSong label, where the first two releases, *Here Comes The Weekend* and *Where Or When* fail to chart. He produces The Flamin' Groovies' LP *Shake Some Action*, which makes US #142.

1977 Feb Edmunds announces the launch of his new band, Rockpile, with a short UK and European tour. The group comprises Lowe°, Terry Williams and guitarist Billy Bremner and the intention, says Lowe, is "playing smelly rock'n'roll in bars and clubs".

Apr LP *Get It* is released as a Dave Edmunds solo, but fails to chart. Rockpile begins a US tour with Bad Company°.

July Edmunds' *I Knew The Bride* reaches UK #26.

Oct Rockpile makes an extensive UK tour.

Nov Edmunds plays on Nick Lowe's° first Stiff Records tour package, "Last Chicken in the Shop".

1978 Sept Lowe° co-writes much of the material on new Edmunds LP *Tracks On Wax*. The LP and the three singles from it fail to chart. Rockpile plays UK's Knebworth Festival. Edmunds takes the stage with Emmylou Harris & The Hot Band at London's Hammersmith Odeon, and he and Tommy Riley back Carl Perkins° for UK TV special "South Bank Show".

Oct Edmunds tours US as part of package tour with Elvis Costello° and Mink De Ville.

1979 July His recording of Elvis Costello's° song *Girls Talk* hits UK #4. LP *Repeat When Necessary* reaches UK #39.

Aug LP *Repeat When Necessary* reaches US #54.

Oct *Queen Of Hearts* makes UK #11. *Girls Talk* climbs to US #56.

Dec *Crawling From The Wreckage* (penned by Graham Parker°)

DAVE EDMUNDS *cont.*

reaches UK #59. Rockpile plays with Wings and Elvis Costello° in a benefit concert for Kampuchea.

1980 Jan Rockpile tours UK, supported by US band The Fabulous Thunderbirds (for whom Edmunds will produce two successful LPs).

Feb Edmunds' version of *Singin' The Blues* (1950s chartmakers for Guy Mitchell and Tommy Steele°) makes US #28.

Sept Rockpile's *Wrong Way*, written by Squeeze's° Difford and Tilbrook, is released on the F-Beat label but fails to chart.

Oct The only Rockpile LP, *Seconds Of Pleasure*, is released and makes UK #34 and US #27.

Nov Rockpile's *Teacher Teacher* fails to chart in UK but makes US #51.

1981 Feb Rockpile breaks up.

Mar Edmunds' *Almost Saturday Night* (a John Fogerty song) reaches UK #58 and US #54.

Apr Edmunds' LP *Twangin'* reaches UK #37 and US #48.

June *The Race Is On* reaches UK #34. It features The Stray Cats° (not those from *Stardust* days but a US rockabilly band, whose debut LP Edmunds has produced).

Dec SwanSong releases LP *The Best Of Dave Edmunds*, which traces his career from *Sabre Dance* on. It fails to chart in UK and proves to be his SwanSong swan song.

1982 LP *The Best Of Dave Edmunds* peaks at US #163.

Apr With a new deal on Arista, LP *D.E.7* makes UK #60 and US #46. It includes Bruce Springsteen's° song *From Small Things Big Things Come*, which fails to chart.

June Edmunds sets off on a nationwide US tour.

July He is rushed to hospital with internal hemorrhaging after endless touring.

Aug Fully recovered, Edmunds plays UK's Reading Festival.

Sept [3-5] Edmunds takes part in the US Festival in San Bernardino, Cal., in front of an estimated 400,000 people.

1983 Apr The Jeff Lynne-produced LP *Information* reaches UK #92 and US #51. *Slipping Away* makes UK #60.

May *Slipping Away* reaches US #39.

June Edmunds produces *On The Wings Of A Nightingale*, the Paul McCartney°-penned comeback for The Everly Brothers°.

1984 Oct LP *Riff Raff*, including six tracks produced by Lynne, peaks at US #140.

1985 July Edmunds appears on the soundtrack LP for film *Porky's Revenge*. It includes a song with The Crawling King Snakes and four of his own, one of which, *High School Nights*, reaches US #91. He embarks on a US tour.

Oct [21] Edmunds co-ordinates Carl Perkins'° UK TV special "Blue Suede Shoes", bringing along friends Eric Clapton° and George Harrison°.

1987 June Arista releases Edmunds' live hits LP *I Hear You Rocking* but it fails to chart. He tours Holland and Germany.

1988 Sept Having spent much of the last 2 years producing (The Everly Brothers°, Mason Ruffner, K.D. Lang) and contributing songs to the Steve Martin/John Candy movie *Planes Trains and Automobiles*, Edmunds signs to Capitol and records a new LP in LA. (He is also slated to produce Nick Lowe's° first LP for Warner Bros., Dion's° debut for Arista and a comeback LP by The Stray Cats°.)

THE ELECTRIC LIGHT ORCHESTRA (ELO)

Roy Wood (vocals and cello)
Jeff Lynne (vocals and guitar)
Bill Hunt (keyboards)
Richard Tandy (bass)
Bev Bevan (drums)
Wilf Gibson (violin)
Hugh McDowell (cello)
Andy Craig (cello)

1967 Wood (b. Nov.8, 1946, Birmingham, UK), ex-local band Mike Sheridan & the Nightriders (now called Idle Race) is guitarist with The Move°, currently Birmingham's biggest band enjoying much top 10 success.

1969 Wood offers friend Jeff Lynne (b. Dec.30, 1947, Birmingham), who joined Idle Race after Wood's departure and is leading the group, a place in The Move°, but Lynne elects to stay with Idle Race.

1970 Oct When Move° singer Carl Wayne leaves for a solo cabaret career, Lynne agrees to join, providing he can also be involved in Wood's separate group within The Move, playing "jazz and classically-influenced free-form music" with instrumentation aligned more to an orchestra than a rock band. The whole idea is financed by manager Don Arden, who gets them a contract with Harvest.

1971 Plans for the first Electric Light Orchestra (ELO) release are delayed as The Move° has hits with *Tonight* and *Chinatown* and LP *Message From The Country*. After a US tour The Move retires from live performance (but will still nominally exist). Drummer Bevan (b. Beverley Bevan, Nov.24, 1946, Birmingham) opens a Birmingham record shop.

1972 Apr [16] ELO makes its live debut at The Greyhound pub in Croydon, Surrey, UK. Its innovative style is not well received.

May The Move's° *California Man* hits UK #7.

Aug ELO's first single, Lynne's *10538 Overture*, hits UK #9. Debut LP *Electric Light Orchestra*, featuring Lynne and Wood and released on Harvest label, reaches UK #32. United Artists in US, having rung Arden to discover the title of the LP and being left a message "No Answer" by a secretary who could not reach him, releases it as *No Answer*. It makes US #196. Having planned ELO for several years, Wood surprises everyone by leaving the group to form his own, more pop-oriented, group Wizzard°. He takes Hunt and McDowell with him while Craig leaves altogether. Lynne recruits cellists Mike Edwards and Colin Walker and bassist Mike D'Albuquerque.

Aug [12] The new line-up debuts at UK's Reading Festival.

1973 Feb The first post-Wood release, a version of Chuck Berry's° *Roll Over Beethoven*, with quasi-classical intro, hits UK #6.

Mar LP *ELO II* is released, making UK #35 and US #62.

June [2] The group begins a 40-date US tour in San Diego, Cal.

July *Roll Over Beethoven* reaches US #42.

Sept McDowell rejoins from Wizzard°. Gibson and Walker leave and Mik Kaminski joins on violin.
Nov *Showdown*, later an R&B hit for Candi Staton, reaches UK #12.
Dec Concept LP *On The Third Day* is released through Warner Bros. in UK but fails to chart. United Artists releases the LP in US where it makes #52.
1974 Feb *Showdown* climbs to US #53.
Mar *Ma-Ma-Ma-Belle* reaches UK #22.
May *Daybreaker* peaks at US #87.
Oct LP *Eldorado*, billed as "A Symphony by The Electric Light Orchestra" makes US #16 and earns a gold disk. It fails to chart in UK.
Nov Live LP *The Night The Light Went On In Long Beach*, is released worldwide, excluding UK and US. Harvest issues LP *Showdown*, a compilation of singles and tracks from the first two LPs. Edwards and D'Albuquerque leave to be replaced by bassist Kelly Groucutt, ex-Barefoot, and cellist Melvyn Gale, ex-London Palladium orchestra.
1975 Mar Using a thirty-piece string section for the first time, *Can't Get It Out Of My Head*, from *Eldorado*, becomes the group's first US top 10 hit at #9. (The group will spend most of the year touring US.)
Oct LP *Face The Music*, much of it recorded at the Musicland studios in Munich, West Germany (where the group will record most of their future work), hits US #8.
1976 Feb *Evil Woman* hits #10 in both UK and US, as a US tour begins. During a 3-week period, the group grosses more than all previous bands and solo artists.
May *Strange Magic* makes US #14.
July *Strange Magic* climbs to UK #38.
Aug Reissued *Showdown* makes US #59.
Sept ELO, signed to Arden's Jet label, releases a US-only greatest hits LP, *Ole ELO*, which reaches US #32.
Oct LP *A New World Record*, written, arranged and produced by Lynne, who is now the main focus in the group, gains immediate radio interest and hits UK #6 and US #5. It sells five million copies worldwide.
Dec *Livin' Thing* hits UK #4
1977 Jan *Livin' Thing* reaches US #13.
Jan [17] ELO begins a major US and Canadian tour at the Veterans' Memorial Auditorium, Phoenix, Ariz. (It will end 3 months later on Apr.6 at the Place de Nationale, Montreal, Canada.)
Mar *Rockaria!* hits UK #9.
Apr ELO's version of The Move's° only US hit, *Do Ya*, reaches US #24, after Todd Rundgren° has used it in his live show. Harvest releases compilation LP *The Light Shines On*, as Lynne, locked away in a chalet in Bassins, Switzerland, writes songs for a new LP.
June *Telephone Line*, from *A New World Record*, hits UK #8. An extensive world tour begins, which, with the year's record sales, will gross the band more than $10 million.
Sept *Telephone Line* hits US #7.
Oct *Turn To Stone* makes UK #18.
Nov With advance orders of four million, double LP *Out Of The Blue*, again written and produced by Lynne, hits #4 in both UK and US. (During its chart run US distribution for Jet switches to CBS/Columbia and the band sues United Artists for allegedly allowing millions of defective copies to reach the market.)
1978 Jan *Mr. Blue Sky* hits UK #6.
Feb *Turn To Stone* makes US #13.
Apr *Sweet Talkin' Woman* reaches US #17.
June *Wild West Hero* hits UK #6.
Aug *Mr. Blue Sky* climbs to US #35. The group begins a tour featuring an elaborate set, with lasers and a huge illuminated "spaceship".
Oct *Sweet Talkin' Woman* hits UK #6, becoming the fourth UK hit from *Out Of The Blue*.
Nov *It's Over* peaks at US #75.
Dec EP *ELO* reaches UK #38. (Tracks are *Can't Get It Out Of My Head, Strange Magic, Ma-Ma-Ma-Belle* and *Evil Woman*.) Lynne's first solo *Doin' That Crazy Thing* is released but, like Bevan's solo *Let There Be Drums*, fails to chart.
1979 Jan Jet releases box set *Three Light Years*, comprising LPs *On The Third Day, Eldorado* and *Face The Music*, which reaches UK #38. Kaminski's solo *Violinski: Clog Dance* makes UK #17.
Mar Harvest issues LP *The Light Shines On Vol. 2*, but it meets with little interest.
May *Shine A Little Love* hits UK #6.
June LP *Discovery* becomes the group's first UK #1, and hits US #5.
July *The Diary Of Horace Wimp* hits UK #8, as *Shine A Little Love* hits US #8.
July [20] ELO advertises in the music press dedicating its forthcoming single *Don't Bring Me Down* to "Skylab".
Sept *Don't Bring Me Down* hits UK #3 and US #4, becoming the band's biggest US single success.
Nov *Confusion* hits UK #8 and US #37.
Dec Concentrating on recording and less on live performance (the band has toured every year since 1972), Lynne pares the full-time band to a core of himself, Bevan, Tandy and Groucutt, calling on Gale when required.
1980 Jan LP *ELO's Greatest Hits* hits UK #7 and US #30.
Feb *Last Train To London* reaches US #39.
May ELO is commissioned to write the songs for film *Xanadu*. First release from the film, *I'm Alive*, makes UK #20.
June Title track *Xanadu* teams ELO with Olivia Newton-John° and hits UK #1 (the band's first UK chart-topper).
July Soundtrack LP *Xanadu*, with one side featuring ELO and the other Olivia Newton-John°, hits UK #2 and US #4. The film, however, is a box-office disaster. *I'm Alive* makes US #16.
Aug *All Over The World*, from *Xanadu*, reaches UK #11.
Oct *Xanadu* hits US #8, as *All Over The World* makes US #13.
Nov *Don't Walk Away* reaches UK #21.
1981 July *Hold On Tight* hits UK #4. (It is the first record credited simply to the ELO acronym. They will revert back to the full name in 1986, when signed to CBS/Epic.)
Aug LP *Time* tops the UK chart and reaches US #16.
Oct *Hold On Tight* hits US #10. The group begins a major tour, but for the first time has less than capacity audiences. *Twilight* becomes their poorest chart showing for years at UK #30.
Nov *Twilight Time* makes US #38.
1982 Jan *Ticket To The Moon/Here Is The News* reaches UK #24.
Mar For the first time since *Nightrider* 6 years earlier, an ELO single (*The Way Life's Meant To Be*) fails to chart in UK and US.
1983 Apr Dave Edmunds'° LP *Information*, produced by Lynne, is released.
June ELO's *Rock'n'Roll Is King* makes UK #13.
July LP *Secret Messages* hits UK #4, but makes only US #36.
Aug *Rock'n'Roll Is King* peaks at US #19.
Sept *Secret Messages* reaches UK #48.
Oct *Four Little Diamonds* falters at US #86. (It will be the group's last hit for 2½ years.) Bevan leaves the group to join Black Sabbath° (but will rejoin in time for the next LP).
1984 Sept Lynne produces six tracks for Dave Edmunds'° LP *Riff Raff*.
1986 Mar Signed to CBS/Epic, ELO, now reduced to three-piece Lynne, Bevan and Tandy, returns to US charts with *Calling America*, which peaks at UK #28.
Mar [15] The group makes its first concert appearance in 4 years, in its home town Birmingham. George Harrison° joins them on stage.
Apr *Calling America* peaks at US #18. The group appears at "Heartbeat '86" charity show in Birmingham (its last live appearance). LP *Balance Of Power* hits UK #9 and US #49, but *So Serious* and *Getting To The Point* taken from the LP, fail to chart.
1987 Lynne produces a track on LP *Duane Eddy*, Eddy's° comeback album on Capitol. Long-time Beatles° fan Lynne works with ex-Beatle George Harrison° on his LP *Cloud Nine* (featuring Lynne's US #1 and UK #2 produced *Got My Mind Set On You*).
1988 July Lynne co-writes and co-produces *Let It Shine* with Brian Wilson for his debut solo LP *Brian Wilson*.
Oct Concentrating more on production, Lynne teams with Randy Newman° for tracks on LP *Land Of Dreams*. Lynne is also part of The Traveling Wilburys with Bob "Lucky" Dylan°, George "Nelson" Harrison°, Roy "Lefty" Orbison° and Tom "Charlie T. Jnr." Petty°. Debut single *Handle With Care* is released with the LP from which it is taken, *Traveling Wilburys*. "Nelson" Harrison and "Otis" Lynne co-produce the project.

ELECTRIC PRUNES

Jim Lowe (guitar, autoharp and vocals)
Ken Williams (lead guitar)
Weasel Spangola (rhythm guitar)
Mark Tulin (bass)
Preston Ritter (drums)

1965 The group forms in Seattle, Wash., US, before moving to Los Angeles, where they sign to Reprise Records.
1966 May First single is *Ain't It Hard*, which does not chart.

ELECTRIC PRUNES *cont.*

1967 Feb Major success comes with the psychedelia-laden *I Had Too Much To Dream (Last Night)*, (unusually, written by a female duo Annette Tucker and Nancie Mantz), which reaches US #11. It also charts briefly in UK at #49.

Apr LP *The Electric Prunes* is released, reaching US #113.

May *Get Me To The World On Time*, from the same writers, taken from the LP, peaks at US #27. *Get Me To The World On Time* makes UK #42.

July *The Great Banana Hoax*, written by Lowe and Tulin, fails to make the charts.

Sept LP *Underground* is a minor US seller, reaching #172.

Dec The group makes a brief trip to Europe, and *Long Day's Flight*, a track from *Underground* not released as a US single, is issued in UK, but does not chart.

1968 Jan The original quintet is augmented by many other musicians on LP *Mass In F Minor*, an electronic rock transposition of a Catholic mass, written and arranged by David Axelrod. It is a minor seller in US, reaching #135, though it will remain a mid-'60s cult LP for many years after. After its release, the original group members depart, but Axelrod keeps the name alive by drawing from the additional musicians who played on *Mass In F Minor*. He records another "serious" rock LP, *Release Of An Oath*, with the revised line-up of Mark Kinkaid (guitar and vocals), Ron Morgan (guitar), Brett Wade (bass, flute and vocals), John Herren (keyboards), and Richard Whetstone (drums, guitar and vocals). The LP does not chart.

1969 May Herren leaves, and the rest of the second line-up record LP *Just Good Old Rock'n'Roll* as a quartet (without David Axelrod input). Neither it nor *Hey Mr. President* sells, and Electric Prunes splits for good.

EMERSON, LAKE AND PALMER (ELP)

Keith Emerson (keyboards)
Greg Lake (bass and vocals)
Carl Palmer (drums)

1970 Apr [11] Emerson (b. Nov.2, 1944, UK), following the break-up of The Nice, teams with Lake (b. Nov.10, 1948, Bournemouth, UK), who has just left King Crimson°. They audition drummers for a new band.

June The band forms, with Palmer (b. Mar.20, 1947, Birmingham, UK) recruited from the just-split Atomic Rooster.

Aug [25] The trio makes its live debut at the Guildhall, Plymouth, UK.

Aug [29] It plays UK's Isle of Wight Festival on the penultimate day, alongside The Doors°, The Who° and Joni Mitchell°.

Dec With the band signed to Island in UK and Atlantic (Cotillion label) in US, debut LP *Emerson Lake & Palmer*, produced (as will be all the band's subsequent LPs) by Lake, hits UK #4. It sets the style for most subsequent work – flashy instrumental virtuosity and rock/classical fusions, and generally grandiose lyrical concepts. (Pete Sinfield of King Crimson° becomes the trio's main lyric writer.)

1971 Mar The eponymous debut LP reaches US #18.

Mar [26] The group is recorded live at City Hall, Newcastle, UK, playing its own arrangement of Mussorgsky's *Pictures At An Exhibition*.

Apr Not released as a UK single, *Lucky Man* (from the debut LP) reaches US #48.

June LP *Tarkus*, a concept LP (though obscurely presented and understood by few: Tarkus appears to be a mechanized armadillo which engages mythical beast the Manticore in battle), hits UK #1 for a week.

Aug LP *Tarkus* hits US #9.

Dec Low-priced live LP *Pictures At An Exhibition* hits UK #3.

1972 Feb The live LP reaches US #10.

Apr The band plays at the Mar-Y-Sol festival in Puerto Rico, where its performance of *Take A Pebble/Lucky Man* is recorded for a live LP of the event. A revival of B. Bumble & The Stingers' *Nut Rocker*, originally included on LP *Pictures At An Exhibition*, is extracted as a US single and reaches #70.

July Fourth LP *Trilogy* hits UK #2.

Sept LP *Trilogy* hits US #5.

Oct A US-only release *From The Beginning*, taken from LP *Trilogy*, makes US #39.

1973 Jan *Lucky Man*, re-promoted in US to coincide with the group's tour, peaks at #50.

Feb [2] Emerson's hands are injured on stage in San Francisco, Cal. during the US tour. His piano, rigged to explode as a stunt during the set, detonates prematurely.

Mar The film *Pictures At An Exhibition*, featuring the band in a concert performance of the title piece, premieres in LA.

Dec The group's debut UK single *Jerusalem*, taken from new LP *Brain Salad Surgery*, fails to chart. Both are released on the band's recently formed label Manticore (named after the *Tarkus* creature). (Other early signings to Manticore will include Pete Sinfield, Little Richard°, and the Italian band P.F.M.)

1974 Jan LP *Brain Salad Surgery* hits UK #2 and US #11.

Aug Live triple LP *Welcome Back My Friends To The Show That Never Ends; Ladies And Gentlemen . . . Emerson, Lake And Palmer* hits UK #5.

Sept The live triple LP hits US #4.

Nov Manticore Records is signed to Motown for US distribution.

1975 Dec Lake's solo *I Believe In Father Christmas*, a grandiose production, hits UK #2. (It will become a standard and will be played and will sell again in UK every succeeding Christmas.) In US, it makes #95 (but will become a seasonal airplay standard).

1976 Apr Emerson's solo *Honky Tonk Train Blues*, a revival of a Meade Lux Lewis classic, reaches UK #21.

1977 Apr Double LP *Works* hits UK #9. It is mostly a showcase for the trio's solo works; they combine as a band only for the fourth side.

May Double LP *Works* makes US #12.

July A racing keyboards/guitar interpretation of Aaron Copland's *Fanfare For The Common Man*, extracted from *Works*, hits UK #2 behind Hot Chocolate's° *So You Win Again*.

Sept Lake's solo *C'est La Vie*, extracted from *Works*, makes US #91.

Dec Compilation LP *Works, Volume Two*, rounding up tracks from singles (including *Honky Tonk Train Blues* and *I Believe In Father Christmas*) and previously unissued out-takes, makes UK #20 and US #37.

1978 Dec LP *Love Beach*, the trio's final studio LP, reaches UK #48 and US #55.

Dec [30] Having played a wide-ranging farewell tour during the latter half of the year, the band announces its official break-up.

1979 Mar Palmer forms P.M., a quintet consisting of himself and four US musicians.

Dec Live LP *Emerson, Lake & Palmer In Concert* is released to fulfill contractual obligations. Recorded during the band's 1978 US tour, it reaches US #73.

1980 While Emerson involves himself with film and TV soundtrack work, Lake signs to Chrysalis as a soloist.

Mar Signed to Ariola, Palmer's group P.M. issues unsuccessful LP *One P.M.*, while struggling to find exposure outside German TV slots.

July P.M. breaks up.

Dec Compilation LP *The Best Of Emerson, Lake & Palmer* reaches US #108.

1981 Jan Palmer joins John Wetton, Steve Howe and Geoff Downes in Asia°.

May Emerson's soundtrack LP from the movie *Nighthawks* reaches US #183.

Oct Solo LP *Greg Lake* makes UK and US #62.

Dec Lake's solo single *Let Me Love You Once* reaches US #48.

1983 Sept Lake reunites with Palmer when he joins Asia° in place of John Wetton for a Far East tour.

Dec [6] Lake and Palmer play in Asia's° major gig at the Budokan theater in Tokyo, Japan, broadcast live via satellite TV and seen by 20 million MTV viewers in US (also later on home video as *Asia In Asia*.

1984 Lake leaves Asia° to make way for Wetton's return, but Asia breaks up.

1985 Emerson and Lake agree to record together, aiming for a comeback like that achieved by contemporaries Yes° a year earlier. The duo cannot interest Palmer in the project, so Cozy Powell is recruited on drums instead.

1986 June Signed to Polydor, the new trio debuts with LP *Emerson, Lake & Powell*, which hits UK #6 and makes US #23.

July *Touch And Go*, extracted from the LP, reaches US #60. The band tours US. (The line-up will not last long and Powell will leave to pursue other projects.)

1987 Asked again to join, Palmer agrees, and the trio spends an extended period rehearsing.

	Oct	After unsuccessful rehearsals, the renewed ELP project is abandoned.
1988	Feb	Emerson, Palmer and Robert Berry (ex-Hush) release LP *To The Power Of Three*, on Geffen and credited to "3", but it fails to chart.

BRIAN ENO

1966		Eno (b. Brian Peter George St. John le Baptiste de la Salle Eno, May 15, 1948, Suffolk, UK) enrols at Winchester School of Art, becomes president of the Students' Union and meets sax player Andy Mackay.
1969		He leaves art school, having become an electronics whizz and learnt to play the synthesizer. He has, however, often described himself as a "non-musician".
1971	Jan	After Mackay has joined Roxy Music°, Eno is brought in, initially as soundman and technical adviser, but then to play Mackay's synthesizer. He is responsible for much of the groundbreaking nature of Roxy's sound and also, bizarre and androgynous in appearance, one element of its colorful image.
1973	July	After two LPs, *Roxy Music* and *For Your Pleasure*, personality clashes result in Eno leaving for a solo career.
	Nov	A first collaboration with King Crimson's° Robert Fripp results in LP *No Pussyfooting*, released by Island Records.
1974	Mar	His first solo LP *Here Come The Warm Jets* reaches UK #26 and US #151. Both Fripp and Roxy Music's° Manzanera play guitar on it.
	June	[1] Eno takes part in a concert at London's Rainbow Theatre with John Cale°, Kevin Ayers°, Nico and others, which is recorded for release later in June as LP *June 1st, 1974*.
	Nov	Second solo LP *Taking Tiger Mountain By Strategy* is released. It continues his inventive and creative style.
1975	Apr	He works with John Cale° on the latter's LP *Slow Dazzle*. (This partnership will continue with LP *Helen Of Troy* released in Nov. During the year he will work on Phil Manzanera's LP *Diamond Head* and Robert Wyatt's *Ruth Is Stranger Than Richard*; produce Robert Calvert's LP *Lucky Lief And The Longships*; issue a boxed set of writings *Oblique Strategy*; make a lecture tour of UK universities and a concert tour with pub-rock band The Winkies.)
	Nov	LP *Another Green World*, a Fripp collaboration, and LP *Evening Star* are released but neither charts.
	Dec	Completing a busy year, he launches his own record label, Obscure, through Island. LP *Discreet Music* marks the beginning of a major departure from his earlier work that will lead eventually to his "ambient" phase.
1976	Aug	Taking advantage of Roxy Music's° hiatus, Manzanera puts together the group 801, with Eno, Bill McCormick (bass and vocals), Francis Monkman (piano and clarinet), Lloyd Watson (guitar and vocals) and Simon Phillips (drums). The group plays 3 times, with the final gig at London's Queen Elizabeth Hall recorded for LP *801 Live*, which will be released in 2 months. Eno spends the latter part of the year working with David Bowie° on his LP *Low*.
1977	Jan	*Low* is released, featuring major contributions from Eno.
	May	New US band Talking Heads° plays London's tiny Rock Garden club after supporting The Ramones° in the UK. Eno is present on one of the 2 nights, meets the band and invites them to his house, thus beginning a significant musical alliance.
	Dec	Eno's first LP in 2 years, *Before And After Science*, is released and reaches US #171.
1978	June	Talking Heads'° LP *More Songs About Buildings And Food* is the beginning of Eno's production collaboration with the band.
	Aug	Devo's° debut LP *Are We Not Men?* is also produced by Eno.
	Oct	LP *Music For Films*, Eno's first true "ambient" LP is released, charting briefly at UK #55. Eno continues to talk about having discovered "a totally new way of listening to music". Critical reactions are mixed, but the LP and its successors develop a faithful cult audience. (During the year Eno also records two LPs with German avant-garde group Cluster: *Cluster And Eno* and *Eno, Moebius And Roedelius – After The Heat*.)
1979	Mar	LP *Music For Airports* is the first LP released on his Ambient label.
	July	The second Eno-produced Talking Heads° LP *Fear Of Music* is released.
1980		Eno's ambient music comes to full fruition with LP *Possible Music* and LP *The Plateaux Of Mirror*. Both are released on Editions EG label, which has been established by and for artists including Eno and, later, Daniel Lanois, Roger Eno and Laraaji. (Roxy Music° will join the label in Dec. 1981.)
	Sept	Talking Heads'° LP *Remain In Light* produces international success for the band and reinforces Eno's production quality.
1981	Feb	LP *My Life In The Bush Of Ghosts*, a collaboration with Talking Heads'° David Byrne, is viewed by critics as an innovative work and reaches UK #29 and US #44.
1982	Mar	Eno's LP *On Land* is released with no chart interest.
1984		U2's° singer Bono phones Eno to ask him to produce its new LP, explaining the band's desire to progress creatively. The sessions (recorded in an old Irish castle) result in the group, inspired by Eno, breaking out of its old sound and experimenting with spontaneous compositions and new sounds. Co-production credit on the subsequent project goes to Daniel Lanois.
	Oct	When U2° LP *The Unforgettable Fire* is issued, much of the experimental material is absent. It goes on to become a major international success.
1987		U2°, Eno and Lanois reunite for LP *The Joshua Tree*. It is U2's most successful LP, particularly in US, and Eno is largely credited with its success.

ERASURE

Vince Clarke (keyboards)
Andy Bell (vocals)

1985		Clarke, who has had success with Yazoo°, The Assemby and Depeche Mode° on Daniel Miller's independent label, Mute, and his producer Eric "E.C." Radcliffe plan to record an LP with 10 different singers but it proves to be impractical and Clarke settles for one vocalist, Bell, an ex-choirboy who has been with UK Peterborough band The Void, whom he finds after auditioning 42 singers answering an ad in UK's *Melody Maker*.
	Oct	Debut single *Who Needs Love Like That*, on Mute, climbs to UK #55.
	Nov	*Heavenly Action* makes only UK #100 and a tour is cancelled.
	Dec	After a short promotional visit to Germany, the duo makes its UK live debut at London's Heaven.
1986	Jan	Clarke calls in vocalists Jim Burkman and Derek Ian for a UK tour.
	Apr	*Oh L'Amour* makes UK #85. (It will later achieve success for Dollar in 1988.)
	June	LP *Wonderland* reaches UK #71.
	Dec	*Sometimes*, an early hit throughout Europe, hits UK #2.
1987	Mar	*It Doesn't Have To Be* reaches UK #12.
	Apr	Second LP *The Circus* hits UK #6. The duo takes "The Circus" tour to Europe, Scandinavia and US.
	June	Erasure is the opening act on UK commercial TV's first "The Roxy" chart show, performing *Victim Of Love*, which hits UK #7.
	Aug	Erasure supports Duran Duran° on US tour.
	Oct	A remixed version of *The Circus* hits UK #6.
	Dec	LP *Two Ring Circus* is released, featuring six remixes and three re-recordings of original LP *The Circus*.
1988	Mar	*Ship Of Fools* hits UK #6.
	Apr	[14] The duo embarks on a sold-out UK tour.
	Apr	LP *The Innocents* tops the UK chart in a week of its release.
	May	*Chains Of Love* reaches UK #11.
	July	[13] Erasure starts extensive US tour, and *Chains Of Love* climbs towards the US top 30 and LP *The Innocents* makes US top 100.
	Sept	[19] *A Little Respect* is released.

DAVID ESSEX

1964		Essex (b. David Cook, July 23, 1947, London, UK), having left school, is the drummer in semi-professional East London group The Everons when Derek Bowman (*Daily Express* theater critic) sees the group play at a pub in Walthamstow, London.
1965	Apr	First recording *And The Tears Come Tumbling Down*, on Fontana Records, fails completely (as will three Fontana singles during 1965 and 1966).
1968		One-off singles for Uni (*Love Story*) and Pye (*Just For Tonight*) also fail to chart.
1969	June	He signs to Decca, but *That Takes Me Back* and follow-up *Day The Earth Stood Still* arouse little interesst.
1971	Oct	Essex gets the leading role as Jesus to Jeremy Irons' Judas Iscariot in Jean Michael Tebelak's religio-rock musical *Godspell* on London's West End stage. (After almost a year of success in the role, he is contacted by UK film producer David Puttnam, who is impressed with his performance and offers him a major movie role.)

DAVID ESSEX *cont.*

1972 Oct [23] Essex begins a 7-week break from *Godspell* to star in film *That'll Be The Day* with Ringo Starr° on UK's Isle of Wight. He plays an aspiring rock star Jim Maclaine in Ray Connolly's drama set in the UK of the late 1950s.

1973 Apr [12] *That'll Be The Day* premieres in London. Well reviewed, the movie will also become a major financial success.

Sept Signed to CBS on the strength of his stage and screen success, Essex's first single for the label, self-penned *Rock On*, which evokes the nostalgic feel of his recent movie, hits UK #3.

Dec *Lamplight* hits UK #7, while Essex' debut CBS LP *Rock On* also peaks at UK #7.

1974 Feb *Rock On* hits US #3, selling over a million in US. LP of the same title makes US #22.

Feb [18] Essex begins filming *Stardust*, the sequel to *That'll Be The Day*, which shows Jim Maclaine rise to the pinnacle of his career in the 1960s before excess plunges him to destruction. It co-stars Adam Faith°, in the Ringo Starr° role, and Larry Hagman.

June *Lamplight* makes only US #71. (Essex will not reach US singles chart again.)

Oct [24] *Stardust* premieres in London (and will be a major money-spinning movie).

Nov LP *David Essex* reaches UK #2, while the self-penned *Gonna Make You A Star* tops the UK chart for 3 weeks.

1975 Jan *Stardust*, the title song from the movie, reaches UK #7.

Aug *Rollin' Stone* reaches UK #5.

Sept LP *All The Fun Of The Fair* reaches UK #3.

Oct *Hold Me Close* tops the UK chart for 3 weeks.

1976 Jan *If I Could* makes UK #13.

Apr *City Lights* reaches UK #24.

June LP *On Tour* peaks at UK #51.

Nov LP *Out On The Street* makes UK #31. Extracted from it, *Coming Home* reaches UK #24.

1977 Oct *Cool Out Tonight* reaches UK #23 and LP *Gold And Ivory* makes #29. (These are his final recordings for CBS.)

1978 Sept Essex plays Che Guevara in Tim Rice and Andrew Lloyd Webber's musical *Evita* on the London West End stage. His featured song, *Oh What A Circus*, is his first release for his new label Mercury and hits UK #3.

1979 Jan CBS compilation LP of all his hit singles, *The David Essex Album*, makes UK #29.

Apr LP *Imperial Wizard*, his first Mercury LP (including *Oh What A Circus*), peaks at UK #12.

1980 May Essex stars in movie *Silver Dream Racer* with Beau Bridges. It is a drama of ambition and jealousy set in the dangerous world of motorbike racing, and has an Essex-penned soundtrack, from which *Silver Dream Machine*, aided by the movie's publicity, hits UK #4.

June LP *Hot Love* reaches UK #75. The title track peaks at UK #57.

1981 Sept LP *Be-Bop-The-Future* fails to chart, as do *Heart On My Sleeve* and *Be-Bop-A-Lula*.

1982 July *Me And My Girl (Night Clubbing)* reaches UK #13 and LP *Stage-Struck* makes UK #31.

Dec TV-advertised LP *The Very Best Of David Essex*, a compilation of CBS and Mercury hits, makes UK #37.

1983 Jan *A Winter's Tale*, co-written with Tim Rice, reaches UK #2.

Oct Essex, as chief mutineer Fletcher Christian, co-stars with Frank Finlay in *Mutiny*, a musical version of *Mutiny On The Bounty*. Initially released as a studio production on record only, with backing by the Royal Philharmonic Orchestra, LP *Mutiny* reaches UK #39. *Tahiti*, taken from it, hits UK #8.

Dec Essex solo LP, *The Whisper*, makes UK #67 and *You're In My Heart*, taken from it, peaks at UK #59.

1984 Nov Entirely self-penned LP *This One's For You* fails to sell, as does extracted *Welcome*.

1985 Mar *Falling Angels Riding* reaches UK #29. *Mutiny* is staged in London's West End, starring Essex, Finlay and new UK girl singer Sinitta.

1986 Dec TV-advertised LP *Centre Stage*, containing Essex' versions of hit songs from stage and screen, makes UK #82.

1987 May *Myfanwy* reaches UK #41. It is taken from the musical *Betjeman*, which consists of works by late UK Poet Laureate Sir John Betjeman, set to music by UK DJ Mike Read.

1988 Oct Essex stars in UK's BBC1 TV six-part sitcom "The River" as a lecherous lock-keeper.

EURYTHMICS

Annie Lennox (vocals)
Dave Stewart (keyboards and guitar)

1971/76 Lennox (b. Dec.25, 1954, Aberdeen, Scotland, UK), having failed to complete a course at London's Royal Academy of Music, is working in Pippins, a restaurant in Hampstead London, where she meets Stewart (b. Sept.9, 1952, Sunderland, UK), who stowed away, at age 15, in the back of a van belonging to folk outfit Amazing Blondel after a gig in his native Newcastle. Having made his first recording with Brian Harrison as Harrison and Stewart, releasing *Deep December* on local Multicord label in Sunderland, UK, he joins Longdancer, helping to record two LPs for Elton John's° Rocket label in the early 70s, and develops major drug dependancy. Stewart proposes to Lennox. (They do not get married but will live together for 4 years.)

1977 Lennox and Stewart record together with his best friend Peet Coombes in trio The Catch releasing *Borderline/Black Blood*, which becomes a minor hit in Holland.

1979 June The band expands, changes name to The Tourists, and releases debut single *Blind Among The Flowers* which reaches UK #52.

Aug *The Loneliest Man In The World* makes UK #32.

Oct The Tourists' remake of Dusty Springfield's° *I Only Want To Be With You* hits UK #4 (their biggest hit).

1980 Jan *So Good To Be Back Home* hits UK #8.

Sept The group switches to RCA and releases *Don't Say I Told You So* which reaches UK #40. (It is The Tourists' final single. Their career also included three LPs: *The Tourists* at UK #72, *Reality Affect* at UK #23 and *Luminous Basement* at UK #75.)

Oct While on tour in Australia, The Tourists disband.

Dec After the band splits Stewart and Lennox go to Conny Plank's studio in Cologne, West Germany and record demos. With the help of former Can members Holger Czukay and Jaki Liebezeit and DAF members Robert Gorl and Gabi, they cut *Never Gonna Cry Again*. A week after their affair ends, Lennox and Stewart form Eurythmics. (The new name comes from a dance and mime form based on Greek formats by Emil Jacques-Dalcrose in the early 1900s, to teach children music through movement.)

1981 July Signed worldwide to RCA Records, their first single as Eurythmics, *Never Gonna Cry Again*, reaches UK #63.

Aug *Belinda* fails to chart.

Oct Debut LP *In The Garden* also fails.

1982 Mar *This Is The House*, with help from Blondie° drummer Clem Burke, again misses the chart.

June *The Walk* also fails.

Dec *Love Is A Stranger* finally makes UK #54. Kiki Dee guests on back-up vocals.

1983 Feb LP *Sweet Dreams (Are Made Of This)* hits UK #3 and will peak at US #15.

Mar *Sweet Dreams (Are Made Of This)* hits UK #2, one place behind Bonnie Tyler's° *Total Eclipse Of The Heart*. It is supported by an innovative video, scripted (as are all their early visuals) by Stewart and Lennox.

Apr *Love Is A Stranger* is re-issued, hitting UK #6.

July *Who's That Girl?* hits UK #3. The accompanying video features Bananarama° (whose Siobhan Fahey will later marry Stewart).

Sept *Sweet Dreams (Are Made Of This)* hits US #1 for a week and is a million-seller.

Nov *Right By Your Side* hits UK #10. *Love Is A Stranger*, belatedly released in US, makes #23.

Dec [8] Lennox flies to Vienna, Austria, to see a throat specialist about a recurring vocal problem.

1984 Jan [27] The duo begins a 175-date world tour in Australia.

Feb *Here Comes The Rain Again* hits UK #8. LP *Touch*, recorded at a disused church in Crouch End, London, which has become the duo's home base, tops the UK chart and hits US #7.

Mar Lennox marries German Hare Krishna devotee Rahda Raman. (It will only last 6 months.) Meanwhile, *Here Comes The Rain Again* hits US #4.

June *Who's That Girl?*, another belated US release, peaks at #21.

July Mini-LP *Touch Dance*, containing four dance remixes from LP *Touch*, reaches UK #31 and US #115.

Sept *Right By Your Side* makes US #29. Already used as the backing track on UK TV commercial for "Kelly Girl", it is reported that *Sweet Dreams* will be used as the theme for forthcoming US TV soap opera "Paper Dolls". Stewart sets up The Church recording studio in London's Crouch End.

Nov *Sex Crime (1984)*, from Virgin Films' movie adaptation of George Orwell's *1984*, hits UK #4 and US #81.

Dec Soundtrack LP *1984 (For The Love Of Big Brother)*, recorded at Compass Point, Nassau, reaches UK #23.

1985 Jan *Julia*, from *1984*, makes UK #44. The soundtrack LP reaches US #93.

May *Would I Lie To You?* reaches UK #17. LP *Be Yourself Tonight* hits UK #3 and US #9. The LP includes a guest appearance from Elvis Costello°.

July *There Must Be An Angel* hits UK #1. *Would I Lie To You?* hits US #5. Scheduled to play Live Aid concert, Eurythmics have to cancel when Lennox's voice problems recur.

Sept *There Must Be An Angel* reaches US #22.

Nov *Sisters Are Doing It For Themselves*, a duet with Aretha Franklin°, hits UK #9 and climbs to US #18.

Dec Lennox makes acting debut in Hugh Hudson's film *Revolution* starring Al Pacino and Donald Sutherland.

1986 Jan *It's Alright (Baby's Coming Back)* reaches UK #12 but only US #78.

June *When Tomorrow Comes* makes UK #30.

July LP *Revenge* hits UK #3, and will stay on chart for 52 weeks.

Sept *Thorn In My Side* hits UK #5.

Oct *Missionary Man* reaches US #14. LP *Revenge* makes US #12.

Dec [2] Lennox rips her bra off in front of 2,000 fans while singing *Missionary Man*.

Dec *The Miracle Of Love*, aimed for the Christmas market, reaches only UK #25. *Thorn In My Side* makes US #68. (By this time Stewart, sometimes credited as David A. Stewart to avoid confusion with another namesake, is an in-demand producer and session man working with many major stars like Bob Dylan°, The Ramones°, Bob Geldof, Daryl Hall°, Tom Petty°, Mick Jagger and Feargal Sharkey.)

1987 Mar *Missionary Man* makes UK #31.

Apr [15] Eurythmics win as Songwriters of the Year at the Ivor Novello Awards in London's Grosvenor House.

Aug [1] Stewart marries Siobhan Fahey at Chateau Dangu, France.

Oct *Beethoven (I Love To Listen To)* reaches UK #25.

Nov LP *Savage* hits UK #7.

1988 Jan *Shame* reaches UK #41. *I Need A Man* makes US #46.

Feb LP *Savage* peaks at US #41.

Apr *I Need A Man* reaches UK #26. All three singles from the LP fail to make the top 20 in both UK and US. Dave Stewart launches his own Anxious Records as Eurythmics begin work on an LP of cover versions.

June *You Have Placed A Chill In My Heart* makes UK #16 and US #64.

THE EVERLY BROTHERS

Don Everly (vocals and guitar)
Phil Everly (vocals and guitar)

1955 Don (b. Isaac Donald Everly, Feb.1, 1937, Brownie, Ky., US) and Phil (b. Jan.19, 1939, Chicago, Ill., US), the sons of radio performers Ike and Margaret Everly, have appeared on family shows, until their parents retired, on stations in Kentucky, Ia., and in Knoxville, Tenn., where they now live. The brothers go to Nashville to attempt to sell some of their songs to country singers and to make a demo in the hope of picking up a recording deal. Don places *Thou Shalt Not Steal* for $600 and, after an initial lack of success, they are offered a session with CBS/Columbia Records.

Nov The Everly Brothers make their first studio recordings, four tracks cut in 22 minutes with country singer Carl Smith's backing band, at Nashville's Old Tulane Hotel.

1956 Feb Columbia releases two original country songs, *Keep A-Lovin' Me* and *The Sun Keeps Shining* as a single. It does not sell well, and the other songs from the session, *If Her Love Isn't True* and *That's The Life I Have To Lead* are shelved. Columbia passes on its option, and the brothers again do the rounds of Nashville labels. They fail to secure a deal until their father contacts old acquaintance Chet Atkins. Via him, they are signed as songwriters by Roy Acuff and Wesley Rose's publishing company, and Rose becomes their manager.

1957 Rose persuades Archie Bleyer at New York-based Cadence Records that The Everly Brothers are the country singers he is looking for. Bleyer requests them to record a song by Felice and Boudleaux Bryant, *Bye Bye Love* (which some thirty acts have rejected). It is recorded at RCA's Nashville studio, in a session supervised by Atkins, but not in a straight country fashion. The style – close harmonies over acoustic guitars and a rock'n'roll beat – becomes The Everly Brothers' trademark.

Apr The brothers tour around Mississippi tent shows as the single is released.

May [11] They make their debut on Nashville's "Grand Ole Opry".

June *Bye Bye Love* hits US #2 for 4 weeks (below Pat Boone's° *Love Letters In The Sand*) and becomes a million-seller. It also hits US C&W #1 and R&B #5.

July [12] The Everly Brothers appear on DJ Alan Freed's new Friday Night Rock'n'Roll on US ABC-TV with Frankie Lymon°, Buddy Knox°, Connie Francis° and others.

Aug *Bye Bye Love*, released in UK on London label, hits #6 during a 16-week top 30 run.

Aug [4] The duo guests on US TV's "Ed Sullivan Show" singing *Bye Bye Love* and *Wake Up Little Susie*. (By the end of the year, they will have been seen on most of US TV's top-rated variety shows, including those of Patti Page, Arthur Murray and Perry Como – the latter, also shown in UK, offers British fans their first view of The Everly Brothers.)

Oct *Wake Up Little Susie*, another Bryants' song with a classic teen-calamity lyric (and, although hardly risque, banned from airplay in Boston), tops the US chart for 2 weeks and is a second million-seller. (It also hits C&W #1 and R&B #2.)

Dec *Wake Up Little Susie* hits UK #2.

1958 Mar *This Little Girl Of Mine* (R&B #9 for Ray Charles° in 1955) reaches US #26. Debut LP *The Everly Brothers – They're Off And Running!* makes US #16.

Apr [5] They begin an 80-day tour of US and Canada at Norfolk, Va., co-starring in Irving Feld's "Greatest Show of Stars" with Sam Cooke°, Paul Anka°, Frankie Avalon° and others.

May *All I Have To Do Is Dream*, a ballad written by the Bryants in some 15 minutes, hits US #1 for 4 weeks and is another million-seller. Contrasting B-side *Claudette*, written by Roy Orbison° about his wife, reaches US #30.

June *All I Have To Do Is Dream/Claudette* hits UK #1 for 8 weeks (their first UK #1).

Aug Rocking *Bird Dog*, which they struggled through 15 studio takes to perfect, is a fourth million-seller and tops the US chart for a week. Ballad B-side *Devoted To You* hits US #10.

Sept The brothers go to the studio with bassist Floyd Chance to record country/folk songs, released as LP *Songs Our Daddy Taught Us*, which fails to chart.

Nov *Bird Dog* tops the UK chart for 2 weeks.

Dec *Problems*, another archetypal teen-dilemma song, hits US #2 and is their fifth million-seller. B-side *Love Of My Life* peaks at US #40.

Dec [30] The Everly Brothers headline Alan Freed's Christmas Rock'n'Roll Spectacular at Loew's State Theater, Manhattan, New York, alongside Chuck Berry°, Bo Diddley°, Jackie Wilson° and others.

1959 Jan [16] They make a brief UK visit (for the first time) to appear on TV show "Cool for Cats", receive a *New Musical Express* award as World #1 Vocal Group and attend a Savoy Hotel reception in their honor – all within 24 hours before flying on to Europe.

Feb *Problems* hits UK #6.

May Folky ballad *Take A Message To Mary* reaches US #16, and B-side *Poor Jenny* (another teen soap opera) makes US #22.

July *Poor Jenny* makes UK #14, while *Take A Message To Mary* peaks at UK #20.

Sept Written by Don, *('Til) I Kissed You* hits US #4, and is another million-seller. Recorded with backing by The Crickets (Sonny Curtis playing lead guitar), it is the first Nashville-recorded rock'n'roll/country record to employ a full drumkit, with tom-toms, in the studio. (Before this, drummers uses a snare drum and brushes.)

Oct *('Til) I Kissed You* hits UK #2, behind Bobby Darin's° *Mack The Knife*.

Oct [25] The Everly Brothers announce that they are considering parting from Cadence, and are talking with both RCA and newly-formed Warner Bros. Records.

Dec [15] They record their first session outside Nashville. *Let It Be Me*, an English translation of Gilbert Becaud's French *J'Appartiens* (a US hit for Jill Corey in 1957), is cut in Bell Sound studios in New York, and is their first session with an orchestral backing (eight violins and a cello, conducted by Bleyer).

1960 Feb *Let It Be Me* hits US #7.

THE EVERLY BROTHERS *cont.*

Feb [17] The Everly Brothers sign to Warner Bros., in a 10-year contract worth $1 million.

Mar *Let It Be Me* makes UK #13. Meanwhile, the duo records eight songs in Nashville for Warner, but none of them is felt strong enough to be a single. Don writes *Cathy's Clown* at home, with finishing-off assistance from Phil, and they cut it 2 days later, for rush single release.

Apr [6] They begin their first UK tour with a concert at London's New Victoria Theatre, backed by The Crickets.

May *Cathy's Clown*, The Everly Brothers' all-time biggest seller, tops the US chart for 5 weeks and the UK chart for 8 (with the catalog number WB 1, it gives Warner Bros. its first UK #1 with its first release). It sells three million copies worldwide. B-side *Always It's You* makes US #56.

June The remaining tracks from the first Warner sessions are released on LP *It's Everly Time!*, which hits US #9 and UK #2 – their most successful chart LP.

July Cadence releases unheard Phil-penned *When Will I Be Loved*, which hits US #8 and UK #4. B-side, a revival of Gene Vincent's° *Be-Bop-A-Lula* makes US #74.

Sept Cadence LP *The Fabulous Style Of the Everly Brothers*, a compilation of hit singles, reaches US #23.

Oct *So Sad (To Watch Good Love Go Bad)*, a country-styled ballad written by Don and extracted from the first Warner LP after strong radio play, hits US #7 and UK #5. B-side is a revival of Little Richard's° *Lucille*, in a new arrangement which features eight top Nashville session guitarists strumming acoustically in unison, and it makes US #21 and UK #14.

Nov UK version of LP *The Fabulous Style*, a compilation with only four songs in common with the US version, hits UK #4.

Dec The final unheard track released on single by Cadence, Boudleaux Bryant ballad *Like Strangers*, reaches US #22.

1961 Jan *Like Strangers* reaches UK #11, while the second Warner LP *A Date With The Everly Brothers* hits US #9. The brothers move from Nashville to Hollywood and, at Rose's suggestion, take acting lessons.

Mar Their most successful double A-side is *Walk Right Back* (written by Sonny Curtis of The Crickets) at UK #1 for 4 weeks and US #7 and *Ebony Eyes* (a John D. Loudermilk ballad with a poignant love and death theme) at US #8 and UK #17. LP *A Date With The Everly Brothers* hits UK #3.

May [19] The brothers launch their own record label, Calliope, designed as a showcase for new acts.

June A revolutionary arrangement of 1934 Bing Crosby oldie *Temptation*, making prominent use of a female chorus, peaks at US #27. It was recorded against manager Rose's advice, and amid some other disagreements the brothers and he part company (the most serious effect will be the denial of Acuff/Rose-signed Bryants' songs). Jack Rael (Patti Page's manager for 15 years) is appointed new manager. B-side of *Temptation*, *Stick With Me Baby* makes US #41.

July *Temptation* hits UK #1 for 2 weeks. Amid a minor spurt of oldie-mania on US radio, original Cadence single *All I Have To Do Is Dream* re-charts at US #96. Also on US chart at #34 is the brothers' rock instrumental version of Elgar's *Pomp And Circumstance*, their only Calliope label success. Credited to "Adrian Kimberly", it is actually arranged and performed by Don with help from Neal Hefti. (Calliope label will soon become inactive.)

Oct *Don't Blame Me*, a ballad first recorded by Ethel Walters in 1933, reaches US #20. Uptempo B-side *Muskrat* makes US #82 but UK #20, where it is A-side.

Nov [25] The brothers are inducted into the US Marine Corps Reserves, which initially means 6 months' active service. They report to Camp Pendleton, Cal., for duty.

1962 Mar *Crying In The Rain*, written for The Everly Brothers by Carole King° and Howard Greenfield, hits #6 in both US and UK. On weekend leave from Marine training, the brothers appear on US TV's "Ed Sullivan Show" to sing it – in uniform and with regulation cropped haircuts.

June *That's Old Fashioned (That's The Way Love Should Be)* hits US #9. B-side *How Can I Meet Her?* makes US #75 and as UK A-side reaches #12. It is announced that The Everly Brothers' record sales top 35 million.

July LP *Instant Party* makes UK #20 (their last UK chart LP for 8 years).

Sept LP *The Golden Hits Of The Everly Brothers*, a compilation of singles since *Cathy's Clown*, reaches US #35, but fails in UK. (This LP will still be on Warner's catalog 26 years later, when it is released on compact disk.)

Oct *I'm Here To Get My Baby Out Of Jail*, from Cadence LP *Songs Our Daddy Taught Us*, is released as a US single and reaches #76.

Oct [13] At the opening of a UK tour, Don Everly collapses on stage at London's Prince of Wales Theatre during rehearsal. He is hospitalized briefly, then flown back to US for medical treatment. Phil continues the tour solo, with the Everlys' guitarist Joey Page helping him on harmony vocals.

Nov *Don't Ask Me To Be Friends*, on Warner, peaks at US #48. In UK, it is B-side to Gerry Goffin/Jack Keller song *No One Can Make My Sunshine Smile* which reaches UK #11.

Dec The duo's only seasonal LP, *Christmas With The Everly Brothers And The Boys Town Choir*, mostly of traditional carols, is released.

1963 Jan With top Nashville session men, the brothers record LP *The Everly Brothers Sing Great Country Hits*, which includes versions of *I Walk The Line, I'm So Lonesome I Could Cry, Oh Lonesome Me, Release Me*, and other C&W classics.

Apr *So It Always Will Be* makes UK #23. Like all the duo's releases this year, it fails to reach US Hot 100.

June *It's Been Nice* makes UK #26.

Sept [29] The duo opens a UK tour, supported by Bo Diddley° and The Rolling Stones°, and later joined by Little Richard°.

Nov Written by Barry Mann and Cynthia Weil, *The Girl Sang The Blues* and *Love Her* (which The Walker Brothers° will later revive as their first hit) climbs to UK #25.

1964 July *The Ferris Wheel* reaches US #72. Also released is LP *The Very Best Of the Everly Brothers*, which looks like a compilation but features new re-recordings of their biggest hits, including six originally on Cadence. (Warner has tried to buy The Everly Brothers' early material from Bleyer, but he has already sold it to his ex-artist Andy Williams – who wants to keep his own early tracks from being reissued outside his control.) The LP does not chart (but will stay on Warner's catalog into the 1980s).

Sept [16] The Everly Brothers appear on US ABC-TV's first edition of "Shindig" singing *Gone Gone Gone*.

Dec Co-written by The Everlys, and in a frantic Bo Diddley°-like arrangement, *Gone Gone Gone* reaches US #31 and UK #36.

1965 Jan LP *Gone Gone Gone* is released. The rift with Rose has been resolved and half the LP's songs are written by the Bryants, as well as two by Loudermilk.

Mar LP *Rock'n'Soul* contains versions of 1950s rock'n'roll hits, including *That'll Be The Day, Hound Dog* and *Kansas City*.

May A revival of Buddy Holly and The Crickets'° *That'll Be the Day*, taken from the LP, reaches UK #30.

June Another Everly co-written R&B/rocker, *The Price Of Love*, recorded in Nashville on April 4, is rush-released to tie in with a UK and European tour. It hits UK #2, but fails to chart in US.

July A West to East Coast US tour follows the European one.

Sept Uptempo country-styled *I'll Never Get Over You* peaks at UK #35. LP *Beat Soul* develops the *Rock'n'Soul* theme but concentrates on R&B oldies. It shows a tougher edge to the duo than any earlier recordings, and features session players Jim Gordon and Billy Preston, and songs like *Hi-Heel Sneakers, People Get Ready* and *Walking The Dog*. It reaches US #141, but fails to chart in UK despite UK's current R&B fixation.

Sept [16] The Everly Brothers appear on US TV's first show of the second season of "Shindig", singing a revival of Mickey and Sylvia's *Love Is Strange*.

Nov Promoted by another UK visit, and appearances on UK TV's "Ready Steady Go" and "Top of the Pops", *Love Is Strange* reaches UK #11.

1966 Mar LP *In Our Image*, with their more accustomed sound, is released. It includes Don's ballad *It's All Over* (a non-selling US single which will be a UK top 10 hit for Cliff Richard° in 1967). The Everly Brothers tour the Far East.

May They record LP *Two Yanks In England*, in London for the first time, which is issued 2 months later. The session musicians include guitarist Jimmy Page and bassist John Paul Jones (both later in Led Zeppelin°). The Hollies° also participate, with the group's Graham Nash, Tony Hicks and Allan Clarke writing eight of the twelve songs under the pseudonym L. Ransford. The brothers also record a solo each.

1967 Feb LP *The Hit Sound Of The Everly Brothers*, consisting mainly of covers and revivals like *Blueberry Hill* and *Let's Go Get Stoned*, fails to chart.

July *Bowling Green*, written by Englishman Terry Slater (despite being a hymn to the Everlys' Kentucky roots), reaches US #40, after a 2½-year chart absence. (Slater, the duo's bass player, has been a friend ever since his group The Flintstones opened The Everly Brothers' 1963 UK tour. He moves to LA and becomes a long-time co-writer with Phil, as the brothers' music moves to the country-rock field – even though they fail to become part of its commercial success.) LP *The Everly Brothers Sing*, featuring five Slater songs, is released.

1968 May Loudermilk-penned *It's My Time* makes UK #39 (The Everly Brothers' last UK hit single for 16 years).

Nov LP *Roots*, with country songs and excerpts from the old Everly family radio show recorded in 1952, as well as new material including *Living Too Close To The Ground* and *Ventura Boulevard*, features a re-recording of 12-year-old *I Wonder If I Care As Much*, a Don and Phil co-composition which was B-side of *Bye Bye Love*.

1969 Despite lack of recording success they continue to tour and are a popular guest act on US network TV shows, including those of The Smothers Brothers, Johnny Cash° and Glen Campbell° – not only singing, but introducing comedy into their act.

Apr *I'm On My Way Home Again/The Cuckoo Bird*, recorded in LA with Clarence White and Gene Pasons of The Byrds°, is issued only in US and fails to chart.

1970 Feb [6] The Everly Brothers record a live LP at the Grand Hotel, Anaheim. The resulting double LP *The Everly Brothers Show* is their last recording for Warner Bros. *Yves* (written by Scott McKenzie of *San Francisco* fame) is the final Warner single.

July [8] They host "The Everly Brothers Show" on US ABC-TV. It is an 11-week peak time summer replacement for "The Johnny Cash Show", and is strongly country music-oriented, with regular comedy relief from Joe Higgins and Ruth McDevitt.

Aug US Barnaby label, owned by Andy Williams, finally makes use of the early Everly tracks purchased from Bleyer in the 1960s. After years off the market, 20 are packaged on double LP *The Everly Brothers' Original Greatest Hits*, with a nostalgic sleeve complete with a 1950s rock'n'roll quiz. It reaches US #180.

Oct CBS issues double LP *Original Greatest Hits* which hits UK #7.

1971 Don Everly is the first of the duo to cut a solo (eponymous) LP on Lou Adler's Ode label, which attracts little attention (the apparently brooding, angst-ridden nature of much of its material is widely thought to reflect turmoil in his personal life).

1972 June Signed to RCA, the brothers release LP *Stories We Could Tell*, recorded at Lovin' Spoonful° John Sebastian's house with guest players including Ry Cooder°, Delaney and Bonnie°, Graham Nash and David Crosby. Songs include Rod Stewart's° *Mandolin Wind*, Jesse Winchester's *The Brand New Tennessee Waltz* and the title track by Sebastian.

1973 Feb LP *Pass The Chicken And Listen*, also on RCA, marks a return to Nashville and to producer Atkins, who brings in top session men, but it fails to chart.

July [14] The personal conflict which has been building between the brothers finally comes to a head at the John Wayne Theater at Knott's Berry Farm in Hollywood, Cal. Entertainment manager Bill Hollinghead stops the show midway through the second of three scheduled sets, unhappy with Don's performance, and Phil smashes his guitar and storms off. Don performs the third set solo and announces their break-up to the audience ("The Everly Brothers died 10 years ago").

Sept Phil signs a solo deal with RCA. LP *Star Spangled Springer*, produced by Duane Eddy° and with musical assistance from Warren Zevon°, Jim Horn, Earl Palmer and James Burton, was recorded just before the split. Critically acclaimed (and including the original version of *The Air That I Breathe* (later a worldwide hit for The Hollies°), it fails to sell.

1974 Oct Don releases another solo LP on Ode, *Sunset Towers*, backed by UK group Heads, Hands & Feet.

1975 Jan Phil signs to UK Pye label, releasing LP *There's Nothing Too Good For My Baby* (US title: *Phil's Diner*).

Nov Phil releases solo LP *Mystic Line* on Pye, then requests that his contract be terminated.

Dec In UK, TV-advertised 20-track compilation LP *Walk Right Back With The Everlys* sparks a major revival of interest, hitting UK #10. This inspires BBC radio to produce a multi-part "Everly Brothers Story" documentary series, which is syndicated around the world.

1977 Feb [10] Don starts work on solo LP *Brother Juke Box*, at Acuff-Rose Sound studios, Nashville, with Rose producing. It will be released on Hickory Records in US and DJM Records in UK.

Apr LP *Living Legends*, a collection of Cadence material on TV-advertised label Warwick Records, reaches UK #12.

Sept Warner Bros. issues *The New Album*, which contains (with a couple of exceptions) previously unreleased Everly Brothers tracks from the 1960s. It fails and Warner does not issue any more of the 60 or so unreleased songs still in the vaults.

1978 Phil appears in Clint Eastwood movie *Any Which Way But Loose*, duetting on his song *Don't Say You Don't Love Me No More* with Eastwood's co-star Sondra Locke.

1979 Phil has a one-off deal with Elektra Records for Snuff Garrett-produced LP *Living Alone*, released only in US.

1981 Signed to Curb Records, Phil releases *Dare To Dream Again*, which collects good airplay in UK (where it is released on Epic), but fails to chart.

1982 Nov Now signed to Capitol, and produced in London by Shakin' Stevens'° producer Stuart Colman, Phil charts at UK #47 with his debut for the label, *Louise*.

1983 Jan In UK, K-Tel's Christmas TV-advertised Everly Brothers compilation LP *Love Hurts* peaks at #31 and has a 22-week UK chart run.

Mar Phil's duet with Cliff Richard°, *She Means Nothing To Me*, hits UK #9. Mark Knopfler of Dire Straits° plays guitar on the track.

May Capitol LP *Phil Everly*, produced by Stuart Colman at Eden Studios, London, charts at UK #61 for a week.

June [30] After 10 years of estrangement, differences are finally settled, and the Everly Brothers announce plans for a reunion concert in Sept. Phil is quoted as saying "We settled it in a family kind of way – a big hug did it!"

Sept [23] The Everly Brothers Reunion Concert is a sell-out at London's Royal Albert Hall, as the duo slips effortlessly back together to perform their repertoire in the classic style. The event is filmed (for TV and later home video release) and recorded. (More concerts will follow in US and elsewhere.)

1984 Jan Live double LP *The Everly Brothers Reunion Concert*, on Impression Records, is the duo's first non-compilation LP to chart in UK for 22 years, and reaches #47.

Mar Double LP *Reunion Concert*, on Passport Records in US, peaks at #162, after a 14-year LP chart absence.

Oct Signed to Mercury, the brothers reach US #50 and hit UK #4 with *On The Wings Of A Nightingale*, written for them by Paul McCartney° and produced by Dave Edmunds°. It is taken from their first studio LP since re-forming, Edmunds-produced *The Everly Brothers*, which reaches UK #36.

THE EVERLY BROTHERS *cont.*

Nov The LP, retitled *EB 84*, climbs to US #38, their best US LP chart placing since 1962.

1986 Apr LP *Born Yesterday*, again produced by Edmunds, is released. The Everly Brothers are inducted into the Rock'n'Roll Hall of Fame.

1987 Feb [1] Phil gives Don a custom-made guitar made from mother-of-pearl African blackwood and a pound of gold on his fiftieth birthday.

1988 Aug A granite statue of The Everly Brothers is unveiled in the duo's home state, at City Hall, Everly Brothers Boulevard, Central City, Ky.

Nov *Don't Worry Baby* (with The Beach Boys° guesting on a revival of their 1964 hit), and LP *Some Hearts* from which it is taken, are released.

EVERYTHING BUT THE GIRL

Tracey Thorn (vocals)
Ben Watt (vocals)

1980 Unknown to each other at the time, Thorn (b. Sept.26, 1962, UK) and Watt (b. Dec.6, 1962, UK), both sign to Cherry Red Records in UK as soloists. Thorn also records as a member of The Marine Girls trio. Her solo LP *A Distant Shore* costs only £120 to record, but is a UK independent chart success and sells over 60,000.

1982 A&R man Mike Alway, a long-time friend, introduces Watt to Thorn while both are studying at Hull University, UK. They form a romantic and artistic union.

1983 Jan [5] The duo performs for the first time as Everything But The Girl (a name taken from a second-hand furniture store in Hull) at London's ICA theatre. Paul Weller of The Style Council° guests on their version of *The Girl From Ipanema*.

July *Night And Day*, a revival of the Cole Porter standard, is their only release as a duo for Cherry Red but does not chart.

1884 Mar Thorn guests on The Style Council's° LP *Café Bleu*.

May After leaving Cherry Red for new label blanco y negro (formed by Alway and Rough Trade's Geoff Travis), their first hit *Each And Everyone* reaches UK #28. The duo is unable to perform it on BBC TV's "Top of the Pops" because both are in the middle of their degree exams.

July Debut LP *Eden* climbs to UK #14, while *Mine* makes UK #58.

Sept The duo embarks on a 24-date UK tour.

Oct *Native Land* reaches only UK #73.

1985 May LP *Love Not Money* hits UK #10, and gains popularity in Europe, particularly Italy and Holland.

1986 Aug *Come On Home* reaches UK #44.

Sept LP *Baby The Stars Shine Bright* peaks at UK #22. It features noted UK jazz musician Peter King in the horn section, beginning a long-term liaison between him and the group.

Oct *Don't Leave Me Behind* reaches UK #72.

1987 The duo concentrates on writing new songs, and Thorn also duets with Lloyd Cole° for one of his LP tracks.

1988 Mar LP *Idlewild* reaches UK #13, but *These Early Days*, taken from it, fails to chart.

July A revival of Rod Stewart's° *I Don't Want To Talk About It*, hits UK #3.

Sept The duo supports Joan Armatrading° on US tour.

FABIAN

1959 Jan After being spotted on a doorstep at the age of 15 by Frankie Avalon's° manager Bob Marcucci and signed up for his looks, Fabian (b. Fabiano Forte Bonaparte, Feb.6, 1943, Philadelphia, Penn., US) comes to national prominence with *I'm A Man*. It reaches US #31 and Fabian is transformed and marketed into a pop idol worshipped by teenagers. After the first two singles had failed, Marcucci and his Chancellor Records partner Peter de Angelis enlisted hot Brill Building writers Doc Pomus and Mort Shuman, who assessed the situation and provided the hit.

Apr The same team provides *Turn Me Loose*, which hits US #9. The close proximity of Dick Clark's "American Bandstand" studio proves beneficial to Fabian, who now provokes hysteria whenever confronting an audience.

May Debut LP *Hold That Tiger!*, with a 5-month chart stay, rises to US #5.

June Chancellor quickly releases tailor-made *Tiger*, his only million-seller, which hits US #3. Publicity is increased and teen magazines, previously preoccupied with "The Fabulous Fabian", now allude to him as "Tiger".

Sept Double-sided *Come On And Get Me*/*Got The Feeling* is rather less successful, reaching US #29 and #54 respectively.

Nov For his big screen debut, Fabian co-stars with Stuart Whitman in Don Siegel movie *Hound Dog Man*. The film title song (by Pomus and Shuman) reinstates Fabian in the top 10, at US #9, and becomes his only UK hit, charting for one week at #46. Also from the film is the B-side *This Friendly World*, which makes US #12.

Dec Second LP *Fabulous Fabian* hits US #3, giving him a total of seven hit singles and two hit LPs in his first year.

1960 Feb Record sales fall but his Hollywood appeal increases, and during the year he plays alongside Bing Crosby in *High Time* and John Wayne in *North To Alaska*. Meanwhile, double-sider *String Along*/*About This Thing Called Love* reaches only US #31 and #39.

Nov *Kissin' And Twistin'*, a Don Kirshner/Al Nevins song, reaches only US #91 and is his last hit (less than 2 years after his chart debut).

1961 Fabian concentrates on his acting. (In the next 25 years he will appear in some two dozen films including *Love In A Goldfish Bowl* with Tommy Sands, *Ride The Wild Surf* with Shelley Fabares and Tab Hunter, and *Dr. Goldfoot And The Girl Bombs* with Vincent Price. He will also make the odd revival show/cabaret tour.)

1988 July/Aug As the 80s continue to revive the 1950s, he tours US with "Fabian's Good Time Rock'n'Roll Revue", also featuring Lesley Gore° and The Marvelettes.

THE FACES

Rod Stewart (vocals)
Ron Wood (guitar)
Ian McLagan (keyboards)
Ronnie Lane (bass)
Kenny Jones (drums)

1969 June The band, formed in UK from ex-members of The Small Faces° and the Jeff Beck° group, signs to Warner Bros. Records, while lead singer Stewart° signs a separate deal for £1,000 to Mercury Records as a solo artist. The band debuts at UK's Cambridge University as Quiet Melon, supplemented by Art Wood (Ron's elder brother), Long John Baldry° and Jimmy Horowitz.

1970 Apr LP *First Step* reaches UK #45 and US #119. The group is billed in US as The Small Faces° for this LP, and tours to promote it, building a solid live following on both sides of the Atlantic with its "lads night out" brand of rock and shambolic stage presence. *Flying* does not chart.

1971 Mar LP *Long Player* reaches US #29.

May LP *Long Player* makes UK #31 but *Had Me A Real Good Time* fails to chart.

Oct Stewart's° solo career explodes with a worldwide chart topper *Maggie May*. The group backs him on his many TV appearances leading to a regular billing of Rod Stewart & The Faces, which causes rancor within the band.

Dec LP *A Nod's As Good As A Wink . . . To A Blind Horse* hits UK #2 and US #6. With assistance from producer Glyn Johns, the group begins to score hit singles. A revival of The Temptations'° hit, *(I Know) I'm Losing You*, more in keeping with Stewart's° solo style, reaches US #24.

1972 Feb *Stay With Me* hits UK #6.

Mar *Stay With Me* climbs to US #17. The group embarks on UK and US tours at large venues but Stewart's° solo success overshadows the band's reputation as a unit.

1973 Mar *Cindy Incidentally* hits UK #2 and makes US #48.

Apr LP *Ooh La La* hits UK #1 and reaches US #21, but is publicly disowned by Stewart° who has shown little interest in the project.

May Lane leaves and is replaced by Japanese bassist Tetsu Yamauchi. (Lane will invest his earnings from the group into a mobile studio and form his own group, Slim Chance.)

1974 Jan Double A-side *Pool Hall Richard*/*I Wish It Would Rain* hits UK #8.

Feb Live LP *Coast To Coast Overture And Beginners*, issued on Mercury rather than Warner with the band credited as Rod Stewart & The Faces, hits UK #3 and US #63.

Dec *You Can Make Me Dance Sing Or Anything* reaches UK #12. The group tours UK.

1975 Apr Stewart° quits the UK for tax reasons.

June Wood tours US playing guitar with The Rolling Stones°.
Sept Remnants of the group back Stewart° on a US tour to promote his LP *Atlantic Crossing*, augmented by guitarist Jesse Ed Davis and a string section.
Dec Stewart° announces he is quitting the group and Wood joins The Rolling Stones°. The group splits when The Small Faces'° *Itchycoo Park* is enjoying renewed chart success at UK #9.
1976 June Jones and McLagan re-form The Small Faces° unsuccessfully with Steve Marriott. (Jones will join The Who° in 1979 as drummer.)
1977 May LP *The Best Of The Faces* reaches UK #24.
June EP *The Faces*, reprising earlier hits, charts in UK at #41.

FAIRPORT CONVENTION

Judy Dyble (vocals)
Ian Matthews (vocals)
Richard Thompson (guitar)
Simon Nicol (guitar)
Ashley Hutchings (bass)
Martin Lamble (drums)

1967 June The first Fairport Convention line-up (ex-Ethnic Shuffle Orchestra members Hutchings and Nicol, with Thompson (b. Apr.3, 1949, London), and drummer Shaun Frater) changes the night they debut, after a short rehearsal period, at a Golders Green, London, UK, church hall when Martin Lamble, from the audience, declares himself a better drummer than Frater and after a rehearsal proves this to be true. Frater is replaced. Librarian Dyble and ex-harmony group Pyramid Matthews are recruited as lead singers. The group plays mainly cover versions at various "underground" venues in London. At one gig they meet Joe Boyd, who is establishing his own production and management company, Witchseason.
Nov In a deal arranged by Boyd, the group's first single, *If I Had A Ribbon Bow* (originally recorded by Maxine Sullivan in 1936) is released on Track Records, but sells poorly.
1968 Jan Fairport Convention plays its first major gig at London's Saville Theatre supporting Procol Harum°.
June The group's eponymous debut LP is released on Polydor. As well as original songs, it contains material by Joni Mitchell° (for whom Boyd has obtained a UK publishing deal earlier in the year) and a musical arrangement of George Painter's poem *The Lobster*.
July Dyble leaves (and spends a brief spell with Giles, Giles and Fripp before joining Trader Horne and then Penguin Dust). Sandy Denny (b. Jan.6, 1941, UK), who has briefly sung with The Strawbs and is becoming a noted folk singer in her own right, joins and Fairport Convention begins to incorporate more traditional English influences.
1969 Jan The group signs to Island Records. LP *What We Did On Our Holidays* includes, through Denny's influence, traditional songs like *Nottamun Town* and *She Moved Through The Fair*. The band guests on Al Stewart's° LP *Love Chronicles*. Matthews leaves after contributing to only track, unhappy with the traditional drift.
May [14] Lamble is killed when the band's van crashes on the way back to London after a gig in Birmingham.
Aug LP *Unhalfbricking* is their first chart album, reaching UK #12. Taken from it, *Si Tu Dois Partir*, a French version of Dylan's° *If You Gotta Go, Go Now*, is the group's only UK hit single at #21.
Sept Dave Mattacks replaces Lamble, while trad-folk violinist Dave Swarbrick, who played on the last LP, becomes a full-time member. The new line-up begins a UK tour.

1970 Feb LP *Liege And Lief*, promoted as "the first British folk-rock album ever", reaches UK #17. Six of the eight tracks are traditional tunes played in contemporary electric fashion. A new versus old argument begins to split the band, with Denny eager to be more contemporary, while Hutchings wants to play only traditional music: the result is that they both leave. (Hutchings will form Steeleye Span and then The Albion Band, while Denny forms Fotheringay with husband Trevor Lucas and Jerry Donahue). The band decides not to replace Denny, but recruits bassist Dave Pegg ex-rock bands like The Uglies, The Exception and The Way of Life (in the latter two with future Led Zeppelin° members Robert Plant° and John Bonham).
July LP *Full House* makes UK #13. The group begins a US tour.
Oct *Now Be Thankful* is released with B-side *Sir B. McKenzie's Daughter's Lament For The 77th Mounted Lancers' Retreat From The Straits Of Loch Knombe In The Year Of Our Lord 1727, On The Occasion Of The Announcement Of Her Marriage To The Laird Of Kinleakie*, which makes *Guinness Book of Records* as the longest-ever song title.
1971 Jan The group is reduced to a four-piece when Thompson leaves to go solo.
July LP *Angel Delight* hits UK #8 and manages US #200 for a week.
Nov LP *Babbacombe Lee*, a concept album based on the story of Victorian-era condemned prisoner John Lee ("the man they couldn't hang") fails to chart in UK but creeps to US #195. Thompson and Denny join the band on stage during a show at London's Rainbow Theatre. Nicol leaves (and will found The Albion Country Band).
1972 Mar The Rainbow concert prompts Trevor Lucas to bring Denny, Hutchings, Thompson and Mattacks together as The Bunch to record an LP of rock'n'roll covers, *Rock On*. Mattacks leaves to drum with The Albion Country Band and temporary members Roger Hill (guitar), David Rea (guitar) and Tom Farnall (drums) are recruited.
Aug Mattacks rejoins the group and brings with him guitarists Trevor Lucas and Jerry Donahue (both ex-Fotheringay).
Nov Double compilation LP *The History Of Fairport Convention* is released.
1973 Mar LP *Rosie*, recorded chiefly under Swarbrick's direction aiming at the pop market, fails to chart as does the title track.
Oct LP *Nine* is released.
Nov Fairport Convention sets out on a world tour as Denny rejoins the band, having joined them on stage in Auckland, New Zealand for a gig in Jan.
1974 Jan The group is recorded live at Australia's Sydney Opera House.
Oct LP *Live Convention (A Moveable Feast)*, featuring the Sydney recordings, as well as performances from London's Rainbow Theatre and Fairfield Hall, Croydon, UK, is released.
1975 Jan Mattacks leaves again and is replaced by Bruce Rowlands after Paul Warren drums temporarily on a European tour.
July LP *Rising For The Moon* reaches UK #52 and US #143.
1976 Jan Denny, Lucas and Donahue leave at the end of a US tour.
Mar Ex-Wizzard° keyboard player Bob Brady, Dan Ars Bras (guitar) and Rodger Burridge (mandolin/fiddle) are recruited for 2 months to play UK and European tours, after which they leave again. (The band abbreviates its name to Fairport.)
May LP *Gottle O'Geer*, intended as a Swarbrick solo LP, is recorded as a group LP to fulfill the Island contract.
1977 Jan Island releases 1971-recorded live LP *Live At The LA Troubadour*.
Feb The band's first LP for Vertigo Records, *A Bonny Bunch Of Roses* does not chart. Nicol returns to complete a four-man line-up with Pegg, Swarbrick and Rowland.
May Denny releases solo LP *Rendezvous*.
1978 Apr [21] Denny dies of a brain hemorrhage, after falling downstairs at a friend's house.
May LP *Tipplers Tales* is released.
1979 Although the Vertigo LPs have been well received, the band announces its intention to split after playing a farewell tour, having gone through fifteen different line-ups and twenty members.
Aug [4] An opening spot for Led Zeppelin° at UK's Knebworth Festival is followed the same night by a gig at Cropredy in Oxfordshire. (The band will re-form annually, to play either at Cropredy or in the grounds of nearby Broughton Castle.)

FAIRPORT CONVENTION *cont.*

Dec LP *Farewell, Farewell* is released in an initial pressing of 3,000 to be sold from Pegg's home, but when the pressing runs out it is reissued on Simons Records.

1980 Aug A reunion concert features Richard and Linda Thompson.

1981 Aug Dyble returns for the group's second reunion concert. (A recording of the show will be released in 1982 as Fairport's fourth live LP *Moat On the Ledge*. In between reunions, the members all find success elsewhere.)

1987 Aug Matthews joins the band's latest reunion line-up to celebrate its 20th Anniversary.

Oct LP *Heyday*, consisting of tracks from UK BBC radio sessions, is released on Hannibal Records, which is owned by the band's ex-manager Boyd.

ADAM FAITH

1955 July Faith (b. Terence Nelhams, June 23, 1940, London, UK) leaves school wanting to enter the film world, which leads him to Rank Screen Services where he is employed as a messenger boy (and will eventually progress to assistant film editor).

1956 When the Lonnie Donegan°-led skiffle craze strikes UK, he starts to play with some fellow workers in skiffle group The Worried Men.

1957 The Worried Men, still a semi-professional group, are playing a residency at the 2 I's coffee bar in Soho, London, from where an edition of BBC TV's "6.5 Special" pop show is broadcast live. The show's director, Jack Good, notes Nelhams in the group and suggests he could succeed as a soloist, with a change of name. A more likely one is picked out of a book of boys' (Adam) and girls' (Faith) names. After a second "6.5 Special" appearance towards the end of the year, he is signed to EMI Records.

1958 Jan *(Got A) Heartsick Feeling*, on EMI's HMV label, flops completely.

Nov The Bacharach/David song *Country Music Holiday* is also a failure, and HMV drops him. Faith, disillusioned, involves himself in his film editing job at Rank, temporarily abandoning his musical career.

1959 Apr Recommended by John Barry (with whom he worked on "6.5 Special") for the new BBC TV pop show "Drumbeat", Faith is offered a residency on the weekly show. (He will stay with the series through its 22-week run, performing mainly covers of US rock hits like *C'mon Everybody* and *Believe What You Say*. *Ah! Poor Little Baby*, on Top Rank, fails to chart. He gains a dynamic manager, Eve Taylor.

Oct Songwriter Johnny Worth, who, while performing as a member of The Raindrops, met Faith on "Drumbeat", believes the singer to be the ideal interpreter for his song *What Do You Want*, which he and arranger Barry conceive in the mode of Buddy Holly's° recent chart-topper *It Doesn't Matter Any More*. They interest EMI/Parlophone producer John Burgess, who agrees to record Faith.

Dec *What Do You Want* hits UK #1 in only its third charted week, topping the chart for 4 weeks. It is the Parlophone label's first #1 hit, selling 50,000 copies a day at its peak, and a total of over 620,000 in UK alone. Establishing Faith's vocal trademarks like his hiccoughing Hollyish phrasing and exaggerated pronunciation of "buy-bee" (baby), it marks the start of a long partnership between songwriter Worth (under his pen-name of Les Vandyke), Barry (whose pizzicato string arrangement is the record's other notable feature) and Faith.

1960 Mar *Poor Me*, a clone of the first hit, also tops the UK chart. (Faith will later borrow this title for his early autobiography.) Sell-out tours follow, teen mag coverage proliferates, and Faith quickly becomes the UK's biggest teenage idol behind Cliff Richard°.

Apr He appears in his first movie, the slightly controversial (and X-certificated) *Beat Girl*, which also stars Shirley Ann Field in a story of teenage rebellion. Music for the movie is written by Barry, and Faith sings three songs.

May *Someone Else's Baby* hits UK #2, behind The Everly Brothers'° *Cathy's Clown*.

June He appears in second film, *Never Let Go*, a crime thriller starring Richard Todd and Peter Sellers.

July *Made You*, from *Beat Girl*, reaches UK #5. UK's BBC radio declines to play it because the lyric is felt to be too explicit, so B-side, a revival of traditional *When Johnny Comes Marching Home* (sung over the credits in *Never Let Go*) gets airplay instead and makes UK #11.

Oct *How About That* hits UK #4.

Dec Faith appears on UK BBC TV's "Face to Face", a penetrating interview program featuring the incisive John Freeman, and acquits himself intelligently. Meanwhile, Faith's debut LP *Adam* hits UK #6 and stays in the UK top 20 for 36 weeks. Seasonal *Lonely Pup (In A Christmas Shop)* hits UK #4.

1961 Feb *Who Am I* hits UK #5. Soundtrack LP from *Beat Girl* belatedly charts in UK, reaching #11.

May *Easy Going Me*, written by Lionel Bart, reaches UK #12.

Aug *Don't You Know It* also makes UK #12.

Oct He stars in film *What A Whopper!*, a low-budget UK comedy concerning a Loch Ness Monster hoax.

Nov *The Time Has Come*, from *What A Whopper!*, hits UK #4.

1962 Feb *Lonesome*, Faith's first slow ballad A-side, reaches UK #12.

Mar LP *Adam Faith* makes UK #20.

May *As You Like It*, Faith's last single backed by Barry (now heavily committed to film work), hits UK #5.

Sept Faith stars with Anne Baxter and Donald Sinden in film *Mix Me A Person*, a drama in which he plays a man wrongly imprisoned for murder.

Oct *Don't That Beat All*, with new arranger Johnny Keating, is a notable break from the familiar sound. It hits UK #8.

Dec After 13 consecutive UK top 20 singles, *Baby Take A Bow* makes only UK #22.

1963 Feb *What Now* reaches UK #31, as Faith, like most of his pre-Beatles° contemporaries, reels under the chart onslaught of Merseybeat sounds.

July *Walkin' Tall* makes only UK #23. Faith decides to recruit The Roulettes – Russ Ballard (lead guitar), Pete Salt (rhythm guitar), John Rodgers (bass) and Bob Henrit (drums) – as his backing group, adding a hard, beat group edge to his vocal sound, which becomes less mannered and more aggressive.

Oct He commissions singer-songwriter Chris Andrews to write new material and *The First Time*, with The Roulettes backing and a newly-contemporary sound, hits UK #5.

1964 Jan *We Are In Love*, from the same team, reaches UK #11.

Apr Andrews-penned *If He Tells You* reaches UK #25.

June *I Love Being In Love With You* peaks at UK #33.

Sept Andrews' song *Only One Such As You*, an unaccustomedly chest-thumping ballad, fails to chart in UK. Meanwhile, he has discovered Sandie Shaw°, and impressed by her vocal talent, persuades Taylor to sign her. (Shaw covers Lou Johnson's US Bacharach/David hit *(There's) Always Something There To Remind Me* which hits UK #1.)

Dec Faith's cover of Johnson's *A Message To Martha (Kentucky Bluebird)* (also written by Bacharach and David) reaches UK #12.

1965 Feb *Stop Feeling Sorry For Yourself* reaches UK #23. Meanwhile, the Andrews-penned, Roulettes-backed *It's Alright* (originally UK B-side of *I Love Being In Love With You*) belatedly reaches US #31, a beneficiary of the "British Invasion" of US charts.

Apr *Talk About Love* reaches US #97 (his last US chart entry). In UK the reflective *Hand Me Down Things* is the second chart failure on Parlophone.

June *Someone's Taken Maria Away*, a pastiche of the Bacharach/David style by Andrews and *Concrete And Clay*-influenced, reaches UK #34.

Sept LP *Faith Alive* recorded on stage with The Roulettes, makes UK #19.

1966 Oct Following three more flop singles (including a revival of Perry Como's *Idle Gossip* and the later P.J. Proby°/Tom Jones°-flavored *To Make A Big Man Cry*), a cover of Bob Lind's *Cheryl's Goin' Home* reaches UK #46, and will be Faith's final UK singles chart entry.

1967 Nov Unsuccessful *To Hell With Love* is Faith's final Parlophone release. (Faith has already given up cabaret appearances and will cease recording, determined to take up acting full time. Over the next 3 years, he will work from the bottom up in repertory theater around UK, progressing to the lead in a touring revival of *Billy Liar*, the part of Festus in *Twelfth Night*, and a role as a murderer (opposite Dame Sybil Thorndike) in Emlyn Williams' *Night Must Fall*.

1971 He takes the title role in UK ITV's drama series "Budgie", playing a constantly-stymied working-class small-timer attempting to be a wide boy. The series is both a critical and huge public success.

1972 Faith discovers singer/songwriter Leo Sayer° and becomes his manager.

1973 Apr He produces LP *Daltrey*, the first solo LP by The Who's° Roger Daltrey, which includes several compositions by Sayer°. (Shortly afterwards, he has a serious auto accident. He will later describe the near-fatal crash as a major turning point in his life.)

1974 Feb [18] Recovered from his accident apart from a slight limp, Faith begins filming with David Essex° on *Stardust*, the sequel to Essex' previous success *That'll Be The Day*. He takes the rock star manager role played by Ringo Starr° in the earlier movie.

July After 7 years without recording, Faith releases LP *I Survive*, co-produced by himself and David Courtney, with contributions from Paul McCartney°. Rated by the critics, both it and two extracted singles fail to chart, and Faith retires to concentrate on acting, management (Leo Sayer°) and production.

Oct *Stardust* premieres in London, and Faith's performance gains critical plaudits.

1975 He appears on London's West End stage in Stephen Poliakoff's play *City Sugar*.

1978 Feb Faith produces Lonnie Donegan's° LP *Puttin' On The Style*, a star-studded nostalgia/comeback set.

1979 He stars with Ian McShane in soccer drama movie *Yesterday's Hero*, playing a third division club manager.

1980 Apr [30] The film *McVicar*, in which Faith stars alongside Roger Daltrey in the true story of prison escapee John McVicar, premieres in London.

1981 Dec TV-advertised compilation LP *24 Golden Greats* reaches UK #61.

1988 Oct Faith opens on the London West End stage in a musical version of *Budgie*, in which he reprises his old TV role while also refurbishing his singing talent for live stage work.

MARIANNE FAITHFULL

1964 June Faithfull (b. Dec.29, 1946, Hampstead, London, UK), daughter of a British university lecturer and an Austrian Baroness, and an ex-pupil at St. Joseph's convent school in Reading, UK, is taken to a party in London by boyfriend, artist John Dunbar, where she is introduced to The Rolling Stones'° manager Andrew Loog Oldham. He is impressed by her looks and, learning that she has aspirations to be a folk singer, offers to sign and record her.

Sept Faithfull is signed by Oldham to Decca and records the Mick Jagger/Keith Richard ballad *As Tears Go By*, which hits UK #9.

Nov A version of Bob Dylan's° *Blowin' In The Wind*, more obviously folky than her debut, fails to chart.

1965 Jan *As Tears Go By* reaches US #22.

Mar *Come And Stay With Me*, written by Jackie DeShannon, is more commercial and is her biggest hit at UK #4.

Apr *Come And Stay With Me* reaches US #26.

May Faithfull is married to John Dunbar. She parts from Oldham after disagreements and releases *This Little Bird*, which hits UK #6. A simultaneous cover (also on Decca), by Oldham-produced Nashville Teens, peaks at UK #38. She appears in one-off Brighton Song Festival in UK with Lulu°, Manfred Mann°, Dave Berry° and others, singing *Go Away From My World*.

June *This Little Bird* reaches US #32. Two LPs are issued simultaneously in UK: folk package *Come My Way*, which reaches UK #12, and *Marianne Faithfull*, which includes her first two hit singles and makes UK #15. She appears at the Uxbridge Blues and Folk Festival in UK with several R&B bands.

July LP *Marianne Faithfull* reaches US #12.

Aug *Summer Nights* hits UK #10.

Oct *Summer Nights* reaches US #24.

Nov A cover of The Beatles'° *Yesterday* loses out at UK #36 to Matt Monro's competing version. Faithfull gives birth to a son, Nicholas.

Dec *Go Away From My World* (only released in UK on EP) climbs to US #89.

1966 Feb LP *Go Away From My World* reaches US #81. (Its title seems prophetic as Faithfull and Dunbar will shortly separate. She will become Mick Jagger's constant companion and they will remain together for almost 4 years.)

Apr Folk-flavored LP *North Country Maid* fails to chart in UK.

Nov LP *Faithfull Forever* reaches only US #147.

1967 Feb LP *Love In A Mist* fails to chart in UK.

Feb [12] She is with Jagger at Keith Richard's house in West Wittering, Sussex, UK, when police raid the premises, but is not charged with drug possession as Jagger and Richard later are.

Mar A revival of The Ronettes'° *Is This What I Get For Loving You*, with Oldham as producer, reaches UK #43.

June [25] She sings in the chorus of The Beatles'° *All You Need Is Love*, recorded live during "Our World" global TV broadcast.

1968 May She co-stars with Alain Delon in film *Girl On A Motorcycle*, which is savaged by the critics.

Nov [22] Faithfull miscarries the baby she is expecting by Mick Jagger.

Dec [12] She participates in filming of The Rolling Stones'° "Rock And Roll Circus" musical extravaganza, intended as a TV film but never shown.

1969 Feb *Something Better* is Faithfull's last single for Decca. B-side *Sister Morphine*, a drug-weary song written with Jagger and Richard, is later regarded as one of her most notable disks. This is to be her last recording for several years, as she develops her acting ambitions and plays in Chekhov's *Three Sisters* at London's Royal Court Theatre.

Apr Compilation LP *Marianne Faithfull's Greatest Hits* reaches US #171.

May Faithfull and Jagger are arrested at their shared London home on charges of marijuana possession.

July [8] On the Australian set of film *Ned Kelly*, in which she is to co-star with Mick Jagger, Faithfull is discovered in a coma, suffering from a self-inflicted overdose. She is dropped from the movie and goes to hospital for treatment of heroin addiction.

1970 Faithfull and John Dunbar are divorced after several years of separation. She stars as Ophelia with Nicol Williamson in film production of Shakespeare's *Hamlet*.

1975 Nov She returns to recording after a lengthy break with a version of Waylon Jennings' *Dreaming My Dreams* for independent NEMS label. It charts in Ireland but fails in UK.

1978 Mar LP *Faithless* is released, with backing by The Grease Band and C&W leanings in its material. It does not chart.

1979 Faithfull marries punk bass player Ben Brierly of The Vibrators.

Nov [23] She is arrested at Oslo airport, Norway, for possession of marijuana.

Dec Faithfull signs to Island Records and LP *Broken English* reaches UK #57, despite a boycott by Island's distributor EMI over objections to its lyrical content. Extracted from the LP, *The Ballad Of Lucy Jordan* is her first UK hit single for over 12 years, reaching #48.

1980 Mar LP *Broken English* reaches US #82.

1981 Oct LP *Dangerous Acquaintances* makes UK #45 and US #104.

1983 Mar LP *A Child's Adventure* reaches UK #99 and US #107.

1987 July LP *Strange Weather* is released, featuring songs by Jagger/Richard, Dr. John° and Tom Waits°. Its gloomy nature denies it airplay and it meets with little success.

1988 Living in Cambridge, Mass., US, Faithfull has a deporation order served on her by the US immigration authorities.

GEORGIE FAME

1959 Aug/Sept On holiday at Butlins in Pwllheli, Wales, Fame (b. Clive Powell, June 26, 1943, Leigh, Lancs., UK) stands in for injured pianist in resident group Rory Blackwell & The Blackjacks. Blackwell convinces the 16-year-old to quit his cotton factory job and move to London as a full-time Blackjack. Within a month the band folds, leaving him stranded. Rather than go home ingloriously, he lands a gig playing piano in an East End London pub.

Oct Songwriter Lionel Bart spots him and recommends an audition for top UK rock'n'roll manager Larry Parnes. With pianists at a premium, Powell is hired and given his new name. (This is a penchant of Parnes, creator of Tommy Steele°, Marty Wilde°, Vince Eager, Duffy Power and others.)

1960 Feb In addition to backing Parnes' stars, Fame is allowed to develop his own vocal talents by opening the second half of the Gene Vincent°/Eddie Cochran° tour.

Apr Fame makes his disk debut playing piano on Gene Vincent's° *Pistol Packin' Mama*.

1961 June Fame joins Parnes' billtopper Billy Fury's° permanent backing group, The Blue Flames.

Dec Fury replaces The Blue Flames with The Tornados as his backing band. Fame and The Blue Flames get a residency at the Flamingo, a Soho jazz cellar in London's West End. At first they play the regular "Twist Sessions" but soon amass a following for their heady jazz/rock/blue beat melange.

1962 July R&B rivals to Alexis Korner's Blues Inc at nearby Marquee club, The Blue Flames expand from four to seven, playing brassy jazz-rock.

Nov Inspired by Booker T.° and Jimmy McGriff, Fame gets a Hammond organ – one of the first in London.

1963 Sept EMI's Columbia label signs The Blue Flames. Debut live LP *Rhythm And Blues At The Flamingo*, cut at the Flamingo and produced by ex-Cliff Richard° sidekick Ian Samwell, spreads their reputation and they play 40 gigs a month.

1964 *Do The Dog Shop* and *Do-Re-Mi* fail to chart.

Aug *Bend A Little* fails to chart.

Oct Second LP *Fame At Last* reaches UK #15.

Dec Fame re-works *Yeh Yeh*, an Afro-Cuban song by Lambert, Hendricks and Ross, and it hits UK #1 and reaches US #21, making it a million-seller.

1965 Jan With John Mayall°, The Rolling Stones°, The Animals° and The Yardbirds°, Fame leads the R&B boom. Like Mayall's Bluesbreakers, The Blue Flames is an academy for aspiring musicians. John McLaughlin, Mickey Waller and Mitch Mitchell are among those passing through.

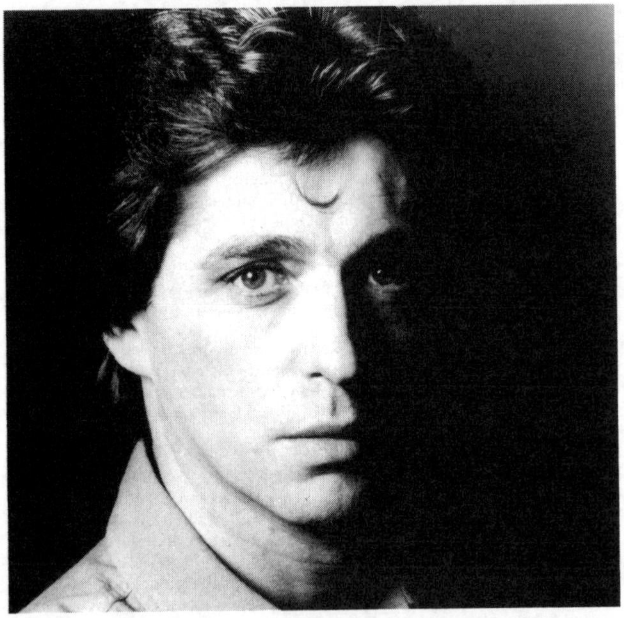

Mar Written by jazzman Johnny Burch, *In The Meantime* takes Fame to UK #22 and US #97. Appearances on American TV shows are taped in UK because his band contains two blacks – a prime reason they never tour US.

July Fame wins jazz, pop and vocal polls, but his new single *Like We Used To Do* makes only UK #33.

Oct *Something* reaches only UK #23 but live work remains sold-out.

1966 May LP *Sweet Things* hits UK #6.

June His own composition *Get Away* hits UK #1 but makes only US #70.

Sept A cover of Bobby Hebb's hit *Sunny* makes UK #13, one place behind the original.

Oct LP *Sound Venture* hits UK #9 but Fame disbands his Blue Flames to pursue a more flexible career. (Over the years, he will front many combos and orchestras of varying composition and size.)

Dec Fame reaches UK #12 with his version of Billy Stewart's *Sitting In The Park*.

1967 Mar LP *Hall Of Fame* peaks at UK #12 and his own composition *Because I Love You*, on CBS/Columbia, makes UK #15.

July LP *Two Faces Of Fame* peaks at UK #22.

Sept *Try My World* reaches UK #37.

Dec Inspired by the movie, Mitch Murray and Peter Callender write *The Ballad Of Bonnie And Clyde*, which becomes Fame's third UK chart topper. It also hits US #7 to become his biggest (but last) US hit. Sales earn him another gold disk.

1968 Fame spends most of the year touring, but finds time to release LP *The Third Face Of Fame*.

1969 July His cover of Kenny Rankin's *Peaceful* reaches UK #16.

Dec *Seventh Son* peaks at UK #25 but LP of the same name fails to chart.

1971 Fame teams up with ex-Animals° veteran Alan Price for *Rosetta*, which makes UK #11, LP *Fame And Price, Price And Fame Together*, which fails to chart, and a short-lived TV series.

1974/88 Following his subterranean heyday, Fame moves increasingly towards adult oriented material. He sings with the Count Basie Orchestra at London's Royal Albert Hall, performs a tribute to songwriter Hoagy Carmichael, appears on numerous television variety shows, makes TV commercials, fronts various bands he calls The Blue Flames and continues to record.

FAMILY

Roger Chapman (vocals)
Charlie Whitney (guitar)
John "Poli" Palmer (keyboards)
John Weider (bass)
Rob Townsend (drums)

1962 The band is formed by Whitney as The Farinas, while at art college in Leicester, UK.

1964 Aug They record *You'd Better Stop* without success for Fontana Records, and play widespread club and college dates.

1967 Moving to London, they change name again to Family, at the suggestion of US producer Kim Fowley. The line-up is Chapman (b. Apr.8, 1944, Leicester) and Whitney (b. June 4, 1944, UK), with Jim King on sax and flute, Rick Grech (b. Nov.1, 1946, Bordeaux, France) on bass and Harry Ovenall on drums.

July They make their London debut at The Royal Albert Hall as support to Tim Hardin.

Sept Another one-off deal, with Liberty Records, results in first Family single *Scene Through The Eye Of A Lens*, which does not sell.

1968 July A new recording deal with Reprise Records results in LP *Music In A Doll's House*, featuring new drummer Rob Townsend (b. July 7, 1947). Produced by Dave Mason of Traffic°, it reaches UK #35, but *Me My Friend*, taken from it, is not a hit.

Jenny Fabian's cult novel *Groupie* is published, allegedly based on Family's touring exploits.

1969 Mar LP *Family Entertainment* charts in UK, hitting #6.

Apr John Weider (b. Apr.21, 1947, UK), formerly with Eric Burdon & The Animals°, joins on bass when Grech quits to join Blind Faith° on the eve of Family's first US tour (cancelled after a few dates when Chapman's visa is revoked).

July [5] They support The Rolling Stones° at their free concert in Hyde Park, London.

Oct Jim King leaves, to be replaced by ex-Eclection keyboardist John "Poli" Palmer (b. May 25, 1943).

Nov *No Mule's Fool* is their first UK hit single, reaching UK #29.

1970 Jan LP *A Song For Me*, the first to be produced by the band, hits UK #4.

Sept EP *Strange Band*, featuring stage favorite *The Weaver's Answer*, reaches UK #11.

Nov LP *Anyway*, a part-live and part-studio-recorded set, hits UK #7.

1971 Mar LP *Old Songs, New Songs* fails to chart, since it consists mainly of previously released material, now remixed to their own satisfaction.

June John Weider leaves to form Stud and play guitar: his replacement is John Wetton (b. July 12, 1949, Derby, UK) from Mogul Thrash.

Aug *In My Own Time* becomes Family's most successful single, hitting UK #4.

Oct LP Fearless returns them to UK LP chart at #14 – and Family's best US showing, at #177.

1972 Sept LP *Bandstand* yields UK #13 hit *Burlesque* and makes UK #15 itself, but Palmer and Wetton both quit, the latter going on to join King Crimson°. Replacements are Tony Ashton (b. Mar.1, 1946, Blackburn, UK) and Jim Cregan, ex-Stud.

1973 Sept LP *It's Only A Movie*, released on the band's own new Raft label, proves to be their last. It makes UK #30.

Oct Family splits up after a farewell tour: Chapman and Whitney, the songwriters, will stay together in Streetwalkers, before Chapman pursues an active solo career, and Cregan moves to Cockney Rebel and then to Rod Stewart's° band, and Townsend will join Medicine Head.

CHRIS FARLOWE

1959 Farlowe (b. John Deighton, Oct.13, 1940), an ex-member of The John Henry Skiffle Group who won the All England Skiffle Championship at Tottenham Mecca, London, UK, in 1957, widens his musical horizons to R&B and rock'n'roll and forms The Thunderbirds, with Albert Lee (guitar), Dave Greenslade (keyboards), Bruce Waddell (bass) and Ian Mague (drums).

1962 Nov Their first release, *Air Travel*, a one-off for Decca, fails to chart.

1963 Sept *I Remember*, penned by Farlowe, is released on EMI's Columbia, but also fails.

1965 June Mod-aimed *Buzz With The Fuzz* (the final Columbia single) is withdrawn when EMI objects to the mod slang of the lyrics.

Aug Farlowe releases *Stormy Monday Blues* under the name Little Joe Cook, on Guy Stevens' Sue label. The authenticity of the performance fools most into believing that it is by an obscure black US blues singer.

Oct Farlowe and the group sign to Immediate Records but *The Fool*, produced by Eric Burdon of The Animals°, fails to chart.

1966 Feb Mick Jagger produces Farlowe's *Think* (a Jagger/Richard song due to be included on The Rolling Stones'° LP *Aftermath*). It makes UK #37.

Apr LP *14 Things To Think About* reaches UK #19.

July *Out Of Time*, another Jagger/Richard song, already featured by The Stones° on *Aftermath* in a sparser arrangement than the orchestral swirl Jagger created for Farlowe, tops the UK chart for 1 week.

Nov Third Jagger/Richard composition, *Ride On Baby* reaches UK #31. (The Stones' version had been rejected from *Aftermath*.)

Dec LP *The Art Of Chris Farlowe*, more soul/R&B-oriented than its predecessor, reaches UK #37.

1967 Feb *My Way Of Giving* charts briefly at UK #48.

June A revival of jazz standard *Moanin'* reaches UK #46.

Dec *Handbags And Gladrags*, penned by Manfred Mann's° Mike D'Abo, reaches UK #33.

1968 May Farlowe disbands The Thunderbirds, deciding to take a rest from the music scene. (He will concentrate on his small London antiques business, specializing in World War II Nazi memorabilia.)

1970 Sept Farlowe returns from semi-retirement to lead the band The Hill before handling vocals in Jon Hiseman's jazz-rock band Colosseum.

1971 Nov Colosseum folds, and Farlowe joins Atomic Rooster as vocalist.

1975 Oct *Out Of Time* is reissued on revived Immediate label and reaches UK #44.

Nov Comeback LP *Chris Farlowe And His Band Live* is released but fails to chart.

1978 Jan Farlowe sings the theme song from UK BBC's crime drama series "Gangsters"; it is released in UK on the BBC's own label.

1982 Feb He sings the tracks *Who's To Blame* and *Hypnotising Ways* on Jimmy Page's score for Charles Bronson film *Death Wish II*.

Sept [21] Farlowe, along with a host of 1960s hitmakers, appears in the "Heroes and Villains" charity concert at London's Hammersmith Odeon.

Oct Following his success at the "Heroes and Villains" concert, Farlowe releases *Let The Heartaches Begin*, but it fails to chart.

1988 July Having had occasional recording and performing activities, Farlowe is used by Jimmy Page as one of his featured vocalists on LP *Outrider*.

JOSE FELICIANO

1963 Blind since birth, Feliciano (b. Sept.10, 1945, Puerto Rico), who has lived in Harlem, New York, since the age of 5, discovering and mastering the acoustic and 12-string guitar in his teens, leaves home to become a regular on the Greenwich Village coffee house circuit, singing with guitar in a style which encompasses Latin-American, folk and R&B influences.

1964 Signed to RCA Records, after being spotted playing at Gerde's Folk City by an A&R man visiting the club to check out another act, Feliciano releases debut single *Everybody Do The Click* and LP *The Voice And Guitar Of José Feliciano*. Neither charts, but the latter brings him his first airplay.

1965/67 A series of Latin-American recordings, sung in Spanish, are a major success in Central and South America, as well as among the US Hispanic community.

1968 Aug Feliciano's early revival of The Doors'° 1967 million-seller *Light My Fire* is his first chartmaker, hitting US #3 and selling a million. Its slowed-down, sparse acoustic-with-woodwind arrangement and soul-inflected vocal defines Feliciano's style. It is taken from LP *Feliciano!*, on which familiar songs by Lennon°/McCartney°, Tom Paxton, Bacharach/David, Bobby Hebb and Gerry & The Pacemakers°, are similarly customized. His first chart LP and also his biggest seller, it hits US #2, earns a gold disk and stays on chart for 59 weeks.

Nov *Light My Fire* hits UK #6 (The Doors'° original peaked at UK #49). LP *Feliciano!* also hits UK #6. US follow-up customizes Tommy Tucker's *Hi-Heel Sneakers*, which reaches US #25 while B-side *Hitchcock Railway* makes US #77. Rush-released *The Star-Spangled Banner*, recorded live at the fifth game of The Baseball World Series (Detroit Tigers vs. St. Louis Cardinals) in Detroit, Mich., reaches US #50.

Dec [28] He appears at the Miami Pop Festival in Hallendale, Fla., before 100,00 people, with Chuck Berry°, Marvin Gaye°, The Grateful Dead°, Joni Mitchell° and others.

1969 Jan LP *Souled* reaches US #24.

Feb Taken from the LP, revivals of Bruce Channel's *Hey! Baby* and The Supremes'° *My World Is Empty Without You* are a minor double-sided US hit at #71 and #87 respectively.

Mar [12] He receives two Grammy awards as Best New Artist of 1968 and for *Light My Fire* voted Best Contemporary Male Pop Vocal Performance.

May Feliciano's version of The Bee Gees'° *Marley Purt Drive* reaches US #70.

Aug LP *Feliciano/10 To 23* (the title arising from the inclusion of a recording taped at age 10) reaches US #16, and is his second gold disk.

Sept Self-composed *Rain* reaches US #76.

Nov LP *Feliciano/10 To 23* reaches UK #29. Taken from it, *And The Sun Will Shine* (another Bee Gees° cover) is his second and last UK hit single, at #25.

1970 Jan Double LP *Alive Alive-O!*, recorded in concert at the London Palladium, reaches US #29, earning a third gold disk. (Feliciano had a tussle with UK authorities before performing at The Palladium, due to UK's 6-month quarantine rule for animals entering UK, which meant that his guide dog could not accompany him.)

June LP *Fireworks* reaches US #57.

July Double A-side *Destiny/Susie-Q* peaks at US #83.

Aug LP *Fireworks* makes UK #65, Feliciano's final UK chart LP.

1971 May Compilation LP *Encore! José Feliciano's Finest Performances* reaches US #92.

Nov LP *That The Spirit Needs* peaks at US #173.

1973 June LP *Compartments*, recorded with Steve Cropper (ex-Booker T. & The MG's°), reaches US #156.

1975 Jan *Chico And The Man*, the theme from the Freddie Prinze/Jack Albertson TV comedy series (sung by Feliciano over the credits), stalls at US #96 while LP *And The Feeling's Good* makes US #136.

JOSE FELICIANO *cont.*

Sept LP *Just Wanna Rock 'N' Roll* reaches US #165.

1976 Sept Leaving RCA, he records LP *Angela* for Private Stock label, but without chart success.

1977 Feb LP *Sweet Soul Music* on Private Stock is co-produced by Jerry Wexler, and touches some of Feliciano's early R&B/soul fire, but still fails to sell.

1981 He signs to Motown Latino, to concentrate on Spanish-language recordings. An LP in English, *José Feliciano*, fails to chart.

1982 Aug [2] Feliciano marries Susan Omillion in Cal.

1983 Apr Motown Latino LP *Escenas De Amor* creates interest in the Hispanic market, but second Motown English-language LP *Romance In The Night* fares no better than the first and he will not remain with the label. (Feliciano will continue regular US live and TV work in the 80s, always a popular club draw with his individualizations of familiar material, but will have no chart success.)

BRYAN FERRY

1964 June Ferry (b. Sept.26, 1945, Washington, County Durham, UK) forms his first band, The Banshees, in Sunderland, UK.

Sept He moves to Newcastle to study fine arts at the university. A fan of US soul music, he becomes vocalist with The Gas Board, a soul/R&B band and works as a DJ.

1968 July He leaves university with a fine arts degree, moving to London to work as a van driver, antiques restorer and a ceramics teacher at a Hammersmith girls' school. He teaches himself piano and writes songs, occasionally dabbling in the visual arts.

1970 Ferry loses his teaching job when school authorities object to his turning classes into music sessions. He decides to form a band to play the songs he has been writing.

1971 Nov Roxy Music° is formed (the name is inspired by a cinema, with Music added as there is a US group called Roxy).

1972 The first regular line-up of Roxy Music° begins playing and Ferry, the inspiration behind the band, will remain its central character throughout the group's successful career.

1973 Oct Ferry's first solo LP *These Foolish Things*, backed by a session group which includes Roxy drummer Paul Thompson, is released by Island. It is a collection of Ferry covers of his favorite oldies. Aided by success of Roxy Music°, the LP hits UK #5, while extracted single, reviving Bob Dylan's° *A Hard Rain's Gonna Fall*, hits UK #10.

1974 June A revival of Dobie Gray's *The "In" Crowd* reaches UK #13.

Aug LP *Another Time, Another Place* comprises, apart from Ferry-composed title track, more pop and R&B oldies by Willie Nelson°, Joe South°, Bob Dylan°, Ike Turner and others. It hits UK #4, but like Roxy Music° releases, fails to chart in US.

Sept His version of The Platters'° *Smoke Gets In Your Eyes*, taken from the LP, reaches UK #17.

Dec After spending most of the year on a Roxy Music° world tour, Ferry plays three solo dates, including one at London's Royal Albert Hall, with backing by the group (in evening dress) and an orchestra. The dinner-jacket look has become Ferry's trademark, even though his current image with Roxy is military chic.

1975 July *You Go To My Head* peaks at UK #33.

1976 June [26] As a Roxy Music° "sabbatical" is announced, Ferry's solo LP *Let's Stick Together*, a more even mix of oldies and his own material, makes UK #19. The title track, a Wilbert Harrison° R&B number, is extracted and hits UK #4.

Aug EP *Extended Play* comprises four assorted revivals from the recent LP: *Heart On My Sleeve, The Price Of Love, Shame Shame Shame* and *It's Only Love*. The second track (originally a 1965 UK hit for The Everly Brothers°) gains most airplay, and hits UK #7 – the first EP to make UK top 10 since The Beatles'° *Magical Mystery Tour* 9½ years earlier. With Roxy Music ° drummer Paul Thompson and the group's ex-bassist John Wetton, plus session guitarist Chris Spedding, The Bryan Ferry Band is formed for live work.

Oct LP *Let's Stick Together* is Ferry's first US chart entry at #160.

Dec *Heart On My Sleeve*, issued as a US single on Atlantic, makes #86. Ferry is romantically linked to US model Jerry Hall (featured on the sleeve of Roxy Music's° LP *Siren* and on the video vocals of *Let's Stick Together*) (she will later leave him for Mick Jagger).

1977 Jan Ferry announces the full touring line-up of his new band, which includes Roxy Music's° Phil Manzanera on second guitar, Ann Odell on keyboards, a brass section and three backing singers.

Feb The new group tours UK as the prelude to a world tour, helping *This Is Tomorrow* to hit UK #9.

Mar As the tour moves on through Europe, LP *In Your Mind*, solely of Ferry compositions, hits UK #5.

Apr Ferry sings *She's Leaving Home* on the soundtrack of Lou Reizner's record and film *All This And World War II*.

May After a short break, the second half of the world tour begins, taking in Australia, Japan and US. LP *In Your Mind* reaches US #126. After the tour, the band disperses and Ferry bases himself in LA, where he writes songs for a new LP.

June *Tokyo Joe*, taken from LP *In Your Mind*, reaches UK #15.

Dec Ferry moves to a hotel in Montreux, and over the next 3 months will record LP *The Bride Stripped Bare* at the Montreux Casino Studio. Instrumentals are handled by a session crew including Waddy Wachtel and Neil Hubbard (guitars), Rick Marotta (drums) and Alan Spenner (bass).

1978 May *What Goes On* peaks at UK #67.

Aug *Sign Of The Times* makes UK #37, but a projected summer UK tour to preface the new, Montreux-recorded LP, is cancelled when ticket sales are poor.

Oct LP *The Bride Stripped Bare*, a mixture of new songs and R&B oldies like Sam and Dave's° *You Don't Know Like I Know* and Al Green's° *Take Me To The River*, reaches UK #13.

Nov LP *The Bride Stripped Bare* makes US #159. Ferry reassembles Roxy Music° to record LP *Manifesto*.

1982 June [26] Ferry marries Lucy Helmore at a society wedding in Sussex (his son will be named after Otis Redding).

1985 June After two chart-topping Roxy Music° LPs (*Flesh And Blood* and *Avalon*) and a live mini-LP (*The High Road*), Ferry re-emerges as a solo artist with LP *Boys And Girls*, which tops the UK chart. It features guest musicians including Mark Knopfler, David Sanborn, Nile Rodgers and David Gilmour. During its recording Ferry tells writer/producer Keith Forsey that he is too busy to record a new song *Don't You (Forget About Me)*. (It is later a US #1 for Simple Minds°.) *Slave To Love* hits UK #10.

July [13] Ferry and the band play in the Live Aid concert at Wembley,UK.

Aug LP *Boys And Girls* makes US #65 on Warner Bros.

Sept *Don't Stop The Dance* reaches UK #21.

Dec *Windswept* peaks at UK #46.

1986 Apr *Is Your Love Strong Enough?*, featured in Ridley Scott's film *Legend*, reaches UK #22, while TV-advertised compilation LP *Street Life – 20 Greatest Hits*, containing both Roxy Music° and Ferry solo successes, tops the UK chart for 5 weeks. becoming one of the best selling LPs of the year.

1987 Oct After another lengthy spell in the studio, Ferry's first new recording in 2 years is *The Right Stuff*, co-written with The Smiths'° guitarist Johnny Marr. It reaches UK #37.

Nov Marr also features on LP *Bête Noire*, which hits UK #7. Released in US on Reprise, it peaks at #65.

1988 Feb *Kiss And Tell* reaches UK #41.

Apr Now featured in Michael J. Fox movie *Bright Lights Big City*, *Kiss And Tell* moves to US #31.

Oct *Let's Stick Together* is released as a prelude to greatest hits LP *The Ultimate Collection*.

THE 5TH DIMENSION

Marilyn McCoo (vocals)
Florence LaRue (vocals)
Lamonte McLemore (vocals)
Billy Davis, Jr. (vocals)
Ron Townson (vocals)

1966 The group forms as The Versatiles in LA with McLemore (b. Sept.17, 1939, St. Louis, Mo., US) and McCoo (b. Sept.30, 1943, Jersey City, N.J., US), both ex-members of The Hi-Fis (along with Floyd Butler and Harry Elston, later in Friends of Distinction), Davis (b. June 26, 1940, St. Louis) and Townson (b. Jan.20, 1933, St. Louis), who have known McLemore in hometown vocal groups, and LaRue (b. Feb.4, 1944, Penn., US), a Cal. State graduate and ex-teacher. They tour US with the Ray Charles° revue for 6 months and Marc Gordon becomes their manager. He takes them back to LA and introduces them to Johnny Rivers°, who has started his own Soul City label, through Liberty Records.

1967 Feb Signed by Rivers°, the group becomes The 5th Dimension, the name suggested by Townson and his wife Babette because Rivers says The Versatiles is dated. They cut (with Rivers producing) a cover of a Mamas and Papas'° LP track, *Go Where You Wanna Go*, which is released and reaches US #16.

May *Another Day, Another Heartache*, a P.F. Sloan/Steve Barri song, climbs to US #45. Producer Rivers° has to re-schedule sessions for a first LP in order to take part in The San Remo Song Festival. During the break, rehearsal pianist Jim Webb spends a weekend at a fair, where he sees a hot air balloon in action and is inspired to write *Up, Up And Away*. Back at the studio, he plays it to the others, who insist on recording it and ask to hear other Webb songs, from which they choose four more to complete the LP.

July *Up, Up And Away* is the group's first top 10 hit at US #7.

Aug Debut LP *Up, Up And Away* hits US #8, earning a gold disk and staying on chart for 83 weeks.

Dec *Paper Cup*, written by Webb, reaches US #34.

1968 Jan LP *The Magic Garden*, produced by Bones Howe and with all but one song (Lennon°/McCartney's° *Ticket To Ride*) by Webb, is a polished, harmony-rich concept LP, but with poor marketing it peaks at US #105 (though sales are consistent and it stays on chart for 31 weeks).

Feb [29] The 5th Dimension and *Up, Up And Away* sweep the 10th annual Grammy awards with Record of the Year, Song of the Year, Best Contemporary Single, Best Contemporary Group Performance and Best Performance by a Group of Two to Six Persons. (The Johnny Mann Singers also win Best Performance Grammy for a larger group with their UK hit choral version of it.)

Mar *Carpet Man*, from LP *The Magic Garden*, reaches US #29.

July A cover of Laura Nyro's laid-back summer song *Stoned Soul Picnic* hits US #3, selling over a million and becoming the group's first gold single.

Sept LP *Stoned Soul Picnic* reaches US #21.

Nov *Sweet Blindness*, another Nyro song from the LP, reaches US #13.

1969 Feb *California Soul* reaches US #25.

Apr *Aquarius/Let The Sunshine In* is the group's biggest hit, topping the US chart for 6 weeks and selling 2 million copies in 3 months. The medley from Broadway rock musical *Hair* was cut after the group saw Ronnie Dyson sing *Aquarius* in the show. Producer Howe linked the two instrumental tracks in the LA studio and the group overdubbed the final vocals in Las Vegas (where they have been appearing at Caesar's Palace with Frank Sinatra).

May *Aquarius/Let the Sunshine In* reaches UK #11, the group's first UK hit. (Due to a misunderstanding, an abridged version intended for US AM radio, which omits much of *Aquarius*, is released in UK, but does not affect sales and is not corrected.)

July LP *The Age Of Aquarius* hits US #2 and remains charted for 72 weeks, earning a gold disk.

Aug *Workin' On A Groovy Thing*, a Neil Sedaka° co-composition taken from the LP, reaches US #20.

Nov *Wedding Bell Blues*, another Nyro song also from LP *Aquarius*, is the group's second #1 and third million-selling single, topping the US chart for 3 weeks. (The group has had its most successful year. McCoo married Davis, and LaRue and manager Gordon also married.)

1970 Jan The group leaves Soul City Records and signs to Bell label. LP *The Age Of Aquarius* passes a million US sales (in later years, this would qualify it for a platinum disk).

Feb *Wedding Bell Blues* makes UK #16 (the group's second and final UK hit), while the last extract from the LP, Nyro's song *Blowing Away*, reaches US #21.

Mar First Bell single, *A Change Is Gonna Come/People Gotta Be Free*, a medley of Sam Cooke's° 1965 hit and The Young Rascals'° 1968 #1, reaches US #60, dually credited with B-side, *The Declaration*.

Mar [11] *Aquarius/Let The Sunshine In* wins a Grammy award as Record of the Year for 1969.

May *The Girls' Song*, the final Soul City release, reaches US #43, while Bell single *Puppet Man* (another Sedaka° song) makes US #24.

June LP *Portrait*, on Bell, reaches US #20, while Soul City compilation LP *The 5th Dimension/Greatest Hits* overtakes it to hit US #5. Both LPs gain gold disks.

July *Save The Country* (again by Nyro) reaches US #27.

Sept Another Soul City compilation LP, *The July 5th Album*, reaches US #63, while *On The Beach (In The Summertime)*, from LP *Portrait*, makes US #54.

Dec A Bacharach/David ballad, *One Less Bell To Answer* hits US #2 for 2 weeks (behind George Harrison's° *My Sweet Lord*), and is another million-seller.

1971 Apr LP *Love's Lines, Angles And Rhymes* reaches US #17, while the title track makes US #19.

June *Light Sings*, from Broadway musical *The Me Nobody Knows*, reaches US #44.

Nov Double live LP *The 5th Dimension Live!!* reaches US #32, while a revival of The Association's° *Never My Love*, taken from the live LP, makes US #12. Compilation LP *Reflections* peaks at US #112.

1972 Feb *Together Let's Find Love* reaches US #37.

Apr LP *Individually And Collectively*, featuring group and solo performances, reaches US #58.

June *Last Night I Didn't Get To Sleep At All*, penned by UK writer Tony Macaulay, hits US #8, and is the group's fifth and last million-selling single.

Nov *If I Could Reach You* hits US #10. Compilation LP *Greatest Hits On Earth* (containing the hits from both Soul City and Bell catalogs), makes US #14. (It is the group's last gold LP.) The group performs at the White House at the invitation of President Nixon.

1973 Feb *Living Together, Growing Together*, from movie *Lost Horizon*, peaks at US #32.

Apr LP *Living Together, Growing Together* reaches US #108, while *Everything's Been Changed* climbs to US #70.

Sept *Ashes To Ashes* makes US #52.

1974 Jan *Flashback* peaks US #82, and is the group's last Bell release.

1975 Sept Signed to ABC Records, the group is reunited with Jim Webb for LP *Earthbound*, a concept-packaged set of his songs. It reaches US #136.

Nov McCoo and Davis leave the group for solo careers (though remain with ABC Records). Producer Don Davis puts them together to work on an LP of duets.

1976 Apr *Love Hangover* is the last 5th Dimension hit single, at US #80 (Diana Ross'° version on Motown hits #1). (The group has no more chart hits, but retreats to the supper club circuit where it has always had a solid following.)

May McCoo and Davis peak at US #91 with their first duet *I Hope We Get To Love In Time*.

1977 Jan McCoo and Davis hit US #1 with *You Don't Have To Be A Star (To Be In My Show)*, selling over a million copies, while their LP *I Hope We Get To Love In Time* reaches US #30, and earns a gold disk.

Feb [19] *You Don't Have To Be A Star (To Be In My Show)* wins a Grammy award, as Best R&B Vocal Performance by a Duo.

Apr The duo scores its only UK success as *You Don't Have To Be A Star (To Be In My Show)* hits UK #7.

May *Your Love* by McCoo and Davis reaches US #15.

June [15] The duo co-hosts a US CBS TV summer variety series of six programs, "The Marilyn McCoo and Billy Davis Jr. Show".

Sept *Look What You've Done To My Heart* is McCoo and Davis' last hit, peaking at US #51. Their second (and last) ABC LP *The Two Of Us* makes US #57.

1978 Mar The 5th Dimension signs to Motown, but LP *Star Dancing* arouses little interest.

Oct McCoo and Davis sign to CBS/Columbia Records for LP *Marilyn And Billy*, which peaks at US #146.

1979 Apr Second 5th Dimension Motown LP *High On Sunshine* fails to chart, and the group is dropped from the label.

1980 McCoo and Davis split professionally. She moves to RCA to record solo (plus the occasional duet with Davis), but finds no chart success, and fares better on TV, hosting the show "Solid Gold". (All former members of The 5th Dimension continue performing, in various combinations or alone, into the 80s, but the group will only be successful on the nightclub nostalgia circuit, where its hit repertoire adapts neatly to the MOR atmosphere.)

THE FIVE SATINS

Fred Parris (vocals)
Bill Baker (vocals)
Al Denby (vocals)
Jim Freeman (vocals)
Ed Martin (vocals)
Jessie Murphy (piano)

1953 While at high school in New Haven, Conn., US, the group originally forms as The Scarlets.

1954/55 They make four ballad singles for Red Robin Records, none of which are chart hits.

1956 Parris (b. Mar.26, 1936, Conn.), now in the US Army in the Far East, has written *In The Still Of The Night* during a long night of military guard duty. When he returns to US on leave, the group records it with other songs on a 2-track machine in a New Haven church basement. They are now renamed The Five Satins, and signed to local label Standord Records.

July First Standord single *All Mine* fails, but second, *In The Still Of The Night*, begins to sell in the New York area, prompting Ember Records to buy the rights and reissue it.

Nov *In The Still Of The Night* reaches US #24, and #1 in New York, where it will remain a perennial radio favorite. The single remains charted for 19 weeks.

1957 Feb [15] to May 5, the group tours the US on Irving Feld's "Greatest Show of 1957" rock package show, with Chuck Berry°, Fats Domino°, LaVern Baker and many others.

Aug After unsuccessful releases *Wonderful Girl* and *Oh Happy Day*, they return to US chart with *To The Aisle*, reaching #25 in a long stay of 17 weeks. Baker sings lead, Parris having returned to Japan and army duty soon after the release of *In The Still Of The Night*.

1958 Parris returns to the group on discharge, but there are no hits this year.

1959 Dec *Shadows* is a minor US chart success at #87.

1960 Jan *In The Still Of The Night*, still being played by East Coast US DJs, returns to US chart, reaching #81.

May *I'll Be Seeing You* reaches #79 in US.

1961 Jan *In The Still Of The Night* makes another fleeting return to US chart at #99, but newer singles on Ember have failed to chart, and the group will move through the 1960s with releases on Cub, Chancellor, Red Bird and United Artists labels with no success. (Parris will then try a solo career on Checker, Atco and RCA, again with no hits.)

1973 After reforming (with original member Freeman in the line-up) as Fred Parris & The Five Satins, and finding success on the now-burgeoning US oldie revival circuit, the group appears with other 1950s hitmakers in the movie *Let The Good Times Roll*, partly filmed at "Madison Square Garden Rock Revival Show". Songs performed include *In The Still Of The Night* and an a cappella *I'll Be Seeing You*.

1974 The new line-up signs to Kirshner Records and resumes recording, without charting.

1975 Oct Under the name Black Satin, recording in contemporary style, they have US R&B top 40 entry with *Everybody Stand Up And Clap Your Hands*. It fails to cross over to the pop chart.

1982 Mar As Fred Parris & The Five Satins, they have first US Top 100 entry for 21 years with the nostalgic *Memories Of Days Gone By*, reaching #71.

FIVE STAR

Deniece Pearson (lead vocals)
Doris Pearson (vocals)
Stedman Pearson (vocals)
Lorraine Pearson (vocals)
Delroy Pearson (vocals)

1983 The group forms first as a trio in Romford, Essex, UK, when the three daughters of Buster (Stedman) and Dolores Pearson, Doris (b. June 8, 1966, Romford), Lorraine (b. Aug.10, 1967, Romford) and Deniece (b. June 13, 1968, Romford) beg their father to let them record his newly-demoed song *Problematic*. (Pearson, originally from Jamaica, is an ex-professional guitarist, who played during the 1960s in tour bands behind many overseas acts working in UK, including soulsters Wilson Pickett° and Lee Dorsey°, and reggae singers Desmond Dekker° and Jimmy Cliff°. Having produced and written songs and run independent reggae label K&B, he launched Tent Records to focus on commercial dance music.) Impressed by his daughters' recording, he realizes they have potential as a professional act and records a second demo of Lorraine's song *Say Goodbye*. Dolores Pearson prompts the idea of brothers Stedman (b. June 29, 1964, Romford) and Delroy (b. Apr.11, 1970, Romford) also joining, though they are at college and school respectively. Stedman agrees readily and, through his design and choreographic skills, the group begins to fashion its own costumes, dance steps and visual image. Delroy is in line for a place in West Ham's junior soccer team when he leaves school, but lets it go to join the group. Pearson becomes their manager.

Sept The group makes its UK TV debut on BBC's "Pebble Mill At One", singing *Say Goodbye*. RCA Records is interested and Pearson begins to negotiate with them, stressing that Five Star is already contracted, but that Tent Records as a whole is a negotiable deal.

Oct *Problematic* is released by Tent, independently distributed through PRT. Club reaction is good, but sales small.

1984 Apr Pearson signs Tent Records to RCA, and the group's recordings appear on a joint Tent/RCA label, the main advantage being superior promotion and distribution. *Hide And Seek* is released and just misses UK top 100.

Oct *Crazy* also fails to chart.

1985 June *All Fall Down*, produced by Nick Martinelli and co-written by 1970s UK hitmaker Barry Blue, reaches UK #15. It is promoted via a hectic schedule of lip-synch personal appearances in UK clubs and discos. (B-side *First Avenue*, written by Deniece, will receive a Grammy nomination as Best R&B Instrumental of the Year.)

Aug A second Martinelli production, *Let Me Be The One*, reaches UK #18. First LP *Luxury Of Life*, including all the singles plus some new tracks (the work of six producers and nine different studios), reaches UK #25. (It will climb further up the chart to accompany each succeeding single, eventually peaking at #12. By 1987, it will have sold over 300,000 copies in UK, earning a platinum disk.)

Oct *Love Take Over*, extracted from the LP but remixed by 19 hitmaker Paul Hardcastle, makes UK #25. *All Fall Down* reaches the US chart at #65 and makes R&B #16.

Nov *R.S.V.P.*, also from the LP, reaches UK #45. The group visits US for the first time, on a promotional trip. The Walt Disney organization, noting Five Star's youth appeal, offers them a TV show of their own, but Pearson declines on the grounds that the group is not yet well-enough established. LP *Luxury Of Life* climbs to US #57.

Dec The group appears in the "Celebration of Youth" concert in London, attended by HM Queen Elizabeth.

1986 Jan They spend 6 weeks in LA, recording a second LP and doing club, TV and radio promotional work.

Feb *System Addict*, seventh single from the debut LP, is the group's first UK top 10 hit at #3.

Mar *Let Me Be The One* reaches US #59.

May *Can't Wait Another Minute*, recorded in LA, hits UK #7.

June The group accepts an invitation to write the theme for UK youth TV series "How Dare You", but declines George Michael's° invitation to support Wham!° at its farewell concert at Wembley.

Aug *Find The Time* hits UK #7. It and the previous single are included on LP *Silk And Steel*, which tops the UK chart. (It will be a long-term seller, eventually passing triple platinum and selling over a million in UK alone.)

Sept [14] The group's "Children of the Night" UK tour (sponsored by Crunchie Bars), with an 8-piece band accompanying it, opens at Poole, Dorset.

Oct *Rain Or Shine*, from LP *Silk And Steel*, hits UK #2 and earns a gold disk for a half-million-plus sales.

Nov *Can't Wait Another Minute* reaches US #41, and hits US R&B top 10.

Dec *If I Say Yes*, from LP *Silk And Steel*, reaches UK #15, while the group makes a short US tour.

1987 Jan The Pearson family moves from Romford to a much larger house in Sunningdale, Berks., UK, where electronic gates and security cameras safeguard their privacy.

Feb [9] Five Star wins a BPI award from UK record industry as Best British Group.

Feb *Stay Out Of My Life*, the fifth single from second LP and written by Deniece, hits UK #9. *If I Say Yes* makes US #67.

May *The Slightest Touch*, the last extract from *Silk And Steel*, hits UK #4.

Aug *Whenever You're Ready* reaches UK #11.

Sept LP *Between The Lines*, recorded in London and US, hits UK #7.

Oct *Strong As Steel*, from the LP, makes UK #16.

Oct [26/27] Major dates on the "Children of the Night, 1987" tour (this time sponsored by Ultrabrite toothpaste), at Wembley Arena, London, are filmed for UK home video release.

Dec *Somewhere, Somebody*, extracted from the third LP, makes UK #2

1988 June *Another Weekend* peaks at UK #18.

Aug LP *Rock The World*, the work of several producers including Leon Sylvers III from the US and Delroy Pearson, reaches UK #17, while extracted *Rock My World* peaks at UK #28.

THE FIXX

Cy Curnin (vocals and piano)
Jamie West-Oram (guitar)
Charlie Barrett (bass)
Rupert Greenall (keyboards)
Adam Woods (drums)
Dan K. Brown (bass)

1980 Jan The band begins in UK as The Portraits, formed by Curnin (b. Dec.12, 1957) and Woods, who recruit Greenall and release *Hazards In The Home* as a one-off for Ariola Records.
1981 Apr With the line-up now stabilized to include Barrett and West-Oram, they change name to The Fix and have *Lost Planes* issued by the 101 Label, marketed by Polydor Records. They also have tracks on 101's compilation LPs *Beyond The Groove* and *Live Letters*.
1982 Jan They sign a full record deal with major label MCA, which demands partial change of name to the potentially less controversial Fixx. *Some People* is released in UK, but fails to sell.
Apr *Stand Or Fall* is UK chart debut, at #54.
May LP *Shuttered Room* has only a brief UK chart showing, also at #54.
July *Red Skies* is their second and last UK hit, only reaching #57.
Nov *Stand Or Fall* charts at US #76, and LP *Shuttered Room* begins an 18-month US chart residency, but only peaking at #106. Barrett leaves, and will be replaced by a sequence of semi-permanent session men on bass.
1983 May LP *Reach The Beach* is released, tailored specifically for the US market. It hits #8 in US LP chart.
Aug *Saved By Zero* reaches #20 in US.
Sept *One Thing Leads To Another* enters US singles chart and hits #4.
1984 Jan *The Sign Of Fire* reaches US #32.
Oct *Are We Ourselves* reaches US #15. LP *Phantoms* reaches US #19.
Nov Tina Turner's° version of Curnin and West-Oram's *Better Be Good To Me* hits US #5.
1986 July *Secret Separation* reaches US #19.
Oct Fourth LP *Walkabout* is released.
1987 June LP *React*, a hits collection plus three new tracks, is released in US only.

ROBERTA FLACK

1968 Flack (b. Feb.10, 1939, Asheville, N.C., US), having graduated in music from Howard University in Washington, D.C., then worked as a high school music teacher in North Carolina, returns to Washington to teach, and also begins singing in local clubs during the evenings. Atlantic recording artist Les McCann sees her performing and arranges an audition with label boss Ahmet Ertegun and producer Joel Dorn, which results in her signing to the label.
1970 Jan Debut LP *First Take*, produced by Dorn, is released, initially a middling US chartmaker.
Oct LP *Chapter Two* reaches US #33.
1971 Aug *You've Got A Friend*, a cover duet with Donny Hathaway° of a Carole King° song (simultaneously a US #1 hit for James Taylor°), reaches US #29.
Nov Another duet with Hathaway°, reviving *You've Lost That Lovin' Feelin'* reaches US #71.
1972 Jan LP *Quiet Fire* makes US #18.
Feb A revival of The Shirelles'° 1961 hit *Will You Love Me Tomorrow* peaks at US #76.
Apr Through its exposure in Clint Eastwood movie *Play Misty For Me*, a track from Flack's debut LP, reviving Ewan MacColl's folk ballad *The First Time Ever I Saw Your Face*, tops the US chart for 6 weeks, selling two million copies. It is the longest running #1 hit by a solo female artist since Gogi Grant's *The Wayward Wind* in 1956. LP *First Take* (released in 1970) tops the US chart for 5 weeks and earns a gold disk.
June Duet LP *Roberta Flack And Donny Hathaway* hits #3 and is another gold disk.
July *The First Time Ever I Saw Your Face* reaches UK #14 and LP *First Take* makes UK #47.
Aug A third duet with Hathaway°, *Where Is The Love*, hits US #5 (selling over a million), and makes UK #29.
Dec [10] Flack and two members of her backing group, bassist Jerry Jemmott and guitarist Cornell Dupree, are injured when Jemmott crashes their car driving into Manhattan, N.Y. The men both have fractured and broken bones, while Flack needs surgery on her lip.
1973 Feb *Killing Me Softly With His Song*, which Flack heard sung by Lori Lieberman (for whom it was written – about singer Don McLean°) while on a TWA flight from LA to New York, hits US #1 for 5 weeks and is a million-seller. (Flack has spent 3 months perfecting it in the studio prior to release.)
Mar [3] Flack wins Grammy awards for *The First Time Ever I Saw Your Face*, which is voted both Song of the Year and Record of the Year, and for *Where Is The Love*, which is named Best Pop Vocal Performance by a Duo.
Mar *Killing Me Softly With His Song* hits UK #6.
Oct LP *Killing Me Softly* hits US #3 (earning another gold disk) and makes UK #40, while *Jesse*, written by Janis Ian°, reaches US #30.
1974 Mar [2] *Killing Me Softly With His Song* wins Record of the Year and Song of the Year at the annual Grammy awards. In addition, Flack wins Best Pop Vocal – Female.
Mar Dorn leaves Atlantic Records during the recording of Flack's new LP *Feel Like Makin' Love*. (Flack takes over production herself but, due to her production inexperience and artistic perfectionism, it will take 8 months to complete. On release, Flack will use the production pseudonym Rubina Flake.)
Aug *Feel Like Making Love* tops the US chart for a week, selling over a million, and reaches UK #34.
1975 May LP *Feel Like Makin' Love* makes US #24.
June *Feelin' That Glow* peaks at US #76.
1978 Feb After a lengthy absence from the chart (during which she has cut down live performances to pursue other concerns, like her work in various educational programs for disadvantaged US youth), Flack's LP *Blue Lights In The Basement* hits US #8 and is another gold disk.
May Taken from the LP, *The Closer I Get To You*, a ballad duet with Donny Hathaway° (written by James Mtume and Reggie Lucas), hits US #2 and UK #42.
July *If Ever I See You Again*, the title song from the Joe Brooks film, reaches US #24.
Oct LP *Roberta Flack* reaches US #74.
1979 Jan [13] Donny Hathaway° dies after falling from a New York hotel room window. (He had been working on more duet material with Flack, which will eventually emerge in 1980 in LP and single form. Grieving the loss, Flack will remain out of the public eye for much of the year.)
1980 Mar *You Are My Heaven*, duetted with Hathaway°, reaches US #47.
June Uptempo *Back Together Again*, another Flack/Hathaway° duet, penned by Mtume and Lucas, reaches only US #56 but hits UK #3. LP *Roberta Flack Featuring Donny Hathaway* makes US #25 and UK #31.
Sept *Don't Make Me Wait Too Long* reaches UK #44.
1981 Jan Double live LP *Live And More*, recorded with Memphis singer Peabo Bryson°, reaches US #52.
July LP *Bustin' Loose*, the Flack-performed soundtrack from the film of the same title (released on MCA) reaches US #161. She also records a popular US TV commercial for Kentucky Fried Chicken.
1982 June The title song from Kate Jackson/Harry Hamlin film *Making Love* reaches US #13.
Aug LP *I'm The One* reaches US #59, while its extracted title track makes US #42.
1983 Jan Flack announces a tour which will take her and Bryson° through Europe, the Middle East, The Far East, Australasia, South America and US. She moves from Atlantic to Capitol Records.
Sept Flack and Bryson's° duet *Tonight I Celebrate My Love* reaches US #16 and hits UK #2 – Flack's biggest-selling UK single. LP *Born To Love* with Bryson makes US #25 (it is Flack's last US chart LP) and UK #15. She moves into a New York apartment in the Dakota building – the block in which John Lennon° lived at the time of his death.
1984 Jan *You're Looking Like Love To Me*, another duet with Bryson°, taken from the LP, reaches US #58.
Mar Flack is honored with an hour-long musical tribute on the steps of New York's City Hall. (Washington has also given her a public honor, declaring April 22 Roberta Flack Day.)
Apr TV-advertised compilation LP *Roberta Flack's Greatest Hits* reaches UK #35.
1988 Aug [20] Flack plays a benefit concert on Nantucket Island, Mass., for the island's only health care facility, The Nantucket Cottage Hospital.
Oct LP *Oasis*, her first new solo album in 6 years is released.

FLEETWOOD MAC

Peter Green (guitar)
Mick Fleetwood (drums)
John McVie (bass)
Jeremy Spencer (guitar)

1967 Apr Fleetwood (b. June 24, 1942, London, UK), ex-The Cheynes, The Bo Street Runners, Peter B's Looners and Shotgun Express (the latter with Rod Stewart°) joins John Mayall's° Bluesbreakers. The group comprises Mayall, Fleetwood, McVie (b. Nov.26, 1945, London, UK) and Green (b. Peter Greenbaum, Oct.29, 1946, London, UK), who has played with Fleetwood as a member of both the Looners and Shotgun Express and replaced Eric Clapton° in The Bluesbreakers in July 1966. Fleetwood, Green and McVie form a close alliance, but within a month Fleetwood and Green are fired.

July Without Mayall°, The Bluesbreakers have recently worked for Blue Horizon label owner Mike Vernon as a backing band for US bluesman Eddie Boyd. Vernon is keen to sign a domestic blues outfit for his label. After auditioning (and rejecting) Midlands-based band The Levi Set, he introduces their guitarist Spencer (b. July 4, 1948, West Hartlepool, Lancs., UK) to Green and Fleetwood. Fleetwood Mac is formed comprising Green, Fleetwood, Spencer and bassist Bob Brunning.

Aug [12] They make their debut at The Windsor Jazz and Blues Festival. McVie, fired from The Bluesbreakers, joins to replace Brunning, who leaves to form The Sunflower Brunning Blues Band.

Nov The group releases its debut single *I Believe My Time Ain't Long* billed as Peter Green's Fleetwood Mac. They become resident house band for the Blue Horizon label backing Otis Spann, Duster Bennett and others on a variety of LPs.

1968 Mar A new blues boom hits UK and the band's debut LP *Fleetwood Mac*, mixing originals with blues classics by Robert Johnson and Howlin' Wolf°, hits UK #4 and makes US #198.

Apr *Black Magic Woman*, written by Green, reaches UK #37. (Santana's° version will hit US #4 in Jan. 1971.)

July A cover of Little Willie John's blues *Need Your Love So Bad*, highlighted by Mickey Baker's (of Mickey and Sylvia) string arrangement, reaches UK #31.

Sept LP *Mr. Wonderful* hits UK #10. (On it, Christine Perfect (later McVie) plays piano, although still a member of the group Chicken Shack. Green expands the group, adding a third guitarist, ex-Boilerhouse Danny Kirwan (b. Mar.13, 1950, London).

1969 Jan *Albatross*, written by Green, tops the UK chart. A haunting guitar instrumental, it lifts the group out of the blues bracket and establishes its name throughout Europe.

Feb LP *English Rose* reaches US #184.

May Green's *Man Of The World* hits UK #2. The group's contract with Blue Horizon ends and it signs a one-off deal with ex-Rolling Stones° manager Andrew Loog Oldham's Immediate label.

Aug *Need Your Love So Bad* is reissued, this time reaching UK #32.

Sept LP *Pious Bird Of Good Omen* reaches UK #18. While the group negotiates a new contract, Blue Horizon releases a collection of old material, and re-promotes *Need Your Love So Bad*, which charts for a third time at UK #42.

Oct LP *Then Play On* hits UK #6 and makes US #109, marking their debut on Reprise label.

Nov *Oh Well* hits UK #2. The song's religious overtones reflect Green's renouncement of his Jewish faith and his involvement with Christianity (he begins to appear on stage in a long white robe underlining a new messianic image).

Dec LP *Blues Jam At Chess* is released featuring the group and a selection of Blues greats recorded in 1968.

1970 Jan Spencer releases an eponymously titled debut solo LP backed by the group.

Mar *Oh Well* reaches US #55.

Apr [11] Green quits the band in Munich during a European tour, the pressures of stardom now proving intolerable. To avoid breach of contract, he agrees to finish the tour and then leave.

June *The Green Manalishi (With The Two-Prong Crown)* hits UK #10. In his last single for the group, Green gives a heart-rending graphic description of the terrors that are haunting him.

Aug [17] McVie's wife, Christine Perfect, joins the line-up on keyboards, having been voted *Melody Maker*'s Female Vocalist of the Year in 1969.

Oct LP *Kiln House* reaches UK #39 and US #69. Spencer becomes creative lead on their first LP release without Green (but it will be 6 years before they have another major hit album).

Nov Green's solo LP *The End Of The Game* fails to chart.

1971 Feb Spencer leaves during a US tour after telling the group at its LA hotel he is "just popping out for a bit". (It is the last they see of him for 2 years. It later transpires he too has suffered the pressures that affected Green, and relinquishing his pop career, he joins the religious cult The Children of God.) Green flies to US to help the group complete the tour but returns to his self-imposed retirement at its end. (Spencer will record an LP *Jeremy Spencer And The Children Of God* in 1973 for CBS and LP *Flee* for Atlantic in 1979.)

Apr At the end of the tour, the group is in disarray having lost its two main songwriters and guitarists. Judy Wong, wife of Jethro Tull's° Glenn Cornick introduces the group to LA musician Bob Welch (b. July 31, 1946, Cal.) who replaces Spencer. They begin recording a new album of Welch, Kirwan and Christine McVie compositions.

July LP *Fleetwood Mac In Chicago*, recorded in Jan. 1969, reaches US #190.

Oct LP *Black Magic Woman* makes US #143.

Nov LP *Future Games* peaks at US #91. They continue to tour US extensively.

1972 Feb LP *Greatest Hits* reaches UK #36.

May LP *Bare Trees* makes US #70.

Aug Kirwan leaves the band. (After refusing to appear on stage he becomes the first member of the group to be fired. In the mid 70s he will record unsuccessfully for DJM before being admitted to a psychiatric hospital.) He is replaced by Long John Baldry° side-man Bob Weston, while vocalist Dave Walker also joins, recruited from Savoy Brown. The group returns to UK to record its next LP.

1973 May LP *Penguin* reaches US #49. It features a guest appearance from Green but fails to chart in UK. The Fleetwood Mac penguin association is John McVie's idea. (He is a member of The London Zoological Society and becomes a keen student of the species.)

June Reissued *Albatross* hits UK #2. Walker's departure leaves the group as a five-piece once more.

Dec LP *Mystery To Me* reaches US #67. The group begins a tour to promote the LP and Weston begins an affair with Fleetwood's wife Jenny. Romantic entanglements wreck the tour and the group pulls out of all further engagements, Weston is sacked. The group's manager Clifford Davis, angered at group's decision to cut short the tour, assembles a bogus Fleetwood Mac to fulfill the dates resulting in a bitter legal battle. (The impostors later form Stretch and have a hit with *Why Did You Do It*.)

1974 Nov LP *Heroes Are Hard To Find* reaches US #34. As legalities are resolved, the band decides to settle permanently in Cal.

1975 Jan Welch leaves. (He will form the band Paris and enjoy later solo success with LPs *French Kiss* and *Three Hearts*.) Fleetwood visits Sound City studios in Van Nuys, Cal. to preview it as a future recording venue. As a demonstration, producer Keith Olsen plays Fleetwood a track from an LP by duo Buckingham and Nicks. By chance, Lindsey Buckingham is in another part of the studio and strikes up a rapport with Fleetwood, who later meets his partner and lover Stevie Nicks. The duo is invited to join Fleetwood Mac, forming the tenth line-up since 1967. (Buckingham and Nicks were members of Bay Area group Fritz. When the group split in 1971, the duo moved to LA in 1973 and recorded eponymously titled debut LP on Polydor. It flopped, and in order to finance further songwriting efforts, Buckingham worked as a sessionman and toured with Don Everly, while Nicks worked as a waitress in Hollywood.)

Mar LP *Vintage Years*, recordings from 1967-69, reaches US #138.

Aug LP *Fleetwood Mac* enters the US chart. The songwriting talents of Christine McVie and Buckingham/Nicks begin to flower as airplay and sales increase in the next year.

Dec Reissued LP *Fleetwood Mac In Chicago* reaches US #118.

1976 Jan *Over My Head* reaches US #20.

June *Rhiannon (Will You Ever Win)*, also from the eponymous LP, peaks at US #11.

Sept *Say You Love Me* makes US #11.

Nov 15 months after the record enters the US chart, LP *Fleetwood Mac* hits #1, going platinum, and reaches UK #23, aided by a white vinyl format. *Say You Love Me* climbs to UK #40.

1977 Jan [26] Weeks before the group launches its new LP, Peter Green

attacks his accountant, who is trying to deliver a £30,000 royalty cheque, with an air rifle. Green insists that he wants no royalty and is later committed to a mental hospital. (He has been working as a gravedigger and hospital porter in recent years.)
Feb Affected by personal problems within the group (the McVies are separating, the Buckingham and Nicks relationship is unsteady and the Fleetwoods' divorce proceedings begin), LP *Rumours* is finally released. Creatively reflecting much of this turmoil, it will connect with radio and public alike, eventually topping both UK and US charts, with worldwide sales in excess of 15 million, spending more than 130 weeks on US chart and more than 400 weeks on UK chart.
Feb [28] The group begins a 7-month US tour at the University of California, Berkeley, Cal. (The tour will end at The Hollywood Bowl, LA on Oct.4.)
Mar *Go Your Own Way* hits US #10 and UK #38.
May *Don't Stop* reaches UK #32.
Aug *Dreams* tops the US chart and makes UK #24.
Sept *Don't Stop* hits US #3.
Oct *You Make Loving Fun* peaks at UK #45.
Dec *You Make Loving Fun* hits US #9.
1978 Feb [23] LP *Rumours* wins a Grammy for Album of the Year.
Mar Reissued *Rhiannon* reaches UK #46.
July [17] The group begins a summer US tour at Alpine Valley Music Theater, Troy, Wis.
1979 July Green's comeback, an instrumental LP *In The Skies*, on Creole Records, makes UK #32.
Nov *Tusk*, recorded (and filmed) with The U.S.C. Trojan Marching Band at LA's Dodger Stadium, hits US #8 and UK #6, creating a record for the number of musicians to appear on a single. The group spends $1 million on double LP *Tusk*, which tops the UK chart and hits US #4. Its main creative force is Buckingham who has resisted record company pressure to repeat the *Rumours* formula.
Nov [26] The group begins a lengthy US tour in Pontacello, Id.
1980 Jan Nicks-penned *Sara* reaches UK #37.
Feb *Sara* hits US #7.
May *Think About Me* makes US #20. Green releases LP *Little Dreamer*, on PVK Records. It peaks at UK #34 (after which Green will again fade into obscurity and live as a recluse).
June *Sisters Of The Moon* peaks at US #86.
Sept [1] The group finishes a tour at LA's Hollywood Bowl. (A long period of solo activity begins before Fleetwood Mac records together again.)
Oct [4] Buckingham, Nicks and Fleetwood present The U.S.C. Marching Band with a platinum disk for its contribution on *Tusk* at half-time during a game at Dodger Stadium.
Dec LP *Fleetwood Mac Live* reaches UK #31 and US #14.
1981 Feb *Fireflies* peaks at US #60.
July Mick Fleetwood's LP *The Visitor*, recorded at great cost in Ghana, West Africa, makes US #43. (It recoups little in sales and the losses incurred will, together with real estate ventures, contribute to Fleetwood's eventual bankruptcy.)
Aug Nicks' debut solo LP *Bella Donna* tops the US chart and makes UK #11.
Sept Nicks' *Stop Draggin' My Heart Around*, with help from Tom Petty and The Heartbreakers°, hits US #3 and UK #50.
Nov Buckingham's solo LP *Law And Order* makes US #32.
1982 Jan Buckingham's *Trouble* hits US #9 and UK #31, while Nicks' duet with The Eagles'° Don Henley, *Leather And Lace*, written for Waylon Jennings and Jessi Colter by Nicks, hits US #6.
Apr Nicks' *Edge Of Seventeen (Just Like The White Winged Dove)* climbs to US #11.
July After a 3-year studio gap, group LP *Mirage* is released. It will top the US chart and hit UK #5. Nicks' solo *After The Glitter Fades* makes US #32.
Aug Fleetwood Mac's *Hold Me* hits US #4.
Oct *Gypsy* reaches US #12 and UK #46.
1983 Jan Fleetwood Mac's *Love In Store* makes US #22.
Jan [29] Nicks marries Kim Anderson outside her LA home.
Feb UK-only release, *Oh Diane*, penned by Buckingham, hits #9.
May Nicks sings backing vocals on Robbie Patton's US #52 *Smiling Islands*.
July Nicks' solo LP *The Wild Heart* hits US #5 and UK #28.
Aug Her single from the LP, *Stand Back* hits US #5. Buckingham's solo *Holiday Road*, from the movie *National Lampoon's Vacation* peaks at US #82.
Nov Nicks' *If Anyone Falls* reaches US #14.
1984 Jan Nicks' *Nightbird* makes US #33.
Feb Christine McVie's solo LP *Christine McVie* reaches US #26.
Mar Taken from the LP, her *Got A Hold On Me* hits US #10.
May [1] Mick Fleetwood files for bankruptcy.
June *Love Will Show Us How* climbs to US #30 for Christine McVie.
Sept LP *Go Insane*, a Buckingham solo, makes US #45.
Oct *Go Insane* reaches US #23.
1985 Dec Nicks' third solo LP *Rock A Little* peaks at US #12 and UK #83.
1986 Nicks has a succession of hit singles from the LP: *Talk To Me* (US #4/UK #68), *I Can't Wait* (US #16/UK #54), *Needles And Pins* (US #37) and ballad *Has Anyone Ever Written Anything For You* (US #60).
1987 Apr The group reunites when Christine McVie, working on the soundtrack to Blake Edwards' film *A Fine Mess*, and trying to record a version of Presley's° *Can't Help Falling In Love*, enlists the help of Buckingham and John McVie. This leads to new Fleetwood Mac recordings. Having led a nomadic studio existence in the past, the new LP is overdubbed and mixed in Buckingham's own studio at his Bel Air home. LP *Tango In The Night* is released, and becomes the band's biggest seller since *Rumours*.
May *Big Love* hits US #5 and UK #9. B-side features part 1 of LP cut *You And I Part 2*. LP *Tango In The Night* hits US #7.
Aug *Seven Wonders* reaches US #19 and UK #56.
Oct *Little Lies* hits US #4 and UK #5. LP *Tango In The Night* tops the UK chart.
1988 Jan *Family Man* peaks at UK #54.
Feb *Everywhere* makes US #14 and hits US #4.
Apr *Family Man* peaks at US #90.
June *Isn't It Midnight* reaches UK #60. A press conference announces that Buckingham, particularly unhappy at the prospect of touring, is to quit the group.
Aug The group's "Shake The Cage" tour of Europe and Australia opens without Buckingham. He is replaced by Johnny Burnette's son, Billy, and Rick Vito.

EDDIE FLOYD

1956 Having moved to Detroit in his teens, Floyd (b. June 25, 1935, Montgomery, Ala., US) helps to form The Falcons.
1959 July As a member of The Falcons, Floyd's chart debut *You're So Fine* reaches US #17.
1960 Wilson Pickett° replaces Joe Stubbs as lead singer and The Falcons, originally R&B/doo-wop specialists, develops a more soulful, gospel style.
1962 May *I Found A Love* reaches US #75. After Pickett leaves and the group breaks up, Floyd settles in Washington, D.C., where he starts Safice Records with local disk jockey Al Bell and former Moonglow Chester Simmons, but the venture is not immediately successful. He also writes songs and *Comfort Me*, penned for Carla Thomas (at university in Washington), is his introduction to the Stax label.
1965 Oct After Bell moves to Memphis to become national sales director for Stax, Floyd is signed as a staff songwriter. *634-5789*, a smash for ex-colleague Pickett° (and later covered by James Brown°, Ry Cooder° and Tina Turner° among others) is his first collaboration with MG's guitarist Steve Cropper, followed by another hit for Pickett, *Ninety Nine And A Half*, and an Otis Redding° classic *Don't Mess With Cupid*.
1966 Sept Floyd's demo of his own *Knock On Wood*, originally written with Cropper for Redding°, is polished up and issued as a single. The archetypal Stax record and the acme of 60s soul, it shoots to #1 on the R&B chart, crosses to US #28 on the pop list and peaks at UK #19.
1967 Mar *Raise Your Hand*, with Floyd formally contracted as an artist too, reaches US #79 and UK #42. (It will become a Springsteen° stage staple and be included on his 1987 boxed set. Janis Joplin° and The J. Geils Band° will cut interim covers.)
Apr Floyd tours Europe with the warmly received Stax package which includes Otis Redding°, Booker T & The MG's°, Sam & Dave°, Arthur Conley and The Mar-Keys.
May LP *Knock On Wood* makes UK #36.
July *Don't Rock The Boat* is a minor US hit at #98.
Aug *Love Is A Doggone Good Thing* reaches US #97 and *Things Get Better* becomes his final UK hit at #31.
Oct *On A Saturday Night* falters at US #92.

EDDIE FLOYD *cont.*

1968 Sept *I've Never Found A Girl* makes US #40.
Dec *Bring It On Home To Me*, a Sam Cooke° song and his first non-original chart entry, peaks in Christmas week at US #17.
1969 Aug *Don't Tell Your Mama (Where You've Been)* reaches US #73.
Nov *Why Is The Wine Sweeter* makes US #98.
1970 Apr *California Girl* peaks at US #45, his last chart entry. During his recording and singing career he will continue to write songs for other Stax acts, including Sam & Dave°, Rufus Thomas and The Mad Lads.
1988 After 30 years on the road, Floyd's enduring popularity, especially in Europe, allows no question of retirement. His hobby is collecting cover versions of *Knock On Wood*, which has so far attracted over 60, by acts as diverse as David Bowie°, Cher, Count Basie, Eric Clapton° and the biggest hit version by Amii Stewart.

THE FLYING BURRITO BROTHERS

Gram Parsons (guitar and vocals)
Chris Hillman (guitar, mandolin and vocals)
Chris Ethridge (bass)
Sneaky Pete Kleinow (pedal steel)
Michael Clarke (drums)

1968 Oct Parsons (b. Cecil Connor, Nov.5, 1946, Winterhaven, Fla., US), quits The Byrds° before their South African tour because of his anti-apartheid views. They split shortly after (to be re-formed by Roger McGuinn with new players), and Parsons recruits other ex-Byrds°, Hillman and Kleinow, plus Ethridge and (temporarily) drummer Jon Corneal, to form The Flying Burrito Brothers in LA.
1969 Feb Signed to A&M Records, they record LP *The Gilded Palace Of Sin*, though Corneal leaves during sessions to join Dillard and Clark. He is replaced by Michael Clarke, another ex-Byrd° who, ironically, has just left Dillard and Clark.
May LP *The Gilded Palace Of Sin* sells disappointingly, reaching US #164. The band begins a US tour with Three Dog Night°.
Sept Ethridge leaves just before sessions commence for their next LP, *Burrito Deluxe*; Hillman switches to bass, and Bernie Leadon (also from Dillard and Clark) is added on guitar and dobro. Parsons begins to drift apart from the others (who are becoming frustrated by apparent lack of commercial progress of their country-rock style), and spends much time with old friends, the temporarily LA-domiciled Rolling Stones°.
1970 Apr Parsons leaves amongst much bad feeling after LP *Burrito Deluxe*, and Rick Roberts joins. The LP fails to chart in US or UK.
1971 June LP *Flying Burrito Brothers* returns them to US chart, but only at #176. Parsons, meanwhile, has moved to London, where for 2 years he spends much time with The Rolling Stones° and even more time drinking, but does not record or perform.
July Leadon leaves, joining with members of Linda Ronstadt's° backing group to form The Eagles°, while Kleinow returns to session work and is replaced by Al Perkins on pedal steel. Byron Berline (fiddle), Kenny Wertz (guitar) and Roger Bush (bass) all join, though the morale of remaining original members is low.
Oct After recording live LP *Last Of The Red-Hot Burritos* this line-up disintegrates; Clarke goes to Hawaii, and Hillman and Perkins leave for Stephen Stills' band, Manassas. Roberts reorganizes the band by bringing in Don Beck (pedal steel), Alan Munde (banjo and guitar) and Erik Dalton (drums), and they play a tour of Europe from which live LP *Live In Amsterdam* will eventually emerge in 1975.
1972 June LP *Last Of The Red-Hot Burritos* reaches US #171, by which time the group is no more, with Roberts staying with A&M as a soloist.
1973 Mar Returned to LA from London, Gram Parsons signs to Reprise Records and releases solo LP *GP*, which does not chart. He tours US to promote it, with a new four-man backup band plus singer Emmylou Harris, who has been discovered in Washington, D.C., by Burrito Brothers' members, Roberts and Hillman.
Sept [19] Parsons is found dead in a room at the Joshua Tree Inn, Joshua Tree, Cal. Death is ascribed to heart failure following a drug overdose. In a weird epilog, his body in its coffin is stolen by his road managers, Phil Kaufman and Michael Martin, taken out into the desert and burned. The two men are apparently carrying out Parsons' own wishes.
1974 Jan Parsons' solo LP *Grievous Angel* appears posthumously, though again does not chart.
July A&M releases Burritos' double compilation LP *Close Up The Honky Tonks*, which includes 11 previously unissued songs.
1975 Oct Original group members Chris Ethridge and Sneaky Pete Kleinow revive the Flying Burrito Brothers' name, signing to CBS/Columbia Records and releasing LP *Flying Again*, with a line-up completed by former Canned Heat° member Joel Scott Hill (bass), Floyd "Gib" Guilbeau (fiddle) and ex-Byrds° Gene Parsons (drums) – the latter unrelated to Gram Parsons. This, ironically, is their highest-placed LP on US chart, reaching #138.
1976 May Gram Parsons' retrospective LP *Sleepless Nights* includes nine previously unheard Burritos' tracks recorded in 1970, shortly before Parsons left the band.
June Second CBS/Columbia LP *Airborne* is released, minus Ethridge but with the addition of Skip Battin (bass) from The New Riders of the Purple Sage.
1979 May The band, now Kleinow, Guilbeau, Battin, Greg Harris (guitar) and Ed Ponder (drums), plays Tokyo, Japan, resulting in a live LP titled *Live In Tokyo* in US, and *Close Encounters To The West Coast* in Japan.
1981 LP *Hearts On The Line* is credited to The Burrito Brothers, "Flying" being dropped from the name. The band consists of Battin, Guilbeau and Kleinow, plus John Beland on guitar and vocals.
1982 Jan LP *Sunset Sundown* is released on Curb Records in US, featuring only Beland and Guilbeau as The Burrito Brothers.
1985 Oct A tour yields two US LPs on Relix Records, *Cabin Fever* and *Live From Europe*, both credited to The Flying Brothers. This line-up includes original member Kleinow, plus Skip Battin, Greg Harris and Jim Goodall.

DAN FOGELBERG

1971 Fogelberg (b. Aug.13, 1951, Peoria, Ill., US), a songwriter/guitarist since age 14, is studying art at the University of Illinois, Champaign, US, but drops out to work the folk circuit.
1972 He tours in US as support to Van Morrison°, before moving to LA to work as a session guitarist.
1973 Signed to CBS/Columbia, his debut LP *Home Free*, recorded in Nashville, Tenn., with producer Norbert Putnam, does not chart.
1974 He signs a management deal with Irving Azoff (whom he first met in Ill. managing R.E.O. Speedwagon°) and Azoff persuades another of his acts, Joe Walsh°, to produce Fogelberg's second LP *Souvenirs*, for which he switches to Epic label. Uneasy with LA lifestyle, he leaves, eventually settling in Boulder, Col.
1975 Feb LP *Souvenirs* reaches US #17.
Mar *Part Of The Plan* hits US #31 and he goes on a major US tour with The Eagles°. He contributes two songs, *Old Tennessee* and *Love Me Through And Through*, to his backing band Fools Gold's eponymous debut LP.
Nov Self-produced LP *Captured Angel* climbs to US #23.
1977 July LP *Nether Lands*, co-produced by Putnam, reaches US #13 and becomes his first million-seller.
1978 May Fogelberg contributes *There's A Place In The World For A Gambler* to the soundtrack LP *FM*.
Oct LP *Twin Sons Of Different Mothers*, recorded with jazz flautist Tim Weisberg, hits US #8 and is a second million-seller.
Dec From LP *Twin Sons Of Different Mothers*, *The Power Of Gold* reaches US #24.
1980 Mar His biggest US chart successes are *Longer* at US #2 and LP *Phoenix*, from which the single is taken, at US #3. Both are million-sellers. In UK, *Longer* reaches #59 and LP *Phoenix* makes #42. (They will be his only UK hits.) Fogelberg donates the royalties from *Face The Fire* to the Campaign for Economic Democracy Education Fund, which promotes the use of solar energy in favor of nuclear energy.
May *Heart Hotels* reaches US #21 and is featured on soundtrack LP *Urban Cowboy*.
1981 Feb *Same Old Lang Syne* hits US #9.
Oct LP *The Innocent Age*, a 17-part song cycle, which features his previous chart single, hits US #6 and is his fourth million-selling LP. It includes *Hard To Say*, which hits US #7.
1982 Mar *Leader Of The Band* is the third US top 10 single from *The Innocent Age*, hitting #9.
May *Run For The Roses* reaches US #18.
June [6] He appears at the anti-nuclear rally "Peace Sunday – We Have A Dream", before 85,000 people at the Rose Bowl, Pasadena, Cal., with Bob Dylan°, Jackson Browne°, Joan Baez°, Stevie Wonder° and others.

Dec Compilation LP *Dan Fogelberg/Greatest Hits* reaches US #15. *Missing You* reaches US #23.

1983 Mar *Make Love Stay* reaches US #29. Fogelberg produces the debut solo LP *Beauty Lies* for Michael Brewer (ex-Brewer and Shipley).

1984 Mar LP *Windows And Walls* peaks at US #15, while *The Language Of Love*, taken from it, makes #13.

May *Believe In Me*, also from the LP, reaches US #48.

1985 Apr *Go Down Easy* reaches US #85.

June Gaining inspiration from a visit to The Telluride Bluegrass Festival, Col. in 1983, Fogelberg records a traditional country music LP *High Country Snows*, which makes US #30.

1987 June Clean shaven for the first time since *Souvenirs*, Fogelberg returns to more familiar territory with LP *Exiles*. Recorded in LA and co-produced with Russ Kunkel, the LP reaches US #48. *She Don't Look Back* makes US #84.

WAYNE FONTANA AND THE MINDBENDERS

Wayne Fontana (vocals)
Eric Stewart (guitar)
Bob Lang (bass)
Ric Rothwell (drums)

1961 While working as an apprentice telephone engineer, Fontana (b. Glyn Ellis, Oct.28, 1940, Manchester, UK) forms The Jets, a semi-professional outfit playing the Manchester club circuit.

1963 The group gets its first break at The Oasis, with Fontana Records producer Jack Baverstock. Only Fontana and Lang (b. Jan.10, 1946) show so substitute locals, Eric Stewart (b. Jan.20, 1945, Manchester) and Ric Rothwell (b. Mar.11, 1944, Manchester) are recruited at the last minute. Despite a disastrous performance, Baverstock sees enough potential to sign them. Fontana christens his new group "The Mindbenders", taken from the title of a UK psychological horror film starring Dirk Bogarde, which is playing at his local cinema.

June The group debuts with revivals of Bo Diddley's° *Road Runner*, which fails to chart, and Fats Domino's° *Hello Josephine*.

July *Hello Josephine* charts in UK at #46.

Oct *For You, For You*, backed with current beat favorite *Love Potion No. 9*, also fails to chart.

1964 Feb *Little Darlin'* is released but does not make the chart.

June Cover of Ben E. King's *Stop Look And Listen* reaches UK #37.

Nov The group's cover version of Major Lance's US hit *Um Um Um Um Um Um*, written by Curtis Mayfield°, is its first major UK chart success, hitting #5.

1965 Feb *The Game Of Love*, Clint Ballard Jr.'s song, brings international fame. It hits UK #2 while LP *Wayne Fontana And The Mindbenders* makes UK #18.

Apr US chart debut *The Game Of Love* climbs to #1 and is a million-seller. The group visits US for promotion, but is refused performance visas by US officials concerned about the flood of UK groups entering and working where US bands might play instead. Before being allowed in, The Mindbenders has to obtain proof from *Billboard* and *Cash Box* magazines that its single is the top-selling US record and that the visit is justifiable on popularity grounds.

May US LP *The Game Of Love*, a variation on the UK release, makes US #58.

July Ballard composition *Just A Little Bit Too Late* reaches UK #20 and US #45.

Oct *She Needs Love* reaches UK #32, the last single released by Fontana with the group.

Nov Fontana and The Mindbenders split by mutual consent to pursue separate careers, a move prompted actively by Fontana. Both parties continue to record for the same label.

Dec Fontana's first solo hit *It Was Easier To Hurt Her*, a US hit for Garnett Mimms, makes UK #36.

1966 Jan LP *Eric, Rick, Wayne And Bob* recorded immediately prior to the split is released.

Mar The Mindbenders rapidly outsells its former "tambourine player" (as Fontana is referred to after the split) with *A Groovy Kind Of Love*, which hits UK #2.

May *A Groovy Kind Of Love* also hits US #2, while The Mindbenders' UK follow-up *Can't Live With You, Can't Live Without You* makes #28. Fontana's *Come On Home* also charts in UK at #16.

July LP *The Mindbenders* reaches UK #28.

Aug The Mindbenders' US LP *A Groovy Kind Of Love* peaks at US #92, while Fontana's single *Goodbye Bluebird* makes UK #49.

Sept The Mindbenders' *Ashes To Ashes* peaks at UK #14 and US #55, and is its final US hit.

Nov Fontana's *Pamela Pamela* reaches UK #11, his biggest solo hit, but also his last. (It is written by Graham Gouldman, who will later team up with Stewart in 10cc°.)

1967 Fontana releases *24 Sycamore* (Apr.), *Impossible Years* (Sept.) and *Gina* (Nov.) but none reaches the charts.

Sept The Mindbenders appears as a beat group at a school dance in UK-made Sidney Poitier film *To Sir With Love*. The group's cover of The Box Tops'° *The Letter*, far outsold by the original, is its last UK hit single, reaching only #42.

1968 Lang leaves the group and is replaced for the final weeks of the band's life by Graham Gouldman, a successful songwriter for artists including The Yardbirds°, Herman's Hermits°, Jeff Beck° and The Hollies°. Rothwell also departs and The Mindbenders finally dissolves. (Fontana will release six more singles during the next 18 months before his recording career will end. Stewart will play sessions for 2 years, before joining Lol Creme and Kevin Godley in Hotlegs, to have a hit with *Neanderthal Man* at #2 in 1970, and will re-recruit Gouldman for 10cc. Lang will drop out of music and re-emerge in Racing Cars in 1976, and quit again to run a stereo equipment business. Rothwell will establish an antique business.)

1970 Fontana gives up his singing career and works for Chappell music publishers as a resident songwriter.

1973 The "English Invasion Revival" tour of the US brings Fontana back to the live arena.

1976 Aug Fontana makes an unsuccessful comeback with *The Last Bus Home* for Polydor.

1979 A further rock'n'roll revival tour encourages Fontana to put together a new Mindbenders group to perform his old 1960s hits.

1988 Fontana continues to work live, performing much of his own material, and sees fame return when *The Game Of Love* is featured in the Robin Williams' movie *Good Morning Vietnam*.

EMILE FORD AND THE CHECKMATES

Emile Ford (vocals)
Ken Street (guitar)
Alan Hawkshaw (keyboards)
George Ford (bass)
John Cuffley (drums)

1955 Having grown up in the West Indies and intending to become a sound engineer, Ford (b. Emile Sweetman, Oct.16, 1937, St Lucia, Windward Islands) is sent to London to complete his education. He studies at Paddington Technical College and Tottenham Polytechnic but becomes increasingly distracted by the rumbling beat scene.

1959 Jan The Checkmates, formed by Ford with brother George and fellow student Ken Street, is one of the earliest self-contained groups to enter the coffee bar/club circuit.

Aug The group wins a Soho Fair talent competition, which leads to a Pye recording contract and overnight stardom. John Cuffley joins as drummer and Alan Hawkshaw will join on keyboards.

Oct The group's upbeat revival of 1916 vaudeville song *What Do You Want To Make Those Eyes At Me For?* hits UK #1 for 6 weeks and is charted for 6 months. It earns a gold disk.

1960 Feb A follow-up upbeat revival of Frank Loesser's 1948 composition *On A Slow Boat To China*, hits UK #3.

May The group turns to contemporary material and personalizes a Ricky Nelson° LP track *You'll Never Know What You're Missing* (written by Baker Knight), which peaks at UK #12.

Sept *Them There Eyes*, a 1930s jazz standard popularized by Billie Holliday, takes Ford to UK #18. Pye banishes The Checkmates from the session and uses The Johnny Keating Orchestra, which leads to tension between label and star.

Dec The group's *Counting Teardrops*, a Barry Mann/Howard Greenfield collaboration, restores them to the top five, hitting UK #4.

1961 Mar *What Am I Gonna Do?*, a minor US hit for Jimmy Clanton, written by Neil Sedaka°, reaches UK #33.

May *Half Of My Heart*, a Denmark Street confection, reaches only UK #42.

1962 Mar Reverting to well-worn oldies, Ford attempts to revitalize *I Wonder Who's Kissing Her Now*, once a Joe Loss hit, but it only makes UK #43 and is his last chart appearance.

EMILE FORD AND THE CHECKMATES *cont.*

Apr The group plays the Tower Ballroom, New Brighton, Lancashire, UK. Further down the bill is emerging Liverpool beat combo The Beatles°.

1963 Mar The Checkmates leaves Ford and releases *You've Got To Have A Gimmick Today*. (The group never finds one and splits up after three Decca and three Parlophone singles flop. George Ford will become a popular session player, recording and touring with Cockney Rebel and The Shadows°; Hawkshaw will also play with The Shadows; Cuffley will spend most of the 1970s in The Climax Blues Band; while Street will become manager of Love Affair. Emile Ford will continue to play the cabaret circuit, also working as a studio engineer and developing his ideas for audio equipment.)

1988 Heading his own electronics company, Ford patents a new design of speaker which is taken up and marketed by a major manufacturer.

FRANKIE FORD

1959 After forming his own band The Syncopators at High School in New Orleans, Ford (b. Frank Guzzo, Aug.4, 1940, Gretna, La., US), records for Johnny Vincent's Ace label, based in Jackson, Miss. Vincent has already scored major US hits with New Orleans acts, notably Huey "Piano" Smith and The Clowns.

Apr Ford reaches US #14 with *Sea Cruise*, his voice having been overdubbed on Huey Smith's backing track. (The song will become a minor rock classic, with later versions including another US chart entry by Johnny Rivers° in 1971.)

Aug *Alimony*, again recorded with Huey Smith and The Clowns, peaks at only US #97. Both this record and *Sea Cruise* have been recorded by dubbing new vocals by Ford on to existing backing tracks by The Clowns – after erasing the original vocals by the band's own singer Bobby Marchan.

1960 Feb *Time After Time* reaches #75 in US.

Oct Signing to Imperial Records, he charts in US with a cover version of fellow New Orleans artist Joe Jones' *You Talk Too Much*. But Ford's version stalls at #87, completely eclipsed by Jones' original which hits US #3.

1961 Apr His revival of the Boyd Bennett/Fontane Sisters' 1955 hit *Seventeen* reaches US #72.

1962 Ford begins a 3-year stint in US Army, which takes him to Korea, Vietnam, Guam and Thailand as part of a special entertainment unit that has him writing and directing stage shows and casting musical talent.

1966 Out of the army, he has a local New Orleans hit with *I Can't Face Tomorrow*.

1971 Jan He buys a New Orleans club which will henceforth be the base for his activities, and starts to record again, for the Paula label in Shreveport, La. (Ford will never again have a national hit, but continues regular performing on the New Orleans live circuit right through into the late 1980s, when he appears on US and UK TV in a live Mardi Gras concert transmitted from New Orleans.)

FOREIGNER

Lou Gramm (vocals)
Mick Jones (guitar)
Rick Wills (bass)
Dennis Elliot (drums)

1976 Feb The band is formed by ex-Spooky Tooth°, Jones (b. Dec.27, 1944, London, UK), after he meets ex-King Crimson° multi-instrumentalist Ian McDonald (b. June 25, 1946, London, UK) in New York at a studio session for singer Ian Lloyd. He recruits Elliott (b. Aug.18, 1950, London, UK), whom he had met at an Ian Hunter session, and three Americans: Ed Gagliardi (b. Feb.13, 1952, New York, US) on bass, Al Greenwood on keyboards, and Black Sheep singer Lou Gramm (b. May 2, 1950, Rochester, N.Y., US) on lead vocals. The bi-nationality of the personnel leads to the band's name.

1977 Feb After a year in rehearsals, during which the group signs to Atlantic, LP *Foreigner* is released. Likened to the sound of Bad Company°, it hits US #4 but does not chart in UK.

June *Feels Like The First Time*, taken from the LP, hits US #4 and reaches UK #39.

Oct *Cold As Ice* hits US #6 and UK #24.

1978 Feb *Long Long Way From Home* peaks at US #20.

Mar Foreigner plays the "California Jam II" festival in Ontario, Cal. Also on the bill are Aerosmith°, Heart° and Santana°.

Aug Second LP *Double Vision* is released and hits US #3 and makes UK #32.

Aug [27] The group plays UK's Reading Festival on the last day.

Sept *Hot Blooded*, from LP *Double Vision*, hits US #3 and is a million-seller, while making only UK #42.

Nov Title track from *Double Vision* is another million-seller, hitting US #2, but not charting in UK.

1979 Mar *Blue Morning, Blue Day* peaks at US #15 and UK #45.

Aug [27] The group headlines at Reading Festival, UK.

Aug Jones replaces Gagliardi with ex-Roxy Music° and Small Faces° bass player Rick Wills before recording LP *Head Games*.

Oct *Dirty White Boy* reaches US #12.

Dec *Head Games*, the title track from the new LP, reaches US #14.

1980 Jan LP *Head Games* makes US #11.

Mar *Women* reaches US #41.

Sept Greenwood and McDonald leave the band and it stabilizes as a four-piece.

1981 Aug After a lengthy gap, LP *4* tops the US chart. Co-produced by noted rock producer Robert "Mutt" Lange, and with keyboardist Thomas Dolby°, it hits UK #5 and spends 62 weeks on chart.

Sept *Urgent*, featuring Motown sax-man Junior Walker, makes US #4 and UK #54.

Oct *Juke Box Hero* reaches UK #48.

Nov The uncharacteristic ballad *Waiting For A Girl Like You*, written by Jones, becomes a US million-seller. It fails to make US #1, but spends an unprecedented 10 weeks at #2. It is also their first UK top 10 hit single at #8.

1982 Apr *Juke Box Hero* reaches US #26.

May *Urgent* re-charts in UK, climbing this time to #45.

June *Break It Up* makes US #26.

Aug *Luanne* reaches only US #75.

Dec Greatest hits collection *Records: The Best Of Foreigner* reaches UK #58.

1983 Feb Greatest hits collection *Records: The Best Of Foreigner* makes US #10.

1984 Dec After another gap, Foreigner returns with synthesizer-dominated sound on a new LP, *Agent Provocateur*.

1985 Jan The gospel-influenced and choir-accompanied *I Want To Know What Love Is*, created by Jones, hits #1 in both US and UK and is another million-seller. It features guest contributions from The Thompson Twins'° Tom Bailey, Jennifer Holliday and the New Jersey Mass Choir.

Feb LP *Agent Provocateur* hits US #5 and UK #1.

May *That Was Yesterday* makes US #12 and UK #28.

June A remixed version of *Cold As Ice* is released in UK and makes #64. *Reaction To Action* and *Down On Love* both reach US #54.

1987 Feb Gramm solo LP *Ready Or Not* and solo US top 10 hit *Midnight Blue* hint at the dissolution of the band or Gramm's departure.

Dec *Say You Will* from new LP *Inside Information* hits US #6 but reaches only UK #71.

1988 Feb Release of LP *Inside Information* confounds the breakup rumors. It reaches US #15 and UK #64.

May *I Don't Want to Live Without You*, from the LP, hits US #5, but makes only UK #84.

THE FORTUNES

Glen Dale (guitar and vocals)
Barry Pritchard (guitar and vocals)
David Carr (keyboards)
Rod Allen (Bainbridge) (bass and vocals)
Andy Brown (drums)

1963 Sept Originally formed as The Cliftones in Birmingham, UK, it is one of the first provincial beat groups signed to Decca Records in UK. A revival of the Jamies' *Summertime, Summertime* is issued, but is not a hit.

1964 Jan *Caroline* does not chart but becomes a familiar radio sound in UK for some years, adopted by UK pirate station Radio Caroline as its theme tune and given daily plays.

1965 Aug After two more unsuccessful singles, *You've Got Your Troubles* hits UK #2.

Oct *You've Got Your Troubles* hits US #7.

Nov *Here It Comes Again* hits UK #4.

Dec LP *The Fortunes*, containing the hits, is released but does not chart. *Here It Comes Again* reaches US #27.

1966 Mar *This Golden Ring* makes UK #15, but only US #82 even though the group has just played a US tour with Peter and Gordon° and The Moody Blues°. (It is their last hit in US or UK for more than 5 years.)

July Dale leaves to go solo, replaced by Scotsman Shel MacRae. *Is It Really Worth Your While?*, first single by the new line-up just fails to make UK chart.

1967 Aug The group moves from Decca to United Artists Records. Several UA singles between now and late 1970 all fail to sell, and the group makes considerably more money recording ad jingles (*It's The Real Thing*) for Coca Cola and playing northern UK club dates.

1968 Aug Carr leaves and the group continues as a four-piece.

1970 June A cover of Pickettywitch's (US #67) *That Same Old Feeling* is released in US on World Pacific Records in competition with the original and reaches US #62.

1971 May The Fortunes sign a new deal with Capitol Records and team with writer/producers Roger Cook and Roger Greenaway, releasing *Here Comes That Rainy Day Feeling Again*.

July *Here Comes That Rainy Day Feeling Again* fails to chart in UK, but reaches US #15.

Oct *Freedom Come Freedom Go* hits UK #6 but peaks at only US #72.

1972 Feb *Storm In A Teacup* hits UK #7, but fails to chart in US. Another Scot, George McAllister, joins to bring them up to a quintet again. (Further singles on Capitol are unsuccessful and later isolated 70s singles, on Mooncrest and Target, fare no better. The group will use its harmonic vocal strengths and back-catalog of familiar hits to continue as a supper club act in UK, without ever finding its way back into the rock/pop mainstream.)

THE FOUR SEASONS

Frankie Valli (lead vocals)
Bob Gaudio (vocals and organ)
Nick Massi (vocals and bass)
Tommy DeVito (vocals and guitar)

1953 Valli (b. Frank Castelluccio, May 3, 1937, Newark, N.J., US) cuts his first record, a version of George Jessel's *My Mother's Eyes* for Mercury Records' subsidiary Corona, via a connection made by fellow Newark Central High student Paul Kapp. It is credited to Frank Valley and The Travelers, and flops (as does follow-up *Somebody Else Took Her Home*).

1954/56 Valli joins The Variety Trio, a vocal group comprising Hank Majewski and Nick and Tommy DeVito (b. June 19, 1936, Montclair, N.J.). The group, no longer a trio, changes name to The Variatones, and works solidly on the N.J. club circuit (including the Broadway Lounge in Passaic and Newark's Silhouette Club).

1956 June Signed to RCA, The Variatones are renamed The Four Lovers and record Otis Blackwell's *(You're The) Apple Of My Eye*, which reaches US #62. Despite an appearance on US TV's "Ed Sullivan Show" and several follow-ups, The Four Lovers' career goes no further.

1959 Under the name Frank Tyler, Valli records solo *I Go Ape* (written by Bob Crewe and Frank Slay), on Okeh. It fails to sell. Gaudio (b. Nov.17, 1942, New York, N.Y., US), formerly with *Short Shorts* hitmakers The Royal Teens, joins the group in place of Nick DeVito, and the name changes again, to Frank Valle & The Romans, for *Come Si Bella* on Cindy label – again, to poor sales.

1960 Massi (b. Nicholas Macioci, Sept.19, 1935, Newark), ex-local group Hugh Garrity & The Hollywood Playboys, replaces Majewski. The group teams with independent New York producer Bob Crewe, acting as his session vocal group for 2 years on productions released under such names as The Village Voices (*Redlips*) and Billy Dixon & The Topics (*I Am All Alone*) on Crewe's Topix label.

1961 Gaudio, whose developing talent as a songwriter is giving the group a solid (if as yet hit-less) repertoire of original material, records keyboard instrumental *10 Million Tears*, as Turner Di Centri. (He plays a stand-up electronic organ with the group on stage.)

1962 Jan The group guests on back-up vocals on Danny and The Juniors'° collaboration with Freddy Cannon *Twistin' All Night Long*, which makes US #68.

Feb Crewe leases the group's recording of a Bell Sisters oldie, *Bermuda*, to George Goldner's Gone label, which releases it as by The Four Seasons (the name of a top New York restaurant opposite Goldner's office, and also – according to Gaudio – of a bowling alley at which the group almost got a lounge residency). It fails to sell.

July The group spends the summer performing at Martell's Sea Breeze in Point Pleasant Beach. Crewe and arranger Charles Calello, meanwhile, analyze all the notable gimmicks which have sparked major recent hits and decide to record a track by The Four Seasons incorporating as many as possible. Gaudio offers his recently-penned ballad *Sherry* (written in 15 minutes).

Aug Gimmick-laden *Sherry* is released, featuring the prominent piercing falsetto end of Valli's three-octave tenor voice range (the group is billed as The Four Seasons featuring the "Sound" of Frankie Valli on most of its LPs). Crewe almost puts the disk on Perry, a label in which he has an interest but then leases it to Vee Jay in Chicago when Randy Wood shows interest. The day after the group appears singing it on Dick Clark's "American Bandstand" on TV, Vee Jay gets orders for 180,000 copies.

Sept *Sherry* hits US #1 in just 4 weeks, and stays at the top for 5. It sells two million copies in US and tops the R&B chart for a week.

Nov *Big Girls Don't Cry*, a similar commercial blend jointly penned by Crewe and Gaudio, also tops the US chart for 5 weeks (and the R&B chart for 4), and is a second million-plus seller. *Sherry*, meanwhile, hits UK #8.

Dec [9] The group appears on US TV's "Ed Sullivan Show".

Dec Debut LP *Sherry And 11 Others*, including the two #1 singles, plus an update of The Four Lovers' *Apple Of My Eyes*, several oldies like *Peanuts*, *La Dee Dah*, *Teardrops* and *Oh Carol*, hits US #6. Seasonal LP (of carols and secular Christmas songs) *The Four Seasons Greetings* is also released, and extracted from it, a *Sherry*-styled revival of *Santa Claus Is Coming To Town*, reaches US #23.

1963 Feb *Big Girls Don't Cry* makes UK #13.

Mar Hymnal *Walk Like A Man* tops the US chart for 3 weeks, the group's third million-seller. (When this completes its #1 run, The Four Seasons have been at #1 on the US chart for 13 of the preceding 27 weeks.)

Mar [2] The group guests in Chubby Checker's° "Limbo Party" spectacular at the Cow Palace, San Francisco, along with Marvin Gaye°, The Crystals° and others.

Apr *Walk Like A Man* reaches UK #12, while LP *Big Girls Don't Cry And Twelve Others*, a collection mainly of vocal group oldies like *Sincerely*, *Silhouettes* and *Goodnight My Love*, hits US #8.

May A revival of Fats Domino's° *Ain't That A Shame* peaks at US #22. A lot of airplay is stolen by its Crewe/Gaudio-penned ballad B-side, *Soon (I'll Be Home Again)*, which reaches US #77.

July *Ain't That A Shame* makes UK #38, while LP *Sherry And 11 Others* reaches UK #20.

Aug LP *Ain't That A Shame And 11 Others*, a mixture of new songs and more vocal group revivals, reaches US #47. Taken from it, *Candy Girl*, written by Larry Santos, hits US #3, while B-side, Gaudio's *Sherry*-like *Marlena*, reaches US #36.

Oct Compilation LP *Golden Hits Of The Four Seasons* climbs to US #15. Taken from the previous LP, Latin-styled Gaudio/Calello song *New Mexican Rose* makes US #36 and B-side *That's The Only Way* reaches US #88.

Dec Crewe and the group are at loggerheads with Vee Jay, mainly over alleged non-payment of royalties. (The label is a victim of its successful marketing of the group, selling millions of records with the costs this incurs, and then suffering cashflow problems while having to wait months for distributors' payments.) The group threatens to withhold future products.

1964 Feb Crewe and the group sign a new deal with another Chicago-based label, Mercury, for release on its Philips subsidiary. *Dawn (Go Away)*, written by Gaudio with Sandy Linzer, hits US #3 (kept from the top by The Beatles'° *I Want To Hold Your Hand* and *She Loves You*), and is another million-seller.

Mar LP *Born To Wander*, the group's first on Philips, follows the current US folk "hootenanny" craze by being a collection of quieter, mainly folk-influenced harmonic songs (mostly Gaudio originals), but reaches only US #84. (It includes West Coast-styled death ballad *No Surfin' Today*, which moves them into the territory of their chief US competitors The Beach Boys°, and Crewe/Gaudio's *Silence Is Golden*, later a worldwide hit for The Tremeloes.)

Apr Vee Jay, retaining the rights to earlier group recordings, issues a revival of Maurice Williams & The Zodiacs' *Stay* (from LP *Ain't That A Shame*, and also a current UK hit for The Hollies°), which reaches US #16. The Four Seasons' current and former labels match each other with single and LP releases. LP *Dawn (Go Away) And 11 Other Great Songs* hits US #25.

May *Ronnie*, a new Crewe/Gaudio song, hits US #6.

June LP *Stay And Other Great Hits*, a compilation of earlier tracks on Vee Jay, reaches US #100.

July *Rag Doll*, recorded in a rush Sunday session in a Broadway basement studio, the day before the group goes on a US tour, tops the US chart for 2 weeks and is another million-seller. Meanwhile, on Vee Jay, a revival of The Shepherd Sisters' oldie *Alone* (taken from LP *Big Girls Don't Cry*) reaches US #28.

Sept *Rag Doll* hits UK #2. In US, LP *Rag Doll* hits #7 and Vee Jay compilation LP *More Golden Hits By The Four Seasons* makes #105.

Sept [5] It is reported that President Lyndon Johnson has invited the group to perform at the upcoming Democratic Party national convention.

Oct *Save It For Me*, a Crewe/Gaudio song from LP *Rag Doll* hits US #10, while *Sincerely*, another Vee Jay reissue, reaches US #75. Also on Vee Jay, double LP *The Beatles Vs. The Four Seasons*, which repackages LPs *Introducing The Beatles* and *Golden Hits Of The 4 Seasons*, reaches US #142.

Nov *Big Man In Town* reaches US #20.

1965 Feb *Bye Bye Baby (Baby Goodbye)* reaches US #12 (it will be a UK #1 in 1975 for The Bay City Rollers°).

Apr *Toy Soldier* peaks at US #64. This is the fourth Four Seasons single in a row not to be a hit in UK, despite the success of *Rag Doll*.

May LP *The 4 Seasons Entertain You*, including the recent hits, makes US #77. Massi leaves the group and is replaced temporarily by the group's arranger Charlie Calello, before Joe Long (b. Sept.5, 1941) joins.

Aug *Girl Come Running* reaches US #30.

Dec An adaptation of the group's sound to incorporate a brassy, Motown-like dance beat on the ultra-commercial Sandy Linzer/Denny Randell/Crewe song *Let's Hang On* hits US #3 and is the group's first million-seller since *Rag Doll*. A novelty falsetto version of Bob Dylan's° *Don't Think Twice, It's Alright*, credited to The Wonder Who, reaches US #12. It soon transpires that this is The Four Seasons under a pseudonym. (Valli clowned with a "Rose Murphy" voice during recordings of some Dylan songs for LP use, with a result so outrageous and commercial it was felt worthy of release – though not at the expense of *Let's Hang On*, hence the pseudonym.)

1966 Jan *Let's Hang On* hits UK #4. In US, *Little Boy (In Grown Up Clothes)* reaches #60.This unheard track is on Vee Jay, along with LP *On Stage With The Four Seasons* (which does not chart) as part of the legal settlement between Crewe and the group and Vee Jay, which has concluded that the former were free to continue releasing records on Philips, but owed Vee Jay an LP in lieu. (Vee Jay will be bankrupt within months and all recorded masters will revert to producer and group.) Philips' first compilation LP, *The Four Seasons' Gold Vault Of Hits* hits US #10 and earns a gold disk. LP *Big Hits By Burt Bacharach, Hal David And Bob Dylan*, a set of mainly straight covers of familiar songs plus The Wonder Who hit *Don't Think Twice*, reaches US #106.

Feb Valli's first solo *(You're Gonna) Hurt Yourself* reaches US #39. When this charts, the group has three simultaneous hits on the US singles chart under three different names.

Mar *Working My Way Back To You* (later revived by The Spinners°) hits US #9 and makes UK #50, while LP of the same title reaches US #50.

June Classical adaptation *Opus 17 (Don't You Worry 'Bout Me)* reaches US #13 and UK #20.

July The Wonder Who's double A-side gimmick, *On The Good Ship Lollipop* and *You're Nobody Till Someobdy Loves You*, makes US #87 and #96 respectively.

Oct A new arrangement of Cole Porter standard *I've Got You Under My Skin* with an inventive use of strings, hits US #9 and reaches UK #12.

Nov Valli's second solo *The Proud One* (later revived by The Osmonds°) reaches US #68.

1967 Jan Crewe and The Four Seasons acquire the early tracks from Vee Jay, and they are repackaged into compilation LPs *2nd Vault Of Golden Hits* (which also features the recent Philips successes) and *Lookin' Back* which reach US #22 and #107 respectively.

Feb *Tell It To The Rain*, by new Petrillo/Cifelli writing team, hits US #10 and peaks at UK #37.

May *Beggin'* reaches US #16. It fails to chart in UK (but will later be a minor UK hit for Timebox).

July Compilation LP *New Gold Hits* reaches US #37. Included on it is *C'mon Marianne* which hits US #9 (later revived by Donny Osmond°). The Wonder Who's *Lonesome Road* (also on the LP) reaches US #89. In another triple chart representation, Valli has his biggest solo hit, a million-seller with *Can't Take My Eyes Off You*, which hits US #2. (Andy Williams' cover will take UK honors.)

Sept Valli's *I Make A Fool Of Myself* reaches US #18.

Nov Mildly psychedelic *Watch The Flowers Grow* reaches US #30.

1968 Feb Valli's *To Give (The Reason I Live)* makes US #29.

Mar A revival of The Shirelles'° *Will You Love Me Tomorrow* reaches US #24.

1969 Jan After a lengthy period with no Four Seasons disks on the US chart (their *Saturday's Father* in mid-1968 having flopped), *Electric Stories* reaches US #61.

Feb Double compilation LP *Edizione D'Oro (The Four Seasons Gold Edition – 29 Gold Hits)* reaches US #37 and earns a gold disk.

Mar The group's concept LP *The Genuine Imitation Life Gazette*, a lyrically serious work on sociological themes, climbs to US #85. Both sides of the single from it, *Something's On Her Mind/Idaho* chart briefly at US #98 and #95 respectively. Gaudio pacts with CBS/Columbia Records for his own Gazette label. Its first release is Lock Stock & Barrel's *Happy People*.

July Valli's *The Girl I'll Never Know (Angels Never Fly This Low)* makes US #52.

Oct The group's *And That Reminds Me (My Heart Reminds Me)*, a revival of an old Della Reese number, is released on Crewe label while contract renegotiations are proceeding with Philips. It reaches US #45.

1970 Apr Gaudio and Jake Holmes (who co-operated on *Imitation Life*) write and produce concept LP *Watertown* for Frank Sinatra.

May *Patch Of Blue* peaks at US #94. It is the first chart single to bear the credit Frankie Valli & The Four Seasons (and will be their last to make the US chart for 5 years).

June LP *Half And Half*, ten tracks split evenly between Valli solos and The Four Seasons songs, reaches US #190. (It marks the end of the group's period with Philips.)

1971 Jan DeVito retires because of hearing difficulties. His temporary replacement is Bob Grimm and drummer Gary Wolfe also joins. (The group has never until now used a full-time drummer on stage.) The new line-up begins the group's first UK tour for 7 years.

Feb *You're Ready Now*, a 1966 track by Valli which failed, is reissued in UK after Northern dancefloor success and reaches #11.

Apr Double compilation LP *Edizione D'Oro* reaches UK #11.

Sept *Whatever You Say*, a Gaudio song recorded in London in a one-off deal with UK Warner Bros., is released in a very limited UK pressing and flops.

Nov UK compilation LP *The Big Ones* reaches UK #37. Grimm and Wolfe leave and are replaced by bassist/vocalist Demetri Callas and Paul Wilson. Keyboards player Al Ruzicka also joins.

1972 Jan The Four Seasons sign to Motown Records subsidiary Mowest, but only LP *Chameleon* and a few singles are released, none of which charts. Gaudio gives up performing to concentrate on writing and production; he is first replaced by Clay Jordan, a Motown session man, and then by Billy De Loash.

1973 Moving to Motown, The Four Seasons release two movie singles: *How Come* (from *Tom Sawyer*) and *Scalawag Song* (from *Scalawag*). The Motown deal ends with no chart success.

1975 Mar Valli and Gaudio lease Valli's solo of Bob Crewe/Kenny Nolan-penned ballad *My Eyes Adore You*, which was recorded for Motown but since bought from the label, to Private Stock Records. It tops the US chart for a week, becoming a million-seller, and hits UK #5.

May Motown in UK reissues *The Night*, which was unsuccessful in 1982, but has since become in demand in discos. It hits UK #7. Valli's disco-flavored *Swearin' To God* hits US #6. Gaudio recruits a new Four Seasons around Valli: John Paiva (guitar), Lee Shapiro (keyboards), ex-Critters lead singer Don Ciccone (bass) and Gerry Polci (drums and vocals), and starts writing new material with girlfriend Judy Parker. He secures a deal with Warner-Curb Records.

Oct *Who Loves You* hits UK #6.

Nov *Who Loves You* hits US #3. Valli's revival of Ruby & The Romantics' *Our Day Will Come*, produced by Hank Medress and Dave Appell, makes US #11.

Dec LP *Who Loves You* reaches US #38.

1976 Jan Double LP *The Four Seasons Story*, a best-of compilation on Private Stock, reaches US #51.

Feb From LP *Who Loves You*, Gaudio and Parker's *December '63 (Oh, What A Night)*, (a song originally written about prohibition, as *December '33*), featuring shared lead vocals from Valli and Polci, tops the UK chart for 2 weeks.

Mar *December '63 (Oh, What A Night)* tops the US chart for 3 weeks and. after many years, is another million-seller for the group. LP *Who Loves You* reaches UK #12, while double compilation LP *The Four Seasons Story*, on Private Stock, reaches UK #20.

May Gerry Polci-sung *Silver Star* hits UK #3 and US #38, while Valli's *Fallen Angel* reaches US #36 and UK #ll.

Aug Valli's *We're All Alone* (written by Boz Scaggs°) peaks at US #78.

Nov UK TV-advertised compilation LP *Greatest Hits*, on K-Tel, hits UK #4.

Dec *We Can Work It Out*, from Lou Reizner's *All This And World War II* record and film documentary, makes UK #34.

1977 May LP *Helicon* reaches US #168.

June *Rhapsody* makes UK #37.

Aug *Down The Hall* peaks at US #65 and UK #34.

Sept Valli announces he is leaving The Four Seasons to pursue a wholly MOR oriented career. (During their years together, The Four Seasons have sold more than 85 million records and had more chart disks than any other US group.)

1978 Aug Valli tops the US chart for 2 weeks with Barry Gibb's title song from movie *Grease*. It is his all-time biggest solo, earning a platinum disk for two million US sales and hits UK #3.

1979 Feb Valli's *Fancy Dancer*, produced by Gaudio, reaches US #77.

1980 Valli has three ear operations to cure a problem brought on by otosclerosis, a rare disease which had rendered him deaf.

Aug Valli's *Where Did We Do Wrong*, a duet with Chris Forde, stalls at US #90.

Dec The Four Seasons' *Spend The Night In Love* makes US #91.

1984 Valli and The Four Seasons team with Californian Beach Boys° on the appropriately titled single *East Meets West* for FBI Records.

1985 Sept Valli and The Four Seasons are reunited on Curb/MCA LP *Streetfighter*, which involves many old collaborators including Calello, Linzer and Gaudio (who produces).

1988 Oct After a successful summer US tour, Valli and The Four Seasons return to the UK charts with a Ben Leibrand re-mix of *December '63 (Oh, What A Night)* and *Big Girls Don't Cry* featured on the soundtrack of *Dirty Dancing II*.

THE FOUR TOPS

Levi Stubbs (lead vocals)
Renaldo "Obie" Benson (vocals)
Abdul "Duke" Fakir (vocals)
Lawrence Payton (vocals)

1953 Benson, Fakir, Payton and Stubbles (later Stubbs) are asked to sing together at a friend's birthday party in Detroit, Mich., US. The combination works so well that they meet to repeat it at Fakir's house the next day and form The Four Aims. They begin singing at high school graduation parties, church and school functions, and local one-nighters.

1954/55 After several auditions they are accepted by a talent agency which books them first into small clubs in Detroit, then further afield, beginning with a week at the Ebony Lounge, Cleveland, Oh., which earns $300.

1956 As The Four Aims, the group sings back-up or opens for such acts as Brook Benton°, Count Basie, Della Reese and Billy Eckstine. The name is changed to The Four Tops (at the suggestion of their musical conductor) to avoid confusion with The Ames Brothers. Stubbles has also shortened his name to Stubbs.

May They record *Kiss Me Baby/Could It Be You*, for Chess in Chicago, but it fails to attract attention so they decide to concentrate on their club act, polishing dance routines and vocal arrangements.

1958/59 They tour throughout US with the Larry Stelle Revue. Another one-off record for the Red Top label also fails.

1960 Sept Signed by John Hammond to Columbia, the group stays only long enough to release *Ain't That Love*, another poor seller.

1962 The group tours with Billy Eckstine's revue, frequently working in Las Vegas. They release a version of the standard *Where Are You?*, which is also a current hit for Dinah Washington, on Riverside label.

1963 Mar The group meets Berry Gordy Jnr., head of fast-growing Motown Records in Detroit, and signs to his label for an advance of $400. The first recordings are jazz-oriented and Gordy plans to put the group on the specialist Workshop label. They spend the rest of the year singing back-up on other Motown artists' records, including The Supremes'° first top 30 hit *When The Lovelight Starts Shining Through His Eyes*.

1964 The Four Tops are singing at Detroit's 20 Grand club when Motown producers Holland, Dozier and Holland, call them to the studio after their performance. Eddie Holland sings them a song he thinks will suit them, and through the small hours the group records *Baby I Need Your Loving*.

Oct *Baby I Need Your Loving* hits US #11. (Mersey group The Fourmost° make UK #24 with their cover.)

Dec *Without The One You Love* peaks at US #43.

1965 Feb Ballad *Ask The Lonely* reaches US #24.

Apr Debut LP *Four Tops* climbs to #63.

June Holland-Dozier-Holland's *I Can't Help Myself* tops the US chart for 2 weeks, and the R&B chart for 9 (deposing on both another Motown/H-D-H production, The Supremes'° *Back In My Arms Again*) and is the group's first million-seller.

July *I Can't Help Myself* is the first UK Four Tops hit (reaching #23), and the group begins a sold-out club tour of UK and Europe, with the UK leg arranged by The Beatles° manager, Brian Epstein.

Aug Speedy Motown follow-up *It's The Same Old Song* is recorded on a Thursday, in shops by the next Monday, and hits US #5. Columbia reissues *Ain't The Love*, which peaks at US #93.

Sept *It's The Same Old Song* reaches UK #34.

Dec LP *The Four Tops' Second Album* climbs to US #20, while *Something About You* reaches US #19.

1966 Apr *Shake Me, Wake Me (When It's Over)* makes US #18.

June Slower-paced *Loving You Is Sweeter Than Ever* peaks at US #45.

Sept LP *Four Tops On Top* reaches US #32, while in UK *Loving You Is Sweeter Than Ever* makes #21.

Oct Revolutionary *Reach Out I'll Be There*, with an unorthodox instrumental blend of flutes, oboes and arab drums, tops the US chart for 2 weeks and is the group's second million-seller. Within 2 weeks, it is also at UK #1 (for 3 weeks) and seals the group's worldwide success.

Dec LP *Four Tops On Top* is the group's first UK LP success, hitting #9.

1967 Jan Live LP *Four Tops Live!*, recorded at The Roostertail in Detroit, and containing versions of songs like *If I Had A Hammer* and *Climb Every Mountain*, displays the group's more MOR side. It reaches US #17, while *Standing In The Shadows Of Love*, a highly-commercial near-clone of *Reach Out*, hits #6 in both US and UK.

Mar The live LP hits UK #4 (and will be an consistent seller, remaining on chart for 72 weeks).

Apr *Bernadette* hits US #4 and UK #8, becoming another million-seller.

May Another cabaret-styled LP, *Four Tops On Broadway*, containing mainly show tunes, reaches US #79.

THE FOUR TOPS *cont.*

June *Seven Rooms Of Gloom* reaches US #14 and UK #12, while B-side *I'll Turn To Stone* makes US #76.
Sept LP *Four Tops Reach Out* makes US #11.
Oct *You Keep Running Away* reaches US #19 and UK #26. (Holland, Dozier, and Holland leave Motown over royalty disputes and the group will have other Motown house producers like Frank Wilson, Smokey Robinson°, Ivy Hunter and Johnny Bristol.)
Nov LP *The Four Tops Greatest Hits*, a compilation of singles, hits US #4.
1968 Jan A revival of The Left Banke's° 1966 hit *Walk Away Renée*, taken from LP *The Four Tops Reach Out*, hits UK #3. The LP hits UK #4.
Feb Compilation LP *Greatest Hits* tops the UK chart for a week. The Tops are the first black act to achieve this distinction (stablemates The Supremes'° repeat it a week later).
Mar Following its UK success, *Walk Away Renée* is extracted as a US single and reaches #14.
Apr Another LP extract, the group's version of Tim Hardin's *If I Were A Carpenter* (a 1966 hit for Bobby Darin°), hits UK #7.
June *If I Were A Carpenter* makes US #20.
Sept *Yesterday's Dreams* climbs to US #49 and UK #23.
Oct LP *Yesterday's Dreams* reaches US #93, while *I'm In A Different World* (a belatedly-released Holland-Dozier-Holland song/production) makes US #51.
Dec *I'm In A Different World* climbs to UK #27.
1969 Feb LP *Yesterday's Dreams* reaches UK #37.
June *What Is A Man* makes US #53 and UK #16.
July LP *Four Tops Now!* climbs to US #74.
Oct Jim Webb-penned *Do What You Gotta Do* reaches UK #11.
Dec *Don't Let Him Take Your Love From Me* makes US #54, while LP *Soul Spin* reaches US #163.
1970 Apr *I Can't Help Myself* is reissued in UK and hits #10.
June A revival of much-recorded *It's All In The Game* makes US #24 and hits UK #5. LP *Still Waters Run Deep* reaches US #21 and UK #29.
Oct Taken from the LP, mellow-grooving *Still Water (Love)*, produced by Frank Wilson, reaches US #11 and hits UK #10.
Nov LP *Changing Times* makes US #109. The Four Tops team with The Supremes° for LP *The Magnificent 7*, which makes US #113.
1971 Jan The Four Tops and The Supremes'° duetted version of *River Deep, Mountain High* peaks at US #14.
Feb *Just Seven Numbers (Can Straighten Out My Life)* makes US #40.
Apr Benson's collaboration with Al Cleveland and Marvin Gaye°, *What's Going On*, hits US #2.
May *Just Seven Numbers* climbs to UK #36.
June Another teaming with The Supremes on *You Gotta Have Love In Your Heart* makes US #55. *River Deep, Mountain High* reaches UK #11.
July *In These Changing Times* peaks at US #70, and a further collaboration with The Supremes° on LP *The Return Of The Magnificent Seven* reaches US #154.
Oct The group's revival of Webb's *MacArthur Park* makes US #38.
Nov The Four Tops record a dynamic version of a Moody Blues' B-side *A Simple Game*, with The Moody Blues'° producer Tony Clarke, who interested the group in the song when he gave them a demo during a UK tour. Among the backing musicians on the track (and another Moody Blues song *So Deep Within You* cut at the same time), are uncredited Moody Blues members. It is the biggest UK Four Tops hit (at #3) since *Walk Away Renée*. Compilation LP *Greatest Hits Vol. 2* reaches US #106 and UK #25. From it, the duet with The Supremes°, *You Gotta Have Love In Your Heart*, reaches US #25.
1972 Jan The third Four Tops/Supremes° collaboration LP, *Dynamite*, climbs to US #160.
Feb *A Simple Game* makes only US #90.
Apr UK reissue, *Bernadette* reaches #23.
June LP *Nature Planned* makes US #50. Gordy moves Motown's base from Detroit to Hollywood. The Four Tops decide not to move with the company. They are negotiating with Dunhill when the label's writer/producers Dennis Lambert and Brian Potter walk in with demos of two songs they composed with The Four Tops in mind, *Keeper Of The Castle* and *Ain't No Woman*. The quality of these prompts the group to sign to Dunhill.
July *In These Changing Times* peaks at US #70.
Aug *Walk With Me Talk With Me Darling* makes UK #32.
Oct *(It's The Way) Nature Planned It* reaches US #53.
Dec Debut Dunhill label LP *Keeper Of The Castle* climbs to US #33.
1973 Jan *Keeper Of The Castle*, the group's first single for Dunhill, hits US #10 and UK #18 (on Probe).
Apr *Ain't No Woman (Like The One I've Got)* hits US #4 and earns a gold disk for millon-plus sales.
May Motown LP *The Best Of The Four Tops* peaks at US #103.
Aug *Are You Man Enough*, taken from the soundtrack of film *Shaft in Africa*, hits US #15.
Oct Second Dunhill LP *Main Street People* makes US #66.
Nov *Sweet Understanding Love* peaks at US #33 and UK #29. Motown's UK double compilation LP *The Four Tops Story, 1964-72*, makes UK #35 (the last UK chart entry in the 70s).
1974 Feb *I Just Can't Get You Out Of My Mind* reaches US #62.
May LP *Meeting Of The Minds* peaks at US #118.
June *One Chain Don't Make No Prison* reaches US #41.
Sept *Midnight Flower* climbs to US #55.
Nov Live LP *Live And In Concert* peaks at US #92.
1975 May *Seven Lonely Nights*, the first release on ABC (which absorbed its Dunhill subsidiary) peaks at US #71.
June LP *Night Lights Harmony* peaks at US #148.
Dec *We All Gotta Stick Together* charts at US #97 for 1 week.
1976 Nov *Catfish* peaks at US #71 (the group's last hit with ABC/Dunhill). The LP of same title reaches US #124.
1978 Apr The Four Tops perform Stevie Wonder's° *Isn't She Lovely* at Aretha Franklin's° wedding.
1981 Nov The group stages a comeback on its new label, disco-oriented Casablanca Records. First single for the label, *When She Was My Girl*, peaks at US #11 and hits UK #3.
Dec LP *Tonight!*, on Casablanca, reaches US #37.
1982 Jan *Don't Walk Away*, taken from the LP, makes UK #16 but fails in US.
Mar UK TV-advertised K-tel compilation LP *The Best Of The Four Tops* climbs to UK #13. *Tonight I'm Gonna Love You All Over*, third single from LP *Tonight!*, reaches UK #43.
June *Back To School Again*, from the soundtrack of movie *Grease 2*, makes US #71 and UK #62.
Aug LP *One More Mountain*, on Casablanca, is released to coincide with the group's first UK tour for some time but fails and the group leaves the label.
Sept *Sad Hearts*, the final release on Casablanca, peaks at US #84.
1983 The Four Tops return to Motown for the company's 25th Anniversary NBC TV special, re-signing with Berry Gordy shortly after. The "Battle of the Bands" with The Temptations° during the special leads the two groups to tour together, initially in US and then internationally.
Nov *I Just Can't Walk Away*, on Motown, reaches US #71. (It will be the group's final US chart single.) LP *Back Where I Belong* is not a strong seller.
1985 July LP *Magic*, on Motown, reaches US #140.
1986 Stubbs provides the voice for the man-eating plant Audrey II in the film version of musical *The Little Shop of Horrors*.
July Stubbs is immortalized by UK singer Billy Bragg° in *Levi Stubbs' Tears*, which makes UK #29.
Oct LP *Hot Nights* is the group's last of its second spell with Motown.
1987 July [29] Michigan State Governor, James Blanchard, declares an annual state-wide "Four Tops Day", honoring the group for its contribution to American music and its civic activities in Detroit.
1988 Sept The Four Tops sign to Arista Records, releasing LP *Indestructible* which makes US #149. It includes contributions from Phil Collins°, Aretha Franklin°, Kenny G, Huey Lewis° and Narada Michael Walden. Title track *Indestructible* makes US #35 and UK #55. The band contributes *Going Loco In Acapulco* to the soundtrack of Phil Collins° movie *Buster*.

THE FOURMOST

Brian O'Hara (guitar and vocals)
Mike Millward (guitar and vocals)
Billy Hatton (bass)
Dave Lovelady (drums)

1958/60 O'Hara (b. Mar.12, 1942, Liverpool, UK) and Hatton (b. June 9, 1941, Liverpool) are in a group with two friends while still at Bluecoat Grammar School, Liverpool. For 3 years, the quartet plays gigs on a part-time basis around Liverpool, as The Four Jays.
1961 Mar [1] The Four Jays, still an amateur group, make their debut at Liverpool's Cavern club, 20 days before The Beatles'° first

performance there.
Nov Millward (b. May 9, 1942, Bromborough, Cheshire, UK), an old friend of O'Hara and Hatton, moves to Liverpool to join the group when a guitar slot falls vacant.
1962 Sept Lovelady (b. Oct.16, 1942, Liverpool) replaces an earlier drummer, joining from another semi-professional band in Crosby, Liverpool. All four still have day jobs: accountant's clerk (O'Hara), solicitor's clerk (Millward), apprentice engineer (Hatton) and student architect (Lovelady).
Nov Deciding to turn professional, and now with a stable line-up, the group changes its name to The Four Mosts.
1963 June Brian Epstein takes over the band's management, amends the name to The Fourmost, and signs it to EMI's Parlophone label.
July [3] Debut single *Hello Little Girl* is recorded at Abbey Road studios. It is an early Lennon°/McCartney° song which The Beatles° have chosen not to record commercially. As in his launch of Billy J. Kramer°, Epstein encourages full exploitation of this Beatles connection.
Oct *Hello Little Girl* hits UK #9.
Dec [24] The group begins a short season supporting The Beatles° at their Christmas show at Finsbury Park Astoria, London.
1964 Feb A second Lennon°/McCartney° song, the soft-rock ballad *I'm In Love*, reaches UK #17.
Apr The group plays the *New Musical Express* Poll Winners Concert at Wembley, UK, with The Beatles°, The Hollies°, The Rolling Stones° and others.
May The group starts an 8-month residency, with stablemate Cilla Black°, in the "Startime" variety show at the London Palladium. *A Little Loving*, written by Russ Alquist, hits UK #6.
Aug *How Can I Tell Her*, an upbeat Carter/Lewis song in unusual march time, reaches UK #33.
1965 Jan *Baby I Need Your Lovin'*, a cover of The Four Tops'° first US hit, climbs to UK #24 (causing some dissension between US Motown and EMI, since it inadvertantly breaks an agreement that EMI, as UK Motown distributor, will not release cover versions of the latter's singles). The group makes a cameo appearance in Gerry & The Pacemakers'° film *Ferry Cross The Mersey*, performing *I Love You Too*.
Apr The Fourmost tours UK with Cilla Black° and P.J. Proby°.
July *Everything In The Garden* fails to chart as the commercial appeal of the Merseybeat sound rapidly fades.
Sept The group's only LP, *First And Fourmost*, with 14 tracks which are mostly covers of US rock and pop originals, fails to chart.
Dec *Girls Girls Girls*, a Leiber/Stoller song previously recorded by The Coasters° and Elvis Presley°, reaches UK #33 and is the group's final chart success.
1966 Millward falls ill and is replaced by Bill Parkinson when it becomes clear he is no longer fit to play gigs. (Millward has developed leukemia and dies later in the year.)
Aug *Here, There And Everywhere*, a cover of The Beatles'° LP *Revolver* song, does not chart.
Nov The group's last Parlophone single is a revival of George Formby's *Auntie Maggie's Remedy*, which fails to chart.
1967 July A cover of Jay & The Techniques' US hit *Apples, Peaches, Pumpkin Pie* on CBS Records fails. (Two further CBS singles, including *Rosetta*, produced by Paul McCartney°, will also fail. The group will move into musical/comedy cabaret in UK Northern clubs during the remainder of the 1960s, before eventually splitting.)

PETER FRAMPTON

1972 May Ex-Herd and Humble Pie° guitarist Frampton (b. Apr.22, 1950, Beckenham, UK), after leaving latter group in Oct. 1971, signs to A&M Records as a soloist and releases LP *Wind Of Change*, which features Ringo Starr°, Billy Preston and other star session men.
Sept [16] First stage performance in New York, supporting The J. Geils Band°, with his own new band, Frampton's Camel: Mike Kellie (ex-Spooky Tooth°) on drums, Mickey Gallagher (ex-Bell & Arc) on keyboards and Rick Wills (ex-Cochise) on bass, all three having just left Parrish & Gurvitz.
Oct LP *Wind Of Change* reaches US #177.
1973 May LP *Frampton's Camel* sees Kellie replaced by US drummer John Siomos, formerly with Mitch Ryder°. The LP does not chart in UK, and reaches only #110 in US.
1974 June After another UK non-chart LP, but US #25, *Somethin's Happening* (on which the "Camel" appendix is dropped), Gallagher leaves to join Glencoe and is replaced by former Herd member Andy Bown, who also doubles on bass when Wills leaves to play with Roxy Music°.
1975 May LP *Frampton*, recorded with Siomos and Bown, sells well in US, reaching #32.
1976 Apr LP *Frampton Comes Alive!*, a double set recorded on stage at Winterland, San Francisco, is released. With blanket US rock radio support it will become the most successful live LP in rock history, eventually selling 10 million copies. It tops US chart for a week. It will return to US #1 in July (1 week), Aug. (3 weeks) and Sept./Oct. (5 weeks).
May *Show Me The Way*, taken from the LP, hits US #6. It features a Frampton trademark sound: the "voicebox" guitar technique of forming words by channelling the sound through a mouthpiece.
June *Show Me The Way* hits UK #10, with LP *Frampton Comes Alive!* hitting UK #6.
Aug *Baby, I Love Your Way*, also from the live LP, reaches US #12.
Sept *Baby, I Love Your Way* makes only #43 in UK.
Nov *Do You Feel Like We Do* hits US #10 and UK #39.
1977 July A new studio recording, *I'm In You* is Frampton's biggest US hit single, spending 3 weeks at #2, though in UK it climbs only to #41 and is his final chart single. LP *I'm In You* also hits US #2, and reaches UK #19.
Oct A revival of Stevie Wonder's° *Signed, Sealed, Delivered (I'm Yours)*, with Wonder guesting on harmonica, reaches US #18.
1978 Jan *Tried To Love* reaches US #41.
June [29] Frampton suffers a broken arm and cracked ribs in a car crash in the Bahamas, which will put him out of action for months.
July Robert Stigwood's film *Sergeant Pepper's Lonely Hearts Club Band* is released, co-starring Frampton (as Billy Shears) and the Bee Gees°. The film is a failure both critically and commercially.
Aug Soundtrack LP from *Sergeant Pepper's Lonely Hearts Club Band* hits US #5 and UK #38.
1979 July LP *Where I Should Be* climbs to US #19. *I Can't Stand It No More*, from the LP, makes US #14, and is Frampton's last US hit single.
1981 July The sleeve of LP *Breaking All The Rules* features new short-haired image, which fails to help him regain former glory, as the LP reaches US #47.
1982 Sept LP *The Art Of Control* peaks at only US #174, and its poor sales prompt Frampton to leave the A&M label after more than a decade.
1985 After a period of inactivity, Frampton signs to Virgin Records.
1986 Synthesizer-laden LP *Premonition* is released on Virgin (UK)/Atlantic (US), but it fails to return him to the chart, although single *Lying* is a minor US hit (#74).
1987 He joins one-time schoolfriend David Bowie° as guitarist for Bowie's world-wide "Glass Spider" tour.
1988 July Increasingly inclined to session work, Frampton features on new Karla Bonoff LP *New World*.

CONNIE FRANCIS

1955/57 Connie Francis (b. Concetta Rosa Maria Franconero, Dec.12, 1938, Newark, N.J., US), a child accordianist and a star turn at family gatherings and neighborhood shows, graduating to local television at age 10, having appeared on Arthur Godfrey's networked talent show (he suggests the name change), divides her time between schooling and singing (4 years as a regular on NBC-TV's "Star Time"). She signs at age 16 to MGM Records and makes demos singing soundalikes of Kay Starr and Jo Stafford and dubs Tuesday Weld's singing voice for Alan Freed's film *Rock Rock Rock*. Her first nine singles fail to chart and she is about to enrol at New York University when her fortunes change.
1957 Nov She makes her chart debut supporting country singer Marvin Rainwater on *The Majesty Of Love* – a 1 week hit at US #93 which becomes an accredited million-seller.
1958 Mar To please her father, she uses the last 20 minutes of a session to record one of his favorite songs, *Who's Sorry Now*. Featured on the first broadcast of Dick Clark's "American Bandstand" and plugged on the program, it hits US #4, becoming a million-seller. In UK it hits #1 for 6 weeks, displacing Rainwater's *Whole Lotta Woman*.
June A 1918 oldie, *I'm Sorry I Made You Cry*, makes US #36 and UK #11.
July *Heartaches/I Miss You So* misses the Hot 100. (No other Connie Francis single will miss the US top 50 until 1965.)

CONNIE FRANCIS *cont.*

Sept *Stupid Cupid*, by Neil Sedaka° (before his own hits) and Howard Greenfield, reaches US #17. Coupled with the 30-year-old Guy Lombardo standard *Carolina Moon*, it hits UK #1 for 6 weeks.

Nov Another Sedaka/Greenfield composition, *Fallin'* reaches US #30 and UK #20. The oldie B-side *I'll Get By* reaches UK #19.

1959 Jan A 1933 weeper, *My Happiness* hits US #2 and UK #4 to become another million-seller. Unreleased in US, *You Always Hurt The One You Love* (a 1944 smash for the Mills Brothers) reaches UK #13.

Apr *If I Didn't Care*, a Jack Lawrence standard from the 30s, reaches US #22.

May Francis asks Sedaka° and Greenfield to write a song called *Bobby* to celebrate her romance with Bobby Darin°. Instead they give her a paean to Frankie Avalon°, *Frankie*, which hits US #9. B-side *Lipstick On Your Collar* becomes one of her most memorable hits at US #5 and UK #3, and her third gold disk.

Sept *You're Gonna Miss Me* makes US #34, paired with her own composition *Plenty Good Lovin'*, which makes US #69 and UK #18.

Dec Francis personalizes a gloomy 1927 ballad, *Among My Souvenirs*. It hits US #7 and makes UK #11. The patriotic B-side, *God Bless America*, reaches US #36 and is another million-seller.

1960 Mar LP *Rock'n'Roll Million Sellers* makes UK #12 and *Valentino*, unreleased in US, makes UK #27.

Apr [2] Francis wins Best Selling Female Artist at first annual NARM awards.

Apr Recorded in UK, *Mama*, a sentimental ballad learned from her grandmother and sung in Italian, hits US #8 and UK #2 to become her fifth gold disk. It is included in her first US chart LP, *Italian Favorites*, which hits #4. LP *Connie's Greatest Hits* simultaneously reaches US #17. The B-side of *Mama*, *Teddy*, written by Paul Anka°, makes US #17.

May Written by Greenfield and his new partner Jack Keller, the countryish *Everybody's Somebody's Fool* hits US #1 and UK #5.

June The B-side, another Italian song, *Jealous Of You*, hits US #19, becoming gold disk number six. *Mama/Robot Man*, a UK-only release, hits #2.

Sept The same duo provides *My Heart Has A Mind Of Its Own*, which hits US #1, displacing Chubby Checker°. (Francis becomes the only female singer to have successive #1s.) It hits UK #3 and earns another gold disk. The B-side *Malaguena* reaches US #42.

Dec Hitting US #7 and UK #12, Winfield Scott's bouncy *Many Tears Ago* brings her fourth million-seller of the year. The B-side *Senza Mamma (With No One)* charts for 1 week at US #87. LP *More Italian Favorites* reaches US #9.

1961 Feb LP *Connie's Greatest Hits* climbs to UK #16. (It will be her last UK chart LP for 16 years.)

Mar Francis hits US #4 and UK #5 with another Sedaka/Greenfield-penned million-seller, *Where The Boys Are*, also the title of her first MGM movie starring George Hamilton. The B-side *No-One* reaches US #34.

May Greenfield/Keller's country-flavored *Breakin' In A Brand New Broken Heart* hits US #7 and UK #12. Live LP *Connie At The Copa* reaches US #65. LP *Jewish Favorites* makes US #69.

Aug Reverting to oldies, she releases a 1928 song, *Together*. It hits #6 in US and UK and is gold disk number 10. Its B-side, *Too Many Rules*, also charts at US #72. LP *More Greatest Hits* climbs to US #39.

Oct Double-sided *(He's My) Dreamboat/Hollywood* (both written by John D. Loudermilk) reaches US #14 and #42 respectively but fails in UK. LP *Never On Sunday*, a collection of movie themes, her fourth hit LP of the year, reaches US #11.

Dec Double-sided *When The Boy In Your Arms (Is The Boy In Your Heart)/Baby's First Christmas* hits US #10 and #26. Only *Baby's First Christmas* charts in UK at #30. (Cliff Richard° has already hit UK #3 with a male version of the A-side.)

1962 Feb *Don't Break The Heart That Loves You* is her third US #1 but reaches only UK #39.

Apr LP *Do The Twist* reaches US #47.

June *Second Hand Love* (co-written by Phil Spector) hits US #7 but fails in UK.

Aug Containing five of her recent top 10 hits, LP *Connie Francis Sings* reaches only US #111.

Sept Co-written by Francis, *Vacation* hits US #9 and UK #10. (It will be her last significant UK hit.)

Oct *I Was Such A Fool (To Fall In Love With You)/He Still Thinks I Care* reaches US #24 and #57. The B-side, taken from her US #22 LP *Country Music Connie Style*, was originally a George Jones C&W item.

1963 *I'm Gonna Be Warm This Winter* reaches US #18 but only UK #48. The B-side, *Al Di La*, reaches US #90. Francis maintains her US popularity, reaching the top 50 with five singles: *Follow The Boys* (the title song from her second movie – #17), *If My Pillow Could Talk* (#23), *Drownin' My Sorrows* (#36), *Your Other Love* (#28) and the President Kennedy tribute *In The Summer Of His Years* (#46). Chart LPs include: *Modern Italian Hits* (#103), *Follow The Boys* (#66), *Award Winning Motion Picture Hits* (#108), *Great American Waltzes* (#94), *Big Hits From Italy* (#70) and *The Very Best Of Connie Francis* (#68).

1964 Francis places four hit singles: *Blue Winter* (#24), *Be Anything (But Be Mine)* (#25), *Looking For Love* (the theme song from her third movie) (#45) and *Don't Ever Leave* (#42). LPs are: *In The Summer Of His Years* (#126), *Looking For Love* (#122) and *A New Kind Of Connie* (#149).

1965 June *My Child* reaches UK #26. Six singles miss the US top 40 but all make the top 80. LP *Connie Francis Sings For Mama* reaches US #78.

1966 Jan *Jealous Heart* reaches UK #44. LP *When The Boy Meets The Girls* makes US #61 and is also the title of her fourth and last movie in which she co-stars with Harve Presnell.

1967/74 In 1969, *The Wedding Cake* becomes her last hit, peaking at US #91, but Francis continues to headline on the night club/cabaret circuit, taking time out for charity shows and entertaining troops in Vietnam.

1974 Nov [8] After an appearance at The Westbury Music Fair in New York, Francis is attacked and raped in a second floor room at Howard Johnson's Motel. Emotionally shattered, she retreats from public view. (She will be awarded $3 million in damages.)

1977 June Compilation LP *20 All Time Greats* hits UK #1 and earns a platinum disk.

1978 Sept Francis appears on "Dick Clark's Live Wednesday" TV show singing a medley of her hits.

1981 Nov She returns to the concert stage for the first time in 7 years.

1984 Sept After some seventy singles and sixty LPs, Francis titles her autobiography after her first hit *Who's Sorry Now*.

FRANKIE GOES TO HOLLYWOOD

"Holly" Johnson (vocals)
Paul Rutherford (vocals)
Brian "Nasher" Nash (guitar)
Peter "Ged" Gill (drums)
Mark O'Toole (bass)

1980 Aug The five members of the band come together and play their first gig, as support to Hambi & The Dance. Johnson (b. William Johnson, Feb.19, 1960, Khartoum, Sudan) has been with Big In Japan, appearing on their eponymous single and their EP *From Y To Z And Never Again*, leaving to go solo and releasing singles *Yankee Rose* on Eric's Records and *Hobo Joe* before forming band Hollycaust. Rutherford (b. Dec.8, 1959, Liverpool, UK) has been with The Spitfire Boys, singing on their only single *Mein Kampf* and briefly with The Opium Eaters, before moving to live temporarily in US. O'Toole (b. Jan.6, 1964, Liverpool) has been playing in local groups, while his cousin Nash (b. May 20, 1963, Liverpool) has played with Dancing Girl and then Sons Of Egypt with Gill (b. Mar.8, 1964, Liverpool).

Sept The band changes name to Frankie Goes To Hollywood taking inspiration from a headline about Frank Sinatra's move into the film business.

1982 Nov They make their national debut on UK radio with a live session for DJ David "Kid" Jensen. Their TV first is an appearance on UK Channel 4's "The Tube", including a rough video version of their track *Relax*. Their performance attracts record company interest, particularly from "The Tube" theme composer and noted producer Trevor Horn.

1983 Nov *Relax* is released as the first single on the Zang Tumb Tumm label, produced by company co-owner Horn. The B-side is a cover of fellow Merseyside act Gerry & The Pacemakers'° *Ferry Cross The Mersey*. "Relax" and "Frankie Says . . ." T-shirts, the idea of journalist Paul Morley, start to appear. The initial video is banned by UK TV and a second version is filmed.

1984 Jan UK BBC Radio DJ Mike Read initiates a ban on *Relax* claiming it to be "obscene", as the rest of the BBC, both radio and TV follow.

Jan [28] *Relax* tops the UK chart, after a 10-week climb. BBC's "Top of the Pops" is unable to feature the disk while it is still banned.

Mar Sales of *Relax* reach 1¾ million, spurred by the ban and the myriad issues and seven remixes of the single on 7", 12", picture disk and "cassingle". It will later hit US #10 (and will be featured in US movie *Police Academy*).

June With much media and public anticipation, the Horn-produced follow-up, *Two Tribes*, enters at UK #1. It goes silver in 2 days and gold in 7. Frankie Goes To Hollywood becomes the first band to achieve this with its second release. BBC Radio receives the airplay premiere. The record intro includes an impersonation of Ronald Reagan by UK mimic Chris Barrie. A video directed by Godley & Creme° features Reagan and Chernenko lookalikes wrestling and keeps sales alive. The record stays at #1 for 9 weeks, and sells 1½ million in UK. (The group is the only act to have platinum singles with first two releases.) *Relax* returns to the chart where it eventually settles at UK #2, with *Two Tribes* still at UK #1.

Oct Double LP *Welcome To The Pleasure Dome* enters UK at #1, with the UK's biggest LP ship-out to date. (It will be their only LP produced by Horn.)

Dec [8] Festive ballad *The Power Of Love* reaches UK #1, with the help of Godley & Creme° nativity video, and Frankie Goes To Hollywood becomes the first band since Gerry & The Pacemakers° to have a UK #1 with its first three singles. In typical ZTT promotion, the pre-release posters for the single have proclaimed: "*The Power Of Love* – Frankie Goes To Hollywood's third number one."

Dec LP *Welcome To The Pleasure Dome* reaches US #33.

1985 Feb *Welcome To The Pleasure Dome* hits UK #2.

Mar [12] The band begins a 3-week tour, opening at RDS Simmons Court, Dublin, and covering UK.

Apr [9] A major tour of Europe opens in Copenhagen, and the group has to spend the rest of 1985 exiled from UK for tax reasons.

Nov Recording begins in Amsterdam for a new LP.

1986 May The band appears at Montreux Rock Festival and destroys its equipment in front of a later TV audience of 20 million.

Aug *Rage Hard*, from the forthcoming LP, hits UK #4.

Oct LP *Liverpool* is released. It cost over twice as much to record as double LP *Welcome To The Pleasure Dome*.

Dec *Warriors Of The Wasteland* makes UK #19.

1987 Jan [11] The group begins what will be a final tour at Manchester's Grand Metropolitan Centre.

Mar *Watching The Wildlife* reaches UK #28. Condoms are given away free as a promotional gimmick. The group's last public appearance is on UK TV show "Saturday Live", after which a split is announced, and then denied.

Apr Johnson appears solo at an AIDS benefit concert in London. The band's break-up is finally made official.

July Johnson signs a solo deal with MCA in UK, who supports him during forthcoming litigation.

Aug ZTT serves an injunction against Johnson. Johnson counters. The rest of Frankie Goes To Hollywood form a new outfit called The Lads (who fail to release any material).

Oct *The Power Of Love* is used as a backing track to first UK TV condom commercial.

1988 Jan The ZTT and Perfect Songs case against "Holly" Johnson in London's High Court attracts much media attention.

Feb In its outcome Johnson wins an important test case for British recording artists relating to contracts and royalty payments and wins substantial costs.

Aug Rutherford signs a solo deal with the 4th & Broadway label. Newspaper reports state that the remainder of the band (with new lead singer Dee Harris), desperate to make a comeback, indulges in an orgy of alcohol, drugs and vandalism during recording sessions at The Music Works studio, London.

Sept Rutherford's debut "house" single *Get Real* is released.

ARETHA FRANKLIN

1950 Franklin (b. Mar.25, 1942, Memphis, Tenn., US), the fourth of six children raised by her father after her mother left (and later died), begins to learn piano by listening to Eddie Heywood records, but rejects the offer of professional lessons from her father. Rev. C.L. Franklin, pastor of the 4,500-member New Bethel Church, Detroit, Mich., and the most famous gospel preacher of the 50s – commanding $4,000 a sermon, and dubbed the "Million Dollar Voice". Franklin has been taught to sing by family friends Mahalia Jackson and The Ward Sisters, Frances Steadman and Marion Williams.

1952 Gospel star James Cleveland comes to live with the Franklin family and encourages her musical ambitions, but her biggest influence is her father's friend, hymn writer and gospel singer Clara Ward. Having heard Ward sing *Peace In The Valley* at a relative's funeral, she resolves on a singing career.

1956 Franklin's first recordings, for Checker label, are live versions of Ward hymns, recorded at her father's church.

1960 After dropping out of school, Franklin tours as a gospel vocalist. Then, encouraged by Sam Cooke°, she tailors her style to the secular field. Leaving the family home in Detroit, she moves to New York, taking dance and vocal lessons, and gets a manager, Joe King.

Aug [1] She makes her first secular recordings in a New York demo studio, cutting four tracks: *Right Now*, *Over The Rainbow*, *Love Is the Only Thing* and *Today I Sing The Blues*. The latter comes to the attention of CBS/Columbia Records veteran A&R man John Hammond, who signs her after watching her rehearse.

Oct Her first Columbia LP, *The Great Aretha Franklin*, is released. Produced by Hammond, it is a mixture of jazz, R&B and standards. *Today I Sing The Blues* is issued as a single and hits US R&B #10.

Dec [11] Franklin makes her New York stage debut at The Village Vanguard, with a program of standards.

1961 Mar Her chart debut, at US #76, is *Won't Be Long*, recorded with The Ray Bryant Trio.

Nov A revival of *Rock-A-Bye Your Baby With A Dixie Melody* reaches US #37 (and will be Franklin's only sizeable US hit on Columbia).

1962 Feb *I Surrender, Dear* reaches US #87 and B-side *Rough Lover* makes US #94. Meanwhile LP *The Electrifying Aretha Franklin* is released and she marries Ted White, now her manager.

July *Don't Cry, Baby* peaks at US #92.

Sept *Try A Little Tenderness* reaches US #100.

Dec LP *The Tender, The Moving, The Swinging Aretha Franklin* climbs to US #69.

1963 Jan *Trouble In Mind* peaks at US #86 and LP *Laughing* is released.

1964 Oct *Runnin' Out Of Fools* reaches US #57 and LP *Unforgettable: A Tribute To Dinah Washington* is released.

1965 Jan *Can't You Just See Me* peaks at US #96, while LP *Runnin' Out Of Fools* reaches US #84.

July LP *Yeah!!!* makes US #101.

1966 Aug LP *Soul Sister*, her last LP for Columbia, climbs to US #132.

Sept Dissatisfied with the artistic direction and lack of commercial success (which has made a $90,000 loss over 6 years), Franklin is unwilling to re-sign to Columbia. Atlantic Records outbids CBS for her, producer Jerry Wexler believing her Mitch Miller-guided recording path has been wrong and that she needs a tough R&B frame to recapture her gospel vocal fire. (This leads to a long and fruitful working relationship between Franklin and Wexler, later assisted by Arif Mardin and Tom Dowd.)

1967 Jan For her first Atlantic sessions, Wexler takes Franklin to Rick Hall's

ARETHA FRANKLIN *cont.*

Florence Alabama Music Emporium (FAME) studios in Muscle Shoals, Alabama, using the rhythm section he paired with Wilson Pickett°. A week's sessions to cut an LP are planned; but after 1 day's recording which produces just *I Never Loved A Man (The Way I Love You)* (a song Franklin has discovered herself and told Wexler she wanted to record) and a backing track for *Do Right Woman – Do Right Man*, a heated exchange between her husband and one of the horn players results in a quick return to New York.

Feb [8] With Wexler-distributed acetates of *I Never Loved A Man* already getting airplay on top US R&B stations, Franklin, with the help of sisters Erma and Carolyn, finishes recording *Do Right Woman, Do Right Man* in New York, so that the single has a B-side and can be released.

May *I Never Loved A Man (The Way I Loved You)* tops the US R&B chart for 9 weeks and crosses over to hit US #9. It earns Franklin her first gold disk for million-plus sales. The LP of same title hits US #2 (also earning a gold disk), and the media and music business dub her "Lady Soul".

June A new arrangement of Otis Redding's° R&B hit *Respect* tops the US chart for 4 weeks and the R&B chart for 8 weeks, and is a second million-seller.

July *Respect* hits UK #10. In US, Columbia releases a compilation LP of earlier material, *Aretha Franklin's Greatest Hits*, which makes US #94.

Aug LP *I Never Loved A Man* reaches UK #36.

Sept *Baby I Love You* is Franklin's third million-selling single, hitting US #4 (and topping the R&B chart for 6 weeks). It climbs to UK #39.

Oct LP *Aretha Arrives*, recorded in New York in June, hits US #5, while another Columbia compilation LP, *Take A Look*, peaks at US #173 and its title track makes US #56.

Nov *(You Make Me Feel Like A) Natural Woman*, written by Carole King°, hits US #8.

Dec Two more Columbia singles chart briefly in US: *Mockingbird* (US #94) and *Soulville* (US #83). Franklin is named *Billboard* magazine's Top Female Vocalist of the Year.

1968 Feb *Chain Of Fools*, a revival of an R&B hit by Don Covay, hits US #2 and earns another gold disk. Paired with her revival of The Rolling Stones'° *(I Can't Get No) Satisfaction*, it makes UK #43. LP *Aretha: Lady Soul*, mostly recorded just before Christmas, also hits US #2. (Eric Clapton° guests on track *Good To Me As I Am To You*.)

Feb [29] Franklin wins her first Grammy awards as *Respect* is named Best Female R&B Vocal Performance of 1967 (a category introduced this year) and Best R&B Recording.

Apr *(Sweet Sweet Baby) Since You've Been Gone* hits US #5 (and is another million-seller), while B-side *Ain't No Way* reaches #16. The A-side also makes UK #47, while LP *Lady Soul* reaches UK #25.

May [7] On her first tour of Europe, Franklin performs at The Olympia Theatre in Paris, France, and her concert is recorded for future LP release.

July *Think* hits US #7 (Franklin's first self-penned million-seller) and makes UK #26. B-side, reviving Sam Cooke's° *You Send Me*, reaches US #56.

Aug LP *Aretha Now* hits US #3, as LP *Lady Soul* is certified gold.

Sept While Franklin spends time in the studio working on her next LP, her revival of Dionne Warwick's° *I Say A Little Prayer* hits UK #4. In US, where it is a double A-side with *The House That Jack Built*, it hits #10 and #6 respectively, and is another million-seller. LP *Aretha Now* hits UK #6.

Nov LP *Aretha In Paris*, recorded at the Olympia concert in May, reaches US #13.

Dec Another Covay revival, *See Saw*, peaks at US #14 and B-side *My Song* makes US #31. This is another US million-seller.

1969 Mar LP *Soul '69*, from the Sept. sessions, and including some pop-jazz fusions, reaches US #15. She tours US, but some of her performances are described as patchy (attributed to a collapsing marriage that is heading for divorce).

Mar [12] *Chain Of Fools* wins a Grammy award as Best Female R&B Performance of 1968.

Apr A revival of The Band's° *The Weight* reaches US #19 and B-side, reviving The Miracles' *Tracks Of My Tears*, reaches #71.

May She works on another LP in the studio, with slide guitarist Duane Allman (later of The Allman Brothers Band°) joining the regular session musicians for some tracks.

June *I Can't See Myself Leaving You* reaches US #28. B-side, John Hartford's much-covered *Gentle On My Mind*, makes US #76.

June [13] She headlines a major R&B music spectacular, Soul Bowl '69, at Houston Astrodome, Tex., with Ray Charles°, The Staple Singers°, Sam and Dave° and many others – including Franklin's old friend, gospel singer James Cleveland.

July [22] Franklin is arrested for causing a disturbance in a Detroit parking lot, a symptom of the personal difficulties she is facing as her 7-year marriage to White fragments.

Aug Compilation LP *Aretha's Gold* reaches US #18.

Oct *Share Your Love With Me* reaches US #13, while Franklin records for the first time at Criteria Studios in Miami, Fla., cutting 9 tracks (again with Allman in attendance) including a revival of The Beatles'° *Eleanor Rigby* and her own composition *Call Me*.

Dec *Eleanor Rigby* reaches US #17.

1970 Mar LP *This Girl's In Love With You*, a mixture of the year's New York and Miami recordings, reaches US #17. It includes a version of The Beatles'° *Let It Be*, recorded in Dec. 1969 before the release of The Beatles' own version. Franklin returns to Miami for further sessions at Criteria, mostly to cut strong R&B and blues oldies with The Dixie Flyers.

Mar [11] She wins a Grammy award for *Share Your Love With Me* as Best Female R&B Vocal Performance of 1969.

May *Call Me*, coupled with a revival of Dusty Springfield's° *Son Of A Preacher Man*, also recorded in Miami, makes US #13.

July *Spirit In The Dark* reaches US #23.

Aug Returning to New York to record, she cuts a version of *Bridge Over Troubled Water*, with Billy Preston among the session musicians. (It will be released in 1971.)

Sept A revival of Ben E. King's° *Don't Play That Song* reaches US #11 and UK #13, and is her first million-selling single since *See Saw* in 1968. Remarried, and with a new backing band led by saxman King Curtis (comprising Cornell Dupree on guitar, Richard Tee on piano, Jerry Jemmott on bass and Bernard Purdie on drums), Franklin begins a series of well-received US concerts.

Oct LP *Spirit In The Dark* reaches US #25.
Dec A cover of Elton John's° *Border Song (Holy Moses)* reaches US #37.
1971 Mar [5-7] Franklin plays 3 nights at the Fillmore West in San Francisco, with Ray Charles° (they do an encore duet on the third night), King Curtis and Tower of Power.
Mar [16] She wins another Grammy award for *Don't Play That Song*, named Best Female R&B Vocal Performance of 1970.
Apr A revival of Marvin Gaye° and Tammi Terrell's *You're All I Need To Get By* reaches US #19.
June Franklin's version of Paul Simon's° *Bridge Over Troubled Water* (he had already claimed to have had her in mind when writing the song, prior to Simon & Garfunkel's° own version in 1970) hits US #6. Coupled with *A Brand New Me*, it is another million-seller.
July LP *Aretha Live At Fillmore West* hits US #7.
Aug [17] Franklin sings at the funeral of King Curtis (who was stabbed to death in the street 4 days earlier) in New York, along with Stevie Wonder°, Cissy Houston and others, as the Rev. Jesse Jackson preaches the sermon.
Oct Compilation LP *Aretha's Greatest Hits* reaches US #19. Meanwhile, her revival of Ben E. King's° *Spanish Harlem* hits US #2 and UK #14, and is another million-seller.
Dec *Rock Steady*, a further million-seller, hits US #9.
1972 Feb [1] Franklin sings *Take My Hand, Precious Lord* at the funeral of her old friend and one-time mentor Mahalia Jackson, in Chicago.
Mar LP *Young Gifted And Black* reaches US #11, and is a gold disk. She wins another Grammy award when *Bridge Over Troubled Water* is named Best Female R&B Vocal Performance of 1971.
June *Day Dreaming*, Franklin's fourth consecutive million-seller, hits US #5.
July Double gospel LP *Amazing Grace*, made with James Cleveland and The Southern California Community Choir, and recorded at a church in Watts, LA, in Jan. hits US #7. Her last Wexler-produced LP, it earns a gold disk for a half million sales. Columbia compilation LP *In The Beginning/The World Of Aretha Franklin 1960-1967* reaches US #160.
Aug *All The King's Horses* makes US #26.
Sept *Wholy Holy*, with James Cleveland, peaks at US #81.
1973 Mar *Master Of Eyes (The Deepness Of Your Eyes)* makes US #33.
Mar [3] Franklin wins two Grammy awards: *Young, Gifted And Black* is named Best Female R&B Vocal Performance of 1972 and *Amazing Grace* Best Soul Gospel Performance.
Apr Franklin begins a major US stadium tour.
Aug Jazz-tinged LP *Hey Now Hey (The Other Side Of The Sky)*, recorded in LA with producer Quincy Jones, makes US #30.
Sept A revival of Jimi Hendrix'° *Angel* reaches US #20 and UK #37.
1974 Mar A revival of Stevie Wonder's° *Until You Come Back To Me (That's What I'm Gonna Do)* hits US #3 (selling over a million) and makes UK #26.
Mar [2] She wins a further Grammy for *Master Of Eyes (The Deepness Of Your Eyes)*, which is named Best Female R&B Vocal Performance of 1973.
Apr With Wexler, Mardin and Dowd producing again, LP *Let Me In Your Life* reaches US #14. Franklin is made an Honorary Doctor of Law at Bethune-Cookman College, Oh., US.
June *I'm In Love* makes US #19.
Sept *Ain't Nothing Like The Real Thing*, another Gaye°/Terrell revival, climbs to US #47.
Dec *Without Love* reaches US #45.
1975 Jan LP *With Everything I Feel In Me* peaks at US #57.
Mar [1] She wins her tenth Grammy award for *Ain't Nothing Like The Real Thing*, named Best Female R&B Vocal Performance of 1974, her eighth successive win in the category.
Oct *Mr. D.J. (5 For The D.J.)* reaches US #53.
Dec LP *You* peaks at US #83.
1976 July Franklin and Curtis Mayfield° co-produce the soundtrack LP for movie *Sparkle*, which makes US #18.
Aug *Something He Can Feel* (from *Sparkle*) reaches US #28.
Oct *Jump*, also from the film soundtrack, peaks at US #72.
1977 Jan [19] Franklin performs an a cappella *God Bless America* at Jimmy Carter's Inaugural Eve Gala in Washington, D.C., US.
Jan Compilation LP *Ten Years Of Gold* reaches US #135.
Feb *Look Into Your Heart* makes US #82.
June *Break It To Me Gently* peaks at US #85, but hits US R&B #1 for 1 week.
July Lamont Dozier-produced LP *Sweet Passion* reaches US #49.
1978 Apr Franklin marries actor Glynn Turman.
June LP *Almighty Fire* makes US #63.
June [21] She begins a 5-date appearance at Las Vegas, her first engagement there in 8 years.
July [9] Franklin upsets the audience at the Rev. Gibson's 18th annual "Youth on Parade Program" at LAs' Good Shepherd Baptist Church with a lackluster performance.
1979 Feb [13] She opens a cabaret season at Harrah's Restaurant in Lake Tahoe, Nev.
Oct LP *La Diva* reaches US #146.
1980 June Franklin appears in film *The Blues Brothers* as a waitress, singing *Think*. Shortly afterwards, she ends her 15-year association with Atlantic and signs to Arista, under the executive production of Clive Davis.
Nov LP *Aretha*, produced by Mardin, is her Arista debut, and reaches US #47.
Dec A cover of The Doobie Brothers'° *What A Fool Believes* peaks at UK #46.
1981 Jan *United Together* makes US #56.
June *Come To Me* peaks at US #84.
Sept *Love All The Hurt Away*, a duet with George Benson°, reaches US #46 and UK #49. The LP, of which the duet is the title track, climbs to US #36.
1982 Feb [24] After 7 years, she wins another Grammy award for *Hold On, I'm Coming*, named Best Female R&B Vocal Performance of 1981.
Sept Luther Vandross° produces Franklin's third Arista LP *Jump To It*, which reaches US #23 and earns a gold disk.
Oct The title track from *Jump To It* makes US #24, tops the R&B chart for 4 weeks and reaches UK #42.
Nov [25] She performs at the Jamaica World Music Festival, to an audience of 45,000 at the Bob Marley Performing Center in Montego Bay, with The Clash°, The Grateful Dead°, Gladys Knight° and others.
1983 July *Get It Right* peaks at US #61 and UK #74.
Aug LP *Get It Right*, again produced by Vandross°, reaches US #36.
1984 Franklin wins US *Ebony* magazine's annual award for American Black Achievement.
1985 May Franklin's voice is proclaimed "one of Michigan's natural resources" by the state's government.
July LP *Who's Zoomin' Who?*, produced by Narada Michael Walden, is released: it will reach US #13 and become her first certified million-selling LP, gaining a platinum disk. The Rev. C.L. Franklin is shot during a civil rights campaign. (He survives, but goes into a coma.)
Oct *Freeway Of Love* hits US #3 but makes only UK #68.
Nov *Who's Zoomin' Who* hits US #7 and reaches UK #11.
Dec Franklin duets with Annie Lennox of Eurythmics° on *Sisters Are Doin' It For Themselves*, which makes US #18 and hits UK #9.
1986 Jan LP *Who's Zoomin' Who* reaches UK #49.
Mar *Another Night* peaks at US #22 and UK #54.
May A reissue of *Freeway Of Love* reaches UK #51, while TV-advertised compilation LP, *The First Lady Of Soul*, makes UK #89.
Nov The title song from the Whoopi Goldberg movie *Jumpin' Jack Flash*, produced by its original co-writer Keith Richard, reaches US #21 and UK #58.
1987 Feb *Jimmy Lee* peaks at US #28. LP *Aretha*, produced by Walden, makes US #32 and UK #51. Also from the LP, a duet with George Michael°, *I Knew You Were Waiting (For Me)*, written by Climie Fisher and Dennis Morgan, tops both the US and UK charts, selling over a million.
July [27] Over a 3-day period, Franklin records gospel songs at the New Bethel Baptist Church on C.L. Franklin Boulevard, Detroit, with guests the Rev. Jesse Jackson, The Franklin Sisters and Mavis Staples. Meanwhile, her father dies, having never come out of his coma.
1988 Feb Double LP *One Lord, One Faith*, from the sessions commemorating Rev. Franklin, makes US #106.
Mar [2] At the 30th annual Grammy ceremonies, Franklin picks up her thirteenth and fourteenth awards, for Best R&B Vocal, Duo/Group and Best R&B Vocal Female.
Aug [22] US Public Broadcasting Services TV airs "Aretha Franklin: The Queen of Soul", a 1-hour documentary with contributions from Ray Charles°, Eric Clapton°, Whitney Houston° and Smokey Robinson°.
Sept Franklin performs on stage for the first time in several years, amid rumors that she is about to re-sign to Atlantic Records.

FREDDIE & THE DREAMERS

Freddie Garrity (vocals)
Derek Quinn (lead guitar)
Roy Crewsdon (rhythm guitar)
Pete Birrell (bass)
Bernie Dwyer (drums)

1961 The group is formed by Garrity (b. Nov.14, 1940, Manchester, UK), a former milkman, who has previously sung in local skiffle group Red Sox, followed by the John Norman Four and then The Kingfishers, in which Crewsdon (b. May 29, 1941, Manchester) also played. Quinn (b. May 24, 1942, Manchester), Birrell (b. May 9, 1941, Manchester) and Dwyer (b. Sept.11, 1940) all join as the new group evolves from The Kingfishers.

Oct First UK TV and radio appearances, on BBC's "Let's Go" and "Beat Show" respectively.

1963 Mar After a year of growing popularity in northern England, followed by seaside dates at Dreamland, Margate, UK, and then a stint in Hamburg, West Germany (at the Top Ten club), they are signed to EMI's Columbia label after intense talent scouting by the company in Manchester/Liverpool following the rapid success of The Beatles°.

June Debut recording, reviving James Ray's *If You Gotta Make A Fool Of Somebody*, hits UK #2. They quickly become popular UK TV favorites, thanks to a zany, low-comedy stage act focused on Garrity's kicks, jumps and giggles while performing.

Aug A Mitch Murray (writer of first two Gerry & The Pacemakers° chart-toppers) song *I'm Telling You Now* also hits UK #2.

Dec *You Were Made For Me*, another Murray composition, makes a UK hit hat-trick at #3, while debut LP *Freddie And The Dreamers* hits UK #5. The group makes its film debut in *What A Crazy World*, starring Joe Brown.

1964 Feb *Over You* hits #10 in UK.

May A revival of Paul Anka's° *I Love You Baby* makes UK #19.

July *Just For You* makes UK #41.

Nov A revival of G-Clefs' 1961 hit *I Understand* returns them to UK top 10, hitting #6.

1965 Feb During a world tour, a timely US visit places them on national TV shows "Shindig" and "Hullaballoo", where their stage antics and catchy songs are an immediate success, prompting Tower Records to reissue *I'm Telling You Now*, and Mercury Records (to which their latest material is signed) to release *I Understand*.

Apr *I'm Telling You Now* tops US chart for 2 weeks, taking its total sales over a million, while *I Understand* reaches US #36.

May *A Little You* climbs to UK #26, while LP *Freddie And The Dreamers* reaches US #19.

June *Do The Freddie* and *You Were Made For Me*, released on Mercury and Tower respectively, are simultaneous US hits. The former is recorded specifically for US market, creating a teen dance based on Garrity's stage movements, and reaches #18, while the latter reissue makes #21.

July LP *Do The Freddie* reaches US #85.

Aug *A Little You* is their final US hit, at #48.

Nov Final UK hit revives Dick And Deedee's *Thou Shalt Not Steal*, and peaks at #44. The group appears in the low-budget UK musical film *Every Day's A Holiday* (*Seaside Swingers* in US) as a bunch of singing holiday camp chefs. (They will then move into club and cabaret work, including regular winter pantomime and summer seaside residency, where a family audience will replace the rock fans.

1968 Oct The group splits up, with Garrity and Birrell moving on to UK children's TV in weekly show "Little Big Time".

1970 Children's LP *Oliver In The Overworld* is the final group release after 4 years of unsuccessful singles and LPs.

1976 Garrity reforms the group with new personnel, to play UK 60s revival concerts. They also join oldies tours in US and Australia.

1988 Garrity debuts as a serious stage actor in a UK production of *The Tempest*.

FREE

Paul Rodgers (vocals)
Paul Kossoff (guitar)
Andy Fraser (bass)
Simon Kirke (drums)

1968 May The group is formed in London, UK, by two ex-members of R&B band Black Cat Bones: Kossoff (b. Sept.14, 1950, London, UK), the son of actor David Kossoff, and Kirke (b. Aug.7, 1952, Shrewsbury, UK). They recruit Rodgers (b. Dec.17, 1949, Middlesborough, UK), ex-Roadrunners and Brown Sugar, after hearing him at The Fickle Pickle, an R&B club in Finsbury Park, London. Fraser (b. July 28, 1948, Shropshire, UK) joins after being fired by John Mayall's° Bluesbreakers. Alexis Korner watches their first gig and names them Free, after his own 60s trio Free At Last.

Nov Signed to Island Records, who wants the group to be called The Heavy Metal Kids, it releases LP *Tons Of Sobs*, which does not chart in UK (but makes US #197 almost a year on).

1969 July Debut single *Broad Daylight* also fails but the group builds a huge live reputation through constant UK touring.

Sept It tours US, supporting Blind Faith°.

Nov LP *Free* is UK chart debut at #22, but *I'll Be Creepin'* fails to chart.

1970 July *All Right Now*, a highly commercial riff-based rocker, tops UK chart for 3 weeks and establishes Free as a major act.

Aug LP *Fire And Water*, including the hit, climbs to UK #2, after the group makes a major impact at the Isle of Wight Festival.

Oct *All Right Now* hits US #4 and LP *Fire And Water* makes US #17.

1971 Jan Follow-up single *Stealer* climbs to US #49 after failing to chart in UK.

Feb LP *Highway* reaches UK #41 but only US #190.

May [9] At the end of a Pacific tour, the group splits to pursue individual projects, frustrated by intra-group frictions and disappointed by lack of sales consistency.

June *My Brother Jake*, released 2 weeks before the split, hits UK #4.

July LP *Free Live!*, released as a souvenir of the band, also hits UK #4.

Oct LP *Free Live!* climbs to US #89.

Nov Kossoff and Kirke release LP *Kossoff, Kirke Tetsu And Rabbit*, with bassist Tetsu Yamauchi (b. Oct.21, 1947, Fukuoka, Japan) and keyboardist John "Rabbit" Bundrick. It is not a big seller. Rodgers forms Peace with Stewart McDonald (bass) and Mick Underwood (drums), which tours UK supporting Mott The Hoople°. Andy Fraser forms an unsuccessful trio, Toby, (with Adrian Fisher on guitar and Stan Speake on drums).

1972 Jan Free re-forms after Rodgers and Fraser's projects (Peace and Toby) fail. It tours UK and recommences recording.

June LP *Free At Last* reaches UK #9 and US #69. *Little Bit Of Love* makes UK #13. The group tours US but Kossoff suffers drug abuse-associated health problems which cause him to miss several dates.

July [22] Fraser leaves to form Sharks, on the eve of Free's tour of Japan.

July Kossoff's drug problems render him unavailable for the tour, so Tetsu and Rabbit are recruited for the trip, on which Rodgers plays guitar.

Oct Kossoff, fit again, rejoins for a UK tour and to record an LP, but leaves Free officially to make his own LP, *Back Street Crawler*. (He will form a band of that name in 1974, signing to Atlantic Records and releasing LPs *The Band Plays On* and *Second Avenue*.)

1973 Jan Wendell Richardson of Osibisa joins temporarily on guitar for a UK tour.

Feb *Wishing Well* hits UK #7, while LP *Heartbreaker* climbs to UK #9 and US #47.

July Free announces its final split. Rodgers, after turning down an offer to join Deep Purple°, stays with Kirke to form Bad Company°, while Tetsu replaces Ronnie Lane in The Faces°. (Rabbit will join The Who° as sideman.)

Aug *All Right Now* is reissued in UK and returns to the chart, reaching #15.

1974 Mar Compilation LP *The Free Story* hits UK #2.

1975 May LP *The Best Of Free* is released in US only. It reaches #120.

1976 Mar [19] Kossoff dies of heart failure on a flight to London after a history of drug abuse.

1978 Mar *The Free EP*, compiling *All Right Now*, *My Brother Jake* and *Wishing Well*, reaches UK #11. (This will remain a steady seller in Island Records' UK catalog and will chart a second time, reaching #57, in Oct. 1982.)

1982 Mar Fraser has a minor US hit with *Do You Love Me*, reaching #82, having worked with Robert Palmer° on LP *Clues* and Eno° on LP *Before And After Science*.

BOBBY FREEMAN

1955 Freeman (b. June 13, 1940, San Francisco, Cal., US) is at high school in San Francisco when, as a singer and pianist, he has first taste of recording with vocal group The Romancers, who record briefly and unsuccessfully for Dootone Records.

1958 Apr Still at high school, he is spotted playing in a club and signed to Josie Records, recording his own composition *Do You Wanna Dance*.

June *Do You Wanna Dance* hits US #5, and becomes a much-revived rock standard: there will be later hit versions in US or UK by Cliff Richard° (1962), Del Shannon° (1964), The Beach Boys° (1965), The Mamas and The Papas° (1968), Bette Midler° (1973) and The Ramones° (1978).

Aug *Betty Lou Got A New Pair Of Shoes* reaches US #37.

Dec *Need Your Love* peaks at #54 in US.

1959 Feb Freeman graduates from high school, turning professional with three US hits already under his belt, but two Josie singles during this year will be less successful: *Mary Ann Thomas* reaching US #90 in June and *Ebb Tide* #93 in Dec.

1960 Oct He resurges with the dance-craze song *(I Do The) Shimmy Shimmy* on the King label, which reaches US #37 and stays on chart for 3 months.

1964 Jan After a long recording silence, and while resident at a club in North Beach, San Francisco, Freeman becomes the first act to work with local DJs Tom Donahue and Bob Mitchell when they set up Autumn Records. He cuts Autumn's debut single *Let's Surf Again*, but it is not successful.

Aug Freeman's *C'mon And Swim* is Autumn's second release, and a US #5 smash, equalling *Do You Wanna Dance*. The single is produced by another local DJ, Sylvester Stewart (later to find fame as Sly Stone of Sly & The Family Stone°).

Nov *S-W-I-M*, another Stone production, is less successful, peaking at US #56, and becoming Freeman's last US chart hit. (He continues working, still mainly around the San Francisco area. In the later 60s and early 1970s he will record intermittently in a less rock-oriented soul style, for labels such as Double Shot and Touch.)

THE FUGS

Ed Sanders (guitar and vocals)
Ken Weaver (drums and vocals)
Tuli Kupferberg (vocals)

1965 After a string of performances at a tiny theater in Greenwich Village, New York, N.Y., US, focusing on poetry with beat bards Allen Ginsberg and Gregory Corso joining in, The Fugs becomes a rock group with Sanders and Kupferberg (writer of much of the material) on vocals, accompanied by Peter Stampfield and Steve Weber (ex-Holy Modal Rounders), with Ken Weaver (drums, vocals), Vinnie Leary (guitar), Lee Crabtree (piano), Pete Kearney (guitar) and John Anderson (bass). The band signs to avant-garde jazz label ESP and releases LP *The Fugs' First Album*. With downright offensive lyrics (*Kill For Peace* and *Coca Cola Douche* being prime examples), the group becomes known for the taboo-breaking severity of its gigs (which sometimes offends audiences who exit en masse) but also performs versions of William Blake poems.

1966 Aug LP *The Fugs* gives the band its first chart appearance, reaching US #95.

Nov The LP's success boosts sales of earlier *The Fugs' First Album*, which charts at US #142.

1967 Although it is acknowledged that the group's "appeal" lies mainly in live performance, The Fugs signs to Reprise Records and goes on tour with Stefan Grossman on guitar and Charlie Larkey on bass.

1968 Jan First Reprise LP *Tenderness Junction* is released. *Out Demons Out*, taken from it, becomes something of an anthem and will later be adopted in the UK by The Edgar Broughton band. The abrasive lyrical approach, referencing sex, drugs and Vietnam makes audiences feel uncomfortable.

Oct LP *It Crawled Into My Hand, Honest* reaches US #167, the band's last chart LP. It contains a pastiche of highly commercial psychedelic pop single *Crystal Liaison* which gains some airplay but fails to chart. The group line-up is now Sanders, Kupferberg, Weaver and Larkey with Bob Mason as second drummer.

1969 Nov LP *The Belle Of Avenue A* is released, and the group splits up. (Sanders will remain visible into the 1970s as a writer, reporting for the underground press and writing a book on the Charles Manson case and trial, and will record solo LPs *Sanders' Truck-Stop* and *Beer Cans On The Moon*, neither of which charts.)

1970 Reprise releases Fugs live LP *Golden Filth*, earlier recorded on stage at the Fillmore East in New York.

THE BOBBY FULLER FOUR

Bobby Fuller (vocals, guitar)
Randy Fuller (bass)
Jim Reese (rhythm Guitar)
Dwayne Quirico (drums)

1960-63 Fuller (b. Oct.22, 1942, Goose Creek, Tex., US) builds a studio in his parents' home in El Paso, Texas, records a number of tracks and places them with local labels like Yucca and Todd. He also runs a local teen nightclub, the Rendezvous, and plays there with a group called The Embers, who will later become The Fanatics, and eventually (after many personnel changes) The Bobby Fuller Four.

1964 He closes the Rendezvous in the summer, forms his own label, Exeter Records, and releases a new single on it every few weeks, including surf music and an early version of *I Fought the Law* by Bobby Fuller & The Fanatics.

Nov The group leaves Texas for Hollywood and hoped-for stardom, taking tapes of Fuller's songs. The name is changed to Bobby Fuller & The Cavemen for a gig at La Cave Pigalle, then to The Bobby Fuller Four when they acquire a residency at PJ's, breaking all attendance records at their first gig.

Dec They sign with Bob Keene, owner of a group of small LA record labels, who decides to try them in different guises on several of his outlets. First release is *Those Memories Of You*, as Bobby Fuller & The Fanatics, on Donna Records.

1965 Feb *Take My Word*, with the group as The Bobby Fuller Four, is released on another of Keene's labels, Mustang Records.

Mar They sign to appear as a surf band in the movie *Ghost In The Invisible Bikini*. Producer Phil Spector sits in with the group on piano at gigs and attempts, unsuccessfully, to sign them to his Philles label.

July They have an LA area hit with *Let Her Dance*, (its riff a re-working of *La Bamba*), leased to Liberty Records for national distribution, though it fails to sell outside California, and appear on several US TV shows like "Shindig", "Shebang" and "Hollywood A Go-Go". First LP *KRLA King Of Wheels* is released, in co-operation with an LA radio station.

Sept *Never To Be Forgotten* also sells well in LA but fails to chart nationally.

Oct Fuller revamps *I Fought The Law*, a revival of a Crickets' song which he has attempted before. This time it is a powerful guitar-driven version which will be his breakthrough success.

1966 Mar *I Fought The Law* reaches #9 in US.

Apr *I Fought The Law* climbs to #33 in UK, while second LP *The Bobby Fuller Four: I Fought The Law* reaches US #144.

May Another revived Crickets' song in similar style, *Love's Made A Fool Of You*, reaches US #26 as the band embarks on their first national tour.

June As *The Magic Touch* is issued, Fuller falls out with Keene over the choice of A-side, plus Keene's decisions not to record a live LP at PJ's (a project close to Fuller's heart), and to cancel a projected UK visit. He decides to quit the tour and go solo, while the single fails to chart.

July [18] Fuller is found dead in his car in LA, his body badly beaten and reeking of gasoline. The circumstances of his death are never uncovered, and Keene releases a statement dismissing police reports which call it accidental death or suicide. The question of foul play never arises, despite the odd mode of death. (The group continues for a while under Bobby's brother as The Randy Fuller Four, but with no chart success they will split up in 1968).

BILLY FURY

1958 Oct Ronald Wycherley (b. Apr.17, 1941, Liverpool, UK), following a childhood fraught with illness (including rheumatic fever which has left him with a weak heart), is working as a deckhand on River Mersey tug boats and writing songs with his guitar as a hobby, when Larry Parnes' "Rock Extravaganza" rock package show, headlined by Marty Wilde°, comes to the Birkenhead Essoldo, across the Mersey from his home. Wycherley talks his way into

BILLY FURY *cont.*

Wilde's dressing room in the hope of interesting him in some songs. Parnes is so impressed by the teenager's obvious vocal talent and the strength of his on-the-spot demos, that he offers to sign him up if Wycherley will go on stage and sing a couple of his songs as a "local addition" to the bill. Although petrified, Wycherley complies, and the audience reaction is enough to make Parnes realize his hunch is right. He signs the singer to a management contract, and re-christens him Billy Fury, quickly getting him on tour and on UK TV in "Jack Good's Oh Boy!"

Nov [26] Fury is signed by Parnes to Decca Records, and records his first session at the company's studio in West Hampstead, London.

1959 Feb Self-penned *Maybe Tomorrow* charts in UK, reaching #18, aided by Fury's success in nationwide tour exposure.

June *Margo Don't Go* reaches UK #28.

Oct The curtain is dropped during Fury's act at Dublin's Theatre Royal: his wild, Presley°-like stage movements are deemed "offensive" by the management.

1960 Apr *Colette*, dual-tracked in an Everly Brothers'° style untypical of Fury, is nevertheless his first UK top-tenner, climbing to #9.

June *That's Love*, another Fury original, makes UK #19. By now, he is also a huge TV success in UK, starring weekly on the rock music shows "Boy Meets Girls" (with Marty Wilde°) and "Wham!" (which he headlines).

10" LP *The Sound Of Fury* reaches UK #18. It features self-penned tracks (under the name Wilbur Wilberforce) and material is Elvis-styled rockabilly, produced by Jack Good, and backed by Joe Brown and other top session players. It will later be regarded by critics as the great early UK rockabilly LP, but Decca does not see Fury's recording career in this direction, sensing the commercial potential of strong rock ballads and carefully-chosen US cover versions.

Oct *Wondrous Place*, a personal favorite of Fury's, reaches UK #25.

1961 Feb *A Thousand Stars*, a cover of US hit by Kathy Young & The Innocents, makes UK #14.

Apr A cover of Marty Robbins' *Don't Worry* reaches only UK #40, and Decca quickly looks for a stronger follow-up.

Aug A cover of Goffin/King ballad *Halfway To Paradise* (a US hit by Tony Orlando°), is Fury's biggest UK hit yet, reaching #3 and staying on chart for over 5 months. With a big orchestral backing, this confirms him as a teen heartthrob rather than rockabilly hero.

Oct Dramatically-backed revival of the oldie *Jealousy* also hits UK #3. LP *Halfway To Paradise* hits UK #5.

1962 Jan *I'd Never Find Another You* (another Goffin/King/Tony Orlando° cover) hits UK #2, also winning a Carl-Alan award in UK as favorite dancefloor record.

Mar Eager to record some R&B, Fury covers Gladys Knight & The Pips'° *Letter Full Of Tears*. It reaches UK #17, a poor seller by his now-established standards, and ensures the return of ballads.

June Big production rock ballad *Last Night Was Made For Love* hits UK #5.

Aug Promised an Elvis-like career in films, Fury stars in Michael Winner's *Play It Cool*, essentially playing himself. The movie is lightweight but popular. *Once Upon A Dream*, from the film, hits UK #7, while the other movie songs are gathered on EP *Play It Cool*, which sits at #2 on UK EP chart for many weeks.

Nov *Because Of Love*, also sung by Elvis Presley° in movie *Girls! Girls! Girls!*, makes UK #18.

1963 Mar *Like I've Never Been Gone* takes him back into the UK top 5, peaking at #3.

June *When Will You Say I Love You* hits UK #3. By now Fury is flanked in UK top 10 by a whole new wave of UK hitmakers from his native Liverpool – Billy J Kramer° (at #1), The Beatles° (#2), and Gerry And The Pacemakers (#6). LP *Billy* reaches UK #6.

Aug [9] He tops the bill on the first edition of UK TV's major mid-1960s pop show "Ready Steady Go".

Aug Untypically lightweight *In Summer* is last of a trio of consecutive UK top 5 hits, at #5. With the beat boom on the ascendant, Fury is now associated with the old school of balladeers (even though he performs much rock in similar style to most beat groups on stage, backed by The Tornados°), and will henceforth have a tougher time commercially. (He survives, however, as a major chart name longer than any of his pre-beat contemporaries, apart from Cliff Richard°.)

Oct *Somebody Else's Girl* reaches UK #20.

Nov Live LP *We Want Billy* peaks at #14 in UK.

1964 Jan Uptempo *Do You Really Love Me Too (Fool's Errand)* reaches UK #13.

May Ballad *I Will*, a cover of a US hit by Vic Dana, also makes UK #13.

Aug Fury revives Conway Twitty's former #1 *It's Only Make Believe*, taking it to UK #10.

1965 Jan *I'm Lost Without You*, a Teddy Randazzo ballad which is the most startlingly melodramatic of all Fury's recordings, reaches UK #16.

Aug *In Thoughts Of You* makes UK #9, and is his final UK top 10 hit. His second film *I've Gotta Horse* (Fury actually owns the co-starring racehorse Anselmo, which finished fifth in the 1964 Derby), proves a non-starter.

Oct *Run To My Lovin' Arms*, covered from Jay and The Americans, reaches UK #25.

1966 Feb *I'll Never Quite Get Over You* reaches UK #35, Fury's poorest UK chart performance for 5 years.

Aug Revival of Tennessee Ernie Ford's *Give Me Your Word* reaches UK #27, bringing to an end Fury's hit run and also his contract with Decca. His remarkable total of 20 UK top 20 entries is surpassed in the 1960s only by The Beatles°, Elvis Presley° and Cliff Richard°.

1967 Jan He signs a new recording contact with EMI's Parlophone label, which will produce 11 singles before the end of 1970, but no hits at all. Fury, wary of his recurring heart problems which have occasionally hospitalized him and caused mid-tour cancellations, takes a back seat from most live performance and spends much time on his farm, devoting efforts to horse breeding and pursuing his animal conservation interests.

1972 May He releases a one-off single, *Will The Real Man Please Stand Up*, on his own label, Fury Records, but it is not a hit.

1973 Apr [12] London première of the movie *That'll Be The Day* starring David Essex° and set in 1958. Fury has a cameo role as Stormy Tempest, a clone of his younger self, and sings several songs including *Long Live Rock*, written for him by Pete Townshend of The Who°.

1981 Oct He decides to regenerate his recording career, signing to Polydor Records and working with Shakin' Stevens'° producer Stuart Colman. First release is *Be Mine Tonight*, which is not successful.

1982 Sept *Love Or Money* returns him to UK singles chart after 16-year gap, though it peaks at only #57.

Nov A revival of Bobby Vee's° *Devil Or Angel* is another minor UK chart entry, at #58.

1983 Jan [28] Fury dies from heart failure, the nemesis that has dogged him all his adult life.

Feb Compilation LP *The Billy Fury Hit Parade* reaches UK #44.

Mar LP *The One And Only*, completed with Stuart Colman only shortly before Fury's death, reaches UK #54.

June *Forget Him* provides an inappropriately-titled posthumous UK chart swan song, climbing to #59.

PETER GABRIEL

1975 May Gabriel (b. May 13, 1950, Cobham, Surrey, UK) leaves Genesis° after a final concert as lead vocalist at St. Etienne, France. He remains with Charisma Records as a solo artist, though will not record or perform live for almost 2 years.

Aug [16] He makes a belated press announcement concerning his departure from Genesis° for personal reasons.

Nov He co-writes and produces *You'll Never Know* for UK comedian/actor Charlie Drake, and sings a version of Lennon°/McCartney's° *Strawberry Fields Forever* on compilation LP *All This And World War II*, which makes UK #23.

1976 July He begins recordings for a solo LP at Nimbus Studios, Toronto, Canada.

1977 Mar LP *Peter Gabriel*, produced by Bob Ezrin and the first of four eponymously-titled LPs, hits UK #7. Gabriel begins his first solo tour in US and Canada.

Apr *Solsbury Hill* reaches UK #13. He makes his London solo stage debut backed by, among others, Robert Fripp of King Crimson° on guitar. A short European tour follows.

May LP *Peter Gabriel* reaches US #38 but *Solsbury Hill* makes only US #68.

July *Modern Love* is released in UK but fails to chart.

1978 May *DIY* is issued in UK, again without charting.

June Second LP *Peter Gabriel*, produced by Robert Fripp, hits UK #10.

Aug LP *Peter Gabriel* reaches US #45.

Sept A remix of *DIY*, issued as a UK single, fails to chart. He appears at Knebworth, UK, with Frank Zappa°.

1979 Gabriel spends part of the year working with writer Atejanmdo Jodorowsky on the screenplay for a movie version of Genesis'° concept LP/stage show *The Lamb Lies Down On Broadway*, due to be financed by Charisma, but the movie never materializes.

Mar The Tom Robinson Band's *Bully For You*, co-written by Gabriel, reaches UK #68.

May [12] Gabriel joins Kate Bush° and Steve Harley° in a benefit concert at London's Hammersmith Odeon, for the family of Bush's lighting engineer Billy Duffy, who died in an accident. He also sings guest vocals on Robert Fripp's LP *Exposure*.

1980 Mar *Games Without Frontiers* is his first solo top 10 single, hitting UK #4. Kate Bush° guests on backup vocals.

May *No Self Control* makes US #33.

June Third LP *Peter Gabriel*, produced by Steve Lillywhite and including guest appearances by Phil Collins°, Paul Weller of The Jam°, and Kate Bush°, tops UK chart for 2 weeks. Charisma has leased it to US Mercury after Atlantic, US licensee of the two previous *Peter Gabriel* LPs, turned it down. Noting the UK chart success of (the included) *Games Without Frontiers*, Atlantic tries to buy the LP back, but to no avail. (On a special release of the LP in Germany, Gabriel sings in German.)

July Jimmy Pursey (ex-Sham 69) releases *Animals Have More Fun* in UK, co-written and co-produced by Gabriel.

Aug Third LP *Peter Gabriel* peaks at US #22. *Biko*, a protest song concerning the death in South Africa of black activist Steve Biko, reaches UK #38.

Sept *Games Without Frontiers*, released by Mercury in US, climbs to #48.

1982 July Gabriel inaugurates the "World of Music Arts and Dance" (WOMAD) festival at Shepton Mallet, UK. It becomes a regular event for many years, bringing together artists from around the world and predates the later "World Music" trend. He loses money on the venture.

Sept Fourth LP *Peter Gabriel*, produced by Gabriel and David Lord and the last to use this title, hits UK #6. The German market receives a German-language version.

Oct [2] A reunion with Genesis° at Milton Keynes Bowl, UK, for a WOMAD benefit concert, helps offset some of the losses of the Shepton Mallet festival.

Oct *Shock The Monkey*, taken from the new LP, makes UK #58.

Nov The fourth LP *Peter Gabriel* reaches US #28. Geffen, his new label in the US, stickers the sleeve with the word "Security" to give it a separate identity from the earlier three.

Dec *I Have The Touch* is released from the LP as a UK single, without charting.

1983 Jan *Shock The Monkey* reaches US #29 and is his first single to perform better in US than UK.

June Double LP *Peter Gabriel Plays Live*, instigated by US Geffen, to satisfy fans in the absence of new studio material (though in fact Gabriel adds new studio overdubbing on the tracks), hits UK #8.

July *I Don't Remember*, taken from the live LP, reaches UK #62.

Aug Double LP *Peter Gabriel Plays Live* peaks at US #44. A live version of the early hit *Solsbury Hill*, taken from it, makes US #84.

Nov Tom Robinson reaches UK #39 with *Listen To The Radio: Atmospherics*, co-written with Gabriel.

1984 June *Walk Through The Fire*, taken from film soundtrack of *Against All Odds* (but actually an unheard out-take from the third LP), makes UK #69.

1985 Apr The soundtrack LP from film *Birdy*, composed and performed by Gabriel and co-produced with Daniel Lanois, reaches UK #51.

1986 May *Sledgehammer*, accompanied by an acclaimed promo video by Steve Johnson, using stop-motion techniques with revolutionary flair, hits UK #4. LP *So*, co-produced by Gabriel and Lanois, enters the UK chart at #1.

June He plays on the "Conspiracy of Hope" tour of US, for Amnesty International.

July *Sledgehammer* tops the US chart for a week, becoming a million-seller internationally and LP *So* hits US #2.

Oct *In Your Eyes*, taken from the LP, reaches US #26.

Nov Gabriel's duet with Kate Bush° on *Don't Give Up*, taken from LP *So*, hits UK #9 and is promoted by two different videos. *Biko* is included on all-star compilation LP *Conspiracy Of Hope*, released in aid of Amnesty International.

1987 Feb [9] Gabriel is voted Best British Male Artist at the UK Record Industry's BPI awards. *Sledgehammer* wins as Best Video, the first of many video awards.

Mar *Big Time* reaches UK #13 and hits US #8, accompanied by another eye-catching video. He performs live in Japan for the "Hurricane Irene" benefit.

Nov A new live version of *Biko*, taken from the soundtrack LP of film *Cry Freedom*, makes UK #49. Gabriel contributes to ex-Band° member Robbie Robertson's eponymous first LP.

1988 Gabriel begins recording a soundtrack for new David Bowie° movie. His impressive collection of video hits, released as *CV*, tops the UK music video charts.

June [11] Gabriel appears at the Nelson Mandela 70th Birthday Party at Wembley, UK, performing his anti-apartheid anthem *Biko*.

July It is announced that he will participate with other major acts (including Sting°, Bruce Springsteen° and Tracy Chapman°) in the Amnesty International world tour.

Aug The Martin Scorsese-directed film *The Last Temptation Of Christ*, with a Gabriel score, opens in US and UK with much controversy.

GALLAGHER & LYLE

Benny Gallagher (vocals and guitar)
Graham Lyle (vocals and guitar)

1966 The duo, both from Largs, Scotland, moves to London to secure a publishing deal.

1967 June Under the name Gallagher-Lyle, *Trees* is released in UK on Polydor but makes no impression.

1969 The duo signs to The Beatles°-owned Apple Music Publishing, where two songs, *International* and *Sparrow*, are covered by Mary Hopkin° and Noel Harrison respectively.

1970 Apr Contract with Apple expires and the duo meets Tom McGuinness (ex-Manfred Mann°), who invites them to join his recently-formed band McGuinness Flint, as vocalist/guitarists and resident songwriters.

Dec McGuinness Flint's *When I'm Dead And Gone*, written by the duo, hits UK #2.

1971 Feb *When I'm Dead And Gone* peaks at US #47.

May McGuinness Flint's *Malt And Barley Blues*, written by the duo, hits UK #5.

Sept After 18 months in the band, having written two LPs' worth of songs (on Capitol LPs *McGuinness Flint* and *Happy Birthday Ruthie Baby*), Gallagher and Lyle leave to pursue a distinct career.

1972 Apr They remain on Capitol for their debut LP *Gallagher And Lyle*, which proves to be their only effort for the label.

1973 Mar The duo signs to A&M Records for LP *Willie And The Lapdog*, produced by Glyn Johns. A&M also reissues the Capitol LP, assumed under the new contract. Neither charts, but reviews are positive.

Sept They join Slim Chance, a 9-piece touring band led by ex-Faces° bassist Ronnie Lane.

Nov [5] Slim Chance makes its live debut at Chipperfield's Circus on Clapham Common, London.

Dec LP *Seeds*, produced by Johns, is released and the duo contributes five songs to Dennis Coulson's eponymous Elektra LP.

1974 May Both leave Slim Chance on the eve of its "Passing Show" UK tour to continue as Gallagher & Lyle.

Sept LP *The Last Cowboy* fails to chart.

1975 Oct Art Garfunkel° records the title track from their LP *Breakaway*.

1976 Apr *I Wanna Stay With You* is their first chart single, hitting UK #6. LP *Breakaway* hits UK #6.

June *I Wanna Stay With You* reaches US #49. *Heart On My Sleeve* hits UK #6.

Sept Garfunkel's° version of title song from LP *Breakaway* reaches UK #35.

Dec *Heart On My Sleeve* makes US #67. Bryan Ferry's° cover version of it is his only US solo hit at #86.

1977 Feb *Every Little Teardrop* reaches UK #32 and is their last UK single hit. LP *Love On The Airwaves* makes UK #19.

1978 Jan LP *Showdown*, the duo's last for A&M, is released without charting.

1979 Oct LP *Lonesome No More* is a one-off recording for Mercury and arouses little interest.

1980 The duo splits to pursue separate careers.

1981 Sept Garfunkel° records Gallagher & Lyle's *A Heart Of New York*, which reaches US #66, and includes it on his LP *Scissors Cut*, which makes US #113 and UK #51.

1983 June Lyle releases a solo, *Marley*, on Red Bus Records in the UK and collaborates with Tom McGuinness on LP *Acting On Impulse*

GALLAGHER & LYLE *cont.*

(credited to the Lyle-McGuinness Band). Gallagher concentrates on TV and movie scores.

1984 Sept Tina Turner° hits US #1 and UK #3 with *What's Love Got To Do With It*, written by Lyle with Terry Britten. (It will be voted Song Of The Year at the Grammy awards in 1985).

1985 Aug Tina Turner° hits US #2 and UK #3 with another Lyle-Britten song, *We Don't Need Another Hero*, the theme from film *Mad Max – Beyond Thunderdome*.

1986 Aug Tina Turner's° LP *Break Every Rule* contains five Lyle-Britten songs and hits US #2 and UK #33. It includes *Typical Male*, which is released as a single.

1988 Apr Gallagher & Lyle re-forms and releases *Putting The Heart Back Into The City* on A&M in UK to commemorate the opening of the Glasgow International Garden Exhibition.

THE GAP BAND

1950s The three Wilson brothers, Ronnie, Charles and Robert, become mainstays of the choir in their father's church in Tulsa, Ok., US. Their job is to warm up the congregation before he speaks.

1967 Ronnie, the oldest brother, forms The Gap Band with other local musicians. (Robert and Charles are still at school and do not join until several years later.)

1970 The Gap Band (the group gets its name from the three main streets of Tulsa's black business community; Greenwood, Archer and Pine) builds its reputation supporting acts such as Ike Turner, The Rolling Stones° and Leon Russell°, on whose Shelter label its first two LPs are released. The other two Wilsons are added to the group as they come of age.

1974 Ronnie plays horns on Leon Russell's° LP *Stop All That Jazz*.

1978 The Gap Band is reduced to the three Wilson brothers. The group signs to Mercury and strikes success immediately with its eponymous debut LP which makes US #77 and enters the R&B charts. *Shake* hits US R&B #1, as does follow-up *Open Up Your Mind (Wide)*.

1979 June LP *The Gap Band* reaches US #77.

1980 Jan LP *Gap Band II* reaches US #42 and is successful internationally.

Aug *Oops Upside Your Head* becomes a dance standard, hitting UK #6.

Oct *Party Lights* reaches UK #30.

Dec LP *Gap Band III* makes US #16 and achieves platinum status. Taken from it, *Burn Rubber On Me (Why You Wanna Hurt Me)* spends 11 weeks on the UK chart, reaching #22, and is regarded as one of the group's definitive funk hits.

1981 Apr *Humpin'*, also from the third LP, achieves UK #36, while *Burn Rubber On Me* reaches US #84.

June *Yearning For Your Love* reaches UK #47 and US #60. A soulful ballad, it marks a significant new direction for the group after the uptempo funk of previous hits. The group makes a short UK visit.

1982 June LP *Gap Band IV* is released and becomes another million-seller (UK #14). Under Lonnie Simmons' production, who by this time has signed The Gap Band to his fledgling Total Experience label, the group records more ballad-style songs including *Season No Reason To Change* and *Outstanding*, as well as more familiar uptempo tracks like *You Dropped The Bomb On Me* and *Talkin' Back*, which continue to popularize its sound on dancefloors. The LP's opening track, *Early In the Morning*, peaks at US #24 and UK #55.

Sept *You Dropped A Bomb On Me* reaches US #31.

1983 Feb *Outstanding* is released, but despite another tour, it stalls at UK #68 and US #51.

Sept LP *Gap Band V – Jammin'* reaches US #28, and earns a gold disk.

1984 Apr *Someday* makes UK #17.

June Follow-up *Jammin' In America* makes only UK #64, despite guest harmonica work from Stevie Wonder°.

1985 Jan LP *Gap Band VI* makes US #58.

Apr LP *Gap Gold – The Best Of The Gap Band* reaches US #103.

1986 Mar LP *Gap Band VII* makes US #159.

Apr *Going In Circles*, taken from the LP, reaches US R&B #2, but fails to cross over.

1987 Jan *Big Fun* hits UK #4.

Feb LP *Gap Band VIII* climbs to UK #47, but fails to cross over in US where it reaches R&B #30.

Mar *How Music Came About (Bop B Da B Da Da)* climbs to UK #61.

May US follow up to *Big Fun*, *Zibble, Zibble (Get The Money)* makes R&B #15.

Aug A re-mix of *Oops Upside Your Head* peaks at UK #20.

1988 Aug The group returns with *You Told Me That* and LP *Straight From The Heart/IX*.

ART GARFUNKEL

1970 Garfunkel (b. Oct.13, 1942, New York, N.Y., US) and long-time musical partner Paul Simon°, whom he met at school in Queens, New York, at age 11, have established the most successful duo since The Everly Brothers°. They split for professional reasons but remain firm friends. Garfunkel's first solo project is acting in Mike Nichols' black comedy war drama movie *Catch 22*.

1971 He appears opposite Ann-Margret and Candice Bergen with Jack Nicholson in film *Carnal Knowledge*.

1973 Oct Having spent a characteristically long period of time crafting his music, Garfunkel emerges with debut solo single *All I Know* which rises quickly to hit US #9 and LP *Angel Clare*, co-produced with ex-Simon and Garfunkel° producer Roy Halee, which hits US #5 and reaches UK #14.

1974 Feb *I Shall Sing* reaches US #38.

Oct The third and last US single to chart under the artist name "Garfunkel" is Tim Moore's *Second Avenue*, which makes US #34.

1975 Sept Revival of The Flamingos' 1959 hit *I Only Have Eyes For You* reaches US #18 but tops the UK chart.

Nov LP *Breakaway*, produced by Richard Perry, climbs to hit #7 in both US and UK. It includes a first reunion cut with, and written by, Simon°, *My Little Town* which hits US #9.

1976 Feb Third single and title cut, written by Gallagher & Lyle°, from LP *Breakaway*, reaches US #39 but all follow-up attempts fail in UK.

1977 Aug From forthcoming LP project recorded mostly at Muscle Shoals studio, *Crying In My Sleep* falls short of both charts.

1978 Feb LP *Watermark* is released, making US #19 and UK #25. It includes current US hit (#17), a cover of Sam Cooke° classic *(What A) Wonderful World* recorded as a trio with James Taylor° and Paul Simon°. (CBS/Columbia insist on the extra song to boost the commerciality of the LP.) One other cut is recorded with Irish folk band The Chieftains, while the remaining ten compositions are all penned by songwriter Jimmy Webb with whom Garfunkel develops a lasting professional relationship.

Nov He begins a 50-city US tour, his first since Simon and Garfunkel° days. It includes two sold-out dates at New York's Carnegie Hall, one performed with Webb.

1979 Feb Garfunkel hosts popular US TV show, NBC's "Saturday Night Live" in which Paul Simon° also appears.

Apr During a busy period, fourth LP *Fate For Breakfast* reaches US #67 and hits UK #2, aided considerably by a surprise UK #1 single, *Bright Eyes*. Written by UK composer Mike Batt, it is heavily featured in cartoon film of Richard Adams' *Watership Down*. Enjoying a 19-week stay on the UK chart, it becomes a rare UK million-seller. In US it disappears without trace.

July A cover of The Skyliners' 1959 hit *Since I Don't Have You* reaches US #53 and UK #38.

Sept His acting career flourishes with a lead role in Nicholas Roeg-directed *Bad Timing*. While he is filming it in Europe, his girlfriend commits suicide in New York. He also makes the more modest film *Illusions*.

1981 Sept LP *Scissors Cut* reunites him with Roy Halee. It reaches US #113 and UK #51 but, with the exception of the minor US charting of *A Heart In New York* (#66), it fails to produce any hit singles, despite songwriting contributions from Gallagher & Lyle°, Jules Shear, Clifford T. Ward and Jimmy Webb.

Oct Simon & Garfunkel unite for an historic reunion concert in New York's Central Park. Following its success (documented on film, TV and video), the duo continues around the world for a 12-month tour. Press reports indicate growing personality friction as the tour progresses.

1984 Nov A UK compilation, *The Art Garfunkel Album*, with the help of a TV campaign, climbs to UK #12. It is not released in US.

1986 July Garfunkel is featured in the role of a teacher in a "go-go rap" movie *Good To Go*.

Dec Having performed a Jimmy Webb seasonal work, *The Animals Christmas*, in London and New York, Garfunkel releases a non-charting LP of it with gospel singer Amy Grant also featured.

1988 *So In Love*, a reworking of The Tymes' 1963 hit, is released from forthcoming LP. While promoting it in UK, Garfunkel is visibly upset by the interviewer's probing emotional questioning on BBC

TV show "Wogan" and refuses to perform the song. It fails to chart.

Mar LP *Lefty* peaks at US #134 but fails in UK.

May A cover version of Percy Sledge classic *When A Man Loves A Woman* fails to score.

Sept Plans are announced by manager Ken Greengrass for Garfunkel to return to live European work including a scheduled appearance at the Prince's Trust charity concert in London with James Taylor°.

MARVIN GAYE

1957 Gaye (b. Apr.2, 1939, Washington, D.C., US), the son of an apostolic minister, returns to Washington with an honorable discharge from the US Navy and joins doo-wop group The Marquees who record, via an introduction from friend and adviser Bo Diddley°, *Hey Little School Girl* (produced by Diddley) and *Baby You're My Only Love* for Okeh.

1958 The Marquees are recruited by Harvey Fuqua, who is re-forming his seminal doo-wop group The Moonglows in Washington.

1959 Moving to Chicago, Ill., the group, as Harvey & The Moonglows, records *Almost Grown* for Chess Records.

1960 Fuqua and Gaye leave The Moonglows and move to Detroit, where Fuqua sets up Tri-Phi and Harvey labels. He signs as an artist to Gwen Gordy's Anna label, a subsidiary of her brother Berry Gordy's Motown Records, into which his own labels are also then absorbed. Through this connection, Gaye finds work as a session drummer (for The Miracles) and back-up vocalist (for The Marvelettes) at Anna and Motown.

1961 Gaye signs to Motown as a solo artist and marries Berry Gordy's younger sister Anna.

May He records his first solo, *Let Your Conscience Be Your Guide*, and LP *The Soulful Moods Of Marvin Gaye*, a collection of ballads and only the second LP released by Motown. Neither charts.

1962 Oct With The Motown Revue (including The Miracles, The Contours, Mary Wells, The Supremes° and Little Stevie Wonder°), Gaye begins a 2-month US tour.

Dec In a change of pace with new producer William "Mickey" Stevenson, *Stubborn Kind Of Fellow*, with backing vocals by Martha & The Vandellas°, is Gaye's US chart debut at #46. It also makes R&B top 10. An LP of the same title follows.

Dec [19] Gaye begins a 10-day run at the Apollo Theater in Harlem, New York, with The Motown Revue.

1963 Mar *Hitch Hike* (covered 2 years later by The Rolling Stones°) reaches US #30.

July *Pride And Joy* hits US #10. LP *Live On Stage* is released.

Dec *Can I Get A Witness* (again covered by The Rolling Stones°) makes US #22, and B-side *I'm Crazy 'Bout My Baby* climbs to US #77.

1964 Apr Under Gordy's direction, Gaye is teamed with Mary Wells to record LP *Together*.

May *You're A Wonderful One* reaches US #15.

June *Once Upon A Time*, a duet with Wells, makes US #19. It is taken from LP *Together*, which reaches US #42.

July *Once Upon A Time* is Gaye's UK chart debut, at #50 for 1 week. In US, B-side *What's The Matter With You Baby* makes US #17. LP *Greatest Hits*, a compilation of Gaye's singles to date, reaches US #72.

Sept *Try It Baby* peaks at US #15. Gaye performs on Murray The K's "Rock'n'Roll Extravaganza" at the Brooklyn Fox theater, alongside fellow Motown acts The Temptations°, The Supremes°, The Miracles, The Contours and Martha & The Vandellas°, plus UK group The Searchers° and others.

Oct *Baby Don't You Do It* (later revived by The Who°) climbs to US #27.

Oct [28] Gaye participates in US TV's "TAMI Show" with The Beach Boys°, The Rolling Stones°, Chuck Berry° and others.

Nov Motown pairs Gaye with another girl singer, Kim Weston, on *What Good Am I Without You*, which makes US #61.

Dec *How Sweet It Is (To Be Loved By You)* is Gaye's first solo UK hit, at #49.

1965 Jan *How Sweet It Is (To Be Loved By You)* hits US #6.

Mar LP *How Sweet It Is To Be Loved By You* makes US #128.

May *I'll Be Doggone* hits US #8, becoming Gaye's first US R&B #1 and million-seller.

Aug *Pretty Little Baby* reaches US #25.

Nov *Ain't That Peculiar* hits US #8 and R&B #1, and is another million-seller. Gaye releases two LPs which reveal different sides of his style: *A Tribute To The Great Nat "King" Cole* and *Hello Broadway* (a collection of show tunes).

1966 Mar *One More Heartache* peaks at US #29.

July *Take This Heart Of Mine* reaches US #44.

Aug LP *Moods Of Marvin Gaye*, mostly a singles compilation, climbs to US #118.

Sept *Little Darlin' (I Need You)* makes US #47 and UK #50.

Oct Another compilation LP, *Marvin Gaye Greatest Hits, Vol.2*, peaks at US #178.

1967 Mar Gaye and Weston duet on LP *Take Two*, from which *It Takes Two* makes US #14 and UK #16.

July Gaye duets with Philadelphia singer Tammi Terrell on *Ain't No Mountain High Enough*, which reaches US #19. (This will be Gaye's most enduring collaboration; he and Terrell will record together until her tragic death.)

Aug *Your Unchanging Love* makes US #33.

Nov Gaye and Terrell's *Your Precious Love* hits US #5, while duet LP *United* reaches US #69.

1968 Jan The duo enjoys its second US top 10 success with *If I Could Build My Whole World Around You* which hits US #10 and makes UK #41. B-side *If This World Were Mine* reaches US #68.

Feb Gaye's solo *You* makes US #34.

May Another Gaye/Terrell duet, *Ain't Nothing Like The Real Thing*, hits US #8 and UK #34.

Sept *You're All I Need To Get By*, with Terrell, hits US #7.

Oct Terrell collapses on stage in Gaye's arms during a concert at Hampton-Sydney College in Virginia. Doctors diagnose a brain tumor. Meanwhile, the duo's LP *You're All I Need* reaches US #60.

Nov Gaye's solo *Chained* makes US #32, while *You're All I Need To Get By* climbs to UK #19. Another duet with Terrell, *Keep On Lovin' Me Honey*, makes US #24.

Dec Gaye's first US #1 (for 7 weeks) is *I Heard It Through The Grapevine*, a Norman Whitfield/Barrett Strong song (a million-seller for Gladys Knight & The Pips° on Motown in 1967). After lying unused for some months after he recorded it, Gaye's dramatically different version becomes the biggest-selling single of Motown's first 20 years of operations. It is taken from LP *In The Groove*, which reaches US #63.

Dec [28] Gaye performs at the Miami Pop Festival in Hallendale, Fla., with Chuck Berry°, Junior Walker°, Fleetwood Mac° and others.

MARVIN GAYE *cont.*

1969 Feb *You Ain't Livin' Till You're Lovin'*, a Terrell duet, climbs to UK #21.

Mar *I Heard It Through The Grapevine* hits UK #1 for 3 weeks and is a worldwide hit. Gaye and Terrell's duet *Good Lovin' Ain't Easy To Come By* makes US #30.

June *Too Busy Thinking About My Baby* hits US #4 and is another million-seller. (B-side *Wherever I Lay My Hat* will be a UK #1 in 1983 for Paul Young°.)

July *Good Lovin' Ain't Easy To Come By* reaches UK #26. LP *M.P.G.* is Gaye's first US LP top 50 placing at #33. At the same time, compilation LP *Marvin Gaye And His Girls*, featuring duets with Terrell, Wells and Weston, peaks at US #183.

Sept *Too Busy Thinking About My Baby* hits UK #5.

Oct Duet LP *Easy* with Terrell makes US #184, while solo *That's The Way Love Is* hits US #7, but fails to chart in UK. The LP of the same title reaches US #189.

Dec *What You Gave Me*, with Terrell, reaches US #49. Another Terrell duet, *The Onion Song* hits UK #9 (the last hit for the duo). (It will reach US #50 five months later.)

1970 Feb *How Can I Forget* reaches US #41.

Mar [16] Terrell dies, aged 24, in Graduate Hospital, Philadelphia. She has had six brain operations in 18 months. Grief-stricken, Gaye retires from the public eye.

June *Abraham, Martin And John*, written by Dick Holler (a US hit for Dion° and on Motown for The Miracles), hits UK #9. Compilation LP *Marvin Gaye And Tammi Terrell's Greatest Hits* reaches US #171 and UK #60.

July *The End Of Our Road* makes US #40.

Dec Compilation LP *Marvin Gaye Super Hits* climbs to US #117.

1971 Apr Gaye returns to the spotlight with a creative tour-de-force in a new, subtler style (the result of his own writing and production), voicing concern about poverty, pollution and the Vietnam War. *What's Going On* hits US #2 for 3 weeks (behind Three Dog Night's° *Joy To The World*) and is a million-seller.

July LP *What's Going On* hits US #6.

Aug *Mercy Mercy Mercy (The Ecology)*, from the LP, hits US #4 and is another million-seller.

Nov Third US single from the LP, *Inner City Blues (Make Me Wanna Holler)*, hits US #9. In UK, where the new style has not met the same reaction, both LP and single of *What's Going On* fail to chart. *Save The Children* is extracted from the LP and reaches UK #41.

1972 June *You're The Man* reaches US #50.

1973 Feb Following the success of Isaac Hayes° and Curtis Mayfield° in similar ventures, Gaye writes and performs the soundtrack for a detective movie, *Trouble Man*. The title track hits US #7, while the soundtrack LP (with three vocals and ten instrumental tracks) reaches US #14.

Sept *Let's Get It On*, again self-produced (with Ed Townsend), but this time in an earthier R&B style than the ethereal *What's Going On*, tops the UK chart for 2 weeks and is another million-seller.

Oct LP *Let's Get It On*, a celebration of sexuality, performed in appropriate muscular, steamy style, hits US #2.

Dec Motown teams Gaye with his fourth female singing partner, Diana Ross°, and they record LP *Diana And Marvin*, which climbs to US #26. The duet single *You're A Special Part Of Me* reaches US #12, while Gaye's solo *Come To Get This*, from LP *Let's Get It On*, makes US #21.

1974 Feb *You Sure Love To Ball*, also from the LP, reaches US #50.

Apr *You Are Everything*, a Gaye/Ross° revival of The Stylistics° US hit, hits UK #5.

May Another Ross°/Gaye duet, *My Mistake (Was To Love You)*, reaches US #19. Triple compilation LP *Marvin Gaye Anthology*, containing most of his hit singles to date, reaches US #61.

Aug Gaye/Ross° duet *Don't Knock My Love* reaches US #46, while LP *Marvin Gaye Live!*, recorded in concert at Oakland, Cal., (a return to live stage after a 6-year absence) hits US #8.

Nov Gaye's solo *Distant Lover* (later a favorite stage performance) reaches US #28.

1976 June LP *I Want You* hits US #4 and makes UK #22, while extracted title track reaches US #15.

Aug *After The Dance*, also from the LP, reaches US #74.

Sept Gaye plays sold-out and rave-reviewed concerts in London, UK, at the Royal Albert Hall and the Palladium. The latter is recorded for LP release.

Nov Compilation LP *Marvin Gaye's Greatest Hits* reaches US #44. It is retitled *The Best Of Marvin Gaye* in UK, where it reaches #56.

1977 Apr Though they have not lived together for years, Gaye and Anna Gordy are only now divorced. Gaye marries Janis Hunter.

June Dance-oriented *Got To Give It Up*, another million-seller, tops the US chart and hits UK #7. Double live LP *Marvin Gaye Live At The London Palladium*, which includes *Got To Give It Up* as its only studio track, hits US #3.

1978 Oct It is reported that Gaye is in financial collapse, with unsecured debts of $7 million.

Nov Janis Hunter files for divorce.

1979 Feb Double LP *Here, My Dear*, a tortured reflection on the break-up of Gaye's marriage to Anna Gordy, reaches US #26. Gaye teams with Stevie Wonder°, Diana Ross° and Smokey Robinson° for *Pops We Love You* a tribute to Berry Gordy's late father. It reaches US #59. Gaye, beset by problems, including hard drugs (especially free-base cocaine), and pursued by US Internal Revenue Service with an unpaid tax bill over $2 million, moves to self-imposed exile and seclusion in Hawaii (where he reportedly tries to commit suicide with a cocaine overdose) and lives in a trailer.

1981 Mar LP *In Our Lifetime*, Gaye's last new LP for Motown, issued without his approval, reaches US #32 and UK #48. Now increasingly erratic as a performer and suffering from paranoid delusions brought on by years of drug abuse, Gaye divides his time between London and Ostend, Belgium. He severs his contract with Motown.

1982 Nov Signed, after lengthy negotiations (involving the IRS, which is due most of Gaye's royalties), to CBS/Columbia, Gaye's *(Sexual) Healing*, a sensual progression from his *Let's Get It On* bag, hits UK #4.

Dec LP *Midnight Love*, recorded in Belgium, with old friend Fuqua, hits US #7 and UK #10, achieving million-plus sales. *(Sexual) Healing* tops the US R&B chart for 10 weeks, the first disk to do so since Ray Charles'° *I Can't Stop Loving You* in 1962. Gaye returns to US, living in Hollywood and then Palm Springs.

1983 Jan *(Sexual) Healing* hits US #3 (also selling a million), while *My Love Is Waiting* reaches UK #34.

Feb [25] Gaye wins his first Grammy award for *(Sexual) Healing* named Best Male Vocal Performance of the Year.

June A US tour to promote the new material is not a financial success, and the pressure pushes Gaye into retreat with drugs again.

Sept Gaye's version of *I Heard It Through The Grapevine* is used over the credits of movie *The Big Chill*.

Nov LP *Every Great Motown Hit Of Marvin Gaye* reaches US #80. Gaye moves into his parents' house (purchased by him for them in the 1960s) in Crenshaw, LA.

Dec TV-advertised compilation LP *Greatest Hits* reaches UK #13.

1984 Feb Gaye sings *The Star Spangled Banner* at the National Basketball Association (NBA) All-Star Game.

Mar Gaye announces more than once to relatives that he intends to take his own life – on one occasion having a gun forcibly removed from his grasp.

Apr [1] Gaye, still living at his parents' LA home, and with family and friends concerned over his mental state, is shot dead by his father, Marvin Gaye Sr., during a violent argument.

Apr [5] Gaye is buried at Forest Lawn Cemetery in LA. The funeral service is attended by Smokey Robinson°, Stevie Wonder°, Motown's Berry Gordy, Harvey Fuqua, Quincy Jones, Ray Parker Jr.°, producers Norman Whitfield and Eddie and Brian Holland. Robinson reads the *23rd Psalm*, and Wonder sings *Lighting Up The Candle* in dedication to Gaye.

Nov Gaye's father is sentenced to 5 years imprisonment for voluntary manslaughter.

1985 Apr Lionel Richie° writes Gaye tribute *Missing You*, a US #10 for Diana Ross°.

May *Sanctified Lady* reaches UK #51.

June LP *Dream Of A Lifetime*, a compilation of tracks recorded shortly before his death and unreleased material from Gaye's time at Motown, reaches UK #46.

Dec LP *Romantically Yours*, drawn from unissued 1979 jazz-oriented big band sessions, is released, without charting.

1986 May *I Heard It Through The Grapevine* is reissued in UK after being used on a TV advertisement for Levi's jeans, and hits UK #8.

THE J. GEILS BAND

Peter Wolf (vocals)
J. Geils (guitar)
Danny Klein (bass)
Seth Justman (keyboards and vocals)
Magic Dick (harmonica)
Stephen Jo Bladd (drums and vocals)

1965/67 Geils (b. Jerome Geils, Feb.20, 1946, New York, N.Y., US), and Klein (b. May 13, 1946, New York, N.Y.) perform in a jug band in Worcester Tech, Mass. They drop out of college to go professional, moving to Boston and switching from jug band music to blues, playing in local band The Hallucinations, with Magic Dick (b. Richard Salwitz, May 13, 1945, New London, Conn., US). Wolf (b. Peter Blankfield, Mar.7, 1946, New York, N.Y.), an ex-DJ on Boston's WBCN with an encyclopedic knowledge of R&B music, and Bladd (b. July 13, 1942, Boston, Mass.). The J. Geils Blues Band is formed and Geils, Dick, Klein, Wolf and Bladd will provide the band's nucleus for 16 years.

1969 Justman (b. Jan.27, 1951, Washington D.C., US) joins and "Blues" is dropped from the name. The group's reputation builds performing at local club The Catacombs, followed by much success at The Boston Tea Party. It is discovered by an Atlantic talent scout who attends the gig expecting to find a black soul group.

1971 Jan The group cuts eponymous first R&B LP (including covers of John Lee Hooker° and Otis Rush songs) for Atlantic, which wins it the Most Promising New Band award from *Rolling Stone* magazine. Critics praise the band as the best white blues/R&B act since Paul Butterfield°. The LP reaches only US #195.

June [27] The band plays the final night of the Fillmore East with The Beach Boys°, The Allman Brothers° and Mountain.

Dec It releases second LP *The Morning After*, which reaches US #64.

1972 Jan The group's first chart entry is a cover of Bobby Womack's° *Looking For A Love*, which makes US #33.

Apr [1] Four people die, including a 16-year-old hacked to death in his sleeping bag, during The Mar Y Sol Festival, Puerto Rico, at which The J. Geils Band is performing.

Nov LP *Live – Full House* makes US #54.

1973 Apr The band appears on ABC TV's "In Concert" but is censored due to the offensive lyrics of a song.

May LP *Bloodshot* hits US #10.

June *Give It To Me* reaches US #30 and pushes sales of *Bloodshot* to gold status.

Sept *Make Up Your Mind* makes only US #98.

1974 Jan LP *Ladies Invited* makes US #51 and LP *Nightmares . . . And Other Tales From The Vinyl Jungle* reaches US #26. They represent a departure from the band's traditional R&B base.

Aug [7] Wolf marries actress Faye Dunaway in Beverly Hills, LA. (The marriage will end in divorce.)

1975 Jan *Must Of Got Lost* reaches US #12.

Oct LP *Hotline* peaks at US #36.

Nov The band records gigs in Boston and at Detroit's Cobo Arena for the next LP.

1976 May *Where Did Our Love Go* makes US #68.

June Double live LP *Blow Your Face Out* climbs to US #40.

1977 July The J. Geils Band changes name to Geils for self-produced LP *Monkey Island*, which is its final Atlantic LP and reaches US #51.

Aug *You're The Only One* reaches US #83.

1979 Feb The group leaves Atlantic for EMI America. LP *Sanctuary* reaches US #49 and earns another gold disk. It includes *One Last Kiss*, which makes US #35.

Apr *Take It Back* reaches US #67.

June *One Last Kiss* makes UK #74.

July Atlantic issues LP *Best Of The J. Geils Band*, which peaks at US #129.

1980 Feb LP *Love Stinks* makes US #18 and earns a gold disk. The title track reaches US #38, while *Come Back* makes US #32.

July *Just Can't Wait* reaches US #78.

1982 Feb *Centerfold* and LP *Freeze Frame* both top the US charts.

Apr Title track of *Freeze Frame* hits US #4, while *Centerfold* becomes the group's biggest UK hit at #3. LP *Freeze Frame* reaches UK #12.

May *Freeze-Frame* makes UK #27.

July *Angel In Blue*, the third single from LP *Freeze Frame*, makes US #40 and UK #55. The band tours UK supporting The Rolling Stones°.

1983 Jan Live LP *Showtime!* reaches US #23. *I Do* climbs to US #24. Wolf leaves for a solo career; the press reports he has been sacked.

Mar *Land Of A Thousand Dances* reaches US #60.

1984 Aug Wolf's solo LP *Lights Out* reaches US #24 and the title track peaks at US #12.

Nov Wolf's *I Need You Tonight* reaches US #36.

Dec The group's *Concealed Weapons* reaches US #63. Its first post-Wolf LP *You're Getting Even While I'm Getting Odd* reaches US #80.

1985 May *Oo-Ee-Diddley-Bop!* makes US #61.

Aug *Fright Night* from the film of the same name, reaches US #91.

1987 May Wolf's LP *Come As You Are* peaks at US #53.

GENESIS

Tony Banks (keyboards)
Mike Rutherford (guitars)
Phil Collins (drums and vocals)

1965 May Two groups are formed at public school Charterhouse in Godalming, Surrey, UK: Peter Gabriel° (b. May 13, 1950, London, UK) and Tony Banks (b. Mar.27, 1951, East Heathly, Sussex UK) are in The Garden Wall, with Chris Stewart (drums); Michael Rutherford (b. Oct.2, 1950, Guildford, Surrey) and Anthony Phillips are members of The Anon with Rivers Job (bass), Richard MacPhail (vocals) and Rob Tyrell (drums).

1966 Sept Joining forces as The (New) Anon after some pupils have left the school, Phillips, Rutherford, Gabriel°, Banks and Stewart make a 6-track demo tape of mostly Phillips/ Rutherford songs.

1967 Jan They send the tape to ex-Charterhouse pupil Jonathan King° at Decca Records, who is impressed and finances more demos and renames the group Genesis.

Dec Still at school, the group signs a 1-year contract to Decca and King produces its first session at Regent Sound studio in London.

1968 Feb Debut single *The Silent Sun* is released, but does not chart.

May Chris Stewart departs and John Silver joins on drums. *A Winter's Tale* is released by Decca but fails to chart.

Aug King books studio time in the school summer holidays to produce and record a Genesis LP.

1969 Mar LP *From Genesis To Revelation* is released, an orchestra having been added after the sessions to make them sound like The Moody Blues°. (The LP allegedly sells just 650 copies.)

June *Where The Sour Turns To Sweet*, the last Decca release, fails to sell.

July With all members now finished at school (though Banks has begun a physics course at Essex University), the group decides to go professional. Silver leaves and is replaced on drums by John Mayhew, recruited through a *Melody Maker* classified ad.

Sept After rehearsing in August, Genesis plays its first paid gig (at a private party: fee £25), moving on to a series of youth club, social club and college bookings (Twickenham Technical College pays a princely £50).

Oct For 5 months the group lives together in a cottage near Dorking, Surrey, practising and rehearsing its stage act and writing songs for the second LP.

1970 Mar Charisma Records owner Tony Stratton-Smith sees Genesis live, signs them to his label and becomes their manager.

July After completing the new LP, Phillips and Mayhew leave. (Phillips will record several guitar-based solo LPs in the late 70s.)

Aug Phil Collins° (b. Jan.31, 1951, Chiswick, London) joins on drums after auditioning with 14 others in reply to another *Melody Maker* ad.

Oct LP *Trespass* is released in UK but fails to chart.

Dec Mick Barnard, a temporary replacement for Phillips, is in turn replaced by ex-Quiet World member Steve Hackett (b. Feb.12, 1950, London) on guitar.

1971 Jan Two-part single *The Knife*, taken from LP *Trespass*, does not sell. The band begins to gig constantly in UK, building a solid live following.

June Gabriel° breaks his ankle, which halts touring for a while, and the group works in the studio on a new LP.

Nov LP *Nursery Cryme*, on which Collins° sings his first lead vocal on one track, does not chart. In live shows Gabriel's° props and masks attract the attention of the music press, though these and his between-songs stories are initially there to cover up the band's tuning and to settle Gabriel's own nerves.

1972 Jan First live gig outside UK is in Brussels, Belgium.

May *Happy The Man* is released but does not chart.

GENESIS *cont.*

Oct LP *Foxtrot* reaches UK #12. Its 24-minute track *Supper's Ready* becomes the band's live anthem.

Dec [11] The group plays its first US gig, at Brandeis University near Boston, Mass.

1973 Jan First headlining tour of major UK venues.

Mar The band begins its first full US tour.

Aug LP *Genesis Live*, recorded on tour in Leicester and Manchester, UK, and originally taped for a US radio broadcast, hits UK #9.

Oct LP *Selling England By The Pound*, co-produced by Genesis and John Burns, hits UK #3. Promoter Tony Smith takes over from Tony Stratton-Smith (no relation) as manager.

Nov Another major UK tour is followed by second extensive US trek.

1974 Jan Five sell-out nights in London's Drury Lane theater.

Feb LP *Selling England By The Pound*, their first US chart entry, reaches #70.

Apr *I Know What I Like (In Your Wardrobe)*, an edited version of a track from LP *Selling England By The Pound* is Genesis' first hit single, at UK #21.

May 18-month-old LP *Nursery Cryme* makes a belated UK chart showing at #39.

June LP *Genesis Live* reaches US #105.

Oct London Records in US releases the 1969 LP *From Genesis To Revelation*, which crawls to US #170.

Nov *Counting Out Time* does not chart. The group begins a world tour, with a show based around new double LP, *The Lamb Lies Down On Broadway*, which it will perform 102 times.

Dec Double LP *The Lamb Lies Down On Broadway*, recorded on the Island Studios mobile, hits UK #10.

1975 Jan Double LP *The Lamb Lies Down On Broadway* reaches US #41.

Apr *The Carpet Crawlers* does not chart.

May At the end of the "Lamb Lies Down" world tour, in St. Etienne, France, Gabriel° plays his last show with the band before departing for unrevealed personal reasons (eventually to embark on a successful solo career).

Nov Hackett releases LP *Voyage Of The Acolyte* which peaks at UK #26.

1976 Mar LP *A Trick Of The Tail*, produced by David Hentschel, hits UK #3 with Collins° on lead vocals as well as drums since the search for a new singer to replace Gabriel° has proved unsuccessful. The title track fails to chart as a single.

Mar [28] Ex-Yes° and King Crimson° drummer Bill Bruford joins for a US tour, freeing Collins° for vocal duties.

Apr LP *A Trick Of The Tail* makes US #31. The group has decided on individual writing credits for this LP.

Dec After a series of UK gigs, Bruford returns to session work and is replaced by American session drummer Chester Thompson. On a further UK tour, Genesis is the first band to play the re-opened Rainbow Theatre in London.

1977 Jan LP *Wind And Wuthering*, produced by Hentschel and Genesis and recorded in Holland the previous Nov. hits UK #7.

Feb [1] The film *Genesis In Concert* is premiered in London, with HRH Princess Anne in attendance.

Feb The band begins a 3-month, 45-city North American tour.

Mar *Your Own Special Way* reaches UK #43. It is also their first US hit single, at #62. LP *Wind And Wuthering* makes US #26.

June Three-track EP *Spot The Pigeon* reaches UK #14. Genesis plays three sold-out nights at Earls Court, London. Hackett leaves. (He will have six hit solo LPs in the UK and US in six years.)

Nov Double live LP *Seconds Out* (with Hackett) hits UK #4. The remaining members work on a new LP as a trio, recording in Holland with Hentschel.

1978 Jan LP *Seconds Out* reaches US #47.

Feb American guitarist Daryl Steurmer replaces Hackett as a guest for stage work only.

Mar [29] The band arrives in US for a 20-date tour, the first leg of "World Tour 78", which will keep them on the road for most of the year.

Apr First trio release, *Follow You, Follow Me*, hits UK #7. LP *And Then There Were Three* hits UK #3.

May [15] The band begins European leg of its world tour.

May LP *And Then There Were Three* earns the band its first gold disk, reaching US #14. *Follow You, Follow Me* makes US #23.

June [24] The band shares top billing with Jefferson Starship° at the Knebworth Festival in UK.

July *Many Too Many* peaks at UK #43.

1979 After months of arduous live work, Genesis is put on hold as Banks and Rutherford record solo LPs and Collins° tries to resolve marital difficulties.

Nov Banks' LP *A Curious Feeling*, featuring Chester Thompson and singer Kim Beacon, charts at UK #21 and US #171.

1980 Mar [29] The band begins a 7-month world tour in Vancouver, Canada.

Mar Rutherford's solo LP *Smallcreep's Day* reaches UK #13 and US #163.

Apr LP *Duke*, recorded at Abba's° Polar Studios in Stockholm, Sweden, tops the UK chart for 2 weeks: the band's first UK #1. *Turn It On Again* hits UK #8.

May [24] Collins°, Banks and Rutherford amuse LA fans by turning up at the Roxy club box office to sell tickets personally for their performance.

June *Duchess* climbs to UK #46. LP *Duke* reaches US #11 and will earn the band's second US gold disk.

July Taken from the LP, *Misunderstanding* reaches US #14.

Sept *Misunderstanding* stalls at UK #42. *Turn It On Again* makes US #58.

1981 Feb With Collins'° parallel solo career now underway, Genesis launches its own Duke Records label, distributed by Atlantic in the US. John Martyn, Leo Kosmin and the band Nine Ways To Win are all signed, but the project is short-lived.

Sept LP *Abacab*, featuring the horn section from Earth, Wind & Fire°, is the group's second UK #1 (for 2 weeks), while the title track hits UK #9.

Nov LP *Abacab* hits US #7. Their first US top 10 success, it earns the group a platinum disk. *Keep It Dark* reaches UK #33 and *No Reply At All* makes US #29.

1982 Feb The title track from *Abacab* makes US #26.

Mar *Man On The Corner* makes UK #41.

May In US *Man On The Corner* outperforms UK by one place to US #40.

June Three-track EP *3 x 3*, featuring *Paperlate*, hits UK #10. Double LP *Three Sides Live* (the fourth side has unreleased studio cuts from 1979-81), hits UK #2.

July *Paperlate* reaches US #32 and double LP *Three Sides Live* hits US #10, earning a gold disk.

Oct The "Six of the Best" concert at Milton Keynes Bowl, UK, has the present Genesis line-up reunited with Gabriel°, while Hackett also joins for the encore *I Know What I Like*. Rutherford's second solo LP *Acting Very Strange* climbs to UK #23 and US #145.

1983 June Banks releases two LPs, his soundtrack for Michael Winner film *The Wicked Lady* (on Atlantic) and his own *The Fugitive*, which reaches UK #50.

Oct *Mama* hits UK #4, taken from LP *Genesis* and co-produced with Hugh Padgham, tops UK chart.

Nov LP *Genesis* hits US #9 and is the group's second US million-seller. *Mama* reaches only US #73.

Dec *That's All!* reaches UK #16 and hits US #6 a few weeks later.

1984 Feb *Illegal Alien* climbs to UK #46.

Mar LPs *Nursery Cryme* and *Trespass* are reissued in UK, charting briefly at #68 and #98 respectively.

Apr *Illegal Alien* makes US #44.

July *Taking It All Too Hard* reaches US #50.

1985 Feb Rutherford's extra-curricular band Mike & The Mechanics, featuring Paul Carrack (ex-Ace°, Squeeze°, Nick Lowe° among others) and Paul Young° (ex-Sad Café) hits US #6 and UK #21 with *Silent Running*, the theme from film *On Dangerous Ground*.

Mar LP *Mike & The Mechanics* reaches UK #78.

May A second Mike & The Mechanics single, *All I Need Is A Miracle*, hits US #5 but stalls in UK at #53.

1986 June LP *Invisible Touch* tops the UK chart, while the title track single makes UK #15.

July *Invisible Touch* tops the US chart, becoming their first #1 single on both sides of the Atlantic, while the LP hits US #3.

Aug Third Mike & The Mechanics single, *Taken In*, reaches US #32.

Sept *In Too Deep*, from movie *Mona Lisa*, climbs to UK #30.

Oct *Throwing It All Away*, taken from LP *Invisible Touch*, hits US #4.

Nov Collection of recent video promos released as *Visible Touch* tops UK music video chart.

1987 Jan *Land Of Confusion* benefits from a popular video, created by UK TV puppet masters Fluck and Law from the "Spitting Image" series, and peaks at UK #14 and hits US #4.

Feb *Tonight, Tonight, Tonight* reaches UK #18, and through its exposure as a TV beer commercial, will top the US chart.

May *In Too Deep* hits US #3 as the group completes a lengthy world tour.

June *Throwing It All Away* reaches UK #22.

GERRY & THE PACEMAKERS

Gerry Marsden (vocals and lead guitar)
Les Chadwick (bass)
Les Maguire (piano and saxophone)
Freddie Marsden (drums)

1959 The group is formed by Gerry (b. Gerard Marsden, Sept.24, 1942, Liverpool, UK), his brother Freddie (b. Oct.23, 1940, Liverpool) and Chadwick (b. John Leslie Chadwick, May 11, 1943, Liverpool), with pianist Arthur Mack, initially as a part-time skiffle and rock oufit. The original name is The Mars Bars (a naive ploy to seek sponsorship from the confectionary maker – instead, the company insists that it is changed). The Pacemakers is settled on as an alternative.

1960 June [6] The group plays, along with The (Silver) Beatles°, at Wallasey's Grosvenor Ballroom.

Dec Mack leaves and Chadwick switches from lead to bass guitar. The group is offered a 4-month contract to play in Hamburg, West Germany. The trio gives up its day jobs (Gerry is a tea-chest maker) to turn professional.

1961 May Maguire (b. Dec.27, 1941, Wallasey, UK), ex-The Undertakers, joins on piano and occasional saxophone, rounding off the group's sound, which (with a repertoire of 300 songs acquired prior to and during the German trip) is now wholly rock/R&B-based.

Oct [19] The group makes a one-off tie-up with The Beatles°, playing at Litherland Town Hall, Merseyside, as "The Beatmakers". (The two groups will constantly play alongside each other on engagements at the Cavern club and other Liverpool venues throughout 1961 and 1962.)

1962 June Brian Epstein, already managing The Beatles°, signs the group to a management contract.

Nov EMI's George Martin sees the group playing at a Birkenhead ballroom and signs it to the Columbia label.

1963 Jan [22] The first recording session in London produces Gerry's own *Away From You*, the standard *Pretend* (saved for an LP), and Mitch Murray's *How Do You Do It* (a song Martin has wanted The Beatles° to cut, but which they rejected and wrote *Please Please Me* to replace).

Apr *How Do You Do It* hits UK #1 for 3 weeks, selling half a million copies.

June *I Like It*, this time custom-written for the group by Murray, tops the UK chart for 4 weeks.

Oct An anthemic revival of Rodgers and Hammerstein's *You'll Never Walk Alone* (from *Carousel*) tops the UK chart for 4 weeks and is the group's biggest UK seller (776,000 copies). It also gives them the unique distinction of having hit UK #1 with their first three singles. (The record will stand for 21 years until equalled in 1984 by another Liverpool group, Frankie Goes To Hollywood°. The B-side of Frankie's first chart-topper *Relax* will be a revival of Gerry's *Ferry Cross The Mersey*.)

Nov LP *How Do You Like It?*, featuring *You'll Never Walk Alone* hits UK #2.

Dec [13] The group tops the bill on UK TV's "Sunday Night at the London Palladium" (but this particular show comes from the Prince of Wales theater). This appearance is followed by a 4-week starring role in the pantomime "Babes in the Wood", which plays in Hanley, Ipswich and Cheltenham, UK.

1964 Feb Written by Gerry, *I'm The One* hits UK #2 for 2 weeks, held from the top by The Searchers'° *Needles And Pins*. The group plays a sold-out UK tour with US visitor Ben E. King.°

Apr Gerry & The Pacemakers tour Australia and New Zealand.

May [3] Their US TV debut, singing *Don't Let The Sun Catch You Crying*, is on "The Ed Sullivan Show". The song, a ballad written by Gerry, peaks at UK #6, the group's first single not to make the UK top 5.

June The group starts work on its own feature film and Gerry writes a batch of new songs for the soundtrack.

July *Don't Let The Sun Catch You Crying* hits US #4, the group's first and biggest US hit. *I'm The One*, having failed to sell in US earlier, makes US #82.

Aug *How Do You Do It*, issued in US to follow up the top 10 success, hits #9. US LP *Don't Let The Sun Catch You Crying* (compiled from UK singles and LP tracks) reaches US #29.

Sept *It's Gonna Be Alright*, an uptempo taster of music from their movie, makes only UK #24 – a chart disaster by the group's previous standards, but also a sign that pop music in UK is rapidly developing away from the Pacemakers' pure Merseybeat style.

Oct *I Like It*, a late issue in US, makes #17.

Dec US LP *Gerry And The Pacemakers' Second Album*, another compilation from UK singles and LP tracks, peaks at US #129.

1965 Jan The film *Ferry Cross The Mersey*, written by Tony Warren, creator of UK TV's "Coronation Street", opens in UK. The movie stars Gerry & The Pacemakers as a facsimile of themselves, rising to success in a beat contest. Cilla Black°, The Fourmost° and some lesser-known Liverpool acts make cameo appearances in the largely location-shot movie. The ballad title song, written by Gerry, returns the group to the UK top 10 at #8. In US a revival of Bobby Darin° ballad *I'll Be There* is released and reaches US #14.

Feb Soundtrack LP from *Ferry Cross The Mersey* makes UK #19.

Mar As the movie is released in US, *Ferry Cross The Mersey* gives the group its last US top 10 success (as it already has in UK), hitting #6. The soundtrack LP reaches US #13, while simultaneously-released US LP *I'll Be There* (pairing the ballad hit with revived 1950s rock numbers) makes US #120.

Apr *I'll Be There* reaches UK #12.

Apr [29] An appearance at the Brooklyn Fox Theater, New York, launches a month-long US tour.

May *It's Gonna Be Alright* makes US #23.

June *You'll Never Walk Alone* is finally promoted as a US single and reaches #48.

July Compilation LP *Gerry And The Pacemakers' Greatest Hits*, not released in UK, makes US #44.

Sept *Give All Your Love To Me*, a ballad not released in UK, reaches US #68.

Dec A revival of 1950s ballad *Walk Hand In Hand*, an attempt to recapture the *You'll Never Walk Alone* spirit, climbs to UK #29. (It is the group's final UK chart entry.)

1966 Feb *La La La*, an *I Like It*-styled beater, and now unfashionable, is the group's first single to miss the UK chart.

Apr *La La La* makes US #90.

Oct The group decides to split, recognizing that it can no longer keep pace with the rapidly-changing UK rock scene. Gerry announces he will continue as a solo vocalist. One of the final group recordings, *Girl On A Swing*, peaks at US #28 but fails in UK.

GERRY & THE PACEMAKERS *cont.*

1967 Jan Gerry signs to CBS as a soloist, but first solo *Please Let Them Be* fails to chart. (A fate which will be shared by 6 more solo releases on CBS, NEMS, Decca, Phoenix and DJM over the next 10 years, despite success in other showbiz areas.)

July Gerry leads a team of UK vocalists to victory in the annual Knokke-Le-Zoute song festival in Belgium.

1968 Jan Gerry takes over the leading role from Joe Brown in the musical *Charlie Girl* on London's West End stage. (He will stay with the show for 2 years.)

1970 Gerry gains a regular slot on UK children's TV on the "Sooty and Sweep Show".

1973 June [28] Gerry puts a new Pacemakers line-up together for the British Re-Invasion Show at Madison Square Garden, New York, US, playing with The Searchers°, Herman's Hermits° and Wayne Fontana and The Mindbenders°.

1975 Nov With the new Pacemakers, Gerry plays a successful 8-week nostalgia tour of Australia. (He will subsequently divide his time between solo live and TV work, and nostalgic tours and hit re-recordings with new Pacemakers groups. LP *20 Year Anniversary* containing new versions of old group favorites will appear in UK in 1983.)

1985 June With *You'll Never Walk Alone* having been adopted as a crowd anthem by Gerry's own favorite soccer team, Liverpool FC, soon after his 1963 hit, he has been asked to perform the song on several special occasions such as the memorial service following the death of Bill Shankly, Liverpool's former manager. When a fire at the ground of Bradford City football club kills over 50 spectators, a multi-artist recording of the song is arranged by 10cc's° Graham Gouldman, money from its sales contributing to a fund for the victims' families. Gerry takes the lead vocal in the hymnal style of his original recording and the record tops the UK chart – making him the first-ever act to hit #1 with two different versions of the same song.

ANDY GIBB

1973 Gibb (b. Mar.5, 1958, Manchester, UK), after moving to Australia at age 6 months with his family and returning to London 9 years later, after his brothers' success as The Bee Gees° in the 1960s, moves with his parents to Ibiza, Spain, and plays in local clubs before moving to Isle of Man, UK.

1975 He returns to Australia and has a huge hit with *Words And Music*. He supports The Bay City Rollers° on tour and opens for The Sweet° in Sydney.

1976 He marries Kim Reeder. (It will only last 2 years.)

1977 Gibb signs to Robert Stigwood's RSO label (to whom his brothers, The Bee Gees° are also signed).

July *I Just Want To Be Your Everything*, written by brother Barry, tops the US chart after a 14-week climb. It peaks at UK #26. LP *Flowing Rivers* reaches US #19.

1978 Mar *(Love Is) Thicker Than Water*, co-written with Barry and featuring Joe Walsh° on guitar, replaces The Bee Gees'° *Stayin' Alive* at US #1, but is replaced a week later by The Bee Gees' *Night Fever*.

June Gibb becomes the first artist to hit US #1 with his first three releases when *Shadow Dancing*, penned by all four Gibbs, tops the chart. It reaches UK #42. LP *Shadow Dancing* hits US #7 and UK #15.

July Gibb is joined on stage by The Bee Gees° at a concert in Miami, Fla. It is the first time all four brothers have appeared live together.

Sept *An Everlasting Love* hits UK #10 and US #5.

Dec Ballad *(Our Love) Don't Throw It All Away* hits US #9.

1979 Feb *(Our Love) Don't Throw It All Away* reaches UK #32.

1980 Mar *Desire* hits US #4. LP *After Dark* reaches US #21.

May *I Can't Help It*, a duet with Olivia Newton-John°, reaches US #12.

Dec LP *Andy Gibb's Greatest Hits* reaches US #46.

1981 Feb *Time Is Time* makes US #15.

Apr *Me (Without You)* reaches US #40.

June [10] Gibb opens in the role of Frederic in Gilbert and Sullivan's *The Pirates of Penzance* at LA's Ahmanson Theater.

Sept *All I Have To Do Is Dream*, a duet with "Dallas" TV star Victoria Principal, makes US #51.

1982 Gibb is fired as TV host on US show "Solid Gold" for missing several tapings. (He will be replaced by Rex Smith, who originally played the role of Frederic in the New York production of *The Pirates of Penzance*.) He is also dismissed from the Broadway production (he had already starred in LA and Canadian productions) of *Joseph and the Amazing Technicolor Dreamcoat*, for missing 12 performances in a month.

1985 Gibb is treated for drug dependency at the Betty Ford Clinic in Cal. following a well-publicized addiction to cocaine, which he blames on the break-up of his affair with Ms Principal.

1987 He files for bankruptcy in Miami claiming less than $50,000 in assets and debts of more than of $1 million.

1988 Jan Gibb signs to Island Records to record a new LP in UK.

Mar [7] While working on the LP, Gibb is admitted to the John Radcliffe Hospital, Oxford, UK, with severe stomach pains.

Mar [10] Gibb dies of unspecified causes.

DEBBIE GIBSON

1983 Gibson (b. Aug.31, 1970, Long Island, N.Y., US) has been writing songs since childhood (including *Make Sure You Know Your Classroom* at age 6) and learning piano (with Morton Estrin, who has also taught Billy Joel°) from age 5. Her parents, recognizing her skills (she has already won $1,000 in a songwriting contest with *I Come From America*) and her perfect pitch singing voice, invite Doug Breithart to become her manager. Under his guidance she learns to play, write, arrange, engineer and produce songs, and will demo-record over 100 of her own in a multi-track home studio.

1985 Gibson is offered lead role in US production of *Les Miserables* but is turned down when producers discover she is only 15. Her prior acting experience has been as an extra in movies *Ghostbusters* and *Sweet Liberty*.

1986 Sept [2] Still at school, she signs worldwide to Atlantic and begins recording LP *Out Of The Blue* with producer Fred Zarr.

1987 Sept Chart debut *Only In My Dreams*, written by her, hits US #4.

Oct *Only In My Dreams* peaks in UK at #54.

Dec *Shake Your Love* hits US #4.

1988 Feb *Shake Your Love* hits UK #7, while debut LP *Out Of The Blue*, featuring ten songs written by Gibson and four tracks produced by her, hits at US #7. US critics hail her as the most versatile and talented of a sudden crop of successful teenage female singers. (The LP will sell over 2 million copies.)

Mar *Only In My Dreams* is reissued in UK to tie in with Gibson's short promotional and mini-concert tour. It reaches UK #11.

Apr Title track from LP *Out Of The Blue* hits US #3.

May *Out Of The Blue* reaches UK #19, while LP of the same title peaks at #26.

June *Foolish Beat* is her first #1, topping US chart for a week. Gibson becomes the youngest artist ever to write, produce and perform a US #1 single. She graduates, with honors, from Calhoun High School.

July *Foolish Beat* hits UK #9. She begins her first headlining major US concert tour, supported by label-mates, Times Two.

GARY GLITTER

1958/59 Taking his stepfather's surname to front Paul Russell & His Rebels, Glitter (b. Paul Gadd, May 8, 1940, Banbury, Oxon, UK) and his group secure a residency at the Safari Club in Trafalgar Square, London, where he meets film producer Robert Hartford Davis, who becomes his manager and arranges a contract with Decca Records.

1960 Jan Ballad *Alone In The Night* is released on Decca under the name Paul Raven. It fails to sell, despite an airing on UK TV's "Cool for Cats".

Feb He tours at the bottom of a bill including Anthony Newley, Mike Preston and Mike & Bernie Winters. The Rebels accompany him but quit when the manager suggests they go professional.

1961 Glitter (as Raven) has a small part in Davis' film *Stranger in the City*, and tours Scandinavia.

Aug Second single, *Walk On Boy* is released on Parlophone, but is only successful in the Middle East.

Nov *Tower Of Strength* is a version of a Bacharach/Hilliard song but Frankie Vaughan hits UK #1 with it, and Parlophone drops Glitter (Raven). He shelves a recording career and works as a warm-up man for UK TV's "Ready, Steady, Go!" He links up with the Mike Leander Orchestra, making a short tour as vocalist before it breaks up. He forms Paul Raven & Boston International, later The Bostons. (The group becomes a popular live act in Germany where it will spend much of the next five years.)

1968 Leander is made UK head of MCA Records, and signs him to the label.

June Written by Leander, *Musical Man* is released by Raven under the name Paul Monday but it flops.

Aug Reverting to Paul Raven, his next MCA single, *Soul Thing*, also flops.

1969 Oct Released under the name Rubber Bucket, *We Are All Living In One Place* features a chanting chorus of 3,000 people assembled in front of the MCA offices to watch police evict squatters next door. Despite heavy publicity, it fails to sell. A version of George Harrison's° *Here Comes The Sun* (released as Paul Monday) flops.

1970 July A version of Sly Stone's *Stand*, as Paul Raven, is his last MCA single.

Oct He appears on LP *Jesus Christ Superstar*.

1971 With a switch of image and musical direction he records a 15-minute dance stomp, *Rock'n'Roll*, under the new name Gary Glitter (chosen after considering Terry Tinsel, Stanley Sparkle and Vicky Vomit).

1972 Mar Bell UK releases *Rock'n'Roll*, split between both sides of a single (with *Rock'n'Roll Part 2* as the featured side). Initially it looks like being yet another flop, but UK discos, then Radio Luxembourg, and finally Radio 1, pick up on it.

June *Rock'n'Roll* hits UK #2, where it stays for 3 weeks.

Sept *Rock'n'Roll* hits US #7.

Oct Second Gary Glitter single, *I Didn't Know I Loved You (Till I Saw You Rock'n' Roll)* hits UK #4.

Nov First LP, *Glitter* hits UK #8, but makes only US #186.

Dec *I Didn't Know I Loved You (Till I Saw You Rock'n'Roll)* reaches US #35. (Bell will release 5 more Glitter singles in US but this will be his last US chart entry.)

1973 Jan Glitter buries his Paul Raven persona when he ceremoniously places old records and photos of his former self in a coffin which he sinks in the river Thames.

Feb *Do You Wanna Touch Me (Oh Yeah)*, with the established Glitter style, hits UK #2.

Apr *Hello Hello I'm Back Again* also hits UK #2.

July *I'm The Leader Of The Gang (I Am)* hits UK #1 for 4 weeks. Second LP, *Touch Me* hits UK #2.

Nov *I Love You Love Me Love* enters the UK chart at #1 where it will stay for 4 weeks, eventually selling more than a million copies in UK alone. Glitter's shows at London's Rainbow Theatre are filmed for documentary *Remember Me This Way*.

1974 Mar Glitter's backing band begins a separate career as The Glitter Band and debut *Angel Eyes* hits UK #4. (They will score several more hits in their own right in 18 months.) As well as touring and recording on their own, they continue to work with Glitter, whose *Remember Me This Way* hits UK #3.

June *Always Yours* hits UK #1.

July LP *Remember Me This Way* hits UK #5.

Dec *Oh Yes! You're Beautiful* hits UK #2.

1975 Jan Glitter bows out of concert performance with a televised "farewell" show. (For the next few years his live appearances will be sporadic.)

May *Love Like You And Me* hits UK #10.

June *Doin' Alright With The Boys* hits UK #6.

Nov A remake of The Rivingtons' *Papa Oom Mow Mow* makes only UK #38.

1976 Mar *You Belong To Me* reaches UK #40. Compilation LP *Greatest Hits* makes UK #33.

1977 Feb *It Takes All Night Long* reaches UK #25.

May The Glitter Band splits.

July *A Little Boogie Woogie In The Back Of My Mind* reaches UK #31. (Glitter will spend much of the next few years touring outside UK on the strength of his 70s fame. He has a stint as a very portly Frank-N-Furter in Antipodean production of *The Rocky Horror Show* and, unable to trim his spending, he will be declared bankrupt.)

1980 Sept GTO releases 4-track EP *Gary Glitter*, which makes UK #57.

Nov [13] Glitter launches a comeback tour at Cromwell's Club, Norwich, UK. He releases *What Your Momma Don't See (Your Momma Don't Know)*.

1981 Oct A Bell track, *And Then She Kissed Me*, reaches UK #39. With a reunited Glitter Band he completes a UK tour which is not a financial success. He signs to Arista.

Dec *All That Glitters*, a segued mix of Glitter's biggest hits, reaches UK #39.

1982 July Joan Jett & The Blackhearts' version of *Do You Wanna Touch Me* makes US #20. In UK, Glitter is increasingly regarded as a fatherly figure who, by his own admission, will never go away.

1984 July *Dance Me Up*, an updated version of his 1970s style, reaches UK #25 and Glitter appears on BBC TV's "Top of the Pops".

Dec *Another Rock'n'Roll Christmas* hits UK #7.

1986 Mar [1] Glitter is admitted to hospital suffering from an accidental overdose of sleeping pills.

1988 June The Timelords' *Doctorin' The Tardis* which borrows from Glitter's *Rock'n'Roll*, hits UK #1 and Glitter teams with the group to record a remix. He appears on the cover of UK music paper *New Musical Express* and has his own chat segment on UK ITV's late-night show "Night Network". Always a larger than life image, he continues to provide popular cult entertainment, increasingly for UK's advertising industry.

GODLEY & CREME

Kevin Godley (vocals and drums)
Lol Creme (vocals and guitar)

1964/69 Both Godley (b. Oct.7, 1945, Manchester, UK) and Creme (b. Sept.19, 1947, Manchester), while attending art school in Manchester, have been in local band The Sabres, when The Whirlwinds, featuring Graham Gouldman, releases a single with Creme-penned B-side *Baby Not Like Me*. Gouldman's next band, The Mockingbirds, featuring Godley as drummer, releases *That's The Way It's Gonna Stay*, the first of many over the next 2 years on EMI/Columbia, Decca and Immediate labels. Gouldman, by now a successful songwriter (*For Your Love*, *Bus Stop* and *No Milk Today*) listens to demos made by Godley & Creme and invites them to join him on a project to be financed by Giorgio Gomelsky's Marmalade Records in London. Four songs are recorded and released, including two on a single credited to Frabjoy & Runcible Spoon.

1969 Godley & Creme are signed as writers by the London office of the Kasenatz-Katz production house.

GODLEY & CREME *cont.*

1970 Aug They team with Gouldman and ex-Mindbender Eric Stewart to form Hotlegs, and release *Neanderthal Man*, which hits UK #2.

1971 Godley & Creme become staff producers and writers at the Stewart part-owned Strawberry Studios in Stockport, Cheshire, UK.

1972/76 After recording a demo of *Donna* for Apple, the quartet signs to Jonathan King's° UK Records. He christens them 10cc° and they have eight top 10 UK hits in 4 years.

1976 Nov Godley & Creme split from 10cc° and begin work on a 3-minute track which will eventually evolve into a three LP set. (Gouldman and Stewart stay together and continue as 10cc.)

1977 Nov Triple box set LP *Consequences*, (featuring Sarah Vaughan and Peter Cook) reaches UK #52. *Five O'Clock In The Morning*, taken from the LP flops. Their guitar attachment the "Gizmo", featured on the LP, also fails to take off, despite promotion as a major new musical innovation. (An excerpt from *Consequences* will later be used in a UK cinema cigarette commercial.)

1978 Aug LP *L*, with assistance from Andy Mackay on saxes and US DJ Paul Gambaccini playing the role of "The Bad Samaritan" on the track *The Sporting Life*, reaches UK #47.

1979 Jan *Sandwiches Of You* is released, but fails to chart.

Feb LP *Music From Consequences* is released, featuring selected songs from the triple set.

Oct The duo, signed to Polydor, releases *An Englishman In New York*, but despite radio play it fails to chart.

Nov Paul McCartney° guests on LP *Freeze Frame*, but this also fails to score.

1981 Two further unsuccessful singles are followed by production work on Mickey Jupp's LP *Long Distant Romancer*.

Oct Reverting to the commercial direction of 10cc°, *Under Your Thumb* hits UK #3.

Nov LP *Ismism* reaches UK #29.

Dec *Wedding Bells* hits UK #7. Concurrently running an increasingly successful career as video directors/producers, their work includes clips for Visage, Duran Duran° and Toyah.

1982 They direct a TV commercial for a UK jeans company.

Sept A video for *Save A Mountain For Me* is shot on Alcatraz Island, San Francisco, Cal., but fails to help sales.

1983 Apr LP *Birds Of Prey* and single *Samson* are released to indifferent reaction. They direct three videos from Police's° *Synchronicity* LP (including award-winning *Every Breath You Take*), moving on to Herbie Hancock's *Rockit* and a brief reunion with Gouldman and Stewart directing 10cc's° *Feel The Love* promo clip.

Nov The video for *Rockit* wins awards for Most Innovative Video and Best Art Direction at *Billboard* magazine's Video Music Awards ceremony in Pasadena, Cal., the latest in a long series of video trophies.

1984 Much of the year is spent directing videos for hot new UK act, Frankie Goes To Hollywood°. They also complete the "Rebellious Jukebox" series for US MTV and release *Golden Boy*, which fails to score.

1985 Apr *Cry*, produced by Trevor Horn, makes UK #19 and US #16, aided by their own highly acclaimed, and later copied, video, featuring continuous 3-second face changes. (The song will rechart the following year at UK #66 after being featured in an edition of US TV show "Miami Vice".) Horn remixes 10cc° and Godley & Creme material for LP *The History Mix Volume I*. A video of *History Mix* compiled from promo clips and others they have directed is issued in US.

1986 *Mondo Video*, an experimental project, is made and set to be released on their Videola label in 1988.

1987 They direct NYNEX *Yellow Pages* TV commercial for the US market.

Sept Compilation LP *The Changing Faces Of 10CC And Godley And Creme* hits UK #4, and achieves gold status.

1988 Feb LP *Goodbye Blue Sky*, featuring songs using harmonicas of all shapes and sizes, is released to critical acclaim, as is *A Little Bit Of Heaven*, but neither charts. They begin work on debut feature film *Howling at the Moon*.

ANDREW GOLD

1964/67 After taking up piano, guitar and drums simultaneously at age 13, Gold (b. Aug.2, 1951, Burbank, Cal., US), son of composer Ernest Gold and singer Marni Nixon, forms his first band to play high school dances and parties with Peter Bernstein (son of film composer Elmer Bernstein) and Wendy Waldman. They variously call themselves The Doberman, The Herd and The Wails. Gold and friend Charlie Villiers secure a contract with Polydor, releasing self-penned *All The Little Girls*.

1969 Gold forms Bryndle with Bernstein, Waldman, ex-Stone Poney Kenny Edwards and his girlfriend Karla Bonoff, and drummer Dennis Wood. The band signs to A&M, spending 6 months working with producer Chuck Plotkin on a never-to-be-released LP.

1971 Bryndle splits and Gold spends a few months working at A&M studios as an assistant engineer. He reunites with Bernstein and Edwards, and with drummer Gene Garfin forms The Rangers.

1973 Aug The Rangers split and Linda Ronstadt° calls Gold, saying she needs a guitarist and piano player for a gig at LA's Roxy.

1974 He tours with Ronstadt° for 9 months before going into the studio to work on her LP *Heart Like A Wheel*. He contributes lead guitar, electric piano, drums and percussion to Ronstadt's US chart topping remake of Clint Ballard's *You're No Good*.

1975 Plotkin, now A&R chief at Asylum Records, signs Gold to a solo contract and he begins work on his solo debut, with friends Edwards, Garfin and Bernstein.

Oct Gold plays guitar, piano and drums on Garfunkel's° UK #1 *I Only Have Eyes For You*.

1976 Jan *That's Why I Love You* reaches US #68. LP *Andrew Gold* makes only US #190, but songs from it are later covered by Judy Collins°, The James Gang, Cliff Richard° and Leo Sayer°.

Mar Gold starts work on second LP with producer Peter Asher.

1977 May LP *What's Wrong With This Picture?* makes US #95.

June Autobiographical *Lonely Boy* hits US #7 and UK #11.

1978 Mar LP *All This And Heaven Too* peaks at US #81 and UK #31.

Apr *Thank You For Being A Friend* reaches US #25.

May *Never Let Her Slip Away* hits UK #5.

July *How Can This Be Love* makes UK #19. *Never Let Her Slip Away* stalls at US #67.

Oct *Thank You For Being A Friend* reaches UK #42.

1980 LP *Whirlwind* fails to chart, and Gold and Asylum part company. When his marriage to singer Nicolette Larson ends, Gold moves to UK where he teams with ex-10cc° Graham Gouldman to form Common Knowledge. (Larson becomes a country singer in Nashville, Tenn.)

1982 Gold co-produces and writes three songs for 10cc's° LP *Ten Out Of 10*. Common Knowledge records *Victoria* for Vertigo.

1985 After achieving little success as Common Knowledge, Gold and Gouldman change labels, from Vertigo to RCA, and band name to Wax.

Oct Wax debut single *Ball And Chain* is released, but fails to chart.

1986 Apr *Right Between The Eyes* reaches UK #60 and US #43 from Wax.

June Debut LP *Magnetic Heaven* fails to chart.

1987 May Gold co-produces Japan superstar E (Eikichi) Yazawa's English-speaking debut LP *Flash In Japan*.

Sept Wax single *Bridge To Your Heart* reaches UK #12 and LP *American English* makes UK #59.

LESLEY GORE

1962 While still studying at the Dwight Preparatory School for Girls, Englewood, N.J., Gore (b. May 2, 1946, New York, N.Y., US) sings with a 7-piece jazz group at the Prince George Hotel, Manhattan, N.Y. The group sends demos via its booking agent Joe Glaser to Mercury Records' Irving Green. He is unimpressed by the group, but sees potential for Gore as a soloist, and agrees to a contract guaranteeing the release of some singles.

1963 Feb Armed with more than 250 demos, Mercury staff producer Quincy Jones visits Gore at her home in Tenafly, N.J. to choose material for her first single.

June Released 3 days after Gore's 17th birthday, *It's My Party* tops the US chart and is a million-seller. (The song will receive a Grammy nomination for Best Rock'n'Roll Record the following year.)

July *It's My Party* hits UK #9.

Aug Follow-up *Judy's Turn To Cry*, continuing the storyline of the first single, hits US #5. LP *I'll Cry If I Want To* reaches US #24.

Dec *She's A Fool* hits US #5. Gore undertakes a pre-Christmas UK tour. She receives several awards: The National Association of Record Merchants (NARM) votes her the Most Promising Female Vocalist of 1963; she wins the Most Promising Female Vocalist Popularity Poll of 1963 by the American Disk Jockeys and 16 magazine votes her Best Female Vocalist.

1964 Feb *You Don't Own Me*, Gore's second million-seller, hits US #2, held off the top spot for 3 weeks by The Beatles'° *I Want To Hold Your Hand*. LP *Lesley Gore Sings Of Mixed-Up Hearts* peaks at US #125.

Apr *That's The Way The Boys Are* reaches US #12.

June *I Don't Wanna Be A Loser* makes US #37. Gore graduates from high school.

Aug LP *Boys, Boys, Boys* reaches US #127. Gore flies to California to appear in first annual "TAMI Show" (Teenage Awards Music International) at the Santa Monica Civic Auditorium. She makes a cameo appearance in film *Girls on the Beach*.

Sept Gore enrolls at Sarah Lawrence College. Jeff Barry and Ellie Greenwich-penned *Maybe I Know* reaches US #14.

Oct *Maybe I Know* makes UK #20.

Nov *Hey Now* reaches US #76. B-side *Sometimes I Wish I Were A Boy* reaches only US #86.

Dec LP *Girl Talk* reaches US #146. US trade magazines *Cashbox*, *Music Business* and *Record World* all name her the year's Best Female Vocalist.

1965 Feb *Look Of Love* makes US #27.

Apr *All Of My Life* reaches US #71.

Aug *Sunshine, Lollipops And Rainbows*, penned by Marvin Hamlisch from movie *Ski Party* in which Gore makes a cameo appearance, climbs to US #13. LP *The Golden Hits Of Lesley Gore* reaches US #95.

Oct *My Town, My Guy And Me* makes US #32.

Dec LP *My Town, My Guy And Me* reaches US #120. Gore's self-penned, with brother Michael, *I Won't Love You Anymore (Sorry)* reaches US #80.

1966 Feb *We Know We're In Love* peaks at US #76.

Apr [11] Gore appears on the final broadcast of US NBC-TV's "Hullabaloo" with Paul Anka°, The Cyrkle and Peter and Gordon°. *Young Love* reaches US #50.

July During her summer vacation, Gore makes her TV acting debut in "The Donna Reed Show", and guests as Catwoman's assistant Pussycat in "Batman".

1967 Mar *California Nights* reaches US #16.

May LP *California Nights* makes US #169.

July *Summer And Sandy* peaks at US #65.

Oct *Brink Of Disaster* stalls at US #82.

1968 May Gore receives a B.A. degree in English and American literature.

1969 Having recorded Laura Nyro's *Wedding Bell Blues*, Gore leaves the Mercury label.

1970 Gore signs to ex-Four Seasons° producer Bob Crewe's label, cutting four singles, none of which charts, and recording a duet with Oliver under the name Billy & Sue.

1972 She signs to Mowest Records cutting LP *Someplace Else Now*, but returns to the nightclub circuit, where she has made her living over the past few years. She also turns to stage work, appearing in summer stock productions of *Finian's Rainbow*, *Funny Girl* and *Half A Sixpence*.

1975 Gore appears on the bill of "Richard Nader's Rock'n'Roll Revival" at New York's Madison Square Garden. She reunites with Quincy Jones who signs her to A&M to record LP *Love Me By Name*. Produced by Jones, musical assistance comes from The Brothers Johnson, Dave Grusin, Herbie Hancock, Tom Scott and Toots Thielemans.

1980 Nov She contributes lyrics (*Out Here On My Own*, a US #19 for Irene Cara), to brother Michael's Academy Award-winning score for *Fame*.

1981 Oct Dave Stewart and Barbara Gaskin's cover of *It's My Party* hits UK #1.

GRAND FUNK RAILROAD

Mark Farner (vocals and guitar)
Craig Frost (keyboards)
Mel Schacher (bass)
Donald Brewer (drums)

1967 Brewer (b. Sept.3, 1948, Flint, Mich., US), ex-leader of a band called The Jazz Masters, and Farner (b. Sept.29, 1948, Flint) join Terry Knight and The Pack and *I (Who Have Nothing)*, on local Flint label Lucky Eleven, makes US #46.

1968 They are joined by bassist Schacher (b. Apr.3, 1951, Owosso, Mich., US), ex-? & The Mysterians. Knight becomes manager and changes the group's name, using inspiration from The Grand Trunk Railroad.

1969 July Capitol Records signs the band after seeing it play the Atlanta Pop festival in front of 125,000 people.

Aug The group participates in the 3-day "Texas International Pop Festival" at Dallas. A reported 120,000 see Grand Funk perform with Chicago°, Led Zeppelin°, Janis Joplin° and many others.

Oct *Time Machine* makes US #48.

Nov LP *On Time* climbs to US #27.

Dec *Limousine Driver* makes US #98.

1970 Feb *Heartbreaker* stalls at US #72. LP *Grand Funk* reaches US #11.

June The band spends $100,000 on a block-long billboard in New York's Times Square to promote new LP *Closer To Home*.

Aug LP *Closer To Home* hits US #6.

Sept *Closer To Home* makes US #22.

1971 Jan *Mean Mistreater* reaches US #47. LP *Live Album* hits US #5.

Feb *Inside Looking Out* makes UK #40. (It will be the group's only UK chart single.)

May [3] 150 reporters are invited to New York's Gotham Hotel to meet the band; only 6 show. *Feelin' Alright* makes US #54.

June [5] Breaking The Beatles'° box-office record, Grand Funk sells out an appearance at New York's Shea Stadium in 72 hours.

June LP *Survival* hits US #6.

Sept *Gimme Shelter* reaches US #61.

1972 Jan LP *E Pluribus Funk* hits US #5.

Mar [27] The group fires manager Knight, setting off a series of multi-million dollar lawsuits between the two parties. John Eastman, Paul McCartney's° brother-in-law, takes over.

Mar *Footstompin' Music* makes US #29.

Apr *Upsetter* reaches US #73.

June Compilation LP *Mark, Don & Mel 1969-71* climbs to US #17.

Nov *Rock 'N' Roll Soul* reaches US #29. LP *Phoenix* hits US #7. The band drops "Railroad" from its name. LP *Mark, Don And Terry 1966-67* charts briefly at US #192.

Dec [23] Accompanied by two deputy sheriffs, Knight turns up at a charity concert, with a court order giving him the right to seize $1 million in money or assets pending the settlement of several outstanding lawsuits.

1973 Keyboardist Frost (b. Apr.20, 1948, Flint, Mich.) joins the group.

Sept LP *We're An American Band*, produced by Todd Rundgren, is the group's first as Grand Funk and hits US #2. *We're An American Band* hits US #1.

1974 Jan *Walk Like A Man* reaches US #19.

May A cover of Little Eva's° *The Locomotion* hits US #1 in 8 weeks. For only the second time in rock history a cover version tops the chart after the original has hit #1. (The first was *Go Away Little Girl*. A third time will occur when The Carpenters° hit US #1 with *Please Mr. Postman* after The Marvelettes have done the same.) LP *Shinin' On* hits US #5.

Sept *Shinin' On* reaches US #11.

1975 Jan *All The Girls In The World Beware!!!* hits US #10. Jimmy Ienner takes over as producer. *Some Kind Of Wonderful* hits US #3 and *Bad Time* hits US #4.

Oct The group reverts to its original name Grand Funk Railroad, but LP *Caught In The Act* makes only US #21. LP *Born To Die*, intended to be the group's last, reaches US #47.

1976 Feb *Take Me* reaches US #53.

Apr *Sally* reaches US #69.

Sept Frank Zappa° offers to produce the band and it stays together to record LP *Good Singin' Good Playin'*, signing to MCA. The LP reaches US #52. *Can You Do It* makes US #45. The group splits when Farner goes solo, cutting one LP for Atco. The rest form Flint with guitarist Billy Elworthy.

Nov Capitol issues LP *Grand Funk Hits* which reaches US #126.

1981 Jan Grand Funk re-forms with Farner, Brewer and bassist Dennis Bellinger (Frost is with Bob Seger°). They cut LP *Grand Funk Lives* for Full Moon label. It reaches US #149.

1983 *What's Funk?* is released. It is the second and last LP from the re-formed group who appeared on *Heavy Metal* film soundtrack. The group finally splits, having sold in excess of 20 million records. Brewer joins Frost in Bob Seger's° Silver Bullet Band.

GRANDMASTER FLASH, MELLE MEL & THE FURIOUS FIVE

Joseph Saddler (Grandmaster Flash)
Melvin Glover (Melle Mel)

1977/78 Flash (b. Joseph Saddler, Jan.1, 1958, New York, N.Y.,US), having worked as a mobile DJ in the Bronx area of New York, begins developing the scratch mixing technique originated by Bronx DJ Jamaican Kool Herc, adding rappers Cowboy, Kid Creole and Melle Mel to his road show, he forms Grandmaster Flash & The 3 MCs. He adds two more rappers, Duke Bootee (b. Ed Fletcher) and Kurtis Blow°, who is later replaced by Raheim, and the group becomes Grandmaster Flash & The Furious Five.

1979 Following the success of The Sugarhill Gang's *Rapper's Delight*, New York labels sign other rap outfits, and Flash makes his recording debut on Enjoy label with *Superrappin'*, whose rapid fire rap exchanges by The Furious Five galvanize the street scene. Disappointed by lack of chart success, Flash seeks an alternative label deal, releasing *We Rap More Mellow* for Brass label (as The Younger Generation) and *Flash To The Beat* for Bozo Meko (as Flash & The Five) before signing to Sylvia Robinson's Sugarhill label.

1980 The group's debut on Sugarhill, *Freedom*, despite not making the Hot 100, is awarded a gold disk and is popular in their native New York.

1981 They follow this with *The Adventures Of Grandmaster Flash On The Wheels Of Steel* which also goes gold. It is hailed as a definitive disk in rap history and features serious sampling for the first time. Follow-up *Flash To The Beat* fails to attract the same attention.

1982 May Robinson asks the group to record *The Message*, written by her and Bootee.

Aug Interest from New York clubs spreads to UK where *The Message* hits #8.

Nov *The Message*, having gone gold in 25 days, climbs only to US #62, failing to cross over completely from its specialist market. LP *The Message* makes US #53 and UK #77.

1983 June Discord within the group affects recording. Melle Mel, the dominant voice in The Furious Five, begins to emerge in his own right and records *The Message II (Survival)* with Bootee but it fails to chart.

Nov Earlier recorded *White Lines (Don't Don't Do It)*, a combination of Grandmaster Flash and Melle Mel, is an anti-cocaine rap anthem. It becomes a US dance hit but fails to chart. Flash leaves the group and begins a lengthy $5 million court case against Sugarhill to use the full group name (which he will lose). Mel, still on Sugarhill, is with rapping buddies, Scorpio and Cowboy but Raheim and Kid side with Flash.

1984 Feb *White Lines (Don't Don't Do It)* re-enters the UK chart to hit #7.

June Sugarhill compilation LP *Greatest Messages* climbs to UK #41. Now established as Grandmaster Melle Mel & The Furious Five, their contribution to the breakdance movie *Beat Street* titled *Beat Street Breakdown Part 1*, on Atlantic, peaks at UK #42.

Sept Mel's *We Don't Work For Free* reaches UK #45.

Oct Mel is featured as intro rapper on worldwide Chaka Khan° smash *I Feel For You* which hits US #3 and UK #1. *Beat Street Breakdown Part 1* reaches only US #86. Sugarhill LP *Work Party*, released only as Grandmaster Melle Mel, climbs to UK #45.

1985 Jan Mel hits UK #8 with *Step Off (Part 1)*. Grandmaster Flash signs a worldwide solo contract with Elektra.

Feb Grandmaster Flash solo release *Sign Of The Times* charts briefly at UK #72, as debut solo LP *They Said It Couldn't Be Done* makes a 1-week appearance at UK #95.

Mar Grandmaster Melle Mel's *Pump Me Up* makes UK #45.

1986 Apr Flash releases non-charting LP *The Source*.

1987 Mar LP *Ba Dop Boom Bang* and single *U Know What Time It Is?* both fail to chart for Flash. A lack of commercial success encourages all parties involved to reunite as Grandmaster Flash, Melle Mel & The Furious Five at a charity concert hosted by Paul Simon° at New York's Madison Square Garden.

1988 Feb Still contracted as a solo artist to Elektra, Grandmaster Flash releases LP *On The Strength*.

EDDY GRANT

1960 Grant (b. Edmond Montague Grant, Mar.5, 1948, Plaisance, Guyana) moves with his parents to London, UK, where his first musical experience is as a trumpeter in the Camden Schools' Orchestra. He later takes up piano and guitar.

1965 He forms a group with two friends from Acland Burghley school in Hornsey Rise, London: Pat Lloyd (b. Mar.17, 1948, London, UK) and John Hall (b. Oct.25, 1947, London). They are joined by twin brothers Derv and Lincoln Gordon (b. June 29, 1948, Jamaica), and rehearse for almost a year, since Grant is the only one who plays any instrument.

1966 The group emerges as The Equals (Derv Gordon on lead vocals, Grant on lead guitar, Lincoln Gordon on rhythm guitar, Lloyd on bass and Hall on drums), with a repertoire of ska-influenced R&B songs mostly written by Grant. Some demos of these are heard by UK independent label President Records, which signs the group. Debut single *I Won't Be There* gets UK pirate radio airplay, but does not sell. As a sideline from the group, Grant makes one of the first English ska LPs, *Club Ska*, using a string of pseudonyms to give the impression of a compilation LP.

Dec *Hold Me Closer* again fails to chart. Several DJs pick up instead on the riff-driven Grant-penned B-side, *Baby Come Back*.

1967 The Equals spend 6 months working in Europe, particularly Holland and West Germany. Ariola Records in Germany releases *Baby Come Back*. It becomes a major hit, bringing the group extensive TV work, which spreads the popularity of *Baby Come Back* to hit #1 in Holland and Belgium.

Dec Low-price LP *Equals Explosion*, promoted on pirate station Radio Caroline as an ideal party LP, hits UK #10 and puts the group in the odd position of having a UK chart LP before a single.

1968 Feb Supported by pirate stations (Caroline in UK and Radio Veronica from Holland, much heard in UK), *I Get So Excited* makes UK #44.

Mar LP *Equals Explosion* reaches UK #32. (It includes Grant's *Police On My Back*, which will be revived by The Clash° on their 1980 LP *Sandanista*.)

July *Baby Come Back*, reissued in UK as an A-side, tops the UK chart for 3 weeks (deposing The Rolling Stones'° *Jumpin' Jack Flash*). UK sales top 250,000 and The Equals receive a gold disk for total European/UK sales of over a million.

Sept *Laurel And Hardy* reaches UK #35.

Oct *Baby Come Back* is the group's only US hit, at #32.

Dec *Softly Softly* peaks at UK #48.

1969 Apr Concerned not to lose commercial touch, the group pares its style to a hook-filled bubblegum/R&B blend on *Michael And The Slipper Tree*, which makes UK #24.

Aug In similar style, *Viva Bobby Joe* hits UK #6. (It is taken up by football crowds, who sing the adaptation "Viva Bobby Moore" at appearances by the England soccer team captain.)

1970 Jan *Rub-A-Dub-Dub* reaches UK #34.

1971 Jan Less bubblegum-like *Black Skin Blue-Eyed Boys*, an indication of Grant's later writing style, gives the group its third (and last) top 10 UK hit, at #9.

1972 Following an illness which keeps him off the road, Grant leaves The Equals to set up his own production company, the first step towards his own complete recording operation. (He will continue for a while to produce the group, in which he is replaced by Jimmy Haynes. Haynes will leave in mid-1973, to be replaced by Dave Martin, while Hall will quit early in 1975 and Neil McBain will take over on drums. The Equals will never again have any commercial impact on record, despite remaining a popular UK and Continental live attraction until the mid-70s.)

1973/76 Grant works as a producer (for The Pioneers and others), using the songwriting and performing royalties from his Equals days to set up his own label Ice Records (initially in Guyana) and The Coach House recording studio in London.

1977 Grant's debut solo LP is *Message Man*, on which he studio-overdubs every voice and instrument himself (setting a pattern for later recordings).

1979 July His solo career is launched via a deal between Ice and UK Ensign label (which also has The Boomtown Rats°); totally self-performed LP *Walking On Sunshine* is released, and from it, *Living On The Front Line*, a hard-edged reggae/funk blend is a major disco hit and reaches UK #11.

Nov *Walking On Sunshine*, does not chart in UK as a single, but is Grant's debut US R&B at #86.

1980 Dec *Do You Feel My Love*, taken from LP *Love In Exile*, hits UK #8.

1981 May *Can't Get Enough Of You*, his first single with an Ice/Ensign label co-credit, reaches UK #13.

June LP *Can't Get Enough*, featuring its near-namesake hit, is his first UK chart LP, at #39.

Aug *I Love You, Yes I Love You* makes UK #37.

1982 Grant relocates his home and Ice recording studio to the Caribbean at St. Phillip, Barbados.

Sept The title track of Grant's LP *Walking On Sunshine*, revived by US group Rocker's Revenge, hits UK #4.

Nov With Ice Records signed in a new marketing and distribution deal to RCA, *I Don't Wanna Dance* tops the UK chart for 3 weeks, becoming one of the UK's biggest-selling singles of 1982.

1983 Feb LP *Killer On The Rampage* is Grant's biggest-selling UK LP, hitting #7. Taken from it, *Electric Avenue* hits UK #2.

Mar Double A-side reissue, *Living On The Frontline/Do You Feel My Love* on Mercury (which still holds the rights originally leased to Ensign), reaches UK #47.

Apr *War Party* peaks at UK #42.

July Via a deal with Portrait Records, *Electric Avenue* hit US #2 and earns a gold disk for over a million sales. LP *Killer On The Rampage* hits US #10 and is another gold disk.

Sept *I Don't Wanna Dance* reaches US #53.

Nov *Till I Can't Take Love No More* makes UK #42.

1984 May *Romancing The Stone*, written by Grant for the film of the same title (though not used in it) peaks at UK #52.

July LP *Going For Broke*, not a UK chart success, reaches US #64, while *Romancing The Stone* climbs to US #26.

Nov TV-advertised compilation LP *All The Hits: The Killer At His Best* reaches UK #23.

1988 Mar His Ice label is marketed in UK by PRT Records and Grant returns to the UK chart after a 4-year absence with *Gimme Hope Jo'anna*, an anti-apartheid song, dressed as reggae-funk, aimed at South Africa. It hits UK #7.

Apr Parlophone Records releases new LP *File Under Rock*.

Oct Grant appears alongside U2°, Aztec Camera°, Joan Armatrading° and others in the televised "Smile Jamaica" benefit concert at London's Dominion Theatre, to raise money to aid Jamaica's recovery after Hurricane Gilbert. *Put A Hold On It* is released.

THE GRASS ROOTS

Warren Entner (vocals and guitar)
Creed Bratton (guitar)
Rob Grill (bass and vocals)
Ricky Coonce (drums)

1966 Songwriters/producers P.F. Sloan and Steve Barri initiate The Grass Roots name as a label of convenience for a studio project as a Byrds°/Turtles°-type folk-rock duo, when working for Lou Adler's Dunhill label. Their first release is a cover of Bob Dylan's° *Mr. Jones (Ballad Of A Thin Man)*, which does not sell.

July Sloan and Barri's own song *Where Were You When I Needed You*, in a strident folk-rock arrangement, gives The Grass Roots a US chart debut, reaching #28. An LP of the same title, played, sung and mostly written by the duo, is released, without charting.

Sept *Only When You're Lonely*, again performed by Sloan and Barri as The Grass Roots, reaches US #96.

1967 Sloan and Barri recruit Entner (b. July 7, 1944, Boston, Mass., US), Bratton (b. Feb.8, 1943, Sacramento, Cal., US), Grill (b. Nov.30, 1944, Los Angeles, Cal.) and Coonce (b. Aug.1, 1947, Los Angeles), already playing together as LA bar band, The Thirteenth Floor, to become The Grass Roots. The duo continues to produce and write for the group.

July *Let's Live For Today*, a cover of an Italian hit by Italy-based UK group The Rokes, hits US #8.

Sept LP *Let's Live For Today*, with Sloan and Barri singing and playing alongside the new members (and featuring seven of their songs), peaks at US #75. Extracted from it, *Things I Should Have Said* reaches US #23. Sloan severs his connections with the group but Barri continues as producer.

Nov *Wake Up, Wake Up* reaches US #68.

Dec LP *Feelings* fails to chart.

1968 Nov *Midnight Confessions* hits US #5 and earns a gold disk for million-plus US sales. (Like their entire output, it fails completely in UK.)

Dec Compilation LP *Golden Grass* reaches US #25, earning a gold disk for a half million US sales.

1969 Jan *Bella Linda* makes US #28.

Mar A cover of *Lovin' Things*, Marmalade's° 1968 UK hit, reaches US #49.

Apr LP *Lovin' Things* climbs to US #73. Bratton leaves and is replaced on guitar and vocals by Denny Provisor, who has recorded as a soloist for Valiant Records.

May *The River Is Wide*, a revival of The Forum's US #45 hit of almost 2 years earlier, reaches US #31.

Sept *I'd Wait A Million Years* makes US #15.

Dec *Heaven Knows* reaches US #24.

1970 Jan LP *Leaving It All Behind* peaks at US #36.

Mar *Walking Through The Country* reaches US #44.

June *Baby Hold On* climbs to US #35.

Oct *Come On And Say It* reaches US #61.

Dec LP *More Golden Grass*, a compilation of hit singles since the original volume, peaks at US #152.

1971 Mar *Temptation Eyes* reaches US #15.

Jul *Sooner Or Later* hits US #9.

Nov Compilation LP *Their 16 Greatest Hits* reaches US #58 and earns a gold disk for a half million US sales.

Dec *Two Divided By Love* reaches US #16.

1972 Mar *Glory Bound* reaches US #34. Extensive personnel changes lead to a new 5-piece line-up for the next LP. Entner and Grill remain, but Coonce and Provisor depart, and are replaced by Reed Kailing and Virgil Webber (guitars) and Joel Larson (drums).

July *The Runway* makes US #39, while LP *Move Along* peaks at US #86.

1973 Mar *Love Is What You Make It* reaches US #55 (the group's last single for Dunhill).

1975 Sept Now signed to Haven label, *Mamacita* reaches US #71 (their final hit single). Also on Haven, LP *Grass Roots* fails to chart. (The group fades from the chart, but continues to work regularly on the live circuit.)

1983 Apr [5] US Interior Secretary James Watt announces that The Beach Boys° and The Grass Roots are being banned from performing at the annual "Fourth of July" celebration in Washington, D.C., citing that the acts attract "the wrong element of people."

THE GRATEFUL DEAD

Jerry Garcia (lead guitar)
Bob Weir (rhythm guitar)
Ron "Pigpen" McKernan (organ and harmonica)
Phil Lesh (bass)
Bill Kreutzmann (drums)

1963 Garcia (b. Jerome John Garcia, Aug.1, 1942, San Francisco, Cal., US), McKernan (b. Sept.8, 1945, San Bruno, Cal.), Weir (b. Robert Hall, Oct.6, 1947, San Francisco), Tom Stone, Marshall Leicester, David Parker and Bob Matthews, all veterans of varied Northern California folk, bluegrass and blues outfits, come together in Palo Alto, Cal, as Mother McCree's Uptown Jug Champions. (Matthews and Parker will remain part of the later Grateful Dead "family", as soundman and accountant respectively.)

1965 Apr As the jug band formula hardens into a rock/R&B mix, the personnel fluctuates until the group re-emerges as The Warlocks, with Garcia, Pigpen and Weir, joined by Kreutzmann (b. Apr.7, 1946, Palo Alto, Cal.), Lesh (b. Philip Chapman, Mar.15, 1940, Berkeley, Cal.) and bassist Dan Morgan, playing R&B around the Bay Area bars.

July The Warlocks become involved with Ken Kesey's Merry Pranksters commune in La Honda and, as the regular band, accompany Kesey's "Acid Tests", a series of public experimentations with still-legal hallucinogenic LSD. The LSD experience changes The Warlocks' music profoundly, moving it towards high amplification and intensity, and also their audience, from R&B fans to members of the new drug culture. The group is renamed The Grateful Dead after Garcia finds the name in the Oxford Dictionary while at a pot party at Lesh's house. They also acquire a financial benefactor in Stanley Owsley, wholesale manufacturer of LSD, who designs them a customized hi-tech PA system. Designer Rick Griffin and lyricist Robert Hunter (an ex-folk group colleague of Garcia's) also link up with the band.

Nov [6] Alongside Jefferson Airplane°, The Grateful Dead play the opening night at Bill Graham's Fillmore Auditorium in San Francisco.

1966 June The group moves to the Haight-Ashbury neighborhood of San Francisco, center of the new hippy culture, to live communally at

710, Ashbury Street. It becomes the base for an exhaustive series of free concerts, played in addition to their paid performances. A one-off single, *Don't Ease Me In*, is recorded for Scorpio label, a subsidiary of Berkeley-based Fantasy Records.

Oct The band plays at the LSD Made Illegal meeting in San Francisco.

1967 Jan [14] They play at the first Human Be-In, at Golden Gate Park, San Francisco, along with Jefferson Airplane°, Dizzy Gillespie's band, and Quicksilver Messenger Service°. The Grateful Dead are signed to Warner Bros.

May LP *Grateful Dead* is recorded in 3 days. Gaining muted critical response, since it clearly does not capture the group's live essence in the studio, it reaches US #73. (It will sell consistently over some years and eventually earn a gold disk.)

June [16] The band plays the Monterey Pop Festival (though disagreements with music industry executives will mean they are left out of the film documentary of the event, despite being one of its main attractions).

Oct [2] All members of the band are charged with possession of cannabis, following a police raid on the Ashbury Street house.

1968 Feb Recordings begin for a second LP, which in sharp contrast to the debut, will take 6 months to complete. During this time the Haight-Ashbury scene begins to dissolve, while the band acquires a second drummer, Mickey Hart (a fan who became friendly with Kreutzman, jammed with the group and was recruited), and a keyboardist, Tom Constanten, whose use of prepared tapes arouses the band's interest. Hart's father Lenny becomes their manager.

Aug [4] The group plays the Newport Pop Festival in Costa Mesa, Cal., alongside Steppenwolf°, Sonny and Cher°, Canned Heat°, Jefferson Airplane° and many more.

Sept LP *Anthem Of The Sun*, featuring live and studio recordings, sells fairly well, reaching US #87, but not well enough to cover the considerable recording costs (halfway through, they fired producer Dave Hassinger and took over the recording themselves), which will leave the band in debt to Warner until the early 1970s.

Dec [28] The band plays the Miami Pop Festival in Hallendale, Fla., with a host of acts including Chuck Berry°, Joni Mitchell°, The Box Tops° and Country Joe & The Fish°.

1969 Continuing financial problems lead The Grateful Dead to accept Bill Graham's long-standing offer to handle their bookings. They still play free gigs but Graham books them into packed clubs around the nation.

Aug LP *Aoxomoxa* reaches US #73, but they still owe Warner $100,000 and one more LP.

Aug [15] The Grateful Dead play the Woodstock Festival, to more than 400,000 people.

Aug [31] They play the New Orleans Pop Festival in Prairieville, La., with Country Joe & The Fish° and Jefferson Airplane°.

Dec [6] They play at the ill-fated Rolling Stones° concert at Altamont Speedway, Livermere, Cal., where a murder occurs during the Stones' act. (The event is later recalled by the group in *New Speedway Boogie* on LP *Workingman's Dead*.)

1970 Feb The band at last releases a full live recording, double LP *Live/Dead* (recorded "live" in the studio before an audience of friends), which reaches US #64. It includes a 25-minute version of stage favorite *Dark Star*. Constanten leaves to concentrate on Scientology studies.

May [23] The band plays its first gig outside US, a 4-hour set at the Hollywood Rock festival in Newcastle-Under-Lyme, UK.

Aug On LP *Workingman's Dead*, the complexity of earlier LPs is dropped in favor of Garcia's country-rock roots and harmony vocals, though a psychedelic sensibility remains. It reaches US #27 (earning a gold disk) and UK #69, and extracted *Uncle John's Band* makes US #69.

Nov On Sunflower label, LP *Vintage Dead*, with live recordings from the Avalon Ballroom, San Francisco, in 1966, reaches US #127.

Dec In a similar vein to LP *Workingman's Dead*, LP *American Beauty* reaches US #30 and earns another gold disk. Manager Lenny Hart is fired when it is discovered he has embezzled some of the group's funds. The younger Hart feels obliged to leave (though will later rejoin).

1971 July LP *Historic Dead*, of early 1966 recordings on Sunflower, reaches US #154.

Sept Lenny Hart is arrested and charged with embezzlement of $70,000 dollars from the group.

Dec Double live LP *Grateful Dead* makes US #25, while *Truckin'*, taken from it, reaches US #64.

1972 Members begin to splinter off into other projects, Garcia in particular playing on many sessions. His first solo LP is *Garcia*, and from it, *Sugaree*, reaches US #92. Weir cuts LP *Ace* (the track *One More Saturday Night* will become a staple of The Grateful Dead's concerts) and Hart's LP is *Rolling Thunder*. Meanwhile, Pigpen has sustained serious liver damage and is forced to rest and stop drinking. Husband and wife Keith (keyboards) and Donna Godchaux (backing vocals) are added to the band, and they tour Europe for 2 months.

1973 Jan Triple live LP *Europe '72*, a celebration of the group's 2-month European tour, reaches US #24.

Feb *Sugar Magnolia* peaks at US #91.

Mar [8] Pigpen dies from a stomach hemorrhage in a friend's back yard.

Mar With the Warner Bros. contract fulfilled, the group sets up Grateful Dead Records for the band's work, and Round Records for more esoteric releases from the "family". (These will lead eventually to the band's own studio, publishing company, booking agency and travel agency, but the labels will fail.)

July [28] With The Band° and The Allman Brothers Band°, the group co-headline the Watkins Glen Festival, which draws the all-time high festival audience of 600,000 people.

Sept Live LP *History Of The Grateful Dead Volume 1 (Bear's Choice)*, recorded at the Fillmore East, New York, in Feb. 1970, reaches US #60.

Dec LP *Wake Of The Flood*, first LP on The Grateful Dead's own label, indicates attempts to place their improvization in more of a jazz context. It reaches US #18.

1974 Apr Compilation LP *The Best Of/Skeletons From The Closet*, on Warner, makes US #75.

Aug LP *Grateful Dead From The Mars Hotel* reaches US #16 and UK #47. The band decides to cut down on touring.

1975 Sept [28] The band plays a free concert in Lindley Park, San Francisco, to end a year's lay-off from live work.

Oct LP *Blues For Allah* reaches US #12 and UK #45. Hart returns to the band.

Nov *The Music Never Stopped* makes US #81.

1976 July Double live LP *Steal Your Face*, recorded at Winterland, San Francisco in Sept. 1974, reaches US #56 and UK #42. It is released chiefly to recoup losses made on a disastrous group film project.

1977 June Documentary film *The Grateful Dead* premieres.

Sept The group headlines an 11-hour concert at Old Bridge, N.J., with New Riders of the Purple Sage and The Marshall Tucker Band.

Sept [16] The group plays three dates at the Great Pyramid in Cairo, Egypt, the last of which is timed to coincide with a total eclipse of the moon.

Oct The record label experiment fails, due mainly to problems with distribution, and the band signs to Arista. First release is LP *Terrapin Station*, which reaches US #28 and UK #30.

Dec Warner double retrospective LP *What A Long Strange Trip It's Been: The Best Of The Grateful Dead* reaches US #121. (The title will be borrowed 9 years later by *Rolling Stone* magazine, for a book of its own finest moments.)

1979 Jan LP *Shakedown Street*, produced by Lowell George of Little Feat°, reaches US #41. Weir's second solo LP, *Heaven Help The Fool*, is also released by Arista.

Apr The Godchauxs are asked to leave the band because of musical differences. (Keith Godchaux will die in a car accident on July 21.) The band is rumored for two large UK festivals but fails to confirm for either. Brent Mydland joins on keyboards and vocals.

1980 Jan [13] The Grateful Dead co-headline a benefit concert for the people of Kampuchea with The Beach Boys° and Jefferson Starship°, at Alameda Coliseum, Oakland, Cal.

June LP *Go To Heaven* reaches US #23 and *Alabama Getaway* makes US #68.

June [5] The band celebrates its 15th Anniversary with a commemorative concert at Compton Terrace in Phoenix, Ariz.

July [2] Weir and Hart are arrested on suspicion of inciting a riot, after they intervene in an attempted drug arrest during a Grateful Dead concert at San Diego Sports Arena.

1981 Mar The group plays its first UK gig for 5 years, at London's Rainbow Theatre.

May Double live LP *Reckoning*, recorded in New York in 1980, and

featuring a totally acoustic set, reaches US #43.
Oct Double live LP *Dead Set*, from a San Francisco concert, makes US #29.

1982 The group abandons recording and tours periodically. The treks are by now communal experiences for "Deadheads" (the fans who follow their heroes around US – the fan tours are arranged by the "family" business). Fans also begin to write to the group expressing concern at Garcia. He has become addicted to heroin, and both his health and standard of contribution to the band deteriorate.

May [28] The group plays at a benefit concert for the Vietnam Veterans Project at San Francisco's Moscone Center. Country Joe & The Fish° and Jefferson Starship° also take part.

Sept [3] The Grateful Dead play the US Festival in San Bernardino, Cal., where 400,000 people watch them alongside Fleetwood Mac°, The Cars°, Police° and many others.

Nov [25] The band plays the Jamaica World Music Festival at The Bob Marley Performing Center near Montego Bay.

1985 Jan Garcia's drug problem comes to a head: the others tell him the band cannot continue if he stays addicted. He agrees to take treatment, but several days later is busted in his car and is put into a drug diversion program.

1986 July With Garcia off drugs, the band resumes full-time touring, including summer dates with Tom Petty and The Heartbreakers°, but it proves too much for the still-fragile guitarist.

July [10] Garcia lapses into a 5-day diabetic coma. (He recovers and begins to play with R&B keyboardist Merle Saunders.)

July The Grateful Dead tour again, supporting Bob Dylan°. At his insistence, encouragement of tape-recording by the audience is suspended.

1987 The Grateful Dead complete a video and record a long-overdue studio LP. The initial plan is to record old songs, but Hunter becomes involved and the LP takes on a theme of ageing and redirection. Extracted *Touch Of Grey* hits US #9 (the band's first major hit single).

Aug LP *In The Dark* hits US #6.

Aug [23] An escapée from a drug treatment center shoots a policeman and is then shot to death at a Grateful Dead "Summer of Love" 20th anniversary celebration concert.

Sept [15] The Grateful Dead receive a platinum disk – their first – for LP *In The Dark*, as it makes UK #57.

1988 Sept [24] The group closes a 9-concert series at New York's Madison Square Garden with an extra benefit show for Cultural Survival, Greenpeace and Rainforest Action Network. They are joined on stage by Bruce Hornsby & The Range°, Daryl Hall and John Oates°, Suzanne Vega°, former Stone Mick Taylor and ex-Hot Tuna Jack Casady. The ten concerts gross $3,768,244.

AL GREEN

1959 Green (b. Al Greene, Apr.13, 1946, Forrest City, Ark., US), having formed gospel quartet with brothers Walter, William and Robert, gradually moves to secular pop. (Sam Cooke° is also making a similar gospel to pop transition.) His father reportedly fires him from the quartet after catching him listening to the "profane" music of Jackie Wilson°.

1964 He moves with his family to Michigan, where, with high school friends Palmer James, Curtis Rogers and Gene Mason, he forms The Creations, playing the "chitlin' circuit" and enjoying local success with recordings on Zodiac label.

1967 As Al Greene & The Soul Mates, they form their own record company, Hot Line Music Journal, to release their debut single, *Back Up Train*.

1968 Feb *Back Up Train* climbs to US #41 and wins the group a spot at the prestigious Apollo Theater in New York. Follow-up *Don't Hurt Me No More* fails to chart and, unable to keep up their momentum, they break up and Green goes solo, dropping the last letter of his surname to become Al Green, and returning to club singing.

1969 In Midland, Tex., Green meets bandleader Willie Mitchell, also chief producer and vice president of Hi Records in Memphis, who, after hearing Green sing, signs him to the label. He takes him to Memphis to record with the Hi label house band, comprising Al Jackson (drums), Leroy Hodges (bass), Mabon Hodges (guitar), Charles Hodges (organ), Wayne Jackson (trumpet), James Mitchell (baritone sax), Andrew Love (tenor sax), Ed Logan (tenor sax) and Jack Hale (trombone). (With minor variations, they play on all Al Green records until 1978.) The first two releases are a version of The Beatles'° *I Want To Hold Your Hand*, which flops, and *You Say It* which is a minor R&B hit.

1971 Jan Green's slowed-down version of The Temptations'° hit *Can't Get Next To You* makes US #60.

Nov *Tired Of Being Alone* reaches US #11 and hits UK #4. LP *Al Green Gets Next To You* makes US #58.

1972 Feb LP *Let's Stay Together* enters the US chart, hitting #8, and goes gold. It also tops the R&B chart for 10 weeks.

Feb [12] *Let's Stay Together* tops the US chart at the beginning of a 9-week stay and hits UK #7. (Tina Turner° will revive it in 1983.)

May *Look What You Done For Me* hits US #4 and will reach UK #44. LP *Let's Stay Together* hits US #8 and is another gold disk.

Sept *I'm Still In Love With You* hits US #3, Green's third consecutive US million-seller, and reaches UK #35. LP *Al Green*, recorded during Green's Soul Mates days, reaches US #162 on Bell label.

Oct *Guilty* makes US #69.

Dec *You Ought To Be With Me* hits US #3 and is a fourth million-seller. LP *I'm Still In Love With You* hits US #4 during a 67-week chart stay.

1973 Feb *Hot Wire*, another Soul Mates track, makes US #71. LP *Green Is Blues* reaches US #19.

Apr *Call Me (Come Back Home)* hits US #10.

July LP *Call Me* also hits US #10.

Oct *Here I Am (Come And Take Me)* hits US #10 again.

1974 Feb *Livin' For You* makes US #19. LP of same title peaks at US #24.

May *Let's Get Married* reaches US #32.

Oct [25] While Green is taking a shower at his Memphis home, ex-girlfriend Mary Woodson bursts in and pours boiling hot grits over him and then shoots herself fatally with his gun. Green is hospitalized with second-degree burns. (Rumors persist that the incident prompts Green to become a born-again Christian, but Green claims his spiritual rebirth had already taken place, in 1973. His Christianity becomes more evident from this point.)

Dec *Sha-La-La (Make Me Happy)* hits US #7 and UK #20.

1975 Jan LP *Al Green Explores Your Mind* reaches US #15, becoming his twelfth gold disk. (Included is *Take Me To the River*, which will become Talking Heads'° first hit in 1978.)

Apr *L-O-V-E (Love)* reaches US #13 and UK #24. LP *Al Green's Greatest Hits* makes US #17 and UK #18, becoming Green's first UK chart LP.

July *Oh Me, Oh My (Dreams In My Arms)* climbs to US #48.

Oct LP *Al Green Is Love* reaches US #28.

Dec *Full Of Fire* makes US #28.

1976 Apr LP *Full Of Fire* peaks at US #59. Green buys a church building in Memphis and becomes its minister, having been ordained a pastor of the Full Gospel Tabernacle. (He will continue his pop career and preach at the church when he is not away on tour.)

Dec LP *Have A Good Time* climbs to US #93.

1977 Jan *Keep Me Cryin'* reaches US #37 (his final collaboration with producer Mitchell).

July LP *Al Green's Greatest Hits, Volume II* reaches US #134. Green breaks from Mitchell and forms a band to record at his own American Music Recording Studio in Memphis. It comprises Reuben Fairfax (bass), James Bass (guitar), Johnny Toney (drums), Buddy Jarrett (alto sax), Fred Jordan (trumpet) and Ron Echols (tenor and alto sax).

1978 Jan Following non-charting LP *Truth 'N' Time*, LP *The Belle Album* reaches US #103. *Belle* peaks at US #83. The song's lyric confirms Green's inner conflict between a sexual life and a more overwhelming spiritual religious one.

Feb [13] LA declares the day "Al Green Day" as Green performs at the Dorothy Chandler Pavilion.

June [17] Green wins the Grand Prize, and $14,000, for his performance of *Belle* at the seventh Tokyo Music Festival in Japan.

1979 After a bad fall from a stage in Cincinnati, Oh., Green decides to make a full commitment to his church.

1980 He releases LP *Cream Of Al Green*. *The Lord Will Make A Way* is Green's first of a string of pure gospel releases, which only find success in the specialist area.

1982 Feb LP *Higher Plane*, including versions of *Amazing Grace* and *Battle Hymn Of The Republic*, is released.

Sept [9] Green opens on Broadway with Patti Labelle° in a production of Vinnette Carroll's gospel musical *Your Arms Too Short To Box With God*. (The show will run until Nov.)

Nov LP *Precious Lord*, a mix of standard hymns and songs written by

AL GREEN *cont.*

Green with Moses Dillard, is released and begins a new series of gospel LPs.

1988 June Green appears at the Nelson Mandela 70th Birthday Party concert and reaches new fans.

Oct Following a biography interview on UK TV show "Wired", Green, making a commercial comeback, links with Eurythmics'° Annie Lennox for duet 45 *Put A Little Love In Your Heart* from Bill Murray movie *Scrooged*. Meanwhile, LP *Hi-Life – The Best Of Al Green*, a UK compilation is still climbing at UK #34, and old hit *Let's Stay Together*, used on a UK TV aftershave commercial, is reissued.

GUESS WHO

Burton Cummings (vocals and keyboards)
Randy Bachman (guitar)
Jim Kale (bass)
Garry Peterson (drums)

1962 The group forms in Winnipeg, Canada, as Chad Allan & The Reflections, from members of two local teenage bands with Allan Kobel (guitar and vocals), Bob Ashley (piano) and Kale, all ex-Allan & The Silvertones, and Bachman and Peterson, ex-The Velvetones. Kobel changes his name to Chad Allan. The group's first release is a cover of Mike Berry's UK hit *Tribute To Buddy Holly*, recorded in Minneapolis for Canadian-American Records. Much of the group's early repertoire is Cliff Richard° songs and Shadows° instrumentals, learned from imported UK singles, and this material makes them unique in southern Canada.

1963 Mar *Tribute To Buddy Holly* makes Winnipeg radio station CKY's chart top 10 and attracts the attention of Canada's largest label, Quality, to whom the group signs.

Dec *Shy Guy*, on Quality, is another local CKY hit at #20.

1964 Jan Through Allan's UK friends, the group has obtained and learned The Beatles'° first UK LP, and moved into the Merseybeat style. Allan and Bachman trade in their old Gretsch and Jazzmaster guitars for more appropriate Rickenbackers.

May When Detroit group The Reflections has a US and Canadian top 10 hit with *(Just Like) Romeo And Juliet*, the group changes its name to Chad Allan & The Original Reflections, releasing *A Shot Of Rhythm And Blues* in an arrangement similar to Gerry & The Pacemakers'° version. To avoid confusion as both Reflections groups are on Quality, the name is changed to Chad Allan & The Expressions.

1965 May The group's revival of Johnny Kidd's° *Shakin' All Over* (learned from an old UK single) becomes Canadian #1. With the "British Invasion" in full swing, and the group's style a close approximation of the UK sound, Quality credits *Shakin' All Over* to "Guess Who?" and the publicity semi-implies a major UK group moonlighting. US licensee Scepter Records follows suit, and this ploy seems to work.

June *Shakin' All Over* reaches US #22 and the band tours US with The Turtles° and The Crystals°. The pressure of constantly appearing on stage causes Ashley to suffer increasing nervous problems. One night, when The Crystals mischievously pull him on stage during their act, he cracks and quits the group. Burton Cummings (b. Dec.31, 1947, Winnipeg, Canada), ex-Winnipeg group The Deverons, replaces Ashley and becomes joint lead vocalist with Allan. *Tossin' And Turnin'*, under the group's real name, becomes Canadian #1.

July LP *Shakin' All Over* has a sleeve credit to "Guess Who? – Chad Allan & The Expressions". The name sticks because the group has had a hit single and is adopted by the group, at the request of Scepter Records, which transports the group to New York to cut follow-up material for the US market. *Hey Ho, What You Do To Me* fails, as does ballad *Hurting Each Other* (later revived by The Carpenters°), and the group fades from US view.

1966 Allan leaves, after suffering voice problems which are aggravated whenever he forces his vocals during live gigs. He is briefly replaced by Bruce Dekker, an ex-Deverons colleague of Cummings. The group reduces to a quartet, with Cummings handling all vocals.

1967 Feb After wide pirate radio airplay, *His Girl*, leased from Quality by independent UK King label, enters the UK chart at #45. The group visits UK for promotion but falls out with King label, who wants a direct UK signing before organizing a tour. The group refuses and returns to Canada, $25,000 in debt. One recording is held in UK, with the group cutting some songs by UK writers Jimmy Stewart and Jerry Langley.

1968 The Quality contract has lapsed and the group takes a regular TV slot on CBC show "Where It's At" (with Allan rejoining). Through this, they meet producer Jack Richardson, who is working for an ad agency. Impressed by the band, he has them record a promotional LP for Coca-Cola, then mortgages his house to pay for the recording of an LP which will become *Wheatfield Soul*, and sets up the Nimbus 9 label to release it.

1969 Jan The third Guess Who single on Nimbus 9, the Cummings/Bachman composition *These Eyes*, is a hit in Canada and gains the group and the label a US deal with RCA.

May Having topped the Canadian chart, *These Eyes* hits US #6.

June LP *Wheatfield Soul* makes US #45. The group is urged to move to LA (but will remain based in Winnipeg and provide an example to Canadian rock talent which has always felt the need to move to US to succeed).

June [25] *These Eyes* wins a gold disk for a million-plus US sales.

Aug *Laughing*, another Cummings/Bachman ballad, reaches US #10 and is a second million-seller.

Nov LP *Canned Wheat Packed By The Guess Who* reaches US #91. *Undun*, B-side of *Laughing*, climbs to US #22.

1970 Feb *No Time* hits US #5, the third consecutive million-seller.

May Double A-side *American Woman/No Sugar Tonight* tops the US chart for 3 weeks – the fourth gold disk and the band's biggest US seller. (Because the song's lyric is a put-down of less desirable US attitudes, from a Canadian point of view, when the group is invited to play at the White House, it is specifically requested not to play *American Woman*.) The LP of the same title, also a gold disk winner, hits US #9.

July *American Woman* reaches UK #19; apart from *His Girl*, it is the band's only UK hit single. Bachman leaves the group, his Mormon religion proving impossible to reconcile with the high-living band style which arrives with success. (He will team again with Allan, plus two other Bachman brothers, to form Brave Belt, emerging later – minus Allan – as Bachman-Turner Overdrive°.) A new Guess Who LP featuring Bachman is shelved. Cummings takes control of the band and recruits two guitarists – Kurt Winter (ex-Brother, another Nimbus 9 act) and Greg Leskiw (ex-Wild Rice).

Sept *Hand Me Down World* reaches US #17.

Dec *Share The Land* hits US #10 and LP of the same title reaches US #14 (earning another gold disk).

1971 Feb *Hang On To Your Life* peaks at US #43.

June Compilation LP *The Best Of The Guess Who* reaches US #12. Double A-side *Albert Flasher/Broken* makes US #29.

Sept LP *So Long, Bannatyne*, lacking Cummings' lyrics and Bachman's music, reaches US #52.

Oct *Rain Dance*, from the LP, reaches US #19.

Dec *Sour Suite* peaks at US #50.

1972 Apr *Heartbroken Bopper* makes US #47. LP *Rockin'* reaches US #79. Leskiw leaves the group (to form Mood Jga Jga and record for Warner Bros.) and is replaced on guitar by Don McDougall.

June *Guns, Guns, Guns* makes US #70.

Oct *Runnin' Back To Saskatoon* reaches US #96. LP *Live At The Paramount*, recorded at a Seattle, Wash., concert, reaches US #39. Bassist and founder member Kale leaves (to record with Scrubaloe Caine and later front his own Jim Kale Band in Winnipeg). He is replaced by Bill Wallace, an ex-colleague of Winter's in Brother.

1973 Feb LP *Artificial Paradise* reaches only US #112.

Mar *Follow Your Daughter Home*, extracted from the LP, makes US #61.

Aug LP *#10* reaches US #155. (The title is not strictly accurate: this is the 10th LP since *Wheatfield Soul*.)

1974 Jan LP *The Best Of The Guess Who, Volume II*, a compilation of hits from where the first volume ended, makes US #186.

Apr *Star Baby* reaches US #39. Winter and McDougall are fired by Cummings. The replacement for both is Toronto-born Domenic Troiano, who has been playing guitar with the James Gang. He is the first (and will be the last) member of Guess Who not to hail from Winnipeg.

June LP *Road Food*, recorded before Winter and McDougall's departure, reaches US #60.

Sept *Clap For The Wolfman*, from LP *Road Food*, including snatches of dialogue from renowned US radio DJ Wolfman Jack, hits US #6.

Dec *Dancin' Fool* reaches US #28 (and will be the group's final US hit single).

1975 Feb LP *Flavors* reaches US #48.

Aug LP *Power In The Music* makes US #87. Cummings disbands the group, signs to Portrait as a soloist and moves to LA. Troiano returns to Toronto and forms his own band. Peterson forms the unsuccessful Delphia and Wallace plays with various groups around Winnipeg.

Dec Cummings' self-penned first solo on Portrait, *Stand Tall*, hits US #10 and is a million-seller. His first solo LP *Burton Cummings*, produced by Richard Perry, makes #30. (He will have three minor hits, all failing to reach US top 60, during 1977 and 1978. Second solo LP *My Own Way To Rock* will reach US #51. *You Saved My Soul*, on Alfa, will make US #37 in 1981.)

1977 May Compilation LP *The Greatest Of The Guess Who* reaches US #173.

1979 Kale and McDougall, along with Allan (vocals), David Inglis (guitar), Vince Masters (drums) and David Parasz (horns), regroup as Guess Who, recording LP *All This For A Song*. Neither the LP, single *Sweet Young Thing* or the reunion are a success (and other attempted regroupings will also fail).

1985 Apr Cummings is featured with countrymen like Neil Young°, Bryan Adams°, Joni Mitchell°, Anne Murray and Gordon Lightfoot° on *Tears Are Not Enough*, the charity record made by Canadian artists under the name Northern Lights, in aid of African Famine relief.

GUNS 'N' ROSES

W Axl Rose (lead vocals)
Slash (guitar)
Izzy Stradlin (guitar)
Duff Rose McKagan (bass)
Steven Adler (drums)

1985 The group forms in LA, Cal., US, around Rose (b. William Bailey, 1962 – later to discover his real surname is Rose) from Lafayette, Ind. The members, drawn from Seattle, Wash., Hollywood, Cal., and Stoke-on-Trent, Staffs., UK, are united by a desire to play earthy, gutsy rock'n'roll and settle on the band name after groups they have been in (LA Guns and Hollywood Rose – rejected names include Heads of Amazon and AIDS). They become local cult favorites matching their vision of punk nihilism with traditional heavy metal.

1986 May Guns 'N' Roses release EP *Live . . . Like A Suicide*, which fails to chart.

July Following intensive live work in Cal. and record label competition, the band is signed worldwide to Geffen Records by A&R head Teresa Ensenat.

1987 Apr The group supports Iron Maiden's° US tour, but pulls out half way through when Rose loses his voice. At the same time, Slash is sent to Hawaii to recuperate from ongoing chemical abuse. Most band members openly acknowledge drug and drink problems.

June On a first UK visit, Guns 'N' Roses play the Marquee, London.

July They begin a US tour, this time behind Motley Crue°.

Aug Debut LP *Appetite For Destruction* is released. Produced by Mike Clink, it is written, arranged and performed by Guns 'N' Roses. It begins a slow rise up the US LP chart.

Nov Guns 'N' Roses visit UK for their first major venue tour inviting heavy metal group Faster Pussycat to support. The dates include a sell-out performance at London's Hammersmith Odeon.

1988 May In the middle of an unbroken 14-month touring period, Guns 'N' Roses begin a major venue US tour behind Aerosmith°, but soon become the main attraction. A rider in contract insists that Guns 'N' Roses confine chemical abuse to the dressing room, so as not to tempt Aerosmith.

July *Sweet Child O' Mine*, written about Axl's girlfriend, is released in US and climbs to hit US #1, despite Axl's anger that Geffen edited it from 6 to 4 minutes.

Aug The band interrupts a US tour to play UK's Castle Donington Monsters of Rock. Their third major festival appearance is marred as "slam dancing" crowd antics result in two deaths during their performance of *It's So Easy*. The band had already stopped playing three times in an attempt to calm the situation.

Sept *Sweet Child O' Mine* peaks at UK #24. Meanwhile, their debut LP finally hits US #1 after 57 weeks on chart, having sold more than 5 million copies. It also peaks at UK #15.

Oct *Welcome To The Jungle*, used in latest Clint Eastwood "Dirty Harry" movie *Dead Pool*, enters the US chart at #57 and UK at #31, where it is released as double A-side with *Night Train*. Rose helps Don Henley on his third solo LP.

Nov Finishing a US tour with Aerosmith°, during which Rose was arrested in Atlanta, Chicago and Philadelphia, the band cancels plans for a follow-on UK visit with Metallica° in favor of a long rest.

Dec 8-track LP *G 'N' R Lies*, featuring four tracks from earlier EP *Live – Like A Suicide* with four new cuts, is released as the group visits Japan for live dates.

HAIRCUT 100

Nick Heyward (guitar and vocals)
Graham Jones (guitar)
Les Nemes (bass)
Phil Smith (saxophone)
Mark Fox (percussion and congas)
Blair Cunningham (drums)

1980 Heyward (b. May 20, 1961, UK), while working by day in an ad agency, teams with friends, Nemes (b. Dec.5, 1960, UK), a commercial artist, and Jones (b. July 8, 1961, UK), a photographic printer, to form a part-time group in suburban Beckenham, Kent, UK.

1981 Jan They play local gigs around South London, with friend Patrick Hunt on drums.

Mar They recruit US session drummer Cunningham (b. Oct.11, 1957, Memphis, Tenn., US), currently gigging round UK, as a permanent member to replace Hunt and to help record a studio demo with engineer Karl Adams (who will become their manager). French teacher Smith (b. May 1, 1959, UK) also joins after helping out on the demo as a session player.

May Adams hawks their demo around UK record companies. Interest increases as the group plays higher-profile gigs attracting music press attention with their perky, clean-cut pop sound and ingenuous visual image. Some UK media are hailing them as the new Monkees°.

Sept Having considered and rejected the names The Blatant Beavers, Marine Boy and Captain Pennyworth, they sign to Arista Records as Haircut 100 and link with producer Bob Sargeant.

Nov Debut single *Favourite Shirts (Boy Meets Girl)* hits UK #4.

Dec German teacher Fox (b. Feb.13, 1958, West Germany), after sitting in on studio rehearsals, joins the group.

1982 Mar *Love Plus One* hits UK #3. LP *Pelican West* confirms the group as UK teen idols of the moment, hitting #2 and selling over 300,000 in its first week. It will remain on UK chart for 34 weeks.

May *Fantastic Day* hits UK #9.

Aug As the group makes its first US visit, LP *Pelican West* peaks at #31. *Love Plus One* reaches US #37 (but is its only US hit single).

Sept *Nobody's Fool* hits UK #9.

Nov Second LP release is postponed. Heyward splits from the others amid general acrimony and Fox (who had left because of a personality clash with singer/songwriter Heyward) returns to take up lead vocals.

1983 Jan Heyward is retained by Arista as a solo and Haircut 100 moves to Polydor Records. The new label aims the group at an older market, with a college tour and less emphasis on a wide-eyed youthful image.

Apr Heyward UK solo debut *Whistle Down The Wind* reaches #13.

July *Take That Situation*, written originally by Heyward for second Haircut 100 LP, becomes his second UK solo hit, peaking at #11.

Aug Haircut 100's *Prime Time*, without Heyward, reaches UK #46, but later singles such as *Two Up Two Down* fail to sell.

Oct Heyward's solo *Blue Hat For A Blue Day* reaches UK #14. His solo LP *North Of A Miracle*, which uses noted session players including Steve Nieve (from Elvis Costello's° Attractions) and Tim Renwick (Quiver), is acclaimed for its maturity of performance and songwriting and hits UK #10.

Dec *On A Sunday*, taken from the LP, reaches only UK #52.

1984 June Heyward's *Love All Day* makes UK #31.

July Haircut 100 LP *Paint On Paint* is released. It flops and the group splits.

Nov Heyward's *Warning Sign*, a shift from schoolboy-type pop into funk, reaches UK #25.

1985 June His *Laura* climbs to UK #45.

1986 May *Over The Weekend* is Heyward's second in a row to miss UK top 40, stalling at #43.

Oct Second Heyward solo LP *Postcards From Home*, aimed at a more mature audience, flops despite critical raves.

HAIRCUT 100 *cont.*

1987 Heyward, marooned between teen and adult audiences, but disillusioned with Arista, signs a new worldwide deal with Warner Bros.

1988 June While recording debut LP for Warner Bros., Heyward contributes to Groove Train's cover version of *Why Did You Do It*, with Heaven 17's° Martyn Ware.

Sept *You're My World* reaches UK #67.

Oct As third solo LP *I Love You Avenue* hits record stores, Heyward has his temporary moustache removed live on UK TV show "The Last Resort".

BILL HALEY & HIS COMETS

Bill Haley (vocals and guitar)
Frannie Beecher (lead guitar)
Al Pompilli (bass)
Rudy Pompilli (sax)
Ralph Jones (drums)

1942 After leaving school in Booth-Win, Pa., US, Haley (b. July 6, 1925, Highland Park, Detroit, Mich., US), who has shown musical aptitude since his early youth, and has played guitar and yodelled, Jimmie Rodgers-style, with his own C&W band in school (playing at dances, fairs and local clubs) hits the road as a musician. He works first as a yodeller with a traveling show, then with country bands, including The Down Homers and The Range Drifters.

1948 Forming The Four Aces of Western Swing, Haley makes his first record, *Too Many Parties, Too Many Pals*, for small Cowboy label in Philadelphia, Pa.

1949 He joins radio station W-PWA in Chester (near Booth-Win) as a DJ, also playing on air with The Four Aces.

1950 He disbands The Four Aces and recruits guitarist Billy Williamson and pianist Johnny Grande to form The Saddlemen. They record for country labels Keystone and Centre and cut one single for Atlantic Records, backing singer Lou Graham.

1951 Haley is asked by Essex Records boss Dave Miller to record *Rocket 88*, an R&B hit for Jackie Brenston for Chess. Haley's version, released on Essex subsidiary label Holiday, sells about 10,000 copies. The similar *Green Tree Boogie*, a Haley original, fares no better.

1952 Haley moves on to Essex, and C&W *Icy Heart*, coupled with *Rock The Joint*, another R&B cover of a 1949 Jimmy Preston record, sells 75,000 copies.

1953 Haley drops the cowboy image and renames his group Bill Haley & His Comets, bringing in a new drummer, Dick Richards. The first release under the new name is Haley's own *Crazy Man Crazy*. The song is promptly covered by Ralph Marterie and receives considerable airplay in that form, but Haley's version benefits in sales. It becomes the first rock'n'roll disk to enter *Billboard*'s pop chart, reaching #15.

1954 Apr [12] Signed to Decca Records, Haley's first session at Pythian Temple studios, New York, produces *Thirteen Women* backed with *Rock Around The Clock*. The A-side attracts little attention. *Shake, Rattle And Roll*, Haley's second Decca single, reaches US #12.

Dec Released on Brunswick in UK, *Shake, Rattle And Roll* hits #4, while *Rock Around The Clock* charts briefly at UK #17.

1955 Jan *Dim, Dim The Lights (I Want Some Atmosphere)* makes US #11.

Mar *Mambo Rock* reaches US #17, while *Birth Of The Boogie* makes US #26.

Apr *Mambo Rock* peaks at UK #14.

May *Rock Around The Clock*, featured in film *The Blackboard Jungle*, enters the US chart. (Climbing steadily, it will hit #1 on July 9 and stay there for 7 weeks, becoming one of the biggest-selling singles in chart history. It spends 24 weeks in US top 40 – 19 in top 10.)

Sept *Razzle Dazzle/Two Hound Dogs* reach US #15 and #9 respectively.

Oct *Rock Around The Clock* re-enters the UK chart, to spend 5 weeks at #1 in two separate spells. Film *The Blackboard Jungle* is on UK release and youths rip up cinema seats and dance in the aisles, in the country's first experience of post-war hooliganism.

Nov *Burn That Candle* makes US #16. B-side *Rock-A-Beatin' Boogie* peaks at US #41.

1956 Jan *Rock-A-Beatin' Boogie* hits UK #4.

Feb *See You Later, Alligator* hits US #6. A million-seller, it will be

Haley's last US top 10 hit.

Mar *See You Later, Alligator* hits UK #7.

Apr *R-O-C-K*, which makes US #29, features in the first rock'n'roll exploitation movie, *Rock Around The Clock*, which has Haley starring with Alan Freed and Little Richard°. The film and its hasty follow-up, *Don't Knock The Rock*, are hugely popular worldwide (although some countries ban them), causing unprecedented scenes in cinemas. They are a major boost to Haley's stardom, but also serve to undermine it – revealing the chubby family man who is sharing the screen with outrageously-imaged Little Richard°. *The Saints Rock'n'Roll*, a rock version of the traditional *When The Saints Go Marching In*, reaches US #18.

May *The Saints Rock'n'Roll* hits UK #5.

June *Hot Dog Buddy Buddy* peaks at US #60. B-side *Rockin' Through The Rye*, an update of Scottish folk tune *Comin' Through The Rye* reaches US #78.

Aug *Rockin' Through The Rye*, Haley's fifth consecutive UK top 10, hits #3. His version of Little Richard's° *Rip It Up* peaks at US #25, while B-side *Teenager's Mother (Are You Right?)* makes US #68.

Sept *Razzle Dazzle* reaches UK #13. Given impetus by Haley's movie appearances, *Rock Around The Clock* (#5) and *See You Later, Alligator* (#12) re-enter the UK chart.

Oct LP *Rock'n'Roll Stage Show* reaches UK #18.

Nov *Rip It Up* hits UK #4. In the same week LP *Rock'n'Roll Stage Show* makes UK #30 (there will be no separate LP chart until 1958). *Rudy's Rock* makes US #34 and UK #30.

Dec The title track from *Don't Knock The Rock/Choo Choo Ch'Boogie* reaches US #45. *Rudy's Rock* (at #26) and *Rock Around The Clock* (at #24) both re-enter the UK chart.

1957 Jan Both *Rockin' Through The Rye* and *Rock Around The Clock* re-enter UK chart at #19 and #25 respectively, the latter dropping out for a week before making its fifth and final re-entry on Brunswick at #22.

Feb [5] Haley arrives by liner at Southampton, for his long-awaited UK concert debut. The first US rock artist to tour UK, he is mobbed for 20 minutes by fans when his train reaches London.

Feb [6] The UK tour opens at the Dominion Theatre in London, where fan mania is again rife. 1952-recorded *Rock The Joint* is issued and peaks at UK #20. The title track from *Don't Knock The Rock* hits UK #7.

Apr *Forty Cups Of Coffee/Hook, Line And Sinker* peaks at US #70.

June *(You Hit The Wrong Note) Billy Goat* makes US #60.

1958 May *Skinny Minnie* reaches US #22.

Aug *Lean Jean* peaks at US #67.

1959 Oct *Joey's Song* makes US #46.

1960 *Skokiaan (South African Song)* is Haley's last US hit for Decca, at #70. He signs to new Warner Bros. label, and releases a re-recording of his 1948 *Candy Kisses*, but it and subsequent singles for the label fail to chart, despite heavy promotion. (After Warner drops him he will record for a series of small labels.)

1964 Haley briefly returns to Decca and records *Green Door/Yeah, She's Evil*, which again fails. (Haley achieves success with some Latin dance hits in South America, records for Mexican Orfeon label, and tours Europe regularly.)

1968 Apr MCA reissues *Rock Around The Clock* and it reaches UK #20. With a current rock'n'roll revival in UK, Haley tours the country, including an appearance at London's Royal Albert Hall. (He will continue his career on the increasingly successful rock'n'roll revival circuits in US and UK.)

May LP *Rock Around The Clock*, on Ace of Hearts label, reaches UK #34.

1969 Haley is given an 8-minute ovation at Richard Nader's Rock'n'Roll Revival show in New York's Madison Square Garden (but in the years to come it will be UK and German fans who will remain the most faithful).

1973 Haley stars in *Let The Good Times Roll*, a film compiled from Nader's concerts of the past 4 years.

1974 Apr *Rock Around The Clock* re-enters the UK chart, reaching #12, coinciding with a visit by Haley. It also re-enters the US chart, peaking at #39.

1976 Feb [5] Former Comets sax player Rudy Pompilli dies.

1979 Nov Despite having been ill for much of the decade, Haley gives a spirited performance in his last UK appearance, at The Royal Variety Show.

1980 A UK tour is cancelled as Haley is reported seriously ill with a brain tumor.

1981 Feb [9] Haley dies of a heart attack in Harlingen, Tex. (He has sold an estimated 60 million records in his seminal rock'n'roll career.)

Apr *Haley's Golden Medley* makes UK #50.

DARYL HALL AND JOHN OATES

Daryl Hall (vocals and guitar)
John Oates (vocals and guitar)

1967 Students at Temple University, Hall (b. Daryl Franklin Hohl, Oct.11, 1949, Pottstown, Penn., US) and Oates (b. Apr.7, 1949, New York, N.Y., US) first meet while fleeing in the same freight elevator from a gang fight at a dance in Philadelphia's Adelphi Ballroom, where Hall has been leading his own band, The Temptones, and Oates his band, The Masters. (Hall has had piano and vocal training as a child, while Oates has been playing guitar since age 8, and begun his music career with a Motown covers band in the sixth grade. Both have been raised in the suburbs of Philadelphia, but have frequented the ghetto areas, absorbing music influences and later joining R&B/doo-wop groups. Hall has recorded a single as part of Kenny Gamble & The Romeos (with Gamble, Leon Huff and Thom Bell, who will all become major soul producers) and done regular session work for Gamble and Huff at Sigma Sound Studios.) Discovering shared interests, they team to sing in various R&B and doo-wop outfits, before going their separate ways – Oates to a new college, and Hall to his first serious band, Gulliver.

1969 Oates also joins Gulliver (which has recorded an LP for Elektra), just before it disbands. He makes a trip to Europe, while Hall finds studio work in Philadelphia, singing back-up for The Stylistics°, The Delfonics, The Intruders and others.

1972 They sign to Atlantic as a duo, but debut LP, *Whole Oats*, produced by Arif Mardin, fails. The duo plays around Philadelphia, building a solid live following.

1974 Jan Having moved to Greenwich Village, New York, R&B-styled LP *Abandoned Luncheonette*, also produced by Mardin, (since described by Hall as "our first real album") is released.

Feb The LP reaches US #33 and extracted *She's Gone* makes US #60, unaided by their first video, produced by John's sister Diane. (The song will be a US R&B #1 6 months later for Tavares.)

June The duo begins work on a new LP, with Todd Rundgren° producing, at Secret Sound studios, New York.

Nov LP *War Babies* climbs to US #86. Overtly rock-oriented, it is a departure from previous work: Atlantic terminates the duo's contract, citing stylistic inconsistency.

1975 Sept The duo signs to RCA, where LP *Daryl Hall And John Oates* (generally known as "The Silver Album" because of the silver make-up sleeve shot of the duo, created by Mick Jagger's make-up man Pierre LaRoche) is a slow US chart mover until extracted *Sara Smile* (written by Hall for girlfriend Sara Allen) takes off.

1976 June *Sara Smile* hits US #4 after 5 months on the chart and is a million-seller, while LP *Daryl Hall And John Oates* makes US #17, earning a gold disk for a half million sales.

July LP *Daryl Hall And John Oates* spends 1 week at UK #56.

Oct *She's Gone*, reissued by Atlantic, hits US #7 and reaches UK #42.

Nov LP *Bigger Than Both Of Us*, recorded at Cherokee Studios and Sound Labs in LA with producer Chris Bond, peaks at US #13 (Hall and Oates' first platinum LP) and UK #25.

Dec *Do What You Want, Be What You Are*, from the LP, reaches US #39.

1977 Mar *Rich Girl* (written about a friend of Sara Allen's whose father is a fast food king) is the third single from *Bigger Than Both Of Us*, and becomes the duo's first #1 hit, topping the US chart for 2 weeks, but fails to chart at all in UK. (The notorious serial killer David Berkowitz, known as "Son of Sam", will later claim the song as a motivation for his murders.)

Apr LP *No Goodbyes*, a collection of early Atlantic tracks, peaks at US #92.

June *Back Together Again* reaches US #28.

Aug *It's Uncanny*, on Atlantic, reaches US #80. Hall records tracks for a solo LP with Robert Fripp producing. (It will not be released until 1980.)

Oct LP *Beauty On A Back Street* (which Oates will later claim as the duo's only recording he hates) peaks at US #30 and UK #40.

Nov *Why Do Lovers (Break Each Other's Heart?)* reaches US #73.

1978 June LP *Livetime*, recorded on the road with the duo's regular band – Caleb Quaye (lead guitar), Kenny Passarelli (bass), Roger Pope (drums), David Kent (keyboards and backing vocals) and Charles DeChant (sax, keyboards and percussion), reaches US #42. They spend much of the year playing live, including a tour, sponsored by Care-Free chewing gum, of high schools which have sent Care-Free the most gum wrappers.

Sept LP *Along The Red Ledge* makes US #27. (Hall will later comment that producer David Foster "tried to make us sound like Earth, Wind & Fire°".)

Oct *It's A Laugh*, taken from the LP, reaches US #20.

1979 Jan *I Don't Wanna Lose You* climbs to US #42.

Nov LP *X-Static* peaks at US #33. The duo has spent much of the year touring, concentrating on club dates. Oates writes soundtrack for film *Outlaw Blues*.

1980 Jan *Wait For Me*, taken from *X-Static*, reaches US #18.

Mar Hall and Oates hire Studio C at New York's Electric Lady studios and start producing themselves, using their own road band for backup – now comprising G.E. Smith (lead guitar), Tom "T-Bone" Wolk (bass, synthesizers and guitar), Mickey Curry (drums) and Charlie DeChant (sax).

May Hall's solo LP *Sacred Songs*, recorded in 1977 with Robert Fripp, reaches US #58.

June *Running From Paradise* (from *X-Static*, and not released as a US single) makes UK #41 (the duo's first UK hit single for almost 4 years).

Sept Self-produced LP *Voices*, from the New York sessions, reaches US #17 in a 100-week chart run in which it will go platinum. It includes *Every Time You Go Away*, which Paul Young° will revive as a hit single, and *Diddy Doo Wop (I Hear The Voices)*, which is Hall's reaction to the "Son of Sam" revelations. The first single extracted, *How Does It Feel To Be Back* peaks at US #30, while a revival of The Righteous Brothers'° *You've Lost That Lovin' Feelin'* makes UK #55.

Nov On US release, *You've Lost That Lovin' Feelin'* reaches #12.

Dec *Kiss On My List*, also from LP *Voices*, climbs to UK #33.

1981 Apr *Kiss On My List* (written by Hall with Sara Allen's younger sister Janna, who reputedly has never written a song before), tops the US chart for 3 weeks, selling over a million.

July *You Make My Dreams* hits US #5.

Sept LP *Private Eyes*, self-produced in 4 more months of sessions at Electric Lady studios, is Hall and Oates' first US top 10 LP, hitting #5 and earning a platinum disk. The title track tops the US chart for 2 weeks, and is another million-seller.

1982 Jan *I Can't Go For That (No Can Do)* also tops the US chart, deposing Olivia Newton John's° *Physical* (which had toppled *Private Eyes* 10 weeks earlier). It is their third million-seller in four releases and it also spends a week at US R&B #1 (extremely rare for a white act – only the fourth instance since 1965). In addition, they are listed under "Black Music" in *World Book Encyclopedia*.

Feb *I Can't Go For That (No Can Do)* (written by the duo with Sara Allen in the studio, and recorded on the spot) is its biggest UK single success to date, hitting #8.

Apr *Private Eyes*, reissued as UK follow-up, makes #32.

May *Did It In A Minute* is the third top 10 US single from LP *Private Eyes*, hitting #9.

DARYL HALL AND JOHN OATES *cont.*

Aug *Your Imagination* reaches US #33, as the duo works on a new LP at Electric Lady studios (being filmed by MTV for a documentary, during the final recording work).

Dec *Maneater*, the duo's fifth US #1 (and sixth million-seller) tops the chart for 4 weeks, while in UK it hits #6 – their highest UK chart placing. It is taken from their tenth LP *H2O*, which hits US #3 (also a million-seller) and reaches UK #24.

1983 Jan Also from *H2O*, ballad *One On One* reaches UK #63.

Apr *One On One* hits US #7.

May *Family Man*, the fourth single from the LP, and a cover of a 1982 UK hit by Mike Oldfield°, makes UK #15.

June *Family Man* hits US #6.

Nov *Say It Isn't So* peaks at UK #69. The duo releases LP *Rock 'N' Soul (Part 1)*, a compilation of 11 US top 10 hits (including the current single and forthcoming release *Adult Education*), which hits US #7 and UK #16 and will become another platinum disk.

Dec *Say It Isn't So* hits US #2, where it spends 4 weeks behind Paul McCartney° and Michael Jackson's° *Say Say Say*.

1984 Mar *Adult Education* reaches UK #63.

Apr With *Adult Education* at its US chart peak of #8, the Recording Industry Association Of America (RIAA) confirms suggestions in *Billboard* and *Newsweek* that Hall and Oates are now the most successful duo in US recording history, amassing a total 19 US gold and platinum awards. The duo, meanwhile, takes a rest from the road prior to the next round of recording, with Hall collaborating with other acts, and Oates honing his skiing and race driving skills.

Aug Hall duets on Elvis Costello's° second US chart success, *The Only Flame In Town*, which peaks at #56.

Oct Hall writes and produces *Swept Away* for Diana Ross°, which peaks at US #19. LP *Big Bam Boom* is released, their first new LP in 2 years, and mostly containing songs built up during work in the studio. After self-producing for some time, they bring in New York electro producer Arthur Baker to help with mixing and production on the LP.

Nov *Out Of Touch* tops the US chart for 2 weeks (the duo's sixth US #1 single) and makes UK #48. LP *Big Bam Boom* hits US #5 (their fifth consecutive platinum LP) and reaches UK #28.

1985 Jan [28] Both Hall and Oates take part in the all-star session in LA which produces charity single *We Are The World*.

Feb *Method Of Modern Love* hits US #5 and reaches UK #21.

May Hall and Oates pay tribute to the soul music that inspired them in their teen years when the legendary Apollo Theater in Harlem is reopened and they conceive a show featuring David Ruffin and Eddie Kendricks of The Temptations°, to benefit the United Negro College Fund. Meanwhile, *Some Things Are Better Left Unsaid*, third single from the LP, reaches US #18.

June UK RCA releases a remixed version of *Out Of Touch*, which peaks at UK #62.

July *Possession Obsession*, again taken from LP *Big Bam Boom*, reaches US #30.

Sept Live single, *A Night At The Apollo Live!*, a medley of two of The Temptations's° 60s hits *The Way You Do The Things You Do* and *My Girl*, taken from the Apollo benefit concert, reaches US #20.

Oct *A Night At The Apollo Live!* makes UK #58, while the live LP of the May concert, *Live At The Apollo With David Ruffin And Eddie Kendricks*, reaches US #21 and UK #32.

1986 Sept Rumors of a split seem confirmed as Hall releases his second solo LP, *Three Hearts In The Happy Ending Machine*, produced by Eurythmics'° Dave Stewart, which reaches US #29 and UK #26. His solo single *Dreamtime*, taken from it, hits US #5 and peaks at UK #28. Oates produces an LP for The Parachute Club and co-writes *Electric Blue* (which will be a major US hit for Australian band Icehouse°).

Nov Hall's solo *Foolish Pride* reaches US #33.

1988 June Reunited and signed to Clive Davis' Arista Records, the duo releases LP *Ooh Yeah!*, co-producing it with T-Bone Wolk, the only remaining member of the previous band. It reaches US #24. From it, Hall-penned *Everything Your Heart Desires* hits US #3.

Aug Also from the LP, *Missed Opportunity* reaches US #29.

Sept [24] Hall and Oates, together with Suzanne Vega° and Bruce Hornsby & The Range°, join The Grateful Dead° for the end of their series of nine concerts at New York's Madison Square Garden, in a benefit show to help save the world's tropical rain forests. The duo performs *Every Time You Go Away* and Marvin Gaye's° *What's Going On* with The Grateful Dead, plus the finale, *Good Lovin'*, with the whole assembled company.

STEVE HARLEY & COCKNEY REBEL

1973 Jan Harley (b. Steven Nice, Feb.27, 1951, London, UK), an ex-local newspaper journalist and folk singer, advertises in the music press for musicians to form a band, and selects Milton Reame James (keyboards), Jean Paul Crocker (electric violin and guitars), Paul Jeffreys (bass) and Stuart Elliott (drums). With Harley on lead vocals, they become Cockney Rebel, and debut at the Beckenham Arts Lab before working on the London club circuit.

June The group signs to EMI Records.

Aug Harley-penned *Sebastian* is the debut single, but does not chart.

Nov LP *Human Menagerie* is released, also failing to chart.

1974 Jan *Big Big Deal* is another non-chartmaker.

June *Judy Teen*, again written by Harley, is the group's breakthrough single, hitting UK #5.

July LP *The Psychomodo* hits UK #8.

Aug By the time *Mr. Soft* hits UK #8, the group has broken up, following internal friction (partly over Harley's obsession with self-promotion and his provocative stance against UK music press).

Oct For a concert at London's Rainbow, Harley assembles a new group, retaining Elliott from the original Cockney Rebel, and adding Jim Cregan (guitar), Duncan MacKay (keyboards) and George Ford (bass).

Nov The new line-up begins work on an LP at EMI's Abbey Road studios and AIR studios in London.

1975 Feb With the new label credit of Steve Harley & Cockney Rebel, *Make Me Smile (Come Up And See Me)* is Harley's biggest UK seller, topping the chart for 2 weeks.

Mar *Make Me Smile (Come Up And see Me)* is the band's only US hit, reaching #96. They tour US to promote it.

Apr Harley co-produces LP *The Best Years Of Our Lives* with Alan Parsons, and it hits UK #4.

June *Mr. Raffles (Man It Was Mean)* reaches UK #13.

Oct *Black Or White* fails to chart, giving UK's music press the chance to predict Harley's commercial eclipse.

Dec The group supports The Kinks° on a US tour.

1976 Feb LP *Timeless Flight* reaches UK #18 as the band tours UK to promote it. Extracted *White White Dove*, however, does not sell.

Aug A revival of George Harrison's° *Here Comes The Sun*, credited just to Harley, hits UK #10.

Nov *Love's A Prima Donna* reaches UK #41.

Dec LP *Love's A Prima Donna* reaches UK #28. Harley breaks up the band again, and moves to live in US, while continuing to record for EMI.

1977 Aug Live LP by the mark two Cockney Rebel, *Face To Face – A Live Recording*, reaches UK #40.

1978 Aug LP *Hobo With A Grin* fails to chart.

1979 Oct Having released three more unsuccessful singles, Harley returns to UK. His solo *Freedom's Prisoner* reaches UK #58. Steve Harley/Jimmy Horowitz-produced LP *The Candidate* fails to sell and EMI drops him.

1980 EMI releases compilation LP *The Best Of Steve Harley & Cockney Rebel*.

1981 Mar A one-off on Chrysalis Records, *I Can't Even Touch You*, fails to chart.

1983 Aug Comeback single *Ballerina (Prima Donna)*, on Stiletto label, makes UK #51.

1986 Feb After a period of apparent inactivity, Harley teams with Sarah Brightman on a specially-recorded duet of the title song from Andrew Lloyd Webber's forthcoming musical *The Phantom of the Opera*. It hits UK #7.

Apr Harley signs to RAK as a solo artist, releasing *Heartbeat Like Thunder* and *Irresistible* without success.

Oct Video *Live From London*, featuring many of Cockney Rebel's hits from a 1984 performance, is released.

1988 Mar Use of *Mr. Soft* in a UK TV commercial leads to EMI re-releasing it and a greatest hits compilation.

HARPERS BIZARRE

Ted Templeman (guitar and lead vocals)
Dick Scoppettone (guitar and vocals)
Eddie James (guitar and vocals)
Dick Yount (bass and vocals)
John Peterson (drums and vocals)

1966 Nov The group is formed in Santa Cruz, Cal., US, by four former members (Templeman, Scoppettone, James and Yount) of The Tikis, who have recorded for Autumn and Warner Bros. Records for 3 years without success. Joined by Peterson, formerly with The Beau Brummels°, they sign to Warner Bros. with new name Harpers Bizarre. They will have access to many of LA's best writers, session players, arrangers and producers.

1967 Apr *The 59th Street Bridge Song (Feelin' Groovy)*, a cover of the Paul Simon° song, reaches US #13 and UK #34.

May Debut LP *Feelin' Groovy*, arranged by Leon Russell° and leaning heavily on the writing and arranging talents of Randy Newman°, is a moderate US seller, reaching #108. It highlights their close five-part harmonic vocal style, echoing other contemporary groups.

June *Come To The Sunshine*, covering a 1966 Van Dyke Parks' single, makes US #37.

Sept Parks himself plays piano with the group on a revival of Cole Porter's *Anything Goes*, which peaks at US #43 and UK #33.

Dec LP *Anything Goes* includes revivals of standards like the title track and *Three Babes In The Wood*, with new material by Parks and Newman°. It reaches US #76. Another revival, Glenn Miller's *Chattanooga Choo-Choo*, makes US #45.

1968 Sept *Battle Of New Orleans* is their final (minor) US hit at #95, and LP *The Secret Life Of Harpers Bizarre* fails to chart. By this time, Eddie James has left, and they continue as a foursome.

1969 June LP *Harpers Bizarre 4* features Ry Cooder° guesting on guitar. It does not sell, and the group splits shortly afterwards. Templeman stays with Warner Bros. as a producer (notably for The Doobie Brothers° and Van Halen°.)

1976 Scoppettone, James and Yount reunite as Harpers Bizarre for the one-off LP *As Time Goes By*, on US Forest Bay label.

GEORGE HARRISON

1968 Nov Harrison (b. Feb.25, 1943, Wavertree, Liverpool, UK) becomes the first Beatle to issue material independently of the group with LP soundtrack of film *Wonderwall*, which reaches US #49.

1969 May LP *Electronic Sound*, which makes US #191, consists of Harrison experimenting with new acquisition, a moog synthesizer.

Oct He produces various Apple artists, including Radha Krishna Temple on *Hare Krishna Mantra*, which reaches UK #12.

Nov Having become the second writing force behind Lennon° and McCartney° within The Beatles°, the group releases the first single he has penned, *Something* which hits UK #4 and US #1. (It will become a show biz standard with hundreds of cover versions recorded in the coming years.)

Dec Harrison plays a number of concerts with Delaney and Bonnie°.

1970 Dec LP *All Things Must Pass* is released and hits UK #4 and US #1. After The Beatles° split, Harrison is the first to secure a chart-topping LP. Released to tie in with the first non-Beatle Christmas since 1962, it achieves worldwide sales of 3 million copies. The triple LP box set is a showcase of his talent and will never be equalled by future releases. Co-produced by Phil Spector, Harrison is backed by an all-star band, including Ringo Starr°, Ginger Baker, Billy Preston, Badfinger° and debut of Derek & The Dominoes, featuring Eric Clapton°. Bob Dylan° contributes two songs to the LP, *I'd Have You Anytime*, co-written with Harrison, and *If Not For You*, later covered by Olivia Newton-John° (1971 UK #7, US #25). Third record in the set is a loose session entitled *Apple Jam*. At one point, the musicians break into Cliff Richard's° 1968 chart-topper *Congratulations* and UK songwriters, Bill Martin and Phil Coulter, successfully claim a royalty entitlement from Harrison.

1971 Jan *My Sweet Lord* hits UK and US #1, giving Harrison a second accolade as the first ex-Beatle with a chart-topping single. Originally given away by Harrison to Billy Preston for his Apple LP *Encouraging Words* and even scheduled as a Preston single release, it becomes a worldwide #1, selling over 5 million copies.

Mar Bright Tunes, who owns copyright of the late Ronnie Mack's song *He's So Fine*, a hit for The Chiffons° (1963 UK #16, US #5), makes a legal claim that *My Sweet Lord* plagiarizes its former clients' hit,

and all royalty payments are frozen. Harrison claims that his song is inspired by The Edwin Hawkins Singers' hit *Oh Happy Day* (1969 UK #2, US #4) and almost 5 years later in the US, District Court Judge, Richard Owens, will rule in favor of the plaintiff, but will allow that Harrison perhaps subconsciously adapted the song. (Bright Tunes is paid $587,000 and is taken over by ex-Beatles' manager, Allen Klein, who continues a damage suit.) The Chiffons° releases a cover version of *My Sweet Lord*. *What Is Life* hits US #10.

Aug After a personal plea for help from friend Ravi Shankar, Harrison organizes two concerts to aid victims of famine and war in Bangladesh. Held at New York's Madison Square Garden, the line-up of artists includes Bob Dylan°, Eric Clapton° and Ringo Starr°. Due to legal problems, the proceeds are frozen and Harrison writes his own check to maintain the fund. *Bangla Desh* hits UK #10 and makes US #23.

1972 Jan LP *The Concert For Bangla Desh*, another triple box-set, tops UK chart and hits US #2.

1973 June LP *Living In The Material World* hits UK #2 and tops US chart. *Give Me Love (Give Me Peace On Earth)* hits UK #8 and tops US chart. Harrison returns to his own career, having recently appeared on LPs for Nilsson° and Ringo Starr°.

1974 June Harrison announces the formation of his own record label, Dark Horse. Its first signing is Ravi Shankar but Splinter is the only success for the label, other than Harrison himself, with *Costafine Town* which will reach UK #17 and US #77 in Nov.

July Harrison announces a US tour supported by Ravi Shankar and Billy Preston. It is pounded by critics as audiences expect some sprinkling of Beatle-magic, but instead are treated to a handful of Fab Four songs with changed lyrics.

Dec LP *Dark Horse* hits US #4, but fails to chart in the UK. An introspective set, it includes a version of The Everly Brothers'° *Bye Bye Love*, a farewell to his former wife, Patti Boyd, who has recently left him for Eric Clapton°. (Patti provides backing vocals on the track.)

1975 Jan *Ding Dong* makes UK #38. Harrison becomes the first ex-Beatle who fails to make UK top 30. The B-side *I Don't Care Anymore* reflects his mood of the time. *Dark Horse* makes US #15.

GEORGE HARRISON *cont.*

Feb *Ding Dong* peaks at US #36.

Oct LP *Extra Texture (Read All About It)* peaks at UK #16 and hits US #8. It proves to be his last Apple LP and the label features a partly eaten apple core. *You* reaches UK #38 and US #20.

Nov EMI/Capitol LP *The Best Of George Harrison* makes US #31.

Dec LP *Thirty-Three And A Third* climbs to UK #35 and reaches US #11, but its sales are impaired by the release of LP in Nov.

1977 Jan *This Song* reaches US #25. It offers wry comment on the *My Sweet Lord* court case, referring in its lyrics to the publishers of *He's So Fine*.

Mar *Crackerbox Palace* makes US #19.

1979 Mar LP *George Harrison* peaks at UK #39 and US #14. His major new interest in Formula One motor racing is highlighted by the track *Faster*, inspired by racing driver Jackie Stewart's book of the same name and Niki Lauda's fight to overcome his crash injuries. *Blow Away* reaches UK #51 and US #16. Harrison's film company, Handmade Films, launched with US businessman, Denis O'Brien, scores an unexpected hit during the year: EMI drops out of backing Monty Python film *The Life Of Brian*. Harrison, friendly with the Pythons after appearing on US TV's "Saturday Night Live" with Eric Idle in 1977, raises money with his partner to continue the project and it becomes one of the biggest grossers in the US that year. Harrison appears in the film in a very brief cameo role. EMI also lands Handmade another success when they sell on the rights to *The Long Good Friday* which is deemed too violent. (Films in the 1980s will include *The Time Bandits*, *The Missionary*, *Mona Lisa* and *A Private Function*, among many hits.)

1980 His autobiography *I Me Mine* is published in a limited edition of 2,000 copies at £148 each.

1981 June LP *Somewhere In England* reaches UK #13 and US #11. *All Those Years Ago* makes UK #13 and hits US #2, and Harrison returns to single success with his tribute to John Lennon°, which features the two other remaining Beatles°.

1982 Nov LP *Gone Troppo* reaches only US #108 and misses UK altogether. Harrison shows no interest in promoting this LP and his label, Warner Bros., lets it slip with similar lack of interest.

Dec *Wake Up My Love* reaches US #53.

1985 Disillusioned with the music business, Harrison has spent the past 3 years involved in film production and setting up a second home in Australia.

May He appears in Handmade Films' *Water* with Eric Clapton° and Ringo Starr° in a scene set at the United Nations in New York.

July He performs an unreleased Bob Dylan° song *I Don't Want To Do It* on the soundtrack of film *Porky's Revenge*.

Dec He joins forces with Ringo Starr°, Eric Clapton°, Dave Edmunds° and others to pay tribute to rockabilly legend, Carl Perkins°, for a UK Channel 4 TV special, and performs a succession of solos, including *Everybody's Trying To Be My Baby*.

1986 Mar He performs at "Heartbeat 86", a charity concert, sharing vocals on *Johnny B. Goode* with Robert Plant° and Denny Laine.

Sept Harrison contributes on two tracks for Duane Eddy° comeback LP *Duane Eddy*. Handmade Films' *Shanghai Surprise* flops. Harrison had publicly attempted to appease its two stars Madonna° and Sean Penn.

1987 Feb He returns to the old days with a jam session at Hollywood's Palamino Club with Bob Dylan°, Taj Mahal, and John Fogerty.

June With Ringo Starr°, he performs *While My Guitar Gently Weeps* and *Here Comes The Sun* at the Prince's Trust concerts at Wembley Stadium.

Nov LP *Cloud Nine* hits UK #10. Harrison collaborates with The Beatles'° afficianado, ELO's° Jeff Lynne, and together they create a highly commercial confection of songs far removed from Harrison's 1970s persona. He wins over a whole new generation of fans, many of whom were born after The Beatles split. *Got My Mind Set On You*, a cover of Rudy Clark's R&B classic, hits UK #2.

1988 Jan In one of the greatest comebacks in rock history, Harrison tops the US chart with *Got My Mind Set On You*. It is nearly 24 years since he first topped the chart with The Beatles° and *I Want To Hold Your Hand*. LP *Cloud Nine* hits US #10.

Feb *When We Was Fab* reaches UK #25 and US #23. Harrison gives a tongue-in-cheek nod to The Beatles° sound with a Godley & Creme° produced video that includes Ringo Starr°.

Aug Reports emanate from US that Harrison, Starr and Lynne plan an LP and may tour. *USA Today* reports that a mystery group, The Traveling Wilburys, will release its debut LP in Oct. and that the group comprises Harrison with Roy Orbison°, Tom Petty°, Bob Dylan° and Jeff Lynne.

WILBERT HARRISON

1954 After serving in the US Navy, Harrison (b. Jan.6, 1929, Charlotte, N.C., US), said to have been born into a family of 23, becomes a nomadic, idiosyncratic R&B singer, recording one-off singles for the Rockin' (*This Woman Of Mine*) and Duluxe (*Gin And Coconut Milk*) labels, before having a regional R&B hit in Miami, Fla., with *Don't Drop It*, cut for Savoy Records.

1958 Dec In New York, during studio time paid for by Fury Records' owner Bobby Robinson (with the agreement of Savoy's Herman Lubinsky, to whom Harrison is still officially contracted), he records from memory *K.C. Lovin'*, with guitarist Jimmy Spruill and other session players. Harrison recalls the song, written by Jerry Leiber and Mike Stoller, from the original version by Little Willie Littlefield, an R&B chart hit in 1952, but since he knows it as *Kansas City*, that is the title used on his single.

1959 May *Kansas City*, released on Fury, tops US chart for 2 weeks and R&B chart for 7 weeks, selling over a million. Other minor US chart versions of the song are by Rocky Olson (#60), Hank Ballard° (#72) and Little Richard° (#95). Littlefield's *K.C. Lovin'* is reissued (now retitled *Kansas City*) but does not chart.

June Little Richard's° version of the song charts at UK #26; Harrison's fails to show. (Also on the R&B charts during 1959 will be his final Savoy release *Baby Don't You Know*.) *C.C. Rider*, his Fury follow-up, fails to chart.

1960/69 On the move on small club and roadhouse tours, Harrison develops a one-man-band act, playing drum and harmonica with his guitar (and occasionally piano), since he cannot afford to maintain a traveling band. He records one-offs on labels like Seahorn, Neptune, Doc, Port and Vest, which fail to chart.

1970 Jan Long written off as a one-hit wonder, Harrison resurfaces in New York again, on Juggy Murray's also believed-dormant Sue label with *Let's Work Together*, which reaches US #32. It is his own composition, a revised version of *Let's Stick Together*, originally recorded without success for Fury in the early 1960s. (This earlier version will be revived by Bryan Ferry° in 1976, hitting UK #4.) LP *Let's Work Together* reaches US #190.

Feb Canned Heat's° cover version of *Let's Work Together* hits UK #2 (and will make US #26 in Nov.), bringing Harrison financial reward through songwriting royalties.

1971 Mar *My Heart Is Yours* makes US #98 and is his final chart entry. On Nashville label SSS International, it is produced in New Orleans by Allen Toussaint and Marshall Sehorn (and is a song cut years before without success for Fury). Creedence Clearwater Revival° takes Harrison on tour to open its shows with his novel act, but this raised profile fails to bring him further record success. Assorted 70s releases on Buddah, Hotline and Brunswick Records fail to sell.

DONNY HATHAWAY

1964 Hathaway (b. Oct.1, 1945, Chicago, Ill., US), having been raised in St Louis, Mo., and been a gospel singer throughout his childhood and teens, majors in music theory at Howard University, Washington D.C., where he meets singer Roberta Flack°, while playing keyboards with the Ric Powell Jazz Trio in Washington clubs.

1968 Back in Chicago, he meets Curtis Mayfield°, who invites him to work as a producer for fledgling Curtom label, where he works with singer June Conquest and records some duets with her. He moves on to work at Chess Records with Woody Herman, and then freelances on production work for Stax with Carla Thomas and The Staple Singers°.

1969 He becomes friendly with session saxophonist King Curtis, who recommends him to Atlantic, to whom Hathaway signs as a producer, writer and recording artist.

1970 Feb *The Ghetto (Part 1)* makes US #87. Hathaway records his debut LP, *Everything Is Everything*, which initially does not chart.

1971 June LP *Donny Hathaway* reaches US #89 and is followed by *Everything Is Everything*, which peaks at US #73.

Aug His duet with Roberta Flack° on a cover of Carole King's° *You've*

Got A Friend reaches US #29. (James Taylor° is currently at US #1 with the same song.)
Nov Also duetted with Flack°, a revival of The Righteous Brothers'° 1965 #1 *You've Lost That Lovin' Feelin'* makes US #71.
1972 May Live LP *Donny Hathaway Live* is his first top 20 entry, peaking at US #18. It earns a gold disk for a half million US sales.
June *Giving Up* peaks at US #81, while his duet with June Conquest, on Curtom, on a revival of Sam and Dave's° *I Thank You*, reaches US #94.
Aug *Where Is The Love*, a duet with Flack°, hits US #5 and sells over a million, earning a gold disk. It also makes UK #29 – Hathaway's first UK hit. Their joint LP *Roberta Flack And Donny Hathaway* hits US #3 and also goes gold.
Sept Hathaway composes and performs the music for Godfrey Cambridge film *Come Back Charleston Blue*. The soundtrack LP makes US #198.
Sept [2] He sings the theme song for US TV comedy series "Maude" (a spin-off from "All In The Family", which will run until 1978).
Nov *I Love You More Than You'll Ever Know* makes US #60.
1973 Aug *Love, Love, Love* reaches US #44 and LP *Extension Of A Man* peaks at US #69.
1974/77 He forms his own freelance production company, and work in the control booth (for Aretha Franklin°, Jerry Butler° and others) keeps him out of the studio as an artist for some time (as do recurrent personal problems).
1978 May After 6 years, he duets with Roberta Flack° again, on *The Closer I Get You*, a James Mtume/Reggie Lucas song from her LP *Blue Lights In The Basement*. It hits US #2 (a million-seller) and UK #42.
Sept Hathaway's solo *You Were Meant For Me* reaches US R&B #17 but does not cross over. (It will be his last hit during his lifetime.)
1979 Jan [13] Hathaway dies, aged 33, after falling from the fifteenth floor of the Essex House Hotel, New York. The death is officially registered as suicide, though some close friends are sceptical.
1980 Apr His duet with Flack°, *You Are My Heaven*, reaches US #47.
May LP *Roberta Flack Featuring Donny Hathaway*, on which Hathaway was completing work at the time of his death, climbs to US #25 and earns a gold disk.
June Uptempo *Back Together Again*, taken from the LP with Flack°, reaches US #56 and hits UK #3. Boosted by it, LP *Roberta Flack Featuring Donny Hathaway* reaches UK #31, the final chart monument to Hathaway.

RICHIE HAVENS

1962 Havens (b. Jan.21, 1941, Brooklyn, New York, N.Y., US), a former street corner singer and teenage member of the McCrea Gospel singers, starts to sing and play guitar on the burgeoning Greenwich Village folk scene, having first come to the area as a painter. His unique guitar style uses open E-chord tuning and a rapid strumming style which uses the instrument as percussion.
1965 He signs to small label Douglas Records, releasing debut LP *A Richie Havens Record*, which sells only to his Greenwich Village underground following.
1966 LP *Electric Havens* is also only a cult favorite, but his reputation as an individual club and café entertainer, leads him, and several contemporaries from the same Village scene, to a contract with MGM's new progressive Verve Forecast label.
1967 Debut Verve Forecast LP *Mixed Bag* sets the pattern for almost all subsequent releases; open-strumming style and intense vocals in a personalized selection of traditional songs and covers like *Just Like A Woman* (Bob Dylan°) and *Eleanor Rigby* (Lennon°/McCartney°). It does not chart initially, but gains wide notice.
1968 Jan [20] Havens appears with Bob Dylan°, Judy Collins°, Arlo Guthrie, Pete Seeger and others in a tribute concert to Woody Guthrie, at New York's Carnegie Hall.
Mar LP *Something Else Again* is his US chart debut, peaking at #184.
July LP *Mixed Bag* reaches US #182.
Dec Revived by his growing popularity, the second Douglas LP *Electric Havens* also finally charts, making US #192.
Dec [28] He plays the Miami Pop Festival at Hallendale, Fla., to 100,000 people, along with Chuck Berry°, Three Dog Night°, Fleetwood Mac°, Marvin Gaye° and many others.
1969 Feb Double LP *Richard P. Havens, 1983*, highlighted by Beatles° and Dylan° adaptations, reaches US #80.
Aug [16] Havens appears at the Woodstock Festival, N.Y., where his late-night, impassioned set is rapturously received. His song *Freedom* becomes one of the anthems of the festival and is included in the *Woodstock* movie.
1970 Jan [28] He takes part in a 7-hour benefit concert at Madison Square Garden, along with Jimi Hendrix°, Judy Collins°, The Young Rascals° and others, to raise funds for the Vietnam Moratorium Committee.
Feb Havens forms his own Stormy Forest label, the first release is LP *Stonehenge*, which includes an offbeat version of The Bee Gees'° *I Started A Joke*. It reaches US #155.
Aug [28] He appears at UK's Isle of Wight Pop Festival, with Joni Mitchell°, Joan Baez° and Jimi Hendrix° (whose last public performance this is).
Nov An MGM reissue of LP *Mixed Bag* puts the title back on the US chart, at #190.
1971 Feb LP *Alarm Clock* is his most successful chart LP, climbing to US #29.
May Taken from *Alarm Clock*, a revival of George Harrison's° *Here Comes The Sun* (the original is on The Beatles'° LP *Abbey Road*) is his only single to gain widespread US airplay and only US top 20 entry, making US #16.
Oct [19] On a UK visit, Havens is recorded live at BBC TV Theatre, London, for a TV special on his music (also to be released on his live LP in 1972).
Dec LP *The Great Blind Degree* peaks at US #126.
Dec [9] Havens has a role in the orchestral stage version of The Who's° rock opera *Tommy*, a one-off show at London's Rainbow Theatre, which also includes Roger Daltrey, Steve Winwood° and Peter Sellers.
1972 Oct Double live LP *Richie Havens On Stage* is his second-biggest seller, reaching US #55. It includes three stage performances, from London (BBC TV Theatre), Santa Monica Civic Center, Cal., and The Westbury Music Fair, Westbury, N.Y. This reprises mainly material from earlier LPs, including his Woodstock highlight *Freedom*.
1973 June LP *Portfolio* reaches US #182.
1974 Havens appears as Othello in the Patrick McGoohan-directed movie of Jack Good's musical *Catch My Soul*, which is based on Shakespeare's *Othello*. He co-stars with Tony Joe White, Lance LeGault and Delaney and Bonnie°, and sings six songs.
1975 Oct LP *Mixed Bag II* peaks at US #186.
1976 Oct After a year's hiatus, Havens signs to A&M Records for LP *The End Of The Beginning*, which reaches US #157, his last US LP chart entry.
1977 Apr [5] Havens appears with Jackson Browne°, John Sebastian, Country Joe McDonald and others in a 3-day rally in LA which raises $150,000 to help preserve whales and dolphins from the international fishing industry. Second A&M LP *Mirage* fails to sell, and the label drops him. Havens writes and performs the music for, and appears in, the Richard Pryor-starring movie *Greased Lightning*.
1980 Havens is signed to Elektra for LP *Connections*, which fails to chart. (During the 80s, little will be seen or heard of him in the music field, though he will occasionally appear in films.)

RONNIE HAWKINS

1952/58 Hawkins (b. Jan.10, 1935, Huntsville, Ark., US), having assembled his first backing group, The Hawks (a name he will retain despite constant personnel changes), at the University of Arkansas, plays local hillbilly gigs. As fashions change, he modifies into a journeyman rock'n'roller, relying on Berry°/Diddley° songs. Unable to arouse much enthusiasm in US, he moves from Fayettsville in the Ozark Mountains to Hamilton, Ont., Canada, on the advice of Conway Twitty, and becomes a successful fixture on the Canadian scene, making his recording debut *Bo Diddley* on Quality.
1959 June Signed to Roulette label, his workmanlike revision of Chuck Berry's° *Thirty Days*, now called *Forty Days*, makes US #45. Among his current Hawks are drummer Levon Helm and guitarist Jimmy Ray Paulman.
Sept An 1955 R&B hit for Young Jessie, *Mary Lou* becomes Hawkins' biggest seller, peaking at US #26. (17 years later, Bob Seger° will revive it on his platinum LP *Night Moves*.) Roulette's sobriquet, "Mr. Dynamo", proves an overstatement when Hawkins fails with his next three singles: *Southern Love*, *Lonely Hours* and *The Ballad Of Caryl Chessman*.

RONNIE HAWKINS *cont.*

1960 16-year-old Robbie Robertson becomes The Hawks' roadie, then joins on bass. When Fred Carter goes to Nashville, he takes over lead guitar.

1963 Mar Featuring Robertson's incandescent guitar, Hawkins' version of Bo Diddley's° *Who Do You Love* is widely regarded as his recording zenith. It fails to sell. Later in the year, his current Hawks members (Helm, Robertson, Rick Danko, Richard Manuel and Garth Hudson) desert him and move to US. They record as Levon & The Hawks, backing John Hammond and then Bob Dylan°. (They will later surface as The Band° in 1968.)

1964/68 Hawkins spends most of his time in the Canadian club circuit, reminiscing about his sexual excesses and sitting out his 10-year contract with Roulette.

1969 Media interest arising from the ascent of The Band°, and bon mots from John Lennon° reflate Hawkins' reputation. Jerry Wexler signs him to Atlantic subsidiary Cotillion and he records with Duane Allman and other Muscle Shoals acts in Ala.

Dec John Lennon° stays with Hawkins while in Canada on his peace trip.

1970 Jan Cotillion releases a promotional single, on which Lennon° exhorts the virtues of Hawkins' upcoming LP. It lasts all of 90 seconds.

Feb Hawkins' comeback single *Down In The Alley* reaches US #75, but the LP from which it is taken, *Ronnie Hawkins*, fails.

1971 A second Cotillion LP *The Hawk* excites even less interest and he moves to Monument for LP *Rock And Roll Resurrection* and *Ain't That A Shame*.

1976 Nov [25] Hawkins sings *Who Do You Love* at The Band's° farewell concert "The Last Waltz". He also appears in Bob Dylan's° *Renaldo And Clara*, before returning to obscurity, occasionally plaguing some company to record his latest offerings.

SCREAMIN' JAY HAWKINS

1947 Hawkins (b. Jalacy Hawkins, July 18, 1929, Cleveland, Oh., US) wins a national Golden Gloves amateur boxing competition and begins to box professionally, while also playing piano in R&B bands Tiny Grimes, Lynn Hope and others.

1954 After making his first record *Coronet Boogie*, for Timely label, Hawkins retires from boxing to concentrate on music, adopts the stage name of Screamin' Jay Hawkins, and cuts several more disks for various labels, including Apollo and Grand.

1956 Feb [12] Signed to Okeh, he records *I Put A Spell On You* in New York, reputedly during a drinking spree – hence the abandoned grunts and groans (the most suggestive of which are edited out to ensure radio play).

Apr *I Put A Spell On You* is an R&B chart success. Hawkins develops his nascent cod voodoo stage persona, which now includes emerging on stage from a coffin and carrying skulls and other voodoo impedimenta. Unable to find a chart follow-up, despite (or perhaps because of) continuous label hopping, Hawkins' compelling stage act nonetheless assures him steady work on the club circuit.

1962 Hawkins has minor regional chart success with *I Hear Voices*.

1965 Feb [5] *Poor Folks* is another minor local hit. Hawkins makes his first UK visit. On arriving in London he expresses a wish to meet UK vocalist Screaming Lord Sutch, who has borrowed many elements of Hawkins' stage act, including the entrance in a coffin, but apparently declines media prompting to put a spell on him.

1967 Two more minor local hits follow with *Feast Of The Mau Mau* and *Constipation Blues*.

1978 Mar Hawkins is featured in Floyd Mutrux's *American Hot Wax* movie, about a week in the life of Alan Freed, in a specially staged concert sequence. (Other than remakes and reissues of *I Put A Spell On You*, Hawkins' chart profile is now behind him. He continues live work throughout US and Europe.)

HAWKWIND

Dave Brock (guitar and vocals)
Nick Turner (sax, flute and vocals)
Mick Slattery (guitar)
John Harrison (bass)
Terry Ollis (drums)
Dik Mik (electronics)

1969 July Brock and Slattery are in Famous Cure and Turner is in Mobile Freakout when, having met by chance on tour in Holland, they meet again after their return to UK. They debut as Group X (but change name to Hawkwind Zoo) at a 10-minute gig at All Saint's Hall, Notting Hill, London, UK.

Oct Manager Doug Smith secures the band, now shortened to Hawkwind, a deal with Liberty. Huw Lloyd Langton replaces Slattery. Occasional drummer Viv Prince (ex-Pretty Things°) brings extra police attention through his membership of Hell's Angels.

1970 Dick Taylor, (also ex-Pretty Things) is brought in to produce the group and ends up playing on the sessions.

July Hawkwind's first release is *Hurry On Sundown/Mirror Of Illusion*. Harrison leaves and is replaced on bass by Thomas Crimble.

Aug Debut LP *Hawkwind* is released. True to their "people's band" tag, they play at Canvas City, a series of free gigs performed on the perimeter of UK's Isle of Wight Festival.

Sept Langton leaves the group (he will return 9 years later), as does Crimble.

1971 May Dave Anderson (ex-Amon Duul) is recruited. Soundman Del Dettmar plays synthesizer, replacing Dik Mik (who will rejoin 3 months later).

June The group plays Glastonbury Fayre, with dancer Stacia appearing for the first time and poet Robert Calvert as vocalist.

Aug Lemmy (b. Ian Kilmister) joins on bass after Anderson leaves. (Initially on 6-months' trial, he stays nearly 4 years.)

Oct LP *In Search Of Space* reaches UK #18. Its "space-rock" image is partially inspired by Calvert.

1972 Jan Simon King replaces Ollis on drums.

Feb The group plays the Greasy Truckers Party at London's Roundhouse. The performance is recorded and excerpts appear on LPs *Greasy Truckers Party* and *Glastonbury Fayre*. Calvert joins the band full-time and sings many of the lead vocals.

Aug One of Calvert's songs, *Silver Machine*, taken from the Greasy Truckers recordings and remixed with Calvert's original vocal re-recorded by Lemmy, begins a UK chart rise, eventually hitting UK #3.

Dec Third LP *Doremi Fasol Latido* reaches UK #14. The success of *Silver Machine* enables Hawkwind to create a lavish 30-date touring show entitled "The Space Ritual".

1973 June Double LP *Space Ritual Alive*, based on the live show, hits UK #9.

Aug Dik Mik quits. *Urban Guerilla* makes UK #39 but is withdrawn because the band is worried about association with current IRA activity.

Dec LP *Space Ritual Live* makes US #179 during the band's first US tour.

1974 Jan On its return, the group begins a full UK tour.

Feb Hawkwind begins a second US tour and plays a benefit for acid guru Timothy Leary, back in jail after escaping and being recaptured in Switzerland.

Apr Simon House, who played on recent US tour, joins on keyboards, synthesizer and violin. Dettmar leaves the stage line-up to operate his synthesizer from the mixing desk.

May Calvert's solo LP, *Captain Lockheed & The Starfighters*, is released on United Artists.

June Dettmar leaves the group and emigrates to Canada.

July Simon King breaks ribs playing soccer and Alan Powell (ex-Chicken Shack, Stackridge, Vinegar Joe) is brought in temporarily. (He stays when King recovers and the group has two drummers.)

Sept Fifth LP, *Hall Of The Mountain Grill* reaches UK #16 and US #110. The band plays UK's Harrow Free Festival and begins a US tour, which is halted in Indiana when state police impound their gear under a new tax law. They return home.

Oct Hawkwind returns to US to play 21 re-scheduled dates.

Dec The group begins a US tour (which will run until Feb.).

1975 June LP *Warrior On The Edge Of Time* reaches UK #13 and US #150. The group tours US again and includes Canada. At the border, Canadian customs mistakenly identify amphetamine pills Lemmy has in his luggage for cocaine. The offence is elevated to a felony from a misdemeanor and he spends 5 days in a police cell and, on release, finds the band has sacked him. Paul Rudolph (ex-Deviants, Pink Fairies, Uncle Dog) is flown out to complete the tour (and will join full-time).

Back in UK, Lemmy announces plans for his new group, Motorhead°. Hawkwind tours France.

Aug The group tops the bill at UK's Reading Festival. Calvert joins for a one-off appearance and decides to stay. His second solo LP, *Lucky*

Leif And The Longships, produced by Brian Eno°, fails to chart. Stacia leaves to get married. (The band has a period of stability and ends the year with a UK tour.)

1976 Jan Hawkwind signs to Charisma Records.

Apr Compilation LP *Road Hawks* makes UK #34.

June *The Time of the Hawklords*, a sci-fi novel by Michael Butterworth with the band as fantasy heroes, is published.

July *Kerb Crawler/Honky Dorky*, on Charisma, fails to chart.

Sept LP *Astounding Sounds, Amazing Music* makes UK #33.

1977 Jan Turner leaves to form Sphynx.

Feb Rudolph and Powell leave and a new band, with Adrian Shaw on bass, debuts at London's Roundhouse. United Artists releases compilation LP *Masters Of The Universe*.

July LP *Quark Strangeness And Charm* makes UK #30. The group tours UK again.

Oct House leaves to join David Bowie's° world tour and is replaced by Paul Hayles.

1978 Feb Hawkwind is on an unhappy US tour. Calvert sells his guitar minutes after the final concert finishes. They return home and Shaw forms a group with House.

June Calvert forms The Hawklords (the name changed for legal reasons) with Smith returning as manager. Shelving *PXR-5*, the new group records LP *25 Years On*. The line-up is Calvert, Brock, Martin Griffiths (drums), Steve Swindell (ex-Pilot and String Driven Thing, keyboards) and Harvey Bainbridge (bass).

Oct LP *25 Years On* makes UK #48. *Psi Power* is released. The group tours UK. United Artists re-releases *Silver Machine* which makes UK #34.

Dec Griffiths quits the band.

1979 Jan Calvert leaves to go solo. King rejoins on drums and the 4-piece band reassumes the name Hawkwind and rehearses and records in Wales. Swindell leaves soon after.

May LP *PXR-5*, released by Charisma, makes UK #59. Tim Blake (ex-Gong) replaces Swindell and Langton rejoins. The group plays UK's Leeds Science Fiction Festival.

1980 July *Shot Down In The Night* reaches UK #59.

Aug Smith arranges a deal which includes Hawkwind, Motorhead° and Girlschool, with Bronze Records. LP *Live 1979*, recorded in St Albans in Nov., makes UK #15. The group begins a tour of UK and Europe (which will last the rest of the year).

Sept Ginger Baker (ex-Cream° and Blind Faith°) joins, replacing King.

Nov LP *Levitation* reaches UK #21.

1981 Mar Baker is sacked before a scheduled Italian tour, which is cancelled. Griffiths rejoins and the group plays UK's Stonehenge and Glastonbury festivals.

Oct LP *Sonic Attack* is released on RCA and makes UK #19.

1982 May LP *Church Of Hawkwind* reaches UK #26.

Oct LP *Choose Your Masques* reaches UK #29.

1983 Jan *Silver Machine* makes its third UK chart appearance at #67.

Nov LP *Zones* makes UK #57.

1984 Feb EMI reissues LP *Hawkwind*. It reaches UK #75.

1985 Nov LP *Chronicle Of The Black Sword* makes UK #65.

1986 Aug Hawkwind plays UK's annual Reading Festival.

1987 The group makes the "Chronicles of the Black Sword" tour.

1988 Apr Hawkwind begins an extensive UK tour with a new line-up: Brock, Langton, Bainbridge (now on keyboards), Allan Davis (bass) and Danny Thompson (drums).

Aug [14] Calvert dies after a heart attack at his home in Kent.

ISAAC HAYES

1958 Hayes (b. Aug.20, 1942, Covington, Tenn., US) moves from rural Tennessee, where he has been brought up by his sharecropper grandparents and sung in church for many years, to Memphis, Tenn. He plays in his high school band, and on saxophone and keyboards with various local amateur groups including The Teen Tones and The Swing Cats.

1964 Some gigs in Memphis with Gene "Bowlegs" Miller and a meeting with musicians from Stax Records group The Mar-Keys leads to an invitation from Stax president Jim Stewart for session work at the label's studios.

1965 Now a regular member of the Stax house band, but holding down a day job in a Memphis meat-packing plant, Hayes meets David Porter, an insurance salesman with songwriting aspirations. The two form a partnership which produces successful material for Stax.

1966/67 Hayes plays on many of the label's most successful releases of the mid-60s, including Otis Redding°, Carla Thomas, William Bell and Eddie Floyd° hits. Hayes and Porter also co-write and produce a string of Sam and Dave° hits, including *You Don't Know Like I Know, Hold On I'm Coming, Soul Man* and *When Something Is Wrong With My Baby*.

1968 Debut LP *Presenting Isaac Hayes* is the result of a post-party late-night session by Hayes with MG's bassist "Duck" Dunn and drummer Al Jackson, Jr. Sales are unspectacular.

1969 Oct Stax simultaneously releases 27 LPs to tie in with a publicity campaign following its new link with Paramount and Gulf & Western. It introduces subsidiary Enterprise label, on which LP *Hot Buttered Soul* is initially marketed as a makeweight alongside more obviously commercial items by Booker T. & The MG's°, Eddie Floyd°, Johnnie Taylor and others. DJs are hooked by the unique formula which Hayes introduces on the 4-song LP – familiar songs in extended, personalized versions, an intimate "rap" monologue, and arrangements with wah-wah guitars and muscular funk rhythm sections in symphonic layers of strings. The LP is by far the biggest success of the 27, hitting US #8 and earning a gold disk. Double-sided *Walk On By/By The Time I Get To Phoenix*, in sharply edited form, also makes US #30 and #37 respectively.

1970 May LP *The Isaac Hayes Movement*, in similar style to the first (with which Hayes, with refinements and some exceptions, will stick throughout his recording career), hits US #8. Its sleeve promotes Hayes' striking visual image: shaven headed, shaded and bearded, stripped to the waist and garlanded with gold chains. He maintains this appearance on his tours (undertaken with a 40-piece orchestra).

Sept From *Movement*, a reworking of Jerry Butler's° *I Stand Accused* climbs to US #42.

1971 Jan LP *To Be Continued* makes US #11.

Mar A revival of *The Look Of Love*, from the third LP, reaches US #79.

June A personalized cover of The Jackson 5's° *Never Can Say Goodbye* reaches US #22 only weeks after the original hit #2.

Sept MGM's film *Shaft*, starring Richard Roundtree as a black New York private eye, opens in US, with a soundtrack composed and performed by Hayes.

Nov *Theme From Shaft* tops the US chart for 2 weeks, becoming Hayes' only million-selling single. The double soundtrack LP also hits US #1 and earns a gold disk.

1972 Jan Double LP *Black Moses* is packaged in a sleeve which folds out to form a large cross and illustrates a biblically-attired Hayes by a riverbank. It hits US #10 and earns another gold disk. *Theme From Shaft* hits UK #4, while the soundtrack LP makes UK #17. The music from the film is the chief factor in spreading the commercial success of Hayes' music outside US.

Feb LP *Black Moses* reaches UK #38.

Mar Hayes wins two Grammy awards: Best Instrumental Arrangement for *Theme From Shaft* and Best Original Score Written for a Motion Picture for the *Shaft* soundtrack. The theme also wins an Oscar for Best Film Song, and a similar honor at the Golden Globe Awards. Meanwhile, his 1968 debut LP, reissued by Atlantic Records as *In The Beginning*, makes US #102.

Apr *Do Your Thing*, an edited version from *Shaft* soundtrack, climbs to US #30. Hayes' sax-playing instrumental cover of Al Green's° *Let's Stay Together* reaches US #48.

May Hayes and Porter duet on soul ballad *Ain't That Loving You (For More Reasons Than One)*, which makes only US #86.

Aug Hayes plays at Wattstax '72 in LA, a benefit concert by Stax artists (others include The Staple Singers°, Carla Thomas, Luther Ingram and Albert King) for the 7th annual Watts Festival.

Dec *Theme From The Men*, written by Hayes for US ABC-TV anthology series of spy and police thrillers "The Men", reaches US #38.

1973 Jan Hayes makes his first live UK appearance.

July Double live LP *Live At The Sahara Tahoe*, which features his full, orchestra-backed cabaret act, makes US #14, earning another gold disk.

Dec LP *Joy* reaches US #16.

1974 Jan Hayes completes work on two movie soundtrack projects for release later in the year, while *Joy, Part 1* makes US #30.

June *Wonderful* peaks at US #71, while Hayes' soundtrack LP from film *Tough Guys* makes US #146.

Aug Double soundtrack LP from movie *Truck Turner*, in which Hayes

ISAAC HAYES *cont.*

also has a star acting role, peaks at US #156.

1975 After an altercation with Stax over royalty payments, Hayes moves from Enterprise to set up his own Hot Buttered Soul label through ABC Records. (He will tailor his output more closely to prevailing disco styles.)

Aug LP *Chocolate Chip* reaches US #18 (and earns a further gold disk), though the extracted title track peaks at US #92. Enterprise releases compilation LP *The Best Of Isaac Hayes*, which makes US #165.

1976 Jan [25] Hayes plays alongside Stevie Wonder° and Bob Dylan's° "The Rolling Thunder Revue" at "Night of the Hurricane 2" in front of 40,000 people at Houston Astrodome, Tex. The concert is a benefit show for imprisoned boxer "Hurricane" Carter.

Feb LP *Disco Connection*, billed as by The Isaac Hayes Movement, reaches US #85.

Mar LP *Groove-A-Thon* peaks at US #45.

May The instrumental title track from *Disco Connection* hits UK #10 (Hayes' only UK hit single in addition to *Shaft*).

Aug LP *Juicy Fruit (Disco Freak)* reaches US #124.

Dec [22] Hayes files for bankruptcy.

1977 Mar Double LP *A Man And A Woman*, recorded live with Dionne Warwick°, reaches US #49. This is the last release on Hot Buttered Soul, and the end of Hayes' association with ABC. He and Warwick also make a joint guest appearance on an episode of TV's "The Rockford Files".

June Declared a bankrupt with $6 million debts, Hayes moves from Memphis to Atlanta (where he will work regularly at Master Sounds studios) and signs a new deal with Polydor.

1978 Jan His first Polydor LP *New Horizon* makes US #78.

Dec LP *For The Sake Of Love* reaches US #75. From it, *Zeke The Freak* is a big disco success but fails to chart.

1979 Nov LP *Don't Let Go* reaches US #39 and stays on chart for 30 weeks (it will be his final gold disk for a half million US sales).

Dec Hayes duets with Millie Jackson° on LP *Royal Rappin's*, which makes US #80.

1980 Jan The title track from LP *Don't Let Go*, an updated hustling disco-style revival of Jesse Stone's R&B standard peaks at US #18 (his final hit).

June LP *And Once Again* reaches US #59.

1981 Apr Hayes appears as the villain in John Carpenter's film *Escape from New York*.

1985 Feb Two dancefloor-aimed revivals of *Theme From Shaft*, by Eddy & The Soul Band and Van Twist, bring the Hayes composition back into the UK chart, reaching #13 and #57 respectively.

1986 Hayes has TV cameo acting roles in "The A-Team" and "Hunter" (in his archetypal black tough guy role), and co-stars with Paul Sorvino and Barry Bostwick in TV movie *Betrayed By Innocence*.

Dec Hayes, signed to CBS/Columbia, releases a revival of Freddie Scott's 1963 hit *Hey Girl* which incorporates a topically-relevant anti-crack rap, with *Ike's Rap* on the flip. It hits US R&B #9. LP *U-Turn* makes US R&B #37.

1987 Feb Hayes embarks on a US promotional tour for his LP *U-Turn*, co-produced with the members of Surface. Hayes plays all instruments, replacing the symphony orchestras with synth-created "orchestral" arrangements. He appears in movie *Counter Force* with George Kennedy and Andrew Stevens, and also completes *The Sofia Conspiracy* with Ed Marinaro from US TV's "Hill Street Blues". Meanwhile, US R&B group The Fabulous Thunderbirds revive Hayes' early composition *Wrap It Up*.

HEART

Ann Wilson (lead vocals)
Nancy Wilson (guitar and vocals)
Roger Fisher (guitar)
Howard Leese (keyboards and guitar)
Steve Fossen (bass)
Michael Derosier (drums)

1970 Ann Wilson (b. June 19, 1951, San Diego, Cal., US), living in Seattle, Wash., US, and ex-local bands Ann Wilson & The Daybreaks and Bordersong with sister Nancy (b. Mar.16, 1954, San Francisco, Cal.), joins Seattle-based group The Army, formed by Fossen and brothers Mike and Roger Fisher in 1963, who play the local bar circuit. She takes over lead vocals, but the group's music mix remains hard-rock covers of material by Led Zeppelin° and others. Wilson and Roger Fisher also strike up a romantic relationship.

1972 The Army renames itself White Heart and continues on the club circuit in the Pacific North-West.

1974 After college and a spell as a solo folk singer, Nancy Wilson also joins the band, which abbreviates its name to Heart. She replaces Mike Fisher in the playing line-up, as he becomes sound engineer and manager, and her boyfriend.

1975 The group relocates to Vancouver, British Columbia, Canada, primarily to avoid Mike Fisher being drafted. After establishing a renewed live reputation in Canada, Heart signs to Shelly Siegal's Vancouver-based independent Mushroom label, which records LP *Dreamboat Annie*, a mixture of folky ballads and hard rock. It sells 30,000 copies in Canada.

1976 June With independent distribution, Mushroom releases LP *Dreamboat Annie* in US, with extracted *Crazy On You*, which is the group's US chart debut at #35.

Oct *Magic Man* hits US #9, and after a slow chart climb, LP *Dreamboat Annie* hits US #7 (eventually spending 100 weeks on chart and selling over 2 million).

Dec The group returns to Seattle, signing a new US deal with CBS/Portrait Records. Mushroom sues for breach of contract, and the group countersues to prevent the release of a second Mushroom LP made up of allegedly unfinished demos.

1977 Jan The title song from *Dreamboat Annie* reaches US #42.

Feb LP *Dreamboat Annie* is released by Arista in UK and makes #36.

May [28/30] Heart plays two concerts at Oakland Stadium, Cal., in front of 100,000 people, as part of a bill featuring The Eagles°, Foreigner° and Steve Miller°.

July Debut Portrait LP *Little Queen* hits US #9 (a second million-seller) and climbs to UK #34.

Aug *Barracuda*, taken from the LP, reaches US #11.

Oct The title track from *Little Queen* makes US #62.

Dec *Kick It Out* reaches US #79.

1978 Feb Reissued Mushroom single *Crazy On You* re-charts in US, reaching #62.

Mar [18] The band plays the California Jam 2 festival in Ontario, Cal., to 250,000 people, together with Aerosmith°, Santana°, Ted Nugent° and others.

June LP *Magazine*, the second Mushroom LP, reaches US #17. It has finally been issued after a Seattle judge decides that Mushroom may release the LP, but that Heart first had the right to re-mix and re-record the material. The sleeve bears a disclaimer. Despite the group's reluctance to acknowledge it, it becomes a million-selling platinum LP. From it, *Heartless* reaches US #24.

Nov *Straight On* reaches US #15. It is taken from second Portrait LP *Dog And Butterfly*, which reaches US #17 and is their fourth million-seller.

1979 Mar Title track from LP *Dog And Butterfly* reaches US #34.

1980 Jan While the band is completing the recording of its next LP, the Wilson sisters/Fisher brothers relationships sour. Roger Fisher leaves, later to form his own band in Seattle.

Apr Portrait is absorbed into Epic label for LP *Bebe Le Strange*, which hits US #5 as they play a lengthy, 77-date, US tour, with Leese and Nancy Wilson jointly covering Fisher's guitar role. The LP is another million-seller and extracted *Even It Up* makes US #34.

Dec Double LP *Greatest Hits/Live*, a compilation of hit singles with six tracks recorded live on the tour earlier in the year, reaches US #13.

1981 Jan *Tell It Like It Is*, a revival of Aaron Neville's 1967 million-seller, hits US #8 – Heart's first US top 10 hit since *Magic Man* in 1976.

Apr Heart's *Unchained Melody* becomes the eighth version of the song to make the US Hot 100, at US #83.

May The group begins an extensive 6-month US tour. (At the end of it, Fossen and Derosier will leave and the Wilson sisters will take a sabbatical before recruiting new musicians and planning the next LP.)

Oct [2] Ann and Nancy Wilson perform, alongside Paul Simon°, Joan Baez° and others in the Bread & Roses festival at the Greek Theater, Berkeley, Cal., to benefit a prisoners' aid group operated by Baez' sister Mimi Farina.

1982 June Nancy Wilson appears in film *Fast Times At Ridgemount High* (and *The Wild Life*).

July LP *Private Audition* reaches US #25 and UK #77. The group line-up is now the Wilson sisters and Leese, plus newcomers Mark Andes (ex-Spirit°, Jo Jo Gunne, and Firefall) on bass, and Denny

Carmassi (ex-Montrose and Gemma) on drums. *This Man Is Mine*, taken from the LP, reaches US #33.

1983 Sept *How Can I Refuse*, from the forthcoming LP, reaches US #44.

Oct LP *Passionworks*, their last for Epic, reaches US #39.

Nov Final Epic single, *Allies* peaks at US #83.

1984 July Ann Wilson duets with Loverboy's Mike Reno on *Almost Paradise*, love theme from movie *Footloose*, which hits US #7. (Reno replaces the film's producers' original male choice, Foreigner's° Lou Gramm, who rejects the project.)

1985 Jan Now signed to Capitol Records, the group begins work on a new LP.

Aug First Capitol single *What About Love?* hits US #10.

Nov [11] The group opens a UK tour at the Apollo, Manchester, supporting Tears For Fears°.

Dec LP *Heart*, the group's first for Capitol, tops the US chart, going platinum, and reaches UK #50. At the same time, *Never*, extracted from it, hits US #4.

1986 Mar *These Dreams* tops the US chart for a week, displacing Starship's *Sara*.

Apr *These Dreams* reaches UK #62, Heart's first UK chart single.

June *Nothin' At All* hits US #10.

Aug *If Looks Could Kill* reaches US #54.

1987 Jan Ann Wilson's solo *The Best Man In The World* is featured in Eddie Murphy movie *The Golden Child*, and makes US #61.

July *Alone* becomes the group's biggest hit single, topping the US chart for 3 weeks. Written by Billy Steinberg and Tom Kelly, it gives the songwriting duo a third US #1 (the previous two being Madonna's° *Like A Virgin* and Cyndi Lauper's° *True Colors*).

Aug *Alone* hits UK #3, their first UK top 10 single, and prompts UK visit for promotion and major tour dates. UK press becomes obsessed with Ann's weight problems. LP *Bad Animals*, which includes *Alone*, hits US #5 (another platinum disk) and UK #7.

Oct *Who Will You Run To*, also taken from the LP, hits US #7 and reaches UK #30.

Dec *There's The Girl* climbs to UK #34.

1988 Jan *There's The Girl* peaks at US #12.

Mar *These Dreams/Never* hits UK #8, and is double UK A-side reissue of two tracks from 1985 LP *Heart*, which peaks at UK #19. *I Want You So Bad* reaches US #49.

June Still using the back catalog, *What About Love* climbs to UK #14.

Oct Reissued *Nothin' At All* makes UK #38.

HEATWAVE

Johnnie Wilder Jr. (vocals)
Keith Wilder (vocals)
Rod Temperton (keyboards)
Eric Johns (guitars)
Mario Mantese (bass)
Ernest "Bilbo" Berger (drums and percussion)

1975 The Wilder brothers, both born in Dayton, Oh. US, having served in the US Army in West Germany, decide to remain in Europe and form a band when discharged. UK-born Temperton, who has been playing in Germany, answers the Wilders' music paper ad, as does Johns (from LA). While in Switzerland, Johnnie Wilder recruits Spanish-born Mantese and Czech refugee Berger. Guitarist Jessie Whitten, from Chicago, Ill., completes the Heatwave line-up.

1976 The band begins touring the UK club circuit and UK and European USAF bases, where its strong reputation attracts GTO label. They sign a deal and are teamed with producer (and former hitmaker) Barry Blue.

1977 Mar *Boogie Nights*, produced by Blue, hits UK #2.

June Double A-side *Too Hot To Handle/Slip Your Disc To This* reaches UK #15. The band's debut LP *Too Hot To Handle* makes UK #46.

Nov *Boogie Nights* hits US #2, and becomes one of the year's four biggest-selling singles in US, earning a platinum disk for sales of over 2 million. LP *Too Hot To Handle* peaks at US #11 and is also certified platinum. While on a visit home to Chicago, Whitten is fatally stabbed. Roy Carter, ex-UK group The Foundations, replaces him on guitar and keyboards.

1978 Temperton retires from live work to concentrate on his songwriting for Heatwave and others (he will write hits for Aretha Franklin°, George Benson°, Herbie Hancock and Michael Jackson°).

Feb *The Groove Line* reaches UK #12.

Apr A change of pace from the group's previous solid funk hits, soul ballad *Always And Forever* peaks at US #18, later becoming a US million-seller.

June LP *Central Heating* makes UK #26 and hits US #10, again certified platinum.

July *Mind Blowing Decisions*, another soul ballad, reaches UK #12. Meanwhile, *The Groove Line* hits US #7. It is the band's third US million-seller but also its final US hit single. Mantese is involved in a car accident which causes him partial paralysis, and forces him to leave. Carter and Johns also quit. In a major reshuffle, ex-Fatback band member Calvin Duke (organ and keyboards), Derek Bramble (bass), Keith Harrison (guitar and vocals) and the Wilders' cousin William L. Jones (guitar), are all recruited as replacements, in time for a major US tour.

Dec Double A-side *Always And Forever* (a US hit not previously a UK single) and a new version of *Mind Blowing Decisions* which includes an extended reggae groove, hits UK #9.

1979 June *Razzle Dazzle* reaches UK #43. LP *Hot Property*, recorded in New York with producer Phil Ramone and arrangements by Dave Grusin, fails in UK but makes US #38 and earns a gold disk. In an accident-prone band history, Johnnie Wilder is paralyzed from the neck down in an auto accident, but after initial hospitalization, he fights back to active life with the help of a specially-designed, multi-function wheelchair with facial movement controls. This allows him to continue work with the band, producing and singing in the studio. J.D. Nicholas (b. Apr.12, 1952, UK) joins to take over Wilder's vocal role on stage.

1981 Feb After a 2-year absence, Temperton's song *Gangsters Of The Groove* makes UK #19. LP *Candles*, from which *Gangsters* is taken (produced by James Guthrie and Johnnie Wilder and recorded in LA), reaches UK #29 and US #71.

Apr *Jitterbuggin'*, also from *Candles*, reaches UK #34, and is Heatwave's last UK hit single.

1982 July Berger and Nicholas leave (Nicholas joining The Commodores° on lead vocals). LP *Current*, produced in LA by Blue and Wilder, makes US #156. (The group will fade from commercial view though Temperton will remain a successful songwriter.)

Dec Michael Jackson's° LP *Thriller*, the best-selling album of all time, includes the Temperton-penned title track.

HEAVEN 17

Glenn Gregory (vocals)
Ian Craig Marsh (synthesizer)
Martyn Ware (synthesizer)

1980 Oct One-time computer operators, Marsh (b. Nov.11, 1956, Sheffield, UK) and Ware (b. May 19, 1956, Sheffield), quit The Human League° and establish British Electric Foundation (soon abbreviated to B.E.F.), a production umbrella for several projects. The first to get underway is Heaven 17 (named after a group in Anthony Burgess' book *A Clockwork Orange*), an electronic dance-styled outfit, with ex-photographer Gregory (b. May 16, 1958, Sheffield), whom they met at Sheffield's Meatwhistle drama center, recruited as vocalist.

1981 Apr *Music For Stowaways*, an entirely instrumental limited edition cassette, is the first B.E.F. UK release, on Virgin. Heaven 17 debuts on the same label with *(We Don't Need This) Fascist Groove Thing*, which overcomes a UK BBC Radio ban (because of the title) and climbs to UK #45.
Follow-up *I'm Your Money* fails to chart.

Oct LP *Penthouse And Pavement* climbs to UK #14, and *Play To Win* reaches UK #46. (*Let's All Make A Bomb* was rejected as a third single as the title was open to misinterpretation and another possible ban.) B.E.F. LP *Music For Listening To* is released, to moderate sales.

Nov The title track from LP *Penthouse And Pavement*, with Josie Jones guesting on vocals, reaches UK #57. John Wilson joins the group on bass.

Dec Ware and Marsh produce, and write several songs for, Hot Gossip's LP *Geisha Boys And Temple Girls*.

1982 Feb *Height Of The Fighting (He-La-Ho)*, a re-recording (from LP *Penthouse And Pavement*) with jazz-funk band Beggar & Co.'s horn section, fails to chart.

Apr B.E.F. LP *Music Of Quality And Distinction, Vol.1*, with guest singers (including Paul Jones, Tina Turner°, Sandie Shaw° and Gary Glitter°) of mainly classic pop oldies, reaches UK #25, but the expensive project loses £10,000. Gregory sings on two tracks: *Perfect Day* and a revival of Glen Campbell's° *Wichita Lineman*. It is the last B.E.F. project, and Marsh and Ware concentrate their energies on Heaven 17.

HEAVEN 17 *cont.*

Nov *Let Me Go* reaches UK #41.

1983 Mar *Let Me Go*, released in US by Arista, reaches #74 and LP *Heaven 17* makes US #68.

May *Temptation*, on which Gregory duets lead vocals with Carol Kenyon, is the group's biggest UK hit at #2. LP *The Luxury Gap* hits UK #4.

July *Come Live With Me* hits UK #5, while LP *The Luxury Gap* makes US #72.

Sept *Crushed By The Wheels Of Industry* peaks at UK #17.

Dec Tina Turner's° first solo hit *Let's Stay Together* is co-produced by Ware, with Gregory on backing vocals. It hits UK #6 and will peak 3 months later at US #26.

1984 Sept *Sunset Now* reaches UK #24.

Oct LP *How Men Are* makes UK #12.

Nov *This Is Mine* reaches UK #23.

Nov [25] Gregory takes part in the all-star recording for Band Aid's° *Do They Know It's Christmas?*

1985 Jan *. . . (And That's No Lie)* makes UK #52.

1986 Apr *The Foolish Thing To Do* fails to chart. The group is now hardly seen or heard. Marsh and Ware always shunned the spotlight, and Gregory's TV guest slots and magazine profiles are also less frequent.

July LP *Endless*, a compilation of hit singles and earlier LP tracks, is released only on cassette and CD. It is a minor UK success, peaking at #70.

Nov LP *Pleasure One*, the group's first new recording for 2 years, makes a brief UK chart showing at #78.

1987 Jan *Trouble*, taken from LP *Pleasure One*, peaks at UK #51.

Aug Ware co-produces LP *Introducing The Hardline According To Terence Trent D'Arby*, which hits UK #1.

1988 Aug After a year off the recording scene, Heaven 17 releases *The Ballad Of Go Go Brown*.

JIMI HENDRIX

1954 Hendrix (b. James Marshall Hendrix, Nov.27, 1942, Seattle, Wash., US), his mother a full-blooded Cherokee Indian, is given an electric guitar at age 12. Being left-handed, he turns his guitar upside down and teaches himself to play it by listening to the records of bluesmen Muddy Waters°, Elmore James and B.B. King° and rockers Chuck Berry° and Eddie Cochran°, devoting more attention to this than his school studies.

1959 Hendrix enlists as a paratrooper in the 101st Airborne Division, to avoid being drafted in the army.

1961 He is discharged after back injuries suffered during a parachute jump. He had already played in high school groups before enlisting and decides to use his obvious talent for the guitar. Adopting the stage name Jimmy James, he starts with an obscure R&B group, but moves to more prestigious work behind Sam Cooke°, B.B. King°, Little Richard°, Ike and Tina Turner°, Wilson Pickett° and Jackie Wilson°.

1964 Hendrix relocates to New York, where he plays the club circuit with The Isley Brothers°, King Curtis and John Paul Hammond. He strikes up a relationship with soul singer Curtis Knight and they write and record together. (One of the songs they record is the prophetic *Ballad Of Jimi*, written by Knight in 1965 after Hendrix tells him he will die in exactly five years time.)

1965 Hendrix forms his own group, Jimmy James & The Blue Flames, who play a mix of R&B standards and original material.

1966 Hendrix's reputation begins to spread in New York and his band is recommended by Keith Richard's girlfriend, Linda Keith, to The Animals'° Chas Chandler, now turned to management. After seeing Hendrix play at the Café Wha?, Chandler persuades him to go to London with him to form a new band.

Sept [21] Hendrix and Chandler arrive in London and recruit drummer Mitch Mitchell (b. John Mitchell, June 9, 1947), who has been playing in UK TV's "Ready, Steady, Go!" session band and with Georgie Fame's Blue Flames, and Noel Redding (b. David Redding, Dec.25, 1945) to form the 3-piece Jimi Hendrix Experience. (Mitchell has a background in the arts, having worked as a child actor in TV commercials and appeared in UK BBC TV series "Jennings at School", before moving on to music in his teens.) Redding, having been to art school and played with the Modern Jazz Group, joins on bass, despite having been auditioned for The Animals° on guitar.

Oct The Jimi Hendrix Experience's first gig is as support for French pop star Johnny Hallyday at the Paris Olympia. Chandler spends much of his own money publicizing the new group.

Dec The first Jimi Hendrix Experience single, a cover of The Leaves hit although Hendrix prefers Tim Rose's version, *Hey Joe*, is released on Polydor after being rejected by Decca.

1967 Jan [11] Chandler's high-profile press reception at the Bag O' Nails club coincides with *Hey Joe*'s entry into the UK chart.

Feb It hits UK #6 and Hendrix's "wild man" image is promulgated in the press. The group supports The Who° at the Savile Theatre, its first non-club outing.

Mar *Purple Haze* is released on new Track label after a deal with Kit Lambert. Amid allusions to mind-expanding drugs, it is taken up as an anthem for the new "love generation".

Mar [31] The group begins its first UK tour as part of a package including Cat Stevens°, The Walker Brothers° and Engelbert Humperdinck. (Hendrix will make a nightly habit of setting fire to his guitar at the end of the group's set and playing the instrument with his teeth. Rank theaters warn Hendrix to tone down his act during the tour.)

Apr During an appearance on UK BBC-TV's "Top of the Pops", a technician inadvertently puts on the backing track of Alan Price's *Simon Smith And His Amazing Dancing Bear* instead of *Watchtower*, to which Hendrix responds "I don't know the words to that one, man."

May *Purple Haze* hits UK #3. Debut LP *Are You Experienced?* is released. It hits UK #2 during a 33-week chart stay, held off the top by The Beatles'° LP *Sgt. Pepper*. By this time the group's month-long European tour is breaking attendance records at many venues.

June Plans for a live EP are shelved in favor of ballad *The Wind Cries Mary*, which hits UK #6, Hendrix's third successive top 10 hit.

June [18] The Jimi Hendrix Experience makes its US debut at the Monterey Pop Festival in Cal., having been booked at the urging of Paul McCartney°. Although the band only plays four original songs, Hendrix's versions of *Wild Thing* and *Like A Rolling Stone* get a tumultuous reception (but at their next performance on a bill with The Mamas & The Papas° at the Hollywood Bowl, they are booed).

June As in UK, Hendrix quickly gains fame (and notoriety) through the media. He takes up an invitation to support The Monkees° on a US tour. The group's music and Hendrix's outrageous showmanship are entirely inappropriate for The Monkees' teenybop audience and they are pulled off after only seven gigs. (Chandler claims that protests from the right-wing Daughters of the American Revolution have brought this action about, but in reality Chandler planned the support spot as a publicity stunt knowing the outrage Hendrix's act will cause.)

July The group records *Burning Of The Midnight Lamp* in New York, which features Hendrix on harpsichord and Aretha Franklin's° backing group, The Sweet Inspirations, on backing vocals.

Sept *Burning Of The Midnight Lamp* makes UK #18.

Oct Hendrix achieves his first US chart entries, on Reprise, when *Purple Haze* makes #65 and LP *Are You Experienced?* hits #5 during a 101-week run.

Dec Second LP, *Axis: Bold As Love*, is issued in UK and enters the chart to hit #5. The trio tours UK, including the "Christmas on Earth" concert with The Who°, The Move° and Pink Floyd°. Capitol Records releases LP *Get That Feeling*, a UK #39 and US #75, featuring Hendrix with Curtis Knight, recorded in the summer in US to appease ex-manager Ed Chalpin, who claims Hendrix has broken his contract.

1968 Jan The group plays European dates, but tensions develop, both within the group and with the management. Hendrix ends up in a Swedish jail after an argument with Redding. *Foxy Lady* makes US #67.

Feb *Axis: Bold As Love* hits US #3 during a year-long chart stay. Hendrix cuts out his stage antics and concentrates on the music during the group's US tour – audience reaction is often negative. The "wild man" is proving hard to escape.

Mar *Up From The Skies* peaks at US #82. The group begins a 47-day US tour.

Apr LP *Smash Hits*, comprising both sides of the first four singles and four tracks from the first LP, hits UK #4 and US #6.

May [20] Hendrix signs to US Reprise.

June After finishing the tour, the trio begins sessions for a new LP that

will stretch to 6 months. Hendrix brings in other musicians, and Steve Winwood° (keyboards) and Jefferson Airplane's° Jack Casady play on *Voodoo Chile*.

Sept A revival of Dylan's° *All Along The Watchtower* hits UK #5 and is Hendrix's first US top 20 success, at #20.

Oct Double LP *Electric Ladyland*, with a controversial sleeve picturing Hendrix surrounded by naked women, is released. Some shops refuse to display it, but despite this it hits UK #6 and tops the US chart.

Oct [10-12] Hendrix plays three concerts at San Francisco's Winterland Arena.

Dec *Crosstown Traffic* peaks at US #52. Pressures on Hendrix increase, with disagreements between his management team, Chandler and more commercially-minded Mike Jeffrey, resulting in Chandler selling his share in the band to Jeffrey. The group splits when Mitchell and Redding return to UK without Hendrix. (Redding will later form his own band Fat Mattress.)

1969 Jan Hendrix performs on UK TV show "Lulu"° and plays an unrehearsed *Sunshine Of Your Love* as a tribute to recently-split Cream°, to the annoyance of the progam's producers.

Feb [24] Jeffrey reverses an apparent split by convincing the group to play London's Royal Albert Hall, followed by European dates and a spring US tour.

Apr *Crosstown Traffic* reaches UK #37.

May Hendrix is arrested in Toronto, Canada, charged with possession of heroin. He denies hard drug use (but a cloud will hang over him until his acquittal in Dec.).

May [24] The Jimi Hendrix Experience plays at the International Sports Arena, San Diego, Cal.

June [27] The group plays its final concert on the last day of the 3-day Denver Pop Festival.

June Hendrix spends the summer recording in New York, with Electric Flag drummer/vocalist Buddy Miles and bassist Billy Cox, a friend from his army days.

July [2] Mitchell and Redding announce their split from Hendrix is permanent (but Mitchell is back with him the same month for a performance at the Newport Jazz Festival).

Aug Hendrix plays the Woodstock Festival, backed by the Electric Sky Church, drawn from musicians he has played with during the year, including Mitchell, Cox, Larry Leeds (rhythm guitar), Juma Lewis and Jerry Velez (both percussion). The set is highlighted by *The Star Spangled Banner* and his performance is captured on the *Woodstock* film and LP.

1970 Jan Hendrix, Miles and Cox go on stage for the first time as The Band of Gypsys at the Fillmore East, New York. (The concert is recorded for live LP *Band Of Gypsys*.) Their second performance, in front of 19,000 people at New York's Madison Square Garden, ends abruptly when Hendrix walks off stage in the middle of the second number. The group splits. (Hendrix keeps Cox and recalls Mitchell for subsequent concerts.) Hendrix travels to Hawaii to work on film *Rainbow Bridge*.

Mar [30] The new Jimi Hendrix Experience, with Cox replacing Redding, plays two concerts at the Community Center in Berkeley, Cal.

May LP *Band Of Gypsys* hits US #5, given to Capitol in a one-off deal to compensate ex-manager Chalpin, who also receives $1 million payment and percentage on future Hendrix earnings.

June [20] Hendrix earns $125,000 playing the Newport Jazz Festival.

July [1] Hendrix records his first session at Electric Lady(land) Studios in New York. (A great deal of money and effort was spent in creating a state-of-the-art "dream" studio.)

Aug [17] Hendrix takes part in the Randall Island Rock Festival with Grand Funk Railroad,°, Jethro Tull°, Little Richard° and Steppenwolf°.

Aug [28] A gig in his hometown Seattle ends with him abusing the audience.

Aug [30] He plays UK's Isle of Wight Festival as LP *Band Of Gypsys* hits UK #6.

Sept After bad experiences in Denmark (he leaves stage with the words "I've been dead for a long time") and Germany (the audience boo his late appearance), the group returns to London.

Sept [16] Hendrix joins Eric Burdon and War° on stage at Ronnie Scott's.

Sept [18] Hendrix is found dead after leaving the tragic message "I need help bad, man" on Chandler's answering machine. The coroner's verdict states that death was caused by inhalation of vomit following barbiturate intoxication. (A shared LP with Otis Redding°, one side each, from Monterey Pop Festival has already entered the US chart and reaches #16. It will not be released in UK.)

Oct [1] Hendrix is buried in Seattle.

Oct LP *Monterey Pop* reaches US #16.

Nov *Voodoo Chile* tops the UK chart.

1971 Mar *The Cry Of Love*, the last LP sanctioned by Hendrix himself, is released and hits US #3 and UK #2. It contains songs he had been working on for his planned concept LP, *The First Rays Of The Rising Sun*. The US chart also sees the first cash-in LP, *Two Great Experiences Together!* on Maple Records, featuring Hendrix and sax player Lonnie Youngblood. It peaks at #127. (Due to Hendrix's complicated contractual affairs the market will be flooded throughout the early 70s by LPs bearing his name, the majority are jam sessions never intended for release.)

May *Freedom* peaks at US #59.

Sept Ember label LP *Experience*, drawn from Royal Albert Hall Performances in Feb. 1969, hits UK #9.

Oct LP *Rainbow Bridge*, containing more recordings from the 1968-70 period, makes US #15. Taken from it, *Dolly Dagger* makes US #74.

Nov *Gypsy Eyes/Remember* peaks at UK #35. LP *Jimi Hendrix At The Isle Of Wight* makes UK #17.

Dec LP *Rainbow Bridge* reaches UK #16.

1972 Feb LP *Hendrix In The West*, a collection of live performances highlighted by Chuck Berry's° *Johnny B. Goode* which makes UK #35, hits UK #7 and US #12.

Dec LP *War Heroes*, a curious mix of studio material including a version of Henry Mancini's *Peter Gunn Theme*, makes UK #23 and US #48.

1973 July LP *Soundtrack Recordings From The Film Jimi Hendrix*, a documentary of Hendrix's life, reaches UK #37 and US #89.

1975 Mar LP *Jimi Hendrix* makes UK #35.

Aug *Crash Landing* is the first of three posthumous LPs produced by Alan Douglas, who had been given stewardship of the 600 hours of tapes that were part of Hendrix's estate. (On some cuts Douglas has used session musicians to overdub existing parts so only the original guitar and vocal remain.) The LP hits US #5 and UK #35.

Nov The second Douglas release, LP *Midnight Lightning*, reaches US #43 and UK #46.

JIMI HENDRIX *cont.*

1978 Aug *The Essential Jimi Hendrix* peaks at US #114.
1979 Aug *The Essential Jimi Hendrix Volume 2* makes US #156.
1980 Apr The final Douglas release, LP *Nine To The Universe*, featuring Hendrix's jamming on sessions during recording of his final LP in 1969, climbs to US #127.
May [22] Four Hendrix gold LPs are stolen from Electric Ladyland studios.
1982 Aug LP *The Jimi Hendrix Concerts*, another selection of live recordings from 1968-70, makes US #79 and UK #16.
1983 Feb LP *The Singles Album* climbs to UK #77.
1984 Nov LP *Kiss The Sky*, recordings from 1967-69, reaches US #148.
1988 Oct U2's° LP of their 1987 US tour *Rattle And Hum* highlights Hendrix's version of *The Star Spangled Banner* from *Woodstock* as the intro to *Bullet The Blue Sky*.

HERMAN'S HERMITS

Peter Noone (vocals)
Derek "Lek" Leckenby (lead guitar)
Keith Hopwood (rhythm guitar)
Karl Green (bass)
Barry "Bean" Whitwam (drums)

1961 Noone (b. Nov.5, 1947, Manchester, UK), having studied at the Manchester School of Music and Drama and appeared in UK TV soap serial "Coronation Street", is offered a part in a film starring Judy Garland, but his parents veto it.
1963 Noone joins Manchester beat group The Heartbeats as vocalist, using the name Peter Kovak. They work in youth clubs and teen dancehalls and are signed by managers Harvey Lisberg and Charlie Silverman. The group's name changes after bass player Green (b. July 31, 1947, Salford, UK) notes a likeness between Noone and the character Sherman in TV cartoon "The Rocky and Bullwinkle Show". "Sherman" becomes "Herman" and the group name develops to Herman and His Hermits, later shortened to Herman's Hermits. The line-up is Noone, Green, Leckenby (b. May 14, 1946, Leeds, UK), Hopwood (b. Oct.26, 1946, Manchester) and Whitwam (b. July 21, 1946, Manchester).
1964 Lisberg and Silverman persuade producer Mickie Most to see the group on stage in Bolton, UK. Most sees a facial resemblance between Noone and a young John F. Kennedy and decides that the singer's "little boy lost" look would make him the ideal frontman for a pop act to be aimed as much at mums and dads as teenagers.
Sept Signed to Most, and via him to EMI's Columbia label, the group tops the UK chart for 2 weeks with debut single *I'm Into Something Good*, a cover of Earl-Jean's US #38 hit. (Like most of the records which follow, it includes little of The Hermits themselves; Noone's vocals are backed by sessionmen such as guitarists Jimmy Page and Big Jim Sullivan, with John Paul Jones (later to form Led Zeppelin° with Page) taking care of the bass and most of the arrangements.)
Dec *Show Me Girl*, submitted by *Something Good* writers Goffin and King° who are impressed by the Hermits' cover version, reaches UK #19. *I'm Into Something Good* climbs to US #13. A million-seller, it earns the group's first gold disk.
1965 Jan On first US visit, the group makes a cameo appearance in teen movie *When The Boys Meet The Girls*, starring Connie Francis° and Harve Presnell.
Mar A revival of The Rays' 1957 million-seller *Silhouettes* hits UK #3. The John Carter/Ken Lewis (Ivy League) *Can't You Hear My Heartbeat* hits US #2 and is the group's second million-seller.
Apr The group appears at the *New Musical Express* Poll Winners Concert at the Empire Pool, Wembley, UK, with The Beatles°, The Rolling Stones°, The Kinks° and many others.
May The group embarks on its first full US tour. *Mrs Brown You've Got A Lovely Daughter* tops the US chart for 3 weeks, having entered at #12, the highest first-week placing for a single in 7 years, due to unprecedented airplay. It is extracted from US LP *Introducing Herman's Hermits* which hits US #2. *Mrs Brown You've Got A Lovely Daughter* earns a gold disk on a million-plus US sales but is not released as a single in UK; the group is not enamored of it and thinks the arrangement too corny for the UK market. *Silhouettes* hits US #5 and is a million-seller on combined US/UK sales. An update of Sam Cooke's° *Wonderful World* hits UK #7.
July Noone is voted one of the ten best-dressed men in UK. The group's second US LP *Herman's Hermits On Tour* climbs to US #2 while the first LP is still in the top 10. *Wonderful World* hits US #4.
Aug *I'm Henry VIII, I Am*, a revival of 1911 music hall song, extracted as a US-only single from LP *Herman's Hermits On Tour*, again after strong pre-release airplay, hits #1. It is another US million-seller. On holiday in Hawaii, Noone meets (and "interviews", for *NME*) Elvis Presley°, who is on location for film *Paradise, Hawaiian Style*.
Sept *Just A Little Bit Better* reaches UK #15. LP *Herman's Hermits*, a belatedly-released UK compilation of two US LPs, makes #16.
Oct *Just A Little Bit Better* hits US #7.
Nov The group plays a UK tour with The Fortunes°, Billy Fury° and Wayne Fontana and The Mindbenders°.
Dec Compilation LP *The Best Of Herman's Hermits* reaches US #5.
1966 Jan *A Must To Avoid*, often referred to by Noone as *Muscular Boy*, a dig at his own indistinct phrasing of the lyrics, hits UK #6 and US #8, and is another million-seller.
Mar US-only *Listen People*, the group's first A-side slow ballad, hits US #3 and earns another gold disk.
Apr UK-only *You Won't Be Leaving*, with *Listen People* on the B-side, reaches UK #20. The group sings 11 songs in teen movie *Hold On!*. Soundtrack LP *Hold On!* reaches US #14.
May Extracted from LP *Hold On!*, *Leaning On A Lamp Post*, a revival of George Formby oldie, hits US #9. The group signs a movie deal with MGM Pictures.
July *This Door Swings Both Ways* reaches UK #18.
Aug *This Door Swings Both Ways* makes US #12.
Sept LP *Both Sides Of Herman's Hermits* peaks at US #48.
Nov *No Milk Today*, written by Graham Gouldman later of 10cc°, hits UK #7. *Dandy*, written by Ray Davies of The Kinks°, hits US #5. Noone appears in US TV movie "The Canterville Ghost" with Sir Michael Redgrave amd Douglas Fairbanks Jr.
Dec *East West*, also by Gouldman, reaches UK #37 and US #27.
1967 Jan Compilation LP *The Best Of Herman's Hermits, Volume II* peaks at US #20.
Mar *There's A Kind Of Hush (All Over The World)* hits UK #7 and US #4, and is a US million-seller. US B-side is former UK hit *No Milk Today*, which makes #35.
May LP *There's A Kind Of Hush All Over The World* reaches US #13.
July [14] The group opens US tour, with The Who° (on their first US tour) as support act. *Don't Go Out Into The Rain (You're Going To Melt)* reaches US #18 but is not released as a UK single.
Sept *Museum*, written and also recorded by Donovan° (Mickie Most later admits he used the same backing track for both versions) reaches US #39. It is released in UK but is the group's first chart failure.
Oct LP *Blaze* reaches US #75 but is not released in UK.
1968 Jan Compilation LP *The Best Of Herman's Hermits, Volume III* reaches US #102.
Feb *I Can Take Or Leave Your Loving* climbs to UK #11 and US #22.
June *Sleepy Joe* reaches UK #12 but only US #61 as a new generation of US bands has eclipsed Herman's Hermits, though they have lasted longer than most of their contemporaries.
Aug *Sunshine Girl* hits UK #8.
Sept The group, with Noone as romantic lead opposite Sheila White, stars in film *Mrs. Brown You've Got A Lovely Daughter*, inspired by the hit single. Soundtrack LP fails to chart in UK but reaches US #182.
Nov [5] Noone marries French girl, Mireille Strasser.
Nov He enters into business partnership with Graham Gouldman, which includes studio production work and the opening of a New York boutique named Zoo.
1969 Jan *Something's Happening*, a rewrite of a continental song, hits UK #6.
May *My Sentimental Friend* hits UK #2 and is the group's second-biggest UK success.
Nov *Here Comes The Star*, a cover of an Australian hit noted during a tour there, peaks at UK #33.
1970 Mar *Years May Come, Years May Go* reaches UK #7 and is the group's last release on UK Columbia.
June *Bet Yer Life I Do*, on Most's newly-formed RAK label and written by members of Hot Chocolate°, makes UK #22.
Dec *Lady Barbara*, another Hot Chocolate° song, which reaches UK #13, is the group's final UK hit single. It is credited to Peter Noone & Herman's Hermits, which leads to speculation of a split, which occurs once the record is a hit. The Hermits base themselves in US

to work the nostalgia circuit, while Noone stays in UK, recording on Most's RAK label.

1971 June Noone's only hit at UK #12 is David Bowie's° *Oh You Pretty Thing*, featuring Bowie playing piano. (The follow-up, another Bowie song, *Right On Mother*, will fail to chart as will later 70s solos on RAK, Philips, Casablanca and Bus Stop.)

Oct Compilation LP *The Most Of Herman's Hermits* reaches UK #14. The Hermits without Noone sign to RCA Records and release *She's A Lady*, which fails to sell. (Occasional later UK singles without Noone will also flop, though the group will continue to play as a live act for several years.)

1973 June [28] Noone briefly reunites with The Hermits to top the bill of the "British Invasion" nostalgia concert at New York's Madison Square Garden, to 13,000 people. Also playing are The Searchers°, Gerry & The Pacemakers° and Wayne Fontana and The Mindbenders°. (Noone and the group will permanently part company later in the year, with Noone continuing in cabaret and on theatrical stage.)

1977 Oct TV-advertised compilation LP *Greatest Hits* reaches UK #37.

1980 Living in LA, Noone forms The Tremblers, with Gregg Inhofer and Gee Connor on guitars, Mark Browne on bass and Robert Williams on drums, and records LP *Twice Nightly* and single *Steady Eddy*, but with no chart success.

1983 Noone has his biggest stage success with starring role (as Frederic) in a new version of Gilbert and Sullivan's *The Pirates Of Penzance* in London, having taken over the role from Rex Smith on Broadway in 1982.

THE HOLLIES

Allan Clarke (vocals)
Graham Nash (guitar)
Tony Hicks (guitar)
Eric Haydock (bass)
Bobby Elliott (drums)

1961 The group is formed in Manchester, UK, by former schoolfriends Clarke (b. Apr.5, 1942, Salford, UK) and Nash (b. Feb.2, 1942, Blackpool, UK), who were The Two Teens duo, joined by Haydock (b. Feb.3, 1943) and Don Rathbone (drums), becoming The Fourtones, then The Deltas, and with another guitarist, becoming The Hollies.

1963 Jan EMI producer Ron Richards, checking out the UK beat scene in the wake of The Beatles'° initial success, sees the group perform at the Cavern club in Liverpool, and invites them for an EMI audition in London. The second guitarist does not want to turn professional, so group manager Allan Cheetham invites Hicks (b. Dec.16, 1943, Nelson, Lancs., UK), from local group The Dolphins, to audition instead. When EMI accepts the group, Hicks joins full-time.

Apr [4] The first Hollies recording session produces the first single, a revival of The Coasters'° *(Ain't That) Just Like Me*.

June *(Ain't That) Just Like Me* reaches UK #25.

July Rathbone moves from drums to the group's management, and is replaced by Elliott (b. Dec.8, 1942), an ex-colleague of Hicks' who has been playing with Shane Fenton and The Fentones. The new line-up tours widely in UK.

Oct *Searchin'*, a revival of another Coasters° oldie, reaches UK #12 (despite a unanimous thumbs-down review from BBC TV's "Juke Box Jury", on which panellist Pat Boone° advises viewers to go out and buy the original version).

Oct [29] The group begins sessions for its first LP.

1964 Jan Third single, a revival of Maurice Williams & The Zodiacs' *Stay*, is the group's first UK top 10 entry, hitting #8.

Mar LP *Stay With The Hollies* hits UK #2.

Apr A revival of Doris Troy's *Just One Look* hits UK #2, as the group begins recording its second LP.

May *Just One Look* is the group's first US chart entry, at #98.

June *Here I Go Again* hits UK #4.

Oct *We're Through*, The Hollies' first self-written A-side (by Clarke, Hicks and Nash under the name L. Ransford), hits UK #7.

Nov LP *In The Hollies Style* is released in UK, without charting.

1965 Mar The Goffin/King° song *Yes I Will* (later recorded by The Monkees° as *I'll Be True To You*) hits UK #9.

Apr The group visits US for the first time, playing the New York Broadway Paramount, with Little Richard° and others.

May [5] On return from US, the group records *I'm Alive* at Abbey Road studios.

July *I'm Alive*, written by Clint Ballard Jr., tops the UK chart for 3 weeks, deposing Elvis Presley's° *Crying In The Chapel* and yielding to The Byrds'° *Mr. Tambourine Man*.

Oct Graham Gouldman's song *Look Through Any Window* hits UK #4, while LP *The Hollies* hits UK #8.

1966 Jan At George Martin's suggestion, the group covers George Harrison's° *If I Needed Someone* (from The Beatles'° *Rubber Soul* LP). Harrison publicly denounces their interpretation as "soul-less", and it halts at UK #20. Meanwhile, *Look Through Any Window* reaches US #32.

Feb LP *Hear! Here!* makes US #145.

Mar *I Can't Let Go*, a Chip Taylor composition selected by Hicks from two demos at Dick James Music (the other is John Phillips' *California Dreamin'*), hits UK #2.

Apr After missing several gigs, Haydock is asked to leave.

May *I Can't Let Go* reaches US #42.

May [10] The group records the theme for Peter Sellers film *After The Fox* at Abbey Road studios, with Sellers doing a spoken part. Between bass players, they hire Jack Bruce for the session, while the track's composer Burt Bacharach plays piano.

May [18] Bernie Calvert, previously with Hicks in The Dolphins, joins the group on bass, playing on another Gouldman song, *Bus Stop*, on his first day.

June Clarke, Hicks and Nash are invited by The Everly Brothers° to submit songs for an LP to record in UK. After a day sifting material at the London Mayfair Hotel, The Hollies join The Everly Brothers in the studio for recording, along with sessioneers Jimmy Page and John Paul Jones (later both of Led Zeppelin°).

July *Bus Stop* hits UK #5, while LP *Would You Believe* reaches UK #16.

Sept *Bus Stop* hits US #5, the group's US breakthrough.

Nov *Stop Stop Stop*, written by the group, and powered by an unusual six-string banjo riff, hits UK #2.

Dec LP *For Certain Because* reaches UK #23.

1967 Jan [11] The group begins sessions for a new LP at Abbey Road, while LP *Bus Stop* reaches US #75.

Feb Elliott suffers a burst appendix while touring in Germany. He is hospitalized for several weeks, and when the group returns to London to complete the LP, session drummers Clem Cattini and Dougie Wright deputize.

Mar *On A Carousel*, taken from the LP sessions, hits UK #4, while LP *Stop! Stop! Stop!* (US equivalent of *For Certain Because*) reaches US #91.

May *On A Carousel* reaches US #11.

June *Carrie-Anne*, another Clarke/Hicks/Nash song, almost 2 years in the writing (and finished during rehearsals at a TV studio), hits UK #3.

July LP *Evolution* reaches UK #13 and US #43. US distribution switches from Imperial Records to Epic. As Imperial exercises its sell-off period (with additional releases), product from the two labels overlaps. *Pay You Back With Interest*, on Imperial, reaches US #28, while *Carrie-Anne*, on Epic, hits US #9. Imperial compilation LP *The Hollies' Greatest Hits* reaches US #11.

Sept The group begins recording LP *Butterfly*, an admittedly *Sergeant Pepper*-influenced set, with the prevailing "Summer of Love" psychedelic aura of mid-1967.

Oct *King Midas In Reverse*, chiefly written by Nash, and released as a single against the advice of producer Richards (who feels its more experimental structure and lyric will alienate traditional Hollies fans), reaches UK #18 and US #51.

Nov Imperial reissues *Just One Look* in US, which makes #44.

Dec *Dear Eloise*, released as a US-only single to tie in with the group's US tour, reaches #50. In LA, Nash meets David Crosby, ex-The Byrds°, while attending a recording session by The Mamas and The Papas°.

1968 Jan The group records Clarke/Nash song *Wings* for inclusion on World Wildlife Fund charity LP *No One's Gonna Change My World*.

Mar Work starts in the studio on a new LP, but most of the material is not used or left unfinished (including Nash's *Marrakesh Express*, later a hit for Crosby, Stills & Nash°).

Apr *Jennifer Eccles*, written by Clarke and Nash as a deliberate contrast to the complexity of *King Midas*, hits UK #7.

May *Jennifer Eccles* makes US #40.

May [24] A concert at London's Lewisham Odeon is recorded by EMI for a live LP (but never used).

July The Hollies' management announces that Nash and Bernie Calvert

THE HOLLIES *cont.*

are both planning solo LPs. Nash has grown unhappy with the group's musical direction since *King Midas*, and speculation is already rife that he will leave.

Aug The group plays a UK cabaret season, wearing matching suits and widening the stage repertoire to include songs like *Puff (The Magic Dragon)* and Roger Miller's° *Dang Me*.

Sept *Do The Best You Can* reaches US #93.

Oct In disagreement with a Hicks-proposed plan to record an LP entirely of Bob Dylan° songs, Nash announces that he will leave in Dec. Meanwhile, compilation LP *The Hollies' Greatest* tops the UK chart for 7 weeks and *Listen To Me* makes UK #11.

Dec [8] Nash leaves at the end of a charity concert at the London Palladium (and goes into rehearsal in London with David Crosby and Stephen Stills for their new trio project).

1969 Jan The group auditions for a new singer/guitarist, and Terry Sylvester, ex-The Escorts and The Swingin' Blue Jeans° is recruited.

Feb Sylvester's first studio session with the group is for *Sorry Suzanne*, after which the group proceeds with LP *Hollies Sing Dylan*.

Apr *Sorry Suzanne* hits UK #3 but stalls at US #56.

June LP *Hollies Sing Dylan* hits UK #3.

June [25] The group records *He Ain't Heavy, He's My Brother*, with Elton John° playing piano. Sessions continue for LP *Hollies Sing Hollies*, a set entirely of compositions by group members.

Oct The group appears on "The Bobbie Gentry Show" on UK TV, singing several unaccustomed country-style songs.

Nov *He Ain't Heavy He's My Brother* hits UK #3, while LP *Hollies Sing Hollies* is released without charting.

1970 Mar *He Ain't Heavy, He's My Brother* hits US #7, and total world sales top a million.

Mar [10] Elton John° joins the group again at Abbey Road, playing piano on *I Can't Tell The Bottom From The Top*.

May *I Can't Tell The Bottom From The Top* hits UK #7.

June LP *He Ain't Heavy, He's My Brother* reaches US #32, while *I Can't Tell The Bottom From The Top* peaks at US #82.

Oct *Gasoline Alley Bred* reaches UK #14.

Dec LP *Confessions Of The Mind* makes UK #30.

1971 Feb LP *Moving Finger* (US equivalent of *Confessions Of The Mind*) reaches US #183, while the group plays a Far East tour.

Mar [16] The Hollies' first session at AIR studios in London produces *Hey Willy*.

June *Hey Willy* reaches UK #22, while LP *Distant Light* is released without charting in UK.

Aug Clarke, determined to cut a solo LP, leaves the group. He signs to RCA and records LP *My Real Name Is 'Arold*, which is not a success. Swedish singer Mikael Rickfors, ex-Bamboo, is recruited on lead vocals.

1972 Mar *The Baby*, written by Chip Taylor, the first with Rickfors' lead vocal, and the only hit, reaching UK #26. It is also the group's first release on new UK label, Polydor.

Sept LP *Distant Light* makes US #21. *Long Cool Woman In A Black Dress*, a Creedence Clearwater Revival°-styled near-solo track by Clarke, taken from LP *Distant Light*, belatedly hits US #2, earning the group a gold disk for million-plus sales, and, re-promoted by EMI, also reaches UK #32.

Nov *Magic Woman Touch* is the first Hollies UK single chart failure.

Dec Also from *Distant Light*, *Long Dark Road* reaches US #26.

1973 Mar *Magic Woman Touch* reaches US #60 and LP *Romany* makes US #84.

July Clarke is invited back into the group, having cut two solo LPs with little success, and Rickfors returns to Sweden. Clarke's new agreement with the others will allow him to make solo LPs alongside the group's work.

Oct Clarke's song *The Day That Curly Billy Shot Crazy Sam McGhee*, in similar style to *Long Cool Woman* reaches UK #24.

Nov [15] The group records *The Air That I Breathe* after being introduced to Phil Everly's version of the song. Meanwhile, compilation LP *The Hollies' Greatest Hits* reaches US #157.

1974 Mar *The Air That I Breathe* hits UK #2 and LP *Hollies* reaches UK #38.

May *Son Of A Rotten Gambler* fails to chart in UK (as does *I'm Down*, 6 months later).

June LP *Hollies* makes US #28.

Aug *The Air That I Breathe* hits US #6 and is a million-seller, collecting another gold disk.

1975 Apr *Sandy*, a Bruce Springsteen° song found by Clarke (who is an early champion of the US artist in UK, recording several of his songs on later solo LPs), reaches US #85. LP *Another Night* makes US #123. Both miss the UK chart.

July Title track from *Another Night* reaches US #71.

1976 LPs *Write On* and *Russian Roulette*, and four singles from them, all fail to chart. The group splits from producer Richards.

1977 Apr Live LP *The Hollies Live Hits*, recorded on stage in Christchurch, New Zealand, in Feb. 1976, hits UK #4.

1978 Mar LP *A Crazy Steal* fails to chart, and Clarke leaves the group again to concentrate on his solo career.

July TV-advertised compilation LP *20 Golden Greats*, on EMI, hits UK #2.

Aug Clarke rejoins, and the group begins its first studio sessions for over a year.

1979 Mar The group is reunited with Richards for LP *Five Three One – Double Seven O Four* (the title comes from its Polydor catalogue number). It fails to chart.

1980 June The group links with producer Mike Batt for *Soldier's Song*, recorded with the London Symphony Orchestra. It is the group's first UK hit single since *The Air That I Breathe*, but peaks at #58.

Oct LP *Buddy Holly*, a return to the *Hollies Sing Dylan*-concept, this time featuring entirely Buddy Holly° songs, is advertised on UK TV by Polydor but fails to chart.

1981 May Sylvester leaves after an acrimonious argument. Within days, Calvert follows him, leaving Clarke, Hicks and Elliott as a trio.

June Attempts to work with other musicians and vocalists include never-released *I Don't Understand You*, with Labi Siffre, and *Carrie*, with its writer John Miles. (*Carrie* will be released in 1988 as B-side of hit reissue *He Ain't Heavy, He's My Brother*.)

July [30] At EMI's invitation, Hicks and Elliott put together the segued tracks *Holliedaze* and *Holliepops*, a variation on the currently huge "Stars On 45" craze.

Sept *Holliedaze (A Medley)* reaches UK #28. Hicks, Clarke and Elliott reunite with Graham Nash (who flies to UK from Hawaii) and Eric Haydock to perform it on UK TV's "Top of the Pops".

1982 Nash decides he would like to record with the group again, and he and Clarke make a deal with WEA Records in US, for a Nash-

Hollies reunion LP. Instrumental parts for the tracks are recorded in London and LA in March, May and June.

1983 Feb Nash, Clarke, Hicks and Elliott record the vocals and final tracks for LP *What Goes Around* at Nash's Rudy Records studios in LA.

July A revival of The Supremes'° *Stop! In The Name Of Love* reaches US #29. It is taken from LP *What Goes Around* which makes US #90. Both fail to chart in UK. A US tour follows, compiling Hollies classics with later Nash material, before the reunion ends as Nash returns to his solo career and work with David Crosby.

1984 Nov The Hollies re-sign to EMI, this time to appear on the Columbia label. The line-up comprises the Clarke/Hicks/Elliott core, plus keyboards player Denis Haines, Alan Coates on harmony vocals, and Ray Stiles (a member of Mud° during the 1970s) on bass.

1985 May *Too Many Hearts Get Broken* is released without charting.

1987 Jan Further Columbia singles *This Is It* and *Reunion Of The Heart* fail to chart.

Oct On tour in West Germany, the group is approached to record *Stand By Me* (not the Ben E. King° song), which makes the German chart on release, but is not issued in UK.

1988 Sept *He Ain't Heavy, He's My Brother*, reissued following exposure in a UK Miller Lite Beer TV commercial, tops the UK chart, finally giving the group its second UK #1 single. It holds off a challenge from Bill Medley's version, from the film *Rambo III*. The group begins a major UK tour, and EMI releases a double-LP anthology rounding up all Hollies hit singles and an LP of rare tracks.

BUDDY HOLLY AND THE CRICKETS

1949 Sept Holly (b. Charles Hardin Holley, Sept.7, 1936, Lubbock, Tex., US) enters Hutchinson Junior High School, where he meets Bob Montgomery and they form a duo, Buddy & Bob, playing mainly country and bluegrass, but also influenced by major R&B/doo-wop vocal groups. They become a popular attraction around Lubbock.

1953 Sept Buddy & Bob perform on radio for the first time, on local country station K-DAV. Adding Larry Welborn on bass, the group earns a regular Saturday afternoon slot "The Buddy and Bob Show".

1954 At K-DAV, they record several demos (which will eventually appear as LP *Holly In The Hills* after Holly's death).

1955 Growth of rockabilly in the wake of tumultuously-received tours by Elvis Presley°, encourages Holly to move his music from its pure country base. Drummer Jerry Allison joins the line-up.

Oct [14] Buddy & Bob appear supporting Bill Haley & His Comets° on a show booked by K-DAV, where the group is spotted by Nashville-based agent Eddie Crandall.

Oct [15] Buddy & Bob open a show for Elvis Presley° at Lubbock's Cotton Club.

Dec Crandall wires K-DAV's Dave Stone from Nashville, asking if Holly can cut some demos and send them to him.

1956 Jan Via talent scout Jim Denny, Crandall interests Decca Records in Nashville in recording Holly but not Montgomery. The trio splits up, with Montgomery insisting that Holly grab the opportunity. (Montgomery will stay in music on the production and publishing side, and will still have a thriving career in the 1980s.) Holly recruits Sonny Curtis (guitar) and Don Guess (bass) for a promised session in Nashville.

Jan [26] At Bradley's Barn studio, Nashville, the group records as Buddy Holly & The Three Tunes.

Apr [16] Holly's first single, *Blue Days, Black Nights* is released.

May The group (still Holly, Allison, Curtis and Guess) tours the South-Eastern states.

July [22] The group cuts a second Nashville session. (Decca will sit on these recordings and release them after Holly's success with The Crickets, as LP *That'll Be The Day*, credited to Buddy Holly & The Three Tunes.)

Sept Holly leaves Decca, following mutual dissatisfaction. He and Allison drive to New Mexico to see independent producer Norman Petty, who has a studio in Clovis.

1957 Feb Holly forms a new band with Allison, Niki Sullivan (rhythm guitar) and Joe B. Mauldin (bass). They tape several demos for Petty, naming themselves The Crickets in the process.

Feb [25] The Crickets record a new, tighter version of Holly's composition *That'll Be The Day* at Petty's Clovis studio.

May [27] *That'll Be The Day* is released by Brunswick Records (an associate company of Decca).

July Petty becomes the group's manager, and it begins a wide-ranging tour to promote the new single, including a date at the Apollo in Harlem (which has booked them unseen as a black R&B act on the strength of *That'll Be The Day*).

Sept *That'll Be The Day* tops the US chart for a week, selling over a million. At the end of the month, a second single is released on Brunswick's sister label Coral, and credited just to Buddy Holly (a dual release ploy which will continue for the next year). The song is *Peggy Sue*, originally written by Holly as *Cindy Lou*, then renamed after Allison's girlfriend.

Nov *That'll Be The Day* tops the UK chart for 3 weeks. LP *The Chirping Crickets* is released in US.

Dec [1] The group appears on US TV's "Ed Sullivan Show", performing *That'll Be The Day* and *Peggy Sue*, and Sullivan interviews Holly.

Dec *Peggy Sue* hits US #3 and is a million-seller.

1958 Jan Follow-up *Oh Boy!* hits US #10, while *Peggy Sue* hits UK #6.

Jan [26] The group makes a second appearance on US TV's "Ed Sullivan Show" performing *Oh Boy*, and follows it with a 6-day tour of Australia, playing in Melbourne, Sydney and Brisbane, with Jerry Lee Lewis° and Paul Anka°.

Feb *Oh Boy!* hits UK #3.

Mar [1] The group opens its only UK tour with a show at The Trocadero, Elephant & Castle, London.

Mar [2] Holly and The Crickets appear on peak-time UK TV in the live variety show "Sunday Night At The London Palladium". (During the tour, they will also be seen on TV in Jack Payne's "Off The Record" show, while *Listen To Me* reaches UK #16, giving them four simultaneous UK top 20 hits for a week.)

Mar [25] The UK tour closes at London's Hammersmith Gaumont.

Apr *Maybe Baby* reaches US #17 and UK #4. Holly solo LP *Buddy Holly* is issued in US.

June Holly records his first sessions without The Crickets, covering two Bobby Darin° songs, *Early In The Morning* and *Now We're One* in New York, backed by a small group (including saxophonist Sam "The Man" Taylor) organized by Coral A&R man Dick Jacobs. While in New York, Holly meets Maria Elena Santiago when visiting a music publisher, and they form a romantic attachment.

July *Rave On* reaches US #37 and hits UK #5. Holly fails an initial medical which might have led to military call-up, because of a stomach ulcer.

Aug [15] Holly and Santiago marry at Holly's parents' home in Lubbock.

Aug *Think It Over/Fool's Paradise* reach US #27 and #58 respectively.

Sept Holly solo *Early In The Morning* reaches US #32 and UK #17. In Clovis, while recording more solo material, Holly produces the first single by his friend Waylon Jennings, *Jole Blon*.

Oct Following a decision by Holly to end his association with Norman Petty (the two have not been on the best of terms over recording and career matters for some time), and also to set up a base in New York with his wife, Holly and The Crickets separate. Allison (also recently married, to Peggy Sue) and Mauldin return to Texas, and Holly gives them full rights to The Crickets' name so they can continue recording. Allison, meanwhile, has a solo US hit (#68) under the pseudonym Ivan, with a song picked up on the Australian tour, Johnny O'Keefe's *Real Wild Child*.

Oct [21] In a New York studio session, Holly records for the first time accompanied by a string section, the Dick Jacobs Orchestra.

Nov *It's So Easy* (one of the last recordings made by the team, with the addition of Tommy Allsup on guitar) reaches UK #19, having failed to chart in US.

1959 Jan Holly agrees to head a package tour, with back-up band comprising Tommy Allsup (guitar) Carl Bunch (drums) and Waylon Jennings (bass). "The Winter Dance Party" sets out around the Mid-Western states, traveling by bus in mostly poor weather. Ritchie Valens°, Dion & The Belmonts°, The Big Bopper° and Frankie Sardo are also on the tour. Meanwhile, *Heartbeat*, a Holly solo (with the original version of the much-revived *Well All Right* on the B-side) reaches US #82 and UK #30.

Feb [2] The tour plays a date at the Surf Ballroom in Clear Lake, Io. Tired of bus travel, they hire a light plane to take them to the next date at Moorhead, Minn., to give them time to rest. In bad weather, the plane crashes in a field only minutes after take-off near Mason City, Io. Holly, Valens°, The Big Bopper° and all on board are killed.

Feb [4] Bobby Vee°, a local singer with a style closely modelled on Holly's, fills in on the tour at Moorhead; Jimmy Clanton and Frankie Avalon° also join to make up the decimated troupe.

Feb [7] Holly's funeral is held at the Tabernacle Baptist Church in Lubbock, with over 1,000 people attending. The pallbearers are

Montgomery, Allison, Mauldin, Sullivan, Curtis and Phil Everly. He is buried in Lubbock City Cemetery.

Apr The ironically-titled *It Doesn't Matter Anymore*, a song written for Holly by Paul Anka°, and recorded at his final New York sessions, with an innovatory pizzicato string arrangement, reaches US #13, with B-side *Raining In My Heart* reaching US #88. In UK, *It Doesn't Matter Anymore* tops the chart for 3 weeks, while The Crickets, on their first recording without Holly, make US #26 with *Love's Made A Fool Of You* (a Holly composition, first cut by him as a demo for The Everly Brothers°).

May A memorial LP, *The Buddy Holly Story*, compiling most of his hits both solo and with The Crickets, reaches US #11 and hits UK #2. (It will stay charted in both countries for over 3 years.)

Aug Holly will have no more hit singles in US, but a long series of posthumous UK chart successes with either reissued or discovered material begins with *Midnight Shift*, which reaches UK #26.

Oct *Peggy Sue Got Married*, a lyrical sequel to his first solo hit, and taken from one of Holly's demos (with extra over-dubbing by The Jack Hansen Combo), makes UK #13.

1960 Jan The (post-Holly) Crickets, rejoined by Sonny Curtis, reach UK #27 with *When You Ask About Love*.

May *Heartbeat*, promoted in competition with a new cover version, re-enters the UK chart, making #30. The Crickets' *Baby My Heart* makes UK #33.

June *True Love Ways*, one of Holly's final New York studio recordings (and later one of his most-covered ballads) peaks at UK #25.

Oct *Learning The Game*, another overdubbed home demo, reaches UK #36, while compilation LP *The Buddy Holly Story Vol.2* hits UK #7.

1961 Feb *What To Do* reaches UK #34.

Apr LP *In Style With The Crickets* makes UK #13.

Aug A cover of Elvis Presley's° *Baby I Don't Care*, originally on Holly's 1958 solo LP, is issued as a UK single, and peaks at #12.

Nov LP *That'll Be The Day* (a compilation of 1956 Decca recordings, reissued at low price) hits UK #5.

1962 Norman Petty, after agreements between himself, Coral Records, and Holly's parents, acquires control of Holly's released and unreleased recordings. Taking the large number of solo home demos, he works in the studio with The Fireballs (already hitmakers with instrumentals *Torquay* and *Bulldog*, and later to be bigger still with *Sugar Shack* and *Bottle Of Wine*), replacing the early over-dubbings with backing more sympathetic to Holly's style and intentions.

Mar *Listen To Me* re-enters UK chart at #48.

Aug The Crickets, now comprising Allison, Curtis, pianist Glenn D. Hardin, and new vocalist Jerry Naylor, have their biggest post-Holly hit with the Goffin/King° song *Don't Ever Change*, which hits UK #5 but fails in US.

Oct *Reminiscing*, an unreleased track made with sax star King Curtis in Holly's final sessions, reaches UK #17.

1963 Feb LP *Reminiscing*, compiled by Petty from unissued material with Fireballs backing tracks, is released after long rumors of its coming and several apparent delays. Reviews, 4 years after Holly's death, are excellent. The Crickets reach UK #17 with the Holly-like Sonny Curtis song *My Little Girl*, which they feature in UK pop movie *Just For Fun*.

Apr A racing version of Chuck Berry's° *Brown-Eyed Handsome Man* hits UK #3. It is taken from LP *Reminiscing*, which reaches US #40 and hits UK #2 (behind The Beatles° *Please Please Me*).

July *Bo Diddley*, another rocking cover version from the LP, hits UK #4.

Sept *Wishing*, a newly-dubbed version of another demo cut by Holly for The Everly Brothers°, hits UK #10.

1964 Jan *What To Do* re-enters UK chart, making #27.

May *You've Got Love* makes UK #40.

June LP *Buddy Holly Showcase* hits UK #3, while The Crickets' country-styled *Don't Try To Change Me* reaches UK #37.

Aug The Crickets' final hit single, at UK #21, is a re-write of Ritchie Valens'° *La Bamba*, titled *(They Call Her) La Bamba*. (The Crickets will continue to exist in on-off fashion through the late 1980s. Line-up changes are extensive and continuous, but always revolving around Jerry Allison, who owns the name, and usually Sonny Curtis.)

Sept *Love's Made A Fool Of You*, Holly's original demo for The Everly Brothers°, reaches UK #39.

1965 July LP *Holly In The Hills*, compiling the early Holly and Montgomery radio station recordings, reaches UK #13.

1967 July Compilation LP *Buddy Holly's Greatest Hits* hits UK #9.

1968 Apr In the middle of a general rock'n'roll revival, a reissue of *Peggy Sue/Rave On* reaches UK #32.

1969 Apr LP *Giant*, made up of Holly's home recordings, reaches UK #13.

Dec LP *The Buddy Holly Story* is finally certified gold for a half million US sales.

1971 Aug Reissued LP *Buddy Holly's Greatest Hits* reaches UK #32.

1975 July LP *Buddy Holly's Greatest Hits* is reissued again, reaching UK #42.

1976 Sept [7] Paul McCartney° commemorates Holly's 40th birthday with the inauguration of "Buddy Holly Week" in UK. (McCartney has purchased the publishing rights to Holly's song catalog.) At the same time, The Buddy Holly Memorial Society is formed in US.

1977 Sept Allison, Mauldin and Curtis perform at the second "Buddy Holly Week" celebration.

1978 Mar LP *20 Golden Greats* tops the UK chart, and reaches US #55.

May [18 The biopic *The Buddy Holly Story*, with Holly played by Gary Busey, has its world premiere in Dallas, Tex.

1979 Feb [3] A concert, hosted by Wolfman Jack, at the Surf Ballroom in Clear Lake commemorates the final performances of Buddy Holly, The Big Bopper° and Ritchie Valens° exactly 20 years previously. Acts appearing include Jimmy Clanton, Del Shannon° and The Drifters°.

Mar A six-LP box set *The Complete Buddy Holly*, containing every one of Holly's recordings, is released in UK.

1980 Mar [24] Holly's spectacles, recovered from the scene of the plane crash, are discovered (along with The Big Bopper's° wristwatch) in files by coroner's court officials in Mason City.

Mar A statue of Holly is erected in front of Lubbock Civic Center.

1983 LP *For The First Time Anywhere*, containing original recordings without dubbing or the later backing tracks, is released.

1984 Sept LP *Greatest Hits* reaches UK #100.

1988 Apr The Crickets release LP *Three Piece* on Allison's Rollercoaster label, their first LP in over a decade.

Sept The Crickets sign to CBS and are to record *Got The T-Shirt*, winner of the 1987 Buddy Holly Week Song Contest.

THE HONEYCOMBS

Denis D'Ell (vocals and harmonica)
Martin Murray (lead guitar)
Alan Ward (rhythm guitar and keyboards)
John Lantree (bass)
Ann "Honey" Lantree (drums)

1963 The group is formed by Murray (b. Oct.7, 1941, London, UK), a former guitarist in various skiffle and rock groups and a hairdresser by day, who recruits Ward (b. Dec.12, 1945, Nottingham, UK) and persuades hairdresser colleague Ann Lantree (b. Aug.28, 1943, Hayes, Middx., UK), whose hobby is playing drums, to join. A bass player comes and goes, and Ann's brother John Lantree (b. Aug.20, 1940, Newbury, Berks., UK) fills the gap, while D'Ell (b. Denis Dalziel, Oct.10, 1943, London) is recommended by a friend of Murray's as a vocalist. Initial gigs around North London are as The Sherabons. The catchier Honeycombs comes from Ann's nickname Honey and the group's hair stylist background.

1964 Playing the local club and dancehall circuit, the group is spotted at the Mildmay Tavern by songwriters Ken Howard and Alan Blaikley, who become their managers. They sign the group to Pye Records and team it with independent producer Joe Meek.

Sept First release, the Howard/Blaikley composition *Have I The Right?* tops the UK chart.

Oct Murray suffers a fall during a ballroom gig, and breaks bones in his leg and right hand. With both in plaster, he is unable to play, and is replaced for a while on guitar by 16-year-old Peter Pye. The group plays its first major UK tour with Lulu°, Millie Small and The Applejacks.

Nov *Have I The Right?* hits US #5 and is a million-seller. UK DJ Jimmy Savile presents the group with a gold disk on BBC TV's "Top Beat" show, staged at London's Royal Albert Hall. *Is It Because?* peaks at UK #38.

Dec [26] The group appears on the Christmas edition of UK TV's "Thank Your Lucky Stars", playing *Eyes*, which fails to chart.

1965 Jan The group leaves for a 4-week tour of Australia and New Zealand. *I Can't Stop*, not released in UK, is US follow-up at #48 (and the group's only other US hit single). LP *Here Are The Honeycombs* reaches US #147.

May *Don't Love You No More* is cancelled as a single release after the group records Ray Davies' (of The Kinks°) song *Something Better Beginning*. It reaches UK #39.

Sept *That's The Way*, with Honey duetting with D'Ell on vocals, strongly supported by UK pirate radio ships who give it blanket airplay, makes UK #12.

1966 Jan LP *All Systems Go* gives belated UK release to *I Can't Stop* as its opening track, but receives scant attention.

Feb *Who Is Sylvia?* has good UK airplay, but fails to chart. (Two more singles will be released by Pye, to no success, and the group, now badly adrift of changing pop music fashions, drifts into club/variety work before breaking up. D'Ell will attempt a comeback as a solo singer during the 1970s, appearing on UK TV's "Opportunity Knocks".)

JOHN LEE HOOKER

1943 Hooker (b. Aug.22, 1917, Clarksdale, Miss., US), having learned guitar as a teenager from his musician stepfather Will Moore, been a gospel singer and played the blues (sitting in with local musicians like Robert Nighthawk) while living in Memphis, Tenn., during the mid-1930s, moves to Detroit, Mich. He works as a janitor at a car plant by day and plays at night in clubs like the Forest Inn and Club Basin, with a 3-or 4-piece blues band (typically, Bob Thurman on piano, Otis Finch on sax, and Tom Whitehead on drums), making a name as a popular blues act.

1948 Oct Modern Records talent scout Lee Sensation hears Hooker play in a Detroit Bar and signs him. A debut recording session is held in a local studio with just Hooker and guitar. Self-penned *Boogie Chillun* sets the pattern for his primitive, intense blues style and is a huge US hit nationally in the burgeoning "race" (later R&B) market (and over the next 5 years will sell a million copies).

Dec His second session is for independent producer Joe Von Battle, who circumvents the Modern contract by selling *Black Man Blues* to King records for release as by "Texas Slim". (Hooker will record for anyone who shows interest, avoiding contractual complications by using a new name. Between 1949 and 1954 he

will issue about 70 singles on 21 different labels, under 10 different pseudonyms, including Delta John, Johnny Lee, Johnny Williams and John Lee Booker.)

1949 *Crawlin' King Snake*, on Modern, sells strongly and will be much covered by late-1960s electric blues bands.

1951 *I'm In The Mood* is his second major R&B hit, another estimated million-seller over a period of some years.

1952 He makes his debut as a radio DJ in Detroit.

1955 Oct He signs to Vee Jay Records in Chicago, which recognizes his potentially wider appeal and molds him into a tighter, more commercial performer on disk, backing him with disciplined R&B session men like guitarist Eddie Taylor.

1956 Mar [27] He records *Dimples*. (It will be a UK hit 8 years later.)

1960 June [24] He is one of the few purely blues performers at the second annual Newport Folk Festival. The performance is recorded by Vee Jay, for later release as LP *Concert At Newport*.

1961 Apr [11] Hooker has folk singer Bob Dylan° as his opening act at Gerde's Folk City in New York (Dylan's New York stage debut).

1962 Hooker tours Europe and UK with the "American Blues Folk Festival 1962" concert package.

July Self-composed *Boom Boom* is his only crossover success, reaching US #60. (It will be a hit cover by The Animals° in 1964.)

1964 July With the UK R&B boom in full swing, and many of Hooker's songs revived by UK bands, familiar oldies by his contemporaries like Howlin' Wolf° and Jimmy Reed° are making the UK singles chart. Hooker's *Dimples* (also covered by The Animals°) climbs to UK #23. He visits UK and plays it on TV's "Ready Steady Go".

1966 He signs to ABC Records, recording LPs for its Impulse (jazz) and Bluesway (blues) subsidiary labels as well as ABC itself, over the next 8 years. One of the first releases is an LP recorded in concert, *Live At The Cafe Au Go-Go*.

1967 Feb LP *House Of The Blues*, a budget-price reissue of tracks recorded for Chess in the early 1950s, is Hooker's only UK chart LP, reaching #34.

1970 Aug [11] He headlines the Ann Arbor Blues and Jazz Festival in Mich., with Buddy Guy, Johnny Winter° and others.

1971 Apr Double LP *Hooker'n'Heat*, recorded with Canned Heat° for Liberty, reaches US #73 (his first US chart LP).

May LP *Endless Boogie*, on ABC, makes US #126.

1972 Apr LP *Never Get Out Of These Blues Alive* reaches US #130.

1974 He signs to Atlantic Records, cutting LPs *Detroit Special* and *Don't Turn Me From Your Door*.

1978 Double LP *The Cream*, a selection of classic songs recorded live at the Keynote Club in Palo Alto, Cal., is recorded for US

JOHN LEE HOOKER *cont.*

independent blues label Tomato Records.

1979 Apr Hooker, with Lightnin' Hopkins, Big Mama Thornton and others, appears at "The Boogie'n'Blues Concert" at New York's Carnegie Hall.

1980 June Like several other blues and R&B performers (including Ray Charles°, James Brown° and Aretha Franklin°), Hooker has a cameo part in movie *The Blues Brothers*.

1982 He plays in UK on a bill with B.B. King° and Bobby Bland, to critical acclaim.

1986 Hooker's music is featured in Steven Spielberg's movie *The Color Purple*.

1988 At age 71, Hooker continues to tour US and overseas. His style, and some of his repertoire, is virtually unchanged over more than 30 years; the stark, fierce vocal/guitar combination still making him unique, as well as a rare survivor among his late 1940s blues contemporaries. In mid-88, he records an LP with a cast of long-time admirers, including Robert Cray°, Carlos Santana° and George Thorogood.

THE HOOTERS

Rob Hyman (vocals and keyboards)
Eric Bazilian (vocals and lead guitar)
John Lilley (rhythm guitar)
Andy King (bass)
David Uosikkinen (drums)

1978 Hyman, having worked with producer Rick Chertoff to release two LPs under the name Baby Grand, teams with Bazilian in Philadelphia, Pa., US, to form the nucleus of The Hooters (taken from the nickname they gave to their keyboard harmonica) and they recruit other local musicians.

1980 The Hooters release their first single on a local independent label. The ska-flavored *Fighting On The Same Side* gains regional popularity, as does debut LP *Amore*.

1983 Hyman and Bazilian provide the singing, playing and arranging backbone to Cyndi Lauper's° debut LP *She's So Unusual*. (Their particular assistance on *Time After Time* will help the disk top the US chart in June 1984.)

1984 With local popularity at fever pitch, The Hooters sign a major contract with CBS/Columbia.

1985 June Their debut for CBS/Columbia, *All You Zombies*, climbs to US #58.

July [13] Due to the group's local status, it is given the privilege of opening the US side of Live Aid in its native Philadelphia.

Sept LP *Nervous Night* climbs to US #12. It fails in UK as do all current single releases.

Oct *And We Danced* reaches US #21. It coincides with the group's first major venue US nationwide tour.

1986 Feb *Day By Day*, released in 1985, reaches US #18.

June *Where Do The Children Go* peaks at US #38.

Sept Bazilian and Hyman retreat to a cabin in Virginia to write songs. (The subsequent material will be recorded in New York during the winter.)

1987 May Bryan Adams° invites The Hooters to support him on his forthcoming spring/summer tour.

July *Johnny B* peaks at US #64.

Aug Second CBS/Columbia LP *One Way Home* is released. It climbs to US #27 but fails in UK.

Nov *Satellite*, taken from the recent LP, climbs to US #61.

1988 Jan *Satellite* makes UK #22 but fails to lift the LP into the UK chart. Follow-ups *Karla With A K* and *Johnny B* also fall short.

MARY HOPKIN

1967 After singing in church choirs since early childhood, then moving to folk club performances and regular spots on Welsh television, Hopkin (b. May 3, 1950, Pontardawe, South Wales, UK), makes her first recording, *Llais Swynol Mary Hopkin*, a Welsh language EP on Cambrian label.

1968 May She wins UK TV talent show "Opportunity Knocks", is spotted by model Twiggy who recommends her to Paul McCartney°, and signs to The Beatles'° new Apple label.

Aug [27] *Those Were The Days*, produced by McCartney° and based on the melody of traditional Russian folk song *Darogoi Dlimmoyo*, launches Apple in UK alongside The Beatles'° own *Hey Jude*.

Sept *Those Were The Days* replaces *Hey Jude* at UK #1, topping the UK chart for 6 weeks and selling over 750,000 copies.

Oct Hopkin appears on "The Ed Sullivan Show" in US, singing *Those Were The Days*.

Nov *Those Were The Days* spends 3 weeks at US #2 and is a million-seller. (She also records it in Spanish, French, German, Italian and Hebrew and by early 1969 the cumulative worldwide sales will be over 8 million.)

1969 Mar LP *Post Card*, produced by McCartney° and including covers of songs by Harry Nilsson° and Donovan°, hits UK #3.

Apr *Goodbye*, written and produced by McCartney°, hits UK #2. Hopkin meets her future husband, record producer Tony Visconti, while recording more foreign language versions of her songs. She sings the theme to movie *Where's Jack* for Paramount Pictures.

May *Goodbye* makes US #13, while LP *Post Card* reaches US #28.

1970 Feb *Temma Harbour*, produced by Mickie Most, hits UK #6. Hopkin appears on Cilla Black's° UK BBC TV show, singing six songs from which UK's entry for the 1970 Eurovision Song Contest will be selected.

Mar *Temma Harbour* reaches US #39.

Apr *Knock Knock Who's There*, having been selected as the UK Eurovision entry, is released and hits UK #2. (The Eurovision contest is won by Irish entry, Dana's *All Kinds Of Everything*.)

July A McCartney°-produced revival of Doris Day's *Que Sera, Sera (Whatever Will Be, Will Be)* reaches US #77.

Nov *Think About Your Children*, written by Hot Chocolate's° Errol Brown, reaches UK #19 and US #87.

1971 July *Let My Name Be Sorrow* makes UK #46.

Oct Hopkin's own favorite recording, LP *Earth Song – Ocean Song*, produced by Tony Visconti and including contributions from Ralph McTell and Dave Cousins of The Strawbs , fails to sell.

Dec *Water, Paper And Clay* is her last release on Apple and does not chart. Hopkin marries Tony Visconti, and will work with him through the 70s, often singing backup vocals on his productions for David Bowie° and others.

1972 Aug A UK single made for Bell with Visconti, under the name Hobby Horse, reviving The Jamies' 1958 US hit *Summertime Summertime*, fails to attract attention.

Nov Compilation LP *Those Were The Days*, collating the Apple singles, is released but fails to chart in UK or US.

Dec The seasonal *Mary Had A Baby* is released in UK on Regal Zonophone but fails to chart. (Mary is pregnant in real life at this time, and son Morgan is born shortly afterwards.) In US Apple issues *Knock Knock Who's There*, which makes #92.

1976 Mar *If You Love Me*, recorded for Visconti's Good Earth label, reaches UK #32.

1977 May *Wrap Me In Your Arms*, also on Good Earth, fails to chart. Hopkin features with various artists on Chrysalis fantasy concept LP *The King Of Elfland's Daughter* and takes lead vocal on extracted single *Lirazell*. Neither charts.

Dec *Beyond The Fields We Know*, another single from the concept LP, with Hopkin's vocals, fails to chart.

1980 After devoting time to her children, Hopkin teams with Mike Hurst (ex-Springfields) and Mike D'Albuquerque (ex-ELO°) as Sundance, a harmony trio which signs to Bronze Records.

1981 Oct *What's Love* fails to chart. The group plays support to Dr. Hook° on a UK tour, after which Hopkin leaves, unwilling to move into the MOR cabaret circuit. Her marriage to Visconti ends and a relationship with Dr. Hook vocalist Dennis Locorriere develops.

1984 May She returns to UK chart as lead vocalist with Oasis, a group which includes Peter Skellern on piano and vocals and Julian Lloyd Webber on cello. *Hold Me* fails but LP *Oasis* makes UK #23. The group does not continue on a permanent basis because Hopkin becomes ill and leaves in advance of a planned tour.

1988 She participates with other artists in EMI recording of Dylan Thomas' *Under Milk Wood*, produced by George Martin.

BRUCE HORNSBY & THE RANGE

Bruce Hornsby (vocals, keyboards and accordion)
David Mansfield (violin, mandolin and guitar)
George Marinelli (guitar and vocals)
Joe Puerta (bass and vocals)
John Molo (drums)

1978 Having excelled at piano in high school and studied music at the University of Miami and The Berklee School of Music, Hornsby (b. Nov.23, 1954, Williamsburg, Va., US) forms a home town band and begins playing endless bars and lounges on the road around the southern states. He also begins a 7-year habit of recording demo tapes of his newly-written material, sending them regularly to record companies.

1980 He moves to Los Angeles with his brother John, where both will work for 3 years at 20th Century Fox Publishing, jointly writing production-line pop songs.

1981 In Hollywood, Hornsby meets Huey Lewis° who is impressed by his writing and playing abilities.

1983 Hornsby, recommended as a keyboardist by friend and bass player Joe Puerta, is invited to join the backing band being formed for a lengthy US tour by Sheena Easton°.

1985 Years of writing, recording and submitting dozens of demo tapes to over seventy record companies finally pay off when Hornsby and his newly-formed band, The Range, are signed worldwide to RCA.

1986 Aug Chart debut *Every Little Kiss* reaches US #72. The group starts its first nationwide US tour and dates sell out when LP *The Way It Is* is released. The title track receives heavy airplay and is released as a single.

Sept *The Way It Is* also receives immediate heavy UK radio attention and reaches UK #15. LP of the same title (which includes three tracks produced by Lewis) climbs to #16.

Oct Hornsby & The Range tour UK as support to Huey Lewis & The News°, making a strong UK TV impact on primetime show "Wogan".

Dec *The Way It Is*, after a steady climb on US chart since Sept., hits #1 for a week and will remain charted for 22.

1987 Mar *Mandolin Rain* hits US #4, while LP *The Way It Is*, after a 6-month US chart climb, peaks at #3. Huey Lewis & The News top the US chart with *Jacob's Ladder*, written by Bruce and John Hornsby. The track is relegated to a B-side in UK.

Apr Hornsby wins Grammy award as Best New Artist Of 1986. ASCAP also gives *The Way It Is* an award as Most Played Song. Meanwhile, *Mandolin Rain* makes a fleeting UK chart showing at #70.

July *Every Little Kiss* is reissued in US, this time reaching #14.

July/ Oct Increasingly in demand for his distinctive keyboard style, Hornsby guests on Clannad's° LP *Sirius*, and on an LP by Tom Wopat (former "Dukes of Hazzard" star turned country singer). LP *The Way It Is* tops 2 million.

Oct/ Dec The band works on second LP, with Neil Dorfsman sharing production credits with Hornsby. Peter Harris replaces Mansfield in The Range.

1988 June LP *Scenes From The Southside*, a musical biography of the Hornsby brothers' adolescence in America's South, includes their own version of *Jacob's Ladder*. It hits US #5, as does the simultaneously-extracted *The Valley Road*. In UK, the LP makes #18, and the single #44.

July Hornsby also plays accordion on LPs by Patti Austin° (*The Real Me*), Kim Carnes° (*View From The House*) and Huey Lewis (*Small World*). *Look Out Any Window*, extracted from LP *Scenes From The Southside*, is released.

HOT CHOCOLATE

Errol Brown (vocals)
Tony Wilson (bass and vocals)
Harvey Hinsley (guitar)
Larry Ferguson (keyboards)
Patrick Olive (percussion)
Tony Connor (drums)

1969 The group is formed in Brixton, London, UK, by Olive (b. Mar.22, 1947, Grenada) with drummer Ian King and guitarist Franklyn De Allie. Songwriters Brown (b. Nov.12, 1948, Kingston, Jamaica) and Wilson (b. Oct.8, 1947, Trinidad) join shortly afterwards, followed by Ferguson (b. Apr.14, 1948, Nassau, Bahamas). De Allie departs.

Oct The group's reggae-styled adaptation (with his agreement) of John Lennon's° *Give Peace A Chance* is a one-off on Apple but fails to chart. Mavis Smith of Apple names them The Hot Chocolate Band.

1970 The group signs to Mickie Most's RAK Records after Brown and Wilson approach Most with three of their songs. Most agrees that *Bet Yer Life I Do* is ideal for Herman's Hermits° and takes *Think About Your Children* for Mary Hopkin°. He suggests that Hot Chocolate (to which the name is now shortened) should record *Love Is Life*.

Aug Hot Chocolate debuts at the Nevada Ballroom, Bolton, UK.

Sept *Love Is Life* hits UK #6, introducing a trademark sound characterized by Brown's distinctive pop/soul voice and a percussive, commercial instrumental backing. Brown's shaved head becomes a visual focus.

Oct Hinsley (b. Jan.19, 1948, Northampton, UK), ex-Cliff Bennett's° Rebel Rousers, joins on guitar.

1971 Apr *You Could Have Been a Lady* reaches UK #22.

Sept *I Believe (In Love)* hits UK #8.

1972 Mar *Mary-Anne* fails to chart.

Nov *You'll Always Be A Friend* reaches UK #23.

1973 Mar Connor (b. Apr.6, 1947, Romford, Essex, UK), ex-Audience and Jackson Heights, replaces King on drums.

May *Brother Louie*, lyrically the group's most notable song yet about inter-racial love and racism, hits UK #7.

Aug *Rumours* peaks at UK #44, while Stories' cover version of *Brother Louie* tops the US chart. The group signs to the MAM agency for live work (and will play a UK tour roughly every 18 months, organized by MAM's Ian Wright).

1974 Apr *Emma* hits UK #3.

June The group's debut LP *Cicero Park* fails to chart.

Dec *Cheri Babe* makes UK #31.

1975 Mar *Blue Night* fails to chart in UK.

Apr Released in US by Big Tree Records, *Emma* hits US #8. LP *Cicero Park* makes US #55.

June *Disco Queen* reaches UK #11 and US #28.

Sept *A Child's Prayer* hits UK #7.

Nov Wilson leaves to sign a solo deal with Bearsville Records. Percussionist Olive takes over on bass. LP *Hot Chocolate* is their first UK chart LP, making #34.

Dec *You Sexy Thing*, a harder dance number, hits UK #2.

1976 Feb *You Sexy Thing* hits US #3. (It is the group's all-time biggest US hit, selling over a million.) LP *Hot Chocolate* peaks at US #41.

Apr *Don't Stop It Now* reaches UK #11 and US #42.

July *Man To Man* climbs to UK #14.

Aug LP *Man To Man* reaches UK #32.

Sept *Heaven Is The Back Seat Of My Cadillac* reaches UK #25.

Oct LP *Man To Man* peaks at US #172.

Dec Compilation LP *Hot Chocolate 14 Greatest Hits* hits UK #6, selling 500,000 copies in UK alone.

1977 July *So You Win Again*, a rare outside composition for the group written by ex-Argent° singer Russ Ballard, is its biggest UK hit, topping the chart for a week.

Sept *So You Win Again* reaches US #31.

Dec *Put Your Love In Me* reaches UK #10.

1978 Apr *Every 1's A Winner* makes UK #12 and LP of the same title climbs to #30.

Dec *I'll Put You Together Again*, from the musical *Dear Anyone*, peaks at UK #13.

1979 Feb *Every 1's A Winner*, released via a new deal with Infinity Records in US, hits #6 and earns the group's second gold disk for a million-plus sales. LP of the same title reaches US #31.

June *Mindless Boogie*, the group's first UK 12" single, reaches UK #46.

July The group plays its first headlining US tour of 12 auditorium dates, followed by a 45-date UK trek.

Aug *Going Through The Motions* reaches UK and US #53. LP of the same title makes US #112 but fails in UK. The group follows its UK tour with a long tour of Europe, concentrating on West

HOT CHOCOLATE *cont.*

Germany, where its popularity is enormous.
Dec TV-advertised compilation LP *20 Hottest Hits* hits UK #3 and is another half-million seller.
1980 June *No Doubt About It*, written for the group by Steve Glen, Mike Burns and Mickie Most's brother Dave, about a real-life UFO sighting by Glen and Burns, hits UK #2.
Aug *Are You Getting Enough Of What Makes You Happy* reaches UK #17.
Dec *Love Me To Sleep* peaks at UK #50. LP *Class* fails to chart.
1981 Feb *Losing You* fails to chart.
June *You'll Never Be So Wrong* reaches UK #52.
1982 May *Girl Crazy* hits UK #7.
Aug *It Started With A Kiss* hits UK #5.
Oct *Chances* peaks at UK #32 and LP *Mystery* reaches UK #24.
1983 Jan *Are You Getting Enough Happiness*, released in US after the group signs to EMI America, reaches US #65, but is its last US chart hit.
June *What Kinda Boy You Looking For (Girl)* hits UK #10.
Oct *Tears On The Telephone* peaks at UK #37.
1984 Mar *I Gave You My Heart (Didn't I)* reaches UK #13, and is the last new recording by Hot Chocolate to chart.
1987 Feb Dutch disco DJ Ben Liebrand creates a new dance remix of the group's *You Sexy Thing*, adding 80s percussion and rhythm tracks to the original recording. Released as a single, it climbs to UK #10.
Mar 16-track TV-advertised compilation LP *The Very Best Of Hot Chocolate* tops the UK chart with sales of half a million. It continues the tradition that the group's only really big-selling LPs are collections of its hit singles.
Apr A "Groove Mix" of *Every 1's A Winner* is created by Liebrand in similar fashion to *You Sexy Thing*, and reaches UK #69.
May After a long musical silence (apart from reissues), it is confirmed that Hot Chocolate has split when Brown signs to WEA Records as a soloist and records with producers Tony Swain and Steve Jolley.
Aug Brown's solo *Personal Touch* reaches UK #25.
Dec Brown's *Body Rockin'* makes UK #51.
1988 Sept Following a rest in the Caribbean, Brown returns with new single *Maya*.

THE HOUSEMARTINS

Norman Cook (vocals)
Paul Heaton (vocals and guitar)
Stan Cullimore (bass)
Hugh Whitaker (drums)

1984 The band forms in Hull, Humberside, UK, around Heaton (b. May 9, 1962), who arrives in the town after a year traveling around Europe. He places a postcard in his front-room window, requesting young musicians to get in touch with him. Cullimore (b. Apr.6, 1962), who lives in the same street, quickly does. Whitaker and Ted Key are recruited from Hull band The Gargoyles. The group gains local live experience, then tours widely for 7 months playing small gigs throughout the UK, eventually coming to the attention of record labels.
1985 Oct The Housemartins sign to Go! Discs Records in London and are promoted as "the fourth best band in Hull". Debut single *Flag Day* does not chart.
Nov Norman Cook (b. July 31, 1963), an ex-club DJ from Brighton, UK, replaces Key who departs to open a vegetarian restaurant in Hull.
1986 Mar *Sheep* receives substantial airplay in UK, and is the band's chart debut, reaching UK #54.
June *Happy Hour*, helped by strong airplay and an inventive semi-animated promotional video showing the band in similar light to early Madness° promos, hits UK #3.
June [20-22] The band appears at the annual Glastonbury Festival in UK, alongside The Cure°, The Pogues°, Lloyd Cole° and others.
July Debut LP *Hull 4, London 0* (a title play on the band's continual promotion of its home town and provincial working-class pride) hits UK #3.
Sept [30] The band begins a UK tour in Birmingham.
Nov *Think For A Minute* reaches UK #18.
Dec With two well-timed UK TV specials heavily plugging the new single, the group tops the UK chart at Christmas with its biggest seller, a capella version of Isley Jasper Isley's *Caravan of Love*. The original reached US #51 and UK #52 the previous Dec. An a capella vocal set featured on The Housemartins' UK tour in an unusual fashion, with the band adopting an alter ego identity as The Fish City Five and opening the act.
1987 Feb [9] The group wins the Best Newcomers award at the annual BPI awards in UK.
Mar The popular UK tabloid press reveals that some members of the band are gay and not the cheeky, affable, working-class lads from Hull they pertain to be, and that Cook's real forename is Quentin and his background relatively wealthy South of England instead of his Housemartin image.
June *Five Get Over Excited*, reaching UK #11, is the first release with drummer Dave Hemmingway in place of Whitaker who quit due to ideological differences with the rest of the group.
The group appears in the "Red Wedge" concerts, encouraging the young left-wing vote, in the run-up to the UK General Election.
Aug *Me And The Farmer* reaches UK #15.
Oct LP *The People Who Grinned Themselves To Death* hits UK #9.
Dec *Build* peaks at UK #15.
1988 Feb The band announces that it is to split, claiming The Housemartins was only planned as a 3-year project. Cook is already finding parallel success as a dance record re-mixer, using his club DJ background to remix tracks by James Brown°, Nitro Deluxe and Eric B & Rakim among others.
May *There Is Always Something There To Remind Me* (not Sandie Shaw's° 1964 hit of the same title but a new song by Heaton and Cullimore, taken from a BBC Radio 1 session) is the final single, reaching UK #35. Double LP *Now That's What I Call Quite Good*, a compilation of hits, rarities and out-takes, is the band's farewell hit at UK #8.

WHITNEY HOUSTON

1974/80 Houston (b. Aug.9, 1963, N.J., US), like her singing mother Cissy and cousin Dionne Warwick°, begins her vocals career, at age 11, in a gospel setting – The New Hope Baptist Junior Choir. Within 4 years she is sought for backing vocals for such recording artistes as Chaka Khan° and Lou Rawls. In the meantime, Houston sings with her mother at nightclub and concert engagements and develops her own solo numbers.
1981 She also pursues a career as a model and is featured in US magazine *Glamor* and on the front cover of *Seventeen*.
1983 Clive Davis, head of Arista Records, sees and hears potential in Houston and signs her to a worldwide contract.
1984 June Although an early commercial glimpse of her is witnessed on a duet with Teddy Pendergrass° (*Hold Me* peaks at US #46), Davis continues to protect, teach and nurture his prodigy in a quest to record the perfect debut LP. He enlists the help of many significant songwriters (Michael Masser, Peter McCann, Linda Creed and Gerry Goffin) and producers (Narada Michael Walden, Michael Masser and Kashif).
1985 Mar LP *Whitney Houston* is finally released in US. Its early progress is quiet (it will take 9 months to top the US chart).
July Debut single *You Give Good Love* slowly climbs to hit US #3. Its release in UK sparks some club/dance interest but fails to make the chart.
Oct [26] Released in August, ballad *Saving All My Love For You* hits US #1. (It will win a 1985 Grammy Award for Best Female Pop Vocal Performance.)
Dec *Saving All My Love For You* becomes an international smash and hits UK #1. Debut LP *Whitney Houston*, although destined to spend over 100 consecutive weeks on the UK chart, peaks at #2.
1986 Feb Uptempo Walden-produced *How Will I Know* hits US #1 and peaks at UK #5.
Mar Having collected five US music awards, Houston's next single *The Greatest Love Of All* (originally B-side of *You Give Good Love*) is a cover version of the 1977 hit by George Benson°. It is her third consecutive US #1 and hits UK #8.
Aug She wins a US Emmy award for Outstanding Individual Performance in a Variety Program on US TV and announces her first major live US dates. She celebrates her 23rd birthday.
Nov Houston arrives in UK for her first European live dates, which are all sell-outs.
1987 Jan With Davis again assuming role of Executive Producer, a similar grouping of writers and producers is recruited to attempt to repeat the formula.
Apr She completes early promotion work for new single with a live appearance at Montreux Rock Festival, Switzerland.

June *I Wanna Dance With Somebody (Who Loves Me)* climbs rapidly to hit both US and UK #1.

June [18] Her second LP *Whitney* becomes the only LP by a solo artiste to debut on top of the Billboard chart. Continuing a familiar mix of dance pop numbers and ballads (including a duet version, with mother Cissy, of the *Chess* musical standard *I Know Him So Well*), it hits UK #1 in its first week of release.

Aug Ballad *Didn't We Almost Have It All* continues the US run as another #1, but only reaches UK #14. A world tour in support of the second LP is announced.

Dec *So Emotional* tops the US chart and hits UK #5.

1988 Apr [23] Following two more US music awards and a Grammy for Best Female Pop Performance for *I Wanna Dance With Somebody (Who Loves Me)*, Houston breaks a chart record: *Where Do Broken Hearts Go* climbs to US #1, pipping Billy Ocean's° *Get Outta My Dreams (Get Into My Car)*, to become her seventh consecutive US chart-topper, overtaking the previous record of six achieved by The Beatles° and The Bee Gees°. In UK, it makes only #14.

June [11] Already in the middle of a sell-out world tour, Houston headlines the Nelson Mandela 70th Birthday Party celebration at London's Wembley Stadium. Fifth single from LP *Whitney*, *Love Will Save The Day*, is released to tie-in with UK visit and hits UK #10.

Sept *Love Will Save The Day* breaks the chart-topping run in US by hitting only #9. On the way down the chart, it passes her newly-recorded and climbing *One Moment In Time*, a ballad headlining Davis' current project – a special 1988 Olympics various artists musical tribute LP *One Moment In Time*. As producers invite songs for a third Houston LP, Hollywood beckons with dazzling film offers including a strongly tipped project with Robert De Niro and ongoing rumors of a *Dreamgirls* movie.

HOWLIN' WOLF

1948 Following some years of farm labor and then US Army service, Wolf (b. Chester Arthur Burnett, June 10, 1910, West Point, Aberdeen, Miss., US), moves to West Memphis, Ark., to try to earn a living as a musician. He forms The House Rockers, who build a local reputation as a hot electric blues band.

1949 Wolf and the band secure a daily half-hour live music spot on local West Memphis radio station KWEM. (By now he is known as Howlin' Wolf. The "Howlin'" refers to his early singing style, a personal adaptation of Jimmie Rodgers' "blue yodel" and legend suggests he was called "The Wolf" by his family, from *Little Red Riding Hood*, when he misbehaved as a child.)

1951 Via his radio slot, Wolf comes to the attention of Ike Turner, working in the area as field A&R man for LA-based Modern Records, and Memphis-based producer Sam Phillips, a regular supplier of local recordings to Modern and to Chess Records in Chicago.

May [14] Phillips records Wolf at his Sun studio, leasing the results to Chess – which annoys Modern, who claims rights to Wolf and arranges for Turner to record him independently at KWEM.

Nov Different recordings of the same Wolf composition, *Moanin' At Midnight*, are released both on Modern's subsidiary RPM, and on Chess. The song is incorrectly labelled *Mornin' At Midnight* on RPM, while Chess avoids split sales by promoting the other side, *How Many More Years*. The RPM release reaches US R&B top 20 first, to be quickly replaced by the Chess single.

1952 Feb Modern relinquishes its claims to Wolf when Phillips produces a contract signed the previous August – though two more Turner-produced records appear on RPM anyway.

July [10] Phillips records the last of five Howlin' Wolf sessions. Wolf signs directly to Chess, persuaded by a cash advance, and takes his guitarists Hubert Sumlin and Willie Johnson with him.

1953 In Chicago, he secures his first club dates with the help of Muddy Waters°, and starts to record at Chess studios, with house musicians Willie Dixon (bass), Otis Spann (piano) and Earl Phillips (drums) augmenting the band. (Over the next 10 years he will record most of his classic repertoire for the label, including his own compositions *Smokestack Lightnin'*, *No Place To Go*, *Sitting On Top Of The World*, *Evil*, *Killin' Floor*, *I Ain't Superstitious* and *Who's Been Talking*, and Willie Dixon's *Spoonful*, *Down In The Bottom*, *Back Door Man*, *The Red Rooster* and *Wang Dang Doodle*.)

1961 Nov [24] He arrives in UK for his first tour. *Little Baby* is released by Pye Records as his first UK single, but does not sell.

1963 July Wolf is recorded live with Spann, Buddy Guy and Muddy Waters°, at Chicago's Copa Cabana club. (The recordings appear in 1964 as LP *Folk Festival Of The Blues*.)

1964 June His first (and only) pop hit is *Smokestack Lightnin'*, which belatedly reaches UK #42 (it was recorded in 1956). (Wolf's songs have become staple repertoire for new UK R&B groups: *Smokestack Lightnin'* will be covered by The Yardbirds° and Manfred Mann°; *Spoonful* by Cream° and Ten Years After°; *The Red Rooster* (as *Little Red Rooster*) by The Rolling Stones°, and *I Ain't Superstitious* by Jeff Beck°,Rod Stewart° and Savoy Brown. In US, *Back Door Man* is revived by The Doors°, *Killin' Floor* by Electric Flag and *How Many More Years* by Little Feat°.)

1965 May [26] At the group's invitation, he appears with The Rolling Stones° on a US TV "Shindig" slot.

1967 Sept With Bo Diddley° and Muddy Waters°, Wolf records LP *The Super Super Blues Band*, which includes new versions of several familiar songs.

1969 Apr Envious of the success of Waters'° "psychedelic" LP *Electric Mud*, Wolf records similarly-conceived LP *The Howlin' Wolf Album*, which in private Wolf calls "birdshit".

1971 Sept Wolf travels to London with Sumlin to record with a UK superstar line-up including Eric Clapton°, Ringo Starr°, Steve Winwood°, and Bill Wyman and Charlie Watts of The Rolling Stones°. LP *The London Howlin' Wolf Sessions*, compiled from the UK recordings, is his only US chart hit, reaching #79.

1972 Sept [8] Wolf appears at Ann Arbor Jazz and Blues Festival (organized in memory of blues pianist Otis Spann), with Muddy Waters°, Dr. John°, Bobby Bland and many others.

1973 Shortly after suffering two heart attacks, Wolf is badly injured in a car crash and is hospitalized for weeks with kidney damage. He continues to gig and record sporadically, and releases LP *The Back Door Wolf*.

1975 Nov He performs live at the Chicago Amphitheater, with B.B. King°, Bobby "Blue" Bland and Little Milton, but he returns to hospital with kidney complications.

1976 Jan [10] He dies in hospital near Chicago, Ill., following brain surgery.

THE HUMAN LEAGUE

Philip Oakey (vocals)
Martin Ware (synthesizer)
Ian Craig Marsh (synthesizer)
Adrian Wright (onstage slides and films)

1977 Ware (b. May 19, 1956, Sheffield, UK) and Marsh (b. Nov.11, 1956, Sheffield), both computer operators, form dual synthesizer band The Dead Daughters in Sheffield, the name coming from a sci-fi game, Star Force. Their synthesizer and tape-oriented approach is well out of step with the Punk times.

June Addy Newton joins and the band becomes The Future, recruiting Oakey (b. Oct.2, 1955, Sheffield), a hospital porter and friend of Ware's.

Sept They re-name the group The Human League (a name taken from a computer game). Newton leaves to join Clock DVA and Wright (b. June 30, 1956, Sheffield) joins to handle "stage visuals".

1978 Jan A demo of *Being Boiled*, *Circus Of Death* and *Toyota City* is recorded in Sheffield and sent to independent UK labels.

Mar On the strength of the demo, the group signs to Edinburgh-based Fast Product Records, and label owner Bob Last becomes their manager.

June Debut on Fast is *Being Boiled*, Oakey's first composition. Ex-Sex Pistol° Johnny Rotten hears it and dubs them "trendy hippies".

1979 Mar The group tours UK as support to Siouxsie & The Banshees°.

Apr Virgin Records negotiates with Fast, and announces a long-term deal with The League. Instrumental EP *Dignity Of Labour* is released on Fast.

May The band supports Iggy Pop° on a European tour.

July First Virgin single, 12-inch *I Don't Depend On You*, is credited to The Men.

Oct Debut LP *Reproduction* (containing a new recording of original demo *Circus Of Death*) and *Empire State Human* are released. The League sets up its own Monumental Pictures recording studios in Sheffield.

Dec The group is dropped from the supporting slot on a Talking Heads° UK tour because its "remote-controlled entertainment" concept goes down badly with the public.

1980 May Two-single package *Holiday '80*, with a new recording of *Being Boiled*, makes UK #56. The League's clean-edged weirdness

THE HUMAN LEAGUE *cont.*

begins to make inroads into post-Punk UK charts, as a new movement of synth-based "New Romantic" bands.

May LP *Travelogue* makes UK #16. (The League comments that it has always been aiming for pop stardom, and has already trademarked its name.)

June *Empire State Human* is reissued, reaching UK #62. Wright, previously slide projectionist and lightshow operator, appears on stage as a full band member. The band appears in the new wave rock showcase movie *Urgh! A Music War*.

Oct After internal disagreements, Ware and Marsh leave the group to form the British Electric Foundation (and later Heaven 17°). Oakey and Wright are left with the rights to the band's name, and an already-planned European tour. Bassist Ian Burden (b. Dec.24, 1957, Sheffield) is recruited from local band Graf, and Oakey brings in two teenage girl dancers, Joanne Catherall (b. Sept.18, 1962, Sheffield) and Suzanne Sulley (b. Mar.22, 1963, Sheffield), whom he spotted dancing in a Sheffield club where they are working as cocktail waitresses. The new group sets off for a month-long tour of Europe to fulfill contractual obligations.

1981 Mar The new line-up introduces a simpler, poppier and less quirky sound with producer Martin Rushent. *Boys & Girls*, featuring the new girls' vocals, makes UK #48.

May *The Sound Of The Crowd* reaches UK #12. Jo Callis (b. May 2, 1955, Glasgow, Scotland, UK), ex-guitarist for Scottish pop-punk band The Rezillos, is added to the line-up on synthesizer.

July *Love Action (I Believe In Love)* (credited to Human League Red) hits UK #3.

Aug Debut LP *Reproduction* finally charts in UK (and will climb to #49 in an almost 6-month chart stay).

Oct The group announces its biggest UK tour from the end of Nov. *Open Your Heart* (credited to Human League Blue) hits UK #6. LP *Dare* tops the UK chart and will remain charted for 71 weeks. (Containing the recent and future singles, this LP will sell over 5 million copies worldwide.)

Dec *Don't You Want Me*, taken from the LP, and featuring traded vocals between Oakey and Catherall, hits UK #1 for 5 weeks. It is the biggest-selling UK single of 1981, topping a million, and is also Virgin's first UK #1 single.

1982 Jan Capitalizing on the group's success, the original *Being Boiled* is reissued through EMI. Despite its dissimilarity to current League material, it hits UK #6.

Feb *Holiday '80* double-pack is reissued in UK and makes #46.

July *Don't You Want Me* hits US #1 for 3 weeks, and is a million-plus seller. LP *Dare*, on US chart since Feb., peaks at #3. In UK, mini-LP *Love And Dancing* of dance-oriented re-mixes from LP *Dare* hits UK #3.

Sept LP *Love & Dancing* makes only US #135.

Nov *Mirror Man* hits UK #2.

1983 May *(Keep Feeling) Fascination* also hits UK #2. (It will be the group's last recording for a year as it spends much studio time working on a new LP.)

Aug *(Keep Feeling) Fascination* hits US #8. Mini-LP *Fascination!*, only released in US, makes #22.

Nov *Mirror Man*, belatedly released in US, reaches #30.

1984 May *The Lebanon* reaches UK #11. It is a departure for the group in its highlighting of Callis' guitar and for its lyric. LP *Hysteria* hits UK #3 but stays charted for just 18 weeks, partly because the group refuses to tour or do any promotion for it (but later admits this was a mistake: "We thought we were so popular we didn't have to").

June *The Lebanon* peaks at US #64.

July *Life On Your Own* makes UK #16.

Aug LP *Hysteria* reaches US #62.

Oct Oakey teams with disco producer Giorgio Moroder for *Together In Electric Dreams*, the theme from movie *Electric Dreams*. It hits UK #3, and is more successful than the film (which will later perform well on home video, aided by public familiarity with the music). The single has a guitar solo by Peter Frampton°.

Dec *Louise* makes UK #13 and is followed by a period of public silence.

1985 The group retires to Oakey's 24-track home studio and begins recording with Colin Thurston, producer of their first LP (and Magazine, Duran Duran° and Kajagoogoo). Callis departs to work with Feargal Sharkey and the sessions are joined by Associates° drummer Jim Russell and members of Comsat Angels.

July A second Oakey/Moroder collaboration, *Goodbye Bad Times*, makes UK #44.

Aug LP *Philip Oakey And Giorgio Moroder* makes only UK #52.

Sept On the assigned released date, the new Human League LP does not appear (the sessions with Thurston have been ditched).

1986 The group, minus Wright and Callis, but with Jim Russell a full member, travels to Minneapolis, Minn., US, to work with Jimmy Jam and Terry Lewis, the men behind Janet Jackson's° successful LP *Control*, and the hottest producers of the moment. 4 months are spent in recording a new LP.

Sept *Human*, the first release from the Jam/Lewis sessions, hits UK #8. LP *Crash* hits UK #7. It emerges that Jam and Lewis have laid down the law as producers and brought in session singers and players as seen fit during the recordings. Oakey admits that the sessions had ended in acrimony, but the LP re-establishes the group in the international marketplace.

Nov *Human* hits US #1, while LP *Crash* peaks at US #24. Following this re-establishment of its public profile, the group plans its first live performances in 4 years. *I Need Your Loving* spends only 1 week at UK #72.

1987 Jan *I Need Your Loving* reaches US #44.

1988 Sept *Love Is All That Matters*, remixed from 2-year-old LP *Crash*, is released as a UK single, a prelude to a TV-advertised compilation LP designed to hit the 1988 Christmas market.

HUMBLE PIE

Peter Frampton (guitar and vocals)
Steve Marriott (guitar and vocals)
Greg Ridley (bass)
Jerry Shirley (drums)

1969 Apr The group is formed in London, UK, by guitarists/vocalists Frampton° (b. Apr.22, 1950, Beckenham, UK) and Marriott (b. Jan. 30, 1947, London, UK), who have just left The Herd and The Small Faces° respectively. They recruit Ridley (b. Oct.23, 1947, UK) from Spooky Tooth, and Shirley (b. Feb.4, 1952, UK) from Little Women.

Sept After a secluded rehearsal period at Marriott's country cottage, they sign to Immediate Records and debut with LP *As Safe As Yesterday Is*, which reaches UK #32. *Natural Born Bugie* hits UK #4, and is their only UK smash.

Dec Rapid follow-up LP, the acoustic-flavored *Town And Country*, fails to chart.

1970 July They switch to A&M Records for LP *Humble Pie*, which again fails to chart.

1971 Mar LP *Rock On* is released without charting, though it sells reasonably (#118) in US, where the group tours ceaselessly.

Oct Frampton° leaves to go solo, and will emerge as a mid-70s star in his own right. He is replaced by Dave "Clem" Clempson (b. Sept.5, 1949, UK) from Colosseum. The group has minor US hit (#73) with *I Don't Need No Doctor*.

1972 Jan Live LP *Performance – Rockin' The Fillmore*, recorded in US and featuring Frampton°, restores them to UK chart at #32, and marks their US breakthrough, climbing to #21.

May LP *Smokin'* becomes their most successful release, making UK #28 and hitting US #6. *Hot 'N' Nasty* reaches US #52.

Nov The two early Immediate LPs are repackaged together in US by A&M as *Lost And Found*, and chart at #37.

1973 Apr Double LP *Eat It*, featuring black vocal trio The Blackberries, signals a move towards soul music. It reaches US #13 and UK #34.

1974 Apr LP *Thunderbox* reaches US #52, but does not chart in UK.

1975 Mar Tired of touring, the group splits, as final LP *Street Rats* reaches US #100.

July Marriott records unsuccessful solo LP *Marriott*, then forms The Steve Marriott All-Stars (which includes Clempson and Ridley) for a year, before completing the cycle in 1976 when The Small Faces° re-forms.

1980 Apr After a further low-key solo career, Marriott reforms Humble Pie with Jerry Shirley, adding Bobby Tench (formerly with Jeff Beck°) on guitar and vocals, and Anthony Jones on bass. Signed to Atco in US and Jet Records in UK, they release LP *On To Victory*, but it sells only moderately. *Fool For A Pretty Face (Hurt By Love)* reaches US #52.

1981 Apr While the group is in Chicago on a US tour, Marriott crushes his fingers in a hotel door. Dates are cancelled while his hand heals sufficiently for him to play guitar again.

June His hand recovered, Marriott is now hospitalized with an ulcer when the tour reaches Dallas, and more shows are cancelled. The new line-up's second LP *Go For The Throat* also fails to sell in great numbers (US #154), and the group disbands again. (Marriott will eventually return to his roots with UK pub band Packet of Three.)

BRIAN HYLAND

1960 Hyland (b. Nov.12, 1943, Queens, New York, N.Y., US) is still attending Franklin K. Lane High School in Brooklyn when Dave Kapp signs him – first to his Leader subsidiary, then to his Kapp label.

Aug His debut single *Rosemary* fails but *Itsy Bitsy Teenie Weenie Yellow Polka Dot Bikini* hits US #1 and UK #8, is a million-seller and makes an overnight star of the 16-year-old singer.

Oct From the same songwriters, Lee Pockriss and Paul Vance, follow-up *Four Little Heels* makes only US #73 and UK #29. B-side *That's How Much* reaches only US #74.

Dec *Lop-Sided Overloaded And It Wiggled When We Rode It* (about a donkey, not a woman) is a worldwide flop.

1961 Sept After leaving Kapp, Hyland signs to ABC Paramount to represent him in the Avalon°/Fabian°/Vee° market. *Let Me Belong To You* reaches US #20 (and is the first of many specially-tailored adolescent love songs which keep Hyland on chart and bring rewards to songwriters Peter Udell and Gary Geld).

Nov *I'll Never Stop Wanting You* charts for 1 week at US #83.

1962 Apr Udell and Geld write three teen romance classics. The first *Ginny Come Lately* reaches US #21 but hits UK #5.

July *Sealed With A Kiss* hits US and UK #3, winning Hyland a second gold disk.

Nov *Warmed Over Kisses (Left Over Love)* makes US #25 and UK #28.

1963 Jan *I May Never Live To See Tomorrow* reaches only US #69.

Mar *If Mary's Not There* stalls at US #88.

Oct *I'm Afraid To Go Home* makes US #63 (and will be his final Paramount hit).

1966 Apr Hyland makes a surprise chart comeback on Philips, but *3000 Miles* charts for only 1 week at US #99.

Sept Produced by Snuff Garrett and arranged by Leon Russell°, *The Joker Went Wild* makes US #20.

Dec *Run Run Look And See* reaches US #25.

1967 Hyland has three minor hits: *Hung Up In Your Eyes* (US #58), *Holiday For Clowns* (US #94) and *Get The Message* (US #91).

1969 Mar Hyland resurfaces with *Tragedy*, on Dot. A top 10 hit for both Thomas Wayne and The Fleetwoods, it reaches US #56.

Apr A cover of Jimmy Charles' 1960 top 5 hit, *A Million To One* reaches US #90. Dot links *Tragedy/A Million To One* as an LP title and it charts at US #160.

July *Stay And Love Me All Summer* reaches US #82.

1970 Dec Hyland hits US #3 and UK #41 with a third million-seller, a version of Curtis Mayfield's° classic *Gypsy Woman*. Released on Uni (his sixth label), it is produced by early 1960s contemporary Del Shannon°, and was a 1961 top 20 hit for The Impressions°.

1971 Jan Uni LP *Brian Hyland* reaches US #171.

Mar A cover of Jackie Wilson's° *Lonely Teardrops* becomes Hyland's US chart swan song at #54. (He has had 22 Hot 100 hits over 11 years.)

1975 Aug Reissued in UK, *Sealed With A Kiss* hits #7. (Unable to locate Hyland to promote the single, rumors suggest that his label ABC has a dozen doppelganging Hylands in response to its appeal. The real Hyland will spend the next decade as a country artist.)

JANIS IAN

1963 Ian (b. Janis Fink, Apr.7, 1951, New York, N.Y., US), already a competent guitarist and pianist, begins her folk-styled, observational songwriting while still in junior high school, and her song *Hair Of Spun Gold* is published in the folk music magazine *Broadside*.

1965 July While starting to play regularly live at New York folk haunts like the Village Gate (where she is spotted by Elektra Records, which wants to sign her as a songwriter, but passes on her as a singer) and Gaslight clubs, Ian writes *Society's Child (Baby I've Been Thinking)*, a song dealing with older-generation hypocrisy and discrimination when faced with teenage inter-racial love.

1966 She is signed to Verve Folkways Records, which releases *Society's Child* as her debut single. Initial progress is slow, with many US radio stations banning it because of its lyrical content.

1967 Apr Leonard Bernstein features *Society's Child* in a TV special, which results in renewed airplay and a US singles chart debut.

July *Society's Child (Baby I've Been Thinking)* reaches US #14, and debut LP *Janis Ian* peaks at US #29.

1968 Jan LP *For All The Seasons Of The Mind*, released on progressive Verve Forecast label, reaches US #179. LP *The Secret Life Of J. Eddy Fink* is released (with Richie Havens° playing drums), but fails to chart. Extensive US club and college touring and the demands of the pop marketplace leave her disillusioned, so she retires to live in Philadelphia, where she marries.

1971 She returns to live appearances, and signs to Capitol Records. LP *Present Company* is released, but does not sell.

1973 Oct Ian's song *Jesse*, recorded by Roberta Flack°, reaches US #30.

1974 Jan Ian signs to CBS/Columbia, where her work will develop a matured, sensitive style incorporating her folk roots with acquired jazz and blues influences.

July First CBS/Columbia LP *Stars*, which includes her own version of *Jesse*, reaches US #83. (Its title track will be covered by Cher° and Glen Campbell°, among others.)

1975 Aug *At Seventeen* hits US #3, her first million-seller. (It will win two Grammy awards in 1976.)

Sept LP *Between The Lines*, which includes the hit single, tops the US chart for a week, earning a gold disk for a half million sales.

1976 Feb LP *Aftertones* reaches US #12.

1977 Mar LP *Miracle Row*, self-produced with Ron Frangipane, reaches US #45.

1978 Oct Joe Wissert-produced LP *Janis Ian* peaks at US #120.

1979 Dec *Fly Too High*, which reaches UK #44 is her first UK success. It was written and recorded by Ian and producer Giorgio Moroder for Jodie Foster film *Foxes*, with rhythm section Keith Forsey and Harold Faltermeyer, and taken from LP *Night Rains* which fails to chart in US and UK, despite Chick Corea, Ron Carter and Bruce Springsteen's° E Street Band saxophonist Clarence Clemmons guesting.

1980 July *The Other Side Of The Sun*, also from LP *Night Rains* makes UK #44.

1981 July *Under The Covers* reaches US #71, while LP *Restless Eyes*, recorded in LA with producer Gary Klein, peaks at US #156. This is Ian's final chart appearance, though she will remain a popular live performer in the singer-songwriter ranks through the 1980s.

ICEHOUSE

Iva Davies (guitar and vocals)
Guy Pratt (bass)
Andy Qunta (keyboards)
Michael Hoste (keyboards)
Bob Kretschmer (guitar)
John Lloyd (drums)

1980 Jan The band, formed by Davies (b. May 22, 1955), ex-teenage member of the ABC National Training Orchestra in Sydney, Australia, (with Lloyd on drums, Keith Welsh bass and Anthony Smith keyboards) under its original name Flowers, signs to independent Australian label, Regular Records.

May/Aug Debut single *Can't Help Myself* written by Davies, and follow-up *We Can Get Together* are Australian top 10 hits.

Oct LP *Icehouse*, produced by Davies and Cameron Allan, hits #4 in Australia and will be one of the year's biggest sellers there and in New Zealand.

1981 Feb The band signs worldwide to Chrysalis Records, changing its name to Icehouse (after the LP) to avoid conflict with Scots group The Flowers, and embarks on a short UK tour followed by a longer one in the US and Canada.

July Icehouse tours the UK again, as support to Simple Minds°.

Aug *We Can Get Together* reaches US #62.

Sept LP *Icehouse* climbs to US #82.

Nov Simple Minds supports Icehouse on Australian tour. *Love In Motion*, recorded by Davies alone, but credited to the band, hits Australian top 10.

1982 Jan The original line-up splits, and Davies carries on under the Icehouse name.

May Davies records LP *Primitive Man* on his own, working in Sydney and Los Angeles with co-producer Keith Forsey.

Aug Needing a band to tour in support of LP *Primitive Man* (which hits Australian top 10 along with *Great Southern Land*), Davies recruits Pratt (ex-Killing Joke) and Qunta in London, and Kretschmer in Australia. Drummer Lloyd and keyboardist Hoste

ICEHOUSE *cont.*

(who played in the early Flowers before leaving to complete his studies) rejoin.

Oct LP *Primitive Man* reaches US #129.

Dec *Hey Little Girl* taken from the LP becomes another local top 10 hit as the band plays an extensive Australian tour.

1983 Mar A remix of *Hey Little Girl* reaches UK #17 and the band appears on UK TV's "Top of the Pops". LP *Primitive Man* is reissued in UK as *Love In Motion* to include the new version of the hit and makes #64.

May *Street Cafe* reaches only UK #62.

June Icehouse supports David Bowie° on a major tour in UK, followed by dates in Holland.

Dec Davies completes work on soundtrack music for video director Russell Mulcahy's first feature film *Razorback*, made in Australia.

1984 June LP *Sidewalk* is released, but fails to chart in UK or US.

1985 Dec *Boxes*, a ballet written by Davies and Kretschmer, opens at Sydney Opera House.

1986 May *No Promises* reaches UK #72, extracted from LP *Measure For Measure*, which does not chart.

Aug *No Promises* reaches US #79.

1988 Jan The band's US chart debut, reaching #14, is extracted from LP *Man Of Colours*, which topped Australian chart while single hit #4.

Mar *Crazy* reaches UK #38.

May *Electric Blue*, also from the LP *Man Of Colours*, finally gives the band a US top 10 hit, making #7, but reaches only UK #53.

BILLY IDOL

1976 Idol (b. William Broad, Nov.30, 1955, Stanmore, Middx., UK) is studying English at Sussex University when friend Steve Severin (later of Siouxsie & The Banshees°) suggests they go to London and get involved in the very early London punk rock scene, because it seems like fun. The pair becomes part of the "Bromley Contingent", a group of fans which follows The Sex Pistols° around and numbers later stars like Siouxsie, Marco Pirroni (of Adam and The Ants°) and club impresario Philip Sallon. He changes his name to Billy Idol when the group Chelsea is formed, but he leaves with fellow guitarist Tony James.

Sept The Idol-James band becomes Generation X, having its first hit with *Your Generation* which reaches UK #36. (The band is named after a 1964 book found in Idol's mother's bookcase.)

Dec The band, with Idol on vocals, Bob Andrews on guitar, Tony James on bass and Mark Laff on drums, is the first to play the seminal punk venue, The Roxy.

1978 Mar *Ready Steady Go* reaches UK #47.

Apr LP *Generation X* enters UK chart and climbs to #29.

1979 Feb Generation X makes UK #11 with *King Rocker*. LP *Valley Of The Dolls* reaches UK #51.

Apr *Valley Of The Dolls* peaks at UK #23.

June *Friday's Angels* reaches UK #62.

Oct *Dancing With Myself* makes UK #62.

1981 Jan EP *Dancing With Myself* climbs to UK #60. By the time Generation X splits up, the name has been shortened to Gen X. It has had six hits and has been the first punk band to appear on "Top of the Pops", but much of its career has been tied up in a long-running management dispute. James has already departed.

Feb Idol goes to New York, where he meets manager Bill Aucoin, who had helped Kiss's° career. Aucoin arranges for the New York office of Chrysalis Records (Generation X's UK label) to place him on a $200 a week retainer. He records LP *Don't Stop*, which includes a version of Generation X's *Dancing With Myself* and of Tommy James'° *Mony Mony*. It becomes popular on the New York dance scene. Aucoin introduces Idol to young guitarist Steve Stevens. They form a group and start writing and recording. Keith Forsey is brought in to produce.

Nov LP *Don't Stop* reaches US #71.

1982 May LP *Billy Idol* is released.

Sept *Hot In The City* reaches UK #58 and US #23. LP *Billy Idol* makes US #45, after considerable promotion from Chrysalis.

1983 July *White Wedding* reaches US #36.

Dec LP *Rebel Yell* hits US #6, eventually turning double platinum.

1984 Mar *Rebel Yell* reaches only US #46 and UK #62.

July Idol finally has a UK hit when *Eyes Without A Face* reaches #18. It also becomes his biggest US single, hitting #4.

Sept *Flesh For Fantasy* is a disappointing UK #54, but US #29.

Dec *Catch My Fall* reaches US #50.

1985 Jan Idol is featured on the cover of the Jan. 31 issue of *Rolling Stone* magazine, wearing even less of his rockin' bondage gear than usual and showing a considerable area of buttock. The issue is the lowest-selling *RS* of recent times and in some states can only be sold in a brown paper bag.

June Chrysalis UK releases compilation *Vital Idol*. It spends 26 weeks on chart, hitting UK #7.

July The old standard *White Wedding* is re-released in UK and hits #6.

Sept A reissue of *Rebel Yell* single and LP in UK pays off. The single hits #6 and the LP, shaded somewhat by the compilation, climbs to #36.

1986 Oct *To Be A Lover* makes UK #22 and hits US #6.

Nov Idol's UK pop renaissance is confirmed when LP *Whiplash Smile* enters the UK chart at #9 and peaks the next week at #8.

1987 Mar *Don't Need A Gun* reaches UK #26 and US #37.

July *Sweet Sixteen* climbs to UK #17, having peaked at US #20 in June.

Oct A remake of Tommy James & The Shondells'° *Mony Mony* hits UK #7. It top the US chart in Nov.

1988 Jan The "exterminator" mix of *Hot In The City* returns it to the UK chart at #13.

June Idol and his girlfriend Perri Lister have a son, Willem Wolf Broad.

July Compilation LP *Idol Songs – 11 Of The Best* hits UK #2.

Aug A belated release of *Catch My Fall* makes UK #63.

THE IMPRESSIONS

Jerry Butler (vocals)
Curtis Mayfield (vocals)
Arthur Brooks (vocals)
Richard Brooks (vocals)
Sam Gooden (vocals)

1957 Three members of a Tennessee vocal quintet, The Roosters, Brooks brothers Arthur (b. Chattanooga, Tenn., US) and Richard (b. Chattanooga) with Sam Gooden (b. Sept.2, 1939, Chattanooga), relocate to Chicago, Ill., leaving behind Fred Cash (b. Oct.8, 1940, Chattanooga) and Emanuel Thomas. Songwriter/producer Jerry Butler° (b. Dec.8, 1939, Sunflower, Miss., US.) joins as a temporary replacement and recruits his friend Curtis Mayfield° (b. June 3, 1942, Chicago, Ill., US) to make the line-up a quintet. Their releases on small Chicago labels, Bandera *Listen To Me* and *Swirl Don't Leave Me*, fail to chart.

1958 The group demos *Pretty Baby* and *My Baby Loves Me* for Vee Jay label. Vi Muszynski, having heard the group, decides to make them the first act on her label, which she is trying to link up with Vee Jay, but negotiations break down and the group signs directly to Vee Jay.

Apr Under the supervision of Vee Jay A&R man Calvin Carter, and rechristened The Impressions, the group records four songs, two written by Butler° and the Brooks brothers.

May One of these, *For Your Precious Love*, is the group's first single, credited to Jerry Butler° & The Impressions.

Aug *For Your Precious Love* peaks at US #11. Its success prompts Butler° to go solo and he is replaced by original Rooster Cash. But, without Butler's name, the group fades into obscurity and two further Vee Jay singles fail. The Impressions temporarily split and Mayfield° earns a living playing guitar on Butler's records and writing songs for him, including hits *Let It Be Me* and *He Will Break Your Heart*.

1959 Mayfield° re-forms the group, now clearly the leader and songwriter, and it moves to New York.

1960 He secures The Impressions a contract with ABC/Paramount.

1961 Dec More than a year after signing with the label, *Gypsy Woman* makes US #20.

1962 Feb *Grow Closer Together* spends a week at US #99.

July *Little Young Lover* reaches US #96.

1963 Feb *I'm The One Who Loves You* stalls at US #73. Mayfield° returns to Chicago, taking Cash and Gooden with him. The Brooks brothers stay in New York.

May The first single as a trio, *Sad, Sad Girl And Boy*, peaks at US #84.

Sept Debut LP *The Impressions*, featuring Johhny Pate's arrangement of a strong horn section and gospel-style vocal interplay, reaches US #43.

Nov The Impressions' biggest success is *It's All Right*, which hits US #4. They begin to influence other acts; Major Lance and Gene Chandler° record Mayfield's° songs (chiefly through his role as staff producer at Okeh Records), as do UK R&B groups.

1964 Feb *Talking About My Baby* reaches US #12.

May *I'm So Proud* makes US #14, while LP *The Never-Ending Impressions* climbs to US #52.

July Gospelly *Keep On Pushing* hits US #10.

Oct *You Must Believe Me* makes US #15, while the group's biggest-selling LP, *Keep On Pushing*, hits US #8.

1965 Jan Taken from the LP, Mayfield°-penned gospel song *Amen* hits US #7 and is featured in film *Lilies of the Field*.

Mar *People Get Ready*, reflecting Mayfield's° increasing social awareness, makes US #14. (It will be a hit for Aretha Franklin° and covered by dozens of artists.)

Apr LP *People Get Ready* makes US #23 and LP *The Impressions' Greatest Hits* reaches US #83.

May Upbeat R&B *Woman's Got Soul* reaches US #29.

June *Meeting Over Yonder* peaks at US #48.

Sept *I Need You* stalls at US #64.

Oct *Just One Kiss From You* falters at US #76. LP *One By One* makes US #104.

1966 Jan *You've Been Cheatin'* makes US #33. Mayfield° sets up his own record label, Windy C. (He signs The Five Stairsteps and June Conquest, but after only seven releases, the label folds.)

Feb *Since I Lost The One I Love* peaks at US #90.

Mar LP *Ridin' High* reaches US #79.

Apr *Too Slow* peaks at US #91.

Sept *Can't Satisfy* makes US #65.

1967 Mar *You Always Hurt Me* reaches US #96.

July LP *The Fabulous Impressions* makes US #184.

Sept *I Can't Stay Away From You* peaks at US #80.

Dec With *We're A Winner*, Mayfield° explicitly confronts black politics and the disk is partly banned by US radio.

1968 Feb Despite radio censorship, *We're A Winner* reaches US #14. It is the group's last single for ABC. When the contract expires Mayfield° and Thomas establish their Curtom label.

Apr ABC continues to release existing Impressions material. LP *We're A Winner* makes US #35, the group's best placing in 3 years.

May *We're Rolling On (Part 1)* reaches US #59.

Aug *I Loved And I Lost* climbs to US #61.

Oct *Fool For You*, the first Curtom single, makes US #22. ABC compilation LP *The Best Of The Impressions* peaks at US #172.

Dec On Curtom, *This Is My Country* makes US #25, while on ABC *Don't Cry My Love* reaches US #71.

1969 May *Seven Years* peaks at US #84.

June LP *The Young Mods' Forgotten Story* reaches US #104.

Aug *Choice Of Colors*, from the LP, makes US #21.

Nov Also from the LP, *Say You Love Me* reaches US #58.

1970 Mayfield° quits The Impressions to go solo but continues to oversee all aspects of their career, writing and producing some of their Curtom releases and recruiting his replacement, Leroy Hutson.

June *Check Out Your Mind* makes US #28.

Sept *(Baby) Turn On To Me* climbs to US #56.

1971 Mar *Ain't Got Time* reaches US #53. ABC compilation LP *16 Greatest Hits* peaks at US #180.

Aug *Love Me* is the last Mayfield°-penned Impressions song to chart, reaching US #94.

1972 Apr LP *Times Have Changed* spends 2 weeks at US #192.

1973 Mar LP *Curtis Mayfield/His Early Years With The Impressions* makes US #180. Hutson leaves for a solo career. Cash and Gooden bring in Reggie Torian and Ralph Johnson and this line-up records the soundtrack for movie *Three The Hard Way*. Chicago TV station WTTW reassembles most of the original Impressions, the 1960s line-up and the current group for TV special "Curtis". (Most of the sound recordings will later be released on LP *Curtis In Chicago*.)

1974 July Still with Curtom, The Impressions reach US #17 with *Finally Got Myself Together*, written and produced by Ed Townsend. LP *Finally Got Myself Together* makes US #176.

1975 July *Sooner Or Later* peaks at US #68.

Aug LP *First Impressions* peaks at US #115.

Nov *Same Thing* stalls at US #75.

Dec The title track from LP *First Impressions* becomes the group's only UK chart entry – reaching #16.

1976 Johnson leaves to form his own group, Mystique. Nate Evans replaces him.

Mar LP *Loving Power* makes US #195.

1977 Feb LP *The Vintage Years*, featuring thirteen hits by The Impressions and thirteen by Jerry Butler° solo, reaches US #199.

1981 Sept LP and single *Fan The Fire*, released through 20th Century, fail to sell. (Mayfield° is now working for Neil Bogart's Boardwalk label.)

1982 LP *In The Heat Of The Night* is released on MCA.

1983 Butler° and Mayfield° briefly rejoin the group for a reunion tour.

JAMES INGRAM

1973/79 Ingram moves to LA from Akron, Oh., US, with band Revelation Funk. He spends 2 years touring with Ray Charles° playing piano and singing background vocals, before becoming Leon Haywood's musical director, playing on his hit single *Don't Push It Don't Force It*. He also plays keyboards for The Coasters° on Dick Clark's oldies package tours, and begins working for publishing company ATV, singing on demos.

1980 Russ Titelman sends Quincy Jones a demo of Barry Mann and Cynthia Weil's *Just Once* with Ingram the vocalist. Jones invites Ingram to be one of the featured vocalists on his LP *The Dude*.

Aug Ingram sings backing vocals on Carl Carlton's US #22 hit *She's A Bad Mama Jama*.

Nov *Just Once*, from LP *The Dude*, credited to Quincy Jones, but sung by Ingram, reaches US #17.

1981 Feb [25] Ingram performs *Just Once* at the 23rd annual Grammy awards. He is nominated in three categories: Best New Artist, Best Pop Male Vocal and Best R&B Vocal. Jones invites him to tour Japan, where he performs in front of 20,000 people backed by Jones' 50-piece orchestra.

1982 Feb Ingram song *Hold On* is covered by sax man Ernie Watts on his LP *Chariots Of Fire*.

Feb [24] Ingram wins a Grammy for Best R&B Vocalist at the 24th annual Grammy awards, the only artist to do so without having released an LP.

Mar *One Hundred Ways*, from Jones' LP *The Dude*, reaches US #14.

May *Baby Come To Me*, a duet with Qwest labelmate Patti Austin°, peaks at US #73.

Dec Ingram joins a star cast of singers to back Donna Summer° on *State Of Independence*.

1983 Feb *Baby Come To Me*, used and revived as the love theme for US TV soap "General Hospital", tops the US chart for 2 weeks, prior to Michael Jackson's° *Billie Jean*.

Apr Ingram joins Austin° on stage at the 1982 Academy Awards presentation to sing *How Do You Keep The Music Playing?*. Producer Quincy Jones assembles an all-star cast of musicians and writers for Ingram's debut LP including Larry Carlton (guitar),

JAMES INGRAM *cont.*

David Paich, Michael McDonald°, David Foster, Greg Phillinganes, Jimmy Smith (keyboards and synthesizers), Louis Johnson and Nathan East (bass), Harvey Mason (drums) and Watts and Tom Scott (reeds). Work starts on the LP at Westlake Audio studios, LA.

Aug *How Do You Keep The Music Playing?*, the theme to Goldie Hawn/Burt Reynolds movie *Best Friends*, reaches US #45.

Nov Debut LP *It's Your Night* is released, and goes gold despite peaking at only US #46.

Dec Michael Jackson's° *P.Y.T. (Pretty Young Thing)*, written by Ingram, hits US #10.

1984 Jan Ingram guests on a 2-hour Quincy Jones US TV special.

Mar *Yah Mo B There*, a inspirational duet with Michael McDonald°, reaches US #19.

Apr Barry Mann-penned *There's No Easy Way* peaks at US #58. LP *It's Your Night* reaches UK #25. Michael Jackson's° *P.Y.T. (Pretty Young Thing)* hits UK #11.

Dec *What About Me?*, sung with Kenny Rogers° and Kim Carnes°, reaches US #15.

1985 Feb A remixed *Yah Mo B There* reaches UK #12, after two false starts the previous year (#44 Feb. and #69 Apr.).

1986 Aug Second LP *Never Felt So Good* is released. Produced by Billy Ocean°-collaborator Keith Diamond, it makes US #123 and UK #72, but sees no UK or US chart singles action.

1987 Mar Ballad *Somewhere Out There*, with Linda Ronstadt°, from Spielberg-produced movie *An American Tail*, hits US #2 and UK #8.

1988 Mar *Somewhere Out There* wins a Grammy for Song of the Year at 30th annual Grammy awards.

July Ingram guests on Patti Austin's° LP *The Real Me*.

INXS

Michael Hutchence (vocals)
Kirk Pengilly (guitar, sax and vocals)
Garry Beers (bass and vocals)
Tim Farriss (guitar)
Andy Farriss (keyboards)
Jon Farriss (drums and vocals)

1977 The group forms as The Farriss Brothers in Sydney, Australia.

1978 Fresh from school, they move to Perth, where they spend 10 months writing, rehearsing and playing local gigs.

1979 The group returns to Sydney where it is renamed INXS.

Sept [1] The group makes its live debut at The Oceanview Hotel, Toukley.

1980 May *Simple Simon/We Are The Vegetables* is released in Australia on Deluxe label.

Oct Debut LP *INXS* is released and the group has its first Australian hit with *Just Keep Walking*.

1981 INXS plays 300 dates in Australia during the "Fear and Loathing Tour", "The Campus Tour", "Stay Young Tour" and "The Tour With No Name".

Mar *The Loved One* (which will be re-recorded in 1987 for LP *Kick*) is released.

Oct The group signs to RCA, releasing its second Australia-only LP *Underneath The Colours*, which includes Australian hits *Stay Young* and *Loved One*.

1982 Jan The group tours New Zealand, and on its return records *The One Thing*.

Apr Hutchence, Pengilly and Andrew Farriss travel to UK and US to consider the next stage in INXS' career.

July WEA signs the group for Australasia, releasing its third LP *Shabooh Shoobah*.

1983 Jan INXS signs to Atlantic in US and embarks on a tour as guests of The Kinks° and Adam and The Ants°.

Mar The group makes its US debut with *The One Thing* which, with a heavy rotation promo video on MTV, reaches #30. LP *Shabooh Shoobah* makes US #46, while *Don't Change* is the group's first (unsuccessful) UK release.

May The group's first New York headlining date is at The Ritz.

July *Don't Change* reaches US #80.

Sept *Original Sin* is recorded at New York's Power Station studio, with Nile Rodgers producing and Daryl Hall° and Dave Stewart guesting on vocals.

Oct Mini-LP *Dekadence*, with remixes of four tracks from LP *Shabooh Shoobah*, reaches US #148.

1984 Jan The group plays a sell-out Australian tour as *Original Sin* tops the local chart.

May INXS' UK live debut is at London's Astoria. *Original Sin* reaches US #58.

June LP *The Swing* makes US #52.

July The first two LPs, *INXS* and *Underneath The Colours*, are belatedly released in US.

Aug *I Send A Message* peaks at US #77 and LP *INXS* reaches US #164.

Sept The group sets out on a 3-month US tour concluding with a sold-out show at The Hollywood Palladium.

Nov Returning home, INXS stops off at Guam in the Pacific, becoming the first international group to play there.

1985 Mar The group starts work on fifth LP *Listen Like Thieves* at Sydney's Rhinoceros Studios, with Chris Thomas producing. LP *The Swing* achieves double-platinum status in Australia.

July [13] The group appears at the Australian venue of the Live Aid Concert, beamed worldwide by satellite.

Aug Work finishes at London's AIR Studios on LP *Listen Like Thieves*.

Aug [28] "The 1985 INXS World Tour" commences in Australia.

Nov Breaking its tour, the group briefly returns home to perform at the "Rockin' The Royals" charity concert in the presence of HRH Prince Charles and Princess Diana.

Dec *This Time* reaches US #81. Video *The Swing And Other Stories* is issued in US by Atlantic Video, and in UK by Channel 5.

1986 Apr *What You Need* hits US #5 and UK #51. Hutchence makes his acting debut in movie *Dogs In Space*, and has a solo top 10 hit in Australia with *Rooms For The Memory*, from the film.

May The group embarks on "If You Got It, Shake It!" world tour, highlighted by two sell-out shows supporting Queen° at London's Wembley Stadium.

June LP *Listen Like Thieves* reaches US #54 and UK #46.

Sept *Kiss The Dirt (Falling Down The Mountain)* makes UK #54. The group returns home for "Si Lo Tienes Muevelo" tour.

Oct Video *What You Need* is released.

1987 Jan The group heads a major Australian tour with eight other bands under the banner "Australian Made".

Oct *Need You Tonight* reaches UK #58.

Oct [16] INXS' 1987-88 world tour opens in East Lansing, Mich., US.

Dec [2-14] The group tours UK.

1988 Jan *Need You Tonight* becomes its first US #1 hit. LP *Kick* hits US #3 and UK #9. *New Sensation* makes UK #25.

Mar *Devil Inside* reaches UK #47, hitting US #2 4 weeks later.

July *Never Tear Us Apart* peaks at UK #24 and hits US #3.

Aug Video compilation *Kick Flicks* is released, while *New Sensation*, the fourth single from LP *Kick*, enters the US chart at #86.

IRON BUTTERFLY

Doug Ingle (vocals and keyboards)
Erik Braunn (guitar and vocals)
Lee Dorman (bass)
Ronald Bushy (drums)

1966 Formed in San Diego, Cal., by Ingle (b. Sept.9, 1946, Omaha, Neb., US), the son of a church organist, Bushy (b. Sept.23, 1945, Washington, D.C.), bassist Jerry Penrod (b. San Diego, Cal.), guitarist Danny Weis (b. San Diego) and vocalist Darryl DeLoach (b. San Diego), Iron Butterfly relocates to LA.

1967 The group works at LA's Bido Lito's, The Galaxy and The Whisky A-Go-Go and signs to Atlantic Records' subsidiary Atco.

1968 Mar LP *Heavy* reaches US #78 during a 49-week stay on the chart, sustained by touring as the opening act for The Doors° and Jefferson Airplane°. DeLoach quits and Penrod and Weis leave to form Rhinoceros. Dorman (b. Sept.19, 1945, St. Louis, Mo., US) and Braunn (b. Aug.11, 1950, Boston, Mass., US) replace them.

May Iron Butterfly's *Possession* and *Unconscious Power* are featured with material from Cream° in film *Savage Seven*.

July LP *In-A-Gadda-Da-Vida* enters the US chart and will climb to #4.

Aug Iron Butterfly takes part in the Newport Pop Festival at Costa Mesa, Cal., US.

Oct *In-A-Gadda-Da-Vida*, edited from the 17-minute LP version, reaches US #30.

Dec The group joins a star bill for the 3-day Miami Pop Festival at Hallendale, Fla., US.

1969 Feb LP *Ball* enters the US chart and will hit #3.

Mar *Soul Experience* stalls at US #75.

June The group joins Joe Cocker°, Creedence Clearwater Revival°, Jimi

Hendrix° and many others on the bill of the Denver Pop Festival held at the Mile High Stadium, Denver, Col.

July *In The Time Of Our Lives* reaches US #96.

Aug Iron Butterfly performs at the 3-day Atlantic City Pop Festival in N.J., US.

Sept Braunn quits, later forming Flintwhistle with DeLoach and Penrod. Guitarists Larry Reinhardt and ex-Blues Image Mike Pinera replace him.

1970 May LP *Iron Butterfly Live* reaches US #20.

Aug LP *Metamorphosis*, with new members Pinera and Reinhardt, makes US #16. Pinera proclaims: "You gotta change, you better get hip."

Nov *Easy Rider (Let The Wind Pay The Way)*, from movie *Easy Rider*, on which Iron Butterfly sings the title track, reaches US #66.

1971 Apr LP *In-A-Gadda-Da-Vida* drops off the US chart after 140 weeks, selling in excess of 3 million copies and is Atlantic Records' biggest seller. (It will remain so until the advent of Led Zeppelin°.)

May [23] The group splits after its farewell live appearance.

1972 Jan LP *The Best Of Iron Butterfly/Evolution* makes US #137.

1973 Compilation LP *Star Collection* is released.

1975 Feb Braunn and Bushy regroup with Phil Kramer (b. July 12, 1952, Youngtown, Oh., US) and Howard Reitzes (b. Mar.22, 1951, Southgate, Cal.) to sign with MCA Records, releasing LPs *Scorching Beauty* (US #138) and *Sun And Steel* before splitting again.

IRON MAIDEN

Bruce Dickinson (vocals)
Dave Murray (lead and rhythm guitar)
Adrian Smith (guitar)
Dennis Stratton (guitar)
Steve Harris (bass)
Nicko McBrain/Clive Burr (drums)
Eddie

1976 May Harris (b. Mar.12, 1957, London, UK) having formed pub band Smiler, meets Murray (b. Dec.23, 1958, London) and forms new band Iron Maiden (named after the instrument of torture), determined to keep heavy metal alive in face of new punk wave. The line-up features Harris (the only original member to remain in future line-ups), Murray, vocalist Paul Di'anno (b. May 17, 1959, Chingford, Essex, UK) and drummer Doug Sampson. The group's live debut is at The Cart and Horses pub, Stratford, in London's East End.

1977 The new band bases itself in Leytonstone, UK, and plays local live gigs in the summer.

1978 The band plays a regular stint at London pubs The Bridgehouse, Canning Town, and Ruskin Arms, East Ham. Despite constant gigging, it is unable to interest any A&R men. Cult following develops and Iron Maiden releases an EP of demos featuring *Iron Maiden*, *Prowler* and *Strange World* on its own label. DJ Neal Kay of The Bandwaggon Soundhouse in London is sent a copy and the tape becomes a massive heavy metal club hit. Iron Maiden appears regularly at The Soundhouse in the next 12 months.

1979 Feb The band has £12,000 worth of equipment stolen from its van. (Ilkay Bayram from London is later convicted of theft, and most of the equipment is returned.)

May DJ Kay organizes his "Heavy Metal Crusade" at London's Music Machine. Iron Maiden appears in what is remembered as the first concert of the "New Wave of British Heavy Metal" (NWBHM), a phrase coined by *Sounds* music magazine editors Alan Lewis and Geoff Barton.

June Roderick Smallwood from the MAM Agency hears the demo and invites the band to play at The Windsor Castle and The Swan pubs, then finds the band UK gigs nationwide. Di'anno is arrested for carrying a knife.

Oct A showcase at London's Marquee is ignored by every major label.

Nov EP *The Soundhouse Tapes* is released through mail-order, having been recorded a year earlier in Cambridge. New guitarist Tony Parsons joins and they record two tracks for compilation LP *Metal For Muthas*, released through EMI.

Dec A sell-out gig at London's Marquee clinches a deal with EMI Records.

1980 Jan Parsons is replaced by Dennis Stratton (b. Nov.9, 1954, London) ex-Remus Down Boulevard.

Feb Debut single *Running Free* reaches UK #34. The band refuses to mime on UK BBC TV's "Top of the Pops", becoming the first act to play live on the show since The Who° in 1973.

Apr Debut LP *Iron Maiden* hits UK #4, helped by a UK tour with Judas Priest°. Sampson is replaced by Clive Burr.

June *Sanctuary* reaches UK #29. On the sleeve, Derek Riggs, the group's artistic designer, depicts Iron Maiden's mechanical psycho-killing mascot Eddie knife-slashing PM Margaret Thatcher. After legal threats, her eyes are blacked out. EMI holds a special Iron Maiden party at Madame Tussaud's Chamber of Horrors.

Aug Iron Maiden is featured on UK TV show "20th Century Box" special on NWBHM, as it begins a European tour backing Kiss°.

Nov *Woman In Uniform*, with picture sleeve featuring PM Thatcher waiting for revenge on Eddie holding a machine gun, climbs to UK #35. Eddie is introduced as part of the live act (and will grow in physical and popular stature over the coming years). Stratton is fired, replaced by ex-Urchin guitarist Adrian Smith (b. Feb.27, 1957, London).

1981 Feb Half live, half studio LP *Killers*, containing four new tracks, reaches UK #12 and US #78.

Mar *Twilight Zone/Wrath Child* makes UK #31.

May Iron Maiden begins a sold-out Japanese tour, followed by its first US tour, opening for Judas Priest°.

June *Purgatory* makes UK #52.

Sept Di'anno is replaced by ex-Samson vocalist and private school educated Bruce Dickinson (b. Aug.7, 1958, Sheffield, Yorks., UK). (Di'anno continues to record with Lone Wolf and Battlezone.)

Oct Live EP *Maiden Japan* peaks at UK #43 and US #89.

Dec The group plays a pub gig as Genghis Khan.

1982 Feb "The Beast on the Road" tour begins in Dunstable, UK (ending 11 months later in Niggata, Japan).

Mar *Run To The Hills* hits UK #7. It is also their first video to be shown on US MTV.

Apr Iron Maiden knocks Barbra Streisand off the top spot as LP *The Number Of The Beast* hits UK #1. It reaches US #33 (where it will have a 65-week chart run and earn a gold disk). The group relocates to The Bahamas for tax purposes.

May *The Number Of The Beast* makes UK #18. The group begins a 6-month "The Beast on the Road" US tour including a sold-out date at The Palladium, New York, where a larger (12 feet) than life Eddie holds aloft a "bitten-off" head of Ozzy Osbourne°.

July A soccer match with The Scorpions ends in 0-0 tie.

1983 Jan Drummer Burr quits the line-up amicably, to be replaced by Michael "Nicko" McBain (b. June 5, 1954), ex-Trust and Streetwalkers.

May *Flight Of Icarus* peaks at UK #11. LP *Piece Of Mind*, recorded in Nassau, hits UK #3 and US #14 (where it will become platinum).

June A 4-month "World Piece" universal tour, including their first headlining US dates, commences.

July *The Trooper* reaches UK #12.

Dec Readers of UK heavy metal magazine *Kerrang* vote *Piece Of Mind* and *The Number Of The Beast* as top two heavy metal LPs of all time. Iron Maiden wins a soccer match against Def Leppard° in West Germany 4-2.

1984 Aug *2 Minutes To Midnight* reaches UK #11. The "World Slavery" tour begins in Poland (running through to July 1985 ending in Southern California after 200 shows).

Nov *Aces High* peaks at UK #20. LP *Powerslave*, recorded at Le Chalet, France, hits UK #2 and reaches US #21.

1985 Apr The "World Slavery" tour continues through South East Asia.

June LP *Iron Maiden* is reissued, reaching UK #71.

Oct Live *Running Free* makes UK #19. Their recent 11-month, 26-country tour is documented by double LP *Live After Death*, which will hit UK #2 and US #19.

Dec Live *Run To The Hills* makes UK #26. The group plays a gig at the Marquee in London as The Entire Population of Hackney.

1986 Sept *Wasted Years* peaks at UK #18. LP *Somewhere In Time* hits UK #3 and US #11, and marks the beginning of yet another tour.

Nov *Stranger In A Strange Land* reaches UK #22. The band plays a charity gig at London's Hammersmith Odeon with special guests, the heavy metal pastiche combo Bad News.

1987 Jan Dickinson is arrested in Lubbock, Tex., for allegedly hitting someone with a microphone and then strangling him with the cord back in March 1985.

May Iron Maiden finishes a 7½-month world tour and begins work on a new studio project.

1988 Apr LP *Seventh Son Of A Seventh Son* enters UK charts at #1 and peaks at US #12. *Can I Play With Madness* hits UK #2. Both confirm Maiden's position as UK's top metal act.

Aug *Evil That Men Do* hits UK #5.

Aug [20] Uncharacteristically, the band plays only one UK date of the year at The Donington Festival.

Oct A tape by Iron Maiden wakes fan Gary Dobson from a coma 8 weeks after he was crushed at Donington.

THE ISLEY BROTHERS

Ronald Isley (lead vocals)
Rudolph Isley (vocals)
O'Kelly Isley (vocals)

1950s Four Isley brothers, Rudolph (b. Apr.1, 1939, Cincinnati, Oh., US), Ronald (b. May 21, 1941, Cincinnati), O'Kelly (b. Dec.25, 1937, Cincinnati) and Vernon leave the church choir in their native Cincinnati to form a vocal quartet. They begin church touring but quit when Vernon is killed in a bicycle accident. After a year's break, their parents, Kelly and Sallye Bernice Isley, persuade the three brothers to re-form.

1957 The Isley Brothers travel to New York looking for a record deal. Their first single, doo-wop *The Cow Jumped Over The Moon* is released on Teenage label, but fails to chart, as do subsequent releases on Mark-X, Gone and Cindy labels.

1958 Although they have yet to succeed as recording artists, The Isleys' polished live work secures a contract with the influential General Artists' Corporation management agency.

1959 During a summer appearance at the Howard Theater in Washington, D.C., they are seen by RCA's Howard Bloom, who signs them. Bloom brings in production duo Hugo and Luigi to supervise The Isley Brothers' recording. First effort *Turn To Me* fails.

July [29] The Isleys record their second RCA single, *Shout*. An adaptation of stage favorite *Lonely Teardrops*, with the line "you know you make me want to shout", it features their church organist Professor Herman Stephens.

Sept *Shout* makes only US #47 but is a huge R&B hit. (It will become a standard and a million-seller.) Its success allows the brothers to move the rest of the family from Cincinnati to N.J.

Oct LP *Shout* is released, but sells poorly, as does *Respectable*.

1960 The Isleys leave RCA for Atlantic, where they are teamed up with writer/producers Jerry Leiber and Mike Stoller (fresh from their successes with The Coasters°), but Leiber and Stoller are unable to work The Isleys' gospel energy into a commercial package and their four singles all fail to sell.

1962 The Brothers move to Wand Records, where they team with producer Bert Berns. Blues ballad *Right Now* is another flop but, for the follow-up, Berns presents his own song *Twist And Shout*, originally recorded by The Top Notes in 1961.

July *Twist And Shout* tops the R&B chart and peaks at US #17, and becomes a classic reaching a wider audience through The Beatles'° version.

Oct With the current Twist dance craze, Wand has The Isleys record *Twistin' With Linda*, which reaches US #54. LP *Twist And Shout* makes US #61.

1963 After the release of *Hold On Baby*, essentially a rewrite of *Twist And Shout*, The Isleys leave Wand for United Artists, continuing to work with Berns. UA debut *Tango* flops and the label instructs the group to record *Surf And Shout*.

July *Twist And Shout* reaches UK #42.

1964 Hardened by record company demands, the brothers set up their own label, T-Neck (named after Teaneck, N.J., where the family now lives). First release, *Testify*, fails to chart. (The record features Jimi Hendrix°, a member of the Isleys' touring band, on guitar.) The group re-signs to Atlantic.

1965 Sept After more flop singles, Atlantic drops the group.

Dec The Isleys are signed by Berry Gordy's Tamla-Motown where they are teamed with writers and producers Holland, Dozier & Holland.

1966 Apr The group's first Tamla single, *This Old Heart Of Mine*, makes US #12 and UK #47.

June *Take Some Time Out For Love* reaches US #66. LP *This Old Heart Of Mine* peaks at US #140.

Aug *I Guess I'll Always Love You* makes US #61 and UK #45.

1967 May *Got To Have You Back*, their last US pop hit on Tamla, spends 2 weeks at #93.

1968 Parting with Motown in US, the Isleys visit UK.

Nov *This Old Heart Of Mine* is reissued and hits UK #3.

Dec LP *This Old Heart Of Mine* makes UK #23.

1969 Jan Encouraged by their UK success, the brothers return to US and revive T-Neck, with Ronald as president, Rudolph vice-president and O'Kelly secretary/treasurer. They begin writing and producing their own material (and will produce other artists on the label, including The Brothers Three, Dave Cortez, Privilege and Judy White).

Feb *I Guess I'll Always Love You* reaches UK #11.

Apr *Behind A Painted Smile*, another old Tamla cut, hits UK #5.

June The first single on T-neck label, *It's Your Thing* hits US #2 (held off #1 by The Beatles'° *Get Back*) and makes UK #30.

July LP *It's Our Thing* enters the US chart to peak at #22. Despite not making the US top 20, it will sell over 2 million copies.

Aug *I Turned You On* makes US #23 and *It's Your Thing* reaches UK #30.

Sept *Black Berries* peaks at US #79. From Tamla back catalog, *Put Yourself In My Place* reaches UK #13. Ronnie, Rudolph and Kelly (he has dropped the "O") invite brothers Ernie (guitar, drums) and Marvin (bass, percussion) and cousin Chris Jasper (keyboards) to form an extended Isley Brothers, continuing to use brass sections live and in the studio. They later recruit (non-related) drummer Everett Collins.

Oct *Was It Good To You* peaks at US #83. LP *The Brothers: Isley* reaches US #180. The group is featured on one side of double LP *Live At Yankee Stadium* (US #169), with The Edwin Hawkins Singers and Brooklyn Bridge on the other.

1970 Oct *Get Into Something* peaks at US #89, after two previous singles *Keep On Doin'* (Feb.) and *Girls Will Be Girls, Boys Will Be Boys* (Aug.) climb no higher than US #75.

1971 Feb *Freedom* peaks at US #72.

Aug The Isleys' cover of Stephen Stills' *Love The One You're With* is their biggest hit in 2 years, reaching US #18.

Oct *Spill The Wine* climbs to US #49. LP *Givin' It Back*, comprising only cover versions, including James Taylor's° *Fire And Rain*, two Stephen Stills songs, and a medley of Neil Young's° *Ohio* and Jimi Hendrix's° *Machine Gun*, makes US #67.

1972 Jan A cover of Dylan's° *Lay Lady Lay* peaks at US #71.

Apr *Lay-Away* climbs to US #54.

Aug LP *Brother, Brother, Brother* begins a 33-week US chart run, peaking at #29.

Sept *Pop That Thang* reaches US #24.
Nov *Work To Do* makes US #51.
1973 Apr LP *The Isleys Live* climbs to US #139.
July *That Lady*, with T-Neck switching distribution from Buddah to CBS, begins a 20-week chart run, hitting US #6 and selling over 2 million copies.
Sept *That Lady* makes UK #14. Rock-tinged LP *3+3*, recorded at Record Plant West in Hollywood, enters the US chart to hit #8, but fails in UK.
Dec LP *The Isleys' Greatest Hits* makes US #195.
1974 Jan *What It Comes Down To* reaches US #55.
Feb *Highway Of My Life* makes UK #25.
Apr A revival of Seals & Crofts' smash *Summer Breeze* peaks at US #60.
June *Summer Breeze* makes UK #16.
Sept *Live It Up* reaches US #52, as live LP *Live It Up* makes US #14 and goes platinum.
1975 Jan *Midnight Sky* peaks at US #73.
June LP *The Heat Is On* begins a 40-week US chart run, during which it will top the US chart, giving the group its second platinum LP.
July *Fight The Power* hits US #4. The Isleys play the Bay area Kool Jazz Festival, Cal.
1976 Jan *For The Love Of You (Part 1 & 2)* reaches US #22.
May LP *Harvest For The World* sells a half million copies in its first 3 days of US release. It hits US #9 and makes UK #50, The Isley Brothers' third consecutive platinum LP.
June *Who Loves You Better* reaches US #47.
July The title track from *Harvest For The World*, an anti-hunger peace song, makes US #63 but hits UK #10.
1977 Apr LP *Go For Your Guns* begins a 34-week US chart run. It hits #6 and earns another platinum disk.
May *The Pride* makes US #63, as LP *Go For Your Guns* reaches UK #46.
June *Livin' In The Life* climbs to US #40.
Sept Second T-Neck compilation, *Forever Gold*, reaches US #58.
1978 Apr LP *Showdown* is released. It will hit US #4 and be the fifth consecutive platinum album.
May Disco single *Take Me To The Next Phase* peaks at UK #50.
June LP *Showdown* makes UK #50.
1979 June LP *Winner Takes All*, recorded at Bearsville studio, New York, enters the US chart to peak at #14.
Dec *It's A Disco Night (Rock Don't Stop)*, stalls at US #90 but makes UK #14.
1980 Apr LP *Go All The Way* hits US #8 and goes platinum. *Don't Say Goodnight (It's Time For Love)* makes US #39.
1981 Mar LP *Grand Slam* peaks at US #28.
May *Hurry Up And Wait* reaches US #58.
Oct The Isleys' second LP of the year, *Inside You*, peaks at US #45, the first to fall after nine successive gold or platinum LPs.
1982 Aug LP *The Real Deal* stalls at US #87.
1983 June LP *Between The Sheets* returns the group to gold status, reaching US #19.
July The title track from *Between The Sheets* makes UK #52.
1984 After 15 years together, the two younger Isley brothers and Chris Jasper split from the group to form Isley, Jasper, Isley, and negotiate a separate deal with CBS/Epic. (The split is apparently acrimonious and the two groups will have little do with each other.)
1985 Feb Isley, Jasper, Isley's debut LP *Broadway's Closer To Sunset Boulevard* reaches US #135, while *Kiss And Tell* peaks at US #63. They almost exclusively reflect the rock side of The Isley Brothers and soul fans reject the LP.
Nov Isley, Jasper, Isley's gospel-styled *Caravan Of Love* makes US #51 and UK #52. The LP of the same title peaks at US #77 with Isley, Jasper, Isley having returned to soul. In their promotion they claim they were responsible for all The Isley Brothers'hits of the past 10 years.
Dec LP *Masterpiece*, with The Isley Brothers signed to Warner Bros., peaks at US #140 but *Colder Are My Nights* fails to chart.
1986 Mar [31] Kelly Isley dies of a heart attack, aged 48.
Dec UK group The Housemartins° top the UK chart with an a cappella version of *Caravan Of Love*.
1987 June Third Isley, Jasper, Isley LP *Different Drummer* fails to chart.
July The Isley Brothers LP *Smooth Sailin'* makes US #64. It is written and produced by US soul singer Angela Winbush.
1988 Feb Chris Jasper solo LP *Superbad* peaks at US #182.
Mar The Isley Brothers LP *Greatest Hits*, including cuts by Isley, Jasper, Isley, is a UK-only compilation and makes #41.
Sept The Christians'° revival of *Harvest For The World* hits UK #8, taken from summer Olympics LP *One Moment In Time*.

IT'S A BEAUTIFUL DAY

David LaFlamme (electric violin)
Pattie Santos (vocals)
Bill Gregory (guitar)
Tom Fowler (bass)
Val Fuentes (drums)

1967 July The group is formed in San Francisco, US, by classically-trained LaFlamme (b. Apr.5, 1941, Salt Lake City, Ut., US). Their name is inspired by the weather condition on the day they form.
1968 The group signs to local label Sound Records after becoming a popular live attraction, mainly through LaFlamme's distinctive efforts on unique five-string violin, and the appeal of song *White Bird*, written by LaFlamme and his wife Linda.
1969 May LP *It's A Beautiful Day*, originally released on Sound, is picked up for national distribution by CBS/Columbia Records, together with the group's recording contract.
Aug LP *It's A Beautiful Day* reaches US #47.
1970 May LP *It's A Beautiful Day* climbs higher in UK to #28, boosted by a group tour.
June [28] Visiting UK and Europe, the group plays the Bath Festival, alongside Led Zeppelin°, Pink Floyd°, Santana°, Donovan° and others.
July LP *Marrying Maiden* makes US #28 and UK #45.
1972 Jan After personnel changes, LP *Choice Quality Stuff/Anytime* reaches US #130.
Dec LP *Live At Carnegie Hall* reaches US #144.
1973 Apr LP *It's A Beautiful Day . . . Today* reaches US #114, and is their final chart success. They will disband in 1974 after one further LP, *1001 Nights*.
1977 Jan David LaFlamme re-emerges as a soloist on Amherst Records. LP *White Bird* reaches US #159, while the extracted title track (an updating of the original It's *A Beautiful Day* favorite) makes US singles chart where that original failed, peaking at #89.

THE JACKSON 5/THE JACKSONS

Sigmund "Jackie" Jackson (vocals)
Toriano "Tito" Jackson (vocals)
Jermaine Jackson (vocals)
Marlon Jackson (vocals)
Michael Jackson (vocals)

1963 The group is first formed as a trio in Gary, Ind., US, by Jackie (b. May 4, 1951, Gary), Tito (b. Oct.15, 1953, Gary) and Jermaine (b. Dec.11, 1954, Gary), the three oldest sons of steelworks crane driver Joe Jackson (an ex-guitarist for The Falcons) and wife Kathy. Initially known as The Jackson Family, the trio recruits cousins Johnny Jackson and Ronnie Rancifer as drummer and pianist, and begins to play dates around Gary.
1964 Younger brothers Marlon (b. Mar.12, 1957, Gary) and Michael (b. Aug.29, 1958, Gary) join the group in place of the cousins (who stay as backing musicians), and they become The Jackson 5.
1965 They enter and win a local talent contest at Roosevelt High School in Gary, performing The Temptations'° *My Girl*.
1966 The group begins to play further afield, with father Joe Jackson as manager driving them to other cities (most frequently Chicago) in a Volkswagen van. On a trip to New York, they compete in another talent contest at Harlem's Apollo Theater, and win.
1967 The group supports Gladys Knight & The Pips° at an Indiana gig, and Knight, recently signed to Motown, notes to label boss Berry Gordy Jr. that the act is worth considering.
1968 *Big Boy*, produced by Gordon Keith, is recorded for Ben Brown's Gary-based Steeltown label, without success. The group is again noted by a Motown act, Bobby Taylor & The Vancouvers, which also recommends that the label should check it out.
1969 After seeing the brothers perform, while attending with Diana Ross° a campaign benefit concert for Gary's mayor Richard Hatcher, Berry Gordy Jr. signs them and moves them to Hollywood for grooming and rehearsals. The Jackson family moves to Cal.
Oct [18] The group's first live performance as a Motown act is at The Hollywood Palace, with Diana Ross° and The Supremes° and others. Their first Motown recording is a song written by Freddie

Perren, Fonce Mizell and Deke Richards, (collectively, with Berry Gordy, The Corporation), originally intended for Gladys Knight & The Pips°. Gordy suggests it should be re-written with the new, young group in mind.

1970 Jan *I Want You Back*, with Michael on lead vocal, tops the US chart for 4 weeks and is a million-seller.

Feb Debut LP *Diana Ross Presents The Jackson 5*, a Berry Gordy PR exercise giving the impression that it is Ross° who has discovered the brothers, hits US #5, as *I Want You Back* hits UK #2.

Apr *ABC*, written by the same team in a similar style to *I Want You Back*, affirms the popularity of the group's sound – unlike anything else heard on Motown – and is a second million-seller. It tops the US chart for 2 weeks, deposing The Beatles'° *Let It Be*. The debut LP, meanwhile, reaches UK #16.

June The group becomes the first act to top the US Hot 100 with its first three chart entries, as *The Love You Save*, a third million-seller, hits #1 for 2 weeks. Meanwhile, *ABC* hits UK #8.

Aug *The Love You Save* hits UK #7. The brothers' second LP, *ABC*, hits US #4 and UK #22.

Sept [26] Motown announces that The Jackson 5 have sold 10 million disks in 9 months.

Oct *Mama's Pearl*, written by The Corporation in a similar uptempo style to the three previous chart-toppers, intended as the fourth single, is passed over by Gordy in favor of a complete contrast – ballad *I'll Be There*, co-written by the group's producer, Hal Davis. It tops the US chart for 5 weeks, and is Motown's biggest-selling single to date, in excess of 4 million copies. LP *Third Album*, which includes the single, hits US #4.

Dec LP *The Jackson 5 Christmas Album*, combining traditional and contemporary seasonal songs, is 1970's top-selling Christmas disk (#1 on *Billboard*'s annual Christmas LPs chart, it will re-chart during the festive seasons of the next 3 years).

1971 Jan *I'll Be There* hits UK #4.

Mar *Mama's Pearl* is issued as follow-up and hits US #2, held from #1 by The Osmonds'° *One Bad Apple* – an imitation of The Jackson 5 sound by a group which had earlier specialized in country-styled harmony singing. *Mama's Pearl* is a further million-seller and also makes UK #25.

June *Never Can Say Goodbye*, another slower-paced song written by Clifton Davis, is the brothers' sixth consecutive million-seller, hitting US #2 (behind Three Dog Night's° *Joy To The World*) and reaching UK #33. Their third LP, *Maybe Tomorrow*, reaches US #11.

Aug The title track from *Maybe Tomorrow* peaks at US #20.

Sept [11] An animated "Jackson 5" series airs on US ABC TV.

Nov LP *Goin' Back To Indiana* reaches US #16. It is the soundtrack of a US TV Jackson 5 special.

1972 Feb *Sugar Daddy* hits US #10, but fails to chart in UK. Meanwhile, LP *Jackson 5 Greatest Hits*, a compilation of the singles to date, reaches US #12.

May A revival of Thurston Harris' *Little Bitty Pretty One* (a close musical relative of Michael Jackson's° solo US #13 revival of *Rockin' Robin*) reaches US #13.

Aug LP *Lookin' Through The Windows* hits US #7. The title track makes US #16.

Oct Compilation LP *Jackson 5 Greatest Hits* reaches UK #26.

Nov Following Michael's solo successes for Motown, the label releases Jermaine's first solo single *That's How Love Goes*, which reaches US #46 with LP *Jermaine* peaking at US #27.

Dec *Corner Of The Sky*, from Broadway musical *Pippin*, makes US #18. In UK, LP *Lookin' Through The Windows* reaches #16 and the extracted title track hits #9 – their first UK hit single for almost 18 months. At the same time, the brothers' version of seasonal *Santa Claus Is Coming To Town* is released in UK and reaches UK #43.

1973 Mar The group's version of Jackson Browne's° *Doctor My Eyes*, recorded as an LP track, is released as a UK single after the writer's own US hit version has failed in UK, and hits #9. In US, Jermaine follows his hit debut with a revival of Shep & The Limelites' 1961 doo-wop ballad hit *Daddy's Home*, taken from his debut LP after strong radio play. It hits US #9 and earns him a solo gold disk.

May LP *Skywriter* reaches US #44, while *Hallelujah Day*, taken from it, makes US #28.

July The Jacksons are the first major US black group to tour Australia. Meanwhile, *Hallelujah Day* peaks at UK #20, and Jermaine's solo LP *Come Into My Life* makes US #152.

Sept The title track from LP *Skywriter*, not used as a US single, reaches UK #25.

Oct *Get It Together*, the title track from the brothers' forthcoming LP, makes US #28.

Nov LP *Get It Together* peaks at US #100, while Jermaine's single *You're In Good Hands* makes US #79. (It will be his last solo success for 3 years.) Motown tries out another brother, Jackie, as a soloist, but his LP *Jackie Jackson* fails and the experiment is not repeated.

Dec [15] Jermaine marries Berry Gordy's daughter Hazel, in LA. (This will have important ramifications when the group later leaves Motown.)

1974 Feb A tour of Africa is cut short after only a week when the brothers are unable to adjust to the food and water.

May *Dancing Machine*, taken from LP *Get It Together*, hits US #2 behind Ray Stevens'° *The Streak*, and is the group's biggest-selling US single since *Never Can Say Goodbye*.

May [13] 43 arrests are made at a concert by the group at RFK Stadium, Washington, D.C., after bottles are hurled by youths outside the venue, injuring over 50 people.

Nov LP *Dancing Machine* (the second consecutive Jackson 5 LP to contain the title track) makes US #16. Meanwhile, the group sings backing vocals on Stevie Wonder's° *You Haven't Done Nothin'*, which tops the US chart.

Dec Taken from the LP, *Whatever You Got, I Want* peaks at US #38.

1975 Mar A two-part single, *I Am Love* (7 mins. 56 secs. in total), reaches US #15.

May The Jackson 5 leave Motown to sign to Epic Records in a deal which will allow more recording freedom. It is revealed that they were receiving only 2.7% royalties on Motown sales and were not allowed to write their own material. Motown files a $20 million suit for breach of contract (the case will finally be settled in 1980). Jermaine, married into the Gordy family, remains at Motown as a soloist and leaves the group. Younger brother Randy (b. Oct.29, 1962, Gary) replaces him and sisters LaToya (b. May 29, 1956, Gary) and Rebbie (b. Maureen Jackson, May 29, 1950, Gary) join the line-up temporarily.

July LP *Moving Violation*, the group's last Motown recording, reaches US #36, while *Forever Came Today*, a revival of former Motown stablemates The Supremes° 1968 US hit, peaks at US #60.

1976 June [16] "The Jacksons", a 4-week summer variety show, begins on US CBS TV. The shows feature the group plus sisters LaToya, Rebbie and Janet, plus guests and a regular comedy sketch team.

Aug Motown triple compilation LP *Jackson Five Anthology* (which also includes Michael's and Jermaine's solo hits on the label) reaches US #84.

Nov Jermaine's solo LP *My Name Is Jermaine*, on Motown, makes US #164, and extracted *Let's Be Young Tonight* reaches US #55.

1977 Jan US CBS TV series "The Jacksons" has a second and longer run (through Mar.).

Feb *Enjoy Yourself*, the group's first Epic single (as The Jacksons, since Motown owns The Jackson 5 name) is their biggest seller since *Dancing Machine* 3 years earlier, hitting US #6 and earning a gold disk. Debut Epic LP *The Jacksons* reaches US #36.

Apr *Enjoy Yourself* peaks at UK #42.

May On tour in UK for the first time in 5 years, The Jacksons participate in the celebrations for Queen Elizabeth II's Silver Jubilee at the King's Theatre, Glasgow, Scotland. Meanwhile, written by and recorded with producers Kenny Gamble and Leon Huff at Philadelphia International Records, *Show You The Way To Go* climbs to US #28.

June Boosted by the group's just-completed UK concert tour, *Show You The Way To Go* tops the UK chart for a week, the group's first and only UK #1 hit.

July LP *The Jacksons* reaches UK #54.

Sept *Dreamer*, taken from the LP, makes UK #22, while Jermaine's solo LP *Feel The Fire* peaks at US #174.

Nov *Goin' Places*, the title track from the group's forthcoming LP, reaches US #52 and UK #26.

Dec LP *Goin' Places* makes US #63 and UK #45.

1978 Feb *Even Though You've Gone* reaches UK #31.

Mar [1-3] Jackie Jackson wins four trophies at the first annual "Rock'n'Roll Sports Classic", a charity event to be televised in May, pitting celebrities against each other in sporting contests.

Nov *Blame It On The Boogie* reaches US #54 and hits UK #8,

outselling a competing version on Atco by its writer Mick Jackson (no relation).

1979 Feb LP *Destiny*, the first self-produced brothers LP, reaches US #11, is a million-seller and earns a platinum disk. The title track makes UK #39.

May *Shake Your Body (Down To The Ground)*, taken from LP *Destiny*, hits US #7 and sells over 2 million copies in US, earning a platinum disk. It also hits UK #4, while LP *Destiny* reaches UK #33.

1980 The Motown 1975 suit is finally settled, with The Jacksons making a payment of $600,000 (Motown having claimed $20 million), and the label retaining all rights to use of The Jackson 5 name.

July Jermaine returns after a 3-year chart absence, with Stevie Wonder°-written and produced *Let's Get Serious*, which hits US #9. It is his first UK solo success, hitting #8. Simultaneously, LP of the same title hits US #6 (earning a gold disk) and reaches UK #22.

Aug *Burnin' Hot*, extracted from Jermaine's solo LP as a UK single, reaches #32.

Sept In US, *You're Supposed To Keep Your Love For Me*, also Wonder°-penned, is Jermaine's solo follow-up and reaches US #34.

Oct The Jacksons' self-produced LP *Triumph* reaches UK #13.

Nov *Lovely One* reaches US #12 and UK #29. It is taken from LP *Triumph*, which hits US #10 and is the group's second consecutive platinum LP.

Dec LaToya Jackson, the fifth oldest in the family (and the second daughter), signed as a solo artist to Polydor, reaches US #116 with her eponymous debut LP.

1981 Jan The group's *Heartbreak Hotel*, also from LP *Triumph*, reaches US #22 and UK #44. Meanwhile, Jermaine's solo LP *Jermaine* – his second for Motown by this title – makes US #44.

Apr The group's *Can You Feel It* hits UK #6 but stalls at US #77.

May Jermaine's *You Like Me, Don't You?* reaches US #50 and UK #41.

July The group begins a 36-city US tour, during which live recordings are made for LP *Jacksons Live*. (It will be released at the end of the year and the tour will gross $5½ million, $100,000 being donated to Atlanta Children's Foundation after a gig at The Omni in Atlanta, Ga.)

Aug *Walk Right Now* makes only US #73, but is a second consecutive UK top 10 hit at #7.

Sept LaToya Jackson's LP *My Special Love* peaks at US #175.

Nov Jermaine's solo LP *I Like Your Style* makes US #86, while extracted *I'm Just Too Shy* reaches US #60.

1982 Jan Double live LP *Jacksons Live* makes US #30.

Sept Jermaine's *Let Me Tickle Your Fancy*, with backing vocals by Devo°, reaches US #18, while the LP of the same title (his last for Motown) makes US #46.

1983 May [16] Michael and Jermaine reunite with the brothers to perform on Motown's televised 25th Anniversary spectacular on US NBC TV.

Aug UK TV-advertised compilation LP *18 Greatest Hits*, on Telstar label, tops the UK chart for 3 weeks.

Nov [21] A press conference called by promoter Don King, at the Tavern on the Green in New York, announces an 18-city, 40-date US tour by The Jacksons (six-strong, with Jermaine rejoining his brothers after leaving Motown), to commence the following summer.

1984 Feb [27] The Jacksons' Pepsi ad premieres on US MTV.

Feb Jermaine signs as a soloist to Arista Records.

May Following a promotional UK visit, during which Jermaine performs tracks from his forthcoming first LP for Arista to delegates at the World DJ Convention in London, his UK-only single release *Sweetest, Sweetest* makes #52.

June [13] *State Of Shock*, taken from the group's new LP, and featuring Mick Jagger duetting on guest vocals with Michael Jackson°, is released. LA radio station K-IQQ plays it for 22 hours continuously. LP *Jermaine Jackson*, Jermaine's Arista solo debut, reaches US #19 (and UK #57 where it is retitled *Dynamite*), while sister LaToya signs to Private I label. Her only solo hit single is *Heart Don't Lie* at US #56. Her LP of the same title reaches US #149.

July [6] The "Victory" 40-concert tour opens in Kansas City, Mo. (and will gross $5½ million). It marks the first time in 8 years that all six Jackson brothers have performed together on the live stage.

July Meanwhile, Motown capitalizes on the reunion and releases compilation LP *Michael Jackson & The Jackson 5 – 14 Greatest Hits* (on a picture disk), which reaches US #168.

Aug *State Of Shock* hits US #3, earning a gold disk, and reaches UK #14. It is taken from LP *Victory* which hits UK #3.

Sept *Torture*, also from the LP, makes US #17 and UK #26. LP *Victory* hits US #4, and earns the group's third LP platinum disk. Meanwhile, Jermaine's first US single for Arista, *Dynamite*, makes US #15.

Nov *Body*, a third single from the LP, peaks at US #47. It is The Jacksons' final hit single as a group.

Dec Michael Jackson° writes and produces *Centipede*, the only hit single for older sister Rebbie who is signed to CBS/Columbia. It reaches US #24, and the LP of the same title makes US #63.

Dec [9] The Jacksons play their last show together at LA's Dodger Stadium.

1985 Jan Jermaine's *Do What You Do* reaches US #13.

Jan [28] Michael, Jackie, Marlon, Randy, Tito, and LaToya Jackson all participate in the recording of USA For Africa's° *We Are The World*, in aid of African famine relief, which will be a worldwide #1 and multi-million seller.

Mar Jermaine duets with actress/singer Pia Zadora on *When The Rain Begins To Fall*, taken from film *Voyage of the Rock Aliens*. It makes US #54 and UK #68, while *Do What You Do* is Jermaine's biggest-selling UK single, hitting #6.

July Jermaine's *(Closest Thing To) Perfect*, from Jamie Lee Curtis movie *Perfect*, reaches US #67.

1986 Apr *I Think It's Love* by Jermaine is his biggest solo seller for 2 years, peaking at US #16.

July Jermaine's solo *Do You Remember Me?* makes US #75.

1987 Oct Marlon releases debut LP, *Baby Tonight*, which makes US #188. Singles *Don't Go* and *Baby Tonight* both have success on the R&B chart, but fail to cross over.

FREDDIE JACKSON

1976/83 Jackson (b. Oct.2, 1956), the middle of five children raised by his mother in Harlem, having sung in his local White Rock Baptist church, where he met Ashford and Simpson°, and earned dollar bills given by old ladies who thought he was cute, after leaving high school, works in a bank as a computer operator until he has saved enough to pursue an artistic career. Teaming up with Paul Laurence, he forms a band called LJE, playing top 40 cover versions in New York nightclubs. Jackson moves to the West Coast, where he joins Mystic Merlin.

FREDDIE JACKSON *cont.*

1984 On his return to New York, Jackson begins vocal backing on tours for Evelyn King, Lillo Thomas, Angela Bofill and others including Harry Belafonte° and Melba Moore. She signs him to her Hush Productions management company and gets a worldwide deal with Capitol.

Oct Jackson starts recording his debut LP.

1985 May Debut LP *Rock Me Tonight* is released. It will hit US #10 and reach UK #73. Jackson sets out on an 89-date US tour with Melba Moore.

Aug *Rock Me Tonight (For Old Times Sake)* reaches US #18 and tops the US R&B chart for 6 weeks.

Nov *You Are My Lady* reaches US #12.

Dec *You Are My Lady* makes UK #49.

1986 Feb *He'll Never Love You (Like I Do)* peaks at US #25.

Mar *Rock Me Tonight (For Old Times Sake)* reaches UK #18.

Sept Jackson and Joe Cocker° guest on syndicated TV "Melba and Friends" 1-hour special.

Sept [23] Jackson, James Brown° and Melba Moore headline an anti-crack rally at New York's Plaza Hotel.

Oct *Tasty Love* peaks at UK #73.

Oct [30] Jackson begins a 55-city tour at the Civic Center, Saginaw, Mich. as US leg of worldwide "Tasty" tour, with Levert and Meli'sa Morgan.

Nov Jackson and Melba Moore top the R&B chart with *A Little Bit More*. The following week Jackson replaces himself at #1 with *Tasty Love*. He becomes the first artist to achieve this feat since Dinah Washington's *This Bitter Earth* replaced her duet with Brook Benton°, *A Rockin' Good Way*.

Dec *Tasty Love* makes US #41. Second LP *Just Like The First Time* reaches UK #30.

Dec [31] Jackson joins Air Supply°, Gladys Knight & The Pips° and Melba Moore for CBS-TV's "Happy New Year America".

1987 Feb LP *Just Like The First Time* spends 26 weeks at the top of the R&B chart, crosses over to make US #23 and is certified platinum (Jackson's second). He becomes the first black artist in the 80s to have five #1s on the US R&B chart when *Have You Ever Loved Somebody* hits the top.

Mar *Have You Ever Loved Somebody* makes US #69.

Aug *Jam Tonight* tops the R&B chart and he becomes the only artist in the 80s to have six #1s. It also reaches US #32.

Nov *Look Around* makes US R&B #69.

1988 July *Nice 'N' Slow*, featuring Najée on sax, makes UK #56.

Aug LP *Don't Let Love Slip Away*, produced by Paul Laurence, reaches US #48 and UK #24. Jackson begins a world tour in US as part of the Budweiser Music Festival.

Sept Jackson visits UK to play 4 sell-out concerts at London's Hammersmith Odeon, before embarking on a tour of Japan. *Crazy (For Me)* is extracted from LP *Don't Let Love Slip Away* as a UK single, and makes #41. *Nice 'N' Slow* reaches US #61.

JANET JACKSON

1973 Jackson (b. May 16, 1966, Gary, Ind., US), the youngest in a family of 9 and sister of The Jackson 5°, appears in her brothers' stage show for the first time at age 7, at MGM Grand Hotel, Las Vegas, Nev.

1977 Sept She appears on US TV as Penny Gordon Woods in CBS sitcom series "Good Times". This leads to further appearances in "Different Stokes" and "Fame".

1982 Nov Signed to A&M Records, she promotes her debut LP *Janet Jackson* by touring high schools and encouraging kids to stay in school. The LP reaches US #63.

1983 Jan *Young Love*, taken from the LP, reaches US #64.

Mar *Come Give Your Love To Me* makes US #58.

1984 Aug She elopes with James DeBarge in Michigan Falls. (The marriage is annulled 7 months later and she returns to the Jackson family home, shared with Michael, Tito, and mother Katherine, in Encino, Cal.)

Nov LP *Dream Street* reaches US #147, with help from Jesse Johnson, Giorgio Moroder and Cliff Richard°.

1986 Jan LP *Control*, produced by Jimmy Jam and Terry Lewis, is released.

Mar Jackson begins a 13-city promo tour.

Apr *What Have You Done For Me Lately* hits US #4.

May *What Have You Done For Me Lately* hits UK #3.

June *Nasty* climbs to UK #19.

July *Nasty* hits US #3. LP *Control* tops the US chart, achieving platinum status. Jackson, just turned 20, becomes the youngest artist, since 13-year-old Little Stevie Wonder°, to top the LP chart.

Sept *When I Think Of You* hits UK #10.

Oct *When I Think Of You* tops the US chart for 2 weeks. 14 years since brother Michael Jackson° topped the charts with *Ben*, they become the first siblings in the rock era to have solo #1s.

Nov *Control* peaks at UK #42. *Control – The Videos* is released.

Dec Jackson begins a US tour. She tops *Billboard*'s year end survey in six categories: Top Black Artist, Top Pop Singles Artist, Top Pop Singles Artist Female, Top Dance Sales Artist, Top Dance Club Play Artist and Top Black Singles Artist.

1987 Jan *Control* hits US #5 and tops the R&B chart.

Jan [26] Jackson is nominated in nine categories at the 14th annual American Music Awards at LA's Shrine Auditorium. She wins two: Best R&B Single (*Nasty*) and Best Female R&B Video Artist.

Feb [1] Jackson guests on the first "Hitline USA", TV show.

Feb [24] Jackson makes an impressive live appearance at the 29th annual Grammy awards singing *What Have You Done For Me Lately* with help from producers Jam and Lewis, but fails to win any awards.

Mar *Let's Wait Awhile* hits US #2, making five top 10 hits from one LP.

Apr A remix of *Let's Wait Awhile* launches A&M's dance-oriented Breakout label in UK, and hits #3.

June Jackson guest-vocals on Herb Alpert's° Jam and Lewis-produced *Diamonds*. It hits US #5 and tops the R&B chart.

Aug A remix of *The Pleasure Principle* tops the R&B chart as it drops from its peak position of US #14 on Hot 100. *Control – The Videos Part II* is released.

Sept [11] *Nasty* video wins an award for its choreographer Paula Abdul at MTV Video Music awards at LA's Universal Amphitheater.

1988 Nov Jackson records a new LP with producers Jam and Lewis.

JOE JACKSON

1971 Sept Jackson (b. Aug.11, 1954, Burton-on-Trent, UK), having left school with an S-level examination pass in music, goes to the Royal College of Music in London on a piano scholarship.

1974 After leaving college, he joins pub and covers band Edward Bear.

1976 Jackson joins Arms & Legs, recording three unsuccessful singles for UK MAM, penned by him. (Mark Andrews is lead singer, later to emerge on A&M as Mark Andrews & The Gents.)

1977 Jackson leaves Arms & Legs to go to Portsmouth, UK, and becomes a featured performer at the local Playboy Club, and then musical director for TV show "Opportunity Knocks" winners, Coffee and Cream, who are popular on the cabaret circuit.

1978 Moving to London, he records a demo LP of his own songs. Through this recording he nearly signs to United Artists, but the LP is passed to Albion Music. David Kershenbaum of A&M hears it and signs him.

Oct *Is She Really Going Out With Him?* is released. Jackson forms a regular band; himself on vocals and keyboards, Gary Sandford on guitar, Graham Maby ex-Arms & Legs on bass and Dave Houghton on drums.

1979 Jan LP *Look Sharp!*, produced by Kershenbaum, reaches UK #40 and US #20. *Sunday Papers* and *One More Time* fail to sell.

May Jackson tours US where *Is She Really Going Out With Him?* reaches US #21. Reissued in UK, it climbs to #13.

Oct LP *I'm The Man*, produced by Kershenbaum, reaches UK #12 and US #22.

1980 Feb *It's Different For Girls* hits UK #5.

Mar *Kinda Kute* and *The Harder They Come* both fail to chart.

July Jackson produces UK reggae act The Rasses' LP *Natural Wild*.

Oct LP *Beat Crazy*, credited to The Joe Jackson Band, reaches UK #42 and US #41. It is the last LP with his regular rock line-up. *Mad At You* is released but fails to chart.

1981 *Beat Crazy* and *One To One* flop.

June LP *Joe Jackson's Jumpin' Jive* featuring 1940s and 1950s bop and jive music, makes UK #14 and US #42. The title track reaches UK #43. Jackson tours with the band featured on the LP, which includes an extensive horn section. Jackson produces LP by Portsmouth-based band The Keys.

1982 After the break-up of his marriage, he moves to New York.

June LP *Night And Day* becomes his biggest UK hit at #3, after beginning as a poor seller, and hits US #4.

Oct *Steppin' Out* hits US #6. (It will hit UK #6 in 1983.)

1983 Feb *Breaking Us In Two* reaches UK #59 and US #18.

Sept Soundtrack LP *Mike's Murder* reaches US #64. It is his first attempt at movie scoring. He was originally commissioned to write one song but completed an entire LP (though much of the music is excised from the film itself). *Memphis*, from the movie, reaches US #85.

1984 Mar LP *Body And Soul*, another Jackson and Kershenbaum production and the last to feature Graham Maby on bass, peaks at UK #14 and US #20.

Apr *Happy Ending*, with vocals from Elaine Caswell, makes UK #58.

June *Be My Number Two* reaches UK #70 and *You Can't Get What You Want* climbs to US #15.

Aug *Happy Ending* peaks at US #57.

1985 Jackson composes music for Japanese movie *Shijin No Ie (House Of The Poet)*.

1986 Apr Three-sided live LP *Big World*, recorded direct to 2-track in New York, is released to limited appeal and reaches US #34 and UK #41.

1987 Apr LP *Will Power*, mainly instrumental with orchestra and jazz session players, makes only US #131.

1988 May Double LP *Live 1980/86*, featuring live material covering four differing line-ups, reaches UK #66 and US #91. He produces LP for reggae outfit The Toasters.

Aug Movie soundtrack *Tucker* and single *(It's A) Shape In A Drape*, written and performed by Jackson, are released.

MICHAEL JACKSON

1963 Jackson (b. Aug.29, 1958, Gary, Ind., US) is found by his mother Katharine practising dance steps in front of the mirror. She and husband, Joe, are keen to promote their nine offspring's musical ability. Michael, age 5, also performs *Climb Every Mountain* to his kindergarten class. (With Joe as manager, Michael will join four of his brothers, Jackie, Tito, Jermaine and Marlon to form The Jackson 5°.)

1969 As Berry Gordy has signed the group to his Motown label, the Jackson family moves to LA, Cal., the label's new headquarters. At a Sammy Davis Jr. showbiz gathering, Quincy Jones meets 10-year-old Jackson for the first time (although Jackson will not recall the event).

1970 The Jackson family settles in Encino, Cal.

1971 Dec 2 years after the first Jackson 5° hit, Jackson, signed as a solo to Tamla Motown, hits US #4 with ballad *Got To Be There*. He also appears on labelmate (and life-time friend) Diana Ross'° US TV special "Diana".

1972 Mar *Got To Be There* hits UK #5, while the LP of the same name peaks at US #14. Jackson spends much time with Diana Ross° on the set of her current movie, *Lady Sings the Blues*.

May *Rockin' Robin* hits US #2, kept off the top by Roberta Flack's° *The First Time Ever I Saw Your Face*.

June *Rockin' Robin* hits UK #3, as UK release of LP *Got To Be There* climbs to #37.

July *I Wanna Be Where You Are* reaches US #16.

Sept With the Bill Withers° original a flop in UK, Motown releases Jackson's version of *Ain't No Sunshine* in UK only. It hits #8. Meanwhile, LP *Ben* hits US #5.

Oct [14] Extracted title track *Ben* hits US #1. Written by American composer Walter Scharf and UK lyricist Don Black, the ballad was written for movie *Ben* (a follow-up to *Willard*). Black is responsible for suggesting that Jackson vocalizes the song.

Dec *Ben* hits UK #7, as parent LP climbs to UK #17.

1973 May Tamla releases LP *Music And Me*, which peaks at US #92, while *With A Child's Heart* makes US #50.

1975 Mar *We're Almost There* reaches US #54, but Jackson's final official solo Motown LP release, *Forever, Michael*, makes only US #101. (He will not release another LP for 4 years.)

May Although brother Jermaine will stay at the label, the remaining group quits Motown and re-starts as The Jacksons° on Epic. Still in the family line-up, Michael also signs a solo deal with Epic which allows creative freedom and a considerable rise in The Jackson 5° 2.7% Motown royalty.

July Tamla 45, *Just A Little Bit Of You*, peaks at US #23.

Oct The first of many Motown Jackson compilation LPs, *The Best Of Michael Jackson* falters at US #156.

1977 July Rehearsals begin in New York for a movie version of musical *The Wiz*, already a stage success adapted from *The Wizard of Oz*, Jackson is chosen to play the Scarecrow opposite Diana Ross'° Dorothy and Richard Pryor's Wiz. While filming, Jackson stays at sister LaToya's Manhattan apartment. The project links Michael professionally with producer Quincy Jones, responsible for its soundtrack.

1978 Oct A film LP *The Wiz* is released through MCA, on which Diana Ross° and Michael Jackson duet on *Ease On Down The Road*, which reaches US #41 and UK #45. Jackson spends 6 months recording his debut solo LP for Epic.

1979 Mar First single for Epic, *You Can't Win*, peaks at US #81 but fails to chart in UK.

Oct Released on July 28th, Jackson-penned dance number, *Don't Stop 'Til You Get Enough* hits US #1, his first for 7 years. It also hits UK #3 and propels parent LP, *Off The Wall* (released in Aug. and produced by Jones) to hit US #3 and UK #5. (It will sell over 10 million copies worldwide.)

Dec *Off The Wall* title track hits UK #7.

1980 Jan *Rock With You* also hits US #1, nudging KC & The Sunshine Band's° *Please Don't Go*.

Feb [27] Jackson is awarded his first Grammy as *Don't Stop 'Til You Get Enough* wins as Best R&B Performance.

Mar *Rock With You* hits UK #7.

Apr Title cut from *Off The Wall* hits US #10.

May Ballad *She's Out Of My Life* hits UK #3 and peaks at US #10 within a month. Jackson becomes the first solo artist to enjoy four hits from one LP (a record he himself will break).

Aug *Girlfriend*, penned by Paul McCartney°, reaches UK #41, as Michael rejoins The Jacksons° to promote new LP *Triumph*.

1981 May Motown issues unreleased tracks compilation LP *One Day In Your Life*. It peaks at US #144. During The Jacksons'° "Triumph" tour, Jackson collapses from exhaustion in New Orleans, La.

June Becoming an instant middle-of-the-road airplay favorite, *One Day In Your Life* tops the UK chart (his first UK #1).

Aug Motown follow-up *We're Almost There* reaches UK #46. Repromoted LP *Best Of Michael Jackson* makes UK #11 while LP *One Day In Your Life* peaks at UK #29.

Dec [25] Jackson calls Paul McCartney° and suggests they write and record songs together, so McCartney flies to LA to cut *The Girl Is Mine*.

1982 June Jackson and Jones work on a story-telling record book of Spielberg's hit movie *E.T.*

Aug Jackson and Jones begin work on a new LP, to be called *Thriller* at Westlake studios, LA. In addition to a formidable session musician line-up, Jones invites song contributions from ex-Heatwave° writer Rod Temperton, who offers the title track.

Oct Recorded earlier in the year, Diana Ross° releases Jackson-written *Muscles*, which will hit US #10. (The title is also the name of

Jackson's pet snake, one of an increasing number of unusual animal companions Jackson will choose to share his Encino mansion.)

Nov Jackson joins Jones-created all-star chorus on Donna Summer's° US #41 *State Of Independence*.

Dec [1] LP *Thriller* is released. (With demos originally recorded at Jackson's 24-track Encino home, some with Temperton present, the LP, produced by Jones and engineered by Bruce Swedien, will break all sales records and become the most celebrated and successful LP of all time. It will sell over 40 million copies worldwide and hit #1 in every Western country including UK and US, where it will spend a record 37 weeks at #1. From it will come an unprecedented seven top 10 US hit singles. It will sell over 1 million copies in LA alone and receive a record 12 Grammy nominations.)

Dec First extract from the LP, McCartney° duet, *The Girl Is Mine* hits UK #10.

1983 Jan *The Girl Is Mine* hits US #2. Jackson makes a quick visit to London to link with McCartney° once more to complete further songs for release on McCartney's new LP.

Feb LP *E.T. – The Extra-Terrestrial*, released on MCA, peaks at UK #82. It includes a previously unreleased Jackson track and a souvenir booklet featuring pictures of Jackson cuddling E.T.

Mar [5] Jackson-penned *Billie Jean* hits US #1. (It stays there for 7 weeks and coincides for 1 week with its UK #1 position. Having entered the US chart in Jan., it transforms the fortunes of LP *Thriller*, Jackson's career, the financial status of Epic Records and the fabric of modern music itself. Only when it hits US #1, does MTV, previously reluctant to air "black videos", begin showing the *Billie Jean* clip. Featuring self-choreographed dancesteps, the visuals combine with audio innovation to provide what many critics regard as the perfect modern single project. In contrast to future recording, Jackson's vocals for *Billie Jean* were made in one take.)

Apr [30] In an unprecedented chart feat, and separated only by Dexy's Midnight Runners'° *Come On Eileen*, Jackson's follow-up *Beat It* hits US #1, failing to replace himself at the top spot by only 1 week, the shortest gap registered since The Beatles° in 1964. (It also hits UK #3.) The song features Jones-invited Eddie Van Halen° on lead guitar, which Van Halen offers free of charge. The accompanying video, directed by Bob Giraldi at a cost of $160,000, boosts the disk's success. It features group dance routines led by Jackson, co-created with *Dreamgirls* choreographer Michael Peters.

May [16] Jackson links with his brothers to perform both group and solo spots for "25 Years of Motown" on US NBC TV. It includes a specially-choreographed performance of *Billie Jean* which is nominated for an Emmy TV award.

June *Wanna Be Startin' Something* hits UK #8 and US #5.

Aug Motown tries to cash in with *Happy*, which peaks at UK #52.

Sept Ballad *Human Nature*, still from LP *Thriller*, hits US #7. Meanwhile, opportunist female singer Lydia Murdock records "answer" disk to accusatory *Billie Jean*: *Superstar* fails in US but makes UK #14, borrowing heavily from the *Billie Jean* riff.

Nov Title track, *Thriller*, featuring a ghostly rap from horror movie veteran Vincent Price (who will not appear in the Jon Landis directed mini-epic video, the peak of Jackson's current video triumphs), hits UK #10, 6 months ahead of its US release. Meanwhile, *Say Say Say*, another McCartney° duet hits UK #2. From McCartney's LP *Pipes Of Peace*, Jackson also co-leads on track *The Man*.

Dec [2] US MTV airs the full-length *Thriller* video for first time.

Dec At the end of his most successful year to date, Jackson announces a $5 million sponsorship deal with Pepsi Cola. A rider in the contract ensures that Jackson will not have to hold or drink a can of Pepsi in any promotion. Meanwhile, *P.Y.T. (Pretty Young Thing)* hits US #10, as *Say Say Say* now tops the US chart. A UK-only released singles pack of nine records makes UK #66.

1984 Jan [26] Jackson is hospitalized with scalp burns following an accidental flare explosion on the set filming a Pepsi commercial. A spark ignites his hair on the sixth take of the Giraldi-directed ad.

Jan Doubleday Publishers announce that they will be producing a Jacqueline Onassis-edited Jackson autobiography. It will be written with the help of author Stephen Davis.

Feb Jackson features strongly on Berry Gordy Jr.'s son Kennedy's (aka Rockwell) hit single *Somebody's Watching Me* (US #2 and UK #6). Norris McWhirter bestows several Guinness World Records on Jackson for sales of *Thriller*.

Feb [27] The Pepsi ad premieres on US MTV.

Feb [28] Jackson collects an unprecedented eight Grammy awards, all linked to *Thriller* projects.

Apr [5] Jackson wins the latest in a string of Best Video awards at the second annual American Video Awards. Appropriately, video *The Making Of Michael Jackson's Thriller* is released in UK and US and becomes the best-selling music video to date. In addition to featuring the full length Landis-directed *Thriller* video, it also includes *Beat It, Billie Jean* and previously unseen rehearsal clips. As *P.Y.T.* reaches UK #11, *Thriller*, the seventh and final LP single hits US #4.

Apr [27] Philadelphia radio station W-WSH broadcasts a "No Michael Jackson" weekend in protest to his airwave saturation of the past year.

Apr Jackson returns to hospital to undergo further scalp and facial laser surgery. Song parody specialist Weird Al Yaonkovic reaches US #12 and UK #36 with novelty *Eat It*, with Rick Derringer assuming Eddie Van Halen's° solo.

May During a New York stay, Jackson expresses interest in a jacket worn by elevator operator, Hector Cormana, who gives Michael a spare.

June Jackson dons Cormana's jacket on a visit to The White House to receive a Presidential Award from President and Mrs. Reagan. Motown vault issues *Farewell My Summer Love* which reaches US #38 and UK #7. LP of same name makes US #46 and hits UK #9. Compilation LP *Michael Jackson & The Jackson 5 – 14 Greatest Hits* reaches US #168 from Motown. Jackson, meanwhile, rejoins The Jacksons° for newly-announced LP *Victory* and subsequent tour. (Completed by Jackson as a favor to his brothers, the tour will be dogged by financial and organizational problems from the moment boxing promoter Don King offers $3 million upfront advances. Michael's dissatisfaction with the reunion and the subsequent money squabbles leads him to donate his portion to children's charities.) Jackson duets with Mick Jagger on the LP's lead-off single *State Of Shock* (US #3 and UK #14).

July The official Michael Jackson doll, complete with white glove, is launched.

Aug Jackson receives death threats during the "Victory" tour and his personal security is doubled. *Girl You're So Together* reaches UK #33 on Motown. He appears as duet vocalist on brother Jermaine's new LP, on track *Tell Me I'm Not Dreaming*.

Nov Jackson unveils his Hollywood Star on the Walk of Fame, LA.

1985 Jan Following UK success of Band Aid's° single, Jackson co-writes US version, *We Are The World* for star group USA For Africa°, with Lionel Richie°, in 2½ hours.

Mar [3] Jackson visits UK to attend Madame Tussaud's Waxworks in London which is inaugurating his waxwork lookalike. Traffic comes to a standstill as Jackson jumps on to his car to wave to crowds. He also visits legendary Abbey Road recording studios.

May Jackson receives $58 million in royalties from Epic Records.

July During a year which will see no new singles or LP releases, Jackson's 15-minute space fantasy film, produced with George Lucas, begins shooting in Cal. *Captain Eo*, starring Jackson and featuring new material will take over a year to premiere, during which time exclusive distributor Disneyland/World will build a movie theater on both sites specifically to show the project.

Aug [14] Competing with both Paul McCartney° and Yoko Ono, Jackson outbids everyone to secure the ATV music publishing catalog. At $47.5 million, he gains rights to more than 250 songs written by Lennon°/McCartney°. Reports indicate that it sours relationships between McCartney and Jackson. Jackson has also bought rights to all Sly Stone° songs.

1986 Feb 14-year-old heart transplant patient Donna Ashlock, a devoted Jackson fan, receives a surprise phone call from the star, who invites her to his home for lunch and movies the following month.

Mar Jackson's manager Frank DiLeo, business affairs adviser John Branca and Pepsi president Roger Enrico complete Jackson's second contract for the soft drinks giant. This time for $15 million, it will include two further commercials and sponsorship of a world solo tour.

Aug [4] Jackson and co-producer Jones move into studio D at Westlake studios to record a follow-up to *Thriller*. Jackson has already written 62 songs for consideration and Jones invites outsiders to offer more. (The Beatles'° *Come Together* is recorded, but rejected.) Jackson insists that his 300-pound snake, Crusher, and constant chimp companion, Bubbles, are present at recording sessions. (Bubbles will enjoy studio rides on back of engineer Bruce Swedien's Great Dane.)

Sept As increasingly health-conscious Jackson buys an oxygen chamber to prolong his lifespan, a Jackson-written and produced track is released as title cut for new Diana Ross° LP *Eaten Alive*. After more than a year's preparation, Jackson's *Captain Eo*, produced by sci-fi film maker George Lucas, premieres at Disneyland. It includes never-released dance number *We Are Just Here To Save The World*, written and performed by Jackson.

Nov Shooting begins in New York on video for the title cut from new LP *Bad*. A 17-minute mini-film, directed by Martin Scorsese, its locations include the Bronx subway and the Dobbs Ferry School.

1987 Feb As recording of LP *Bad* begins the final stage, Jackson tapes video clips for two planned singles, *The Way You Make Me Feel* and *Smooth Criminal* (at a reported cost of over $5 million).

Mar During the US televised Grammy awards, Pepsi airs the new Michael Jackson teaser commercial: "This Spring . . . The Magic Returns".

May [29] Jackson offers $50,000 to buy the remains of the "Elephant Man", John Merrick. Eventually doubling his offer, the London Hospital rejects it.

June [6] Jackson severs ties with Jehovah's Witnesses, for whom he has been a long-term supporter.

June Cabaret artist Valentino Johnson spends $40,000 in plastic surgery to look like Jackson and subsequently mimics his act. DiLeo considers legal action.

July [13] Fifty of America's biggest record retail heads are invited to Jackson's Encino home to preview LP *Bad*. Hosted mainly by LaToya and Joe Jackson, dinner and a tour of the mansion are included with Michael appearing only briefly to pose for photos.

Aug [8] First single from the LP, a ballad duet with Siedah Garrett, *I Just Can't Stop Loving You* debuts on US and UK charts. It will top both charts in the coming weeks. (The duet was initially rejected by Whitney Houston° and Barbra Streisand.)

Aug [27] Jackson's LP *Bad* is previewed 4 days ahead of release on an LA radio station.

Aug [31] On a US CBS TV special, "Michael Jackson – The Magic Returns", the 17-minute *Bad* video is aired for the first time. It is clear that, with tour and promotion efforts surrounding *Bad*, Jackson intends to outsell *Thriller*, aiming for the first 50 million-selling LP. LP *Bad* is released and is the biggest-shipped LP ever worldwide. It enters US and UK charts at #1. Extensive sleeve notes include thanks to Cary Grant and Marlon Brando.

Sept [12] Having promised a solo world tour to both Pepsi and his fans, Jackson chooses 38,000-capacity Korakuen stadium, Toyko, Japan to begin a tour that will take over 1 year to complete. (It will be the biggest grossing tour of all, and will take in Japan, Australia, where some dates will be cancelled through poor ticket sales, US, Canada, UK and Europe. Jackson's personal entourage will be more than 250-strong including a chef, hairdresser and manager DiLeo, who will handle all interviews. Also included are two recent business managers, Jimmy Osmond and Marlon Brando's son, Miko.)

Oct Title cut *Bad*, written and co-produced by Jackson, hits US #1 and UK #3. UK TV compilation, credited to Michael Jackson and Diana Ross°, *Love Songs*, climbs to UK #15.

Dec *The Way You Make Me Feel* hits UK #3 and US #1. Another UK-only mix LP of old Jackson and Jackson 5° hits, *The Michael Jackson Mix*, is released. It will peak at UK #27.

1988 Feb Siedah Garrett-penned social conscience song, *Man In The Mirror*, makes UK #21.

Mar [26] *Man In The Mirror* hits US #1.

Apr A UK-remix by Stock-Aitken-Waterman studio PWL of Motown hit *I Want You Back '88* hits UK #8 for a surprised Michael Jackson & The Jackson 5°.

May From recent Stevie Wonder° LP *Characters*, Jackson duet *Get It* reaches US #80 and UK #37.

June Video compilation *The Legend Continues* immediately becomes the best-selling UK music video of all time, out-shipping *The Making Of Michael Jackson's Thriller*. As all Jackson's Epic LPs re-enter the UK chart, old Motown compilation *18 Greatest Hits* peaks at UK #85. With press silence still maintained, the much-anticipated autobiography, *Moonwalk*, is released but fails to satisfy public thirst for Jackson trivia. An immediate best-seller, he makes the point that he believes he is one of the loneliest people in the world.

July [2] *Dirty Diana* is fifth US #1 from LP *Bad*, as Jackson becomes the only artist ever to pull five chart-topping singles off one album.

July He arrives in London, UK, for a series of dates, including a record seven sold-out Wembley Stadium (72,000-capacity) performances. (At one of them, he will present audience members Prince Charles and Princess Diana with a six-figure check for The Prince's Trust Charity.) Chimp Bubbles is refused entry to UK under strict quarantine laws, but tour companion US TV actor Jimmy Safechuck is allowed in. He has appeared with Jackson in a recent Pepsi commercial and will also perform on stage. During the trip, Jackson visits London toy store, Hamleys, (where he buys a doll of himself) and record store HMV, when both agree to open for him after hours. Meanwhile a limited UK-only 5-singles souvenir pack, *Bad*, enters the UK LP chart for 1 week at #99, and *Dirty Diana* hits UK #4. It features Billy Idol's° guitarist Steve Stevens.

Sept Jackson returns to UK for more dates, including a concert at Liverpool's Aintree race course. UK press over-reacts to serious crowd problems caused by the number of fans. *Another Part Of Me* peaks at US #11 and UK #15.

Oct [23] Jackson joins Berry Gordy Jr. to tour the house where Gordy launched Motown Records in 1959. Jackson donates $125,000 to the Motown Museum as he prepares for two Detroit concerts in Nov.

Nov *Smooth Criminal*, the seventh single from LP *Bad*, is released.

Dec *Moonwalker*, starring Jackson and featuring Sean Lennon among others, opens in movie theaters throughout US and UK.

MILLIE JACKSON

1964 Jackson (b. July 15, 1943, Thompson, Ga., US), having run away from life with her preacher grandfather at age 14, and lived in New York, working mainly as a model, makes her live vocal debut with an impromptu performance at Harlem's Palm Cafe, the result of a wager with friends. Persuaded that she could make a success of singing, she begins to take it seriously, obtaining her first booking at Club Zanzibar, Hoboken, N.J., US. (For 8 years she will work as a club singer part-time in the evenings, while continuing her day job. Her unique stage act, mixing raunchy and sometimes X-rated raps with soul ballads, is slowly honed during this period.)

1969 A one-off deal with MGM Records produces just one single which does not sell.

1972 Jan She signs to Spring Records and *A Child Of God (It's Hard To Believe)*, co-written by Jackson, makes US R&B #22.

June Second single *Ask Me What You Want*, also co-written by her, crosses over to make US #27.

Sept *My Man, A Sweet Man*, written by Raeford Gerald reaches US #42.

Oct Debut LP *Millie Jackson*, mostly a showcase for Gerald's songs plus the singles so far, and recorded in New York and Washington, D.C., makes US #166.

Nov *My Man, A Sweet Man* is the only UK hit single of Jackson's Spring years, reaching #50.

1973 Jan The last extract from the LP, *I Miss You Baby*, makes US #95.

Oct *Hurts So Good*, from movie *Cleopatra Jones*, reaches US #24 and is an R&B hit. It is included on LP *It Hurts So Good*, which peaks at US #175.

1974 July *How Do You Feel The Morning After* reaches US #77.

Dec LP *Caught Up*, co-produced by Jackson with Brad Shapiro, and recorded at Muscle Shoals and at Criteria Studios in Miami, is her commercial breakthrough, reaching US #21 and earning a gold disk for a half million sales. A concept LP on the theme of the eternal triangle, it blends new songs with oldies by writers as diverse as Bobby Womack° and Bobby Goldsboro. It earns Jackson a nomination as Best Female R&B Vocalist at the 1974 Grammy awards. She describes her own romantic stance as "happily divorced", with two children from a marriage which was over within months, and has a quiet, reclusive offstage lifestyle which contrasts sharply with her public persona.

1975 Feb A revival of Luther Ingram's *(If Loving You Is Wrong) I Don't Want*

MILLIE JACKSON *cont.*

To Be Right, taken from LP *Still Caught Up* (punctuated by the soul-searching "rap" which is becoming her stage trademark), reaches US #42.

Aug LP *Still Caught Up*, another Muscle Shoals recording, continues the eternal triangle theme, with one side illustrating the wife's side and the other devoted to the mistress' angle. It peaks at US #112, but includes one of Jackson's later most popular (and covered) performances, *Loving Arms*.

Oct *Leftovers*, taken from LP *Still Caught Up*, charts briefly at US #87.

1977 Mar LP *Lovingly Yours* reaches US #175.

Dec LP *Feelin' Bitchy*, a no-holds-barred sample of the raunchier material which attracts notice to Jackson's live performances (like *All The Way Lover* and *A Little Taste Of Outside Love*), is marketed by Spring with the caution of an airplay warning sticker on the sleeve for DJs. It reaches US #34 and earns a second gold disk.

Dec [25] Jackson participates in the Christmas night re-opening of the Apollo Theater in Harlem, New York.

1978 Jan *If You're Not Back In Love By Monday*, taken from LP *Feelin' Bitchy*, reaches US #43, and is her final US singles chart entry.

Sept LP *Get It Out'cha System* makes US #55, and is Jackson's third gold LP. She tours UK, where her colorful onstage language causes some controversy among some unfamiliar with her raunchy performing reputation (but gains her plenty of publicity, including a cover story in *Time Out* magazine).

1979 May LP *A Moment's Pleasure*, on the same lines as LP *Feelin' Bitchy* and including *Never Change Lovers In The Middle Of The Night* and a sensuous cover of Exile's *Kiss You All Over*, peaks at US #144. She is now managing and producing a soul/funk quartet, The Facts of Life, as well as administering her own music publishing company, Double Ak-Shun Music.

Nov LP *Royal Rappin's*, consisting of duets with Isaac Hayes° (often considered her close male counterpart), reaches US #80. Their duetted revival of Foreigner's° *Feels Like The First Time* is extracted but fails to sell outside the R&B market.

1980 Jan Double live LP *Live And Uncensored*, also marketed with a sticker warning of its explicitness, reaches US #94.

July LP *For Men Only* reaches US #100. From it, her version of Kenny Loggins/Michael McDonald's° *This Is It* is released, but fails to chart.

1981 Feb LP *I Had To Say It* makes US #137.

1982 Apr LP *Live And Outrageous (Rated XXX)*, repeats the formula (and cautious marketing) of LP *Live And Uncensored* and reaches US #113.

1983 Dec LP *E.S.P.* (which stands for Extra Sexual Persuasion), produced at Muscle Shoals by the longstanding Jackson/Shapiro team, fails to cross over but peaks at US R&B #40. (It will be Jackson's final US chart LP.) Extracted *I Feel Like Walking In The Rain* makes R&B #58, and is her last US chart entry.

1984 Mar LP *E.S.P.* is released on Sire in UK, and reaches UK #59, her first UK chart LP. From it, *I Feel Like Walkin' In The Rain* is her second and last UK hit single, making UK #55.

1985 Apr LP *Live And Uncensored* is reissued in UK by Important Records, and makes #81.

June She duets with Elton John° on his *Act Of War*, which reaches UK #32.

1987 Jan Jackson signs to UK label Jive Records, releasing LP *An Imitation Of Love*, which fails to chart.

Feb She begins a tour of US Mid-West.

Apr Jive releases *Love Is A Dangerous Game* in UK. It finds only disco support but is notable in being Jackson's first single to be released as a compact disk.

May *Wanna Be Your Lover*, on Jive, is also a popular dance number but fails to chart.

THE JAM

Paul Weller (vocals and bass)
Bruce Foxton (guitar)
Rick Buckler (drums)

1975 Weller (b. May 25, 1958) meets Buckler (b. Paul Richard Buckler, Dec.6, 1955) at school in Woking, Surrey, UK, where they jam together during lunch hour in the music room. Using the session as group name inspiration, they link with Foxton (b. Sept.1, 1955) and Steve Brookes to play local social and working men's clubs. Brookes leaves, Foxton moves to bass, with Weller now on lead guitar and vocals. (The Jam will remain a trio for the rest of its career.)

1976 Concentrating on live work in London, The Jam plays gigs at the Marquee, 100 Club and regular jaunts at the Red Cow pub, where the group is viewed and dismissed by EMI Records.

1977 Feb [25] Following a month's Red Cow residence and a frenzied gig at the Marquee, The Jam, managed by Weller's father, John, signs to Polydor Records for £6,000 advance offered by A&R man Chris Parry. (A 4-year deal, it will be re-negotiated after 90 days.) UK music press links the band with the burgeoning punk movement but The Jam moves to its own niche and a latter spotlight in a UK mod revival. The trio currently sports mohair suits and Rickenbacker guitars.

May Debut single *In The City*, produced by Parry, reaches UK #40.

June With all songs penned by the group's leader, 19-year-old Weller, LP *In The City* makes UK #20. It has taken 11 days to record. The Jam begins a 42-date UK debut tour in the group car, a red Ford Cortina.

Aug Aided by a first appearance on UK TV's "Top of the Pops", *All Around The World* peaks at UK #13.

Nov *The Modern World* makes UK #36. The group visits US for a 16-date club tour, which is not successful.

Dec Parent LP *This Is The Modern World* reaches UK #22 and is criticized by UK press. A major UK tour starts, highlighted by a brawl between the band and rugby players at a Leeds Hotel. Leeds Crown Court subsequently acquits Weller, who moves to London with his first love, Gill.

1978 Mar While the band supports Blue Oyster Cult° on an ill-billed US tour, *News Of The World* makes UK #27.

Aug *David Watts*, a cover of a Kinks'° track, backed with *'A' Bomb In Wardour Street* peaks at UK #25.

Aug [25] The Jam plays Reading Festival, as the punk "small venue" ideal fades.

Oct *Down In The Tube Station At Midnight* climbs to UK #15.

Nov LP *All Mod Cons*, produced by Vic Coppersmith-Heaven and featuring eleven Weller compositions, hits UK #6. It coincides with the start of a European tour.

1979 Mar *Strange Town* peaks at UK #15. The Jam begins its first world tour, visiting US, Canada and Europe.

Sept *When You're Young* makes UK #17.

Nov Firmly established as a "quick" singles band, *The Eton Rifles* hits UK #3 and the LP from which it is taken, *Setting Sons*, hits UK #4.

1980 Mar Their first US chart appearance, LP *Setting Sons* peaks at US #137 (major US success will always elude this particularly British band). Meanwhile *Going Underground/The Dreams Of Children* becomes the first UK single of the 80s to debut at #1. Ironically, the band is in LA when the news breaks.

Aug *Start* also hits UK #1.

Dec LP *Sound Affects* hits UK #2. The band begins a major UK tour ending in sell-out dates at favored venue, London's Rainbow Theatre. (Weller is using his royalties to set up a publishing company, Riot Stories, for political works.)

1981 Jan UK magazine *Melody Maker* arranges for Weller to meet former hero The Who's° Pete Townshend. During the interview, both artists confirm that they do not like the other's band.

Feb German import single, *That's Entertainment*, makes UK #21. LP *Sound Affects* reaches US #72, as The Jam sets off on another world tour incorporating Japan.

June *Funeral Pyre* hits UK #4.

Aug Weller makes a program on class awareness for UK BBC TV series "Something Else".

Oct *Absolute Beginners* hits UK #4 as Weller finances two new enterprises: *Jamming* magazine, to be run by Jam devotee Tony Fletcher, and his own Respond record label.

Dec The Jam sweeps *New Musical Express* Readers' Poll, as it plays four standing-room-only Christmas dates in London.

1982 Jan LP *The Jam*, a mini-collection of five UK hits, reaches US #176. During new recording, Weller has a breakdown and quits heavy drinking.

Feb *Town Called Malice/Precious*, released as a 12" single, hits UK #1. The Jam becomes the first band since The Beatles° to perform two numbers on the same edition of BBC TV's "Top of the Pops" when it plays both sides.

Mar LP *The Gift*, featuring a new soul slant, tops the UK chart and

reaches US #82. As the group sets off on another UK, Europe, Canada, US and Japanese 4-month tour called "Trans Global Unity Express", an early gig at Bingley Hall, Stafford is filmed for video release.

July Import 45, *Just Who Is The Five O'Clock Hero*, hits UK #8. Weller takes 2 weeks vacation in Italy with Gill and, disillusioned with The Jam formula and keen to seek new soul direction, decides to disband The Jam.

Sept With the public still unaware, and the group recently committed to CND anti-nuclear cause, The Jam's *The Bitterest Pill (I Ever Had To Swallow)*, with Belle Star Jenny McKeowen duetting with Weller, hits UK #2.

Oct [28] The Jam officially announces its split, but will honor a last UK tour.

Dec *Beat Surrender* enters at UK #1, as the band plays farewell dates. The disk is censored by US radio and fails, as with every Jam 45 release, to make the Hot 100. LP *Dig The New Breed*, a 14-track live compilation from 1977-82, hits UK #2, while UK hits compilation LP, released in US only, *The Bitterest Pill (I Ever Had To Swallow)* reaches US #135.

1983 Jan Polydor re-issues all of The Jam's 16 singles, which establishes the precedent of all re-charting simultaneously in UK. Weller folds *Jamming* magazine.

Feb LP *Dig The New Breed* peaks at US #131.

Apr US-only EP, *Beat Surrender* reaches US #171.

Oct While Weller has formed The Style Council° with ex-Merton Parka Mick Talbot, his Respond label signs Questions and Tracie. Buckler joins new group Time UK and Foxton releases solo LP *Touch Sensitive* on Arista. The Jam's double hits LP *Snap!* hits UK #2. A similar video tops the UK music video chart. (Weller, always politically active, will join "The Red Wedge Tour" in time for next UK General Election.)

RICK JAMES

1967 James (b. James Johnson, Feb.1, 1952, Buffalo, N.Y., US) goes AWOL from US Navy and settles in Toronto, Canada, where his room mate is local singer Neil Young°, with whom he forms rock/soul band, The Mynah Birds.

1968 The group goes to Detroit. It signs to Motown, but no material is released. James does some production work for Bobby Taylor, The Spinners and The Marvelettes.

1970 He moves to London, UK, and forms blues band, The Main Line. (For the next 7 years he will commute between London, Canada and US. Rumors persist that he spends time in a US prison for desertion from the Navy.)

1977 James returns to US where he forms The Stone City Band. Inspired by George Clinton° he develops a rock/funk-style he dubs "funk'n'roll". Impressed by his demo tapes, Motown signs him to a worldwide deal.

1978 July *You And I* reaches UK #46, while debut LP *Come Get It!* eventually climbs to US #13.

Sept *You And I* reaches US #13, and is awarded a gold disk.

Oct *Mary Jane*, a barely disguised hymn to marijuana, hits US R&B #3 and initially fails to cross over. Second LP *Bustin' Out Of L Seven* is released. James, with The Stone City Band and vocal trio, The Mary Jane Girls, embarks on his first US tour. His wildly extrovert show gets wide media attention and enthusiastic audiences.

Nov He is out of action for several months with hepatitis. Official sources give "exhaustion" as the cause of the illness. (There are also rumors of drug-related causes.)

1979 Jan *Mary Jane* finally reaches US #41.

Mar LP *Bustin' Out Of L Seven* makes US #16.

Apr *High On Your Love Suite* stalls at US #72.

May *Bustin' Out* falters at US #71.

July James produces new Motown artist Teena Marie's debut LP *Wild And Peaceful* and single *I'm A Sucker For Your Love*, with James featured as co-vocalist, which makes US #43. (James and Marie will continue to contribute to each other's recordings.)

Dec Third LP *Fire It Up* reaches US #34.

1980 Apr James-produced debut LP by The Stone City Band, *In 'N' Out*, reaches US #122.

Sept *Big Time* peaks at UK #41. Fourth LP *Garden Of Love* is released. An uncharacteristic ballad set, it reaches only US #83.

1981 Apr James-produced second Stone City Band LP, *The Boys Are Back*, is released.

June Fifth LP *Street Songs* is released. An extrovert return to funk'n'roll, it hits US #3 and achieves double platinum status. (It will stay in the top 100 LP chart for 54 weeks, and hit US R&B #1, staying on top for 20 weeks.)

July *Give It To Me Baby*, taken from LP *Street Songs*, tops US R&B chart for 5 weeks and makes US #40 and UK #47.

Sept *Super Freak (Pt 1)*, also from the LP, reaches US #16. James embarks on a successful US tour with Teena Marie, Cameo° and The Sugarhill Gang.

1982 June James guests on The Temptations'° *Standing On The Top* which climbs to US #53. Sixth LP *Throwin' Down* is released.

July *Dance Wit' Me* reaches US #64 and UK #53. LP *Throwin' Down* reaches US #13 and UK #93.

Nov [25-27] James joins Aretha Franklin°, Gladys Knight°, The Clash° and others performing to 45,000 people at the Jamaica World Music Festival.

Dec James visits UK for promotion-only work.

1983 June James-produced Mary Jane Girls LP *Mary Jane Girls* is released.

Aug *Cold Blooded*, on Motown, hits US R&B #1. Unable to get exposure on MTV, like all James' singles, it stalls at US #40.

Sept LP *Cold Blooded* hits US R&B #1. James-produced Stone City Band LP *Out From The Shadow* is released.

Oct LP *Cold Blooded* reaches US #16.

1984 Jan *Ebony Eyes*, a sweet-soul duet with Smokey Robinson°, reaches US #43.

Aug *17* reaches US #36.

Oct LP *Reflections*, a retrospective compilation, reaches US #41.

Dec James has stayed out of the public eye all year.

1985 Apr *Can't Stop* reaches US #50.

Sept LP *The Flag* is released. James' contract with Motown ends in acrimony and he retreats to work in his Le Joint recording studios at home in Buffalo.

Dec His first project is to write, arrange and produce US comedian Eddie Murphy's debut LP. *Party All The Time* hits US #2 while Murphy's LP *How Could It Be* will reach US #26.

1987 James signs to Reprise Records.

1988 June First release featuring rap lady Roxanne Shante, *Loosey's Rap*, hits US R&B #1 but fails to cross over. LP *Wonderful*, featuring traditional sexual over-and undertones, peaks at US #148.

TOMMY JAMES & THE SHONDELLS

Tommy James (vocals)
Eddie Gray (guitar)
Mick Jones (guitar)
Mike Vale (bass)
Peter Lucia (drums)
Ronnie Rosaman (organ)
Paul Reaney (vocals)

1960 At age 12, Tommy James (b. Thomas Jackson, Apr.29, 1947, Dayton, Oh., US) forms a group at school in Niles, Mich.

1962 The group cuts *Long Pony Tail* for a local label.

1963 Some months after the disk first appears, DJ Jack Douglas on station W-NIL hears it, contacts James, and asks if he has any other material. James has heard *Hanky Panky* performed in a night club in South Bend, Indiana. (It is the B-side of a single by The

Raindrops, who are actually its writers, Jeff Barry and Ellie Greenwich.) When he records the song for Douglas' Snap label, James ad-libs most of the lyrics. It sells well in Michigan, Illinois and Indiana.

1965 Dec Out of work following high school graduation, James receives a phone call from a DJ in Pittsburgh, who has been playing the 2-year-old *Hanky Panky*. James flies there to appear on local TV and radio. He forms a new Shondells, after the original group refuses to move from Indiana, by hiring local band The Raconteurs. The line-up is Rosman (b. Feb.28, 1945), Vale (b. July 17, 1949), Vince Pietropaoli, drums, and George Magura, sax. The latter three soon leave, to be replaced by Gray (b. Feb.27, 1948) and Lucia (b. Feb.2, 1947).

1966 July Picked up for national release by Roulette Records in New York, *Hanky Panky* hits US #1, sells a million, and makes UK #38. James signs to Roulette.

Sept LP *Hanky Panky* reaches US #46. R&B-style *Say I Am (What I Am)* reaches US #21. The label teams the group with songwriter/producers Bo Gentry and Richie Cordell, in a partnership which will produce a melodic, exhilarating and commercial style.

Dec *It's Only Love* makes US #31.

1967 Apr *I Think We're Alone Now*, a distinctive bubbling arrangement, hits US #4.

June *Mirage* hits US #10 and LP *I Think We're Alone Now* reaches US #74.

July *I Like The Way* peaks at US #25.

Sept *Gettin' Together* makes US #18.

Nov *Out Of The Blue* reaches US #43.

1968 Feb *Get Out Now* climbs to US #48, marking the end of the group's lightweight pop period.

Mar Compilation LP *Something Special! The Best Of Tommy James And The Shondells* reaches US #174.

June *Mony Mony*, written by Gentry and Cordell with Bobby Bloom (later of *Montego Bay* fame) and James himself, with the group's sound hardened into a rock-solid dance beat, hits US #3.

July LP *Mony Mony* reaches US #193.

Aug In spite of the group's long record of UK non-success, *Mony Mony* hits UK #1 for 4 weeks and is UK's most popular dancefloor disk of the summer. US follow-up *Somebody Cares* peaks at #53 but is not used as UK follow-up.

Nov *Mony Mony*-like *Do Something To Me* makes US #38. Issued as the UK follow-up, it flops. The group has developed strong ideas of what its new records should be sounding like, and persuades Roulette to let it self-produce the next LP.

1969 Feb *Crimson and Clover*, a shortened version of the 5½-minute LP title track, launches the new self-produced Shondells sound: a complex weave of vocal and instrumental sounds with an ethereal, layered melody, hints of psychedelia, and a solid commercial hook. It tops the US chart and wins a gold disk, becoming the group's biggest US seller.

May *Sweet Cherry Wine*, a similar production with innovative tempo and rhythm changes, hits US #7. LP *Crimson And Clover* hits US #8.

July *Crystal Blue Persuasion*, a laid-back summer sound which is James' favorite of his own recordings, hits US #2 and is another million-seller.

Nov *Ball Of Fire* climbs to US #19. LP *Cellophane Symphony* reaches US #141.

1970 Jan *She* makes US #23.

Feb Compilation LP *The Best Of Tommy James And The Shondells* peaks at US #21.

Mar *Gotta Get Back To You*, a shift back to R&B style, makes US #45.

May LP *Travelin'* reaches US #91.

June *Come To Me* makes US #47. James collapses on stage in Alabama. The Shondells quit to become the (unsuccessful) Hog Heaven, while James recuperates on his farm in upstate New York.

Aug James produces US #7 hit *Tighter And Tighter* for Brooklyn group Alive & Kicking (a song he intended to cut as his first solo, but did not complete due to remaining nervousness about his vocal performance).

Sept Encouraged by the group's success, James records solo *Ball And Chain*, which makes US #57.

1971 Jan *Church Street Soul Revival* reaches US #62.

Mar *Adrienne* peaks at US #93.

Aug James' biggest solo success, *Draggin' The Line*, hits US #4 and is another million-seller.

Sept LP *Christian Of The World* reaches US #131.

Oct *I'm Comin' Home* makes US #40.

Dec *Nothing To Hide* reaches US #41.

1972 Feb *Tell 'Em Willie Boy's A'Comin'* peaks at US #89.

June *Cat's Eye In The Window* climbs to US #90.

Sept *Love Song* makes US #67.

Nov *Celebration* reaches US #95.

1973 Mar *Boo, Boo, Don't 'Cha Be Blue* makes US #70 and James turns to the club circuit after 18 months of minor US chart placings.

1977 James signs to Fantasy Records and releases Jeff Barry-produced LP *Midnight Rider*. He covers several UK hits by Gary Glitter°, who briefly serves as an influence.

1980 Mar James, signed to Millenium Records, makes US #19 with *Three Times In Love*, after a 7-year chart absence.

Apr LP *Three Times In Love* reaches US #134.

1981 May *You're So Easy To Love* peaks at US #58.

1982 May Joan Jett's version of *Crimson and Clover* hits US #7, and begins an era in which many old James hits will be rediscovered by several acts.

1987 Nov Billy Idol's° cover of *Mony Mony* knocks Tiffany's° cover of *I Think We're Alone Now* off the top of the US chart. (Tiffany will hit UK #1, while Idol will hit UK #7.)

JAN AND DEAN

Jan Berry (vocals)
Dean Torrence (vocals)

1957 Berry (b. Apr.3, 1941, Los Angeles, Cal., US) and Torrence (b. Mar.10, 1940, Los Angeles) meet while members of LA's Emerson Junior High School football team, where, discovering that the showers are a great place to sing, they form a vocal group named The Barons with four friends. When this also moves outside school, neighbors Bruce Johnston and Sandy Nelson° join in on piano and drums.

1958 The group splits, leaving only Berry, Torrence and Arnie Ginsburg. Ginsburg becomes infatuated with a stripper at the nearby Follies Burlesque and the trio, with Torrence on lead vocals, records *Jennie Lee*, inspired by her, in Berry's garage. While Torrence is away for 6 months following call-up to the Army Reserves, this tape comes to the attention of Joe Lubin at Arwin Records (a tiny LA label owned by Doris Day's husband Marty Melcher), who offers to release it. In Torrence's absence, Berry and Ginsburg sign and the disk is issued credited to Jan & Arnie.

Aug *Jennie Lee* hits US #8.

Oct Torrence returns from service shortly after Jan & Arnie's follow-up *Gas Money* peaks at US #81. Arwin releases one more Jan & Arnie single, *I Love Linda*, but it flops, and Ginsberg drops out. The remaining duo starts recording again in Berry's garage.

1959 They meet Lou Adler and Herb Alpert°, two youth veterans of the LA music business who work frequently with Sam Cooke°, and also manage the small Dore label, which has just had a million-seller with *To Know Him Is To Love Him* by The Teddy Bears. Adler and Alpert become Jan and Dean's managers and work with them on recordings, taking the basic garage-cut tracks and overdubbing fuller arrangements (written by Alpert) in a professional 2-track studio.

Sept [7] The duo performs, along with Frankie Avalon°, Duane Eddy°, The Coasters° and many others, in Dick Clark's stage show at the Michigan State Fair, to an audience of 15,000 over four performances.

Oct *Baby Talk*, a cover of an original by an obscure Californian group, and the first under the new work arrangement with Alpert° and Adler, hits US #10. Early copies are marketed as by Jan & Arnie, to capitalize on the earlier success; once it begins to sell, the credit becomes Jan and Dean. The duo appears on Dick Clark's "American Bandstand" on US TV for the first time.

Nov Alpert° and Adler write the follow-up, *There's A Girl*, which reaches US #97.

1960 Mar A revival of traditional *Clementine* (credited as a Berry/Torrence composition) peaks at US #65, losing out to Bobby Darin's° coincidental swing-style revival which reaches US #21.

Sept After *White Tennis Sneakers* has failed, a revival of The Moonglows' oldie *We Go Together* makes US #53.

Dec Another revival, The Crows' *Gee*, falters at US #81. (Two further

Dore singles over the next 7 months, *Baggy Pants* and *Let's Fly Away*, plus an LP which includes 12 singles tracks, will all fail.)

1961 May Determined to sign to a major label and benefit from fuller promotion, the duo cuts a revival of Hoagy Carmichael and Frank Loesser's *Heart And Soul* in a gimmicky uptempo vocal treatment. With Adler, they try to gain a deal with Liberty Records. (Alpert° despises the track, and drops out of the team and his business partnership with Adler to develop his ideas for instrumental music with his trumpet – he will co-found A&M Records in 1962.) Liberty, though interested in Jan and Dean, agrees with Alpert about *Heart And Soul*. Adler and the duo sign an interim two-record deal with independent Challenge label, owned by Gene Autrey.

July *Heart And Soul*, released on Challenge, hits US #25, their biggest success for 2 years.

Sept *Heart And Soul* is the first of only two UK Jan and Dean hits, reaching #24. In US, quick follow-up *Wanted One Girl* fails, and the duo signs to Liberty.

1962 Jan Liberty debut, a revival of oldie *A Sunday Kind Of Love*, peaks at US #95.

May Staff producer Snuff Garrett is brought in to work on *Tennessee*, written by Leon Russell° and Buzz Cason, and it makes US #69.

Aug The duo meets The Beach Boys° for the first time, when both groups play at the same teen hop. (The Beach Boys will occasionally back Jan and Dean live during the fall of 1962, and each group becomes familiar with the other's repertoire.)

1963 Feb *Linda*, a revival of Jack Lawrence's 1944 song about his lawyer's daughter Linda Eastman (later to become Mrs. Paul McCartney°) borrows some of the beat and falsetto vocalizing of the recent Four Seasons° hits, and reaches US #28. Adler recommends that the duo should get involved in the burgeoning California surf music scene (until now mainly instrumental) since both are keen surfers. For LP *Jan And Dean Take Linda Surfin'*, mainly of cover versions, they record two surfing songs they know from singing them live – Brian Wilson's *Surfin'* and *Surfin' Safari*, enlisting the help of Wilson and the other Beach Boys° to back them in the studio.

July Constant musical and social fraternization with Brian Wilson and The Beach Boys° leads to Wilson giving the duo *Surf City* to complete and record. With The Beach Boys' voices as back-up, it tops the US chart for 2 weeks (a year before The Beach Boys' own first #1 with *I Get Around*), and sells over a million, the duo's biggest-selling single. LP *Jan And Dean Take Linda Surfin'* reaches US #71.

Sept *Surf City* is the second and last Jan and Dean UK hit, making #26.

Oct *Honolulu Lulu*, written by Berry with LA DJ Roger Christian, reaches US #11, while LP *Surf City And Other Swingin' Cities* reaches US #32. Featuring mostly Jan and Dean versions of oldies with US city names in their titles, the LP is (like *Honolulu Lulu*) arranged and produced by Berry, and features what will become the duo's staple studio backing crew: the Phil Spector school of with-it session musicians like drummer Hal Blaine, guitarists Tommy Tedesco, Glen Campbell° and Billy Strange, keyboardists Leon Russell° and Larry Knechtel, and sax player Steve Douglas.

1964 Jan Like The Beach Boys°, Jan and Dean expand their lyrical concerns to include cars and the hot rod craze: Berry/Wilson/Christian-penned *Drag City* hits US #10.

Mar LP *Drag City*, featuring mostly original material, plus The Routers' *Sting Ray* and The Beach Boys'° *Little Deuce Coupe*, reaches US #22.

May *Dead Man's Curve*, a car race melodrama in a pounding arrangement with car horns and crash effects, hits US #8. B-side *The New Girl In School*, originally a Brian Wilson song titled *Gonna Hustle You*, with new lyrics by Berry, reaches US #37.

June LP *Dead Man's Curve/The New Girl In School* peaks at US #80. It eschews surfing concerns in favor of car and girl songs, and has P.F. Sloan and Steve Barri (AKA The Fantastic Baggys) as back-up vocalists, together with Berry's girlfriend Jill Gibson, (who will later replace Michelle Phillips in The Mamas & The Papas°).

Aug *The Little Old Lady (From Pasadena)* hits US #3. It is penned by Roger Christian with Don Altfield, a medical student colleague of Berry's at the California College of Medicine (both Berry and Torrence continue their education throughout these hitmaking years; the latter initially in medicine, then switching to architecture and graphic design at USC).

Sept [4] The duo appears with The Animals°, Chuck Berry°, and Del Shannon°, in a 10-day stand at the Paramount Theater in Brooklyn, New York.

Oct Theme from Fabian movie, *Ride The Wild Surf*, another Berry/Christian/Wilson collaboration, reaches US #16. Its B-side is the near-nonsensical *The Anaheim, Azusa And Cucamonga Sewing Circle, Book Review And Timing Association*, which climbs to US #77.

Nov The LPs *The Little Old Lady From Pasadena* and movie soundtrack *Ride The Wild Surf* are released within a week of each other, and peak at US #40 and #66 respectively. Both feature Sloan and Barri as backing vocalists and as writers. Both LPs contain *Sidewalk Surfin'*, which is also extracted as a single. A reworking of The Beach Boys'° *Catch A Wave* with new lyrics about skateboarding, makes US #25 (and promotes sales of the Jan and Dean "Little Old Lady" skateboard, merchandised at the same time).

1965 Mar *(Here They Come) From All Over The World*, a Sloan/Barri song. reaches US #56. It is the theme from "The TAMI Show", a videotaped TV spectacular (later released as movie *Gather No Moss* in UK) hosted by the duo, and including performances from The Rolling Stones°, Chuck Berry°, The Beach Boys°, Marvin Gaye°, James Brown° and many others. Jan and Dean's own slot on the show is captured on live LP *Command Performance/Live In Person*, which makes US #33.

July Ballad *You Really Know How To Hurt A Guy*, written by Berry and Christian with Jill Gibson, climbs to US #27. Torrence hates the song, and Berry ejects him from the session during recording, so he is not heard on it.

Oct At another Jan and Dean session, brought to a halt by a technical hitch, Torrence relieves his boredom by walking to a nearby studio where The Beach Boys° are holding "live-in-studio" sessions with friends for an off-the-cuff style LP, *Beach Boys Party*. Asked if he wants to sing something, he suggests the old Regents hit *Barbara Ann*. After a few minutes' rehearsal, the song is recorded with Torrence on lead vocal. (The track appears on the LP, and will also be the next Beach Boys hit at US #2 and UK #3, but for contractual and inter-label political reasons, Torrence is not credited on it.)

Nov *I Found A Girl*, a near-psychedelic arrangement of a Sloan/Barri song, reaches US #30, as LP *Jan And Dean Golden Hits, Volume 2*, a compilation of singles from *Linda* onward, peaks at US #107.

Dec *The Universal Coward*, a patriotic and apparently right-wing song borrowed from Buffy Saint-Marie's *The Universal Soldier*, is released as a Jan Berry solo after Torrence refuses to have anything to do with it. It fails to chart, as does Jan and Dean's opportunistic (cashing in on the folk-rock boom) *Folk City* which follows close behind.

1966 Jan LP *Folk'n'Roll*, including the recently unsuccessful singles, several covers of hits, and some Sloan/Barri items including *Eve Of Destruction*, reaches US #145.

Feb Familiar in concert, and partially present on most LPs, Jan and Dean's surreal comedy bent is given full rein on LP *Jan And Dean Meet Batman*, a cash-in on the new cult-appeal TV series. The LP fails to chart, but extracted *Batman* makes US #66.

Mar The duo prepares to film *Easy Come, Easy Go* with Elvis Presley°, and signs to do a weekly ABC TV show. The contract with Liberty expires, and although the label wants it to re-sign, the duo plans its own Jan & Dean Records as a subsidiary of Lou Adler's Dunhill label.

Apr [12] Berry, preoccupied with his just-received draft notice and with an imminent medical school exam, crashes his Corvette into a parked truck on Whittier Boulevard in LA, and is almost killed. (He will be initally in a coma and then totally paralysed for several months, suffering partial paralysis for long after. He will also suffer brain damage which will necessitate re-learning processes. Recovery will be slow over many years.)

June LP *Filet Of Soul*, consisting of out-takes from the duo's TAMI Show performance and unused studio rejects, is released to Torrence's displeasure, and reaches US #127. Unhappy with Liberty's plunder-the-vaults policy, but with Berry out of action for the forseeable future (if not for good), Torrence decides to keep the duo's name active on his own terms, while also helping pay Berry's hospital bills. Setting up independent J&D Records and Magic Lamp Productions, he puts a new lyric over *The Little Old Lady*'s instrumental track, titling it *Tijuana*, but it fails to chart.

July *Popsicle*, originally on LP *Drag City*, reaches US #21. An LP of the

JAN AND DEAN *cont.*

same title, compiled entirely from old tracks, fails to sell.

Aug Second J&D release, a revival of The Jamies' oldie *Summertime, Summertime*, coupled with *California Lullaby*, produced by Torrence, with poor promotion fails to sell.

Sept Unissued *Fiddle Around*, released by Liberty, reaches US #93, and is Jan and Dean's last chart entry.

1967 Mar Torrence concludes a 1-year deal with CBS/Columbia to take Jan and Dean releases from Magic Lamp Productions. *Yellow Balloon* is released, but is defeated by the original version by the group also called Yellow Balloon.

Apr Torrence cuts LP *Save For A Rainy Day* with Jan and Dean's old studio session musicians. A collection of new and old songs around a general theme of rain, it is released in LA on J&D, and scheduled for national distribution by Columbia. Berry, who is slowly recovering, refuses to be a sleeping party to it, and CBS cancels, not being interested in only half of Jan and Dean to promote it.

June Torrence puts his graphic design degree to use, and launches Kittyhawk Graphics, getting an assignment from White Whale Records to design The Turtles'° *Golden Hits* LP sleeve, and later White Whale's display advertising and other corporate artwork.

Oct After collaborating with Brian Wilson on some tracks for The Beach Boys'° LP *Smiley Smile*, Torrence is given the song *Vegetables* and records a version of it with help of session men Joe Osborn and Larry Knechtel. White Whale releases it under the name The Laughing Gravy, but it does not sell.

Nov Berry signs a deal with Warner Bros., supposedly as a therapeutic measure after pressure from his father and doctors. Torrence declines to take part, feeling that Berry is being ill-served by not having full-time professional help, but does not object to the use of his name. (Three unsuccessful singles are released as by Jan and Dean on Warner. Berry later states that the vocals on them were actually the work of session singers, mainly Ron Hicklin.) Torrence quits recording and sets up his Kittyhawk Graphics company, designing LP sleeves and record company artwork.

1971 Aug With United Artists Records (the inheritors of Liberty) as a client of Kittyhawk Graphics, Torrence works closely with the company on double LP *Jan & Dean Anthology Album*, which includes all the hits and a live performance side, from *Jennie Lee* in 1958 to The Laughing Gravy's *Vegetables* in 1964.

1972 Jan Berry signs a solo deal with Lou Adler's Ode label, releasing self-penned *Mother Earth*.

Mar In a short-term deal with United Artists, Torrence forms The Legendary Masked Surfers with Bruce Johnston and Terry Melcher (once both The Rip Chords and Bruce & Terry, as well as their Beach Boys° connections). They use old Jan and Dean backing tracks for *Gonna Hustle You* (*The New Girl In School* with the original, raunchier lyrics).

May Berry revives Huey "Piano" Smith & The Clowns' *Don't You Just Know It* on Ode.

July The second Legendary Masked Surfers release updates Bruce & Terry's 1964 hit *Summer Means Fun*, written by Sloan and Barri. (After this, the group becomes California, and later California Music, involving varied personnel including Curt Becher, Gloria Grinel, Kenny Hinkle and Chad Stuart. Torrence's involvement ends here.)

1973 Jan and Dean re-form for a California Surfer's Stomp Festival and a projected US tour, miming to backing tracks because of Berry's uncertainty about performing, but it turns out to be a disaster.

1974 July Berry releases solo *Tinsel Town*, co-written with Roger Christian and Joan Jacobs.

1975 June The duo performs on stage again at a rock revival show put together by DJ Jim Pewter, this time with no embarrassing disasters.

Aug Jan and Dean reunite on Ode to record *Fun City*, written by Berry with Alan Wolfson and Jim Pewter.

1978 Feb [3] ABC-TV's "Dead Man's Curve" biopic, starring Bruce Davison and Richard Hatch as Jan and Dean, airs in US. Interest in the duo rekindles, and Berry's health improves to the point where they embark on a lengthy coast-to-coast US tour.

1980 July LP *The Jan And Dean Story* reaches UK #67. Torrence joins The Beach Boys'° Mike Love to record several tracks for a cassette-only release of 1960s hits.

1982 Rhino Records releases live Jan & Dean LP *One Summer Night – Live*.

JAPAN

David Sylvian (vocals and guitar)
Rob Dean (guitar)
Richard Barbieri (keyboards)
Steve Jansen (drums)
Mick Karn (saxophone)

1974/77 The band forms in Lewisham, London, UK, with Sylvian (b. David Batt, Feb.23, 1958, Lewisham), his brother Jansen (b. Steve Batt), and school friends Barbieri and Karn (b. Anthony Michaelides, July 24, 1958, London), and plays Roxy-influenced music locally. A music press ad for a second guitarist brings in Dean. The band wins a talent contest sponsored by German record company Ariola-Hansa (which has just opened London offices), and is signed to the label. The Batt brothers and Michaelides adopt their stage names.

1978 Mar Debut UK release *Don't Rain On My Parade* (an oldie from musical *Funny Girl*) fails to chart.

Apr LP *Adolescent Sex* is issued. To promote it, the band tours UK as support to Blue Oyster Cult°, but it sells only moderately.

Aug *Be Unconventional* is released.

Nov *Sometimes I Feel So Low* and LP *Obscure Alternatives* are released in UK to little success, while the group suffers negative reviews from UK's music press.

1979 May *Life In Tokyo*, produced by Giorgio Moroder, fails to chart in UK (but the band has some chart success in Japan).

1980 Feb LP *Quiet Life* is the UK chart debut, reaching #53.

Mar A cover of Smokey Robinson's° *I Second That Emotion* is the band's last recording on Ariola-Hansa.

July The band signs to Virgin Records, and works with producer John Punter.

Oct Virgin debut *Gentlemen Take Polaroids* reaches UK #60 (helped by being a twin-single package for the price of one). A change of working environment boosts the band and a rise in fashion of the New Romantic movement (which Japan's style has in many ways anticipated) is a key element in Japan's increased UK airplay, press coverage and consequent chart success.

Dec LP *Gentlemen Take Polaroids* makes UK #45.

1981 May Dean leaves, moving to LA. *The Art Of Parties*, with Gary Numan° guesting, makes UK #48.

Sept Karn exhibits his sculpture work in Japan.

Oct The title track from LP *Quiet Life*, released on Hansa after the group's departure, reaches UK #19. A compilation LP of early material, *Assemblage*, makes UK #26.

Nov Newly-recorded *Visions Of China*, on Virgin, makes UK #32 and LP *Tin Drum*, on the same label, reaches UK #12. Both reveal oriental influences.

1982 Feb A Hansa reissue of *European Son* (B-side of *Life In Tokyo*) climbs to UK #31.

Apr Ballad *Ghosts* gains widespread UK airplay and hits UK #5.

June *Cantonese Boy* makes UK #24, amid reports of constant disagreements between Sylvian and Karn, and rumors concerning the band's break-up. These are further fuelled by news of solo projects. Karn is the first to release a solo for Virgin, *Sensitive*, which fails to chart.

July A Hansa reissue of *I Second That Emotion* hits UK #9.

Aug Karn and Jansen play on an LP by Japanese act Akiko Yano, and Barbieri produces Swedish band Lustans Lakejer. Sylvian teams with Japanese musician Ryuichi Sakamoto of The Yellow Magic Orchestra, on *Bamboo Houses*. Released under the name Sylvian Sakamoto, it reaches UK #30.

Oct *Life In Tokyo*, reissued by Hansa, makes UK #28 while the band tours UK.

Nov [22] Japan officially announces its break-up, following a final UK concert at London's Hammersmith Odeon. Karn's solo LP *Titles* charts in the same week, making UK #74.

Dec *Night Porter*, a late Virgin release, reaches UK #29.

1983 Mar Hansa's final Japan release, a revival of The Velvet Underground's° *All Tomorrow's Parties* (originally on LP *Quiet Life*), reaches UK #38.

May A live version of *Canton* is Japan's final UK singles hit, reaching #42.

June Double live LP *Oil On Canvas*, recorded during the group's final tour, hits UK #5.

July Sylvian and Ryuichi Sakamoto collaborate on *Forbidden Colours*, the theme to David Bowie°/Tom Conti movie *Merry Christmas Mr. Lawrence* (in which Sakamoto also stars). It climbs to UK #16.

1984 Jan Sylvian solo *Red Guitar* reaches UK #17.
June Sylvian exhibits his Polaroid photo montages at London's Hamilton's Gallery.
July His solo LP *Brilliant Trees* hits UK #4.
Aug Sylvian's *The Ink In The Well* makes UK #36.
Nov His *Pulling Punches* reaches UK #56. Karn teams with former Bauhaus° lead singer Peter Murphy as Dali's Car. Signed to Paradox Records, they debut with *The Judgement Is The Mirror* which reaches UK #66.
Dec Double LP *Exorcising Ghosts*, a compilation of Japan's Virgin material, peaks at UK #45, and Dali's Car LP *The Waking Hour* reaches UK #84.
1985 Dec Sylvian solo *Words With The Shaman* briefly makes UK #72. His LP *Alchemy – An Index Of Possibilities* is released only as a cassette and fails to chart.
1986 Aug Sylvian's *Taking The Veil* reaches UK #53.
Sept Sylvian double LP *Gone To Earth* makes UK #24.
1987 Jan Karn's *Buoy*, featuring Sylvian on guest vocals, reaches UK #63.
Feb Karn solo LP *Dreams Of Reason Produce Monsters* charts briefly at UK #89.
Oct Sylvian's *Let The Happiness In* reaches UK #66.
Nov Sylvian's third LP *Secrets Of The Beehive* makes UK #37.
1988 Apr Sylvian's *Orpheus* fails to chart.

JEAN-MICHEL JARRE

1967 Abandoning his studies at the Conservatoire de Paris to work in his self-created studio experimenting with synthesizers, Jarre (b. 1949, Lyon, France), the son of composer Maurice Jarre and a child prodigy playing piano and guitar at age 5, makes his first professional recording, the soundtrack to film *Des Garçons et des Filles*.
1969 Debut LP *Cage – Erosmachine* is only released in France and sells poorly.
1971 Jarre makes his public debut at the Paris Opéra. He becomes youngest composer to appear at Palais Garnier before writing jingles as well as film and ballet scores.
1972 LP *Deserted Palace* is again only released in France.
1973 Jarre composes the music for film *Les Granges Brûlées*.
1977 He signs to Francis Dreyfus' label Disques Dreyfus and begins working on a new LP.
Sept *Oxygène Part IV* hits UK #4 and becomes familiar as a popular instrumental for TV programs. LP *Oxygène*, with multi-layered synthesizers and sound effects, is released worldwide through a Dreyfus license to Polydor. It hits UK #2 and US #78, selling 6 million copies worldwide.
1978 Jarre composes the score for film *La Maladie de Hambourg*.
Dec LP *Equinoxe*, following a similar musical path to the previous LP, reaches UK #11 and US #126. Jarre becomes the most popular solo instrumentalist in Europe.
1979 Jan *Equinoxe Part 5* reaches UK #45.
July One million spectators attend Jarre's concert at Place de la Concorde, Paris (the first in a decade of mega-concerts Jarre will perform worldwide). It features lasers, synthesizers and fireworks, controlled by computers, and will be the basis for all his live work.
1981 June LP *Magnetic Fields* hits UK #6 and US #98.
Oct Jarre becomes the first western rock artist to play China with major concerts in Beijing. The event is filmed for a TV special and recorded for LP release to offset the phenomenal costs involved.
1982 May Subsequent double LP *The Concerts In China* hits UK #6.
1983 Jarre records LP *Music For Supermarkets*, made expressly to voice his distaste and disregard for the music business. Only one copy of the LP is pressed.
July The LP is auctioned in Paris. The successful bidder is unknown. Jarre destroys the master, but the project is given a public airing on Radio Luxembourg.
Nov LP *The Essential Jean-Michel Jarre*, a compilation of his most celebrated works, reaches UK #14.
1984 Nov LP *Zoolook* peaks at UK #47.
1985 Jarre performs in his home town Lyon, during the Papal visit.
1986 Apr The latest in his increasingly grand live spectaculars is held in Houston, Tex., US for the city's 150th anniversary. Jarre plays to an estimated 1.3 million people while the largest light, laser and firework show plays around him, illuminating Houston's glass skyscrapers. It is the biggest event of its kind, despite his less than superstar status in US. "Rendez Vous Houston" is filmed by video director Bob Giraldi, for worldwide showing on TV. LP *Rendez-Vous* hits UK #9. (The set is inspired by the Challenger space shuttle disaster. Included is *Ron's Song*, which had been intended to be played by shuttle crew member Ron McNair on his saxophone while in space.)
Aug *Fourth Rendez-Vous* peaks at UK #65.
1987 July LP *In Concert Lyon/Houston* reaches UK #18.
1988 Sept Jarre plans another stage spectacular, this time in London's Docklands. It is intended to coincide with the release of his new LP, and to attract 3 million people. The local council of Newham objects on the grounds of public safety and refuses to grant a license to allow the concert to go ahead. LP *Revelations* hits UK #3. It includes guest guitarist Hank Marvin of The Shadows° on track *London Kid*.
Oct [8-9] "Destination Docklands" extravaganza proceeds, despite wind, rain, traffic and Newham council, but as two smaller shows instead of one large event. Marvin is flown in by Jarre from Australia to perform at the event.

AL JARREAU

1968 Jarreau (b. Mar.12, 1940, Milwaukee US) having begun singing at age 4, influenced by his older brothers' interest in jazz and singing, begins improvizing vocal style singing along to radio songs. Choosing music over a career in sports (he is a gifted basketball and baseball player), he works with guitarist Julio Martinez in a Sausalito, Cal. club. (He will spend the next 4 years developing his improvizing vocal style in LA clubs including Dino's, The Troubadour and The Bitter End.)
1972 He plays concerts at The Improvization in New York, where he meets other artists, including Quincy Jones, Bette Midler° and comedian Richard Pryor.
1973/74 Jarreau plays a residence at LA coffee house, The Bla Bla Café, where he develops his writing and performs his own material.
1975 Spotted by Warner Bros. playing at The Troubadour, he is signed up and releases critically-acclaimed debut LP *We Got By*.
Dec During a promotional tour of Europe, he wins a German Grammy award for Best International Soloist (reflecting his early popularity in Europe).
1976 Sept LP *Glow* reaches US #132.
1977 Jan He begins his first world tour.
Aug Double live LP *Look To The Rainbow/Live In Europe*, recorded on his world tour, makes US #49.
1978 Feb [23] Jarreau wins a Grammy for Best Jazz Vocal Performance for LP *Look To The Rainbow* at the 20th annual Grammy ceremonies.
Nov LP *Ally Fly Home* peaks at US #78.
1980 Mar Jarreau wins the Silver Award at the Tokyo Music Festival.
Aug LP *This Time* reaches US #27.
1981 Mar Jarreau wins a Grammy for Best R&B Vocalist, and begins another world tour including Brazil, The Philippines and Japan.
Sept *We're In This Love Together* makes US #15. LP *Breakin Away* hits US #9 and UK #60.
Oct *We're In This Love Together* makes UK #55.
1982 Jan *Breakin' Away* reaches US #43. He plays standing-room-only dates in UK and Scandinavia.
Feb [24] Jarreau wins an award as Best Male Pop Vocalist at the 24th annual Grammy awards.
Apr *Teach Me Tonight* peaks at US #70.
1983 May *Mornin'* makes US #21. LP *Jarreau* reaches US #13 and UK #39.
June *Mornin'* makes UK #28.
July *Boogie Down* peaks at US #77. *Trouble In Paradise* reaches UK #36.
Oct *Boogie Down* falters at UK #63.
Nov *Trouble In Paradise* stalls at US #63.
1984 Nov *After All* peaks at US #69. LP *High Crime* makes US #49 and UK #81, as Jarreau plays sold-out US and UK dates.
1985 Oct LP *Al Jarreau In London*, recorded during his 1984 visit, makes US #125.
1986 June Guesting on Bob James and David Sanborn's LP *Double Vision*, Jarreau revives Lenny Welch's 1963 hit *Since I Fell For You*. Featured in US TV series "Moonlighting", it will later be included on the TV soundtrack LP. Video *Live In London*, filmed during his 1984 UK tour, is released.
Sept LP *L Is For Lover*, his tenth for Warner Bros. and the first in 2 years, reaches US #81 and UK #45.
1987 Mar The title theme for "Moonlighting" TV series makes US #23 and UK #8.
July LP *Moonlighting*, featuring Jarreau on two tracks, is released.
1988 Sept *So Good*, produced by George Duke from forthcoming LP *Heart's Horizon*, is released.

JEFFERSON AIRPLANE/STARSHIP

Grace Slick (vocals)
Marty Balin (vocals)
Paul Kantner (guitar)
Jorma Kaukonen (guitar)
Jack Casady (bass guitar)
Spencer Dryden (drums)

1965 July Jefferson Airplane is formed in San Francisco, Cal., by Balin (b. Jan.30, 1942, Cincinnati, Oh., US), who has previously cut solo singles *Nobody But You* and *I Specialize In Love* for Challenge label and spent some time in LA folk group The Town Criers. First recruit is guitarist Kantner (b. Mar.12, 1942, San Francisco, Cal., US), whom Balin meets at local club The Drinking Gourd. Upright bass player Bob Harvey, singer Signe Toly Anderson, guitar/vocalist Kaukonen (b. Dec.23, 1940, Washington, D.C., US) and drummer Jerry Peloquin also join. Peloquin is soon replaced by Skip Spence. (Jefferson Airplane is a paper match split at one end to act as an instant "roach clip" for a marijuana cigarette.)

Aug [13] The group debuts at the first night of the Matrix Club, which is co-owned by Balin.

Oct [16] Jefferson Airplane plays on the same bill as another local group, The Great Society, at the first Family Dogg dance at Longshoreman's Hall. Kantner is much taken with the other band's singer, Slick (b. Grace Wing, Oct.30, 1939, Chicago, Ill., US) and follows the band just to hear her sing.

Nov Harvey is replaced by Kaukonen's friend, Casady (b. Apr.13, 1944, Washington, D.C.), with whom he had played in The Triumphs. The band signs to RCA Records, for a reported $25,000. (The Great Society signs to CBS/Columbia for an even bigger sum.)

1966 Feb Jefferson Airplane's debut single, *It's No Secret*, is released.

Oct Spence leaves to form Moby Grape°, and is replaced by jazz-schooled drummer Spencer Dryden (b. Apr.7, 1938, New York, N.Y.) from The Peanut Butter Conspiracy.

Nov Debut LP *Jefferson Airplane Takes Off*, recorded in Dec. 1965, is released in US by RCA, and makes US #128 (it will not get a UK release until 1971). Anderson leaves to have a baby and Slick joins, bringing with her two songs she performs with The Great Society – *White Rabbit* and *Somebody To Love*. (The Great Society have recorded two live LPs but Columbia will not release them until Slick finds fame with Jefferson Airplane.)

1967 Jan The band plays its first East Coast tour.

Jan [14] They play at the first Human Be-In, in Golden Gate Park, San Francisco.

June LP *Surrealistic Pillow*, the first to feature Slick's vocal, is produced by Rick Jarrard, with The Grateful Dead's° Jerry Garcia as musical adviser. It hits US #3, earning a gold disk, while *Somebody To Love* (written by Darby Slick, Grace's brother-in-law) hits US #5 and is a million-seller.

June [16] The group takes part in the Monterey Pop Festival in Cal.

Aug *White Rabbit*, written by Slick, and a surreal interpretation of *Alice in Wonderland*, hits US #8, also a million-seller.

Sept LP *Surrealistic Pillow* is released in UK, in an edited form which excludes major tracks like *White Rabbit* and *Plastic Fantastic Lover*, and substitutes tracks from the unissued-in-UK first LP.

Oct *Ballad Of You And Me And Pooneil* reaches US #42.

Dec *Watch Her Ride* makes US #61.

1968 Feb LP *After Bathing At Baxter's*, the beginning of a working relationship with producer Pat Ieraci, reaches US #17. Casady plays on Jimi Hendrix's° LP *Electric Ladyland* and Country Joe & The Fish's° LP *Together*.

Apr *Greasy Heart* makes US #38.

July The group buys a house at 2400 Fulton in San Francisco, which will become its HQ.

Aug Jefferson Airplane begins its first European tour, which includes a well-received appearance at UK's Isle of Wight festival, a free gig at Parliament Hill Fields in London, and two nights at the Roundhouse with The Doors°.

Nov LP *Crown Of Creation* hits US #6, and the extracted title track makes US #64. French movie director Jean-Luc Godard films the band playing on a rooftop, for his projected *One American Movie* film. After Godard drops his plans, the footage is picked up by documentary film-maker D.A. Pennebaker and used in *One P.M.*. Kaukonen and Casady begin an offshoot group, at first called Hot Shit, then renamed Hot Tuna.

1969 Apr Live LP *Bless Its Pointed Little Head* makes US #17.

June LP *Bless Its Pointed Little Head* becomes the group's first UK chart entry, spending a week at #38.

Aug [15] Jefferson Airplane plays an early morning set at the Woodstock Festival.

Dec LP *Volunteers*, the band's most overtly political work, reaches US #13, while its title track makes US #65.

Dec [6] The band takes part in The Rolling Stones'° ill-fated concert at Altamont Speedway, Cal. Balin is attacked halfway through a song by one of the Hells Angels handling security.

1970 Feb LP *Volunteers* reaches UK #34. After an argument with Balin, Dryden leaves to join New Riders of the Purple Sage. He is replaced by Joey Covington, who has been drumming with Hot Tuna.

Feb [27] The group is fined for obscenity in Oklahoma.

May [16] Balin is arrested for drug possession.

Oct Slick, now pregnant by Kantner, is unable to make live appearances. Casady and Kaukonen, who have for some time been playing occasional support gigs to Jefferson Airplane as Hot Tuna, either with other musicians or as an acoustic duo, formalize the offshoot group. They bring in violinist Papa John Creach (b. May 28, 1917, Beaver Falls, Pa., US), who also becomes a member of Jefferson Airplane. Kaukonen switches to electric guitar and Covington plays drums. A Hot Tuna gig at the New Orleans House, Berkeley, is recorded and given a low-key LP release.

Nov Kantner and Slick invite Jerry Garcia, David Crosby and Graham Nash to contribute to LP *Blows Against The Empire*, billed as by Paul Kantner and Jefferson Starship (the first use of this name). The LP reaches US #20 and is the first to be nominated for the sci-fi writers' Hugo Awards.

1971 Jan [25] Slick and Kantner's daughter China is born.

Feb Compilation LP *The Worst Of Jefferson Airplane* reaches US #12.

Apr Balin leaves the group. He retires from music, apart from producing the band Grootna for Columbia.

May [13] Slick crashes her Mercedes in San Francisco. Her injuries are slight, but cause Jefferson Airplane recording sessions to be cancelled.

July Hot Tuna's second LP *First Pull Up Then Pull Down* makes US #43.

Aug The band launches its own RCA-distributed label, Grunt Records.

Oct The first Grunt release, Jefferson Airplane LP *Bark*, climbs to US #11 (earning a gold disk) and UK #42.

Nov *Pretty As You Feel*, an edit from a 30-minute studio jam featuring Jerry Garcia, Carlos Santana° and Creach, is taken from LP *Grunt* and makes US #60.

1972 Jan Slick and Kantner's LP *Sunfighter*, which features baby China on the cover, makes US #89. Creach also releases his first solo LP on Grunt, featuring guest spots from Airplane members, while Hot Tuna appears on David Crosby's LP *If Only I Could Remember My Name*.

1972 Apr The Jefferson Airplane members regroup for LP *Long John Silver*. During the sessions, Covington leaves, and is replaced by ex-Turtles° drummer John Barbata.

May Hot Tuna's LP *Burgers* makes US #68.

Sept LP *Long John Silver* reaches US #20 and UK #30.

Oct The group begins a US tour, with guitarist David Frieberg added. On the last date of the tour Balin takes the stage for three songs. The Hot Tuna members make a final break and resist any attempts to woo them back. (The band will make six more LPs before breaking up in 1978.)

1973 Apr LP *30 Seconds Over Winterland*, a live album recorded during the last US tour, is released.

July Kantner, Slick and Frieberg's LP *Baron Von Tollbooth And The Chrome Nun* reaches US #52.

1974 Feb Slick's debut solo LP, *Manhole*, makes US #127, while Hot Tuna's LP *The Phosphorescent Rat* reaches US #148. Slick, Kantner, Creach, Barbata, 19-year-old guitarist Craig Chaquico (b. Sept.26, 1954) (ex-Steelwind and the Kantner-Slick solo efforts) and Kaukonen's bass-playing younger brother Peter (under the name Peter Kangaroo) begin rehearsing under the name Jefferson Starship.

Mar [19] Jefferson Airplane becomes Jefferson Starship.

Apr Jefferson Starship begins its first US tour. Peter Kaukonen leaves after it and is replaced by UK session player Pete Sears, who had worked on *Manhole*.

June *Early Flight*, an LP of unreleased and rare Jefferson Airplane

material, peaks at US #110.
July The new group goes into the studio for the first time.
Nov *Ride The Tiger* peaks at US #84.
Dec LP *Dragonfly* reaches US #11, and earns a gold disk.
1975 Jan Earlier differences fully resolved, Balin rejoins.
May Hot Tuna's LP *America's Choice* reaches US #75.
Aug Creach leaves the group to settle in LA and front his own band.
Sept LP *Red Octopus* tops the US chart for 4 weeks, and sells more than 2½ million copies.
Sept [30] Jefferson Starship joins The Grateful Dead° for a free concert at San Francisco's Lindley Park.
Oct Balin's song *Miracles* hits US #3, and is a million-seller.
Dec *Play On Love* reaches US #49. Hot Tuna's LP *Yellow Fever* makes US #97.
1976 Before the band returns to the studio, Slick breaks with Kantner. (She will marry the group's 24-year-old lighting engineer, Skip Johnson, in Nov.)
July LP *Spitfire* reaches UK #30.
Sept *With Your Love* makes US #12. It is taken from LP *Spitfire* which hits US #3, achieving platinum status.
Dec *St. Charles* peaks at US #64. Hot Tuna's LP *Hoppkorv* makes US #116.
1977 Mar LP *Flight Log (1966-1976)*, an anthology of Airplane, Starship, Hot Tuna, Slick and Kantner material, reaches US #37.
1978 Apr Hot Tuna's LP *Double Dose* reaches US #92.
May *Count On Me* hits US #8 as its parent LP *Earth* hits US #5.
June [17] Slick's alcohol problem prevents her from taking the stage at the Lorelei Festival in Hamburg, West Germany. As a result, fans riot, stealing or destroying much of the band's equipment.
June [24] The group appears at UK's Knebworth Festival, without Slick (who has effectively quit the band).
July *Runaway* reaches US #12.
Sept *Crazy Feelin'* makes US #54. Balin leaves the band, leaving Kantner as the only original member.
1979 Apr [12] The vocal gap is filled by Mickey Thomas (who sang lead vocal on Elvin Bishop's *Fooled Around And Fell In Love*). Barbata leaves and is replaced by Aynsley Dunbar (b. 1946, Liverpool, UK). Second hits LP collection *Jefferson Starship Gold* reaches US #20.
May [12] The new line-up debuts live at a free concert in Golden Gate Park, San Francisco.
Nov *Jane* reaches US #14.
Nov [12] Balin presents a rock opera, *Rock Justice*, in a 4-day run at the Old Waldorf club, San Francisco.
Dec [31] Jefferson Starship's New Year's Eve concert at X6s Club, San Francisco, is widely broadcast live on US radio.
1980 Jan The group plays a benefit concert at Almeda Coliseum, Oakland, Cal., in aid of the people of Kampuchea, with The Grateful Dead° and The Beach Boys°.
Feb *Girl With The Hungry Eyes* makes US #55. Parent LP *Freedom At Point Zero* hits US #10 and UK #22. *Jane* reaches UK #21.
May Slick releases solo LP *Dreams*, which makes US #32 and UK #28.
Oct [25] Kantner suffers a stroke. (He will recover fully.)
1981 Mar Slick rejoins Jefferson Starship, just as her solo LP *Welcome To The Wreckers' Ball* peaks at US #48.
Apr The group's *Find Your Way Back* reaches US #29.
May Balin's ballad *Hearts* hits US #8.
June Group LP *Modern Times* reaches #26. Balin's first solo LP, *Balin*, peaks at US #35.
Aug The group's *Stranger* reaches US #48.
Sept The second single from Balin's LP, *Atlanta Lady (Something About Your Love)* enters the US chart, reaching #27.
1982 May [28] The group takes part in a benefit concert for the Vietnam Veterans' Project, at Moscone Center in San Francisco, with Boz Scaggs°, Country Joe° McDonald and The Grateful Dead°.
Aug [8] Mickey Thomas marries Sara Kendrick, in San Francisco.
Oct Drummer Don Baldwin (ex-Elvin Bishop Band) joins, Dunbar having left after LP sessions have been completed. *Be My Lady* reaches US #28.
1983 Jan LP *Winds Of Change* makes US #26, and the extracted title track makes US #38.
Feb Balin single, *What Love Is*, reaches US #63.
Mar His second solo LP, *Lucky*, makes US #165.
Aug Kantner releases solo LP, *The Planet Earth Rock And Roll Orchestra*, in US only.
1984 Jefferson Starship begins an extensive US tour.
May *No Way Out* reaches US #23.
June The group begins a US tour to promote LP *Nuclear Furniture*, which enters the US chart, reaching #28.
Sept *Layin' It On The Line* peaks at US #66.
Oct Kantner appears on stage with Balin's band at Golden Gate Park to perform old Jefferson Airplane song *It's No Secret*.
1985 After much legal wrangling, Kantner departs from the band with a lump sum of $250,000 and the provision that Jefferson is dropped from the band's name. Frieberg follows him. Thomas goes on MTV to state that the two have been sacked. The group plays as Starship Jefferson but soon settles on just Starship.
Mar The Kantner, Balin and Casaday Band debuts at the 8th Annual Bay Area Music Awards. After club appearances and a free gig in Golden Gate Park, Balin leaves his own band to join the KBC Band full time.
Nov First Starship single, *We Built This City* tops the US chart for 2 weeks and reaches UK #12. Parent LP *Knee Deep In The Hoopla* hits US #7, but fails to chart in UK.
Dec The KBC Band makes its official debut at the re-opening of the Fillmore. Signe Anderson takes the stage for *It's No Secret*.
1986 Mar *Sara* tops the US chart for a week, but stalls at UK #66.
Apr [23] Starship cancels a tour of Europe.
May *Tomorrow Doesn't Matter Tonight* reaches US #26.
July China Kantner makes a guest appearance on US MTV. The group becomes the first national spokesgroup for the National Network of Runaway Youth Services. Meanwhile, Starship's *Before I Go* peaks at US #68.
1987 Apr *Nothing's Gonna Stop Us Now*, used as the theme for film *Mannequin*, tops the UK chart for 2 weeks.
May Starship's first UK chart-topper finally comes more than 2 decades after the original formation of Jefferson Airplane: *Nothing's Gonna Stop Us Now* hits UK #1 for 4 weeks, and is the second-biggest selling single of the year in UK. Meanwhile, in US double compilation LP *2400 Fulton Street*, credited to Jefferson Airplane, and including re-mastered versions of songs from the group's first six studio LPs, reaches US #138.
June [20] Starship participates in the 20th anniversary "Summer of Love" concert in San Francisco.
Aug *It's Not Over ('Til It's Over)* hits US #9.
Sept LP *No Protection*, which includes both recent top 10 hits, reaches US #12.
Nov *Beat Patrol*, taken from the LP, reaches US #46.
1988 Nov Slick, Kantner, Kaukonen and Casady begin writing and rehearsing for a forthcoming LP and tour.

THE JESUS & MARY CHAIN

William Reid (guitar and vocals)
Jim Reid (guitar and vocals)
Douglas Hart (bass)
Bobby Gillespie (drums)

1984 June The brothers Reid, (b. East Kilbride, Scotland), decide to form a band after writing and recording songs at home on a portastudio, bought by their father with severance pay. They recruit Hart and Gillespie.
Aug Moving to London, the band meets Alan McGee, owner of small independent Creation label, who signs them and becomes their manager.
Nov *Upside Down*, produced by McGee's friend "Slaughter" Joe Foster, is released with no success. (The B-side revives Syd Barrett's° *Vegetable Man*). McGee's expert promotion of the band brings media attention. As the band plays live sets sometimes consisting of only two songs, UK music press becomes increasingly interested.
1985 Feb *Upside Down* tops the UK independent chart for two weeks. McGee signs the band to WEA-marketed label blanco y negro.
Mar *Never Understand*, produced by the Reids themselves, spends 4 weeks on the UK chart, peaking at #47. It is compared with the 1977 original by The Sex Pistols°. McGee's publicity operation has the group claiming to be 18 and 19 when in fact they are in their mid-20s. A riot follows an ultra-short gig at North London Polytechnic, increasing their notoriety.
June *You Trip Me Up* reaches only UK #55.
Oct *Just Like Honey*, an unexpected ballad, makes UK #45.
Nov Debut LP *Psychocandy*, reflecting 4 years of the Reids' musical development, peaks at UK #31.
1986 Jan The group takes a 6-month lay-off and Gillespie leaves to form his

own band Primal Scream.

Aug The more mainstream *Some Candy Talking* is the band's first major UK hit, reaching #13. They now try to discourage their rebel/riot image but controversy persists when UK Radio 1 DJ Mike Read refuses to play it because of apparent drug references in the lyrics. Live performances follow (mainly more responsible, at major venues to wider audiences), and various stand-in drummers are used, but no one joins permanently.

1987 May *April Skies* hits UK #8, the group's biggest-seller yet.

Aug *Happy When It Rains* peaks at UK #25.

Sept LP *Darklands* features William Reid writing and singing lead vocal for the first time and hits UK #5. The group tours without a drummer, employing a roadie to play a drum tracks cassette through the PA. The gigs are poorly received.

Nov US and Canada tour is surrounded by gig violence: in Toronto, Jim Reid is arrested after allegedly hitting troublesome fans with a mike stand. He is charged with assault but later acquitted. Extracted *Darklands* reaches UK #33.

Dec The group is banned from appearing on the US TV version of "Top of the Pops" because its name is considered blasphemous.

1988 Apr *Sidewalking* peaks at UK #30. Meanwhile, LP *Barbed Wire Kisses*, a compilation of B-sides, out-takes and unreleased material, covers for the absence of a newly-recorded LP, and hits UK #9.

JETHRO TULL

Ian Anderson (vocals and flute)
Mick Abrahams (guitar)
Glenn Cornick (bass)
Clive Bunker (drums)

1963 Anderson (b. Aug.10, 1947, Edinburgh, Scotland, UK) forms The Blades (named after James Bond's club) in Blackpool, UK, with fellow blues-minded school friends, Jeffrey Hammond-Hammond (b. July 30, 1946) on bass and John Evans (a.k.a. Evan, b. Mar.28, 1948) on drums. Their first gig at a youth club nets £2.

1965 They play jazz-blues and danceable soul music for northern club audiences and change names to The John Evan Band and then John Evan's Smash (apparently to please Evans' mother, who paid for the group's van).

1967 Cornick (b. Apr.24, 1947, Barrow-in-Furness, UK) replaces Hammond-Hammond on bass.

Nov The group travels to London, hoping to succeed at the heart of the UK blues boom. Within days the road-weary crew has split but Anderson and Cornick stay in London.

Dec The duo forms a new band with guitarist Abrahams (b. Apr.7, 1943, Luton, UK) and drummer Bunker (b. Dec.12, 1946), and signs to Terry Ellis and Chris Wright's booking agency, playing two gigs a week under a variety of names like Navy Blue and Bag Of Blues. Jethro Tull, after the 18th-century agriculturalist, receives most audience enthusiasm, and sticks.

1968 Feb MGM releases Abrahams' *Sunshine Day*, taken from a Derek Lawrence-produced demo, with an earlier Lawrence recording of The John Evan Band on the B-side. The first pressing mistakenly credits the band as Jethro Toe, but it fails to chart.

June The band gains a residency at London's Marquee club. Ellis and Wright suggest that Anderson should abandon his flute, giving the focus to lead guitarist Abrahams, but this is resisted.

June [29] The band supports Pink Floyd° at the first free rock festival in London's Hyde Park.

Aug Jethro Tull becomes the sensation of UK's Sunbury Jazz & Blues Festival, gaining rapturous music press notices. On the strength of this, Island Records offers a recording contract.

Nov Debut LP *This Was* hits UK #10, but *A Song For Jeffrey* (dedicated to ex-member Hammond-Hammond) fails to chart.

Dec A personality clash develops between Anderson and Abrahams, who leaves to form Blodwyn Pig.

Dec [12] The band takes part in The Rolling Stones'° "Rock'n'Roll Circus" (filmed as a TV spectacular but never screened).

1969 Jan *Love Story*, the last featuring Abrahams, reaches UK #29. Tony Iommi (later of Black Sabbath°) and Davy O'List of The Nice are interim members, before Martin Barre (b. Nov.17, 1946) joins permanently.

Jan [24] Jethro Tull opens its first US tour with a concert in New York City.

Apr Reprise issues LP *This Was* in US. It reaches #62.

May *Living In The Past*, the first featuring Barre, hits UK #3. The group appears on UK TV's "Top of the Pops" for the first time.

June [20-22] Jethro Tull participates in the '69 Pop Festival at Northridge, Cal., US.

July [3] The band performs at the Newport Jazz Festival, Rhode Island, US.

Aug LP *Stand Up*, packaged in a gatefold sleeve from which card figures of the band actually "stand up" when opened, tops the UK chart. All songs are written by Anderson, apart from his arrangement of Bach's *Bouree*.

Nov LP *Stand Up* climbs to US #20, while *Sweet Dream* hits UK #7. It is the band's first release on Ellis and Wright's Chrysalis label (Island will still handle the next two LPs).

1970 Jan Double A-side *The Witch's Promise/Teacher* hits UK #4.

Apr LP *Benefit* has John Evan guesting. (Joining initially on a temporary basis, he will stay for 10 years.)

May LP *Benefit* hits UK #3 and US #11.

July [3-5] Jethro Tull plays The Atlanta Pop Festival, at Middle Georgia Raceway, Byron, Ga., US.

Nov [4] The band plays a benefit concert at New York's Carnegie Hall in aid of Phoenix House, a drug rehabilitation center.

Dec Cornick leaves to form his own band, Wild Turkey, and Hammond-Hammond rejoins.

1971 Apr LP *Aqualung* hits UK #4.

May [10] The band plays in a cloud of tear gas at the Red Rock Amphitheater, Denver, Col., after police fire canisters into the audience. On return to UK, Bunker leaves to get married (going on to form Jude with Robin Trower, Frankie Miller and Jim Dewar), and is replaced by Barriemore Barlow (b. Sept.10, 1949).

June LP *Aqualung* hits US #7, the group's first US top 10 success.

Aug From LP *Aqualung*, *Hymn 43* is the group's first US chart single at #91. It receives heavy FM airplay, as do the LP cuts *Locomotive Breath* and *Crosseyed Mary*.

Sept A 5-song EP headed by *Life Is A Long Song* reaches UK #11.

1972 Apr LP *Thick As A Brick* hits UK #5.

June LP *Thick As A Brick* hits US #1 for 2 weeks.

July Double compilation LP *Living In The Past*, featuring mostly unreleased or singles-only material, plus a live side recorded at New York's Carnegie Hall, hits UK #8.

Nov LP *Living In The Past* hits US #3.

1973 Jan *Living In The Past*, extracted for the first time as a US single, makes US #11.

July LP *A Passion Play* is released after being premiered as a live show, which is poorly received by many critics. Anderson announces that the group will cease playing live. The LP still makes UK #13 and hits US #1 (a single edit of the title track has already peaked at US #80).

1974 Nov Largely orchestral (but song-based) LP *War Child* reaches UK #14 and hits US #2. (The LP had been developed in conjunction with a planned film which never surfaces.) The long world tour to promote the LP includes a string quartet augmenting the band.

1975 Jan Taken from the LP, *Bungle In The Jungle* makes US #11.

Sept Recorded in the band's new mobile studio, LP *Minstrel In the Gallery* reaches UK #20 and hits US #7.

Oct The LP title track reaches US #79.

Dec Hammond-Hammond leaves to concentrate on art, and is replaced by John Glascock (b. 1953, London).

1976 Jan LP *M.U. – The Best Of Jethro Tull Vol. 1* contains a previously unreleased track, *Rainbow Blues*. It reaches US #13 and UK #44.

Mar *Locomotive Breath*, issued as a US single, reaches #62.

May LP *Too Old To Rock'n'Roll, Too Young To Die* makes UK #25 and US #14. It contains material taken from a play planned by Anderson and David Palmer and never staged, but forms the basis of the band's UK London Weekend Television TV special.

Dec Seasonal EP *Ring Out Solstice Bells* reaches UK #28. Jethro Tull appears again on UK BBC TV's "Top of the Pops" (as a last-minute replacement for Rod Stewart°).

1977 Feb The group's first UK tour in 3 years introduces LP *Songs From The Wood* which reaches UK #13 and will hit US #8. The LP explores Anderson's interest in folk music (he has recently produced an LP for Steeleye Span°).

May *The Whistler* peaks at US #59. Keyboards player David Palmer joins the band.

Oct LP *Repeat: The Best Of Jethro Tull Vol. 2* is released. With only one new track, it stalls at US #94 and fails to make UK top 50.

1978 Apr LP *Heavy Horses* reaches UK #20 and US #19. The group promotes the LP with an extensive UK tour.

Oct LP *Live: Bursting Out* reaches UK #17 and US #21. The band's US tour is highlighted by a concert at New York's Madison Square Garden, broadcast live to several countries.

1979 Oct [12] Anderson is pierced in the eye by a thorn thrown by an over-zealous fan at a concert in New York's Madison Square Garden.

Oct LP *Stormwatch* reaches UK #27 and US #22. Glascock, who has never played live with the band, has become too ill to record, leaving Anderson to play the bass.

Nov [17] Glascock dies after open heart surgery, aged 26.

Nov Dave Pegg (ex-Fairport Convention°) joins the band.

1980 June Anderson records a solo LP. As well as Barre and Pegg from Jethro Tull, he brings in Eddie Jobson (ex-Roxy Music°) on keyboards and violin and Mark Craney on drums. Bowing to company pressure, Anderson releases it as a Jethro Tull LP, but discards Barlow, Evan and Palmer in favor of the new line-up.

Sept The resultant LP, *A*, with Jobson's influence evident, reaches UK #25 and US #30. Jobson stays only for the subsequent tour before leaving to go solo. (He will feature on the 1981 full-length video *Slipstream*.)

1982 Apr LP *Broadsword And The Beast*, with new drummer Gerry Conway and keyboard player Peter John Vetesse, reaches UK #27, after the band tours UK to promote it.

May LP *Broadsword And The Beast* makes US #19.

1983 Nov Anderson's debut solo LP *Walk Into Light*, with help only from Vetesse, is released but reaches only UK #78.

1984 Sept LP *Under Wraps* makes UK #18 and US #76. It features new drummer Doane Perry with Vetesse making another important contribution. The band tours UK and Europe, but during a US tour Anderson develops a throat infection serious enough to postpone dates. *Lap Of Luxury* reaches UK #70.

1985 The band performs a one-off for German TV, with Jobson (temporarily) back on keyboards, and features in a London Symphony Orchestra presentation of Jethro Tull's music, which plays in Europe and US.

Oct LP *Original Masters*, a compilation of the band's best up to 1977, is released with a small UK TV campaign, but it reaches only UK #63.

1987 Sept LP *Crest Of A Knave* makes UK #19.

1988 June The group, with Anderson, Barre, Pegg, Perry and Martin Allcock (keyboards), embarks on a 4-week US tour as part of its 20th anniversary celebration.

July Chrysalis releases *Jethro Tull Compilation: Twentieth Anniversary*, a 65-track collection documenting the band's history, available in 5-LP, 3-cassette, or 3-CD format. The band plays a major anniversary concert at London's Wembley Arena.

BILLY JOEL

1964 Feb Joel (b. May 9, 1951, Hicksville, Long Island, N.Y., US), whose major preoccupations while growing up have been studying the piano and boxing (he has broken his nose as a local young welterweight champ) is inspired by seeing The Beatles° on US TV's "Ed Sullivan Show", and looks for a band to join, finding The Echoes, who become a popular local live attraction with a repertoire built around UK group hits.

1965/66 He finds work playing piano on sessions at a studio at Levittown, notably for Artie Ripp's Kama Sutra Productions, and producer George "Shadow" Morton. He also continues to play with The Echoes, who become The Emeralds, and then The Lost Souls.

1967 He joins Long Island group The Hassles as keyboard player. Signed to United Artists, their first single is a cover of Sam and Dave's° *You Got Me Hummin'* (their only UK release, which Joel will still perform live during the 1980s). The Hassles release four singles and two LPs, *The Hassles* and *Hour Of The Wolf*, over 18 months.

1969 When The Hassles split, keyboard player Joel and drummer Jon Small form an organ/drums hard rock duo called Attila. Joel also briefly becomes a rock critic for the arts magazine *Changes*.

1970 LP *Attila* is released by Epic in US, with Joel and Small dressed as barbarians for the sleeve picture. The LP bombs and the band splits immediately. Joel enters a period of acute depression (aggravated by the ending of a serious romance), and checks himself into Meadowbrook Hospital, where he is placed under psychiatric observation.

1971 Joel signs as a soloist to Family Productions, owned by Ripp. The deal involves a lifetime agreement (Ripp will still receive royalties from Joel's hit career in the 1980s).

Nov LP *Cold Spring Harbor*, recorded in Cal., is released on Family Productions, through Paramount. Due to mixing/mastering incompetence the LP is pressed sounding too fast (an error not corrected until it is re-mixed in 1984). Joel puts together a band to begin a promotional tour.

1972 Embarrassed by the LP, despite good live reviews, he leaves for LA with girlfriend Elizabeth Weber (ex-wife of Jon Small), where he spends 6 months at the Executive Room on Wilshire Boulevard playing bar piano in a lounge, using the name Bill Martin (the experience produces his song *Piano Man*).

Apr [1] Still an unknown, he plays the Mar Y Sol Festival in Vega Baja, Puerto Rico, where he first comes to the interest of CBS/Columbia records.

1973 Joel and Weber marry, and she attends UCLA's Graduate School of Management. He is sought by several major labels after *Captain Jack* is played constantly on station W-MMR FM (having been taken from a Philadelphia show broadcast live over the station in 1972). CBS/Columbia's chief executive Clive Davis goes to see Joel in the piano bar in LA. The label signs him, but to pacify Ripp has to retain the Family Products Romulus and Remus logo on future Joel releases (for which Ripp will receive some 25 cents from each LP sold).

1974 Apr Debut Columbia LP *Piano Man* makes US #27 (and earns a gold disk for a half million sales 2 years later), while the title track reaches US #25.

July *Worse Comes To Worst*, also from the LP, makes US #80.

Aug *Travelin' Prayer* peaks at US #77. Joel puts together a stage band comprising guitarist Don Evans, bass player Pat McDonald, steel guitar and banjo player Tom Whitehorse and drummer Rhys Clark, and plays dates supporting The Beach Boys°, The J. Geils Band° and The Doobie Brothers°. His first major live success is in Philadelphia, where he is a headliner.

1975 Jan *The Entertainer* reaches US #34, while LP *Streetlife Serenade* climbs to US #35. Joel joins James William Guercio and Larry Fitzgerald's Caribou management company. He and his wife move back from Cal. to New York, where Joel finds renewed songwriting creativity (he claims to have written *New York State Of Mind* within 20 minutes of entering his New York home).

1976 July LP *Turnstiles* peaks at US #122. It includes *Say Goodbye To Hollywood*, a celebration of the Joels' move and a Phil Spector tribute, which will later be covered by Ronnie Spector, as well as the E Street Band. Produced by Joel, it was recorded in New York with Elton John's° sidemen Nigel Olsson and Dee Murray, and the sessions have not, in Joel's opinion, been entirely successful. Having fired producer Guercio early in the recording, Joel also leaves Guercio's Caribou management, appointing his wife

BILLY JOEL *cont.*

Elizabeth as manager. She renegotiates his contract with Columbia, fixing a new and more favorable royalty rate of $1 an LP.

1977 Sept He makes a rare US TV appearance, playing new song *Just The Way You Are* on "Saturday Night Live" to a viewing audience of 20 million.

Dec Also recorded in New York, LP *The Stranger* hits US #2 and earns a platinum disk. (It will become Columbia Records' second biggest selling album of all time after Simon & Garfunkel's° *Bridge Over Troubled Water*.)

1978 Feb *Just The Way You Are*, taken from the LP, hits US #3 (selling over a million) and makes Joel's UK chart debut at #19. (The song will attract over 200 cover versions, including another million-selling version by Barry White°.)

May *Movin' Out (Anthony's Song)*, also taken from LP *The Stranger*, makes US #17 (and UK #35 a month later). LP *The Stranger* reaches UK #25.

July *Only The Good Die Young* makes US #24. The song causes Joel to be banned by Catholic radio stations in US, due to its apparent anti-Catholic views – which he denies.

Oct *She's Always A Woman*, the fourth single from LP *The Stranger*, reaches US #17

1979 Jan *My Life*, Joel's second million-selling single, hits US #3 and UK #12. It is taken from LP *52nd Street*, which tops the US chart for 8 weeks, selling more than 2 million copies in its first month of release. It also hits UK #10.

Feb [15] Joel wins two Grammy Awards for *Just The Way You Are*, which is named both Record of the Year and Song of the Year.

Mar *Big Shot*, also from LP *52nd Street*, reaches US #14.

May *Until The Night*, a track from LP *52nd Street* arranged as a tribute to The Righteous Brothers°, is issued as a UK single and makes #50. Meanwhile, *Honesty* reaches US #24.

1980 Feb [27] At the 22nd Grammy Awards, Joel's LP *52nd Street* is named Best Album of the Year, and wins him a second Grammy for Best Male Pop Vocal Performance.

May *You May Be Right* hits US #7, while *All For Leyna* makes UK #40.

June LP *Glass Houses* tops the US chart for 6 weeks, (another platinum disk) and hits UK #9.

July *It's Still Rock'n'Roll To Me* tops the US chart for 2 weeks, selling over a million.

Sept *It's Still Rock'n'Roll To Me* makes UK #14, while *Don't Ask Me Why*, also from the LP, reaches US #19.

Nov *Sometimes A Fantasy*, the last extract from LP *Glass Houses* peaks at US #36.

1981 Feb [25] Joel wins a Grammy award for LP *Glass Houses*, which is named Best Male Rock Vocal Performance of the Year.

Nov Live LP *Songs From The Attic*, consisting mostly of earlier, pre-*Stranger* songs, hits US #8 and UK #57. It is the first digitally-recorded live LP. Extracted from it, a new version of *Say Goodbye To Hollywood* hits US #17.

1982 Jan *She's Got A Way* reaches US #23.

Apr [15] Joel breaks his left wrist when a car hits his motorcycle, in Long Island, N.Y. (He will remain in hospital more than a month for surgery on his hand.)

July Joel and his wife Elizabeth are divorced.

Nov LP *The Nylon Curtain* hits US #7 (a further million-seller) and reaches UK #27. Taken from it, *Pressure* makes US #20. Meanwhile, on vacation in St. Barthélemy in the Caribbean, Joel, playing piano in the bar of a hotel, meets model Christie Brinkley. *Allentown* enters the US chart.

Dec [27] Joel plays a benefit concert in Allentown, Pa.

Dec [29] Another benefit concert, at the Nassau Coliseum in Uniondale, N.Y., raises $125,000 for Joel's own Charity Begins At Home organization, which will distribute the sum between over 60 different causes.

1983 Feb *Allentown* reaches US #17.

Apr *Goodnight Saigon* makes US #56.

Sept *Tell Her About It*, from his new LP, tops the US chart for a week, and is a million-seller.

Oct LP *An Innocent Man*, with tracks as individual tributes to musical styles and stars which influenced Joel's formative years, hits US #4 (selling over 2 million copies) and UK #2.

Nov *Uptown Girl*, a track from LP *An Innocent Man* in the mold of the early Four Seasons° hits, sells a million and hits US #3. In UK, it tops the chart for 5 weeks, and is by far his biggest seller with sales topping 900,000. The promotional video features Christie Brinkley, now Joel's fiancée.

1984 Feb The title track from LP *An Innocent Man* is released, and hits US #10 and UK #8. LP *Cold Spring Harbor* is reissued in remixed form by Columbia, and reaches US #158 and UK #95.

May Fourth single from LP *An Innocent Man*, *The Longest Time*, reaches US #14 and UK #25.

Aug *Leave A Tender Moment Alone*, featuring a Toots Thielemans harmonica solo, reaches US #27 and UK #29. As Joel arrives in UK for a concert tour, he has five LPs in UK top 100.

1985 Jan [28] Joel takes part in the recording of USA For Africa's° *We Are The World* in LA. All proceeds go to African famine relief. (The single will be a multi-million seller and worldwide chart-topper.)

Mar *Keeping The Faith* reaches US #18.

Mar [23] Joel marries Christie Brinkley.

Aug *You're Only Human (Second Wind)* hits US #9. It is one of two new recordings included on double compilation LP *Greatest Hits Volumes 1 & 2*, which hits US #6 and UK #7.

Nov *The Night Is Still Young* makes US #34.

1986 Feb Double A-side reissue of *She's Always A Woman/Just The Way You Are* reaches UK #53.

June *Modern Woman*, taken from the soundtrack of film *Ruthless People*, hits US #10.

Oct *A Matter Of Trust* hits US #10 and reaches UK #52.

Aug LP *The Bridge*, with *Nylon Curtain*-style songs, includes a guest appearance by Ray Charles° on *Baby Grand*. It reaches US #7 and UK #38.

Sept [29] "The Bridge" tour starts at Civic Center, Glens Fall, N.Y.

1987 From LP *The Bridge*, *Big Man On Mulberry Street*, later becomes the central theme of an episode of US TV series "Moonlighting".

Apr *Baby Grand*, the duet with Ray Charles°, makes US #75. He plays a series of concerts in USSR, including a date at Leningrad which is recorded for LP release.

Nov Live double LP *Kohyept*, taken from his Leningrad show, reaches US #38 and UK #92.

1988 Nov Joel is featured on various artists' LP *Oliver And Company*, singing *Why Should I Worry?* from the forthcoming Disney movie of the same name.

ELTON JOHN

1951 John, (b. Reginald Kenneth Dwight, Mar.25, 1947, Pinner, Middx, UK), son of an ex-Royal Air Force trumpeter, begins taking piano lessons.

1958 He receives a part-time scholarship to London's Royal Academy of Music.

1961 R&B outfit Bluesology is formed, with him on piano, Stuart Brown on guitar, Rex Bishop on bass and Mick Inkpen on drums, and begins to play locally.

1963 He becomes "gofer" for Mills Music Publishers in London.

1965 Bluesology turns professional and for 18 months backs major US R&B artists playing UK club dates, including Major Lance, who recommends it to other US acts, including Wilson Pickett°, Patti Labelle° & The Blue Belles, The Drifters°, Doris Troy and Billy Stewart, for tours throughout Europe.

July He writes Bluesology's first release, on Fontana, *Come Back Baby*.

1966 Dec Long John Baldry° becomes front man for Bluesology. He expands the group into a 9-piece, adding American guitarist Caleb Quaye and Elton Dean on sax, plus Pete Gavin, Mark Charig and Neil Hubbard. It becomes known as The John Baldry Show, and moves to the cabaret circuit.

1967 June Disillusioned with the music he is playing for Baldry, John auditions for Liberty Records (currently establishing an independent London office, and advertising in music paper *New Musical Express* for artists and writers) at Regent Sound Studios in London where he sings Jim Reeves' songs *I Love You Because* and *He'll Have To Go*, too nervous to do his own. He fails, but is given lyrics sent to Liberty by Lincolnshire writer Bernie Taupin. They begin to write by correspondence (and do not meet until about 20 songs have been completed). They sign to The Hollies° publishing company.

Oct Baldry's° *Let The Heartaches Begin* is released and hits UK #1. B-side *Lord You Made The Night Too Long*, written by John and Taupin, is the first disk to bear this credit. (He has changed his name from Dwight, borrowing Elton Dean and John Baldry's forenames.)

1968 Baldry° Show member Quaye finds work as an engineer at Dick James Music's newly-opened 2-track studio in London's West End. John and Taupin sign to Dick James Music publishing (DJM) for £10 a week each as staff writers. (They will write together, with one break, for over 20 years.)

Mar The first Elton John solo single, *I've Been Loving You Too Long* is produced by Quaye and released on Philips, but fails to chart. Meanwhile Roger Cook records John and Taupin's *Skyline Pigeon* on UK Columbia.

1969 Jan *Lady Samantha*, John's second and final Philips release, like everything up until now, fails to chart, but finds significant UK airplay. Meanwhile, John auditions for lead singer with Robert Fripp's new group King Crimson°, but is turned down.

Feb Lulu° performs John and Taupin's *I Can't Go On Living Without You* on her BBC TV show, as one of the British entries for the Eurovision song contest.

May *It's Me That You Need* is John's first release on DJM Records.

June DJM debut LP *Empty Sky* is released, containing all John and Taupin songs.

June [25] John plays piano on The Hollies'° session for *He Ain't Heavy He's My Brother*, at Abbey Road studios, London. He contributes *From Denver To L.A.* to movie *The Games*. (It will be released as a US single on Viking in 1970.) He begins to do work on sessions for budget cover version UK labels including Music for Pleasure and Pickwick, as well as playing on other artists' demos and sessions.

1970 Mar *Border Song*, featuring The Barbara Moore Choir, receives UK airplay, but fails to reach UK top 50.

May [9] He again plays piano on an Abbey Road studio session for The Hollies°, on *I Can't Tell The Bottom From The Top* (and will guest with the group, on organ, on *Perfect Lady Housewife* for inclusion on LP *Confessions Of The Mind*).

May LP *Elton John* reaches UK #11. It is produced by Gus Dudgeon, and features the first Elton John band, with John on vocals and keyboards, Quaye on guitar, Dee Murray on bass and Nigel Olsson on drums.

Aug John signs to Uni Records in US, and *Border Song*, from LP *Elton John*, is his first US singles chart debut at #92.

Aug [25] John makes his first live appearance in US, opening at the 20th Anniversary celebrations for Doug Weston's Troubadour in LA, followed by a 17-day tour.

Oct LP *Elton John* enters the US chart, and will hit #4.

Nov [17] A concert in New York forms a live radio broadcast for station W-PLJ FM (and is recorded for LP release in 1971).

1971 Feb Ballad *Your Song* hits UK #7 and US #8. LP *Tumbleweed Connection*, featuring Dusty Springfield° as a backing vocalist, hits UK #6 and US #5.

Apr John's title song from film *Friends* makes US #34.

May Soundtrack LP *Friends* reaches US #36, while LP *17-11-70* (US title: *11-17-70*), from the Nov. concert, reaches UK #20 and US #11.

Nov John begins a tour of US, Japan and Holland.

1972 Feb Ex-Magna Carta guitarist, Davey Johnstone joins John's band. *Levon* reaches US #24.

Apr *Tiny Dancer* climbs to US #41.

May *Rocket Man* hits UK #2. LP *Madman Across The Water* makes UK #41 but hits US #8.

June LP *Honky Chateau* hits UK #2 and US #1. It is his sixth consecutive LP produced by Gus Dudgeon.

July *Rocket Man* hits US #86.

Sept *Honky Cat* makes UK #31 and hits US #8 as he begins a US tour.

Oct He makes a guest appearance in Marc Bolan's° movie *Born To Boogie*.

Oct [30] John appears in the Royal Variety Show in London.

Nov *Crocodile Rock* hits UK #5.

1973 Feb *Crocodile Rock* tops the US chart for 3 weeks, earning a gold disk, while *Daniel* hits UK #4. Parent LP *Don't Shoot Me, I'm Only The Piano Player* tops both UK and US charts.

June *Daniel* hits US #2, and is another gold single.

July *Saturday Night's Alright For Fighting* hits UK #7.

Sept *Saturday Night's Alright For Fighting* reaches US #12.

Sept [7] John plays LA's Hollywood Bowl, where he is introduced by porn movie star Linda Lovelace.

Oct *Goodbye Yellow Brick Road* hits UK #6.

Dec Double LP *Goodbye Yellow Brick Road* hits both US and UK #1 (his second successive #1) and earns a US gold disk. The title track hits US #2 for 3 weeks, and earns another gold disk.

Seasonal *Step Into Christmas* makes UK #24. He sets up his own company Rocket Records, initially to provide an outlet for other artists.

1974 Mar A Taupin ode to Marilyn Monroe, *Candle In The Wind*, peaks at UK #11.

Apr UK B-side to *Candle In The Wind*, *Bennie & The Jets* is issued as US A-side and hits #1, again a million-seller. It also becomes his first US R&B chart hit, at #15.

June *Don't Let The Sun Go Down On Me* makes UK #16 and hits US #2 (another million-seller).

July LP *Caribou* recorded at James William Guercio's studio, the Caribou Ranch, with help from The Beach Boys°, tops both UK and US charts. John re-signs with MCA in US for $8 million.

Aug [5] His popularity in US is proven when tickets for three Oct. concerts in LA sell out in minutes, causing a fourth show to be added.

Sept *The Bitch Is Back* reaches UK #15 and US #4. John duets with John Lennon° on *Whatever Gets You Through The Night* (which climbs to UK #36 and hits US #1).

Nov Compilation LP *Elton John's Greatest Hits* hits US #1 (for 10 weeks) and UK #1.

Nov [28] John and Lennon° sing *I Saw Her Standing There* at a Thanksgiving concert at New York's Madison Square Garden.

Dec A revival of The Beatles° *Lucy In The Sky With Diamonds*, with a guest appearance by Lennon°, hits UK #10 and US #1, becoming another million-seller.

1975 Jan Neil Sedaka's° *Laughter In The Rain* is released on John's Rocket Records in US (and will become a chart-topper).

Feb Ringo Starr° releases John/Taupin song *Snookeroo*.

Apr *Philadelphia Freedom*, written for John's friend Billie Jean King (after her Philadelphia-based tennis team The Freedoms), and credited to The Elton John Band with an arrangement by Thom Bell, reaches UK #12 and tops the US chart for 2 weeks (also becoming his second R&B hit at #32). John's first LP *Empty Sky* is reissued in US and hits #6. He appears in Ken Russell's movie version of The Who's° *Tommy*.

Apr [19] John fires band members Murray and Olsson on the eve of the release of autobiographical LP *Captain Fantastic And The Brown Dirt Cowboy*.

June LP *Captain Fantastic And The Brown Dirt Cowboy* hits UK #2, held off the top by *The Best Of The Stylistics*, and becomes the first LP ever to go straight to US #1. The songs were written on a cruise liner.

ELTON JOHN *cont.*

June [29] At an Oakland Coliseum concert by The Doobie Brothers° and The Eagles°, John jams on stage with both bands on *Listen To The Music* and Chuck Berry's° *Carol*.

July *Someone Saved My Life Tonight*, a partly autobiographical account of John's recent suicide attempt, reaches UK #22 and US #4.

Aug [25] He plays two benefit shows at LA's Troubadour, scene of his US live debut 5 years earlier, for UCLA's Jules Stein Eye Institute, raising over $150,000.

Nov *Island Girl* makes UK #14 and hits US #1 for 3 weeks, selling a million (and deposing Neil Sedaka's° Rocket single *Bad Blood*, with John on backing vocals). LP *Rock Of The Westies* hits UK #5 and US #1. John becomes godfather to John and Yoko Lennon's° son Sean.

Nov [21] John receives a star on Hollywood's Walk of Fame as LA declares it "Elton John Day".

Nov [26] He concludes US "West of the Rockies" tour at LA's Dodger Stadium (the first artist to play there since The Beatles° in 1966), dressed in a sequined Dodgers uniform.

1976 Feb Double A-side *Grow Some Funk Of Your Own/I Feel Like A Bullet (In The Gun Of Robert Ford)* reaches US #14, but fails to chart in UK.

Mar [7] John is immortalized in wax at Madame Tussaud's in London (the first rock star since The Beatles° to be so honored).

Apr *Pinball Wizard*, from film *Tommy*, released in re-recorded form, hits UK #7.

May LP *Here And There*, recorded live in London and New York, becomes his final DJM LP and hits UK #6 and US #4.

June John's first UK singles chart-topper (a duet with Kiki Dee) is *Don't Go Breaking My Heart*, which stays at #1 for 6 weeks. Pseudonymously credited to Ann Orson and Carte Blanche, it also tops the US chart for 4 weeks, and earns a gold disk. (He will perform the song on TV's "The Muppet Show" with Miss Piggy.)

Aug [10] John begins a 7-date series of sell-out shows at New York's Madison Square Garden (breaking the house record set a year earlier by The Rolling Stones°).

Oct *Bennie And The Jets*, re-issued on DJM as a UK A-side, reaches UK #37.

Nov Double LP *Blue Moves*, with backing vocal assistance from David Crosby, Bruce Johnston, Toni Tennille and Graham Nash, hits both UK and US #3. (It will be the last album for the time being produced by Dudgeon and written totally with Taupin.)

Dec *Sorry Seems To Be The Hardest Word* makes UK #11 and hits US #6.

1977 Mar *Crazy Water*, recorded with help from The Captain & Tennille°, reaches UK #27.

June *Bite Your Lip (Get Up And Dance)* makes both UK and US #28. John achieves a lifetime ambition when he becomes chairman of Watford Football Club.

Oct [1] He becomes the first rock artist to be honored in Madison Square Garden's Hall of Fame in New York.

Oct Compilation LP *Elton John's Greatest Hits Volume Two* hits UK #6 and US #21. He records several tracks with US producer Thom Bell, at Kay Smith studio in Seattle, Wash., and Sigma and Sound studios, Philadelphia, Pa.

Nov [3] John announces his retirement from live work, during a concert at Empire Pool, Wembley, UK.

1978 Apr *Ego*, his first collaboration with lyricist Gary Osbourne, makes both UK and US #34.

Dec *Part Time Love* makes UK #15 and US #22. First album without Taupin lyrics, LP *A Single Man*, produced by John with Clive Franks, hits UK #8 and US #15. (One track features Watford soccer players as backing vocalists.)

1979 Jan *Song For Guy*, an instrumental dedicated to Rocket's motorcycle messenger boy who died in an accident, hits UK #4.

Feb [3] He makes his first live appearance since "retiring", in Sweden.

Mar John begins his comeback tour, his first since 1976, of 30 dates around UK, accompanied only by percussionist Ray Cooper.

May The Thom Bell sessions are released as EP *Are You Ready For Love*, reaching UK #42. In US, treated as a mini-LP, it makes #51 on the LP chart. John plays concerts in Israel, the first Western rock star to do so, as part of the country's independence celebrations.

May [21] John plays the first of eight unique concerts in Leningrad. He is the first Western solo pop star to tour USSR. (The trip is filmed for documentary *To Russia With Elton*.)

Aug *Mama Can't Buy You Love*, taken from the mini-LP, hits US #9.

Sept [27] He collapses on stage at Hollywood's Universal Amphitheater, suffering from exhaustion due to a bout of 'flu. After recovering and resting for 10 minutes, he re-takes the stage for a 3-hour show.

Oct Dance-oriented LP *Victim Of Love*, produced by Pete Bellotte and with vocal support from The Doobie Brothers°, Michael McDonald° and Patrick Simmons, peaks at UK #41 and US #35.

Nov The title track reaches US #31 (the only single from the LP to chart).

1980 Mar Compilation LP *Lady Samantha*, containing DJM label rarities, makes UK #56.

June *Little Jeannie* peaks at UK #33 and hits US #3. LP *21 At 33*, referring to his 21st LP in his 33rd year, makes UK #12 and US #13. Co-writers include Judie Tzuke, Tom Robinson, Gary Osbourne and Taupin, with backing vocals from Bruce Johnston, Toni Tennille, Glenn Frey, Timothy Schmit and Peter Noone.

Sept *(Sartorial Eloquence) Don't You Wanna Play This Game No More* peaks at UK #44 and US #39. John co-writes Tom Robinson's *Never Gonna Fall In Love Again*, while John's *Dear God* fails to chart.

Sept [21] John signs to Geffen Records in US.

Oct K-Tel TV-advertised LP *The Very Best Of Elton John* reaches UK #24.

1981 Mar *I Saw Her Standing There Live*, a live track recorded with John Lennon° in 1974, released as a tribute, makes UK #40.

June *Nobody Wins*, a re-write of a French song, peaks at UK #42 and US #21. LP *The Fox*, produced by Chris Thomas, reaches UK #12 and US #21. (*Just Like Belgium*, the UK follow-up single, will fail to chart).

Sept *Chloe* makes US #34.

1982 Mar [8] John's first tour for 2 years opens in New Zealand.

Apr *Blue Eyes* hits UK #8. LP *Jump Up!* makes UK #13 and US #17.

June *Empty Garden (Hey Hey Johnny)*, a tribute to John Lennon°, makes UK #51 and US #13.

Oct *Blue Eyes* reaches US #12.

Nov Compilation LP *Love Songs* climbs to UK #39. 45s *Princess* and *All Quiet On The Western Front* both fail to chart.

1983 May *I Guess That's Why They Call It The Blues* hits UK #5.

June LP *Too Low For Zero*, his first LP written entirely with Taupin since *Blue Moves* in 1976, hits UK #7 and US #25.

Aug *I'm Still Standing*, helped by an innovative video, hits UK #4 and US #12.

Oct *Kiss The Bride* reaches UK #20 and US #25.

Dec Seasonal *Cold As Christmas* makes UK #33.

1984 Jan *I Guess That's Why They Call It The Blues* hits US #4.

Feb [14] John marries a studio engineer, Renate, in Darling Point, Sydney, Australia.

May Watford Soccer Team loses 2-0 to Liverpool in F.A. Cup Final.

June *Sad Songs (Say So Much)* hits UK #7. LP *Breaking Hearts* hits UK #2 and makes US #20.

Aug *Sad Songs (Say So Much)* hits US #5.

Sept *Passengers* hits UK #5.

Nov *Who Wears These Shoes?* makes UK #50 and US #16.

1985 Jan *In Neon* makes US #38.

Feb *Breaking Hearts (Ain't What It Used To Be)* released for Valentine's Day and John's own first wedding anniversary, reaches UK #59.

Mar [13] John presents George Michael° with the Best Songwriter award at the annual Ivor Novello ceremony at London's Grosvenor House, proclaiming Michael to be a "major songwriter in the tradition of Paul McCartney° and Barry Gibb".

June A duet with Millie Jackson°, *Act Of War*, makes UK #32. (Tina Turner° has been offered the song but turned it down.)

June [28] John duets with Michael° on *Candle In The Wind* in Wham!'s° farewell concert at Wembley Stadium, London.

July [13] John participates in Live Aid, with Michael° duetting on *Don't Let The Sun Go Down On Me*.

Nov *Nikita*, with vocal help from Michael°, hits UK #3 and US #7. LP *Ice On Fire* hits UK #3.

Dec *Wrap Her Up*, again featuring Michael° on vocals (and in the video), reaches UK #12 and US #20.

1986 Jan John joins Gladys Knight° and Stevie Wonder° on Dionne Warwick° & Friends' AIDS fund-raising single *That's What Friends Are For*, which hits US #1 and makes UK #16.

Jan [29] John and Taupin are awarded £5 million in back royalties from Dick James Music, after a lengthy and bitter court case.
Mar *Nikita* hits US #7, while *Cry To Heaven* makes UK #47.
June [20] John participates in the first Prince's Trust concert in London, with Bryan Adams°, Eric Clapton° and Tina Turner°.
Aug [15] He begins a US tour in Detroit, Mich.
Nov *Heartbreak All Over The World* peaks at UK #45 and US #55 as parent LP *Leather Jackets* makes UK #24 and US #91.
Dec [9] John collapses on stage during a concert in Sydney, Australia.
Dec John duets with Cliff Richard° on *Slow Rivers* which peaks at UK #44.
1987 Jan [5] John enters a Sydney hospital for throat surgery, planning to cancel all concerts for the coming year.
Mar John and his wife Renate announce they have split up. He re-signs with MCA in US.
Apr John appears at an AIDS benefit show in London, his first live show since his throat operation.
June He duets with Jennifer Rush on *Flames Of Paradise*, which makes US #36 but fails in UK.
Sept Boxed double LP *Live In Australia*, chronicling his 1986 tour, makes UK #70 and US #24. LP *Greatest Hits Volume Three*, on Geffen, reaches US #84.
Nov Live *Candle In The Wind*, recorded with the Melbourne Symphony Orchestra, hits UK #5.
Dec John tries to sell his soccer club, Watford, but backs out at the last minute.
1988 Jan *Candle In The Wind* hits US #6.
Mar Re-promoted double LP *Live In Australia* (without its boxed packaging) peaks at UK #43.
June *I Don't Want To Go On With You Like That* reaches UK #30.
July LP *Reg Strikes Back* makes UK #11 and US #17. *Town Of Plenty* peaks at UK #74
Sept [6-9] 2,000 of John's personal memorabilia are auctioned at Sotheby's in London. His giant "Pinball Wizard" boots from film *Tommy* sell for $11,000, as dozens of other items, from gold disks to personalized spectacles, contribute a seven figure sale.
Sept *I Don't Want To Go On With You Like That* hits US #2, behind George Michael's° *Monkey*.
Sept [23] John concludes five sell-out performances, supported by Wet Wet Wet°, at New York's Madison Square Garden. (His final concert breaks The Grateful Dead's° career record of 25 sell-out Madison Square Garden concerts.)
Oct John produces and writes for an Olivia Newton-John° LP.
Nov *A Word In Spanish* reaches US #19, as Elton and Renate John announce an "amicable" divorce.

JOHNNY & THE HURRICANES

Johnny Paris (tenor saxophone)
Paul Tesluk (organ)
Dave Yorko (guitar)
Lionel "Butch" Mattice (bass)
Tony Kaye (drums)

1957 Paris (b. 1940, Walbridge, Oh., US) forms an instrumental group at Rossford Catholic High in Toledo, Oh., initially called The Orbits, it includes schoolfriends Tesluk and Yorko.
1959 Feb As premier backing group in the region, it successfully auditions for managers Irving Micahnik and Harry Balk during engagements in Detroit, Mich. Joined by Mattice and Kaye, The Orbits cuts its first single *Crossfire*, dominated by Johnny's booting, rasping sax.
May After the managers re-name the group and negotiate a lease deal with New York-based Warwick label, *Crossfire* hits US #23.
Aug With new drummer Don Staczek, the group records *Red River Rock*, establishing a precedent that most later hits will follow: a swirling, organ-dominated instrumental based on a familiar, usually traditional, tune. The Hurricanes' version of ancient cowboy ballad *Red River Valley* hits US #5 and UK #3, and is a million-seller.
Nov With third drummer, Little Bo Savitch, the group cuts *Reveille Rock*, inspired by the military bugle call. It rises to US #25 and #14 in UK, where, like Duane Eddy°, Buddy Holly° and Eddie Cochran°, the group fares better than at home.
1960 Feb The folk song *Gimme Crack Corn* becomes *Beatnick Fly*, reaching US #15 and hitting UK #8.
June A new deal sees the group's masters issued on Big Top and *Down Yonder* peaks at US #48 and hits UK #8.
Sept *Rocking Goose* reaches only US #60 but hits UK #3. B-side *Revival* charts briefly at US #97.
Dec *You Are My Sunshine* makes US #91 but fails to chart in UK. LP *Stormsville* makes the UK top 20, peaking at #18 and later inspires the name of British rock group The Stormsville Shakers.
1961 Mar *Ja Da* at #86 is their US chart swan song, but it makes UK #14.
Apr Second LP *The Big Sound of Johnny & The Hurricanes* reaches UK #14.
June *Old Smokey/High Voltage* rises to UK #24 and is the group's last hit.
1963 Feb Johnny and an entirely new set of Hurricanes, Eddie Wagenfeald (organ), Billy Marsh (guitar), Bobby Cantrall (bass) and Jay Drake (drums), tour UK. Paris refutes the popular notion that the group's name was merely a trademark for a marketable sound and that several of its hits had been recorded by session men while The Hurricanes toured.

JOHNNY HATES JAZZ

Clark Datchler (vocals)
Calvin Hayes (guitars)
Mike Nocito (keyboards)

1985 Hayes (b. Aug.5, 1960), son of producer Mickie Most, is A&R head at Most's RAK label, and begins working at its London, UK, studios with US-born engineer Nocito (b. Nov.23, 1962), who has previously engineered for The Thompson Twins°, Police° and Duran Duran°. They team up with vocalist Datchler (b. Mar.27, 1961), who has been signed to RAK as a soloist by Most, but whose *I Don't Want You* and *Things Can't Get Worse* have failed. The trio's first single *Me And My Foolish Heart* is released but fails to sell.
1986 Oct An acoustic showcase performance at Ronnie Scott's club in London excites other record company interest.
Dec The group signs to Virgin Records.
1987 May New label debut is Datchler-written *Shattered Dreams* which hits UK #5 (and will also become a major hit throughout Europe and in Australia during the summer).
Sept *I Don't Want To Be A Hero* reaches UK #11. (The rest of the year will be spent writing and recording the band's debut LP.)
Dec *Turn Back The Clock*, title song from the forthcoming LP, peaks at UK #12.
1988 Jan LP *Turn Back The Clock* enters UK LP chart at #1, selling over 100,000 in its first week. It is produced by Hayes and Nocito, and mostly written by Datchler.
Mar The LP passes 300,000 UK sales even though the group has yet to tour (astutely selling itself through widespread UK TV appearances), while *Heart Of Gold* reaches UK #19.
May *Shattered Dreams* hits US #2.
July *Don't Say It's Love* peaks at UK #48, their smallest chart success to date. LP *Turn Back The Clock* climbs to US #56.

GRACE JONES

1976 Jones (b. May 19, 1953, Spanishtown, Jamaica, West Indies), having spent her teenage years in Syracuse, N. Y., US, has been an elite fashion model in Paris (appearing on the covers of *Vogue*, *Elle* and *Stern*), and studied acting and had a part in movie *Gordon's War*, when she turns to singing as the disco music boom hits Europe. Recording in France, her early releases are signed to Beam Junction Records in US and Polydor in UK.
1977 Feb Debut Double A-side *Sorry/That's The Trouble* reaches US #71.
May *I Need A Man* makes US #83. Both this and its predecessor are gigantic hits on the New York club/disco circuit, where she concentrates her early outrageous live performances, cultivating a decadent androgynous image, mostly carefully designed by her French artist/photographer husband, Jean-Paul Goode.
Oct She signs to Island Records and cuts the first of three disco LPs, *Portfolio*, which makes US #109.
1978 Aug LP *Fame* reaches US #97. She becomes the first artist to perform a live set at New York's most exclusive disco, Studio 54.
1979 Sept LP *Muse* features the club hits *What I Did For Love* and *I Need A Man*, and peaks at US #156.
1980 Aug LP *Warm Leatherette* marks a transition in sound from glossy disco to a sparse, relaxed reggae-funk. Produced by Island's owner Chris Blackwell at Compass Point studios in Nassau, Bahamas, it features top Jamaican reggae sessioneers Sly & Robbie° on instrumentation, and includes a cover of a Motown oldie (The Marvelettes' *The Hunter Gets Captured By The Game*), plus new wave material by The Normal (the title track) and The Pretenders°

GRACE JONES *cont.*

(*Private Life*). It reaches UK #45 and US #132, while *Private Life* is extracted and is her first UK hit single, at #17.

Oct Jones takes umbrage with UK TV chat show host Russell Harty while being interviewed on his program, and physically attacks him before a prime-time audience.

1981 June LP *Nightclubbing* repeats the previous team and formula and introduces Jones as writer, as well as including songs by David Bowie°/Iggy Pop° and Vanda and Young. It reaches US #32 and UK #35. *Pull Up To The Bumper*, taken from the LP, makes UK #53 and hits the US R&B chart.

1982 Nov Double A-side *The Apple Stretching/Nipple To The Bottle* peaks at UK #50.

Dec LP *Living My Life* features more of Jones' own lyrics, and makes US #86 and UK #15.

1983 Apr *My Jamaican Guy* reaches UK #56.

1984 June Jones stars with Arnold Schwarzenegger in the fantasy action movie *Conan The Destroyer*, in the role of Zula.

1985 May She appears as May Day, a sophisticated martial artist villainess, opposite Roger Moore, in James Bond film *A View To A Kill*.

Nov Trevor Horn-written and produced *Slave To The Rhythm* is released in UK on ZTT/Island, and is Jones' biggest hit single, peaking at UK #12. The LP of the same title also reaches UK #12, while in US, it marks the beginning of a deal with EMI/Manhattan and reaches #73.

1986 Feb Compilation LP *Island Life* hits UK #4, her most successful UK LP. *Pull Up To The Bumper* (backed with *La Vie En Rose*) is reissued after being included on the LP, and climbs to UK #12.

Mar A revival of Roxy Music's° *Love Is The Drug*, also from LP *Island Life*, makes UK #35.

Nov Jones signs to EMI/Manhattan for UK as well as US. *I'm Not Perfect (But I'm Perfect For You)* reaches UK #56, climbing to US #69 a few weeks later. Nile Rodgers-produced LP *Inside Story*, from which the single is taken, peaks at UK #61.

1987 Mar LP *Inside Story* makes US #81, while *Party Girl* is issued as a UK single, without charting. An extended period of recording inactivity follows.

1988 Aug Jones claims that police drag her and her two children off an American Airlines jet in Kingston, Jamaica, after her boyfriend, Chris Stanley, demands an apology from the pilot for the delay of the flight.

HOWARD JONES

1970 Jones (b. Feb.23, 1955, Southampton, UK), already an accomplished pianist, begins to write songs and joins his first group while living temporarily with his parents in Canada, where his father's lecturing job keeps the family on the move.

1973/78 He attends music college in Manchester, UK, but leaves to work in a factory and later becomes a full-time piano teacher (one of his pupils is his future wife Jan) and plays in amateur bands.

1979 He buys a synthesizer with damages received after a road accident and begins to sing, with his own synth accompaniment, in pubs and clubs around his home in High Wycombe, UK, and meets Jed Hoile, a mime artist who will later become his partner on stage.

1983 As the result of a 24-track demo tape of *New Song* and *What Is Love*, Jones signs to WEA Records in UK and Elektra in US.

Oct Debut *New Song*, produced by Colin Thurston, hits UK #3. He makes his UK TV debut with pre-programmed synthesizer backing.

1984 Jan *What Is Love* hits UK #2.

Mar *Hide And Seek* makes UK #12 and debut LP *Human's Lib*, produced by Rupert Hine and featuring Hine's own drummer Trevor Morais and Jones' brother Martin playing bass, enters UK chart at #1, selling 100,000 copies in its first week. *New Song* charts in US, reaching #27.

June *Pearl In The Shell* hits UK #7. *What Is Love* peaks at US #33 and LP *Human's Lib* at US #59.

July He tours US with Eurythmics°.

Aug *Like To Get To Know You Well*, issued also as title track of a long-form performance video, hits UK #4.

Dec Low-priced LP *The Twelve Inch Album* reaches UK #15. It is a compilation mini-LP of re-mixes and extended versions of earlier singles, with two unheard tracks. Jones tours UK, supported by Strawberry Switchblade, culminating in major London shows on Christmas Eve.

1985 Feb *Things Can Only Get Better*, with the help of The TKO Horns and Afrodiziak, hits UK #6. Jones appears on UK TV for the first time with a group calling itself The Howard Jones Big Band.

Mar LP *Dream Into Action*, produced by Hine, hits UK #2.

Apr [16] He plays a major London concert date at Wembley Arena.

May *Look Mama* hits UK #10.

June *Things Can Only Get Better* hits US #5 and LP *Dream Into Action* hits US #10.

July [13] He performs in Live Aid concert at Wembley, UK.

July *Life In One Day* peaks at UK #14.

Sept *Life In One Day* reaches US #19.

Nov Belatedly released in US, *Like To Get To Know You Well* reaches #49.

1986 Mar Re-recorded version of *No One Is To Blame* (of original on LP *Dream Into Action*), produced by Phil Collins°, reaches UK #16.

July Revamped *No One Is To Blame* proves a bigger success in US, where it peaks at #4, his highest-placed US hit. A 6-track mini-LP *Action Replay*, including *No One Is To Blame*, climbs to US #34.

Oct *All I Want* reaches UK #35. LP *One To One*, made with US producer Arif Mardin, hits UK #10.

Nov He contributes *Little Bit Of Snow* to Anti-Heroin Project charity LP *Live-In World*. Proceeds from it go to Phoenix House rehabilitation center for drug and alcohol addicts. LP *One To One* peaks at US #56.

Dec *You Know I Love You . . . Don't You?* reaches UK #43 and peaks at US #17.

1987 Mar *Little Bit Of Snow* reaches only UK #70. Jones, a lacto-vegetarian, eating dairy products but no fish or meat, opens a vegetarian restaurant in New York, which burns down within 12 months. (He continues to support various causes with performances during 1987, including more anti-drug projects and the Hurricane Irene concerts but does not record. His future in the restaurant business is uncertain.)

RICKIE LEE JONES

1961 One of 4 children, Jones (b. Nov.8, 1954, Chicago, Ill., US), at age 7 writes her first song, *I Wish*.

1965 She breaks a tooth riding a mare in an amateur rodeo.

1969 Jones runs away from home for the first time, fleeing with a girlfriend from Phoenix, Ariz. to San Diego, Cal. They steal a car, but the adventure only lasts 3 days.

1970 Having moved to Olympia, Wash., she is asked to leave three schools in succession, including Timberline High in Olympia where she is removed for insubordination.

1973 Jones arrives in LA, Cal., and begins waitressing in an Echo Park area Italian restaurant. She starts playing her own songs, some in spoken word monologues, at clubs including the Comeback Inn, Venice, A La Carte, Hollywood and The Troubadour.

1976 Jones writes *Easy Money* while working (and part-time singing) at Venice coffee house, Suzanne's.

1977 Aug She composes *The Last Chance Texaco* and *Chuck E.'s In Love*, the second about fabled LA figure Chuck E. Weiss, whom Jones has met in the kitchen at the Tropicana Motel, LA. They then meet Tom Waits°, a Tropicana resident who becomes Jones' sometime beau.

1978 Linking with manager Nick Mathe, they send Warner Bros. label a four-song EP, *Company*, *Young Blood*, *The Last Chance Texaco* and *Easy Money*, recorded as a demo originally for A&M. Warner's A&R producer Lenny Waronker also sees Jones at a Troubadour showcase. Little Feat's° Lowell George tips the scales when he chooses to record *Easy Money* on his solo LP *Thanks, I'll Eat Here*, having heard it sung down the phone. Warner Bros. signs Jones to a worldwide contract, on her stipulation that Waronker co-produce her debut.

Nov Jones appears as the blond on the cover of Tom Waits'° LP *Blue Valentine*.

1979 Apr Debut LP *Rickie Lee Jones* is released simultaneously with single *Chuck E.'s In Love*. (The single will hit US #4 and UK #18 in July.) The LP hits US #3, earning a platinum disk, and makes UK #18.

May Following a limited showcase US tour of small clubs, Jones appears on NBC TV's "Saturday Night Live", despite arguing with producers over her choice of song. She wins out performing *Coolsville*.

June Jones takes part in a 3-hour jam with Bruce Springsteen° and Boz Scaggs° at LA's Whisky A Go-Go club.

Aug As follow-up *Young Blood* makes US #40, Jones begins on her first major tour, including sell-out dates at New York's Carnegie Hall.

1980 Feb [27] Jones is named Best New Artist of 1979 at the 22nd Grammy awards.

1981 Aug After a 2-year gap, Jones returns with her second LP *Pirates*. It will hit US #5, selling gold, but make only UK #37.

Oct *A Lucky Guy* peaks at US #64.

1982 Jones moves from LA to New York, then to Paris in an attempt to cope with pressures of fame.

1983 July After another 2-year retreat, 10" 7-track mini-LP *Girl At Her Volcano* is released, peaking at US #39 and UK #51. With two live cuts, it features revivals of *On Broadway* and *Walk Away Renée* and a new Tom Waits° number *Angel Wings*. Another Jones-performed Waits ballad will also feature in Martin Scorsese's movie *King of Comedy*.

1984 Feb Jones returns to live in LA with a new boyfriend and a cat.

Oct New single *The Real End* peaks at US #83 while parent LP *The Magazine* is released. Co-produced by James Newton Howard, it only makes US #44 and UK #40 and features musical assistance from Toto° band members.

Nov "The Magazine" tour begins in US Mid-West.

1985 Jan Jones plays her first Australian dates, followed by a European visit including sell-out UK concerts and Eastern bloc gigs.

1988 Oct Pregnant with her first child, Jones records her bi-annual LP, produced by Walter Becker, in the studio.

TOM JONES

1963 Jones (b. Thomas Jones Woodward, June 7, 1940, Pontypridd, South Wales, UK) forms his first band, Tommy Scott and the Senators. They record some tracks for EMI with producer Joe Meek.

1964 He is spotted supporting Mandy Rice-Davies at Pontypridd, by Gordon Mills, an ex-member of UK vocal group The Viscounts, who becomes his manager and changes his name to Tom Jones, after the film of the same name.

Aug Jones is signed to Decca Records, where his first release is a revival of Ronnie Love's 1961 US hit *Chills And Fever*, which fails to chart.

1965 Mar Second single *It's Not Unusual*, written by Mills and Les Reed (originally with Sandie Shaw° in mind) tops the UK chart for a week, instantly establishing Jones as a leading male solo vocalist in a scene dominated by groups.

Apr Jones appears at the *New Musical Express* poll winners concert at the Empire Pool, Wembley, London, backed by new stage group The Squires (who will play with him live throughout the mid-60s) on a bill which includes The Beatles°, The Rolling Stones°, The Animals° and many others.

May *Once Upon A Time* reaches UK #32, while *It's Not Unusual* hits US #10. (It also makes the R&B chart, many programmers on black radio stations hearing the record "blind" assume Jones is American and black.)

June Debut LP *Along Came Jones* reaches UK #11. *Little Lonely One*, a pre-Decca track recorded with Meek, is released in US by Tower Records (a subsidiary of Capitol/EMI), to cash in on the success of *It's Not Unusual*. It makes US #42.

July A revival of Billy Eckstine's *With These Hands* reaches UK #13.

Aug *What's New Pussycat*, a Bacharach/David song which is the theme to movie of the same title, reaches UK #11 and US #3. US LP *It's Not Unusual* (a re-titling of *Along Came Jones*) reaches US #54.

Sept *With These Hands* reaches US #27. Jones says in an interview that, having spent most of the year in Britain, he faces the fact that "my long-term career will be in Britain".

Oct LP *What's New Pussycat?*, compiled specifically for the US market, makes US #114.

1966 Jan *Thunderball*, the theme from the fourth James Bond film and written in similar style to highly successful *Goldfinger* from the previous Bond movie, reaches UK #35 and US #25.

Mar *Promise Her Anything*, another movie theme, reaches US #74.

June *Not Responsible*, in Jones' *It's Not Unusual* style, reaches UK #18.

July *Not Responsible* makes US #58.

Aug *This And That* peaks at UK #44.

Oct LP *From The Heart* reaches UK #23.

Dec *Green Green Grass Of Home*, based on Jerry Lee Lewis'° version, becomes Jones' all-time biggest-selling single. It tops the UK chart for 7 weeks, and sells over 1,220,000 copies in UK.

1967 Feb *Green Green Grass Of Home* reaches US #11.

Mar Jones stays with country music on a revival of Bobby Bare's *Detroit City*, which hits UK #8 and reaches US #27.

Apr LP *Green Green Grass Of Home* hits UK #3 and reaches US #65.

May *Funny Familiar Forgotten Feelings* hits UK #8 and makes US #49.

July [4] Jones appears on the first telecast of US CBS TV show "Spotlight", recorded in London as a summer replacement for "The Red Skelton Show". (He will star regularly on the show during its 2-month run.)

July Live LP *Live At The Talk Of The Town*, recorded at the London supper club, hits UK #6.

Aug Jones revives a ballad written and originally recorded by Lonnie Donegan°, though never a hit: *I'll Never Fall In Love Again*. It hits UK #2. Meanwhile, a rock revival of Tennessee Ernie Ford's *Sixteen Tons* makes US #68.

Oct *I'll Never Fall In Love Again* reaches US #49.

Dec *I'm Coming Home* hits UK #2.

1968 Jan LP *13 Smash Hits* (not a compilation, but a selection of covers of familar songs by other artists, plus *I'll Never Fall In Love Again*, hits UK #5. *I'm Coming Home* reaches US #57.

Mar *Delilah*, a dramatic uptempo song of passion and revenge (which becomes the archetypical spoof number for Jones impressionists) hits UK #2.

May *Delilah* reaches US #15.

July LP *The Tom Jones Fever Zone* makes US #14.

Aug *Help Yourself* hits UK #5. LP *Delilah* tops the UK chart.

Sept *Help Yourself* makes US #35.

Dec *A Minute Of Your Time* reaches UK #14.

1969 Jan LP *Help Yourself* hits UK #4 and US #5. *A Minute Of Your Time* reaches US #48.

Feb [7] The weekly musical variety show "This is Tom Jones" first airs on US ABC TV. (Originated variously in London and Hollywood, and with guest stars who normally duet with Jones on at least one song, the series, at Friday evening peak time, will bring in high ratings and cement Jones' stature as an "all-round entertainer" in US. This in turn will lead him to settle in US and play for many years in Las Vegas during the 1970s and much of the 1980s. The TV show will run for 2 years.)

May *Love Me Tonight* hits UK #9. LP *Tom Jones Live!* reaches US #13.

July *Love Me Tonight* makes US #13. LP *This Is Tom Jones* hits UK #2 and US #4.

Sept Following a good response to *I'll Never Fall In Love Again* on the TV show, it is reissued in US and hits #6, earning a gold disk.

Sept [22] Jones appears with The Beatles°, James Brown°, Crosby, Stills, Nash & Young°, Three Dog Night° and others on the first telecast of US ABC TV's "The Music Scene".

Nov Live LP *Tom Jones Live In Las Vegas* hits both UK and US #3.

1970 Jan A revival of Clyde McPhatter oldie *Without Love (There Is Nothing)* hits UK #10.

Feb *Without Love (There Is Nothing)* hits US #5.

May *Daughter Of Darkness* hits UK #5 and US #13. LP *Tom* hits UK #4 and US #6.

Sept A revival of Ben E. King°/Shirley Bassey oldie *I (Who Have Nothing)* reaches UK #16 and US #14. Jones wins *Playboy* magazine's Entertainer of the Year and Top Male Singer awards in its annual readers' poll.

Nov LP *I (Who Have Nothing)* hits UK #10 and reaches US #23.

Dec *Can't Stop Loving You*, never released in UK, reaches US #25.

1971 Jan [15] Jones' weekly TV series "This is Tom Jones" airs for the last time on US ABC TV.

Feb *She's A Lady* reaches UK #13.

Apr *She's A Lady* hits US #2 and is a US million-seller.

June *Puppet Man*, written by Neil Sedaka°, reaches UK #49 and US #26. LP *She's A Lady* hits UK #9 and US #17.

Nov *'Til*, a 1962 top 20 hit for The Angels, hits UK #2 and makes US #41.

Dec Live LP *Live At Caesar's Palace*, recorded in Las Vegas, reaches UK #27 and US #43.

1972 May *The Young New Mexican Puppeteer* hits UK #6 and reaches US #80.

June LP *Close Up* reaches UK #17 and US #64.

1973 May *Letter To Lucille* makes UK #31 and US #60.

June LP *The Body And Soul Of Tom Jones* reaches UK #31 and US #93.

1974 Jan Compilation LP *Greatest Hits* peaks at UK #15 and US #185.

TOM JONES *cont.*

Sept *Something 'Bout You Baby I Like* reaches UK #36.

1975 Mar Double compilation LP *20 Greatest Hits* tops the UK chart for 4 weeks.

1977 Apr *Say You'll Stay Until Tomorrow* makes UK #40 and US #15, while LP of the same title reaches US #76. LP *Tom Jones Greatest Hits* climbs to US #191.

1978 Oct LP *I'm Coming Home* reaches UK #12.

1981 May LP *Darlin'* peaks at US #179.

1983 Apr With his style out of vogue on the pop charts, Jones concentrates on recording country music, signing a new deal with Mercury Records in Nashville. *Touch Me (I'll Be Your Fool Once More)* hits US C&W #4. (All Jones' future US success will be on the C&W chart.)

Sept *It'll Be Me* makes US C&W #34.

Dec Country-flavored LP *Don't Let Our Dreams Die Young* hits US C&W #9.

1984 Feb *I've Been Rained On Too* reaches US C&W #13.

June *This Time* makes US C&W #30.

Dec LP *Love Is On The Radio* makes US C&W #40.

1985 Jan *I'm An Old Rock'n'Roller (Dancin' To A Different Beat)* makes US C&W #67.

1987 Apr Jones returns to UK for the first extended period since settling in US in the early 1970s. The main reason is to promote his role in the LP version of the new musical by Mike Leander, *Matador*, released by Epic. Based on the true story of a star of the Spanish bullring who rose from poverty in Andalucia, the work is mooted for a London stage production, and Jones is keen to take the lead role should it materialize – notwithstanding it would mean ending his Las Vegas appearances.

May *A Boy From Nowhere*, a ballad in traditional powerful Jones' style from *Matador*, hits UK #2, his first UK top 10 for 15 years, held off the top by Starship's *Nothing's Gonna Stop Us Now*.

June To capitalize on Jones' chart success, Decca reissues his original chart-topper *It's Not Unusual* (which is already getting plays in some UK discos because its distinctive rhythm matches a current Euro-beat dance trend), and it re-charts at UK #17. Also cashing in on the revival of Jones' interest is TV-promoted compilation LP *Tom Jones – The Greatest Hits* on Telstar Records, which also makes UK #17. Meanwhile, studio cast-recorded LP *Matador* makes UK #26.

1988 Jan Second cut from *Matador*, *I Was Born To Be Me*, makes UK #61.

Oct Following a performance by Jones of Prince's° number *Kiss* on Jonathan Ross' late-night UK TV show "The Last Resort", he is contacted by Anne Dudley of UK instrumental group The Art of Noise°, suggesting that he record the song as guest vocalist on a version by the group. Vocal and instrumental tracks are eventually recorded on opposite sides of the Atlantic, and then meshed into the finished production by Dudley. (She and the rest of the group do not actually meet Jones until the disk is in the shops.) Released on China Records (to which The Art of Noise is contracted), it is an instant UK smash, hitting #5, promoted by an appearance on UK TV variety show "Live from the London Palladium".

Nov Jones appears with a variety of other Welsh entertainers on the George Martin-produced music version of Dylan Thomas' *Under Milk Wood*, which is released on LP by EMI. Meanwhile, as a soloist, Jones signs a new recording contract with Jive Records, and begins work on an LP for Spring 1989 release, to be followed by a major UK tour at Easter 1989.

JANIS JOPLIN

1960 Saving money to make a trip to California, Joplin (b. Jan.19, 1943, Port Arthur, Tex., US) earns a living singing in clubs in Austin and Houston, Tex, and becomes part of The Waller Creek Boys trio, together with R. Powell St. John (later a member of Mother Earth), a songwriter for the 13th Floor Elevators.

1963 Jan Joplin hitch-hikes to San Francisco, Cal., where she sings in North Beach clubs, either solo or with Jorma Kaukonen (later of Jefferson Airplane°) or Roger Perkins. Her three-octave vocal range impresses those close to her, but she does not progress beyond sporadic singing jobs.

1966 Joplin returns to Texas to straighten out from the hippy, druggy, California lifestyle. She enrolls at college, makes marriage plans and gives up singing.

June With marriage plans abandoned, she is about to join the 13th Floor Elevators but returns to San Francisco as lead singer with Big Brother & The Holding Company, the house band at The Avalon Ballroom.

Aug During a visit to Chicago, Ill., Big Brother signs to Mainstream Records.

1967 June The group plays a show-stopping performance at the Monterey Pop Festival. Joplin is clearly the star and Dylan's° manager Albert Grossman signs the group.

Aug Mainstream releases the band's debut LP, which reaches US #60.

1968 Feb Big Brother & The Holding Company, now a major draw on the West Coast, makes its New York debut at the Anderson Theater on Second Avenue.

Mar [8] Big Brother plays on the opening night of The Fillmore East in an old movie theater on New York's Second Avenue and Sixth Street.

Mar CBS/Columbia Records buys the group's Mainstream contract and books it into Studio E in New York to record its label debut.

Aug Producer John Simon, unhappy with the quality of the recordings, is over-ruled by CBS/Columbia, which releases LP *Cheap Thrills* (the title shortened, at the label's insistence, from *Dope, Sex And Cheap Thrills*).

Sept Grossman announces that Joplin is to split from the group at the end of the year.

Oct LP *Cheap Thrills*, after 7 weeks on the chart, hits US #1, where it will stay for 8 weeks. Mainstream releases *Down On Me*, from the LP, which reaches US #43.

Nov *Piece Of My Heart* makes US #12. Also on Mainstream, *Coo Coo* reaches US #84.

Dec [1] Joplin makes her last official appearance with Big Brother & The Holding Company. The group breaks up for a time.

Dec [21] Joplin, backed by The Kozmic Blues Band, appears at the "Stax-Volt Yuletide Thing" for the company's annual convention in Memphis, Tenn.

1969 Feb [11-14] Joplin plays four nights at New York's Fillmore East.

Feb Ex-Big Brother Sam Andrews (b. Dec.18, 1941, Taft, Cal.) joins Joplin's new group, initially called Janis & The Joplinaires. Other members include Brad Campbell (bass), Terry Clements (sax) and Marcus Doubleday (trumpet). The line-up changes throughout the year, and Andrews leaves. Joplin develops an alcohol and drug addiction.

Apr [21] Joplin and The Kozmic Blues Band perform in UK at London's Royal Albert Hall.

Aug Having performed recently at the Texas International Festival and the Atlanta Pop Festival, Joplin plays the 2-day New Orleans Pop Festival in Prairieville, La.

Oct LP *I Got Dem Ol' Kozmic Blues Again Mama!* is released and hits US #5.

Nov [15] Joplin is arrested at a gig in Tampa, Fla., after allegedly badmouthing a policeman. Charges are eventually dropped.

Dec The soul-based Kozmic Blues Band has been unsuccessful with live appearances since LP *I Got Dem Ol' Kozmic Blues Again Mama!* and disbands. *Kozmic Blues* reaches US #41.

1970 Peter Albin (b. June 6, 1944, San Francisco, Cal., US) and David Getz (b. Brooklyn, N.Y., US), who played with Country Joe & The Fish°, bring in James Gurley (b. Detroit, Mich.), Andrews and guitarist Dave Shallock to re-form Big Brother & The Holding Company.

Apr Joplin appears with Big Brother at the Fillmore West and the Winterland.

May Joplin's new group, the Full-Tilt Boogie Band, makes its debut at a Hells Angels benefit in San Rafael. The line-up is Campbell, John Till (guitar), Richard Bell (piano), Ken Pearson (organ) and Clark Pearson (drums). Joplin and the group will tour constantly in the coming months.

Aug [6] She participates in a 12-hour antiwar rock festival at New York's Shea Stadium on the 25th anniversary of the dropping of the first atom bomb on Hiroshima.

Aug [8] Joplin buys a headstone for the grave of her greatest influence Bessie Smith at the Mount Lawn cemetery in Philadelphia, Pa. (Smith died in 1937 after being refused admission to a whites-only hospital.)

Sept Joplin begins recording a new LP (which is not finished) at Columbia's West Coast Studios in Hollywood.

Oct [4] Joplin is found dead at the Landmark Hotel, Hollywood, with fresh needle marks in her arm. An inquest rules that death is due to an accidental heroin overdose. (She had been scheduled to record the vocal for *Buried Alive In The Blues* the following day.)

Nov Big Brother & The Holding Company's LP, *Be A Brother*, featuring uncredited contributions from Joplin, reaches US #134.

1971 Feb LP *Pearl*, drawn from the unfinished sessions, hits US #1 for 9 weeks.

Mar Joplin's much-praised version of Kris Kristofferson's° *Me And Bobby McGee* hits US #1.

Apr LP *Pearl* reaches UK #50.

June *Cry Baby* (one of several Jerry Ragavoy songs on LP *Pearl*) reaches UK #42. B-side is her better-known *Mercedes Benz*. The re-packaged CBS/Columbia debut LP, peaks at US #185.

Sept *Get It While You Can*, by Ragavoy, peaks at #78. Big Brother LP, *How Hard It Is*, featuring occasional vocals from new singer Kathi McDonald, reaches US #157.

1972 May LP *Janis Joplin In Concert* hits US #4.

July Taken from the LP, *Down On Me*, a live version from the first Big Brother LP, reaches UK #91. LP *Janis Joplin In Concert* makes UK #30.

1973 Aug LP *Janis Joplin's Greatest Hits* reaches US #37.

1975 May LP *Janis*, the soundtrack from Joplin documentary of the same name featuring early recordings from 1963-65, reaches US #54. It contains live and TV recordings with her two post-Big Brother bands and folk-blues material recorded in Texas before she joined Big Brother.

1979 Oct [10] *The Rose*, starring Bette Midler°, supposedly based on Joplin's life, premieres in LA.

1982 Feb LP *Farewell Song* reaches US #104. It contains a song with The Kozmic Blues Band, one with Full-Tilt, one recorded live in LA with the Paul Butterfield° Blues Band and six from Big Brother & The Holding Company. The Big Brother tracks feature added instrumentation from 80s session musicians.

JOURNEY

Steve Perry (vocals)
Neal Schon (guitar)
Ross Valory (bass)
Jonathan Cain (keyboards)
Steve Smith (drums)

1973 Feb The band is formed in San Francisco, at the suggestion of Santana's° ex-production manager Walter Herbert, by ex-Santana guitarist Schon (b. Feb.27, 1954, San Mateo, Cal., US), who recruits ex-Fruminous Bandersnatch and Steve Miller° Band member Valory (b. Feb.2, 1949, San Francisco, Cal.), Tubes° drummer Prairie Prince (b. May 7, 1950, Charlotte, N.C., US) and George Tickner on guitar. Originally The Golden Gate Rhythm Section, a San Francisco radio station holds a competition to find the band a new name, and Journey wins. Herbert becomes the band's manager.

June Keyboards player and vocalist Gregg Rolie (b. 1948), also ex-Santana°, joins the line-up as the band begins to play large venue support to bigger groups, as well as local club work.

Sept Prince leaves to join The Tubes°.

1974 Feb After thirty drummers have been tried, ex-Jeff Beck°, Frank Zappa° and John Mayall° sideman Aynsley Dunbar (b. 1946, Liverpool, UK), is persuaded to join.

Nov The band signs to CBS/Columbia Records.

1975 Apr Tickner leaves to go to medical school after completing work on the first LP. He is not replaced and the band continues with a single guitarist.

May Debut LP *Journey* reaches US #138.

1976 Apr LP *Look Into The Future* makes US #100.

Nov The band plays a UK tour, supporting Santana°.

1977 Mar LP *Next* peaks at US #85. The band feels it is failing to develop in commercial terms because of the lack of a strong front-focus vocalist (Rolie is handling most vocals from behind his keyboards), and a search is instituted.

June Robert Fleischmann is recruited as frontman and plays a summer US tour with Journey, but he proves incompatible and is asked to leave.

Oct [10] Fleischmann is replaced by Steve Perry.(b. Jan.22, 1953, Hanford, Cal.), ex-Tim Bogert's band Alien Project, who has sent an audition tape to manager Herbert.

1978 Apr LP *Infinity*, with Perry on lead vocals and Roy Thomas Baker producing, reaches US #21, and will stay charted for 123 weeks, earning a platinum disk for a million-plus sales.

May From the LP, *Wheel In The Sky* is the band's first US chart single, reaching #57.

July *Anytime*, also from LP *Infinity*, makes US #83.

Sept Third single from the LP, *Lights*, reaches US #68.

Nov Dunbar leaves to join Jefferson Starship°, and is replaced on drums by Steve Smith (b. Aug.21, 1954, Los Angeles), from Ronnie Montrose's group.

1979 Feb Journey signs an advertising deal with Budweiser beer.

Mar The band plays seven dates in UK, where, as yet, it has made no chart progress.

May LP *Evolution* reaches US #20 and is a second million-seller. Extracted from it, *Just The Same Way*, peaks at US #58.

July [28] Journey takes part in the "World Series of Rock" at Cleveland Stadium. Also on the bill are Aerosmith°, Ted Nugent° and Thin Lizzy°.

Oct First top 20 hit single is *Lovin', Touchin', Squeezin'*, which reaches US #16.

1980 Jan *Too Late* reaches US #70, while a retrospective LP of tracks from the first three LPs *In The Beginning* peaks at US #152.

Apr *Any Way You Want It* reaches US #23, while LP *Departure* hits US #8, the third million-seller.

July *Walks Like A Lady* reaches US #32.

Sept Double A-side *Good Morning Girl/Stay Awhile* makes US #55. The band flies to UK for a one-off concert at London's Rainbow.

1981 Mar Live double LP *Captured* hits US #9, and earns the band's fourth platinum disk.

Apr *The Party's Over (Hopelessly In Love)*, from LP *Captured*, reaches US #34. Rolie, tired of touring, leaves the band and is replaced on keyboards by Jonathan Cain (b. Feb.26, 1950, Chicago, Ill., US), ex-The Babys.

Sept LP *Escape*, the most successful to date, hits US #1, staying charted for a total of 146 weeks (and for more than a year in top 20), and selling over 2 million copies. Taken from it, *Who's Crying Now*, is the band's biggest-selling single, hitting US #4.

Nov Schon releases LP *Untold Passion* in collaboration with keyboards player Jan Hammer. It peaks at US #115.

Dec *Don't Stop Believin'*, from LP *Escape*, hits US #9.

1982 Feb *Open Arms* hits US #2 for 6 weeks behind Joan Jett's *I Love Rock'n'Roll*, and is the band's first million-selling single.

Mar A minor UK breakthrough comes when *Don't Stop Believin'* reaches UK #62, and LP *Escape* makes a belated first entry into the UK chart.

July *Still They Ride* reaches US #19.

Sept LP *Escape* peaks at UK #32, while reissued *Who's Crying Now* reaches UK #46.

Oct Perry duets with Kenny Loggins on his single *Don't Fight It*, peaking at US #17.

1983 Feb Second Schon/Hammer collaboration, LP *Here To Stay*, climbs to US #122.

Mar *Separate Ways (Worlds Apart)* hits US #8. It is taken from LP *Frontiers*, which hits US #2 for 9 weeks (behind Michael Jackson's° *Thriller*, and is a further platinum disk, spending 85 weeks on chart. It also hits UK #6; the band's most successful LP in UK. Meanwhile, a video game is marketed in US, inspired by Journey's LP *Escape*.

June *Faithfully*, from LP *Frontiers*, reaches US #12.

Aug *After The Fall* reaches US #23, while in UK the 1979 LP *Evolution* charts briefly at #100.

Nov *Send Her My Love* reaches US #23.

1984 Apr Schon's live LP *Through The Fire*, in collaboration with Sammy Hagar, Kenny Aaronson, and Santana's° Mike Shrieve, climbs to US #42.

June Perry records a solo LP, *Street Talk*, which reaches US #12 and UK #59. *Oh Sherrie*, extracted from it, hits US #3.

Aug His second solo single *She's Mine* reaches US #21.

Oct Perry's solo *Strung Out* makes US #40.

1985 Jan [28] Perry joins a host of major US rock acts in LA at the recording session for USA For Africa's° *We Are The World*, on which he contributes a line of the lead vocal.

Feb The last single from Perry's solo LP, *Foolish Heart*, peaks at US #18.

Mar *Only The Young*, from the soundtrack of movie *Vision Quest*, hits US #9. This is the first Journey release for 2 years, the band having relaxed its earlier formidable touring and recording schedule for an extended rest while members have pursued solo projects.

JOURNEY *cont.*

1986 May Regrouped as just a three-man core of Perry, Schon and Cain, Journey releases concept LP *Raised On Radio*, produced by Perry, which hits US #4 and also makes UK #22. *Be Good To Yourself*, taken from the LP, hits US #9.

Aug *Suzanne*, also from the LP, reaches US #17. Mike Baird and Randy Jackson are added to the line-up.

Nov Third LP extract *Girl Can't Help It* also reaches US #17.

1987 Feb A last single from the LP, *I'll Be Alright Without You* reaches US #14. (After this, the group members will pursue solo careers and the break-up appears to be permanent. Perry will spend much of 1988 working on a second solo LP.)

JOY DIVISION

Ian Curtis (vocals)
Bernard Albrecht (Barney Sumner) (guitar)
Peter Hook (bass)
Steven Morris (drums)

1977 May [29] Having come together in Manchester, UK, as The Stiff Kittens some 6 months earlier, but without any live exposure, the band renames itself Warsaw (from a track on David Bowie's° LP *Low*) for a live debut at Manchester's Electric Circus, bottom of the bill to The Buzzcocks° and Penetration.

July [18] It records a demo of 4 songs at Pennine Sound studios.

Dec The band becomes Joy Division (a name taken from Nazi concentration camp novel *House of Dolls*) to avoid confusion with London punk band Warsaw Pakt, which has just released its first LP.

1978 Apr [14] The band plays the Stiff Test/Chiswick Challenge, an audition night organized by the two UK independent labels at Manchester's Rafters Club. It performs last, at 2am, but impresses the club DJ, and future manager, Rob Gretton. Journalist Tony Wilson, boss of the new Factory Records label (known for his Manchester-based TV music show "What Goes On") also sees the band's performance.

June The 1977 demos are released as EP *An Ideal For Living* on the band's own Enigma label (the fold-out sleeve is inscribed "this is not a record – it is an enigma"). Virgin Records issues a 10" various artists LP *Cross Circuit: Live At The Electric Circus*, which features Joy Division's *At A Later Date*.

1979 Jan Joy Division's *Digital* and *Glass*, both produced by Martin "Zero" Hannett, appear on Factory Records double compilation EP *A Factory Sample*, with Cabaret Voltaire, John Dowie and Durutti Column.

June Joy Division contributes *From Safety To Where* and *Autosuggestion* to the Fast Product compilation EP *Earcom 2: Contradiction*. The group signs to Factory and debut LP *Unknown Pleasures* is released after Wilson uses his life savings of £8,500 to record 10,000 copies. The band increases its live performances, putting inevitable pressure on Curtis, who suffers from epilepsy.

Oct *Atmosphere/Dead Souls*, under the title *Licht Und Blindheit*, and *Transmission/Novelty* are released.

1980 Apr *Love Will Tear Us Apart* is released, to overwhelming critical praise, but initially it reaches only the UK independent chart. Factory takes the innovatory step of providing record shops with a flexi-disc containing the tracks *Komakino*, *Incubation* and *As You Said*; not to be sold, but to be given away to fans. The group completes a new LP with Hannett and plays a series of impromptu live UK dates, several of which have to be cancelled as Curtis falls ill.

May [18] In the early hours of the morning Curtis hangs himself, 4 days before the group is due to fly to US. (Joy Division's greatest success will come after the singer's death.)

July *Love Will Tear Us Apart* reaches UK #13 and second LP *Closer* hits UK #6. LP *Unknown Pleasures* spends 1 week at UK #71.

1981 Jan Joy Division re-emerges as New Order, with Albrecht on vocals.

Oct Joy Division's double LP *Still*, a collection of live and studio material, hits UK #5.

1982 Aug Factory's video division Ikon issues *Here Are The Young Men*, a 60-minute live Joy Division video.

1983 Nov *Love Will Tear Us Apart* re-enters the UK chart, peaking at #19.

1988 July A reissue of Joy Division's *Atmosphere* reaches UK #34 but is a top independent seller. (New York group The Swans release a version of *Love Will Tear Us Apart*; it has also been covered by Paul Young° and P.J. Proby°, with assistance from Hook.) Factory issues Joy Division double compilation LP *Substance*, which hits UK #7.

JUDAS PRIEST

Rob Halford (vocals)
K.K. Downing (guitar)
Glenn Tipton (guitar)
Ian Hill (bass)
Dave Holland (drums)

1969 The original Judas Priest (the name is taken from Bob Dylan's° *The Ballad Of Frankie Lee And Judas Priest* on his LP *John Wesley Harding*) is formed in Birmingham, UK, as a pop/rock covers band playing around the Midlands clubs. (Only Downing and Hill will survive from the initial line-up to the band's recording days.)

1971 The band gains a strong vocalist and frontman in ex-theatrical lighting engineer Halford, (b. Aug.25, 1951, Birmingham, UK) the brother of Hill's girlfriend. Drummer John Hinch also joins, and the quartet's music hardens into the rock mode currently successful for Deep Purple° and fellow Birmingham group Black Sabbath°.

1974 Tipton joins as second guitarist. After more than 4 years of playing clubs, the band signs to Gull Records. Debut LP, produced by Rodger Bain, *Rocka Rolla*, with the title track also released as a single, fails to chart. Hinch is replaced on drums by Alan Moore.

1976 Mar *The Ripper* is released, trailering the band's second Gull LP.

Apr LP *Sad Wings Of Destiny* sells only marginally better than its precedecessor, but marks the band's US debut release, via Janus Records.

1977 Jan With the aid of Halford's flamboyant stage act the band is developing a strong grass-roots following with consistent UK touring, and gains a new, major contract with CBS/Columbia (as well as a new drummer, ex-sessionman Simon Phillips.)

May LP *Sin After Sin*, the first for CBS, is produced by ex-Deep Purple° bassist Roger Glover, and provides the group's first chart entry, at UK #23. From the LP, their rock version of Joan Baez's° *Diamonds And Rust* is released as a single, but fails to chart. Tours of UK and Europe follow, in support of the LP, and new drummer Les Spinks joins in place of Phillips.

July [23] On a first US tour, Judas Priest supports Led Zeppelin° at Oakland Coliseum, Cal.

1978 Jan A revival of Spooky Tooth's *Better By You, Better By Me*, from the next LP, fails to chart.

Mar LP *Stained Class*, produced by Dennis Mackay, reaches UK #27. Gull, meanwhile, compiles LP *Best Of Judas Priest* from its two earlier LPs, but this fails to chart.

Apr LP *Stained Class* makes US #173, the band's US chart debut.

Nov LP *Killing Machine*, produced by James Guthrie, reaches UK #32.

1979 Feb Judas Priest's first hit single is *Take On The World*, extracted from LP *Killing Machine*, which reaches UK #14.

Apr The LP is retitled *Hell Bent For Leather* (a deliberate play on the group's leather-clad image) in US, and includes an additional track, reviving Fleetwood Mac's° *The Green Manalishi (With The Two-Prong Crown)*. It makes US #128.

May *Evening Star* peaks at UK #53. The band tours abroad again, finding huge success in the Far East.

Oct Live LP *Unleashed In The East*, recorded at the Koseinenkin and Nakano Sunplaza Halls in Tokyo, Japan, proves to be a chart breakthrough, hitting UK #10 and reaching US #70. It is produced by Tom Allom – a partnership which will become lasting. Drummer Binks has left, physically and mentally exhausted by the band's gruelling international tour schedule. His place is taken by Dave Holland.

1980 Mar [9] The group begins a 17-date UK tour at Bristol's Colston Hall.

Apr *Living After Midnight* makes UK #12. It is taken from LP *British Steel* (the first to feature Holland on drums), which is the group's biggest UK success, hitting #4 (and will reach US #34).

June *Breaking The Law*, also from LP *British Steel*, peaks at UK #12.

July LP *British Steel* reaches #34, earning the band a US gold disk for a half million sales.

Aug Judas Priest appears at the first Castle Donington Monsters of Rock festival in UK, second on the bill to Rainbow°.

Sept *United*, the third single from LP *British Steel*, makes UK #26.

1981 Feb *Don't Go*, from the next LP, peaks at UK #51.

Mar LP *Point Of Entry* reaches UK #14.

May *Hot Rockin'* peaks at UK #60, while LP *Point Of Entry* makes US #30.

1982 July LP *Screaming For Vengeance* reaches UK #11.

Aug From the LP, *You've Got Another Thing Comin'* peaks at UK #66.

Oct LP *Screamin' For Vengeance* makes US #17 for several weeks and is a million-seller, earning the group's first platinum LP. The 9-year-old LP *Rocka Rolla* also finally gets a US release. The group continues to tour intensively, the live show often highlighted by Halford roaring across the stage on a Harley Davidson motorbike.

Nov *You've Got Another Thing Comin'* is the group's only US singles chart entry, at #67. (Huge demand for Judas Priest in US in the wake of this single, and the LP from which it is taken, will involve the group in touring there for much of 1983.)

1984 Feb LP *Defenders Of The Faith*, recorded in Ibiza and mixed by Allom in Miami, peaks at UK #19, with extracted *Freewheel Burnin'* making UK #42.

Apr LP *Defenders Of The Faith* is another US gold LP, peaking at #18. After some live dates to promote it, the band members take a break for much of this year and the next, settling in their new home in Phoenix, Ariz., US.

1985 July [13] Judas Priest emerges from its lengthy lay-off to play the Live Aid concert in Philadelphia, Pa.

1986 Apr The group returns to record LP *Turbo*, with the sound broadened with synth guitars and electronic effects. It makes UK #33 and US #17.

May Halford takes part in the Hear'N'Aid heavy metal charity single *Stars* to benefit Famine Relief in Ethiopia, which reaches UK #26. The band begins a world tour in US, moving on to Japan and Europe before playing their first UK live dates at the end of the year.

Dec [3] Judas Priest and CBS Records have a lawsuit filed against them by James Vance and the family of Raymond Belknap, contending that Vance and Belknap formed a suicide pact and shot themselves in the head after listening to the band's records for 6 hours in 1985.

1987 June Recordings made on the 1986 tour are released as LP *Priest Live*, which reaches UK #47.

1988 Apr The band's revival of Chuck Berry's° *Johnny B. Goode*, from the Anthony Michael Hall film of the same title, reaches UK #64.

June LP *Ram It Down*, the first studio set for 2 years, makes UK #24.

KANSAS

Steve Walsh (vocals and keyboards)
Kerry Livgren (guitar)
Rich Williams (guitar)
Dave Hope (bass)
Phil Ehart (drums)
Robby Steinhardt (violin)

1970 Livgren (b. Sept.18, 1949), Hope and Ehart, all friends from West Topeka High School, Kan., US, form a Frank Zappa°-inspired band with other local musicians. They play mainly dances and club dates locally, but with frequent personnel changes, the original trio remains the only constant.

1971 The trio recruits classically-trained violinist Steinhardt (son of a senior University of Kansas music lecturer), and relaunches as White Clover, playing around Kansas until the end of the year when Ehart leaves and the band splits.

1972 Ehart goes to UK in search of musical inspiration. He returns home 4 months later, disappointed with the stark pop/rock divide of early 70s UK, where progressive bands like Yes° and King Crimson° are afforded less exposure than in US. Back in Topeka, he re-forms White Clover, with Hope and Steinhardt, and they recruit vocalist Walsh and guitarist Williams. Livgren rejoins shortly afterwards, and the name is changed to Kansas. Kansas begins gigging again, developing a style which blends UK progressive influences with a refined form of early US heavy metal.

1973 The group records a $300 demo in a Liberal, Kan., studio, and Ehart mails a copy to an East Coast friend with record industry contacts. Months later, while the band is gigging in Dodge City, Kirshner Records' Wally Gold calls from New York, saying he wants to see the band live.

1974 July Signed to Kirshner, the group releases its debut LP *Kansas*, which makes US #174, and with constant touring eventually sells 100,000 copies.

1975 May LP *Songs For America* reaches US #57, earning a gold disk for a half million sales. The band continues to tour constantly all over US.

1976 Feb LP *Masque* reaches US #70, earning another gold disk in a 20-week chart run.

1977 Apr LP *Leftoverture*, produced by Jeff Glixman, is the band's commercial breakthrough. It hits US #5 and is a million-seller, going platinum. Extracted *Carry On Wayward Son*, penned by Livgren (now their chief songwriter), is Kansas' US singles debut at #11.

1978 Jan LP *Point Of Know Return* hits US #4, and is a second platinum seller, while the title track reaches US #28.

Mar *Dust In The Wind*, also from LP *Point Of Know Return*, hits US #6. Kansas' only top 10 single, it earns a gold disk for million-plus sales.

May Walsh is guest vocalist on ex-Genesis° guitarist Steve Hackett's second solo LP *Please Don't Touch*.

June [27] In a ceremony at New York's Madison Square Garden, Kansas is the first group to be chosen by UNICEF as its Deputy Ambassadors of Goodwill.

July *Carry On Wayward Son* reaches UK #51, more than a year after its US success. (It will be the band's only UK hit. No Kansas LPs will make the UK chart.) Meanwhile, *Portrait (He Knew)* peaks at US #64.

Aug [26] The band plays the first Canada Jam festival in Ontario, to 80,000 people, with The Commodores°, Earth, Wind & Fire°, The Village People°, Dave Mason and Atlanta Rhythm Section°.

1979 Jan Double live LP *Two For The Show*, recorded on tour, makes US #32 and is the group's third consecutive platinum LP.

Feb *Lonely Wind* reaches US #60.

July LP *Monolith*, the first self-produced by the band, hits US #10 and goes gold. Kansas plays an 80-city US tour to support the LP, opening at Von Braun Civic Center, Huntsville, Ala.

Aug *People Of The South Wind* peaks at US #23.

Oct *Reason To Be* makes US #52.

1980 Mar Walsh's solo LP *Schemer Dreamer*, on which other members of Kansas also play, reaches US #124. Livgren becomes a born-again Christian, as, shortly afterwards, does Hope. Livgren expresses his new-found faith through solo LP *Seeds Of Change* which does not chart.

Oct *Hold On*, from the forthcoming Kansas LP, peaks at US #40.

Nov LP *Audio-Visions* reaches US #26.

1981 Jan Another track from the LP, *Got To Rock On*, peaks at US #76. Walsh leaves the group, and is replaced by John Elefante.

1982 July LP *Vinyl Confessions*, with Elefante on lead vocals, makes US #16, while extracted *Play The Game Tonight* climbs to US #17.

Sept Second single from the LP, *Right Away*, peaks at US #73.

1983 Sept The group moves from Kirshner to CBS Associated label, and LP *Drastic Measures* reaches US #41. (The lower chart placing is a reflection of the year's tour results: like most US stadium-filling bands of the previous 2 or 3 years, Kansas has experienced a sharp downturn in audience attendance which is leaving venues unfilled.)

Oct *Fight Fire With Fire*, taken from the LP, makes US #58. The group comes off the road and, for a while, calls it a day.

1984 Sept Compilation LP *The Best Of Kansas* peaks at US #154.

1986 Oct Walsh, Ehart and Williams reunite to resurrect Kansas. New recruits are Steve Morse (ex-Dixie Dregs) on guitar and Billy Greer on bass. The group signs to MCA and records a comeback LP.

1987 Jan Kansas' reunion LP *Power* reaches US #35.

Feb *All I Wanted*, extracted from LP *Power*, makes US #19.

KC & THE SUNSHINE BAND

Harry Wayne Casey (vocals and keyboards)
Richard Finch (bass)
Jerome Smith (guitar)
Robert Johnson (drums)
Fermin Goytisolo (congas and percussion)

1973 Casey (b. Harold Wayne Casey, Jan.31, 1951, Hialeah, Fla., US) working as a record store assistant, collects records as part of his job from Tone Distributors. He works part-time in their studios for free, and begins to learn the ins and outs of production, also meeting bass player and TK Records' engineer, Finch (b. Jan.25, 1954, Indianapolis, Ind., US). Together they form KC (from Casey's nickname) & The Sunshine Junkanoo Band ("junkanoo" being a style of local dance music). The band plays locally with a line-up varying between 9 and 11.

1974 They sign to Henry Stone's Miami-based TK label, and release debut single *Blow Your Whistle* (recorded by Casey, Finch and session musicians, and inspired by the whistle flute sound which the duo first heard at a wedding reception for local R&B artist Clarence Reid), which sells locally and becomes a club hit in Europe.

KC & THE SUNSHINE BAND *cont.*

July For TK, Casey and Finch write and produce George McCrae's *Rock Your Baby*, which tops both US and UK charts and is a million-seller.

Sept The band makes its UK chart debut with *Queen Of Clubs* (released earlier in US to no reaction), which hits UK #7, licensed from TK by President Records and released on disco-oriented Jay Boy label.

Dec *Sound Your Funky Horn* makes UK #17, while Casey and Finch write and produce McCrae's second UK hit *You Can Have It All*, which peaks at #23.

1975 Apr *Get Down Tonight*, recorded by a now-permanent group line-up which goes on tour, (and includes female back-up singers Beverley Champion and Jeanette Williams) reaches UK #21.

Aug *Get Down Tonight* is KC & The Sunshine Band's US chart debut. After climbing for several weeks while they are on a European tour, it hits #1 for a week as they return home. Simultaneously, Casey/Finch-written and produced *That's The Way (I Like It)* hits UK #4. As resident house band at TK studios, they also back Betty Wright on her UK #25 hit *Where Is The Love* and George McCrae on his UK #23 *It's Been So Long*.)

Sept Debut LP *KC And The Sunshine Band* reaches UK #26, while instrumental single *Shotgun Shuffle*, credited only to The Sunshine Band, charts briefly at US #88.

Nov *That's The Way (I Like It)* (according to Casey, a toned-down re-cut of an original more lascivious version on which the repeated "a-has" were sensual moans), tops the US chart for 2 weeks, and is a million-seller. Meanwhile, *I'm So Crazy* reaches UK #34. The group becomes a major live touring attraction in US, pulling critical praise for its melding of R&B and gospel with a white rock sound.

Dec LP *KC And The Sunshine Band* hits US #4, while instrumental LP *The Sound Of Sunshine*, credited to The Sunshine Band, makes US #131.

1976 Apr *Queen Of Clubs* is re-promoted in US, and this time charts at #66.

Aug After an 8-month hiatus between UK releases, *(Shake Shake Shake) Shake Your Booty* makes UK #22.

Sept In US, *(Shake Shake Shake) Shake Your Booty* tops the chart for a week (deposing The Bee Gees'° *You Should Be Dancing*), and is another million-seller.

Dec LP *Part 3* peaks at US #13.

1977 Jan *Keep It Comin' Love* reaches UK #31, while in US *I Like To Do It* makes #37.

May Taken from LP *Part 3*, *I'm Your Boogie Man* makes UK #41.

June *I'm Your Boogie Man* tops the US chart for a week, making The Sunshine Band only the second group after The Jackson 5° to achieve four US #1 singles in the 70s.

Sept Released months after its UK chart run, *Keep It Comin' Love* (also from LP *Part 3*, on which it was segued with *I'm Your Boogie Man*) hits US #2 and tops the R&B chart.

1978 Jan *Wrap Your Arms Around Me*, B-side of 6-month-old *I'm Your Boogie Man*, picks up US airplay, and is elevated to A-side, making US #48.

Mar *Boogie Shoes*, originally released as B-side of *Shake Your Booty*, is reissued as an A-side and makes US #35. The track is included on the soundtrack LP of movie *Saturday Night Fever*, which spends 25 consecutive weeks at US #1 between Jan. and July, and 18 weeks at UK #1. With the total sales of LP *Saturday Night Fever* exceeding 25 million copies, it means that *Boogie Shoes* sells to more people than the combined total of everything else released by KC & The Sunshine Band.

May *Boogie Shoes* reaches UK #34.

June A revival of The Four Tops'° *It's The Same Old Song* climbs to US #35.

Aug *It's The Same Old Song* peaks at UK #49.

Sept LP *Who Do Ya (Love)* makes US #36.

Oct *Do You Feel All Right* reaches US #63.

1979 Jan *Who Do Ya love*, the title track from the band's recent LP, peaks at US #68.

July *Do You Wanna Go Party*, a deliberate effort to move back from the prevailing disco sound to a more basic funk mixture, peaks at US #50, and is followed by an LP of the same title which also climbs to US #50.

1980 Jan The untypical ballad *Please Don't Go*, a Casey/Finch song written in the studio during recordings for the previous LP, on which it was included, is extracted to provide the group with its final US chart-topper and million-seller. It is the first US #1 of the 80s (for 1 week, after 19 weeks' climbing the Hot 100), and hits UK #3.

Feb Casey duets with Casablanca Records' girl singer Teri DeSario, on a revival of Barbara Mason's 1965 hit *Yes, I'm Ready*. Credited to Teri DeSario with KC, it hits US #2 only weeks after *Please Don't Go* has left the top, and earns the duo a gold disk for a million-plus sales.

Mar Compilation LP *Greatest Hits* reaches US #132. An LP of the same title, though with a different track listing, hits UK #10.

July A second DeSario/KC duet, *Dancin' In The Streets*, makes US #66.

1981 TK Records goes bankrupt and the group disbands. Casey signs to Epic, where he records LP *The Painter* (under the group name) and LP *Space Cadet* (as a solo), but without much promotion both fail to chart.

1982 Jan [15] Casey is seriously injured in a head-on collision near his home in Hialeah, Fla. (He loses all feeling on the right side of his body as the result of injury to a nerve, and is confined to a wheelchair, before spending most of the year recuperating while learning to walk again. When he is fit enough to re-enter the studio, he cuts LP *All In A Night's Work*, for Epic, but it does not chart.)

1983 Aug *Give It Up* is extracted from LP *All In A Night's Work* by Epic in UK, and becomes KC's first hit in over 3 years and biggest-ever in UK. After 10 years of UK chart entries, it is his first UK #1 (for a week). US Epic declines to issue the single, leading Casey to negotiate his release from the label along with the rights to the track. He launches his own independent US label, Meca Records (Musical Enterprise Corporation of America), and releases *Give It Up*.

Sept LP *All In A Night's Work* makes UK #46.

Oct *(You Said) You'd Gimme Some More*, taken from the LP, reaches UK #41.

1984 Mar *Give It Up* reaches US #18, while LP *KC Ten*, also on Meca, peaks at US #93. (Despite having no further chart entries, KC will continue to tour US playing the party-type R&B music in which The Sunshine Band specialized.)

CHAKA KHAN

1969 Khan (b. Yvette Marie Stevens, Mar.23, 1953, Great Lakes, Ill., US), having performed since age 12 when she and some girl friends from school entered local talent shows as The Crystalettes, and later been a member of the Afro-Arts Theater in Chicago, adopting her new name while working for the Black Panther movement's Breakfast Program ("Chaka" meaning fire), joins the group Shades of Black.

1970 She marries at 17, and sings in the group Lock and Chain, before joining soul/dance band Lyfe.

1971 Khan meets Chicago-based funk/jazz group Ask Rufus, formed out of the remnants of pop band The American Breed, former million-sellers with *Bend Me, Shape Me*.

1972 When lead singer Paulette McWilliams leaves Ask Rufus, Khan is invited to replace her.

1973 Aug Signed to ABC Records, the group shortens its name to Rufus. The other members with Khan are Tony Maiden (guitar), Kevin Murphy (keyboards), Nate Morgan (keyboards), Bobby Watson (bass) and Andre Fischer (drums). Debut LP *Rufus* makes US #175.

1974 Aug Rufus' singles chart debut is with a Stevie Wonder° song, *Tell Me Something Good*, which hits US #3 and earns a gold disk for a million sales. LP *Rags To Rufus* hits US #4, and also goes gold.

Dec *You Got The Love* makes US #11.

1975 Apr *Once You Get Started* hits US #10, and the LP from which it is taken, *Rufusized*, hits US #7, the band's second gold LP. It also makes UK #48, Rufus' first UK chart entry.

May [22] The band joins Joe Cocker°, Pure Prairie League and Earl Scruggs in the "Music – You're My Mother" concert at Fort Campbell, Ky., to 17,000 US Army troops and their families.

June *Please Pardon Me (You Remind Me Of A Friend)* peaks at US #48.

June [21] On tour in UK, Rufus supports Elton John° at Wembley, along with The Beach Boys°, The Eagles° and Joe Walsh°.

1976 Apr Rufus' second million-seller is *Sweet Thing*, which hits US #5. It is extracted from LP *Rufus Featuring Chaka Khan*, which hits US #7, and is a third gold disk.

June *Dance With Me* makes US #39.

1977 Apr *At Midnight (My Love Will Lift You Up)* peaks at US #30. LP *Ask Rufus* is the band's biggest-selling LP to date, reaching US #12 and topping a million sales, to earn a platinum disk.

June *Hollywood* reaches US #32.

Sept [27] Khan participates in the Rock'n'Bowl benefit for US Special Olympics at South Bay Bowl, Redondo Beach, Cal.

1978 Jan Khan duets with Joni Mitchell° on her LP *Don Juan's Restless Daughter*.

Apr LP *Street Player* reaches US #14, and earns another gold disk.

June The group billing changes to Rufus & Chaka Khan, beginning with *Stay*, which reaches US #38.

July Khan sings lead vocals on Quincy Jones' hit single *Stuff Like That*.

Dec Amid some bad feeling between herself and the rest of Rufus, Khan signs a solo deal with Warner Bros. Her first solo LP *Chaka* reaches US #12, earning a gold disk for a half million sales. Produced by Arif Mardin, it features instrumental help from Average White Band°, George Benson° and Rufus.

1979 Jan Taken from the LP, *I'm Every Woman*, written by Ashford and Simpson°, makes US #21 (having already topped the R&B chart for 3 weeks) and UK #11.

Mar Rufus' LP *Numbers* is the band's smallest seller since its debut, peaking at US #81.

Mar [22] Just a day before her 26th birthday, Khan has a son, Damien Holland.

Aug Now split from Rufus (though she is contracted to make two further LPs for ABC with the group), Khan guests on Ry Cooder's° LP *Bop Till You Drop*. Rufus, meanwhile, recruits David Wolinski for lead vocals, alongside existing member Tony Maiden.

1980 Feb Fulfilling her contract, Khan cuts *Do You Love What You Feel* with Rufus, which climbs to US #30. Rufus LP *Masterjam* reaches US #14, and earns another gold disk.

Aug Solo LP *Naughty* climbs to US #43.

1981 May Rufus' LP *Party 'Til You're Broke* makes US #73.

June Khan's solo LP *What Cha' Gonna Do For Me* reaches US #17 and earns a gold disk, while the title track makes US #53.

Dec A Rufus & Chaka Khan single, *Sharing The Love*, creeps to US #91. It is taken from LP *Camouflage*, which makes US #98.

1982 Feb With their differences behind them, Chaka Khan and Rufus perform together at New York's Savoy Theater, the show being recorded for a live LP. Meanwhile, Khan contributes vocals to Lenny White's LP *Echoes Of An Era*. Along with Chick Corea, Stanley Clarke and Freddie Hubbard, she records new versions of jazz classics.

1983 Feb A revival of Michael Jackson's° hit *Got To Be There* makes US #67. It is taken from LP *Chaka Khan*, which reaches US #52.

Nov Double LP *Live – Stompin' At The Savoy*, a recording of the Feb. 1982 Khan/Rufus reunion concert, is released by Khan's label Warner Bros., and climbs to US #50.

Dec *Ain't Nobody*, taken from the live LP, reaches US #22.

1984 May *Ain't Nobody* hits UK #8 (Rufus' only UK hit single), while LP *Live – Stompin' At The Savoy* makes UK #64.

Nov Khan's revival of *I Feel For You*, written by Prince° and originally on his second LP *Prince* in 1979, features a rap intro by Grandmaster Melle Mel° and harmonica fills by Stevie Wonder°. It tops the UK chart for 3 weeks, and hits US #3, selling over a million to earn a gold disk. Mardin-produced LP of the same title reaches US #14 and UK #15, and is a US million-seller, earning a platinum disk.

1985 Feb *This Is My Night*, exemplifying the electro-funk feel of the LP, hits UK #14, but peaks at US #60. Khan's UK tour which follows is plagued by her throat problems.

May *Eye To Eye* reaches UK #14, while ballad *Through The Fire* makes US #60.

Oct Khan's *Can't Stop The Street* is featured in the break dance/rap movie *Krush Groove*.

Dec *Own The Night*, featured in an episode of US TV's "Miami Vice", makes US #57.

1986 May Khan arranges the vocals for Robert Palmer's° US #1 *Addicted To Love*.

July Written by Scritti Politti°, *Love Of A Lifetime* climbs to US #53 and UK #52. Khan duets with David Bowie° on *Underground*, from the soundtrack of *Labyrinth*.

Aug LP *Destiny* makes UK #77. Producer Mardin is assisted on it by son Joe, and it includes a song written by Genesis'° Mike Rutherford. Khan contributes vocals to Steve Winwood's° US #1 *Higher Love*.

1988 Nov [5] Khan begins a month's tour of Europe in Hamburg, as new single *It's My Party*, produced by Russ Titelman, is released.

KID CREOLE & THE COCONUTS

August Darnell (vocals)
Andy Hernandez (percussion)

1976 Oct Darnell (b. Thomas Browder) and Hernandez, with lead singer Cory Day, find initial success in Dr. Buzzard's Original "Savannah" Band, a 1930s-styled disco outfit formed by Darnell's half-brother, Stoney Browder Jr. Signed to RCA Records, the group's *I'll Play The Fool* reaches US #80, and its eponymous debut LP makes US #22. The LP, mixing latin and salsoul rhythms with 1930s dance band material, earns a gold disk for a half million US sales.

1977 Jan Dr. Buzzard reaches US #27 hit with a medley of the standards *Whispering-Cherchez La Femme-C'est Si Bon*.

Mar LP *Dr. Buzzard Meets King Pennett*, on similar lines to the debut, makes US #36.

1979 Their last LP, *Dr. Buzzard Goes To Washington*, is issued on US Elektra, but fails to chart.

1980 After Dr. Buzzard breaks up, Darnell becomes staff producer for Michael Zilkah's Ze Records, producing and arranging Don Armando's Second Avenue Rhumba Band, The Aurral Exciters and Christina, among others. Kid Creole & The Coconuts are formed using a similar musical formula to Dr. Buzzard, but dropping the orchestra. Darnell adopts the name Kid Creole, while Andy "Sugar Coated" Hernandez becomes Coati Mundi. The Coconuts are a female vocal trio, featuring Darnell's wife Adrianna. The visual image is taken from the nightclub scenes in 1930s movie *King Kong*. Debut LP *Off The Coast Of Me* is released in US by Ze Records, to good reviews, but without charting.

1981 July *Me No Pop I* is the group's first UK release, on Ze/Island, and climbs to #32. Meanwhile, second LP *Fresh Fruit In Foreign Places* reaches US #180.

Sept Darnell produces UK funk band Funkapolitan for London Records in UK, and also Machine for US RCA.

1982 June *I'm A Wonderful Thing, Baby* hits UK #4 and establishes the group as a major UK club dancefloor favorite. At the same time, LP *Fresh Fruit In Foreign Places* climbs to UK #99.

Aug *Stool Pigeon* hits UK #7, while LP *Tropical Gangsters* hits UK #3. (This will be the group's best-selling LP in UK, charting for 40 weeks.) In US, a revised version appears as LP *Wise Guy*, making #145.

Oct *Annie, I'm Not Your Daddy* is the group's biggest UK single, hitting #2 behind Culture Club's° *Do You Really Want To Hurt Me*. "In The Jungle", a TV special featuring the group, is screened in UK.

Dec EP *Christmas At B'Dilly Bay*, featuring lead track *Dear Addy*, makes UK #29.

1983 May Coati Mundi solo LP *The Former Twelve Year-Old Genius* is released on Virgin in UK, but fails to chart.

June *Did You Have To Love Me Like You Did?* recorded by The Coconuts in their own right, peaks at UK #60.

Sept Kid Creole & The Coconuts' *There's Something Wrong With*

KID CREOLE & THE COCONUTS *cont.*

Paradise reaches UK #35 and LP *Doppelganger* makes UK #21. Meanwhile, The Coconuts release their own LP *Don't Take My Coconuts* on EMI-America, but it fails to chart.

Nov *(Welcome To) The Lifeboat Party* makes UK #49, and is the group's final UK hit single.

1984 Feb Darnell produces Elbow Bones & The Racketeers' *A Night In New York* on EMI America, which reaches UK #33.

Apr Kid Creole's *My Male Curiosity*, from the soundtrack of film *Against All Odds*, is issued as a UK single, without charting.

Oct LP *Cre-Ole*, a compilation of the group's hits on Ze, makes UK #21.

Dec The Kid Creole concept TV special "There's Something Wrong in Paradise" is shown on UK TV.

1985 The group signs to Sire Records for UK and US.

July LP *In Praise Of Older Women And Other Crimes* and single *Endicott* both fail to sell.

1986 Apr *Caroline Was A Dropout* is another unsuccessful single.

1987 June LP *I Too Have Seen The Woods* fails to chart.

1988 Mar Kid Creole & The Coconuts duet with Barry Manilow° on *Hey Mambo*, a track on Manilow's LP *Swing Street*, co-produced by Emilio Estefan Jr. of Miami Sound Machine°.

JOHNNY KIDD AND THE PIRATES

Johnny Kidd (vocals)
Alan Caddy (guitar)
Brian Gregg (bass)
Clem Cattini (drums)

1959 Jan The group is formed in London by Kidd (b. Frederick Heath, Dec.23, 1939, London, UK), former leader of skiffle group The Five Nutters. Caddy (b. Feb.2, 1940, London, UK) is also an ex-Nutter. The rest of the early line-up is variable, with session men playing on first three singles.

June A booking on BBC radio's "Saturday Club" show leads to a contract with EMI's HMV label and debut single *Please Don't Touch* (written by Kidd and manager Guy Robinson), which makes UK #25.

Dec A revival of music hall standard *If You Were The Only Girl In The World* flops.

1960 Jan Gregg and Cattini, former session men in the Larry Parnes' tour back-up band The Beat Boys, join to complete a powerful live group: all in pirate gear playing in front of a galleon backdrop, and Kidd in a eye-patch which he later admits temporarily upsets his eyesight after every show.

Feb A cover of Marv Johnson's US hit *You Got What It Takes* reaches UK #25.

Aug *Shakin' All Over*, almost issued as a B-side, hits UK #2 beneath Cliff Richard° and The Shadows'° *Please Don't Tease*. Driven by a powerful guitar riff from session player Joe Moretti, the rock song becomes a UK standard.

Oct *Restless*, in similar style to *Shakin'*, makes UK #19.

1961 Apr A cover of Ray Sharpe's US hit *Linda Lu* reaches UK #47.

July The Pirates leave Kidd to back Tommy Steele's° brother Colin Hicks as The Cabin Boys, before becoming the basis of producer Joe Meek's studio house band the Tornados°. They are replaced by Frank Farley (drums), Johnny Spence (bass) and Johnny Patto (guitar), previously Cuddly Dudley's backing group The Redcaps.

1962 Mar Guitarist Mick Green, also formerly with The Redcaps (whose ability to play simultaneous lead and rhythm mark him as Britain's answer to James Burton), replaces Patto.

1963 Jan A cover of Arthur Alexander's *A Shot Of Rhythm & Blues*, firmly in an R&B mold, creeps into UK chart at #48 after two flop singles.

Sept Merseybeat-flavored *I'll Never Get Over You* is Kidd's second-biggest UK single, hitting #4.

Dec *Hungry For Love*, a stage favorite with many UK beat groups, makes UK #20.

1964 Jan The Pirates, minus Kidd, release an R&B single with Spence vocalizing, a revival of Little Walter's *My Babe*, which is not a hit.

Apr Kidd adds Vic Cooper on organ to the group. *Always And Ever*, an unlikely rock adaptation of Latin standard *La Paloma*, is Kidd's last UK chart entry, reaching #46.

July Green leaves to join Billy J. Kramer° and The Dakotas. He is replaced by John Weider.

Oct A revival of Marvin Rainwater's *Whole Lotta Woman* fails to sell, as do all later Kidd records.

1966 Apr Acknowledging his depression about declining interest in his music, seen as outdated, Kidd splits from The Pirates. Spence and Farley keep the latter name, and with guitarist Jon Morshead, record *Casting My Spell* unsuccessfully for Polydor before splitting.

May Kidd recruits The Regents, former backing group of Buddy Britten, as The New Pirates. They play UK one-nighters continuously, favorites of the Ted audience who hate most UK beat groups with rare venom.

Oct [7] While on tour, Kidd dies in a car crash in Radcliffe, near Manchester, UK. (Nick Simper, a member of The New Pirates, survives the crash and later will be a founding member of Deep Purple°.) The group carries on for a while as The Pirates, but bookings dry up without Kidd's name, and they will split in May 1967.

1976 Dec Former Kidd sidemen Mick Green, Johnny Spence and Frank Farley re-form as The Pirates, and become one of the most highly-rated UK live acts of the late 70s in pubs, clubs and larger venues. Debut LP *Out Of Their Skulls* charts in UK at #57 (but three later LPs and a plethora of singles will sell less well despite continuous onstage success, and the lack of record sales will lead again to a break-up in 1982).

THE GREG KIHN BAND

Greg Kihn (vocals and guitar)
Greg Douglas (guitar)
Gary Phillips (keyboards and vocals)
Steven Wright (bass and vocals)
Larry Lynch (drums and percussion)

1974 Kihn (b. Baltimore, Md., US) moves to Berkeley, Cal., where he signs to new, independent Beserkley label.

1975 He sings with labelmates Earth Quake and Jonathan Richman (backing vocals on hit single *Roadrunner*), and cuts two tracks for compilation LP *Beserkley Chartbusters, Vol.1*, before forming the first version of The Greg Kihn Band, with Wright and Lynch. The trio hones its material on club gigs around the San Francisco area, with a Sunday night residency at the San Pablo Avenue music hall, usually with Earth Quake's Robbie Dunbar as guest guitarist. Debut LP *Greg Kihn*, produced (like its follow-ups) by Matthew King Kaufman, is released, but does not chart.

1976 Mar Dave Carpenter joins the band on guitar, filling the slot which Dunbar has been caretaking. This line-up becomes the definitive version of The Greg Kihn Band, and records LP *Greg Kihn, Again*, which fails to chart, but features a critically-rated version of Bruce Springsteen's° *For You* in a folk-rockish arrangement which the writer admires and later adopts (crediting Kihn).

1978 Aug [26] On tour in UK, the band plays the Reading Festival, alongside Status Quo°, Spirit° and others.

Oct Third LP *Next Of Kihn*, consisting wholly of Kihn's own songs, is the first band disk to chart, reaching US #145.

1979 Sept LP *With The Naked Eye*, which includes another highly-rated Springsteen° cover, *Rendezvous*, reaches US #114.

1980 May LP *Glass House Rock* peaks at US #167.

Nov The band becomes a quintet with Gary Phillips (ex-Copperhead and Earth Quake) joining on keyboards and vocals.

1981 Sept The band's first hit single is *The Breakup Song (They Don't Write 'Em)*, which reaches US #15, and stays on chart for over 5 months. It is taken from LP *Rockihnroll*, which is Kihn's best-selling LP to date, reaching US #32 and charting for 32 weeks.

1982 May LP *Kihntinued* reaches US #33.

June *Happy Man*, extracted from the LP, reaches US #62.

July *Every Love Song*, also from LP *Kihtinued*, makes US #82.

1983 Apr *Jeopardy* becomes Kihn's only UK chart success, peaking at #63.

May *Jeopardy* is a US smash, peaking at #2 (behind Michael Jackson's° *Beat It*), and giving Kihn his first million-seller. LP *Kihnspiracy*, from which the hit is taken (and which also includes an unlikely revival of Patsy Cline's° country ballad *I Fall To Pieces*), reaches US #15 at the same time. Greg Douglas replaces Carpenter.

1984 June *Love Never Fails* makes US #59; it is extracted from LP *Kihntagious*, which peaks at US #121. It is Kihn's final Beserkley release before signing to major label EMI America.

1985 Apr LP *Citizen Kihn* reaches US #51. It credits Kihn as a soloist, though Wright is still on hand on several instruments, as well as co-arranging the tracks and co-writing all eleven songs with Kihn. *Lucky* is extracted and reaches US #30.

1986 Apr *Love And Rock And Roll* spends 5 weeks on the US chart, but reaches only #92.

B.B. KING

1949 King (b. Riley King, Sept.16, 1925, Itta Bena, nr. Indianola, Miss., US), cousin of bluesman Bukka White, has been playing blues guitar professionally since his US Army service, mostly around Miss. and Tenn. While leading a trio in Memphis, Tenn., his local popularity is noted by radio station W-DIA, and he secures his own regular show. The station's publicity man dubs King "The Beale Street Blues Boy", which is shortened to Blues Boy and eventually B.B. Towards the end of the year, King signs to Bullet label, debuting with *Miss Martha King*.

1950 King is signed to the Kent/Modern/RPM group of labels by talent scout Ike Turner. (He will remain with the company until 1962.)

1951 King hits US R&B #1 with *Three O'Clock Blues*, his eighth single. Ike Turner is featured on piano, Willie Mitchell on trumpet and Hank Crawford on alto sax.

1952 *You Didn't Want Me* is another R&B chart-topper. (King will continue to enjoy regular R&B chart success for the next 5 years.)

1954 Aug [19] King and his band play at the Savoy Ballroom in Hollywood, with Johnny Otis° and The Platters°, to a packed audience of 2,400.

1955 He is now averaging 300 gigs a year (a rate he will maintain until the late 1970s).

1957 May [29] King plays with Ray Charles°, The Drifters°, Ruth Brown, Jimmy Reed° and others at an outdoor R&B festival at Herndon Stadium in Atlanta, Ga.

July *Be Careful With A Fool* is King's first crossover success at US #95.

Nov *I Need You So Bad* makes US #85.

1960 Feb *Sweet Sixteen* hits US R&B #2 but does not cross over.

1962 King moves from Kent to larger ABC label (with which he will stay until it is absorbed into MCA in 1979).

1964 Mar *How Blue Can You Get It*, his first ABC success, peaks at US #97.

May *Rock Me Baby*, recorded for Kent before the label move, is King's first sizeable pop hit, reaching US #34. (It will be much covered and adapted by the UK R&B fraternity.)

June *Help The Poor*, on ABC, climbs to US #98.

Nov *Beautician Blues* peaks at US #82 as *Never Trust A Woman* makes US #90.

Nov [21] King plays a concert at the Regal Theater, Chicago, Ill. (which will be released as LP *Live At The Regal* in 1965).

1965 July *Blue Shadows* peaks at US #97.

1966 Oct *Don't Answer The Door* makes US #72.

1967 Apr *The Jungle*, another stockpiled oldie from Kent, reaches US #94.

1968 Apr *Paying The Cost To Be The Boss*, on ABC's Bluesway label, is his second US top 40 hit, at #39. King is in dispute with his manager Lou Zito over financial affairs. It is moderated by King's accountant Sidney Seidenberg, and when the dispute concludes, King appoints Seidenberg his new manager.

Apr [4] On the night after Martin Luther King is shot, King, Buddy Guy and Jimi Hendrix° gather in a club to play the blues all night and pass a hat around to collect money for King's Southern Christian Leadership.

July *I'm Gonna Do What They Do To Me* climbs to US #74.

Aug *The Woman I Love* stalls at US #94.

Oct Double A-side *The B.B. Jones/Put It On Me*, featured on the soundtrack to movie *For the Love of Ivy*, makes US #98 and #82 respectively. King's first LP chart success is with *Lucille*, on Bluesway, which makes US #192. (Lucille is the name King gives to his customized Gibson guitar.)

1969 May *Why I Sing The Blues* makes US #61.

July LP *Live And Well*, produced by Bill Szymczyck, with one a studio side and the other recorded at New York's Village Gate club, climbs to US #56.

Aug [1] King plays at the Atlantic City Pop Festival, to 110,000 people, alongside Creedence Clearwater Revival°, Jefferson Airplane°, The Byrds° and others.

Aug *Get Off My Back Woman* peaks at US #74.

Aug [30] He plays the International Pop Festival at Dallas Speedway in Lewisville, Tex., along with Janis Joplin°, Canned Heat°, Santana°, Led Zeppelin° and many more.

Oct *Just A Little Love* peaks at US #76. Under Seidenberg's encouragement, King starts to widen his following from the traditional (and declining) black audience towards a young, international white one, booking rock-oriented venues like the Fillmores East and West, and audiences already weaned on blues-derived rock bands. (King and Seidenberg will maintain this successful direction into the late 1980s, to the chagrin of a few blues purists.)

Dec *The Thrill Is Gone*, using an imaginative string arrangement, is King's biggest hit single, making US #15.

1970 Feb LP *Completely Well*, which includes *The Thrill Is Gone*, reaches US #38.

Apr *So Excited* peaks at US #54. LP *The Incredible Soul Of B.B. King* peaks at US #193. King begins work on a new LP, and in an attempt to repeat the pop chart success of *Completely Well*, features leading white rock musicians, including Carole King°, Leon Russell° and Joe Walsh°.

July [3] He plays the Atlanta Pop Festival in Byron , Ga., to 200,000 people, with Jimi Hendrix°, Jethro Tull°, Johnny Winter° and others.

July *Hummingbird* makes US #48.

Nov LP *Indianola Mississippi Seeds*, with King's star sidemen, reaches US #26. *Chains And Things* climbs to US #45.

1971 Feb *Ask Me No Questions* peaks at US #40.

Mar [16] King wins a Grammy award for *The Thrill Is Gone*, named Best Male R&B Vocal Performance of 1971.

Apr LP *Live In Cook County Jail* reaches US #25. King is taking an active interest in prisoner welfare (and will become co-chairman of F.A.I.R.R. – Foundation for the Advancement of Inmate Rehabilitation and Recreation). *That Evil Child* peaks at US #97.

June *Help The Poor*, an instrumental version of the 1964 release, makes US #90.

Sept *Ghetto Woman* climbs to US #68.

Oct LP *Live At The Regal*, reissued from 1965, reaches US #78.

Nov LP *B.B. King In London*, featuring sidemen Peter Green, Alexis Korner, Steve Marriott and Ringo Starr°, reaches US #57, as *Ain't Nobody Home* makes US #46.

Nov [19] King marks his 25th anniversary in the music business by opening a European tour in London.

1972 Mar LP *L.A. Midnight* reaches US #53. From it, a new version of *Sweet Sixteen* makes US #93.

Apr [1] King plays at the Mar Y Sol festival in Vega Baja, Puerto Rico, with Black Sabbath°, The Allman Brothers Band°, Emerson, Lake and Palmer° and many more.

May *I Got Some Help I Don't Need It* peaks at US #92.

Aug LP *Guess Who* reaches US #65. Taken from it, *Guess Who* makes US #62.

1973 Mar Compilation LP *The Best Of B.B. King* makes US #101.

Aug *To Know You Is To Love You* peaks at #38 as LP of the same title climbs to US #71.

Dec *I Like To Live The Love* reaches US #28.

1974 June *Who Are You* peaks at US #78.

B.B. KING *cont.*

Aug LP Friends makes US #153.
Nov *Philadelphia* peaks at US #64.
Dec LP *Together For The First Time . . . Live*, a collaboration with King's old friend and associate Bobby Bland, reaches US #43.
1975 Nov LP *Lucille Talks Back* climbs to US #140.
1976 Aug A further collaboration with Bobby Bland, LP *Together Again . . . Live*, reaches US #73.
1977 Feb LP *King Size* makes US #154.
1978 Apr King joins top defense lawyer F. Lee Bailey, his fellow co-chairman of F.A.I.R.R., for a joint rap session and concert for the inmates of Norfolk prison in Boston, Mass. Parts of it are filmed by US ABC TV for showing on "Good Morning America".
May LP *Midnight Believer* peaks at US #124. King switches labels as ABC is absorbed into parent company MCA.
1979 Apr King plays a month-long, 30-date USSR tour.
Aug LP *Take It Home* makes US #112, and gives King his first UK LP chart success at #60.
Aug [24] King celebrates his 30th anniversary making music by performing at LA's Roxy.
1980 May Live LP *Now Appearing At Ole Miss* climbs to US #162.
1981 Mar LP *There Must Be A Better World Somewhere* peaks at US #131.
1982 Jan [21] King donates his entire record collection (20,000, including 7,000 rare blues 78s) to the University of Mississippi's Center for the Study of Southern Culture.
May LP *Love Me Tender* makes US #179.
Sept [16] He records LP *Blues 'N' Jazz* on his 57th birthday.
1983 June [23] King plays at the Kool Jazz festival in New York, alongside Ray Charles°, Miles Davis° and others.
July LP *Blues 'N' Jazz* reaches US #172.
1985 Feb King appears in John Landis' movie *Into The Night*, playing himself (with his guitar).
1987 Feb [24] He wins a Grammy lifetime achievement award, and joins a star line-up of blues musicians who make a tribute to the blues at the 29th annual Grammy awards.

BEN E. KING

1957 King (b. Benjamin Earl Nelson, Sept.23, 1938, Henderson, N.C., US), after moving to Harlem as a boy, graduates from church choir to street corner doo-wop, singing with The Four Bs and The Moonglows before joining The Crowns. *Kiss And Make Up* is released and is a minor R&B success.
1958 May The Crowns share an Apollo Theater bill In New York with The Drifters°.
1958/59 The Drifters' manager George Treadwell fires The Drifters' members and, owning the trademark, hires The Crowns to become The Drifters. King is featured vocalist on *There Goes My Baby*, *Dance With Me*, *This Magic Moment*, *Save The Last Dance For Me* and *I Count The Tears* – smash hits which make The Drifters the hottest vocal group of the era. Treadwell fires King after he complains about low wages.
1960 Oct Signing a solo deal with Atlantic subsidiary Atco, King, with producers Leiber and Stoller, cuts four sides in 3 hours. (*Spanish Harlem*, *First Taste Of Love*, *Young Boy Blues* and *Stand By Me*, become the basis of a lifelong career.)
1961 Mar King's double-sided *Spanish Harlem*, a rare collaboration between Jerry Leiber and his apprentice Phil Spector, hits UK #10; *First Taste Of Love*, written by Spector and Doc Pomus, reaches US #53 but its B-side reaches UK #27. (On a par with King's and superior to over 150 versions, Aretha Franklin's° revival of *Spanish Harlem* will hit US #2 10 years later.)
June *Stand By Me*, polished up by Leiber and Stoller in The Drifters'° Latin style, hits US #4 and UK #27. (John Lennon° will revive it for a US top 20 hit in 1975.)
Aug LP *Spanish Harlem* climbs to US #57.
Sept King's version of the standard *Amor* makes US #18 and UK #38 (it will be his last UK chart appearance for 25 years).
Oct Pomus/Spector-written *Young Boy Blues* is finally released, rising to US #66. B-side *Here Comes The Night* charts at US #81. (In 1984, Robert Plant° will revive *Young Boy Blues* on his LP *Honeydrippers*.)
1962 Mar Another Pomus/Spector composition, *Ecstasy*, peaks at US #56.
June Co-written by King (under his wife's name) and Atlantic boss Ahmet Ertegun, *Don't Play That Song* climbs to US #11. (Aretha Franklin's° version will be a million-seller in 1970.)
Aug *Too Bad* charts for only 2 weeks, at US #88.
1963 Apr *How Can I Forget*, a King original, reaches US #85.
Aug King's version of Leiber and Stoller's (later much-recorded) *I (Who Have Nothing)* makes US #29 (and will be his last top 40 hit for 12 years).
Nov From musical *My Fair Lady*, *I Could Have Danced All Night* reaches US #72.
1964 As soul becomes more synonymous with the modern sounds of Motown and Stax, King's pioneering brand loses impetus. During the year, he has only two modest hits: *That's When It Hurts* (#63) and *It's All Over* (#72).
1965 Jan *Seven Letters* reaches US #45.
Apr *The Record (Baby I Love You)* peaks at US #84.
1966/67 Three minor hits conclude his 7-year solo run on Atco: *Goodnight My Love* (US #91), *So Much Love* (#96) and *Tears Tears Tears* (#93).
1967 July LP *Spanish Harlem* spends 3 weeks on the UK chart, climbing to #30.
1968/74 King works cabaret, club and supper circuits – mixing his own hits with those of current stars.
1974 Dec King makes a cameo appearance on Genesis° LP *The Lamb Lies Down On Broadway* – singing the phrase "on Broadway" (even though his was not the voice on The Drifters'° recording!)
1975 Apr Ahmet Ertegun, seeing King perform in a Miami nightclub, convinces him to re-sign with Atlantic rather than Atco. Produced by Bert DeCoteaux, *Supernatural Thing* hits US #5.
June LP *Supernatural* makes US #39.
1977 July King joins Average White Band° for LP *Benny And Us*, which makes US #33.
1978/86 King experiences more lean years as his popularity dwindles. After an unsuccessful union with Don Covay, Joe Tex, Wilson Pickett° and Solomon Burke as The Soul Clan, King rejoins The Drifters° for European tours. He releases one LP, *Street Tough*, for Atlantic in May 1981.
1986 Dec Featured as the title of a film based on a Stephen King novella, *Stand By Me* charts again at US #16 after a 27-year gap. Its undated sound and production values testify to Leiber and Stoller's studio innovation and King's vocal prowess.
1987 Feb Before the film premieres in UK, an advertising agency uses part of the song in a TV commercial promoting Levi 501 jeans. Its nightly exposure in UK takes *Stand By Me* to UK #1. King's cover of Percy Sledge's *When A Man Loves A Woman*, featured in the same ads, also hits UK #1.
Mar LP *Stand By Me (The Ultimate Collection)*, featuring both King solos and Drifters° tracks, including *Spanish Harlem*, makes UK #14.
June EMI releases *Dancing In The Night* through its dance label Syncopate.
July On the strength of revived fortunes, EMI Manhattan Records sign King and release LP *Save The Last Dance For Me*, which reaches UK #69. It is an updated version by King, with help from producers Mick Jones, John Paul Jones, Preston Glass and Lamont Dozier and features Mark Knopfler on guitar.

CAROLE KING

1958 While at Queen's College, New York, King (b. Carole Klein, Feb.9, 1942, Brooklyn, New York, N.Y., US) meets Paul Simon°, and begins writing songs professionally. She also meets lyricist Gerry Goffin, and the two write together for Don Kirshner and Al Nevin's Aldon Music based in New York's Brill Building.
1959 Mar King releases debut single *Baby Sittin'*, on ABC-Paramount, followed by *Short-Mort* on RCA-Victor and *Oh Neil!* (her response to Neil Sedaka's° *Oh! Carol*), on Alpine.
1960 Jan Goffin and King have their first success as writers of The Shirelles° US chart-topper *Will You Love Me Tomorrow*. (During the next 6 years, Goffin and King will write dozens of US Hot 100 hits.)
1962 Aug Kirshner hears a demo of *It Might As Well Rain Until September* King has made for Bobby Vee° and persuades her to release her own version. After an initial pressing on Companion Records, Aldon Music establishes its own Dimension label, specifically to release Goffin/King compositions and releases the track. Meanwhile, Goffin and King's *The Locomotion* tops the US chart, sung by their babysitter, Little Eva°.
Oct King-sung *It Might As Well Rain Until September* reaches US #22 and hits UK #3.
1967 Goffin and King separate (and later divorce). King forms

Tomorrow Records with journalist Al Aronowitz. She releases her own version of *Some Of Your Lovin'* (previously a hit for Dusty Springfield°) and an LP by The Myddle Class, which includes bass player Charles Larkey (who will become King's second husband).

1968 King forms new band The City with Larkey and guitarist Danny "Kootch" Kortchmar. Their LP *Now That Everything's Been Said* is released on Lou Adler's Ode label. Because of King's nerves, the band does not tour (and will soon break up).

1969 King plays piano on James Taylor's° LP *Sweet Baby James*.

1970 Mar King records debut LP *Writer: Carole King* at Crystal Sound studio in LA, where she now lives, which fails to sell.

Oct King records LP *Tapestry* with Larkey, Kortchmar and drummer Russ Kunkel, who will become her regular band, with James Taylor° playing guitar and singing backing vocals.

1971 May *It's Too Late* hits US #1.

June *Tapestry* tops the US chart. It will stay at #1 for 15 weeks and on chart for over 300 weeks, selling over 15 million worldwide. Re-promoted LP *Writer: Carole King* reaches US #84. James Taylor's° version of King's *You've Got A Friend* tops the US chart.

July LP *Tapestry* enters the UK chart as it goes gold in US. It will hit UK #4. King is the first artiste to perform at New York's Philharmonic Hall at Lincoln Center, traditionally a classical venue.

Aug *So Far Away/Smackwater Jack* makes US #14.

Sept *It's Too Late* hits UK #6.

1972 Jan *Sweet Seasons* hits US #9, as LP *Music*, with lyrics by Toni Stern, tops the US chart and reaches UK #18. Overcoming her fear of playing live, King tours US and UK.

Mar [9] King performs with James Taylor° and Barbra Streisand at a benefit for Presidential candidate George McGovern.

Mar [14] King wins four Grammys at the annual awards: Best Song, Best Record, Best Album and Best Female Vocalist.

Nov *Been To Canaan* reaches US #24. *It Might As Well Rain Until September* is reissued and makes UK #43.

Dec LP *Rhymes And Reasons* hits US #2 and climbs to UK #40.

1973 May [25] King performs a free concert in New York's Central Park to an audience of 100,000. Soundman Chip Monck ensures that everyone can hear the performance.

July *Believe In Humanity/You Light Up My Life*, from the forthcoming LP, reaches US #28.

Aug LP *Fantasy* hits US #6.

Oct *Corazon* peaks at US #37.

1974 Feb [14] King joins Dylan° at the last of his 39-date US tour in LA.

Apr [29] King gives birth to her fourth child, Levi.

Aug *Jazzman*, with Tom Scott guesting on sax, hits US #2.

Nov LP *Wrap Around Joy*, with lyrics by David Palmer, tops the US chart.

1975 Jan *Nightingale* hits US #9.

Apr Original TV soundtrack LP *Really Rosie*, which includes background vocal contributions from King's daughters Sherry and Louise Goffin, reaches US #20.

1976 Feb *Only Love Is Real* makes US #28.

Mar King teams with ex-husband Goffin to work together for the first time since 1967 on songs for LP *Thoroughbred*, which has vocal support from David Crosby, Graham Nash, James Taylor° and J.D. Souther. The LP hits US #3.

1977 Jan LP *Tapestry* leaves the US chart after 302 consecutive weeks.

Apr King, newly-signed to Capitol Records, where she forms her own Avatar label, starts work on LP *Simple Things* in LA. Self-produced with Norm Kinney, King uses recently Capitol-signed band Navarro, which includes Rick Evers (who becomes her third husband), to back her.

July *Hard Rock Café* makes US #30.

Sept LP *Simple Things* reaches US #17.

1978 Jan Again using Navarro, King records LP *Welcome Home* at Sound Labs, Hollywood.

Mar Evers dies from an apparent drug overdose.

Apr LP *Her Greatest Hits* reaches US #47.

June LP *Welcome Home* reaches US #104.

1979 Mar King records LP *Touch The Sky* at Pecan Street studios, Austin, Tex., with a group of musicians she had heard on Jerry Jeff Walker's LP *Jerry Jeff*.

July LP *Touch The Sky* peaks at US #104.

1980 Jan King records ten of her most famous early songs for LP *Pearls – Songs Of Goffin and King*, using the studios at Pecan Street, Austin. Ex-husband Larkey plays bass, and recent Warner Bros. signing Christopher Cross° plays rhythm guitar on *The Locomotion*, *Chains* and *Hi De Ho*.

July LP *Pearls – Songs Of Goffin And King* reaches US #44.

1982 Apr Now signed to Atlantic Records, King releases LP *One To One*, which reaches US #119. Despite a brief promotional visit, it fails to chart in UK.

1983 LP *Speeding Time* reunites King with producer Adler, musicians Kortchmar and Kunkel and lyricist Goffin. King records, for the first time, her own version of The Everly Brothers° 1961 hit *Crying In The Rain*, which she wrote with Howard Greenfield, with a sax solo from Plas Johnson.

1985 Mar *Care Bears* movie premieres. It includes songs by King and John Sebastian, and is later a popular video.

1987 Mar [9] King is inducted into the 18th annual Songwriters Hall of Fame awards at New York's Plaza Hotel.

Apr [23] King sues Lou Adler for breach of contract. She claims that over $400,000 in royalties is owed to her, and requests the rights to all of her old recordings.

1988 Feb In a rare live appearance, King joins a star group of musicians, including Billy Joel°, Joe Walsh°, Duane Eddy°, Warren Zevon, Robert Cray°, Roberta Flack°, Cyndi Lauper°, Ben E. King° and Ashford and Simpson°, to make up the house band for US TV show "David Letterman's Sixth Anniversary Special" at New York's Radio City Music Hall.

July A celebration of King's music, *Tapestry*, opens a 2-month run at the Cincinnati Playhouse, Oh.

JONATHAN KING

1965 Aug King (b. Kenneth King, Dec.6, 1944, London, UK) is studying English at Cambridge University when he writes *Everyone's Gone To The Moon* and records it for Decca. With major airplay from UK pirate radio stations, it hits UK #4.

Sept Follow-up *Green Is The Grass* fails to chart.

Nov *Everyone's Gone To The Moon* reaches US #17. King writes and produces *It's Good News Week* for a band of Royal Air Force servicemen whom he names Hedgehoppers Anonymous; it hits UK #4 – after Decca chief Sir Edward Lewis has insisted that he changes part of the original lyric to avoid offence.

Dec Debut LP *Or Then Again* is released, without charting.

1966 Jan Having failed in UK, *Where The Sun Has Never Shone* charts at US #97.

1967 King begins a career in journalism, as UK pop press columnist in *Disc and Music Echo*.

Dec King produces *The Silent Sun*, the first single by Genesis°. The group had sent him a demo tape made while at Charterhouse school – which King had also attended – and he had paid for a second demo, and signed it to Decca under a 1-year contract.

1968 Jan King hosts Saturday evening UK TV pop/chat show "Good Evening".

1970 Jan His revival of The Hombres' 1967 US hit *Let It All Hang Out* reaches UK #26.

1971 Feb King revives The Four Tops'° *It's The Same Old Song*, under the pseudonym The Weathermen, on B&C Records. It makes UK #19.

May Under another pseudonym, Sakkarin, King covers The Archies'° *Sugar Sugar*, which climbs to UK #12.

June Under his own name, *Lazy Bones* reaches UK #23.

July King produces St. Cecilia's *Leap Up And Down And Wave Your Knickers In The Air*, which makes UK #12.

Dec *Hooked On A Feeling*, a 1969 B.J. Thomas US (but not UK) hit, is

revived by King in an arrangement borrowed from Johnny Preston's 1960 #1 hit *Running Bear*, and reaches UK #23. (This same rearrangement will be borrowed by Swedish group Blue Swede 2½ years later, to top the US chart.) A novelty item produced by King using actress Adrienne Posta on exaggerated cockney lead vocals, *Johnny Reggae* by The Piglets hits UK #3.

1972 Feb *Flirt*, a cover of a continental hit, reaches UK #22. This will be his last hit single for Decca. He launches his own label, UK, through Decca. (Its major signing will be 10cc°, who will have a string of UK top 10 hits on UK before moving to Mercury.)

Aug King releases *The Official Munich Games Theme 1972* under the name Athlete's Foot, to the tune of *Deutschland Uber Alles*.

Nov On his own UK label, and under the pseudonym Shag, King's cover of continental hit *Loop Di Love* hits UK #4.

1974 Feb His revival of The Rolling Stones'° *(I Can't Get No) Satisfaction*, under the pseudonym Bubblerock, makes UK #29.

1975 Oct King's only hit single of his own on UK is *Una Paloma Blanca*, which hits UK #5, outselling Dutchman George Baker's UK #10 version. King also sings on a revival of Daddy Dewdrop's US hit *Chick A Boom (Don't Ya Jes Love It)* by 53rd & 3rd on UK; it makes UK #36.

1976 Feb Under the pseudonym Sound 9418, King's revival of Glenn Miller's *In The Mood* makes UK #46.

July As One Hundred Ton and a Feather, King's cover of Tavares' *It Only Takes A Minute* hits UK #9.

1978 King stands for the British Parliament as a Royalist candidate at a by-election in Epsom. (He is not elected, despite receiving 2,000 votes, one of the highest returns ever for an independent candidate.)

Oct *One For You, One For Me*, a cover of a continental hit by La Bionda, reaches UK #29.

Dec King's last hit under a pseudonym is Father Abraphart & The Smurps' *Lick A Smurp For Christmas (All Fall Down)*, which makes UK #58 and is a put-down of Belgian "act" The Smurfs (recent UK hitmakers with *The Smurf Song*), based on reports that the plastic Smurf toys intended for children are covered in leaded paint. King releases it on the one-off Petrol label, as a giveaway flexi-disk.

1979 June *You're The Greatest Lover*, under his own name, makes UK #67.

Nov King covers another continental hit, *Gloria* (originally by Dario Balden Bembo), which reaches UK #65.

1980/88 King mostly shelves his recording career to become a media superstar. He will present UK BBC TV shows "Entertainment USA" and "No Limits" (releasing a single of the themes on both sides), write a novel *Bible Two*, pen a weekly pop column for UK daily newspaper *The Sun*, and commute between his homes in London and New York, where he will broadcast a daily radio station talk show, while supporting the New York Mets. He will also broadcast on rival UK radio and TV networks, and re-establish his UK label, but fail to secure chart positions for a number of acts. King will also be associate publisher for UK heavy metal magazine *Raw*.

KING CRIMSON

Robert Fripp (guitar)
Greg Lake (bass and vocals)
Ian McDonald (saxophone)
Mike Giles (drums)
Pete Sinfield (lyricist)

1967 Aug Giles, Giles & Fripp is formed in Bournemouth, Dorset, UK, by Giles brothers Pete on bass and Mike on drums/vocals with guitarist Robert Fripp (b. 1946, Wimborne, Dorset).

Sept The trio moves to London but finds gigs hard to obtain.

1968 June McDonald (b. 1946, UK) joins with ex-Fairport Convention° singer Judy Dyble, and the group signs to Deram Records. Sinfield arrives as lyricist a few weeks later and Dyble departs.

Sept LP *The Cheerful Insanity Of Giles, Giles And Fripp* is released by Deram to little reaction (sales are supposedly less than 600 copies) and the band splits.

1969 Jan [13] Disillusioned, Pete Giles leaves and the group changes its name to King Crimson, recruiting Lake (b. Nov.10, 1948, Bournemouth, UK) from The Gods, and signing for management to fledgling E.G. company.

Apr [9] After a week's limber-up in Newcastle (still as Giles, Giles & Fripp), the first King Crimson gig is at The Speakeasy in London, followed by a lengthy residency at the Marquee club.

July [5] The band supports The Rolling Stones° at London's Hyde Park concert in front of 650,000 people.

Nov Self-produced debut LP *In The Court Of The Crimson King*, on Island, hits UK #5. The group plays an 18-date US tour, opening at Goddard College in Plainfield, Vt., to support the LP's US Atlantic release.

Dec The group returns to UK and McDonald and Giles leave. (They will record LP *McDonald And Giles* in 1970 and McDonald will help form Foreigner° in 1978.)

1970 Feb LP *In The Court Of The Crimson King* reaches US #28. The extracted title track makes US #80.

Mar Lake leaves to form Emerson, Lake and Palmer (ELP)° with Keith Emerson and Carl Palmer. Left as a duo, Fripp and Sinfield recruit assorted friends to record a second LP. Meanwhile *Cat Food*, made with help from both Giles brothers and jazzman Keith Tippett, is released. It fails to chart but gets the temporary line-up an appearance on UK TV's "Top of the Pops". Fripp is invited to join Yes° after Emerson turned him down for ELP° but decides to re-form King Crimson instead.

May Following LP sessions, Fripp and Sinfield keep vocalist/bassist Gordon Haskell (ex-Fleur De Lys) and saxophonist Mel Collins (ex-Circus) in the band. LP *In The Wake Of Poseidon* hits UK #4.

Aug Andy McCulloch joins as drummer.

Oct Haskell and McCullogh leave after recording the third LP while LP *In The Wake Of Poseidon* climbs to US #31.

Nov Ian Wallace joins on drums and Boz Burrell, recruited as a singer, is taught bass parts to the group's stage repertoire by Fripp and becomes bass player also.

1971 Jan LP *Lizard* reaches UK #30. Tippett guests again and Jon Anderson of Yes° sings guest vocals on one track.

Apr LP *Lizard* peaks at US #113. The band plays live for the first time since late 1969 on four dates in West Germany.

May The band begins playing live in UK (and will continue until Oct.).

Dec After second US tour Fripp asks Sinfield to leave. (He will produce the first Roxy Music° LP and write for ELP°.)

1972 Jan LP *Islands* reaches UK #30.

Feb The group returns to tour US and LP *Islands* makes US #76.

Apr Back in UK, all the band except Fripp depart, having failed to agree with him over the structure of King Crimson's stage act. (Burrell will later co-found Bad Company°.)

June Live LP *Earthbound* recorded in US in March, fails to chart in UK and US Atlantic refuses to release it.

July Fripp puts together a new band with Bill Bruford (ex-Yes°) on drums, John Wetton (ex-Family°) on bass and vocals, Jamie Muir on percussion and David Cross on flute and violin.

Oct [13] The new line-up makes its live debut in West Germany, and plays there and in UK for 3 months.

1973 Feb Muir leaves, supposedly to enter a Tibetan monastery, and is not replaced.

Apr LP *Larks' Tongues In Aspic* reaches UK #20. It is generally hailed as the group's best effort for years, with strong lyrics written by Richard Palmer-James.

June With the band midway through a 5-month US tour, LP *Larks' Tongues In Aspic* makes US #61.

Oct A short UK tour ends in Bristol, which is the last King Crimson UK gig for 8 years.

Nov Fripp releases LP *No Pussyfootin'*, a collaboration with Brian Eno (ex-Roxy Music°), which does not chart.

1974 Apr LP *Starless And Bible Black* makes UK #28.

June The band is again on a lengthy (38-date) US tour when LP *Starless And Bible Black* peaks at US #64.

May [1] The current line-up plays live for the last time, in New York's Central Park. Cross leaves the band.

Sept [25] After completing LP sessions with help from ex-members Collins, Cross and McDonald, they decide not to play together again. (Wetton moves to join Uriah Heep ; he will later form UK with Bruford and eventually join Asia°.)

Oct [18] Fripp announces that King Crimson has disbanded for good. LP *Red* charts briefly in UK the following week at #45.

1975 June Live LP *USA*, recorded on 1974 US tour, fails to chart in UK but reaches US #125.

Nov Fripp and Eno° collaborate on second LP, *Evening Star*, which does not chart.

1976 Feb Fripp compiles a retrospective of the band's career, double compilation LP *A Young Person's Guide To King Crimson*, issued with a companion booklet and including two previously unissued tracks.

May Fripp solo LP *Exposure* charts at UK #71 and US #79.

1980 May Fripp LP *God Save The Queen/Heavy Manners* makes US #110, having failed to chart in UK. The set is entirely instrumental, featuring an electronic style dubbed "Frippertronics".

Nov Fripp forms a one-off band, The League Of Gentlemen, with Barry Andrews (keyboards), Sarah Lee (bass) and Johnny Toobad (drums). *Heptaparaparshinokh* does not sell, but is notable for its B-side solo by Fripp, *Marriagemuzic*, which plays at 33rpm and is 11 mins 45 secs long.

1981 Apr The League Of Gentlemen's all instrumental eponymous LP does not chart in UK but reaches US #90.

May Fripp reunites with Bruford to form the band Discipline, with top New York session man Tony Levin (who has played on John Lennon's° LP *Double Fantasy* and Peter Gabriel's° solo LPs) on bass and Adrian Belew (who has previously worked with Frank Zappa° and Talking Heads°) on vocals and guitar. The band plays 2 months' live dates in UK and Europe, combining traditional Crimson repertoire with new material.

Oct By the time its first LP is released, Discipline's name has changed to King Crimson and the LP title becomes *Discipline*. It charts in UK at #41.

Nov *Matte Kudasai*, released as a UK single, just misses the chart. The LP peaks in US at #45.

1982 July LP *Beat*, which includes song lyrics by Belew based on US beat poet Jack Kerouac's work, reaches UK #39 and US #52. Its recording marks a widening rift between Fripp and the others which will lead to another split. Meanwhile the band embarks on a lengthy tour which takes in most of the UK. A gig at London's Hammersmith Odeon marks its final UK appearance, but further European dates will follow into 1983.

Dec Fripp records instrumental LP *I Advance Masked* with Andy Summers of The Police°. It does not chart in UK but makes US #60.

1984 Mar *Sleepless*, extracted from the forthcoming LP and remixed into a 7-minute-plus 12" dance version, reaches UK #79, finally giving King Crimson an (albeit minor) UK hit single.

Apr The final King Crimson LP *Three Of A Perfect Pair* reaches UK #30 and US #58. The band is inactive after its release and has effectively broken up after completing the recording. (Fripp will continue a production relationship with The Roches, three sisters recording for Warner Bros. Belew will record two solo LPs for Island and form The Bears on IRS. Bruford will record solo, with Patrick Moraz of The Moody Blues°, and with the band Earthworks, while Levin will concentrate on session work.)

Nov Second LP collaboration between Fripp and Summers, *Bewitched*, reaches US #155 but fails to chart in UK. (Fripp will go on to make LP *God Save The King* with The League Of Gentlemen in 1985, an eponymous LP as The League Of Crafty Guitarists in 1986, and LP *The Lady Or The Tiger* in 1987 in collaboration with Toyah .)

1986 May [16] Fripp and Toyah are married.

THE KINGSMEN

Lynn Easton (sax and vocals)
Jack Ely (guitar and vocals)
Mike Mitchell (lead guitar)
Bob Nordby (bass)
Don Gallucci (organ)
Gary Abbott (drums)

1958 Easton and Ely meet as teenagers when playing in local groups in Portland, Ore., US. Ely joins Easton's band, The Journal Juniors, when their guitarist fails to show for a gig. The two eventually form a duo to play locally, then add Mitchell on guitar.

Sept Nordby joins. Another local band breaks up and Easton's parents arrange for the acquisition of their name, The Kingsmen.

1962 Having built a live reputation playing R&B songs and rock instrumentals, and now joined from a rival group by Don Gallucci on keyboards, they are firmly part of the US Northwest touring scene which also includes Paul Revere & The Raiders°. A revival of Richard Berry's 1956 R&B song *Louie Louie*, learned from a popular local version by Seattle group, The Wailers, is added to their repertoire and becomes their most in-demand live item, sometimes leading to outrageous 45-minute stage versions.

1963 May *Louie Louie* is recorded for $50 in a small Portland studio, with Ely on lead vocals. The following day, Paul Revere & The Raiders° record their version in the same studio. The Kingsmen version is placed with local label Jerden, while Revere's is picked up (from Jerden) by major label CBS/Columbia Records, along with the group's recording contract. Both are good sellers in Northwest US, with the better-distributed Raiders having the airplay edge.

Aug Frictions occur in the band when Easton announces that he owns the name (because his parents had arranged the paperwork that way), and wants to assume frontman vocal duties, moving Ely to drums. Instead, Ely and Nordby leave, to be replaced by Gary Abbott (drums) and Norm Sundholm (bass). At the same time The Kingsmen's version of Louie Louie becomes a big hit in Boston, prompting Wand Records to acquire it from Jerden for national distribution.

Dec *Louie Louie* hits #2 in US, selling over a million copies. The group appears on TV with Easton miming to Ely's vocals.

1964 Feb [1] Widespread controversy over whether Ely's indistinct vocal on *Louie Louie* is masking off-color lyrics comes to a head when Matthew Welsh, Governor of Indiana, delares the song "pornographic", and asks the State's radio stations to ban it. Berry and Ely are called in to testify as to what they wrote and sang respectively. An FCC investigation concludes "the record to be unintelligible at any speed we played it". *Louie Louie* reaches UK #26, and is their sole UK hit. It is a huge underground success with London's mod dancers, whose reaction to it in clubs spurs most UK sales, since BBC radio shuns the record.

Mar LP *Louie Louie: The Kingsmen In Person*, recorded (apart from the hit single) live at a Portland club, reaches US #20. It will stay on chart for 131 weeks.

May A revival of Barrett Strong's *Money* reaches US #16.

Aug *Little Latin Lupe Lu*, a revival of The Righteous Brothers'° US hit of 14 months previously, peaks at US #46.

Oct *Death Of An Angel* makes #42 in US.

Nov LP *The Kingsmen – Vol.2* reaches US #15. It repeats first LP's formula of familiar cover versions.

1965 Mar *The Jolly Green Giant*, based on a TV ad for canned produce, hits US #4, their second-biggest hit after *Louie Louie*.

Apr LP *The Kingsmen – Vol.3* climbs to US #22.

May *The Climb* (about a dance), reaches US #65.

Sept *Annie Fannie*, celebrating a *Playboy* magazine cartoon character, peaks at US #47.

Dec Live LP *The Kingsmen On Campus* makes US #68.

1966 Apr *Killer Joe*, reviving a 1963 US hit by The Rocky Fellers, climbs only to US #77.

May A continuing seller since 1963 because it has been US radio's most-played "oldie", *Louie Louie* briefly re-enters US chart, reaching #97.

Sept Compilation LP *15 Great Hits* reaches #87 in US, and is their final chart entry.

1967 Easton leaves The Kingsmen, which by now has been through numerous other personnel changes. The band splits permanently 6 months later.

THE KINKS

Ray Davies (vocals and guitar)
Dave Davies (vocals and guitar)
Mick Avory (drums)
Pete Quaife (bass)

1958 Ray Davies (b. June 21, 1944, London, UK) persuades his parents to buy a guitar for younger brother Dave (b. Feb.3, 1947, Muswell Hill, London, UK). The brothers play together at a variety of gigs, including a local pub.

1963 Ray meets Alexis Korner after a gig and through his contacts becomes part of London's growing R&B scene led by The Rolling Stones°. (Interest in Muddy Waters° and Chuck Berry° will be a major influence in the early period of Kinks' hits.) Ray splits his time between gigging with blues combo, The Dave Hunt Band, and brother Dave's R&B outfit, The Ravens, which includes Quaife (b. Dec 31, 1943, Tavistock, Devon, UK).

Sept Ray quits The Ravens, who attract the interest of businessmen Robert Stace and Grenville Collins. They become their managers, booking them at society gatherings and country parties. Stace also arranges a meeting with pop impresario Larry Page.

Nov The group records a 5-track demo. Page places one song but fails to interest record companies. The demo comes to the attention of

THE KINKS *cont.*

American producer Shel Talmy, who has a contract with Pye. Page provides the band's new name, The Kinks and Avory (b. Feb.15, 1944) is added as drummer.

1964 Jan Contractual problems arise, with Kinks management now including Stace, Collins, Page, tour promoter Arthur Howes and Talmy.

Jan [23] The Kinks sign to Pye and record four songs for the label within a week of signing.

Feb First single *Long Tall Sally* is released, without charting. Intense hype earns the band an appearance on UK TV's "Ready Steady Go!" and much press coverage.

Apr Follow-up single *You Still Want Me* also fails to chart.

Sept The group's third single *You Really Got Me* rockets to hit UK #1 and US #7. Its insistent riff lays the base for all Kinks' singles during this period.

Oct Debut LP *Kinks*, comprising R&B covers and Ray Davies compositions, hits UK #3.

Nov *All Day And All Of The Night* hits UK #2.

Dec Ray marries 17-year-old Kinks' fan Rasa Dicpetri. LP *You Really Got Me* reaches US #29.

1965 Feb *Tired Of Waiting For You* is the band's second UK #1. The Kinks make their US TV debut on "Shindig", as *All Day And All Of The Night* hits US #7.

Mar LP *Kinda Kinks* hits UK #3.

Apr *Tired Of Waiting For You* hits US #6. LP *Kinks-Size* makes US #13. The band plays the 1965 *New Musical Express* Poll Winners Concert. *Everybody's Gonna Be Happy* peaks at UK #17. It sees a change of style, influenced by Earl Van Dyke, who has recently toured with The Kinks.

Apr [30] The group begins its first UK tour.

May [25] Dave Davies is knocked unconscious during a London concert leading to cancellation of the rest of the tour.

June *Set Me Free*, written originally for Cilla Black°, hits UK #9 and US #23.

July The Kinks begin their first US tour, as they split from Page.

Aug LP *Kinda Kinks* makes US #60. They fail to perform at one US gig (and will be blacklisted from playing in the country for 4 years).

Sept *See My Friend* hits UK #10. *Who'll Be The Next In Line* reaches US #34. The Kinks change management, setting up their own company. (This leads to court cases which will not be resolved until 1970.)

Dec LP *Kinks Kontroversy* hits UK #9 as LP *Kinks Kinkdom* makes US #13.

1966 Jan *Till The End Of The Day* hits UK #8. The Kinks appear on the last broadcast of US TV's "Shindig!"

Feb *A Well Respected Man* reaches US #13.

Apr With a softer songwriting style, *Dedicated Follower Of Fashion* hits UK #4. The group makes a promo film to support it in the clothes shops of London's Carnaby Street. LP *Kinks Kontroversy* makes US #95.

May *Till The End Of The Day* peaks at US #50.

June *Dedicated Follower Of Fashion* reaches US #36.

July *Sunny Afternoon* knocks The Beatles'° *Paperback Writer* off the UK top spot.

Aug LP *The Kinks Greatest Hits!* hits US #9.

Sept Budget compilation LP *Well Respected Kinks* hits UK #5. Quaife leaves temporarily, his absence covered by John Dalton.

Oct *Sunny Afternoon* reaches US #14.

Nov LP *Face To Face* peaks at UK #12.

Dec *Dead End Street* hits UK #5, but falters at US #73. UK BBC bans the promo film for it, which features the group leaping in and out of coffins.

1967 Feb LP *Face To Face* peaks at US #135.

Apr The group records UK concerts for a future live LP.

May *Waterloo Sunset* hits UK #2.

July *Mr. Pleasant* peaks at US #80. (It will be their last US chart appearance for 3 years.)

Aug Dave Davies, in brother Ray's shadow for so long, hits UK #3 with solo *Death Of A Clown*. It is, however, written by Ray.

Sept LP *The Live Kinks* climbs to US #162.

Oct LP *Something Else* makes UK #35. (It will be the group's last original LP to chart in UK.)

Nov *Autumn Almanac* hits UK #3.

Dec Dave Davies' *Susannah's Still Alive* makes UK #20. LP *Sunny Afternoon*, a budget compilation hits UK #9.

1968 Jan LP *Live At Kelvin Hall* reflects the rawness of The Kinks' live performance, but sells poorly.

Mar LP *Something Else By The Kinks* makes US #153.

Apr *Wonderboy* reaches UK #36.

Aug *Days* makes UK #12.

Nov LP *(The Kinks Are) The Village Green Preservation Society* is released. Ray's homage to England, it sells poorly. The group plays the Fiesta, Stockton, regarded as a "cabaret circuit graveyard". (It is a fate which will befall The Bee Gees° in 1974.)

1969 Apr *Plastic Man* reaches only UK #31, partly due to a UK BBC ban for inclusion of the word "bum" in the lyric. Quaife leaves the band permanently, and is again replaced by Dalton. Ray produces LP *Turtle Soup* for The Turtles°, and writes a song a week to feature in UK BBC TV series "Where Was Spring?" starring Eleanor Bron.

Oct LP *Arthur (Or The Decline And Fall Of The British Empire)* is released. Commissioned as a UK Granada TV play but never produced, its subject is an ordinary man reflecting on his life. It fails to chart in UK, but makes US #105. The group begins its first US tour in 4 years as support to Spirit° after resolving problems with American Federation of Musicians for The Kinks' "unprofessional conduct".

1970 Jan *Victoria* makes UK #33.

Mar *Victoria* peaks at US #62.

June Ray flies from New York to London and back during The Kinks' US tour to re-record lyric in the song, changing Coca-Cola to cherry cola to appease the BBC and copyright holders.

July Ray announces he is quitting the band, but changes his mind.

Aug The Kinks' *Lola* hits UK #2 and matches *All Day And All Of The Night*'s 14-week stay. John Gosling joins the band on keyboards.

Dec LP *Lola Vs. Powerman And The Moneygoround, Part One* reaches US #35.

1971 Jan *Apeman* also spends 14 weeks on chart, hitting UK #5 and climbing to US #45. Again Ray has to re-record a lyric.

Mar Soundtrack LP for film *Percy*, about a penis transplant, is released.

Oct LP *Golden Hour Of The Kinks* reaches UK #21.

Nov The group signs to RCA Records.

1972 Jan LP *Muswell Hillbillies*, eulogizing Ray's North London childhood, reaches US #100. The group is now re-gaining a large US following, already nostalgic for the 1960s. For touring it expands the live line-up, adding a horn section and female backing vocalists.

Apr LP *The Kinks Kronikles* reaches US #94, a greatest hits package reflecting the group's revived interest in US.

June *Supersonic Rocket Ship* reaches UK #16.

Aug LP *Everybody's In Showbiz, Everybody's A Star*, a double set with a live LP showcasing their US oldies act and a studio LP augmented by The Mike Cotton Sound brass ensemble, reaches US #70.

Oct The group previews new work as a West End stage show *The Kinks Are The Village Green Preservation Society*, and plays London's Rainbow Theatre at end of a short UK tour.

1973 Mar LP *The Great Lost Kinks Album* reaches US #145.

May The group opens its own Konk studios in Hornsey, London.

July Ray Davies walks out on his wife and children. After two drug overdoses, he announces at a rainy pop festival at London's White City stadium, that he is retiring. He returns within a week.

Dec LP *Preservation Act 1* reaches US #177. The LP is an extension of the themes first introduced in *Village Green*.
1974 July LP *Preservation Act II* makes US #114.
Oct The Kinks launch their own short-lived label, Konk, with Claire Hammill's LP *Stage Door Johnnies*.
1975 June LP *Soap Opera*, based on TV musical "Starmaker" which Ray had written last year, peaks at US #51.
Dec LP *Schoolboys In Disgrace* reaches US #45. It will be the group's last for RCA.
1976 June LP *The Kinks Greatest – Celluloid Heroes* climbs to US #144. The group relocates to US, and signs a deal with Arista.
Nov Dalton leaves the group, and is temporarily replaced by Andy Pyle.
Dec Press reports a fight between Ray and a Konk act, Cafe Society's Tom Robinson.
1977 Mar Arista debut LP *Sleepwalker* reaches US #21.
May *Sleepwalker* makes US #48.
July Ray Davies announces yet again that he is quitting.
Nov *Father Christmas* is released.
Dec The group plays a Christmas show at London's Rainbow Theatre.
1978 Apr Pyle leaves. (He will form the group United with Gosling.)
May The group begins a 1-month tour to tie in with release of LP *Misfits*.
June LP *Misfits* reaches US #40. Having recently rejoined, Dalton now leaves permanently. Gosling also quits. They are replaced by Gordon Edwards (keyboards) and Jim Rodford (bass).
Sept The Kinks' first US top 40 chart success in 8 years is *Rock'N'Roll Fantasy* which climbs to #30.
Oct LP *20 Golden Greats* makes UK #19.
1979 Feb The Pretenders° have a debut hit with *Stop Your Sobbing*, originally a Kinks LP track. (They will also chart with *I Go To Sleep*, another Kinks LP track.)
June *(I Wish I Could Fly Like) Superman* reaches US #41. The group begins its first major tour for 3 years.
July Ian Gibbons joins on keyboards.
Sept LP *Low Budget* makes US #11.
1980 June LP and video *One For The Road* are released simultaneously. The LP reaches US #14.
July Dave releases first solo LP *PL 13603* (*AFL1-3603* in UK; both titled after the disk's catalog number).
Sept LP *Second Time Around* peaks at US #177.
Dec The Kinks begin a short UK tour.
1981 July Dave releases second solo LP *Glamour*. It makes US #152, as The Kinks' single *Better Things* reaches US #46.
Sept Ray is divorced from his second wife, Yvonne.
Oct The band plays New York's Madison Square Garden for the first time. The public learns of Ray's romance with The Pretenders'° Chrissie Hynde.
Nov LP *Give The People What They Want* reaches US #15. *Destroyer* peaks at US #85.
1982 Jan Ray begins work on project *Return To Waterloo* which will provide a TV play for UK Channel 4 TV, a prerecorded video and LP.
Sept The Kinks participate in the 3-day US Festival at San Bernardino, Cal.
1983 Feb Hynde's (and Ray's) daughter Natalie is born.
May *Come Dancing* hits US #6, aided by exposure on MTV.
Aug LP *State Of Confusion* reaches US #12.
Sept *Come Dancing* makes UK #12, the group's first UK single success in 11 years.
Oct Old *You Really Got Me*, at UK #47, wins out over new *Don't Forget To Dance*, which makes UK #58 (but also US #29).
Nov LP *Kinks Greatest Hits – Dead End Street* peaks at UK #96. Dave releases third solo LP *Chosen People*.
1984 May Hynde leaves Ray for Simple Minds'° Jim Kerr. An unofficial biography of The Kinks by Johnny Rogan is published. LP *Word Of Mouth* is released.
Nov An official biography of The Kinks by Jon Savage is published.
1986 Ray appears in film *Absolute Beginners* as Patsy Kensit's father. The band signs a deal with London Records, releasing LP *Think Visual*.
July LP *Come Dancing With The Kinks* makes US #159.
1987 Virgin Video releases a compilation of Kinks promotional videos. PRT releases all of the Kinks' Pye LPs on CD.
1988 Mar LP *Live – The Road* is released.

KISS

Gene Simmons (bass and vocals)
Paul Stanley (guitar and vocals)
Ace Frehley (guitar and vocals)
Peter Criss (drums and vocals)

1972 The band is formed part-time in New York City by Simmons (b. Gene Klein, Aug.25, Queens, New York, N.Y., US), a teacher, and Stanley (b. Paul Eisen, Jan.20, Queens, New York), acquaintances from an earlier part-time group. Criss (b. Peter Crisscoula, Dec.27, 1947, Brooklyn, New York) is discovered through his own ad in *Rolling Stone*, and they rehearse as a trio while continuing day jobs. Frehley (b. Paul Frehley, Apr.22, 1951, Bronx, New York) is recruited as guitarist from an ad in *Village Voice*.
1973 Jan [30] The band plays its first gig, at the Coventry Club in Queens. Deliberately, its immediate impact is visual and theatrical.
1974 Jan [8] Casablanca Records signs the band.
Feb Debut LP, *Kiss*, is launched with nationwide promotion – including marathon kissing competitions. It reaches only US #87 (but will stay on chart for 23 weeks).
June *Kissin' Time* makes US #83.
Nov LP *Hotter Than Hell* peaks at US #100.
1975 Apr Through constant touring, Kiss builds a strong following. LP *Dressed To Kill* climbs to US #32.
May *Rock'N'Roll All Nite* reaches US #68.
Nov LP *Alive!*, recorded on tour, hits US #9. Extracted from it, *Rock'N'Roll All Nite* reaches US #12.
1976 Feb [20] Four sets of Kiss footprints are placed on the sidewalk outside Grauman's Chinese Theater in Hollywood, Cal.
Apr LP *Destroyer* reaches US #11 and is the group's first platinum selling disk. *Shout It Out Loud* climbs to US #31.
June *Flaming Youth* reaches US #74. LP *Destroyer* makes UK #22 and LP *Alive!* reaches UK #49.
Aug LP *The Originals*, a repackaging of the first three LPs and containing a comic book history of Kiss, peaks at US #36.
Nov Atypical ballad, written and sung by Criss, *Beth*, with B-side *Detroit Rock City*, hits US #7. The group makes its UK debut but interest is limited and its image is taken less seriously as the band only conducts interviews in full make-up. LP *Rock And Roll Over* enters the US chart. It will make #11, go platinum, and have a 45-week stay on the chart.
Dec [11] Frehley receives an electric shock during a concert at Lakeland, Fla. He is not seriously hurt.
1977 Feb *Hard Luck Woman* makes US #15.
May *Calling Dr. Love* reaches US #16.
June Marvel Comics publishes *The Kiss Comic Book* based on the masked men.
July *Christine Sixteen* makes US #25.
Aug [25-27] Kiss plays three shows at LA's Forum, which are recorded for forthcoming LP *Kiss Alive II*.
Sept LP *Love Gun* hits US #4, but the title track falters at #61.
Nov LP *Alive II* hits US #7 and becomes the group's fourth platinum disk. It charts for 1 week in UK, at #60.
1978 Jan A live version of 1976 hit *Shout It Out Loud* reaches US #54.
Apr *Rocket Ride* makes US #39.
May LP *Double Platinum*, a two record set of Kiss "classics", climbs to US #24.
Oct The four members simultaneously issue solo LPs which are launched in a high profile campaign, with each cover featuring a matching portrait of the artist in full make-up. Each LP is shipped platinum, but sales fail to match expected demand. Simmons' effort fares best, reaching US #22, followed by Frehley (#26), Stanley (#40) and Criss (#43).
Oct [30] US NBC-TV airs the animated cartoon *Kiss Meets the Phantom of the Park*, in which the heroes foil a mad scientist gone berserk in an amusement park.
1979 May *I Was Made For Lovin' You* makes US #11 and UK #50 (and is Kiss' UK singles debut).
June LP *Dynasty* hits US #9 and reaches UK #50.
Sept *Sure Know Something* makes US #47.
1980 May [17] Criss leaves the group to pursue a solo career.
June LP *Kiss Unmasked*, the first to miss the US top 30, peaks at #35 and makes UK #48. *Shandi*, from the LP, reaches US #47.
July [25] The group plays New York's Palladium, with new drummer Eric Carr.
Aug Kiss embarks on a European tour.
1981 Jan [12] The R.I.A.A. donates some 800 rock LPs to the Library of

Congress. Included is Kiss' *Alive!*.
Jan Casablanca releases LP *Best Of The Solo Albums*.
Dec LP *Music From The Elder*, a concept album unlike much of the band's previous material, reaches US #75 and fails to go gold. It makes UK #51. Taken from it, *A World Without Heroes* reaches US #56 and UK #55.
1982 Frehley leaves the group and is replaced by Vinnie Vincent. (Frehley will resurface with his own group, Frehley's Comet.)
Nov LP *Creatures Of The Night* reaches US #45 and UK #22. The band dedicates the LP to Casablanca label boss Neil Bogart, who died from cancer.
1983 Apr *Creatures Of The Night* makes UK #34.
Aug Kiss cancels a 3-day tour of Argentina when the extremist Free Fatherland Nationalist Commando movement threatens to stop the tour even if it "goes so far as to cost the very lives of that unfortunate band".
Sept [18] Kiss reveals all when the members appear on US MTV without make-up.
Oct LP *Lick It Up* earns a gold disk. It climbs to US #24 and hits UK #7. Kiss is signed to Mercury label and the LP sleeve features the group without make-up.
Nov *Lick It Up* makes US #66 and UK #31.
1984 Mark St. John replaces Vincent (who will later form Vinnie Vincent's Invasion).
Oct LP *Animalize*, returns the group to platinum status, making US #19 and UK #11. *Heaven's On Fire* reaches US #49 and UK #43.
Dec Simmons stars as the villain opposite Tom Selleck's hero in film *Runaway*.
1985 St. John leaves, and is replaced by Bruce Kulick.
Oct LP *Asylum* makes US #20 and UK #12. *Tears Are Falling* reaches US #51 and UK #57.
1986 May Kiss contributes *Runaway* on the various artists LP *Hear 'N' Aid*, for heavy metal music's fund-raising activities for famine relief.
June Simmons stars in film *Never Too Young To Die*, with Robert Englund and George Lazenby.
Oct Simmons' second film role is in *Trick Or Treat* with Ozzy Osbourne°.
1987 Nov Kiss' biggest UK hit at #4 is *Crazy Nights* which falters at US #65. LP *Crazy Nights* reaches US #18 and hits UK #4.
1988 Jan Ballad *Reason To Live* makes US #68 and UK #33.
Aug Simmons starts the Simmons record label.
Sept *Turn On The Night* reaches UK #41. Kiss plays the opening night of the newly relocated Marquee in London's Charing Cross Road.

THE KNACK

Doug Fieger (vocals and guitar)
Berton Averre (guitar)
Prescott Niles (bass)
Bruce Gary (drums)

1978 May The group forms in Los Angeles, US, with the intention of presenting a tight update of the mid-1960s beat group style – a sound which comes to be dubbed "power pop". Fieger (b. Detroit, Mich., US) is former bassist of Detroit group Sky, and Gary (b. Apr.7, 1952, Burbank, Cal., US) is ex-Jack Bruce Band. Niles (b. May 2, New York, US) and Averre (b. Dec.13, Van Nuys, Cal., US) are fellow veterans of LA session work.
1979 Feb Huge live success on Southern California club scene has 13 record labels bidding to sign them, with Capitol succeeding. They are teamed with Blondie's° producer Mike Chapman, with whom they produce an LP's-worth of songs, with little overdubbing (early mid-1960s style) in only 11 days, and for $18,000.
Aug Debut *My Sharona* is an instant US smash, topping the chart for 6 weeks. It sells over a million inside 2 weeks, and tops a second million in less than a month in the US. In UK it hits #6. LP *Get The Knack* performs similarly, topping US chart for 5 weeks. It will sell over 5 million copies worldwide by the end of 1979. UK sales are comparatively meager: it stalls at #65.
Nov *Good Girls Don't*, also from debut LP, reaches US #11, though only UK #66.
1980 Mar Constant Beatles° comparisons and associations contribute to a critical backlash against the group, which in turn hits their record sales: LP *But The Little Girls Understand* reaches US #15, and sales of 600,000 are only a fraction of first LP's total. *Baby Talks Dirty* is extracted, making equally disappointing US #38.
Apr Hasty follow-up *Can't Put A Price On Love* climbs to only US #62.
1981 Nov *Pay The Devil (Ooo Baby Ooo)* reaches US #67. Taken from LP *Round Trip*, it fizzles out at US #97, convincing the group members that they have lost the knack. They play a final US tour, then disband. Fieger forms Taking Chances, and the others stay together as The Game, but these ventures will not renew commercial success.
1983 Aug Fellow Detroiters Was (Not Was) employ Fieger as a guest vocalist on their LP *Born To Laugh At Tornados*, by which time The Knack is all but forgottten.

GLADYS KNIGHT & THE PIPS

Gladys Knight
Merald "Bubba" Knight
William Guest
Edward Patten

1951 Knight (b. May 28, 1944, Atlanta, Ga., US), whose parents are singers in Wings Over Jordan Gospel choir, wins $2,000 for singing *Too Young* on US TV's "Ted Mack's Original Amateur Hour". She has already sung gospel widely around the South with The Morris Brown Choir.
1952 Sept [4] After an impromptu performance together at a 10th birthday party for Merald Knight (b. Sept.4, 1942, Atlanta), Gladys, he and sister Brenda form a vocal group with cousins William (b. June 2, 1941, Atlanta) and Elenor Guest, singing gospel and ballads at family and church functions (they perform at the Mount Mariah Baptist Church in Atlanta).
1957 Having been persuaded by another cousin, James "Pips" Woods (whose nickname they purloin and who becomes their manager), to turn professional, the quintet cuts its first (unsuccessful) disk, *Whistle My Love*, for Brunswick. The Pips also tour with Sam Cooke°, B.B. King° and Jackie Wilson°.
1959 Brenda Knight and Elenor Guest both leave the group to get married, and are replaced by two male vocalists: a further cousin, Edward Patten (b. Aug.2, 1939, Atlanta) and Langston George.
1960 The group records a 1952 Johnny Otis° song, *Every Beat Of My Heart*, for Atlanta-based Huntom label, initially with little success, but eventually with enough sales interest for Huntom to sell the master to larger R&B independent Vee Jay in Chicago.
1961 May The group is signed by Bobby Robinson's New York-based Fury label, and re-records *Every Beat Of My Heart*.
June Both versions of *Every Beat Of My Heart* chart at the same time. The newer recording on Fury peaks at US #45, but the Vee Jay original, credited to The Pips, is still climbing.
July *Every Beat Of My Heart* on Vee Jay hits US #6 and tops the R&B chart for a week. The group is in huge demand for tour and club dates.
1962 Feb *Letter Full Of Tears*, on Fury, reaches US #19. (Coincidentally, it will be covered by UK singer Billy Fury°, who will have a UK top 20 hit with it a few weeks later.)
Apr *Operator* peaks at US #97, and shortly afterwards George quits, leaving the group as a quartet. (It will subsquently remain a quartet. Knight herself will depart for some 2 years to marry and have a baby. The Pips will work as back-up session singers.)
1964 June Knight returns to the group which signs to another independent R&B label, Maxx Records. *Giving Up*, written by Van McCoy, climbs to US #38.
Sept *Lovers Always Forgive* makes US #89, following which the label goes bankrupt and leaves the group without an outlet.
1966 Still extremely busy on the live circuit, with a tight, sharply-choreographed act behind Knight's gospelly soul leads, Gladys Knight & The Pips are booked as special guests on a Motown touring package, and on the strength of audience reception, offered a recording contract by label boss Berry Gordy Jr. A democratic vote goes 3-1 for acceptance, and they sign to Motown Records, which places them on Soul label, alongside Jimmy Ruffin° and Junior Walker & The All-Stars°. First release *Just Walk In My Shoes*, produced by Harvey Fuqua and Johnny Bristol, fails to chart.
1967 May The group switches to producer Norman Whitfield for *Take Me In Your Arms And Love Me*, which makes US #98.
July The group's UK chart debut is *Take Me In Your Arms And Love Me* which, aided by massive airplay on (imminently-departing) UK pirate radio stations, reaches #13.
Aug *Everybody Needs Love* makes US #39.

Dec Gladys Knight & The Pips' major chart breakthrough comes with their original version of Whitfield and Barrett Strong's *I Heard It Through The Grapevine* (later one of the most successful and re-recorded songs in the Motown catalog). It hits US #2 and sells over 1½ million copies, held from the top by The Beatles''° *Hello Goodbye*. It also tops the US R&B chart for 6 weeks, but makes only UK #47. The group also has its first US hit LP, *Everybody Needs Love*, which includes *Grapevine* and reaches #60.

1968 Mar Another Whitfield/Strong song, *The End Of Our Road* (like *Grapevine* later also to be revived as a hit single by Marvin Gaye°) reaches US #15.

July *It Should Have Been Me* peaks at US #40, while LP *Feelin' Bluesy* reaches US #158.

Sept *I Wish It Would Rain*, released only 7 months after The Temptations''° US #4 version, climbs to US #41.

1969 Feb LP *Silk'n'Soul* makes US #136.

Apr Ashford and Simpson°-penned and produced *Didn't You Know (You'd Have To Cry Sometime)* makes US #63.

Sept The group's unexpected, gospelly revival of Shirley Ellis' 1964 dance hit, *The Nitty Gritty*, makes US #19.

Dec Another gospel-tinged song, Whitfield/Strong's *Freedom Train*, reaches US #17. Both it and the previous hit are included on LP *Nitty Gritty*, which climbs to US #81.

1970 Apr *You Need Love Like I Do (Don't You)*, again penned by Whitfield and Strong, makes US #25.

May Compilation LP *Gladys Knight & The Pips' Greatest Hits* reaches US #55.

1971 Feb After a gap between releases, during which the group has ceased working at Motown with Whitfield (producer of nine of their last ten hits), it is teamed with producer Clay McMurray for *If I Were Your Woman*, written by McMurray with Pam Sawyer and Leon Ware. The new team proves a provident one, as the single hits US #9 and becomes the group's second US million-seller.

June [6] The group guests on the final edition of US CBS TV's "Ed Sullivan Show".

July *I Don't Want To Do Wrong*, the first single A-side to be part-written by group members (with producer Bristol and Catherine Schaffner), reaches US #17. It is taken from LP *If I Were Your Woman*, which reaches US #35 – their highest-placed LP to date.

1972 Jan McMurray-penned and produced *Make Me The Woman That You Go Home To* climbs to US #27.

Feb LP *Standing Ovation* reaches US #60.

Apr *Help Me Make It Through The Night*, the group's revival of Kris Kristofferson's° ballad (a million-seller for Sammi Smith in 1971), reaches US #33.

July First Motown single *Just Walk In My Shoes* is reissued in UK, and reaches #35 – the group's first UK chart entry in 4½ years.

Dec *Help Me Make It Through The Night* hits UK #11 (their biggest UK hit to date).

1973 Jan Having nursed a growing feeling that they have not been getting the support and career-development from Motown which has been accorded to its other leading acts, despite a string of hits, they decide to leave when their contract expires. They are quickly signed by Buddah Records, based in New York.

Mar A 1968 LP track, Bacharach/David ballad *The Look Of Love*, is picked by UK Motown as follow-up to *Help Me Make It Through The Night*, and reaches UK #21.

Apr A number by Mississippi songwriter Jim Weatherly, *Neither One Of Us (Wants To Be The First To Say Goodbye)*, produced by Joe Porter, is released as the group leaves Motown. It is their second-biggest success on the label, and third million-seller, hitting US #2 (behind Vicki Lawrence's *The Night The Lights Went Out In Georgia*).

May LP *Neither One Of Us* is the group's first top 10 LP, hitting US #9.

June From the LP, *Daddy Could Swear, I Declare*, co-written by Gladys and Bubba Knight with producer Bristol, reaches US #19, while *Neither One Of Us (Wants To Be The First To Say Goodbye)* makes UK #31.

July Buddah label debut is Weatherly's *Where Peaceful Waters Flow*, which reaches US #28.

Sept Another LP on Soul, *All I Need Is Time*, featuring tracks cut shortly before the group's Motown exit, reaches US #70. The title track, produced by Porter, reaches US #61.

Oct *Midnight Train To Georgia*, another Weatherly-written song (originally as *Midnight Plane To Houston*, in which form he has cut it himself), tops the US chart for 2 weeks, and spends 4 weeks at R&B #1. It is another million-seller, and the first of four consecutive gold singles on Buddah.

1974 Jan *I've Got To Use My Imagination*, a million-seller, hits US #4. It is taken from the group's debut Buddah LP *Imagination*, which hits US #9, and also includes *Midnight Train To Georgia*. The LP earns a gold disk for a half million sales, and is the first to feature the group as co-producers (with Tony Camillo, Kenny Kerner and Richie Wise).

Mar [2] The group receives two Grammy awards, for its two most successful singles of the previous year: *Neither One Of Us (Wants To Be The First To Say Goodbye)* is named Best Pop Vocal Performance by a Group, and *Midnight Train To Georgia* is Best R&B Vocal Performance by a Group.

Apr *Best Thing That Ever Happened To Me*, another Weatherly song from *Imagination*, hits US #3 and is a further million-seller. Double compilation LP *Anthology*, on Motown, reaches US #77, while Soul issues LP *Knight Time*, containing unissued material by the group. It makes US #139.

May The group's soundtrack LP from film *Claudine*, featuring songs written and produced by Curtis Mayfield°, reaches US #35 and earns another gold disk.

July *On And On* is taken from *Claudine* soundtrack, and hits US #5 to become the group's fourth consecutive gold single.

Aug *Between Her Goodbye And My Hello* is a final single on Soul, and climbs to US #57.

Dec *I Feel A Song (In My Heart)* reaches US #21, and is taken from LP *I Feel A Song*, which peaks at US #17 and earns a gold disk.

1975 Apr *Love Finds Its Own Way* makes US #47. Knight gets married, for the second time, to ex-social worker Barry Hankerson, and moves her family home to Detroit.

May Final Soul LP, *A Little Knight Music*, makes only US #164.

June A medley of *The Way We Were/Try To Remember*, from the long-running off-Broadway musical *The Fantasticks!*, recorded live at a club in Detroit, and prefaced by a spoken passage from Knight, hits UK #4 and reaches US #11. LP *I Feel A Song* becomes the group's first UK chart LP, reaching UK #20.

July [10] The group begins a 4-week run of "The Gladys Knight and The Pips Show" on US NBC TV in a summer replacement slot. The 1-hour shows mix music with comedy and guest stars.

Aug After UK top 10 hit medley *The Way We Were* (which sets the standard of sophisticated supper club soul on which the group will concentrate for the rest of its Buddah career), the label's UK licensee tries the UK market with earlier US Buddah hits which originally failed in UK. First of these is *Best Thing That Ever Happened To Me*, which now hits UK #7.

Oct *Money* makes US #50.

Dec David Gates-penned *Part Time Love* reaches US #22 and UK #30, while LP *2nd Anniversary* (a reference to completing 2 successful years with Buddah) reaches US #24.

1976 Mar LP *The Best Of Gladys Knight And The Pips*, a compilation of Buddah singles, hits UK #6 and reaches US #36.

June *Midnight Train To Georgia* belatedly hits UK #10 after being extracted from the compilation LP – the second Buddah single UK

GLADYS KNIGHT & THE PIPS *cont.*

hit long after its original US success.

Aug *Make Yours A Happy Home* reaches UK #35.

Oct Knight makes her movie acting debut in *Pipe Dreams*, a film produced by and co-starring husband Hankerson. A romantic drama set in the Alaskan oilfields, The Pips do not feature in acting roles, but join her in singing eight songs on the soundtrack.

Nov *So Sad The Song*, taken from *Pipe Dreams*, reaches US #47 and UK #20.

Dec Soundtrack LP *Pipe Dreams* peaks at US #94.

1977 Jan *Nobody But You*, another song from *Pipe Dreams*, reaches UK #34.

June [10-11] The group plays the 3rd Kool Jazz Festival in San Diego, Cal.

July LP *Still Together* reaches US #51 and UK #42. The title is ironic since throughout 1977-79 Gladys Knight & The Pips will be unable to record together, even though they continue to perform live as a team. The forced separation on disk is due to complex legal problems involving several record labels (the group is trying to move to CBS, and still has a suit hanging over it from the end of the Motown days, as well as a dispute over royalties with Motown). Previously recorded material is released and the untypical and uptempo *Baby Don't Change Your Mind* (the group's last US hit single on Buddah), a blend of traditional Motown with a hint of the new disco style, reaches US #52 and hits UK #4, their biggest UK hit.

Oct *Home Is Where The Heart Is* reaches UK #35.

Nov TV-advertised double compilation LP *30 Greatest*, on K-Tel, hits UK #3.

1978 Apr *The One And Only*, theme song from the Henry Winkler film of the same title, reaches UK #32.

July *Come Back And Finish What You Started*, in the uptempo mode of *Baby Don't Change Your Mind*, reaches UK #15.

Sept LP *The One And Only* peaks at US #145.

Oct *It's A Better Than Good Time* reaches UK #59.

1979 Knight records an enforced solo LP, *Miss Gladys Knight* for Buddah, while The Pips find a deal with Casablanca Records and release two LPs, *At Last . . . The Pips* and *Callin'*, without her. All fail to chart.

1980 July Complex legalities finally solved, Gladys Knight & The Pips reunite for recording and sign a new deal with CBS/Columbia. (Much of their earlier stature on disk has been eroded by 3 years' absence, and success on the new label will prove sparse by comparison with Buddah years.) *Landlord*, one of only two Columbia US singles successes, peaks at US #46 and hits R&B #3. Ashford and Simpson°-produced Columbia LP *About Love* reaches US #48.

Sept *Taste Of Bitter Love* makes UK #35.

Oct LP *A Touch Of Love*, another UK TV-advertised compilation on K-Tel, this time of the group's ballads, reaches UK #16.

Dec Dance-oriented track *Bourgie Bourgie* reaches UK #32, after finding major success in UK discos, but fails in US.

1981 Oct LP *Touch* reaches US #109.

1982 Nov [25] Knight appears at the World Music Festival in Jamaica at the Bob Marley Performing Center near Montego Bay. Also on the bill are Aretha Franklin°, The Clash°, Squeeze°, The Grateful Dead° and many others.

1983 May *Save The Overtime (For Me)* hits US R&B #1 for a week (the group's first R&B #1 in over 8 years). It makes US #66 but fails in UK.

July LP *Visions* is the group's biggest-selling album in US for 8 years, reaching US #34 and earning a gold disk.

1984 Feb A third UK TV-advertised compilation LP, *The Collection – 20 Greatest Hits*, on Starblend Records, reaches UK #43.

1985 Apr LP *Life* reaches US #126. Knight stars with Flip Wilson in US TV sitcom "Charlie and Company". The group leaves CBS and signs to MCA Records.

1986 Jan Knight, along with Stevie Wonder° and Elton John°, is one of the "friends" to contribute a short duet to Dionne Warwick's° *That's What Friends Are For*, which tops the US chart for 4 weeks, selling over a million, and reaches UK #16.

1987 Sept [28] Knight joins Smokey Robinson° to guest for a week on US TV show "$10,000 Pyramid" (known in UK as "The Pyramid Game").

1988 Mar With *Love Overboard* reaching US #13, having topped the R&B chart, Gladys Knight & The Pips celebrate 30 years of recording.

BUDDY KNOX

1955 Knox, (b. Wayne Knox, Apr.14, 1933, Happy, Tex., US), Jimmy Bowen (b. Nov.30, 1937, Santa Rita, N.M., US) and Don Lanier, all students on athletics scholarships at West Texas University, form The Rhythm Orchids to play college dances and parties, with Knox and Lanier on guitars and Bowen stand-up bass.

1956 In a 3-day session at Norman Petty's recording studio in Clovis, N.M., where they meet and recruit drummer Dave Alldred, the trio records three of its own songs. Local Dumas, Tex., businessman Chester Oliver presses 1500 copies of a single, coupling *Party Doll*, sung by Knox (and written by him at age 15) and *I'm Sticking With You*, sung by Bowen. The record sells out around Dumas and Amarillo, helped by Amarillo DJ Dean Kelly playing *Party Doll*, and the trio decides to form its own label, Triple-D after KDDD in Dumas where Bowen has been a DJ, to fill continuing local demand for it.

1957 Jan Lanier's sister in New York sends a copy of the single to Phil Kahl at Roulette Records, which signs the group and flies it to New York to record additional tracks. Roulette markets both sides of the original separately with new B-sides, so *Party Doll* is released, credited to Buddy Knox & The Rhythm Orchids, while *I'm Sticking With You* credits Jimmy Bowen & The Rhythm Orchids.

Mar *Party Doll* hits US #1, selling over a million. It is joined on the US chart by three hasty cover versions by Steve Lawrence (#10), Wingy Manone (#56), and Roy Brown (#89). *I'm Sticking With You* reaches US #14.

Apr [12] The group stars in Alan Freed's Rock'n'Roll Easter Jubilee show at New York's Brooklyn Paramount.

Apr [18] Knox joins the Tank Corps for 6 months' active duty as a US Army reserve lieutenant. (Roulette organized a 20-song session in New York with him and the group, to avoid a future shortage of tracks.)

May *Party Doll* peaks at UK #29.

June With Knox in the Army, the follow-up is credited to "Lieutenant Buddy Knox". Another group original, *Rock Your Little Baby To Sleep*, reaches US #23.

Oct The Hawaiian-flavored *Hula Love*, written by Knox as a teenager and closely based on the 1911 song *My Hula, Hula Love*, makes US #12.

Nov Knox and The Rhythm Orchids perform *Hula Love* in rock movie *Jamboree*.

Dec Alldred leaves the group to become "Dicky Doo" in Dicky Doo & The Don'ts and is replaced by Chico Hayak.

1958 Mar *Swingin' Daddy* reaches only US #80.

Aug *Somebody Touched Me*, a revival of 1954 Ruth Brown R&B hit, reaches US #22. It is the last single to credit The Rhythm Orchids. (Bowen will move to record production, initially with Chancellor. In the mid-1960s, he will become an MOR producer working with Bing Crosby, Frank Sinatra, Dean Martin, Kenny Rogers° and others, later running his own Amos label and by the 1980s becoming Nashville president of MCA Records.)

1959 Jan Double-sided *That's Why I Cry/Teasable Pleasable You*, with Bobby Darin° guesting on piano, peaks at US #88 and #85 respectively.

May *I Think I'm Gonna Kill Myself* reaches US #55, his last hit for Roulette. A Knox original, it will be covered by Waylon Jennings.

1961 Jan After two flops, Knox moves to Liberty, where Snuff Garrett produces a remake of the 6-year old Clovers R&B hit *Lovey Dovey*, which makes US #25.

Mar Knox unearths *Ling Ting Tong*, a 1955 Charms/Five Keys R&B novelty, which peaks at US #65 and is his last US chart appearance.

1962 Aug Knox makes a surprise return to the UK chart, reaching #45 with *She's Gone*.

1968 May After unsuccessful recording on Ruff and Reprise labels, Knox signs to United Artists with his style more firmly aimed at the C&W market. *Gypsy Man* is a US country hit, without crossing to the pop chart, and a fair-selling LP of the same title follows.

1972 He appears in country music movie *Travelling Light*, with Waylon Jennings, Bobby Bare, and Jerry Allison of The Crickets, with whom he co-writes the soundtrack.

1974 Knox becomes a Canadian citizen and settles on a farm near Winnipeg, Manitoba, with his family, but spends much of the year touring the country and rock'n'roll nostalgia circuits. He becomes an active businessman, co-owning a club in Vancouver, British Columbia and having real estate in Seattle, Wash.

1977 Apr He tours UK with contemporaries Jack Scott, Warren Smith and Charlie Feathers and is recorded live with them at London's Rainbow Theatre by EMI, for LP *Four Rock'n'Roll Legends*. (He will later record for Redwood Records and his own Sunnyhill label but releases will be sporadic. In the 1980s he will work regularly and successfully as a live act in Canada, Europe and the US.)

KOOL & THE GANG

James "J.T." Taylor (lead vocals)
Robert "Kool" Bell (bass)
Ronald Bell (saxophones)
Claydes Smith (guitar)
George Brown (drums)
Dennis "Dee Tee" Thomas (sax)
Robert "Spike" Mickens (trumpet)

1964 The group is formed by Bell (b. Oct.8, 1950, Youngstown, Oh., US), whose father has played with jazz pianist Thelonious Monk, with fellow students at Lincoln High School, Jersey City, N.J., as jazz combo The Jazziacs. The original line-up features Bell, his brother Ronald (b. Nov.1, 1951, Youngstown), Brown (b. Jan.5, 1949, Jersey City), Mickens (b. Jersey City), Thomas (b. Feb.9, 1951, Jersey City), with Woody Sparrow (guitar) and Rick Westfield (keyboards).

1967 Sparrow leaves, and is replaced on guitar by Smith (b. Sept.6, 1948, Jersey City). Finding little earning power in jazz, the band moves toward R&B, and a local Jersey City promoter finds it regular gigs backing soul acts, under the name The Soul Music Review. The band still plays jazz in its spare time in churches and coffee bars, frequently jamming with jazzmen Leon Thomas and Pharoah Saunders.

1968 The group becomes an R&B attraction first as The New Dimensions, then The New Flames, known colloquially on the local scene as Kool & The Flames. To avoid confusion with James Brown's° Famous Flames, a switch is made to Kool & The Gang.

1969 While playing New York club dates, the band meets writer/producer Gene Redd, who is setting up his own label, De-Lite Records. Impressed with the group's tightness as a live unit, and its original material, Redd offers a recording deal.

Oct With the youngest members just graduated from high school, the band debuts for De-Lite with self-penned funk instrumental *Kool And The Gang*, which makes US #59 (and R&B #19).

1970 Jan Another instrumental, *The Gang's Back Again*, peaks at US #85. Debut LP *Kool And The Gang* is released.

July *Let The Music Take Your Mind* reaches US #78.

Oct *Funky Man* makes US #87 (and R&B #16).

1971 Apr Live LP *Live At The Sex Machine* is the band's first charted LP, at US #122. It includes group compositions and versions of Dionne Warwick's° *Walk On By* and Jim Webb song *Wichita Lineman*.

Oct LP *The Best Of Kool And The Gang*, a compilation of singles to date, peaks at US #157.

1972 Jan Another live LP, wholly instrumental *Live At P.J.'s*, reaches US #171.

1973 Apr LP *Good Times* makes US #142.

Oct *Funky Stuff*, the band's first major commercial breakthrough, makes US #29 (and R&B #5).

Dec LP *Wild And Peaceful*, including *Funky Stuff*, is entirely written, produced and arranged by the band, and reaches US #33, earning a gold disk for a half million sales. (It will also spin off the band's two biggest-selling singles of the 70s and remain on chart for 60 weeks.)

1974 Jan Instrumental LP *Kool Jazz*, gathering up the most jazz-oriented tracks from three previous LPs, reaches US #187.

Mar From LP *Wild And Peaceful*, the band's first million-selling single is *Jungle Boogie*, which hits US #4.

June *Hollywood Swinging* hits US #6, and is a second million-seller.

Oct *Higher Plane*, from the band's next LP, peaks at US #37.

Dec LP *Light Of Worlds* reaches US #63, earning the band's second gold LP in a 34-week chart run.

1975 Jan The band visits Europe for the first time, playing at the MIDEM music industry festival in Cannes, France, following with a UK tour. Tracks from their gig at London's Rainbow Theatre are recorded for LP release.

Feb *Rhyme Time People*, co-written by the band with their early live collaborators Thomas and Saunders, and taken from LP *Light Of Worlds*, peaks at US #63.

May Compilation LP *Kool And The Gang Greatest Hits!* reaches US #81.

July *Spirit Of The Boogie*, the title track from forthcoming LP, reaches US #35. B-side *Summer Madness*, also from LP *Light Of Worlds*, collects airplay in its own right, and is later chart-listed as a dual A-side.

Oct LP *Spirit Of The Boogie*, again written and produced by the band, reaches US #48.

Dec *Caribbean Festival*, another extract from the LP, makes US #55.

1976 May LP *Love And Understanding*, which couples five new tracks with live versions of *Hollywood Swinging*, *Summer Madness* and *Universal Sound* from the early 1975 London Rainbow concert, reaches US #68. Taken from it, the title track makes US #77. Otha Nash and Larry Gittens join the band for a while, on trombone and trumpet respectively.

1977 Jan LP *Open Sesame* peaks at US #110, while the title track makes #55. (It is the group's last US hit single for 3 years – a symptom of the early hit sound being eclipsed by the exploding disco genre, with which Kool & The Gang's jazz-rooted tightness proves out of sympathy as hustling rhythm takes over from funk. Rather than veering in a disco direction, the band determines to ride out the craze.)

July [2-4] The group plays the Brute Music Festival, Callaway, Md., in front of 100,000 fans.

1978 Jan The band's *Open Sesame* is included on the soundtrack LP of movie *Saturday Night Fever*, which hits US #1 for 25 weeks and UK #1 for 18 (eventually selling over 25 million copies).

Feb LP *The Force* reaches US #142, the band's lowest chart ebb. Westfield leaves. The looked-for new musical direction begins to take form as Bell meets soul vocalist James Taylor (b. Aug.16, 1953, S.C.), and invites him to join the line-up. The band has never featured a recognized solo voice, and with Taylor the incorporation of ballads into the repertoire becomes a more realistic proposition. An accidental meeting in the studio with jazz-funk keyboardist and producer Eumir Deodato (1973 hitmaker with *Also Sprach Zarathustra*), provides the other key: the band and Deodato share similar backgrounds and ideas, and a desire to experiment with a simpler, more laid-back approach. Deodato becomes the group's producer (a role he will hold through 1982). Earl Toon, Jr. also joins the band on keyboards in Westfield's place (but will not remain a permanent member).

1979 Dec The first Deodato-produced, Taylor-fronted Kool & The Gang LP, *Ladies Night*, reaches US #13 and is the group's first million-selling platinum LP. The title track hits US #8, selling over a million to earn a gold disk, and hits UK #9.

1980 Mar *Too Hot*, also from the LP, hits US #5 and reaches UK #23.

July A third single from LP *Ladies Night*, *Hangin' Out* makes UK #52.

Dec *Celebration* hits UK #7.

1981 Feb *Celebration* hits US #1 for 2 weeks and is the band's biggest-selling single, earning a platinum disk for over 2 million US sales. (The song has been used as the welcoming-home anthem for the American hostages returned from captivity in Iran on Jan.26, and the theme song of the 1981 US Superbowl.) LP *Celebrate*, from which it is taken, hits US #10 and is also a platinum-seller.

Mar *Jones Vs. Jones*, also from LP *Celebrate*, reaches UK #17.

June *Take It To The Top*, a third single from from the million-selling LP, reaches UK #15, while *Jones Vs. Jones* makes US #39.

Dec *Steppin' Out* reaches UK #12, while *Take My Heart (You Can Have It If You Want It)* climbs to US #17.

1982 Jan *Get Down On It* hits UK #3, their first UK top 5 success. LP *Something Special*, which includes both this and the two Dec. US/UK hit singles, reaches US #12 (the band's third consecutive platinum LP), and hits UK #10 – their first UK chart LP.

Feb *Steppin' Out* peaks at US #89.

Mar *Take My Heart (You Can Have It If You Want It)* reaches UK #29.

May *Get Down On It* hits US #10.

Aug *Big Fun* reaches UK #14.

Oct *Big Fun* makes US #21.

Oct [15-18] The band plays four nights at London's Apollo Victoria theater, followed by live UK dates in Manchester and Birmingham.

Nov LP *As One*, the band's last produced by Deodato, reaches US #29 (a gold LP) and UK #49, while *Ooh La La La (Let's Go Dancin')* hits UK #6.

1983 Jan *Hi De Hi, Hi De Ho* reaches UK #29, as *Ooh La La La (Let's Go Dancin')* makes US #30.

KOOL & THE GANG *cont.*

June UK-only compilation LP *Twice As Kool*, of the group's hit singles to date, hits UK #4.

1984 Jan *Straight Ahead* reaches UK #15, and is taken from LP *In The Heart*, produced by the group itself, which makes US #29 (another gold disk) and UK #18.

Feb *Joanna*, a Taylor/Smith ballad from LP *In The Heart*, hits US #2 (behind Culture Club's° *Karma Chameleon*) and is a million-seller, becoming the band's biggest US singles success after *Celebration*.

Mar *Joanna/Tonight* is released as a UK double A-side from the LP, and hits #2, the group's highest-placed UK single.

May *Tonight*, released independently of *Joanna* in US, climbs to #13, while the LP's title song *(When You Say You Love Somebody) From The Heart* hits UK #7.

Nov While the band is on tour in UK, Bell and Taylor take part in the recording of Band Aid's° *Do They Know It's Christmas?*, in aid of African famine relief. (This will top the UK chart over Christmas and become the biggest-selling single of all time in UK – over 3½ million copies.)

Dec *Fresh* reaches UK #11.

1985 Jan LP *Emergency* reaches US #28 and UK #47.

Mar *Misled* hits US #10 and reaches UK #28.

June *Fresh*, belatedly issued as a US single, hits #4.

Sept Bell/Taylor ballad *Cherish* hits US #2 for 3 weeks, behind Dire Straits'° *Money For Nothing*. It is another million-seller and hits UK #4.

Nov Extracted title track from LP *Emergency* reaches US #18 and UK #50.

Dec The band tours UK, with major dates at Brighton Centre, Birmingham's National Exhibition Centre and London's Wembley Arena.

1987 Jan *Victory* hits US #10 and reaches UK #30. It is taken from LP *Forever*, which reaches US #25. Both are produced by Khalis Bayyan (who is actually Ronald Bell, having adopted a Moslem name in accordance with his faith). Curtis "Fitz" Williams is now on keyboards, with Clifford Adams and Michael Ray as trombonist and second trumpeter respectively. The LP sleeve also notes the death of ex-member Rick Westfield.

Feb The group begins a US tour.

Mar *Stone Love* reaches UK #45.

1988 Feb Taylor leaves the band to pursue a solo career. He is replaced by a trio of new lead singers – Gary Brown, Skip Martin (ex-Dazz Band) and Dean Mays.

Aug Compilation LP *Greatest Hits* is released, including three new tracks, one of which is the band's new single *Rags To Riches*.

Nov UK-only LP *The Singles Collection* is released.

KRAFTWERK

Ralf Hutter (keyboards, drums, vocals, woodwind and strings)
Florian Schneider (keyboards, drums, vocals, woodwind and strings)
Wolfgang Flur (electronic drums)
Klaus Roeder (violin and guitar)

1970 Hutter and Schneider, having met while at Dusseldorf Conservatory, West Germany, join Organisation, influenced by the new wave of German keyboard groups. Their debut LP *Tone Float*, produced by Conny Plank and recorded at a studio set in a Dusseldorf oil refinery, is released through RCA. It fails and Hutter and Schneider leave to form their own band, Kraftwerk (German for "Powerplant").

1971 Kraftwerk's debut LP *Highrail*, released by German Philips label, attracts attention, but few sales.

1972 LP *Var* is again released in Germany. UK Vertigo releases LP *Kraftwerk*, a compilation of material from the group's first two LPs.

1973 Nov LP *Ralf And Florian* is released. Self-produced, it contains a mix of experimental synthesizer music with traditional string and woodwind parts.

1974 Hutter and Schneider add Flur and Roeder to create a 4-piece.

Nov LP *Autobahn* is released. Its centerpiece is the 22-minute title track about a journey on the German highway system.

1975 May Receiving unexpected airplay in both UK and US, an edited version of *Autobahn* reaches UK #11 and US #25. The LP hits UK #4 and US #5. (Its rhythmic synthesized style will open the door for many futurist and Eurodisco acts in the next 10 years.)

Oct Reissued LP *Ralf And Florian* makes US #160. Roeder is replaced by Karl Bartos. The group leaves Philips/Vertigo to form its own Dusseldorf-based Kling Klang label licensed through EMI.

Nov LP *Radio Aktivitaet* is released in Germany.

1976 Jan Its English language equivalent LP *Radio-Activity*, released by Capitol, reaches US #140. Vertigo issues compilation LP *Exceller 8*.

1977 May LP *Trans-Europe Express* peaks at US #119. The group tours UK, appearing on stage in robotic style, wearing mannequin outfits.

1978 May LP *The Man-Machine* (German title: *Mensch Maschine*) hits UK #9, but makes only US #130.

June *Trans Europe Express* makes a belated US #67.

Nov *Neon Lights* climbs to UK #53.

1981 May After a 2½-year UK chart absence, *Pocket Calculator* reaches UK #39. LP *Computer World* makes UK #15 and US #72. (It will later influence Neil Young's° LP *Trans*.)

July Double A-side *Computer Love/The Model* reaches UK #36.

1982 Jan Re-issued, and by now both a dancefloor and airplay favorite, *Computer Love/The Model* tops the UK chart.

Feb LP *Trans-Europe Express* climbs to UK #49.

Mar *Showroom Dummies* makes UK #25 as the group begins a UK tour.

1983 With the boom in rhythm boxes and portable tape machines, many electro pop bands emulate Kraftwerk's rhythm patterns. (One of the more successful is Afrika Bambaataa's° *Planet Rock*, which borrows the *Trans Europe Express* riff.)

Apr LP *Techno Pop* is scheduled for release, but cancelled without official reason. The group also cancels a UK tour in its traditional anonymous style.

Aug *Tour De France*, commissioned by the organizers of the European bicycle race as the official theme, is released from four-song LP *Set* and reaches UK #22.

1984 Sept Following its exposure in movie *Breakdance*, *Tour De France* is remixed and makes UK #24.

1985 June LP *Autobahn*, reissued by Parlophone, reaches UK #61.

1986 Nov First EMI LP *Electric Café* climbs to UK #58. Released in US through Warner Bros., it falters at #156. Its sleeve features computer graphics from the New York Institute who subsequently produce an entirely computer-generated video for the title cut.

1987 Jan Kraftwerk performs well-received UK live dates as second single *Telephone Call* joins unsuccessful *Musique Non-Stop*.

BILLY J. KRAMER AND THE DAKOTAS

Billy J. Kramer (vocals)
Mike Maxfield (lead guitar)
Robin MacDonald (rhythm guitar)
Ray Jones (bass)
Tony Mansfield (drums)

1962 Dec Kramer (b. William Ashton, Aug.19, 1943, Bootle, Lancs., UK), a British Railways apprentice fitter during the day, is spotted singing at Liverpool's Cavern club with The Coasters°, which has just been voted #3 favorite group in local *Mersey Beat* magazine poll, by Brian Epstein, who buys Kramer's contract from his manager, promoter Ted Knibbs, for £50.

1963 Jan [6] Kramer signs to a 6-year management deal with Epstein's NEMS company. The Coasters°, who want to keep their day jobs, leave to team up with local singer Chick Graham. Failing to obtain the services of Liverpool's Remo 4 as a backing group, Epstein teams Kramer with Manchester group The Dakotas. Maxfield (b. Feb.23, 1944, Manchester), MacDonald (b. July 18, 1943, Nairn, Scotland), Jones (b. Oct.22, 1939, Oldham, Lancs.) and Mansfield (b. Anthony Bookbinder, May 28, 1943, Salford, Lancs.) have been playing professionally since Feb. 1962.

Feb After rapid rehearsals and one show at the Cavern, Kramer and The Dakotas leave for a 3-week season at the Star Club in Hamburg, West Germany. They hone their stage act before returning to UK.

Mar The group is signed to Parlophone by EMI's George Martin. Liverpool songwriter Ralph Bowdler gives it *She's My Girl* to record, but because of the Epstein connection, the group has access to John Lennon° and Paul McCartney's° songs and chooses *I'll Be On My Way*, on which The Beatles° have passed, and *Do You Want To Know A Secret*, just recorded by The Beatles for their first LP.

June Debut single *Do You Want To Know A Secret?* hits UK #2 behind The Beatles'° own *From Me To You*. On the single, the "J." is inserted into Kramer's name for the first time to distinguish him from other singers named Billy. (This idea is credited to John Lennon°.) The group tours UK as support to The Beatles°.

Aug *Bad To Me*, written by Lennon° specifically for Kramer, tops the UK chart for 2 weeks but is dethroned by The Beatles'° *She Loves You*. The Dakotas hits UK #18 with its instrumental *The Cruel Sea*, written 18 months earlier by Maxfield who chose the title at random when he spotted Nicholas Monserrat's novel on a bookshelf.

Sept Kramer wins *Melody Maker* poll award as UK's Best Newcomer of the Year.

Oct [27] The group appears on UK TV's variety show, "Sunday Night at the London Palladium", 2 weeks after The Beatles° have made their debut.

Nov *I'll Keep You Satisfied*, its third Lennon°/McCartney°-penned single, hits UK #4, promoted by a 20-date UK tour titled "The Billy J. Kramer Pop Parade".

Dec LP *Listen . . .* reaches UK #11. The group joins The Beatles'° Christmas stage show at Finsbury Park Astoria, London.

1964 Mar Released on single against Epstein's advice but at Kramer's insistence, US song by Mort Shuman and John McFarland, *Little Children*, gives the group its biggest UK seller so far, topping the UK chart after selling 78,000 copies in 1 day. It dethrones another of Epstein's acts, Cilla Black°, but is displaced by The Beatles'° *Can't Buy Me Love*.

Apr [26] The group plays the New Musical Express Poll Winners Concert at Wembley, UK, with The Beatles°, Cliff Richard° and The Shadows°, The Rolling Stones°, and other major UK names.

June *Little Children* hits US #7 and is a worldwide million-seller.

July *Bad To Me*, having originally flopped in US, is reissued as B-side to *Little Children*. It picks up airplay in its own right and replaces its A-side in the US top 10, at #9. Jones leaves The Dakotas, MacDonald switches to bass and Mick Green, ex-Johnny Kidd and The Pirates°, joins on rhythm guitar.

Aug *From A Window*, a new Lennon°/McCartney° song, hits UK #10. *I'll Keep You Satisfied* reaches US #30 and LP *Little Children* makes US #48.

Oct *From A Window* makes US #23.

1965 Jan *It's Gotta Last Forever* proves an ironic title when it is unexpectedly a UK chart failure.

Feb *Billy J. Plays The States*, a 4-track live EP recorded on stage at Long Beach, Cal. is released in UK, to moderate sales. *It's Gotta Last Forever* reaches US #67.

June The group's last hit is Burt Bacharach's *Trains And Boats And Planes* which reaches UK #12 in a losing battle with Bacharach's own version, which hits UK #4 but is not released as a single in US, where Kramer's reaches US #47.

Nov *Neon City* fails to chart. Relying on outside songwriters for its material and closely associated with the now-lapsed Mersey boom, the group is failing to develop with the rapid changes on the pop scene and among its audience.

1966 Aug The group finds more of its live work on northern UK club and cabaret circuit where recent nostalgia proves a strong popularity factor. Mansfield leaves and Frank Farley (ex-Johnny Kidd° sideman) joins. *You Make Me Feel Like Someone* is the last release credited to the group.

1967 Jan *Sorry*, a solo by Kramer although he still plays live with The Dakotas, fails and his contract is not renewed by EMI.

Apr Kramer covers The Bee Gees° *The Town Of Tuxley Toy Maker* on a one-off release for Reaction Records.

1968 Mar The Dakotas split and Kramer continues his cabaret career as a soloist. He marries shortly afterwards and releases a cover of Nilsson's° *1941* on NEMS Records, which gains much UK airplay but no chart place. (He will also revive Lennon° and McCartney's° *A World Without Love* on NEMS later in the year, before moving to MGM Records for another unsuccessful one-off, *The Colour Of My Love*).

1971 June A cover of Neil Diamond's° *And The Grass Won't Pay No Mind*, is released on Polydor under Kramer's real name, William Howard Ashton.

1973 Kramer tours US with a new group of Dakotas as part of Richard Nader's "British Re-invasion Show".

1974/88 Maintaining his performing career in clubs in UK and Europe, and joining the occasional major nostalgia concert, Kramer remains an active performer. Despite lack of chart success, he continues to record: 11 singles appear on 7 different UK labels, including two in a brief return to EMI, between 1973 and 1983.

KRIS KRISTOFFERSON

1958 Kristofferson (b. June 22, 1936, Brownsville, Tex., US) leaves Pomona College in Texas with a Ph.D, to study in UK at Oxford University on a Rhodes Scholarship. He starts writing songs while in UK, and changes his name to Kris Carson, signing with Larry Parnes' stable of talent.

1960 On his return home, Kristofferson joins the US Army (where he will learn to fly and spend much time in West Germany as a helicopter pilot).

1963 In Germany, he begins songwriting again, and also performing, singing in clubs on US bases. Several new songs are sent back to US to publisher Marijon Wilkin in Nashville.

1965 He leaves the army with the rank of Captain, with an invitation to take up a teaching post at West Point military academy. By now writing songs regularly, Kristofferson is about to take up the academic post teaching literature when he meets Johnny Cash°, who encourages him to take his songwriting seriously. He moves to Nashville, living cheaply and employed as a cleaner at CBS Records studios while he tries to get his songs accepted by publishers and artists.

1969 Cash° gives Roger Miller° Kristofferson's *Me And Bobby McGee*, which becomes a country hit, and helps (along with Cash's unpaid PR work) to establish the writer's name.

1970 Kristofferson signs a recording deal with Nashville-based Monument Records.

June Debut LP *Kristofferson* is released, without charting.

July [26] He visits UK to play the Isle of Wight Festival, alongside acts like Joni Mitchell° and Jimi Hendrix°.

1971 Mar Sammi Smith hits US #8 with Kristofferson's song *Help Me Make It Through The Night*. It becomes his first million-selling composition, rapidly followed by Janis Joplin's° cover of his *Me And Bobby McGee*, which tops the US chart for 2 weeks, and is another million-seller.

July Kristofferson makes his US chart debut with LP *The Silver-Tongued Devil And I*, which peaks at #21 and is certified gold.

Oct *Loving Her Was Easier (Than Anything I'll Ever Do Again)* makes US #26.

Nov LP *Me And Bobby McGee* reaches US #43. Kristofferson makes his movie acting debut (also singing four songs) in *Cisco Pike*, co-starring Gene Hackman. (By the early 1980s, he will be better-known for his film acting than for his music.)

1972 Apr *Josie* climbs to US #63, while Gladys Knight & The Pips'° version of *Help Me Make It Through The Night* makes US #33 (and will reach UK #11 in Nov.).

May LP *Border Lord* makes US #41.

1973 Jan LP *Jesus Was A Capricorn* reaches US #31, earning another gold disk, while its title track makes US #91.

July Kristofferson co-stars with Bob Dylan° in Sam Peckinpah's movie *Pat Garrett and Billy The Kid*.

Aug [19] Kristofferson marries singer Rita Coolidge, in Malibu. His father, a minister, presides over the ceremony.

Oct Another extract from *Jesus Was A Capricorn*, ballad *Why Me* (later often revived by Elvis Presley° in concert), makes US #16 and is Kristofferson's only million-selling single, during a 38-week chart run (only a week shy of Johnny Mathis' *Wonderful, Wonderful* 39-week record).

Nov Kristofferson teams with his wife for LP *Full Moon*, (on Coolidge's label, A&M) which reaches US #26 and earns another gold disk.

Dec From the LP, duet *A Song I'd Like To Sing* makes US #49.

1974 Apr Duet *Loving Arms* peaks at US #86.

July Solo LP *Spooky Lady's Sideshow* reaches US #78.

Dec [18] 1971 LP *Me And Bobby McGee* passes a half million US sales and Kristofferson is awarded a gold disk.

1975 Jan LP *Breakaway*, with Coolidge, makes US #103.

1976 Jan LP *Who's To Bless . . . And Who's To Blame* peaks at US #105. Kristofferson stars with Sarah Miles in film *The Sailor who Fell from Grace with the Sea*, made and set in UK. (Their explicit love scenes are rumored to cause trouble between him and Rita Coolidge.)

Aug LP *Surreal Thing* proves a poor seller, peaking at US #180.

Dec Kristofferson co-stars with Barbra Streisand° in a remake of *A Star is Born*. (His performance will win him a Golden Globe award as Best Actor in a Motion Picture Comedy or Musical.)

1977 Feb Soundtrack LP from *A Star is Born*, on which Kristofferson sings five tracks, tops the US chart for 6 weeks.

June *Watch Closely Now*, from the movie soundtrack, makes US #52 –

KRIS KRISTOFFERSON *cont.*

his last US single chart entry.

July A compilation LP of early material, *Songs Of Kristofferson* reaches US #45, while soundtrack LP *A Star Is Born* tops the UK chart for 2 weeks.

Sept Kristofferson participates in the New York Pop Arts Festival at Radio City Music Hall.

Nov He co-stars with Burt Reynolds in film *Semi-Tough*.

1978 May LP *Easter Island* reaches US #86.

June Kristofferson stars as Rubber Duck in movie *Convoy*, based on C.W. McCall's hit of the same name.

1979 Jan [9] He takes part with Coolidge in "A Gift of Song", the UNICEF benefit concert in aid of world hunger relief, at UN General Assembly in New York. Like other writer/performers on the bill (including Abba°, John Denver° and The Bee Gees°), he will pledge all future royalties from a new composition to UNICEF.

Mar LP *Natural Act*, with Coolidge, reaches US #106. He finally kicks a 20-year heavy-drinking habit, but at the same time separates from Coolidge.

May LP *Natural Act* makes UK #35 (his only UK chart LP).

Dec Kristofferson and Rita Coolidge's 6-year marriage ends in divorce.

1980 Nov Kristofferson stars in Michael Cimino's epic movie *Heaven's Gate*.

1981 Dec He co-stars with Jane Fonda in *Rollover*.

1983 Jan LP *The Winning Hand* features duets with Brenda Lee°, Willie Nelson° and Dolly Parton.

1984 Aug He stars in film *Flashpoint* with Treat Williams.

Sept Kristofferson is reunited with *A Star is Born* co-star Barbra Streisand on film, when he appears as a bartender in her video *Left In The Dark*.

Nov He teams with Willie Nelson° on LP *Music From Songwriter* (from the film *Songwriter*, in which they co-star), which reaches US #152.

1985 Sept LP *Highwayman*, a collaboration with Johnny Cash°, Waylon Jennings and Willie Nelson°, tops the US C&W chart.

Dec Kristofferson stars in Alan Rudolph's film *Trouble in Mind*

1986 July [22] At a BMI lunch in Nashville, Tenn., it is announced that *Help Me Make It Through The Night* has now received its 3-millionth play.

1987 Jan [13-18] Kristofferson and Coolidge reunite, professionally, for a week at the Las Vegas Hilton.

July [4] Kristofferson participates in "Welcome Home" a benefit for Vietnam Veterans, with John Fogerty, Neil Diamond° and Stevie Wonder°.

July [6] He apologizes after a memorial plaque given to him by Veterans at the "Welcome Home" benefit is discovered in a trash can.

Sept [19] Kristofferson participates in the Farm Aid II charity benefit with Neil Young°, John Cougar Mellencamp°, Lou Reed° and others, at the University of Nebraska's Memorial Stadium.

PATTI LaBELLE

1961 LaBelle (b. Patricia Holt, May 24, 1944, Philadelphia, Pa., US), forms girl vocal group The Blue Belles in Philadelphia, with Nona Hendryx, Sarah Dash and Cindy Birdsong. (Holt and Birdsong have been members of The Ordettes in high school, and Dash and Hendryx of The Del Capris). Together, they perform at local gigs organized by promoter Bernard Montague, which leads to them meeting producer Bobby Martin and signing via him to new label Newtown Records.

1962 May *I Sold My Heart To The Junkman*, first recorded unsuccessfully by The Four Sportsmen for Newtown, whose vocal track Martin wipes from the original and adds new vocals by the girls, climbs to US #15.

1963 Nov Holt is on lead vocals so Martin boosts her billing in the group, and she becomes Patti LaBelle. After some unsuccessful singles, ballad *Down The Aisle (The Wedding Song)*, credited to Patti LaBelle & The Blue Belles, makes US #37.

1964 Feb Parkway Records, part of Cameo, Philadelphia's leading independent label, signs the group. Their version of standard ballad *You'll Never Walk Alone*, from musical *Carousel* (and a UK chart-topper by Gerry & The Pacemakers° only 3 months earlier), climbs to US #34.

Dec Another standard ballad, Irish *Danny Boy (Londonderry Air)*, makes US #76.

1965 Dec After a year of non-action, the group signs to Atlantic and records new material. *All Or Nothing* climbs to US #68.

1966 Dec *Take Me For A Little While* reaches US #89. (It will be covered by several UK groups, including The Koobas, who just miss the UK top 50 with it, and will also be revived by another Atlantic act, Vanilla Fudge°.)

1967 Dec Birdsong leaves the group to join The Supremes° in place of Florence Ballard. The Blue Belles continue as a trio, but leave Atlantic when no more hits are forthcoming.

1970 With the trio's career at a low ebb, Vicki Wickham, a UK ex-patriot who first met the girls as a UK TV "Ready Steady Go" executive when they guested on the show during a 1966 promotional visit, becomes their manager. She abbreviates the group name to LaBelle and updates its image and material.

1971 Oct In a new deal with Warner Bros., the trio cuts LP *LaBelle*, which gains good reviews but does not chart, despite a US tour supporting The Who°. More successful is the LP on which they sing back-ups to Laura Nyro on a collection of group oldies, *Gonna Take A Miracle*, which reaches US #46.

1972 On second Warner LP *Moonshadow*, six of the songs are written by Hendryx, and the group's sound has developed into a sleek rock/funk hybrid. It still fails to chart.

1973 The group unveils a new visual image while headlining at New York's Bottom Line club: tight, shiny lamé "space" suits, reminiscent of the glitter-pop costumes sported by many groups currently on UK chart.

1974 July They sign to Epic and record LP *Nightbirds* with producer Allen Toussaint in New Orleans, backed by The Meters.

Dec LP *Nightbirds* is released in US, with single *Lady Marmalade*, which becomes a big club and disco hit.

1975 Mar *Lady Marmalade*, with its distinctive French-language chorus line "voulez-vous coucher avec moi ce soir?" tops the US chart for a week and is a million-seller. It is written by Bob Crewe and Kenny Nolan, (who, almost uniquely, have also penned the song it has deposed at US #1, Frankie Valli's *My Eyes Adored You*). LP *Nightbirds* hits US #7 and earns the group a gold disk.

Apr *Lady Marmalade* is the group's only UK hit, peaking at #127.

June *What Can I Do For You?* reaches US #48.

Oct LP *Phoenix* peaks at US #44.

1976 Oct LP *Chameleon* makes US #94, after which the trio splits, with LaBelle and Hendryx following diametrically opposed musical directions. (All three will have subsequent solo careers; Dash finding least success.)

1977 Nov Remaining signed to Epic, LaBelle's solo LP *Patti LaBelle* reaches US #62.

1978 July LP *Tasty* peaks at US #129.

1979 May LP *It's Alright With Me* creeps to US #145.

1980 May Her last Epic LP, *Released*, makes US #114.

1981 Oct She signs to Gamble and Huff's Philadelphia International label, but despite hometown support (LaBelle still lives in Philadelphia with her husband and three children), LP *The Spirit's In It* only climbs to US #156.

1982 Sept [9] She opens on Broadway, co-starring with Al Green° in Vinnette Carroll's gospel musical *Your Arm's Too Short To Box With God*, at the Alvin Theater. (The scheduled limited engagement of 30 shows will be extended to 80 after rave reviews.)

1984 Mar After a long quiet period, but still signed to Philadelphia International, LaBelle's *If You Only Knew* reaches US #46. Its parent LP *I'm In Love Again* makes US #40, and in a 35-week chart stay sells over a half million copies in US, earning a gold disk.

Apr LaBelle guest duets with Bobby Womack° on *Love Has Finally Come At Last*, extracted from his LP *The Poet II* on Beverly Glen label. It reaches US #88.

Sept LaBelle plays Big Mary in film *A Soldier's Story*.

1985 May She signs to MCA Records, and records two tracks for the soundtrack of film *Beverly Hills Cop*, starring Eddie Murphy. From the soundtrack LP, *New Attitude* is released as a single, and reaches US #17.

July [13] She performs at the Live Aid spectacular in her hometown of Philadelphia.

Aug Her second *Beverly Hills Cop* track, *Stir It Up*, makes US #41.

1986 June *On My Own*, a Burt Bacharach/Carole Bayer Sager ballad duetted with Michael McDonald° (in separate studios on separate coasts – they do not meet until performing the song together on Johnny Carson's "Tonight Show" on US TV), tops the US chart for 3 weeks, and hits UK #2, behind Spitting Image's novelty *The Chicken Song*.

July LP *Winner In You*, her first LP for MCA, which includes the duet, also tops the US chart for a week, turning platinum, and reaches UK #30.
Aug *Oh, People*, with a video shot by Godley and Creme°, makes US #29 and UK #26.
Oct LaBelle stars in US NBC-TV movie *Unnatural Causes*.
Dec [1] LaBelle receives an Award of Merit from the Philadelphia Art Alliance.
Dec *On My Own* is named Top Black Single on *Billboard* magazine's year end survey.
1987 Feb *Something Special (Is Gonna Happen Tonight)*, from Bette Midler°/Shelley Long-starring film *Outrageous Fortune*, makes #50 on US Hot Black Singles chart.
Aug *Just The Facts*, written and produced by Jimmy Jam and Terry Lewis for Dan Aykroyd/Tom Hanks film *Dragnet*, is another US Hot Black Singles hit at #33.

CYNDI LAUPER

1958 Lauper (b. June 20, 1953, New York, N.Y., US) is relocated from Williamsburg suburb to Queens with her mother, brother and sister, after her parents divorce.
1970 She leaves education and home to hitch-hike through Canada with her dog Sparkle.
1971 She spends a year at Vermont College studying art.
1974 Back in New York, Lauper first joins Long Island band, Doc West, as lead singer, then covers band Flyer, with whom she will spend the next 3 years.
1977 Lauper loses her voice after intense vocal performing. Doctors say she will never sing again, but she regains her voice through vocal training with Katie Ayresta.
1978 She meets sax and keyboards player John Turi and together they form band Blue Angel.
1979 Blue Angel signs to Polydor.
1980 LP *Blue Angel* is released, but fails to chart. The band splits after management and label squabbles. Lauper finds work in clothes store, Screaming Mimi's.
1981 Lauper meets David Wolff, her future manager and lover, while working at Miho's bar in New York, singing current top 40 songs.
1982 She is declared bankrupt in a court case, relating to her Blue Angel days.
1983 Wolff secures Lauper a deal with CBS subsidiary, Portrait, and she begins work on her debut LP, with help from Philadelphia band The Hooters°.
Dec Debut LP *She's So Unusual* is released.
1984 Mar *Girls Just Want To Have Fun* hits US #2, held off #1 by Van Halen's° *Jump*, and UK #2, where it is beaten by Frankie Goes To Hollywood's° *Relax*.
Apr [5] Lauper's video *Girls Just Want To Have Fun* wins Best Female Video at the second annual American Video Awards.
June *Time After Time*, written by Lauper and The Hooters'° Rob Hyman, hits US #1 and UK #3, held off #1 by Frankie Goes To Hollywood's° *Two Tribes* and *Relax*. Its video features her mother Catrine, boyfriend Wolff and mentor, wrestling administrator, Lou Albano. (Her first two singles will both be used in UK TV commercials.) Parent LP *She's So Unusual* hits US #4 and UK #16 (and will sell over 4 million copies).
Sept *She Bop* hits US #3, but stalls at UK #46.
Dec A cover of Jules Shear's *All Through The Night* hits US #5, but peaks at UK #64. It is her fourth consecutive top 5 US hit in a year.
1985 Feb *Money Changes Everything* reaches US #27. Lauper wins Best New Artist award at the 27th annual Grammy ceremony.
Mar She contributes vocals to USA For Africa's° #1 hit *We Are The World*.
May Shear's *Steady*, written by Shear and Lauper when she was with Blue Angel, makes US #57.
July *The Goonies 'R' Good Enough*, from movie *The Goonies*, hits US #10.
1986 Aug Ballad *True Colors*, penned by Tom Kelly and Billy Steinberg, tops the US chart and reaches UK #12.
Sept LP *True Colors* hits US #4 and UK #25. It includes Lauper originals and covers of *What's Goin' On* and *Iko Iko*. Lauper begins a tour of Australia and Japan.
1987 Jan *Change Of Heart* hits US #3 but peaks at UK #74.
Aug Video *Cyndi Lauper In Paris*, filmed at Le Zenith Concert Hall, Paris, France, is released. Lauper becomes a born again Christian having spent 2 years heavily involved in the promotion of professional US wrestling.
1988 She begins work on her motion picture debut.
Oct Lauper joins several US writers and performers at the "Music Speaks Louder Than Words" summit in USSR.

LED ZEPPELIN

Robert Plant (vocals)
Jimmy Page (guitar)
John Paul Jones (bass)
John Bonham (drums)

1968 Mar The Yardbirds°, on their final US tour, perform *I'm Confused* (later titled *Dazed And Confused*) and *White Summer* (both become part of Led Zeppelin's repertoire).
July The Yardbirds° split after a UK gig at Luton. Page (b. Jan.9, 1944, Heston, Middx., UK) and bassist Chris Dreja decide to form The New Yardbirds and are booked for a 10-day tour of Scandinavia, but Page decides to launch the group with a new line-up and Dreja quits to become a photographer. Jones (b. John Baldwin, June 3, 1946, Sidcup, Kent, UK), an ex-session man and arranger like Page, joins on bass. Terry Reid and B.J. Wilson of Procol Harum° reject the group, but Reid recommends 19-year-old Midlands R&B vocalist Plant° (b. Aug.20, 1948, West Bromwich, Staffs, UK). Page and group manager Peter Grant see Plant perform with a band called Hobbstweedle in Birmingham. Plant is invited to join and leaves the Midlands with only his rail fare in his pocket. Plant suggests Bonham (b. May 31, 1948, Bromwich, Staffs., UK), who is backing acts like Joe Cocker°, Chris Farlowe° and Tim Rose on the club circuit, and he joins.
Sept The New Yardbirds tour Scandinavia, having recorded their debut LP in 2 weeks.
Oct The Who's° drummer Keith Moon had often used the phrase "going down like a lead Zeppelin" to describe disastrous gigs, Page likes the phrase, drops the "a" and the group is renamed Led Zeppelin.
Oct [15] They make their live debut at Surrey University.
Dec [26] The group begins its first US tour in Boston, Mass., with Vanilla Fudge° and the MC5, and are an immediate success.
1969 Feb LP *Led Zeppelin* hits US #10.
Apr LP *Led Zeppelin* hits UK #6. The group appears on UK TV's "How It Is". A decision not to release singles in UK (at Grant's insistence) leads to lack of airplay on UK radio and only rare TV appearances. The group begins its second US tour, this time as bill-toppers. *Good Times Bad Times* makes US #80.
June [27] Led Zeppelin performs at London's Playhouse Theatre for UK BBC Radio's "In Concert" show.
June [28] They play the Bath Festival of Blues and Progressive Music.
June [29] The group tops the bill at the Pop Proms at London's Royal Albert Hall.
July They participate in the Newport Jazz and Blues Festival, Newport, Rhode Island, US.
Oct The group appears at a "Sunday Lyceum" concert promoted by Tony Stratton-Smith, and receives the highest fee ever paid to a UK band for a one-off concert.
Nov LP *Led Zeppelin 2* hits #1 in UK and US, and stays charted for 138 weeks and 98 weeks respectively. Recorded and written in hotel rooms and during rehearsals on tour, it features *Whole Lotta Love*, which will become a group anthem.
Dec UK newspaper *Financial Times* announces the group has made $5 million in US sales, and comments that, unlike The Beatles°, they have not been awarded MBE's for their export achievements. The group is awarded two platinum disks and one gold disk at London's Savoy Hotel by Mrs. Gwyneth Dunwoody, Parliamentary Secretary to UK Board of Trade.
1970 Jan *Whole Lotta Love* hits US #4, as the group begins a UK tour.
Feb They are refused admission to Singapore because of the length of their hair and cancel a concert. They change their name to Nobs for a concert in Copenhagen, Denmark, after Count Evan von Zeppelin objected to the use of his family name on a German tour.
Mar Led Zeppelin plays the Montreux Jazz Festival.
Apr The group returns home after almost a year and a half of touring and recording. *Living Loving Maid (She's Just A Woman)*, B-side of *Whole Lotta Love*, stalls at US #65.
June They tour Iceland and turn down $200,000 to play two US concerts, so they can play UK's Bath Festival for a second time.
Aug A US tour begins.

LED ZEPPELIN *cont.*

Sept Their appearances in New York's Madison Square Garden gross over $100,000 per performance. The band is voted Top Group in UK music weekly *Melody Maker* poll after years of Beatles'° domination. With The Rolling Stones° in tax exile and The Beatles split, Led Zeppelin is #1 group in the world.

Oct LP *Led Zeppelin 3*, with a change of style and a more acoustic feel, hits #1 in UK and US.

1971 Jan *Immigrant Song* reaches US #16.

Mar Led Zeppelin plays a "thank you" tour for its UK fans in the clubs and ballrooms they played in their early days in 1968. They agree to play for their original 1968 fee if the promoter charges the 1968 admission fee.

Nov Fourth LP is released untitled and hits UK #1 and US #2. It becomes known as *Led Zeppelin 4* or *Four Symbols* after the runic images on its inner sleeve. The group's selling power is underlined by the lack of any title or name on the album cover. The LP contains *Stairway To Heaven*, which becomes the group's new anthem and will later be regarded as a landmark in rock history. A UK tour includes two nights at London's Wembley Arena with circus and novelty acts.

1972 Feb *Black Dog* makes US #15.

Apr *Rock And Roll* climbs to US #47.

July Manager Peter Grant tries to organize a Led Zeppelin concert at London's Waterloo train station, but fails.

Dec The group plays two concerts at London's Alexandra Palace.

1973 Apr LP *Houses Of The Holy* hits UK and US #1. The sleeve again has no title or name.

May *Financial Times* quotes Grant as saying that Led Zeppelin will earn $30 million in US in the coming year. The group's concert at Tampa Stadium, Fla. grosses $309,000, breaking the US box office record held by The Beatles° (for their 1965 Shea Stadium performance).

July A Madison Square Garden concert is filmed for inclusion in movie *The Song Remains The Same*. The band is robbed of $180,000 from New York's Drake Hotel deposit box; it is never recovered. *Over The Hills And Far Away* reaches US #51.

Oct The group works on fantasy film sequences for a forthcoming movie. Page appears on Maggie Bell's LP *Suicide Sal* and Jones writes, produces and plays on Madeleine Bell's LP *Comin' Atcha*.

Dec *D'yer Mak'er* makes US #20.

1974 Jan The formation of Led Zeppelin's own label, SwanSong, named after an unreleased Page instrumental, is announced. (The label logo is based on William Rimmer's *Evening Fall Of Day*.)

May SwanSong is launched with parties in US and London.

1975 Mar First SwanSong LP, the double *Physical Graffiti* is released and tops UK and US charts.

Apr 51,000 tickets for three UK concerts at Earls Court, London, sell out in 2 hours.

May US President Gerald Ford's daughters tell Dick Cavett on his talk show that Led Zeppelin is their favorite group. *Trampled Underfoot* reaches US #38. The group plays five 4-hour shows at Earls Court, London.

June They go into tax exile in Switzerland.

Aug Plant° and his wife are badly injured in a car crash on holiday in Rhodes, Greece. He is flown to UK for treatment in plaster casts, but is flown out again on a stretcher to Jersey to recuperate when the time limit on his UK visit, before paying full income tax for the year, is about to expire.

1976 Apr LP *Presence* hits US and UK #1.

Oct Led Zeppelin's film *The Song Remains The Same* is premièred in New York, and the soundtrack double LP hits both US and UK #1. The group makes its first US TV appearance playing *Black Dog*, a former US release, on "Don Kirshner's Rock Concert".

1977 July On a US tour, Bonham, manager Peter Grant, and a bodyguard are arrested and charged with assault on a security employee of promoter Bill Graham. The tour is cancelled when Plant's° son becomes ill and dies. Rumors spread that the group, appalled by its bad luck, is to split up.

1978 July After a quiet year with his family, Plant° re-emerges to play with local musicians, and Led Zeppelin regroups to prepare a new LP.

Dec They record at Abba's° Polar studios, Stockholm, Sweden during their tax exile.

1979 Aug Zeppelin tops the bill for two dates at Knebworth Fair, a major UK outdoor festival.

Sept LP *In Through The Out Door* is released worldwide and tops UK and US charts, selling over 4 million copies in US.

Dec Plant°, Jones and Bonham join the all-star line-up of UNICEF "Rock for Kampuchea" concert at London's Hammersmith Odeon.

1980 Feb *Fool In The Rain* reaches US #21.

May Led Zeppelin announces its first full-scale European tour for 7 years.

June They close their European tour with a concert in West Berlin.

Sept The group meets at Page's Windsor, UK, house to rehearse for a US tour.

Sept [25] Bonham is found dead in bed, having choked in his sleep after a drinking bout.

Oct [10] Bonham's funeral takes place at his local Rushnock parish church, Worcs., UK.

Dec [4] A statement is released announcing the group's decision not to continue after "the loss of our dear friend".

1982 Feb Page-composed soundtrack LP *Death Wish II* reaches UK #40 and US #50.

Dec LP *Coda*, compiled by Page from unissued Zeppelin material, hits UK #4.

1983 Jan LP *Coda* hits US #6.

Sept Page appears at ARMS concert in aid of Multiple Sclerosis victims at London's Royal Albert Hall with Eric Clapton°, Steve Winwood° and Jeff Beck°, and performs *Stairway To Heaven*.

1984 July Page appears with Roy Harper at UK's Cambridge Folk Festival.

1985 Mar Page joins Harper for LP *Whatever Happened To Jugula?* which makes UK #44. Page, having formed a new combo, The Firm, with Bad Company's° vocalist Paul Rodgers, bassist Tony Franklin and drummer Chris Slade, releases LP *The Firm*. It makes UK #15 and US #17.

Apr Firm's *Radioactive* reaches US #28.

May Firm's *Satisfaction Guaranteed* stalls at US #73.

July Zeppelin re-forms (with Phil Collins° on drums) for Live Aid extravaganza at JFK Stadium, Philadelphia.

Nov Multi-national group The Far Corporation takes *Stairway To Heaven* into the UK chart for the first time, hitting #8.

1986 Jan The group rehearses for a week with Chic's° Tony Thompson on drums, but decides not to re-form.

Mar Firm's *All The Kings Horses*, a trailer for its new LP, peaks at US #61.

Apr Firm's LP *Mean Business* peaks at US #22 and UK #46.

1988 May Zeppelin regroups, with Jason Bonham filling his father's role, and performs *Stairway To Heaven* and *Whole Lotta Love* at New

York's Madison Square Garden as part of Atlantic Records' 40-year celebration concert.

June Plant's° solo career continues, and Page releases first solo LP *Outrider*, which makes UK #27 and US #26.

BRENDA LEE

1956 Mar Lee (b. Brenda Mae Tarpley, Dec.11, 1944, Lithonia, Ga., US), after many local talent contests, makes her debut at age 11 on "Ozarek Jubilee" TV show, hosted by country singer Red Foley, and also tours with Foley's road show, before making national TV appearances on the "Perry Como Show" and the "Ed Sullivan Show".

July She signs to Decca Records, which promotes her as "Little Miss Brenda Lee" because of her young age and diminutive stature.

1957 Mar After some country success with *Jambalaya* and *I'm Gonna Lassoo Santa Claus*, her chart debut is *One Step At A Time*, backed by the Anita Kerr Singers, which reaches US #43.

Aug *Dynamite* makes US #72 and leads to her revamped billing as "Little Miss Dynamite" – a reference to her dynamic stage presence, which will stay with her until the mid-1960s.

1959 Mar She is booked to play the Olympia in Paris, France (partly to help drum up publicity in US). The original show is cancelled when the promoter discovers her age, but her manager leaks a story to the local press that she is a 32-year-old midget, and then gains publicity denying it. Held over at the Olympia for 5 weeks, Lee becomes an in-demand name in Europe. She follows French dates with shows in West Germany, Italy and UK.

1960 Apr After 2 years without hits, Lee records Ronnie Self's rock ballad *Sweet Nothin's* which hits US #4 and is a million-seller.

May *Sweet Nothin's* hits UK #4. Also written by Self, country-styled *I'm Sorry* tops the US chart for 3 weeks and is another million-seller. B-side *That's All You Gotta Do* hits US #6.

July *I'm Sorry* makes UK #12.

Oct Italian-originated ballad *I Want To Be Wanted* tops the US chart for a week and is her third consecutive million-seller. B-side *Just A Little* makes US #40. Debut LP *Brenda Lee*, which includes the hit singles, hits US #5 (and will spend 13 months on chart).

Nov *I Want To Be Wanted* peaks at UK #31.

Dec *Rockin' Around The Christmas Tree* reaches US #14 (and becomes a Christmas standard).

1961 Jan LP *This Is . . . Brenda* hits US #4.

Feb Ballad *Emotions* hits US #7 while B-side *I'm Learning About Love* peaks at US #33.

Mar An early rocker, *Let's Jump The Broomstick* is reissued in UK and makes UK #12.

Apr *Emotions* reaches UK #45, reflecting a decreasing interest in UK of her ballad style despite US top 10 consistency.

May *You Can Depend On Me* hits US #6.

June LP *Emotions* reaches US #24.

June [25] Lee performs in Alan Freed's show at the Hollywood Bowl with Bobby Vee°, Jerry Lee Lewis°, The Shirelles° and others.

Aug A return to uptempo material with Jackie DeShannon-penned gimmick-rocker *Dum Dum* hits US #4 and makes UK #22. Ballad B-side *Eventually* reaches US #56.

Oct LP *All The Way*, including *Dum Dum* makes US #17.

Nov Country ballad *Fool #1* hits US #3 (another gold disk) and makes UK #38. Uptempo B-side *Anybody But Me* climbs to US #31.

Dec *Rockin' Around The Christmas Tree* is repromoted in US and makes US #50.

1962 Mar Ballad *Break It To Me Gently* hits US #4 and UK #46. Uptempo B-side *So Deep* reaches US #52.

Apr LP *Sincerely* reaches US #29.

May Not released in US, uptempo *Speak To Me Pretty* is Lee's biggest UK hit at #3. It is taken from children's movie *Two Little Bears* in which Lee has a small cameo role. Meanwhile, ballad *Everybody Loves Me But You* hits US #6 and rock B-side *Here Comes That Feeling* peaks at US #89.

Aug Uptempo *Here Comes That Feeling* is chosen instead of the A-side by Decca as UK follow-up to *Speak To Me Pretty* and hits UK #5. In US, slow DeShannon song *Heart In Hand* reaches US #15 and uptempo B-side *It Started All Over Again* makes US #29.

Oct Uptempo *It Started All Over Again* is again picked as UK A-side and reaches UK #15.

Nov *All Alone Am I* hits US #3 and is another million-seller. B-side *Save All Your Lovin' For Me* makes US #53. LP *All The Way* belatedly reaches UK #20.

Dec *Rockin' Around The Christmas Tree* is released in UK for the first time and hits #6. On its third US release, it makes #59. LP *Brenda, That's All* reaches US #20.

Dec [30] Lee is slightly injured when fire guts her Nashville home and she attempts to rescue her pet poodle Cee Cee, who dies of smoke inhalation.

1963 Feb *All Alone Am I* breaks Lee's UK "ballad jinx" hitting #7. In US, double A-side *You Used To Be*/*She'll Never Know* makes #32 and #47. LP *Brenda, That's All* reaches UK #13.

Apr LP *All Alone Am I* makes US #25.

Apr [24] Lee is married to considerably taller Ronnie Shacklett in Nashville.

May *Losing You* hits US #6 and UK #10, while LP *All Alone Am I* hits UK #8.

May [3] After only 8 days' honeymoon, Lee opens at New York's Copacabana.

July She signs a 20-year contract with Decca, guaranteeing her $35,000 a year. It also includes a two-film deal with Universal Pictures.

Aug Double A-side *My Whole World Is Falling Down*/*I Wonder* makes US #24 and #25. This time UK issues ballad *I Wonder* as A-side and it makes UK #14.

Nov *The Grass Is Greener* makes US #17 and uptempo B-side *Sweet Impossible You* reaches US #70 and UK #28.

1964 Jan LP *Let Me Sing*, which includes *Break It To Me Gently* and *Losing You*, reaches US #39. New ballad *As Usual* climbs to US #12.

Feb *As Usual* hits UK #5.

Apr *Think* makes US #25 and UK #26. (This is the first indication that Lee's chart consistency is being affected by the rise of Merseybeat and group-oriented music which has swept many contemporaries from the chart.)

July *Alone With You* makes US #48 and fails in UK. LP *By Request* reaches US #90.

Sept *When You Loved Me* makes US #47.

Oct Lee records in UK with The Animals'° and Herman's Hermits'° producer Mickie Most in an effort to meet the new musical trends head-on. *Is It True*, written by John Carter and Ken Lewis, is rush released in UK and makes #17.

Nov *Is It True* also makes US #17.

Dec Extracted from LP *Merry Christmas*, *Christmas Will Be Just Another Day* reaches UK #29.

1965 Feb Second Most production, *Thanks A Lot* makes US #45 and UK #41. B-side, a cover of Dave Berry's° 1964 UK hit *The Crying Game*, makes US #87.

May *Truly, Truly, True* peaks at US #54.

July A return to country ballad-style, *Too Many Rivers* makes US #13, her biggest hit single for over 2 years.

Aug *Too Many Rivers* reaches UK #22 (her final UK singles chart entry).

Oct LP *Too Many Rivers* makes US #36.

Nov *Rusty Bells* reaches US #33.

1966 July LP *Bye Bye Blues* makes US #94 and UK #21, while *Ain't Gonna Cry No More* peaks at US #77.

Aug Compilation LP *10 Golden Years*, featuring a hit from each year from 1956-65, reaches US #70.

Dec Now uncharacteristic rock *Coming On Strong* makes US #11.

1967 Feb LP *Coming On Strong* reaches US #94 and, taken from it, *Ride, Ride, Ride* makes US #37.

June LP *For The First Time*, with jazzman Pete Fountain, reaches US #187.

1969 Apr *Johnny One Time*, after a 2-year chart absence, makes US #41. In her country ballad-style, it has much in common with mainstream late 60s country music, into which Lee is inevitably drawn.

May *You Don't Need Me For Anything Anymore* makes US #84.

June LP *Johnny One Time* reaches US #98.

1973 Apr Kris Kristofferson°-penned *Nobody Wins* is her last US Hot 100 entry at US #70. It tops the US country chart (and Lee will work in this field from now on).

1977 July Released from Decca before official contract expiry, Lee moves to Elektra (her only recording for the label is a country single).

1979 Lee re-signs to MCA Records (Decca's successor) in Nashville.

1980 TV-promoted compilation LP *Little Miss Dynamite*, on Warwick Records, makes UK #15.

1981 Mar Lee appears in Burt Reynolds/Jackie Gleason film *Smokey and the Bandit II* as the Nice Lady.

1984 Jan Double compilation LP *25th Anniversary* reaches UK #65.

1985 Apr Another TV-promoted compilation LP *The Very Best Of Brenda Lee* reaches UK #16.

1988 Lee begins legal action against MCA Records.

THE LEFT BANKE

Michael Brown (keyboards)
Steve Martin (vocals)
Jeff Winfield (guitar)
Tom Finn (bass)
George Cameron (drums)

1964 Working in New York as an assistant at his father's World United Recording studio and playing piano for Reparata & The Delrons, classically-trained musician Brown (b. Michael Lookofsky, Apr.25, 1949, New York, US) first meets Martin, Cameron and Finn (the latter a member of The Magic Planets).

1965 Brown and friends form The Left Banke while experimenting in World United studio with a sound blending classical influences with "British invasion"-style pop-rock. Brown's father Harry Lookofsky grooms what he recognizes as a talent for harmony singing and unusual arrangements, and builds their tracks to professional production standards.

1966 Mar They record *Walk Away Renée*, a baroque-styled arrangement of a ballad written by Brown, which will prove sufficiently offbeat to be turned down by several labels before it is released by Mercury's subsidiary label, Smash Records, in July.

Oct *Walk Away Renée* hits #6 in US.

1967 Feb *Pretty Ballerina* climbs to US #15. Like *Walk Away Renée*, it fails to chart in UK. Rick Brand replaces Winfield on guitar while they are recording tracks for debut LP.

May LP *Walk Away Renée/Pretty Ballerina* peaks at US #67, by which time there has been a rift in the group, and as owner of the name Left Banke, Brown retires to the studio to record *Ivy Ivy* alone. This fails to chart when Smash declines to promote it while the two group factions are at loggerheads. By the time they reconcile, both *Ivy Ivy* and rapidly-issued follow-up *She May Call You Up Tonight* are lost causes.

Oct *Desirée* creeps to US #98 and is their last chart entry. Brown leaves for good, followed by Brand.

1968 The Left Banke name this time is left with Finn, Martin and Cameron, who record four more unsuccessful singles, and the LP *Left Banke, Too* (released in 1969) as a trio.

Jan A cover version of *Walk Away Renée* by The Four Tops° hits UK #3, then US #14, 2 months later.

Aug A more unexpected cover version of *And Suddenly* (the B-side of ill-fated *Ivy Ivy*) by the Cherry People reaches US #45.

1969 Brown joins forces with a group named Montage, producing, playing keyboards, vocally arranging, and writing most of their one LP *Montage* for Laurie Records.

1971 Steve Martin releases *Two By Two/Love Songs In The Night*, both written by Brown, but it is a one-off reunion. Brown and vocalist Ian Lloyd then form Stories, with Steve Love (guitar) and Brian Madey (drums), and they sign to Kama Sutra Records.

1972 Aug Stories' *I'm Coming Home* reaches US #42, while their debut LP *Stories* makes #182.

1973 Aug Stories have their biggest hit with a cover of Hot Chocolate's° *Brother Louie*, which tops US chart and sells over a million. Brown leaves the group during the recording sessions for this and LP *Stories About Us*, which reaches US #29.

1976 Brown forms The Beckies, who release one (unsuccessful) LP on Sire Records. Tom Finn provides vocals for one song on the LP.

1978 Feb Martin, Finn and Cameron attempt to reform The Left Banke. They record an LP's worth of material which will remain unreleased until 1986, and *And One Day*, a single issued in US during the autumn by Camerica Records. (In the mid-1980s, US and UK archive labels Rhino and Bam Caruso will reissue all Left Banke material, including originally unreleased tracks and obscurities.)

JOHN LENNON

1967 Oct Lennon (b. Oct 9, 1940, Liverpool, UK) makes his first and only solo appearance (as Private Gripweed) in a feature film, *How I Won The War* directed by Richard Lester.

1968 Nov LP *Unfinished Music No 1 – Two Virgins* is released. A melange of sound effects and disjointed music, it is made famous by its cover of Lennon and Yoko Ono in a naked, full-frontal pose. Lennon takes the photo himself on a delayed shutter release, reportedly too embarrassed to employ a professional photographer. EMI refuses to distribute the LP and it is handled by Track which wraps it in brown paper bags for retail.

Dec [10] Lennon makes his first solo TV performance, at the filming of "The Rolling Stones' Rock 'N' Roll Circus", singing *'Yer Blues*.

1969 Feb LP *Unfinished Music No 1 – Two Virgins* makes US #124.

Mar [20] Lennon marries Ono in Gibraltar.

May LP *Unfinished Music No 2 – Life With The Lions* makes US #174. A continuation of the first LP, it has a free-form live concert on one side while the other is recorded on a cassette player at Queen Charlotte Hospital, Hammersmith, London, during Ono's pregnancy (which ends in miscarriage).

July *Give Peace A Chance* hits UK #2, and becomes the definitive peace anthem for pacifists worldwide. It is recorded during a "bed-in", a form of protest invented by Lennon and Ono in which they stayed in bed to protest for world peace and asked the media to film and interview them in Room 1742 of Hotel La Reine, Montreal, Canada. The disk is credited to The Plastic Ono Band (a name Lennon will use for the musicians he is recording with over the next few years). Appearing on it are Lennon, Tommy Smothers, Petula Clark°, Timothy Leary and Allen Ginsberg.

Sept *Give Peace A Chance* reaches US #14.

Sept [13] The Plastic Ono Band, with a line-up of Eric Clapton°, Klaus Voorman and Alan White, appears in a hastily-arranged slot at The Toronto Rock 'N' Roll Festival. The group rehearses on the flight to Toronto and performs a shaky set of rock'n'roll classics and Lennon originals.

Nov *Cold Turkey*, about the agonies of drug withdrawal, makes UK #14. Its failure to make the top 10 prompts Lennon to return his MBE in protest to Buckingham Palace, although he also claims he is protesting against Britain's involvement in the Biafran War and support of US in Vietnam. This action alienates him with the British Establishment and prompts his emigration to America.

Dec LP *The Wedding Album*, an avant-garde recording which includes souvenirs of the event, makes US #178. *Melody Maker*'s Richard Williams reviews a pre-release copy of the LP pressed on two disks, each with a blank B-side, and notes that these B-sides contain single tones maintained throughout, reproduced electronically and altering by a microtone or semitone to produce an uneven beat. (They are in fact an engineer's test signal.) Lennon and Ono send him a telegram saying: "We both feel that this is the first time a critic topped the artist."

Dec [15] Lennon makes his last live appearance in UK at a UNICEF benefit at London's Lyceum Ballroom.

1970 Jan *Cold Turkey* peaks at US #30 as LP *The Plastic Ono Band – Live Peace In Toronto 1969* hits US #10.

Feb *Instant Karma*, recorded in a day and produced by Phil Spector, hits UK #5 and US #3. George Harrison° plays guitar and Allen Klein and assorted club-goers from London's Hatchetts Club provide the chorus.

Mar Lennon and Ono begin an intensive 6-month course of primal scream therapy conducted by its originator, Dr. Arthur Janov. During this, Lennon writes most of the material for his first solo LP.

1971 Jan LP *John Lennon And The Plastic Ono Band* traces themes from Lennon's troubled adolescence and topics brought to the surface during his primal therapy treatment. It makes UK #11 and hits US

#6 (acclaimed in later years a creative pinnacle). *Mother* climbs to US #43.

Apr *Power To The People* hits UK #7 and US #11.

Sept Lennon and Ono set up home in New York, US.

Oct LP *Imagine*, commercially his most successful LP, features a melodic pop sound and is acclaimed as his best solo work. The LP, containing two thinly-veiled attacks on Paul McCartney° in *Crippled Inside* and *How Do You Sleep?*, tops both UK and US charts.

Nov *Imagine* hits US #3, but Lennon resists its UK release.

Dec *Happy Xmas (War Is Over)* is released in US only and fails to chart (which it will continue to do on subsequent re-releases).

1972 Feb Lennon and Ono co-host US TV's "The Mike Douglas Show" for a week and Lennon jams with his rock'n'roll hero Chuck Berry°.

June *Woman Is The Nigger Of The World* peaks at US #57.

July For double LP *Some Time In New York City*, Lennon teams for one disk with group Elephant's Memory (who contributed to the soundtrack of *Midnight Cowboy*) to record an overtly-political LP commenting on causes ranging from Northern Ireland to the imprisonment of radicals, Angela Davis and John Sinclair. The other disk is concert recordings with The Mothers of Invention. The LP makes US #48. The Beatles'° song publishing arm, Northern Songs, refuses to recognize some of Yoko Ono's composer credits with Lennon, and release of the LP is delayed in UK.

Aug Lennon makes his only major appearance at a concert in New York's Madison Square Garden for the One To One charity. Critics regard it as his first solo performance. He is joined on stage by Stevie Wonder° and Roberta Flack° for *Give Peace A Chance* finale.

Oct LP *Sometime In New York City* reaches UK #11.

Dec *Happy Xmas (War Is Over)* hits UK #4, and makes the first of many chart visits having been held up from UK release due to the Ono song-credit dispute.

1973 Mar Lennon is ordered to leave US by Immigration Authorities and begins his long fight to gain the necessary green card to enable him to remain in the country.

Nov *Mind Games* climbs to UK #26 and US #18. LP *Mind Games*, a return to the commercial era of *Imagine*, makes UK #13 and hits US #9.

1974 Jan Lennon asks H.M. The Queen for a Royal pardon in connection with his UK drug conviction to enable him to leave US and be guaranteed return entry.

Mar Lennon enters a dark period of his life, embarking on a drunken LA lifestyle after a temporary split from Ono. He is seen in the company of his former personal assistant, May Pang, and at an infamous incident at LA's Troubadour Club, he throws insults at The Smothers Brothers and punches their manager and a cocktail waitress before being forcibly removed from the premises. The incident makes headlines worldwide.

Aug He produces Nilsson's° LP *Pussycats*, a mixture of cover versions which adds little to either reputation.

Oct LP *Walls And Bridges* hits UK #6 and tops the US chart.

Nov *Whatever Gets You Through The Night* hits US #1, but makes only UK #36. He becomes the last of the four ex-Beatles° to hit US #1. Elton John° plays on the session for the single and, recognizing the song's potential, makes a bargain with Lennon that if the disk got to #1, Lennon would have to appear in concert with him. Lennon accepts, confident of the record's non-#1 status.

Nov [28] On Thanksgiving Night, Lennon makes what will be his final concert appearance at New York's Madison Square Garden joining Elton John° for three songs, *Whatever Gets You Through The Night*, *Lucy In The Sky With Diamonds* and *I Saw Her Standing There* (released as an EP in UK in Mar. 1981, it makes UK #40).

1975 Jan *Happy Xmas (War Is Over)* belatedly makes UK #48.

Feb *#9 Dream* reaches UK #23 and hits US #9.

Mar For LP *Rock 'N' Roll*, Lennon finally achieves his aim to record an LP of his favorite rock'n'roll songs. (The project was begun in 1973 with Phil Spector producing. After disagreements between the two, Spector disappeared with the master tapes and Lennon, unhappy with the production work, re-recorded the set.) It is reported that Lennon has struck up an agreement with Morris Levy, Chuck Berry's° publisher, that he would cover certain Berry songs for a new LP as Levy threatened a lawsuit against Lennon for using Berry's song *You Can't Catch Me* in the shape of *Come Together* on LP *Abbey Road*. Lennon subsequently gives Levy some master tapes of songs which, without Lennon's authorization, he releases as TV-advertised mail order LP *Roots – John Lennon Sings The Great Rock & Roll Hits* on Adam VIII label. Apple promptly releases LP *Rock 'N' Roll* to kill off the disk and Lennon successfully sues Levy, winning compensation of $45,000. The LP hits both UK and US #6. Lennon co-writes *Fame* with Luther Vandross° and David Bowie° (which reaches UK #17 and tops the US chart), for Bowie's LP *Young Americans*. On this LP, he also plays guitar with Bowie on The Beatles'° song *Across The Universe*.

Apr Lennon's remake of Ben E. King's° *Stand By Me* makes UK #30 and US #20.

June [13] He makes his last TV appearance on "Salute to Sir Lew Grade", performing *Slippin' And Slidin'* and *Imagine*.

Oct [9] Sean Taro Ono Lennon is born. His only child by Ono, the birth has a profound effect on Lennon. (He retires for 5 years to become a househusband in his Manhattan apartment building, The Dakota, while Ono runs their business empire.)

Nov Greatest hits compilation LP *Shaved Fish* hits UK #8 and US #12. Released as a UK single for first time, *Imagine* hits #6.

1976 Mar Lennon receives his green card allowing permanent residence in US (but never returns to UK).

1980 Aug After his hiatus, Lennon begins songwriting again on a holiday in Bermuda and records sessions for forthcoming LP *Double Fantasy* (named after a flower Lennon saw in a botanical garden in Bermuda). Lennon is not signed to any label, but David Geffen offers to release the LP without hearing any of the material.

Nov LP *Double Fantasy* is released and will top both UK and US charts. It receives positive reviews as Lennon returns to the limelight.

Dec [8] Lennon and Ono return home from the recording studio at 10:50 EST. As they enter the courtyard of The Dakota building, Lennon turns around when he hears a voice say "Mr. Lennon?" He is shot five times by Mark Chapman and dies of blood loss shortly after at the Roosevelt Hospital.

Dec Record sales soar immediately. *(Just Like) Starting Over* hits #1 in UK and US. EMI in UK receives orders from record shops for over 300,000 copies of *Imagine* single.

Dec [14] Ono calls for a 10-minute silent vigil around the world at 2:00 p.m. EST.

1981 Jan [10] *Imagine* tops the UK chart, with *Happy Xmas (War Is Over)* at #2. *Give Peace A Chance* reaches UK #33.

Jan [22] A picture of Lennon naked next to a fully-clothed Ono appears in an obituary issue of *Rolling Stone* magazine.

Feb *Woman* completes a hat trick of UK #1s in a 9-week period. Roxy Music's° version of *Jealous Guy* hits UK #1.

Mar *Woman* hits US #2.

May *Watching The Wheels* reaches UK #30 and US #10.

Dec *Happy Xmas (War Is Over)* makes UK #28.

1982 Nov Compilation LP *The John Lennon Collection* hits UK #1 and US #33. *Love* climbs to UK #41.

Dec *Happy Xmas (War Is Over)* makes UK #56.

1984 Jan *Nobody Told Me* hits UK #6. LP *Heart Play – Unfinished Dialogue*, featuring excerpts from a *Playboy* magazine interview given shortly before his death, reaches US #94.

Feb LP *Milk And Honey*, featuring six of Lennon's songs recorded just before his death in 1980, hits UK #3 and US #11.

Mar *Nobody Told Me* reaches UK #32 and hits US #5.

Apr *Borrowed Time* reaches UK #32 as *I'm Stepping Out* peaks at US #55.

Nov Son Julian, from Lennon's marriage to Cynthia Twist, has his first hit with *Too Late For Goodbyes*, at UK #6 and LP *Valotte*, which reaches UK #20 and US #17. Many critics note a similar vocal style to his father's. Lennon's *Jealous Guy* peaks at UK #65.

1986 Mar LP *Live In New York City* makes UK #55 and US #41. His Aug. 1972 US concert is released on video.

Dec LP *Menlove Avenue*, of studio sessions from the *Rock 'N' Roll* and *Walls And Bridges* period, makes US #127.

1988 Sept Ono produces a syndicated series for radio on Lennon's life which features many unheard songs and interviews. A biography by Albert Goldman, who has previously written a book on Elvis Presley°, outrages fans with its claims.

Oct A movie and soundtrack, under the generic title *Imagine* and produced by Ono, are simultaneously released. They include out-takes, videos, home movies and previously unheard material.

LEVEL 42

Mark King (vocals and bass)
Mike Lindup (keyboards and vocals)
Boon Gould (guitar)
Phil Gould (drums)

1980 The band forms in London, UK, but three of its members are from the Isle of Wight, where King has been a drummer with various holiday camp groups, before switching to bass and moving to London. The name is taken from Douglas Adams' book *The Hitch-hiker's Guide to the Galaxy*, in which "42" is the answer to question "What is the meaning of life?" First London club gigs are played as a purely instrumental jazz-funk band.

May Debut single *Love Meeting Love*, featuring a vocal by King (urged by producer/label owner Andy Sojka as a vital selling-point) is recorded for Sojka's UK dance-oriented independent label, Elite Records. It receives strong UK disco play and makes the dance chart, interesting larger record companies in the group.

Aug The band signs to Polydor, which reissues its first single (the Elite pressing having sold out).

Sept *Love Meeting Love* makes UK #61.

Nov *(Flying On The) Wings Of Love* is released. It again makes the UK dance chart but fails to cross over.

1981 May *Love Games*, from the band's debut LP, reaches UK #38.

Aug *Turn It On* reaches UK #57, as debut LP *Level 42*, produced by Mike Vernon, peaks at UK #20.

Nov *Starchild*, also from the LP, makes UK #47. The band tours West Germany supporting Police°.

Dec Elite releases a limited-edition LP, *Strategy*, containing the rest of the material recorded prior to the band's Polydor signing.

1982 Apr LP *The Early Tapes, July-August 1980*, a reissue by Polydor of the Elite limited-edition LP, makes UK #46.

May *Are You Hearing (What I Hear?)* reaches UK #49.

Oct *Weave Your Spell* peaks at UK #43. It is taken from LP *The Pursuit Of Accidents*, which makes UK #17. The band follows with a "Pursuit of Accidents" tour of UK and Europe, which brings it in contact with Larry Dunn and Verdine White of Earth, Wind & Fire°, who offer to produce the next LP.

1983 Feb *The Chinese Way* is the group's first UK top 30 single, reaching UK #24.

Apr *Out Of Sight, Out Of Mind*, written by all four band members, makes UK #41.

Aug *The Sun Goes Down (Living It Up)* hits UK #10.

Sept LP *Standing In The Light*, produced in LA by Dunn and White, hits UK #9. The band follows with a 6-week US tour.

Oct *Micro Kids*, taken from the LP, reaches UK #37. Following the band's return from US, it plays another UK tour into the new year.

1984 July King releases solo LP *Influences* which makes UK #77. He also releases *Freedom*, with Lindup but credited to Thunderthumbs and the Toetsenman (their nicknames).

Oct *Hot Water* becomes a live highlight and reaches UK #18. It is taken from LP *True Colours*, which makes UK #14.

Nov *The Chant Has Just Begun*, also from LP *True Colours*, makes UK #41.

1985 July Double live LP *A Physical Presence*, mostly recorded at small UK club tour venues, climbs to UK #28.

Oct *Something About You* hits UK #6, the group's biggest-selling UK single.

Nov LP *World Machine*, produced by Wally Badarou, widens the group's sound into more commercial pop and hits UK #10.

Dec Ballad *Leaving Me Now*, from LP *World Machine*, reaches UK #15.

1986 Apr *Something About You* is the group's US chart debut, hitting #7.

June *Lessons In Love*, with Gary Barnacle on saxophone (and coupled with a live version of stage favorite *Hot Water*), hits UK #3. (It is the group's highest chart placing and will be the second biggest-selling single of the year in Europe, reaching #1 in eight countries.) It is followed by a successful long-running world tour.

Aug *Hot Water* is the band's second US chart entry, at #87. The group tours US supporting Steve Winwood°.

1987 Jan King is voted Best Bass Player in *Making Music* magazine's poll.

Feb Uptempo *Running In The Family* hits UK #6. The group tours UK and Europe promoting it.

Apr *To Be With You Again* hits UK #10.

June *Lessons In Love* reaches US #12, while LP *Running In The Family*, including the two previous singles, and again produced by Badarou, hits UK #2 and US #23. In support, the band plays a UK tour, which includes two dates at Birmingham NEC and eight at Wembley Arena, and follows with a tour of Europe and US.

Aug *Running In The Family* peaks at US #83.

Sept *It's Over*, another ballad, hits UK #10. As well as the usual 7" and 12" singles formats, it is released experimentally as one of UK's first CD video disks and sells out its pressing despite the fact that CD video players are not yet on the UK market.

Dec Both Gould brothers leave the group, Boon suffering from an ulcer and Phil from nervous exhaustion. (Boon Gould will later release a solo LP.) Neil Conti from Prefab Sprout° joins temporarily on drums. *Children Say*, another track from the LP (and promoted by a video which features just King and Lindup), reaches UK #22. All proceeds are donated to London's Great Ormond Street children's hospital appeal fund.

1988 Oct [29] Level 42 begins a European tour in Hamburg, West Germany. (The 10-date tour will end in Barcelona on Nov.12.)

GARY LEWIS AND THE PLAYBOYS

Gary Lewis (vocals and drums)
Al Ramsey (guitar)
John West (guitar)
David Costell (bass)
David Walker (keyboards)

1964 Aug Lewis (b. Gary Levitch, July 31, 1946, New York, N.Y., US), the son of movie comedian Jerry Lewis, having played drums since age 14, forms a band in Hollywood, Cal., with neighbors Ramsey (b. July 27, 1943, New Jersey, US), West (b. July 31, 1939, Uhrichsville, Oh., US), Costell (b. Mar.15, 1944, Pittsburgh, Pa., US) and Walker (b. May 12, 1943, Montgomeryville, Ala., US). Initially together to play just local parties, they audition at Disneyland, and are hired for a summer season at the park. They also have a cameo musical role in the Raquel Welch movie *A Swingin' Summer*.

1965 Feb Signed to Liberty Records by producer Snuff Garrett, the group's debut is Leon Russell°-arranged *This Diamond Ring*, co-written by Al Kooper and previously turned down by Bobby Vee°. An instant hit, it tops the US chart for 2 weeks and is a million-seller. The group performs on US TV's "Ed Sullivan Show".

May *Count Me In*, written by Glen D. Hardin of The Crickets, hits US #2 behind Herman's Hermits'° *Mrs. Brown You've Got A Lovely Daughter*. Debut LP *This Diamond Ring* reaches US #26.

Aug The sing-a-long *Save Your Heart For Me* (on which Lewis whistles as well as singing), hits US #2 behind Sonny and Cher's° *I Got You Babe*.

Oct *Everybody Loves A Clown*, a joint composition by Lewis, Garrett and Russell°, hits US #4. LP *A Session With Gary Lewis & The Playboys*, which includes the previous two hit singles, reaches US #18.

Dec LP *Everybody Loves A Clown* makes US #44.

1966 Jan The Beach Boys°-like *She's Just My Style*, again jointly penned by singer, producer and arranger, hits US #3. The group appears in the pop/espionage B-movie *Out of Sight*, with The Turtles°, The Knickerbockers, and Freddie & The Dreamers°.

Apr *Sure Gonna Miss Her* hits US #9, while LP *She's Just My Style* reaches #71.

June *Green Grass*, a UK song by Roger Cook and Roger Greenaway (themselves hitmakers as David and Jonathan), hits US #8 (the last of Lewis's seven consecutive US top 10 hits).

July LP *Gary Lewis Hits Again!* makes US #47.

Aug *My Heart's Symphony*, another Hardin song, reaches US #13.

Nov *(You Don't Have To) Paint Me A Picture* reaches US #15.

Dec Compilation LP *Golden Greats*, containing all the group's top 10 singles, hits US #10. It is Lewis' most successful LP, earning a gold disk for a half million sales, and staying on chart for 46 weeks.

1967 Jan [1] Lewis is drafted into the US Army, and the band is forced to split. (Bitter at the interruption to his career, he will refuse to form a Special Services band to entertain troops, and instead spends his time as a clerk/typist in Korea.) *Where Will The Words Come From*, released just before his call-up, reaches US #21.

Apr Liberty continues to issue earlier-recorded Lewis disks, but with the band off the road and unavailable for TV promotion, *The Loser (With A Broken Heart)* reaches only US #43, while LP *You Don't Have To Paint Me A Picture* peaks at #79.

June *Girls In Love* makes US #39.

July LP *New Directions* climbs to US #185.
Sept *Jill* reaches UK #52.
1968 Aug Out of the army, and with a new group of Playboys, Lewis' revival of Bryan Hyland's° *Sealed With A Kiss* reaches US #19.
Sept Newly-recorded LP *Gary Lewis Now!* sells moderately, reaching US #150, but will be Lewis' last successful LP.
1969 June Lewis tries another revival, of The Cascades'° *Rhythm Of The Rain*, but it halts at #63 (although it charts for 12 weeks). It will be his final US singles chart entry.
Sept LP *Rhythm Of The Rain* fails to chart.
1970/72 Lewis tries to escape the teenybop appeal of his earlier hits by evolving a more serious singer/songwriter style, but makes little headway.
1973/74 With the advent of 1960s nostalgia shows and tours in US, Lewis re-forms The Playboys to concentrate on playing his early hits on the oldies circuit, and finds regular touring work.
1975 Feb In an unexpected postscript, *My Heart's Symphony* is reissued in UK, where Lewis and The Playboys made no impression during the 1960s, after dancefloor success (as a "rare oldie") on the Northern Soul scene, and it makes UK #36.

HUEY LEWIS & THE NEWS

Huey Lewis (vocals)
Sean Hopper (keyboards)
Chris Hayes (lead guitar)
Johnny Colla (saxophone and guitar)
Mario Cipollina (bass)
Bill Gibson (drums)

1976 Nov Lewis (b. Hugh Cregg, July 5, 1950, New York, US), a latecomer member (on harmonica and occasional vocals) to San Francisco band Clover when it signs to Vertigo Records in UK, sings lead vocal on the band's debut single *Chicken Funk*, produced by Nick Lowe°.
1977 Clover releases four singles and two LPs (*Unavailable* and *Love On The Wire*), none of them chart successes. The band also backs Elvis Costello° on LP *My Aim Is True*, and tours supporting Thin Lizzy° and others.
1979 May After leader John McFee leaves to join The Doobie Brothers°, Clover breaks up. Lewis plays briefly in London on sessions for Nick Lowe° and Dave Edmunds° (LPs *Labour Of Lust* and *Repeat When Necessary*), then returns to Mill Valley, Cal., US, involving himself in a yoghurt business by day, and joining regular Monday night jam sessions at Uncle Charlie's club in Marin County with a group of musicians (who will form the core of his next band). They record a disco version of the *Exodus* theme, titled *Exodisco*, which is picked up by Mercury Records, and issued under the name American Express.
1980 May After playing informally together for some months, The News is formed on a permanent basis after Chrysalis signs the group on the strength of demos recorded by the Monday night jammers at Different Fur studio in Marin County. Lewis and Sean Hopper (b. Mar.31, 1953, Cal., US) are both ex-Clover, Hayes (b. Nov.24, 1957, Cal.) has been with California jazz bands, and Colla (b. July 2, 1952, Cal.), Gibson (b. Nov.13, 1951, Cal.), and Cipollina (b. Nov.10, 1954, Cal.) are all ex-members of Soundhole, which backed Van Morrison°.
July LP *Huey Lewis And The News*, produced by Bill Schnee and of almost all self-penned material, fails to sell.
1982 Apr *Do You Believe In Love*, written by Clover's producer Robert John Lange, is the band's debut US hit, climbing to #7, but does not chart in UK.
June LP *Picture This* makes US #13 and fails in UK. It has more non-Lewis compositions than the first LP and covers of songs by Wet Willie, Phil Lynott, and The Hollywood Flames (their 1957 hit *Buzz Buzz Buzz*). The song from Wet Willie's Michael Duke, *Hope You Love Me Like You Say You Do*, is extracted and makes US #36. Lynott's song *Tattoo (Giving It All Up For Love)* is issued in UK, but fails to chart.
Sept *Workin' For A Livin'*, also from the second LP, peaks at US #41.
1983 Sept LP *Sports* is released and initially hits US #6. (It is destined to be a long-term US seller, topping 7 million.)
Nov *Heart And Soul*, a Chinn/Chapman song earlier recorded by Exile, hits US #8 (the first US hit from LP *Sports*).
1984 Mar *I Want A New Drug (Called Love)* hits US #6. (Lewis later sues Ray Parker Jr.°, writer of the similarly-styled *Ghostbusters* theme, for alleged plagiarism of this song; the case will be settled out of court to Lewis' satisfaction.)
June LP *Sports* hits US #1 for a week, having been on chart for 8½ months. Third extract, *The Heart Of Rock And Roll*, hits US #6 for 4 weeks.
Sept *If This Is It*, also from LP *Sports*, peaks at US #6. It finally gives Lewis a UK chart debut, reaching #39.
Dec Final *Sports* extract, *Walking On A Thin Line*, makes US #18.
1985 Jan [28] Lewis and the band participate in the recording of USA For Africa's° *We Are The World*, in LA. Lewis takes a solo vocal line on the single.
July Lewis opts out of playing at Live Aid, resenting the over-publicity involved in the event.
Aug *The Power Of Love*, written for movie *Back To The Future* (in which Lewis has a cameo acting role as a music teacher) tops the US chart for 2 weeks, becoming a million-seller.
Sept LP *Sports* finally charts in UK, reaching #23, while *The Power Of Love* is the band's first UK top 20 hit, climbing to #11.
Dec EP *Heart And Soul*, a compilation of US top 10 hits *The Heart Of Rock And Roll* and the title track, plus *Hope You Love Me Like You Say You Do* and *Buzz Buzz Buzz* from LP *Picture This*, reaches UK #61.
1986 Feb [10] The band wins a BPI award from the UK record industry as Best International Band of the Year, and performs live at the awards ceremony in London.
Mar Following the release in UK of film *Back To The Future*, *The Power Of Love* is reactivated (as a double A-side with a reissue of the band's first US hit *Do You Believe In Love*), and hits UK #9.
May *The Heart Of Rock And Roll*, released for the third time in UK, finally makes #49.
Sept *Stuck With You* tops the US chart for 3 weeks and reaches UK #12.
Oct LP *Fore!*, which includes *Stuck With You* and *The Power Of Love*, hits US #1 and UK #8.
Dec *Hip To Be Square* reaches US #3 and UK #41.
Dec [7] Lewis & The News sing the US national anthem a cappella before the San Francisco 49ers v. New York Jets football game.
1987 Mar *Jacob's Ladder*, the fourth single from LP *Fore!*, hits US #1. Written by Bruce Hornsby° (whose first LP Lewis has partly produced, and whose group has supported The News on tour), the song is a swipe at US TV evangelists.
Apr *Simple As That*, released in UK in place of *Jacob's Ladder*, makes #47.
May *I Know What I Like* hits US #9.
Sept *Doing It All (For My Baby)* hits US #6; the LP *Fore!* has generated six US top 10 hits.
1988 Aug LP *Small World* enters US and UK charts. First single from the LP, *Perfect World* makes its way towards the US top 10 but struggles in UK.

JERRY LEE LEWIS

1949 Lewis (b. Sept.29, 1935, Ferriday, La., US) shows an early talent for music, so his parents mortgage their house to buy him a piano, which he teaches himself to play in 2 weeks. He is exposed to a rich mix of musical cultures – jazz (through his parents), hillbilly (and its more commercial offspring, country and western), gospel and cajun. He makes his first public performance at an auto show featuring the year's new model Fords in Natchez, La. When he earns $9 singing *Hadacol Boogie* with a local C&W band, his father encourages his musical career, loading the piano on the family truck and driving his son to shows.
1950 Lewis attends a fundamentalist Bible school in Waxahachie, Tex. (He is later expelled.)
1951 Lewis, at age 16, marries preacher's daughter Dorothy Barton (whom he soon abandons in favor of club life).
1952 Lewis gets married, bigamously, to Jane Mitcham at a shotgun wedding, encouraged by her brothers.
1954 Jane gives birth to Jerry Lee Lewis Jr.
1956 Lewis and his father sell 33 dozen eggs to finance a trip to Memphis, Tenn., hoping to audition for Sun Records. They arrive to find label head Sam Phillips has just left for Nashville, Tenn. Lewis threatens to sit on the doorstep until he is allowed in to perform. Eventually Jack Clement lets him in to cut a tape and tells him to return in a month. When he does so, Phillips invites him to record *Whole Lotta Shakin' Goin' On* and *Crazy Arms* for a Sun single. Released near the end of the year, it is promptly banned by most of the country's radio stations because of its vulgarity.

JERRY LEE LEWIS *cont.*

Dec [4] Lewis joins Elvis Presley° and Carl Perkins° in an impromptu recording session at Sun studios in Memphis. (These recordings will become known as *The Million Dollar Quartet*. Johnny Cash° leaves the session just before its start, at the insistence of his wife, who wants to go shopping.)

1957 Lewis, now touring extensively, meets Sam Phillips' brother Judd at a show in Alabama. He offers Lewis national TV exposure and takes him to New York and gets a contract for two appearances on the "Steve Allen Show".

Mar [31] He begins a major tour of Southern states with Perkins° and Cash° at Little Rock, Ark.

July [28] Lewis makes his US TV debut on the "Steve Allen Show". (His second appearance is the only time Allen's show is ever to top Ed Sullivan's in the national ratings. Before it *Whole Lotta Shakin' Goin' On* had sold about 30,000 copies, mainly in the South. Afterwards, it sells more than 6 million nationally, not reaching its #3 chart peak until Sept., when Sun is shipping 50-60,000 copies a day. It tops C&W and R&B charts simultaneously.)

Oct *Whole Lotta Shakin'*, released on London label, hits UK #8.

Nov [12] *Jamboree* (UK title: *Disc Jockey Jamboree*) with Lewis, Fats Domino°, Carl Perkins° and many others, premieres in US.

Dec [11] Still married to Jane Mitcham, Lewis secretly marries his 13-year-old cousin Myra Gale Brown, daughter of his bass player, in Hernando, Tenn. (Lewis' other cousins include country singer Mickey Gilley and TV evangelist Jimmy Swaggart.)

1958 Jan *Great Balls Of Fire* hits US #2 for a month, kept from the top by Danny & The Juniors'° *At The Hop*. It sells a million copies in its first 10 days of release (and will sell over 5 million in US). It tops the UK chart.

Feb Hank Williams' *You Win Again* (a 1952 US #13 for Tommy Edwards), B-side of *Great Balls Of Fire*, makes US #95.

Apr *Breathless* hits both US and UK #7, as Lewis is legally divorced from Jane Mitcham.

May [22] Lewis' unorthodox marriage has earned some condemnation from the church in US but the real storm hits when he arrives for his first UK tour. Waiting reporters ask who his young companion is and he tells them she is his wife and cousin and that he has been married twice before. Newspapers seize on the story. The resulting hysteria leads to his being booed off stage and forced to cancel 34 of the scheduled 37 concerts. On his return he finds that Sun, panicked by the scandal, has not serviced his new record, *High School Confidential*, to DJs.

June [9] Lewis takes out a 5-page trade ad to explain his recent divorce. He writes "I hope that if I'm washed up as a performer, it won't be because of this bad publicity."

June He also re-weds Myra in a ceremony of impeccable legality. *High School Confidential*, from the film of the same name in which Lewis appears, makes US #21, selling a half million copies. (Sales of Lewis' subsequent Sun releases will be limited by lack of radio play and the label's hesitancy in promoting its artist.)

Sept *Break Up* makes US #52 as B-side *I'll Make It All Up To You* peaks at US #85. (Both songs are written by Charlie Rich.)

1959 Jan *I'll Sail My Ship Alone* stalls at US #93.

Feb *High School Confidential* makes UK #12. Myra gives birth to Lewis' second son, Steve Allen.

May *Lovin' Up A Storm* reaches UK #28.

1960 Constantly touring, Lewis develops a serious problem with alcohol and pep pills.

June *Baby Baby Bye Bye* climbs to UK #47.

1961 May *What'd I Say* makes US #30 and UK #10.

1962 Apr [24] Lewis' son Steve Allen drowns in their home swimming pool.

Apr [29] Lewis returns to UK for the first time in 4 years amid favorable public response.

June LP *Jerry Lee Lewis Vol. 2* reaches UK #14.

Sept Lewis' version of Chuck Berry's° *Sweet Little Sixteen* stalls at US #95, but makes UK #38.

1963 Mar His version of Little Richard's° *Good Golly Miss Molly* makes UK #31.

Sept [6] Lewis leaves Sun and signs to Mercury Records subsidiary Smash.

1964 Mar LP *The Golden Hits Of Jerry Lee Lewis*, a re-recording of his Sun hits for Smash, becomes Lewis' first US chart LP, reaching #116 during an 8-week chart stay.

Apr Lewis' first single for Smash, *I'm On Fire* stalls at US #98.

Nov *High Heel Sneakers* peaks at US #91.

Dec LP *The Greatest Live Show On Earth*, recorded in Birmingham, Ala. on July 1, 1964, makes US #71.

1965 June LP *The Return Of Rock* makes US #121.

1966 May LP *Memphis Beat* reaches US #145.

Aug [21] Lewis is signed to play Iago in Jack Good's London stage production of *Catch My Soul*, his rock opera adaptation of Shakespeare's *Othello*.

1968 Mar Lewis switches to recording country music, and *Another Place, Another Time* peaks at US #97 but hits US C&W #1.

July *What Made Milwaukee Famous (Has Made A Loser Out Of Me)* stalls at US #94, but is another big country hit (one of more than 30 by Lewis in the next 10 years). LP *Another Place, Another Time* peaks at US #160, during a 12-week stay.

Nov *To Make Love Sweeter For You* hits US C&W #1.

1969 Feb LP *She Still Comes Around (To Love What's Left Of Me)* makes US #149.

May Two Smash LPs, *Jerry Lewis Sings The Country Music Hall Of Fame, Volume 1* and *Volume 2*, reach US #127 and US #124.

Sept Two Sun compilation LPs simultaneously make the US chart. *Original Golden Hits Vol.1* (including the first three singles) reaches #119 and *Vol.2* makes #122.

Sept [13] Lewis takes part in "The Rock'n'Revival Concert" in Toronto, Canada, with fellow rockers Chuck Berry°, Gene Vincent°, Bo Diddley°, Little Richard° and (making its live debut) John Lennon's° Plastic Ono Band.

1970 Feb LP *She Even Woke Me Up To Say Goodbye* spends 2 weeks in US chart, making #186.

May LP *The Best Of Jerry Lee Lewis*, a collection of his country hits, peaks at US #114.

Oct LP *Live At The International, Las Vegas*, his first for main label Mercury, reaches US #149. Myra, Lewis' wife, files for divorce. She will later claim that she only spent 3 nights alone with Lewis in 13 years of marriage. He is shocked into embracing the church and shunning alcohol, cigars and the pursuit of young women. (This abstinence will only last 2 months.)

1971 Jan LP *There Must Be More To Love Than This* makes US #190. The title track tops US country chart.

Apr Lewis' mother dies.

Aug LP *Touching Home* reaches US #152.

Dec LP *Would You Take Another Chance On Me* makes US #115. The title track hits US C&W #1.

Dec [18] Lewis divorces his wife Myra Brown, as he prepares to marry Memphis divorcée, 29-year-old Jaren Elizabeth Gunn Pate.

1972 Jan Lewis' version of Kris Kristofferson's° *Me And Bobby McGee* becomes his biggest pop hit in more than 13 years, climbing to US #40.

Apr Lewis returns to rock'n'roll covering The Big Bopper's° *Chantilly Lace*, which reaches US #43. It also tops US country chart. LP *The "Killer" Rocks On* begins a 12-week US chart run, peaking at #105.

May *Chantilly Lace* makes UK #33 (his first UK hit in 9 years and his last to date).

July *Turn On Your Love Light* stalls at US #95.

1973 Mar LP *The Session* enters US chart and at #37 is his best LP chart result. It is a collection of oldies recorded in London with the help of Peter Frampton°, Rory Gallagher, Albert Lee, Alvin Lee and others.

May Extracted from the LP, *Drinkin' Wine Spo-Dee O'Dee*, a cover of 1949 R&B #2 for Stick McGhee and one of the first songs Lewis ever performed, reaches US #41 (and will be his last US pop hit).

Nov [13] Lewis' 19-year-old son Jerry Lewis Jr., the drummer in his band, is killed in an auto accident in DeSoto county. He has recently been in mental hospitals and suffered from drug abuse.

1976 Sept [29] Lewis accidentally shoots his bass player Norman Owens in the chest, while blasting holes in his own office door. Owens survives but sues his boss.

Nov [22] Lewis drives his Rolls Royce into a ditch and is arrested for drunk driving.

Nov [23] 10 hours later, he is arrested for brandishing a Derringer pistol outside Elvis Presley's° Gracelands home in Memphis, demanding to see the "King".

1977 Lewis hits US C&W #4 with aptly-titled *Middle Age Crazy*.

1978 Lewis signs to Elektra Records. *Rockin' My Life Away* receives some FM radio play but the relationship between artist and company is soon strained and ends in mutual lawsuits.

1979 May Elektra LP *Jerry Lee Lewis* makes US #186.

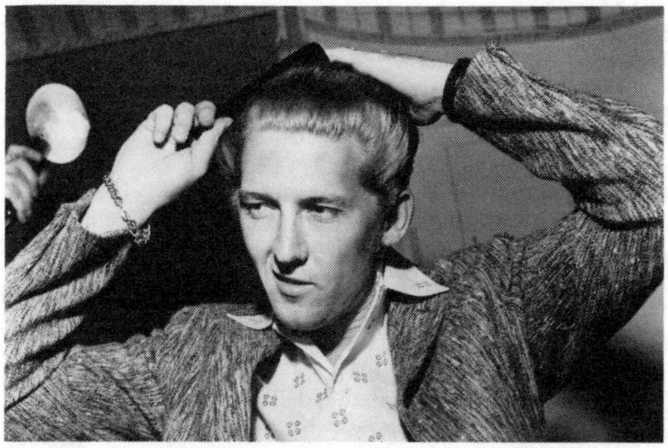

1980 June Lewis is featured on *Roadie* film soundtrack.

1981 Apr [23] A concert for German TV in Stuttgart reunites the three surviving members of Sun's 1956 "Million Dollar Quartet"; Lewis, Carl Perkins° and Johnny Cash°, who this time is not whisked away by his wife to shop. (Recordings from the show will be released in 1982 on CBS LP *The Survivors*.)

June [30] Lewis is hospitalized in Memphis Methodist Hospital with a hemorrhaging stomach ulcer. From his bed, he countersues Elektra Records for $5 million as label dispute ends his contract. (After two serious operations doctors estimate his chances of survival at 50-50. He is back on the road within 4 months and recording for his new label, MCA.) Lewis hits US C&W #4 with *Thirty Nine And Holding*.

1982 Lewis appears on the year's Grammy Awards telecast with cousin Mickey Gilley, as ex-wife Myra's book *Great Balls of Fire* is published.

June [8] Lewis' estranged fourth wife, Jaren, drowns in a swimming pool.

1983 Feb LP *My Fingers Do The Talkin'* makes US C&W #62. (Two singles also make C&W chart later in the year: *Come As You Were* (US #66) and *Why You Been Gone So Long* (US #69).)

June [7] Lewis marries his fifth wife and companion of 2 years, Shawn Michelle Stevens.

Aug [24] Shawn is found dead at Lewis' Mississippi home. An autopsy finds the cause of death to be a methadone overdose and a grand jury finds no reason to suspect foul play, despite widespread media interest.

1984 Feb [16] Lewis surrenders himself to federal authorities in Memphis for arraignment and to plead not guilty to charges of evading federal income taxes for 1975-80.

Apr [24] Lewis marries wife number six, 22-year-old Kerrie McCarver.

Oct After a long battle with the Internal Revenue Service, a Federal Court jury acquits Lewis of tax evasion. A *Rolling Stone* article by Pulitzer Prize winner Richard Ben Cramer points to disturbing circumstantial evidence surrounding Shawn's death – broken glass on the floor, a sack of bloodstained clothes in the room where she died and blood and bruises on her body. Her mother claims Shawn had called her the day before her death and said she was going to leave Lewis after the two had had physical fights. "The Killer" survives the scandal.

1985 Lewis recovers from another spell on the critical list, with two bleeding ulcers. Rhino Records releases LP *Milestones*, a collection of Lewis' work from 1956-77. He begins recording an LP with Gilley.

1986 Feb Lewis is inducted into the Rock'n'Roll Hall of Fame.

June [5] Lewis joins Ray Charles° as Fats Domino's° guests at the Storyville Jazz Hall, New Orleans, La., recording a US HBO TV special "Fats Domino and Friends". Ron Wood plays guitar for Lewis.

Dec [2] Lewis checks into the Betty Ford Clinic to overcome a painkiller addiction.

1987 Jan [28] Jerry Lee Lewis III is born in Memphis, Tenn.

1988 Production begins on filming of Lewis' life in movie *Great Balls of Fire* starring Dennis Quaid, who receives piano lessons from Lewis.

GORDON LIGHTFOOT

1958 Lightfoot (b. Nov.17, 1938, Orillia, Ontario, Canada), having shown musical talent since age 8 and later learned the piano, moves from his hometown on the shore of Lake Simcoe to study orchestration and harmony at Westlake College, Los Angeles, Cal., but becomes homesick after 14 months and returns to Canada. While turning out piano pieces for a living, he starts to take a deep interest in folk and country music.

1960 He begins to play the guitar, inspired by listening to Pete Seeger and Bob Gibson. He teams with Terry Whelan as The Two Tones and has a local hit with Nashville-cut *Remember Me, I'm The One*, on Chateau Records.

1963 Having spent a year working in UK, Lightfoot performs folk-styled material around Toronto clubs with his guitar and, hearing Bob Dylan° for the first time via records, begins to absorb his influence.

1964 Singing at Steel's Tavern in Toronto, he meets Ian & Sylvia Tyson, a leading Canadian folk duo, who decide to record his *For Lovin' Me* and *Early Morning Rain*. (The two songs are passed on for consideration by Peter, Paul & Mary, who also record them and have US hits with both during 1965.) Lightfoot is signed by Albert Grossman, manager of both the Tysons and Peter, Paul & Mary (as well as Bob Dylan°).

1965 He recruits two back-up musicians, Red Shea (guitar) and John Stockfish (bass) for his live gigs, and signs to United Artists Records. (He will record five LPs in 4 years for the label, starting with *Lightfoot*, but none will chart.) Country singer Marty Robbins hits US C&W #1 with his *Ribbon Of Darkness*. Lightfoot receives the first of many Juno awards, the Canadian music industry's Grammy equivalent.

1967 He makes his debut at New York's Town Hall, as his growing popularity takes his touring further afield.

1969 Dec His last LP for UA is *Sunday Concert*, recorded live at Massey Hall, Toronto.

1970 Jan He signs to the Warner Bros. subsidiary label Reprise, working with producer Lenny Waronker.

1971 Feb Lightfoot's singles chart debut *If You Could Read My Mind* hits US #5, while the LP of the same title (originally called *Sit Down Young Stranger* and retitled after the single's success) reaches US #12, selling over a half million copies to earn a gold disk.

July *If You Could Read My Mind* reaches UK #30. Follow-up *Talking In Your Sleep* peaks at US #64, while LP *Summer Side Of Life* makes US #38. United Artists compilation LP *Classic Lightfoot (The Best Of Gordon Lightfoot, Vol.2)* makes US #178.

Sept *Summer Side Of Life* peaks at US #98.

1972 May LP *Don Quixote* reaches US #42 and UK #44.

July *Beautiful*, taken from *Don Quixote*, makes US #58.

Dec LP *Old Dan's Records* makes US #95.

1974 June *Sundown* tops the US chart, going gold with million-plus sales, as does the LP of the same title, which hits US #1 for 2 weeks.

Aug *Sundown* reaches UK #33, while LP of the same title reaches UK #45. In US, United Artists compilation *The Very Best Of Gordon Lightfoot* makes US #155.

Nov *Carefree Highway*, taken from LP *Sundown*, hits US #10.

1975 Apr LP *Cold On The Shoulder* hits US #10.

May Extracted from the LP, *Rainy Day People* reaches US #26.

1976 Jan Double compilation LP *Gord's Gold* (the first component LP which has new re-recordings of songs from his United Artists days) makes US #34, and earns a gold disk. By now, Lightfoot is playing some 70 concerts a year in US and Canada, backed by a stage band consisting of Red Shea and Terry Clements (guitars), Pee Wee Charles (steel guitar) and Rick Haynes (bass). (There is no drummer on live shows, though Jim Gordon plays drums on recording sessions.)

Nov *The Wreck Of The Edmund Fitzgerald*, the true account of the sinking of an ore vessel on Lake Superior in Nov. 1975, hits US #2 for 2 weeks (behind Rod Stewart's° *Tonight's The Night*), and is Lightfoot's second gold single.

Dec LP *Summertime Dream*, which includes *The Wreck Of The Edmund Fitzgerald*, hits US #12 and is a million-seller, earning a platinum disk.

1977 Jan *The Wreck Of The Edmund Fitzgerald* reaches UK #40.

Mar *Race Among The Ruins* makes US #65.

1978 Mar He moves to Warner Bros. for LP *Endless Wire*, which climbs to US #20, earning another gold disk.

Apr *The Circle Is Small (I Can See It In Your Eyes)*, taken from *Endless*

GORDON LIGHTFOOT *cont.*

Wire, reaches US #33.
Oct *Daylight Katy*, not issued as a US single, reaches UK #41.
1980 May LP *Dream Street Rose* reaches US #60.
1982 Mar LP *Shadows* makes US #87.
May *Baby Step Back*, taken from LP *Shadows*, reaches US #50, and is Lightfoot's final US singles chart entry.
1983 Jan Lightfoot presents five songs to Kenny Rogers°. He turns them down, but Lightfoot will re-work them to record on a future LP.
1985 Apr He sings on *Tears Are Not Enough* by Northern Lights, the Canadian multi-artist recording in aid of the USA For Africa° trust, sharing vocals with fellow countrymen like Neil Young°, Joni Mitchell°, Bryan Adams°, Baron Longfellow and many others.
Aug LP *Salute* peaks at US #175.
1986 Sept LP *East Of Midnight*, produced with help from compatriot David Foster, climbs to US #165.
1987 Nov Lightfoot ends his North American tour in Atlantic City, N.J.
1988 Apr Lightfoot and The Lightfoot Band, now comprising Terry Clements, Rick Haynes and recent additions Barry Keane on drums and Mike Heffernan on keyboards, begin re-recording 13 Lightfoot songs at Eastern Sound studios, Toronto, Canada. The songs, plus previously unrecorded *If It Should Please You*, will be released as LP *Gord's Gold Volume II* at the end of the year.

LITTLE EVA

1962 May Eva (b. Eva Boyd, June 29, 1945, Bellhaven, N.C., US) is working in Brooklyn, New York, as babysitter to Louise Goffin, infant daughter of songwriters Gerry Goffin and Carole King°, when her employers suggest she sings on a demo version of their newly-written dance song *The Loco-Motion*, to be submitted to Dee Dee Sharp, a recent US hitmaker with *Mashed Potato Time*.
June Sharp's producer rejects the song, but Eva's demo impresses Goffin and King's° boss, music publisher Don Kirshner, who makes it the first release on his new Dimension label.
Aug *The Loco-Motion* hits US #1 and is a million-seller. It is also #1 on the R&B chart for 3 weeks. The dance itself is invented belatedly for Eva to perform on TV while singing the hit.
Oct *The Loco-Motion* hits UK #2, held from the top by The Tornados'° *Telstar*.
Nov LP *L-L-L-L-Locomotion* peaks at US #97.
Dec *Keep Your Hands Off My Baby* reaches US #12 and UK #30.
1963 Mar *Let's Turkey Trot*, reviving a 1920s dance, reaches US #20.
Apr *Let's Turkey Trot*, coupled in UK with US follow-up *Old Smokey Locomotion*, reaches #13, with the sides sharing equal popularity.
June *Old Smokey Locomotion* peaks at US #48 and is Eva's last hit under her own name.
July She duets with Big Dee Irwin (though uncredited on the label) on his revival of *Swinging On A Star*, which reaches US #37.
1964 Jan *Swinging On A Star* hits UK #6. This is Eva's last chart appearance in the 60s (though she will have a few more singles on Dimension, move to Amy and later Spring Records during the decade).
1972 Sept *The Loco-Motion*, reissued in UK, becomes a hit again at #10. (It will continue to be a perennial steady UK seller, never deleted from catalog, and even appearing in 12" form for disco DJs in the mid-1980s.)
1974 May *The Loco-motion* returns to US #1 in a revival by Grand Funk, produced by Todd Rundgren°. This song is only the second in history to be a US chart-topper in two different versions. (The other, *Go Away Little Girl* is also a Goffin/King° composition.)
1988 Aug *The Loco-Motion* proves popular once more as Australian actress/singer Kylie Minogue takes a new Stock/Aitken/Waterman-produced revival to UK #2, having already chart-topped in Australia with it in 1987. The success focuses interest on Little Eva who reveals that she made virtually no money out of her early hit career and is living on welfare and singing gospel in Kinston, N.C.

LITTLE FEAT

Lowell George (vocals and guitar)
Paul Barrere (lead guitar)
Bill Payne (keyboards)
Fred Tackett (guitar)
Kenny Gradney (bass)
Richie Hayward (drums)
Sam Clayton (percussion)

1970 Mar Guitarist George (b. Apr.13, 1945), ex-Factory, The Standells and The Seeds, having briefly joined Frank Zappa's° Mothers of Invention to replace Ray Collins (his rhythm guitar and vocals preserved on Zappa track *Didja Get Any Onya* from *Weasels Ripped My Flesh*), is encouraged by Zappa to form his own band after Zappa hears George's song *Willing*. George takes Zappa's advice and his bass player, Roy Estrada. The two link up with Payne (b. Mar.12, 1949, Waco, Tex., US) and Hayward, ex-The Fraternity Of Man. (Jimmy Carl Black from The Mothers of Invention supplies the band its moniker when making fun of George's small shoe size.)
May Little Feat signs to Warner Bros. and *Strawberry Flats/Hamburger Midnight* is released to critical acclaim.
1971 Debut eponymous LP, completed for some time, is released. Produced by Russ Titelman, Ry Cooder° and Sneaky Pete Kleinow guest on it.
1972 Second LP *Sailin' Shoes* is released. Estrada leaves to join the Magic Band of Captain Beefheart°.
1973 Third LP *Dixie Chicken* includes Gradney on bass and percussionist Clayton, both ex-Delaney and Bonnie°. Ex-Lead Enema Barrere also joins and the new line-up plays its first gig at the Easter Festival, Hawaii, US. The cycle of touring and destructive personal habits becomes too much and the band breaks up. Payne joins The Doobie Brothers° then leaves them mid-tour to join Bonnie Raitt's band. The rest of the band signs to Zappa's° Discreet label to provide backing for unknown LA singer Kathy Dalton. Freddie White joins from Donny Hathaway's° band on drums. There are rumors that ex-Vinegar Joe singer Robert Palmer° will be asked to replace the increasingly erratic George, who in turn is rumored to be forming a band with John Sebastian and Phil Everly.
1974 Nov Warner Bros. offers the band money to re-form and it re-enters its Blue Seas studio in Hunts Valley, Md., to cut LP *Feats Don't Fail Me Now*. Bonnie Raitt, Emmylou Harris and Van Dyke Parks guest on the LP, which reaches US #36 and is the band's first gold disk.
1975 Jan [12] The group embarks on a 9-city, 18-show European tour under the banner "The Warner Brothers Music Show". The other bands on the tour, The Doobie Brothers°, Tower of Power, Bonaroo, Graham Central Station and Montrose are upstaged by Little Feat who picks up the rave reviews.
Jan As the band records LP *The Last Record Album*, George contracts hepatitis.
Dec LP *The Last Record Album* reaches US and UK #36.
1977 June LP *Time Loves A Hero* is released with George only contributing one song. The LP reaches US #34 and hits UK #8.
1978 Mar Live shows around double LP *Waiting For Columbus* are considered lackluster, but it reaches US #18 and UK #43, becoming the band's second gold disk.
1979 Apr As George mixes Little Feat's LP, Payne and Barrere tour with Nicolette Larson. It is well-received, Warners signs the backing band and Payne announces Little Feat is disbanded. George sets out on a tour with his solo LP *Thanks, I'll Eat It Here*, which reaches US and UK #71.
June [29] 2 months after Little Feat's break up and the day after a sell-out solo performance in Washington, George, aged 34, is found dead from a heart attack brought on by drug abuse in a motel in Arlington, Va.
Aug [4] The surviving members of Little Feat are joined by Jackson Browne°, Emmylou Harris, Nicolette Larson, Michael McDonald°, Bonnie Raitt and Linda Ronstadt° in a benefit concert at LA's Forum. The 20,000 crowd raises over $230,00 for George's widow.
Dec Little Feat LP *Down On the Farm* (originally titled *Duck Lips*) reaches US #29 and UK #46.
1981 Aug Compilation LP *Hoy-Hoy!* reaches UK #76.
Sept LP *Hoy-Hoy!* reaches US #39.
1988 Apr The original line-up with Craig Fuller assuming George's position re-signs with Warner Bros., and the group records a new LP.
Aug LP *Let It Roll* is released, but meets with scant interest.

LITTLE RICHARD

1950 Little Richard (b. Richard Wayne Penniman, Dec.5, 1935, Macon, Ga., US) having grown up with 11 brothers and sisters, the children of Charles and Leva Mae, and the Seventh Day Adventist faith (his father and grandfather are preachers), and sung in church, with the family Penniman Singers, developing strong gospel links, as The Tiny Tots Quartet, after running off with Dr. Hudson's Medicine Show, selling snake oil at fairs and carnivals, he then sings with Sugarfoot Sam's Minstrel Show. Adopted by the white family of Ann and Johnny Johnson, who run Macon's Tick Tock Club, he begins performing R&B numbers. He also picks up a job washing dishes in a bus station and sings with the B. Brown Orchestra.

1951 Oct [16] Richard makes his first recordings in Atlanta, Ga., for RCA, arranged after singer Billy Wright has introduced him to a Georgia DJ with RCA connections, who had entered him in a radio audition contest at Atlanta's Eighty One Theater. Wright, with his heavy make-up and gelled hair, is to be a major visual influence on Richard. (Tracks from this session and another in Jan. 1952, including *Every Hour* and *Get Rich Quick*, are released in 1952 on four US singles and on LP in US and UK in 1959 and 1970.)

1953 Richard moves to Houston to record eight tracks for Don Robey's Peacock label, initially credited to the sessions vocal group, The Tempo-Toppers, but after 1955 the billing is changed to feature Little Richard.

1954 Richard meets Lloyd Price°, who suggests sending blues demos recorded at Macon radio station W-BML, to Art Rupe at Specialty Records in LA.

1955 Feb Richard auditions for Specialty. Tracks recorded include the a cappella gospel piece *He's My Star* and piano boogie *Chicken Shack Baby*. He fronts the Johnny Otis° Orchestra for two singles and tours small black nightclubs, where he mainly sings the blues.

Sept [14] Specialty contacts Richard, while he is working in Fayetteville, Tenn., and he enters the studio for a 48-hour session in New Orleans with the Crescent City rhythm section (who feature on many of Fats Domino's° disks) and producer Robert "Bumps" Blackwell, who is also Richard's manager. Richard plays piano and sings. After recording blues numbers *Kansas City* and *Directly From My Heart*, he records a version of a live number he has written – *Tutti Frutti*. (The lyrics are cleaned up by local songwriter Dorothy La Bostrie.) The histrionic vocal and bashing piano style sets the mold for Little Richard's image as Blackwell insists on a live feel to studio recordings. Richard signs to Specialty (the deal gives him half a cent for every record sold).

1956 Feb *Tutti Frutti*, its publishing rights sold to Specialty for $50, reaches US #17. It stays on chart for 12 weeks but will sell over 3 million copies.

Mar Richard enters the recording studio again. (He will record six more sessions between now and Feb. 1957, using a band based around Earl Palmer (drums), Red Tyler and Lee Allen (saxes), Frank Fields (bass), Ernest McLean and Justin Adams (guitars); and supplementary pianists Huey Smith, Edward Frank, Little Booker and Salvador Doucette.) Pat Boone's° version of *Tutti Frutti* reaches US #12.

May *Long Tall Sally* makes US #13. Originally titled *The Thing*, then *Bald Headed Sally*, the song was sanitized for Boone° to record his own version (US #8).

June B-side *Slippin' And Slidin'*, based on the ribald New Orleans blues number *I Got The Blues For You*, reaches US #33.

Aug *Rip It Up* reaches US #17. B-side *Ready Teddy* peaks at US #44.

Dec *Rip It Up*, released on London label, makes UK #30 (his UK chart debut).

1957 Feb Richard heads for LA with his own band, the Upsetters, beginning an intensive schedule of touring and film work (including movie *Mr. Rock'n'Roll*).

Mar *The Girl Can't Help It*, from Jayne Mansfield-starring film of the same name, peaks at US #49. (Richard appears in the film, and also appeared in Bill Haley° movie *Don't Knock The Rock* the previous year.) *Long Tall Sally* hits UK #3 during a 16-week stay. B-side *Tutti Frutti* spends a week at UK #29.

Apr *Lucille*, penned by Richard, peaks at US #27. B-side *Send Me Some Lovin'* climbs to US #54. *She's Got It* reaches UK #15.

May *The Girl Can't Help It* hits UK #9, as its A-side *She's Got It* re-enters UK chart for 2 weeks, reaching #28.

July *Jenny, Jenny* makes US #14, while B-side *Miss Ann* peaks at US #56.

Aug *Lucille* hits UK #10. Richard's only US chart LP in the 50s, *Here's Little Richard*, enters the chart to peak at #13 during a 5-week run. (He will never have a UK chart LP.)

Sept *Jenny, Jenny* reaches UK #11.

Oct *Keep A Knockin'*, from film *Mr. Rock'n'Roll*, hits US #8.

Oct [12] After a year of whirlwind success, Little Richard, on the fifth date of a 2-week Australian tour in Sydney, publicly renounces rock'n'roll and embraces God. (He will later tell the story of dreaming of his own damnation, and praying to God after one of the engines in a plane he is in catches fire.)

Oct [13] On his return to US, Specialty arranges a final eight-song session before he enters theological college. Specialty tries to keep his conversion quiet. (Label artist Joe Lutcher has been warning Richard for some time that pop music is "evil". Richard and Lutcher will tour US as the "Little Richard Evangelistic Team".)

Dec *Keep A Knockin'* reaches UK #21.

1958 Jan [27] Richard enters Oakwood theological college in Huntsville, Ala., (where he will receive a BA and become ordained as a Seventh Day Adventist minister).

Mar *Good Golly, Miss Molly*, from the final Specialty session, hits US #10 and UK #8. (B-side *Hey Hey Hey Hey* will be revived in 1964 by The Beatles° on LP *Beatles For Sale*, in a medley with *Kansas City* which fails to credit Richard's song. Several years later, after strong approaches by the song's publisher, it is fully credited on the LP and back royalties are paid by EMI.)

June *Ooh! My Soul* makes US #35.

July B-side *True Fine Mama* climbs to US #68.

Aug *Ooh! My Soul* reaches UK #22.

Oct Richard's version of *Baby Face*, written in 1926, peaks at US #41.

1959 Jan *Baby Face* hits UK #2, behind Elvis Presley's° *I Got Stung/One Night*.

Apr Richard's version of *By The Light Of The Silvery Moon* reaches UK #17.

May *Kansas City*, his last US chart hit for 5 years, reaches US #95, eclipsed by Wilbert Harrison's° #1 version of it.

June *Kansas City* makes UK #26. During the summer Richard returns to the studio to record gospel tracks for Gone/End Records. (The basic vocal/piano/organ tracks are overdubbed with a choir and have extra instrumentation added when they are re-released on Coral and Guest Star labels in the 1960s.)

1960/62 Having sold an estimated 18 million singles during the 1950s, Richard records 20 gospel songs with Quincy Jones producing, for release on LPs on Mercury label. Seven more gospel tracks, including *Crying In The Chapel*, are cut for Atlantic, with Jerry Wexler producing.

1962 Late in the year, the Rev. Little Richard returns to rock'n'roll with a UK comeback tour promoted by Don Arden. Paul McCartney° asks Richard to teach him his singing style. Brian Epstein books Richard into the Cavern, Liverpool, and he headlines a concert with The Swinging Blue Jeans°, Cilla Black° and Gerry & The Pacemakers°.

Oct On Mercury, *He Got What He Wanted* makes UK #38.

1963 Richard tours Europe with The Beatles° (with whom firm mutually respecting relationships have been formed), The Rolling Stones° and others. He later notes that the young groups know his records better than he does.

Oct [5] Little Richard joins The Everly Brothers'° UK tour, ostensibly to boost poor ticket sales.

1964 Mar He records the first of seven sessions for Vee Jay label. Early tapings produce versions of *Whole Lotta Shakin' Goin' On* and *Good Lawdy Miss Clawdy*.

June On his second UK tour, *Bama Lama Bama Loo* reaches UK #20, his last UK hit for 13 years.

Aug *Bama Lama Bama Loo* peaks at US #82.

Dec Richard re-records his greatest hits for Vee Jay. (In UK, various combinations of the tracks appear on Stateside, Fontana, Sue, President and Joy labels over the next 4 years.)

1965 Vee Jay issues LPs *Little Richard Is Back* and *Little Richard's Greatest Hits*, released in UK on Fontana.

Nov *I Don't Know What You've Got But It's Got Me* is the only Vee Jay single to chart, spending a week at US #92.

Dec Richard records seven studio tracks for Modern Records, including *Holy Mackerel*, *Don't You Want A Man Like Me* and *Baby What You Want Me To Do*.

1966 Jan He records Modern label LP *Little Richard Sings His Greatest Hits – Recorded Live*. Songs from it are combined with studio tracks

LITTLE RICHARD *cont.*

and released, with overdubbed applause, in UK on Polydor and Contour labels. Richard begins recording five sessions for soul label Okeh.

1967 As a rock'n'roll revival in Europe gains momentum, Richard revisits for successful tours. He becomes increasingly involved in drug abuse (which will dog his career into the 1970s).

Aug Another live compilation, *Little Richard's Greatest Hits*, on Okeh, peaks at US #184, and is his first chart LP in 10 years.

1968 Richard records six tracks for Brunswick, which are released as US singles. The first two, *Try Some Of Mine* and *She's Together* (produced by Don Covay) are also issued by MCA in UK.

1969 Sept [13] Little Richard takes part in the "Rock'n'Revival Concert" in Toronto, Canada, with Jerry Lee Lewis°, Gene Vincent°, Bo Diddley° and John Lennon's° newly-formed Plastic Ono Band.

Sept Now living in Riverside, Cal. he signs to Warner/Reprise Records.

1970 July *Freedom Blues*, recorded for Reprise at Muscle Shoals, makes US #47.

July [18] Richard takes part in the Randall Island Rock Festival with Jimi Hendrix°, Jethro Tull°, Grand Funk Railroad°, Steppenwolf and others.

Sept *Greenwood Mississippi* stalls at US #85. He appears at the Toronto Pop Festival, documented in D.A. Pennebaker's film *Keep On Rockin'*.

1971 Nov LP *The King Of Rock'n'Roll* makes US #184.

1972 Apr Richard sings on Canned Heat's° *Rockin' With The King*, which makes US #88. He contributes two tracks to the soundtrack of Warren Beatty/Goldie Hawn-starring movie $ (UK title: *The Heist*) and reunites with Blackwell, Earl Palmer and Lee Allen to record LP *The Second Coming*.

Aug [5] Little Richard takes part in an ill-conceived "Rock'n'Revival" concert in London.

1973 After leaving Reprise (and an unissued country LP *Southern Child*), he records for ALA with Blackwell (his last work with the producer).

June [20] Richard rises from his sickbed to make an appearance on Dick Clark's retrospective 20th anniversary "Bandstand" show on US ABC-TV.

1975 He records a one-off single, *Call My Name*, for Emerson, Lake & Palmer's° Manticore label.

1976 He re-records 20 of his greatest hits in London for SJ Records. After the death of his brother Tony, Richard is reborn to Christianity for the second time and works temporarily for Memorial Bibles International.

1977 July Creole's release of SJ recordings of *Good Golly Miss Molly/Rip It Up* makes UK #37.

1979 Richard becomes a fully-fledged evangelist, preaching the story of his salvation throughout US, but based mainly in LA. (He will relate the experience of his redemption in lengthy *Little Richard's Testimony*, included on his gospel LP *God's Beautiful City*.)

1985 Charles White publishes book *The Life and Times of Little Richard*.

1986 Feb Little Richard is inducted into the Rock'n'Roll Hall of Fame.

Apr From forthcoming movie, *Great Gosh A'Mighty (It's A Matter Of Time)* makes US #42.

June He appears in Richard Dreyfuss/Bette Midler°-starring movie *Down and Out in Beverly Hills*. From the movie, *Great Gosh A'Mighty (It's A Matter Of Time)* reaches UK #62.

Oct He signs to WEA Records, which releases LP *Lifetime Friend*. Extracted *Operator* makes UK #67. Vigorous media promotion mixes gospel attitude with legendary Little Richard style.

Dec He teams with The Beach Boys° for *Happy Endings* from film *The Telephone*.

1988 Sept He contributes *Rock Island Line* to the Leadbelly/Woody Guthrie tribute LP *Folkways: A Vision Shared*.

Nov Now seen as a media evangelist, Richard duets with Phillip Bailey on the title track for Arnold Schwarzenegger/Danny DeVito film *Twins* on new CBS subsidiary WTG Records.

THE LITTLE RIVER BAND

Glenn Shorrock (vocals)
David Briggs (guitar)
Beeb Birtles (guitar)
Graham Goble (guitar)
George McArdle (bass)
Derek Pellicci (drums)

1974 When London-based Australian band Mississippi breaks up after 2 years, three of its members Goble (b. May 15, 1947, Adelaide, South Australia), Birtles (b. Gerard Birtlekamp, Nov.28, 1948, Amsterdam, Netherlands) and Pellici meet Shorrock (b. June 30, 1944, Rochester, Kent, UK, raised in Elizabeth, Australia), late of Esperanto, and fellow Australian Glenn Wheatley, working in management in London. The five decide to meet in Australia in the New Year.

1975 Mar Back in Australia, they re-form as Mississippi, with Wheatley as manager. Criticized for having an American name, they become The Little River Band, chosen at random from a small community 30 miles outside Melbourne.

May Adding guitarist Rick Formosa and bassist Roger McLachlan, they cut debut LP *Little River Band*. (Released in Australia, it will be voted Album of the Year.)

1976 Apr They sign to EMI's Harvest label, which releases LP *Little River Band* worldwide. The group begins a tour of Europe, Canada and US, without Formosa and McLachlan, who have left to be replaced by Briggs (b. Jan.26, 1951, Melbourne, Australia) and McArdle (b. Nov.30, 1954, Melbourne).

Dec *It's A Long Way There* is the group's first US hit single, reaching #28. LP *Little River Band* makes US #80.

1977 Mar *I'll Always Call Your Name* makes US #62. LP *Diamantina Cocktail*, a compilation of two previous Australian LPs (*After Hours* and *Diamantina Cocktail*), reaches US #49, and is the first US gold LP by an Australian group.

Nov *Help Is On Its Way*, taken from *Diamantina Cocktail* and produced by American John Boylan, reaches US #14.

1978 Mar *Happy Anniversary* makes US #16.

Oct *Reminiscing* hits US #3, earning a gold disk, while LP *Sleeper Catcher* reaches US #16 (and will earn a platinum disk). The band returns home from its second world tour, to find it has swept the first Australian Rock Awards, and Wheatley has been named Manager of the Year.

1979 Jan The group tours US again. After it, McArdle leaves, giving away all his money and retreating to the Blue Mountains to undertake a 3-year Bible study course. He is replaced on bass by Barry Sullivan, and New Zealander Mal Logan joins on keyboards.

Apr *Lady* hits US #10.

Sept *Lonesome Loser*, marking a change of label from Harvest to Capitol, hits US #6.

Oct LP *First Under The Wire*, on Capitol and including *Lonesome Loser*, hits US #10, and also achieves platinum status.

1980 Jan *Cool Change*, taken from *First Under The Wire*, hits US #10.

Apr Briggs is replaced by Chicago-born Wayne Nelson, and guitarist Stephen Housden also joins.

May *It's Not A Wonder* peaks at US #51.

June Double live LP *Backstage Pass* makes US #44.

1981 Nov *The Night Owls* hits US #6. It is taken from LP *Time Exposure*, produced by George Martin, which reaches US #21 and earns a gold disk.

1982 Mar *Take It Easy On Me*, also from *Time Exposure*, hits US #10.

May Third extract *Man On Your Mind* reaches US #14.

1983 Feb *The Other Guy* reaches US #11, while compilation LP *Little River Band/Greatest Hits* makes US #33.

June *We Two* makes US #22. Shorrock leaves to go solo, to be replaced by John Farnham, from Adelaide, Aus.

Aug LP *The Net*, which includes *We Two*, makes US #61.

Sept *You're Driving Me Out Of My Mind*, also taken from *The Net*, reaches US #35.

Oct Shorrock's solo single *Don't Girls Get Lonely* reaches US #69, but his solo LP fails to chart.

1985 Mar After more personnel changes, Goble is left as the only original member and the band's credit changes to LRB on LP *Playing To Win*, which reaches US #75. The title track makes US #60.

1987 Farnham leaves to go solo (and will have a major international hit with *You're The Voice*, which tops the Australian chart and hits UK #6).

1988 After a 2-year recording hiatus, Little River Band signs to MCA, its renewed activity due in large part to Shorrock reuniting with the band. The new line-up appears on a TV concert from the World Expo in Brisbane, Australia.

Apr The band plays a concert in Melbourne to launch new LP *Monsoon* and single *Love Is A Bridge*.

Aug Glenn Frey joins the band on stage at the Sydney Entertainment Centre, Australia. The reunited LRB joins Frey on The Eagles° hits *Desperado*, *Lyin' Eyes* and *Take It Easy* as well as their own hits *Cool Change* and *Night Owls*.

LOS LOBOS

Cesar Rosas (guitar and vocals)
David Hidalgo (guitar, accordian and vocals)
Conrad Lozano (bass)
Steve Berlin (sax)
Luis Perez (drums)

1974/77 Rosas, Hidalgo, Lozano and Perez, all Spanish-Americans living in LA's Chicano community and refugees from top forty cover bands, decide to form an acoustic group to rediscover and revitalize traditional Chicano folk music. They name the quartet Los Lobos (The Wolves) and spend 2 years researching and rehearsing before performing at Chicano weddings, bars and benefits in the LA area. An immediate success with the older generation of Chicanos, Los Lobos are also popluar among members of their own generation anxious to retain elements of Mexican culture.

1978 The group records (and finances) its debut LP *Just Another Band From L.A.*.

1980 Los Lobos supports Public Image Ltd° at a concert in LA. Its acoustic set receives a hostile reception from the hardcore punk audience, but the band comes to the attention of the local Anglo-American music industry. Los Lobos begins to integrate an electric sound into the previously acoustic-only Spanish and American tunes.

1983 Signing to LA independent label Slash, Los Lobos records EP *And A Time To Dance*. (It will receive a Grammy award the following year.)

1984 Saxophonist Berlin, ex-LA band The Blasters, joins the line-up.

Dec LP *How Will The Wolf Survive?* enters the US chart and will climb to #47.

1985 Mar *Will The Wolf Survive?* reaches US #78.

Apr Released in UK via London Records, double A-side *Don't Worry Baby/Will The Wolf Survive?* makes UK #57. LP *How Will The Wolf Survive?* climbs to UK #77.

1986 Los Lobos receives increasing media attention in US and UK, cited as a leading roots band. The group excels on live stage and develops substantial mainstream followings, but the year passes without any US or UK chart entries.

1987 Mar LP *By The Light Of The Moon* makes US #47 and UK #77. The band contributes eight tracks to the soundtrack (and subsequent LP) of movie *La Bamba*, based on the life of 1950s Chicano pop star Ritchie Valens°. It includes versions of Valens' compositions *Come On Let's Go*, *Ooh! My Head*, *Donna* and his 1959 hit *La Bamba* (a traditional Mexican song).

Aug Los Lobos' version of *La Bamba* hits US and UK #1 for 2 weeks, becoming the first all-Spanish sung record to do so. Valens'° original version charts briefly at UK #49.

Sept Soundtrack LP *La Bamba* hits US #1 and reaches UK #24.

Oct *C'mon On, Let's Go* makes UK #18.

Nov *C'mon On, Let's Go* reaches US #21.

1988 Oct LP *La Pistola Y El Corazon* is released, containing traditional Chicano songs, it avoids deliberate commercial exploitation of *La Bamba* success.

NILS LOFGREN

1969 Lofgren (b. June 21, 1951, Chicago, Ill., US), of Italian and Swedish parents, having been a classical music student for 10 years, and played in Beatles°/Kinks°-influenced high school bands like The Waifs and The Grass, in Maryland, D.C., before running away from home (or, more specifically, from school) with $100 in his pocket and sleeping for 2 weeks in doorways in Greenwich Village, New York, after returning home, forms the band Paul Dowell & The Dolphin, which successfully auditions for Sire Records and releases two singles, but splits after both fail and the group is beset by management and contract problems. New group Grin is formed, with Lofgren on vocals, keyboards and guitar, Bob Berberich (b. 1949, Md., US), ex-Reekers, on drums, and Bob Gordon (b. 1951, Ok., US), ex-Paul Dowell & The Dolphin, on bass.

1970 Feb Having seen him playing with Grin at the Cellar Door club in Washington in 1969, Neil Young° invites Lofgren to play piano (and some uncredited guitar) on his LP *After The Goldrush*. He plays frequently with Young and his band Crazy Horse after the LP, but does not join the group full-time, being keen to make a success of Grin.

1971 Feb He plays on and writes songs for the eponymous debut LP by Crazy Horse.

Aug Grin signs to Spindizzy/Columbia, and debut LP *Grin* reaches US #192. The group tours supporting Edgar Winter°.

1972 Feb Second Grin LP *1+1* peaks at US #180, and extracted *White Lies* is Grin's only US hit single, reaching #75.

1973 Mar Lofgren's younger brother Tom is recruited on second guitar for Grin's third LP *All Out*, which makes US #186.

Nov Signing a new deal with A&M, the band records LP *Gone Crazy*, which does not chart. Disillusioned, Grin splits, and after playing briefly with The Dubonettes and producing their debut A&M LP (released under a new name, Charlie & The Pep Boys), Lofgren accepts another invitation to join Crazy Horse for Neil Young's° "Tonight's The Night" tour.

1974 Mar He leaves Crazy Horse to go solo again, and the press speculates that The Rolling Stones° will recruit Lofgren as lead guitarist in place of departed Mick Taylor.

1975 Apr He re-signs to A&M as a soloist, and LP *Nils Lofgren*, including a homage to Keith Richards in *Keith Don't Go (Ode To The Glimmer Twin)*, reaches US #141. He follows it by extensive touring (including a UK visit), with a band including Tom Lofgren (guitar), Scotty Ball (bass) and Mike Zack (drums).

1976 Jan The "official bootleg" LP *Back It Up*, a recording of a live show broadcast on radio station K-SAN in San Francisco, is acclaimed by the press, despite limited availability.

Mar He begins a US club and concert tour to introduce a new studio LP.

May LP *Cry Tough*, part produced by Al Kooper, and part by David Briggs, reaches US #32 and hits UK #8. It includes a revival of The Yardbirds'° *For Your Love*.

1977 Apr LP *I Came To Dance* climbs to US #36 and UK #30. On it, Wornell Jones and Andy Newmark are his new bass player and drummer, while Newmark also co-produces with Lofgren. Patrick Henderson joins the live band on keyboards.

Nov Double live LP *Night After Night*, recorded on tour earlier in the year, reaches US #44 and UK #38.

1979 Aug LP *Nils* features three songs with lyrics by Lou Reed°, and also Randy Newman's° *Baltimore*; it fails to chart in UK, but makes US #54.

Aug [19] Along with The Stranglers° and AC/DC°, he supports The Who° in a concert at Wembley, UK.

1981 Oct He signs to new MCA-distributed Backstreet label for LP *Night Fades Away*, which makes US #99 and UK #50.

1982 May Compilation LP *A Rhythm Romance* (on A&M) reaches UK #100.

1983 Feb He tours again with Neil Young° and plays on Young's controversial synthesizer-based LP *Trans*.

Aug LP *Wonderland* is released and sells poorly, after which Lofgren loses his MCA/Backstreet recording contract.

1984 He joins Bruce Springsteen's° E Street Band as guitarist, replacing Steve Van Zandt, and tours with Springsteen (whom he first met during a Fillmore East audition night in 1972) into 1985.

1985 June Lofgren is signed as a soloist by UK independent label Towerbell and LP *Flip*, recorded at Philadelphia's Warehouse studios with producer Lance Quinn, reaches UK #36. Taken from it, *Secrets In The Street* is his only UK solo hit single at UK #53.

1986 Apr Following the release of his third live set, double LP *Code Of The Road* (which makes UK #86), Towerbell label hits financial problems and folds, and Lofgren puts his solo career on ice in favor of a supporting role to Springsteen°.

1987 Nov He appears on only two tracks of Springsteen's LP *Tunnel Of Love* (but remains a full stage member of The E Street Band and plays on early 1988 "Tunnel of Love Express" US and European tour).

1988 Sept He plays the "Human Rights Now!" Amnesty International tour with Springsteen.

KENNY LOGGINS & JIM MESSINA

1963/67 Messina (b. Dec.5, 1947, Maywood, Cal., US) forms a high school surf instrumental group, Jim Messina & The Jesters, which becomes popular on the California "Battle of the Bands" circuit, and records two LPs, *Jim Messina And The Jesters* for Thimble Records and hot rod-oriented *The Dragsters* for Audio Fidelity. *Drag Bike Pookie* is a hit in parts of Cal. only. When the surf craze evaporates, Messina moves to studio work in LA, as a guitarist and as an engineer and producer.

1967 Sept From being the group's studio engineer, Messina joins Buffalo Springfield° on bass, in place of Bruce Palmer.

1968 Loggins (b. Jan.7, 1948, Everett, Wash., US), having moved to Cal. with his family as a child, and majored in Music at Pasadena City College, Cal., leaves to join studio group Gator Creek, which records unsuccessfully for Mercury, and then joins (equally unsuccessful) Second Helping.

Aug Messina and fellow ex-Buffalo Springfield° member Richie Furay form Poco°, with George Grantham, Rusty Young, and Randy Meisner. Messina assembles LP *Last Time Around* from latter-day studio tapes after Buffalo Springfield has split.

1969 After joining (for one tour) ex-hitmakers The Electric Prunes°, Loggins becomes a full-time songwriter (on $100 a week) at Wingate Music, a division of ABC Records.

1970 Nov Messina leaves Poco° to concentrate on production work at Columbia Records.

1971 June Loggins' first hit composition is *House At Pooh Corner* for The Nitty Gritty Dirt Band, which reaches US #53. It is one of four Loggins songs cut by the band on its LP *Uncle Charlie And His Dog Teddy*.

Sept At the instigation of friend and A&R man Don Ellis, Loggins signs to CBS/Columbia as a soloist. He meets Messina, now a staff producer, who works with him to prepare a debut solo LP. Their collaboration is such that LP *Kenny Loggins With Jim Messina Sittin' In* is released as a joint effort and they decide to continue to work together, making a live debut at the Troubadour billed as The Kenny Loggins Band with Jim Messina.

1972 May The debut LP reaches US #70 (and in a 113-week chart stay will earn a gold disk), while extracted *Vahevala* makes US #84.

June *Nobody But You*, written by Messina, stalls at US #86. Both this and the previous single are credited to Kenny Loggins with Jim Messina.

1973 Jan *Your Mama Don't Dance* hits US #4 and is a million-seller, earning the duo's only gold single. (The song will be covered by Elvis Presley°, among others.) It is included on LP *Loggins And Messina* (also produced by Messina), which reaches US #16, and also earns a gold disk.

Apr Anne Murray's version of *Danny's Song* (written by Loggins for his brother Dan's son) hits US #7.

May *Thinking Of You* reaches US #18 and is credited to Loggins & Messina, which is how the credit will remain on subsequent duo releases.

Dec LP *Full Sail* hits US #10, while *My Music*, taken from it, climbs to US #16.

1974 Mar *Watching The River Run*, a joint composition, peaks at #71.

July Double live LP *On Stage* hits US #5, and is another gold disk.

Dec LP *Mother Lode* hits US #8 and earns another gold disk.

1975 Feb *Changes*, taken from *Mother Lode*, makes US #84.

May *Growin'* reaches US #52.

Sept A revival of Chris Kenner/Dave Clark Five° hit *I Like It Like That* peaks at US #84. It is extracted from LP *So Fine*, a nostalgic set of R&B oldies from the 1950s and early 1960s, which reaches US #21.

Oct Also from the oldies LP, a revival of Clyde McPhatter's *A Lover's Question* reaches US #89, and is the final Loggins & Messina hit single.

1976 Jan Loggins turns down an offer to co-star with Barbra Streisand in film *A Star is Born*. Shortly after, he cuts his hand with a craft knife while practicising his wood-carving hobby at home – a serious injury which requires surgery.

Mar LP *Native Sons* makes US #16 and earns a gold disk. A lengthy tour begins, with a new back-up band. Loggins has a cast on his injured hand and is unable to play guitar.

Nov The duo splits following a final concert in Hawaii (both are, in any case, signed individually to Columbia, the hitmaking liaison having always been on an unformalized basis). Loggins marries Eve Ein, a long-time friend of Messina's wife Jenny.

1977 Jan LP *The Best Of Friends*, a compilation of their hit singles, reaches US #61.

July LP *Celebrate Me Home*, Loggins' first solo, reaches US #27. (In a 33-week chart stay, it will sell over a million to earn a platinum disk.) He tours US for the first time as a soloist, backed by a new band (Mike Hamilton on guitar, Brian Mann on keyboards, Vince Denham on saxes, Jon Clarke on woodwinds, George Hawkins on bass and Tris Imboden on drums), supporting Fleetwood Mac°.

Sept Loggins' first solo hit single is *I Believe In Love*, which peaks at US #66.

1978 Jan A second double live LP by Loggins & Messina, *Finale*, assembled after the duo's break-up, makes US #83.

Sept LP *Nightwatch*, produced by jazzman Bob James, hits US #7 and is Loggins' second consecutive platinum LP. It includes a revival of Billy Joe Royal's 1965 hit *Down In The Boondocks*, and also Loggins/Michael McDonald°-penned *What A Fool Believes* (which will be a US #1 hit for McDonald's band The Doobie Brothers° in 1979).

Oct From the LP, *Whenever I Call You Friend*, with Stevie Nicks of Fleetwood Mac° guest-duetting (and co-written by Loggins with singer Melissa Manchester), hits US #5.

1979 Jan *Easy Driver* makes US #60.

Nov Messina's solo LP *Oasis* reaches US #58.

1980 Feb Loggins' LP *Keep The Fire*, with new producer Tom Dowd, makes US #16, earning a gold disk. It includes songs co-written with Michael McDonald°, Stephen Bishop, and Loggins' wife Eve, and has guest appearances by McDonald and Michael Jackson°.

Oct *I'm Alright*, the theme from movie *Caddyshack*, hits US #7. Loggins also performs half the film's soundtrack LP, which makes US #78.

Nov Double live LP *Kenny Loggins: Alive* makes US #11 and is a further gold disk winner.

1981 July Messina moves to Warner Bros. for his second solo hit LP *Messina*, which peaks at US #95.

1982 Oct Loggins' LP *High Adventure* reaches US #13, and earns a gold disk, while *Don't Fight It*, a duet with Steve Perry from Journey°, makes US #17.

1983 Jan *Heart To Heart* climbs to US #15.

May *Welcome To Heartlight*, a song inspired by writings of children from Heartlight school, makes US #24.

1984 Mar *Footloose*, the Loggins/Dean Pitchford-penned theme from the film of the same title, tops the US chart for 3 weeks, and is a million-seller. (The song has been written in a hotel room in Lake Tahoe, Nev., where Loggins has been performing – despite broken ribs still mending after a fall off stage at a concert in Provo, Utah.)

Apr Soundtrack LP *Footloose*, which Loggins shares with Deniece Williams°, Bonnie Tyler° and others, tops the US chart for 10 weeks and is a million-seller.

May *Footloose* hits UK #6, Loggins' first UK chart success. The film soundtrack LP hits UK #7.

July Also taken from the movie, *I'm Free (Heaven Helps The Man)* reaches US #22.

1985 Jan [28] Loggins contributes to the recording of USA For Africa's° *We Are The World*, which will be a US and UK chart-topper, and a multi-million seller.

May LP *Vox Humana* reaches US #41, while the title track makes US #29.

July *Forever* peaks at US #40.

Oct *I'll Be There* stalls at US #88.

1986 July *Danger Zone*, theme from the Tom Cruise movie *Top Gun*, hits US #2.

Sept *Playing With The Boys*, also taken from *Top Gun*, makes US #60. The soundtrack LP tops the US chart for 2 weeks.

Nov Soundtrack LP *Top Gun* hits UK #4.

Dec *Danger Zone* reaches UK #45.

1988 Sept LP *Back To Avalon* peaks at US #69, while extracted *Nobody's Fool* (the theme from film *Caddyshack 2*) hits US #8.

LOVE

Arthur Lee (guitar, vocals)
Bryan MacLean (guitar, vocals)
John Echols (lead guitar)
Ken Forssi (bass)
Alban "Snoopy" Pfisterer (drums, keyboards)

1965 The group, originally formed in Los Angeles, Cal., as The Grass Roots, comprising Lee (b. 1945, Memphis, Tenn., US), ex-Byrds°

roadie MacLean (b. 1947, Los Angeles), Echols (b. 1945, Memphis), Johnny Fleckenstein and Don Conka, changes name to Love (Grass Roots° being taken up by another LA band, who become major US hitmakers), and original members Conka and Fleckenstein are replaced by Forssi (b. 1943, Cleveland, Oh.) and Pfisterer (b. 1947, Switzerland).

Apr Love makes its live debut in LA and builds a strong reputation playing clubs on Sunset Strip.

1966 Having established itself with the West Coast underground, Love takes up a residency at Bido Lito's club in Hollywood. It becomes the first rock group to sign to Elektra Records.

May Debut LP *Love* climbs to US #57.

June *My Little Red Book*, a Bacharach/David song originally cut by Manfred Mann° for film *What's New Pussycat?*, reaches US #52.

Sept *7 And 7 Is* peaks at US #33.

1967 Mar LP *Da Capo*, recorded with the addition of Tjay Cantrelli on flute and sax and Michael Stuart on drums, makes US #80. Pfisterer and Cantrelli depart, leaving the band with Lee, Forssi, MacLean, Echols and Stuart.

Nov LP *Forever Changes* is regarded as the group's (and Lee's) masterwork. It makes UK #24 but only US #152.

1968 Jan *Alone Again Or*, taken from the LP, reaches only US #99.

Aug Lee emerges with a restructured band, bringing in Frank Fayad on bass, George Suranovich on drums and Jay Donnellan on lead guitar.

1969 Sept LP *Four Sail*, the band's last for Elektra, makes US #102.

Dec Love moves to Blue Thumb Records and uses material remaining from *Four Sail* sessions for double LP *Out Here* which reaches US #176. Suranovich is fired and replaced by Drachen Theaker, ex-Crazy World of Arthur Brown, who leaves shortly thereafter.

1970 May *Out Here* climbs to UK #29.

Sept Compilation LP *Love Revisited* on Elektra, containing tracks mostly from the first three LPs, peaks at US #142.

Dec Lee re-forms the band again, with Fayad, Suranovich, Gary Rowles and Nooney Rickett on guitars, for LP *False Start*. Jimi Hendrix° guests on one track. Soon after the LP's release, Lee dismisses the rest of the band.

1972 Aug Lee releases solo LP *Vindicator* for A&M.

1973 Feb Compilation LP *Love Masters* is released. Lee records solo LP *Black Beauty* which is never released.

1974 Dec Lee forms yet another version of Love, which includes Melvan Whittington (guitar), John Sterling (guitar) and Joe Blocker (drums), with Sherwood Akuna and Robert Rozelle sharing bass duties. It records soul-influenced LP *Reel To Reel* for RSO Records. Lee returns to playing occasional one-off dates.

1977 Sterling convinces Lee to re-form Love and attempt to recapture the spirit of earlier times. The band's line-up is Lee, MacLean, Sterling, Kim Kesteron (bass) and George Suranovich (drums), with The Knack's° drummer Bruce Gary also playing at one point, but it never releases any recordings.

1979 Various late 70s/early 80s Love reunions include one with Lee and MacLean on a Southern California tour.

1980 Rhino Records re-releases *Best Of Love* to cater for ongoing cult demand.

1981 July Rhino and Beggars Banquet in UK release LP *Arthur Lee*, a solo effort made up from earlier left-over tracks.

1982 Two Love LPs are released: Rhino's *Love Live*, a compilation of onstage recordings, and MCA's *Love*.

1986 The Damned° revives Love's 1968 single *Alone Again Or* which makes UK #27.

THE LOVIN' SPOONFUL

John Sebastian (vocals, guitar, harmonica and autoharp)
Zal Yanovsky (guitar and vocals)
Steve Boone (bass and vocals)
Joe Butler (drums and vocals)

1964 Feb Among friends invited to Cass Elliot's house to watch The Beatles'° US TV debut on the "Ed Sullivan Show" are Sebastian (b. John Benson Sebastian, Mar.17, 1944, New York, N.Y., US) and Yanovsky (b. Zalman Yanovsky, Dec.19, 1944, Toronto, Ontario, Canada). They discuss the possibility of a rock group and play duet guitar until dawn. Sebastian, whose father recorded harmonica singles for Archie Bleyer's Cadence label in the 1950s, is a college drop-out Greenwich Village folkie who backed local heroes Fred Neil and Tom Rush, and made sporadic appearances (including on their Elektra LP) as a member of the Even Dozen Jug Band. Yanovsky is guitarist with The Halifax Three, a sharp-suited folk group from Nova Scotia.

June In the height of Beatlemania The Halifax Three folds. Yanovsky and founder member Denny Doherty join Elliot and James Hendricks – ex-The Big Three (completed by Tim Rose). As The Mugwumps, they become prototypical electric folkies. Gigs are disastrous and recordings so inept that Warners releases their LP only after they become famous elsewhere. Between studio gigs backing Judy Collins°, Jesse Colin Young and Tim Hardin, Sebastian becomes a Mugwump, but the group disbands.

Dec Doherty, having joined The Journeymen for 7 months before they split, goes with Elliott to the Virgin Islands, where they join The Mamas And The Papas°. Their song *Creeque Alley* chronicles the comings and goings of the clique.

1965 Jan With producer Erik Jacobsen, Sebastian and Yanovsky plan a group – to be called The Lovin' Spoonful (after a phrase from Mississippi John Hurt's *Coffee Blues*). They find Boone (b, Sept.23, 1943, N.C., US) and Butler (b, Sept.16, 1943, Glen Cove, Long Island, N.Y, US) and rehearse in the basement of the rundown Albert Hotel. Early attempts at gigging and recording are unsuccessful.

June After a residency at the Night Owl in Greenwich Village, they work on Sebastian's innovative compositions. Jacobsen secures a deal with the recently formed Kama Sutra label.

Oct A celebration of rock'n'roll, *Do You Believe In Magic* hits US #9.

Dec Debut LP *Do You Believe In Magic* makes US #32. They evolve their own style – a light, lyrical synthesis they call Good Time Music. Others call it Folk Rock. With their striped jerseys and mischievous image, they become America's answer . . . mop tops from Manhattan.

1966 Jan *You Didn't Have To Be So Nice* hits US #10.

Apr *Daydream* hits US and UK #2 and is a million-seller. LP *Daydream* hits US #10 and UK #8. Compilation LP *What's Shakin'*, on Elektra, includes four Spoonful tracks – given to them in early 65 in return for musical equipment. One track *Good Time Music* defines the group's raison d'être.

July Written in a taxi en route to the studio, *Did You Ever Have To Make Up Your Mind* hits US #2.

Aug Featuring atmospheric streetnoise and engineer Roy Halee's booming drum experiments (which he continues on Simon and Garfunkel's° *Bookends*), *Summer In The City* becomes their biggest hit, tops the US chart for 3 weeks and hits UK #8. They win their second gold disk.

Oct Soundtrack LP for movie *What's Up Tiger Lily* reaches only US #126 but the film, a Japanese thriller on to which Woody Allen and Louise Lasser dub unrelated American dialogue, remains a cult item.

Nov *Rain On The Roof* hits US #10.

Dec Their third LP of the year, *Hums Of The Lovin' Spoonful* makes US #14.

1967 Jan *Nashville Cats* becomes their sixth consecutive top 10 success, hitting US #8, and making UK #26. B-side *Full Measure* makes US #87.

Mar With full orchestral backing, *Darling Be Home Soon* reaches US #15 and UK #44 (their last UK hit). LP *The Best Of The Lovin' Spoonful* is the first of many compilations. It hits US #3 and spends a year on the LP chart.

May Their second soundtrack LP, for Francis Ford Coppola's *You're A Big Boy Now*, reaches US #118.

June Joe Wissert becomes their producer, and *Six O'Clock* makes US #18.

Aug Yanovsky leaves after media indignation over a marijuana bust where he allegedly incriminated others to avoid prosecution. His replacement is Jerry Yester, ex-The Modern Folk Quartet, who produced *Goodbye And Hello* for Tim Buckley°.

Nov *She's Still A Mystery* reaches US #27.

1968 Feb *Money* peaks at US #48. LP *Everything Playing* reaches only US #118.

Apr *The Best Of The Lovin' Spoonful Vol 2* makes US #156.

Aug *Never Going Back* reaches US #73. (It is written by John Stewart and produced by Chip Douglas who did The Monkees'° *Daydream Believer*.)

Oct After "2 glorious years and a tedious one", Sebastian leaves the group, which soon crumbles. Subsequent individual output confirms that, to all intents and purposes, he was The Lovin' Spoonful. Sebastian's first solo venture is writing songs for *Jimmy*

THE LOVIN' SPOONFUL *cont.*

Shine, a Broadway musical starring Dustin Hoffman but his score is rejected, the show fails and he moves to California.

Nov A final LP, *Revelation Revolution 69* mentions only Joe Butler. Any Spoonful ingenuity is absent.

1969 Jan *She's A Lady*, Sebastian's solo debut, reaches US #84.

Feb The Lovin' Spoonful's *Me About You* reaches US #91. It is a lackluster swan song for one of the era's top US pop groups.

Aug Clad in the tie-dyes which will become his trademark, Sebastian appears at the Woodstock Festival. He performs Spoonful song *Younger Generation*, which becomes a highlight of the movie, and *I Had A Dream*, the opening track on LP *Woodstock*.

1970 Mar While MGM and Warner/Reprise argue about who owns his contract, Sebastian's first LP *John B. Sebastian* (issued on both labels!) rises to US #20. Paul Rothchild produces.

Sept At UK's Isle of Wight Festival Sebastian reunites with Yanovsky (there as part of Kris Kristofferson's° band). Yanovsky's solo LP *Alive And Well In Argentina* (co-produced with Jerry Yester) finds only cult acceptance. He returns to Ontario, Canada to open his Chez Piggy's restaurant. Yester cuts LPs with his wife Judy Henske, and the group Rosebud, and joins his brother Jim in The Association° for a brief spell. He will re-form The Modern Folk Quartet in the 1980s, but wins more acclaim as a producer (Aztec Two Step and Tom Waits°) and as a string arranger in LA. Butler appears on Broadway in *Hair* and Boone moves to Baltimore where he works as a musician.

Oct Losers in the contract battle, MGM issues an unauthorized live LP, *John Sebastian Live*, recorded during Lovin' Spoonful days. It peaks at US #129.

1971 Apr Reprise retaliates with a bona fide live LP *Cheapo Cheapo Productions Presents . . .* It reaches US #75.

Sept Sebastian's LP *The Four Of Us*, inspired by a cross-country vacation, reaches US #93.

1971/74 Sebastian tours as a one-man show and between times plays harmonica on LPs by Stephen Stills, Ohio Knox, Rita Coolidge and The Everly Brothers°.

1974 Sept Sebastian's first LP in 3 years, *The Tarzana Kid* fails to chart but marks a reunion with Spoonful producer Erik Jacobsen.

1976 May After five singles fail, Reprise are on the point of dropping Sebastian when his song for John Travolta's° TV series "Welcome Back Kotter", *Welcome Back* hits US #1. Double LP *The Best Of The Lovin' Spoonful* reaches US #183. Sebastian's LP *Welcome Back* makes US #79.

Aug Sebastian's *Hideaway* makes only US #95.

1980 Oct 15 years after The Lovin' Spoonful's inception, the four original members reunite for a cameo appearance in Paul Simon's° movie *One Trick Pony*.

1981/88 Sebastian continues to tour, with friends, with NRBQ and solo; and writes mainly for TV and films (*The Care Bears*, *Strawberry Shortcake* and NBC-TV's *The Jerk II*).

NICK LOWE

1965 Lowe (b. Mar.24, 1949, Woodchurch, Suffolk, UK) joins group Kippington Lodge, based in Tunbridge Wells, Kent, as bassist, with Bob Andrews (keyboards), Brinsley Schwarz° (guitar), Pete Whale (drums) and Barry Landerman (keyboards). Lowe and Schwarz have previously been together in schoolboy groups Sounds 4 plus 1 and Three's A Crowd.

1966 The group signs to Parlophone, releasing five singles over 4 years, none of which charts.

1969 Oct Minus Landerman and Whale but with Billy Rankin on drums, the group changes name to Brinsley Schwarz°.

1974 Feb The band makes a brief appearance in film *Stardust*.

1975 Mar Brinsley Schwarz° splits, having cut several critically-appreciated LPs with no commercial recognition.

July Lowe becomes a producer, working over the next 9 months on The Kursaal Flyers' LP *Chocs Away*, Dr. Feelgood's° second LP *Malpractice* and Graham Parker's° LP *Howling Wind*. He also records two glam-rock one-off singles under pseudonyms The Disco Brothers and The Tartan Horde (whose single *Rollers Show* is a parody of current teen rage The Bay City Rollers°).

1976 Aug [14] Lowe's own debut solo single *So It Goes*, co-produced by Lowe and Jake Riviera, is the first release (with catalog number BUY 1) on UK independent label Stiff, where Lowe becomes an in-house producer. (He will be responsible for The Damned's° debut LP and Elvis Costello's° first single *Less Than Zero*. Away from the label, he also produces Clover's (including Huey Lewis°) *Chicken Funk* and Dave Edmunds'° LP *Get It*.)

1977 May On Stiff, Lowe releases 4-track EP *Bowi*, the title a tongue-in-cheek response to David Bowie's° LP *Low*.

June Edmunds'° *I Knew The Bride* is written by Lowe in the style of Chuck Berry's° *You Never Can Tell*.

July Lowe joins Edmunds'° group Rockpile, while continuing his parallel solo career (often using the same musicians) and producing Costello's° debut LP *My Aim Is True* and The Rumour's LP *Max*, among others.

Oct Lowe revives Billy Fury's° *Halfway To Paradise* on Stiff. He also performs in the Stiff tour package "Live Stiffs", with labelmates Costello°, Ian Dury° and Wreckless Eric. Following this, he leaves Stiff, with Costello and Riviera, moving to Riviera's new Radar Records.

1978 Mar LP *Jesus Of Cool*, illustrating his bass guitar collection on the sleeve, is Lowe's first solo effort (US title: *Pure Pop For Now People*). It reaches UK #22 and US #127. Taken from it, the first Radar single *I Love The Sound Of Breaking Glass* hits UK #7. (For Radar he also produces Costello's° second LP *This Year's Model*.)

May Lowe's *Little Hitler*, co-written by Dave Edmunds°, fails to chart. Meanwhile, Mickey Jupp's LP *Juppanese*, a Lowe co-production, is his last Stiff assignment.

Nov *American Squirm* again fails to chart. He contributes to the soundtrack of film *Rock'n'Roll High School*.

1979 Jan Lowe produces The Pretenders° debut *Stop Your Sobbin'* and another Costello° LP, *Armed Forces*.

June *Crackin' Up* makes UK #34, while LP *Labour Of Lust*, recorded in London and Helsinki with Rockpile, peaks at UK #43 and US #31.

July [4] Rockpile opens a 2-month US tour supporting Blondie°, at the Central Youth Center, Scranton, Pa.

Aug [15] Film *Americathon*, with soundtrack contributions from Lowe, premieres.

Aug [18] Lowe marries Johnny Cash's° step-daughter Carlene Carter, in LA, Cal.

Sept [1] Documentary *Born Fighters*, devoted to Lowe and Dave Edmunds°, is shown on UK TV.

Sept *Cruel To Be Kind* a re-recording of an old B-side (co-written by ex-Brinsley Schwarz° colleague Ian Gomm), climbs to #12 in both UK and US.

1980 In a year spent mostly working on the road and in the studio with Rockpile, Lowe also produces Costello's° LP *Get Happy* and his wife Carlene's LP *Musical Shapes*.

Oct Rockpile releases its only LP, *Seconds Of Pleasure*.

1981 Jan Costello's° LP *Trust* is the last which Lowe will produce for him for 5 years.

Feb Rockpile splits, leaving Lowe working solo before forming his own touring and recording band, Nick Lowe and The Chaps (with ex-Ace° keyboard player Paul Carrack, ex-Rumour guitarist Martin Belmont and Bobby Irwin on drums).

Sept Lowe produces Carlene Carter's LP *Blue Nun*.

1982 Feb Nick Lowe and The Chaps tour US, then change name to Noise To Go. LP *Nick The Knife* is Lowe's first for F-Beat Records, and uses an assortment of musicians from Rockpile and Noise To Go. It spends a disappointing 2 weeks at UK #99 but makes US #50. *Burnin'* is extracted from the LP, without charting.

Oct Lowe produces The Fabulous Thunderbirds' LP *Rhythm*.

1983 June LP *The Abominable Showman* is co-produced by Roger Bechirian, and among its guest players is Simon Climie, (later of Climie Fisher°). It does not chart in UK, but peaks at US #129.

1984 Jan John Hiatt's LP *Riding With The King* is co-produced by Lowe.

June *Half A Boy, Half A Man* reaches UK #53.

July LP *Nick Lowe And His Cowboy Outfit* features *L.A.F.S. (Love At First Sight)*, and a duet with Costello° on *Baby It's You* (also the single B-side). The LP makes US #113 but fails in UK.

Sept Lowe's compilation LP *Sixteen All-Time Hits* is released on Demon Records.

1985 Sept LP *Rose Of England* is Lowe's last for F-Beat, and also his final recording with Cowboy Outfit.

1986 Jan *I Knew The Bride*, produced by Huey Lewis° and backed by The News, makes US #77.

Mar Another Lowe compilation LP, *Nick's Knack*, is released in UK by Demon Records.

Sept He produces Elvis Costello's° LP *Blood And Chocolate* on Demon.

1988 Feb LP *Pinker And Prouder Than Previous* features material recorded over an 18-month period, and its guest musicians include Lowe's long-time collaborator Dave Edmunds°.

LULU

1963 Lulu (b. Marie McDonald Lawrie, Nov.3, 1948, Lennoxcastle, near Glasgow, Scotland, UK) joins Glasgow group The Gleneagles, which begins to play regularly at Lindella and Le Phonographe clubs. The latter's owner Tony Gordon, impressed by audience reactions, introduces the group to his sister Marion Massey, who is involved in showbiz management in London. Massey becomes the group's manager and changes the name to Lulu & The Luvvers. The line-up is Lulu (vocals), Ross Nelson (lead guitar), Jim Dewar (rhythm guitar), Alec Bell (keyboards), Jimmy Smith (saxophone), Tony Tierney (bass) and David Miller (drums).

1964 June Massey negotiates a contract with Decca, and the group debuts with a revival of The Isley Brothers'° *Shout*, which hits UK #7. (Similar follow-up *Satisfied* will fail to chart.)

Aug *Shout* makes a minor US chart showing at #94.

Nov *Here Comes The Night* (a UK top 5 hit for Them°, also on Decca, a few months later) charts briefly at UK #50.

1965 July Partly thanks to her adaptability to musical styles and her easy TV demeanor, Lulu begins to be booked as a solo performer (while still doing regular club and package show gigs with The Luvvers) and also records solo. (The Luvvers do not appear on disk after the first unsuccessful singles.) Lulu performs *Leave A Little Love* as a soloist at the televised Brighton Song Festival. The Les Reed-penned song is placed second (behind Kenny Lynch's *I'll Stay By You*) and is her biggest hit since *Shout*, at UK #8.

Sept *Try To Understand* reaches UK #25.

1966 Feb Lulu splits from The Luvvers.

Mar She is the first UK girl singer to appear behind the Iron Curtain, performing in Poland.

1967 May Moving from Decca to Columbia, she is paired with producer Mickie Most. First collaboration, on a cover of a Neil Diamond° B-side, *The Boat That I Row*, hits UK #6. She tours UK supporting The Beach Boys°.

July *Let's Pretend* reaches UK #11. B-side is the Don Black/Mark London song *To Sir With Love*, the theme from a UK movie starring Sidney Poitier, in which Lulu also plays a rebellious London schoolgirl. The song is not promoted in UK, despite good box office for the film.

Oct *To Sir With Love*, issued as US A-side to coincide with US release of the movie, tops the chart for 5 weeks, and becomes her only million-selling single.

Nov *Love Loves To Love Love* makes UK #32. A reissue of *Shout* (due to popularity of *To Sir With Love*) makes US #96.

Dec LP *To Sir With Love* peaks at US #24.

1968 Feb *Best Of Both Worlds* reaches US #32.

Mar *Me The Peaceful Heart* hits UK #9.

June *Boy* reaches UK #15.

Sept A cover of Tim Rose's *Morning Dew* makes US #52.

Nov *I'm A Tiger* hits UK #9.

Dec [27] She hosts her own musical variety show on UK TV. Special guests are The Jimi Hendrix° Experience and Hendrix causes production consternation when he switches in mid-act to an unscheduled number, Cream's° *Sunshine Of Your Love*.

1969 Feb [18] Lulu marries Maurice Gibb of The Bee Gees°, at Gerrards Cross, Bucks., UK, with Bee Gee Robin Gibb as best man.

Apr She represents UK in the Eurovision Song Contest with *Boom Bang-A-Bang*. In the most bizarre result in the history of the contest, it ties for first place with the entries from France, Spain and Holland. *Boom-Bang-A-Bang* hits UK #2.

Nov Lulu leaves Mickie Most and Columbia, and signs to Atlantic subsidiary Atco Records, debuting with *Oh Me Oh My (I'm A Fool For You Baby)*, penned by Glaswegian Jim Doris, and recorded in Muscle Shoals, Ala., US, with production by Jerry Wexler, Tom Dowd and Arif Mardin. It makes UK #47.

1970 Feb *Oh Me Oh My (I'm A Fool For You Baby)* climbs to US #22.

Mar LP *New Routes* on Atco makes US #88.

May Lulu teams with The Dixie Flyers on *Hum A Song (From Your Heart)*, which reaches US #54.

1971 Oct Compilation LP *The Most Of Lulu* makes UK #15.

1973 Lulu and Maurice Gibb separate (and will later divorce).

1974 Feb Now signed to Polydor, she revives David Bowie's° *The Man Who Sold The World*, with Bowie producing and featuring on saxophone and back-up vocals. It hits UK #3.

1975 Apr *Take Your Mama For A Ride*, on Wes Farrell's Chelsea label, makes UK #37.

1976 Lulu marries hairdresser John Frieda.

1977 June [18] Lulu gives birth to a son.

1981 Oct She signs to Alfa Records (marketed by CBS), and releases *I Could Never Miss You (More Than I Do)*, which reaches US #18. LP *Lulu* peaks at US #126.

Dec *I Could Never Miss You (More Than I Do)* makes UK #62.

1982 Jan *If I Were You* makes US #44.

1985 Dec Lulu takes part in Carol Aid, an all-star Christmas carol concert to raise money for the Band Aid Trust, at London's Heaven nightclub. Others singing with her include Chris De Burgh°, Sandie Shaw° and Cliff Richard°.

1986 Aug She signs to Jive records and re-records *Shout*, in a similar but updated arrangement to the original, which hits UK #8. The original version is later reissued by Decca, and the sales of this are added to those of the new recording for UK chart purposes.

FRANKIE LYMON & THE TEENAGERS

Frankie Lymon (lead vocals)
Sherman Garnes (vocals)
Joe Negroni (vocals)
Herman Santiago (vocals)
Jimmy Merchant (vocals)

1955 Lymon (b. Sept.30, 1942, Washington Heights, N.Y., US), a fellow student at Edward W Stitt Junior High in the Bronx, joins The Premiers, a quartet formed at the school, consisting of two blacks, tenor Jimmy Merchant (b. Feb.10, 1940) and bass man Sherman Garnes (b. June 8, 1940) and two Puerto Ricans, lead singer Herman Santiago (b. Feb.18, 1941) and baritone Joe Negroni (b. Sept.9, 1940).

Nov The Premiers impress Richard Barrett, leader of The Valentines, who use the same school for rehearsal, and talent scout/A&R man for George Goldner.

Dec Goldner, a dance instructor and multiple label owner, signs the group to Gee, named after his recent Crows' smash. The soprano-voiced Lymon assumes lead role and the group records *Why Do Fools Fall In Love*, a Lymon composition. At the suggestion of a session saxophonist the name is changed to The Teenagers.

1956 Feb Credited to The Teenagers featuring Frankie Lymon, *Why Do Fools Fall In Love* reaches the top of the R&B chart and crosses into the pop list, hitting US #7, with sales exceeding a million.

Apr Sidelining academic pursuits, the group embarks on a hectic non-stop touring schedule. A second single, *I Want You To Be My Girl*, giving Lymon billing over the group, reaches US #17.

July *I Promise To Remember* makes only US #57 but *Why Do Fools Fall In Love* hits UK #1. 13-year old Lymon becomes an unlikely teen heart-throb.

Oct *The ABCs Of Love*, the group's fourth release, makes only US #77.

1957 Mar Designed as a riposte to the growing body of rock'n'roll detractors, *I'm Not A Juvenile Delinquent* fails in US despite promotion in Alan Freed movie *Rock Rock Rock* but it reaches UK #12. The group's UK tour includes two weeks topping the bill at the London Palladium. At 14, Lymon is the youngest ever headliner, having already been the youngest chart topper at 13.

Apr *Baby Baby*, the flip of *I'm Not A Juvenile Delinquent*, also in the Freed film, attracts UK airplay in the wake of The Teenagers' tour and outsells the A-side, hitting UK #4.

July Lymon is encouraged to break from The Teenagers but his first solo effort, *Goody Goody*, recorded in England, reaches only US #22 and #24 in UK, where it is his last hit.

1960 Aug After 3 years in the doldrums, during which time Roulette absorbs the bankrupt Goldner's labels, *Little Bitty Pretty One*, originally recorded for a 1958 LP, returns Lymon to the US chart at #58. The comeback is short-lived as his broken voice has robbed him of his major asset.

1961 On the advice of distraught friends, Lymon submits to a drug rehabilitation program.

1964 Following the failure of a redesigned night club act, Lymon is arrested and found guilty of narcotics offences. He is unable to shake his heroin addiction.

1968 Feb [28] Lymon's body is discovered in the 165th Street house in which he grew up. A nearby syringe figures in every news report. A star at 13, all but spent at 14, and dead at 25.

1981 Oct Diana Ross° revives *Why Do Fools Fall In Love* for a top 10 hit and

FRANKIE LYMON & THE TEENAGERS *cont.*

dedicates her LP to Lymon's memory. (The original endures as one of rock's most popular oldies and a reconstituted group of The Teenagers, led by Santiago and Merchant (both Negroni and Garnes died in the late 1970s), with Pearl McKinnon duplicating Lymon's soprano, continues to gather momentum on the rock revival and lounge circuits.)

LYNYRD SKYNYRD

Ronnie Van Zant (vocals)
Gary Rossington (guitar)
Allen Collins (guitar)
Billy Powell (keyboards)
Leon Wilkeson (bass)
Bob Burns (drums)

1965 The group is formed in high school in Jacksonville, Fla., US, under the name My Backyard, later changed to immortalize school gym teacher Leonard Skinner, a legendary antagonist of long-haired students.

1968 Debut single *Need All My Friends* is released on Jacksonville-based Shade Tree label.

1971 After some years of touring in the South, the group releases second single *I've Been Your Fool*.

1972 Al Kooper (ex-Blood, Sweat & Tears°) is touring with Badfinger° and looking for suitable talent for his new label Sounds of the South, marketed by MCA, when he spots the group playing at Funocchio's bar in Atlanta, Ga. Kooper is impressed by Skynyrd's "Dixie Rock" style, and signs it.

1973 Nov Debut LP *Pronounced Leh-Nerd Skin-Nerd* is produced by Kooper and features a new third guitarist, Ed King (ex-Strawberry Alarm Clock, and more recently a session man), whose joining gives the group a near-unique three-guitar stage line-up. The LP reaches US #27 and earns a gold disk, its big airplay track is *Free Bird*, a tribute to the late Duane Allman of The Allman Brothers Band°.

Dec Skynyrd tours US and Canada as support on The Who's° "Quadrophenia" tour.

1974 Oct *Sweet Home Alabama* is the group's first US chart single, hitting #8. (The song is seen as a Southerners' answer to Neil Young's° 1971 *Southern Man*.) It is taken from LP *Second Helping*, again produced by Kooper, which reaches US #12 and earns a second gold disk.

Dec Burns leaves, and is replaced on drums by Artimus Pyle.

1975 Jan *Free Bird*, belatedly issued as a single (soon to become the band's anthem and a perennial on FM radio), reaches US #19. King leaves after playing in sessions for the next LP.

May LP *Nuthin' Fancy* hits US #9, earning another gold disk, and reaches UK #43, following the group's UK live debut as support to Dutch group Golden Earring.

July *Saturday Night Special* reaches US #27.

1976 Mar *Double Trouble* makes US #80, while LP *Gimme Back My Bullets*, produced by Tom Dowd, reaches US #20 (the fourth gold disk) and UK #34. The band gains an English manager, Peter Rudge. Van Zant is being arrested continually for brawling – usually in bars – as the group begins to develop a reputation for in-fighting and general physical aggravation.

Aug [21] The group appears at UK's Knebworth Festival, alongside The Rolling Stones°, Todd Rundgren° and 10cc°.

Sept 3-track EP comprising *Free Bird*, *Sweet Home Alabama* and *Double Trouble* reaches UK #31.

Sept [5] Rossington is injured in a car crash in Jacksonville.

Nov New third guitarist Steve Gaines joins and a female back-up trio is added for Skynyrd's double live LP *One More For The Road*, recorded in Atlanta, Ga. It hits US #9 and UK #17 and is the group's biggest seller, earning a platinum disk for a million US sales.

Dec A live version of *Free Bird*, from the double LP, makes US #38.

1977 Apr [15] Van Zant and Collins present the gold disk awarded them for LP *One More For The Road* to Maynard Jackson, mayor of Atlanta, in appreciation of the band's Atlanta fans. Another gold disk goes to Fox Theater, Atlanta, where the LP was recorded. Several group members, plus James Brown° and other celebrity Georgians are honored at a ceremony in the Atlanta Braves' baseball stadium, prior to the team's opening home game.

Oct [20] Van Zant, Steve Gaines, his sister Cassie Gaines (one of the three female back-up singers) and personal manager Dean Kilpatrick are killed when Skynyrd's rented single-engined Convair 240 plane, short of fuel, crashes into a swamp in Gillsburg, Miss., while en route from Greenville, S.C., to Baton Rouge, La., to play at Louisiana University, on a 50-city tour. Rossington, Collins, Powell and Wilkeson are all seriously injured (but will eventually recover). MCA withdraws the sleeve of just-released LP *Street Survivors*, which pictures the group standing amid flames.

Nov LP *Street Survivors*, is a second platinum disk, hitting US #5 and UK #13.

1978 Mar *What's Your Name*, taken from LP *Street Survivors*, reaches US #13.

Apr The group's last US hit single is *You Got That Right*, which makes US #69.

Nov LP *Skynyrd's First And Last*, containing unreleased 1970-72 recordings, reaches US #15 and UK #50, and becomes another platinum LP.

1979 Oct With the exception of Pyle, the surviving Lynyrd Skynyrd members form a new group, The Rossington-Collins Band, with female lead vocalist, Dale Krantz, who has earlier been a back-up singer for .38 Special, the band fronted by Van Zant's brother Donnie. Guitarist Barry Harwood (to give a three-guitar line-up again) and drummer Derek Hess also join. The group remains signed to MCA.

1980 Jan EP *Free Bird* re-charts in UK, reaching #43.

Feb Double compilation LP *Gold And Platinum* reaches US #12 and UK #49, earning a final platinum disk.

Aug The first Rossington-Collins Band LP *Anytime, Anyplace, Anywhere* reaches US #13, and earns a gold disk, while extracted *Don't Misunderstand Me* is the band's only hit single, peaking at US #55. On stage, the group plays an instrumental version of *Free Bird* to close its act, the tune now being a dedication to Ronnie Van Zant.

1981 Nov LP *This Is The Way* by The Rossington-Collins Band makes US #24. It is dedicated to Collins' wife Katy, who died a year earlier. Shortly after, the band breaks up.

1982 Feb [13] The inscribed 300lb marble slab is stolen from the grave of Ronnie Van Zant in a cemetary at Orange Park, Fla. (Police will find it 2 weeks later in a partially dried-up river bed.)

Mar Pyle forms a new quintet, The Artimus Pyle Band, which begins touring US.

June EP *Free Bird* charts for the third time in UK, this time hitting its highest position of #21.

Dec LP *Best Of The Rest*, a compilation of Skynyrd rare tracks and out-takes, reaches US #171.

1986 Powell joins a Christian band, Vision, after being released from 30 days in jail.

1987 Vision joins ex-Grand Funk Railroad° singer Mark Farner on a club tour. They perform Lynyrd Skynyrd material, and the audience response convinces them that Skynyrd should re-form.

Sept A new Lynyrd Skynyrd is formed, comprising Rossington, Powell, Pyle, Wilkeson, King, Johnny Van Zant (vocals) and Randall Hall (guitar), with Dale Krantz Rossington and Carol Bristow (The Honkettes) on backing vocals. The group plays Charlie Daniels' 13th Volunteer Jam Reunion in Georgia, and a 32-date reunion tour, marking the 10th anniversary of the fatal plane crash.

Nov Compilation LP *Legend* by the original Lynyrd Skynyrd is released by MCA, containing previous B-sides and unreleased and uncompleted songs. The material is produced by Dowd with the surviving members.

1988 Sept The new Lynyrd Skynyrd's double live LP *For The Glory Of The South* is released on MCA, consisting of tracks recorded on the Sept. 1987 reunion tour.

MADNESS

Graham "Suggs" McPherson (vocals)
Mike Barson (keyboards)
Chris "Chrissie Boy" Foreman (guitar)
Mark "Bedders" Bedford (bass)
Lee "Kix" Thompson (sax and vocals)
Dan "Woody" Woodgate (drums)
Carl "Chas Smash" Smyth (horns)

1976 Barson (b. May 21, 1958), Thompson (b. Oct.5, 1957, London, UK) and Foreman (b. Aug.8, 1958), all from Gospel Oak school in Camden and living in Kentish Town, London, form bluebeat-based band The Invaders.

1977 June [30] The group makes its first public appearance with John Hasler on drums and Smyth (b. Cathal Smyth, Jan.14, 1959) on bass, and adopts its "Nutty Sound".

1978 Feb Temporary vocalist Dikron is replaced by McPherson (b. Jan.13, 1961, Hastings, Sussex, UK).

Sept The constantly changing line-up settles around original trio with McPherson, Bedford (b. Aug.24, 1961, London) and Woodgate (b. Oct.19, 1960, London).

1979 Jan [1] The Invaders play their last gig at the London Film-makers Co-op, after which they change name to Madness.

Mar McPherson strikes a friendship with The Specials AKA° after seeing them perform at the Hope & Anchor pub, Islington, London, and Madness signs to Specials' leader Jerry Dammers' 2-Tone label.

Oct Debut single, *The Prince*, a tribute to ska hero Prince Buster written by Thompson, makes UK #16, 2-Tone's second release. Madness signs to Dave Robinson's Stiff Records in UK after a wedding party and Sire in US.

Nov LP *One Step Beyond*, produced by Clive Langer and Alan Winstanley (who will produce most of the band's records), hits UK #2, during a 78-week chart stay. Meanwhile, the band completes 3 week US tour of N.Y., Cal. and Tex.

Dec *One Step Beyond* hits UK #7.

Dec [30] Madness headlines a concert at the London Lyceum.

1980 Jan *My Girl* hits UK #3. (It is later covered by another Stiff artist Tracey Ullman as *My Guy*.)

Feb Madness returns from a European tour and plays a Saturday morning gig at London's Hammersmith Odeon for "Under 16s".

Mar The group's progress is marred by unwanted attentions of National Front extremists while on tour with The Specials°. LP *One Step Beyond* reaches US #128, released on Sire Records.

Apr EP *The Work Rest And Play* hits UK #6, with *Night Train To Cairo* as the lead track and a cut rebutting the National Front.

July The group begins a 30-date tour of Europe.

Oct *Baggy Trousers* hits UK #3 (helped by a Dave Robinson-produced video featuring sax player Thompson), as parent LP *Absolutely* hits UK #2, during a 46-week chart stay.

Oct [8] A UK tour begins in Blackpool.

Nov LP *Absolutely* makes US #146. (The group is subsequently released from Sire, under an agreement which stated that if the second LP did not sell a certain amount, Madness could leave the label.) The group begins a "Twelve Days of Madness" tour. At each date, it plays an Under 16s matinee, where all tickets sell for £1, as well as doing an evening show. (The tour ends in five sell-out gigs at London's Hammersmith Odeon, including a Christmas Eve charity show.)

Dec *Embarrassment* hits UK #4, as Madness is voted Singles Artists of the Year by *New Musical Express*, having spent 46 weeks on chart during 1980.

1981 Feb Instrumental *Return Of The Los Palmas Seven* hits UK #7. The group appears in 2-Tone movie *Dance Craze*.

Mar/Apr Madness make full-length feature movie *Take It or Leave It*, directed by Stiff Records' boss Dave Robinson. The group begins the "Absolutely Madness One Step Beyond Far East Tour" of Australasia, Japan and US.

May *Grey Day* hits UK #4.

Oct *Shut Up* hits UK #7, as parent LP *Seven*, recorded at Compass Point Studios in Nassau, The Bahamas, hits UK #5. *Take It or Leave It* movie premieres to poor reviews. The group sets out on a 36-date UK tour.

1982 Jan The group's revival of Labi Siffre's 1972 hit *It Must Be Love* hits UK #4. (Siffre makes a cameo appearance in a Madness video, on which children are warned on UK TV not to copy the band who throw themselves into a swimming pool, clutching electric guitars.) Suggs marries singer Bette Bright.

Mar *Cardiac Arrest* makes UK #14, the group's first single since *The Prince* to miss the top 10. There is resistance from radio on the grounds of bad taste.

May *House Of Fun* hits UK #1, with another original video filmed at a fun fair, toppling Eurovision winner Nicole's *A Little Peace*. Compilation LP of hits *Complete Madness* also hits UK #1.

July *Driving In My Car* hits UK #4.

Nov LP *The Rise And Fall* hits UK #10.

Dec *Our House* hits UK #5.

1983 Feb [21] Madness begins its annual UK tour.

Mar *Tomorrow's (Just Another Day)* hits UK #8.

Apr The group, now with Geffen Records for US, has its biggest US LP chart success with LP *Madness*. It reaches US #41.

July *Our House* becomes the group's biggest US hit at #7.

Sept *Wings Of A Dove* hits UK #2, held off the top by UB40's° *Red Red Wine*.

Oct *It Must Be Love* makes US #33.

Nov *The Sun And The Rain* hits UK #5.

Dec [21] Founding member and writer Barson announces his intention to leave and settle in Holland with his Dutch wife, Sandra.

1984 Feb *Michael Caine*, with a guest appearance by Michael Caine, reaches UK #11.

Mar Parent LP *Keep Moving* hits UK #6. *The Sun And The Rain* stalls at US #72.

Apr LP *Keep Moving* peaks at US #109, and is the group's US chart swan song.

June *One Better Day* makes UK #17, and is the group's last release for Stiff, on which the band hits top 20 with every UK release.

Oct The group forms its own label, Zarjazz (derived from its favorite comic *2000 AD*), through Virgin. First release is Feargal Sharkey's *Listen To Your Father*, written by Madness and originally intended as a group release. It makes UK #23.

1985 Feb Smyth and McPherson as The Fink Brothers (characters in *2000 AD*), peak at UK #50 with *Mutants In Mega City*.

Mar Madness, with UB40°, The Specials°, General Public and others, assemble as Starvation to record *Starvation Tam-Tam Pour L'Ethiope*, to raise funds for the starving in Ethiopia, Eritrea and The Sudan. The single makes UK #33.

Sept Madness' *Yesterday's Men*, the band's first on Zarjazz, reaches UK #18.

Oct LP *Mad Not Mad* makes UK #16.

Nov *Uncle Sam*, with a return to "Nutty Sound" video style, makes UK #21 – the first to fail to make top 20 in 21 attempts.

Dec [21] Madness participates in Greater London Council Christmas party for the unemployed with Marc Almond, Ian Dury° and others.

1986 Feb *Sweetest Girl*, a revival of Scritti Politti's° hit, reaches UK #35.

Sept [1] Madness officially announces that it will split.

Nov *Waiting For The Ghost Train* makes UK #18.

Dec A second hits LP *Utter Madness* is released and reaches UK #29.

1987 Mar The Voice of the Beehive's *Just A City* features Bedders and Woody. (Bedders will later begin work on film scores.)

1988 Feb Madness re-forms as The Madness, but as a four-piece, and signs to Virgin.

Mar *I Pronounce You* stalls at UK #44.

May LP *The Madness* makes US #65.

June *What's That* is the first Madness disk to fail to chart in UK.

MADONNA

1977 After a year at the University of Michigan, to which she wins a scholarship, Madonna (b. Madonna Louise Ciccone, Aug.16, 1959, Rochester, Detroit, Mich., US) heads for New York, at the urging of her ballet teacher. Subsequently moving to university in North Carolina, she is awarded another scholarship (having completed a 6-week dance workshop) to Alvin Ailey's prestigious New York studio, to work with choreographer Pearl Lang. (She has initially studied piano before switching to ballet, but finds theater her forte when studying at Rochester Adams High School and playing lead roles in school productions.)

MADONNA *cont.*

1979 She lands a place in The Patrick Hernandez Revue, working in Paris, France. Hernandez is a disco star looking to capitalize on his worldwide hit, *Born To Be Alive*. She leaves the revue to form a band with her boyfriend Dan Gilroy. Calling the band The Breakfast Club, they play local venues, with Madonna starting behind the drum kit, but soon stepping out front to sing.

1980 Madonna leaves the band and starts her own group Emmenon, shortened later to Emmy. When the first drummer leaves, an old boyfriend from Detroit, Steve Bray, joins and she leaves the dance company and begins working with him on demo tapes at his home studio. She also lands a part in Stephen Jon Lewicki's low-budget 60-minute movie thriller *A Certain Sacrifice*. Late in the year she signs to rock manager Adam Alter's Gotham Productions.

1982 She splits from Gotham having spent a wasted year, recording in studios and waiting for a record deal. (Gotham will later sue her and receive an insubstantial settlement.) Madonna's big break comes when she gives DJ/producer Mark Kamins at Danceteria club a tape of the dance material she has made with Bray. Kamins introduces her to Sire Records' executive Michael Rosenblatt, who hears the cassette and agrees to sign her subject to label boss Seymour Stein's approval. Stein, hospitalized, agrees and the deal is signed. Kamins produces *Ain't No Big Deal*, intended as the first single but dropped in favor of *Everybody*, which breaks on dance radio stations and climbs the dance chart. Lip-synching, she debuts at the Danceteria.

Dec *Everybody* is released in UK, but fails to chart.

1983 *Physical Attraction*, penned by Reggie Lucas, is another big club hit.

June *Holiday*, written by current flame "Jellybean" Benitez, is released. During a UK promo trip, Madonna lip-synchs at London's Music Machine.

Sept LP *Madonna*, produced by Lucas, enters the US chart to hit #8. *Lucky Star* is released in UK.

Oct *Holiday* peaks at US #16. The video for *Burning Up* is added to the MTV playlist.

1984 Feb *Holiday* hits UK #6. Madonna performs on UK BBC TV's "Top of the Pops". LP *Madonna* hits UK #6.

Apr Re-released *Lucky Star* makes UK #14.

June *Borderline* hits US #6, but stalls at UK #56.

Oct *Lucky Star* hits US #4, giving a boost to the LP and pushing its sales over a million. Madonna begins work on her first major film role, in Susan Seidelman's *Desperately Seeking Susan*, alongside Rosanna Arquette.

Nov LP *Like A Virgin*, produced by Nile Rodgers and featuring Chic's° rhythm section (Rodgers, Bernard Edwards and Tony Thompson), enters the UK chart.

Dec *Like A Virgin*, written by Tom Kelly and Billy Steinberg, tops the US chart for 6 weeks.

1985 Jan *Like A Virgin* hits UK #3.

Feb LP *Like A Virgin* tops the US chart.

Mar *Material Girl* hits US #2 and UK #3.

Apr Madonna begins her first tour. Titled "The Virgin Tour", it plays to 355,000 fans in 27 cities. Up and coming rap act The Beastie Boys° support her. On the final tour date, she is carried off stage by her father, Tony.

May Ballad *Crazy For You* from film *Vision Quest*, tops the US chart. Madonna is syndicated worldwide in beachwear for fashion magazines.

June *Angel* hits US #5 as *Crazy For You* hits UK #2.

July *Desperately Seeking Susan* is premiered, while movie release of earlier soft-porn *A Certain Sacrifice* is planned.

Aug [3] From *Desperately Seeking Susan* movie and co-written by Madonna and Bray, *Into The Groove* is Madonna's first UK chart-topper. (In US, it will only appear on the B-side of 12" *Angel* so will never make *Billboard* Hot 100.) Sire later adds the song to LP *Like A Virgin* and also repackages LP *Madonna* as *The First Album*. *Holiday* re-enters the UK chart, this time hitting #2 – kept out by *Into The Groove* (only The Beatles°, John Lennon° and Frankie Goes To Hollywood° have also filled the top 2 places simultaneously).

Aug [13] Madonna performs solo and with The Thompson Twins° in the Philadelphia leg of Live Aid. She is introduced by Bette Midler° who claims that Madonna is "a woman who pulled herself up by her bra-straps".

Aug [16] Madonna marries actor Sean Penn on her 26th birthday. As the cliffside coastal wedding takes place, news crews fly overhead in a fleet of helicopters.

Aug *Dress You Up* enters the US chart to hit #5. After her honeymoon, she begins working on a new LP which she will dedicate to her husband, "the coolest guy in the universe".

Sept After nearly a year on chart, LP *Like A Virgin* hits UK #1. Meanwhile *Angel* hits UK #5. *Penthouse* and *Playboy* magazines publish nude spreads she sat for while penniless in New York in 1977.

Oct *Dress You Up* hits US #5 as *Gambler* hits UK #4.

Dec *Dress You Up* hits UK #3 and becomes Madonna's eighth top 10 hit of the year. (She becomes the only woman to have three disks in UK top 15 for nearly 30 years, joining Ruby Murray.)

1986 Jan *Borderline* and *Gambler* both re-enter the UK chart, hitting #2 and #61 respectively. Madonna and Penn travel to China to film scenes for a new movie. She wins Best Selling Video award in UK for *Like A Virgin The Video EP*.

Mar While filming *Shanghai Surprise*, press harassment causes Madonna and Penn to over-react. *The Sun*'s photographer Dave Hogan is knocked down by the Penns' car. The UK tabloid press picks up on the incident and on general rumblings of discontent on the film set. Producer George Harrison° calls a press conference to defuse the situation.

Apr Due to recording commitments Madonna is unable to appear opposite Bruce Willis in scheduled movie *Blind Date*. *Like A Virgin – Live* video documentary is released.

June *Live To Tell*, a ballad from film *At Close Range*, starring Sean Penn, hits US #1 and UK #2. At a post-movie party, Madonna rejects actor Don Johnson's request to duet on his forthcoming LP.

July Produced by Madonna, with Stephen Bray and Patrick Leonard, LP *True Blue* enters the UK chart at #1 and will also climb to US #1. *Papa Don't Preach*, from the LP, tops both US and UK charts.

Aug She shoots a video in LA's Echo Park district featuring UK youngster Felix Howard.

Oct *True Blue* tops the UK chart, tying Sandie Shaw's° record of most UK number #1s (three) by a female act.

Nov *True Blue* hits US #3. *Shanghai Surprise* premieres to savage reviews. LP *You Can Dance*, a collection of continuously sequenced remixes and dub versions, hits UK #5.

Dec *Open Your Heart* hits UK #4.

1987 Feb *Open Your Heart* becomes Madonna's fifth US chart-topper, and her third from LP *True Blue*.

Mar Madonna receives the dubious distinction of being voted "favorite artist of record pirates" by a special *Billboard* panel, a measure of her worldwide popularity.

Apr Madonna becomes the only female artist to have four UK #1s when *La Isla Bonita* tops the chart.

June [14] A record-breaking Japanese tour begins in Osaka.

July *Who's That Girl*, the title of the new movie in which she stars with Griffin Dunne and Sir John Mills, hits both UK and US #1. The film fails to match the single's success. Madonna tours UK for the first time, playing one show in Leeds and three at London's Wembley Stadium under the banner "The True Blue Tour".

Sept LP *Who's That Girl* hits US #7 and UK #4.

Oct *Causin' A Commotion* hits US #2 and UK #4.

Dec *The Look Of Love* hits UK #9. LP of dance remixes, *You Can Dance*, hits UK #4. Madonna guests on A&M's *A Very Special Christmas*, reviving Eartha Kitt's *Santa Baby*.

1988 Jan LP *You Can Dance* reaches US #14. Madonna stars on Broadway in *Speed The Plow*.

Sept Against her wishes, a video of film *A Certain Sacrifice* becomes publicly available as a new Patrick Leonard produced-LP is recorded in LA.

Oct Press reports state that Meryl Streep wins the title role in the film version of *Evita*, after Madonna is turned down, for demanding a $5-million fee and refusing to do a screen test.

MANFRED MANN

Paul Jones (vocals and harmonica)
Manfred Mann (keyboards)
Mike Vickers (guitar)
Tom McGuinness (bass)
Mike Hugg (drums)

1962 Dec The group is formed in London as The Mann-Hugg Blues Brothers, after Mann (b. Michael Lubowitz, Oct.21, 1940, Johannesburg, South Africa) and Hugg (b. Aug.11, 1942, Andover, Hants., UK), have met in the summer while playing piano and vibes respectively at a Butlin's holiday camp. They recruit Jones (b. Paul Pond, Feb.24, 1942, Portsmouth, Hants.), Vickers (b. Apr.18, 1941, Southampton, Hants.), and Dave Richmond on bass.

1963 Mar They play London's Marquee club, one of a series of notable engagements which attracts record companies' attention.

May With a change of name to Manfred Mann, the group signs to EMI's HMV label.

July Debut single, jazz/R&B instrumental *Why Should We Not?* fails to chart.

Oct *Cock-A-Hoop* is an uptempo R&B vocal, and again does not chart.

1964 Jan Richmond leaves for session work, and is replaced by McGuinness (b. Dec.2, 1941, Wimbledon, London, UK), who has played with Eric Clapton° in The Roosters. The group is asked to write a new theme tune for UK TV pop show "Ready Steady Go!", and comes up with *5-4-3-2-1*.

Feb With promotion of the TV show (on which the group frequently also guests), *5-4-3-2-1* hits UK #5. (Its lyric reverses several thousand years of Greek mythology – in this song, the Trojans wait at the gates of Troy, and the Greeks are inside!)

May *Hubble Bubble Toil And Trouble*, in uptempo R&B style, reaches UK #11.

Aug The group covers *Do Wah Diddy Diddy*, an obscure Jeff Barry/Ellie Greenwich song originally cut without success by The Exciters. It deposes The Beatles'° *A Hard Day's Night* to top the UK chart for 2 weeks, and sells 650,000 copies in UK.

Oct Debut LP *The Five Faces Of Manfred Mann*, a collection mainly of R&B covers with a few originals, hits UK #3. Meanwhile, *Do Wah Diddy Diddy* is their US chart debut, hitting #1 for 2 weeks.

Nov A revival of The Shirelles'° *Sha La La* hits UK #3.

Dec US compilation LP *The Manfred Mann Album* reaches US #35.

1965 Jan *Sha La La* makes US #12.

Feb The group's first down-tempo A-side, *Come Tomorrow*, hits UK #4.

Mar *Come Tomorrow* reaches US #50, while LP *The Five Faces Of Manfred Mann* peaks at US #141.

May *Oh No Not My Baby*, a revival of Maxine Brown's US hit, reaches UK #11.

June The group appears in the televised Brighton Song Festival in UK, performing *The One In The Middle*, an autobiographical song. They also perform Bacharach/David's *My Little Red Book* on the soundtrack of movie *What's New, Pussycat?*; released as a US single, it fails to chart.

July *The One In The Middle* is the title song of a 4-track EP, which sells as strongly as a single in UK, and hits #6. (The main selling point of the EP is the inclusion of a version of Bob Dylan's° *With God On Our Side*, which receives wide airplay.)

Oct Another Dylan° song, *If You Gotta Go, Go Now* (unrecorded by Dylan himself), hits UK #2 behind Ken Dodd's *Tears*.

Nov LP *Mann Made*, again a mix of covers and originals, hits UK #7. Vickers leaves to concentrate on arranging and studio work, and McGuinness switches to guitar. The group recruits new bassist Jack Bruce (b. May 14, 1943, Lanarkshire, Scotland), but he has to work out a month's notice with John Mayall°, so Pete Burford and David Hyde each fill in on bass for 2 weeks.

1966 Jan [26] The Animals'° Eric Burdon sings lead vocals for Manfred Mann at a London gig, while Paul Jones is recovering from a minor car crash.

May *Pretty Flamingo* tops the UK chart for 3 weeks.

July *You Gave Me Somebody To Love* peaks at UK #36.

July [31] Jones leaves the group, having given a year's notice of his intention. Bruce departs at the same time, to form Cream° with Eric Clapton° and Ginger Baker.

Aug After the group has considered Rod Stewart°, Long John Baldry° and Wayne Fontana°, Jones is replaced by Mike D'Abo (b. Mar.1, 1944, UK), ex-A Band of Angels, and Bruce by Klaus Voorman (b. Apr.29, 1942, West Berlin, West Germany) from Paddy, Klaus & Gibson. *Pretty Flamingo* peaks at US #29. Meanwhile, the group changes record labels in UK from HMV to Fontana, and links with producer Shel Talmy.

Sept A cover of Bob Dylan's° *Just Like A Woman*, from his LP *Blonde On Blonde*, is the group's first Fontana single (and first with D'Abo on lead vocals). It hits UK #10 but is not released in US where Dylan himself has the hit single, and Dylan's version is not on a UK single.

Oct Compilation LP *Mann Made Hits* on HMV reaches UK #11.

Nov *Semi-Detached Suburban Mr. James* hits UK #2. (The title

MANFRED MANN *cont.*

originally used the more commonplace name Jones; but was changed while recording in case it should be interpreted as a reference to Paul Jones.) Meanwhile, Jones, who has remained contracted to HMV as a soloist, releases his first single *High Time*, which hits UK #4. Manfred Mann's first Fontana LP *As Is* reaches UK #22.

1967 Jan LP *Soul Of Mann*, a compilation LP on HMV of the group's instrumental tracks, makes UK #40.

Feb Jones' solo *I've Been A Bad Bad Boy* hits UK #5.

Apr The group's *Ha! Ha! Said The Clown* hits UK #4.

May Jones stars in Peter Watkins' film *Privilege*, with model Jean Shrimpton. An EP of the songs from the movie tops the UK EP chart, but does not register on the singles chart.

June Manfred Mann's instrumental revival of Tommy Roe's° *Sweet Pea* makes UK #36.

Sept Jones' *Thinkin' Ain't For Me* reaches UK #32, while the group's version of Randy Newman's° *So Long Dad* fails to chart.

1968 Jan UK movie *Up The Junction* has songs and music written and performed by the group. The soundtrack LP fails to chart.

Feb The group covers another Dylan° song (as yet unrecorded by him), *The Mighty Quinn (Quinn The Eskimo)*, which tops the UK for 2 weeks.

Apr *The Mighty Quinn* hits US #10.

June LP *The Mighty Quinn* makes US #176; in UK titled *Mighty Garvey*, it fails to chart.

July A cover of John Simon's *My Name Is Jack* hits UK #8.

1969 Jan *Fox On The Run* peaks at US #97.

Feb *Fox On The Run* hits UK #5, while Jones' final UK solo chart success, at UK #45, is *Aquarius* (from musical *Hair*). (He drops out of music to concentrate on theatre work for the next 10 years, including appearances in *Conduct Unbecoming* (a 2-year stint), *Hamlet* and *Joseph and the Amazing Technicolor Dream Coat*.)

May Manfred Mann's *Ragamuffin Man* hits UK #8.

June The group splits after a series of farewell gigs. Mann forms a jazz group named Emanon ("no name" backwards), but this soon disbands. He and Hugg work together on advertising jingles and similar projects, working for Michelin, Ski Yogurt, and other commercial products.

Oct McGuinness forms McGuinness Flint, with Hughie Flint (drums), Benny Gallagher (guitar and vocals), Graham Lyle (guitar and vocals) and Dennis Coulson (keyboards and vocals).

Nov Mann and Hugg re-group with session musicians as Manfred Mann Chapter Three, issuing an eponymous LP on Philips' "progressive" label Vertigo. It fails to sell.

1970 Oct *Manfred Mann Chapter Three, Volume Two* also fails, after which the group splits.

Dec McGuinness Flint's *When I'm Dead And Gone* hits UK #2, but the band is mainly studio-bound and rarely plays live gigs.

1971 Feb LP *McGuinness Flint* hits UK #9 and US #155, while *When I'm Dead And Gone* reaches US #47.

May *Malt And Barley Blues* by McGuinness Flint hits UK #5.

Sept McGuinness Flint LP *Happy Birthday, Ruthy Baby* makes US #198.

1972 Mar Mann forms Manfred Mann's Earth Band, with Mick Rogers (vocals and guitar), Colin Pattenden (bass) and Chris Slade (drums). The new group's debut LP *Manfred Mann's Earth Band* makes US #138.

Apr Earth Band's *Living Without You* climbs to US #69.

1973 June Earth Band LP *Get Your Rocks Off* (the title track another Dylan° song) peaks at US #196.

Oct The group hits UK #9 with *Joybringer*, based on *Jupiter*, from Holst's *The Planets*.

1974 Apr The group signs a new recording deal with Bronze Records and LP *Solar Fire* reaches US #96.

Dec LP *The Good Earth* makes US #157.

1975 Feb McGuinness Flint splits after two further unsuccessful LPs. McGuinness and keyboards player Lou Stonebridge (latter-day replacement for Coulson) continue as Stonebridge McGuinness, but will have no chart success.

Oct Earth Band LP *Nightingales And Bombers* reaches US #120.

1976 Apr The band's version of Bruce Springsteen's° *Spirit In The Night* reaches US #97.

Sept Another Springsteen cover, *Blinded By The Light* hits UK #6.

Oct The first Earth Band LP to chart in UK is *The Roaring Silence* (including *Blinded By The Light*), which hits UK #10. Chris Thompson replaces Mick Rogers as lead vocalist.

1977 Feb *Blinded By The Light* tops the US chart for a week and is a million-seller.

Mar LP *The Roaring Silence* hits US #10, earning the band its only gold LP.

June *Spirit In The Night* is reissued in a remixed version and climbs to US #40.

1978 Apr LP *Watch* reaches US #83.

June *Davy's On The Road Again* hits UK #6, as LP *Watch* makes UK #33.

1979 Feb Jones and McGuinness reunite to form The Blues Band, initially only part-time, with Dave Kelly on guitar and vocals, Gary Fletcher on bass and Hughie Flint on drums. (Rob Townsend will replace Flint midway through the band's existence.)

Mar Earth Band's version of Dylan's° *You Angel You* peaks at UK #54, and its parent LP *Angel Station* reaches UK #30.

Apr The Blues Band makes its live debut at The Bridge House, Canning Town, London.

June Earth Band's *You Angel You* makes US #58, while LP *Angel Station* peaks at US #144.

July *Don't Kill It Carol*, also from LP *Angel Station*, peaks at UK #45.

Oct TV-advertised LP *Semi-Detached Suburban*, a compilation of Manfred Mann's 1960s hits, demonstrates their enduring appeal by hitting UK #9.

1980 Mar The Blues Band LP *Official Bootleg Album* makes UK #40.

July The Blues Band's eponymous EP (featuring *Maggie's Farm*, *Ain't It Tuff*, *Diddy Wah Diddy* and *Back Door Man* reaches UK #68.

Nov LP *Ready* by The Blues Band climbs to UK #36.

1981 Mar Earth Band LP *Chance* reaches US #87.

Oct The Blues Band LP *Itchy Feet* makes UK #60.

1982 Dec After 4 years of over 600 gigs in UK, Canada and Europe, The Blues Band splits following farewell concerts at The Venue in London. (Jones will return to stage work, appearing in *Cats* in 1982, followed by long residencies in *Guys and Dolls* and *The Beggar's Opera*.)

1983 Feb Earth Band LP *Somewhere In Africa*, a concept LP about Mann's homeland of South Africa, makes UK #87.

Apr [30] The original Manfred Mann reunites for the 25th anniversary of London's Marquee club.

1984 Mar *Runner* reaches US #22, while a new, amended version of LP *Somewhere In Africa* (on the band's new US label Arista) peaks at US #40.

1986 July With Bronze Records having gone into liquidation 2 years earlier, the band re-emerges after a lengthy silence on 10 Records with LP *Criminal Tango*, consisting of revivals of other's oldies. It does not chart.

1987 Nov Second 10 LP *Masque* offers a new sound without vocalist Thompson, but also fails to chart.

THE MAMAS AND THE PAPAS

John Phillips (vocals)
Denny Doherty (vocals)
Cass Elliot (vocals)
Michelle Gilliam (vocals)

1964 The group comes together as trio The New Journeymen in St. Thomas in the Virgin Islands, when Doherty teams with the two remaining Journeymen, Phillips and Gilliam. Phillips (b. Aug.30, 1935, Parris Island, S.C., US) has been a member of folk trio The Journeymen (with Scott McKenzie and Dick Weissman), releasing three LPs on Capitol, Gilliam (b. Holly Michelle Gilliam, June 4, 1945, Long Beach, Cal., US), whom Phillips married after meeting at San Francisco's Hungry I club in 1962, has joined The Journeymen, and Doherty, (b. Nov.29, 1941, Halifax, Nova Scotia, Canada), has sung with similar group The Halifax Three, recording for Epic, before joining Elliot (b. Ellen Naomi Cohen, Sept.19, 1941, Baltimore, Md., US), ex-lead singer of The Big Three, in The Mugwumps (with Zalman Yanovsky and John Sebastian who form The Lovin' Spoonful°). The Mugwumps release *I Don't Wanna Know*, on Warner Bros., cut some more material not issued at the time, and after working on *Freak Out* movie soundtrack, split. The New Journeymen rehearse to fulfill contractual obligations.

1965 Jan Elliot has become a waitress, but joins them briefly in the Virgin Islands, and then full time when the group relocates to California. Here they meet up with an old friend, ex-New Christy Minstrel

Barry McGuire, who introduces them to his producer, and owner of the new Dunhill label, Lou Adler.

Oct Adler hires the group to sing back-ups on sessions for McGuire's LP *This Precious Time* and uses Phillips' song *California Dreamin'* for McGuire. The New Journeymen sign to Dunhill in their own right, and after toying with The Magic Circle as a name, they become The Mamas and The Papas.

Dec *Go Where You Wanna Go* is recorded as a debut single, but Adler changes his mind and puts out the group's own version of *California Dreamin'* instead (it uses the same backing track as McGuire's LP version).

1966 Mar *California Dreamin'* hits US #4 and earns a gold disk for a million-plus US sales.

May *Monday Monday*, another Phillips song (which everyone apart from him in the group dislikes), is the follow-up. It tops the US chart for 3 weeks, and is another million-seller. Meanwhile, *California Dreamin'* makes UK #23 and LP *If You Can Believe Your Eyes And Ears*, which contains both songs, tops the US chart for a week, selling over a million copies in its 105-week chart stay.

June *Monday Monday* hits UK #3.

July *I Saw Her Again* hits US #5, while the LP (retitled *The Mamas And The Papas* in UK) hits UK #3.

July [8] Gilliam leaves the group, in need of a rest (and also because of friction with husband Phillips), and is replaced temporarily by Jill Gibson, long-time girlfriend of Jan Berry from Jan and Dean°. (She will return before the end of the year.)

Sept *I Saw Her Again* makes UK #11.

Nov *Look Through My Window* reaches US #24 (but fails to chart in UK), while the group's second LP *The Mamas And The Papas* hits US #4 and earns another gold disk. They make a US TV special.

1967 Jan *Words Of Love*, a lead vocal showcase for Elliot, hits US #5 and is a third million-selling single. The B-side, a revival of Martha & The Vandellas'° *Dancing In The Street*, makes US #73.

Feb The second LP (retitled *Cass, John, Michelle And Denny* in UK) peaks at UK #24. *Words Of Love* makes UK #47.

Mar [2] *Monday Monday* wins a Grammy award as the Best Contemporary Group Performance of 1966.

Apr A revival of The Shirelles'° *Dedicated To The One I Love* hits US #2 for 3 weeks (behind The Turtles'° *Happy Together*, and is the group's fourth million-selling single. It is taken from LP *The Mamas And The Papas Deliver*, which spends 7 weeks at US #2, and is another million-seller.

May *Dedicated To The One I Love* also hits UK #2, while uptempo *Creeque Alley*, the story-song of the group's history up to its first successes, hits US #5.

June [16] With Lou Adler, the group are prime movers in the organization of the Monterey International Pop Festival, in Cal. The Mamas and The Papas appear on the bill alongside The Who°, Jimi Hendrix°, Simon and Garfunkel°, Otis Redding°, The Grateful Dead°, and many more. The event is filmed by D.A. Pennebaker for movie *Monterey Pop*.

July LP *The Mamas And The Papas Deliver* hits UK #4. Meanwhile, Phillips' composition *San Francisco (Be Sure To Wear Some Flowers In Your Hair)*, recorded by ex-Journeyman Scott McKenzie, hits US #4.

Aug *Creeque Alley* hits UK #9 (and is the group's last UK hit single), while Scott McKenzie's *San Francisco* tops the UK chart for 4 weeks.

Sept *Twelve Thirty (Young Girls Are Coming To The Canyon)* reaches US #20.

Oct [7] Elliot spends a night in jail in London, after a dispute over a hotel bill. Plans for concerts and TV appearances by the group in UK are cancelled.

Nov *Glad To Be Unhappy*, originally recorded by the group for a Rodgers and Hart TV tribute show, peaks at US #26.

Dec Compilation LP *Farewell To The First Golden Era* hits US #5, and is the group's last gold LP, while *Dancing Bear* is their first not to enter the US top 50, peaking at #51.

1968 Mar [8] The group is included for the first time in the new publication of *Who's Who in America*.

June *Safe In My Garden* peaks at US #53.

July LP *The Papas and The Mamas* makes US #15. After its release, the group breaks up, while Phillips and Gilliam also head for a personal split.

Aug A live track with Elliot taking a solo vocal, *Dream A Little Dream*, and credited to Mama Cass, reaches US #12 and UK #11.

Sept The theme from film *For the Love of Ivy* peaks at US #81.

Oct Dunhill Records sues Phillips, Doherty and Gilliam, charging that they have not met their contractual obligations to the label since disbanding the group.

Oct [8] Elliot opens as a soloist at Caesar's Palace in Las Vegas, but suffering from tonsilitis and hampered by an under-rehearsed band, she cancels the 2-week engagement after the opening night.

Nov Second compilation LP, *Golden Era, Vol.2*, makes US #53, while first Mama Cass solo LP *Dream A Little Dream* reaches US #87, and her second solo single *California Earthquake* makes US #67.

Dec A revival of Bobby Freeman's *Do You Wanna Dance* climbs to US #76.

1969 Apr UK Compilation LP *Hits Of Gold* hits UK #7. Mama Cass' *Move In A Little Closer, Baby* makes US #58.

June Mama Cass' LP *Bubblegum, Lemonade, And . . . Something For Mama* peaks at US #91.

Aug Mama Cass' *It's Getting Better* reaches US #30 and hits UK #8 (her last UK hit).

Nov US compilation LP *16 Of Their Greatest Hits* makes US #61, while Mama Cass' *Make Your Own Kind Of Music* reaches US #36. On it (and subsequent singles) she is billed as Mama Cass Elliot.

Dec Mama Cass' LP *Make Your Own Kind Of Music* is a reissue of her previous solo set, with the addition of the hit title track. It reaches US #169.

1970 Feb Mama Cass' *New World Coming* climbs to US #42.

May Phillips' solo LP *John Phillips (John The Wolfking Of L.A.)* makes US #181.

July *Mississippi*, from Phillips' LP, climbs to US #32, his only solo hit single. Phillips also co-produces, with Lou Adler, Robert Altman's film *Brewster McCloud*.

Aug Mama Cass' *A Song That Never Comes* peaks at US #99 (her last US solo hit).

Oct [31] After Gilliam and Phillips have divorced, she marries actor Dennis Hopper, co-star of *Easy Rider*. (It will last 8 days.)

1971 Mar Mama Cass' compilation LP *Mama's Big Ones* peaks at US #194.

Apr LP *Dave Mason And Mama Cass*, duetted by Elliot with the ex-member of Traffic°, makes US #49. Doherty's solo LP *Whatcha Gonna Do?* fails to sell.

Nov The group attempts a reunion with LP *People Like Us*, but it peaks at US #84 after lukewarm reviews, and they decide to split again.

1972 Feb *Step Out*, taken from the reunion LP, makes US #81.

1973 Mar Double compilation LP *20 Golden Hits* reaches US #186.

July [30] At a press conference organized by New York Senator James Buckley, the former group members announce a $9 million suit against ABC-Dunhill Records. Phillips claims in a press statement that the label has been guilty of "systematic, cold-blooded theft of perhaps up to $60 million, stolen from each and every artist who recorded for it during a 7-year period". The label claims that the charges are "without foundation".

1974 July [29] Elliot dies while staying in London, aged 32, from a heart attack while choking on food and inhaling vomit.

1977 Michelle Phillips (she has kept her original married surname as her professional name) becomes a successful actress and appears in cinema and TV movies such as *Dillinger* and *Valentino*. She also records solo LP, *Victim Of Romance* for A&M, which fails to chart.

July TV-promoted compilation LP *The Best Of The Mamas And The Papas* hits UK #6.

1980 July [30] Phillips is arrested in LA by federal narcotics agents for possession of cocaine.

1981 Apr [20] Phillips is jailed for 5 years after pleading guilty in an LA court to drug possession charges. (The sentence will be suspended after 30 days, in exchange for 250 hours of community service by Phillips. He will tour US, lecturing against drugs.)

1982 Mar [3] Phillips and Doherty re-form the group for a reunion tour, which opens at New York's Other End club. The female group members are both new: Phillips' daughter MacKenzie (who has starred in film *American Graffiti*) and Spanky McFarlane (ex-lead singer of Spanky & Our Gang). This new line-up releases nothing new on disk but remains on the oldies touring circuit in US.

1986 July The re-formed Mamas and The Papas are hired by the Florida Panhandle real estate company to play a beach gig at Destin, Fla. in order to attract prospective condominium buyers.

1988 Nov Phillips co-writes The Beach Boys'° US #1 Kokomo.

THE MANHATTAN TRANSFER

Tim Hauser (vocals)
Alan Paul (vocals)
Janis Siegel (vocals)
Laurel Massé (vocals)

1972 The group forms in New York, US, as a tight vocal harmony unit (the descendants of an earlier The Manhattan Transfer which had featured Hauser with a jug band-type backing, recording briefly for Capitol). Hauser has been in teenage doo-wop groups in New York, while Paul has been a child actor, played on Broadway in *Oliver* and toured in *Grease*, and featured in TV commercials. Siegel and Massé have worked in commercials and done session vocal work. (In the mid-1960s, Siegel was in girl group The Young Generation, on Leiber and Stoller's Red Bird label.)

1973 A sound incorporating elements from (and material out of) several vocal group genres, plus a visual style embodying 1930s and 1940s swing era kitsch, is first honed in New York's gay clubs and baths (the same circuit which helped Bette Midler° to fame a year or two earlier).

1974 Mainstream cabaret work develops the group's spectacularly-staged live show, and it signs to Atlantic Records.

1975 July Debut LP *The Manhattan Transfer* reaches US #33, and has the longest group US LP chart run at 38 weeks. Hauser co-produces it with Atlantic boss Ahmet Ertegun.

Aug [10] The group's musical/comedy variety show "Manhattan Transfer" begins a 4-week run on US CBS TV on Sunday evenings, in a summer replacement slot.

Nov Taken from the debut LP, *Operator* makes US #22. It is the group's US single chart debut (and will be its sole US hit single until 1980),

1976 Feb *Tuxedo Junction* reaches UK #24.

Oct LP *Coming Out*, produced by Richard Perry, makes US #48.

1977 Mar Taken from LP *Coming Out*, the group's revival of Art and Dotty Todd's 1958 US top 10 hit *Chanson D'Amour*, sung in French, tops the UK chart for 5 weeks (having dethroned another Perry production, Leo Sayer's° *When I Need You*). It is also a major hit in France, and establishes the group all over Europe, but fails in US.

Apr LP *Coming Out* makes UK #12, while debut LP *Manhattan Transfer* belatedly charts in UK, reaching #49.

June *Don't Let Go*, taken from LP *Coming Out*, climbs to UK #32.

1978 Mar LP *Pastiche* reaches US #66 and hits UK #10.

Apr *Walk In Love*, from LP *Pastiche*, reaches UK #12. The group begins a UK tour.

June Also from the LP, *On A Little Street In Singapore* makes UK #20.

Sept Double A-side extract from LP *Pastiche*, a revival of The Supremes'° *Where Did Our Love Go* and the French-sung *Je Voulais Te Dire (Que Je T'Attends)*, climbs to UK #40.

Dec Live LP *Live*, recorded in Manchester, Bristol and London during the group's April/May tour, hits UK #4.

1979 Jan A further single from LP *Pastiche*, *Who What When Where Why* makes UK #49. Massé leaves the group, and is replaced by Cheryl Bentyne.

Nov LP *Extensions*, produced by Jay Graydon, includes *Birdland*, a vocal version of Weather Report's tribute to Charlie Parker and a highlight of the group's stage act, and makes UK #63. (*Birdland* is also used for a TV ad jingle by Akai Hi-Fi.)

1980 Jan LP *Extensions* peaks at US #55. The group updates its sound and its image changes from pure swing era to more modern slick chic.

June *Twilight Zone-Twilight Tone* (incorporating the instrumental riff from the old TV series theme) peaks at US #30 and UK #25.

Dec *Trickle Trickle* makes US #73, as *Downbeat* magazine names them the Best Vocal Group of 1980 in its annual poll.

1981 Feb [25] The group wins a Grammy award for *Birdland*, named Best Vocal or Instrumental Jazz Fusion Performance of 1980.

Aug LP *Mecca For Moderns* reaches US #22, while from it the group's revival of The Ad Libs' 1965 US top 10 hit *Boy From New York City* hits US #7 and is its biggest-selling US single. It fails to chart in UK, where it has been a top 5 success for Darts only 3 years previously.

1982 Jan Compilation LP *The Best Of The Manhattan Transfer* reaches US #103.

Feb [24] The group wins two further Grammy awards: *Boy From New York City* is named Best Pop Performance by a Duo or Group with Vocal, while LP track *Until I Met You (Corner Pocket)* is voted Best Duo or Group Jazz Vocal Performance.

June A revival of *Route 66*, featured in Burt Reynolds film *Sharkey's Machine*, makes US #78.

1983 Oct Disco-flavored club favorite *Spirit Of Life*, penned by Rod Temperton and Derek Bramble, climbs to US #40.

Dec LP *Bodies And Souls*, produced by Richard Rudolph and including *Spice Of Life*, peaks at US #57, in a 6-month chart stay.

1984 Feb *Spice Of Life* reaches UK #19 as LP *Bodies And Souls* makes UK #53.

1985 Feb The group's last hit single is *Baby Come Back To Me (The Morse Code Of Love)*, which creeps to US #83. It is taken from part-live, part-studio-recorded LP *Bop Doo-Wop*, a minor US chart entry at #127. (The group will continue to work steadily in concert and cabaret.)

BARRY MANILOW

1957/61 Manilow (b. Barry Alan Pinkus, June 17, 1946, Brooklyn, New York, N.Y., US), raised by his mother and grandparents, acquires a stepfather, Willie Murphy, and a piano. After leaving Eastern District high school in Brooklyn, where he was voted best musician, Manilow moves to Greenwich Village, marries and goes to work in the CBS mailroom in Manhattan. He enters New York City College to study advertising, with the aim of becoming a television executive. Within a year, he has moved to the New York College of Music, which leads to spending 2 years at the Juillard School of Music.

1962 Having spent a short time as a film editor at CBS, Manilow is asked by an off-Broadway producer to write some music arrangements on current projects. He writes an original score for *The Drunkard*.

1967 Recently divorced, Manilow is asked by CBS to be musical director on show "Callback", a syndicated showcase for newcomers.

1970/71 Manilow spends 2 years on "Callback", and also writes many TV and radio commercials.

1972 Mar Having spent two seasons working as one half of the duo Jeanne & Barry in cabaret at Upstairs At The Downstairs in New York opening for Joan Rivers (and playing piano for auditioning actors), Manilow is about to quit when a girl singer asks him to accompany her audition at the Continental Baths, a nightclub set up in the basement by a Turkish Bath establishment. She fails the audition, but Manilow is taken on as house pianist on Saturday nights. 2 weeks later, young singer Bette Midler° turns up for an audition. Manilow arranges and produces Midler's *Boogie Woogie Bugle Boy* single and its parent LP *The Divine Miss M.* He cuts his own demo which he sells to Bell Records, on the condition that he will tour to promote a debut LP.

1973 Midler° asks Manilow to be her musical director on a US tour. Manilow, his debut LP completed, obliges, opening the second half of her show with three of his own songs.

1974 Apr While Midler° takes a year's sabbatical, Manilow tours US and, without a hit single, performs some of the material his audience may be familiar with: Manilow-performed or penned commercials for products such as McDonalds, Kentucky Fried Chicken, Pepsi, Dr. Pepper and many others.

1975 Jan *Mandy* (originally *Brandy* when its lyricist Scott English made US #91 with it in Mar. 1972) hits US #1 for 1 week.

Feb LP *Barry Manilow II* hits US #9.

Mar *Mandy* makes UK #11, Manilow's UK debut.

Apr *It's A Miracle*, on Arista, reaches US #12.

Aug *Could It Be Magic*, based on Chopin's *Prelude In C Minor*, hits US #6.

Oct LP *Barry Manilow I* reaches US #28.

1976 Jan *I Write The Songs*, written by The Beach Boys° Bruce Johnston, tops the US chart, for 1 week. (Arista president Clive Davis had heard David Cassidy's° version during a UK visit.)

Feb LP *Tryin' To Get The Feelin'* hits US #5 (and will be Manilow's longest charted US LP at 87 weeks).

May Title cut ballad *Tryin' To Get The Feelin'* hits US #10.

July [30] Manilow begins an 8-month 98-city US tour.

Oct *This One's For You* makes US #29.

Dec [21] *Barry Manilow On Broadway* opens for a 2-week sold-out season at New York's Uris Theater. (The show will receive a special Tony award.)

1977 Feb *Weekend In New England*, penned by Randy Edelman, hits US #10.

Feb [19] *I Write The Songs* wins the Grammy for Song of the Year at

the 19th annual awards.

Mar [2] US ABC TV airs "The Barry Manilow Special".

Apr [13] Manilow ends his US tour at the MGM Grand Hotel, Las Vegas, Nev.

Apr LP *This One's For You* hits US #6, earning his first platinum disk.

July *Looks Like We Made It* hits US #1 for 1 week. LP *Barry Manilow Live*, recorded at Uris Theater, tops the US chart. (He has five LPs on chart and by the year's end will have sold 7 million LPs in a year in US.)

Sept [11] "The Barry Manilow Special" wins an Emmy award in Comedy, Variety or Music Special category.

Nov *Daybreak* reaches US #23.

1978 Feb LP *Even Now* enters the US chart to hit #3 and earn another platinum disk.

Feb [24] US ABC TV airs "The Second Barry Manilow Special" from the Hollywood Pantages, with guest Ray Charles°.

May *Can't Smile Without You* hits US #3 and makes UK #43.

July *Even Now* reaches US #19.

Aug *Copacabana (At The Copa)*, from Chevy Chase/Goldie Hawn film *Foul Play*, hits US #8 and UK #42, although in UK the song is double A-side with *Somewhere In The Night*.

Oct [7] Manilow begins a European tour with a concert at London's Royal Albert Hall.

Oct He has his first LP success in UK with LP *Even Now* which reaches #12.

Nov *Ready To Take A Chance Again*, from LP *Foul Play* (and an Academy Award nominee), makes US #15.

1979 Jan *Could It Be Magic* peaks at UK #25.

Feb *Somewhere In The Night*, written by Richard Kerr and Will Jennings, hits US #9.

Feb [15] Manilow wins a Grammy award for *Copacabana*, which is named Best Male Pop Vocal Performance of 1978.

Mar LP *Manilow Magic* hits UK #3 (and will have a 151-week chart stay). Double compilation LP *Greatest Hits* hits US #7 and earns another platinum LP.

May [23] US ABC TV airs "The Third Barry Manilow Special".

Nov *Ships* hits US #9.

1980 Feb *When I Wanted You* reaches US #20. LP *One Voice* hits US #9, and again earns a platinum disk. (Its title cut will become a popular live number as successive audiences learn to light candles during its opening bars. Manilow will contribute the song as the national theme for United Way of America.)

May *I Don't Want To Walk Without You* climbs to US #36.

Oct LP *One Voice* makes UK #18. Manilow writes and performs *We Still Have Time* for Jack Lemmon film *Tribute*.

Nov *Lonely Together* reaches UK #21.

1981 Jan *I Made It Through The Rain* hits US #10 as parent LP *Barry* reaches US #15, his sixth consecutive platinum LP. *Lonely Together* makes UK #21. LPs *Manilow Magic* and *Barry* both hit UK #5. Manilow embarks on "In The Round World Tour".

Feb *I Made It Through The Rain* makes UK #37.

Apr *Lonely Together* breaks a run of 18 consecutive top 40 hits, stalling at US #45. Boxed LP *Gift Set* makes UK #62.

May Uptempo *Bermuda Triangle* reaches UK #15. 78,000 tickets are sold within hours of a Manilow UK tour.

Oct *Let's Hang On* makes UK #12 as parent LP *If I Should Love Again*, the first solely produced by Manilow, hits UK #5.

Nov *The Old Songs* reaches US #15 as parent LP *If I Should Love Again* makes US #14.

Dec *The Old Songs* peaks at UK #48.

1982 Jan Manilow sells out five nights at London's Royal Albert Hall at the start of a 15-date UK tour.

Feb *Somewhere Down The Road* reaches US #21 as *If I Should Love Again* stalls at UK #66. LP *Greatest Hits* makes US #147.

Apr [19] UK BBC TV airs the first of two "Barry in Britain" TV specials.

May A revival of The Four Seasons'° *Let's Hang On* makes US #32. LP *Barry Live In Britain* tops the UK chart for 1 week. *Stay*, from the LP, makes UK #23.

Sept *Oh Julie!* reaches US #38.

Oct [6] Manilow begins "Around the World in 80 Dates" tour, including dates in 52 US cities and first visits to Japan and Australia.

Oct LP *Oh Julie!* reaches US #69.

Nov *I Wanna Do It With You* hits UK #8 as parent LP *I Wanna Do It With You* hits UK #7.

Dec *I'm Gonna Sit Right Down And Write Myself A Letter* peaks at UK #36.

1983 Jan *Memory*, from the musical *Cats*, reaches US #39, and LP *Here Comes The Night* makes US #32.

June *Some Kind Of Friend* stalls at UK #48.

Aug [27] Manilow embarks on UK leg of "Around the World" tour, performing before 40,000 fans at an outdoor concert at Blenheim Palace, Oxfordshire, UK. (Showtime TV channel will air "Barry Manilow: The Concert at Blenheim Palace".)

Sept *You're Looking Hot Tonight* climbs to UK #47.

Oct [6] The world tour ends with a gala charity concert at London's Royal Albert Hall in the presence of the Prince and Princess of Wales.

Oct LP *A Touch More Magic* hits UK #10.

1984 Jan *Read 'Em And Weep*, written and produced by Jim Steinman (and originally recorded by Meat Loaf°) reaches US #18 and UK #17 as parent LP *Barry Manilow/Greatest Hits, Volume II* makes US #30.

Dec LP *2.00 AM Paradise Café*, with guests Sarah Vaughan, Mel Tormé and Gerry Mulligan, makes UK #28.

1985 Jan LP *2.00 AM Paradise Café* reaches US #28.

July Compilation LP *The Manilow Collection – 20 Classic Hits* reaches US #100.

Nov LP *Manilow* climbs to UK #40.

1986 Jan [4/6] Manilow plays three sell-out dates at Wembley during his UK tour.

Aug Now signed to RCA Records, Manilow's *I'm Your Man* peaks at US #86. He releases his first Spanish language LP, *Barry Manilow, Grandes Exitos En Espanol.*

1987 Manilow has a tumor on his tongue removed by surgery.

Nov "Big Fun on Swing Street" with Kid Creole°, Gerry Mulligan, Stanley Clarke and Phyllis Hyman, and produced by Steve Binder, airs on US TV.

Nov [25] Manilow begins major worldwide tour "Big Fun Tour De Force" in Milwaukee, Wis.

1988 Feb LP *Swing Street* reaches US #70 and UK #81.

Nov [11] Manilow continues his world tour with the European leg in Mainz, West Germany. A fan in East Germany writes to Manilow: "Please tell me when you're coming to West Germany. I plan to

BARRY MANILOW *cont.*

steal a hot-air balloon and sail over the Berlin Wall."

Nov [27] Manilow takes part in the fifth anniversary, and final, edition of UK TV variety show "Live from the Palladium", before playing a week of sell-out concerts at London's Alexandra Palace.

THE MARCELS

Cornelius "Nini" Harp (lead vocals and guitar)
Ronald "Bingo" Mundy (first tenor vocal)
Gene Bricker (second tenor vocal)
Dick Knauss (baritone vocal)
Fred Johnson (bass vocal)

1960 The multi-racial vocal quintet (three black vocalists and two whites, with a name taken from a hairstyle) is based in Pittsburgh, Pa., where its club act consists mainly of versions of R&B and doo-wop group oldies. It disbands and re-forms more than once before manager Julius Kruspir sends a sampler tape of the group's vocal efforts to producer Stu Phillips at New York-based Colpix Records.

1961 Feb Phillips calls in the group for an after-hours recording session. After cutting three tracks, they experiment with the Rodgers and Hart oldie *Blue Moon*, eventually turning in an outrageous version which kicks the tempo high and buries the original melody under bass singer Johnson performing an exaggerated parody of the traditional bass doo-wop role. This proves to be the gimmick which hooks first radio DJs and then record buyers. Murray The K at station W-INS in New York plays a borrowed advance tape 26 times in one show, creating a demand in the city overnight.

Apr *Blue Moon* tops the US chart for 3 weeks (displacing Elvis Presley's° *Surrender*), and is a US million-seller. (It also hits R&B #1 for 2 weeks.)

May Licensed by Pye International Records, *Blue Moon* also tops the UK chart for 2 weeks, despite attacks on it from panelists on UK BBC TV's "Juke Box Jury" and in most of the press.

June A straighter, gimmick-free revival of George Gershwin's *Summertime* makes US #78 and UK #46. The group's two white vocalists Bricker and Knauss leave, and are replaced by Walt Maddox and Fred Johnson's brother Allen. The next single, a revamp of another oldie, *You Are My Sunshine*, fails to chart.

Dec A revival of Ted Weems' 1947 million-seller *Heartaches*, given the *Blue Moon* treatment, hits US #7 but fails in UK. The group appears alongside Chubby Checker° and Dion° in the low-budget twist craze exploitation movie *Twist Around The Clock*, singing *Merry Twistmas*.

1962 Feb *My Melancholy Baby* (on which the group parodies itself, starting with *Blue Moon* bass man intro, halting proceedings with a hammy "oh no, not that ole thing again – sing *Melancholy Baby*", and then doing just that, but in *Blue Moon* style), makes US #58. The gimmick approach is wearing thin, and it will be the group's last hit. Mundy leaves, followed by Harp, as the group encounters managerial problems. A final Colpix single, *I Wanna Be The Leader* has the once-again highlighted bass vocalist bewailing his restriction to singing "ba-ba-ba's" – he wants to be lead vocalist and handle real lyrics. The group cuts its final single, *How Deep Is The Ocean*, for Kyra label, and disbands afterwards.

1963 Apr Johnny Cymbal pays tribute to The Marcels' sound on his *Mr. Bass Man*, which reaches US #16 and UK #24.

1970s The five original Marcels reunite on several occasions for Ralph Nader's "Rock'n'Roll Revival" shows.

1980 The Marcels' version of *Blue Moon* is used over the closing credits of John Landis' movie *An American Werewolf in London*.

MARILLION

Fish (vocals)
Steve Rothery (guitar)
Mark Kelly (keyboards)
Peter Trewavas (bass)
Mick Pointer (drums)

1978 Dec Silmarillion, named after the book by J.R.R. Tolkien, is formed in Aylesbury, Bucks., UK by Doug Irvine (bass) and Mick Pointer (b. July 22, 1956) (drums) as an instrumental group, playing a 1-hour set at the Hanborough Tavern in Southall, Middx.

1979 Aug Rothery (b. Nov.25, 1959, Brampton, South Yorkshire, UK), answering a music paper ad, is chosen from 30 applicants and joins the band on guitar.

Oct Brian Jelliman is added on keyboards, and the group shortens its name to Marillion.

1980 Nov Irvine leaves. While the group advertises for a bassist/vocalist, it records instrumental *The Web* at Leyland studio in Buckingham, Bucks., and sends the tape to two musicians from Scotland, who had been in touch with them.

1981 Jan [2] Fish (b. Derek William Dick, Apr.25, 1958, Dalkeith, near Edinburgh, Scotland) and Diz Minnitt arrive, with lyrics to *The Web*, to audition. (Fish, the son of a garage proprietor, having left school to do a 4-year degree course with the Forestry Commission in Cumbria, has sung with small bands in Scotland. His nickname has stuck when a landlady accuses him of wallowing in the bath like a fish.)

Mar [14] The new line-up debuts at the Red Lion pub, Bicester, Oxfordshire.

July Marillion records a 3-track demo at Roxon studio, Oxfordshire, which is later sold at gigs.

Aug The band supports Spirit° at local venue, The Friars, Aylesbury.

Nov Kelly (b. Apr.9, 1961, Dublin, Eire), playing with Romford-band Chemical Alice, replaces Jelliman.

1982 Jan [25] The band plays its first headlining gig at London's Marquee.

Feb The group records a session for UK BBC Radio 1's Tommy Vance's "The Friday Rock Show". A Marillion fan club called "The Web" is established.

Mar Minnitt quits the band and is replaced by Trewavas (b. Jan.15, 1959, Middlesborough, Cleveland, UK) from local group The Metros.

May Marillion begins a 25-date 6-week tour of Scotland.

July It headlines The Friars, Aylesbury, the first unsigned band to do so.

Aug The band takes part in the Theakston and Reading festivals.

Sept The group signs a worldwide contract with EMI Records.

Nov *Market Square Heroes* makes UK #60, as the group tours UK.

Dec Marillion plays 3 sell-out dates at London's Marquee.

1983 Feb *He Knows You Know* reaches UK #35. The readers of UK music paper *Sounds* vote Marillion the Best New Band of 1982.

Mar [15] Marillion begins a major UK tour at Norwich University.

Mar LP *Script For A Jester's Tear*, recorded at London's Marquee Studios in Dec. with producer Nick Tauber, hits UK #7. Lyrics are all penned by Fish, who has now adopted a central live role.

Apr [18] Marillion ends its 29-date UK tour at London's Hammersmith Odeon.

Apr *Market Square Heroes* re-enters at UK #53. The group sacks Pointer replacing him with ex-Camel drummer Andy Ward.

May [20] The group makes its UK BBC TV debut on "The Old Grey Whistle Test".

June *Garden Party* reaches UK #16. Marillion makes its first appearance on BBC TV's "Top of the Pops".

June [17] The group headlines the Glastonbury Festival.

July Marillion embarks on a 5-week tour of North America, during which *Script For A Jester's Tear*, released through Capitol, makes US #175. The tour is curtailed when Ward leaves the band.

Aug The band plays the Reading Festival for the second year, with John Marter temporarily on drums.

Sept Marillion supports Rush° for five nights at New York's Radio City Music Hall.

Oct Video *Recital Of The Script*, filmed at the Apr.18 Hammersmith Odeon concert, is released. Jonathan Mover is recruited as drummer, but leaves almost immediately.

Nov The group starts work on its new LP at the Manor studios, Oxfordshire, with drummer Ian Mosley (b. June 16, 1953, Paddington, London, UK), who has been a student at the Guildhall School of Music, before playing with Curved Air, The Gordon Giltrap Band and Steve Hackett.

Dec Taking a break from recording, Marillion plays a 5-date "Farewell to '83" tour and invites Mosley to join the band full-time.

1984 Feb *Punch And Judy* reaches UK #29.

Mar LP *Fugazi*, again produced by Tauber, hits UK #5. Video *Grendel And The Web* is released.

Apr The group begins a 24-date sell-out tour of UK, before touring Europe and North America.

May *Assassing* reaches UK #22.

July [21] Marillion plays the Milton Keynes Bowl, on a bill with Status Quo°, Nazareth and Jason & The Scorchers.

Aug The group tours Europe, playing a series of festivals in Germany.

Nov [3] Marillion plays the Royal Court Theatre, Liverpool at the start of a short UK and Europe "Real to Reel" tour.

Nov Budget-priced live LP *Real To Reel*, recorded in Leicester, UK, and Montreal, Canada, is released to counter the many bootlegs available and in response to requests from Marillion's fan club "The Web". It hits UK #8.

Dec [22] Marillion ends a 9-date sell-out tour at The Friars, Aylesbury.

1985 Mar The group starts work on new LP at the Hansa studios in Berlin, West Germany with producer Chris Kimsey.

May [25] Marillion starts a European tour.

June Ballad *Kayleigh* hits UK #2, behind The Crowd's charity chart-topper *You'll Never Walk Alone* as parent LP *Misplaced Childhood*, the last of a trilogy of concept LPs, enters the UK chart at #1.

Aug [17] The group supports Z.Z. Top° at Castle Donington, UK.

Sept *Lavender* hits UK #5 as Fish loses his voice, causing cancellation of a 23-date UK tour.

Oct *Kayleigh* makes US #74.

Nov *Heart Of Lothian* reaches UK #29.

1986 The group starts recording its fourth studio LP, and begins another tour of North America, releasing *Brief Encounter*, a mini-album of live tracks and B-sides.

June Video *1982-1986 The Videos*, featuring seven of the band's hits and B-side *Lady Nina*, is released.

Oct Fish and Tony Banks, from Genesis°, team for *Shortcut To Somewhere* which makes UK #75.

1987 May *Incommunicado* hits UK #6.

June Parent LP *Clutching At Straws* hits UK #2.

July *Sugar Mice* makes UK #22. LP *Clutching At Straws* peaks at US #103.

Sept [18] Marillion begins a US tour.

Nov *Warm Wet Circles* peaks at UK #22.

1988 July *B-Sides Themselves*, a CD-only collection of non-album material, makes UK #64.

Sept Marillion and Fish announce they are to split, citing musical differences.

Nov *Freaks (Live)* reaches UK #24.

Dec LP *The Thieving Magpie*, recorded during the 1984 "Fugazi" and 1987 "Clutching at Straws" tours, hits UK #25.

BOB MARLEY & THE WAILERS

Bob Marley (vocals and guitar)
Peter Tosh (vocals and guitar)
Bunny Wailer (vocals and percussion)
Aston "Family Man" Barrett (bass)
Carlton Barrett (drums)

1961 Marley (b. Robert Nesta Marley, Feb.6, (Passport date: Apr.6), 1945, Rhoden Hall, St. Ann's, Jamaica) the son of an English army captain from Liverpool, UK, and Jamaican Cedella Booker, comes to the attention of Kingston, Jamaica, label owner and producer Leslie Kong and records original pop song *Judge Not (Unless You Judge Yourself)* for Kong's Beverley label.

1962 Marley cuts a second single for Kong, *One Cup Of Coffee*.

1964 Marley forms The Wailin' Wailers with childhood friends from the Trenchtown ghetto of West Kingston, Tosh (b. Winston Hubert McIntosh, Oct.19, 1944, Westmoreland, Jamaica), Livingston (soon known as Bunny Wailer, b. Neville O'Riley, Apr.10, 1947, Kingston, Jamaica), Junior Braithwaite and Beverley Kelso, and begins a prolific 4-year recording relationship with top Kingston producer Clement (Sir Coxsone) Dodd, owner of the Studio One label.

1965 The Wailin' Wailers' first Studio One single, *Simmer Down*, is a big Jamaican hit (said to have sold 80,000 copies on the island). (Recording as The Wailin' Wailers and The Wailin' Rudeboys, the group will cut some 80 sides for Studio One between now and 1966 – notably *Put It On*, *The Ten Commandments Of Love* and *Love And Affection*.)

1966 The Wailers start their own Wailin' Souls label, but it soon founders when Livingston is imprisoned for possessing marijuana. Marley leaves the country, joining his mother in Delaware, US, and working in the town's Chrysler car factory.

.967 Marley returns to Jamaica to sign a deal with Johnny Nash, releasing *Reggae On Broadway*. (Nash will later have hits with *Stir It Up* and *Guava Jelly*, both written by Marley.) He reunites with Tosh and Wailer and will record 11 singles for Kong's Beverley label from late 1967 to early 1968.

969/71 Now committed Rastafarians, The Wailers leave Kong to work with similarly-inclined producer Lee "Scratch" Perry on their newly-formed Tuff Gong label. With Perry, The Wailers record successful singles, some will become reggae standards – *Soul Rebel*, *Duppy Conqueror*, *400 Years* and *Small Axe*.

1972 Island Records head Chris Blackwell signs the group, aiming to break it in the international market. With the rhythm section of the Barrett brothers, Aston "Family Man" (b. Nov.22, 1946, Kingston) and Carlton (b. Dec.17, 1950, Kingston) (who have been working with the group since the Lee Perry sessions), The Wailers release LP *Catch A Fire* which, with unprecedented promotional support, establishes them as strong contenders for mainstream pop stardom – a promise fulfilled later in the year with second Island LP *Burnin'*.

1974 Despite growing international recognition, Tosh and Wailer leave The Wailers, unhappy with the Island-generated public perception of Bob Marley & The Wailers. Female vocal trio the I-Threes (Judy Mowatt, Marcia Griffiths and Marley's wife, Rita), Bernard "Touter" Harvey and Earl "Wire" Lindo (keyboards) and Al Anderson (guitar) join the line-up.

Sept Eric Clapton° tops the US chart with Marley's *I Shot The Sheriff*. (Marley's own version is included on LP *Burnin'*.)

1975 May A US breakthrough comes with the group's third Island LP, *Natty Dread* which makes US #92.

Aug Bob Marley & The Wailers begin a UK tour with a new line-up of Tyrone Downie (keyboards), Alvin "Seeco" Patterson (percussion) and Julian "Junior" Murvin (guitar), who replace Harvey and Lindo.

Oct *No Woman No Cry*, extracted from forthcoming LP *Live!*, reaches UK #22. LP *Natty Dread* makes UK #43 while LP *Burnin'* makes US #151.

Nov LP *Catch A Fire* peaks at US #171.

Dec LP *Live!*, recorded during a summer concert at London's Lyceum Ballroom, makes UK #38.

1976 May LP *Rastaman Vibrations* reaches UK #15.

July *Roots Rock Reggae*, written by Vincent Ford, makes US #51. LP *Rastaman Vibrations* hits US #8, during a 22-week stay on chart.

Dec [3] An attempt is made on Marley's life when seven gunmen burst into his Kingston home, and injure Marley, his wife and his manager Don Taylor. (Believing it to be politically motivated, Marley leaves Jamaica for an 18-month exile in Miami, Fla., US, where LP *Exodus* will be partly recorded.)

Dec LP *Live!* makes US #90.

1977 Marley has an operation at Cedars Lebanon Hospital, Miami, Fla. to remove a toe after a cancerous growth is found. The media is informed that he has received a foot injury while playing his favorite game, soccer.

June LP *Exodus* hits UK #8.

July *Exodus* reaches UK #14.

Aug LP *Exodus* makes US #20.

Oct *Waiting In Vain* reaches UK #27, as the group plays a week at London's Rainbow Theatre.

1978 Feb Double A-side *Jamming/Punky Reggae Party* hits UK #9.

Apr *Is This Love* also hits UK #9. LP *Kaya*, which sees Lindo rejoin, hits UK #4.

Apr [22] Returning to Jamaica, the group headlines the "One Love Peace Concert" in Kingston, where Marley unites Prime Minister Michael Manley and his opponent Edward Seaga on stage in avowals of unity and common purpose.

May LP *Kaya* makes US #50.

July *Satisfy My Soul* reaches UK #21.

Dec Live double LP *Babylon By Bus*, recorded on tour, makes UK #40.

1979 Feb LP *Babylon By Bus* makes US #102. The group headlines at New York's Apollo Theater in Harlem, the first reggae band to do so.

Oct LP *Survival* reaches UK #20.

Nov *So Much Trouble In The World* makes UK #56.

Dec LP *Survival* reaches US #70.

1980 Apr [17] Marley performs at the Independence Day celebrations in Salisbury, Zimbabwe, 2 years after his first trip to Africa, visiting Kenya and Ethiopia.

Apr The group begins a major European tour, including a 100,000 sell-out show in Milan, Italy.

July *Could You Be Loved* hits UK #5 as parent LP *Uprising* hits UK #6.

July [10] Marley opens a tour in Dublin, Eire.

Aug LP *Uprisin'* reaches US #45.

BOB MARLEY & THE WAILERS *cont.*

Sept [20/21] Marley & The Wailers play New York's Madison Square Garden with The Commodores°.

Oct *Three Little Birds* reaches UK #17.

Oct [8] Marley, preparing for a major US tour with Stevie Wonder°, collapses in New York. (Cancer is diagnosed and Marley attends The Sloan-Kettering Hospital in New York as an out-patient. The tour is cancelled.)

Dec Marley flies to Dr. Josef Issels Clinic in Bavaria, Germany, for treatment. Stevie Wonder° hits US #5 with his tribute to Marley, *Master Blaster (Jammin')*.

1981 Apr Marley is awarded Jamaica's Order of Merit. In his absence, his son Ziggy accepts the honor.

May [11] Marley dies of lung cancer and a brain tumor, age 36, at the Cedars of Lebanon Hospital, Miami, Fla., having flown to his mother's home in Miami.

May [20/21] His body lies in state at the National Arena in Kingston.

May [21] A Jamaican legend, Marley is buried with full state honors in St. Ann's, after an Ethiopian Orthodox Festival is held in Kingston, attended by thousands.

July *No Woman No Cry* hits UK #8. LP *Live*, re-titled *Live At The Lyceum*, re-enters UK chart at #68.

Aug [6] The Fourth International Reggae Sunsplash Festival in Jarrett Park, Montego Bay, Jamaica, billed as a tribute to Marley, is attended by 20,000 people. Four of Marley's children appear as The Melody Makers.

Nov LP *Chances Are*, on Cotillion, recorded between 1968 and 1972, makes US #117.

1982 Dec [29] Jamaica issues a Bob Marley commemorative stamp.

1983 June *Buffalo Soldier* hits UK #4 and LP *Confrontation* hits UK #5.

July LP *Confrontation* reaches US #55.

1984 May Island releases compilation LP and video *Legend* to commemorate the third anniversary of Marley's death. The LP hits UK #1 in its week of entry. It will stay there for 12 weeks and on chart for 2 years. Double A-side *One Love/People Get Ready* hits UK #5.

July Third single from the LP, *Waiting In Vain* reaches UK #31.

Oct LP *Legend* reaches US #54.

Dec *Could You Be Loved* makes UK #71.

1986 July LP *Rebel Music* makes UK #54.

1987 Apr [17] Carlton Barrett is shot dead outside his home in Kingston.

May [19] The Wailers, having ousted Rita Marley as executor of Marley's will, call for an investigation of his estate.

MARMALADE

Dean Ford (lead vocals and harmonica)
William "Junior" Campbell (guitar, piano and vocals)
Patrick Fairley (guitar)
Graham Knight (bass)
Raymond Duffy (drums)

1961 The group is initially formed in Glasgow, Scotland, by friends Fairley (b. Apr.14, 1946) and Campbell (b. May 31, 1947), who has spent 2 years playing clarinet in the local East Bank Academy Orchestra. They are joined by apprentice plater Ford (b. Thomas McAleese, Sept.5, 1946), Knight (b. Dec.8, 1946) and trainee chef, Duffy, and call themselves The Gaylords, occasionally prefacing this with Ford's name, and concentrating on Cliff Richard° and The Shadows° as role models for image and repertoire.

1964/65 With the beat group boom in full swing, they broaden their output into US soul covers, hiring Brian Poole & The Tremeloes'° manager, Peter Walsh, to oversee all business matters, and begin playing south of the border, primarily at US Air Force bases. They are voted #1 group in Scotland, (a title they will retain in 1965 and 1966), and their professionalism draws attention from major record companies. Norrie Paramor, Cliff Richard's° mentor and head of EMI's Columbia label, is the first to sign them. Debut single in the spring of 1964 is a cover of Chubby Checker's° *Twenty Miles*, backed with an example from the Campbell/McAleese catalog, *What's The Matter With Me*. It sells in Scotland, but nowhere else. The group continues touring, releasing *Mr. Heartbreak's Here Instead* and a workout of Shirley Ellis' nonsense-rhyme novelty *The Name Game*, which also fail.

1966 Fourth, and final, Columbia single *He's A Good Face, But He's Down And Out* receives wider appreciation, but fails to chart. Disillusioned, the group decides to change name, manager, record company and relocate to London. Duffy declines and quits, later to re-surface in Matthews Southern Comfort°. The remaining quartet becomes Marmalade and places an ad for a drummer in *Melody Maker* magazine. Alan Whitehead (b. July 24, 1946), an ex-work-study trainee joins.

1967 The group earns a solid reputation in London but is unable to interest anyone in its own compositions. Despite a well received showing at the Windsor Jazz Festival, and a Thursday night residency at London's Marquee club, the group still has only support slots on tours and plays other's hits on the ballroom circuit. The members agree to "sell out" – going totally commercial in an attempt to break into the big time. They sign to CBS, but first 45 *It's All Leading Up To A Saturday Night* fails to change their fortunes.

Dec Their next single *I See The Rain*, makes the Dutch chart, peaking at #23 during a 5-week showing. Marmalade sets off on a tour of The Netherlands. Jimi Hendrix° expresses the opinion that it is the best single of 1967, but the public remains unimpressed.

1968 *Man In A Shop* fails to chart.

June They cover The Grass Roots'° *Lovin' Things* for their next single, and it hits UK #6.

Oct Follow-up *Wait For Me Marianne* peaks at UK #30 during a 5-week chart run.

1969 Jan Marmalade's cover of the bouncy reggae-tinged track from The Beatles° *White Album*, *Ob-La-Di Ob-La-Da*, tops the UK chart for 3 weeks, despite competition from The Bedrocks #20 version. LP *There's A Lot Of It About It* is released, but fails to chart.

July *Baby Make It Soon*, the group's finale for CBS, hits UK #9.

Oct [15] The band begins recording for Decca.

Nov [14] They sign to Decca. The deal allows them complete freedom to write, arrange, produce and record whatever material they wish, free from corporation interference. Campbell/McAleese-written *Reflections Of My Life* is released the same day.

1970 Jan *Reflections Of My Life* hits UK #3.

May *Reflections Of My Life*, released through sister company London, hits US #10.

June LP *Reflections Of The Marmalade* (US title: *Reflections Of My Life*) is issued. It fails in UK but climbs to US #71.

Sept Follow-up single *Rainbow* hits UK #3 and US #51. Decca claims one million sales. Campbell assumes studies at The Royal College of Music.

1971 Apr *My Little One* makes UK #15, but fails in US. Campbell quits shortly after group triumphs in Thailand at the Bangkok Music Festival, frustrated at restrictions imposed by working within a group. Effectively he had been musical director to his colleagues for some time. Guitarist/composer Hughie Nicholson, ex-Decca-signed Scots group The Poets, is recruited. Whitehead also quits and is replaced by second ex-Poets, Dougie Henderson.

Oct *Cousin Norman*, written by Nicholson, hits UK #6.

Nov Fairley announces his "retirement" as a performer, to work as promotion manager for the group's three music publishing companies, Catrine, Carnbro and J.G.K. Marmalade remains a quartet. *Reflections Of My Life* earns a gold disk (and will ultimately sell over 2 million copies).

Dec *Back On The Road* makes UK #35, as parent LP *Songs* fails to chart.

1972 The band gains unfortunate publicity when a popular UK Sunday newspaper reveals details of supposed goings-on backstage involving female fans.

May *Radancer*, the group's final release, hits UK #6. Nicholson quits to join Cody.

Oct Junior Campbell signs to Decca offshoot, Deram, and hits UK #10 with his own *Hallelujah Freedom*.

1973 June Campbell has a second hit with *Sweet Illusion*, which makes UK #15.

1974 Oct Ford, Knight and Henderson, the only remaining members, as Marmalade issue LP *Our House Is Rockin'* for EMI. The line-up is augmented by Mike Japp (guitar, keyboards and vocals), Joe Breen (bass) and Howie Casey (drums), as Knight departs.

1975 Ford quits and emigrates to US, where he cuts an eponymous LP with Alan Parsons°. It includes a cover of Jimmy Webb's *Crying In My Sleep*, extracted as a 45. A critical but not commercial success, both are released in UK by EMI. Fairley also goes to US, working still in publishing, especially for the group Yes°.

1976 Knight and Whitehead resurrect the name Marmalade, bringing in guitarist/keyboardist Sandy Newman, from Scots group The Chris McClure Section.

1977 Mar Signed to Tony Macaulay's Target Records, Marmalade's *Falling Apart At The Seams* hits UK #9. On Ariola America in US, it makes #49. Further singles and LP *Only Light On My Horizon Now* all fail to sell. The group is joined by Garth Watt Roy on vocals and keyboards.

1978 Watt Roy joins The Q-Tips and is replaced by ex-Federation member, Bristol-born Alan Holmes.

1979 Marmalade records LP *Doing It All For You*, for Sky. It fails to chart.

1980 Marmalade, now comprising Knight, Newman, Holmes and ex-Love Affair drummer Glenn Taylor, flourish on the cabaret circuit, making LPs and singles sporadically for the European market, where a loyal following is maintained.

1984 Marmalade sets up its own Just Songs label, and releases Newman composition *Heartbreaker* as a 45. It attracts few sales but other acts cover it, including The Tremeloes' Chip Hawkes, using the pseudonym Maxwell Silver.

1988 The band is successfully touring UK, with White Plains and several other acts, on the nostalgic "Sound of the 60s" package shows.

M/A/R/R/S

Martyn Young (Colourbox)
Steve Young (Colourbox)
Alex (AR Kane)
Rudi (AR Kane)
Russell (AR Kane)
C.J. Mackintosh (scratch DJ)
Dave Dorrell (scratch DJ)

1987 Two rock acts recording for UK independent label 4AD Records, the trio AR Kane and the duo Colourbox, decide on a temporary recording collaboration because both bands are keen to make a dance record. The name M/A/R/R/S is obtained from the first-name initials of all five musicians.

May Two tracks are recorded, but diametrically opposite approaches to recording make real collaboration difficult, so *Anitina* is almost all by AR Kane, and *Pump Up The Volume* is Colourbox with AR Kane's guitars. Martyn of Colourbox calls in two top London club DJs, C.J. Mackintosh and Dave Dorrell, to give their track stronger dance ingredients.

July A 12" version of the record is circulated in an anonymous white label form to club DJs around UK, gauging reactions (which are ecstatic). *Pump Up The Volume*, the side enhanced by Mackintosh and Dorrell with sampling, cutting and scratching, becomes the track that dancers demand.

Sept [11] Production team Stock Aitken and Waterman obtains a High Court injunction to prevent M/A/R/R/S and 4AD selling *Pump Up The Volume* in UK because of alleged copyright infringement of UK hit *Roadblock*, which has been "sampled" on the track. The injunction is withdrawn after 4 days, while the record stands at #11. It is subsequently thought that Phil Harding and Pete Waterman "borrow" a snippet of the M/A/R/R/S track for Sybil's *My Love Is Guaranteed*, leading to a reverse injunction, but these legalities are dropped. However, long-term European royalties will be held in abeyance further to a more serious and lengthy injunction served on M/A/R/R/S and 4AD by Stock Aitken and Waterman.

Oct *Pump Up The Volume* tops UK chart for 2 weeks, eventually becoming the UK's biggest-selling 12" single of 1987.

1988 Feb *Pump Up The Volume* (released without the offending *Roadblock*) makes US #13, the first major international scratch sample hit, which marks the beginning of a new era of many similar attempts at sample mixes.

June AR Kane releases EP *Up Home!* and LP *69* which tops the independent chart.

Aug Martyn Young produces The Isley Brothers'° classic *Harvest For The World* for The Christians°.

MARTHA & THE VANDELLAS

Martha Reeves (lead vocals)
Annette Sterling (vocals)
Rosalind Ashford (vocals)

1960 Martha Reeves (b. July 18, 1941, Ala., US), having moved to Detroit, Mich., in her teens, does some solo club singing as Martha LaVelle, and performs with ex-high school friends Sterling and Ashford (b. Sept.2, 1943, Detroit) as vocal trio The Del-Phis. They record an unsuccessful single for Checkmate label. Reeves then joins Tamla Motown Records as a secretary in the A&R department. Among the more usual tasks, since she is known to have a good voice, one of her jobs is to sing new song lyrics on to tapes for artists (normally back-up singers) who need to learn the words prior to recording sessions.

1961 When a backing singer is absent from a recording session through illness, the producer, familiar with Reeves' voice from the demo tapes, suggests she fills the role. This is the first of many such appearances.

1962 July Getting regular studio opportunities, Reeves mentions her two former singing partners, and Motown tries out all three as an integrated back-up trio. The first session on which they sing is for Marvin Gaye's° *Stubborn Kind Of Fellow*, which also becomes his first hit single, reaching US #46.

Sept After also backing Gaye° on *Hitch Hike* (which will make US #30 in Mar.1963), the trio is signed as an act in its own right, to Motown's Gordy label, and renamed Martha & The Vandellas (partly inspired by Reeves' favorite singer, Della Reese). Debut single *I'll Have To Let Him Go* fails to chart.

1963 June Second single, mid-tempo beat-ballad *Come And Get These Memories*, climbs to US #29. The debut LP, titled after the hit, does not chart.

Sept Bounding dance number *Heat Wave*, written by Holland/Dozier/Holland, hits US #4 and tops the R&B chart for 5 weeks (replacing fellow new Motown star Stevie Wonder's° *Fingertips*), to sell over a million.

Dec The same writing team's *Quicksand*, in similar dance-oriented style, hits US #8. First chart LP is *Heat Wave* which makes US #125. In spite of their new-found success, Sterling leaves to get married, and is replaced by Betty Kelly (b. Sept.16, 1944, Detroit).

1964 Mar *Live Wire* reaches US #42.

May *In My Lonely Room* makes US #44.

Sept The group plays 10 days at the Fox Theater in Brooklyn, New York, in Murray The K's rock'n'roll extravaganza, along with Marvin Gaye°, The Supremes°, The Searchers°, The Shangri-Las° and many others.

Oct The group's version *Dancing In The Street*, co-written by Marvin Gaye° and turned down by Mary Wells, becomes one of the most consistently-played dance records of all time. Their second million-seller, it hits US #2 for 2 weeks, behind Manfred Mann's° *Do Wah Diddy Diddy*.

Nov *Dancing In The Street* is their UK chart debut, reaching #28.

1965 Jan *Wild One* makes US #34.

Mar [20] The group arrives in UK as part of the first Motown package tour. Also on the bill are Stevie Wonder°, The Supremes°, The Miracles and The Temptations°.

Apr The trio returns to US top 10 with *Nowhere To Run* which hits US #8. It also reaches UK #25 (one of the first batch of three singles released in UK launch of the Tamla Motown label).

June LP *Dance Party* (including *Dancing In The Street* and *Nowhere To Run*) makes US #139.

Sept *You've Been In Love Too Long* reaches US #36.

Dec After many DJs have turned A-side *You've Been In Love* over, B-side Holland/Dozier/Holland's ballad *Love (Makes Me Do Foolish Things)* reaches US #70.

1966 Mar *My Baby Loves Me* climbs to US #22.

Mar [29] The group begins a UK tour.

June *What Am I Gonna Do Without Your Love?* makes US #71.

July LP *Greatest Hits*, a compilation of the trio's singles to date, reaches US #50.

Dec *I'm Ready For Love*, written by Holland/Dozier/Holland for The Supremes° but turned down, hits US #9 and reaches UK #29.

1967 Feb LP *Watchout!*, including *I'm Ready For Love*, peaks at US #116.

Apr *Jimmy Mack*, extracted from LP *Watchout!*, hits US #10, and tops the R&B chart for a week, becoming another million-seller. It reaches only UK #21 (but will be a consistent seller in UK because of its universal danceability and the equal popularity of B-side *Third Finger, Left Hand*, for the next 15 or so years).

Sept *Love Bug Leave My Heart Alone* reaches US #25.

Oct Live LP *Martha And The Vandellas Live!* peaks at US #140.

Dec The group's name is amended to Martha Reeves & The Vandellas on *Honey Chile*, which climbs to US #11.

1968 Jan Kelly leaves and is replaced by Reeves' younger sister Lois, previously with The Orlons.

Feb *Honey Chile* reaches UK #30.

MARTHA & THE VANDELLAS *cont.*

May Double A-side *I Promise To Wait, My Love/Forget Me Not* makes US #62 and #93 respectively.
June LP *Ridin' High* peaks at US #167.
Sept *I Can't Dance To That Music You're Playin'* reaches US #42.
Sept [15] The trio appears on the first edition of US NBC TV's black audience-targetted music show "Soul", alongside Lou Rawls and comedian Red Foxx.
Nov *Sweet Darlin'* stalls at US #80.
1969 Feb *Dancing In The Street* is reissued in UK and, with the particular support of Alan Freeman's major national radio show "Pick of the Pops", is a bigger UK success than first time around, hitting #4.
Apr *Nowhere To Run*, reissued as UK follow-up, reaches #42.
May *(We've Got) Honey Love* makes US #56. Reeves suffers a breakdown, which puts the group off the road and out of the studio for a time.
1970 Sept *Jimmy Mack* re-charts in UK at #21.
Nov *I've Gotta Let You Go* reaches US #93.
1971 With Reeves recovered, they regroup, but without founder member Ashford, who has left to be replaced by Sandra Tilley, ex-Motown group The Velvelettes.
Mar *Forget Me Not*, a minor 1968 US hit, is released in UK and climbs to #11.
May The group plays a comeback show at P.J.'s club in LA.
Nov *Bless You* reaches US #53, and is the group's last US chart single.
1972 Jan *Bless You* is also the final UK chart entry, making #33.
Apr LP *Black Magic* is the group's final US chart LP, reaching #146.
Dec [1] The group gives its farewell performance in Detroit.
Dec Reeves begins a solo career, and her sister Lois joins Quiet Elegance, recording for Hi in Memphis, Tenn.
1973 Signed as a soloist to MCA, Reeves works with J.J. Johnson on the music for black action movie *Willie Dynamite*. On the soundtrack, she sings three songs, *Willie D*, *King Midas* and *Keep On Movin' On*, backed by The Sweet Things.
1974 Apr Reeves' only solo hit single is *Power Of Love*, on MCA, which makes US #76. It is taken from LP *Martha Reeves*, produced by Richard Perry, which does not chart, despite the musicianship of Billy Preston, Joe Sample, Nicky Hopkins and Ralph McDonald.
1976 She moves to Arista Records, but solo LP *The Rest Of My Life* fails to chart.
1978 Reeves releases disco-oriented LP *We Meet Again* on Fantasy Records, reuniting her with Motown producer Henry Cosby. It fails to chart.
July [1] Martha & The Vandellas re-form for the first time in 10 years in a benefit for actor Will Geer at the Santa Cruz Catalyst, Cal.

RICHARD MARX

1982 At age 18, Marx (b. 1964, Chicago, Ill., US), having been brought into music from an early age by his father (Richard Sr., a jazz pianist and top jingle writer) and sung on TV commercials since his pre-teens, receives a call from Lionel Richie°. Richie has heard a demo tape of four Marx songs, and invites him to sing some LP backing vocals. One of these is Richie's million-seller *All Night Long*. (Richie will also introduce him to many industry figures and contacts.)
1984 June With producer David Foster and Kenny Rogers°,
Dec he co-writes *What About Me?* a US #15 by Rogers with Kim Carnes° and James Ingram°, and Rogers' *Crazy*, which makes US #79. (From this highly successful springboard, Marx will collaborate with many artists over the next two years, writing for Chicago° (*We Are The World* LP track *Good For Nothing*), Philip Bailey (*The Goonies* LP track *Love Is Alive*), and others.)
1986 Friend Bobby Colomby (ex-Blood, Sweat & Tears°, now an A&R executive) introduces Marx to the president of EMI Manhattan who sees solo artist potential in his songs and signs Marx to the label worldwide. Colomby also teams him with producer David Cole, who will co-produce his debut LP.
1987 Aug Marx begins a lengthy US tour supporting R.E.O. Speedwagon°, and *Don't Mean Nothing*, with Joe Walsh° guesting, is his US chart debut, hitting #3.
Dec *Should've Known Better* hits US #3.
1988 Mar Marx is nominated for (though does not win) a Grammy award for Best Rock Vocal Performance. Meanwhile, *Should've Known Better* is a middling UK hit, reaching #50, while *Endless Summer Nights* becomes his biggest US smash yet, hitting #2.
Apr LP *Richard Marx* peaks at UK #68, and is still climbing in US.
May *Endless Summer Nights* equals his previous UK peak, reaching #50.
July *Hold On To The Night* tops the US chart and Marx becomes the first male singer to notch four top 3 hits from a debut LP. His solo career hits a new peak, and Marx continues to pursue writing for and producing projects with other artists, including Randy Meisner (ex-Eagles°), Fee Waybill (ex-Tubes°) and new all-girl rock group Vixen.

MATTHEWS SOUTHERN COMFORT

1966 Matthews (b. Ian Matthew McDonald, 1946, Lincs., UK) joins London-based harmony vocal group Pyramid, having turned down a career as a professional soccer player.
1967 Jan Pyramid's only single *Summer Of Last Year* is released by Deram, without success.
Nov Matthews leaves Pyramid to join Fairport Convention° as joint lead vocalist.
1969 Jan He leaves Fairport Convention° after recording two LPs with the band, to form his own group Matthews Southern Comfort. He recruits Mark Griffiths (guitar), Carl Barnwell (guitar), Gordon Huntley (pedal steel), Andy Leigh (bass) and Ray Duffy (drums). They sign to EMI Records.
1970 Jan Debut LP *Matthews Southern Comfort* is released and shows Matthews veering away from his previous folk-rock sound toward a country style.
July LP *Second Spring* makes UK #52.
Oct A smooth, steel guitar-backed country style version of Joni Mitchell's° *Woodstock* tops the UK chart for 3 weeks. (It has already been a US top 20 hit in the spring for Crosby, Stills, Nash & Young°.)
Dec Matthews leaves the group just before the last Matthews Southern Comfort LP *Later That Same Year* is released.
1971 Jan Matthews signs a solo deal with Vertigo, releasing LP *If You Saw Thru' My Eyes*.
Mar *Woodstock* makes US #23.
Apr The band becomes Southern Comfort following Matthews' departure, signing to Harvest Records for eponymous LP *Southern Comfort*. Meanwhile, LP *Later That Same Year* makes US #72.
July LP *Frog City* by Southern Comfort is released and makes US #196. The group's single *Mare, Take Me Home* peaks at US #96.
Oct *Tell Me Why* by Southern Comfort reaches US #98.
1972 Feb Matthews' LP *Tigers Will Survive* climbs to US #196, while his a cappella revival of The Crystals'° *Da Doo Ron Ron* makes US #96. He forms Plainsong, with singer/guitarist Andy Roberts, keyboards player Dave Richards and bassist Bobby Ronga.
Sept Plainsong LP *In Search Of Amelia Earhart* is issued on Elektra, but fails to chart. Meanwhile, Southern Comfort's LP *Stir Don't Shake* is its last, after which the group disbands.
Dec Ronga leaves Plainsong as the group records a second LP for Elektra (which is never released, although five tracks will be heard on Matthews' solo albums). Plainsong splits after the sessions and Matthews moves (at the suggestion of Elektra boss Jac Holzman) to LA to work with Michael Nesmith.
1973 Sept His first solo Elektra LP *Valley Hi*, produced by Nesmith at his Countryside studios, reaches US #181. Matthews tours US, supporting America°, with his own band comprising ex-Nazz drummer Tom Mooney and the Curtis brothers from Crazy Horse.
1974 Matthews tours US under the name Ian Matthews & Another Fine Mess, with a band comprising Tommy Nunes (guitar), Joel Tepp (harmonica), Don Whaley (bass) and John Ware (drums).
June LP *Some Days You Eat The Bear . . . Some Days The Bear Eats You* is his last LP for Elektra.
Aug LP *Journey From Gospel Oak*, a compilation of unreleased 1971-72 material recorded in Nov. 1972 and scheduled for release by Vertigo, is issued by Mooncrest in UK, with Matthews unaware of its release.
Oct LP *The Best Of Matthews Southern Comfort* is released, again without Matthews' knowledge.
1975 Matthews draws up a contract with Arista Records, but decides not to sign.
Aug Matthews' contract with Elektra expires.
1976 May LP *Go For Broke*, released by CBS/Columbia, is produced by Norbert Putnam.
Oct *Distilled* by Southern Comfort, is a compilation LP released on UK Harvest.

1977 May LP *Hit And Run*, Matthews' second and final album for Columbia, includes a remake of *Tigers Will Survive*.
1978 Oct LP *Stealin' Home*, issued by Mushroom Records, reaches US #80. Folk label Rockburgh, owned by Sandy Robertson, releases it in UK. *Shake It* gets considerable airplay in US and climbs to #13, his first hit for 8 years.
1979 Mar *Give Me An Inch* (later a hit for Robert Palmer°) makes US #67.
Aug LP *Siamese Friends* fails to chart.
1980 Mar LP *Discreet Repeat*, a double compilation of solo material, is his last for Mushroom and Rockburgh.
June On RSO, LP *A Spot Of Interference* is released and again fails to sell.
1981/83 Matthews, living in Seattle, Wash., is involved in a legal dispute with Mushroom, which he claims owes him more than $500,000 in royalties. He releases two poor-selling LPs *Moods For Mallard* and *Shook*.
1983/86 Abandoning his own recording career, Matthews moves to LA and takes up a post as A&R man for Island Records.
1987 He moves to an A&R post at new age pioneering label, Windham Hill. LPs *Meet Southern Comfort* and *Fairport Convention's Heydays*, an album of UK BBC radio broadcasts from 1968-69, both featuring Matthews' work, are released in UK.
Aug Matthews participates in Fairport Convention's° 20th anniversary celebrations by appearing live with the band. He leaves his A&R post at Windham Hill to begin recording a new LP for the same label, some view this as perfect A&R.
1988 Apr LP *Walking A Changing Line – The Songs Of Jules Shear* is released on Windham Hill. This is the label's first all-vocal set and receives significant critical acclaim.

JOHN MAYALL

1962 Mayall (b. Nov.29, 1943, Macclesfield, Cheshire, UK), having studied art in Manchester, done National Service in the British Army (including some time in Korea), and then worked in a Manchester art studio attached to an advertising agency, forms his first group, The Blues Syndicate. Gigging mostly at Manchester's Twisted Wheel club, the group (a quintet featuring guitar, piano, trumpet, alto sax, and Hughie Flint on drums) plays raw R&B, inspired by Alexis Korner's London-based Blues Incorporated.
1963 Jan Encouraged by Korner, Mayall moves to London, where he gets a job as a draughtsman, and tries to form a new R&B band.
July After trying out many musicians, Mayall debuts The Bluesbreakers with himself on vocals, keyboards and harmonica, Bernie Watson on guitar, John McVie on bass and Peter Ward on drums (replaced once full-time gigging starts by Martin Hart).
1964 Apr Mayall signs a short-term deal with Decca, and records single *Crawling Up A Hill*. Almost immediately after it, the band's personnel changes, reducing to a quartet comprising Mayall, McVie, Roger Dean on guitar and Flint on drums again.
1965 Mar Debut LP is *John Mayall Plays John Mayall*, recorded live at Klook's Kleek R&B club in West Hampstead, London. Second single *Crocodile Walk* is also released, after which the Decca deal expires.
Apr Hearing that Eric Clapton° has left The Yardbirds°, Mayall invites him to join The Bluesbreakers. Clapton, keen to play blues (the reason why he split from The Yardbirds), agrees. He is hired in place of Dean, who is dismissed in a fashion which will become a Mayall trademark. Clapton's presence in the group is sufficient to boost the audiences at Mayall's gigs enormously.
June [19] The Bluesbreakers play the Uxbridge Blues and Folk Festival, alongside The Who°, Long John Baldry°, The Spencer Davis Group°, and others.
Aug Clapton°, tired of one-night gigs and wanting some sunshine, departs without notice, with a car full of friends, for 3 months to Greece. Mayall muddles through with temporary replacement guitarists, but audience attendances begin to wane as word gets around of Clapton's exit.
Oct McVie is fired by Mayall for being drunk once too often, and Jack Bruce, ex-The Graham Bond Organization, replaces him on bass.
Nov Mayall finds Peter Green, a guitarist good enough to step into Clapton's° shoes, when Clapton himself returns with a tan and slips back into his job. Green is forced out again after only 3 days as a Bluesbreaker. Shortly after Clapton's return, Bruce leaves because Mayall is unable to pay him enough. McVie rejoins the line-up. With Clapton, The Bluesbreakers record *I'm Your Witchdoctor* in a one-off deal with Immediate Records.
1966 Mar Producer Mike Vernon convinces Decca that Mayall should be re-signed, and the group cuts its first studio LP *Blues Breakers* (having also made another one-off single, *Lonely Years* for small Purdah label between contracts).
July LP *Blues Breakers*, credited to John Mayall with Eric Clapton° for maximum commercial appeal, becomes Mayall's first major success, hitting UK #6. While the LP is in the top 10, Clapton leaves for the second and final time, to join Jack Bruce and Ginger Baker in Cream°.
July [17] Mayall persuades an initially-uncertain Peter Green to replace Clapton, this time on a firm basis.
Sept Flint leaves, and is replaced on drums by Aynsley Dunbar, ex-The Mojos.
Oct Two singles on Decca, *Parchman Farm* and *Looking Back* (the first featuring Clapton°, the second Green) are issued in rapid succession, neither charting.
1967 Mar LP *A Hard Road*, the only studio LP featuring Green, with a sleeve painting by Mayall, hits UK #10.
Apr Dunbar leaves to join Jeff Beck's° group, and is replaced first by Mickey Waller, then by ex-Shotgun Express drummer Mick Fleetwood.
June Fleetwood is fired by Mayall for excessive drinking, and Green follows him (they will form Fleetwood Mac°). Mayall, left with just himself and McVie (who has already been approached re Fleetwood Mac, but refused) hires several new musicians: Mick Taylor (ex-Gods) on guitar, Chris Mercer on sax, Keef Hartley (ex-Artwoods) on drums and second sax player Rip Kant (who vanishes after 2 months). This line-up is the first to tour US.
Sept LP *Crusade* hits UK #8. McVie is tempted away to Fleetwood Mac° and is followed in The Bluesbreakers by a succession of short-lived bassists lasting 8 months between them: Paul Williams, Keith Tillman and Andy Fraser. At the same time, the brass section of the band is enlarged, as Henry Lowther on trumpet and Dick Heckstall-Smith on sax join existing sax player Mercer.
Dec LP *The Blues Alone*, a solo by Mayall (with Hartley playing drums on some tracks), makes UK #24.
1968 Jan The band begins a US tour at the Cafe Au-Go-Go club in New York.
Mar LP *Diary Of A Band Vol.1*, recorded live on the road during 1967, reaches UK #27. Its companion volume, *Diary Of A Band Vol.2* makes UK #28. Meanwhile, Mayall has his first US chart LP with *Crusade*, which makes #136.
Apr Hartley leaves to form his own band. Mayall asks an initially very sceptical Jon Hiseman (ex-Graham Bond Organization) to replace him on drums for an extended US tour. Tony Reeves from The New Jazz Orchestra joins on bass.
June Solo LP *The Blues Alone* makes US #128.
Aug LP *Bare Wires*, recorded by the extended, brass-featuring band line-up, hits UK #3. At the end of a lengthy US tour, Mayall breaks up the band and settles in LA, retaining Taylor on guitar, and recruiting bassist Steve Thompson and drummer Colin Allen to return to his old quartet format.
Oct LP *Bare Wires* reaches US #59.
1969 Jan LP *Blues From Laurel Canyon*, recorded in LA by the quartet, makes UK #33.
Apr LP *Blues From Laurel Canyon* reaches US #68.
Apr [6] Mayall's band plays the Palm Springs Pop Festival in Cal., where a riot breaks out when police helicopters try to disperse an audience too large for the festival site.
May Taylor leaves to join The Rolling Stones°, and Allen departs to Stone The Crows.
June Mayall forms a new band (dropping the Bluesbreakers tag), featuring a revolutionary line-up without drums. Thompson remains on bass, while Marianne Faithfull's° former stage guitarist Jon Mark is recruited, with Duster Bennett (guitar) and Johnny Almond (sax).
Aug Compilation LP *Looking Back*, with tracks recorded between 1964 and 1967 (including some with Clapton°), reaches UK #14.
Oct *Don't Waste My Time* makes US #81, Mayall's only US hit single, taken from LP *The Turning Point*.
Nov LP *The Turning Point*, recorded by the drumless line-up, and the first result of a new recording deal with Polydor, peaks at UK #11 and US #32. In a 55-week stay on US chart, it becomes Mayall's only gold disk.
1970 Apr LP *Empty Rooms*, recorded by the same band line-up, hits UK #9,

JOHN MAYALL *cont.*

while LP *Diary Of A Band* (the same as UK *Diary Of A Band, Vol.1*) makes US #93.

May LP *Empty Rooms* reaches US #33.

June The band splits, with Mark and Almond forming the duo Mark-Almond, and the others moving to sessions or solo work.

Dec LP *U.S.A. Union*, on which Mayall collaborates with an entirely US-originated group (Harvey Mandel on guitar, Larry Taylor on bass and Don "Sugarcane" Harris on violin) for the first time, reaches UK #50 and US #22.

1971 May LP *John Mayall – Live In Europe* (equivalent to UK *Diary Of A Band, Vol.2*) creeps to US #146.

June Double LP *Back To The Roots*, a reunion with previous Bluesbreakers Clapton°, Taylor and Hartley, alongside Mayall's current US players, makes UK #31 and US #52. This is Mayall's last LP to chart in UK.

Dec Double compilation LP *Thru The Years*, containing mostly unreleased 1960s Bluesbreakers material, makes US #164. New LP *Memories*, cut by a trio comprising Mayall, Larry Taylor on bass and ex-Ventures° lead guitarist Jerry McGee on guitar, climbs to US #179.

1972 July Live LP *Jazz Blues Fusion*, recorded in New York and Boston with guitarist Freddie Robinson, reaches US #64.

Nov LP *Moving On* makes US #116.

1973 Mar Double LP *Down The Line*, combining an LP of mid-1960s studio cuts with the original *John Mayall Plays John Mayall* live LP, peaks at US #158.

Oct Double LP *Ten Years Are Gone* makes US #157.

1975 Mar Mayall signs to ABC/Blue Thumb Records for LP *New Year, New Band, New Company*, which makes US #140, and is his final US chart entry. The new band of the title includes earlier cohorts Taylor and Don Harris, plus Rick Vito (guitar), Jay Spell (keyboards), Soko Richardson (drums), and for the first time, a female vocalist, Dee McKinnie.

1976/77 Three more LPs on the label follow, none rating much interest from either critics or record buyers.

1979 May Mayall signs to DJM Records, issuing LP *Bottom Line*, to minimal sales.

Dec Second DJM LP *No More Interviews* is again a minor seller. (Mayall will not record a new LP for some years, but continues to live in Cal., playing with musicians of his choice from time to time.)

1988 Dec After a lapse of almost a decade, Mayall signs to Island and records some new material, released as LP *Chicago Line*.

CURTIS MAYFIELD

1970 Oct [1] Mayfield (b. June 3, 1942, Chicago, Ill., US), after 13 years as a member of The Impressions° (11 years as leader, chief songwriter and producer), leaves for a solo career – after finding his own replacement, Leroy Hutson. (The Impressions remain on his Curtom label and he will continue to direct their career.)

Dec Debut solo LP *Curtis* reaches US #19. It includes two lengthy funk pieces, *Move On Up* and *(Don't Worry) If There's A Hell Down Below, We're All Going To Go*. The latter is edited as a US single and makes US #29.

1971 July Double live LP *Curtis/Live!*, with a mixture of new and recent songs and Impressions° oldies, recorded live at the Bitter End in New York, reaches US #21. (In contrast to his rich studio productions, Mayfield's 70s live band will be his own guitar and vocals, plus drummer, percussionist and bass player, and occasionally a second guitarist.)

Aug *Move On Up*, edited from the first LP, becomes a UK dancefloor hit, and his UK chart debut, reaching #12. (Neither LP charts in UK.)

Dec LP *Roots* peaks at US #40. It contains the anti-war song *We Got To Have Peace*, but is mostly concerned with romantic themes. Extracted *Get Down* makes US #69. Mayfield devotes the next few months to work on his first film soundtrack.

1972 Oct His soundtrack LP from film *Superfly* (one of the rash of "blaxploitation" movies which appear in the wake of 1971's highly successful *Shaft* with its innovative Isaac Hayes° score) tops the US chart for 4 weeks, and earns a gold disk. Much of the music is downbeat, despairing at the violence and drug culture in the film rather than glorifying it. Cautionary tale *Freddie's Dead* is extracted and hits US #4, his first solo million-seller.

1973 Jan The title track from *Superfly* hits US #8, a second consecutive million-seller.

Mar Soundtrack LP *Superfly* reaches UK #26, Mayfield's only UK chart LP.

Aug LP *Back To The World*, featuring mainly social consciousness songs, with rich, layered production, makes US #16, and is his third and final gold LP. Taken from it, *Future Shock* makes US #39.

Oct Chicago's WTTW-TV produces a musical special based around Mayfield, titled "Curtis in Chicago". It features both the original and current Impressions° line-ups, plus Jerry Butler°, Gene Chandler°, and other artists with whom Mayfield has been involved, and following various solo and group spots, the show ends with an ensemble rendition of The Impressions' *Amen*.

Nov *If I Were Only A Child Again*, taken from the TV show, reaches US #71.

Dec LP *Curtis In Chicago*, soundtrack of the TV show, makes US #135.

1974 Jan *Can't Say Nothin'* peaks at US #88.

May Mayfield produces and plays on Glady Knight° & The Pips' soundtrack LP from film *Claudine*, which reaches US #35.

Aug LP *Sweet Exorcist* makes US #39. It contains a collaboration with Donny Hathaway° on *Suffer*, while extracted *Kung Fu* reflects a current media craze and peaks at US #40.

Dec LP *Got To Find A Way*, lyrically negative and musically stark-sounding, reaches US #76.

1975 July LP *There's No Place Like America Today*, another downbeat set dealing with racial prejudice, violence and deprivation, peaks at US #120.

Oct From the LP, uniquely upbeat ballad *So In Love* makes US #67 – his last US hit single.

Dec He works with The Staple Singers° on their soundtrack LP from film *Let's Do It Again*, which reaches US #20.

1976 July LP *Give, Get, Take And Have* peaks at US #171, with no hit singles from it (but sees an about-turn in attitude from Mayfield, embracing disco music and only hinting at earlier concerns with *Mr. Welfare Man*, first recorded by Gladys Knight° for *Claudine* soundtrack).

Aug Mayfield produces Aretha Franklin's° LP *Sparkle*, which makes US #18.

1977 Apr LP *Never Say You Can't Survive* (featuring his own version of *Sparkle*) creeps to US #173.

Oct Soundtrack LP *Short Eyes*, from a low-budget prison movie featuring both Mayfield and Tex-Mex country singer Freddy Fender, follows the *Superfly* mold, but with no commercial success.

1978 June He produces Aretha Franklin° again, on LP *Almighty Fire*, which makes US #63, but marks the final collaboration between the two.

Oct LP *Do It All Night*, entirely disco-styled, fails to chart in US and is not given UK release.

Dec *No Goodbyes*, a lengthy disco track which is Mayfield's first UK single for 3 years, is issued only on 12" and reaches UK #65.

1979 The Curtom label hits financial difficulties and Mayfield sells out to RSO, which insists he find an outside producer for his next record. He chooses Philadelphia team Norman Harris, Ronald Tyson and Bunny Sigler.

Sept LP *Heartbeat*, part-produced by the trio, and partly (three tracks) by Mayfield himself, reaches US #42. It includes *Between You Baby And Me*, a duet with his recent discovery Linda Clifford.

1980 July LP *The Right Combination*, duetted with Clifford, stalls at US #180.

Aug Mayfield's solo LP *Something To Believe In* charts for 10 weeks in US, reaching #128. It is his last LP with RSO, and his final US chart entry.

1981 Mayfield transfers to Neil Bogart's Boardwalk label. Disco producer Dino Fekaris produces LP *Love Is The Place*, which fails to sell and is deleted in US (and not issued in UK). (Mayfield's prospects seem even gloomier when Bogart dies shortly after, and label affairs are plunged into confusion.)

1982 Oct LP *Honesty*, also on Boardwalk, is released in US. Self-produced, it has some political comment amid romantic material.

1983 Mar LP *Honesty* is released on Epic in UK, where reviews are good, and he tours twice in quick succession – his concerts featuring no material recorded after *Superfly*. (Later in the year, both Mayfield and Jerry Butler° rejoin The Impressions° for a brief US tour. A studio LP from the reunion is rumored, but none emerges.)

1985 Sept With Curtom defunct, Mayfield forms new label CRC. It releases

US-only LP *We Come In Peace With A Message Of Love.*

1986 Nov Single *Baby It's You* is released in both US and in UK (on the 98.6 label); an LP is announced, but does not appear.

1987 May Still without a recording contract, Mayfield makes a short UK tour, and during the visit is invited to record with The Blow Monkeys, one of the young UK groups who regard his early 1970s work as an inspiration.

June The Blow Monkeys' *Celebrate (The Day After You)*, featuring Mayfield, is released. As an apparent pre-election attack on the UK Prime Minister, it is banned by the BBC as possibly prejudicial, until after the event, thus limiting its chances of a high chart position (it peaks at UK #52).

1988 June Mayfield tours UK, Switzerland, Austria, West Germany, Holland, and France, as his Curtom label is revived internationally by independent soul label Ichiban Records. Soundtrack LP *Superfly* is reissued in UK.

July *Move On Up*, always Mayfield's most popular recording in UK (and subsequently repromoted by Mayfield fan Paul Weller, who revived it with The Jam°), is reissued as a UK 12" single, and charts briefly at #87.

PAUL McCARTNEY

1969 Mar [12] McCartney (b. June 18, 1942, Liverpool, UK) marries Linda Eastman (b. Sept.24, 1942, Scarsdale, N.Y., US) at Marylebone Register Office, London.

1970 Apr [11] McCartney announces that he will not record with John Lennon° again.

May Home-recorded LP *McCartney* hits UK #2 and tops the US chart. His solo debut adds to tension between members of The Beatles° as it is released almost simultaneously with the group's LP *Let It Be*.

1971 Mar Debut solo single *Another Day* hits UK #2 and US #5.

June LP *Ram* hits UK #1 and US #2. While his former writing partner Lennon° bases his early solo career on songs of personal angst and political commentary, McCartney settles into a simpler pop groove which will remain a constant for most of his recording career.

Sept *Back Seat Of My Car* makes UK #39, as US-only release *Uncle Albert/Admiral Halsey* tops the US chart.

Nov As a member of The Beatles°, McCartney was reluctant to stop live performance and so sets up a group to perform under the name Wings, comprising Paul and Linda McCartney, Denny Laine on guitars and vocals and Denny Seiwell on drums.

Dec LP *Wings Wildlife* reaches UK #11 and US #10. His second LP in 6 months, it is savaged by the critics.

1972 Feb The group, augmented by Henry McCullough on guitar and vocals, tours UK, arriving at colleges unannounced and asking social secretaries if they would like Wings to perform in their hall that evening.

Mar *Give Ireland Back To The Irish* reaches UK #16 and US #21. Written after the "Bloody Sunday Massacre" in Northern Ireland in Jan., it is banned by the BBC and the IBA.

June Embittered by the ban on his single, McCartney puts music to nursery rhyme *Mary Had A Little Lamb*. It hits UK #9 and US #28.

July [9] Wings makes its formal concert debut at Chateauvillon, France.

July The McCartneys are arrested for possession of drugs in Sweden during a Wings European tour.

Sept They are arrested again for drug possession at their Scottish farmhouse.

1973 Jan *Hi Hi Hi* is banned by the BBC, claiming that the record endorses drug use. It is subsequently promoted with its B-side *C Moon*, and hits UK #5.

Mar [8] McCartney is arrested again for growing marijuana on his farm in Scotland.

Apr Ballad *My Love* hits UK #9 as McCartney hints at a possible Beatles° reunion.

May LP *Red Rose Speedway*, credited to Paul McCartney & Wings, hits UK #5 and tops the US chart. Wings begins a UK tour.

May [10] "James Paul McCartney" special airs on UK TV. A musical extravaganza, it features McCartney in a crowded Liverpool pub for a singalong, performing a Fred Astaire-style dance routine and ending with a solo performance of *Yesterday*.

June *My Love* hits US #1, and is later deposed by George Harrison's° *Give Me Love (Give Me Peace On Earth)*. *Live And Let Die*, the theme to forthcoming James Bond film, hits UK #9. Music

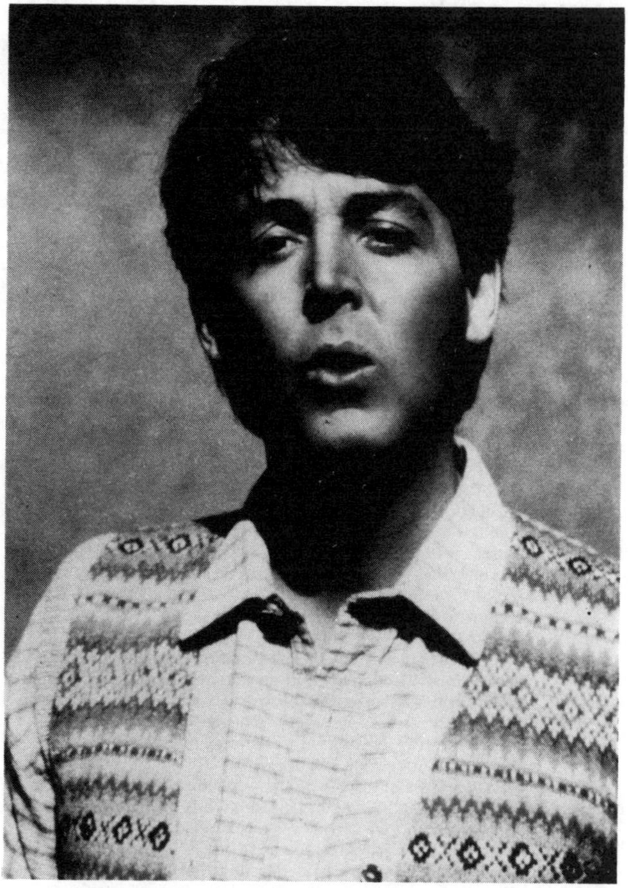

producer George Martin has played the song in its finished form to the film's producer Harry Saltzmann, who assumes it is a demo and suggests that Thelma Houston should cut the song. Martin reassures Saltzmann that this a finished item by an ex-Beatle. (The song stands but Brenda Arnau will cover it on the film's soundtrack LP.)

Aug *Live And Let Die* hits US #2, kept off the top by Diana Ross'° *Touch Me In The Morning* and then by Stories' *Brother Louie*. McCullough and Seiwell quit the group and the remaining three fly to Ginger Baker's ARC studios in Lagos, Nigeria to begin recording LP *Band On The Run*.

Dec *Helen Wheels*, a song written about McCartney's Landrover jeep – known affectionately as "Hell On Wheels" – reaches UK #12 and US #10. LP *Band On The Run*, his first post-Beatles° LP receives rave reviews. It tops both UK and US charts and will sell 6,000,000 copies worldwide and spend over 2 years on both UK and US charts. (The cover features personalities Michael Parkinson, James Coburn, Kenny Lynch, Clement Freud, Christopher Lee and John Conteh posing with the group as escaped convicts caught in a searchlight. McCartney had invited them to lunch, and then asked them to pose for the photo.) After many refusals, due to drug convictions, McCartney finally gets a US visa.

1974 Mar *Jet*, inspired by McCartney's pet labrador puppy, hits both UK and US #7.

May The group becomes a five-piece again, joined by Jimmy McCulloch (ex-Thunderclap Newman and Stone The Crows) on guitar and vocals and former UK karate champion Geoff Britton on drums.

June McCartney writes and produces UK #7 hit *Liverpool Lou* for brother Mike McGear's group Scaffold. *Band On The Run* tops the US chart. The group travels to Nashville, Tenn. to record, and for McCartney to produce Peggy Lee's LP *Let's Love*.

Aug *Band On The Run* hits UK #3, backed with the theme to UK TV series "The Zoo Gang".

Oct Wings release *Walking In The Park With Eloise*, written by McCartney's father James, under the pseudonym The Country Hams. (When McCartney appears on BBC radio program "Desert Island Discs", he chooses it as one of his favorite records.)

Dec *Junior's Farm*, written during McCartney's stay in Nashville at Junior Putnam's farm, makes UK #16 and US #3.

1975 Feb Joe English (b. Rochester, N.Y., US) replaces Britton on drums.

June *Listen To What The Man Said* hits UK #6 and US #1. LP *Venus And Mars*, which contains a version of the theme to popular UK TV soap opera "Crossroads" (and which will be later adopted by the TV show for a period), tops both UK and US charts.

Sept [9] At the Gaumont, Southampton, UK, Wings begins a 13-month world tour of 10 countries and will play to over 2 million people.

Sept After buying Buddy Holly's° song catalog, McCartney institutes an annual "Buddy Holly Week", held around Holly's birthday.

Oct *Letting Go* makes UK #41 and US #39.

Dec *Venus And Mars Rock Show* reaches US #12, but fails in UK, his first chart miss in 13 years.

1976 Apr LP *Wings At The Speed Of Sound* hits UK #2, behind the soundtrack to UK TV show "Rock Follies", and tops the US chart. McCartney's democratic approach to Wings affords each member a lead vocal cut.

May *Silly Love Songs* hits UK #2, kept from the top by labelmates The Wurzels with the novelty *Combine Harvester*, but hits US #1.

May [3] The Wings world tour arrives in US as "Wings over America", and McCartney makes his first US stage appearance in 10 years at Tarrant County Convention Center, Fort Worth, Tex.

Sept *Let 'Em In* hits UK #2 and US #3.

Sept [25] Wings play a UNESCO concert in St. Mark's Square, Venice, Italy to draw attention to the decay and neglect in the historic city. The concert is a success but the weight of equipment used by the group causes areas of subsidence damage in the square.

Dec [21] The world tour ends with 3 standing-room-only nights at Wembley Empire Pool, UK.

1977 Jan LP *Wings Over America*, a 30-track documentary of the group's US tour – including five Beatles° songs, hits UK #8 and US #1.

Mar *Maybe I'm Amazed*, a live version of a song from McCartney's debut solo LP, reaches UK #28 and US #10.

Apr LP *Thrillington*, an orchestral interpretation of McCartney's LP *Ram*, is released, featuring orchestra leader Percy "Thrills" Thrillington, a pseudonym for McCartney.

Nov McCulloch leaves to join the re-formed Small Faces°, while English joins Sea Level,reducing Wings to a trio again.

Dec Waltz *Mull Of Kintyre* tops the UK chart for 9 weeks. It is co-written by Laine about the southern tip of the Kintyre peninsula, 11 miles from McCartney's farmhouse in Campbelltown, Scotland. (Laine later sells McCartney his rights to the song after being declared bankrupt.) The disk fails in US, where B-side *Girls School* is promoted and reaches US #33.

Dec [17] Mr. David Ackroyd purchases the 1-millionth copy of *Mull Of Kintyre* in UK and becomes the first record buyer in the world to receive a gold disk for his purchase. It becomes the biggest-selling UK single of all time at 2.5 million, replacing The Beatles° *She Loves You* (and will remain the biggest seller until Band Aid's° 1984 *Do They Know It's Christmas?*).

1978 Apr *With A Little Luck* hits UK #5 and tops the US chart, as parent LP *London Town*, recorded in London and on the yacht, Fair Carol, in the Virgin Islands, hits UK #4 and US #2. The LP features *Girlfriend*, later covered by Michael Jackson° on LP *Off The Wall*.

July *I've Had Enough* makes UK #42 and US #25. Wings becomes a five-piece, joined by Laurence Juber on guitar and vocals and ex-session man Steve Holly on drums.

Sept *London Town* peaks at UK #60 and US #39.

Dec LP *Wings Greatest Hits* hits UK #5 and US #29.

1979 Mar [16] "Wings over the World" airs on US TV.

May *Goodnight Tonight* hits UK and US #5, where it is released on Columbia label, with which McCartney signs a multi-million dollar deal.

June *Old Siam Sir* makes UK #35 as parent LP *Back To The Egg* hits UK #6 and US #8.

July *Getting Closer* reaches US #20.

Aug *Haven't We Met Somewhere Before?*, written by McCartney for film *Heaven Can Wait* but rejected, is featured as the opening song in film *Rock'n'Roll High School*, performed by The Ramones°.

Linda McCartney releases *Seaside Woman*, under the name Suzy & The Red Stripes. Despite McCartney's production, the single fails to chart.

Sept *Getting Closer/Baby's Request* makes UK #60. Wings appear on stage at London's Hammersmith Odeon with The Crickets.

Oct *Arrow Through Me* reaches US #29.

Oct [24] McCartney receives a medallion cast in rhodium from the UK arts minister after being declared the most successful composer of all time. From 1962-78, he has written or co-written 43 songs that have sold over a million copies each. He has sold 100 million singles and 100 million LPs.

Dec [29] Wings appear on the last night as part of the "Concerts for the People of Kampuchea" at London's Hammersmith Odeon, with *Rockestra Theme* revived with an all-star band, most of whom featured on the disk.

1980 Jan Festive *Wonderful Christmastime*, McCartney's first solo single since 1971, hits UK #6.

Jan [16] McCartney is jailed in Tokyo for marijuana possession. (Laine later sympathetically relates McCartney's experience in *Japanese Tears*.)

Jan [25] He is released and extradited from Japan.

May *Coming Up* hits UK #2. The single features a live version of the A-side on the flip, recorded at Glasgow Apollo in Dec. 1979, which becomes popular on US radio and tops the US chart, so different forms of the song chart in US and UK. In the video promoting it, McCartney takes on the role of five stars, which include Frank Zappa°, Ron Mael, Buddy Holly°, Andy Mackay and himself as a Beatle, complete with collarless suit, in a group dubbed The Plastic Macs.

June Like his solo debut, LP *McCartney II* is recorded at home, using microphones plugged directly into the tape machines. It hits UK #1 and US #3.

July Ballad *Waterfalls* hits UK #9.

Sept *Temporary Secretary*, released as a limited edition 12" single, fails to chart.

Oct [24] McCartney receives a rhodium disk from *Guinness Book of Records* for being the all-time best-selling songwriter and recording artist.

Nov [26] Film *Rockshow*, a Wings concert from their 1976 US tour, premieres at New York's Ziegfeld Theater.

1981 Feb LP *McCartney Interview*, originally a promotional record for US radio stations, is released due to public demand. It is deleted on the day of release in UK, but still reaches #34. It makes US #158.

Mar [3] McCartney guests on UK radio show "Desert Island Discs".

Apr [21] He attends the wedding of Ringo Starr° and Barbara Bach.

1982 Apr *Ebony And Ivory*, calling for racial harmony and written specifically by McCartney as a duet with Stevie Wonder°, tops both UK and US charts. McCartney becomes the first of The Beatles° to gain an entry in *Who's Who*.

May LP *Tug Of War*, recorded with help from Stevie Wonder°, Eric Stewart, Ringo Starr° and Carl Perkins°, hits both UK and US #1.

Aug *Take It Away* reaches UK #15 and US #10.

Oct *Tug Of War* makes both UK and US #53.

Nov *The Girl Is Mine*, a duet with Michael Jackson° on his LP *Thriller*, hits UK #8.

1983 Jan *The Girl Is Mine* hits US #2.

Oct McCartney makes a cameo appearance in Tracey Ullman's video *They Don't Know*.

Nov *Say Say Say*, another duet with Michael Jackson° promoted by a $500,000 video, hits UK #2 and US #1, as parent LP *Pipes Of Peace* hits UK #4 and US #15. McCartney writes the theme to Richard Gere film *The Honorary Consul*.

1984 Jan Another costly video recreating the famous Christmas Day truce during the Great War in 1914, helps *Pipes Of Peace* top the UK chart.

Feb *So Bad*, with *Pipes Of Peace* on the B-side, makes US #23.

Oct *No More Lonely Nights*, trailering McCartney's first feature film, hits UK #2. The A-side features a ballad version with an uptempo re-recording of it on the flip.

Nov LP *Give My Regards To Broad Street* forms the soundtrack to film, based on a script by McCartney and starring him and described as a "musical fantasy drama". LP comprises re-recordings of Beatles° tracks and McCartney hits and is overseen by ex-Beatle producer George Martin. The film is a critical and box-office failure, but the LP hits UK #1 and US #21. McCartney is awarded the Freedom o Liverpool in a ceremony at Liverpool's Picton Library.

Dec *No More Lonely Nights* hits US #6. McCartney, who now owns the rights to the Rupert Bear cartoon stories, which have appeared in UK's *Daily Express* newspaper for over 50 years, makes a short pilot film featuring song *We All Stand Together*, credited to Paul McCartney & The Frog Chorus. It hits UK #3, and will become an annual Christmas favorite.

1985 July [13] McCartney sings *Let It Be* as climax to Live Aid spectacular.

Dec *Spies Like Us*, the theme to Dan Aykroyd/Chevy Chase film, hits UK #13. *We All Stand Together*, repromoted at Christmas, reaches UK #37.

1986 Feb *Spies Like Us* hits US #7.

Aug *Press* makes UK #25 and US #21.

Sept LP *Press To Play* hits UK #8 and US #30.

Nov *Stranglehold* stalls at US #81.

Dec [17] The McCartneys escape injury when their car bursts into flames on the way to a recording of UK TV show "The Tube" in Newcastle, UK.

Dec *Only Love Remains* reaches UK #34.

1987 Nov Greatest hits LP *All The Best!* hits UK #2.

Dec *Once Upon A Long Ago* hits UK #30. (CD version of single harks back to McCartney's first love with versions of *Don't Get Around Much Anymore* and *Kansas City*.) B-side *Back On My Feet* is co-written with Elvis Costello°.)

1988 Jan LP *All The Best!* makes US #62, where it features different track listing.

June It is reported that McCartney has been asked to record an LP of his rock'n'roll favorites for exclusive release in USSR on the state Melodiya label.

Aug Moscow News reports that plans are being laid for McCartney to play eight concerts in Moscow in 1989, as work continues on new LP.

Nov McCartney produces *Let The Children Play*, the profits of which will go to the annual Children In Need fund-raising event.

THE McCOYS

Rick Zehringer (lead guitar and vocals)
Bobby Peterson (organ)
Randy Hobbs (bass)
Randy Zehringer (drums)

1962 The group is formed in Union City, Ind., US, by brothers Rick (b. May 8, 1947, Fort Recovery, Oh., US) and Randy Zehringer, with friends Dennis Kelly (bass) and Ronnie Brandon (keyboards), while all are at high school. They name themselves after The Ventures'° 1960 rock instrumental *The McCoy*, the B-side of US #2 hit *Walk Don't Run*.

1965 After name changes from Rick & The Raiders to The Rick Z Combo, under which they release *You Know That I Love You* during early post-high school gigs, they revert to being The McCoys again, with Hobbs and Peterson replacing college-bound Kelly and Brandon.

June The McCoys sign to producer/songwriter Bert Berns' new New York label Bang Records, after opening for Bang artists The Strangeloves (aka producers Feldman/Goldstein/Gottehrer) at a gig in Dayton, Oh. The Strangeloves put The McCoys into the studio to record one of Berns' own songs, *Hang On Sloopy*, a 1964 US hit for The Vibrations as *My Girl Sloopy*.

Oct *Hang On Sloopy* tops the US chart, selling over a million copies, and hits UK #5 where it is the first release on independent label Immediate Records, owned by The Rolling Stones'° manager Andrew Loog Oldham.

Dec A revival of Peggy Lee's 1958 hit *Fever* in a *Hang On Sloopy*-based arrangement hits US #7 and reaches UK #44. (B-side *Sorrow* will be revived in UK a few months later by The Merseys and hit UK #4. David Bowie° will revive it again in 1973.) LP *Hang On Sloopy* climbs to US #44.

1966 Feb *Up And Down* reaches only US #46 and makes no impression in UK.

Mar A revival of Ritchie Valens'° *Come On Let's Go* reaches US #22, the group's last US top 30 hit.

Aug Second LP *(You Make Me Feel) So Good* fails to chart, but the title track climbs to US #53.

Oct Eschewing previous R&B-based style, The McCoys record psychedelic *Don't Worry Mother, Your Son's Heart Is Pure* in a first attempt to expand their image but sales disappoint, with highest US placing at #67.

1967 Jan *I Got To Go Back* recalls the *Sloopy*-R&B style but makes only US #69.

May *Beat The Clock* reaches US #92, after which the group splits from Bang Records to seek a new recording deal.

1968 Oct Signed to Mercury Records in search of wider artistic freedom, the group issues LP *Infinite McCoys*. Fashionably psychedelic, it features Blood Sweat & Tears'° brass section and is produced by singer/guitarist Rick Zehringer but fails to chart. *Jesse Brady*, which makes a brief showing at US #98, is the last McCoys chart entry. Second Mercury LP *Human Ball* fails to chart.

1969 After the group has become a regular feature at Steve Paul's Scene Club in New York, Paul takes over The McCoys' management and links them (minus Peterson, who leaves) with albino blues guitarist Johnny Winter°, whom he also manages.

1970 Oct Rick Zehringer changes surname to Derringer to produce LP *Johnny Winter And . . .*, which reaches US #154 but makes UK #29. Rick, Randy and Hobbs are the backing group on it (and on Winter's° follow-up LP *Live – Johnny Winter And . . .*, also produced by Derringer, which will climb to US #40 and UK #20 in 1971).

1972 May When Winter stops touring to cure a drug habit, Derringer joins brother Edgar Winter's band White Trash on the road and plays on LP *Roadworks* which makes US #23.

1973 May Derringer produces Edgar Winter's group's *Frankenstein*, which tops US chart and makes UK #18, and LP *They Only Come Out At Night*, which hits US #3.

Dec Signed to Steve Paul's Blue Sky label as a soloist, Derringer releases LP *All American Boy*, which reaches US #25.

1974 Mar *Rock And Roll Hoochie Koo*, taken from solo LP, peaks at US #23 and is Derringer's only major solo hit single. While recording solo, he continues to play with and produce LPs for both Winter brothers.

1975 May Solo LP *Spring Fever* reaches only US #141.

1976 Aug Derringer forms hard rock quartet, Derringer, with Danny Johnson (guitar), Kenny Aaronson (bass) and Vinnie Appice (drums), but LP *Derringer* makes only US #154. (Later LPs *Sweet Evil*, *Live* (both 1977) and *If I Weren't So Romantic, I'd Shoot You* (1978) will fail to crack US top 100, though the group will constantly tour in US.)

1979/80 Derringer returns to solo recording with moderately-selling LPs *Guitars And Women* and *Face To Face* and turns to smaller club venues. He continues to get credits as a well-respected session musician, appearing on LPs by Steely Dan°, Donald Fagen, Todd Rundgren°, Bette Midler° and others.

1984 Apr He produces Weird Al Yankovic's LP *In 3-D*, a selection of hit parody/pastiches, which reaches US #17. Taken from the LP, *Eat It*, a parody of Michael Jackson's° *Beat It*), hits US #12 and UK #36.

1986 Derringer returns to the live stage as guitarist for Cyndi Lauper°.

1988 Aug For Weird Al Yankovic, Derringer produces *Fat*, a parody of Michael Jackson's *Bad*, timed to coincide with Jackson's world tour. It charts briefly in UK at #91.

MICHAEL McDONALD

1964 McDonald (b. 1952, St. Louis, Mo., US), son of a St. Louis bus driver, while at high school forms his first band, Mike & The Majestics, which proves popular at local fraternity parties and is the first of a string of bands McDonald will play with including Jerry Jay & The Sheratons, The Del Rays and Blue.

1972 McDonald signs his first recording deal with RCA Records. Self-penned *God Knows I Love My Baby* fails and RCA passes on the option to release an LP. His session work includes songs and vocals for acts including David Cassidy° and Jack Jones.

1973 Now signed to Bell Records, McDonald releases some unsuccessful singles, all produced by Rick Jarrard, including *Dear Me* and *When I'm Home*.

1974 Without a solo contract again, McDonald joins Steely Dan° on live keyboards and vocals.

1975 He auditions for The Doobie Brothers° in New Orleans, La., and is chosen to replace exiting Tom Johnston. McDonald is required to learn and rehearse the live Doobies repertoire for a solid 48 hours prior to an immediate band tour. Established as the reviver of The Doobie Brothers'° fortunes, McDonald enjoys his first #1 as a songwriter, with Kenny Loggins°, as *What A Fool Believes* hits #1 for the group, and wins two Grammies at the annual award ceremonies. His lead vocal work, songwriting and keyboard playing dominates The Doobie Brothers' output for his 7-year stay.

MICHAEL McDONALD *cont.*

1978 June Always looking to collaborate his songwriting skills (including efforts with Kenny Loggins°, Michael Johnson, Brenda Russell and others), McDonald co-writes, via the US mail service, *You Belong To Me* with and for Carly Simon°, which will hit US #6.

1979 Aug [4] McDonald performs at a memorial concert for Lowell George's family at LA's Forum alongside Jackson Browne°, Linda Ronstadt° and others.

Aug He provides vocal assistance on Christopher Cross'° successful debut LP, particularly prominent on hit *Ride Like The Wind*.

1980 Jan His first solo success of any kind is a duet with Nicolette Larson on his *Let Me Go Love*. It reaches US #35. He cuts original track *If You Remember Me* for Jon Voight/Faye Dunaway-starring movie *The Champ*, which will later be a hit for Chris Thompson.

Oct McDonald co-produces, with Patrick Henderson, debut LP for his wife, Amy Holland.

1982 Mar Arista LP *That Was Then – The Early Recordings Of Michael McDonald* is released. A collection of material recorded in his days at Bell, it features seven previously released cuts and rough versions of four unreleased tracks including a cover of The Allman Brothers° *Midnight Rider*.

Mar [31] The Doobie Brothers° announce that they are splitting. (McDonald will immediately sign a solo deal with Warner Bros. and resume his solo career.)

Aug *I Keep Forgettin' (Every Time You're Near)* is released as first Warner single. It will hit US #4 and remain his biggest solo success. (He will later be sued by Leiber and Stoller for "using" their Chuck Jackson hit *I Keep Forgettin'* – he loses the case and future royalties will be split as Leiber/Stoller/McDonald/Sanford.) Debut LP *If That's What It Takes* is released simultaneously. It begins a 32-week chart stay and will hit US #6. Produced by Ted Templeman and Lenny Waronker, it features many guest session players including members of Toto° and Steve Gadd, Greg Phillinganes, Willie Weeks, Kenny Loggins° and Lenny Castro.

Nov McDonald joins an all-star chorus on Quincy Jones-created Donna Summer° hit *State Of Independence*.

Dec From his LP, *I Gotta Try* makes US #44. This year's Kenny Loggins° LP *High Adventure* features strong songwriting and vocal contributions from McDonald, particularly hit *Heart To Heart*. It is the latest in a long and fruitful relationship.

1983 Spending much of the year composing and collaborating, McDonald writes and produces a second Holland LP, *On Your Every Word*, for Capitol.

May McDonald joins Chris Thompson to help ex-Doobie Brother° Patrick Simmons revive The Chi-Lites'° *Have You Seen Her* on his solo debut LP *Arcade*.

1984 Feb A duet with James Ingram° for his debut LP is the inspirational *Yah Mo B There* which peaks at US #19 and makes UK #44 (it re-enters in Apr. at UK #69).

1985 Jan "Jellybean" Benitez' remix of *Yah Mo B There* makes UK #12.

July *No Lookin' Back* is released and will make US #34.

Sept Parent LP *No Lookin' Back* begins a 4-month US chart stay where it peaks at #45 (but will fail in UK). Produced by McDonald and Templeman, it features a similar session line-up to first Warner LP. *Our Love*, featured in Richard Gere/Kim Basinger movie *No Mercy*, is released as a single.

1986 June [14] His duet with Patti LaBelle°, Bacharach/Sager-penned ballad *On My Own* hits US #1. It is included on LaBelle's LP *The Winner In You*, for which she cut her vocal track in Philadelphia, Pa., and sent the tape to McDonald to add vocals in LA. They have yet to meet and even tape the promotional video on opposite coasts. It also hits UK #2.

July UK re-issue *I Keep Forgettin'* climbs to UK #43.

Sept Released on MCA for film soundtrack *Running Scared*, starring Billy Crystal and Gregory Hines, *Sweet Freedom*, penned by Rod Temperton, peaks at UK #12, prompting a UK promotional visit including a BBC TV "Top of the Pops" appearance, and hits US #7. McDonald also links with James Ingram° again as they join ex-Ambrosia front man David Pack on his *I Can't Let Go* for Pack's Warner LP *Anywhere You Go*.

Nov McDonald vocalizes on Toto's° US #11 hit *I'll Be Over You*.

Dec UK-only compilation LP *Sweet Freedom* hits UK #6, staying on chart for over 6 months. A premature greatest hits package, it features The Doobie Brothers'° *What A Fool Believes*, plus specially licensed *On My Own* and *Sweet Freedom*, from MCA, and *Yah Mo B There*, from Qwest.

1987 McDonald shares lead vocals on gospel group The Winans' *Decisions* LP cut *Love Has No Color*.

Apr McDonald visits UK for sell-out dates, including 2 nights at London's Hammersmith Odeon, where he is joined by UK singer Jaki Graham for *On My Own* (prompting McDonald to provide her with a song for her next LP) and encores with soul classic *When A Man Loves A Woman*.

Dec [29] McDonald becomes father to son Dylan Michael.

1988 Aug McDonald appears again on a Christopher Cross° LP *Back Of My Mind*.

Nov [12-13] McDonald returns to UK for two live concerts in preparation for a third Warner LP and major touring activity in 1989.

DON McLEAN

1961 McLean (b. Oct.2, 1945, New Rochelle, N.Y., US), an asthmatic child who has been interested in music from an early age, decides to pursue a career in music after the death of his father.

1963 Having played concerts while at high school and as a student at Villanova University (where he has played with Jim Croce), he starts performing in clubs around N.Y., Baltimore, Philadelphia and Canada, and meets and works with Lee Hays, Brownie McGhee and Josh White.

1968 McLean makes New York's Café Lena his base, and through the club's owner, Lena Spencer, he is appointed "The Hudson River Troubadour" by the New York State Council on the Arts. He plays in 50 river communities, 3 times a day for a month, earning $200 a week.

1969 Having heard about McLean hitch-hiking from Mount Marcy in the Adironacks to Riverside Park on 125th St., New York, giving impromptu concerts on the way, Pete Seeger invites him to join an expedition to sail the Hudson River, to tell people living on the waterway about the dangers of industrial pollution. The sloop, Clearwater, with McLean as a crew member and part of The Sloop Singers, sails from South Bristol, Me., to New York in 6 weeks, singing 25 concerts. A TV special, "The Sloop at Nyack", chronicling the trip, airs on US NET's "Sounds of Summer" series.

1970 McLean spends 6 weeks singing at elementary schools in Mass. While staying at Mrs. Sedgewich's lodging house, McLean reads a book about painter Vincent Van Gogh and, inspired by the subject, writes *Vincent*, one of only six songs penned during the year. Debut LP *Tapestry*, rejected by 34 labels, is released on Mediarts label. Produced by The Youngbloods° Jerry Corbitt, and dedicated to The Weavers, it fails to chart.

1971 United Artists releases title track from forthcoming LP *American Pie*, an 8-minute 36-second track divided into two parts. The single, against all conventions, picks up airplay across US. (At the end of the year, radio station W-ABC in New York names it the most-played record of 1971.)

1972 Jan *American Pie* tops the US chart, as LP of same title, dedicated to Buddy Holly°, hits US #1 for 7 weeks.

Mar *Vincent*, coupled with *Castles In The Air*, reaches US #12 and McLean's first LP *Tapestry* belatedly makes US #111. *American Pie* hits UK #2, kept from the top by Chicory Tip's *Son Of My Father*. LP *American Pie* hits UK #3.

June *Vincent*, played daily at the Van Gogh Museum in Amsterdam, Holland, tops the UK chart for 2 weeks. Performing at LA's The Troubabour, McLean is seen by singer Lori Lieberman. Inspired by his performance, she asks her writers and producers Charles Fox and Norman Gimbel to write a song about him. They write *Killing Me Softly With His Song*, which she records for her debut LP *Lori Lieberman*. (It is later a big hit for Roberta Flack°.)

July LP *Tapestry* reaches UK #16 as McLean begins a UK tour.

1973 Feb *Dreidel* makes US #21 as parent LP *Don McLean* reaches US #23.

Apr A revival of Buddy Holly's° *Everyday*, from forthcoming LP *Playin' Favorites*, makes UK #38.

May *If We Try*, from LP *Don McLean*, stalls at US #58.

June Perry Como makes US #29 with McLean ballad *And I Love You So*, having hit UK #3 in May.

Nov LP *Playin' Favorites*, a collection of non-originals, fails to chart in US but makes UK #42. From it, *Mountains O' Mourne* tops the chart in Ireland.

1974 Dec LP *Homeless Brother*, produced by Joel Dorn with top New York session musicians, Richard Tee, Hugh McCracken, David Spinozza and Willie Weeks, makes US #120. McLean covers George Harrison's° *Sunshine Life For Me (Sail Away Raymond)*

and *Crying In The Chapel*, a US #3 in 1965 for Elvis Presley°, with vocals from The Persuasions.

1975 June *Wonderful Baby*, later recorded by Fred Astaire, makes US #93.

1976 Sept LP *Solo*, a live double album recorded on his earlier UK tour, including a free concert in London's Hyde Park attended by 85,000 people, is released.

1977 Apr *The Pattern Is Broken*, from new LP *Prime Time*, is featured in film *Fraternity Row*.

1978 June [26] Signed to Millennium Records, McLean commences work on new LP at the Jack Clement Recording Studio, Nashville, Tenn.

1980 June *Crying*, reviving Roy Orbison's° 1961 US #2, tops the UK chart for 3 weeks. Parent LP *Chain Lightning* makes UK #19. Both records are on EMI International in UK.

Sept LP *The Very Best Of Don McLean* hits UK #4, as McLean tours extensively in UK. (A concert at London's Dominion Theatre is recorded for 1982 LP release *Dominion Recorded Live*.)

1981 Mar *Crying* hits US #5. LP *Chain Lightning* reaches US #28.

May *Since I Don't Have You*, reviving The Skyliners' 1959 US #12, reaches US #23.

Aug *It's Just The Sun* stalls at US #83.

Dec *Castles In The Air*, a new recording of his 1972 hit, makes US #36.

1982 Jan LP *Believers*, dedicated to the memory of The Weavers' Lee Hays, who died in Aug. 1981 after a long battle with diabetes, peaks at US #156.

May *Castles In The Air* makes UK #47.

1984 Jan Video *The Music Of Don McLean*, featuring McLean in concert and being interviewed by DJ Paul Gambaccini, is released.

Apr [18] McLean begins a UK tour in Cardiff, Wales. (It will end at the Royal Festival Hall in London on May 12.)

1987 Apr EMI America releases LP *Don McLean's Greatest Hits – Then And Now*, coupling five McLean hits with five new tracks recorded in New York and Berkeley, Cal. with producer Dave Burgess (ex-member of The Champs°), who is now acting as McLean's manager. Extracted *He's Got You* makes US C&W #73.

Nov McLean concludes another sell-out UK tour at London's Royal Festival Hall. (McLean will have toured the UK almost every other year since his first visit in 1972.)

Dec *You Can't Blame The Train*, from forthcoming LP *Love Tracks*, reaches US C&W #49.

1988 Now firmly settled in the country field, McLean, signed to Capitol Records, releases LP *Love Tracks*, recorded at Nightingale Studios, Nashville, Tenn., which unusually for the artist features new songs by outside writers.

MEAT LOAF

1961 Born to a gospel-singing family, Marvin Lee Aday (b. Sept.27, 1948, Dallas, Tex., US) steps on the foot of his high school football coach, who gives him the nickname Meat Loaf.

1967 Having left his home in Dallas for Los Angeles, Cal., Meat Loaf builds a reputation with LA band Meat Loaf Soul, now Popcorn Blizzard, which stays together for 3 years, opening for acts including The Who°, Ted Nugent°, Iggy Pop° and Johnny and Edgar Winter°.

1969 Living in a communal home in Echo Park, LA, he applies for a job as a parking-lot attendant at the Aquarius Theater, when he meets an actor appearing in musical *Hair*. He auditions at the actor's suggestion, and is cast as Ulysses S. Grant in the LA production.

1970 June The production opens at the Vest Pocket Theater, Detroit, Mich. Playing Sheila in the show is female singer Stoney, with whom Meat Loaf will record one LP for Rare Earth, and tour with Alice Cooper° and labelmates Rare Earth. The duo splits shortly after (Stoney later joins Bob Seger's° band as backing singer).

1971 Mar Meat Loaf rejoins the road tour of *Hair* at the Hanna Theater, Cleveland, Oh.

June While still with the show, Meat Loaf makes his first US chart appearance (with Stoney) as *What You See Is What You Get* reaches US #71.

Sept Having moved to New York with *Hair*, the show closes.

1972 Dec Meat Loaf is cast as Buddha in musical *Rainbow*.

1974 Jan *More Than You Deserve*, a musical written by Jim Steinman, opens off Broadway, with Meat Loaf in the roles of Perrine and Rabbit. (Steinman, a New Yorker raised in California, is in high school band, Clitoris That Thought It Was A Puppy, when he writes play *Dream Engine* which impresses New York producer Joseph Papp. Steinman relocates to New York to work frequently with Papp.)

1975 Mar Meat Loaf opens at the Belasco Theater on Broadway in Richard O'Brien's *The Rocky Horror Show* as Eddie and Dr. Scott. (He will recreate the role for the film version of *The Rocky Horror Picture Show*.) Meat Loaf and Steinman tour US with the *National Lampoon Road Show*.

1976 Feb Meat Loaf plays the priest in *Rockabye Hamlet*, a musical version of *Hamlet*, at New York's Minskoff Theater.

Aug He sings on Ted Nugent's° LP *Free For All*.

1977 Jan Steinman and Meat Loaf start rehearsing at the Ansonia Hotel, New York, on songs Steinman has written for musical *Neverland*, a futuristic version of *Peter Pan*, which has recently been presented at Washington's Kennedy Center. After extensive rehearsal, they sign a deal with RCA Records, but pull out when the label refuses to include producer Todd Rundgren° as part of the package. Bearsville Records funds the project for a period, as does Rundgren, before Warner Bros. steps in and agrees to release the LP, but with limited promotion. Meat Loaf, Steinman and Rundgren reject the offer. In desperation, manager David Sonenberg plays the tapes to fledgling Cleveland International

MEAT LOAF *cont.*

company, which persuades Epic to release the project. Meat Loaf performs at the CBS Records convention in New Orleans. (His appearance will result in CBS commissioning promotional films for tracks *Bat Out Of Hell*, *Paradise By The Dashboard Lights* and *You Took The Words Right Out Of My Mouth*.

Oct LP *Bat Out Of Hell* is released in US and makes #14 during an 88-week chart stay.

1978 Jan LP *Bat Out Of Hell* is released in UK. Sales soar after a promo video clip of the title track is shown on BBC TV's "The Old Grey Whistle Test". The LP will hit UK #9, selling over 2 million copies during a record 395 weeks on chart.

June *You Took The Words Right Out Of My Mouth* makes UK #33.

July Meat Loaf tours Australia, where LP *Bat Out Of Hell* knocks LP *Saturday Night Fever* off the top of the chart. *Two Out Of Three Ain't Bad* reaches US #11.

Aug *Two Out Of Three Ain't Bad* makes UK #32,

Sept *Paradise By The Dashboard Lights*, with Ellen Foley on female vocals and Phil Rizzuto as the baseball announcer, peaks at US #39.

Oct Meat Loaf ends his North American tour in Cleveland, his 170th date in under a year as the LP goes platinum. (In Toronto, an over-exuberant Meat Loaf falls off stage and tears ligaments in his leg, leaving him in a wheelchair for a month.)

1979 Jan *You Took The Words Right Out Of My Mouth* makes US #39.

Feb *Bat Out Of Hell* reaches UK #15.

June [13] Film *Roadie*, in which Meat Loaf stars with Blondie's° Debbie Harry, premieres in US.

Aug [15] Meat Loaf's second film of the year, *Americathon*, premieres in LA.

1981 May Intended as follow-up to *Bat Out Of Hell*, Steinman releases solo LP *Bad For Good*, having tired of waiting for Meat Loaf, who has had vocal chord problems brought about through too much touring, to lay down vocal tracks. It reaches US #63 and hits UK #7.

Sept Meat Loaf's second LP *Deadringer*, with all songs written by Steinman, enters UK chart and spends 2 weeks at #1. It reaches US #45. Extracted *I'm Gonna Love Her For Both Of Us* makes US #84 and UK #62.

1982 Feb *Dead Ringer For Love*, a duet with Cher°, hits UK #5, helped by a duo video. Meat Loaf begins a major tour.

1983 Mar Now pursued by other acts, Steinman writes and produces Bonnie Tyler's° UK #1 *Total Eclipse Of The Heart*.

May Meat Loaf's LP *Midnight At The Lost And Found*, produced by Tom Dowd without Steinman, hits UK #7, as extracted *If You Really Want To* peaks at UK #59.

Oct *Midnight At The Lost And Found* reaches UK #17. *Total Eclipse Of The Heart* hits US #1.

1984 Jan *Razor's Edge* makes UK #41. Meat Loaf appears in TV show "Rebellious Jukebox" with Jools Holland.

Oct *Modern Girl*, Meat Loaf's first for new label Arista, reaches UK #17.

Nov *Bad Attitude*, with Roger Daltrey guesting, hits UK #8, as Meat Loaf begins a tour.

1985 Jan *Nowhere Fast* peaks at UK #67. Epic's compilation LP *Hits Out Of Hell* hits UK #2, as a simultaneous video package also sells.

Apr *Piece Of The Action* peaks at UK #47.

1986 July Meat Loaf appears as Gil in film *Out of Bounds*.

Sept *Rock'N'Roll Mercenaries*, a duet with John Parr, reaches UK #31.

Oct LP *Blind Before I Stop*, recorded in Rosbach, West Germany with producer Frank Farian, reaches UK #28.

1987 June Increasingly a UK TV media favorite, Meat Loaf plays for The Duchess of York's team in the fund-raising "The Grand Knockout Tournament" at Alton Towers, UK.

Nov LP *Live At Wembley* makes UK #60, as his contract with Arista expires.

MELANIE

1967 Melanie (b. Melanie Safka, of Ukranian-Italian parents, Feb.3, 1947, Astoria, Long Island, N.Y., US) is a student at New York's Academy of Fine Arts, and occasional singer/guitarist in clubs in Long Branch, N.J. (to where the family moved during her teens) and Greenwich Village, New York, when she signs her first publishing agreement and cuts debut single *Beautiful People*, for CBS/Columbia Records. It fails to sell.

1969 Misdirected when going to audition for a part in a production of *Dark Side of the Moon*, and allegedly going into the wrong office, she meets Peter Schekeryk, who invites her to perform an impromptu vocal audition. He is sufficiently impressed to become her manager (and later producer and husband), and gain her a deal with Neil Bogart's Buddah label. Debut LP *Born To Be* and single *Beautiful People* attract little sales but the latter gains some airplay.

Aug [16] She appears during a rainstorm at the Woodstock festival, where she is as appreciative of the audience as they are of her (the inspiration for her song *Lay Down (Candles In The Rain)*).

Nov Second LP *Affectionately Melanie* makes US #196.

1970 July Her first chart single is hymnal *Lay Down (Candles In The Rain)*, backed by The Edwin Hawkins Singers, which hits US #6 but fails in UK. It is taken from LP *Candles In The Rain*, which reaches US #17 and earns a gold disk.

Sept *Peace Will Come (According To Plan)* climbs to US #32.

Nov Live LP *Leftover Wine*, recorded at New York's Carnegie Hall, reaches US #39. Following a highly successful UK tour, Melanie's revival of The Rolling Stones'° *Ruby Tuesday* hits UK #9.

Dec LP *Candles In The Rain* hits UK #5. Spurred by its UK success, *Ruby Tuesday* is issued as a US single and makes #33. Her soundtrack LP from movie *All The Right Noises* is also released, to little interest.

1971 Jan Previously a minor UK hit as a cover version by The New Seekers 4 months earlier, Melanie's own version of her *What Have They Done To My Song Ma* makes UK #39.

Feb Live LP *Leftover Wine* climbs to UK #22.

Mar LP *The Good Book* peaks at US #80. (She becomes noted for her musical adaptations of children's stories, including *Alexander Beetle* and *Christopher Robin*, and becomes an active ambassador for UNICEF, touring the world on its behalf.)

June LP *The Good Book* hits UK #9. Meanwhile, Melanie, at odds with Buddah Records and its insistence that she deliver LPs on demand, forms her own label, Neighborhood Records, in partnership with Schekeryk (to whom she is now married).

Dec The first Neighborhood release, light-hearted *Brand New Key* tops the US chart for 3 weeks, and becomes a million-seller. Written in 15 minutes and intended as an uptempo concert relief, its lyric nonetheless attracts misinterpretations of its overt innocence, and even sparks some radio bans. LP *Gather Me*, also on Neighborhood and including the single, reaches US #15 and earns a gold disk. Former label Buddah gathers up previously unissued tracks as LP *Garden In The City* in competition, which falters at US #115 but, in a novel marketing move, is packaged in a flower-scented "scratch and sniff" sleeve.

1972 Jan *Brand New Key* hits UK #4, while LP *Gather Me* makes UK #14. (UK West Country rural novelty group The Wurzels will take their comic adaptatation of *Brand New Key*, titled *Combine Harvester*, to UK #1 in 1975.)

Mar Competing Melanie singles *The Nickel Song* (on Buddah) and *Ring The Living Bell* (on Neighborhood) peak at US #35 and #31 respectively.

Apr Buddah double LP *The Four Sides Of Melanie*, a compilation of her earliest material, peaks at US #103, while LP *Garden In The City* makes UK #19.

Oct Double LP *The Four Sides Of Melanie* reaches UK #23.

Nov After a lengthy gap between releases, *Together Alone* peaks at US #86.

Dec LP *Stoneground Words* climbs to US #70.

1973 Mar *Bitter Bad* makes US #36.

June Double live LP *Melanie At Carnegie Hall*, her second set to be recorded at the New York venue, makes US #109. (She has now retreated from full-time performing to spend time at home in N.J. and will become a mother three times in 3 years.)

Dec *Will You Love Me Tomorrow*, a remake of The Shirelles° 1961 classic, stalls at US #82.

1974 Mar *Will You Love Me Tomorrow* reaches UK #37.

May LP *Madruguda* peaks at US #192, her final chart entry.

May [9] Along with Bob Dylan°, Pete Seeger and others, she takes part in a "Friends of Chile" benefit concert at New York's Felt Forum, which raises $30,000 towards legal aid fees for Chilean refugees and political prisoners.

1975 With her career noticeably slowing, Melanie releases two unsuccessful LPs, *As I See It Now* and *Sunset And Other Beginnings*, after which Neighborhood label closes.

1976 LP *Photograph*, released on Atlantic and co-produced by label boss Ahmet Ertegun, fails to sell.

1977 LP *Photogenic – Not Just A Pretty Face* is issued on Midland International label, while a second new LP, *Ballroom Streets*, is released by independent label Tomato. (Melanie will disappear from the recording scene but will continue to play live.)

1982 Aug Comeback LP *Arabesque*, on RCA, garners little interest.

1983 Sept *Every Breath Of The Way*, on revitalized Neighborhood label, makes UK #70. This minor success leads to some UK live dates. A show at London's Royal Albert Hall is cancelled due to poor ticket sales, so Melanie performs outside the venue to an enthusiastic audience.

Nov LP *Seventh Wave* is her last Neighborhood release.

1987 LP *Am I Real Or What* is released only in Canada.

JOHN COUGAR MELLENCAMP

1962 Mellencamp (b. Oct.7, 1951, Seymour, Ind., US), the second of five children, joins his first band in fifth grade, miming to current hits.

1965/66 He links with his first live band, Crepe Soul, with whom he plays for a year and a half before joining Snakepit Banana Barn, playing fraternities for $30 a weekend.

1967 He is sacked by the band because they claim he cannot sing, and buys his first acoustic guitar.

1970 Having graduated from Seymour High School, Mellencamp leaves the family home, moving to an apartment in the small town of Valonia. He marries and becomes a father, finds work as a carpenter's helper, while his wife Priscilla works as a telephone operator.

1971 He forms glitter-rock group Trash, with guitarist friend Larry Crane, covering mainly 1960s hits.

1975 After graduating from Vincennes University, Mellencamp (now separated from his wife and child) works for a telephone company, before being laid off. With a year's severance pay, he sets out for New York with a demo he has made of Paul Revere & The Raiders'° *Kicks*. An admirer of David Bowie°, Mellencamp calls his management company, MainMan. He meets Tony De Fries, who offers to record him and arranges a deal with MCA Records.

1976 Mellencamp records his first LP *Chestnut Street Incident*, mainly comprising cover versions. When the disk, still in demo form, is released, Mellencamp discovers that De Fries has re-named him Johnny Cougar, and he has to participate in De Fries-inspired "Johnny Cougar Day", driving through his hometown, Seymour, in an open-top car motorcade.

1977 Parting company with MainMan, he moves to Bloomington, Ind., where he rehearses self-written material with his newly-formed band, The Zone, and records a second LP, *The Kid Inside*. He meets Billy Gaff, president of Riva Records and manager of Rod Stewart°, who signs him to the label.

1978 Mar LP *A Biography*, not released in US, is issued in UK, as Mellencamp begins a UK tour, heralded by Gaff as the next Springsteen°. Despite a massive publicity campaign (posters spring up bearing the legend "Cougar" and little else), the disk and promotion fail.

1979 Aug LP *John Cougar* featuring some of the material from LP *A Biography*, makes US #64.

Dec *I Need A Lover* reaches US #28.

1980 Feb *Small Paradise* stalls at US #87. After nearly 3 years on the road, Mellencamp returns to the studio to cut a new LP.

Oct LP *Nothing' Matters And What If It Did*, produced by Steve Cropper, reaches US #37.

Dec *This Time* makes US #27.

1981 May *Ain't Even Done With The Night* reaches US #17.

1982 Mellencamp, now divorced, remarries. He begins a major US tour with his own band, comprising Larry Crane, Mike Wanchic (guitar), Toby Meyers (bass) and Kenny Aronoff (drums), supporting Heart° before headlining later in the year.

July [3] He gives a free concert for 20,000 high school students in Fort Wayne, Ind., who had sandbagged for 8 days in Mar. 1982, during the state's worst flood crisis.

Aug *Hurts So Good* hits US #2 for 4 weeks and is a million-seller, kept off the top by Human League's° *Don't You Want Me*.

Sept [11] As LP *American Fool* tops the US chart, *Jack And Diane* hits US #4 and *Hurts So Good* falls to US #8, Mellencamp becomes the only male artist to have two US top 10 hits and a #1 LP simultaneously. *American Fool* stays at US #1 for 9 weeks, achieving platinum sales.

Oct *Jack And Diane* hits US #1 for 4 weeks.

Nov *Jack And Diane* reaches UK #25. LP *American Fool* makes UK #37. (It becomes the biggest-selling LP of the year in US, selling over 3 million copies.)

1983 Jan *Hand To Hold On To* hits US #9. Mellencamp cancels an appearance at the US Festival, after promoters insist on all video rights to his performance.

Oct *Crumblin' Down* hits US #9 as he changes his name to John Cougar Mellencamp. LP *Uh-huh* hits US #9 and is his second platinum-seller.

1984 Feb *Pink Houses* hits US #8.

Mar LP *Uh-huh* peaks at UK #92.

May *Authority Song* reaches US #15.

July Susan Miles wins US MTV "Party House with Mellencamp" competition. She paints her house pink. He writes screenplay *Ridin' The Cage* in which Warner Bros. shows interest.

1985 Mar Mellencamp produces *Colored Lights* for The Blasters' LP *Hard Line*.

July [13] Mellencamp turns down the opportunity to participate in Live Aid, stating "concerts that just raise money aren't a good idea".

Sept [22] He organizes Farm Aid with Willie Nelson° and Neil Young°. (During the show he asks the audience to write to their congressmen demanding action to help American farmers.)

Oct *Lonely Ol' Night* hits US #6.

Nov Recorded in his newly-built studio, LP *Scarecrow*, dedicated to his grandfather Speck, hits US #2.

Dec [6] At a concert at New York's Madison Square Garden, the sound system breaks down twice. Mellencamp waits patiently for the problem to be resolved. When he returns to the stage, he plays for 2 hours and tells the audience that anyone with a ticket stub can get their money back if they so wish.

Dec *Small Town* hits US #6.

1986 Feb *Small Town* makes UK #53.

Apr *R.O.C.K. In The USA* hits US #2.

May *R.O.C.K. In The USA* peaks at UK #67.

June *Rain On The Scarecrow* makes US #21.

July [4] Mellencamp participates in Farm Aid II at Manor Downs, Austin, Tex.

Aug *Rumbleseat* makes US #28.

Sept Mellencamp and his band start work with producer Don Gehman on a new LP at Belmont Hall Studio, Belmont, Ind.

1987 Sept [19] Mellencamp participates in Farm Aid III at the University of Nebraska's Memorial Stadium with Neil Young°, Joe Walsh°, Lou Reed° and others.

Oct *Paper In Fire*, his first release on Mercury, hits US #9 as parent LP *The Lonesome Jubilee* hits US #6 and UK #31.

Oct [30] Mellencamp begins a 6-week US tour in Terre Haute, Ind. (ending Dec.15).

Dec He contributes *Run Rudolph Run* to the Various Artists' Special Olympics charity LP *A Very Special Christmas*.

Dec [16] Mellencamp performs two free concerts for the people of Chilicothe, Oh., after local radio station W-FBC has initiated a petition.

1988 Jan *Cherry Bomb* hits US #8.

Jan [25/26] Mellencamp returns to UK to play two concerts at London's Hammersmith Odeon.

Apr *Check It Out* climbs to US #14.

May [26] He opens a US tour at Irvine Meadows, LA.

June *Rooty Toot Toot* peaks at US #61.

July [3] The US tour ends in Milwaukee, Wis.

Aug Mellencamp is one of the featured artists on Woody Guthrie/Leadbelly tribute LP *Folkways: A Vision Shared*.

Sept [13] Mellencamp appears with Paul Simon° on US NBC TV's "Coca Cola Presents Live: The Hard Rock".

MEN AT WORK

Colin Hay (vocals)
Ron Strykert (guitar)
Greg Ham (sax, keyboards and flute)
John Rees (bass)
Jerry Speiser (drums)

1979 The band forms in Melbourne, Australia, after Hay (born in Scotland, UK, but emigrated at age 14 with his parents to Australia) and Strykert, who have met while performing in musical *Heroes* in Sydney, decide to form an acoustic duo. They are joined first by Rees and then by Hay's former buddies from Melbourne's La Troube University, Speiser and Ham.

1980 They work regularly as the house band at The Cricketer's Arms, a Richmond, Melbourne pub, where they are noted by customer Peter Karpin, who works for CBS Records' Australian office. Through his persistence, CBS signs them.

1982 Debut single *Who Can It Be Now?* (written by Hay, as will be all the subsequent hit singles) and LP *Business As Usual* are produced by Peter Mclan, an American. Both top the Australian charts (the LP for 10 weeks, beating a record established by Split Enz'° *True Colours*) and Men At Work becomes the highest-paid band in Australia.

Oct Following a US tour supporting Fleetwood Mac°, *Who Can It Be Now?*, with its promo video getting saturation MTV play, tops the US chart for a week and is a million-seller.

Nov LP *Business As Usual* also tops the US chart, and sells over 4 million copies in US to rank quadruple platinum. It holds #1 for 15 weeks (beating the record of 12 weeks for a debut LP, established by The Monkees° in 1967), before surrendering to Michael Jackson's° *Thriller*. The group begins a 50-date headlining US tour, supported by fellow Australians Mental As Anything. Meanwhile UK debut is *Who Can It Be Now?* which makes UK #45.

1983 Jan LP *Business As Usual* hits UK #1 for 6 weeks. Taken from it, *Down Under* (another Australian #1 during 1982) tops both US and UK charts, for 4 and 3 weeks respectively. For 2 weeks, the group has both best-selling single and LP in US and UK simultaneously – a feat only previously achieved by a few performers, including The Beatles°, Rod Stewart° and Simon & Garfunkel°. *Down Under* is a second US million-selling single.

Feb [25] Men At Work is named Best New Group at the 25th US Grammy awards.

May LP *Cargo*, originally cut the previous summer but held over because of the success of its predecessor, hits US #3 (a second platinum LP) and UK #8, while *Overkill*, taken from it, makes UK #21.

May [28] The group appears on the first of the 3-day US '83 Festival in San Bernardino, Cal. They co-headline the day's bill with The Clash° and The Stray Cats°.

June *Overkill* hits US #3.

July Also extracted from the second LP, *It's A Mistake* makes UK #33.

Aug *It's A Mistake* is the group's fourth consecutive US top 10 hit at #6.

Oct *Dr. Heckyll And Mr. Jive*, third single from LP *Cargo*, reaches US #28 and UK #31 (and is the group's last UK chart entry).

1984 Rees and Speiser leave the group and are not replaced; session men take the bass and drum roles for the band's third LP.

1985 June After a lengthy period with no releases, the group makes US #47 with Hay's *Everything I Need*.

July LP *Two Hearts*, containing the hit single, earns a US gold disk, reaching US #50.

1987 Mar Recorded in London with producer Robin Millar, Hay's solo LP *Looking For Jack*, released under the name Colin James Hay, reaches US #126. Extracted *Hold Me* reaches US #99.

METALLICA

James Hetfield (vocals and guitar)
Kirk Hammett (guitar)
Cliff Burton (bass)
Lars Ulrich (drums)

1981 Formed by Danish-born Ulrich and Hetfield, club appearances in LA, the Bay area of San Francisco and New York, establish Metallica as leading exponents of "thrash metal" style inspired by the new wave of UK heavy metal.

1983 They sign to independent label Megaforce and release debut LP *Kill 'Em All*. The LP is released in UK on fledgling Music for Nations independent label and meets with cult interest.

1984 Aug Second LP *Ride The Lightning* is released on Megaforce in US, but picked up by Elektra 3 months later. The group signs with management team Q-Prime, which handles Def Leppard°. The LP sells a half million copies before the end of the year and reaches US #100. On Music for Nations in Europe, it reaches UK #87.

1985 Aug Metallica performs at UK heavy metal festival, Castle Donington.

1986 Mar LP *Master Of Puppets* is released and climbs to US #29, while the group spends 6 months touring as guests on Ozzy Osbourne's° US tour. The tour also helps sales of two earlier LPs. Unusually for a metal band in the age of MTV, they achieve all this without the aid of a promo video. The tour's only hitch comes when Hetfield breaks his wrist skateboarding, a favored band activity.

Sept Metallica begins a European tour with successful UK dates.

Sept [27] Between Scandinavian dates, the tour bus leaves the road, killing Burton instantly. No one else is seriously injured. (The band returns to Cal. and attends Burton's funeral in San Francisco.)

Nov The band tours Japan and US, with new bass player Jason Newsted, from Phoenix-based Flotsam and Jetsam.

1987 Jan Metallica returns to Europe to finish off the cancelled tour, playing its last date in Gothenburg, Sweden – ending nearly a year on the road.

Mar The group goes to an expensive Marin County rehearsal studio to write material for a new LP. But, unaccustomed to a plush studio, the band plays outside the studio, instead of inside it, and Hetfield breaks his arm skating in an empty pool. The group leaves the studio and decides to soundproof Ulrich's home garage in San Francisco. When Hetfield is fit to play, rather than writing songs, the group works on favorite covers of UK metal bands.

July They move into Ulrich's garage and cut five tracks in 6 days, covering band favorites Budgie, Diamondhead, Killing Joke and The Misfits. Released as *The $5.98 EP – Garage Days Revisited*, it reaches UK #27.

Aug Metallica appears at UK's Castle Donington metal festival again. After two more dates at German festivals it returns to Ulrich's garage to work on a new LP.

Oct *The $5.98 EP – Garage Days Revisited* makes #28 on US LP chart.

1988 Metallica joins Van Halen°, The Scorpions and others as part of the "Monsters of Rock" package tour in US and Europe.

Aug *Harvester Of Sorrow* enters the UK chart at #20, but drops 12 places the following week.

Sept LP *... And Justice For All* released simultaneously in US and UK precedes a headlining US tour scheduled to begin mid-November.

MIAMI SOUND MACHINE

Gloria Estefan (lead vocals)
Emilio Estefan (keyboards)
Juan Avila (bass)
Enrique (Kiki) Garcia (drums)

1973 The band forms in Miami, Fla., as a trio comprising Emilio Estefan, Avila and Garcia, all born in Cuba and raised in Miami, under the name The Miami Latin Boys. They play regular dates at restaurants, weddings and parties.

1974 Gloria (b. Sept.1, 1957, Havana, Cuba) attends the wedding of a friend at which The Miami Latin Boys play at the reception. She is invited to sing some songs with them, and Estefan offers her a permanent slot as vocalist (there being no other band on the Miami circuit with a female lead vocalist). She turns him down, being more concerned with studying for a psychology degree at the University of Miami. Her mother persuades her to compromise, singing with the band at weekends, and studying during the week.

1975 Gloria starts to collaborate with Estefan on the group's material and, with her as lead singer, "Boys" is dropped from the name and they become Miami Sound Machine. A local Hispanic label, Audio Latino, releases the group's first single, *Renecer*.

1978 After 2 years of increasing romantic as well as musical involvement, Emilio and Gloria are married.

1979 The group records its first, self-financed, LP. It is eventually picked up by CBS International, which puts it onto the US Latin market.

1984 Sept *Dr. Beat*, the band's first single in English (and only its second track recorded in the language), is released as B-side to a Spanish-language song in US, but becomes popular in UK clubs and crosses over to hit UK #6. The group visits UK to play it on BBC TV's "Top of the Pops". (This success pre-dates any outside the Latin market in US.)

1985 The group appears in Japan at the 15th Annual Tokyo Music Festival, where its performance wins the Grand Prize. In Miami, the city renames the street on which the Estefans live Miami Sound Machine Boulevard, in honor of the group's success and the good PR it brings to Miami.

1986 Feb *Conga*, based on a traditional Cuban street dance, is the group's first US chart entry, and hits #10.

Apr Sylvester Stallone asks them to write and perform the theme for a movie he is working on, and they are also requested to do a song in Tom Cruise film *Top Gun*.

May *Bad Boy* hits US #8, while the group's first all-English LP *Primitive Love*, which contains both *Conga* and *Bad Boy*, reaches US #23.

June *Bad Boy* reaches UK #16.

Sept *Words Get In The Way*, the group's first ballad in English, hits US #5.

Dec *Billboard* magazine lists the band as Top Pop Singles Act of the year.

1987 Jan Last single from LP *Primitive Love*, *Falling In Love (Uh-Oh)* makes US #25. The group begins a Pepsi-sponsored world tour.

Aug In deference to Gloria's clear star status at the front of the group, its billing changes to Gloria Estefan & Miami Sound Machine on *Rhythm Is Gonna Get You*, which hits US #5, and LP *Let It Loose*, which makes US #16. (It will be maintained on subsequent releases.)

Oct *Betcha Say That* peaks at US #36.

1988 Mar *Can't Stay Away From You* hits US #6.

May Ballad *Anything For You*, written by Gloria, is the band's biggest hit to date, topping the US chart for a week. It is taken from LP *Let It Loose* which climbs the US chart again, hitting #6 and earning a platinum disk.

Aug *Anything For You* makes UK #27.

Nov *1-2-3*, taken from LP *Let It Loose* as a UK single, hits #9 following a promotional visit to UK, on which they perform the single on nationally-aired peak-time TV variety show "Live from the Palladium". UK-compiled LP *Anything For You* follows it onto the UK chart.

GEORGE MICHAEL

1975 Michael (b. Georgios Panayiotou, June 25, 1963, Finchley, Middx., UK) meets Andrew Ridgeley at Bushey Meads Comprehensive School, Herts., UK.

1979 Michael and Ridgeley form their first band, The Executive, with other friends.

1981 Michael begins serious songwriting and co-pens, with Ridgeley, future hits including *Careless Whisper*. Supporting themselves with casual jobs, they form Wham!° (which will become the most successful UK pop band of the 80s).

1982 Michael, set to become the only songwriting force in the band in the next 4 years, signs a publishing contract with Morrison Leahy.

1983 Aug As Wham!° mania grips Europe, Michael travels to Muscle Shoals studios in Alabama to record a solo version of *Careless Whisper* with Jerry Wexler producing. Sessions are instructive but unsuccessful and Michael returns to London to re-record it for later release.

1984 June He flies to Miami, Fla., US to cut his first solo video for *Careless Whisper*.

July He produces and co-writes a single for friend David Austin, *Turn To Gold* which makes UK #68.

Aug *Careless Whisper* is released in UK as Michael's debut solo while Wham!° is rising in popularity. Ridgeley and Michael feel the ballad, strikingly opposed to Wham!'s fun uptempo style, will benefit as a solo release. It hits UK #1, selling over 1 million copies, and is viewed as a middle-of-the-road classic. Michael dedicates the song to his parents, to whom he will remain very close: "5 minutes in return for 21 years."

Dec Invited by Bob Geldof to sing on Band Aid's° *Do They Know It's Christmas?*, Michael performs a lead vocal section.

1985 Feb [16] With Wham!° at the peak of its success, the members elect to release *Careless Whisper* in US credited to "Wham! featuring George Michael". It hits US #1 for 3 weeks.

Mar Michael is named Songwriter of the Year at the Ivor Novello awards in London, UK. Presented with the award by Elton John°, Michael becomes its youngest ever recipient.

May Increasingly independent musically from Ridgeley, Michael sings two duets with Smokey Robinson° and Stevie Wonder° at a Motown celebration in New York.

July [13] Michael sings lead vocals to Elton John's° performance of *Don't Let The Sun Go Down On Me* at the Live Aid spectacular, Wembley, UK.

Nov Continuing the association, Michael completes falsetto backing on John's° hit *Nikita* and duets on *Wrap Her Up*, both for John's LP *Ice On Fire*.

Dec Michael and Ridgeley decide to split Wham!° in 1986, leaving both free to pursue solo directions.

1986 Apr While the split announcement is made, second Michael solo single, *A Different Corner*, chronicling Michael's current fragile emotional state, hits UK #1 and US #7.

June [28] Wham!° plays "The Final" date at Wembley Stadium, UK. (Following a rest, Michael will begin work on his debut solo LP, recording in SARM studios, Notting Hill, London and PUK studios, Denmark, and will sign with management team Michael Lippman and Rob Kahane.)

Sept Michael flies to US to record a duet with Aretha Franklin° and film a video. The song will only appear on her new LP.

1987 Feb Michael/Franklin° *I Knew You Were Waiting (For Me)*, written by Simon Climie and Dennis Morgan and produced by Narada Michael Walden, appears on Arista (Franklin's label) in US and Epic (Michael's label) in UK. It hits both UK and US #1.

June First post-Wham!° Michael solo single, *I Want Your Sex*, is released ahead of debut LP. Featured on soundtrack LP *Beverly Hills Cop II* starring Eddie Murphy, the song causes protest particularly in UK where reactionary radio prohibits airplay in the AIDS era. US MTV re-edits the video three times before it is acceptable. Michael insists that the lyrics promote monogamous relationships and spells this out on the accompanying video which stars his current girlfriend, US make-up artist Kathy Jueng. Despite the ban, it hits UK #3 and US #2 (#1 on *Billboard* sales only chart).

July Speculation in UK will remain unconfirmed that Michael is at least a backing vocalist on a version, reportedly recorded by his cousin, of The Bee Gees° *Jive Talkin'* released under the name Boogie Box High. It hits UK #7.

Oct The title cut from forthcoming LP *Faith* hits UK #2 and begins to climb the US chart.

Nov Debut solo LP *Faith* is released. It is written, arranged and produced by Michael and features him on most instruments. It

GEORGE MICHAEL *cont.*

hits US #1 and UK #1 and will stay on US chart for over a year.

Dec [12] Benefitting from heavy US MTV rotation of the video, *Faith* hits US #1 for 4 weeks.

1988 Jan *Father Figure* hits UK #11 as Michael prepares for forthcoming live work. On discovering that his accountants are investing in US arms company, he instructs all stock to be sold.

Feb [19] Michael opens a world "Faith" tour at Budokan, Tokyo, Japan, to a wildly enthusiastic reception.

Feb [27] On only its 7th week on chart *Father Figure* hits US #1 as LP *Faith* holds for its 5th consecutive week on US LP list. Including Wham!° hits, *Father Figure* becomes Michael's sixth US #1.

Mar During Australian dates, Michael unveils a giant white stage cage which opens and closes the show in dramatic fashion. He can only use the device at appropriate venues, including all US gigs (which are divided between spring and fall).

May Ballad *One More Try* hits UK #8.

May [28] *One More Try* becomes third US chart-topper from his debut LP, which has also returned to pole position, now quadruple platinum in 6 months.

June As the tour reaches Europe, some dates are cancelled and postponed when Michael is admitted for a minor throat operation in London.

June [11] Having resumed the tour at Earls Court in London, Michael plays an early slot for Nelson Mandela's 70th Birthday Party concert at Wembley. He performs only cover versions by black artists including Marvin Gaye's° *Sexual Healing*. 6 hours later, Michael is performing at another sold-out Earls Court date.

July Fifth extracted single, *Monkey*, remixed by producers Jimmy Jam and Terry Lewis, is his least successful authorized UK single (including Wham!° releases) at #13.

Aug [27] *Monkey* tops the US chart and is his eighth US #1 of the 80s, a record beaten only by Michael Jackson° with nine.

Aug Second section of US tour begins with sold-out dates and more rave reviews. Michael announces that he will donate proceeds of his forthcoming single *If You Were My Woman*, a remake of Gladys Knight's° *If I Were Your Woman*, to anti-apartheid groups. (The record will, however, not be released.)

Oct [31] The "Faith" tour ends at Pensacola, Fla., US.

Nov Another ballad from his LP, *Kissing A Fool*, climbs to hit US top 10 in its UK release week.

BETTE MIDLER

1965 Midler (b. Dec.1, 1945, Paterson, N.J., US), named after Bette Davis by her film fan mother, and raised in Oahu, Hawaii, harbors acting ambitions while studying at the University of Hawaii, and has her first part as an extra in locally-filmed movie *Hawaii*.

1966 She moves to New York, earning a living from bit stage parts, then auditions for the Broadway production of *Fiddler on the Roof* and gets a chorus role.

1969 Leaving *Fiddler on the Roof* after advancing to the lead female role of Tevye, she attempts a parallel singing career, while appearing in rock musical *Salvation*, and hones her act as a song stylist with small gigs in Greenwich Village clubs.

1970 One of her drama teachers at Herbert Berghof Studio, Bob Elston, helps her obtain a regular singing engagement in the offbeat venue of the Continental Baths, a Turkish bath with a largely gay male clientele. Here she hones a multi-element act which includes earthy comedy with a variety of musical styles, from show tunes to Andrews Sisters pastiches and 1960s girl group repertoire. Her piano accompanist is Barry Manilow°.

1971 Cult fame at the Turkish bath attracts US media and Midler appears on TV on both David Frost's and Johnny Carson's shows – initially as a gimmick and then as a guest vocalist. She also plays Mrs. Walker and The Acid Queen in a stage production of The Who's° *Tommy* by the Seattle Opera Association, Wash.

1972 Midler moves into mainstream cabaret and widespread TV slots, and signs to Atlantic Records.

Dec [31] She marks the end of her "arrival" year with two capacity major-venue concerts at the Philharmonic Hall in Lincoln Center, New York.

1973 Mar Debut LP *The Divine Miss M*, featuring accompaniment by Manilow°, hits US #9 and earns a gold disk, while extracted *Do You Want To Dance?*, a revival of Bobby Freeman's hit, reaches US #17.

July Also taken from the debut LP, a revival of The Andrews Sisters' *Boogie Woogie Bugle Boy* hits US #8.

Nov *Friends*, coupled with Midler's revival of The Dixie Cups'° *Chapel Of Love*, makes US #40.

1974 Feb LP *Bette Midler* hits US #6, earning a second gold disk. From it, her revival of Glenn Miller's *In The Mood* makes US #51. (Manilow° also plays piano on these, but starts his solo career soon after.)

Mar [2] Midler wins a Grammy award as Best New Artist of the Year for 1973.

1975 Dec [1] Midler is hospitalized to have her appendix removed.

1976 Feb [17] Harvard University's Hasty Pudding Theatrical Society votes Midler its Woman of the Year award. Her acceptance speech claims that the award "characterizes what the American male wants in a woman – brains, talent and gorgeous tits".

Mar LP *Songs For The New Depression* reaches US #27.

1977 June After a 3-year absence from the singles charts, *You're Moving Out Today*, co-written by Midler, Bruce Roberts and Carole Bayer Sager, makes US #42. (Simultaneously, Sager's version hits UK #6.)

July Double live LP *Live At Last* makes US #49.

1978 Feb *Storybook Children (Daybreak)* climbs to US #57, while its parent LP *Broken Blossom* reaches US #51.

Nov [25] Midler hosts "Rolling Stone . . . The 10th Anniversary" on US CBS TV.

1979 July *Married Men*, a cover of Bonnie Tyler's° UK hit, reaches US #40.

Oct Midler stars in movie *The Rose*, the rags-to-riches-to-rags again story of a Janis Joplin°-type rock singer. Midler's performance as the central character is highly rated (at the following year's Academy Awards, it will bring her an Oscar nomination).

Nov LP *Thighs And Whispers* makes US #65.

1980 Feb A revival of Percy Sledge's *When A Man Loves A Woman*, featured in *The Rose*, climbs to US #35. The soundtrack LP from the film reaches US #12, and becomes Midler's only platinum LP.

May Midler's first book, *A View from a Broad*, is published.

June Title song from *The Rose* is Midler's biggest single, hitting US #3 and selling over a million.

Sept [17] *Divine Madness*, a movie built around a Midler concert in 1979 at Pasadena Civic Auditorium, Cal., premieres in LA.

1981 Jan *My Mother's Eyes*, from *Divine Madness*, reaches US #39, while the movie's live soundtrack LP peaks at US #34.

Feb [25] *The Rose* brings Midler her second Grammy award as Best Female Pop Vocal Performance of 1980. (Following this, she has the additional accolade of appearing on the cover of *Newsweek*.)

1982 She appears in movie *Jinxed*, directed by Don Siegel.

1983 Sept *All I Need To Know* climbs to US #77, after an almost 2½-year chart absence.

Oct LP *No Frills*, including the single, reaches US #60.

Nov Another *No Frills* extract, *Favorite Waste Of Time* peaks at US #78.

1984 Mar A revival of The Rolling Stones'° *Beast Of Burden* peaks at #71, and is Midler's last hit single.

Sept [14] Midler co-hosts, with Dan Aykroyd, the first US MTV awards from New York's Radio City Music Hall.

1985 Jan [28] She is one of the host of US stars contributing vocals to USA For Africa's° recording *We Are The World*, in aid of African famine relief. (The single will be a multi-million-seller, and top charts all around the world).

Jan Midler's musical career takes a back seat, as she signs a contract with Touchstone Pictures to make a series of films. The first three, *Down And Out In Beverly Hills* (with Richard Dreyfus), *Ruthless People* (with Danny De Vito) and *Outrageous Fortune* (with Shelley Long) are major box office hits, and will turn her into an ongoing hot property as a movie actress.

1986 Nov Midler becomes a mother for the first time at age 40, when she has a daughter.

ROGER MILLER

1956 Miller (b. Jan.2, 1936, Fort Worth, Tex., US), after 3 years in the US Army in Korea, in which he has been assigned to Special Services and played in a country band, settles in Nashville, Tenn., attempting to become a successful songwriter while working at assorted day jobs.

1957/61 In Nashville, he records for RCA without success, but finds better luck via his songs, writing *Invitation To The Blues* for Ray Price (US #92 in 1958) and *(In The Summertime) You Don't Want My*

Love for Andy Williams (US #64 in 1960), among others.

1962 He joins Faron Young's band as drummer and back-up vocalist and writes *Swiss Maid* for Del Shannon°, which hits UK #2.

1964 May He is taking acting lessons and preparing to move to LA in an attempt to break into films, when he signs to Mercury Records' Smash label, and his debut release, self-penned novelty *Dang Me*, starts to get airplay and sales.

July *Dang Me*, produced in Nashville by Jerry Kennedy, hits US #7 and becomes a million-seller. (It will also win Miller three Grammy awards, including Best Country Performance of 1964.)

Aug LP *Roger And Out* makes US #37. It will stay on chart for 46 weeks, earning a gold disk for a half million US sales.

Oct Novelty country rocker *Chug-A-Lug*, taken from the LP, hits US #9.

Dec *(And You Had A) Do-Wacka-Do* makes US #31.

1965 Mar *King Of The Road*, in a more restrained, jazzy style, sells 550,000 copies in its first 18 days on release. It hits US #4 and is his second million-seller. (It will also win five Grammy Awards: Best Rock'n'Roll Recording, Best Rock'n'Roll (Male) Performance, Best Country Recording, Best Country Song and Best Country Performance of 1965.) LP *The Return Of Roger Miller* hits US #4, and is another gold disk and Grammy (Best Country and Western Album) winner.

May *King Of The Road* tops the UK chart for a week. (Miller will later open a hotel in Nashville, named The King of the Road).

June *Engine Engine No.9*, a close melodic relative of The Everly Brothers'° *Walk Right Back*, hits US #7 and UK #33.

Aug *One Dyin' And A Buryin'* makes US #34, while LP *The 3rd Time Around* reaches US #13.

Oct Bittersweet *Kansas City Star* reaches US #31 and UK #48.

Dec *England Swings*, naively-written but catchily commercial, about London trendiness, hits US #8. LP *Golden Hits*, a compilation of his singles to date, hits US #6, and is his third gold LP, remaining on chart for 13 months.

1966 Jan Despite UK reviews dismissing it as "pure corn", *England Swings* makes UK #13.

Mar Introspective *Husbands And Wives* makes US #26.

July Nonsense song *You Can't Roller Skate In A Buffalo Herd* climbs to US #40.

Sept [12] "The Roger Miller Show", a musical variety half-hour on US NBC TV, starts a weekly run on Monday evenings.

Oct Another novelty, *My Uncle Used To Love Me But She Died*, reaches US #58.

Nov A revival of Elvis Presley's° *Heartbreak Hotel* (Miller's first hit single not written by him) peaks at US #84.

Dec [26] Miller's US TV show ends its run after moderate success, while LP *Words And Music* peaks at US #108.

1967 Apr *Walkin' In The Sunshine* reaches US #37.

July LP *Walkin' In The Sunshine* makes US #118, as Miller's record sales enter a steep decline from his 1964/65 peak.

1968 Apr Reflectively sentimental *Little Green Apples*, written by Bobby Russell, reaches US #39. (It will win two Grammy awards as Best Song and Best Country Song of 1968.)

May *Little Green Apples* makes UK #19, after a 2-year UK chart absence, (but will be his last UK hit).

Sept LP *A Tender Look At Love* stalls at US #173.

Dec *Vance* peaks at US #80, and will be Miller's last US top 100 entry (although he will continue to make the C&W chart).

1969 May *Little Green Apples* re-enters the UK chart and reaches #39.

Sept LP *Roger Miller* makes US #163.

1970 Feb LP *Roger Miller 1970* reaches US #200 for 2 weeks. (It will be his last US chart LP but he will be an active songwriter and live performer in US throughout the 70s and 1980s, despite a lack of hits.)

1985 Apr [25] *Big River*, a musical written by Miller, based on Mark Twain's *Huckleberry Finn*, opens on Broadway, New York, and will win a Tony theater award as Best Musical of the Year.

THE STEVE MILLER BAND

Steve Miller (vocals and guitar)
James "Curley" Cooke (guitar and vocals)
Lonnie Turner (bass and vocals)
Tim Davis (drums and vocals)

1948 Miller (b. Oct.5, 1943, Milwaukee, Wis., US), son of a pathologist raised in Dallas, Tex., receives his first guitar lesson from family friend Les Paul.

1955 While at Woodrow Wilson high school, he forms his first band The Marksmen Combo, with schoolfriend Boz Scaggs°, playing around Texas, Louisiana and Oklahoma.

1957 Aged 14, he backs blues legend Jimmy Reed° in a Dallas bar.

1961 Miller and Scaggs attend the University of Wisconsin, Madison, where they play in R&B/Motown covers band, The Ardells, which becomes The Fabulous Night Train with Ben Sidran.

1963 Miller leaves college, returning to Texas to write songs, which will provide much of the material for LP *Children Of The Future*, before studying at the University of Copenhagen, Denmark.

1964 He returns to US and moves to Chicago, Ill. where he works with Muddy Waters°, James Cotton, Howlin' Wolf° and The Butterfield Blues Band, among others.

1965 He joins Barry Goldberg to form The World War Three Band, which becomes The Goldberg Miller Blues Band, releasing one single for Epic Records, *The Mother Song*.

1966 Nov Miller moves to Cal., forming The Miller Band, with Cooke, Turner (b. Feb.24, 1947, Berkeley, Cal.) and Davis. The band starts gigging, making its live debut at The Matrix in San Francisco.

1967 Apr The band participates in the San Francisco Stage College Folk Festival. Jim Peterman joins on organ and vocals.

June The group performs at the Monterey Pop Festival.

Sept Scaggs° returns and joins the band, which backs Chuck Berry° on his live LP *Live At The Fillmore*. Cooke leaves to form Curley Cooke's Hurdy Gurdy Band.

Oct The band signs to Capitol Records, before setting off on a major US tour.

1968 Jan The Steve Miller Band arrives in UK to record its debut LP with producer Glyn Johns at Olympic studios in Barnes, London.

Feb Three Steve Miller Band tracks are featured on the soundtrack to movie *Revolution* on United Artists.

May [18] The band appears at Northern California Rock Festival with The Doors°, The Grateful Dead° and others.

June LP *Children Of The Future* reaches US #134.

Aug Scaggs° leaves shortly after completion of the group's new LP *Sailor*, as does Peterman. The group continues as a trio. (Ben Sidran will join the band briefly on keyboards.)

Nov *Living In The USA* makes US #94 as parent LP *Sailor* reaches US #24.

1969 Mar Nicky Hopkins, ex-Jeff Beck's° group, joins on keyboards.

June LP *Brave New World*, like the previous two recorded in UK with Glyn Johns, reaches US #22. (Track *My Dark Hour* features Paul McCartney° on bass using the pseudonym Paul Ramon.)

Nov LP *Your Saving Grace* peaks at US #38. Turner and Hopkins both leave; Hopkins to join Quicksilver Messenger Service°. Bob Winkelman joins on bass and vocals.

1970 July LP *Number Five*, recorded in Nashville, Tenn. and produced by the band, reaches US #23. Davis leaves for a solo career, cutting two LPs for Metromedia.

Aug Miller recruits Ross Valory on bass and vocals and Jack King on drums and vocals.

Sept *Going To The Country* reaches US #69.

1971 Oct LP *Rock Love* makes US #82.

Dec Valory leaves. (He will later join San Francisco rock group Journey°.)

1972 Jan After the poor showing of *Rock Love*, Miller augments the band with keyboardist Dicky Thompson, bassist Gerald Johnson and second drummer Roger Alan Clark.

Feb The band makes its UK debut at London's Rainbow Theatre, where it previews its forthcoming LP.

Mar Clark and King both leave, the latter being replaced by namesake John King.

Apr LP *Recall The Beginning . . . A Journey From Eden* peaks at US #109. After its release, Miller contracts hepatitis, forcing a 6-month layoff.

Oct The group begins a 50-city US tour, for which Turner returns, replacing Johnson, who leaves to join Boz Scaggs'° band. (Cooke joins for some gigs at the latter end of the tour.)

Dec Capitol releases double LP *Anthology* which climbs to US #56, the band's first gold disk.

1973 Apr The Steve Miller Band returns to London to play at the Rainbow Theatre.

Oct LP *The Joker* hits US #2.

1974 Jan *The Joker*, featuring an innovative acoustic guitar track becomes a radio hit, and climbs steadily to US #1, displacing Jim Croce's

THE STEVE MILLER BAND *cont.*

Time In A Bottle, but fails to chart in UK.

Apr *Your Cash Ain't Nothing But Trash* reaches US #51.

May Thompson and King depart.

June Reissued *Living In The USA* makes US #49. Miller takes a sabbatical, buying a 312-acre farm in Medford, Ore., and installing a 24-track studio.

1975 July [5] Miller, making his first appearance in 14 months, assembles a new Steve Miller Band, comprising Turner, Les Dudek on guitar and vocals and Doug Clifford on drums, for the Knebworth Festival, Herts., UK, where Pink Floyd° tops the bill.

Oct The band reverts to a trio with Miller and Turner, with new drummer Gary Mallaber (b. Oct.11, 1946, Buffalo, N.Y.).

1976 After returning from a break, Miller forms his own Sailor Records, licensed to Capitol in US and Mercury in UK and Europe.

May LP *Fly Like An Eagle*, his first album in 2½ years, hits US #3, going platinum during a 97-week chart stay.

June LP *Fly Like An Eagle* reaches UK #11, his first UK LP success.

July *Take The Money And Run* reaches US #11.

Oct Miller assembles another Steve Miller Band comprising Turner, Mallaber, David Denny (b. Feb.5, 1948, Berkeley, Cal.) (guitar), Norton Buffalo (harmonica and vocals), Greg Douglas (b. Oct.11, 1949, Concord, Cal) (guitar and vocals) and Byron Allred (b. Oct.27, 1948, Logan, Ut.) (keyboards).

Nov *Rock 'N' Me* is his second US #1 and makes UK #11.

1977 Mar *Fly Like An Eagle* hits US #2, kept off the top by Barbra Streisand's *Evergreen*. (*Rolling Stone* magazine will vote *Fly Like An Eagle* best LP of the year.)

May LP *Book Of Dreams*, recorded at the same sessions as LP *Fly Like An Eagle* hits US #2, his second platinum LP.

June LP *Fly Like An Eagle* reaches UK #12.

July *Jet Airliner* hits US #8.

July [24] Miller begins a US tour (ending on Aug.18) at The Omni, San Francisco.

Oct *Jungle Love* reaches US #27.

Dec *Swingtown* peaks at US #17.

1978 Dec LP *Greatest Hits 1974-1978* is released and will climb to US #18 and go platinum.

1981 Nov LP *Circle Of Love* is released. Despite a 4-year layoff, it will reach US #26 and earn a gold disk, but fails to chart in UK.

Dec *Heart Like A Wheel* reaches US #24.

1982 Feb *Circle Of Love* peaks at US #55.

June LP *Abracadabra*, produced by Miller and Mallaber, hits US #3 (earning a platinum disk) and UK #10 (and is a worldwide hit).

June [19] Miller begins an extensive US tour with new guitarists Kenny Lewis and John Massaro.

Aug *Abracadabra* hits UK #2, held off the top by Captain Sensible's *Happy Talk*.

Sept *Abracadabra* becomes Miller's third US chart-topper, in an edited form, while *Keeps Me Wondering Why* climbs to UK #52.

Nov *Cool Magic* stalls at US #57.

1983 Jan *Give It Up* falters at US #60.

May LP *The Steve Miller Band Live!*, recorded on UK tour in 1982, stalls at US #125 and UK #79. A live video is simultaneously issued.

1984 Oct *Shangri-La* makes US #57.

Nov LP *Italian X-Rays* reaches US #101 but fails to chart in UK, where it will be his last release for Mercury.

1985 Feb *Bongo Bongo* stalls at US #84.

1986 Nov *I Want To Turn The World Around*, from the forthcoming LP, peaks at US #97.

Dec LP *Living In The 20th Century* is released, climbing to US #66. It is dedicated to Jimmy Reed° with whom Miller had played as a teenager. His first for Capitol in UK under a new Sailor deal, it includes familiar Miller associates including Mallaber, Buffalo and guitarist Les Dudek, and one side has covers of blues classics.

1988 Oct LP *Born 2 B Blue* reaches US #108. It celebrates his 20th year at Capitol with a set of blues and jazz standards, and includes a jazz version of *Zip-A-Dee-Doo-Dah* and a cover of Lee Dorsey's° *Ya Ya*.

Nov [10] Miller begins his first tour in 6 years in Burlington, Vt.

KYLIE MINOGUE

1979 Mar Minogue (b. May 28, 1968, Melbourne, Australia), daughter of Australian accountant Ron and Welsh mother Carol, gets her first acting role, as a Dutch girl in Australian TV soap opera, "The Sullivans".

Oct Supported by her parents, Minogue is offered the character of Robin in another soap, "Skyways", which also features future colleague and Stock, Aitken and Waterman protegé, Jason Donovan.

1984 Having successfully completed her High School Certificate, Minogue joins another soap, "The Hendersons", as Charlotte Kernow.

1985 Two further TV shows, "Fame and Misfortune" and "The Zoo Family" feature Minogue.

1986 She quits school and accepts the role of Charlene in new soap "Neighbours", again linking with Donovan.

1987 Apr Minogue wins Australian TV Logie award as "Neighbours" tops the nation's ratings.

July At an Australian Rules Football game in Sydney, Minogue is invited to sing. She performs Little Eva's° hit *The Locomotion*. It attracts the attention of Australian label Mushroom, which signs her to record the song.

Aug *The Locomotion* hits AUS #1 for 7 weeks before being deposed by Los Lobos'° *La Bamba*.

Sept Spotted by UK producer Pete Waterman, Minogue is invited to record at SAW's London studios during a 10-day visit and cuts *I Should Be So Lucky*. Meanwhile, UK ratings of "Neighbours" approach 14 million viewers per episode.

Nov *The Locomotion* is certified Australia's biggest-selling single of the 80s and is a hit in New Zealand and the Far East.

1988 Jan *I Should Be So Lucky*, written and produced by SAW, is released on its own independent PWL label, after all major record companies have turned it down.

Feb [20] *I Should Be So Lucky* hits UK #1 on its way to becoming the UK's first gold single of the year. It also hits AUS #1. Minogue is awarded four further TV Logie awards.

May As *I Should Be So Lucky* tops charts in 12 other territories, follow-up *Got To Be Certain* hits UK #2, held off the top by Wet Wet Wet's° *With A Little Help From My Friends*.

July Debut LP *Kylie*, written and produced by SAW, enters at UK #1, on its way to platinum sales. Signed to Geffen in US, *I Should Be So Lucky* peaks at US #28.

Aug Remixed by SAW for UK and US release, *The Locomotion* hits UK #2 in its first week of release.

Sept Minogue begins a US promotional visit.

Oct Fourth single from debut LP, *Je Ne Sais Pas Pourquoi* hits US #2 (confirming Minogue as the most successful debut solo female singer). *The Locomotion* tops the US chart.

Nov LP *Kylie* hits US #3 while rumors of a Christmas duet with Jason Donovan, masterminded by SAW, are denied.

THE MISSION

Wayne Hussey (guitar and vocals)
Simon Hinkler (guitar)
Craig Adams (bass)
Mick Brown (drums)

1985 Dec Hussey (b. May 26, 1959, UK) and Adams, after the break-up of The Sisters of Mercy° plan a follow-on band named The Sisterhood, but legalities prevent use of this name. Hinkler (ex-Artery) and Brown (ex-Red Lorry Yellow Lorry) are recruited, and the quartet becomes The Mission.

1986 Jan The band plays its first live dates (still billed as The Sisterhood), supporting The Cult° on a European tour.

Feb First radio sessions are broadcast, on UK BBC Radio 1's "Janice Long Show".

May Signed to independent label Chapter 22, based in Solihull, UK, the band begins its first headlining UK tour "Expedition 1 – Keeping The Faith", supported by Pauline Murray and The Storm.

June Debut single *Serpents Kiss* tops the UK independent chart, and climbs to UK #70.

July Several major UK labels are interested and the band's contract is bought from Chapter 22 by Phonogram while they tour Italy and West Germany.

Aug Double A-side *Garden Of Delight* and a revival of Neil Young's° *Like A Hurricane*, released on Chapter 22 prior to the new deal, tops the independent chart and makes UK #50. The band plays a mini-tour of Holland and Belgium, and UK's Reading Festival.

Oct *Stay With Me*, the band's debut on Phonogram's Mercury label, reaches UK #30.

Nov The Mission plays a UK tour to launch LP *God's Own Children*, which reaches UK #14.

1987 Jan *Wasteland*, edited from its LP version, reaches UK #11, as the band plays overseas dates titled "The World Crusade".

Mar *Severina*, also from the LP, peaks at UK #25. The band returns to tour UK.

Apr The band makes its live US debut on a 2-month coast-to-coast tour, billed as Mission UK to avoid a name-clash with an existing US band.

July The band tours Europe briefly between two major UK dates supporting U2° in Leeds and Edinburgh. Compilation LP *The First Chapter*, rounding up nine tracks recorded for Chapter 22 (including the first two hit singles), makes UK #35.

Sept The band plays UK's Reading Festival, this time as headliners, then begins recording a new LP at Manor studios in Oxford, UK, with ex-Led Zeppelin° John Paul Jones producing.

1988 Feb *Tower Of Strength* reaches UK #12.

Mar LP *Children* hits UK #2, supported by a UK tour.

Apr The Mission begins a headlining world tour, while *Beyond The Pale*, taken from the LP, reaches UK #32.

May LP *Children* peaks at US #126.

MR. MISTER

Richard Page (vocals and bass)
Steve George (keyboards and saxophone)
Steve Farris (guitar)
Pat Mastelotto (drums)

1981 The group is formed in Los Angeles, Cal., US, by Page and George, who have been together since high school, and in the Phoenix Boys Choir (of which Page's mother was the director), later both playing in high school band Andy Hardy as vocalist and keyboards player respectively. Prior to Mr. Mister, they have been in the group Pages on Epic, and then settled into session work while writing songs for Michael Jackson°, Kenny Loggins° and others.

1982 Jan The first guitarist to audition for the duo, Farris, is also recruited. Several would-be drummers come and go before Mastelotto joins, and with no sign of a suitable bassist to fill out the projected quintet, Page decides to take on bass as well as vocals. Mr. Mister settles as a quartet.

Mar Following rehearsals, the band plays a showcase for record companies at S.I.R. studios in LA.

June The band is signed to RCA.

1983 Mr. Mister spends the year rehearsing, writing, playing on tour, and eventually recording a debut LP.

1984 Apr *Hunters Of The Night* marks the group's US chart debut, reaching #57. Its parent LP *I Wear The Face* does not chart, and the band later admits that the set was written to formularized ideas and lacked the spontaneity to succeed. Page is offered the chance to replace Bobby Kimball as lead singer with Toto°, but turns the offer down, believing Mr. Mister can still make it.

1985 Dec *Broken Wings*, written in 20 minutes by Page, George and Page's cousin John Lang, tops the US chart for 2 weeks (having failed to sell in its first 2 months on the market).

1986 Jan *Broken Wings* hits UK #4. Page is offered the chance to replace Peter Cetera as vocalist in Chicago° but again turns the offer down.

Mar LP *Welcome To The Real World* tops the US chart, selling over a million copies to earn a platinum disk. Simultaneously, *Kyrie*, an anthemic song originally written a year earlier while the band was touring as support to Adam Ant°, and taken from the LP, also hits US #1, for 2 weeks, and makes UK #11.

May *Is It Love*, from the LP, hits US #8.

1987 Oct *Something Real (Inside Me/Inside You)* reaches US #29.

Nov LP *Go On . . .* makes US #55.

JONI MITCHELL

1962 Mitchell (b. Roberta Joan Anderson, Nov.7, 1943, Fort McLeod, Alberta, Canada) enters Alberta College of Art, Calgary, having shown an early aptitude for visual arts, aiming for a career as a commercial artist. She also sings and plays the ukelele, which she has learnt from a Pete Seeger teach-yourself record. Gradually, music becomes more important than her art studies, and at a friend's suggestion she sings at the local Depression coffee house with Peter Albling.

1964 On her way to perform at the Mariposa Folk Festival in Ontario she writes her first song, blues number *Day After Day*. After the festival she does not go back to school, but enters Toronto's Yorktown folk scene and starts playing in local coffee bars.

1965 June She marries fellow folk singer Chuck Mitchell and they begin working as a duo on the Northeastern US circuit.

1966 The Mitchells move to Detroit but their marriage dissolves soon after. Keeping her married name, she relocates to New York. Tom Rush, having met Mitchell in Detroit, records her *Urge For Going*, after failing to persuade Judy Collins° to do so.

1967 Mitchell bases herself in New York, looking after her own bookings and finances until she meets Elliot Roberts, who sees her opening for Richie Havens° at the Café Au Go Go in Greenwich Village. He becomes her manager and secures a deal with Reprise Records. After a period in London, Mitchell moves to LA to record an LP produced by David Crosby, who had "discovered" her singing in a club in Coconut Grove, Fla. Judy Collins° records Mitchell's *Both Sides Now* and *Michael From Mountains* on her LP *Wildflowers*.

1968 June Mitchell's debut LP *Joni Mitchell* (sometimes known as *Song For A Seagull*), produced by Crosby and featuring Mitchell on piano and guitar with Stephen Stills on bass, makes US #189.

Dec [28] She participates in the Miami Pop Festival, in Hallendale, Fla. with Fleetwood Mac°, Marvin Gaye° Three Dog Night° and Canned Heat°. It is the start of a 40-week spell on the road, playing festivals in Atlanta, Newport, Big Sur, New York and Monterey and opening for Crosby, Stills & Nash°.

1969 Feb [1] Mitchell makes her debut at New York's Carnegie Hall.

Oct Second LP *Clouds*, featuring Mitchell's own versions of *Both Sides Now* and *Chelsea Morning*, reaches US #31, aided by her appearances on Johnny Cash's° TV show, where she meets Bob Dylan° for the first time.

1970 Feb [17] Mitchell announces that she is quitting live performance during a concert at London's Royal Albert Hall.

Mar [11] Mitchell wins the Best Folk Performance for *Clouds* at the 12th annual Grammy awards in New York.

May LP *Ladies Of The Canyon*, recorded while she is living with Graham Nash in Laurel Canyon, reaches US #27 and is her first gold LP. Crosby, Stills, Nash & Young° make US #11 with her *Woodstock*.

July *Big Yellow Taxi* reaches UK #11 as parent LP *Ladies Of The Canyon* hits UK #8.

Aug *Big Yellow Taxi* makes US #67.

Aug [26] Mitchell participates in the Isle of Wight Festival, UK.

Oct Matthews Southern Comfort° tops the UK chart with Mitchell's *Woodstock*.

1971 July Mitchell tours US and Europe with Jackson Browne°, and sings backing vocals on James Taylor's° US #1 *You've Got A Friend*.

Aug LP *Blue*, recorded at A&M studios LA with Stephen Stills (bass),

JONI MITCHELL *cont.*

James Taylor (guitar), Russ Kunkel (drums) and "Sneaky" Pete Kleinow (pedal steel), reaches US #15 and hits UK #3.

Sept *Carey*, from LP *Blue*, spends 1 week on US Hot 100, at #93.

1972 Dec After a sabbatical, spent in the woods of Canada where she writes material for her new album, she releases LP *For The Roses*, her first for Asylum Records.

1973 Jan *You Turn Me On, I'm A Radio*, from LP *For The Roses*, makes US #25.

Feb LP *For The Roses* reaches US #11.

Nov Nazareth's version of Mitchell's *This Flight Tonight* reaches UK #11.

1974 Jan *Raised On Robbery* stalls at US #65.

Mar LP *Court And Spark* is Mitchell's first fully-electric album, with help from Larry Carlton, Joe Sample, Wilton Felder, Robbie Robertson and L.A. Express. It reaches UK #14.

May *Help Me* hits US #7. Parent LP *Court And Spark* hits US #2 for 4 weeks.

Sept *Free Man In Paris*, with José Feliciano° guesting on guitar, reaches US #22.

Sept [11] Mitchell performs at London's Wembley Stadium, on a bill with Crosby, Stills, Nash & Young° and The Band°.

Dec [24] Mitchell joins Linda Ronstadt°, Carly Simon° and James Taylor° singing christmas carols on the streets of LA.

1975 Feb A live version of *Big Yellow Taxi* makes US #24. Double LP *Miles Of Aisles*, from a concert with L.A. Express – Tom Scott (woodwinds/reeds), Robben Ford (guitar), Larry Nash (piano), Max Bennett (bass) and John Guerin (drums) – hits US #2 and makes UK #34. (The concert comprises familiar Mitchell material with only two new songs, *Love Or Money* and *Jericho*.)

Mar [1] Mitchell and Tom Scott win the Grammy for Best Arrangement Accompanying Vocalists for *Down To You* from LP *Court And Spark*.

Mar She joins Bob Dylan's° "Rolling Thunder Revue", initially as a spectator, but then taking part at certain gigs.

1976 Jan LP *The Hissing Of Summer Lawns*, again using L.A. Express, hits US #4 and reaches UK #14.

Feb Extracted *In France They Kiss On Main Street* peaks at US #66.

Nov LP *Hejira*, mostly written in her car while driving through US and strongly jazz-oriented, is released.

Nov [20] Mitchell, with John Sebastian, Country Joe McDonald and Fred Neil, takes part in "California Celebrates The Whales Day" at Sacramento's Memorial Auditorium.

Nov [25] She participates in The Band's° farewell concert "The Last Waltz" at the Winterland, San Francisco.

Dec LP *Hejira* reaches UK #11.

1977 Jan LP *Hejira* reaches US #13.

1978 Feb LP *Don Juan's Reckless Daughter*, with guests Chaka Khan°, Wayne Shorter, Jaco Pastorius, Glenn Frey and J.D. Souther, reaches US #25, earning her eighth and final gold disk, and makes UK #20.

Apr Jazz giant Charles Mingus, fighting Lou Gehrig's disease, contacts Mitchell to ask whether she would assist him on T.S. Eliot's *Four Quartets*. It comes to nothing but Mingus contacts Mitchell to write and sing lyrics to six melodies he has written. She accepts his offer, and begins work in her Regency Hotel apartment in New York.

1979 Jan [5] Charles Mingus dies, age 56, in Cuernavaca, Mexico.

July LP *Mingus*, using jazz musicians Gerry Mulligan, John McLaughlin, Jan Hammer and Stanley Clarke, is released. (Mitchell is quoted as saying "Mingus wanted his stock to go up before he died, there was an element of choosing me to write his epitaph, help ensure he got a bigger funeral.") It makes US #17 and UK #24.

Sept A concert at Santa Barbara County Bowl is recorded for forthcoming LP *Shadows And Light*. Mitchell's band for the show is Pat Metheny (lead guitar), Jaco Pastorius (bass), Don Alias (drums), Lyle Mays (keyboards), Michael Brecker (sax) and The Persuasions (vocals).

1980 Oct Double live LP *Shadows And Light* makes US #38 and UK #63.

Dec [2] "Shadows and Light" concert special airs on cable TV Showtime channel.

1981 Feb [5] Canadian Prime Minister Pierre Trudeau inducts Mitchell into Canada's Juno Hall of Fame.

1982 During recording of her new LP *Wild Things Run Fast* she parts company with Roberts, her manager for 17 years. After a few weeks' handling her own affairs, she teams with Peter Asher.

Nov [21] Mitchell marries her bassist Larry Klein in Malibu, Cal.

Dec *(You're So Square) Baby, I Don't Care*, originally sung by Elvis Presley° in 1957 film *Jailhouse Rock*, makes US #47. Parent LP *Wild Things Run Fast*, with guest vocalists Lionel Richie° and James Taylor°, makes US #25 and UK #32.

1985 Mitchell changes direction yet again for LP *Dog Eat Dog*, using UK synthesizer-directed Thomas Dolby° as co-producer. (Rod Steiger is featured as an evangelist on track *Tax Free*.)

Nov LP *Dog Eat Dog* peaks at UK #57.

Dec LP *Dog Eat Dog* makes US #63.

1986 Jan *Good Friends*, with guest vocalist Michael McDonald°, stalls at US #85.

1988 Apr LP *Chalk Mark In A Rainstorm*, self-produced with Klein and recorded in US and UK, features guests Peter Gabriel°, Don Henley, Thomas Dolby°, Tom Petty°, Willie Nelson°, Wendy & Lisa and Billy Idol°. It makes US #45 and UK #26.

MOBY GRAPE

Alexander "Skip" Spence (guitar and lead vocals)
Peter Lewis (guitar and vocals)
Jerry Miller (guitar)
Bob Mosley (bass)
Don Stevenson (drums)

1966 Sept The band is formed in San Francisco, Cal., US by Lewis (b. July 15, 1945, Los Angeles , Cal.) and Mosley (b. Dec.4, 1942, Paradise Valley, Cal.), originally with Joel Scott Hill (guitar) and Kent Dunbar (drums) but Hill and Dunbar drop out and Spence (b. Apr.18, 1946, Windsor, Canada), ex-Jefferson Airplane° and Quicksilver Messenger Service°, Stevenson (b. Oct.15, 1942, Seattle, Wash., US), and Miller (b. July 10, 1943, Tacoma, Wash.), both ex-The Frantics, join.

Nov [25-27] After two months rehearsing in Sausalito, Cal., and developing a local reputation, the group plays at the Fillmore, San Francisco, where 14 record labels express interest. David Rubinson of Columbia/CBS signs it.

1967 Mar Debut LP *Moby Grape* is accompanied by a publicity hype involving the release of five singles at the same time. The band tours with record label backing and the LP reaches US #24.

May *Omaha*, one of the five simultaneously-released singles, charts briefly at US #88.

Nov After disastrous LA sessions for a follow-up LP, the band is sent to record LP *Wow* in New York, where Columbia insists on discipline.

1968 June LP *Wow*, with a track playing at 78rpm, plus the bonus live LP *Grape Jam*, and guests Al Kooper and Mike Bloomfield°, reaches US #20. Shortly after its release, Spence leaves with drug problems and checks into hospital for 6 months. (He will re-emerge with solo LP *Oar* in Oct. 1969.)

July The band almost splits but re-groups to record a third LP as a quartet.

1969 Feb Four-piece group undertakes a short UK and European tour.

Mar Mosley leaves, dropping out to become a school janitor. LP *Moby Grape '69* reaches US #113.

Apr Remaining trio records a contractual obligation-filling LP in Nashville, with session man Bob Moore playing bass. The trio splits and Miller and Stevenson join Bill Champlin's Rhythm Dukes. (Champlin will later join Chicago°.)
Oct LP *Truly Fine Citizen*, from the Nashville recordings, reaches only US #157.
1970 Jan Mosley enlists in the US Marines. (He will last 9 months before being discharged for fighting an officer.)
Dec A fake Moby Grape, put on the road by manager Matthew Katz, who owns the name, plays some dates including a gig outside the gates of the Rolling Stones°/Jefferson Airplane° concert at Altamont, Cal.
1971 Apr The original quintet reunites, adding Gordon Stephens (viola and mandolin) and signs to Reprise Records.
Aug The band splits again without playing any live gigs.
Oct LP *20 Granite Creek*, titled after the house where it was recorded, is released 6 weeks after the band's final split, making US #177.
1972 Mar Bob Mosley releases an eponymous solo LP, which does not chart.
1973 Oct Lewis, Mosley and Miller team again, with drummer John Craviotta and guitarist Jeff Blackburn, who have both been with Miller for 2 years in Silver Wings, based in Santa Cruz, Cal. Since Katz still owns the Moby Grape name, the band calls itself The (Original) Grape.
1974 The group plays small-time live dates but is unable to attract a record deal, meanwhile LP *Great Grape* is issued by a fake Katz-backed aggregation.
1975 May The group splits again and Mosley, Miller and Craviotta form Fine Wine with ex-H.P. Lovecraft guitarist Michael Been. LP *Fine Wine* is released in Germany only.
1977 May Mosley, Craviotta and Blackburn link as Ducks and are joined briefly by Neil Young°, gaining live prestige in Santa Cruz but not recording.
July Spurred by Ducks' growing reputation, Lewis and Miller form yet another Grape, joined by long-absent Spence, plus drummer Jon Oxendine, who played with Miller in The Rhythm Dukes in 1969, Christian Powell on bass, and Cornelius Bumpus (who will join The Doobie Brothers° late on in their career) on sax.
1978 Feb Mosley rejoins after Ducks folds.
Apr LP *Live Grape* is released by the new group in US on Escape label but it finds little success. (Lewis and Spence will leave during the year but with now ever-fluctuating personnel, Grape continues into 1980s obscurity in minor Southern California live circuits.)

EDDIE MONEY

1977 Money (b. Edward Mahoney, Mar.2, 1949, Brooklyn, New York, N.Y., US), the son of a New York policeman, attending the NYPD police academy, also fronts a Long Island rock band by night under the pseudonym of Eddie Money. Faced with a choice of careers, he quits the force and moves to Berkeley, Cal., where he becomes a regular vocalist on the San Francisco Bay bar circuit. Concert promoter Bill Graham spots his potential and becomes his manager, negotiating a recording deal with CBS/Columbia.
1978 May Debut LP *Eddie Money* reaches US #37 (it will sell over a million copies to earn a platinum disk in almost a year on chart), boosted by *Baby Hold On*, which is extracted and makes US #11. (Following this success, Money begins to tour US as support to The Rolling Stones°, Ted Nugent°, and Cheap Trick°, and then headlining in his own right.
Sept *Two Tickets To Paradise*, also from the debut LP, reaches US #22.
1979 Jan A revival of The Miracles' *You've Really Got A Hold On Me* peaks at US #72.
Mar *Maybe I'm A Fool* reaches US #22. It is extracted from his second LP *Life For The Taking*, which climbs to US #17 and earns a gold disk for a half million sales.
June *Can't Keep A Good Man Down*, also from LP *Life For The Taking*, makes US #63.
Sept Money sings *Get A Move On* on the soundtrack of film *Americathon*; as a single, it peaks at US #46.
1980 Sept *Runnin' Back* makes US #78. It is taken from his third LP *Playing For Keeps*, which peaks at US #35.
Nov A duet with Valerie Carter, *Let's Be Lovers Again* reaches US #65.
1982 Sept Money returns to the US chart after a 2-year absence with *Think I'm In Love*, which climbs to #16, trailering his fourth LP.
Sept [3] He features in the US Festival in San Bernardino, Cal., playing to over 400,000 people alongside Fleetwood Mac°, The Police°, Santana°, Talking Heads° and many others.
Oct LP *No Control*, produced by Tom Dowd, reaches US #20 and earns a gold disk.
Nov Taken from the LP, *Shakin'* peaks at US #63.
1983 Dec LP *Where's The Party?* makes US #67, his smallest-selling LP to date.
1984 Jan *The Big Crash*, taken from the LP, makes US #54.
Mar Also from LP *Where's The Party?*, *Club Michelle*, peaks at US #66.
1986 Nov Following a gap between recordings of almost 3 years, during which he battles to overcome a drug problem, Money returns with his biggest-selling single, as *Take Me Home Tonight* hits US #4. It features guest vocalist Ronnie Spector, singing the opening line of *Be My Baby*, her 1963 million-seller with The Ronettes°.
Dec LP *Can't Hold Back*, including the top 5 single, peaks at US #20, earning a gold disk.
1987 Mar *I Wanna Go Back*, taken from LP *Can't Hold Back*, reaches US #14.
June *Endless Nights* makes US #21.
Sept *We Should Be Sleeping* peaks at US #90.
1988 Dec *Walk On Water* climbs into the US top 10, to bring Money his second biggest hit, from new LP *Nothing To Lose*.

THE MONKEES

Davy Jones (vocals and guitar)
Mike Nesmith (vocals and guitar)
Peter Tork (vocals, keyboards, bass and guitar)
Mickey Dolenz (vocals and drums)

1965 Writer/director/producer Bob Rafelson teams with Bert Schneider to form Raybeat company in US to produce, for Screen Gems, a pilot episode of a sitcom based around a Beatles°-type group using Richard Lester's film *A Hard Day's Night* as its framework.
Sept [8] An ad appears in LA's *Daily Variety*: "Madness!! Running parts for four insane boys, aged 17 to 21. Wanted spirited Ben Franks'-type." 437 hopefuls are auditioned including Stephen Stills, who is allegedly turned down because of bad teeth, Paul Williams, Charles Manson and future leader of Three Dog Night°, Danny Hutton, who makes the last eight.
Oct The four signed are Jones, Nesmith, Dolenz and Tork. Jones (b. Dec.30, 1946, Manchester, UK), ex-apprentice jockey and actor, has starred as Ena Sharples' grandson Colin in UK TV show "Coronation Street"; in the first episode of "Z-Cars" and in both London and New York productions of *Oliver* as The Artful Dodger. He has also appeared on US TV's "Ed Sullivan Show" with The Beatles° on their US TV debut. He is already a minor teen sensation in US, where he has made an LP and hit US #93 with *What Are We Going To Do?* Nesmith, a member of LA's folk circuit, has released singles for the Colpix label under the name Michael Blessing. Dolenz, son of Hollywood character actor George Dolenz, and child star of US TV show "Circus Boy", under the name Mickey Braddock playing the lead role Corky, has made an unsuccessful single. Tork, recommended to the producers by his friend Stephen Stills, has also drifted around LA's folk circuit playing in the Au Go Go Singers with Ritchie Furay.
Nov The pilot episode, in its mixture of silent comedy and slow and fast motion film technique, is a big success with a test audience of teenagers and the show is placed with NBC for its 1966 fall schedule.
1966 Mar Acting and grooming lessons begin. The group members are encouraged to record and write themselves, but their efforts are found wanting. Songwriters Tommy Boyce and Bobby Hart, who have already written *Last Train To Clarksville* and *The Monkees Theme*, are passed over as musical producers for the show. Mickie Most passes and a combination of Leon Russell° and Snuff Garrett is a failure.
July With the show due to start in Sept., Screen Gems music chief Don Kirshner takes over and appoints Boyce and Hart as producers, and with Lester Sill is responsible for molding The Monkees' sound and musical persona. Gerry Goffin and Carole King°, Neil Diamond°, Barry Mann and Cynthia Weil and Neil Sedaka°, all signed to Kirshner's Aldon Music company, are brought in to write songs.
Sept [12] The Monkees TV show premieres on US NBC-TV.
Nov [5] Despite a hesitant start for the TV show, debut single *Last Train To Clarksville* hits US #1, providing the perfect counterpoint to The Beatles'° "yeah yeah yeah" with "no no no", and earns a gold disk.

THE MONKEES *cont.*

Nov Debut LP *The Monkees*, released on Colgems, tops the US chart for 13 weeks and earns a gold disk, selling 3,200,000 copies in 3 months.

Nov [26] *I'm A Believer*, written by Neil Diamond°, is released with advance orders of 1,051,280.

Dec The band hits US #1 with *I'm A Believer*. Try-out concerts in Hawaii erupt in riots, confirming Beatlemania-like success.

1967 Jan [20] The TV series premieres on UK BBC TV as *I'm A Believer* tops the UK chart for 4 weeks, selling over 750,000 copies.

Feb LP *More Of The Monkees*, released with advance orders of over 1.5 million, tops the US chart for 18 weeks. LP *The Monkees* hits UK #1. *Last Train To Clarksville* belatedly charts in UK, reaching #23. A successful US concert tour gives the group more confidence as musicians in a real band. Nesmith insists that The Monkees should be allowed to play on their own records with more of their own songs (at this point, James Burton, Glen Campbell°, Leon Russell°, David Gates and Hal Blaine are regular players on their disks) and insists that either he or Don Kirshner goes. Schneider gives him backing and Kirshner resigns as chief executive of Screen Gems Music. UK magazine *Monkees Monthly* is launched.

Mar Another Neil Diamond° composition, *A Little Bit Me, A Little Bit You* hits US #2 (a third million-selling single) and UK #3. Jones forms short-lived record company, Davy Jones Presents.

Apr The group starts a brief tour of Canada.

May LP *More Of The Monkees* tops the UK chart, unseating *The Sound Of Music* (which had dethroned LP *The Monkees*).

May [16] LP *Headquarters*, their third consecutive LP to sell over a million copies, is released. Nesmith brings in producer Chip Douglas. The group plays on the LP supplemented by only three outsiders.

June LP *Headquarters* hits US #1 for 1 week, before being displaced by The Beatles'° *Sgt. Pepper*.

June [4] The Monkees win an Emmy award for Outstanding Comedy Series 1966-1967.

June [9/10] They play The Hollywood Bowl, LA.

June [30] The group plays the first of three sold-out concerts at The Empire Pool, Wembley, London.

July [7] The Monkees tour US with Jimi Hendrix° as opening act. (He quits the tour within 2 weeks.)

July *Alternate Title* hits UK #2. (Its original title *Randy Scouse Git* had been heard by Dolenz on UK TV show "Till Death Us Do Part".) LP *Headquarters* hits UK #2, kept from the top by *Sgt. Pepper*.

Aug *Pleasant Valley Sunday* hits US #3 and UK #11. B-side *Words* reaches US #11.

Nov LP *Pisces, Aquarius, Capricorn & Jones Ltd.* is released.

Nov [17] Jones opens a boutique, Zilch I, in New York.

Nov Nesmith gathers together 54 of LA's top session men to give his songs a big band treatment and self-finances LP *The Wichita Train Whistle Sings*, on Dot.

Dec LP *Pisces, Aquarius, Capricorn & Jones Ltd.* tops the UK chart for 5 weeks. *Daydream Believer*, written by ex-Kingston Trio member John Stewart, tops the US chart for 4 weeks and hits UK #5. (Jones had trouble interpreting the lyrics, so the engineer used a code to number different takes. Jones asks at the beginning of the record "what number is this?" To which everyone in the studio replies "7a".) The band completes filming of a second TV series. Tim Buckley° and Frank Zappa° make guest appearances.

1968 Jan LP *Pisces, Aquarius, Capricorn & Jones Ltd.* hits UK #5.

Feb [15] Shooting begins for feature film *Head*, directed by Bob Rafelson.

Mar *Valleri* becomes the band's sixth million-selling single, hitting US #3 and UK #12. The Monkees collect their tenth gold disk in 18 months.

Mar [25] The 58th (final) episode of the TV series is broadcast.

May LP *The Birds, The Bees And The Monkees*, on which each group member contributes individual tracks, hits US #3. The band performs a free concert in Salt Lake City, Ut., to be filmed for live segments of *Head*.

June The TV series (along with "Batman") is axed.

July The Monkees' revival of The Coasters'° *D.W. Washburn* reaches US #19 and UK #17.

Oct *Porpoise Song* peaks at US #62.

Nov [20] *Head* premieres in LA. Given a budget of $750,000 by Columbia Pictures, Rafelson, expected to deliver a standard teen flick, has instead, with Jack Nicholson (who has become part of The Monkees' clique), created a film about the manipulation of The Monkees, mixed in with a tribute to classic Hollywood movies. The resultant bizarre pot-pourri features a variety of guest appearances, from boxer Sonny Liston to Victor Mature as The Big Victor representing capitalism. It includes scenes of The Monkees committing suicide by jumping from a bridge, and a concert intercut with Vietnam war atrocities. (It is a box-office disaster and will not be shown in UK until Mar. 1977.)

Dec Soundtrack LP *Head* makes US #45.

Dec [30] Tork quits, buying out his contract for $160,000, and after years of conspicuous living is left completely broke. The remaining members are also keen to call it a day, but are scared off by Tork's highly-priced contract buy-out.

1969 Feb *Tear Drop City* reaches US #56 and UK #46.

Mar LP *Instant Replay* makes US #32.

Apr [14] TV special "33 1/3 Revolutions Per Monkee", recorded in 1968, is aired.

June *Listen To The Band*, written by Nesmith, and using musicians who will become Area Code 615, climbs to US #63. *Someday Man* peaks at UK #47. LP *The Monkees Greatest Hits* makes US #93, as the group tours US as a trio.

Oct *Good Clean Fun* falters at US #82.

Nov LP *The Monkees Present* makes US #100.

1970 Mar [1] Nesmith, his contractual obligations complete, quits The Monkees to form his own group, The First National Band. Dolenz and Jones carry on recording LP *Changes*, but it fails to sell. (The industry joke is that the next LP will be by The Monkee.)

June *Oh My My* peaks at US #98 and Dolenz and Jones decide to end The Monkees.

Oct Nesmith's solo *Joanne* makes US #21 and his LP *Magnetic South* reaches US #143.

1971 Jan Nesmith's *Silver Moon* makes US #42, while parent LP *Loose Salute* peaks at US #159.

May *Nevada Fighter*, also by Nesmith, reaches US #70.

July Jones makes US #52 with *Daisy Jane*.

1975 The group meets to discuss re-forming. McDonald's have offered a TV commercial, but Tork declines as he is a vegetarian. Nesmith is only interested if a feature film is part of the package. Dolenz and Jones re-form the band with writers Tommy Boyce and Bobby Hart, and begin a 2-year tour, "The Golden Great Hits of The Monkees Show – The Guys Who Wrote 'Em and The Guys Who Sang 'Em". They sign a deal with Capitol, which issues LP *Dolenz, Jones, Boyce And Hart*.

Aug Compilation LP *The Monkees Greatest Hits* capitalizes on the group's tour, reaching US #58.

1977 Mar Nesmith's first UK success is with *Rio* at #28, in part due to the creation of his Pacific Arts Corporation, a video company which films a promo for the single. (He will subsequently produce films including *Elephant Parts*, *Time Rider* and *Repo Man*. The National Film Theatre in UK imports a copy of *Head* to meet cult demand. It runs for a season at The Electric Cinema in London.

1978 Dec Dolenz and Jones star in Harry Nilsson's° *The Point* at London's Mermaid Theatre.

1979 Dolenz stays in UK, to work as a freelance director in TV ("Metal Mickey") and stage (*Bugsy Malone*). (Nesmith's mother Bette sells her patent for Liquid Paper to the Gillette Corporation for $47 million. She will die in 1980, leaving Nesmith as her sole beneficiary.) Nesmith's LP *Infinite Rider On The Big Dogma* makes US #151.

1980 Jones tours Japan after *Daydream Believer* is used in a Kodak commercial, and Monkeemania breaks loose once again in Japan.

Mar Four-track EP *The Monkees*, containing *I'm A Believer*, *Daydream Believer*, *Last Train To Clarksville* and *A Little Bit Me, A Little Bit You*, reaches UK #33.

1981 Tork tours Japan with his group The New Monks, after working as a waiter and telling *National Enquirer* that he is a "professional has-been".

Nov LP *The Monkees* makes UK #99.

1982 Rhino inadvertently creates the foundation for a Monkees revival with the release of the first in a series of LPs. The label reissues all the band's LPs along with much previously unavailable material.

May Jones and Tork undertake a tour of Australia, which is a smash success. US MTV repeats The Monkees TV series. Arista releases LP *Then And Now . . . The Best Of The Monkees*, which includes some new tracks.

1986 Feb [22/23] To celebrate the 20th anniversary of the group, US MTV airs "Pleasant Valley Sunday", a 22½ hour broadcast of every Monkees TV episode.

Feb Dolenz, Jones and Tork re-form the group to begin a US summer tour.

June [22/23] MTV repeats "Pleasant Valley Sunday".

Aug [1/3] The Monkees convention is held in Philadelphia, Pa.

Aug Monkeemania explodes in US again with the group occupying seven positions on US LP chart: *Then And Now . . . The Best Of The Monkees* (#21), *The Monkees* (#92), *More Of The Monkees* (#96), *Headquarters* (#121), *Pisces, Aquarius, Capricorn & Jones Ltd.* (#124), *The Birds, The Bees And The Monkees* (#145) and *Changes* (#152). *That Was Then This Is Now* single makes US #20 and UK #68.

Aug [12] Auditions are held for The New Monkees. Jason Nesmith and Bobby Darin's° son Dodd both fail to make the final four.

Oct [18] As the group plays Atlanta, the mayor Andrew Young declares it Monkees Day.

Nov *Daydream Believer* peaks at US #79.

1987 Rhino releases two LPs of rare material, *Missing Links* and *Live 1967*.

Sept Newly-recorded LP *Pool It!* makes US #72.

Oct *Heart And Soul* peaks at US #87.

THE MOODY BLUES

Denny Laine (vocals and guitar)
Ray Thomas (flute, harmonica, vocals)
Mike Pinder (keyboards)
Clint Warwick (bass)
Graeme Edge (drums)

1964 May [4] Laine (b. Oct.29, 1944) disbands Denny Laine & The Diplomats and forms a new group in Birmingham, UK, comprising Thomas (b. Dec.29, 1942, Stourton-on-Severn, UK) and Pinder (b. Dec.12, 1942, Birmingham, UK), both from local rock group El Riot & The Rebels, and Edge (b. Mar.30, 1944, Rochester, Kent, UK), from Gerry Levene & The Avengers and Warwick (b. June 25, 1940). They adopt the name The Moody Blues and sign with London manager Tony Secunda, who secures them a contract with Decca Records.

Aug The group performs its debut single *Lose Your Money* on UK TV show "Ready Steady Go!", but it fails to chart.

1965 Jan *Go Now*, a cover of Bessie Banks' US R&B hit, tops the UK chart.

Mar *I Don't Want To Go On Without You*, a revival of a Drifters'° B-side, makes UK #33.

Apr [11] The Moody Blues take part in the annual *New Musical Express* poll winners concert at the Empire Pool, Wembley, London, with The Beatles°, The Rolling Stones°, The Kinks°, The Animals° and many others.

Apr *Go Now* hits US #10, in a unique US top 10 in which nine of the singles are from UK.

July *From The Bottom Of My Heart* makes UK #22 and US #93, while LP *The Magnificent Moodies*, produced by Denny Cordell, fails to chart.

Nov *Everyday* makes UK #44.

1966 Apr *Stop!* spends 1 week on US Hot 100, at #98.

Aug Laine and Warwick leave. (Laine signs a solo deal with Deram, then joins ex-Move° member Trevor Burton in the band Balls before joining Wings in 1973. Warwick quits the music business.)

Sept John Lodge (b. July 20, 1945, Birmingham), ex-El Riot & The Rebels with Thomas and Pinder, (before playing with The Carpetbaggers, the John Bull Breed and The Falcons), and Justin Hayward (b. Oct.14, 1946, Swindon, Wilts., UK), who has previously recorded singles on UK Pye and Parlophone and been a member of The Wilde Three with husband and wife Marty° and Joyce Wilde, are recruited as replacements. The band moves to Belgium, to avoid the UK taxman.

Oct Their only release this year is flop single *Boulevard De La Madelaine*.

1967 Apr [14] Laine releases his first solo single *Say You Don't Mind* which fails (but is later a hit for Colin Blunstone).

Sept The group begins a 3-month US tour.

1968 Jan Hayward-penned *Nights In White Satin* reaches UK #19. It is taken from their first LP *Days Of Future Passed*, a concept LP based around a theme of different times of the day and night,

THE MOODY BLUES *cont.*

which makes UK #27. The London Festival Orchestra, a group of session musicians conducted by Peter Knight also plays a major part, though its orchestrated passages are edited between and around The Moody Blues tracks so the orchestra does not actually accompany the group. (The original idea, abandoned early on, was for band and orchestra to record Dvorak's *New World Symphony* together. The LP is also the start of a long-term relationship between The Moody Blues and producer Tony Clarke.

May LP *Days Of Future Passed* hits US #3, and will give the band its first gold disk during a 102-week chart stay.

Aug *Voices In The Sky* makes UK #27, as parent LP *In Search Of The Lost Chord*, another concept album, hits UK #5.

Sept *Tuesday Afternoon*, taken from LP *Days Of Future Passed*, makes US #24. LP *In Search Of The Lost Chord* makes US #23 and earns a second gold disk.

Nov The band makes its US live debut as *Ride My See Saw*, extracted from LP *In Search Of The Lost Chord*, peaks at US #61.

Dec *Ride My See Saw* makes UK #42. Its B-side is little heard *A Simple Game* (later a UK #3 for The Four Tops° with Clarke producing).

1969 May LP *On The Threshold Of A Dream* tops the UK chart for 2 weeks and reaches US #20 during a 136-week chart run, and becomes third gold disk.

July *Never Comes The Day* stalls at US #91.

Oct *Watching And Waiting* is the first single release on the band's own Threshold label.

Dec LP *To Our Children's Children* hits UK #2. The band moves to Cobham, Surrey and opens a chain of Threshold record stores.

Dec [12] The group performs at London's Royal Albert Hall. The concert is recorded (and released as part of LP *Caught Live Plus Five* in June 1977).

1970 Jan LP *To Our Children's Children* makes US #14 and is the group's fourth gold LP.

May Hayward's *Question*, the group's first release on its own Threshold label, hits UK #2, kept off the top by the England World Cup Squad's *Back Home*.

June *Question* reaches US #21.

Aug LP *A Question Of Balance*, written and recorded in 5 weeks, hits UK #1 for 3 weeks.

Sept LP *A Question Of Balance* hits US #3, and becomes the group's fifth gold disk.

Oct [30] The Moody Blues play London's Royal Festival Hall.

1971 Aug LP *Every Good Boy Deserves Favour*, the acronym for the notes on a treble stave, tops the UK chart.

Sept *The Story In Your Eyes* reaches US #23. (The UK equivalent is withdrawn, at the band's request.) Parent LP *Every Good Boy Deserves Favour* hits US #2, becoming the group's sixth consecutive gold disk.

1972 June Lodge-penned *Isn't Life Strange* reaches UK #13 and US #29.

Nov Re-issued *Nights In White Satin* hits US #2, passing a million sales, as parent LP *Days Of Future Passed* hits US #3 while the group tours US. LP *Seventh Sojourn* hits UK #5.

Dec LP *Seventh Sojourn* tops the US chart for 5 weeks and earns a further gold disk

1973 Jan *Nights In White Satin* hits UK #9, 10 places higher than its previous appearance 5 years earlier.

Feb *I'm Just A Singer (In A Rock'n'Roll Band)* makes UK #36. (This will be their last new release for some time as they remain dormant until 1978, although not actually announcing a split.)

Mar *I'm Just A Singer (In A Rock'n'Roll Band)* reaches US #12.

1974 Feb The group ends a 9-month world tour in US, and decides to split for the time being.

June Hayward and Lodge start recording at The Moody Blues' new, as yet unopened, studio backed by three-piece Idaho group Providence.

July [17] The Moody Blues open their own studio (the first quadrophonic in the world) in West Hampstead, London.

Nov Double compilation LP *This Is The Moody Blues* reaches UK #14 and US #11, earning a gold disk.

1975 Mar [10] Hayward and Lodge's LP *Blue Jays* is launched in US at a listening party in New York's Carnegie Hall. It hits UK #4.

Aug Thomas' solo LP *From Mighty Oaks* makes US #68.

Oct Hayward and Lodge's *Blue Guitar*, co-produced by 10cc°, hits UK #8. The Graeme Edge Band featuring Adrian Gurvitz makes US #107 with LP *Kick Off Your Muddy Boots*.

1976 Aug Thomas' second LP *Hope Wishes And Dreams* makes US #147.

1977 Feb Lodge's solo LP *Natural Avenue* reaches UK #38.

Mar Hayward's solo LP *Songwriter* makes UK #28 and US #37.

May Lodge's LP *Natural Avenue* reaches US #121.

June Double LP *Caught Live + 5*, featuring three sides of the Dec. 1969 Royal Albert Hall concert and a fourth side of unreleased studio recordings from the late 1960s, makes US #26, and is the group's first LP not to be certified gold.

July Second Graeme Edge Band LP *Paradise Ballroom* makes US #164.

1978 June The Moody Blues re-unite for new LP *Octave*, their first disk for 6 years, which they record at the Record Plant, LA. Midway through the recording producer Clarke leaves, having been effectively the sixth Moody Blue for over a decade, and closely identified with the development of their symphonic sound of the 70s.

July LP *Octave* hits UK #6 and reaches US #13, and becomes the group's first platinum disk. Pinder quits the band and the music business, and is replaced by Patrick Moraz (b. Switzerland), ex-Refugee and Yes°. Hayward's solo *Forever Autumn*, extracted from Jeff Wayne's concept LP *War Of The Worlds*, hits UK #5.

Aug *Steppin' In A Slide Zone*, written by Lodge, makes US #39.

Oct The group begins its first live appearances in 4 years, for a sell-out world tour. *Driftwood* peaks at US #59.

1979 Dec *Nights In White Satin* is re-issued for a second time and reaches UK #14. TV-promoted K-tel compilation LP *Out Of This World* reaches UK #15.

1980 July Hayward's second solo LP *Night Flight*, produced by Jeff Wayne, reaches UK #41 and US #166.

1981 May LP *Long Distance Voyager*, on Threshold, hits UK #7.

July LP *Long Distance Voyager* tops the US chart for 3 weeks, turning platinum.

Aug *Gemini Dream*, from LP *Long Distance Voyager*, reaches US #12.

Oct *The Voice* makes US #15.

Dec *Talking Out Of Turn* stalls at US #65.

1983 Sept *Blue World* makes UK #35 as parent LP *The Present* reaches UK #15 and US #26.

Oct *Sitting At The Wheel* makes US #27.

Dec *Blue World* peaks at US #62.

1985 Apr Retrospective LP *Voices In The Sky/The Best Of The Moody Blues*, including the group's hits from 1967-83, reaches US #132.

Oct Hayward's third solo LP *Moving Mountains*, on Towerbell Records, reaches UK #78.

1986 May The group switches to Polydor for LP *The Other Side Of Life*, which makes UK #24 and hits US #9.

June [19] The Moody Blues open a major US tour in Chastain Park, Atlanta, Ga. (ending on Oct.7).

July *Your Wildest Dreams* hits US #9.

Sept *The Other Side Of Life* reaches US #58.
1988 June LP *Sur La Mer* peaks at UK #21.
July LP *Sur La Mer* reaches US #38.
Aug *I Know You're Out There Somewhere* makes US #30 and UK #52.

VAN MORRISON

1960 Morrison (b. Aug.31, 1945, Belfast, N. Ireland), having left school to concentrate on a career in music, encouraged from an early age by his parents to have an interest in blues and jazz, plays guitar and soprano sax with local rock'n'roll and jazz groups, including the country-rock group Deanie Sands & The Javelins.
1961 He tours UK and Europe with local R&B group The Monarchs, and then forms Them°, from members of The Monarchs and some old schoolfriends.
1964 Them° begins a tour of England, where they attract the attention of producer Bert Berns, writer of *Twist And Shout, Shout* and *Hang On Sloopy*.
July Berns produces *Don't Start Crying Now/One Two Brown Eyes* for Them°.
1966 Aug Morrison retires to Belfast to rest and write songs and consider his future, after a gruelling US tour.
1967 Mar He disrupts Them° by signing a solo contract with Berns, traveling to New York to record for his Bang label. The group continues without Morrison, replacing him with vocalist Ken McDowell.
June *Brown Eyed Girl*, the first of four Berns-Morrison singles, hits US #10.
Oct Berns issues an LP of Morrison's recordings, *Blowin' Your Mind* without the singer's knowledge. It reaches US #182.
Dec Berns dies of a heart attack. Morrison negotiates with other companies and signs to US Warner Bros.
1968 July He records LP *Astral Weeks* in 48 hours in New York. (Without a hit single, the LP will take time to generate sales, but will move into the US charts by the end of the year.)
1970 Apr LP *Moondance* peaks at US #29 and UK #32, aided in US by *Come Running* which makes #39.
Sept LP *His Band And The Street Choir* is released (and will climb to US #32 in 1971).
Dec *Domino* hits US #9.
1971 Feb *Blue Money* makes US #23. Morrison becomes a much-respected live act in US, assembling an 11-piece Caledonia Soul Orchestra, including string players and guitarist John Platania, a mainstay of his studio work.
June *Call Me Up In Dreamland* makes US #95.
Oct *Wild Night* reaches US #28. LP *Tupelo Honey* is released, making US #27. It is conceived as a suite of love songs to Morrison's wife, Janet Planet.
1972 Jan *Tupelo Honey* title track peaks at US #47.
Aug *Jackie Wilson Said (I'm In Heaven When You Smile)* makes US #61. LP *St. Dominic's Preview* enters the US chart, staying 6 months there and peaking at #15.
Oct *Redwood Tree* reaches US #98.
1973 Aug LP *Hard Nose The Highway* makes UK #22 and US #27. Morrison's personal life, always kept from public view, hits trouble and he is divorced. He returns to Ireland to write songs.
1974 Jan LP *T.B. Sheets*, of tracks from the *Blowin' Your Mind* sessions, is released but reaches only US #181.
Mar Double live LP *It's Too Late To Stop Now*, with Morrison and the Caledonian Soul Orchestra in top form, makes only US #53. Morrison disbands the orchestra and tours Europe with a 5-piece band, playing sax and harmonica himself.
Nov LP *Verdon Fleece*, an intensely personal record of songs written in Ireland in 1973, makes only US #53 and UK #41.
1975/76 Morrison makes a number of unsuccessful recordings – including one with The Crusaders°.
1976 Nov [25] Morrison is one of many special guests at The Band's° farewell concert "The Last Waltz".
1977 May Morrison's "comeback" LP, *A Period Of Transition*, makes UK #23 and US #43. It features Dr. John° on piano.
Nov *Moondance* is re-released and briefly makes US #92.
1978 Oct Soul-tinged LP *Wavelength* is released, making US #28 and UK #27. The title track peaks at US #42. *Bright Side Of The Road*, Morrison's only UK chart single, reaches #63.
1979 Sept LP *Into The Music* makes UK #21 and US #43. His records are now distributed by Warners in US and by PolyGram elsewhere.
1980 Sept LP *Common One*, with Morrison edging towards his old mystical self, reaches UK #53 and US #73.
1982 Feb After another break of more than a year, LP *Beautiful Vision*, with Morrison again the soul mystic, reaches UK #31 and US #44.
1983 Mar LP *Inarticulate Speech Of The Heart* is released. Striking a chord with fans of his earlier solo recordings, and aided by instrumental *Celtic Swing* (for which Morrison makes a promo video), it makes UK #14 and US #116
1984 Mar LP *Live At The Grand Opera House*, recorded in Belfast, reaches UK #44.
July Morrison receives a big reception when he joins Bob Dylan° at Wembley Stadium, London, in front of 72,000 people. They perform Dylan's *It's All Over Now, Baby Blue*, a song Morrison recorded in the early 1960s.
Nov Morrison leaves his base in Marin County, Cal., to begin nomadic traveling between Dublin, Belfast and London.
1985 Feb LP *A Sense Of Wonder*, back in the realms of poetry and spirituality, reaches UK #25 and US #61. (The credits include a thank you to Scientology founder L. Ron Hubbard.)
1986 Morrison undertakes a tour ending at London's Dominion Theatre.
May [17] He joins U2°, Elvis Costello° and The Pogues° for Dublin's Self-Aid concert, a post Live Aid effort at raising funds for the unemployed in the Irish Republic.
July LP *No Guru, No Method, No Teacher* (the title Morrison's rebuttal of press attempts to characterize his spirituality and cast him as a devotee of scientology) peaks at UK #27 and US #70.
1987 Sept LP *Poetic Champions Compose* reaches UK #26 and US #90.
1988 July LP *Irish Heartbeat*, an exploration of his Celtic musical roots recorded with The Chieftains, Ireland's top traditional music group, makes UK #18. Morrison is in his most cheerful form and is even seen to smile in concert.

THE MOTELS

Martha Davis (vocals)
Jeff Jourard (guitar)
Marty Jourard (keyboards and saxophone)
Michael Goodroe (bass)
Brian Glascock (drums)

1978 July The group is formed in LA by Davis (b. Jan.15, 1951, Berkeley, Cal., US), who has led a three-piece version for some 5 years (initially as The Warfield Foxes in Berkeley, and then as The Motels in LA) and Jeff Jourard. They recruit the latter's brother, ex-classical guitarist-turned-jazz/rock bassist Goodroe, and (after rejecting dozens of other drummers) UK ex-patriot Glascock, once in Toe Fat with Cliff Bennett°, and since a session man for Joan Armatrading°, The Bee Gees° and others.
1979 Jan Regular work at the Whiskey A-Go-Go in Hollywood, and dates around other LA clubs, attract a strong live following, and also initiate record company interest.
Mar Capitol Records signs the group.
Sept Debut LP *Motels*, produced by John Carter, initially does not chart.
Oct/Nov The group tours extensively in support of the LP, playing Canada, Australia and UK, as well as US.
Dec The LP belatedly reaches US #175 following the tour exposure. Jeff Jourard leaves after disagreements with Davis, and is replaced on lead guitar by Tim McGovern from The Pop.
1980 Sept LP *Careful* reaches US #45.
Oct *Whose Problem?*, taken from LP *Careful*, reaches UK #42 following a successful UK tour and strong radio play, though the LP fails to chart in UK.
1981 Jan *Days Are O.K.*, also from the LP, makes UK #41 (completing the band's UK singles chart career before its US equivalent has even begun).
1982 Jan After Capitol rejects third LP *All Four One*, McGovern leaves (later to join The Burning Sensations), and is replaced by ex-Elephant's Memory member Guy Perry. The LP is re-recorded with Perry and additional session musicians, produced by Val Garay, and is accepted by Capitol.
July LP *All Four One* reaches US #16, earning a gold disk for a half million sales in a 41-week chart run. Extracted *Only The Lonely* is US singles chart debut, hitting #9.
Oct *Take The L (Out Of Lover)*, also from the third LP, peaks at US #52.
Dec *Forever Mine* reaches US #60.
1983 Nov *Suddenly Last Summer* hits US #9, helping parent LP *Little Robbers*, also produced by Garay, to US #22 (and a second gold disk).

THE MOTELS *cont.*

1984 Jan *Remember The Nights*, extracted from LP *Little Robbers*, makes US #36.

1985 Sept *Shame* reaches US #21. It is taken from the band's fifth LP *Shock*, which climbs to US #36.

Nov Extracted title track from *Shock* makes US #84.

1987 Dec Having overcome cancer, which had brought about the break-up of The Motels, Davis, still signed to Capitol, returns with *Don't Tell Me The Time* which makes US #80 and is taken from LP *Policy* which reaches US #127.

MOTLEY CRUE

Nikki Sixx (bass)
Vince Neil (vocals)
Mick Mars (guitar)
Tommy Lee (drums)

1981 Jan [17] Frank Carlton Serafino Ferrano (b. Dec.11, 1958) begins calling himself Nikki Sixx.

Jan Sixx leaves US group London, to start new band Christmas and recruits Lee (b. Oct.3, 1962) from local LA band, Suite 19. They link with guitarist Bob Deal (b. Apr.4, 1955), who changes his name to Mick Mars. Firing an early vocalist, Neil (b. Vincent Wharton, Feb.8, 1961) is recruited from Cheap Trick° covers group, Rock Candy, and they form Motley Crue.

1982 They begin playing increasingly outrageous gigs in the LA area, including dates at the Starwood Club, where they chainsaw mannequins and set their trousers on fire. Signed to their own independent Leathur label, they release first LP *Too Fast For Love*, recorded for under $20,000.

1983 May Impressed by live performances, Elektra signs Motley Crue and puts them into the studio to record songs penned mainly by Sixx.

Nov Second LP *Shout At The Devil*, produced by veteran rock producer Tom Werman, is released. Accompanied by nationwide US tour supporting Kiss°, it eventually peaks at US #17.

Dec Debut LP *Too Fast For Love*, now licensed to Elektra, climbs to US #77.

1984 Jan [12] The group opens its US tour, supporting Ozzy Osbourne°, at New York's Madison Square Garden.

Feb *Looks That Kill* makes US #54.

June *Too Young To Fall* peaks at US #90.

Aug [18] The group makes its UK debut at the "Monsters of Rock" concert at Castle Donington.

Dec [8] Vocalist Neil, while driving a Pantera sports car, is involved in a serious accident in Redondo Beach, Cal., which kills Hanoi Rocks member Nick Dingley and injures two others. (Neil is charged with vehicular manslaughter and released on $2,500 bail. He will serve 20 days in jail, pay $2.6 million compensation to the injured parties, serve 200 hours of community service and begin school and college lectures on the dangers of drugs and alcohol.)

Dec *Hit Parader* magazine readers' poll votes Motley Crue #1 Rock Act of 1984.

1985 Feb LP *Shout At The Devil* is voted #1 LP by readers of *Circus* magazine.

June Third LP *Theater Of Pain*, with the group reunited, ships gold in US, eventually hits US #6 and makes UK #36 (their UK chart debut). (The LP's liner notes convey the message: "To all Crue fans – if, and or when, you drink, don't take the wheel. Live and learn so we can all rock our asses off together for a long time to come. The Crue. We love you!")

July A revival of Brownsville Station's *Smokin' In The Boys Room* is Motley Crue's biggest single to date, making US #16 and UK #71. Much of its success is due to heavy rotation of video on US MTV. Neil and Mars participate in heavy metal charity single *Stars*, to raise money for Ethiopian famine relief.

Sept Motley Crue begins world "Theater of Pain" tour, and drops *Kill 'Em Dead Kid* from its live act.

Nov Japanese dates are a sell-out, as *Home Sweet Home* peaks at US #89.

1986 Mar *Home Sweet Home* is double A-side in UK with reissued *Smokin' In The Boys Room* and makes UK #51. The band finishes its world tour with sell-out US dates.

May [10] Tommy Lee marries Heather Locklear from US TV show "Dynasty" and has "Heather" tattooed on his left forearm. (He first met her at an REO Speedwagon° concert.)

July Sixx kicks his heroin addiction after the shock of his grandmother's death.

1987 May Epitomizing the group's musical and personal attitude, LP *Girls Girls Girls* is released and will hit US #2 and UK #14. Its title track makes US #12 and UK #26.

June Embarking on a world "Girls" tour, they use their own Lear jet for US dates.

July Sixx announces plans to marry ex-Prince° girlfriend Vanity in Dec.

1988 Jan Matthew John Trippe sues the group's management, claiming he was asked to masquerade as Sixx after the latter was injured in a serious car accident in 1983. Trippe claims he wrote and performed as Sixx for 2 years before Sixx rejoined the group in summer 1985 and demands royalty payments for songs he has written under Sixx's name.

MOTORHEAD

Lemmy (bass and vocals)
Eddie Clarke (guitar)
Phil Taylor (drums)

1964/71 Lemmy (b. Ian Kilmister, Dec.24, 1945, Stoke-on-Trent, UK), having begun his musical career in Manchester as a member of soul bands The Rainmakers and The Motown Sect, moves to London playing in bands Sam Gopal's Dream and Opal Butterfly, and is a roadie for Jimi Hendrix°.

1971 Aug He joins Hawkwind° after bassist Dave Anderson leaves, initially for 6 months but stays for nearly 4 years. He does not even own a bass guitar.

1975 May Lemmy is dismissed from Hawkwind° after spending 5 days in a Canadian jail for drug possession.

June On return to UK, Lemmy announces plans for a new band. Initially the name is to be Bastard, but is changed to Motorhead (the title of the last song he wrote for Hawkwind°). The song itself becomes the group's theme tune. Other members are Larry Wallis (still with The Pink Fairies) on guitar and Lucas Fox on drums. Lemmy's description of his musical approach is: "We're the kind of band that if we moved in next to you, your lawn would die."

July Motorhead debuts at London's Roundhouse, supporting Greenslade.

Sept The band conflicts with producer Dave Edmunds° in studio sessions for debut LP on United Artists, and Fritz Fryer takes over.

Oct They support Blue Oyster Cult° at London's Hammersmith Odeon.

Dec Fox is replaced by Lemmy's friend Philthy Animal (b. Phil Taylor, Sept.21, 1954, Chesterfield, UK), who has not played professionally before.

1976 Jan United Artists rejects Motorhead's debut LP and they decide to split. (The tapes will be released in 1979 as *On Parole*.)

Feb "Fast" Eddie Clarke joins as second guitarist, and after one rehearsal as a 4-piece Wallis walks out. (The remaining trio, generally regarded as the definitive Motorhead line-up, will stay together for 6½ years.) For 7 months the group has no manager, no recording contract and no income.

Dec Two tracks, *White Line Fever* and *Leavin' Here*, are recorded for Stiff Records, but not released. (Stiff will release the tracks 2 years later in a singles box set, and on compilations *A Bunch Of Stiffs* and *Hits Greatest Stiffs*.)

1977 Apr The band records a gig at the Marquee, London. The recording goes wrong and is unusable. Chiswick Records boss Ted Carroll offers them 2 days in the studio as a consolation. They record 11 songs and Chiswick puts up money to finish an LP.

June Motorhead supports Hawkwind° on tour. Taylor breaks bones in his hand punching someone in a fight after the third gig, but carries on. Chiswick releases *Motorhead/City Kids* and then LP *Motorhead*, which makes UK #43.

Aug On a headlining UK tour, Taylor breaks bones again when he hits the tour manager's face. The tour is cancelled.

1978 Taylor and Clarke gig with Speedy Keen and Billy Rath as The Muggers.

July Motorhead signs to Bronze Records, as part of a deal which includes Hawkwind° and Girlschool.

Sept First Bronze single, a cover of *Louie Louie*, makes UK #68.

1979 Mar LP *Overkill* reaches UK #24 and the title track peaks at UK #39.

July *No Class* makes UK #61.

Oct LP *Bomber* reaches UK #12, while the title track climbs to UK #34.

Dec Liberty/UA releases the rejected 1976 LP *On Parole*. It makes UK #65.

1980 May EP *The Golden Years* hits UK #8.

Oct *Ace Of Spades* reaches UK #15 and LP of the same name hits UK #4 as the group tours constantly.

Dec Chiswick releases EP of old material, *Beer Drinkers And Hell Raisers* which makes UK #43. Taylor's broken bone for this year is in his neck.

1981 Feb Motorhead unites with its feminine counterpart Girlschool as Headgirl and cover each other's songs (*Bomber* and *Emergency*) and Johnny Kidd and The Pirates'° *Please Don't Touch* on EP *St. Valentine's Day Massacre* which hits UK #5. Lemmy collaborates with The Nolan Sisters, Cozy Powell and others on *Don't Do That*.

Apr The group begins its first US tour.

June *No Sleep Till Hammersmith*, a live LP recorded at London's Hammersmith Odeon in 1980, becomes possibly the noisiest UK #1 LP, and proves a career peak.

July Live single *Motorhead/Over The Top* hits UK #6. Motorhead has become the clear ascendant of New Wave of British Heavy Metal (NWBHM), a movement which will inspire US bands including Metallica°.

1982 Mar *Iron Fist* reaches UK #29.

Apr LP *Iron Fist* hits UK #6.

May Motorhead begins a major US tour. Lemmy's plan to record a version of Tammy Wynette's *Stand By Your Man* with The Plasmatics' Wendy O. Williams is the final straw for Clarke, who quits the tour. (He will later form Fastway.) Brian Robertson (ex-Thin Lizzy°) is brought in as replacement.

June LP *Iron Fist* makes US #174.

1983 Feb Big Beat releases LP *What's Words Worth*, recorded live at London's Roundhouse early in the band's career. It reaches UK #71.

May *I Got Mine* makes UK #46.

June LP *Another Perfect Day* peaks at UK #20.

July *Shine* makes UK #59.

Aug LP *Another Perfect Day* reaches US #153. Robertson and Taylor both leave. Lemmy auditions guitarists, and Phil Campbell and Wurzel join. Ex-Saxon drummer Pete Gill also joins the new 4-piece Motorhead.

1984 May The new Motorhead plays its first gig at London's Hammersmith Odeon.

Sept *Killed By Death* reaches UK #51 and double LP compilation of mainly old material *No Remorse* makes UK #14. The group leaves Bronze. (The label serves an injunction on them and the band will be unable to record for nearly 2 years.)

Oct The new line-up tours UK – to rave reviews. A lack of funds means the band has to stop touring. They move into a house in suburban London (next door to a clergyman).

1985 June Lemmy records a single with 19-year-old UK model Samantha Fox (her first) but an injunction means the record is never released.

1986 May Motorhead contributes to a post-Live Aid heavy metal fund-raising LP *Hear N' Aid*, which makes UK #50. Single *Stars* reaches UK #26.

June *Deaf Forever* reaches UK #67. It is the first collaboration with Bill Laswell and new label GWR re-releases the Motorhead back catalog.

July LP *Orgasmatron*, written in 2 days and recorded in 3 weeks, reaches UK #21.

Dec LP *Orgasmatron* peaks at US #157.

1987 Apr Lemmy contributes to Ferry Aid's *Let It Be*, released to benefit those bereaved by the Zeebrugge ferry disaster. The record sells over a half million copies, topping the charts for 3 weeks.

Sept Lemmy plays in comic strip movie *Eat The Rich*. His performance wins no awards but the Motorhead theme tune for the film appears on Motorhead LP *Rock'n'Roll* which makes UK #34.

1988 Lemmy and the band release another live LP, *No Sleep At All*.

MOTT THE HOOPLE

Ian Hunter (vocals and guitar)
Mick Ralphs (guitar)
Verden Allen (keyboards)
Peter "Overend" Watts (bass)
Dale "Buffin" Griffin (drums)

1968 Watts (b. May 13, 1949, Birmingham, UK), Griffin (b. Oct.24, 1948, Ross-on-Wye, Hereford, UK), Allen (b. May 26, 1944, Hereford, UK) and Ralphs (b. May 31, 1944, Hereford) come together as The Shakedown Sound after meeting as members of The Doc Thomas Group. They switch names to Silence (previously used by Watts and Griffin for a post-school band), and vocalist Sam Tippins joins.

1969 Ralphs sends a demo tape to Guy Stevens at Island Records, and he becomes their manager and producer. Tippins is sacked and Stevens places an ad in UK music paper *Melody Maker* for a new singer/keyboards player. Hunter (b. June 3, 1946, Shrewsbury, UK) replies and wins the audition. He is a veteran of Hamburg clubs, and has played on singles by the 1958 Rock 'n' Roll Show and Charlie Wolfe in 1968.

June Stevens renames the group Mott The Hoople (after a 1967 novel by Willard Manus).

Oct First single on Island is *Rock 'N' Roll Queen* which fails to chart.

Nov Debut LP *Mott The Hoople* (originally to have been titled *Talking Bear Mountain Picnic Massacre Disaster Dylan Blues* but overruled by Island) includes covers of The Kinks°, Sonny Bono and Doug Sahm (Sir Douglas Quintet°) material, and highlights Hunter's strongly Dylan°-like vocals. (In 1970, it will reach UK #66 and US #185.)

1970 Oct LP *Mad Shadows* makes UK #48. The band tours widely in UK, becoming a major live attraction to a degree not reflected by record sales. Rather more chaotic US visits help bring the name to the US market.

1971 Apr LP *Wild Life* climbs to US #44. It includes a live version of Little Richard° oldie *Keep A Knockin'*.

July [8] They play London's Royal Albert Hall and cause a minor riot, leading to a temporary ban on rock gigs at the venue.

Aug LP *Brain Capers*, the band's last for Island, fails to chart.

Oct *Midnight Lady*, produced by George "Shadow" Morton, is final Island single and again does not sell.

1972 Mar [26] After a show in Zurich, Switzerland, they decide to split. Long-time Mott fan David Bowie°, hearing of the decision, offers them one of his new songs to continue recording. After turning down *Suffragette City*, they choose *All The Young Dudes*.

July Extracting itself from the Island contract, the band signs a new deal with CBS.

Sept *All The Young Dudes*, produced by Bowie°, hits UK #3, causing a minor controversy over the line "stealing clothes from Marks and Sparks" (later changed to "unmarked cars").

Oct LP *All The Young Dudes* reaches UK #21. It includes contributions from both Bowie° and his guitarist Mick Ronson. Island issues LP *Rock 'N' Roll Queen*, a compilation of earlier tracks.

Nov As *All The Young Dudes* makes US #37 and the LP reaches US #89, the group begins its first major US tour (which Hunter chronicles in a diary).

Nov [25] The band plays the Woodstock of the West festival in LA, with Stevie Wonder°, The Eagles° and The Bee Gees° among others.

Dec On return from US, Allen quits to pursue solo projects. He is not replaced and the band continues as a quartet.

1973 Jan *One Of The Boys*, taken from the LP, reaches US #96. The band plays its first UK gigs as a four-piece.

July *Honaloochie Boogie* peaks at UK #12. It is their first release with new members Morgan Fisher (ex-Love Affair) on piano and Mick Bolton on organ.

Aug The band headlines a highly successful US tour, including a sell-out week at Broadway's Uris Theater, New York. LP *Mott* hits UK #7 and reaches US #35. Ralphs leaves to form new band Bad Company°, and is replaced by Luther Grosvenor from Spooky Tooth°, now calling himself Ariel Bender.

Sept *All The Way From Memphis* hits UK #10.

Dec *Roll Away The Stone* hits UK #8.

1974 Apr *The Golden Age Of Rock And Roll* reaches UK #16 and LP *The Hoople* UK #11.

June LP *The Hoople* reaches US #28, while *The Golden Age Of Rock And Roll* peaks at US #96 (the band's last US hit single). Hunter's book, the revealing *Diary of a Rock'n'Roll Star* (based on the band's touring exploits), is published.

July *Foxy Foxy* peaks at UK #33. Bolton leaves, apparently on religious grounds, and is replaced by ex-Amen Corner° keyboardist Blue Weaver. Meanwhile, early compilation LP *Rock And Roll Queen*, issued in US on Atlantic, makes US #112.

Sept [21] Bender quits, to be replaced on guitar by Mick Ronson.

MOTT THE HOOPLE *cont.*

Oct Hunter collapses from exhaustion in US, prior to planned UK and European dates.

Nov *Saturday Gig* reaches UK #41, while live LP *Mott The Hoople – Live*, recorded in Nov. 1973 at London's Hammersmith Odeon and in New York in May 1974, reaches UK #32 and US #23.

Dec [16] With Hunter not fully recovered, and problems looming over rescheduling of gigs, the band decides to split.

1975 Jan Hunter and Ronson put together The Hunter-Ronson Band, designed to tour to promote the solo LPs on which both are working.

Mar Ronson's solo LP *Play, Don't Worry* reaches UK #29 and US #103.

May Buffin, Watts and Fisher regroup under the truncated name Mott, adding new members Ray Major (guitar) and Nigel Benjamin (vocals), while Hunter's solo LP *Ian Hunter* reaches UK #21 and US #50. The Hunter-Ronson Band plays a sell-out UK tour, and then makes a short visit to US, before splitting.

June Hunter's solo single *Once Bitten, Twice Shy* reaches UK #14.

Oct Mott's LP *Drive On* reaches UK #54 and US #160, and will be the group's last chart success.

1976 June Hunter's LP *All American Alien Boy* makes UK #29 and US #177, while Mott's LP *Shouting And Pointing* fails to chart.

Nov Benjamin leaves Mott and the band splits.

1977 May Mott regroups again, with the addition of John Fiddler from Medicine Head, as British Lions. (This band will last some 2 years, after which Fisher will form his own Pipe label, and Buffin and Watts form their own Grimstone Productions, producing Slaughter & The Dogs and Department S, among others. Buffin will revert to his real name and occasionally produce live sessions for BBC's Radio 1. Allen and Grosvenor will release material through Jet and Spinet Records over the next 5 years.) After 2 years' living and working in US (re-publishing an updated version of his book, as *Reflections of a Rock'n'Roll Star*), Hunter returns to UK with a new four-piece backing band named Overnight Angels (after his new LP). The band plays 10 well-received dates around UK, but the LP fails to chart in UK and is not issued in US. (Hunter will follow it with 18 months' resting in New York, though will produce Generation X's LP *Valley Of The Dolls* during 1978.)

1979 May Hunter's LP *You're Never Alone With A Schizophrenic*, his first for new label Chrysalis, reaches UK #49 and US #35.

June [28] Hunter appears at the Palladium Theater, New York with Mick Ronson and Ellen Foley.

Sept Hunter's *Just Another Night* reaches US #68.

1980 Apr Hunter's double live LP *Ian Hunter Live: Welcome To The Club*, recorded during a record-breaking 7-night sell-out at LA's The Roxy, reaches UK #61 and US #69.

1981 Sept Hunter's LP *Short Back And Sides*, which includes contributions from Todd Rundgren° and two of The Clash°, reaches UK #79 and US #62.

1983 Aug Hunter switches back to CBS/Columbia for LP *All Of The Good Ones Are Taken*, which fails to chart in UK but makes US #125, his last chart entry. (Little will be heard from him over the subsequent 5 years.)

THE MOVE

Carl Wayne (vocals)
Roy Wood (vocals and guitar)
Trevor Burton (lead guitar)
Christopher "Ace" Kefford (bass)
Bev Bevan (drums)

1966 Feb The group is formed in Birmingham, UK, by members of three of the city's best existing beat groups: Wood (b. Nov.8, 1946, Birmingham) ex-Mike Sheridan and The Nightriders; Wayne (b. Aug.18, 1944, Birmingham), Chris Kefford (b. Dec.10, 1946, Birmingham) and Bevan (b. Nov.24, 1944, Birmingham) ex-Carl Wayne and The Vikings and Burton (b. Mar.9, 1944, Birmingham) ex-Danny King and The Mayfair Set. Stabilizing as a quintet after initial jams at Birmingham's Cedar Club, the group builds a big local reputation, links with manager Tony Secunda and moves to London.

Dec With a cult following gained by several Secunda-initiated PR stunts and from regular outrageous behavior during a residency at London's Marquee club (taken over from The Who°), the group signs with producer Denny Cordell, and via him to Deram Records.

1967 Jan *Night Of Fear*, a Roy Wood song with a riff based on the 1812 Overture, hits UK #2.

Apr [29] The group plays the "14-Hour Technicolour Dream" at London's Alexandra Palace, with Pink Floyd°, Tomorrow and John's Children (featuring Marc Bolan°).

May *I Can Hear The Grass Grow*, developing Wood's flirtation with psychedelia, hits UK #5. The group begins to gain a reputation for Who°-type destruction (usually smashing TV sets or obliterating effigies of people like Adolf Hitler) in its stage act and on TV appearances.

Sept [30] BBC Radio 1 is launched in UK, with The Move's *Flowers In The Rain* as the first record played.

Oct *Flowers In The Rain* hits UK #2. The group has switched, with other Cordell-produced acts, to Regal Zonophone Records (a label previously reserved for Salvation Army music).

Nov The Move is successfully sued by UK Prime Minister Harold Wilson over a nude caricature of him on promotional postcard for *Flowers In The Rain*. All the royalties earned by the record go to charity as part of the settlement. *Cherry Blossom Clinic*, scheduled as the next single, is dropped since its lyric (concerning a mental asylum) is considered likely to create more unfavorable publicity. (The track will appear on the group's first LP.)

1968 Mar *Fire Brigade* climbs to UK #3.

Apr Debut LP *Move* makes UK #15. Kefford leaves to pursue a solo career. (He will record one single as The Ace Kefford Stand for Atlantic, reviving The Yardbirds'° *For Your Love*.) Burton switches to bass and the group continues as a quartet. Richard Tandy (who will later play with Burton in Balls and with Wood and Bevan in ELO°) occasionally joins on keyboards and bass.

July *Wild Tiger Woman* fails to chart in UK.

Sept Live *Something Else* is released in UK. It is an unusual 5-track 33rpm 7" EP, later to become an expensive collector's item, but it fails to chart.

1969 Feb *Blackberry Way* tops the UK chart for a week, The Move's only #1 hit. Burton, tired of the group's commercial material, quits on the eve of a US tour, which has to be cancelled. (Burton will join The Uglys and then form Balls with ex-Moody Blues'° vocalist Denny Laine.)

Mar Jeff Lynne (b. Dec.30, 1947, Birmingham) of The Idle Race and Rick Price (b. June 10, 1944, Birmingham) of Sight and Sound are invited to join The Move. Lynne decides against it but Price comes in as bassist.

Aug *Curly* reaches UK #12.

Oct The Move's only US tour is unsuccessful and the northern UK cabaret gigs which follow cause a rift between Wayne and the others.

1970 Jan Wayne leaves for a solo cabaret and TV career which will see moderate success (but not on record) during the 70s. Lynne agrees to join in his place, admitting to being more interested in the "Electric Light Orchestra" project currently being mooted by Wood.

Feb LP *Shazam* fails to chart but Wood's track *Hello Susie* is covered by Amen Corner° and hits UK #4.

May *Brontosaurus*, an uncharacteristically heavy rocker, hits UK #6.

Oct LP *Looking On* fails to chart, as does *When Alice Comes Back To The Farm*, taken from it.

1971 July The band moves to EMI's Harvest label, with Wood and Lynne jointly producing. *Tonight* reaches UK #11 but LP *Message From The Country* fails to chart.

Oct The Move makes its final live appearances, after which Price leaves. (He will form Sheridan/Price and then Mongrel, but will later rejoin Wood in Wizzard°. The only Move performances will be on UK TV, promoting its final two singles.)

Nov *Chinatown* peaks at UK #23. Plans are made for transforming The Move into The Electric Light Orchestra° (later known as ELO), with the recruitment of five (mostly strings) players, including ex-Move part-timer Richard Tandy.

1972 Feb Wood releases solo single *When Grandma Plays The Banjo* but it does not chart. (Later sideline solo efforts in Wizzard° will net him four UK top 20 hits.)

Apr [16] First live appearance of ELO°, in Croydon, UK, signifies the end of The Move.

June Final Move single *California Man* hits UK #7.

Aug Wood leaves ELO° to form Wizzard°.

Nov *Do Ya*, by Lynne on UK B-side of *California Man*, is issued as an A-side in US and gives The Move its only US chart entry, reaching #93. (The song will later be a bigger US hit for ELO°.)

ALISON MOYET

1982 Jan Moyet (b. Genevieve Alison Moyet, June 18, 1961, Essex, UK), nicknamed "Alf" from childhood by her French father, having sung with Southend R&B groups the Vicars and the Screaming Abdabs, joins ex-Depeche Mode° keyboardist and songwriter Vince Clarke to form Yazoo°. The unlikely combination of Moyet's bluesy vocals and Clarke's synthesizers is successful and provides 18 months of UK hit singles and LPs.

1983 July Yazoo° splits after completing its second LP. Clarke remains with Yazoo's label Mute but Moyet signs as a soloist to CBS, using the name Alison Moyet rather than the "Alf" she has been throughout Yazoo's career. Recording is delayed until contractual difficulties are sorted out with US Sire, to which Moyet is still tied via Yazoo's US deal.

1984 Moyet marries long-time boyfriend Malcolm Lee and moves from Essex to Hertfordshire, UK.

Aug CBS debut *Love Resurrection*, with a lusher sound than the sparse electronics of Yazoo°, hits UK #10.

Nov Traditional soul-styled *All Cried Out* reaches UK #8. LP *Alf*, produced and written by Tony Swain and Steve Jolley, with one song, *Invisible*, by Lamont Dozier, hits UK #1 and will stay on chart for a year. Moyet begins a major UK tour to promote the LP.

Dec *Invisible* reaches UK #21.

1985 Feb [10] She heads the bill of a benefit concert at the London Palladium for National Jazz Centre, on a varied bill which includes Jools Holland from Squeeze° and The Humphrey Lyttleton Band.

Apr In a change of style to acknowledge her original musical preferences, Moyet revives Billie Holiday's jazz standard *That Ole Devil Called Love* and has her biggest UK hit at #2. She gives birth to her first child (but her marriage will fail within the year).

June She follows her Billie Holiday revival with a UK tour accompanied by a jazz band, but receives much criticism for over-reaching herself, and does not commit the stage set to record.

July [13] She appears in Live Aid at Wembley, duetting with Paul Young° on *That's The Way Love Is*.

1987 Jan After a long silence, *Is This Love* reaches UK #3.

Apr LP *Raindancing* hits UK #2 and *Weak In The Presence Of Beauty* hits UK #6.

June *Ordinary Girl* proves a disappointing UK seller, peaking at #43.

Dec A revival of the Ketty Lester oldie *Love Letters*, remaining true to Lester's hit arrangement, hits UK #4.

MUD

Les Gray (vocals)
Rob Davis (lead guitar and vocals)
Ray Stiles (bass and vocals)
Dave Mount (drums and vocals)

1966 Feb Gray (b. Apr.9, 1946, Carshalton, Surrey, UK), a veteran of skiffle and trad jazz bands, and Mount (b. Mar.3, 1947, Carshalton), both from different local groups, team to form Mud. They recruit local musicians, Davis (b. Oct.1, 1947, Carshalton) and Stiles (b. Nov.20, 1946, Carshalton), ex-Trolls and Remainder.

Apr They make their first live appearance at Streatham Ice Rink, South London, and release debut single *Flower Power*, for CBS.

Oct The band makes its radio debut on UK BBC's "Monday Monday".

1968 Apr After 2 years' gigging as a semi-professional band, Mud turns professional and releases second single for CBS, *Up The Airy Mountain*.

1969 May They make their UK TV debut on BBC's "The Basil Brush Show", as Philips Records releases the band's third single *Shangri-La*.

1970 June *Jumping Jehosaphat*, also on Philips, like the first three singles, fails to chart.

1973 Feb Mud begins a UK tour as support to US singer Jack Jones.

Apr *Crazy* reaches UK #12.

July *Hypnosis* makes UK #16.

Dec *Dyna-Mite* hits UK #4.

1974 Feb *Tiger Feet* tops the UK chart for 4 weeks, and starts a short-lived UK dance craze. (Labelmate Suzi Quatro° will knock them from the top with *Devil Gate Drive*.)

May *The Cat Crept In* hits UK #2.

Aug *Rocket* hits UK #6.

Sept LP *Mud Rock* hits UK #8. Mud signs to Private Stock Records. (The first single for the label will not be released until Oct. 1975.)

Dec *Lonely This Christmas*, on which Gray indulges his passions for Elvis Presley° vocal inflections, tops the UK chart over the Christmas period.

1975 Mar *The Secrets That You Keep* (another Presley° pastiche), released on St. Valentine's Day, hits UK #3.

May *Oh Boy*, a revival of The Crickets 1957 UK #3, tops the UK chart, deposing The Bay City Rollers'° *Bye Bye Baby*.

July *Moonshine Sally* hits UK #10 while LP *Mud Rock Vol.2* hits UK #6.

Aug *One Night* makes UK #32.

Oct *L-L-Lucy*, the group's first release on Private Stock, hits UK #10.

Nov LP *Mud's Greatest Hits* reaches UK #25.

Dec Ballad *Show Me You're A Woman* hits UK #8 and LP *Use Your Imagination* makes UK #33.

1976 June *Shake It Down* reaches UK #12.

Dec *Lean On Me*, a 1972 UK #18 for its writer Bill Withers, hits UK #7. (This will end Mud's chart-making career, but the group will subsequently record for RCA.)

1977 Mar Gray, signed to Warner Bros. as a solo artist, reaches UK #32 with a revival of The Mindbenders 1966 UK #2 *A Groovy Kind Of Love*.

1985 Dec Re-issued *Lonely This Christmas* makes UK #61, as Mud continues on the UK cabaret circuit.

1988 Sept Stiles makes his first "Top of the Pops" appearance in almost 12 years as a member of The Hollies°, performing *He Ain't Heavy, He's My Brother*.

RICKY NELSON

1957 Apr [10] Nelson (b. Eric Hilliard Nelson, May 8, 1940, Teaneck, N.J., US), second son of US showbiz couple Ozzie and Harriet Nelson (formerly a bandleader and band vocalist), has played "himself" in the family radio show "The Adventures of Ozzie and Harriet" since Mar. 1949, and since its switch to ABC TV in Oct. 1952. He sings Fats Domino's° *I'm Walking* for the first time on the show, eliciting a huge teenage response. In real life, Nelson has told a girlfriend that he intends to record a single, as a defensive reaction to her adulation of Elvis Presley°. Ozzie Nelson arranges through contacts at Verve Records to have the song recut in a studio session (arranged by guitarist Barney Kessel), along with two other tracks.

May Verve releases single *A Teenager's Romance* coupled with *I'm Walking* and, with instant TV exposure, it sells 60,000 copies in 3 days.

June *A Teenager's Romance* hits US #8 and *I'm Walking* makes US #17, with total sales topping a million.

Sept The third track from the debut session, *You're My One And Only Love*, is issued coupled with Kessel's instrumental *Honey Bop* and makes US #14. No contract has been signed with Verve and, when it becomes clear that the label is withholding royalties, Ozzie Nelson initiates legal proceedings, and agrees to Lou Chudd of Imperial Records (which had Fats Domino's° original *I'm Walking*) signing Ricky. Additionally, one of his songs is included in each subsequent episode of "The Adventures of Ozzie and Harriet" (which will guarantee maximum exposure through to 1966, when the series ends).

Oct *Be-Bop Baby*, his Imperial debut (and a self-confessed try at a Carl Perkins°-type rockabilly track), hits US #5 and is a second million-seller. B-side cover of Elvis Presley's° recent version of *Have I Told You Lately That I Love You* reaches US #29.

1958 Jan Uptempo *Stood Up* hits US #5 (earning another gold disk) and B-side *Waiting In School*, written by Johnny and Dorsey Burnette°, makes US #18. Debut LP *Ricky*, a mixture of familiar rock songs and ballads, tops the US chart for 2 weeks.

Feb Nelson forms his own full-time band for live work and for recording sessions as well as "Ozzie and Harriet" TV slots. He recruits James Burton (guitar) and James Kirkland (bass) after hearing them play in the studio with Bob Luman, plus Gene Garf (piano) and Richie Frost (drums). (Kirkland will later be replaced by Joe Osborn.) Meanwhile, *Stood Up* is his UK chart debut, at #27.

Apr *Believe What You Say*, another Johnny and Dorsey Burnette° composition, hits US #8, and is coupled with country-flavored *My Bucket's Got A Hole In It*, which makes US #18.

Aug *Poor Little Fool*, written by Sharon Sheeley, becomes Nelson's

RICKY NELSON *cont.*

first #1 single, topping the US chart for 2 weeks, and selling well over a million.

Sept Second LP *Ricky Nelson*, which includes *Poor Little Fool*, hits US #7.

Oct *Poor Little Fool* hits UK #4.

Nov Introspective ballad *Lonesome Town*, the first song submitted to Nelson by songwriter Baker Knight, hits US #7, while B-side *I Got A Feeling*, also penned by Knight, hits US #10, combining to make a further million-seller.

Dec UK follow-up to *Poor Little Fool* is familiar oldie *Someday (You'll Want Me To Want You)*, which competes with a simultaneous UK chart version by Jodi Sands. It hits UK #9, while B-side *I Got A Feeling* makes UK #27.

1959 Jan He co-stars in movie *Rio Bravo*, a western directed by Howard Hawks, with John Wayne and Dean Martin.

Mar LP *Ricky Sings Again*, another compendium of rockers and country-style ballads, reaches US #14.

Apr Two tracks taken from the LP form the next million-selling double A-side single: Knight's ballad *Never Be Anyone Else But You* hits US #6, while rocking Dorsey Burnette° composition *It's Late* hits US #9.

May *It's Late* hits UK #3.

June *Never Be Anyone Else But You* reaches UK #14.

Aug Another double A-side US top 10 has both *Sweeter Than You* (a Knight ballad) and *Just A Little Too Much* (a Burnette rocker) independently hitting US #9.

Sept *Sweeter Than You* makes UK #19 and *Just A Little Too Much* reaches UK #11.

Nov LP *Songs By Ricky*, including both sides of the last hit, reaches US #22.

Dec Offbeat and laid-back *I Wanna Be Loved* reaches US #20 and B-side *Mighty Good* makes US #38.

1960 Jan I Wanna Be Loved reaches UK #30.

May *Young Emotions* makes US #12, with B-side *Right By My Side* peaking at US #59.

July *Young Emotions* stalls at UK #48.

Sept *I'm Not Afraid* peaks at US #27 and B-side revival of *Yes Sir, That's My Baby* at US #34.

Oct LP *More Songs By Ricky* makes US #18. He appears in comedy film *The Wackiest Ship in the Army*, with Jack Lemmon.

1961 Jan *You Are The Only One* reaches US #25. Its B-side is *Milk Cow Blues* (one of the earliest songs recorded by Elvis Presley°), which peaks at US #79.

May Jerry Fuller-penned *Travelin' Man* (originally offered to Sam Cooke°, but rejected) tops the US chart for 2 weeks, giving Nelson another million-seller after a long run of smaller successes. B-side *Hello Mary Lou*, a Gene Pitney° composition, hits US #9.

May [8] On his 21st birthday, Nelson officially changes his performing name from Ricky to Rick.

July LP *Rick Is 21*, containing both sides of the recent single, hits US #8, while *Hello Mary Lou* gets A-side promotion in UK and hits #2.

Nov *A Wonder Like You* reaches US #11 and B-side *Everlovin'* makes US #16.

Dec *Everlovin'* is UK A-side and peaks at #23.

1962 Apr *Young World*, written by Fuller, hits US #5; its B-side, a revival of Gershwin's *Summertime*, reaches US #89.

May *Young World* makes UK #19.

June LP *Album Seven By Rick* reaches US #27.

Sept *Teenage Idol*, a pseudo-autobiographical lament on the isolation of fame, hits US #5 and climbs to UK #39.

1963 Feb Nelson's last new single for Imperial, *It's Up To You*, another Fuller song, hits US #6 and makes UK #22. Nelson signs a new $1 million contract with Decca Records, to last 20 years.

Mar Compilation LP *Best Sellers By Rick* makes US #112.

Apr Both sides of Decca debut single *You Don't Love Me Anymore/I Got A Woman* chart at US #47 and #49, while Imperial's *That's All/I'm In Love Again* makes US #48 and #67. Nelson has time to promote neither: he marries Kristin Harmon, daughter of American football star Tom Harmon, and she joins him (also playing his wife) in the cast of "Ozzie and Harriet".

June *String Along*, previously recorded by Fabian°, and given the same guitar riff by Burton as *Poor Little Fool*, reaches US #25.

July LP *For Your Sweet Love* makes US #20.

Oct First major Decca hit is a Latin-rhythm revival of Glenn Miller's *Fools Rush In*, which makes both US and UK #12.

1964 Jan Imperial releases an old LP track, Gene Pitney° song *Today's Teardrops*, which reaches US #54.

Feb Another revival on Decca, 1930 song *For You*, repeating the Latin arrangement, hits US #6 and UK #14. It is his last US top 10 disk, and last UK chart entry, for 8 years. LP *Rick Nelson Sings For You* makes US #14, and will be his last LP chart entry until 1970.

May Another Latin-styled revival, *The Very Thought Of You*, reaches US #26.

Sept *There's Nothing I Can Say* peaks at US #47.

Nov He features in movie *Love and Kisses* (adapted from a Broadway play), co-starring with wife Kristin, but it arouses little attention in an entertainment world where The Beatles° and the "British Invasion" have swept aside much that was previously established.

Dec *A Happy Guy* reaches US #82.

1965 Mar Billy Vera composition, *Mean Old World*, peaks at US #96, and will be his last US single chart entry for almost 5 years.

1966 May He enters the country music phase of his career with critically-acclaimed LP *Bright Lights And Country Music* but it fails to chart.

Sept [3] "The Adventures of Ozzie and Harriet" finally ends on US TV after 14 years.

1967 Apr Second country LP *Country Fever* again reaps critical plaudits but small sales.

1968 Nov LP *Another Side Of Rick*, with folkier country material, includes a trio of Tim Hardin compositions.

1969 May Nelson forms a new road and recording band, with Allen Kemp (guitar), Tom Brumley (steel guitar), ex-Poco° member Randy Meisner (bass) and Pat Shanahan (drums). (This will become The Stone Canyon Band.)

1970 Jan LP *Rick Nelson In Concert* features the still-unnamed Stone Canyon Band. It is recorded at LA's The Troubadour and features three Bob Dylan° songs, plus Nelson's own oldies *I'm Walking* and *Hello Mary Lou*. Dylan's *She Belongs To Me*, is also released as a single in a studio-recorded version, and puts Nelson back on US singles chart, reaching #33.

Apr Nelson's own composition *Easy To Be Free* makes US #48.
Nov LP *Rick Sings Nelson* peaks at US #196.
1971 June LP *Rudy The Fifth* fails to chart but is regarded as one of his best, highlighted by The Rolling Stones° song *Honky Tonk Women* (a Nelson concert favorite around this time) and *Gypsy Pilot*, which is also issued (unsuccessfully) as a single. Meisner leaves The Stone Canyon Band after the recording, to co-found The Eagles°.
Oct [15] Booed at an oldies concert at New York's Madison Square Garden when he plays new material alongside his early hits, Nelson pens *Garden Party* as a response.
1972 Oct *Garden Party* hits US #6 (in a top 10 which includes Elvis Presley° and Chuck Berry°) and is Nelson's first million-seller since 1961.
Nov *Garden Party* makes UK #41 – his first UK hit single for 8½ years, but also his last. He makes his first visit to UK, playing mainly at US bases with The Stone Canyon Band.
1973 Jan LP *Garden Party* reaches US #32.
Feb *Palace Guard*, taken from the LP, peaks at US #65. This is his first release on MCA, as US Decca Records is renamed.
1974 Mar LP *Windfall*, the last with The Stone Canyon Band, makes US #190. Following this, the MCA contract (officially with 9 years to run) is terminated.
1977 Sept Nelson signs to Epic, releasing self-produced LP *Intakes*, which does not chart. (His short period with Epic is unsuccessful but he experiments with material from a wide range of sources like John Fogerty and UK's Gallagher & Lyle°. His personal life suffers a blow when his wife Kristin divorces him.)
1981 Feb He signs a new deal with Capitol and releases LP *Playing To Win* (produced by Jack Nitszche), which is his last US chart entry, at #153. (He will continue to gig widely, both in US and overseas, during the early-to-mid 80s, mixing new material and old in audience-pleasing fashion. He also has guest acting roles on TV drama series like "McCloud" and "Petrocelli".)
1983 He features in US NBC TV movie *High School USA*, playing a school principal, with his mother Harriet portraying his secretary.
1985 Aug [22] Nelson co-stars with Fats Domino° in a live spectacular at Universal Amphitheater in LA. (The show is taped as a TV special for syndicated airing throughout US in Jan. 1986. Following his death, it will be re-edited as a tribute show. A subsequent show, also recorded, features Nelson singing John Fogerty's *Big Train (From Memphis)* with Johnny Cash°, Jerry Lee Lewis°, Roy Orbison° and Carl Perkins°.)
Nov He tours UK on a well-received nostalgia package which co-stars Bobby Vee°, Bo Diddley° and Del Shannon°.
Dec [31] Nelson dies, along with his fiancée Helen Blair, his sound engineer Clark Russell and back-up band members Bobby Neal, Patrick Woodward, Rick Intveld and Andy Chapin, when a chartered DC3 carrying them between concert dates in Guntersville, Ala., and Dallas, Tex., catches fire and crashes near De Kalb, Tex. (Rumors ensue that the fire was caused by the plane's occupants freebasing cocaine.)
1986 Jan [6] A memorial service for Nelson is held in the Church of the Hills at Forest Lawn Memorial Park, Hollywood, Cal.
Jan A posthumous LP, *All The Best*, is released, consisting of recent re-recordings of his hits.

SANDY NELSON

1958 Nelson (b. Sander Nelson, Dec.1, 1938, Santa Monica, Cal., US), inspired at age 7 to play drums after seeing Gene Krupa live, is a neighbor of Dean Torrence (later of Jan and Dean°), and in a high school-based group with both Jan and Dean and future Beach Boys° member Bruce Johnston, though he leaves before the recording of Jan & Arnie-credited hit *Jennie Lee*. With Johnston, he joins local club/dance band Kip Tyler & The Flips as their drummer, and plays on some singles recorded for Ebb and Challenge labels. He begins regular session work on small-label productions around LA (notably those involving the Kim Fowley/Bruce Johnston/Gary "Skip" Paxton "brat pack"), and makes his first major hit appearance drumming on Phil Spector's first disk, The Teddy Bears' *To Know Him Is To Love Him*.
1959 July Nelson finances the recording of his own drums-highlighting instrumental, *Teen Beat* (with Johnston playing piano), at DJ Art Laboe's Original Sound studio in Hollywood. Laboe, who has just launched Original Sound Records (and has a current US #14 hit with its fourth release, Preston Epps' *Bongo Rock*), hears commercial potential and decides to release *Teen Beat* as a one-off.
Aug [3/6] As part of a session band including Jackie Kelso (sax) and Red Callender (bass), Nelson backs Gene Vincent° on tracks for his LP *Crazy Times* in Capitol Tower studios, Hollywood.
Oct *Teen Beat* hits US #4 and is a million-seller, interesting other labels in Nelson (who has no contract with Laboe) and he signs to Imperial Records.
Nov Imperial debut *Drum Party* fails to chart (as will three singles which follow it in 1960-61).
Dec *Teen Beat* hits UK #7.
1960 Jan Gene Vincent's° *Wild Cat*, with Nelson on drums, reaches UK #21. Meanwhile, Nelson's first LP *Teen Beat* features a re-recording of the title track (Original Sound holds on to the hit version, and will continue to profit from it on reissues and compilation LPs for the next 2 decades), plus a mixture of Nelson originals and cover versions, but does not chart.
July Nelson drums and sings (screams) back-up vocals on The Hollywood Argyles' *Alley-Oop*, which tops the US chart and is a million-seller.
1961 Dec *Let There Be Drums*, featuring Richie Allen (Richard Podolor) on guitar, hits US #7 and is Nelson's second million-seller.
1962 Jan *Let There Be Drums* hits UK #2, behind Cliff Richard's° *The Young Ones*.
Mar *Drums Are My Beat* reaches US #29, while B-side *The Birth Of The Beat*, at US #75, is edited from its 10-minute version on Nelson's LP *Let There Be Drums*, which is his best-selling LP, hitting US #6 and remaining on chart for 46 weeks.
Apr *Drums Are My Beat* climbs to UK #30.
May *Drummin' Up A Storm* makes US #67 and B-side *Drum Stomp* peaks at US #86. LP *Drums Are My Beat* reaches US #29.
July *All Night Long* reaches US #75, while *Drummin' Up A Storm* makes UK #39.
Aug Both are featured on LP *Drummin' Up A Storm*, which peaks at US #55.
Oct *And Then There Were Drums* reaches US #65.
Nov LP *Compelling Percussion*, including *And Then There Were Drums* and offbeat *Drums – For Strippers Only*, climbs to US #141.
Dec LP *Golden Hits*, not a compilation of his own successes but a collection of instrumental versions of oldies like *Splish Splash*, *Kansas City* and *What'd I Say*, makes US #106.
1963 Following a motorcycle accident, Nelson has his right foot and part of his leg amputated. After recuperation, he returns to drumming despite this disability. (His 1963 LP *Beat That Drum*, released by Imperial during his absence, reissues earlier tracks under new titles to give the false impression of being new material.)
1964 Oct *Teen Beat '65*, an update of his original hit, with a dubbed-on audience to give it a live feel, makes US #44.
Dec LP *Live! In Las Vegas* (actually dubbed in LA) reaches US #122.
1965 Mar LP *Teen Beat '65* makes US #135.
July Another "live" LP, *Drum Discotheque*, including the updated *Let There Be Drums '66*, peaks at US #120.
Oct LP *Drums A-Go-Go* (the title track has hovered just below US Hot 100 with the original version by The Hollywood Persuaders) reaches US #118.
1966 Jan LP *Boss Beat*, mainly covers of recent pop hits, reaches US #126.
Apr Nelson's final US chart entry is LP *"In" Beat*, another set of pop covers, which makes #148.
1966/71 He will remain with Imperial until the early 1970s, releasing two or three LPs per year of either current cover versions, or on stylistic themes like jazz or country, or reviving the big band sound – like *Manhattan Spiritual* in 1969.
1972 June Nelson visits UK with producer Nik Venet. Some recordings are made in London, and he gives a detailed radio interview to DJ Charlie Gillett about his career, on BBC Radio London's show "Honky Tonk".
1982 After a decade of playing regularly around LA, usually with a small jazz group, in which he is able to improvise on drums more freely than within earlier rock/pop constraints, Nelson returns to recording via his own label, Veebltronics. *A Drum Is A Woman* becomes a cult favorite in rock instrumental circles (notably in UK, where it is imported), but runs foul of a feminist organization in LA. Nelson, taken aback ("I only meant a drum is sensual and sexy"), reissues it under the non-controversial title *Drum Tunnel*. (His small group work will continue through the 80s, with occasional releases for devotees on his own label.)
1988 Nov UK combo Boss Beat releases *Let There Be Drums* in a typical contemporary vein.

WILLIE NELSON

1939/42 Nelson (b. Apr.30, 1933, Abbott, Tex., US) is bought a Stella guitar by his mother and at age 6 is surrounded by music. His grandparents are learning music through mail-order courses and passing their knowledge on to Willie (they help raise him following the divorce of his parents Ira and Myrle) and his older sister Bobbie Lee. Willie begins writing songs at age 7 and spends much time listening to the radio, favoring the Grand Ole Opry concerts and Texas western swing (particularly Bob Wills) while his family's dedication to the church and gospel music also makes a profound impression.

1943 At age 10, Nelson joins John Paycheck's Bohemian Polka Band on a part-time basis.

1946 His sister Bobbie marries fiddle player Bud Fletcher, and both she and Willie play for Fletcher's friend Bud Wills.

1952 Nelson joins the airforce but has to leave the same year with a bad back.

1953 He marries Martha Matthews and they have first daughter Lana. Still writing songs, he begins playing small clubs and bars in Fort Worth, Tex.

1955 He begins broadcasting a radio show in Washington state which features a half-hour live set by his own band.

1956 Second daughter, Susie, is born. With composing skills maturing, he finances his own recording of *No Place For Me*, which he sells to his radio listeners (2,000 copies) in Vancouver, Wash., where he is currently a successful DJ.

1958 After 3 years away from Texas trying various jobs ranging from encyclopedia selling, DJ and vacuum cleaner salesman, Nelson returns to Houston where he works as a DJ and also performs at the Esquire nightclub. His songwriting has become prolific, but his dire financial position forces him to sell songs cheaply, including future country standard *Family Bible* for $50 and *Night Life* (later a hit for Ray Price) for $150. Son Billy is born.

1960 The Nelsons move to Nashville, where he meets other struggling musicians including Mel Tillis, Roger Miller° and Kris Kristofferson°, who hang out in Tootsie's Orchid Lounge.

1961 With the help of Hank Cochran, Nelson signs a publishing contract with Pamper Music. His song *Crazy* is picked up by Patsy Cline° and hits #1 on the country chart and later hits US #9, her first top 10. He also pens *Hello Walls*, a US #2 for Faron Young, the biggest hit of his career. With his songwriting a success, Nelson, again aided by Cochran, secures a recording deal with Liberty.

1962 Debut LP *. . . And Then I Wrote* is released. Nelson has success on the country chart with Shirley Collie on *Willingly* and solo *Touch Me*. As other artists including Perry Como, Eydie Gormé and Jimmy Elledge enjoy hits with Nelson material, crossover success will elude him. He replaces Danny Young in Ray Price's Cherokee Cowboys as a working musician, but the strains of touring result in divorce for Willie and Martha.

1963 Jan Second LP *Here's Willie Nelson* is released featuring Leon Russell° on piano. It achieves little in sales, and Nelson moves to Monument, while Liberty closes down its country operations.

Dec Nelson's *Pretty Paper* is a big Christmas hit for Roy Orbison°, peaking at US #15 (and UK #6 a year later).

1964 Nov [28] Nelson achieves a childhood ambition and makes his debut at Nashville's Grand Ole Opry, performing initially as an opening act for Roger Miller° and later forming a band with Wade Ray.

Dec Nelson signs to RCA Records, which insists that he conforms to its traditional country requirements. First LP *Country Willie – His Own Songs* fails to chart.

1965 Nelson marries Shirley Collie and they settle in Ridgetop, Tenn., taking up hog-farming. (Ray Price asks Nelson to raise one of his fighting roosters. Nelson shoots it when it kills two of his hens and Price refuses to record any Nelson song ever again.) RCA LP *Country Favorites Willie Nelson Style* collects few sales.

1966 A performance at Panther Hall, Fort Worth, Tex. is recorded for release as LP *Country Music Concert*.

1967 Nelson divorces Collie, who has recently become a martial arts expert.

1968 Nelson marries glass factory worker Connie Koepke, whom he has met at a concert in Cut'n'Shoot, Tex.

1969 Daughter Paula is born.

1970 Through showbusiness lawyer, Neil Rushen, Nelson signs to Atlantic Records, which allows him the creative freedom that had frustrated him at RCA. Atlantic debut is gospel-tinged LP *The Troublemaker* (later issued by CBS/Columbia in 1976).

Dec [23] The Nelsons' house in Ridgetop, on the outskirts of Nashville, Tenn., burns to the ground. (Nelson will move his family back to Texas and will live there (and in Colorado) for the next 20 years.)

1971 Atlantic LP *Shotgun Willie* becomes his best-selling vocal project to date (it includes a version of Leon Russell's° *A Song For You*) and Nelson begins his biggest tour with a major date in every state.

1972 July [4] Nelson inaugurates his annual "Fourth of July Picnic" (to be held every year until 1980 at different Texas locations) at Dripping Springs, Tex.

1973 Daughter Amy Lee is born. Still without a solo hit single or LP, Nelson is inducted into the Nashville Songwriters Hall of Fame.

1974 LP *Phases And Stages*, recorded at Muscle Shoals studio and produced by Jerry Wexler, is released but fails to sell beyond the country market.

1975 After 14 unsuccessful years, CBS/Columbia Records signs Nelson to a worldwide deal.

July First CBS/Columbia LP *Red Headed Stranger* climbs to top the country chart as *Blue Eyes Crying In The Rain* crosses over to peak at US #21. Its success will help the LP climb to US #28. As Nelson's pioneering and innovative "outlaw" country style becomes more popular, *Red Headed Stranger* begins a run of US LP success which will see at least one Nelson project chart every year for 14 years. With its simple instrumentation and sparse production, his first Columbia LP is against current Nashville style and will spend 43 weeks on the pop chart.

Nov RCA begins extensive re-releasing and repackaging of old Nelson material: LP *What Can You Do To Me Now* reaches US #196. LP *Wanted: The Outlaws*, recorded with Waylon Jennings, Tompall Glaser and Jessi Colter, is the first country LP to be a million-seller. It tops the country chart, but fails to cross over.

1976 Jan *Remember Me* makes US #67.

Mar Nelson receives a Grammy award for Best Country Vocal Performance for *Blue Eyes*, as Columbia LP *The Sound In Your Mind* is released, making US #48. Meanwhile, RCA single *Good Hearted Woman*, recorded with Waylon Jennings, climbs to US #25.

May [8] Nelson performs at Bob Dylan's° second benefit gig for convicted boxer Rubin Hurricane Carter. Following the Houston gig, Nelson is served with a subpoena for grand jury investigation into drug offences.

May RCA LP *Willie Nelson Live* (originally *Country Music Concert*) peaks at US #149.

June Atlantic reissues LP *Phases And Stages*, which reaches US #187.

Oct Fourth chart LP of the year, newly-licensed LP *The Troublemaker* climbs to US #60.

1977 May LP *Before His Time*, released by RCA, is a compilation of earlier recordings remixed by Waylon Jennings, and peaks at US #78.

July A tribute to Lefty Frizzell, who died in 1975, Columbia LP *To Lefty From Willie* peaks at US #91.

1978 Feb Nelson teams with Jennings for LP *Waylon And Willie*. Released through Jennings RCA contract (Columbia will be flexible with Nelson's contract for many years), it benefits from single *Mamas Don't Let Your Babies Grow Up To Be Cowboys* (US #42) and climbs to US #12. Nelson sets up his own short-lived label Lone Star, to record other artists.

May Columbia LP *Stardust*, featuring US #84 version of Hoagy Carmichael's *Georgia On My Mind*, is released. An album of pop standards from 1926-55 and produced by Booker T. Jones, it begins a 2-year chart stay and will peak at US #30. It also stays on the country chart for over 500 weeks.

Dec Recorded live at Harrah's, Lake Tahoe, Nev., double LP *Willie And Family Live* begins a rise to US #32 and a 1-year chart stay.

1979 Mar Nelson is awarded Grammys for *Georgia On My Mind* named Best Country Vocal Performance Male and *Mamas Don't Let Your Babies* named Best Duo or Group Vocal Performance. He also wins CMA Entertainer of the Year award. RCA LP *Sweet Memories* peaks at US #154.

June New studio LP *One For The Road* is released by Nelson and Leon Russell° and peaks at US #25.

Nov Columbia LP *Willie Nelson Sings Kristofferson* unites him with another old friend and makes US #42.

Dec Seasonal LP *Pretty Paper* hits *Billboard* top 10 Christmas chart and US #73.

1980 Jan Nelson makes his movie debut, alongside Robert Redford and Jane Fonda in *Electric Horseman*. The soundtrack LP, featuring one side of Nelson songs and another of instrumental themes by Dave Grusin, makes US #52.

Feb A single from the film, digging at his 1978 hit, *My Heroes Have Always Been Cowboys* reaches US #44.

Mar Finding ever-inventive ways of using old material, RCA invites Danny Davis to score orchestral backing for earlier Nelson recordings. Subsequent LP *Danny Davis And Willie Nelson With The Nashville Brass* peaks at US #150.

June Nelson and Ray Price finally settle their 15-year feud, recording LP *San Antonio Rose* together. It begins a 25-week run peaking at US #70.

Sept Nelson appears in a second movie, country dominated *Honeysuckle Rose*. As single *On The Road Again*, from the film, climbs to US #20, the soundtrack LP featuring a Nelson duet with Emmylou Harris will make US #11.

1981 Mar *On The Road Again* wins Nelson another Grammy for Best Country Song. Studio LP *Somewhere Over The Rainbow* is released, rising to US #31.

June Nelson is taken sick in Hawaii with a collapsed lung. He spends his hospital stay writing songs.

July [4] The "Fourth of July Picnic" is held at Caesar's Palace, Las Vegas, Nev.

Aug RCA issues LP *The Minstrel Man* which stalls at US #148.

Sept LP *Willie Nelson's Greatest Hits (And Some That Will Be)* is released by Columbia. During a 93-week chart stay, it will make US #27.

1982 Mar LP *Always On My Mind* is released. The title track, a version of Presley's° live favorite, becomes the biggest success of Nelson's career, hitting US #5, and propelling sales of parent LP to hit US #2 for 4 weeks during a 99-week chart stay.

June Nelson appears with Gary Busye in movie *Barbarosa* and also in TV movie *In The Jailhouse Now* with John Savage. Two LPs released for the country market, *Old Friend* with Roger Miller° and the TV movie soundtrack recorded with Webb Pierce, fail to chart.

July His only solo UK chart single is *Always On My Mind* which makes UK #49 during a 3-week stay. (No LP will chart in UK.)

Aug *Let It Be Me* makes US #40. Nelson is now performing as many as 250 concerts per year including dates with Frank Sinatra, Waylon Jennings, The Stray Cats°, Z.Z. Top°, Neil Young°, Dolly Parton° and Linda Ronstadt°, with live success in all territories including New Zealand, Australia, Europe, Canada and Japan.

Oct Jennings and Nelson re-appear on RCA for LP *WWII* which makes US #57 and includes *Just To Satisfy You* (US #52 in Mar.).

1983 Feb LP *Poncho And Lefty*, on Epic Records through Merle Haggard's new contract, is credited to Haggard/Nelson. It tops the country chart and makes US #37.

Mar Nelson wins a Grammy for *Always On My Mind* named Best Country Vocal Performance Male. (It will also win an award as CMA's Single of the Year.) Meanwhile, new solo studio LP *Tougher Than Leather* is released, set to make US #39.

Mar [7] Nelson receives a Lifetime Achievement award from the Songwriters' Hall of Fame.

Apr Third LP with Waylon Jennings, *Take It To The Limit*, their first for Columbia, makes US #60.

May Nelson becomes the first country artist to receive the National Academy of Popular Music's Lifetime Achievement Award.

July [4] After a 3-year gap, Nelson reinstates his annual "Fourth of July Picnic", but will extend it to a 3-day event held in different US locations, including Syracuse, N.Y. and Atlanta, Ga.

Nov LP *Without A Song* reaches US #54. It features Nelson's first duet with Julio Iglesias on their version of *As Time Goes By*.

Dec Further RCA songs reappear on LP *My Own Way* which peaks at US #182.

1984 May Another duet with Iglesias, ballad *To All The Girls I've Loved Before* hits US #5 and UK #17.

June LP *Angel Eyes*, featuring guitarist Jackie King, is released stalling at US #116.

Aug LP *City Of New Orleans* begins a 6-month US chart stay, peaking at #69.

Nov Nelson appears opposite Kristofferson° in movie *Songwriter*, while LP soundtrack, released by both artists, climbs to US #152.

1985 Jan [28] Nelson joins 44 other artists at A&M studios, Hollywood, to record *We Are The World*, to raise funds to help feed the starving in Africa and US.

Mar LP *Me And Paul*, referring to his long serving drummer Paul English, peaks at US #152. The year's collaboration LP *Funny How Time Slips Away* with Faron Young only makes the country chart.

Apr Nelson and Iglesias win CMA Vocal Duo of the Year award for *To All The Girls I've Loved Before*.

Sept Inspired by Band Aid's° idea, Nelson becomes a main organizer and president of Farm Aid, aimed to raise funds and help the plight of US farmers. Farm Aid I is held amid massive US media interest and the concerts will pool over $10 million in donations. LP *Highwayman*, a collaboration between Nelson, Johnny Cash°, Waylon Jennings and Kristofferson°, tops the country chart and climbs to US #92.

Oct LP *Half-Nelson*, comprising only duets, peaks at US #178.

Nov His *Time Of The Preacher* is used in UK BBC TV thriller "Edge of Darkness" and he writes *They're All The Same* for Johnny Cash°, having been told by Cash that he dreamt Nelson has written a song with that title.

1986 May LP *The Promiseland* fails to chart but hits C&W #1, joining five LPs already on the country chart.

June He begins sold-out UK dates, including a performance attended by Prince Charles.

July [4] His annual "Fourth of July Picnic" turns into a Farm Aid II benefit concert in Austin, Tex.

Sept Nelson receives Roy Acuff Community Service Award from the Country Music Federation.

Nov [7] Nelson appears as a corrupt lawman in US TV series "Miami Vice".

1987 Feb He appears in a film based on his early Columbia concert LP *Red Headed Stranger*.

July [4] The "Fourth of July Picnic" is held at Carl's Corner, Tex. His live band is still Bobbie Nelson (piano), Jody Payne (guitar), Grady Martin (guitar), Mickey Raphael (harmonica), Bee Spears (bass) and Paul English (drums).

July LP *Island In The Sea* only makes US C&W #14.

Sept Nashville's Country Hall of Fame opens a multi-media exhibition of the life and career of Willie Nelson.

1988 Oct LP *What A Wonderful World*, of oldie cover versions in *Stardust* mode is released. It is his 30th LP for Columbia in 13 years, of which 15 have earned gold disks and 8 have earned platinum ones.

THE NEVILLE BROTHERS

Art Neville (vocals and piano)
Aaron Neville (vocals)
Charles Neville (sax)
Cyril Neville (vocals and percussion)

1955 Eldest brother Art (b. Dec.17, 1937, New Orleans, La., US) records *Mardi Gras Mambo*, as vocalist and pianist with seven-piece New Orleans R&B band The Hawketts, which becomes a local standard, reissued annually by Chess for the Mardi Gras celebrations. Shortly afterwards, younger brother Aaron (b. 1941, New Orleans) joins vocal group The Avalons.

1957 Still performing with The Hawketts, Art signs a solo deal with Specialty Records and releases several singles (including *Zing Zing* and *Cha Dooky-Doo*) popular in the R&B market. Third brother Charles, who left home at age 14 to get married, joins the house band at New Orleans' Dew Drop Inn club and tours the South with various blues players.

1958 Art joins the US Navy and Aaron fills his place in The Hawketts.

1959 Aaron's adventures outside the band include getting married and serving six months in prison for car theft.

1960 Out of prison, Aaron records *Over You* with Allen Toussaint for Minit, beginning a long-working relationship between the duo. It reaches #21 on US R&B chart.

1962 Jan Back with The Hawketts after military service, Art has a regional hit with *All These Things*. (He will follow Aaron to Toussaint as a soloist but neither will have any major chart success with Minit.) Charles leaves New Orleans to play in New York with Joey Dee & The Starliters°, while baby brother Cyril starts showing an interest in music. (He will shortly join Art and Aaron in an eight-piece New Orleans gig circuit band named The Neville Sounds.)

1966 Aaron records blues ballad *Tell It Like It Is* for New Orleans label, Parlo. Written by Lee Diamond and ex-Hawketts member George Davis, it reputedly sells 40,000 copies in New Orleans in its first week of release. (It will later be adapted as the anthem of the US Black Power movement.)

THE NEVILLE BROTHERS *cont.*

1967 Jan *Tell It Like It Is* hits US #2 and is a million-seller. It tops the R&B chart for 4 weeks.

Feb On the strength of his hit, Aaron begins several months of live work around the US, including an appearance at the prestigious Apollo Theater in Harlem, New York. His backing band for the tour is The Neville Sounds with Art on keyboards.

Apr Aaron's follow-up *She Took You For A Ride* reaches US #92.

1968 The Neville Sounds splits, with Aaron and Cyril branching off as The Soul Machine, and Art keeping the rhythm section ("Ziggy" Modeliste on drums, George Porter on bass, Leo Nocentelli on guitar, and himself on keyboards) to form The Meters, who rapidly become New Orleans' equivalent of Memphis' Booker T. and The MG's°, playing as house band behind many Allen Toussaint and Marshall Sehorn productions.

1969 Mar Toussaint and Sehorn decide to emulate Booker T.° by recording The Meters as an R&B instrumental group in its own right and leasing it to New York's Josie Records. Debut single *Sophisticated Cissy* makes US #34.

June The Meters' *Cissy Strut* reaches US #23.

July LP *The Meters*, a wholly instrumental collection, peaks at US #108.

Aug The Meters' *Ease Back* reaches US #61.

1970 Jan The Meters' *Look-Ka Py Py* climbs to US #56 but LP of the same title makes only US #198.

May The Meters' *Chicken Strut* reaches US #50.

July The Meters' *Hand Clapping Song*, the last Sehorn and Toussaint single, reaches US #89. LP *Struttin'* makes only US #200.

1972 The group signs to Reprise, releasing LP *Cabbage Alley* which does not chart. (The Meters' own hit career will now fade, but its session work will include major acts like Dr. John° on LP *In The Right Place*, LP *Desitively Bonaroo* and 1973 US top 10 hit *Right Place, Wrong Time*, and Robert Palmer° on his first solo LP *Sneakin' Sally Through The Alley*.)

1974 LP *Rejuvenation* includes slide guitar from Lowell George of Little Feat°, whom the group met during the Robert Palmer° sessions.

1975 Sept Cyril joins The Meters as percussionist vocalist and the band tours Europe as support for The Rolling Stones°. LP *Fire On The Bayou* reaches US #179.

1976 Art brings in the two remaining brothers and the group performs and releases, on Island, an eponymous LP as The Wild Tchoupitoulas (the name is from the Mardi Gras tribe of their Indian uncle). It also records LP *Trick Bag* as The Meters.

1977 Oct Final Meters LP *New Direction* is released. It does not chart but extracted *Be My Lady* reaches US #78. The band changes its name to The Neville Brothers. Charles leaves again, but only temporarily.

1978 Mar LP *The Neville Brothers* is released by Capitol.

1981 Sept LP *Fiyo On The Bayou*, a play on an earlier Meters title, on A&M, reaches US #166.

1984 June LP *Neville-ization*, recorded live in 1982 at New Orleans' Tipitina's, is released but fails to chart.

1986 Rhino Records in US releases *Treacherous*, a 30-year retrospective double LP of the brothers, without success.

1987 LP *Uptown*, featuring a more mainstream soul music production than previous releases, fails to chart.

NEW ORDER

Barney Sumner (guitar and vocals)
Peter Hook (bass)
Stephen Morris (drums)
Gillian Gilbert (keyboards)

1980 May [18] Joy Division° comes to an end suddenly after lead singer Ian Curtis commits suicide.

May The remaining group members, Sumner (b. Bernard Dicken, Jan.4, 1956, Salford, Lancs., UK, known as Bernard Albrecht in Joy Division), Hook (b. Feb.13, 1956, Salford) and Morris (b. Oct.28, 1957, Macclesfield, Cheshire, UK) announce their intention to stay together under a new name. While previously completed and scheduled Joy Division recordings, *Love Will Tear Us Apart* and LP *Closer* are released in the months following Curtis' death, the group remains silent for some time.

July [29] Having changed name to New Order (to some controversy in UK rock press which sees Nazi connotations), the trio plays a first gig at The Beach Club in home base of Manchester, UK.

Sept [20/30] New Order fills four US East Coast dates which Joy Division° had been booked to play in May.

Oct Gilbert (b. Jan.27, 1961, Manchester), a long-time friend of Morris, ex-all-girl punk band The Inadequates, having just completed a course at Stockport technical college, agrees to join New Order on keyboards and occasional guitar.

Oct [25] The band plays its first gig as a quartet, at The Squat club, Manchester.

Dec First New Order single *Ceremony* is recorded at Strawberry Studios, Stockport.

1981 Feb [9] First London date is at the Heaven club (originally designed as a secret gig, but a very badly-kept secret which sees 1,000 tickets sell out instantly), supported by Section 25 and The Stockholm Monsters.

Feb [16] First UK radio session is broadcast on "The John Peel Show" on BBC Radio 1.

Mar *Ceremony*, released by UK independent Factory Records, for which Joy Division° had recorded, reaches UK #34.

Apr [24] The group begins 2 weeks of recording at Strawberry Studios with producer Martin Hannett, for its first LP.

May A short European tour takes in France, Belgium, West Germany, Denmark, Sweden and Norway.

June [20] The group plays Glastonbury Fayre, benefitting the Campaign for Nuclear Disarmament.

Oct Double A-side *Procession/Everything's Gone Green* peaks at UK #38.

Dec Debut LP *Movement* reaches UK #30.

1982 Jan [4] The group appears on UK TV on BBC-2's "Riverside", playing *Temptation* and *Death Rattle*.

Apr [8] An audience riot occurs at the end of a New Order gig in Rotterdam, Holland, and Hook is knocked unconscious. (Further European tour dates in Holland, Belgium and France follow.)

June *Temptation*, released as a 33rpm single, reaches UK #29.

June [1] A session by the group on UK BBC Radio 1's "The John Peel Show" includes unrecorded *Turn The Heater On*, written by reggae artist Keith Hudson.

June [16/22] The group plays a tour of Italy.

June [26] The Hacienda Club in Manchester, owned by Factory Records, and in which New Order also has a financial interest, opens with a free members' evening highlighted by a performance by the group.

Sept [11] They headline the first day of the fourth Futurama Festival in Leeds, UK.

Sept [19] The group plays in a basketball stadium in Athens, Greece, as part of the first Festival of Independent Rock'n'Roll.

Oct [22] Recordings begin for the next LP, at Britannia Row studios, London.

Nov 6-track mini-LP *New Order, 1981-1982*, compiling tracks from UK singles, is released in US.

Nov [25] The group begins a 10-date tour of Australia and New Zealand, opening at the Palais Theatre, Melbourne.

1983 Feb The group records for 2 weeks in New York with US dance producer/mixer Arthur Baker.

Apr *Blue Monday*, released only as a 12″ single, and based around a hypnotic electronic dance rhythm, climbs to UK #12.

May LP *Power, Corruption And Lies*, self-produced by the group, hits UK #4.

Sept *Confusion*, produced and co-written by Baker and released only on 12″ single, reaches UK #12. The group is now a huge success in the US rock-oriented dance field, mainly thanks to *Blue Monday*, which is released on Baker's dance-based Streetwise label in US.

Oct Having never left UK top 100 since its release, *Blue Monday* climbs the chart again (aided by having been a hit in European holiday resort clubs in the summer and purchased by UK holiday makers returning home). It hits UK #9. (By 1987, the 12″-only release will have sold over 600,000 copies in UK to become the biggest-selling 12″ single.)

1984 Apr The group makes its first visit to Japan, playing sell-out shows in Tokyo and Osaka. A brief recording session in Tokyo produces *State Of The Nation* for a future single.

May *Thieves Like Us* reaches UK #18, again produced and co-written by Baker. At the same time, *Murder* is issued as a single in Belgium – one of Factory's Benelux-only releases.

1985 June Rapid follow-up (released only 4 weeks later) *The Perfect Kiss*, disco-based in *Blue Monday* mode, makes UK #46. It is the group's first release on Quincy Jones' Qwest label in US. LP *Low Life* hits UK #7.

July The group makes its US LP chart debut with *Low Life*, reaching US #94.

Aug The group appears in UK BBC TV's marathon rock show "Rock Around The Clock", which is simultaneously broadcast in stereo on Radio 1.

Nov *Sub-Culture* peaks at UK #63.

1986 Apr *Shellshock*, featured on the soundtrack of movie *Pretty in Pink*, reaches UK #28. Factory's Ikon video label releases New Order's controversially-titled (though not controversial in itself) live long-form home video *Pumped Full Of Drugs*.

Sept The June 1982 "John Peel Show" UK BBC radio session, released on a 12" EP as part of an archive series by Strange Fruit Records, reaches UK #54. New Factory single *State Of The Nation* peaks at UK #30.

Oct LP *Brotherhood*, recorded in London, Dublin and Liverpool, hits UK #9.

Nov *Bizarre Love Triangle*, in a version remixed by Shep Pettibone from the original on LP *Brotherhood*, reaches UK #56.

1987 Aug *True Faith*, co-produced by Stephen Hague, is New Order's highest-placed UK chart single, hitting #4. Double LP *Substance*, consisting of 12-inch single mixes, hits UK #3. It is one of the first rock LPs to be also released in DAT (digital audio tape) format.

Nov The group has its first US top 40 LP chart success with *Substance*, which makes #36. Another Strange Fruit 12" EP of BBC recordings, *Peel Sessions Volume II* is released in UK. Sumner announces his intention to work as a soloist during 1988.

Dec *True Faith* is New Order's first US hit single, reaching #32, while in UK *Touched By The Hand Of God* makes #20.

1988 Feb [8] In the British Record Industry awards at London's Royal Albert Hall, the group wins the year's Best Music Video award, with *True Faith* video.

May The perennial *Blue Monday* is reissued in UK in a new version, its re-mix overseen by Quincy Jones, and re-titled *Blue Monday 1988*. It hits UK #3, its highest chart position in 5 years of consistent sales, and US #68.

Nov *Fine Time* is released as a trailer to LP *Technique*, to be released in 1989.

Dec The group plays its only gig of 1988 at the G-Mex, Manchester, UK.

RANDY NEWMAN

1961 Newman (b. Randolph Newman, Nov.28, 1943, New Orleans, La., US), nephew of Alfred and Lionel Newman (heads of music at 20th Century-Fox Pictures) and a graduate in music composition at UCLA, releases US debut single *Golden Gridiron Boy* on Dot, produced by Pat Boone°. It does not sell.

1962 He joins the staff at Metric Music, Liberty Records' music publishing division, writing songs full-time for $50 a week.

Nov The Fleetwoods record *They Tell Me It's Summer* as B-side of US #36 hit *Lovers By Night, Strangers By Day*; it is Newman's first song to be covered.

Dec Another composition, *Somebody's Waiting*, is B-side of Gene McDaniels' *Spanish Lace*, which makes US #31.

1964 July Newman's first song to reach the US chart in its own right is Jerry Butler's° version of *I Don't Want To Hear It Anymore*, which makes US #95.

1965 May His first composition to chart in UK is Cilla Black's° recording of *I've Been Wrong Before*, which reaches UK #17. (Over the next 2 years, he establishes himself as a major popular writer, with hit covers of his songs by Alan Price (*Simon Smith And His Amazing Dancing Bear*) and Gene Pitney° (*Nobody Needs Your Love* and *Just One Smile*), as well as recordings by Judy Collins°, Manfred Mann°, Frankie Laine, Jackie DeShannon, The Walker Brothers°, The Nashville Teens, Harpers Bizarre°, and many more.)

1966 He releases instrumental LP *The Randy Newman Orchestra Plays Music From The Hit Television Series "Peyton Place"*, on US Epic, with help from his uncles at 20th Century-Fox.

1967 He becomes a staff arranger-producer at Warner Bros., working with The Beau Brummels°, Van Dyke Parks and Harpers Bizarre°.

1968 June Debut vocal LP *Randy Newman* is released on Warner's Reprise label, along with single *Bee Hive State*. It includes already-covered songs like *Love Story* and *So Long Dad*, plus *Cowboy* (which Newman has submitted unsuccessfully after being invited to write a theme song for film *Midnight Cowboy*). Many copies of the LP are allegedly given away as a loss-leader publicity stunt by Warner, and the LP does not chart.

1969 Nov He arranges Peggy Lee's Leiber/Stoller-penned *Is That All There Is?*, which hits US #10.

1970 Mar Harry Nilsson° releases LP *Nilsson Sings Newman*, with covers of 10 Newman songs, including some not yet recorded by Newman but he guests on vocals on two tracks.

Apr LP *Twelve Songs* features guest musicians Ry Cooder°, Clarence White and Gene Parsons of The Byrds°, and includes *Mama Told Me (Not To Come)*, left off the previous LP because Newman has not rated it that highly.

July His first #1 song is Three Dog Night's° version of *Mama Told Me (Not To Come)*, which tops the US chart for 2 weeks. Meanwhile, Newman contributes to the music of film *Performance*, starring Mick Jagger (on the soundtrack of which he sings *Gone Dead Train*), and to the Dick Van Dyke/Bob Newhart comedy *Cold Turkey* (for which he writes the score).

1971 Oct Live LP *Randy Newman Live*, recorded at the Bitter End club, is his US chart debut, at #191.

1972 July LP *Sail Away*, with a much-covered title track, peaks at US #163, selling 100,000 copies in an 18-week chart stay.

1974 Oct [5] Newman plays the Atlanta Symphony Hall accompanied by an 87-piece orchestra conducted by another musician uncle, Emil Newman.

Dec LP *Good Old Boys*, with guest backing vocals by Glenn Frey and Don Henley of The Eagles°, reaches US #36, his biggest-selling LP to date, which stays on chart for 5 months. He promotes it with a 20-city US tour, accompanied by The Atlanta Symphony Orchestra.

1978 Jan *Short People*, his singles chart debut, hits US #2 and is a million-seller. A parody on bigotry (a familiar Newman theme), it makes him a target for hatred by short people throughout US for a while, though he (measuring 5' 11") is publicly unrepentant. The song comes from LP *Little Criminals*, his first to hit US top 10, at #9, earning a gold disk for a half million sales. The LP back-up band includes members of The Eagles°. (Neither the LP nor single charts in UK, but Newman makes a UK tour during the year, and his live set is taped for a UK TV show.)

1979 Sept LP *Born Again*, one of the first digitally-recorded LPs (and for which he has commuted to LA and written the songs in an office, 9 to 5 fashion), peaks at US #41. It has guest harmony vocals by Stephen Bishop, and includes the (non-chart) single *Story Of A Rock'n'Roll Band*, a send-up of the Electric Light Orchestra° story.

1980 July UB40° revives Newman's *I Think It's Going To Rain Today*, from his first LP. A double A-side single with the group's own *My Way Of Thinking*, it hits UK #6.

1982 Feb His soundtrack to Milos Forman movie *Ragtime*, starring James Cagney, is released on Elektra, and peaks at US #134. (*One More Hour* is nominated for an Oscar as Best Original Song.)

1983 Feb A duet with Paul Simon°, *The Blues*, is Newman's second US singles chart entry, reaching #51.

Mar LP *Trouble In Paradise* reaches US #64. As well as the duet with Simon, it also has guest appearances by Bob Seger°, Rickie Lee Jones°, Linda Ronstadt°, Jennifer Warnes°, and Lindsay Buckingham and Christine McVie from Fleetwood Mac°.

1984 Aug His song *I Love L.A.*, from LP *Trouble In Paradise*, is used for US TV ads promoting the Los Angeles Olympics.

Oct He writes and performs the soundtrack to Robert Redford movie *The Natural*, released as an LP on Warner Bros., but without charting.

1985 Sept Newman plays the Farm Aid benefit in US.

1986 Nov He writes and records the soundtrack music for Steve Martin/Chevy Chase comedy film *The Three Amigos* (which also has his first screeplay work, in collaboration with Martin).

1987 May Compilation LP *Lonely At The Top*, surveying a variety of his work, is released in Europe to promote a tour.

1988 Oct *Land Of Dreams*, Newman's first LP in 5 years, part-produced by Jeff Lynne and Mark Knopfler, is released.

OLIVIA NEWTON-JOHN

1964 Newton-John (b. Sept.26, 1948, Cambridge, UK), having moved to Melbourne, Australia, with her family at age 5, and sung in a folk vocal group in her early teens, becoming a frequent performer on local TV with singing partner Pat Carroll, wins a Johnny O'Keefe national talent contest, for which the prize is a trip to UK.

1965 Having postponed the prize trip a year to complete school, she travels to UK with Carroll, to perform as a duo in pubs and clubs.

1966 May After Carroll's visa has expired and she has returned to Australia,

OLIVIA NEWTON-JOHN *cont.*

Newton-John remains in UK performing solo, and makes an unsuccessful one-off single for Decca, recording Jackie DeShannon's *Till You Say You'll Be Mine.*

Sept Meeting Bruce Welch of The Shadows° at a concert in Bournemouth, she is offered the chance to star in the Cliff Richard° and The Shadows° London Palladium pantomime *Cinderella*, but declines to return to Australia for Christmas.

1967 Back in UK, she sets up home with Bruce Welch in West London.

1970 Newton-John is recruited by producer Don Kirshner to join the group Toomorrow, with Ben Thomas, Karl Chambers and Vic Cooper, formed to star in a movie of the same title.

Aug Two Toomorrow singles are issued simultaneously in UK, on different labels (Decca and RCA); neither sells.

Sept The movie *Toomorrow* (a science fiction musical comedy) opens in UK, and RCA releases a soundtrack LP by the group. Both fail, and after spending some time on promotional work for the film, the quartet disbands.

1971 Jan Newton-John duets with Cliff Richard° on *Don't Move Away*, B-side of his UK hit *Sunny Honey Girl*, after which she joins Richard's tour of Holland, Belgium, West Germany and Switzerland.

Apr Her belated second solo single, made for UK Pye International via a deal signed with Festival Records in Australia, covers Bob Dylan's° *If Not For You*, and hits UK #7. It is produced by John Farrar, now married to her ex-partner Pat Carroll, and also a member of Marvin, Welch & Farrar with Bruce Welch, to whom she is engaged.

June *Love Song* fails to chart.

Aug [30] She appears on UK TV guesting in Cliff Richard's° holiday special "Getaway with Cliff".

Sept *If Not For You* is her US debut at #25.

Oct [25] She begins a season at the London Palladium on a bill topped by Cliff Richard°.

Dec Her revival of folk standard *Banks Of The Ohio*, produced by Welch and Farrar, hits UK #6, and creeps to US #94. LP *If Not For You* makes US #158.

1972 Jan She begins a 13-week guest residency on Cliff Richard's° BBC TV series "It's Cliff Richard".

Apr A cover of George Harrison's° *What Is Life* reaches UK #16. Shortly after, Newton-John and Welch break up.

Aug *Just A Little Too Much* fails to chart.

1973 Feb Another cover, of John Denver's° *Take Me Home, Country Roads*, makes UK #15.

June *Let Me Be There*, written by ex-Shadows° member John Rostill, fails to chart in UK.

Aug She plays a recorder solo on Marvin, Welch & Farrar's *Music Makes My Day*.

1974 Feb *Let Me Be There* hits US #6 (after topping the country chart), her first major US success, and the first of five consecutive US million-seller singles. The LP of the same title makes US #54.

Mar Her third LP, *Music Makes My Day*, is the first to chart in UK, reaching #37.

Apr She represents UK in the Eurovision Song Contest, held in Brighton, UK, with *Long Live Love*. The song fails in the competition (won by Abba° with *Waterloo*), but reaches UK #11.

June LP *Long Live Love* marks a move to EMI Records in UK, and peaks at UK #40. *If You Love Me (Let Me Know)* fails to chart in UK, but after the US success of *Let Me Be There* it hits US #5, earning a gold disk.

Oct *I Honestly Love You* reaches UK #22, while in US it is her first chart-topper, holding #1 for 2 weeks and selling over a million. Her US LP *If You Love Me, Let Me Know* also tops the US chart for a week, earning a gold disk.

1975 Newton-John, new boyfriend Lee Kramer (who becomes her manager in US, at the suggestion of original manager Peter Gormley) and her writer/producer Farrar move from UK to US, to capitalize on her huge 1974 US success. (She will take up residence in Malibu, Cal.)

Mar *Have You Never Been Mellow*, written and produced by Farrar, tops the US chart for a week, and is another million-seller. The LP of the same title also hits US #1 for a week, and earns a further gold disk.

Mar [1] *I Honestly Love You* wins a Grammy award as Record of the Year for 1974, and Newton-John has a second award for Best Female Pop Vocal Performance. (She is also voted Female Vocalist of the Year by the Country Music Association, the first UK performer to be so honored. The choice angers many prominent CMA members, who leave to form the Association of Country Entertainers. She surmounts the criticism by heavily playing the country music circuit, and recording in Nashville.)

Apr LP *Have You Never Been Mellow* makes UK #37.

Aug *Please Mr. Please* (written by Welch and originally his only solo single in 1974) hits US #3, her fifth million-selling single in a row.

Nov LP *Clearly Love* reaches US #12 and earns another gold disk. From it, *Something Better To Do* makes US #13.

1976 Jan *Let It Shine/He Ain't Heavy . . . He's My Brother* climbs to US #30. She duets with John Denver° on *Fly Away*, which reaches US #13.

May LP *Come On Over* makes US #13 and UK #49. The title track reaches US #23. Kramer resigns as her manager, and the couple's personal relationship also breaks up.

Sept *Don't Stop Believin'* makes US #33.

Nov [17] Her first US TV special is aired on ABC-TV, with guests including Elliot Gould and Lynda Carter.

Dec LP *Don't Stop Believin'* reaches US #30. Taken from it, *Every Face Tells A Story* climbs to US #55.

1977 Apr *Sam*, taken from LP *Don't Stop Believin'*, reaches US #20.

Apr [14] Newton-John begins a US tour.

May [8] She makes her New York live debut at the Metropolitan Opera House, and is approached to play the lead role of Sandy in a movie adaptation of the Broadway hit musical of 1950s nostalgia, *Grease*.

May [28] As part of The Queen's Silver Jubilee celebrations, she stars in The Big Top Show at Windsor Castle, UK, with Elton John° and Leo Sayer°.

June *Making A Good Thing Better* stalls at US #87.
July *Sam* hits UK #6.
Aug LP *Making A Good Thing Better* peaks at US #34 and UK #60.
Oct Newton-John and Kramer are reunited both professionally and personally.
Dec A reissue of *I Honestly Love You* peaks at US #48.
1978 Jan Compilation LP *Olivia Newton-John's Greatest Hits* makes US #13 and UK #19, selling over a million in US.
May TV special *Olivia* is aired on ABC-TV in US. She sues her US label, MCA Records, for $10 million, alleging "failure to adequately promote and advertise" her records.
June *You're The One That I Want*, a duet with co-star John Travolta° from movie *Grease*, tops the US chart for a week, selling over 2 million to earn a platinum disk. It is UK #1 for 9 weeks, where it sells over 1,870,000 copies, making it the third best-selling single in UK pop history to date.
June [16] Movie *Grease* opens across the US.
July Soundtrack LP *Grease* tops the US chart for 12 weeks, and is a multi-million seller.
Sept *Summer Nights*, a second *Grease* duet with Travolta°, hits US #5, topping a million sales. It tops the UK chart for 7 weeks, selling over 1,500,000 copies in UK, and giving the duo a second entry among UK's 10 best-selling singles of all time. Her solo from *Grease*, *Hopelessly Devoted To You*, hits US #3, and is a further million-seller.
Dec *Hopelessly Devoted To You* hits UK #2.
1979 Jan *A Little More Love* hits US #3 and UK #4, while parent LP *Totally Hot* hits US #7 and is another million-seller. It also makes UK #30.
Jan [9] Newton-John appears in the UNICEF "A Gift of Song" concert at the United Nations in New York.
June *Deeper Than The Night* makes US #11 and UK #64.
Aug *Totally Hot*, the title track from the last LP, makes US #52. B-side *Dancin' Round And Round* reaches US #82.
1980 May She duets with Andy Gibb° on *I Can't Help It*, which makes US #12. (She also appears on Gibb's LP *After Dark*.)
July Newton-John stars with Gene Kelly in fantasy musical movie *Xanadu*, which is slaughtered by the critics and a box office failure, but spins off a highly successful music soundtrack. The title track *Xanadu*, with The Electric Light Orchestra°, tops the UK chart for 3 weeks, and the movie's soundtrack LP is UK #1 for 2 weeks.
Aug Her solo *Magic*, from *Xanadu*, tops the US chart for 4 weeks.
Sept Soundtrack LP *Xanadu*, shared between Newton-John and ELO, hits US #4, while *Magic* peaks at UK #32.
Nov *Suddenly*, a ballad duet with Cliff Richard° from *Xanadu*, reaches UK #15.
1981 Jan The duet with Richard° makes US #20.
Nov *Physical*, banned by some radio stations for supposed sexual innuendo, hits US #1 for 10 weeks, selling over 2 million copies. It also hits UK #7.
Dec LP *Physical*, promoted by a US TV special based around the songs on the LP, hits US #6, and is another million-seller, also making UK #11.
1982 Feb *Landslide* reaches UK #18.
Apr *Make A Move On Me* hits US #5 and peaks at UK #43.
July *Landslide* makes US #52. She makes a rare US tour, partly filmed for video release.
Nov *Heart Attack* hits US #3 and makes UK #46. TV-promoted compilation LP *20 Greatest Hits* hits UK #8. A different compilation, LP *Olivia's Greatest Hits, Vol.2* reaches US #16.
1983 Jan A re-issue of *I Honestly Love You*, from the compilation, makes UK #52.
Feb *Tied Up* peaks at US #38.
Nov *Twist Of Fate*, from film *Two of a Kind*, in which she stars again with John Travolta°, reaches UK #57.
1984 Jan Soundtrack LP *Two Of A Kind*, containing four Newton-John songs, peaks at US #26, while *Twist Of Fate* hits US #5.
Mar Also from the movie, *Livin' In Desperate Times* peaks at US #31.
Aug She hosts a reception in LA for the Australian 1984 Olympic team.
1985 Newton-John marries actor/dancer Matt Lattanzi, whom she first met while working on *Xanadu*.
Nov *Soul Kiss* makes US #20, while the LP of the same title peaks at US #29.
1986 Mar LP *Soul Kiss* reaches UK #66.
July She sings guest vocal on David Foster's *The Best Of Me*, which makes US #80.
1988 Sept LP *The Rumour* makes US #67. The title track, written by Elton John° and Bernie Taupin, reaches US #62.

NILSSON

1967 Nov Nilsson (b. Harry Nelson, June 15, 1941, Brooklyn, New York, US), having lived in California since childhood, is (as Harry Nelson) a computer specialist at the Security First National Bank in Van Nuys, and has been for many years (as Nilsson) a part-time songwriter (with some unsuccessful early 60s singles on Mercury and Capitol), when The Monkees° record his song *Cuddly Toy* on their LP *Pisces, Aquarius, Capricorn And Jones Ltd*. With interest in his material running high, RCA signs him as a singer/songwriter.
1968 Mar Debut LP *Pandemonium Shadow Show*, produced by Rick Jarrard, has six Nilsson originals (including *Cuddly Toy*), plus covers including The Beatles'° *You Can't Do That* and *She's Leaving Home*, and a carbon-copy of Phil Spector's arrangement of Ike & Tina Turner's° *River Deep, Mountain High*. The LP does not chart, but gets wide airplay: John Lennon° hears it and names Nilsson his favorite US singer. Three of the new songs are quickly covered: *1941* (Tom Northcott and Billy J. Kramer°), *Without Her* (Jack Jones) and *It's Been So Long* (Kenny Everett).
Sept LP *Aerial Ballet* contains all Nilsson originals apart from Fred Neil's *Everybody's Talkin'*, which is issued as a single without success.The LP does not chart, but the single, plus *Together* (covered by Sandie Shaw°) and *One* gain extensive radio play.
1969 Jan He writes the score for Otto Preminger's film *Skidoo*, including a vocal version of the movie's credits. He also has a small role in the movie (which stars Jackie Gleason and Carol Channing) as a security guard.
June Three Dog Night's° revival of *One*, a Nilsson composition from LP *Aerial Ballet*, hits US #5, becoming his first million-selling song.
July He writes and plays piano on The Turtles'° *The Story Of Rock And Roll*, which reaches US #48.
Sept LP *Harry* is his first to chart, reaching US #120. Mainly self-produced, it contains *The Puppy Song* (later a hit for David Cassidy°) and his first Randy Newman° cover, *Simon Smith And The Amazing Dancing Bear*. He writes *Best Friend*, the theme tune of new TV comedy series "The Courtship of Eddie's Father" and also composes incidental music for the show.
Oct Nilsson's version of Fred Neil's *Everybody's Talkin'*, from LP *Aerial Ballet*, is chosen as the theme tune to film *Midnight Cowboy*, despite prospective songs having been commissioned from several writers, including Bob Dylan's° *Lay Lady Lay* and Nilsson's own *I Guess The Lord Must Be In New York City* (included on LP *Harry*). The resulting exposure belatedly turns it into his first US chart single, hitting #6.
Nov *Everybody's Talkin'* makes UK #23. Follow-up *I Guess The Lord Must Be In New York City* peaks at US #34.
1970 Mar He releases *Nilsson Sings Newman*, a collection of 10 songs written by Randy Newman° (who also plays piano). It does not chart.
Mar [11] He wins his first Grammy award, when *Everybody's Talkin'* is named Best Male Contemporary Vocal Performance of 1969.
1971 Apr Nilsson writes, narrates and sings the songs in *The Point*, an animated children's fantasy produced by Murakami-Wolf Films for US TV. The soundtrack LP reaches US #25, his biggest-selling LP to date.
May *Me And My Arrow*, from *The Point*, reaches US #34.
July LP *Aerial Pandemonium Ballet*, a compilation of tracks from the first two LPs, makes US #149.
1972 Jan LP *The Point* makes UK #46.
Feb Recording in UK with producer Richard Perry, Nilsson hears Badfinger's° *Without You*, written by the group's Pete Ham and Tom Evans, and determines to record it. Released as a single, it tops the US chart for 4 weeks, and is his only million-seller. Its Perry-produced parent LP *Nilsson Schmilsson* hits US #3, and collects a gold disk for a half million sales.
Mar *Without You* tops the UK chart for 5 weeks, selling almost 800,000 copies in UK, while LP *Nilsson Schmilsson* hits UK #4.
Apr *Jump Into The Fire*, also from the LP, makes US #27.
June *Coconut*, a third single from LP *Nilsson Schmilsson* peaks at UK #42.
Aug LP *Son Of Schmilsson*, a second gold LP, makes US #12 and UK

#41, while *Coconut* hits US #8.

Nov Self-penned *Spaceman*, from LP *Son Of Schmilsson*, makes US #23.

1973 Jan *Remember (Christmas)*, also self-written, reaches US #53.

Mar Nilsson wins a Grammy award for *Without You*, named Best Male Pop Vocal Performance of 1972.

Aug LP *A Little Touch Of Schmilsson In The Night*, a set of standard ballad revivals with an orchestra conducted by Gordon Jenkins, reaches US #46 and UK #20 (his last UK chart LP).

Sept From the LP, a revival of *As Time Goes By* peaks at US #86.

1974 Mar [12] Nilsson and John Lennon° are thrown out of LA's Troubadour club after heckling comedian Tommy Smothers' act.

May Self-penned *Daybreak* reaches US #39, his last US hit single. It is taken from film *Son of Dracula*, a horror-spoof-musical directed by Freddie Francis in which Nilsson and Ringo Starr° appear. The soundtrack LP, containing Nilsson's songs and Paul Buckmaster's incidental music, makes US #160.

Oct LP *Pussy Cats*, produced by Nilsson's close friend and drinking partner John Lennon°, reaches US #60. It includes offbeat revivals of rock standards like *Rock Around The Clock* and Bob Dylan's° *Subterranean Homesick Blues*.

1975 Apr LP *Duit On Mon Dei* makes US #141.

1976 Adapted for the stage, *The Point* runs successfully at London's Mermaid Theatre.

Feb LP *Sandman* peaks at US #111.

Aug LP *Nilsson . . . That's The Way It Is* stalls at US #158.

Nov *Without You* is reissued in UK and climbs to #22.

1977 Aug *All I Think About Is You* makes UK #43, and is Nilsson's last UK chart entry. It is taken from LP *Knnillssonn*, which makes US #108, and is his last new LP for RCA.

1978 July Compilation LP *Greatest Hits* is his final US chart LP, reaching #140.

1980 Sept He signs a new deal with Mercury Records, releasing (for the first time credited to his full name Harry Nilsson) LP *Flash Harry*, produced by Steve Cropper. It has song collaborations with John Lennon°, Ringo Starr° and Van Dyke Parks, among others, plus two items by new Nilsson acquaintance Eric Idle. One track on the LP, *Harry*, is a tribute to Nilsson, sung by Idle and Charlie Dore. A commercial failure, the LP is not followed up.

1981 Apr [27] He attends the wedding of Ringo Starr° and Barbara Bach. (Otherwise, his activities during the 80s are low-key to the apparent point of retirement).

TED NUGENT

1966 Nugent (b. Dec.13, 1948, Detroit, Mich., US), having played guitar since age 9, and led local bands The Royal High Boys and The Lourdes in his early and mid-teens, forms heavy garage band The Amboy Dukes in Detroit, with himself and Steve Farmer on guitars, John Drake on vocals, Rick Lober on keyboards, Bill White on bass and Dave Palmer on drums (although the personnel will change frequently throughout the group's existence. Vehemently anti-drugs Nugent will summarily dismiss any group member he suspects of indulging).

1967 The Amboy Dukes sign to Mainstream Records, and find local success with their first single, a revival of Them's° *Baby Please Don't Go*.

1968 Feb The group's first LP *The Amboy Dukes* is also a US chart debut, reaching #183.

Aug *Journey To The Center Of The Mind* is the group's only US hit single, reaching #16, while LP of the same title makes US #74. (A third LP for Mainstream, *Migration*, will fail to chart.) The band tours almost continuously, with some 150 dates a year, mostly in the North-West and in the South (and a stage act which starts out as quasi-psychedelic punk rock will become ever more dominated by Nugent's flashy Jimi Hendrix°-inspired guitar fireworks).

1970 Mar The group signs to Polydor, and LP *Marriage On The Rocks/Rock Bottom* creeps to US #191.

1971 Mar Second Polydor LP, live *Survival Of The Fittest*, recorded at the Eastown Theater in Detroit, reaches US #129. On it, the name of the band changes to Ted Nugent & The Amboy Dukes.

1973 In an ongoing campaign of self-publicity while touring between record deals, Nugent stages live "guitar battles" with other heavy feedback merchants like Iron Butterfly's° Mike Pinera (currently with the New Cactus Band), The MC5's Wayne Kramere, and Frank Marino of Mahogany Rush.

1974 With another label change to Frank Zappa's° Discreet label, and credited as Ted Nugent's Amboy Dukes, two LPs *Call Of The Wild* and *Tooth, Fang And Claw* fail to chart. (Both titles are indicative of Nugent's highly-publicized passion for blood-sports and hunting. He is adept with firearms and bow and arrow, and an active supporter of the National Rifle Association. From his Michigan farm he hunts wild game which becomes food for the Nugent household of himself, wife and daughter.)

Oct Nugent wins the US National Squirrel-Shooting Archery Contest, downing a squirrel at 150 yards. Over the 3-day event, he also shoots over two dozen other live moving targets.

1975 The Amboy Dukes split, and Nugent is signed to a solo deal by Epic, teaming with producer Tom Werman, retaining bass player Rob Grange from the final Dukes line-up, and adding Derek St. Holmes from Detroit band Scott on rhythm guitar and vocals and Cliff Davies on drums, to make up his new backing band. He is also taken over by Aerosmith's° managers, Leber-Krebs, who organize his live tours into commercially successful operations.

Dec [28] He is threatened on stage in Spokane, Wash., by a member of the audience, David Gelfer, who aims a .44 Magnum at him before being taken away to be charged with "intimidating with a weapon". Nugent carries on with the show.

1976 Apr Nugent's first solo hit single is *Hey Baby*, which peaks at US #72. It is taken from his debut Epic LP *Ted Nugent*, which provides his first US top 30 LP, peaking at #28, and collecting a gold disk during its 62 weeks on chart.

Sept LP *Ted Nugent* makes UK #56, his UK chart debut.

Nov LP *Free For All*, with guest vocals by Meat Loaf°, reaches US #24 and UK #33, and becomes Nugent's first million-seller, earning a platinum disk. *Dog Eat Dog*, taken from the LP, makes US #91.

1977 July LP *Cat Scratch Fever* peaks at US #17 (his second platinum LP) and UK #28.

Sept The title track from LP *Cat Scratch Fever* is Nugent's biggest-selling solo single, reaching US #30.

1978 Jan Nugent causes controversy when he signs his autograph on a fan's arm with the tip of a Bowie knife.

Feb Instrumental single *Home Bound* reaches US #70.

Mar Double live LP *Double Live Gonzo!* makes US #13 (his third in a row to go platinum) and UK #47.

Mar [18] He plays at the California Jam II festival in Ontario, Cal., to an audience of 250,000, alongside Heart°, Santana°, Aerosmith°, Dave Mason and others.

Apr *Yank Me, Crank Me*, from the live LP, climbs to US #58.

Dec LP *Weekend Warriors* is Nugent's fourth consecutive (and last) platinum LP, reaching US #24. It fails to chart in UK, where Nugent is suddenly regarded as anachronistic in the post-punk New Wave atmosphere.

1979 Jan *Need You Bad*, taken from LP *Weekend Warriors*, peaks at US #84.

Apr [7] Nugent plays the California Music Festival, at the Memorial Coliseum, LA, to 110,000 people, sharing the bill with Van Halen°, Cheap Trick°, Aerosmith° and The Boomtown Rats°.

June LP *State Of Shock* peaks at US #18 and earns a gold disk.

July [28] He co-headlines the World Series of Rock, at Cleveland Stadium, Oh., with Journey° and Thin Lizzy°.

1980 June LP *Scream Dream* reaches US #13 (his last gold LP) and UK #37.

July [6] More than 30 people at a Nugent concert in Hollywood are arrested in the audience, for violence and drug offences.

Aug *Wango Tango*, extracted from LP *Scream Dream*, makes US #86, and is Nugent's final hit single.

1981 Apr Live LP *Intensities In 10 Cities* peaks at US #36 and UK #75.

1982 Jan Compilation LP *Great Gonzos! The Best Of Ted Nugent* makes US #140. It is Nugent's final release on Epic, as he signs a new deal with Atlantic Records. He also revamps his band, bringing in one-time Vanilla Fudge° drummer Carmine Appice and recruiting previous accompanists Derek St. Holmes (vocals) and Dave Kiswiney (bass).

Aug Debut Atlantic LP *Nugent* makes US #51.

1984 Apr LP *Penetrator*, on Atlantic, peaks at US #56.

1985 Jan [10] Nugent appears in US TV series "Miami Vice".

1986 Apr He plays on *Stars*, the single made to profit the USA For Africa Foundation by heavy metal star aggregation Hear 'N' Aid.

1988 Nugent sings *Love Is Like A Chain Saw* in horror film *State Park*.

GARY NUMAN

1977 Numan (b. Gary Webb, Mar.8, 1958, Hammersmith, London, UK), the son of a British Airways bus driver, whose former groups have included Meanstreet (who appeared on punk compilation LP *Live At The Vortex*), assumes the name Tubeway Army, calling himself "Valerium", drafting in Paul Gardiner aka "Scarlett" (bass) and Numan's uncle, Gerald Lidyard, aka "Rael" (drums) for live appearances. As he discovers synthesizers, his sound moves away from guitars towards electronic rock.

1978 Feb Numan quits his job at W.H. Smith on the day the first Tubeway Army single *That's Too Bad* (funded by his father Tony) is released on Beggars Banquet.

Aug Second single *Bombers* fails to chart. Numan sings a TV commercial for Lee Cooper jeans.

1979 Apr *Down In The Park* also flops.

May Numan makes his UK BBC TV "Top of the Pops" debut, singing *Are Friends Electric?*

June *Are Friends Electric?*, from Tubeway Army's LP *Replicas*, tops the UK chart, boosted by a first pressing of 20,000 picture disks. Numan assembles a touring band, comprising Paul Gardiner (bass), Russell Bell (guitar/synthesizer), Chris Payne (synthesizer), Cedric Sharpley (drums) and Ultravox° moonlighter Billy Currie (keyboards/synthesizer).

Sept The Tubeway Army name is dropped, and *Cars* is released credited to Gary Numan, topping the UK chart. LP *The Pleasure Principle* enters the UK chart at #1, a week after LP *Tubeway Army*, Numan's 1978 debut album, reaches UK #14. Numan begins a UK tour. After selling out London's Hammersmith Odeon he announces a second show there, with proceeds going to the Save the Whales Fund.

Oct LP *Replicas*, released on Atco Records, makes US #124.

Dec *Complex* hits UK #6.

1980 Numan's tour continues through Europe, US, Japan, Australia and New Zealand.

May *We Are Glass* hits UK #5. Video *The Touring Principle*, filmed at Numan's Hammersmith Odeon concert on Sept.28, 1979, is released. LP *The Pleasure Principle* reaches US #16.

June *Cars*, Numan's only US chart success, hits #9.

Sept *I Die: You Die*, premiered on UK BBC TV's "Kenny Everett Video Show", hits UK #6, as parent LP *Telekon* enters the UK chart at #1. Numan begins his second tour, "The Gary Numan Teletour 80".

Nov LP *Telekon* makes US #64.

1981 Jan *This Wreckage* reaches UK #20.

Apr He plays three sell-out shows at London's Wembley Arena, and on the final night announces his retirement from live work.

May Boxed LP *Living Ornaments 1979-1980* hits UK #2, while LP *1979* makes UK #47 and LP *1980* reaches UK #39.

July Numan sings vocals on Paul Gardiner's UK #49 *Stormtrooper In Drag*.

Sept *She's Got Claws* hits UK #6. LP *Dance*, written about the aftermath of his first real love, hits UK #3, with guests Mick Karn of Japan° and Roger Taylor from Queen°.

Nov LP *Dance* makes US #167.

Dec Numan sings vocals on touring backing band Dramatis' *Love Needs No Disguise*, which makes UK #33.

1982 Mar *Music For Chameleons*, with Dollar's Therese Bazar guesting, reaches UK #19.

Apr Numan begins his first tour since announcing his stage retirement.

June *We Take Mystery (To Bed)* hits UK #9.

Aug *White Boys And Heroes* makes UK #20.

Sept LP *I, Assassin* hits UK #8.

Nov While attempting to fly solo round the world, Numan is arrested on suspicion of spying and smuggling after flying his Cessna plane over a militarily sensitive area in India. The charges are subsequently dropped. This is the latest in a series of interesting events surrounding his flying career – he also crash lands his plane on at least one occasion, but is unhurt. Dramatis makes UK #57 with *I Can See Her Now*.

Dec Compilation LP *New Man Numan – The Best Of Gary Numan* peaks at UK #45.

1983 Sept *Warriors* makes UK #20 as LP of the same title, produced by Bill Nelson°, reaches UK #12.

Oct *Sister Surprise*, Numan's last release for Beggars Banquet, makes UK #32.

1984 Numan forms his own label, Numa Records, signing Hohokam, Steve Braun, John Webb (Numan's brother) and model Caroline Munro.

Oct LP *The Plan*, credited to Tubeway Army & Gary Numan, makes UK #29.

Nov First Numa release *Beserker* reaches UK #32, as LP of the same title climbs to UK #45.

Dec *My Dying Machine* peaks at UK #66.

1985 Mar Numan teams with Shakatak's Bill Sharpe for *Change Your Mind*, from Sharpe's forthcoming Polydor LP *Famous People*, which makes UK #17.

Apr LP *White Noise Live* peaks at UK #29.

May EP *The Live* reaches UK #27.

Aug *Your Fascination* makes UK #46.

Sept *Call Out The Dogs* climbs to UK #49. LP *The Fury* reaches UK #24.

Oct Sharpe and Numan's *New Thing From London Town* makes UK #52.

Nov *Miracles* makes UK #49.

1986 Apr *This Is Love* reaches UK #28.

June *I Can't Stop* makes UK #27.

Nov LP *Strange Charm* peaks at UK #59.

Dec *I Still Remember*, with all proceeds going to the Royal Society for the Prevention of Cruelty to Animals (R.S.P.C.A.), falters at UK #74.

1987 Apr Radio Heart, with Gary Numan, reach UK #35 with *Radio Heart*.

June Second Radio Heart single, *London Times*, makes UK #48.

Sept *Cars (E Reg Mix)*, a re-mix of Numan's 1979 #1 hit, reaches UK #16.

Oct Double LP *Exhibition*, a Beggars Banquet compilation of hits, makes UK #43, as early Numan LPs are released on CD.

1988 Oct With his own label defunct, Numan signs to Miles Copeland's Illegal label, and makes UK #48 with LP *Metal Rhythm*.

Nov Single *America* peaks at UK #49.

BILLY OCEAN

1959/73 Ocean (b. Leslie Sebastian Charles, Jan.21, 1950, Trinidad, West Indies), having become interested in music at age 4 when he is given a toy ukelele, moves with his family (including five brothers and sisters) to London, UK. On leaving Stepney Green school, he becomes an apprentice tailor's cutter, and his boss, Benjamin Sollinger, lends him £30 to buy a piano. Ocean sings with local London East End band Shades of Midnight at a pub in Petticoat Lane, and with groups The Go and Dry Ice.

1974 Working at a Savile Row tailors, he releases first single under pseudonym Scorched Earth. It flops. He goes to work at Ford Motors in Dagenham, Essex, where he works by night so he can write and record during the day.

1975 Dec He quits and signs to Dick Leahy's GTO label. Teaming with producer Ben Findon, his first single *Whose Little Girl Are You* fails to sell.

1976 Apr *Love Really Hurts Without You* hits UK #2 and reaches US #22.

Aug *L.O.D. (Love On Delivery)* makes UK #19.

Dec *Stop Me (If You've Heard It All Before)* peaks at UK #12.

1977 Apr He meets Laurie Jay, who becomes his manager. GTO rejects his latest song *Who's Gonna Rock You*. (It will become a 1980 UK #12 for The Nolan Sisters.) *Red Light Spells Danger*, his second UK top 10 success, hits #2.

1979 Sept *American Hearts* peaks at UK #54.

1980 Feb *Are You Ready* makes UK #42.

Oct La Toya Jackson's debut LP includes two Ocean-penned songs, *Are You Ready* and *Stay The Night*.

1981 May He self-finances GTO-rejected *Nights (Feel Like Getting Down)* which makes US R&B top 5. (It will later appear without permission on Jane Fonda's first "workout" LP, and Ocean will be awarded substantial royalties.)

July LP *Nights (I Feel Like Getting Down)* fails in UK but climbs to US #152, his previous two having failed to chart in either territory.

1982 GTO is sold to CBS/Epic as LP *Inner Feeling* fails to chart.

1984 After 2 years of inactivity, Ocean signs to Jive in UK, where he is teamed with producer, and fellow Trinidadian, Keith Diamond.

May First Ocean/Diamond collaboration, *European Queen (No More Love On The Run)*, flops.

Nov [3] *European Queen*, retitled, at his manager's suggestion, and reissued as *Caribbean Queen (No More Love On The Run)* hits US #1, US R&B #1 and #1 on the dance chart. (It will also receive a

BILLY OCEAN *cont.*

third title and version as *African Queen* in the relevant territories.) LP *Suddenly* hits US #9, earning a US platinum disk. *Caribbean Queen (No More Love On The Run)* hits UK #6 and LP *Suddenly* hits UK #9.

1985 Feb *Loverboy*, penned by Ocean with producer Robert "Mutt" Lange, hits US #2, held off #1 by Foreigner's° *I Want To Know What Love Is*. Ocean begins a 2-month US tour, playing his first live dates with a band in 10 years. *Loverboy* makes UK #13.

Mar Ocean wins a Grammy for Best R&B Vocal Performance.

May Ocean begins his first major tour, "Ocean Across America", including a performance at Live Aid, Philadelphia, Pa.

June Ballad title track from LP *Suddenly* hits #4 in both UK and US.

July *Mystery Lady* peaks at US #24.

Aug *Mystery Lady* stalls at UK #49.

Nov *When The Going Gets Tough, The Tough Get Going* hits US #2. It is featured on the soundtrack for Michael Douglas movie *The Jewel of the Nile*.

1986 Mar *When The Going Gets Tough, The Tough Get Going* gives Ocean his first UK #1, despite a UK video ban for featuring US non-Musicians Union members Douglas, Kathleen Turner and Danny De Vito.

May *There'll Be Sad Songs (To Make You Cry)* is Ocean's second US #1, and reaches UK #12. LP *Love Zone* hits UK #2.

July The title cut hits US #10.

Aug *Love Zone* peaks at UK #49 while LP *Love Zone* hits US #6.

Oct *Love Is Forever* reaches US #16 but *Bittersweet* stalls at UK #44. Ocean begins a sell-out UK tour. Having received two American Music Awards, *Sad Songs* is nominated for a Grammy.

1987 Jan *Love Is Forever* makes UK #34. He spends the year creating third Jive released LP with writers and producers Lange, Keith Diamond and Wayne Braithwaite.

1988 Mar *Get Outta My Dreams (Get Into My Car)* hits UK #3 and LP *Tear Down These Walls* also hits UK #3.

Apr [9] Ocean's third US chart-topper *Get Outta My Dreams* deposes Michael Jackson's° *Man In The Mirror*.

May LP *Tear Down These Walls* makes US #18. Ocean begins a UK tour, leading to world venues until the fall as *Calypso Crazy* climbs to UK #35.

June *The Colour Of Love* hits US #17, but stalls at UK #65, as the tour reaches US and Canada.

Oct *Stand And Deliver* fails to chart in UK.

THE OHIO PLAYERS

Leroy "Sugarfoot" Bonner (guitar and vocals)
Billy Beck (keyboards)
Clarence Satchell (saxophones and flute)
Marvin "Merv" Pierce (trumpet)
Ralph "Pee Wee" Middlebrooks (trumpet)
Marshall Jones (bass)
Jimmy "Diamond" Williams (drums and percussion)

1969 Originally formed in 1959 in Dayton, Oh., US, as an R&B instrumental unit named Greg Webster & The Ohio Untouchables, the group (with several personnel changes) has played as back-up band to The Falcons, contributing to 1962 hit *I Found A Love*, and becoming the studio house band at Compass Records in the mid-60s, before signing to Capitol Records in LA, helped by a Compass-recorded demo tape. LP *Observations In Time* fails and the Capitol contract expires without any success.

1971 The band signs to Westbound Records in Detroit, Mich.

1972 Jan Slightly funky *Pain*, which sets the tone for the band's hit style, is US chart debut at #64.

Mar LP *Pain*, recorded in Nashville and self-financed by the band (the completed recordings having gained the Westbound deal) makes US #177.

1973 May *Funky Worm*, with a novelty lyric, makes US #15 and tops the R&B chart for a week, selling over a million to earn a gold disk. Second Westbound LP *Pleasure* (with a sexist sleeve picture – to become a notable band trademark) reaches US #63.

Oct *Ecstasy* makes US #31.

Nov LP *Ecstasy* peaks at US #70. It is the band's last new recording for Westbound, prior to signing with major label Mercury Records.

1974 July *Jive Turkey* reaches US #47. It is taken from LP *Skin Tight*, the band's first for Mercury, which reaches US #11, and is the group's first gold LP, selling over a half million copies.

Oct The title track from LP *Skin Tight* reaches US #13 (and R&B #2), the group's second million-selling single. Like most Ohio Players singles, it is co-written by the entire band.

Nov LP *Climax*, a compilation of early Westbound tracks, makes US #102.

1975 Feb LP *Fire* (its sleeve showing a naked model in a fireman's helmet and entwined in a fire hose) and its extracted title song both hit US #1 for a week, and both earn gold disks. The single also hits R&B #1 for 3 weeks.

Mar Westbound compilation LP *The Ohio Players' Greatest Hits* makes US #92.

May Also from the LP, *I Want To Be Free* peaks at US #44.

Sept LP *Honey* (the sleeve this time showing a nude model getting sticky) hits US #2, the group's second gold LP.

Oct *Sweet Sticky Thing*, taken from LP *Honey*, climbs to US #33 (and tops the R&B chart for a week).

1976 Jan *Love Rollercoaster*, a second extract from LP *Honey*, is the group's second US #1, and its fourth million-selling single.

Feb LP *Rattlesnake*, a compilation of early material from Westbound, makes US #61. The instrumental title track makes US #90.

Apr *Fopp*, from the band's forthcoming LP, reaches US #30.

July LP *Contradiction* peaks at US #12, earning another gold disk. *Who'd She Coo?*, taken from the LP, is the band's first and only UK hit single, reaching #43.

Sept *Who'd She Coo?* makes US #18 (and is another R&B #1 for 1 week).

Dec LP *Ohio Players Gold*, a compilation of Mercury hit singles, reaches US #31, going gold.

1977 Feb *Feel The Beat* makes US #61.

May LP *Angel* climbs to US #41.

Aug Instrumental track *O-H-I-O*, taken from LP *Angel*, climbs to US #45, and is the band's final US single chart entry.

1978 Jan LP *Mr. Mean* reaches US #68, as the group's more traditional funk style loses popularity in the current disco music genre peak (which the band does not attempt to adopt, but new song titles will borrow from the idiom for topicality).

Oct LP *Jass-Ay-Lay-Dee* ("Jazzy Lady"), the group's last for Mercury, reaches US #69.

1979 May The Ohio Players move to Arista for LP *Everybody Up*. It reaches US #80, but is a one-off release.

1981 Apr The band signs to Neil Bogart's Boardwalk label, and records LP *Tenderness* in a mellower style than previously. It peaks at US #165.

Dec Second Boardwalk LP *Ouch* is the group's first LP not to chart in US since pre-Westbound days. (The band will have no more disk success, but it will remain together to tour and maintain a depleted though still loyal following – particularly in its home town of Dayton, where the group has helped local community needs, and where it still gives occasional concerts for free at its old high school.)

THE O'JAYS

Eddie Levert (vocals)
Walter Williams (vocals)
William Powell (vocals)

1958 The Mascots form as an R&B/doo-wop group at McKinley High School, Canton, Oh., US, with Levert, Williams and Powell, plus Bobby Massey and Bill Isles.

1961 They record for the first time, cutting *Miracles* for Wayco label, and come under the wing of Cleveland, Oh., DJ Eddie O'Jay, who hones their stage act to professionalism, and gives career guidance. As a return gesture, they rename themselves The O'Jays. Further singles follow on King, but without charting.

1963 Sept The group signs to Imperial Records, and US chart debut, at #97, is *Lonely Drifter*, produced by H.B. Barnum.

1965 June A revival of Benny Spellman's 1962 hit *Lipstick Traces (On A Cigarette)* reaches US #48.

Aug *I've Cried My Last Tear* makes US #94.

Nov Debut LP *Comin' Through*, on Imperial, fails to chart.

1966 Aug Isles leaves to work as a songwriter, but maintaining links with the group, which continues performing as a quartet and moves back to Cleveland.

Oct *Stand-In For Love* peaks at US #95. The group leaves Imperial, moving to associated Minit label.

1967 May Second LP *Soul Sounds*, released on Minit, again fails and has no spin-off hit singles.

1968 Jan Signed to New York-based Bell Records, *I'll Be Sweeter Tomorrow (Than I Was Today)* climbs to US #66.
July *Look Over Your Shoulder* makes US #89.
Sept Last success on Bell is *The Choice*, which creeps to US #94.
1969 The group plays the Apollo Theater in Harlem, New York, with The Intruders, who are working with Kenny Gamble and Leon Huff, and recommend their producers to check out The O'Jays.
Sept The group links with Gamble and Huff's independent production company, with releases appearing on Philadelphia-based Neptune label. The first of these, *One Night Affair*, reaches US #68.
1970 May *Deeper (In Love With You)* makes US #64.
Sept *Looky Looky (Look At Me Girl)* stalls at US #98, and is the last group Neptune release.
1971 Massey leaves to go into record production, and the group continues as a trio. (Massey will find success as a producer with Cleveland group The Ponderosa Twins.) A revival of Sam Cooke's° *You Send Me* makes US #78.
1972 Gamble and Huff form their own label, Philadelphia International Records, and suggest to Levert that he might like to sign to it as a soloist. Levert is only interested in working as part of the group, so The O'Jays are signed as a unit (having also been approached by Motown and Invictus Records).
Oct *Backstabbers*, a departure for the group into a hard-hitting, socially aware lyric (penned by Gamble and Huff), hits US #3, becoming the group's first million-seller, and reaches UK #14. The LP of the same title hits US #10, and is both The O'Jays' and Philadelphia International's first gold LP.
Dec Taken from the LP, *992 Arguments* makes US #57.
1973 Mar The group tops the US chart for a week with its second million-selling single, *Love Train*, again written and produced by Gamble and Huff, and also from LP *Backstabbers*.
Apr *Love Train* hits UK #9.
May LP *The O'Jays In Philadelphia*, rounding up Neptune recordings, makes US #156.
July *Time To Get Down* makes US #33.
1974 Jan LP *Ship Ahoy*, written and produced by Gamble and Huff, reaches US #11, and earns another gold disk.
Mar *Put Your Hands Together*, taken from LP *Ship Ahoy*, hits US #10.
June The group's third million-seller, also from LP *Ship Ahoy*, is *For The Love Of Money*, which hits US #9.
Aug Live LP *The O'Jays Live In London*, recorded on the first UK and European tour, reaches US #17. It becomes the group's third gold LP.
1975 Jan *Sunshine* peaks at US #48.
June *Give The People What They Want* makes US #45. It is taken from LP *Survival*, which reaches US #11 and earns another gold disk.
Aug *Let Me Make Love To You* peaks at US #75.
1976 Jan The group's fourth million-selling single, *I Love Music*, hits US #5. It is taken from LP *Family Reunion*, which hits US #7 and is a million-seller.
Feb *I Love Music* reaches UK #13. Prior to the group's biggest US tour, Powell leaves. (He has had cancer diagnosed, and his health has deteriorated so he has no strength to face the rigors of the road.) Replacement is Sammy Strain, who has previously sung for 12 years with Little Anthony & The Imperials. The group also forms its own Shaker Records in Cleveland, designed as a "community-style" label to help nurture new talent in its home region.
Apr *Livin' For The Weekend* makes US #20.
Oct *Message In Our Music* peaks at US #49, while parent LP *Message In The Music* reaches US #20.
1977 Feb *Darlin' Darlin' Baby (Sweet Tender Love)* makes US #72 and UK #24.
May Powell dies of cancer, at home in Canton.
July LP *Travelin' At The Speed Of Thought* reaches US #27.
1978 Jan Double compilation LP *The O'Jays: Collectors' Items* peaks at US #132.
Apr A remixed reissue of *I Love Music*, released to capitalize on a new lease of UK disco success by the song, makes UK #36.
June LP *So Full Of Love* hits US #6, earning another platinum disk, and marks a return from social consciousness and rock crossover fusions to the romantic R&B of The O'Jays' roots.
July *Used Ta Be My Girl*, taken from the LP, hits US #4, and is The O'Jays' fifth and last million-selling single. In UK, it reaches #12.
July [12] The group celebrates its 20th anniversary at LA's Greek Theater.
Oct Ballad *Brandy* makes US #79 and UK #21.
1979 Oct *Sing A Happy Song* peaks at UK #39, while parent LP *Identify Yourself* is another platinum disk-earner, reaching US #16.
1980 Feb *Forever Mine* makes US #28 – the group's first US top 30 entry in almost 4 years.
Oct The group switches from Philadelphia International to the associated TSOP label for *Girl, Don't Let It Get You Down*, which is its last US singles chart entry, at #55. On the same label, LP *The Year 2000* makes US #36.
1982 July LP *My Favorite Person* climbs to US #49.
1983 The group celebrates its 25th anniversary playing a 75-city US tour on a bill with Rufus and Johnny "Guitar" Watson.
Aug *Put Our Heads Together* reaches UK #45, while LP *When Will I See You Again* makes US #142.
1987 Dec The group returns to the recording scene via a new deal with EMI Manhattan Records and LP *Let Me Touch You* climbs to US #66.

MIKE OLDFIELD

1968 Nov Oldfield (b. May 15, 1953, Reading, Berks., UK) releases LP *Children Of The Sun* as Sallyangie, with his sister Sally, on UK Transatlantic label.
1969 Sept After single *Two Ships* fails, Sallyangie splits and Oldfield forms short-lived band Barefeet, which does not record.
1970 Mar Oldfield joins Kevin Ayers'° backing band, The Whole Wide World, as bass player.
Oct He plays on Ayers'° Harvest label LP *Shooting At The Moon*.
1971 Aug He goes solo when The Whole Wide World breaks up (Harvest releases another LP, *Whatevershebringswesing*, after the split.)
1972 With financial backing from Virgin record shops' owner Richard Branson, who is planning his own label, Oldfield begins work at Abbey Road studios in London on a 50-minute instrumental composition. Virgin signs him and gives studio time at the newly-opened Manor complex.
1973 May Virgin label launches with an LP of Oldfield's lengthy *Tubular Bells*, which enters the UK chart a few weeks later. Not entirely solo (it has contributions from Jon Field on flute, Steve Broughton on drums and ex-Bonzo Dog Doo-Dah Band° vocalist Viv Stanshall as occasional narrator, among others), the LP also has hundreds of studio overdubs by Oldfield playing different parts.
1974 Apr LP *Tubular Bells* hits US #3 and earns a gold disk (eventually selling 3 million copies).
May A segment from side one of *Tubular Bells* is used as the main theme to movie *The Exorcist* and, extracted as a US single, hits US #7 (Oldfield's only US single success).
July Bowing to public request, Virgin issues *Mike Oldfield's Single*, containing an edit from *Tubular Bells* similar to the US release. It reaches UK #31. Meanwhile, the LP, after a year on UK chart, much of it up and down the top 10, reaches its highest placing to date – #2 behind Paul McCartney° & Wings' LP *Band On The Run*.
Sept Oldfield's second LP, similarly-constructed *Hergest Ridge*, enters the UK LP chart at #1. After 3 weeks, it is deposed by *Tubular Bells*, finally peaking at #1 after 16 months on sale. (It will spend a total of 264 weeks on the UK chart.)
Oct LP *Hergest Ridge* reaches US #87.
Nov Oldfield guests on guitar on friend David Bedford's LP *Stars End*, played by The Royal Philharmonic Orchestra.
1975 Feb LP *The Orchestral Tubular Bells* is arranged by Bedford and played by The Royal Philharmonic Orchestra, with Oldfield on guitar. It makes UK #17. Second Oldfield single *Don Alfonso* fails to chart.
Mar [1] Oldfield wins a Grammy award for *Tubular Bells*, named Best Instrumental Composition of 1974.
Nov LP *Ommadawn*, incorporating wider influences (Celtic and African) than the two previous works, hits UK #4.
1976 Jan Seasonal double A-side, combining traditional *In Dulce Jubilo* with (vocal) *On Horseback*, hits UK #4. Meanwhile LP *Ommadawn* peaks at US #146.
Dec *Boxed*, a 4-LP box-set containing remixed versions of his first three LPs and a compilation of singles and guest appearances, reaches UK #22.
1977 Jan *Portsmouth*, a traditional tune arranged by Oldfield, hits UK #3.
Feb Oldfield's arrangement of the *William Tell Overture* fails to chart (as will its follow-up *The Cuckoo Song*).
1978 Dec Double LP *Incantations*, 3 years in the writing and making, reaches UK #14. For the first time, Oldfield is willing to give interviews and spend time promoting an LP, after receiving a

MIKE OLDFIELD *cont.*

course of Exegesis training in self-assertiveness.

1979 Jan 4-track *Take Four*, reprising *Portsmouth*, *In Dulce Jubilo* and two traditional re-arrangements, makes UK #72.

May *Guilty*, made with a New York rhythm section, surprises many with its disco leanings, but reaches UK #22. Its release is followed by Oldfield's first tour, with a 50-piece accompaniment which includes string players and a choir. The shows are audio/visual events, incorporating films by Ian Eames.

Aug Double live LP *Exposed*, recorded during the tour, reaches UK #16.

Dec LP *Platinum*, a less serious and more varied collection than its predecessors, peaks at UK #24.

1980 Jan Oldfield's version of the theme from UK BBC TV children's show "Blue Peter" makes UK #19.

July Live group Oldfield Music is formed for a UK and European tour to promote LP *Platinum*.

Sept Oldfield's version of Abba's° *Arrival*, with a parody of Abba's "helicopter" LP sleeve, fails to chart.

Nov LP *QE2* reaches UK #27, but his revival of The Shadows'° *Wonderful Land* fails.

1981 July LP *QE2*, on Epic in US, makes #174. Virgin announces that worldwide sales of LP *Tubular Bells* have passed 10 million. (Oldfield will subsequently sue Richard Branson over royalty payments throughout his time with Virgin. They settle their differences out of court.) Oldfield is entered in the UK edition of *Who's Who* – the only rock musician included apart from Paul McCartney°.

July [28] Oldfield plays a free concert in London on the eve of Prince Charles and Lady Diana Spencer's wedding, composing new music for the occasion. (This helps him gain the award of the Freedom of the City of London in 1982 in recognition both of his charity works and his export contribution from overseas sales and earnings.)

1982 Mar The Mike Oldfield Group is formed for live work, with Maggie Reilly (vocals), Tim Cross (keyboards), Maurice Pert (percussion and keyboards), Rick Fenn (bass) and Pierre Moelen (drums).

Apr LP *Five Miles Out*, partly inspired by his experiences as a private pilot, hits UK #7. The title track climbs to UK #43.

May Oldfield's last US chart entry, at #164, is LP *Five Miles Out*.

June *Family Man*, a vocal track from LP *Five Miles Out*, reaches UK #45. (The song will be revived as a US top 10 hit in 1983 by Daryl Hall and John Oates°.)

1983 June LP *Crises* hits UK #6.

July *Moonlight Shadow*, extracted from LP *Crises*, and with a vocal by Maggie Reilly, hits UK #4. (It is a thinly-disguised reference to John Lennon's° murder.)

Sept *Shadow On The Wall*, also from LP *Crises*, with a guest vocal by ex-Family° singer Roger Chapman, fails to chart.

1984 Jan *Crime Of Passion* reaches UK #61.

July LP *Discovery* makes UK #15, while *To France*, taken from it, peaks at UK #48.

Dec Oldfield's soundtrack LP of his music from movie *The Killing Fields* peaks at UK #97.

1986 Apr *Shine*, with Yes° singer Jon Anderson on guest vocals, fails to chart. (Oldfield will spend the rest of the year producing a video LP, which will eventually appear in 1988 as *Wind Chimes*.)

1987 Oct LP *Islands* reaches US #29. The title track (also issued as a UK single) features vocals by Bonnie Tyler°.

ALEXANDER O'NEAL

1972 Raised and based in Minneapolis, Minn., ex-North Natchez high school footballer and active civil rights supporter, O'Neal (b. 1954) settles on a musical direction, starting out on the local club scene.

1978 He links up with the black Minneapolis music mafia to form Flyte Time. Co-members include future production force Jimmy Jam and Terry Lewis. Prince°, head of the local music scene, invites them to become his full time backing band. Apparently due to his arrogance and unwillingness to conform, O'Neal is fired and sets up a temporary and unsuccessful rival band.

1984 Maintaining an association with Jam and Lewis, O'Neal, now solo, accepts their offer to write and produce a debut LP to be released on Jam/Lewis controlled label Tabu (licensed through CBS/Columbia). The producers invite other stable member Monte Moir to oversee three cuts. Moir, Jam and Lewis also form O'Neal's backing band, The Secret, for the LP.

1985 Apr Debut LP *Alexander O'Neal*, recorded at Creation Audio, Minneapolis, is released, peaking at US #91. It features three US Hot Black Singles hits (*Innocent*, a duet with Tabu artiste Cherrelle, *A Broken Heart Can Mend* and *If You Were Here Tonight*), but none crosses over.

June The debut LP climbs to UK #19 after strong import demand.

Dec His duet with Cherrelle on *Saturday Love* hits UK #6, but fails again to lift O'Neal out of US specialist charts.

1986 Feb *If You Were Here Tonight*, written and produced by Monte Moir, reaches UK #13.

Apr *A Broken Heart Can Mend* peaks at UK #53, while reissued *Saturday Love* makes US #26.

July Suffering from severe cocaine and alcohol addiction, O'Neal enters Minnesota's Hazelden Clinic. During his treatment, Jam and Lewis promise they will produce a follow-up LP after his rehabilitation and also contribute half the cost of O'Neal's hospital bills.

1987 Aug Having recovered and married for a second time (O'Neal already has three children), he releases second LP, *Hearsay*. All tracks bar one are written and produced by Jam and Lewis after their recent success with Janet Jackson°. It will hit UK #4 and US #29, earning a platinum in both territories. Meanwhile, first cut from the LP, *Fake* tops US R&B chart and makes US #25 and UK #33, helped by an energetic black and white video.

Sept [16] O'Neal begins a co-headlining US tour with Force MD's.

Oct Co-written by O'Neal and Jellybean Johnson, *Criticize* peaks at US #70, but hits UK #4.

Dec O'Neal performs sold out dates in London, UK.

1988 Feb From LP *Hearsay*, a duet with Cherrelle, *Never Knew Love Like This* climbs to UK #26 and US #28. *The Voice On Video* hits #3 on the UK music video chart.

May Ballad *The Lovers* reaches UK #28.

July *What Can I Say To Make You Love Me*, released to coincide with standing-room-only UK dates, makes UK #27. One of his Wembley performances is filmed for later TV showing.

Oct With parent LP *Hearsay* now on US and UK charts for over a year,

UK-only reissue (and remix) of *Fake*, titled *Fake '88*, peaks at UK #16. UK BBC-TV airs the full Wembley Arena concert recorded in July.

Nov Seasonal LP *My Gift To You*, featuring traditional Christmas songs and Jam/Lewis originals, is released. O'Neal guests on labelmate Cherrelle's new LP *Affair*, on tracks *Keep It Inside* and *Everything I Miss At Home*. UK-only LP *Hearsay All Mixed Up*, featuring remixed tracks from *Hearsay* is released, to boost Christmas sales.

ROY ORBISON

1954 Orbison (b. Apr.23, 1936, Vernon, Tex., US) brought up in Wink, Tex., where he has sung in his teens with local hillbilly group The Wink Westerners, goes to West Texas State University (where a classmate is Pat Boone°), with ambitions to be a geologist.

1955 Singing with The Teen Kings, he records at Norman Petty's studio in Clovis, N.M. *Trying To Get To You* is released on Jewel Records, but does not sell.

1956 July Having auditioned in Memphis, Tenn., for Sam Phillips at Sun Records, his first Sun single, uptempo rockabilly *Ooby Dooby*, makes US #59.

1957 Several further unsuccessful singles are released on Sun, all in rockabilly mode, which is not the best forte for Orbison's high, expressive voice. Orbison moves to Nashville to concentrate on his songwriting.

1958 May Writing songs for Acuff-Rose Music, he places *Claudette*, written for his wife (which he has recorded as a demo at Sun, but will be released 2 decades later), with The Everly Brothers°. Released as B-side of *All I Have To Do Is Dream*, it reaches US #30 and shares in worldwide sales of several million.

1959 Jan In Nashville, he signs to RCA, but *Almost 18* fails to register and, guided by manager Wesley Rose, he parts from the label to sign to newer, smaller outfit: Monument Records, owned by Fred Foster.

1960 Feb Orbison's Monument debut *Up Town* charts at US #72.

July Self-penned *Only The Lonely*, written for Elvis Presley° and also offered to The Everly Brothers°, is his breakthrough, hitting US #2 and selling over a million. Its wordless vocal accompaniment becomes a much-covered gimmick.

Oct *Only The Lonely*, his UK chart debut, tops the UK chart for 2 weeks, dethroned by the year's biggest-seller, Elvis Presley's° *It's Now Or Never*.

Nov *Blue Angel*, similarly styled to *Only The Lonely*, hits US #9.

Dec *Blue Angel* reaches UK #11.

1961 Jan *I'm Hurtin'* makes US #27.

June Starkly melodramatic *Running Scared* is another million-seller, topping the US chart for a week, and hitting UK #9.

Oct *Cryin'*, his third million-seller, hits US #2 and makes UK #25. B-side *Candy Man* makes US #25. (Both titles will be much revived by other acts.)

1962 Mar Orbison's fourth million-seller is uptempo (and also frequently revived) *Dream Baby*, which hits US #4.

Apr *Dream Baby* hits UK #2, below The Shadows'° *Wonderful Land*.

June LP *Crying* is his first LP to chart, reaching US #21.

July Less commercial *The Crowd* makes US #26 and UK #40.

Nov Double A-side ballad/beat combination *Leah/Working For The Man* reaches US #25 and #33. In UK, only *Working For The Man* is promoted and peaks at UK #50. Meanwhile, compilation LP *Roy Orbison's Greatest Hits* reaches US #14.

1963 Mar Self-penned ballad *In Dreams* (which will become one of Orbison's most enduring songs) hits US #7.

Apr *In Dreams* hits UK #6.

May Orbison, who needs always to wear glasses to see properly, leaves his only regular pair on a plane while flying to Alabama to perform and has to wear his dark-tinted sunglasses. Due to fly to UK for a tour immediately, he has to keep on wearing these and they become such a trademark during his widely-photographed and reported trek with The Beatles° that Orbison accepts them as his new image (which he will keep).

May [18] He begins a UK tour with The Beatles° and Gerry & The Pacemakers°, opening at the Granada, Slough.

June After the UK tour, LP *Lonely And Blue* reaches UK #15, while LP *Crying* makes UK #17.

July *Falling* reaches US #22 and hits UK #9, entering the top 20 while *In Dreams* is also still present. (B-side *Distant Drums* is covered by, and will be a posthumous hit for, Jim Reeves.)

Oct Another double A-side couples Elvis Presley° oldie *Mean Woman Blues*, which hits US #5, with Orbison/Joe Melson ballad *Blue Bayou*, which reaches US #29. Meanwhile, LP *In Dreams* peaks at US #35.

Nov *Blue Bayou* hits UK #5, while the rock side peaks at UK #19. LP *In Dreams* hits UK #6.

Dec Seasonal ballad *Pretty Paper* makes US #15. (It is not released in UK at this time, due to the continuing success of *Blue Bayou*.)

1964 Mar *Borne On The Wind*, issued only in UK as a single, reaches #15.

May *It's Over*, another enduring ballad, hits US #9.

June *It's Over* tops the UK chart for 2 weeks – the first time a US act has had a UK #1 since the beginning of Aug. 1963, when Elvis Presley° topped with *(You're The) Devil In Disguise*.

July LP *Exciting Sounds Of Roy Orbison*, a compilation of his early Sun tracks on Ember Records, reaches UK #17.

Sept Distinctive uptempo arrangement of *Oh, Pretty Woman*, written by Orbison and Bill Dees, tops the US chart for 3 weeks and is another million-seller.

Oct *Oh, Pretty Woman* tops the UK chart for 3 weeks.

Nov Compilation LP *More Of Roy Orbison's Greatest Hits* reaches US #19, while LP *Early Orbison*, which compiles tracks from his first two (non-charting) Monument LPs, peaks at US #101.

Dec *Pretty Paper*, released one Christmas late in UK, hits #6. LP *Oh Pretty Woman*, a compilation of singles tracks released only in UK, hits UK #4.

1965 Jan Orbison tours Australia with The Rolling Stones°.

Mar *Goodnight* reaches US #21 and UK #14.

Aug Latin-styled *(Say) You're My Girl* makes US #39 and UK #23. Meanwhile, Orbison's contract with Monument expires. He signs a new deal for US with MGM Records, which offers movie as well as recording opportunities. He is satisfied with the way London Records has marketed his Monument repertoire in UK and many other territories around the world and signs a new direct international deal with London, which automatically gives it the product recorded for MGM. *Ride Away* is the first single under the new arrangement: it peaks at US #25 and UK #34. LP *There Is Only One Roy Orbison*, also his first recorded for MGM, reaches US #55 and hits UK #10.

Nov A revival of R&B standard *Let The Good Times Roll*, released by Monument in competition with newer releases, makes US #81.

Dec Ballad *Crawling Back* reaches US #46 and UK #19. Monument compilation LP *Orbisongs* makes US #136.

ROY ORBISON *cont.*

1966 Feb Uptempo *Breakin' Up Is Breakin' My Heart* peaks at US #31 and UK #22. LP *The Orbison Way* reaches US #128 and UK #11.

Apr *Twinkle Toes*, another uptempo rocker, peaks at US #39 and UK #29.

June [6] Tragedy strikes when his wife Claudette is knocked off her motorbike while they are riding together, and dies.

July *Lana*, previously an LP track, now issued as a UK single, reaches #15.

Aug *Too Soon To Know*, a highly personalized ballad widely recognized as referring to the loss of his wife, hits UK #3 but stalls at US #68. LP *The Classic Roy Orbison* reaches UK #12.

Sept Compilation LP *The Very Best Of Roy Orbison* makes US #94, and is Orbison's final US chart LP.

Dec Orbison stars in movie *The Fastest Guitar Alive* for MGM, a musical western in which he plays an offbeat gunfighter. This will be his only major film role.

1967 Jan *There Won't Be Many Coming Home*, taken from the film, makes UK #18. Meanwhile, in US *Communication Breakdown* reaches #60.

Mar *So Good* makes UK #32.

July LP *Orbisongs* peaks at UK #40.

Aug *Cry Softly Lonely One* reaches US #52, and will be Orbison's final US solo hit single.

Sept Compilation LP *Roy Orbison's Greatest Hits* climbs to UK #40.

1968 Aug *Walk On*, a dramatic ballad, makes UK #39.

Sept While Orbison is on tour in UK, performing at Bournemouth, his home in Nashville catches fire, and the two eldest of his three sons, Roy Jr. and Tony, die in the blaze.

Oct *Heartache* peaks at UK #44.

1969 Orbison marries German-born Barbara, whom he met in a club in Leeds, UK.

May *My Friend* climbs to UK #35.

Oct Gimmicky uptempo *Penny Arcade* reaches UK #27.

1973 Jan Compilation LP *All-Time Greatest Hits* makes UK #39.

1976 Jan TV-promoted compilation LP *The Best Of Roy Orbison* tops the UK chart for a week.

1978 Jan Orbison undergoes open heart surgery in Nashville, Tenn.

1980 July He returns to the US singles chart for the first time in 13 years, duetting with Emmylou Harris on *That Lovin' You Feelin' Again*, from the soundtrack of film *Roadie*.

1981 Feb [25] *That Lovin' You Feelin' Again* wins a Grammy award as 1980's Best Country Performance by a Duo or Group with Vocal.

July [19] Odessa, Tex., announces "Roy Orbison Day". He plays there for the first time in 15 years.

July LP *Golden Days* makes UK #63.

1986 Sept Orbison's *In Dreams* features strongly in the plot and on the soundtrack of movie *Blue Velvet*.

1987 Jan [21] He is inducted into the Rock'n'Roll Hall of Fame. Orbison is joined by Bruce Springsteen° to sing *Oh, Pretty Woman*.

July Orbison signs to Virgin Records in UK, for which he records new versions of his best-known songs. The resulting LP, *In Dreams: The Greatest Hits*, makes UK #86. Virgin also releases, through its video division, *Roy Orbison: A Black And White Night*, a film of a club concert at which Orbison is backed by a cast of star admirers, including Bruce Springsteen°, Elvis Costello° and Tom Waits°. The musical content mostly features his familiar hits of the 1960s.

1988 Nov Orbison participates in George Harrison's° all-star recording ensemble The Traveling Wilburys°, which also features Bob Dylan°, Tom Petty° and Jeff Lynne of ELO°. The group's eponymous LP, with major contributions from Orbison, races up both US and UK charts, as does extracted single *Handle With Care*.

Dec [4] Orbison makes what will be his last performance in Cleveland, Oh.

Dec [7] Orbison is rushed to hospital in Hendersonville, Nashville, after suffering a heart attack while visiting his mother. He dies within minutes of admittance.

Dec Virgin Records announce that his just-completed LP *Mystery Girl* will be released on Feb.14, 1989.

ORCHESTRAL MANOEUVRES IN THE DARK (OMD)

Andy McCluskey (vocals)
Paul Humphreys (synthesizers)

1977 Sept Liverpool, UK, schoolfriends McCluskey (b. June 24, 1959, Wirral, Cheshire, UK) and Humphreys (b. Feb.27, 1960, London, UK) having played together and separately in various short-lived school bands (for one of these, Equinox, McCluskey has written *Orchestral Manoeuvres In The Dark*), jointly form The Id, with Gary Hodgson (guitar), Steve Hollis (bass) and Malcolm Holmes (drums). The group performs several songs which will later be part of the OMD repertoire and also has eight transient members during its year of existence. One Id track, *Julia's Song* (words by ex-member Julia Kneale) is recorded for inclusion on Open Eye label compilation LP *Street To Street – A Liverpool Album* (which will be released in July 1979).

1978 Aug The Id splits, and McCluskey joins local experimental band Dalek I Love You as vocalist, but will stay for only a month before becoming disillusioned by the band's chaotic approach, and leaving to work in the Customs and Excise office at Liverpool docks. Following this, he and Humphreys decide to start a new group, initially named VCL XI.

Oct First gig – regarded by the duo more as a self-indulgent experiment in non-group music – is at Liverpool club Eric's. They perform, with the help of backing tracks provided by their tape recorder "Winston", and rename themselves for the evening Orchestral Manoeuvres In The Dark (after McCluskey's old song) because it is the most self-indulgent name they can think of. To their surprise, their performance is a success with Eric's audience, and they realize that the group has a viable future.

1979 June OMD's *Electricity* is released on Manchester-based independent Factory label, in a 5,000 pressing which quickly sells out. OMD signs to DinDisc, a label set up by Richard Branson to have an all-female staff. DinDisc reissues *Electricity*, but it fails to chart.

Sept [20] The group begins a 13-date UK tour supporting Gary Numan° at Glasgow's Apollo Theatre.

Dec [7/8] OMD supports Talking Heads° at the Electric Ballroom, London.

1980 Feb OMD's second single, *Red Frame White Light* debuts at UK #67.

Feb [15] The group's first headlining tour opens at Eric's, Liverpool.

Mar Debut LP *Orchestral Manoeuvres In The Dark*, recorded in their own Liverpool studio, peaks at UK #27.

May *Messages* reaches UK #13.

Oct *Enola Gay*, titled after the plane which dropped the atomic bomb on Hiroshima, hits UK #8.

Nov Second LP *Organisation* hits UK #6. Augmented by Dave Hughes on synthesizer and Malcolm Holmes on drums, OMD tours UK, Europe and US (through early 1981, during which Hughes leaves and is replaced by Martin Cooper).

1981 Oct After almost a year's chart absence, OMD hits UK #3 with *Souvenir*.

Nov LP *Architecture And Morality* also hits UK #3, during 39 weeks on chart.

Dec *Joan Of Arc* hits UK #5.

1982 Feb *Maid Of Orleans*, a sequel to *Joan Of Arc*, hits UK #4. LP *Architecture And Morality* peaks at US #144. McCluskey and Humphreys spend most of the year in their studio, working on a fourth LP.

1983 Mar *Genetic Engineering* makes UK #20 as LP *Dazzle Ships* hits UK #5. (DinDisc is now absorbed by Virgin which releases OMD's product.)

Apr *Telegraph* makes UK #42.

May LP *Dazzle Ships* climbs to US #162.

1984 May *Locomotion* hits UK #5. LP *Junk Culture* begins a UK chart run of 27 weeks, during which it hits #9.

July *Talking Loud And Clear* reaches UK #11.

Sept *Tesla Girls* makes UK #21. (Nikolai Tesla is one of the pioneers of electrical technology.)

Nov *Never Turn Away* peaks at UK #70. LP *Junk Culture*, through A&M, makes US #182.

Dec After touring Europe, US, Japan and Australia in the past 2 years, Humphreys decides the pressure is too great and that he will quit and settle down with his American wife. A week and a half later he has changed his mind and is back in OMD.

1985 June *So In Love* reaches UK #27. LP *Crush* makes UK #13.

July [7] OMD, with Aswad° and Working Week, plays a free concert in London's Battersea Park, as part of Greater London Council's "Jobs For A Change" scheme.
Aug *Secret* makes UK #34. The group becomes more popular in US, partly as a result of support tours for acts including The Thompson Twins° and Power Station.
Oct *So In Love* is OMD's first US singles success, peaking at #26. The group begins a series of anti-racism concerts with other artists in Europe.
Dec *La Femme Accident* makes UK #42.
1986 Jan *Secrets* peaks at US #63.
May *If You Leave*, featured on the soundtrack of John Hughes' film *Pretty in Pink*, hits US #4 and makes UK #48. McCluskey says in an interview, "America is the only place where we're still hip."
Oct *(Forever) Live And Die* makes UK #11 and US #19. LP *The Pacific Age* reaches UK #15 and US #47.
Nov *We Love You* peaks at UK #54.

TONY ORLANDO & DAWN

Tony Orlando (vocals)
Joyce Vincent Wilson (vocals)
Telma Hopkins (vocals)

1957 Orlando (b. Michael Anthony Orlando Cassivitis, Apr.3, 1944, Manhattan, New York, US), of Greek/Puerto Rican heritage, has been singing with local doo-wop group The Five Gents, and is currently cutting demos for a music publisher.
1960 Having met Don Kirshner at Aldon Music, Orlando is teamed with young writer Carole King° to sing demos of her compositions. An early King song, written with Gerry Goffin, *Halfway To Paradise* is sold to Epic Records.
1961 June Epic releases Orlando's demo of *Halfway To Paradise* and it makes US #39. (In UK Billy Fury° will hit #3 with it.)
Oct Barry Mann/Cynthia Weil-penned *Bless You* reaches US #15.
Nov *Bless You* hits UK #5.
Dec *Happy Times (Are Here To Stay)*, Orlando's last for Epic, reaches only US #82.
1963 Having had little further success, Orlando goes to work at music publishers Robbins, Feist and Miller and also gets married.
1968 Completing 5 years in music publishing, Orlando is working for Clive Davis at April-Blackwood publishers involved with writers James Taylor° and Laura Nyro.
1970 Bell Records is interested in releasing *Candida*, produced by Hank Medress and Dave Appell with unknown trio Dawn, but is unhappy with the lead singer. They keep the backing vocal track by Hopkins (b. Oct.28, 1948, Louisville, Ky., US) and Wilson (b. Dec.14, 1946, Detroit, Mich., US). Medress and Appell ask Orlando to record the lead vocal. He hears the results 2 months later on New York radio as the disk is taking off.
Oct *Candida* hits US #3.
Dec LP *Candida* reaches US #35.
1971 Jan Follow-up *Knock Three Times* hits US #1. It features Orlando on lead vocals and is released under the group name Dawn, but Orlando has still not met Hopkins and Wilson, who recorded the backing vocals in Cal. Orlando finally meets the girls and insists on forming a full-time unit to promote and tour.
Feb *Candida* hits UK #9.
Apr *I Play And Sing* makes US #25.
May *Knock Three Times* tops the UK chart.
July *Summer Sand* reaches US #33.
Aug *What Are You Doing Sunday* hits UK #3.
Nov *What Are You Doing Sunday* peaks at US #39.
Dec LP *Dawn Featuring Tony Orlando* stalls at US #178.
1972 Feb *Runaway/Happy Together* reaches US #79.
July *Vaya Con Dios* makes only US #95.
1973 Jan *You're A Lady* peaks at US #70, beaten by Peter Skellern's original version at US #50.
Mar LP *Tuneweaving* reaches US #30 and is the group's first gold LP.
Apr Dawn records *Tie A Yellow Ribbon Round The Old Oak Tree*, based on a true tale of a convict returning home to White Oak, Ga., hoping to see a sign that his wife still loves him. The song begins a 4-week stay on top of the US chart. (It is the year's best-selling single, sells over six million internationally and will have over 1,000 cover versions.)
Sept *Say, Has Anybody Seen My Sweet Gypsy Rose* hits US #3 and makes UK #12.
Oct LP *Dawn's New Ragtime Follies* is released, making US #43.
1974 Feb Head of programming for CBS TV, Fred Silverman, sees Dawn perform *Tie A Yellow Ribbon* at the sixteenth annual Grammy Awards and gives the trio a 4-week summer tryout variety series. ("Tony Orlando and Dawn" will air for 2 seasons.)
Mar Now credited as Tony Orlando & Dawn, *Who's In The Strawberry Patch With Sally* makes UK #37.
Apr *It Only Hurts When I Try To Smile* reaches US #81.
May LP *Golden Ribbons* makes UK #46.
Oct *Steppin' Out (Gonna Boogie Tonight)* hits US #7.
Dec *Who's In The Strawberry Patch With Sally* reaches US #27 and LP *Prime Time* makes US #16, bringing the group's worldwide sales to over 25 million.
1975 Jan The trio's first and second LPs are reissued, *Candida & Knock Three Times*, making US #170, and *Tony Orlando & Dawn II* US #165.
Feb *Look In My Eyes Pretty Woman* reaches US #11.
May Dawn moves with Bell promotion man and friend Steve Wax from Bell to Elektra. The group's cover of Jerry Butler's° 1960 US top 10 smash *He Don't Love You (Like I Love You)* tops the US chart for 3 weeks. LP *He Don't Love You (Like I Love You)* is released, reaching US #20.
June LP *Tony Orlando and Dawn's Greatest Hits* reaches US #16 on its way to gold status.
Aug *Mornin' Beautiful* reaches US #14.
Sept *You're All I Need To Get By*, a 1968 US #7 for Marvin Gaye° and Tammi Terrell, makes US #34.
Nov LP *Skybird* makes US #93. The title track makes US #49.
1976 Mar A cover of Sam Cooke's° 1961 US #7, *Cupid*, reaches US #22.
Apr LP *To Be With You* makes US #94.
1977 Apr *Sing* peaks at US #58.
July [22] During a show at "The Music Show" in Cohasset, Mass., Orlando stuns Hopkins and Wilson announcing to the audience that "this is my last day as a performer". (He recently suffered when close friend comedian Freddie Prinze committed suicide and his 21-year-old sister Rhonda died.)
Nov No longer with Dawn, Orlando returns to playing the Las Vegas circuit.
1979 Aug Orlando, signed to Casablanca, makes US #54 with *Sweets For My Sweet*.
Sept Hopkins embarks on TV acting career in US ABC-TV's "A New Kind of Family". (She will appear regularly in "Bosom Buddies" and "Gimme A Break"). Orlando begins an acting career in TV movie *Three Hundred Miles For Stephanie*" and guests on "The Cosby Show".
1981 Jan When American hostages are returned from 444 days in captivity in Iran, US revives Dawn's lasting image of yellow ribbons. Orlando takes over the leading role in *Barnum* on Broadway, while Jim Dale is on vacation.
Nov [15] Orlando joins a star cast in "Hey, Look Me Over!", a one-off benefit for the American Musical and Dramatic Academy at The Avery Fisher Hall, New York.
1988 Aug Orlando, Hopkins and Wilson re-form to perform at Trumps in Atlantic City, N.J.

JEFFREY OSBORNE

1970 Osborne (b. Mar.9, 1948, Providence, R.I., US), having taught himself to play drums at age 15, then sung and drummed with local bands, is offered the chance to join L.T.D. (the name stands for Love, Togetherness and Devotion), a 10-man funk group from Greensboro, N.C., after he sits in with the group on a tour date in Providence. Despite being married with two small daughters, he follows his mother's advice to grab the opportunity, and becomes L.T.D.'s lead singer.
1971/73 Before finding any commercial success, L.T.D. tours the R&B circuit just to make a living. Osborne supplements his income by doing session work (drums and back-up vocals) for acts like The Sylvers and Smokey Robinson°. The road work and consequent absence from home takes its toll on his marriage, which ends in divorce.
1974 L.T.D. signs to A&M Records, but debut LP *Love, Togetherness And Devotion* fails to chart. (Follow-up *Gettin' Down* will fare similarly.)
1976 Nov The group's breakthrough is *Love Ballad*, written by Skip Scarborough, which makes US #20 and tops the R&B chart for 2 weeks.
Dec LP *Love To The World* reaches US #52.

JEFFREY OSBORNE *cont.*

1977 Feb Extracted title track from LP *Love To The World* peaks at US #91.
Nov *(Every Time I Turn Around) Back In Love Again* dethrones Barry White° on the US R&B chart for 2 weeks, and a month later crosses over to hit US #4. The band's biggest hit single, it earns a gold disk for a million-plus sales.
1978 Jan LP *Something To Love* reaches US #21 and turns gold, with sales of a half million.
Apr *Never Get Enough Of Your Love* peaks at US #56.
Sept The group has its third US R&B #1 for 2 weeks with *Holding On (When Love Is Gone)*, which also crosses over to US #49 and makes UK #70 (the group's only UK chart entry). The track is taken from LP *Togetherness*, which is their biggest-selling LP yet, reaching US #18 and going platinum with sales of over a million.
1979 Aug LP *Devotion* climbs to US #29, and earns another gold disk.
1980 Oct LP *Shine On* makes US #28.
1981 Jan Extracted title song from LP *Shine On* reaches US #40, the group's last chart single.
1982 Jan LP *Love Magic* makes US #83, following which Osborne leaves and the group splits up. He remains with A&M as a soloist.
Aug Osborne's debut solo LP *Jeffrey Osborne*, produced by George Duke, reaches US #49. *I Really Don't Need No Light*, taken from it, makes US #39.
Dec Another extract from the LP, *On The Wings Of Love*, climbs to US #29.
1983 Apr *Eenie Meenie* makes US #76.
Sept *Don't You Get So Mad* from Osborne's second LP, reaches US #25 and UK #54, his first solo UK chart entry.
1984 Jan *Stay With Me Tonight*, the title song from the second LP, reaches US #30.
Mar LP *Stay With Me Tonight* peaks at US #25 after more than 6 months on chart. It becomes Osborne's first solo gold LP.
Apr *We're Going All The Way*, taken from the LP, makes US #48.
May *Stay With Me Tonight* climbs to UK #18, while LP of the same title makes UK #56.
July *On The Wings Of Love* reaches UK #11.
Oct Osborne duets with Joyce Kennedy on *The Last Time I Made Love*, which makes US #40. (Kennedy is ex-soul group Mother's Finest, whose first solo LP *Lookin' For Trouble*, is Osborne's first venture into production. The LP peaks at US #79, and will earn him a producer's Grammy nomination.) *Don't Stop* peaks at UK #61, and LP of the same title at UK #59.
Dec LP and single *Don't Stop* peak at US #39 and #44 respectively.
1985 Mar A second extract from the LP, *The Borderlines*, reaches US #38.
1986 Aug *You Should Be Mine (The Woo Woo Song)* reaches US #13, while *Soweto* makes UK #44. Both tracks are from LP *Emotional*, on which Osborne has worked with several producers in addition to long-time collaborator George Duke, Richard Perry, Michael Masser and Rod Temperton. Three of the tracks are self-produced, as Osborne builds on the studio experience gained from working with Joyce Kennedy. The LP peaks at US #26, but does not chart in UK.
1987 Feb Osborne sings *The Star-Spangled Banner* prior to the National Basketball Association All-Star game in Seattle, Wash.
1988 Aug After a 2-year recording hiatus, during which Osborne has spent more time with second wife Sheri and daughter Tiffany, he returns with LP *One Love – One Dream*, again with a variety of co-producers, including Bruce Roberts (who also co-writes with Osborne), Andy Goldmark, Ross Vanelli, and David "Hawk" Wolinski. The dance-tempo *She's On The Left* is extracted as a single.

OZZY OSBOURNE

1967 Osbourne (b. John Michael Osbourne, Dec.3, 1948, Aston, Birmingham, UK), whose early career as a burglar is halted by 2 months served in Winson Green Prison following conviction, on release takes a job in a slaughterhouse, but soon becomes unemployed. With three other Birmingham youths, he forms Polka Tulk, which takes the name of one of their early songs and becomes Black Sabbath°.
1970 After the release of their eponymous debut LP, Black Sabbath° will become hugely successful and help create a new genre – heavy metal. The group and Osbourne in particular also set standards for hard rock musicians in their consumption of alcohol and drugs.
1978 Osbourne leaves Black Sabbath° after seven LPs, following a major row with group member Tony Iommi. He is replaced by ex-Savoy Brown vocalist Dave Walker before returning briefly later in the year after plans to form a band with guitarist Gary Moore and ex-Deep Purple° bassist Glenn Hughes fail.
1980 July Osbourne signs a solo deal with Jet Records, with an LP already recorded with his new band, The Blizzard of Ozz, comprising ex-Quiet Riot Randy Rhoads, ex-Rainbow° bassist Bob Daisley and ex-Uriah Heep drummer Lee Kerslake. Jet is owned by Don Arden, who has recently ceased to handle Black Sabbath°.
Sept *Crazy Train* makes UK #49 as parent LP *Ozzy Osbourne's Blizzard Of Ozz* hits UK #7. The group begins its first UK tour.
Nov *Mr. Crowley*, written about occultist Aleister Crowley, reaches UK #46.
1981 Apr LP *Blizzard Of Ozz* enters the US chart, where it will stay for 2 years and peak at #21, also going platinum.
May Osbourne begins a US tour with a new Blizzard of Ozz. Kerslake and Daisley leave to join Uriah Heep, and are replaced by Tommy Aldridge on drums and Rudy Sarzo on bass. (In a notorious incident Osbourne bites the head off a live dove before assembled Columbia executives at a meeting in LA. He will attempt to repeat the trick with a live bat thrown on to the stage by a fan – the bat bites back and Osbourne reportedly undergoes a series of rabies injections.)
Aug The group returns to UK to headline the "Heavy Metal Holocaust" at Stoke-On-Trent – following Black Sabbath's° withdrawal.
Nov Osbourne's second LP *Diary Of A Madman* (title taken from Crowley's autobiography) reaches UK #14 and US #16, earning a second US platinum disk.
1982 Dailey returns, replacing Aldridge, and Don Airey (ex-Rainbow°) is added on keyboards. The band begins a US tour.
Mar [19] During high jinks near Orlando, Fla., the party's tour plane is buzzing their bus, making mock dive-bomb runs. On the last run the wing of the plane clips the bus and it is thrown out of control and crashes into a house, killing 25-year-old Randy Rhoads, Osbourne's hairdresser Rachel Youngblood and pilot Andrew Aycock. (Osbourne decides to complete the tour, bringing in ex-Gillan guitarist Bernie Torme as a temporary replacement for Rhoads.)
May *Mr. Crowley*, a live picture disk EP, enters the US LP chart, reaching #120 during an 18-week stay. Black Sabbath° is preparing to release *Live At Last*, which features performances of old songs with Dio on vocals, who claims the songs are his own. Osbourne books two nights at the New York Ritz and, with Aldridge, Sarzo and Brad Gillis (guitar) records a double LP's worth of old Sabbath numbers, which will be released as *Talk Of The Devil*.
June Osbourne marries Don Arden's daughter Sharon, his personal manager. Jake E. Lee, ex-LA band Rough Cutt joins the group on guitar.
Nov LP *Talk Of The Devil* enters UK chart, peaking at #21.
1983 Jan LP *Talk Of The Devil* reaches US #14.
May The Ozzy Osbourne Band plays the US festival in Cal. Following a tour and new recording sessions, Aldridge leaves again. He is replaced by Carmine Appice, ex-Vanilla Fudge°, as Sharon and Don Arden quarrel. She assumes full management control of Osbourne's affairs, taking him to sign up with CBS in US and Epic in UK. Family relations will remain difficult.
Dec *Bark At The Moon* enters the UK chart at the end of the month, to peak at #21, aided by a werewolf transformation video, a device which also becomes popular on stage. Parent LP *Bark At The Moon* reaches US #19 and UK #24.
1984 Splintered glass from a broken mirror used in the filming of the video for single *So Tired* lodges in Osbourne's throat, but there are no permanent ill effects.
Mar Appice leaves the group and Aldridge returns for another extensive tour.
June Ballad *So Tired* reaches UK #20 as Osbourne is urged by his wife to enter the Betty Ford Clinic for treatment of drug and alcohol dependency.
1985 Jan Osbourne and The Blizzard of Ozz play Rock in Rio festival. Airey is no longer with the group and after the festival Aldridge quits, never to return. Daisley follows, but will continue to help in studio recordings. Osbourne recruits drummer Randy Caspillo, from Lita Ford's band, and bassist Phil Soussan.
July Osbourne, Tony Iommi, Geezer Butler and Bill Ward re-form for a

day as Black Sabbath° to play Live Aid in Philadelphia. (The day before the concert Osbourne has been served with a writ from Don Arden, charging that he is trying to re-form Sabbath as a performing unit and claiming $1.5m in damages. The band plays on and Arden loses the suit.)

1986 Jan Ozzy Osbourne biography *Diary of a Madman* is published.

Feb *Shot In The Dark* reaches UK #20 as parent LP *The Ultimate Sin* hits UK #8.

Apr *Shot In The Dark* makes US #68. Osbourne begins his first full UK tour in 3 years, following it with tours of US and Japan.

June LP *The Ultimate Sin* hits US #6.

Aug Title track from *The Ultimate Sin/Lightning Strikes* spends a week at UK #72. Osbourne takes a break from his US tour to play UK's Castle Donington heavy metal festival.

Dec [19] A California Superior court judge denies a motion to reinstate a lawsuit served on Jan.13 against Osbourne and CBS Inc. which had sought to implicate Osbourne in the suicide of Californian teenager John McCollum, who it was claimed had been influenced by the lyrics of Osbourne's *Suicide Solution*. Judge John L. Cole states that the case involved areas "clearly protected by the First Amendment".

1987 In a parody of the attention he has received from fundamentalist US Christian groups, Osbourne plays a Bible-bashing preacher in heavy metal film *Trick or Treat*.

May LP *Tribute*, dedicated to Randy Rhoads and consisting of live recordings from 1981 featuring Rhoads' guitar playing, reaches UK #13.

June LP *Tribute* hits US #6.

1988 Osbourne recruits a new guitarist, 21-year-old Zakk Wylde who has been teaching guitar in N.J. During preparations for a new LP Soussan quits, leaving Castillo on drums, John Sinclair on keyboards and Daisley as studio-only bassist.

Oct LP *No Rest For The Wicked*, produced by Roy Thomas Baker, is released, to peak at UK #23 and US #13. Osbourne embarks on a 2-month US tour, opening in Omaha, Ne. (and ending in Long Beach, Cal., after which he will return to domestic security with his wife and three children at their 18th-century Buckinghamshire, UK home).

THE OSMONDS

Alan Osmond (vocals)
Wayne Osmond (vocals)
Merrill Osmond (vocals)
Jay Osmond (vocals)
Donny Osmond (vocals)

1959 The group is formed as a barber shop-style harmony quartet by four of the sons of George and Olive Osmond, Alan (b. June 22, 1949, Ogden, Ut., US), Wayne (b. Aug.28, 1951, Ogden), Merrill (b. Apr.30, 1953, Ogden) and Jay (b. Mar.2, 1955, Ogden) in their hometown,Ogden, where they sing at their Mormon church's Family Nights.

1962 On a visit to LA, the group meets a professional barber shop quartet in Disneyland and, after performing impromptu harmonies with them, is introduced to the park's talent booker, who signs it for the "Disneyland After Dark" show.

Dec [20] As The Osmond Brothers, the group appears for the first time on new weekly "Andy Williams Show" on US NBC-TV, harmonizing on *I'm A Ding Dong Daddy From Dumas* and *Side By Side*. (They will remain regulars on the show throughout its first 5-year run.)

1963 Dec 6-year-old Donny (b. Dec.9, 1957, Ogden) joins the group, joining his brothers on their numbers and soloing on *You Are My Sunshine* on the "Andy Williams Show".

1967 May The weekly "Andy Williams Show" comes to an end.

Sept The group begins regular guest appearances on US ABC-TV's "The Jerry Lewis Show" (which will last until mid-1969).

1967/70 The Osmond Brothers record for Barnaby, Andy Williams' own label, and Uni Records, but without success.

1971 Feb Now known as The Osmonds, they debut on the US chart after being signed to MGM Records by Mike Curb, who sees their potential as an answer to The Jackson 5°. Curb sends them to Fame studios in Muscle Shoals, Ala., where producer Rick Hall records them on the Jacksons-cloning *One Bad Apple* (written by George Jackson – no relation), which tops the US chart for 5 weeks and is a million-seller. LP *Osmonds*, which includes the hit, makes US #14 and earns a gold disk.

Mar *I Can't Stop*, a reissue from their previous label Uni, makes US #96.

June Aware of the teen idol appeal of his youthful good looks (he has had the major share of US teen magazine coverage since the success of *One Bad Apple*), MGM records Donny as a solo act, beginning with *Sweet And Innocent*, which hits US #7, and is the first solo million-seller by a solo member of the family.

July *Double Lovin'* makes US #14.

Aug LP *Home-Made* reaches US #22, and earns a gold disk, while Donny's first solo LP *The Donny Osmond Album*, which includes *Sweet And Innocent*, makes US #13 and earns a gold disk.

Sept A revival of Goffin and King°-penned Steve Lawrence/Mark Wynter 1963 hit *Go Away Little Girl*, recorded solo by Donny, tops the US chart for 3 weeks – his second million-seller in two solo releases.

Oct *Yo-Yo*, written by Joe South°, hits US #3, the group's second million-selling single.

Dec Donny's LP *To You With Love, Donny* reaches US #12 and earns a gold disk.

1972 Jan Donny's revival of Freddie Scott's *Hey Girl*, released as a double A-side with a new version of Billy Joe Royal's *I Knew You When*, hits US #9 and is another million-seller.

Mar *Down By The Lazy River*, written by Merrill and Alan, hits US #4 and is another million-seller. The group's LP *Phase Three*, including both this hit single and *Yo-Yo*, hits US #10 and is a million-seller.

Apr *Down By The Lazy River* is the group's UK chart debut, reaching #40, while in US, Donny's revival of Paul Anka's° 1960 million-seller *Puppy Love* hits #3, and is Donny's fourth gold disk out of four singles.

May LP *Portrait Of Donny* is released, set to hit US #6 and become his third gold LP.

June Little Jimmy Osmond (b. Apr.16, 1963, Canoga Park, Cal., US), the youngest of the family (and notably overweight though he will lose the surplus pounds in his teenage years), makes his recording debut on a solo novelty, *Long-Haired Lover From Liverpool*, which climbs to US #38, but will score its biggest sales in UK at the end of the year. (Interviewed, the 9-year-old admits that he has no idea where Liverpool actually is.)

July Donny's *Puppy Love* is his UK chart debut. It tops the chart in its second week, holding #1 for 5 weeks, and is the start of Osmond fan mania in UK, which will outstrip its US counterpart and give the group and solo members huge UK live, TV and record success over the next 5 years. Donny's revival of Nat "King" Cole's *Too Young* reaches US #13. LP *Too Young* enters the US chart to rise to #11.

Aug The group's *Hold Her Tight* makes US #14, while live LP *The Osmonds Live* reaches US #13 and earns a gold disk.

Sept Donny's LP *Portrait Of Donny* hits UK #5.

Sept [16] The Osmonds cartoon TV series starts on UK's ITV.

Oct Donny's *Too Young* hits UK #5, while his double A-side *Why/Lonely Boy* (revivals of Frankie Avalon° and Paul Anka° hits respectively) hits US #13.

Nov Live LP *The Osmonds Live* reaches UK #13, while the group sings guest vocals (and is dually credited) on Steve Lawrence and Eydie Gormé's *We Can Make It Together*, which reaches US #68.

Dec Little Jimmy tops the UK chart for 5 weeks with *Long-Haired Lover From Liverpool*, which becomes the year's biggest UK seller, shifting over 985,000 copies. He is the youngest individual (age 9) ever to hit UK #1. The group's rock original *Crazy Horses* lines up at UK #2 behind it, while it peaks at US #14. Donny's *Why* hits UK #3, while the group's LP *Crazy Horses* makes US #14 (their fifth and last gold LP) and hits UK #9. Donny's solo LP *Too Young* hits UK #7, as his LP *My Best To You* begins a climb to US #29.

1973 Feb Little Jimmy's LP *Killer Joe* makes UK #20 and peaks at US #105, while his revival of LaVern Baker's 1950s hit *Tweedle Dee* reaches US #59.

Apr Donny's revival of Johnny Mathis/Cliff Richard° hit *The Twelfth Of Never* hits US #8, selling over a million, and tops the UK chart, while Little Jimmy's *Tweedle Dee* hits UK #4.

May Donny's LP *Alone Together* makes US #26 and hits UK #6.

July The group's rocker *Goin' Home* reaches US #36.

Aug *Going Home* hits UK #4, while the group's concept LP *The Plan*, an expression of their Mormon faith, hits US #58 and UK #6.

Sept Donny's revival of Tab Hunter's *Young Love* tops the UK chart for

THE OSMONDS *cont.*

4 weeks, having peaked at US #23, released as a double A-side with a revival of Jimmy Charles' *A Million To One*.

Oct The group's harmony ballad *Let Me In* reaches US #36.

Nov Marie Osmond, the group's younger sister (b. Oct.13, 1959, Ogden), who has recently begun singing in concert with her brothers, debuts on the US chart with a country-style ballad (produced by country star Sonny James), reviving Anita Bryant's 1960 million-seller *Paper Roses*. It hits US #5 and is a million-seller as parent LP *Paper Roses* makes US #59.

Dec *Let Me In* hits UK #2 (behind Gary Glitter's° *I Love You Love Me Love*). Marie's *Paper Roses* hits UK #2 for Christmas (behind *Merry Christmas Everybody* by Slade°). Donny's *When I Fall In Love* hits UK #4, and his solo LP *A Time For Us* also hits UK #4, while heading for US #58.

1974 Jan Donny's double A-side revival of Elvis Presley's° *Are You Lonesome Tonight?* and Nat "King" Cole's *When I Fall In Love* makes US #14.

Feb Marie's LP *Paper Roses* peaks at UK #46.

Apr Little Jimmy revives Eddie Hodges' 1961 hit *I'm Gonna Knock On Your Door*, reaching UK #11.

May The group's *I Can't Stop* climbs to UK #12.

July Marie's LP *In My Little Corner Of The World* enters the US chart, set to make #164.

Aug LP *Our Best To You* hits UK #5.

Aug [12] The group begins six evenings of live UK TV shows on BBC 1, aired at peak time from BBC Television Theatre.

Sept The group's *Love Me For A Reason*, a ballad penned by Johnny Bristol, tops the UK chart for 3 weeks. Donny & Marie begin a series of duets with a revival of Dale & Grace's *I'm Leaving It (All) Up To You*, which hits US #4 (selling over a million) and UK #2. Donny & Marie's LP *I'm Leaving It All Up To You* enters charts, set to reach US #35 and UK #13.

Oct *Love Me For A Reason* hits US #10.

Dec The group's *Where Did All The Good Times Go* makes UK #18, while LP *Love Me For A Reason* makes US #47 and UK #13. LP *Donny* enters the US chart, reaching #57.

1975 Jan Donny & Marie's *Morning Side Of The Mountain*, a revival of Tommy Edwards' 1959 success, hits US #8 and UK #5.

Feb Donny's LP *Donny* makes UK #16.

Mar The group's *Having A Party*, not released as a US single, makes UK #28, while Donny's solo *I Have A Dream* reaches US #50.

Apr Marie's solo revival of Connie Francis'° *Who's Sorry Now* reaches US #40 as same titled LP makes US #152.

June LP *I'm Still Gonna Need You* makes UK #19.

July A revival of Frankie Valli's *The Proud One* hits UK #5. Donny & Marie's revival of Eddy Arnold's country ballad *Make The World Go Away* makes US #44 and UK #18, and the duo's LP of the same title makes US #133 and UK #30.

Sept *The Proud One* reaches US #22, while the group's LP of the same title reaches US #160.

Dec *I'm Still Gonna Need You* makes UK #32.

1976 Jan LP *Around The World – Live In Concert* makes US #148 and UK #41.

Jan [16] "Donny & Marie", a one-hour musical/comedy/variety show, heavily featuring all the Osmond family, debuts on US ABC-TV.

Feb Donny & Marie's revival of Nino Tempo & April Stevens' *Deep Purple* reaches US #14 and UK #25.

May LP *Donny & Marie – Featuring Songs From Their Television Show* peaks at US #60.

June Donny & Marie's LP *Deep Purple* makes UK #48. The group has a short UK BBC-TV series (through July).

July Donny revives The Four Seasons'° *C'mon Marianne*, which makes US #38.

Oct Donny's LP *Discotrain* makes US #145 and UK #59, while the group has another short UK BBC-TV series (through December).

Nov The group's *I Can't Live A Dream* reaches US #46 and UK #37, and is The Osmonds' last singles chart entry. LP *Brainstorm* makes US #145.

1977 Jan LP *Donny & Marie – A New Season* makes US #85 while festive LP *The Osmonds Christmas Album* peaks at US #127.

Feb Donny & Marie revive Marvin Gaye°/Tammi Terrell's duet *Ain't Nothing Like The Real Thing*, reaching US #21.

May LP *This Is The Way That I Feel*, by Marie, makes US #152.

June Marie's *This Is The Way That I Feel* reaches US #39, and is her last solo US hit single.

June [6] A US tour begins in Tucson, Ariz.

Oct Aiming at an older market, LP *Donald Clark Osmond* stalls at US #169.

Dec The "Donny & Marie" TV show, previously made in Hollywood, originates (in a Christmas Special edition) from the family's present home town of Orem, Utah, where the Osmonds have built their own $2½ million studio facility to house all their subsequent film, TV and video projects. This show features 28 Osmond family members, and has The Mormon Tabernacle Choir guesting.

1978 Jan Donny & Marie revive The Righteous Brothers'° *(You're My) Soul And Inspiration*, reaching US #38. LP *The Osmonds Greatest Hits* reaches US #192.

Mar LP *Winning Combination*, by Donny & Marie, makes US #99.

Nov Donny & Marie's *On The Shelf* is their final duetted chart entry, reaching US #38.

Dec Soundtrack LP *Goin' Coconuts*, from feature film starring Donny & Marie, climbs to US #98.

1980 Feb The group has its final UK BBC TV series (through March).

Aug The group breaks up.

Dec [12] Marie begins her own US NBC-TV series "Marie", produced by Osmond Productions. (The music/comedy hour will run for 2 months, and will briefly return to the screen the following Sept., but will not find the success of the "Donny & Marie" show.)

1982 The four older Osmonds re-form, without Donny, to concentrate on country music, and sign to Mercury Records.

Mar [21] Donny stars in the title role in a Broadway revival of musical *Little Johnny Jones* at the Alvin Theater. (It closes after only one performance.)

1983 The Osmond family's film and video studio center in Utah is sold to a Texan banker. (It will be repurchased 5 years later by Jimmy Osmond, from profits of his many successful businesses – including promoting Prince's° Far East tour).

1984 Apr The Osmonds, their repertoire now wholly country music (and signed to Warner Bros.), visit UK to play at Mervyn Conn's annual Country Music Festival at Wembley, London.

1985 Apr The group returns to play the Wembley festival for the second year running.

1987 Sept Having not recorded for a decade (he has meanwhile married Debra Glenn and the couple have two children in Provo, Utah), Donny signs a new recording deal with Virgin Records in UK. First single *I'm In It For Love* peaks at UK #70. Marie, now signed to Capitol Records, makes the country chart with *Everybody's Crazy 'Bout My Baby* (#24) and *Cry Just A Little* (#50), from LP *I Only Wanted You*.

1988 Sept Donny's *Soldier Of Love* reaches US #29 – the first top 30 pop hit by any of The Osmonds in the 80s.

Nov Donny's *If It's Love That You Want* reaches UK #70. (He has spent much of 1988 on touring and TV work in UK, rebuilding a rock career, though both he and Jimmy are also busy in other fields: Donny as a TV producer and director and satellite TV entrepreneur, and Jimmy as a rock impresario, restaurateur, and owner of the Oz-Art advertising and design company.)

GILBERT O'SULLIVAN

1968 Apr O'Sullivan (b. Raymond Edward O'Sullivan, Dec.1, 1946, Waterford, Ireland), having moved to Swindon, UK, with his family at age 13, where he has played in bands The Doodles and Rick's Blues while at Swindon Art College studying graphic design, releases his first single, *What Can I Do*, for CBS, under the name Gilbert. It does not chart.

1970 After a second one-off single, *Mr. Moody's Garden* on Major Minor, has also failed, O'Sullivan sends a demo tape and a photo of himself looking unusual enough to be sure to attract attention, to Gordon Mills, manager of Tom Jones° and Engelbert Humperdinck. Mills is impressed, signs him to his newly-formed MAM record label and becomes his producer on disk.

Dec Debut MAM single with his surname added, self-penned (as will be all his subsequent hits) *Nothing Rhymed* hits UK #8. O'Sullivan begins to make TV and personal appearances with a strikingly obtuse visual image: short trousers, sleeveless sweater, flat cap and pudding basin haircut (the image in the photo which had caught Mills' attention, but will be retained only for the first couple of releases).

1971 Apr *Underneath The Blanket Go* makes UK #40. EMI's Columbia label reissues the Major Minor single as by Gilbert O'Sullivan, but flipped over to feature *I Wish I Could Cry*. It gains some airplay, but fails to chart.

Sept *We Will* reaches UK #16.

Oct LP *Gilbert O'Sullivan – Himself* hits UK #5, and will stay on UK chart for 82 weeks.

Dec *No Matter How I Try* hits UK #5.

1972 Apr *Alone Again (Naturally)* hits UK #3.

July *Ooh-Wakka-Doo-Wakka-Day* hits UK #8, while *Alone Again (Naturally)* is his US debut (complete with new, longer-haired, college sweater image) and tops the chart for 6 weeks, selling over a million copies.

Sept LP *Gilbert O'Sullivan – Himself* (amended to include *Alone Again (Naturally)*, not on the UK version a year earlier) hits US #9.

Nov *Clair* tops the UK chart for 2 weeks. The song is written about Mills' daughter (for whom O'Sullivan used to babysit).

Dec *Clair* hits US #2, held off the top by Billy Paul's *Me And Mrs. Jones* and then by Carly Simon's° *You're So Vain*. It is O'Sullivan's second gold disk.

1973 Jan LP *Back To Front* hits UK #1 for a week, and stays on chart for 64 weeks. O'Sullivan has his own BBC TV special in UK, to coincide with its release.

Feb LP *Back To Front* reaches US #48.

Apr He switches from acoustic to electric piano on *Get Down*, which tops the UK chart for 2 weeks. ("Get down" is an admonition to his dog with regard to furniture, not an instruction for dancers.)

May *Out Of The Question*, not released as a UK single, and taken from LP *Back To Front*, makes US #17.

Aug *Get Down* hits US #7, and is O'Sullivan's third US gold disk.

Sept *Ooh Baby* reaches UK #18.

Oct LP *I'm A Writer Not A Fighter* hits UK #2.

Nov *Ooh Baby* makes US #25, while the LP creeps to US #101, and is O'Sullivan's final US chart LP.

Dec *Why Oh Why Oh Why* hits UK #6.

1974 Mar *Happiness Is Me And You* climbs to UK #19.

Apr *Happiness Is Me And You* peaks at US #62, and is O'Sullivan's final US chart single.

Aug O'Sullivan incurs the wrath of the feminist movement with *A Woman's Place*, which makes UK #42.

Nov LP *Stranger In My Own Back Yard* hits UK #9.

Dec Seasonal *A Christmas Song* reaches UK #12.

1975 July *I Don't Love You But I Think I Like You* peaks at UK #14.

1976 Dec Compilation LP *Greatest Hits* reaches UK #13.

1977 Nov LP *Southpaw*, his last for MAM, fails to chart.

1979 June [8] O'Sullivan begins legal proceedings against MAM and Mills for unpaid royalties, despite continuing to record for the label.

1980 Oct Debut CBS release, *What's In A Kiss?* reaches UK #19. LP *Off Centre* is released, to poor sales. O'Sullivan by now has become a resident of Jersey in the Channel Islands.

1981 Sept Compilation LP *20 Golden Greats*, a TV-promoted release on K-tel, makes UK #98.

1982 May At the case of O'Sullivan versus MAM/Mills, the judge rules in favor of the plaintiff, agreeing that his original contract with Mills had been unreasonable, and that he had not received his due share of the revenue created by his songs and records. The court awards him payment of substantial back royalties. (Mills will die in 1986.)

Oct LP *Life And Rhymes*, produced by Graham Gouldman, is released on CBS, without charting.

1988 After a long absence from record and retirement from live performances, LP *Frobisher Drive*, named after his old address in Swindon, is released in West Germany, with a UK release and tour planned.

JOHNNY OTIS

1948 Otis (b. John Veliotes, Dec.28, 1921, Vallejo, Cal., US) has been a musician since his teens, playing drums in Count Otis Matthews' West Oakland House Rockers, in San Francisco, Cal. He has drummed and played piano and vibes with several bands in Denver, Col., Kansas City, Kan. and LA, Cal., before forming his own band in 1945 (featuring later successful solo talent like Bill Doggett, Jimmy Rushing and Big Jay McNeely), and having a US hit with *Harlem Nocturne*. Sensing musical changes, he pioneers the development of R&B on US West Coast when he opens the Barrelhouse Club in LA. It is LA's first major venue to feature exclusively R&B music, mostly local acts whom Otis – with an unerring ear for talent – has discovered. These include the teenage Little Esther (Phillips) and The Robins (later to become The Coasters°).

1950 He tours with The Johnny Otis Show, an R&B revue featuring the pick of talent from the Barrelhouse. Several R&B-oriented record companies have noted Otis' ear for finding strong performers, and he becomes a traveling talent scout while on the road with his show. (Legend has him note and recommend to King Records three future major acts in one night, while visiting Detroit, Mich.: Jackie Wilson°, Little Willie John and The Royals, later to become Hank Ballard° & The Midnighters.)

1952/55 Otis discovers and works with (among others) Big Mama Thornton (producing her original version of *Hound Dog*), Bobby Bland, Little Richard° and Johnny Ace° (producing *Pledging My Love*).

1957 Otis signs to Capitol, to record as The Johnny Otis Show, with various featured singers taking the vocals.

1958 Jan *Ma! He's Making Eyes At Me*, with Marie Adams on lead vocal, hits UK #2.

Feb *Bye Bye Baby* reaches UK #20.

Aug *Willie And The Hand Jive* hits US #9. (This will be covered 2 years later by Cliff Richard° and The Shadows°, and be a UK and international hit.)

Nov *Crazy Country Hop* peaks at US #87.

1959 May *Castin' My Spell*, featuring Marci Lee on lead vocal, reaches US #52.

1960 Feb *Mumblin' Mosie* makes US #80. The run of Capitol hits ceases. (Otis will move to King Records, but will not chart again in the 60s.)

1969 Blues-based LP *Cold Shot*, recorded for Kent Records and highlighting Otis' son Shuggie (a talented slide guitarist) and blues vocalists Gene Connors and Delmar "Mighty Mouth" Evans, gains positive reviews and good sales, and includes R&B hit *Country Girl*. The same team, thinly anonymous, concocts a pornographic blues LP, *Snatch And The Poontangs*.

1970 Mar LP *Here Comes Shuggie Otis* reaches US #199. The Otis band plays the Monterey Jazz Festival, and is recorded for a live LP by Epic Records.

1974 Otis launches his own Blues Spectrum label, concentrating on R&B recordings, including Charles Brown and Joe Turner, backed by the Otis band.

1975 Mar LP *Inspiration Information* by Shuggie Otis makes US #181.

1982 After a lengthy absence from disk, Otis signs to US independent Alligator label with a new version of The Johnny Otis Show. The new line-up includes Shuggie and Delmar Evans, plus drummer Nicky Otis, two new vocalists, Barbara Morrison and Charles Williams, and guest players like Plas Johnson on sax. The revue tours and records ensemble-fashion much as it did in the 1950s.

ROBERT PALMER

1969 After a services' childhood based mostly in Malta, and a post-schooldays' "apprenticeship" in semi-pro Scarborough, UK, rock'n'roll band Mandrake Paddle Steamer, Palmer (b. Alan Palmer, Jan.19, 1949, Batley, Yorks., UK) moves to London to join The Alan Bown Set as vocalist, replacing Jess Roden.

Nov He sings on Bown's Deram label single *Gypsy Girl*, and also records new vocals to replace Roden originals on LP *The Alan Bown!* (though US release on Music Factory retains Roden's vocals).

1970 He joins avant garde jazz rockers Dada in place of Paul Korda, who has sung (with Elkie Brooks°) on their LP *Dada* for Atco Records. They splinter before recording again.

1971 Palmer sticks with ex-Dada musicians who form Vinegar Joe, aiming in a more blues-rock direction. He shares vocals with Elkie Brooks°, and other members are Pete Gage (guitar), Mike Deacon (keyboards), Steve York (bass) and Pete Gavin (drums).

1972 Apr Signed to Island Records, they release LP *Vinegar Joe*, but like all their records, it fails to chart in UK or US.

Dec LP *Rock'n'Roll Gypsies* is released.

1973 Oct *Six Star General* is Vinegar Joe's final release, and they split soon afterwards.

1974 Sept Retained by Island as a soloist, Palmer records LP *Sneakin' Sally Through The Alley* in New Orleans, with assistance from The Meters and Little Feat's° Lowell George. It fails to chart in UK, but receives much US airplay, and eventually makes US #107 in July 1975.

ROBERT PALMER *cont.*

1975 Palmer and his wife leave London to live in New York.

Dec LP *Pressure Drop*, released after he has toured in US as support and backup singer with Little Feat°, features the group and a Motown rhythm section, with string settings by Barry White's° arranger Gene Page. It reaches US #136, but does not chart in UK.

1976 Palmer moves from New York to Nassau, Bahamas, where he will live and do most of his songwriting until 1987.

Nov LP *Some People Can Do What They Like* reaches US #68, and is a UK chart debut at #46.

1977 Jan First hit single is LP extract *Man Smart, Woman Smarter*, which reaches US #63.

1978 Apr LP *Double Fun* makes US #45 but fails to chart in UK.

June *Every Kinda People*, extracted from LP *Double Fun*, is Palmer's breakthrough single: it reaches US #16, and gives him a UK singles chart debut at #53.

1979 July LP *Secrets* reaches UK #54, while *Bad Case Of Loving You (Doctor Doctor)*, from the LP, makes #61.

Sept He continues to sell better in US, as LP *Secrets* reaches #19, and *Bad Case Of Loving You (Doctor Doctor)* hits #14.

1980 Feb A revival of Todd Rundgren's° *Can We Still Be Friends* makes US #52, but flops in UK.

Sept LP *Clues*, which includes collaborations with Gary Numan°, reaches UK #31, his highest LP chart placing yet in UK, while the extracted *Johnny And Mary* makes UK #44.

Nov LP *Clues* reaches US #59. In contrast to UK, there are no US hit singles to boost it this time. A concert at the Dominion Theatre in London, UK, is recorded for live LP project.

Dec *Looking For Clues*, from LP *Clues*, climbs to UK #33.

1982 Apr Combined concert (from the Nov. 1980 recording) and studio recorded LP *Maybe It's Live* reaches UK #32. One of the non-live tracks revives The Persuaders' 1973 US hit *Some Guys Have All The Luck*, and is a UK hit for Palmer, reaching #16.

May LP *Maybe It's Live* sells poorly in US, reaching only #148.

1983 Apr LP *Pride* reaches UK #37 and US #112, and contains minor UK hit single *You Are In My System*, a cover of a US dance hit by The System. The original makes US #64 while Palmer is hitting UK #53.

June *You Can Have It (Take My Heart)* reaches UK #66.

July After a long absence, he returns to US singles chart with *You Are In My System*, which makes #78.

1985 Jan He joins Duran Duran's° John and Andy Taylor on a temporary basis in Power Station, designed as a one-LP studio project.

July He leaves Power Station after dispute with other members, who want to continue the project, tour, and play at Live Aid. Michael Des Barres replaces him.

Nov *Discipline Of Love (Why Did You Do It)* makes US #82, but fails in UK on first release, while LP *Riptide* makes a poor initial UK showing, reaching #69 before dropping.

1986 May *Addicted To Love*, from LP *Riptide*, hits US #1, and is Palmer's first worldwide million-selling single, aided by a striking video shown widely on TV. LP *Riptide* boosted by *Addicted To Love's* presence, peaks at #8.

June *Addicted To Love* hits UK #5.

July *Hyperactive* climbs to #33 in US.

Aug *I Didn't Mean To Turn You On* hits UK #9, while LP *Riptide*, boosted back into UK chart by the singles' success, finally reaches #5.

Nov *I Didn't Mean To Turn You On* hits US #2. *Discipline Of Love (Why Did You Do It)*, reissued in UK, now charts briefly at #68.

1987 Palmer and his family move to Lugano, Switzerland, where he works on music for the soundtrack of film *Sweet Lies*.

Sept He begins commuting from Lugano to Milan, Italy, to work at Logic studios on tracks for next LP.

1988 Apr It is announced that he will sign to EMI/Manhattan Records, while Island releases *Sweet Lies* in UK. It is a minor hit, reaching #58.

July LP *Heavy Nova* enters at its peak of UK #17, and climbs to US #25. *Simply Irresistible* continues US success at #20, and reaches UK #44. As Palmer makes plans for a worldwide tour, he teams up with Teo Macero and Clare Fischer to work on a musical *Don't Explain*.

GRAHAM PARKER & THE RUMOUR

Graham Parker (vocals)
Brinsley Schwarz (guitar)
Bob Andrews (keyboards)
Andrew Bodnar (bass)
Steve Goulding (drums)

1975 Having returned to UK from a tomato-picking and drug-abusing stay in Guernsey, the Channel Islands, Parker (b. Nov.18, 1950) is introduced to his eventual backing band, The Rumour (comprising members from UK roots band Ducks DeLuxe, Brinsley Schwarz° and Bontemps Roulez) through future Stiff Records boss, Dave Robinson. Parker has sent a demo tape of original R&B cuts to Hope & Anchor pub above which Robinson runs a small studio.

1976 Jan [9] Parker signs to Phonogram Records.

Apr Debut LP *Howlin' Wind*, produced by Nick Lowe°, is released to much critical acclaim and accompanied by a well-received sell-out club tour, but with sales of only 30,000.

Sept Official bootleg LP *Live At Marble Arch* secures a US deal with Mercury. With only 1,000 pressed, it is much bootlegged.

Oct Third LP of the year, *Heat Treatment*, produced by Robert "Mutt" Lange, features a semi-permanent brass section, and sells 60,000 copies.

1977 Mar EP *The Pink Parker* is his first UK singles hit at #24. The lead track is a cover of The Trammps' disco classic *Hold Back The Night*, featuring guest guitarist Thin Lizzy's° Brian Robertson.

July The Rumour releases first "solo" LP *Max*.

Oct Lowe°-produced LP *Stick To Me* makes UK #19.

1978 May *Don't Ask Me Questions* makes UK #32 as live double parent LP *The Parkerilla* reaches UK #14.

July [15] Parker & The Rumour support Bob Dylan° at Blackbushe Aerodrome, UK, open-air concert.

1979 Feb The Rumour has a minor hit with its cover of Duke Ellington's *Do Nothing Till You Hear From Me*. They sign to Stiff, while Parker remains at Vertigo and releases *Frozen Years*.

Mar LP *Squeezing Out Sparks*, produced by Jack Nitzsche, the band's most accomplished studio recording to date, makes UK #18 and, through Arista, US #40, with the aid of promo LP *Live Sparks*, a concert version of the studio disk. Graham Parker & The Rumour begin a major US tour suppporting Cheap Trick°, including a sell-out date at New York's Palladium. During the tour, Parker dedicates anti-Mercury Records song *Mercury Poisoning* to his new record boss, Arista's Clive Davis. Rumour releases its second LP without Parker on Stiff, *Frogs, Sprouts, Clogs And Krauts*.

May *Emotional Traffic*, pressed in red, amber and green vinyls, is later flipped but *Hard Enough To Show* also fails to chart.

Nov *Issues*, under the pseudonym The Duplicates is released on Stiff.

1980 Apr Parker signs to Stiff and releases *Stupefaction* and Jimmy Iovine-produced LP *The Up Escalator*, which includes Bruce Springsteen° on backing vocals. The LP reaches UK #11 – Parker's biggest UK success.

Aug *Purity Of Essence*, Rumour's third and last LP, is released, along with single *My Little Red Book*. With Andrews already gone, the group splits from Parker and disbands after backing US singer/songwriter Garland Jeffreys on his LP *Escape Artist*. Parker publishes sci-fi book *The Great Trouser Mystery*.

1982 Mar Parker's RCA LP *Another Grey Area*, produced by Jack Douglas, makes UK #40.

1983 Sept LP *The Real Macaw* fails to chart.

1985 Apr Parker signs to Elektra and releases LP *Steady Nerves* with backing band The Shot (including Schwarz°).

June *Wake Up (Next To You)* makes US #39, Parker's only US top 40 single.

1986 June He begins a European tour, backed by Schwarz° and Bodnar.

1988 May At Atlantic's 40th Birthday concert at New York's Madison Square Garden, Bob Geldof performs Parker's abortion song, *You Can't Be Too Strong* from LP *Squeezing Out Sparks*.

July LP *The Mona Lisa's Sister* appears on Demon (RCA in US), having been rejected by A&R-confused Atlantic. It costs $60,000 to record, less than his last video with Elektra.

Sept [24] Parker begins a solo acoustic US tour at the University of Rhode Island.

RAY PARKER JR.

1970 Parker (b. May 1, 1954, Detroit, Mich., US), having played the guitar since age 12, and toured supporting The Spinners° with his post-high school group Jeep Smith & The Troubadours, becomes a guitarist in the house band at Detroit's biggest club, the Twenty Grand, which leads to studio sessions for Motown and for Holland/Dozier/Holland's Invictus and Hot Wax labels.

1972 May After working with Parker in the studio (on sessions for LP *Talking Book*, Stevie Wonder° invites him to join the road band for his North American tour with The Rolling Stones°.

1973 After playing on Stevie Wonder's° LP *Innervisions*, Parker moves to LA, where he begins songwriting in earnest (inspired by working with Wonder), and becomes a regular session guitarist, playing with Barry White° (and White's various groups), Boz Scaggs° and LaBelle°, among others.

1974 Dec Parker's first hit composition is *You Got The Love*, recorded by Rufus, which reaches US #11. He also has a bit part in movie *Uptown Saturday Night*.

1976 Apr Barry White's° *You See The Trouble With Me*, which Parker co-writes and plays on, hits UK #2.

1977 Parker opens his own Ameraycan recording studio in LA and, after a demo tape impresses Arista Records chief Clive Davis, he is signed to the label as a recording act. He puts together the band Raydio, with himself on vocals and guitar, Arnell Carmichael on synthesizer, Charles Fearing on guitar, Vincent Bonham on keyboards, Jerry Knight on bass and Larry Tolbert on drums – all previous studio cohorts from the early 70s in Detroit.

1978 Apr Raydio's debut single *Jack And Jill*, written and produced by Parker, hits US #8 and is a million-seller, while LP *Raydio* makes US #27 and earns a gold disk for a half million sales. Bonham leaves the group, which tours US with Bootsy Collins.

May *Jack And Jill* reaches UK #11.

Aug *Is This A Love Thing*, also from the LP, makes UK #27.

1979 Aug Raydio's second LP *Rock On* peaks at US #45 (also a gold disk), while extracted *You Can't Change That* hits US #9.

1980 June The group changes name to Ray Parker Jr. & Raydio for its third LP *Two Places At The Same Time*, which makes US #33 and is Parker's third gold LP. The title track peaks at US #30.

1981 June LP *A Woman Needs Love*, fourth consecutive gold disk, reaches US #13. From it, *A Woman Needs Love (Just Like You Do)* hits US #4, the highest-placed single yet.

Sept *That Old Song*, also from the fourth LP, reaches US #21. Parker produces soul songstress Cheryl Lynn's *Shake It Up Tonight*, which reaches US #70, and its parent LP *In The Night*, which makes US #104.

1982 June Parker disbands the group to record as a soloist, and his LP *The Other Woman* reaches US #11 (again earning a gold disk). The title track (inspired, according to Parker, by listening to Rick Springfield's° *Jessie's Girl*), hits US #4.

Aug *Let Me Go*, also from the LP, peaks at US #38.

1983 Jan Third single from LP *The Other Woman*, *Bad Boy* peaks at US #35. Compilation LP *Greatest Hits*, covering both Parker's Raydio and solo career to date, makes US #51.

1984 Jan *I Still Can't Get Over Loving You* reaches US #12. It is taken from LP *Woman Out Of Control*, which peaks at US #30.

Aug Parker's theme for Bill Murray/Dan Aykroyd film *Ghostbusters*, written and recorded within 2 days of being requested by the producers, tops the US chart for 3 weeks, and is Parker's second US million-selling single. Its promo video is directed by Ivan Reitman, and includes Murray and Aykroyd, plus guest cameos by Danny De Vito, Peter Falk and others. (The song will earn Parker an Academy Award nomination, but he will be successfully sued by Huey Lewis° on the basis that it plagiarizes Lewis' *I Want A New Drug*.)

Sept *Ghostbusters* hits UK #2 for 3 weeks below Stevie Wonder's° million-selling *I Just Called To Say I Love You*.

1985 Jan *Jamie* reaches US #14. It is taken from Parker's LP *Ghostbusters*, which makes US #60 (though is overshadowed by the movie soundtrack LP, which along with the theme song also has tracks by Elmer Bernstein, The Thompson Twins°, Air Supply° and others, and hits US #6 and UK #24).

Dec *Girls Are More Fun* makes US #34, and the LP *Sex And The Single Man* reaches US #65.

1986 Jan As the film opens in UK to repeat its US box office success, *Ghostbusters* re-charts in UK, hitting #6. (Total UK sales will top 800,000.)

Feb Parker's duet with UK singer Helen Terry on *One Sunny Day/Dueling Bikes From Quicksilver*, from the soundtrack of film *Quicksilver*, is released on Atlantic and peaks at US #96. Meanwhile, *Girls Are More Fun* makes UK #46.

1987 Sept Parker signs a new deal with Geffen Records, his debut single *I Don't Think That Man Should Sleep Alone* peaking at US #68.

Oct Geffen LP *After Dark* reaches US #86 and UK #40.

Nov *I Don't Think That Man Should Sleep Alone*, taken from LP *After Dark*, climbs to UK #13.

1988 Jan *Over You* makes UK #65.

Dec Parker pursues his long-term ambition to win an acting role in the sequel movie *Ghostbusters 2* as the original stars agree to make the film.

THE ALAN PARSONS PROJECT

1974 Parsons, who has engineered many historic LPs including The Beatles'° *Abbey Road* and Pink Floyd's° *Dark Side Of The Moon*, forms a group with his partner, lyricist, singer and keyboard player Eric Woolfson, while working at Abbey Road Studios in London, UK,producing groups like Pilot and Steve Harley's° Cockney Rebel.

1976 July His first LP as an artist/producer, intended as a one-off project, is *Tales Of Mystery And Imagination*, based on Edgar Allan Poe's book. Like all subsequent Parsons releases, it is a concept LP packaged in an elaborate sleeve and instrumentally-based, but features Woolfson on vocals with a selection of guest vocalists (Arthur Brown, John Miles and The Hollies'° Terry Sylvester are on this). Released on 20th Century in US, it reaches US #38, after being premiered at Griffith Park Observatory's planetarium, accompanied by one of the first specially-commissioned laser shows.

Aug On Arista UK, the LP makes UK #56.

Sept Taken from the LP, *(The System Of) Doctor Tarr And Professor Fether* makes US #37.

Oct *The Raven*, also from LP *Tales Of Mystery And Imagination*, peaks at US #80.

1977 Aug LP *I, Robot*, taken from a concept by science fiction writer Isaac Asimov, and titled after his book, makes UK #30.

Oct *I Wouldn't Want To Be Like You*, with vocals by Lenny Zakatek, makes US #36. It is taken from LP *I, Robot*, which hits US #9, and earns Parsons his first platinum disk.

1978 Jan *Don't Let It Show*, with vocals by David Townshend, peaks at US #92.

June LP *Pyramid* makes UK #49.

Aug LP *Pyramid* reaches US #26, earning a gold disk.

Sept *What Goes Up*, taken from LP *Pyramid*, creeps to US #87.

1979 Sept LP *Eve* represents a musical battle of the sexes and makes UK #74. The music is supplied by a nucleus of ex-Pilot players David Paton (bass) and Ian Bairnson (guitar), Cockney Rebel's Stuart Elliott (drums) with Lesley Duncan as a featured vocalist.

Oct LP *Eve* reaches US #13, earning another gold disk.

Dec *Damned If I Do*, with Zakatek on vocals, is taken from LP *Eve* and makes US #27.

1980 Nov LP *The Turn Of A Friendly Card* reaches UK #38.

1981 Feb LP *The Turn Of A Friendly Card* makes US #13 and earns Parsons a second platinum disk for a million-plus sales. Zakatek contributes lead vocals to *Games People Play*, which is extracted to reach US #16.

Aug *Time*, with Woolfson singing lead vocal, reaches US #15.

Nov *Snake Eyes*, with vocals by Chris Rainbow, climbs to US #67.

1982 June LP *Eye In The Sky*, concerned with the misuse of technology (the title taken from a Philip K. Dick novel), reaches UK #28. Colin Blunstone is among its featured vocalists.

Oct LP *Eye In The Sky* hits US #7 and is a third platinum-seller. The title track, with Woolfson on vocal, hits US #3.

Dec *Psychobabble*, with vocals by Elmer Gantry, makes US #57.

1983 Jan *Old And Wise*, a third extract from LP *Eye In The Sky*, makes UK #74.

Nov Compilation LP *The Best Of The Alan Parsons Project* makes UK #99.

Dec *You Don't Believe*, with Zakatek on vocals, makes US #54.

1984 Jan LP *The Best Of The Alan Parsons Project* reaches US #53.

Mar *Don't Answer Me*, with Woolfson on vocals, makes UK #58, its parent LP *Ammonia Avenue* reaching UK #24.

May *Don't Answer Me*, with Woolfson on vocals, reaches US #15, as does LP *Ammonia Avenue*, which earns a gold disk.

THE ALAN PARSONS PROJECT *cont.*

June *Prime Time*, with Woolfson again on vocals, makes US #34.
1985 Feb LP *Vulture Culture* makes UK #40.
Mar Taken from the LP, *Let's Talk About Me*, with vocals by David Paton, makes US #56.
Apr LP *Vulture Culture* makes US #46.
May *Days Are Numbers (The Traveller)*, with vocals by Rainbow, peaks at US #71.
1986 Feb Parsons and his label Arista dispute royalty payments over compact disk releases. (It will be a year before his product is available on CD.) LP *Stereotomy* (the title another Edgar Allan Poe reference) features Procol Harum's° singer Gary Brooker among others and makes US #47.
Mar *Stereotomy*, with John Miles on lead vocals, peaks at US #82.
1987 Feb LP *Gaudi*, based on the life of the Spanish painter, makes UK #66. Simultaneously, most of Parsons' back-catalog is released for the first time on compact disk by Arista (their dispute now resolved). Compilation LP *Limelight: The Best Of, Vol.2*, featuring 10 tracks from previous LPs, most of them also former US hit singles, is released.
June Parsons and Woolfson digitally re-master the original LP *Tales Of Mystery And Imagination* for compact disk release by Mercury, adding some new touches with synthesizer and guitar, and inserting a narration by Orson Welles (commissioned at the time of the original release).

DOLLY PARTON

1946 Jan [19] Parton, the fourth of Robert and Avie Lee Parton's 12 children is delivered by Dr. Robert F. Thomas (whom she later immortalizes in song) in Locust Ridge, Sevier County, Tenn. The family is so poor, they pay the doctor with a sack of corn meal.
1957 Having already appeared on Cass Walker's Knoxville, Tenn., radio show, Parton takes a Greyhound bus to Lake Charles, La., to record her first single *Puppy Love*, penned with her uncle, for local Gold Band label.
1958 Drumming with the Sevier County High School marching band, Parton makes her debut at "The Grand Ole Opry".
1962 She records *It's Sure Gonna Hurt* for Mercury, credited to Dolly Parton with The Merry Melody Singers, which includes three members of The Jordanaires.
1964 June [1] Parton relocates to Nashville the day following her high school graduation, staying with relatives.
June Parton signs with Monument Records, which, with Ray Stevens producing, initially aims her at the pop market, but her first success is as a songwriter – Bill Phillips' US C&W top 10 hit with *Put It Off Until Tomorrow*.
1966 May [30] Parton marries Carl Dean (whom she had met in the Wishy Washy laundromat on her first day in Nashville), in Catoosa County, Ga.
1967 Oct [7] "Dolly Parton Day" is celebrated in Sevier County. 7,000 locals attend her concert at the courthouse to celebrate her signing to RCA and replacing Norma Jean (to whom she had earlier sent some songs) on "The Porter Wagoner Show" TV program. (Parton's RCA debut *Just Because I'm A Woman* makes US C&W #19.)
1968 Parton becomes a regular on "The Grand Ole Opry" show. She and Wagoner are named Best Duet of the Year by the Country Music Association (CMA). They also receive the first of three Grammy nominations.
1969 Mar LP *Just The Two Of Us*, with Porter Wagoner, makes US #184. (The partnership will produce 18 country hits – the first a cover of Tom Paxton's *The Last Thing On My Mind*.)
Aug Parton/Wagoner LP *Always, Always* peaks at US #162.
Nov Solo LP *My Blue Ridge Mountain Boy* climbs to US #194.
1970 Apr Parton/Wagoner LP *Porter Wayne And Dolly Rebecca* climbs to US #137.
Aug LP *A Real Live Dolly*, recorded at Parton's high school, makes US #154.
Oct LP *Once More*, again with Wagoner, makes US #191.
1971 Mar LP *Two Of A Kind*, Parton's last chart LP with Wagoner, climbs to US #142.
June Solo LP *Joshua* creeps to US #198. (The title track gave Parton her first US C&W #1 in 1970.)
1974 Mar *Jolene* makes US #60 and tops the US country chart – the second of four consecutive country #1s.
Apr [21] Parton and Wagoner perform their last live show together in Salinas, Kan.
Apr Parton forms The Traveling Family Band, which includes four siblings and two cousins.
1975 Oct Parton, having been nominated on five previous occasions, is voted Female Vocalist of the Year by the CMA.
1976 Feb Syndicated TV series "Dolly", recorded in Nashville and featuring country stars, airs in US.
June *Jolene* hits UK #7. Vocal problems will result in her cancelling 65 dates in the latter part of the year. She is named CMA Female Vocalist of the Year for a second successive year.
1977 Parton signs to West Coast management team Ray Katz and Sandy Gallin.
May [6] She makes her New York debut at The Bottom Line club.
May Parton participates in a concert in Scotland at Glasgow's King Theatre to celebrate Queen Elizabeth's Silver Jubilee. She is introduced to Prince Philip, the Duke of Edinburgh, backstage.
July *Light Of A Clear Blue Morning* stalls at US #87, while parent LP *New Harvest . . . First Gathering*, which features a shift away from country, makes US #71.
1978 Jan Mainstream pop song, *Here You Come Again*, written by Barry Mann and Cynthia Weil, hits US #3. LP *Here You Come Again* reaches US #20, and is Parton's first platinum LP.
May *Two Doors Down* reaches US #19.
Sept *Heartbreaker* makes US #37.
Oct Parton appears on the front cover of *Playboy* magazine, in bunny costume. She is named Entertainer of the Year by the CMA as LP *Heartbreaker* makes US #27.
Dec Compilation LP *Both Sides* makes UK #45.
1979 Feb Parton becomes the first country artist to have a disco hit, with *Baby I'm Burnin'*, which also makes US #25 and tops the country chart.
Feb [15] Parton wins Best Country Female Vocal Performance at the 21st annual Grammy ceremonies.
July *You're The Only One* peaks at US #59 as parent LP *Great Balls Of Fire* makes US #40.
Oct *Sweet Summer Lovin'* stalls at US #77.
1980 May *Starting Over Again* makes US #36, while parent LP *Dolly Dolly Dolly* makes US #71.
Dec *Nine To Five*, in which Parton makes her movie debut with Jane Fonda and Lily Tomlin, premieres in US.
1981 Feb *9 To 5* tops the US chart, but stalls at UK #47.
Mar LP *9 To 5 And Odd Jobs* reaches US #11.
May *But You Know I Love You* makes US #41.
Sept *The House Of The Rising Sun* peaks at US #77.
1982 Feb [24] Parton wins her second Best Country Vocal Performance Grammy, for *9 To 5*.
Mar [25] TV version of "9 To 5" airs, with Parton's sister Rachel Dennison reprising her role.
May LP *Heartbreak Express* makes US #106.
July Parton stars with Burt Reynolds in movie *The Best Little Whorehouse in Texas*, which premieres in US.
Sept *I Will Always Love You*, from *The Best Little Whorehouse in Texas* and a remake of Parton's 1974 country chart-topper, makes US #53 and is her 15th country #1 as *The Best Little Whorehouse* soundtrack LP climbs to US #63. (Parton duets with Burt Reynolds on *Sneakin' Around* cut.)
Dec LP *Greatest Hits* climbs to US #77.
1983 June LP *Burlap And Satin* makes US #127.
Oct *Islands In The Stream*, a duet with Kenny Rogers° and written by The Bee Gees°, tops the US chart, the only platinum single in the year.
1984 Jan *Save The Last Dance For Me* makes US #45 as parent LP *The Great Pretender*, reprising hits of the 1950s and 1960s, reaches US #73.
Apr *Downtown* peaks at US #80, while *Here You Come Again* makes UK #75.
June Sylvester Stallone/Dolly Parton-starring picture *Rhinestone*, based on Larry Weiss' song *Rhinestone Cowboy*, opens in US. (The project is Parton's first since major stomach surgery.) Soundtrack LP *Rhinestone*, featuring Parton songs, reaches US #135.
Dec Festive LP *Once Upon A Christmas*, with Kenny Rogers°, is released, set to make US #31.
1985 Jan *Once Upon A Christmas*, from Parton and Kenny Rogers'° Christmas TV special, makes US #81, as she prepares for a US tour with Rogers.

June *Real Love*, another duet with Rogers°, peaks at US #91. Construction begins on Dollywood, an 87-acre theme park near her birthplace in the Smoky Mountains.

Sept LP *Greatest Hits* makes UK #74.

Dec US ABC-TV airs "A Smoky Mountain Christmas". It becomes the network's highest-rated Sunday night program in over 2 years.

1986 Jan [19] Parton begins work on often-postponed LP project with Emmylou Harris and Linda Ronstadt°.

1987 Mar Parton's collaboration with Emmylou Harris and Linda Ronstadt°, LP *Trio*, makes UK #60.

May LP *Trio* tops the US country chart for 5 weeks, and is set to hit US #6. (Extracted *To Know Him Is To Love Him* tops the country chart.)

Sept [27] US ABC TV premieres "Dolly", a variety show scheduled as the network's prime-time Sunday evening show. (Despite attempts to re-vamp the program, it fails to achieve ratings, and ABC pulls it off the air.)

Dec LP *Rainbow*, a mainstream pop album and Parton's first for CBS/Columbia, stalls US #153.

1988 Mar [2] *Trio* wins Parton, Ronstadt° and Harris a Grammy for Country Vocal – Duo/Group at the annual ceremonies. It is Parton's fourth.

Mar Parton visits UK to promote LP *Rainbow* and appears on TV show "Aspel & Co."

TEDDY PENDERGRASS

1969 Pendergrass (b. Mar.26, 1950, Philadelphia, Pa., US), whose mother was a nightclub performer, has taught himself the drums in his early teens after a childhood steeped in gospel music, and is drumming with local group The Cadillacs when they are invited to become the instrumental back-up team for Harold Melvin & The Blue Notes, a Philadelphia R&B group with a 13-year history and its roots in doo-wop, and a minor hit single, *My Hero* (US #78 in 1960).

1970 On a French West Indies tour, The Blue Notes lead singer John Atkins leaves and Pendergrass replaces him as front man.

1971 The group signs to Kenny Gamble and Leon Huff's Philadepphia International label, based in its own home town.

1972 Aug The group's first hit is *I Miss You*, which reaches US #58.

Dec *If You Don't Know Me By Now*, a ballad written and produced by Gamble and Huff, hits US #3 and sells over a million, establishing the group firmly in the pop field as well as R&B, where it has previously been known. Debut LP *Harold Melvin and The Blue Notes* reaches US #53.

1973 Feb *If You Don't Know Me By Now* hits UK #9.

Mar *Yesterday I Had The Blues* peaks at US #63.

Dec *The Love I Lost*, again a Gamble/Huff composition, hits US #7, and is the group's second million-seller. Second LP *Black And Blue* peaks at US #57.

1974 Feb *The Love I Lost* makes UK #21.

May *Satisfaction Guaranteed (Or Take Your Love Back)* makes US #58 and UK #32.

Nov Penned by Gene McFadden and John Whitehead, *Where Are All My Friends* reaches US #80.

1975 May LP *To Be True* makes US #26, earning a gold disk for a half million sales during its 32-week chart run.

June *Bad Luck*, also by McFadden and Whitehead, makes US #15, while UK-only reissued oldie on Route label, *Get Out*, makes UK #35.

Aug *Hope That We Can Be Together Soon*, featuring guest vocalist Sharon Paige duetting on lead with Pendergrass, reaches US #42.

1976 Feb The group's last major US hit single is ballad *Wake Up Everybody* (penned by McFadden and Whitehead), which reaches US #12. The LP of the same title hits US #9 earning a second gold disk.

Mar *Wake Up Everybody* reaches UK #23.

Apr *Tell All The World How I Feel About 'Cha Baby* stalls at US #94. It is the group's last single for Philadelphia International and also last with Pendergrass' lead vocal. He leaves for a solo career, staying with Gamble and Huff's label, while Harold Melvin and The Blue Notes move to ABC Records, with new lead singer David Ebo.

Aug Group compilation LP *All Their Greatest Hits* reaches US #51.

1977 Mar To compete with Thelma Houston's revival, Harold Melvin and The Blue Notes' version of Gamble/Huff/Gilbert song *Don't Leave Me This Way*, previously an LP track, is issued as a UK single, and outsells Houston's, hitting UK #5.

July Pendergrass' first solo hit single is Gamble and Huff's *I Don't Love You Anymore*, which makes US #41. It is taken from his debut solo LP *Teddy Pendergrass*, which peaks at US #17 and spends 35 weeks on chart, selling over a million copies to earn a platinum disk. A different single, *The Whole Town's Laughing At Me*, is extracted in UK and reaches #44. Having taken a year's absence from live performance after splitting with Melvin, he begins to tour with the 15-piece Teddy Bear Orchestra (the name taken from Pendergrass' nickname). His sultry ballads, addressed directly to the females in the audience, quickly bring him a reputation as a ladies' man entertainer.

Aug Pendergrass joins Lou Rawls, Billy Paul, Archie Bell and others on The Philadelphia All-Stars' *Let's Clean Up The Ghetto* (all profits will go to a 5-year charity product in areas of urban decay). It reaches US #91 and UK #34.

Aug [22/27] Pendergrass participates in "Let's Clean Up The Ghetto Week" in LA, at the instigation of the mayor, Tom Bradley.

1978 Sept Second solo LP *Life Is A Song Worth Singing* and extracted *Close The Door* are both US million-sellers, reaching US #11 and #25 respectively.

Sept [2] Pendergrass performs a "For Women Only" midnight concert at Avery Fisher Hall, New York. The audience are handed white chocolate teddy bear-shaped lollipops. (Further "ladies only" concerts (invariably standing-room-only) follow: a PR exercise by manager Shep Gordon to capitalize on the perception of Pendergrass as an aural seducer.

Nov In UK, *Close The Door* is double A-side with *Only You* and reaches #41.

1979 Aug LP *Teddy* hits US #5 and earns another platinum disk. *Turn Off The Lights*, taken from it, peaks at US #48.

1980 Feb Double live LP *Teddy Live! Coast To Coast*, with three sides recorded in concert and a fourth containing interviews and new studio tracks, makes US #33, reaching gold status. A UK tour is cancelled, partly because of Pendergrass' liaison with the wife of Marvin Gaye° – who is touring UK for the same promoter at the same time.

Sept LP *T.P.* reaches US #14, and is Pendergrass' fourth LP to turn platinum with US sales over a million. It includes a duet with Stephanie Mills on *Feel The Fire*.

Oct *Can't We Try*, taken from LP *T.P.*, climbs to US #52.

1981 Jan Another extract from the LP, *Love T.K.O.*, reaches US #44.

Apr He tours UK for the first time as a soloist and, as in US, his shows are hugely successful with female audiences in particular.

July Pendergrass duets again with Stephanie Mills on her single *Two Hearts* on 20th Century. It peaks at US #40 and UK #49.

Oct LP *It's Time For Love* reaches US #19, earning another gold disk. The first single from it, *I Can't Live Without Your Love*, just fails to chart.

1982 Feb *You're My Latest, My Greatest Inspiration* makes US #43. He makes his movie debut in *Soup For One* and sings *Dream Girl* on the soundtrack, produced by Nile Rodgers and Bernard Edwards of Chic°. He also makes a second successful UK visit.

Mar [18] On the way home from a basketball game, Pendergrass crashes his Rolls Royce into a barrier after skidding off the road in Philadelphia. He is pulled from the wreck with a severely injured spinal chord, and hospitalized in a critical condition. (He is paralyzed from the neck down for some time and gradually recovers only partial movement, but it will keep him from recording and performing for over 2 years.)

Oct LP *This One's For You*, consisting of material recorded before the accident, makes US #59.

1984 Jan LP *Heaven Only Knows*, his last for Philadelphia International, stalls at US #123.

July Pendergrass, confined to a wheelchair, returns to recording and signs to Asylum Records, where his debut is LP *Love Language*, peaking at US #38.

Aug From the LP, *Hold Me* reaches US #44. The single is a duet with Whitney Houston° (her first chart entry).

1986 Feb *Hold Me*, having failed in 1984, is reissued in UK after Whitney Houston° tops the chart with *Saving All My Love For You*, and this time climbs to UK #44.

1988 June New LP *Joy* reaches UK #45.

July Single and LP *Joy* make US #77 and US #54 respectively.

CARL PERKINS

1950 Perkins (b. Carl Lee Perkings, Apr.9, 1932, Ridgely, Tenn., US), from a poor sharecropping family, whose father Buck is an invalid with a lung disorder, begins to play bars and honky tonks around Tennessee, with brothers Jay and Clayton as The Perkins Brothers Band, to earn extra money.

1953 Jan [24] He marries Valda Crider in Corinth, Miss., and she encourages him to make a career in music. (During their first year together, he picks cotton and she takes in laundry to make ends meet.)

1954 Perkins begins to play professionally, still on the honky tonk circuit, singing and playing electric guitar, with his brothers backing him on acoustic guitar and double bass. They mix country and hillbilly music with the occasional blues and uptempo R&B number, and earn around $30 a month. Perkins relocates to Jackson, Miss., where he and his wife move into a government housing project.

Aug He hears Elvis Presley's° first single *Blue Moon Of Kentucky* on the radio, and recognizes a similar blend of styles to those he is playing himself. After watching Presley at a high school dance in Betthel Springs, Miss., The Perkins Brothers Band decides to travel to Memphis, Tenn., to audition for Presley's record company, Sun.

Oct The three brothers, together with new drummer W.S. Holland, impress Sam Phillips at Sun, particularly with Perkins' original material. Phillips offers Perkins a contract if he can come up with more new songs.

1955 Jan [22] The first Sun recording session produces *Movie Magg* and *Turn Around*, which are issued as a single on Phillips' new label Flip Records, to little success.

Feb Perkins supports Elvis Presley° on a tour of the South.

July [11] *Gone Gone Gone*, an uptempo rockabilly track, is recorded for Perkins' second single, on Sun label itself.

Nov When Presley's° contract is sold to RCA, Phillips decides to mold Perkins into a suitable replacement, and encourages him to play up the emerging rock'n'roll elements in his writing and recording. The band is signed to Phillips' Stars Inc. promotional agency.

Dec [19] Perkins and the band record his own composition *Blue Suede Shoes* (based on a true incident spotted in a gig audience). Sensing its commercial potential, Phillips rush-releases it and gives it heavy promotion.

1956 Mar [3] *Blue Suede Shoes* enters the US top 100 simultaneously with Presley's° first national hit *Heartbreak Hotel*.

Mar [17] Perkins makes his first TV appearance, on Red Foley's country show "Ozark Jubilee".

Mar [22] The Perkins brothers are driving to New York for an appearance on "The Perry Como Show" on NBC-TV when their car hits a pick-up truck near Wilmington, Del. Perkins and brother Jay are both hospitalized with their injuries, and media promotion made possible by *Blue Suede Shoes*' success slips away while they are recovering.

Apr *Blue Suede Shoes* hits US #3, and sells over a million. Presley's° cover is released as the lead song on an EP after he, rather than Perkins, sings it on national TV, and it reaches US #24.

Apr [10] When Perkins leaves hospital and returns to Memphis, he is presented with a new 1956 Cadillac Fleetwood by Sam Phillips, in celebration of *Blue Suede Shoes*' million sales.

June *Blue Suede Shoes* hits UK #10 (his only UK chart single), but Presley's cover hits UK #9.

July Perkins' follow-up *Boppin' The Blues* stalls at US #70.

Dec [4] While Perkins and the band are in Sun studios in Memphis recording *Matchbox* (with the label's newcomer Jerry Lee Lewis° playing piano on the session), they are visited by Johnny Cash° (on the way downtown to shop for Christmas with his wife), and then by Elvis Presley°, who has just returned to Memphis for Christmas. After Cash leaves, the other three settle down to a studio jam session on familiar gospel, country and R&B numbers, while Phillips leaves the studio tape running. (These impromptu recordings become legendary as "The Million Dollar Quartet" tapes and segments will be released in the late 1970s and mid-1980s, after Presley's death.)

1957 Mar *Your True Love* peaks at US #67, and is Perkins' last hit for Sun.

Mar [31] Perkins opens a tour of the US South, co-headlining with Johnny Cash° (and supported by Jerry Lee Lewis°, among others), in Little Rock, Ark.

Nov [12] Rock'n'roll movie *Jamboree* (released as *Disc Jockey Jamboree* in UK) premieres in Hollywood, and features Perkins performing *Glad All Over*.

1958 Jan [3] *Disc Jockey Jamboree* opens in UK.

Feb [19 Perkins leaves Sun to sign a new recording deal with CBS/Columbia. (Johnny Cash° will follow within months.)

May *Pink Pedal Pushers* reaches US #91.

Oct Jay Perkins, never fully recovered from the car crash 2 years before, and since diagnosed as having cancer, dies.

1959 June *Pointed Toe Shoes* peaks at US #92, and will be his last US pop chart entry.

1963 He leaves Columbia for US Decca (but will have no successful recordings on the label). He tours Europe for the first time, playing US bases in France, Italy and West Germany.

1964 May [9] He opens his first major UK tour, co-headlining with Chuck Berry°, at Finsbury Park Astoria, London. Also on the bill are The Animals° and The Nashville Teens. (His arrival at London airport has been greeted by fans holding a banner proclaiming "Welcome Carl 'Beatle Crusher' Perkins". In fact, The Beatles° are ardent fans and play a jam session with him the first time their touring paths cross, which inspires the group to cut three Perkins compositions (of the many they have traditionally played on stage) before the end of the year.)

May Perkins records *Big Bad Blues* with backing by The Nashville Teens, in London. It does not chart, despite his touring success.

Oct The Beatles'° revival of Perkins' *Matchbox* reaches US #17.

Oct [18] Perkins returns to UK for a second successful tour, with The Animals° and Gene Vincent°.

Dec The Beatles° revive two more Perkins songs – *Honey Don't* (original B-side of *Blue Suede Shoes*) and *Everybody's Trying To Be My Baby* – on their chart-topping LP *Beatles For Sale* (*Beatles '65* in US). These covers earn Perkins more in songwriter royalties than he has earned from all his own post-*Blue Suede Shoes* recordings.

1966 Perkins signs to country label Dollie Records, where he will cut a series of highly-rated, but non-charting, singles like *County Boy's Dream* and *Lake County Cotton Country*.

1967 He joins Johnny Cash's° touring revue (and will spend several years playing back-up guitar for Cash and performing in his own right in the shows). He is featured in Cash's weekly TV show, and in his documentary movie and million-selling LP recorded at San Quentin prison, among other notable appearances. Both Cash and Perkins forswear alcohol and pills which have been threatening to blight their lives and support each other with a joint "dry" pact. They also become born-again Christians.

1969 Feb *Daddy Sang Bass*, a Perkins song recorded by Cash°, reaches US #42.

1970 Jan Back with CBS, he collaborates on LP *Boppin' The Blues* with rock revival band NRBQ, which backs him on several remakes of his early hits.

1971 He writes songs for the soundtrack of Robert Redford movie *Little Fauss and Big Halsy*.

1974 Perkins signs to Mercury Records' country label, cutting LP *My Kind Of Country*, and singles which include a revival of Kenny Rogers'° *Ruby (Don't Take Your Love To Town)*.

Dec His brother Clayton, troubled with a severe drink problem, takes his own life (shortly before Perkins' father dies of cancer).

1976 He launches his own production company and label, Suede Records, in US. He also leaves the Johnny Cash° troupe after 9 years on the road, and launches his own new road band which includes his two sons.

1977 Oct Following Elvis Presley's° death, he releases tribute single *The EP Express*, largely made up from titles of Presley hits.

1978 Apr In a brief deal with UK Jet label, Perkins records LP *Ol' Blue Suedes Is Back*, containing remakes of his early material, which is given TV promotion (and also supported by a tour), and reaches UK #38 – the only hit LP of his career.

1981 Apr [23] Perkins, Johnny Cash° and Jerry Lee Lewis° record a joint session in Stuttgart, Germany, which will result in LP *The Survivors* (a reference to the Dec. 1956 "Million Dollar Quartet" session).

Apr Paul McCartney° invites Perkins to the sessions for his LP *Tug Of War*, writing one song, *Get It*, as a duet for the pair.

1985 Feb Perkins appears as Mr. Williams, a nightclub bouncer, in John Landis' film *Into the Night*.

Mar He cuts a new version of *Blue Suede Shoes* for the soundtrack of film *Porky's Revenge*, backed by Lee Rocker and Slim Jim Phantom of The Stray Cats°.

Oct [21] At Limehouse Studios, London, a TV special is taped to mark the 30th anniversary of *Blue Suede Shoes*. It consists of a performance by "Carl Perkins and Friends", the latter including George Harrison°, Ringo Starr°, Eric Clapton°, Dave Edmunds° (who co-ordinates the band and music), and The Stray Cats'° Rocker and Phantom.

1986 Jan [1] "Blue Suede Shoes" TV special has its first showing, on UK Channel 4 TV. (It will also be released as a home video.)

Dec [1] A Coca-Cola commemorative bottle goes on sale in Perkins' hometown of Jackson, Miss., at $10 apiece. Proceeds go to the Carl Perkins Child Abuse Center, founded in 1982.

1987 Jan [21] Perkins is inducted into the Rock'n'Roll Hall of Fame.

PETER AND GORDON

Peter Asher (vocals)
Gordon Waller (vocals)

1959/63 Asher (b. June 22, 1944, London, UK) and Waller (b. June 4, 1945, Braemar, Scotland) both sons of doctors, meet at Westminster Boys' School and are part of a quasi-Shadows° trio, playing school events and coffee bars.

1964 Jan EMI's A&R chief Norman Newell hears them during a 2-week booking at London's Pickwick Club. They are summoned to EMI to record one of their own compositions, *If I Were You*.

Jan [21] Cajoling Paul McCartney°, then Asher's sister Jane's boyfriend, into finishing a song he had started, the duo rushes to record it at EMI.

Mar *A World Without Love* enters UK chart and gives the duo a #1 debut with 2 weeks in the top slot.

May *A World Without Love* hits US #1 and tops charts in 9 other countries.

June *Nobody I Know*, written by McCartney°, hits UK #10 and US #12. LP *A World Without Love* reaches US #21.

June [15] The duo flies to US, playing at New York's World Fair 4 days later.

Aug LP *Peter And Gordon* makes UK #18. EP *Just For You* reaches UK #20.

Sept Second EP *Nobody I Know* is released.

Oct *I Don't Want To See You Again* reaches US #16. Also a McCartney° composition, it surprisingly fails to make the UK top 50.

Nov Peter and Gordon appear on "The Ed Sullivan Show".

Dec LP *In Touch With Peter And Gordon* is released in UK. LP *I Don't Want To See You Again* makes US #95.

1965 Feb *I Go To Pieces*, given to them by Del Shannon° while on tour together in Australia, hits US #9 but has no UK success.

Apr *True Love Ways* hits UK #2 but only US #14. LP *I Go To Pieces* is released in US and climbs to #51.

July *To Know You Is To Love You* hits UK #5 and peaks at US #24. LP *True Love Ways*, released in US only, makes #49.

Oct LP *Hurtin' 'n' Lovin'* is released.

Nov Van McCoy song *Baby I'm Yours* reaches UK #19. A Barbara Lewis #11 hit 3 months previously in US, it is the flipside of *Don't Pity Me*, which reaches only US #83.

1966 Feb US-only LP *Peter And Gordon Sing And Play The Hits Of Nashville* is released.

Mar The duo releases *Woman*. Paul McCartney°, growing tired of people assuming his songs are only hits because he has written them, pens the song as Parisian student Bernard Webb. It reaches UK #28. In US, McCartney adds co-writing credit of A. Smith. It reaches US #14. LP *Woman*, released in US only, peaks at #60.

Apr The duo appears on final episode of NBC-TV's "Hullabaloo". *There's No Living Without Your Love* is a US-only hit at #40.

June *Don't Pity Me* is released in UK without success. LP *Peter And Gordon* is released.

July LP *The Best Of Peter And Gordon* is released in US making #72, while *To Show I Love You* reaches US #98.

Oct *Lady Godiva* makes UK #16, despite being banned in Lady Godiva's hometown of Coventry and being branded obscene by the city's mayor.

Nov *Lady Godiva* climbs to US #6. Its sales will total a million by 1967, the duo's fourth million-seller.

Dec LP *Somewhere . . .* is released.

1967 Jan *Knight In Rusty Armour* reaches US #15. LP *Lady Godiva* is released in US, making #80.

Mar LP *Knight In Rusty Armour* is released in US.

Apr *Sunday For Tea* makes US #31 and *The Jokers* makes US #97. They are the duo's final US chart entries and neither charts in UK.

June LP *In London For Tea* is released in US. Waller releases a US solo single *Speak For Me*.

1968 Jan Waller releases his first UK solo single, a cover of Jim Webb's *Rosecrans Boulevard*.

Feb *Never Ever* is released in US.

Apr *I Feel Like Going Out* is released in UK.

June *Every Day*, Waller's second solo single, will be followed at Christmas by *Weeping Analeah*, but both fail commercially.

Aug *You've Had Better Times*, released in UK in July, is the duo's last US single release. LP *Hot, Cold And Custard* is released in US.

Sept The duo splits. Asher becomes A&R manager at The Beatles'° Apple Records; Waller pursues a solo career.

Dec James Taylor's° eponymous debut LP is released, produced by Asher. Asher leaves Apple to develop his career as producer and manager (starting with James Taylor° in the 60s, through a host of artists in the 1970s, and is still producing acts in the 1980s, including 10,000 Maniacs). Waller releases a second US solo single *Every Day*.

1969 Apr Waller signs to Bell, releasing *I Was A Boy When You Needed A Man*. Like its three predecessors on Columbia, it fails to chart.

May *I Can Remember (Not Too Long Ago)* is the duo's final UK release.

1970 May Waller's *You're Only Gonna Hurt Yourself* is his final single release.

1972 Apr Waller's only solo LP *Gordon* is released. (It will be prefixed . . . *And Gordon* when released in US in May.)

1973 May Waller is cast as Pharaoh in the London production of Tim Rice and Andrew Lloyd Webber's musical *Joseph And His Amazing Technicolor Dreamcoat*.

THE PET SHOP BOYS

Neil Tennant (vocals)
Chris Lowe (keyboards)

1981 Aug Tennant (b. July 10, 1954, Gosforth, Northumberland, UK), who has already been in Newcastle-based folk outfit Dust and has a degree in history, is assistant editor of UK pop magazine *Smash*

THE PET SHOP BOYS *cont.*

Hits when, in a hi-fi shop in London's King's Road, he meets Lowe (b. Oct.4, 1959, Blackpool, UK), son of a jazz trombonist, who has been in 7-piece band One Under The Eight, where he learned keyboards, but is studying architecture. They write songs and record demos for 2 years and name themselves The Pet Shop Boys after friends who worked in an Ealing pet shop.

1983 Aug On assignment to interview Sting° for *Smash Hits* in New York, Tennant meets long-time hero, disco producer Bobby "O" Orlando, who offers to produce them.

1984 June Orlando-produced debut *West End Girls* becomes a cult success in France and Belgium but its UK release on Epic goes unnoticed and the duo is dropped.

Nov They sign with manager Tom Watkins.

1985 Feb After competitive bidding over new demos, EMI signs the duo.

July *Opportunities (Let's Make Lots Of Money)* fails to chart despite strong airplay.

Oct Re-recorded version of *West End Girls*, produced this time by Stephen Hague, is released and takes 3 months to make top 10 breakthrough.

1986 Jan *West End Girls* tops the UK chart for 2 weeks. The association with Hague is successful.

Apr Debut LP *Please* hits UK #3 while *Love Comes Quickly* makes UK #19.

May Remixed *Opportunities (Let's Make Lots Of Money)* is re-released and reaches UK #11, while *West End Girls* soars to US #1 and is a #1 hit in eight countries.

Aug *Opportunities (Let's Make Lots Of Money)* hits US #10. Despite pressure from the public, press and record company, the group refuses to tour anywhere, a policy it will always maintain. LP *Please* hits US #7.

Sept Extracted from it, fourth single *Suburbia* hits UK #8.

Oct *Love Comes Quickly* stalls at US #62.

Nov Six special 12"-mixes of hits from LP *Please* are repackaged as UK mini-LP *Disco*, which reaches UK #15.

1987 Jan A video collection of promo clips, *Television*, tops the UK music video chart. LP *Disco* makes US #95.

June After 6 months' writing and recording an LP, the duo releases *It's A Sin* which tops the UK chart and has similar success worldwide.

Aug [14] The duo performs *Always On My Mind* on UK TV special "Love Me Tender", marking the 10th anniversary of Elvis Presley's° death.

Aug A collaboration with Dusty Springfield° on 3-year old Tennant/Lowe composition *What Have I Done To Deserve This?*, produced by Hague, hits UK #2.

Sept LP *Actually* hits UK #2.

Oct *Rent*, The Pet Shop Boys' fifth UK top tenner, hits #8 and they spend 2 weeks promoting it in Japan.

Nov *It's A Sin* climbs to US #9 and LP *Actually* makes US #25.

Dec *Always On My Mind* is finally released as a single. It is the duo's first non-original single and becomes UK Christmas #1.

1988 Feb [8] The Pet Shop Boys win BPI Award as Best British Group. Dusty Springfield° joins them to sing *What Have I Done To Deserve This?* live at awards ceremony, as it hits US #2.

Feb The duo wins an Ivor Novello award for *It's A Sin* as International Hit of the Year.

Apr *Heart* tops the UK chart.

May *Always On My Mind* hits US #4. The repackaged US version of LP *Actually* is released in UK, including the previously omitted *Always On My Mind*.

June A Pet Shop Boys feature film, *It Couldn't Happen Here*, co-starring Joss Ackland, Neil Dickson, Barbara Windsor and Gareth Hunt, is released in UK, but interest is short-lived.

Sept *Domino Dancing* is released, followed by a 6-track LP containing *I'm Not Scared* (a song they wrote and produced for Eighth Wonder), a Frankie Knuckles house mix of *I Want A Dog*, a new version of *Always On My Mind* and two tracks produced by Trevor Horn.

TOM PETTY AND THE HEARTBREAKERS

Tom Petty (vocals and guitar)
Mike Campbell (guitar)
Ron Blair (bass)
Benmont Tench (keyboards)
Stan Lynch (drums)

1971 Petty (b. Oct.20, 1953, Gainesville, Fla., US), inspired by Elvis Presley°, whom he saw filming *Follow that Dream* on location near his home in Gainesville at age 7, leaves high school to join top local band Mudcrutch, which plays the Florida bar circuit successfully for 2 years.

1973 Petty takes a Mudcrutch demo tape to LA, and finds interest from seven record labels, including Denny Cordell's Shelter Records, which signs the band.

1974 Two Mudcrutch singles are released, but after moving to LA and recording an LP for Shelter, the band breaks up. (The LP is not released.)

1975 Cordell retains Petty on Shelter and suggests working solo, but he forms a new back-up band, The Heartbreakers, with ex-Mudcrutch members Campbell (b. Feb.1, 1954, Panama City, Fla.) and Tench (b. Sept.7, 1954, Gainesville), and recruiting Blair (b. Sept.16, 1952, Macon, Ga.) and Lynch (b. May 21, 1955, Gainesville).

1976 Nov Debut LP *Tom Petty And The Heartbreakers* is released, but initially sells poorly (only 6,500 after 3 months on release).

1977 May Petty's song *American Girl* is recorded by ex-Byrds° member Roger McGuinn (another of Petty's early influences). The group works hard on the road to promote itself and the debut LP (playing more than 200 dates in 1977 around US, Europe and UK). First notable sales of Petty's records are in UK.

June LP *Tom Petty And The Heartbreakers* makes UK #24.

July *Anything That's Rock'n'Roll*, taken from the LP, reaches UK #36.

Aug *American Girl*, also from the LP, peaks at UK #40.

1978 Feb A further LP extract, *Breakdown*, is the group's US chart debut at #40, while debut LP *Tom Petty And The Heartbreakers*, having entered the chart in Sept., makes US #55.

May The group appears in movie *FM*, about a California radio station. The Petty track *Breakdown* is included on the soundtrack LP, which hits US #5 and makes UK #37.

July Second LP, *You're Gonna Get It!*, reaches UK #34.

Aug LP *You're Gonna Get It!* makes US #23, and earns Petty's first gold disk. Extracted *I Need To Know* peaks at US #41.

Oct *Listen To Her Heart* reaches US #59.

1979 May [23] Petty files for Chapter XI Bankruptcy – the right to work out a reorganization of his debts. (This has partly arisen out of a record company dispute: Shelter has been sold to ABC, which has now been bought by MCA Records, and Petty is said to owe MCA $575,000 which will only be automatically repaid if he remains one of its acts and cuts six further LPs. MCA sues for breach of contract, but the bankruptcy declaration, revealing assets of only $56,000, causes the suit to be withdrawn as pointless. A solution is reached via the establishment of a new MCA-controlled label, Backstreet Records, to be run by Danny Bramson and devoted wholly to Petty and The Heartbreakers.)

Sept Petty hands over the tapes for a new LP, and tours US under the banner "Why MCA?".

Nov LP *Damn The Torpedoes* peaks at UK #57.

1980 Feb *Don't Do Me Like That* hits US #10, while its parent LP *Damn The Torpedoes* hits US #2 for 7 weeks (behind Pink Floyd's° *The Wall*), earning Petty his first platinum disk.

Mar *Refugee*, also from the LP, reaches US #15.

May The third extract from LP *Refugee*, *Here Comes My Girl* peaks at US #59.

1981 May LP *Hard Promises* makes UK #32. Petty has initially withheld the tapes for this, until MCA agrees not to implement a proposed one-dollar price rise to $9.98 on the US release. Petty (whose sales had accounted for almost 25% of MCA's 1980 profits) accuses the label of greed, and it backs down.

June *The Waiting* reaches US #19. Parent LP *Hard Promises* hits US #5, Petty's second platinum disk.

Aug *A Woman In Love (It's Not Me)* peaks at US #79.

Sept Stevie Nicks' *Stop Draggin' My Heart Around* with Petty and The Heartbreakers backing her, hits US #3 and makes UK #50.

1982 Blair leaves The Heartbreakers, to be replaced by Howard Epstein.

June [6] Petty plays at "Peace Sunday: We Have A Dream", an anti-nuclear concert to launch Peace week, at The Rose Bowl,

Pasadena, Cal. Also on the bill are Bob Dylan°, Jackson Browne°, Stevie Wonder°, and many more.

Sept [3] Petty plays the US Festival in San Bernardino, Cal., alongside Fleetwood Mac°, The Police°, Talking Heads°, and a host of other acts.

Nov LP *Long After Dark* makes UK #45.

1983 Jan LP *Long After Dark* hits US #9 (earning a gold disk), while extracted *You Got Lucky* reaches US #20.

Apr *Change Of Heart*, also from LP *Long After Dark*, makes US #21.

May Del Shannon° releases LP *Drop Down And Get Me*, produced by Petty and backed by The Heartbreakers.

1985 Apr LP *Southern Accents*, co-produced by Petty, Jimmy Iovine and Dave Stewart of Eurythmics°, reaches UK #23. *Don't Come Around Here No More*, taken from it, makes UK #50.

May LP *Southern Accents* hits US #7, earning another gold disk, while *Don't Come Around Here No More* reaches US #13.

July *Make It Better (Forget About Me)* makes US #54.

July [13] Petty and The Heartbreakers play at Live Aid in Philadelphia, Pa., US.

Sept *Rebels* peaks at US #74.

Sept [22] Petty plays at Farm Aid in US.

1986 Feb The group tours Australia, New Zealand and Japan, backing Bob Dylan°, as double live LP *Pack Up The Plantation* reaches US #22.

Mar *Needles And Pins*, with Stevie Nicks on backing vocals, makes US #37. Meanwhile, Bob Dylan°, with Petty and The Heartbreakers backing, releases *Band Of The Hand* (the theme song to the movie of the same title) on MCA.

June Petty begins a 40-date US "True Confessions" tour with Dylan°, preceded by a major concert for Amnesty International.

1987 Mar [4] Petty obtains a restraining order against B.F. Goodrich from exposing a song similar to Petty's *Mary's New Car*.

May [17] A fire damages Petty's house in LA – damage is estimated at $800,000.

May LP *Let Me Up (I've Had Enough)* peaks at UK #59.

July LP *Let Me Up (I've Had Enough)* reaches US #20.

Oct Petty and The Heartbreakers open a tour with Bob Dylan° in Israel, moving to Europe and UK.

1988 Nov Petty joins George Harrison°, Bob Dylan°, Roy Orbison° and Jeff Lynne of ELO° as The Traveling Wilburys. Their eponymous LP climbs the charts in both US and UK, as does extracted *Handle With Care*. Lynne co-produces new Petty LP *Songs From The Garage*, with contributions from Harrison and Orbison.

WILSON PICKETT

1961 Pickett (b. Mar.18, 1941, Prattville, Ala., US), having moved to Detroit as a teenager in 1955, has sung in gospel groups, before joining R&B band The Falcons, veterans of 1959 US #17 hit *You're So Fine*.

1962 May The Falcons' *I Found A Love*, with Pickett on lead vocal, reaches US #75.

1963 May Falcons producer Robert Bateman suggests that Pickett should go solo and arranges an audition with singer Lloyd Price°, owner of Double L label. Price signs him, and *If You Need Me*, a Bateman/Pickett composition, reaches US #64 (but a cover by better-known Solomon Burke° makes US #37).

Sept *It's Too Late* reaches US #49.

Nov *I'm Down To My Last Heartbreak*, his third on Double L, makes US #96.

1965 May Atlantic Records buys Pickett's contract, and after two unsuccessful releases (*I'm Gonna Cry* and *Come Home Baby*), producer Jerry Wexler records him at Stax studio in Memphis, with Booker T. and The MG's°.

Sept *In The Midnight Hour*, co-written by Pickett with MG's guitarist Steve Cropper, reaches US #21. It becomes a much-covered soul classic and Pickett gains the nickname "The Wicked Pickett" at Atlantic (often used in his publicity) – supposedly because of his interest in the ladies at the record company.

Oct *In The Midnight Hour* is his UK chart debut, at #12.

Dec *Don't Fight It* makes US #53 and UK #29, while LP *In The Midnight Hour* climbs to US #107.

1966 Jan *634-5789* reaches US #13 and UK #36, and is Pickett's first US R&B #1 (for 7 weeks).

Mar Pickett tours UK for live appearances, causing a sensation among the burgeoning UK mod and R&B audience.

July Staying with numbers for titles, *Ninety Nine And A Half (Won't Do)* makes US #53.

Sept Recorded at Muscle Shoals studios, Ala., Pickett's revival of Chris Kenner's *Land Of 1,000 Dances* (also a 1965 US top 20 for Cannibal & The Headhunters) is the only top 10 hit of this much-covered song, at US #6. It climbs to UK #22.

Oct LP *The Exciting Wilson Pickett* reaches US #21.

Dec *Mustang Sally*, written by Mack Rice (ex-The Falcons) peaks at US #23 and UK #28.

1967 Mar LP *The Wicked Pickett* makes US #42, while his revival of Solomon Burke's° *Everybody Needs Somebody To Love* reaches US #29.

Apr Pickett records a solo version of his Falcons success *I Found A Love*, which makes US #32.

July US radio airplay is divided on double-sided *Soul Dance Number Three/You Can't Stand Alone* which reaches US #55 and #70 respectively.

Sept Pickett's cover of Dyke & The Blazers' *Funky Broadway* (a minor hit in the spring) hits US #8 and R&B #1 (for 1 week). LP *The Sound Of Wilson Pickett*, containing the hit, reaches US #54.

Oct *Funky Broadway* reaches UK #43.

Nov A revival of former mentor Price's° million-seller *Stag-O-Lee* makes US #22, but is replaced by radio DJs playing B-side *I'm In Love*, which climbs to US #45. These are among several tracks cut at renewed sessions in Memphis, in partnership with Bobby Womack°.

Dec LP *The Best Of Wilson Pickett*, a compilation of his hit singles to date, peaks at US #35 (in a year-long chart run).

1968 Mar *Jealous Love* makes US #50, while LP *I'm In Love* reaches US #70.

May *She's Lookin' Good* makes US #15.

July *I'm A Midnight Mover*, a return to the style of *Midnight Hour*, makes US #24.

Aug LP *The Midnight Mover* peaks at US #91.

Oct *I Found A True Love* (not to be confused with *I Found A Love*) reaches US #42, while *I'm A Midnight Mover* makes UK #38 (after a year's absence on UK chart).

Dec *A Man And A Half* makes US #42.

1969 Jan Recording at Muscle Shoals again, Pickett covers The Beatles'° *Hey Jude* (at the suggestion of Duane Allman of The Allman Brothers°, who plays guitar on it), and it reaches US #23 while the original version is still on chart. It climbs to UK #16 (and will be Pickett's final UK chart entry).

Apr LP *Hey Jude* makes US #97 and *Minnie Skirt Minnie* peaks at US #50.

1970 May Pickett's rock cover (again with Duane Allman) of Steppenwolf's° *Born To Be Wild* reaches US #64.

June A cover of The Archies'° *Sugar Sugar*, a double A-side with tribute song *Cole, Cooke And Redding*, reaches US #25.

Aug A further rock cover, *Hey Joe*, reaches US #59, but its follow-up, a revival of *You Keep Me Hanging On*, makes only US #92.

Nov Recorded in Philadelphia with producers Kenny Gamble and Leon Huff and with a sharp new Pickett sound on original material, *(Get Me Back On Time) Engine Number 9* makes US #14 (and R&B #3). The LP from these sessions, *Wilson Pickett In Philadelphia*, reaches US #64.

1971 Mar Another Philadelphia production, *Don't Let The Green Grass Fool You*, makes US #17 (and R&B #2), and is his first certified million-selling single.

Apr Pickett headlines with other artists on a tour of Ghana, Africa, to celebrate the country's independence. (He features prominently in the movie and LP of the event, *Soul To Soul*.)

June *Don't Knock My Love, Pt 1*, recorded with Brad Shapiro and Dave Crawford in Miami, reaches US #13, and is Pickett's second million-seller.

July Compilation LP *The Best Of Wilson Pickett, Vol.II* reaches US #73.

Sept *Call My Name, I'll Be There* peaks at US #52.

1972 Feb A cover of UK band Free's° *Fire And Water* reaches US #24, while LP *Don't Knock My Love* peaks at #132.

July *Funk Factory* makes only US #58.

Nov Pickett's revival of the Randy Newman° song (and Three Dog Night° million-seller), *Mama Told Me Not To Come*, charts briefly at US #99, after which Pickett and Atlantic Records part company.

1973 Apr Pickett signs to RCA, but *Mr. Magic Man* manages a week at US #98, while LP of the same title reaches only US #187.

WILSON PICKETT *cont.*

Oct *Take A Closer Look At the Woman You're With* makes US #90 (Pickett's last US top 100 entry). (Three LPs and many singles follow on RCA in the next 3 years, none of them successful – but *Pickett In The Pocket*, another Pickett/Shapiro Miami production, is critically rated.)

1974 Nov [21] Pickett is arrested in Andes, New York, for possession of a dangerous weapon, after he pulls a gun during an argument. Frequently temperamental, especially when indulging his appetite for alcohol, Pickett has an offstage reputation to match his fiery passion while performing.

1978 Pickett makes widely vocal his contempt for the disco explosion, for its emasculation of the traditional soul style. He attempts to blend artistic preference with commercial necessity on LP *A Funky Situation*, produced by Rick Hall in Muscle Shoals, but it finds few sales.

1979 Pickett signs to EMI America, which will release two disco-influenced LPs, *I Want You* and *The Right Track*. Both fail. He is more successful on the US live circuit, reverting to his best-known material, and often touring with "The Soul Clan", an aggregation of his 1960s contemporaries like Eddie Floyd°, Don Covay and Joe Tex.

1988 Oct Pickett signs to Motown, cutting a new version of *In The Midnight Hour*, which reaches UK #62, and LP *American Soul Man*.

PINK FLOYD

Roger Waters (vocals, bass)
Rick Wright (keyboards)
David Gilmour (vocals, guitar)
Nick Mason (drums)

1965 Waters (b. Sept.9, 1944, Great Bookham, Cambridge, UK), Wright (b. July 28, 1945, London, UK) and Mason (b. Jan.27, 1945, Birmingham, UK) meet as students at the Regent Street Polytechnic in London. They are members of various college bands. Waters invites friend Syd Barrett (b. Roger Barrett, Jan.6, 1946, Cambridge) to join the trio in a new band, which Barrett names Pink Floyd after Georgia bluesmen Pink Anderson and Floyd Council. Late in the year the group plays its first gig, a mix of R&B and 12-bar blues, at The Countdown Club in London.

1966 Mar London's Marquee Club begins the "Spontaneous Underground", a Sunday afternoon psychedelic groove with Pink Floyd as regulars. The group drops its blues sound and begins playing extended musical numbers with Barrett writing the material. It quickly become the hippest band among London's early psychedelic set and experiments with feedback and electronic sound with back-projected film shows and lights.

Dec The group's reputation for experimentation and innovation continues with the establishment of The UFO Club which becomes the focal point of British psychedelia. Despite the name, the club is an Irish dance hall on other nights called The Blarney Club in a basement on London's Tottenham Court Road. Here the group verifies its future recorded sound with songs like *Interstellar Overdrive* and *Astronomie Domine*.

1967 Feb Pink Floyd records its first single *Arnold Layne*, but still has no record contract.

Mar EMI signs the group and purchases *Master Of Song*. (Legend has it that when introduced to label executives, one asked "Which of you is Pink?" – referred to on later LP *Wish You Were Here*.)

Apr *Master Of Song* peaks at UK #20. Surprisingly, despite the transvestite subject matter, BBC radio continues to play the record while pirate station, Radio London, bans it.

July *See Emily Play* hits UK #6. British DJ Pete Murray describes the group as a "con" on TV's "Juke Box Jury". They will not have another hit single for 12 years.

Aug Debut LP *The Piper At The Gates Of Dawn* hits UK #6.

Nov The group visits US for the first time. Barrett is developing LSD drug dependency. He appears on "The Pat Boone Show" to be interviewed and replies to questions with a blank stare. The group releases *Apples And Oranges* which fails to chart.

1968 Jan Barrett's behavior causes concern, and Waters invites friend Dave Gilmour (b. Mar.6, 1944, Cambridge) to join the group, excusing Barrett from live appearances to concentrate on songwriting.

Mar Barrett's attitude worsens as the group goes into commercial decline. He is asked to leave and the group reverts to a 4-piece minus its main songwriter.

Apr *It Would Be So Nice* is released but fails to chart.

June LP *A Saucerful Of Secrets* hits UK #9. The group plays the first-ever free concert in London's Hyde Park with Jethro Tull° and Roy Harper.

Dec *Point Me At The Sky* fails to chart.

1969 July Soundtrack LP of Barbet Schroeder's film *More* reaches UK #9.

Oct Double-set LP *Ummagumma*, consisting of one record of live performances and the other contributions from each member of the group, hits UK #5.

Dec Barrett releases his first solo single *Octopus* which fails to chart.

1970 Jan Barrett releases debut LP *The Madcap Laughs*, with help from Gilmour and Waters. It reaches UK #40. *Ummagumma* climbs to US #74.

Mar The group performs three songs on the soundtrack of Michaelangelo Antonioni's film *Zabriskie Point*.

Oct LP *Atom Heart Mother* defines the sound which will elevate Pink Floyd to worldwide superstar status in the next decade. It becomes the group's first UK chart-topper but reaches only US #55.

Nov Barrett releases LP *Barrett*. It proves to be his swan song and he returns to his hometown of Cambridge to become a recluse, resisting all efforts by Pink Floyd members and others to step back into the limelight. A sad, shambolic figure, he is a victim of drug abuse.

1971 Aug EMI releases compilation LP *Relics*. It contains first two singles which had been deleted and reaches UK #32 and US #152, .

Nov LP *Meddle* is released. Side two is taken up by *Echoes* which becomes a live favorite. The LP hits UK #3, climbing to US #70. In a *Melody Maker* poll, the group is voted second in best group category. The winners are Emerson, Lake and Palmer°.

1972 June Another soundtrack for Barbet Schroeder's film *Obscured By Clouds* hits UK #6 and becomes Pink Floyd's highest-charting LP in US at #46.

Sept Film (made for European TV) *Pink Floyd Live At Pompeii* receives its premiere at The Edinburgh Theatre. (It is released in 1974 in the cinema.)

1973 Mar LP *Dark Side Of The Moon* is released, a concept project dealing with madness which has taken most of the previous year to record. Sound effects and music are molded into Pink Floyd's most commercial outing. It sells more than 13 million copies worldwide and is the group's first US #1 (and still on the Billboard chart in 1988, 736 weeks later). It reaches only UK #2 despite a 294-week chart run. (In the 1980s CD boom, it is reported that there is a pressing plant in Germany that only produces *Dark Side Of The Moon* and no other CDs.) The group spends the rest of the year touring to perform the LP in its entirety with an appropriately grandiose stage production.

July Extracted track *Money* is released in US (but not UK), reaching #13.

1974 Jan *A Nice Pair*, a re-package of their first two LPs, makes UK #21 and US #36.

1975 July The group plays Knebworth Festival, Herts., UK and performs one of its most spectacular shows including real spitfire planes and quadrophonic sound.

Sept LP *Wish You Were Here* tops both UK and US charts. It contains a tribute to Syd Barrett, *Shine On You Crazy Diamond*, which is sung by Roy Harper. Violinist Stephane Grappelli makes an uncredited contribution on the LP.

1976 Dec The group makes headlines when film shoot for sleeve of LP *Animals* goes disastrously wrong. A 40' tall inflatable pig is moored above Battersea Power Station but breaks loose from its mooring. The Civil Aviation Authority issues a warning to all pilots in London airspace that a pig is on the loose. It is last sighted at 18,000' over Chatham, Kent, but is never seen again.

1977 Feb LP *Animals* hits UK #2 and US #3. The group spends the rest of the year touring with the "Animals" stage show.

1978 The group members concentrate on solo projects. Mason produces British punk band The Damned's° second LP *Music For Pleasure* and Steve Hillage's *Green*.

June Gilmour releases eponymously titled debut LP which reaches UK #17 and US #29. Wright releases his *Wet Dreams* debut, but it fails to chart.

1979 Despite enormous earnings, the group is in perilous financial state due to the collapse of investment company, Norton Warburg, which has handled its business affairs. Waters comes to the forefront as a writer, composing almost all of the group's forthcoming LP *The Wall*.

Dec LP *The Wall* hits UK #3 and tops US chart for 15 weeks. Taken from it, *Another Brick In The Wall (Part II)* is UK Christmas #1, and will top the US chart in Jan.

1980 The group tours with a "Wall" show which explores the theme of the group's alienation from its audience. One of the most celebrated stage spectaculars in rock history, a 160' long, 30' high wall is built between group and audience and then ceremoniously destroyed after the intermission. Due to its enormous financial outlay, the show is only performed 29 times and is a loss. Wright leaves the band after the tour due to personal differences with Waters.

May *Run Like Hell* reaches US #53.

1981 May Mason releases solo LP *Nick Mason's Fictitious Sport*.

Dec Greatest hits collection *A Collection Of Great Dance Songs* makes UK #37 and US #31.

1982 Movie version of *The Wall*, directed by Alan Parker and starring Bob Geldof, premieres.

Aug *When The Tigers Break Free* climbs to UK #39.

1983 Apr LP *The Final Cut* is released, giving the group its third UK #1 and hitting US #6. The LP, co-produced with Michael Kamen, has an anti-war theme and is almost entirely the work of Waters.

May *Not Now John* reaches UK #30. In a career spanning 16 years, it is only Pink Floyd's fifth UK hit. The division between Waters and the other two members proves divisive and they split acrimoniously.

1984 Mar Gilmour releases second solo LP *About Face*, which reaches UK #21 and US #32.

May Waters releases his first solo opus *The Pros And Cons Of Hitch Hiking* which makes UK #13 and US #31. He embarks on a major tour which will be a financial disaster, lacking the Pink Floyd brand name. Gilmour plays a variety of sessions including Bryan Ferry's° LP *Bete Noire*, Grace Jones'° *Slave To The Rhythm* and Arcadia's *So Red The Rose*.

1987 Gilmour and Mason reunite to record again. They decide their project should be under the Pink Floyd banner, but Waters claims in court they have no right to use the name. Wright returns to the group on a salary and the group wins temporary rights against Waters to continue with the name.

Sept The group releases LP *A Momentary Lapse Of Reason* which hits UK and US #3. Extracted *Only Learning To Fly* is released on CD only in UK, but fails to chart.

Sept [7] "The Momentary Lapse of Reason" world tour starts in Ottawa, Canada.

Dec *On The Turning Away*, extracted from LP *A Momentary Lapse Of Reason*, peaks at UK #55.

1988 Jan Waters reaches UK #54 with *The Tide Is Turning (After Live Aid)*. His LP *Radio K.A.O.S.* stalls at UK #85.

June *1 Slip*, taken from LP *A Momentary Lapse Of Reason*, makes UK #50.

Aug "The Momentary Lapse of Reason" tour visits UK with sold out dates at Wembley Stadium, London. At Manchester City Football Club's Maine Road ground concert, video cameras spy on the crowd to spot drug use. Nine arrests are made.

Sept The tour concludes at The Nassau Coliseum, New York. In the 12 months on the road, the band will have been seen by more than 10 million people at 155 concerts in 15 different countries as a new generation of Pink Floyd fans tunes in to its music.

GENE PITNEY

1959 Pitney (b. Feb.17, 1941, Hartford, Conn., US), having grown up in Rockville, Conn., where he started writing songs while still at high school, makes his first single, self-penned *Classical Rock And Roll*, as half of the duo Jamie and Jane, with Ginny Mazarro, on Decca. It does not sell.

1960 Regularly making demos of his songs and sending them to a New York music publisher, Pitney has his first cover, when The Kalin Twins (of *When* fame) record *Loneliness*.

Nov Pitney's *Today's Teardrops* is recorded by Roy Orbison° as B-side of *Blue Angel*, which hits US #9.

1961 Jan His first top 10 success as a writer is with *Rubber Ball*, recorded by Bobby Vee°. The song is credited to "Orlowski" (his mother's maiden name) because of publishing complications.

Feb He quits the University of Connecticut, where he has been studying electronics, to concentrate on music. *(I Wanna) Love My Life Away*, recorded as a demo on 4-track equipment, with Pitney singing all parts and playing most of the instruments (and costing $30 – the session fee to the bass player), is placed with Musicor Records, distributed through United Artists. It is Pitney's US chart debut, reaching #39 after heavy promotion touring around radio and TV stations.

Apr *I Wanna Love My Life Away* makes UK #26.

May Ricky Nelson° has a US and UK top 10 hit with Pitney's song *Hello Mary Lou*. (It will become one of his most revived songs.)

June *Louisiana Mama* fails to chart.

Sept Goffin/King° song *Every Breath I Take*, co-produced at Bell Sound Studios in New York by Phil Spector (part of a fully orchestral four-song session which costs an astronomical $13,000), makes US #42, and will be best remembered by its extended falsetto ending – a product of Pitney's heavy cold during the session.

1962 Jan *Town Without Pity*, the Ned Washington/Dmitri Tiomkin-penned theme from Kirk Douglas film of the same name, reaches US #13.

Mar *Town Without Pity* makes UK #32.

June *(The Man Who Shot) Liberty Valance*, written by Bacharach and David as the theme to John Wayne/James Stewart western movie of the same title (though not used on the soundtrack because the film is released early without it), hits US #4.

Nov Another Bacharach/David song, *Only Love Can Break A Heart*, hits US #2, and is Pitney's first million-seller. It is kept from the top by his own composition *He's A Rebel*, which he has given to Phil Spector for The Crystals°. *Only Love*'s B-side, *If I Didn't Have A Dime (To Play The Jukebox)*, peaks at US #58.

1963 Feb LP *Only Love Can Break A Heart* reaches US #48, while *Half Heaven – Half Heartache*, co-written by Pitney's publisher Aaron Schroeder, reaches US #12.

May *Mecca* makes US #12, while LP *Gene Pitney Sings Just For You* peaks at US #85.

Aug *True Love Never Runs Smooth*, another Bacharach/David ballad, makes US #21, while LP *World Wide Winners* climbs to US #41.

Sept He begins acting lessons.

Dec *24 Hours From Tulsa* reaches US #17, while LP *Blue Gene* makes US #105.

1964 Jan Boosted by a promotional visit to UK, in which Pitney appears widely on TV, Bacharach/David's *24 Hours From Tulsa* becomes his first major UK success, hitting UK #5. After having to return to US because of illness, he visits UK again after the single is established on the chart for a full UK tour.

Feb *That Girl Belongs To Yesterday*, written by The Rolling Stones'° Keith Richard and Mick Jagger, makes US #49. (Pitney has met The Rolling Stones via their manager Andrew Oldham, who is also his UK publicist, and has also been present at the sessions for their first LP and played piano on *Not Fade Away*.)

Apr *That Girl Belongs To Yesterday* hits UK #7, as does his LP *Blue Gene*. Compilation LP *Gene Pitney's Big Sixteen* makes US #87.

May *Yesterday's Hero* peaks at US #64, and is not released in UK. (Its substitute *I'm Gonna Find Myself A Girl* fails to chart in UK.)

Oct *It Hurts To Be In Love* hits US #7 and makes UK #36.

Nov LP *It Hurts To Be In Love* climbs to US #42.

Dec *I'm Gonna Be Strong*, written by Barry Mann and Cynthia Weil,

GENE PITNEY *cont.*

hits US #9 and UK #2, where it is held off the top by The Rolling Stones'° *Little Red Rooster* and then The Beatles'° *I Feel Fine*. It becomes one of his most celebrated records because of its falsetto final notes (which Pitney will always reproduce on stage).

1965 Feb Compilation LP *Gene Pitney's Big 16* reaches UK #12.

Mar *I Must Be Seeing Things* makes US #31 and hits UK #6. LP *I'm Gonna Be Strong* reaches UK #15, while a Nashville-recorded LP of country songs duetted with George Jones, *George Jones And Gene Pitney*, makes US #141.

Apr *I've Got Five Dollars And It's Saturday Night*, a duet with Jones from the LP, stalls at US #99.

June *Last Chance To Turn Around* reaches US #13.

July Another Mann/Weil song, *Looking Through The Eyes Of Love* (with *Last Chance To Turn Around* on the B-side) hits UK #3. LP *I Must Be Seeing Things* makes US #112.

Aug *Looking Through The Eyes Of Love* makes US #28.

Sept LP *Looking Through The Eyes Of Love* climbs to US #43 and heads for UK #15.

Dec *Princess In Rags* makes US #37 and hits UK #9.

1966 Jan Pitney comes second in the San Remo Song Contest in Italy, with *Nessuno Mi Puo Guidicare*.

Mar *Backstage* hits UK #4, as compilation LP *Big Sixteen, Volume 3* climbs to US #123.

May *Backstage* makes US #25. A film role is mooted for Pitney in movie *Sweet Wind of Spring*, but the Italian-based production does not materialize.

July Having failed to chart in US, *Nobody Needs Your Love*, written by Randy Newman°, hits UK #2, behind The Kinks'° *Sunny Afternoon*.

Oct LP *Nobody Needs Your Love* reaches UK #13.

Nov He appears in the Royal Variety Show at the London Palladium in UK.

Dec A second Newman° composition, *Just One Smile*, hits UK #8, while new compilation LP, *Greatest Hits Of All Times*, climbs to US #61.

1967 Jan *Just One Smile* stalls at US #64. Meanwhile, while in San Remo for the annual song festival, Pitney marries Lynne Gayton. (They will have two sons, Christopher and Todd.)

Mar LP *Young, Warm And Wonderful* climbs to UK #39.

Apr Compilation LP *Gene Pitney's Big Sixteen* peaks at UK #40.

Nov *(In The) Cold Light Of Day* makes UK #38.

Dec *Something's Gotten Hold Of My Heart*, a British song by Roger Cook and Roger Greenaway, hits UK #5.

1968 Apr *Somewhere In The Country* makes UK #19.

July *She's A Heartbreaker*, an outright R&B performance of a song written by Charlie Foxx and Jerry Williams ("Swamp Dog"), reaches US #16.

Sept LP *She's A Heartbreaker* creeps to US #193.

Nov *Billy You're My Friend* stalls at US #92, while *Yours Until Tomorrow*, a Goffin/King° song, makes UK #34.

1969 Mar UK-composed (by Tony Hazzard) *Maria Elena* reaches UK #25.

Oct Compilation LP *Best Of Gene Pitney* hits UK #8.

1970 Jan *She Lets Her Hair Down (Early In The Morning)*, an adaptation of the Silvikrin shampoo TV ad, stalls at US #89.

Mar *A Street Called Hope*, another Cook/Greenaway song, makes UK #37.

Oct *Shady Lady* reaches UK #29.

1973 May *24 Sycamore*, written by Les Reed and Barry Mason, and previously recorded by UK singer Wayne Fontana°, makes UK #34.

1974 May Pitney signs a new worldwide recording deal with UK label Bronze Records.

Aug His first Bronze release, *Blue Angel*, peaks at UK #39. After voice strain and some bouts of ill-health, he cuts down on his previously almost continuous worldwide touring, restricting it to 6 months in each year, to spend the other half at home with his family.

1975 Apr [10] The Gene Pitney Appreciation Society presents him with a plaque in honor of his regular twice-annual UK tours. The presentation is made during a tour, on stage at the Fiesta club, Sheffield, UK.

Oct Alan O'Day-penned *Train Of Thought* on Bronze collects good UK airplay, but fails to chart, as does Bronze LP *Pitney '75*.

Nov He opens a UK concert tour to promote both records, at Batley Variety Club, Yorks.

1976 Oct TV-promoted compilation LP *His 20 Greatest Hits* hits UK #6.

1977 Jan He signs to Epic Records, but three singles during the year all fail, and the deal is not extended.

1978 Dec Still a twice-annual UK visitor, he plays the London Palladium supported by Co-Co, the group which has performed UK's entry in the 1978 Eurovision Song Contest.

1988 Dec After many years away from recording (though still touring all over the world for between 6 and 8 months each year), Pitney adds guest vocals to a new version of his hit *Something's Gotten Hold Of My Heart*, by UK singer Marc Almond, formerly of Soft Cell°.

ROBERT PLANT

1966 Nov Plant (b. Aug.20, 1948, West Bromwich, Staffs., UK) makes his recording debut as a member of Birmingham, UK-based band Listen, on *You Better Run* for CBS Records.

1967 He cuts two solo singles for CBS, but neither *Our Song* nor *Long Time Coming* sells. He also sings on The Exceptions' *The Eagle Flies On Friday*, another chart failure. He joins Birmingham group Band of Joy, which releases no records (an LP of its archive material will be issued by Polydor in 1978).

1968 While debating whether to join Alexis Korner's new band as singer, he is asked by Jimmy Page to join The New Yardbirds (who become Led Zeppelin°). Plant is lead singer with Led Zeppelin (until the band splits after the death of drummer John Bonham in Dec.1980).

1979 Dec [29] Plant sings with Dave Edmunds'° band Rockpile in the third "Concert for the People of Kampuchea" at London's Hammersmith Odeon.

1981 Apr Plant begins a solo career, playing live with his part-time band, The Honeydrippers. The band will make occasional appearances in London and Birmingham, playing R&B and blues covers, and he will also work with The Big Town Playboys.

1982 July Plant's first solo LP *Pictures At Eleven*, released on Led Zeppelin's° SwanSong label, hits UK #2 and US #5.

Oct Extracted from it, *Burning Down One Side* makes UK #73 and US #64.

Nov *Pledge Pin* peaks at US #74.

1983 June Due to have his live set shown on UK TV show "The Tube", Plant, dissatisfied with his performance, vetoes its transmission.

July *Big Log* reaches UK #11 and US #20 and he appears on BBC TV's "Top of the Pops" (which Led Zeppelin° would never agree to do) to sing it. LP *The Principle Of Moments* hits UK #7 and US #8.

1984 Jan *In The Mood* reaches US #39.

Nov After Plant tours with The Honeydrippers, mini-LP *The Honeydrippers, Vol.1* hits US #4 and UK #56. The group line-up on it is Plant, Jimmy Page, Jeff Beck° and Chic's° Nile Rodgers, who also produces.

1985 Jan The Honeydrippers' revival of Phil Phillips' *Sea Of Love*, from the mini-LP, hits US #3 and makes UK #56.

Feb The Honeydrippers' *Rockin' At Midnight* reaches US #25.

June LP *Shaken 'N' Stirred* makes UK #19 and US #20.

July *Little By Little*, taken from the LP, reaches US #36.

July [13] Plant plays Live Aid in Philadelphia in a one-off Led Zeppelin° reunion (with Phil Collins° on drums).

1986 Jan Plant, Page, Jones and Tony Thompson rehearse in a small hall near Bath, UK, with the idea of reviving Led Zeppelin°, but after a few days the rehearsals are abandoned.

Mar With several other Birmingham-based acts, he plays the "Heartbeat 86" benefit show for a children's hospital.

1988 Feb Plant plays live in Folkestone, Kent, UK, with his new band, credited as The Band of Joy (for one night only). The line-up is Plant, Doug Boyle (guitar), Phil Johnstone (keyboards) and Chris Blackwell (drums). All are young Led Zeppelin° fans who have sent Plant a demo tape which impressed him. (Johnstone is also the writer of the group's material and he and Plant have collaborated on *Heaven Knows* and *Tall Cool One* for Plant's new LP.) *Heaven Knows* reaches UK #33.

Apr LP *Now And Zen*, with a guest appearance from Jimmy Page and sampled Led Zeppelin° tracks, hits UK #10 and US #7.

May Plant plays with Led Zeppelin° on another one-off reunion at Atlantic Records' 40th Anniversary concert at New York's Madison Square Garden (with John Bonham's son Jason on drums).

July Plant guests on Page's LP *Outrider*. *Tall Cool One*, used in US TV ads for Coca-Cola, reaches US #25.

Sept *Ship Of Fools* makes US #84.

THE PLATTERS

Tony Williams (lead vocals)
David Lynch (vocals)
Paul Robi (vocals)
Herb Reed (vocals)
Zola Taylor (vocals)

1953 The group is formed as a doo-wop quartet in Los Angeles, Cal., US, by lead singer Williams (b. Apr.5, 1928), Lynch, Reed and Alex Hodge, and while performing in LA clubs they meet manager/producer Buck Ram.

1954 Feb [15] Ram signs The Platters to a management agreement.

May At Ram's instigation, female singer Taylor from The Teen Queens joins the group to widen and sweeten the vocal blend.

July Hodge has a run-in with the law and is forced to leave the group. Ram recruits Robi, completing the line-up of The Platters, which will become the most successful black group of the 50s. The group is signed to Federal Records, an R&B subsidiary of King, but debut release *Only You (And You Alone)* fails to chart. Ram provides the group with excellent live bookings, and their financial success persuades another LA vocal group, The Penguins, to sign to Ram's management company.

1955 After The Penguins score a million-seller on independent Dootone label with *Earth Angel*, Mercury Records approaches Ram in an attempt to sign them. He agrees on condition that Mercury makes it a package deal and signs The Platters too.

Nov Signed to Mercury, the group debuts with a new version of *Only You (And You Alone)*, which hits US #5. Given an initial push by DJ Hunter Hancock, its success is stronger in the pop field than R&B, to Mercury's surprise – but not to Ram's, who is concerned that The Platters should be considered a popular ballad, rather than R&B, group. The first successful single enables him to persuade the label's A&R and promotional departments likewise.

1956 Feb *The Great Pretender* tops the US chart for 2 weeks, selling over a million, and B-side *I'm Just A Dancing Partner* makes US #87. (Ram has told Mercury that *The Great Pretender* will be the next hit before he has even written a song to go with the title.)

May *(You've Got) The Magic Touch* hits US #4 and is a second million-seller. B-side *Winner Take All* makes US #50.

July The group's debut LP *The Platters* hits US #7.

Aug *My Prayer* (offered by its English lyricist Jimmy Kennedy to Ram after he has heard *The Great Pretender*) tops the US chart for 5 weeks, earning another gold disk, while B-side *Heaven On Earth* makes US #39.

Sept In UK, *The Great Pretender* is coupled with *Only You*, and is the group's debut, hitting UK #5.

Nov *You'll Never Never Know* reaches US #11, while B-side *It Isn't Right* makes US #23. Meanwhile, *My Prayer* hits UK #4.

1957 Jan *On My Word Of Honor* reaches US #20 and B-side *One In A Million* makes US #31. Double A-side *You'll Never Never Know/It Isn't Right* peaks at UK #23.

Feb LP *The Platters, Volume Two* reaches US #12.

Apr *I'm Sorry* reaches US #19 and B-side *He's Mine* makes US #23.

June *I'm Sorry* reaches UK #18.

July *My Dream* makes US #24.

Nov *Only Because*, peaking at US #65, is the group's first US top 50 failure since signing to Mercury.

1958 Mar *Helpless* peaks at US #56.

Apr *Twilight Time*, co-written by Ram in 1944 with The Three Suns (who had a major hit with it at the time), and originally issued as B-side of *Out Of My Mind*, is premiered on "Dick Clark's Saturday Night TV Show", from which it goes on to top the US chart for a week, and become another million-seller. Mercury also produces a film clip of the group singing the song, which it promotes to US TV shows – an early ancestor of the music video.

July B-side *You're Making A Mistake* makes US #50. *Twilight Time* hits UK #3.

Oct The group plays an extended European tour and, while performing in Paris, records *Smoke Gets In Your Eyes*. Meanwhile, *I Wish* makes US #42 and B-side *It's Raining Outside* creeps to US #93.

1959 Jan *Smoke Gets In Your Eyes*, originally a 1934 chart-topper for Paul Whiteman and a Jerome Kern/Otto Harbach song from 1933 musical *Roberta*, is another million-seller, topping the US chart for 3 weeks.

Feb *Smoke Gets In Your Eyes* topples Elvis Presley's° *I Got Stung/One Night* from UK #1, where it stays for 5 weeks.

Apr LP *Remember When?* reaches US #15.

May *Enchanted* peaks at US #12.

July The title song from LP *Remember When* makes US #41.

Aug *Remember When* reaches UK #25.

Aug [10] The four male members of the group are arrested in Cincinnatti, Oh., having been found in flagrante delicto with four 19-year-old women (three of them white). The wide coverage of the arrest results in radio stations across US removing Platters records from playlists.

Oct *Where*, an adaptation of Tchaikovsky's *Symphonie Pathétique*, makes US #44. B-side *Wish It Were Me*, from film *Girls' Town*, peaks at US #61.

Dec [10] The male group members are acquitted of the charges of lewdness, assignation, and aiding and abetting prostitution, arising from their Aug. arrest. Judge Gilbert Bettman lectures them in court about responsibility to their public.

1960 Feb Another oldie, *Harbor Lights*, hits US #8 and UK #11. B-side *Sleepy Lagoon* peaks at US #65. Compilation LP *Encore Of Golden Hits* enters the US chart, on its way to hitting #6 during a 174-week stay in which it is certified gold.

May *Ebb Tide*, credited as by "The Platters featuring Tony Williams", makes US #56.

Aug *Red Sails In The Sunset* reaches US #36.

Nov *To Each His Own* makes US #21.

Dec Compilation LP *More Encores Of Golden Hits* reaches US #20.

1961 Williams leaves the group (and will sign as a soloist to Frank Sinatra's Reprise label later in the year). Sonny Turner replaces him as lead vocalist.

Feb *If I Didn't Care* makes US #30.

Feb [14] Ram and the group sue Mercury Records after the label refuses to accept recordings without Williams' lead vocal. Ram states that the contract does not stipulate who should sing lead, and that other members have previously done so on some 25% of Platters tracks.

Apr *Trees* peaks at US #62.

Sept *I'll Never Smile Again* makes US #25.

1962 Feb *It's Magic* stalls at US #91, and is the group's last hit for Mercury, and also its last chart entry for more than 4 years. Taylor leaves to go solo, as does Paul Robi. They are replaced by Sandra Dawn and Nate Nelson (ex-The Flamingos) respectively.

1966 June Now signed to Musicor Records, and with the traditional ballad style modified to more contemporary soul, The Platters make US #31 with *I Love You 1,000 Times* (also an R&B success).

July Musicor LP *I Love You 1,000 Times* climbs to US #100.

Dec *I'll Be Home*, a revival of 1956 Moonglows/Pat Boone° hit, peaks at US #97.

1967 Apr Motown-influenced *With This Ring* is the biggest chart success for the new-style Platters, reaching US #14.

Aug Also uptempo, *Washed Ashore On A Lonely Island In The Sea* makes US #56.

Nov *Sweet, Sweet Lovin'* peaks at US #70, and is the final Platters US chart entry. (The group will continue as a worldwide live nightclub attraction through the next 2 decades, still with Ram until Jean Bennett takes over in the mid-1980s.)

1969 Oct [18] The group appears on Richard Nader's first Rock'n'Roll Revival Concert at Madison Square Garden, New York, alongside Chuck Berry°, Bill Haley & His Comets°, and others.

1978 Apr Compilation LP *20 Classic Hits*, featuring 1950s Mercury repertoire and promoted via a nostalgic TV campaign, hits UK #8.

POCO

Richie Furay (guitar and vocals)
Jim Messina (guitar and vocals)
Rusty Young (pedal steel)
Randy Meisner (bass and vocals)
George Grantham (drums and vocals)

1968 Aug After the break-up of Buffalo Springfield°, the band forms as Pogo around ex-members Furay (b. May 9, 1944, Yellow Springs, Oh., US) and Messina (b. Dec.5, 1947, Maywood, Cal., US) who join Young (b. Feb.23, 1946, Long Beach, Cal.), Grantham (b. Nov.20, 1947, Cordell, Ok., US), both ex-Colorado band Boenzee Cryque, and Meisner (b. Mar.8, 1946, Scottsbluff, Neb., US) ex-Poor, and sign to Epic.

Nov The group makes its debut at LA's The Troubadour.

1969 Because of difficulties with owners of *Pogo* comic strip, they change name to Poco.

POCO *cont.*

Apr Meisner quits after a personality clash, and joins Rick Nelson's Stone Canyon Band. Timothy Schmit (b. Oct.30, 1947, Sacramento, Cal.) is invited to replace him, but turns it down to stay in college and avoid the draft. Poco continues as a four-piece.
June Debut LP *Pickin' Up The Pieces* enters US chart and reaches #63.
1970 Feb Invited a second time, Schmit joins. (He has been in Sacramento folk trio, Tim, Tom & Ron in 1962, becoming surf band The Contenders in 1963, before joining New Breed and then Glad.)
July Second LP *Poco* reaches US #58.
Nov *You Better Think Twice* makes US #72. Messina leaves for a solo career, replaced by Paul Cotton, (b. Feb.26, 1943) who joins from Illinois Speed Press, recommended by Chicago's° Peter Cetera.
1971 Feb Live LP *Deliverin'* reaches US #26.
May *C'mon* peaks at US #69.
Dec LP *From The Inside*, the group's first with Cotton, makes US #52.
1972 Feb Poco makes its live UK debut at London's Rainbow Theatre.
Nov The band appears on debut program of US ABC TV's "In Concert".
1973 Jan LP *Good Feelin' To Know* reaches US #69.
Sept Furay leaves to join Souther-Hillman-Furay Band.
Nov LP *Crazy Eyes* reaches US #38.
1974 June LP *Seven*, with the band as a four-piece, makes US #68.
Dec LP *Cantamos*, the last for Epic, peaks at US #76.
1975 July The group signs to ABC and releases *Head Over Heels*, which reaches US #43.
Aug Epic releases *The Very Best Of Poco*, which makes US #90.
Nov *Keep On Tryin'* reaches US #50.
1976 Apr Also on Epic, *Poco Live*, from their 1974 winter tour, peaks at US #169.
May LP *Rose Of Cimarron* makes US #89. The group begins a major US tour, supporting the Stills-Young band. When Young causes the tour to close and new member Al Garth quits, Poco comes close to disbanding.
Aug The title track from LP *Rose Of Cimarron* stalls at US #94.
Dec The group starts recording at Scoring Two studios, but leaves 3 weeks later to assess its future.
1977 May LP *Indian Summer*, with Poco virtually cutting its country roots and using the synthesizer playing of Steely Dan's° Donald Fagen, reaches US #57.
Sept Schmit leaves to join The Eagles° (replacing Meisner again), as *Indian Summer* makes US #50.
1978 Jan Grantham also leaves, to join Secrets.
Mar After exhaustive auditions, Britons Charlie Harrison and Steve Chapman are chosen.
Dec Kim Bullard (b. Atlanta, Ga., US), ex-Crosby, Stills & Nash's° US tour, joins on keyboards.
1979 Jan LP *Legend* earns the group its first gold disk, reaching US #14.
Mar *Crazy Love* is the band's biggest hit at US #17.
July *Heart Of The Night* makes US #20.
1980 July The band, now on MCA Records which has absorbed ABC label, releases LP *Under The Gun*. It reaches US #46.
Aug *Under The Gun* peaks at US #48.
Oct *Midnight Rain* stalls at US #74.
1981 July LP *Blue And Gray* makes US #76.
1982 Mar LP *Cowboys And Englishmen* climbs to US #131.
Dec Poco move to Atlantic Records for LP *Ghost Town*, which makes US #195.
1983 Feb *Shoot For The Moon* reaches US #50.
1984 June Furay reunites the early line-up for LP *Inamorata*, which makes US #167, as *Days Gone By* peaks at US #80.

THE POGUES

Shane McGowan (guitar and vocals)
Jem Finer (banjo)
James Fearnley (accordian)
Spider Stacy (tin whistle)
Caitlin O'Riordan (bass)
Andrew Ranken (drums)

1983 The band is formed in London by McGowan (b. Dec.25, 1957, Kent, UK), ex-punk band The Nipple Erectors (later The Nips), originally under the name Pogue Mo Chone ("kiss my arse" in Gaelic). It plays a mixture of country, rockabilly and assorted Scots and Irish folk.
1984 May Forming its own Pogue Mahone label, with independent distribution by Rough Trade, the band releases debut single *The Dark Streets Of London*, which is banned from daytime UK BBC radio play when the meaning of the group's name becomes apparent.

June Stiff Records picks up the single and signs the band, but insists the name is abridged (or censored) to The Pogues.
Nov Debut LP *Red Roses For Me*, produced by Stan Brennan, mixes group originals with traditional folk songs, and charts briefly at UK #83. Extracted *Boys From The County Hell* fails, despite the band's growing reputation as a live act.
1985 Apr *A Pair Of Brown Eyes*, produced by Elvis Costello°, reaches UK #72. The promotional video is filmed by Alex Cox (with whom the band will make a feature film).
June *Sally Maclennane* peaks at UK #51, aided by a special limited pressing in the shape of a shamrock.
Aug Following a successful UK Cambridge Folk Festival appearance and a headlining slot at a benefit concert for Nicaragua in Brixton, London, Costello°-produced LP *Rum, Sodomy And The Lash* (a title reportedly taken from Winston Churchill's description of life in the Royal Navy) reaches UK #13.
Sept *Dirty Old Town*, a revival of Ewan MacColl's folk song, makes UK #62. It is produced by Philip Chevron (ex-Radiators From Space), who joins The Pogues as guitarist.
1986 Jan The band makes its US live debut with a short tour – during which O'Riordan briefly walks out between New York shows, leaving Pogues roadie Darryl Hunt to deputize on bass.
Mar A plan to revive The Lovin' Spoonful's° *Do You Believe In Magic?* is shelved, and the band releases 4-track EP *Poguetry In Motion*, which climbs to UK #29.
Apr McGowan is hit by a London taxicab as he leaves a restaurant and suffers a fractured arm and torn ligaments.
May [16] O'Riordan marries Elvis Costello° in Dublin, Ireland.
May [17] The band appears in Dublin at the Self Aid concert (raising funds to help young Irish unemployed to set up in business), with U2°, Van Morrison°, Elvis Costello°, Chris De Burgh° and others.
June [20] The band plays UK's Glastonbury Fayre with The Cure°, Level 42°, The Housemartins° and many other acts.
Sept *Haunted*, written by O'Riordan and originally used on the soundtrack of Cox-directed film *Sid and Nancy*, peaks at UK #42 while most of the band are in Spain's Sierra Nevada with Cox, filming the surreal western *Straight To Hell*, in which they play the homicidal McMahon gang.
Nov O'Riordan leaves the group and Hunt takes over on bass.
1987 Mar [6] The band appears on Irish TV, with U2° and other guests, in a 25th anniversary celebration of Irish folk group The Dubliners.
Apr *The Irish Rover*, teaming The Pogues with The Dubliners, hits UK #8.
June The band has four songs on the soundtrack LP from *Straight To Hell*. The movie is released to mixed reviews. *The Good, The Bad And The Ugly* (from the film) is scheduled as a single, but then cancelled. Pogues manager Frank Murray persuades a close friend, veteran Irish musician Terry Woods, to join the band on concertina.

Nov After the collapse of Stiff, and its absorption by Trevor Horn's ZTT Records, the band's Pogue Mahone label is revived within the new set-up to release its records.

Dec *A Fairytale Of New York*, with seasonal lyrics (and some ripe language), intended as a McGowan/O'Riordan duet 2 years earlier, features Kirsty MacColl guesting in the female vocals. It hits UK #2 during Christmas week, kept off the top by The Pet Shop Boys'° *Always On My Mind*.

1988 Jan LP *If I Should Fall From Grace With God*, produced by Steve Lillywhite (MacColl's husband), hits UK #3. The band is on a 3-week US tour on which Joe Strummer, ex-The Clash° (and co-star of *Straight To Hell*) joins as a temporary member – adding The Clash hits *London Calling* and *I Fought The Law* to The Pogues' onstage repertoire.

Mar The title track from *If I Should Fall From Grace With God* is extracted but peaks at only UK #58.

Apr LP *If I Should Fall From Grace With God* reaches US #88.

July *Fiesta* makes UK #24.

THE POINTER SISTERS

Ruth Pointer (vocals)
Anita Pointer (vocals)
Bonnie Pointer (vocals)
June Pointer (vocals)

1969 Sisters Bonnie (b. July 11, 1951, East Oakland, Cal., US) and June Pointer, daughters of a minister at East Oakland Church of God, with a background almost entirely in religious music, begin to perform as a duo around San Francisco clubs, calling themselves Pointers. They are joined after a few months by sister Anita (b. Jan.23, 1948, East Oakland), who leaves a day job as a secretary.

1971 San Francisco promoter Bill Graham becomes the trio's manager, and local producer David Rubinson begins to hire them. They work extensively over the next 2 years as stage and session back-up vocalists for Elvin Bishop, Boz Scaggs°, Dave Mason, Taj Mahal and others.

1972 Ruth Pointer leaves an office job to join her sisters and Atlantic signs them to a recording deal, but *Don't Try To Take The Fifth*, produced by Wardell Quezergue, sells only moderately.

1973 Oct Freed from Atlantic and Bill Graham, the group is signed by David Rubinson to Blue Thumb Records, a subsidiary of ABC. *Yes We Can Can*, written by Allen Toussaint and produced by Rubinson, reaches US #11, while the group's first LP, *The Pointer Sisters*, makes US #13 and earns a gold disk.

1974 Feb A revival of Willie Dixon's Chicago standard *Wang Dang Doodle* peaks at US #61.

Apr LP *That's A Plenty*, again produced by Rubinson, makes US #82. They get extensive TV bookings, their visual image based on 1940s-type fashions.

Sept Double LP *Live At The Opera House*, recorded at the San Francisco Opera House, (which the group has been the first pop act ever to play), climbs to US #96.

Dec Country-styled *Fairytale*, written by Anita and Bonnie, reaches US #13 and makes US C&W #37 (with the group playing Nashville's Grand Ole Opry as part of a tour).

1975 Mar *Live Your Life Before You Die* peaks at US #89.

Mar [1] *Fairytale* wins a Grammy award as 1974's Best Country Vocal Performance by a Duo or Group.

Oct *How Long (Betcha' Got A Chick On The Side)* makes US #20 (having topped the R&B chart for 2 weeks), while parent LP *Steppin'* reaches US #22.

Dec *Going Down Slowly* peaks at US #61.

1976 Dec Double compilation LP *The Best Of The Pointer Sisters* makes US #164.

1977 Feb [4] The group takes part in the 25th anniversary edition of Dick Clark's "American Bandstand" on US ABC TV.

1978 Jan LP *Having A Party* climbs to US #176, as the group leaves Rubinson and Blue Thumb, suing the label for unpaid royalties. Meanwhile, Bonnie leaves her sisters to go solo, and signs to Motown.

1979 Feb The remaining trio signs to Richard Perry's new Planet label, where debut *Fire*, written by Bruce Springsteen° and produced by Perry (as will be the remainder of the group's output), hits US #2 (selling over a million), and parent LP *Energy* reaches US #13, earning a gold disk. Bonnie's Motown solo debut *Free Me From My Freedom/Tie Me To A Tree (Handcuff Me)*, peaks at US #58, and her LP *Bonnie Pointer* at US #96. *Everybody Is A Star*, a revival of Sly & The Family Stone's° 1970 hit, is the group's UK chart debut, at #61.

Apr *Fire* reaches UK #34.

May *Happiness*, written by Toussaint and taken from LP *Energy*, makes US #30.

Oct The sisters' LP *Priority* peaks at US #72 (spinning off no hit singles, though it has songs by Bob Seger°, Graham Parker°, Bruce Springsteen° and Jagger/Richard), while Bonnie revives The Elgins' *Heaven Must Have Sent You*, which reaches US #11.

1980 Feb A revival of The Four Tops'° *I Can't Help Myself (Sugar Pie, Honey Bunch)*, Bonnie's final solo hit, makes US #40, while her second solo LP (titled, like the first, *Bonnie Pointer* peaks at US #63. (She enters a legal dispute with Motown, which will prevent release of further solo material on the label.) Jerry Weintraub takes over the sisters' management.

Oct *He's So Shy* hits US #3 and is the group's second million-selling single, while parent LP *Special Things*, with session contributions from Ollie Brown, Nate Watts and Greg Phillinganes, makes US #34.

Dec *Could I Be Dreaming*, also from LP *Special Things*, peaks at US #52.

1981 Aug *Slow Hand* hits US #2 (their third gold single). It is taken from LP *Black And White*, which reaches US #12 and earns a gold disk.

Sept *Slow Hand* hits UK #10 and LP *Black And White* makes UK #21.

Dec Also from the LP, *Should I Do It* peaks at UK #50.

1982 Apr *Should I Do It* reaches US #13.

Aug *American Music* makes US #16. It is taken from LP *So Excited!*, which peaks at US #59 (and also includes a version of Prince's° *I Feel For You*, later a hit for Chaka Khan°).

Nov *I'm So Excited*, co-written by the sisters, and extracted from its near-namesake LP, reaches US #30, while compilation LP *The Pointer Sisters' Greatest Hits*, on Planet, creeps to US #178.

1983 Apr *If You Wanna Get Back Your Lady* peaks at US #67.

Nov *I Need You* heralds a new LP, and makes US #48.

1984 Apr *Automatic* hits US #5. It is also taken from LP *Break Out*, which hits US #8 (the sisters' only platinum LP) and UK #9.

May *Automatic* hits UK #2, behind Duran Duran's° *The Reflex*.

June *Jump (For My Love)*, also from LP *Break Out*, hits US #3 and UK #6.

Aug *I Need You*, belatedly released in UK, reaches #25.

Oct *I'm So Excited*, a remix of their 1982 chart success, hits US #9.

Nov Remixed *I'm So Excited* reaches UK #11.

1985 Jan *Neutron Dance*, from LP *Break Out* and also heard in film *Beverly Hills Cop*, makes UK #31.

Jan [28] The Pointer Sisters take part in the recording of USA For Africa's° *We Are The World*.

Feb *Neutron Dance* hits US #6.

Mar [2] The group wins a Grammy award for *Jump (For My Love)*, which is named Best Group Pop Vocal Performance of 1984.

Apr *Baby Come And Get It* makes US #44.

Aug *Dare Me* reaches US #11 and UK #17. It is from LP *Contact*, which makes UK #34.

Nov *Freedom* peaks at US #59.

1986 Jan The Pointer Sisters join Eddie Murphy, Bill Cosby, Bob Dylan° and Stevie Wonder° in concerts to celebrate the first observance of Martin Luther King Jr.'s birthday as a US national holiday.

Mar *Twist My Arm*, from LP *Hot Together*, stalls at US #83.

Dec Also from the LP, *Goldmine* makes US #33.

1987 Feb *All I Know Is The Way I Feel* stalls at US #93.

Sept *Be There*, from the soundtrack of film *Beverly Hills Cop II*, peaks at US #42.

Dec The Pointer Sisters contribute *Santa Claus Is Coming To Town* to the Special Olympics charity LP *A Very Special Christmas*.

1988 Dec Ruth contributes *Streets Of Gold* to the soundtrack of cartoon movie *Oliver and Company* with fellow artists Billy Joel°, Huey Lewis° and Bette Midler° among others.

THE POLICE

Sting (vocals and bass)
Andy Summers (guitar and vocals)
Stewart Copeland (drums, percussion and vocals)

1977 Jan [9] Copeland (b. July 16, 1952, Alexandria, Egypt), a US citizen drumming with progressive rockers Curved Air, (who are managed by Copeland's brother Miles) and bassist/vocalist Sting (b. Gordon Sumner, Oct.2, 1951, Wallsend, Northumberland, UK), an ex-primary school teacher, from jazz combo Last Exit, meet in London.

Jan [12] They begin rehearsing with guitarist Henri Padovani (b. Corsica) at Copeland's studio in his Mayfair apartment.

Feb [12] The Police records its first single, *Fall Out*, at Pathway studios. (The two sides cost £150 to record.)

Feb [21] The band begins rehearsals with New York singer Cherry Vanilla, to back her on a UK tour.

Mar [3] Cherry Vanilla, Johnny Thunders & The Heartbreakers and The Police tour starts at London's Roxy Club in Covent Garden.

Mar [19] The Police begins a tour of Holland, supporting Wayne County & The Electric Chairs.

May *Fall Out* is released on Copeland's Illegal label, selling out its initial pressing of 2,000 copies immediately and entering the UK independent chart.

May [28] After Gong reunites to play at the Circus Hippodrome in Paris, France, ex-Gong member Mike Howlett invites Copeland and Sting to join guitarist Summers (b. Andrew Somers, Dec.31, 1942, Poulton Le Fylde, Lancashire, UK) to play as Strontium 90. (Summers is ex-New Animals, Soft Machine, Kevin Ayers°, and has contributed to Neil Young's° LP *Everybody Knows This Is Nowhere*.) Summers adds an echo unit which, combined with Copeland's inverted reggae drum style, provides rhythm back-drop to forthcoming Sting lyrics.

June The Police plays London's Marquee, after which Summers is formally added to the line-up.

Aug [10] The Police records a session with producer John Cale°.

Aug [12] Padovani quits the band.

Aug [18] The Police plays its first gig as a trio at Rebecca's, Birmingham, UK.

Oct [22] The Police travels to Munich, West Germany, to record and play with Eberhard Schoener, for his EMI LP *Video Flashback*.

1978 Jan [13] The band begins recording its first LP at Surrey Sound studios with Nigel and Chris Gray engineering.

Feb [22] The Police appears in a Wrigley's Chewing Gum ad for US TV, having to dye their hair blond for it. (Mistakenly associated as part of UK's punk movement, the blond visual image will give the group a strong identity for the next 2 years.)

Mar [10] The Police supports US group Spirit° at the start of a UK tour promoted by Miles Copeland.

Mar [22] Miles Copeland secures an option deal with A&M Records to release *Roxanne*.

Apr *Roxanne* is released in UK but fails as the band, currently working with Schoener's Laser Theatre in West Germany, is unable to promote it.

July Copeland releases *Don't Care* under the name of Klark Kent. An eponymous 10-inch LP, on green vinyl, also fails.

Sept Sting, with many acting roles in TV commercials behind him, begins filming *Quadrophenia*, based on The Who's° LP. He plays the character Ace.

Oct The group's second A&M single, *Can't Stand Losing You*, makes UK #42.

Oct [16] The Police appears on UK BBC Radio 1's "Kid Jensen Show" before setting off on its first US tour.

Oct [20] US debut is at New York's CBGB's, at the start of a 23-date North American tour.

Nov First LP *Outlandos D'Amour* is released, with single *So Lonely*. The LP hits UK #6.

Dec A&M America does not release debut A&M single *Roxanne* and it is available only on import from UK. The single and other tracks from LP *Outlandos D'Amour* (recorded for only £3000) become popular with college radio. The band begins a UK tour, supporting Alberto Y Los Trios Paranoias.

1979 Feb [13] The Police begins work on its second LP at Surrey Sound studios.

Mar [1] The group embarks on a 29-date US tour at LA's The Whiskey.

Apr [25] The Police makes its debut on UK BBC TV's "Top of the Pops" as re-released *Roxanne* climbs the UK chart. The band heads back to US for its third tour, where the single reaches #32.

May *Roxanne* makes UK #12 as parent LP *Outlandos D'Amour* hits UK #6 and US #23.

June The group begins its first headlining UK tour.

July [24] The Police headlines Reading Rock Festival.

Aug Re-released *Can't Stand Losing You* hits UK #2, behind The Boomtown Rats'° *I Don't Like Mondays*.

Aug [11] Sting appears on UK BBC TV show "Juke Box Jury".

Aug [16] *Quadrophenia* premieres, as Sting turns down numerous film offers, including the villain in Bond film *For Your Eyes Only*. (He will, however, frequently appear in other films.)

Sept [10] *Message In A Bottle* is released as the group begins an 11-date UK tour, at The Assembly Rooms, Derby (ending at London's Hammersmith Odeon). It tops the UK chart after 2 weeks of release.

Sept [27] The Police plays New York's Diplomat Hotel at the start of a 2-month US tour (which will include a visit to Kennedy Space Center in Houston to film a video for forthcoming single *Walking On The Moon*).

Oct Second LP *Reggatta De Blanc*, co-produced by the group with Nigel Gray, hits UK #1 for 4 weeks. It will also reach US #25, where it will be issued as a double 10"-LP.

Nov *Fall Out*, originally released through Illegal label in 1977, makes UK #47.

Dec *Walking On The Moon* hits UK #1. Like every Police single released on A&M, it is written by Sting who now visually and musically dominates the line-up. *Message In A Bottle* stalls at US #74.

Dec [18] In the middle of a West German and UK tour, The Police plays London's Hammersmith Palais and Odeon on the same night. (The group makes the short journey between venues in an army personnel carrier, with 40 police officers on standby to maintain order.)

1980 Jan [20] The group plays the State University of New York, Buffalo, N.Y. at the start of its first world tour (which takes in 37 cities in 19 countries, ending in Sting's home town Newcastle, where it plays two charity concerts for the Northumberland Association of Boys' Clubs. The group sets up its own charity called The Outlandos Trust, headed by Conservative Member of Parliament Anthony Steen.)

Mar Re-issued *So Lonely*, the group's fourth UK top 10, hits #6.

June *Six Pack*, a collection of first Police singles, now on blue vinyl, makes UK #17, as Sting and Summers move to Eire for tax purposes.

July [7] The Police begins work on its third LP at Wisseloord studio in Hilversum, Holland.

July [26] The group headlines the "Reggatta De Bowl" charity gig at Milton Keynes, Beds., UK.

Aug [8] The band begins a month's tour of Europe at Wechter Festival in Belgium.

Sept [27] *Don't Stand So Close To Me* hits UK #1 for 4 weeks.

Oct [3] UK BBC TV airs "Police in the East" documentary.

Oct LP *Zenyatta Mondatta*, produced by Police and Nigel Gray, hits UK #1 for 4 weeks.

Oct [21] The Police begins a 33-date North American tour at the Winnipeg Arena, Canada.

Dec *De Do Do Do, De Da Da Da* hits UK #5.

Dec [14/16] The Police plays three concerts at Buenos Aires and Mar Del Plata in Argentina.

1981 Jan *De Do Do Do, De Da Da Da* hits US #10. LP *Zenyatta Mondatta* is the group's first US top 10, at #5. The Police begins a 2-month tour of North America, Japan, Australia and New Zealand in Montreal, Canada.

Feb [25] *Reggatta De Blanc* is named Best Rock Instrumental Performance at the 23rd annual Grammy awards ceremonies.

Mar [1] Sting begins work on UK BBC TV play "Artemis 81".

Apr *Don't Stand So Close To Me* hits US #10.

June [15] The Police begins recording its fourth LP at AIR studios in Montserrat, the Caribbean, with Hugh Padgham co-producing. The project is again filmed by UK BBC TV. (Hosted by Squeeze° member and TV presenter Jools Holland, it will air in UK at Christmas.)

Oct *Invisible Sun*, inspired by the troubles in Northern Ireland, hits UK #2, kept off the top by Adam and The Ants'° *Prince Charming*. Parent LP *Ghost In The Machine*, co-produced by Padgham, hits UK #1 at the start of a 3-week run.

Nov *Every Little Thing She Does Is Magic* tops the UK chart, the only cut from the LP recorded at Le Studio, Quebec, Canada.

Dec *Every Little Thing She Does Is Magic* hits US #3. *Spirits In The Material World* reaches UK #12.

1982 Jan LP *Ghost In The Machine* hits US #2 for 6 weeks.

Feb [24] The Police wins two awards at the 24th Grammy ceremonies: Best Rock Vocal Performance by a Duo or Group for *Don't Stand*

So Close To Me and Best Rock Instrumental Performance for *Behind My Camel.*

Mar *Spirits In The Material World* reaches US #11.

May *Secret Journey* makes US #46.

June [27] An out of court settlement is reached between Sting and Virgin Music over the contract concerning the copyright to Sting's early songs, originally signed in 1977.

July Copeland scores Francis Ford Coppola's movie *Rumble Fish*.

Sept [3] The group plays the US Festival in San Bernardino, Cal., alongside Fleetwood Mac°, Jackson Browne°, Talking Heads° and others.

Sept Sting's first solo single, a revival of *Spread A Little Happiness* from soundtrack of *Brimstone & Treacle*, makes UK #16.

Oct Summers releases solo instrumental LP *I Advance Masked* with King Crimson's° Robert Fripp.

1983 June *Every Breath You Take*, a Sting song concerning obsessive love, hits UK #1 for 4 weeks as parent LP *Synchronicity*, again recorded in Montserrat and Le Studio, Quebec, Canada, enters UK chart at #1, where it will stay for 2 weeks. Sting bases its lyrical direction strongly on written works by Arthur Koestler.

July *Every Breath You Take* hits US #1 for 8 weeks, helped by a Godley & Creme°-shot video on heavy US MTV rotation. LP *Synchronicity* hits US #1 for 17 weeks, achieving multi-platinum status.

Aug *Wrapped Around Your Finger* hits UK #7 and US #8.

Nov *Synchronicity II* reaches UK #17. *King Of Pain* hits US #3.

Dec *Synchronicity II* makes US #16. *Every Breath You Take* is named *Billboard*'s Top Single of the Year.

1984 Jan *King Of Pain* peaks at UK #17.

Feb [28] *Every Breath You Take* is named Song of the Year and Best Pop Performance by a Duo, or Group with Vocal and *Synchronicity* is named Best Rock Performance by a Duo or Group with Vocal at the 26th annual Grammy awards.

Mar *Wrapped Around Your Finger* hits US #8.

Apr [5] *Every Breath You Take* is awarded Best Group Video at the second annual American Video Awards.

Sept Summers and Fripp release *Bewitched*.

1985 May Copeland cuts African-influenced LP *The Rhythmatist*.

June Sting releases first solo LP *Dream Of The Blue Turtles*.

1986 June [11] The Police reunites at an Amnesty International concert in Atlanta, Ga., performing five songs.

July [21] The group begins recording for the follow-up to *Synchronicity*, but abandons the sessions soon after, as Sting insists on pursuing solo musical and acting interests.

Oct A revised edition of earlier hit *Don't Stand So Close To Me '86* makes UK #24, as a prelude to a greatest hits package.

Nov LP *Every Breath You Take*, reprising the group's career, is its fifth successive UK #1, and contains all its hits singles.

Dec *Don't Stand So Close To Me '86* makes US #46.

1987 July Summers' LP *XYZ* is released, the first to feature his vocals.

1988 Jan Copeland releases instrumental LP *The Equalizer And Other Cliff Hangers*, which includes US TV's "The Equalizer" theme, as a prelude to future new age LPs on brother Miles' newly-established specialist label, No Speak.

BRIAN POOLE AND THE TREMELOES

Brian Poole (vocals)
Rick West (lead guitar)
Alan Blakely (rhythm guitar)
Alan Howard (bass)
Dave Munden (drums)

1959 The group is formed in Dagenham, Essex, UK, by ex-schoolfriends Poole (b. Nov.3, 1941, Barking, Essex, UK), initially on vocals and guitar, Blakely (b. Apr.1, 1942, Bromley, Kent, UK) on drums and Howard (b. Oct.17, 1941, Dagenham) on saxophone, before Munden (b. Dec.12, 1943, Dagenham) joins on drums, allowing Blakely to switch to rhythm guitar and Poole to sing. Howard then changes from sax to bass guitar, and the group begins as a dancehall band playing cover versions, including impersonations of Buddy Holly° and The Crickets (Poole wears Holly-type horn-rimmed glasses).

1961 July After 2 years of solid gigging, during which West (b. Richard Westwood, May 7, 1943, Dagenham) has joined as lead guitarist making it a quintet, UK BBC radio producer Jimmy Grant spots the group playing in Southend, Essex, and books it for a run of featured spots on the popular "Saturday Club" show.
The group also plays a summer season as a successful rock ballroom band at Butlin's holiday camp at Ayr, Scotland.

Dec The group turns professional after it is offered an audition by Decca Records.

1962 Jan The group is signed to Decca, after being selected in preference to The Beatles°, both groups auditioning almost simultaneously, but local availability swings it for producer Mike Smith when he has to choose between these two.

Mar Debut single *Twist Little Sister* fails to chart, but picks up good UK airplay and earns them a spot on TV's "Thank Your Lucky Stars".

Sept An LP of cover versions, *Big Hits Of '62*, is released on Decca's low-price Ace of Clubs label. The group backs The Vernons Girls on their cover of Little Eva's° *The Loco-Motion*.

1963 Mar With the advent of the Merseybeat boom, they adapt a harder rocking stance. Poole abandons his Holly° specs in favor of contact lenses, and through energetic marketing by Decca, they become part of the new R&B/beat movement, but *Keep On Dancing* still fails to chart (though is featured in UK pop movie *Just For Fun*).

Aug The group hits UK #5 with its cover of *Twist And Shout*, hugely popular on The Beatles° debut LP but not available as a Beatles single. Further progress is halted by The Beatles' EP *Twist And Shout*, which is a bigger-seller.

Oct The group's revival of The Contours' *Do You Love Me?* tops the UK chart for 3 weeks, fighting off a version by The Dave Clark Five°. The hit is followed by a major UK tour supporting Roy Orbison°.

Dec *I Can Dance*, almost an exact clone of *Do You Love Me?* peaks at UK #31.

1964 Mar A fast-rocking revival of a Roy Orbison° B-side, *Candy Man*, hits UK #6.

Apr The band appears at the *New Musical Express* Poll Winners concert at Wembley, UK, with The Beatles°, Cliff Richard° and many others. Tours of South Africa and Australia will follow.

June First ballad hit, a revival of a Crickets B-side, *Someone Someone*, hits UK #2. The group spends time in Ireland filming a spot in movie *A Touch of Blarney*.

Sept The group returns to the beat with *Twelve Steps To Love*, which makes UK #32. Meanwhile, *Someone Someone* reaches US #97 – the group's only US chart entry with Poole.

1965 Feb Another ballad, reviving The Browns' *The Three Bells*, reaches UK #17.

Aug A cover of The Strangeloves' US hit *I Want Candy* makes UK #25, and will be the group's last hit in its present form.

Nov *Good Lovin'* (later a US #1 for The Young Rascals°) does not chart.

Poole decides to leave for a solo career, and Howard quits both band and showbiz, to be replaced temporarily on bass by Mick Clark.

1966 Jan [28] The split between Poole and The Tremeloes is officially announced.

May Poole releases solo *Hey Girl* which fails to chart. (He will move to CBS, but *Everything I Touch Turns To Tears* also fails. His solo live career will also fail to take off, and he will return to the family's butchery business in Dagenham.)

June The Tremeloes' solo (without Poole) cover of Paul Simon's° *Blessed* fails to sell.

July The group moves to CBS but its cover of The Beatles'° *Good Day Sunshine* from the LP *Revolver*, fails. New front man Len "Chip" Hawkes (b. Nov.11, 1946, Shepherds Bush, London, UK), replacing Clark on bass, helps develop a strong harmony vocal blend which will highlight subsequent records.

1967 Mar A "good-time" cover of Cat Stevens'° *Here Comes My Baby* begins the group's second and stronger lease of chart life, hitting UK #4.

May A revival of a Four Seasons° B-side, *Silence Is Golden*, showcasing the group's perfected harmony vocals, is its biggest-seller, topping the UK chart for 3 weeks. Meanwhile, *Here Comes My Baby* reaches US #13.

July LP *Here Come The Tremeloes* (re-titled *Here Comes My Baby* in US) makes UK #15 and US #119 (the group's only LP success).

Aug Uptempo *Even The Bad Times Are Good* hits UK #4, as *Silence Is Golden* makes US #11 and is a million-seller.

Oct *Even The Bad Times Are Good* reaches US #36.

Nov Although the group is now a familiar sight on UK TV and the live circuit, its record success varies, its material aligning it away from the progressing rock scene. More subtle and less commercial ballad *Be Mine* makes only UK #39.

1968 Feb *Suddenly You Love Me* sees the group identifying its pop market by blending strongly commercial ingredients. It hits UK #6.

Mar *Suddenly You Love Me* reaches US #44, the group's final US chart entry.

May Latin-tinged uptempo *Helule Helule* reaches UK #14.

Oct *My Little Lady*, another exuberant harmony rocker, hits UK #6.

Dec The band changes pace with a more serious cover of Bob Dylan's° *I Shall Be Released*, reaching UK #29.

1969 Apr *Hello World* makes UK #14.

Nov *(Call Me) Number One* hits UK #2 and is one of the group's biggest UK sellers.

1970 Apr *By The Way* peaks at UK #35.

Oct *Me And My Life* hits UK #4, the group's final top 10 entry.

1971 July *Hello Buddy* makes UK #32 and is the group's last hit single, as it becomes eclipsed by newcomers in the UK teen market, like T.Rex, Sweet° and Slade°. With almost a decade's worth of familiar hits to draw upon, The Tremeloes join the cabaret and northern UK club circuit, where the nostalgia factor ensures a consistently lucrative living.

1974 Nov Hawkes leaves for a solo vocal career, concentrating on country music (but will find no greater success).

1975 Jan Blakely leaves the group.

1988 The Tremeloes, having made a brief recording comeback covering F.R. David's hit *Words*, are still on the cabaret circuit and on 1960s nostalgia tours around UK, sometimes with their original leader as Brian Poole & The Tremeloes, performing early beat-era material, and sometimes as The Tremeloes, playing later hits.

IGGY POP

1964 Pop (b. James Jewel Osterburg, Apr.21, 1947, Muskegan, Ann Arbor, Mich., US) joins The Iguanas as drummer and singer, and has one-off jobs drumming for Junior Wells, Buddy Guy, The Shangri-Las° and others.

1965 The Iguanas release a cover of Bo Diddley's° *Mona*, of which 1,000 copies are made and sold at gigs. He meets Ron Asheton and James Williamson, and leaves The Iguanas to join The Prime Movers with Asheton on bass (who is sacked after 2 weeks and later joins The Chosen Few). He adopts the name Iggy Pop: Iggy after The Iguanas, Pop after local junkie Jim Popp.

1966 Pop moves to Chicago, Ill., with friend Sam Lay, drummer with The Butterfield Blues Band.

1967 He returns to Michigan and forms The Psychedelic Stooges with Asheton and his brother Scott on drums.

Nov The band makes its debut at a Halloween party.

Dec Dave Alexander joins on bass. Pop appears in an obscure art movie with Nico.

1968 The band continues to play live, mostly around Michigan, supporting Blood, Sweat & Tears° at one gig. Pop is also busted for indecent exposure.

1969 Elektra A&R employee Danny Fields, in Detroit, Mich. to sign The MC5, sees the group, now abbreviated to The Stooges, and signs it. The Stooges are advanced $25,000 to record a debut LP.

Aug LP *The Stooges* reaches US #106. It is produced by John Cale° and recorded in 4 days.

1970 The band adds Steve Mackay on sax and ex-roadie Bill Cheatham on guitar.

July LP *Fun House* is released, produced by Don Gallucci (who produced The Kingsmen's° *Louie Louie*). James Williamson joins on guitar.

Aug Alexander and Cheatham quit, while Zeke Zettner, another ex-roadie, joins.

1971 Aug The band splits due to drug related problems and Pop moves to Florida to improve his golf and cuts lawns for a living.

1972 He turns down an offer to return to Elektra. He meets admirer David Bowie° and his then manager Tony DeFries in New York. They persuade Pop to sign with MainMan Management and he re-forms The Stooges.

July Iggy & The Stooges, featuring Pop, the Asheton brothers and Williamson, play UK debut at a King's Cross cinema, London. They begin sessions for a new LP.

1973 Apr LP *Raw Power* is released, the first of a two-LP deal with CBS, and reaches US #182. A new LP is planned, but disagreements between band and management prevent its release. (Out-takes and sessions from it are later issued by US Bomp and French Siamese Records in the late 70s.) DeFries sacks Williamson over drug problems and Scott Thurston joins on keyboards.

Oct The band moves back to US for a tour which ends in violence at two gigs in Detroit. One of the shows, recorded on a cassette machine, is issued as *Metallic K.O.*

1974 The Stooges split from MainMan, and then disband.

1975 Williamson becomes a recording engineer in LA, while Asheton forms new short-lived US band The New Order, and later Destroy All Monsters with ex-MC5 members.

May New sessions for Pop are sponsored by rock journalist Bob Edmonds and songwriter Jimmy Webb. Pop, Williamson and Thurston begin to record nine tracks, which remain incomplete as Pop disappears. (He has checked himself into an L.A. psychiatric institute for drug rehabilitation. Reportedly David Bowie° is his only visitor.)

1976 Mar [21] Pop and Bowie are involved in a drug bust in their hotel room in Rochester, N.Y., US.

1977 Jan Pop appears on Bowie's° LP *Low*.

Apr Pop's first solo LP *The Idiot* is released by Bowie's° current label RCA and is "recorded" by Bowie, rather than produced. It reaches US #72 and UK #30, and includes the first version of future Bowie hit *China Girl* co-written by the pair. Pop tours (with Bowie playing keyboards) and support band Blondie°. Throughout summer, old Stooges numbers become regular features of punk live sets including those by The Sex Pistols°, The Damned° and others.

June LP *Raw Power* is re-issued and reaches UK #44. (The track *Hard To Beat* is re-titled *Your Pretty Face Has Gone To Hell*.)

Sept LP *Lust For Life* reaches US #120 and UK #28, produced by Bowie°. It was recorded and mixed in 13 days in Berlin and includes *The Passenger*, inspired by a Jim Morrison poem.

1978 *Skydog In France* and LP *Kill City* from the May 1975 sessions are released on Bomp in USA and Radar in UK. Live LP, taken from the two most recent tours, is issued as *TV Eye (1977 Live)* on RCA, produced by Bowie°.

June He plays shows at London's Music Machine.

1979 Pop signs to Arista Records and begins work on a new LP.

Mar He forms a new touring band, including ex-Sex Pistols° Glen Matlock, ex-Ike & Tina Turner° band leader Jackie Clark and regular Pop keyboardist Scott Thurston.

Apr The tour strikes problems because of associations with Matlock's former band and several gigs are cancelled by authorities.

May LP *New Values* and single *I'm Bored* are released.

June *Five Foot One* is released.

Oct LP *New Values* reaches US #180 and UK #60. It is produced by

Williamson and reunites Pop with Thurston, Scott Asheton, Williamson and MC5's guitarist Fred "Sonic" Smith. They tour UK with guest Matlock on bass. The inclusion of an ex-Sex Pistol° leads to a ban by Dunstable Council which has still not lifted its ban on The Sex Pistols.

1980 Mar LP *Soldier* peaks at US #125 and UK #62. XTC's° Barry Andrews replaces Thurston, who leaves to join The Motels°. Other guests include Simple Minds°, Bowie°, Ivan Kral of The Patti Smith° Group and Glen Matlock.

Aug LP *No Fun*, a Stooges compilation on Elektra, is released.

1981 Sept LP *Party*, his last for Arista, makes US #166, and track *Bang Bang* becomes a popular US dance hit.

1982 Pop publishes a book of anecdotes, *I Need More*, and moves to Brooklyn, New York.

Sept LP *Zombie Birdhouse* is issued on Blondie° Chris Stein's Animal label. It fails to chart. Pop and Stein work on the soundtrack to movie *Rock 'N' Rule*.

1984 Pop sings the title song on the soundtrack to Alex Cox movie *Repo Man*.

1985 He appears in another Cox movie *Sid And Nancy*.

1986 Pop signs to A&M worldwide.

Oct Debut single for the label is *Cry For Love* co-written by Steve Jones. LP *Blah Blah Blah*, produced by Dave Richards and Bowie°, reaches US #98 and UK #43.

1987 Jan A cover of 1957 Johnny O'Keefe song *Real Wild Child* is Pop's first major single success, hitting UK #10. He also makes a cameo appearance in Paul Newman film *The Color of Money*.

1988 He appears on the soundtrack of Australian movie *Dogs in Space*.

June LP *Instinct*, produced by Bill Laswell, reaches US #110 and UK #61, while single *Cold Metal* fails to chart.

PREFAB SPROUT

Paddy McAloon (guitar and vocals)
Martin McAloon (bass)
Wendy Smith (vocals and guitar)

1982 Prefab Sprout forms as a trio in Consett, County Durham, UK, based around Newcastle University English student Paddy McAloon (who has wanted to use the band name since he first thought of it in 1973). The early line-up, performing only Paddy McAloon songs, includes his brother Martin, Smith and drummer Mick Salmon, and plays local pub gigs in the Durham area.

Aug Rejected by all major labels, Prefab Sprout releases *Lions In My Own Garden* on its own Candle label. One of the 1,000 copies issued impresses Newcastle record store owner and label head Keith Armstrong.

1983 Mar Armstrong signs Prefab Sprout to his Kitchenware label.

Oct *The Devil Has All The Best Tunes*, on Kitchenware, becomes a UK independent hit.

1984 Jan *Don't Sing*, with Kitchenware signing the band to a distribution deal with CBS/Epic, makes UK #62.

Mar Debut LP *Swoon* is released. Produced by Prefab Sprout and David Brewis, it makes UK #22. Graham Lant has replaced Salmon . From it, *Couldn't Bear To Be Special* fails to chart.

Nov Ballad *When Love Breaks Down* also fails, but features another new drummer, Neil Conti.

1985 Mar *When Love Breaks Down* re-mix is released again, but fails.

June LP *Steve McQueen*, produced by Thomas Dolby°, reaches UK #21. It is re-titled *Two Wheels Good* in US, after objections over the original title from Steve McQueen's daughter, and features extra cuts.

July From the LP, *Faron Young* makes UK #74.

Sept *Appetite* fails to chart.

Nov *When Love Breaks Down*, issued for the third time, reaches UK #25.

1986 Feb *Johnny Johnny* makes UK #64. The group plays a one-off gig at London's Hammersmith Odeon, before beginning a tour of Japan.

1987 Prefab Sprout retreats to create a new LP around Paddy McAloon's compositions.

1988 Feb *Cars And Girls*, a McAloon commentary on Bruce Springsteen° songs, reaches UK #44.

Mar LP *From Langley Park To Memphis* hits UK #5. Produced by Paddy McAloon with Jon Kelly, Andy Richards and Thomas Dolby° (who was scheduled to produce the whole LP but could not because of illness), it features Stevie Wonder°, Pete Townshend and The Andrae Crouch Gospel Singers. The LP sells a half million copies in Europe in its first 10 weeks of release.

Apr *The King Of Rock'n'Roll* hits UK #7, but the band is unwilling to tour.

June McAloon, still living in his parents' home in Consett, begins work on the soundtrack to an unwritten movie, *Zorro The Fox*.

July *Hey Manhattan!* peaks at UK #72.

Nov Ballad *Nightingales*, featuring Stevie Wonder° on harmonica, is released in UK.

ELVIS PRESLEY

1948 Sept [12] Presley (b. Jan.8, 1935, Tupelo, Miss., US), one of twin sons (brother Jesse being stillborn), moves with his parents to Memphis, Tenn., where father Vernon finds a job at a paint company and mother Gladys works at a hospital as a nurse's aide. He goes to L.C. Humes high school by day, mowing lawns or cinema ushering in the evening to help make ends meet.

1949 Aug After a year in a cramped one-room apartment, the family qualifies for a federal housing apartment. Presley, naturally shy, makes few friends at school and does not shine academically.

1953 June [14] Having become noted in his final year as a performer in the Christmas 1952 school show, and as an eye-catching dresser, Presley gains his high school diploma and leaves.

July Employed by Crown Electric Co. as a truck driver, he calls one lunch hour at Memphis Recording Service at 706, Union Ave., paying $4 to make a private recording for his mother's birthday. Marion Keisker, office manager for Sam Phillips, who owns the company and associated Sun Records label, finds his voice interesting, and keeps a tape of *My Happiness* and *That's When Your Heartaches Begin* to play for Phillips.

1954 Jan [4] Presley returns to cut a second private record, singing *Casual Love Affair* and *I'll Never Stand In Your Way*. This time, Phillips asks for Presley's address and a phone number, promising to contact him to try something in the studio.

Apr Looking for a vocalist to record *Without You*, a song he has received on an anonymous Nashville demo, Phillips agrees to Keisker's suggestion of Presley. He has several attempts but finds no empathy with the song, so Phillips lets Presley try out his gospel, country, R&B and Dean Martin ballad material, and suggests some rehearsal sessions with other musicians. He calls guitarist Scotty Moore who runs local club band The Starlight Wranglers and, with the band's bass player Bill Black, they begin practice sessions.

July [5] Phillips tries a formal recording session with Presley, Moore and Black on country ballad *I Love You Because*. During a break, Presley fools with an uptempo romp through Arthur Crudup's blues number *That's All Right Mama*, and is joined by the other two in an impromptu jam session. Phillips, hearing the individual "something" for which he has been trying in vain with Presley, has them repeat it with his tapes running, and after a handful of run-throughs, a satisfactory master is made.

July [6] Similar experimentation marks the next day's song – Bill Monroe's bluegrass *Blue Moon Of Kentucky*, which is accelerated to a racing tempo. Moore suggests the strange hybrid of (black) blues and (white) country will offend the Southern radio and musical community, but Phillips hears commercial potential, and couples *That's All Right Mama* with *Blue Moon Of Kentucky* as a Sun single.

July [10] Phillips takes acetates of the recorded tracks to DJ Dewey Phillips (unrelated) at Memphis radio station WHBQ. The DJ rates *That's All Right Mama* and plays it on his R&B show "Red Hot and Blue" at 9.30pm. The switchboard immediately lights up with requests for repeat spins. Phillips phones Presley's home to ask him to come to the studio for a interview but Presley, forewarned by Sam Phillips of the single's likely airing, is at a movie, unable to face the embarrassment of hearing his voice on the radio. His parents seek him out and take him to WHBQ, where Phillips puts him at his ease, and Memphis learns that this hot new R&B singer is a local white 19-year-old.

July [12] Presley signs a recording contract with Sun and a management deal with Scotty Moore, and gives notice to quit Crown Electric.

July [19] With over 5,000 orders from the Memphis area, the single is released as Presley's Sun debut. (It will top the local chart by the end of the month, with action on both sides: Dewey Phillips plays *That's All Right Mama*, while Sleepy Eye John on WHEM and most other Memphis DJs play *Blue Moon Of Kentucky*.)

July [20] The trio's first public performance is playing on a flatbed truck outside a new drugstore on Lamar Ave., Memphis, to mark its opening, to a swelling and increasingly excited crowd. (Local engagements at the Eagle's Nest and Bel Air clubs follow, and Moore and Black leave The Starlight Wranglers to work with Presley full-time.)

Aug [10] Local agent Bob Neal books Presley low on the bill of a two-performance show at Overton Park Shell auditorium in Memphis, headlined by Slim Whitman. After a polite reception to two country ballads during the afternoon show, he is advised by Dewey Phillips to perform uptempo material in the evening. He sings *Good Rockin' Tonight* and *That's All Right Mama*, with leg and body movements. The sensual performance drives the audience wild; Presley exits the stage bewildered by screams and shouts which all but drown the music and is pushed back by Phillips to encore, to a similar reception. Established country artist Webb Pierce, waiting to follow him, stands stunned and uncomprehending.

Sept [9] *Good Rockin' Tonight* (with *I Don't Care If The Sun Don't Shine*) is recorded as a follow-up single.

Sept [25] Sam Phillips gains a booking for Presley on Nashville's "Grand Ole Opry", aired live from Ryman Auditorium. He is introduced by Hank Snow and sings *Blue Moon Of Kentucky*, but fails to impress the staid audience, or the talent booker Jim Denny, who suggests he take up truck driving again.

Oct [16] He gets a better reception on country music radio show "The Louisiana Hayride", on KWKH in Shreveport, La. After he sings *That's All Right Mama* to an enthusiastic live audience, station director Horace Logan signs Presley to a year's contract, for $18 per weekly slot. He is also contracted to sing a radio commercial for one of the show's sponsors, a doughnut manufacturer.

Nov Neal (with Moore's agreement) takes over management and books the trio (billed as Elvis Presley, The Hillbilly Cat, and His Blue Moon Boys), into one-night dates all over the South.

Dec [18] Third single, *Milk Cow Blues Boogie/You're A Heartbreaker* is recorded at Sun, with several versions of *I'm Left, You're Right, She's Gone*.

1955 Jan Oscar Davis, right-hand man to talent entrepreneur Col. Tom Parker (manager of Eddy Arnold and Hank Snow), is impressed by Presley's power over an audience when he sees him at Memphis Airport Inn while visiting Neal. He reports the local phenomenon back to Parker, who negotiates with Neal to have Presley on his "Hank Snow Jamboree" package shows of country acts playing the Southern states. Parker views Presley performing in Texarkana, Ark., then sets up a meeting in Memphis with Neal and Presley, where he offers guidance and suggests that Presley should be recording elsewhere than at Sun – a notion rejected both by Neal and Presley. *Milk Cow Blues Boogie* is released, but proves a poor seller.

Feb [5] Presley records a cover of Arthur Gunter's *Baby Let's Play House*, for which he invents a hiccuping rockabilly vocal style which will characterize many later impersonations of his singing. It is his first recording with drums, played by Johnny Bonnero from local Dean Beard Band.

Mar [5] Presley has his first TV exposure when the weekend edition of "The Louisiana Hayride" is televised locally.

Mar Neal also gains the group an audition on Arthur Godfrey's "Talent Scouts" show in New York. Having to fly to the audition unnerves Presley and tryout performance of *Good Rockin' Tonight* is not his best. Godfrey's producers turn him down, (and will pick up instead on his biggest 1950s rival in popularity, Pat Boone°).

Apr *Baby Let's Play House/I'm Left ,You're Right, She's Gone* is released by Sun, to better sales than its predecessor.

Apr [5] Parker pays for Presley's parents to travel to see him on a "Hank Snow Jamboree" in Chattanooga and suggests that their son is being overworked (having previously ascertained Gladys Presley's fears on the same subject) and that he needs more professional management. Gladys is cautious, mentioning Presley's obligations to Neal, Sun and "The Louisiana Hayride" (a contract now extended to 18 months), but Parker finds an ally in Vernon Presley (who will later give him signed permission to negotiate a new recording deal on his son's behalf).

May [13] Presley's stage act causes an audience riot for the first time, in Jacksonville, Fla. He has much of his clothing ripped off, but escapes uninjured.

July *Baby Let's Play House* is Presley's first national chart entry, reaching #10 on *Billboard*'s country chart, and Presley buys his first Cadillac. Parker begins to promote Presley outside the South, impressing New York music publisher Arnold Shaw with Presley's records and reputation, and via Shaw, top Cleveland, Oh., DJ Bill Randle, who gives him heavy airplay which slowly spreads to New York.

Aug *Mystery Train/I Forgot To Remember To Forget*, Presley's final Sun single, is released. Parker spreads word that his contract with Sun may be for sale. Decca Records bids $5,000 and is turned down by Phillips, as is Dot Records' offer of $7,500. Parker hears that Mercury Records is considering a $10,000 bid, and makes it known to CBS/Columbia's Mitch Miller, who says he will up it to $15,000. Parker hints that RCA is considering £20,000, and Miller intimates that "no singer is worth that much". Ahmet Ertegun of Atlantic disagrees, and is willing to risk $25,000, but Parker insists that nearly twice as much is "more realistic".

Oct [15] Presley plays Lubbock, Texas, where the opening act is local hillbilly duo Buddy (Holly°) and Bob.

Nov With Neal's management contract about to expire, Parker takes up the negotiating power granted him by Presley's parents and works out a deal in New York with RCA Records and Aberbach publishing, which will pay Sun $35,000 for the Presley contract and all previously-recorded material, and Presley himself $5,000 as a past royalty settlement. (The publisher pays $10,000 of the sum for Presley's future song publishing on its Hill and Range subsidiary.)

Nov [12] Presley is voted Most Promising Country and Western Artist in the annual US DJ poll, and Parker has him in prominent attendance at the Country Music DJ's Convention in Nashville.

Nov [22] Neal's contract with Presley expires, and RCA/Aberbach/Parker's offer to Sam Phillips becomes official. In need of expansion capital (and with only a year of Presley's contract still to run), Phillips accepts. (Phillips begins investing in the fledgling Holiday Inn hotel chain, which will make him a bigger fortune than the record industry.) RCA reissues all five Presley singles on its own label, though Sun still has a sell-off period for existing stock.

1956 Jan [10/11] Presley has his first RCA recording sessions, in Nashville. First cut is a cover of Ray Charles'° *I Got A Woman*, and the second a new song, *Heartbreak Hotel*. The session uses more musicians than the Sun recordings, including Dominic ("D.J.") Fontana on drums, ex-housedrummer with "The Louisiana Hayride", who has also been touring regularly with Presley.

Jan [27] *Heartbreak Hotel* is released to tie in with his debut on US network TV.

Jan [28] The William Morris agency books Presley into the first of six weekly guest slots (for $1,250 each) on Tommy and Jimmy Dorsey-hosted "Stage Show", aired live from New York on CBS. He performs *Heartbreak Hotel* and a cover of Carl Perkins'° *Blue Suede Shoes*.

Jan [30/31 and Feb 1] In RCA's New York studios, Presley records his own version of *Blue Suede Shoes*, plus seven more tracks for his debut LP.

Feb [4] On his second "Stage Show" appearance he sings *I Was The One* (B-side of *Heartbreak Hotel*) and Little Richard's° *Tutti Frutti*.

Feb [11] On "Stage Show" he performs *I Got A Woman* and a medley of *Shake, Rattle & Roll/Flip, Flop And Fly* and is introduced by Bill Randle, the first DJ to have played his records on the East Coast.

Feb [18] Another "Stage Show" slot features *Baby Let's Play House* and a repeat of *Tutti Frutti*.

Mar *Heartbreak Hotel* debuts on the US chart.

Mar [17] Presley returns to "Stage Show", singing *Blue Suede Shoes* and *Heartbreak Hotel*.

Mar [24] His final "Stage Show" appearance features *Money Honey* and *Heartbreak Hotel*.

Apr *Heartbreak Hotel* tops the US chart for 8 weeks, becoming Presley's first million-seller (it also hits C&W #1 and R&B #5). B-side *I Was The One* makes US #23. *Blue Suede Shoes*, released as the lead track on an EP, climbs to US #20 (Carl Perkins'° original hits #2, behind *Heartbreak Hotel*).

Apr [1] A screen test at Paramount studios in Hollywood for producer Hal Wallis results in a 3-film contract guaranteeing $450,000.

Apr [3] Presley returns to US TV on NBC's "Milton Berle Show", aired live from the aircraft carrier USS Hancock, moored at San Diego. 25,000 people apply for tickets, and an estimated 40 million (a quarter of the US population) watch him sing *Heartbreak Hotel*, *Money Honey* and *Blue Suede Shoes*. He earns $5000 from the show.

Apr [10] Presley buys his parents a new $40,000 home in Audubon Park, Memphis.

Apr [11] Presley is flying to Nashville for a recording session when his plane develops engine trouble and has to make an emergency landing. Shaken, he records *I Want You, I Need You, I Love You* later in the day, but the incident creates an aversion to flying which lasts for years.

Apr [23] Parker books Presley into an unsuitable Las Vegas residency – 2 weeks at the Venus Room of the Frontier Hotel, paying $8,500 a week. Middle-aged audiences are cool (and Presley will not return to Vegas for 13 years). However, he appropriates an uptempo arrangement of R&B oldie *Hound Dog* from the hotel's lounge group, Freddie Bell and The Bell Boys.

May Debut LP *Elvis Presley* tops the US chart for 10 weeks (with advance orders of 362,000, making it RCA's biggest-selling LP to date before it is even issued). Meanwhile, a cover of The Drifters'° *Money Honey*, lead track on Presley's second EP, reaches US #76.

June *Heartbreak Hotel* is UK chart debut, hitting #2 (behind Pat Boone's° *I'll Be Home*), while *Blue Suede Shoes* hits UK #9.

June [5] On a second "Milton Berle Show", Presley does a comedy routine with Berle, sings *I Want You, I Need You, I Love You* and introduces *Hound Dog* in a hip-shaking performance which brings in a storm of protest to the show.

July [1] Presley returns to US NBC TV on "The Steve Allen Show" in New York, where the producers attempt to quieten the criticism by involving him in more comedy, and insisting on more sedate performances of *I Want You, I Need You, I Love You* and *Hound Dog* (the latter sung in white tie and tails to an actual (unmoved) hound.

July [2] Presley records *Hound Dog* at RCA's New York studio, finally satisfied after 31 takes. He also cuts *Don't Be Cruel* and *Any Way You Want Me* much more quickly, with The Jordanaires on backing vocals for the first time.

July [4] He returns to Memphis (by train) to play a charity concert at the 14,000-seater Russwood Auditorium.

July *I Want You, I Need You, I Love You* tops the US chart for a week and is his second million-selling single. B-side *My Baby Left Me* (like *That's All Right Mama* an Arthur Crudup song), reaches US #31.

Aug Presley's most successful single is released, coupling *Don't Be Cruel* (which hits US #1 for 7 weeks) and *Hound Dog* (which lines up behind it at #2). US sales top 5 million.

Aug [22] Filming begins in Hollywood on *The Reno Brothers*, for which Hal Wallis "loans" his new movie property to 20th Century Fox. A Civil War western starring Richard Egan and Debra Paget, it is adapted to feature Presley and to include four songs, all period-style written by Ken Darby (whose trio backs Presley on them). Ballad *Love Me Tender* (based on traditional *Aura Lee*), is sufficiently strong and the producers re-title the movie after it.

Sept *I Want You, I Need You, I Love You* makes UK #14 (in the same week *Heartbreak Hotel* drops out of UK top 10, having already spent 18 weeks in the top 30).

Sept [1/3] At Radio Recorders studios in Hollywood, with his usual musicians, Presley records 13 songs for his second LP. In Hollywood, he also buys his mother a pink Cadillac.

Sept [9] A Presley segment aired from Hollywood is slotted into the New York-transmitted "Toast of the Town" show hosted by Ed Sullivan on CBS. (Sullivan is originally on record as saying he would never have Presley on his show, but Steve Allen's success in direct competition has changed his mind, and Parker negotiates $50,000 for three slots.) It is watched by an estimated 54 million people (a third of the US population), and features *Don't Be Cruel*, *Love Me Tender*, *Ready Teddy* and *Hound Dog*. Sullivan himself is ill, and the show is hosted by Charles Laughton.

Sept [10] On Monday after the Sullivan show, record stores are deluged with requests for *Love Me Tender*, not scheduled for release for many weeks.

Sept [26] He returns to Tupelo, Miss., to perform at the annual Mississippi-Alabama Fair and Dairy Show. Tupelo declares it "Elvis Presley Day" in his honor, and he plays afternoon and evening open-air shows, donating his $10,000 fee to the town.

Oct *Blue Moon*, one of six simultaneously-released singles comprising the whole debut LP in 45rpm form, reaches US #55 while Sun track *I Don't Care If The Sun Don't Shine*, released by RCA on an EP, makes US #74. RCA, unable to resist huge advance orders (856,237 by the end of Sept.), releases *Love Me Tender* before the movie premiere. It tops the US chart in its second week and holds #1 for 5 weeks, selling over 2 million. In UK, *Hound Dog* hits #2.

Oct [16] *Love Me Tender* premieres at New York's Paramount Theater. Critics slay it but it recoups its $1-million budget in little more than a week and 20th Century Fox releases a record 550 prints around US.

Oct [28] Presley appears on Ed Sullivan's "Toast of the Town" show for a second time, performing *Don't Be Cruel*, *Love Me Tender*, *Love Me* and *Hound Dog*.

Nov *Any Way You Want Me*, B-side of *Love Me Tender*, reaches US #27.

Nov [10] *Billboard*'s national DJ poll reveals that Presley is the most-played male artist and country artist of 1956.

Dec Second LP *Elvis* tops the US chart for 5 weeks, while *Love Me*, lead track on EP *Elvis, Vol.1* (extracts from the LP) hits US #6. Also from the EP, *When My Blue Moon Turns To Gold Again* and *Paralyzed* make US #27 and #59 respectively. From a similar EP of extracts, *Elvis, Vol.2*, sentimental ballad *Old Shep* reaches US #47. *Don't Be Cruel* peaks at UK #17, *Blue Moon* hits UK #9 and B-side *I Don't Care If The Sun Don't Shine* makes UK #23. At home in Memphis for Christmas, Presley visits Sun studios, where Carl Perkins° and his group are recording a session, with Jerry Lee Lewis° guesting on piano. Johnny Cash° is also present but his wife draws him away to go shopping. The others settle down to a jam session, mostly on gospel songs and recent hits.

Phillips tapes these and they become the legendary "Million Dollar Quartet Session" (issued on disk after Presley's death).

Dec [13] Movie *Love Me Tender* premieres in London, UK.

1957 Jan In Hollywood, he films his first contracted movie for Hal Wallis, *Loving You* (originally titled *Lonesome Cowboy*), co-starring with Lizabeth Scott and Wendel Corey. Presley's parents stay with him at Hollywood's Knickerbocker Hotel during filming. Meanwhile, *Poor Boy*, from the EP of songs from *Love Me Tender*, reaches US #35 and *Love Me Tender* single hits UK #10.

Jan [4] Presley has a medical check-up at Kennedy Veterans Hospital. It is a preliminary to his call-up by the US Army.

Jan [6] His last appearance on Network TV for some years is the third contracted Ed Sullivan slot in New York. He sings *Hound Dog*, *Love Me Tender*, *Heartbreak Hotel*, *Don't Be Cruel*, *When My Blue Moon Turns To Gold Again*, his new single *Too Much* and spiritual *Peace In The Valley*. During the uptempo numbers, he is shown on screen only from the waist up.

Jan [12/13 and 19] Three sessions at Radio Recorders produce 12 new tracks, including *Peace In The Valley* and *All Shook Up*.

Feb *Too Much*, introduced on his last Ed Sullivan appearance, tops the US chart for 3 weeks and is another million-seller. B-side *Playing For Keeps* makes US #34.

Mar Sun single *Mystery Train* is released for the first time in UK and peaks at #23 while *Rip It Up*, from LP *Elvis*, is also extracted as a UK single, and makes #27.

Mar [19] He buys Graceland, a large house in 13 acres of ground in Memphis suburb Whitehaven.

Apr *All Shook Up*, written by Otis Blackwell (who also penned *Don't Be Cruel*), tops the US chart for 8 weeks, selling 2 million copies. B-side ballad *That's When Your Heartaches Begin* (which includes a short spoken recitation) reaches US #58.

Apr [30] The songs for forthcoming *Jailhouse Rock* are cut at Radio Recorders studios, with songwriters Jerry Leiber and Mike Stoller attending the sessions.

May In Hollywood, he films *Jailhouse Rock* for MGM, co-starring Judy Tyler and Mickey Shaughnessy. Meanwhile, *Peace In The Valley*, now on an EP of four religious songs, reaches US #25 (and #3 on US LP chart).

June *Too Much* hits UK #6.

July *(Let Me Be Your) Teddy Bear*, from film *Loving You*, tops the US chart for 7 weeks, and is another 2-million-plus seller. The film's ballad title song is B-side and reaches US #28. LP *Loving You*, which has the soundtrack recordings on one side and a second side of new non-movie songs (including a cover of Bing Crosby/Grace Kelly hit ballad *True Love*), hits US #1 for 10 weeks, earning a gold disk for a half million sales. Meanwhile, *All Shook Up* is released in UK, and becomes Presley's first UK #1, topping the chart for 7 weeks and selling over a half million copies.

July [9] Movie *Loving You* is released in US.

Aug The UK outlet for Presley's recordings changes, as RCA's own label is launched through Decca. EMI, which has previously issued RCA product on the HMV label, has a lengthy sell-off period for recordings already licensed, and for several months the UK chart is flooded by competing Presley singles on two labels. One of the first UK RCA singles released is *(Let Me Be Your) Teddy Bear*, which hits UK #2 for 2 weeks (behind *All Shook Up*, which is on HMV).

Aug [2] The Official UK Elvis Presley Fan Club is launched. (In US, there are already thousands of Presley fan clubs.)

Aug [23] Film *Loving You* opens in London, UK.

Aug [31] He plays his first Canadian live date, at the Empire Stadium in Vancouver, where fans rush the stage during the show. Presley and his band have to flee to avoid being trampled.

Sept EP *Loving You, Vol.1*, a four-song extract from the soundtrack, reaches US LP chart #18, while EP *Just For You*, which has four songs from the LP's non-film side, makes US #16 on the LP chart. In UK, HMV (in its sell-off period) releases *Paralyzed*, from LP *Elvis*, and it hits UK #8, giving Presley three simultaneous UK top 20 entries.

Oct *Jailhouse Rock*, the Leiber/Stoller-written title song from the film, tops the US chart for 7 weeks, selling over 2 million. Also from the movie, B-side *Treat Me Nice* makes US #27.

Oct [21] Film *Jailhouse Rock* opens in US.

Nov With the movie not yet scheduled for UK release, RCA holds *Jailhouse Rock* back until the New Year in UK, and releases instead *(Let's Have A) Party*, another rocker from *Loving You*. It hits UK #2 and B-side *Got A Lot O' Livin' To Do* makes UK #18. At the same time, *Loving You*, B-side of *Teddy Bear*, reaches UK #24, while HMV pushes out yet another single, coupling *Lawdy Miss Clawdy* and *Trying To Get You*. Both sides chart, at UK #15 and #16 respectively. In the week ending Nov.2, Presley has eight titles in UK top 30 (at 3, 11, 17, 19, 21, 24, 26, and 30).

Dec LP *Elvis' Christmas Album* tops the US chart for 4 weeks. Initially packaged as a deluxe gift item, with a sleeve incorporating 10 pages of photos, it has a side of secular Christmas material (including *Blue Christmas* and an appropriation of Clyde McPhatter and The Drifters'° arrangement of *White Christmas*) and a side of carols and hymns which incorporates four songs from EP *Peace In The Valley*. It earns a gold disk (and over 2 decades of repeat Christmas sales will sell well over a million copies). In UK, where LP sales are still minimal, RCA extracts *Santa Bring My Baby Back (To Me)* and it hits UK #7.

Dec [20] Against nationwide teenage protest, Presley's draft notice for the US Army is served to him (at home at Graceland, where he has returned for Christmas with his parents) by Milton Bowers, Chairman of the Memphis Draft Board.

Dec [21] Paramount Pictures petitions the Army to defer Presley's induction date, so that movie *King Creole* can be completed. The draft board agrees to a 2-month delay, which incurs a barrage of public comment alleging "special treatment".

1958 Jan Presley travels from Memphis to Hollywood by train, to film *King Creole*, co-starring Walter Matthau and Carolyn Jones. He records the songs for the film soundtrack at Radio Recorders, with his usual Nashville musicians.

Jan [10] *Jailhouse Rock*, due for release as a UK single on this day, is put back for a week because Decca's pressing plant is unable to have enough copies ready to meet advance orders of 250,000.

Jan [16] Film *Jailhouse Rock* premieres in London, UK.

Jan [17] *Jailhouse Rock* is released in UK and sells 500,000 copies in its first 3 days.

Jan [25] *Jailhouse Rock* enters the UK chart at #1, the first time this feat has been achieved, and stays at the top for 3 weeks, selling 750,000 copies. Meanwhile, last UK HMV single, old Sun track *I'm Left, You're Right, She's Gone*, peaks at UK #18.

Feb *Don't*, Presley's first slow ballad A-side since *Love Me Tender*, tops the US chart for 5 weeks, topping 2 million sales – aided by B-side *I Beg Of You*, which hits US #8. In UK, the five-song EP from *Jailhouse Rock* joins the single on the chart, reaching #15.

Feb [1] His last recording session prior to Army induction produces four songs, including *Your Cheating Heart* (not issued until 1965) and *Wear My Ring Around Your Neck* (his next single).

Feb [17] Movie *Jailhouse Rock* goes on general UK release, while in US production of *King Creole* moves to New Orleans for location filming. Presley takes over a floor of the Roosevelt Hotel with his entourage. The city declares it "Elvis Presley Day" as he arrives, and the streets are so choked with people that filming is initially impossible.

Mar *Don't* hits UK #2 for 3 weeks, held from the top by Perry Como's *Magic Moments*.

Mar [24] Presley is sworn in as US private 53310761 at 5pm at the Memphis draft office, then leaves by bus for Fort Chaffee, Ark., for full induction.

Apr *Wear My Ring Around Your Neck* peaks at US #2, behind David Seville's *Witch Doctor*. US sales are over a million, and B-side *Doncha' Think It's Time* makes US #21.

May LP *Elvis' Golden Records*, a compilation of singles from *Heartbreak Hotel* to *Jailhouse Rock*, hits US #3, earning a gold disk, and staying in US top 25 for 74 weeks. Meanwhile, *Wear My Ring Around Your Neck* hits UK #2 for 2 weeks, behind Connie Francis'° *Who's Sorry Now?*.

June [4] Film *King Creole* opens in US.

June [10/11] On his first weekend's leave from US Army, Presley records two sessions in Nashville (which will provide his hit singles of late 1958 and 1959). New guitarist Hank Garland plays in place of Moore, who is busy with other recording projects since Presley's draft has ended his live work. Black is also not present (bass is played by Bob Moore); he too is working in Memphis on his own projects since finishing work with Presley in Feb. (and will have success with his instrumental Bill Black Combo).

June [25] Presley's parents celebrate their 25th wedding anniversary while living in a house he has rented for them in Texas, close to

Fort Hood, where he is undergoing basic training.

July *Hard-Headed Woman*, from the soundtrack of *King Creole*, tops the US chart for 2 weeks, selling over a million. In keeping with the movie's setting, its arrangement incorporates elements of Dixieland jazz in rock backing. B-side *Don't Ask Me Why*, also from the film, reaches US #28.

Aug *Hard-Headed Woman* hits UK #2 for 2 weeks, held from #1 by The Everly Brothers'° *All I Have To Do Is Dream/Claudette*.
Gladys Presley falls ill, and is returned to Memphis and admitted to Methodist Hospital where the family doctor and four specialists diagnose acute hepatitis. After 3 days, her condition worsens and the hospital advises Presley to return home. After initial reluctance (the Army fearing press allegations of "preferential treatment") he is granted compassionate leave. Against Gladys' wishes, he flies from Texas by plane to speed the journey.

Aug [12] He visits his mother in hospital, staying the night and much of the following day.

Aug [14] He has returned home to rest when Gladys dies of heart failure at 3.15am, with Vernon Presley at her bedside.

Aug [15] Her funeral is held at the National Funeral Home in Forest Hill, Memphis. Presley is so overcome with grief that he is unable to stand for much of the proceedings and has to be supported. 500 policeman keep a gigantic crowd at bay.

Aug [28] Film *King Creole* opens in London, UK.

Sept Its sell-off period expired, EMI deletes all Presley and other RCA product from its HMV catalog.

Sept [22] After giving a press conference at Brooklyn Army Terminal, New York (by special dispensation of the military), Presley sets sail for a tour of duty in West Germany, on troopship USS Randall.

Oct [1] Presley arrives in West Germany at Bremerhaven and is transported to the US Army base at Friedburg, near Frankfurt. (He will buy a house in nearby Bad Neuheim, taking advantage of a military rule which allows him to live off camp if he has family to support. He will move his father, grandmother, some friends and staff into it. On the base, he will be a jeep driver for his platoon sergeant.)

Oct Soundtrack LP from *King Creole* hits US #2, behind Frank Sinatra's *Only The Lonely*. In UK, the title song is extracted and hits #2, again behind Connie Francis° with *Stupid Cupid/Carolina Moon*. (Moving it aside from #2 the following week is newcomer Cliff Richard° with *Move It*, which is also held at #2 by Francis).

Nov The introduction of a UK LP chart sees LPs *Elvis' Golden Records* and *King Creole* hit UK #3 and #4 respectively.

Dec *One Night*, a heavy blues-rock treatment of a 1956 Smiley Lewis R&B hit (with lyrics altered from the suggestive originals to ensure radio play), hits US #4, as double A-side frantic rocker *I Got Stung* hits US #8. US sales again top a million.

1959 Jan *I Got Stung/One Night*, combined for chart purposes in UK, enters the UK chart at #1, and holds for 5 weeks.

Mar RCA releases the pre-Germany press conference and interviews as a spoken-word EP, *Elvis Sails*.

Apr Compilation LP *For LP Fans Only*, rounding up singles B-sides and EP tracks, including some Sun recordings, reaches US #19. UK equivalent (with extra tracks) is titled *Elvis*, and hits #4.

May Another double A-side release, *A Fool Such As I* (a revival of a 1953 country hit by Hank Snow) hits US #2 and wild rocker *I Need Your Love Tonight* hits US #4. The coupling sells over 2 million in US. In UK, the sides are combined, like the previous single, for one chart listing, and it tops the UK chart for 6 weeks (dethroning Buddy Holly's° *It Doesn't Matter Anymore*).

Aug *A Big Hunk O' Love*, one of Presley's fastest-paced rockers, tops the US chart for 2 weeks, selling over a million, while B-side ballad *My Wish Came True* peaks at US #12. In UK, *A Big Hunk O' Love* hits #3. These are the last of the June 1958 recordings to be issued on single. (A dearth of new Presley records will follow until after his 1960 Army release – with the approval of Parker, who wants fans well starved of product to prepare for the post-Army releases.)

ELVIS PRESLEY *cont.*

Sept In Bad Neuheim, he is introduced to a young American girl, 14-year-old Priscilla Beaulieu, stepdaughter of a US Air Force captain, who lives nearby. (A friendship develops which will become a romance.)

Oct Compilation LP *A Date With Elvis*, another gathering of singles and EP tracks, makes US #32 and hits UK #4 (the UK version has an amended and expanded track listing). Its sleeve includes a calendar for counting down the days to Presley's US Army release.

1960 Jan [20] Presley is promoted to Sergeant.

Feb 4-song EP *Strictly Elvis*, featuring sentimental *Old Shep* (unavailable in UK since 1958), reaches UK #26.

Mar Compilation LP *50 Million Elvis Fans Can't Be Wrong – Elvis Gold Records, Vol.2* makes US #31, earning a gold disk.

Mar [1] The US Army hosts a "Farewell Elvis" press conference at Friedburg base in West Germany.

Mar [2] He flies home for demobilization from Frankfurt. The plane makes a refuelling stop at Prestwick Airport, Scotland, and while it is on the ground, Presley talks to fans through an airport fence. This is the only occasion on which he sets foot on UK soil.

Mar [3] At 7.42am, he lands in a snowstorm at McGuire Air Force Base, US.

Mar [5] Presley is demobbed from the US Army at Fort Dix, N.J.

Mar [7] He arrives home in Memphis, having come from N.J. by train.

Mar [20/21] His first post-Army recording session takes place in Nashville, with Moore back in the band (Black will never play again with Presley). His regular studio pianist is now Floyd Cramer (who will become a hitmaker in his own right). Six tracks are recorded, including *Stuck On You* and *Fame And Fortune*, which are rush-scheduled by RCA.

Mar [23] He travels by train from Nashville to Miami, to tape a TV show slot with Frank Sinatra.

Mar [26] The Timex-sponsored Frank Sinatra show is recorded at Fontainebleu Hotel, Miami Beach. Presley guests with Sammy Davis Jr. and Sinatra's daughter Nancy. He sings *Fame And Fortune* and *Stuck On You* in a solo slot, and duets with Sinatra on a traded duet of *Love Me Tender* and *Witchcraft*. Parker has negotiated $125,000 for the appearance.

Apr [3/4] A longer Nashville session is later rated one of Presley's most artistically successful, producing material for LP *Elvis Is Back*, and two million-selling singles, *It's Now Or Never* and *Are You Lonesome Tonight*.

Apr [18] He travels with his father from Memphis to Hollywood on the Missouri Pacific Railroad's Texas Eagle Express, to begin filming *G.I. Blues*.

Apr [25] *Stuck On You*, released with advance US orders of 1,275,077, tops the US chart for 4 weeks. B-side *Fame And Fortune* makes US #17. In UK, *Stuck On You* hits #2 (behind Lonnie Donegan's° *My Old Man's A Dustman*).

Apr [26] Filming begins for Wallis and Paramount on *G.I. Blues*, which co-stars Juliet Prowse, and typecasts Presley as a young US soldier in West Germany (though in an entertainment unit, from which the Army had withheld Presley for fear of more "special treatment" accusations).

May [6] The songs for *G.I. Blues* soundtrack are recorded in Hollywood.

May [12] "Frank Sinatra – Timex Show" is aired on US ABC TV.

June Presley has his tonsils removed in hospital in Memphis. Meanwhile , LP *Elvis Is Back*, with tracks from the Apr. Nashville session, hits US #2 (behind The Kingston Trio's *Sold Out*) and earns a gold disk. In UK, it hits #1, while compilation LP *Elvis' Gold Records, Vol.2* hits UK #4.

July [3] Vernon Presley marries divorcee Dee Stanley, whom he has met while living in West Germany (her ex-husband having been a master sergeant in US Army).

July [25] Filming of *Flaming Star* (originally titled *Flaming Lance*) begins at 20th Century Fox studios in Hollywood. Co-starring Steve Forrest and Barbara Eden, it is a western directed by Don Siegel, with Presley in a troubled role as a half-breed into which he throws himself enthusiastically – in contrast to his bored acceptance of *G.I. Blues*' near-caricature of himself.

Aug *It's Now Or Never*, recorded at the Apr.3 session but not used on the LP, tops the US chart for 5 weeks. It is an adaptation of 1901 Italian song *O Sole Mio* and, with its semi-operatic Latin sound, stands apart from anything Presley has ever recorded before. (Worldwide, it will become his biggest-selling single, with total sales over 20 million.) B-side, the contrasting *A Mess Of Blues* reaches US #32. In UK, a copyright wrangle over *It's Now Or Never* temporarily prevents its release, so RCA promotes *A Mess Of Blues* and pairs it with *The Girl Of My Best Friend* from LP *Elvis Is Back*. Both sides chart, and for the first time both sides of a Presley single obtain UK top 10 positions, with *A Mess Of Blues* hitting #3 and *The Girl Of My Best Friend* hitting #5.

Aug [8/12] Four songs intended for film *Flaming Star* are recorded at 20th Century Fox studios, Hollywood. (Only the title song and one other will be used in the movie.)

Oct [20] Film *G.I. Blues* opens in US.

Oct [28] Copyright problems resolved, *It's Now Or Never* is released in UK, having built up advance orders of 500,000, the largest ever known in UK.

Oct [30/31] In Nashville, Presley records his first lengthy gospel music session. (It will form much of his 1961 inspirational LP *His Hand In Mine*.)

Nov *It's Now Or Never* enters the UK chart at #1, holding for 9 weeks. On the Saturday following the single's Friday release, many UK shops report selling more copies of *It's Now Or Never* than everything else in stock combined. *Are You Lonesome Tonight*, a ballad originally popular in the mid-1920s via Al Jolson, hits US #1 for 6 weeks, selling 2 million copies. In it, Presley updates the mid-song narration technique originally employed on *That's When Your Heartaches Begin* in 1957, which splits listeners into love-or-hate camps. B-side *I Gotta Know* makes US #20.

Nov [7] The songs for movie *Wild in the Country* are recorded in Hollywood.

Nov [10] *G.I. Blues* premieres in London, UK.

Dec With her parents' permission, Priscilla Beaulieu flies to Memphis to spend Christmas with Presley and his family at Graceland. Meanwhile, the soundtrack LP from *G.I. Blues* tops the US chart for 10 weeks, earning a gold disk, and tops the UK chart for 25 weeks (well into mid-1961).

Dec [13] *It's Now Or Never* passes the million sales mark in UK in 6½ weeks: the one-millionth copy leaves Decca's pressing plant at 3.30pm. This is a new record time for a disk achieving this total in UK – the previous holder, Harry Belafonte's *Mary's Boy Child* in 1957, took 8 weeks.

Dec [20] Film *Flaming Star* opens in US, to diasappointing box office returns compared with *G.I. Blues*.

1961 Jan *Are You Lonesome Tonight?* tops the UK chart for 4 weeks, having entered in its first week at #2.

Jan [13] Film *Flaming Star* opens in UK.

Feb LP *His Hand In Mine*, his first wholly religious LP (made up of most of the gospel songs recorded at the end of Oct.), reaches US #13 and will earn a gold disk for a half million sales.

Feb [25] Presley performs a benefit concert in Memphis in aid of local charities, raising $51,000. During the show, he is presented with a plaque by RCA which marks record sales of 76 million worldwide.

Mar The only secular recording at the Oct. 1960 gospel session, *Surrender*, another dramatic adaptation of old Italian ballad *Come Back To Sorrento*, hits US #1 for 2 weeks, and is a million-seller. B-side is *Lonely Man*, written for *Wild in the Country* but cut from the completed film. In UK, *Wooden Heart* from *G.I. Blues* is released as a single (in common with most of the world, but not US). It tops the UK chart for 4 weeks, staying in UK top 50 for 27 weeks. Some location filming is done for movie *Blue Hawaii*.

Mar [25] Presley plays another benefit show, at Bloch Arena in Pearl Harbor, Hawaii, raising $53,000 for the USS Arizona Memorial Fund. (His 17-song set will be his last stage appearance for nearly 8 years.)

May EP *Elvis By Request*, an experimental 4-track release at 33rpm, headed by the title song from *Flaming Star*, reaches US #14. In UK, *Surrender* enters the chart at #1 and holds for 4 weeks.

June Gospel LP *His Hand In Mine* hits UK #3. Presley turns to R&B for a revival of Chuck Willis' *I Feel So Bad*, which hits US #5. B-side is ballad title song from *Wild in the Country*, which makes US #26.

June [15] Film *Wild in the Country*, a drama co-starring Presley with Tuesday Weld and Hope Lange, opens in US. Like *Flaming Star*, it has few songs and is serious in intent. It is also not a huge money-maker, inevitably leading Col. Parker back to lighter, more lucrative *G.I. Blues*-type films.

Aug LP *Something For Everybody*, divided into ballad and beat sides, and recorded with *I Feel So Bad* in Nashville on Mar.12/13, tops the US chart for 3 weeks, earning a gold disk. At the last minute, *I Slipped, I Stumbled, I Fell*, an aggressive rocker recorded for *Wild in the Country*, is added to the LP.

Sept The popularity of *Wild In The Country* and *I Feel So Bad* is reversed in UK, as the former hits #2 and the latter reaches #20.

Oct The coupling of two classic-style rockers, *(Marie's The Name) His Latest Flame* and *Little Sister*, proves to be Presley's most potent double A-side since *A Fool Such As I/I Need Your Love Tonight*, hitting US #4 and #5 respectively, and topping a million sales.

Nov *(Marie's The Name) His Latest Flame* tops the UK chart for 3 weeks, while *Little Sister* reaches UK #20. LP *Something For Everybody* hits UK #2 (behind *Another Black And White Minstrel Show* by The George Mitchell Minstrels).

Nov [14] Film *Blue Hawaii*, a romantic musical with 14 songs and co-starring Presley with Joan Blackman and Angela Lansbury, is released in US. (It will be a huge box office success, setting the seal on a money-making Presley movie formula.)

Dec Soundtrack LP from *Blue Hawaii* tops the US chart for 20 weeks, and is Presley's biggest-selling LP to date, topping 2½ million sales. In UK, it tops the chart for 18 weeks (and will remain in UK top 20 for 65 weeks). Meanwhile at Christmas, LP *Elvis' Christmas Album* re-charts at US #120.

1962 Jan *Can't Help Falling In Love*, from *Blue Hawaii*, hits US #2 (behind Chubby Checker's° *The Twist*), and is another million-seller. (This will become one of Presley's most enduring and much-covered ballads, and during the 1970s will be the song with which he will invariably close his live appearances.) B-side *Rock-A-Hula Baby*, also from the movie, peaks at US #23.

Feb *Rock-A-Hula Baby*, initially promoted as UK A-side, hits #3.

Mar *Can't Help Falling In Love*, having overtaken *Rock-A-Hula Baby* on UK chart, hits #1 for a week (dethroning Cliff Richard's° *The Young Ones* after 8 weeks at the top). This makes the single Presley's all-time most successful double-sided hit in UK.

Mar [29] Film *Follow that Dream*, a romantic comedy partly filmed on location in the rural deep South, opens in US, again to good box office receipts. It co-stars Presley with Anne Helm and Arthur O'Connell, and features only five songs.

Apr Loping rockaballad *Good Luck Charm* tops the US chart for 2 weeks (and will be Presley's last US chart-topping single for 9 years). Its sales top a million, and B-side ballad *Anything That's Part Of You* reaches US #31.

May *Good Luck Charm* tops the UK chart for 5 weeks.

June The EP of four songs from *Follow that Dream*, led by the title track, reaches US #15. (25 years later, *Follow That Dream* will often be revived in concert by Bruce Springsteen°. Presley will never sing it during his live touring.)

July LP *Pot Luck* hits US #4, and tops the UK chart for 10 weeks. EP *Follow That Dream* reaches UK #12, making it Presley's highest-charting EP in UK.

July [25] Film *Kid Galahad*, a remake of 1937 Humphrey Bogart/Edward G. Robinson movie, and starring Presley as a potential boxing champion (with Gig Young and Charles Bronson also featuring), opens in US.

Sept *She's Not You* hits US #5, another million-seller, and tops the UK chart for 3 weeks. B-side *Just Tell Her Jim Said Hello* reaches US #55.

Oct The 6-song soundtrack EP from *Kid Galahad*, led by rocker *King Of The Whole Wide World*, makes US #30.

Nov *Return To Sender*, a traditionally-styled (Otis Blackwell co-penned) medium-pace Presley rocker from movie *Girls! Girls! Girls!*, hits US #2 for 5 weeks (held off #1 by The Four Seasons'° *Big Girls Don't Cry*), its sales topping 2 million. B-side ballad *Where Do You Come From?*, also from the movie, peaks at US #99. In UK, EP *Kid Galahad* reaches #16.

Nov [2] *Girls! Girls! Girls!*, a romantic musical co-starring Presley with Stella Stevens and Laurel Goodwin, opens in US.

Dec *Return To Sender* tops the UK chart for 3 weeks, selling 700,000 copies. LP *Elvis' Christmas Album* re-charts in US at #59 while in UK, Presley's second LP *Elvis* (subtitled in UK *Rock'n'Roll No.2*) is reissued after several years' unavailability since its deletion by HMV, and hits UK #3.

1963 Jan The soundtrack LP from *Girls! Girls! Girls!* hits US #3 and earns a gold disk. Priscilla Beaulieu returns to Memphis to stay at Graceland with Vernon and Dee Presley. Presley has arranged with her parents that she should complete her education in Memphis. She attends the Immaculate Conception High School, joining in Presley's social life when he is at home during breaks between filming.

Feb Soundtrack LP from *Girls! Girls! Girls!* hits UK #2, behind Cliff Richard's° soundtrack LP *Summer Holiday*.

Mar Blackwell/Scott co-penned short uptempo *One Broken Heart For Sale*, from film *It Happened at the World's Fair*, sets a precedent for a new Presley single by not entering the US top 10 – it peaks at #11, while hitting UK #8. Also from the film, ballad B-side *They Remind Me Too Much Of You* peaks at US #53.

Apr [3] Film *It Happened at the World's Fair*, featuring Presley with Joan O'Brien and Gary Lockwood in another romantic musical, partly filmed on location at the Seattle World Fair, opens in US.

May Soundtrack LP *It Happened At The World's Fair* hits both US and UK #4.

Aug *(You're The) Devil In Disguise* hits US #3 and is a million-seller. In UK, it tops the chart for a week. (It will be Presley's last UK chart-topper until mid-1965 and the last single by any US act to reach UK #1 until Roy Orbison's° *It's Over* in 1964.)

Oct LP *Elvis' Gold Records, Volume 3*, a compilation of most hit singles from *Stuck On You* to *She's Not You*, hits US #3 and earns a gold disk.

Nov Leiber/Stoller's *Bossa Nova Baby*, taken from film *Fun in Acapulco*, hits US #8 and tops a million sales. R&B-rocker *Witchcraft* (a revival of little-known 1956 R&B hit by The Spiders) makes US #32. In UK, *Bossa Nova Baby* reaches #11.

Nov [21] Movie *Fun in Acapulco* opens in US, co-starring Presley with Ursula Andress, previously known for her role in James Bond film *Dr. No*.

1964 Jan Soundtrack LP *Fun In Acapulco*, almost entirely Latin-influenced, hits US #3 and UK #9, earning another gold disk. *Kiss Me Quick*, from LP *Pot Luck*, belatedly issued as a single after being a major hit in Ireland and several European countries, reaches UK #11.

Mar *Kissin' Cousins*, the title song from the film, reaches US #12. B-side soul-style ballad (later regarded a Presley classic), *It Hurts Me* makes US #29. It is one of just three cut recently in a now-rare Nashville studio session, on Jan.12.

Mar [6] Movie *Kissin' Cousins*, a hillbilly comedy in which Presley plays dual roles as an Air Force officer and his mountain boy cousin (the latter in a blonde wig), opens in US. In UK, location-filmed *Viva Las Vegas*, which has also been completed for the same company (MGM) is released instead, with the title amended to *Love in Las Vegas*. (A musical titled *Viva Las Vegas* has been released in UK in the early 1950s by MGM.) Presley's *Las Vegas* co-star is Ann-Margret, better-known than most of his leading ladies. (Off-screen, a romance between the two is rumored, which comes to nothing, though both will remain close friends. Ann-Margret will attend his funeral.)

Apr *Viva Las Vegas* reaches UK #17, while compilation LP *Elvis' Gold Records, Volume 3*, released belatedly in UK, hits #6.

Apr [20] Movie *Viva Las Vegas* is released in US (both it and *Kissin' Cousins* will show in the top 20 US box office takers of 1964).

May *Kiss Me Quick*, released in US as a special double A-side "Gold Standard Series" coupling with *Suspicion* (to catch spin-off sales from Terry Stafford's US #3 hit revival of the latter), makes US #34. Soundtrack LP *Kissin' Cousins* hits US #6.

June A revival of Ray Charles'° *What'd I Say*, cut in gospel-rock style with The Carol Lombard Quartet on back-up vocals, makes US #21. It is taken from *Viva Las Vegas* and the film's title song is on the B-side, reaching US #29.

July The 4-track soundtrack EP from *Viva Las Vegas* (not including the two songs already on a single) charts briefly at US #92, while *Kissin' Cousins* hits UK #12, and the soundtrack LP hits UK #5.

Aug *Such A Night*, a revival of 1954 Johnnie Ray hit which Presley had recorded in Apr. 1960 (and originally issued on LP *Elvis Is Back*) is released and makes US #16.

Sept *Such A Night* reaches UK #13.

Nov For the first time since 1961, both sides of a Presley single reach US top 20. First is rocker *Ain't That Loving You Baby*, which is released for the first time (but was recorded during Presley's Army leave weekend session in June 1958, along with *I Got Stung*, *A Fool Such As I* and others). It reaches US #16, but is overtaken by organ-backed ballad *Ask Me*, an Italian-originated song recorded in Jan. this year at the same time as *It Hurts Me*. This makes US

#12, and combined sales give Presley another million-seller. In UK, *Ain't That Loving You Baby* reaches #15, while *Ask Me* gets no UK exposure.

Nov [12] Film *Roustabout*, a romantic drama teaming Presley with established actress Barbara Stanwyck, opens in US. Much of it features him riding a motorcycle and a minor accident while shooting has to be written in to the script to accommodate a facial cut.

Dec *Blue Christmas*, extracted from the 1957 Christmas LP as a UK seasonal single, climbs to #11.

1965 Jan Soundtrack LP from *Roustabout* (which does not spin off a single release) tops the US chart for 1 week (dethroned by LP *Beatles '65*), earning another gold disk. In UK, it reaches #12.

Jan [22] Movie *Girl Happy*, co-starring Presley with actress/singer Shelley Fabares (whose *Johnny Angel* his *Good Luck Charm* replaced at US #1 in 1962), opens in US.

Mar Presley and Parker note the 10th anniversary of their partnership, with the announcement that they have made $150 million from sales of 100 million records, and a further $135 million from Presley's first 17 movies.

Apr *Do The Clam*, a dance number from *Girl Happy*, makes US #21 and UK #19.

May Soundtrack LP *Girl Happy* hits both US and UK #8.

June Originally released to coincide with Easter, Presley's revival of gospel ballad *Crying In The Chapel* (recorded in 1960 with the tracks which formed LP *His Hand In Mine*, but held for release until now) becomes his first US top 10 hit since *Bossa Nova Baby*, hitting #3 and selling a million. It also tops the UK chart for 3 weeks.

June [15] Film *Tickle Me*, co-starring UK actress Jocelyn Lane, opens in US. None of its nine songs are purpose-written: it uses tracks from earlier Presley LPs, back to his first post-army days.

July Presley travels to Hawaii to film movie *Paradise, Hawaiian Style*, staying at the Ilikai Hotel, Waikiki. Meanwhile, *(Such An) Easy Question*, originally from LP *Pot Luck* and now included in *Tickle Me*, makes US #11, but is not released in UK. B-side *It Feels So Right*, which makes US #55, is also from the movie, though originally a 1960 cut from LP *Elvis Is Back*. At the same time, an EP of five further *Tickle Me* songs, all from earlier Presley LPs, climbs to US #70 (his last EP to make the US chart – the format is all but dormant in US by now).

Aug [27] Presley plays host to The Beatles°, who are on a break in LA from a US tour, at his house in Perugia Way, Bel Air. They talk and play together for hours late into the night, jamming along to records, while managers Tom Parker and Brian Epstein play pool.

Sept LP *Elvis For Everyone*, a collection of unissued studio and film recordings cut between Presley's Sun days and 1964, and released to mark his 10th anniversary with RCA, hits US #10.

Oct *I'm Yours*, from LP *Pot Luck* but also revived for *Tickle Me*, makes US #11, with a narration on the original LP cut removed. This again is not issued in UK, but LP *Flaming Star And Summer Kisses*, a UK compilation made up of tracks from deleted LP *Loving You* and unissued-in-UK EP *Elvis By Request*, reaches UK #11.

Oct [22] Bill Black dies in Memphis at the Baptist Hospital, having not recovered from surgery on a brain tumor.

Dec *Puppet On A String*, a light ballad from film *Girl Happy*, which has sustained airplay ever since the movie soundtrack's release, is finally issued as a US single for the Christmas market, and reaches #14. In UK, *Tell Me Why*, an unreleased song recorded in 1957 (at the same session as *All Shook Up*) is released with *Puppet On A String* as its B-side, and makes UK #15. Meanwhile, soundtrack LP *Harem Scarum* hits US #8 and LP *Elvis For Everyone* hits UK #8.

Dec [15] Movie *Harem Scarum*, which co-stars Presley and Mary Ann Mobley in an unlikely *Desert Song*-type setting, is released in US. In UK, it is retitled *Harem Holiday*. The film is ill-received even by fans and UK publication *Elvis Monthly* advises Presley followers to complain to producer Sam Katzman about the poor quality of the production.

1966 Jan *Tell Me Why* makes US #33, while B-side *Blue River* makes US #95. In UK, soundtrack LP *Harem Holiday* reaches #11. Having left Graceland to live with her parents again after graduating from high school, Priscilla Beaulieu returns, to live again with Presley's grandmother. Rumors of a secret engagement ensue when she is seen regularly with Presley on his between-films breaks throughout the year.

Mar *Blue River* is UK A-side and peaks at #22.

Apr Presley's revival of standard *Frankie And Johnny*, also the title song from his next film, reaches US #25 and UK #21, though much US airplay goes to ballad B-side *Please Don't Stop Loving Me* (also from the movie), which climbs to US #45.

Apr [20] Movie *Frankie and Johnny*, a romantic musical/comedy based on the traditional song, opens in US. It co-stars Presley with Donna Douglas from TV's "The Beverly Hillbillies".

May Soundtrack LP *Frankie And Johnny* reaches US #20 and UK #11.

May [25] At a 4-day recording session in Nashville, Presley works with producer Felton Jarvis for the first time.

June [8] *Paradise, Hawaiian Style*, a largely location-shot romantic musical designed to re-create the magic (and money-making power) of *Blue Hawaii*, opens in US, featuring Presley with another UK actress, Suzannah Leigh. With inferior songs and a considerably dulled charisma, the movie does only a fraction of the earlier Hawaiian picture's box office.

July *Love Letters*, one of 18 tracks cut in a productive return to the Nashville studios at the end of May, is rush-released, reaching US #19 and hitting UK #6. It is an exact revival of Ketty Lester's 1962 voice/piano arrangement.

Aug Soundtrack LP *Paradise, Hawaiian Style*, reaches US #15 and hits UK #7.

Nov *Spinout*, the movie title song, peaks at US #40, while its double A-side coupling *All That I Am*, also from the film, makes US #41 and, as the only promoted side in UK, reaches UK #18. (It is significant in being the first Presley recording to feature strings in the accompaniment.)

Dec *If Every Day Was Like Christmas*, a new seasonal song recorded in Nashville on June 10, reaches UK #13. (It does not chart in US because of a policy of restricting Christmas records to a special Christmas chart at this time). Meanwhile, soundtrack LP *Spinout* makes US #18, and (as *California Holiday*) UK #17. The LP is most notable for the three non-movie bonus tracks it includes: a revival of The Clovers' R&B rocker *Down In The Alley*, Hawaiian ballad *I'll Remember You* and a lengthy version of Bob Dylan's° *Tomorrow Is A Long Time* (which Dylan will, 3 years later, quote as being his favorite cover version of one of his songs).

Dec [14] Musical comedy film *Spinout*, co-starring Shelley Fabares again, opens in US. In UK, it is re-titled *California Holiday*.

1967 Feb *Indescribably Blue*, recorded at the same June session as *If Every Day Was Like Christmas*, reaches US #33 and UK #21.

May Presley's second religious LP *How Great Thou Art*, including *Crying In The Chapel*, and recorded in Nashville alongside *Love Letters*, reaches US #18, earning a gold disk, and UK #11. (It will also win Presley's first Grammy award, for Best Religious Recording of 1967.) In UK, double A-side *You Gotta Stop/The Love Machine* is taken from film *Easy Come, Easy Go*, and makes UK #38.

May [1] Presley marries Priscilla Beaulieu at the Aladdin Hotel, Las Vegas, before 100 invited guests, in a civil ceremony conducted by Nevada Supreme Court Justice David Zenoff. Presley's assistant Joe Esposito is his best man, and the bride's sister Michelle is her maid of honor. After a reception in the hotel, they fly to Palm Springs to begin a honeymoon.

May [4] After a day in Hollywood where Presley puts finishing touches to movie *Clambake*, they fly home to Memphis to complete their honeymoon.

May [14] Film *Easy Come, Easy Go* opens in US, featuring a cameo role from veteran actress Elsa Lanchester (best remembered as *The Bride of Frankenstein*).

May [29] A second wedding reception is held at Graceland, for 125 friends and relatives unable to attend in Las Vegas.

June *Long Legged Girl (With The Short Dress On)*, a novelty rocker from *Double Trouble*, peaks at US #63. Its B-side *That's Someone You Never Forget*, a revival of a *Pot Luck* LP track, makes US #92.

July Soundtrack LP *Double Trouble* reaches US #47.

July [24] Movie *Double Trouble*, a comedy thriller, is released in US. Much of it is set in UK and Europe (though all shot in Hollywood), and features some UK supporting actors like Norman Rossington and leading lady Annette Day.

Aug *Long Legged Girl (With The Short Dress On)* makes UK #49.

Sept Two tracks taken from 1961 LP *Something For Everybody*, *There's Always Me* and *Judy*, peak at US #56 and #78 respectively. The coupling fails to chart in UK, but soundtrack LP *Double Trouble* peaks at UK #34.

Nov Cut at a rare Nashville studio session of R&B and country numbers on Sept.10/11, Presley's revival of bluesman Jimmy Reed's° *Big Boss Man*, with Charlie McCoy playing harmonica, reaches US #38. From the same session, B-side *You Don't Know Me* (a 1962 hit for Ray Charles°) reaches US #44, but fails in UK.

Dec [4] Film *Clambake* opens in US, co-starring Presley for the third time with Shelley Fabares. TV actors Will Hutchins and Bill Bixby are also featured.

1968 Jan Parker announces that Singer Sewing Machine Company is to sponsor Presley's first TV spectacular, to be made by NBC TV for year-end telecast.

Feb *Guitar Man*, written by country-rock singer-guitarist Jerry Reed (and featuring him on guest guitar), reaches US #43. Soundtrack LP *Clambake* (which also includes a side of non-movie bonus songs, including *Guitar Man*, *You Don't Know Me* and *Big Boss Man*) reaches US #40.

Feb [1] Daughter Lisa Marie is born at 5.01 pm at the Baptist Memorial Hospital, Memphis.

Mar *Guitar Man* makes UK #19.

Mar [11] Presley records four songs for film *Live a Little, Love a Little* at MGM Sound studios in Hollywood. (One of the songs, *Wonderful World*, by UK songwriting team Fletcher and Flett, has also just been recorded by Cliff Richard° with slightly different lyrics as one of UK's six shortlisted songs for the Eurovision Song Contest.)

Mar [14] Film *Stay Away Joe*, a comedy western made on location in Arizona, and starring Presley as an American Indian, opens in US.

Apr Released as a special single for Easter, Presley's revival of inspirational *You'll Never Walk Alone* (originally from musical *Carousel*, but best known via Gerry & The Pacemakers'° interpretation) makes US #92. Compilation LP *Elvis' Gold Records, Volume 4*, anthologizing mostly post-1962 hit singles, reaches US #33, while soundtrack LP *Clambake* makes UK #39.

May *U.S. Male*, another Reed° song in similar style to *Guitar Man* (and again with him playing guitar), reaches US #28 and UK #15. Its B-side is *Stay Away*, taken from film *Stay Away Joe*, and sung to the traditional tune of *Greensleeves*.

June Movie *Speedway* opens in US, co-starring Presley with Nancy Sinatra (as a tax inspector, out to get him). They duet on one song on the soundtrack.

June [27] Work begins on the Singer/NBC TV special, produced and directed by Steve Binder (whose previous credits include the all-star T.A.M.I. show in 1964). Binder has fought and won a lengthy running battle with Parker over the format of the show, which he sees as an opportunity to relaunch the magnetism of Presley as a live performer. (Parker had wanted Presley to sing 20 Christmas songs and say goodnight.)

June [28] Taping continues for the special at NBC's studios in Burbank, where for two extended sessions, Presley, Scotty Moore, Charlie Hodge and D.J. Fontana play in the round with an audience gathered about them, jamming on familiar material. These sessions continue the next day, interspersed with choreographed set pieces involving such Presley songs as *Trouble*, *Guitar Man*, *It Hurts Me*, *Little Egypt* and a gospel medley. A new song, *If I Can Dream*, is specially written for the show's finale by Earl Brown. (By June 30, Binder and NBC have hours of tape to edit into a 1-hour program.)

July The coupling of *Let Yourself Go*/*Your Time Hasn't Come Yet, Baby* from *Speedway*, peaks at US #71 and #72 respectively. It fails in UK, but *You'll Never Walk Alone*, appearing some months after its US release, makes UK #44.

July [7] Presley cuts the title song from *Charro*, with a backing track by the Hugo Montenegro Orchestra, in Hollywood. (It will be released in 1969 as B-side to *Memories*.)

Aug Soundtrack LP *Speedway* makes US #82. This is unique in being the only Presley LP on which a track is sung entirely by somebody else – in this case, co-star Nancy Sinatra's *Your Groovy Self*. In UK, the LP fails to chart, but *Your Time Hasn't Come Yet, Baby* climbs to #22.

Oct The coupling of *A Little Less Conversation*/*Almost In Love*, both from *Live a Little, Love a Little*, makes US #69 and #95 respectively.

Oct [9] Film *Live a Little, Love a Little* opens in US, a slightly more adult comedy than usual, co-starring Presley (as a photographer) with Michele Carey.

Dec The Singer TV special "Elvis" is aired on US NBC. It draws rave critical reactions, and also the year's largest viewing figures for a musical special.

1969 Jan The critically-rated closing number from the TV special, *If I Can Dream*, restores Presley to the US top 20, reaching #12.

Jan [13] Presley begins lengthy recording sessions at Chips Moman's American Recording Studios in Memphis, the first time he has recorded in his home town since working with Sam Phillips. Between Jan.16/17 and Jan.20/23, he will record 20 songs which will form the basis of a highly-rated series of singles and an LP.

Jan [25] Recording complete, Presley flies to Aspen, Col., with his wife and entourage, for a skiing vacation.

Feb LP *Elvis*, the soundtrack from the NBC TV special, hits US #8, his highest-placed LP in US since 1965, and the first since *How Great Thou Art* to pass half-million sales and earn a gold disk.

Feb [17/22] More recording sessions at American studios produce a further 14 new tracks, including revivals of many favorites from other artists' repertoires.

Mar *If I Can Dream* reaches UK #11.

Apr *Memories*, an orchestrally-backed ballad extracted from the TV show, makes US #35.

May LP *Elvis Sings Flaming Star*, a collection of tracks either unissued or (like the title track) not previously on LP, is released at low price and reaches US #96. (This is actually a reissue by RCA of an LP titled *Singer Presents Elvis*, pressed up for sale only through Singer Sewing Machine shops at the time of the TV special, as a promotional tie-in. Copies of the original LP will become high-priced collectors' items, because of scarce availability.) In UK, the NBC TV show LP *Elvis* hits #2. After completing work on film *Change of Habit* in Hollywood, Presley and Priscilla vacation for 2 weeks in Honolulu, Hawaii.

June Mac Davis' song *In The Ghetto*, with a stark socially-conscious lyric and a subtle, arresting arrangement, is the first release from the Memphis sessions and hits US #3 (his first top 10 in 4 years), selling over a million (again, his first since *Crying In The Chapel*, 4 years earlier).

June [10] Presley flies to Las Vegas to discuss arrangements for what is to be his comeback to the live stage after 8 years.

July LP *From Elvis In Memphis*, a varied collection from the Jan. session, receives the best reviews of a Presley LP since *Elvis Is Back* and reaches US #13, earning another gold disk. In UK, low-priced LP *Elvis Sings Flaming Star* tops the chart for 2 weeks, while *In The Ghetto* hits #1 for a week before giving way to The Rolling Stones'° *Honky Tonk Women*.

July [5] Presley flies to Las Vegas to begin rehearsals for his comeback show.

July [26] Presley opens at the Showroom of the International Hotel, Las Vegas, the beginning of a 4-week engagement which nets him $1 million. (The concerts are universally acclaimed a triumph, with the magnetic Presley stage presence of old still intact and doing justice to both 1950s material and new songs.) His new live back-up band includes Rick Nelson's° ex-guitarist James Burton, bassist Jerry Scheff, guitarists John Wilkinson and Charlie Hodge, keyboards player Larry Muhoberac (who will be replaced on future engagements by ex-Crickets Glen D. Hardin) and drummer Ronnie Tutt. Back-up vocal groups are The Imperials (The Jordanaires having turned down the gig because of Nashville commitments) and The Sweet Inspirations.

Aug *Clean Up Your Own Back Yard*, taken from film *The Trouble with Girls*, reaches US #35.

Aug [17] The TV special is re-shown on US NBC, with *Blue Christmas* edited out and replaced by *Tiger Man*, in deference to the midsummer season.

Aug [28] After 57 shows at the International, Presley's season closes. He and Priscilla fly to Palm Springs for a 3-week vacation.

Sept LP *From Elvis In Memphis* tops the UK chart for a week, while *Clean Up Your Own Back Yard* makes UK #21.

Sept [3] Movie *Charro*, a spaghetti-type western in which Presley plays a drifter with a constant 4-day stubble growth, opens in US, largely to indifference.

Nov For the first time in 7 years, Presley tops the US singles chart, with Mark James' *Suspicious Minds*, another recording from the Jan. Memphis session. It holds #1 for a week, and sells almost 2 million copies (but will be his last US chart-topper).

Dec *Suspicious Minds* hits UK #2 (behind Rolf Harris' *Two Little Boys*).

ELVIS PRESLEY *cont.*

Dec [10] Film *The Trouble with Girls (and How To Get into It)* opens in US, featuring cameo appearances by John Carradine and Vincent Price. Again, it has little action at the box office, and the low-budget Presley movie era is over.

1970 Jan *Don't Cry Daddy* hits US #6 and is another million-seller. B-side *Rubberneckin'*, taken from film *Change of Habit*, reaches US #69. Double LP *From Memphis To Vegas/From Vegas To Memphis*, featuring two sides of live performance and two from the Memphis sessions, reaches US #12 and earns a gold disk.

Jan [21] Film *Change of Habit*, in which Presley co-stars as a ghetto doctor with Mary Tyler Moore as a nun, opens in US.

Jan [26] Presley returns to the International Hotel for a second season, earning $1 million for a month's shows.

Feb [27] He begins 6 days of performances at Houston Astrodome, to a total of 200,000 people.

Mar *Kentucky Rain* reaches US #16, as *Don't Cry Daddy* hits UK #8.

Apr Double LP *From Memphis To Vegas/From Vegas To Memphis* hits UK #3.

May Budget LP *Let's Be Friends* makes US #105.

June *The Wonder Of You*, a live revival of old Ray Peterson hit, recorded in Las Vegas, hits US #9, and earns a gold disk for a million US sales. Meanwhile, *Kentucky Rain* reaches UK #21.

July Live LP *On Stage – February 1970*, recorded at the second International Hotel season, reaches US #13, earning a gold disk, and hits UK #2.

Aug *The Wonder Of You* tops the UK chart for 6 weeks, selling over 700,000 copies in UK, while double A-side *I've Lost You/The Next Step Is Love* makes US #32.

Aug [22] It is announced that Presley will play his first US live tour since the mid-1950s (6 dates opening in Phoenix, Ariz.).

Sept 4-LP boxed compilation set *Worldwide 50 Gold Award Hits, Vol.1*, anthologizing most of his major hits, reaches US #45 and UK #49, earning a gold disk.

Nov A live-recorded revival of Dusty Springfield's° *You Don't Have To Say You Love Me* makes US #11, while B-side fast country-rocker *Patch It Up* reaches US #90.

Dec *I've Lost You* hits UK #9. Budget LP *Almost In Love*, mostly collating film songs from earlier EPs, reaches US #65, while LP *Elvis' Golden Records, Vol.1* is reissued in UK, and makes #21.

Dec [15] Movie *Elvis – That's the Way it is*, a documentary of his summer 1970 Las Vegas shows, is released in UK.

1971 Jan *You Don't Have To Say You Love Me* hits UK #9, as soundtrack LP *Elvis: That's The Way It Is* reaches US #21 and UK #12, and earns another gold disk. Meanwhile, from forthcoming LP *Elvis Country*, a revival of *I Really Don't Want To Know* reaches US #21.

Jan [9] Presley receives the Jaycee's Award as one of the Ten Outstanding Young Men of the Year. (The other winners are all from outside the entertainment field and include President Richard Nixon's press secretary, Ronald Ziegler.)

Mar LP *Elvis Country (I'm 10,000 Years Old)*, recorded during a lengthy Nashville session in June 1970, reaches US #12, earning a further gold disk, and hits UK #6.

Apr *Where Did They Go, Lord?* makes US #33, while B-side *Rags To Riches* (originally a 1953 R&B hit for Jackie Wilson° and The Dominoes, and a pop #1 for Tony Bennett) reaches US #45, while religious compilation LP *You'll Never Walk Alone*, released for Easter, makes US #69. In UK, a revival of Engelbert Humperdinck's *There Goes My Everything* (B-side of *I Really Don't Want To Know* in US) hits UK #6.

June *Rags To Riches* hits UK #9, while *Life* climbs to US #53 and B-side *Only Believe* makes US #95.

June [1] The two-room shack in Tupelo, Miss., Presley's birthplace, is opened as a tourist attraction.

Aug Unusual folk-styled *I'm Leavin'* peaks at US #36, while LP *Love Letters From Elvis*, recorded at the same sessions as *Elvis Country*, reaches US #33 and UK #7. Budget LP *C'mon Everybody*, with more tracks from earlier film EPs, makes US #70 and hits UK #5. In UK, LP *You'll Never Walk Alone* reaches #20, while *Heartbreak Hotel* is reissued on a maxi-single (coupled with *Hound Dog* and *Don't Be Cruel*) in UK, and hits #10.

Sept [8] Presley receives the Bing Crosby Award, from US National Academy of Recording Arts and Sciences, given to people who "during their lifetimes, have made creative contributions of outstanding artistic or scientific significance to the field of phonograph records". (He is the sixth recipient, predecessors being Bing Crosby, Frank Sinatra, Duke Ellington, Ella Fitzgerald and Irving Berlin.)

Oct *It's Only Love* reaches US #51, but is not released in UK at this time. 4-LP boxed compilation *Worldwide Gold Award Hits, Vol.2* (each copy contains a small rectangle cut from an item of Presley's clothing) makes US #120. *I'm Leavin'* reaches UK #23.

Dec Budget LP *I Got Lucky*, with another set of film EP tracks, reaches US #104 and UK #26, while LP *Elvis' Christmas Album* is reissued in UK at budget price and hits UK #7.

1972 Jan A revival of B.J. Thomas' *I Just Can't Help Believing*, taken from the soundtrack of *Elvis: That's the Way it is*, hits UK #6, while UK maxi-single reissue *Jailhouse Rock*, in the wake of *Heartbreak Hotel*'s success, makes UK #42.

Feb [23] Presley and Priscilla are legally separated.

Mar A revival of Buffy Saint-Marie's ballad *Until It's Time For You To Go* reaches US #40 and hits UK #5. It is taken from LP *Elvis Now*, which peaks at US #43 and UK #12.

May Live-recorded revival of Mickey Newbury's *An American Trilogy* (combining traditional *Dixie*, *All My Trials* and *Battle Hymn Of The Republic*) reaches US #66, while third gospel LP, *He Touched Me*, climbs to US #79 and UK #38.

June [9/11] He plays his first concerts in New York: four shows at Madison Square Garden to a total of 80,000 people, earning $730,000.

July *An American Trilogy* hits UK #8.

Aug Live LP *Elvis As Recorded At Madison Square Garden* reaches US #11, earning a gold disk, and hits UK #3, while compilation LP *Elvis Sings Hits From His Movies, Vol.1* peaks at US #87. Divorce proceedings begin between Presley and Priscilla.

Oct Presley has his first US top 10 and first million-selling single since *The Wonder Of You* in 1970, with Dennis Linde's R&B rocker *Burning Love* (originally recorded by Arthur Alexander). It hits US #2, behind Chuck Berry's° *My Ding-A-Ling*, and UK #7.

Dec LP *Burning Love And Hits From His Movies, Vol.2*, combining the recent hit with earlier film songs, reaches US #22.

1973 Jan [14] "Aloha from Hawaii" TV show is aired live via satellite from the Honolulu International Center, to Japan and the Far East. (US and Europe see a taped version, but UK declines to take it. Its total worldwide audience is estimated as 1½ billion – the largest ever for any TV show.) The concert is a benefit for Kuiokalakani Lee Cancer Fund and raises $75,000; Presley sings Lee's best-known song *I'll Remember You* during the telecast.

Jan Ballad *Separate Ways*, taken from film *Elvis on Tour* (and widely interpreted as having been recorded because of his recent separation from Priscilla), reaches US #20. In UK, it is flipped to make *Always On My Mind* A-side and hits UK #9.

Feb Budget LP *Separate Ways*, again compiling the recent hit with earlier material, makes US #46.

Mar [3] *He Touched Me* wins Presley his second Grammy award (and second for a religious LP), as Best Inspirational Performance of 1972.

May Double LP *Aloha From Hawaii Via Satellite*, a recording of the Jan. telecast, tops the US chart for a week, earning another gold disk. (It is Presley's first #1 LP in 9½ years – and his last.) In UK, it reaches #11.

June A live version of James Taylor's° *Steamroller Blues*, taken from the "Aloha from Hawaii" show, reaches US #17, while his live revival of Tony Joe White's *Polk Salad Annie* (an onstage favorite) reaches UK #23 as a UK-only single.

June [6] Movie *Elvis on Tour*, filmed on the road the previous year, opens in US. (It will win a Golden Globe award as Best Documentary of the Year.)

Aug LP *Elvis*, with recently-recorded material, peaks at US #52 and UK #16.

Sept *Fool* (US B-side of *Steamroller Blues*) makes UK #15.

Oct Double A-side *Raised On Rock/For Ol' Times Sake* makes US #41.

Oct [9] Presley and Priscilla are divorced at a courthouse in Santa Monica, Cal. (The tension between them will evaporate and they will remain close friends.)

Dec *Raised On Rock* reaches UK #36.

1974 Jan LP *Raised On Rock/For Ol' Times Sake*, combining recently-cut rock and country material, reaches US #50.

Mar A revival of Billy Lee Riley's *I've Got A Thing About You, Baby* peaks at US #39 and UK #33.

Apr LP *Elvis – A Legendary Performer, Vol.1*, compiled as a historical overview and combining notable hits with unreleased material and interviews, reaches US #43, earning a gold disk, and UK #20.

May LP *Good Times* makes US #90 and UK #42.

Aug *If You Talk In Your Sleep* reaches US #17 and UK #40. Two of his Las Vegas Hilton (as the International Hotel has now been renamed) shows are cancelled due to Presley having 'flu. During the month, he also receives his 8th degree Black Belt in Karate.

Sept Live LP *Elvis Recorded Live On Stage In Memphis* reaches US #33 and UK #44.

Nov LP *Having Fun With Elvis On Stage*, containing clips of Presley's between-songs stage patter and jokes, makes US #130. (It had originally been sold by Parker as a souvenir item at concerts.)

Dec A hard-rocking revival of Chuck Berry's° *Promised Land* reaches US #14, while a revival of ballad *My Boy*, originally recorded by Richard Harris, hits UK #5.

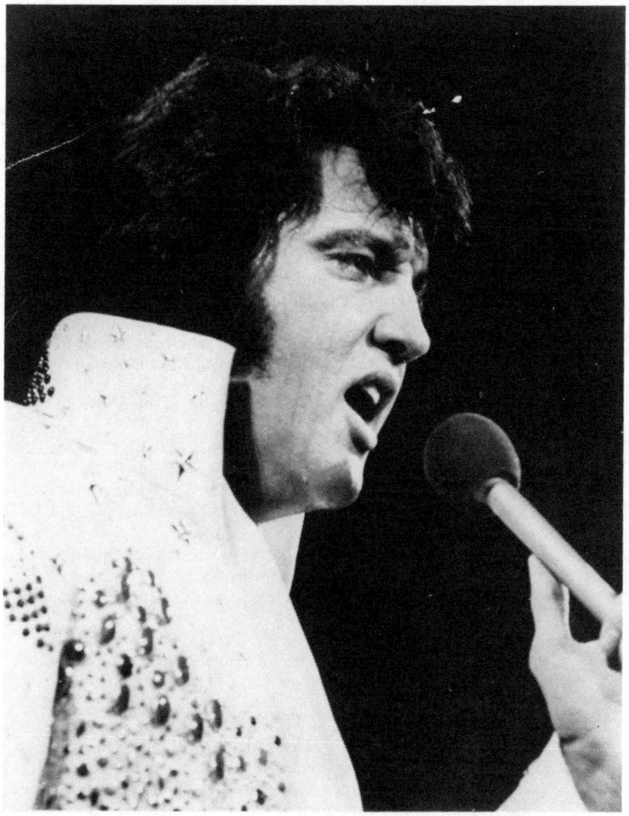

1975 Jan He is hospitalized in Memphis. A stomach complaint is diagnosed, and he is ordered a special diet and a treatment of cortisone, which has the side-effect of causing a notable weight gain. (He will fight to maintain a balance between his health and weight for the rest of his life, with prescription drugs in often grossly over-prescribed amounts.)

Feb *Promised Land* hits UK #9.

Mar [1] Presley wins his third Grammy award, as his 1974 live version of *How Great Thou Art* is named Best Inspirational Performance.

Mar *My Boy* reaches US #20, while LP *Promised Land* reaches US #47 and UK #21.

June *T-R-O-U-B-L-E* makes US #35 and UK #31. It is taken from LP *Today*, which climbs to US #57 and UK #48.

July TV-advertised double LP *40 Greatest Hits*, marketed in UK by Arcade Records, tops the UK chart.

Sept LP *The Elvis Presley Sun Collection* (the first time the early tracks have all been released on one LP) makes UK #16.

Nov *Bringing It Back* peaks at US #65.

Dec *Green, Green Grass Of Home*, a revival of Tom Jones's° hit, is issued as a UK-only single, and makes #29.

1976 Mar LP *Elvis – A Legendary Performer, Vol.2*, another historical overview, reaches US #46 and earns a gold disk.

Apr [29] Bruce Springsteen°, on tour in Memphis, attempts to see Presley by climbing the fence at Graceland. He is escorted off the premises by security guards while still trying to explain who he is. Presley is not disturbed.

May A revival of Timi Yuro's 1961 hit *Hurt* reaches US #28 and UK #37, while compilation LP *The Sun Sessions* makes US #76.

July LP *From Elvis Presley Boulevard, Memphis, Tennessee* (recorded in Feb. at his new studio at Graceland) reaches US #41 and earns a gold disk. In UK, it makes #29.

Oct 1960 hit *The Girl Of My Best Friend* is reissued in UK and hits #9.

Nov Jerry Lee Lewis° is arrested outside Graceland when he appears, drunk and with a .38 Derringer pistol, demanding to see Presley.

1977 Feb LP *Elvis In Demand*, a UK fan club-compiled set of hard-to-find tracks, reaches UK #12. On it is 1962 track *Suspicion*, which is also issued as a UK single, and hits #9.

Mar *Moody Blue* reaches US #31 and hits UK #6, while B-side ballad *She Thinks I Still Care* (a revival of a George Jones song) is a top 10 country chart hit.

Apr He makes his final recordings, in a session following a concert at the Civic Center, Saginaw, Mich.

May Compilation LP *Welcome To My World*, mixing live and studio country songs, makes US #44 and UK #7. (It will earn a platinum disk for million-plus sales, after his death.)

June [26] Presley's final concert is at the Market Square Arena in Indianapolis, Ind.

Aug [1] Book *Elvis: What Happened?*, written by former Presley payroll members Red and Sonny West and Dave Hebler, exposing the apparent darker side of Presley's private personality, is published.

Aug [16] Presley is discovered lying on the floor in a bathroom at Graceland by girlfriend Ginger Alden. He fails to respond to resuscitation attempts by aide Joe Esposito and is rushed to hospital, but pronounced dead at 3.30pm. His death of heart failure makes major headlines throughout the world.

Aug [17] Thousands of fans from all over US and even overseas arrive in Memphis to pay their respects (25,000 file past his coffin at Graceland during the afternoon). In Washington, President Jimmy Carter issues a tribute statement: "Elvis Presley's death deprives our country of a part of itself. He was unique and irreplaceable." Carter notes how Presley's unique meld of styles "changed the face of American popular culture . . . he was a symbol to people the world over, of the vitality, rebelliousness and good humor of this country".

Aug [18] Presley's funeral service is held at Graceland, with 150 people attending, and 75,000 more outside the gates. His body is moved by hearse in a 19-Cadillac cortege to Memphis' Forest Hill Cemetery, for entombment at 4.30pm in a mausoleum alongside his mother.

Sept *Way Down* reaches US #18, and sells over a million in US, while topping the UK chart for 5 weeks and selling more than 600,000. LP *Moody Blue*, containing his final recordings (including *Way Down*), is also a million-seller, hitting both US and UK #3. (The UK chart is flooded by Presley back-catalog LPs, resulting in top 30 positions for *G.I. Blues*, *Blue Hawaii*, *Hits Of The 70s*, *Loving You* and *Elvis' Golden Records, Vol.2*, and by old singles, of which *It's Now Or Never*, *Jailhouse Rock*, *All Shook Up*, *Crying In The Chapel*, *Are You Lonesome Tonight*, *The Wonder Of You*, *Wooden Heart* and *Return To Sender* all make the top 50. Double LP *40 Greatest Hits* tops the UK chart again.)

Oct The bodies of Presley and his mother are removed from Forest Hill Cemetery and re-buried side-by-side in the Meditation Garden at the rear of Graceland, because of an attempt to steal his body from the public cemetery. US CBS TV shows "Elvis in Concert", a special filmed during his final tour in June in Omaha and Rapid City.

Nov Double LP *Elvis In Concert*, combining the soundtrack from the TV show with June 1977 tour recordings, hits US #5 and reaches UK #13, and is another platinum disk.

Dec *My Way*, a 1977 live recording of the Frank Sinatra standard, reaches US #22 and hits UK #9, and is Presley's final million-selling single.

1978 June Gospel compilation LP *He Walks Beside Me* reaches US #113 and UK #37, while UK compilation of early tracks *The '56 Sessions, Vol.1* makes UK #47.

ELVIS PRESLEY *cont.*

July *Don't Be Cruel* is reissued as a UK single to tie in with the LP, and reaches #24.

Nov LP *Elvis – A Canadian Tribute* includes all his recordings by Canadian writers and makes US #86.

1979 Jan LP *Elvis – A Legendary Performer, Vol.3* makes US #113 and UK #43 (and will earn a gold disk).

Apr LP *Our Memories Of Elvis*, on which producer Felton Jarvis re-edits tapes to remove horns and strings and highlight Presley's voice more strongly against small-group accompaniment, makes US #132 and UK #72.

June [26] Vernon Presley dies in Tupelo of a heart attack, aged 63. (He will be buried beside his wife and son at Graceland.)

Dec TV-promoted double compilation LP *Love Songs* hits UK #4, while seasonal *It Won't Seem Like Christmas (Without You)* reaches UK #13.

1980 Mar At a Sotheby's auction in London, a paper napkin from the Las Vegas Riviera hotel with Presley's authenticated signature on it, sells for $500.

May [16] Dr. George Nichopoulous is indicted in Memphis on 14 counts of overprescription of drugs, notably to Presley, Jerry Lee Lewis°, and nine other patients.

July Compilation LP *Elvis Presley Sings Leiber And Stoller* makes UK #32.

Sept 8-LP boxed set *Elvis Aron Presley* reaches US #27 and UK #21. It consists largely of unheard material, including Presley's Apr. 1956 Las Vegas appearance and the 1961 charity concert in Hawaii. Only 250,000 copies are produced worldwide.

Oct *It's Only Love*, released on single for the first time in UK after inclusion on the boxed set, is his final UK top 10 hit, at #3.

Dec TV-promoted gospel compilation *Inspirations* hits UK #6, while seasonal *Santa Claus Is Back In Town* (from the 1957 Christmas LP) makes UK #41.

1981 Mar *Guitar Man*, in a version with updated accompaniment added by Jarvis, peaks higher than its first appearance in 1968, at #28. In UK, it reaches #43. The LP of the same title, also with updated accompaniment, reaches US #49 and UK #33.

Apr Warner Bros. film *This is Elvis*, a documentary of his life using original concert and movie footage, plus specially-filmed linking material using actors, opens in US.

May Double soundtrack LP *This Is Elvis* makes US #115 and UK #47, while *Loving Arms* (from LP *Guitar Man*) reaches UK #47.

1982 Feb Compilation LP *The Sound Of Your Cry*, rounding up rare tracks, makes UK #31.

Mar A live version of *Are You Lonesome Tonight* on which Presley breaks up laughing in mid-song is issued as a UK single, reaching #25.

June The title track from *The Sound Of Your Cry* makes UK #59.

Dec Presley's final US hit single is *The Elvis Medley*, assembled from clips taken from *Jailhouse Rock, Teddy Bear, Hound Dog, Don't Be Cruel, Burning Love* and *Suspicious Minds*. It makes US #71. An LP of the same title, coupling the medley with nine hits, reaches US #133.

1983 Feb A further UK reissue of *Jailhouse Rock* on its 25th anniversary re-charts at UK #27.

Apr LP *Jailhouse Rock/Love In Las Vegas*, compiling songs from both films, reaches UK #40. *Baby I Don't Care*, taken from the LP, makes UK #61.

May [9] Bob Neal, former manager of Presley, dies in Nashville, aged 65.

June LP *I Was The One*, with additional modern accompaniment to several 1950s hits, makes US #103 and UK #83.

1984 Jan Presley's version of Billy Swan hit *I Can Help* is released as a single for the first time, and reaches UK #30.

Mar LP *Elvis – The First Live Recordings* gathers extremely early tapes of Presley performing on "The Louisiana Hayride" and makes US #163 and UK #69.

Nov His version of Roger Whittaker's ballad *The Last Farewell* makes UK #48.

Dec To mark the 50th anniversary of Presley's birth, 6-LP boxed set *Elvis – A Golden Celebration* is issued and climbs to US #80. It concentrates on unreleased live and TV show material from 1956-57, together with posthumously-discovered tapes of Presley singing at home with friends.

1985 Priscilla Beaulieu, now a successful actress (and a star of TV show "Dallas") publishes *Elvis and Me*, her account of love and life with Presley.

Feb LP *A Valentine Gift For You*, compiling Presley love songs, makes US #154, while *The Elvis Medley* finally appears as a UK single, and reaches #51.

May LP *Reconsider Baby*, a collection of Presley's best blues recordings, makes UK #92.

Aug A little-heard version of *Always On My Mind*, from the soundtrack of *This is Elvis*, reaches UK #59.

1987 Apr *Bossa Nova Baby* is reissued in UK to tie in with a Latin music fad in dance clubs, and makes UK #47. A new extended mix of it is produced by UK DJ/producer Simon Harris.

Sept To mark the 10th anniversary of Presley's death, double LP *Presley – The All-Time Greatest Hits*, compiling 45 hit tracks, hits UK #4. (Parallel US double LP *The Top 10 Hits* reaches #117.) *Love Me Tender/If I Can Dream* is extracted as a double A-side and makes UK #56.

1988 Jan Following its use on a TV ad for glue, Presley's *Stuck On You* is reissued and charts at UK #58.

Nov Presley's only child Lisa Marie marries in Hollywood.

THE PRETENDERS

Chrissie Hynde (vocals and guitar)
Pete Farndon (bass)
James Honeyman-Scott (guitar)
Martin Chambers (drums)

1965 Hynde, heavily influenced by current US soul stars and also practising on a baritone ukelele, attends a Mitch Ryder° & The Detroit Wheels concert at a local amusement park.

1967 She begins playing guitar and joins band Sat.Sun.Mat which includes future Devo° keyboardist Mark Mothersbaugh.

1973 Having spent 3 years at Kent State University, studying art, Hynde leaves for London, UK. She sells leather handbags in Oxford Street and models at St. Martin's School of Art. She also meets *New Musical Express* magazine journalist Nick Kent, who invites her to become a contributing writer. (Her first review is of a Neil Diamond° LP.)

1974 Hynde works part-time at future punk guru Malcolm McLaren's clothes shop Sex. She then relocates to Paris to join The Frenchies, and meets session guitarist Chris Spedding.

1975 Hynde returns to Cleveland, Oh., US, and joins R&B group Jack Rabbit.

1976 She returns to UK and forms short-lived band, Berk Brothers, but is deposed by Johnny Moped as lead singer.

1977 Feb Hynde sings backing vocals on Spedding's LP *Hurt*, produced by Chris Thomas.

Aug She cuts a demo tape of *The Phone Call* and links with Anchor Records' Dave Hill, who is forming new Real Records and invites her to join on an ad-hoc basis and helps fund further demo sessions.

1978 Mar Hynde puts together a band with Hereford-based musicians Farndon on bass, drummer Gerry Mackleduff (who will be replaced by Chambers following the recording of the first single) and Honeyman-Scott on guitar. The group, still nameless, records Ray Davies' *Stop Your Sobbing*, with producer Nick Lowe° for the Real label. Hynde settles on The Pretenders, inspired by The Platters° hit *The Great Pretender*.

1979 Feb *Stop Your Sobbing* is UK chart debut at #34. The group begins club touring, including dates at London's Marquee club and The Moonlight.

July Produced by Thomas, follow-up *Kid* climbs to UK #33 as the group begins a month's UK tour, including a headline concert at London's Lyceum.

Oct [22] The Pretenders begin four consecutive Monday night gigs at the Marquee club, as Hynde/Honeyman-Scott-penned *Brass In Pocket* begins a climb to hit UK #1.

Dec Christmas is celebrated with two festive dates at favored Marquee. The band also performs in the Concert for Kampuchea at London's Hammersmith Odeon.

1980 Jan Hill leaves Real to become The Pretenders' full-time manager (the label is bought by US company Sire, which retains the band). As the group begins a 30-date UK tour, debut LP *Pretenders* enters the UK chart at #1 and begins a US rise to hit #9.

Apr *Talk Of The Town* hits UK #8 as The Pretenders visit US for the first time and Hynde meets former hero Ray Davies at a New York club (they begin a 3-year relationship). The LP has already sold over a half million and *Brass In Pocket (I'm Special)* makes US #14. The band plays 3,500-seater Santa Monica Civic Auditorium, sold out in 2 hours, and a benefit gig for the United Indian Development Association in Hollywood.

May Towards the end of a US mini-tour, Hynde is involved in a fight with a Memphis bouncer and spends a night in jail.

June *Stop Your Sobbing* stalls at US #65.

July Grace Jones° covers Hynde's *Private Life*.

Aug A North American tour includes a performance at the 50,000 attended New Wave Festival in Toronto, Canada.

Oct [6] A 15-date UK tour begins in Newcastle, Tyne & Wear.

1981 Feb *Message Of Love* makes UK #11.

Apr US EP *Extended Play*, featuring *Message Of Love, Talk Of The Town, Porcelain, Cuban Slide* and *Slide*, makes #27 on the LP survey but remains unreleased in UK.

Apr [10] Honeyman-Scott marries US model Peggy Sue Fender, in London.

May [16] Chambers marries Tracey Atkinson.

Aug LP *Pretenders II* is released, set to hit US #10 and UK #7. The group begins a 3-month US tour, during which Chambers smashes a lamp in his hotel room and injures his fist. The rest of the tour is cancelled.

Sept *Day After Day* peaks at UK #45.

Nov *I Go To Sleep* hits UK #7.

Dec Shortly before planned UK Christmas dates, Chambers damages his other hand and more concerts are postponed.

1982 Jan The Pretenders resume US dates, followed by concerts in Japan, Hong Kong and Australia.

Mar Farndon and Honeyman-Scott return to Japan to meet respective model girlfriend and wife.

Apr On their planned wedding day, Davies and Hynde are refused marriage by a registrar concerned that they are rowing too much.

May Honeyman-Scott plays for The Beach Boys° on a US tour.

June [14] Farndon is fired – he is viewed as incompatible with the other members.

June [16] Honeyman-Scott dies following a period of cocaine and heroin addiction.

July Hynde flies to US to be with Ray Davies on The Kinks° US tour.

Sept Tony Butler fills on bass temporarily (he will rejoin Big Country°), while Billy Bremner (ex-Rockpile) joins on lead guitar.

1983 Jan *Back On The Chain Gang* hits US #5 (where it is used in DeNiro film *King of Comedy*) and makes UK #17.

Feb Hynde gives birth to her and Davies' daughter, Natalie. Mick Green of The Pirates (Johnny Kidd & The Pirates°) helps audition new guitarists and Robbie McIntosh (ex-Manfred Mann's° Earth Band and Night) becomes new lead guitar while he recommends Malcolm Foster, who is hired as bassist.

Apr [14] Farndon, who had been in the process of forming a group with Rob Stoner and ex-Clash° Topper Headon, dies of a drug overdose in the bathtub.

May [28/30] The Pretenders participate in the 3-day US Festival at San Bernardino, Cal.

Nov Festive *2000 Miles* reaches UK #15.

1984 Jan LP *Learning To Crawl* makes UK #11 and is set to hit US #5. The band begins "The Pretenders World Tour". Natalie joins her mother on the trek but Davies' Kinks° commitments keep the family apart.

Feb *Middle Of The Road* reaches US #19.

May [5] *Show Me* peaks at US #28 as, following a whirlwind romance, Hynde marries Simple Minds° vocalist Jim Kerr.

July *Thin Line Between Love And Hate*, reviving The Persuaders 1971 hit, now with Paul Carrack on keyboards, stalls at US #83 and UK #49.

1985 July [13] The Pretenders perform at Live Aid spectacular in Philadelphia, Pa., following Simple Minds°.

Sept UB40° invites Hynde to co-vocal a revival of Sonny & Cher° hit *I Got You Babe*. It tops the UK chart and makes US #28.

1986 Nov Following a lengthy recording session featuring a variety of musicians, based around Hynde, new LP *Get Close* produced by Jimmy Iovine, is released, set to hit UK #6 and US #25.

Dec Extracted *Don't Get Me Wrong*, aided by UK TV show "Avengers"-style black and white video, hits both UK and US #10.

1987 Jan *Hymn To Her* hits UK #10.

Jan [14] The Pretenders begin an 8-month world tour in Plattsburgh, N.Y., US. The line-up Hynde assembles comprises Robbie McIntosh (guitar), T.M. Stevens (bass), Bernie Worrell (keyboards) and Blair Cunningham, ex-Haircut 100°, (drums).

Mar *My Baby* (following an addition to the Kerr family) peaks at US #64.

Sept *If There Was A Man*, recorded for soundtrack LP for James Bond movie *The Living Daylights*, under the name Pretenders For 007, peaks at UK #49.

Nov Compilation LP *The Singles* hits UK #6 and US #69, as re-mixed version of *Kid* fails to chart.

1988 July A second collaboration between UB40° and Hynde, after performing together in June at the Nelson Mandela 70th Birthday Party concert in Wembley, London, *Breakfast In Bed*, hits UK #6.

THE PRETTY THINGS

Phil May (vocals)
Dick Taylor (lead guitar)
Brian Pendleton (rhythm guitar)
John Stax (bass)
Viv Prince (drums)

1962 Taylor (b. Jan.28, 1943), a student at Sidcup Art College with Keith Richard, is a member of Little Boy Blue & The Blue Boys (an embryonic Rolling Stones°) but quits the group when it changes name to Rollin' Stones and is about to turn professional, to begin a course at the Royal College of Art instead.

1963 Taylor forms a group with fellow R&B fan May (b. Nov.9, 1944, Kent, UK) taking the name from Bo Diddley's° *Pretty Thing*.

Dec The line-up, comprising Taylor, May, Prince (b. Aug.9, 1944), Pendleton (b. Apr.13, 1944) and Stax (b. Apr.6, 1944), is signed to Fontana after a gig at London's Central School of Art, and in the next few months will appear on UK TV's "Ready Steady Go" and feature in *The Sunday Times* color supplement.

1964 June The group creates media interest with its no-holds-barred style of R&B, long-haired, unkempt image which takes The Rolling Stones° persona one step further. May holds claim to having the longest hair on a man in UK. Bryan Morrison and James Duncan take over the group's management and Duncan writes debut hit *Rosalyn* (based on Benny Spellman's *Fortune Teller*), which makes UK #41.

Nov *Don't Bring Me Down* hits UK #10, as the group's image reaches its peak of notoriety when attempts are made to evict the members from their communal home in Belgravia. Newspapers are filled with tales of their exploits on the road and moral outrage is voiced by the establishment.

1965 Mar LP *The Pretty Things* hits UK #6, as extracted *Honey I Need* reaches UK #13.

July *Cry To Me*, written by Bert Berns, makes UK #28.

Sept The Pretty Things appear on US TV show "Shindig!" alongside The Yardbirds°, Jerry Lee Lewis° and Raquel Welch.

Nov Skip Alan (b. Alan Skipper, June 11, 1948, London) replaces Prince.

Dec LP *Get The Picture* fails to chart as the group's popularity begins to wane together with the R&B boom.

1966 Jan *Midnight To Six Man* makes UK #46.

May *Come See Me* peaks at UK #43.

July The group makes its final UK chart entry with Ray Davies-penned *A House In The Country*.

1967 Jan Wally Allen and Jon Povey (b. Aug.20, 1944, London) from Bern Elliott's Fenmen, replace Stax and Pendleton.

May LP *Emotions* completes the contract with Fontana, with basic tracks smothered with strings against the group's wishes. The group signs to EMI, releasing three singles without success.

1968 Mar John "Twink" Alder replaces Alan.

Dec LP *SF Sorrow* is a rock opera with a continuous thematic story. The group is now involved in London's flourishing psychedelic underground scene, far removed from its R&B origins. Despite critical acclaim, the LP is not a hit.

1969 Jan The group performs the LP in its entirety at London's Camden Roundhouse. The group makes a cameo appearance in Norman Wisdom film *What's Good For The Goose*.

Nov Taylor quits to become a producer with drummer Alder. (They will later work together when Alder becomes a member of The Pink Fairies.) Alan returns and Vic Unitt, from The Edgar Broughton Band, replaces Taylor.

1970 June LP *Parachute* is a critical success, but only makes UK #43. *Rolling Stone* magazine will vote it Album of the Year.

1971 June The group splits.

Nov The Pretty Things are prompted to re-form by manager Bill

THE PRETTY THINGS *cont.*

Shepherd and sign to Warner Bros. May, Povey and Alan are joined by Peter Tolson (b. Sep.10, 1951, Bishops Stortford, UK) on guitar, Stuart Brooks on bass and Gordon Edwards (b. Dec.26, 1946, Southport, Lancs., UK) on keyboards.

1973 The group tours US for first time.

Nov David Bowie° pays homage to the group on his LP of cover versions *Pin Ups*, which includes *Rosalyn* and *Don't Bring Me Down*.

1974 Oct The group signs to Led Zeppelin's° SwanSong label, and makes US #104 with LP *Torpedo*.

Dec Jack Green (b. Mar.12, 1951, Glasgow, Scotland) replaces Brooks and the group undertakes a long US tour.

1976 May LP *Savage Eye* makes US #163.

June The group disbands for a second time, when May, the only surviving original member, quits. It plays a few final gigs supporting Uriah Heep and Bad Company° at London's Wembley Empire Pool.

July May forms Phil May & The Fallen Angels which includes Bill Lovelady and ex-T. Rex man Mickey Finn with ex-Pretty Thing Wally Allen. The group releases an LP in Holland only, where The Pretty Things still enjoy cult status.

1977 The remaining members continue under the name Metropolis (until quitting at the end of the year).

1980 Aug The group re-forms to work part-time, playing clubs and pubs and releases LP *Cross Talk*. They appear performing the title theme in Vincent Price horror movie *The Monster Squad*.

1984 Members of the group provide music for an episode of UK TV series "Minder" under the name Zac Zolan & Electric Banana.

Aug The group begins a residency at a club in London's Little Venice and records "live" LP *Live At Heartbreak Hotel*, in front of an invited audience.

LLOYD PRICE

1950 Pianist, composer and vocalist Price (b. Mar.9, 1933, Kenner, La., US) begins leading an R&B quintet in New Orleans and writing and performing jingles and songs for local radio station W-BOK. One of these, *Lawdy Miss Clawdy*, results in Price signing to Specialty Records. (He had been rejected by Imperial label in favor of Fats Domino°.)

1952 *Lawdy Miss Clawdy* (with Domino° on piano) hits US R&B #1 (and will have numerous cover versions, including one by Elvis Presley°).

1953 Price advises fellow singer Little Richard° to send tapes to his producer Art Rupe. *Ain't It A Shame* is another top 10 R&B success. Drafted into the US Army, Price forms a band which entertains troops in Japan, Korea and the Far East.

1956 Discharged from the Army, Price moves to Washington, D.C., where he sets up his own Kent Record Company.

1957 Apr He leases *Just Because* to ABC-Paramount and it makes US #29. (Like every further chart success, except *Never Let Me Go* and *Misty*, *Just Because* is an original Price composition.)

Sept *Lonely Chair*, on KRC, reaches US #88.

1959 Feb On ABC-Paramount, Price's *Stagger Lee*, his R&B rewrite of folk tune *The Ballad Of Stack-O-Lee*, hits US #1 for 4 weeks.

Mar *Stagger Lee* hits UK #7. With Bo Diddley°, The Coasters°, Clyde McPhatter and Little Anthony & The Imperials, Price begins a 7-week "Biggest Show of Stars" package tour in Richmond, Va. *Where Were You (On Our Wedding Day)* reaches US #23.

Apr *Personality* hits US #2 for 3 weeks, held from the top by Johnny Horton's *The Battle Of New Orleans*.

May *Where Were You* reaches UK #15.

June Price's first UK top 10 is *Personality* at #9.

Aug *Personality* re-enters the UK chart and climbs to #25.

Sept *I'm Gonna Get Married* hits US #3 and reaches UK #23.

Nov *Wont'cha Come Home* reaches US #43.

Dec Its A-side, *Come Into My Heart*, makes US #20, as Price completes the year on US R&B package tours and TV appearances.

1960 Mar *Lady Luck* makes US #14, while B-side *Never Let Me Go* peaks at US #82.

May *No Ifs No Ands* climbs to US #40 as *Lady Luck* makes UK #45.

Aug *Question* makes US #19.

Sept *Just Call Me (And I'll Understand)* reaches US #79.

Dec *(You Better) Know What You're Doin'* makes only US #90.

1963 Nov A cover of Errol Garner's standard *Misty* is Price's first US Hot 100 single in almost 3 years at #21. It is released on his own Double-L label, which issues the first solo recording by Falcons' lead vocalist Wilson Pickett°.

1964 Jan *Billie Baby*, also on Double-L, reaches US #84. Price concentrates on other music business interests and investments and establishes a fund for black students, providing them with scholarships to attend college.

1967 Dec Wilson Pickett's° remake of *Stag-O-Lee* makes US #22.

1969 Price, based in New York, establishes a new label, Turntable, and opens a club of the same name (at former jazz venue Billboard). (This follows the murder of his Double-L partner Harold Lugan at their New York office, whose body is found while the record player spins a Lloyd Price disk.)

1971 Oct *Stagger Lee* makes the US chart (#25) for a third time with Tommy Roe's° cover.

1972 Price releases LP *The Roots And Back* on GSF label.

1974 Sept With boxing promoter Don King, Price co-promotes the 3-day "Zaire 74" music festival in Zaire, Africa.

1976 Price and King form LPG label in New York, having unsuccessfully dabbled in Muscle Shoals soul (on Scepter) and versions of Broadway hits (on Ludix label).

PRINCE

1965 Prince (b. Prince Rogers Nelson, June 7, 1958, Minneapolis, Minn., US), named after Prince Roger Trio, led by his jazz pianist father John Nelson (and occasionally featuring his mother Mattie as vocalist), develops into a private, sometimes lonely individual, like his father, who leaves his family following years of trying to reconcile his musical and home lives. A loner at school, where he is nicknamed "Princess" and "Butcher Dog" (supposedly because he looks like an alsatian dog), Prince teaches himself piano and plays in school talent shows, but never considers singing to an audience.

1968 His mother remarries, and stepfather Hayward Baker (with whom he has a generally strained relationship) takes him to his first James Brown° concert (a seminal musical experience which will retain some of its influence throughout his career).

1970 At age 12, Prince runs away from home and drifts, sometimes staying with his father (who buys him a guitar which he teaches himself to play). He is eventually adopted by the Anderson family, whose son André (later André Cymone) becomes a close friend and future musical collaborator. Prince begins writing songs and starts to play saxophone, drums and bass guitar. (He will master over two dozen instruments.)

1972 Drummer Charles Smith, a cousin, invites Prince to play guitar (and Cymone bass) in his junior high school-based band, Grand Central, which has Cymone's sister Linda on keyboards. Their repertoire is mainly current hit covers, which Prince arranges.

1973 Prince goes to Minneapolis Central High School, where fellow students include Mark Brown (later bassist Brown Mark) and Terry Lewis (later of Time). Grand Central becomes Champagne, Morris Day replaces Smith on drums, and Prince becomes band leader, although most of his own songs fall flat with audiences. His writing influences include, alongside several major R&B names, folk singer Joni Mitchell° and similar white performers.

1974 Even before he leaves school at 16, Prince and his mainly black local peers have developed their own individual Minneapolis musical scene and sound, known to its young adherents as "Uptown", around Prince's outfit and band Flyte Tyme, which includes drummer Jellybean Johnson, bassist Terry Lewis and singer Alexander O'Neal°. (The influential "Minneapolis Sound" of the 1980s is rooted here.)

1976 Prince is invited to play guitar on sessions at Sound 80 studios in Minneapolis by Brooklyn artist Pepe Willie, produced by Motown's Hank Cosby, and also featuring Colonel Abrams. (This is the source of instrumental out-takes LP *The Minneapolis Genius: 94 East*, released in 1986 by Willie on Hot Pink label.) Meanwhile, a demo tape is produced by English sound engineer Chris Moon, who recognizes Prince's talent and teaches him studio technique in return for half the proceeds from items on which they collaborate (mainly lengthy funk workouts on sexual themes).

June While Prince heads for New York to seek a recording deal, his demo made with Moon attracts the attention of Minneapolis businessman Owen Husney.

Sept Prince returns to Minneapolis, and Husney forms management company American Artists with attorney Gary Levinson. Convincing Prince to mold his songs into more accessible form, he puts up money for high-quality demos.

1977 Mar Record company negotiations start from the premise that Prince will produce himself. After a studio audition, Warner Bros. agrees to the terms and offers a long-term contract.

1978 Nov Debut LP *For You*, which has taken 5 months to produce (and used double the money advanced by Warner for three LPs), is almost entirely played by Prince himself, on synthesizers (an identifiable element of the Minneapolis Sound), and makes US #163. Taken from it, *Soft & Wet* (a title of which many radio stations are wary), reaches US #92 and R&B #12, selling almost 350,000 copies, mainly in the R&B market. (Follow-up *Just As Long As We're Together*, from the LP, fails to chart.)

1979 Jan At Minneapolis' Capri Theater (and chiefly to assembled Warner executives), Prince debuts live the band he has formed locally after completing the first LP (with Cymone on bass, keyboard player Gayle Chapman and drummer Bobby Z, plus rock guitarist Dez Dickerson and keyboardist Matt Fink, the result being a cross-breed of black/white, male/female and rock/funk influences).

Feb Prince leaves Husney and American Artists, turning variously and unsatisfactorily for management to Hollywood-based Perry Jones and Bob Marley's° ex-manager Don Taylor, before his Warner-appointed agent Steve Fargnoli introduces him to Cavallo & Ruffalo (managers of Earth, Wind & Fire° and Ray Parker Jr.°) where Fargnoli takes on responsibility for him personally.

June Recording begins for a new LP (which this time will take only 6 weeks to complete).

Oct LP *Prince* peaks at US #22, initially selling a half million copies (it will later sell double, going platinum). From it comes another R&B (but not crossover) hit (#13), *Why You Wanna Treat Me So Bad?*, and it also contains *I Feel For You* (which Chaka Khan° will revive for a #1 hit in 1984).

Nov From the new LP, *I Wanna Be Your Lover* tops the R&B chart for 2 weeks and makes US #11, his first major hit single.

1980 Jan Now fast gaining a press reputation for arrogance, Prince begins a feud with Motown punk-funker Rick James° while supporting him on tour. Meanwhile, *I Wanna Be Your Lover* is his UK chart debut at #41.

Feb [9] Prince plays a showcase in Minneapolis, but the venue is far from full and reactions are mixed to the rock assault and sexual shock tactics on stage.

Feb Gayle Chapman leaves and is replaced by Lisa Coleman (daughter of LA session veteran Gary Coleman), who has auditioned via a demo (and will stay with Prince for 6 years).

Mar Writing a batch of songs in short order, mostly on his Fender Telecaster guitar, Prince begins recording another LP; a rough-edged, one-man affair cut on his own 16-track equipment, which will become *Dirty Mind*.

Dec After being remixed in LA, LP *Dirty Mind* makes US #45 and earns a gold disk. Though it breaks Prince to a wider, young white audience, seemingly indecent tracks like *Head* and *Sister* outrage many in the black music industry. From the LP, *Uptown* makes US R&B #5, but does not cross over, due to an expected lack of pop airplay for the whole LP.

1981 Jan Prince and the band (later becoming known as The Revolution) begin to tour widely in US.

June [2] Prince plays his first UK date, at the London Lyceum. The attendance is poor and the rest of the tour is cancelled. (He will not play UK again for 5 years.)

June On returning to US, André Cymone quits the band for solo projects. (He signs with American Artists and will release two LPs, before concentrating on production.)

July Warner releases an eponymous LP by Minneapolis group Time, with all songs credited to Jamie Starr (an early Prince pseudonym). The LP had originated when Prince invited Morris Day to sing over six tracks he had already completed. The band has been formed only after the LP was completed and includes former Flyte Tyme members Lewis and Johnson, plus keyboardists Jimmy Jam and Monte Moir. (The members will later pay tribute to Prince's role as motivator in shaping the group.)

Dec Prince's fourth LP *Controversy* reaches US #21, while the extracted title track peaks at US #70. (Another extract, *Let's Work* hits R&B #9, but does not cross over.) This LP will also turn platinum, spending 63 weeks on US chart. Prince takes Time with him on a new US tour.

1982 Mar He buys a mansion in suburban Minneapolis, from which base he will henceforth permanently snub the traditional US music centers.

Oct A 6-month tour begins in support of new LP *1999*. It is a Minneapolis revue, with Prince & The Revolution following Time and Prince's new all-girl protegée group Vanity 6 (blonde Bostonian Brenda Bennett, Canadian Dee Dee Winters who is Vanity, and 16-year-old Minneapolis native Susan Moonsie).

Dec The title track from LP *1999* reaches US #44. The double LP initially slowly climbs up the chart (but will be a hit during 1983). Although Prince has played and produced most of its tracks by himself, the LP credits Prince & The Revolution for the first time.

1983 Jan Prince breaks on to the white act-dominated MTV playlist with his video for *Little Red Corvette*, from LP *1999*. Always uneasy with interviews, he now stops talking to the press.

Feb LP *1999* finally picks up real momentum, aided by wide exposure for *Little Red Corvette*, now issued as a single, while the *1999* title track makes UK #25. However, the tour does not go well. Time, despite a successful second LP in *What Time Is It?* (which has reached US #26), is relegated to backing Vanity 6 from behind a curtain, while Jam and Lewis are fired by Prince after missing a show (through being stranded by snow in Atlanta, where they were producing The SOS Band).

Apr The tour finishes and Prince begins work on a film with Hollywood scriptwriter William Blinn, while UCLA film graduate Albert Magnoli is brought to Minneapolis to discuss directing the project. Dickerson leaves The Revolution, and is replaced by Wendy Melvoin (daughter of session keyboardist Mike Melvoin), who will appear in the film.

May *Little Red Corvette* hits US #6 and makes UK #54, while LP *1999* finally peaks at US #9, and earns a platinum disk for million-plus sales, staying on chart for more than 2½ years.

July The title song from *1999* re-charts in US, this time at #12.

Oct *Delirious*, third single from the LP, hits US #8.

Nov Filming of *Purple Rain* begins (and will take 7 weeks, at a cost of $7 million). Wendy and Lisa begin contributing as a songwriting team as part of the project. *Purple Rain*, *Baby I'm A Star* and *I Would Die 4 U* are recorded live at Minneapolis' First Avenue club, where the movie's performance scenes are filmed.

Dec *Little Red Corvette* is reissued in UK, but peaks at #66.

PRINCE *cont.*

1984 Jan Double A-side *Let's Pretend We're Married/Irresistible Bitch* peaks at US #52.

July *When Doves Cry*, taken from the forthcoming movie and LP *Purple Rain*, gives Prince his first chart-topper, hitting US #1 for 5 weeks, and selling over 2 million copies to earn a rare single platinum disk (it will be the biggest-selling single of 1984). In UK, it is also his biggest success to date, hitting #4.

July [27] Film *Purple Rain* opens nationwide in US (and in UK 4 days later), its plot taking romantic liberties with Prince's past, his relationship with his parents and his rise through the Minneapolis scene. It is well received despite its cast of non-actors, and takes $60 million in 2 months at the US box office.

Aug Soundtrack LP *Purple Rain* sells over a million in its first week in US (eventually selling 9 million in US). It stays at US #1 for 24 weeks and hits UK #7.

Sept *Let's Go Crazy*, also from LP *Purple Rain*, tops the US chart for 2 weeks, selling a million (but is not issued in UK at this time).

Oct The title song from *Purple Rain* hits US #2 (another million-seller) and UK #8.

Nov A 100-date US tour gets underway. (By the time it ends in Apr. 1985 more than 1,692,000 tickets will have been sold. In the midst of the schedule Prince plays unpublicized free concerts for handicapped children.) The 2-hour show features his latest protegée, percussionist/singer Sheila E. (daughter of Santana° percussionist Pete Escovedo, and introduced to Prince by Carlos Santana), with whom he has already recorded LP *The Glamorous Life* in June 1984.

1985 Jan *I Would Die 4 U*, also from the movie, hits US #8 and makes UK #58.

Jan [28] Although expected to join the all-star session for USA For Africa's° *We Are The World*, he declines on the grounds that he does not record with other acts – but offers to donate an exclusive track to the follow-up charity LP (he gives *4 The Tears In Your Eyes*).

Feb Double A-side *1999/Little Red Corvette* becomes Prince's most successful UK single, hitting #2 behind Elaine Paige and Barbara Dickson's *I Know Him So Well*, while LP *1999* also makes UK #30.

Feb [11] Prince visits UK briefly to receive a BPI award as Best International Artist, at a nationally-televised London ceremony. He makes an extremely short, faltering acceptance speech, with his huge bodyguard at his side. The UK press is not kind to him, and he reportedly flies home vowing never to return.

Mar *Take Me With You*, duetted with another female protegée, Apollonia (who replaces Vanity, to lead Apollonia 6), is the only single from LP *Purple Rain* not to hit US top 10, peaking at #25. It is bettered by Sheena Easton's° *Sugar Walls*, which Prince has written for her under the pseudonym Alexander Nevermind, which hits US #9. In UK, *Take Me With You* is issued as double A-side with *Let's Go Crazy* and hits UK #7.

Mar [2] Prince wins a Grammy award for LP *Purple Rain*, named 1984's Best Group Rock Vocal Performance. His *I Feel For You* is also named R&B Song of the Year.

Mar [25] Prince wins the Best Original Score Oscar for *Purple Rain* at the Academy Awards.

May LP *Around The World In A Day* tops the US chart for 3 weeks and hits UK #5. The LP has evolved from rehearsals for Prince's next tour, and has been recorded at the newly-built Paisley Park studios at his HQ, the Warehouse. In striking contrast to its predecessor, it is released with minimal promotion, and Prince reportedly has to be talked by Warner into releasing singles from it. Tracks include spiritual *The Ladder* (co-written with his father) and *Temptation*, which features a conversation with God. Prince instructs Fargnoli to announce that he is retiring from live performance. Paisley Park (the studio and now the label) will become the center of Prince-orchestrated projects and acts, including The Family (featuring his regular sax player Eric Leeds and Susannah Melvoin) and Madhouse (a jazzy project, also featuring Leeds), in addition to independent protegées like Sheila E. and Jill Jones.

June Prince goes to Paris to plan and write songs for a new movie, after which he and Fargnoli travel to the South of France to schedule shooting for *Under the Cherry Moon*. When work starts, Prince relegates director Mary Lambert to an advisory role, and takes control himself. Meanwhile, *Paisley Park* is released as a single in UK and reaches #18.

July The first US single extracted from LP *Around The World In A Day*, *Raspberry Beret*, hits US #2. It is also the first single released on his own Paisley Park label.

Aug *Raspberry Beret* makes UK #25.

Sept *Pop Life*, from LP *Around The World In A Day*, hits US #7. Prince breaks his press silence to talk to Neal Karlen for *Rolling Stone*. The interview, vetted by Prince and his management, is as unrevealing as ever.

Oct *Pop Life* peaks at UK #60.

Nov *America*, a further single from LP *Around The World In A Day*, peaks at US #46.

1986 Apr *Kiss*, taken from the forthcoming movie and soundtrack LP *Parade*, tops the US chart for 2 weeks, selling over a million. Behind it at #2 is *Manic Monday* by The Bangles°, written by Prince under the pseudonym Christopher. In UK, *Kiss* hits #6.

May LP *Parade – Music From Under The Cherry Moon* hits US #3 and UK #4, earning a platinum disk. Prince decides to return to live work and the "Parade" tour is launched, with a big band, choreography replacing technoflash, and a greater R&B emphasis. Reviews are ecstatic.

June [7] Prince's birthday show in Detroit is filmed.

June Lisa Barber, a Sheridan, Wy., motel chambermaid, is the 10,000th caller to an MTV contest number. She wins a date with Prince to attend the premiere of *Under the Cherry Moon* in her hometown.

July [1] *Under the Cherry Moon* film premieres in Sheridan, Wy. Barber tells Prince she enjoys the movie. After the showing, at the assembled crowd party at the Holiday Inn, Prince plays an impromptu 45-min. set.

July [2] *Under the Cherry Moon* opens nationwide at 941 US theaters.

July *Mountains*, written by Wendy and Lisa and taken from *Parade*, makes US #23 and UK #45.

Aug *Anotherloverholenyohead*, from *Parade*, peaks at US #63. Prince submits a song to one of his long-time favorite artists, Joni Mitchell°, but she finds it unsuitable and declines to record it.

Aug [12/14] Prince plays three sold-out nights at London's Wembley Arena, his first UK dates in 5 years. (These are among his final live appearances with The Revolution, which he will disband before the end of the year.)

Sept *Girls And Boys*, released only as a UK single, reaches #11.

Nov *Anotherloverholenyohead* peaks at UK #36.

1987 Mar Prince prepares a new stage show, recruiting musicians and dancers. He retains Fink, Leeds, Greg Brooks and Wally Safford from The Revolution, recalls Sheila E. and adds guitarist Mico Weaver, keyboardist Boni Boyer, bassist Seacer and dancer/singer Cat Glover.

Apr *Sign O' The Times*, the title song from the forthcoming LP, hits US #3 and UK #10, as rehearsals for a European tour take place at Birmingham, UK, National Exhibition Centre.

May Double LP *Sign O' The Times* hits US #6 and UK #4, earning a platinum disk.

June *If I Was Your Girlfriend* (on which Prince's alter-ego "Camille" is credited with lead vocal), makes US #67 and UK #20, as the European tour begins.

July Prince's two UK Wembley Stadium dates are cancelled. The official reason given is poor weather (and hoped-for alternative dates at the indoor Earl's Court arena cannot be arranged in time), but rumors cite inter-promoter politics as a factor. No attempt is made to stage the "Sign o' the Times" tour in US (because, it is assumed, of the huge costs involved), but a movie of the same title, largely consisting of the tour show as filmed in Rotterdam, Holland, serves as a substitute for both US and UK audiences. (It will also be issued as a home video.)

Sept *U Got The Look*, a duet from *Sign O' The Times* with Sheena Easton°, hits US #2 and reaches UK #11. Rumors of a romance circulate at the same time, and the video for the single seems to (or possibly tries to) suggest a sexual chemistry between them.

Dec *I Could Never Take The Place Of Your Man*, another track from *Sign O' The Times*, hits US #10 and makes UK #29. Meanwhile, the music press runs stories concerning a mysterious Prince LP which he is apparently asking Warner to rush out on the carefully-planned Christmas release schedules. Warner staff admit to knowing less about it than the press, but rumors suggest Prince having directed that it should ship in a plain black sleeve, carrying no credits.

1988 Jan [1] Prince performs an after-midnight concert to benefit Minnesota

Coalition for the homeless. He is joined on stage by Miles Davis°.

Jan Wendy and Lisa's LP *Sideshow* is released by Virgin Records. The Christmas and New Year rush passes without the Black Album appearing. Several thousand are pressed in Europe and, when the recall notice comes, 100 copies slip out of WEA Records' German pressing plant. These (directly, or via a German radio broadcast) and advance promo cassettes, are the sources for a subsequent flood of bootlegs. The LP itself is a series of hardcore erotic funk out-takes; the track listing is: *Le Grind, Cindy C, Dead On It, When 2 R In Love, Bob George, Supercalifragisexi, 2 Nigs United 4 West Compton* and *Hard Rock In A Funky Place*.

Feb *Hot Thing*, B-side of *I Could Never Take The Place Of Your Man*, makes US #63.

May *Alphabet St.*, from the forthcoming LP (which is announced as definitely not being the Black Album), hits US #8 and UK #9.

June LP *Lovesexy*, an unlikely blend of sexy R&B and spiritual concerns, reaches US #11 and gives Prince his first UK #1 hit. It also concerns itself with the "battle" between Camille (the good or positive side of Prince's personality) and Spooky Electric (the bad). A Prince-penned Warner press release suggests that the Black Album was Spooky Electric's idea, but that Camille won over and stopped the "evil" record. (Cynics suggest that the whole business of the mystery LP was merely an elaborate pre-release scam for *Lovesexy*.) Meanwhile, Prince's sister Tyka Nelson signs to Chrysalis Records, and releases an LP, to no great success.

July The "Lovesexy" tour begins in Paris, France, and includes seven nights at London's Wembley Arena, UK. The visual emphasis is on technoflash and showbiz: Prince enters the circular stage on an outsize pink Cadillac. Cat disrobes him on a neon bed and then ties him to a chair, as an indication of his continuing obsession with sex. (After some of the gigs, Prince adjourns to small clubs, where he performs an additional late-night 3-hour set for invited guests. The tour is accompanied by rumors concerning Prince, such as the story that he is to star in the title role of a biographical movie about Jimi Hendrix° (firmly denied).

Aug *Glam Slam*, from *Lovesexy*, reaches UK #29.

Sept [14] A 20-date US tour – Prince's first in 4 years – sets out from the Met Center, Bloomington, Minn. (scheduled to end in Worcester, Mass., on Oct.22).

Sept Prince plays a benefit concert in Boston, Mass., to establish a scholarship in the name of 17-year-old Frederick Weber, who was killed when hit by an automobile while waiting in line for Prince concert tickets outside Boston's Tower Records store.

Nov *I Wish U Heaven*, again from LP *Lovesexy*, makes UK #24. Prince ends the year collaborating with other artists – once again working with Sheena Easton°, duetting with Madonna° on her forthcoming LP and signing George Clinton° to Paisley Park and paying off the latter's tax bill.

P.J. PROBY

1957 Proby (b. James Marcus Smith, Nov.6, 1938, Houston, Tex., US), after an education at a military school, moves to LA with ambitions to become a star. Taking the name Jett Powers, he has singing and acting lessons and picks up bit parts in B-movies and on TV.

1958 As Powers, he records two solo singles (*Go Girl Go* and *Loud Perfume*) for small LA labels, without success. He also forms The Moondogs with Marshall Leib (later one of Phil Spector's Teddy Bears), Larry Taylor (later of Canned Heat°) and Elliott Ingber (later in Frank Zappa's° Mothers of Invention); despite its later credentials, this quartet achieves little.

1959/60 Working as a demo singer, he signs to Liberty Records as a songwriter (his *Clown Shoes* will be Johnny Burnette's° last UK hit in 1962).

1961/62 He records for Liberty, both as Jett Powers and as Orville Wood, but a series of singles fails to make any impression.

1963 Fellow songwriter Jackie DeShannon introduces him to UK TV producer Jack Good (of "Oh Boy!" fame), currently working in Hollywood. Good earmarks him for the role of Iago in a rock version of *Othello* which he is hoping to stage with Cassius Clay as Othello, but the project founders.

1964 Apr Good is commissioned by Brian Epstein to produce a Beatles° TV special in London for UK BBC TV, and invites Powers – now using the name P.J. Proby, which meets with Good's approval – to UK as a guest act for the show. Good, who engineered Gene Vincent's° moody black leather image for UK TV 5 years earlier, molds a startling visual appearance for Proby, with tight trousers, loose smock top, and 18th-Century-type ponytailed hairstyle.

May [6] The show "Around The Beatles" is screened in UK and Proby's rocking guest slot arouses great interest. In anticipation, Good produces *Hold Me*, a 1939 ballad revived as a raucous rave-up, with Proby self-duetting in abandoned style. He sells it to Decca for release.

July *Hold Me* hits UK #3, rocketing Proby to stardom in UK, where he settles to take advantage of a flood of TV and live work.

Sept Marketed in US as part of the "British Invasion", *Hold Me* reaches US #70.

Oct *Together*, a 1961 top 20 hit for Connie Francis°, is rocked up in similar style to *Hold Me* (with Jimmy Page, later of Led Zeppelin°, on guitar), and hits UK #8. Liberty Records, to which Proby is still contracted in US, enforces its contract and wins a court action to prevent Decca releasing further Proby material. He transfers to Liberty in UK. (The label has already released *Try To Forget Her*, from his Jett Powers days, in competition with *Together*. Despite a reported large advance order figure, it failed to chart in UK.)

1965 Jan His first new Liberty recording, *Somewhere*, from *West Side Story*, is a melodramatic arrangement with Proby in quivering, over-the-top ballad vocal form. It hits UK #6.

Feb [1] While on a UK tour with Cilla Black°, Proby is forcibly "rested" when he is banned by the ABC chain from any further live appearances at its theaters, after he apparently deliberately splits his tight velvet pants on stage to excite the female audience. (The first such incident, at Croydon Castle Hall on January 29, was accepted as an accident.)

Feb [8] ABC TV follows its theater chain namesake with a ban on Proby screen appearances, because of the trouser-splitting.

Feb [24] UK BBC TV bans Proby from appearance on any shows.

Feb *Somewhere* peaks at US #91.

Mar A revival of Billy Eckstine's *I Apologise*, with another exaggeratedly dramatic vocal performance, reaches UK #11. LP *I Am P.J. Proby* climbs to UK #16 (his only chart LP).

June Affected by the bans, Proby begins to lose his performing reliability and becomes eccentric off stage, with a penchant for outrageous pronouncements to the media (he informs a *Sunday Times* interviewer that he aims to star in a movie "about a pop star who goes off his head and believes he's Jesus Christ").

July *Let The Water Run Down*, a rocking R&B performance, makes UK #19.

Oct A Lennon°/McCartney° ballad not recorded by The Beatles°, *That Means A Lot*, reaches UK #30.

Dec Proby's straight and sensitive version of *Maria*, from *West Side Story*, hits UK #8.

1966 Feb *You've Come Back* makes UK #25.

June *To Make A Big Man Cry*, having failed as a single for Adam Faith°, peaks at UK #34.

Nov *I Can't Make It Alone*, a Goffin/King° ballad with Spectoresque production by Jack Nitzsche, reaches UK #37.

1967 Mar *Niki Hoeky*, a R&B-rocker written by Pat and Lolly Vegas (later to find fame as Redbone with *Witch Queen Of New Orleans*), reaches US #23. It is Proby's biggest but last US hit (it fails to chart in UK).

1968 Mar MOR/country ballad *It's Your Day Today* makes UK #32, and is Proby's final UK hit single. Shortly afterwards, he is declared a bankrupt, with debts of £60,000, and returns to US, reputedly to Tex. to breed horses, which also fails. (He will continue recording for Liberty, much of it country-styled material, with the occasional oddity like 7-minute *Mery Hopkins Never Had Days Like These*, but no disk will chart.)

1970 Aug *It's Goodbye* is, appropriately, Proby's last Liberty release.

1971 He returns to UK, again at Jack Good's request, to play Iago on the London stage in Good's rock musical version of *Othello*, titled *Catch My Soul*. This has a successful West End run.

1972 Mar A one-off single for EMI's Columbia label coupling the standard *We'll Meet Again* with his own song *Clown Shoes* makes no impact. (Similar one-offs for a variety of labels like Ember, Seven Sun and Rooster will characterize his sparse recorded output through the next decade. Live work will mainly be in UK cabaret, playing a nostalgic show to appeal to those with memories of the mid-1960s. In contrast to his earlier public eccentricities, he will be reclusive off stage.)

1977 Proby is signed, again by Jack Good, to portray the 1970s Elvis Presley° in stage musical *Elvis* in London's West End. (Presley at younger periods of his life is played by other singers, including

Shakin' Stevens°. The musical will run successfully for 19 months and pick up a theater award as Best Musical of the Year. Proby's performance will deteriorate after excellent initial reviews, and he will be sacked.)

1985 Sept After living in UK in comparative obscurity for several years (though regularly playing small club and cabaret dates), Proby signs to Manchester independent label Savoy Records, releasing a revival of Soft Cell's° *Tainted Love* on a 12"-only single, which generates music press interest, but is not a hit.

Nov A rapid follow-up on Savoy, a revival of Joy Division's° *Love Will Tear Us Apart*, has more positive reviews than sales. (Further, often eccentric, releases on the label – including a recitation from T.S. Eliot's poem *The Waste Land* – will also only remain cult items, despite the fact that in the late 1980s Proby is recording more regularly than at any time since his chart heyday.)

PROCOL HARUM

Gary Brooker (vocals and piano)
Matthew Fisher (keyboards)
Robin Trower (guitar)
Dave Knights (bass)
Barry J. Wilson (drums)

1959 While Brooker (b. May 29, 1945, Southend, Essex, UK), Trower (b. Mar.9, 1945, Southend) and bass player Chris Copping (b. Aug.29, 1945, Southend) are still at secondary school in Southend, they team with singer Bob Scott and drummer Mick Brownlee to form The Paramounts. The group becomes popular locally, playing covers of rock hits in local youth clubs, and when Scott drops out, pianist Brooker takes over vocals.

1962 After the group leaves school and gains a manager, Peter Martin, its gigs (still semi-professional) expand, as does the repertoire, which includes covers of US R&B singles by Ray Charles°, James Brown°, Bobby Bland and others. The group becomes resident band at Southend's Shades club.

1963 Jan Brownlee, the only one who does not wish to turn professional, leaves, and is replaced by Wilson (b. Mar.18, 1947, Southend) on drums, recruited through a small ad in *Melody Maker*.

Sept Copping leaves to go to Leicester University, and is replaced on bass by Diz Derrick.

Oct A demo coupling covers of The Coasters'° *Poison Ivy* and Bobby Bland's *Further On Up The Road* gains the group an EMI audition, and it signs to Parlophone label, working with The Hollies'° producer, Ron Richards.

1964 Jan *Poison Ivy* is released as the first single, and hits UK #35. It receives a boost from The Rolling Stones°, who name The Paramounts their favorite UK R&B group after the two bands have worked together on TV's "Thank Your Lucky Stars" pop show.

Mar A revival of Thurston Harris' *Little Bitty Pretty One* is plugged via a "Ready Steady Go!" TV appearance, but fails to chart (as will three more singles released to the end of 1965).

1966 Sept The group splits after its live gigs have reduced in quality (i.e. backing Sandie Shaw° and Chris Andrews on tours of Europe). Derrick leaves the music business, Trower and Wilson play with other R&B circuit bands, and Brooker decides to concentrate on songwriting, teaming with lyricist Keith Reid, whom he has met via a mutual acquaintance, R&B producer Guy Stevens.

1967 Apr With a batch of material in need of a band to play it, Brooker and Reid advertise for musicians in *Melody Maker*, and the first version of Procol Harum (after the Latin (procul) for "far from these things") is formed, with Brooker on piano and vocals, Fisher (b. Mar.7, 1946) on organ, Ray Royer (b. Oct.8, 1945) on guitar, Knights (b. June 28, 1945) on bass and Bobby Harrison (b. June 28, 1943) on drums. Producer Denny Cordell, a long-time acquaintance of Brooker, produces the first recording: Reid's surreal poem *A Whiter Shade Of Pale*, set by Brooker to music adapted from one of the movements of Bach's *Suite No.3 in D Major (Air On The G String)*.

May The band performs *A Whiter Shade Of Pale* at London's Speakeasy club, and Cordell places the record with Decca's Deram label, also sending a demo to pirate radio ship Radio London to see how it sounds on the radio.

May [12] The rave listener reaction to the first few exclusive plays of it on "Big L" prompt Deram to rush-release it in UK.

June *A Whiter Shade Of Pale* tops the UK chart for 6 weeks, selling 606,000 copies, dethroned by The Beatles'° *All You Need Is Love*. (Procol Harum becomes only the sixth act to top the UK chart with a debut release.)

July *A Whiter Shade Of Pale* hits US #5, taking its sales over a million (eventual worldwide sales will top 6 million). Meanwhile, after dissension within the group (plus panic that there is no act and no other repertoire with which to tour on the back of the hit), Royer and Harrison are asked to leave (they form their own band, Freedom), and Brooker recruits his old Paramounts cohorts Trower and Wilson to take over on guitar and drums.

Oct Cordell's production company moves its outlet from Deram to EMI's Regal Zonophone label, and *Homburg*, in similar style to the first single, hits UK #6. Meanwhile, LP *Procol Harum*, not a chart item in UK, reaches US #47. The US pressing includes *A Whiter Shade Of Pale* among the tracks, unlike the UK version, and all but one of the other tracks are Brooker/Reid collaborations.

Nov *Homburg* peaks at US #34.

1968 Apr *Quite Rightly So* makes UK #50.

Nov The group is signed to A&M Records in US for second LP *Shine On Brightly*, which reaches US #24 but on Regal Zonophone in UK it fails to chart.

Dec [28] On tour in US, the group plays the Miami Pop Festival, in Hallendale, Fla., to 100,000 people, along with Chuck Berry°, Fleetwood Mac°, The Turtles°, Canned Heat°, and many more.

1969 Mar Knights and Fisher both leave, to take up management and production respectively. Copping, his university studies at Leicester complete, rejoins his former Paramounts co-members, on both bass and organ. The line-up of the early 1969 Procol Harum is now the same as the early 1963 Paramounts.

Apr [6] The group plays with Ike and Tina Turner°, John Mayall° and others at Palm Springs Pop Festival, Cal., where an audience too large for the drive-in car park venue riots when police helicopters try to disperse it.

June LP *A Salty Dog* (recorded before the departure of Fisher and Knights, and produced by the former) makes US #32, while the title track reaches UK #44.

June [22] The group plays the Toronto Rock Festival, Canada, to 50,000 people, alongside The Band°, Chuck Berry°, Steppenwolf° and Blood, Sweat & Tears°.

July LP *A Salty Dog* is the first Procol Harum LP to chart in UK, reaching #27.

Aug [1] The group plays the Atlantic City Pop Festival, N.J., with Creedence Clearwater Revival°, Janis Joplin°, B.B. King°, The Byrds° and others, to 110,000 people.

1970 June LP *Home*, on which Chris Thomas takes over as producer (also for the next few LPs), makes UK #49.

July The band plays the 3-day Atlanta Pop Festival, in Byron, Ga., to 200,000 people, along with Jimi Hendrix°, Captain Beefheart°, Jethro Tull°, The Allman Brothers Band° and others.

Aug LP *Home* peaks at US #34.

Aug [28] Procol Harum plays on the second day of UK's Isle of Wight Festival.

1971 July The group signs a new contact with Chrysalis Records in UK, for release (via Island) of LP *Broken Barricades*, which makes UK #41 and US #32.

July [16] Trower leaves for a solo career. (He will become successful as a guitarist heading his own group through the 70s, with big LP sales in US.) Dave Ball (b. Mar.30, 1950) joins on guitar, while Alan Cartright (b. Oct.10, 1945) comes in on bass to allow Copping to concentrate on keyboards.

Aug [6] The group plays a concert with the Edmonton Symphony Orchestra and the Da Camera Singers, in Edmonton, Alberta, Canada. Mostly consisting of newly-arranged versions of earlier LP tracks, the show is recorded for live LF release.

1972 May Live LP *Procol Harum In Concert With The Edmonton Symphony Orchestra*, from the Canadian concert, makes UK #48. A double-pack reissue combining LPs *A Whiter Shade Of Pale* (the debut LP with the title track added) and *A Salty Dog* reaches UK #26.

June *A Whiter Shade Of Pale* is reissued in UK as lead track on a maxi-single (with *Homburg* and *A Salty Dog*), and climbs to UK #13.

July The live LP is more successful in US, where it is Procol Harum's best-selling LP, hitting US #5 and earning a gold disk for a half million-plus sales. Taken from it, a new orchestra-backed version of *Conquistador* (originally a track on the debut LP) makes US #16.

Aug Live *Conquistador* reaches UK #22.

Sept Ball leaves to work with Long John Baldry° and is replaced by ex-Plastic Penny and Cochise member Mick Grabham.
1973 May LP *Grand Hotel*, featuring guest vocal back-up by The Swingle Singers, reaches US #21.
Nov US compilation LP *The Best Of Procol Harum*, on A&M, creeps to US #131.
1974 May LP *Exotic Birds And Fruit* (its title a reference to the sleeve painting by Jakob Bogdani) fails to chart in UK but makes US #86.
1975 Mar [16] Along with Kevin Coyne and John Martyn, Procol Harum headlines "Over The Rainbow" closing down concert at London's Rainbow Theatre in Finsbury Park.
Sept LP *Procol's Ninth* reaches UK #41 and US #52. It is produced, at Brooker's request, by Jerry Leiber and Mike Stoller, and includes their song *I Keep Forgettin'* (formerly a hit for Chuck Jackson), as well as a revival of The Beatles'° *Eight Days A Week*. Extracted from it, *Pandora's Box* makes UK #16, but (with the LP) will be the group's last UK chart records.
1976 July Cartright leaves, and Copping moves back to bass, as Pete Solley joins on keyboards.
1977 Apr LP *Something Magic* peaks at US #147 (failing to chart in UK), and is the final Procol Harum LP. The group decides to split, considering that its particular strand of music has been fully explored, and recognizing a less favorable musical climate as punk rock catches hold in UK. A round of live dates in support of the last LP also becomes a farewell tour.
Oct [18] *A Whiter Shade Of Pale* is named the joint winner (with Queen's° *Bohemian Rhapsody*) as Best British Pop Single 1952-1977 at the British Record Industry Britannia Awards, to mark the Queen's Silver Jubilee. Held at the Wembley Conference Centre, London, (and shown on UK TV 2 days later) Procol Harum re-forms for the occasion to perform the song live.
1979 Brooker releases solo LP *No Fear Of Flying* on Chrysalis, which fails to chart.
1982 Moving to Mercury, Brooker releases second unsuccessful solo LP *Lead Me To The Water*. (He will be less visible on disk through the rest of the 80s.)

PUBLIC IMAGE LTD.

John Lydon (vocals)
Keith Levene (guitar)
Jah Wobble (bass)
Jim Walker (drums)

1978 Apr After The Sex Pistols° split at the end of their Dec. 1977 US tour, lead singer Johnny Rotten reverts to his real name John Lydon (b. Jan.31, 1956, Finsbury Park, London, UK) and, having taken a short holiday in Jamaica, returns to UK and forms a new band with ex-Clash° member Levene, novice bass player Wobble (b. John Wardle) and Canadian Walker, who has played drums with The Furys, and is recruited through an ad and auditions. The quartet's name is chosen because it claims to see itself as an alternative band espousing "anti-rock'n'roll". It signs to Virgin (The Sex Pistols' label).
July [25] The formation of the group is officially announced by Lydon.
Nov Debut single *Public Image*, released in a mock-newspaper sleeve, hits UK #9. The group is billed on this as Public Image Ltd. (but all subsequent singles will simply credit PiL).
Dec LP *Public Image Ltd.* reaches UK #22.
Dec [25] First live gig is a Christmas Day showcase at London's Rainbow Theatre. (Scattered live dates will follow in early 1979, but PiL will not mount a full tour. Walker will leave, to be replaced on drums by Richard Dudanski and then by Martin Atkins.)
1979 June [30] Lydon guests on UK BBC TV's "Juke Box Jury", along with Joan Collins.
July *Death Disco* reaches UK #20.
Oct *Memories* peaks at UK #60.
Dec LP *Metal Box* makes UK #18, so titled because the original release is packaged in a round 12-inch metal container with the album inside in the form of three 12-inch singles.
1980 Feb [13] Lydon's London house is raided by the police, who smash open the front door to find him waving a ceremonial sword at them from the top of the stairs. After a search, the only illegal item found on the premises is a canister of tear gas, claimed to be for defense against intruders.
Mar *Metal Box* is reissued in conventional form as double LP *Second Edition* and reaches UK #46. The band plays some European dates, including a Paris concert which is recorded for a live LP.
May Double LP *Second Edition* makes US #171.
June Returning from a short US tour which has had a mixed reception, the band announces that it will not play live again, and Atkins leaves to join Brian Brain.
Aug Wobble departs for a solo career (and will later form Human Condition).
Oct [6] Lydon is arrested for assault, after a pub brawl in Dublin, Ireland. (Sentenced to 3 months in jail for disorderly conduct, he will be acquitted on appeal.)
Nov Live LP *Paris Au Printemps (Paris In The Spring)*, from the concert earlier in the year (and released mainly to counter bootleg LPs of PiL's live show), reaches UK #61. Jeanette Lee joins the group for "visual assistance" – she organizes its video projections.
1981 Mar From new recordings by Lydon, Levene and Lee, *Flowers Of Romance* reaches UK #24.
Apr LP *The Flowers Of Romance*, with Atkins drumming on three tracks, makes UK #11.
May [15] PiL plays a show at New York's Ritz club (deputizing for Bow Wow Wow) posing behind a video screen while the music is played from tapes. They are showered with missiles and booed off stage by the 1,500 audience, whom Lydon insults in return. (The band considers the show successful, having videoed the debacle for movie use – begging suggestions that it has all been stage-managed.) A second show the following night is cancelled.
June LP *The Flowers Of Romance* reaches US #114.
1982 Lydon sets up permanent home in New York, and Lee leaves the group.
1983 July Levene departs, leaving Lydon as PiL's only full-time member.
Oct *This Is Not A Love Song* hits UK #5 and is the group's biggest hit single, while double LP *Live In Tokyo*, its second live set, makes UK #28. Lydon appears in movie *Cop Killer* with Harvey Keitel.
1984 May Lydon assembles a new band for *Bad Life* which peaks at UK #71.
July LP *This Is What You Want . . . This Is What You Get* makes UK #56.
1985 Feb Lydon teams with New York hip-hop artist Afrika Bambaataa° under the name Time Zone. on *World Destruction*, which reaches UK #44.
1986 Feb *Rise*, on which Ginger Baker plays drums, reaches UK #11. It is taken from LP *Album*, produced by Material member Bill Laswell (and also featuring Baker on drums and percussion), which makes UK #14.
May *Home*, also from LP *Album* creeps to UK #75.
1987 Sept *Seattle* peaks at UK #47 as parent LP *Happy?* makes UK #40.
1988 Aug After a long absence from performing, Lydon puts together a new stage version of PiL comprising himself on vocals, John McGeogh (guitar), Lu Edmonds (keyboards and guitar), Alan Dias (bass) and Bruce Smith (drums), which tours supporting Big Country°.
Sept 500 fans storm the stage in Athens, Greece, during a PiL set, destroying equipment and setting fire to trees in the park. Greek anarchists join in throwing rocks and petrol bombs. A reported £1 million-worth of damage is caused.
Dec Recording begins for a new Public Image Ltd. LP, scheduled for Spring 1989 release.

SUZI QUATRO

1958/64 Quatro (b. June 3, 1950, Detroit, Mich., US) having played bongos in her father's semi-professional Art Quatro Trio at age 8, and been taught to play drums and piano by her father, who makes sure his four daughters and one son get a good grounding in music, forms her own group at school.
1964 Determined to make a career in music, she leaves school and forms The Pleasure Seekers with her sisters, Arlene, Patti and Nancy, appearing on local TV as Suzi Soul. They become regulars at Detroit's Hideout club, the main venue for new young rock talent.
1965 The Pleasure Seekers' *Never Thought You'd Leave Me* is released on Dave Leone and Punch Andrews' (later Bob Seger's° manager) Hideout label, but not distributed outside Michigan.
1966 Mar *Light Of Life*, on Mercury, is the second (and last) Pleasure Seekers single.
1967 Suzi and her sisters travel to Vietnam to tour casualty wards.
1968 Suzi and Nancy form Cradle, playing hard-edged progressive rock.
1969 UK producer Mickie Most, in Detroit to work with Jeff Beck° at Motown studios, sees Cradle at a club and, impressed by Suzi,

invites her to come to UK and record for his RAK label.

1970 Cradle splits, and Suzi takes up Most's offer to move to UK. She arrives with Arlene, who is acting as her manager but returns to Detroit, after Most signs her.

1972 July After 18 months of writing and rehearsing, Quatro's *Rolling Stone* is released.

1973 June Quatro's second single, *Can The Can*, written for her by RAK's newly-signed writing team, Nicky Chinn and Mike Chapman, hits UK #1 for a week. She tours UK, supporting Slade°. A touring band is assembled comprising Len Tuckey (guitar), Dave Neal (drums) and Alastair McKenzie (keyboards), who is soon replaced by Mike Deacon from Vinegar Joe.

Aug *48 Crash* hits UK #3.

Oct Debut LP *Suzi Quatro* makes UK #32.

Nov *Daytona Demon* reaches UK #14.

Dec Quatro is named Best-selling Female Artist of the Year in UK.

1974 Feb *Devil Gate Drive* is her second UK #1 for 2 weeks, dethroning labelmate Mud's° *Tiger Feet*.

Apr Debut LP *Suzi Quatro* makes US #142.

July *Too Big* reaches UK #14.

Sept *All Shook Up*, on Bell, peaks at US #85. (She receives a message from Elvis Presley° complimenting her on her version of it and inviting her to Graceland – an offer she does not have the nerve to take up.)

Sept [30] She begins a tour of West Germany, supported by The Arrows.

Oct LP *Quatro* climbs to US #126.

Nov *The Wild One* hits UK #7.

1975 Feb *Your Mama Won't Like Me* makes UK #31.

Apr After seven consecutive chart singles, *I Bit Off More Than I Could Chew* fails.

May LP *Your Mama Won't Like Me* reaches US #146. Quatro undertakes a 3-month US tour, supporting Alice Cooper°.

1976 Mar Nearly 3 years after its UK release, *Can The Can*, on Big Tree, climbs to US #56.

1977 Mar Quatro's first release since Aug. 1975, *Tear Me Apart* makes UK #27. The producers of US TV series "Happy Days", having spotted Quatro on the cover of *Rolling Stone*, cast her as female rocker Leather Tuscadero. She is written into further episodes, but declines the offer to star in a spin-off series and settles in UK with her husband, Len Tuckey.

1978 Apr After another non-chart single, Quatro hits UK #4 with *If You Can't Give Me Love*.

July *The Race Is On* reaches UK #43.

Nov *Stumblin' In*, a duet with Smokie's lead singer Chris Norman, makes UK #41.

1979 May *Stumblin' In*, on RSO, hits US #4.

June *If You Knew Suzi*, the Chapman-produced LP which contains *Stumblin' In*, reaches US #37. *If You Can't Give Me Love* makes US #45.

Oct *I've Never Been In Love* peaks at UK #44. LP *Suzi . . . And Other Four Letter Words* climbs to US #117.

Nov *She's In Love With You* is Suzi's only UK hit for the year, reaching UK #11. *She's In Love With You* makes US #41.

1980 Jan *Mama's Boy* reaches UK #34.

Apr TV-advertised LP *Suzi Quatro's Greatest Hits* hits UK #4. *I've Never Been In Love* makes US #56.

Oct After leaving RAK signing to Chinn and Chapman's new Dreamland label, *Rock Hard*, on Dreamland, peaks at UK #68. It is featured in movie *Times Square*.

Nov LP *The Rock Hard* reaches US #165.

1981 Feb *Lipstick* makes US #51.

1982 Quatro quits recording and touring and daughter, Laura, is born.

Nov Signed to Polydor following the demise of Dreamland, her *Heart Of Stone* peaks at UK #60 but parent LP *Main Attraction* fails to chart.

1983 Quatro re-signs to RAK (but future chart action will not be forthcoming. She will be seen on television, hosting a UK daytime program "Gas" among other frequent appearances, and will continue her acting career, starring in London's West End stage production of *Annie Get Your Gun*.

QUEEN

Freddie Mercury (vocals)
Brian May (guitar)
John Deacon (bass)
Roger Taylor (drums)

1963/64 May (b. July 19, 1947, Twickenham, Middx., UK) and his father make a guitar, hand-carved from a 19th-century fireplace. Using a moving pick-up arrangement, a wide number of tones and echoes are created, with May using a coin as a pick (the genesis of the future distinctive Queen guitar sound). He leaves school, with 10 "O-level" and 3 "A-level" examination passes, to study at Imperial College, London to become an infra red astronomer. (He has been in teenage band The Others, releasing *Oh Yeah* in both UK and US on Fontana.)

1966 He is invited by Sir Bernard Lovell to work at Jodrell Bank, but chooses a music career instead.

1967 May forms band Smile with Taylor (b. Roger Meddows-Taylor, July 26, 1949, King's Lynn, Norfolk, UK) and Tim Staffell, whom he met at Imperial College, on bass.

1969 Smile's only single is US-only *Earth*, on Mercury.

1970 During the summer Staffell leaves to join ex-Bee Gee° Colin Petersen's group Humpy Bong but persuades his flatmate Mercury (b. Frederick Bulsara, Sept.5, 1946, Zanzibar, Africa) to join May and Taylor in a new group. (Mercury has moved to England in 1959 with his family, living less than 100 yards from May's home in Feltham, Middx., although they do not meet until 1970, and has sung for unrecorded group, Wreckage.) Queen is formed but the group still seeks a regular bass player.

1971 Feb Science graduate Deacon (b. Aug.19, 1951, Leicester, UK) joins on bass. They begin playing clubs and colleges (their debut gig is at the College of Estate Management, London) but continue to pursue individual ambitions. May is working towards a doctorate, Taylor is reading for a biology degree, Deacon is teaching and Mercury is studying design and running a clothes stall at Kensington Market.

1972 Queen is invited to showcase new recording hardware at De Lane Lea studios. Present while they record a demo tape are engineers Roy Thomas Baker and John Anthony (who had worked on the Smile single). They are impressed with the group and suggest to their employers, Trident Audio Productions, that Queen should be signed.

Nov After Trident executives have attended a Queen concert, the company signs the band to a production, publishing and management deal. While Baker and Anthony start work on a debut at Trident's studios, recording in vacant studio time, the company employs US A&R man Jack Nelson to negotiate a record deal. He hawks a 24-track demo and EMI signs the group.

1973 Apr [9] EMI launches Queen with a gig at London's Marquee.

June While Queen awaits launch of its first LP, Mercury, as Larry Lurex, releases a revival of *I Can Hear Music*.

July EMI releases Queen's debut single *Keep Yourself Alive* and eponymous LP. (The single will fail to chart.) The band supports Sparks at London's Marquee.

Nov [12] Queen begins a UK tour as support to Mott The Hoople° at Leeds Town Hall.

1974 Mar [1] The group begins its first headlining UK tour at Blackpool's Winter Gardens (ending in a gig at London's Rainbow. The flamboyant Mercury is becoming the main character in the line-up.)

Mar LP *Queen II* hits UK #5 during a 29-week chart stay. (The group utilizes state of the art studio technology during its recording.) The debut LP charts, peaking at UK #24 and is US debut on Elektra at #83.

Apr [12] Queen begins a US tour, again supporting Mott The Hoople°, in Denver, Col.

Apr Second single *Seven Seas Of Rhye*, a reworking of a track from the first LP, hits UK #10. (Queen makes its UK BBC TV "Top of the Pops" appearance when a David Bowie° promo film is unavailable and the group is slotted into the show, making a major impact.)

May A US tour is abandoned when May contracts hepatitis followed by a duodenal ulcer. LP *Queen II* makes US #49.

Nov With May fully recovered, LP *Sheer Heart Attack* hits UK #2, and charts for 42 weeks. Extracted *Killer Queen* also hits UK #2.

Nov [30] The group begins another UK tour, at Manchester's Palace Theatre (ending with a performance at London's Rainbow Theatre).

1975 Feb [5] Queen begins a US tour in Columbus, Oh.

Feb *Now I'm Here* peaks at UK #11 as Queen are voted "Band of the Year" in UK music paper *Melody Maker*.

May *Killer Queen* is Queen's first US hit, reaching #12, as does parent LP *Sheer Heart Attack*. After touring US and the Far East (a territory to which Queen will pay much attention), the group begins recording a new LP, with Baker producing, using six different studios.

Sept [19] The group splits acrimoniously with Trident, and signs with Elton John's° manager John Reid.

Nov First product of the sessions is classical pastiche *Bohemian Rhapsody*, the pinnacle of Baker's lavish production and Mercury's rock operatic writing style. EMI is reluctant to release the 7-minute single, but a copy is leaked to DJ Kenny Everett at London's Capital Radio, which creates a sales demand through heavy airplay.

Dec *Bohemian Rhapsody* tops the UK chart for 9 weeks, the longest run at #1 since Paul Anka's *Diana* in 1957. Bruce Gowers' promotional film helps make it a hit in other territories. (Although the promo costs only £5,000, it begins a new trend in the music industry to produce videos to promote records.) LP *A Night At The Opera* hits UK #1 in a chart run of nearly a year and hits US #4.

Dec [14] A UK tour begins at the Empire Theatre, Liverpool.

Dec [24] The group ends its most successful year with a live simultaneous broadcast on UK's BBC TV and Radio 1 of its London's Hammersmith Odeon show.

1976 Jan [27] Queen begins a 4-month tour of US, Japan and Australia at the Palace Theater, Waterbury, Conn., US.

Apr *Bohemian Rhapsody* hits US #9. *Queen at The Rainbow* film is released in UK, supporting Burt Reynolds' *Hustle*.

July Second single from the LP, *You're My Best Friend*, reaches US #16 and hits UK #7. Recording for a new LP begins. The band breaks from sessions to play a free concert in London's Hyde Park, plus dates in Edinburgh and Cardiff.

Dec [1] Queen, scheduled to appear on UK TV show "Today", pulls out at the last minute. EMI replaces it with recent signing The Sex Pistols°, who cause a furore with their behavior.

Dec *Somebody To Love* hits UK #2. (The group members have moved into other activities during the year: Mercury producing Eddie Howell's LP *Man From Manhattan* (on which he and May also play) and all members, bar Deacon, play on Ian Hunter's LP *All American Alien*.)

1977 Jan LP *A Day At The Races* enters UK chart at #1 and eventually hits US #5 as Queen begins a tour of US and Canada, in an outrageous visual style led by Mercury's stage costumes. *Somebody To Love* reaches US #13.

Mar *Tie Your Mother Down* makes UK #31.

Apr *Tie Your Mother Down* peaks at US #49.

May As the group tours UK and Europe, *Queen's First EP*, with lead track *Good Old Fashioned Lover Boy*, reaches UK #17.

July Recording for a new LP begins. Taylor, the first group member to cut a solo, releases *I Wanna Testify*.

Oct With the LP completed, Queen begins a US tour that will last until Christmas.

Oct [18] *Bohemian Rhapsody* ties with Procol Harum's° *A Whiter Shade Of Pale* as Best British Pop Single, 1952-1977 at the British Record Industry Britannia Awards, honoring The Queen's Silver Jubilee and the centenary of recorded sound at London's Wembley Conference Centre.

Nov Anthemic *We Are The Champions* hits UK #2. It is released as a double A-side with *We Will Rock You*. Parent LP *News Of The World* hits UK #4, and starts a climb to US #3.

1978 Feb *Spread Your Wings* reaches UK #34. *We Are The Champions* hits US #4, and goes platinum. Meanwhile, Queen completes a tour of Europe, including only two large UK dates. May contributes guitar to one-time skiffle king Lonnie Donegan's° comeback LP, *Puttin' On The Style*.

May *It's Late* peaks at US #74.

July The band begins a 3-month stay at Montreux, Switzerland, recording a new LP at its own studio.

Nov Double A-side *Bicycle Race/Fat Bottomed Girls* reaches UK #11. Queen starts a 6-month tour of US, Japan and Europe. LP *Jazz* hits UK #2 and eventually US #6.

Nov [16] The audience at New York's Madison Square Garden is treated to the sight of semi-nude female cyclists during Queen's performance of *Fat Bottomed Girls*.

1979 Mar *Don't Stop Me Now* hits UK #9, but stalls at US #86.

June *Bicycle Race/Fat Bottomed Girls* makes US #24, as the group begins a UK tour.

July LP *Live Killers*, recorded in UK on tour, is released, with extracted *Love Of My Life*. They hit UK #3 and #63 respectively.

Aug LP *Live Killers* reaches US #16.

Nov Light-hearted rockabilly *Crazy Little Thing Called Love* hits UK #2. It represents a diversion for Queen, including Mercury's debut as a rhythm guitarist, and was recorded in Munich, West Germany, with a producer known only as Mack, the first outside producer other than Baker to work with Queen. The group makes a full UK tour.

Dec Elektra in US finally releases *Crazy Little Thing Called Love* after US stations begin playing imported copies.

1980 Feb *Save Me* enters the UK chart, reaching #11. It is not released in US. *Crazy Little Thing Called Love* tops the US chart.

July *Play The Game* makes UK #14 and US #42. Parent LP *The Game* tops the UK chart. Queen begins a US tour that will last until September.

Sept Third single from LP *The Game*, Deacon's *Another One Bites The Dust*, with its distinctive Chic°-style disco bass line, hits UK #7. LP *The Game* is the group's first US #1, where it will stay for 5 weeks.

Oct *Another One Bites The Dust* tops the US chart. Unexpected support for the single has come from black radio stations and it hits #2 on US Hot Black Singles chart.

Nov *Need Your Loving Tonight* reaches US #44. The group tours UK and Europe.

Dec Queen's soundtrack for film *Flash Gordon* hits UK #10 and US #23.

1981 Jan Extracted *Flash* hits UK #10.

Feb Queen plays Japan again, before setting off on a groundbreaking South American tour, taking in Argentina and Brazil, under the banner "Gluttons for Punishment Tour". (Their South American popularity will soar throughout the decade.) *Flash* makes US #42.

Apr Taylor's second solo *Future Management* peaks at UK #49, as parent LP *Fun In Space* reaches UK #18 and US #121.

June Taylor's *Man On Fire* fails to chart.

Nov LP *Greatest Hits* tops the UK chart, beginning a 312-week chart run, and reaches US #14. Queen collaborates with David Bowie° for *Under Pressure*, which hits UK #1 (the group's first UK chart-topper since *Bohemian Rhapsody*).

1982 Jan *Under Pressure* reaches US #29.

June Queen's *Body Language* reaches UK #25 and US #11. Dance-

QUEEN *cont.*

based LP *Hot Space* hits UK #4 and US #22. The group, in the middle of a European tour, plays a concert at Milton Keynes Bowl, Beds., UK, which is filmed by Channel 4 TV. (The tour will continue to North America, followed by Japan in the fall.)

July *Las Palabras De Amor* reaches UK #17.

Aug Elektra releases *Calling All Girls* as the US single but it stalls at #60. *Back Chat* makes UK #40.

1983 Queen begins a year-long group sabbatical.

Apr [21/22] May gathers a group of friends for a session at Record Plant studios in LA, including Eddie Van Halen° (guitar), Fred Mandel (keyboards), Phil Chen (bass) and REO Speedwagon° drummer Alan Gratzer.

Nov First product of May's star-session is *Star Fleet*, based on a Japanese children's puppet sci-fi series theme, which reaches UK #65. Mini-LP *Star Fleet Project* reaches UK #35 and US #125. (During the year a change of US distribution to EMI-owned Capitol Records is negotiated.)

1984 Feb Queen's *Radio Ga Ga* enters the UK chart at #4 and then climbs to #2, held off the top by Frankie Goes To Hollywood's° *Relax*, which is boosted by a further 12" remix to increase its sales for the week. The single is an apparent criticism of contemporary radio programming. Its video effectively integrates a backdrop of scenes from film *Metropolis*. Composed by Taylor, this hit completes a unique chart feat as all four group members have now individually penned a top 10 hit.

Mar LP *The Works* hits UK #2 and US #23. It stays on UK chart for 93 weeks and is the group's second largest-selling UK LP, after *Greatest Hits*.

Apr *I Want To Break Free* hits UK #3, as *Radio Ga Ga* reaches US #16.

May *I Want To Break Free* makes US #45.

July *It's A Hard Life* hits UK #6, but stalls at US #72. Taylor's second solo LP, *Strange Frontier*, reaches UK #30.

Aug After a month of rehearsals, Queen begins a European tour which will include four nights at Wembley Arena. The European dates are followed by a controversial eight-show visit to Sun City in South Africa, putting them on the United Nations cultural blacklist.

Oct *Hammer To Fall*, fourth single from LP *The Works*, reaches UK #13. Mercury's first solo *Love Kills*, taken from the new soundtrack by Giorgio Moroder to Fritz Lang's classic 1926 film *Metropolis*, hits UK #10. (Footage from *Metropolis* has already been used in the promo video for *Radio Ga Ga*.)

Dec Queen's seasonal *Thank God It's Christmas* reaches UK #21.

1985 Jan Queen plays the "Rock in Rio" festival in Rio de Janeiro, Brazil.

May Mercury's second solo *I Was Born To Love You* reaches UK #11 and US #76. (While the other band members' solos have been with EMI, he has signed to CBS.) His solo LP *Mr. Bad Guy*, also self-produced and all songs self-written, including *Foolin' Around*, from movie soundtrack *Teachers*, hits UK #10. Taylor produces actor Jimmy Nail's UK #3 *Love Don't Live Here Anymore*, a revival of Rose Royce's° 1978 hit.

July [13] Queen performs at Live Aid at Wembley Stadium, UK.

July Mercury's second single from LP *Mr. Bad Guy*, *Made In Heaven*, stalls at UK #57. Taylor co-produces Feargal Sharkey's UK #26 *Loving You*.

Sept Mercury's *Living On My Own* makes UK #50.

Nov Queen's *One Vision*, from the soundtrack of film *Iron Eagle*, hits UK #7. May and Deacon guest on Elton John's° LP *Ice On Fire*.

Dec *The Complete Works*, a 14-LP boxed set, containing all the group's LPs except *Greatest Hits*, plus a bonus disk of previous single-only tracks, is released.

1986 Jan *One Vision* stalls at US #61.

Mar *A Kind Of Magic* hits UK #6. (The song and its flipside, *A Dozen Red Roses For My Darling*, are written for film *Highlander*.)

Apr Mercury contributes three tracks to the cast recording of Dave Clark's stage musical *Time*.

May Deacon temporarily forms The Immortals, to provide *No Turning Back* for film *Biggles*.

June Mercury's *Time*, from the LP, makes UK #32. LP *A Kind Of Magic* enters the UK chart at #1 and makes US #46.

July Extracted *Friends Will Be Friends* reaches UK #14. A UK Wembley Stadium concert is taped for simultaneous broadcast on UK independent TV and radio. Mercury releases a video EP of his four singles.

July [27] Queen plays Budapest's Nepstadion in Hungary in front of 80,000 fans during a European tour. The concert, filmed as *Magic in Budapest*, is the first by a Western act since Louis Armstrong in 1964.

Aug [9] Queen returns to UK to play Knebworth Festival.

Aug *A Kind Of Magic* makes US #42.

Oct *Who Wants To Live Forever* reaches UK #24.

Dec LP *Live Magic* hits UK #3.

1987 May Mercury's version of The Platters'° *The Great Pretender* hits UK #5.

Oct Taylor, playing guitar rather than drums, forms The Cross, which signs to Virgin, and *Cowboys And Indians* makes UK #75.

Nov Increasingly operatic over the years, Mercury duets with Spanish opera singer Monserrat Caballé on *Barcelona*, which hits UK #8.

Dec A three-volume video compilation, *The Magic Years*, chronicles Queen's extensive recording and visual career, and supersedes previous Queen video collections, all of which have been worldwide best-sellers.

1988 Feb The Cross LP *Shove It!* makes UK #58 as the group begins a mini-tour. May produces *Bohemian Rhapsody* by The Young Ones comic troupe Heavy Metal alter egos Bad News. (He will also produce singles for current flame, actress Anita Dobson.)

Oct Mercury and Caballé highlight a star-studded show to launch Barcelona's successful bid for the 1992 Olympic Games at the Avinguda De Maria Cristina Stadium. The pair's LP, also titled *Barcelona*, makes UK #25.

QUICKSILVER MESSENGER SERVICE

Gary Duncan (guitar)
John Cipollina (guitar)
Greg Elmore (drums)
David Freiberg (bass)

1964 Dec The group forms in San Francisco, US, with Murray on vocals and harmonica, Cipollina (b. Aug.24, 1943, Berkeley, Cal., US) on guitar, Freiberg (b. Aug.24, 1938, Boston, Mass., US) on bass and Casey Sonoban on drums. Skip Spence is briefly involved during early rehearsals at the Matrix Club, while Dino Valenti is lead vocalist, but a drugbust and imprisonment quickly put him out of the picture.

1965 June Elmore (b. Sept.4, 1946, San Diego, Cal.) and Duncan (b. Gary Grubb, Sept.4, 1946, San Diego, Cal.), both ex-Brogues, join in a new version of the group.

Dec First public performance, after several months of rehearsal in a North Beach basement.

1967 Jan [14] The group performs at the first "Human Be-In" at the Polo Fields, Golden Gate Park, San Francisco, alongside Jefferson Airplane° and Big Brother & The Holding Company.

June The band plays the Monterey Pop Festival.

July Having become a huge live attraction around San Francisco (75 gigs at the Avalon ballroom), the group makes a cameo appearance, performing two songs, in the hippie exploitation movie *Revolution*.

Oct Murray leaves and the group signs to Capitol. It is one of the last Bay Area bands to sign a recording contract, having held out until Capitol has agreed to all its conditions.

1968 Aug Eponymous debut LP, strong on instrumental passages due to lack of a strong lead vocalist, reaches US #63. The group appears at the 2-day Newport Festival in Costa Mesa, Cal.

1969 Jan Duncan leaves to form a band with Valenti.

May LP *Happy Trails*, consisting partly of live performances from the Fillmores East and West, with Cipollina and Duncan dual guitar-led improvisations on Bo Diddley's° *Who Do You Love* and *Mona*, reaches US #27.

Aug Nicky Hopkins on piano (ex-Steve Miller° band and Rolling Stones° sideman) joins just in time to prevent the remaining three-piece band from splitting. *Who Do You Love* is extracted in shortened form from the previous LP and reaches US #91.

Dec With Hopkins, the band records LP *Shady Grove*, which climbs to US #25.

1970 Jan [1] Valenti finally joins fully and Duncan returns, after playing a New Year's Eve reunion gig.

July Hopkins leaves, and is replaced on keyboards by Mark Naftalin, ex-Paul Butterfield°.

Oct LP *Just For Love*, recorded in Hawaii, displays a new style with more vocals. It reaches US #27, as Cipollina, disillusioned by the new Valenti-dominated direction, leaves to produce a Jim Murray solo LP, the sessions for which result in the band Copperhead.

Nov *Fresh Air*, taken from the LP, is the group's biggest US hit single, peaking at #49.

1971 Mar LP *What About Me* reaches US #26 and extracted title track (later covered by Moving Hearts) makes US #100.

July Freiberg is arrested for drug possession, fined $5000 and jailed for 2 months. He is replaced on bass by Mark Ryan. (Freiberg will join Jefferson Airplane° in Aug. 1972.)

Oct Naftalin leaves and is replaced by Chuck Steaks.

Dec LP *Quicksilver* peaks at US #114.

1972 May LP *Comin' Thru* reaches US #134.

Aug The group is scheduled again to play a UK tour but for the third time it is cancelled, as the members consider splitting up after playing a week-long "closing down celebration" concert series in San Francisco. Triple LP set *Last Days Of The Fillmore* includes three Quicksilver tracks and reaches US #40.

1973 June The group does not split but virtually ceases activity, while compilation LP *Anthology* reaches US #108. Ryan leaves and John Nicholas (ex-It's A Beautiful Day°) joins on bass.

1974 A seven-man version of the group maintains the low live profile and does not record. New members are Harold Aceves (drums), Bob Hogan (keyboards) and Bob Flurie (bass), with Duncan, Elmore and Valenti remaining.

1975 Dec Reunion of a Valenti/Duncan/Elmore line-up, with Skip Olsen on bass and Michael Lewis on Keyboards, records LP *Solid Silver*, which makes US #89. After this, the group finally disbands.

1987 Gary Duncan exhumes the Quicksilver Messenger Service name for LP *Peace by Piece*.

GERRY RAFFERTY

1968 Rafferty (b. Apr.16, 1947, Paisley, Scotland, UK) quits the last of a series of Scottish-based rock cover groups and joins The Humblebums, a folk-based group featuring singer/comedian Billy Connolly and Tam Harvey, which signs to Transatlantic Records.

1970 The Humblebums split after two poorly-received LPs, *Humblebums* (1969) and *Open Up The Door* (1970).

1971 Rafferty records his first solo LP, *Can I Have My Money Back?*, also for Transatlantic, but it makes little commercial impact.

1972 In London, he forms Stealers Wheel, conceived as "a Scots version of Crosby, Stills, Nash & Young°", with Joe Egan, a colleague from Paisley, Rab Noakes (guitar), Ian Campbell (bass) and Roger Brown (drums and vocals). By the time the group is signed to A&M, this line-up has already splintered, and the eponymous debut LP, produced by Jerry Leiber and Mike Stoller, has Rafferty and Egan as joint lead vocalists, playing guitar and keyboards respectively, Rod Coombes (drums), Tony Williams (bass) and ex-Big Three guitarist Paul Pilnick. Rafferty leaves the group shortly after the LP is recorded and, dissatisfied with the music business, returns to Scotland with his wife and baby. He is replaced by Luther Grosvenor, ex-Spooky Tooth, and Delisle Harper replaces Williams.

1973 May *Stuck In The Middle With You* hits US #6. It is taken from the debut LP, which makes US #50.

June *Stuck In The Middle With You* hits UK #8 and Rafferty is persuaded to rejoin the group.

Sept *Everyone's Agreed That Everything'll Turn Out Fine* reaches US #49 and UK #33. It proves inappropriate, as Pilnick, Coombes and Williams all leave the band. Rafferty and Egan record a second LP as a duo, with session help from Joe Jammer (guitar), Gary Taylor (bass) and Andrew Steele (drums).

1974 Feb *Star*, from the forthcoming second LP, reaches UK #25 and US #29.

Apr LP *Ferguslie Park*, named after a district of Paisley, fails to chart in UK but reaches US #181.

1975 Mar *Right Or Wrong*, recorded by Rafferty and Egan with Bernie Holland (guitar) and Dave Wintour (bass), and produced by Mentor Williams, fails to sell. Rafferty and Egan split.

1978 Feb Rafferty resurfaces after an enforced absence through management and label problems. Signed to United Artists as a soloist, he releases LP *City To City*.

Apr The LP title track is issued as a single and fails to sell, but self-penned *Baker Street*, driven by an arresting sax riff from session player Raphael Ravenscroft, is released. With massive UK airplay, it hits #2, and the LP hits UK #6. (Its total worldwide sales will be 4½ million copies.)

June *Baker Street* also hits US #2 for 6 weeks behind Andy Gibb's° *Shadow Dancing*, and earns a gold disk for million-plus US sales. In UK, ballad cut *Whatever's Written In Your Heart* is follow-up but fails to chart despite good airplay (as does a competing reissue of old Transatlantic track *Mary Skeffington*).

July LP *City To City* tops the US chart, displacing *Saturday Night Fever* soundtrack (which has held #1 for almost 6 months). The LP earns a platinum disk for a million US sales. He makes a US promotional visit, but declines (and will continue to refuse) to tour US.

Oct *Right Down The Line*, is US follow-up, reaching US #12.

1979 Jan *Home And Dry*, third US single from LP *City To City*, reaches #28.

June Rafferty's second United Artists LP, *Night Owl*, hits UK #9.

July LP *Night Owl* peaks at US #29, earning a gold disk for a half million US sales. The title track is extracted as a UK single, hitting #5, while in US, *Days Gone Down (Still Got The Light In Your Eyes)* is taken from the LP, reaching US #17.

Sept *Get It Right Next Time*, also from LP *Night Owl*, reaches UK #30 and US #21.

1980 Apr *Bring It All Home*, from Rafferty's next LP, makes UK #54.

May LP *Snakes And Ladders* reaches UK #15.

June *The Royal Mile (Sweet Darlin')*, taken from LP *Snakes And Ladders*, reaches UK #67 (his last UK hit single).

July LP *Snakes And Ladders* peaks at US #61.

Aug *The Royal Mile (Sweet Darlin')* reaches US #54 (his last US hit).

1982 Oct LP *Sleepwalking* reaches UK #39.

1983 Feb He contributes to Mark Knopfler's soundtrack of movie *Local Hero*.

1987 Nov Rafferty produces Scottish twins The Proclaimers' *Letter From America*, which hits UK #3.

1988 May He signs a new recording deal with London Records, producing LP *North And South*, which reaches UK #43. It is recorded with long-term friend and producer Hugh Murphy and reveals unsuccessful single, *Shipyard Town*.

RAINBOW

Ritchie Blackmore (lead guitar)
Ronnie James Dio (vocals)
Tony Carey (keyboards)
Jimmy Bain (bass)
Cozy Powell (drums)

1975 Apr [7] Blackmore (b. Apr.14, 1945, Weston-Super-Mare, UK) leaves Deep Purple° after a show in Paris. (He has become disillusioned by the band's direction, despising just-completed LP *Stormbringer*, and has recorded *Black Sheep Of The Family*, rejected by Deep Purple, with American band Elf, which has toured as Deep Purple's support band and recorded its second LP *Carolina County Ball* for Purple records.)

May After Elf has recorded final LP *Trying To Burn The Sun*, in London with producers Roger Glover and Martin Birch, the group (minus its guitarist Steve Edwards, who departs to Florida), with Dio on vocals, Mickey Lee Soule on keyboards, Craig Gruber on bass and Gary Driscoll on drums, teams with Blackmore as Ritchie Blackmore's Rainbow. He takes the band to Musicland studios, Munich, West Germany, to record LP *Ritchie Blackmore's Rainbow*.

July Gruber leaves as soon as the LP sessions are complete, and is replaced on bass by Bain, ex-Harlot.

Sept LP *Ritchie Blackmore's Rainbow* is released on Purple's offshoot Oyster label and reaches UK #11 and US #30. As it charts, Soule and Driscoll leave the band, and Blackmore recruits Powell (ex-Bedlam and solo success with *Dance With The Devil*, but more recently driving racing cars for Hitachi) and Carey (from LA country group Blessings) to join himself, Dio and Bain.

1976 July LP *Rainbow Rising*, recorded by the new line-up, reaches UK #11 (on Polydor) and US #40.

Aug [31] The group makes its UK stage debut to promote the LP (and will tour US, Canada, Europe and the Far East for the remainder of the year).

1977 Jan Bain is fired by Blackmore for being out of step, musically, with the band (or at least with its leader). His replacement on bass is Mark Clarke, ex-Uriah Heep among other groups.

May The group records a new LP at Le Château studio in Paris, France. During the sessions, Blackmore becomes disenchanted with both Carey and Clarke, and elbows both from the band. LP recordings are halted, and Blackmore decides to assemble a live LP instead.

July David Stone, keyboards player with Canadian band Symphonic

RAINBOW *cont.*

Slam, joins after auditioning in LA for Blackmore, while Australian bassist Bob Daisley, ex-Steve Ellis' band Widowmaker, is also recruited.

Aug Double live LP *On Stage*, recorded by the band's second line-up during its late 1976 tours, with the billing shortened to Rainbow, hits UK #7 and makes US #65.

Sept *Kill The King* is Rainbow's first chart single, making UK #44. A UK tour is postponed while the new players are being broken in, and rescheduled for Nov.

Dec The band returns to the Paris studios and completes the third studio LP.

1978 Jan Rainbow tours Japan (then around US for much of the year).

Apr *Long Live Rock'n'Roll*, trailering the new LP, climbs to UK #33.

May Produced by Martin Birch, LP *Long Live Rock'n'Roll* hits UK #7 and US #89.

Oct Extracted from the LP and pressed on red vinyl, *L.A. Connection*, reaches UK #40.

Nov After a long time on the road, perfectionist Blackmore has become more disillusioned with most of his band. At the end of a US tour, he unloads everybody but Powell (Dio will re-emerge as vocalist with Black Sabbath°). He settles to rest in his US home in Conn. before attempting more recruitment.

Dec Blackmore plays at London's Marquee club with ex-Deep Purple° colleague Ian Gillan's band over Christmas. He fails to persuade Gillan to become Rainbow's vocalist, but recruits Don Airey, ex-Colosseum, on keyboards.

1979 Apr Blackmore recruits vocalist Graham Bonnet, one-time hitmaker as half of The Marbles but later less successful as a solo singer, and Roger Glover, ex-Deep Purple° with Blackmore and now mainly producing, joins on bass.

Sept LP *Down To Earth*, made by the new line-up and produced by Glover, hits UK #6 and reaches US #66.

Oct Taken from the LP, *Since You Been Gone*, written by ex-Argent° singer and writer Russ Ballard (and a 1978 US chartmaker for Head East), hits UK #6. The band's most commercial recording yet, the song causes some controversy among its more metal-minded followers.

Dec *Since You Been Gone* makes US #57.

1980 Mar *All Night Long*, a Blackmore/Glover composition, also from LP *Down To Earth*, hits UK #5.

Aug [16] Powell quits the band following its starring appearance at the first UK Castle Donington Monsters of Rock festival.

Oct [1] Bonnet also leaves, to pursue a solo career signed to Vertigo records. Joe Lynn Turner, ex-US group Fandango, joins as lead singer, while Bobby Rondinelli is recruited on drums.

1981 Feb *I Surrender*, another Russ Ballard song, gives Rainbow its highest singles hit at UK #3. It is taken from LP *Difficult To Cure*, produced by Glover, which also hits UK #3.

Apr LP *Difficult To Cure* makes US #50, while the band tours US to promote it.

July *Can't Happen Here*, a remixed version of a Blackmore/Glover song from LP *Difficult To Cure*, reaches UK #20.

Aug Polydor in UK reissues both the band's first hit single *Kill The King* and its original LP *Ritchie Blackmore's Rainbow* and they re-chart at UK #41 and #91 respectively.

Nov Airey leaves (later to join Ozzy Osbourne's° group), and is replaced on keyboards by Dave Rosenthal in time for a UK tour.

Dec Compilation LP *The Best Of Rainbow* reaches UK #14, while 4-track 12"-EP *Jealous Lover* (the title track having been UK B-side of *Can't Happen Here*, recorded at a leisurely tour break session in a church hall) peaks at US #147.

1982 Apr *Stone Cold* climbs to UK #34. It is taken from LP *Straight Between The Eyes*, which hits UK #5.

June *Stone Cold* makes US #40 and LP *Straight Between The Eyes* reaches US #30. The band plays a world (excluding UK) tour to promote the LP.

1983 Sept Rondinelli is replaced by former Brand X drummer Chuck Burgi for LP *Bent Out Of Shape*, which reaches UK #11. Taken from it, *Street Of Dreams* peaks at UK #52. (MTV in US bans the promo video for it, since it demonstrates hypnosis.)

Oct The band plays its first UK tour since 1981, playing a set mainly from the recent LP.

Nov *Can't Let You Go*, also from LP *Bent Out Of Shape*, reaches UK #43, while the LP makes US #34.

Dec *Street Of Dreams* peaks at US #60.

1984 Mar Blackmore decides to fold the band when both he and Glover are invited to join the most successful line-up of Deep Purple° (with Jon Lord, Ian Gillan and Ian Paice), and Rainbow plays its final tour in Japan.

Mar [14] In Rainbow's final live show, in Japan, it is accompanied by a Japanese symphony orchestra, and the set includes Blackmore's adaptation of Beethoven's *Ninth Symphony*.

Apr Deep Purple° re-forms, with Blackmore and Glover as members, and Rainbow splits.

1986 Mar Double compilation LP *Finyl Vinyl*, remixed for release by Glover, and containing many unheard live items by Rainbow, plus scarce tracks previously only on singles B-sides, reaches UK #31, a successful coda to the band's career.

THE RAMONES

Joey Ramone (vocals)
Johnny Ramone (guitar)
Dee Dee Ramone (bass)
Tommy Ramone (drums)

1974 Aug [16] After a first gig at a private party, The Ramones, having formed in Forest Hills, New York, begin a residency at New York's CBGB's club. The original line-up is Johnny Ramone (b. John Cummings, Oct.8, 1948, Long Island, N.Y., US) Ritchie Ramone, soon to be replaced by Dee Dee Ramone (b. Douglas Colvin, Sept.18, 1952, Fort Lee, Va., US) and Joey Ramone (b. Jeffrey Hyman, May 19, 1952, Forest Hills, N.Y.). Tommy Ramone (b. Thomas Erdelyi, Jan.29, 1949, Budapest, Hungary) takes over on drums to let Joey sing. They all adopt the working surname Ramone.

1975 June The band auditions for Rick Derringer and Blue Sky Records by opening for Johnny Winter° at Waterbury, Conn., in front of a 20,000 audience. The label does not sign them.

Nov Danny Fields becomes the band's manager, and negotiates a recording contract with Sire Records.

1976 Feb The group records its debut LP on a $6400 budget.

May *Blitzkrieg Bop* fails to chart. LP *The Ramones* makes US #111.

July [4] The group celebrates the US bicentennial by making its debut at London's Roundhouse with fellow patriots The Flamin' Groovies.

July They appear in punk film *Blank Generation*.

1977 Mar LP *Leave Home* reaches US #148.

May LP *Leave Home* makes UK #45 while the group begins its first UK tour, popularizing its no-frills "1-2-3-4" intros to every song and the "Gabba gabba hey!" catchphrase.

June *Sheena Is A Punk Rocker* reaches UK #22.

July The Heartbreakers release *Chinese Rocks*, co-written by Dee Dee Ramone. The band is invited to Phil Spector's home, as its winter UK tour is cancelled.

Aug *Swallow My Pride* peaks at UK #36.

Sept *Sheena Is A Punk Rocker* makes US #81.

Dec LP *Rocket To Russia* climbs to US #49 and UK #60.

1978 Jan *Rockaway Beach* makes US #66.

May Tommy Ramone leaves the band (but remains its producer, credited as T. Erdelyi). He is replaced by Marc Bell from Richard Hell's Voidoids, who takes the name Marky Ramone. *Do You Wanna Dance* peaks at US #86.

Oct *Don't Come Close* makes UK #39. LP *Road To Ruin*, on which the group makes an effort to write songs lasting more than the usual 2 minutes, reaches US #103 and UK #32.

1979 Apr [25] Roger Corman's film *Rock'n'Roll High School* premieres in LA. The Ramones are featured in the film, performing the title track and a new Paul McCartney° song *Did We Meet Somewhere Before*.

June Live LP *It's Alive*, recorded at London's Rainbow, reaches UK #27.

Aug Soundtrack LP *Rock'n'Roll High School*, with The Ramones tracks re-mixed by Phil Spector, is released.

Sept *Rock'n'Roll High School* makes UK #67. (Spector has reportedly listened to the opening chord for 10 hours.)

1980 Jan LP *End Of The Century*, produced by Spector, makes US #44 and UK #14. (Recorded in five different studios, the band will later denounce *Century* as its worst LP.)

Feb *Baby I Love You*, a cover of Spector-produced Ronettes° hit from 1964, hits UK #8.

Apr *Do You Remember Rock'N'Roll Radio* reaches UK #54.

Aug [19] The group begins a short UK tour at London's Hammersmith Odeon.

1981 Aug LP *Pleasant Dreams*, produced by Graham Gouldman in New York and England, makes US #58.
Sept [3-5] The Ramones perform in front of almost 500,000 at the US festival in San Bernardino, Cal.
1983 Apr LP *Subterranean Jungle*, produced by Bezerkley Records' Ritchie Cordell and Glen Kolotkin, makes US #83. Marky Ramone leaves and is replaced by Richard Beau from The Velveteens, who becomes the second Ritchie Ramone.
Aug [15] Joey Ramone is rushed to St. Vincent's Hospital, New York, where he undergoes emergency brain surgery. (He was involved in a fight with fellow musician Seth Macklin over his girlfriend Cynthia Whitney.)
1984 Nov LP *Too Tough To Die*, with contributions from Talking Heads'° Jerry Harrison and Tom Petty and The Heartbreakers'° Benmont Tench, makes US #171.
1985 Jan Signed to Beggars Banquet in UK, The Ramones' LP *Too Tough To Die* reaches UK #63.
Feb *Howling At The Moon*, co-produced by Eurythmics'° Dave Stewart, makes UK #85.
June *Bonzo Goes To Bitburg*, a reference to a controversial visit by President Ronald Reagan to a Nazi war grave, fails to make the UK top 75.
June [22] The Ramones perform at UK's Milton Keynes Bowl, supporting bill-toppers U2°.
1986 May *Somebody Put Something In My Drink/Something To Believe In* makes UK #69. LP *Animal Boy* reaches UK #38.
1987 Oct LP *Halfway To Sanity* spends 1 week at UK #78.
1988 June Retrospective LP *Ramones Mania* is released in UK.
Aug Johnny Ramone joins Debbie Harry for duet *Go Lil' Camaro Go*, but it fails to chart.

CHRIS REA

1970 Rea (b. Mar.4, 1951, Middlesborough, UK), while working in his family's ice cream parlor in Middlesborough, and doing part-time laboring, buys his first guitar after being inspired by Joe Walsh° and Ry Cooder° LPs.
1973 He becomes a proficient enough guitarist to join local professional band, Magdelene (whose singer David Coverdale has just left to join Deep Purple°), and begins to develop his songwriting skills.
1974 May Rea cuts *So Much Love*, a one-off for Magnet Records, but to little notice.
1975 Magdelene changes its name to The Beautiful Losers, and wins *Melody Maker*'s Best Newcomers of 1975 award, but little comes of this accolade.
1977 Rea splits from the group to sign to Magnet as a soloist, and works with producer Gus Dudgeon on a debut LP. The Beautiful Losers splits. (Rea will later estimate that by the end of the band's time, around 30 members have passed through its ranks.)
Nov He is one of many guitarists guesting on LP *The Hank Marvin Guitar Syndicate*, a solo instrumental by The Shadows'° lead guitarist.
1978 Apr *Fool (If You Think It's Over)* is released and initially does nothing.
June Dudgeon-produced LP, *Whatever Happened To Benny Santini?*, with session contributions from Pete Wingfield, Rod Argent and others, is released. (The title refers to Magnet having considered at one time re-christening Rea Benny Santini.) Rea claims the LP sounds "too American", and that Dudgeon has smoothed away all the rough edges of his style. In the post-punk UK musical climate, it is also dismissed as wimpish MOR by most reviewers.
Sept In the less new wave-obsessed US market, *Fool (If You Think It's Over)*, released on United Artists, gets airplay and climbs to US #12, pulling LP *Whatever Happened To Benny Santini?* to US #49 and a gold disk for a half million sales. Rea is offered a major US tour, but turns it down to concentrate on further recording in UK.
Oct The single's US success prompts Magnet to repromote it in UK, and this time *Fool (If You Think It's Over)* makes UK #30. (Elkie Brooks'° 1982 revival of it will make UK #17.)
Nov The title track from LP *Whatever Happened To Benny Santini?* reaches US #71.
1979 Feb *Fool (If You Think It's Over)* is nominated for (but does not win) a Grammy at the 1978 awards in US.
Apr *Diamonds*, a track taken from Rea's second LP *Deltics*, makes both UK and US #44.
May LP *Deltics*, produced by Dudgeon, is Rea's UK LP chart debut at #54, but fails in US.
1980 Apr Rea's first self-produced LP, *Tennis*, reaches UK #60. (Two singles, *Tennis* and *Dancing Girls* are extracted from it, but neither charts.) (He spends most of the next 2 years on the road in UK, continuing to write songs, but eschewing recording in favor of stage work. He also marries long-time girlfriend Joan.)
1982 Mar LP *Chris Rea* reaches UK #52. In US, it marks a new deal with CBS/Columbia, but does not chart.
Apr *Loving You*, the opening track from LP *Chris Rea*, is his first hit single in 3 years, reaching UK #65 and US #88.
1983 June LP *Water Sign* makes UK #64.
Oct *I Can Hear Your Heartbeat*, taken from LP *Water Sign*, climbs to UK #60, but is a bigger hit in Ireland and on the Continent, hitting top 20 in several countries, as does the LP. This helps build his European reputation to a level far exceeding his still cult-sized UK following. He undertakes a successful tour of Europe, and West Germany, particularly, affords him near superstar status.
1984 Mar *I Don't Know What It Is But I Love It*, a taster from his next LP, climbs to UK #65.
May LP *Wired To The Moon* peaks at UK #35, but *Bombollini*, the second single taken from it, fails.
1985 May *Stainsby Girls*, following strong UK airplay, reaches UK #27.
June LP *Shamrock Diaries*, which includes *Stainsby Girls*, is Rea's first UK top 20 LP, reaching #15.
July *Josephine*, second single from the LP, peaks at UK #67.
1986 Mar *It's All Gone* reaches UK #69.
May LP *On The Beach* is Rea's best-seller in UK, making #11 with a 24-week chart run.
June A remixed version of *On The Beach*, title song from the LP, reaches UK #57.
1987 July Rea's self-penned *Let's Dance* (the third different UK hit single by this title, following Chris Montez's 1962 #2 and David Bowie's 1983 #1) reaches UK #12, to become his all-time biggest-selling UK single. LP *On The Beach* also re-charts in UK, reaching #75, its sales revitalized by the success of *Let's Dance*.
Aug *Loving You Again* climbs to UK #47.
Sept Self-produced LP *Dancing With Strangers* which includes *Let's Dance* hits UK #2, behind Michael Jackson's° *Bad*, earning a gold disk in its first week of release, and confirming Rea's star status in UK comparable to that in which he operates on the Continent. In US, *Let's Dance*, Rea's first release via a new deal with Motown, makes US #81, but parent LP, on the same label, fails to chart. Meanwhile, he makes his first concert tour of Australia, followed by another European trek, supported by a now-regular road band: Robert Ahwaii (guitar), Max Middleton (keyboards), Kevin Leach (keyboards), Dave Kemp (saxophone), Eogham O'Neil (bass), Dave Mattacks (drums) and Rea's brother Kevin (percussion and vocals).
Dec Seasonal *Joys Of Christmas* fails to make UK top 75.
1988 Feb *Que Sera* peaks at UK #73.
Aug *On The Beach Summer '88*, a re-mixed version of the earlier hit, is Rea's first single for WEA, which has acquired Magnet, and makes UK #12. WEA repromotes LP *On The Beach* which reaches UK #37.
Oct *I Can Hear Your Heartbeat* peaks at UK #74.
Nov Compilation LP *The Best Of Chris Rea – New Light From Old Windows* hits UK #5.

OTIS REDDING

1957 Redding (b. Sept.9, 1941, Dawson, Ga., US) leaves school in Macon, Ga., to take a variety of day jobs, and sing in talent shows at every opportunity, frequently finding success with his Little Richard° imitation.
1959 He begins to gig regularly in clubs with R&B band Johnny Jenkins & The Pinetoppers, and makes his first recording locally with the group backing him. *She's Alright*, a Little Richard° pastiche, remains initially unreleased.
Dec During a talent contest at Macon's Douglas Theater, he meets his future wife Zelda.
1960 Sept After 6 months in LA looking for a break in music (but finding only a car wash job), Redding returns to Macon and records *Shout Bamalama* (again in Little Richard° style) for Confederate label, distributed by King Records. It is released, but does not sell well.
1961 Redding gains a residency at Macon's Grand Dukes club, and cuts another single, *Gettin' Hip*, for Alshire Records. Phil Walden, The Pinetoppers' manager, takes over Redding's management.
Aug Redding marries Zelda and they set up home in Macon.

OTIS REDDING *cont.*

1962 Feb Still associated with The Pinetoppers (he regularly chauffeurs the group to gigs and is given vocal spots in its act), Redding accompanies Jenkins and the group on a college tour of Tenn. and Ala. In Atlanta, they record *Love Twist* for local Gerald label, which is picked up by Atlantic and sells well in Southern states.

Oct At the suggestion of Atlantic's Joe Galkin, Jenkins & The Pinetoppers (with Redding again driving) travel to Memphis, Tenn., to record a session at Atlantic-distributed Stax Records. At the end of the (unproductive) Jenkins session, with studio time in hand, Redding persuades Stax's owner Jim Stewart to have him record two of his own songs: Little Richard°-styled *Hey Hey Baby* and slow, pleading *These Arms Of Mine*, in which Stewart hears commercial potential. Atlantic which has paid for the session, and technically has Redding contracted, allows Stax to issue it as a single on new Volt label.

1963 Mar After local Memphis success, *These Arms Of Mine* makes US R&B #20.

June *These Arms Of Mine* debuts Redding on the US Hot 100, reaching #85.

June [24] With his debut finally peaking, Redding's second recording session is held at Stax. He is now officially an Atco (Atlantic subsidiary) artist, but by special arrangement records as part of the Stax set-up and continues to have feature releases issued on Volt.

Oct *That's What My Heart Needs*, cut in June, makes US R&B #27 but does not cross over.

Nov On the strength of two hits and the fast-climbing third release *Pain In My Heart*, Redding is invited to play (for $400) a week at New York's Apollo Theater in Harlem (his performance being recorded for Atco's live compilation LP *Saturday Night At The Apollo*, released in 1964).

1964 Feb *Pain In My Heart*, an adapted cover of Irma Thomas' current Southern R&B hit *Ruler Of My Heart*, makes US #61, and is his biggest seller to date.

Apr Redding/Walden song *Come To Me*, recorded with Booker T. & The MG's° (as will be virtually every Redding track) but with Jenkins playing additional guitar, peaks at US #69.

May Debut LP *Pain In My Heart* makes US #103 while, taken from it, *Security* stalls at US #97 (though is much-covered by UK R&B groups).

Nov Self-penned *Chained And Bound* peaks at US #70.

1965 Mar *Mr. Pitiful* makes US #41 as B-side *That's How Strong My Love Is* climbs to US #74.

Apr LP *The Great Otis Redding Sings Soul Ballads* makes US #147.

June Deep soul ballad *I've Been Loving You Too Long (To Stop Now)* becomes his breakthrough release on the US pop chart, reaching US #21 (and R&B #2).

July [3] Though Redding has not yet had a UK hit, when the UK R&B chart is launched he has two top 20 placings, with *Mr. Pitiful* (#6) and *Pain In My Heart* (#16).

Oct Uptempo *Respect*, penned by Redding, makes US #35 (and R&B #4). (2 years later, the song will be revived in a still more commercial arrangement by Aretha Franklin° and become a million-selling US chart-topper.)

Nov LP *Otis Blue/Otis Redding Sings Soul* (often cited by later critics as one of the all-time great soul LPs) makes US #75.

Dec *Just One More Day* stalls at US #85.

1966 Jan UK Atlantic's Tony Hall selects Redding's version of Smokey Robinson°-penned *My Girl* (a US #1 for The Temptations° in 1965, but not a big UK seller) as a UK single from LP *Otis Blue*. It gets strong airplay and is his UK chart debut, reaching #11.

Mar LP *Otis Blue/Otis Redding Sings Soul* gives him his first UK chart LP, hitting UK #6, and staying in the top 30 for 21 weeks.

Apr LP *The Great Otis Redding Sings Soul Ballads* finds belated UK sales, peaking at #30. Meanwhile, Redding's version of The Rolling Stones'° *(I Can't Get No) Satisfaction* reaches US #31 (R&B #4) and UK #33. (Redding will tour UK and Europe to great success later in the year, and in UK will record "Ready, Steady, Otis!", an entire edition of UK TV pop show "Ready, Steady, Go!".)

June *My Lover's Prayer* peaks at US #61 (and R&B #10) while LP *The Soul Album*, from which it is taken, makes US #54.

Aug LP *The Soul Album* makes UK #22 and *My Lover's Prayer* climbs to UK #37. Redding launches his own label, Jotis Records. Among its acts is Arthur Conley, for whom Redding writes and produces *Sweet Soul Music* (a reworking of Sam Cooke's° *Yeah Man* which

will hit US #2 and UK #7 in 1967).

Sept R&B dance track *I Can't Turn You Loose* makes UK #29 (having hit US R&B #11).

Nov *Fa-Fa-Fa-Fa-Fa (Sad Song)* reaches US #29 and UK #23.

1967 Jan LP *Complete And Unbelievable . . . The Otis Redding Dictionary Of Soul* makes US #73 and UK #23 while, taken from it, a revival of standard ballad *Try A Little Tenderness* is his second-biggest US hit single to date, reaching #25.

Feb A UK reissue of LP *Otis Blue* (following a change of Atlantic's UK licensee), after an extended absence from the shops, hits UK #7, while *Try A Little Tenderness* makes UK #46.

Mar [17] The Stax label package tour plays a date at London's Hammersmith Odeon, UK.

Apr *I Love You More Than Words Can Say* peaks at US #78, while his revival of The Beatles'° *Day Tripper* reaches UK #43. Redding's live performance at LA's Whiskey A-Go-Go club is recorded by Atlantic (and will be released after his death).

May Redding's debut LP *Pain In My Heart* is belatedly released for the first time in UK and reaches #28, while *Let Me Come On Home* peaks at UK #48.

June Redding duets with Stax artist (and daughter of Rufus *Walking The Dog* Thomas) Carla Thomas on an adaptation of Lowell Fulson's *Tramp*, which reaches US #26, while his solo revival of Sam Cooke's° *Shake!* makes US #47. Redding's duet LP with Thomas, *King And Queen*, reaches US #36.

June [16] Redding participates in the Monterey Pop Festival – seen as a deliberate move to capture the attention of the young, white rock audience. Redding's biggest asset is the passionate strength of his live performance, and he gets a rapturous reception from the largely hippy audience. (Part of his set will be included in D.A. Pennebaker's film *Monterey Pop*.)

July *Shake* reaches UK #28.

Aug *Glory Of Love* peaks at US #60, while LP *King And Queen* with Carla Thomas reaches UK #18 and their duetted single *Tramp* makes UK #18.

Sept Live LP *Otis Redding Live In Europe*, recorded on the Stax/Volt tour, reaches US #32. Meanwhile, Redding's second duet single with Thomas, a version of Eddie Floyd's° much-covered *Knock On Wood*, reaches US #30.

Oct *Knock On Wood* makes UK #35.

Dec [7] Redding goes to the studio to record a song he has written with Stax guitarist Steve Cropper, *(Sittin' On) The Dock Of The Bay*. (A relaxed soul ballad, it will become his biggest hit, but Redding will not live to see its release.)

Dec [10] En route to a concert in the Mid-West, the twin-engined chartered plane carrying Redding and his road band, The Bar-Kays, goes down in the icy waters of Lake Monoma, near

Madison, Wis. The only survivor is Memphis-born Ben Cauley – at 20, the oldest of The Bar-Kays. (At Redding's funeral, the pall-bearers are fellow soul singers Joe Tex, Joe Simon, Johnnie Taylor, Solomon Burke°, Percy Sledge, Don Covay and Sam Moore, of Sam and Dave°.)

1968 Jan Compilation LP *History Of Otis Redding* hits US #9, a bigger seller than any LP during his lifetime.

Mar Posthumously-released *(Sittin' On) The Dock Of The Bay* tops the US chart for 4 weeks, selling over a million, and hits UK #3. Meanwhile, another Otis & Carla single, *Lovey Dovey* makes US #60, and a UK reissue of *My Girl* reaches #36.

Apr Compilation LP *History Of Otis Redding* hits UK #2 (below Bob Dylan's° *John Wesley Harding*), while live LP *Otis Redding In Europe* reaches UK #14.

May LP *Dock Of The Bay*, a collection of tracks from his final sessions in late 1967, hits US #4 while, taken from it, *The Happy Song (Dum Dum)* reaches US #25.

June LP *Dock Of The Bay* tops the UK chart for a week, while *The Happy Song (Dum Dum)* reaches UK #24.

July Also taken from the LP, a revival of The Impressions'° *Amen* makes US #36 and B-side *Hard To Handle* peaks at US #51. This, like subsequent posthumous singles, is released on Atco rather than Volt. *Love Man* enters the UK chart.

Aug *Hard To Handle*, elevated to A-side in UK, makes #15, while LP *The Immortal Otis Redding*, assembling more of his last recordings, reaches US #58.

Nov Ballad *I've Got Dreams To Remember* makes US #41, while parent LP *The Immortal Otis Redding* reaches UK #19.

Dec Live LP *Otis Redding In Person At The Whiskey A-Go-Go*, recorded in Apr. 1966, reaches US #82, while a revival of James Brown's° *Papa's Got A Brand New Bag* makes US #21 – his biggest US hit since *(Sittin' On) The Dock Of The Bay*.

1969 Mar A revival of Clyde McPhatter's 1950s hit *A Lover's Question* climbs to US #48.

Mar [12] *(Sittin' On) The Dock Of The Bay* wins two Grammy awards, named Best Male R&B Vocal Performance of 1968 and Best R&B Song.

June *Love Man* makes US #72.

July *Love Man* reaches UK #43 (Redding's final UK chart single), while the LP of the same title makes US #46.

1970 Aug LP *Tell The Truth*, containing Redding's last unissued recordings from 1967, creeps to US #200.

Nov Reprise Records issues live LP *Monterey International Pop Festival*, on which one side each is devoted to the acts of Redding and Jimi Hendrix° at the June 1967 festival. It climbs to US #16.

1972 Oct Double anthology LP *The Best Of Otis Redding* peaks at US #76 and is his final US chart entry.

1973 Nov Redding's 12-year-old son Dexter releases *God Bless*, on Phil Walden's Capricorn label.

1980 Dec Brothers Dexter (vocals, bass) and Otis Redding III (guitar) and their cousin Mark Locket (vocals, drums, keyboards), now a trio named The Reddings and signed to Believe label, have their first chart entry with *Remote Control*, which makes US #89.

1981 Jan The Reddings' LP *The Awakening* makes US #174.

Aug Second Reddings' LP *Class* reaches US #106.

1982 July The Reddings' version of *(Sittin' On) The Dock Of The Bay* makes US #55 (and R&B #21), and is taken from their third LP *Steamin' Hot*, which reaches US #153.

JIMMY REED

1955 Feb Having moved to Chicago, where his laid-back, boogie-influenced style makes him a popular figure on the Southside club and bar scene, Reed (b. Mathis James Reed Leland, Sept.6, 1925, Dunleith, Miss., US) signs to newly formed label, Vee-Jay, and *You Don't Have To Go Boogie In the Park* hits US R&B #9.

1956 *Ain't That Loving You Baby* is another R&B success.

1957 July Reed's first hot 100 pop hit is *The Sun Is Shining* at US #65.

Nov *Honest I Do* makes US #32. Reed is now the biggest draw on the Southside club scene (eclipsing even Muddy Waters°).

1958 Apr [5] Irvin Feld's "Greatest Show of Stars" opens its 80-date US tour in Norfolk, Va. Reed stars with Sam Cooke°, The Everly Brothers°, Clyde McPhatter and many others.

Aug *Down In Virginia* charts briefly at US #93.

1959 May [29] Reed performs in pouring rain at an outdoor festival in the Herndon Stadium, Atlanta, Ga. Other artists on the bill include Ray Charles°, The Drifters° and B.B. King°.

1960 Mar *Baby What You Want Me To Do* makes US #37.

May *Found Love* peaks at US #88.

Oct *Hush-Hush* reaches US #75.

1961 *Big Boss Man* (the description by which Reed will become known) reaches US #78 and *Bright Lights Big City* makes US #58 (both are big R&B hits). The blues declines in popularity in favor of R&B/soul, and the UK R&B/beat boom emerges. Double LP *Jimmy Reed At Carnegie Hall*, comprising a studio re-creation of Reed's Carnegie Hall concert and a best of selection, makes US #46.

1962 *Aw Shucks, Hush Your Mouth* reaches US #93 and *Good Lover* makes US #77. Both are big R&B hits. LP *Just Jimmy Reed* reaches US #103.

1963 Apr *Shame Shame Shame* makes US #52.

1964 Sept *Shame Shame Shame* climbs to UK #45.

Oct Reed begins an extensive UK club and concert tour. The Rolling Stones° cover his *Honest I Do* on their first LP. Other UK groups to cover Reed tracks include The Pretty Things°, The Animals° (both record *Big Boss Man*) and Them° (*Bright Lights Big City*). Reed is unable to capitalize on this due to increasing ill-health (epilepsy and alcoholism). (He remains inactive for most of the late 60s and early 1970s.)

1976 Aug [29] Reed dies in San Francisco from an epileptic seizure after completing a three-night engagement at the Bay area's Savoy Club.

LOU REED

1965 Reed (b. Louis Firbank, Mar.2, 1942, Freeport, Long Island, N.Y., US), after playing in local teenage bands like The Shades, attending Syracuse University, and working for Pickwick Records as a writer and recorder of low-budget cash-in records for supermarket racks (and getting a near-hit single in New York with *The Ostrich* by The Primitives), becomes a founder member of The Velvet Underground° with John Cale° and Sterling Morrison. (During his time with the band he will be its lead singer and most prominent songwriter.)

1970 Sept Following a Velvet Underground° residency at Max's Kansas City club, New York, Reed leaves the group and returns to his parents' home in Long Island.

1971 He is signed to RCA as a solo artist.

1972 June Debut solo LP *Lou Reed*, recorded in London with Yes° members Steve Howe and Rick Wakeman (among others), reaches US #189. He tours UK with a backing band named The Tots.

1973 Jan [9] Reed marries a cocktail waitress, Betty, in New York.

Mar [24] Reed is bitten on the posterior by a fan who leaps on stage at a concert in Buffalo, N.Y. The man is seized and ejected from the theater, leaving Reed to end the show and contemplate a sore bum.

Apr LP *Transformer*, produced in London by David Bowie° and Mick Ronson, reaches US #29. Extracted *Walk On The Wild Side* reaches US #16, and is Reed's only solo US chart single.

June *Walk On The Wild Side* hits UK #10, and does not draw a half-anticipated BBC radio ban over its lyrics, because the producers fail to understand street idioms like "giving head" used by Reed. As in US, it is his only UK chart single. LP *Transformer* makes UK #13, and stays on UK chart for 6 months.

Sept [22] Reed headlines the annual Crystal Palace Garden Party in London.

Nov LP *Berlin*, the third in a row to be recorded in London, produced this time by Bob Ezrin, makes US #98 and hits UK #7.

1974 Apr Live LP *Rock'n'Roll Animal*, recorded at New York's Academy of Music, with a line-up of Reed (guitar, vocals), Dick Wagner (guitar), Steve Hunter (guitar), Prakash John (bass), Josef Chirowsky (keyboards) and Whitney Glen (drums), climbs to US #45 and UK #26, and with consistent sales earns Reed his first gold disk.

Nov LP *Sally Can't Dance* hits US #10; his only LP to enter the US top 10 or top 20.

1975 Apr Live LP *Lou Reed Live* contains another section of the previous year's Academy of Music concert, and is a companion to live LP *Rock'n'Roll Animal* from the same occasion.

July Double LP *Metal Machine Music* is the most controversial of Reed's career, and the least accessible, having four sides of white noise, whines, whistles, feedback and screams. The sleeve implies that it is a live set, but this is not the case. Originally to have been released by Red Seal (RCA's classical music division) as an experimental piece of music, the set fails to sell after poor (and

LOU REED *cont.*

bewildered) reviews, and is withdrawn by RCA within a few months.

1976 Mar LP *Coney Island Baby*, in Reed's normal style, peaks at US #41 and UK #52.

Nov Reed signs a new deal with Arista Records, producing LP *Rock And Roll Heart*, which makes US #64.

1977 May Compilation LP *Walk On The Wild Side: The Best Of Lou Reed*, on RCA, halts at US #156.

1978 May LP *Street Hassle* makes US #89.

May [17] Reed begins a week of concerts at New York's Bottom Line club, which are recorded for planned live LP *Take No Prisoners*.

1979 Mar Double live LP *Take No Prisoners*, due to a contractual wrangle, is released by Arista in US and by RCA elsewhere. It fails to chart.

June Arista LP *The Bells* has a brief 4-week US chart run, peaking at #130.

1980 Feb [14] On St. Valentine's Day, Reed marries Sylvia Morales, in a ceremony at his apartment on Christopher Street, Greenwich Village, New York. (His previous marriage had foundered early on.)

May LP *Growing Up In Public* stalls at US #158.

Oct Reed has a cameo role as a record producer in Paul Simon's° film *One Trick Pony*.

Dec Last Arista LP is *Rock And Roll Diary, 1967-80*, a history of Reed's earlier career, with most tracks by The Velvet Underground°. It creeps to US #178.

1982 Mar He returns to RCA with LP *The Blue Mask*, which makes US #169.

July LP *Transformer* is reissued in UK at mid-price, and charts again at #91.

1983 Apr LP *Legendary Hearts* peaks at US #159.

1984 Aug LP *New Sensations* makes US #56 and UK #92.

1985 Oct *September Song* is released on A&M, taken from compilation *Lost In The Stars*, as a tribute to Kurt Weil.

Dec He appears with 48 other acts on the Artists United Against Apartheid single *Sun City* on Manhattan Records, which reaches US #38 and UK #21.

1986 May LP *Mistrial* makes UK #69.

1987 Feb Sam Moore and Reed duet on a re-working of Sam and Dave's° million-seller *Soul Man*, now used as the theme to the movie of the same name. It reaches UK #30.

R.E.M.

Michael Stipe (vocals)
Peter Buck (guitar)
Mike Mills (bass)
Bill Berry (drums)

1978 Stipe (b. Decatur, Ga., US), a student of painting and photography at University of Georgia, meets Buck in their native Athens, Ga., record store, where Buck works. Both are keen on the UK new wave music.

1980 Apr They meet Berry (b. Hibbing, Minn., US) and Mills at a party and R.E.M. is formed soon after (the letters mean Rapid Eye Movement – a physiological term for the sleep cycle stage at which dreaming begins).

1981 1,000 copies of first single *Radio Free Europe* are released on local Hib-Tone label. It is picked up by US college radio network and becomes a favorite. *Village Voice* magazine votes it Best Independent Single of the Year. Jefferson Holt becomes manager and invites Mitch Easter to produce recordings at Drive-In studios, N.C.

1982 Impressed by *Radio Free Europe*, R.E.M. is signed by Miles Copeland's I.R.S. label. Five-track mini-LP *Chronic Town* is released and is very popular with rock critics. Dense layers of guitars add to Stipe's often inaudible lyrics, adding an air of mystique to the band which is developing into cult status.

1983 May First LP *Murmur*, co-produced by Easter and Don Dixon, is released on I.R.S. It peaks at US #36 during a 30-week chart stay. Live performances now mix original material with covers of songs including *Born To Run*, *In The Year 2525* and *Paint It Black*.

July A re-recorded version of *Radio Free Europe* is US chart single debut, at #73, but fails in UK. The band plays a series of seven stadium dates opening for The Police°.

1984 May LP *Reckoning*, featuring a more melodic and accessible style, will spend over 1 year on US chart, peaking at #27 and is UK debut at #91.

June From it *S. Central Rain (I'm Sorry)* peaks at US #85. Follow-up *(Don't Go Back To) Rockville* gains airplay in both US and UK but fails to chart.

1985 Jan R.E.M. travels to UK for live dates and to record a new LP with producer Joe Boyd. Stipe suffers mental and physical breakdown during the sessions.

June LP *Fables Of The Reconstruction* enters the US chart, selling over 300,000 copies in 3 months and reaching US #28. All attempts at hit singles fail, but with a growing fan following (with worship by a group of "Distiples" who believe that Stipe is a guru) and critical enthusiasm, some thrown by Boyd's addition of lush strings and horns, it makes UK #35.

1986 Sept LP *Life's Rich Pageant*, produced by John Cougar Mellencamp's° collaborator Don Gehman, reaches US #21 and UK #43.

Oct *Fall On Me* makes US #94.

1987 Jan R.E.M. begins a successful US tour.

Feb LP *Life's Rich Pageant* is certified gold.

May A collection of out-takes and B-side material is released as LP *Dead Letter Office*.

June LP *Dead Letter Office* reaches US #62, selling over 250,000 copies, and makes UK #60 for 2 weeks. (All band members, except Stipe, back Warren Zevon on LP *Sentimental Hygiene*.)

Sept Fifth LP *Document*, the last of new material for I.R.S., is released. It hits US #10 and UK #28, on MCA. A collection of plot-free videos, *Succumbs*, tops *Billboard*'s video chart.

Oct R.E.M. plays its first UK concerts in 2 years.

Nov *The One I Love*, from LP *Document*, climbs to hit US #9.

Dec *The One I Love* makes UK #51.

1988 Jan UK magazine *New Musical Express* readers vote four R.E.M. LPs into the all-time top 100. *Rolling Stone* magazine devotes its front cover to R.E.M. with the heading "America's Best Rock'n'Roll Band".

Mar *It's The End Of The World As We Know It* peaks at US #69.

Apr *Finest Worksong* makes UK #50.

June R.E.M. signs worldwide to Warner Bros. for a reported seven figure sum.

Oct Stipe, with 10,000 Maniacs'° girlfriend Natalie Merchant and The Roches, contributes *Little April Shower* to various artists Walt Disney compilation LP *Stay Awake*. I.R.S. releases the remaining product on LP *Eponymous*, which makes US #105 and UK #69.

Nov Warner debut LP *Green* is released.

REO SPEEDWAGON

Gary Richrath (guitar)
Kevin Cronin (vocals)
Neal Doughty (keyboards)
Bruce Hall (bass)
Alan Gratzer (drums)

1968 The group is formed in Champaign, Ill., US, (named after a make of antique fire engine) with local University of Illinois students Gratzer (b. Nov.9, 1948, Syracuse, New York, US) and Doughty (b. July 29, 1946, Evanston, Ill.), who recruit the band's chief songwriter Richrath (b. Oct.18, 1949, Peoria, Ill.), vocalist Terry Luttrell and bass player Craig Philbin. REO Speedwagon becomes Champaign's most popular live band.

1972 Feb Irving Azoff becomes the group's manager (he will later also manage The Eagles°) and Cronin (b. Oct.6, 1951, Evanston, Ill.), whom Richrath has discovered via a "Musicians' Referral Service" in Chicago, replaces Luttrell on lead vocals as the band signs to Epic and records debut LP *REO Speedwagon*, which fails to chart. The band begins to tour extensively (as it will throughout the 70s, often sharing major treks with fellow Mid-Western acts like Bob Seger's° band and Kansas°).

Dec On LP *R.E.O. T.W.O.*, Mike Murphy takes over on lead vocals, Cronin having left to become a solo singer/songwriter, after differences with Richrath.

1974 Feb LP *Ridin' The Storm Out* is the group's first to chart in US, reaching #171.

Dec LP *Lost In A Dream* reaches US #98.

1975 Aug LP *This Time We Mean It*, the last to feature Murphy as lead vocalist, makes US #74. The band splits from manager Azoff.

1976 July Hall (b. May 3, 1953, Champaign) replaces Philbin on bass and Cronin rejoins on lead vocals for LP *R.E.O.*, which makes US #159. Cronin and Richrath will co-produce the group from here on, and jointly provide most of its songs.

1977 Apr Live double LP *You Get What You Play For* reaches US #72.

Staying on chart for 2 weeks short of a year, it will earn the band its first platinum LP for million-plus sales. The heavy touring schedule continues.

June First US chart single is a live version of *Ridin' The Storm Out*, taken from the double LP, which creeps to US #94.

1978 May The group makes a cameo appearance in movie *FM*, performing *Ridin' The Storm Out*.

June LP *You Can Tune A Piano, But You Can't Tuna Fish*, makes US #79 and is a second platinum LP, spending 11 months on chart. Extracted from it, *Roll With The Changes* climbs to US #58.

Aug *Time For Me To Fly* makes US #56.

1979 Sept LP *Nine Lives* (also the band's ninth LP) makes US #33, earning a gold disk.

1980 June Double compilation LP *A Decade Of Rock'n'Roll, 1970 To 1980*, rounding up tracks from the group's first 10 years, makes US #55, and also goes gold. A reissue of *Time For Me To Fly* (also on the compilation) from 2 years earlier, makes US #77.

1981 Feb LP *Hi Infidelity* finally achieves the band's major chart breakthrough, toppling John Lennon's° *Double Fantasy* from US #1 and holding #1 for a total of 15 weeks to the end of June (in three separate runs). It sells 7 million copies and earns another platinum disk.

Mar Cronin's song *Keep On Loving You*, the first single from LP *Hi Infidelity*, also tops the US chart (for a week) and is another million-seller. After a decade as one of the busiest and most continually-mobile tour support bands in US, REO Speedwagon becomes one of the biggest stadium-fillers.

May *Take It On The Run*, also from LP *Hi Infidelity*, hits US #5, while *Keep On Loving You* is UK chart debut, hitting #7.

July Third single from the LP, *Don't Let Him Go*, makes US #24.

Aug [8] US MTV features REO Speedwagon live from Denver, Col., for its first stereo concert broadcast.

Aug *Take It On The Run* is a second UK hit single, reaching #19, while LP *Hi Infidelity* hits UK #6 during a 29-week chart run.

Oct *In Your Letter* makes US #20.

1982 Aug LP *Good Trouble* hits US #7 (the group's fourth platinum LP) and reaches UK #29. Taken from it, *Keep The Fire Burnin'* also hits US #7.

Oct Also from the LP, *Sweet Time* makes US #26.

1984 Dec After more than 2 years since the band's last single, *I Do Wanna Know* reaches US #29.

1985 Jan LP *Wheels Are Turnin'* hits US #7 and earns a platinum disk.

Mar *Can't Fight This Feeling*, written by Cronin on Hawaiian island Molokai, and taken from LP *Wheels Are Turnin'*, hits US #1 for 3 weeks, and is the band's second million-selling single.

Apr *Can't Fight This Feeling* reaches UK #16.

June Another track from the LP, *One Lonely Night*, makes US #19.

Aug *Live Every Moment* reaches US #34.

Nov UK-only compilation LP *Best Foot Forward* is released, but fails to chart.

1987 Feb First new LP in nearly 2 years, *Life As We Know It* enters the US chart. It will reach #28 during a 48-week chart stay.

Apr *That Ain't Love* reaches US #16.

June *Variety Tonight* stalls at US #60.

Oct *In My Dreams* makes US #19.

1988 Aug Compilation LP *The Hits* peaks at US #61.

PAUL REVERE & THE RAIDERS

Paul Revere (keyboards)
Mark Lindsay (vocals and saxophone)
Mike "Smitty" Smith (drums)
Philip "Fang" Volk (bass)
Drake "Kid" Levin (guitar)

1959 The band is formed in Caldwell, Ida., as an instrumental group named The Downbeats by Revere (b. Jan.7, 1942, Boise, Ida., US), a drive-in restaurant owner and ex-hairdresser, and Lindsay (b. Mar.9, 1942, Cambridge, Ida., US), who meets Revere when making bakery deliveries to him.

1960 Renamed Paul Revere & The Raiders (though still heavily instrumentally-oriented), the group signs to local Gardena label, where its first instrumental single *Beatnik Sticks* is a small regional seller.

1961 Apr The group's local hit *Like, Long Hair* (another instrumental) makes US #38 on the national chart. Shortly after, Revere will be drafted and the group disbands. An LP and four follow-up singles, on Gardena, fail through lack of live promotion.

1963 Revere and Lindsay regroup in Portland, Ore., where Smith, Volk and Levin join the re-vamped line up. The group becomes part of the buoyant Portland/Seattle live scene, alongside groups like The Wailers, The Sonics and The Kingsmen. It signs to leading North-Western label Jerden and the resulting single *So Fine* fails to sell, but brings the group to the notice of CBS/Columbia, which buys its contract.

June The first Columbia single is a version of the staple of every North-Western band's live act, Richard Berry's *Louie Louie*, with a vocal by Lindsay. (The Kingsmen's° version is released nationally by Wand Records almost simultaneously and, despite Columbia's promotion, The Kingsmen's will hit US #2 and sell over a million at the end of 1963.)

1964 Lindsay leaves the group, while follow-up *Louie – Go Home* also fails to chart.

1965 Apr The Raiders move to LA and Lindsay rejoins. A revival of *Ooh Poo Pah Doo* also fails.

June Impressed by their showmanship and teen appeal (and their startling Revolutionary War stage outfits, a band trademark), "American Bandstand" presenter Dick Clark adopts the group as house band for his new TV show "Where The Action Is", which launches on June 27. (This constant national exposure turns them into teen idols, and guarantees excellent promotion for subsequent records. Photogenic Lindsay becomes a pin-up heart-throb in US.)

Oct Columbia pairs the group with producer Terry Melcher, and *Steppin' Out* reaches US #46. LP *Here They Come*, featuring mostly familiar rock standards and released to coincide with the TV show launch, peaks at #71 – the group's first chart LP.

1966 Jan The Kinks°-influenced *Just Like Me* reaches US #11.

Apr Levin is drafted, and is replaced on guitar by Jim Valley.

May Propelled by an arresting guitar riff, *Kicks*, an anti-drug song penned by Barry Mann and Cynthia Weil, hits US #4, and LP *Just Like Us!* hits US #5. (It will stay charted for 43 weeks, earn a gold disk and become the first Columbia LP by a rock group to sell a million.)

July *Hungry*, another Mann/Weil song in hard rock style, hits US #6, while mostly group-written LP *Midnight Ride*, its second gold disk, hits US #9.

Oct The first hit single written from within the group is *The Great Airplane Strike*, penned by Lindsay and producer Melcher. It makes US #20.

1967 Jan Lindsay and Melcher's *Good Thing* hits US #4.

Feb LP *The Spirit Of '67*, which includes *Hungry* and *Good Thing*, hits US #9 (third consecutive top 10 LP) and again goes gold.

Mar *Ups And Downs* makes US #22.

June *Him Or Me – What's It Gonna Be?* hits US #5. With influences from The Monkees° and The Rolling Stones° clearly showing, this is later selected by many critics as the group's finest.

July Compilation LP *Greatest Hits* reaches US #15, and is the group's last gold LP.

Sept *I Had A Dream*, a heavy rocker with a hint of psychedelia, makes US #17. Meanwhile, Volk and Smith leave to join Levin (now out of the service) and form Brotherhood, while Valley departs to work as a soloist. Their replacements are Freddy Weller (b. Sep.9, 1947, Ga., US) on guitar, Charlie Coe (b. Nov.19, 1944) on bass and Joe Correro (b. Nov.19, 1946, Greenwood, Miss., US) on drums.

Oct LP *Revolution!*, highlighted by *Him Or Me – What's It Gonna Be?*, reaches US #25.

Dec *Peace Of Mind* peaks at US #42. It is the group's last single produced by Melcher.

1968 Jan The group has its own TV show, "Happening '68", which will last for much of the year. Its still-strong teen appeal makes it more unfashionable with rock fans drifting in the direction of West Coast, psychedelic and progressive sounds, but the music is much less out on a limb, credibility-wise, than the group's image and presentation.

Mar Lindsay produces The Rolling Stones°-influenced *Too Much Talk*, which makes US #19. (Lindsay will continue to be the group's producer until the end of its chart days, but will also have a parallel solo vocal career.)

Apr LP *Goin' To Memphis* reaches US #61.

July *Don't Take It So Hard* climbs to US #27.

Oct *Cinderella Sunshine* peaks at US #58, while LP *Something Happening* climbs to US #122.

1969 Apr *Mr. Sun, Mr. Moon* reaches US #18.

PAUL REVERE & THE RAIDERS *cont.*

May LP *Hard'n'Heavy (With Marshmallow)* makes US #51. Lindsay announces his solo career.

July *Let Me* reaches US #20.

Aug Lindsay's first solo single *First Hymn From Grand Terrace*, part of Jimmy Webb's epic *Hymn From Grand Terrace* featured on Richard Harris' LP *The Yard Went On Forever*, is a minor US success at #81.

Oct LP *Alias Pink Puzz* reaches US #48, while from it, *We Gotta All Get Together* makes US #50. These are the last disks credited to Paul Revere & The Raiders.

1970 Feb *Just Seventeen*, credited to The Raiders, peaks at US #82. Lindsay's biggest solo success is *Arizona*, a song recorded by Steve Rowland's UK group Family Dogg as follow-up to 1969 hit *Way Of Life*. Lindsay's revival hits US #9, and earns a gold disk for million-plus sales. (It is also a typical example of Lindsay's solo output, which tends to be tuneful ballads in Glen Campbell° mold, which would not fit into the invariably uptempo and rocking Raiders group style.)

Apr Lindsay's first solo LP *Arizona* makes US #36.

May LP *Collage*, the first LP credited just to The Raiders, peaks at US #154. Lindsay's solo *Miss America*, from his debut LP, reaches US #44.

July Lindsay has another solo hit with *Silver Bird*, which reaches US #25.

Oct Lindsay's solo LP *Silver Bird* climbs to US #82.

Nov Lindsay's version of Neil Diamond's° *And The Grass Won't Pay No Mind* reaches US #44.

1971 Jan *Problem Child*, another Lindsay solo, halts at US #80.

June Lindsay's cover of Bread's° *Been Too Long On The Road* scrapes the US Hot 100 at #98.

July A revival of John D. Loudermilk's *Indian Reservation (The Lament Of The Cherokee Reservation Indian)*, previously a US and UK top 20 hit for Don Fardon, hits US #1 for a week, The Raiders' only US chart-topper. Freddy Weller sings lead vocal (he will later have a successful career as a solo country singer) and Lindsay still produces. (The group has now split as a live unit and has session men playing most of the instrumental parts on the current recordings.)

July [20] Musical variety show "Make Your Own Kind of Music", with Lindsay a regular feature, airs on US NBC TV.

Aug LP *Indian Reservation* reaches US #19.

Oct The group's version of Joe South's° *Birds Of A Feather* makes US #23, while Lindsay's solo LP *You've Got A Friend* stalls at US #180 and single *Are You Old Enough* falters at US #87.

1972 Feb The Raiders' *Country Wine* peaks at US #51.

June *Powder Blue Mercedes Queen* makes US #54.

Aug Double compilation LP *All-Time Greatest Hits*, rounding up the chart singles, makes US #143.

Nov *Song Seller* creeps to US #96.

1973 Feb The last Raiders chart single is *Love Music*, which peaks at US #97.

June [20] The group appears on the 20th anniversary special edition of Dick Clark's "American Bandstand", alongside Little Richard°, Three Dog Night° and others.

1974 *Ain't Nothin' Wrong* is released by the group on Drive label, but without success.

1976 July *The British Are Coming* is released on 20th Century during USA's bi-centennial celebrations. A new group of Raiders put together for live work by Revere and Lindsay re-dons the old revolutionary uniforms, to take full advantage of the promotion the bicentennial is giving to the group. (Regular tour and Cal. club work will follow, though no renewed disk success is forthcoming.)

1983 Edsel in UK releases compilation LP *Kicks*. With Revere and Lindsay having enjoyed many successful years singing TV and radio jingles and now touring regularly on the rock'n'roll/oldies circuit, LP *Paul Revere Rides Again* is released in US.

CLIFF RICHARD

1948 Sept Richard (b. Harry Rodger Webb, Oct.14, 1940, Lucknow, India) arrives in England on the wartime troopship S.S. Ranghi to live in Carshalton, Surrey with his parents, Rodger and Dorothy, and sisters, Donella and Jacqueline.

1952 His family moves to Enfield, Middx., where he attends Cheshunt Secondary Modern School. (While there, he will form 5-piece vocal group, The Quintones, which will split when the three girl members go to secretarial college.)

1957 Aug After leaving school with an O-level in English, he finds work as a credit control clerk at Atlas Lamps factory in Enfield. He also joins The Dick Teague Skiffle Group, playing pubs in Ware, Cheshunt and Hoddesdon.

1958 He and the group's drummer Terry Smart leave to form a rock'n'roll band with Norman Mitham on guitar, calling themselves Harry Webb & The Drifters. Teddy Boy John Foster, employed at the local sewage works, sees the band at The Five Horseshoes pub in Hoddesdon and offers to manage them. Foster persuades his parents to finance the recording of a demo. For £10, they cut *Breathless* and *Lawdy Miss Clawdy* at HMV Records store in London's Oxford Street. They play a week's engagement at the 2 I's coffee bar in London's Soho district. After a gig they are approached by Ian Samwell, wishing to join the group as its lead guitarist. He is accepted, and proves also to have songwriting talent. Promoter Bob Greatorex books the group for a one-night stand at a dance hall in Ripley, Derbys, but is unhappy with the lead singer's name. After a discussion at The Swiss pub near the 2 I's, they settle upon Cliff Richard & The Drifters. (Samwell suggests leaving the "s" off Richards, which is the initial suggestion, pointing out that when Richard corrects people who get it wrong, they will keep his name in mind.)

July Foster arranges for Richard & The Drifters to take part in a talent contest at the Gaumont Cinema on Shepherd's Bush Green in London. He persuades variety agent George Ganjou to see the band and Ganjou takes Richard's demo tape to Norrie Paramor, head of A&R at EMI Records' Columbia label, who invites the group to audition for him.

Aug [9] Richard signs to EMI and leaves his job at Atlas. With The Drifters, he begins a 4-week residency at Butlins holiday camp in Clacton-on-Sea, Essex. Mitham quits the band, Samwell switches to bass and Ken Pavey, a professional player working at the holiday camp, fills in the guitar slot.

Aug [29] Debut single *Schoolboy Crush* (a cover of a US release by Bobby Helms) backed with *Move It* (a rock number written by Samwell and completed on a bus on the way to the studio) is released in UK. Two session players, guitarist Ernie Shear and bassist Frank Clark, are on the tracks at Paramor's insistence, to ensure a strong sound.

Sept The group is signed to appear on a UK package tour headed by *When* hitmakers The Kalin Twins. Minus a lead guitarist since Mitham's departure, Foster visits the 2 I's to recruit singer/guitarist Tony Sheridan, but cannot find him. Instead, he spots Hank Marvin, a regular at the club and known to be an excellent player. Marvin agrees to join Richard on tour provided his rhythm guitar-playing partner Bruce Welch is taken on too.

Sept [13] Richard makes his UK TV debut in Jack Good's "Oh Boy" (where he will become a program resident). Good has heard the single, disregarded *Schoolboy Crush*, but raved over *Move It*. He orders Richard to sing without his customary guitar and minus his sideburns. (He also encourages a sexy stage act which will have newspapers complaining about TV depravity and the corruption of the young.) At the same time, *Move It*, now promoted to A-side after most radio DJ's have shared Good's judgement of it, makes its debut on the UK chart.

Oct [5] Richard & The Drifters, comprising Marvin (lead guitar), Welch (rhythm guitar), Samwell (bass) and Smart (drums), make their concert debut at The Victoria Hall, Hanley, Stoke-on-Trent, UK, at the start of The Kalin Twins' UK tour, which also features trumpeter Eddie Calvert and The Most Brothers. (Teen reaction to Richard will be such that, almost from the outset, The Kalin Twins will find it hard to follow his act.)

Oct [25] Richard makes his UK radio debut, on BBC Light Programme's "Saturday Club".

Nov *Move It* hits UK #2, behind Connie Francis'° *Stupid Cupid*. By the end of the tour, Samwell has been eased to a songwriting/management role to make way for a stronger bass player – Jet Harris, who was touring with The Most Brothers but has been helping The Drifters on most dates. Smart leaves, feeling he is not up to the standard of the more recent recruits, and announces his intention to join the Merchant Navy. He is replaced by Harris' drummer friend, Tony Meehan.

Dec Follow-up *High Class Baby*, another Samwell composition, hits UK #7, though Richard hates the song (and will never perform it again).

1959 Jan [24] Richard, with the new line-up, begins his first headlining UK tour at York's Rialto Theatre, on a bill with Wee Willie Harris and Tony Crombie & His Rockets.

Feb *Livin' Lovin' Doll* makes UK #20, as Richard wins the Best New Singer award in the annual *New Musical Express (NME)* poll.

May *Mean Streak* hits UK #10 while B-side *Never Mind* makes UK #21 (both are written by Samwell). Debut LP *Cliff* hits UK #4.

May [14] Film *Serious Charge*, starring Anthony Quayle, premieres in London. Richard features as a young semi-delinquent trying to make it as a rock singer, and sings three songs.

Aug *Living Doll*, written by Lionel Bart for *Serious Charge*, but revamped for single release as a mid-tempo, slightly country song, tops the UK chart for 5 weeks, selling over a half million copies. The song wins an Ivor Novello award, and the single, on international sales, earns his first gold disk.

Oct *Travellin' Light*, in similar style to *Living Doll*, tops the UK chart for 5 weeks, while rocking B-side, Samwell's *Dynamite*, makes UK #16 (and will be a popular concert item throughout Richard's career and be re-recorded more than once).

Nov Second LP *Cliff Sings* hits UK #2, while *Living Doll*, issued in US on ABC Records, reaches US #30.

Nov [27] Film *Expresso Bongo* premieres in London, UK. Based on Wolf Mankowitz' stage play, it stars Laurence Harvey, with Richard as the manipulated teenage rock star Bongo Herbert.

Dec Richard and The Shadows° (to which The Drifters have changed their name to avoid confusion with the US Drifters°), open at Stockton's Globe Theatre, UK, in pantomime *Babes in the Wood*.

1960 Jan Richard and The Shadows° begin a 5-week US package tour with Freddy Cannon, Bobby Rydell°, Clyde McPhatter and bill-topper Frankie Avalon°.

Jan [21] Richard guests on "The Pat Boone Show" on US ABC TV, singing five songs including *Living Doll*.

Feb *A Voice In The Wilderness*, a ballad from *Expresso Bongo*, hits UK #2 for 3 weeks (held from the top by Anthony Newley's *Why*), while the EP of four songs from the film reaches UK #11 (representing uncommonly large sales for the time by an EP).

Feb [21] Richard wins Top British Male Singer award in *NME* poll, and takes a 2-day break from the US tour to attend the presentation in UK.

Apr *Fall In Love With You* hits UK #2, while B-side revival of Johnny Otis'° *Willie And The Hand Jive* makes UK #18. Meanwhile, Richard and his family move into their first owned home in Percy Road, Winchmore Hill, North London.

May [16] Richard participates in The Royal Variety Performance at London's Victoria Palace, in the presence of HM The Queen, appearing in a "youth" segment alongside Adam Faith° and Lonnie Donegan°.

June Richard and The Shadows° open a 6-month season at the London Palladium, in *Stars in your Eyes*.

July *Please Don't Tease*, written by Welch of The Shadows° with Pete Chester (son of comedian Charlie), is chosen by members of Richard's fan club, invited to a preview hearing of recently-recorded tracks, as the best bet for a hit single. It tops the UK chart for 4 weeks but is deposed by The Shadows' first instrumental hit, *Apache*.

Oct Fast rocker *Nine Times Out Of Ten* (the fans' third choice) is released as follow-up and hits UK #3.

Oct [14] Richard receives more than 5,000 cards on his 20th birthday.

Nov LP *Me And My Shadows* hits UK #2, behind soundtrack LP *South Pacific*.

1961 Jan *I Love You* hits UK #2, behind Johnny Tillotson's° *Poetry In Motion*.

Feb [4] It is announced that Richard and his manager Tito Burns are parting, amicably. (The following month, Australian Peter Gormley, who is already handling The Shadows°, becomes Richard's manager.)

Mar *Theme For A Dream* hits UK #2, behind The Everly Brothers'° *Walk Right Back*.

Apr [8] Richard sits on the panel of UK TV show "Juke Box Jury".

May *Gee Whiz It's You* (from LP *Me And My Shadows*), pressed as a single for export, begins to sell in UK and is made generally available. Hitting the top 20 while *Theme For A Dream* is still in the top 5, it climbs to UK #5. Meanwhile, LP *Listen To Cliff* hits UK #2.

May [15] Richard's father dies in hospital, aged 56.

May [20] Richard makes his debut on UK TV show "Thank Your Lucky Stars", singing *A Girl Like You*.

June *A Girl Like You* hits UK #3.

Aug [17] Richard and The Shadows° open a European tour at the Tivoli Gardens, Copenhagen, Denmark.

Aug [28] Richard opens a 6-week summer season at UK's Blackpool Opera House.

Oct *When The Girl In Your Arms Is The Girl In Your Heart*, a ballad from forthcoming film *The Young Ones*, hits UK #2 (behind Helen Shapiro's° *Walkin' Back To Happiness*, while LP *21 Today* tops the UK chart for a week.

1962 Jan As the movie opens in UK (it will be the second-biggest box office grosser of the year, after *The Guns of Navarone*), the title song from *The Young Ones* enters the UK chart at #1, and holds for 8 weeks, selling more than a million copies in UK. Soundtrack LP *The Young Ones* knocks Elvis Presley's° LP *Blue Hawaii* from UK #1, and tops the chart for 6 weeks before surrendering again to the Presley soundtrack. Press reports state that Richard is to marry 17-year-old Valerie Stratford, but are quickly dismissed.

Feb Richard wins *NME*'s Top British Male Singer award for the second consecutive year.

Mar [13] Richard receives an award as Show Business Personality of the Year from the Variety Club of Great Britain.

May *I'm Looking Out The Window*, a revival of a Peggy Lee ballad, hits UK #2 (behind Elvis Presley's° *Good Luck Charm*), while B-side revival of Bobby Freeman's *Do You Want To Dance?* hits UK #10.

May [5] Richard is awarded a gold disk for UK million sales of *The Young Ones*.

Sept A revival of Jerry Lee Lewis'° rocker *It'll Be Me* hits UK #2, behind Elvis Presley's° *She's Not You*.

Sept [21] Richard pays a swift visit to US to appear on TV's "Ed Sullivan Show".

CLIFF RICHARD *cont.*

Sept [28] Richard appears on UK BBC TV's "The Billy Cotton Band Show", singing *It'll Be Me*.

Oct Richard begins a week of concerts at the London Palladium, while LP *32 Minutes And 17 Seconds With Cliff Richard* hits UK #3.

Dec On UK TV's "Sunday Night at the London Palladium", Richard premieres both sides of *The Next Time/Bachelor Boy* (the latter Richard's first co-writing credit, and both taken from forthcoming film *Summer Holiday*).

1963 Jan *The Next Time* tops the UK chart for a week (before being deposed by The Shadows'° *Dance On*), while *Bachelor Boy* hits UK #3. Total UK sales approach 950,000.

Jan [10] *Summer Holiday*, filmed largely on European locations in summer 1962, premieres in London, UK.

Jan [21] Radio Luxembourg devotes its entire "ABC of the Stars" program to Richard.

Feb Soundtrack LP *Summer Holiday* tops the UK chart for 14 weeks.

Feb [11] Richard appears at a charity concert in Nairobi, Kenya, Africa.

Mar The title song from *Summer Holiday* tops the UK chart for 2 weeks, replacing The Beatles'° *Please Please Me*.

Apr [14] Richard and The Shadows° appear on US TV's "Ed Sullivan Show", singing *Summer Holiday*.

May A revival of Ruth Brown's *Lucky Lips* hits UK #4.

June Richard and The Shadows star in *Holiday Carnival*, a summer variety show at Blackpool (ending Sept.).

July LP *Cliff's Hit Album*, a compilation of singles from *Move It* to *Do You Want To Dance?*, hits UK #2.

Aug US teen magazine 16 votes Richard Most Promising Singer in its annual poll.

Sept A revival of Tommy Edwards' *It's All In The Game* hits UK #2, behind The Beatles'° *She Loves You* while in US (where he is now signed to Epic) *Lucky Lips* becomes Richard's first chart single since *Living Doll*, and climbs to US #62.

Oct LP *When In Spain*, recorded in Barcelona and sung in Spanish, hits UK #8.

Oct [20] Richard appears again on US TV's "Ed Sullivan Show", singing *It's All In The Game*.

Nov [3] Richard and The Shadows° appear on UK TV's "Sunday Night at the London Palladium", singing *Don't Talk To Him*.

Nov *Don't Talk To Him* hits UK #2, held from the top by The Beatles'° *She Loves You* (enjoying its second run at #1).

1964 Feb *I'm The Lonely One* hits UK #8, while *It's All In The Game* reaches US #25 – his biggest US hit to date.

Apr *I'm The Lonely One* stalls at US #92.

Apr [2] Richard and The Shadows open a UK tour at Kingston-upon-Thames, Surrey.

May *Constantly*, an English-lyric version of an Italian ballad, hits UK #4, while US-compiled LP *It's All In The Game* makes US #115.

May [26] Richard and The Shadows perform at the *NME* Poll Winners' Concert at Wembley, UK.

June *On The Beach*, from film *Wonderful Life*, hits UK #7.

July [2] Richard attends the world premiere of his new film *Wonderful Life* in London, UK.

July Soundtrack LP *Wonderful Life* hits UK #2, behind The Beatles'° *A Hard Day's Night*.

Aug *Bachelor Boy* spends a week at US #99.

Aug [10] Richard receives a gold disk for a million sales of *Bachelor Boy/The Next Time* on UK TV show "Thank Your Lucky Stars".

Aug [19/21] At the invitation of Epic Records, Richard records in Nashville, Tenn., US, with producer Billy Sherrill and vocal backing from The Jordanaires.

Oct A revival of Johnny Mathis' *The Twelfth Of Never* hits UK #8.

Nov Richard and The Shadows° perform at The Royal Variety Show in London.

Dec *I Could Easily Fall (In Love With You)* hits UK #9. It is taken from the London Palladium pantomine *Aladdin and his Wonderful Lamp*, which stars Richard and The Shadows° with Arthur Askey and Una Stubbs.

1965 Jan LP *Aladdin And His Wonderful Lamp* reaches UK #13.

Feb Richard denies rumors that he is quitting show business.

Apr *The Minute You're Gone*, cut in Nashville, tops the UK chart for a week. (B-side *Just Another Guy* is one of the first covers of a song by Neil Diamond°.) Meanwhile, LP *Cliff Richard* hits UK #9.

June [8/14] Richard and The Shadows° play a week of concerts in Birmingham, UK.

July *On My Word* reaches UK #12.

Aug Compilation LP *More Hits By Cliff* makes UK #20.

Sept *The Time In Between* makes UK #22, while LP *When In Rome*, sung in Italian, fails to chart.

Oct [3] Richard and The Shadows° open a UK tour in Derby.

Oct [9] Richard comperes "Sunday Night at the London Palladium" on UK TV.

Nov Richard and The Shadows° participate in the annual Royal Variety Show.

Dec *Wind Me Up (Let Me Go)*, another ballad from the Nashville sessions, hits UK #2 for 3 weeks, behind The Beatles'° *We Can Work It Out/Day Tripper*.

Dec [7] Richard appears on UK TV show "Cinema", discussing his films.

1966 Jan LP *Love Is Forever*, a collection of romantic ballads, reaches UK #19.

Feb [21] Richard and The Shadows° make their cabaret debut at London's Talk of the Town.

Apr *Blue Turns To Grey*, written by Mick Jagger and Keith Richards of The Rolling Stones°, reaches UK #15.

Apr [3] Richard and The Shadows° takes part in the Stars' Organization for Spastics concert at London's Empire Pool, Wembley.

May Richard and The Shadows participate in the annual *NME* Poll Winners Concert at the Empire Pool, Wembley, London, on a bill with The Beatles°, The Rolling Stones°, Roy Orbison°, Dusty Springfield°, The Yardbirds°, The Spencer Davis Group° and many others.

June LP *Kinda Latin* hits UK #9.

June [16] Richard joins evangelist Billy Graham on stage at Earls Court, London, and talks of his discovery of the Christian faith, before singing *It Is No Secret*.

Aug Ballad *Visions* (later used as the closing theme for his TV series) hits UK #7.

Oct *Time Drags By*, from forthcoming movie *Finders Keepers*, hits UK #10.

Oct [8] Richard attends the premiere of film *Finders Keepers* in London, UK.

Dec [10] Richard opens in the London Palladium pantomime *Cinderella*, with music entirely written by The Shadows°.

Dec [12] Richard and The Shadows attend the premiere of film *Thunderbirds Are Go!* in which their puppet likenesses appear, singing *Shooting Star*.

1967 Jan *In The Country*, taken from *Cinderella*, hits UK #6, while soundtrack LP *Finders Keepers* hits UK #6 and LP *Cinderella* makes UK #30. Richard states in an *NME* article that he intends to give up showbiz and teach religious instruction in school.

Apr *It's All Over*, previously cut by The Everly Brothers°, hits UK #9.

May LP *Don't Stop Me Now* reaches UK #23.

May [7] Richard participates in the annual *NME* Poll Winners Concert at Wembley's Empire Pool, on a bill with The Beach Boys°, Stevie Winwood°, Georgie Fame°, Lulu° and Dusty Springfield°.

June *I'll Come Running*, penned by Neil Diamond° (as is B-side *I Got The Feelin'*), makes UK #26.

Sept *The Day I Met Marie*, written by Hank Marvin, hits UK #10. (For many years, Richard will cite this as his favorite of his own recordings).

Sept [23] Richard is voted Top Male Singer by the readers of *Melody Maker* magazine.

Nov Gospel LP *Good News*, his first religious release, peaks at UK #37.

Dec Ballad *All My Love* hits UK #6.

Dec [6] He is confirmed into membership of the Church of England by Graham Leonard, Bishop of Willesden, at St. Paul's church, Finchley, London.

1968 Apr *Congratulations*, Bill Martin/Phil Coulter's song chosen to represent UK in the Eurovision Song Contest, tops the UK chart for 2 weeks – his first #1 hit in 3 years (and last until 1979). It will be a worldwide million-seller, partly thanks to being cut in several languages.

Apr [6] Richard, representing UK, sings *Congratulations* in the Eurovision Song Contest held at London's Royal Albert Hall. He comes second to Spain's Massiel, with *La La La*.

Apr Richard appears in UK TV drama "A Matter of Diamonds".

May Richard and The Shadows° participate in the annual *NME* Poll Winners Concert at Wembley's Empire Pool, on a bill with Lulu°, The Rolling Stones°, Dusty Springield°, Scott Walker and many others.

June Live LP *Cliff In Japan*, recorded at Sankei Hall, Tokyo, makes UK #29. *Congratulations* spends 3 weeks on US singles chart, but peaks at #99.

June [28] He appears in a TV concert special on ITV, "Talk of the Town", taped at the London venue of the same name.

July *I'll Love You Forever Today*, co-written by Richard for his forthcoming film *Two a Penny*, peaks at UK #27.

July [11] UK TV airs a Cliff Richard and The Shadows special to celebrate their 10 years together.

Aug LP *Two A Penny* fails to chart. It is partly the soundtrack of the film, a morality drama, which Richard has made, without a fee, for the Billy Graham organization.

Oct *Marianne*, written by actor Bill Owen (of 1980s "Last of the Summer Wine" fame) makes UK #22.

Oct [11] Richard and The Shadows° begin a season at the London Palladium.

Nov LP *Established 1958*, half Cliff Richard and half Shadows tracks, celebrating their 10th anniversary in show business, climbs to UK #30.

Dec *Don't Forget To Catch Me*, from the 10th anniversary LP, climbs to UK #21.

1969 Mar *Good Times (Better Times)* reaches UK #12.

May [12] Richard guests on UK children's TV "Sooty" show.

June *Big Ship*, written by Raymond Froggatt, hits UK #8.

Aug Compilation LP *The Best Of Cliff* hits UK #5.

Oct *Throw Down A Line*, a duet with Hank Marvin, hits UK #7, while LP *Sincerely* makes UK #24.

Oct [7] Richard and The Shadows° begin a Japanese tour at The Alaska, Tokyo.

Nov [7] Richard and The Shadows commence a UK tour in Finsbury Park, London.

Dec *With The Eyes Of A Child* makes UK #20.

Dec [10] Richard participates in a special gala midnight performance at the London Palladium in aid of the Royal Society for the Prevention of Cruelty to Animals (RSPCA).

1970 Jan [3] Richard's own UK TV series starts on BBC 1.

Mar A second duet with Marvin, *The Joy Of Living*, (also the theme of the TV series) peaks at UK #25.

May [11] Richard makes his straight stage acting debut in Peter Shaffer's *Five Finger Exercise* at the New Theatre, Bromley, Kent, UK.

July *Goodbye Sam, Hello Samantha*, widely promoted as his 50th single, hits UK #6. While live-recorded LP *Cliff Live At The Talk Of The Town* fails to chart.

Aug [31] UK BBC TV airs a Cliff Richard special with guest Aretha Franklin°.

Sept *I Ain't Got Time Anymore* makes UK #21.

Oct Religious LP *About That Man* fails to chart.

Oct [21] Richard and The Shadows° begin a UK tour in Golders Green, London.

Dec LP *Tracks'n'Grooves* climbs to UK #37.

1971 Jan [2] UK BBC TV airs the first of a 13-week series "It's Cliff Richard", with resident guests Hank Marvin and Una Stubbs.

Feb *Sunny Honey Girl* reaches UK #19.

Apr Marvin-penned (with ecological concerns) *Silvery Rain* peaks at UK #27.

May [17] Richard opens at the Sadlers Wells Theatre in London in play *The Potting Shed*. (The show had been scheduled to open a week earlier at Bromley, but the New Theatre was gutted by fire before the opening night.)

June [13] Richard and The Shadows° take part in "A Night with the Stars", a tribute to recently deceased UK singer Dickie Valentine, at the London Palladium. (Richard joins Petula Clark° in a duet of *I Want To Hold Your Hand*.)

July [5] Richard receives an Ivor Novello award for outstanding service to UK music, at the Rose d'Or Festival in Juan Les Pins, in which he performs with Olivia Newton-John°.

Aug *Flying Machine* climbs to UK #37.

Oct [25] Richard and The Shadows° start a season at the London Palladium.

Dec *Sing A Song Of Freedom* reaches UK #13.

1972 Jan UK TV airs the first of 13-week series "It's Cliff Richard", with resident guests Olivia Newton-John° and The Flirtations.

Mar *Jesus* makes UK #35.

Apr [14] Richard is voted the Top Male Pop Personality by *The Sun* newspaper for the third year running.

Sept *Living In Harmony* reaches UK #12.

Sept [2] UK TV airs "The Case", a musical comedy-thriller starring Richard, Newton-John° and comedian Tim Brooke-Taylor.

Nov [17] Richard begins a UK tour, at Fairfield Hall, Croydon. He is joined on stage by Olivia Newton-John°.

Dec LP *The Best Of Cliff, Volume Two* peaks at UK #49, while *A Brand New Song* becomes his first single to fail to reach UK top 50.

1973 Jan [10] Richard appears on UK BBC TV's "Cilla Black Show", singing six entries chosen to represent UK in the Eurovision Song Contest. *Power To All Our Friends* is chosen as UK entry by TV viewers.

Apr [7] *Power To All Our Friends* comes second in the Eurovision Song Contest, before going on to hit UK #4.

May *Help It Along*, a 4-track EP containing the Eurovision entry songs, makes UK #29.

Dec *Take Me High* peaks at UK #27. It is the theme from Richard's movie of the same title, co-starring Debbie Watling and George Cole, filmed on location in Birmingham, UK.

1974 Jan Soundtrack LP *Take Me High* climbs to UK #41.

Mar Richard is awarded the Silver Clef for outstanding services to the music industry by the Nordoff-Robbins Music Therapy Charity.

Apr [3/11] Richard plays the London Palladium. He falls ill, and Rolf Harris deputizes for three performances.

June *(You Keep Me) Hangin' On* reaches UK #13. Meanwhile, live LP *Help It Along* is released with all profits going to TEAR Fund (an international Christian aid organization), but the LP does not chart.

July [3] Richard plays Bottom in a production of *A Midsummer Night's Dream* with past and present members of his old school at Cheshunt.

July [9] The International Cliff Richard Movement meets for the first time at the United Reform Church in Crouch End, London.

Oct [27] Richard and The Shadows° play together for the first time in 6 years in a charity concert at the London Palladium.

Nov LP *The 31st Of February Street*, produced by Dave Mackay, fails to chart.

1975 Mar *It's Only Me You've Left Behind* also fails to chart.

June [5] Richard participates in a charity concert in Manchester, UK's Free Trade Hall for the families of two policemen who had died in the course of duty.

July [9] UK TV airs "Jim'll Fix It", in which fan Helen Moon from Cromer, Norfolk, meets Richard.

Sept [6] UK TV series "It's Cliff and Friends" airs for the first time.

Oct *(There's A) Honky Tonk Angel (Who Will Take Me Back In)* fails to chart, after Richard belatedly becomes aware of the implications of the song's lyric and refuses to promote it.

1976 Feb Bruce Welch of The Shadows° takes over as Richard's producer, and *Miss You Nights* restores him to UK singles chart after a 20-month absence, reaching #15. EMI Records releases LP *I'm Nearly Famous* and *The Best Of Cliff Richard* in USSR. He becomes the third UK artist to achieve such an honor.

May *Devil Woman* hits UK #9.

June Welch-produced LP *I'm Nearly Famous*, including the two recent top 20 singles, hits UK #5.

Sept Also from the LP, *I Can't Ask For Anything More Than You, Babe* reaches UK #17, while *Devil Woman* becomes his first US top 10, peaking at #6 (higher than it attained in UK). It earns a US gold disk for a million-plus sales.

Sept [16] Richard begins a USSR tour with a concert at The Hall of the October Revolution, Leningrad, to a rapturous audience.

Sept [25] Richard is invited to a reception at the British Embassy in Moscow.

Oct LP *I'm Nearly Famous* makes US #76.

Dec *Hey, Mr. Dream Maker* peaks at UK #31, while *I Can't Ask For Anymore Than You, Babe* stalls at US #80. Richard travels to his birthplace, India, where he meets Mother Teresa.

Dec [7/8] He appears in concert at the Kalamandir Auditorium, New Delhi, India.

1977 Mar *My Kinda Life* reaches UK #15.

Apr LP *Every Face Tells A Story* hits UK #8.

July *When Two Worlds Drift Apart* climbs to UK #46, while *Don't Turn The Light Out* makes US #57.

Sept [5] Richard's book *Which One's Cliff?*, written with Bill Latham, is published.

Oct [18] The British Phonographic Institute (BPI) awards Richard the Britannia Award as Best British Male Solo Artist of the last 25

years, to coincide with HM The Queen's Silver Jubilee celebrations.
Oct [28] Richard receives the Gold Badge Award from the Songwriters' Guild of Great Britain.
Nov TV-advertised double compilation LP *40 Golden Greats* tops the UK chart for a week – his first #1 LP since *Summer Holiday*.
1978 Feb [27] Richard and The Shadows° begin 2 weeks of reunion concerts at the London Palladium.
Mar Gospel LP *Small Corners* makes UK #33, but *Yes! He Lives*, taken from it, fails to sell.
Aug *Please Remember Me*, coupled with a new version of the former #1 hit *Please Don't Tease*, fails to chart.
Oct LP *Green Light* reaches UK #25.
Nov Extracted *Can't Take The Hurt Anymore* misses UK top 50.
1979 Feb [1] EMI Records organizes a special lunch at Claridge's, London, to celebrate its 21-year relationship with Richard.
Feb [13] Richard and The Shadows° receive a special award at the annual Music Week awards, celebrating 21 years as hitmaking artists.
Mar TV-promoted live LP *Thank You Very Much*, featuring highlights of the previous year's Palladium concerts with The Shadows°, hits UK #5.
Apr The title song from *Green Light* stalls at UK #57.
July [5] Richard is guest of honor at the Variety Club of Great Britain lunch at The Dorchester, London.
Aug *We Don't Talk Anymore*, an Alan Tarney song produced by Welch, tops the UK chart for 4 weeks, his first UK #1 after more than 11 years. It will become his biggest-selling single worldwide, with total sales of over 5 million.
Sept LP *Rock'n'Roll Juvenile* hits UK #3. Norrie Paramor, Richard's original producer, dies.
Sept [22] Richard participates in "Hosannah '79", an anti-racist festival in Birmingham, UK.
Oct [4] Richard and Kate Bush° perform with the London Symphony Orchestra at London's Royal Albert Hall, as part of the Hall's 75th Birthday Appeal.
Nov *Hot Shot*, from LP *Rock'n'Roll Juvenile*, peaks at UK #46.
Dec [2] Richard participates in a carol concert in Camberley, Surrey, UK, in aid of the International Year of the Child.
Dec [16] Richard leads an estimated 30,000 people in carol singing outside Buckingham Palace, as part of the International Year of the Child activities.
1980 Jan [1] Richard is included in HM The Queen's New Year Honours List, being awarded an OBE (Order of the British Empire).
Jan *We Don't Talk Anymore* hits US #7, while the LP of the same title (a revised version of *Rock'n'Roll Juvenile*) makes US #93.
Feb *Carrie*, from the LP, hits UK #4.
Apr *Carrie* makes US #34.
Apr [16] Mother-of-two Kim Kayne pays £1,400 for the privilege of having lunch with Richard as part of the fund raising activities of London's Capital Radio "Help a London Child" charity.
July [23] Richard receives his OBE from The Queen at Buckingham Palace.
Aug *Dreamin'* hits UK #8.
Sept LP *I'm No Hero* hits UK #4.
Oct Richard plays five nights at London's Apollo Theatre.
Nov *Suddenly*, a duet with Olivia Newton-John° from the soundtrack of film *Xanadu*, reaches UK #15, while *Dreamin'* hits US #10.
1981 Jan *Suddenly* peaks at US #20.
Feb *A Little In Love* reaches UK #15, while LP *I'm No Hero* peaks at US #80.
Feb [24] Richard receives *The Daily Mirror* newspaper's readers' award as Outstanding Music Personality of the Year at London's Café Royal.
Mar [3] Richard begins a 7-week 35-date North American tour, opening in Seattle, Wash., as *A Little In Love* reaches US #17.
Mar [16] Richard appears on US TV show "Solid Gold".
Mar [20] While he is away, "Cliff in London" airs on UK BBC TV.
Mar Richard's first home video, *The Young Ones*, is released by Thorn EMI Video.
Apr [18] Richard ends his US tour in LA, Cal.
May The "Cliff Richard Rock Special" takes place at London's Hammersmith Odeon – all audience members dress in 1950s clothes.
June *Give A Little Bit More* makes US #41.
July Compilation LP *Love Songs*, featuring familiar ballads, tops the UK chart for 5 weeks.
Sept *Wired For Sound* hits UK #4.
Oct LP *Wired For Sound* hits UK #4 and US #132, as the title track peaks at US #71.
Dec *Daddy's Home*, a revival of Shep & The Limelites' 1961 US smash recorded live in concert, hits UK #2, behind The Human League's° *Don't You Want Me*.
1982 Mar *Daddy's Home* reaches US #23.
Aug *The Only Way Out* hits UK #10.
Sept LP *Now You See Me . . . Now You Don't*, including his previous and next singles, hits UK #4.
Oct *Where Do We Go From Here?* peaks at UK #60, while *The Only Way Out* climbs to US #64.
Dec Seasonal *Little Town*, a new uptempo arrangement of Christmas carol *O Little Town Of Bethlehem*, reaches UK #11.
1983 Mar Richard duets with Phil Everly on the Stuart Colman-produced rocker *She Means Nothing To Me*, which hits UK #9.
May A revival of Buddy Holly's° *True Love Ways*, recorded live with the London Philharmonic Orchestra, hits UK #8. It is taken from live LP *Dressed For The Occasion* with the LPO, which hits UK #7.
June *Drifting*, a ballad duetted with Sheila Walsh, reaches UK #64.
Sept Dance-oriented *Never Say Die (Give A Little Bit More)* reaches UK #15. This is the first Richard single to have an extended 12" dance version.
Oct LP *Silver*, marking 25 years as a recording artist, hits UK #7. It is briefly available as a boxed set which includes a second LP, *Rock'n'Roll Silver*, with versions of several 1950s oldies. Meanwhile, *Never Say Die (Give A Little Bit More)* peaks at US #73.
Dec *Please Don't Fall In Love*, taken from LP *Silver*, hits UK #7.
1984 Apr *Baby You're Dynamite*, a rocker also from the LP, makes UK #27.
May After heavy radio play of B-side ballad *Ocean Deep*, it charts at UK #72 in place of the A-side.
July LP *20 Original Greats*, featuring Richard and The Shadows°, peaks at UK #43.
Sept *Two To The Power*, a duet with Janet Jackson° on her label A&M, fails to chart.
Nov *Shooting From The Heart* peaks at UK #51.
Dec LP *The Rock Connection* (including several rock tracks first heard on *Rock'n'Roll Silver*, plus *She Means Nothing To Me*), makes UK #43. (This compilation is released because Richard's EMI contract has lapsed and will take time to renegotiate; meanwhile, he is not available for recording.)
1985 Feb *Heart User* climbs to UK #46.
Oct It is announced that Richard is to star in London's West End in 1986 in the first stage production of Dave Clark's° musical *Time*. The first recording of a song from the show is *She's So Beautiful*, produced by Stevie Wonder° and featuring him on all instruments, with Richard handling the vocals. It reaches UK #17.
Dec *It's In Every One Of Us*, penned by US writer David Pomeranz several years earlier but from *Time*, peaks at UK #45.
Dec [19] Richard joins Chris De Burgh°, Lulu°, Sandie Shaw° and others for Carol Aid, a carol-singing event at London's Heaven club to raise funds for the Band Aid Appeal.
1986 Mar Richard returns to UK #1 with a revival of his own former chart-topper *Living Doll*, recorded with alternative TV comedy team The Young Ones, with all proceeds going to the Comic Relief charity. Featuring Hank Marvin guesting on guitar, it tops the UK chart for 3 weeks and sells over a half million copies in UK.
Apr [6] Richard opens at London's Dominion Theatre as lead in Dave Clark's° musical *Time* (which also features an electronic/holographic "cameo" by Lord Olivier). (The show and star are well reviewed and draw constant capacity audiences; Richard will stay in it for a year, after which David Cassidy° will take over.)
May *Born To Rock'n'Roll*, taken from *Time*, fails to chart, while the original all-star LP of the show, featuring Richard and other guest performers including Freddie Mercury, Dionne Warwick° and Julian Lennon, makes UK #21.
Sept *All I Ask Of You*, from rival West End musical (Andrew Lloyd Webber's *The Phantom of the Opera*), Richard's duet with the show's female lead Sarah Brightman, hits UK #3.
Dec *Slow Rivers*, a duet with Elton John°, reaches UK #44.
1987 July Richard re-signs to EMI and records a new LP with

writer/producer Alan Tarney. From it, *My Pretty One* hits UK #6.

Sept *Some People* hits UK #3, while parent LP *Always Guaranteed* hits UK #5 – eventually outselling all previous Richard LPs to turn platinum.

Oct A 50-date European tour is followed by 6 sold-out nights at the National Exhibition Centre, Birmingham, UK.

Nov *Remember Me*, also from LP *Always Guaranteed*, reaches UK #15.

Dec He hosts a Pro-Celebrity charity tennis tournament.

1988 Feb *Two Hearts*, a final extract from the previous year's LP, makes UK #34.

Sept The 30th anniversary of his first hit with *Move It* is noted by tributes in a variety of media, and a 30th anniversary 47-date UK tour begins at the end of Sept. ending mid-Dec. Every ticket sells out within 3 days, giving him a combined tour audience of over 200,000.

Nov LP *Private Collection*, a double compilation LP rounding up a decade of hits from *We Don't Talk Anymore* to new *Mistletoe And Wine* (and including most of Richard's duets with other artists), tops the UK chart and turns triple platinum, with sales of over 900,000.

Dec Richard's 99th single, seasonal *Mistletoe And Wine*, tops the UK chart for 4 weeks, to become the biggest-selling single of 1988 in UK.

LIONEL RICHIE

1967 Richie (b. Lionel Brockman Richie Jr., June 20, 1949, Tuskegee, Ala., US), the son of a retired army captain and a teacher, having been raised in a religious environment and been singing in the Episcopal Church Choir, is encouraged to seek a career in the ministry, but his Uncle Bertram buys him a saxophone and his grandmother encourages him to practise the piano. Now studying economics at predominantly black Tuskegee Institute (where he was born – his grandfather having worked on campus), he meets other ambitious musicians including Thomas McClary and William King to form The Commodores°. He also meets his future wife, Brenda Harvey.

1974 Delayed by touring and disk success of The Commodores°, he finally graduates in economics.

1978 Aug Richie has become the dominant creative and vocal force within The Commodores°, and writes and sings lead on their first US #1, *Three Times A Lady*.

1979 Oct The Commodores'° ballad *Still*, written and sung by Richie, hits US #1. Relying increasingly on his ballad-writing skills, The Commodores will enjoy eight Richie-penned top 10 hits prior to his departure from the group.

1980 Nov [15] Richie's first composition outside The Commodores°, *Lady*, sung by Kenny Rogers°, reaches UK #12 and hits US #1 for 6 weeks. Richie also produces the song, which is recorded in only 4 hours, and he meets Rogers' manager, Ken Kragen.

1981 Mar Still with The Commodores°, but increasingly in demand as a solo, Richie enters the studio with Rogers° to produce LP *Share Your Love* (US #6), which will spring Richie-penned US #3 hit *I Don't Need You*.

Apr While working on Rogers'° project and a new Commodores° LP, Richie is contacted by film producer, Franco Zeffirelli, who needs a song for his forthcoming Brooke Shields movie *Endless Love*. He offers Diana Ross° as a possible co-vocalist. Richie accepts and flies to Reno, Nev., for a 3 a.m. recording session with Ms. Ross.

July He appears on his final new Commodores° LP *In The Pocket*. From it, Richie-penned and performed *Oh No* makes US #4 and UK #44.

Aug [15] Richie/Ross° duet *Endless Love* hits US #1 for 9 weeks, and UK #7. (The song becomes the most successful Motown single and soundtrack single. Its achievements coincide with Richie signing a solo management deal with Kragen, although he is still officially with The Commodores°.)

1982 Mar Richie begins work in LA on his debut solo LP with producer James Carmichael who enlists top session musicians including Greg Phillanganes, Paulinho DaCosta, Michael Boddicker. Joe Walsh°, Kenny Rogers° and even tennis star Jimmy Connors also guests. On many tracks Richie plays on the same studio piano used by Carole King° on her LP *Tapestry*.

Mar [29] Richie performs *Endless Love* at the Annual Academy Awards ceremony in LA.

Aug With his debut LP completed, Richie and The Commodores°, still theoretically together, are shocked by the death of their manager Benny Ashburn at age 54.

Oct Richie formally announces his solo split from the band. First single, *Truly*, a ballad from Motown LP *Lionel Richie*, is released. The LP will hit US #3 and UK #9 and is dedicated to Ashburn.

Nov [27] *Truly* hits US #1 and UK #6.

1983 Feb *You Are* peaks at UK #43 as Richie appears on the Motown 25th Anniversary TV celebration.

Mar *You Are* hits US #4 while Richie, with 17 previous nominations for a Grammy, finally wins one for *Truly*. LP sales now exceed 3 million.

May Ballad *My Love* hits US #5 and UK #70. Richie is already recording a follow-up LP and planning a first solo tour.

Sept He begins a 48-date world tour, including 3 weeks in the Far East, opening at Lake Tahoe, Nev. Supported by The Pointer Sisters°, his backing band includes Prince° percussionist Sheila E. For *Endless Love*, Richie uses a life-like Diana Ross° laser projection.

Oct [29] The Mayor of Tuskegee proclaims it "Lionel Richie Day".

Nov [12] Uptempo dance cut *All Night Long (All Night)* hits US #1 during a 5-month chart stay (4 weeks at #1) and UK #2. It outsells *Endless Love* to become Motown's biggest single worldwide to date and is helped by Richie's first solo video produced by ex-Monkee° Mike Nesmith. LP *Can't Slow Down* is released, set to hit both US and UK #1, and beginning chart stays of nearly 3 years. It features co-written tracks with Cynthia Weil and David Foster, and includes session help from Toto's° Steve Lukather and Jeff Porcaro.

Nov [22] Los Angeles mayor Bradley pronounces it "Lionel Richie Day".

Dec Richie and his wife move house from Kenny Rogers'° estate to a Bel Air, LA mansion. During tour dates, Richie's plane crashlands in Phoenix, Ariz., but no one is hurt.

1984 Jan *Running With The Night*, spurred by Bob Giraldi-directed video, hits US #7 and UK #9.

Feb Richie hosts US TV American Music Awards and also wins two himself.

Mar Pepsi-Cola announces an $8.5 million sponsorship deal with Richie, for which he will record a series of song-associated TV commercials, and will fund two tours in 2 years.

Apr *Hello* hits UK #1 (his first UK chart-topper).

May [12] With a second major tour underway (with opening act Tina Turner°), *Hello* hits US #1. (Originally slated for inclusion on the debut LP, the typical Richie ballad is supported by emotive video using the dramatic effect of a blind girl, directed by Giraldi. Richie plays the part of Mr. Reynolds, a teacher.)

Aug [4] LP extract *Stuck On You* hits US #3 and UK #12.

Aug [12] Richie is asked by Los Angeles Olympic Games producer David Wolper to perform the final song at the closing ceremony. In a larger than life extravaganza, Richie performs *All Night Long*, featuring an occasion-written extra verse. Helped by 200 dancers, Richie is seen by an estimated TV audience of 2.6 billion.

Nov From LP *Can't Slow Down*, *Penny Lover*, co-written with his wife Brenda, hits US #8 and UK #18.

Dec Diana Ross° hits US #10 with Richie-written and produced *Missing You*, a tribute to the late Marvin Gaye°.

1985 Jan Encouraged by Kragen, Richie is asked by Quincy Jones to co-write a song with Michael Jackson° for USA For Africa° supergroup effort to raise money for famine relief. Prepared over a 3-day period, they take only 2½ hours to write *We Are The World* – a worldwide #1 which also features Richie's vocal contributions.

Mar At the Annual Grammy Awards, Richie receives Album of the Year for *Can't Slow Down*, now selling over 10 million copies worldwide.

Dec [21] Hitting UK #8, *Say You Say Me* hits US #1 for Christmas period. Although not written specifically for the movie, it features as the theme to Gregory Hines/Mikhael Baryshnikov film *White Nights*. Motown does not allow the song to appear on the Atlantic movie soundtrack LP. The US chart-topper sets a new record as Richie becomes the only songwriter in history to achieve nine #1s in 9 consecutive years.

1986 Jan Richie returns to the studio to cut his long-awaited third LP.

Mar [24] *Say You Say Me* wins an Oscar for Best Original Song at the Academy Awards ceremony.

May Richie is named ASCAP's Writer of the Year.

LIONEL RICHIE *cont.*

Aug LP *Dancing On The Ceiling* is released, with its title cut already heading to hit US #2 and UK #7. Repeating his proven formula, Richie adds the talents of Eric Clapton°, Alabama and others. *Dancing On The Ceiling* video, featuring Richie dancing round all four sides of a room, is directed by Stanley Donen.

Nov *Love Will Conquer All* hits US #9, but UK #45.

Dec Ballad *Ballerina Girl* hits US #7 and UK #17.

1987 Jan Unusual for the 80s, B-side of *Ballerina Girl*, country-flavored *Deep River Woman* reaches US #71 as it is flipped by radio. The song features Alabama on backing vocals.

Jan [26] Richie wins Favorite Male Vocalist (Pop), Favorite Male Vocalist (R&B) and Favorite Pop Video Single categories at the 14th annual American Music Awards.

Feb Richie concludes a 3-month US tour, seen by more than 1 million people.

Apr From the last LP, *Se La* reaches US #20 and UK #43. Richie's world tour hits UK with standing-room-only dates in major cities.

1988 June Richie's wife Brenda is arrested for "investigation of corporal injury to a spouse, resisting arrest, trespassing, vandalism, battery and disturbing the peace". Ms. Richie is apparently upset when she discovers her husband with model-actress Diane Alexander in the latter's apartment.

JONATHAN RICHMAN AND THE MODERN LOVERS

1969 Richman, (b. May 16, 1951, Boston, Mass., US), a writer for Boston-based music papers *Vibrations* and *Fusion*, puts together his first group, usually called The Modern Lovers, influenced by mid-60s US garage rock and the hard, monotone style of Lou Reed° with The Velvet Underground°.

1971 Mar The first stable version of The Modern Lovers is formed in Boston (where the group will be based, although playing frequently in New York, where its name and music start to become noticed), with Richman on vocals and guitar, Ernie Brooks on bass, Jerry Harrison (later to join Talking Heads°) on keyboards, John Felice (later to join The Real Kids) on rhythm guitar and David Robinson (later of The Cars°) on drums.

1972 Apr The group is flown to LA at the joint expense of A&M and Warner Bros. to record demos with Kim Fowley producing (to be released years later on Bomp Records), before signing a recording deal with Warner.

1973 An LP is recorded for Warner Bros., with John Cale° producing. Richman feels that the sessions are unsatisfactory, and has doubts about some of the material. There is some dissension within the group, and the label, sharing the uncertainty, decides not to release the LP. (The tapes will later be bought for issue by Beserkley Records.)

Nov Warner Bros. drops the group. Robinson leaves and is replaced by Bob Walker on drums for only a few final gigs.

1974 Jan The Modern Lovers disband and Richman returns to Boston, gigging with local musicians.

1975 June Richman signs to new independent label Beserkley Records, based in Berkeley, Cal., debuting with self-penned two-part *Roadrunner*. (It is also released by United Artists in UK.)

July Beserkley buys from Warner the tapes of the John Cale°-produced recordings, which are released as LP *The Modern Lovers*. Richman contributes tracks to compilation LP *Beserkley Chartbusters*.

1976 LP *Jonathan Richman And The Modern Lovers*, the title easily confused with the previous Beserkley LP, consists of new recordings produced by Beserkley's directors Greg Kolotkin and Matthew "King" Kaufman. For the LP, Richman puts together a new line-up of The Modern Lovers, consisting of himself, Leroy Radcliff on guitar, Greg "Curly" Kerane on bass and David Robinson back on drums.

1977 June The Beserkley label is launched in UK, and reissues Richman's *Roadrunner* as its first single. With eager UK music press reviews, it climbs to UK #11, the group's first singles chart entry (a feat it will never achieve in US).

Sept LP *Rock'n'Roll With The Modern Lovers* is the group's only UK chart LP, reaching #50.

Oct The group tours UK for the first time, with a new line-up including D. Sharpe on drums and Asa Breuner on bass.

Dec *Egyptian Reggae*, an offbeat but highly commercial guitar instrumental from LP *Rock'n'Roll With The Modern Lovers*, hits UK #5.

1978 Feb *The Morning Of Our Lives*, a live-recorded single credited to just The Modern Lovers, reaches UK #29. (It is Richman's final chart entry. Subsequent singles released during the year by Beserkley, *New England*, *Abdul And Cleopatra* and *Buzz Buzz Buzz*, all sell poorly.) Richman disbands The Modern Lovers, ostensibly in order to go solo. (Although he continues to record on his own for a while, he will effectively retire for 2 years from live work.)

1979 Jan LP *The Modern Lovers Live* is an onstage set recorded on the group's late 1977 UK tour.

Feb Following the break-up of the group, an LP, to have been titled *Modern Love Songs* before the split, is released as Richman solo LP *Back In Your Life*. *Lydia*, Richman's final Beserkley single, fails to sell.

1980 Jan LP *The Jonathan Richman Songbook* is Richman's last LP for Beserkley.

Mar Following a 2-year period of self-imposed seclusion in New England, Richman tours US with a new-look Modern Lovers, including two female back-up singers.

1981 Oct LP *The Original Modern Lovers*, of archive material recorded in 1972 with Kim Fowley producing, is released on Bomp label.

1982 Solo Richman LP *Jonathan Sings!* is released on US Sire.

1985 June The Modern Lovers re-form to record LP *Rockin' And Romance*, released on US Sire and in UK by Rough Trade. (Two singles, *That Summer Feeling* and *I'm Just Beginning To Live*, are taken from it in UK but fail to chart.)

1986 Feb LP *It's Time For . . .* appears on Rough Trade.

1988 Jan The Modern Lovers play live dates in UK with a new trio line-up consisting of Richman on vocals and guitar, Brendan Totten on guitar and Johnny Avila on drums.

Mar LP *Modern Lovers '88*, by the new line-up, is released by Rounder label in US and by Demon in UK.

THE RIGHTEOUS BROTHERS

Bill Medley (vocals)
Bobby Hatfield (vocals)

1962 Medley (b. Sept.19, 1940, Santa Ana, Cal., US), having been a member of The Paramours and recorded *There She Goes* on Moonglow, meets Hatfield (b. Aug.10, 1940, Beaver Dam, Wis., US), who had been with The Variations and released a solo, *Hot Tamales*, also on Moonglow, and they form a duo. They debut at a high school prom in Anaheim, Cal. (They are dubbed The Righteous Brothers by black marines who see them perform at The Black Derby in Santa Ana – the name sticks.)

1963 June Moonglow releases *Little Latin Lupe Lu*, a Medley-penned R&B/dance number, which reaches US #49, after being used as a commercial by LA radio station KRLA. Two further Moonglow singles, *Koko Joe* and *My Babe* are released, the latter reaching US #75.

1964 Phil Spector expresses an interest in producing them, after seeing them perform on a package bill at San Francisco's Cow Palace, but they are still contracted to Moonglow. Spector makes a deal whereby they appear on his own Philles label in US and London in UK while other territories receive their masters through Moonglow. They become Philles' first white act. Spector commissions husband and wife team Barry Mann and Cynthia Weil to write a song for the brothers.

Aug [19] The Righteous Brothers support The Beatles° as they begin their US tour at the Cow Palace, San Francisco..

Sept [16] They are featured with real-life brothers, Don and Phil Everly°, and Sam Cooke° on the premiere of US ABC-TV show "Shindig!".

Dec Their first Philles single, *You've Lost That Lovin' Feelin'*, will top both US and UK charts. (Earning the description "classic" over a period of time, the pop record will later be a hit in US or UK for Dionne Warwick°, Daryl Hall and John Oates° and actor Telly Savalas. Many critics feel it is the definitive Spector "Wall of Sound" disk.)

1965 Jan *You've Lost That Lovin' Feelin'* is featured on UK BBC-TV's *Juke Box Jury*. The four panelists dismiss it, one questioning whether it has been played at the right speed, and vote it a "miss". A UK cover by Cilla Black° charts the following week, but producer Andrew Loog-Oldham places a self-paid ad in the UK music press extolling the virtues of the original over the cover. It works. The Righteous Brothers leap-frog Black's version and hit UK #1. LP

You've Lost That Lovin' Feelin' hits US #4. Moonglow releases their early material on LP *Right Now!*, which makes US #11, and *Bring Your Love To Me*, which reaches US #83. (Moonglow follows with LPs *Some Blue-Eyed Soul* (US #14) and *This Is New!* (US #39).)

May The duo's legitimate follow up, *Just Once In My Life*, penned by husband and wife team Gerry Goffin and Carole King°, hits US #9. (Two further Moonglow singles chart – *You Can Have Her* (US #67) and *Justine* from the film *A Swingin' Summer* (US #85).)

June LP *Just Once In My Life* hits US #9.

Aug Another Goffin/King° song, *Hung On You*, is the follow-up and makes US #47, but DJs prefer its B-side, the 1950s smash *Unchained Melody*, which hits US #4 and UK #14.

1966 Jan Spector chooses another oldie for the follow-up. *Ebb Tide* hits US #5, but makes only UK #48. LP *Back To Back* reaches US #16. (Moonglow has its final success with the duo, as *Georgia On My Mind* peaks at US #62.) MGM Records offers $1 million for The Righteous Brothers' contract. Spector, now interested in Ike & Tina Turner°, sells.

Apr MGM debut, on subsidiary Verve, is *(You're My) Soul And Inspiration*, which Mann and Weil had intended as a follow-up to *You've Lost That Lovin' Feelin'*. It hits US #1 and makes UK #15. Medley's production, to some, differs little from Spector's work. LP *Soul And Inspiration* hits US #7.

June Moonglow releases LP *The Best Of The Righteous Brothers*, compiled from four LPs recorded from 1962-63. It makes US #130.

July *He* makes US #18. B-side *He Will Break Your Heart* reaches US #91.

Sept *Go Ahead And Cry* peaks at US #30. LP *Go Ahead And Cry* climbs to US #32.

Nov *White Cliffs Of Dover*, a re-issue of a Philles LP track, makes UK #21. *On This Side Of Goodbye* reaches US #47. *Soul And Inspiration* is certified gold.

Dec *Island In The Sun* climbs to UK #36.

1967 Apr LP *Sayin' Somethin'* stalls at US #155.

May *Melancholy Music Man* reaches US #43.

June *Stranded In The Middle Of No Place*, their last single for Verve, makes only US #72.

Oct LP *Greatest Hits* reaches US #21, while LP *Souled Out* spends 2 weeks at US #198.

Nov Medley leaves to pursue a solo career (on MGM/Verve until 1969 but has no notable success). He is replaced by Jimmy Walker, ex-Knickerbockers. For legal reasons, the new duo is not allowed to use the name The Righteous Brothers on record for 1 year.

1968 Verve issues two LPs by The Righteous Brothers featuring unreleased titles and singles. Hatfield records solo singles for Verve while he waits out the legal delay. Medley releases debut LP *100+* on MGM, which makes US #188, having already had three minor solo hits with *I Can't Make It Alone* (US #95), *Brown Eyed Woman* (US #43) and *Peace Brother Peace* (US #48).

Dec Live LP *One For The Road* reaches US #187.

1969 Jan *You've Lost That Lovin' Feelin'* is re-issued in UK and hits #10. Medley releases another two LPs. Hatfield and Walker, now recording as The Righteous Brothers, release LP *Re-Birth*, which fails to chart.

Mar Hatfield's solo *Nothing Is Too Good For You* makes US #84.

Apr LP *Greatest Hits, Vol.2* reaches US #126. Medley's solo LP *Soft And Soulful* peaks at US #152.

1970 The Righteous Brothers split.

1971 Medley releases the Herb Alpert°-produced, Michel Colombier-arranged LP *A Song For You* for A&M, which despite impressive title track, *The Long And Winding Road* and a new version of *You've Lost That Lovin' Feelin'* fails to sell.

1974 July With the production team of Lambert and Potter, Medley and Hatfield re-form to hit US #3 with Alan O'Day-penned *Rock'n'Roll Heaven* on Capitol's Haven subsidiary. The song is a tribute to dead rock'n'roll stars.

Aug LP *Give It To The People* makes US #27.

Sept *Give It To The People* makes US #20.

Dec *Dream On* peaks at US #32.

1977 Nov *You've Lost That Lovin' Feelin'*, reissued again, makes UK #42.

1981 Medley resumes his solo recording career after a 5-year absence (following the murder of his wife Karen in 1976) and records LP *Sweet Thunder* in Berry Hill, Tenn., with producers Michael Lloyd, Brent Maher and Randy Goodrum. He signs with top management team Kragen & Company. *Don't Know Much* makes US #88.

1982 Medley releases LP *Right Here And Now*, produced by Richard Perry on his Planet label. The title track makes US #58. He opens Medleys club in LA. He and Hatfield re-form again for a US TV special celebrating the 30th anniversary of "American Bandstand". They sing an updated version of *Rock'n'Roll Heaven*.

1986 *You've Lost That Lovin' Feelin'* reaches a new audience through its exposure in Tom Cruise film *Top Gun*. It is B-side of the main hit, Berlin's *Top Gun*.

1987 Sept Medley duets with Jennifer Warnes° on *(I've Had) The Time Of My Life*. Taken from the *Dirty Dancing* film soundtrack, it tops the US chart as the film's popularity spreads. The LP is the most successful soundtrack LP since *Saturday Night Fever*, selling more than 14 million copies worldwide.

1988 Aug Medley records *He Ain't Heavy He's My Brother* for the soundtrack to Sylvester Stallone's *Rambo III*. (He has already recorded a duet with Gladys Knight° for a previous Stallone movie *Cobra*.) It reaches UK #25, but The Hollies'° reissue tops the UK chart.

JOHNNY RIVERS

1960 Rivers (b. John Ramistella, Nov.7, 1942, New York, N.Y., US), having grown up in Baton Rouge, La., where he formed his first rock'n'roll groups in high school, then commuted in his later teens between New York and Nashville trying to gain an entry into the music business, has met DJ Alan Freed, who has been impressed by his songs and helped him get a one-off deal with Gone Records, also suggesting the new name Rivers from the river bayou country of his upbringing. After playing in Las Vegas and Lake Tahoe with Louie Prima's band, he moves to LA, where he has had *I'll Make Believe* recorded by Ricky Nelson° in 1958.

1961 A revival of *Blue Skies* for Chancellor label gains some airplay, but fails to chart.

1963 He gets a live residency at LA's Gazzari's club, which first gains him notice as a performer.

1964 Rivers moves to newly-opened Whiskey A Go-Go club, where his live rock oldie sets intersperse record sessions, all the music being aimed primarily at the dancefloor. He becomes a success with regular patrons and the buzz reaches Imperial Records, which signs him to a recording contract and tapes his live stage act.

June Live debut LP *Johnny Rivers At The Whiskey A Go-Go* reaches US #12.

July Extracted from the LP, a revival of Chuck Berry's° *Memphis* (also a major hit in instrumental form for Lonnie Mack a year previously) hits US #2, behind The Four Seasons'° *Rag Doll*.

Sept Another Berry° revival recorded live, *Maybelline*, reaches US #12.

Oct LP *Here We A Go Go Again!*, another live set of mainly oldies from the club act, makes US #38.

Dec Rivers' revival of Harold Dorman's R&B oldie *Mountain Of Love* hits US #9.

1965 Feb LP *Johnny Rivers In Action!* peaks at US #42.

Mar *Midnight Special*, a rocked-up version of Paul Evans' 1960 US hit, reaches US #20 (and in 1973 will be used as the theme to US NBC TV's music series of the same title), while B-side revival of Sam Cooke's° *Cupid* peaks at US #76.

June LP *Meanwhile Back At The Whiskey A Go Go* reaches US #21.

July *Seventh Son* is his third US top 10 hit, at US #7.

Sept LP *Johnny Rivers Rocks The Folk* makes US #91.

Nov Taken from the folk/rock LP, a revival of The Kingston Trio's *Where Have All The Flowers Gone?* makes US #26.

1966 Jan *Under Your Spell Again* reaches US #35.

Apr Rivers records *Secret Agent Man*, the theme from Patrick McGoohan TV spy series "Secret Agent" (a re-titling of UK series "Danger Man"), which hits US #3. The LP *. . . And I Know You Wanna Dance* peaks at US #52.

July A revival of *(I Washed My Hands In) Muddy Water* (cut by Charlie Rich as B-side to his 1965 hit *Mohair Sam*) reaches US #19.

Sept LP *Johnny Rivers' Golden Hits*, a compilation of his hit singles to date, reaches US #29.

Nov *Poor Side Of Town*, an original ballad written by Rivers and producer Lou Adler, is his all-time biggest-selling single, topping the US chart for a week, and selling over a million.

Dec LP *Changes*, featuring *Poor Side Of Town* and other material with a similar, more contemporary sound, makes US #33. Rivers sets up his own music publishing company Rivers Music (signing Jim

JOHNNY RIVERS *cont.*

Webb, among others), and while in renegotiation of his recording contract with Imperial, launches his own Liberty/Imperial-distributed label, Soul City Records (which will be a production base for Rivers' scouting for new talent, including The 5th Dimension° in 1967). He puts together a regular studio band of acclaimed sessioneers Hal Blaine (drums), Joe Osborn (bass – an old friend from Baton Rouge) and Larry Knechtel (keyboards).

1967 Mar Passing over Webb's song *By The Time I Get To Phoenix* as a single (which he suggests instead for Glen Campbell°), Rivers cuts a lush revival of The Four Tops'° *Baby I Need Your Lovin'*, and hits US #3.

June LP *Rewind* reaches US #14.

June [16] Rivers is a co-organizer, with Lou Adler and The Mamas and The Papas°, of the Monterey Pop Festival.

July A second Motown revival, The Miracles' *The Tracks Of My Tears*, hits US #10.

1968 Jan *Summer Rain*, with hints of flower power in arrangement and lyric (which refers to The Beatles'° *Sergeant Pepper's Lonely Hearts Club Band*), reaches US #14.

Feb [29] He wins a Grammy award as co-producer of The 5th Dimension's° *Up, Up And Away*, which is named Record of the Year for 1967.

May *Look To Your Soul* makes US #49.

June LP *Realization* hits US #5.

Dec *Right Relations*, with a socially-conscious lyric, peaks at US #61.

1969 Rivers retires almost completely from live concert appearances to spend more time at his retreat in Carmel, Cal.

Mar A cover of Joe South's° *These Are Not My People* makes US #55.

June LP *A Touch Of Gold* peaks at US #26.

Aug *Muddy River* reaches US #41.

Nov *One Woman*, an excursion into soul music, stalls at US #89. Rivers sells Soul City Records for $2½ million. (Now a rare performer, he will spend much time traveling in India and Japan, investigating disciplines such as yoga, transcendental meditation and vegetarianism.)

1970 June A cover of Van Morrison's° *Into The Mystic* makes US #51.

Aug LP *Slim Slo Slider* reaches US #100.

Sept *Fire And Rain*, a cover of James Taylor's° ballad, stalls at US #94.

1971 May A revival of Frankie Ford's *Sea Cruise*, back in his original straightforward rock style, makes US #84. This is Rivers' first release on United Artists, which has absorbed Imperial and Liberty Records.

Sept *Think His Name*, an inspirational number backed by The Guru Ram Das Ashram Singers, peaks at US #65, while LP *Home Grown* makes US #148.

Dec He sells his Rivers Music publishing house, with a stock of valuable copyrights, for over $1 million.

1972 Nov LP *L.A. Reggae*, on which he is backed by members of The Crickets and other guests, and which showcases mainly rock and R&B covers, peaks at US #78.

1973 Jan From the LP, a revival of Huey "Piano" Smith's *Rockin' Pneumonia And The Boogie Woogie Flu* hits US #6, and sells over a million to earn a gold disk.

May In similar style, a revival of Carl Perkins'° *Blue Suede Shoes* makes US #38 (though the LP of the same title, a mixture of new and old songs, fails to chart).

1975 Aug Rivers leaves UA (disgreements with the label over contracts disincline him from re-signing), to record on a one-off (and unsuccessful) basis for Atlantic, and then to sign to Epic Records for *Help Me Rhonda* (a revival of The Beach Boys'° 1965 US #1, on which Brian Wilson assists with back-up vocals). It reaches US #22 and LP *New Lovers And Old Friends* makes US #147.

1977 Feb *Ashes And Sand*, issued on his own revived Soul City label (to which he has re-acquired the title rights), stalls at US #96.

Feb [4] Rivers takes part in the all-star celebrity band (with Chuck Berry°, Gregg Allman and others) on the 25th anniversary special of Dick Clark's "American Bandstand" on US ABC TV.

Oct A cover of Jack Tempchin & The Funky Kings' *Swayin' To The Music (Slow Dancin')*, recorded for Big Tree label, hits US #10, and is his final million-selling single.

1978 Jan LP *Outside Help* on Big Tree reaches US #142.

Feb Rivers' final US chart entry is a revival of a Major Lance hit, *Curious Mind (Um, Um, Um, Um, Um, Um)*, which makes US #41. (Following this, he will take little active part in music making (except for a religious LP in the mid 1980s), content in retirement against a background of having sold some 30 million records over 15 years – though he leaves a whole generation of successful songwriters and acts for whom he was original sponsor and champion.)

SMOKEY ROBINSON

1954 Robinson (b. William Robinson, Feb.19, 1940, Detroit, Mich., US) puts together a vocal group from friends at Northern Night School: Ronnie White (b. Apr. 5, 1939, Detroit), Bobby Rogers (b. Feb.19, 1940, Detroit) and Pete Moore (b. Nov.19, 1939, Detroit), plus guitarist Marv Tarplin. (Rogers' sister Claudette (b. 1942) joins the group during the next 2 years, replacing another brother, Emerson, who goes into the US Army, and will marry Robinson in 1963.)

1957 Having become established on the Detroit club scene, initially as The Matadors, and then as The Miracles, they audition for Jackie Wilson's° manager (who turns them down). They are heard by Berry Gordy Jr., who has just written *Reet Petite* for Wilson°, but is still working at Ford Motors while trying to break into the music business full-time. He sees potential in the young group and helps it get a deal with End Records.

1958 End releases The Miracles' first single, *Got A Job*, a Robinson/Gordy/Tyrone Carlo-penned "answer" to The Silhouettes' hit *Get A Job*. It creeps on to the R&B chart, but does not cross over.

1959 Oct Gordy, now closely involved with the group, leases Robinson-penned ballad *Bad Girl* to Chess Records. It is The Miracles' US pop chart debut, at #93.

1960 Using royalties from work with Jackie Wilson° and Marv Johnson, and a loan of $800, Gordy forms his own company, Motown Records, and sets up the Tamla label to feature The Miracles. First Tamla release is The Miracles' dance tune *Way Over There*, which does not chart.

1961 Feb *Shop Around*, an early model of the ultra-commercial dance sound (and later much-covered), hits US #2, and is the group's and Motown's first million-seller.

Apr Follow-up *Ain't It Baby* peaks at US #49.

Aug *Mighty Good Lovin'* climbs to US #51.

Nov *Everybody Gotta Pay Some Dues* makes US #52 (and like all immediate post-*Shop Around* releases, is a bigger hit on local R&B charts.) Robinson is by now becoming an increasingly important part of the growing Motown operation, both arranging and writing for young artists on the label, and Gordy makes him company vice-president.

1962 Feb *What's So Good About Goodbye* makes US #35.

June *I'll Try Something New* reaches US #39.

Sept A reissue of *Way Over There* this time peaks at US #94.

1963 Feb *You've Really Got A Hold On Me* is the group's second US top 10 hit, at #8. (It will be covered by The Beatles° on their second LP and a staple of UK beat groups' repertoires.)

May *A Love She Can Count On* peaks at US #31.

June LP *The Fabulous Miracles* makes US #118.

Sept Robinson-penned dance number *Mickey's Monkey* is The Miracles' second US top 10 of the year, hitting #8. (Reportedly, it is also the first disk Michael Jackson° buys.)

Oct Live LP *The Miracles On Stage* reaches US #139.

1964 Jan *I Gotta Dance To Keep From Crying* peaks at #35, while LP *Doin' Mickey's Monkey* makes US #113. Claudette Robinson retires from performance with the group, to look after home and family (though will later guest with it on occasion).

Apr Now adept at writing songs for other Motown acts, Robinson pens The Temptations'° first major hit, *The Way You Do The Things You Do*, which reaches US #11. At the same time, The Miracles' *(You Can't Let The Boy Overpower) The Man In You* makes US #59.

May Robinson has his first #1 as a writer, when Mary Wells' version of his and Ronnie White's *My Guy* tops the US chart.

Aug *I Like It Like That* reaches US #27.

Oct *That's What Love Is Made Of* peaks at US #35.

1965 Jan *Come On Do The Jerk* makes US #50.

Mar Another Temptations' release of Robinson/White song, *My Girl*, tops the US chart and is a million-seller. (On various songs, both for The Miracles and other acts, Robinson collaborates with one or another of the group: Moore, White or Tarplin. Like the label's other chief writers, he also oversees production and arrangement, using the Hitsville USA house band.)

Mar [20] The Miracles begins a UK package tour to launch Motown's own label identity in UK, with labelmates Martha & The Vandellas°, The Supremes°, The Temptations° and Stevie Wonder°.

May Ballad *Ooh Baby Baby* reaches US #16.

June Double compilation LP *Greatest Hits From The Beginning* is the group's first big LP seller, reaching US #21.

Sept Another Robinson ballad, *The Tracks Of My Tears*, makes US #16 (and will later be much covered).

Nov *My Girl Has Gone* peaks at US #14.

1966 Feb A return to the dance idiom, *Going To A Go-Go* makes US #11 and is the group's UK chart debut, reaching #44. The LP of the same title hits US #8. Robinson begins to produce Marvin Gaye°, renewing Gaye's US top 10 status with *Ain't That Peculiar.*

July Another dance number, *Whole Lot Of Shakin' In My Heart (Since I Met You)* reaches US #46.

Dec *(Come Round Here) I'm The One You Need* makes US #17 and UK #45.

1967 Jan LP *Away We A Go-Go* peaks at US #41.

Apr Robinson's status within the group is recognized by Motown when, with *The Love I Saw In You Was Just A Mirage* (which makes US #20), the billing becomes Smokey Robinson & The Miracles.

July *More Love* (later revived by Kim Carnes°) peaks at US #23.

Nov LP *Make It Happen* reaches US #28.

Dec *I Second That Emotion*, later also much covered, is the group's first US top 10 hit in 4 years, at #4.

1968 Jan *I Second That Emotion* is their first top 30 UK hit, making #27.

Apr *If You Can Want* makes US #11 and UK #50, while compilation LP *Greatest Hits, Vol.2* hits US #7. (Robinson's golden songwriting period of the 60s is now drawing to a close, as his Motown corporate duties draw him away from writing. The group's later LPs will contain many songs from outside sources.)

July *Yester Love* makes US #31.

Sept *Special Occasion* peaks at US #26.

Nov LP *Special Occasion* makes US #42.

1969 Mar *Baby, Baby Don't Cry* hits US #8, while LP *Live!* makes US #71.

June *The Tracks Of My Tears*, not a hit first time around in UK, is reissued and becomes the group's biggest UK success to date, hitting #9.

July *Doggone Right* reaches US #33 while the group's rush-released version of Dion° hit *Abraham, Martin And John*, originally an LP track, makes US #33 (in competition with a simultaneous US #35 version by black comedienne Moms Mabley).

Sept LP *Time Out For Smokey Robinson And The Miracles* reaches US #25.

Oct *Here I Go Again*, B-side of *Doggone Right*, makes US #37.

1970 Jan *Point It Out* also reaches US #37, while LP *Four In Blue* peaks at US #78.

June *Who's Gonna Take The Blame* peaks at US #46, while LP *What Love Has Joined Together* makes US #97.

Sept *The Tears Of A Clown*, originally recorded in 1967 and released on LP *Make It Happen*, is released in UK and tops the chart for a week, selling almost 900,000 copies.

Nov LP *A Pocketful Of Miracles* reaches US #56.

Dec Motown releases *The Tears Of A Clown* in US on the strength of its UK success. It tops the US chart for 2 weeks (their first US #1) and sells well over a million, becoming the group's most successful single ever.

1971 Feb Another former UK non-hit, *(Come 'Round Here) I'm The One You Need*, is reissued as follow-up to *The Tears Of A Clown* and makes UK #13.

May New recording *I Don't Blame You At All* makes US #18 and UK #11.

July Dance song *Crazy About The La La La* reaches US #56.

Oct LP *One Dozen Roses* makes US #92.

1972 Jan *Satisfaction* peaks at US #49.

July [16] At the end of a 6-month farewell US tour, Robinson, who has wanted to leave the group to pursue his own projects since 1970, makes his last appearance with The Miracles in Washington, D.C., prior to launching his solo career via Motown. (William Griffin replaces him in the group.)

Aug *We've Come Too Far To End It Now* reaches US #46, while LP *Flying High Together* makes US #46.

1973 Jan *I Can't Stand To See You Cry*, the last single released by Robinson with The Miracles, makes US #45. Double compilation LP *1957-1972* reaches US #75.

Sept The Miracles' *Don't Let It End ('Til You Let It Begin)* peaks at US #56 (the first of only four hit singles the group will have without Robinson). Robinson's first solo LP *Smokey* peaks at US #70 (critics feel it lacks the assurance of his best work with The Miracles). Extracted *Sweet Harmony* makes US #48.

1974 Feb *Baby Come Close* is his first solo top 30 hit, reaching US #27, while *Just My Soul Responding* is released as a UK single and makes #35.

June LP *Pure Smokey*, an overtly romantic set, reaches US #99, while extracted *It's Her Turn To Live* makes US #82.

Oct The Miracles' *Do It Baby* reaches US #13.

Nov *Virgin Man* makes US #56.

1975 Jan The Miracles' *Don't Cha Love It* peaks at US #78, while Robinson's *I Am I Am* climbs to US #56.

May LP *A Quiet Storm* sees Robinson deepening his vocal register and experimenting musically.

June From LP *A Quiet Storm*, *Baby That's Backatcha* reaches US #26 and tops the R&B chart for a week.

Nov Also from the LP, *The Agony And The Ecstasy* reaches US #36.

1976 Feb The title song from *A Quiet Storm* makes US #61.

Mar *Love Machine* by The Miracles tops the US chart, selling over a million, and hits UK #3 (but is the group's final hit).

Apr LP *Smokey's Family Robinson* makes US #57.

July *Open* peaks at US #81.

Oct A reissue of *The Tears Of A Clown* reaches UK #34.

1977 Apr LP *Deep In My Soul* peaks at US #47, while extracted *There Will Come A Day (I'm Gonna Happen To You)* makes US #42.

Aug Robinson is executive producer of, and writes and produces the music for, movie *Big Time*.

1978 May LP *Love Breeze* makes US #75.

July *Daylight And Darkness* reaches US #75.

1979 Feb Double live LP *Smokin'* makes US #165, while Robinson teams with Diana Ross°, Marvin Gaye° and Stevie Wonder° on *Pops We Love You*, a tribute for Berry Gordy's father's 90th birthday. It reaches US #59 and UK #66.

Oct LP *Where There's Smoke* reaches US #17.

1980 Feb Taken from it, *Cruisin'* is Robinson's first top 10 hit as a soloist, at US #4.

May LP *Warm Thoughts* makes US #14 while, taken from it, *Let Me Be The Clock* reaches US #31.

1981 May *Being With You*, produced by George Tobin (to whom Robinson has originally submitted it for Kim Carnes° after she revived *More Love* successfully) hits US #2 and earns a gold disk for million-

SMOKEY ROBINSON *cont.*

plus sales. The LP of the same title hits US #10 and also earns a gold disk.

June *Being With You* tops the UK chart for 2 weeks, while the LP makes UK #17 – his only UK chart LP.

July *You Are Forever* makes US #59.

Dec [12] US TV program "American Bandstand" airs "Smokey Robinson 25th Anniversary Special".

1982 Mar LP *Yes It's You Lady* reaches US #33, as does extracted *Tell Me Tomorrow* (which also makes UK #51).

May *Old Fashioned Love* reaches US #60.

1983 Mar LP *Touch The Sky* climbs to US #50.

May [16] Robinson is reunited with The Miracles on the Motown 25th Anniversary US NBC-TV special.

Aug *Blame It On Love*, a duet with Barbara Mitchell of High Inergy, climbs to US #48.

Sept Compilation LP *Blame It On Love And All The Great Hits* makes US #124.

1984 Jan Robinson duets with fellow Motown hitmaker Rick James° on *Ebony Eyes*, which reaches US #43.

July LP *Essar* peaks at US #141.

1985 Jan [28] Robinson takes part in the recording of USA For Africa's° single *We Are The World*.

1986 Mar LP *Smoke Signals* peaks at US #104.

1987 Jan [21] Robinson is inducted into the Rock'n'Roll Hall of Fame.

Mar *Just To See Her* reaches UK #32, following Robinson's performance of it at TV-aired Montreux Rock Festival from Switzerland.

July *Just To See Her* hits US #8, Robinson's first top 10 single in 6 years, while LP *One Heartbeat* peaks at US #26.

Sept [28] Robinson and Gladys Knight° guest on US TV show "$10,000 Pyramid" for a week.

Oct The title song from *One Heartbeat* hits US #10.

Dec *What's Too Much* stalls at US #79.

1988 Mar [2] Robinson wins his first Grammy award, when *Just To See Her* is named Best Male R&B Vocal.

Mar New single *Love Don't Give No Reason* peaks at US R&B #35, while Robinson features in a duet with Dolly Parton° on *I Know You By Heart*.

TOMMY ROE

1958 Roe (b. May 9, 1943, Atlanta, Ga., US) forms rock group Tommy Roe & The Satins, while still at Brown High School, Atlanta. Heavily influenced by Buddy Holly° and The Crickets, they play school hops and fraternity parties at the University of Georgia.

1960 Offered a recording deal by local Judd Records (run by Judd Phillips, brother of Sun Records' Sam Phillips), the band records *Sheila*, written by Roe at age 14. It gains local sales but is not promoted nationally.

1961 Roe graduates from school and works for General Electric Company, still performing at evenings and weekends. Atlanta DJ Paul Drew (with whom The Satins have played many live gigs) recommends him to Felton Javis, a producer at ABC-Paramount Records (and later to produce Elvis Presley°), who likes his style and self-penned material, and signs him.

1962 June *Sheila* is re-recorded for ABC (originally as a B-side) in an arrangement similar to Holly's° *Peggy Sue*, in line with Roe's Holly-like vocal treatment. When it picks up major airplay in US, the label advances him $5,000 to quit his GEC job and tour to promote it.

Sept *Sheila* tops the US chart for 2 weeks and is Roe's first million-seller.

Oct *Sheila* hits UK #2 (behind The Tornados'° *Telstar*), having aroused interest in UK by entering the top 30 simultaneously with Buddy Holly's° posthumous *Reminiscing*.

Nov A revival of Robin Luke's *Susie Darlin'* reaches US #35, while LP *Sheila* makes US #110.

Dec *Susie Darlin'* makes UK #37.

1963 Mar [9] Roe begins a month-long UK tour at East Ham Granada, London, co-headlining with *Let's Dance* hitmaker Chris Montez. The Beatles° are the main support act.

Apr Rush-released in UK because of the tour, Merle Kilgore's slow ballad *The Folk Singer* hits UK #4.

May *The Folk Singer* makes US #84. (His next two singles, including a revival of Russ Hamilton's 1957 hit *Rainbow*, will fail to chart.)

Oct *Everybody*, a gospelly rocker written by Roe on his UK tour, is also released first in UK, where it hits #9.

Dec *Everybody* hits US #3, and is his second million-seller.

1964 Feb *Come On*, in similar style to *Everybody*, reaches US #36.

May *Carol* makes US #61.

Dec *Party Girl* also peaks at US #61. Roe is serving 2 years in the US Army, and thus unable to promote his records. (He remains under contract to ABC, and bides his time while the "British Invasion" of US pop music puts many contemporaries out of the charts.)

1966 July Out of the army, he writes and records *Sweet Pea* in a chunky pop style (presaging the "bubblegum" pop phase 2 years later). It hits US #8 and is Roe's third million-seller.

Nov *Hooray For Hazel*, in similar style, hits US #6.

Dec Compilation LP *Sweet Pea*, rounding up the year's two hits and earlier singles back to *Everybody*, makes US #94.

1967 Feb *It's Now Winter's Day* reaches US #23.

Apr *Sing Along With Me* charts for a week at US #91.

June *Little Miss Sunshine* also charts for only a week at US #99. LP *It's Now Winter's Day* peaks at US #159.

1968 With no recording in the year, Roe tours in Dick Clark's "Caravan of Stars".

1969 Mar Steve Barri becomes Roe's producer, with the intention of resurrecting his "Buddy Holly" sound, but instead the two concoct *Dizzy*, co-written by Roe with hometown friend Freddy Weller (a member of Paul Revere & The Raiders°) while they were on tour together in 1968. Driven by a sledgehammer Hal Blaine drum track and an off-beat sawing violin arrangement by Jimmy Haskell, the song is a very sophisticated bubblegum blend which tops the US chart for 4 weeks. It is Roe's biggest seller, topping 2 million copies in US, with similar sales worldwide.

May *Heather Honey* makes US #29 and LP *Dizzy* reaches US #25.

June *Dizzy* tops the UK chart for a week, deposing The Beatles'° *Get Back* and being replaced by The Beatles' *The Ballad Of John And Yoko*.

Aug *Heather Honey* makes UK #24 (his last UK hit).

Oct *Jack And Jill* peaks at US #53.

Dec *Jam Up Jelly Tight* hits US #8, and is Roe's fifth and last million-seller.

1970 Feb Compilation LP *12 In A Roe: A Collection Of Tommy Roe's Greatest Hits*, peaks at US #21.

Mar *Stir It Up And Serve It* reaches US #50.

July *Pearl* also peaks at US #50.

Oct *We Can Make Music* makes US #49, while LP of the same title climbs to US #134.

1971 Oct Following a summer US tour with long-time friends Joe South° and Billy Joe Royal, Roe has his last hit for ABC and his last US top 30 entry with a revival of Lloyd Price's° *Stagger Lee*, which makes US #25.

1972 Sept Dissatisfied with West Coast life, and no longer with ABC Records, Roe returns to Georgia, where he signs with Atlanta-based MGM South, and reaches US #92 with *Mean Little Woman, Rosalie*.

1973 May *Working Class Hero*, also on MGM South, makes US #97, and is Roe's final hit single.

1976/78 Returning to LA after 4 years in Atlanta, Roe records two LPs for Monument Records, *Energy* and *Full Bloom*, but neither is successful. (He will drift out of the public eye in the later 70s and the 1980s.)

KENNY ROGERS

1944 Rogers (b. Kenneth Donald Rogers, Aug.21, 1938, Houston, Tex., US) earns his first dollars as a 6-year-old, singing *You Are My Sunshine* for the residents of a nursing home near his home in Houston.

1955 While at Jefferson Davis High School, Rogers forms doo-wop combo The Scholars, who record *Poor Little Doggie* and *Spin The Wheel* for Jimmy Duncan's local Cue label and *Kangewah*, written by Hollywood gossip columnist Louella Parsons, for Imperial Records.

1958 Through his brother Lelan, a promoter for Decca Records, Rogers meets Ray Doggett (who has recently had success writing *On My Mind Again* for Gale Storm) and records Doggett's *That Crazy Feeling* at ACA Recording Studio in Houston. Originally released on local Lynn label, Carlton Records picks up the record and has Rogers (credited on it as Kenneth Rogers The First) make a major promotional tour, which includes an appearance on Dick Clark's TV show "American Bandstand".

May [15] Rogers, at age 19, marries for the first time.

1959 He cuts further Carlton singles concurrently with releases on Ken-Lee, a label set up with brother Lelan.

Sept [15] Rogers' wife Janice gives birth to a daughter, Carole Lynne.

Sept Rogers joins jazz-styled Bobby Doyle Trio (its front man is a blind pianist) as a stand-up bassist and singer.

1960 Jan [26] Janice files for divorce.

Oct Rogers marries Jean Laverne Massey.

1961 The Bobby Doyle Trio tours US extensively, frequently as support to The Kirby Stone Four.

1962 Mar The trio starts work in New York on a debut album for CBS/Columbia.

July LP *In A Most Unusual Way* is released.

1963 Oct [22] Rogers' third marriage is to Margo Gladys Anderson.

1964 May [24] Rogers becomes a father for a second time when son Kenneth Ray Rogers II is born.

1965 June [24] Rogers with fellow Bobby Doyle member, Don Russell and Anthony Navarro open The Act Three Club on Main Street in Houston, where the trio will play regularly.

June Rogers cuts solo single *Take Life In Stride* for Mercury.

Dec Rogers and Russell decide not to renew their license for The Act Three Club.

1966 Having spent a short period with four-part harmony group The Lively Ones (Rogers, Russell, Paula Chase and Paul Mussarra) and working at The Houstonaire supper club, Rogers joins The New Christy Minstrels, earning $750 a week. He records one LP with the group *New Kick! (The New Christy Minstrels Sing The Hits Of Today And Tomorrow)*.

1967 July [10] The contracts of Rogers and fellow Minstrels Mike Settle, Terry Williams and Thelma Camacho expire.

July [11] Rogers, Settle, Williams and Camacho start recording a debut LP as The First Edition, for Reprise Records, having auditioned for producer Jimmy Bowen during their time with The Minstrels.

July Ken Kragen, co-manager of The Smothers Brothers and co-producer of their US TV show "The Smothers Brothers' Comedy Hour", sees the group at Ledbetter's in LA and signs them to a management deal.

Dec LP *The First Edition* is released.

1968 Jan The First Edition makes its TV debut on "The Smothers Brothers' Comedy Hour".

Mar *Just Dropped In (To See What Condition My Condition Was In)*, with a heavy rock arrangement and mock-"psychedelic" lyric, written by Mickey Newbury (and rejected by Jerry Lee Lewis°), hits US #5. Debut LP *The First Edition* reaches US #118.

1969 Mary Arnold replaces Camacho in The First Edition. (Karen Carpenter also auditioned for the slot.)

Mar *But You Know I Love You*, written by Settle in a more country music direction, reaches US #19.

Apr LP *The First Edition '69* makes US #164.

Aug *Ruby, Don't Take Your Love To Town*, concerning a Korean War veteran, written several years earlier by country singer Mel Tillis, hits US #6. Highlighting Rogers' solo vocal, it credits the group for the first time as Kenny Rogers & The First Edition.

Nov *Ruben James*, in similar style to *Ruby*, makes US #26.

Dec *Ruby, Don't Take Your Love To Town* hits UK #2 for 5 weeks, behind Rolf Harris' *Two Little Boys*. Meanwhile, the LP of the same title (and first LP credited to the extended group name) reaches US #48.

1970 Settle leaves the band, to be replaced by Kin Vassy.

Feb *Something's Burning*, penned by Mac Davis, reaches US #11 and hits UK #8.

June LP *Something's Burning* makes US #26.

Aug *Tell It All Brother* reaches US #17.

Nov *Heed The Call* makes US #33.

Dec Featuring both the previous hit singles, LP *Tell It All Brother* peaks at US #61.

1971 Apr *Someone Who Cares*, from James Caan/Katharine Ross film *Fools*, peaks at US #51. The group's compilation LP *Greatest Hits* makes US #57.

July *Take My Hand*, a gospel-flavored Rogers-penned song, stalls at US #91.

Sept Canadian-produced syndicated TV program "Rollin' on the River", starring The First Edition, airs on US TV. Filmed in a riverboat setting, it features music guests, including Kris Kristofferson°, Mac Davis and B.J. Thomas.

Oct LP *Transition* reaches US #155.

1972 Apr *School Teacher*, with Vassy on lead vocal, stalls at US #91. It is taken from double LP *The Ballad Of Calico*, a concept album concerning the 1889 mining town of Calico, Cal., which reaches US #118.

1973 May [27] Compilation LP *Greatest Hits* is certified gold after more than 2 years on sale.

1974 The First Edition splits, leaving Rogers $65,000 in debt.

1975 He signs to United Artists Records as a solo artist.

Mar His first UA single, *Love Lifted Me*, stalls at US #97.

1977 June *Lucille* hits US #5, selling a million, and tops the UK chart.

July Debut solo LP *Kenny Rogers* makes US #30 and UK #14

Aug *Daytime Friends* makes US #28.

Oct *Daytime Friends* reaches UK #39, while the LP of the same title peaks at US #39. Rogers gets married, for the fourth time, to Marianne Gordon, an actress on US TV show "Hee Haw". He also has his first book *Making it with Music*, written with Len Epand, published.

Nov Rogers begins a UK concert tour with UA label-mate Crystal Gayle.

1978 Jan *Sweet Music Man* peaks at US #44. *Lucille* is named Country Single of 1977 at the American Music Awards in Santa Monica, Cal.

Feb [23] Rogers wins his first Grammy award, as *Lucille* is named Best Male Country Vocal Performance of 1977.

Apr LP *Ten Years Of Gold*, one side featuring re-recorded solo versions of The First Edition hits, reaches US #33. (In 103 weeks on US chart, it will sell over a million copies, earning Rogers' first platinum disk.)

July *Love Or Something Like It* reaches US #32.

Sept LP *Love Or Something Like It* makes US #53, and earns a gold disk.

1979 Mar *The Gambler* reaches US #16, while the LP of the same title peaks at US #12, and becomes Rogers' second platinum LP.

June LP *Classics*, an album of duets between Rogers and country singer Dottie West, makes US #86.

July *She Believes In Me*, taken from LP *The Gambler*, hits US #5 and peaks at UK #42.

KENNY ROGERS *cont.*

Aug [16] Rogers performs at the Ohio State Fair to 80,000 fans.

Sept [14] "Kenny Rogers Day" is proclaimed in Los Angeles, as Rogers receives a star on the Hollywood Walk of Fame.

Nov *You Decorated My Life* hits US #7, while parent LP *Kenny* hits US #3 and is another million-seller. Rogers' footprints are immortalized in cement at The Country Palace in Toledo, Oh.

Nov [12] Rogers begins filming *The Gambler*, a TV movie based on the song of the same title, which marks his acting debut.

Dec US CBS-TV airs the documentary "Kenny Rogers and the American Cowboy". UK compilation LP *The Kenny Rogers Singles Album* makes UK #12.

1980 Jan LP *Every Time Two Fools Collide*, another duetted set with West, reaches US #186.

Feb *Coward Of The County*, taken from LP *Kenny*, hits US #3, earning a gold disk, and tops the UK chart for 2 weeks.

Feb [27] *The Gambler* wins Rogers a Grammy award as Best Male Country Vocal of 1979.

Apr TV movie *The Gambler* airs on CBS-TV.

May *Don't Fall In Love With A Dreamer*, a duet with Kim Carnes°, hits US #4. It is taken from LP *Gideon*, which reaches US #12, earning another platinum disk. Meanwhile, LP *Kenny* hits UK #7.

Aug *Love The World Away* reaches US #14.

Nov *Lady*, penned by Lionel Richie°, tops the US chart for 6 weeks, selling over a million, and hitting #1 on US R&B, C&W and Adult Contemporary charts. It will also reach UK #12, and is Rogers' first release on Liberty label (as United Artists Records is renamed).

Dec Rogers shares the Top Male Vocalist of 1980 award with Michael Jackson° in *Record World* magazine. His compilation LP *Kenny Rogers' Greatest Hits*, of hit singles up to *Lady*, tops the US chart for 2 weeks, and is his fifth platinum LP, spending 181 weeks on US chart.

1981 Feb UK-compiled LP *Lady* makes UK #40.

June *What Are We Doin' In Love*, a duet with West, reaches US #14.

Aug *I Don't Need You* hits US #3. It is taken from LP *Share Your Love*, produced by Richie°, which hits US #3 and earns another platinum disk. Rogers also stars in TV movie *Coward of the County*, in which he plays a Southern preacher.

Aug [17] Rogers headlines a benefit concert at the Nassau Coliseum, Long Island, N.Y., for singer Harry Chapin°, killed a month earlier in a car crash.

Oct *Share Your Love With Me*, from LP of the same title, reaches US #14.

Dec *Blaze Of Glory*, again from the LP, stalls at US #66, while seasonal LP *Christmas* makes US #34.

Dec [4] Kenny and Marianne Rogers have a son, Christopher Cody.

1982 Mar *Through The Years*, from LP *Share Your Love*, peaks at US #13.

Aug Film *Six Pack*, starring Rogers, opens in US. From the movie, *Love Will Turn You Around* reaches US #13, while LP of the same title peaks at US #34 and earns a gold disk.

Nov *A Love Song* peaks at US #47.

Nov [23] Rogers and his wife Marianne present the first World Hunger Media Awards at the UN in New York.

Dec LP *Christmas* re-charts at US #149, now passing the platinum sales mark.

1983 Mar Rogers duets with Sheena Easton° on a revival of Bob Seger's° *We've Got Tonight*, which hits US #6 and UK #28.

Apr LP *We've Got Tonight* reaches US #27, earning a gold disk. This is his last new LP for Liberty, as he signs to RCA Records in a deal worth more than $20 million.

June *All My Life*, from LP *We've Got Tonight*, makes US #37.

Aug *Scarlet Fever*, also from the LP, and Rogers' last Liberty single, stalls at US #94.

Sept [18] Kenny Rogers' "HBO" special airs on US TV.

Oct *Islands In The Stream*, a duet with Dolly Parton° written by The Bee Gees°, tops the US chart and becomes the only platinum (US million-selling) single of 1983. It is also awarded an American Music Award (AMA) as Best Country Single (Rogers' 15th), and named Vocal Duet of the Year and Single Record of the Year by the Academy of Country Music. The single is taken from his debut RCA LP *Eyes That See In The Dark*, co-produced by Barry Gibb, which hits US #6 and earns a platinum disk as he and Parton host the annual CMA Awards. Meanwhile, LP *Eyes That See In The Dark* reaches UK #53 and the extracted title track makes UK #61.

Nov *Islands In The Stream* hits UK #7. TV movie *The Gambler II*, starring Rogers, Bruce Boxleitner and Linda Evans, airs on US TV.

1984 Jan Liberty compilation LP *Twenty Greatest Hits* makes US #22, and is another platinum LP.

Mar *This Woman*, taken from LP *Eyes That See In The Dark*, makes US #23.

May The title track from *Eyes That See In The Dark* stalls at US #79.

June Liberty LP *Duets*, compiling Rogers' hits with Sheena Easton° and Kim Carnes° with eight cuts duetted with Dottie West, climbs to US #85.

Oct LP *What About Me?* peaks at US #31 (a further platinum seller) and UK #97.

Nov *What About Me?*, sung with Carnes° and James Ingram°, reaches US #15.

Dec [2] Rogers and Dolly Parton's° "A Christmas to Remember" special airs on US TV. The duo's LP of seasonal duets, *Once Upon A Christmas*, reaches US #31, selling over a million, while *The Greatest Gift Of All*, taken from it, makes US #81.

1985 Jan [28] Rogers takes part in the recording of USA For Africa's° *We Are The World* in LA, the session having been largely co-ordinated by his manager Ken Kragen, after initial approaches by Harry Belafonte°. The single will top the US and UK charts, selling several million worldwide.

Feb *Crazy* makes US #79, as Rogers and Parton° begin a joint US tour.

June Rogers duets on *Real Love*, the title cut from Parton's° new album, which peaks at US #91.

Aug TV-promoted compilation LP *The Kenny Rogers Story*, on Liberty, hits UK #4.

Sept *Make No Mistake, She's Mine*, a duet between Rogers and country singer Ronnie Milsap, tops the US country chart for a week but does not cross over.

Oct LP *I Prefer The Moonlight* stalls at US #163, but reaches US C&W #18.

Nov The title song from LP *I Prefer The Moonlight* hits US C&W #2 for 2 weeks, again without crossing over.

Dec *Morning Desire*, taken from LP *I Prefer The Moonlight*, reaches US #72.

1986 Mar [2] Rogers wins his third Grammy, for *Make No Mistake, She's Mine*, sharing the Best Country Vocal Duet award with co-singer Ronnie Milsap.

THE ROLLING STONES

Mick Jagger (vocals and harmonica)
Keith Richard (rhythm guitar)
Brian Jones (lead guitar)
Bill Wyman (bass)
Charlie Watts (drums)

1949 Jagger (b. July 26, 1943, Dartford, Kent, UK) and Richard (b. Dec.18, 1943, Dartford) become friends while attending Maypole County Primary School, but lose contact.

1960 Jagger is a student at London School of Economics and Richard is attending Sidcup Art School when they meet again on a train. Friendship is rekindled when they discover a joint love of R&B and a passion for records on Chess label, particularly Chuck Berry°, and Richard joins R&B group, Little Boy Blue & The Blue Boys, with which Jagger sings.

1962 Jones (b. Feb.28, 1942, Cheltenham, Glos., UK), under the alias of Elmo Lewis, advertises in *Jazz News* for R&B musicians to form a band. An all-round musician, he frequently guests with Alexis Korner's Blues Incorporated which has a Saturday residency at the Ealing Blues Club. Pianist Ian Stewart answers the ad and begins to rehearse with Jones. Jagger and Richard become friendly with Jones after visiting the club and the nucleus of a group is formed comprising Jagger, Richard, Jones, Stewart, Geoff Bradford and Dick Taylor, with a variety of drummers sitting in. Jagger also becomes vocalist with Blues Incorporated and plays with the group on his nights off from Alexis Korner's band.

July Blues Incorporated is booked to appear on UK BBC Radio's "Jazz Club", broadcast live on Thursday evenings, but the contract only extends to six musicians, so Jagger is left on the sidelines. Blues Incorporated, however, needs a group to sub for its Thursday night Marquee club sessions and Jagger and cohorts eagerly accept the gig.

July [12] The Rollin' Stones, comprising Jagger, Richard, Jones, Taylor and traveling salesman Tony Chapman on drums, make their debut, taking their name from a Muddy Waters° song.

Oct The group makes its first studio recordings, *Soon Forgotten, Close Together* and *You Can't Judge A Book (By Looking At The Cover)*, which are submitted to record companies with little success.

Dec Wyman (b. William Perks, Oct.24, 1936, Lewisham, London, UK), from The Cliftons, becomes bassist after Taylor leaves, the rest of the group being impressed by his amplifier at his audition.

1963 Jan Watts (b. June 2, 1941, Islington, London), a designer with a Regent Street ad agency, who has been a regular drummer with Blues Incorporated and approached several times to join the fledgling Stones, but resisting for financial security, replaces Chapman. The six-piece group records a further demo tape at IBC Studios, but is still unable to gain a record contract, and begins a Sunday residency at Crawdaddy Club at the Station Hotel, Richmond, Surrey.

Apr The group begins to attract large audiences at the club and receives its first press write-up in *The Richmond & Twickenham Times*.

Apr [28] Andrew Oldham, age 19, an ex-PR man for The Beatles°, travels to Richmond with business associate Eric Easton.

May [3] Oldham signs the group to a management contract, and it becomes The Rolling Stones (adding the "g"). (Stewart, pushed to a backseat role of roadie and backing musician in the studio, with his straight image seen by Oldham at odds with the style he intends to create for the group, becomes an integral part of the group, unseen by the public, and is known as the sixth Stone until his death in 1985.)

May [11] *New Record Mirror* writer, and R&B fan, Norman Jopling writes a piece entitled "The Rolling Stones – Genuine R&B".

May Decca A&R man Dick Rowe signs The Rolling Stones (having recently rejected The Beatles°) and they enter the studio to record their first single.

June They decide to cover an obscure Chuck Berry° song, *Come On*, never released in UK. The line "Some stupid jerk" is altered to "Some stupid guy" to ensure radio play on UK's BBC.

June [7] The group makes its UK TV debut on ABC-TV's "Thank Your Lucky Stars", but this does not aid disk sales.

Aug *Poison Ivy*, recorded as a follow-up, is never released.

Sept *Come On* peaks at UK #21. With The Rolling Stones failing to decide on a second single, a chance meeting between Oldham and his former employers Lennon° and McCartney° leads to their visiting the Studio S1 jazz club, where they play part of a new song they have written, *I Wanna Be Your Man*, and within minutes complete the rest of the number. The Rolling Stones are now armed with something more valuable than gold in the pop world of 1963 – an unrecorded Lennon/McCartney composition.

Sept [29] The group starts its first national tour supporting The Everly Brothers° and Bo Diddley° at London's New Victoria Theatre.

Dec *I Wanna Be Your Man* (now also on LP *With The Beatles* sung by Ringo), reaches UK #12. The Stones make the song a hard-driving R&B number, with whining steel guitar. Jagger/Richard meet Gene Pitney° on UK TV program "Thank Your Lucky Stars" and present him with *That Girl Belongs To Yesterday*, which hits US and UK charts, beginning a songwriting partnership which will provide other artists with songs, but it will be almost a year before they write an original for a Stones' single.

Dec [20] The group is voted Sixth Best British Vocal Group in *New Musical Express* annual readers' poll.

1964 Jan [6] The group begins its first tour as bill-toppers at the Granada Harrow supported by The Ronettes° and Marty Wilde°. *NME* describes the group as a "caveman-like quintet". The Stones are now attracting a major following with screaming fans and press reports of their wild concerts. The image of long-haired tearaways becomes compounded as an antidote to The Beatles° clean showbiz image.

Feb EP *The Rolling Stones* reaches UK #19, and will stay in UK singles chart for 20 weeks.

Mar The group remodels Buddy Holly's° *Not Fade Away* in Bo Diddley° style, with Phil Spector lending a hand on maracas and co-writing B-side *Little By Little* with Jagger, and it hits UK #3.

Apr [18] They cause a minor riot at the "Ready Steady Go! Rave Mad Mod Ball".

Apr [22] The president of The National Federation of Hairdressers offers a free haircut to the next group to reach #1 claiming The Rolling Stones are the worst of the lot – "one of them looks as if he's got a feather duster on his head".

May Released with 100,000 advance orders, debut LP *The Rolling Stones* tops the UK chart. Oldham makes the first of many marketing ploys by leaving the group's name off the LP's front cover, unheard of in the history of record releases.

May [12] The Rolling Stones are refused lunch at a Bristol hotel because they are not wearing ties.

May The group performs in a UK TV ad for Rice Krispies breakfast cereal.

May [27] 11 boys are suspended at a school in Coventry, for having Mick Jagger haircuts.

June [1] The Stones arrive in US for a debut tour.

June [2] The tour, with The Chiffons°, Bobby Goldsboro, Bobby Vee° and Bobby Comstock, opens at the Manning Bowl, Lynn, Mass.

June [3] US TV debut is on "The Hollywood Palace" show where the group is subjected to quips from host Dean Martin. After a trampolinist's act, Martin tells the audience: "That's the father of The Rolling Stones; he's been trying to kill himself ever since."

June [10] The Stones record at Chess Studios in Chicago, Ill., where they meet Chuck Berry°, Muddy Waters° and Willie Dixon.

June [16] They break off the US trip to fly to UK for 1 day to fulfill a gig booked a year earlier at a Commemoration Ball at Magdalen College, Oxford. The cost of the flight home amounts to £1,500, their fee for the gig is £100.

June [27] The Stones appear on UK BBC TV's "Juke Box Jury" (the only time the show has five panelists rather than four), and cause controversy over their languid comments and hair.

July A cover of The Valentinos' *It's All Over Now*, recorded at Chess Studios, tops the UK chart. With assistance from engineer Ron Malo, The Rolling Stones begin to define a harder rock sound which will become their trademark. *Not Fade Away* reaches US #48.

July [24] They cause a riot at Blackpool's Empress Ballroom, and 30 fans are treated in hospital.

Aug LP *England's Newest Hit Makers – The Rolling Stones*, the UK LP with added US single *Not Fade Away*, reaches US #11. *Tell Me (You're Coming Back)* makes US #24.

Aug [7] The group stars at the Fourth National Jazz and Blues Festival, Richmond, Surrey, UK.

Aug [10] Jagger is fined £32 for driving without insurance and breaking the speed limit. His solicitor explains Mr. Jagger was on an errand of mercy visiting two fans injured in a car crash.

Sept [5] The group tours UK with Charlie & Inez Foxx, The Mojos and Mike Berry.

Sept EP *Five By Five*, recorded in Chicago, is released with 180,000 advance orders and hits UK #9. Jagger/Richard's *As Tears Go By* hits UK #9 for Marianne Faithfull° (US #22 in Jan.1965). *It's All*

Over Now makes US #26.

Oct [14] Watts marries Shirley Ann Shepherd in Bradford. Jones takes an overdose of sleeping pills.

Oct [23] The Stones begin a second US tour.

Oct [25] The group is banned from the "Ed Sullivan Show" after riotous scenes in the audience. Sullivan announces that he will in future only book groups like The Dave Clark Five° who have a wholesome image.

Oct [28] The Stones appear in US TV's "TAMI Show" in LA with Chuck Berry°, James Brown°, The Beach Boys° and Marvin Gaye°.

Nov [13] Official biography *Our Own Story* is published.

Nov [23] The Stones are temporarily banned by UK BBC after arriving late for "Saturday Club" and "Top Gear".

Nov [27] Jagger is fined £16 for driving offences. His solicitor tells the court not to be prejudiced by his client's long hair, advising that such a reputable figure as the Duke of Marlborough had hair longer than Jagger.

Dec LP *12 x 5* hits US #3. In UK, the group revives Willie Dixon's *Little Red Rooster* against critics' scepticism that a purist blues record will be a hit. It hits UK #1 in 2 weeks. A cover of Irma Thomas' *Time Is On My Side* hits US #6.

Dec [6] The Stones are voted #1 UK R&B group and Best New Group in *NME* annual readers' poll. Jagger is voted Best New Disc or TV Singer.

Dec [21] Watts' book *Ode to a High Flying Bird* is published, a tribute to jazz giant Charlie Parker.

Dec [22] In an *NME* ad, the group wishes starving hairdressers and their families a Happy Christmas.

1965 Jan LP *The Rolling Stones No. 2*, again with no title or artist name on the sleeve, hits UK #1. It includes a few covers and has versions of US R&B hits including Otis Redding's° *Pain In My Heart* and Solomon Burke's *Everybody Needs Somebody To Love*.

Jan [21] They begin an Australian tour with Roy Orbison°, Rolf Harris and Dionne Warwick°.

Feb *Heart Of Stone* reaches US #19. *The Last Time*, recorded at RCA's Hollywood studios with engineer Dave Hassinger (and with Phil Spector and Jack Nitzsche providing production assistance), tops the UK chart in its second week.

Mar [5] The group begins a UK tour with The Hollies° and Dave Berry°.

Mar [12] Portuguese pianist Sergio Varella-Cid vents his anger to the press after his recital is drowned out by The Stones playing in another part of Sheffield City Hall.

Mar [19] *Tailor and Cutter* magazine carries a plea to The Rolling Stones to wear ties to save tie-makers from financial disaster.

Apr LP *The Rolling Stones, Now!* hits US #5. On a Scandinavian tour in Odense, Wyman is knocked unconscious by a 220 volt shock on stage. They make their fifth refusal to appear on UK TV show "Sunday Night at The London Palladium".

Apr [10] A schoolteacher in Wrexham attacks parents who allow their children to wear Rolling Stones' "corduroy" trousers.

Apr [22] The group begins a tour of North America.

May *The Last Time* hits US #9 and B-side *Play With Fire* makes US #96.

June Live EP *Got Live If You Want It*, documenting their UK Mar. tour (recorded by engineer Glyn Johns hanging a microphone over theater balconies), hits UK #7.

July *(I Can't Get No) Satisfaction*, held back in UK because of the EP's success, tops the US chart for 4 weeks, the group's first US #1. Based around a definitive riff which entered Richard's head after waking up in the middle of the night in a hotel room, it is notable for its use of a fuzz box distorting the sound, and its risqué lyrics about female monthly cycles. (Richard will later claim that probably the most famous riff in rock history is based on Martha & The Vandellas° *Dancing In The Street*.)

July [22] Jagger, Wyman and Jones are fined £3 each for insulting behavior on Mar.18 when, denied use of the private toilet at a service station by a mechanic, they urinated against the garage wall and drove off "making a well-known gesture".

Aug LP *Out Of Our Heads* hits US #1 for 3 weeks. Press reports state that The Stones are set to sign a £5 million deal to make five films.

Aug [28] Allen Klein becomes co-manager of the group with Oldham.

Sept *(I Can't Get No) Satisfaction* tops the UK chart.

Sept [10] The Stones star in their own edition of UK TV's "Ready Steady Go!"

Sept [18] Wyman's wife Diane writes "My Life as a Stone's Wife" in UK music paper *Disc*.

Sept [26] They embark on sixth UK tour with The Spencer Davis Group° and Unit 4+2.

Oct LP *Out Of Our Heads*, the first LP recorded entirely in US, featuring covers of soul classics rather than R&B and four Jagger/Richard originals, hits UK #2, held off the top by *The Sound Of Music* soundtrack. Jimmy Tarbuck covers Jagger/Richard song *Wasting Time* on B-side of his non-hit *Someday*.

Oct [15] The group, scheduled to appear on Eamonn Andrews' UK TV talk show, bows out.

Nov *Get Off Of My Cloud* tops UK and US charts.

Dec [3] Richard is knocked unconscious by an electric shock on stage in Sacramento, Cal.

Dec [10] *Satisfaction* is voted Best Record of the Year in *NME* readers' poll.

Dec LP *December's Children (And Everybody's)* hits US #4.

1966 Jan From the US LP, the group's version of *As Tears Go By* hits US #6. It is intended as lead track on the next UK EP, but is cancelled.

Feb *19th Nervous Breakdown* hits UK #2 for 3 weeks, behind Nancy Sinatra's *These Boots Are Made For Walkin'*.

Mar Decca vetoes release of The Stones' projected LP *Could You Walk On The Water*. The original track line-up is also abandoned, and the project develops into *Aftermath* (hence its title).

Apr *19th Nervous Breakdown* hits US #2. LP *Aftermath*, the first Stones LP composed entirely of Jagger/Richard songs, tops the UK chart. Notable is the track *Going Home* which lasts 11 minutes, 35 seconds (the final 7 minutes studio-improvized while the tapes still rolled). Greatest hits LP *Big Hits (High Tide And Green Grass)* hits US #3.

Apr [30] Otis Redding° names The Stones his favorite group (he covers *Satisfaction*).

May *Paint It Black* hits UK #1.

June *Paint It Black* hits US #1.

June [29] The group begins its fifth US tour.

July Jagger/Richard song *Out Of Time* hits UK #1 for Chris Farlowe°. LP *Aftermath* hits US #2.

July [25] Jones plays his last US gig with The Stones in San Francisco.

Aug US-only release *Mother's Little Helper* hits US #8. B-side *Lady Jane* makes US #24.

Oct *Have You Seen Your Mother, Baby, Standing In The Shadow?*, suffering from bad studio mix due to Decca's haste to release it, hits UK #5 and US #9. (The group appears in drag at a photo call to promote the single on New York's Park Avenue.)

Oct [23] A UK tour with Ike & Tina Turner° begins at London's Royal Albert Hall, their last for 4 years.

Nov Compilation LP *Big Hits (High Tide And Green Grass)* hits UK #4. (Noticeable omission is Lennon°/McCartney's° *I Wanna Be Your Man*.)

Dec Live LP *Got Live If You Want It!* hits US #6.

1967 Jan [13] The Stones appear on the "Ed Sullivan Show" and are forced to change the lyrics of *Let's Spend The Night Together* to "Let's Spend Some Time Together".

Jan LP *Between The Buttons* hits UK #3. It is a pop-oriented LP and will lead to a split from manager/producer Oldham in order to guide their own career.

Jan [22] They make their first and last appearance on UK TV's "Sunday Night at The London Palladium". Showbiz tradition in UK dictates that artists wave to the audience on a revolving stage during the program's fade out. The Stones refuse and incur the wrath of press and public.

Jan [29] Comedians Peter Cook and Dudley Moore, at the close of "Sunday Night at The London Palladium", wave to the audience with paper dummies of the group.

Feb [5] Sunday newspaper *News of the World* names Mick Jagger in an article about drug-taking pop stars.

Feb *Let's Spend The Night Together* hits UK #3 while LP *Between The Buttons* hits US #2.

Feb [12] Police make a drug raid on "Redlands", Richard's Sussex home (and charges are made against him and Jagger).

Mar *Ruby Tuesday* tops the US chart, as B-side *Let's Spend The Night Together* makes US #55.

Apr [13] The Stones play their first gig behind the Iron Curtain at the Palace of Culture, Warsaw, Poland.

May [10] Jones is arrested for drug possession.

June [29] Jagger and Richard are found guilty of illegal possession of drugs at Chichester. Jagger goes to Brixton jail, Richards to Wormwood Scrubs. (They are released on bail the next day, and the prison sentences quashed on appeal on July 31.)

July [1] *The Times* newspaper prints an editorial by William Rees-Mogg, protesting against the punishment meted out on the two group members.

July [6] Jones is admitted to hospital for nervous strain.

July LP *Flowers*, a compilation of singles and studio out-takes, hits US #3.

Aug *We Love You*, the group's thank you to fans after events of the last few months, hits UK #8. It opens with the sound of footsteps and cell doors being slammed and features backing vocals from Lennon° andMcCartney°. They make a promotional film for it based on *The Trials of Oscar Wilde*, but it is banned by UK's BBC.

Aug [26] Jagger and girlfriend Marianne Faithfull° visit the Maharishi Mahesh Yogi with The Beatles°.

Sept [29] Oldham quits as the group's manager.

Oct *Dandelion* reaches US #14 and B-side *We Love You* makes US #50.

Oct [30] Jones is sentenced to 9 months in prison for drug possession and sent to Wormwood Scrubs. (He is released on bail, pending appeal, the following day.)

Dec [12] Jones' sentence is quashed after three psychiatrists concur he is in a poor mental state and has suicidal tendencies.

Dec [16] *NME* reports that Marianne Faithfull° is the first signing to The Stones' new Mother Earth label.

Dec LP *Their Satanic Majesties Request* hits UK #3 and US #2. (This contribution to psychedelia is delivered months after the "Summer of Love" and suffers from comparison with The Beatles'°, who reached the peak of their creative power with *Sgt. Pepper* in the summer when The Stones fell behind due to personal problems.) The LP's complex 3-D sleeve photo was designed to outdo *Sgt. Pepper*.

1968 Jan *She's A Rainbow* makes US #25. Wyman hits US #87 with *In Another Land*, also from the LP.

May [12] Jones is again arrested for drug possession.

June *Jumping Jack Flash* hits UK #1. The Stones team with Traffic° producer Jimmy Miller and return to R&B/rock.

July *Jumping Jack Flash* hits US #1.

Aug LP *Beggars Banquet*, ready for release, is put on hold by Decca because the sleeve depicts a graffiti-covered toilet.

Sept *Street Fighting Man*, banned by many US cities fearing that the lyrics may incite civil disorder, makes US #48. Jagger begins work on his first film role in *Performance*.

Sept [26] Jones is fined £50 on a drugs charge.

Nov Jones buys Cotchford Farm in Sussex, former home of *Winnie the Pooh* author A.A. Milne.

Dec LP *Beggars Banquet* is released in a plain white sleeve depicting an invitation. Produced by Miller, with mainly acoustic overtones, the LP is regarded as their finest achievement and includes *Sympathy For The Devil*. It hits UK #3 and US #3. Jones is gradually being excised from the group's activities, drug abuse and life in the fast lane having taken their toll on him. Since the sleeve argument, the group's relationship with Decca has also worsened (when the LP is re-promoted in the 1980s by Decca, it will only be available in the toilet sleeve).

Dec [10] TV show "Rock and Roll Circus", created by the group, is filmed in a London studio, with performances from artists including The Who°, Eric Clapton° and John Lennon°. (The show is never transmitted.)

1969 June [9] Jones, in poor mental and physical shape, quits the group. He is quoted as saying "I no longer see eye to eye with the disks we are cutting" – when the group is recording some of its purest blues sounds (Jones' first love).

June [13] The Rolling Stones announce Jones will be replaced by Mick Taylor (b. Jan 17, 1948, Herts., UK), guitarist with The John Mayall° Band.

June [25] Taylor makes his live debut with the band at Rome's Coliseum.

July [3] Jones is found dead in his home swimming pool by girlfriend Anna Wohlin after taking a midnight swim. (The coroner records a verdict of misadventure "drowning while under the influence of alcohol and drugs".)

July [5] The Rolling Stones play a free concert in London's Hyde Park attended by 250,000 fans. Jagger pays tribute to Jones by reciting Shelley's *Adonais*, and 3,000 butterflies are released. The event is filmed by UK's Granada TV as "The Stones in the Park".

July [6] Jagger flies to Australia with Marianne Faithfull° to work on film *Ned Kelly*.

July [8] Faithfull° attempts suicide after Jagger says their relationship is over.

July [10] Jones is buried in Cheltenham. Canon Hugh Evan Hopkins reads Jones' own epitaph: "Please don't judge me too harshly."

July *Honky Tonk Women* tops the UK chart for 5 weeks.

Aug [10] Richard's girlfriend Anita Pallenberg gives birth to a son, Marlon. (Richard and Pallenberg will be seen starring with David Warner in film *Michael Kohlhaas*, which will be withdrawn shortly after release.)

Aug *Honky Tonk Women* tops the US chart for 4 weeks.

Sept LP *Through The Past Darkly (Big Hits Volume 2)*, a second greatest hits set, dedicated to the memory of Brian Jones, hits #2 in both UK and US. Jean Luc Godard's impressionistic film of the group at work, *Sympathy of the Devil* premieres at the Edinburgh Festival.

Nov [7] The Stones begin their sixth US tour. Writer (and later rock biographer) Albert Goldman compares Jagger to Adolf Hitler in *The New York Times*.

Dec [6] Aiming to repeat their successful Hyde Park Concert, The Stones close their US tour with a free concert at Altamont Speedway, Livermore, Cal. Having employed UK Hells Angels to act as security men in London, the group hire their San Francisco counterparts, who prove to be less placid and, due to a mixture of drink and drugs, provoke angry scenes. In a confused atmosphere, 18-year-old black youth Meredith Hunter is stabbed to death by bikers when he pulls a gun at the front of the stage midway through the group's set. The group rushes through its numbers before escaping in a helicopter. The disastrous concert is seen by many as an epitaph to the good times of the 60s and the closing of an era.

Dec LP *Let It Bleed* hits UK #1 and US #3. It includes guest artists ranging from Ry Cooder° to Merry Clayton, and is highlighted by *Midnight Rambler*, with Jagger portrayed in the role of the Boston Strangler Albert de Salvo, and closes with The London Bach Choir singing the introduction to *You Can't Always Get What You Want*.

1970 July [28] *Ned Kelly* film is premiered in Australia.

July [31] The Stones' contract with Decca ends. (Still to deliver a single to complete the deal, they provide unreleasable *Cocksucker Blues*.)

Aug [1] Film *Performance* premieres, having been delayed for 2 years because of worries over its excessive violence. Jagger receives critical accolades for his performance as retired rock star Turner.

Sept Live LP *Get Yer Ya-Ya's Out!*, recorded at New York's Madison Square Garden in 1969, hits UK #1.

Oct The live LP hits US #6.

Nov Jagger's solo *Memo From Turner*, taken from *Performance* soundtrack, reaches UK #32.

Dec [6] *Gimme Shelter* concert film opens in New York. (It documents their 1969 US tour ending with the events at Altamont.)

1971 Mar [4] The group begins a UK tour at City Hall, Newcastle, and announces a decision to live in the South of France as tax exiles.

Mar [18] Ticket touts charge up to £10 for tickets at their farewell concert at London's Roundhouse.

Apr [7] They form their own label Rolling Stones Records to be distributed worldwide by the Kinney/Warner Bros. group.

Apr LP *Stone Age* hits UK #4 as Decca begins re-packaging Stones' material. (This will extend into the mid-70s and cause anger from the group who publicly decry the process.)

May *Brown Sugar*, the first release on Rolling Stones label, hits UK #2 and tops the US chart. LP *Sticky Fingers*, with an Andy Warhol-designed sleeve of a male torso from the waist down clad in jeans, complete with a real zip fastener, uses a horn section filling out their sound with heavy brass inflections. It tops both UK and US charts.

May [12] Jagger marries Nicaraguan Bianca Rosa Perez-Mora, member of the European jet set,in St. Tropez, France. The civil ceremony is followed by a Roman Catholic service. Selections from film *Love Story* are played on the chapel harmonium at the bride's request.

July *Street Fighting Man* reaches UK #21 as *Wild Horses* makes US #28.

July [23] The group files a $7½ million lawsuit against Klein, alleging "mismanagement of funds".

Aug [31] The Stones file a High Court writ against Andrew Oldham and Eric Easton for "royalty deprivation".

Sept LP *Gimme Shelter* reaches UK #19.

Oct [1] Mick and Bianca Jagger become parents to daughter Jade.

1972 Jan Double compilation LP *Hot Rocks 1964-1971*, put together by Klein, hits US #4.

Apr [17] Richard's and Pallenberg's daughter Dandelion is born.

May *Tumbling Dice* hits UK #5 and US #7.

June [3] A North American tour with Stevie Wonder° and Martha Reeves opens in Vancouver, B.C., Canada.

June LP *Exile On Main Street*, the group's only double studio set, heavily brass oriented, is released and tops both UK and US charts. Clean-up TV campaigner Mary Whitehouse claims BBC radio should not air the LP due to its obscene nature. Chairman Lord Hill listens to the LP and claims to hear nothing wrong, although it is littered with swear words.

Aug *Happy* reaches US #22.

Nov Decca compilation LP *Rock'n'Rolling Stones* makes UK #41.

Dec Another Klein double compilation LP *More Hot Rocks (Big Hits And Fazed Cookies)* hits US #9.

Dec [26] The Jaggers fly to Nicaragua to search for Bianca's relatives, missing after the earthquake.

1973 Jan [18] The group plays a benefit concert at LA's Forum in aid of victims of the Nicaraguan earthquake disaster. It raises over $400,000.

May *You Can't Always Get What You Want* (originally B-side of 1969 #1 *Honky Tonk Women*) makes US #42.

June [26] Richard and Pallenberg are arrested on charges of drugs and firearms possession.

July [31] Richard's house "Redlands" is razed to the ground.

Sept *Angie*, an acoustic love song, hits UK #5, amid great press interest in its subject, David Bowie's° wife Angie. LP *Goat's Head Soup*, recorded at Byron Lee's Dynamic Sound Studios, Kingston, Jamaica, tops both UK and US charts.

Sept [11] The group begins a UK tour.

Oct *Angie* hits US #1 for 1 week.

1974 Feb *Doo Doo Doo Doo Doo (Heartbreaker)*, also from LP *Goat's Head Soup*, reaches US #15.

June Wyman LP *Monkey Grip* makes US #99 and UK #39.

Aug *It's Only Rock'n'Roll* hits UK #10. Its release is heralded by an outbreak of graffiti across London bearing the title, and marks the debut of production credits to "The Glimmer Twins" – a pseudonym for Jagger/Richard.

Sept *It's Only Rock'n'Roll* reaches US #16.

Nov LP *It's Only Rock'n'Roll* hits UK #2 and US #1.

Dec [12] Taylor quits, suffering from the pressure of being a member of the world's most popular group, as The Stones prepare to start work on their new LP in Munich, West Germany.

Dec A revival of The Temptations'° *Ain't Too Proud To Beg*, from LP *It's Only Rock'n'Roll*, reaches US #17.

Dec [31] Ron Wood of The Faces° denies rumors that he is joining the group, stating The Faces are more important to him.

1975 Apr [14] Wood is confirmed as Taylor's replacement for touring purposes only.

May [31] During a press conference at a Fifth Avenue hotel in New York to announce a Stones US tour, the group comes into view performing live on a flat-bed truck, to the surprise of journalists.

June [3] A US tour begins, with Wood guesting.

June Compilation LP *Made In The Shade* reaches UK #14 and US #6. Decca releases an LP of unreleased material, but against the wishes of The Stones. LP *Metamorphosis*, mainly a collection of Jagger/Richard songs demoed for other artists during the 1960s, makes UK #45, and (with slightly fewer tracks) hits US #8.

July A version of Stevie Wonder's° *I Don't Know Why*, from LP *Metamorphosis* peaks at US #42.

Sept *Out Of Time*, also from the LP, featuring a Jagger solo over the backing track to his 1966 production for Chris Farlowe°, makes UK #45 and US #81.

Nov Double compilation LP *Rolled Gold – The Very Best Of The Rolling Stones* hits UK #7.

Dec [19] Wood is officially confirmed as a full member of the group.

1976 Mar Wyman solo LP *Stone Alone* makes US #166.

May LP *Black And Blue*, more dance-slanted than usual, hits UK #2 and US #1. Extracted ballad *Fool To Cry* hits UK #6 and US #10.

May [19] Richard crashes his automobile near Stafford, UK. Drugs are found in it (and he will later be fined).

June [4] Richard's 6-week-old son Tara dies from pneumonia in Geneva, Switzerland.

July US B-side *Hot Stuff* makes US #49.

Aug [21] The Stones headline Knebworth Festival, Herts., UK, in front of 200,000 fans, and perform a retrospective set tracing their roots back to their debut LP in 1964.

1977 Feb [27] Richard is arrested for drug possession at Toronto's Harbour Castle Hotel by The Royal Canadian Mounted Police. (A charge of trafficking in heroin will hang over him for 18 months.)

Mar [4] The group performs an intimate club set at El Mocambo night club in Toronto. (The set later appears on LP *Love You Live*.)

Aug [2] Richard and Pallenberg embark on a drug rehabilitation course.

Sept [30] The Stones begin recording a new LP in Paris, France.

Oct LP *Love You Live* hits UK #3 and US #5. Keith Richard adds an "s" to his surname.

Nov LP *Get Stoned* reaches UK #13.

1978 June LP *Some Girls* causes controversy for its attitude towards women and use of photos of Lucille Ball, Raquel Welch and Farrah Fawcett-Majors in a mock wig ad on the sleeve. After litigation threats, it is changed. The LP hits UK #2 and tops the US chart. The group embarks on its ninth US tour.

July *Miss You*, influenced by the current disco trend and the group's first 12" single, hits UK #3 and tops the US chart.

July [24] Marsha Hunt presses a paternity suit against Jagger, claiming maintenance for her child Karis.

Oct *Respectable* makes UK #23. *Beast Of Burden* hits US #8.

Oct [23] Richards is fined and ordered to play two charity concerts for his Toronto drug offence in 1978.

1979 Feb *Shattered* makes US #31. Richards releases solo single, a revival of Chuck Berry's° *Run Rudolph Run*.

Apr [22] Richards escapes imprisonment on his drug conviction, on condition he performs a benefit concert for the Canadian National Institute for the Blind at the Civic Auditorium, Oshawa, Ontario. He forms group The New Barbarians with Ron Wood (guitar), Ian McLagan (keyboards), Stanley Clarke (bass), Ziggy Modeliste (drums) and Bobby Keyes (sax).

May The New Barbarians begin a US tour.

Nov [2] Jagger is divorced from Bianca.

1980 Feb Wyman is quoted that he will leave The Stones in 1982.

Feb [23] Wood and girlfriend Josephine Carslake are imprisoned on drugs charges in St. Martin in the Caribbean.

July [3] Richards and Pallenberg separate. (He begins a new relationship with Patti Hansen.)

July LP *Emotional Rescue*, continuing the band's dance-oriented feel, tops UK and US charts. Extracted title track hits UK #3 and US #9.

Oct *She's So Cold* makes UK #33 and US #26.

1981 Mar Jagger walks out of the filming of Werner Herzog's *Fitzcarraldo* in Peru, after five members of the crew are killed.

Apr Compilation LP *Sucking In The Seventies* reaches UK #15.

July [22] Ross gives a free concert in New York's Central Park, abandoned the previous night after only three songs, due to a torrential downpour and strong winds.

Aug LP *Ross* makes US #32 and UK #44 while, from it, *Pieces Of Ice* peaks at US #31 and UK #46. Double compilation LP *Diana Ross Anthology*, on Motown, reaches US #63.

1984 Jan TV-advertised compilation LP *Portrait* hits UK #8, while *Let's Go Up* peaks at US #77.

Sept *All Of You*, a ballad duetted with Julio Iglesias, reaches US #19, while *Touch By Touch* peaks at UK #47.

Oct *Swept Away*, written and produced by Daryl Hall of Hall and Oates°, makes US #19. It is taken from the LP of the same title, which reaches US #26 and UK #40.

1985 Jan [28] Ross participates in USA For Africa's° recording of *We Are The World*.

Apr *Missing You*, taken from LP *Swept Away*, hits US #10. The song, dedicated to Marvin Gaye°, is written and produced by Lionel Richie°.

Oct *Eaten Alive*, featuring Michael Jackson° on back-up vocals, makes US #77 and UK #71.

Nov LP *Eaten Alive*, produced by Barry Gibb of The Bee Gees°, reaches US #45 and UK #11.

Dec *Chain Reaction*, written by The Bee Gees°, stalls at US #95.

1986 Feb [1] Ross marries Norwegian shipping magnate Arne Naess, in Geneva, Switzerland.

Mar *Chain Reaction* is Ross' biggest UK single since *I'm Still Waiting*, topping the UK chart for 3 weeks.

May A new mix of *Chain Reaction* peaks at US #66, while *Experience*, also from LP *Eaten Alive*, makes UK #47.

Nov Compilation LP *Diana Ross And Others: Their Very Best Back To Back* makes UK #21.

1987 Jan [26] Ross hosts the American Music Awards in LA.

June LP *Red Hot Rhythm'n'Blues*, containing versions of R&B oldies, makes US #73 and UK #47. Taken from it, *Dirty Looks* makes US R&B #12, failing to cross over, but reaches UK #49.

Oct Ross gives birth to her fourth child, Ross Arne.

1988 Aug [26] Ross gives birth to her fifth child, a boy.

Oct Ross' revival of The Bobettes' 1950s hit *Mr. Lee*, taken from LP *Red Hot Rhythm'n'Blues*, makes UK #58.

Nov With Peter Asher producing, Ross sings *If We Hold On Together*, the theme from Steven Spielberg-produced cartoon film *The Land Before Time*.

ROXY MUSIC

Bryan Ferry (vocals)
Andy Mackay (saxophone and woodwinds)
Phil Manzanera (guitar)
Brian Eno (keyboards)
Rik Kenton (bass)
Paul Thompson (drums)

1970 Nov Ferry° (b. Sept.26, 1945, Washington, County Durham, UK), a fine arts graduate, former R&B vocalist and spare-time songwriter, and ex-university colleague (and bass player) Graham Simpson decide to form a band to play the songs Ferry has been writing.

1971 Jan Mackay (b. July 23, 1946, London, UK), introduced to Ferry by a mutual friend, joins and brings with him electronics expert and synthesizer player Eno° (b. May 15, 1948, Woodbridge, Suffolk, UK), an acquaintance from Reading University.

June Following ads in UK music paper *Melody Maker*, Roger Bunn joins on guitar and American classically-trained tympanist Dexter Lloyd on drums. The band plays no live dates but records demos of Ferry's° material, which he hawks, initially without success, around London record companies.

July Bunn and Lloyd leave. Ferry recruits a guitarist he has long admired, Davy O'List (formerly with Keith Emerson in The Nice), while another *Melody Maker* ad brings in drummer Thompson (b. May 13, 1951, Jarrow, Northumberland, UK), who has backed Billy Fury°.

Dec Following positive press coverage from *Melody Maker*'s Richard Williams on the strength of the early demos, the band plays two try-out live gigs, at the Friends of the Tate Gallery Christmas show and the Union Ball at Reading University.

1972 Jan [21] Roxy Music is heard in session on UK BBC Radio 1's "Sounds of the Seventies", the early demo tape having impressed presenter John Peel.

Feb O'List leaves and Manzanera (b. Philip Targett-Adams Manzanera, Jan.31, 1951, London, UK), who has been doing the group's sound mixing but was previously guitarist with experimental band Quiet Sun, joins in his place. EG Management signs the band to a contract which includes recording and leasing product to a record company.

Mar Debut LP is recorded for £5,000 at Command Studios, London, with ex-King Crimson° lyricist Pete Sinfield producing.

May Simpson is dismissed from the group and Kenton, a bass-playing friend of Sinfield, replaces him.

May [30] With Kenton, the band plays its first major gig, at the Great Western Express Festival in Lincs., UK.

June Roxy Music's first tour is as support to Rory Gallagher around the North of England.

June [20] The group's TV debut is on UK BBC 2's "The Old Grey Whistle Test".

July The band supports Alice Cooper° at the Empire Pool, Wembley, UK. Press reviews applaud Roxy Music's act at Cooper's expense.

Aug Following a release deal signed by EG with Island Records, debut LP *Roxy Music*, following ecstatic reviews, hits UK #10.

Sept Ferry°-penned *Virginia Plain* (not included on the LP) hits UK #4.

Oct During Roxy Music's first headlining UK tour, Ferry's° voice begins to suffer (he has a history of tonsilitis) and a break in the tour follows while he is hospitalized to have his tonsils removed.

Dec The band plays its first US tour, opening for Jethro Tull°, Humble Pie°, The Allman Brothers Band°, and others.

1973 Jan Kenton is fired and not replaced. During recordings for the second LP, session man John Porter plays bass.

Apr *Pyjamarama* hits UK #10, though the band claims it as a hasty

ROXY MUSIC *cont.*

release pressured by Island. It is not included on LP *For Your Pleasure*, which hits UK #10, promoted by a sell-out UK tour.

July Eno° quits the band after personality clashes with Ferry°, who recruits Curved Air's violinist Eddie Jobson (b. Apr.28, 1955, Billingham, Teesside, UK) as a replacement (initially a controversial move, as he does not consult the rest of the band).

Aug LP *For Your Pleasure* is the band's US chart debut, at #193.

Oct Ferry° releases his first solo LP *These Foolish Things* (for some time, his solo projects will continue in tandem with Roxy Music).

Nov The band tours UK, with Jobson handling all keyboards (Ferry° and Eno° had previously shared them), and Ferry moves to center stage as vocalist without an instrument.

Dec *Street Life* hits UK #9. It is taken from Chris Thomas-produced LP *Stranded*, which tops the UK chart for a week – the band's first #1 hit. For the first time, two tracks are co-written (by Manzanera and Mackay). Bass player on the LP is John Gustafson, ex-The Big Three° and The Merseys, while the sleeve model is *Playboy* Girl of the Year Marilyn Cole. A successful European tour follows.

1974 May Mackay releases solo, largely instrumental, LP *In Search Of Eddie Riff*, which does not chart.

June The band plays another US tour, where its appeal is still cult-fashionable rather than commercial. Concerts in New York, Boston, Baltimore, Detroit, Cleveland and Philadelphia are successful. LP *Stranded* creeps to US #186.

Oct *All I Want Is You*, heralding a new LP (recorded in Aug. with John Porter, who had produced Ferry's° solo LPs), reaches UK #12 as the band plays another sold-out UK tour, with John Wetton joining temporarily on bass. Ferry introduces new stage images, appearing in gaucho attire and US military-style uniform.

Dec LP *Country Life*, again with Ferry co-writing material with other members of the band, hits UK #3. (Its sleeve, showing two scantily-clad models, causes controversy, notably in US where it has to be sold in opaque green shrinkwrap.)

1975 Feb/May The band tours US, Japan, Australia and New Zealand, still retaining Wetton on bass. While the band is on the road in US, LP *Country Life* becomes its first major US seller, reaching #37.

Oct A UK tour is mounted to promote the next LP, this time without Wetton (who has joined Uriah Heep) and with Gustafson playing bass (he will stay in the group on a semi-permanent basis for several months).

Nov LP *Siren*, produced again by Thomas and with co-writing credits for Mackay, Jobson and Manzanera, hits UK #6. The sleeve photo is of Texan fashion model Jerry Hall (with whom Ferry° will later become romantically linked). Extracted *Love Is The Drug*, an R&B-based dance number, hits UK #2 – the band's biggest hit single to date.

Dec The band tours US again, as LP *Siren* climbs to US #50.

1976 Jan *Both Ends Burning*, also from LP *Siren*, makes UK #25.

Mar *Love Is The Drug*, the band's first US hit single, reaches US #30 as it tours US again.

May On return to UK, Mackay follows a solo project with music for UK TV series "Rock Follies", Manzanera works with new outfit 801, Ferry does more solo work and Jobson returns to US to play with Frank Zappa°. It is decided to rest Roxy Music indefinitely.

June [26] After frequent press rumors, the band finally announces: "We have all decided to go our separate ways, for the rest of the year at least, to have a rest from Roxy Music for a while."

Aug With the band still inactive, live LP *Viva! Roxy Music*, assembled from concert recordings made from 1972-75, is released, hitting UK #6 and making US #81.

1977 Nov EG transfers the Roxy Music catalog from Island to Polydor Records in UK. Earlier material is repromoted and *Virginia Plain*, reissued as a single (coupled with *Pyjamarama*), reaches UK #11.

Dec Compilation LP *Greatest Hits* reaches UK #20.

1978 Nov After an 18-month hiatus (the recent months having seen Ferry's° solo chart success dwindle), Ferry, Mackay, Manzanera and Thompson regroup to cut a new Roxy Music LP at Basing Street studios, London. Keyboards player Paul Carrack (ex-Ace°) and bassist Gary Tibbs (ex-new wave band The Vibrators) are recruited.

1979 Mar *Trash*, heralding the new LP, peaks at UK #40.

Apr LP *Manifesto*, produced by the band, hits UK #7. The band supports it with a reunion tour of UK and Europe (with Tibbs on bass and David Skinner on keyboards), then moves on to play US and Japan.

May LP *Manifesto* reaches US #23.

June From the LP, *Dance Away* hits UK #2 and makes US #44.

Sept *Angel Eyes*, a disco-flavored excerpt from LP *Manifesto* (and also available in a dance-floor-aimed extended 12" version) hits UK #4. (It is on UK chart simultaneously with similarly-titled but different song *Angeleyes* by Abba°.)

1980 A new LP is recorded in London by Ferry°, Mackay and Manzanera, who co-produce with Rhett Davies, with other players (including Tibbs, Carrack, guitarist Neil Hubbard, and drummers Andy Newmark and Allan Schwartzberg) being hired for work on specific tracks. Two oldies, Wilson Pickett's° *In The Midnight Hour* and The Byrds'° *Eight Miles High*, are included among the new Ferry and Ferry/Manzanera songs.

May *Over You* hits UK #5, as LP *Flesh And Blood* tops the UK chart for a week.

Aug *Oh Yeah (On The Radio)* hits UK #5. It is taken from LP *Flesh And Blood* which returns to UK #1 for 3 weeks and makes US #35, while *Over You* makes US #80, the band's third and final US singles chart entry.

Nov *The Same Old Scene*, third single from the LP, reaches UK #12.

1981 Mar A specially-recorded version of John Lennon's° *Jealous Guy*, cut as a tribute following Lennon's murder, tops the UK chart for 2 weeks – Roxy Music's only #1 single.

1982 Apr After a lengthy recording hiatus, *More Than This* hits UK #6, heralding what will be the band's last studio LP – again recorded by Ferry/Mackay/Manzanera with session musicians. Mackay publishes a book – *Electronic Music*, written while the band was inactive.

June LP *Avalon*, produced by Davies, tops the UK chart for 3 weeks. The sleeve features Lucy Helmore, whom Ferry° marries on June 26.

July The extracted title song from *Avalon* makes UK #13.

Aug LP *Avalon* reaches US #53.

Oct *Take A Chance With Me*, also from the LP, reaches UK #26, and is Roxy's last hit single.

1983 Mar Mini-LP *Musique/The High Road*, recorded live at Glasgow's Apollo Theatre (and the soundtrack to a live home video of the same title featuring the band), reaches UK #26.

May Mini-LP *Musique/The High Road* makes US #67 as the band tours US for the last time, in an 8-piece line-up.

Nov Compilation LP *The Atlantic Years 1973-1980* (US-originated by the band's US label Atlantic) reaches UK #23.

1984 June Mackay and Manzanera re-emerge in The Explorers, with Ferry-like vocalist James Wraith, but debut single on Virgin Records, *Lorelei*, fails to chart.

1985 June Eponymous debut LP by The Explorers is released, again without chart success. At the same time, Ferry° re-launches his solo career with LP *Boys And Girls*, which tops the UK chart.

1986 Apr TV-promoted double compilation LP *Street Life – 20 Great Hits*, containing both Roxy Music and Ferry solo singles, tops the UK chart for 5 weeks, earning a platinum disk.

1988 Nov TV-promoted compilation LP *The Ultimate Collection*, again mixing Roxy Music and Ferry solo material, hits UK #6.

JIMMY RUFFIN

1960 Ruffin (b. May 7, 1939, Colinsville, Miss., US) moves to Detroit with his family to work in a car assembly plant.

1961 Recommended to Berry Gordy Jr. at Motown by a member of The Contours, he is signed to the subsidiary Miracle label, but spends much time singing back-up for other acts.

1963 He declines an invitation to join The Temptations° (though brother David does), preferring to sing solo.

1966 Oct After 5 years of waiting for the Motown promotional machine to roll around to him, Ruffin is moved to Soul label (alongside Junior Walker & The All-Stars°), and records commercial ballad *What Becomes Of The Broken Hearted*, which hits US #7.

Dec *What Becomes Of The Broken Hearted* hits UK #10.

1967 Jan *I've Passed This Way Before* reaches US #17.

Mar *I've Passed This Way Before* reaches UK #29.

Apr *Gonna Give Her All The Love I've Got* makes US #29 and UK #26.

May LP *The Jimmy Ruffin Way* reaches UK #32.

June LP *Top Ten*, containing the hits to date plus new material, peaks at UK #133.

Aug *Don't You Miss Me A Little Bit Baby* makes US #68.
1968 Apr *I'll Say Forever My Love* peaks at US #77.
1969 Aug *I've Passed This Way Before* is reissued in UK, as part of a campaign to re-promote Motown oldies, and reaches UK #33. Ruffin visits UK to aid promotion, and begins a period during which he will be more active in UK than US, as reissued and new singles are UK chart successes.
1970 Jan LP *Ruff'N Ready* reaches US #196.
May *Farewell Is A Lonely Sound* hits UK #8 but fails in US.
Aug *I'll Say Forever My Love* (not a UK chartmaker on first 1968 release) hits UK #7.
Nov He duets with brother David (now a soloist, having left The Temptations°) on a revival of Ben E. King's° *Stand By Me*, which makes US #61. The song is taken from an LP of duets, *I Am My Brother's Keeper*, which fails to chart. Meanwhile *It's Wonderful (To Be Loved By You)* hits UK #6.
1971 Feb *Maria (You Were The Only One)* reaches US #97, and is his last US success on Soul.
1974 June Compilation LP *Jimmy Ruffin's Greatest Hits* reaches UK #41.
Aug Ruffin's original success, *What Becomes Of The Broken Hearted*, is pulled from successful LP *Greatest Hits* and reissued as a UK single. It hits UK #4, his all-time highest chart placing, with aggregate sales now well over 1 million.
Nov *Farewell Is A Lonely Sound*, also reissued, charts for the second time in UK, reaching #30. It coincides with release of Ruffin's debut on new label Polydor, to which he has signed while based in UK, *Tell Me What You Want* makes UK #39.
1980 Apr *Hold Onto My Love*, recorded for RSO Records and written and produced by Robin Gibb of The Bee Gees°, hits US #10 and UK #7, but will be Ruffin's final US hit single.
June LP *Sunrise* on RSO, containing the hit, climbs to US #152 (after which Ruffin disappears from the US chart and, seemingly, the music scene).
1985 Jan He re-emerges after 4 years' silence, signed to EMI in UK. *There Will Never Be Another You* is a UK club hit and spends a week at UK #68. (Ruffin, unable to find the momentum or the material to maintain his re-emergence, is dropped by EMI. He participates on Paul Weller-assembled Council Collective, which reaches UK #24 with *Soul Deep*.)

THE RUNAWAYS

Cherrie Currie (vocals)
Lita Ford (lead guitar)
Joan Jett (rhythm guitar)
Jackie Fox (bass)
Sandy West (drums)

1976 After a gig on the roof of an LA apartment block, all-girl teen rock'n'roll group, The Runaways, signs to Mercury Records. The group was formed when record producer and entrepreneur Kim Fowley, looking for a female Ramones°, introduced Jett (b. Sept.22, 1960, Philadelphia, Pa., US) to West (b. 1960). The line-up includes Currie (b. 1960, LA), Fox (b. 1960) and Ford (b. 1959, London, UK).
Aug Debut LP *The Runaways*, produced and co-written by Fowley, reaches US #194.
Sept The group makes its New York debut at CBGB's with Television° and Talking Heads°.
1977 Feb Kim Fowley/Earle Mankey-produced LP *Queens Of Noise* makes US #172.
June The group tours Japan (which will produce LP *Live In Japan*). Jett assumes lead vocals when Currie leaves.
July [1] Fox, suffering from exhaustion (she has recently attempted suicide) leaves and is replaced by Vickie Blue.
Dec LP *Waitin' For The Night*, again produced by Fowley, fails to chart.
1978 Currie releases solo LP *Beauty Is Only Skin Deep*. (She will later form a duo with sister Marie and record for Capitol, achieving some success in Japan. After the sisters split, she will pursue an acting career.) Laurie McAlister joins the band.
Dec [31] The band plays a concert in San Francisco (it will be its last one).
1979 Apr They have no funds and no recording deal. Jett wants to keep the band strictly rock'n'roll, while Ford favors a move towards heavy metal. The band is due to appear in movie *We're All Crazy* but splits prior to the commitment. Jett moves to London, UK, where she cuts tracks with ex-Sex Pistols° Paul Cook and Steve Jones.
July LP *And Now . . . The Runaways* is issued on Cherry Red Records in UK.
1980 Feb Currie appears with Jodie Foster in the film *Foxes*. Cherry Red releases Runaways LP *Flaming Schoolgirls* a half live/half studio set from the original line-up.
July [15-16] Jett performs at the 2-day new wave festival "Urgh!" in Santa Monica, Cal. Her performance is filmed for movie *Urgh! A Music War*.
July Jett, having been in hospital suffering from a heart-valve infection and pneumonia, forms her own backing band The Blackhearts with Ricky Byrd (guitar), Gary Ryan (bass) and Lee Crystal (drums). She records LP *Joan Jett* with producers Kenny Laguna and Ritchie Cordell. Unable to arouse record company interest, Laguna releases the LP himself.
1981 Jan Joan Jett & The Blackhearts sign to Boardwalk Records.
Feb Jett opens at New York's Peppermint Lounge as a prelude to a US tour to promote her forthcoming LP.
Apr Jett's group's debut LP *Bad Reputation* reaches US #51.
Dec Jett releases a hard rock version of *Little Drummer Boy*.
1982 Mar Jett releases a cover of The Arrows' *I Love Rock'n'Roll*, which she had seen them perform on UK TV during a UK tour, but had failed to convince The Runaways of its potential. It tops the US chart and LP of the same name will hit US #2. Currie stars in horror film *Parasite*.
May *I Love Rock 'N' Roll* hits UK #4. LP *I Love Rock 'N' Roll* reaches UK #25.
June For a follow-up, Jett covers Tommy James & The Shondells'° 1969 chart topper *Crimson And Clover*. It hits US #7 but makes only UK #60.
Sept A cover of Gary Glitter's° *Do You Wanna Touch Me (Oh Yeah)* is Jett's third US hit at #20. LP *I Love Rock 'N' Roll* is certified US platinum.
1983 Aug Jett's *Fake Friends* reaches US #35. LP *Album* makes US #20.
Oct Jett cuts Sly & The Family Stone's° 1969 #1 *Everyday People*, which peaks at US #37.
1984 Aug Ford's solo LP *Dancin' On The Edge* makes US #66, having been at UK #66 for 1 week.
Nov Jett's LP *Glorious Results Of A Misspent Youth* reaches US #67.
1986 Oct Jett's *Good Music*, with vocal backing from The Beach Boys°, reaches US #83.
1987 Jett stars with Michael J. Fox in movie *Light and Day*, as leader of rock band, The Barbusters.
1988 June Ford, having recorded hard rock-oriented LPs for Mercury and Vertigo, reaches US #12 on RCA with solo *Kiss Me Deadly*. Her LP *Lita* peaks at US #29.
Sept Jett's *I Hate Myself For Loving You* hits US #8 and UK #46 while LP *Up Your Alley* still climbs the US chart.

RUN DMC

Jason Mizel, Jam Master Jay (DJ)
Joseph "Run" Simmons (voice)
MC Darryl "D" McDaniels (voice)

1982 Having all grown up in New York suburb Hollis, Simmons (b. 1964, New York, N.Y., US), McDaniels (b. 1964, New York) and Mizel (b. 1965, New York) start rap trio Run DMC after graduating from St. Pascal's Catholic School, New York.
1983 Managed by Simmons' brother Russell, who has set up Rush Productions, Run DMC signs a recording deal with Profile Records in New York for $2,500, after rejections by all major labels.
June Spurred by early specialist interest in first rap singles, debut LP *Run – D.M.C.* is released. It will peak at US #53, spend over 1 year on chart and become the first US gold rap LP.
July Run DMC begins a rap package tour which includes L.L. Cool J°.
1985 Feb Still without crossover singles, follow-up LP *King Of Rock* is released, set to peak at US #52.
May Run DMC appears in first rap movie *Krush Groove*. It is based on the life-story of Russell Simmons who has now also become co-chairman of Run DMC producer Rick Rubin's new label, Def Jam.
Nov Run DMC contributes to Artists Against Apartheid protest song and video *Sun City* which makes US #38 and UK #21.
1986 July Run DMC, having become closely allied to a training shoe manufacturer, debuts on UK chart at #62 with new single *My Adidas/Peter Piper*. Meanwhile US release is *Walk This Way*, a mix of rap and heavy metal as provided by Aerosmith's° vocalist

RUN DMC *cont.*

Steve Tyler and guitarist Joe Perry. Attracting heavy US MTV rotation, it hits US #4. It ties in with release of third LP *Raising Hell* which also benefits. (It will hit US #3 in Sept., with sales over 2 million, and UK #41. It also becomes rap's first platinum LP.)

Aug At the end of a mini promotion summer European visit, Run DMC signs a six-figure sponsorship update deal with Adidas in Munich, West Germany.

Aug [17] Following five 1986 US gigs where crowd trouble has been prevalent (Pittsburgh, Cleveland, Atlanta, Cincinnati and New York), a riot between rival gangs erupts at a Long Beach, LA concert; 42 of the 14,500 audience are seriously injured. The incident sparks outbursts and future bans from many other US venues.

Sept Still promoting recent LP, the group appears on US TV shows "Saturday Night Live" and co-raps with the hostess on "The Late Show Starring Joan Rivers". The City of Los Angeles rescinds an invitation for Run DMC to take part in the LA Street Scene Festival because of recent troubles at the rap trio's gigs.

Oct *Walk This Way* hits UK #8, as mini-tour dates sell-out in UK.

Nov As *You Be Illin'* climbs to US #29, Run DMC accepts an invitation from Michael Jackson° to have dinner at Jackson's studio to discuss possible collaboration on his forthcoming LP, but plans will fizzle.

Dec Strengthening group resolve to make teenagers more aware of gang and drug-related problems, Run DMC travels to LA to hold street seminars, some of which are co-hosted by band hero Barry White°.

1987 Jan Run DMC begins writing and producing its own feature length movie, *Tougher Than Leather*, planned as a rapping adventure thriller, and will also finance the project at an unexpected $10m.

Feb *It's Tricky* stalls at US #57, while *You Be Illin'* peaks at UK #42.

Apr As a prelude to a UK tour with similar Rubin-produced Beastie Boys°, both bands appear at Montreux Pop Festival, Switzerland.

May *You Be Illin'* reaches UK #16.

Dec Run DMC contributes nativity rap song *Christmas In Hollis* to Jimmy Lovine seasonal compilation LP *A Special Christmas*. It stalls at UK #56.

1988 Jan Release of (12 months in the making) movie and LP is delayed as a legal dispute opens between the band and its label, Profile.

May *Run's House* is released and makes UK #37, but fails in US.

June With the dispute settled (Run DMC have to pay legal costs, but are now tied to a ten-LP deal with Profile), LP *Tougher Than Leather* is finally released to lukewarm response. It makes UK #13 (but only spends 5 weeks on chart) and hits US #9, also falling off quickly.

July Run DMC headlines "Run's House" US tour with DJ Jazzy Jeff and Fresh Prince, Public Enemy and others. At an LA gig, Run DMC is joined on stage by The Beastie Boys°.

Aug *Mary Mary*, a cover of the Mike Nesmith-penned Monkees° song, makes US #75 but fails in UK.

TODD RUNDGREN

1965 Rundgren (b. June 22, 1948, Upper Derby, Pa., US), while still at high school joins Money, a UK-style R&B band, on guitar.

1966 His first post-school group is Woody's Truck Stop, a blues band in the Paul Butterfield° mold, in Philadelphia.

1967 With Woody's Truck Stop's bassist Carson Van Osten, Rundgren leaves to form The Nazz (the name's probable inspiration being The Yardbirds'° B-side *The Nazz Are Blue*). Designed to inherit a pre-psychedelic sound (and notably the UK influence of The Beatles°, The Small Faces° and The Move°), the group includes Robert "Stewkey" Antoni on vocals and keyboards and Thom Mooney on drums, and makes its live debut supporting The Doors°.

1968 Signed to Screen Gems/Columbia (which also has The Monkees°), The Nazz is placed on new subsidiary label SGC.

Nov Debut LP *Nazz* stalls at US #118, but remains on chart for 26 weeks.

1969 Jan The group visits UK for promotion and to cut a second LP in London but because of a lack of clearances with the UK Musicians' Union, work permits are declared invalid, and The Nazz flies to LA to record instead.

Mar Debut single *Open My Eyes*, a riff-driven rocker released prior to the LP without charting, is overtaken in US airplay by its Association°-styled harmony ballad B-side, *Hello It's Me*, which makes US #71.

June Second LP *Nazz Nazz*, compiled from two LPs-worth of material cut at the LA sessions, reaches US #80, but following continual disagreements with Mooney, Rundgren has left the band before the LP's release (along with Van Osten). He returns for one promotional US tour before being replaced by future Cheap Trick° member Rick Nielsen.

1970 Feb *Hello It's Me* is released again as an A-side, following continuing airplay, and climbs to US #66. Rundgren becomes an in-house producer for Albert Grossman's Bearsville Studios and engineers The Band's° LP *Stage Fright*.

Nov After producing Bearsville's first LP, by The American Dream, Rundgren is given studio time as payment, and cuts LP *Runt* for Bearsville subsidiary Ampex, with the aid of Tony Sales (bass) and Hunt Sales (drums). ("Runt" is a nickname given him by Patti Smith°.) From the LP, *We Gotta Get You A Woman* is his first solo single, reaching US #20.

1971 Jan LP *Runt* makes US #185, while final Nazz LP, *Nazz III*, from the leftover second LP tracks, is released as a cash-in, without charting.

May The second LP credited to Runt, *The Ballad Of Todd Rundgren*, sells poorly, but extracted *Be Nice To Me* makes US #71.

Sept *A Long Time, A Long Way To Go*, also from the LP, makes US #92. He follows with a working visit to UK, taking over production of Badfinger's° LP *Straight Up* from George Harrison°.

1972 Apr Bearsville signs for distribution to Warner Bros. Rundgren is moved from Ampex to Bearsville itself, and begins to record under his own name, starting with double LP *Something/Anything*, on which three sides are recorded solo and the fourth with a group, live with no overdubs.

June LP *Something/Anything* peaks at US #29, earning Rundgren a gold disk, and *I Saw The Light*, taken from it, reaches US #16.

July *I Saw The Light* is Rundgren's only UK hit single, reaching #36.

Aug Also from LP *Something/Anything*, *Couldn't I Just Tell You* stalls at US #92. Rundgren's name becomes known as a producer and engineer, as he works extensively with Bearsville acts like Foghat, Jesse Winchester, Ian & Sylvia and Paul Butterfield°.

1973 June LP *A Wizard, A True Star*, recorded at his own Secret Sounds studios in New York is a near-psychedelic potpourri, with 26 songs presented in a style similar to *Abbey Road*'s side 2. It makes US #86, but the Philly-soul single *Sometimes I Don't Know What To Feel*, taken from it, flops.

Sept Rundgren produces Grand Funk's° single and LP *We're An American Band*, which hit US #1 and #2 respectively, both becoming million-sellers.

Dec Rundgren's solo revival of Nazz song *Hello It's Me* is belatedly taken from LP *Something/Anything* and becomes his biggest-selling single, hitting US #5.

1974 May Another 2-LP set, *Todd*, half-solo and half-group effort, climbs to US #54. It includes *Sons Of 1984*, recorded live in New York's Central Park and featuring a 3,000-strong chorus, overdubbed from the New York audience and another at San Francisco's Golden Gate Park, recorded in Sept. 1973.

June The Beach Boys°-styled ballad *A Dream Goes On Forever*, from LP *Todd*, reaches US #69.

Dec Rundgren forms the band Utopia (with Mark Klingman and Ralph Shuckett on keyboards, Roger Powell on synthesizer, John Siegler on bass, John Wilcox on drums and Kevin Elliman on percussion) to develop his symphonic art-rock ideas and more metaphysical lyrical concerns. The band's debut LP *Todd Rundgren's Utopia*, an hour-long set, reaches US #34.

1975 May *Real Man*, heralding a new solo LP, peaks at US #83.

June Solo LP *Initiation* is a 68-min. single album, with cosmically-inclined songs (including *Real Man*) on one side and a 30-min. instrumental on side two. Players include members of Utopia, plus Edgar Winter°, Rick Derringer and Dan Hartman.

Dec Utopia's second LP, recorded live, *Another Live*, includes a version of The Move's° *Do Ya*, plus a song from *West Side Story*. Reaching US #66, this is the last LP to feature the original Utopia line-up. Rundgren makes his first playing visit to UK to promote the LP with a series of successful concerts.

1976 July LP *Faithful*, credited to Rundgren solo but future "Utopians" play on it, on side one features close re-creations of six (other acts') 1960s classics, including two Lennon°/McCartney° songs, and one each by Bob Dylan°, The Yardbirds° and Jimi Hendrix°, plus The Beach Boys'° *Good Vibrations*, which is released as a single and reaches US #34.

Aug [21] Rundgren performs at UK's Knebworth Festival with 10cc°, Lynyrd Skynyrd°, Hot Tuna and bill-toppers The Rolling Stones°.

1977 Mar A new line-up of Utopia is put together for Egyptology/pyramids-obsessed LP *Ra*, comprising Rundgren (vocals and guitar), Kasim Sulton (bass and vocals), Roger Powell (keyboards and vocals) and John "Willie" Wilcox (drums). The LP becomes the group's biggest UK hit, reaching UK #27, and peaks at US #79. (Rundgren has planned to release it on his own label, Etheric Records, but does not get the label beyond the planning stage.)

Oct Utopia LP *Oops! Wrong Planet* features shorter, more radio-oriented songs (including *Love Is The Answer*, later a hit for England Dan & John Ford Coley) and reaches US #73 and UK #59. Rundgren produces Meat Loaf's° LP *Bat Out Of Hell*. (It will hit both US and UK top 10 in 1978, selling several million worldwide and staying on UK chart for 7 years, and will be Rundgren's most successful production project, on which he will receive a producer's royalty.)

1978 May He returns to solo recording with LP *Hermit Of Mink Hollow*, on which he plays all instruments.

July From the LP, Rundgren's first US top 30 single since *Hello It's Me* in 1973 is *Can We Still Be Friends?* (later covered by Robert Palmer°), which makes US #29.

1979 Jan Double live LP *Back To The Bars*, credited as a Rundgren solo but featuring a variety of group line-ups including guests Hall and Oates° (for whom he had previously produced LP *War Babies*), Stevie Nicks of Fleetwood Mac° and Spencer Davis°, reaches US #75. Press reports state that Rundgren is to take the UK Musicians' Union to court over its "restrictive strangleholds" over visiting musicians. (The union had refused him permission to broadcast a live show from London's The Venue.)

1980 Feb Utopia LP *Adventures In Utopia*, conceived as the soundtrack to a TV/video special, reaches US #32 and UK #57 (the group's last UK chart entry).

Apr *Set Me Free*, from LP *Adventures In Utopia*, is the group's first US hit single, making #27.

June Also from the LP, *The Very Last Time* peaks at US #76.

Aug [13] Rundgren's home in Woodstock, N.Y., is broken into by four masked men, who bind and gag Rundgren, his girlfriend and three guests, then strip the house of valuable art treasures and stereo equipment.

Nov Utopia LP *Deface The Music*, entirely consisting of 1960s Beatles° soundalike pastiches, written and recorded in 2 weeks, climbs to US #65.

1981 Apr LP *Healing*, totally solo and quasi-religious, peaks at US #48. It includes a free single, *Time Heals* (which some months later is released in its own right, without success, despite being regarded as one of his best singles, but its Rundgren-produced promotional video will win Flo & Eddie's Golden Hippo Award.)

1982 Mar Utopia LP *Swing To The Right* is the band's last for Bearsville, reaching US #102. From it, *One World* gets plenty of airplay, but fails to chart.

Apr Rundgren makes a solo US tour to promote the LP, despite it being a band recording.

Dec Utopia signs to US Network label for LP *Utopia*, which is made into a double package by including a 5-track 12" single, and it reaches US #84. In UK, it is issued by Epic with a free 7" single instead.

1983 Jan Taken from the LP, *Feet Don't Fail Me Now* makes US #82, Utopia's last hit single.

Mar Rundgren's final solo Bearsville LP, *The Ever Popular Tortured Artist Effect*, makes US #66. He releases a 90-min. video special based on the LP, recorded in his own computer-video studio in Woodstock, N.Y.

May Taken from the LP, *Bang The Drum All Day* is Rundgren's last solo US hit single, reaching #63.

Oct Rundgren co-writes and plays on Will Powers' *Kissing With Confidence*, which reaches UK #17.

1984 Mar With a change of label to US Passport, Utopia LP *Oblivion* makes US #74, and includes the near-hit single *Cry Baby*.

1985 May Utopia LP *P.O.V.*, on Passport, includes the group's version of *Mated*, later a UK hit single for David Grant & Jaki Graham.

Nov Rundgren's LP *A Capella*, recorded for Warner Bros., uses just his voice with help from the keyboard emulator to make a variety of vocal-based sounds. Extracted *Something To Fall Back On* gains much radio play, and he undertakes a US tour with gospel-style vocal group support.

Dec Rundgren duets with Bonnie Tyler° on *Loving You Is A Dirty Job (But Somebody's Gotta Do It)*, which makes UK #73.

1986 Utopia splits. Roger Powell records solo for New Age label.

Nov Utopia LP *Trivia* is a compilation of tracks from earlier LPs.

1987 Aug Rhino Records in US (having previously reissued extremely rare Nazz LPs) begins a re-issue program covering all Rundgren and Utopia Bearsville releases, bringing Rundgren's work out on compact disk for the first time.

RUSH

Alex Lifeson (guitar)
Geddy Lee (vocals and bass)
Neil Peart (drums)

1969/72 Lifeson (b. Aug.27, 1953, Fernie, British Columbia, Canada) and Lee (b. July 29, 1953, Willowdale, Toronto, Canada) meet in the Toronto suburb of Sarnia while at high school, and team with drummer John Rutsey to form a band playing Cream°, Hendrix° and Led Zeppelin°-influenced music. They begin performing the bar and club circuit when the legal drinking age is reduced from 21 to 18.

1973 The band supports The New York Dolls in Toronto. They recruit producer Terry Brown, (who has worked with Procol Harum° and fellow Canadians April Wine) and at Toronto's Sound studios cut an LP for $9,000. Unable to interest record labels, they set up their own Moon label to release debut LP *Rush*. A copy of it is sent to Cleveland, Oh., radio station W-MMS DJ Donna Halper, who brings the band to the attention of Mercury Records. The group signs to Mercury with a two-album deal worth $200,000.

1974 July LP *Rush* is released. Rutsey quits and Peart (b. Sept.12, 1952, Hamilton, Ontario, Canada) auditions and takes his place.

Aug [19] Rush embarks on its debut US tour, playing support dates until Christmas.

Oct LP *Rush* reaches US #105.

1975 Jan The group starts work on its second LP at Toronto Sound.

Feb Rush receives the Juno award as Most Promising Group.

Mar LP *Fly By Night* makes US #113, as the group begins a US tour supporting Aerosmith° and Kiss°.

Nov LP *Caress Of Steel* peaks at US #148.

1976 May Fourth LP in 2 years, *2112* reaches US #61.

June [11-13] Rush sells out three nights at Toronto's 4,000-seater Massey Hall.

Sept The group begins a tour of Canada.

Nov Double LP *All The World's A Stage*, recorded live in Toronto, makes US #40.

Dec The band plays selected dates in New York, Chicago, Indianapolis and Boston.

1977 Jan *Fly By Night/In The Mood* charts briefly at US #88.

Apr Determined to break nationwide, the band begins a US tour of the North East and Mid West.

June [2] The band opens its first UK tour at the Manchester Free Trade Hall. The first seven dates are sold out.

July Work commences on a new LP at Rockfield Studios, Monmouthshire, Wales, UK.

Oct LP *A Farewell To Kings* reaches US #33 and marks the group's UK debut at #22.

Nov LPs *2112*, *All The World's A Stage* and *A Farewell To Kings* are all certified gold.

Dec *Closer To The Heart* makes US #77.

1978 Jan The group's first UK chart single, *Closer To The Heart*, reaches UK #36.

Feb [12] Rush opens its second sell-out UK tour at the Odeon, Birmingham.

Feb They win a second Juno award, for Best Group.

Apr LP *Archives*, a triple set reissue of the group's first three LPs, makes US #121.

Oct Rush embarks on the "Hemispheres" tour covering Canada, US, UK and Europe. (It will last until June and include 113 dates.)

Dec LP *Hemispheres* reaches US #47 and UK #14.

1979 Jan [8] The Canadian government names Rush official Ambassadors of Music.

Feb Rush wins the Juno award for second year running.

Apr The band embarks on a 3-month tour of UK and Europe.

1980 Jan Rush sets out on 5-month "Permanent Waves" tour of US.

RUSH *cont.*

Feb LP *Permanent Waves* hits US #4 and UK #3.
Mar *Spirit Of The Radio* makes US #51 and UK #13.
June Rush visits UK for another sell-out tour, including five nights at London's Hammersmith Odeon.
1981 Feb The band starts "Moving Pictures" US tour to promote new LP.
Mar LP *Moving Pictures* hits both US and UK #3.
Apr *Limelight* reaches US #55. *Vital Signs/A Passage To Bangkok* makes UK #41.
Aug *Tom Sawyer* climbs to US #44.
Nov *Tom Sawyer* reaches UK #25. LP *Exit . . . Stage Left*, a second live double, hits US #10 and UK #6.
1982 Jan A live version of *Closer To The Heart* makes US #69.
Mar Lee guests on vocals for fellow Canadians Dave Thomas and Rick Moranis (Bob and Doug McKenzie from Canadian TV comedy show "SCTV") on *Take Off* which reaches US #16. LP *Great White North* hits US #8 and earns a gold disk.
Oct *New World Man* makes US #21 and UK #42. LP *Signals* hits US #10 and UK #3.
Nov *Subdivisions* reaches UK #53.
1983 May *Countdown*, with a live version of *New World Man* on the flipside, makes UK #36.
1984 May *The Body Electric* peaks at UK #56. LP *Grace Under Pressure* hits US #10 and UK #5.
1985 Oct *The Big Money* makes UK #46.
Nov LP *Power Windows*, produced by the band and Peter Collins, hits US #10 and UK #9.
1987 Jan *Big Money* makes US #45.
Oct *Time Stand Still*, with guest vocal by Til Tuesday's Aimee Mann, reaches UK #41, but fails to make US Hot 100. LP *Hold Your Fire*, recorded in England, Monserrat, Toronto and Paris with Collins again producing with the band, hits US #13 and UK #10.

LEON RUSSELL

1958 Russell (b. Hank Wilson, Apr.2, 1941, Lawton, Okla., US), a child piano prodigy who has learned to play the trumpet and formed his own band in his mid-teens (lying about his age to get a job in a Tulsa nightclub and playing with visiting Ronnie Hawkins° and Jerry Lee Lewis°), moves to LA. Still lying about his age, he starts a career as a sessionman, learning guitar from James Burton and playing in studios alongside Glen Campbell°, Dorsey Burnette° and others.
1962 He becomes a regular member of Phil Spector's "Wall of Sound" session crew, playing on hits by The Crystals°, Bob B. Soxx & The Blue Jeans, and others, sometimes using the pseudonym Russell Bridges. He also plays on Herb Alpert's° *A Taste Of Honey* and The Byrds'° *Mr. Tambourine Man*.
1965 At Liberty Records, he begins arranging for Gary Lewis & The Playboys° and is rewarded with a gold disk for Lewis' first single, *This Diamond Ring*.
1966 Russell's own recording career gets off to a false start with a one-off single for A&M, which quickly disappears.
1967 He builds a recording studio, and his session work includes playing on ex-Byrd° Gene Clark's solo LP, and arranging LP *Feelin' Groovy* for Harper's Bizarre°.
1968 Russell teams with guitarist Marc Benno for LP *Asylum Choir*. Released on Mercury subsidiary Smash, it is critically rated, but does not sell. He joins "Delaney & Bonnie° and Friends" tour and comes to the attention of Joe Cocker's° manager Denny Cordell, following which Cocker's second LP is recorded at Russell's studio; it includes *Delta Lady* (originally written by Russell for Rita Coolidge).
1969 Apr A second Asylum Choir LP is recorded, but Smash declines to release it. Cordell suggests that Russell records with him in UK. The sessions go well, and they return to Cal. to apply finishing touches to the LP, and set up their own label, Shelter Records.
1970 June Russell organizes the band for Cocker's "Mad Dogs and Englishmen" US tour. His high profile in these live shows establishes a personal following, which benefits LP *Leon Russell*, Shelter's first release; it reaches US #60. (He also plays with Bob Dylan°, The Rolling Stones° and Eric Clapton° during the year). His own show airs on National Educational TV in US – a relaxed affair filmed in his recording studio and featuring a variety of friends, musicians, girlfriends and children.
1971 Jan [22] Movie *Mad Dogs and Englishmen*, documenting the tour of the same name, with Russell in a prominent role, premieres in London.
July LP *Leon Russell And The Shelter People*, recorded throughout 1970, climbs to US #17, earning a gold disk, and also reaches UK #29 – his only UK chart entry.
Aug [1] He plays in George Harrison's° "Concert for Bangla Desh" at New York's Madison Square Garden.
1972 Jan Russell buys the tapes of LP *Asylum Choir II* from Smash. Released on Shelter, it reaches US #70.
Sept LP *Carney* is Russell's most successful, hitting US #2 (for 4 weeks) and going gold, with a 35-week chart stay.
Oct *Tight Rope*, taken from LP *Carney*, reaches US #11.
1973 Sept Triple live LP *Leon Live*, recorded at Long Beach Arena in Cal. in front of 70,000 people, hits US #9 and earns another gold disk. *Queen Of The Roller Derby*, from the live LP, reaches US #89.
Oct Double A-side Hank Wilson single *Roll In My Sweet Baby's Arms/I'm So Lonesome I Could Cry* makes US #78. Both come from Russell's "pseudonymous" (it uses his real name) country LP *Hank Wilson's Back*, which climbs to US #28. (His future wife Mary McCreary's LP *Butterflies In Heaven* is also released on Shelter.)
1974 May Russell's revival of Tim Hardin's *If I Were A Carpenter* reaches US #73.
Aug LP *Stop All That Jazz* peaks at US #34.
1975 July LP *Will O' The Wisp* makes US #30, earning Russell's fourth gold disk.
Nov *Lady Blue*, extracted from LP *Will O' The Wisp*, reaches US #14.
1976 Jan *Back To The Island* makes US #53. Russell marries Mary McCreary (vocalist with the Sly & The Family Stone° spin-off group Little Sister). He also cuts his ties with Shelter Records and establishes new label Paradise Records.
July *The Wedding Album*, recorded with his wife, climbs to US #34.
Sept *Rainbow In Your Eyes* by Leon and Mary Russell, released on Paradise, makes US #52. (This will be Russell's last chart single).
Dec Shelter compilation LP *Best Of Leon* makes US #40 and is another gold disk.
1977 Feb [19] Russell's song *This Masquerade* wins a Grammy in the hit version by George Benson°, which is named Record of the Year for 1976.
July Another duetted LP with Mary Russell, *Make Love To The Music*, peaks at US #142.
1978 Sept Solo LP *Americana* makes US #115.
1979 Aug Russell moves closer to his country-blues roots on double LP *Willie And Leon*, recorded with Willie Nelson° for his label, Columbia. It reaches US #25 and earns another gold disk.
1981 Apr Live LP *The Live Album*, recorded by Russell with bluegrass band The New Grass Revival, creeps to US #187, and is his last chart LP.

THE RUTLES

Ron Nasty (rhythm guitar and vocals)
Dirk McQuickly (bass and vocals)
Stig O'Hara (lead guitar and vocals)
Barry Wom (drums and vocals)

1978 Apr The LP and TV movie *The Rutles: All You Need Is Cash* are released. The project is a spoof on the career of The Beatles°, masterminded by (and starring) Eric Idle, former Monty Python and UK comedy series "Rutland Weekend Television" actor (from which The Rutles' name originates). The project includes pastiches of Beatles music by Neil Innes (ex-Bonzo Dog Doo-Dah Band°), with George Harrison° among the performers (but not playing himself). Taken from the LP, *I Must Be In Love*, reaches UK #39 (giving the fictitious Rutles a real-life hit single), while LP *The Rutles* climbs to UK #12 and US #63. The story it tells is as follows:
1959 Jan [21] Nasty and McQuickly meet at 43, Egg Lane, Liverpool, UK, when McQuickly knocks Nasty to the floor. Soon joining with O'Hara, they will gig for 18 months as a trio before discovering Wom (b. Barrington Womble) hiding in their van.
1960 Arthur Scouse becomes their manager and sends them to Hamburg to play various clubs on the infamous Reeperbahn. On this trip a fifth member, Leppo, joins the group, mainly standing at the back as he can't play guitar. He is lost in transit when the group returns to Liverpool. The group, however, will claim his influence immeasurable.
1961 The group returns to the Liverpool club circuit.

Oct Leggy Mountbatten, a one-legged retail chemist from Bolton, accidentally falls down steps to the Cavern and falls in love with the fit of the boys' trousers. He smartens up their image and does the rounds of London record companies.

1962 The group signs to Parlourphone after a recommendation from music publisher Dick Jaws, who signs their publishing for the rest of their natural lives.

1963 Their debut LP is recorded in 20 minutes and Rutlemania breaks out in UK.

Nov Nasty causes a controversy at The Royal Variety Show when he bows to the Royal Box and dedicates the next number to a very special lady in the audience, "Barry's mum".

Dec The nation takes The Rutles to its heart, with the top 20 containing nineteen of their records, including *Rut Me Do, Twist And Rut* and *Please Rut Me.*

1964 Feb The Rutles arrive to conquer US. 10,000 fans await their arrival at Kennedy Airport, but their plane lands at La Guardia. 73 million people see the group perform live on US TV's "Ed Sullivan Show", while New York DJ Bill Murray The K stakes a claim as the fifth Rutle.

Mar Nasty has his first book of comic prose, *Out of Me Head*, published to worldwide acclaim.

July [10] Debut feature film *A Hard Day's Rut*, directed by Richard Leicestershire, is premiered in London.

Nov Mountbatten's autobiography *A Cellarful of Goys* is published.

1965 July Their second feature film *Ouch!* opens.

Aug [14] The group plays Ché Stadium (named after Cuban guerilla leader Ché Stadium) in New York, arriving at the gig a day early to enable them to leave before the audience arrives.

1966 Aug Nasty is widely quoted in an interview that The Rutles are bigger than God. The story makes the front page all over US and fans turn against the group. At a hurriedly arranged press conference, Nasty claims he has been misquoted, and actually said that The Rutles are bigger than Rod (Rod Stewart° who will not be famous for another 5 years).

1967 June [1] Their meisterwork *Sergeant Rutter's Only Darts Club Band* is released and re-shapes the world's attitude to pop music.

June The group claims it is influenced by the effects of tea, to which it was introduced 2 years earlier by Bob Dylan°. McQuickly makes public his tea addiction and admits to enjoying biscuits too. Nasty is arrested for possession of tea by Detective Inspector Brian Plant, causing a national outcry. In London, *The Times* prints an editorial calling for the legalization of tea.

Aug O'Hara falls under the spell of Surrey mystic Arthur Sultan. He convinces the rest of the group to join him at Sultan's retreat in Bognor, Sussex, UK. While there, they hear the shock news that Mountbatten has resigned as their manager and accepted a teaching post in Australia.

Dec [26] The group faces its first failure when its TV film about four Oxford history professors on a tour of English tea shops – *The Tragical History Tour* – is panned by the critics, despite the soundtrack's classic *W.C. Fields Forever* and *I Am The Waitress.*

1968 Apr Nasty and McQuickly launch The Rutle Corps at a press conference in New York. Its aim is to promote new artists. Early signings include Les Garçons De La Plage and Arthur Hodgeson & The Kneecaps. The company fails, its only success being the animated feature film *Yellow Submarine Sandwich.*

Dec Wom completes a year in bed as a tax dodge.

1970 May The group falls into disarray. The Rutle Corps crumbles. Nasty calls in the world's most feared promoter, Ron Decline, to settle financial affairs. Their last LP *Let It Rot* is released with an accompanying film which shows the group's sad break-up.

Dec The final split occurs. McQuickly sues Nasty and O'Hara, Wom sues McQuickly, Nasty sues O'Hara and Wom, and O'Hara accidentally sues himself. McQuickly joins The Punk Floyd and releases LP *White Dopes On Punk.* Wom also releases solo LP *When You Find The Girl Of Your Dreams In The Arms Of Some Scotsman From Hull.* After this, the group members drift into obscurity.

1978 Mar Interest is re-awakened in the group through the NBC-TV documentary "All You Need Is Cash", and the group is once more in the public eye, despite claims made in the film by blues singers Blind Lemon Pye and Rambling Orange Peel that The Rutles stole their music.

BOBBY RYDELL

1957 Rydell (b. Robert Ridarelli, Apr.26, 1942, Philadelphia, Pa., US), having entered Paul Whiteman's amateur talent TV show and become a regular (singing and playing drums for 3 years), joins local Philadelphia rock band Rocco & His Saints as drummer (the line-up includes Frankie Avalon° on trumpet).

1958 Leaving the Saints to pursue a solo career as a vocalist, Rydell is rejected by Capitol, Decca and RCA, and releases his first two singles on manager Frankie Day's Veko label. Neither charts and Rydell signs to Cameo label.

1959 June His sixth single (and fourth for Cameo), *Kissin' Time* peaks at US #11 and is the start of a successful 4 years (Rydell will have nineteen US top 30 entries).

Sept [4-7] Rydell performs at Dick Clark's 4-day Michigan State Fair which includes teen idols Frankie Avalon° and Freddy Cannon.

Dec *We Got Love/I Dig Girls* hits US #6 and #46 respectively.

1960 Feb *Wild One* hits US #2. It also hits UK #2 and is his first UK hit on EMI's Columbia label. B-side *Little Bitty Girl* makes US #19.

May *Swinging School*, taken from movie *Because They're Young*, hits US #5, but makes only UK #44. B-side *Ding-A-Ling* reaches US #18.

July *Volare* hits US #4.

Sept *Volare* reaches UK #22.

Dec *Sway* makes US #14 and UK #12. B-side *Groovy Tonight* reaches US #70. Rydell appears with a host of stars in the "Christmas Rock'n'Roll Show" at the Paramount Theater, Brooklyn, N.Y.

1961 Jan *Good Time Baby/Cherie* climb to US #11 and #54 respectively.

Jan [24] Rydell represents the US at the first "French International Rock'n'Roll Festival" in Paris, France.

Feb LP *Bobby's Biggest Hits* peaks at US #12. (No LPs will chart in UK.)

Mar *Good Time Baby* reaches UK #42.

May *That Old Black Magic*, a cover of Glenn Miller's hit, makes US #21.

July *The Fish* reaches US #25.

July [29] "The Dick Clark Caravan of Stars" opens at Steel Pier, Atlantic City, N.J. (During its 6-week run ending in Detroit in Sept. Rydell plays some dates.)

Oct Live LP *Rydell At The Copa* reaches US #56.

Dec *I Wanna Thank You* reaches US #21, while B-side *The Door To Paradise* peaks at US #85. *Jingle Bell Rock*, a duet with Chubby Checker°, makes US #21. Following its success, they release LP *Bobby Rydell/Chubby Checker*, which hits US #7.

1962 Feb *I've Got Bonnie* makes US #18, and the flipside *Lose Her* reaches US #69.

June *I'll Never Dance Again* makes US #14.

Sept LP *All The Hits* peaks at US #88.

Oct *The Cha-Cha-Cha* hits US #10.

Dec LP *Biggest Hits Volume 2* makes US #61.

1963 Feb *Butterfly Baby* reaches US #23.

May *Wildwood Days* makes US #17. Rydell stars in films *Bye Bye Birdie* and *That Lady From Peking.*

Sept *Let's Make Tonight* reaches US #98.

Nov *Forget Him* is Rydell's last major hit, at US #4 and UK #13.

1964 Jan LP *The Top Hits Of 1963* reaches US #67.

Mar *Make Me Forget* reaches US #43. LP *Forget Him* peaks at US #98.

May A cover of Peter and Gordon's° *A World Without Love* reaches US #80.

Sept Rydell is one of many acts on the bill which reopens the Paramount Theater, Brooklyn.

Dec *I Just Can't Say Goodbye* spends 1 week at US #94.

1965 Feb *Diana* reaches US #98.

1978 Rydell has the honor of having the high school in film *Grease* named after him. (He will enjoy many successful years on the US oldies circuit with his contemporary teen idols.)

MITCH RYDER & THE DETROIT WHEELS

Mitch Ryder (vocals)
John Badanjek (drums)
Jim McCarty (guitar)
Joe Kubert (guitar)
Jim McCallister (bass)

1963 Having left R&B vocal group The Peps, Ryder (b. William Levise Jr., Feb.26, 1945, Detroit, Mich., US) forms Billy Lee & The Rivieras, with Badanjek, McCarty, Kubert, and Earl Elliott on bass,

MITCH RYDER & THE DETROIT WHEELS *cont.*

in Detroit. They headline regularly at the Village club and record *Fool For You* on local gospel-oriented Carrie label.

1964 With Ryder having built a reputation as a white soul singer, the group becomes the house band at Detroit's Walled Lake Casino, attracting audiences of 3000, and records a version of *Do You Want To Dance* for local label, Hyland Records.

1965 Producer Bob Crewe signs The Rivieras to his New Voice label, taking the group to New York for 6 months to rehearse and adapt its live repertoire for recording.

July The name Mitch Ryder is picked out of a phone book and the band becomes The Detroit Wheels to sound more "contemporary". *I Need Help* is released but does not chart.

1966 Jan *Jenny Take A Ride*, a medley of two rock oldies, *See See Rider* and Little Richard's° *Jenny Jenny*, hits US #10.

Mar *Jenny Take A Ride* reaches UK #27, while LP *Take A Ride* makes US #78.

Apr A revival of The Righteous Brothers'° *Little Latin Lupe Lu* reaches US #17 and UK #48.

June *Break Out* climbs to US #62. (It will become a cult favorite on Northern UK dancefloors in the mid-1970s but will never chart in UK.)

July *Takin' All I Can Get* reaches only US #100.

Sept LP *Breakout . . . !!!* hits US #3.

Nov *Devil With A Blue Dress On/Good Golly Miss Molly*, another medley taken from LP *Breakout . . . !!!*, is the band's biggest hit at US #4 and a million-seller. Crewe decides that Ryder's future is as a solo artist and he splits singer and band after the sessions which produce the next LP and two hit singles.

1967 Mar *Sock It To Me – Baby!* hits US #6.

May LP *Sock It To Me!* climbs to US #36, while medley single, *Too Many Fish In The Sea/Three Little Fishes*, makes US #24. Crewe puts Ryder on the road solo in extravagant costumes, with a 40-piece orchestra, grooming him for the Las Vegas circuit. (The Detroit Wheels, without Ryder, will release three further singles before disbanding.)

July First solo *Joy*, a more subdued production than the exuberant group efforts, peaks at US #41.

Oct Solo revival of *What Now My Love* reaches US #30.

Nov Another revival, *You Are My Sunshine*, peaks at US #88 but solo LP *What Now My Love* fails to chart.

Dec Compilation LP *All Mitch Ryder Hits!*, rounding up both group and solo singles, climbs to US #37.

1968 Feb Ryder returns to the medley formula with two 1959 revivals, *(You've Got) Personality/ Chantilly Lace*. It is his last Crewe-produced solo and falters at US #87. Ryder splits from Crewe and signs to Dot Records.

1969 LP *The Detroit-Memphis Experiment*, produced by Steve Cropper of Booker T. and The MG's°, has good reviews but it and *Sugar Bee* sell poorly.

1970 Reunited with Detroit Wheels drummer Badanjek, Ryder forms the 7-man hard rock band Detroit, signing to Dot associate label Paramount Records.

1972 Feb LP *Detroit*, the band's only LP release, reaches US #176.

1978 With a new 8-piece backing band, Ryder releases the critically acclaimed but non-charting LP *How I Spent My Vacation*, for US independent label Seeds & Stems and Line Records in Germany.

1979 Live EP *Rock'n'Roll Live* is issued in Germany by Line.

1980 Line/Seeds & Stems release another LP, *Naked But Not Dead* while an EP *We're Gonna Win* is released in Germany.

1981 Ryder, now a cult figure in Germany, has the double LP set *Live Talkies*, which includes a bonus maxi-single, issued on Line.

1982 Sept Ryder solo LP *Smart Ass* is released by Line and in UK by Safari but fails to chart.

1983 After more than 15 years, Ryder returns to the US chart at #120 with solo LP *Never Kick A Sleeping Dog*, produced by John Cougar·Mellencamp° for Riva Records. Extracted *When You Were Mine*, written by Prince°, climbs to US #87.

1988 LP *Detroit* is reissued in CD form, with previously unreleased material included.

SADE

Sade Adu (vocals)
Stewart Matthewman (sax)
Paul Denman (bass)
Andrew Hale (keyboards)
Paul Cook (drums)

1963 Sade Adu (b. Helen Folasade Adu, Jan.16, 1959, Ibadan, Nigeria, Africa) is brought with her family by her mother to Clacton, Essex, UK, where she will be raised.

1978/80 Working part-time at London rock venue, The Rainbow, she attends St. Martin's School of Art.

1980 She joins her first group, Arriva, having written songs for some years (her first composition is *Kisses From The Karma Sutra*), and Arriva's most popular live number will be *Smooth Operator*, penned by Adu and guitarist Ray St. John.

1981 She joins eight-piece North London funk band Pride, where she links with manager Lee Barrett and future Sade band members Denman, Hale and Matthewman.

1983 With little record company interest, she quits Pride and forms her own band, Sade, inviting Cook to join the other three. Barrett invests £8,000 in the project and secures enthusiasm from several labels, particularly Virgin, with the help of several gigs at Ronnie Scott's club, Soho, London, a venue well suited to the band's smokey jazz-tinged soul material.

1984 Jan She signs to CBS/Epic as a solo artist for an advance of £60,000 and 14¾% of LP sales. The Sade band members in turn sign to her.

Feb Sade's debut single *Your Love Is King* is released and hits UK #6, helped by the first UK BBC TV "Top of the Pops" appearance.

Mar The band begins recording debut LP with producer Robin Millar as Adu moves into a converted fire station in North London with current beau, journalist Robert Elms.

May Follow-up *When Am I Gonna Make A Living?* makes UK #36.

July First LP *Diamond Life* is released in UK and hits #2, confirming her as a predominently LP-selling artiste. The LP spends 98 weeks on chart and will sell over 6 million copies worldwide.

Aug Starting with selected UK dates, the band begins a hectic promotional tour of Europe, taking in Switzerland, Germany and Italy. Sade donates money to striking UK coalminers' families.

Sept As *Smooth Operator* reaches UK #19 and becomes a big European hit, the band performs five shows in Tokyo. During her Japanese stay, Sade experiences an earthquake in bed. Although the earth moves, she is unhurt.

Nov She sings and chats on UK TV show "Wogan". She also moves apartment to Camden, London.

Dec She returns to Nigeria for Christmas to see her 82-year-old grandmother.

1985 Feb A US campaign is launched by her US label, CBS subsidiary Portrait, as LP *Diamond Life* enters the chart. It will peak at US #5 with platinum sales and win the group the BPI Best New Album award.

Apr The band rejects an offer to perform at the annual Montreux pop festival to concentrate instead on recording follow-up LP.

May *Smooth Operator* finally hits US #5 after months of airplay.

July [13] Sade performs at the "Live Aid" spectacular at Wembley, UK, as *Your Love Is King* stalls at US #54.

Sept *Diamond Life* video is released in US.

Nov With recording over, the band begins a UK tour, followed by selected gigs at small US venues. First single from the new LP, *Sweetest Taboo*, is released to hit US #5 and UK #31.

Dec Second LP, *Promise*, again featuring group originals, hits both UK and US #1, and wins a multi-platinum award.

1986 Jan The band begins a lengthy world tour to support the LP. (It will include major US dates in May.)

Feb *Is It A Crime* peaks at UK #49.

Feb [25] Sade receives Best Newcomer award at the 28th annual Grammy ceremony in LA.

Apr She joins a select number of performers who have featured on the front cover of US magazine *Time*. As elsewhere, it is assumed that Sade is not a band but only a solo performer. *Never As Good As The First Time* peaks at US #20.

1987 Apr She appears in cult film *Absolute Beginners* as torch singer Athene Duncannon and contributes *Killer Blow* to the soundtrack. She relocates to Spain and will subsequently begin work with the band members on third LP.

1988 Apr Sade re-emerges with *Love Is Stronger Than Pride* which makes UK #44.

May Third LP, *Stronger Than Pride*, hits UK #3.

June *Paradise* makes UK #29.

July Sade begins a 40-date US tour, joined by vocalist Leroy Osbourne. *Paradise* reaches US #16 as parent LP *Stronger Than Pride* hits US #7.

Nov [21/22] Sade plays sold-out dates at London's Wembley Arena as part of the European leg of a world tour.

SAM AND DAVE

Sam Moore (vocals)
Dave Prater (vocals)

1961 Moore (b. Oct.12, 1935, Miami, Fla., US), son of a Baptist deacon and ex-member of gospel group The Melonaires, now a secular soloist, is joined spontaneously on stage at the King of Hearts Club in Miami by Prater (b. May 9, 1937, Ocilla, Ga., US), a jobbing vocalist working at the club as a chef. Audience reaction is favorable so they decide to form a duo.

1962 Signed by Morris Levy of Roulette Records in New York, the duo records gospel-flavored R&B for 4 years without much success. (An eponymous LP will be compiled from these Roulette singles after Sam and Dave have become successful.)

1965 They leave Roulette to sign with Atlantic, where Jerry Wexler arranges recording sessions in Memphis at Stax Records. The deal with Stax owner Jim Stewart is that their records are released on his label. The duo is teamed with songwriters Isaac Hayes° and David Porter, with backing provided by The Memphis Horns.

1966 Jan *You Don't Know Like I Know* reaches US #90 and #7 on the R&B chart.

June *Hold On, I'm Comin'* climbs to US #21 and tops the R&B chart for a week.

Sept LP *Hold On, I'm Comin'* reaches US #45.

Oct *Said I Wasn't Gonna Tell Nobody* peaks at US #64.

Dec *You Got Me Hummin'* makes US #77.

1967 Feb LP *Double Dynamite* reaches US #118.

Mar [17] Now signed to Otis Redding's° manager Phil Walden, Sam and Dave play Hammersmith Odeon, London, on the Stax/Volt European Tour, along with Redding and Booker T. and The MG's°.

Mar The success of the UK dates puts LP *Hold On, I'm Comin'* on the UK chart at #37. *When Something Is Wrong With My Baby*, an intense soul ballad, in contrast to previous uptempo funk hits, reaches US #42.

Apr A revival of Sam Cooke's° *Soothe Me* is the duo's first UK chart single at #35.

May LP *Double Dynamite* reaches UK #28.

July *Soothe Me* makes US #56.

Oct *Soul Man* hits US #2 and tops the R&B chart for 7 weeks. It sells over a million and earns a gold disk.

Dec *Soul Man* climbs to UK #24.

1968 Jan LP *Soul Men* reaches US #62.

Feb [29] The duo wins a Grammy award with *Soul Man* for Best Rhythm And Blues (Group) Performance of 1967.

Mar *I Thank You* hits US #9 and is another international million-seller. In UK it peaks at #34 while LP *Soul Men* makes UK #32.

May Stax splits from Atlantic after its distribution deal expires and the duo's recordings revert to the Atlantic label, with its recording sessions relocating to Miami. Prater shoots his wife during a domestic argument but, because of the circumstances of the incident, he avoids prosecution or imprisonment.

June *You Don't Know What You Mean To Me* reaches US #48. LP *I Thank You* is released in US but does not chart.

Aug *Can't You Find Another Way (Of Doing It)* peaks at US #54.

Nov *Everybody Got To Believe In Somebody* makes US #73.

1969 Jan *Soul Sister, Brown Sugar* reaches US #41.

Mar *Born Again* makes only US #92 and is Sam and Dave's last US chart single (though Atlantic will release a further eight, after the duo itself splits, up to June 1971). Compilation LP *The Best Of Sam And Dave* winds up their US chart career, reaching #87. *Soul Sister, Brown Sugar* is their last but biggest UK hit at #15.

June Sam and Dave appear at the "Soul Bowl '69" festival at Houston Astrodome, Tex., alongside Aretha Franklin°, The Staple Singers°, Ray Charles° and other major R&B names.

1970 Now on notoriously bad terms with each other, Sam and Dave split up for solo careers. Moore stays with Atlantic and releases three solo singles, none of them hits. Prater signs to Alston.

1971 With no solo success, they team up again, signing to United Artists.

1975 LP *Back Atcha'* is released without chart success. The duo drifts apart again.

1979 Feb With popularity renewed because of The Blues Brothers' revival of *Soul Man* (which makes US #14), the duo is reactivated again.

Sept Sam and Dave tour in the US as support to The Clash°. LP *Sweet And Funky Gold*, consisting of re-recordings of their (and others') hits, is released on US Gusto label.

1980 Oct The duo appears as Sam and Dave in Paul Simon's° semi-autobiographical movie *One Trick Pony*.

1981 The duo finally splits for good after a decade of its on-off relationship.

1982 Prater tours with singer Sam Daniels as Sam and Dave.

1987 Feb Moore re-records *Soul Man* with Lou Reed° as the title theme to a teen comedy film. Released as a single, it reaches UK #30. Prater is arrested for selling crack to an undercover drug squad officer.

1988 Apr [9] Prater is killed when his car leaves the road and hits a tree near Syracuse, Ga.

May [14] Moore appears at Atlantic Records' 40th Anniversary Show at Madison Square Garden, New York, with "Blues Brother" Dan Aykroyd duetting.

SANTANA

Carlos Santana (guitar and vocals)
Tom Frazer (guitar)
Gregg Rolie (keyboards)
David Brown (bass)
Rod Harper (drums)

1966 Oct Carlos Santana (b. July 20, 1947, Autlan de Navarro, Mexico), having grown up in Tijuana and then San Francisco (where he first discovers R&B and the blues) meets keyboards player Rolie after leaving high school, and with him forms The Santana Blues Band, which includes Brown (bass), Frazer (guitar) and Harper (drums). They play extensively at San Francisco club and park gigs.

1968 The band debuts at the Fillmore in San Francisco, shortens its name to Santana, and undergoes personnel shifting, as its sound begins to encompass the Latin music of Santana's own background into its blues-based approach. Percussionists Mike Carabello and Jose Chepito Areas are added to the line-up. Frazer and Harper leave, and Michael Shrieve joins on drums.

Sept [2] The band plays the Sky River Festival in Sultan, Wash., with The Grateful Dead°, Muddy Waters°, Country Joe & The Fish°, and others.

1969 Feb Carlos Santana plays on LP *The Live Adventures Of Al Kooper And Mike Bloomfield*.

Aug [1] The band takes part in the Atlantic City Pop Festival in N.J. alongside Jefferson Airplane°, B.B. King°, Creedence Clearwater Revival° and others.

Aug [15] Now signed to CBS/Columbia, the band appears at the Woodstock Festival, which brings it national notice. (*Soul Sacrifice*, from the festival, is included in *Woodstock* movie and triple LP.)

Aug [30] The band plays a third major festival in a month, the Texas International Pop Festival, at Dallas International Motor Speedway, Lewisville, Tex.

Nov Debut LP *Santana*, boosted by the Woodstock appearance and positive critical response, hits US #4. (It will spend over 2 years on US chart and earn a gold disk.)

Dec *Jingo*, a percussive highlight from the LP, makes US #56.

Dec [6] Santana is on the bill of The Rolling Stones'° concert at Altamont Speedway, Livermore, Cal., where a murder is committed during The Stones' act.

1970 Mar *Evil Ways*, also from the debut LP, hits US #9.

May LP *Santana* makes UK #26.

Oct Second LP *Abraxas* tops the US chart for 6 weeks, selling over a million copies.

Dec LP *Abraxas* hits UK #7 (and will spend a year on UK chart).

1971 Jan A cover of Fleetwood Mac's° *Black Magic Woman*, from LP *Abraxas*, hits US #4, and is the band's biggest hit single. Neal Schon joins on guitar and vocals.

Apr *Oye Como Va*, also from LP *Abraxas*, and a Latin-rock adaptation of a salsa number by Tito Puente, reaches US #13.

Nov LP *Santana III* tops the US chart for 5 weeks, earning another gold disk, and hits UK #6.

SANTANA *cont.*

Dec The band breaks up as a live unit and, although it will regroup for recording, founder member Rolie and Schon leave. (After an 18-month rest, Rolie will join Schon in Journey°.) Meanwhile, *Everybody's Everything*, taken from LP *Santana III*, reaches US #12.

1972 Mar *No One To Depend On*, also from the third LP, makes US #36.

Sept Carlos Santana cuts a live LP at Hawaii's Diamond Head volcano with drummer Buddy Miles, from which double A-side *Evil Ways/Them Changes* creeps to US #84. LP *Carlos Santana And Buddy Miles, Live!* hits US #8 and makes UK #29.

Dec LP *Caravanserai*, moving the band's music into freer, jazzier forms, hits US #8 (another gold disk) and UK #6.

1973 Feb The group plays with The Rolling Stones° at the latter's LA benefit concert for victims of the Nicaraguan earthquake, to 19,000 people.

Apr Carlos Santana marries Urmila, a Sri Chinmoy adherent.

Aug LP *Love Devotion Surrender*, a duetted instrumental between Carlos Santana and guitarist Mahavishnu John McLaughlin, reaches US #14 and hits UK #7. (Like his wife and McLaughlin, Santana has now become a devotee of Sri Chinmoy, and taken the additional religious name Devadip – which means "The light of the lamp of the Supreme".)

Dec LP *Welcome* reaches US #25, earning another gold disk, and hits UK #8. The band's personnel is changing extensively with every new LP, but its music continues in a more jazzy direction.

1974 Sept Compilation LP *Santana's Greatest Hits* reaches US #17 and UK #14.

Oct *Samba Pa Ti*, an instrumental from LP *Abraxas*, is issued as a UK single, and makes UK #27.

Nov Carlos Santana teams with Alice Coltrane (another disciple of Sri Chinmoy) for instrumental LP *Illuminations*, which makes UK #40.

Dec LP *Borboletta*, with guest appearances from Stanley Clarke and Brazilian musicians Airto Moriera and Flora Purim, reaches US #20 and UK #18.

1975 June Bill Graham, the first man to book the band in the 1960s, becomes its manager.

Dec Triple live LP *Lotus*, a deluxe package recorded and originally only released in Japan, appears belatedly in US and UK, but its expensive nature prevents it from charting.

1976 Jan [25] Carlos Santana guests with Bob Dylan's° Rolling Thunder Review at the "Night of the Hurricane II" concert at Houston Astrodome, a benefit show for Ruben "Hurricane" Carter. He duels on guitar with fellow guest Stephen Stills on *Black Queen*.

May LP *Amigos* hits US #10 (earning a gold disk, which *Borboletta* had failed to do), and reaches UK #21. Taken from the LP, *Let It Shine* makes US #77.

Dec The band plays London's Royal Albert Hall, the concert broadcast simultaneously by UK BBC TV and stereo radio.

1977 Feb LP *Festival* makes both US and UK #27, and is another US gold disk.

Apr The band plays with Joan Baez° and others, at a free concert for the inmates of Soledad Prison in Cal., organized by the Bread and Roses charitable foundation.

Nov A revival of The Zombies'° 1964 hit *She's Not There* becomes the group's biggest UK hit at #11.

Dec *She's Not There* makes US #27. Double live LP *Moonflower* hits US #10 (a further gold disk) and UK #7.

1978 Mar The band plays at California Jam II in Ontario, Cal., to 250,000 people, alongside Ted Nugent°, Aerosmith°, Heart°, and others.

Oct After a summer US tour, the band begins a European tour.

Dec LP *Inner Secrets* makes US #27 (another gold disk) and UK #17. Taken from it, a revival of Buddy Holly's° *Well All Right* peaks at US #69 and UK #53.

1979 Feb Also from LP *Inner Secrets*, a revival of The Classics IV's° *Stormy* makes US #32.

Apr Carlos Santana's instrumental solo LP *Oneness/Silver Dreams – Golden Reality*, half studio cuts and half live recording from Osaka, Japan, peaks at UK #55.

May *One Chain (Don't Make No Prison)*, extracted from LP *Inner Secrets* (and a 1974 middling US hit for The Four Tops°), makes US #59.

Nov LP *Marathon* reaches US #25 and UK #28.

1980 Feb *You Know That I Love You*, taken from LP *Marathon*, makes US #35.

Mar *All I Ever Wanted*, also from the LP, peaks at US #57.

Sept Another Carlos Santana instrumental solo double LP, *The Swing Of Delight* (with guest appearances by jazzmen Herbie Hancock, Wayne Shorter and Ron Carter), makes US #74.

1981 Apr LP *Zebop!* reaches UK #33.

June LP *Zebop!* hits US #9 and earns the band a gold disk.

July *Winning*, a Russ Ballard song extracted from LP *Zebop!*, reaches US #17.

Aug Also from the LP, *The Sensitive Kind* makes US #56.

1982 Sept [3] The band plays the US Festival in San Bernardino, Cal., to 400,000 people, along with Fleetwood Mac°, The Grateful Dead°, The Cars°, Jackson Browne°, and many others.

Oct *Hold On* reaches US #15. It is taken from LP *Shango*, which makes US #22 and UK #35.

Dec *Nowhere To Run*, also from LP *Shango*, makes US #66.

1983 Apr LP *Havana Moon*, a Carlos Santana solo with guest support from Willie Nelson°, Booker T. Jones, and The Fabulous Thunderbirds, reaches UK #84.

July The group tours Europe and UK, supporting Bob Dylan°.

1985 Apr LP *Beyond Appearances* peaks at US #50 and UK #58 while, taken from it, *Say It Again* makes US #46.

July [13] The band plays Live Aid in Philadelphia, Pa.

1986 July [20] Santana celebrates its 20th anniversary with a concert in San Francisco. All previous group members come on stage to make a 17-piece band.

Nov UK-compiled TV-promoted LP *Viva! Santana – The Very Best* peaks at UK #50.

1987 Apr LP *Freedom* reaches US #95. The band plays a lengthy Freedom World Tour, with founder member Rolie rejoining the current line-up of Carlos Santana (guitar), Chester Thompson (keyboards), Alfonso Johnson (bass), Tom Coster (synthesizers), Graham Lear (drums), Armando Peraza, Raul Rekow and Orestes Vilato (all percussion) and Buddy Miles (vocals).

Nov Carlos Santana's instrumental solo LP *Blues For Salvador* creeps to US #195.

1988 July Santana plays a 1988 summer tour with jazz saxophonist Wayne Shorter as a guest player.

LEO SAYER

1968 Sayer (b. Gerard Hugh Sayer, May 21, 1948, Shoreham-by-Sea, Sussex, UK), having studied at Worthing Art College and worked in London as a magazine illustrator, playing harmonica in folk clubs by night, returns to Sussex after a nervous breakdown, and works in a factory while starting to write songs.

1972 He joins rock group Patches, who record one-off single *Living In America*. Their agent/manager is Dave Courtney (an ex-drummer for Adam Faith°), who becomes Sayer's co-writer. They take their songs and the group to Faith, who signs them to a management contract and, when Patches split up, takes over Sayer as a soloist. Gerard becomes Leo from a nickname given him by Faith's wife Jackie; with his wide mane of thick curly hair, she calls him the "little (he is only 5'4" tall) lion".

1973 Mar Faith° and Courtney record Sayer at a studio owned by Roger Daltrey, ex-lead singer of The Who°. Daltrey's own debut LP, *Daltrey*, is almost entirely written by Sayer (lyrics) and Courtney (music). (It gives Daltrey his biggest solo hit, at UK #5, with extracted *Giving It All Away*.)

Aug Faith° has Sayer signed to a solo deal with Chrysalis, which releases his debut single *Why Is Everybody Going Home*, but it fails to chart. Sayer marries a librarian, Janice.

1974 Jan Second single *The Show Must Go On* hits UK #2 (Three Dog Night's° cover will hit US #4 in May), and is extensively promoted by Sayer on TV and live appearances (with Roxy Music°), on which he wears pierrot costume and make-up.

Feb Debut LP *Silver Bird* hits UK #2. He makes a promotional US tour, after which the pierrot costume is abandoned because of negative US reaction.

July *One Man Band* is belated follow-up and hits UK #6.

Oct *Long Tall Glasses* (originally written as *I Can Dance*, but amended in the studio after he has forgotten some of the original lyrics) hits UK #4. Second LP *Just A Boy* (the title comes from a line in *Giving It All Away*) hits UK #4.

1975 Feb He begins a 2-month US tour, where he is signed to Warner Bros., which releases LP *Just A Boy*.

May Sayer's US chart debut is LP *Just A Boy*, which reaches US #16, and *Long Tall Glasses (I Can Dance)* which hits US #9.

June *One Man Band* creeps to US #96.
Sept *Moonlighting* hits UK #2, behind Rod Stewart's° *Sailing*.
Oct LP *Another Year* hits UK #8. Courtney leaves as Sayer's producer and co-writer to work solo. He is replaced by ex-Supertramp° member Frank Farrell.
Nov LP *Another Year* stalls at US #125. Sayer has to cancel a follow-up US tour when he is hospitalized for a wisdom tooth operation.
1976 Nov *You Make Me Feel Like Dancing*, an R&B-styled song written by Sayer with Vini Poncia, and recorded in LA with new producer Richard Perry, hits UK #2. Sayer promotes it and his forthcoming LP with a tour of UK and Australia.
1977 Jan *You Make Me Feel Like Dancing* tops the US chart for a week, selling over a million copies.
Feb *When I Need You*, written by Albert Hammond and Carole Bayer Sager, tops the UK chart, while parent LP *Endless Flight* hits UK #4.
Apr Sayer contributes *I Am The Walrus* to the all-star *All This And World War II* LP/movie project, which features cover versions of Beatles° songs.
May *When I Need You* tops the US chart for a week, while *How Much Love* hits UK #10. Sayer plays a 56-city US tour, which grosses $2½ million.
June LP *Endless Flight* hits US #10, selling over a million copies to earn Sayer a platinum disk.
Aug *How Much Love* reaches US #17.
Oct *Thunder In My Heart* makes UK #22, while parent LP of the same title hits UK #8.
Nov *Thunder In My Heart* peaks at US #38, as the LP makes US #37.
1978 Jan *Easy To Love* reaches US #36.
Feb [23] *You Make Me Feel Like Dancing* wins Sayer and Vini Poncia a Grammy for R&B Song of 1977, at the 20th annual ceremony.
July Sayer hosts the "Midnight Special" show on US NBC TV.
Sept LP *Leo Sayer* reaches UK #15, but stalls at US #101. He begins a weekly UK series "Leo" on BBC TV.
Oct *I Can't Stop Lovin' You (Though I Try)* hits UK #6.
Nov A revival of Buddy Holly's° *Raining In My Heart* peaks at US #47.
Dec *Raining In My Heart* makes UK #21.
Dec [14] Sayer guests on the "Perry Como Christmas Show" on US TV.
1979 Apr Compilation LP *The Very Best Of Leo Sayer* tops the UK chart for 3 weeks.
Oct LP *Here* makes UK #44.
1980 Aug A revival of 1961 Bobby Vee° hit *More Than I Can Say*, produced by Alan Tarney, hits UK #2.
Sept LP *Living In A Fantasy* reaches UK #15.
Dec *More Than I Can Say* hits US #2.
1981 Mar *Living In A Fantasy* makes US #23, while LP of the same title reaches US #36.
1982 Apr *Have You Ever Been In Love* hits UK #10.
July *Heart (Stop Beating In Time)* makes UK #22.
Aug LP *World Record* reaches UK #30.
1983 Jan Sayer has another UK BBC TV series, "Leo Sayer".
Apr *Orchard Road* makes UK #16.
Oct *Till You Come Back To Me* peaks at UK #51.
Nov LP *Have You Ever Been In Love*, promoted by a TV campaign, reaches UK #15.
1984 May Sayer embarks on a 50-date 2-month UK tour.
1986 Feb A revival of *Unchained Melody*, included on the soundtrack of film *Car Trouble*, makes UK #54.
1988 July He plays a self-financed UK tour with no recording contract; and is reported as intending to release future recordings himself on an independent basis.
Nov His former manager Faith° pays Sayer a reported £650,000. Details are not revealed, but the payment appears to be in settlement of owed earnings and record royalties.

BOZ SCAGGS

1959 Scaggs (b. William Royce Scaggs, June 8, 1944, Oh., US), having grown up in Texas, meets Steve Miller° at school in Dallas and joins his band The Marksmen on vocals and tambourine. Miller teaches him the guitar.
1961 Scaggs and Miller are together at the University of Wisconsin, Madison, Wis., where they play in R&B/Motown covers group The Ardells, which becomes The Fabulous Night Train.
1963 He returns to Texas and forms R&B band The Wigs with John "Toad" Andrew on guitar, Bob Arthur on bass and George Rains on drums.
1964 The band quits college and travels to UK to find work, but fails to make an impression. As The Wigs split, Scaggs moves to Europe.
1965 He arrives in Stockholm, Sweden, where he records debut LP *Boz* for Polydor, released only in Sweden.
1965/67 Scaggs continues his world tour which reaches India before returning to US.
1967 Sept [1] On arrival back in San Francisco, Cal., he rejoins The Steve Miller° Band, replacing singer/guitarist James Cooke.
1968 Scaggs is featured on The Steve Miller° Band's two US chart LPs *Children Of The Future* (#134) and *Sailor* (#24), both recorded in UK with producer Glyn Johns. Following the sessions, he leaves the band due to musical differences with Miller.
1969 With the help of *Rolling Stone* editor Jann Wenner, Scaggs gains a solo deal with Atlantic, and records at Muscle Shoals studios in Alabama with top session players, including Duane Allman.
Aug LP *Boz Scaggs*, produced by Wenner, is released to critical acclaim, but few sales. He is dropped by Atlantic.
1970 After several months in the Southern states, Scaggs moves back to the West Coast and forms The Boz Scaggs Band, which signs to CBS/Columbia at the end of the year.
1971 May Debut Columbia LP *Moments* reaches US #124, while extracted *We Were Always Sweethearts* makes US #61.
July *Near You*, also from the LP, stalls at US #96.
Dec LP *Boz Scaggs And Band*, recorded in London, falters at US #198.
1972 Oct *Dinah Flo* peaks at US #86, while parent LP *My Time* reaches US #138. Scaggs tours US with guest band members Steve Miller° and George Rains.
Dec He forms a new band, with Les Dudek (guitar), Tom Rutley (bass), Jimmy Young (keyboards), Rick Schlosser (drums) and Jack Schroer (sax).
1974 Apr [27] Scaggs plays the Cherry Blossom Music Festival in Richmond, Va., alongside The Steve Miller° Band.
May LP *Slow Dancer* reaches US #81.
July Capitalizing on Scaggs' recent success, Atlantic reissues his only LP for the label, *Boz Scaggs*. It reaches US #171.
1976 Apr [16] When he attempts to see Bobby Bland backstage after a show at Antone's club in Austin, Texas, Scaggs is hurled into the street by bouncers.
May *It's Over*, from his next LP, reaches US #38.
Sept LP *Silk Degrees*, produced by Joe Wissert and arranged by David Paich, is Scaggs' most successful LP. It hits US #2, spending 115 weeks on chart and selling over a million copies in US, to earn a platinum disk. Back-up session players include future members of Toto°.
Oct *Lowdown*, from the LP, hits US #3 and is a million-seller.
Nov *Lowdown* is Scaggs' UK chart debut, at #28. Third LP extract *What Can I Say?* reaches US #42.
1977 Feb [19] At the 19th Grammy awards, Scaggs' *Lowdown* is named Best R&B Song of 1976.
Mar *What Can I Say?* hits UK #10.
May Fourth single from the LP, *Lido Shuffle*, makes US #11 and UK #13.
July LP *Silk Degrees* finally makes UK #20.
July [13] A Scaggs concert at New York's Avery Fisher Hall is concluded midway by a power cut in the city.
Aug Rita Coolidge's cover of *We're All Alone*, a Scaggs song from LP *Silk Degrees*, hits US #7 and UK #6, her biggest solo single.
Nov *Hard Times* makes US #58.
Dec LP *Down Two Then Left* makes US #11 (his second platinum LP) and UK #55. (The LP title was originally announced as *Still Falling For You*.)
1978 Jan *Hollywood* makes US #49 and UK #33, and is his last UK hit single.
1979 June [3] Scaggs and Rickie Lee Jones° join Bruce Springsteen° and The E. Street Band for a jam session on stage at The Whiskey A-Go-Go in LA, at the wedding reception of Sprinsgsteen's lighting man Mark Brickman.
1980 May *Breakdown Dead Ahead* climbs to US #15.
June LP *Middle Man* hits US #8 (his third consecutive platinum LP) and UK #52.
Aug *Jo Jo*, taken from LP *Middle Man*, makes US #17.
Oct *Look What You've Done To Me* peaks at US #14.
1981 Feb Compilation LP *Hits*, dominated by tracks from LP *Silk Degrees*, reaches US #24. Scaggs' last US chart single is *Miss Sun*, a duet with Lisa Dal Bello, which makes US #14.
1982 May [28] Scaggs plays a benefit concert for the Vietnam Veterans

BOZ SCAGGS *cont.*

Project at Moscone Center, San Francisco, with Jefferson Starship° and The Grateful Dead°.

1983/87 Scaggs retires from the music scene. He opens his own Southern-style restaurant in San Francisco.

1988 He is persuaded by CBS/Columbia to return to the studio to record a new LP.

Apr Scaggs appears at the Montreux Pop Festival in Switzerland.

July LP *Other Roads* is released. The set includes three songs co-written with singer/poet Jim Carroll and features assistance from members of Toto°. It climbs to US #47, but fails in UK. From it, *Heart Of Mine* climbs to US #35. Scaggs announces plans to open a jazz/blues club in San Francisco.

SCRITTI POLITTI

Green Gartside (vocals)
Nial Jinks (bass)
Tom Morley (Linn drums)

1977 The group is formed by Gartside (b. Green Strohmeyer-Gartside, June 22, 1956, Cardiff, Wales, UK), an ex-schoolmate of Soft Cell's° Marc Almond, Jinks and Morley, all friends at Leeds art school, after Green is inspired by The Sex Pistols'° concert in Leeds.

1978 The group, with temporary members including Matthew Kay, relocates to London and begins low-key gigging at mainly punk venues.

1979 The band supports Joy Divison° and Gang of Four on tour, but suffers a setback when Green collapses with a heart complaint.

Oct EP *Four 'A' Sides* is released on Scritti Politti's own St. Pancras label and features a photocopied sleeve, but goes unnoticed.

Nov Further EP *John Peel Session* is released.

1980 Green spends the year convalescing at home with his parents and begins writing new songs, now heavily influenced by R&B music. Meanwhile Jinks leaves the band.

1981 The group's first new track, *The Sweetest Girl*, appears on *New Musical Express* music newspaper cassette.

Nov Rough Trade releases it and it reaches UK #64. Jinks rejoins shortly afterwards.

1982 May *Faithless* makes UK #56 and tops UK independent chart.

Aug Double A-side *Asylums In Jerusalem/Jacques Derrida*, with guest Robert Wyatt on keyboards, is the group's first UK top 50 entry at #43.

Sept Debut LP *Songs To Remember*, produced by Adam Kidron, reaches UK #12, and again tops UK independent chart.

Nov Morley quits.

1983 Green signs to Virgin Records and moves to New York to work on an LP with new members David Gamson (keyboards) and Fred Maher (drums) and producer Arif Mardin.

1984 Apr *Wood Beez (Pray Like Aretha Franklin)* hits UK #10.

July *Absolute* reaches UK #17.

Nov *Hypnotise* makes UK #68.

1985 May *The Word Girl* hits UK #6.

June Mardin-produced LP *Cupid And Psyche '85*, containing the first five Virgin singles, hits UK #5.

Sept *The Perfect Way* is the group's first US hit at #11. (Miles Davis° will later cover it.)

1986 Feb Madness'° version of *The Sweetest Girl* reaches UK #35.

Aug Chaka Khan° makes US #53 and UK #52 with Green-penned *Love Of A Lifetime*.

Sept Green and Gamson write the title cut for Al Jarreau's° LP *L Is For Lover*.

1987 Aug Scritti Politti contributes a song for Madonna's° *Who's That Girl* soundtrack.

1988 Mar The group takes part in the annual Montreux pop festival in Switzerland.

May *Oh Patti (Don't Feel Sorry For Loverboy)*, with Miles Davis° guesting on trumpet, reaches UK #13.

June LP *Provision*, recorded in New York, hits UK #8 and US #113. It has taken 3 years to complete, delayed by Green's need always to use the latest state-of-the-art studio technology.

July *First Boy In This Town (Lovesick)* makes UK #63.

Aug *Boom! There She Was* peaks at US #53.

Oct Maher produces Information Society's US #3 *What's On Your Mind (Pure Energy)*, having also produced Marlon Jackson's debut LP.

Nov *Boom! There She Was* climbs to UK #55 as *Oh Patti* is released in US.

SEALS & CROFTS

Jim Seals (vocals, guitar, sax and violin)
Dash Crofts (vocals, guitar, mandolin)

1958 Both Seals (b. Oct.17, 1941, Sidney, Tex., US) and Crofts (b. Aug.14, 1940, Cisco, Tex., US) are playing guitar and drums respectively in the backing group of rock singer/pianist Dean Beard (and have cut some unsuccessful singles with him for Edmoral and Atlantic), when Beard is invited to join The Champs° (who have had a million-selling rock instrumental with *Tequila* earlier in the year) and they join with him, relocating from Texas to LA.

1965 They both leave the fragmenting Champs°; Seals staying in Cal. to write songs and play sessions and Crofts returns to Tex.

1966 Seals teams with guitarist Louie Shelton, bassist Joseph Bogan and, in need of a drummer, persuades Crofts back to LA. This quartet becomes The Dawnbreakers, which is augmented by the three Day sisters as vocalists. (Crofts marries one of them, Billie Lee Day.)

1969 Following the example of group manager Marcia Day, The Dawnbreakers are converted to the Baha'i faith (founded by Persian prophet Baha'u'llah in the 19th Century). Seals marries Ruby Anderson, a member of the community living with the group at its manager's LA home.

1970 The Dawnbreakers split, with Shelton turning to production and Bogan to studio engineering. With their help, Seals and Crofts remain together as a duo, and record an eponymous debut LP for Talent Associates label. It does not chart, but their extensive live work gains a following.

Nov LP *Down Home*, their second and last on Talent Associates, makes US #122, and attracts Warner Bros., which signs them.

1972 Jan Warner debut LP *Year Of Sunday*, produced by Shelton, and augmenting the duo's harmony vocal blend with horn and string accompaniment, reaches US #133.

Nov *Summer Breeze* (later revived by The Isley Brothers°) is their first singles chart entry, hitting US #6. It is taken from the LP of the same title, which hits US #7 and earns a gold disk. Crofts and his wife have a daughter.

Dec Seals and his wife Ruby have a son.

1973 Mar *Hummingbird*, with lyrics strongly influenced by Baha'i, reaches US #20.

June LP *Diamond Girl* hits US #4, earning a second gold disk.

July The LP's extracted title song *Diamond Girl* (jointly written in tribute to their wives, both new mothers) hits US #6.

Nov *We May Never Pass This Way (Again)* makes US #21.

1974 Apr LP *Unborn Child* reaches US #14, while the title track peaks at US #66.

June *King Of Nothing*, from LP *Unborn Child* makes US #60. The duo tours constantly, punctuating its middle of the road harmony material on stage with mandolin features by Crofts, and sax pieces and dance reels on the violin by Seals.

Sept Warner acquires release rights to the duo's first two LPs from Talent Associates, and reissues them as double LP *Seals And Crofts I And II*, which peaks at US #86.

1975 May LP *I'll Play For You* makes US #30, earning the duo's fourth gold disk.

June Extracted title track *I'll Play For You* reaches US #18.

Dec LP *Seals And Crofts' Greatest Hits*, a compilation of hit singles to date, reaches US #11 and earns another gold disk.

1976 July *Get Closer*, featuring Carolyn Willis (from hitmaking group The Honey Cone), hits US #6.

Sept LP *Get Closer* makes US #37, earning another gold disk.

Dec *Baby, I'll Give It To You*, from LP *Get Closer*, makes US #58.

1977 Jan LP *Sudan Village* peaks at US #73.

Feb [9] Seals & Crofts take part in US ABC-TV's "American Bandstand's 25th Anniversary Special".

Nov *My Fair Share*, from film *One on One*, makes US #28, while Seals/Crofts-composed and performed soundtrack LP from the movie peaks at US #118.

1978 The 32-track Dawnbreaker Studios is financed by Seals & Crofts' earnings, and is built to the duo's specifications at the HQ of manager Marcia Day's management company Day Five Productions, in San Fernando Valley, Cal. (The Baha'i religious community is also based there.)

June LP *Takin' It Easy*, the first recorded at Dawnbreaker Studios, makes US #78 and is the duo's last LP to chart, while *You're The Love*, taken from it, reaches US #18.

Sept The title song from *Takin' It Easy* stalls at US #79 (and is the duo's last chart entry).

Sept [9] Drama series "The Paper Chase", a spin-off from the film of the same title, first airs on US CBS TV, with Seals & Crofts performing theme song *The First Years*. (Seals & Crofts will quit the music business to devote their full-time efforts to the Baha'i community, although rumors will, from time to time, suggest a reunion.)

THE SEARCHERS

Mike Pender (vocals and lead guitar)
John McNally (vocals and rhythm guitar)
Tony Jackson (vocals and bass)
Chris Curtis (vocals and drums)

1961 McNally (b. Aug.30, 1941, Liverpool, UK) and Pender (b. Mike Prendergast, Mar.3, 1942, Liverpool) form an instrumental duo and perform at their local pub in Kirkdale, Liverpool, naming themselves The Searchers after a John Wayne movie. They meet Jackson (b. July 16, 1940, Liverpool) and drummer Norman McGarry, and the group begins regular work backing singer Johnny Sandon.

1962 Mar Sandon leaves to front The Remo Four, and they continue as a quartet, perfecting their harmony vocal style. Regularly playing clubs like the Cavern, the Casbah, and The Hot Spot, they build a reputation at The Iron Door, whose owner becomes their manager.

Sept McGarry leaves to replace Ringo Starr° in Rory Storme & The Hurricanes, and Curtis (b. Chris Crummy, Aug.26, 1941, Oldham, UK) joins on drums. While playing clubs in Hamburg, West Germany, several tracks are recorded live at the Star Club by Philips Records.

1963 May Having heard a demo by the group, Pye Records A&R man Tony Hatch views them in action at The Iron Door and signs them to Pye.

Aug Debut single, reviving The Drifters'° *Sweets For My Sweet*, tops the UK chart for 3 weeks, deposing Elvis Presley's° *Devil In Disguise*.

Aug [31] The group appears at B-Day, a 13-hour outdoor rock festival in Liverpool, with The Hollies°, Billy J. Kramer and The Dakotas° and more than 20 other bands.

Sept LP *Meet The Searchers* hits UK #2.

Oct *Ain't Gonna Kiss Ya*, a 4-track EP from which the title song receives wide UK airplay, reaches UK #12. *Sugar And Spice* hits UK #3, while *Sweet Nothin's*, from the live Hamburg recordings released on Philips, makes UK #48.

Nov LP *Sugar And Spice* hits UK #5.

1964 Jan [24] The group starts its own 15-minute weekly show on Radio Luxembourg.

Feb *Needles And Pins*, a cover of Jackie DeShannon's minor US hit, written by Jack Nitzsche and Sonny Bono, tops the UK chart for 3 weeks. It is the group's biggest hit, with total UK sales of over 850,000.

Apr *Needles And Pins* reaches US #13 (taking sales over a million), and The Searchers guest on US TV's "Ed Sullivan Show".

Apr [26] The group appears in *New Musical Express* Poll Winners concert at Wembley, UK, with Cliff Richard°, The Beatles° and others.

May *Don't Throw Your Love Away*, a revival of a Shirelles° song, is the group's third UK #1. *(Ain't That) Just Like Me* reaches US #61 and LP *Meet The Searchers – Needles And Pins* is the first US LP chartmaker at #22.

June LP *It's The Searchers* hits UK #4.

July *Don't Throw Your Love Away* peaks at US #16. Live LP *Hear! Hear!*, a compilation of early tracks recorded in Hamburg, makes US #120.

Aug *Some Day We're Gonna Love Again*, a cover of a Barbara Lewis track, reaches UK #11. Jackson departs for a solo career, signing to CBS, and is replaced by Frank Allen (b. Dec.14, 1943, Hayes, Middx., UK), ex-Cliff Bennett's° Rebel Rousers.

Sept *Some Day We're Gonna Love Again* makes US #34.

Oct *When You Walk In The Room*, another Jackie DeShannon cover, hits UK #3, while LP *This Is Us* reaches US #97.

Nov *When You Walk In The Room* reaches US #35.

Dec *What Have They Done To The Rain?*, an anti-nuclear protest song written by Malvina Reynolds, highlights the group's softer, folk-influenced side, normally restricted to LP tracks (and influential on many mid-1960s folk-rock groups). It reaches UK #13.

1965 Jan A revival of The Clovers' *Love Potion #9*, only released in UK as an LP track, hits US #3 and is a million-seller.

Feb *What Have They Done To The Rain?* reaches US #29.

Mar *Goodbye My Love* hits UK #4.

Apr *Bumble Bee*, a revival of a LaVern Baker hit, is a US-only release (though it finds UK success as leading track on an EP) and reaches US #21. The band plays *New Musical Express* Poll Winners Concert at The Empire Pool, Wembley. LP *Sounds Like The Searchers* hits UK #8 (and is the group's last UK chart LP). LP *The New Searchers LP* makes US #112.

May *Goodbye My Lover Goodbye* (a US re-titling, for copyright reasons, of *Goodbye My Love*), peaks at US #52.

July *He's Got No Love* makes UK #12.

Aug *He's Got No Love* reaches US #79.

Oct *When I Get Home* peaks at UK #35. In US, LP *The Searchers No.4* reaches #149.

Dec A harder folk-rock style on P.F. Sloan's *Take Me For What I'm Worth* makes UK #20.

1966 Mar *Take Me For What I'm Worth* reaches US #76.

Apr Curtis leaves and is replaced on drums by John Blunt.

May A cover of The Rolling Stones'° *Take It Or Leave It* makes UK #31.

Oct *Have You Ever Loved Somebody?* reaches UK #48 (while Paul And Barry Ryan's version makes #49). (It will be the group's last UK chart single.)

Dec *Have You Ever Loved Somebody?* peaks at US #94.

1968 The group leaves Pye for Liberty for two singles, then joins RCA.

1969 Dec Blunt is replaced on drums by Billy Adamson.

1971 Sept *Desdemona* reaches US #94.

1972 LP *Second Take* is released on RCA.

1973 June The group tours US in the "British Re-Invasion Show", with Wayne Fontana°, Herman's Hermits° and Gerry & The Pacemakers°.

1979 The group signs to Sire Records and, given a free recording hand, uses material from a variety of songwriters such as Tom Petty°.

1980 Mar LP *The Searchers* on Sire reaches US #191.

1981 LP *Play For Today* (US title: *Love's Melodies*) is released, but fails to chart.

Nov [23] The group performs at The Royal Variety show with Adam and The Ants°, Lonnie Donegan° and Cliff Richard° reunited with The Shadows°.

1985 Dec [23] Pender plays his last gig with the group, before leaving to form his own touring band, Mike Pender's Searchers. He is replaced by Spencer James.

1987 May The group begins a successful UK "Solid 60s Silver" tour with Gerry & The Pacemakers° and Peter Sarstedt. (It will run until June.) PRT reissues all the Pye material on LP and CD in UK.

1988 June The Searchers take action against Mike Pender's use of The Searchers name.

NEIL SEDAKA

1952 Sedaka (b. Mar.13, 1939, Brooklyn, N.Y., US), a piano student since age 9, begins to write songs with his 16-year-old lyricist neighbor and Lincoln High School colleague Howard Greenfield, their first composition being *My Life's Devotion*.

1955 Impressed by The Penguins' hit *Earth Angel*, Sedaka and Greenfield write their first semi-rock'n'roll song, doo-wop ballad *Mr. Moon*, which Sedaka performs with great success at a school talent show. He joins high school vocal group, The Tokens°, with Hank Medress (who will later co-found another group of that name and have several hits in the 1960s). Also a school colleague and romantic attachment at this time is Carol Klein, who later becomes hit singer/songwriter Carole King°.

1957 Sedaka wins a piano scholarship to New York's Juilliard School of Music (with the recommendation of Arthur Rubinstein, who judged him the winner of a Lincoln High School piano competition a few months earlier). Studying serious music does not affect his pop interests and he and Greenfield continue to write regularly, while Sedaka records one-off single *Fly, Don't Fly On Me* for Philadelphia-based Legion label, which flops.

1958 Songwriters Doc Pomus and Mort Shuman put Sedaka and Greenfield in contact with Don Kirshner and Al Nevins, publishers at Aldon Music in Broadway's Brill Building in New York, who sign them to an exclusive contract and start placing their songs with recording acts. The first to be recorded is *Passing Time*, cut by Atlantic all-girl group The Cookies.

Feb Sedaka releases his own second single *Laura Lee* on Decca, but still with no success.

NEIL SEDAKA *cont.*

Sept Connie Francis° records Sedaka/Greenfield composition *Stupid Cupid* (originally written for The Shepherd Sisters), reaching US #14 and topping the UK chart.

Dec [1] After Nevins has played Sedaka's demo of *The Diary* to Steve Scholes of RCA, he signs Sedaka to RCA as a recording artist.

1959 Feb *The Diary*, Sedaka's first RCA single, climbs to US #14.

May Follow-up *I Go Ape*, a wild rocker, is his UK chart debut, hitting #9. It peaks at US #42 following a ban by several US radio stations. Sedaka tours UK for the first time, to promote the single.

June Busy with session work, as well as writing and recording (and studying at Juilliard), Sedaka plays piano on Bobby Darin's° US and UK chart-topper *Dream Lover*. His own single *Crying My Heart Out For You* flops.

Dec *Oh! Carol*, a public display of affection for Carol Klein (to which she responds with little-heard *Oh Neil*), hits US #9 and UK #3. His debut LP *Rock With Sedaka* is released, but does not chart.

1960 May *Stairway To Heaven* hits US #9 and UK #8.

Sept Ballad *You Mean Everything To Me* reaches US #17 and UK #45, while uptempo B-side *Run Samson Run* makes US #28.

1961 Feb *Calendar Girl* hits US #4 and UK #8.

June *Little Devil* reaches US #11 and hits UK #9.

Oct *Sweet Little You* peaks at US #59, but fails to chart in UK.

Dec *Happy Birthday Sweet Sixteen*, one of Sedaka and Greenfield's most enduring songs, hits US #6.

1962 Feb *Happy Birthday Sweet Sixteen* hits UK #3.

May March-tempo *King Of Clowns* reaches US #45 and UK #23.

Aug Sedaka has his first US chart-topper and first million-seller with *Breaking Up Is Hard To Do*, which holds US #1 for 2 weeks, and hits UK #7. The distinctive gibberish chorus line was conceived after the rest of the song, coming in a flash of inspiration during a sleepless night. Sedaka is touring UK while the single is on the charts.

Nov *Next Door To An Angel*, almost a clone of *Breaking Up*, hits US #5 and reaches UK #29, where soundalike follow-ups are generally ill-regarded.

1963 Jan Compilation LP *Neil Sedaka Sings His Greatest Hits*, rounding up major singles from *Oh Carol* to *Next Door To An Angel*, makes US #55.

Mar *Alice In Wonderland* reaches US #17, but fails in UK (where the Merseybeat boom is just stirring on chart and the subsequent "British Invasion" will be instrumental in Sedaka's decision to retire from recording during the second half of the 60s).

May *Let's Go Steady Again* makes US #26 and UK #42.

Aug *The Dreamer* peaks at US #47 but fails in UK.

Nov Skeeter Davis, a million-seller earlier in the year with *The End Of The World*, hits US #7 with Sedaka's *I Can't Stay Mad At You*.

Dec *Bad Girl* makes US #33, with no UK success.

1964 Aug *Sunny* stalls at US #86.

1965 Oct *The World Through A Tear* makes US #76.

1966 Feb *The Answer To My Prayer* proves anything but, ending Sedaka's run of hits on RCA. Aware that he is now out of fashion with pop mainstream, Sedaka gives up recording and live performances at around the same time. He and Greenfield are contracted as staff writers, via Kirshner, for Screen Gems Music.

1968 Sept He signs to Screen Gems' label SGC Records in US, releasing two unsuccessful singles. Meanwhile, his song *Workin' On A Groovy Thing* takes Patti Drew to US #62.

1969 Aug The 5th Dimension's° revival of *Workin' On A Groovy Thing* reaches US #20.

1970 May The 5th Dimension's° version of Sedaka/Greenfield's *Puppet Man* makes US #24.

1971 June Tom Jones° revives *Puppet Man*, taking it to US #26 and UK #50. Sedaka visits UK for the first time in several years, for a 4-month tour, mostly of Northern clubs, where his act proves immensely popular.

1972 Jan Tony Christie's version of Sedaka/Greenfield's *Is This The Way To Amarillo* reaches UK #18. Sedaka signs to Kirshner's new eponymous label and, inspired by the success of friend Carole King's° LP *Tapestry*, he records LP *Emergence*, credited simply as Sedaka. *I'm A Song (Sing Me)* and *Superbird* from the LP are given strong airplay in UK and another lengthy tour follows, including a major date at London's Royal Albert Hall. Sedaka moves his wife Reba and children Dara and Marc to UK, and sets up a new working base from a flat in Mayfair, London. This move splits him from Greenfield and he begins to write with new lyricist, Phil Cody.

June He records self-produced LP *Solitaire* for Kirshner Records at Strawberry Studios, Stockport, UK, with the four musicians who will shortly be known as 10cc°. Eric Stewart engineers the sessions, while Lol Creme, Kevin Godley and Graham Gouldman all back Sedaka.

Nov *Beautiful You* reaches UK #43, but LP *Solitaire*, from which it is taken, does not chart. Sedaka appears on UK TV's "Top of the Pops".

Dec A UK reissue of *Oh! Carol* (on a maxi-single with *Breaking Up Is Hard To Do* and *Little Devil*) reaches UK #19.

1973 Mar *That's When The Music Takes Me*, also from LP *Solitaire*, reaches UK #18.

June *Standing On The Inside*, his first release under a new UK and European recording deal with MGM Records, reaches UK #26.

Sept It is taken from LP *The Tra-La Days Are Over*, on MGM, again recorded at Strawberry Studios with 10cc°. Also extracted as a UK single is *Our Last Song Together*, written as a swan song with Greenfield, which makes UK #31.

1974 Feb *A Little Loving*, released on Polydor (which has now absorbed subsidiary MGM label), reaches UK #34. Meanwhile, Andy Williams' cover of *Solitaire* hits UK #4.

July Sedaka/Cody composition *Laughter In The Rain* climbs to UK #15, while LP of the same title (this time recorded in LA with producer Robert Appere and sessioneers including David Foster, Danny Korthchmar and Russ Kunkel) makes UK #17.

Aug At a party in the Sedakas' London flat to celebrate the UK success of *Laughter In The Rain*, Sedaka discusses with guest Elton John° his current lack of a US recording contract. (His recent UK successes have not been released in US.) John, a long-time fan, offers a deal to issue the Polydor recordings in North America on his own Rocket label.

Nov Live LP *Live At The Royal Festival Hall*, recorded with the Royal Philharmonic Orchestra, peaks at UK #48.

1975 Feb Released on Rocket, *Laughter In The Rain* tops the US chart for a week, and gives Sedaka his second million-selling single, more than 12 years after the first. It is also included on US LP *Sedaka's Back*, a compilation from the last three UK LPs, which makes US #23 and earns a gold disk for a half million US sales.

Mar LP *Overnight Success* reaches UK #31, while LP *Neil Sedaka Sings His Greatest Hits*, a reissue of the 1963 compilation, makes US #161. Sedaka plays Las Vegas, opening for The Carpenters° at the Riviera Hotel, but is asked to leave the show halfway through the 2-week engagement when his act starts getting a better response. (The Riviera will invite him back as a headliner.)

Apr *The Queen Of 1964*, from LP *Overnight Success*, peaks at UK #35, and is Sedaka's final UK hit single.

May *The Immigrant*, from LP *Laughter In The Rain* which is dedicated to John Lennon° (currently fighting US authorities to stay in US), reaches US #22.

June The Captain & Tennille's° cover of *Love Will Keep Us Together*, originally from LP *The Tra-La Days Are Over*, tops the US chart for 4 weeks and reaches UK #32.

Aug A belated US release of *That's When The Music Takes Me* climbs to US #27.

Sept Uptempo *Bad Blood*, on which Sedaka is joined by Elton John° on backing vocals, tops the US chart for 3 weeks, and is his biggest-selling single, topping 1.4 million in US. (It is deposed by John's *Island Girl*.)

Nov LP *The Hungry Years*, a revised version of *Overnight Success*, and including *Bad Blood*, reaches US #16 and earns a second gold LP.

Dec A re-recording of *Breaking Up Is Hard To Do*, in a slow ballad format, hits US #8 (the only former US #1 to return to the top 10 in a different version by the same artist).

1976 May *Love In The Shadows* makes US #16.

June LP *Steppin' Out* climbs to US #26.

July 18-track compilation LP *Laughter And Tears: The Best Of Neil Sedaka Today*, promoted on TV, hits UK #2. (It will be his last UK chart LP.) Meanwhile, the title song from *Steppin' Out* (with Elton John° on backing vocals) makes US #36.

Oct His last hit single on Rocket is *You Gotta Make Your Own Sunshine*, which reaches US #53 as a reissue on RCA of Kirshner LP *Solitaire* peaks at US #159.

1977 June Sedaka signs a new recording deal with Elektra, debuting with a new version of *(Is This The Way To) Amarillo*, which makes US

#44. Debut Elektra LP *A Song* reaches US #59.

Nov On Rocket, compilation LP *Neil Sedaka's Greatest Hits*, anthologizing the 70s material, peaks at US #143.

1980 June A duet with his daughter Dara, *Should've Never Let You Go*, reaches US #19, and is his last US singles chart entry. It is taken from LP *In The Pocket*, which peaks at US #135.

1984 He signs a new deal with MCA/Curb Records, and releases LP *Come See About Me*, which does not chart.

1987 Sedaka's autobiography, *Laughter in the Rain* is published.

BOB SEGER

1964 Seger (b. May 6, 1945, Dearborn, Mich., US), who has led his own rock trio, The Decibels, in high school, then played full-time in Ann Arbor, Mich., with The Town Criers, joins Doug Brown & The Omens (the city's leading group) on keyboards. He begins to write songs with vocalist Brown, and they record several demos, paid for by local-based hitmaker Del Shannon°, who becomes their publisher.

1966 Mar The Omens, under the pseudonym of The Beach Bums, record *The Ballad Of The Yellow Beret* (a parody of Barry Sadler's US chart-topper *Ballad Of The Green Berets*) on Are You Kidding Me? label. The gimmick is a favorite with local college students, but is withdrawn when Sadler threatens legal action.

May The result of a $1,200 recording session is *East Side Story*, Seger's first release under his own name, billed as Bob Seger & The Last Heard (the band being the remnants of The Omens). It is a sizeable hit in Detroit on Hideout Records (selling 50,000 copies), and is picked up for national distribution by Cameo – as is follow-up *Persecution Smith*.

Dec Cameo buys out his contract and issues seasonal rocker *Sock It To Me, Santa*.

1967 Seger & The Last Heard continue to record for Cameo, cutting *Vagrant Winter* and *Heavy Music Parts 1 & 2*, the latter being a major hit in Detroit but prevented from nationwide success by the sudden demise of Cameo. Brown splits from Seger to pursue his own music, while Punch Andrews, who has produced *Heavy Music*, becomes Seger's manager.

1968 Jan Seger re-forms his band as The Bob Seger System and signs to Capitol Records. First Capitol single, *2 + 2 = ?*, an anti-war heavy rocker, only sells in Michigan.

1969 Feb *Ramblin' Gamblin' Man* becomes Seger's US chart success, reaching #17, while debut LP, titled after the single, makes US #62.

May *Ivory* peaks at US #97.

1970 Apr After completing work on second LP, *Noah*, Seger breaks up The System (which has been increasingly prone to internal strife), and announces that he is quitting music for a year to return to college. (He will enroll, but not stay.) The LP does not chart but, from it, *Lucifer* peaks at US #84.

Nov LP *Mongrel*, recorded after a shorter-than-expected layoff, with new musicians, climbs to US #171.

1971 Without a band, Seger records solo, acoustic, singer/songwriter-style LP *Brand New Morning*, which fails to sell. He experiments with a new band named STK, including Oklahoma duo Dave Teegarden and Skip "Van Winkle" Knape. (STK is not successful, but its members will form the core of Seger's next stage group.)

Nov *Looking Back* makes US #96, after which Seger leaves Capitol. He and Andrews form Palladium Records, which is signed to Warner/Reprise.

1972 Aug A cover version of Tim Hardin's *If I Were A Carpenter* makes US #76. It is taken from first Palladium LP *Smokin' O.P.'s* ("O.P.'s" refers to smoking other people's cigarettes), which makes US #180 and includes a remake of *Heavy Music*.

1973 Mar LP *Back In '72*, part-recorded at Muscle Shoals studios, Ala., with guests including J.J. Cale°, stalls at US #188.

1974 Aug *Get Out Of Denver* reaches US #80. A Chuck Berry° soundalike, (later revived by UK acts Dave Edmunds° and Eddie & The Hot Rods), it is taken from LP *Seven/Contrasts*, which fails to chart.

1975 May Seger re-signs to Capitol after Warner/Reprise turns down LP *Beautiful Loser*. On Capitol, it reaches US #131.

Oct *Katmandu*, from LP *Beautiful Loser*, makes US #43 (and is a top 10 hit in Detroit). Seger tours US with newly-formed backing group, The Silver Bullet Band, featuring Drew Abbott (guitar), Robyn Robbins (keyboards), Alto Reed (saxophones), Chris Campbell (bass) and Charlie Allen Martin (drums). (The band membership will change many times during subsequent years, with bassist Campbell the only enduring member. First to go will be drummer Martin, after being injured in a car accident, replaced by Teegarden, who played in STK with Seger.)

1976 Apr First LP to credit The Silver Bullet Band is double live LP *Live Bullet* recorded on stage at Cobo Hall, Detroit, during the previous year's tour. It reaches US #34, and will sell over a million copies in a 140-week chart stay.

June *Nutbush City Limits*, a live cover of Ike and Tina Turner's° hit, taken from the double LP, reaches US #69.

1977 Jan [23] Seger plays in Tampa, Fla, supported by The Patti Smith° Group, but loses his support star for the remainder of the tour when Smith falls off stage and is badly injured.

Mar LP *Night Moves*, featuring The Silver Bullet Band on one side and The Muscle Shoals Rhythm Section on the flip, hits US #8, earning Seger's second consecutive platinum disk. The title track is extracted and gives Seger his first top 10 single, hitting US #4.

May *Mainstreet*, also from LP *Night Moves*, reaches US #24.

Aug Another track from the LP, *Rock 'N' Roll Never Forgets* climbs to US #41.

1978 June A year in the making, LP *Stranger In Town* is released, hitting US #4, and is his third million-selling LP, staying on US chart for over 2 years. It also marks Seger's UK chart debut at #31. The LP uses both The Silver Bullet Band and The Muscle Shoals Rhythm Section, and has guest appearances by The Eagles'° vocalist Glenn Frey (whom Seger has known since youth in Detroit) and Bill Payne of Little Feat°.

July *Still The Same*, first single from the LP, hits US #4.

Oct *Hollywood Nights*, also from LP *Stranger In Town*, reaches US #12, and is his first UK chart single, peaking at #42.

1979 Jan From the LP, ballad *We've Got Tonight* is third extracted single, reaching US #13.

Feb *We've Got Tonight* makes UK #41.

May Final single from the LP, *Old Time Rock'n'Roll*, peaks at US #28.

1980 Mar [19] A US tour to promote forthcoming LP *Against The Wind* opens in Fayetteville, N.C.

May LP *Against The Wind*, produced by Bill Szymczyk, is the product of almost 2 years' work. Another million-seller, it tops the US chart for 6 weeks during a 110-week chart stay. In UK, it makes #26. *Fire Lake*, the first extracted single. hits US #6.

June The title song from the LP, *Against The Wind*, hits US #5.

Oct Third single from the LP, *You'll Accomp'ny Me* reaches US #14.

Oct [3] During a concert by Bruce Springsteen° in Ann Arbor, Seger joins him on stage for a duet on *Thunder Road*.

Dec *The Horizontal Bop*, final extract from LP *Against The Wind*, climbs to US #42.

1981 Oct A second double live LP, *Nine Tonight*, recorded in Boston and Detroit, hits US #3 and UK #24. From it, a live version of *Hollywood Nights* makes US #49.

Nov Also from the live LP, *Tryin' To Live My Life Without You* hits US #5.

1982 Feb *Feel Like A Number* climbs to US #48, while a live version of *We've Got Tonight*, from LP *Nine Tonight*, reaches UK #60.

1983 Feb *Shame On The Moon*, a song by Rodney Crowell, is Seger's biggest-selling single, hitting US #2. It is taken from LP *The Distance*, produced by Seger and Jimmy Iovine over 14 months (and originally intended as a double LP), which hits US #5 (his sixth consecutive platinum LP) and reaches UK #45. On the LP, Seger uses new musicians: Russ Kunkel (drums), Waddy Wachtel (guitar) and Roy Bittan from Bruce Springsteen's° E. Street Band (piano), alongside bassist Chris Campbell, keyboardist Craig Frost and saxophonist Alto Reed from the current Silver Bullet Band. This angers the band's regular guitarist, Drew Abbott, who leaves the line-up.

Mar Kenny Rogers° and Sheena Easton's° cover of *We've Got Tonight* hits US #6 and UK #28, bettering Seger's original in both territories.

May *Even Now*, also from the LP, climbs to US #12 and UK #73.

June *Roll Me Away* reaches US #27.

Nov *Old Time Rock'n'Roll* is reissued as a single due to its inclusion in Tom Cruise movie *Risky Business*, and this time peaks at US #48.

1985 Jan *Understanding*, taken from the soundtrack of movie *Teachers*, reaches US #11.

1986 May *American Storm* makes US #13. It is taken from LP *Like A Rock*, again a platinum seller, which hits US #3 and UK #35. For the first time, Seger has a co-writer, Craig Frost, on his songs.

July Extracted title song from *Like A Rock* climbs to US #12.

BOB SEGER *cont.*

Sept *It's You*, also from LP *Like A Rock*, makes US #52.
Dec Last single from the LP, *Miami*, peaks at US #70. (It will later be used in US TV series "Miami Vice".)

1987 Aug *Shakedown*, recorded for movie *Beverly Hills Cop II* (and originally intended for Michigan buddy, ex-The Eagles'° Glenn Frey, whom laryngitis prevented from recording it) gives Seger his first US chart-topper. It is not released on Capitol, but MCA, which holds the soundtrack rights. Seger rewrites some of Keith Forsey's original lyrics before recording it.
Dec Seger is one of the artists on the Special Olympics benefit LP *A Very Special Christmas*, with a version of *The Little Drummer Boy*.

1988 Aug He makes a guest appearance on Little Feat's° comeback LP *Let It Roll*, and files for divorce after a brief marriage.

THE SEX PISTOLS

Johnny Rotten (vocals)
Steve Jones (guitar)
Sid Vicious (bass)
Paul Cook (drums)

1971 London schoolfriends Cook (b. July 20, 1956, London, UK) and Jones (b. Sept.3, 1955, London), developing an interest in music, meet Fine Arts graduate Malcolm McLaren who is opening up a shop called "Let It Rock" in King's Road, Chelsea, London.

1972 Cook, Jones and friend Wally Nightingale decide to form a band. Cook scrapes together money for a drumkit and Jones and Nightingale steal equipment for the latter to use, while Jones is the singer.

1973 McLaren renames his shop "Too Fast To Live, Too Young To Die". He takes an interest in the band and Glen Matlock, an assistant at the shop, hearing of an opening for a bassist, joins the band.

1974 They rehearse throughout the year as The Swankers, learning a variety of 60s covers, and begin to write their own material.

1975 The Swankers makes its only public performance, singing three songs at a party above Tom Salter's Café in the King's Road.
May McLaren returns from 6 months in US, working with The New York Dolls, and decides that Nightingale will not fit into his scheme for the group. Jones moves to guitar, leaving the band looking for a singer.
June McLaren suggests ex-Television° Richard Hell (who has already invented the punk look for himself), but the band wants an unknown London vocalist.
Aug John Lydon (b. Jan.31, 1956) meets the group at McLaren's shop, now renamed "Sex", and is asked to join as singer. His audition is to stand by the shop's juke box and sing along to Alice Cooper's° *School's Out*. The group becomes The Sex Pistols, and Jones christens Lydon "John Rotten", after his catchphrase, "You're rotten, you are."
Nov [6] The Sex Pistols play their first gig at St. Martin's School of Art in London, following with a series of small gigs, mainly at art schools.

1976 Apr The Sex Pistols support Joe Strummer's band The 101ers at the Nashville Rooms. The group spends the summer building a cult reputation in London, playing in a variety of venues.
Aug The Sex Pistols are banned from the European Punk Rock Festival in Mont De Marsan, France, by organizers who dislike their image. (They have already been banned from several London venues, including Dingwalls and the Rock Garden.)
Aug [29] The group plays the Screen on the Green, Islington, London, supported by The Buzzcocks° and The Clash°.
Sept [3] The group plays the Club de Chalet du Lac in Paris. Devoted followers of the band, Billy Idol° drives to France in his ex-Post Office van with Siouxsie and Steve Severin of The Banshees to see the gig.
Sept [17] They play a concert for inmates at Chelmsford Prison, Essex, UK.
Sept The Sex Pistols make their first UK TV appearance singing *Anarchy In The UK* on "So It Goes". They headline The 100 Club punk rock festival which sees the debuts of Subway Sect and Siouxsie & The Banshees°, featuring Vicious on drums.
Oct [8] A week after Rotten appears on the cover of music paper *New Musical Express*, The Sex Pistols are signed to EMI for a £40,000 advance. (Chrysalis, RAK and Polydor have all made bids.)
Oct They record *Anarchy In The UK* with producer Chris Thomas.

Nov [26] *Anarchy In The UK* is released.
Nov [28] The Sex Pistols appear on UK TV programs "Nationwide" and "London Weekend Show".
Dec [1] The group appears on UK Thames TV early evening magazine program "Today". Taunted by interviewer Bill Grundy, they respond with verbal abuse and make the cover of every newspaper the next day, establishing the group's name across the country.
Dec [5] The "Anarchy in the UK Tour" (also featuring The Clash°, The Damned° and The Heartbreakers) is due to start, but many dates are cancelled. (Only three out of 19 gigs go ahead.)
Dec [7] The Sex Pistols are discussed at EMI's AGM. Chairman Sir John Read apologizes for the group's behavior.
Dec *Anarchy In The UK* makes UK #38.

1977 Jan [6] EMI issues a statement saying it feels unable to promote The Sex Pistols' records in view of the adverse publicity generated over the last 2 months, but that press reports of their behavior seem to have been exaggerated. (EMI honors the group's contract, promising the £40,000 advance, and *Anarchy In The UK* sells 55,000 copies before being withdrawn.)
Feb Vicious (b. John Simon Ritchie, May 10, 1957, London), a member of Flowers of Romance, is auditioned as bass player to replace Matlock, and joins despite his rudimentary playing skills. (Matlock takes with him the songwriting ability that The Sex Pistols never replace.)
Mar Matlock forms band The Rich Kids, with Steve New (guitar) and Rusty Egan (drums).
Mar [10] The Sex Pistols sign to A&M Records in a ceremony outside Buckingham Palace.
Mar [16] Due to pressure from other A&M artists and the LA head office, A&M fires the band, having pressed 25,000 copies of *God Save The Queen*. The Sex Pistols have earned £75,000 for their 6 days with the label.
May The group signs to Virgin for £15,000. Virgin strikes problems pressing the group's new single *God Save The Queen* at the CBS plant when workers threaten to walk out, but problems are smoothed over. Jamie Reid's sleeve depiction of HM The Queen with a safety pin through her mouth causes a furore in the press.
May [27] *God Save The Queen* is released, and reportedly sells 150,000 copies in 5 days, despite being banned from daytime play by UK BBC Radio 1 and leading chainstores.
June [7] Virgin Records hires a boat called "Queen Elizabeth" for a party on the River Thames. The Sex Pistols perform *Anarchy In The UK* outside the Houses of Parliament and members of the party are arrested when the boat docks.
June *God Save The Queen* hits UK #2. Claims are made that the record is outselling Rod Stewart's° #1 *I Don't Want To Talk About It*. Virgin Records, trying to buy airtime during "Today" commercial breaks to advertise the record, are turned down by UK Thames TV.
June [18] Rotten, producer Thomas and engineer Bill Price are attacked with razors as they leave a public house in North London on their way back to nearby Wessex studio.

June [19] Cook is attacked by five men wielding knives and an iron bar outside Shepherds Bush underground station.

July *Pretty Vacant* hits UK #6, while the group tours Scandinavia. McLaren meets film director Russ Meyer to discuss making a Sex Pistols film. (Meyer will pull out of the project.)

Aug The group undertakes an "undercover" UK tour as Spots (an acronym for Sex Pistols On Tour Secretly), and also plays as The Tax Exiles, Special Guest, The Hampsters and Acne Rabble.

Oct *Holidays In The Sun* hits UK #8. The Belgian Travel Service issues a summons claiming the sleeve infringes copyright of one its brochures. (The sleeve is withdrawn from sale.)

Nov [12] LP *Never Mind The Bollocks – Here's The Sex Pistols* enters the UK chart at #1, displacing Cliff Richard's° *40 Golden Greats*. It stays on top for 2 weeks, before being dethroned by Bread's° *The Sound Of Bread*.

Nov A policewoman sees the LP sleeve in a shop window and informs the retailer he is contravening the 1889 Indecent Advertsing Act because of the word "bollocks" on the sleeve. (Magistrates "reluctantly" declare 2 weeks later that it is not an offence to display the record.) The Sex Pistols sign to Warner Bros. for US.

Dec Vicious and his US girlfriend Nancy Spungen are arrested on suspicion of possessing illegal substances, but are released without charge. The Sex Pistols return from a tour of Holland, to play UK dates. (Their last UK gig is in Huddersfield, Yorks., on Christmas Day at Ivanhoe's Club, in front of local children in aid of charity.) Listeners to Israeli Radio vote *God Save The Queen* the worst single of the year.

1978 Jan [5] The Sex Pistols begin a US tour at the Great Southeast Music Hall, Atlanta, Ga.

Jan [10] The group makes its US TV debut on "Variety".

Jan [14] After gigs in Memphis, Baton Rouge, Dallas and Tulsa, the group plays what will be its last live show, at the San Francisco Winterland Ballroom. Rotten quits the tour and heads for New York.

Jan [16] Vicious overdoses and goes into hospital. McLaren returns to London, while Cook and Jones use plane tickets to Rio de Janeiro, previously purchased for a planned one-off concert. Virgin declares there will be "no more Sex Pistols releases".

Jan LP *Never Mind The Bollocks* makes US #106.

Feb Cook and Jones stay in Rio as guests of great train robber Ronald Biggs.

Feb [23] Vicious and Spungen are arrested for possession of drugs.

Apr Cook and Jones play dates with Johnny Thunders at London's Speakeasy Club. Vicious also performs as a vocalist with Thunders.

May Rotten, having reverted to his real name Lydon, announces the formation of his new band.

July Virgin refuses to release the single Cook and Jones recorded with Biggs under the title *Cosh The Driver*. Instead it is released as *No One Is Innocent (A Punk Prayer By Ronnie Biggs)*, as a double A-side with Vicious' version of *My Way*. Vicious plays a farewell gig at the Electric Ballroom, London, under the banner "Sid Sods Off" with The Vicious White Kids – Rat Scabies, Glen Matlock and Steve New.

Oct [11] Vicious, living at the Chelsea Hotel in New York with Spungen, calls the police to say someone has stabbed her. He is arrested, charged with murder and placed in the detoxification unit of a New York prison. (McLaren eventually bails him out with money from Virgin.)

1979 Feb [2] Vicious dies at a New York party from an accumulation of fluid on the lungs caused by a heroin overdose.

Feb The Sex Pistols, McLaren and Virgin go to court in an attempt to resolve the group's financial affairs. The High Court judge appoints a receiver to sort out finances, including money tied up in the movie and LP *The Great Rock'n'Roll Swindle*, currently in production. He tells those concerned to sort out who owns the name The Sex Pistols and whether Lydon is still under contract to McLaren. (In the course of the week Cook and Jones change sides, joining Lydon/Virgin against McLaren.)

Mar The Sex Pistols' revival of Eddie Cochran's° *Something Else*, coupled with *Friggin' In The Riggin'*, hits UK #3. LP *Great Rock'n'Roll Swindle*, a double set of out-takes and jokey songs, hits UK #7. (It is later re-released as a single LP.)

Apr *Silly Thing*, double A-side with Tenpole Tudor's *Who Killed Bambi*, hits UK #6.

July *C'mon Everybody* makes UK #21.

Aug LP *Some Product – Carri On Sex Pistols*, containing interviews, commercials and the "Today" interview, but no music, hits UK #6.

Oct *The Great Rock'n'Roll Swindle* movie premieres. Julien Temple's film is a collection of early Pistols footage and comic situations, with McLaren tongue-in-cheek claiming the whole phenomenon was no more than his inspired hype. Rotten is largely absent from the movie. *The Great Rock'n'Roll Swindle*, double A-side with Tenpole Tudor's *Rock Around The Clock*, reaches UK #21. Cook and Jones' band The Professionals make UK #43 with *1-2-3*.

Dec LP *Sid Sings* makes UK #30.

1980 Feb Last Virgin LP, *Flogging A Dead Horse*, reaches UK #23.

July *(I'm Not Your) Stepping Stone*, reviving The Monkees'° hit, makes UK #21.

1986 Jan [13] Lydon, Jones, Cook and Vicious' mother sue McLaren for £1 million. (They will settle out of court.) The official receiver awards the three remaining band members and Vicious' mother £1,000,000. (Lydon is a member of Public Image Ltd.° Jones, living in LA, works as a session guitarist, while Cook has disappeared from view.)

July [20] Film *Sid and Nancy*, directed by Alex Cox with Gary Oldman as Sid and Chloe Webb as Nancy, premieres in London.

1988 Nov Rumors circulate that The Pistols are being offered $6 million to re-form and play US dates in 1989.

THE SHADOWS

Hank Marvin (lead guitar)
Bruce Welch (rhythm guitar)
Brian Bennett (drums)

1958 Apr [6] Marvin (b. Brian Rankin, Oct.28, 1941, Newcastle, UK) and Welch (b. Bruce Cripps, Nov.2, 1941, Bognor Regis, UK), having left school in Newcastle, travel to London with their part-time skiffle quintet The Railroaders, to enter a national talent contest and come third.

May The Railroaders split after the contest. Welch and Marvin remain in London and form The Five Chesternuts with comedian Charlie Chester's drummer son Pete, a vocalist and a bass player.

Aug The group records a one-off single for EMI's Columbia label, *Teenage Love*, which leads to an appearance on UK BBC TV's "6.5 Special", but no further success. Welch and Marvin take jobs at the 2 I's coffee bar in Soho, London, where they play guitar in the basement club as "The Geordie Boys", and operate the orange juice and coke machines.

Sept Marvin, having played a 2-week UK tour as temporary guitarist with The Vipers, is seen by Cliff Richard's° manager John Foster playing at the 2 I's. Richard has been offered a UK tour supporting The Kalin Twins, but his group The Drifters has just lost guitarist Ken Pavey and needs a replacement. Foster intended to offer Tony Sheridan the job, but he cannot be found. Marvin is asked to join instead and insists that Welch joins too. Foster agrees after they play for him at home.

Oct [5] Richard° goes on tour backed by a Drifters line-up of Marvin (lead guitar), Welch (rhythm guitar), Ian Samwell (bass) and Terry Smart (drums). Marvin is recruited by The Kalin Twins to play guitar for them too.

Oct [19] As the tour ends, Samwell leaves The Drifters. Fellow 2 I's regular Jet Harris (b. Terence Harris, July 6, 1939, London, UK), on the tour backing The Most Brothers and asked by The Drifters to play along behind the curtain to boost Samwell's hesitant bass playing, is asked by Richard° to replace Samwell.

Dec Smart leaves The Drifters to join the Merchant Navy. Harris suggests Tony Meehan (b. Daniel Meehan, Mar.2, 1943, London, UK), ex-Vipers drummer, with whom he, Marvin and Welch have all played at the 2 I's, as replacement.

1959 Jan The new quartet plays together on record for the first time on Richard's° *Livin' Lovin' Doll* and backs him at Manchester Free Trade Hall.

Feb Offered a recording deal in their own right by Columbia's Norrie Paramor, on the strength of their playing with Richard°, The Drifters release *Feelin' Fine*, a vocal written by ex-member Samwell (who becomes their manager for ventures independent of Richard). B-side *Don't Be A Fool (With Love)*, written by Marvin and Welch's ex-Chesternuts colleague Chester is performed by the group on UK TV's "Oh Boy!", but is a flop.

May The group records its first instrumental, *Chinchilla*, for the soundtrack of Richard's° film *Serious Charge*.

THE SHADOWS *cont.*

June Harris marries Carol DaCosta.

July *Jet Black*, an instrumental written by Harris, is the second Drifters single but does not chart. It is released in US as by The Four Jets, since *Feelin' Fine* had to be withdrawn from the US market when Atlantic group The Drifters° issued an injunction to prevent duplication of their name. The group decides a permanent change is necessary, and Harris suggests The Shadows while drinking at The Six Bells pub in Ruislip, UK.

Aug [29] Welch marries Anne Findley. Cliff Richard° is Best Man.

Dec *Saturday Dance*, another vocal written by Marvin and Chester, is the first single credited to The Shadows, but another flop. The group appears with Richard° in pantomime *Babes in the Wood* in Stockton, UK. Harris' car crashes, injuring himself and Marvin slightly.

1960 Jan They tour US with Cliff Richard° in a package including Frankie Avalon°, Bobby Rydell° and Freddy Cannon.

Apr On a UK tour, the group meets singer/songwriter Jerry Lordan, who demonstrates his composition *Apache* on the ukelele. They record it with Richard° sitting in on bongos.

June Peter Gormley becomes their full-time manager.

Aug *Apache* hits UK #1 for 6 weeks, deposing Richard's° *Please Don't Tease*. (Danish guitarist Jorgen Ingmann's version, recorded without hearing The Shadows', steals US chart honors.)

Sept [25] The group plays its first concert without Richard° in Bristol, UK.

Dec *Man Of Mystery*, a version of the theme from the Edgar Wallace movie series, hits UK #6. B-side *The Stranger* climbs to UK #11. Marvin marries long-time girlfriend Billie, with Welch as Best Man. *Apache* is voted Record of the Year in *New Musical Express*.

1961 Feb *FBI*, credited to manager Gormley because of a publishing wrangle, but a Marvin/Welch/Harris composition, hits UK #4.

Mar The group tours southern Africa, Australasia and the Far East with Richard° and first live recording is a 4-track EP cut at The Colosseum, Johannesburg.

June Film theme *The Frightened City* hits UK #3. The group films movie *The Young Ones* with Richard° at UK's Elstree Studios.

Sept Debut LP *The Shadows*, featuring new instrumentals and vocals, hits UK #1 for 6 weeks.

Oct *Kon-Tiki* hits UK #1. The Shadows hold UK #1 in the first week of the month with their LP, single, and EP *The Shadows To The Fore* (which includes *Apache*). Meehan leaves during a 6-week residency with Richard° at Blackpool, UK. He wants to move into production and starts work for Decca as an A&R man. Bennett (b. Feb.9, 1940, London, UK) an acquaintance from the 2 I's and ex-Marty Wilde's° Wildcats and instrumental group The Krew Kats drummer, is backing Tommy Steele° when Welch phones him. He joins The Shadows in time to tour Australia with Richard°.

Nov *The Savage*, written by producer Norrie Paramor and taken from film *The Young Ones*, hits UK #10.

1962 Mar *Wonderful Land*, a Jerry Lordan composition and the first Shadows track with orchestral backing, tops the UK chart for 8 weeks, but is toppled by another instrumental, *Nut Rocker* by B. Bumble & The Stingers.

Apr Differences between Welch and Harris come to a head, and Harris walks out to pursue a solo career. Brian "Liquorice" Locking, another acquaintance who played with Bennett in groups backing Vince Taylor and Marty Wilde°, joins on bass.

Apr [13] The group is presented belatedly with a gold disk for worldwide million-plus sales of *Apache*.

Apr [27] Harris signs to Decca as a solo singer/guitarist, and Jack Good becomes his manager and producer.

May The group travels to Greece to film *Summer Holiday* with Cliff Richard°. Welch and Bennett write the title song.

June Harris's 6-string bass guitar solo version of *Besame Mucho* (with Meehan on drums) reaches UK #22.

Aug *Guitar Tango*, the first Shadows single to feature acoustic guitars, hits UK #4.

Sept Harris' second solo, a revival of *Main Title Theme*, from 1950s Frank Sinatra film *Man With The Golden Arm*, reaches UK #12.

Oct LP *Out Of The Shadows*, featuring tracks with Harris, hits UK #1 for 3 weeks (it will have further runs at the top in Nov., Dec. and Jan. 1963).

Nov EP *The Boys*, featuring music by the group from UK movie of the same title, tops the UK EP chart. They appear with Cliff Richard° at the Royal Variety Show in London.

1963 Jan The Shadows' *Dance On*, written by vocal group The Avons, hits UK #1 for 2 weeks. It is replaced by *Diamonds*, a Lordan composition co-credited to Jet Harris & Tony Meehan (on top for 3 weeks).

Mar *Foot Tapper*, from *Summer Holiday*, tops the UK chart for 1 week, deposing Cliff Richard's° title song. (This will be the group's final UK #1 single.)

May LP *The Shadows' Greatest Hits*, a compilation of singles to date, hits UK #2 behind The Beatles'° *Please Please Me*, and will stay in UK top 20 for 49 weeks. Harris and Meehan's second duet *Scarlet O'Hara* hits UK #2.

June *Atlantis*, a ballad instrumental with strings, peaks at UK #2 for 2 weeks behind Gerry & The Pacemakers'° *I Like It*. The group plays a 16-week summer season, "Holiday Carnival", in Blackpool with Richard°.

July Harris is slightly injured in a car crash.

Aug Pressures of work begin to fray Welch's nerves and he announces that he will leave the group for a desk job in The Shadows' organization after a tour of Israel and France in Oct.

Sept Harris and Meehan's *Applejack* hits UK #4, but their joint career stops when Harris and girlfriend, singer Billie Davis, are injured in an accident involving their car and a bus. Harris is left in poor physical and mental shape. He leaves Meeham 3 weeks later on a "Ready Steady Go" show on UK TV, goes home and smashes all his guitars.

Oct *Shindig* hits UK #6. EP *Los Shadows*, with four Spanish tunes recorded in Barcelona during the summer, makes UK #42. (EPs by The Beatles° and The Searchers° are in UK singles chart at the same time.) Locking, who has become committed to his Jehovah's Witness faith, announces that he is to leave. Marvin and Welch consider recruiting John Paul Jones, bassist with Harris and Meehan's backing group (and later with Led Zeppelin°), but settle on ex-Interns bass player John Rostill (b. June 16, 1942, Birmingham, UK). Welch has overcome his nervous problems with medical help, and decides not to leave.

Dec The group films *Wonderful Life* in the Canary Islands with Cliff Richard°, while *Geronimo* reaches UK #11 (their first to miss UK top 10).

1964 Jan With Harris out of action, Meehan records *Song Of Mexico* as The Tony Meehan Combo. It reaches UK #39 (but will be Meehan's last hit).

Mar Rostill plays on stage with The Shadows for the first time on a UK tour with Richard°.

Apr *Theme For Young Lovers*, from *Wonderful Life* soundtrack, reaches UK #12. Marvin's 18-month-old twin sons almost drown in the backyard pond, but he saves them with the "kiss of life" and the rescue is widely publicized.

May The group tours Europe while LP *Dance With The Shadows* hits UK #2.

June *The Rise And Fall Of Flingel Bunt*, The Shadows' hardest-rocking single since *The Savage*, hits UK #5. Harris is divorced by wife Carol.

Aug The group makes its own 25-minute musical comedy film, *Rhythm and Greens*, a series of short historical sketches in costume. It is shown in UK as support to Dirk Bogarde's *King and Country*.

Sept Title track *Rhythm And Greens* peaks at UK #22.

Nov The group plays three numbers in the Royal Variety Show, as well as backing Cliff Richard°.

Dec The Shadows write the score for, and have acting and musical roles in, the Cliff Richard°-starring pantomime *Aladdin and His Wonderful Lamp* at the London Palladium, which runs for 15 weeks.

1965 Jan *Genie With The Light Brown Lamp*, from the pantomime, reaches UK #17.

Mar Ballad *Mary Anne*, written by Lordan and the first vocal Shadows single since *Saturday Dance*, climbs to UK #17.

June More familiar sounding instrumental *Stingray* peaks at UK #19. The Shadows support Richard° on another European tour.

July LP *The Sound Of The Shadows* hits UK #4.

Sept Vocal *Don't Make My Baby Blue* (previously recorded by Frankie Laine), hits UK #10 (it will be the last Shadows top 10 single for almost 13½ years).

Dec *The War Lord* theme from a Charlton Heston movie makes UK #18. The group writes (but does not perform) the music for Frank Ifield's pantomime *Babes in the Wood* at the London Palladium.

LP *More Hits!* a compilation of further hit singles, is the group's first LP not to chart in UK.

1966 Apr Vocal *I Met A Girl* reaches UK #22.

June LP *Shadow Music* hits UK #5.

July *A Place In The Sun*, an instrumental in the *Wonderful Land* mode (and written by Lordan's wife Petrina) peaks at UK #24, while the group is filming *Finders Keepers* with Cliff Richard°.

Nov Marvin-penned vocal *The Dreams I Dream* peaks at UK #42.

Dec The Shadows write the music for, and feature in, Cliff Richard's° pantomime *Cinderella* at the London Palladium. Puppet likenesses of Cliff Richard and The Shadows appear in Gerry Anderson's movie *Thunderbirds Are Go!*, in a nightclub scene as "Cliff Richard Jr. and The Sons of The Shadows". The group writes and performs four tracks on the film soundtrack, released as an EP.

1967 May *Maroc 7*, theme from a Gene Barry movie, peaks at UK #24. Welch parts from his wife and moves in with Australian singer Olivia Newton-John°.

July LP *Jigsaw* hits UK #8.

Aug The Shadows win the Split song festival, in Yugoslavia, with *I Can't Forget*. They tour Australia and Spain (without Richard°).

Sept *Tomorrow's Cancelled* is the first Shadows single since before *Apache* not to chart in UK.

Oct Bennett releases LP *Change Of Direction*, with a 6-piece group which includes Rostill.

Dec LP *From Hank, Bruce, Brian And John*, released, by Shadows standards, very hastily after its predecessor (5 months) fails to chart.

Dec [25] The Shadows appear in UK TV's production of pantomime *Aladdin*.

1968 Jan [1] The group begins a 3-week cabaret at the Talk of the Town club, its first in London without Cliff Richard°. (After a week, Rostill suffers a minor nervous breakdown and is ordered to rest, while Bennett is hospitalized with appendicitis. Ex-members Locking and Meehan fill in for the remainder of the booking.)

Jan Marvin releases his first solo single, *London's Not Too Far*, without success.

Mar With the current line-up back together, the group tours Japan, while in UK *Dear Old Mrs. Bell* fails to chart.

May They play a short season at the London Palladium with Tom Jones°.

Oct Cliff Richard° and The Shadows celebrate their 10th Anniversary in the music business with LP *Established 1958*, which contains equal shares of Shadows-backed Richard vocals and group instrumentals. Welch and his wife are divorced, and he is engaged to Olivia Newton-John°. It is reported that Welch and Bennett plan to leave the group at the end of the year

Dec [19] Following bad feeling and arguments within the group, it is admitted between the quartet that tiredness, disenchantment, and a loss of creativity have set in, and that a split is necessary. They play their last (10th anniversary) show with Richard°, at the London Palladium.

1969 Mar Marvin releases solo *Goodnight Dick*, which fails to chart. Bennett plays for 7 days in Washington, D.C. as Tom Jones'° drummer.

Sept Marvin duets with Cliff Richard° on *Throw Down A Line*, which hits UK #7. Bennett releases LP *The Illustrated London Noise*, which fails.

Oct With no plans to re-form the group, but attracted by the offer, Marvin, Rostill and Bennett play a short tour of Japan as The Shadows, with keyboards player Alan Hawkshaw, an old friend of Bennett's. A live LP is recorded by Japanese EMI/Odeon at Sankei Hall, Tokyo. In UK, a lengthy version of Richard Rodgers' *Slaughter On 10th Avenue*, recorded earlier without Welch, is released coupled with Marvin's solo version of *Midnight Cowboy* theme, but does not chart.

Nov Marvin's first solo LP, *Hank Marvin*, reaches UK #14.

1970 Mar The second "Cliff and Hank" duet, *Joy Of Living*, peaks at UK #25. The song is the theme for a weekly Cliff Richard° TV series, on which Marvin is a resident guest, featuring in comedy sketches as well as playing and singing. He declines an invitation by Roy Wood to join The Move°.

Aug Marvin and Welch (back in action after 18 months) consider setting up as a vocal duo, and invite Australian singer/guitarist/songwriter John Farrar, whom they met on tour, to join them for experimental rehearsals.

Oct LP *Shades Of Rock*, a collection of hard-rock oldies (recorded earlier in the year by Marvin, Bennett, Hawkshaw and several different bassists), is released as by The Shadows. It reaches UK #30.

1971 Jan Having settled as a harmony vocal trio, Marvin, Welch and Farrar debut on Cliff Richard's° UK TV show, appearing five times in the series. Marvin gets married again (to Carole).

Mar The trio, backed by Bennett on drums and Dave Richmond on bass, tours West Germany, Switzerland and the Benelux countries and includes several Shadows tracks in its act due to audience demand.

Apr LP *Marvin, Welch And Farrar* reaches UK #30, but *Faithful* flops. Welch amd Farrar begin producing Olivia Newton-John°; her *If Not For You* hits UK #7.

Nov Marvin, Welch and Farrar LP *Second Opinion* fails to chart.

Dec The trio, with Bennett, supports Cliff Richard° on a UK tour.

1972 Mar Newton-John° breaks off her engagement to Welch, which shatters him and he attempts suicide.

Sept Marvin and Farrar, continuing as a duo and backed by Hawkshaw (keyboards), Rostill and Bennett, tour the Far East with Newton-John° and Cliff Richard°.

1973 Apr Marvin and his wife Carole become Jehovah's Witnesses.

Aug LP *Hank Marvin And John Farrar* fails to chart.

Nov Marvin, Welch, Farrar and Bennett record *Turn Around And Touch Me* as The Shadows, but it does not chart. The recording session is Welch's return to working life. (He and Newton-John° had reconciled in April, then parted again in June, by mutual consent.)

Nov [26] Rostill, who played in Las Vegas with Tom Jones°, but returned to UK to work, dies from accidental electrocution while playing guitar in his home studio. Welch, who has been writing songs with him, discovers his body when he arrives for a demo session.

1974 Apr LP *Rockin' With Curly Leads*, is recorded by Marvin, Welch, Farrar and Bennett, with Alan Tarney playing bass, as The Shadows. It reaches UK #45. Welch releases solo *Please Mr. Please*, written by himself and Rostill, but it fails to sell.

May The group's 11-year-old compilation LP *The Shadows' Greatest*

THE SHADOWS *cont.*

Hits is reissued in stereo and re-charts at UK #48.

Aug Bennett joins Georgie Fame's° band The Blue Flames on drums for a UK tour.

Oct At a charity concert at the London Palladium, The Shadows' appearance (meant as a one-off) prompts BBC TV boss Bill Cotton Jr. to ask them to represent UK in the 1975 Eurovision Song Contest. The group plays some UK concerts to regain the feel of live performance together. Brian Goode from Peter Gormley's office becomes their manager.

1975 Apr The Shadows perform *Let Me Be The One* in the Eurovision Song Contest in Stockholm, Sweden, to a TV audience of 300 million. It is beaten into second place by Dutch group Teach-In with *Ding-A-Dong*, but The Shadows peak at UK #12 with it (one place above Teach-In). LP *Specs Appeal*, containing the six Eurovision songs from which UK's entry was selected on UK TV and other new material, reaches UK #30. A demand for more of The Shadows, following all the TV publicity, prompts the recording of a live LP at the Olympia Theatre in Paris (intended as this line-up's final concert).

Nov LP *Live At The Paris Olympia* is released without charting.

1976 May *It'll Be Me Babe* fails to chart. Farrar moves to US to write for and produce Olivia Newton-John°, while Welch produces Cliff Richard° on *Miss You Nights* and *Devil Woman*.

Aug Bennett travels to Russia as Richard's° drummer on a pioneering tour of USSR by a major Western rock act.

1977 Feb Compilation LP *20 Golden Greats*, promoted via an acclaimed TV ad involving young lads doing The Shadows' high kicks with cricket bat "guitars", is the group's first UK top 10 LP for 9½ years. It hits UK #1 for 6 weeks and is the group's biggest seller – over a million copies in UK.

Mar Signed as a soloist to DJM Records (owned by publisher Dick James), Bennett releases concept LP *Rock Dreams*, on which Cliff Richard° sings some guest vocals. It fails to chart.

May The group plays a rapturously-received "20 Golden Dates" UK tour to follow up the hits LP, with Alan Jones on bass and Francis Monkman on keyboards

Aug Marvin wins the CBS Arbiter award for services to British music, with fellow guitarists Joe Brown and Bert Weedon.

Sept LP *Tasty*, of new Shadows material, fails to sell.

Nov Recruiting several noted guitarists, Marvin issues LP *The Hank Marvin Guitar Syndicate*, which fails to chart.

1978 Feb Cliff Richard° and The Shadows reunite for a series of London Palladium concerts to mark their 20th Anniversary. Films and recordings are made of these, for the TV special and live LP *Thank You Very Much*.

Apr Bennett releases his second DJM LP *Voyage*, again without success.

Aug *Love Deluxe* receives good airplay in UK but fails to chart.

Sept The group plays a UK tour, with Jones again on bass, and ex-Cliff Richard° band member Cliff Hall on keyboards.

1979 Jan *Don't Cry For Me Argentina*, an instrumental version of Julie Covington's #1 hit from Rice/Lloyd Webber musical *Evita*, is The Shadows' first top 10 single since 1965, hitting UK #5.

June *Theme From The Deer Hunter (Cavatina)*, in competition with John Williams' solo guitar version (which makes #13), hits UK #9.

Aug [1] Welch marries again, his new wife Lynne has been a close friend for some years.

1980 Mar LP *String Of Hits*, after several months on chart, hits UK #1 for 3 weeks following a TV ad campaign, while *Riders In The Sky*, a disco-flavored revival of The Ramrods' 1961 hit, makes UK #12. The group's recording contract with EMI expires, and is not renewed when the company fails to agree to The Shadows recording independently and leasing the results. Polydor signs a 3-year contract with the group's newly-formed production company Rollover Records, to take three LPs.

Aug Compilation LP *Another String Of Hot Hits* makes UK #16, while the group's first Polydor release, a cover of Jean Michel Jarre's° *Equinoxe, Part 5*, reaches UK #50.

Sept LP *Change Of Address* reaches UK #17.

1981 May A revival of Anton Karas' theme from film *The Third Man* peaks at UK #44, and is the last Shadows hit single.

Sept The group tours UK to promote LP *Hits Right Up Your Street*.

Oct The LP reaches UK #15.

1982 Mar Marvin's solo LP *Words And Music* makes UK #66, while extracted *Don't Talk* reaches UK #49 (his only solo single success).

Oct Double LP (two for the price of one) *Life In The Jungle/Live At Abbey Road*, on which the second disk features a session cut before a live studio audience, peaks at UK #24.

1983 May The group wins an Ivor Novello award from the British Academy of Songwriters, Composers and Authors, to mark 25 years of outstanding contribution to British music.

Oct LP *XXV*, celebrating the group's 25th anniversary, makes UK #34.

1984 Nov LP *Guardian Angel* makes UK #98 for a week.

1986 Mar Marvin reprises his guitar solo on Cliff Richard's° 1959 chart-topper *Living Doll*, on the new charity version by Richard and comedy team The Young Ones, in aid of Comic Relief. It tops the UK chart for 3 weeks.

May LP *Moonlight Shadows* hits UK #6.

1987 Nov LP *Simply Shadows* makes UK #11.

1988 Oct Marvin, who is living in Australia, flies to London to play at Jean-Michel Jarre's° London's Docklands open-air concert, a journey which costs Jarre a reported £20,000.

SHALAMAR

Howard Hewett (vocals)
Jody Watley (vocals)
Jeffrey Daniel (vocals)

1977 May The group name is created by producers Dick Griffey and Simon Soussan to give an identity to *Uptown Festival*, a disco medley incorporating five classic Motown hits, made by session singers and musicians in Los Angeles, Cal., US. It reaches US #25 and UK #30, released on Soul Train label, since Griffey is talent booker for the TV show of the same name, produced by his partner Don Cornelius.

July LP *Uptown Festival*, also cut by sessioneers, hits US #8.

1978 Nov Having formed his own record label, Solar (Sound Of Los Angeles Records), Griffey puts together a group to continue as Shalamar. He recruits "Soul Train" dancers Watley (b. Jan.30, 1959, Chicago, Ill., US) and Daniel (b. Aug.24, 1955, Los Angeles, Cal.) and lead singer Gerald Brown, pairing them with producer Leon Sylvers III to record dance-oriented LP *Disco Gardens*, which stalls at US #171.

1979 Jan *Take That To The Bank*, from the LP, reaches US #79 (and R&B #11) and UK #20. Brown leaves and is replaced by Hewett (b. Oct.1, 1955, Akron, Oh., US), as lead singer.

Nov *The Second Time Around*, from LP *Big Fun*, makes UK #45.

1980 Feb *Right In The Socket*, also from the LP (which does not chart in UK) peaks at UK #44.

Mar *The Second Time Around* becomes the trio's biggest US success, hitting #9 and selling over a million (also topping the R&B chart, dethroning Michael Jackson's° *Rock With You*). LP *Big Fun* makes US #23 and earns a gold disk, Solar's first. Daniel marries soul vocalist and Broadway star of *The Wiz*, Stephanie Mills. (They will divorce in less than a year.)

Oct *I Owe You One* reaches UK #13

1981 Feb *Full Of Fire* makes US #55.

Apr *Make That Move* peaks at UK #30.

May LP *Three For Love* makes US #40, and is the group's second gold LP. Taken from it, *Make That Move* reaches US #55.

Nov LP *Go For It* peaks at US #115.

1982 May LP *Friends* climbs to US #35, and is Shalamar's third and last US gold LP. Extracted from it, *A Night To Remember* makes US #44, while *I Can Make You Feel Good*, the UK extract co-written by Hewett, hits UK #7, and is the group's first of three consecutive UK top 10 hits with songs from LP *Friends*. The group begins "Friends World Tour".

July *A Night To Remember* hits UK #5.

Sept Compilation LP *Greatest Hits* reaches UK #71.

Oct *There It Is* hits UK #5.

Dec The title track from *Friends* reaches UK #12.

1983 Jan [8] Daniel appears on UK TV show "Jim'll Fix It" demonstrating the street dance art of body popping.

Jan LP *Friends* peaks at UK #6 (having been on chart for over 40 weeks), while the trio is touring UK.

July *Dead Giveaway* hits UK #8. It is from LP *The Look* which hits UK #7. (The title cut is written by Hewett with Stanley Clarke.)

Sept *Dead Giveaway* makes US #22, while parent LP *The Look* reaches US #38.

Nov *Over And Over*, also from LP *The Look*, makes UK #23.

1984 Daniel leaves the group, moving to UK to become host of newly-launched UK TV version of "Soul Train". Watley also leaves for a solo vocal career (and will find success in 1987). The group continues, with Hewett being joined by Delisa Davis and Micki Free.

Apr Taken from the soundtrack of film *Footloose* and released on Columbia/CBS, *Dancing In The Sheets* climbs to US #17, their most successful US single for over 4 years, and UK #41, in simultaneous competition with *Deadline USA* (from another movie *Street Fleet*) which makes UK #52.

Nov [25] Watley takes part in the recording of Band Aid's° *Do They Know It's Christmas?* (UK's all-time best-selling single) in London.

Dec *Amnesia* is the trio's last US chart single, making #73. In UK, it reaches #61. Shalamar's *Don't Get Stopped In Beverly Hills* is featured in Eddie Murphy's film *Beverly Hills Cop*.

1985 Jan LP *Heart Break* makes US #90, and is the trio's last LP to chart in US.

Feb *My Girl Loves Me*, from LP *Heart Break*, peaks at US #45.

1986 Feb Shalamar's *Razzle Dazzle* is featured in Goldie Hawn movie *Wildcats*. Hewett is arrested outside a Miami shopping center by FBI agents and charged with four counts of conspiracy to possess cocaine. (He is later acquitted.)

May TV-promoted compilation LP *The Greatest Hits*, surveying the group's entire chart career, hits UK #5. Meanwhile, a remixed version of their biggest UK hit *A Night To Remember* climbs to UK #52, closing the group's UK hit career. Hewett leaves for a solo career. Sidney Justin, an ex-LA Rams football player replaces him, but the group disbands shortly after.

Nov Hewett, signed to Elektra, has a minor US hit with *I'm For Real*, on which he is backed by George Duke, Stanley Clarke and Wilton Felder, from LP *Commit To Love*.

1987 May Signed to MCA as a soloist, Watley hits US #2 for 4 weeks (behind Cutting Crew's *(I Just) Died In Your Arms* and U2's° *With Or Without You*) with *Looking For A New Love*, which also reaches UK #13.

DEL SHANNON

1960 Shannon (b. Charles Westover, Dec.30, 1939, Coopersville, Mich., US) having begun singing and playing guitar in high school, then entertained in Special Services (including several months in "Get Up and Go" forces radio show in West Germany) when drafted into the military, becomes resident guitarist and vocalist in the band of the Hi-Lo club in Battle Creek, Mich., by night, working as a carpet salesman by day. He collaborates on songs with the band's keyboards player, Max Crook, and their promising sound and original material catches the ear of DJ Ollie McLaughlin on radio station W-GRV in nearby Ann Arbor. He introduces Shannon and Crook to Detroit entrepreneurs Harry Balk and Irving Micahnik, who sign Shannon to their Embee Productions, and arrange recording sessions in New York via a deal with Big Top Records. After an unexciting first session, Shannon and Crook write *Runaway*, which is considered by Big Top as commercial enough to be issued as the first single.

1961 Apr *Runaway* tops the US chart for 4 weeks, selling over a million to earn Shannon his only gold disk. Crook plays the song's instrumental break on a patent high-pitched electronic keyboard called a musitron, and this arresting sound is a major factor in the record's success (which will be repeated worldwide).

June *Runaway* also tops the UK chart for 4 weeks, selling a half million copies.

Aug *Hats Off To Larry*, another self-composed song in *Runaway* style and arrangement (with a second hook-laden musitron solo by Crook), hits US #5.

Sept *Hats Off To Larry* hits UK #6.

Oct On *So Long Baby*, an uptempo rocker, the musitron is replaced by a kazoo solo. It peaks at US #28.

Dec *Hey! Little Girl* makes US #38.

1962 Jan *So Long Baby* hits UK #10.

May *Hey! Little Girl* hits UK #2. UK B-side is *You Never Talked About Me*, which Shannon sings in a cameo slot in UK pop/jazz movie *It's Trad, Dad*.

June *Cry Myself To Sleep*, recorded in Nashville with vocal backing by The Jordanaires, peaks at US #99.

Sept *Cry Myself To Sleep* reaches UK #29.

Oct Another Nashville recording, *The Swiss Maid*, written by Roger Miller°, features Shannon yodelling and makes US #64.

Dec *The Swiss Maid* hits UK #2 (behind Frank Ifield's *Lovesick Blues*).

1963 Feb *Little Town Flirt* hits US #12 and UK #4.

May *Two Kinds Of Teardrops* reaches US #50 and hits UK #5. LP *Hats Off To Del Shannon* (a UK compilation of singles A and B-sides) hits UK #9. He tours UK with Johnny Tillotson°, and enthuses to UK press about the new musical boom sweeping UK, and particularly about The Beatles°, whose material he (as a songwriter) rates highly.

May [9] Shannon plays a concert at London's Royal Albert Hall with The Beatles°, and suggests covering one of Lennon° and McCartney's° hits to help give them more exposure in US.

July Returning home, Shannon records his own version of The Beatles'° recent UK chart-topper *From Me To You*. It makes US #77 – the first Lennon°/McCartney° song to chart in US – while LP *Little Town Flirt* reaches US #12.

Sept *Two Silhouettes*, US B-side of *From Me To You*, is UK A-side and peaks at #23.

Nov Attempting to sever ties with Balk and Micahnik after disagreements over royalties and other business practices, Shannon forms his own label, Berlee Records, and issues The Four Seasons°-influenced *Sue's Gotta Be Mine*, which reaches US #71 and UK #21. LP *Little Town Flirt*, belatedly released in UK, makes #15.

1964 Mar *Mary Jane* fails to chart in US, but peaks at UK #35.

Aug Shannon moves to New York-based Amy Records for a high-tempo revival of Jimmy Jones' 1960 million-seller *Handy Man*, which makes US #22 and UK #36.

Sept He plays on an all-star bill supporting current US chart-toppers The Animals° at the Paramount Theater, Brooklyn, New York. Other performers include Jan and Dean° and Chuck Berry°.

Oct *Do You Want To Dance?*, revived in identical style to *Handy Man*, peaks at US #43.

1965 Jan Shannon hits US #9 after a 3½-year top 10 absence with *Keep Searchin' (We'll Follow The Sun)*.

Feb *Keep Searchin' (We'll Follow The Sun)* hits UK #3. Peter and Gordon's° cover of his *I Go To Pieces* hits US #9.

Mar *Stranger In Town* reaches US #30 and UK #40, and is his last UK chart single.

May *Break Up* stalls at US #95.

June Shannon turns down a request from songwriter Tommy Boyce to record *Action*, the theme song to new Dick Clark US TV series "Where The Action Is". (Freddy Cannon makes US #13 with it in Sept.)

1966 Shannon moves from Michigan to LA and signs a new deal with Liberty Records.

May A revival of Toni Fisher's *The Big Hurt* is Shannon's only hit on Liberty, reaching US #94.

1967 Shannon records extensively for Liberty in UK, with Andrew Oldham producing. Intended as an LP, the completed tracks mostly sit on the shelf for more than a decade.

1969 Oct Leaving Liberty, Shannon produces other acts rather than seeking a new deal for himself. His first production success is with the group Smith, whose Shannon-produced revival of The Shirelles'° *Baby It's You* hits US #5. He records himself for Dunhill, the label on which he has worked with Smith, but only two unsuccessful singles result.

1970 Nov Shannon produces Brian Hyland°, a long-time friend, on a revival of The Impressions'° *Gypsy Woman*, which hits US #3 and is a million-seller.

1973 June Live LP *Live In England*, on United Artists, is a recording of a concert in Manchester from his UK tour the previous year.

1974 Oct Dave Edmunds° produces *And The Music Plays On*, recorded in UK (but not a hit).

1975 May He signs to US Island Records, debuting with a revival of The Zombies'° *Tell Her No* which gains excellent reviews, but lacks the promotion to sell.

Aug Second Island single is *Cry Baby Cry*, recorded in collaboration with Jeff Lynne of Electric Light Orchestra°. Again, it is insufficiently exposed to succeed, and Shannon leaves Island after its release.

1978 Mar LP *And The Music Plays On* combines the Dave Edmunds°-produced title track from 1974 with unreleased tracks cut with Andrew Oldham in 1967.

1979 Feb [3] He plays a nostalgia show at the Surf Ballroom, Clear Lake, Ia., to mark the 20th anniversary of the final performances by Buddy

DEL SHANNON *cont.*

Holly°, Ritchie Valens° and The Big Bopper° (before their deaths in a plane crash). Also playing are The Drifters° and Jimmy Clanton (who was on the Winter Dance Party tour of 1959).

1982 Jan LP *Drop Down And Get Me*, produced by Tom Petty° on Elektra, reaches US #123.

Feb Petty°-produced revival of Phil Phillips' *Sea Of Love* is Shannon's first US singles chart entry for 15 years, and peaks at US #33.

1984 He signs to Warner Bros., and records new material in Nashville.

1986 Oct Luis Cardenas, ex-LA band Renegade, revives *Runaway* and takes it to US #83. Shannon (with Donny Osmond°) has a cameo role in Cardenas' promotional video.

1988 May Shannon tours UK on a nostalgic package with his contemporaries Bobby Vee° and Brian Hyland°.

HELEN SHAPIRO

1961 Jan Shapiro (b. Sept.28, 1946, Bethnal Green, London, UK) is still at school and taking weekly vocal classes at the Maurice Berman singing academy in Baker Street, London, when EMI producer John Schroeder hears her and is impressed by her deep, mature voice and phrasing. He arranges a demo session and EMI's Columbia label A&R head Norrie Paramor (who initially refuses to believe he is listening to a 14-year-old girl on the demo) signs her to a recording contract.

May Schroeder writes *Don't Treat Me Like A Child* for her debut and, aided by radio and TV slots (including Saturday prime time "Thank Your Lucky Stars"), it hits UK #3.

Aug *You Don't Know*, a mid-tempo Schroeder/Mike Hawker ballad, in contrast to its bouncy teenbeat predecessor, tops the UK chart for 2 weeks, shifting 40,000 copies in a day at its peak. (It also becomes a major hit in many other territories and worldwide sales will top a million by the end of the year.)

Sept [28] She celebrates her birthday establishing a UK performing record: the first female to make over a dozen radio and TV appearances before the age of 15. This also marks the end of school for her and the beginning of a schedule of live appearances which takes in a short London Palladium season and several European tours.

Oct From the same writing team, teen rocker *Walkin' Back To Happiness*, released with advance orders of 300,000, hits UK top 10 while *You Don't Know* is still in it, and tops the chart for 4 weeks before surrendering to Elvis Presley's° *His Latest Flame*.

Dec *Walkin' Back To Happiness* spends a week at #100 on the US chart, regarded as a major achievement for a UK girl singer at this time. Worldwide sales again top a million. Shapiro is voted Top UK Female Singer in the annual *New Musical Express* poll. This success gives her some leeway to follow her own inclinations over material, and she releases a 4-track EP of standards, from which *Goody Goody* gains considerable airplay and tops the UK EP chart.

1962 Mar Shapiro just fails to achieve three consecutive UK #1 singles – a feat never achieved by a female performer or a UK act – as *Tell Me What He Said*, a US song written by Jeff Barry, peaks at UK #2, held off by The Shadows'° *Wonderful Land*.

Apr Debut LP *Tops With Me*, a collection of personal favorite oldies like *Lipstick On Your Collar* and *Will You Love Me Tomorrow?*, hits UK #2. She has a lead role, opposite Craig Douglas°, in UK pop/jazz movie *It's Trad, Dad*, which is a UK box office success.

May Soundtrack LP *It's Trad, Dad*, on which she sings *Let's Talk About Love* and *Sometime Yesterday*, hits UK #3. *Let's Talk About Love* is also released as a single and peaks at UK #23.

Aug *Little Miss Lonely*, her first slow ballad on single (and a return to Schroeder/Hawker material) hits UK #8, but will be her last major hit single. Meanwhile, she makes a cameo appearance in Billy Fury° film *Play It Cool*, singing *Cry My Heart Out* and *But I Don't Care*.

Nov *Keep Away From Other Girls*, a Bacharach/Hilliard song originally cut in US by Babs Tino, stalls at UK #40.

1963 Feb She begins a UK tour, opening at Bradford Gaumont. The Beatles° are among the supporting acts, and Lennon° and McCartney° tell her that their song *Misery* was written for her, but rejected by Paramor. *Queen For Tonight* reaches UK #33.

Apr LP *Helen's Sixteen* (referring both to her age and its number of tracks) fails to chart.

May *Woe Is Me*, recorded at her first US sessions, in Nashville the previous month, reaches UK #35. (She also cuts the original version of *It's My Party*, but the planned release is cancelled when Lesley Gore's° version appears.)

July *Not Responsible*, another Nashville recording, is her first single not to chart in UK.

Oct *Look Who It Is* makes UK #47, while LP *Helen In Nashville*, from the sessions earlier in the year, fails to chart.

1964 Feb A revival of Peggy Lee's *Fever* reaches UK #38, and is her final hit single. She is one of the large generation of immediately pre-beat boom stars whose styles are now out of public fashion.

1965 June After four unsuccessful singles, Shapiro sings *Here In My Arms* in the UK Song Festival at Brighton, but even the TV coverage fails to help it chart.

1968 With UK hits long gone, but still finding plenty of live work, particularly overseas, she switches labels from Columbia to Pye (rejoining John Schroeder, who has made the same move), and has a near-chartmaker with *Today Has Been Cancelled*.

1970/78 She moves to cabaret work and to the London West End stage in musicals like *The French Have A Word For It* and a new production of *Oliver*. She cuts one-off singles for Phoenix, DJM, Magnet and Arista, including Russ Ballard's *Can't Break The Habit*.

1983 Signing to Oval Records, a label with a reputation for artistic freedom, she records her first LP in almost 2 decades, *Straighten Up And Fly Right*, with mature versions of standards and personal favorites. UK music paper *New Musical Express* gives a rave review to her *Cry Me A River* and UK BBC Radio 2 plays the LP extensively. She showcases the material on stage in a series of dates at Fairfield Hall, Croydon, a major London suburban venue.

1985 She begins to work with jazzman Humphrey Lyttleton and his band, jointly recording LP *Echoes Of The Duke*, a tribute to Duke Ellington.

1986 20-track compilation LP *Helen Shapiro 25th Anniversary Album*, on EMI, celebrates her quarter-century of recording, as she continues a busy career in cabaret and stage musicals.

SANDIE SHAW

1964 Apr Shaw (b. Sandra Goodrich, Feb.26, 1947, Dagenham, Essex, UK) is working as an IBM machine operator and singing in her spare time when she talks her way backstage at an Adam Faith° and his group The Roulettes one-nighter and impresses them with an impromptu vocal demonstration. Their manager Eve Taylor is only marginally impressed, but sees potential in her style, and signs her to a management contract, renaming her Sandie Shaw.

July After recording demos with producer Tony Hatch, Shaw is signed to Pye Records, and debuts with *As Long As You're Happy*, which flops.

Oct A cover of Lou Johnson's US hit *(There's) Always Something There To Remind Me*, written by Bacharach and David, tops the UK chart for 3 weeks, deposing Roy Orbison's° *Oh, Pretty Woman*. Shaw is immediately seen on several UK TV spots and gains as much notoriety from the fact that she always sings barefoot as from her hit single. (The bare feet are a gimmick dreamed up by Taylor, who predicts that this will be a source of interest for the press. Shaw continues to sing barefoot on stage for several years.)

Dec *(There's) Always Something There To Remind Me*, released in US on Frank Sinatra's Reprise label, reaches US #52 (three places lower than Johnson's highest US ranking with it 3 months earlier).

1965 Jan Third single is *I'd Be Far Better Off Without You*, written by Chris Andrews, but several reviewers and DJs note that B-side *Girl Don't Come* is the stronger song. Pye switches its promotion to it and *Girl Don't Come* hits UK #3.

Feb [21] She makes her concert debut, supporting Faith° at De Montfort Hall, Leicester, UK, with a UK tour following.

Mar *I'll Stop At Nothing*, written by Andrews for Faith, is given to Shaw instead and hits UK #4. Debut LP *Sandie* hits UK #3, and will be her only UK chart LP.

Apr *Girl Don't Come* makes US #42, her biggest US chart success. She attempts to visit the US to promote it, but is refused a performing visa by US immigration authorities because of the deluge of UK acts hitting success in US; she is deemed "not of sufficiently distinguished ability". Instead, Shaw makes a short promotional visit to Canada.

May Another Andrews composition, *Long Live Love* (rhythmically reminiscent of Tom Jones'° *It's Not Unusual*, a UK chart-topper 2 months earlier and which Shaw had turned down) is her second

UK #1, for 3 weeks.

June She is finally allowed into US and appears on US TV's "Ed Sullivan Show", singing *Long Live Love* (which stalls at US #97 2 weeks later and is her final US chart entry). LP *Sandie Shaw* peaks at US #100 at the same time.

Oct *Message Understood*, also Andrews-penned, hits UK #6.

Nov LP *Me* is released, but does not chart. She makes her cabaret debut at London's Savoy hotel, backed by The Paramounts, faring moderately well through a 3-week stint after a disastrous opening night.

Dec *How Can You Tell* peaks at UK #21.

1966 Feb *Tomorrow* hits UK #9. She is given the chance to record the theme song to forthcoming Michael Caine film *Alfie* as the follow-up, but Taylor rejects it. (The song will be a hit for Cilla Black° in UK and Cher° in US.)

Apr Low-priced compilation LP *The Golden Hits Of Sandie Shaw* anthologizes her hit singles to date.

June *Nothing Comes Easy* reaches UK #14.

July She performs in the Venice song festival in Italy.

Sept *Run* peaks at UK #32, during a year when Shaw is concentrating her efforts abroad in Europe.

Dec *Think Sometimes About Me* also reaches UK #32.

1967 Jan *I Don't Need Anything* charts for only 1 week at UK #50.

Mar She is named as the "other woman" in a widely publicized divorce case, with the judge delivering her a public reprimand.

Apr [8] Shaw represents UK in the Eurovision Song Contest with Bill Martin and Phil Coulter's *Puppet On A String*. The song wins, Britain's first victory in the contest.

May *Puppet On A String* tops the UK chart for 3 weeks, selling over 500,000 copies. It also becomes her biggest international success, with sales in West Germany exceeding 750,000, and worldwide total estimated at 4 million. The success brings a flood of work offers from all over Europe and elsewhere.

July Martin and Coulter also write her follow-up, *Tonight In Tokyo*, which peaks at UK #21.

Nov *You've Not Changed*, written by Andrews, makes UK #18. Shaw appears in The Royal Variety Show in London.

Dec Despite the year's singles successes, LP *Love Me, Please Love Me* fails.

1968 Feb *Today* reaches UK #27.

Mar [6] She marries fashion designer Jeff Banks, in London.

Apr *Don't Run Away* is Shaw's first since her debut single not to make UK top 50. (*Show Me* in June and a cover of Nilsson's° *Together* in Aug. will fare equally poorly.)

Sept She covers Mary Hopkin's° debut *Those Were The Days* and sings it on UK TV's "Top of the Pops". The Hopkin version, gaining radio play and promotion, shared with The Beatles'° *Hey Jude* and the launch of Apple Records, hits UK #1 and Shaw's flops.

Nov BBC musical series "The Sandie Shaw Supplement" proves popular, but the LP of the same title with music from the show fails.

1969 Apr *Monsieur Dupont* is a notable, if short-lived, UK singles chart comeback, hitting #6.

May *Think It All Over* peaks at UK #42 (and will be Shaw's last hit single for 15 years).

1971 Feb She covers Lynn Anderson's *Rose Garden*, but the US version also gets UK chart success.

Aug After several more flop singles, the last is a cover of Cat Stevens° *Father And Son*, her contract with Pye lapses and is not renewed.

1977 June After 5 years with no records, concentrating on cabaret and overseas work, plus straight theater roles (in Shaw's *St. Joan* and Shakespeare's *Hamlet*), she is signed to CBS. *One More Night* fails to chart, however, and follow-up *Your Mama Wouldn't Like It* also flops. (No LP is recorded before this deal lapses and she will disappear off the recording scene and public eye for 5 years.)

1982 Mar She is a featured vocalist (with Tina Turner°, Gary Glitter°, The Associates'° Billy McKenzie and others) on British Electric Foundation LP . . . *Presents Music Of Quality And Distinction*, singing an updated version of 1964 Dionne Warwick°/Cilla Black° hit *Anyone Who Had A Heart*.

1983 LP *Choose Life*, released on Palace Records in association with the World Peace Exposition, is a Buddhist-inspired set of songs written by Shaw herself. (Shaw is now married to Nik Powell, boss of the Palace record, film and video company and the Video Palace shops.) *Wish I Was*, from the LP, is also released.

1984 May A revival of The Smiths'° first single, *Hand In Glove*, recorded with the group and released on Rough Trade (to which they are contracted), charts at UK #27. (Smiths' lead singer Morrissey is a long-time Sandie Shaw fan, and has satisfied a personal ambition by working with her and having her record one of his compositions.)

1985 Dec [19] She takes part in Carol Aid, an all-star Christmas carol service held at London's Heaven club, to raise money for the Band Aid Appeal, along with Cliff Richard°, Lulu° and Chris De Burgh°.

1986 June Having made a conscious decision to resume her performing career with a higher profile, after several years of mainly domestic life, Shaw signs to Polydor. A revival of Lloyd Cole & The Commotions'° *Are You Ready To Be Heartbroken?* is a minor UK chart entry, at #68 as she makes a successful university tour.

1988 Sept Shaw signs to Rough Trade for LP *Hello Angel*. With musical assistance of George Michael's° bassist Deon Estus, The Communards'° Richard Coles and The Pretenders'° Chrissie Hynde (who plays harmonica on *Nothing Less Than Brilliant*), it features songs written by The Jesus & Mary Chain°, Fairground Attraction's Mark Nevin, Clive Langer and Morrissey with new collaborator Stephen Street. Morrissey and producer Street's song *Please Help The Cause Against Loneliness* trailers the LP.

THE SHIRELLES

Shirley Owens (lead vocals)
Addi "Micki" Harris (vocals)
Doris Coley (vocals)
Beverly Lee (vocals)

1957 The group is formed as The Poquellos, at high school in Passaic, N.J., US, by classmates Owens (b. June 10, 1941, Passaic), Harris (b. Jan.22, 1940, Passaic), Coley (b. Aug.2, 1941, Passaic) and Lee (b. Aug.3, 1941, Passaic), initially to sing at school parties and dances, where their speciality piece is group-composed *I Met Him On A Sunday*. Another schoolfriend, Mary Jane Greenberg, persuades them to audition this for her mother Florence Greenberg, who owns small local label Tiara Records.

1958 Jan Greenberg records *I Met Him On A Sunday* with the group, but insists on a more commercial-sounding name to put on the release; The Shirelles is the girls' own choice.

Apr The single starts to sell well, and Tiara, without the resources to promote a national success, leases it to Decca.

May *I Met Him On A Sunday* reaches US #50. (It will be followed by two more Tiara recordings leased to Decca, *My Love Is A Charm* and *I Got The Message*, but neither will chart.)

1959 May Greenberg forms Scepter Records with writer/producer Luther Dixon, and The Shirelles are signed. Dixon becomes their producer and Greenberg their manager.

July A revival of The Five Royales' ballad *Dedicated To The One I Love* is a moderate success at US #83, but follow-up *A Teardrop And A Lollipop* fails.

1960 Oct After another failure with *Please Be My Boyfriend*, Owens and Dixon co-write *Tonight's The Night*, which makes US #39.

Dec The group appears in a Christmas all-star show at Brooklyn's Paramount Theater, N.Y., alongside Ray Charles°, Dion°, Chubby Checker°, The Coasters°, Neil Sedaka°, and many others.

1961 Feb Owing songwriters Goffin and King° a favor, Dixon produces an uptempo string-backed arrangement of their ballad *Will You Love Me Tomorrow* (with King herself helping with the arrangement and playing drums), which tops the US chart for 2 weeks and is a million-seller. It is the first recording by an all-girl group to hit US #1.

Mar *Dedicated To The One I Love* is reissued as follow-up and this time is a smash, hitting US #3 and becoming the group's second million-seller. Meanwhile, *Will You Love Me Tomorrow* is their UK chart debut, hitting #4.

Apr [2] The group begins a major US tour in Irving Feld's "Biggest Show of Stars, 1961", debuting in Philadelphia, Pa. Also on the bill are Chubby Checker°, Fats Domino°, The Drifters°, Bo Diddley°, and others.

June *Mama Said* hits US #4.

June [25] The group appears at the Hollywood Bowl, in an Alan Freed outdoor spectacular also starring Brenda Lee°, Bobby Vee°, Jerry Lee Lewis°, and others.

Aug *A Thing Of The Past* halts at US #41, much of its airplay is being stolen by the B-side, Goffin and King's° *What A Sweet Thing That Was*, which climbs to US #54.

Nov *Big John* makes UK #21, at the same time as Jimmy Dean's *Big*

THE SHIRELLES *cont.*

Bad John (a different song) is at US #1. LP *The Shirelles Sing To Trumpet And Strings* is released without charting.

1962 Feb A Bacharach/David song, *Baby It's You* (molded for the group at Dixon's urging from its original form as *I'll Cherish You*), hits US #8. (A year later, The Beatles° will revive it on their debut LP, along with a version of *Boys*, B-side of *Will You Love Me Tomorrow*.)

May *Soldier Boy*, in simple, uptempo C&W style with a widely applicable lyric, written by Dixon and Greenberg in a few minutes and recorded as rapidly at the end of a session, becomes the group's third million-seller, topping the US chart for 3 weeks.

June LP *Baby It's You* reaches US #59, while *Soldier Boy* makes UK #23.

July *Welcome Home Baby* peaks at US #22. Greenberg turns down Gene Pitney's° song *He's A Rebel* as the follow-up, when offered it for The Shirelles by publisher Aaron Schroeder. (She is afraid the title will prove controversial in the South, but Phil Spector will record it with The Crystals° and take it to US #1).

Oct *Stop The Music* reaches US #36. (B-side *It's Love That Really Counts* will later be a UK hit for The Merseybeats.)

1963 Jan A revival of Doris Day's 1958 hit *Everybody Loves A Lover* makes US #19. After this, they record without Dixon, who leaves Scepter to work at Capitol Records.

Mar Compilation LP *The Shirelles' Greatest Hits* reaches US #19. Their best-selling LP, it stays charted for 49 weeks.

May *Foolish Little Girl* hits US #4, and is the group's last top 10 success. By now, the girl group sound, of which The Shirelles have been the hitmaking pioneers, has taken a major hold on US charts, and competition from groups like The Angels, The Chiffons° and Phil Spector's The Crystals°, for both songs and chart placings, is intense.

June *Foolish Little Girl* reaches UK #38, the group's third and final UK hit.

July *Don't Say Goodnight And Mean Goodbye* reaches US #26, while LP *Foolish Little Girl* makes US #68.

Sept *What Does A Girl Do?* peaks at US #53.

Oct The group sings the theme song to film *It's a Mad, Mad, Mad, Mad World*, but it makes only US #92.

Nov The Shirelles tour UK for the first time, with Little Richard° and Duane Eddy°. Owens and Coley have both married by this time, and are now Shirley Alston and Doris Kenner respectively. (Dionne Warwick°, also with Scepter Records, often fills in on stage for one or the other of them during 1963 when family commitments call.)

1964 Jan *Tonight You're Gonna Fall In Love With Me* reaches US #57. The group is no longer recording for Scepter, having fallen out with Greenberg and the label after discovering that trust fund money from their hit earnings, supposedly theirs at age 21, does not exist. The group attempts to leave but is prevented from signing elsewhere because of extended legal proceedings. (Meanwhile, Scepter will continue to release Shirelles singles regularly, from already-cut material, until the end of the year – though without any great promotion. Dionne Warwick° has just broken with *Anyone Who Had A Heart* and is now the label's priority act.)

Apr *Sha-La-La* (revived as a bigger hit by Manfred Mann° a few months later) makes US #69.

Aug *Thank You Baby* reaches US #63.

Nov *Maybe Tonight* stalls at US #88.

1965 Jan *Are You Still My Baby?* makes US #91, and is the last Shirelles chart entry for 2½ years.

1967 Aug *Last Minute Miracle* is recorded after legal and other difficulties between the group and Scepter are finally solved. It stalls at US #99 and the group signs to Mercury, where *I'll Stay By Your Side* and *There's A Storm Going On In My Heart* both fail to sell.

1968 Kenner leaves the group because of family commitments (she has married again, and is now Mrs. Doris Jackson). The others continue as a trio.

1969 Feb They sign to Bell Records as Shirley and The Shirelles. *Look What You've Done To My Heart* gains some UK airplay (and later some specialist sales as a Northern dancefloor favorite), but fails to chart in either US or UK.

Oct The group appears in Richard Nader's first Rock'n'Roll Revival Concert at New York's Felt Forum, alongside Bill Haley & The Comets°, Chuck Berry°, The Platters°, The Coasters°, and others.

1972 The trio is signed to RCA, recording LPs *Happy In Love* and *The Shirelles*. Both contain strong songs (by Bill Withers°, Carole King°, Marvin Gaye° and others) but fail to sell.

1973 The group appears in film *Let the Good Times Roll*, a documentary of a New York Madison Square Garden rock revival show interspersed with vintage performance clips, singing *Soldier Boy* and *Everybody Loves A Lover*.

1975 Doris Jackson returns to the group to replace Alston, who leaves for a solo career but is prevented by the other three from billing herself as "Shirley of The Shirelles". She signs to Prodigal Records and records LP *With A Little Help My Friends*, a collection of oldies on which she is joined on individual tracks by artists originally associated with the songs, such as The Drifters° (*Save The Last Dance For Me*, The Five Satins° (*In The Still Of The Night*), Herman's Hermits° (*Silhouettes*) and The Flamingos (*I Only Have Eyes For You*). The LP attracts critical interest, but does not sell.

1976 Jan LP *Let's Give Each Other Love*, on RCA, is the group's last.

1977 Alston records two further solo LPs, *Lady Rose* and *Sings The Shirelles' Biggest Hits*, for US Strawberry label, without success.

1982 Though now without recording contracts, both Alston and the three-piece Shirelles continue performing careers, the latter still popular on nostalgia dates and tours.

June [10] After a live show in Atlanta, Harris collapses and dies of a heart attack. (A memorial service is held in the group's home town of Passaic.)

1983 Oct The Shirelles are invited by Dionne Warwick° to sing *Will You Love Me Tomorrow* on her new LP *How Many Times Can We Say Goodbye*.

SIMON & GARFUNKEL

1953 Paul Simon° (b. Oct.13, 1941, Newark, N.J., US) and Art(hur) Garfunkel° (b. Nov.5, 1941, Queens, N.Y., US) meet at school in New York, playing The White Rabbit and The Cheshire Cat respectively in a production of *Alice in Wonderland*.

1955 Now writing songs together, Simon & Garfunkel apply to the Library of Congress to register their copyright.

1957 They tape a demo of Simon's song *Hey Schoolgirl*, at Sande's Recording Studio in New York and are heard by Sid Prosen, who secures them a deal for the cut.

Nov They adopt the name Tom & Jerry (Tom Graph is Garfunkel and Jerry Landis Simon), and *Hey Schoolgirl* is released on Big Records. The duo appers on Dick Clark's TV show "American Bandstand", performing *Hey Schoolgirl* directly after Jerry Lee Lewis° sings *Great Balls Of Fire*.

1958 Jan *Hey Schoolgirl* reaches US #49, but will be Tom & Jerry's only chart success, despite further singles on Big, including *Don't Say Goodbye* and *Our Song*. Most of the tracks are variations of The Everly Brothers'° style and sound. Simon° releases unsuccessful solo *True Or False*, as True Taylor.

1959 After high school, Tom & Jerry drift apart. Garfunkel° goes to Columbia University to study mathematics and architecture, while Simon° goes to Queens College to study English and starts making demo tapes for other singers and cutting further solo singles as Jerry Landis, including *Anna Belle* on MGM.

1960/63 While both are at college, Simon° continues to record and release singles under such names as Tico, Tico & The Triumphs and Jerry Landis, for labels including MGM, Warwick, Amy and Madison. Garfunkel° releases two singles under the name Artie Garr on Octavia and Warwick labels. Simon's songs become more influenced by the folk song boom in US and he begins playing folk dates in Greenwich Village.

1964 After Simon has traveled to UK and become involved in the folk scene (briefly joined by Garfunkel° for UK club dates during summer vacation), they reunite under their real surnames as Simon & Garfunkel. They are signed by Tom Wilson at CBS/Columbia Records.

Oct Debut LP *Wednesday Morning, 3:AM*, combining some of Simon's° songs with folk standards like *Go Tell It On The Mountain* and Bob Dylan's° *The Times They Are A-Changin'*, is released with no success.

1965 Jan The duo splits again temporarily as Simon returns to UK to play folk clubs and record some BBC radio sessions (for a religious program).

Oct Without informing Simon° or Garfunkel°, Wilson takes *The Sound Of Silence*, an acoustic track from the debut LP, and re-mixes it, adding drums, percussion and stinging electric guitar. The resulting commercial blend is issued as a single.

Nov The record has hit #1 in Boston when Simon°, living at Al Stewart's° house in UK, is contacted by Columbia and informed of the duo's burgeoning success. He returns to US and reunites with Garfunkel° for promotional appearances.

1966 Jan *The Sound Of Silence* tops the US chart for 2 weeks and sells over a million, but struggles in UK, which is a disappointment to Simon, who regards UK as a spiritual home.

Mar Debut LP *Wednesday Morning 3:AM* is re-promoted and reaches US #30, while the duo's newly-recorded LP, *Sounds Of Silence*, including the "electric" re-mix of *The Sound Of Silence*, climbs to US #21. Both earn gold disks. *Homeward Bound*, written on the platform of Wigan Station during Simon's° UK stay, hits US #5, while The Bachelors' cover of *The Sound Of Silence* hits UK #3 (after the original has failed to score – Simon is not amused, as he makes clear in interviews).

Apr *Homeward Bound* is the duo's UK chart debut, hitting #9, while LP *Sounds Of Silence* (with *Homeward Bound* added) reaches UK #13.

June *I Am A Rock*, from the LP and originally recorded solo by Simon° on 1964's LP *The Paul Simon Songbook*, hits US #3.

July *I Am A Rock* makes UK #17, while The Cyrkle's cover version of Simon's *Red Rubber Ball* hits US #2.

Sept *The Dangling Conversation*, a Simon° song about deteriorating relationships (and the duo's first track to feature strings), reaches US #25. It fails to chart in UK, as will the duo's next four US hit singles.

Dec *A Hazy Shade Of Winter* peaks at US #13. (The Bangles'° 1987 revival will hit US #2.) LP *Parsley, Sage, Rosemary and Thyme*, which includes *The Dangling Conversation* and the duo's new arrangement of traditional *Scarborough Fair/Canticle*, hits US #4, earning a gold disk.

1967 Apr *At The Zoo* reaches US #16, while Harper's Bizarre° cover Simon's *59th Street Bridge Song (Feelin' Groovy)* (from LP *Parsley, Sage, Rosemary And Thyme*), making US #13 and UK #34.

June [16] The duo appears at The Monterey Pop Festival in Cal.

Aug *Fakin' It*, with oblique references to Donovan° and (instrumentally) to The Beatles'° *Strawberry Fields Forever*, reaches US #23. B-side *You Don't Know Where Your Interest Lies* becomes the rarest Simon & Garfunkel CBS track since, after its deletion, it is never reissued on LP or in any other form. The duo is commissioned to supply music for Mike Nichols-directed movie *The Graduate*.

1968 Apr *Scarborough Fair/Canticle* climbs to US #11. Originally featured on LP *Parsley, Sage, Rosemary and Thyme*, it is also featured in *The Graduate*. Meanwhile, the soundtrack LP from *The Graduate* (which stars Dustin Hoffman and Anne Bancroft) tops the US chart for 9 weeks, earning a gold disk. Alongside incidental music by Dave Grusin, the LP features five Simon & Garfunkel tracks, of which only *Mrs. Robinson* is a new song.

May LP *Bookends*, compiling new Simon° songs with the duo's recent hit singles and a new, fuller version of *Mrs. Robinson*, tops the US chart for 7 weeks, replacing the movie soundtrack LP, and selling over a million in US.

June *Mrs. Robinson* tops the US chart for 3 weeks and is a million-seller.

July *Mrs. Robinson* restores the duo to the UK singles chart, hitting #4. The duo plays sold-out concerts at London's Royal Albert Hall.

Aug LP *Bookends* tops the UK chart for 5 weeks.

Sept LP *Parsley, Sage, Rosemary and Thyme* is re-released in UK and reaches UK #13.

Nov Soundtrack LP *The Graduate* is released in UK to tie in with the film's UK release and hits #3. The duo's debut LP *Wednesday Morning 3:AM* is also belatedly issued in UK, reaching #24.

1969 Feb 4-track EP *Mrs. Robinson* hits UK #9.

Mar [12] *Mrs. Robinson* wins two Grammy awards, as Record of the Year and Best Contemporary Pop Vocal Performance by a Duo or Group.

May New Simon° song, *The Boxer*, hits US #7 and UK #6. The duo follows it with a US tour, between lengthy sessions for the next LP, only interrupted by Garfunkel's° acting commitments in movie *Catch 22*.

Nov [30] The duo's first TV special airs on US TV.

1970 Feb *Bridge Over Troubled Water* hits US #1 for 6 weeks and UK #1 for 3. The LP of the same title is released and rapidly also tops both US and UK charts (in US for 10 weeks and in UK for 41 weeks in 8 separate runs over an 18-month period). This puts the duo in the very rare company of acts who have topped US and UK singles and LP charts simultaneously. Among the tracks is a revival of The Everly Brothers'° *Bye Bye Love*, recorded live on tour at a concert in Ames, Iowa. (Relations between the two have become increasingly strained throughout the reported 800 hours it has taken to complete recording of the LP with, among other things, Garfunkel° objecting to Simon's° song *Cuba Ci, Nixon No* and Simon becoming frustrated by his partner's film commitment interruptions. By the time the LP is released, the duo has effectively split.)

May Taken from the LP, *Cecilia* hits US #4 and is another million-seller, while folk singer Julie Felix's cover of *El Condor Pasa (If I Could)* (Simon's arrangement of a traditional tune from the Andes) makes UK #19. Also released this month is *Hair* actress/singer Marsha Hunt's version of *Keep The Customer Satisfied* which reaches UK #41.

Oct The duo's own version of *El Condor Pasa (If I Could)* reaches US #18.

1971 Mar [16] Simon & Garfunkel sweep the Grammy awards, as *Bridge Over Troubled Water* single and LP win, collectively, in six categories: Record of the Year, Album of the Year, Song of the Year, Best Contemporary Song, Best Engineered Record and Best Arrangement of Accompanying Vocalists.

1972 Apr They reunite for a one-off concert in aid of Presidential candidate Senator George McGovern, at New York's Madison Square Garden.

Aug Compilation LP *Simon & Garfunkel's Greatest Hits* hits US #5 and UK #2. It includes live versions of some unreleased tracks.

Oct Taken from the compilation, *For Emily, Whenever I May Find Her* reaches US #53. B-side *America* makes US #97 and UK #25.

1975 Oct [18] Simon & Garfunkel reunite on UK NBC-TV show "Saturday Night Live".

Dec After some years of successful solo careers, the duo sings Simon's° *My Little Town*, which is included on the current solo LP by each partner, and also hits US #9 as a single (though fails to chart in UK).

1977 Oct [18] They appear together (in tuxedos) at the Britannia Music Awards in London, where, due to a technical fault with TV cameras, they have to perform *Bookends/Old Friends* for six takes. At the awards (a one-off event marking 25 years of the British Record Industry), *Bridge Over Troubled Water* single and LP are voted the Best International (non-UK) LP and Single released between 1952 and 1977.

1978 Mar Garfunkel's° LP *Watermark*, includes a re-make of Sam Cooke's° *What A Wonderful World* which features Simon° and James Taylor° on guest vocals.

1981 Sept Garfunkel's° LP *Scissors Cut* features Simon° on Jim Webb-written song *In Cars*.

Sept [19] The duo reunites for a concert in New York's Central Park.

SIMON & GARFUNKEL *cont.*

Over 400,000 attend the performance, which is recorded and filmed for subsequent record release and TV/video showing.

Nov UK Compilation LP *The Simon & Garfunkel Collection* hits UK #4.

1982 Apr Double live LP *The Concert In Central Park* is released by Geffen Records and hits both US and UK #6, earning a gold disk.

Apr [19] They announce a further reunion, to tour overseas.

May From the live LP, a revival of The Everly Brothers'° *Wake Up Little Suzie* reaches US #27.

June [8] They open a 9-date European tour (which will end on June 19 with sold-out shows at London's Wembley Stadium) in Paris, France.

1983 July [19] The duo embarks on another US reunion tour. (It will be a major success and a new Simon & Garfunkel LP, *Think Too Much*, is planned but they will drift apart during recording and the LP will appear as Simon's° solo *Hearts And Bones*.)

CARLY SIMON

1964 Apr Carly (b. June 25, 1945, New York, N.Y., US) and older sister Lucy, daughters of Richard L. Simon, co-founder of Simon & Schuster publishers, form singing duo The Simon Sisters and have a minor hit (US #73) on Kapp Records with *Winkin' Blinkin' And Nod*.

1964/65 The sisters record a series of children's and folk songs for Kapp and CBS/Columbia.

1966 The Simon Sisters split when Lucy gets married. Carly moves to France.

1967 She returns to US and meets Bob Dylan's° manager Albert Grossman. She signs a management deal as Grossman hopes to promote her as a female Dylan.

Sept Simon records four tracks with producer Bob Johnston, but she argues with Grossman over her career direction and the songs are not issued. She meets Jacob Brackman, film critic for *Esquire* magazine and the two begin to write songs together.

1969 Simon meets Jac Holzman, founder of Elektra label, via a mutual friend and pop entrepreneur Jerry Brandt. Holzman signs her to the label.

1971 Apr Debut LP *Carly Simon*, produced by Holzman, enters the US chart, eventually reaching #30. It features lyrics by Brackman and, taken from it, *That's The Way I've Always Heard It Should Be* hits US #10.

Nov *Anticipation* peaks at US #13. (It will later be used for a commercial on US TV.) Second LP *Anticipation*, also produced by Holzman, is released, reaching US #30.

1972 Feb Simon wins a Grammy as Best New Artist.

Mar *Legend In Your Own Time* makes US #50.

Nov *You're So Vain* tops the US chart (and will hit UK #3), earning a gold disk. (The song causes considerable conjecture concerning the identity of its subject. It seems unlikely to be the track's backing vocalist Mick Jagger.)

Nov [3] Simon marries James Taylor° in her Manhattan apartment. That evening she joins him on stage, where he announces their marriage.

Dec LP *No Secrets* hits US #1 and UK #3. It is her first LP produced by Richard Perry, who tries to give her voice a harder rock edge. (It will remain her most successful LP.)

1973 Mar *The Right Thing To Do* makes both US and UK #17.

1974 Jan LP *Hotcakes* hits US #3 and UK #19. Again produced by Perry, it includes backing vocals by husband Taylor° and features their first song written together, *Forever My Love*.

Mar *Mockingbird*, a duet with Taylor° on Charlie & Inez Foxx 1963 smash, hits US #5 and UK #34.

May *I Haven't Got Time For The Pain* peaks at US #14. LP *Playing Possum*, again produced by Perry, hits US #10.

June *Attitude Dancing* reaches US #21.

Aug *Waterfall* stalls at US #78.

Oct *More And More* falters at US #94.

Nov LP *The Best Of Carly Simon* reaches US #17.

Dec [24] Simon goes carol singing with Linda Ronstadt°, Joni Mitchell° and James Taylor° in Hollywood, Cal.

1976 June *It Keeps You Running*, a cover of The Doobie Brothers'° hit, makes US #46. LP *Another Passenger*, produced by Ted Templeman and with Brackman as co-writer, reaches US #29.

1977 July *Nobody Does It Better* is issued as theme from James Bond movie *The Spy Who Loved Me*. The song, co-written by Marvin Hamlisch and Carole Bayer Sager, hits US #2 and UK #7.

1978 Apr [19] Simon joins Bruce Springsteen°, Jackson Browne°, The Doobie Brothers° and others in petitioning President Carter to end nuclear power in US. (It precedes her forthcoming involvement in the "No Nukes" project.)

Apr LP *Boys In The Trees*, produced by Arif Mardin, hits US #10. *You Belong To Me*, written with Doobie Brother° Michael McDonald° over a telephone, hits US #6.

Aug Another Simon and Taylor° duet, a cover of The Everly Brothers° 1958 hit *Devoted To You*, reaches US #36.

1979 June LP *Spy* reaches US #45, and will be Simon's last for Elektra. *Vengeance* peaks at US #48.

Sept [19] Simon joins other anti-nuclear musicians singing with Graham Nash, John Hall and Taylor°, on the first of a five night series of Musicians United for Safe Energy (MUSE) concerts at New York's Madison Square Garden. (The show is recorded for LP *No Nukes*.)

1980 July LP *Come Upstairs*, Simon's first for Warner Bros., makes US #36. *Jesse*, from the LP, climbs to US #11.

Oct [4] Simon collapses of exhaustion on stage in Pittsburgh, Pa. (Over the next few years, Simon develops an increasing fear of live performance.)

1981 Sept LP *Torch* is released. A collection of standards from the 1920s, 1930s and 1940s, it makes US #50.

1982 July Written and produced by The Chic° Organization and taken from film *Soup for One*, *Why* hits UK #10, but stalls at US #74. Simon and Taylor° separate.

1983 Aug On Will Powers' UK #17 *Kissing With Confidence*, Simon provides lead vocals on the Lynn Goldsmith pseudonymous novelty hit.

Sept LP *Hello Big Man* reaches US #69, while taken from it, *You Know What To Do* makes US #83.

1985 June *Tired Of Being Blonde* stalls at US #70.

Sept LP *Spoiled Girl*, her only LP for CBS/Epic, fails to chart. She appears in film *Perfect*, in which she tips water over John Travolta°.

1986 Nov *Coming Around Again*, her first single for Arista, reaches US #18 and UK #12. (B-side *Itsy Bitsy Spider* features the vocal debut of her daughter.) Produced by ex-Yardbird° Paul Samwell-Smith, the song is taken from Jack Nicholson/Meryl Streep film *Heartburn*.

1987 May LP *Coming Around Again* peaks at #25 in both US and UK.

1988 Aug At the annual Martha's Vineyard Celebrity Auction, one of the featured items is a private performance of one song by Simon in the home of the winning bidder. Simon sings three songs for $26,000 each for two men, unable to outbid each other.

Sept LP *Greatest Hits Live* makes US #87 and UK #49. The LP is recorded live in front of invited guests at the harbor in Gay Head, Martha's Vineyard, Mass. Simon begins work on the soundtrack to movie *Working Girl*.

PAUL SIMON

1958 Following US chart success with friend Art Garfunkel° as Tom & Jerry, Simon (b. Paul Frederick Simon, Oct.13, 1941, Newark, N.J.), cuts solo single *True Or False* for the same label, Big records, under the name True Taylor, but it flops.

1959 Simon attends Queens College in New York to study English. He makes money cutting demos for music publishers, having been introduced to contacts by fellow demo-maker Carole Klein (later Carole King°). He also adopts the name Jerry Landis to make more solo singles, the first *Anna Belle*, for MGM, is another failure.

1961 Several singles for Warwick Records, including *I Want To Be The Lipstick On Your Collar* and *Play Me A Sad Song*, fail to sell, before Simon moves (still, at this time making more money from demo work than his own releases) to Madison Records where he records as Tico and Tico & The Triumphs.

1962 Jan *Motorcycle* by Tico & The Triumphs reaches US #99 on Amy Records, which has acquired Madison and Simon's contract. He makes another two Tico singles for Amy, neither of them hits. (Some songs from this time are credited to Simon/Landis, the Simon being Paul's brother Eddie.)

1963 Jan As Jerry Landis again, *The Lone Teen Ranger*, on Amy, reaches US #97. He also writes and produces for others, including Ritchie Cordell, The Fashions and Dotty Daniels, and begins to play Greenwich Village clubs like Gerde's Folk City at night, while still plugging songs to publishers during the day. Later in the year, while at law school, he teams up again with Garfunkel°

(completing a Math degree at Columbia University), and they perform folk-style material for the first time as Simon & Garfunkel°.

1964 Dropping out of law school, Simon travels to UK (joined during summer vacation by Garfunkel°), where he plays the folk circuit, and is befriended by London social worker Judith Piepe, with whom he lodges. He records a solo single for UK independent label Oriole Records, still using the name Jerry Landis, *He Was My Brother*, written about a friend killed during the US civil rights disturbances. (It is credited to Paul Kane in US, where it is issued by Tribute Records.)

1965 Jan After the US failure of the first Simon & Garfunkel° LP *Wednesday Morning, 3:AM*, Simon returns to UK, where, with Judith Piepe, he gains some work on BBC radio, contributing songs to a series of Piepe's commentaries on the daily religious series "Five to 10". He also plays the UK folk circuit, with fellow Americans Tom Paxton, Carolyn Hester and Buffy St. Marie.

May Thanks to his US Columbia contract, Simon is able to record solo LP *The Paul Simon Songbook* (showing Simon and Piepe on the sleeve), for UK CBS. (It contains solo acoustic versions of several songs which will later reappear on the next duo LP. The solo LP is not a big seller and will be deleted at Simon's own request in 1979.) While in UK, he also works with other singer/songwriters, including Jackson C. Frank and Al Stewart°.

Dec When Simon & Garfunkel's° *The Sound Of Silence* hits the US chart, Simon is contacted by producer Tom Wilson and returns to US, to re-form the duo (which will have 5 years of huge international success).

1969 Tensions arise between Simon and Garfunkel° during the lengthy recording sessions for LP *Bridge Over Troubled Water*, and they decide to go their separate ways once the project is completed.

1970 Feb While the single and LP *Bridge Over Troubled Water* are #1 worldwide, the duo splits. Simon agrees to continue as a solo artist on CBS, but under his own terms.

Aug [6] Simon takes part in an anti-war festival at New York's Shea Stadium, 25 years after the bombing of Hiroshima.

1971 He writes songs for, and then records (partly in Jamaica) his first post-duo solo LP.

1972 Mar LP *Paul Simon* hits US #4, earning a gold disk, and tops the UK chart for a week. Among the guest players is violinist Stephane Grappelli. The LP is co-produced by Simon & Garfunkel's° former co-producer and engineer, Roy Halee. Taken from it, *Mother And Child Reunion*, a track recorded in Jamaica (and, according to Simon, about a dish of egg and chicken) hits US #4 and UK #5.

May *Me And Julio Down By The School Yard*, also from the LP, reaches US #22 and UK #15.

Aug *Duncan*, a third single from the LP, makes US #52.

1973 May [6] Simon begins his first solo tour since his break with Garfunkel°, in Boston, Mass.

June LP *There Goes Rhymin' Simon* hits US #2 and UK #4, earning a gold disk. Again, it features many guest musicians.

July From the LP, *Kodachrome* hits US #2 and is a million-seller. Another track, *Take Me To The Mardi Gras* hits UK #7 with *Kodachrome* relegated to UK B-side because of the BBC's refusal to play songs which mention commercial brand names.

Oct Gospel-styled *Loves Me Like A Rock*, recorded with The Dixie Hummingbirds, hits US #2 and is another million-seller, also reaching UK #39.

1974 Jan *American Tune*, also from LP *There Goes Rhymin' Simon*, reaches US #35.

Apr Live LP *Paul Simon In Concert/Live Rhymin'* peaks at US #33 but fails to chart in UK. It was recorded on tour the previous year, and features some of the guests from the previous studio set. (Simon spends the rest of this year writing and recording.)

1975 Oct *Gone At Last*, a gospel-style duet with Phoebe Snow, backed vocally by The Jessy Dixon Singers, reaches US #23, and is a taster for the long-in-production new LP.

Dec LP *Still Crazy After All These Years*, Simon's most jazz-flavored set yet, made with top session crew, tops the US chart, selling over a million, and hits UK #6. Among the tracks is Simon & Garfunkel's° duet *My Little Town* (also included on Garfunkel's° new LP), which hits US #9 as a single. Lyrically, the LP contains references to his recently failed marriage (Simon and first wife Peggy are now divorced).

1976 Feb Taken from the LP, *50 Ways To Leave Your Lover* tops the US chart for 3 weeks, selling over a million, and makes UK #23.

Mar *Still Crazy After All These Years* wins two Grammy awards, as Album of the Year and Best Male Pop Vocal Performance of 1975.

May The title song from *Still Crazy After All These Years* reaches US #40, while Simon is on a lengthy international tour to promote the LP (which includes a UK BBC TV special).

1977 Jan [19] Simon participates in the Inaugural Eve Gala Performance for President-elect Jimmy Carter.

1978 Jan *Slip Slidin' Away* hits US #5 and makes UK #36. It is also one of two new songs on compilation LP *Greatest Hits, Etc.*, which is a million-selling LP, reaching US #18 and UK #6. (The other new song is *Stranded In A Limousine*.) Simon makes his acting debut in Woody Allen's movie *Annie Hall*.

Mar Simon and James Taylor° provide guest vocals on Art Garfunkel's° revival of *(What A) Wonderful World*, which reaches US #17.

Mar [22] NBC-TV movie *The Rutles*, in which Simon makes a cameo appearance, airs on US TV. (He will make occasional appearances on NBC-TV's "Saturday Night Live", performing both solo and with Garfunkel° (and on one occasion, with George Harrison°) for the late-night cult comedy show, and will also be best man at its producer's wedding.)

Dec During the year, Simon becomes a part-owner of the Philadelphia Furies soccer team. US NBC-TV airs "The Paul Simon Special".

1979 Feb [15] Simon signs to Warner Bros. (partly for the chance to undertake his own movie project), paying CBS $1.5 million to release him from his contract. He also begins a suit against CBS for non-payment of royalties.

Mar He begins work on the screenplay for his movie *One-Trick Pony*.

1980 Simon devotes most of the first half of the year to the movie: he writes the script and songs for it, and also directs and acts in the production. When the film is completed, Simon embarks on a major US and UK concert tour.

Sept *Late In The Evening*, taken from *One-Trick Pony*, hits US #6 and reaches UK #58. Soundtrack LP *One-Trick Pony*, treated by fans and reviewers as a new Paul Simon LP rather than a movie soundtrack, reaches US #12 and UK #17.

Oct [1] Movie *One-Trick Pony* opens in US (and will be only a moderate success). Included are brief appearances by The B-52's° and a specially re-formed The Lovin' Spoonful°.

Nov The title song from *One-Trick Pony* climbs to US #40.

Nov [6] Simon begins a UK tour at London's Hammersmith Odeon, his first live appearance in UK for 5 years. He buys the audience a drink – a gesture which costs him £1,000 a night.

1982 Apr [19] Simon & Garfunkel° announce a reunion (though it will be mainly for nostalgic live concerts).

1983 Feb *The Blues*, a duet with Randy Newman°, reaches US #51.

Aug [16] Simon marries long-time girlfriend, actress Carrie Fisher.

Dec LP *Hearts And Bones* peaks at US #35 and UK #17. The set is salvaged from what was to be a new Simon & Garfunkel° LP on Geffen, and guests include composer Phillip Glass. From it, *Allergies* reaches US #44.

1984 Simon begins work on a new LP which will take him to South Africa to record both vocal and instrumental groups.

1985 Jan [28] Simon joins the all-star line-up for recording of USA For Africa's° *We Are The World*.

Oct LP *Graceland* hits US #3, earning a platinum disk, and tops the UK chart for 5 weeks. It is chiefly inspired by South African dance music, both traditional and electric, and features the group Ladysmith Black Mambazo (which, as a result of this exposure, becomes an international act, with Simon later co-producing two of its Warner Bros. LPs). The LP also includes contributions from Linda Ronstadt°, The Everly Brothers° and Los Lobos° (who later threaten to sue if their name isn't credited on composer credits). From the LP, *You Can Call Me Al* hits UK #4 and initially US #44 (but will re-chart at US #23 on repromotion in mid-1987). The song's promo video features comedy actor Chevy Chase.

Dec Also from the LP, *The Boy In The Bubble* reaches UK #33.

1987 Jan The title song from *Graceland* peaks at UK #81.

Jan [30] Simon holds a press conference in London to state that both the ANC and the UN have removed him from their blacklists (originally imposed after he broke the boycott on recording in South Africa).

Apr Simon plays UK dates at London's Royal Albert Hall, and is picketed by anti-apartheid protestors. Guests on stage include husband and wife Hugh Masekela and Miriam Makeba. (Simon will play Zimbabwe, Africa, later in the summer, where TV film and best-selling home video *The Graceland Concert* will be shot.)

PAUL SIMON *cont.*

1988 Mar [2] LP *Graceland* is named Record of the Year at the 30th annual Grammy ceremonies.

Sept [13] John Cougar Mellencamp° appears with Paul Simon on US NBC-TV's "Coca Cola Presents Live: The Hard Rock".

Nov Compilation LP *Negotiations And Love Songs, 1971-1986* reaches UK #17 and US #110.

SIMPLE MINDS

Jim Kerr (vocals)
Charlie Burchill (guitar)
Mike McNeil (keyboards)
John Gibbin (bass)
Mel Gaynor (drums)

1977 Nov Johnny & The Self Abusers, a Glasgow, Scotland, UK, septet featuring three guitarists, exhibit true punk nihilism by splitting up on the day their first single *Saints And Sinners* is released on Chiswick. Members of the band divide according to musical interests to form 1960s-flavored Cuban Heels and more psychedelic, experimental Simple Minds.

1978 Feb Simple Minds debut at Glasgow's Satellite Club. The line-up is Kerr, Burchill (b. Nov.27, 1959), Brian McGee (drums) and Duncan Barnwell (guitar), all ex-The Self Abusers.

May Now joined by McNeil (b. July 20, 1958) who has previously played keyboards with a variety of local bands, and Derek Forbes (bass) ex-Subs, the band records a six-song demo at Glasgow's Ca Va studios. This comes to the attention of Ian Cranna (then contributor to UK music paper *New Musical Express*, later manager of Orange Juice). The band gigs heavily in Scotland, including a residency at Glasgow's Mars Bar.

Nov Barnwell quits, and the remaining quintet records another demo at Ca Va, subsequently releasing through Edinburgh independent label, Zoom, a subsidiary of Arista, run by Bruce Findlay. The deal means Arista retains control of Simple Minds regardless of their main deal with Zoom.

1979 May The group enlists the services of John Leckie, whose production work with Magazine had impressed it, and records debut LP *Life In A Day*. It hits UK top 30 in its first week of release, spending a further 5 weeks retreating. The title track reaches UK #62.

June *Chelsea* fails to chart. The group spends the rest of the year gigging extensively in UK and Europe, with two appearances on UK BBC TV's "Whistle Test", (including a session shot live at New York's Hurrah club during the group's first US visit in Oct.) and recording a second, more experimental LP.

1980 Jan LP *Real To Real Cacophony* is released. According to one reviewer it is probably the most uncommercial album ever released by Arista.

Feb The LP fails to chart, as does single *Changeling*. Tension between Zoom and Arista has resulted in the former requesting to be dropped from the latter's roster. Under the terms of the original deal, however, Arista retains Simple Minds and, without its major asset, Zoom folds. Findlay joins business affairs lawyer, Robert White, to form Schoolhouse Management (which will handle Simple Minds' future affairs).

Sept LP *Empires And Dance* charts for 3 weeks, reaching UK #41. It impresses Peter Gabriel° who invites the group to tour.

Oct As *I Travel* fails to chart, the band looks for a new record deal.

1981 Feb Arista releases *Celebrate* which also fails. Simple Minds negotiate their departure from Arista, renouncing their rights to back royalties, and sign to Virgin. They enter the studio with new heart, recording a prodigious amount of material.

May First single for Virgin, *The American*, reaches UK #59. McGee quits to get married and is replaced by Kenny Hyslop (ex-Slik).

Aug *Love Song*, another single from a forthcoming LP, makes UK #47.

Sept Simple Minds release two LPs *Sons And Fascinations* and *Sister Feelings Call*, in an unusual double package, initially made available as a limited-edition double LP, and subsequently released separately. The double LP peaks at UK #11 during a 7-week stay.

Nov *Sweat In Bullet* stalls at UK #52.

1982 Feb Arista releases a compilation of early Simple Minds tracks, *Celebration*, which makes UK #45. *I Travel* is reissued, but fails to chart.

Apr *Promised You A Miracle*, from the next LP, peaks at UK #13 in an 11-week stay. Hyslop quits, to be replaced first by Mark Ogletree, then Mel Gaynor (b. May 29, 1959).

Aug *Glittering Prize* reaches UK #16.

Sept LP *New Gold Dream (81, 82, 83, 84)* is released with work from all three drummers, although Gaynor's contributions predominate. The LP confirms Simple Minds' increasing popularity, spending a year in the UK LP chart, peaking at UK #3. The band begins a sold-out UK tour.

Oct Having bought the entire Arista Simple Minds back catalog, Virgin reissues all four LPs.

Nov Third single from LP *New Gold Dream*; *Someone Somewhere (In Summertime)* reaches UK #36.

1983 Feb Simple Minds begin to make an impression in US, where LP *New Gold Dream* begins a 19-week stay on chart, reaching #69.

Nov *Waterfront* makes UK #13.

1984 Jan *Speed Your Love To Me* peaks at UK #20.

Feb Steve Lillywhite-produced LP *Sparkle In The Rain* begins a 57-week stay on UK chart, and is Simple Minds' first UK #1 album, while reaching US #64.

Mar *Up On The Catwalk* reaches UK #27.

Mar [13] A UK tour is cancelled after Kerr falls ill at end of the opening night in Birmingham, UK.

May [5] Kerr marries The Pretenders'° Chrissie Hynde.

May Simple Minds play 8 consecutive nights at London's Hammersmith Odeon, tying with Elton John's° 1982 record.

1985 Apr Simple Minds achieve a breakthrough in US with *Don't You Forget About Me*, from the soundtrack to US "brat-pack" movie *The Breakfast Club*. Unlike all previous releases, it is not self-penned, and had been offered to Billy Idol° and Bryan Ferry°. It hits US #1, spending 22 weeks on chart, and UK #7, spending more than half a year on UK chart.

May Soundtrack LP *The Breakfast Club* includes the Simple Minds cut.

July Simple Minds are invited to play Live Aid in Philadelphia, Pa.. Their song *Ghostdancing* is dedicated to Amnesty International, an organization for which they tour later in the year.

Aug A consistent seller, *Don't You Forget About Me* re-enters at UK #61.

Oct The group's new UK #1 LP, *Once Upon A Time*, will go platinum during an 82-week chart stay. (Released through A&M deal in US, it will hit US #10 in Mar. 1986.) *Alive And Kicking* hits UK #7 and US #3.

Dec The band begins an extensive massive world tour.

1986 Jan *Sanctify Yourself* hits UK #10 and US #14.

Mar *All The Things She Said* hits UK #9 and US #28.

Apr [20] The combined Simple Minds/Rod Stewart° soccer XI beat Pepperdine 2-0.

June [22] Simple Minds top the bill at UK's Milton Keynes Bowl pop festival.

Aug [12] The final date of a world tour in Paris, France, is recorded for future live LP release.

Nov Their live version of *Ghostdancing* makes UK #13.

1987 June Third successive UK platinum, double LP *Live In The City Of Light*, enters UK chart at #1 and will rise to US #96.

July *Promised You A Miracle* reaches UK #50, taken from the live LP.

1988 June [11] The group plays the Nelson Mandela 70th Birthday Concert at London's Wembley Stadium. They record *Mandela* which they pledge not to release, which is aired on UK radio.

SIMPLY RED

Mick Hucknall (vocals)
David Fryman (guitar)
Fritz McIntyre (keyboards)
Tony Bowers (bass)
Chris Joyce (drums)

1984 Manchester-based band The Frantic Elevators, focused around singer/writer Hucknall (b. 1961, Manchester, UK), an ex-local club DJ, splits after releasing on local UK labels several singles, including *You Know What* (Eric's), *Searchin' For The Only One* (Crackin' Up), *Voices In The Dark* (TJM) and *Holding Back The Years* (No Waiting), between 1979 and 1983. Hucknall forms a new band, Simply Red.

1985 The group signs a worldwide deal with Elektra Records and begins recording in Amsterdam.

July Debut single *Money's Too Tight (To Mention)*, a cover of a 1983 song by The Valentine Brothers, reaches UK #13. The group supports James Brown° in concert in London.

Sept *Come To My Aid* makes UK #66.

Oct Debut LP *Picture Book*, produced by Stewart Levine, reaches UK #34. Tim Kellett joins the band on trumpet.

Nov *Holding Back The Years*, a re-recording of a Frantic Elevators song, reaches UK #51.

1986 Mar *Jericho* climbs to UK #53 and the band embarks on its first US tour.

July *Holding Back The Years* is reissued in the UK hitting #2 and hits US #1 for a week. Sales worldwide top the million mark. LP *Picture Book* reaches US #16.

Aug *Open Up The Red Box* makes UK #61.

Oct *Money's Too Tight To Mention*, released as the US follow-up, reaches #28.

1987 Mar *The Right Thing* reaches UK #11. The band adds new members, Aziz Ibrahim (guitar), replacing Richardson, Ian Kirkham (sax) and Janette Sewell (vocals) as new LP *Men And Women* hits UK #2 and US #31. The LP, including songs by Cole Porter, Sly Stone and Bunny Wailer, is banned in Singapore because of "crude lyrics" in *The Right Thing*. Due to its success, earlier LP *Picture Book* picks up renewed sales and also hits UK #2.

May *The Right Thing* reaches US #27.

June *Infidelity*, co-written by Lamont Dozier, reaches UK #31.

July *Maybe Someday* fails to chart.

Dec *Ev'rytime We Say Goodbye*, a Cole Porter revival previously issued by Simply Red as a bonus track on 12" version of *The Right Thing*, reaches UK #11.

1988 Mar *I Won't Feel Bad* is released to tie in with live shows at London's Wembley Arena but makes only UK #68.

SIOUXSIE & THE BANSHEES

Siouxsie Sioux (vocals)
John McGeoch (guitar)
Steve Severin (bass)
Kenny Morris (drums)

1976 Sept [20] Bromley, Kent, UK punkette Siouxsie (b. Susan Dallion, May 27, 1957, London, UK) takes part in the 100 Club Punk Festival in London, UK, with Sid Vicious on drums, Steve Havoc on bass and Marco Pironi on guitar. Their live set, which features Siouxsie reciting The Lord's Prayer, lasts 20 minutes. The band splits immediately. (Havoc will revert to the name Steve Severin, Vicious will join The Sex Pistols°, and Pironi will join The Models before becoming Adam Ant's songwriting partner in Adam & The Ants°.)

Dec [1] Siouxsie appears with The Sex Pistols° on UK TV show "Today". Morris joins The Banshees on drums.

1977 Feb [24] Pete Fenton joins on guitar.

July [2] John McKay replaces Fenton.

Oct [20] After Johnny Thunders & The Heartbreakers' Rainbow Theatre gig, at which The Banshees are support act, Siouxsie and Morris are arrested and detained overnight at Holloway Road Police Station. They are fined £20 each for obstruction and released the following morning.

Nov The band sings *Make Up To Break Up* on its debut UK TV appearance.

Nov [29] The group records a session for John Peel's radio show.

1978 June [9] The group signs to Polydor Records.

June [21] Siouxsie & The Banshees appear with The Clash°, The Sex Pistols° and Generation X in Don Lett's film *Punk Rock Movie*. (The group was filmed for Derek Jarman's *Jubilee* but the clip was never used.)

Sept After much word-of-mouth and media interest, debut single *Hong Kong Garden* hits UK #7.

Oct [11] The band commences its first major UK tour, with Nico and the Human League° as support.

Dec LP *The Scream*, produced by the band and Steve Lillywhite, reaches UK #12.

1979 Apr [7] The group plays a charity concert for MENCAP and is later faced with a £2,000 bill for seat damage.

Apr *The Staircase (Mystery)* peaks at UK #24.

July *Playground Twist* climbs to UK #28.

Sept LP *Join Hands* reaches UK #13. Morris and McKay leave midway through a tour, and after 5 days of panic, the others are temporarily joined for the balance of the dates by Pete "Budgie" (formerly with The Slits) on drums, and Robert Smith (on loan from The Cure°) on guitar.

Oct [3] Siouxsie is hospitalized with hepatitis.

Oct *Mittageisen (Metal Postcard)* makes a disappointing UK #47.

1980 Jan [16] With Smith committed to The Cure°, John McGeoch (moonlighting from Magazine) joins temporarily on guitar.

Apr *Happy House*, produced by the band and Nigel Gray, reaches UK #17.

June *Christine* makes UK #24.

July McGeoch joins on guitar full-time (but at first still "unofficially", so that he can continue with other projects).

Aug LP *Kaleidoscope* hits UK #5.

Oct The band tours US for the first time.

Nov *Israel* climbs to UK #41.

1981 Feb The year starts with a short UK tour.

Mar Severin produces Altered Images'° *Dead Pop Stars*.

June *Spellbound* makes UK #22.

June [18] The Banshees plays its first Iron Curtain concert in Yugoslavia before embarking on what the group states will be its last UK tour.

July LP *Juju* hits UK #7.

Aug *Arabian Nights* reaches UK #32, while the band is on a major 30-date UK tour.

Aug [10] The group plays a charity concert for the Disabled Children's International Games.

Oct Siouxsie and Budgie start a spin-off project as The Creatures, recording *Mad-Eyed Screamers*, which makes UK #24.

Dec Compilation LP *Once Upon A Time* reaches UK #21 and is also issued as a video collection. The group tours again in US.

1982 June *Fire Works* reaches UK #22. Siouxsie contracts laryngitis and is ordered to rest her voice for 6 months.

Oct *Slow Dive* makes UK #41.

Nov LP *A Kiss In The Dreamhouse*, produced by Mike Hedges (and including the band's first recordings with string accompaniment) reaches UK #11. Smith is borrowed from The Cure° again for the tour to promote the LP when McGeoch falls ill. (Without returning, McGeoch will announce within a few weeks that he has left the group, apparently dissatisfied with Siouxsie's attitude.)

Dec *Melt*, a double A-side with the French-language Christmas song *Il Est Né Le Divin Enfant*, makes UK #49.

1983 Most of the first half of the year is spent on solo/spin-off projects, as Siouxsie and Budgie record The Creatures LP *Feast*, while Severin and Smith (who has stayed on as a Banshee in addition to his Cure° commitments) form The Glove. Both projects will be released on The Banshees' newly-formed Wonderland Records, through Polydor.

May The Creatures reach UK #21 with *Miss The Girl*.

Aug Their follow up *Right Now*, originally recorded by Mel Torme as the B-side to his 1963 *Comin' Home Baby* hit, makes UK #14.

Sept [6] The group plays a concert in Italy for the communist party.

Sept The Glove releases *Blue Sunshine* and plays London's Royal Albert Hall.

Oct A revival of the Lennon/McCartney° song *Dear Prudence* gives the group its biggest UK single success, hitting #3.

Oct [31/Nov 1] The band plays two concerts at the Royal Albert Hall, London, which are recorded for live LP release.

Dec Live double LP *Nocturne*, is the first LP release on the new Wonderland label. It reaches UK #29.

1984 Apr *Swimming Horses* makes UK #28.

May Smith leaves to concentrate on The Cure° and is replaced on guitar by John Carruthers (ex-Clock DVA).

June *Dazzle* peaks at UK #33. LP *Hyena* reaches UK #15, as the band appears in a UK Channel 4 TV special.

July LP *Hyena*, released in US by Geffen Records, becomes the group's first US success, at #157.

Nov EP *Overground*, featuring string-backed (courtesy of The Chandos Players) renditions of songs like *Overground* and *Placebo Effect*, makes UK #47.

1985 Oct The band plays a month-long UK tour, after two attempts at beginning a new studio LP with two different producers, Bob Ezrin and Hugh Jones. Siouxsie spends much of the tour with a leg in plaster, after dislocating a kneecap on stage at London's Hammersmith Odeon.

Nov *Cities In Dust* climbs to UK #21.

1986 Jan The group guests in film *Out Of Bounds*.

Mar *Candy Man* reaches UK #34.

May LP *Tinderbox*, produced by the band with Steve Churchyard, reaches UK #13.

July LP *Tinderbox* makes US #88.

SIOUXSIE & THE BANSHEES *cont.*

1987 Feb A cover of Bob Dylan's° *This Wheel's On Fire*, originally a UK hit for Julie Driscoll and The Brian Auger Trinity, makes UK #14.

Mar Carruthers leaves, to be replaced by John Klein (ex-Specimen) and Martin McCarrick joins on keyboards. LP *Through The Looking Glass*, a set of cover versions, reaches UK #15.

Apr *The Passenger*, a revival of an Iggy Pop° song, makes UK #41.

July The band makes a one-off live London appearance at the Finsbury Park "Supertent".

Aug *Song From The Edge Of The World* reaches UK #39.

1988 Aug *Peek A Boo* shows a shift in the group's musical direction and peaks at UK #16.

Sept LP *Peepshow* maintains the new musical route and the band promotes it with a UK tour.

SIR DOUGLAS QUINTET

Doug Sahm (vocals and guitar)
Augie Meyers (organ)
Jack Barber (bass)
Johnny Perez (drums)
Frank Morin (horns)

1964 Sahm (b. Nov.6, 1941, San Antonio, Tex., US), having recorded *A Real American Joe* as Little Doug for Texas label Sarg in 1955, and turned down a chance to join the "Grand Ole Opry" in order to finish school, spends some years in local bar bands and forms the Sir Douglas Quintet, with Morin, Meyers, Barber and Perez.

1965 May The band signs to Huey Meaux' Tribe label, and *She's About A Mover*, with a British-beat Vox organ riff from Meyers, climbs to US #13.

July *She's About A Mover* reaches UK #15.

Aug Similarly-styled follow-up *The Tracker* fails to chart.

1966 Mar *The Rains Came* reaches US #31. Debut LP *The Sir Douglas Quintet* is released, to limited interest. As the year progresses, the initial novelty of the Quintet wears off, and with a drug bust in Texas hanging over him, Sahm breaks up the band and moves to California.

1968 Sahm cuts *Honkey Blues* with Morin and session musicians, as Sir Douglas Quintet + 2.

1969 Sahm re-forms the original Quintet, with Harvey Kagan replacing Barber, and George Rains replacing Perez, and the band signs to Mercury's Smash label.

Mar Smash debut *Mendocino* makes US #27.

May LP *Mendocino* peaks at US #81.

Aug *Dynamite Woman* reaches US #83.

1970 June LP *Together After Five* is popular in Europe. LP *1+1+1=4* is released but fails to chart.

1971 LP *Return Of Douglas Saldana* is released (the last on Smash), but goes unnoticed.

1973 Mar Sahm breaks up the band again to go solo, and LP *Doug Sahm And Band*, on Atlantic, reaches US #125. Produced by Jerry Wexler and Arif Mardin, it includes contributions by Bob Dylan° (*Wallflower*) and Dr. John°.

1974 He links with Creedence Clearwater Revival's° rhythm section on LP *Groover's Paradise* for Warner Bros.

1976 Sahm, with the quintet's original producer, Meaux, records LP *Rock For Country Rollers* on Dot.

1977 Live LP *Live Love* is released in US on Meyers' Texas label.

1979 Sahm appears in film *More American Graffiti*.

1980 LP *Hell Of A Spell* is released, without success, on Takoma label.

1981 Feb The group re-forms again, with original members Sahm, Meyers and Perez joined by Alvin Crow (guitar and vocals), Speedy Sparks (bass) and Shawn Sahm (guitars and vocals) for LP *Border Wave*, a new wave-flavored comeback on Takoma (Chrysalis in UK), produced by Craig Leon and Cassell Webb. Despite the contemporary sound, it makes only US #184.

1988 Having spent most of the 80s touring, Sahm forms a new group, The Almost Brothers, with guitarist Amos Garrett and ex-Blasters pianist Gene Taylor.

THE SISTERS OF MERCY

Andrew Eldritch (vocals)
Gary Marx (guitar)
Ben Gunn (guitar)
Craig Adams (bass)

1980 The band, initially studio bound, is formed in Leeds, UK, with Eldritch, Marx, and a drum machine named Doktor Avalanche. Debut single *The Damage Done* is released on their own independently-distributed Merciful Release label. In order to play live, Eldritch and Marx recruit Gunn and Adams. They tour, supporting Nico, The Birthday Party, The Clash° and The Psychedelic Furs.

1982 Apr Second release *Body Electric*, on Leeds-based Confederacion Nacional de Trabajo label, sells well to a growing cult following and gets good UK music press reviews.

June The band arranges a distribution deal for Merciful Release with York-based Red Rhino, part of independent distributor The Cartel. While touring UK, The Sisters record a BBC Radio 1 session for "The John Peel Show".

Oct Another Leeds group, The March Violets, is signed to Merciful Release, and the bands begin a UK tour together.

Nov A row between the two bands flares up and The Violets leave the label to form their own Rebirth Records. The Sisters of Mercy release *Alice* which climbs the UK independent chart.

1983 Mar *Anaconda* fails.

May 5-track EP *Reptile House* hits the top of the independent charts and sells on export.

June Gunn leaves after disagreements within the band and is replaced by Wayne Hussey, who has worked with Pauline Murray, Dead or Alive° and ska-punk group The Walkie Talkies.

Oct After the release of *Temple Of Love* the group signs a distribution deal with WEA.

1984 June *Body And Soul* reaches UK #46.

Oct *Walk Away*, written by Eldritch and Hussey, also makes UK #46.

1985 Feb *No Time To Cry* peaks at UK #63.

Apr Debut LP *First And Last And Always* reaches UK #14, with impressive sales in the north of England. More problems arise in the group; Eldritch's lifestyle causes him health problems and Marx, overshadowed by Hussey, refuses to attend soundchecks. On a European tour, Eldritch issues an ultimatum – either Marx leaves or he does. Marx leaves. A concert at London's Royal Albert Hall is filmed (and will be released on video as *Wake* – the title, many assume, alludes to the last Sisters of Mercy concert. Immediately afterwards the group announces its decision to split. Hussey and Adams will form The Mission°, and Eldritch moves to Hamburg, West Germany.

1986 July Amid legal tangles over the use of The Sisters of Mercy name, Eldritch releases LP *Gift* as The Sisterhood. It manages a 1-week stay on UK chart at #95.

1987 Oct Eldritch and Patricia Morrison (ex-Gun Club) return as The Sisters of Mercy, and *This Corrosion* hits UK #7.

1988 Mar The new Sisters' second single, *Dominion*, reaches UK #13. LP *Floodland* hits UK #9.

June *Lucretia My Reflection* makes UK #20.

SLADE

Noddy Holder (guitar and vocals)
Dave Hill (guitar)
Jimmy Lea (bass, piano and violin)
Don Powell (drums)

1964 Hill (b. Apr.4, 1952, Fleet Castle, UK) and Powell (b. Sept.10, 1950, Bilston, UK) play in Wolverhampton band, The Vendors, with Johnny Howells (vocals), Mickey Marston (guitar) and Dave Jones (bass). The band does not record commercially, but makes a four-song demo EP.

1965 The Vendors become The 'N Betweens and record under their new name, with session drummer Bobby Graham producing. The results, only released in France on Barclay label EPs, include versions of The Sorrows' *Take A Heart* and Rufus Thomas' *Can Your Monkey Do The Dog*. Meanwhile, Holder (b. June 15, 1950, Walsall, UK) is guitarist and backing vocalist in Wolverhampton's Steve Brett & The Mavericks, and plays on their Dec. 1965 Columbia single *Chains On My Heart*.

1966 Holder and Lea (b. June 14, 1952, Wolverhampton, UK) join Hill and Powell in The 'N Betweens when the others leave, thus

completing the future Slade line-up.
Nov The 'N Betweens cover The Young Rascals'° *You Better Run* on Columbia; the group's last release under this name.

1969 Feb After playing mostly covers (Motown, Beatles°, ska) on the Midlands club circuit, they move to London. Now named Ambrose Slade, they are seen at Rasputin's Club by Chas Chandler, ex-The Animals°, who launched Jimi Hendrix's° career in UK. Chandler becomes their manager/producer and, in an attempt to cash in on the first UK skinhead cult, dresses them in boots, braces and short-cropped hair. He arranges a recording contract with Fontana.
Apr Ambrose Slade releases its only LP under that name, *Beginnings*. It sells poorly (as does *Genesis/Roach Daddy*, released in May).
Oct At Chandler's suggestion, the band shortens its name to Slade for the next Fontana release, *Wild Winds Are Blowing*, but it fares no better.

1970 Mar *The Shape Of Things To Come*, a cover of a US hit by Max Frost and The Troopers, is the band's last Fontana single, and again fails, despite a grand launch to press and media at London's Bag O' Nails club.
Sept Debut Polydor release, *Know Who You Are*, also fails.
Nov LP *Play It Loud* is released, but fails to chart.

1971 June *Get Down And Get With It*, a revival of a Bobby Marchan song, best known via Little Richard's° version, reaches UK #16.
Nov Follow-up *Coz I Luv You* hits UK #1 for 4 weeks. It is the first of six chart-toppers and a 5-year run of top 20 hits, all penned by Holder and Lea. It also launches the distinctive trademark of personalized spellings of titles.
Dec [24] The group plays a Christmas Eve party gig at London's Marquee club.

1972 Feb *Look Wot You Dun* hits UK #4.
Apr LP *Slade Alive* hits UK #2 (and will remain on UK chart for over a year).
May [10] The group begins its first major headlining UK tour, supported by Status Quo°, in Bradford.
July *Take Me Bak 'Ome* tops the UK chart for a week.
Sept *Mama Weer All Crazee Now* hits UK #1 for 3 weeks.
Oct *Take Me Back 'Ome* is Slade's first US chart entry, at #97, while LP *Slade Alive* makes US #158.
Dec *Gudbuy T'Jane* hits UK #2, behind Chuck Berry's° *My Ding-A-Ling*.

1973 Jan LP *Slayed* tops the UK chart for 3 weeks, as *Mama Weer All Crazee Now* makes US #76.
Feb LP *Slayed* reaches US #69.
Mar *Cum On Feel The Noize* hits UK #1 for 4 weeks, confirming Slade with the most successful run of UK hit singles achieved by a group in the post-Beatles° era.
Apr *Gudbuy T'Jane* makes US #68.
June *Skweeze Me Pleeze Me* tops the UK chart for 3 weeks, while *Cum On Feel The Noize* stalls at US #98.
July [4] Powell is badly injured in a car crash, in which his girlfriend Angela Morris is killed. (He will be hospitalized for 6 weeks, and will suffer memory problems as a result of his head injuries for some months. He will return to his drumkit, eventually fit again.)
Oct LP *Sladest* tops the UK chart for 3 weeks, and makes US #129. *My Friend Stan* hits UK #2, behind Simon Park Orchestra's million-selling *Eye Level*.
Dec *Merry Christmas Everybody* enters the UK chart at #1, staying on top for 5 weeks. After selling over a quarter million copies in its first day, it becomes the group's biggest single, selling over a million in UK (and will re-chart every Christmas from 1981-86).

1974 Mar LP *Old, New, Borrowed And Blue*, is the band's third consecutive UK #1 LP, while US-only LP *Stomp Your Hands, Clap Your Feet* makes US #168.
Apr *Everyday* hits UK #3.
July *Bangin' Man* also hits UK #3. Slade spends the rest of the year working on its feature film, *Flame*.
Oct Hymnal *Far Far Away*, an early taster of *Flame* soundtrack, hits UK #2.
Dec Soundtrack LP *Slade In Flame* hits UK #6 as the movie opens in UK. The title is the name of a mid-1960s band which Slade portrays in the film (which also stars Tom Conti, Alan Lake and UK DJs Tommy Vance and Emperor Rosko).

1975 Mar *How Does It Feel* reaches UK #15, ending a run of 12 top 5 hits.
May *Thanks For The Memory (Wham Bam Thank You Mam)* hits UK #7.
July LP *Slade In Flame* makes US #93.
Sept [12] The group's movie *Flame* has its first US showing, in St. Louis, Mo. (It will make little impression in US.)
Dec *In For A Penny* reaches UK #11.

1976 Feb *Let's Call It Quits* also peaks at UK #11.
Mar *Nobody's Fool* makes UK #14. The group leaves Polydor for manager/producer Chandler's own label, Barn records.

1977 Feb Debut Barn single *Gypsy Roadhog* peaks at UK #48.
Apr *Burning In The Heat Of Love* fails to chart.
Nov A rock medley of two early Elvis Presley° items, *My Baby Left Me/That's All Right Mama* reaches UK #42.

1978 Mar *Give Us A Goal* shows Slade's affinity with UK football terraces, but fails to chart.
Nov *Rock 'N' Roll Bolero* and LP *Slade Alive, Vol.2* fail to chart in UK.
Dec Lea and brother Frankie form The Dummies as a sideline from Slade, releasing three singles, without chart success.

1979 The last three Barn singles, *Ginny Ginny* (May), *Sign Of The Times* (Oct.) and *Okey Cokey* (Dec.) all fail. *Okey Cokey* is reissued a month later by RSO label, but fares little better. There is also an unsuccessful LP, *Return To Base* (Oct.).

1980 June Slade reappears on another Chandler label, Six of the Best, which specializes in six-song 12"-EPs. Tracks include *Night Starvation* and *When I'm Dancin' I Ain't Fightin'*.
Oct *Slade Alive At Reading '80*, a five-track EP recorded at the year's Reading Rock Festival and released on Chandler's Cheapskate label, reaches UK #44, the group's first singles chart entry for 3 years.
Nov Polydor's TV-advertised LP *Slade Smashes* reaches UK #21.
Dec A live version of *Merry Christmas Everybody*, recorded at the Reading Festival, makes UK #70.

1981 Feb *We'll Bring The House Down* hits UK #10, the group's first top 10 for 6 years.
Mar LP *We'll Bring The House Down* reaches UK #25.
Apr *Wheels Ain't Comin' Down* stalls at UK #60.
Sept *Lock Up Your Daughters*, the group's first single in a newly-signed deal with RCA, reaches UK #29.
Nov LP *Till Deaf Us Do Part* makes UK #68.

1982 Apr *Ruby Red* makes UK #51.
Dec *(And Now The Waltz) C'Est La Vie* peaks at UK #50, with a live version of seasonal favorite *Merry Christmas Everybody* on the B-side, in competition to Polydor's annual reissue of it. Live LP *Slade On Stage* makes UK #58.

1983 Sept US heavy metal group Quiet Riot hits US #5 and makes UK #45 with a copycat revival of *Cum On Feel The Noize*, which restores the memory of Slade. (The new wave of US glam-metal bands is influenced by the pop-metal and gaudy image of UK bands like Slade and Sweet° – for whom the US audience was far too serious in the early 1970s.)
Dec Slade produces one of its catchiest and most commercial singles, *My Oh My*, pitched at an ideal tempo for TV-massed swaying and scarf-waving, which it receives on "Top of the Pops" and other shows. It hits UK #2, behind The Flying Pickets' *Only You*. LP *The Amazing Kamikaze Syndrome* makes UK #49.

1984 Mar *Run Run Away*, a more rock-oriented follow-up, hits UK #7.
May US LP *Keep Your Hands Off My Power Supply*, reaches US #33.
June Polydor releases another hits compilation LP, *Slade's Greats*, which makes UK #89. *Run Run Away* reaches US #20, the group's biggest US hit.
Aug *My Oh My*, issued as US follow-up, reaches US #37. Meanwhile, Quiet Riot's second Slade cover, *Mama Weer All Crazee Now*, makes US #51.
Nov *All Join Hands* reaches UK #15.

1985 Feb *Seven Year Bitch* stalls at UK #60.
Apr *Myzsterious Mizter Jones* (a return to title misspelling) makes UK #50. LP *Rogues Gallery* reaches UK #50.
May *Little Sheila* makes US #86.
Dec TV-advertised LP *Crackers: The Slade Christmas Party Album* reaches UK #34, while extracted *Do You Believe In Miracles* makes UK #54.

1987 Feb *Still The Same* makes UK #73.
May LP *You Boyz Make Big Noize* (a title suggested by the tea lady at the recording studio) makes UK #98.

1988 Dec Slade returns with a revival of Chris Montez' 1962 hit *Let's Dance*.

SLY AND ROBBIE

Sly Dunbar (drums)
Robbie Shakespeare (bass)

1969/74 Dunbar (b. Noel Charles Dunbar, May 10, 1952, Kingston, Jamaica), who played his first session in 1969 on Dave & Ansil Collins' *Double Barrel*, a huge Jamaican hit (and later a UK #1 and US #22) and Shakespeare (b. Robert Shakespeare, Sept.27, 1953, Kingston, Jamaica), who played his first major sessions in 1973 for Big Youth on LP *Screaming Target* (released in UK on Virgin) are recruited by leading Jamaican producer Jo Jo Hookim as members of his studio band The Revolutionaries. Among the first sessions is The Mighty Diamonds' LP *Right Time*.

1975 While continuing to work with The Revolutionaries, the duo is recruited into the studio bands of producers Joe Gibbs (The Professionals) and Lee Perry (The Upsetters). (With The Professionals the duo will work with Dennis Brown on the records which first establish him in Jamaica; with The Upsetters the duo plays on Junior Murvin's hit single *Police And Thieves*, which will make the UK pop charts twice, in 1976 and 1980.)

1976 Dunbar and Shakespeare are now the key drum and bass rhythm team in reggae (rivalled only by the Barrett brothers in The Wailers.) They start to play on the sessions of practically every major (and many minor) Jamaican artists, including Peter Tosh, Bunny Wailer, Burning Spear and Jimmy Cliff°.

1977 Dunbar releases two solo LPs *Simple Spyman* and *Slick And Wicked*. Shakespeare is featured on both.

1978 Dissatisfied with the financial returns of working only for other producers, they form Sly and Robbie, producers and musicians, and their own Taxi Records label. Their first major international success is with Gregory Isaacs' LP *Soon Forward*.

1979 A second Isaacs' LP, *Cool Ruler*, is released. They produce Black Uhuru's first major international LP *Showcase*.

1980 They produce Uhuru's LP *Sinsemilla*. They are recruited by Island Records' owner Chris Blackwell as members of the regular session band at Compass Point Studios, Nassau, The Bahamas. Among their first sessions are those for Grace Jones'° LP *Warm Leatherette*. (They will continue to work regularly with Jones. Compass Point is the launchpad for Sly and Robbie session/production work in other areas of music outside reggae – they will go on to work with such stars as The Rolling Stones°, Joe Cocker°, Ian Dury°, Yoko Ono and Bob Dylan°.)

1981 Aug As Bits & Pieces, Dunbar and Shakespeare have a substantial international success with *Don't Stop The Music*.

1985 Sept They release the funk/reggae LP *Language Barrier*, produced by New York avant-funkist Bill Laswell (with whom Dunbar first worked in 1983 on the sessions for Herbie Hancock's LP *Future Shock*.

1986 Aug Dunbar and Shakespeare set off on a lengthy and high-profiled US and European tour with "The Taxi Gang" package (also featuring vocalist Ini Kamoze and Yellowman).

1987 They record a second Laswell-produced LP, *Rhythm Killers*, which features Hancock , Bootsy Collins and Parliament/Funkadelic keyboard player Bernie Worrell among other guests. *Boops (Here To Go)* reaches UK #12 and *Fire* makes UK #60. The LP climbs to UK #35.

1988 Sept LP *The Summit* looks set to make further inroads into the mainstream market.

SLY & THE FAMILY STONE

Sly Stone (vocals, keyboards and guitar)
Freddie Stone (guitar)
Cynthia Robinson (trumpet)
Jerry Martini (saxes)
Rosemary Stone (vocals, piano)
Larry Graham (bass guitar)
Greg Errico (drums)

1966 DJ and producer (The Beau Brummels°, Bobby Freeman) Stone (b. Sylvester Stewart, Mar.15, 1944, Dallas, Tex., US), having earlier formed The Stoners with Robinson (b. Jan.12, 1946), forms The Family Stone in San Francisco, adding brother Freddie (b. June 5, 1946), sister Rosemary (b. Mar.21, 1945) and cousin Graham (b. Aug.14, 1946, Beaumont, Tex). The Family Stone starts gigging in bars and clubs in Oakland.

1967 Their iconoclastic collision of funk, jazz, rock and anarchic humor, soon tagged "psychedelic soul", extends their following to the city's emergent psychedelic movement. The group signs to Epic and releases LP *A Whole New Thing*.

1968 Apr *Dance To The Music* hits US #8.
May LP *Dance To The Music* reaches US #142.
July *Life/M'Lady* peaks at US #93.
Aug *Dance To The Music* hits UK #7.
Sept [11] Arriving in London to begin a tour, UK Customs find cannabis in Graham's possession.
Sept BBC TV cancels a scheduled appearance and a week later the band leaves UK without having performed.
Oct *M'lady* makes UK #32.
Dec LP *Life* reaches US #195.

1969 Feb *Everyday People* hits US #1 for 4 weeks.
Mar *Everyday People* makes UK #36, while B-side *Sing A Simple Song* climbs to US #89.
May *Stand!* reaches US #22.
June LP *Stand!* makes US #13, and becomes the group's first gold disk. *I Want To Take You Higher*, B-side of *Stand!*, peaks at US #60.
July [3-6] For the first time, rock performers take part in the Newport Jazz Festival at Rhode Island, US. Sly & The Family Stone are featured on the bill with Led Zeppelin°, James Brown° and others.
Aug The band performs *I Want To Take You Higher* at the Woodstock Festival. Press reports suggest several members of The Family Stone have drug problems, and the band acquires a reputation for failing to show at scheduled gigs.
Oct *Hot Fun In The Summertime* hits US #2.

1970 Feb *Thank You (Falettinme Be Mice Elf Agin)* coupled with *Everybody Is A Star* hits US #1.
June Reissued *I Want To Take You Higher* makes US #38.
Nov LP *Greatest Hits* is released, hitting US #2 and bringing the group its second gold disk.

1971 Sept [4] *The New York Times* reports that Stone's Hollywood landlord is suing him for $3 million, claiming his building is inundated with "loud, noisy and boisterous persons" and that he wants Stone to leave.
Dec *Family Affair* hits US #1 in 5 weeks. LP *There's A Riot Goin' On* also tops the US chart.

1972 Jan *Family Affair* reaches UK #15. Graham leaves the group (to form Graham Central Station) and is replaced by Rusty Allen. Errico leaves to be replaced by Andy Newmark, and saxophonist Pat Ricco joins.
Mar *Runnin' Away* peaks at US #23. LP *There's A Riot Goin' On* makes UK #31.
May *Runnin' Away* reaches UK #17. *Smilin'* peaks at US #42.
Nov [25] Despite an impressive bill including Sly & The Family Stone, LA radio station K-ROQ's "The Woodstock of the West" only attracts 32,000 to its 100,000-seater LA Coliseum.

1973 June LP *Fresh* hits US #7.
Sept *If You Want Me To Stay* makes US #12.
Dec *Frisky* peaks at US #79.

1974 Feb Graham Central Station's eponymous debut LP reaches US #48.
May Graham Central Station's *Can You Handle It?* makes US #49.
June [5] Stone marries Kathy Silva on stage before a gig at New York's Madison Square Garden.
Aug LP *Small Talk* picturing Stone, Silva and baby Sylvester Bubb Ali Stewart on the sleeve, reaches US #15. *Time For Living* makes US #32.
Oct [30] Silva files for divorce. Graham Central Station LP *Release Yourself* makes US #51.
Nov (Sly & The Family Stone's *Loose Booty* reaches US #84.

1975 Jan [16] Sly & The Family Stone begin a six-night stand at New York's Radio City Music Hall. Attendances at the eight-date residency are less than one-third full.
Aug Graham Central Station LP *Ain't No 'Bout-A-Doubt It* makes US #22 and goes gold. His *Your Love* reaches US #38.
Nov LP *High On You*, credited to Stone as a solo, makes US #45. Graham Central Station's *It's Alright* peaks at US #92.

1976 Jan Stone files for bankruptcy.
Mar Instrumental *The Jam* from Graham Central Station makes US #63.
June Graham Central Station LP *Mirror* reaches US #46.

1977 Apr Graham Central Station LP *Now Do U Wanta Dance* makes US #67.

1978 July Now credited as Larry Graham & Grand Central Station, LP *My Radio Sure Sounds Good To Me* reaches US #105.

1979 July Graham's last LP with Grand Central Station, *Star Walk*, reaches US #136.
Nov Sly & The Family Stone LP *Back On The Right Track* makes US #152.
1980 June Graham's solo LP *One In A Million You* enters the US chart on its way to #27 and a gold certification. The ballad title track also goes gold, hitting US #9.
Nov Graham's *When We Get Married* makes US #76.
1981 Mar Stone is featured on George Clinton° and Funkadelic's LP *The Electric Spanking Of War Babies*.
Aug Graham's LP *Just Be My Lady* makes US #46.
Sept His *Just Be My Lady* reaches US #67.
1982 July Graham's LP *Sooner Or Later* peaks at US #142. Single of same name makes UK #54.
1983 Aug Graham's LP *Victory* makes US #173.
1984 Bobby Womack°, having persuaded Stone to seek treatment for his drug addiction, invites him on a 2-month US tour.
1986 Reports say Stone has kicked his drug addiction and that several record labels are interested in signing him. There is also talk of an LP with George Clinton°.
1987 Jan [29] Stone helps launch "Fight for Literacy Day" in California.
1988 *Family Affair* is reissued on CBS' dance label Upfront.

THE SMALL FACES

Steve Marriott (vocals and guitar)
Ronnie "Plonk" Lane (bass)
Jimmy Winston (organ)
Kenny Jones (drums)

1965 June The group is formed in London when pub-playing trio Lane (b. Apr.1, 1946, Plaistow, London, UK), Jones (b. Sept.16, 1948, Stepney, London) and Winston (b. James Langwith, Apr.20, 1945, Stratford, London), looking for a strong singer or guitarist, find both in Marriott (b. Jan.30, 1947, Bow, London), whom they meet working in a music shop in East Ham, London. He has been in showbiz since age 12 as an actor (appearing in the London production of *Oliver* and UK radio and TV plays and shows) and has cut a solo single (*Give Her My Regards* for Decca in 1963). They adopt the name Small Faces because of their lack of height and the Mod connotations of "Face". All are R&B fans, and they pitch the group directly at the Mod/R&B scene recently opened up by The Who°.
Oct Signed to Decca, their debut is Ian Samwell-written/produced *Whatcha Gonna Do About It*, which borrows its rhythm structure from Solomon Burke's° *Everybody Needs Somebody To Love* and adds some sawing pop-art guitar. It reaches UK #14.
Nov Winston leaves, to be replaced by Ian McLagan (b. May 12, 1945, London), who comes recommended via a glowing review in *Beat Instrumental* magazine of his playing in Boz & The Boz People. At the same time, follow-up single *I've Got Mine* just misses the chart, and the group begins live work (notably in a London West End residency at The Cavern club, off Leicester Square) to build a firm following on which to launch subsequent disks.
1966 Mar *Sha La La La Lee*, written by Kenny Lynch and Mort Shuman, hits UK #3.
May *Hey Girl*, which hits UK #10, is the group's first Marriott/Lane-composed chartmaker.
June LP *The Small Faces* hits UK #3, staying on chart for 6 months.
Sept The group has its first #1 when another Marriott/Lane song, *All Or Nothing*, tops the UK chart for a week (deposing The Beatles'° *Yellow Submarine/Eleanor Rigby*).
Dec *My Mind's Eye*, again written by Marriott and Lane, hits UK #4 at Christmas (part of its melody is lifted from the Christmas carol *Angels From The Realms Of Glory*). Already aware that Decca is trying to push a more polished version of the group on record than that seen in its raucous, stomping live gigs, they are amused when Decca releases a rough mix of the single instead of a more polished take – apparently in error.
1967 Mar *I Can't Make It* peaks at UK #26, after which the group announces that it is to leave Decca for Andrew Oldham's Immediate label.
May Decca releases a final single *Patterns* but, with no promotion from the group, it fails to chart.
June Compilation LP *From The Beginning*, on Decca, reaches UK #17.
July *Here Comes The Nice* (with some oblique drug references, in tune with the rock mood of the time) reaches UK #12 and LP *Small Faces* also peaks at UK #12.
Sept *Itchycoo Park*, the group's most experimental production yet, with phased drums and spacey harmonies, hits UK #3.

1968 Jan *Tin Soldier*, another complex production, hits UK #9. *Itchycoo Park* is the group's first US hit single, peaking at #16. The group tours Australia with The Who° (both groups are thrown off an aircraft for rowdy behavior while preparing to fly between Australian gigs).
Mar LP *There Are But Four Small Faces* makes US #178.
Apr *Tin Soldier* reaches US #73.
May *Lazy Sunday*, eschewing the psychedelic tendencies of the two previous Lane/Marriott-penned singles, is a loping good-time rocker in Ray Davies/Kinks° style, with Marriott vocalizing in an exaggerated cockney accent. It is their biggest UK hit since *All Or Nothing*, hitting #2.
June Concept LP *Ogden's Nut Gone Flake* tops the UK chart for 6 weeks. One side features tracks linked by comedian Stanley Unwin, while the LP's round cover (representing the lid of the Ogden's tobacco tin) is a gimmick selling point. The group subsequently refuses to play most of tracks from the LP when performing live.
Aug *The Universal*, almost free-form in approach, reaches UK #16.
Oct LP *Ogden's Nut Gone Flake* peaks at US #159. The Small Faces begin a UK package tour with The Who° and Joe Cocker°.
Oct [19] Peter Frampton° of The Herd sits in on guitar at a Small Faces gig, and ignites a rapport with Marriott. (They begin to make plans to form a new group (which will become Humble Pie°); with Marriott in particular wanting to gain rock credibility, aware of the teen tag still attaching to The Small Faces despite their more recent progressions.)
1969 Feb Marriott leaves and The Small Faces disband. Lane, Jones and McLagan stay together (to link up in June with guitarist Ron Wood and vocalist Rod Stewart°, and re-launch their career as The Faces°).
Mar The final "new" Small Faces single, *Afterglow (Of Your Love)* (coupled with heavy rock spoof *Wham! Bam! Thank You Ma'm*), makes UK #36. Double LP *The Autumn Stone* is released at the same time, summarizing the group's career via both old and new material.
1972 Aug LP *Early Faces*, compiled as a cash-in on the success of The Faces°, and actually containing Small Faces Decca tracks, makes US #176.
1973 Mar A US reissue of LP *Ogden's Nut Gone Flake* reaches US #189.
1976 Jan *Itchycoo Park* is reissued in UK, picks up strong airplay, and makes the top 10 for the second time, hitting #9.
Apr *Lazy Sunday*, also reissued on the strength of the previous success, makes UK #39.
June Spurred by the interest in the group's old hits, Marriott (who has just disbanded Steve Marriott's All-Stars after a long US tour) re-forms the group, with Jones and McLagan rejoining, but Lane

THE SMALL FACES *cont.*

declining. Rick Wills comes in on bass instead.

1977 Apr [13] The group begins its 11-date reunion tour of UK with a show in Sheffield. (The group's resurrection has only been officially announced in March, though they have been rehearsing for some months while contractual wrangles were worked out.)

Aug LP *Playmates* by the new line-up fails to chart.

Sept A second UK tour is undertaken to promote the LP, for which Jimmy McCulloch (ex-Paul McCartney's° Wings) joins temporarily on guitar.

1978 May The group splits again after recording the material for a second LP. (Jones will join The Who° after Keith Moon's death, Wills will move to US to join Foreigner°, McLagan will become a member of The Rolling Stones'° augmenting road band and Marriott will continue to lead R&B groups into the 1980s, mostly in small clubs and pubs.)

Sept LP *78 In the Shade* fails to chart, and – unlike The Small Faces material of the 1960s – is quickly forgotten.

1983 Sept [20] A benefit concert is held at London's Royal Albert Hall for Ronnie Lane, now suffering from multiple sclerosis. The superstar line-up includes Eric Clapton°, Jeff Beck°, Steve Winwood° and Jimmy Page.

PATTI SMITH

1969 Smith (b. Dec.30, 1946, Chicago, Ill., US), having moved with her family from New Jersey to Paris, then to London and New York, starts a small local newspaper before working for *Rock* magazine.

1970 She hangs out at Village Oldies record store with clerk Lenny Kaye, who has previously recorded as Link Cromwell (and in 1973 will compile the legendary compilation LP *Nuggets* for Elektra records).

1971 Feb Smith invites Kaye to accompany her poetry readings on guitar. They play support to Andy Warhol/Velvet Underground° follower Gerard Malanga, at St. Mark's Church, New York. She begins to write for rock monthly *Creem*.

1972 May Playwright Sam Shepard becomes a personal and professional collaborator, while she works as the opening act for artists at Mercer Art Center for $5 a night. One of the bands she supports is The New York Dolls. Two volumes of her poetry are published, *Witt* and *Seventh Heaven*.

1973 She re-unites with Kaye for more readings at Le Jardin in New York, while a piano player, Richard (DNV) Sohl, also joins. They play in an "improv" style. Todd Rundgren's° LP *A Wizard A True Star* includes a dedication to Patti Lee Smith, who had earlier nicknamed him "Runt".

1974 June Smith records *Hey Joe/Piss Factory* for Robert Mapplethorpe's Mer label. Initially released locally, Sire Records picks it up for nationwide release. After dates at LA's The Whiskey, she recruits new guitar player, Ivan Kral. She plays a 3-week stint at New York's CBGB's and invites the club DJ, Jay Dee Daugherty, to play drums. He stays and The Patti Smith Group is formed.

1975 Jan [1] Smith participates in New York poetry project New Year's Day Extravaganza with Yoko Ono.

Jan The group signs to Arista Records.

Dec Debut LP *Horses* is released, produced by John Cale°. Cale and Smith differ over musical direction, with Cale preferring more improvization. The LP includes cover versions of *Gloria* and *Land Of A Thousand Dances*, as well as references to rock idols Jimi Hendrix° and Jim Morrison. It reaches US #47.

1976 Apr A censored version of *My Generation* is released as a single.

May [17] The group makes its UK debut at The Roundhouse in London, supported by The Stranglers°.

Oct The Patti Smith Group tours Europe.

Dec LP *Radio Ethiopia* makes US #122.

1977 Jan Smith breaks vertebrae in her neck as she falls off stage at a gig in Tampa, Fla., supporting Bob Seger° and she needs 22 stitches.

Sept The full version of *My Generation* is released on a 12" format.

1978 Apr *Because The Night*, co-written with Bruce Springsteen°, hits UK #5 and US #13. (It is the first time that Springsteen's name appears in the top 20 singles charts.) Parent LP *Easter*, produced by Jimmy Iovine, reaches UK #16 and US #20.

Aug [27] The Patti Smith Group plays UK's Reading Festival, while *Privilege (Set Me Free)* makes UK #72.

1979 Feb *Babel*, Smith's fifth book of poetry, is published.

May LP *Wave* makes UK #41 and US #18. Produced by long-time friend, Todd Rundgren°, called in by Arista to encourage her to record again, it will be her last LP in 9 years. It includes minor hit *Frederick*, *Dancing Barefoot* (UK #63) and a cover version of The Byrds'° *So You Wanna Be A Rock'N'Roll Star*.

1980 Mar [1] She marries Fred "Sonic" Smith, ex-MC5. (Although she retires from music, she occasionally gives unannounced poetry readings.)

1988 July Living in Detroit raising her two children Jesse and Jackson, Smith comes out of retirement with *People Have The Power* and LP *Dream Of Life*, produced by Fred Smith and Jimmy Iovine. Both Sohl and Daugherty are still with her. The LP reaches US #65 and UK #70.

THE SMITHS

Morrissey (vocals)
Johnny Marr (guitar)
Andy Rourke (bass)
Mike Joyce (drums)

1982 May Marr, a veteran of several Manchester-based bands, looking for someone to write lyrics to his tunes, meets Morrissey (b. Stephen Patrick Morrissey, May 22, 1959, Manchester, UK), whose book *James Dean Isn't Dead* has been published by locally-based Babylon Books, and who has been UK president of The New York Dolls fan club.

Nov Morrissey and Marr form The Smiths with local musicians Rourke and Joyce (b. June 1, 1963, Manchester).

1983 Apr The group signs a one-off single deal with London-based independent label Rough Trade, after turning down local Factory Records. Recording interest in The Smiths follows increasing popularity from extensive Manchester area gigging. (Most early shows have Morrissey paying tribute to his various influences/obsessions: a bunch of gladioli, often tucked into the seat of his trousers, representing Oscar Wilde, and a hearing aid in tribute to early 1950s vocalist Johnnie Ray. He also styles much of his appearance, and hairstyle, on his favorite vocalist Billy Fury°, recently deceased.)

May Debut single *Hand In Glove* benefits from considerable pre-release anticipation, and tops the UK independent chart.

May [18] A session by the group is broadcast on UK BBC Radio 1's "John Peel Show".

July The group signs a long-term deal with Rough Trade, in the face of potentially more lucrative offers from major companies, and plays London's Hammersmith Palais, supporting Altered Images°.

Dec Second single *This Charming Man*, in a sleeve picturing French actor Jean Marais, is UK national chart debut and reaches #25, promoted by an appearance on BBC TV's "Whistle Test". Morrissey writes an article in weekly UK rock magazine *Sounds* in appreciation of his favorite girl singer, Sandie Shaw°.

1984 Feb Released to coincide with a 20-date UK tour, *What Difference Does It Make* reaches UK #12. The picture sleeve shows actor Terence Stamp in film *The Collector*, but when Stamp objects to the use of such an ancient shot, it is replaced by a similarly-posed picture of Morrissey. (Morrissey, meanwhile, moves from Manchester to London, and contracts laryngitis, which causes cancellation of some tour dates.)

Mar The group's debut LP *The Smiths*, in a sleeve depicting Joe Dallesandro in Warhol's film *Flesh*, hits UK #2.

May Sandie Shaw° releases a version of *Hand In Glove*, with The Smiths backing her; it climbs to UK #27. Morrissey, although not featured on this release, expresses in UK music press his admiration both for Shaw and other 1960s female singers.

June *Heaven Knows I'm Miserable Now* is the group's highest-charting single, hitting UK #10 (despite some major chains' refusal to stock it because of objections to the lyrics of B-side *Suffer Little Children*, after complaints from relatives of victims in UK's 1960s Moors Murders case). LP *The Smiths*, released in US on Sire, makes #150. The band plays another UK tour, and headlines Greater London Council's "Festival for Jobs".

Sept *William, It Was Really Nothing* reaches UK #17. On a brief US visit, the band plays The Danceteria in New York.

Nov Welsh live dates are followed by a tour in Ireland, while low-priced LP *Hatful Of Hollow*, a collection of BBC radio session tracks and B-sides, hits UK #7.

1985 Feb *How Soon Is Now?* makes UK #24.

Feb [23] LP *Meat Is Murder* enters the UK chart at #1, displacing Bruce Springsteen's° *Born In The USA*. (The group begins a

5-week UK tour the next day, supported by fellow Manchester band James.)

Mar *Shakespeare's Sister* climbs to UK #26.

Mar [18] The band's concert at the Apollo Theatre, Oxford, UK, is recorded by the BBC. (A live LP is mooted, though the tracks are eventually released on various single B-sides.)

Apr Rourke and Joyce play on *Incense And Peppermints* the first single by The Adult Net, a band formed as a sideline by Brix Smith, guitarist with The Fall and wife of its leader, Mark E. Smith. (Both will continue to work with The Adult Net on subsequent projects.)

May LP *Meat Is Murder* makes US #110.

July *That Joke Isn't Funny Anymore*, taken from LP *Meat Is Murder*, peaks at UK #49.

Oct *The Boy With The Thorn In His Side* makes UK #23.

1986 Feb The band appears with New Order° and The Fall in the "From Manchester With Love" concert at the Royal Court theater, Liverpool, UK.

Apr The band adds a second guitarist, Craig Gannon.

June *Big Mouth Strikes Again* reaches UK #26. It is taken from LP *The Queen Is Dead*, which hits UK #2 behind Genesis'° LP *Invisible Touch*.

Aug *Panic* makes UK #11.

Nov *Ask* reaches UK #14. Marr is injured in a car crash, forcing the band to cancel an appearance at an Artists Against Apartheid benefit at London's Royal Albert Hall.

Dec Gannon leaves the band (and it plays what will be its last live shows).

1987 Jan Controversy over the lyrics of *Shoplifters Of The World Unite* helps it climb to UK #12.

Mar Compilation LP *The World Won't Listen* hits UK #2 (beneath the *Phantom Of The Opera* London Cast LP). It is announced that The Smiths will sign to EMI Records when their current Rough Trade contract expires.

Apr Originally recorded for a John Peel BBC Radio 1 session, *Sheila Take A Bow* hits UK #10.

May US double compilation LP *Louder Than Bombs* on Sire is imported in to UK by Rough Trade and, despite a high selling price, reaches UK #38. It also climbs to US #63.

Aug *Girlfriend In A Coma* reaches UK #13. Unusually for The Smiths (who had once vowed never to get involved with promotional videos), it has a video – which features a solo Morrissey, and fuels speculation that there will soon be no group for EMI to release, but several weeks will elapse before the official announcement of a split, and the news that Morrissey will go to EMI as a solo artist.

Oct LP *Strangeways, Here We Come*, (the title referring to a prison in Manchester) hits UK #2, behind Michael Jackson's° *Bad*, and is the group's final LP.

Nov *I Started Something I Couldn't Finish* reaches UK #23, following which Morrissey moves to EMI. (Marr will continue working with acts like Bryan Ferry°, Paul McCartney° and Talking Heads°, before becoming involved with The Pretenders°, while Rourke and Joyce remain with The Adult Net.)

Dec *Last Night I Dreamt That Somebody Loved Me*, taken from LP *Strangeways*, makes UK #30, while LP *Strangeways Here We Come* reaches US #55.

1988 Mar Morrissey's debut solo single *Suedehead* on EMI's reactivated HMV label hits UK #5. Its promotion includes a video showing Morrissey at play in James Dean's hometown. Simultaneously, his solo LP *Viva Hate*, recorded with producer Stephen Street (and with assistance from another Manchester musician, Vini Reilly of Durutti Column), enters the UK LP chart at #1.

June Morrissey's second single *Everyday Is Like Sunday* makes UK #13.

June [11] Marr plays guitar in Midge Ure's all-purpose back-up band at the Nelson Mandela Birthday Concert at Wembley, UK.

Sept A live Smiths LP, *Rank* (recorded in Oct. 1986 at a concert at the National Ballroom, Kilburn, London), hits UK #2, behind Kylie Minogue's° *Kylie*.

Oct Strange Fruit Records releases a 12" EP featuring The Smiths' May 1983 BBC "John Peel Show" session. (Amid rumors that Marr will re-form a new version of The Smiths, probably with Rourke and Joyce, and even with Morrissey, the guitarist confirms a permanent liaison with The Pretenders°.)

SOFT CELL

Marc Almond (vocals)
David Ball (keyboards)

1978 Almond (b. Peter Marc Almond, July 9, 1959, Southport, UK) leaves college in Southport and moves to Leeds Polytechnic to study Fine Arts, where he meets Ball (b. May 3, 1959, Blackpool, UK).

1979 Oct Both fans of Northern Soul music, Almond and Ball form a duo, with Ball writing music for Almond's theatrical pieces, and Almond penning lyrics to Ball's instrumentals. With the addition of slide and film special effects, handled by Steven Griffith, they become Soft Cell.

Dec Soft Cell plays its first gig, at Leeds Polytechnic.

1980 June 4-track EP *Mutant Moments*, featuring four joint compositions, is recorded in a local studio (the session and pressing of 2,000 copies paid for by Ball).

Sept [6] Coinciding with release of the EP on its own Big Frock label, Soft Cell plays with great success to a 5,000-plus audience at the Futurama 2 Science Fiction Music Festival in Leeds. The EP, meanwhile, attracts the attention of Some Bizzare Records boss Stevo who invites the duo (Griffith and the multi-media accessories have now dropped out) to contribute a track to his projected compilation LP of new synthesizer-based "futurist" acts. *The Girl With The Patent Leather Face* is recorded on 2-track equipment at practically no cost.

1981 Mar Stevo negotiates a deal for both Soft Cell and Some Bizzare with Phonogram, which includes a £1,000 advance for the duo, and includes distribution of compilation LP *Some Bizzare Album* (which makes UK #58). The duo's first Some Bizzare single *Memorabilia*, produced by Mute Records' Daniel Miller, is released, without charting.

July At London's Advision Studios, Soft Cell resurrects little-known (though long a cult favorite on the UK Northern Soul circuit) Gloria Jones track *Tainted Love*, written by ex-Four Preps and Piltdown Men member Ed Cobb and produced by Mike Thorne.

Sept *Tainted Love* tops the UK chart for 2 weeks, and will become the year's biggest-selling single, also hitting #1 in a score of other territories around the world.

Dec *Bedsitter* hits UK #4, while the duo's debut LP *Non-Stop Erotic Cabaret*, recorded in New York with Thorne, hits UK #5. *Billboard* magazine in US names Soft Cell New Wave Band of the Year.

1982 Jan *Tainted Love* re-charts in UK, reaching #43.

Feb *Say Hello, Wave Goodbye* hits UK #3. The duo follows with a lengthy UK club tour. (After it, Ball will return to Leeds for several months, during which he will write the music for the next LP, leaving Almond to do solo work, for which he becomes Marc and The Mambas, a pseudonym used prior to his Soft Cell days. Keyboards player Annie Hogan assists Almond.)

June *Torch* hits UK #2, behind Adam Ant's *Goody Two-Shoes*. Mini-LP *Non-Stop Ecstatic Dancing*, featuring New York-recorded dance remixes of several of the duo's tracks, hits UK #6.

July *Tainted Love* charts for the third time in UK, reaching #50, and hits US #8, having been climbing the US chart since Jan. (It will set a new longevity record on US top 100, its 43 weeks being the longest consecutive chart run by a single.)

Aug LP *Non-Stop Erotic Cabaret* reaches US #22, while *What*, another Northern Soul revival (the original by Judy Street), hits UK #3.

Sept LP *Non-Stop Ecstatic Dancing* makes US #57.

Oct Almond experiments with a different musical direction via LP *Untitled*, released under the name Marc and The Mambas. It couples original material with revivals of songs by Jacques Brel, Lou Reed° and others, and makes UK #42.

Dec *Where The Heart Is* reaches UK #21. Marc and The Mambas (Almond, Hogan, bass player Tim Taylor and others) play the Theatre Royal, Drury Lane, London.

1983 Jan LP *The Art Of Falling Apart*, recorded in New York the previous Sept., hits UK #5. It is packaged with a free 12-inch Jimi Hendrix° tribute disk, containing Soft Cell's versions of *Hey Joe*, *Purple Haze* and *Voodoo Chile*.

Mar *Numbers/Barriers* reaches UK #25. In a marketing exercise to push the single higher ("Top of the Pops" having ignored it because of *Numbers*' sex-oriented lyric), Phonogram gives away copies of *Tainted Love* with it as a sales booster. This causes friction with Almond, who has the shrink-wrapping stopped. The duo plays another UK tour, while LP *The Art Of Falling Apart* makes US #84.

SOFT CELL *cont.*

June Ball scores the music for a stage revival of Tennessee Williams' play *Suddenly Last Summer*.

Aug Despite scathing reviews (and a chain store ban because of allegedly obscene lyrics), double LP *Torment And Toreros* by Marc and The Mambas makes UK #28. Almond's group now includes a string section, all-girl trio The Venomettes (one of whom, Ginny, marries David Ball).

Oct Soft Cell's *Soul Inside* reaches UK #16.

Nov Ball releases solo LP *In Strict Tempo*, with guest vocals from Genesis P. Orridge of Psychic TV. It fails to chart.

Dec Almond and Ball announce the end of Soft Cell as they complete a final LP together, and play a last US tour.

1984 Jan The duo's final UK live dates are a farewell series at London's Hammersmith Palais.

Feb *Down In The Subway*, extracted from the final LP, makes UK #24.

Mar The final Soft Cell LP *This Last Night In Sodom* reaches UK #12.

June Almond has his first solo success with *The Boy Who Came Back*, reaching UK #52.

Sept Follow-up *You Have* makes UK #57. Almond takes part in a week-long festival at London's Bloomsbury theater, which celebrates the work of French Writer George Bataille. (A mini-LP of material from this, *Violent Silence*, will be released in French-speaking territories in 1986, and imported in to UK.)

Nov Containing both the solo singles, LP *Vermin In Ermine*, credited to Marc Almond and The Willing Sinners (three former Mambas and three new musicians), makes UK #36. *Tenderness Is A Weakness* is extracted, but fails to sell.

1985 Feb *Tainted Love* charts for the fourth time, making UK #43.

May Almond sings guest vocals with Jimi Somerville on Bronski Beat's medley of *I Feel Love/Love To Love You Baby/Johnny Remember Me*, which hits UK #3.

Aug *Stories Of Johnny*, Almond's first release away from Phonogram, through Virgin, brings his biggest solo success to date, at UK #23.

Oct LP *Stories Of Johnny* reaches UK #22, while extracted *Love Letters* (with Westminster City School Choir guesting) makes UK #68. Almond follows its release with a European tour, including UK dates.

1986 Jan *The House Is Haunted (By The Echo Of Your Last Goodbye)*, a Mel Torme number, makes UK #55.

Feb Almond and The Willing Sinners play a series of dates in Japan.

June *A Woman's Story*, a revival of a Cher° song (allegedly recorded after Almond heard the original playing in a London taxi), peaks at UK #41. (The 12-inch version is a multi-track EP, subtitled *Some Songs To Take To The Tomb*, and includes revivals of Procol Harum's° *A Salty Dog* and Johnnie Ray's *The Little White Cloud That Cried*, among others.)

Oct *Ruby Red* makes UK #47.

Dec Soft Cell compilation LP *The Singles Album* reaches UK #58.

1987 Feb Almond's *Melancholy Rose* creeps to UK #71.

Apr LP *Mother Fist And Her Five Daughters*, again credited to Marc Almond and The Willing Sinners, makes UK #41. The extracted title track stalls at UK #93.

June He duets guest vocals on Sally Timms' *This House Is A House Of Tears* (an Almond composition).

Nov Almond compilation LP *Singles* is released, without charting. Following this, his contract with Virgin expires and a new deal is signed with EMI's Parlophone label. The Willing Sinners have now been replaced by new backing group La Magia, though Annie Hogan still remains from the original Mambas, as do Billy McGee and Steve Humphreys from The Sinners.

Dec Almond plays a series of sell-out Christmas concerts at The Astoria, London.

1988 July *Tears Run Rings*, on Parlophone, reaches UK #26.

Sept Almond's debut Parlophone LP, *The Stars We Are*, is released.

SONNY & CHER

1957 Sonny Bono (b. Salvatore Bono, Feb.16, 1935, Detroit, Mich., US), having moved to Hollywood in 1954, at first working at the Douglas Aircraft factory on an assembly line, becomes a record-packer at Specialty Records.

May He writes *High School Dance*, B-side of Larry Williams' hit *Short Fat Fanny* on Specialty. (Sonny later has his own single on the label, *Wearing Black*, under the name Don Christy, and will become a writer, producer and A&R man at Specialty.)

1960/62 After Specialty has curtailed most of its operations, he records as Sonny Christie and Ronny Sommers for an assortment of labels, with no success.

1962 Sonny co-writes *Needles And Pins* with Jack Nitzsche, which is recorded by Jackie DeShannon and makes US #84. (It will be an international hit for The Searchers° in 1964, topping the UK chart and reaching US #13.) Nitzsche introduces Bono to producer Phil Spector, and he begins to work for him as a general assistant and West Coast promotion man – gaining much as a producer by witnessing Spector at work in the studio.

1963 Cher° (b. Cherilyn Sarkasian La Pier, May 20, 1946, El Centro, Cal., US), having moved to LA primarily to act, meets Sonny and, through his introduction, becomes a session singer for Spector, doing back-ups for The Ronettes°. She also begins to sing as a duo with Sonny, and as Caesar & Cleo they release *The Letter* on Vault Records, arranged by Harold Battiste (with whom they will later work at Atco). Meanwhile, The Righteous Brothers° record Bono's song *Koko Joe*, written in 1951.

1964 Sonny and Cher° marry in Tijuana, Mexico. After much prompting from Sonny, Spector agrees to record Cher as a soloist, but only one single is cut: *Ringo I Love You* on Spector's Annette label, under the pseudonym Bonnie Jo Mason. With borrowed money, Sonny produces a Cher session himself at RCA studios in Hollywood, but it emerges as another duet after Cher has an attack of studio nerves and asks him to sing with her. Four tracks are recorded, and after sounding out Spector as to their worth, Sonny sells them to Reprise Records, which issues them under the Caesar & Cleo name as two (initially unsuccessful) singles, *Baby Don't Go* and *Love Is Strange*.

1965 Atlantic's Ahmet Ertegun is impressed by *Baby Don't Go* and, learning that they have no contract with Reprise, offers a recording deal. They are signed to Atlantic's Atco subsidiary (which does not affect Cher's° solo deal, recently signed with Imperial). They decide to use their own names and debut as Sonny & Cher with *Just You* – again to no initial success.

July *I Got You Babe*, written and produced by Sonny (and almost issued as a B-side until he persuades Ertegun otherwise), shoots to US #1, holding for 3 weeks and selling over a million. Their eye-catching, hippy dress style and long hair immediately bring them notice on TV appearances. (Bono is refused admission to New York's Americana Hotel, because of his mode of dress.)

July [31] They arrive amid much publicity in UK for a first promotional visit, which helps *I Got You Babe* to top the UK chart for 2 weeks. (They also film segments for a future TV special "Sonny and Cher in London".)

Sept Sonny releases a solo single, partially-autobiographical *Laugh At Me*, which hits US #10 and UK #9, while Spector-produced Bonnie & The Treasures' *Home Of The Brave*, with Sonny & Cher on back-up vocals, reaches US #77.

Oct *Baby Don't Go* is reissued by Reprise re-credited to Sonny & Cher, and hits US #8 and UK #11. *Just You*, repromoted by Atco, also charts in US, reaching #20. Debut LP *Look At Us* hits US #2 and UK #7.

Nov *But You're Mine*, follow-up to *I Got You Babe* makes US #15 and UK #17, while Vault reissues *The Letter*, which reaches US #75.

Dec A second solo by Sonny, *The Revolution Kind*, peaks at US #70.

1966 Mar A revival of *What Now My Love* reaches US #16 and UK #13.

June *Have I Stayed Too Long* peaks at US #49 and UK #42. It is taken from LP *The Wonderous World Of Sonny And Cher*, which makes US #34 and UK #15.

Oct *Little Man*, in an arresting gypsy-style arrangement by Sonny, reaches US #21 and UK #9. They make their starring movie debut in *Good Times*.

Nov *Living For You* makes US #87 and UK #44.

1967 Feb Uptempo *The Beat Goes On* (later revived by Vanilla Fudge°) is the duo's last major Atco success, hitting US #6 and reaching UK #29.

May *A Beautiful Story* reaches US #53.

June *Plastic Man* peaks at US #74.

Sept *It's The Little Things* makes US #50.

Oct Compilation LP *The Best Of Sonny And Cher* reaches US #23, as they make a guest appearance on US TV's "The Man from U.N.C.L.E."

1968 Jan Their final Atco hit is *Good Combination*, which reaches US #56.

Aug [4/5] Sonny & Cher take part in the 2-day Newport Festival in Costa Mesa, Cal.

1969 A second movie, *Chastity* (titled after their daughter's name) is only moderately successful.

1970 With hit singles no longer coming despite sporadic releases as a duo, they move to the cabaret scene, appearing regularly in Las Vegas in an act which mixes comedy with music. They sign a new recording deal, covering both the duo's and Cher's° solo work, with Kapp Records, a subsidiary of MCA.

1971 Aug [1] They begin their highly successful TV series, "The Sonny and Cher Comedy Hour" on CBS, which mixes songs and comedy with star guests, based on the format of the club/comedy act they have perfected during the previous year.

Dec Bolstered by the popularity of the TV show, *All I Ever Need Is You* hits US #7, while LP *Sonny And Cher Live* makes US #35.

1972 Feb *All I Ever Need Is You* hits UK #8.

Apr *A Cowboy's Work Is Never Done* hits US #8. It is taken from LP *All I Ever Need Is You*, which reaches US #14.

Aug *When You Say Love*, which makes US #32, is taken from a Budweiser beer ad on US TV.

1973 Apr MCA (having absorbed Kapp label) releases two Sonny & Cher singles during the year; but only *Mama Was A Rock And Roll Singer, Papa Used Write All Her Songs* charts, making US #77. It is the duo's last hit together.

1974 Jan The final two singles by Sonny & Cher are released by Warner Bros. but neither charts.

Feb [20] Cher° files for divorce from Sonny.

June [26] Sonny and Cher's divorce is finalized. (She will marry Gregg Allman 2 days later, and in turn file for divorce from Allman 9 days after that.)

Sept [22] A TV show featuring Sonny as a soloist, "The Sonny Comedy Revue", opens on US ABC TV.

1976 Feb Following on from a Cher° solo TV series on US CBS, the network replaces it with a new version of "The Sonny and Cher Show" (which will run until mid-1977).

1980 While Cher is recording for Casablanca, Sonny reappears on the scene as an actor, in both big-screen and TV movies (as he will continue to do throughout the 80s).

1987 Sonny and Cher reunite on US NBC-TV's "Late Night with David Letterman" and perform *I Got You Babe*.

1988 Sonny appears in movie *Hairspray*.

Apr Cher° wins the Best Actress Oscar at the Academy Awards for her performance in *Moonstruck*. In the same week, Sonny is elected Mayor of Palm Springs. (He is also now a restaurant owner, in partnership with his fourth wife.)

JOE SOUTH

1958 South (b. Feb.28, 1940, Atlanta, Ga., US), an accomplished guitarist since age 11, and working in a country band with steel guitarist Pete Drake at age 15, has his first success with the novelty *The Purple People Eater Meets The Witch Doctor* – a cash-in on two recent million-selling novelty hits by Sheb Wooley and David Seville. It reaches US #47, but proves impossible to follow up, so he hones his skills as a songwriter, initially setting poems written by his mother to music.

1961 Aug He becomes a DJ on a country music radio station in Atlanta but continues to record sporadically, and *You're The Reason*, on Fairlane label, reaches US #87 (eclipsed by Bobby Edwards' US #11 version on Crest).

1962 Nov As a session guitarist on the Atlanta studio scene, he begins to place his own songs with local acts, and writes The Tams' *Untie Me*, which reaches US #60. He also plays guitar on several sessions by Tommy Roe°.

1965 Aug South produces his close friend, Atlanta-based singer Billy Joe Royal, who is signed to Columbia/CBS. Royal's debut, South's composition *Down In The Boondocks*, hits US #9 – South's first top 10 success as a writer.

Oct *I Knew You When*, a second South song by Royal, reaches US #14 (while *Down In The Boondocks* makes UK #38). Royal's LP titled after the first hit climbs to US #96; it is produced by South, and he writes six of the 12 tracks, including the two hits and Royal's next (US #38) single, *I've Got To Be Somebody*.

1967 Oct While doing session work for CBS as a guitarist (on Simon and Garfunkel's° *The Sound Of Silence*, to which he helps add a rock backing track to the original acoustic arrangement), South continues to work with Royal, and writes and produces *Hush*, which Royal takes to US #52.

1968 Sept *Hush* is covered, in a heavier arrangement, by Deep Purple°, and this time hits US #4 and is South's first million-selling composition. Meanwhile, he signs to Capitol Records as a vocalist, debuting with his own song *Birds Of A Feather*, which is a regional success but does not make US Hot 100.

1969 Mar South's first LP, *Introspect*, featuring 11 of his own songs, makes US #117. Taken from it, *Games People Play* becomes a major hit, reaching US #12. At the same time, Johnny Rivers° covers South's *These Are Not My People* (also from the LP), reaching US #55.

Apr *Games People Play* hits UK #6, but will be South's only UK success.

July Reissued *Birds Of A Feather* is a disappointing follow-up, peaking at US #96.

Oct *Don't It Make You Want To Go Home* reaches US #41. It co-credits South's group The Believers: Tommy South (drums and back-up vocals), Barbara South (keyboards and back-up vocals), Eddie Farrell (bass and back-up vocals) and Pee Wee Parks (back-up vocals).

1970 Feb *Walk A Mile In My Shoes*, also featuring The Believers, reaches US #12. It is taken from LP *Don't It Make You Want To Go Home*, a collection of 14 more of his own songs (including his own versions of *Hush* and *Untie Me*), which climbs to US #60.

Mar [11] South wins two Grammy awards for *Games People Play*, voted Best Contemporary Song and Song of the Year for 1969.

Apr *Children* peaks at US #51.

Oct Compilation LP *Joe South's Greatest Hits*, with the cream of tracks from his previous two LPs, makes US #125.

1971 Feb Country singer Lynn Anderson covers *Rose Garden* (from LP *Introspect*) and has a million-seller with it, hitting both US and UK #3. (This will become one of South's most-covered compositions, with Elvis Presley°, among many others, also cutting it.)

Dec *Fool Me* makes US #78, and will be South's last hit single. Though his songs continue to attract prolific cover versions, he drops out of the busy work schedule which has given him such a high profile for 2 years, feeling a need for rest from the pressures. He is also affected by the death of his brother Tommy – a member of The Believers. (He will not attempt to maintain further commercial success as an artist, and moves to Maui, Hawaii for 3 years. Later LPs *So The Seeds Are Growing*, *Midnight Rainbows* and *To Have, To Hold And To Let Go* (the latter two on Island label, to which he moves on returning to mainland US in 1975) will fail to chart, and he will slip into obscurity.)

SPANDAU BALLET

Gary Kemp (guitar)
Martin Kemp (bass)
Tony Hadley (vocals)
John Keeble (drums)
Steve Norman (rhythm guitar, sax and percussion)

1969 Oct [16] Gary Kemp (b. Oct.16, 1960, Islington, London, UK) is given his first guitar by his parents. He later plays two songs at his primary school prize-giving day, and the attending Bishop of Stepney is so impressed that he gives Kemp a tape recorder (which he will use in writing songs during the coming years).

1970 Kemp brothers Gary and Martin (b. Oct.10, 1961, Islington), both set to attend Owens Grammar School, Islington, also take lessons at Anna Scher's Children's Theatre for acting.

1974 Hadley (b. Anthony Patrick Hadley, June 2, 1959, Islington), having had vocal lessons for some years, wins a talent contest singing Gary Puckett's *Young Girl*.

1975 Martin Kemp, excelling at soccer, trains with Arsenal Football Club,

1976 Gary Kemp fails his "A" level examinations, and starts a power pop group The Makers with Owens Grammar School friends Hadley, Keeble (b. July 6, 1959, Islington), Norman (b. Mar.25. 1960, Islington) and Richard Miller.

1978 Apr Hadley features photographically in photo-love story "Sister Blackmail" in UK *My Guy* girls' magazine.

1979 Gary Kemp and ex-schoolmate Steve Dagger revive the failed Makers under a new name, which becomes Spandau Ballet. Hadley, Keeble, Norman and Martin Kemp (later bassist but cannot yet play bass) all join, while Dagger becomes manager.

Nov [17] Inspired by frequent Soho, London, night-clubbing at The Blitz, Billy's Le Kilt and Le Beate Route, Spandau Ballet invites 50 friends to an Islington studio to hear new songs.

Dec At a Steve Strange Blitz club party, Island Records boss Chris

Blackwell offers to sign the band. Dagger rejects the overture, and hires a lawyer to organize setting up a label of their own.

1980 Mar [7] Setting their own "new romantic" style (with emphasis on clothing, make-up and clubs), Spandau Ballet, now wearing kilts, selects unusual one-off live dates to intrigue the music media, including a gig at the Scala cinema.

Mar [13] The band is filmed at the Scala cinema for inclusion on "Blitz Kids" club scene documentary on UK TV show "20th Century Box".

Apr Having formed its own Reformation label, the group signs a deal to license its releases and company to Chrysalis Records.

July [26] The band plays aboard H.M.S. Belfast, a Second World War cruiser moored on the River Thames in London.

Dec Debut single *To Cut A Long Story Short*, well marketed, stylishly packaged (as will be all the early releases) and much anticipated following the "buzz" and music press interest around the band, hits UK #5.

1981 Feb *The Freeze* reaches UK #17.

Mar LP *Journey To Glory*, produced by Richard James Burgess, hits UK #5.

Apr The band visits US to spread the "New Romantic" style – playing New York's Underground Club, with a collection of UK fashion designers.

May *Musclebound* hits UK #10.

Aug *Chant #1* (I Don't Need This Pressure On), made with help from UK funk outfit Beggar & Co., hits UK #3. More than previous releases, it shows the soul boy background below the group's stylish rock veneer.

Nov *Paint Me Down* makes UK #30.

1982 Jan Gary Kemp and Burgess work on actress/comedienne Pamela Stephenson's EP *Unusual Treatment*.

Feb *She Loved Like Diamond* peaks at UK #49.

Mar LP *Diamond* reaches UK #15.

Apr The group begins a UK tour in Edinburgh, Scotland.

May *Instinction*, from LP *Diamond*, remixed as a single by Trevor Horn, hits UK #10.

Oct *Lifeline*, produced by Swain and Jolley, hits UK #7.

1983 Mar *Communication* reaches UK #12.

Apr Gary Kemp-penned ballad *True* tops the UK chart in its second week of release, and spends 4 weeks at #1.

May LP *True* tops the UK chart for a week.

July Now a major live attraction, Spandau Ballet play dates at London's Royal Albert Hall, Sadlers Wells Theatre and Royal Festival Hall.

Aug *Gold*, extracted from LP *True*, hits UK #2, held off the top by KC's° *Give It Up*. (The song is used by UK BBC TV as the theme for its Olympics coverage.)

Oct *True*, belatedly, is US chart debut, hitting #4, while LP of the same title reaches US #19.

1984 Jan *Gold* makes US #29.

Apr *Communication* peaks at US #59.

June *Only When You Leave*, taken from the band's forthcoming LP, hits UK #3.

July LP *Parade* hits UK #2, held from the top by Bob Marley's° LP *Legend*.

Sept *I'll Fly For You* hits UK #9, while *Only When You Leave* makes US #34.

Oct LP *Parade* makes US #50 as, taken from it, *Highly Strung* reaches UK #15.

Nov [25] The group takes part in the all-star session for Band Aid's° *Do They Know It's Christmas?*, which will end the year at UK #1. Hadley sings one of the lead lines on it.

Dec *Round And Round* peaks at UK #18.

Dec [4] The group plays the first of six nights of major concerts at Wembley Arena, London.

1985 Feb The band sues Chrysalis for release from its contract, claiming that a lack of consistent US success is due to the label's inefficient promotion of it in US. (The dispute means that no new material can be released by Spandau Ballet until legal matters are resolved.)

July [13] Spandau Ballet appears on the Live Aid bill at Wembley, UK.

Nov Chrysalis releases compilation LP *The Singles Collection*, without the band's co-operation. It hits UK #3, aided by TV promotion – which also angers the group.

1986 Jan [25] Gary Kemp appears solo on the Labour Party Red Wedge UK tour, which opens in Manchester.

Apr [26] The Kemp brothers and Norman all escape serious injury when the car (driven by Norman) in West Berlin, West Germany, crashes.

May Freed from its Chrysalis deal, the group signs the Reformation label to CBS.

July *Fight For Ourselves* reaches UK #15. (The band makes it a condition of the new CBS contract that its records are not to be released in South Africa.)

Nov LP *Through The Barricades*, recorded in France, hits UK #7. The ballad title track hits UK #6.

1987 Feb *How Many Lies*, also from the LP, peaks at UK #34.

1988 May The Kemp brothers attend the Cannes Film Festival, where they officially announce that they are to play the notorious 1960s London gangland leaders Ron and Reggie Kray in a movie.

July *Raw* reaches UK #47, the group's first release since early 1987.

THE SPECIAL AKA

Jerry Dammers (keyboards)
Terry Hall (vocals)
Neville Staples (vocals and percussion)
Lynval Golding (guitar)
Roddy Radiation (guitar)
Sir Horace Gentleman (bass)
John Bradbury (drums)

1977 July The band is formed in UK by Dammers (b. Gerald Dankin), Golding and Gentleman (b. Horace Panter) as The Coventry Automatics, who attempt to forge a punk/reggae fusion, with only marginally successful results. When they start to delve back to the rougher pre-reggae Jamaican ska form, the sound gels.

1978 The line-up expands to include Hall and Staples (initially a roadie) on vocals, a drummer named Silverton and guitarist Radiation (b. Rod Byers). The group is known as The Coventry Specials for a while, before settling as The Special AKA.

June After attracting the attention of Joe Strummer, the band plays UK national dates as support on The Clash's° "On Parole" tour. Clash manager Bernie Rhodes also manages the band, moving it to London for rehearsals in Camden Town, which last for many weeks and this leads to Silverton leaving. Convinced that this approach is wrong, Dammers splits from Rhodes and takes the band back to Coventry, where new manager Rick Rogers takes over.

1979 Dammers conceives the idea of the group recording on its own independent label. £700 is borrowed to pay for recording Dammers-penned *Gangsters*, a tribute to Prince Buster's ska classic *Al Capone*.

Mar Bradbury joins on drums, in time to play on the *Gangsters* session. Because the group cannot afford to record a B-side, Golding suggests to his friend, guitarist Neol Davies, that they use instrumental track *The Selecter*, which Davies has cut with Bradbury on drums, and local trombonist Barry Jones. (This is credited to "The Selecter", though Davies will not form the actual group until the single is selling.)

Apr Dammers makes use of his art college background to design a label. The name 2-Tone comes from his black-and-white creation. A deal is made with Rough Trade in London, which presses 5,000 copies of the single and arranges distribution.

July With the single attracting interest and sales, approaches are made by major record companies. Chrysalis signs The Special AKA and agrees to an autonomous 2-Tone label to be given a budget and marketed by Chrysalis, releasing at least six singles a year. All The Special AKA members, and their managers, become 2-Tone directors.

Sept *Gangsters*, taken over by Chrysalis, hits UK #6. Abridging its name to The Specials, the group tours UK with newly-formed Selecter and 2-Tone's other signing, London group Madness°. Trombonist Rico Rodrigues joins The Specials, while trumpeter Dick Cuthy is added for tour work.

Nov Debut LP *Specials*, produced by Elvis Costello°, hits UK #4, while a revival of *A Message To You, Rudy* hits UK #10.

Dec [28] The group performs alongside The Who° and The Pretenders° at the third of four concerts in aid of the People of Kampuchea, at London's Hammersmith Odeon.

1980 Jan Live EP *The Special AKA Live*, containing four revivals of 1960s/early 1970s ska and reggae hits, plus original song *Too*

Much Too Young (which captures the airplay), tops the UK chart for 2 weeks.

Jan [25] A 6-week US tour by the group opens at New York's Hurrah club, ending in 4 sold-out dates at LA's Whiskey A-Go-Go club, where many fans pose in "2-Tone" black-and-white clothing.

June *Rat Race* hits UK #5.

Sept [13] A UK fall tour opens at the Riviera Lido, St. Austell, Cornwall, with 2-Tone act The Swinging Cats as support group.

Oct *Stereotype* hits UK #6, while the band's second LP, *More Specials*, produced by Dammers and Dave Jordan at Horizon Studios, Coventry, hits UK #5. It moves away from the band's ska roots, into what Dammers describes as "lounge music" – much of it coming from his fascination with film soundtrack music.

Oct [16] The UK tour ends in Birmingham, having played a month of English dates, and two in Scotland at Glasgow and Edinburgh. (At a date in Cambridge, Dammers and Hall have been arrested and charged with incitement to violence, after trouble in the audience causes them to stop the show. They will be fined £1,000 when the case comes to court in Jan.)

1981 Jan *Do Nothing* hits UK #4. A proposed US tour is cancelled by Dammers, who is suffering from exhaustion.

Feb *Dance Craze*, a concert movie based around the music of The Specials and the 2-Tone stable, is released. The soundtrack LP, featuring songs by the bands appearing in the film, hits UK #5.

July *Ghost Town* tops the UK chart for 3 weeks, its lyric topical as riots flare in several UK inner-city areas.

Nov [2] The group fragments. Vocalists Staples, Hall and Golding leave to form Fun Boy Three (they will release two LPs and have five UK hit singles before splitting in 1983). Byers forms his own rockabilly group, Roddy Radiation & The Tearjerkers, while Panter also leaves, initially joining a religious sect, and later re-emerging in General Public. Dammers re-forms the group and reverts to the earlier name of The Special AKA. He and Bradbury alone remain from the earlier line-up, while Gary McManus (bass), John Shipley (guitar) and three vocalists – Rhoda Dakar (ex-The Bodysnatchers), Stan Campbell (ex-The Selecter) and Egidio Newton (ex-Animal Nightlife) join.

1983 Sept *Racist Friend*, the first release by the new line-up, makes UK #60.

Apr *Nelson Mandela*, an anthem demanding freedom for the ANC leader imprisoned in South Africa, hits UK #9.

1984 June LP *In The Studio* reaches UK #34. Long in preparation in the studio, it carries a purposely ironic title.

1985 Mar The members of Special AKA take part, along with Madness°, UB40°, General Public and The Pioneers, in recording *Starvation*, a new version of an old Pioneers song released to raise funds for Ethiopian famine relief. Released on Madness' Zarjazz label, it reaches UK #33.

1986 Apr [23] Dammers forms Artists Against Apartheid in a meeting at Donmar Warehouse, London.

June [28] Dammers and Artists Against Apartheid organize an anti-apartheid concert on Clapham Common in London, featuring Elvis Costello°, Peter Gabriel°, Boy George, Sade°, Sting°, Billy Bragg°, Hugh Masekela, and others. The audience numbers 250,000.

1988 June [11] Dammers is the prime mover behind the Nelson Mandela 70th Birthday Party concert, held at Wembley Stadium, London, and seen all over the world via TV. Artists performing include Dire Straits°, Whitney Houston°, Stevie Wonder°, Simple Minds°, Tracy Chapman°, and many others. The Special AKA's *Nelson Mandela* is the show's anthem, and, retitled *Free Nelson Mandela (70th Birthday Remake)*, is reissued in UK.

THE (DETROIT) SPINNERS

Bobbie Smith (vocals)
Phillipe Wynne (vocals)
Billy Henderson (vocals)
Henry Fambrough (vocals)
Pervis Jackson (vocals)

1961 Aug The Detroit-based US group, signed to Harvey Fuqua's Tri-Phi label, an associate of Motown Records, debuts with *That's What Girls Are Made For*. It is also the label's first release, and features Fuqua on lead vocals.

Nov *Love (I'm So Glad) I Found You* also features Fuqua, and peaks at US #91.

1965 Aug *I'll Always Love You* is released on Motown, and reaches US #35.

1967 G.C. Cameron joins the group as lead singer.

1970 Oct After a lengthy period without success, Motown transfers the group to its V.I.P. subsidiary in search of a new impetus. Stevie Wonder° produces *It's A Shame*, which does the trick, reaching US #14.

Nov LP *2nd Time Around* makes US #199.

Dec The group is dubbed The Motown Spinners in UK to avoid confusion with well-known Liverpool folk group The Spinners. With this billing, *It's A Shame* is UK chart debut, at #20.

1971 Jan Follow-up on V.I.P., again produced by Wonder°, is inappropriately titled *We'll Have It Made*, which stalls at US #89. Following this, the group leaves Motown in search of a new deal. Both Stax and Avco Embassy are interested, but Aretha Franklin°, a long-time friend of the group in Detroit, puts them in touch with her label, Atlantic, to which they sign before the end of the year. Prior to this, Cameron leaves to pursue a solo career at Motown, and is replaced by Wynne as lead vocalist.

1972 Nov Producer Thom Bell, always an admirer of The Spinners, produces them when he is contracting productions in Philadelphia for Atlantic. Debut single is *How Could I Let You Get Away?*, but B-side *I'll Be Around* is superior and more commercial, and steals the airplay until it is made A-side by default. It hits US #3, and is the group's first million-seller.

1973 Mar Follow-up *Could It Be I'm Falling In Love*, produced again by Bell (as will be all The Spinners' Atlantic output until 1979), is a second millon-seller, hitting US #4.

May Cashing in on their current success, Motown reissues 1968 track *Together We Can Make Such Sweet Music*, which makes US #91. A Motown compilation LP, *The Best Of The Spinners*, makes US #124.

June Debut Atlantic LP *Spinners* reaches US #14 and goes gold, while *One Of A Kind (Love Affair)* is the group's third consecutive gold single, and hits US #11. The Spinners also finally re-chart in UK, as *Could It Be I'm Falling In Love* makes UK #11. The change of label has meant a change of UK name for the group, now known as The Detroit Spinners in UK.

Sept Linda Creed's lyrically socially-conscious *Ghetto Child* reaches US #29.

Nov *Ghetto Child* hits UK #7.

1974 Mar *Mighty Love* makes US #20.

May LP *Mighty Love* reaches US #16, and is the group's second gold LP.

June *I'm Coming Home*, taken from the LP, climbs to US #18.

Oct After the group has been the opening act for Dionne Warwick° on a 5-week summer theater tour taking in Las Vegas, Bell suggests a duet between her and the group – not a contractual problem, since Warwick is signed to Atlantic's associate label Warner Bros. The result is *Then Came You*, a million-seller which tops the US chart – the first #1 hit for either side of the partnership (but the duetting is not carried on to any subsequent singles).

Nov *Love Don't Love Nobody* reaches UK #15, while *Then Came You* peaks at UK #29.

1975 Feb LP *New And Improved*, which includes the duet with Warwick°, hits US #9 and earns the group another gold disk.

Apr *Living A Little, Laughing A Little*, makes US #37.

May *Sadie* reaches US #54.

Oct *They Just Can't Stop It (Games People Play)* puts The Spinners back in US top 10, hitting #5 and earning another gold disk – as does LP *Pick Of The Litter*, which includes the single and hits US #8.

1976 Feb *Love Or Leave* makes US #36, while double live LP *Spinners Live!* makes US #20.

Aug *Wake Up Susan* reaches US #56.

Oct LP *Happiness Is Being With The Detroit Spinners* makes US #25, and is their last gold LP.

Dec *The Rubberband Man* is a further million-seller, and holds US #2 for 3 weeks (behind Rod Stewart's° *Tonight's The Night*). It also reaches UK #16 – the group's first UK hit for 2 years.

1977 Wynne leaves for a solo career, and is replaced by John Edwards.

Feb *Wake Up Susan* reaches UK #29.

Apr *You're Throwing A Good Love Away* peaks at US #43.

May A 4-track UK EP, tied in to a UK tour, coupling earlier hit *Could It Be I'm Falling In Love* with three LP tracks, makes UK #32. Meanwhile, UK compilation LP *Detroit Spinners' Smash Hits* peaks at UK #37, and LP *Yesterday, Today And Tomorrow* reaches US #26.

June [10/11] The Spinners take part in the third San Diego KOOL Jazz Festival.

Oct *Heaven And Earth (So Fine)* is a minor US hit at #89.

1978 Jan LP *Spinners 8* climbs to US #57.

June Compilation LP *The Best Of The Spinners* makes US #115.

Aug *If You Wanna Do A Dance* reaches US #49. This is the group's last Bell-produced hit single.

1979 June LP *From Here To Eternity* stalls at US #165.

1980 Mar The group teams with new producer Michael Zager, who records them on a version of The Four Seasons'° *Working My Way Back To You* blended in a medley with a new song of his own, *Forgive Me Girl*. It hits US #2, giving the group its final million-selling single, while parent LP *Dancin' And Lovin'* makes US #32.

Apr *Working My Way Back To You/Forgive Me Girl* is the group's all-time biggest seller in UK, and its only UK #1, topping the chart for 2 weeks.

June *Body Language* reaches UK #40.

July A second medley in similar new-plus-old style, blending a revival of Sam Cooke's° *Cupid* with *I've Loved You For A Long Time*, hits both US and UK #4.

Aug LP *Love Trippin'*, which includes the *Cupid* medley, makes US #53

1981 Mar Another medley, of *Yesterday Once More/Nothing Remains The Same*, reaches US #52.

Apr LP *Labor Of Love* peaks at US #128.

1982 Jan LP *Can't Shake This Feelin'* stalls at US #196.

Mar *Never Thought I'd Fall In Love* creeps to US #95.

1983 Jan A revival of Willie Nelson° standard *Funny How Time Slips Away* is the group's final US hit single, making #67, while LP *Grand Slam* is the last chart LP, peaking at US #167.

1984 July [14] Former group member Phillipe Wynne dies.

1986 Aug [5] The Spinners take part in the "Rock'n'Roll Special" at Meadowlands, East Rutherford, N.J., with The Righteous Brothers°, Frankie Valli & The Four Seasons° and Tommy James & The Shondells°.

1988 May [14] The Spinners participate in Atlantic Records' 40th Anniversary show at New York's Madison Square Garden.

SPIRIT

Randy California (guitar and vocals)
Jay Ferguson (vocals)
John Locke (keyboards)
Mark Andes (bass)
Ed Cassidy (drums)

1966 Dec California (b. Randy Wolfe, Feb.20, 1951, Los Angeles, Cal., US), his stepfather Cassidy, always shaven-headed, (b. May.4, 1931, Chicago, Ill.) and Locke (b. Sept.25, 1943, Los Angeles), form Spirits Rebellious in LA. Locke has played 4 years with Cassidy in New Jazz Trio, while Cassidy and California have been in The Red Roosters in 1965, prior to going to New York for session work.

1967 The trio recruits the two other ex-The Red Roosters members, Ferguson (b. John Ferguson, May 10, 1947, Burbank, Cal.) and Andes (b. Feb.19, 1948, Philadelphia, Pa.), and shortens the name to Spirit.

1968 Apr Signed to Lou Adler's new Ode label, the group releases LP *Spirit*, critically rated as a progressive rock masterpiece. It climbs to US #31, staying on chart for 8 months.

1969 Mar LP *The Family That Plays Together* reaches US #22, their highest LP chart placing. *I Got A Line On You*, extracted from the LP, is their first US hit single, reaching #25.

Oct LP *Clear Spirit* reaches US #55.

1970 Mar *1984*, taken from LP *Clear Spirit*, reaches US #69.

Sept First release on Epic is *Animal Zoo*, which charts briefly at US #97.

1971 Feb LP *The 12 Dreams Of Dr. Sardonicus* is generally considered their commercial peak, although it only reaches US #63.

June California leaves for UK to play solo, while Andes and Ferguson depart to form Jo Jo Gunne, with Matt Andes (guitar) and Curly Smith (drums), which signs to Asylum Records.

1972 Apr LP *Feedback*, recorded by Cassidy and Locke with newly-joined Texas guitarist Chris Staehely and his bassist brother Al, reaches US #63, after which Cassidy and Locke also leave, and a totally non-original Spirit tours US.

May Jo Jo Gunne's *Run Run Run* reaches US #27 and UK #6 – its only chart single. LP *Jo Jo Gunne* makes US #57, but does not chart in UK.

Sept California releases solo LP *Captain Kopter And The Fabulous Twirlybirds*, which fails to chart.

1973 May Jo Jo Gunne LP *Bite Down Hard* makes US #75, featuring Jimmie Randall on bass in place of departed Mark Andes.

Aug Compilation LP *The Best Of Spirit* peaks at US #120.

Oct *Mr. Skin* stalls at US #92.

1974 Jan Jo Jo Gunne LP *Jumpin' The Gunne* peaks at US #169. Cassidy and California re-form Spirit as a trio, with Barry Keene on bass, and sign to Mercury Records.

Dec Final Jo Jo Gunne LP *So . . . Where's The Show?* reaches US #198. Ex-Spirit member Chris Staehely plays guitar on it in place of Matt Andes.

1975 June Locke rejoins the group for double LP *Spirit Of '76* on Mercury, which reaches US #147.

1976 Mark Andes rejoins, bringing his brother Matt from Jo Jo Gunne on guitar, for LP *Son Of Spirit*, which does not chart.

June [18] LP *The 12 Dreams Of Dr. Sardonicus* goes gold with a half million US sales, 6 years after release.

Aug LP *Farther Along* reaches US #179.

Aug [29] The group plays a reunion concert at Santa Monica, Cal., with Neil Young° guesting for the encore version of Bob Dylan's° *Like A Rolling Stone* – though California almost throws him off at first.

1977 Apr The group's last Mercury LP, *Future Games (A Magical Kahvana Dream)*, includes "Star Trek" dialog, but not Locke or the Andes brothers, who have departed, Mark Andes to join Firefall. It does not chart.

1978 Feb Locke joins Nazareth for a US tour.

Apr Ferguson, having stayed with Asylum as a soloist after the demise of Jo Jo Gunne, hits US #9 with *Thunder Island*. Spirit tours UK.

1979 Jan Spirit LP *Live*, recorded on stage in West Germany, is released in US on its own Potato label, and in UK on Illegal Records.

June Ferguson reaches US #31 with solo *Shakedown Cruise*.

1981 Apr Rhino Records in US releases Spirit LP *Journey To Potatoland*, a project from the early 1970s, rejected by Epic as lacking commercial potential. It reaches UK #40 on Beggars Banquet Records – Spirit's only UK chart entry.

June [16] California and Cassidy, with keyboardman George Valuck, perform on UK BBC TV's "The Old Grey Whistle Test" followed the next night by a one-off gig at London's Hammersmith Odeon.

1982 Mark Andes joins Heart°.

1984 Feb Spirit reunites as a five-piece, releasing re-recorded *1984*.

Mar LP *Spirit Of '84/Dream The Thirteenth Dream*, on Mercury Records, features the reunited line-up on re-cuts of old songs *Fresh Garbage*, *I Got A Line On You* and*1984*, plus some new material. (Following this, the group will be inactive again.)

SPLIT ENZ

Tim Finn (vocals and piano)
Phil Judd (vocals and guitar)
Eddie Rayner (keyboards)
Wally Wilkinson (guitar)
Mike Chunn (bass)
Paul Crowther (drums)
Noel Crombie (spoons and design)

1972 Oct The group forms in Auckland, New Zealand as Split Ends, with Finn (b. June 25, 1952), Judd, Chunn, Miles Golding and Michael Howard.

1973 Mar Their first tour, around colleges and universities, is followed by a New Zealand tour supporting John Mayall°.

Apr First single *For You* is released on Vertigo Records.

Sept The group makes the final of the New Zealand NZBC TV "New Faces" talent show, giving their startling image nationwide coverage, and a major brewery offers them touring sponsorship on the pub circuit.

1975 Mar The band moves to Australia and changes name to Split Enz.

May They sign to Mushroom Records, and first LP *Mental Notes* is recorded in Australia. The band supports Roxy Music° in Sydney, and sparks interest from guitarist Phil Manzanera.

1976 May The group moves to UK, where Manzanera produces LP *Second Thoughts* (mainly upgraded re-recordings of songs from the first LP).

1977 May During a US tour Judd leaves and is replaced by Finn's 18-year-old brother Neil (b. May 27, 1958, Te Awamutu, NZ). Wilkinson, Chunn and Crowther also leave to be replaced by Englishmen Nigel Griggs (b. Aug.18, 1949) and Malcolm Green (b. Jan.25, 1953) shortly before third LP *Dizrhythmia* is released.

1978 The group tours UK, usually as a support act. Judd rejoins, then quits again as Chrysalis drops the group. They return to Australia after recording LP *Frenzy* and re-sign with Mushroom. *I See Red* hits top 10 in Australia and New Zealand.

Oct Split Enz plays *Time Out* magazine's "10th Anniversary Concert" in London.

1979 Sept After spending most of the year touring, the band releases LP *True Colours*.

1980 A&M Records offers the group a worldwide contract on the strength of the LP. Led by Neil Finn's catchy single *I Got You*, *True Colours* becomes the group's best-selling LP. Chrysalis releases retrospective LP *Beginning Of The Enz*.

Aug *I Got You* reaches UK #12 and US #40. LP *True Colours* is released in gimmick formats, including different color sleeves and the first commercial use of laser-etched vinyl. It peaks at UK #42 and US #40 during a 6-month chart run.

1981 Mar LP *Waiata* (the title Maori for "song", "party" or "celebration") is released.

May Neil Finn's *History Never Repeats* makes UK #63. LP *Waiata* enters the US charts and peaks at #45 during a 19-week run.

1982 May Green leaves shortly after LP *Time And Tide* is released.

June LP *Time And Tide* enters the US chart, peaking at #53. In UK, *Six Months In A Leaky Boat* is banned by BBC in the event that it might refer to the British fleet preparing to engage Argentina in the Falklands War.

1983 The group celebrates its 10th anniversary with a concert in Te Awamutu, New Zealand.

Sept Tim Finn's solo LP *Escapade* peaks at US #161.

1984 Aug LP *Conflicting Emotions* makes US #137.

1985 As Tim Finn announces he is leaving the group to go solo (on Virgin), he marries actress Greta Scaachi. After the mini-LP *See You Round*, Neil Finn and Hester form a new group with Nick Seymour.

1986 Tim Finn's second solo LP, *Big Canoe*, fails to chart. Neil signs to Capitol Records and moves to LA to work with Mitchell Froom, calling his new band Crowded House, a reference to life at his LA residence.

1987 Apr First Crowded House release, *Don't Dream It's Over*, hits US #2. LP *Crowded House* makes US #12, and will spend the rest of the year on chart.

June *Don't Dream It's Over* reaches UK #27.

July *Something So Strong* hits US #7.

Sept *World Where You Live* falters at US #65.

1988 June [11] Paul Young° sings *Don't Dream It's Over* at "Nelson Mandela 70th Birthday Party Concert".

Aug LP *Temple Of Low Men* reaches US #40. *Better Be Home Soon* makes US #42.

DUSTY SPRINGFIELD

1960 Springfield (b. Mary O'Brien, Apr.16, 1939, Hampstead, London, UK), ex-member of UK vocal trio The Lana Sisters, with her brother Dion O'Brien and friend Tim Field, forms The Springfields, a folk and country music-based vocal/guitar trio. She adopts new stage name Dusty Springfield, while Dion becomes Tom Springfield. They begin working in folk clubs.

1961 May Signed to Philips Records, the trio's debut *Dear John* fails to chart.

Sept *Breakaway* makes UK #31.

Dec Christmas song *Bambino* reaches UK #16. Debut LP *Kinda Folksy* is released, and they are named Best UK Vocal Group in *New Musical Express* readers' poll, on the strength of two minor hits.

1962 June Field leaves and is replaced by Mike Pickworth, who changes name to Mike Hurst.

Sept *Silver Threads And Golden Needles*, having failed to chart in UK, reaches US #20.

Nov *Dear Hearts And Gentle People* is US follow-up and makes #95.

1963 Mar *Island Of Dreams* hits UK #5.

Apr *Say I Won't Be There* also hits UK #5, as the group tours UK supporting US visitors Del Shannon° and Johnny Tillotson°.

Aug The Springfields' *Come On Home* reaches UK #31 and is their last hit.

Sept [24] The group announces that it is to split, and that Dusty Springfield will be signing a solo deal with Philips.

Oct [11] The group plays its farewell concert at the London Palladium. (After the split, Hurst will become a record producer, most notably for Showaddywaddy in the 1970s, while Tom Springfield will write such hits as *The Carnival Is Over* and *Georgy Girl* for The Seekers, and in the early 1970s will launch Springfield Revival.)

1964 Jan [1] *I Only Want To Be With You* is the first record played on new BBC UK TV show "Top of the Pops".

Jan Dusty's solo debut is a change from pop/folk to more Motown-style music and *I Only Want To Be With You* hits UK #4. The Springfields appear in UK movie *It's All Over Town* (a cameo slot filmed before their break-up), singing *If I Was Down And Out*, which is also released as a final Springfields single.

Mar *Stay Awhile*, in similar style to her debut, reaches UK #13, while *I Only Want To Be With You* makes US #12.

Apr She tours Australia with Gerry & The Pacemakers°.

May Debut LP *A Girl Called Dusty* hits UK #6, as *Stay Awhile* climbs to US #38.

July Bacharach/David-written *I Just Don't Know What To Do With Myself* hits UK #3.

Aug *Wishin' And Hopin'*, another Bacharach/David song, from the debut LP is chosen as US single and hits #6. (A version by The Merseybeats charts in UK at the same time.) She visits US briefly to record some tracks in New York.

Oct US-only *All Cried Out* reaches US #41.

Dec *Losing You* hits UK #9.

1965 Feb *Your Hurtin' Kinda Love* halts at UK #37.

Mar *Losing You* stalls at US #91. Meanwhile, she hosts a Rediffusion TV special featuring The Supremes°, Martha & The Vandellas°, Stevie Wonder°, Smokey Robinson° & The Miracles and The Temptations°.

Apr [11] She appears at the *New Musical Express* Poll Winners' concert at Wembley, UK, with The Beatles°, The Rolling Stones° and many others.

July Uptempo *In The Middle Of Nowhere* hits UK #8.

Oct *Some Of Your Lovin'*, a ballad with vocal backing by Madeleine Bell and Doris Troy, hits UK #8.

Nov LP *Everything's Coming Up Dusty* hits UK #6, as she appears in The Royal Variety Show in London.

1966 Feb Uptempo *Little By Little* reaches UK #17.

Apr *You Don't Have To Say You Love Me*, an Italian song with new English lyrics by Simon Napier-Bell, tops the UK chart, and is her all-time best-selling single.

July Goffin/King° ballad *Goin' Back* hits UK #10, as *You Don't Have To Say You Love Me* hits US #4.

Oct Another ballad, *All I See Is You*, hits UK #9 and US #20.

Nov Compilation LP *Golden Hits*, rounding up her singles successes to date, hits UK #2.

1967 Jan She records two movie theme songs, *The Corrupt Ones* for *The Peking Medallion*, and *The Look Of Love* for James Bond movie *Casino Royale*.

Mar *I'll Try Anything* reaches UK #13 and US #40.

June *Give Me Time* makes UK #24 and US #76.

Nov *The Look Of Love*, from *Casino Royale*, is her last hit on Philips in US, reaching #22. LP *Where Am I Going* peaks at UK #40.

Dec *What's It Gonna Be* reaches US #49.

1968 Aug *I Close My Eyes And Count To Ten* hits UK #4.

Sept *I Will Come To You* fails to chart. Now signed to Atlantic records in US, she travels to Memphis to record an LP with the label's Southern session men.

1969 Jan *Son Of A Preacher Man*, recorded in Memphis, hits UK #9, and US #10, while LP *Dusty . . . Definitely* makes UK #30.

Mar *Don't Forget About Me* reaches US #64, while B-side *Breakfast In Bed* makes US #91.

Apr LP *Dusty In Memphis*, from the Memphis sessions and recorded in less than a week (later considered one of her finest), is released and is her first LP not to chart in UK.

May *The Windmills Of Your Mind*, the theme song from film *The Thomas Crown Affair*, reaches US #31.

July A version of Tony Joe White's *Willie And Laura Mae Jones* climbs to US #78.

Sept *Am I The Same Girl* peaks at UK #43.

Nov [30] She appears with David Bowie°, Grapefruit and The Graham Bond Organization, at Save Rave '69, a benefit show in London for the magazine *Rave*.

Dec *A Brand New Me*, written and produced in Philadelphia by Gamble and Huff, reaches US #24. It is not released as a UK single.

1970 Mar *Silly, Silly Fool* stalls at US #76, and is her last US singles chart entry.

DUSTY SPRINGFIELD *cont.*

Sept A revival of The Young Rascals'° *How Can I Be Sure* reaches UK #37, and is her last UK hit single for 9 years.

1972 She leaves UK to live in LA.

Nov LP *See All Her Faces* fails to chart.

1973 May LP *Cameo* is released on Philips in UK and Dunhill in US, without success.

1974 She begins recording her second Dunhill LP *Longings* (but it will not be released).

Mar *What's It Gonna Be* is her last new release for Philips in UK. She becomes a session singer in LA and almost signs to Rocket records.

1975 She sings back-up vocals on recording sessions by Anne Murray.

1978 She attempts a recording comeback, signing new dual deals, with Mercury in UK and United Artists in US.

Feb *A Love Like Yours* and LP *It Begins Again* are produced by Roy Thomas-Baker. The LP is critically acclaimed, but is only a moderate seller, making UK #41.

1979 May *Living Without Your Love* also fails to chart.

Nov *Baby Blue*, on Mercury, reaches UK #61 – her first UK chart single since 1970.

1980 She signs to 20th Century Records in US, releasing only one single *It Goes Like It Goes*, the Oscar-winning song from *Norma Rae*.

Oct [7] She makes her first New York stage appearance in 8 years, at the Grande Finale Club.

1983 LP *White Heat*, an electronic dance-flavored set on US Casablanca, despite some US critical plaudits, is not released in UK.

1984 Mar A Dusty Springfield/Spencer Davis° duet, re-working old William Bell/Judy Clay hit *Private Number*, is released in UK on Allegiance records, without success.

1985 Aug She returns to UK to promote her new single *Sometimes Like Butterflies*, released on Peter Stringfellow's Hippodrome label, but it finds little success.

1987 Aug The Pet Shop Boys° invite Dusty Springfield to guest on their single *What Have I Done To Deserve This*, which is a worldwide hit.

Sept She sings guest vocals on Richard Carpenter's single *Something In Your Eyes*.

Dec *I Only Want To Be With You* is re-issued to tie in with Springfield's brief appearance in a UK soft drink TV ad. The single is backed by her 1968 recording of *Breakfast In Bed* (which will be a hit in 1988 for UB40° & Chrissie Hynde).

1988 Jan Compilation LP *The Silver Collection* on Philips reaches UK #14.

Feb [8] She makes a live UK TV appearance with The Pet Shop Boys° at the BPI annual awards ceremony from London's Royal Albert Hall, performing *What Have I Done To Deserve This*.

Feb Springfield sings on The Pet Shop Boys° forthcoming theme to film *Scandal*.

RICK SPRINGFIELD

1962 Aug [23] Springfield (b. Richard Springthorpe, Aug.23, 1949, Sydney, Australia), the son of an army officer, has led a nomadic military childhood, including some pre-teen years in UK, when he is given a guitar and makes music his first interest.

1970 Having completed school, he has played with groups like Rock House (making a visit to entertain troops in Vietnam) and Wackedy Wak in Sydney, when he joins Zoot, which becomes Australia's most successful teen-idol band, with a string of local hits. As a member of Zoot, he records *Speak To The Sky*, which hits #1 in Australia.

1972 Sept After recording a debut solo LP for Capitol Records in London, he moves to US when *Speak To The Sky* becomes a US hit, reaching #14. The song is written by Springfield (as will be almost every subsequent single).

Oct Splashing his youthful good looks around the teen media, Capitol attempts to make him its answer to Donny Osmond°, as debut LP *Beginnings* makes US #35. (He will not have another hit LP until 1981.)

Dec *What Would The Children Think* makes US #70.

1974 July Leaving Capitol, he signs to CBS/Columbia. LP *Comic Book Heroes* fails to chart, while extracted *American Girls* stalls at US #98. Management and immigration problems (which mean he cannot play live) force him out of active performance, but he remains in US and goes to acting school.

1976 Oct A brief deal with Chelsea Records sees no chart action for LP *Wait For The Night*, but *Take A Hand* makes US #41. He finds TV acting work with Universal in Hollywood, and appears in hit series like "The Rockford Files" and "The Six Million Dollar Man". (TV work will keep his musical career on a back burner, as he guests in "The Incredible Hulk" and appears regularly in soap drama "The Young and the Restless".)

1978 He records without success for Mercury Records. (This material will re-emerge in 1984.)

1981 He signs a new recording contract with RCA, and plays Dr. Noah Drake in another soap, "General Hospital".

Aug With his popularity cemented by a high TV profile, his first RCA hit, self-penned *Jessie's Girl*, tops the US chart for 2 weeks, and is a million-seller.

Sept Debut RCA LP *Working Class Dog* hits US #7, and is also a million-seller.

Nov *I've Done Everything For You*, taken from the LP and written by Sammy Hagar, hits US #8.

1982 Feb *Love Is Alright Tonite* makes US #20.

Feb [24] *Jessie's Girl* earns him a Grammy award, named Best Male Rock Vocal Performance of 1981.

May *Don't Talk To Strangers* hits US #2 for 4 weeks, behind Paul McCartney° and Stevie Wonder's° *Ebony And Ivory*, while parent LP *Success Hasn't Spoiled Me Yet* also hits US #2 (behind Asia's° debut LP), and is his second platinum LP.

July *What Kind Of Fool Am I*, also from the LP, reaches US #21.

Oct *I Get Excited* makes US #32.

1983 Jan RCA reissues 1976 Chelsea LP *Wait For Night*, to minor sales at US #159.

Feb He begins filming in Ray Stark's *Hard to Hold* for Universal – his first starring non-TV movie role.

June *Affair Of The Heart* hits US #9. It is taken from LP *Living In Oz*, which reaches US #12 and is his third million-selling LP.

Sept *Human Touch*, another extract from LP *Living In Oz*, makes US #18.

Dec *Souls* peaks at US #23.

1984 Jan *Human Touch* is his UK chart debut, at #23.

Feb LP *Living In Oz* makes UK #41.

Apr *Jessie's Girl* reaches UK #43.

May The first song taken from the soundtrack of newly-released movie *Hard to Hold* is *Love Somebody*, which hits US #5.

June Soundtrack LP *Hard To Hold* reaches US #16, a further million-seller.

July *Don't Walk Away*, another track from the movie, makes US #26.

Oct *Bop 'Til You Drop*, also from *Hard to Hold*, reaches US #20.

Dec The B-side of *Bop*, *Taxi Dancing* (a duet with Randy Crawford°), makes US #59.

1985 Jan *Bruce*, one of the songs Springfield originally recorded in 1978 for Mercury, is issued to capitalize on the popularity of its subject matter – an autobiographical piece concerning people mistaking him for Bruce Springsteen°. It reaches US #27. Mercury also issues LP *Beautiful Feelings*, containing other 1978 tracks with new accompaniment added, which makes US #78.

May *Celebrate Youth*, from his newly-recorded LP, reaches US #26.

June LP *Tao* makes US #21 (earning a gold disk) and UK #68.

Aug *State Of The Heart*, another song from LP *Tao*, makes US #22.

1988 Apr After an extended absence from recording, Springfield returns with self-penned *Rock Of Life*, which reaches US #22. The parent LP of the same title makes US #55 and UK #80.

BRUCE SPRINGSTEEN

1963 Having tried drumming unsuccessfully at an early age, Springsteen (b. Bruce Frederick Joseph Springsteen, Sept.23, 1949, Freehold, N.J., US), son of Adele and Douglas Springsteen, as a teenager buys a guitar for $18 from a local pawn shop and begins to learn songs from the radio. (He will be influenced by Elvis Presley°, Chuck Berry° and, later on, by The Beatles° and The Rolling Stones°.)

1965 Already composing his own songs, Springsteen discovers sister Ginny's boyfriend George Theiss has a vacancy in his high school band, The Castiles. Springsteen passes two auditions for group manager 32-year-old Tex Vineyard. With the band practising every day after school, Vineyard, an unemployed factory worker, secures The Castiles constant gigs at school dances, Y.M.C.A. parties and clubs around N.J. areas Red Bank, Long Branch and Asbury Park.

1967 Aug Having recorded one demo, *That's What You'll Get*, The Castiles play their final gig at Off Broad Street coffee house, Red Bank. Springsteen moves to live in nearby Asbury Park and joins short-lived trio Earth. He also begins spending many evenings at the Upstage Club, a popular local hangout for aspiring musicians, where he meets Vini Lopez, Southside Johnny and Steve Van Zandt.

1969 Springsteen forms new band Child from club members, which changes name to Steel Mill when they realize another Child already exists. Managed by Tinker West, the group begins constant local gigging, and also a mini club-tour of Cal., which attracts encouraging press reviews.

1971 Steel Mill splits. (Three members, drummer Lopez, keyboardist Danny Federici and bassist Van Zandt will join Springsteen's future backing E. Street Band.) Springsteen forms Dr. Zoom & The Sonic Boom, a collection of Asbury Park musicians not currently affiliated to other line-ups. It plays only three dates, as summer performing is seriously interrupted by Asbury riots.

Sept Springsteen starts 10-piece group, The Bruce Springsteen Band, with a horn section and girl singers. After only two dates, the line-up is cut to David Sancious on keyboards, Garry Tallent on bass, Van Zandt (now on guitar), Lopez and Federici, while Asbury saxophonist Clarence Clemons also joins.

1972 Springsteen auditions for aspiring producers Mike Appel and Jim Cretecos and, after returning from an unsuccessful solo trip to Cal., signs a long-term management contract with Appel's Laurel Canyon Promotion Company, on a car hood in an unlit parking lot. Appel arranges an audition for Springsteen in front of CBS/Columbia A&R head John Hammond who is impressed and arranges a further audition for Columbia colleagues at the Gaslight Club, Greenwich Village, New York.

June [9] Despite difficulties between an aggressive Appel and the label, Springsteen signs a worldwide CBS deal for an advance of $25,000 with a $40,000 recording budget. Springsteen quickly re-forms The Bruce Springsteen Band (now without Van Zandt) against the wishes of CBS which sees him as a solo folk performer. Undaunted, Springsteen takes the band into the studio to record his first LP in 3 weeks.

1973 Jan Debut LP *Greetings From Asbury Park* is released. Selected as a priority by CBS head Clive Davis, critics are encouraged to think of Springsteen as the new Dylan°. Despite a lengthy club tour and a 10-date support role for CBS headliners Chicago° (criticized as a misconceived disaster), the LP only sells 25,000 copies. Relations between artist's management and CBS worsen.

Feb Springsteen's *Blinded By The Light* disappears without trace.

May While Davis is fired, Springsteen plays the CBS Records Annual Convention in San Francisco prior to recording second LP.

Nov LP *The Wild, The Innocent And The E. Street Shuffle* is released. It proves popular with rock critics who pay particular attention to native ballad *Asbury Park Fourth Of July (Sandy)*. A six-city club tour fails to ignite sales, even though Springsteen and the band are now seasoned live performers, commonly playing 2-hour sets. Ernest Carter replaces Lopez as the backing group are named The E. Street Band – after the road where Sancious' mother lives in Belmar, N.J.

1974 May The band plays three nights at Charley's Club in Harvard Square, Cambridge, Mass. One of them is attended by influential rock critic, 26-year-old Jon Landau who writes for *Rolling Stone* and Boston-based *The Real Paper*, and is suitably impressed, particularly by Springsteen's first live performance of new song *Born To Run*.

May [22] After seeing a second date in Cambridge, Landau is moved to write: "I saw rock and roll future – and its name is Bruce Springsteen." The often misquoted sentence immediately sparks intense promotion ideas at CBS and snowballs further similar reviews by other critics. CBS re-promotes the first two Springsteen LPs as a long-term friendship develops between the artist and Landau.

Aug [3] Springsteen & The E. Street Band open for Anne Murray at the Schaefer Festival, N.Y. It is the final gig in the line-up for Carter and Sancious who are replaced by drummer Max Weinberg and pianist Roy Bittan.

Nov With production indecision delaying the third LP, Springsteen asks Landau to help, which he unofficially does.

1975 Feb Landau becomes co-producer of the new LP and invites Steve Van Zandt to relink with Springsteen to provide a rockier edge to the current recordings. Appel, also co-producing with Springsteen, is unhappy with Landau's involvement.

Apr UK act The Hollies° shorten earlier Springsteen song to *Sandy*, peaking at US #85.

July While public and record company await the new LP, his first two releases finally chart, *Greetings* making US #60 and *The Wild, The Innocent* reaching US #59.

Sept [6] Third LP *Born To Run* is released and immediately hailed as a rock classic. It will hit US #3, while the title cut simultaneously climbs to US #23. Springsteen and the band begin their first national tour, a 40-date "Born To Run" trek which gains sensational reviews.

Oct [27] In an unprecedented move, both *Time* and *Newsweek* magazines feature cover stories on Springsteen. Many other critics feel that the hype machine is out of control.

Nov At an LA gig, Springsteen meets Phil Spector. The arrangement of the title track from *Born To Run* was credited as a tribute to the producer. Spector invites Springsteen to a Dion° session, and he plays two dates at London's Hammersmith Odeon, his first UK performances, as part of a European tour also taking in Stockholm and Amsterdam. As LP *Born To Run* makes UK #17, many people, including Springsteen, are outraged by CBS hype which features bill posters of the famous (misquoted) Landau review. A theater hoarding announces "At last London is ready for Bruce Springsteen."

Dec Appel tapes three concerts for a planned live LP. The only cut which will officially emerge is festive *Santa Claus Is Coming To Town*, which highlights a special live rapport between Clarence Clemons and Springsteen.

1976 Jan Follow-up *Tenth Avenue Freeze Out* peaks at US #83.

Feb Van Zandt produces LP *I Don't Want To Go Home* for Southside Johnny & The Asbury Jukes, which includes Springsteen song *The Fever*.

Mar Springsteen enlists the help of Landau and lawyer Mike Mayer in looking at his original Appel contract. Appel is seeking to renegotiate a management contract with Springsteen who realizes for the first time that he only receives 3½% wholesale album sales as opposed to Appel's 14%.

Apr The band begins a US tour as Manfred Mann's° Earth Band's cover of Springsteen's *Spirit In The Night* makes US #97 (it will re-chart a year later to make US #40).

Apr [29] At 3:00 a.m. Springsteen, Van Zandt and publicist Glen

Brunman ask a Memphis cab driver to take them to see Elvis Presley's° Graceland home. Springsteen climbs over the wall but is apprehended by a security guard who assumes that he is just another crank fan.

May [14] Appel's Laurel Canyon company sends Springsteen an outstanding payment check for $67,368.78.

July [2] Appel legally informs Springsteen that he must not use Landau as a producer on his fourth LP.

July [27] Springsteen counters with writs alleging fraud and breach of trust by Appel.

Aug He plays a 1-week engagement in Red Bank, N.J. to earn money during the legal dispute.

Sept Springsteen begins another lengthy tour opening at The Coliseum, Phoenix, Ariz.

1977 Jan Manfred Mann's° Earth Band's cover of Springsteen's *Blinded By The Light* tops the US chart (having hit UK #6 6 months earlier).

May [28] After several legal flurries, an out-of-court settlement is reached with Appel. He reportedly wins substantial monies, but Springsteen is free to seek new management and make his own decisions.

June [1] Springsteen and Landau begin legal recording under a renegotiated deal with CBS at Atlantic Studios, Manhattan, N.Y.

July Always a prolific songwriter, Springsteen gives *Fire* to New York rockabilly Robert Gordon and *Because The Night* to Jimmy Iovine who is producing a Patti Smith° LP in the next door studio (the song will reach US #13 and UK #5).

1978 May [23] Prefacing the finished LP, Bruce Springsteen & The E. Street Band return to stage work at Shea's Buffalo Theater. The beginning of another lengthy series, the performances now extend to 3 hours with the inclusion of many cover versions.

June [3] Springsteen plays Long Island's Nassau Coliseum – his first New York appearance in 2 years.

June LP *Darkness On The Edge Of Town* is finally released and hits US #5 and UK #16, while *Prove It All Night* makes US #33 (he will be without a UK chart single until 1980).

Sept *Badlands* peaks at US #42.

Dec The Pointer Sisters° follow Gordon and record *Fire*, hitting US #2 (and UK #34 in Mar. 1979).

1979 Jan [1] A 7-month tour ends in Cleveland after 109 shows in 86 cities, all sell-outs including dates at New York's Madison Square Garden.

Mar The band enters the Power Station to record a new LP.

Apr During hi-jinks with comic Robin Williams and Springsteen's girlfriend Joyce Heiser, Springsteen damages a leg in a motorbike accident at home, forcing him to take a 3-month break.

May Tapes for a new LP leak out of the studio, aiding increasing pirate/bootleg operations.

July Greg Kihn° cuts Springsteen's *For You* on his LP *With The Naked Eye* while The Knack° record his *Rendezvous*.

Aug CBS and Springsteen file a suit in LA against five bootleggers, seeking $1.75 million in damages.

Sept [23] On his 30th birthday, Springsteen plays the Musicians United For Safe Energy (MUSE) concert at New York's Madison Square Garden at Jackson Browne's° invitation. Springsteen performs on condition that no politicians are present and that photographer Lyn Goldsmith is also barred (Goldsmith had sold private pictures of Springsteen taken during their brief 1978 tour affair). Springsteen is strongly featured in subsequent *No Nukes* triple LP and film.

Oct Springsteen re-enters the studio to work on a new LP.

1980 Nov Double LP *The River* is released, trimmed from an original choice of 60 songs, and set to hit US #1 and UK #2, spending over 1 year on both charts. From the LP, *Hungry Heart* hits US #5 with unavailable elsewhere B-side *Held Up Without A Gun*, and makes UK #44.

Nov [3] "The River" tour begins in Ann Arbor, Mich., with the live set now extended at some dates to 4 hours and including popular encore medley of Mitch Ryder° songs which will remain a long-term habit.

1981 Mar *Fade Away* peaks at US #20.

Mar [19] After initially postponed dates caused by ill-health, Springsteen returns to UK for his first dates since 1975 opening with two nights in London.

May Gary U.S. Bonds° releases LP *Dedication* (US #27 and UK #43) produced by Springsteen and containing four of his songs including *This Little Girl* (US #11, UK #43) and *Jolé Blon* (US #65, UK #51). Springsteen will also convert backing vocals on the LP to live assistance on selected Bonds' dates.

May [11] Springsteen finishes a 32-date European tour in Paris, France.

June The title track from *The River* makes UK #35.

Oct 1975-recorded *Santa Claus Is Comin' To Town* is included on CBS various artists' LP *In Harmony*, released in aid of Children's Television Workshop and children's charities. It becomes a seasonal radio favorite.

1982 Jan Sessions for a new LP begin at Springsteen's home and in the studio – they will dominate the next 2 years of his career.

July Second Springsteen-produced Gary U.S. Bonds° LP *On The Line* is issued (US #52, UK #55), including US #21 *Out Of Work*. Springsteen gives *From Small Things (Big Things One Day Come)* to UK rocker Dave Edmunds°, but it will fail to chart.

Sept With little fanfare, Springsteen releases LP *Nebraska*, a solo set of acoustic compositions recorded by Springsteen and his band at Power Station on a 4-track home tape recorder. It hits both US and UK #3 but no singles will be issued from it. The original home recordings also feature new songs including *Working On The Highway* and the first electric version of future hit *Born In The USA*.

1983 Springsteen spends the year writing and recording over 100 new songs for selection on his next project. With no live dates, he also drives extensively throughout US.

1984 Apr Van Zandt leaves The E. Street line-up amicably and sets up Little Steven & The Disciples of Soul.

May Following a near 2-year wait, new material emerges with *Dancing In The Dark*, helped on its way to hit US #2 and UK #28 by his first formal video, directed by Brian De Palma. Previously shy of the device, his only celluloid promotion has been a live clip of popular number *Rosalita*.

June New LP *Born In The USA* is released to become his most successful multi-platinum LP. It will spend over 2 years on both US and UK charts, hitting #1 on each. The "Born In The USA" tour debuts in St. Paul, Minn., with Nils Lofgren° replacing Van Zandt on guitar. It is Springsteen's first live work since "The River" tour and will take in Europe, Australia, US, Canada and Japan. It also features his first female backing singer, Patti Scialfa.

Oct *Cover Me* hits US #7 and UK #16.

Dec Title cut *Born In The USA*, already an anthemic live number re-identifying Springsteen's harder image, hits US #9.

1985 Jan [25] Springsteen contributes a lead vocal to USA For Africa's° *We Are The World* benefit disk. He will also donate popular live cut (previously unreleased) *Trapped* for inclusion on LP *USA For Africa* (the track was recorded on Aug.6, 1984 at Meadowlands, East Rutherford, N.J. and is part of extensive live recordings accompanying the "Born" tour). Meanwhile, *Dancing In The Dark* is repromoted in UK, hitting #4.

Feb Ballad *I'm On Fire*, supported by his first concept-acted video begins a 5-month US chart stay on its way to hit #6.

Mar Reissued *Cover Me* makes UK #16 as US close-harmony cover band Big Daddy's unrecognizable version of *Dancing In The Dark* makes UK #21.

May [13] Springsteen marries model/actress Julianne Phillips in Oregon.

June As *Glory Days* hits US #5, the tour reaches UK amid unprecedented ticket demand, with sell-outs at 72,000-attendee dates at Wembley Stadium. Double A-side *I'm On Fire/Born In The USA* hits UK #5 as all seven Springsteen LPs either re-enter or enter UK chart simultaneously (*The Wild* peaks at #33, while *Greeting* makes #41).

Aug *Glory Days* reaches UK #17 as sixth extract from LP *Born In The USA*, *I'm Goin' Down* hits US #9.

Oct [2] "Born in the USA" tour ends at LA's Coliseum, Cal.

Nov Springsteen contributes lead vocals to Artists United Against Apartheid single *Sun City* and appears in a video alongside its inspirator, Little Steven Van Zandt (US #38, UK #21).

Dec Still from LP *Born In The USA*, *My Hometown* climbs to hit US #6, while in UK festive *Santa Claus Is Coming To Town/My Hometown* hits UK #9.

1986 Feb Lee Iococa reportedly offers Springsteen $12 million to license *Born In The USA* for a series of Chrysler commercials. Springsteen rejects the offer.

Mar Always concerned at the quality and quantity of live bootleg recordings, Springsteen has ensured that many of the "Born in the USA" dates have been taped to add to other live recordings of the past 10 years for future release. Over 200 LP bootlegs are freely available on the market.

Nov Having performed over 500 shows in the past decade, Springsteen releases personally-compiled unprecedented five LP live set *Live 1975 – 1985*, reflecting the performance glory which has so endeared his live act to his dedicated followers. Dominated by his latest stadium concerts, the set includes four never available Springsteen performances: instrumental *Paradise By The Sea*, his versions of *Because The Night*, *Fire* and new *Seeds* taped at LA's Coliseum in Sept. 1985. Produced by Landau, Springsteen and, Chuck Plotkin and compiled from 21 concerts, the LP enters US chart at historic #1 and hits UK #4.

Dec From it, *War*, a cover of Edwin Starr's hit accompanied by a live video, hits US #8 and UK #18.

1987 Jan [21] Springsteen performs *Oh, Pretty Woman* with its composer Roy Orbison° at the second annual Hall of Fame dinner.

Feb *Fire* makes US #46 and UK #54.

May Live *Born To Run* reaches UK #16.

Oct [9] New studio LP *Tunnel Of Love* is released, immediately hitting US and UK #1, while *Brilliant Disguise* makes UK #20.

Nov *Brilliant Disguise* hits US #5.

Dec *Tunnel Of Love* makes UK #45.

1988 Jan Springsteen plays selected acoustic gigs in aid of Harry Chapin° Memorial Fund.

Feb *Tunnel Of Love* hits US #9.

Feb [25] "Tunnel of Love Express" tour opens at The Centrum, Worcester, Mass., US.

Apr *One Step Up* reaches US #13.

May Natalie Cole° covers previous Springsteen B-side *Pink Cadillac* hitting #5 in US and UK.

June [21] The UK leg of "Tunnel of Love Express" tour opens at Aston Villa Football Club ground, Birmingham.

July *Tougher Than The Rest* reaches UK #13.

Aug Springsteen's wife files for divorce.

Sept [2] Springsteen participates in the opening concert at London's Wembley Stadium of "Human Rights Now!" Amnesty International 6-week world tour with Sting°, Peter Gabriel°, Tracy Chapman° and Youssou N'Dour.

Sept Springsteen contributes *I Ain't Got No Home* and *Vigilante Man* to various artists' LP *A Vision Shared*, a tribute to Woody Guthrie and Leadbelly.

Oct *Spare Parts* makes UK #32.

SQUEEZE

Chris Difford (vocals and guitar)
Glenn Tilbrook (vocals and lead guitar)
Julian "Jools" Holland (keyboards)
Harry Kakoulli (bass)
Paul Gunn (drums)

1974 Mar Difford (b. Nov.4, 1954, London, UK) meets Tilbrook (b. Aug.31, 1957, London, UK) when he answers Difford's music paper ad requesting band members for a new group. With the recruitment of Holland and Gunn, Squeeze is formed, taking its name from a Velvet Underground° LP.

1976 They sign with Miles Copeland's BTM label and management company. Gunn is replaced by Lavis, and Kakoulli joins on bass.

1977 Jan *Take Me I'm Yours*, scheduled for release by BTM, is withdrawn.

July EP *Packet Of Three*, on Deptford Fun City Records, is produced by John Cale°. They sign to A&M worldwide, becoming the company's first "new wave" signing since The Sex Pistols°.

1978 Apr *Take Me I'm Yours*, on A&M, reaches UK #19. Debut LP *Squeeze*, produced by Cale°, fails to chart. The band makes its first visit to US but has to change name temporarily to UK Squeeze to avoid confusion with a US band called Tight Squeeze.

June *Bang Bang* peaks at UK #49.

Aug Squeeze plays UK's Reading Festival.

Nov *Goodbye Girl* reaches UK #63.

1979 Mar Second LP *Cool For Cats* produced by John Wood, makes #45.

Apr *Cool For Cats* hits UK #2, kept from the top by Art Garfunkel's° *Bright Eyes*.

June *Up The Junction* also hits UK #2, this time blocked by Tubeway Army's *Are "Friends" Electric?*

Sept *Slap And Tickle* makes UK #24.

Nov Festive *Christmas Day* fails to chart.

1980 Mar LP *Argy Bargy*, again produced by Wood, and featuring new bassist John Bentley, reaches UK #32. *Another Nail In My Heart* makes UK #17.

Apr The group begins its fourth US tour.

May *Pulling Mussels From A Shell* reaches UK #44.

Aug After returning to UK, Holland quits. (He supports Police° on tour and makes a documentary with them for UK TV, which leads him to become a co-host of UK TV show "The Tube" from 1982-87. He will also front his own band The Millionaires.) He is replaced by Paul Carrack (ex-Ace°).

Nov [30] Squeeze and Elvis Costello° perform a benefit concert at the Top Rank club in Swansea, Wales for the family of Welsh boxer Johnny Owen, who died from injuries sustained during a world title bout in Las Vegas, Nev., US.

1981 Mar Tilbrook teams with Elvis Costello° for one-off *From A Whisper To A Scream*.

May LP *East Side Story*, co-produced by Elvis Costello° and Roger Bechirian, makes UK #19. *Is That Love* climbs to UK #35.

Aug Soulful *Tempted*, with Carrack on lead vocal, reaches UK #41 and US #49.

Oct Country-flavored *Labelled With Love* hits UK #4. Just before its release Carrack leaves to join Carlene Carter's band. Ex-Sincero Don Snow replaces him.

1982 Apr *Black Coffee In Bed*, with guest vocals from Elvis Costello° and Paul Young°, reaches UK #51.

May LP *Sweets From A Stranger* makes UK #37.

June The group tours US, where it sells out New York's Madison Square Garden.

July *When The Hangover Strikes* fails to chart.

Oct Alan Tarney-produced *Annie Get Your Gun* makes UK #43.

Nov The group announces a split and plays what will be its last show at the 3-day Jamaica World Music Festival at the Bob Marley Performing Center near Montego Bay. Compilation LP *Singles 45's And Under* is released, and hits UK #3.

1983 Feb *Labelled With Love*, a musical based on the songs of Difford and Tilbrook, opens in Deptford, London. The pair decides to stay together and write. They also work with Helen Shapiro°, Billy Bremner (ex-Rockpile), Paul Young° and Jools Holland. Lavis joins Chris Rea's° band.

1984 July Difford and Tilbrook release eponymous LP, produced by Tony Visconti and E.T. Thorngren, which reaches UK #47. Two singles from it fail to chart.

SQUEEZE *cont.*

1985 Jan Squeeze re-forms for a charity gig at a pub in Catford, London. The reunion becomes permanent (other commitments allowing). The line-up is Difford, Tilbrook, Holland and Lavis with Keith Wilkinson on bass.
Mar *The Last Time Forever* peaks at UK #45.
Sept LP *Cosi Fan Tutti Frutti*, produced by Laurie Latham, reaches UK #31 and US #57.
1986 Apr [28] Holland and Lavis are involved in a car crash returning to London from Plymouth after performing in a charity concert for a drug and alcohol rehabilitation center. Lavis breaks an arm.
1987 Squeeze embarks on another successful US tour spurred by renewed US chart activity, including sold-out Madison Square Garden concerts in New York.
Aug *Hourglass* reaches UK #17 and US #15.
Sept LP *Babylon And On*, featuring additional keyboard player ex-Soft Boy Andy Metcalfe, reaches UK #14 and US #36.
Oct Taken from it, *Trust Me To Open My Mouth* stalls at UK #72.
1988 Feb *853 5937*, also from the LP, makes UK #32.

THE STAPLE SINGERS

Mavis Staples
Cleo Staples
Pervis Staples
"Pop" Staples

1951 The group forms in Chicago, Ill., US, as a family gospel quartet led by former blues guitarist Roebuck "Pop" Staples (b. Dec.28, 1915, Drew, Miss., US), with son Pervis and daughters Mavis and Cleo.
1956 Now with Vee Jay label (having recorded for United in 1954), the group has its first major US national gospel chart #1 with *Uncloudy Day*.
1964 Signing to CBS/Epic, they decide to mix gospel with more mainstream R&B music, but social and moral issues will continue to play a large part in their material's lyric content.
1967 June Larry Williams-produced *Why? (Am I Treated So Bad)* gives the group its first US Hot 100 single, at #95.
Sept A cover of Stephen Stills' *For What It's Worth* makes US #66.
1968 July The group switches to Stax, where its first producer is house band guitar mainstay Steve Cropper, whose purist production values fail to secure chart success.
1970 Sept Mavis' solo single *I Have Learned To Do Without You* peaks at US #87, while solo LP *Only For The Lonely* makes US #188.
1971 Feb Now produced by Al Bell, the group has its first top 30 single with *Heavy Makes You Happy (Sha-Na-Boom Boom)*, at US #27. (Bell will continue to produce the group throughout its stay with Stax, until 1974.)
Mar LP *The Staple Singers* makes US #117.
Apr The group tours US with The Bee Gees°. Pervis leaves to do his US military service, and is replaced by his sister Yvonne. (He will not return to the line-up.)
June The Staple Singers' appearances in Ghana earlier in the year are included in film *Soul to Soul*, which also features Ike & Tina Turner°, Wilson Pickett° and Santana°.
July *You've Got To Earn It* peaks at US #97.
Oct The group enjoys its first top 20 single with *Respect Yourself*, hitting US #12.
1972 Feb LP *Bealtitude: Respect Yourself* makes US #19.
Apr The band tops the US chart with *I'll Take You There*, earning a gold disk.
June *I'll Take You There* makes UK #30.
Aug *This World* reaches US #38.
1973 Mar *Oh La De Da* peaks at US #33.
June *Be What You Are* stalls at US #66.
Aug LP *Be What You Are* climbs to US #102. The group is featured in movie *Wattstax* alongside Isaac Hayes°, Rufus Thomas and Richard Pryor.
Oct Second single from LP *Be What You Are*, *If You're Ready (Come Go With Me)*, hits US #9.
1974 Feb *Touch A Hand, Make A Friend* makes US #23.
June *If You're Ready (Come Go With Me)* reaches UK #34.
Aug *City In The Sky* peaks at US #79.
Sept LP *City In The Sky* stalls at US #125.
Dec Their last Stax release, *My Main Man* reaches UK #76.
1975 Following the demise of Stax, the group signs to Curtis Mayfield's° Curtom label.
Oct Produced by Mayfield°, the group achieves its second US #1 with *Let's Do It Again*, the title track to Sidney Poitier/Bill Cosby film.
Nov LP *Let's Do It Again* reaches US #20.
1976 Feb Again from *Let's Do It Again* soundtrack, *New Orleans* makes US #70.
Sept LP *Pass It On* peaks at US #155.
1977 Nov The group is featured in *The Last Waltz*, Martin Scorsese's film of The Band's° final concert, filmed the previous year. (With frequent label changes, The Staple Singers no longer enjoy chart success with either singles or LPs, though they will continue regular releases, supported by tours throughout the world.)
1984 Their re-recording of *Slippery People*, now a familiar cut through Talking Heads'° cover version, is a substantial dancefloor success in US and UK, but fails to cross over.
Nov Geordie band The Kane Gang reaches UK #21 with a cover of *Respect Yourself*.
1986 Feb Ruby Turner covers *If You're Ready (Come Go With Me)*, reaching UK #30.

RINGO STARR

1969 Starr (b. Richard Starkey, July 7, 1940, Liverpool, UK) appears in Italian/French film *Candy*, an updated version of Voltaire's *Candide*, as a Mexican gardener.
1970 Feb [22] *The Magic Christian*, in which Starr appears as Youngman Grand, the adoptive son of the world's richest man, Sir Guy Grand, played by Peter Sellers, premieres in New York.
Apr LP *Sentimental Journey* hits UK #7 and US #22. The commercial value of being an ex-Beatle° going solo is exemplified by this George Martin-produced selection of standards, including *Night And Day* and *Bye Bye Blackbird*. Starr claims "I did it for me mum!". Arrangers on the LP include The Bee Gees'° Maurice Gibb, Elmer Bernstein, Johnny Dankworth, Les Reed and Quincy Jones.
Oct LP *Beaucoups Of Blues* makes US #65. Recorded in Nashville using songs commissioned from top C&W writers and produced by pedal steel guitarist, Pete Drake, and engineered by Elvis Presley's° guitarist, Scotty Moore, it features top country musicians, including Jerry Reed, The Jordanaires (Elvis Presley's backing vocalists) and Charlie Daniels.
Nov *Beaucoups Of Blues* title track reaches US #87.
1971 May Self-penned *It Don't Come Easy*, featuring guitar work from producer George Harrison° and Stephen Stills, hits both UK and US #4.
Aug [1] Starr appears with Eric Clapton°, Bob Dylan°, Billy Preston , Leon Russell° and others at the George Harrison°-organized "Concert for Bangla Desh".
Aug *It Don't Come Easy* is certified gold.
Nov He appears in Frank Zappa's° film *200 Motels* in dual role of Larry The Dwarf and Frank Zappa.
1972 Jan He plays an outlaw called Candy in spaghetti western *Blindman*.
Apr George Harrison°-produced *Back Off Boogaloo* hits UK #2 and US #9.
Nov Starr appears as Uncle Ernie in Lou Reizner's all-star LP of The Who's° *Tommy*.
Dec [14] *Born To Boogie*, a film of T. Rex in concert and Starr's debut as director, premieres in London.
1973 Apr He stars as a teddy boy called Mike in film *That'll Be The Day*.
Nov *Photograph*, co-written with George Harrison°, hits UK #8 and US #1. LP *Ringo* hits UK #7 and US #2. It is produced by Richard Perry and includes Beatles'° contributions (notably Lennon's° *I'm The Greatest* which features all but McCartney°).
1974 Jan With Harry Nilsson° on "shoo-wops" and a kazoo vocal by Paul McCartney° *You're Sixteen*, a cover of Johnny Burnette's° 1960 US #8 hit, hits US #1 and UK #3.
Apr *Oh My My* hits US #5.
Dec LP *Goodnight Vienna*, again produced by Perry and using top LA session men, reaches UK #30 and hits US #8.
1975 Jan A cover of The Platters'° 1955 smash *Only You* makes UK #28 and hits US #6. It will be his last UK hit single.
Apr *No No Song*, written by Hoyt Axton, hits US #3.
July [1] Starr and his wife Maureen Cox are divorced.
July *It's All Down To Goodnight Vienna* makes US #31. Starr appears as the Pope in Ken Russell's film *Lisztomania*.
Dec Greatest hits LP *Blast From Your Past* reaches US #30.
1976 Jan [25] Starr joins Bob Dylan° on stage for his "Night of the Hurricane II" benefit concert for boxer Ruben "Hurricane" Carter at the

Houston Astrodome, Tex.

Oct LP *Ringo's Rotogravure*, another all-star session this time produced by Arif Mardin, makes US #28.

Nov *A Dose Of Rock 'N' Roll* climbs to US #26.

Nov [25] Starr appears with a host of stars at The Band's° "The Last Waltz" farewell concert.

1977 Feb A cover of Bruce Channel's 1962 US chart-topper *Hey Baby* stalls at US #74.

Oct LP *Ringo The 4th* reaches US #162.

Dec LP *Scouse The Mouse* is released, with Starr in the title role of this children's story written by British actor, Donald Pleasence.

1978 Apr [25] TV special "Ringo", a musical adaptation of *The Prince and the Pauper* narrated by George Harrison°, is shown on US TV. (The ratings released the following week show that it finished fifty-third out of sixty-five programs.)

May LP *Bad Boy* peaks at US #129. A collection of cover versions, it includes The Supremes'° *Where Did Our Love Go* and Gallagher & Lyle's° *Heart On My Sleeve*. He appears in Mae West's last film *Sextette*, with Timothy Dalton and Tony Curtis.

1979 May [19] Starr teams with Paul McCartney° and George Harrison° to play at Eric Clapton's° wedding reception.

1981 Apr [27] Starr marries actress Barbara Bach, whom he met while appearing in comedy film *Caveman*.

Nov LP *Stop And Smell The Roses* reaches US #98. McCartney° and Harrison° contribute and Van Dyke Parks produces a new version of *Back Off Boogaloo* for the LP which features a medley of Beatles° and Starr songs.

Dec *Wrack My Brain* makes US #38.

1984 Oct Starr narrates UK children's TV series, "Thomas The Tank Engine and Friends" (which will become a worldwide TV hit).

Nov Mr. and Mrs. Starr appear in Paul McCartney's° film *Give My Regards To Broad Street* and in US TV mini-series "Princess Daisy". Starr's LP *Old Wave* is released in Canada only.

1985 July He is the first Beatle° to become a grandfather when his son Zak and his wife Sarah have a daughter, Tatia Jayne.

Dec Starr plays in an all-star band with George Harrison°, Dave Edmunds° and Eric Clapton° for UK TV Channel 4's Carl Perkins° tribute.

1988 Feb He appears in a video for George Harrison's° hit *When We Was Fab*.

Aug Reports emanate from US that Starr, Harrison° and Jeff Lynne are forming a group and will tour.

STATUS QUO

Francis Rossi (guitar and vocals)
Rick Parfitt (guitar and vocals)
Alan Lancaster (bass)
John Coghlan (drums)

1962 Lancaster (b. Feb.7, 1949, Peckham, London, UK) and friend Alan Key join their Beckenham comprehensive school orchestra, playing trombone and trumpet respectively and also form a trad jazz combo. This evolves into a beat group, with Lancaster on bass and Key and his friend Rossi (then calling himself Mike, b. Apr.29, 1949, London) playing guitars. Classmate Jess Jaworski is talked into trading in his new guitar for a Vox organ and joins the group when Key quits. With a friend playing drums, they make their live debut at the Samuel Jones Sports Club in Dulwich. After adding permanent drummer Coghlan (b. Sept.19, 1946, London), they call themselves The Spectres.

1964 After regular working men's club appearances, local gasfitter Pat Barlow offers to manage them and secures them a Monday night residency at the Café des Artistes in London's Brompton Road. He also arranges a gig on the same bill as The Hollies°, which doubles as an audition for a place as a Butlins holiday camp resident group.

1965 They accept a 4-month Butlins summer contract. Jaworski decides to continue his education and is replaced by Roy Lynes. They also meet Parfitt (b. Richard Harrison, Oct.12, 1948, Woking, Surrey, UK), who is playing holiday camps. (He will join the group 2 years later.)

1966 Songwriter Ronnie Scott introduces the group to John Schroeder, Pye Records' recording manager.

July The Spectres sign to Piccadilly, licensed to Pye.

Sept Their first single, a version of Leiber & Stoller's *I (Who Have Nothing)*, fails.

Nov Lancaster's *Hurdy Gurdy Man* is a second unsuccessful single.

1967 Feb The last single as The Spectres is *We Ain't Got Nothin' Yet*.

Mar The Spectres change name to Traffic Jam at the same time as Steve Winwood° forms Traffic, and release *Almost But Not Quite There*.

Nov At Barlow's suggestion, the group name-changes to Status Quo, and is signed to Pye label.

1968 Feb *Pictures Of Matchstick Men*, with Parfitt in the group, hits UK #7, while the group is working as Madeline Bell's backing band and with Barlow still part-time manager.

Apr Follow-up *Black Veils Of Melancholy* fails to chart.

Aug *Pictures Of Matchstick Men* reaches US #12, prompting a US tour.

Sept Debut LP *Picturesque Matchstickable Messages* is released but fails to chart. In addition to the singles, it includes covers of The Bee Gees'° *Spicks And Specks*, The Lemon Pipers' *Green Tambourine* and Tommy Roe's° *Sheila*.

Oct *Ice In The Sun* hits UK #8 and peaks at US #70. The band is currently promoted with smartly chic outfits.

1969 Apr Status Quo supports Gene Pitney° on a UK tour. The group's act mixes its pop sound with its later 12 bar blues sound.

May Ballad *Are You Growing Tired Of My Love* peaks at UK #46.

Oct LP *Spare Parts* fails to chart as the members decide to grow their hair and change musical direction.

1970 July Boogie-tinged *Down The Dustpipe* climbs to UK #12 as Lynes quits the band.

Aug LP *Ma Kelly's Greasy Spoon* is released. Blues-based, it includes *Junior's Wailing*, a cover of a song by blues band Steamhammer, which will become one of the group's most popular live tracks.

Dec *In My Chair*, penned by Rossi and group tour manager Bob Young (who will co-write many of the group's future hits), makes UK #21.

1971 June Follow-up *Tune To The Music* begins 3-year chart absence.

Nov Final Pye LP, *Dog Of Two Head*, is released.

1972 Jan As the band leaves the label, it begins building a solid cult following on the club circuit, playing a heavier brand of blues and boogie, and signs to Phonogram's new rock subsidiary, Vertigo.

May [10] Status Quo begins a UK tour in Bradford, Yorks., as support to Slade°.

July The group receives critical and popular acclaim at the British Great Western Festival in Lincoln (and Reading Festival in Aug.).

1973 Jan Debut Vertigo LP *Piledriver* is self-produced and enters the UK chart, set to hit #5. Status Quo has now defined its classic long-haired image on stage initiating a heads down, no-nonsense act, which sets the style and pose for a myriad of UK heavy metal groups.

Feb *Paper Plane* hits UK #8, as Status Quo tours Australia supporting Slade°.

May *Mean Girl*, from the last Pye LP, reaches UK #20.

June Pye LP *The Best Of Status Quo* peaks at UK #32.

Oct Vertigo single *Caroline*, written in 1970, hits UK #5. Self-produced LP *Hello*, with ex-Herd member Andy Bown guesting on keyboards, enters the UK chart at UK #1.

1974 May *Break The Rules* hits UK #8 as parent LP *Quo* hits UK #2.

1975 Jan *Down Down* is Status Quo's only UK singles chart-topper.

Mar LP *On The Level* hits UK #1. Pye releases LP *Down The Dustpipe*, featuring material from 1970-71, on its Golden Hour label. It reaches UK #20.

Apr LP *Status Quo* is the group's only US chart LP, reaching #148 during a 7-week stay.

June Three-track live EP *Roll Over Lay Down* with *Gerdundula* and *Junior's Wailing*, hits UK #9. (Sleeve notes are provided by UK DJ John Peel.)

1976 Mar *Rain* hits UK #7, as parent LP *Blue For You* hits UK #1, helped by Phonogram's marketing deal with Levi's jeans (a Status Quo trademark), which sees the record advertised in 6,000 clothes shops. (It is one of the first sponsorship tie-ups between the commercial world and rock music in UK.)

Mar [28] After an incident at Vienna airport, Rossi, Parfitt and Lancaster are arrested. Lancaster is charged with assaulting an airport official and the other two with resisting arrest. (They are released on bail.)

Aug *Mystery Song* hits UK #7.

Oct The Rolling Stones'° mobile studio is brought to Glasgow's Apollo Theatre to record three concerts. Tickets for the shows have sold out within hours. Former Herd keyboardist Andy Bown joins the live line-up.

1977 Jan *Wild Side Of Life*, reviving Tommy Quickly's 1964 hit and

STATUS QUO *cont.*

produced by ex-Deep Purple° bassist Roger Glover, hits UK #9. In Vienna, the three Status Quo defendants plead guilty to a reduced charge of obstructing the police and are fined a total of £3,200.

Mar LP *Status Quo – Live* hits UK #3. The band begins a world tour that will take it to Europe, the Far East, Australia and New Zealand.

Nov John Fogerty's *Rockin' All Over The World*, is released for the UK leg of the tour, hitting UK #3. (When Status Quo performs it on UK TV show "Top of the Pops", Lancaster, now semi-resident in Australia, is substituted by a life-size string puppet, discreetly playing bass in the background.) LP *Rockin' All Over The World*, with Pip Williams co-producing, hits UK #5.

1978 For tax reasons, Status Quo will not reside in UK throughout the year. It tours Australia, followed by a studio visit to Hilversum in Holland to record LP *If You Can't Stand The Heat*.

Aug [26] The band makes its only UK appearance of the year, headlining the Reading Rock Festival.

Sept *Again And Again* reaches UK #13.

Nov LP *If You Can't Stand The Heat* hits UK #3.

Dec *Accident Prone* makes UK #36, as Status Quo starts work on a new LP in Hilversum.

1979 Oct *Whatever You Want* hits UK #4, while parent LP *Whatever You Want* hits UK #3. The UK media is beginning to criticize the band's supposed 3-chord rock limitations.

Dec Rare ballad *Living On An Island* reaches UK #16.

1980 Mar LP *12 Gold Bars* hits UK #3.

Oct LP *Just Supposin'* hits UK #4 as extracted *What You're Proposing* hits UK #2.

1981 Jan *Lies* reaches UK #11.

Mar [6] Status Quo begins a UK tour in St. Austell, Cornwall.

Mar LP *Never Too Late* hits UK #2. Extracted *Something 'Bout You Baby I Like* hits UK #9.

Oct *Fresh Quota*, a rarities LP from the PRT label, spends a week at UK #74.

Dec *Rock'n'Roll*, a ballad from LP *Just Supposin'*, hits UK #8.

1982 Coghlan leaves during recording for a new LP in Montreux, to concentrate on his own band, Diesel. He is replaced by Pete Kircher, ex-The Original Mirrors.

Apr *Dear John* hits UK #10, while LP *1982* is the group's fourth UK chart-topper.

May The group plays a UK BBC-televised show at the Birmingham NEC, attended by The Prince and Princess of Wales – all the proceeds go to the Prince's Trust charity. (The show is also recorded for a live LP.)

June *She Don't Fool Me* peaks at UK #36.

Nov *Caroline*, recorded live at the NEC, Birmingham, reaches UK #13. *From The Makers Of . . .*, a three-LP set that includes a live LP from the NEC, as well as a selection of hits on both Pye and Vertigo, hits UK #4.

1983 Lancaster relocates to Australia and suggests the other members follow. Rossi and Parfitt decline and Lancaster continues to play with Status Quo on a loose basis.

Sept *Ol' Rag Blues* hits UK #9.

Nov *A Mess Of The Blues* peaks at UK #15.

Dec LP *Back To Back* hits UK #9.

1984 Jan *Marguerita Time* hits UK #3. The band begins UK-billed "The End of the Road Tour".

June *Going Down Town Tonight*, fourth single from LP *Back To Back*, reaches UK #20.

July [21] The group ends its UK tour topping the bill at Milton Keynes Bowl, filmed for later video release.

Aug A Dutch import LP, *Live At The NEC*, reaches UK #83.

Nov A revival of Dion's° *The Wanderer* hits UK #7. Lancaster quits the line-up.

Dec Vertigo packages a second TV-advertised LP *12 Gold Bars*. It reaches UK #12.

1985 Parfitt records an unissued solo LP, while Rossi works with Bernard Frost on *Modern Romance (I Want To Fall In Love Again)*, which makes UK #54, and *Jealousy*.

July [13] Lancaster rejoins Status Quo to open the Live Aid spectacular at Wembley. They set the tone for the event by opening with *Rockin' All Over The World*.

July By the time the group has gone back to the studio, Lancaster has taken out an injunction to stop the others playing without him as Status Quo. (The court eventually sides with Rossi and Parfitt.)

The group fails to release a single during the year, breaking a run of achieving a top 20 hit each year since 1973.

1986 May Status Quo re-emerges with Dave Edmunds°-produced *Rollin' Home*, which hits UK #9. The line-up is now Rossi, Parfitt, Bown, bassist John Edwards and drummer Jeff Rich.

July [11/12] Status Quo supports Queen° for 2 nights at London's Wembley Stadium.

Aug *Red Sky* hits UK #19.

Sept LP *In The Army Now* hits UK #7.

Nov *In The Army Now*, penned by German pop-writers Bolland and Bolland, hits UK #2.

Dec *Dreamin'* reaches UK #17.

1988 Apr *Ain't Complaining* makes UK #19.

June *Who Gets The Love* peaks at UK #34 as parent LP *Ain't Complaining* reaches UK #12.

Sept *Running All Over The World*, a revised jogging version of *Rockin' All Over The World* altered for Sport Aid, makes UK #17.

Dec *Burning Bridges (On And Off And On Again)*, their 39th consecutive chart single, hits UK #7. In terms of chart records, Status Quo are now the most successful UK group ever, leading The Rolling Stones° (with 34 hits) and The Hollies° (with 31). The band ends a major UK tour, portraying itself as a non-drink and non-drug-taking group, after several recent newspaper stories relating a wild-living past.

TOMMY STEELE

1956 July Steele (b. Thomas Hicks, Dec.17, 1936, Bermondsey, London, UK) having been in the Merchant Navy (since Apr. 1952) and having sung semi-professionally while ashore, including stints as guitarist with C&W group Jack Fallon & The Sons of the Saddle, and a UK tour playing second guitar behind bluesman Josh White, is singing at the 2 I's coffee bar in Soho, London, the day after his ship has docked, when he is approached by photographer and PR man John Kennedy, who sees potential in his singing style and youthful looks. Kennedy is working for manager/agents Roy Tuvey and Geoff Wright, who have already spotted Steele, but after disagreements over financial matters, Kennedy splits from them and teams with Larry Parnes, who is willing to finance Steele's launch while Kennedy handles management. They persuade Hicks to leave the Merchant Navy and sign to them as a professional (they also promise his parents that if nothing comes of his career within a couple of months, they will not hold him to any contract).

Aug Kennedy renames him Tommy Steele, felt to be a "sharper" name than Hicks' own. He launches him on the live circuit in ways calculated to gain publicity; performing at high class, high-profile debutantes' balls, and at the plush Stork Rooms in London's West End. It all makes major (favorable) press copy.

Sept George Martin at EMI Records rejects Steele, but Decca A&R man Hugh Mendl is enthusiastic about him: he becomes Decca's first rock signing.

Oct First recording is *Rock With The Caveman*, written by Steele himself, with Mike Pratt and Lionel Bart. The backing session musicians are mostly jazzmen, led by saxophonist Ronnie Scott, but credited as "The Steelmen" on the disk.

Oct [15] He makes his UK TV debut performing the single on Jack Payne's "Off The Record" show.

Nov *Rock With The Caveman* reaches UK #13. His earnings shoot up from £7 a week 6 months previously, to £700 a week.

Dec [7] A bona fide group of Steelmen (including Roy Plummer on guitar and Alan Stewart on sax) is put together to back him on stage, and he begins stage work in earnest (debuting at London's Finsbury Park Astoria), to fan hysteria reminiscent of that being generated by Elvis Presley° in US. Meanwhile, second single *Elevator Rock* fails to chart, but is allowed to die when Steele covers the current US #1 hit, *Singing The Blues* by Guy Mitchell.

1957 Jan Both Mitchell's and Steele's versions of *Singing The Blues* top the UK chart, the UK single replacing the US one for a week, and then being deposed by it again. This is Steele's biggest UK hit. Meanwhile, his first major cabaret engagement is at London's Café de Paris.

Feb He has a cameo role (as a coffee bar singer) in UK thriller movie *Kill Me Tomorrow*. A starring role in a semi-autobiographical feature film, *The Tommy Steele Story*, is also announced.

Mar Steele also covers Mitchell's follow-up, *Knee Deep In The Blues* (written, like *Singing The Blues*, by Melvin Endsley), but Mitchell hits UK #4 and Steele makes UK #15.

May [3] Rapidly-made low budget film *The Tommy Steele Story* is released in UK. (It will be a UK box office success, released in US as *Rock Around The World*.)

July *Butterfingers*, another Steele/Pratt/Bart song, included in the movie, hits UK #8.

Aug Steele's cover of Andy Williams' *Butterfly* is one of six tracks by various artists on EP *All-Star Hit Parade, No.2*, which reaches UK #15.

Sept Double A-side *Water, Water/Handful Of Songs*, from *The Tommy Steele Story* hits UK #5. (*Handful Of Songs* is also the theme for his TV shows, and for many years will be Steele's signature tune.)

He writes and sings the theme song for another UK film, *The Shiralee*, which reaches UK #11.

Oct He begins filming his second movie, *The Duke Wore Jeans*. In UK music paper *New Musical Express* annual readers' poll, Steele is named runner-up to Elvis Presley° as World Musical Personality.

Nov *Hey You* makes UK #28. Steele appears in The Royal Variety Show in London.

Dec He appears in pantomime for the first time, playing in *Goldilocks* in Liverpool.

1958 Mar Calypso-flavored *Nairobi*, released while Steele is touring South Africa, hits UK #3.

May *Happy Guitar* reaches UK #20.

June Steele becomes engaged to dancer Anne Donati. Kennedy and Parnes try to keep this quiet, believing it will adversely affect his teen following, but already his career has moved from rock'n'roll singer to versatile family entertainer. (Marty Wilde° – another Larry Parnes protegée – arrives on the scene in mid-summer, and Cliff Richard° in mid-autumn, and teenage fans switch to them.)

Aug Steele covers Tony Bennett's US hit *The Only Man On The Island*, reaching UK #16.

Nov [15] Steele and his backing group The Steelmen part company.

Dec He covers Ritchie Valens'° first US release *Come On Let's Go*, hitting UK #10 while Valens' original fails to chart in UK. Steele begins another pantomime season in *Cinderella*.

1959 Aug A cover of Freddy Cannon's *Tallahassie Lassie* just outsells the original in UK – Cannon reaches UK #17, but Steele makes #16, while B-side *Give Give Give* also charts at UK #28.

Sept Steele tours Australia, earning £100,000 from a 10-week stint.

1960 Jan He stars in UK comedy film *Tommy The Toreador*, with Sid James and others. From it, Pratt/Bart/Roy Bennett-penned children's favorite *Little White Bull* hits UK #6.

June [18] Steele marries his fiancée Anne at St. Patrick's Church, Soho Square, London.

July A pure Cockney music hall song, *What A Mouth*, hits UK #5.

Dec Seasonal *Must Be Santa* makes UK #40.

1961 Aug *The Writing On The Wall*, a cover of a US top 5 hit by Adam Wade, reaches UK #30 and is Steele's last chart entry. (He will continue to record for Decca for a year, and will cover Brook Benton's° *Hit Record*, which fails, before switching to Columbia for more sporadic recordings. Steele will leave the record world behind him during the early 60s, and become an international star of stage and film musicals. His movie successes will include *Half A Sixpence*, *The Happiest Millionaire* and *Finian's Rainbow*. He will also triumph on stage in *Half A Sixpence* in London and on Broadway in 1963/64, and in self-directed *Hans Christian Andersen* and *Singing in the Rain* at the London Palladium 10 and 20 years later – well removed from his groundbreaking role as the prototype UK rock star and teen idol.)

STEELY DAN

Donald Fagen (vocals and keyboards)
Walter Becker (bass)
Jeff "Skunk" Baxter (lead guitar)
Denny Dias (rhythm guitar)
Jim Hodder (drums)

1967 Fagen (b. Jan.10, 1948, Passaic, N.J., US) and Becker (b. Feb.20, 1950, New York, N.Y., US) meet as students at Bard's College in upstate New York.

1969 They leave college (only Fagen graduates – in English literature) and begin trying to sell songs they have written at college, with little success. Intent on a musical career, they cut a low-key film soundtrack for an early Richard Pryor movie, *You Gotta Walk It Like You Talk It* (which will not be released on disk until the late 1970s). Despite its failure, it leads to another movie project, a dance video starring Becker's mother, for which they are paid $1,500.

1970 Still writing and trying to sell songs to Brill Building publishers in New York, Becker and Fagen answer an ad in *Village Voice* newspaper from guitarist Dias who is looking for "musicians with jazz chops". They join Dias' band, Demian, and record demos in his basement.

1971 Having sold, through Richard Perry, *I Mean To Shine* for recording on a Barbra Streisand LP, Becker and Fagen quit Demian to join Jay & The Americans, who sing on Brill Building demos and on the New York live circuit. With the band, they meet producer Gary Katz (a 3-year partner in Cloud Nine Productions

STEELY DAN *cont.*

with Richard Perry) and guitarist Baxter.

Nov Katz is offered the house producer's job at ABC-Dunhill Records in LA. He accepts on condition that Fagen and Becker are hired as staff writers, and all parties agree.

1972 Apr After only 6 months, the songwriting contract is cancelled and replaced by Dunhill with an offer for Becker and Fagen to record their own compositions. Katz gathers session help from Dias, Baxter, drummer Hodder and others, including David Palmer, who handles vocals.

June The name Steely Dan is taken from William Burroughs' novel *The Naked Lunch* (in which it refers to a steam-powered dildo), and work begins on a debut LP.

1973 Feb LP *Can't Buy A Thrill* reaches US #17, as *Do It Again*, taken from it, hits US #6.

Apr Palmer departs (to resurface in The Big Wha-Koo on ABC), and Fagen takes over lead vocals, at first unwillingly.

May *Reeling In The Years*, also from the first LP, reaches US #11.

Aug *Show Biz Kids* makes US #61.

Sept LP *Countdown To Ecstacy* reaches US #35, and earns a second gold disk, but yields no major hit singles. The group tours US with two girl backing vocalists, Jenny Soule and Gloria Granola, temporarily added to the line-up.

Nov *My Old School*, taken from the LP, peaks at US #63.

1974 Apr A first UK tour is interrupted by Fagen's throat infection, and only five of 12 dates are completed. The visit boosts newly-released LP *Pretzel Logic* to become the bands's UK debut chart LP, at #37. (On its return to US, the band will play only a selection of Californian dates.)

June LP *Pretzel Logic* hits US #8, and is the band's third gold LP.

July [4] Following an Independence Day gig at Santa Monica Civic Center, Becker and Fagen retire from live work (for 3 years).

Aug [3] With little prospect of further work with Steely Dan, Baxter leaves to join The Doobie Brothers° (with whom he has toured before), and Hodder also leaves. Jeff Porcaro replaces the latter on drums, while Michael McDonald° joins on keyboards (both have augmented the group on tour, with extra vocalist Royce Jones). Meanwhile, *Rikki, Don't Lose That Number* becomes the band's biggest-selling US single, hitting #4.

1975 May LP *Katy Lied* reaches both US and UK #13, and is another US gold disk. (The near-complete recording was almost ruined by faulty studio equipment – which lead producer Katz to storm out of ABC for Warner Bros.) Following its recording, McDonald° leaves to join The Doobie Brothers°, Porcaro returns to sessions (and will eventually form Toto°), while Dias also leaves to move into session work. They are not replaced: Steely Dan will be just Becker and Fagen, with numerous session men on LP recordings.

June *Black Friday*, about the 1929 stock market crash, taken from LP *Katy Lied*, makes US #37.

Sept Debut LP *Can't Buy A Thrill* belatedly charts in UK at #38, as does the single from it, *Do It Again*, at UK #39.

1976 June LP *The Royal Scam* reaches US #15, earning another gold disk, and (following a European promotional tour) peaks at UK #11.

July *Kid Charlemagne*, from LP *The Royal Scam*, peaks at US #82.

Oct *The Fez*, also from the LP, makes US #59.

1977 Jan A UK-only release, taken from LP *The Royal Scam*, *Haitian Divorce*, climbs to UK #17, and is Steely Dan's best-selling UK single.

Mar [31] ABC, irritated by the duo's endless perfectionism in the studio, has set this date for delivery of the next LP. (Becker and Fagen will miss it by months.)

Nov LP *Aja* hits US #3, earning a first platinum disk as a million-selling LP. It is also the first Steely Dan LP to hit UK top 10, at #5, and the first release by Becker and Fagen officially as a duo.

1978 Feb [23] The duo wins a Grammy award for *Aja*, named the Best-Engineered Non-Classical Recording.

Mar *Peg*, extracted from LP *Aja*, reaches US #11.

June *Deacon Blues*, also from LP *Aja*, makes US #19.

July *FM (No Static At All)*, taken from the soundtrack of movie *FM*, reaches US #22.

Aug *FM (No Static At All)* makes UK #49.

Sept *Josie*, a final single from LP *Aja*, climbs to US #26.

1979 Jan Double compilation LP *Greatest Hits* reaches US #30, becoming another million-seller, and makes UK #41. It includes one new song, *Here In The Western World*, and is the first of several Steely Dan compilations.

Mar Taken from the compilation, *Rikki Don't Lose That Number* reaches UK #58.

1980 The duo signs to Warner Bros. and begins work on a new LP titled *Metal Leg*, until it is pointed out that Steely Dan still owes one LP to MCA Records, ABC's new owners.

1981 Jan LP *Gaucho*, on MCA, hits US #9, becoming the third (and last) platinum LP. It makes UK #27.

Feb *Hey Nineteen*, from LP *Gaucho*, hits US #10 (their first US top 10 hit for 6 years).

Apr Also from LP *Gaucho*, *Time Out Of Mind* makes US #22, and is the duo's final US hit single.

June [21] The duo announces its split, but not ruling out working together as Steely Dan again at some future time. (Each begins work on solo projects: Becker as a producer and Fagen as a solo act.)

1982 July Compilation LP *Steely Dan Gold* makes US #115 and UK #4.

Nov Fagen's solo LP *The Nightfly*, on Warner Bros., reaches US #11 and UK #44. The LP is an account of one night at a fictional jazz radio station, WJAZ, with Fagen as the DJ, known as The Nightfly.

Dec Taken from Fagen's LP, *I.G.Y. (What A Beautiful World)* reaches US #26.

1985 May China Crisis° LP *Flaunt The Imperfection* which hits UK #9, is produced by Becker. It also contains three UK hit singles.

Nov TV-promoted compilation LP *Reelin' In The Years – The Very Best Of Steely Dan* makes UK #43.

1987 Feb Rosie Vela's A&M debut LP *Zazu* is produced by Gary Katz, who persuades both Becker and Fagen to play on it, leading to speculation about a reunion.

Oct Another TV-promoted compilation LP, *Do It Again – The Very Best Of Steely Dan*, reaches UK #64.

1988 Apr Fagen takes time off from being music editor for US movie magazine *Première* to release *Century's End*, taken from the movie soundtrack *Bright Lights Big City*.

STEPPENWOLF

John Kay (guitar and vocals)
Michael Monarch (guitar)
Rushton Moreve (bass)
Goldy McJohn (organ)
Jerry Edmonton (drums)

1967 Kay (b. Joachim F. Krauledat, Apr.12, 1944, Tilsit, East Germany), Monarch (b. July 5, 1950, Los Angeles, Cal., US), Moreve (b. 1948, Los Angeles), McJohn (b. May 2, 1945, US) and Edmonton (b. Oct.24, 1946, Canada) form as The Sparrow in Canada. (Kay has been in Canada since 1958, when he arrived with his parents after escaping from East Germany). After recording unsuccessful single *Tomorrow's Ship* for Columbia, the group relocates to Cal. and is noticed playing at a coffee house in Venice Beach. It signs a new recording deal to Dunhill Records and, at producer Gabriel Mekler's suggestion, the name is changed to Steppenwolf (taken from the Herman Hesse novel). After some early recordings and gigs, Moreve is replaced on bass by John Russell Morgan.

1968 Jan Debut LP *Steppenwolf* is released, together with a single reviving Don Covay's *Sookie Sookie*. The single fails to chart, but the LP slowly climbs as the group's hard rock live reputation spreads. (It will hit US #6 when *Born To Be Wild*, the second single extract, becomes a smash.) The LP also contains the band's anti-drug song *The Pusher*, which becomes an onstage anthem.

Aug *Born To Be Wild* hits US #2 for 3 weeks behind The Young Rascals'° *People Got To Be Free*, and sells over a million copies, earning a gold disk. (It will become the archetypal biker song when used in film *Easy Rider* a year later.)

Aug [4] The group plays the Newport Pop Festival in Costa Mesa, Cal., alongside Canned Heat°, Sonny & Cher°, The Grateful Dead°, The Byrds° and others.

Nov *Magic Carpet Ride* hits US #3 and is the group's second consecutive million-selling single. It is taken from LP *Steppenwolf The Second*, which also hits US #3 and earns a gold disk.

Dec [28] The band plays the Miami Pop Festival in Hallendale, Fla., to 100,000 people. The 3-day bill includes The Grateful Dead°, Marvin Gaye°, Chuck Berry°, The Turtles°, Joni Mitchell° and many more.

1969 Mar *Rock Me*, notable for its lengthy polyrhythmic drum/percussion break, hits US #10. It is also featured in sex spoof film *Candy* (premiered in US a month earlier).

Apr LP *At Your Birthday Party*, which includes *Rock Me*, hits US #7. Monarch and Morgan leave the band, and are replaced by Larry Byrom (b. Dec.27, 1948, US) on guitar and Nick St. Nicholas (b. Sept.28, 1943, Hamburg, West Germany) on bass.

May *It's Never Too Late* breaks the run of top 10 singles by peaking at US #51.

June [20] The group plays the Newport '69 festival in Northridge, Cal., along with Jimi Hendrix°, Joe Cocker°, The Byrds°, Creedence Clearwater Revival° and others.

June *Born To Be Wild* is the group's only UK chart entry, at #30.

Aug LP *Early Steppenwolf*, a live recording from 1967 when the group was still known as Sparrow (and including a marathon early 21 min. version of *The Pusher*), reaches US #29. Film *Easy Rider* uses Steppenwolf's *The Pusher* and *Born To Be Wild* as the soundtrack for its opening scenes.

Sept *Move Over* (the first notice of the band's later concern with political matters) makes US #31.

1970 Jan Politically-oriented LP *Monster* reaches US #17, earning a third gold LP, while the title track climbs to US #39.

May Double live LP *Steppenwolf Live* hits US #7 (earning another gold disk), while *Hey Lawdy Mama* peaks at US #35.

June St. Nicholas leaves, and is replaced by George Biondo (b. Sept.3, 1945, Brooklyn, N.Y.).

June [26] The band appears in UK's Bath Festival of Blues and Progressive Music, at Shepton Mallet, Somerset, together with Led Zeppelin°, The Byrds°, Donovan°, Frank Zappa°, Santana° and many more.

Aug [6] Steppenwolf takes part in a 12-hour anti-war rock festival at New York's Shea Stadium, alongside Paul Simon°, Janis Joplin°, Johnny Winter° and others.

Sept *Screaming Night Hog* reaches US #62.

Dec LP *Steppenwolf 7* reaches US #19 and earns a gold disk, while *Who Needs Ya* makes US #54.

1971 Apr Another anti-drug song, *Snow Blind Friend*, makes US #60, while compilation LP *Steppenwolf Gold*, rounding up the hit singles to date, reaches US #24 and earns the band's final gold LP.

May Byrom is replaced on guitar by Kent Henry.

Aug *Ride With Me* peaks at US #52.

Nov LP *For Ladies Only* makes US #54 while the extracted title track reaches US #64.

1972 Feb [14] Kay formally announces the group's dissolution in a press conference at the Hollywood Holiday Inn, explaining: "We were locked into an image and style of music and there was nothing for us to look forward to." (The group has been trapped by its own success, turning over $40 million in disk sales for Dunhill.) The day is declared "Steppenwolf Day" in Los Angeles by the mayor Sam Yorty, commemorating the group's retirement.

May Kay's solo LP *Forgotten Songs And Unsong Heroes*, on Dunhill, makes US #113 and provides him with his only solo hit single, a revival of Hank Snow's *I'm Movin' On*, which reaches US #52. Edmonton and McJohn form their own band, Manbeast, without notable success.

Aug Steppenwolf LP *Rest In Peace*, compiled from earlier material, reaches US #62.

1973 Mar Another compilation LP, *16 Greatest Hits*, creeps to US #152.

July Kay's second solo LP, *My Sportin' Life*, just scrapes the US chart at #200.

1974 Feb Kay re-forms Steppenwolf, with McJohn, Edmonton, Biondo and ex-Flying Burrito Brothers'° guitarist Bobby Cochran, and the band is signed to Mums label.

Oct LP *Slow Flux*, on Mums, reaches US #47. Extracted *Straight Shootin' Woman* is the band's final US hit single at #29, as McJohn is replaced by Wayne Cook.

1975 Oct LP *Hour Of The Wolf*, released on Epic, regains some of the band's old spirit, but Kay's material is generally considered weaker than his early songs. The LP is the band's last chartmaker, at US #155.

1976 Steppenwolf splits again. (Monarch will join heavy metal band Detective.)

1978 Kay records solo LP *All In Good Time* for Mercury, without success.

1980 Kay puts together a new band, which tours US as John Kay and Steppenwolf.

1981 July [1] Moreve is killed in an auto accident in LA.

1988 Sept Kay and a re-formed Steppenwolf release LP *Rock & Roll Rebels*.

CAT STEVENS

1965 Stevens (b. Steven Georgiou, July 21, 1947, Soho, London, UK), son of a Greek London restaurateur and a Swedish mother, begins spare-time songwriting and singing in a folk/rock style while studying at Hammersmith College, London.

1966 July He is heard performing at the college by ex-Springfields member, now record producer, Mike Hurst. Though he has been planning to leave for US to work, Hurst is sufficiently excited by the young student's songs and voice to organize a recording session, at which they cut self-penned *I Love My Dog*. This impresses Tony Hall at Decca, who signs him (now renamed Cat Stevens) as the first act on new Deram label, designed to be a showcase for progressive young UK talent.

Nov *I Love My Dog* is debut single and reaches UK #28, aided by strong pirate radio airplay.

1967 Feb Highly commercial orchestrally-arranged *Matthew And Son* hits UK #2 (behind The Monkees'° *I'm A Believer*) and heightens his reputation as a songwriter. (He is already attracting cover versions – The Tremeloes' first hit without Brian Poole° is a version of his *Here Comes My Baby*, at UK #4.)

Mar [31] He opens a UK package tour at Finsbury Park Astoria, on a bill which includes The Walker Brothers°, Engelbert Humperdinck and The Jimi Hendrix° Experience.

Apr *I'm Gonna Get Me A Gun* (publicized by some gun-toting pictures which Stevens will later disown) is another commercially strong combination of unusual lyric and string arrangement, and hits UK #6. Entirely self-written debut LP, *Matthew And Son*, hits UK #7 at the same time.

June P.P. Arnold's cover of Stevens' *The First Cut Is The Deepest* reaches UK #18.

Aug *A Bad Night* makes UK #20.

Dec *Kitty* peaks at UK #47, while second LP, *New Masters*, fails to chart.

1968 Feb *Lovely City* does not chart. Stevens is unavailable to promote it. He contracts tuberculosis and is hospitalized. Two more singles, *Here Comes My Wife* and *Where Are You* are issued without success while he is convalescing, completing his Deram contract.

1969 Originally reported to be writing a musical, Stevens spends the last months of his recuperation honing more sensitive and less commercial songs, having intensely disliked the whirlwind pop star trappings of his initial rise to fame.

1970 July He signs to Island Records in UK and A&M in US, and LP *Mona Bone Jakon*, produced by ex-Yardbird° Paul Samwell-Smith, showcases the new, more serious singer/songwriter. It makes UK #63.

Aug *Lady D'Arbanville*, taken from the LP and dedicated to ex-girlfriend Patti D'Arbanville, hits UK #8.

Sept Jimmy Cliff's° cover of Stevens-written and produced *Wild World* hits UK #8.

Dec LP *Tea For The Tillerman*, featuring his own version of *Wild World* reaches UK #20.

1971 Apr *Wild World* is US chart debut, reaching #11. LP *Tea For The Tillerman* follows it and hits US #8 (it will remain charted for 79 weeks in US and earn Stevens his first gold disk). LP *Mona Bone Jakon* also belatedly charts in US, at #164.

May A double LP combining his first two LPs, *Matthew And Son/New Masters*, belatedly sells the Deram material in US, reaching #173.

Aug *Moon Shadow*, from his next LP, makes US #30 (and UK #22 a few weeks later).

Oct LP *Teaser And The Firecat* hits UK #3 and US #2, earning a gold disk. It will stay on chart for 93 weeks in UK and 67 weeks in US. The sleeve features his own artwork, and he also produces a sh animated film with the same title as the LP, later to gigs.

Nov *Peace Train*, extracted from the LP only in US, hi

1972 Jan Also from the LP, Stevens' interpretation of Elean children's hymn *Morning Has Broken*, with Rick playing piano, hits UK #9.

Feb Compilation LP *Very Young And Early Songs* is rel Deram in US, reaching #94.

May *Morning Has Broken* hits US #6. Stevens contrib soundtrack of Hal Ashby's cult movie *Harold an*

Sept He begins a 31-date tour of US and Canada at LA Auditorium, backed by an 11-piece orchestra (an folk/blues singer Ramblin' Jack Elliott) to a sold- 6,500.

Nov LP *Catch Bull At Four*, which broadens his instrumentation by using Alun Davies (guitar), Jean Roussel (piano), Alan James (bass) and Gerry Conway (drums), with Stevens himself playing synthesizer on some tracks, hits UK #2 and tops the US chart for 3 weeks, earning a further gold disk.

1973 Jan Different singles are extracted from LP *Catch Bull* in UK and US. *Can't Keep It In* makes UK #13, while *Sitting* reaches US #16.

Aug LP *Foreigner* hits both UK and US #3, and earns a further gold disk. One side is devoted to *Foreigner Suite*, a long and lyrically profound piece indicating Stevens' increasing involvement with philosophical and religious concerns. His live appearances dwindle, and he becomes more reclusive and rarely interviewed. Taken from the LP, *The Hurt* makes US #31, but does not chart in UK. He is now living in Brazil, having left UK for a year's tax exile. The money he would have lost to the UK taxman, he donates to UNESCO and other charities.

Nov [9] He makes his US network TV debut on ABC-TV's "In Concert" show, a 90-minute special taped at The Hollywood Bowl.

1974 May LP *Buddah And The Chocolate Box*, Stevens' sixth US gold disk, hits UK #3 and US #2. *Oh Very Young*, taken from it, hits US #10, but fails to chart in UK (where Island does not promote his singles heavily, being keen to maintain Stevens as its best-selling LP act).

Sept A revival of Sam Cooke's° *Another Saturday Night* makes UK #19, and hits US #6 a few weeks later.

1975 Jan *Ready* climbs to US #26.

Aug Compilation LP *Greatest Hits*, rounding up his Island/A&M singles, hits UK #2 and US #6, and earns another gold disk. *Two Fine People*, included on the compilation, reaches US #33 but fails in UK.

Nov He tours Europe with a five-piece backing band (including a Brazilian percussionist) and a female back-up vocal group, performing in an elaborate and specially-constructed stage set.

1976 Jan LP *Numbers* reaches US #13, but is his first Island LP not to chart in UK. His most complex and lyrically involved LP, it proves inaccessible to many devotees of his light earlier touch.

Mar *Banapple Gas* makes US #41.

1977 June LP *Izitso* makes UK #18 and hits US #7, Stevens' last gold disk.

July *(Remember The Days Of The) Old School Yard*, on which Stevens duets with Elkie Brooks°, is his last hit single in UK, reaching #44, and climbs to US #33.

1978 Jan Instrumental *Was Dog A Doughnut* makes US #70.

1979 Feb LP *Back To Earth*, fails to chart in UK but reaches US #33, while *Bad Brakes* peaks at US #84. Some take the LP title to mean a return to his earlier, earthier pop concerns, but it signifies a return from international celebrity to private person, as he retires from all aspects of making music. By this time, he has totally committed himself to the Muslim faith and life, and changes his name to Yusef Islam.

Sept [9] He marries Fouzia Ali at Kensington Mosque, London.

1981 He finances the establishment of, and begins to teach at, a Muslim school in North London. (He also has the Greek flag removed from the sleeve artwork of his LP *Greatest Hits*). Officially confirming that he has left show business for good, he auctions all the trappings of his pop career, including his gold disks, and donates the money to his current work.

1985 Jan Compilation LP *Footsteps In The Dark*, combining tracks from his nine Island/A&M LPs with three additional songs, makes US #165.

July Rumors persist that Yusef is to appear at Live Aid, and is even willing to go on stage as Cat Stevens.

The Pet Shop Boys'° worldwide hit *It's A Sin* has a melody closely
d on *Wild World*'s (Stevens is reportedly more flattered than
yed), while US band 10,000 Maniacs° revive his *Peace Train*.
Priest hits UK #5 with a revival of *Wild World*.

STEVENS

ns (b. Michael Barratt, Mar.4, 1948, Ely, Wales, UK), one of
ldren, whose chief childhood musical influence has been
rock'n'roll records owned by his elder brothers, begins
g the Cardiff, Wales, club circuit with a rock'n'roll revival
he Sunsets.
aining a strong reputation on the UK rock revival circuit,
' Stevens and The Sunsets sign a recording contract with EMI's Parlophone label, and record LP *A Legend* with producer Dave Edmunds°, at Rockfield studios, Wales. It fails to sell, as does a revival of Big Al Downing's *Down On The Farm*, and EMI drops the group.

1971 A second one-off deal, with CBS, produces another unsuccessful LP, *I'm No J.D.*.

1973 Popular as a live attraction in Europe, the group signs to Dutch label Dureco for an LP (and amid many successful European tours, will continue to record for Dutch labels like Dynamo and Pink Elephant until 1976).

1976 Apr *Jungle Rock*, released on Mooncrest, fails to sell against Hank Mizell's UK #3 version. It is the group's final single, as The Sunsets split shortly afterwards.

1977 Stevens is one of three actors (with P.J. Proby° and Tim Whitnall) signed to play Elvis Presley° at various stages of his life in the Jack Good musical *Elvis* on London's West End stage. (The show runs for 19 months and wins a theater award as Best Musical of 1977.)

Apr Stevens is signed as a soloist to Track Records, but in spite of his West End success, three singles and a first solo LP, *Shakin' Stevens*, fail to chart over a 12-month period with the label.

1978 He becomes a UK TV regtılar, alongside Lulu°, Alvin Stardust and others, in Jack Good's revival of his late 1950s rock show "Oh Boy", and features in Good's "Let's Rock" in US. He also signs with manager Freya Miller.

Aug Stevens is signed to the Epic division of CBS, working with producer Mike Hurst. First Epic single *Treat Her Right* does not chart, and neither do two follow-ups, revivals of Jody Reynolds' *Endless Sleep* and The Classics IV's° *Spooky*.

1980 Mar *Hot Dog*, taken from debut Epic LP *Shakin' Stevens Take One!*, finally gives him a UK singles chart debut at #24, while the LP makes UK #62. Produced by Hurst (his last work with Stevens), the LP features "musical co-ordination" and remixing by Stuart Colman, who also plays bass as part of the eight-man backing group (which includes Albert Lee on lead guitar).

Sept Colman takes over production on *Marie Marie*, a cover of a song by US rockabilly band The Blasters, which reaches UK #19.

1981 Mar A revival of Stuart Hamblen's *This Ole House* (a 1954 UK #1 for Rosemary Clooney) is given a sharp rock arrangement by Colman and proves to be Stevens' major breakthrough, topping the UK chart for 3 weeks.

Apr LP *This Ole House*, with backing by rock revival band Matchbox, hits UK #2.

May *You Drive Me Crazy*, an original song by Ronnie Harwood, hits UK #2 for 4 weeks (behind Adam and The Ants'° *Stand And Deliver*).

July A revival of Jim Lowe/Frankie Vaughan 1956 hit *Green Door* tops the UK chart for 4 weeks.

Aug Budget LP *Shakin' Stevens*, a compilation of early material, makes UK #34.

Oct Stevens' first slow-tempo hit revives Irma Thomas' *It's Raining*, and hits UK #10.

Nov LP *Shaky*, including the three recent hit singles, tops the UK chart for a week.

1982 Jan *Oh Julie*, his first self-penned hit, tops the UK chart for a week.

May *Shirley*, a revival of an obscure 1960s John Fred & The Playboy Band track, hits UK #6.

Sept Uptempo rock ballad *Give Me Your Heart Tonight* reaches UK #11.

Oct LP *Give Me Your Heart Tonight* hits UK #3.

Nov Stevens revives one of Jackie Wilson's° early R&B-rockers, *I'll Be Satisfied*, and hits UK #10.

Dec *The Shakin' Stevens EP*, spotlighting a seasonal revival of Elvis Presley's° *Blue Christmas*, hits UK #2, held from the top by Renée & Renato's *Save Your Love*.

1983 Aug Stevens switches producers to Christopher Neil, and a revival of Ricky Nelson's° Dorsey Burnette°-written 1959 hit *It's Late* reaches UK #11.

Nov *Cry Just A Little Bit*, an original composition by Bob Heatlie, hits UK #3, while parent LP *The Bop Won't Stop* makes UK #21.

1984 Jan Stevens teams with fellow Welsh vocalist Bonnie Tyler°, to revive Brook Benton° and Dinah Washington's 1960 US top 10 hit *A Rockin' Good Way (To Mess Around And Fall In Love)*. Credited to Shaky And Bonnie, it hits UK #5.

Apr *A Love Worth Waiting For* hits UK #2 for 2 weeks, behind Lionel Richie's° *Hello*.

May Stevens' only US chartmaker is *Cry Just A Little Bit*, which reaches US #67.

Sept Dennis Linde's song *A Letter To You* hits UK #10.
Nov Compilation LP *Greatest Hits*, anthologizing 18 singles from *Hot Dog* up to date, hits UK #8.
Dec Self-penned *Teardrops* hits UK #5.
1985 Mar *Breaking Up My Heart*, another Heatlie song, reaches UK #14.
Nov Stevens reunites with his original producer Dave Edmunds° for a revival of *Lipstick, Powder And Paint*, a mid-1950s US R&B hit for bluesman Joe Turner, which makes UK #11. Edmunds-produced LP of the same title reaches UK #37.
Dec Heatlie-penned *Merry Christmas Everyone*, produced again by Edmunds°, tops the UK chart in Christmas week.
1986 Feb *Turning Away* reaches UK #15.
Nov *Because I Love You*, produced again by Neil, reaches UK #14.
Dec *Merry Christmas Everyone* re-charts, making UK #58.
1987 Aug Stevens' revival of Gary Glitter's° *A Little Boogie Woogie (In The Back Of My Mind)* makes UK #12. It is co-produced by Mike Leander, Glitter's former producer.
Oct LP *Let's Boogie*, Stevens' first LP after an unusually long hiatus, makes UK #59. From it comes his first revival of a Motown oldie, The Supremes'° 1964 million-seller *Come See About Me*, which reaches UK #24, and marks a reunion with Stuart Colman.
Dec Self-produced (with Carey Taylor) revival of Emile Ford's° 1959 million-seller *What Do You Want To Make Those Eyes At Me For?* and in an almost identical arrangement, hits UK #5.
1988 Aug A revival of The Detroit Emeralds' mid-1970s soul hit, *Feel The Need In Me*, makes UK #26.
Oct *How Many Tears Can You Hide?* is Stevens' least successful single of the 1980s, peaking at UK #47.
Dec Stevens has one of his rare ballad hits with a revival of Bing Crosby/Grace Kelly oldie *True Love*, while LP *A Whole Lotta Shaky* peaks at UK #42.
Dec [31] Stevens appears on the 25th Anniversary edition of UK BBC TV's "Top of the Pops", singing his first chart-topper *This Ole House*.

AL STEWART

1962 Stewart (b. Sept.5, 1945, Glasgow, Scotland, UK), after learning guitar alongside Robert Fripp (later to found King Crimson°), plays his first live gigs as lead guitarist in a rock/pop band, Tony Blackburn (future UK DJ) & The Sabres, in Bournemouth, UK, (having moved from Scotland with his widowed mother at age 3, and subsequently attended public school until dropping out).
1965 Strongly influenced by Bob Dylan°, he becomes immersed in modern folk music and starts to write his own songs, performing at London area folk club venues like Bunjies and Les Cousins.
1966 Aug His first recording, *The Elf*, a one-off on Decca, does not sell.
1967 Sept Signed to CBS in UK, he releases debut LP *Bedsitter Images*, which has mostly introspective songs for voice and guitar, backed by orchestral arrangements. CBS mounts a concert at London's Royal Festival Hall presenting Stewart with a complete group and orchestra as back-up. His more usual shows are still one-man affairs, and he becomes a popular fixture on the college circuit, where his self-analytical, sometimes acidic, and occasionally controversial lyrics are widely appreciated.
1969 Jan LP *Love Chronicles* (with Jimmy Page on guitar) has an 18-minute title track which includes the word "f---ing" so gets no airplay. It is Stewart's first US release, and his only one on CBS/Columbia.
Dec UK music weekly *Melody Maker* votes LP *Love Chronicles* Folk Album of the Year in its annual survey.
1970 Apr LP *Zero She Flies* is Stewart's UK chart debut, reaching #40.
1972 Feb LP *Orange* shows musical influences outside the folk troubadour style of his first three LPs, but is not a success.
1974 Mar Stewart makes his first major US tour accompanied by members of just-disbanded group Home.
June LP *Past, Present And Future*, a concept album tracing historical events, with inspiration from the book *The Centuries of Nostradamus*, does not chart in UK, but released via a new US deal with Janus Records, makes US #133.
1975 Apr LP *Modern Times* reaches US #30. He tours US again, with a backing band consisting of Gerry Conway, Pat Donaldson, Simon Nicol and Simon Roussell.
1977 Feb Stewart signs a new recording deal with RCA in UK. LP *Year Of The Cat*, produced by Alan Parsons°, reaches UK #37, but hits US #5, selling over a million to earn a platinum disk. The extracted title track makes UK #31, his only UK chart single. It is also his US singles chart debut, and aided by strong US airplay, hits #8.
May *On The Border*, from LP *Year Of The Cat*, reaches US #42.
1978 Nov A new US label deal with Arista Records precedes LP *Time Passages*, also produced by Parsons°. It reaches UK #38 (on RCA) but hits US #10, earning another platinum disk. It is another of his LPs to eschew romantic songs in favor of time-capsule pieces concerned with specific historical events.
Dec The title song from LP *Time Passages* hits US #7.
1979 Mar *Song On The Radio*, another extract from LP *Time Passages*, makes US #29.
1980 Oct LP *24 Carrots* reaches UK #55 and US #37, while, from it, *Midnight Rocks* peaks at US #24, and is Stewart's last US hit single.
1981 Dec Double LP *Live/Indian Summer*, consisting of three sides of live material and one from the studio, makes US #110.
1984 June LP *Russians And Americans* makes UK #83.
1988 Nov After several years of US residency and work, Stewart returns to UK for live dates.

ROD STEWART

1961 Stewart (b. Roderick David Stewart, Jan.10, 1945, Highgate, London, UK), of Scottish parents who moved to London, having attended William Grimshaw school, Hornsey, with Ray and Dave Davies and Pete Quaife (who will achieve success as The Kinks°), signs as an apprentice with professional soccer team Brentford Football Club. After 3 weeks, tired of little more than polishing other players' boots, he quits, heading for Europe, where he becomes a busker. (He is deported from Spain for vagrancy.) He returns to UK and becomes a beatnik, attending CND's Aldermaston marches.
1963 He joins Birmingham, UK, R&B band The Five Dimensions as vocalist and harmonica player. The band plays throughout UK, backing singer Jimmy Powell, who records a single for Pye on which Stewart plays blues harp.
1964 Stewart performs the same duties for Long John Baldry° & The Hoochie Coochie Men, who have just signed with United Artists Records. Baldry had heard Stewart singing, while waiting for a train at Twickenham station.
Aug [6] Stewart makes his UK TV debut on "The Beat Room", with The Hoochie Coochie Men.
Aug Decca Records staff producer Mike Vernon sees Stewart perform at London's Marquee club, and signs him to a solo deal.
Oct Debut single *Good Morning Little Schoolgirl*, despite an appearance on UK TV show "Ready Steady Go!", fails to chart. The Hoochie Coochie Men split, and Stewart joins The Soul Agents.
1965 He joins Steampacket, a group formed by Giorgio Gomelsky, with Stewart sharing vocals with Baldry° and Julie Driscoll with Brian Auger (keyboards), Rick Brown (bass) and Mickey Waller (drums) in the line-up.
July Steampacket supports The Rolling Stones° and The Walker Brothers° on a UK tour, and records an LP (which will not be released until the 1970s).
Nov Stewart signs a solo deal with EMI, releasing *The Day Will Come*, on Columbia. He appears in UK TV documentary "Rod The Mod", a 30-minute portrait of a typical mod.
1966 Mar Steampacket splits. Stewart joins The Shotgun Express with Peter Bardens (keyboards), Beryl Marsden (vocals), Peter Green (guitar), Dave Ambrose (bass) and Mick Fleetwood (drums).
Oct The band releases one single, *I Could Feel The Whole World Turn Around* and appears at the Richmond Rhythm and Blues Festival.
Dec Stewart joins The Jeff Beck° Group.
1967 Apr The Jeff Beck° Group makes UK #14 with *Hi Ho Silver Lining*.
Aug The group plays the 1967 National Rhythm and Blues Festival at Windsor, Berks., UK.
1968 Feb Stewart sings vocals on the B-side, *I've Been Drinking*, of Beck's° hit version of Eurovision song contest entry *Love Is Blue*.
Mar Stewart releases *Little Miss Understood* for Immediate Records, but it fails to chart.
June [22] The Jeff Beck° Group makes its US debut at the Fillmore East, New York, at the start of a tour.
Sept Group LP *Truth* hits UK #8 and US #15. Stewart strikes up a friendship with guitarist Ron Wood.
1969 June Stewart appears with The Small Faces° at Cambridge University as Quiet Melon.
July Beck Group LP *Cosa Nostra – Beck Ola* reaches UK #39 and US #15.

ROD STEWART *cont.*

Oct The Jeff Beck° Group splits and Stewart turns down the chance to join US band Cactus. He stays in UK and joins The Faces° (now without the "Small" adjective), who sign to Warner Bros. He also signs a solo deal with Phonogram, and will run his group and individual careers simultaneously until The Faces split. (Stewart is advanced £1,000 to record his solo debut.)

Nov LP *An Old Raincoat Won't Ever Let You Down*, comprising a mixture of originals and cover versions, fails to chart in UK, but makes US #139. The Faces° play on the LP.

1970 Stewart records guide vocals for Python Lee Jackson's *In A Broken Dream*, for which he is paid enough to buy seat covers for his car. (When the record is released and becomes a hit, Stewart's vocal has not been replaced, but he receives no credit.)

June LP *Gasoline Alley* reaches UK #62 and US #27.

Oct [1] Stewart begins a 28-date US tour at Goddard College, Plainfield, Vt.

1971 June LP *Every Picture Tells A Story* tops the UK chart for 6 weeks and US chart for 4 weeks.

Sept *Reason To Believe*, written by Tim Hardin, reaches UK #19. DJs flip the record, and *Maggie May* becomes A-side.

Oct *Maggie May* tops UK and US charts for 5 weeks. (Stewart tops both UK and US singles and LP charts in the same week.)

Dec *(I Know) I'm Losing You* reaches US #24.

1972 Mar *Handbags And Gladrags*, written by Mike D'Abo, makes US #42.

Aug LP *Never A Dull Moment* hits UK #1 for 2 weeks and US #2.

Sept *You Wear It Well* tops the UK chart.

Oct Python Lee Jackson's *In A Broken Dream* hits UK #3, having already climbed to US #56, while *You Wear It Well* reaches US #13.

Dec [9] Stewart sings *Pinball Wizard* in the London stage production of *Tommy*.

Dec Double A-side *Angel* (a Jimi Hendrix° song) and *What Made Milwaukee Famous* (a hit for Jerry Lee Lewis°) hits UK #4 and US #40.

1973 May Re-released *I've Been Drinking*, credited to Jeff Beck° and Rod Stewart, reaches UK #27.

Aug Compilation LP *Sing It Again Rod* tops the UK chart and makes US #31.

Sept *Oh No Not My Baby*, reviving Manfred Mann's° 1964 smash, hits UK #6 as a revival of Sam Cooke's° *Twisting The Night Away* makes US #59.

Nov *Oh No Not My Baby* makes US #59.

1974 Stewart begins a world tour with The Faces°.

May Stewart guests on the Scotland World Cup Football Squad's LP *Easy Easy*. He duets with soccer star Denis Law on *Angel*.

Oct *Farewell*, incorporating a medley of *Bring It On Home To Me* and *You Send Me*, hits UK #7. Parent LP *Smiler* tops the UK chart, and reaches US #13.

Dec *Mine For Me*, written for LP *Smiler* by Paul McCartney° (along with Elton John° and Bernie Taupin's *Let Me Be Your Car*), stalls at US #91. Stewart signs to Warner Bros., after a legal dispute over whether Phonogram or Warner has the rights to his solo releases.

1975 Mar [5] Stewart meets Swedish actress Britt Ekland at a party in LA, and embarks on a highly publicized love affair. He announces that he is setting up permanent residency in US, and applying for citizenship.

July Press reports claim that Stewart owes the UK taxman over £750,000. On a trip to UK, Stewart refuses to leave the international departure lounge to avoid setting foot in UK.

Aug LP *Atlantic Crossing* hits UK #1 and US #9. The set is produced by Tom Dowd in Muscle Shoals, Ala., using the famed rhythm section, which includes Steve Cropper and Donald "Duck" Dunn.

Sept *Sailing*, penned by Gavin Sutherland, tops the UK chart.

Nov Reviving Motown classic *This Old Heart Of Mine*, Stewart hits UK #4 with his first release on Riva Records, set up by his manager Billy Gaff. *Sailing* makes US #58.

Dec The Faces°, inactive for some time, finally split.

1976 May Compilation LP *The Best Of Rod Stewart* makes US #90.

June *Tonight's The Night (Gonna Be Alright)* hits UK #5. (The song is mostly banned because of its subject matter, the seduction of a virgin.)

July LP *A Night On The Town*, recorded in LA with top session players David Foster, John Jarvis, Steve Cropper and "Duck" Dunn, hits UK #1 and US #2.

Aug UK BBC TV documentary series "Sailor" adopts *Sailing* as its theme, sung by the crew of H.M.S. Ark Royal. It becomes the unofficial anthem of the Royal Navy.

Sept *The Killing Of Georgie (Parts 1 and 2)*, a two-part saga about the death of a gay friend in New York, hits UK #2.

Oct *Sailing*, reissued because of the TV documentary, hits UK #3. A special based on LP *A Night On The Town* airs on UK TV.

Nov *Tonight's The Night* tops the US chart for 7 weeks.

Dec *Get Back*, featured in Lou Reizner's film *All This and World War II* utilizing covers of Lennon°/McCartney° songs, reaches UK #11. A reissue of *Maggie May* makes UK #31.

1977 Apr A revival of Cat Stevens°-penned *First Cut Is The Deepest* reaches US #21.

May Coupled with *I Don't Want To Talk About It* as a double A-side, *First Cut Is The Deepest* tops the UK chart for 4 weeks, holding off The Sex Pistols'° *God Save The Queen*.

July *The Killing Of Georgie* makes US #30. Compilation LP *The Best Of Rod Stewart* reaches UK #18.

Oct *You're In My Heart (The Final Acclaim)* hits UK #3.

Nov LP *Foot Loose And Fancy Free* hits UK #3 and US #2 as Stewart begins a major tour with a band comprising long-term musical associate Jim Cregan (guitar), Gary Grainger (guitar), Billy Peek (guitar), Phil Chen (bass) and Carmine Appice (drums).

1978 Jan *You're In My Heart (The Final Acclaim)* hits US #4.

Feb *Hotlegs/I Was Only Joking* (featuring a reference to *Maggie May*) hits UK #5.

Apr *Hotlegs* reaches US #28.

June Stewart, pursuing his love of soccer, hits UK #4 with *Ole Ola (Muhler Brasileira*, with the Scottish World Cup Football Squad. (After Scotland fails to qualify for the second round, drawing 1-1 with Iran, the record speedily drops down the chart.) *I Was Only Joking* makes US #22.

Dec *D'Ya Think I'm Sexy*, written by Stewart and Appice, tops the UK chart. (Songwriter Jorge Ben will later sue, claiming it is based on his *Taj Mahal*.) LP *Blondes Have More Fun* hits UK #3 and tops the US chart.

1979 Jan [9] Stewart appears in the benefit concert "A Gift of Song – Music for UNICEF", at the UN General Assembly in New York, along with Abba°, The Bee Gees°, John Denver°, Earth, Wind & Fire°, and others. The show is taped for TV showing, and a compilation LP released, while performers each pledge the royalties from one new song to UNICEF, raising $500,000. (Stewart donates *D'Ya Think I'm Sexy*.)

Feb *Ain't Love A Bitch* reaches UK #11 as *D'ya Think I'm Sexy* hits US #1.

Apr Stewart marries Alana Hamilton, ex-wife of actor George Hamilton.

May *Blondes (Have More Fun)* stalls at UK #63.

June *Ain't Love A Bitch* reaches UK #22.

June [21/28] Stewart finishes a 4-month US tour with six performances at the Forum, Ingelwood, Cal.

Nov LP *Rod Stewart's Greatest Hits* tops the UK chart and reaches US #22.

1980 Feb *I Don't Want To Talk About It* makes US #46. (Written by Crazy Horse member Danny Whitten, Everything But The Girl's° version will re-chart in UK in 1988.)

May *If Loving You Is Wrong (I Don't Want To Be Right)* reaches UK #23.

Nov LP *Foolish Behavior* hits UK #4 and US #12. Extracted *Passion* makes UK #17.

Dec A revival of The Temptations'° *My Girl* reaches UK #32.

1981 Feb *Passion* hits US #5.

Mar *Somebody Special* stalls at US #71.

Nov *Tonight I'm Yours (Don't Hurt Me)* hits UK #8. Parent LP *Tonight I'm Yours* hits UK #8 and US #11.

Dec *Young Turks*, aided by a gang dancing video, reaches UK #11 and hits US #5.

1982 Mar Stewart covers Ace's° hit *How Long*, but it peaks at UK #41. It will be his last chart single for Riva. *Tonight I'm Yours (Don't Hurt Me)* reaches US #20.

Apr [26] Stewart is mugged in LA.

May *How Long* makes US #49.

July Stewart records Burt Bacharach and Carole Bayer Sager's *That's What Friends Are For* for Henry Winkler/Michael Keaton film *Night Shift*. (Dionne Warwick's° version will later win a Grammy.)

Nov Double LP *Absolutely Live* reaches UK #35 and US #46.

1983 June LP *Body Wishes*, Stewart's first for Warner Bros., hits UK #5 and US #30.
July *Baby Jane* tops the UK chart, as a prelude to a UK tour, and reaches US #14.
Sept *What Am I Gonna Do (I'm So In Love With You)* hits UK #3.
Oct *What Am I Gonna Do (I'm So In Love With You)* makes US #35.
Dec *Sweet Surrender* reaches UK #23.
1984 Stewart and his wife Alana separate.
June *Infatuation* makes UK #27, while parent LP *Camouflage* hits UK #8 and US #18.
July *Infatuation* hits US #6.
Sept A revival of *Some Guys Have All The Luck* reaches UK #15.
Oct *Some Guys Have All The Luck* hits US #10.
1985 Jan A revival of Free's *All Right Now* stalls at US #72. Stewart headlines two nights at the world's largest rock festival "Rock in Rio" in Rio de Janeiro, Brazil.
July Stewart pairs with old friend Jeff Beck° to release a version of The Impressions'° *People Get Ready*, from Beck's LP *Flash*. It makes US #48.
1986 Apr *Sailing* makes UK #41, with all royalties going to the bereaved families and survivors of the Zeebrugge Ferry Disaster.
June *Love Touch*, produced by Mike Chapman and from Robert Redford/Debra Winger film *Legal Eagles*, reaches UK #27.
July *Every Beat Of My Heart* hits UK #2. A re-recorded version of *Twistin' The Night Away*, featured in Dennis Quaid/Martin Short film *Innerspace*, makes US #80.
Aug *Love Touch* hits US #6.
Sept *Another Heartache*, co-written by Bryan Adams°, makes UK #54 and US #52.
Nov *Every Beat Of My Heart* stalls at US #83. LP *Love Touch*, produced by Bob Ezrin, hits UK #5, and titled *Rod Stewart* in US, it reaches #28.
1988 June LP *Out Of Order*, produced by Duran Duran's° Andy Taylor and Chic's° Bernard Edwards, reaches UK #11 and US #21. Songwriting assistance comes from Simon Climie, whose *Love Changes Everything* Stewart has previously turned down. Extracted *Lost In You* reaches UK #21 and US #12.
Aug *Forever Young* stalls at UK #57.
Oct *Forever Young* reaches US #12, helped by a video co-starring Stewart's son by current girlfriend Kelly Emberg.
Dec Third single from LP *Out Of Order*, *My Heart Can't Tell You No* is released in US.

STING

1971/73 While at teacher training college, Gordon Sumner (b. Oct.2, 1951, Wallsend, Newcastle, UK) plays in semi-professional jazz-rock bands, Earthrise, Phoenix Jazz Band, River City Jazz Band and in 1972 (now teaching under-9s at St. Paul's First School, Cramlington) The Newcastle Big Band, which makes one locally-distributed LP on which Sumner plays bass. He is nicknamed Sting by Newcastle jazz player Gordon Soloman, because of his yellow and black hooped T-shirt, reminiscent of a bee.
1974/77 He plays in another local band, Last Exit, which releases *Whispering Voices*, in 1975, on which Sting plays bass and sings lead on both sides.
1977 Jan Sting joins The Police° (as both lead singer and bass player until 1984), penning all the group's hits and signs a publishing deal with Virgin.
1979 Nov Movie version of The Who's° *Quadrophenia*, with Sting starring as Ace, opens nationwide in US. (He also appears in UK TV movie *Artemis '81*.)
1980 Sept Chris Pettit's film *Radio On*, with Sting appearing as Just Like Eddie, premieres in US.
1981 May *The Secret Policeman's Other Ball*, in which Sting sings an acoustic version of The Police° hit *Roxanne*, opens in US cinemas nationwide.
1982 Aug *Spread A Little Happiness*, from the soundtrack of TV film *Brimstone and Treacle* in which he stars as Martin, is his first solo single, making UK #16. He also records cover versions of *Tutti Frutti* and *Need Your Love So Bad* for *Party Party* soundtrack. Sting splits from his actress wife, Frances Tomelty.
1984 Mar Sting wins a Rock Instrumental Performance Grammy for *Brimstone And Treacle*.
Nov [25] Sting contributes a vocal lead to Band Aid's° *Do They Know It's Christmas?*.
Dec A film of Frank Herbert's novel *Dune*, with Sting starring as Feyd Rautha, opens in US.
1985 Jan With The Police° now effectively disbanded, he holds auditions for a new group in New York, looking for top jazz talent.
Feb Sting's backing group Blue Turtles Band is formed, with Sting (vocals, bass), Darryl Jones (bass), Kenny Kirkland (keyboards), Omar Hakim (drums), Branford Marsalis (various brass and woodwind), Wynton Marsalis (trumpet) and Dollette McDonald and Janice Pendarvis (vocals). It debuts at the New York Ritz.
Mar Phil Collins'° LP *No Jacket Required* features a Sting duet on *Long Long Way To Go*.
June He sings the intro on Dire Straits'° *Money For Nothing*, UK #4 and US #1 single, which he co-writes with Mark Knopfler. Sting's *If You Love Somebody Set Them Free* makes UK #26, as debut LP *The Dream Of The Blue Turtles*, recorded at Eddy Grant's° Blue Wave Studio in Barbados, is released, set to top the UK chart and hit US #2. Sting contributes to Miles Davis'° LP *You're Under Arrest*.
July [13] He plays Live Aid with Phil Collins° and Branford Marsalis.
Aug *Love Is The Seventh Wave* makes UK #41. *If You Love Somebody Set Them Free* hits US #3. *The Bride*, in which Sting stars as Frankenstein, premieres in US.
Sept [13] Sting begins his first solo tour in San Diego, Cal.
Sept The film of David Hare's play *Plenty*, with Sting co-starring opposite Meryl Streep and Sam Neill, opens nationwide in US.
Oct *Fortress Around Your Heart* hits US #8.
Nov *Russians*, aided by black and white Godley & Creme° video, makes UK #12. Director Michael Apted's film of Sting and his band before and during his concert tour in Paris, France, titled *Bring on the Night*, opens in US. Sting sings *Mack The Knife* on A&M various artists compilation LP *Lost In The Stars*, an anthology of Kurt Weil's work.
Dec *Love Is The Seventh Wave* reaches US #17.
1986 Feb Jazz-tinged *Moon Over Bourbon Street* makes UK #44.
Mar *Russians* reaches US #16.
June Live double LP *Bring On The Night* is released to accompany the documentary, which has been edited from 350,000 feet of film.
June [28] Sting takes part in Jerry Dammers-organized anti-apartheid concert on Clapham Common, London.
Nov [14] LP *Conspiracy Of Hope*, in aid of Amnesty International and with contributions from Sting, Peter Gabriel°, Elton John° and Steve Winwood°, is released.
Nov "A Conspiracy of Hope" tour begins in US with Sting, Bryan Adams°, Bob Dylan°, Peter Gabriel°, Tom Petty° and U2°.
1987 Feb [24] *Bring On The Night* wins a Grammy for Best Long-Form Video at the 29th annual ceremonies.
July [2] Sting continues recording in Montserrat during his mother's funeral.
July Sting joins former musical associate Eberhard Schoener in an evening of songs by Bertholt Brecht and Kurt Weil in Hamburg, West Germany. He plays the Umbria Jazz Festival, Italy, with the Gil Evans Orchestra.
Nov *We'll Be Together* makes UK #41 but hits US #7. LP *Nothing Like The Sun*, with guests, Andy Summers, Eric Clapton°, Mark Knopfler, Ruben Blades and Branford Marsalis, hits UK #1 and US #9.
Dec Sting contributes *Gabriel's Message* to the Special Olympics Christmas LP *A Very Special Christmas*.
1988 Jan [20] Sting begins a 46-date US tour in Tampa Bay, Fla.
Feb *An Englishman In New York*, about UK exile Quentin Crisp, falters at UK #51.
Mar *Be Still My Beating Heart* peaks at US #15.
Mar [29] His US tour ends in Portland, Ore.
Apr *Fragile* peaks at UK #70 and is not issued in US. A mini-LP of Spanish versions of songs from the last LP, for the South American market, is released. Sting contributes George Gershwin's *Someone To Watch Over Me*, the theme to Ridley Scott's thriller of the same name.
May *An Englishman In New York* stalls at US #84.
June [11] Sting opens the Nelson Mandela 70th Birthday Party Concert with *If You Love Somebody Set Them Free*.
Aug Sting plays the title role on Stravinsky's *Soldier's Tale*, released on his own Pangaea label. Ian McKellen plays the narrator and Vanessa Redgrave the devil, with the London Sinfonietta. Sting writes the music for Quentin Crisp documentary *Crisp City*.
Sept [2] Sting joins Bruce Springsteen°, Tracy Chapman°, Peter Gabriel° and Youssou N'Dour on Amnesty International's "Human Rights

STING *cont.*

Now! World Tour".

Sept Ballad *They Dance Alone* from LP *Nothing Like The Sun*, written as a protest to Peruvian leader General Pinochet, fails to chart in UK. Sting's *Englishman In New York* is used as the title track to Daniel Day Lewis film *Stars and Bars*. (Sting's own movie appearances in 1988 include *Stormy Monday* and *Julia Julia*.)

Nov A compilation of Sting clips, *The Videos*, is released.

THE STRANGLERS

Hugh Cornwell (vocals and guitar)
Dave Greenfield (keyboards)
Jean-Jacques Burnel (bass)
Jet Black (drums)

1974 Oct The Guildford Stranglers are formed in Chiddingford, Surrey, UK, originally as a trio comprising chemistry graduate and ex-science teacher Cornwell, one-time jazz drummer and ice cream salesman Black (b. Brian Duffy) and Burnel (London-born son of French parents, and a history graduate from Bradford University). The group signs with Albion management.

1975 May Greenfield joins on keyboards after answering an ad placed by the group in UK music magazine *Melody Maker*. A sax player, recruited at the same time, lasts for just 3 days, and the band decides to remain a quartet.

1976 May [17] After a year on the road in minor club gigs, The Stranglers make their major venue debut supporting Patti Smith° at London's Roundhouse.

July [4] The group plays the American Bi-Centennial Show at The Roundhouse, London, with The Ramones° and The Flamin' Groovies.

Sept They support Patti Smith° on a UK tour (followed by a UK tour on their own through Oct. and Nov.).

Dec [17] The group signs a recording deal with United Artists.

1977 Jan [30] Supporting The Climax Blues Band at London's Roundhouse, the group's performance is cut short by a power turn-off after Cornwell reveals his "F**k" T-shirt on stage. (The Greater London Council has warned the management that its performance regulations would not allow this display.)

Feb Group-penned debut single *(Get A) Grip (On Yourself)*, produced by Martin Rushent, makes UK #44 (after being accidentally omitted from the chart by compilers BMRB in its first week of release) while the group is playing live dates in Europe.

Mar The Stranglers record their first live session for "The John Peel Show" on UK BBC Radio 1, after completing a UK mini-tour.

Apr The group plays again at London's Roundhouse, with The Jam° and Cherry Vanilla. First LP *The Stranglers IV: Rattus Norvegicus* hits UK #4.

May Another UK tour begins, lasting into June. Some dates are cancelled when local councils and venue bookers begin banning punk-associated groups.

June The band backs Celia Collin, a female singer found by its manager Dai Davies, who has sung live with them at London's Nashville, on a revival of Tommy James & The Shondells'° *Mony Mony*, credited as Celia and The Mutations. It does not chart.

July *Peaches/Go Buddy Go* hits UK #8. (The A-side is banned by UK BBC for "offensive lyrics", so the B-side is promoted equally. The Stranglers play it on their first major TV appearance, on BBC 1's "Top of the Pops".)

Aug *Something Better Change/Straighten Out* hits UK #9. Burnel is drafted into the French army for military service, but escapes it by providing proof of his permanent residency in UK.

Sept [1] The Stranglers begin a major UK tour, following with another European tour.

Oct *No More Heroes* hits UK #8, while the LP of the same title, again produced by Rushent, hits UK #2.

Nov The group plays a short residency at London's Roundhouse, supported by The Dictators. The act is taped for later live LP use.

Nov [22] The Stranglers perform on the first night of the 3-week Hope and Anchor Front Row Festival in Islington, London.

1978 Feb *Five Minutes* makes UK #11.

Mar [16] The group opens its first US tour (moving on to Canada, Iceland, Scandinavia, and down through Europe).

May *Nice'n'Sleazy* makes UK #18.

June LP *Black And White*, including *Nice'n'Sleazy*, hits UK #2, supported by a UK tour.

Sept A high-speed, keyboard-driven revival of Bacharach/David's *Walk On By* makes UK #21. Jazzman George Melly guests on B-side *Old Codger*.

Oct The group plays London's Battersea Park with Peter Gabriel° (with strippers performing during *Nice'n'Sleazy*), before beginning a series of one-off shows in London using pseudonyms to beat any local council bans.

1979 Mar Live LP *Live (X Cert)*, from a variety of concert appearances, hits UK #7.

Apr Burnel releases solo LP *Euroman Cometh*, which makes UK #40. He also undertakes a solo tour.

June The group records a new LP in Paris, co-producing the tracks with Alan Winstanley (who had engineered previous recordings), and also headlines the Loch Lomond Festival in Scotland.

Aug [18] The Stranglers play Wembley Stadium, London, with AC/DC°, Nils Lofgren° and headliners The Who°.

Sept *Duchess*, from the forthcoming LP, makes UK #14.

Oct LP *The Raven*, the first pressing featuring a 3-D sleeve picture, hits UK #4. Cornwell also releases an LP, *Nosferatu*, in collaboration with Robert Williams, but it fails to chart.

Nov *Nuclear Device (The Wizard Of Aus)*, taken from LP *The Raven*, reaches UK #36, as the band tours UK again.

Dec 4-track EP *Don't Bring Harry* makes UK #41.

1980 Jan [7] Cornwell is found guilty of possession of heroin, cocaine and cannabis. He is fined £300, and sentenced to 3 months' imprisonment in Pentonville jail, London.

Apr *Bear Cage* makes UK #36.

Apr [25] Cornwell is released from prison. (The story of his time spent there will be told in his book *Inside Information*.)

June *Who Wants The World* reaches UK #39.

June [21] The Stranglers are arrested in Nice, France, after allegedly inciting a riot when a concert at the university is cancelled because a generator has not been supplied for electrical power. (Black will chronicle this event in his book *Much Ado About Nothing* – the group members are fined in a Nice court later in the year.)

1981 Feb *Thrown Away* makes UK #42. It is the group's first release on Liberty Records (as parent company EMI renames United Artists).

Mar Self-produced LP *Themeninblack*, also on Liberty, hits UK #8.

Nov *Let Me Introduce You To The Family* peaks at UK #42, as the group tours UK to promote forthcoming LP *La Folie*.

1982 Feb Melodic waltz-time *Golden Brown*, with an arresting harpsichord arrangement, is The Stranglers' most popular single, hitting UK #2 behind The Jam's° *A Town Called Malice*.

Mar LP *La Folie*, which includes *Golden Brown*, makes UK #11.

May The title track from *La Folie*, sung by Burnel in French, reaches UK #47.

Aug *Strange Little Girl* hits UK #7.

Oct Compilation LP *The Collection 1977-1982*, a 14-track singles anthology compiled as a final EMI LP, makes UK #12. Hassles with the label in 1982 ensure that The Stranglers will not re-sign to Liberty as their first contract expires (they have tried to move to Phonogram but an EMI injunction prevented it).

Nov The band signs a new recording deal with Epic.

Apollo Theater in Harlem.

1963 Jan *Let Me Go The Right Way*, written by Gordy, makes US #90.

Aug *A Breath Taking Guy*, penned by Smokey Robinson°, makes US #75.

1964 Jan A Holland/Dozier/Holland song, uptempo dancer *When The Lovelight Starts Shining Through His Eyes*, is the group's top 30 breakthrough, reaching US #23.

Mar *Run, Run, Run*, penned by the same trio, stalls at US #93.

June The group begins a US tour on Dick Clark's "Caravan of Stars", alongside Gene Pitney°, The Shirelles°, Brenda Holloway, and others.

Aug *Where Did Our Love Go* (written by Holland, Dozier and Holland for, but rejected by, The Marvelettes) tops the US chart for 2 weeks, and is the group's first million-seller.

Sept *Where Did Our Love Go* is The Supremes' UK chart debut, hitting #3.

Sept [13] The trio appears in Murray The K's 10-day Rock'n'Roll Spectacular at New York's Fox Theater, Brooklyn, on a bill including Motown labelmates The Temptations°, Marvin Gaye°, The Miracles and Martha & The Vandellas°.

Oct *Baby Love*, also by Holland/Dozier/Holland, hits US #1 for 4 weeks and is a second million-seller. LP *Where Did Our Love Go* hits US #2, staying charted for 89 weeks.

Oct [30] The group appears in the T.A.M.I. show, a stage spectacular videotaped for US TV and UK movie release, alongside The Rolling Stones°, The Beach Boys°, Marvin Gaye°, James Brown°, and others.

Nov The Supremes become the first all-girl group to hit UK #1, when *Baby Love* tops the UK chart for 2 weeks.

Dec *Come See About Me*, by Holland/Dozier/Holland and taken from the LP to compete with Nella Dodds' version (a minor US hit on Wand Records), tops the US chart for a week, but is deposed by The Beatles'° *I Feel Fine*. Meanwhile, LP *Meet The Supremes* hits UK #8 and LP *A Bit Of Liverpool*, featuring covers of UK group hits, makes US #21.

Dec [27] The trio makes its debut on US TV's "Ed Sullivan Show".

1965 Jan *Come See About Me* replaces The Beatles° *I Feel Fine* for a further week at US #1, and is their third consecutive million-seller.

Feb *Come See About Me* makes UK #27.

Mar Again the trio deposes The Beatles° as Holland/Dozier/Holland's *Stop! In The Name Of Love* replaces Lennon°/McCartney's° *Eight Days A Week* at US #1 for 2 weeks.

Mar [20] The Supremes arrive in London, UK, to take part in the Motown package tour which helps launch the label's identity in UK (all previous releases having been licensed on UK labels like London, Oriole and Stateside), with labelmates Martha & The Vandellas°, The Miracles, The Temptations° and Stevie Wonder°.

Apr LP *The Supremes Sing Country, Western And Pop* makes US #79 while *Stop! In The Name Of Love*, the first single released on UK Tamla Motown label, hits UK #7. The trio's characteristic hand-movement choreography for the song is worked out during rehearsals for UK TV's "Ready Steady Go!".

June *Back In My Arms Again* tops the US chart for a week, the trio's fifth consecutive US #1 single and million-seller. In UK, it makes #40 while LP *We Remember Sam Cooke*, featuring songs associated with the recently-deceased Cooke°, makes US #75.

July [29] The trio opens for 3 weeks at New York's Copacabana club.

Aug *Nothing But Heartaches* reaches US #11 but fails to chart in UK.

Sept LP *More Hits By The Supremes* hits US #6.

Oct [10] The Supremes appear again on US TV's "Ed Sullivan Show", introducing *I Hear A Symphony*.

Nov *I Hear A Symphony* tops the US chart for 2 weeks (deposing The Rolling Stones'° *Get Off Of My Cloud*) and is a million-seller.

Dec Live LP *The Supremes At The Copa*, a recording of their club act at New York's Copacabana, reaches US #11.

1966 Jan *I Hear A Symphony* makes UK #39.

Feb *My World Is Empty Without You* hits US #5, and is a further million-seller, but fails in UK.

Apr LP *I Hear A Symphony* hits US #8.

May *Love Is Like An Itching In My Heart* hits US #9. (Though not a UK hit, it will become a classic dance record on the UK Northern Soul scene in the mid-1970s.)

Sept *You Can't Hurry Love* hits US #1 for 2 weeks, selling over a million, and UK #3. (Phil Collins'° 1982 revival of it will be a million-seller.)

Oct LP *The Supremes A' Go-Go* tops the US chart for 2 weeks, deposing The Beatles'° *Revolver*. It is the trio's first #1 LP.

Nov *You Keep Me Hangin' On* tops the US chart for 2 weeks, selling over a million.

Dec LP *The Supremes A' Go-Go* makes UK #15, while *You Keep Me Hangin' On* hits UK #8.

1967 Jan [6] The Supremes begin recording an LP of Disney tunes. (The project is shelved before release and only *When You Wish Upon A Star* appears.)

Mar *Love Is Here And Now You're Gone* tops the US chart for a week (a further million-seller) and makes UK #17. It is taken from LP *The Supremes Sing Holland-Dozier-Holland*, which hits US #6.

Apr After Ballard, unhappy about her role in the group, starts to become unreliable, missing concerts in New Orleans and Montreal, Canada. Cindy Birdsong (b. Dec.15, 1939, Camden, N.J., US) of Patti LaBelle° & The Bluebelles is auditioned as a stand-in.

Apr [29] Birdsong makes her Supremes stage debut at the Hollywood Bowl, at a benefit show for the United Negro College Fund and UCLA School of Music, which also features The 5th Dimension°, Johnny Rivers°, and others.

May *The Happening*, the theme from the Anthony Quinn film of the same name, becomes The Supremes' tenth US #1 (in 13 releases), for 1 week.

June *The Happening* hits UK #6, while LP *The Supremes Sing Motown* (a re-titling of US LP *The Supremes Sing Holland-Dozier-Holland*) makes UK #17.

July LP *The Supremes Sing Rodgers And Hart* makes US #20. During a Las Vegas club engagement at The Flamingo, Ballard is dismissed from the group and fired from Motown (the label flies her back to Detroit, where she is hospitalized with exhaustion). Birdsong steps in, but Gordy announces that lead singer Ross° is to be elevated to featured status in preparation for a solo career, and the group will henceforth be credited as Diana Ross & The Supremes.

Sept *Reflections*, the first release with the new billing (and also one of Motown's first experiments with "progressive" backing music elements, having a characteristically 1967 swirling "psychedelic" intro), hits US #2 (behind Bobbie Gentry's *Ode To Billie Jo*), selling a million, and UK #5.

Oct Double compilation LP *Diana Ross And The Supremes' Greatest Hits* tops the US chart for 5 weeks, while LP *The Supremes Sing Rodgers And Hart* makes UK #25.

Dec *In And Out Of Love* hits US #9 and UK #13.

1968 Jan The trio plays a short nightclub season at London's Talk of the Town. Among those who catch the opening of the act are Paul McCartney°, Cliff Richard° and Michael Caine. They also appear on UK TV's "Sunday Night at the London Palladium".

Feb Compilation LP *Diana Ross And The Supremes' Greatest Hits* (reduced from the US double LP to a 16-track single LP for UK) tops the UK chart for 6 weeks.

Feb [3] TV special "The Supremes Live at the Talk of the Town" airs on UK BBC TV.

Feb [29] Ex-Supreme Ballard marries Thomas Chapman in Detroit.

Mar Ballard signs to ABC Records as a soloist. (She will record two solo singles, but neither will sell.)

Apr UK-recorded live LP *Live At The Talk Of The Town* hits UK #6, while *Forever Came Today*, the last Supremes single written and produced by Holland/Dozier/Holland (who will leave Motown to set up their own successful Invictus and Hot Wax labels), reaches both US and UK #28.

June LP *Reflections* peaks at US #18.

July *Some Things You Never Get Used To*, written and produced by Ashford and Simpson°, makes US #30 and UK #34, while LP *Reflections* makes UK #30.

Aug Rumors that Ross° is shortly to leave The Supremes are reported in both US and UK press.

Oct Live LP *Live At London's Talk Of The Town* peaks at US #57, while LP *Funny Girl*, featuring the group's versions of songs from the show, makes US #150.

Nov *Love Child*, a social-conscience song team-written by Pam Sawyer, Frank Wilson, Deke Richards and R. Dean Taylor tops the US chart for 2 weeks after the trio premieres it on TV's "Ed Sullivan Show". It deposes The Beatles'° *Hey Jude* and is another million-seller.

Nov [19] The Supremes appear before HM The Queen at The Royal Variety Show in London. Ross° does an unrehearsed between-songs monologue urging racial tolerance, which is rapturously applauded.

THE SUPREMES *cont.*

Dec LP *Diana Ross And The Supremes Join The Temptations* hits US #2, while *Love Child* makes UK #15

1969 Jan LP *Love Child* reaches US #14, while a revival of Madeleine Bell's *I'm Gonna Make You Love Me*, duetted with The Temptations° and taken from the two groups' joint LP, is a millon-seller, hitting US #2 (behind Marvin Gaye's° *I Heard It Through The Grapevine*).

Feb *I'm Gonna Make You Love Me* hits UK #3, while LP *Diana Ross And The Supremes Join The Temptations* tops the UK chart for 4 weeks and LP *Love Child* hits UK #8. Meanwhile, LP *T.C.B.*, again with The Temptations°, and featuring the soundtrack of the two groups' TV spectacular of the same title, tops the US chart for a week.

Mar *I'm Livin' In Shame* (said to have been inspired by Lana Turner film *Imitation of Life*) hits US #10.

Apr A revival of The Miracles' *I'll Try Something New*, with The Temptations° (from LP *T.C.B.*), makes US #25.

May *I'm Livin' In Shame* makes UK #14, while *The Composer*, penned by Smokey Robinson°, reaches US #27.

June *No Matter What Sign You Are* makes US #31.

July LP *Let The Sunshine In* makes US #24, while The Supremes/Temptations° LP *T.C.B.* reaches UK #11 and *No Matter What Sign You Are* makes UK #37.

Aug *No Matter What Sign You Are*'s B-side, *The Young Folks*, makes US #69.

Sept A revival of The Band's° *The Weight*, duetted with The Temptations°, peaks at US #46.

Oct A revival of The Miracles' *I Second That Emotion*, again with The Temptations°, makes UK #18.

Nov LP *Together*, a third set with The Temptations°, makes US #28.

Dec *Someday We'll Be Together*, produced and co-written by Johnny Bristol, tops the US chart for a week and sells over a million. It is The Supremes' twelfth and last US #1 (and their last single together before Ross° departs for a solo career). It is taken from LP *Cream Of The Crop*, the last studio set from the Ross-led line-up, which reaches US #33.

Dec [21] Ross° and The Supremes make their last TV appearance together on US TV's "Ed Sullivan Show", singing *Someday We'll Be Together*.

1970 Jan *Someday We'll Be Together* makes UK #13, while LP *On Broadway*, the soundtrack to another Supremes/Temptations° TV special, reaches US #38.

Jan [14] Diana Ross° and The Supremes make their final live appearance together at Las Vegas' Frontier Hotel. (Ross will leave the following day, having introduced her replacement Jean Terrell (b. Nov.26, 1944, Tex., US), the sister of boxer Ernie Terrell, on stage.)

Feb Compilation LP *Diana Ross And The Supremes Greatest Hits, Volume 3*, continuing the hits anthology from the earlier double LP, makes US #31, while LP *Together* with The Temptations° makes UK #28.

Apr The group's billing reverts back to The Supremes for *Up The Ladder To The Roof*, the first release featuring Terrell on lead vocals, which hits US #10. The group is now working with producer Frank Wilson, who has co-written the song with Vincent DiMirco. Meanwhile, *Why (Must We Fall In Love)*, with The Temptations (and featuring Ross°), makes UK #31.

May *Up The Ladder To The Roof* hits UK #6.

June Double live LP *Farewell*, by Diana Ross° and The Supremes, a recording of the trio's final concert on Jan.14, peaks at US #46.

July LP *Right On*, the first featuring Terrell, reaches US #25.

Sept *Everybody's Got The Right To Love*, taken from the LP, makes US #21.

Nov LP *The Magnificent 7*, recorded with The Four Tops°, peaks at US #113, while The Supremes' LP *New Ways But Love Stays* makes US #68.

Dec From the LP, *Stoned Love*, produced and co-written by Frank Wilson, hits US #7, giving the new line-up its first million-seller. Meanwhile, a revival of Ike and Tina Turner's° *River Deep, Mountain High*, with The Four Tops° (from LP *The Magnificent 7*), reaches US #14.

1971 Feb *Stoned Love* hits UK #3.

June *Nathan Jones* reaches US #16, while LP *The Magnificent 7*, with The Four Tops°, hits UK #6.

July *River Deep, Mountain High* peaks at UK #11, while The Supremes' LP *Touch* makes US #85 and LP *The Return Of The Magnificent Seven*, again with The Four Tops, climbs to US #154. The duetted *You Gotta Have Love In Your Heart*, taken from it, makes US #55.

Sept *Nathan Jones* hits UK #5 (and will be revived by Bananarama° in 1988) and LP *Touch* makes UK #40, while the extracted title song stalls at US #71.

Dec *You Gotta Have Love In Your Heart*, with The Four Tops°, makes UK #25.

1972 Jan LP *Dynamite*, with The Four Tops°, makes US #160.

Mar *Floy Joy*, written and produced by Smokey Robinson°, reaches US #16 and hits UK #9.

June Birdsong leaves the group, to devote more time to home and marriage. She is replaced by Lynda Lawrence. LP *Floy Joy* reaches US #54 while, from it, another Robinson° song, *Automatically Sunshine*, makes US #37.

July *Automatically Sunshine* hits UK #10, the group's last top 10 hit. (The song will reappear in a UK TV ad for Persil Automatic washing powder in 1987.)

Sept *Your Wonderful, Sweet Sweet Love* makes US #59.

Nov *I Guess I'll Miss The Man* (from Broadway musical *Pippin*) stalls at US #85.

Dec LP *The Supremes*, written and produced by Jimmy Webb, makes US #129.

1973 May *Bad Weather*, produced and arranged by Stevie Wonder°, makes UK #37.

June *Bad Weather* spends 1 week at US #87. It is the group's last recording to feature Terrell; she leaves shortly after and is replaced by Scherrie Payne (b. Nov.14, 1944, Detroit).

1974 July Triple compilation LP *Anthology (1962-1969)* reaches US #66.

Sept *Baby Love* is reissued in UK and re-charts, making #12. It is their last UK hit single.

1975 July LP *The Supremes* peaks at US #152.

1976 After Laurence has left and Birdsong has returned temporarily, the third slot is filled by Susaye Greene.

Feb [22] Following hard times, including a lost $8.7 million lawsuit against Motown and separation from her husband, which left her on welfare, Ballard dies, aged 32, at Mount Carmel Mercy Hospital, Detroit, from a heart attack brought on by coronary thrombosis.

July LP *High Energy* makes US #42, while extracted *I'm Gonna Let My Heart Do The Walking* makes US #40 (after the group has been absent from the singles chart for 3 years).

Dec *You're My Driving Wheel* stalls at US #85, and is their final US hit single. Wilson, the final original member, leaves and is replaced by Karen Jackson. (Motown sees little commercial potential left in the group and it will disband. Wilson will later perform with new back-up singers as Mary Wilson and The Supremes.)

1977 Sept TV-promoted UK compilation LP *Diana Ross And The Supremes' 20 Golden Greats* tops the UK chart for 7 weeks.

1981 Dec [20] Musical *Dreamgirls*, supposedly based on the story of The Supremes, opens on Broadway at the Imperial Theater.

1983 May [16] Wilson and Birdsong are reunited with Ross° as The Supremes on the Motown 25th anniversary US NBC-TV spectacular.

June The Supremes with Wilson tour US on an oldies package with Frankie Valli & The Four Seasons°, The Righteous Brothers°, The Four Tops° and The Association°.

1984 Wilson writes a book telling her own history of the group – *Dreamgirl: My Life as a Supreme*.

1988 Dec As Bananarama°, now claiming to be the most successful girl trio in rock history, revive *Nathan Jones* in UK top 20, the most successful girl trio in rock history The Supremes are set for compilation LP chart revival through Motown's planned LP *Love Supreme*.

SURVIVOR

Jim Peterik (keyboards, guitar and vocals)
Frank Sullivan (lead guitar and vocals)
Dave Bickler (synthesizers and lead vocals)
Dennis Johnson (bass)
Gary Smith (drums)

1978 The group is formed in Chicago, Ill., US, after Peterik, having been with The Ides of March, whose 1970 million-seller *Vehicle* he also wrote, and (after its split during the early 70s) continued as a soloist, recording LP *Don't Fight The Feeling* with little success, meets Bickler. Sullivan joins the duo from playing with local band Mariah, and Smith and Johnson are recruited before the band starts touring around Chicago and the Pacific North-West.

1979 The band is signed to Scotti Bros. Records.

1980 Mar Peterik and Sullivan write *Rockin' Into The Night* for Florida band .38 Special, which reaches US #43.

Apr Debut LP *Survivor* makes US #169 and extracted *Somewhere In America* climbs to US #70.

1981 Stephan Ellis and Marc Droubay join on bass and drums respectively, replacing Johnson and Smith.

May Peterik and Sullivan write .38 Special's second hit single, *Hold On Loosely*, which reaches US #27.

Aug Peterik writes the theme for animated movie *Heavy Metal*, which is recorded by Don Felder as *Heavy Metal (Takin' A Ride)* and reaches US #43.

Dec Taken from forthcoming second LP, Survivor's *Poor Man's Son* makes US #33.

1982 Jan Second LP *Premonition* makes US #92.

Mar *Summer Nights*, also from the LP, makes US #62.

Apr/May The group records its third LP at Rumbo Recorders, LA, with Peterik and Sullivan co-producing and co-writing. Among the tracks is *Eye Of The Tiger*, which they have written as the theme to Sylvester Stallone's forthcoming third *Rocky* movie. Tony Scotti of their record label has played LP *Premonition* to Stallone, who has indicated that he wants a contemporary, rock-oriented sound with a strong beat and has given the writers a rough cut video of the film for inspiration – which provides the key phrase as Rocky's trainer continually reminds him to "keep the eye of the tiger".

July *Eye Of The Tiger* is released in US as movie *Rocky III* opens, and tops the US chart for 6 weeks, selling over 2 million copies to earn a platinum disk.

Aug Survivor's third LP, titled after *Eye Of The Tiger*, hits US #2 for 4 weeks (behind Fleetwood Mac's° *Mirage*) and is also a million-seller, while the soundtrack LP from the movie (which also includes the single) makes US #15.

Sept *Eye Of The Tiger* is the band's UK chart debut, hitting #1 for 4 weeks and selling 800,000 copies. The LP of the same title reaches UK #12, while the soundtrack LP makes UK #42.

Nov *American Heartbeat*, taken from LP *Eye Of The Tiger*, reaches US #17.

1983 Feb *The One That Really Matters* peaks at US #74.

Nov LP *Caught In The Game* peaks at US #82. The title track stalls at US #77.

1984 July The band performs *The Moment Of Truth* in film *The Karate Kid*. Released as a single on Casablanca (which owns soundtrack rights), it makes US #63.

Dec Jimi Jamison replaces Bickler as Survivor's lead singer, and *I Can't Hold Back* reaches US #13.

1985 Mar *High On You* hits US #8.

July *The Search Is Over* hits US #4, while LP *Vital Signs*, the first to feature Jamison, and including both the current hit and the previous two, reaches US #16 (having steadily climbed the chart since the end of 1984). It earns a platinum disk.

Sept *First Night* peaks at US #53.

1986 Feb *Burning Heart* hits US #2 for 2 weeks (behind Dionne Warwick° and Friends' *That's What Friends Are For*). It is one of the main themes to Sylvester Stallone's movie *Rocky IV*, and is included on the soundtrack LP, which hits US #10. LP *When Seconds Count* makes US #49.

Mar *Burning Heart* hits UK #5, and the soundtrack LP from *Rocky IV* hits UK #3.

1987 Jan *Is This Love* hits US #9.

Mar Follow-up single *How Much Love* reaches US #51.

May *Man Against The World* stalls at US #86.

SWEET

Brian Connolly (vocals)
Andy Scott (guitar)
Steve Priest (bass)
Mick Tucker (drums)

1968 Jan Ex-members of Wainwright's Gentlemen, Connolly (b. Oct.5, 1949, Hamilton, Scotland, UK) and Tucker (b. July 17, 1949, Harlesden, London, UK) form Sweetshop with Priest (b. Feb.23, 1950, Hayes, Middx., UK) and Frank Torpey on guitar.

Feb Sweetshop's live debut is at the Hemel Hempstead Pavilion, Herts.

July Debut single is *Slow Motion*, on Fontana, which fails to chart.

Aug The group makes its first radio broadcast on UK BBC Radio 1's "David Symonds Show".

Sept A move to EMI's Parlophone label for *Lollipop Man* sees minimal sales. (Two more Parlophone singles will also fail to chart in 1970, before the label drops the group.)

1970 Torpey is replaced by Scott (b. June 30, 1951, Wrexham, Wales, UK), who has moved to London after his most recent band Elastic Band has split up. The group abbreviates its name to Sweet.

1971 Jan The group makes its UK TV debut, on juvenile pop show "Lift Off". A new recording deal is signed with RCA, and Sweet links with producer Phil Wainman.

May Wainman-produced Nicky Chinn/Mike Chapman composition *Funny Funny* is UK chart debut, reaching #13.

July *Co-Co* hits UK #2, held from the top by Middle of the Road's *Chirpy Chirpy Cheep Cheep*.

Oct *Alexander Graham Bell* makes UK #33, while *Co-Co* is US chart debut at #91.

1972 Mar *Poppa Joe* reaches UK #11. It begins a series of consecutive UK hits which makes the band "Top of the Pops" regulars on UK TV, and encourages its ever more way-out visual image, with flamboyant costumes, make-up and glitter.

May The group is taken to court in Belgium, by a town objecting to an earlier Sweet concert which involved the use of an allegedly pornographic film clip.

July *Little Willy* hits UK #4. The slight double entendre is exploited by the group (and its audience), especially on live ballroom dates. (Later, for what is considered an overtly sexual stage act, the group is banned from UK Mecca dancehall circuit.)

Oct *Wig Wam Bam* hits UK #4. It is played on TV in American Indian costume and warpaint-like make-up.

1973 Jan *Blockbuster*, using one of the most familiar riffs in rock music (the same one as David Bowie's° *The Gene Genie*, which sits at #2 below it), tops the UK chart for 5 weeks. Like all Sweet hits, it has a hard rock band-composed B-side.

May *Hellraiser* hits UK #2, behind Dawn's *Tie A Yellow Ribbon*. In US, *Little Willy* gives the band its biggest success, hitting #3 and selling over a million.

Aug LP *The Sweet* makes US #191.

Sept *Ballroom Blitz* enters the UK chart at #2, held off the top by Simon Park Orchestra's *Eye Level*.

1974 Jan *Teenage Rampage* is the third consecutive UK #2, behind Mud's° *Tiger Feet*.

May The group begins its first UK tour, while LP *Sweet Fanny Adams* makes UK #27 – the group's only UK chart LP during the 70s. In contrast to the singles, this is entirely self-written.

July *The Six Teens* hits UK #9, while *Blockbuster* makes US #73.

Dec The group splits from Chinn and Chapman, to write and produce itself, and attempts to find greater international rock credibility.

1975 Apr Group-penned *Fox On The Run* hits UK #2, behind The Bay City Rollers'° *Bye Bye Baby*.

Aug *Action* reaches UK #15.

Sept The group begins a 3-month US tour, which heralds its greatest period of US success.

Oct *Ballroom Blitz* hits US #5, a year after its UK success. LP *Desolation Boulevard*, having failed in UK, reaches US #25, earning a gold disk.

1976 Jan *Fox On The Run* hits US #5, and is a second million-selling single, while *Lies In Your Eyes* makes UK #35.

Apr *Action* makes US #20, while entirely group self-penned LP *Give Us A Wink*, recorded in Munich, West Germany, reaches US #27.

1977 May LP *Off The Record* makes US #151.

Aug *Funk It Up (David's Song)*, not issued as a UK single, makes US #88. The group retires to Clearwell Castle in Wales to write another LP, later moving to France to record it.

1978 Feb After a 2-year UK singles chart absence, the group leaves RCA following three flop singles, and signs to Polydor. *Love Is Like Oxygen*, featured in Joan Collins movie *The Bitch*, hits UK #9. Sweet tours UK for the first time in 4 years.

June *Love Is Like Oxygen* hits US #8, while parent LP *Level Headed* makes US #52.

Aug Also from the LP, *California Nights* makes US #74. It is the band's last US hit single (having failed in UK).

1979 May LP *Cut Above The Rest* makes US #151. Connolly leaves to go solo. (He will later form The New Sweet, with no original members.)

SWEET *cont.*

1980 Apr *Give The Lady Some Respect* and LP *Water's Edge* both fail.

1981 The group tours with new guitarist/keyboardist back-up, but finds no recording success, and splits after release of LP *Identity Crisis*.

1984 Oct Retrospective compilation LP *Sweet 16 – It's . . . It's . . . Sweet's Hits*, on UK independent label Anagram, reaches UK #49.

1985 Feb Also on Anagram, segued *It's It's The Sweet Mix*, put together from original hits (*Blockbusters, Fox On The Run, Teenage Rampage, Hellraiser* and *Ballroom Blitz* by UK club DJ/remixer Sanny X, reaches UK #45. Amid the interest this creates, the group re-forms briefly, with Paul Mario Day (ex-Wildfire) replacing Connolly and keyboardist Phil Lanzon (ex-Grand Prix).

1988 Scott tours UK with pub-rockers Paddy Goes To Holyhead.

SWING OUT SISTER

Corinne Drewery (vocals)
Andy Connell (keyboards)
Martin Jackson (percussion)

1982 Ex-Magazine drummer Jackson and ex-A Certain Ratio keyboardist Connell, based in their native Manchester, UK, begin experimenting with electronic dance music.

1984 Having formed a unit named Syncbeat, they are responsible for much of innovative Streetsounds label LP *Electro*.

Aug Jackson and Connell link with St. Martin's School of Art fashion designer Drewery, who has been singing with Working Week and Doug Veitch.

Nov With Drewery having recently survived a collision with a horse, newly-formed Swing Out Sister trio, signed to Mercury, releases debut single *Blue Mood*. It fails to chart as the group sets off as support act for Hipsway on a UK tour.

1986 Oct Second single *Breakout* hits UK #3. The group adds two new members, Johnson brothers Donald (drums) and Derek (bass).

Dec *Surrender* hits UK #7.

1987 Apr *Twilight World* makes UK #32.

May Debut LP *It's Better To Travel*, produced by Paul O'Duffy, enters the UK chart at #1 and achieves UK platinum status.

June *Fooled By A Smile* makes UK #43.

Aug LP *It's Better To Travel* enters the US chart, on its way to #40.

Nov *Breakout* hits US #6, assisted by strong US MTV video rotation.

1988 Feb *Twilight World* reaches US #31.

Mar [2] Swing Out Sister is nominated at the 30th annual Grammy awards for *Breakout* as Best Pop Performance by a Duo or Group with Vocal category.

Sept The group starts recording a second LP.

THE SWINGING BLUE JEANS

Ray Ennis (lead guitar and vocals)
Ralph Ellis (rhythm guitar and vocals)
Les Braid (bass)
Norman Kuhlke (drums)

1958 May The group forms from the nucleus of two Liverpool, UK, skiffle groups who come first and second in a talent contest at Liverpool's Empire theater. The four who decide to regroup to play rock'n'roll rather than skiffle are Ennis (b. May 26, 1942, Liverpool), Ellis (b. Mar.8, 1942, Liverpool), Braid (b. Sept.15, 1941, Liverpool) and Kuhlke (b. June 17, 1942); they name themselves The Bluegenes.

1961 Mar [21] Holding a regular Tuesday night residency at Liverpool's Cavern club, The Bluegenes host the first appearance of a new group at the club, The Beatles°.

1962 They hold residencies at Liverpool's Mardi Gras and Downbeat clubs, becoming synonymous with these venues much as The Beatles° do with the Cavern.

1963 Changing name to more commercial-sounding Swinging Blue Jeans, the group is one of many from Liverpool to gain a recording contract in the wake of The Beatles'° early success, signing to EMI's HMV label.

July Debut single *It's Too Late Now* reaches UK #30.

Sept *Do You Know* fails to chart.

Dec The group has its own weekly 15-minute show, "Swingtime", on Radio Luxembourg, sponsored by a manufacturer of blue jeans, and appears in an episode of UK BBC TV's police drama series "Z Cars", as a Merseyside beat group.

1964 Jan A raucous revival of Chan Romero's *Hippy Hippy Shake* (a long-time stage favorite with the group) hits UK #2, behind The Dave Clark Five's° *Glad All Over*.

Apr A similarly-styled revival of Little Richard's° *Good Golly Miss Molly* reaches UK #11, while *Hippy Hippy Shake* is US debut, climbing to #24.

Apr [26] The group appears at the *New Musical Express* Poll Winners' concert, with The Beatles°, The Dave Clark Five° and others.

May [9] The group starts a UK tour supporting Chuck Berry°, with Carl Perkins° and The Animals°, at Finsbury Park Astoria, London.

June *Good Golly Miss Molly* makes US #43, and LP *Hippy Hippy Shake* reaches US #90.

July A more restrained cover of Betty Everett's *You're No Good* hits UK #3.

Aug *Promise You'll Tell Her*, a self-penned but undistinctive number, fails to chart. *You're No Good* peaks at US #97.

Oct The group's first UK LP, *Blue Jeans A-Swingin'*, is released (the earlier US LP having been a compilation of singles/EP tracks) but sells poorly.

Dec *It Isn't There* also fails.

1965 While continuing to work and tour regularly, the group's music on record loses the pulse of the UK music scene as it moves on from Merseybeat into a tougher R&B stance. Two singles, *Make Me Know You're Mine* and *Crazy 'Bout My Baby* (with a version of *Good Lovin'*, a million-seller for The Young Rascals° in 1966, on the B-side), are released, but without success.

1966 Feb A revival of Dionne Warwick's° *Don't Make Me Over* provides the group's first success for 18 months. It reaches UK #31, but The Blue Jeans will not chart again. Shortly after, Ellis leaves the group and is replaced by Terry Sylvester from The Escorts. Only weeks later, Braid also departs, and another ex-Escort, Mike Gregory, replaces him.

1967 Aug The group covers Herman's Hermits'° US hit *Don't Go Out Into The Rain*, but it fails.

1968 June In an effort to re-define the group's image, follow-up *What Have They Done To Hazel?* is credited to Ray Ennis and The Blue Jeans, and released on Columbia (EMI having closed HMV as a pop label). When this fails too, Sylvester leaves (to join The Hollies° 6 months later) and the group splits.

1973 Ennis re-forms the group with a new line-up, to capitalize on the nostalgic success of events like Herman's Hermits°/Gerry & The Pacemakers°/Searchers° "British Re-Invasion" tour of US. The group finds solid club and cabaret bookings, as well as playing on oldies tours in UK and Europe (particularly popular in Scandinavia). LP *Brand New And Faded*, plus a remake of *Hippy Hippy Shake* on independent Dart label fail to make much impression. (With a name still striking a chord with adult audiences who were teenagers in 1964, The Swinging Blue Jeans will continue to work as a successful club nostalgia act into the 1980s.)

T'PAU

Carol Decker (vocals)
Dean Howard (lead guitar)
Ronnie Rogers (guitar)
Michael Chetwood (keyboards)
Paul Jackson (bass)
Tim Burgess (drums)

1986 Decker (b. Sept.10, 1957, London, UK) and Rogers (b. Mar.13, 1959, Shrewsbury, UK), having met in 1982 when both played in Shrewsbury band The Lazers, have formed a songwriting partnership and are playing support gigs around UK with a small backing group, when they are spotted playing at London's Marquee club by Chris Cooke, ex-manager of Curiosity Killed The Cat°. He offers to manage the duo on the strength of the material and Decker's voice, but does not rate the other musicians, who are released. A demo tape is recorded, with Chetwood (b. Aug.26, 1954, Shrewsbury), Jackson (b. Aug.8, 1961) and Burgess (b. Oct.6, 1961, Shrewsbury) recruited for studio back-up; this secures a recording deal with small UK label Siren Records, marketed by Virgin. The session players agree to become full group members, and the name T'Pau is taken from the "Star Trek" TV series (the name of a Vulcan matriarch played by Celia Lovsky in the episode "Amok Time"). Roy Thomas Baker, ex-producer of Queen° and The Cars°, produces the band at his LA studio.

1987 Jan The group tours UK, supporting Nik Kershaw, as debut single *Heart And Soul* is released (initially without charting in UK).

June Second UK single *Intimate Strangers* also fails to chart, partly because attention is re-focusing on *Heart And Soul*, through its exposure in UK cinemas advertising Pepe clothing and as it climbs the US chart following extensive US airplay.

July With *Heart And Soul* in US top 30, the group plays a US club tour to promote it.

Aug *Heart And Soul* hits US #4, while debut LP *Bridge Of Spies* makes US #33.

Sept Repromoted after the band's US success, *Heart And Soul* hits UK #4. The band expands to a 6-piece, adding Howard on lead guitar (recruited after 18 players have been auditioned).

Oct T'Pau supports Bryan Adams° on a UK tour, including major dates at London's Wembley Arena.

Nov *China In Your Hand* tops the UK chart for 4 weeks, selling over a half million copies. LP *Bridge Of Spies* also hits UK #1 (after first entering the chart in Sept.).

Dec A first major headlining UK tour is extended with additional post-Christmas dates at London's Hammersmith Odeon, to cater for ticket demand.

1988 Feb [8] As *Valentine*, taken from the LP, hits UK #9 in the week which ends with St. Valentine's Day, the group plays *China In Your Hand* at the annual BPI awards ceremony, at London's Royal Albert Hall, broadcast live by UK BBC TV.

Apr A live version of *Sex Talk* (a re-titling of second single *Intimate Strangers*) reaches UK #23.

July *I Will Be With You* makes UK #14.

Oct Just over a year after release, LP *Bridge Of Spies* passes UK sales of 1,200,000, earning a BPI quadruple platinum award. Meanwhile, *Secret Garden* climbs the UK chart as a preface to the group's second LP.

TALK TALK

Mark Hollis (vocals, guitar and keyboards)
Paul Webb (bass)
Lee Harris (drums)

1977 Having left in his second year of studying child psychology at Sussex University and inspired by the current UK punk movement, Hollis (b. 1955, Tottenham, London, UK) begins writing songs, relocating in London. His brother Ed, manager of Eddie & The Hot Rods, secures Hollis studio time backed by Island Records, keen to hear a demo tape. The company signs Hollis' band, The Reaction.

1978 The Reaction releases only one single, *I Can't Resist*, but also records *Talk Talk* (which only appears on Beggars Banquet punk compilation LP *Streets*).

1979 The Reaction folds and Hollis is mainly supported by his wife, Flick.

1981 Ed Hollis brings in two musicians he is currently working with to record new demos with brother Mark: drummer Harris and bassist Webb, friends since schooldays and ex-various Southend R&B bands. They are joined by keyboardist Simon Bremner. Rehearsals on Hollis compositions go well and Talk Talk is formed. Hollis signs a publishing deal with Island Music, which provides 6 months' studio money. Keith Aspden leaves his job at Island Music to manage the group.

Oct UK BBC Radio 1 DJ David "Kid" Jensen attends Talk Talk's debut gig and invites them to record a radio session.

Nov Impressed by demos, EMI signs Talk Talk.

1982 Feb While debut LP is recorded, first single *Mirror Man* appears but fails to chart.

Apr *Talk Talk* single makes UK #52 as the band supports Duran Duran° on an ill-billed UK tour. Both groups are currently using EMI nominated Colin Thurston as LPs producer.

July As *Today* reaches UK #14, synthesizer-based debut LP *The Party's Over* with all songs penned or co-penned by Hollis peaks at UK #21. Talk Talk begins a US visit behind Elvis Costello° & The Attractions.

Oct *Talk Talk* stalls at US #75 as debut LP makes US #132.

Nov UK re-issued *Talk Talk* now rises to UK #23.

1983 Mar The only chart record of the year is *My Foolish Friend* at UK #57. In what will become a familiar band practice, Talk Talk retreats for an entire year to prepare a new LP. Bremner leaves, but his replacement becomes an invisible fourth member: Tim Friese-Green arrives to co-write with Hollis, play keyboards and produce the new songs.

1984 Jan *It's My Life* peaks at UK #46.

Feb LP *It's My Life* also peaks at UK #46, but repays its £250,000 cost by earning a gold disk in every other European territory.

Apr *Such A Shame* makes UK #49, as the band begins a European tour, with particularly popular dates in Italy and Germany.

May Helped by a Steve Thompson US remix, *It's My Life* rises to US #31, while parent LP will spend 5 months on chart peaking at US #42.

Aug *Dum Dum Girl* falters at UK #74. US follow-up *Such A Shame* stalls at US #49.

Oct A remix LP, *It's My Mix*, featuring six cuts from first two Thompson-mixed LPs, emerges from EMI Italy and becomes a UK import favorite.

1985 Jan Talk Talk plays San Remo, Italy, TV festival. Hollis and the band retreat again to work with Friese-Green on the next project.

1986 Jan *Life's What You Make It* is released and becomes their biggest hit in 4 years at UK #16, but falters at US #90.

Mar LP *The Colour Of Spring* hits UK #8, their most successful release eventually going gold, and will peak at US #83. Written and produced by Hollis and Friese-Green, it features Steve Winwood° playing organ on two tracks, and is another big European success.

Apr As *Living In Another World* makes UK #48, Talk Talk begins a major world tour.

May Ballad *Give It Up* peaks at UK #59, with no US follow-ups.

1987 While a further remix mini-LP emerges from EMI Greece, the band retreats to the studio, this time keener to avoid synthesizer-based music. Hollis is enthusiastic to experiment in more abstract form. Together with his wife, Flick and their two children, he also moves from London to rural Suffolk, while Webb and Harris relocate to North London.

1988 Sept Now diverted from EMI main label to UK Parlophone, fourth Talk Talk LP, *Spirit Of Eden*, 14 months in the making, is issued featuring six extended tracks. Confirming its less commercial style, EMI issues a statement that, according to Hollis' wishes, a single will not be extracted. The LP peaks at UK #19, as single *I Believe In You*, an anti-heroin song, is released but fails to chart, and a US release is pondered.

Oct Talk Talk announces it will not tour to promote the LP due to complexities of reproducing *Eden*'s sound, which includes a mini-orchestra and the Chelmsford Cathedral Choir.

TALKING HEADS

David Byrne (guitar and vocals)
Tina Weymouth (bass)
Jerry Harrison (keyboards)
Chris Frantz (drums)

1974 Sept Having first met in Sept. 1970 as freshmen students at the Rhode Island School of Design, Byrne (b. May 14, 1952, Dumbarton, Scotland, UK), Weymouth (b. Martina Weymouth, Nov.22, 1950, Coronado, Cal., US) and Frantz (b. Charlton Christopher Frantz, May 8, 1951, Fort Campbell, Ky., US), form a trio after Frantz and Weymouth graduate, and move to New York. (Byrne has earlier played in Baltimore in a duo called Bizadi, while Frantz has been in The Beans, who had a residency at New York's Electric Circus in 1970. Since their student days together, the two have also played (Oct.1973-June 1974) in The Artistics, a Rhode Island quintet playing mainly 1960s covers, plus Byrne/Franz/Weymouth composition *Psycho Killer*.)

Oct They begin rehearsing, living together in a Chrystie Street garret on Manhattan's Lower East Side, and obtain day jobs.

1975 May After rejecting names like The Portable Crushers and The Vague Dots, Talking Heads is found in an old issue of *TV Guide*.

June Following an audition for Hilly Kristal, owner of New York's CBGB's club, the group is given its first gig, supporting The Ramones°.

Oct Sire Records boss Seymour Stein sees the band and offers a recording deal, which is initially rejected.

Dec First TV appearance is in "Rock from CBGB's", on a Manhattan cable network.

1976 Apr Harrison (b. Jeremiah Harrison, Feb.21, 1949, Milwaukee, Wis., US) sees the band playing in Boston, Mass., and expresses his desire to join. (He has been a member of Jonathan Richman and The Modern Lovers° from 1970-74, and later studied at Harvard and worked in computers in Boston.)

July The group headlines CBGB's bicentennial concert.

Sept Harrison plays with them for the first time, at The Ocean Club in Lower Manhattan. He does not join immediately, having enrolled in an architecture course at Harvard.

TALKING HEADS *cont.*

Nov After considering recording offers from Arista, CBS, RCA and Beserkley Records, the trio signs with Stein at Sire.

Dec Debut single *Love Goes To Building On Fire*, produced by Tony Bongiovi, fails to chart.

1977 Jan The group plays a mini-tour of US North-East (plus Toronto, Canada), with Harrison joining in dates at Boston and Providence.

Feb Harrison, having completed his Harvard degree in architecture, becomes a full-time member. Work on an LP begins with Bongiovi.

Apr [24] The band begins its first European tour, supporting The Ramones° in Switzerland, France, Holland and UK.

May [14] Talking Heads play a night headlining on their own at London's Rock Garden, where they are seen by Brian Eno°, who develops what will be a lasting professional relationship with Byrne.

June [6] The group supports The Ramones° at London's Roundhouse, returning to US the next day.

June [18] Frantz and Weymouth marry in Maysville, Ky.

June [23] The group supports Bryan Ferry° at New York's The Bottom Line club.

July The debut LP is completed, despite disagreements between the group and producer Bongiovi.

Oct While the band is on a 38-day promotional tour of East Coast and Mid-West clubs and colleges, LP *Talking Heads '77* enters the US chart (for a 6-month stay), peaking at #97.

Dec [2/18] The band plays its first West Coast tour, taking in San Francisco and LA.

1978 Jan [9] Talking Heads return to Europe for a 27-day tour of France, Holland, Belgium, West Germany and UK, this time as headliners. Support acts include XTC° in Europe and Dire Straits° in UK.

Jan [31] The band makes its UK TV debut, on BBC 2's "The Old Grey Whistle Test".

Feb *Psycho Killer*, originally performed by Byrne and Frantz in The Artistics, is the group's first singles chart entry, at US #92. LP *Talking Heads '77* spends a week on UK chart at #60.

Mar The group records in the Bahamas, with Eno° producing.

May They make a 2-week tour of North-East US, before playing in Europe (including one UK show in London).

July LP *More Songs About Buildings And Food*, produced by Eno°, reaches UK #21, while the group is on tour in UK.

Nov LP *More Songs About Buildings And Food* makes US #29.

1979 Jan A revival of Al Green's° *Take Me To The River* reaches US #26.

June After completing a new LP, the band plays its first Pacific tour, taking in New Zealand, Australia, Japan and Hawaii.

Aug A US tour opens to promote the new LP, with a slot in the Dr. Pepper festival in New York's Central Park.

Sept LP *Fear Of Music*, again produced by Eno°, reaches US #21 and UK #33. The group plays the Edinburgh Festival in Scotland, alongside Van Morrison° and The Chieftains. (Touring continues through Europe, with 8 more UK dates, until the end of the year.)

Nov *Life During Wartime* makes US #80.

1980 Jan The group returns home after an exhausting tour, and all four take a rest from Talking Heads projects. Byrne records LP *My Life In The Bush Of Ghosts* with Eno.

July After completing a new LP, the band considers touring again, but feels extra musicians are needed to do justice to the new material. Harrison recruits several players with whom he has been working on other projects in New York and Philadelphia.

Aug [23] Talking Heads makes its live debut in the expanded line-up at the Heatwave festival in Toronto, Canada, along with Elvis Costello°, Rockpile, The Pretenders° and others. The augmenting musicians are Busta "Cherry" Jones (bass), Donette MacDonald (back-up vocals), Bernie Worrell (keyboards), Steven Scales (percussion) and Adrian Belew (guitar).

Aug [27] The 9-piece band plays again, at Wollman Rink in New York's Central Park. (This and the Canadian gig were designed to be the only showcases for the larger band, but Sire Records says it will support a tour.)

Nov LP *Remain In Light*, recorded in The Bahamas where the larger line-up has been playing live, peaks at US #19 and UK #33.

Dec [1/2] The group plays two shows in UK at London's Hammersmith Palais and Odeon, during a European tour. New Irish band U2° is support act.

1981 Mar *Once In A Lifetime* reaches UK #14, while Byrne and Eno's LP *My Life In The Bush Of Ghosts* reaches UK #29 and US #44.

May *Houses In Motion* stalls at UK #50. At the end of another major tour, the band members disperse to work on individual projects.

July Frantz and Weymouth's spin-off funk group The Tom Tom Club (including Weymouth's two sisters sharing vocals, plus Steve Scales on percussion, Alex Weir on guitar and Tyron Downie on keyboards) hits UK #7 with *Wordy Rappinghood*.

Sept [22] *The Catherine Wheel*, a ballet choreographed by Twyla Tharp and featuring Byrne's music, premieres at the Broadhurst Theater on Broadway, New York. (The ballet will be shown in Mar. 1983 on US Public Broadcasting TV.)

Oct The Tom Tom Club's *Genius Of Love* reaches UK #65, while the group's eponymous LP makes US #23 and UK #78.

Nov Harrison records solo LP *The Red And The Black*.

1982 Jan *Genius Of Love* by The Tom Tom Club tops the US disco chart. Meanwhile, Byrne's LP of music from *The Catherine Wheel* makes US #104.

Feb Byrne produces The B52's° LP *Mesopotamia*.

Apr The Tom Tom Club's *Genius Of Love* crosses over to make US #31.

May Double LP *The Name Of This Band Is Talking Heads*, a compilation of live performances and out-takes, reaches US #31 and UK #22. The group tours US and Europe as an 8-piece.

July [13] The band plays at UK's Wembley Arena, with The Tom Tom Club as support act.

Aug Tom Tom Club's *Under The Boardwalk* reaches UK #22.

Sept [3/5] Talking Heads take part, along with Fleetwood Mac°, The Police°, Jackson Browne°, and many others, in the 3-day US Festival in San Bernardino, Cal., financed by Apple Computers founder Steven Wozniak.

Nov [4] While the group is in Nassau, The Bahamas, recording at Compass Point studios, Weymouth gives birth to son Robert.

1983 Feb Byrne produces UK trio The Fun Boy Three's LP *Waiting*.

July Self-produced LP *Speaking In Tongues* makes US #15 and UK #21.

Aug Jonathan Demme-directed movie *Stop Making Sense*, a filmed account of Talking Heads on tour, premieres. It includes Byrne performing a version of *Psycho Killer* backed only by a cassette recorder rhythm track.

Sept The Tom Tom Club LP *Close To The Bone* reaches US #73.

Oct *Burning Down The House* hits US #9, the band's biggest hit single to date.

1984 Jan *This Must Be The Place (Naive Melody)* makes US #62 and UK #51.

Oct LP *Stop Making Sense*, recorded alongside the filming of a concert at Hollywood's Pantages Theater in Dec., reaches US #41 and UK #37, staying on chart for 81 weeks.

Nov A cover of The Staple Singers'° *Slippery People* stalls at UK #68.

1985 Jan Byrne stages a solo show, illustrating (with slides) a journey across US, titled "The Tourist Way of Knowledge", at the New York Public Theater.

July LP *Little Creatures* makes US #20 and hits UK #10. Harrison produces Milwaukee's Violent Femmes' LP *The Naked Leading The Blind*, while Frantz and Weymouth work on a third Tom Tom Club LP.

Sept *And She Was* begins a 5-month US chart stay, but climbs no higher than #54. Byrne releases solo LP *Music From The Knee Plays*, a series of musical vignettes linking longer scenes from Robert Wilson's epic opera *The Civil Wars*.

Nov *Road To Nowhere*, aided by an innovative video, brings Talking Heads its only UK top 10 success, hitting #6.

1986 Feb *And She Was* reaches UK #17.

Apr Some 5 years after giving the group its first UK chart success, *Once In A Lifetime* makes the US chart at #91, following its exposure in film *Down and Out in Beverly Hills* (although this single has the live version from LP *Stop Making Sense*).

July Movie *True Stories*, written and conceived by Byrne, premieres. A *True Stories* soundtrack from the film and a separate LP of songs from it played by Talking Heads, are both released.

Sept *Wild Wild Life* makes UK #43.

Oct LP *True Stories* reaches US #17 and hits UK #7.

Nov *Wild Wild Life* reaches US #25. Byrne/Robert Wilson's work *The Knee Plays* premieres in New York.

1988 Apr LP *Naked*, recorded in Paris with producer Steve Lillywhite (and assistance from guitarist Yves N'Djock and keyboardist Wally Badarou) and then completed in New York, makes US #19 and UK #3. The band disperses for a sabbatical to work on individual projects. Harrison's LP *The Casual Gods* (also the name given his backing group) appears almost immediately, but without charting.

Aug Byrne appears live with David Bowie° in London.

Sept The Tom Tom Club plays a 3-week stint at New York's CBGB's. Lou Reed° and Debbie Harry make special guest appearances. Harrison's *Rev It Up*, taken from his LP *Casual Gods*, creeps to UK #90.

Oct The Tom Tom Club's third LP *Boom Boom Chi Boom Boom*, produced by Frantz and Weymouth, is released (following the duo's production work earlier in the year with Bob Marley's° son Ziggy, which resulted in the latter's hit LP and single *Conscious Party* and *Tomorrow's People*). The group (with guitarist Mark Roule and keyboards player Gary Posner) plays a UK club tour.

JAMES TAYLOR

1963 Taylor (b. Mar.12, 1948, Boston, Mass., US), the second of five children in a musically talented family, having spent his childhood between Chapel Hill, N.C., and Milton Academy, Mass. meets Danny Kortchmar in Chilmark, Martha's Vineyard, Mass., where they win the local hootenanny contest.

1964/65 He joins older brother Alex's rock band, The Fabulous Corsairs, but shortly after commits himself to the McLean Psychiatric Hospital in Belmont, Mass., suffering from severe depression. During his 10-month stay there, he starts writing songs.

1966 July He moves to New York and joins Kortchmar's The Flying Machine. They play clubs in Greenwich Village before splitting the following spring.

1968 In an attempt to overcome heroin addiction, Taylor moves to London's Notting Hill. At Kortchmar's suggestion, Taylor takes a demo tape to Apple Records A&R man Peter Asher.

Nov Asher signs Taylor.

Dec Debut LP *James Taylor* is released. Unable to kick his addiction, Taylor returns to US, and enters Austin Riggs mental hospital in Stockbridge, Mass.

1969 July Taylor makes his live debut at LA's Troubadour, but his career is halted when he breaks both hands in a motorcycle accident.

Dec He signs to Warner Bros. and moves to California to work with Asher on a new LP. (Asher becomes his manager and will produce most of his future output.)

1970 Mar LP *Sweet Baby James* enters the US chart to hit #3 (and have a 2-year run).

Oct *Fire And Rain* makes US #3. LP *Sweet Baby James* is certified US gold. Debut LP *James Taylor* is released in US, reaching #62.

Nov *Fire And Rain* reaches UK #42. LP *Sweet Baby James* enters UK chart, where it stays for over a year and hits #7.

Dec *Carolina In My Mind* makes US #67.

1971 Feb Euphoria Records releases LP *James Taylor And The Original Flying Machine – 1967*, which reaches US #74.

Mar Taylor stars in Monte Hellman's movie *Two Lane Blacktop* with Dennis Hopper, Warren Oates and The Beach Boys'° Dennis Wilson. He begins a sell-out 27-city US tour as *Country Road* is released.

May LP *Mud Slide Slim And The Blue Horizon* enters US and UK charts to hit #2 and #4 respectively.

July Carole King°-penned *You've Got A Friend* tops the US chart for 1 week.

Aug *Country Road* climbs to US #37.

Oct *You've Got A Friend* hits UK #4.

Nov Reaching US #31, *Long Ago And Far Away* features harmony vocal contribution from Joni Mitchell°.

1972 Feb Taylor receives a Grammy award for the Best Male Pop Vocal Performance for *You've Got A Friend*, for which writer Carole King° receives the Song of the Year award.

Mar Taylor plays a benefit concert with many others for presidential candidate George McGovern at LA's Forum.

Nov [3] Taylor marries Carly Simon° in her Manhattan apartment. Instead of a honeymoon, Taylor plays New York's Radio City Music Hall that evening.

Dec LP *One Man Dog*, with contributions from Carole King°, Linda Ronstadt°, Carly Simon° and Taylor's brothers Alex and Hugh and sister Kate, hits US #4 and makes UK #27.

1973 Jan *Don't Let Me Be Lonely Tonight* reaches US #14.

Feb *One Man Parade* stalls at US #67.

1974 Mar Taylor duets with wife Carly Simon° on Inez & Charlie Foxx's hit *Mockingbird*, which hits US #5 and reaches UK #34.

Apr Taylor makes a 4-week US tour which ends with a show at the Nassau Coliseum, Long Island, N.Y.

June LP *Walking Man*, produced by David Spinozza, makes US #13.

July He starts a 3-week tour, accompanied by his band The Manhattan Dirt Riders and special guest Linda Ronstadt°.

1975 Apr A 4-week spring tour ends with 3 nights at New York's Carnegie Hall.

May LP *Gorilla*, produced by Russ Titelman and Lenny Waronker, hits US #6. Taken from it, a cover of Marvin Gaye's° 1965 smash *How Sweet It Is* hits US #5.

Nov He makes two short US tours while *Mexico* reaches US #49.

1976 May LP *In The Pocket*, again produced by Titelman and Waronker, peaks at US #16.

Sept *Shower The People* makes US #22.

Dec Aware that Taylor is to leave the company, Warner releases LP *Greatest Hits*. It reaches US #23 and goes platinum. Taylor signs to CBS/Columbia Records.

1977 July His cover of Jimmy Jones' 1960 smash *Handy Man*, and first CBS/Columbia LP, *JT*, from which it is extracted, are produced by Asher and both hit US #4. The LP goes platinum. Taylor begins a month's tour of Eastern US, with a band comprising David Sanborn on saxophone, Kortchmar on guitar, Leland Sklar on bass, Russ Kunkel on drums and Clarence McDonald on percussion.

Oct Taylor produces, plays guitar and sings on sister Kate's CBS/Columbia debut, a cover of Betty Everett's 1964 hit *It's In His Kiss*. It makes US #49.

Nov Taylor begins a brief tour of California and Hawaii.

Dec *Your Smiling Face* reaches US #20. Country singer George Jones releases a cover of *Bartender's Blues* by Taylor, who contributes backing vocals.

1978 Feb [23] Taylor wins his second Best Male Pop Vocal Performance Grammy, this time for *Handy Man*. Asher wins Producer of the Year award.

Mar Taylor joins Paul Simon° to sing on Garfunkel's° *What A Wonderful World*, which makes US #17. Taylor releases *Honey Don't Leave LA*, a disappointing US #61.

Apr Taylor and over forty performers petition President Carter to end US commitment to nuclear power.

May LP *Kate Taylor*, produced by brother James and on which he plays and sings, is released.

July CBS/Columbia issues the original Broadway cast LP *Working*, a musical based on the life of Studs Terkel. It contains three Taylor songs: *Millworker*, *Brother Trucker* (his own versions will appear on LP *Flag*) and *Un Mejor Dia Vendra*.

Sept A second duet with Carly Simon°, a version of The Everly Brothers'° 1958 hit *Devoted To You*, makes US #36.

1979 May LP *Flag* enters the US chart, to hit #10.

July Taken from it, *Up On The Roof*, a cover of The Drifters'° Goffin/King°-penned 1962 smash, hits US #28. Taylor begins a 6-week US summer tour, including 5 nights at LA'S Greek Theater.

Sept [19] Taylor performs in the first of five Musicians United for Safe Energy (MUSE) concerts at New York's Madison Square Garden. The shows are filmed and recorded under the *No Nukes* banner and feature Jackson Browne°, The Doobie Brothers° and Bruce Springsteen°.

Dec Live triple LP *No Nukes* is released, featuring Taylor solo on two songs and others with The Doobie Brothers°, Carly Simon° and John Hall. It makes US #19.

1980 July The *No Nukes* film documentary premieres in New York.

Aug Taylor sets off on a 23-date US tour.

Sept All-star LP *In Harmony*, recorded for children's TV show "Sesame Street", is released. The Taylor and Simon families feature on most of the tracks. *Jelly Man Kelly* is co-written with daughter Sarah. (The LP will win a Grammy for Best Children's Recording.)

1981 Mar Taylor is on a 5-week tour as LP *Dad Loves His Work* hits US #10.

Apr A 10-week tour opens at the Berkeley Greek Theater. The 47 shows will include eight sold-out shows at the New York Savoy.

May *Her Town Too*, a duet with J.D. Souther, reaches US #11.

June *Hard Times* makes US #72.

Sept Singing *Brother Trucker*, Taylor appears as a truck driver in US PBS-TV production of *Working*. Taylor opens a Far East tour in Osaka, Japan, before moving on to Australia.

Oct Taylor performs a sell-out show at the 12,000-seat NBC Arena in Honolulu, Hawaii.

1982 Feb A 6-week tour begins in Cleveland, Oh.

June [9] Taylor appears with Jackson Browne° and Linda Ronstadt° in a

JAMES TAYLOR *cont.*

"Peace Week" benefit concert at the Nassau Coliseum, Long Island, N.Y. (3 days later he will take part in another benefit in New York's Central Park in front of approximately 1 million people.)

1983 Aug Taylor tours US for 6 weeks.

1984 Apr He begins the first of three separate US tours lasting until Sept.

1985 Jan Taylor takes part in the "Rock in Rio" festival.

Dec Taylor self-produces for the first time, with help from engineer Frank Filipetti, LP *That's Why I'm Here*, with guests Joni Mitchell°, Don Henley, Graham Nash, David Sanborn, The Brecker Brothers and Deniece Williams°. The LP reaches US #34 as a cover of Buddy Holly's° *Everyday* makes US #61. He duets with country singer Ricky Skaggs on Christmas song *New Star Shining*, for his LP.

1987 Apr A 16-track UK-only compilation LP *Classic Songs* reaches UK #53.

1988 Mar LP *Never Die Young* makes US #25.

June Taylor makes his first UK appearances in years, before embarking on a major US tour during the summer. He produces his sister's first LP in 10 years and duets on *City Lights*.

THE TEARDROP EXPLODES

Julian Cope (vocals and bass)
Michael Finkler (guitar)
Paul Simpson (keyboards)
Gary Dwyer (drums)

1978 Oct Named after a *Marvel* comic caption, The Teardrop Explodes forms from remnants of several Liverpool, UK bands. Cope (b. Oct.21, 1957, Bargoed, Wales, UK), ex-The Crucial Three with Ian McCulloch (later of Echo & The Bunnymen°) and Pete Wylie (later of Wah!), moves on to The Mystery Girls and The Nova Mob before joining Finkler and Simpson in A Shallow Madness.

Nov The Teardrop Explodes plays its first concert at Liverpool's seminal venue Eric's.

1979 Feb The group's first recording, EP *Sleeping Gas*, is released by Zoo Records.

June Simpson leaves to study, and is replaced by Dave Balfe, ex-Lori & the Chameleons and co-owner of Zoo. Second single *Bouncing Babies* is released.

1980 Feb *Treason (It's Just A Story)*, written by Cope with McCulloch, is the group's third single.

July Alan Gill, ex-Dalek I Love You, replaces Finkler, who leaves to go to college. Zoo signs a distribution deal with Phonogram Records.

Aug The group signs to Phonogram subsidiary Mercury.

Oct First Mercury release *When I Dream* reaches UK #47. Balfe leaves and is replaced by Jeff Hammer. LP *Kilimanjaro* is released, reaching UK #24 during a 35-week chart stay.

1981 Feb *Reward* hits UK #6, featuring added trumpet from "Hurricane" Smith.

Mar LP *Kilimanjaro* is re-issued to include *Reward*.

Apr The group's third single *Treason (It's Just A Story)* is remixed, climbing to UK #18.

Aug *Ha, Ha, I'm Drowning* and *Poppies In The Field* are scheduled for release, but Cope objects and some 30,000 copies are withdrawn.

Sept *Passionate Friend* makes UK #25. Cope reorganizes the band as all but Dwyer depart. Alfie Agius, ex-Interview, briefly joins on bass while Troy Tate, ex-Shake, arrives on guitar. Balfe rejoins taking Hammer's place (who will later join The Stray Cats°). Cope becomes frontman, and switches from bass to rhythm guitar.

Nov Second LP *Wilder* makes UK #29, while *Colours Fly Away* reaches UK #54.

Dec Club Zoo opens in Liverpool with help from the band.

1982 Jan After Agius leaves, ex-Sincero Ron Francois joins on bass.

Mar Three Teardrop Explodes tracks are featured on the various artists compilation LP *To The Shores Of Lake Placid*.

June *Tiny Children* reaches UK #44.

July Francois and Tate leave, making it a trio of Cope, Dwyer and Balfe.

Nov Cope splits the band on its fourth anniversary. Balfe joins The Dumbfounding Two before forming his own management company and the Food label, while Dwyer remains temporarily with Cope.

1983 Mar The group's final single *You Disappear From View* peaks at UK #41.

Nov Remaining contracted to Mercury Records, Cope returns as a soloist on *Sunshine Playroom*, which charts briefly at UK #64.

1984 Mar First solo LP *World Shut Your Mouth* reaches UK #40.

Apr Taken from the LP, *The Greatness And Perfection Of Love* climbs to #52.

Sept He releases a one-off single, *Competition*, on independent UK label Bam Caruso, under the pseudonym Rabbi Joseph Gordan.

Nov Completing his contractual obligation to Mercury, LP *Fried* makes UK #87 for 1 week. Cope retreats, allegedly with a drug problem.

1985 Feb Belated release of Cope's *Sunspots* on Mercury fails to chart.

June Reissue of Teardrop's biggest hits *Reward* with *Treason* is released.

1986 Oct Cope signs to Island Records and releases *World Shut Your Mouth*, the same title as his earlier LP (although the song was not included on the LP). It reaches UK #19.

1987 Feb *Trampolene*, taken from his imminent new LP, reaches UK #31.

Mar Third solo LP *Saint Julian* (the title a reference to a tobacco brand, with allusions to his own cult status) peaks at UK #11.

Apr *Eve's Volcano (Covered In Sin)*, taken from the LP, makes UK #41. (Cope disappears into one of his customary quiet periods.)

1988 Sept As a prelude to a new LP, *Charlotte Anne* is released.

Oct [9] Cope embarks on a 3-week UK tour.

TEARS FOR FEARS

Curt Smith (vocals and bass)
Roland Orzabal (guitar and keyboards)

1980 Smith (b. June 24, 1961, Bath, Avon, UK) and Orzabal (b. Roland Orzabal de la Quintana, Aug.22, 1961, Portsmouth, UK), having first met at age 13 when Smith inducted guitar-playing Orzabal into his school band in Bath, both join Graduate, a 5-piece pop/ska band influenced by the current 2-Tone sound, also including Steve Buck, Andy Marsden and John Baker. Signed to Pye's Precision label in UK, and produced by Tony Hatch, Graduate has a near-hit with *Elvis Should Play Ska* and cuts LP *Acting My Age*, as well as three unsuccessful singles (though they gain some popularity in Spain).

1981 After Graduate splits, Smith and Orzabal stay together and record demos of two Orzabal songs – *Suffer The Children* and *Pale Shelter* at David Lord's studios in Bath, experimenting with synth-pop. The duo's name comes from Arthur Janov's book, *Prisoners of Pain*, concerned with Primal Therapy: confronting fears in order to eliminate them (or shedding "tears for fears"), which Orzabal has read in 1978. Demos of their first two songs interest Phonogram A&R man Dave Bates, who signs them to Mercury label.

Nov First single *Suffer Little Children* is released, without charting. The duo is joined by Manny Elias (drums) and Ian Stanley (keyboards) for live work.

1982 Mar *Pale Shelter* also fails to chart.

Nov *Mad World*, produced by Chris Hughes, hits UK #3, and the band plays its first UK tour as support to The Thompson Twins°.

Dec The band is named Most Promising New Act of 1982 in *Smash Hits* magazine poll.

1983 Feb *Change* hits UK #4.

Mar LP *The Hurting*, further inspired by Janov's theories and produced by Hughes, hits UK #1 in its second week on chart, and will remain charted for 65 weeks in UK.

May *Pale Shelter* is reissued in a re-mixed version included on the LP, and hits UK #5. Meanwhile, the band's US chart debut is with LP *The Hurting*, which peaks at US #73.

Aug *Change* is first US singles chart entry, climbing to #73.

Dec *The Way You Are* peaks at UK #24.

1984 Sept *Mother's Talk* makes UK #14.

Dec Anthemic *Shout* hits UK #4, becoming one of the year's top-sellers.

1985 Mar LP *Songs From The Big Chair*, also produced by Hughes, hits UK #2. Containing only eight tracks, it will eventually go triple-platinum in UK.

Apr *Everybody Wants To Rule The World* hits UK #2, behind USA For Africa's° *We Are The World*.

May The group ends a major headlining UK tour with a concert at London's Royal Albert Hall.

June *Everybody Wants To Rule The World*, written by Orzabal, Smith and Hughes, tops the US chart for 2 weeks, aided by a heavy-rotation video on MTV, and earns the group a gold disk.

July LP *Songs From The Big Chair* tops the US chart for 5 weeks, turning platinum with sales over a million while, in UK, *Head*

Over Heels, taken from the LP, makes UK #12.

Aug *Shout* becomes their second consecutive US chart-topping single (and million-seller), holding #1 for 3 weeks.

Sept The band's first two singles, *Suffer The Children* and *Pale Shelter*, are reissued in UK in their original forms, and chart at #52 and #73 respectively.

Oct *I Believe (A Soulful Re-Recording)*, a new version of a track from the LP, makes UK #23.

Nov *Head Over Heels* hits US #3.

1986 Feb *Everybody Wants To Rule The World* briefly re-charts in UK at #73.

May *Mother's Talk*, belatedly issued as a US single in a re-mixed version, makes #27.

June *Everybody Wants To Run The World*, a re-written version of *Rule The World* with lyrics relating to Sport Aid's "Race Against Time", is used as the theme tune for Sport Aid Week and the worldwide fun run, raising funds for African famine relief. It hits UK #5.

1988 June [11] Smith participates in Nelson Mandela's 70th Birthday Party concert at Wembley Stadium, UK, taking time off from recording a long-awaited new LP.

TELEVISION

Tom Verlaine (vocals and lead guitar)
Richard Lloyd (rhythm guitar)
Richard Hell (bass)
Billy Ficca (drums)

1971 Bassist/vocalist Hell (b. Richard Myers, Oct.2, 1949, Lexington, Ky., US) forms his first group, The Neon Boys, in New York with ex-boarding-school friend Verlaine (b. Thomas Miller, Dec.13, 1949, Mt. Morris, N.J., US), who renamed himself after the French poet, and drummer Billy Ficca. Neither The Neon Boys nor later trio Goo Goo lasts long.

1973 Dec New Jersey guitarist Lloyd, after seeing a Verlaine solo gig, suggests they form a group. Verlaine calls up Hell, Ficca returns from his blues band job and Television is formed.

1974 Mar Television makes its live debut at New York's Townhouse Theater, and picks up a sufficient following in the New York underground for Verlaine to convince the owner of CBGB's club to feature live bands, thus establishing an important base for the city's new wave of music. Verlaine plays guitar on Patti Smith's's° first single, *Hey Joe/Piss Factory*, and collaborates with Smith on a book of poetry, *The Night*.

1975 Brian Eno° produces demos for Island Records but the label does not sign them up. Hell leaves, replaced by Fred "Sonic" Smith. (Hell will later form The Heartbreakers with ex-New York Doll Johnny Thunders.) Television records *Little Johnny Jewel*, on its own Ork records (named after ex-manager William Terry Ork), selling enough copies to attract major record company attention.

1976 Hell leaves The Heartbreakers and forms The Voidoids with Marc Bell on drums and Ivan Julian and Robert Quine on guitars. Television's EP *Blank Generation*, released on Stiff in UK, brings the group UK attention. It signs to Elektra Records.

1977 Feb Debut LP *Marquee Moon*, a critical success but with poor sales in US, is enthusiastically received in UK and makes #28.

Apr *Marquee Moon* reaches UK #30.

May [21] The group opens a US tour supporting Blondie°.

Aug *Prove It* makes UK #25.

Sept Hell & The Voidoids LP *Blank Generation* is released on Sire Records. (Hell tours UK with The Clash°, and will sign to UK label Radar. He replaces Bell (who left to join The Ramones°) with Frank Mauro in The Voidoids.)

1978 Apr *Foxhole* makes UK #36.

May Television LP *Adventure* hits UK #7. Its US sales are promising but it fails to chart.

Aug The group splits. (Smith will play with Blondie°; Verlaine will go solo and later marry Patti Smith°.)

1979 Sept Verlaine releases solo LP *Tom Verlaine* for Elektra, without success.

Dec Lloyd releases LP *Alchemy*, but career efforts are hampered by drug-related problems.

1981 Oct Second Verlaine LP *Dreamtime*, released through Warner Bros., reaches US #177.

1982 May Verlaine releases *Words From The Front*. Hell releases *Destiny Street* on independent Red Star label with Fred Maher on drums.

Nov Hell makes his film debut in *Smithereens*. (He will semi-retire from music and work as a journalist.)

1984 Sept After a long silence, Verlaine releases LP *Cover*, on Virgin, and *Five Miles Of You* and *Let Go The Mansion*.

1985 Nov Lloyd, having overcome his drug problems, releases LP *Field Of Fire*. He plays well-received comeback gigs but soon returns to obscurity.

1987 Feb Phonogram revives the Fontana label for Verlaine's LP *Flash Light*. Three singles are released from the LP, but all fail to sell, leaving the LP with a disappointing 1-week chart stay at UK #99.

Mar *Cry Mercy Judge* fails to make UK top 75. Verlaine plays a well-received gig at London's Town & Country Club (but will slip out of the picture once more).

THE TEMPTATIONS

Eddie Kendricks (vocals)
Otis Williams (vocals)
Paul Williams (vocals)
Melvin Franklin (vocals)
David Ruffin (vocals)

1960 Initially known as The Elgins, the group forms from members of The Primes and The Distants, both based in Detroit, Mich., US. The Primes consisted of Kendricks (b. Dec.17, 1939, Birmingham, Ala., US), Paul Williams (b. July 2, 1939, Birmingham) and Cal Osborne, and were formed in Birmingham. The Distants included Franklin (b. David English, Oct.12, 1942, Montgomery, Ala.), Otis Williams (b. Otis Miles, Oct.30, 1949, Texarkana, Tex., US), Franklin's cousin Richard Street (b. Oct.5, 1942, Detroit), Albert Harrell and Eldridge Bryant. After The Distants have failed with *Come On* on Northern label, Street and Harrell leave (Street will later join The Temptations) and Kendricks and Williams are invited to join the remaining Distants to form The Elgins.

1961 The Elgins are signed by Berry Gordy Jr. to his new Motown subsidiary Miracle Records.

Aug The group is renamed The Temptations (a suggestion from Otis Williams) for their first single *Oh Mother Of Mine*.

1962 Bryant leaves after the failure of second single *I Want A Love I Can See* (now on Gordy label, where the group will remain throughout its tenure with Motown) and is replaced by Ruffin (b. Jan.18, 1941, Meridian, Miss., US). They begin working with writer/producer Smokey Robinson°.

1964 Apr Robinson's° song *The Way You Do The Things You Do*, with Kendricks on lead vocals, is The Temptations' first US hit, making #11.

June LP *Meet The Temptations* reaches US #95.

July *I'll Be In Trouble* makes US #33.

Sept [13] The group appears in Murray The K's Rock'n'Roll Extravaganza at New York's Fox Theater, Brooklyn, with Marvin Gaye°, Martha & The Vandellas°, The Supremes°, The Searchers° and The Ronettes°.

Oct *Girl (Why You Wanna Make Me Blue)*, produced by Norman Whitfield, peaks at US #26.

1965 Mar Ruffin takes over lead vocal on *My Girl*, written and produced by Robinson°. It tops the US chart for a week, selling a million, and makes The Temptations the first male Motown group to have a #1 hit. In UK, *My Girl* makes #43, as the group arrives in London to play on the Motown package tour with labelmates Martha & The Vandellas°, The Supremes° and Little Stevie Wonder°.

May *It's Growing*, another Robinson° song, reaches US #18 and UK #45. It is taken from LP *The Temptations Sing Smokey*, which makes US #35.

Aug *Since I Lost My Baby* makes US #17.

Nov *My Baby* climbs to US #13 while B-side *Don't Look Back* makes US #83.

Dec LP *Temptin' Temptations* reaches US #11.

1966 Apr Robinson's° final production for the group, *Get Ready*, makes US #29 and tops the R&B chart.

July Norman Whitfield and Brian Holland take over production for *Ain't Too Proud To Beg*, which reaches US #13 and again tops the R&B chart.

Aug *Ain't Too Proud To Beg* is their first UK top 30 hit, peaking at #21.

Sept LP *Gettin' Ready* makes US #12.

Oct *Beauty Is Only Skin Deep* hits US #3 and R&B #1, while also making UK #18.

Dec *(I Know) I'm Losing You* hits US #8 and R&B #1, while LP *Getting Ready* is the group's first UK chart LP, reaching #40.

1967 Jan *(I Know) I'm Losing You* makes UK #19.

THE TEMPTATIONS *cont.*

Feb Compilation LP *The Temptations' Greatest Hits* is the group's first US top 10 LP, peaking at #5. In UK, it makes #26.

June Whitfield is now the group's sole producer. *All I Need* hits US #8 and R&B #1 while LP *Temptations Live!* hits US #10.

July LP *Temptations Live!* makes UK #20.

Sept *You're My Everything* hits US #6 and UK #26, as LP *With A Lot O' Soul* hits US #7.

Nov *(Loneliness Made Me Realize) It's You That I Need* reaches US #14, while LP *With A Lot O' Soul* makes UK #19.

1968 Jan LP *The Temptations In A Mellow Mood*, which includes some Broadway standards, makes US #13.

Feb Written by Whitfield and Barrett Strong, ballad *I Wish It Would Rain*, taken from LP *Mellow Mood*, hits US #4 and R&B #1.

Mar *I Wish It Would Rain* makes UK #45. (The Whitfield/Strong writing team will provide the group with their next 13 hits.)

June *I Could Never Love Another (After Loving You)* reaches US #13, tops the R&B chart, and peaks at UK #47, while LP *The Temptations Wish It Would Rain* (which shows them on the sleeve in a desert wearing Foreign Legion uniforms) climbs to US #13.

July Ruffin, after pushing for a change of the group's sound to a deeper soul style, leaves and signs to Motown as a soloist. He is replaced by Dennis Edwards (b. Feb.3, 1943, Birmingham), who has sung with gospel group The Golden Wonders and with Motown's The Contours.

July [9] The Temptations make their first appearance without Ruffin at the Valley Forge Music Fair, Pa.

Aug *Please Return Your Love To Me* reaches US #26, and is the last single in the familiar Temptations style.

1969 Jan Whitfield's ideas for a different direction for the group first take shape on *Cloud Nine*, which has Edwards on lead vocal and adapts the "psychedelic soul" style pioneered by Sly & The Family Stone°. It hits US #6 and R&B #2 (and will win Motown's first Grammy award, as Best Group R&B Performance). Meanwhile, the group teams with The Supremes° on LP *Diana Ross & The Supremes Join The Temptations*, which hits US #2. Taken from this is a duetted revival of Madeleine Bell's hit *I'm Gonna Make You Love Me*, which hits US #2, behind Marvin Gaye's° *I Heard It Through The Grapevine*.

Feb LP *T.C.B.*, the soundtrack of a TV special of the same title featuring The Supremes° and The Temptations, tops the US chart for a week, while the group's own LP, *Live At The Copa*, makes US #15. It is the first LP to feature Edwards.

Mar *Runaway Child, Running Wild*, a similar sound to *Cloud Nine* with a further socially-conscious lyric, hits US #6 and R&B #1. *Get Ready*, not a hit on original UK release, is reissued and hits UK #10.

Apr A revival of The Miracles' *I'll Try Something New*, duetted with Ross° & The Supremes°, reaches US #25.

May LP *Cloud Nine* hits US #4.

May [10] The Temptations perform at The White House in Washington, D.C.

June *Don't Let The Joneses Get You Down*, again dealing with social issues, reaches US #20 and R&B #2.

Sept *Cloud Nine*, belatedly issued in UK (it was originally considered "too progressive"), reaches UK #15. The LP of the same title makes UK #32. Meanwhile, the TV soundtrack LP *The Temptations Show* peaks at US #24.

Oct *I Can't Get Next To You*, which has each member of the group singing lead in succession, tops the US chart for 2 weeks, selling over a million, while a revival of The Band's° *The Weight*, with Ross° & The Supremes°, makes US #46.

Dec LP *Puzzle People*, including *I Can't Get Next To You*, hits US #5, while LP *Together*, with Ross & The Supremes, makes US #28.

1970 Jan TV soundtrack LP *On Broadway*, featuring The Temptations and The Supremes° performing show tunes, reaches US #38.

Feb *Psychedelic Shack* hits US #7 and R&B #2 while *I Can't Get Next To You* reaches UK #13 and LP *Puzzle People* makes UK #20.

May LP *Psychedelic Shack* hits US #9.

June *Ball Of Confusion (That's What The World Is Today)* is another million-seller, hitting US #3 (and R&B #2).

July *Psychedelic Shack* makes UK #33 and the LP of the same title reaches UK #56.

Sept Live LP *The Temptations Live At London's Talk Of The Town*, recorded in UK, reaches US #21.

Oct *Ungena Za Ulimwengu (Unite The World)* continues the formula of recent hits with sound and lyric, but peaks at US #33. Whitfield decides on a change of pace for the next release. Meanwhile, *Ball Of Confusion* is the group's highest-placed UK single to date, hitting #7.

Nov Compilation LP *The Temptations' Greatest Hits, II* reaches US #15.

1971 Jan LP *The Temptations' Greatest Hits, II* makes UK #35.

Apr With Kendricks on lead vocal, *Just My Imagination (Running Away With Me)*, a slow ballad in the group's traditional style, tops both US pop and R&B charts for 2 weeks, becoming another million-seller.

June *Just My Imagination (Running Away With Me)* hits UK #8. Kendricks leaves for a solo career (like Ruffin, staying with Motown). Paul Williams is also forced to quit the group because of poor health (he has an alcoholism problem and a serious liver complaint). They are replaced by Damon Harris (b. July 3, 1950, Baltimore, Md.) and ex-The Distants' Street.

July LP *The Sky's The Limit*, including *Just My Imagination*, makes US #16.

Aug *It's Summer*, from the LP, peaks at US #51.

Dec *Superstar (Remember How You Got Where You Are)* reaches US #18.

1972 Feb *Superstar (Remember How You Got Where You Are* peaks at UK #32.

Mar LP *Solid Rock* makes both US and UK #24.

Apr *Take A Look Around*, from LP *Solid Rock*, reaches US #30 and UK #13.

July *Mother Nature* stalls at US #92.

Dec *Papa Was A Rollin' Stone*, edited from an 11-min.-plus LP track with Edwards on lead vocal, tops the US chart for a week, selling over a million. (The instrumental section of the song on the single's B-side will win a Grammy as Best R&B Instrumental.) LP *All Directions*, containing the full version, hits US #2.

1973 Feb *Papa Was A Rollin' Stone* peaks at UK #14, and LP *All Directions* at UK #19.

Apr *Masterpiece* hits US #7 and R&B #1, while the LP of the same title also hits US #7.

July *The Plastic Man*, from LP *Masterpiece*, peaks at US #40 as the LP reaches UK #28.

Aug [17] Paul Williams, in ill health since leaving the group in 1971, though he has continued to supervise the group's choreography, is found dead in his car. (In financial and matrimonial troubles as well as having serious health problems, he has shot himself in the head.)

Sept *Hey Girl (I Like Your Style)* makes UK #35.

Oct *Law Of The Land*, released as a single in UK but not US, reaches UK #41.

Nov Triple compilation LP *Anthology* makes US #65.

1974 Jan *Let Your Hair Down* reaches US #27, while parent LP *1990* makes US #19.

Feb *Masterpiece* wins a Grammy award as Best Group R&B Performance of 1973.

May *Heavenly* climbs to US #43.

July *You've Got My Soul On Fire* makes US #72, (and is the group's last single to be produced by Whitfield for nearly 10 years).

1975 Feb *Happy People*, with new producer Jeffrey Bowen, makes UK #40.

Mar LP *A Song For You* reaches US #13.

June *Shakey Ground* makes US #26.

Aug *Glasshouse* reaches US #37. Damon Harris leaves the group and is replaced by Glenn Leonard.

1976 Feb *Keep Holding On* makes US #54. It is taken from LP *House Party*, which peaks at US #40.

June LP *Wings Of Love* reaches US #29.

July *Up The Creek (Without A Paddle)* creeps to US #94.

Oct LP *The Temptations Do The Temptations*, on which the group cuts members' own compositions, reaches US #53.

1978 Jan Without Edwards, who leaves to go solo and is replaced by Louis Price, The Temptations sign a new deal with Atlantic. LP *Hear To Tempt You*, produced by Norman Harris and Brian Holland, and mostly written by Ron Tyson (who will join the group in 1983) creeps to US #113, but with no hit singles. The group, out of the public eye at a time when new disco acts abound on the charts, settles into steady work on the club and cabaret circuits.

Nov LP *Bare Back*, also on Atlantic, makes R&B #46 but fails to cross over.

1980 June Berry Gordy, having lured the Temptations back to Motown, writes and produces their first top 50 hit in 5 years. Edwards returns to sing the lead and *Power* makes US #43. The LP of the same title reaches US #45.

1981 Oct *Aiming At Your Heart* makes US #67, while parent LP *The Temptations* reaches US #119.

1982 June LP *Reunion* and its accompanying tour sees the brief return of Ruffin and Kendricks to the group. The LP reaches US #37, while extracted *Standing On The Top, Part 1* makes US #66 and UK #53. It is written and produced by, and features, Rick James°.

1983 New member Ron Tyson, a successful writer and producer, joins the group, which appears on US NBC-TV's Motown 25th anniversary show. A team-up on the show with The Four Tops°, during which they trade medleys of oldies, leads to a joint international tour.

Apr *Love On My Mind Tonight* peaks at US #88, while LP *Surface Thrills* makes US #159.

1984 May The group is reunited with Whitfield for *Sail Away*, which makes US #54. LP *Back To Basics* climbs to US #152.

Dec *Treat Her Like A Lady*, with new lead vocalist Ali Ollie Wodsin (who has replaced Edwards), reaches UK #12. Parent LP *Truly For You* makes US #55 and UK #75.

1985 Feb *Treat Her Like A Lady* peaks at US #48.

Oct Ruffin and Kendrick join Daryl Hall and John Oates° at the re-opening of New York's Apollo Theater. They perform The Temptations' classics *The Way You Do The Things You Do* and *My Girl*, which reach US #20 and UK #58 as a medley titled *A Nite At The Apollo Live!*. The LP from which the tracks come, *Live At The Apollo With David Ruffin And Eddie Kendrick*, makes US #21 and UK #32.

1986 Nov *Lady Soul* reaches US #47.

Nov [15] The Temptations appear on US TV show "227" performing *Get Ready* and *Lady Soul*.

1987 Aug *Papa Was A Rollin' Stone* is given an updated remix for the UK dance market, and climbs to UK #31.

Nov With Edwards back in the line-up, LP *Together Again* stalls at US #112.

Dec Signed as a duo to RCA, Ruffin and Kendricks issue LP *Ruffin And Kendricks*, which makes US R&B #60.

1988 Feb Nearing the end of their third decade, The Temptations release *Look What You Started*, which makes UK #63.

10CC

Graham Gouldman (vocals and guitar)
Eric Stewart (vocals and guitar)
Lol Creme (vocals and guitar)
Kevin Godley (vocals and drums)

1963 All four are members of groups in Manchester's booming beat scene. Creme (b. Lawrence Creme, Sept.9, 1947, Manchester, UK) and Gouldman (b. May 10, 1945, Manchester) rehearse reguarly as members of The Sabres and The Whirlwinds respectively. Brian Franks, a member of The Sabres introduces his cousin Godley (b. Oct.7, 1945, Manchester) to Creme, who immediately strikes up a rapport. Stewart (b. Jan.20, 1945, Manchester) is a member of Jerry Lee & The Staggerlees.

1964 Apr Stewart joins Wayne Fontana & The Mindbenders° who enjoy success in UK and US with major hits including *The Game Of Love* and *Um Um Um Um Um Um*. Godley and Creme begin studying graphic design at art college.

June Gouldman's group signs to HMV label releasing an unsuccessful cover of Buddy Holly's° *Look At Me* with Creme-penned B-side *Baby Not Like Me*.

1965 Feb Gouldman forms The Mockingbirds, with Godley on drums. They sign to Columbia label and begin a regular spot as warm-up band for UK BBC TV program "Top of the Pops", transmitted from Manchester. Gouldman's first song for the group *For Your Love*, written during his lunchbreak while working at a gentlemen's outfitters, Bargains Unlimited in Salford, is rejected by Columbia, but becomes a major hit for The Yardbirds°. The Mockingbirds release a clutch of singles which all flop but for The Yardbirds Gouldman writes *Heart Full Of Soul* and *Evil Hearted You*. The Hollies° hit with his *Bus Stop* and *Look Through Any Window*, and Herman's Hermits° enjoy a string of Gouldman-penned songs including *No Milk Today*.

Oct The Mindbenders split from Wayne Fontana° and have a major hit with *A Groovy Kind Of Love*.

1966 Feb Gouldman attempts a solo career again, signing to Decca for *Stop Or Honey I'll Be Gone*, but without success.

Nov Gouldman pens *Pamela Pamela* for Wayne Fontana° based on an idea for a stage production by Godley & Creme°.

1967 Mar Another Gouldman single *Bony Maronie At The Hop* by studio aggregate Manchester Mob fails.

Apr Gouldman writes a track for The Mindbenders' LP *With Woman In Mind* called *Schoolgirl*, which is released as a single but is banned by UK BBC on grounds of suggestive lyrics.

1968 Feb Gouldman signs to RCA but three singles and an LP *The Graham Gouldman Thing*, co-produced by Gouldman and John Paul Jones (later of Led Zeppelin°) all fail to chart.

Mar Gouldman steps in as a temporary replacement for Bob Lang in The Mindbenders.

Aug He writes the group's last single *Uncle Joe, The Ice Cream Man*.

Nov After The Mindbenders split, Stewart and Gouldman invest in Inter-City recording studio in Manchester, renamed Strawberry by Stewart, from The Beatles° song *Strawberry Fields Forever*.

1969 Sept Godley and Creme having been working as designers for Pan Books on cut-out books based around films such as *The Railway Children* and *The Charge of the Light Brigade*, sign a contract with ex-Yardbirds° manager Giorgio Gomelsky's short-lived Marmlade label and release *I'm Beside Myself*, billed as Frabjoy and Runcible, with Gouldman and Stewart playing on the session, bringing together the future members of 10cc for the first time.

Oct Gouldman spends time in New York as a staff writer for Kasenatz-Katz production team which specializes in creating "bubblegum" music for teenagers. Gouldman writes *Sausalito (Is The Place To Go)* as Ohio Express and sings lead vocal on it. He also writes *Have You Ever Been To Georgia* which is a hit for a number of artists.

Nov Kasenatz-Katz books Strawberry Studios for 3 months as UK branch of its operation. Gouldman and Stewart call in Godley and Creme° to help on the sessions and the fledgling members of 10cc embark on a marathon bout of writing, producing and playing on records which are released worldwide under different names. Godley and Creme pen a minor US hit (under the name Crazy Elephant) *There Ain't No Umbopo*, while Gouldman writes and sings on a million-seller in France for Freddie & The Dreamers°, *Susan's Tuba*.

1970 Aug With money from Kasenatz-Katz work, the group re-equips Strawberry Studios and writes heavy rhythmic African-styled *Neanderthal Man*, to test out the new equipment. When Dick Leahy of Philips Records hears the test tape he offers the group £500 as an advance. The disk sells over 2 million copies worldwide, hitting UK #2 and US #22, under the group name Hotlegs. Two further singles and an LP *Thinks: School Stinks* fail and a spot on a Moody Blues° tour is cancelled when The Moody Blues' John Lodge goes down with a viral infection.

1971 The four concentrate on writing, producing and playing on a variety of sessions at Strawberry Studios (including records by soccer teams Manchester City and Leeds United, John Paul Jones' hit *The Man From Nazareth*, and writing the material for LP *Space Hymns* by a central heating salesman from Sheffield called Ramases, who believes he is a reincarnation of an Egyptian god). Their most successful venture is in reviving Neil Sedaka's° career with work on his LPs *Solitaire* and *The Tra La La Days Are Over* and singles *That's When The Music Takes Me*, *Standing On The Inside*, *Dimbo Man* and *Our Last Song Together*.

1972 They record demos of *Donna* and *Waterfall* and Jonathan King°, an old friend of Stewart's, signs them to his UK label. He names them 10cc (after the average male sperm ejaculation 9cc, adding 1cc to indicate they are above average).

Oct *Donna*, a Godley & Creme° pastiche of 1950s US pop, hits UK #2. The group makes its UK TV "Top of the Pops" debut.

Nov Follow-up *Johnny Don't Do It*, another 1950s pastiche, but a teen death song, sinks without trace.

1973 June The group's first UK #1 hit is with jail-riot song *Rubber Bullets*, despite little radio play because of the British Army's controversial use of rubber bullets in Northern Ireland.

Aug [26] 10cc makes its stage debut at the Douglas Palace Lido, Isle of Man, at the beginning of a UK tour.

Sept *The Dean And I* hits UK #10 as parent LP *10cc* makes UK #36.

Oct *Rubber Bullets* is the group's US chart debut, at #73.

1974 Feb [21] The group begins its first US tour at Club Richard, Atlanta, Ga.

Mar [14] Godley is taken ill and the tour is cancelled.

10CC cont.

May [28] A rescheduled US tour begins.
June LP *Sheet Music*, continuing the group's innovative writing style with subject matter ranging from a talking bomb to voodoo, hits UK #9 and makes US #81.
July *Wall Street Shuffle* hits UK #10.
Aug [23] 10cc plays UK's Reading Festival.
Sept [1] The group begins a UK tour.
Oct *Silly Love* makes UK #24.
1975 Feb The group signs to Phonogram in a deal allegedly worth more than $1 million.
Mar LP *The Original Soundtrack* hits UK #4 and US #15.
Mar [5] The group embarks on another UK tour.
May *Life Is A Minestrone* hits UK #7.
June *I'm Not In Love* hits UK #1 and US #2, where it will stay for 3 weeks, behind three different #1s. (The group was reticent about releasing this plaintive Stewart-sung ballad, with a multiplicity of overdubbed backing vocals, but UK airplay forces its release and radio listeners will consistently vote it into all-time top 10 lists in coming years.) LP *10cc – The Greatest Hits* hits UK #9 and climbs to US #161.
July The group appears at Cardiff Castle supported by Steeleye Span and Thin Lizzy°.
Oct 10cc begins a third US tour, and appears on The Moody Blues'° Justin Hayward and John Lodge's *Blue Guitar*.
1976 Jan *Art For Art's Sake* hits UK #5, but stalls at US #83.
Feb LP *How Dare You?* hits UK #5 and makes US #47.
Apr *I'm Mandy Fly Me* hits UK #6 and reaches US #60.
Aug [21] The group appears at UK's Knebworth Festival, Herts., with The Rolling Stones°.
Oct Godley and Creme° announce they are quitting the group to develop a new musical instrument – the "Gizmo", a guitar attachment which can hold notes and create orchestral sounds for a long period. They plan to record a single showcasing its effect, but recording leads to a triple LP *Consequences* and a long-term duo career. Gouldman and Stewart carry on with 10cc and open Strawberry South Studio in a former cinema in Dorking, Surrey. They become a trio when drummer Paul Burgess is invited to join full time after working on previous tours.
1977 Jan *Things We Do For Love* hits UK #6.
Apr *Things We Do For Love* hits US #5.
May *Good Morning Judge* hits UK #5 as parent LP *Deceptive Bands*, with Stewart and Gouldman playing all instruments, hits UK #3 and makes US #31. The group begins a UK tour, adding Stuart Tosh on drums, Rick Fenn on guitar and Tony O'Malley on keyboards.
June *People In Love* makes US #40.
Sept *Good Morning Judge* reaches US #69.
Dec Double live LP *Live And Let Live*, from the May tour, highlighting LP *Deceptive Bends* and of Stewart/Gouldman compositions from the classic 10cc era, reaches UK #14 and US #146.
1978 Mar Duncan Mackay joins on keyboards.
Sept *Dreadlock Holiday* hits UK #1. The reggae song is inspired by Justin Hayward's experience on holiday in the Caribbean. LP *Bloody Tourists* hits UK #3 and makes US #69.
Nov *Dreadlock Holiday* makes US #44.
1979 Feb *For You And I*, from John Travolta°/Lily Tomlin film *Moment by Moment*, stalls at US #85.
July Gouldman makes UK #52 with the title theme to Farrah Fawcett film *Sunburn*.
Oct LP *Greatest Hits 1972-1978* hits UK #5, but stalls at US #188.
1980 Apr LP *Look Hear?* makes UK #35 and US #180. Gouldman releases music from the animated feature LP *Animalympics* (and will later produce The Ramones° and Gilbert O'Sullivan°.) Stewart writes music for French film *Girls* and produces Sad Café.
1982 Apr Stewart teams with Paul McCartney° to play on the latter's LP *Tug Of War*, and appears in the group line-up for the video of McCartney's hit *Take It Away*.
Aug *Run Away* is the group's final chart single at UK #50. (It is the only one to chart from 11 releases since *Dreadlock Holiday*.)
1983 Oct LP *Windows In The Jungle* makes UK #70, after which the group splits. (Gouldman will have some success as one half of Wax, with Andrew Gold°.)
1987 Sept 10cc hits are included on LP *The Changing Faces Of 10cc And Godley And Creme* which hits UK #4.

10,000 MANIACS

Natalie Merchant (voices)
Robert Buck (guitars)
John Lombardo (guitars)
Steven Gustafson (bass)
Jerry Augustyniak (drums)
Dennis Drew (keyboards)

1981 The band, taking its name from a B-movie, forms in Jamestown, N.Y., US, around Merchant and Lombardo. They begin performing local gigs, playing mostly cover versions of late 1970s UK new wave acts including Joy Division° and Gang of Four.
1982 Extended to a 6-piece, 10,000 Maniacs add folk and country influences. They release a 5-track EP, *Human Conflict Number 5*, on their own Christian Burial Records, which sells mainly at their concerts.
1983 Commuting between London and New York, the band releases debut LP *Secrets Of The I Ching*, again on its own US label and distributed throughout a US East Coast tour. The LP is licensed for independent UK distribution and tops the UK independent chart.
1984 The band signs a worldwide recording deal with Elektra.
1985 LP *The Wishing Chair* is released. Recorded at Livingstone studios in London, it is produced by Joe Boyd. Comprised entirely of songs written by Merchant and Lombardo, it receives rave critical reviews in US and UK, but fails to chart.
1986 July Founding member Lombardo quits, and the four remaining males will construct music around Merchant's lyrics.
1987 June 10,000 Maniacs tour behind R.E.M.° in US (Merchant is romantically involved with R.E.M.'s Michael Stripe).
July [29/30] The band plays UK's Cambridge Folk Festival.
Aug LP *In My Tribe*, produced by Peter Asher, is released and is again highly rated by critics. It tops the US college charts, becoming a student favorite (and will climb to US #51 in Sept. 1988).
Nov 10,000 Maniacs begin a successful UK tour.
1988 Feb Merchant performs a solo showcase at London's Donmar Warehouse, preceding a similar low-key set by Tracy Chapman°.
June *Like The Weather* reaches US #68.
Oct *What's The Matter Here* makes US #82.

TEN YEARS AFTER

Alvin Lee (guitar and vocals)
Leo Lyons (bass)
Chick Churchill (keyboards)
Ric Lee (drums)

1965 Aug The group forms in Nottingham, UK, as The Jaybirds, when Alvin Lee (b. Dec.19, 1944, Nottingham) and Lyons (b. Nov.30, 1943, Beds., UK), who have both been in a trio of the same name which has played clubs in Hamburg, West Germany, team with Ric Lee (b. Oct.20, 1945, Staffs., UK) from Nottingham group The Mansfields. They play hard, guitar-based R&B around the north of England club circuit.
1966 The band moves to London, playing a 6-week stint as the stage band for play *Saturday Night and Sunday Morning*, then backing The Ivy League on tour.
Nov They contact Chris Wright of Chrysalis agency with a view to management, and he takes them on. Churchill (b. Jan.2, 1949) joins, and the band changes its name to Ten Years After (following a single Marquee gig as The Blues Yard).
1967 Oct Signed via Chrysalis to Decca, the band's debut LP *Ten Years After* is released on new "progressive" Deram label, without charting and no single accompanies it. (The band will release very few singles, particularly in UK, during its career, concentrating on LPs.)
1968 Oct Live LP *Undead* is the band's chart debut, reaching UK #26 and US #115.
1969 Mar LP *Stonedhenge* hits UK #6 and peaks at US #61.
July [3] Ten Years After participates in the Newport Jazz Festival at Newport, R.I., US – the only occasion that rock bands play at the festival.
Aug [15] The band plays the Woodstock Festival in US, where Alvin Lee's lightning guitar technique proves a festival-stopper. The success of the act here has much to do with Ten Years After's subsequent US acceptance (the band will play much of its 8 months per year touring US). Lee's 11-min. guitar trip on *I'm Going Home* is filmed for *Woodstock* movie.
Oct *Ssssh* hits UK #4 and US #20.

1970 May LP *Cricklewood Green* hits UK #4 (the band's most successful UK LP, staying charted for 27 weeks) and US #14, while *Love Like A Man*, extracted from it, peaks at US #98.
Aug *Love Like A Man* is the band's only UK singles chart entry, hitting #10. It couples the studio LP cut of the song with a long B-side live version which plays at 33rpm.
1971 Jan LP *Watt* hits UK #5 (the band's last big-selling UK LP) and makes US #21.
Nov *I'd Love To Change The World* reaches US #40. It is taken from LP *A Space In Time*, which introduces electronics as a counter to the guitar, and is the band's biggest-selling US LP, reaching #17 and earning a gold disk for a half million sales. In UK, where the band's chart presence is fading, it peaks at #36. The LP is also the band's first released via a new deal with CBS/Columbia in US and Chrysalis in UK.
1972 Jan *Baby Won't You Let Me Rock'n'Roll You* reaches US #61.
May Compilation LP *Alvin Lee And Company*, rounding up early tracks, is released by Deram in US and makes #55.
Oct LP *Rock'n'Roll To The World* makes UK #27 and US #43.
Dec *Choo Choo Mama* stalls at US #89, ending the band's short run of hit singles.
1973 July Double live LP *Recorded Live* makes UK #36 and US #39.
1974 Feb Lee records LP *On The Road To Freedom* with US gospel singer Mylon LeFevre, plus guest players Steve Winwood°, Jim Capaldi, George Harrison° and Ron Wood. It reaches US #138. Churchill releases solo LP *You And Me*, which does not chart.
Mar After most of a decade on the road, including 28 lucrative but gruelling US tours, Lee decides that Ten Years After has run its useful course, and it breaks up.
Mar [22] The band plays its final UK concert, at London's Rainbow.
June The band's last LP, *Positive Vibrations*, reaches US #81 but fails to chart in UK.
Sept Lee forms Alvin Lee & Co., initially a one-off band to play the gig which is recorded as LP *In Flight*, and then an augmented unit to tour promoting it.
1975 Feb Double live LP *Alvin Lee & Co: In Flight* reaches US #65.
July Ten Years After regroups for a one-off farewell US tour (40 dates through July and Aug.).
Sept Lee's solo LP *Pump Iron!* makes US #131.
1976 Mar Lee forms another version of Alvin Lee & Co. for a UK and European tour, and to record tracks for an LP (which is not released).
1978 Feb After an inactive year, Lee forms 3-piece Ten Years Later, with Tom Compton on drums and Mick Hawkesworth on bass, and signs to RSO Records.
July Ten Years Later LP *Rocket Fuel* makes US #115.
1979 June LP *Ride On* by Ten Years Later reaches US #158.
1980 May Ten Years Later splits, but Lee is only off the road for a few weeks before he puts together The Alvin Lee Band with Steve Gould (guitar), Mickey Feat (bass) and Tom Compton (drums). The band tours and cuts LP *Freefall* for Avatar Records. (He will continue to tour with short-lived backing groups throughout the early-mid 80s and will record a second non-charting LP for Avatar, *Rx5*.)
1986 Lee cuts LP *Detroit Diesel* with Lyons from Ten Years After, and George Harrison°.
1988 No Speak Records negotiates to sign Lee to record as a New Age artist.

THE THE

1980 East Londoner Matt Johnson, having played in bands since age 11, forms new band The The. He writes, produces, arranges and sings the group's debut single, *Controversial Subject* and it becomes clear that this is a one-man band. He releases LP *Burning Blue Soul*, under his own name. (All future projects will be released as by The The.) LP *The Pornography Of Despair* is recorded but not released.
1982 Dec Johnson signs to CBS/Epic Records which releases *Uncertain Smile*, featuring Squeeze° member Jools Holland on piano. It reaches UK #68.
1983 Feb Follow-up *Perfect* fails to chart.
Nov LP *Soul Mining* makes UK #27, after *This Is The Day* reaches UK #70.
1984 June 4AD Records re-releases his 1980 LP as *Burning Blue Soul*.
1986 When *Sweet Bird Of Truth* is due for release, CBS/Columbia fails to promote it (the song's story of a US fighter pilot lost in Arab territory is close to reality). CBS/Columbia is also advised to take down the US flag at its London offices for fear of a Libyan bomb attack. Further problems with a censored sleeve hinder its chart progress.
July *Heartland* is also controversial, but is Johnson's biggest hit, reaching UK #29.
Sept *Infected* is released as an LP and full-length video, after 2½ years in the making. Johnson used sixty-two musicians, three producers and five video directors filming in four different countries. With extensive promotion, the LP reaches UK #14 and *Infected* single makes UK #48. Johnson announces he is retreating from the forefront once more.
1987 Jan *Slow Train To Dawn* fails to chart.

THEM

Van Morrison (vocals)
Billy Harrison (guitar)
Jackie McCauley (piano)
Alan Henderson (bass)
Patrick McCauley (drums)

1963 The group is formed in Belfast, Northern Ireland, with Morrison° (b. George Ivan, Aug.31, 1945), Harrison, Henderson (b. Nov.26, 1944), Eric Wrixen (piano) and Ronnie Mellings (drums). One of the first R&B/beat groups in Northern Ireland (which is dominated by conservative "showbands"), it builds its reputation as a strong live act during a residency in the R&B Club at Belfast's Maritime Hotel.
1964 July Wrixen leaves to join The Wheels and Mellings quits to become a milkman. McCauley brothers Jackie (piano) and Pat (drums) replace them. The group moves to London and signs to Decca.
Sept Debut single *Don't Start Crying Now* fails to chart, but sells well in Belfast.
1965 Feb Aided by "Ready Steady Go" TV appearances, *Baby Please Don't Go*, a sharp R&B version of a blues standard, hits UK #8. Like most later recordings, it is made without much contribution from the band's own players; the producers Tommy Scott and Bert Berns back Morrison° on vocals with session men like Jimmy Page on guitar and Peter Bardens on piano. The B-side, little-played in UK at the time, is Morrison-penned *Gloria*, a riff-driven group favorite which frequently develops live into a 20-minute jam. It becomes an anthem to the US emerging garage band generation: basic repertoire alongside *Louie Louie*. (It will be Them's most enduring number and one of the most influential records of the 60s, despite lack of early chart success.)
Apr *Here Comes The Night*, written and produced by Berns (writer of *Twist And Shout* and *Hang On Sloopy*), hits UK #2. It is Them's biggest, but last, UK success. (Berns, an American working in London, cut *Here Comes The Night* the previous Nov. with Lulu°. It made UK #50. He will work extensively with Them, mainly because he is impressed with Morrison° as a vocalist. After this hit, he will return to US to launch his own Bang label, bringing success to The Strangeloves, The McCoys° and many others.) LP *(The Angry Young) Them* is released in UK, but does not chart. The group heard is mostly Morrison° and session men, which causes the disillusioned McCauley brothers to quit and form their own similar R&B band, The Belfast Gypsies. Harrison leaves to work for the Irish post office. Bardens joins for a while, and John Wilson (b. Nov.6, 1947) comes in on drums.
Apr [11] The band plays in the *New Musical Express* Poll Winners Concert at Wembley Empire Pool, UK. Morrison's° distinctive vocals are the focus of Them's live appeal, which otherwise suffers from a lack of visual image due to the ever-changing line-up.
May *Gloria* charts for 1 week at US #93, selling mostly in Cal. where it hits top 10 in some West Coast cities.
June Morrison°-penned *One More Time* fails to chart in UK.
July *Here Comes The Night* reaches US #24.
Aug *(It Won't Hurt) Half As Much*, written by Berns, is another UK chart failure.
Sept LP *Them* reaches US #54.
Dec *Mystic Eyes*, a Morrison-penned, harmonica-led rave-up from the LP (and another just-failed UK single), makes US #33. The group line-up has now semi-stabilized as: Morrison, Henderson, Wilson, Jim Armstrong (b. July 24, 1944) on guitar, and Ray Elliott (b. Sept.13, 1943) on piano and saxophone. The group's second LP credits this quintet.
1966 Jan LP *Them Again*, mixing R&B standards with some originals, fails

THEM *cont.*

to chart in UK. Wilson leaves and is replaced on drums by Terry Noone.

Apr The band (with Dave Harvey on drums) tours US, playing mainly Cal. dates, including the Fillmore in San Francisco, and The Troubadour in LA.

May Aided by the group's live presence, *Gloria* climbs to US #71, but a US cover by The Shadows of Knight hits US #10. LP *Them Again* reaches US #138.

June Them's return to UK coincides with the release on Decca of a cover of Paul Simon's° *Richard Cory*. It fails to sell, and the group splits. Morrison° returns to Belfast. (He will play some gigs with friends including Eric Bell, later of Thin Lizzy°, before flying to US at Berns' invitation to sign to Berns' Bang label and begin a successful solo career. Them will re-group in LA in 1967, in its final line-up but with Belfast vocalist Ken McDowell in Morrison's place. Two US LPs on Tower label will appear in 1968 without charting, and the group will continue until the early 70s, but without further success.)

1972 Aug Double LP *Them Featuring Van Morrison*, a compilation of Decca material, reaches US #154.

THIN LIZZY

Phil Lynott (vocals and bass)
Eric Bell (guitar)
Brian Downey (drums)

1969 The group is formed in Dublin, Ireland, by Lynott (b. Aug.20, 1951, Dublin, of Brazilian and Irish parents) and Downey (b. Jan.27, 1951, Dublin), who have been at school together and have played variously or together in Skid Row, Sugar Shack and Orphanage (whose version of *Morning Dew* was a success in Ireland). They recruit Bell (b. Sept.3, 1947, Belfast, Northern Ireland, UK), formerly briefly with Them°, whom they have met while in Orphanage, and begin to play gigs around Ireland.

1970 Nov Alerted by the group's Irish reputation as a strong live act, Decca's A&R man checks it out, and signs Thin Lizzy to the label. The trio moves to London to play club gigs, but the UK debut at The Speakeasy in London is not a success.

1971 Apr Debut LP *Thin Lizzy* is released by Decca, and fails to chart. The trio tours with Arrival and Worth, but dates are poorly attended.

1972 Mar LP *Tales From A Blue Orphanage* also fails.

1973 Feb *Whiskey In The Jar*, a guitar riff-driven rock version of a folk tune, is a surprise UK hit, at #6.

May *Randolph's Tango* fails to chart.

Sept LP *Vagabonds Of The Western World* (which does not include *Whiskey In The Jar*, which the band disowns) has a heavier rock stance but still fails.

1974 Jan Bell leaves to return to Ireland. Gary Moore, ex-Skid Row with Lynott, is recruited as guitar replacement. (He will only stay for 4 months before leaving to join Jon Hiseman's Colosseum.)

May Guitarists Andy Gee (ex-Steve Ellis' band) and John Cann (ex-Bullitt) are brought in for an already-contracted tour of West Germany.

June Full-time guitarists Brian Robertson (b. Sept.12, 1956, Glasgow, Scotland, UK) and Scott Gorham (b. Mar.17, 1951, Santa Monica, Cal., US) are recruited.

Aug A new recording deal is signed with Phonogram's progressive rock label, Vertigo.

Oct Debut Vertigo single *Philomena* and LP *Nightlife* are released, but neither charts.

Oct [4] The group makes its stage debut, at Aberystwyth University and follows with a UK club and college tour.

1975 June The group tours UK, including a major headlining gig at London's Roundhouse.

July [12] Thin Lizzy and 10cc° headline an open-air festival at Cardiff Castle in Wales.

Sept LP *Fighting* is the group's first chart LP, at UK #60. It includes *Still In Love With You*, with guest vocalist Frankie Miller. The band tours UK again to promote the LP.

Nov *Wild One* is released, without success.

1976 July LP *Jailbreak* is the band's breakthrough, hitting UK #10 in a 50-week chart run, and also US chart debut, reaching #18 and earning a gold disk. From it, *The Boys Are Back In Town* hits UK #8 and US #12.

Aug Extracted title song from LP *Jailbreak* makes UK #31.

Oct *Cowboy Song* is the band's second (and last) US hit single, peaking at #77.

Nov LP *Johnny The Fox* reaches UK #11 and US #56.

1977 Jan Robertson is forced to leave after his hand is badly cut after a brawl at The Speakeasy in London. He is unable to play on a 10-week US tour supporting Queen°, and Gary Moore comes back to replace him.

Feb *Don't Believe A Word*, from LP *Johnny The Fox*, reaches UK #12.

May Moore returns to Colosseum (from which he has been "on loan") and Robertson, having recovered and toured with Graham Parker° & The Rumour deputizing for Brinsley Schwarz°, rejoins Thin Lizzy for the recording of LP *Bad Reputation* in Toronto.

July The group headlines UK's Reading Festival.

Sept *Dancin' In The Moonlight (It's Caught Me In The Spotlight)* reaches UK #14.

Oct It is taken from LP *Bad Reputation*, which hits UK #4 and US #39.

Nov The group plays a UK tour (ending with two dates at London's Hammersmith Odeon in Dec.).

1978 June Double live LP *Live And Dangerous* hits UK #2 (and will stay on UK chart for 62 weeks). Frôm it, live medley *Rosalie/Cowgirl's Song* makes UK #20.

Aug Robertson leaves again, to form Wild Horses, and Moore rejoins again.

Sept The double live LP makes US #84.

1979 Mar *Waiting For An Alibi*, from the group's next LP, hits UK #9.

May LP *Black Rose (A Rock Legend)* is the band's second consecutive UK #2 LP, held from the top by *The Very Best Of Leo Sayer*. Meanwhile, Moore's solo single on MCA, *Parisienne Walkways* hits UK #8. Moore plays guitar on the disk, with Lynott as guest vocalist.

July *Do Anything You Want To* makes UK #14, while LP *Black Rose (A Rock Legend)* reaches US #81.

July [17] Moore is sacked by the band's management during a US tour. He is replaced by ex-Slik and Rich Kids (and future Ultravox°) guitarist Midge Ure.

July [28] The group appears at the "World Series of Rock" concert at Cleveland Stadium, Oh., US, along with Journey°, Ted Nugent° and Aerosmith°.

Aug Ure, never intended as a permanent guitarist in the band, stays with it for a tour of Japan after the US visit, before departing to Ultravox°.

Nov *Sarah* reaches UK #24.

Nov [12] Guitarist Snowy White (ex-Pink Floyd° live band) joins in place of Ure.

1980 Feb [13] Lynott marries Caroline Crowther, daughter of UK TV personality Leslie Crowther.

Apr Lynott releases his first solo single, *Dear Miss Lonely Hearts*, reaching UK #32.

May Lynott's solo LP *Solo In Soho* makes UK #28.

June *Chinatown*, the title track from the group's forthcoming LP, reaches UK #21.

July Lynott's solo *King's Call*, a tribute to Elvis Presley°, reaches UK #35.

Oct LP *Chinatown* hits UK #7. Taken from it, *Killer On The Loose* hits UK #10. (Its lyrics cause controversy in the wake of the Yorkshire Ripper killings.)

Dec LP *Chinatown* peaks at US #120.

1981 Mar Lynott's solo *Yellow Pearl* makes UK #56.

Apr TV-promoted compilation LP *Adventures Of Thin Lizzy* hits UK #6.

May EP *Killers Live*, including *Bad Reputation*, *Are You Ready* and *Dear Miss Lonely Hearts*, reaches UK #19.

Aug *Trouble Boys* peaks at UK #53.

Dec LP *Renegade* halts at UK #38. This is the last LP to feature White, who leaves for a solo career, and is replaced by ex-Tygers of Pan Tang guitarist John Sykes.

1982 Jan Lynott's *Yellow Pearl* is reissued, this time climbing to UK #14, when it is selected as the new theme tune to BBC TV's "Top of the Pops". It also appears on his second solo LP, *The Philip Lynott Album*, which does not chart.

Jan [20] Lynott appears with Rick Derringer and Charlie Daniels in a UNICEF benefit show at The Savoy, New York, US.

Mar *Hollywood (Down On Your Luck)*, from LP *Renegade*, peaks at UK #53. In US, LP *Renegade* climbs to #157.

1983 Mar LP *Thunder And Lightning*, the group's final studio set, featuring new member Darren Wharton on keyboards, hits UK #4. Taken from it, *Cold Sweat* makes UK #27.

May The extracted title song from LP *Thunder And Lightning* reaches UK #39.

June LP *Thunder And Lightning* makes US #159.

Aug The band splits up, Lynott feeling that it has become predictable and directionless. The final chart single is *The Sun Goes Down*, which peaks at UK #52.

1984 Dec Double LP *Life – Live*, recorded live before the split, reaches UK #29. Its tracks are chosen to feature all ex-Thin Lizzy guitarists in spotlighted roles.

1985 Feb The double live LP creeps to US #185. Grand Slam, a group including Lynott and Downey, fails to secure a recording deal, and Lynott goes solo again to cut unsuccessful *Nineteen*, with Paul Hardcastle producing (though not the same song as the latter's own hit of that title).

1986 Jan [4] Lynott dies of heart failure and pneumonia. (Following an overdose, he has been in a coma for a week.)

May [17] Thin Lizzy re-forms for a one-off date at the Self Aid concert in Dublin, its act a tribute to Lynott, with Bob Geldof handling vocals.

THE THOMPSON TWINS

Tom Bailey (vocals and keyboards)
Alannah Currie (vocals, saxophone and percussion)
Joe Leeway (percussion)

1977 Bailey (b. June 18, 1957, Halifax, Yorks., UK), having met friends Leeway (b. 1957, London, UK) and John Hadd at teacher training college, initially ignores these associations and forms The Thompson Twins (named after two characters in Hergé's cartoon *Tin Tin*), with guitarists Peter Dodd and John Roog in Chesterfield, Yorks.

1978 They move to London with Hadd as agent and link up with drummer Chris Bell. Equipped with a van and a PA, they begin constant London gigging in pubs and clubs with the pledge that they can play anywhere, anytime (which they do for 2 years), and are active for the "Rock Against Racism" cause.

1980 May The group's first release, *Squares And Triangles*, is on its own independent Dirty Discs label.

Nov Another independent, Latent, releases *She's In Love With Mystery*, which becomes a UK independent chart-topper. Bailey begins dating Currie (b. Sept.20, 1959, Auckland, NZ).

1981 Feb The group signs to Arista Records in UK and first release on the Tee label, *Perfect Game*, fails to chart.

June Ex-Japan° saxophonist Jane Shorter is recruited to help Bailey, Dodd, Roog and Bell record debut LP *A Product Of . . .*, which fails, as does *Animal Laugh*.

Aug During a tour to promote releases, Currie joins the band on percussion. Old friend Leeway, until now a roadie, is also invited by Bailey to join after the group buys him a pair of bongos.

Sept *Make Believe* fails to chart.

1982 Jan Shorter is fired. Bassist Matthew Seligman (ex-Soft Boys) is recruited as Bailey becomes frontman.

Mar LP *Set*, produced by Steve Lillywhite, is promoted by live performances and reaches UK #48. Taken from it, *In The Name Of Love* becomes a hot US club hit (#1 on dance chart). LP *Set* is released in US as LP *In The Name Of Love* and reaches US #148.

Apr Following a successful UK university and college tour, the group is offered a US visit. Manager Hadd turns it down and fires Bell, Dodd, Roog and Seligman. Bailey and the record company realize that The Thompson Twins as a trio is the way ahead. (Seligman will play live with David Bowie° while Bell will join Spear of Destiny, Specimen and Gene Loves Jezebel.)

May After *Runaway* is released without success, Arista drops the Tee subsidiary and releases all future product on the main label.

Oct First Arista release *Lies* makes UK #67, beginning a string of chart hits.

1983 Jan Relying on Bailey's songwriting ability, *Love On Your Side* hits UK #9.

Mar LP *Quick Step And Side Kick*, produced by Alex Sadkin in Nassau with Grace Jones° guesting, hits UK #2. It is released in US as *Side Kicks* and will peak at #34 after a 25-week run. *Lies* reaches US #30, aided by good club and dance support.

Apr *We Are Detective* hits UK #7 and features Currie's vocals for the first time.

May *Love On Your Side* peaks at US #45.

July *Watching* makes UK #33.

Nov *Hold Me Now*, introducing a firm slow style, hits UK #4.

1984 Feb *Doctor Doctor* hits UK #3. Third LP *Into The Gap* hits UK #1. (In US it will be on chart for over a year and peak at #10 after 6 months.)

Mar *You Take Me Up* hits UK #2.

June *Sister Of Mercy* reaches UK #11.

July *Doctor Doctor* makes US #11 while the group is on a world tour.

Sept *You Take Me Up* reaches US #44.

Nov *Lay Your Hands* makes UK #13. US-only release *The Gap* peaks at #69. Bailey contributes keyboards on Foreigner's° future #1, *I Want To Know What Love Is*.

1985 Mar Having toured endlessly for 2 years, and now writing and producing a new LP, Bailey falls sick through exhaustion. Current live work is suspended and US producer Nile Rodgers is recruited to complete the LP.

July Bailey recuperates in time for the group's appearance at Live Aid concert in Philadelphia, Pa. Madonna° joins them for their set, which includes a version of The Beatles'° *Revolution*.

Aug With an anti-drug theme *Don't Mess With Doctor Dream* makes UK #15.

Sept Nearly a year behind its UK success, *Lay Your Hands On Me* hits US #6, and is included on LP *Here's To Future Days* which hits UK #5. Also from it, *King For A Day* reaches UK #22.

Dec A cover of *Revolution* peaks at UK #56.

1986 Feb LP *Here's To Future Days* makes US #20.

Mar *King For A Day* hits US #8.

Sept The Thompson Twins' title track for newly-released American movie *Nothing In Common* makes US #54. Currie is made honorary Cultural Ambassador for New Zealand.

Dec Leeway, frustrated with growing internal friction, quits the group leaving Bailey and Currie as The Thompson Twins.

1987 Jan Major tour dates are postponed as Currie goes through serious personal problems and re-scheduled UK gigs are cancelled.

Mar Following promotion at Montreux Music Festival in Switzerland, first single as a duo, *Get That Love*, peaks at UK #66 and US #31.

May LP *Close To The Bone*, produced by Rupert Hine, reaches UK #90 for 1 week and peaks at US #76.

June *Long Goodbye* is the first UK single for 5 years not to chart.

1988 Apr Currie and Bailey have their first child.

Sept LP *Greatest Mixes*, a collection of hits and remixes, is released in US.

Oct A remix of *In The Name Of Love* is released in UK.

Nov LP *Greatest Mixes* is released in UK.

THREE DOG NIGHT

Danny Hutton (vocals)
Cory Wells (vocals)
Chuck Negron (vocals)
Mike Allsup (guitar)
Jimmy Greenspoon (organ)
Joe Schermie (bass)
Floyd Sneed (drums)

1968 The group is formed in Los Angeles, Cal., US, by Hutton (b. Sept.10, 1946, Buncrana, Ireland, and raised in US), an ex-freelance producer and a session singer with Hanna-Barbera Productions, who has had a solo hit (US #73 in 1965) with self-penned (and produced) *Roses And Rainbows*. After auditioning unsuccessfully for The Monkees°, he conceives the idea of a rock group with a triple lead singer line-up and enlists Wells (b. Feb.5, 1944, Buffalo, N.Y., US), whom he has produced for MGM as a member of The Enemies, and Negron (b. June 8, 1942, The Bronx, New York, N.Y.), who has previously recorded as a soloist (without success) for CBS/Columbia. The backing quartet of Greenspoon, (b. Feb.7, 1948, Los Angeles), Sneed (Nov.22, 1943, Calgary, Canada), Allsup (b. Mar.8, 1947, Modesto, Cal.) and Schermie (b. Feb.12, 1945, Madison, Wis.) is assembled from a variety of background influences, from LA session work to country, gospel and backing José Feliciano°. The group name derives from an Australian expression (in the outback, the colder the night, the more dogs you sleep beside to share warmth: coldest is a three-dog night).

Nov Signed to Lou Adler's Dunhill label, the group records an eponymous debut LP with producer Gabriel Mekler, mainly comprising cover versions. (The group's forté will always be personalized versions of outside writers' material, which sees the

THREE DOG NIGHT *cont.*

group running against the grain of most late 60s/early 1970s rock, but results in it being early champions of writers like Randy Newman°, Harry Nilsson°, Laura Nyro and Leo Sayer°.) First single *Nobody* fails to chart.

Dec [28] The group appears at the Miami Pop Festival in Hallendale, Fla., to 100,000 people, on a bill with Chuck Berry°, Fleetwood Mac°, Country Joe & The Fish°, Joni Mitchell°, Canned Heat° and many more.

1969 Apr From the debut LP, a revival of *Try A Little Tenderness*, based on Otis Redding's° 1967 soul version, is the group's first US chart single, reaching #29.

June A Harry Nilsson° song, *One*, the last single taken from LP *Three Dog Night*, hits US #5 and is the group's first million-seller. During a 62-week chart stay, the LP climbs to US #11 and will be the first of 12 consecutive gold LPs.

Sept The group's version of *Easy To Be Hard* (from rock musical *Hair*) hits US #4, earning the second gold single. It is taken from LP *Suitable For Framing*, which reaches US #16 and sells over a half million copies in US during 74 weeks on chart.

Nov Also from the LP, cover of Nyro's *Eli's Coming* hits US #10.

1970 Jan LP *Captured Live At The Forum*, recorded on stage in LA, hits US #6.

Mar Gospel-styled Bonner/Gordon composition *Celebrate* reaches US #15.

June The group's first #1 is a revival of Randy Newman's° *Mama Told Me (Not To Come)*, previously cut by Eric Burdon as an LP track. It holds #1 for 2 weeks and is the third million-selling single. It is also included on LP *It Ain't Easy*, produced by Richard Podolor (who had engineered the previous LP), which hits US #9.

Sept *Mama Told Me (Not To Come)* is the band's UK chart debut, hitting #3. (It will have no consistent UK chart success.)

Oct *Out In The Country*, also from LP *It Ain't Easy*, reaches US #15.

Dec *One Man Band*, from the band's next LP, reaches US #19.

1971 Jan LP *Naturally* makes US #14 and earns another gold disk.

Apr The closing track from *Naturally*, *Joy To The World* (first presented to the group by its composer Hoyt Axton via a rendition in the recording studio) is their second US #1, holding for 6 weeks (despite the fact that Axton himself is reportedly disappointed by it). With sales over 2 million, it is the biggest-selling single of 1971 in US, and also the biggest seller both for the group and for Dunhill Records. Meanwhile, compilation LP *Golden Bisquits*, rounding up the singles to date, hits US #5.

June *Joy To The World* makes UK #24, the group's second and final UK hit.

July On tour in Europe, the group hears the reggae arrangement of *Black And White* by Greyhound (UK #6 at the time) and determines to record it.

Aug Russ Ballard's song *Liar* (originally cut by Ballard's group Argent°) hits US #7.

Dec *An Old Fashioned Love Song*, written by Paul Williams, hits US #4 and is the group's fifth million-selling single. It is taken from LP *Harmony*, which hits US #8.

1972 Feb Also from the LP, *Never Been To Spain*, another Axton song (and later performed live by both Tom Jones° and Elvis Presley°), is a further million-seller, hitting US #5.

Apr *The Family Of Man* reaches US #12.

Sept The group has its third (and final) US #1 and sixth million-selling single with *Black And White*, the song expressing racial harmony heard in Europe the previous summer (though written in 1955 by Earl Robinson and David Arkin, in response to the 1954 US Supreme Court ruling banning segregation in US schools). It is included on LP *Seven Separate Fools*, which hits US #6.

Dec *Pieces Of April*, written by Dave Loggins, peaks at US #19.

1973 May Double live LP *Around The World With Three Dog Night*, recorded on various worldwide tour dates, makes US #18.

June [20] The group appears on the 20th Anniversary special of Dick Clark's "American Bandstand" on US TV, along with Little Richard° and Paul Revere & The Raiders°.

July *Shambala* hits US #3, becoming their seventh million-selling single. Schermie leaves, and is replaced on bass by Jack Ryland. A new keyboards player, Skip Konte, also joins, making the group 8-piece.

Nov LP *Cyan*, including *Shambala*, peaks at US #26, but earns a gold disk for a half million sales.

Dec *Let Me Serenade You*, from LP *Cyan*, reaches US #17.

1974 May The group covers Leo Sayer's° chart-topper *The Show Must Go On*, hitting US #4. It is the group's final million-selling single and is also on LP *Hard Labor*, which reaches US #20.

Aug *Sure As I'm Sittin' Here* makes US #16.

Nov *Play Something Sweet (Brickyard Blues)* peaks at US #33.

1975 Feb Compilation LP *Joy To The World – Their Greatest Hits* reaches US #15, and is the last of the group's 12 consecutive gold LPs.

July [3] On the opening night of a US tour, Negron is arrested in his hotel room in Luisville, Ky., and charged with cocaine possession. (The charge will be dropped in Oct., on the grounds that the warrant used for the arrest was issued on "unfounded information".)

Aug Dunhill is absorbed into parent company ABC, and the group's first LP on the new label, *Coming Down Your Way*, peaks at US #70. From it, Dave Loggins' song *'Til The World Ends* is the group's final US singles chart entry, peaking at #32.

1976 May LP *American Pastime* stalls at US #123, despite continuing success in live work. Immediately after, Hutton leaves and is replaced by new vocalist Jay Gruska. Three former members of Rufus, Al Ciner, Ron Stocker and Denny Belfield, join the expanded backing band, as the band becomes more a cabaret soul revue but splits before making any more recordings.

1981 June After varied solo work (Hutton has produced new wave bands in LA, including Fear), the group re-forms for live work in US, around the original vocal nucleus of Hutton, Negron and Wells.

1983 Sept Three Dog Night's *Joy To The World* receives exposure again when featured in movie *The Big Chill*.

TIFFANY

1984 Tiffany (b. Tiffany Renee Darwish, Oct.2, 1971, Norwalk, Cal., US) visits producer George Tobin and sings country songs in his office. He is impressed by her raw talent and becomes her manager, producer and general mentor.

1986 She signs a worldwide contract with MCA Records, through Tobin's production company.

1987 Sept LP *Tiffany* is released and promoted across US on a "School Spirit Tour" with The Jets.

Oct First single from the LP, a remake of Tommy James & The Shondells'° *I Think We're Alone Now*, tops US chart. Further promotion, prior to returning to school for her junior year, includes the "Tiffany Shopping Mall Tour '87". It involves three shows each weekend in busy US shopping malls where Tiffany performs free for passing consumers. This innovative idea generates enormous media interest including a popular spot on TV's "Tonight Show".

1988 Jan *I Think We're Alone Now* is released in UK and tops UK chart. Tiffany arrives to great media hoopla but fails to find any malls. LP *Tiffany* tops US chart.

Feb *Could've Been* tops US chart. LP *Tiffany* reaches UK #5.

Mar LP *Tiffany* is confirmed quadruple platinum (4 million units) in US. Tiffany runs away from problems with her mother, Janie Williams, and stays with her grandmother in La Mirada, Cal. A court case follows to establish issues including money, guardianship and an application for Tiffany, now aged 17, to become an adult. *Could've Been* reaches UK #4.

Apr *I Saw Him Standing There*, a remake of The Beatles'° with a change to the male gender, hits US #7.

June *I Saw Him Standing There* reaches UK #8. The court issue is resolved. Janie Williams resumes guardianship over her daughter and royalties already due to Tiffany are placed in trust.

July *Feelings Of Forever* reaches US #50 and UK #52.

JOHNNY TILLOTSON

1958 Tillotson (b. Apr.20, 1939, Jacksonville, Fla., US) is signed to Cadence Records (which also has The Everly Brothers°) after being spotted at the University of Florida and entering a major talent show in Nashville. He has been a teenage DJ on Radio W-WPF and a regular on the "Toby Dowdy" TV variety show in Jacksonville, while in high school, having performed country music for 10 years (Hank Williams being his prevailing influence).

Oct Cadence decides to launch him as a beat/ballad singer in the Ricky Nelson° mold (although his natural country roots will continually emerge through his material). Self-penned *Well I'm Your Man* is his US chart debut, reaching #87 before being eclipsed as DJs start playing the other side, ballad *Dreamy Eyes*.

Dec *Dreamy Eyes* (also self-written) peaks at #63, and brings Tillotson on to national TV shows.

1959 Sept *True True Happiness* makes US #54.

1960 Mar *Why Do I Love You So* reaches US #42.

May He scores a small double-sided US hit with covers of two R&B standards, The Penguins' *Earth Angel* and Johnny Ace's° *Pledging My Love*, which reach US #57 and #63 respectively.

Nov *Poetry In Motion*, a commercial beat-ballad written by New York songwriters Paul Kaufman and Mike Anthony, recorded in Nashville after a first, less successful session in New York, is Tillotson's major chart breakthrough, hitting US #2 and selling a million.

1961 Jan *Poetry In Motion* is both his UK chart debut and biggest success, topping the chart for 2 weeks (deposing Elvis Presley's° *It's Now Or Never* and being replaced by Presley's *Are You Lonesome Tonight?*).

Mar Ballad *Jimmy's Girl* reaches US #25 and UK #43.

Sept Another ultra-commercial teenbeat production, self-penned *Without You*, hits US #7, but fails in UK.

1962 Jan In an unusual move, Cadence re-releases his first single *Dreamy Eyes* as a contrasting follow-up to *Without You*. This time, it reaches US #35.

Feb [12] He begins a 6-month stint in the US Army, under the reserve program, at Fort Jackson, S.C.

Apr LP *Johnny Tillotson's Best*, anthologizing his singles to date, peaks at US #120.

June Tillotson's country roots emerge with his own composition *It Keeps Right On A-Hurtin'*, which hits US #3 and is his second million-seller.

Aug *It Keeps Right On A-Hurtin'* makes UK #31. Just out of Army service, he does a 10-week US tour on the strength of the hit, still in his G.I. crew cut.

Sept Mostly country-styled LP *It Keeps Right On A-Hurtin'* is his biggest-selling LP, hitting US #8 and staying on chart for 31 weeks. From it, another smooth country ballad, *Send Me The Pillow You Dream On*, reaches US #17.

Nov A revival of Hank Williams' *I Can't Help It (If I'm Still In Love With You)* reaches US #24, while *Send Me The Pillow You Dream On* climbs to UK #21.

1963 Jan *I Can't Help It (If I'm Still In Love With You* makes UK #41.

Apr Self-penned *Out Of My Mind*, his fourth country-styled ballad in a row, peaks at US #24. He appears in a cameo slot in UK pop movie *Just for Fun*, singing *Judy Judy Judy*.

May *Out Of My Mind* reaches UK #34, following a UK tour with Del Shannon°, but it will be his last UK chart entry for 16 years. With the aid of show choreographer Lou Spencer, he begins planning an adult-oriented nightclub act for US, intended to replace his previously extensive one-night tours from Dec.

Sept Tillotson takes the unusual step of covering a UK hit and reaches US #18 with Ian Samwell's *You Can Never Stop Me Loving You* (Kenny Lynch's version hit UK #10 in Aug.).

Nov A version of Willie Nelson's° *Funny How Time Slips Away* is his last US hit for Cadence, reaching #50, as he signs to MGM Records.

Dec MGM debut *Talk Back Trembling Lips* hits US #7. It is a country-influenced uptempo number, but his next six hits will all be ballads, a style reflecting the fact that he is performing in clubs now rather than on pop tours.

1964 Mar *Worried Guy* climbs to US #37, while debut MGM LP *Talk Back Trembling Lips* reaches US #48.

June *I Rise, I Fall* makes US #36.

Dec *She Understands Me* reaches US #31.

1965 Feb LP *She Understands Me* stalls at US #148, and is his final chart LP.

Mar *Angel*, the theme from Walt Disney film *Those Calloways*, reaches US #51.

June *Then I'll Count Again* is Tillotson's lowest chart-placed single, at US #86.

Oct A revival of Guy Mitchell's 1959 US chart-topper *Heartaches By The Number* peaks at US #35.

Dec *Our World* makes US #70, and is Tillotson's final US hit single. (He will leave MGM after a couple of hitless years, and in 1969 signs to Jimmy Bowen's Amos label, where his revival of *Tears On My Pillow* will just fail to make the US singles chart.)

1979 Apr A reissue of *Poetry In Motion*, pressed on a picture disk as part of a special oldies promotion, re-charts in UK, at #67. (The 70s have seen him move fully into mainstream country music towards which he has always leaned, and he will remain a regular country ballad performer on TV and live circuits into the 1980s.)

THE TOKENS

Hank Medress (first tenor vocals)
Jay Siegel (lead baritone vocals)
Mitch Margo (second tenor vocals)
Phil Margo (bass vocals)

1955 The group is formed as The Linc-Tones at Lincoln High School, Brooklyn, N.Y., US, by Medress (b. Nov.19, 1938, Brooklyn) and Neil Sedaka°, the other members being Eddie Rabkin and Cynthia Zolitin, and performs at hops and dances.

1956 Siegel (b. Oct.20, 1939, Brooklyn) replaces Rabkin, and the group records *I Love My Baby* for small Melba label, to only minor local interest.

1958 Sedaka° leaves to develop his songwriting career and signs to RCA as a soloist. Zolitin also departs. Medress and Siegel draft in replacements and become Daryl & The Oxfords for a year, to little success.

1959 Dec Margo brothers Phil (b. Apr.1, 1942, Brooklyn) and Mitch (b. May 25, 1947, Brooklyn) join and the group is renamed The Tokens.

1960 July The Margos and Medress write *Tonight I Fell In Love*, a determined effort to create a hit song. The group records it privately, then hawks it around New York record companies.

1961 May Sold as a one-off to Morty Kraft's Warwick label, *Tonight I Fell In Love* climbs to US #15. The Tokens audition for producer/songwriters Hugo (Peretti) and Luigi (Creatore) at RCA.

Oct RCA debut is a revised version of Paul Campbell's African folk-based *Wimoweh*, one of the group's audition songs, for which Hugo and Luigi, with songwriting partner George Weiss, have written English lyrics, re-titling it *The Lion Sleeps Tonight*.

Dec *The Lion Sleeps Tonight* tops the US chart for 3 weeks, earning a gold disk for million-plus sales. Additional vocalist Joseph Venneri joins the group to fill out the sound for live appearances.

1962 Jan *The Lion Sleeps Tonight* reaches UK #11, the group's only UK success. Meanwhile, it signs a production deal with Capitol, independent of its recording contract with RCA, and sets up its own company, Big Time Productions, in New York.

Feb Follow-up *B'Wa Nina*, a similar pseudo-African blend, peaks at US #55 while debut LP *The Lion Sleeps Tonight* makes US #54.

Mar Only weeks after The Tokens' hit, Scottish folk/pop singer Karl Denver takes *Wimoweh* in its traditional form to UK #4.

July *La Bomba*, a re-working of Ritchie Valens'° hit *La Bamba*, makes US #85.

1963 Mar The group's first major production success is with The Chiffons'° *He's So Fine*, which tops the US chart. (Several other Chiffons' production successes will follow.)

Aug *Hear The Bells* stalls at US #94, and is The Tokens' last hit on RCA.

1964 Sept The group forms its own B.T. Puppy label (B.T. standing for Big Time), debuting with The Four Seasons°-influenced *He's In Town*, written by Goffin and King°, which climbs to US #43. (The Rockin' Berries' cover hits UK #3.)

1966 Apr *I Hear Trumpets Blow*, written by the group, reaches US #30, and is its final hit on its own label.

May LP *I Hear Trumpets Blow* creeps to US #148.

Aug The Happenings, a vocal quartet from Paterson, N.J., is signed to B.T. Puppy, and produced by The Tokens on a revival of The Tempos' *See You In September*, which hits US #3. (There will be seven more Tokens-produced Happenings US hits over the next 2 years, including another #3 with *I Got Rhythm*).

1967 May The Tokens are signed to Warner Bros., and reach US #37 with a revival of Steve Lawrence/Matt Monro's ballad hit *Portrait Of My Love*.

Aug *It's A Happening World*, also on Warner, peaks at US #69 while B.T. Puppy LP *Back To Back* offering a side apiece by The Tokens and The Happenings, makes US #134.

1969 Dec After a lean period, the group resurfaces on Buddah Records with *She Lets Her Hair Down (Early In The Morning)*, an adaptation of a Silvikrin TV commercial jingle which it has also performed. It reaches US #61.

1970 Mar The final Tokens hit single, again on Buddah, is a revival of The Beach Boys'° *Don't Worry Baby*, peaking at US #95. The group also records an LP for Buddah, *Both Sides Now*, which includes remakes of most of its earlier hits but does not chart.

THE TOKENS *cont.*

Oct Medress leaves the group to concentrate on production and begins a new string of successes in collaboration with Dave Appell, producing Tony Orlando°-led group Dawn. (The group is named after Dawn Siegal, daughter of Tokens' member Jay.) The Tokens continue performing as a trio.

1972 Mar Medress produces a new version of *The Lion Sleeps Tonight* by Robert John, which hits US #3 and is also a million-seller.

1973 Oct Siegal and the Margo brothers, signed to Atco under the new name of Cross Country, reach US #30 with a harmony update of 1965 Wilson Pickett° hit *In The Midnight Hour*. (This is their only success and they will split a year later, moving into various production and writing areas. Phil Margo into movie work, acting and writing screenplays.)

1981 Oct [3] Several years after the group has quietly dissolved, Margo, Margo, Medress and Siegal are reunited for a final reunion/farewell show as The Tokens, at Radio City Music Hall.

1982 Mar *The Lion Sleeps Tonight* is updated by UK group Tight Fit with a 1980s dance beat, and hits UK #1.

1988 Aug The Tokens revive *The Lion Sleeps Tonight* in 1980s-fashion on small Downtown label.

THE TORNADOS

Alan "Tea" Caddy (lead guitar)
George Bellamy (rhythm guitar)
Roger Lavern (keyboards)
Heinz Burt (bass guitar)
Clem Cattini (drums)

1961 Sept London-based session musicians Caddy (b. Feb.2, 1940, London, UK), Bellamy (b. Oct.8, 1941, Sunderland, UK), Lavern (b. Roger Jackson, Nov.11, 1938, Kidderminster, UK), Burt (b. July 24, 1942, Hargin, West Germany) and Cattini (b. Aug.28, 1939, London) are recruited by independent UK producer Joe Meek. Cattini and Caddy are ex-members of Johnny Kidd's° Pirates, while Burt is a protégé of Meek, who feels his teutonic good looks will give the group's visual image a focus. Meek uses them as session men to back his solo artists on record and plans to record them as an instrumental group with a prominent keyboard sound to challenge The Shadows'° guitar-led grip on the instrumental market.

1962 Feb After playing its first live dates supporting singer John Leyton, the group becomes Billy Fury's° onstage backing unit, and plays on record sessions for Meek behind Leyton and Don Charles.

Apr Meek records The Tornados on his instrumental composition *Love And Fury* (a deliberate reference to their stage "boss"), and signs them to Decca. Released as their debut single, it fails to chart.

July They accompany Fury° during his summer season at Great Yarmouth, UK.

Aug Inspired by the recently-launched (July 10) Telstar communications satellite, Meek writes instrumental *Telstar*, tailored to The Tornados' style, with futuristic sound effects.

Oct *Telstar* tops the UK chart for 5 weeks. (It will sell 910,000 in UK.)

Dec *Telstar* tops the US chart for 3 weeks, the first single by a UK group ever to do so. The chart-topping pattern is repeated worldwide with sales over 5 million.

1963 Jan Burt leaves to go solo as a vocalist, using his first name Heinz, but Meek remains his producer. He is replaced on bass by Chas Hodges of The Outlaws, then by Tab Martin.

Feb *Globetrotter*, a Meek tune with *Telstar*-clone sound and arrangement hits UK #3, making it the third instrumental in UK top 5. (*Diamonds* by Jet Harris and Tony Meehan displaced The Shadows'° *Dance On* at #1.) LP *Telstar*, a US-only release, climbs to #45.

Mar Martin leaves to form another Meek-produced group, The Saints (who back Heinz on stage). Brian Gregg, ex-Johnny Kidd's° Pirates, replaces him. *Ridin' The Wind*, is released in US and peaks at #63.

Apr *Robot* makes UK #17, while the group appears in UK pop movie *Just For Fun*, playing *All The Stars In The Sky*.

May First Heinz single *Dreams Do Come True* (later recorded by The Tornados as an instrumental LP track) is from UK film *Farewell Performance*, in which Heinz features and which has a score by Meek.

June Soundtrack LP *Just For Fun* reaches UK #20. *The Ice Cream Man* makes UK #18.

July EP *Tornado Rock* is released. It is a departure from their usual sound and contains revivals of rock classics *Ready Teddy*, *My Babe*, *Long Tall Sally* and *Blue Moon Of Kentucky*.

Aug Lavern, Bellamy and Gregg leave for solo and session work, and are replaced by Jimmy O'Brien, Brian Irwin and Ray Randell.

Sept Heinz, long an ardent Eddie Cochran° fan, hits UK #6 with tribute song *Just Like Eddie*, written by Meek.

Oct The Tornados' *Dragonfly* makes UK #41. They appear with Billy Fury° on LP *We Want Billy!*, recorded live on stage.

Dec *Country Boy* by Heinz makes UK #26, but his solo LP *Tribute To Eddie* does not chart. The Tornados split with Fury°.

1964 Jan The Tornados' first UK LP *Away From It All* fails to chart. The once revolutionary sound of the group is now, in the context of Merseybeat and Beatlemania, out of date. Caddy leaves and is replaced by Stuart Taylor from Screamin' Lord Sutch's group.

Feb *Hot Pot* fails to chart followed by *Monte Carlo* and *Exodus* (released by Decca in Apr. and Aug.)

Mar Heinz reaches UK #26 with *You Were There*.

Oct On Columbia, Heinz makes UK #39 with *Questions I Can't Answer*.

1965 Jan Also on Columbia, The Tornados release *Granada*, with no success.

Feb Cattini, the last remaining original Tornado, leaves to become drummer and leader of Division Two, the touring band behind UK hitmakers The Ivy League. (He will move to constant session work, drumming on records by most major UK names of the 60s and 70s.)

Mar Heinz reaches UK #49 with *Diggin' My Potatoes*. (He will move into cabaret work, before fading from sight and later returning in 1970s rock'n'roll revival shows.)

Apr Cattini releases *No Time To Think* as the Clem Cattini Orchestra.

June *Early Bird*, named after another communications satellite, is unsuccessful.

Sept The group records the theme from TV puppet adventure series *Stingray*.

1966 Aug Following two more non-chart singles, *Pop Art Goes Mozart* and *Is That A Ship I Hear?*, The Tornados (who have had fluctuating personnel since Cattini's departure) disband, mostly moving to studio session work.

1967 Feb [3] Joe Meek dies (on the 8th anniversary of Buddy Holly's° death), apparently suicidally, from shotgun wounds to the head.

TOTO

Bobby Kimball (lead vocals)
David Paich (keyboards and vocals)
Steve Lukather (lead guitar)
Steve Porcaro (keyboards and vocals)
David Hungate (bass)
Jeff Porcaro (drums and percussion)

1978 The group is formed in Los Angeles by six noted sessionmen: brothers Jeff (b. Apr.1, 1954, Los Angeles, Cal., US) and Steve Porcaro (b. Sept.2, 1957, Los Angeles), sons of jazz percussionist Joe Porcaro, their boyhood friend Paich (b. June 25, 1954, Los Angeles), son of bandleader/arranger Marty Paich, and who has previously played in group Rural Still Life with Jeff. They have performed frequently with Hungate (b. Los Angeles), Lukather (b. Oct.21, 1957, Los Angeles) and Kimball (b. Robert Toteaux, Mar.29, 1947, Vinton, La.) for several years, behind acts including Jackson Browne°, Aretha Franklin° and Barbra Streisand, and as back-up band on Boz Scaggs'° hit LPs *Silk Degrees* and *Down Two Then Left* in 1976 and 1977. The Toto name is partly a simplification of lead singer Kimball's real surname and partly after the dog in *The Wizard of Oz*.

1979 Jan Debut single *Hold The Line*, written by Paich, hits US #5, selling over a million, while eponymous first LP, produced by Toto, hits US #9, and also becomes a million-seller, securing an enthusiastic AOR (adult oriented rock) live following. Recorded in Hollywood, eight of the ten cuts are written by Paich.

Mar *I'll Supply The Love*, taken from the LP, makes US #45, while *Hold The Line* is UK chart debut at #14.

Apr LP *Toto* peaks at UK #37.

June *Georgy Porgy*, with guest vocals by soul songstress Cheryl Lynn, reaches US #48.

Dec Hard rock follow-up LP *Hydra*, produced by the band with Tom Knox, makes US #37, earning a gold disk.

1980 Mar *99*, from the second LP, reaches US #26. (All band members will remain highly respected and in-demand writers and session musicians in between Toto projects and will individually contribute to much of the best-selling mainstream US music of the 80s.)

1981 Feb Self-produced LP *Turn Back* peaks at US #41.

1982 July LP *Toto IV* is the group's most successful, hitting US #4 and selling over a million. From it, *Rosanna* (a tribute to Lukather's girlfriend, actress Rosanna Arquette) stays at US #2 for 5 weeks, behind both Human League's° *Don't You Want Me* and Survivor's° *Eye Of The Tiger*, and is also a million-seller.

Sept *Make Believe*, also from LP *Toto IV*, peaks at US #30.

1983 Feb *Africa*, written by Paich and Jeff Porcaro, tops the US chart for a week, and is another million-seller. It also hits UK #3.

Feb [25] Toto dominates the 25th Grammy ceremonies, winning six awards: Record of the Year, Best Pop Vocal Performance and Best Instrumental Arrangement with Vocal (all for *Rosanna*) and LP of the Year, Best Engineered Recording and Best Producer (the group itself) for LP *Toto IV*.

Apr *Rosanna*, reissued in UK as follow-up to *Africa*, reaches UK #12.

May Ballad *I Won't Hold You Back* hits US #10.

July *Waiting For Your Love* peaks at US #73, while *I Won't Hold You Back* makes UK #37.

1984 Hungate leaves, to be replaced on bass by third Porcaro brother Mike (b. May 29, 1955, Los Angeles). Shortly after, Kimball also departs for a solo vocal career, and is replaced by Dennis "Fergie" Fredericksen (b. May 15, 1951). (Kimball will re-emerge in Frank Farian-masterminded heavy group Far Corporation, which hits with a carbon copy revival of Led Zeppelin's° *Stairway To Heaven*.)

Aug Toto is commissioned to write the theme for the 1984 Los Angeles Olympic Games.

Dec *Stranger In Town* climbs to US #30, but parent LP *Isolation* peaks at US #42 and UK #67.

1985 Jan The band members are instrumental in helping to record the backing track for the historic USA For Africa° recording. The group's wholly instrumental soundtrack LP from science fiction movie *Dune* (on which the group is accompanied by The Vienna Symphony Orchestra) receives poor reviews, and struggles on the chart at US #168.

Feb *Holyanna* peaks at US #71.

1986 Nov LP *Fahrenheit*, the first to feature new singer Joseph Williams (who has previously recorded a solo LP for MCA and has been a backing singer for Jeffrey Osborne°) makes US #40 and UK #99. It also features guest appearances from Miles Davis°, Michael McDonald°, Don Henley and others. Taken from it, ballad *I'll Be Over You*, written by Lukather with Randy Goodrum, reaches US #11.

1987 Feb *Without Your Love*, taken from LP *Fahrenheit*, makes US #38. Keyboardist Steve Porcaro quits the line-up and is not replaced, but will continue to contribute in a reduced capacity.

1988 Apr LP *The Seventh One*, with almost identical LP cover to the first release, reaches US #64. Guest vocalists include Jon Anderson and Linda Ronstadt°. Consistent with the previous six LPs, there is at least one cut named after a woman: *Pamela*, which is extracted as a single and reaches US #22.

TRAFFIC

Steve Winwood (vocals, keyboards and guitar)
Dave Mason (vocals and guitar)
Chris Wood (flute and saxophone)
Jim Capaldi (drums and vocals)

1967 Apr [2] Winwood° (b. May 12, 1948, Birmingham, UK) leaves The Spencer Davis Group° at the height of its success after 3 years and forms a new band with three friends from UK Midlands: former Spencer Davis roadie Mason (b. May 10, 1947, Worcester, UK), ex-Sounds of Blue player Wood (b. June 24, 1944, Birmingham) and Capaldi (b. Aug.24, 1944, Evesham, UK), who has played with Mason in The Hellions. Signed to Island Records, they cut a debut single, then retreat to a cottage in rural Berkshire, UK, to rehearse, write and prepare their first LP.

July *Paper Sun*, written by all four group members, and with lead vocal by Winwood°, hits UK #5.

Sept *Paper Sun* makes US #94 for 1 week.

Oct *Hole In My Shoe*, penned by Mason and featuring his lead vocal, hits UK #2. (It will also be a UK #2 hit 17 years later in a spoof revival by Neil from the "Young Ones" TV series.)

Dec [29] Mason leaves after differences of musical opinion with Winwood° and goes to US to play initially with Delaney & Bonnie° before working solo. He is not replaced and Traffic continues as a trio. Meanwhile, *Here We Go Round The Mulberry Bush* hits UK #8; it is the theme from the UK movie of the same title, a romantic teen drama starring Barry Evans and Judy Geeson. Traffic's *Utterly Simple* is also heard on the film's soundtrack, with contributions from The Spencer Davis Group° and others.

1968 Jan LP *Mr. Fantasy* hits UK #8.

Mar *No Name, No Face, No Number*, from the LP, makes UK #40, and will be the group's last UK hit single.

May Mason rejoins the group to contribute to sessions for the second LP.

June LP *Mr. Fantasy* (which has a different track content from the UK release, and includes *Paper Sun* and *Hole In My Shoe*), reaches US #88.

June [10] The group plays the Zurich rock festival in Switzerland, with Jimi Hendrix° and Eric Burdon & The Animals°.

Sept *Feelin' Alright*, from the forthcoming LP, fails to chart.

Oct Mason quits for the second time.

Nov LP *Traffic* hits UK #9. Its most-aired track, *You Can All Join In*, is not released as a UK single (though sells well on import from Europe), but its wide exposure helps boost the LP sales.

1969 Jan Traffic splits as Winwood° leaves to join Eric Clapton°, Rick Grech and Ginger Baker in Blind Faith°. Keyboards player Wynder K. Frog (Mick Weaver) joins Capaldi, Mason and Wood, and they briefly become Wooden Frog, but split after just 2 months of rehearsal. LP *Traffic* reaches US #17.

Jan [7] Capaldi and Wood both attend Winwood's° first gig with Blind Faith°, a free concert in London's Hyde Park.

July Having failed to chart in UK, LP *Last Exit*, recorded as a farewell package before the split, reaches US #19.

1970 Feb After the demise of Blind Faith°, and having spent a month with Ginger Baker's Airforce, Winwood records a solo LP. Capaldi and Wood join the sessions and, with the results working well, it is decided to make it a Traffic LP. The original producer, Guy Stevens, drops out early on. Meanwhile, compilation LP *Best Of Traffic*, rounding up hit singles and tracks from earlier LPs, reaches US #48.

June [14] Mason breaks a lengthy spell of solo touring in US to join Eric Clapton's° Derek & The Dominos for their first UK live shows.

Aug Rick Grech (b. Nov.1, 1946, Bordeaux, France), an ex-colleague with Winwood° in Blind Faith° and Airforce, joins on bass. Mason, signed in US as a soloist to Blue Thumb Records, reaches US #22 with his debut LP *Alone Together* (recorded with help from Capaldi, Leon Russell°, Delaney & Bonnie°, and others), also earning his first gold disk.

Sept LP *John Barleycorn Must Die* reaches UK #11 and hits US #5, the group's biggest US success and first gold LP. From Mason's LP, his solo version of *Only You Know And I Know* (which will be a US top 20 hit by Delaney & Bonnie° a year later) reaches US #42.

Oct *Empty Pages*, from LP *John Barleycorn Must Die*, makes US #74.

Dec Mason's *Satin Red And Black Velvet Woman* stalls at US #97.

1971 Apr The group returns from an inactive winter spent in Morocco, having ostensibly been writing a movie score (for *Nevertheless*, starring Michael J. Pollard) which has fallen through. Mason has teamed with Mama Cass Elliot, formerly with The Mamas and The Papas°, and their duetted LP *Dave Mason And Cass Elliot* makes UK #49.

May For new recordings and in preparation for UK and US tours, the group expands its line-up, adding Ghanaan percussionist Reebop Kwaku-Baah and Derek & The Dominos' drummer Jim Gordon (freeing Capaldi for more vocal spotlights). Mason also returns for a few months, and is present on the live recordings which produce LP *Welcome To The Canteen*.

June Double compilation LP *Winwood*, bringing together The Spencer Davis Group°, Blind Faith° and Traffic tracks which have Winwood° on lead vocals, reaches US #93. It is not released in UK.

Nov LP *Welcome To The Canteen* makes US #26, while the live single from it, a revival of The Spencer Davis Group's° *Gimme Some Lovin'* with Winwood reprising his lead vocal, reaches US #68.

Dec Grech leaves (later to join KGB), while Mason quits and Gordon returns to session work in US.

1972 Jan LP *The Low Spark Of High Heeled Boys*, made before the break-up of the last line-up (though after Mason's departure) fails to chart in

TRAFFIC *cont.*

UK but hits US #7, and becomes the band's second gold LP. *Rock'n'Roll Stew (Part 1)* makes US #93. Winwood° contracts peritonitis and his illness and recuperation keep Traffic inactive for a while. Capaldi fills the time recording a solo LP in Muscle Shoals, Ala., while Mason records another solo LP.

Apr Capaldi's LP *Oh How We Danced* makes US #82 and extracted *Eve* peaks at US #91, while Mason's half-studio, half-live LP *Headkeeper* reaches US #51.

Nov Muscle Shoals drummer and bassist Roger Hawkins and David Hood, who played with Capaldi at the beginning of the year, are invited to Jamaica to record Traffic's next LP, with Winwood°, Capaldi, Wood and Kwaku-Baah still in the main line-up.

1973 Mar LP *Shoot-Out At The Fantasy Factory* is another UK chart failure, but hits US #6 and earns the band's third gold disk.

May Mason's solo live LP *Dave Mason Is Alive!* makes US #116.

June Hawkins and Hood remain with Traffic for a world tour, while keyboards player Barry Beckett is also recruited to fill out the stage sound on tour. Several tour gigs are recorded for a future live LP.

Aug [23] In mid-tour, the group headlines UK's Reading Festival.

Sept After the tour, Kwaku-Baah, Hood, Hawkins and Beckett all return to session work, and the three principals rest for 2 months.

Nov Bass player Rosko Gee (formerly with Gonzales) joins to augment the trio for some UK live dates (and will stay for the last year of the group's life).

Dec Double live LP *Traffic – On The Road*, recorded on the world tour, reaches UK #40 and US #29, while Mason switches labels to CBS/Columbia and makes US #50 with LP *It's Like You Never Left*, which features Graham Nash and Stevie Wonder°.

1974 July Compilation LP of Mason's Blue Thumb recordings, *The Best Of Dave Mason* makes US #183.

Aug *It's All Up To You*, a Capaldi solo, reaches UK #27.

Sept LP *When The Eagle Flies*, Traffic's final recording together, reaches UK #31 and is the group's last UK chart LP. Meanwhile, Capaldi's solo LP *Whale Meat Again* creeps to US #191.

Nov LP *When The Eagle Flies* hits US #9, earning the group's fourth and final gold disk. They complete a US tour, then decide to split to pursue individual careers.

Dec Mason's solo LP *Dave Mason*, on Columbia, reaches US #25 and earns his second gold disk.

1975 Feb Capaldi's solo *It's All Right* makes US #55.

Mar A revised version on Blue Thumb of compilation LP *The Best Of Dave Mason*, now titled *Dave Mason At His Best* after the substitution of one track, peaks at US #133.

May Compilation LP *Heavy Traffic* makes US #155.

Oct Another compilation LP, *More Heavy Traffic*, creeps to US #193.

Nov Capaldi's solo revival of oldie *Love Hurts* hits UK #4 and reaches US #97, where a competing version by UK group Nazareth hits US #8, selling over a million. Meanwhile, Mason's LP *Split Coconut*, with guest appearances by Manhattan Transfer°, David Crosby and Graham Nash, reaches US #27.

1976 Feb Capaldi's solo LP *Short Cut Draw Blood* peaks at US #193.

1977 Jan Mason's solo live double LP *Certified Live* climbs to US #78.

June Mason's *So High (Rock Me Baby And Roll Me Away)* makes US #89 while his LP *Let It Flow* reaches US #37 and earns a gold disk.

July Winwood° begins his solo career with LP *Steve Winwood*, which reaches UK #12 and US #22.

Nov Mason's *We Just Disagree*, from LP *Let It Flow*, is his biggest solo single success, reaching US #12.

1978 Feb *Let It Go, Let It Flow* by Mason makes US #45.

Mar Mason plays the California Jam 2 rock festival in Ontario, Cal., alongside Santana°, Aerosmith°, and others.

July Mason becomes the sixth act to have a US hit single with The Shirelles° 1961 chart-topper *Will You Love Me Tomorrow*, reaching US #39. It is taken from his LP *Mariposa De Oro*, which peaks at US #41.

Aug [26] Mason takes part in the Canada Jam Festival, a spinoff from California Jam, along with The Doobie Brothers°, The Commodores°, and others.

Nov Yet another Blue Thumb repackage of early solo material, *The Very Best Of Dave Mason*, peaks at US #179.

1980 July The last solo hit single by Mason is *Save Me*, peaking at US #71. It comes from his final chart LP *Old Crest On A New Wave*, which makes US #74. (He will continue to work in US and in the following year will be heard singing Miller Beer ads on US radio.)

1983 June After some time spent in South America, Capaldi is signed to Atlantic for solo LP *Fierce Heart*, which climbs to US #91. Taken from it, *That's Love* makes US #28.

July [12] Chris Wood dies of liver failure after a lengthy illness, in London.

Sept *Living On The Edge* by Capaldi reaches US #75. This will be his last chart record. (Like Mason's, his career will wane, while Winwood's° will soar to peaks beyond those achieved by Traffic.)

1988 Nov Capaldi returns, signed to Island Records, with *Something So Strong* and parent LP *Some Come Running*.

JOHN TRAVOLTA

1975 Sept [9] Travolta (b. Feb.18, 1954, Englewood, N.J., US) plays Vinnie Barbarino in US ABC-TV high school comedy series "Welcome Back, Kotter". (It will run for 3 years and establish him as a rising star.) He makes his film debut in *The Devil's Run*.

1976 July Signed to Midland International Records as a solo singer, he hits US #10 with his first single, *Let Her In*, aided by his appearance on TV. LP *John Travolta*, which includes the hit, reaches US #39. Travolta appears in Stephen King horror pic *Carrie*.

Nov *Whenever I'm Away From You* makes US #38.

1977 Mar *All Strung Out On You* reaches US #34.

Apr LP *Can't Let You Go* reaches US #66.

Dec Travolta appears in film *Saturday Night Fever*, which will be a worldwide box office smash, turning him into an overnight star, and spin off the biggest-selling soundtrack LP of all time, with music by The Bee Gees°.

1978 June *Grease*, the movie version of the hit Broadway musical, opens in US, starring Travolta with Olivia Newton-John°. This too will break box office records all over the world, earning more than *Saturday Night Fever*. *You're The One That I Want*, a John Farrar-penned duet between Travolta and Newton-John from *Grease*, tops the US chart for a week and the UK chart for 9 weeks. It sells over 2 million copies in US, earning a platinum disk, while UK sales are over 1,870,000, which makes it the third best-selling single ever in UK up to this time.

July The soundtrack double LP from *Grease* tops the US chart, holding at #1 for 12 weeks.

Sept *Summer Nights*, Travolta's second duet with Newton-John° from *Grease*, hits US #5 and earns a gold disk for million-plus sales. In UK, it tops the chart for 7 weeks, with total UK sales over 1,501,000. *Grease* soundtrack LP also tops the UK chart, staying at #1 for 12 weeks.

Oct *Greased Lightnin'*, a solo rocker from *Grease*, reaches US #47.

Nov *Sandy*, Travolta's solo ballad from *Grease*, hits UK #2, behind *Summer Nights*.

Dec *Greased Lightnin'* reaches UK #11. Film *Moment by Moment*, in which Travolta stars with Lily Tomlin, premieres.

1979 Jan LP *Sandy*, combining the *Grease* hit with earlier Midland International solo material, reaches UK #40. In US, both the early solo LPs are packaged together as double LP *Travolta Fever*, which makes US #161. (This will be his last chart entry. He will concentrate on movie acting and will sing no hit songs in subsequent film roles.)

1980 June Travolta stars in movie *Urban Cowboy*. (His later film roles will include *Blow Out*, *Two of a Kind*, *Perfect* and *Staying Alive*, an unsuccessful follow-up to *Grease*.)

THE TROGGS

Reg Presley (vocals)
Chris Britton (guitar)
Pete Staples (bass)
Ronnie Bond (drums)

1964 The group forms as The Troglodytes in Andover, Hants., UK, comprising Tony Mansfield on guitar and lead vocals, Dave Wright on guitar, and ex-apprentice bricklayers Reg Ball (b. June 12, 1943, Andover) on bass and Bond (b. May 4, 1943, Andover) on drums.

1965 Mansfield and Wright leave the group, and are replaced by Britton (b. June 21, 1945, Watford, Herts., UK) and Staples (b. May 3, 1944, Andover), both ex-Andover group Ten Foot Five. Staples plays bass, so Ball, with initial reluctance, becomes lead vocalist in Mansfield's place. This new line-up is spotted and signed by The Kinks'° manager Larry Page, after he witnesses their very basic live rendition of The Kinks' *You Really Got Me*. (Their very basic rawness will always be the key to The Troggs' individuality.)

1966 Feb The group abridges its name to The Troggs, and debut single is Ball's song *Lost Girl*, leased by Page to CBS. It fails to sell.

Apr *Wild Thing*, by US writer Chip Taylor and cut (obscurely) in US by The Wild Ones, is sent to Page by his US publishing associate. The group thinks the lyric corny but, once the heavy, innuendo-laden arrangement is worked out, it is recorded in a rapid session, with an unusual ocarina solo in place of a whistling passage on the US original.

May Ball changes his name to Reg Presley (which, as anticipated, gets him press notice once the record is climbing) as the single is released via a new deal between Page's production company Page One and Fontana label. Following UK TV slots on "Thank Your Lucky Stars" and "Top of the Pops", *Wild Thing* hits UK #2.

July *Wild Thing* tops the US chart for 2 weeks, selling over a million. Because of a US rights dispute, it is released in US on both Fontana and Atco labels. Fontana shares the same B-side as the UK release, but Atco couples *Wild Thing* with the UK follow-up, *With A Girl Like You*.

Aug Presley's composition *With A Girl Like You*, cut in slightly lighter, but similar, style to *Wild Thing*, tops the UK chart for 2 weeks. The group's debut LP *From Nowhere . . . The Troggs* hits UK #6.

Sept Fontana issues *With A Girl Like You* in US, but since half the US buyers of *Wild Thing* already own the track, it halts at US #29.

Oct Page launches his own Page One label in UK and *I Can't Control Myself*, penned by Presley, hits UK #2. Meanwhile, LP *Wild Thing* climbs to US #52.

Nov *I Can't Control Myself*, also a dual-label release in US, reaches #43.

1967 Jan Another Chip Taylor song, *Any Way That You Want Me* (also a US hit 3 years later for Evie Sands), hits UK #8.

Mar Chanted *Give It To Me*, also Presley-penned, reaches UK #12, while LP *Trogglodynamite* hits UK #10.

Apr [1] Page announces that he is imposing a "ban in reverse": he is forbidding the Troggs to play London dates, because of the illegal-drug publicity which the city's music venues are receiving. (The date of the ban appears to be significant.)

June *Night Of The Long Grass*, a deliberate change of sound with a hint of psychedelia in lyric and arrangement, makes UK #17.

Aug *Hi Hi Hazel* (a minor UK hit the previous year for soul singer Geno Washington) peaks at UK #42, while compilation LP *Best Of The Troggs* reaches UK #24, and is the group's last UK chart LP.

Nov *Love Is All Around*, a ballad with merely a hint of *Wild Thing*'s jerky rhythm, hits UK #5.

1968 Mar *Little Girl* reaches UK #37, and is The Troggs' last UK chart entry. (The band will continue live work for another year on UK club and college circuits.)

May *Love Is All Around* hits US #7.

June LP *Love Is All Around* makes US #109.

1969 Mar A year after Britton originally planned to leave, the group splits. (Presley and Bond will both record solo singles, *Lucinda Lee* and *Anything For You* respectively, after the break-up, but without success. Britton will cut unsuccessful LP *As I Am*.)

1972 Presley and Bond re-form the group with Britton and Staples replaced in the line-up by Richard Moore and Tony Murray, to resume working college and club dates in UK and in France, Holland and West Germany, where a following for the usually outrageous stage act remains strong. A studio tape made during sessions in their later days at Page One also surfaces in bootleg form under the title *The Troggs Tapes*, its main interset being West Country foul language as the group struggles with the attempted creation of a hit. This revives interest in The Troggs, particularly in US.

1973 Nov [16] The group guests on David Bowie's° first US TV special, "The 1980 Floor Show", taped earlier at London's Marquee club, and aired on NBC TV's "Midnight Special".

1975 Jan The Troggs are reunited with Page when they cut a revival of The Beach Boys'° *Good Vibrations* for his Penny Farthing label. Reviews are more amused than scathing but it fails to chart.

Nov The group revives The Rolling Stones'° *(I Can't Get No) Satisfaction*, again without success.

1976 The group is on a nostalgia tour of US when Sire label releases compilation LP *Vintage Years*, containing The Troggs' 1960s hits.

July Penny Farthing releases LP *The Troggs Tapes* (which capitalizes on the title of the bootleg tape, but has nothing to do with it). Rhythm guitarist Colin "Dill" Fletcher has now made the group up to a quintet. (The inherent unmusicality of The Troggs is cited as an influence by many punk groups, and LA band X revives *Wild Thing* on disk.)

1980 Signed in US to Basement records, the group releases LP *Live At Max's Kansas City*, recorded at the New York club. (With a cult following which is apparently undying, the group will continue regular live work in US and UK into the 1980s.)

THE TUBES

"Fee" Waybill (vocals)
Bill "Sputnick" Spooner (guitar)
Vince Welnick (keyboards)
Rick Anderson (bass)
Michael Cotten (synthesizer)
Roger Steen (guitar)
Prairie Prince (drums)
Re Styles (vocals and guitar)
Mingo Lewis (percussion)

1975 Establishing a reputation as San Francisco's prime theatrical rock band, The Tubes, formed in Phoenix and led by ex-drama student Waybill (b. John Waldo, Sept.17, 1950, Omaha, Neb., US) sign to A&M Records, using their advance to make their stage shows more extravagant.

Aug Al Kooper-produced debut LP *The Tubes*, featuring the band's anthem *White Punks On Dope*, reaches US #113.

1976 June LP *Young And Rich*, produced by Ken Scott, makes US #46.

Aug *Don't Touch Me There*, with Waybill in the guise of glam-rock star "Quay Lewd", makes US #61.

1977 June LP *The Tubes Now* reaches US #122.

Nov The group tours UK for the first time and a ban from playing in Portsmouth probably helps *White Punks On Dope* chart at UK #28.

1978 Mar Double live LP *What Do You Want From Live* reaches US #82 and UK #38.

May [9] While on a UK tour, Waybill falls off stage and breaks a leg. They have to cancel seven nights at London's Hammersmith Odeon. UK BBC's film of the incident shows him apparently wielding a chainsaw.

1979 Mar The band fills large venues but is unable to transfer its live popularity into disk sales. With LP *Remote Control* they announce that future emphasis will be less on theater and more on music. With Todd Rundgren° producing, the LP makes US #46.

May *Prime Time* reaches UK #34.

June LP *Remote Control* climbs to UK #40.

1980 They begin recording follow-up LP, *Suffer For Sound*, but it is blocked by A&M.

Aug The group appears in movie *Xanadu*.

1981 July With sales of Tubes' disks unsatisfactory, A&M drops the band. They sign to Capitol, which releases LP *Completion Backwards Principle*, produced by Canadian David Foster. It becomes The Tubes' highest charting LP at US #36.

Aug *I Don't Want To Wait Anymore* makes US #35 and UK #60.

1982 June While The Tubes are touring UK, a publicity stunt involving young girls dancing on the back of a flat-bed truck in London's Tottenham Court Road gets Waybill arrested for obstruction.

Sept A&M releases LP *T.R.A.S.H. (Tubes Rarities And Smash Hits)*, of hits and out-takes, which peaks at US #148.

1983 May LP *Outside Inside*, including guest appearances from Earth, Wind & Fire's° Maurice White and The Motels'° Martha Davis, reaches US #18 but only UK #77.

July The group's first US top 10 success is *She's A Beauty* at #10.

Aug *Tip Of My Tongue* makes US #52.

Oct *The Monkey Time* reaches US #68.

1984 Nov Waybill releases solo LP *Read My Lips* which makes US #146.

1985 Mar *Piece By Piece* charts briefly at US #87.

1986 Mar LP *Love Bomb*, reuniting the group with producer Rundgren°, reaches US #89.

May PMI Video releases *The Tubes Video* which captures the band performing *White Punks On Dope* and *Mondo Bondage*.

Oct XTC's° LP *Skylarking* is recorded at The Tubes' own Sound Hole studio in San Francisco.

1988 Apr Waybill appears on Richard Marx's° eponymous debut LP.

TINA TURNER

1951 Ike Turner (b. Nov.5, 1931, Clarksdale, Miss.), a self-taught musician who has backed local bluesmen Robert Nighthawk and Sonny Boy Williamson on piano, is a DJ at Clarksdale's W-ROX, which leads to recording work with his band Kings of Rhythm, formed at high school. Their *Rocket 88*, recorded at Sam Phillips' Sun studio in Memphis, with lead vocal by sax player Jackie Brenston, hits R&B #1 (and will often be cited as the first rock'n'roll record).

1952/55 Moving to session guitarwork and production, Ike plays on sessions by B.B. King°, Howlin' Wolf° (both of whom he recruits for Modern Records in LA, having become a roving R&B talent scout for the label around the South), Johnny Ace° and others, as well as touring with his band.

1956 The Kings of Rhythm have settled in a club in East St. Louis, Mo., where Ike first meets Tina (who at this time is still Annie Bullock, b. Nov.26, 1938, Brownsville, Tenn., US) and her older sister Alline. Deserted by their mother and later their father into the care of relatives before their teens, the sisters have moved to St. Louis to work and are regulars at R&B clubs. She has been singing since childhood in church and junior talent contests, and repeatedly asks Ike if she can sing with his band, but he is not interested. One evening at the club, after the drummer has offered the microphone to her sister, who is unwilling to sing, she takes it and jumps on stage with the group. She and Ike become a couple and she becomes a regular band vocalist.

1958 Ike and Tina are married and, at Ike's suggestion, she takes the stage name Tina Turner.

1960 Their first record as Ike & Tina Turner comes about by accident when the session singer booked to record Ike's *A Fool In Love* does not show up and Tina steps in.

Oct Already an R&B success, *A Fool In Love* is the duo's first crossover hit, reaching US #27. Ike's band becomes The Ike & Tina Turner Revue and three female backing singers, The Ikettes, are incorporated to support Tina, around whom the show's routines revolve – she is now a striking and uninhibited live performer.

Dec *I Idolize You* makes US #82 and R&B #5.

1961 Sept *It's Gonna Work Out Fine* is their first US top 20 hit, reaching #14 (and R&B #2).

1962 Jan *Poor Fool* makes US #38 (and R&B #4).

Feb Without Tina, The Ikettes and the band record *I'm Blue (The Gong Gong Song)*, which Ike leases to Atco. It makes US #19.

Apr *Tra La La La La* reaches US #50 (and R&B #9).

July *You Should'a Treated Me Right* makes US #89 and is the duo's last pop hit for Sun Records. (A pattern of R&B successes that do not always cross over is developing: The Ike & Tina Turner Revue will be one of the most popular acts of the 60s on the R&B tour circuit, but will only consistently break to wider audiences towards the end of the decade.)

1964 Oct *I Can't Believe What You Say (For Seeing What You Do)* reaches US #95 while the duo is signed to Kent label.

1965 Feb They move to Warner Bros. on the strength of the recent hit single. No singles chart entries will follow on Warner, but LP *Live! The Ike And Tina Turner Show*, a recording of their highly-rated stage act, makes US #126.

Apr Ike records The Ikettes again for Kent's sister label Modern and their *Peaches'n'Cream* climbs to US #36.

Nov The Ikettes' follow-up *I'm So Thankful* peaks at US #74.

1966 Jan While moving around in one-off record deals with independent labels like Innis and Pompeii, they meet producer Phil Spector, who offers Ike $20,000 dollars to put Tina under a production contract. (Spector admires Tina's voice, but is underwhelmed by Ike's production of her records, so the payment is part of a condition that Ike takes no part in the sessions.) Songwriters Jeff Barry and Ellie Greenwich are called in to pen songs, with Spector, for Tina.

Mar [7] Tina records her vocal on *River Deep, Mountain High* after Spector has already spent over $22,000 creating the "wall of sound" backing track.

June Released on Spector's Philles label, *River Deep, Mountain High* climbs no higher than US #88. (This apparent rejection of what he regards as one of his finest productions is given as a major factor in Spector's shutdown of Philles immediately afterwards, and his short-term retirement from production.)

July By contrast, *River Deep, Mountain High* is a major UK success (the duo's first), hitting #3. Warner Bros. releases an earlier track, *Tell Her I'm Not Home*, in UK and this too charts, reaching #48. After years as an R&B enthusiasts' act in Europe and UK, the Turners are suddenly considered major stars – though still restricted to the R&B circuit in US.

Sept [23] They begin a UK tour as support to The Rolling Stones°, playing a major London date at the Royal Albert Hall, and appearing on UK TV's "Ready, Steady, Go!".

Oct LP *River Deep, Mountain High*, coupling the Spector productions with new Ike Turner-produced versions of oldies by the duo, makes UK #27.

Nov Spector-produced UK (but not released in US) follow-up from the same sessions as *River Deep*, a revival of a Martha & The Vandellas° B-side, *A Love Like Yours*, reaches UK #16.

1969 Feb *River Deep, Mountain High* is reissued in UK, and reaches #33.

May The duo signs a two-LP deal with Blue Thumb Records, cutting mainly blues-based material, and also a longer-term contract with Minit, the R&B subsidiary of Minit Records. A revival of Otis Redding's° *I've Been Loving You Too Long* on Blue Thumb peaks at US #68 and *I'm Gonna Do All I Can (To Do Right By My Man)*, on Minit, reaches US #98. Blue Thumb LP *Outa Season* makes US #91.

June [20] Ike & Tina Turner participate in the 3-day Newport '69 Festival.

Aug *The Hunter*, on Blue Thumb, peaks at US #93, while live Minit LP *In Person*, recorded at Basin Street West, reaches US #142.

Oct LP *River Deep, Mountain High*, finally released in US on A&M after 3 years, peaks at US #102.

Nov Second Blue Thumb LP *The Hunter* makes US #176.

Nov [7] The duo supports The Rolling Stones° on a US tour, which opens in Denver, Col.

1970 Jan Ike's composition *Bold Soul Sister*, a final single on Blue Thumb, peaks at US #59.

Apr A version of The Beatles'° *Come Together* (on Minit) reaches US #57.

June LP *Come Together* makes US #130.

Aug A revival of Sly & The Family Stone's° *I Want To Take You Higher* is their first hit on Liberty, which has absorbed Minit. It reaches US #34 (and will become a highlight of the Turners' live act). With a higher, wider audience profile, The Ike & Tina Turner Revue guests on important US TV shows like Ed Sullivan's and Andy Williams'. They also pick up unhip but lucrative work in Las Vegas casinos. By the end of the year Ike has built his own Bolic Sound recording studio in Inglewood, Cal.

1971 Mar An R&B-style revival of Creedence Clearwater Revival's° *Proud Mary* is their first US top 10 hit, at #4, and also first million-selling single. It is taken from LP *Workin' Together*, which is their biggest-selling LP to date in US, peaking at #25. (Despite a hugely successful European tour, neither single nor LP produce similar chart results in UK.)

June A revival of Jesse Hill's *Ooh Poo Pah Doo* (on United Artists, as Liberty Records has now become) reaches US #60.

Sept Double live LP *Live At Carnegie Hall/What You See Is What You Get* reaches US #25 and is the duo's first gold LP, selling over a half million copies in US.

Dec LP *'Nuff Said* makes US #108.

1972 Mar *Up In Heah* reaches US #83.

Aug LP *Feel Good* makes US #160.

1973 Oct Tina's composition, stomping *Nutbush City Limits* reaches US #22 and hits UK #4.

1974 Jan LP *Nutbush City Limits* makes US #163.

Apr [22] Tina begins filming in the role of the Acid Queen in The Who's° film *Tommy*.

Dec *Sexy Ida* reaches US #65.

1975 June Ike Turner-penned *Baby Get It On* reaches US #88, and is the duo's last hit single together. (Behind the scenes, all is not well with the couple domestically: Tina will later claim to have been regularly beaten and kept a prisoner in the house by her husband.)

Oct On the strength of her Acid Queen performance in *Tommy*, Tina records a solo LP, *The Acid Queen*, which reaches US #155.

1976 Strengthened by her newfound Buddhist faith, Tina walks out on Ike and in July they are divorced. While he continues to produce at his studio (where he will be arrested after rigging electronic equipment to make long distance telephone calls without charge), she has four children to support. After depending for a time on food stamps, she recruits a band and plays cabaret gigs. (She is still a far bigger draw in Europe – where she is regarded as a star – than in US.)

1979 Late in the year Tina meets Roger Davies, a young Australian promoter trying to make it in the US music business. She has no recording deal, is playing the cabaret circuit, and is half a million dollars in debt.

1980 Tina teams with Davies, who makes changes in her band and books her into less middle-of-the-road-oriented clubs (with the occasional Las Vegas stand to pay the bills). Record company interest is minimal, partly because Ike's difficult reputation lingers with Tina.

1981 Tina's career prospects brighten again as she supports The Rolling Stones° on tour. Late in the year Davies has a call from Virgin Records in UK to say that Ian Craig Marsh and Martyn Ware of Heaven 17° and the British Electric Foundation want Tina to sing The Temptations° song *Ball Of Confusion* on their LP of choice revivals, *Music Of Quality & Distinction*. With its electronic backdrop, it is not the kind of rock she now wants to record, but the finished track brings her renewed notice as an active vocalist.

Dec [18] Tina supports Rod Stewart° at an LA Forum concert, broadcast live by satellite around the world.

1982 Davies works out a new solo recording deal with Capitol/EMI. Meanwhile, Ike's studio is destroyed by fire and rumors indicate he has a serious cocaine problem.

Dec Davies promotes a series of Tina Turner dates at the New York Ritz, building up a guest list of notables – though aware that management changes at Capitol during the year have left the company less enthused about its new signing, and that she seems in danger of being dropped. David Bowie° resolves this problem. He is just signed to EMI (Capitol's parent company), and its top executives from around the world have been invited to a listening party for his forthcoming LP *Let's Dance*. When Bowie announces to the party that he is moving on to see his "favorite singer" Tina Turner, EMI's executives follow and witness a storming comeback show. (She will stay with Capitol.)

1983 Dec Marsh and Ware-produced version of Al Green's° *Let's Stay Together* is Tina's first Capitol single. It hits UK #6, with her UK profile raised by packed dates at London's The Venue and an appearance on Channel 4 TV's "The Tube".

1984 Mar *Let's Stay Together* reaches US #26, as various writer-producers, including Rupert Hine and Terry Britten, are brought in to collaborate on a first Capitol LP. It is recorded at UK sessions spread over just 2 weeks, while her revival of The Beatles'° *Help!* reaches UK #40.

Mar [27] Turner begins a UK tour at St. Austell's Coliseum, Cornwall.

Apr She opens as support act on Lionel Richie's° "Can't Slow Down" tour.

July First release from the LP sessions is *What's Love Got To Do With It?*, written by Britten and Graham Lyle (ex-Gallagher & Lyle°), which hits UK #3.

Aug LP *Private Dancer* hits US #3 and UK #2, (and will stay in US top 10 until May 1985 and sell over 10 million copies worldwide).

Sept As the tour with Richie° finishes, *What's Love Got To Do With It* tops the US chart for 3 weeks, selling over a million. It is her first #1 hit, and sets a new record for length of time between an act's first US Hot 100 entry and first #1 record – 24 years. On the same day the single hits #1, she seals a deal with Australian director George Miller to appear in his third *Mad Max* movie, with Mel Gibson (Miller had called offering her a part quite unaware of *Mad Max 2* being one of her favorite films). She performs at a series of McDonalds sales conventions (booked a year earlier in the penniless days). Meanwhile, *Better Be Good To Me*, from LP *Private Dancer*, reaches UK #45.

Nov *Better Be Good To Me* hits US #5.

Dec The title track from *Private Dancer* makes UK #26.

1985 Jan She plays the Rock in Rio festival, Brazil, along with Rod Stewart°, Queen°, Whitesnake° and AC/DC°.

Jan [28] Turner takes part in the recording of USA For Africa's° *We Are The World*.

Feb [26] *What's Love Got To Do With It?* wins Grammy awards as Record of the Year, Song of the Year and Best Female Vocal Performance, while Turner's *Better Be Good To Me* also collects a Grammy as Best Female Rock Vocal.

Mar The title song from *Private Dancer* hits US #7 – her third consecutive US top 10 hit from the LP.

Mar [14] Turner plays London's Wembley Arena as her revival of Ann Peebles' *I Can't Stand The Rain* peaks at UK #57.

May *Show Some Respect* peaks at US #37.

June Movie *Mad Max: Beyond Thunderdome* is released. Tina's performance as Aunty Entity is striking, and leads to further film offers. (She reportedly turns down Steven Spielberg's offer of a role in *The Color Purple* three times.) Meanwhile, her European tour is breaking records, and the original 8 dates in West Germany are extended to 30.

July [13] She appears on the Live Aid bill in Philadelphia, where she duets raunchily with Mick Jagger.

Aug *We Don't Need Another Hero (Thunderdome)*, from *Mad Max: Beyond Thunderdome* soundtrack, hits UK #3.

Sept *We Don't Need Another Hero (Thunderdome)* hits US #2, behind John Parr's *St. Elmo's Fire*.

Oct A second soundtrack single, *One Of The Living*, reaches UK #55.

Nov *It's Only Love*, a duet with Canadian rocker Bryan Adams° (on his label A&M), reaches UK #29.

Dec [8] Turner wins an award as Best Actress from the NAACP for her role in *Mad Max: Beyond Thunderdome*.

Dec *One Of The Living* makes US #15.

1986 Jan Duetted *It's Only Love* makes US #15.

June [20] Turner participates in the Prince's Trust concert in London, alongside Eric Clapton°, Elton John° and Bryan Adams°.

Aug [28] Turner receives her Hollywood Walk of Fame outside Capitol Records' headquarters.

Sept *Typical Male*, from her forthcoming LP, reaches UK #33.

Oct *Typical Male* hits US #2, behind Cyndi Lauper's° *True Colors*. LP *Break Every Rule* hits UK #2.

Nov *Two People*, also from LP *Break Every Rule*, makes UK #43, while the LP hits US #4, earning a platinum disk for million-plus sales.

1987 Jan *Two People* reaches US #30.

Mar [4] Turner embarks on her "Break Every Rule" world tour in Munich, West Germany. (It will break box office records in 13 countries.) Financial backing is provided by her corporate sponsors, Pepsi. LP *Break Every Rule* has now hit #1 in nine territories.

Aug The US leg of the tour begins.

1988 Jan [16] On the South American tour leg, Turner plays to 180,000 people in the Maracana Arena, Rio – the largest audience ever assembled for a single performer.

Mar [28] "Break Every Rule" world tour comes to a close after 230 dates in 25 countries (playing to 3½ millon fans), in Osaka, Japan.

July Ike Turner, sentenced to a year's imprisonment for possession and transportation of cocaine, begins work on LP *My Confessions*, an autobiographical set to be released on Starforce label.

THE TURTLES

Howard Kaylan (vocals and sax)
Mark Volman (vocals and sax)
Al Nichol (guitar, piano and vocals)
Jim Tucker (guitar)
Chuck Portz (bass)
Don Murray (drums)

1963 Kaylan (b. Howard Kaplan, June 22, 1947, New York, US), Nichol (b. Mar.31, 1946, Winston Salem, N.C., US), Tucker (b. Oct.17, 1946, Los Angeles, Cal., US) and Portz (b. Mar.28, 1945, Santa Monica, Cal.) add sax player Volman (b. Apr. 19, 1947, Los

THE TURTLES *cont.*

Angeles) to their Westchester, LA, high school surf band The Nightriders, and change its name to The Crossfires. Playing popular surf instrumentals, the new line-up wins several Battle of the Bands competitions, earning a residency at The Revelaire Club, run by DJ Reb Foster. Debut single is surf instrumental *Fiberglass Jungle*, on local small label Capco Records.

1964 "British Invasion" influence (they frequently impersonate UK groups to gain gigs) inspires them to dispense with the surf instrumentals, and Volman and Kaylan switch from saxes to vocals. As a change of pace, they play some folk music dates at high schools as The Crosswind Singers, gradually electrifying the material as the folk-rock style begins to bite nationally.

1965 Ted Feigen, co-owner of new LA label White Whale, approaches the group at a gig and offers a recording deal, though a change of name is thought advisable. Manager Reb Foster suggests The Tyrtles (having seen The Byrds° around town), but the eventual compromise is The Turtles.

Sept A driving version of Bob Dylan's° *It Ain't Me Babe* hits US #8.

Nov Debut LP *It Ain't Me Babe* reaches US #98, while follow-up single, P.F. Sloan's *Let Me Be* (chosen by the band in preference to his offered *Eve Of Destruction*) makes US #29.

1966 Mar *You Baby*, another Sloan song, reaches US #20.

June *Grim Reaper Of Love*, penned by Nichol and Jim Pons, peaks at US #81 while second LP *You Baby*, recorded hurriedly between tours, fails to chart. Murray quits the band, to be replaced by John Barbata (b. Apr.1, 1946, New Jersey, US), ex-drummer with surf band The Sentinels. Portz also leaves shortly afterwards, replaced first by Chip Douglas (later The Monkees'° producer), then by Jim Pons (b. Mar.14, 1943, Santa Monica, Cal.), ex-The (*Hey Joe*) Leaves.

Nov *Can I Get To Know You Better?* stalls at US #89.

1967 Mar *Happy Together*, written by Gary Bonner and Alan Gordon and acquired when The Turtles are playing New York's Phone Booth club, tops the US chart for 3 weeks and is a million-seller.

Apr *Happy Together* is the band's UK chart debut, reaching UK #12.

June Another Bonner/Gordon song, in a romping good-time arrangement, *She'd Rather Be With Me* hits US #3 and earns the band's second gold disk. LP *Happy Together* reaches US #25.

July *She'd Rather Be With Me* hits UK #4 while the group is on a UK tour. Tucker leaves, and is not replaced.

Sept *You Know What I Mean*, a mid-tempo ballad, reaches US #12.

Dec *She's My Girl*, with a hint of psychedelia, reaches US #14.

1968 Jan Compilation LP *The Turtles! Golden Hits* is the group's biggest-selling LP, hitting US #7 and earning a gold disk for a half million sales.

Mar *Sound Asleep*, the first single produced by the band itself, makes US #57.

July Nilsson° song *The Story Of Rock And Roll* (with the composer on piano) peaks at US #48.

Nov *Elenore* hits US #6 and UK #7 (and will be The Turtles' last UK hit). It is taken from jokey concept LP *The Turtles Present The Battle Of The Bands*, which peaks at US #128.

Dec [28] The Turtles take part in the 3-day Miami Pop Festival at Hallendale, Fla.

1969 Mar *You Showed Me*, originally recorded by The Byrds°, pre-*Mr. Tambourine Man*, and resurrected by The Turtles on the *Battle* LP, is extracted to hit US #6.

May [10] The band plays at The White House as guests of Tricia Nixon. (Stories circulate concerning Kaylan and Volman allegedly snorting cocaine on Abraham Lincoln's desk.)

May Barbata leaves (later to join Jefferson Airplane°) and is replaced by John Seiter, ex-Spanky & Our Gang.

July *You Don't Have To Walk In The Rain* reaches US #51.

Oct *Love In The City* stalls at US #91.

Nov The Kinks'° Ray Davies produces LP *Turtle Soup*, which reaches US #117.

Dec Judee Sill's *Lady-O*, the last official Turtles single, reaches US #78.

1970 May Compilation LP *The Turtles! More Golden Hits* reaches US #146.

June The band refuses to complete its LP *Shell Shock* because of growing displeasure with White Whale, which retaliates by issuing *Eve Of Destruction* (from the first LP) as a single. It spends one week at US #100, while the band dissolves amid dissension within its own ranks, as well as with the label. Kaylan and Volman, (with Pons following), accept Frank Zappa's° invitation to join The Mothers of Invention. They first appear on LP *Chunga's Revenge*, billed as The Phlorescent Leech & Eddie, because of legal restraint against them using their names.

1971 Having befriended Marc Bolan° when Tyrannosaurus Rex supported The Turtles on a US tour, Kaylan and Volman assist on Bolan's new T. Rex material, singing back-up vocals on LPs *T. Rex* and *Electric Warrior*, and on hit singles *Hot Love* and *Get It On (Bang A Gong)*.

June With Zappa°, they record live LP *Fillmore East, June 1971*.

Aug [7] At UCLA, Zappa° records live LP *Just Another Band From LA*, the last to feature Kaylan and Volman, who leave to record as Flo (Volman) and Eddie (Kaylan). The duo also appears in Zappa's movie *200 Motels* and perform on the soundtrack LP.

1972 LP *The Phlorescent Leech And Eddie*, on Reprise, is recorded with Pons, Aynsley Dunbar, Don Preston and Gary Rowles (ex-Love°). The duo also sings back-up vocals on John Lennon's° LP *Some Time In New York City*.

1973 LP *Flo & Eddie* is released; the duo having shortened its name to this form.

1974 Weekly radio show, "Flo and Eddie by the Fireside", goes into national syndication in US.

1975 Jan Double anthology LP *Happy Together Again: The Turtles' Greatest Hits*, compiled and annotated by Kaylan and Volman, and including rare and unissued material as well as the hits, reaches US #194. Meanwhile, Flo & Eddie change labels, releasing LP *Illegal Immoral And Fattening* on CBS/Columbia.

1976 LP *Moving Targets* is released, including a new version of The Turtles' *Elenore*.

1980 Volman and Kaylan sing back-up vocals on LPs by Blondie° (*Autoamerican*) and Alice Cooper° (*Flush The Fashion*).

1981 After a period as guest vocalists and producers, the duo releases LP *Rock Steady With Flo And Eddie* on Epiphany, recorded in Jamaica with top reggae artists.

1982 Rhino Records in US begins a reissue program of the entire Turtles catalog, releasing all the LPs, including the rare *Wooden Head*, various compilations and much previously unavailable material – all with full assistance from Kaylan and Volman. A new touring version of The Turtles, based around the duo, hits the road for a successful series of nostalgia gigs.

1987 Rhino issues unreleased LP *Shell Shock*, which had been abandoned at the end of the group's White Whale career.

1988 Rhino releases four Turtles former hits on a 3-inch compact disk EP.

TWISTED SISTER

Dee Snider (vocals)
Jay Jay French (guitar)
Eddie Ojeda (guitar)
Mark Mendoza (bass)
A.J. Pero (drums)

1976/82 Snider (b. Mar.15, 1955, Massapequa, Long Island, N.Y., US) joins French (b. July 20, 1954, New York, N.Y.) and Ojeda (b. Aug.5, 1954, Bronx, New York) to play their own mix of glam and heavy metal to devoted fans in the New York area. (Ex-Dictator Mendoza (b. July 13, 1956) joins in 1978 and Pero (b. Oct.14, 1959, Staten Island, New York) in 1982.) Even after the band puts up $25,000 to stage a sell-out show at New York's 3400-seat Palladium, record companies fail to show interest. A German company offers a contract which never materializes after the company president has a heart attack on his way home from the concert.

1982 Eventually, staff at UK music paper *Sounds* convince the band to visit London and record an LP for local independent punk label, Secret.

Sept LP *Under The Blade*, produced by UFO's Peter Way, is released but Secret promptly goes bust. It briefly enters the UK chart, reaching #70.

1983 An appearance on UK TV Channel 4's "The Tube" leads to a contract with Atlantic Records in US.

Apr *I Am (I'm Me)* is the group's first release for the label, making UK #18 but failing to chart in US.

May *The Kids Are Back* reaches UK #32.

June LP *You Can't Stop Rock'n'Roll* climbs to UK #14 and makes US #130, selling in excess of 200,000 copies.

Aug [20] Twisted Sister plays the Donington Park Festival, UK. The title track of LP *You Can't Stop Rock'n'Roll* makes UK #43.

1984 June LP *Stay Hungry* reaches US #15 and UK #34. A music video cassette also titled *Stay Hungry*, featuring 11 songs, is released.

July With the considerable aid of a video heavily featured on MTV, *We're Not Gonna Take It* reaches US #21 but only UK #58.
Oct *I Wanna Rock* reaches US #68.
1985 Mar *Price* fails to chart in US or UK. Snider assumes a high profile in the US music industry, with a regular heavy metal slot on MTV and appearances on talk shows and before the PMRC-inspired Senate Committee who are investigating the effect of rock'n'roll on American youth. As a non-smoking teetotalling father, his is a respectable voice.
Nov A cover version of The Shangri-Las'° classic *Leader Of The Pack* makes US #53.
Dec LP *Come Out And Play* has a 1 week stay on the UK chart at #95. It features a duet with Alice Cooper° on *Be Kruel To Your Skuel*.
1986 Jan *Leader Of The Pack* makes UK #47.
Feb LP *Come Out And Play* makes US #53.
Apr *You Want What We Got* is released, but fails to chart.
1987 July LP *Love Is For Suckers* reaches UK #57.
Aug LP *Love Is For Suckers* makes US #74, after which the band splits with Snider, who intends to pursue a solo career.
1988 Aug Snider teams with Bernie Torme, ex-Gillan guitarist, for new band Desperado.

BONNIE TYLER

1970 Tyler (b. June 8, 1953, Skewen, South Wales, UK), having attended Rhydhir school, Neath, wins a local talent contest at age 17, and leaves her shop job when she starts to get bookings singing in local pubs and clubs.
1976 A recurring problem with nodules on her throat is finally cured after an operation, which leaves her with what will be a trademark husky voice tone. Now a veteran of the South Wales club scene, fronting a band named Mumbles which specializes in covers of raunchy soul material, she is spotted at Swansea's Townman Club by producer/songwriters Ronnie Scott and Steve Wolfe, who decide that she has an ideal voice to record a song they have jointly penned, *Lost In France*. They become her managers and producers.
Nov Tyler is signed to RCA and *Lost In France*, produced by Scott and Wolfe, is her first single and chart debut, hitting UK #9.
1977 Apr *More Than A Lover* reaches UK #27.
1978 Jan *It's A Heartache* hits UK #4.
June *It's A Heartache* hits US #3 and is a million-seller.
July LP *It's A Heartache* reaches US #16.
1979 Mar LP *Diamond Cut* makes US #145.
July *Married Men* (from movie *The World is Full of Married Men* adapted from the Jackie Collins novel) makes UK #35.
1981 After several failed singles, Tyler does not renew her contracts with either Scott and Wolfe or RCA when they expire. She signs to CBS/Columbia and David Aspden becomes her manager.
1983 Mar In search of a bigger, more Spectoresque sound, Tyler approaches Jim Steinman (writer of Meat Loaf's° *Bat Out Of Hell*) to produce her, and he records her on his own composition *Total Eclipse Of The Heart*, which tops the UK chart for 2 weeks, deposing Michael Jackson's° *Billie Jean*.
Apr Steinman-produced LP *Faster Than The Speed Of Night* tops the UK chart – only the second LP by a UK female singer (the first being Kate Bush's° *The Kick Inside*) to do so.
May The title song from *Faster Than The Speed Of Night*, also written by Steinman, peaks at UK #43.
July An update of Creedence Clearwater Revival's° *Have You Ever Seen The Rain?* halts at UK #47.
Oct *Total Eclipse Of The Heart* tops the US chart for 3 weeks, and is her second US million-seller, while LP *Faster Than The Speed Of Night* hits US #4, and also sells over a million.
1984 Jan Tyler teams with Shakin' Stevens° on a revival of 1960 US top 10 duet hit by Brook Benton° and Dinah Washington, *A Rockin' Good Way (To Mess Around And Fall In Love)*; it hits UK #5, but is a one-off collaboration. Meanwhile, her solo single *Take Me Back* reaches US #46.
Apr *Holding Out For A Hero*, a Steinman song included on the soundtrack of movie *Footloose*, reaches US #34.
Aug *Here She Comes*, from Giorgio Moroder's soundtrack from the revived silent movie *Metropolis*, makes US #76.
1985 Sept *Holding Out For A Hero* is a belated UK success, hitting #2 behind Mick Jagger and David Bowie's° revival of *Dancing In The Street*.
Dec Another Steinman composition, *Loving You's A Dirty Job But Somebody's Gotta Do It*, stalls at UK #73. It features Todd Rundgren° as guest vocal duettist.
1986 May Rundgren° also features on guest vocals on *If You Were A Woman (And I Was A Man)*, which makes US #77.
1988 Oct She participates, along with a host of other Welsh acting and singing personalities, on the all-star LP version of Dylan Thomas' *Under Milk Wood*.
Nov Tyler embarks on a tour of USSR.

THE TYMES

George Williams (lead vocals)
Albert "Caesar" Berry (first tenor vocals)
George Hilliard (second tenor vocals)
Norman Burnett (baritone vocals)
Donald Banks (bass vocals)

1956 The group forms in Philadelphia, Pa., US, as The Latineers, a close-harmony quartet comprising Berry, Hilliard, Burnett and Banks, and is successful in local clubs, talent shows and dances.
1960 Williams joins to give a distinctive lead voice, and the group renames itself The Tymes (the spelling being "just to be different").
1963 Apr Spotted on a Radio WDAS-sponsored local talent show, the group is signed to Cameo Records and placed on its Parkway label (which has Chubby Checker°, among others), with Billy Jackson producing. For a record debut, Williams suggests his half-complete song *The Stroll*, which is revamped by Williams, Jackson and arranger Roy Straigis, and becomes *So Much In Love*. Jackson cuts it in a breezy, finger-snapping arrangement (with appropriate seashore and bird noises in the background) to sound good on summertime radio.
Aug *So Much In Love* hits US #1 and is a million-seller, also reaching UK #21 (the group's only UK hit in its early career).
Sept A revival of Johnny Mathis' *Wonderful! Wonderful!* hits US #7. It is taken from debut LP *So Much In Love*, a collection of standards, which reaches US #15.
1964 Jan *Somewhere*, its melody borrowed from a classical piece, reaches US #19 while LP *The Sound Of The Wonderful Tymes* makes US #117.
Mar *To Each His Own* stalls at US #78 and LP *Somewhere* at US #122.
June *The Magic Of Our Summer Love* makes US #99, as the group's smooth vocal style becomes dated on a US chart dominated by the "British Invasion" and Motown and other labels forging hit paths away from traditional sounds.
Nov *Here She Comes* reaches US #92. Cameo/Parkway itself is in trouble, having changed ownership and failed to invest in developing talent to meet new trends.
1965 After a failed release, *The Twelfth Of Never*, the group leaves Cameo and sets up its own Winchester Records, in partnership with ex-Cameo songwriters Leon Huff, Dave White and John Madara. The label fails after just two non-hit releases, one of them The Tymes' *These Foolish Things*.
1966 They sign, with producer Jackson, to MGM Records on a short-term deal but *Touch Of Baby* and *Pretend* fail and their option is dropped.
1968 Dec Signed, again on a short-term deal, and still with Jackson, to CBS/Columbia, the group reaches US #39 with a dramatic re-scoring of *People*, from *Funny Girl* and best known as a Barbra Streisand° ballad.
1969 Feb *People* is the group's first UK hit since *So Much In Love*, reaching #16. Columbia decides to prune its black artist roster and drops both group and producer.
1970/72 With its style sharpened into a more contemporary soul group blend, The Tymes work on the soul tour and cabaret circuits. Hilliard leaves, to be replaced as second tenor by Charles Nixon.
1973 Jackson decides to finance new recordings himself and then lease them to a label. He takes the group into Sigma Sound studios, Philadelphia, where four tracks are cut until the money runs out. Jackson takes these to Gamble and Huff at Philadelphia International, who turn them down, but RCA Records buys the recordings, finances their completion, and signs the group.
1974 Oct RCA debut is Jackson's composition *You Little Trustmaker*, which reaches US #12 and UK #13.
Dec LP *Trustmaker* is released; recorded in both Philadelphia and New York, it is the group's first LP of contemporary material (apart from a re-recording of *So Much In Love*). It does not chart but *Miss Grace* (written by John and Johanna Hall of Orleans) is

THE TYMES *cont.*

extracted, re-titled to *Ms. Grace* and makes US #91.

1975 Jan *Ms.Grace* hits UK #1 for a week to give the group its all-time biggest UK seller but, with no strong follow-up, commercial impetus is lost.

1976 Jan *God's Gonna Punish You* reaches UK #41, the group's final UK chart entry.

May *It's Cool* makes US #68. The group is again without a recording contract (and will have no more hits, but its most famous song, *So Much In Love* will be recorded with some success by Timothy B. Schmit and Art Garfunkel°).

UB40

Ali Campbell (lead vocals, rhythm guitar)
Rob Campbell (lead guitar, vocals)
Earl Falconer (bass)
Mickey Virtue (keyboards)
Brian Travers (saxophone)
Jim Brown (drums)
Norman Hassan (percussion)
"Yomi" Babayemi (percussion)

1979 Feb After 6 months of rehearsal, UB40 (named after the number on a UK unemployment benefit form) debuts at The Horse and Hounds in King's Heath, Birmingham, sharing the bill with new local band, The Au Pairs. Most of the group have known each other for up to 10 years and several had attended art school together. Ali and Rob Campbell, sons of Scottish folk singer Ian Campbell, have sung with two other brothers in a barbershop quartet and been reggae fans since childhood. After only one more gig, Babayemi is deported to Nigeria by immigration authorities. The group and its manager, ex-encyclopedia salesman Simon Woods, contact local producer Bob Lamb, an ex-member of Birmingham reggae band The Locomotive (1968 hitmakers with *Rudi's In Love*) who owns an eight-track studio, to make some demos. Before the first sessions, reggae toaster/singer Astro (b. Terence Wilson) joins the group. Their big break comes when The Pretenders'° Chrissie Hynde sees their live show and offers a support slot on The Pretenders' 1979/80 UK tour. Despite major label interest, the group signs to Graduate, run by David and Susan Virr from their record shop in Dudley, Worcs., UK. The deal gives them total control but no advance monies – resulting in debts at the outset of their career.

1980 Apr A-side of the group's first release is *King* (a dedication to Martin Luther King), but radio picks up on the catchy B-side *Food For Thought*. It tops the independent chart for 3 months before hitting UK #4. Recorded in Lamb's studio, it sells over a half million copies. Major record company pressure intensifies during the tour with The Pretenders°.

July Follow-up *My Way Of Thinking*, backed with Randy Newman's° *I Think It's Going To Rain Today*, hits UK #6.

Sept First LP, *Signing Off*, recorded by Lamb in eight-track, hits UK #2 (and will stay on chart for 71 weeks).

Nov *The Earth Dies Screaming* hits UK #10.

Dec UB40 leaves Graduate, apparently due to Graduate deleting anti-apartheid *Burden Of Shame* from the South African release of the LP. The group sets up its own DEP International company. After concerts in Europe and Ireland, it tours UK and appears on a Christmas bill at the Birmingham NEC.

1981 June LP *Present Arms*, the first on DEP International, hits UK #2, spending 38 weeks on chart. Initial copies of it come with a free 12" single containing two instrumentals, *Don't Walk On The Grass* and *Dr. X* (a reworking of the LP's title track). The tracks are produced by the band's sound engineer, Ray "Pablo" Falconer, brother of bassist Earl. *Don't Let It Pass You By/Don't Slow Down* makes UK #16.

Sept *One In Ten*, a commentary on UK unemployment figures, hits UK #7. UB40 plays benefit gigs for those arrested during UK inner-city riots of the summer, which lead to UB40 being banned from venues in some cities. The group begins a major international tour.

Oct *Present Arms In Dub*, a dub reworking of the LP, reaches UK #38.

1982 Feb *I Won't Close My Eyes* peaks at UK #32. B-side *Folitician* features Astro as a toaster and is a highlight of UB40's UK tour.

June *Love Is All Is Alright* makes UK #29 and hits #1 in Zimbabwe, Africa, for 3 weeks.

Sept Funk-tinged *So Here I Am* reaches UK #25. LP *The Singles Album*, a collection of the group's Graduate singles, makes UK #17.

Oct LP *UB44* hits UK #4, despite some negative reviews.

1983 Feb *I've Got Mine* peaks at UK #45 (the poorest group chart position to date).

Mar LP *UB40 Live* makes UK #44.

Sept *Red Red Wine*, their first UK #1 hit, tops the chart for 3 weeks. (The group claims it was unaware the song was a Neil Diamond° composition and had picked it up from Jamaican singer Tony Tribe's 1969 version.) LP *Labour Of Love*, a collection of classic songs given reggae covers, hits UK #1 and stays on chart for 18 months.

Nov *Please Don't Make Me Cry* hits UK #10.

Dec *Many Rivers To Cross* reaches UK #16.

1984 Mar *Red Red Wine* makes US #34, the group's first US hit single.

Apr *Cherry Oh Baby* peaks at UK #12. LP *Labour Of Love* reaches US #39.

Oct *If It Happens Again* hits UK #9 and LP *Geffrey Morgan* hits UK #3.

Dec *Riddle Me* peaks at UK #59. The group plays concerts for the Greater London Council, which is fighting off dissolution by the government. LP *Geffrey Morgan* makes US #60.

1985 Feb UB40 joins Madness°, Special AKA, General Public and The Pioneers to record *Starvation* (the profits go to the Ethiopian appeal).

May *I'm Not Fooled* peaks at UK #79.

Aug Ali Campbell and Chrissie Hynde's duet on a reggae version of Sonny & Cher's° *I Got You Babe*, hits UK #1 for 1 week. The video for it is filmed by Jonathan Demme at a concert at Jones Beach, Long Island, N.Y., during one of UB40's three 1985 US visits.

Sept LP *Baggariddim*, consisting of dub versions of tracks from the previous two LPs, with toasters like Dillinger and Sister V guesting, makes UK #14. In a trimmed-down version in US, *Little Baggariddim*, reaches #40, while *I Got You Babe* (also included on the mini-LP) makes US #28.

Dec *Don't Break My Heart*, taken from the free 12" issued with the LP, hits UK #3.

1986 July *Sing Our Own Song*, an expression of solidarity with black activists in South Africa, hits UK #5.

Aug LP *Rat In The Kitchen*, featuring US label boss Herb Alpert° on guest trumpet, reaches UK #8.

Oct *All I Want To Do* makes a disappointing UK #41.

1987 Jan Single *Rat In Mi Kitchen* peaks at UK #12.

May *Watchdogs* reaches UK #39.

Oct *Maybe Tomorrow* makes UK #14.

Nov Virgin Records releases TV-advertised *The Best Of UB40 Vol.1* for the Christmas market. It hits UK #3. Falconer's Volvo turbo goes out of control and hits a wall, killing his brother Ray. The discovery of twice the legal limit of alcohol in Earl's bloodstream leads to charges.

1988 June Second UB40/Chrissie Hynde team-up, a version of standard *Breakfast In Bed*, hits UK #6.

July A week before the group's world tour is due to start, a Birmingham Crown Court judge jails Earl Falconer for 6 months on charges from the car accident. The group is forced to pick up a stand-in bassist at short notice. Newly-recorded LP *UB40* reaches UK #12.

Sept *Where Did We Go Wrong*, released in UK, reaches #26.

Oct *Red Red Wine* tops the US chart while LP *Labour Of Love* (which contains the single) makes US #14 and LP *UB40* reaches US top 40.

U2

Bono (vocals)
The Edge (guitar)
Adam Clayton (bass)
Larry Mullen Jr. (drums)

1976/77 Dublin school boy band, featuring Bono (b. Paul Hewson, May 10, 1960, Dublin, Ireland), The Edge (b. David Evans, Aug.8, 1961, Wales, UK), Clayton (b. Mar.13, 1960), Mullen Jr. (b. Oct.31, 1961, Dublin) and Dick Evans, forms as Feedback at Mullen's parents' home, in response to Mullen's note on a school notice board. Playing mainly cover versions at small-time local engagements, the group changes name to The Hype and, with Dick Evans departure to form The Virgin Prunes, to U2. (Hewson has adopted the name Bono from a billboard, advertising a hearing aid retailer, Bono Vox.)

1978 Mar [30] After playing pub and club gigs in Dublin, U2 wins a talent contest sponsored by Guinness at the Limerick Civic Week. Still in their final year at school, they win £500 and the chance to audition for CBS Ireland (through contest adjudicator A&R man Jackie Hayden) at the Keystone Studios. Already managed by Paul McGuinness, U2 secures live support slots for The Stranglers° and The Greedy Bastards.

Sept Hayden arranges for UK *Record Mirror* journalist Chas de Whalley to record further demos at the Windmill Lane Studios, Dublin, which leads to signing with CBS Ireland (UK does not take up the option).

Sept [18] The band poses backstage after a gig at Dublin's Project Arts Centre, holding gun and pistol replicas.

1979 Sept Having built considerable Irish fan support, following an RTE Radio 2 Irish demo session tape broadcast, U2 finally releases EP *U2:3*, featuring *Out Of Control*, *Stories* and *Boy – Girl*. Only available in Ireland, it tops the chart.

Dec U2 plays its first UK dates to little interest. Miscredited as "V2" at the Hope & Anchor pub in London, only nine people show to watch them.

1980 Feb As *Another Day*, produced by Whalley, also hits #1 in Ireland, U2 plays sell-out gigs on its home territory.

Mar After more promising UK dates attended by A&R employee Bill Stewart, UK label Island signs the band (it remains on CBS in Ireland).

May Debut Island single, *11 O'Clock Tick Tock* is released, produced by Martin Hannett, but fails to chart in UK.

Aug *A Day Without Me* also fails to chart in UK.

Oct *I Will Follow* fails in UK and also US.

Nov Debut LP *Boy*, produced by Steve Lillywhite, fails to chart. (The boy featured on the front cover is Peter, a brother of Virgin Prunes vocalist Guggi.)

Dec Constantly gigging, U2 support Talking Heads° on a UK tour.

1981 Feb The band embarks on first US tour, to immediate live critical acclaim.

Mar LP *Boy* climbs to US #63.

July *Fire* is released and will be UK chart debut at #35.

Aug LP *Boy* belatedly reaches UK #52.

Oct [1] U2 begins a UK tour.

Oct *Gloria* makes UK #55, supported by a video shot at Dublin docks.

Nov Parent LP *October*, produced by Lillywhite and again recorded at the Windmill Lane Studios, Dublin (their long-term professional base), peaks at UK #11 and US #104.

1982 Mar [17] U2 plays a St. Patrick's Day gig at New York's The Ritz.

Apr Following a sold-out UK tour, *A Celebration* (not available on LP) makes UK #47.

June U2 enters Windmill to spend the rest of the year recording new songs.

Oct During a concert in Belfast, N. Ireland, Bono introduces new song *Sunday Bloody Sunday*. (Written by The Edge, its "peace in Northern Ireland" message becomes a live focal point for the band in coming years and highlights links between lyrics and politics.)

1983 Feb *New Year's Day*, boosted by a snow-bound video, hits UK #10 as parent LP *War*, their last with Lillywhite, climbs to US #12.

Mar LP *War* enters the UK chart at #1.

Apr U2 begins a 2-month US tour while *Two Hearts Beat As One* reaches UK #18.

May Debut US chart single is *New Year's Day* at #53, as remaining US dates draw superlative reviews and large crowds.

May [28] U2 takes part in the 3-day US Festival.

Nov First live LP *Under A Blood Red Sky*, produced by Jimmy Iovine, is released simultaneously with a video of the same title. It hits UK #2 and begins a climb to US #28. Recorded in Boston, Mass., West Germany and at the Red Rocks festival in Colorado, US, it becomes the most successful live LP ever, but does little to offset the growing number of U2 bootleg recordings.

1984 Jan *I Will Follow* reaches US #81.

July Bono duets with Bob Dylan° on *Blowing In The Wind* at Dylan's concert at Slane Castle, Ireland.

Aug U2 establishes its own Mother Records to showcase the recordings of unsigned talent (mostly Irish). The label's first release is In Tua Nua's *Coming Thru'*. Run by Fachtra O'Ceallaigh, Mother will also sign, usually on a one-release basis, bands including Cactus World News, Tuesday Blue, Operating Theatre, Painted Word, The Subterraneans and Hothouse Flowers.

Sept Now produced by Brian Eno° and Daniel Lanois, new studio LP *The Unforgettable Fire* hits UK #1 and US #12 as extracted *Pride (In The Name Of Love)*, dedicated to Martin Luther King Jr., climbs to hit UK #3 and US #33.

Nov [25] Bono contributes a lead vocal part to Band Aid's° *Do They Know It's Christmas?*, while Clayton plays bass.

1985 Jan U2 begins its first US arenas tour following sold-out European dates.

May *The Unforgettable Fire* hits UK #6.

June [22] U2 headlines UK's Milton Keynes Bowl.

July [13] U2 plays the fund-raising Live Aid spectacular at Wembley Stadium, London, UK, introduced by Jack Nicholson in Philadelphia. US import LP *Wide Awake In America*, a live studio collection of five cuts, makes UK #11. (The title track is the only previously unreleased track.)

Oct Released as an EP in US, *Wide Awake In America* reaches US #37.

Nov Bono appears on Little Steven-organized Artists United Against Apartheid single and video *Sun City* (UK #21 and US #38). He also sings the closing number on the accompanying LP, the track *Silver And Gold* recorded with The Rolling Stones'° Keith Richard and Ron Wood.

1986 Jan Bono is a featured vocalist on Irish folk group Clannad's° *In A Lifetime*, which makes UK #20.

Mar U2 resumes world touring (which will include performing on the Amnesty International 25th Anniversary tour).

May [17] U2 joins other Irish rock acts to play Self Aid in Dublin, to raise funds for the unemployed.

June [4] Amnesty International's "A Conspiracy of Hope" 2-week US tour begins, featuring U2, Sting°, Peter Gabriel°, Bryan Adams° and Lou Reed° at Cow Palace, San Francisco.

Aug The band enters the studio, with Eno° and Lanois, to record a new LP. (The Edge also records soundtrack LP *The Captive* with Irish songstress Sinead O'Connor.)

Sept [25] U2 is joined on stage by Bruce Springsteen° during a concert in Philadelphia, Pa.

1987 Feb U2 begins a 110-date arena venue world tour.

Mar *With Or Without You* is released with parent LP *The Joshua Tree*. As the LP heads swiftly to US #1, where it will stay for 9 weeks, and UK #1, where it goes platinum in 48 hours, the single hits UK #4.

Mar [27] The group films a video for *Where The Streets Have No Name* in downtown LA, drawing a crowd of thousands.

Apr With changed US chart eligibility, LP *Wide Awake In America* now makes US #100.

May [16] *With Or Without You* becomes U2's first US #1. With music by U2 and lyrics by Bono, it is typical of their songwriting format, and becomes an immediate airplay and sales smash, staying on top for 3 weeks.

May *I Still Haven't Found What I'm Looking For* hits UK #6, with a video filmed on the streets of Las Vegas.

Aug While *Where The Streets Have No Name*, accompanied by a performance video filmed on top of an LA building, hits UK #4, *I Still Haven't Found What I'm Looking For* hits US #1.

Sept [10] The North American leg of world tour begins at New York's Nassau Coliseum.

Nov *Where The Streets Have No Name* reaches US #13. Book *Unforgettable Fire: The Story of U2* hits UK book best-seller lists. Written by Eamon Dunphy, it was originally authorized by the band who later withdrew their support having negotiated unsuccessfully to change the text, which is claimed to be inaccurate.

Nov [18] U2 opens for itself at LA's Coliseum as country/rock outfit The Dalton Brothers.

Dec U2 contributes *Christmas (Baby Please Come Home)* to Jimmy Iovine's charity LP *Special Christmas*.

1988 Jan *In God's Country* reaches US #44, but remains unreleased in UK.

Feb [8] U2 receives Best International Group award at the British Record Industry Awards ceremony at London's Royal Albert Hall.

Mar [2] The band collects Album of the Year and Rock Vocal – Duo/Group awards at the annual Grammy ceremonies in Radio City Music Hall, New York.

Sept Bono and The Edge make contributions to Roy Orbison° comeback LP *Mystery Girl*.

Oct Double LP *Rattle And Hum* (the title taken from U2 song *Bullet The Blue Sky*), capturing live performances from the past 2 years and including rare studio songs, hits UK #1 (with record ship-out figures) and US #1. Produced by Iovine, it is released simultaneously with theater showcased *Rattle And Hum* film, meticulously chronicling the band's recent career. Directed by Phil Joanou, his brief was to "follow the Joshua Tree tour and make a film". *Desire* becomes U2's first UK #1 single and hits US #3.

Nov U2 plays "Smile Jamaica" benefit gig at London's Brixton Academy to raise money for the Hurricane Gilbert disaster fund, and is joined on stage by Keith Richard.

Dec *Angel Of Harlem*, recorded at the legendary Sun studios, Memphis, Tenn., hits UK #9 and begins a US rise.

ULTRAVOX

John Foxx (guitar and lead vocals)
Billy Currie (synthesizer and piano)
Chris Cross (bass and synthesizer)
Warren Cann (drums)

1973 Foxx (b. Dennis Leigh, Chorley, Lancs., UK) recruits Cross (b. Christopher St. John, July 14, 1952, London, UK), who has moved from London to join Preston band Stoned Rose, to form new band Tiger Lily.

Apr They add Cann (b. May 20, 1952, Victoria, Canada) on drums and Steve Shears on guitar. With Roxy Music° as chief musical inspiration, they begin live gigs and demos.

Aug First major gig is at London's Marquee club supporting The Heavy Metal Kids.

Oct Currie (b. Apr.1, 1952, Huddersfield, Yorks., UK) joins on keyboards.

1975 Mar The group record Fats Waller's *Ain't Misbehavin'*, (for an X-certificate film of the same title, which flops) coupled with *Monkey Jive* on small Gull label. (It will be reissued on Dead Good Records in Aug. 1980.)

1976 July After going through a series of names, including The Zips, The Innocents, London Soundtrack and Fire of London, the group becomes Ultravox.

Aug The group signs to Island Records and spends the year writing and rehearsing its debut LP. First product is *The Wild, The Beautiful And The Damned* which is featured on an Island sampler LP.

1977 Feb Debut single *Dangerous Rhythm*, from the forthcoming LP, is released.

Mar LP *Ultravox!*, co-produced by Brian Eno°, is released and is critically well received.

Oct *Rockwork* and parent LP *Ha! Ha! Ha!* are released, but fail.

1978 Feb *Retro*, a live 4-track EP, is released. The band travels to West Germany to record with Conny Plank. Prior to the sessions, Shears leaves, to be replaced by Robin Simon, ex-Neo.

Aug The group plays UK's Reading Festival (billed second to The Jam°), and five consecutive dates at London's Marquee.

Sept Plank-produced LP *Systems Of Romance* is released, but fails to chart.

Dec [26] The original line-up plays two last UK dates at London's Marquee.

1979 Jan Island Records drops the group.

Mar After some weeks of final gigs in US, Foxx leaves for a solo career on returning to UK. Cann works with New Zealand singer Zaine Griff, while Currie and Simon play with Gary Numan° and Magazine respectively, and Cross writes songs with his brother. Apart from Foxx, the members still wish to continue with Ultravox, and look for a new singer and guitarist.

Apr Guitarist/singer James "Midge" Ure (b. Oct.10, 1953, Gambusland, Glasgow, Scotland, UK) joins. He has been with Currie in Visage and was in Salvation, which became Slik. (In 1976, after teaming with The Bay City Rollers'° producers Bill Martin and Phil Coulter, they become brief pop sensations, hitting UK #1 with *Forever And Ever*. Ure left in 1977 and then teamed with ex-The Sex Pistols'° Glen Matlock in The Rich Kids.) While the group works on new material, Ure stands in for Brian Robertson in Thin Lizzy°.

Nov The new line-up plays four UK gigs, starting at Eric's Liverpool, to prepare for a US tour.

Dec The group begins a US tour.

1980 Jan Foxx, having created his own MetalBeat label, releases *Underpass*, which makes UK #31 as parent LP *Metamatic* reaches UK #18.

Mar Foxx's 4-track EP *No One Driving* makes UK #32.

Apr Ultravox signed to Chrysalis, releases *Sleepwalk*, the group's first with Ure. It reaches UK #29 while Island issues *Three Into One*, a compilation of the best of the three LPs for the label.

July LP *Vienna*, the group's first with Ure and for Chrysalis, hits UK #3 during a 72-week chart stay. Foxx's *Burning Car* reaches UK #35.

Oct Ultravox's *Passing Strangers* makes UK #57, as LP *Vienna* is US debut at #164.

Nov *Burning Car*, by Foxx, makes US #51.

1981 Jan Grandiose ballad *Vienna* attracts heavy UK airplay, hitting UK #2, held off the top by Joe Dolce's novelty *Shaddap You Face*.

Mar Island releases 3-track EP *Slow Motion*, which reaches UK #33.

June *All Stood Still* hits UK #8.

Aug *The Thin Wall*, recorded earlier in the year in West Germany with producer Plank, reaches UK #14. Foxx makes UK #40 with *Europe After The Rain*.

Sept LP *Rage In Eden* hits UK #4.

Oct Foxx's second LP *In The Garden* makes UK #24.

Nov Ultravox's *The Voice* peaks at UK #16, while LP *Rage In Eden* makes US #144.

1982 June Ure releases solo Chrysalis single, *No Regrets*, which hits UK #9. (He will produce Steve Harley°, Atrix and Modern Man, while also working with Visage.)

Sept Ultravox reaches UK #12 with *Reap The Wild Wind*.

Oct LP *Quartet*, recorded in Montserrat with George Martin producing, hits UK #6.

Nov *Hymn* makes UK #11.

1983 Mar *Visions In Blue* peaks at UK #15.

Apr The group has its only US single success with *Reap The Wild Wind* which makes US #71. Parent LP *Quartet* peaks at US #61.

June *We Came To Dance* reaches UK #18.

July Ure's *After A Fashion*, with Japan° bassist Mick Karn, makes UK #39.

Oct LP *Monument – The Soundtrack* hits UK #9. Foxx's LP *The Golden Section* makes UK #27.

1984 Feb *One Small Day* climbs to UK #27.

Apr LP *Lament* hits UK #8.

May *Dancing With Tears In My Eyes* becomes Ultravox's first UK top 10 hit in 3 years, at #3.

June LP *Lament* climbs to US #115.

July The title track *Lament* makes UK #22.

Oct *Love's Great Adventure* reaches UK #12.

Nov Chrysalis issues a retrospective LP of its Ultravox recordings, *The Collection*, which hits UK #2. Ure is approached by Bob Geldof to write a song to be recorded by an all-star band to raise funds for the starving people of Ethiopia.

Dec [15] *Do They Know It's Christmas?*, is recorded by Band Aid°. (It enters UK chart at #1 and will become the UK's biggest-selling single.)

1985 July Continuing his efforts with Geldof to raise money to ease famine in Africa and Ethiopia, Ure is active behind the scenes in organizing the Live Aid spectacular, at which he also performs.

Sept Ure's solo *If I Was* tops the UK chart, as Ultravox remains quiet.

Oct Ure's LP *The Gift* hits UK #2. Foxx's LP *In Mysterious Ways* makes 1 week at UK #85.

Nov Ure's *That Certain Smile* reaches UK #28.

Dec Ure begins his first solo tour, with Zal Cleminson, ex-The Sensational Alex Harvey Band, on guitar and Kenny Hyslop (with whom Ure has worked in Slik), on drums.

1986 Feb Ure's *Wastelands* makes UK #46.

June Ure's *Call Of The Wild* reaches UK #27.

Oct Group LP *U-Vox* hits UK #9.

1988 June [11] Ure assembles the band for Nelson Mandela's 70th Birthday Party concert.

Sept Ure's LP *Answers (Answers To Nothing)* makes UK #30, as the title track single stalls at UK #49.

THE UNDERTONES

Feargal Sharkey (vocals)
John O'Neill (guitar)
Damian "Dee" O'Neill (guitar)
Michael Bradley (bass)
Billy Doherty (drums)

1975 Nov The band is formed by five friends in Londonderry, Northern Ireland, playing pop covers in local pubs. They remain members

throughout its existence.
1977 The band begins to perform more of its own songs and makes a demo which is rejected by Stiff, Chiswick and Radar Records.
1978 Aug After a period of playing regional gigs during which their act and repertoire are finely honed, The Undertones are spotted and recorded by Belfast independent label Good Vibrations Records.
Sept Debut release *Teenage Kicks* receives UK airplay from BBC DJ John Peel, which brings A&R interest from UK labels.
Oct The band flies to London to play "Top of the Pops" as the record climbs the chart. They are still without a manager, so Sharkey (b. Aug.13, 1958) negotiates a 5-year deal with Sire Records. Sire reissues *Teenage Kicks* (only 7,000 copies were pressed on Good Vibrations).
Nov *Teenage Kicks* reaches UK #31 in a 6-week chart run. The band begins its first UK tour with The Rezillos, who split halfway through and leave The Undertones to continue the tour alone.
1979 Feb *Get Over You* makes UK #57.
May *Jimmy Jimmy* is their first UK top 20 hit at #16. Debut LP *The Undertones* is released and climbs to UK #13, the sleeve inspired by The Who's° *My Generation* 1965 debut.
July A re-recorded version of *Here Comes The Summer*, extracted from the LP, makes UK #34. While it is on the chart, the group plays its first US tour, supporting The Clash°.
Oct *You've Got My Number (Why Don't You Use It?)* peaks at UK #32.
1980 Jan The band goes to Holland with producer Roger Bechirian to record its second LP.
Apr LP *Hypnotised* is released and becomes their biggest UK LP, hitting #6. *My Perfect Cousin* is their biggest UK hit single at #9.
July *Wednesday Week*, extracted from the LP in UK, charts at #11.
Aug The Undertones tour US again, this time as headliners, but they fail to chart there and remain cult favorites. A headlining European tour follows.
Oct Dissatisfied with lack of chart progress outside UK, the band does not renew its Sire contract but sets up its own label, Ardeck Records, through EMI.
1981 May New UK single *It's Going To Happen* and LP *Positive Touch* are released displaying a widening of approach and more sophistication than earlier aggressive work. The LP charts at UK #17 and the single peaks at UK #18.
July Rapid UK follow-up *Julie Ocean* makes #41.
1982 Feb *Beautiful Friend* is issued in UK but fails to chart.
Oct *The Love Parade* also fails to sell.
1983 Mar LP *The Sin Of Pride* makes UK #43 but has no hit singles to keep it on chart.
June The group disbands and EMI marks the split by reissuing *Teenage Kicks*. It makes UK #60.
Dec A 30-track compilation LP, *All Wrapped Up*, issued as a memorial to the band, charts at UK #67. Sharkey, always the main focus of the band, joins ex-Depeche Mode° and Yazoo° writer/keyboardist Vince Clarke for The Assembly one-off single, *Never Never*, which hits UK #4, then announces plans to continue as a solo act.
1984 Oct Invited to be the first act on Madness'° Zarjazz label, Sharkey has the band backing him on his solo *Listen To Your Father*, which reaches UK #23.
Dec [7] He performs in a benefit concert for Ethiopia at London's Royal Albert Hall, organized by the Save The Children Fund, along with Nick Heyward, Julian Lennon, Mike Rutherford of Genesis° and others.
1985 July Sharkey signs to Virgin, and debut *Loving You* makes UK #26.
Nov He tops the UK chart for 2 weeks with *A Good Heart*, written by Maria McKee of US group Lone Justice. LP *Feargal Sharkey*, produced by Dave Stewart of Eurythmics°, makes UK #12.
1986 Jan *You Little Thief*, taken from the LP (and first promoted in UK by Sharkey on a live TV slot from a Virgin airliner flying over London on Christmas Day) hits UK #5.
Feb [6] While Sharkey is touring UK and performing in Sheffield, his mother Sybil and sister Ursula, visiting friends in Londonderry, Northern Ireland, are held at gunpoint for 4 hours by terrorists but eventually released.
Apr *Someone To Somebody* makes UK #64. Sharkey separates from his wife and moves to LA to re-start his career.
1988 Jan *More Love*, Sharkey's first recording for over 18 months, reaches UK #44.
Apr *Out Of My System* and LP *Wish* fail to chart in UK.

USA FOR AFRICA

1984 Dec UK superstar line-up group Band Aid°, assembled by Bob Geldof, hits UK #1 with *Do They Know It's Christmas?*, released to raise funds to help feed the starving people of Ethiopia and Africa. Eventually selling over 3 million copies in UK alone, Geldof suggests that the music industry, on a worldwide basis, could raise over $500 million, if motivated.
Dec [20] Inspired by Geldof's efforts, music veteran Harry Belafonte° conceives the idea for a US fund-raising for the same cause. He calls management and TV production company head Ken Kragen, who in turn calls Lionel Richie°.
Dec [21] Richie's wife Brenda spots friend Stevie Wonder° in their local store and asks him to contact her husband about the idea. Meanwhile, Kragen asks Quincy Jones to produce the project, and Jones secures the help of Michael Jackson°.
1985 Jan While Kragen establishes the United Support of Artists Foundation (with himself as President and Jackson°, Richie°, Belafonte°, Jones and Kenny Rogers° on the board of directors) and as major stars are quietly invited to participate, he enlists the financial organizational abilities of Marty Rogol who has already run fund-raisers for Harry Chapin° and Rogers. Kragen also invites Barrie Bergman, head of large US record retailers Record Bar, to organize a committee to ensure that all retail profits from any product will go to the USA For Africa fund.
Jan [28] Kragen has decided to record the USA For Africa disk on the night of the American Music Awards when a concentration of top artists will attend. Following the AMA celebrations at 10.00pm, 45 artists arrive at the A&M studios, Hollywood, Cal., greeted by the warning from Jones to "check your ego at the door". The song to be recorded, *We Are The World*, has been written by Jackson° and Richie° in just 2½ hours, following 3 days of preparation. It is arranged, produced and engineered by Jones, Tom Bahler and Humberto Gatica. Inside the studio, a strip of named tape for each performer has been stuck on the floor forming a semi-circular ensemble. Those chosen for lead vocals will be later grouped close to one of six microphones, as their efforts will be recorded after the choruses have been taped. (Geldof sings as part of the chorus, with a host of stars.) This in turn follows the instrumental tracks, recorded earlier by Jones. The end result features 21 solo vocal segments which are, in order of appearance, Lionel Richie°, Stevie Wonder°, Paul Simon°, Kenny Rogers°, James Ingram°, Tina Turner°, Billy Joel°, Michael Jackson°, Diana Ross°, Dionne Warwick°, Willie Nelson°, Al Jarreau°, Bruce Springsteen°, Kenny Loggins°, Steve Perry, Daryl Hall°, Huey Lewis°, Cyndi Lauper°, Kim Carnes°, Bob Dylan° and Ray Charles°. Prince° has been invited, but fails to show. (He will contribute a song to the subsequent LP.) A video team tapes the historic event resulting in 75 hours of footage, later edited to promote the song. After 10 hours, only Richie and Jones remain, putting the final touches to an extraordinary record.
Feb While efforts are made to ship the disk as soon as possible, Kragen decides on CBS/Columbia for its free manufacturing and distribution (all major record companies have offered the same). Meanwhile, Jim Mazza at EMI suggests that Kragen organize the release of an LP featuring unreleased tracks from some participating USA For Africa artists.
Mar [7] 800,000 copies are distributed to record stores nationwide in US. (Within 2 days they have been sold and re-orders are flooding in.)
Mar [23] *We Are The World* enters the US chart at #21. (It will hit #1 by Apr.13, where it will stay for 4 weeks. It also hits UK #1, tops charts in most Western territories and sells 7.5 million copies in US alone.)
Apr [4] Columbia ships 2.7 million copies of LP *We Are The World* in US. Rush-released, donated cuts are from Springsteen°, Prince° (4 *The Tears In Your Eyes*), Huey Lewis & The News°, Chicago°, Turner°, The Pointer Sisters°, Rogers°, Perry, USA For Africa and Northern Lights. (Inspired by USA For Africa, a Canadian effort under the banner Northern Lights is organized. The track is *Tears Are Not Enough*, produced by David Foster and featuring Bryan Adams°, John Candy, Corey Hart, Dan Hill, Gordon Lightfoot°, Joni Mitchell°, Anne Murray and Neil Young°, among others.) The LP will spend 3 weeks at US #1 and reach UK #31.
Apr [5] At 3.50pm GMT, over 5,000 radio stations worldwide unite for 7 minutes and 2 seconds as *We Are The World* is aired.

USA FOR AFRICA *cont.*

Apr [20] USA For Africa Foundation's legal counsel, Jay Cooper, claims that bootleg merchandise, particularly T-shirts are appearing in many US cities. Authorized merchandisers, Winterland, take measures to clamp down on the pirates.

May [16] An initial cheque of $6.5 million in royalties is handed to Kragen by Columbia executive Al Teller. Associated and combined sales from the song, the LP and merchandising sums will exceed $50 million.

June [10] First airlift of supplies is flown to Africa for relief.

June [14] With various local fund-raising efforts still gathering momentum, video distributor RCA/Columbia ships *We Are The World – The Video Event* to swell USA For Africa funds further. Company president Robert Blattner signs an agreement with Richie° to ensure that all profits from the $14.95 video are donated directly to the foundation.

RITCHIE VALENS

1952 At junior high school, Valens (b. Richard Valenzuela, May 13, 1941, Pacoima, Los Angeles, Cal., US) builds a solid-body electric guitar (which he will use until success pays for a Fender Stratocaster), after learning to play acoustic Spanish guitar (right-handed, despite being left-handed) 2 years earlier. Surrounded by Mexican music (with Mexican-Indian parents), he has been music-obsessed since an early age – initially Chicano folk, then R&B, and eventually Little Richard°-style rock'n'roll.

1957 Nov He joins The Silhouettes, a Mexican band which includes a Japanese tenor sax player and two Afro-Chicanos. He sings R&B and rock'n'roll numbers with the group, and is so popular that he becomes its frontman.

1958 May He auditions for Bob Keene, owner of Hollywood-based Del-Fi label, who decides to record him. The first session produces *Come On, Let's Go*, for which he has a riff worked out, but no lyrics, so he makes up the words on the spot. Coupled with Leiber/Stoller's *Framed* (also recorded by The Coasters°), it is released with his name shortened to Ritchie Valens.

Aug Valens begins his first US tour during which he befriends Eddie Cochran° and appears singing *Come On, Let's Go* on Dick Clark's "American Bandstand" TV show.

Oct *Come On, Let's Go* has a 13-week US chart run, peaking at #42 as he finishes touring (in UK Tommy Steele's° cover hits #10). On his return to LA, Valens records *Donna*, written for his high school sweetheart Donna Ludwig. For the B-side, Keene suggests updating an old Mexican wedding song which, sung in Spanish, becomes *La Bamba*.

Dec [5] Valens returns to his old school, Pacoima Junior High, to play a concert which is recorded by Keene. He films a cameo slot for Alan Freed's movie *Go, Johnny, Go*, lip-synching his *Ooh My Head*.

Dec [25] After a second "American Bandstand" appearance, he plays a 10-day run with Cochran°, Bo Diddley° and The Everly Brothers° in Alan Freed's Christmas Show at New York's Loew's State Theater, as both sides of his second single (*Donna* and *La Bamba*) race each other up the US chart, *La Bamba* initially in the lead.

1959 Jan Valens records tracks for an LP and joins "The Winter Dance Party" tour through the upper Midwest in icy winter weather in a poorly-heated bus.

Feb *La Bamba* peaks at US #22.

Feb [3] After a show at Clear Lake, Iowa, Buddy Holly° charters a plane to take them to the next venue. Holly's guitarist Tommy Allsup gives up his seat to Valens, and bassist Waylon Jennings gives his to The Big Bopper°. Minutes after take-off, the plane crashes in a frozen corn field, killing all on board.

Feb *Donna* hits US #2 and is a posthumous million-seller.

Mar *Donna* charts in UK at #29 for 1 week, overtaken by Marty Wilde's° cover which hits #3.

Apr LP *Ritchie Valens* makes US #23 and *That's My Little Suzie* peaks at US #55.

July *Little Girl* reaches US #92. (Further singles and two LPs – *Ritchie*, made up from the remainder of his unissued studio tapes, including some guitar instrumentals, and *Live At Pacoima Junior High School*, from the Dec. 1958 concert – will be released by Del-Fi over the following 12 months, but none will chart. Valens' songs will be covered by many artists, and his influence as a pioneer of "Chicano rock" will endure despite his short career.)

1987 Taylor Hackford's biopic *La Bamba*, with Lou Diamond Phillips playing Valens, attracts a new audience and Los Lobos° hit US and UK #1 with their interpretation of *La Bamba* featured on the film soundtrack.

VAN HALEN

David Lee Roth (vocals)
Eddie Van Halen (guitar)
Michael Anthony (bass)
Alex Van Halen (drums)

1964 Suffering from hyperactivity, Roth (b. Oct.10, 1955, Bloomington, Ind., US) attends a child guidance clinic. He is also given a radio by his Uncle Manny.

1965 The Van Halen family moves from native Holland to Pasadena, Cal., US. Alex (b. May 8, 1955, Nijmegen, Holland) and Eddie (b. Jan.26, 1957, Nijmegen) begin learning guitar and drums.

1972 The Roth family, led by surgeon father, relocates to Pasadena.

1973 Roth joins local band The Red Ball Jets while the Van Halen brothers form The Broken Combs. The three eventually team to form Mammoth and play the local club circuit as a heavy rock covers band.

1974 They link with Snake bassist Anthony (b. June 20, 1955, Chicago, Ill., US).

1975 Now established as the loudest and heaviest band in the LA area, they reject name Rat Salade and settle on Van Halen. With a growing live reputation, they open for bands including Santana°, UFO and Sparks, mostly at the Gazzari on LA's Sunset Strip.

1976 While playing at LA's The Starwood, Van Halen impresses Kiss° bassist Gene Simmons, who offers to produce a demo tape of live numbers including *Runnin' With The Devil* and *House Of Pain*, but it is rejected by all major labels. A songwriting pattern is emerging with Roth writing lyrics and the other members creating the music.

1977 Again playing at The Starwood club, Van Halen, led as much by Eddie Van Halen's impressive guitar work as by Roth's outrageously extrovert stage antics, is spotted by Warner Bros. producer Ted Templeman, who persuades label boss Mo Ostin to sign the band. The contract allows Van Halen to retain full artistic control and includes paternity insurance clauses.

1978 Feb Debut LP *Van Halen*, produced by Templeman, is released and will hit US #19, with sales over 2 million.

Mar [3] Van Halen embarks on its first US tour at the Aragon Ballroom, Chicago, Ill., with contracts insisting that M&M confectionery provision does not include the brown ones.

Mar Roth's overt performance receives national media attention and Van Halen's cover of The Kinks'° *You Really Got Me* makes US #36.

May *Runnin' With The Devil* peaks at US #84 and, supported by a first UK tour behind Black Sabbath°, makes UK #52. LP *Van Halen* rises to UK #34.

1979 Apr LP *Van Halen II*, produced by Templeman, has taken only 6 days to record. It will hit US #6 (and UK #23) on its way to 5 million sales.

Apr [7] The group plays the California Music Festival at LA's Memorial Coliseum.

Apr [8] Van Halen begins a 10-month world tour, transporting over 22 tons of equipment. At some gigs, Roth invites all fans to backstage parties as media concentrates increasingly on alleged drug-taking and wild rock'n'roll celebration.

Apr [13] Roth collapses on stage in Spokane, Washington, D.C.

June Van Halen headlines the UK leg of the world tour.

July *Dance The Night Away* reaches US #15. As US dates resume, the group hires lookalikes to parachute into LA's Anaheim Stadium as a prelude to the gig.

Oct Roth lyric-led *Beautiful Girls* stalls at US #84.

1980 Apr LP *Women And Children First* hits US #6 and UK #15, and will earn a platinum disk . Van Halen's annual tour begins, now titled "Invasion".

May Roth breaks his nose completing a flying squirrel leap during Italian TV recording.

June *And The Cradle Will Rock* stalls at US #55.

1981 Apr [11] Eddie Van Halen marries actress Valerie Bertinelli.

May LP *Fair Warning* hits US #6 and makes UK #49. Like each Van Halen LP, it outsells its predecessor.

1982 Apr *(Oh) Pretty Woman*, reviving Roy Orbison's° 1964 hit, reaches US #12.

May Fifth LP *Diver Down* is released and will hit US #3 and UK #36.
June Van Halen hires Francis Ford Coppola's soundstage at LA's Zoetrope studios to try out its new touring sound system.
July As *Dancing In The Street* makes US #38, "Hide Your Sheep" tour begins at Steve Wozniak's US Festival in Southern Cal.
Oct [22] Van Halen Day is declared in Worcester, Mass.
1983 Feb In place of a cancelled UK visit, Van Halen embarks on its first South American tour playing Uruguay, Venezuela, Brazil and Argentina.
Apr Eddie Van Halen is acclaimed for his guitar work on Michael Jackson's° *Beat It* US #1. (Eddie completed the session work free of charge, as a favor.)
May [28] The band is paid $1½ million (the largest fee ever) to play a single concert, at the second US Festival in San Bernardino. The organizers need an audience of 750,000 to break even – only 300,000 show.
Dec [31] LP *1984* is released on New Year's Eve at the band's insistence.
1984 Feb LP *1984* hits US #2, behind Michael Jackson's° *Thriller*, and UK #15 (despite a ban in some UK outlets due to baby smoking cover shot). It marks the band's first major use of synthesizers and includes its live favorite from 1976, *House Of Pain*.
Feb [25] *Jump*, written by all band members, tops the US chart for 5 weeks. The promotional video, according to Roth, cost $6,000 to record on home 16mm equipment.
Mar Despite BPI imposing a £6,000 fine on UK Warner Bros. for hyping the single, *Jump* hits UK #7.
Mar [21] Kurt Jefferies of Phoenixville, Pa. wins a "Lost Weekend With Van Halen" competition out of more than 1 million entrants.
May *Panama* falters at UK #61.
June *I'll Wait* reaches US #13.
Aug Van Halen plays UK's heavy metal festival at Castle Donington, as *Panama* makes US #13.
Sept UK act Aztec Camera° records an acoustic ballad version of *Jump* as B-side to *All I Need Is Everything*.
Oct As president of his own "Jungle Studs" club, Roth plans a trip to Papua, New Guinea.
Nov *Hot For Teacher* reaches US #56.
1985 Feb Always the main focus of the band, Roth, still with the band, releases debut solo single, with the help of The Beach Boys'° Carl Wilson, a cover of their *California Girls*. With predictably babe-filled video, it hits US #3, but only UK #68.
Mar Roth's solo LP *Crazy From The Heat* (on Warner Bros.) peaks at US #15 and UK #91.
June A long-time fan of Al Jolson, Roth's medley of *Just A Gigolo* and *I Ain't Got Nobody* reaches US #12, as Roth confirms that he is quitting Van Halen.
1986 Feb Eddie and Alex ignore Warner Bros.' advice not to use the Van Halen name with Roth gone.
May [27] Van Halen re-emerges with Sammy Hagar (b. Oct.13, 1947, Monterey, Cal.) as Roth's replacement (Hagar's most recent solo success has been *I Can't Drive 55* which will be incorporated into future Van Halen dates.)
June First Hagar-featured disk, *Why Can't This Be Love* heads towards US #3 and UK #8 as parent LP *5150* reaches UK #16 and hits US #1. It has been recorded at Eddie's studio in his Hollywood Hills home.
July Roth releases further cover versions on mini-LP *Eat 'Em And Smile* which hits US #4 and UK #28 and includes Sinatra's *That's Life*. Meanwhile, Van Halen's *Dreams* makes US #22 and UK #62.
Aug [16] Roth's *Yankee Rose* reaches US #16, as he begins a 10-month tour at Hampton, Va., US.
Oct Van Halen's *Love Walks In* makes US #22 as Roth's *Goin' Crazy* peaks at US #66.
Dec [20] Linda Duke claims she suffers "acoustic trauma" at Roth's LA Forum concert, as his single *That's Life* falters at US #85.
1987 Feb Hagar's solo single *Winner Takes All* from Sylvester Stallone movie *Over The Top*, reaches US #54.
June Hagar continues a parallel solo career with LP *Sammy Hagar* which makes US #14. From it, *Give To Live* reaches US #23 and *Eagles Fly* makes US #82.
1988 Jan While vacationing on Turtle Island off the Australian coast, Eddie Van Halen suffers from 105° temperature having been bitten by a mosquito.
Feb Roth's third solo LP, *Skyscraper* (featuring a front cover photograph of him hanging on to the side of a mountain) is released, hitting US #6 and UK #11.
Mar From it, *Just Like Paradise* hits US #6 and UK #27.
May His follow-up *Stand Up* stalls at US #64.
May [27] Van Halen returns to live work after a 2-year break, opening its "Monsters of Rock" tour at the Alpine Valley Music Theater, Wis., US. Featuring four other heavy metal acts (Scorpions, Dokken, Kingdom Come and Metallica°), it is the most ambitious HM package tour ever attempted. With 250,000 watts of sound at 20 all-day festival concerts, the events are mostly under-attended and some lose money.
June Van Halen LP *OU812*, featuring Hagar lyrics and vocals, peaks at UK #16, but in less than a month hits US #1. It is produced by long-time band associate Donn Landee.
July Roth's *Damn Good/Stand Up* stalls at UK #72.
Aug Roth plays UK's Castle Donington Festival as Van Halen releases first single from the LP, *When It's Love*, which hits US #5 and UK #28.
Sept [29] The band begins a 45-city US tour.
Nov Roth returns to UK for selected dates including London's Wembley Arena, as *California Girls* is unsuccessfully reissued.
Dec Van Halen's *Finish What Ya Started* heads towards US top 10.

LUTHER VANDROSS

1970/73 Vandross (b. Luther Ronzoni Vandross, Apr.20, 1951, New York, N.Y., US), his father a crooner, his mother a gospel singer and his sister has been a member of 1950s group The Crests, having been influenced by the soul music of the early 1960s and formed his first group with friends, guitarist Carlos Alomar and Robin Clark, while still at high school, becoming Listen My Brother and appearing on the first episode of TV show "Sesame Street", studies music briefly after the group breaks up in the early 70s and disappears into a succession of day jobs.
1974 Alomar, working with David Bowie°, invites Vandross and Clark to Philadelphia's Sigma Sound studios for the recording of LP *Young Americans*. Bowie is impressed with the pair and invites Vandross to arrange all the vocal parts. He also sings backing vocals on most of the tracks as well as contributing the song *Fascination*.
1975 Vandross and Clark join Bowie° on the "Young Americans" tour, with Vandross also becoming the opening act. Vandross' *Everybody Rejoice (A Brand New Day)* is included in forthcoming movie *The Wiz*. (The song will later be used in a Kodak commercial.) Bowie introduces Vandross to Bette Midler° for whom he performs vocals on her LP *Songs For The New Depression*. (Producer Arif Mardin will later use Vandross for sessions with Ringo Starr°, Carly Simon°, Chaka Khan° and The Average White Band°.)
1976 Royalties from *Everybody Rejoice* allow Vandross to record more of his songs with a newly-formed vocal group. Cotillion Records signs the band and calls it Luther. Vandross' style does not mesh with the disco flavor of the times and both the group's LPs, *Luther* and *This Close To You*, fail to interest, but *It's Good For The Soul* and *Funky Music (Is A Part Of Me)* are both top 40 R&B hits.
1977/78 Without a recording contract, Vandross earns a living singing jingles.
1978 June Quincy Jones enlists Vandross' vocals for his LP *Sounds . . . And Stuff Like That!!*.
Dec He also sings back-up vocals on Chic's° *Le Freak* and Sister Sledge's *We Are Family*.
1979 Nov Vandross arranges the vocals on Barbra Streisand° and Donna Summer's° smash *No More Tears (Enough Is Enough)*.
1980 May Vandross is main vocalist for debut LP *The Glow Of Love* by disco group Change, which will earn a gold disk. He is also the featured singer on Change's two hits *Searchin'* and *The Glow Of Love*. Vandross signs to Epic in a deal which allows self-production freedom.
1981 Roberta Flack° sings his song *You Stopped Lovin' Me* from movie *Bustin' Loose* and invites him to tour with her.
Sept LP *Never Too Much*, Vandross' first solo record, is released. It will reach US #19 on its way to platinum sales.
Dec Vandross has first solo hit with *Never Too Much*, which reaches US #33.
1982 Aug Vandross produces Aretha Franklin's° LP *Jump To It*.
Oct LP *Forever, For Always, For Love* is released, and will reach US #20, Vandross' second platinum disk.

LUTHER VANDROSS *cont.*

Dec Vandross reaches US #55 with *Bad Boy/Having A Party*.
1983 Nov He produces Dionne Warwick's° LP *How Many Times Can We Say Goodbye* (UK title: *So Amazing*). He duets with Warwick on the title track, which makes US #27.
Dec LP *Busy Body* enters the US chart. It will reach US #32 and earn a third consecutive platinum disk.
1984 Jan LP *Busy Body* makes UK #42.
May *Superstar*, a reworking of Leon Russell's° song, stalls at US #87.
1985 Apr LP *The Night I Fell In Love* peaks at UK #19.
May *'Til My Baby Comes Home* reaches US #29.
1986 Sept *Give Me The Reason*, from movie *Ruthless People*, makes US #57.
Nov LP *Give Me The Reason* enters the UK chart. It will hit UK #9 and spend over a year on the chart.
1987 Jan *Stop To Love* reaches US #15 and hits R&B #1.
Feb LP *Never Too Much* makes UK #41.
Feb [24] Vandross performs live at the 29th annual Grammy ceremonies. He is nominated in the R&B Vocal (Male) category, but loses to James Brown°.
Mar [24] Vandross and Dionne Warwick° co-host the first annual Soul Train Music Awards at the Hollywood Center Television studios, Cal.
June [8] Vandross' drummer, Yogi Horton, leaps to his death from a 17th-floor hotel window. He tells his wife that he is tired of living in Vandross' shadow.
June [18] Vandross cancels two sell-out concerts in Phoenix, Ariz. as a protest to Governor Mecham's rescinding of the Martin Luther King public holiday.
July LP *Forever, For Always, For Love* reaches UK #23.
1988 Feb Vandross wins Favorite Male Soul and Favorite Male Rhythm and Blues artist categories at the annual American Music Awards.
Sept [28] Vandross begins a 3-month "The Heat" US tour with Anita Baker° in Washington, D.C.
Oct LP *Any Love*, produced (as all previous LPs) by Marcus Miller, enters the UK chart at #3 and hits US top 10, as the title track makes US #44 and UK #31.

VANGELIS

1968 Vangelis (b. Evangelos Papathanassiou, Mar.29, 1943, Valos, Greece), having been a keyboards prodigy in his youth and a member of Greek pop group Formynx in the early 1960s, has teamed with vocalist Demis Roussos and drummer Lucas Sideras as Aphrodite's Child, moving to France to escape the Greek Colonels' right-wing coup, when the trio comes to the attention of Pierre Sberre of French Philips Records, and signs to the label.
Nov After spending 3 months at the top of the French chart and hitting the top 10 in most European countries, Aphrodite's Child's *Rain And Tears*, sung in English by Roussos and using Vangelis' arrangement of a 17th-century German tune by Johann Pachelbel, reaches UK #27. (Further European hits *It's Five O'Clock* and *Break* will follow for the trio, but fail to chart in US or UK.)
1972 Aphrodite's Child splits, following concept LP *666*. (Roussos begins a solo vocal career which will find him international success.) Vangelis remains in Paris and writes the score for French film *L'Apocalypse des Animaux* with director Frederick Rossiff.
1974 Vangelis moves to UK, building his own synthesizer recording studio in London's West End.
1976 Jan LP *Heaven And Hell* is Vangelis' first solo chart entry, hitting UK #3.
Oct LP *Albedo 0.39* reaches UK #18.
1979 After two further LPs for RCA, *Spiral* and *Beauborg*, neither of which charts, he moves to Polydor for LP *China*, which does not sell well.
1980 Feb Vangelis teams with Jon Anderson, lead singer of Yes° (with whom he has maintained a close acquaintance since 1974, when he was mooted as their keyboards replacement for Rick Wakeman), to record as a voice/synthesizer duo for Polydor. The duo's *I Hear You Now* hits UK #8 while LP *Short Stories* hits UK #4.
July LP *Short Stories* reaches US #125.
Sept *I Hear You Now* makes US #58.
1981 June Vangelis is commissioned by producer David Puttnam to compose the score for film *Chariots of Fire* and his soundtrack LP hits UK #5, remaining on UK chart for 97 weeks. The main title theme from *Chariots Of Fire* also becomes Vangelis' first solo hit single, reaching UK #12.
July Used as the theme for Carl Sagan's UK BBC TV series "Cosmos", Vangelis' *Heaven And Hell, Third Movement* is released in UK as a BBC single and climbs to UK #48.
Aug Jon & Vangelis' LP *The Friends Of Mr. Cairo* hits UK #6. (One of its tracks, *State Of Independence*, which proves unsuccessful as a single, will be revived with much greater success by Donna Summer° in 1982.)
Sept LP *The Friends Of Mr. Cairo* climbs to US #64.
1982 Jan Jon & Vangelis' *I'll Find My Way Home* hits UK #6.
Apr Vangelis' soundtrack LP *Chariots Of Fire* tops the US chart for 4 weeks after the music wins an Oscar for Best Original Score at the 1982 Academy Awards. It earns a platinum disk for sales of over a million.
May The main title theme from *Chariots Of Fire* also tops the US chart for 1 week (after climbing the top 100 for 21 weeks) and is a million-seller. It also re-enters the UK chart, reaching #41.
June Jon & Vangelis' *I'll Find My Way Home* makes US #51.
1983 Aug Jon & Vangelis' *He Is Sailing* reaches UK #61. It is taken from the duo's LP *Private Collection*, which reaches UK #22 and US #148.
1984 May Soundtrack LP *Chariots Of Fire* is reissued in UK and climbs to #39.
Aug Compilation LP *The Best Of Jon And Vangelis* reaches UK #42 while reissued *State Of Independence*, also included on the LP, makes UK #67.
Oct Solo LP *Soil Activities* makes UK #55.
1985 Mar Solo LP *Mask* reaches UK #69.
1987 Feb Vangelis is cleared in UK court of using Stavros Logarides' melody of *City Of Violets* for his own *Chariots Of Fire*.
1988 Sept The theme from *Chariots Of Fire* has a new lease of life in UK when Vangelis' original version is used as the theme for BBC TV coverage of the Seoul Olympic Games.
Nov LP *Direct*, Vangelis' first for Arista, which promotes the album as "new age" in US, is released.

VANILLA FUDGE

Mark Stein (vocals and organ)
Vince Martell (guitar)
Tim Bogert (bass)
Carmine Appice (drums)

1966 Bogert (b. Aug.27, 1944, Richfield, N.J., US) and Stein (b. Mar.11, 1947, Bayonne, N.J.), who have been playing in Rick Martin & The Showmen, form their own group, The Pigeons. Martell (b. Nov.11, 1945, New York, N.Y., US) joins as lead guitarist, and Appice (b. Dec.15, 1946, New York) replaces the original drummer.
Dec Renamed Vanilla Fudge, the quartet is one of the few East Coast groups to join ranks with the acid rock West Coast movement, with a style it will later describe as "psychedelic-symphonic rock" (a central element of which is slowed-down rearrangements of other artists' hit singles).
1967 July [22] Signed to Atlantic Records, the group makes its New York debut at The Village Theater (soon renamed The Fillmore East) with The Byrds° and The Seeds. Debut single, a version of The Supremes'° *You Keep Me Hangin' On*, hits US #6 and makes UK #18.
Sept Debut LP *Vanilla Fudge* hits US #6 (and will make UK #31 2 months later). It includes elongated versions of The Beatles'° *Eleanor Rigby* and *Ticket To Ride* and Cher's° *Bang Bang*.
1968 Feb *Where Is My Mind* peaks at US #73.
Mar LP *The Beat Goes On* reaches US #17. A concept set, it is ambitiously presented as a musical record of the past 25 years. The title track professes to include the entire history of music in 12 minutes' playing time.
July Third LP *Renaissance* makes US #20.
Oct *Take Me For A Little While*, from the LP, peaks at US #38.
Dec Also from LP *Renaissance*, a cover of Donovan's° *Season Of The Witch* reaches US #65.
1969 Mar LP *Near The Beginning* (with one side studio, the other live) makes US #16. Taken from it, *Shotgun* peaks at US #68.
July Vanilla Fudge takes part in the 3-day Seattle Pop Festival at Woodenville, Wash., with The Byrds°, The Doors°, Led Zeppelin° and many others.
Oct The band's fifth LP *Rock And Roll* makes US #34.
1970 Internal dissent leads the group to disband. Appice and Bogert form heavy metal band Cactus, before going on to join Jeff Beck° in Beck, Bogert & Appice. Stein forms Boomerang and Martell leaves

the music world.
1982 Vanilla Fudge re-forms and releases LP *Greatest Hits*.
1984 Aug Vanilla Fudge re-forms again and records LP *Mystery* for Atlantic subsidiary Atco. It fails to chart.
1988 June The band re-forms again for Atlantic Records' 40th Anniversary celebration.

BOBBY VEE

1958 Inspired by Buddy Holly's° *That'll Be The Day*, Vee (b. Robert Thomas Velline, Apr.30, 1943, Fargo, N.D., US) forms The Shadows at Central High School in Fargo, with brother Bill, Bob Korum and Jim Stillman. They play mainly instrumentals, with a few Holly and self-penned vocal items by Vee.

1959 Feb [3] The Shadows answer a request over local radio station K-FGO for a group to fill in on the visiting "Winter Dance Party" one-night show in Fargo (which Holly°, The Big Bopper° and Ritchie Valens°, who died in a plane crash in the early hours, would have played). They appear second on the program, performing *Bye Bye Love* and *Long Tall Sally*, and wearing matching outfits which they have rushed out and bought in the afternoon.

Feb [14] Local promoter Bing Bingstrom, who was in the "Winter Dance Party" audience, has offered to find The Shadows some paying gigs. Their first is a Valentine Day dance, earning $60.

June [1] The group pays $500 to record its own session at Soma Records' studio, Minneapolis, and cuts Vee-penned *Suzy Baby* and the group instrumental *Flying*.

July Soma issues the single, to major success in Minneapolis and surrounding areas. The group tours radio stations around Iowa and North Dakota, and sales spread. After a San Diego, Cal., station starts to play it, *Suzy Baby* attracts the attention of Liberty Records, which buys the master and releases it nationally. The band experiments with adding a pianist to expand the live sound, and hires Bob Zimmerman, who is spending the summer in Fargo. (He calls himself Elston Gunn at the time – the name will later change to Bob Dylan°.) He plays two gigs with The Shadows, but his one-key ("C") repertoire proves a compatibility problem. He is paid $30 and asked to leave.

Sept *Suzy Baby* makes US #77. Liberty signs the group, and also Vee himself to a separate deal as a soloist.

1960 Apr Pairing him with producer Snuff Garrett, Liberty has Vee cover Adam Faith's° recent UK chart-topper *What Do You Want?* (which is also in Holly°-influenced style), but it stalls at US #93.

Oct After an LP session at Norman Petty's studio in Clovis, N.M. (where most of Holly's° hits had been recorded), Garrett tries Vee (against the singer's wishes) on an R&B oldie – The Clovers' *Devil Or Angel*. It becomes his first major success, hitting US #6. B-side, a similar revival of Ivory Joe Hunter's *Since I Met You Baby*, makes US #81.

Dec [23] He begins a week at New York's Brooklyn Paramount theater, in Clay Cole's Christmas Rock'n'Roll show, alongside Neil Sedaka°, Dion°, Bo Diddley° and many others.

1961 Jan Garrett is offered material from Don Kirshner's Brill Building Aldon Music stable for Vee and *Rubber Ball*, co-written by Gene Pitney°, hits US #6, becoming his first million-seller.

Feb *Rubber Ball* is his UK chart debut, hitting #4 after holding off a top 10 cover version by the established Marty Wilde°.

Mar A John D. Loudermilk song, *Stayin' In* makes US #33 while B-side revival of The Crickets' (post-Buddy Holly°) *More Than I Can Say* peaks at US #61. He has his first LP chart success with second LP *Bobby Vee*, which reaches US #18.

May *More Than I Can Say*, promoted as UK A-side, hits UK #4.

June *How Many Tears*, the first of a run of Carole King°/Gerry Goffin songs recorded by Vee, makes US #63.

June [25] He appears on Alan Freed's outdoor rock show at the Hollywood Bowl, together with Jerry Lee Lewis°, Brenda Lee°, The Shirelles°, and others.

Sept Goffin and King's° *Take Good Care Of My Baby* becomes Vee's all-time most successful single, topping the US chart for 3 weeks, and selling over a million. Meanwhile, *How Many Tears* hits UK #10.

Nov LP *Bobby Vee Sings Hits Of The Rockin' '50s* peaks at US #85.

Dec *Run To Him*, penned by Goffin with Jack Keller, hits US #2 (behind The Tokens'° *The Lion Sleeps Tonight*). The B-side, Goffin/King's° *Walkin' With My Angel*, makes US #53.

1962 Jan Despite a universal thumbs-down from the "Juke Box Jury" panelists on UK BBC TV, *Run To Him* hits UK #6. (For a while it is available in UK on two labels, as London Records' UK licensing agreement with Liberty runs out, and the US label launches in its own right through EMI.)

Feb LP *Take Good Care Of My Baby* makes US #91, and hits UK #7. Vee begins a UK tour with Tony Orlando° and Gary U.S. Bonds°, and also appears on UK national radio ("Easy Beat") and TV ("Thank Your Lucky Stars").

Mar *Please Don't Ask About Barbara*, issued in UK to coincide with the tour, peaks at UK #29, while LP *Hits Of The Rockin' '50s* reaches UK #20.

Apr *Please Don't Ask About Barbara* reaches US #15. (B-side *I Can't Say Goodbye* has already made US #92 in Feb.)

July *Sharing You*, a Goffin/King° song in similar style to *Run To Him*, hits US #15 and UK #10.

Aug LP *Bobby Vee Meets The Crickets* (Holly's° ex-backing group, at this point consisting of Sonny Curtis, Jerry Allison, Glen D. Hardin and Jerry Naylor, is also recording for Liberty) makes US #42, while LP *A Bobby Vee Recording Session* peaks at US #121. Vee appears in a cameo slot, singing *At A Time Like This* (which he has recorded in UK at EMI), in Billy Fury°-starring film *Play it Cool*

Oct *Punish Her* reaches US #20. (B-side *Someday (When I'm Gone From You)*, taken from the LP with The Crickets, has made US #99 in Sept.)

Nov LP *Bobby Vee Meets The Crickets* is his most successful LP in UK, hitting #2, behind UK group The Shadows'° *Out Of The Shadows*. Vee makes a lengthy UK tour with The Crickets, which lasts the whole of Nov.

Dec Compilation LP *Bobby Vee's Golden Greats* reaches US #24, while seasonal LP *Merry Christmas From Bobby Vee* makes US #136. *A Forever Kind Of Love*, recorded in UK during the summer with producer Norrie Paramor, reaches UK #13 (having not been issued in US as a single – while the UK has not had *Punish Her*).

1963 Jan *The Night Has A Thousand Eyes*, from the movie *Just For Fun* (in which he has a cameo role, singing two songs), hits US #3 and becomes another million-seller.

Feb LP *A Bobby Vee Recording Session* hits UK #10.

Mar *The Night Has A Thousand Eyes* hits UK #3.

Apr LP *The Night Has A Thousand Eyes* makes US #102.

May Compilation LP *Bobby Vee's Golden Greats* hits UK #10, while *Charms* reaches US #13.

June LP *Bobby Vee Meets The Ventures*, pairing the singer with Liberty's top guitar instrumental group, makes US #91.

July *Be True To Yourself* makes US #34. (B-side *A Letter From Betty* peaks at US #85.) *Bobby Tomorrow*, a reversal of *Charms*, which is relegated to UK B-side, makes UK #21. It will be his last UK hit single.

Oct LP *The Night Has A Thousand Eyes* reaches UK #15.

Nov [8] He begins a US tour with Dick Clark's "Caravan of Stars" package, in Teaneck, N.J. Sharing the bill are Brian Hyland°, The Ronettes° and Little Eva°, among others.

Dec *Yesterday And You (Armen's Theme)* climbs to US #55. (B-side *Never Love A Robin* creeps to US #99.)

1964 Feb *Stranger In Your Arms* peaks at US #83.

Apr *I'll Make You Mine* makes US #52.

Apr [11] On tour again in UK, Vee appears on BBC radio show "Saturday Club", with The Searchers°, Adam Faith° and Gerry & The Pacemakers°.

June LP *Bobby Vee Sings The New Sound From England!*, featuring Merseybeat arrangements and recent UK hits (plus *She's Sorry*, written as a straight imitation of The Beatles'° *She Loves You*), reaches US #146. Vee tours US with The Rolling Stones°.

July *Hickory, Dick And Doc* climbs to US #63.

1965 Jan *(There'll Come A Day When) Ev'ry Little Bit Hurts* stalls at US #84 (B-side *Pretend You Don't See Her* having peaked at US #97 in Dec.)

Feb *Cross My Heart* creeps into US Hot 100, at #99. It is his last single with producer Garrett (B-side is titled *This Is The End*); the two cease working together by mutual consent.

June *Keep On Trying*, recorded in UK with George Martin producing, makes US #85.

1966 July *Look At Me, Girl* peaks at US #52.

1967 Sept Folk-tinged ballad *Come Back When You Grow Up*, produced by Dallas Smith and pairing Vee with The Strangers, hits US #3 and is his final million-seller.

Oct LP *Come Back When You Grow Up* reaches US #66.

BOBBY VEE *cont.*

Dec A cover version of Kenny O'Dell's *Beautiful People* makes US #37 (one place ahead of the original).

1968 Mar *Maybe Just Today* reaches US #46.

May A medley of two oldies, Smokey Robinson's° *My Girl* and Goffin/King's° *Hey Girl* makes US #35. LP *Just Today* peaks at US #187.

Sept *Do What You Gotta Do*, reviving The Four Tops° hit, peaks at US #83.

Dec *I'm Into Lookin' For Someone To Love Me* stalls at US #98.

1969 Aug *Let's Call It A Day Girl* makes US #92.

1970 Dec As Liberty Records becomes United Artists Records, *Sweet Sweetheart* peaks at US #88 and is also his last US chart entry.

1972 In a conscious effort to break from his earlier style and image, Vee releases LP *Nothing Like A Sunny Day* under his real name. It is a laid-back country/rock-styled package along the lines of Rick Nelson's° Stone Canyon Band material, with a small combo backing (including pedal steel guitar). Among the tracks is a slowed-down re-creation of *Take Good Care Of My Baby*. The LP does not chart, but is well received critically.

1980 May Compilation LP *The Bobby Vee Singles Album* hits UK #5, demonstrating the nostalgic appeal of his early 1960s recordings.

1985 Mar A regular on the oldies touring circuit in US, Vee tours UK on a nostalgic package with contemporaries Del Shannon° and Rick Nelson°.

1988 May Vee makes another oldies tour of UK, again with Shannon° and also Brian Hyland°. (Returning home for the summer, he will be back in UK in Nov., performing at London's Royal Albert Hall with many UK acts from the early 1960s on a nostalgia spectacular.)

SUZANNE VEGA

1975 Vega, half Puerto Rican, having grown up in a hispanic neighborhood on the Upper West side of New York, N.Y., US, is encouraged by her father, a novelist, to attend the New York High School of Performing Arts (of *Fame* fame) where she studies dance and begins composing songs with the guitar.

1977 While working as an office receptionist during the day, she performs her own compositions on the quiet New York folk circuit, including Folk City, The Speakeasy and The Bottom Line.

1983 She meets lawyer Ron Fiernstein and engineer Steve Addabbo, who offer to manager her. Together, they form publishing units Waifersongs and AGF Music Ltd.

1984 July A *New York Times* review of a recent performance describes Vega as "one of the most promising talents on the New York City folk circuit".

Dec Encouraged by increasingly glowing receptions, A&M signs her to a worldwide recording deal.

1985 Jan She begins 3 months of taping 10 of her own compositions for her first LP at Celestial Studios, New York.

Apr Debut LP *Suzanne Vega* is released to universal critical acclaim. She is viewed as the first of many new folk female stars of the late 80s. Produced by Addabbo and ex-Patti Smith° guitarist Lenny Kaye, the LP will spend 27 weeks on chart, climbing to US #91, and will achieve double gold status in UK (where it peaks at #11).

May With UK reaction breaking faster, Vega takes her band, including Marc Shulman (guitar), Sue Evans (drums), Mike Visceglia (bass), Anton Sauko (keyboards) and Stephen Ferrare (percussion) on a European tour.

1986 Jan From the debut LP, *Small Blue Thing* makes UK #65.

Mar *Marlene On The Wall* becomes her first major chart single, making UK #21.

June New recording *Left Of Center* makes UK #32, with the help of one of the earliest CD single release formats. With Joe Jackson° featured on piano, the song is included on the current John Hughes film soundtrack LP *Pretty In Pink* but will not appear on a Vega studio release.

Nov [18/19] As a climax to a successful touring year in Europe (and on larger US folk circuit) Vega plays selected UK venues including two sold-out dates at London's Royal Albert Hall. They are filmed for UK BBC TV showing and later video release.

1987 While writing songs for her second LP, Vega contributes two compositions for a forthcoming Philip Glass LP *Songs From Liquid Days* – one will be sung by Janice Pendarvis, the other by Linda Ronstadt°. *Luka*, already a UK #23, becomes her first major US hit, peaking at #3 and earning a Grammy nomination.

May LP *Solitude Standing*, again produced by Addabbo and Kaye, will benefit from the international success of *Luka* and hit US #11 and UK #2. Vega embarks on an 11-month "Suzanne Vega World Tour '87", beginning in UK and Ireland (traveling to US and Canada in July and Aug., including sold-out nights at New York's Carnegie Hall, and returning to Europe in the fall, following first visits to Japan and Australia).

July *Tom's Diner* stalls at UK #58.

Oct *Solitude Standing* makes US #94 but fails in UK.

1988 Aug UK CD-only EP is released featuring *Luka* and *Left Of Center*.

Oct Vega contributes the title track to Disney compilation LP *Stay Awake* for A&M Records.

THE VELVET UNDERGROUND

Lou Reed (vocals and guitar)
John Cale (bass, keyboards, viola and vocals)
Nico (vocals)
Sterling Morrison (bass and guitar)
Maureen Tucker (drums)

1964 Cale°, (b. Dec.4, 1940, Garnant, Wales, UK), in New York on a Leonard Bernstein scholarship, has been performing in avant-gardist La Monte Young's ensemble The Dream Academy, when he meets Reed° (b. Mar.2, 1943, New York, N.Y.,US) at a party. Reed plays Cale demos of his songs and the two decide to form a band. Reed brings in Morrison, while Cale adds his neighbor Angus MacLise on percussion. They play mostly free gigs under a variety of names. As The Primitives, they release several singles for Pickwick. (The Velvet Underground is taken from the title of a pornographic paperback.)

1965 Mutual friends draw them to the attention of artist Andy Warhol who becomes the group's manager. He decides that Nico (b. Christa Paffgen, Cologne, West Germany), who is singing at The Blue Angel Lounge on East 55th Street, New York, should join the group. The rest of the band are less enthusiastic and MacLise abruptly leaves for Nepal. (He will die there of malnutrition in 1979, aged 41.) He is replaced by Tucker.

Nov [11] The Velvet Underground debuts live as the opening act for The Myddle Class at a high school dance in Summit, N.J.

1966 Early in the year they begin a residency at Cafe Bizarre in Greenwich Village. They become the house band of Warhol's Factory and then the musical component of his multi-media show "The Exploding Plastic Inevitable". The band signs to MGM's Verve label.

1967 Jan The group plays a week-long series of concerts at the Montreal World Fair, Canada.

Mar Debut LP *The Velvet Underground And Nico*, is released, reaching US 171. Reed° takes control of the band and dispenses with Nico and Warhol. (Nico will record a collection of covers for solo LP *Chelsea Girls*.)

1968 Jan LP *White Light, White Heat*, recorded in 1 day at the end of a tour, charts for 2 weeks at US #199.

Mar Clashes between Reed° and Cale° come to a head, and Cale leaves. Bassist Doug Yule, ex-Boston folk-rock group The Grass Menagerie, replaces him.

1969 Apr LP *The Velvet Underground*, recorded in LA, is released. Atlantic Records signs the band after MGM drops it. Cale° produces Nico's solo LP *Marble Index*.

1970 June The group returns to New York for a month's residency at Max's Kansas City club. Tucker is pregnant, so Yule's brother Billy deputizes.

Aug LP *Loaded* is released. Reed°, having left the band to go solo, complains that it has been remixed without his knowledge. The band tours the East Coast with Yule on lead vocals with singer Walter Powers added to the line-up.

1971 Willie Alexander joins the band in place of Morrison, who leaves to teach English at the University of Texas in Austin. Tucker leaves shortly thereafter and moves to Phoenix, Ariz. to raise a family. Yule will keep The Velvet Underground name (until 1973), recording LP *Squeeze*, an almost solo effort, released in UK only. (He will join West Coast band American Flyer in the mid 70s.) Nico releases LP *Desertshore*, with Cale° again producing.

1972 Atlantic releases LP *Live At Max's Kansas City*, taken from fan Brigit Polk's cassette recording of the group's last gig with Reed°.

1974 Double live LP *1969 – The Velvet Underground Live*, released on Mercury, contains previously unrecorded songs. Reed°, Cale° and

Nico play an impromptu "reunion" concert in Paris, France, which is filmed.

June [1] Nico joins Cale° at his London concert (recorded for LP *June 1st, 1974*). The performance leads to the recording of Nico/Cale LP *The End*.

1979 Apr Film *Rock 'n' Roll High School*, satirizing US 1950s teen movies, uses The Velvet Underground's *Rock And Roll* in its soundtrack.

1980 Tucker releases a home-recorded single, *Playin' Possum*, for Spy Records.

1981 Nico's LP *Drama Of Exile*, containing Reed° and Bowie° covers, is released.

1983 Nico releases live mini-LP *Do Or Die*.

1985 Polydor releases a remixed LP of previously unreleased material as *V.U.*, which makes US #85 and UK #47. While recording himself, Cale° brings Nico into the studio to record LP *Camera Obscura*.

1986 May Polydor UK releases The Velvet Underground box set titled *Another View*.

1988 July [18] Nico, having spent several years living in Manchester, UK, with poet John Cooper Clarke, dies of a brain hemorrhage, having fallen off her bicycle while on holiday in Ibiza.

THE VENTURES

Nokie Edwards (lead guitar)
Don Wilson (guitar)
Bob Bogle (bass and guitar)
Howie Johnson (drums)

1959 Wilson (b. Feb.10, 1937) and Bogle (b. Jan.16, 1937) are working as tuckpointers (mortar removers) for a building construction company in Seattle, Wash., US, when they start to play as a duo at local dances and hops.

1960 Jan Edwards (b. May 9, 1939), initially playing bass, and Johnson (b. 1938) join, and the quartet names itself The Versatones, with Wilson's mother Josie as manager.

Feb After recording some tracks at Custom Recorders in Seattle, they release *Cookies And Coke* on their own label, Blue Horizon.

Apr A second Blue Horizon single, this time with a version of Johnny Smith's *Walk Don't Run*, is pressed in small quantities, with the group name changed to The Ventures. They take the disk to The Fleetwoods' manager Bob Reisdorff, who runs local Dolton label. He turns it down, so The Ventures take it to a DJ acquaintance, Pat O'Day, who has a show on K-JR in Seattle, and he plays it after each news bulletin. Reisdorff, hearing the disk on the radio, reconsiders and buys the master of *Walk Don't Run* and the group (in a deal carefully haggled by Josie Wilson which gives the group artistic control over its releases via Blue Horizon Productions, with Reisdorff and Wilson named as joint producers).

Aug Released nationally, *Walk Don't Run* hits US #2 (behind Elvis Presley's° *It's Now Or Never*) and becomes a million-seller. Because Dolton is marketed nationally by Liberty Records, The Ventures' recording operations are moved to LA, where Liberty has its studios, and the group cuts a debut LP, mainly consisting of its versions of other acts' instrumental hits.

Oct *Walk Don't Run* hits UK #8, in a close race with a UK cover version by The John Barry Seven.

Dec A revival of standard *Perfidia*, given the same guitar treatment as *Walk Don't Run*, reaches US #15.

1961 Jan Debut LP *The Ventures* reaches US #11 while *Perfidia* hits UK #4.

Mar *Ram-Bunk-Shush*, a 1957 hit for R&B organist Bill Doggett, reaches US #29 and UK #45.

May Another revived oldie, *Lullaby Of The Leaves*, peaks at US #69 and UK #43 (it is The Ventures' last UK chart entry).

Aug LP *Another Smash!!!* reaches US #39.

Sept *(Theme From) Silver City*, played with Hank Levine's orchestra, makes US #83.

Nov *Blue Moon*, recently a vocal million-seller by The Marcels°, is put through its guitar paces to US #54.

1962 Mar *Twist With The Ventures*, containing instrumental versions of Twist hits, reaches US #24. (It is the first and most successful of a series of Ventures LPs intended as music for dancing to.)

Sept *Lolita Ya-Ya*, the theme from film *Lolita*, makes US #61. Meanwhile, following an auto accident, Johnson, although not physically injured, feels the need to rest and leaves the group. He is replaced on drums by Mel Taylor.

1963 Jan Historically notable for being the first single recording to use fuzz-box guitar, *The 2,000lb Bee* peaks at US #91.

Feb LP *The Ventures Play Telstar And The Lonely Bull*, which contains covers of those two and several more instrumental hits, is the group's biggest-selling LP, hitting US #8, and earning a gold disk for a half million sales. Edwards, who has been sharing lead guitar on record and stage for some time, officially takes over on lead, with Bogle switching to bass.

June LP *Surfing*, a cash-in on the current California surf instrumental boom (which has gained much of its original inspiration from The Ventures), reaches US #30. The group teams with Liberty artist Bobby Vee° for part-vocal, part-instrumental LP *Bobby Vee Meets The Ventures*, which peaks at US #91.

July Blue Horizon Productions contract clause expires and Josie Wilson drops out of production. The group loses automatic creative control over its releases.

Oct LP *Let's Go!*, headed by a cover of The Routers' hit, makes US #30.

1964 Mar The last Ventures LP produced by Reisdorff, *The Ventures In Space*, combining original material with versions of science fiction movie themes, reaches US #27. (Keith Moon of The Who° will later quote this as one of his favorite LPs.)

Aug The Ventures' new, updated arrangement of *Walk Don't Run*, now under the title of *Walk Don't Run '64*, with ideas borrowed liberally from The Chantays'° *Pipeline* and other surf instrumentals, hits US #8. LP *The Fabulous Ventures*, with new producer Dick Glasser, reaches US #32.

Nov An update of Richard Rodgers' *Slaughter On 10th Avenue* makes US #35. It is taken from LP *Walk Don't Run, Vol.2* (also featuring *Walk Don't Run '64*), which makes US #17.

1965 Feb *Diamond Head*, another surf-style instrumental, makes US #70.

Apr LP *The Ventures Knock Me Out!* reaches US #31.

Aug Live LP *The Ventures On Stage*, recorded at concerts in Japan and US, peaks at US #27. (The group's first visits to Japan coincide with the first mass availablity of electric guitars in Japan, and The Ventures become the model guitar group to the Japanese. Over the next 10 years, although little of it will feed back to the West, the group runs a parallel career in Japan, where its popularity is on a par with The Beatles'°. Regular tours and dozens of LPs recorded specifically for the Japanese market, keep a vast demand satisfied. Their collaboration with Japan's emerging pop culture is such that The Ventures write many tunes designed for Japanese writers to add lyrics to in their own language.)

Sept LP *Play Guitar With The Ventures* is an instructional LP, with four tunes (including *Walk Don't Run* repeated over with lead, rhythm or bass guitar parts missing, and the instructions to enable the guitar-learning listener to fill the part with his own instrument and play along with The Ventures. The LP makes US #96 and stays on chart for 13 weeks.

Nov Joe Saraceno takes over as the group's producer for LP *The Ventures A Go-Go*, an anthology of instrumental dance tunes, which reaches US #16.

1966 Mar The group competes with Johnny Rivers° on *Secret Agent Man*, the theme from TV series "Secret Agent" (a re-titling of UK series "Danger Man"), starring Patrick McGoohan. Rivers' vocal version hits the US top 10 while The Ventures make US #54.

Apr The group cashes in on another TV craze with LP *The Ventures/Batman Theme*, which makes US #42.

1967 Apr The group shares in the vogue for psychedelic sounds with a mainly cover-version LP, *Guitar Freakout*, which reaches US #57.

Oct LP *Golden Greats By The Ventures* (not a compilation of their own, but a collection of other acts' hits) reaches US #50 and, in a 44-week chart stay, earns another gold disk.

1968 June Edwards leaves for solo work and is replaced on lead guitar by Jerry McGee.

1969 May The Ventures hit US #4 with *Hawaii Five-0*, the theme from the police TV series starring Jack Lord, which is another million-seller. The group is now a quintet, having added keyboards player Johnny Durrill (ex-The Five Americans).

June LP *Hawaii Five-0* reaches US #11 and earns the group's third gold LP.

July A revival of Percy Faith's 1960 million-seller *Theme From A Summer Place*, taken from the LP, reaches US #83 but is the group's last chart single.

1970 Jan LP *Swamp Rock* makes US #81.

Nov Double LP *The Ventures' 10th Anniversary Album* reaches US #91.

THE VENTURES *cont.*

1972 Edwards returns to the group, McGee having left to join Delaney & Bonnie's° band.

Mar LP *Joy/The Ventures Play The Classics*, makes US #146, and is the last Ventures US chart LP.

1981 After many years concentrating on their still-buoyant Japanese market, The Ventures record, in US, *Surfin' And Spyin'* (written by Charlotte Caffey of The Go-Gos). It is distributed mainly around the Californian surf music revival circuit, where they play live shows to huge acclaim. (The line-up is back to a quartet: Bogle, Wilson, Edwards and Taylor.)

THE VILLAGE PEOPLE

Victor Willis (lead vocals)
David Hodo (vocals)
Felipe Rose (vocals)
Randy Jones (vocals)
Glenn Hughes (vocals)
Alex Briley (vocals)

1977 The group is formed by Jacques Morali, a French producer working in US, after seeing costumed young men in New York gay discos. He conceives the idea of a group visually representing six American male stereotypes: the cowboy, the Indian, the policeman, the biker, the G.I. and the construction worker. He hires actor/singers to perform his tailor-made disco songs behind lead singer Willis. The name represents Greenwich Village, New York, from which the inspiration has come. Via his Can't Stop Productions, Morali signs the group to Casablanca Records in US and Mercury/Phonogram worldwide, and will produce and co-write (usually with Willis and Henri Belolo) all the material.

Oct An eponymous debut LP is released, reaching US #54. In an 86-week chart stay, it will go gold with sales over a half million.

Dec A disco hit in US, the group's first single *San Francisco (You've Got Me)* makes UK #45.

1978 May The group is heard on the soundtrack of Casablanca/Motown-produced disco movie *Thank God it's Friday*, singing *I Am What I Am* and *Hollywood*.

Aug *Macho Man* reaches US #25 and, despite its self-consciously (though a tongue-in-cheek feature of subsequent singles also) gay idiom, sells over a million copies to earn a gold disk. The LP of the same title makes US #24, staying on chart for 69 weeks to top a million sales and earn a platinum disk.

Aug [26] The group performs in Ontario, Canada, at the first Canada Jam festival, to 80,000 people, sharing the bill with The Commodores°, Kansas°, Earth Wind & Fire°, Dave Mason and Atlanta Rhythm Section°.

1979 Jan *Y.M.C.A.*, a disco smash with the ultimate tongue-in-cheek camp lyric, hits US #2 and sells more than 2 million copies, earning a platinum disk. In UK, it tops the chart for 3 weeks, selling 150,000 copies in one day at its peak, with eventual UK sales of almost 1,300,000 (one of UK's top 25 all-time best-sellers).

Feb LP *Cruisin'*, which includes *Y.M.C.A.*, hits US #3 (another platinum disk) and makes UK #24.

Apr *In The Navy* (which the US Navy considers using as a recruitment song until its full implications are pointed out) hits US #3, again selling over a million, and UK #2.

May LP *Go West*, featuring *In The Navy*, hits US #8 (the group's third consecutive platinum LP) and reaches UK #14.

July The title track from *Go West* reaches US #45 and UK #15.

Sept Billy Connolly makes UK #38 with a comedy version of *In The Navy*, retitled *In The Brownies*.

Dec *Ready For The 80s* peaks at US #52, the group's final US hit single. Double LP *Live And Sleazy*, coupling a live LP with a studio set, makes US #32 and earns the group's final gold disk. Willis leaves, and is replaced as lead singer by Ray Simpson, brother of Valerie Simpson (of writer/producer/performing duo Ashford and Simpson°).

1980 Sept *Can't Stop The Music* reaches UK #11. The group co-stars with Valerie Perrine and Bruce Jenner in the movie of the same title, crammed with its (and others') music, which flops. The soundtrack LP climbs to US #47.

1981 Aug The group signs to RCA but LP *Renaissance*, an attempt to change its visual image with the stereotype macho men disappearing in favor of smooth New Romantic types, peaks at US #138, its last US chart entry.

1982 Simpson leaves and is replaced by Miles Jay. With the fading of disco as a major commercial pop genre, the group loses its niche in the marketplace and disappears.

1985 Feb A renewed version of the group has a disco success and makes UK #59 with *Sex Over The Phone* (but it will be a one-off).

GENE VINCENT

1955 May Vincent (b. Eugene Vincent Craddock, Feb.11, 1935, Norfolk, Va., US) leaves the US Navy with a serious leg injury, after a motorcycle accident as a despatch rider. His broken bones do not heal properly because of too-rapid use and he spends several months in hospital. By the end of the year the leg is still in a plaster cast.

1956 Feb [11] Vincent marries 15-year-old Ruth Ann Hand. (It will not last.)

Mar Vincent hangs out at his local WCMS radio station, and occasionally sits in with the house band, The Virginians. Among the songs he sings is *Be-Bop-A-Lula*, purchased for $25 from fellow hospital patient Donald Graves. WCMS DJ "Sheriff" Tex Davis notices the young singer and arranges for him to make a demo tape containing that song, *Race With The Devil* and *I Sure Miss You*.

Apr Davis sends the demo to Ken Nelson of Capitol Records, who is on the look-out for another Elvis Presley°. Vincent is signed to the label.

May [4] Nelson arranges for a recording session at Owen Bradley's Nashville studio, using the same demo band: guitarists Cliff Gallup and Willie Williams, bass player Jack Neal and drummer Dickie Harrell, who become The Blue Caps. The three demo songs are re-recorded, with *Woman Love*.

June [4] Vincent and The Blue Caps play their first live gig, at Myrtle Beach, N.C.

June *Woman Love* is the first Gene Vincent & The Blue Caps release, but B-side *Be-Bop-A-Lula* enters the US chart.

July *Be-Bop-A-Lula* hits US #7, bringing a sudden demand for extensive live work.

July [28] Their first US national TV appearance is on NBC's "Perry Como Show".

Aug *Woman Love* is banned by UK's BBC because of its suggestive lyrics, but *Be-Bop-A-Lula* climbs to UK #16.

Sept Williams quits The Blue Caps and is replaced by Paul Peek in time for a 2-week residency in Washington D.C.

Oct LP *Blue Jean Bop* reaches US #16 (Vincent's only US LP chart entry). Follow-up single *Race With The Devil* peaks at US #96 but makes UK #28. The strain of performing aggravates Vincent's leg (still in a plaster cast). He ignores medical advice to slow down, and he and The Blue Caps go to Hollywood to film a slot performing *Be-Bop-A-Lula* for movie *The Girl Can't Help It*. (The bottom of his plastercast is disguised as a shoe by the studio's make-up department.)

Nov *Blue Jean Bop* climbs to US #49 and makes UK #16.

Dec Gallup, who left The Blue Caps before the Hollywood movie, but returned to play on the recording of a second LP, leaves for good, taking his influential and original guitar sound with him. (The line-up changes frequently and there will be six different versions of The Blue Caps in 2 years.)

1957 Jan Vincent spends 3 weeks in a US hospital for treatment to his injured leg. He is also prevented from live work while a legal wrangle over management is cleared up.

June Vincent has a metal leg brace (which he will wear for the rest of his life) fitted in place of his plaster cast. The new touring version of The Blue Caps (with drummer Harrell the only original) proves successful with lead guitarist Johnny Meeks.

Sept *Lotta Lovin'* climbs to US #13. He makes an ecstatically-received tour of Australia with Eddie Cochran° and Little Richard°.

Dec *Dance To The Bop* reaches US #43 after being performed on US TV's "Ed Sullivan Show". (It will be Vincent's last US hit.)

1958 Mar Vincent and the band appear in teen movie, *Hot Rod Gang*. They record in Hollywood, with Vincent's friend (since touring together twice in 1957) Eddie Cochran° moonlighting on (uncredited) backing vocals on the sessions.

Apr/ July A US West Coast tour is followed by a 40-date trip around Canada. Vincent has trouble holding his group together, due to the exhausting pace on (and allegedly off) stage, which has players constantly leaving to rest or keep from going crazy. These worries and a growing list of non-hit records take their toll on Vincent (who becomes increasingly moody and unreliable – particularly to DJs and the media – and begins to drink heavily). (In May, however, he gets married for the second time, to Darlene Hicks.)

Nov After a year without hits and with only low-paid LA live gigs, The Blue Caps split when Vincent abandons his group in mid-tour because he is unable to pay them 3 weeks' back wages. The Musicians Union withdraws his union card, and he moves with his new wife to the North-West, playing local gigs with pick-up bands.

1959 June Vincent meets and works with guitarist Jerry Merritt. With a new band, they play one of the first-ever rock tours of Japan, where they are enthusiastically welcomed.

Aug Regaining his card, Vincent returns to LA and records LP *Crazy Times*, with Merritt on guitar and session men like Sandy Nelson° on drums and Jackie Kelso on sax. The LP meets little success at a time when the US record industry is looking for clean, inoffensive pop stars. After more low-key live work, he moves to Europe at the invitation of promoter Larry Parnes and UK TV producer Jack Good.

Dec [5] Vincent arrives in UK, where his reputation remains high despite 3 years without hits, and receives an enthusiastic welcome from fans at London Airport.

Dec [6] He makes his UK live debut at Tooting Granada, London, as a guest on Marty Wilde's° show.

Dec He appears on UK TV rock show "Boy Meets Girls", headlined by Wilde°. In US Vincent was urged to tone down his image, but TV producer Jack Good persuades him to dress entirely in black leather and to emphasize his limp. Good gives him a residency on "Boy Meets Girls", and the image of the tortured black leather rock rebel is created. He plays to a rapturous reception at the Paris Olympia, France, and well-received dates at military bases in West Germany.

1960 Jan *Wild Cat* makes UK #21. Vincent plays a 12-date UK tour. Eddie Cochran° flies to UK at Parnes' invitation to co-headline a 12-week tour with him.

Jan [16] Vincent and Cochran° appear together on "Boy Meets Girls".

Feb While touring in Scotland, Vincent has a kilt and tam o'shanter made in Craddock tartan.

Mar *My Heart* reaches UK #16.

Apr [17] The car taking Vincent and Cochran° to London airport at the end of the UK tour in Bristol, crashes, killing Cochran. With a broken collarbone, broken ribs and further damage to his leg, Vincent also suffers psychologically from the death of his closest professional friend.

May [11] After a short spell in hospital and a rest in US, Vincent returns to UK to make his first UK recording, at EMI's Abbey Road studio in London. Backed by The Beat Boys (with Georgie Fame° on piano), he cuts *Pistol Packin' Mama*.

July *Pistol Packin' Mama* makes UK #15. LP *Crazy Times* peaks at UK #12 (his only UK chart LP)

1961 May He tours South Africa for the first time, playing with The Mickie Most Band.

July To coincide with another UK visit, *She She Little Sheila*, recorded in 1959 at LP *Crazy Times* sessions, is released in UK and reaches #22.

Sept *I'm Going Home*, recorded in London with backing by UK group Sounds Incorporated, makes UK #36 (his last UK hit single despite impressive live form).

1962 Apr He tours UK again, co-headlining with Brenda Lee°, and performs *Spaceship To Mars*, accompanied by Sounds Incorporated (and dressed wholly in white rather than his customary all-black leathers), in UK pop movie *It's Trad, Dad!*

1963 Jan Vincent gets married for the third time, to English girl Margaret Russell.

Apr [22] Vincent's recording contract with Capitol expires, and is not renewed. The last recording is an inferior remake, at Abbey Road with Charles Blackwell's orchestra, of *Be-Bop-A-Lula*.

1964 Oct LP *Shakin' Up A Storm*, recorded in London, is issued on EMI's Columbia label. Vincent tours UK, with Carl Perkins°, on a package headlined by The Animals°.

1965 July He begins a 3-month UK seaside summer season at South Pier theater, Blackpool, backed by UK group The Puppets. Vincent is divorced from his English wife and married to South African singer Jackie Frisco.

1966 July He records in a country style for Challenge Records in LA. (LP *Bird-Doggin'* will be released in UK only in 1967.)

1969 Sept [13] Vincent performs at the Toronto Rock'n'Roll Festival with several of his contemporaries and newer acts like The Doors° and John Lennon's° Plastic Ono Band. He is overshadowed by performances from Chuck Berry° and Jerry Lee Lewis°. He returns to tour UK, backed by The Wild Angels, and is the subject of UK BBC TV documentary, "The Rock'n'Roll Singer".

1970 Feb LP *I'm Back And I'm Proud*, mixing rock and country, is released on Dandelion label, run by lifelong Vincent fan and UK BBC radio DJ John Peel. Critically rated, it fails to chart.

Apr He signs in US to Kama Sutra Records and records two country-styled LPs, *Gene Vincent* and *The Day The World Turned Blue*, which are well reviewed but poor sellers. His personal life declines. Lack of commercial success and ever-present management and ex-wife problems cause constant depression, accentuated by heavier drinking, which adversely affects his previously consistent stage form. His fourth wife leaves him.

Sept He makes a chaotic UK tour.

1971 Oct [1] He records five songs at BBC Radio studios in Maida Vale, London, with backing by UK band Kansas Hook.

Oct [12] Vincent dies in US from a bleeding ulcer, aged 36. (The most eloquent tribute – apart from covers of *Be-Bop-A-Lula* by major artists like John Lennon°, and widespread aping of his leather-clad tough rocker image – will be Ian Dury's° 1977 song *Sweet Gene Vincent*.)

BOBBY VINTON

1960 Vinton (b. Stanley Robert Vinton, Apr.16, 1935, Canonsburgh, Pa., US), the son of a band leader, having formed his own big band in high school, played trumpet in similar groups while at Duquesne University and in the US Army, puts together a band of his own once out of the service. They are engaged to play as a back-up and featured outfit on a Dick Clark "Caravan of Stars" US tour. On a tour stop in Pittsburgh, Pa., Vinton records a single for local DJ Dick Lawrence, who intends to place it with a label. Epic Records passes on the disk, but is interested in Vinton's band and he is signed to a two-LP contract.

1962 Apr Neither band LP has sold and Vinton is to be dropped, but is owed one recording session by Epic. Rather than a band arrangement, he records a country-style version of a song found on a demo, *Roses Are Red*.

July *Roses Are Red* tops the US chart for 4 weeks, selling over a million (Epic's first #1 hit), and Vinton's recording contract is renewed. Although he will do further big band work and feature his trumpet live, on disk he will stick to the middle-of-the-road vocal slot which *Roses Are Red* has established for him.

Aug *Roses Are Red* reaches UK #15, beaten by a cover version from UK's Ronnie Carroll which hits #3.

Sept LP *Roses Are Red* hits US #5.

Oct *Rain Rain Go Away*, from the LP, reaches US #12. It is in competition with another Vinton single, *I Love You The Way You Are*, on Diamond label (his 1960 recording, which Lawrence has dusted off and sold to the label after *Roses Are Red*'s success). It reaches US #38.

1963 Jan Double A-side *Trouble Is My Middle Name/Let's Kiss And Make Up* reaches US #33 and #38 respectively.

Apr A revival of Johnnie & Joe's *Over The Mountain (Across The Sea)* makes US #21.

June *Blue On Blue*, submitted by Burt Bacharach for Vinton, hits US #3 and earns his second gold disk.

Sept *Blue Velvet* (a 1951 hit for Tony Bennett) tops the US chart for 3 weeks, earning another gold disk. The LP of the same title, on which all the songs are concerned with the color blue, hits US #12.

1964 Jan *There! I've Said It Again*, a revival of a 1945 Vaughn Monroe hit, recorded by Vinton in one take, tops the US chart for 4 weeks (holding The Kingsmen's° *Louie Louie* at #2), before being displaced by The Beatles'° *I Want To Hold Your Hand*. It earns Vinton's fourth gold disk and reaches UK #34 – his second and final UK hit.

Mar *My Heart Belongs To Only You* hits US #9 while LP *There! I've Said It Again*, containing both the title track and the new single, hits US #8.

June *Tell Me Why* reaches US #13.

Aug LP *Tell Me Why* climbs to US #31.

Sept *Clinging Vine* makes US #17.

Nov Compilation LP *Bobby Vinton's Greatest Hits* reaches US #12, earning a gold disk for a half million sales.

BOBBY VINTON *cont.*

Dec Self-penned *Mr. Lonely*, originally recorded alongside *Roses Are Red* and used as a track on the LP of that title, is belatedly released after an earlier cover version by Buddy Greco has failed. It tops the US chart for a week and is another million-seller.

1965 Feb LP *Mr. Lonely* reaches US #18.

Apr A revival of Lee Andrews & The Hearts' 1957 doo-wop classic *Long Lonely Nights* reaches US #17.

June *L-O-N-E-L-Y*, Vinton's third single in a row with the word in the title, peaks at US #22.

July *Theme From Harlow (Lonely Girl)*, from Carroll Baker movie *Harlow*, peaks at US #61.

Oct Protest song *What Color (Is A Man?)* makes US #38.

1966 Jan Vinton returns to his most romantic style on *Satin Pillows*, which reaches US #23.

Mar A cover version of Ken Dodd's UK million-seller *Tears* peaks at US #59.

1967 Jan *Coming Home Soldier* hits US #11.

Nov Billy Sherrill becomes Vinton's producer for *Please Love Me Forever*, which reprises his *There! I've Said it Again* style and hits US #6.

1968 Feb *Just As Much As Ever* (a hit for Nat "King" Cole) reaches US #24 while LP *Please Love Me Forever* makes US #41.

Apr Vinton revives Bobby Vee's° 1961 chart-topper *Take Good Care Of My Baby*, but it peaks at US #33.

Aug Another revived 1961 Goffin/King° song, Tony Orlando°/Billy Fury° hit *Halfway To Paradise*, makes US #23.

Dec Vinton's revival of *I Love How You Love Me* (a 1962 Phil Spector-produced US #5 hit by The Paris Sisters) hits US #9. It sells over a million, earning his sixth gold disk.

1969 Feb LP *I Love How You Love Me* reaches US #21.

May Another revived oldie, The Teddy Bears/Peter and Gordon° hit *To Know You Is To Love You*, makes US #34.

1970 Mar His version of *My Elusive Dreams* (a country duet hit by David Houston and Tammy Wynette) reaches US #46.

1972 Apr *Every Day Of My Life* makes US #24.

Aug A revival of Bryan Hyland's° 1962 original, *Sealed With A Kiss* reaches US #19.

1974 Nov After over a decade with Epic, Vinton signs a new recording deal with ABC Records, and returns to his original producer, Bob Morgan. The result is his first million-selling single for 6 years, *My Melody Of Love* (partly sung in Polish – a bow to his own ancestry), which hits US #3.

1975 Jan ABC LP *Melodies Of Love* reaches US #16, earning a gold LP. Vinton begins a syndicated weekly musical variety show on US TV. (It will air until 1978.)

Apr A disco-style revival of *Beer Barrel Polka* makes US #33.

July Vinton revives Elvis Presley's° *Wooden Heart* and it climbs to US #58.

1976 June Vinton's version of *Save Your Kisses For Me*, a cover of Brotherhood of Man's UK million-seller (and winner of the 1976 Eurovision Song Contest), stalls at US #75.

1980 Jan After another quiet period, Vinton, signed to Tapestry label, makes US #78 with *Make Believe It's Your First Time*.

1986 Sept Vinton's version of *Blue Velvet* is used as the theme for the movie of the same title.

TOM WAITS

1972 Having joined The Systems soul group at high school and sung and played professionally in his late teens and early twenties on accordian and piano in San Diego and LA bars and dives, Waits (b. Dec.7, 1949, in the back of a taxi cab in the parking lot at Murphy Hospital, Pamona, Cal., US), now a popular local performer on the LA blues and rock club circuit, is spotted by Asylum Records at the famous Troubadour haunt, playing his own subterranean brand of songs.

1973 Debut LP *Closing Time*, produced by Jerry Yester, is released. It arouses critical acclaim and low sales, but prompts opening live slots for Charlie Rich and Frank Zappa°.

1974 The Eagles° cover Waits' *Ol' 55* for their LP *On The Border* which reaches US #17. It becomes Waits' first compositional success and he will later claim "the only good thing about an Eagles LP is that it keeps the dust off your turntable". He teams with producer Bones Howe for second LP *Heart Of Saturday Night*. Tracks reveal a hardened, throaty vocal-style suggesting a legendary lifestyle of "liquor, girls, liquor and more liquor".

1975 Nov Waits, after 5 years of different motels, settles on permanent residence at The Tropicano Motel in West Hollywood where he has a piano installed in the kitchen. He releases live double LP *Nighthawks At The Diner*, which enters the US chart at #164, and has the word "nighthawk" tattooed on his right arm.

1976 Nov LP *Small Change* is released and makes US #89. It features a mixture of original jazz blues with lush "bad lives and broken heart" ballads. Constant US touring keeps chart-interest alive.

1977 Oct LP *Foreign Affairs*, featuring a duet with Bette Midler°, makes US #113.

1978 June Waits begins an acting career with a bit part in Sylvester Stallone's *Paradise Alley*.

Nov LP *Blue Valentine* peaks at only US #181, despite featuring sometime girlfriend, Rickie Lee Jones°, on the cover.

1980 Oct Waits records his final LP for Asylum, *Heartattack And Vine* which charts at US #96. It features *Jersey Girl* which will become an integral part of Bruce Springsteen's° live sets throughout the decade. Waits is quoted saying: "I'm so broke I can't even pay attention."

1981 Dec [31] He marries Irish playwright, Kathleen Brennan, whom he met while working on the soundtrack to Francis Ford Coppola film *One From The Heart*, at The Always and Forever Wedding Chapel, Manchester Boulevard, LA.

1982 After 18 months' work, the soundtrack LP is released through Columbia/CBS. It is Waits' final work with producer Bones Howe and the end of a certain musical style for the songwriter. The soundtrack receives an Oscar nomination.

1983 Having made various cameo acting appearances since 1978, including *Wolfen, Stone Boy* and *One From The Heart*, Waits features in *The Outsiders*, with Matt Dillon, and Coppola's *Rumblefish*. Asylum releases three compilations during the year: double LP *The Asylum Years*, LP *Bounced Check*, which includes two previously unreleased songs, and *Anthology*.

July Rickie Lee Jones° records Waits' composition *Angel Wings* on her 10-inch mini-LP *Girl At Her Volcano*, which reaches US #39.

Oct Waits' daughter Kellesimone is born. Simultaneously his debut for Island Records, LP *Swordfishtrombones* makes US #167 and UK #62. It is the first of three concept LPs loosely based around *Frank's Wild Years*, a track on the LP, and is a serious change of musical direction which Waits describes as "sounding like a demented parade band".

1984 He appears in another cameo role in Coppola's film *The Cotton Club* and contributes a cover version of *What Keeps Man Alive* to an A&M Kurt Weill tribute LP *Lost In The Stars*.

1985 June Waits moves from LA to New York, claiming "it's a great town for shoes".

Sept Son Casey Xavier is born. Waits' first-choice name, Senator Waits, is rejected by Kathleen.

Oct He undertakes sold out US and European tour to promote second Island LP *Raindogs*, which makes UK #29. Guest musicians on the release include Keith Richards (whom Waits claims is "a relative I met in a lingerie shop"), while boxing legend Jake La Motta appears in the video for unsuccessful single *Downtown Train*.

1986 June His musical *Frank's Wild Years*, written with his wife, opens at The Steppenwolf Theater Company in Chicago and later moves to New York. He plays a jailbreaking, unemployed disk jockey in his first starring role in black and white film *Down By Law*.

1987 Sept LP *Frank's Wild Years*, featuring many songs from the musical, completes the trilogy started in 1983. It makes UK #20 but only US #115. New country-folk artist Mary Chapin Carpenter covers *Downtown Train* on her debut Columbia LP.

Nov Waits visits UK to perform songs from the musical and others at sell-out concerts which receive ecstatic reviews.

1988 He contributes *Heigh-Ho (The Dwarfs' Marching Song)* for Disney compilation of favorites, *Stay Awake*. He begins work on LP *Big Time* and a new film project in Montana. This follows a successful portrayal of a dying street-bum in the Nicholson/Streep movie *Ironweed*. Looking to the future, Waits insists that his gravestone epitaph read: "I told you I was sick."

THE WALKER BROTHERS

Scott Engel (vocals)
John Maus (vocals)
Gary Leeds (drums)

1964 Aug The trio comes together in Los Angeles after Leeds, drumming for P.J. Proby°, befriends Engel and Maus when they are playing bass and lead guitar with The Dalton Brothers, the resident band at Gazzari's Club on Sunset Boulevard, LA. Leeds (b. Sept.3, 1944, Glendale, Cal., US), a drummer since his early teens, studied at The Aerospace Technology School in New York (having to quit after a leg injury), co-founded The Standells in LA in 1963 but left after the first two singles to join first Johnny Rivers° and then P.J. Proby° and visited UK during Proby's UK launch on a Jack Good TV show. Engel (b. Noel Scott Engel, Jan.9, 1944, Hamilton, Oh., US) having made some solo singles for tiny California labels in his teens and learned double bass at high school, majored in music and switched to electric bass to join instrumental group The Routers, playing on its 1963 hit *Let's Go* and follow-up *Make It Snappy*. Maus (b. Nov.12, 1943, New York City, US), a child actor at age 12 in TV series "Hello Mum" with Betty Hutton, moved to the West Coast, already with pseudonym John Stewart, and teamed up with Engel after being cast as brothers in a TV play.

Oct They make their first recordings with producers Jack Nitzsche and Nik Venet (ex-Capitol Records, to which The Dalton Brothers were contracted). Four titles are recorded and a deal signed with Mercury Records' Smash label. They appear in a cameo slot in teen movie *Three Hats For Lisa*. Leeds is keen to return to UK, having seen the potential for success while touring with Proby°. Jack Good also advises the trio to launch itself in London.

1965 Feb The trio arrives in UK, with Barry Clayman and Maurice King as managers, and impresses Johnny Franz, A&R man of Mercury's UK counterpart Philips Records.

Mar The US-recorded uptempo *Pretty Girls Everywhere* is the debut single but does not chart.

June Dramatic ballad *Love Her*, a revival of an Everly Brothers° B-side, reaches UK #20. Another of the tracks made with Venet in LA, with Nitzsche arrangement, establishes the trio's lush, orchestrally-backed hit style, highlighting Engel's rich lead vocals. The Walker Brothers begin to play live in the UK, with Engel and Maus laying aside bass and guitar to front the act on vocals and a stage backing band is formed around Leeds.

Sept Amid regular slots on UK TV's most popular music show "Ready Steady Go", *Make It Easy On Yourself*, a revival of Jerry Butler's° which Franz produces in similar style to that established by *Love Her*, tops the UK chart. The Walker Brothers become major teen favorites, constantly pictured in magazines and subject to hysterical female audiences at live gigs.

Nov *Make It Easy On Yourself* reaches US #16. A show at London's Finsbury Park Astoria is their last before UK work permits are renewed.

1966 Jan *My Ship Is Coming In*, a cover of US soul singer Jimmy Radcliffe, hits UK #3 and debut LP *Take It Easy With The Walker Brothers* hits UK #4. Leeds, who for contractual reasons cannot sing or play on the trio's records, signs as solo singer to CBS.

Feb *My Ship Is Coming In* reaches US #63.

Feb [27] The trio appears on UK TV's "Ready Steady Go" broadcast live from La Locomotive club in Paris, France.

Mar *The Sun Ain't Gonna Shine Anymore*, originally recorded in 1965 by Frankie Valli of The Four Seasons°, tops the UK chart for 4 weeks. *You Don't Love Me*, issued by Leeds on CBS under the name Gary Walker, is launched on UK TV's "Thank Your Lucky Stars" and reaches UK #26.

May *The Sun Ain't Gonna Shine Anymore* peaks at US #13. It is their last US hit single. Capitol in UK releases *I Only Came To Dance With You* as by Scott Engel and John Stewart; it is actually a relic of their days in The Dalton Brothers.

June Another Gary Walker solo release, *Twinkie Lee*, reaches UK #26. The trio is on a lengthy UK tour with The Troggs° and Dave Dee, Dozy, Beaky, Mick and Tich°.

Aug *(Baby) You Don't Have To Tell Me* reaches UK #13.

Sept LP *Portrait* hits UK #3.

Oct A revival of Gene McDaniels' *Another Tear Falls* reaches UK #12.

Dec *Deadlier Than The Male* (the theme from film of the same title) peaks at UK #34. EP *Solo Scott – Solo John* displays the two vocalists' individual talents. Engel and Maus are growing increasingly irritated by each other's company, both off and on stage. The consequent pressures start to pull the trio apart as hit singles lessen in impact.

1967 Feb A cover of Lorraine Ellison's *Stay With Me Baby* reaches UK #26.

Mar [31] The trio starts what will be its last UK tour, at Finsbury Park Astoria. Cat Stevens°, Engelbert Humperdinck and The Jimi Hendrix° Experience make up the highly eccentric bill.

Apr LP *Images* hits UK #6.

May [3] At the end of a concert at Tooting Granada, London, the trio announces its intention to split up because of growing internal incompatibilities.

June [4] Maus makes his post-group live debut with a concert at The Olympia, Paris, France while The Walker Brothers' revival of The Ronettes'° *Walking In The Rain* climbs to UK #26.

Aug Maus has the first post-group solo hit. Released under the name John Walker, *Annabella* reaches UK #24. (He will not be able to maintain his UK chart profile and will return to California. Leeds will drop completely out of sight but will continue to reside in UK.)

Oct Compilation LP *The Walker Brothers' Story* hits UK #9, but its sales are overshadowed by Engel's first solo LP *Scott*, released as by Scott Walker, which hits UK #3.

1968 Jan *Jackie* by Scott Walker, a dramatic version of Jacques Brel's song with a controversial lyric which guarantees it little airplay, reaches UK #22. The trio reunites for a one-off tour of Japan (a live LP from it will be released in UK 19 years later by Bam Caruso Records).

May LP *Scott 2*, like its predecessor a mixture of songs by an eclectic batch of "quality" composers with a large proportion of Jacques Brel numbers, tops UK LP chart.

June *Joanna*, a romantic ballad by Scott Walker which he professes to dislike, is his biggest UK solo hit at #7.

1969 Mar A Scott Walker weekly UK TV show, mostly a straight showcase for his singing, begins a 2-month run.

Apr LP *Scott 3* hits UK #3.

July *Lights Of Cincinnati* is Engel's last solo hit single as Scott Walker. It reaches UK #13 but LP *Scott Walker Sings Songs From His TV Series*, with a strong MOR slant, hits #7. (Scott Walker will follow his "brothers" out of the charts, despite recording LPs regularly, and will spend most of his time in seclusion, making live appearances with little notice once or twice a year. His non-charting LPs in 1970 will be *Scott 4* and *'Til The Band Comes In*, self-penned under the name Noel Scott Engel; film theme set *The Moviegoer* in 1972; *Any Day Now*, anthologizing favorite songwriters, in 1973; and two country-tinged sets for CBS, *Stretch* and *We Had It All*, in 1974.)

1975 Aug Against all expectations, the trio reunites and signs to GTO Records in UK.

1976 Feb A revival of Tom Rush's *No Regrets*, performed in the trio's traditional dramatic style, hits UK #7 and newly-recorded LP of the same title makes UK #49.

Sept *Lines* fails to chart, as does parent LP of the same title.

1978 July LP *Nite Flights* breaks new ground by containing material written entirely by the trio and is more avant-garde in approach and arrangement than any previous Walker Brothers LP. It does not chart. *The Electrician*, written by Engel, also fails to sell. After this, the trio does not record together again.

1984 Mar Scott Walker solo LP *Climate Of Hunter*, recorded for Virgin, reaches UK #60, though the singer himself remains in almost total seclusion.

1987 July Engel appears in UK black-and-white TV and cinema ad for Britvic soft drinks, in a cameo role as his 1960s persona. Also in the ad are 1960s contemporaries Sandie Shaw°, Georgie Fame°, Dusty Springfield° and Dave Dee° among others.

JUNIOR WALKER & THE ALL-STARS

Junior Walker (sax and vocals)
Willie Woods (guitar)
Vic Thomas (organ)
James Graves (drums)

1961 Four high school friends form a jazz/R&B-styled band to play the South Bend, Ind., club circuit. Group leader is Earl Bostic-influenced saxophonist Walker (b. Autry DeWalt II, 1942, Blythesville, Ark., US), called Junior by his stepfather. The group name arises from an occasion when, as they perform a jazz number at a club, a customer shouts out "these guys are all stars" and they dub themselves The All-Stars.

1962 The band is heard in a club by Johnny Bristol, who recommends it to Harvey Fuqua in Detroit. He signs Walker and Co. to his Harvey label, and they release three unsuccessful singles through the year.

1964 After Fuqua's labels are absorbed into Berry Gordy's Motown conglomerate, Junior Walker and The All-Stars are re-signed by Gordy, and placed on Soul label. First single for it also fails to chart.

1965 Jan Playing a benefit show in Benton Harbor, Mich., Walker sees two teenagers dancing an unfamiliar dance they call The Shotgun. Walker pens a booting dance tune with that title in his motel room and records it back in the studio in Detroit.

Mar The record takes off immediately and tops the US R&B chart for 3 weeks.

Apr *Shotgun* crosses over and hits US #4, becoming a million-seller.

July A celebration of another dance, *Do The Boomerang* reaches US #36.

Aug First Soul label LP, *Shotgun* makes US #108.

Sept *Shake And Fingerpop*, in a similar dance groove to the first two singles, reaches US #29.

Nov B-side of *Shake And Fingerpop*, slow, more jazz-influenced *Cleo's Back*, unlike the previous hits, is wholly instrumental and peaks at US #43.

1966 Feb Another instrumental in almost identical style, *Cleo's Mood* reaches US #50.

Apr LP *Soul Session* makes US #130.

June *(I'm A) Road Runner* reaches US #20.

Sept A revival of Marvin Gaye's° *How Sweet It Is (To Be Loved By You)* reaches US #18 and also debuts Walker on UK chart at #22. LP *Road Runner* makes US #64.

Dec Another revival of one of Motown's classics, Barrett Strong's *Money (That's What I Want) Part 1*, reaches US #52.

1967 Mar *Pucker Up Buttercup*, a return to *Shotgun* style, reaches US #31.

Aug *Shoot Your Shot* reaches US #44.

Oct LP *"Live!"* makes US #119.

1968 Jan A mellower than usual single, reviving The Supremes'° *Come See About Me*, reaches US #24.

Oct *Hip City, Pt.2* reaches US #31.

Dec [28] The group plays the Miami Pop Festival in Hallendale, Fla., US., alongside Chuck Berry°, Marvin Gaye°, Three Dog Night°, Fleetwood Mac° and many others.

1969 Feb LP *Home Cookin'* makes US #172, while its extracted title track reaches US #42.

May A reissue of *(I'm A) Road Runner* reaches UK #12.

Aug LP *Greatest Hits*, a compilation of hit singles to date, makes US #43, while new single *What Does It Take (To Win Your Love)*, with a lengthy, distinctive sax intro from Walker, is the group's biggest success since *Shotgun*, hitting US #4 and selling over a million.

Nov *What Does It Take (To Win Your Love)* reaches UK #13.

Dec *These Eyes*, a cover of a hit by Canadian rock band Guess Who°, reaches US #16, as the group starts a production liaison with Johnny Bristol.

1970 Feb LP *What Does It Take To Win Your Love* makes US #92.

Mar *Gotta Hold On To This Feeling*, taken from the LP, reaches US #21.

Aug *Do You See My Love (For You Growing)* reaches US #32.

Oct LP *A Gasssss* makes US #110.

1971 Jan A revival of Neil Diamond's° *Holly Holy* reaches US #75.

Aug LP *Rainbow Funk* makes US #91.

Sept *Take Me Girl, I'm Ready*, extracted from the LP, reaches US #50.

1972 Jan *Way Back Home* reaches US #52.

Feb LP *Moody Jr.* is Walker's final US LP chart entry, peaking at US #142.

June Atmospheric semi-instrumental *Walk In The Night* reaches US #46.

Sept [8] The group takes part in the Ann Arbor Jazz and Blues Festival, a tribute to blues pianist Otis Spann, alongside Muddy Waters°, Howlin' Wolf°, Bobby Bland and others.

Sept *Walk In The Night* makes UK #16.

1973 Feb *Take Me Girl, I'm Ready*, belatedly issued in UK, reaches #16.

July Another belated release, *Way Back Home*, makes UK #35.

1977 Feb [9] Walker participates in US ABC-TV's "American Bandstand's 25th Anniversary Special", as part of an all-star house band which includes Chuck Berry°, Johnny Rivers° and Steve Cropper of Booker T. and The MG's°.

1981 Sept Foreigner's° *Urgent*, featuring a blistering sax solo from Walker, hits US #4.

JOE WALSH

1965 Walsh (b. Nov.20, 1947, New York, N.Y., US), having been raised in New Jersey and played clarinet in junior high, then rhythm guitar in The G-Clefs, a duo playing Ventures'° instrumentals and Beatles°-styled The Nomads, goes to college at Kent State, Oh.

1969 While at Kent, he joins The Measles, who become local favorites. When they split, Walsh is asked to join Cleveland-based The James Gang to replace Glenn Schwartz, who has left to join Pacific Gas & Electric.

Nov The group, comprising Walsh, Tom Kriss on bass and vocals and Jim Fox on drums and vocals, makes US #83 with LP *Yer' Album*.

1970 Jan Dale Peters replaces Kriss.

May [4] Walsh witnesses the killings of four students on the campus of Kent State, Oh. (In 1988, Walsh will campaign to erect a memorial for them.)

May The James Gang, having opened for The Who° in Pittsburgh, Pa., in 1969, is invited to support the band on its European tour.

Sept *Funk #49* makes US #59 as LP *James Gang Rides Again* reaches US #20, earning a gold disk.

1971 June *Walk Away* reaches US #51 as LP *Thirds* makes US #27 and earns another gold disk.

Sept Live LP *James Gang Live In Concert* enters the US chart, and becomes the group's third gold disk, making US #24.

Oct *Midnight Man* stalls at US #80.

1972 Jan Walsh quits The James Gang and, turning down an invitation from Steve Marriott to join Humble Pie°, leaves industrial Cleveland for the open air of Boulder, Col.

Mar Walsh forms Barnstorm trio with Kenny Passarelli on bass and Joe Vitale on drums.

Oct Bill Szymczyk-produced LP *Barnstorm*, recorded at Caribou studios and credited as a Joe Walsh solo, reaches US #79.

Nov Keyboards player Rocke Grace joins as the group begins a major US tour, much of it as support to Stephen Stills.

1973 Feb Compilation LP *The Best Of The James Gang Featuring Joe Walsh* makes US #79.

Apr Walsh moves his base from Boulder to Studio City, LA, Cal.

June Tom Stephenson replaces Grace as LP *The Smoker You Drink, The Player You Get* is released. It hits US #6 and earns Walsh his first gold disk.

Oct *Rocky Mountain Way* makes US #23 and UK #39.

Dec James Gang compilation LP *16 Greatest Hits*, featuring Walsh, makes US #181. Barnstorm splits after touring for most of the year.

1974 Jan Walsh solo *Meadows* stalls at US #89. He will spend much of the year working on LP *So What*. He also plays sessions for The Eagles°, B.B. King°, Rod Stewart° and Stephen Stills.

Feb The James Gang has a final hit at US #54 with *Must Be Love*.

Dec Walsh produces Dan Fogelberg's° LP *Souvenirs*.

1975 Jan LP *So What*, including five tracks recorded with Barnstorm, enters the US chart. It will reach US #11 and earn Walsh a second gold disk.

Mar *Turn To Stone* stalls at US #93.

June [21] Walsh plays on the "Midsummer Madness" bill at London's Wembley Stadium, UK, with The Beach Boys°, The Eagles° and Elton John°.

Dec [20] Walsh replaces Bernie Leadon in The Eagles°. He makes an impression with a lengthy guitar lead on the title cut for forthcoming LP *Hotel California*.

1976 Apr Walsh's live solo LP *You Can't Argue With A Sick Mind* reaches US #20 and UK #28.

1977 July EP *Rocky Mountain Way*, including *Turn To Stone*, *Meadows*, *Walk Away* and the title track, reaches UK #39.

1978 June He continues his solo career with *Life's Been Good* reaching US #12 and UK #14 as parent LP *But Seriously, Folks . . .* makes US #8, earning Walsh his first platinum disk, and reaches UK #16.

Nov LP *The Best Of Joe Walsh*, including James Gang tracks, makes US #71.

1979 Sept [22] Walsh announces he will run for president in 1980.

1980 July Walsh's *All Night Long*, from the soundtrack LP for John Travolta-starring movie *Urban Cowboy*, makes US #19.

1981 July *A Life Of Illusion* reaches US #34. Walsh switches to Warner

Bros. for LP *There Goes The Neighborhood* which makes US #20.
1983 July *Space Age Whiz Kids* reaches US #52.
Aug LP *You Bought It – You Name It* climbs to US #48.
1985 July LP *The Confessor* makes US #65.
1987 Aug LP *Got Any Gum*, on Warner Bros., makes US #113.
Sept [19] Walsh participates in the Farm Aid II benefit with John Cougar Mellencamp°, Neil Young°, Lou Reed° and others at the University of Nebraska's Memorial Stadium.

WAR

Lonnie Jordan (keyboards and vocals)
Howard Scott (guitar and vocals)
Charles Miller (saxophone and clarinet)
B.B. Dickerson (bass and vocals)
Harold Brown (drums and percussion)
"Papa Dee" Allen (keyboards and vocals)
Lee Oskar (harmonica)

1969 The band forms from the remnants of early 1960s Long Beach, Cal., group The Creators, who became Night Shift and were only successful on the local circuit. As Night Shift, Jordan (b. Leroy Jordan, Nov.21, 1948, San Diego, Cal., US), Scott (b. Mar.15, 1946, San Pedro, Cal.), Miller (b. June 2, 1939, Olathe, Kan., US) and Brown (Mar.17, 1946, Long Beach), with bassist Peter Rosen, are backing football star turned soul singer Deacon Jones, when noted by ex-The Animals° lead singer Eric Burdon, harmonica player Oskar (b. Mar.24, 1946, Copenhagen, Denmark) and producer Jerry Goldstein, who are looking for a blues-based black band to accompany Burdon.
June Burdon, Oskar and the band meet at Goldstein's home and decide to work together with Goldstein as producer. The name War is chosen as being in stark contrast with current peace preoccupations in music and therefore memorable. Shortly after, Rosen dies from a drug overdose, and ex-Creators bassist Dickerson (b. Morris Dickerson, Aug.3, 1949, Torrance, Cal.) replaces him, while Allen (b. Thomas Allen, July 18, 1931, Wilmington, Del.) also joins on keyboards to make it a 7-piece instrumental unit. Burdon is already signed to MGM, and the new team continues with the label.
1970 The band tours US, then moves to UK and Europe.
July War jams with Jimi Hendrix° in an impromptu session at Ronnie Scott's jazz club in London.
Aug Debut LP *Eric Burdon Declares War* reaches US #18. Taken from it, group-composed *Spill The Wine* hits US #3 and sells over a million, to earn a gold disk. The LP also contains musical tributes to Roland Kirk and Memphis Slim, and a version of John D. Loudermilk's much-revived *Tobacco Road*.
Oct LP *Eric Burdon Declares War* makes UK #50.
1971 Jan *They Can't Take Away Our Music* reaches US #50. It is taken from double LP *The Black Man's Burdon*, which makes US #82.
Feb The LP makes UK #34, and another European tour follows but Burdon drops out, exhausted, and returns to LA. The band completes all contracted dates on its own and, at tour's end, it is decided not to continue the partnership with Burdon. The group's manager Steve Gold negotiates a new recording deal with United Artists Records.
May LP *War*, the debut without Burdon, creeps to US #190.
June [30] The band plays the Hollywood Bowl in United Artists' 99 Cent Spectacular, a low entry price showcase for the label's new acts.
Sept *All Day Music*, written by Goldstein and the band, reaches US #35.
Nov LP *All Day Music* enters the US chart and will reach #16.
1972 May *Slippin' Into Darkness* also reaches US #16, spending 22 weeks on chart and selling over a million to give the band its first "solo" gold disk. The track is an edited version of a cut on LP *All Day Music*, which also peaks at US #16, and is the band's first gold LP (selling over a half million copies).
Aug [19] The band plays on the first edition of US NBC TV's "Midnight Special", performing *Slippin' Into Darkness*.
1973 Jan *The World Is A Ghetto* reaches US #7 and is another million-seller.
Feb LP *The World Is A Ghetto*, written by the band and produced by Goldstein (he and the band have formed their own Far Out production company, which leases all recordings to UA), tops the US chart for 2 weeks, becoming its second gold LP. It includes a 10-min. version of the title track and 13½-min. *City, Country, City*.
Apr *The Cisco Kid*, from the LP, hits US #2, the band's third consecutive million-selling single.
Sept *Gypsy Man* hits US #8. It is taken from LP *Deliver The Word*, which hits US #6 and earns another gold disk.
1974 Jan Also from LP *Deliver The Word*, *Me And Baby Brother* reaches US #15.
May Double live LP *War Live!* reaches US #13.
July Instrumental *Ballero*, extracted from the live LP, climbs to US #33.
1975 Aug LP *Why Can't We Be Friends?* hits US #8, becoming the band's fifth gold LP, while the title track hits US #6 and sells over a million. (The song is beamed into space to US and Russian astronauts during the summer 1975 link-up in Earth orbit.)
Nov Sparse Latin funk track *Low Rider*, also from LP *Why Can't We Be Friends?*, hits US #7.
1976 Feb The group signs a new deal for UK distribution with Island Records and *Low Rider* is its UK chart debut, reaching #12.
July *Me And Baby Brother*, belatedly issued in UK as follow-up, reaches UK #21. Oskar has solo success with US #29 LP *Lee Oskar*. (Two further solo LPs, *Before The Rain* (US #86) and *My Road Our Road* (US #162) will chart in 1978 and 1981.)
Sept *Summer* hits US #7, and is another million-seller. The group writes and performs the music for Krishna Shah's movie *The River Niger*, starring Cicely Tyson and James Earl Jones.
Oct Compilation LP *Greatest Hits*, rounding up all the successful singles, hits US #6. It is the band's biggest-selling LP, earning a platinum disk for million-plus sales. Meanwhile, War and United Artists are at loggerheads (or with "philosophical differences", as the statements quote) over matters of direction and marketing of the band's music. The agreed solution is that the band's production company will move elsewhere, but will deliver a final LP to UA, to be a departure from the mainstream for release on subsidiary Blue Note jazz label.
1977 Jan ABC Records releases LP *Love Is All Around*, a collection old early tracks recorded with Burdon in 1969-70. It reaches US #140.
Aug *L.A. Sunshine*, the rare appearance of a single on Blue Note (and a sampler for the new LP) peaks at US #45.
Sept Double LP *Platinum Jazz*, the set owed to UA, makes US #23 and earns a gold disk.
1978 Feb The band's Far Out Productions signs a new deal with MCA Records. First MCA release, LP *Galaxy* reaches US #15, while the title track makes US #39 and UK #14. Alice Tweed Smyth joins on additional vocals.
Apr *Hey Senorita*, from LP *Galaxy*, reaches UK #40. Dickerson leaves and is replaced on bass by Luther Rabb.
Aug War's soundtrack LP from film *Youngblood*, a drama of ghetto gang warfare, reaches US #69.
1979 May LP *The Music Band* peaks at US #41, earning War's final gold LP. The group adds Pat Rizzo on horns and Ron Hammond on percussion.
1980 Jan LP *The Music Band 2* reaches US #111.
1982 Apr The band moves labels again, signing to RCA for LP *Outlaw*, which reaches US #48. *You Got The Power*, taken from the LP, reaches US #66 and UK #58. Smyth leaves.
July The title track from *Outlaw* makes US #94.
1983 July RCA LP *Life (Is So Strange)* reaches US #164.
1985 Apr *Groovin'*, a revival of The Young Rascals'° 1967 chart-topper, leased by the band and Goldstein to UK independent black music label Bluebird Records, reaches UK #43.
1987 July Goldstein launches the band's own Lax label in UK. First release is an updated remix of *Low Rider* on 12"-single, which makes UK #98.

JENNIFER WARNES

1956 Warnes (b. Seattle, Wash., US), having been raised in Orange County, Cal., makes her professional debut wrapped in the US flag singing *The Star Spangled Banner*, accompanied by 300 accordians.
1967 Feb Warnes, as Jennifer Warren, becomes a regular on US CBS TV's "The Smothers Brothers Comedy Hour". One of the show's writers, Mason Williams invites Warnes to duet with him on *Cinderella Rockefella* for his LP *The Mason Williams Ear Show*.
1968 Nov [22] Warnes stars as Sheila in a West Coast production of *Hair*, which opens at LA's Aquarius Theater.
1969 Now a veteran of the LA folk scene, gaining a reputation for singing Canadian poet Leonard Cohen's° songs, Warnes signs to

JENNIFER WARNES *cont.*

Warner Bros. Records.

1972 She releases her first LP *Jennifer* for Reprise, produced by John Cale° and featuring songs by Jackson Browne°, Jimmy Webb, Donovan° and Barry Gibb.

1975 Warnes signs to Arista Records.

1977 May LP *Jennifer Warnes*, produced by Jim Ed Norman and Jim Price, reaches US #43.

1978 Mar Peter McCann-penned *Right Time Of The Night* hits US #6.

Sept *I'm Dreaming* makes US #50.

1979 Aug LP *Shot Through The Heart*, self-produced with Rob Fraboni, makes US #94.

Nov *I Know A Heartache When I See One* reaches US #19.

1980 Jan A revival of Dionne Warwick's° 1963 Bacharach/David-penned hit *Don't Make Me Over* reaches US #67.

Apr [14] Warnes' *It Goes Like It Goes*, from Sally Field film *Norma Rae*, wins an Oscar for Best Original Song at the annual Academy Awards.

May *When The Feeling Comes Around* reaches US #45.

1981 Dec *One More Hour*, written by Randy Newman° for his score to movie *Ragtime*, receives an Oscar nomination.

1982 Jan *Could It Be Love*, one of three new tracks from LP *Best Of Jennifer Warnes*, reaches US #47.

Nov *Up Where We Belong*, a duet with Joe Cocker° from movie *An Officer and a Gentleman*, tops the US chart for 3 weeks.

1983 Feb *Up Where We Belong* hits UK #7.

Apr [11] Cocker° and Warnes perform *Up Where We Belong* at the Academy Awards. It wins an Oscar for Best Original Song.

Nov *All The Right Moves*, a duet with Chris Thompson from movie of same name, reaches US #85.

1987 Jan Warnes, the first signing to new Cypress label, releases LP *Famous Blue Raincoat*, featuring only Leonard Cohen° songs and self-produced with Roscoe Beck. It reaches US #72.

July Warnes is one of the featured friends on *The Black And White Night – Roy Orbison And Friends*, a filmed concert with Orbison backed by Bruce Springsteen°, Elvis Costello°, James Burton, Tom Waits° and many others. Warnes duets with country singer Gary Morris on *Simply Meant To Be*, penned by Henry Mancini with George Merrill and Shannon Rubicam (husband and wife writers of Whitney Houston's° *I Wanna Dance With Somebody* and *How Will I Know*), for Bruce Willis/Kim Basinger film *Blind Date*.

Aug LP *Famous Blue Raincoat* reaches UK #33.

Nov Warnes' duet with Bill Medley *(I've Had) The Time Of My Life*, from film *Dirty Dancing*, tops the US chart and hits UK #6.

1988 June Warnes guests with Harry Belafonte° on his LP *Paradise In Gazankulu*.

DIONNE WARWICK

1960 After singing in her church choir from age 6, Warwick (b. Marie Dionne Warrick, Dec.12, 1940, East Orange, N.J., US), daughter of Chess Records' gospel promotion department head, is a regular performer with The Drinkard Singers gospel group, managed by her mother. While studying music in Hartford, Conn., she forms The Gospelaires, with sister Dee Dee, cousin Cissy Houston and friend Doris Troy. The girls sing gospel and make ends meet by performing vocal back-up on New York studio pop and R&B recording sessions.

1961 July While working with The Gospelaires on a Leiber/Stoller-produced session for The Drifters"°, Warwick is first heard by composer Burt Bacharach, whose song *Mexican Divorce* The Drifers are cutting. He invites her to become the regular singer on demos he and lyricist partner Hal David are making of their songs for playing to record companies.

1962 Via demos made for Scepter Records' group The Shirelles°, Warwick begins regular studio back-up work for the label's acts, including the successful Chuck Jackson and Tommy Hunt, and is signed to Scepter as a solo vocalist, with Bacharach/David as writers and producers.

1963 Jan Debut single *Don't Make Me Over*, written (as will be virtually all her Scepter output) by Bacharach/David, reaches US #21.

Apr *This Empty Place* peaks at US #84 (its B-side is *Wishin' And Hopin'*, later successfully revived by Dusty Springfield° and The Merseybeats). Marlene Dietrich introduces Warwick on her debut at the Olympia Theatre in Paris, France.

Aug *Make The Music Play* reaches US #81.

1964 Feb *Anyone Who Had A Heart* hits US #8. In UK, it makes #42, eclipsed by Cilla Black's° #1 cover version.

May *Walk On By*, rush-released in US and UK to prevent cover versions, and promoted by Warwick on UK TV shows during a promotional visit, marks her UK breakthrough, hitting #9.

June *Walk On By* hits US #6, becoming her first international million-seller while LP *Presenting Dionne Warwick* reaches UK #14.

Aug *You'll Never Get To Heaven (If You Break My Heart)* (which will be revived later by The Stylistics°) reaches UK #20.

Sept *You'll Never Get To Heaven (If You Break My Heart)* makes US #34 while B-side *A House Is Not A Home* (theme from the movie of the same title) reaches US #71, in competition with an equally strong version by Brook Benton°.

Oct *Reach Out For Me* reaches UK #23.

Nov *Reach Out For Me* makes US #20 and LP *Make Way For Dionne Warwick* reaches US #68.

1965 Mar LP *The Sensitive Sound Of Dionne Warwick* peaks at US #107.

Apr *Who Can I Turn To*, from musical *The Roar of the Greasepaint – The Smell of the Crowd*, makes US #62.

May An uncharacteristic uptempo R&B single, *You Can Have Him* reaches US #75 and UK #37.

Aug *Here I Am*, from Bacharach/David-penned soundtrack of movie *What's New Pussycat?*, reaches US #65. (Its B-side is Warwick's original recording of *(They Long To Be) Close To You*, which will be a million-seller 5 years later by The Carpenters°.)

Nov *(Here I Go Again) Looking With My Eyes* makes US #64.

1966 Jan *Are You There (With Another Girl?)* reaches US #39.

Feb LP *Here I Am* peaks at US #45.

May Live LP *Dionne Warwick In Paris*, recorded on stage at the Olympia, makes US #76, while *A Message To Michael*, a gender-switched revival of Bacharach/David's hit by both Lou Johnson and Adam Faith° as *A Message To Martha (Kentucky Bluebird)*, hits US #8.

June Compilation LP *Best Of Dionne Warwick* hits UK #8.

Aug *Trains And Boats And Planes* (a 1965 UK hit for Bacharach himself and a US and UK hit by Billy J. Kramer°) reaches US #22.

Nov *I Just Don't Know What To Do With Myself*, an LP cut covered as a UK hit by Dusty Springfield° in 1964, reaches US #26.

1967 Jan *Another Night* reaches US #49, as Warwick begins a 4-month European tour.

Feb LP *Here, Where There Is Love* reaches US #18 and UK #39, and earns Warwick's first gold LP. It contains her version of *Alfie*, the film theme which has hit for Cher° and Cilla Black° the previous year.

June LP *On Stage And In The Movies* reaches US #169.

June [10] Warwick appears at the 2-day Fantasy Faire and Magic Mountain Music Fest in Mt. Tamilpais, Cal., with an audience of 15,000. She is billed alongside The Miracles and several of California's new breed of rock bands including The Doors° and Jefferson Airplane°.

July After strong airplay as an LP track, *Alfie* is released as a single and reaches US #15, while B-side *The Beginning Of Loneliness* makes US #79.

Sept *The Windows Of The World* reaches US #32.

Nov LP *The Windows Of The World* makes US #22.

Dec From the LP, *I Say A Little Prayer* hits US #4.

1968 Jan LP *Dionne Warwick's Golden Hits, Part One* hits US #10.

Feb B-side of *I Say A Little Prayer*, movie theme *(Theme From) Valley Of The Dolls*, penned by André and Dory Previn, hits US #2 behind Paul Mauriat's *Love Is Blue*, making the single Warwick's biggest double-sided chartmaker of her career, and a million-seller in US alone. Issued in UK as an A-side, *(Theme From) Valley Of The Dolls* makes UK #28.

Apr LP *Valley Of The Dolls* hits US #6 and earns a gold disk.

May *Do You Know The Way To San José*, taken from the LP, and written by Bacharach/David, hits US #10 while B-side *Let Me Be Lonely* makes US #71.

June LP *Valley Of The Dolls* hits UK #10 while *Do You Know The Way To San José* hits UK #8.

Sept *Who Is Gonna Love Me?* reaches US #33. Its B-side revives Warwick's original *(There's) Always Something There To Remind Me* (a 1964 hit for Sandie Shaw° and Lou Johnson) and makes US #65.

Dec *Promises Promises*, from Bacharach/David's Broadway musical of the same title, reaches US #19.

1969 Jan LP *Promises Promises* makes US #18.

Mar *This Girl's In Love With You*, from LP *Promises, Promises* (and a gender-switch revival of Herb Alpert's° million-seller of the previous summer) hits US #7.

Mar [12] She wins a Grammy award for *Do You Know The Way To San José*, named Best Female Contemporary Vocal Performance of 1968.

May LP *Soulful* reaches US #11.

June *The April Fools*, theme from Jack Lemmon/Catherine Deneuve film of the same title, reaches US #37. Warwick makes her own film acting debut in *Slaves*, a historical drama, opposite Stephen Boyd. (She also sings the movie's theme song.)

Sept LP *Dionne Warwick's Greatest Motion Picture Hits* makes US #31 and earns a gold disk while *Odds And Ends* reaches US #43.

Nov A revival of The Righteous Brothers'° *You've Lost That Lovin' Feelin'* reaches US #16.

Dec Compilation LP *Dionne Warwick's Golden Hits, Part 2* makes US #28.

1970 Feb *I'll Never Fall In Love Again*, from Broadway musical *Promises Promises* (a UK hit for Bobbie Gentry in 1969), hits US #6.

May *Let Me Go To Him* reaches US #32.

June Compilation LPs *Greatest Hits Vol.1* and *Greatest Hits Vol.2* make UK #31 and #28 respectively. In US, LP *I'll Never Fall In Love Again* makes #23.

Aug *Papier Mâché* reaches US #43.

Nov *Make It Easy On Yourself*, a revival of Bacharach/David's 1962 hit for Jerry Butler°, reaches US #37.

1971 Jan LP *Very Dionne* makes US #37 while, taken from it, *The Green Grass Starts To Grow* reaches US #43.

Mar [16] Warwick wins her second Grammy award, as *I'll Never Fall In Love Again* is named Best Female Contemporary Vocal Performance of 1970.

Apr *Who Gets The Guy* reaches US #57.

Aug *Amanda* stalls at US #83, and is Warwick's last hit single on Scepter. She signs to Warner Bros.

Dec Double LP *The Dionne Warwicke Story*, featuring live versions of her hits, makes US #48. (For a short period, she changes the spelling of her surname on all billing, to include the extra "e" in Warwicke, but will revert back to its original form.)

1972 Mar LP *Dionne*, her debut on Warner, peaks at US #54 while, from it, *If We Only Have Love* reaches US #84. This hit marks the end of her long collaboration with Bacharach and David, who will no longer write for her when they also split professionally. Warwick sues the duo, alleging the breaking of a contractual obligation.

Apr LP *From Within*, a collection of reissued Scepter material, makes US #169.

1973 Feb Second Warner LP *Just Being Myself* peaks at US #178 and, like most of Warwick's Warner LPs, fails to spin off a hit single.

1974 Oct *Then Came You*, duetted with The Spinners°, tops the US chart for a week, selling over a million. It is the first chart-topper for both Warwick and the group. (The Spinners° have been her opening act on a 5-week theater tour during the summer and producer Thom Bell has suggested her voice would blend well with the group's lead singer Phillipe Wynne.)

Nov *Then Came You* makes UK #29.

1975 Mar LP *Then Came You*, including the duet with The Spinners°, peaks at US #167.

1976 Jan LP *Track Of The Cat*, produced by Thom Bell and mostly written by him and Linda Creed, makes US #137.

Feb From the LP, *Once You Hit The Road* reaches US #79.

1977 Mar Double live LP *A Man And A Woman*, on which Warwick duets with Isaac Hayes°, released on his Hot Buttered Soul label, makes US #49 and coincides with the opening of a joint US tour by Warwick and Hayes.

1979 Jan Her Warner Bros. contract expired, Warwick signs to Arista Records.

Oct *I'll Never Love This Way Again* hits US #5 and sells over a million. It is taken from her debut Arista LP *Dionne*, produced by labelmate Barry Manilow°, which reaches US #12 and, in over a year's stay on chart, will sell a million.

1980 Feb *Déjà Vu*, also from LP *Dionne*, reaches US #15.

Feb [27] Warwick wins Grammy awards for *I'll Never Love This Way Again*, named Best Female Pop Vocal Performance of 1979, and *Déjà Vu* as Best Female R&B Vocal Performance.

Apr *After You*, theme from the film of the same title, and also produced by Manilow°, peaks at US #65.

Sept Warwick hosts the first season of the US syndicated-TV pop show "Solid Gold".

Oct LP *No Night So Long* makes US #23, while the extracted title song reaches US #23.

Dec *Easy Love*, also from the LP, reaches US #62.

1981 July Double LP *Hot! Live And Otherwise*, which has three live (recorded at Harrah's in Reno, Nev.) and one studio-recorded side, makes US #72. From it, Michael Masser-produced *Some Changes Are For Good* climbs to US #65.

1982 June LP *Friends In Love* makes US #83 while the title song, a duet with Johnny Mathis, reaches US #38.

Dec LP *Heartbreaker*, produced by Barry Gibb of The Bee Gees° with Albhy Galuten and Karl Richardson, and mostly co-written by Gibb (apart from revived oldie *Our Day Will Come*) reaches US #25 and hits UK #3, while the title track, written by The Bee Gees and with Barry Gibb on backing vocals, hits UK #2.

1983 Jan *Heartbreaker* hits US #10 while UK follow-up, The Bee Gees°-penned *All The Love In The World*, hits UK #10.

Feb *Yours*, another Bee Gees° composition, makes UK #66.

Apr *Take The Short Way Home*, written by Gibb and Galuten, is Warwick's 50th US hit single and reaches US #41.

May UK compilation LP *The Collection* reaches UK #11.

June A reissue of *I'll Never Love This Way Again*, taken from LP *The Collection*, makes UK #62.

Nov LP *So Amazing* makes UK #60.

Dec LP *How Many Times Can We Say Goodbye*, (the US title of *So Amazing*) produced by Luther Vandross°, peaks at US #57 as the title song, a duet with Vandross, reaches US #27.

1984 Warwick performs in the US Gala, in the presence of HM Queen Elizabeth II.

Nov Warwick contributes to Stevie Wonder's° soundtrack LP for movie *The Woman in Red*, which hits US #4 and UK #2.

1985 Jan [28] Warwick takes part in the recording of the all-star charity single *We Are The World* by USA For Africa°, which will top charts throughout the world.

Feb LP *Without Your Love*, containing duets with Barry Manilow°,

DIONNE WARWICK *cont.*

Glenn Jones and Stevie Wonder°, makes UK #86.

Mar In US, the LP is given the alternative title *Finder Of Lost Loves* and peaks at US #106.

Nov *That's What Friends Are For*, written by Bacharach/Carole Bayer Sager for 1982 film *Night Shift* and sung by Rod Stewart°, is revived initially to provide a duet for Warwick and Stevie Wonder°. When it is decided to donate its profits to the American Foundation for AIDS Research, Warwick asks first Gladys Knight° and then Elton John° to add vocal parts. The song is released as a single, credited to Dionne Warwick and Friends, and reaches UK #16.

Dec LP *Friends* reaches US #12.

1986 Jan *That's What Friends Are For* tops the US chart for 4 weeks, selling over a million.

Feb *That's What Friends Are For* wins a Grammy award as Song of the Year for 1985.

Apr *Whisper In The Dark*, from LP *Friends*, reaches US #72.

1987 Mar Warwick co-hosts (with Luther Vandross°) the First Annual Soul Train Music Awards at the Hollywood Center television studios.

Aug *Love Power*, a duet with Jeffrey Osborne°, reaches US #12. Parent LP *Reservations For Two*, containing duets with Kashif, Howard Hewett (ex-Shalamar°), Osborne, Smokey Robinson° and June Pointer of The Pointer Sisters°, makes US #56.

Sept [23] The city of New York honors Warwick for her work in raising $1 million for AIDS research.

Nov *Reservations For Two*, from the LP of the same title and duetted with Kashif, peaks at US #62.

1988 Sept Warwick sings *Champagne Wishes And Caviar Dreams*, the theme for the sixth season of Robin Leach's US TV show "Lifestyles of the Rich and Famous".

MUDDY WATERS

1943 Waters (b. McKinley Morganfield, Apr.4, 1915, Rolling Fork, Miss., US), having moved to Chicago from a plantation in Clarksdale on the Mississippi Delta where he grew up, is introduced by fellow bluesman, Big Bill Broonzy, to the South Side clubs and bars where he begins to develop a strong local reputation.

1945 Chicagoans Leonard and Phil Chess sign Waters to their Aristocrat Records label, where he begins work as a sideman for other artists.

1948 After working as a sideman at Columbia Records, Waters moves back to Aristocrat to record his first own-name single *I Can't Be Satisfied*.

1949 He records *Screamin' And Cryin'*, followed by *Rollin' And Tumblin'*.

1950 Aristocrat is renamed Chess. Waters' first single on Chess is *Rollin' Stone* which features the group he will use on many of his best releases over the next decade. (Little Walter (harmonica), Otis Spann (piano) and Jimmy Rogers (second guitar). Bass player and composer, Willie Dixon, will be another regular in the line-up.)

1951 Waters' first big national R&B success is *Louisiana Blues*. (Between now and 1958, he will have a further eleven national R&B hits, of which the most successful will be *She Moves Me* (1952), *Hoochie Coochie Man* (1954), *Mannish Boy* (1955), *I've Got My Mojo Working* (1957) and *Close To You* (1958).)

1958 Waters on his first UK tour makes a big impression on white London bluesmen, Cyril Davies and Alexis Korner, who will be pioneers of UK's emergent R&B movement. (By the end of the decade, the mass black American audience for the blues will largely disappear, favoring the more sophisticated R&B/soul styles. Waters will be able to avoid the limbo into which many US bluesmen are cast thanks to marketing initiatives by Chess, who successfully project him as an LPs artist, selling increasingly to white audiences.)

1961 Sept Live LP *Muddy Waters At Newport* introduces him to the mainstream jazz audience.

1964 May *Muddy Waters Folk Singer*, a solo acoustic LP, gives him a new folk following. Waters is championed by UK R&B/beat groups, including The Rolling Stones° and The Yardbirds°, and re-issued LPs of his 1950s singles start selling to a new generation of fans.

1968 May LP *The Super Super Blues Band*, with Bo Diddley° and Howlin' Wolf°, is released, followed by two controversial "psychedelic" LPs: *Electric Mud*, which reaches US #127, and *After The Rain*.

1969 Oct LP *Fathers And Sons*, featuring white US bluesmen Paul Butterfield° and Mike Bloomfield°, climbs to US #70.

1972 July LP *The London Sessions* is released.

1973 Oct [11] A serious car accident, in which three people are killed, forces Waters into semi-retirement for 2 years.

1976 Nov [25] His first major live appearance following the accident is at The Band's° farewell "Last Waltz" concert in San Francisco.

1977 Mar Bluesman and rock star, Johnny Winter°, signs Waters to his Blue Sky label, producing Waters on two LPs, *Hard Again*, which makes US #143, and *I'm Ready*, which peaks at US #157.

1978 Third Blue Sky set, LP *Muddy Waters Live* is released. Consistent recognition for Waters' dominance of the blues is confirmed as he collects a Grammy for Best Ethnic Or Traditional Recording for 3 consecutive years: *Hard Again* (1977), *I'm Ready* (1978) and *Muddy Waters Live* (1979).

Aug Waters is invited to play at a White House picnic organized by President Jimmy Carter.

1981 May LP *King Bee* reaches US #192.

1982 He plays a concert in Miami with guest Eric Clapton°.

1983 Apr [30] Waters dies of a heart attack at home in Chicago.

1988 July Waters receives posthumous UK success when *Mannish Boy* reaches UK #51 through exposure on a Levi's 501 jeans TV commercial.

BERT WEEDON

1956 Weedon (b. May 10, 1921, East Ham, London, UK), having begun to play classical guitar at age 12 and later, during the Second World War and early post-war years, played widely with dance bands and with the jazz group fronted by Stephane Grappelli and Django Reinhardt, becomes resident guitarist with UK's BBC Showband led by Cyril Stapleton and begins regular radio sessions. He signs to EMI's Parlophone label as a soloist and debut *Stranger Than Fiction* is released only as a 78rpm single.

1957/58 He becomes an in-demand session player on the expanding UK recording scene, backing UK stars and US visitors including David Whitfield, Alma Cogan, Frank Sinatra, Nat "King" Cole and Judy Garland. With UK rock'n'roll growing, he also works with Marty Wilde°, Laurie London and Cliff Richard°, plus many more. Five more solo guitar singles are released by Parlophone but none charts.

1959 June Signed to new Top Rank label, he covers The Virtues' US rock instrumental hit *Guitar Boogie Shuffle* (an upbeat update of Arthur Smith's 1945 country tune *Guitar Boogie*). It hits UK #7. (The Virtues' version makes only UK #24.)

Nov After self-penned *Teenage Guitar* fails to chart, *Nashville Boogie* makes UK #29.

1960 Mar *Big Beat Boogie*, coupled with a cover of Percy Faith's hit *Theme From A Summer Place*, peaks at UK #37.

June *Twelfth Street Rag* makes UK #47.

July LP *King Size Guitar* reaches UK #18.

Aug The Shadows' version of Jerry Lordan composition *Apache* tops the UK chart while Weedon's less dramatic rendition peaks at UK #24. (Weedon has actually recorded it first but EMI, which markets Weedon's Top Rank label and The Shadows' Columbia, has chosen the group's for major promotion.) The Shadows have composed *Mr. Guitar* for him and acknowledge the debt they – and almost all other guitarists in UK – owe to Weedon, who has been the major role model during the 1950s and whose *Play in a Day* teach-yourself guitar booklet is used by almost every newcomer to the instrument. (The booklet, seldom out of print, becomes a far more significant memorial of Weedon's influence than any of his recordings.)

Nov *Sorry Robbie* (credited to Weedon, but with hints of a traditional Scottish air, hence the title) reaches UK #28.

1961 Feb Self-written *Ginchy* makes UK #35.

May *Mr. Guitar*, written by The Shadows°, creeps to UK #47 and is Weedon's last UK singles chart entry.

Nov He moves to EMI's HMV label. He will record 14 singles between now and 1967 but none will chart, though both *Some Other Love* and *South Of The Border* in 1962 just fail to make UK top 50. Still doing regular sessions, as well as concert appearances in UK and Europe, he will be a familar face on UK TV variety and children's shows, and in a long-running series of his own.

1967 June His last single for HMV, a remake of *Stranger Than Fiction*, will be his last release for 3 years.

1970 He signs to MOR budget label Contour Records, eschewing singles for "theme" LPs like *The Romantic Guitar Of Bert Weedon*, *The*

Gentle Guitar Of Bert Weedon and *Bert Weedon Remembers . . .* of Nat "King" Cole and Jim Reeves hits.

1971 LP *Rockin' At The Roundhouse*, recorded after he is the surprise show-stealer at a vintage rock'n'roll revival concert at London's Roundhouse, includes some of his own old hits plus rock guitar standards like The Ventures'° *Walk Don't Run* and Duane Eddy's° *Shazam* and *40 Miles Of Bad Road*. Sales of this and other Contour LPs are huge (all in six figures), though as budget releases they are excluded from the UK chart.

1976 Nov Weedon records LP *22 Golden Guitar Greats* for Warwick Records which, promoted via a TV campaign,strikes a nostalgic chord with UK audiences and tops the UK chart for a week, his biggest hit. (Weedon will remain a steady seller in the nostalgia market, occasionally dipping back into rock – as on *Rockin' Guitars*, a 1977 single with a medley of six rock classics, on Polydor – and will continue to release LPs at an average rate of two a year into the 1980s. By the mid-1980s he will have appeared on more than 5,000 TV and radio programs.)

WET WET WET

Marti Pellow (vocals)
Graeme Clark (bass)
Tom Cunningham (drums)
Neil Mitchell (keyboards)

1982 Clark (b. Apr.15, 1966, Glasgow, Scotland), Cunningham (b. June 22, 1965, Glasgow) and Mitchell (b. June 8, 1967, Helensborough, Scotland), having formed a group while attending Clydebank High School, Glasgow, approach Mark McLoughlin (b. Mar.23, 1966, Clydebank, Scotland) to front as vocalist and, as The Vortex Motion, plays Clash° cover versions, with its first gig at Clydebank Community Centre. McLoughlin changes his name to Marti Pellow and the group settles on Wet Wet Wet as a name, taken from a line in Scritti Politti° song *Getting Having And Holding*.

1984 Dec Having gigged locally in Scotland all year, the group meets Elliot Davis who becomes its manager. Together they establish their own label, The Precious Organisation, and record a demo tape which they send to major record companies in London.

1985 From their demo alone, nine major companies compete to sign them. Dave Bates A&R at Phonogram wins, but only after guaranteeing that the manager will receive a monthly supply of Whiskas cat food – a small sign of faith. Phonogram proposes a string of producers, including Stephen Hague and John Ryan, who do not suit the band's white soul aspirations, but eventually allows the group to record a session with its choice, Al Green° production maestro Willie Mitchell.

1986 Jan Debut TV performance is on UK music show "The Tube".

June The band records several tracks with Mitchell in Memphis, Tenn. Despite creative satisfaction on both sides, Phonogram refuses to use material for debut LP. Increased promotion work includes sessions for Glasgow's Radio Clyde and an appearance at London's Royal Albert Hall for a Greenpeace charity concert.

1987 Apr The group and management insist that remixed original demo of *Wishing I Was Lucky* is released as debut cut. It hits UK #6, with Phonogram conceding defeat on trying to force production ideas on the group.

June Prior to their own headline tour, the group undertakes a supporting role on Lionel Richie° UK dates.

Aug *Sweet Little Mystery* hits UK #5.

Sept Debut LP *Popped In Souled Out* enters UK chart at #2. (Recorded in April with another American producer, Michael Baker, it will reach the top in 1988.)

1988 Feb *Angel Eyes (Home And Away)* hits UK #5. The group receives a BPI Award for Best Newcomer at London's Royal Albert Hall.

Mar The group travels to New Orleans to film the video for *Temptation*, which reaches UK #12.

June The newly re-activated Uni label releases *Wishing I Was Lucky* in US, where it reaches #58. Both Van Morrison° and Squeeze° reach out of court settlements when lyrics are "found" in *Sweet Little Mystery*, from Morrison's *Sense Of Wonder* and *Angel Eyes* and Squeeze's *Heartbreaking World*. *With A Little Help From My Friends*, a track from LP *Sgt. Pepper Knew My Father* is released to raise funds and awareness for the Childwatch charity. It tops UK chart. As plans to release an EP of the Mitchell Memphis sessions are shelved, the group maintains a high profile, singing *Wishing I Was Lucky* at The Nelson Mandela 70th Birthday Party concert and *Twist And Shout* at the Prince's Trust concert, while undertaking more sold out UK dates.

WHAM!

George Michael (vocals)
Andrew Ridgeley (guitar)

1975 Michael (b. Georgios Panayiotou, Jan.26, 1963, Finchley, London, UK) and Ridgeley (b. June 25, 1963, Windlesham, Surrey, UK) meet each other on the first day of term at Bushey Meads Comprehensive School, Hertfordshire, UK.

1979 Together with Ridgeley's brother, Paul, David Austin and Andrew Leaver, Michael and Ridgeley form ska-based band, The Executive, which gigs locally but disbands within 18 months.

1981 Concentrating on songwriting and rehearsing for demos at home, the duo has already written *Careless Whisper* and *Club Tropicana*. Ridgeley is unemployed, Michael has several casual jobs and both enjoy the hectic London nightclub scene, where they create the Wham! name and image and are inspired to write *Wham Rap! (Enjoy What You Do?)*.

1982 Hiring a Portastudio for £20, Wham! records demos of *Wham Rap!*, *Come On!*, *Club Tropicana* and *Careless Whisper* in Ridgeley's parents' front room. Record companies are universally uninterested. The duo is introduced to ex-Phonogram employee, Mark Dean, who recently established small dance-based label Innervision. Through a loan-arrangement with CBS, he offers Wham! a contract which will later prove highly restrictive.

Apr Wham! signs a publishing contract with Morrison/Leahy Music Group. Club appearances to promote debut 45 *Wham Rap!*, with new girl recruits Shirlie Holliman and Mandy Washburn (soon replaced by Diane Sealey (Dee C. Lee), fail to lift it into UK 100.

Oct *Young Guns (Go For It)* is released and enters UK chart, but will take 2 months to hit UK #3. It is helped by a startling dance performance on BBC TV's "Top of the Pops".

1983 Feb Re-release of *Wham Rap! (Enjoy What You Do?)* hits UK #8. Wham! is joined by session players Dean Estus, Robert Anwai and Anne Dudley, who help record *Bad Boys*, the first release written solely by Michael.

May *Bad Boys* hits UK #2, accompanied by a black and white video which Michael describes as the lowest point in Wham!'s career.

July Experiencing serious difficulties with Innervision, Wham! seeks management assistance from 1960s pop entrepreneur, Simon Napier-Bell. Debut LP *Fantastic* hits UK #1, while fourth single from LP *Club Tropicana* hits UK #4. Michael assumes control of musical direction, particularly writing and producing, with Ridgeley concentrating on style, image, visuals and direction.

Aug First Wham! concert tour is announced, sponsored by Fila sportswear. Prior to its start, Michael flies to Muscle Shoals studios in Alabama, US, to record solo version of *Careless Whisper* with Jerry Wexler. Sessions are instructive but unsuccessful and Michael decides to re-record the song in London with help of keyboardist, Andy Richards, for later release. *Bad Boys*, poorly promoted, stalls at US #60.

Oct Dee C. Lee leaves to join The Style Council° and is replaced by singer/dancer, Pepsi (later to realize success with current co-backing performer Shirlie). "Club Fantastic" tour is launched in Aberdeen, Scotland.

Nov With a major legal battle looming, Innervision releases a mix of LP cuts titled *Club Fantastic*. Although Wham! denounces the single in the UK press, it climbs to UK #15.

1984 Jan Wham! visits Japan on promotional tour.

Apr Released from wrangle with Innervision, Wham! is signed to Epic. Michael is busy writing and producing new songs, one of which *Wham! Shake* is rejected by Ridgeley.

May First Epic release *Wake Me Up Before You Go Go*, inspired by a note Ridgeley left lying in his bedroom, makes UK #1.

June Michael flies to Miami to shoot solo video for *Careless Whisper*. Ridgeley receives much publicized plastic surgery to his nose.

Aug *Careless Whisper* is released in the UK as a solo by Michael, despite co-writing credit with Ridgeley. It hits UK #1 and is Epic's first UK million-seller, earning a platinum disk. Michael dedicates the ballad to his mother and father, "5 minutes in return for 21 years". It will top charts around the world over the next 6 months.

Sept *Wake Me Up Before You Go Go* is released in US and takes 10 weeks to top *Billboard* survey. Michael and Ridgeley, in the South of France to record second LP, with Michael assuming full responsibility in all areas and Ridgeley providing quality control, advice and guitar-work, meet Elton John° and develop a long-term friendship.

WHAM! *cont.*

Nov LP *Make It Big*, which includes *Careless Whisper*, is released to phenomenal worldwide success and hits UK and US #1. *Fantastic* also charts at US #83.

Dec A world tour starts at UK's Whitley Bay Ice Rink. Michael is featured singing on Band Aid's Christmas chart-topper *Do They Know It's Christmas?*, which prevents Wham!'s own *Last Christmas* from hitting top spot.

1985 Jan *Last Christmas* is changed to double-A with *Everything She Wants*. It holds UK #2 position for another 4 weeks and earns a platinum disk. *Careless Whisper* is released in US, this time as "Wham! featuring George Michael". It becomes their second US chart-topper and earns a gold disk. The world tour continues throughout Australia, Japan and US.

Mar *Everything She Wants* begins climb to US #1 and Michael receives Songwriter of the Year award at prestigious Ivor Novello Ceremony, London, the youngest ever recipient.

Apr Wham! is the first western pop group invited to perform live in China, following lengthy negotiations between Napier-Bell and the Chinese government.

Apr [7] Wham! plays 10,000-seater Workers' Gymnasium in Peking.

May Michael, becoming increasingly independent musically, performs duets with Smokey Robinson° and Stevie Wonder° at Motown celebration in New York.

July While Ridgeley fund-raises and sings backing vocals, Michael sings *Don't Let The Sun Go Down On Me* to Elton John's° piano accompaniment at Live Aid, Wembley, UK. Wham! undertakes stadium tour of US.

Aug *Freedom* hits US #3, breaking a run of three consecutive US chart-toppers.

Nov Michael records backing vocals on new Elton John° LP *Ice On Fire*, while latest Wham! single *I'm Your Man* hits US #3, but tops in UK. Privately, Michael and Ridgeley, still very close friends, decide that Wham! will split in 1986.

Dec Michael features on four top 20 records in UK Christmas chart: *I'm Your Man*, re-entered *Last Christmas*, Band Aid's *Do They Know It's Christmas?* and as backing vocalist on Elton John's° *Nikita*.

1986 Apr Michael releases second solo single, ballad *A Different Corner*, which hits UK #1 and US #7. It coincides with official announcement that Wham! is to quit as a band having achieved far more than its original goals. They simultaneously dissolve management links with Napier-Bell.

June Final Wham! single is four-track EP, featuring double-A *The Edge Of Heaven/Where Did Your Heart Go*. It tops UK chart in the same week as Wham!'s farewell concert "The Final" is performed in front of 72,000 fans at Wembley Stadium, London. LP *The Final*, a best of hits compilation, tops the UK chart.

July The US post script *The Edge Of Heaven* is released and hits US #10. Michael actively pursues solo career, while Ridgeley concentrates on a future of semi-retirement, unsuccessful motor racing and acting. Both continue solo contracts with Epic Records.

Oct *Where Did Your Heart Go*, written and originally recorded by Was (Not Was) , makes US #50. The US version of greatest hits package LP *Music From The Edge Of Heaven* hits US #10.

Dec Re-promotion of LP *The Final* as a boxed set, complete with Wham! pencil, paper pad and poster, revives its UK chart fortune for the festive season.

BARRY WHITE

1960 White (b. Sept.12, 1944, Galveston, Tex., US), having lived since infancy in East Side Los Angeles, singing in church choir and learning a variety of instruments in his early teens, after troubles in high school which sent him to the Reese School, a center for incorrigible youth, joins LA R&B quintet, The Upfronts, which records for Lummtone Records, without success.

1964 Feb Bob and Earl's *Harlem Shuffle*, arranged by White for Rampart label, reaches US #44. He also plays keyboards on many small label R&B recording sessions, while performing solo in LA clubs.

1966 Jan Earl Nelson of Bob and Earl reaches US #14 under the pseudonym Jackie Lee with *The Duck*, and White tours with him as drummer and road manager.

1967 He becomes involved in A&R for Mustang Records in LA, writing and producing for Felice Taylor, whose *It May Be Winter Outside* reaches US #42 and *I Feel Love Comin' On* makes UK #11.

1968 While working for Mustang, White discovers female vocal trio Love Unlimited (sisters Glodean and Linda James, and Diane Taylor) from San Pedro, Cal. He becomes their manager and producer.

1972 May Having signed Love Unlimited to UNI Records, White produces its *Walkin' In The Rain With The One I Love*, which reaches #14 in both US and UK and sells over a million. (His own voice is heard in the "telephone break" midway through the disk.) The trio's LP *Love Unlimited* makes US #151. He also launches, with Larry Nunes, his own production company, Soul Unlimited Productions (originally MoSoul, which was felt too similar to Motown).

Dec White signs himself, his production house, and Love Unlimited to newly re-launched 20th Century Records.

1973 June White records as a soloist for the first time, in a variation of Isaac Hayes'° style of deep, intimate vocals in lush orchestral arrangements. Debut LP *I've Got So Much To Give* reaches US #16 while extracted *I'm Gonna Love You Just A Little More, Baby* hits US #3 (earning a gold disk for a million sales) and makes UK #23.

Sept The title song from *I've Got So Much To Give* reaches US #32.

Dec Love Unlimited's revival of Felice Taylor's *It May Be Winter Outside* peaks at US #83.

1974 Jan White's second LP *Stone Gon'* makes US #20, as extracted *Never, Never Gonna Give You Up* hits US #7 and earns a gold disk.

Feb *Never, Never Gonna Give You Up* reaches UK #14, while Love Unlimited's LP *Under The Influence Of . . .* hits US #3 and goes gold. The trio's *It May Be Winter Outside* is its second and last UK hit single, reaching #11. Also taken from the Love Unlimited LP is instrumental *Love's Theme*, a dance piece played by a White-conducted 40-piece orchestra. On the LP it serves as the lengthy (8 min.) introduction to the trio's vocal track *I'm Under The Influence Of Love* but, after it becomes a hit with disco DJs, White releases it as a single with the musicians credited as The Love Unlimited Orchestra. It tops the US chart, earning a gold disk, and hits UK #10.

Mar White's *Honey Please, Can't Ya See* makes US #44 while his LP *Stone Gon'* reaches UK #18.

Apr LP *Rhapsody In White*, an instrumental set by The Love Unlimited Orchestra and featuring *Love's Theme*, hits US #8 and makes UK #50.

May Love Unlimited's *I'm Under The Influence Of Love*, the vocal "sequel" to *Love's Theme* (and another song originally recorded by White with Felice Taylor) makes US #76.

June The title track from The Love Unlimited Orchestra's *Rhapsody In White* reaches US #63.

Aug LP *Together Brothers*, soundtrack to the film of the same title performed by The Love Unlimited Orchestra (and including two vocal tracks by White and Love Unlimited), reaches US #96.

Sept White's *Can't Get Enough Of Your Love, Babe* hits US #1 for 1 week (his third million-selling single) and UK #8.

Oct LP *Can't Get Enough* tops the US chart for a week, and is his biggest-selling LP.

Nov LP *Can't Get Enough* is also White's biggest LP seller in UK, where it hits #4.

Dec *You're The First, The Last, My Everything*, taken from LP *Can't Get Enough*, tops the UK chart for 2 weeks. Love Unlimited Orchestra's LP *White Gold* reaches US #28, and Love Unlimited's LP *In Heat* makes US #85.

1975 Jan *You're The First, The Last, My Everything* hits US #2 (his fourth gold single) behind Elton John's° *Lucy In The Sky With Diamonds*, while Love Unlimited's *I Belong To You* reaches US #27 and is the trio's final hit single. White marries Glodean James from Love Unlimited.

Apr White's *What Am I Gonna Do With You?* hits UK #5 and US #8 while The Love Unlimited Orchestra instrumental track *Satin Soul* makes US #22.

June LP *Just Another Way To Say I Love You* reaches US #17 and UK #12. Extracted *I'll Do For You Anything You Want Me To* makes US #40 and UK #20.

Dec Compilation LP *Greatest Hits* reaches US #23 and UK #18.

1976 Jan *Let The Music Play* hits UK #9 and reaches US #32.

Feb Love Unlimited Orchestra instrumental LP *Music Maestro Please* reaches US #92.

Mar White's LP *Let The Music Play* makes UK #22.

Apr *You See The Trouble With Me* hits UK #2 (held from the top by Brotherhood of Man's *Save Your Kisses For Me*). LP *Let The Music*

Play makes US #42.

July *Baby, We Better Try To Get It Together* stalls at US #92.

Sept *Baby, We Better Try To Get It Together* reaches UK #15.

Nov Love Unlimited Orchestra's LP *My Sweet Summer Suite* reaches US #123 and is the group's last chart LP. The extracted title tune makes US #48.

Dec White's *Don't Make Me Wait Too Long* reaches UK #17. LP *Is This Whatcha Wont?* makes US #125.

1977 Feb The Love Unlimited Orchestra's US singles chart swan song is *Theme From King Kong*, a disco variation of the movie theme, which peaks at US #68.

Mar *I'm Qualified To Satisfy* makes UK #37. Love Unlimited's LP *He's All I've Got* (on White's own new Unlimited Gold label) makes US #192.

Apr Compilation LP *Barry White's Greatest Hits Vol.2* reaches UK #17.

Oct *It's Ecstasy When You Lay Down Next To Me* makes UK #40.

Nov *It's Ecstasy When You Lay Down Next To Me* hits US #4, becoming his fifth and last solo gold single. It is taken from LP *Barry White Sings For Someone You Love*, which hits US #8 and is also a million-plus seller, earning a platinum disk.

1978 June *Oh What A Night For Dancing* makes US #24.

Dec LP *Barry White The Man* peaks at US #36 (earning another platinum disk in 6 months on chart) while extracted *Your Sweetness Is My Weakness* peaks at US #60 and is his last US hit single.

1979 Jan White's revival of Billy Joel's° 1978 hit *Just The Way You Are* reaches UK #12 (but is not issued as a US single).

Feb LP *The Man* (including *Just The Way You Are*) makes UK #46.

Apr *Sha La La Means I Love You* peaks at UK #55.

May White moves to his own Unlimited Gold label (which he has signed to CBS Associated Labels for distribution) with LP *The Message Is Love*, which peaks at US #67.

Sept LP *I Love To Sing The Songs I Sing*, a swan song release from 20th Century, makes US #132.

1980 Apr [11] White receives an honorary degree in Recording Arts and Sciences from UCLA's Faculty Club.

Aug LP *Barry White's Sheet Music* reaches US #85.

1982 Oct LP *Change* peaks at US #148.

1985 Dec TV-promoted compilation LP *Heart And Soul*, anthologizing White's major hits of the 1970s, makes UK #34.

1987 Oct After a rest from recording, during which he has updated his home studio R.I.S.E. (Research In Sound Excellence) in Sherman Oaks, Cal., to state-of-the-art 80s specifications, White signs a new recording deal with A&M Records. With a new group of musicians – keyboard players Jack Perry and Eugene Booker (White's godson) and guitarist Charles Fearing (ex-Ray Parker Jr.'s° Raydio) – he produces LP *The Right Night And Barry White*, which makes UK #74.

Nov LP *The Right Night And Barry White* peaks at US #159 while *Sho' You Right*, taken from the LP, reaches US R&B #17.

1988 Jan *For Your Love (I'll Do Most Anything)* makes US R&B #27 while a re-mixed reissue of *Never Never Gonna Give You Up* makes UK #63.

July Compilation LP *The Collection*, a new anthology of White's 20th Century label singles, hits UK #5 as he plans a UK tour.

WHITESNAKE

David Coverdale (vocals)
Bernie Marsden (guitar)
Micky Moody (guitar)
Neil Murray (bass)
David Dowle (drums)

1976 Mar Coverdale (b. Sept.22, 1949, Saltburn-on-Sea. Yorks., UK), the son of a steel-worker, leaves Deep Purple° following a disastrous UK tour, after which the band itself splits up. Contractual ties make it impossible for him to work live or record solo in UK during the forseeable future, so he moves to West Germany with his family, writing material for future use while legal complexities are being untangled.

1977 May Solo LP *Whitesnake*, a set of rock ballads, is released in a snakeskin-style sleeve, but fails to sell in a UK market dominated by the punk explosion. (Coverdale, still in Germany, has recorded his vocals in Munich over backing tracks cut in UK.)

1978 Jan His enforced exile over, Coverdale returns to UK to form a band to promote his second solo LP *Northwinds*, again split-recorded between London and Germany. He recruits sessioneers who have provided his backing tracks: Moody (guitar), Marsden (guitar), Murray (bass), Brian Johnston (keyboards) and Dowle (drums).

Feb [23] As David Coverdale's Whitesnake, the band begins its debut UK tour at Nottingham's Sky Bird Club.

Mar LP *Northwinds* is released, without charting.

June With Pete Solley replacing Johnston on keyboards, the band records 4-track EP *Snake Bite*, highlighted by a revival of Bobby Bland's 1974 soul classic *Ain't No Love In The Heart Of The City* (which will become a Coverdale stage favorite). Released by EMI International at budget price on white vinyl, the EP is the band's chart debut, reaching UK #61.

Aug Coverdale's ex-Deep Purple° colleague Jon Lord joins on keyboards, replacing Solley who is not keen to tour (and will become a successful producer).

Sept *Lie Down (A Modern Love Song)* is taken from the band's forthcoming LP, but fails to chart.

Oct [26] Lord plays his first gig with Whitesnake at Newcastle, Tyne & Wear, UK, on a tour to promote the first full group LP.

Nov LP *Trouble* makes UK #50.

Nov [23] The final UK tour gig at Hammersmith Odeon, London, is recorded for a live LP.

1979 Mar *Time Is Right For Love*, from LP *Trouble*, is issued in UK to tie in with a headlining charity show (at London's Hammersmith Odeon on Mar.3, in aid of the Gunnar Nilsson Cancer Treatment Campaign). (Most of the first half of this year is spent touring overseas.)

July Ex-Deep Purple° drummer Ian Paice replaces Dowle.

Aug [26] The band plays UK's Reading Festival.

Oct LP *Love Hunter* (on which Dowle plays throughout) reaches UK #29. It has a sleeve illustrating a naked woman astride a gigantic snake, which is over-stickered in some territories, including US.

Nov *Long Way From Home*, a 33rpm maxi-single also including two live tracks, makes UK #55.

1980 Mar The band plays its first tour of Japan, where live LP *Live At Hammersmith*, recorded in 1978, is first released.

May *Fool For Your Loving*, a new Coverdale/Moody/Marsden composition, becomes the first major Whitesnake hit single, reaching UK #13.

June The band plays London's Hammersmith Odeon (again recorded for live LP use), on a UK tour to support new LP *Ready An' Willing*, which hits UK #6.

July Taken from the LP, *Ready An' Willing (Sweet Satisfaction)* makes UK #43.

Aug The band headlines UK's Reading Festival.

Sept Released on Mirage label, LP *Ready An' Willing* marks the band's US chart debut, peaking at #90 while *Fool For Your Loving* makes US #53.

Oct Whitesnake develops its initial US success with several months of US touring, supporting AC/DC°, Jethro Tull°, and other major names.

Nov A live version of *Ain't No Love In The Heart Of The City*, from the June Hammersmith Odeon show, makes UK #51, while double live LP *Live In The Heart Of The City* (combining both the 1978 and 1980 Hammersmith Odeon gigs) hits UK #5.

1981 Jan Live LP *Live In The Heart Of The City* (in US a single LP with just the 1980 gig) makes US #146.

May LP *Come An' Get It* hits UK #2 while, from it, *Don't Break My Heart Again* reaches UK #17.

June LP *Come An' Get It* makes US #151 while second extract, *Would I Lie To You*, makes UK #37. On another UK tour to promote the LP, the band sells out 5 nights at London's Hammersmith Odeon.

Aug The band headlines UK's Monsters of Rock festival at Castle Donington (completing its UK live work for the year, before returning to the recording studio, where sessions will be abandoned).

Oct After a tour of Germany leads to friction within the band. Whitesnake is put on indefinite hold. Coverdale devotes time to nursing his sick daughter. Lord completes a solo LP, while Murray and Paice play with Gary Moore (and will later join his band).

1982 Coverdale reassembles Whitesnake without Marsden, Murray and Paice. He invites Cozy Powell (drums) to join, while Lord and Moody remain, and recruits Mel Galley (guitar) and Colin "Bomber" Hodgkinson (bass). The previous year's unfinished recordings are salvaged, with Coverdale re-recording the vocals and Galley overdubbing fresh guitarwork.

WHITESNAKE *cont.*

Nov *Here I Go Again*, from the band's forthcoming LP, makes UK #34.
Dec LP *Saints'n'Sinners*, comprising the revamped tracks from a year earlier, hits UK #9.

1983 Aug The band again headlines the Castle Donington Monsters of Rock festival, its only UK live appearance of the year (which is filmed by EMI for release on home video). *Guilty Of Love*, from a new studio LP in progress, produced by Eddie Kramer and released to tie in with the festival appearance, makes UK #31. (Shortly after, Coverdale will fire his producer and re-cut all the remaining LP vocals. The strain of this will prove too much, and he will collapse from exhaustion.)
Nov Moody leaves the band prior to a year-end tour, and Hodgkinson follows him. The latter is replaced by a returning Murray, while new guitarist is ex-Thin Lizzy° and Tygers of Pan Tang member John Sykes.

1984 Jan *Give Me More Time*, from the forthcoming LP, makes UK #29.
Feb LP *Slide It In* hits UK #9, as the group opens a 17-date tour of the British Isles in Dublin, Ireland (ending with a show at London's Wembley Arena).
Mar While on tour in West Germany, Galley breaks his arm.
Apr *Standing In The Shadow*, taken from LP *Slide It In*, makes UK #62.
May Lord leaves the band to join re-forming Deep Purple°.
July With a change of US label to Geffen Records, LP *Slide It In* reaches US #40 as Whitesnake tours US supporting Dio.
Aug The group tours Japan, with Richard Bailey filling Lord's keyboards slot on stage. Another US tour follows, supporting Quiet Riot.

1985 Jan Whitesnake participates in world's largest rock festival "Rock in Rio", Brazil.
Feb *Love Ain't No Stranger*, a belated single from LP *Slide It In*, makes UK #44.
Oct Whitesnake starts work on a new LP with producer Mike Stone, in Vancouver, Canada. Coverdale, Murray and Sykes are joined by Aynsley Dunbar on drums and Don Airey on keyboards.

1986 Jan Sykes leaves the LP sessions to fly home when his former Thin Lizzy° colleague Phil Lynott dies. Coverdale, meanwhile, is having major problems with his voice, which bring the sessions to a halt. Stone suggests a substitute vocalist, and is fired.
Apr With a deviated septum diagnosed, Coverdale is forced to have an operation and to rest his voice.
Aug Coverdale returns to the studio with new producer Keith Olsen to finish the LP. Dutch guitarist Adrian Vandenburg and keyboardist Bill Cuomo help out, along with Mark Andes and Denny Carmassi from Heart°.

1987 Apr Finally completed, LP *Whitesnake 1987* hits UK #8 while extracted *Still Of The Night* makes UK #16. For touring to promote the LP, Coverdale puts together a new line-up of Whitesnake, retaining Vandenburg on guitar, and adding Vivian Campbell (guitar), Rudy Sarzo (bass) and Tommy Aldridge (drums).
June LP *Whitesnake* hits US #2, the first million-seller and first platinum disk. (The LP will eventually sell over 8½ million copies worldwide.)
June [20] Whitesnake plays the 10th Annual Texas World Music Fest, with Boston°, Aerosmith°, Poison and others.
July *Still Of The Night* makes US #79 while *Is This Love*, a Coverdale/Sykes composition also from the LP, hits UK #9.
Aug The group begins a US tour supporting Motley Crue°.
Oct *Here I Go Again*, originally a track on the 1982 LP *Saints'n'Sinners* (and a UK #34 hit single at the time), now re-cut with a new backing track under Coverdale's vocal (during the late 1986 LP sessions, at Geffen Records' suggestion), tops the US chart for a week.
Oct [30] The group begins a headlining US tour (through to Dec.6).
Nov Re-recorded *Here I Go Again* hits UK #7.
Dec *Is This Love* hits US #2 (behind George Michael's° *Faith*). Coverdale co-stars in the song's promo video with actress Tawny Kittaen.

1988 Feb *Give Me All Your Love*, a re-recorded version of a track from the LP, featuring the new band, reaches UK #18.
Dec Campbell leaves due to reported "musical differences". No replacement is announced, but the remaining quartet begins recording an LP for mid-1989 release.

THE WHO

Pete Townshend (guitar)
Roger Daltrey (vocals)
John Entwistle (bass)
Keith Moon (drums)

1959 Townshend (b. May 19, 1945, London, UK) and Entwistle (b. Oct.9, 1944, London) form The Confederates while still at Acton Grammar School. Townshend comes from a musical background (his father a member of RAF dance band The Squadronaires and his mother a singer with the Sidney Torch Orchestra). He is determined to become a pop star and spends most of his time studying guitar. Entwistle is an accomplished musician studying piano and playing french horn with the Middlesex Youth Orchestra.

1961 They leave school. Townshend goes to art college – the classic training for British 60s rock stars. Entwistle becomes a civil servant.

1962 Daltrey (b. Mar.1, 1945, London, UK), an ex-pupil of Acton Grammar School, invites Townshend and Entwistle to join his band, The Detours. Semi-professional drummer Doug Sandom, who is 10 years older than the others, also joins.

1963 The group supports a wide range of artists from Wee Willie Harris to The Rolling Stones°. Their material ranges from covers of James Brown° to Bo Diddley°.

1964 The group meets freelance publicist, Pete Meaden, who introduces them to the blossoming world of "mod" in London. (A youth cult in reaction to rockers who revelled in motorbike oil and rock'n'roll; mods were opposite, dressed and behaved well, held steady jobs, rode scooters but indulged in drugs.) He molds them into *the* mod band. Sandom leaves the band and various drummers fill in. One night a drunk, dressed completely in ginger with a Wayne Fontana° haircut, sits in on drums during an interval. His wild style clicks with the band and Moon (b. Aug.23, 1947, Wembley, Middx., UK) becomes their drummer. Meaden changes their name to The High Numbers (a mod term for style), and secures a record deal with Fontana.
July *I'm The Face*, a re-write of Slim Harpo's *Got Love If You Want It* with lyrics by Meaden, is released on Fontana but fails.
Sept Film director Kit Lambert, looking for a group to appear in a film, goes to a High Numbers gig. He and his partner, Chip Stamp (brother of actor Terence), take up group management paying off Meaden with £500. They make a promo film of a gig and work on the group's image. The abiding image of the group destroying its equipment originates at its regular venue, The Railway Hotel, Harrow, where the ceiling is so low that Townshend's swinging-guitar style takes chunks out of it until one evening the top of his guitar neck disappears, leading to complete destruction of the instrument, with crowds arriving weekly to witness the mayhem.
Nov Lambert changes the group's name to The Who (a name they had used before) as he is worried that posters featuring The High Numbers give the image of advertising a bingo session. The group begins a Tuesday night residency at the Marquee club as The Who-Maximum R&B.

1965 Jan The group's demo is rejected by EMI, but expatriate American producer, Shel Talmy, shows interest and secures a contract with Brunswick. His reputation is based on his hits with The Kinks° and his hard-edged raw production sound. Townshend's *I Can't Explain*, is selected for a single and Talmy augments The Who with leading session man, Jimmy Page, to bolster Townshend's guitar, and The Ivy League to provide high-backing voices.
Apr After a 2-month struggle, *I Can't Explain* hits UK #8 and reaches US #93.
June *Anyway Anyhow Anywhere* is released. Townshend describes it as "anti-middle age, anti boss-class and anti-young marrieds". Its melange of feedback causes US label Decca to return the master-tape claiming it to be faulty. It hits UK #10, but misses in US. UK TV program, "Ready Steady Go!", adopts it as its theme tune.
Aug [6] The Who plays the Richmond Jazz & Blues Festival with Manfred Mann°, Rod Stewart° and The Yardbirds°.
Nov *My Generation* hits UK #2 (reaching US #74 in Feb. 1966). It establishes a landmark in rock history in reflecting the thoughts of a generation. *The Carnival Is Over* by The Seekers° prevents it from reaching UK #1. Daltrey threatens to leave the group after onstage bust-ups and Boz Burrell (later of Bad Company°) is lined up to take over, but Daltrey stays. He is quoted as saying "when I'm 30 I'm going to kill myself, 'cos I don't ever want to get old".

Dec Debut LP *My Generation* hits UK #5. With The Beatles'° and The Rolling Stones'° debuts, it becomes the final piece of the triumvirate of British rock music, invading international markets.

1966 Jan The Who appears on US TV's "Shindig!"

Mar The group breaks with Brunswick and signs to Robert Stigwood's newly-formed Reaction label.

Apr *Substitute*, on Reaction, hits UK #5. Brunswick releases *A Legal Matter* which makes UK #32. Talmy, represented by Quentin Hogg, sues the group (and gets a royalty on The Who's next 5 years of recorded output).

May [20] Townshend and Daltrey go on stage at The Ricky Tick Club, Windsor, Berks., UK with a stand-in bassist and drummer when Entwistle and Moon fail to show up. When they arrive during the show, Townshend hits Moon over the head with his guitar, who quits the band – for 1 week.

Oct *I'm A Boy* hits #2 while Brunswick releases *The Kids Are Alright* which makes UK #41. The group appears on "Ready Steady Go" UK TV special.

Nov The "Ready Steady Go" performance is re-recorded in studio and released on The Who's only EP *Ready Steady Who* as a tribute to the program. Tracks include *The Batman Theme*, *Bucket T* and *Barbara Ann*, the latter covers of The Beach Boys°. Brunswick, meanwhile, releases *La La La Lies*. Neither disk charts.

Dec LP *A Quick One* hits UK #4 (US #67 in May 1967 as *Happy Jack*). Townshend breaks with musical convention pre-dating *Sgt. Pepper* by linking songs into a mini-opera called *A Quick One While He's Away*, laying the ground for their grand opus *Tommy*.

1967 Jan *Happy Jack* hits UK #3 (US #24 in June).

Mar [25] The Who makes its US stage debut as part of Murray The K's "Easter Rock'n'Roll Extravaganza" package.

May *Pictures Of Lily* hits UK #4 (US #51 in August), released on newly-formed offshoot from Polydor called Track (which Lambert and Stamp run).

June The Who plays the Monterey pop festival.

July [14] The band begins its first US tour, as support to Herman's Hermits°.

Aug The group releases covers of The Rolling Stones'° *The Last Time/Under My Thumb* as a gesture of support to imprisoned Mick Jagger and Keith Richard. It makes UK #44. The Who appears on "The Smothers Brothers" US TV show. Moon overdoes a flash powder explosion in his drum kit which leaves Townshend with singed hair and damaged ears, Moon is cut on the leg by a broken cymbal while fellow guest, Bette Davis, faints into Mickey Rooney's arms.

Nov *I Can See For Miles* hits UK #10 and US #9 (their first US top 10 hit).

1968 Jan LP *The Who Sell Out*, with tracks linked by commercial radio ads, reaches UK #13 and US #48.

May *Call Me Lightning* makes US #40.

June *Dogs* climbs to UK #25. Townshend becomes enamored of the teachings of Meher Baba, an Indian Perfect Spirtual Master, which will profoundly alter his life and his writing of *Tommy*.

Sept *Magic Bus* makes US #25.

Oct LP *Magic Bus, The Who On Tour* reaches US #39.

Nov *Magic Bus* makes UK #26.

Dec The group performs at "The Rolling Stones Rock and Roll Circus".

1969 Apr *Pinball Wizard* hits UK #4 and reaches US #19. It is released as a curtain raiser to *Tommy*, which UK BBC Radio 1 DJ Tony Blackburn describes as "sick".

May LP *Tommy* is given a press launch at Ronnie Scott's club with The Who performing the double LP in full. The story is of a deaf, dumb and blind boy, a genius or wizard at pinball who is elevated to prophet status and then turned on by his followers.

June LP *Tommy* hits UK #2 and US #4. The Who begins a major US tour performing the opera in its entirety.

July Townshend produces Thunderclap Newman's UK #1 *Something In The Air*.

Aug The Who's performance at Woodstock is critically regarded as one of its greatest, capturing the image of a generation. They perform with Bob Dylan° at the Isle of Wight festival, using one of the largest sound systems ever erected in UK. A notice on the speakers warns the audience not to come within 15 feet. *I'm Free* reaches US #37.

Dec The group begins a tour of European opera houses to perform *Tommy*.

1970 Jan Moon, a non-driver, accidentally runs over and kills his chauffeur Neil Boland, when trying to escape from a group of skinheads outside a club in Hatfield, Herts., UK.

May *The Seeker* reaches UK #19 and US #44.

June [7] The Who performs *Tommy* at New York's Metropolitan Opera House.

June LP *Live At Leeds*, recorded at Leeds University, hits UK #3 and US #4.

Aug Taken from the live LP, a cover of Eddie Cochran's° classic *Summertime Blues* reaches UK #38 and US #27.

Nov *See Me, Feel Me* climbs to US #12.

1971 Aug *Won't Get Fooled Again* hits UK #9 and reaches US #15.

Aug [31] During a US tour, security guard George Byrington is stabbed to death at The Who's concert at Forest Hills, New York.

Sept LP *Who's Next* is their first UK chart-topper. It hits US #4.

Oct Entwistle is the first group member to achieve solo success with LP *Smash Your Head Against The Wall* (at US #126).

Nov [4] The group opens new rock venue The Rainbow, Finsbury Park, London, performing three nights.

Dec *Let's See Action* climbs to UK #16, as *Behind Blue Eyes* makes US #34. Greatest hits LP *Meaty Beaty Big And Bouncy* hits UK #9 and US #11.

1972 The group takes time out from recording and touring to concentrate on solo projects releasing just one single during the year.

July *Join Together* hits UK #9.

Aug Moon appears as a nun in Frank Zappa's° film *200 Motels* and as J.D. Clover, a drummer with a group backing Billy Fury°, in film *That'll Be The Day*.

Sept *Join Together* climbs to US #17.

Oct Townshend releases first solo LP *Who Came First* which reaches UK #30 and US #69.

Oct [28] The United States Council for World Affairs adopts *Join Together* as its anthem.

Nov Entwistle's second solo LP *Wistle Rymes* peaks at US #138.

Dec An all-star cast performs a fully orchestrated version of *Tommy* with The Who at The Rainbow. Lou Reizner releases an all-star cast version of *Tommy* with orchestration and Daltrey in the central role. It hits US #5.

1973 Jan *Relay* makes UK #21 and US #39. Masterminded by Townshend, Eric Clapton° makes his comeback at The Rainbow after his heroin addiction.

Apr Daltrey opens a barn studio. One of his first clients is singer/songwriter Leo Sayer°, who co-writes songs with Dave Courtney for Daltrey's debut solo LP *Daltrey*. The LP fails to chart in UK but reaches US #45.

May Daltrey's *Giving It All Away* hits UK #5, but peaks at US #83.

June Entwistle solo LP *Riger Mortis Sets In* reaches US #174.

Sept Daltrey's *I'm Free* reaches UK #13.

Oct *5:15* makes UK #20.

Nov LP *Quadrophenia* hits #2 in both UK and US. Inevitably compared with *Tommy*, it relates the story of Jimmy, an adolescent mod on a spiritual search. The use of sound effects on the LP created a problem as most FX libraries kept only mono recordings so The Who had to record every effect, including bribing the driver of a UK rail train to blow his whistle when leaving Waterloo Station. Moon collapses during a concert after his drink is spiked with horse tranquilizer. 19-year-old Scott Halpin from the audience volunteers to replace him on drums for the remaining three numbers.

Dec [2] The Who is jailed in Montreal for vandalizing a hotel suite.

Dec *Love, Reign O'er Me* peaks at US #76.

1974 Feb *The Real Me* reaches US #92.

Apr Shooting begins on a film version of *Tommy* directed by Ken Russell and starring The Who with Oliver Reed, Ann-Margret, Jack Nicholson and Elton John° among others.

Apr [14] Townshend makes his live solo debut at London's Roundhouse.

June The Lambert/Stamp partnership breaks up and Bill Curbishley unofficially takes over as manager. (Lambert will die after a fall at his mother's house in Fulham in Apr. 1981.)

Oct LP *Odds And Sods* hits UK #10 and US #15. It is a collection of unreleased material compiled by Entwistle. Moon appears in film *Stardust*, the follow-up to *That'll Be The Day*.

1975 Feb [21] Entwistle starts a 5-week US tour with his band Ox in Sacramento, Cal.

Mar [1] Daltrey celebrates his 30th birthday.

THE WHO *cont.*

Mar Film soundtrack LP *Tommy* makes UK #21. Entwistle LP *Mad Dog* peaks at US #192.
May Moon releases his only solo, LP *Two Sides Of The Moon.*
July Daltrey's LP *Ride A Rock Horse* reaches UK #14 and US #28.
Aug Daltrey stars in the title role of Ken Russell's film *Lisztomania.*
Oct LP *The Who By Numbers* hits UK #7 and US #8. Moon becomes a UK "lollipop man" to promote a road safety campaign for a zebra crossing outside Battersea Primary School.
Nov Daltrey's *Come And Get Your Love* makes US #68.
1976 Feb *Squeeze Box* hits UK #10 and US #16.
Mar [9] A US tour is cancelled when Moon collapses during a performance at The Boston Garden, Boston, Mass. The tour is rescheduled.
May [31] The Who's concert at Charlton Athletic Football Club enters *Guinness Book of Records* as the loudest performance (at 120 decibels) by a rock group.
Oct Compilation LP *The Story Of The Who* hits UK #2.
Nov *Substitute* re-released in the wake of the LP hits UK #7.
1977 May Daltrey's *Written On The Wind* makes UK #46.
July Daltrey's LP *One Of The Boys* peaks at UK #45 and US #46.
Oct Townshend, with Ronnie Lane, releases LP *Rough Mix*, which makes UK #44 and US #45. Daltrey's *Avenging Annie* stalls at US #88.
Dec [15] The band plays the first of two "behind closed doors" concerts for its fan club members at Shepperton TV Studios, UK. The show is filmed for use in *The Kids Are Alright* film documentary.
1978 Aug *Who Are You* reaches UK #18.
Aug [5] Pete Meaden commits suicide.
Sept [8] Keith Moon dies of an overdose of Heminevrin prescribed to combat alcoholism, in the same Park Street apartment as Mama Cass had died 4 years earlier.
Sept *The Times* obituary describes Moon as "among the most talented rock'n'roll drummers in contemporary music". LP *Who Are You* hits UK #6 and US #2.
Nov *Who Are You* climbs to US #14.
1979 Jan Despite the group's claim that Moon is irreplaceable, ex-Small Faces° and Faces° drummer, Kenney Jones (b. Sept.16, 1948, London, UK), takes over. He begins a 3-month crash course learning Who material. John "Rabbit" Bundrick (b. Tex., US) is unofficially added to the line-up on keyboards.
May [2] The new line-up makes its debut at London's Rainbow as film *Quadrophenia* premieres. The feature film, based on the original LP, is directed by Franc Roddam and creates new interest in The Who.
June LP *The Kids Are Alright*, a compilation of live cuts tying in with the documentary feature film of the same name directed by The Who, makes UK #26 and hits US #8.
July *Long Live Rock* peaks at UK #48 and US #54.
Oct Soundtrack LP *Quadrophenia* reaches UK #23 and US #46. Daltrey appears in horror film *The Legacy*.
Nov *5:15* makes US #45.
Dec [3] A concert at Riverfront Coliseum, Cincinnati, Oh., US, turns into disaster when eleven members of the audience are trampled to death after a stampede to claim unreserved seats.
Dec [28] The group plays the "Concert for Kampuchea" at London's Hammersmith Odeon.
1980 Apr Townshend's solo *Rough Boys* makes UK #39.
Apr [30] Film *McVicar*, with Daltrey in the title role, premieres in London.
May Townshend's LP *Empty Glass* makes UK #11 and hits US #5.
June Townshend's *Let My Love Open Your Door* peaks at UK #46.
Aug Soundtrack LP *McVicar* makes UK #39 and US #22. Taken from it, *Free Me* climbs to UK #39 and US #53. Townshend's solo *Let My Love Open Your Door* hits US #9.
Oct Daltrey's *Without Your Love* makes UK #55 and US #20. Townshend's *A Little Is Enough* reaches US #72. Virgin re-releases long-deleted LP *My Generation*, which makes UK #20.
Nov *Rough Boys* reaches US #89.
1981 Mar LP *Face Dances*, the first to be recorded by the new line-up, and produced by Bill Szymczyk, hits UK #2 and US #4.
Apr *You Better You Bet* hits UK #9 and US #18.
May *Don't Let Go The Coat* makes UK #47 and US #84.
Oct Entwistle's LP *Too Late The Hero* reaches US #71.
1982 Mar Daltrey's LP *Best Bits* peaks at US #185.
July Townshend's *All The Best Cowboys Have Chinese Eyes* makes UK #32 and US #26.
Aug Townshend's *Uniforms (Corps D'Esprit)* climbs to UK #48.
Sept Final Who studio LP *It's Hard* reaches UK #11 and hits US #8.
Oct *Athena* makes UK #40 and US #28.
Dec [17] The group performs the last gig of its North American farewell tour at Maple Leaf Gardens, Toronto, Canada. It is filmed for later TV screenings.
1983 Jan *Eminence Front* makes US #68.
Mar Townshend solo LP of Who demos and unfinished work *Scoop* reaches US #35.
Dec [16] The Who officially splits.
1984 Mar Daltrey's LP *If Parting Should Be Painless* climbs to US #102. His *Walking In My Sleep* makes UK #62 and US #56.
Nov LP *Who's Last* documenting The Who's final concert makes UK #48 and US #81.
1985 July [13] The Who re-forms for one-off appearance at Live Aid concert in London.
Oct Daltrey's *After The Fire* makes UK #50 and US #48.
Nov Daltrey's LP *Under A Raging Moon* makes UK #52, while Townshend's LP *White City* makes UK #70.
1986 Jan Townshend's *Face The Face* reaches US #26. Daltrey's *Let Me Down Easy* peaks at US #86.
Mar Daltrey's *Under A Raging Moon* makes UK #43.
1988 Feb The group re-forms to receive BPI Award for lifetime achievement and agrees to perform live on UK TV. The program overruns and the group is faded out mid-number after a week of intensive rehearsal. *My Generation* re-charts in UK at #68.
Mar Greatest hits package on LP and video, *Who's Better, Who's Best* hits UK #10.

KIM WILDE

1980 Wilde (b. Kim Smith, Nov.18, 1960, London, UK), daughter of 1950s UK hitmaker Marty Wilde°, has been singing backing vocals on her father's live appearances since leaving art school, when she records a demo with her brother Ricky, who has a production deal with Mickie Most's RAK Records. Most, attracted by her vocals and visual appeal, signs her to RAK. Her mother Joyce Smith, ex-The Vernons Girls, becomes her manager, while Most reportedly puts £250,000 of RAK's money into launching and developing her as a major act.
1981 Mar Debut single *Kids In America*, written by Ricky and produced by him and Marty, hits UK #2 for 2 weeks.
May *Chequered Love* hits UK #4. Wilde does no UK touring to promote this or other early singles, relying on videos and TV appearances, stating that she will need to strengthen her voice to do a satisfactory live performance with a band.
July Debut LP *Kim Wilde*, mostly written by her brother and including the two earlier singles, hits UK #3, and stays on chart for over 3 months.
Aug Taken from the LP, double A-side *Water On Glass/Boys* makes UK #11.
Dec *Cambodia* reaches UK #12.
1982 Mar She announces in a magazine interview her desire to write her own material, but for the moment continues to cut more of her brother's songs.
May *View From A Bridge* reaches UK #16. LP *Select* spends 1 week at UK #19.
Aug RAK announces that in 18 months, Wilde has sold over 6 million disks worldwide – more than her father achieved during his 14-hit UK (just 2 in US) chart career. *Kids In America*, following a deal with EMI America, peaks at US #25. LP *Kim Wilde* reaches US #86.
Oct *Child Come Away* peaks at UK #43. Wilde begins a European tour which includes sell-out dates. (In Germany, her glamorous image has her nicknamed "The Bardot of Rock".)
1983 Feb Wilde receives a BPI Award from the UK record industry as Best British Female Vocalist of 1982. She moves from the family home to an apartment in London, where she begins to tackle her own songwriting.
Aug *Love Blonde* reaches UK #23.
Nov *Dancing In The Dark* reaches UK #67. LP *Catch As Catch Can* peaks at UK #90.
1984 May Wilde signs a new contract with MCA.
Nov MCA debut *The Second Time* peaks at UK #29, and LP *Teases And Dares* reaches UK #66.

Dec *The Touch* makes UK #56.

1985 Jan Her US MCA debut is Marty and Ricky's *Go For It*, which makes US #65, while LP *Teases And Dares* makes US #84.

Apr Rockabilly-flavored *Rage To Love*, remixed by Dave Edmunds°, makes UK #19.

May RAK releases a retrospective singles collection LP, *The Very Best Of Kim Wilde*, which reaches UK #78.

1986 Aug [29] A Kim Wilde mini-dress is sold at Christie's Rock Memorabilia auction in London for £400.

Nov LP *Another Step* charts briefly at UK #88.

Dec After a year out of the record-buying public's eye (though she has done some live performances in Europe) Wilde's version of The Supremes'° 1966 million-seller *You Keep Me Hangin' On* hits UK #2. It is also a big hit in most of Europe, where she has almost reached superstar status.

1987 Apr Wilde performs on the Ferry Aid single *Let It Be*, for the victims of the Zeebrugge ferry disaster, which is a UK #1. She sings at the AIDS benefit concert at Wembley, UK, performing Elton John's° *Sorry Seems To Be The Hardest Word* with Marty and Ricky Wilde.

May Wilde duets with UK soul singer Junior on *Another Step (Closer To You)*, which hits UK #6.

June With heavy airplay and rotation on MTV, *You Keep Me Hangin' On* tops the US chart for a week, making Wilde only the fifth UK female artist to achieve a US #1. She receives a telex from Lamont Dozier, one of the song's writers, congratulating her. LP *Another Step* climbs to US #40.

Aug *Say You Really Want Me*, accompanied by a controversial video which eliminates Wilde's girl-next-door image, peaks at UK #29, despite its talented production team of Rod Temperton, Richard Rudolph and Bruce Swedien. In US it reaches #44.

Sept Reissue of LP *Another Step*, in a new sleeve and with a bonus record of singles remixes, reaches UK #29.

Dec She teams with comedian Mel Smith (as "Mel and Kim") on a remake of Brenda Lee's° *Rockin' Around The Christmas Tree* (all proceeds go to Comic Aid charity). It hits UK #3.

1988 May *Hey Mr. Heartache*, written by Ricky and Marty Wilde° and recorded at the family's home studio in Herts. reaches UK #31.

June LP *Close* makes UK #70.

July Wilde supports Michael Jackson° in Europe and UK on his 1988 "Bad" world tour.

Aug Dance-styled *You Came* hits UK #3.

MARTY WILDE

1957 Wilde (b. Reginald Smith, Apr.15, 1939, Greenwich, London, UK) is spotted singing in London's Condor Club (under the name Reg Patterson) by impresario Larry Parnes. He also sings in UK rockabilly group The Hound Dogs. Parnes signs him and renames him Marty Wilde (in keeping with Tommy Steele° and his later signings – a "soft" forename with a "hard" surname).

Oct He signs to Philips Records where his debut, a cover of Jimmie Rodgers' US hit *Honeycomb*, sets a pattern: many of his singles will cover US originals. *Honeycomb* fails to chart, as will the next two releases, but Wilde gains teen popularity in live one-night stands around the country.

Oct [18] He makes his UK TV debut singing *Honeycomb* on Jack Payne's "Off the Record".

1958 Aug *Endless Sleep*, a cover of Jody Reynolds' US top 5 hit 2 months earlier, is his UK chart debut, hitting UK #4.

1959 Apr His cover of Ritchie Valens'° *Donna* hits UK #3 (the original just scrapes into UK top 20). Wilde's version has plenty of exposure as a resident on Jack Good's UK TV show "Oh Boy!", as well as on tour. He hires a backing group, The Wildcats (Big Jim Sullivan and Tony Belcher on guitars, Brian "Liquorice" Locking on bass and Brian Bennett on drums), for regular support on live dates.

July *A Teenager In Love* crashes into the UK top 10 as *Donna* leaves it, to hit UK #2, and win a three-cornered chart fight with competing versions by Craig Douglas° and Dion & The Belmonts° (the original), both of which make the UK top 30.

Sept [12] Wilde begins a run as host of UK TV rock show "Boy Meets Girls" (which will provide a UK showcase for Eddie Cochran°, Gene Vincent° and UK guitarist Joe Brown.

Nov *Sea Of Love*, a cover of a US million-seller by Phil Philips, hits UK #3.

Dec [2] He marries Joyce Baker, a member of TV vocal group The Vernons Girls, in London.

1960 Jan Self-written *Bad Boy* hits UK #7.

Mar *Johnny Rocco* peaks at UK #30, while *Bad Boy* makes US #45. He tours US to capitalize on this, but will have no further US hits. On his return, UK sales are slipping badly. His marriage and increasing involvement in acting, plus the rise of Cliff Richard° as UK's major teen idol, are seen as factors.

May *The Fight* peaks at UK #47.

Nov [2] His daughter Kim is born.

1961 Jan *Little Girl* makes UK #16.

Feb A rush-released cover of Bobby Vee's° *Rubber Ball*, despite being beaten by the original, hits UK #9. Wilde stars in the London production of *Bye Bye Birdie* (and will appear in action movie *The Hellions*). His former backing group, The Wildcats, change their name to The Krew Kats, and record as an instrumental group.

July *Hide And Seek* reaches UK #47.

Nov Self-penned *Tomorrow's Clown* reaches UK #33.

1962 June A rocking revival of Frankie Laine's *Jezebel* reaches UK #19.

Nov *Ever Since You Said Goodbye* makes UK #31, and is Wilde's final UK hit single.

1963 When his Philips contract expires, he signs to EMI's Columbia label, but with no notable success.

1964 Jan [6] After featuring in UK musical comedy film *What a Crazy World* with Joe Brown and Susan Maughan, he begins "Group Scene 1964"UK tour, supporting The Rolling Stones°, along with The Ronettes° and Johnny Kidd°.

1965 Apr He forms The Wilde Three, a vocal trio also including his wife Joyce and singer/guitarist Justin Hayward (who will later join The Moody Blues°). They record *Since You've Gone* and *I Cried* for Decca, but without success.

1969 Aug Signed again to Philips, bouncy *Abergavenny* is released without success under his own name in UK but, issued in US by Heritage Records under the pseudonym Shannon, it climbs to US #47.

1973/75 He records for Magnet label, under his own name and under pseudonyms Shannon and The Dazzling All Night Rock Show.

1981 He returns to an active pop scene role as songwriter and producer (with son Ricky, a failed teen pop star of the 1970s) for daughter Kim Wilde°.

1982 Feb He signs to Kaleidoscope Records, reviving Roy Orbison's° *In Dreams* and Don Gibson's *Sea Of Heartbreak*.

1987 Apr Wilde joins his son and daughter on stage at Wembley, London, UK, in an AIDS benefit concert, singing Elton John's° *Sorry Seems To Be The Hardest Word*.

DENIECE WILLIAMS

1967 Having grown up in a religious environment, singing in the gospel choir at a local church, Williams (b. Deniece Chandler, June 3, 1951, Gary, Ind., US), while working in a record shop, makes contact with a rep from provincial Chicago record label, Toddlin' Town, which releases *Love Is Tears*, the first of a number of singles, with only limited local success.

1969 Williams goes to Baltimore Morgan State College and becomes a nurse, moonlighting as a nightclub singer.

1971 Stevie Wonder° hears Toddlin' Town recordings and invites Williams to Detroit to audition for his backing vocal group, Wonderlove. She gigs with them for a month but gets homesick and returns to Chicago Mercy Hospital. Wonder persists and Williams becomes a permanent member of Wonderlove, contributing on support spot of The Rolling Stones'° 1972 tour. During the next 3 years, she also contributes Wonderlove vocals to Wonder's LPs, *Talking Book* (1972), *Innervisions* (1973), *Fulfillingness' First Finale* (1974) and *Songs In The Key Of Life* (1976).

1975 Nov Williams leaves Wonderlove to settle in California and concentrate on a solo career. She writes, records and sends demos, one of which comes to the attention of Earth, Wind & Fire° leader, Maurice White, who arranges her signing to Columbia/CBS.

1976 Nov Debut solo LP *This Is Niecy* is released. Produced by White, it immediately scores in soul circles (US #33) and first hit single *Free* follows at US #25. She embarks on a 6-month period of touring, supporting Earth, Wind & Fire° at major US and UK venues.

1977 Apr *Free* hits UK #1 and promotes LP *This Is Niecy* to UK #31.

Aug *That's What Friends Are For* hits UK #8, but does not chart in US.

Nov Second LP *Songbird* is released. It reaches US #66 but fails in UK. A stray cut *Baby Baby My Love's All For You* makes UK #32.

DENIECE WILLIAMS *cont.*

1978 Mar Williams teams with her childhood heart-throb, Johnny Mathis, to record duet *Too Much Too Little Too Late*. Radio and public find it irresistible. It hits US #1 and UK #3, providing a first ever chart-topper for Mathis on his first duet attempt. Williams makes extensive UK promotion visit including a live spot on BBC TV's "Val Doonican Show".

July LP *That's What Friends Are For*, all Mathis/Williams duets, reaches US #19 and UK #16. It includes follow-up cover of Gaye°/Terrell classic *You're All I Need To Get By*, which makes US #47 and UK #45. Compositions by Williams now begin to be covered by acts which will include Frankie Valli, The Whispers, The Emotions and Merry Clayton.

1979 Aug Williams signs to Maurice White's new ARC label (through Columbia) and LP *When Love Comes Calling* is released. It is produced by David Foster and Ray Parker Jr.°, but falters at US #96. *I've Got The Next Dance* reaches only US #73, and Williams will have no further UK attention for 5 years.

1981 Apr Written and produced with Thom Bell (Stylistics°, Delfonics°, Spinners), a new mature soul direction is realized on LP *My Melody*.

Aug LP *My Melody* reaches US #74 and extracted ballad *Silly* makes US #53.

1982 Apr The second Bell collaboration LP *Niecy* makes US #20, aided by her biggest hit for 6 years, a remake of The Royalettes' 1965 hit *It's Gonna Take A Miracle* which reaches US #10.

1983 Apr Returning to mainstream Columbia, LP *I'm So Proud* charts for 19 weeks, but slows to peak at US #54.

1984 Jan Williams re-unites with Mathis to record two duets. A cover of Major Harris' *Love Won't Let Me Wait* fails, but new song *Without Us* becomes popular theme tune to top-rated US TV series "Family Ties".

Feb Hugely successful film soundtrack LP *Footloose* is released and makes US #1 and UK #7.

May *Let's Hear It For The Boy* hits US #1 and UK #2 and becomes an international smash.

June Hastily prepared LP *Let's Hear It For The Boy* makes US #26. A second single from the LP, *Next Love* reaches only US #81.

1986 LP *Hot On The Trail* fails to chart.

1987 LP *Water Under The Bridge* receives no chart success.

1988 July Retreating to gospel roots after a 4-year chart absence, she releases specialist inspirational LP *So Glad I Know* on Sparrow label.

Aug It is announced that Williams has finished work on new LP *This Is As Good As It Gets* and extracted single *I Can't Wait*, both scheduled for release in 1988.

JACKIE WILSON

1950 Wilson (b. Jack Leroy Wilson, June 9, 1934, Detroit, Mich., US), while at high school in Detroit, wins the American Amateur Golden Gloves Welterweight boxing title by posing as an 18-year-old under the name Sonny Wilson. Set for a boxing career, his mother persuades him to finish school and develop his singing talent instead. He joins The Ever Ready Gospel Singers, and sings with R&B quartet The Thrillers (alongside Hank Ballard°) once he completes school and goes to work at a car assembly plant.

1951 Wilson is discovered in a talent show at Detroit's Paradise Theater, by Johnny Otis° who mentions him to Billy Ward, vocal teacher and leader of successful doo-wop group Billy Ward & The Dominoes. Ward notes Wilson's vocal talent and later hires him as a back-up singer. (In the meantime, Wilson records *Danny Boy* on a one-off single for Dizzy Gillespie's Dee Gee label, without success.)

1953 Apr Wilson's own idol Clyde McPhatter, The Dominoes' lead singer, is fired from the group (and will shortly form The Drifters°), and Ward invites Wilson (who has toured with the group) to replace him as lead tenor vocalist. (He is to sing lead on 2 years' worth of the group's recordings on King and Federal labels, one of which, *Rags To Riches*, hits R&B #3 in early 1954.)

1956 June After leaving King/Federal and recording briefly for Jubilee, Ward & The Dominoes are signed to major label Decca.

Sept Wilson sings lead on *St. Therese Of The Roses*, The Dominoes' first Decca single, and the group's first US pop chart hit, peaking at #13. It is his last recording with the group.

1957 Despite The Dominoes' popularity and his own high status among other vocalists (Elvis Presley° raves about his stage performance of *Don't Be Cruel* on the preserved tape of the Dec. 1956 Sun Records Presley/Carl Perkins°/Jerry Lee Lewis° jam session), Wilson is feeling stifled as an individual since, because of the group's billing and the fact that he sings lead, audiences believe him to be Ward. Encouraged by Al Green, a Detroit publisher and agent who becomes his manager, Wilson leaves to go solo and signs to Brunswick Records, a Decca subsidiary, to work with producer/orchestra leader Dick Jacobs in New York.

Sept [8] His solo career begins with release of *Reet Petite (The Finest Girl You Ever Want To Meet)* (co-written by Berry Gordy Jr., future founder of Motown, and Tyran Carlo, a pseudonym for Wilson's cousin Billy Davis), on Brunswick.

Nov Uptempo *Reet Petite* is a moderate solo chart debut in US, making #62.

1958 Jan *Reet Petite* hits UK #6.

May Contrasting (but also penned by Gordy/Carlo) dramatic ballad *To Be Loved* makes both US and UK #23.

Sept Gordy-penned *We Have Love* stalls at US #93.

Oct Wilson's first LP, *He's So Fine* , is released but fails to chart. (He will not have a US chart LP until 1962.)

Dec *Lonely Teardrops* tops the US R&B chart for 7 weeks – both his and writer Gordy's first chart-topper.

Dec [25] Wilson begins a 10-day residency in Alan Freed's Rock'n'Roll Spectacular at Loew's State Theater, Manhattan, New York, alongside 16 other acts including Eddie Cochran°, Bo Diddley° and The Everly Brothers°.

1959 Feb *Lonely Teardrops* is Wilson's first US top 10 hit, at #7, selling over a million copies to earn his first gold disk.

Apr [22] Freed's film *Go Johnny Go*, in which Wilson appears singing *You Better Know It*, premieres in US.

May *That's Why (I Love You So)* reaches US #13.

Aug *I'll Be Satisfied* (UK rocker Shakin' Stevens° will revive it in the 1980s) reaches US #20. It is his last hit penned by Gordy/Carlo.

Oct *You Better Know It* (premiered earlier in the year in *Go Johnny Go*) makes US #37, and spends a week at R&B #1.

1960 Jan *Talk That Talk* peaks at US #34 (hitting the top 3 on the R&B chart). Wilson is now managed by Nat Tarnopol, former assistant to the deceased Al Green, who steers both his recordings and live performances (which include engagements at major Hollywood, Las Vegas and New York nightclubs) in the direction of the majority white middle-class audience.

May Wilson's second million-seller is double A-side *Night* (which hits US #4, and is an almost operatic rendition of a ballad set to the melody of *My Heart At Thy Sweet Voice* from Camille Saint-Saens' *Samson And Delilah*) and *Doggin' Around* (a blues groover which reaches US #15). *Doggin' Around* also hits US R&B #1 for 3 weeks and is issued as UK A-side with *The Magic Of Love* on the B-side, the classical adaptation of *Night* being felt likely to fall foul of a BBC ban (academic, since it fails to sell in UK).

Aug Another double A-side, *(You Were Made For) All My Love* reaches #12 and *A Woman, A Lover, A Friend* makes US #15 and R&B #4 for 4 weeks. He also releases one of his most acclaimed LPs, *Jackie Sings The Blues*.

Sept *(You Were Made For) All My Love* makes UK #33.

Nov *Alone At Last*, with a melody based on Tchaikovsky's *Piano Concerto #1 in b flat*, hits US #8 while B-side *Am I The Man* makes US #32.

Dec *Alone At Last* makes UK #50, and will be Wilson's last UK chart entry for over 8 years. In US, he is voted Entertainer of the Year by *Cash Box* magazine.

1961 Feb *My Empty Arms*, another classical adaptation (from Leoncavallo's *On With The Motley*) hits US #9 and B-side *The Tear Of The Year* makes US #44 and is reissued as a UK A-side after *My Empty Arms* is deleted at time of release for similar reasons as *Night*.

Feb [15] Wilson is shot by Juanita Jones, a female fan who invades his New York apartment and demands attention. Her gun (with which she has threatened to shoot herself) goes off as he tries to disarm her, and leaves him with a stomach wound and a bullet lodged in his back. He is rushed to Roosevelt Hospital.

Mar [31] Wilson is discharged from hospital, the bullet is still lodged in a not dangerous, but not easily-operable, spot.

Apr *Please Tell Me Why* reaches US #20 and B-side *Your One And Only Love* makes US #40.

July *I'm Coming Back To You* reaches US #19 and B-side *Lonely Life* makes US #80.

Sept *Years From Now* makes US #37 while B-side *You Don't Know*

What It Means (co-written by Wilson) peaks at US #79.
Nov *The Way I Am* makes US #58 as B-side *My Heart Belongs To Only You* peaks at US #65.
1962 Jan [21] Wilson appears on US TV's "Ed Sullivan Show".
Feb *The Greatest Hurt* reaches US #34 and B-side *There'll Be No Next Time* makes US #75.
Apr *I Found Love*, a duet with Linda Hopkins co-written by Wilson and Alonzo Tucker, stalls at US #93.
May *Hearts* makes US #58.
July *I Just Can't Help It*, also by Wilson/Tucker, peaks at US #70.
Oct *Forever And A Day* makes US #82.
Nov LP *Jackie Wilson At The Copa*, recorded at New York's Copacabana, is Wilson's first US chart LP, reaching #137.
1963 Apr Wilson/Tucker-penned *Baby Workout*, a strong R&B dance performance with big band-type arrangement and a contrast to his ballads, hits US #5.
May *Baby Workout* tops the US R&B chart for 3 weeks, while the LP of the same title reaches US #36.
June A revival of Faye Adams' *Shake A Hand*, in another duet with Linda Hopkins, makes US #42.
Aug *Shake! Shake! Shake!*, continuing the dance groove of *Baby Workout*, reaches US #33.
Oct *Baby Get It (And Don't Quit It)* makes US #61.
1964 May *Big Boss Line* stalls at US #94.
Aug *Squeeze Her – Tease Her (But Love Her)* peaks at US #89.
1965 Mar A return to middle-of-the-road ballads with traditional Irish *Danny Boy* falters at US #94.
Aug *No Pity (In The Naked City)*, Wilson's last hit co-written with Tucker, makes US #59.
Oct *I Believe I'll Love One* creeps to US #96.
1966 Jan *Think Twice*, a duet with LaVern Baker on a revival of Brook Benton's° 1961 hit, reaches US #93.
Dec Carl Davis-produced *Whispers (Gettin' Louder)*, cut in Chicago rather than New York, moves Wilson into the emerging soul field and reaches US #11. (Davis will continue as Wilson's producer.)
1967 Jan LP *Whispers* makes US #108.
Feb *Just Be Sincere* reaches US #91; its B-side *I Don't Want To Lose You* peaks at US #84.
May *I've Lost You* reaches US #82.
Oct Wilson finally scores his third million-selling single with *(Your Love Keeps Lifting Me) Higher And Higher*, which hits US #6 (and tops the R&B chart for a week).
Dec *Since You Showed Me How To Be Happy* reaches US #32 as LP *Higher And Higher* makes US #163.
1968 Mar A revival of Jerry Butler° and The Impressions'° *For Your Precious Love*, on which Wilson sings with Count Basie's band, reaches US #49.
May *Chain Gang*, also with Basie, creeps to US #84.
June Wilson/Basie collaboration LP *Manufacturers Of Soul*, including the two hit singles, peaks at US #195.
Sept *I Get The Sweetest Feeling*, co-written by arranger Van McCoy, reaches US #34.
Nov A revival of standard *For Once In My Life* reaches US #70.
1969 June Unsuccessful in UK on its original release, *(Your Love Keeps Lifting Me) Higher And Higher* reaches UK #11 – Wilson's first UK chart entry since *Alone At Last* in 1960.
1970 May *Let This Be A Letter (To My Baby)* reaches US #91.
1971 Dec *Love Is Funny That Way* stalls at US #95.
1972 Mar *You Got Me Walking*, written by Eugene Record of The Chi-Lites°, reaches US #93, and is Wilson's final US hit single.
Sept A reissue of *I Get The Sweetest Feeling* hits UK #9.
1975 May Double A-side reissue of *I Get The Sweetest Feeling/Higher And Higher* makes UK #25.
Sept [29] Wilson has a heart attack while singing *Lonely Teardrops* in a Dick Clark revue at the Latin Casino in Camden, N.J. Hitting his head as he falls, he lapses into a coma, suffering severe brain damage due to oxygen starvation. (He is hospitalized and will recover consciousness, but with all faculties, including speech, impaired. Barry White° and The Spinners° will be among those who perform benefits to raise money for his care.)
1978 Mar [15] Wilson's *That's Why (I Love You So)* is included on the soundtrack of movie *American Hot Wax*, based on the life of DJ Alan Freed, which premieres in US.
1984 Jan [21] Wilson dies, having been immobile and in permanent care since his heart attack. His funeral is held at the Chrysler Drive Baptist church in Detroit, where Wilson once sang gospel music; The Four Tops°, The Spinners° and Berry Gordy Jr. all attend.
1986 Dec Wilson's first single *Reet Petite*, reissued in UK and promoted via an inventive model-animation video, dethrones The Housemartins'° *Caravan Of Love* to top the UK chart at Christmas for 4 weeks, 29 years after its original release, this time selling over 700,000 copies.
1987 Mar A third UK reissue of *I Get The Sweetest Feeling* is follow-up to *Reet Petite* and hits UK #3.

JOHNNY & EDGAR WINTER

1959 Albino guitarist/vocalist Johnny Winter (b. Feb.23, 1944, Leland, Miss., US) cuts his first single *Schoolday Blues* on Dart label in Texas, as Johnny & The Jammers.
1968 After several years playing Chicago clubs in groups like Black Plague (with brother Edgar) and Gene Terry & The Down Beats, Winter forms his own group, with brother Edgar (b. Dec.28, 1946, Beaumont, Tex., US) on keyboards, Tommy Shannon on bass and John Turner on drums. They are recruited as regular group at New York's The Scene, after owner Steve Paul has read an effusive article about Winter's blues guitar playing in *Rolling Stone* magazine. Paul also becomes Winter's manager.
1969 Feb Winter is signed to CBS/Columbia, on a 5-year contract worth $300,000.
May Imperial Records releases a one-off LP by Winter, *The Progressive Blues Experiment*, which makes US #49. Recorded some time earlier, it is released in competition with the first Columbia LP.
June Columbia debut LP *Johnny Winter* reaches US #24.
June [20] He plays the 3-day Newport '69 Festival, in Cal.
June [27] He appears in another festival, at Denver's Mile High Stadium, to 50,000 people.
July [3] He takes part in the Newport Jazz Festival on Rhode Island, US.
Aug [30] He plays to 120,000 people at the 3-day Texas International Pop Festival at Dallas International Motor Speedway.
Oct LP *The Johnny Winter Story*, a compilation of early tracks cut during his days in Chicago and released by GRT Records, peaks at US #111.
1970 Jan Columbia LP *Second Winter* makes US #55, while a revival of Chuck Berry's° *Johnny B. Goode*, taken from it, makes US #92. (The LP is a double, but only three sides have material, the fourth is blank.)
May LP *Second Winter* is his UK chart debut, at #59.
June After appearing on his brother's LP *Second Winter*, Edgar Winter signs to CBS/Columbia and LP *Entrance*, featuring Edgar on almost all instruments, makes US #196.
July [3] Johnny Winter takes part in the 3-day Atlanta Pop Festival.
Aug [6] He plays in an anti-war 12-hour festival at New York's Shea Stadium, alongside Paul Simon°, Janis Joplin°, Steppenwolf° and many others.
Oct LP *Johnny Winter And*, featuring Edgar and Rick Derringer's group The McCoys° as back-up band, makes US #154.
Nov LP *Johnny Winter And* reaches UK #29.
1971 May Live LP *Johnny Winter And/Live*, consisting mainly of rock and R&B standards, played by the same line-up as the previous LP, reaches US #40 and UK #20, while a cover of The Rolling Stones'° *Jumpin' Jack Flash* on a single makes US #89. (Johnny Winter's increasing heroin dependency forces him out of action for a period following an early 1971 tour.)
June Edgar Winter forms the brass-based group White Trash, featuring Floyd Radford (guitar), Bobby Ramirez (drums), George Sheck (bass), Mike McLellan (trumpet and vocals), Jon Smith (saxophone) and Jerry La Croix, (lead vocals and saxophone). The group's debut LP *Edgar Winter's White Trash* makes US #111.
1972 Feb *Keep Playin' That Rock'n'Roll* by Edgar Winter's White Trash, makes US #70.
May White Trash's double live LP *Roadwork* reaches US #23 while extracted revival of Otis Redding's° *I Can't Turn You Loose* peaks at US #81. Winter disbands White Trash shortly after to form rock band The Edgar Winter Group, which includes ex-Van Morrison° sideman Ronnie Montrose (guitar), Chick Ruff (drums) and Dan Hartman (bass).
July [24] White Trash's drummer Bobby Ramirez is killed in a brawl in a Chicago bar. (Drug problems keep Johnny Winter musically inactive through this year.)
1973 Jan LP *They Only Come Out At Night*, the first by The Edgar Winter Group, produced by Derringer, hits US #3, earning a gold disk.

JOHNNY & EDGAR WINTER *cont.*

Apr Johnny Winter returns to record with the (deliberately) ironically-titled LP *Still Alive And Well*, which reaches US #22.

May *Frankenstein*, an instrumental by The Edgar Winter Group, tops the US chart for a week, selling over a million. It has originally been B-side of *Hangin' Around*, until airplay prompted Columbia to turn the single over. The title *Frankenstein* comes from the fact that the track is heavily cut, patched and edited from the original master.

June *Frankenstein* reaches UK #18.

Oct *Free Ride*, also from LP *They Only Come Out At Night*, reaches US #14 and features a driving acoustic guitar. (It will be the band's last major hit; Montrose will leave to form his own eponymous group. He will be replaced first by Jerry Weems, then by the group's producer Derringer.)

1974 Jan Edgar Winter Group's *Hangin' Around* makes US #65.

Feb Johnny Winter is one of the celebrities attending the opening of New York's The Bottom Line club.

Apr His LP *Saints And Sinners* peaks at US #42.

June 96 people are arrested after trouble in the audience of an Edgar Winter concert at The Omni in Atlanta.

Aug Edgar Winter's LP *Shock Treatment*, with Derringer on lead guitar, reaches US #13, earning a gold disk, while solo single *River's Risin'* makes US #33.

Nov *Easy Street*, by The Edgar Winter Group, stalls at US #83.

1975 Jan LP *John Dawson Winter III* makes US #78, his first release on new CBS-distributed Blue Sky label.

July LP *Jasmine Nightdreams*, a solo album by Edgar, also on Blue Sky, makes US #69.

Nov LP *The Edgar Winter Group With Rick Derringer* peaks at US #124.

1976 Apr Johnny's LP *Captured Live!* makes US #93. Hartman and Derringer leave Edgar's group. (Hartman will become first a disco artist, with a major hit in *Instant Replay*, then a successful solo performer with more mainstream material like *I Can Dream About You*, and a producer for James Brown° and others.)

July The Winter brothers combine for LP *Together*, a collection of live tracks and revivals, which makes US #89.

1977 Mar Johnny produces acclaimed comeback LP *Hard Again* for blues legend Muddy Waters° and tours as a member of his group.

Sept Johnny returns to his roots for LP *Nothin' But The Blues*, which makes US #146.

1978 Sept Johnny's LP *White, Hot And Blue* makes US #141. It will be his last US chart entry for 6 years.

1979 LP *The Edgar Winter Album* is released, without success.

1980 Edgar Winter recruits a new band, including Jon Paris (bass) and Bobby Torello (drums), for LP *Raisin' Cain*, which fails.

1981 LP *Standing On Rock* is Edgar Winter's final LP. (He will concentrate on session work for Meat Loaf°, Dan Hartman, Bette Midler° and others.)

1984 Aug Johnny Winter's LP *Guitar Slinger*, on independent blues label Alligator Records, makes US #183.

1985 Oct His LP *Serious Business* on Alligator makes US #156.

1987 Sept [12/13] Johnny Winter plays the 15th San Francisco Blues Festival.

1988 Nov [5] He ends a 23-date US tour at the Riverwalk Blues Fest in Fort Lauderdale, Fla., part of the live promotion for his new LP *Winter Of '88*, released on Voyager Records through MCA.

STEVE WINWOOD

1963 Winwood (b. May 12, 1948, Birmingham, UK) joins The Spencer Davis Group° as vocalist, guitarist and keyboards player at age 15.

1967 Apr He leaves The Spencer Davis Group and forms Traffic°.

1967/74 Between two incarnations of Traffic, he has also been a member of Blind Faith° and Ginger Baker's Airforce. His first solo LP would have been *Mad Shadows* in mid-1970, but it was released as Traffic's LP *John Barleycorn Must Die* after Jim Capaldi and Chris Wood helped him record it, and Traffic re-formed. Under his own name in June 1971, double LP *Winwood*, a compilation of tracks featuring him with his previous bands, reached US #93.

1974 Dec After Traffic° has dissolved following a US tour in support of LP *When The Eagle Flies*, Winwood retires home to Gloucestershire, UK, where he builds his own Netherturkdonic Studio. (He will spend the next 2 years quietly experimenting, while also working on sessions for others, notably fellow Island label acts like Sandy Denny, The Sutherland Brothers and Toots and The Maytals.)

1976 Oct Winwood joins Michael Shrieve to guest on Stomu Yamashta's LP *Go*, which makes US #60. He appears with Yamashta in a concert at London's Royal Albert Hall.

1977 July His solo LP *Steve Winwood* is released just as punk is getting into its commercial stride in UK and is dismissed by some reviewers as passé. One track from it, *Midland Maniac* which features Winwood playing all instruments, reaches UK #12.

Oct LP *Steve Winwood* makes US #22.

1978 While not active in live work, he decides to cut an LP on which he will fill every role, playing all instruments, producing and engineering. (It will take over 2 years to complete *Arc Of A Diver*.)

1981 Jan LP *Arc Of A Diver*, with music by Winwood and varied lyric contributions from Will Jennings, Vivian Stanshall and George Fleming, reaches UK #13. Extracted *While You See A Chance*, Winwood's first solo single, makes UK #45. Winwood's contract with Island has expired and the LP's success enables him to negotiate a new deal on favorable terms, including gaining all the publishing rights to his earlier material.

Mar UK follow-up *Spanish Dancer* fails.

Apr LP *Arc Of A Diver* hits US #3, earning a gold disk for a half million sales, and *While You See A Chance* hits US #7.

June US follow-up single, the title song from *Arc Of A Diver*, reaches US #48.

Nov *There's A River*, the last extract from the LP, fails to chart.

1982 Aug LP *Talking Back To The Night*, made in a similar way to (though much faster than) the previous LP, with Winwood playing everything but collaborating (with Jennings, who moves from Nashville to UK to co-write) on the songs, hits UK #6.

Sept *Still In The Game*, from LP *Talking Back To The Night*, reaches US #47 having failed in UK, while the LP makes US #28.

Oct *Valerie*, second single from the LP, reaches UK #51.

Nov *Valerie* peaks at US #70.

1983 Winwood contributes songs to the soundtrack of film *They Call it an Accident*.

Apr [30] His manager Andy Cavaliere dies in New York after a heart attack, aged 36.

Sept [20] He appears at the ARMS benefit concert for multiple sclerosis-suffering former Faces° member Ronnie Lane, at London's Royal Albert Hall, alongside Eric Clapton°, Jeff Beck°, Jimmy Page and others. (He also undertakes a rare short US tour with this charity line-up.)

1986 With his marriage to first wife Nicole in difficulties (the couple will divorce during the year), Winwood moves to New York, US, and, renouncing one-man recording, makes LP *Back In The High Life*, with producer Russ Titelman and local musicians. Five of its eight songs are again collaborations with Jennings.

July *Higher Love*, featuring guest vocals from Chaka Khan°, reaches UK #13. It is taken from LP *Back In The High Life*, which hits UK #8.

Aug *Higher Love* tops the US chart for a week.

Sept LP *Back In The High Life* hits US #3, earning a platinum disk, while *Freedom Overspill*, also from the LP, peaks at UK #69.

Nov *Freedom Overspill* reaches US #20.

1987 Jan [18] Winwood marries Eugenia Grafton in Nashville, Tenn. (The couple will commute between Nashville and Winwood's UK farm.)

Feb [24] Winwood wins two Grammys at the 29th annual awards for *Back In The High Life* (named Record of the Year) and *Higher Love* (Best Rock Vocal). (These complete his Island contract and, with the singer a hot property following his 1986 successes, the label is outbid. He signs a new deal with Virgin Records, reported as being worth $13 million, and carrying a royalty rate of 18%.)

Oct In UK, Island reissues, from its retrospective compilation, Winwood/Jennings composition *Valerie* (a minor hit in late 1982), which reaches UK #19.

Nov Compilation LP *Chronicles* reaches UK #12.

1988 June *Roll With It*, the title song from his first LP for Virgin, makes UK #53. Winwood promotes the LP with an appearance at the Montreux Rock Festival in Switzerland, televised worldwide.

July LP *Roll With It*, recorded in Dublin and Toronto and co-produced by Winwood and Tom Lord Alge, hits UK #4. Most of the songs are Winwood/Jennings collaborations, but *Hearts On Fire* is co-written with ex-Traffic's° Jim Capaldi.

July [7] Winwood begins a 2-month US tour, backed by a band recruited in Nashville, and sponsored by a brewery. (It will be followed by a European tour.)

Aug Roll With It tops the US chart for 4 weeks while the LP of the same title also hits US #1 for a week, earning a platinum disk.

BILL WITHERS

1967 Withers (b. July 4, 1938, Slab Fork, W.Va., US), having spent 9 years in the US Navy, then worked as a mechanic for Ford and IBM while writing songs in his spare time, moves to California and has a day job at the Lockheed Aircraft Corporation. He slowly saves $2,500 to pay for studio time to make demos of his songs, but gets little response from them.

1970 He is working in a factory manufacturing jumbo jet toilet seats, and learning the guitar, when he meets Booker T. Jones, ex-Booker T. & The MG's° and now recording, writing and producing in LA for A&M Records. Jones, impressed by Withers' latest material, aids him in getting a recording deal with A&M-distributed Sussex Records.

1971 June [26] On the release of his first LP, Withers makes his first professional live appearance, in LA.

Sept Withers' debut LP *Just As I Am*, produced by Jones, climbs to US #39 as extracted (self-penned) *Ain't No Sunshine* hits US #3, selling over a million.

Dec *Grandma's Hands*, also from the LP, makes US #42.

1972 Mar Withers wins a Grammy award for *Ain't No Sunshine*, named Best R&B Song of 1971.

July Self-produced LP *Still Bill* reaches US #4, earning a gold disk while, from it, self-penned *Lean On Me* hits US #1 for 3 weeks, his second million-selling single.

Oct Also from the LP, *Use Me* hits US #2 and is another million-seller. Meanwhile, *Lean On Me* is his UK chart debut, reaching #18. (*Ain't No Sunshine* did not sell in UK and Michael Jackson's° LP track cover version was extracted as a UK single, hitting the top 10.)

1973 Jan *Let Us Love* makes US #47.

Mar *Kissing My Love* reaches US #31.

June Double live LP *Bill Withers Live At Carnegie Hall* reaches US #63.

July *Friend Of Mine* reaches US #80. Withers and his actress wife Denise Nicholas (currently starring in US ABC TV's series "Room 222") become parents for the first time.

1974 May LP *'Justments* (a title based on a phrase frequently used by his grandmother, who partially raised him) reaches US #67 while, from it, *The Same Love That Made Me Laugh* reaches US #50.

1975 Jan *Heartbreak Road* makes US #89.

May Compilation LP *The Best Of Bill Withers* reaches US #182. This is his last release on Sussex, with which he is now in legal dispute. Soon afterwards, Sussex folds and Withers signs a new deal with CBS/Columbia (which will also purchase his earlier Sussex material for reissue).

Dec Columbia debut LP *Making Music* reaches US #81.

1976 Feb *Make Love To Your Mind*, taken from LP *Making Music*, reaches US #76.

Nov LP *Naked And Warm* stalls at US #169.

1977 Dec LP *Menagerie* reaches US #39, earning Withers his second gold LP.

1978 Feb LP *Menagerie* reaches UK #27 while, from it, *Lovely Day* reaches US #30 and hits UK #7.

1979 Apr *'Bout Love* reaches US #134.

1981 May Grover Washington Jr.'s *Just The Two Of Us* featuring Withers on vocals, hits US #2 (behind Sheena Easton's° *Morning Train (Nine To Five)*, and is a million-seller. (Withers' own recording career is quiet but he is an eagerly-sought guest vocalist.) Compilation LP *Bill Withers' Greatest Hits* (which includes *Just The Two Of Us*) reaches US #183.

1982 Feb [24] Along with Grover Washington Jr., Withers wins a Grammy award for *Just The Two Of Us*, named Best R&B Song of 1981.

1984 Oct Ralph McDonald's *In The Name Of Love*, with Withers on guest vocal, reaches US #58.

1985 June *Oh Yeah!* peaks at UK #60. It is taken from LP *Watching You, Watching Me*, which reaches UK #60.

1987 Mar A revival of Withers' song *Lean On Me* by US quintet Club Nouveau, tops the US chart (earning a gold disk) and hits UK #3. Withers sends a telegram to the group thanking and congratulating them.

1988 Mar Withers wins another Grammy for *Lean On Me* when Club Nouveau's version is named R&B Song of the Year.

Sept *Lovely Day*, remixed with new instrumental and rhythmic additions by Dutch DJ Ben Leibrand, hits UK #4. His LP *Greatest Hits* also re-charts, making UK #90.

Sept [18] On the strength of his remixed hit, Withers travels to UK to play at London's Hammersmith Odeon, where he is introduced on stage by his son Todd.

Dec Withers returns to UK for a full national tour, as a reissue of *Ain't No Sunshine* makes UK #82.

WIZZARD

Roy Wood (vocals and guitar)
Rick Price (bass)
Hugh McDowell (cello)
Nick Pentelow (sax)
Mike Burney (sax)
Bill Hunt (keyboards and French horn)
Keith Smart (drums)
Charlie Grima (drums)

1972 July Wood, having embarked on a new venture, with guitarist Jeff Lynne, after their Birmingham, UK, group The Move° has had its last hit (UK #7 in May) with *California Man*, originally the Wood-Lynne project but now called the Electric Light Orchestra (ELO), which hits UK #9 with its first single, *10538 Overture*, loses interest in the concept and announces the formation of his new group, Wizzard.

Aug Wizzard debuts at London's Wembley "Rock'n'Roll Festival", on a mismatched bill with Chuck Berry° and Bill Haley°.

1973 Jan Debut single *Ball Park Incident* hits UK #6. The Move's° contract with EMI/Harvest officially has 2 years to run, but the company continues with both splinter groups.

Apr Wood writes, produces and plays on *Farewell*, a single by UK children's TV presenter Ayshea.

May *See My Baby Jive* tops the UK chart, as Wood's multi-colored hair and clothes become part of Wizzard's image.

June LP *Wizzard Brew* reaches UK #29.

Aug *Dear Elaine*, a Wood solo, reaches UK #18. (B-side *Songs Of Praise* had been shortlisted for the previous year's UK entry in the Eurovision Song Contest.)

Sept *Angel Fingers* tops the UK chart. Wood's solo LP *Boulders* reaches UK #15.

Nov LP *Boulders* makes US #173. (Wizzard will never achieve US chart success.)

Dec Harvest celebrates Christmas with Wizzard's *I Wish It Could Be Christmas Every Day*, which hits UK #4, and Wood's *Forever*, which hits UK #8. (*I Wish It Could Be Christmas Everyday* will re-chart at Christmas 1981 (#41) and 1984 (#23).)

1974 Wood begins the year in poor health. The demands of touring and recording lead to ulcers and he is advised to slow down.

May Wizzard signs to Warner Bros. and first single *Rock'n'Roll Winter (Looney's Tune)* hits UK #6.

July Wood's solo *Going Down The Road* reaches UK #13.

Aug *This Is The Story Of My Love (Baby)* makes UK #34. LP *Introducing Eddy And The Falcons* reaches UK #19. Each track on the LP is in the style of a 1950s rock'n'roll hero; Gene Vincent°, Duane Eddy°, Cliff Richard°, Del Shannon°, etc.

Nov Wizzard begins an unsuccessful US tour.

1975 Jan Featuring Wood's favorite new instrument, the bagpipes, *Are You Ready To Rock* hits UK #8.

May Wood's solo *Oh What A Shame*, released on Jet label, reaches UK #13.

Oct Wizzard's management refuses to finance a second US tour and the band splits.

Nov Wood's second LP, *Mustard*, is released. Despite vocal contributions from Phil Everly and girlfriend Annie Haslam, it flops. It is repackaged as *Roy Wood The Wizzard*, with the addition of *Winter*, *Ready To Rock* and *Oh What A Shame*.

1976 Wood signs to EMI/Harvest, Warner and Jet at the same time, with little idea which he is most bound to. He also has managerial difficulties.

Mar On Jet, *Indiana Rainbow*, credited to Roy Wood's Wizzard, is drawn from planned LP *Wizzo* (which will never be released). The Beach Boys° release *It's OK*, on which Wood and two other members of Wizzard had played during their 1974 US tour.

1977 Apr Wood re-emerges with The Wizzo Band. Its LP *On The Road Again* features contributions from Led Zeppelin's° John Bonham, Andy Fairweather-Low and original Move° vocalist Carl Wayne. The LP is deleted soon after release and the band ceases to be. Wood will write and produce for other acts, including Darts, and

WIZZARD *cont.*

forms a live band, The Helicopters, as well as releasing several unsuccessful singles.

1982 July Speed Records releases a compilation LP of Wood's work with The Move° and beyond, *The Singles*, which reaches UK #37.

1983 He sings *Message In A Bottle* on LP *Arrested*, a collection of The Police° songs performed by various rock musicians and the Royal Philharmonic Orchestra.

1985 Wood signs to Legacy Records.

1986 Mar He joins other Birmingham musicians including Robert Plant°, ELO°, The Moody Blues° for "Heartbeat '86" benefit gig.

Nov He helps out Doctor & The Medics with their version of Abba's° first hit, *Waterloo*, which reaches UK #45.

BOBBY WOMACK

1959 The Womack Brothers, consisting of Bobby (b. Mar.4, 1944, Cleveland, Oh., US), Cecil, Curtis, Harris and Friendly Jr., become popular favorites on the gospel circuit and, while touring, meet Sam Cooke° & The Soul Stirrers.

1960 June While continuing his career with his brothers, Bobby Womack is recruited by Cooke° as a guitarist in his band.

1961 Cooke signs The Womack Brothers to his own SAR label, as The Valentinos and The Lovers.

1962 Sept *Lookin' For A Love* is an R&B hit and charts at US #72. It is quickly followed by *I'll Make It Alright* which reaches US #97. Chart success prompts a support slot on James Brown's° US tour.

1964 July *It's All Over Now* is The Valentinos' final chart entry together (US #94). Written by Bobby, it will later become a worldwide smash for The Rolling Stones° (at UK #1 and US #26), with whom Bobby will develop a long-term relationship.

1965 Feb Following the murder of Sam Cooke° in Dec. 1964, Bobby marries his widow, Barbara. He embarks on an unsuccessful stint on Him label and starts a period of heavy session work. As a guitarist, he will contribute to recordings for artists including King Curtis, Ray Charles°, Joe Tex, Wilson Pickett°, The Box Tops°, Aretha Franklin°, Dusty Springfield° and Janis Joplin°.

1966 As a songwriter, Womack begins writing hits for Wilson Pickett°, who will cover 17 Womack songs over 3 years, including *I'm A Midnight Mover* (US #24) and *I'm In Love* (US #45).

1968 Sept Following brief stints at Chess and Atlantic, Womack signs to Minit label for his first solo success at US #52 with *Fly Me To The Moon*, taken from debut solo LP of the same name, which makes US #174.

1969 Jan An R&B cover of The Mamas & The Papas° classic *California Dreamin'*, also from the LP, makes US #43.

Dec *How I Miss You Baby* reaches US #93.

1970 May *More Than I Can Stand* (US #90) is his final Minit hit. Divorce from Barbara coincides with his meeting R&B superstar, Sly Stone. Together they become immersed in a drugs and groupie wilderness which will dominate their lives throughout 70s.

1971 May A one-off live recording LP *The Womack Live* (actually recorded some 3 years earlier at the California Club, LA) is released on United Artists' subsidiary Liberty and reaches US #188.

1972 Jan Debut single for UA *That's The Way I Feel About Cha* makes US #27 and promotes sales for simultaneously released LP *Communication*, which reaches US #83.

June *Woman's Gotta Have It* reaches US #60 and LP *Understanding* makes US #43.

Sept A cover of Neil Diamond's° *Sweet Caroline (Good Times Never Seemed So Good)* charts at US #51.

Dec Flipside *Harry Hippie*, a popular Womack live number, reaches US #31.

1973 Jan He completes film soundtrack LP *Across 110th Street*, starring Anthony Quinn. The LP makes US #50, while title track single reaches US #56.

July Beginning a trilogy of LPs which will all be recorded in Memphis, LP *Facts Of Life* achieves US #37 and includes *Nobody Wants You When You're Down And Out*, which makes US #29.

1974 Mar Simultaneous release of new Memphis LP *Lookin' For A Love Again* reaches US #85 and title song *Lookin' For A Love* gives Womack his biggest career hit at US #10.

June He produces long-time friend, Rolling Stone° Ron Wood's debut LP *Now Look*, which reaches US #118.

July *You're Welcome, Stop On By* makes US #59.

Dec UA releases LP *Bobby Womack's Greatest Hits* which shows signs of his career slowing up (US #142).

1975 May *Check It Out* reaches US #91 with only 3 weeks on the survey. Taken from LP *I Don't Know What The World Is Coming To*, it is his final UA chart single at US #126.

1976 Jan Critics pan new LP *Safety Zone* and it only climbs to US #147.

May Final UA LP *B.W. Goes C&W* is released. The label dumps Womack after his attempt to go country (original working title of LP is, according to Womack, *Move Over Charley Pride And Give Another Nigger A Chance*).

Sept He signs a new deal with CBS/Columbia who releases his final Memphis recording, LP *Home Is Where The Heart Is*, which fails to chart.

1978 July LP *Pieces*, the second CBS/Columbia effort, again fails. The murder of his brother, Harry, compounds Womack's depression as he retreats further into drugs.

1980 Nov Currently without a contract, Crusader°, Wilton Felder enlists Womack as his lead vocal assistance on single and LP, both titled *Inherit The Wind*. The LP reaches US #142; the single makes UK #39, his first artist chart entry in UK.

1981 Dec Recovered from narcotics, Womack returns triumphantly with LP *The Poet*, released on small California soul label, Beverly Glen. It becomes a best-selling R&B/black LP and reaches US #29.

1982 Womack takes label owner, Otis Smith, to court claiming that he is receiving no royalties. Consistently claiming throughout his career that, like James Brown° and many other black artists, he has been short-changed, tempers flare as Womack punches Smith in the courtroom.

1984 Apr With legal wrangles finally over, Womack is free to release second part of Poet project, *The Poet II*. A one-off LP deal with Motown, it reaches US #60 and becomes the first UK LP chart entry at #31.

June As Womack undertakes major US tour, a duet from LP *Love Has Finally Come At Last* with Patti Labelle° climbs to US #88, while *Tell Me Why* makes UK #60.

Dec He organizes benefit concert for Sly Stone, now seeking rehabilitation and visits UK for a mini-tour. Brother Cecil begins scoring hits as one-half of Womack & Womack, with his wife, Linda. As Sam Cooke's° daughter, she now becomes Bobby Womack's sister-in-law, having previously been his step-daughter.

1985 Feb Womack renews his connection with Felder for the latter's second LP *Secrets* which makes US #91 and #77 in UK, where Womack unites with Altrina Grayson for *(No Matter How High I Get) I'll Still Be Lookin' Up To You*, which reaches UK #63

Sept He signs a million-dollar recording contract with MCA worldwide. First release, soul LP *So Many Rivers*, makes UK #28.

Oct *I Wish He Didn't Trust Me So Much*, taken from the LP, reaches UK #64.

Nov LP *So Many Rivers* makes US #66.

1986 June The Rolling Stones° invite Womack to contribute guitar and vocals on their new LP *Dirty Work*. He is prominent as co-vocalist with Jagger on *Going Back To Memphis*.

July LP *Womagic* is released but fails to chart.

1987 Nov Having recently recorded a cover version of UK band Living In A Box's *Living In A Box*, the LP *Womagic* is deleted and replaced by new LP *The Last Soul Man*, including the single, two other new cuts and the majority of tracks on LP *Womagic*. Neither charts.

STEVIE WONDER

1960 Blind since birth, Wonder (b. Steveland Judkins, May 13, 1950, Saginaw, Michigan, US), a member of the Whitestone Baptist Church Choir with his mother, four brothers and sister, is recommended by friend John Glover (with whom he has formed a duo) to Glover's cousin Miracle Ronnie White, who takes Wonder to meet Motown Records' president, Berry Gordy, and producer, Brian Holland. Gordy signs the child prodigy to a long-term contract with Tamla label.

1962 Aug [16] First single, credited to Little Stevie Wonder, *I Call It Pretty Music (But The Old People Call It The Blues)*, featuring Marvin Gaye° on drums, is released, but fails to chart.

Oct [16] Wonder begins a 2-month Motown Records package tour in Washington, D.C. with Marvin Gaye°, The Miracles, The Supremes° and Mary Wells.

1963 May [21] A Stevie Wonder concert is recorded in Detroit for forthcoming LP *12 Year Old Genius*.

Aug Fourth single, *Fingertips – Pt. 2* sells over a million and tops the US chart. LP *Recorded Live – The 12 Year Old Genius* tops the US chart. Wonder becomes the first artist to top the Hot 100, R&B singles and LP charts simultaneously. Meanwhile, he enrols at the Michigan School for the Blind in Lansing, now unable to continue school in Detroit because of his success.

Nov *Workout Stevie, Workout* reaches US #33.

Dec [26] Wonder visits UK for promotional spots on TV shows "Ready, Steady, Go!" and "Thank Your Lucky Stars".

1964 Apr *Castles In The Sand* makes US #52.

July *Hey Harmonica Man* reaches US #29. Wonder drops his "Little" prefix. Wonder makes his movie debut in B-pictures *Bikini Beach* and *Muscle Beach Party*.

1965 Mar [18] Wonder and other Motown artists fly to London, UK, for recording of Associated Rediffusion's hour-long TV show "The Sound of Tamla Motown".

Mar [20] Motortown review, featuring Wonder, commences a UK tour. Acts include Martha & Vandellas°, The Miracles, The Supremes° and The Temptations° with special UK guest stars Georgie Fame° & The Blue Flames.

Oct *High Heel Sneakers* makes US #59.

1966 Jan [21] Wonder flies to London for a UK tour.

Feb *Uptight (Everything's Alright)* hits US #3 and R&B #1, selling over a million.

Mar *Uptight* reaches UK #14, his UK chart debut.

May *Nothing's Too Good For My Baby* reaches US #20.

June LP *Up Tight Everything's Alright* is released, making US #33.

Sept A revival of Bob Dylan's° *Blowin' In The Wind*, duetted with Henry Cosby, hits US #9 and makes UK #36.

Dec *A Place In The Sun* hits US #9.

1967 Jan *A Place In The Sun* reaches UK #20.

Feb LP *Down To Earth* enters the US chart, rising to #92.

Apr *Travlin' Man* makes US #32. (B-side *Hey Love* will make US #90 in May.)

July *I Was Made To Love Her* hits US #2 and is a million-seller.

Aug *I Was Made To Love Her* hits UK #5. Parent LP *I Was Made To Love Her* will make US #45.

Nov *I'm Wondering* reaches US #12 and UK #22.

1968 Apr Compilation LP *Greatest Hits* is released and will make US #37 and UK #25.

May *Shoo-Be-Doo-Be-Doo-Da-Day* hits US #9 and makes UK #46.

Aug *You Met Your Match* reaches US #35.

Sept LP *Stevie Wonder's Greatest Hits* makes UK #25.

Nov Wonder, credited as Eivets Rednow, reaches US #66 with *Alfie*, a piano instrumental. (He also records an instrumental LP under this reversal of his own name.)

Dec An updating of standard *For Once In My Life* hits US #2, behind Marvin Gaye's° *I Heard It Through The Grapevine*, and is another million-seller.

1969 Jan *For Once In My Life* hits UK #3, as parent LP *For Once In My Life* heads for US #50.

Mar [7] He embarks on an 18-day UK concert tour.

Mar *I Don't Know Why* makes US #39.

Apr *I Don't Know Why* reaches UK #14.

May [5] Wonder meets President Nixon at The White House and is presented with the President's Committee on Employment of Handicapped People's "Distinguished Service Award".

July *My Cherie Amour*, B-side of *I Don't Know Why*, hits US #4 and tops a million sales.

Aug *My Cherie Amour* hits UK #4 as parent LP *My Cherie Amour* rises to US #34.

Dec *Yester-me, Yester-you, Yesterday* hits US #7 and UK #2. LP *My Cherie Amour* reaches UK #17.

1970 Jan [10] Wonder is awarded 1969 Show Business Inspiration Award by "Fight for Sight", an organization promoting research into eye diseases.

Mar *Never Had A Dream Come True* reaches US #26 and hits UK #6.

Apr LP *Stevie Wonder Live* makes US #81.

Aug *Signed Sealed Delivered I'm Yours* hits US #3 and reaches UK #15 as LP *Signed Sealed And Delivered* is released, set to make US #25.

Sept [14] Wonder marries Syreeta Wright, a former secretary at Motown Records.

Nov *Heaven Help Us All* hits US #9 and reaches UK #29.

1971 May [13] On his 21st birthday, Wonder receives all his childhood earnings. Despite having earned in excess of $30 million, he receives only $1 million. (His renegotiations with Motown result in the formation of autonomous Taurus Productions and Black

Bull Publishing companies.)

May *We Can Work It Out*, a revival of Lennon°/McCartney's° song, reaches US #13 and UK #27. LP *Where I'm Coming From*, written by Wonder and Syreeta, makes US #62.

July *Never Dreamed You'd Leave In Summer* makes US #78.

Aug [17] Wonder sings at the funeral of legendary session musician King Curtis.

Oct *If You Really Love Me*, written with Syreeta, hits US #8.

Nov LP *Greatest Hits, Vol.2* makes US #69.

1972 Feb *If You Really Love Me* reaches UK #20. LP *Greatest Hits Vol.2* makes UK #30.

Mar LP *Music Of My Mind*, recorded with synthesizer specialists Robert Margouleff and Malcolm Cecil, reaches US #21.

June [3] Wonder begins a 50-date 8-week tour as support to The Rolling Stones° in Vancouver, B.C. Canada.

July *Superwoman (Where Were You When I Needed You)* reaches US #33.

Aug [30] Wonder joins John and Yoko Lennon° for a "One on One" benefit for the Willowbank Hospital at New York's Madison Square Garden.

Sept *Keep On Running* stalls at US #90.

Nov LP *Talking Book* hits US #3.

1973 Jan *Superstition*, written for Jeff Beck°, tops the US chart, selling over a million, and reaches UK #11.

Feb LP *Talking Book* reaches UK #16.

May *You Are The Sunshine Of My Life* tops the US chart, becoming another million-seller.

June *You Are The Sunshine Of My Life* hits UK #7.

Aug [6] While traveling from Greenville, N.C. to Durham, N.C. during a US tour, Wonder is seriously injured in a car accident near Winston-Salem, N.C. (He suffers multiple head injuries and lies in a coma for 4 days.)

Aug [18] *Higher Ground* tops *Billboard*'s soul charts.

Aug Rufus' *Tell Me Something Good*, written by Wonder, hits US #3.

Sept LP *Innervisions* hits US #4, selling over 1 million, and UK #8.

Sept [25] Wonder makes his first post-accident appearance jamming on *Honky Tonk Women* with Elton John° at the Boston Garden, Boston, Mass.

Oct *Higher Ground* hits US #4 and reaches UK #29.

Nov [9] Wonder receives Nederlands Edison Award for *Talking Book*.

1974 Jan *Living For The City* hits US #8 and UK #15.

STEVIE WONDER *cont.*

Mar [2] Wonder wins Grammys in four categories: Pop Vocal Performance – Male (for *You Are The Sunshine Of My Life*), R&B Song and R&B Vocal Performance – Male (both for *Superstition*) and Album of the Year (for LP *Innervisions*).

Mar Wonder plays his first US concert since his accident at New York's Madison Square Garden. He is joined on stage by Roberta Flack°, Eddie Kendricks, Sly Stone° and Wonderlove, and sells out concerts at London's Rainbow.

May *He's Misstra Know It All* hits UK #10.

June *Don't You Worry 'Bout A Thing* reaches US #16.

Sept LP *Fulfillingness' First Finale* tops the US chart for 2 weeks and hits UK #5.

Sept [13] Wonder begins a US tour at the Nassau Coliseum, Long Island, N.Y.

Nov *You Haven't Done Nothin'*, with The Jackson 5° on back-up vocals, hits US #1 and UK #30.

Nov [22] "Stevie Wonder Day" is celebrated in Los Angeles.

1975 Feb *Boogie On Reggae Woman* hits US #3 and UK #12.

Mar [1] Wonder again wins four Grammys: Best Pop Vocal Performance – Male and Album of the Year (both for *Fulfillingness*), R&B Vocal Performance – Male (for *Boogie On Reggae Woman*) and R&B Song (for *Living For The City*).

Mar [6] Wonder is awarded the NARM Presidential Award "in tribute to a man who embodies every facet of the complete musical artist: composer, writer, performer, recording artist, musician and interpreter through his music of the culture of his time . . ."

Apr Minnie Riperton's *Lovin' You*, written by Wonder, tops the US chart. Having recently moved to Manhattan, Wonder and his new companion Yolanda Simmons become parents to a daughter, Aisha Zakia.

May [10] Wonder headlines a concert in front of 125,000 people at the Washington Monument to celebrate "Human Kindness Day".

May Wonder performs in Jamaica with Bob Marley° & The Wailers.

1976 Jan [25] Wonder joins Bob Dylan° and Isaac Hayes° for the "Night of the Hurricane II" benefit show for convicted murderer, boxer Ruben "Hurricane" Carter in the Houston Astrodome.

Jan Stevie Wonder Home for Blind and Retarded Children opens, confirming ongoing personal interest in a wide number of charity and human rights causes.

Apr [14] Wonder and Motown Records announce the signing of a $13-million-dollar contract renewal – the largest ever negotiated in recording history.

Oct LP *Songs In The Key Of Life* debuts at US #1, where it stays for 14 weeks, and hits UK #2.

1977 Jan *I Wish* hits US #1 and UK #5, and is another million-seller.

Feb [19] *Songs In The Key Of Life* is named Album of the Year at the annual Grammy ceremonies. It is also awarded Best Producer and Best Pop Vocal Performance: Male.

May *Sir Duke*, a tribute to Duke Ellington, is a further million-seller, topping the US chart and hitting UK #2, behind Deniece Williams'° *Free*.

Sept *Another Star* makes UK #29.

Oct *Another Star* reaches US #32.

1978 Jan *As* reaches US #36.

1979 Feb *Pops We Love You*, a tribute to Berry Gordy's father on his 90th birthday, with Diana Ross°, Marvin Gaye° and Smokey Robinson°, reaches US #59 and UK #66. Compilation LP *Looking Back* makes US #34.

Apr The Wonders become parents to daughter, Kita Swan Di.

Apr [27] Wonder makes a surprise appearance, performing *Sir Duke*, at a Duke Ellington tribute at UCLA's Royce Hall, LA.

Nov LP *Journey Through The Secret Life Of Plants* hits UK #8.

Dec [2] Wonder, accompanied by the National Afro-American Philharmonic Orchestra, performs material from his forthcoming LP *Journey Through The Secret Life Of Plants* at New York's Metropolitan Opera House.

Dec *Send One Your Love* hits US #4 and UK #52 as parent LP *Journey Through The Secret Life Of Plants*, the soundtrack for a documentary film of the same title, hits US #4.

1980 Feb *Black Orchid* makes UK #63.

Mar *Outside My Window* reaches both US and UK #52.

Sept Wonder returns for a UK tour after a 6-year absence, including six sold-out Wembley Arena dates.

Oct *Master Blaster (Jammin')* hits UK #2, behind The Police's° *Don't Stand So Close To Me*.

Nov LP *Hotter Than July*, dedicated to Martin Luther King Jr., hits US #3 and UK #2. (Wonder will conduct a campaign to have King's January 15th birthdate celebrated as a US national holiday. After marches on Washington in 1981 and 1982, he will have his wish granted in 1983.)

Dec *Master Blaster (Jammin')* hits US #5.

1981 Jan *I Ain't Gonna Stand For It* hits UK #10.

Mar *I Ain't Gonna Stand For It* reaches US #11.

May *Lately* makes US #64 and hits UK #3.

June Wonder contributes to gospel singer Andrae Crouch's *I'll Be Thinking Of You* single.

Aug *Happy Birthday* hits UK #2, behind Shakin' Stevens'° *Green Door*.

Aug [15] Wonder gives his *Hotter Than July* gold disk to Tami Ragoway, whose boyfriend had been shot and killed returning home after Wonder's concert at LA's Forum.

1982 Mar *That Girl* hits US #4 and makes UK #39.

May *Ebony And Ivory*, a duet with Paul McCartney° recorded in Montserrat, West Indies, tops US and UK charts, selling over a million. LP *Stevie Wonder's Original Musiquarium 1* hits UK #8. It is a compilation LP spiced with new tracks.

June [6] Wonder participates in the "Peace Sunday: We Have a Dream" anti-nuclear rally at the Rose Bowl, Pasadena, Cal., with Jackson Browne°, Crosby, Stills & Nash°, Bob Dylan°, Linda Ronstadt° and others.

June *Do I Do* hits UK #10. LP *Stevie Wonder's Original Musiquarium 1* hits US #4.

July *Do I Do* reaches US #13.

Oct *Ribbon In The Sky* makes US #54 and UK #45.

Dec *Used To Be*, a duet with Charlene, reaches US #46.

1983 May [7] Wonder plays tennis while hosting US NBC-TV's "Saturday Night Live".

Aug Wonder sings on and co-writes Gary Byrd's *The Crown*, which hits UK #6 as a 12"-only single.

1984 Jan Wonder guests on Elton John's° *I Guess That's Why They Call It The Blues*.

June Wonder begins a UK and European tour.

Sept *I Just Called To Say I Love You* (taken from soundtrack LP *The Woman In Red* which hits US #4 and UK #2) tops the UK chart for 6 weeks, selling more than 1¾ million copies – it is Wonder's first solo UK #1, and one of the 10 best-selling UK singles of all time.

Oct *I Just Called To Say I Love You* tops the US chart.

Nov Wonder guests on Chaka Khan's° US and UK hit *I Feel For You*. Compilation LP *Love Songs – 16 Classic Hits* reaches UK #20.

Dec *Love Light In Flight* makes UK #44.

Dec [24] Wonder is given the key to the city of Detroit, Mich. (He will later announce plans to run for Mayor of Detroit.)

1985 Jan *Don't Drive Drunk* makes UK #62.

Jan [28] Wonder participates in the recording of USA For Africa's° *We Are The World*.

Feb *Love Light In Flight*, also from LP *The Woman In Red*, reaches US #17.

Mar [25] *I Just Called To Say I Love You* wins the Oscar for Best Song at the annual Academy Awards ceremony. Wonder dedicates the award to Nelson Mandela.

Mar [26] South African radio stations ban the playing of all Wonder's records in response to his Mandela tribute.

July Wonder plays harmonica on Eurythmics'° *There Must Be An Angel (Playing With My Heart)* UK chart-topper.

Sept *Part-Time Lover* hits UK #3 as parent LP *In Square Circle* hits UK #5. He writes and plays *She's So Beautiful* with vocal by Cliff Richard° for the LP of Dave Clark's° *Time*. Released as a Cliff Richard single, it reaches UK #17.

Oct LP *In Square Circle* hits US #5.

Nov *Part-Time Lover* becomes the first single to top the US pop, R&B, adult contemporary and dance/disco charts. *Go Home* peaks at UK #67.

1986 Jan Wonder joins Elton John° and Gladys Knight° as Dionne Warwick's° guests on US #1 *That's What Friends Are For*.

Jan [15] To celebrate the first observance of Martin Luther King Jr.'s birthday as a US national holiday, Wonder organizes concerts in Washington, D.C., New York and Atlanta.

Feb *Go Home* hits US #10.

Apr *Overjoyed* reaches US #24 and UK #17.

June *Land Of La La* makes US #86.

June [17] Wonder begins a US tour to promote *In Square Circle* in Seattle, Wash.
July [31] Wonder is nominated for an Emmy for his appearance in top-rated US NBC-TV's "The Cosby Show".
1987 Jan *Stranger On The Shore Of Love* stalls at UK #55.
Feb Wonder announces a boycott of the state of Arizona, until Governor Evan Meacham reinstates Martin Luther King Jr.'s birthday as a state holiday. (Several other artists support his boycott.)
Mar Wonder records anti-drug song *Stop, Don't Pass Go* in an audio visual experiment, linking Nile Rodgers in a New York studio with Quincy Jones and Wonder in his own LA studio Wonderland 3,000 miles away.
Aug Wonder begins a UK and European tour.
Sept During an 8-day stint at London's Wembley Arena, fan Barry Betts answers Wonder's request to help courier a tape of a new song, *Get It*, to Michael Jackson° in LA.
Nov LP *Characters* makes UK #33.
Dec *Skeletons* reaches US #19 and hits R&B #1, having faltered at UK #59. LP *Characters* reaches US #17 and hits R&B #1.
1988 May *Get It*, a duet with Michael Jackson°, makes US #80 and UK #37.
June [11] Wonder, despite having synthesizer programs stolen, plays at the Nelson Mandela 70th Birthday Party concert at London's Wembley Stadium.
Aug Wonder's duet with Julio Iglesias, *My Love* hits UK #6, after stalling at US #80. He plays an eight-date series of concerts at New York's Radio City Music Hall, as he prepares for a US tour.

XTC

Andy Partridge (guitar and vocals)
Colin Moulding (bass and vocals)
Barry Andrews (keyboards)
Terry Chambers (drums)

1977 Sept Partridge, Moulding and Chambers, all ex-members of Swindon, Wiltshire, UK-based Star Park rock band, changing name to Helium Kidz at the height of the punk boom, are joined by ex-King Crimson° keyboard player Barry Andrews. Having earlier auditioned for CBS Records, XTC signs to Virgin.
Oct EP *3-D* is released.
1978 Jan LP *White Music*, recorded in a week, reaches UK #38, as the band is linked to the current popular UK new wave movement.
Feb *Statue Of Liberty* is released but fails to chart.
May *This Is Pop*, produced by Robert John Lange, is released.
Nov *Are You Receiving Me?* is an unsuccessful prelude to LP *Go Two*. which reaches UK #21.
1979 Jan Andrews quits the band on its return from a 10-date US mini-tour. (He teams with Robert Fripp to form The League of Gentlemen and to record as a soloist for Virgin.) The rest of the band approach longtime friend Dave Gregory as a replacement.
May *Life Begins At The Hop* reaches UK #54. Andrews' first solo *Town And Country* is released.
July The band tours Australia, New Zealand and Japan.
Aug Third LP *Drums And Wires* reaches UK #34 as the band begins a brief UK tour.
Nov *Making Plans For Nigel* makes UK #17.
1980 Feb Partridge releases John Leckie-produced solo LP *Takeway/The Lure Of Salvage* under the name of Mr. Partridge. LP *Drums And Wires* climbs to US #176.
Mar *Wait Till Your Boat Goes Down* is released.
Sept Double A-side *Generals And Majors/Don't Lose Your Temper* peaks at UK #32. LP *Black Sea* reaches UK #16.
Oct *Towers Of London* peaks at UK #31.
Nov *Take This Town*, from *Times Square* movie soundtrack, is released.
1981 Feb *Sgt. Rock (Is Going To Help Me)* makes UK #16. LP *Black Sea* reaches US #41.
Mar *Respectable Street* fails to chart, partly due to its ban on UK BBC Radio for reference to Sony. The group begins a tour of Venezuela, and will also tour US, the Middle East, South-East Asia and Australia during the year.
1982 Feb *Senses Working Overtime*, the group's biggest success, hits UK #10. Double LP *English Settlement*, produced by Hugh Padgham, hits UK #5 (and will reach US #48 in May).
Mar Partridge collapses on stage in Paris from exhaustion.
Apr *Ball And Chain* makes UK #58. Partridge collapses again (with a stomach ulcer), having given himself less than a month to recover from his earlier illness. He later claims it is "a phobia about being in front of people". A tour is cancelled and Chambers leaves.
May *No Thugs In Our House* is released, but fails to chart.
Nov Partridge announces the band will never play live again. LP *Waxworks – Some Singles (1977-1982)* reaches UK #54.
1983 May *Great Fire* fails to chart.
July *Wonderland* also fails to chart.
Aug LP *Mummer*, featuring songs written during Partridge's convalescence, reaches UK #51. Pete Phipps (ex-Glitter Band) plays drums on tracks on which Chambers does not appear. Refusal to promote the LP with live work causes friction between the band and Virgin. Geffen releases the LP in US where it climbs to #145.
Oct *Love On A Farmboy's Wages*, peaks at UK #50.
Nov XTC, as The Three Wise Men, releases *Thanks For Christmas*. Partridge begins producing other acts including Peter Blegvad (ex-Slapp Happy).
1984 Mar LP *Mummer* reaches US #145.
Oct LP *The Big Express* peaks at UK #38 and US #178. It includes three singles: *All You Pretty Girls* (UK #55), and *This World Over* and *Wake Up*, neither of which charts.
1985 Apr Mini-LP *The Dukes Of Stratosphear: 25 O'Clock* is released by the group's psychedelic alter-ego, The Dukes of Stratospheer.
1986 Oct LP *Skylarking*, produced by Todd Rundgren° at The Tubes'° Soundhole Studios in San Francisco, reaches UK #90. The LP will spend over 6 months on US chart, reaching #70.
1987 Aug The second Dukes of Stratospheer LP, *Psonic Psunspots* and CD-only compilation *Chips From The Chocolate Fireball* are released. Remaining a trio, they continue to work as a studio band only, releasing both XTC and alias issues, including Partridge's singles as "Buster Gonad" and "The Jolly Josticles".

THE YARDBIRDS

Keith Relf (vocals and harmonica)
Paul Samwell-Smith (bass)
Chris Dreja (guitar)
Jim McCarty (drums)
Anthony "Top" Topham (guitar)

1963 Relf (b. Mar.22, 1943, Richmond, Surrey, UK), Samwell-Smith (b. May 8, 1943, Richmond, Surrey), Dreja (b. Nov.11, 1945, Surbiton, Surrey, UK), McCarty (b. July 25, 1943, Liverpool, UK) and Topham, having been in local groups in the burgeoning London area R&B scene, come together at The Kingston Art School, Surrey, UK, initially as The Metropolitan Blues Quartet. They play pubs and clubs in the local Richmond area, before moving on to bigger London clubs. They take over the residency from The Rolling Stones° at Giorgio Gomelsky's Crawdaddy Club. Topham leaves to return to college and is replaced by Eric Clapton°.
Dec The group is recorded live, backing Sonny Boy Williamson on his UK tour.
1964 Feb Gomelsky takes demos to various labels. Decca turns them down, feeling it already has too many R&B bands. The group signs to EMI's Columbia label and cuts three songs at its first recording session.
Feb [28] They play the first Rhythm & Blues Festival at UK's Birmingham Town Hall.
June Debut single, a revival of Billy Boy Arnold's *I Wish You Would*, fails to chart but gets exposure on TV and in the pop press.
Oct Despite a BBC ban, a revival of Don & Bob's R&B standard *Good Morning Little Schoolgirl* makes UK #44.
Dec Debut LP, recorded live at the Marquee club in London, is *Five Little Yardbirds*. The band plays on The Beatles'° Christmas show at London's Hammersmith Odeon.
1965 Mar *For Your Love*, written by Graham Gouldman, is the group's first major hit, at UK #3.
Mar [13] Clapton° leaves, unhappy with the move away from blues and towards pop. He joins John Mayall's° Bluesbreakers and Jeff Beck° (b. June 24, 1944) replaces him.
Apr [30] The group supports The Kinks° on a UK tour.
June *Heart Full Of Soul*, also written by Gouldman, hits UK #2. *For Your Love* hits US #6, while LP *For Your Love* reaches US #96.
June [20] They support The Beatles° at the Olympia, Paris.
Aug [6] The Yardbirds play the third annual Richmond Jazz & Blues Festival.
Aug The group begins its first US tour.
Sept *Heart Full Of Soul* hits US #9.

THE YARDBIRDS *cont.*

Sept [23] They sing *Heart Full Of Soul* on US TV's "Shindig". Also featured is Raquel Welch singing *Dancing In The Street*.

Oct Double A-side *Evil Hearted You/Still I'm Sad* hits UK #3.

Dec *I'm A Man* reaches US #17, and LP *Having A Rave Up With The Yardbirds*, including tracks from the UK live LP, makes US #53.

1966 Fontana in UK releases LP *The Yardbirds With Sonny Boy Williamson*, recorded live in Dec. 1963. The band changes managers, replacing Gomelsky with Simon Napier-Bell.

Mar *Shapes Of Things* hits UK #3.

Apr [9] Beck° collapses on stage during a gig in Marseilles, France.

Apr *Shapes Of Things* reaches US #11.

May Relf's first solo, a cover of Bob Lind's *Mr. Zero* is released.

June Samwell-Smith leaves for a career as a producer; his replacement is UK session guitarist Jimmy Page. Dreja moves to bass, while Page shares lead duties with Beck°. *Over Under Sideways Down* hits UK #10.

July *Over Under Sideways Down* reaches US #11. The band releases its first studio LP *Yardbirds*, which makes UK #20.

Sept LP *Over Under Sideways Down* reaches US #52, while the band starts a UK tour supporting The Rolling Stones°.

Oct [19] The Yardbirds arrive in US for a tour.

Oct Beck° departs after the first two gigs, to form a band with Rod Stewart° and Ron Wood. The group continues as a 4-piece. *Happenings Ten Years Time Ago* peaks at UK #43.

Dec *Happenings Ten Years Time Ago* reaches US #30.

1967 Jan The Yardbirds tour Australasia. Columbia decides to pair them in the studio with producer Mickie Most (but there will be no more UK hits).

Mar The group appears in a club scene performing *Stroll On*, with Beck° (still in the band at the time) being required to smash his guitar, in film *Blow Up*.

May LP *The Yardbirds' Greatest Hits* reaches US #28, while Most-produced *Little Games* makes US #51.

Aug A cover of Manfred Mann's° UK hit *Ha Ha Said The Clown* reaches US #45.

Sept LP *Little Games* makes US #80.

Nov *Ten Little Indians*, written by Harry Nilsson°, reaches US #96. The group successfully stops release of LP *Little Games* in UK, though it appears in US despite their opposition.

Dec The group flies to New York for one gig at Madison Square Garden.

1968 Mar [30] The Yardbirds allow recording of a US gig at Anderson Theater, New York, for possible release as live LP by their US label, Epic, but retain final approval of the project. (On hearing the tapes, they convince the label not to issue it.)

July [7] The group splits up. (Page forms The New Yardbirds (later to become Led Zeppelin°), Dreja becomes a photographer. Relf and McCarty plan their own bands. Relf and sister Jane will form the nucleus of the first version of Renaissance.)

1970 Oct Compilation LP *The Yardbirds Featuring Performances By Jeff Beck, Eric Clapton, Jimmy Page* reaches US #155.

1971 Epic releases the March 1969 concert LP, but it is withdrawn when Page, now with Led Zeppelin°, serves an injunction.

1975 Relf joins Armageddon.

1976 May [14] Relf dies, aged 33, electrocuted while playing guitar at home.

1977 McCarty joins Illusion.

1982 The Yardbirds' 1963 sessions with Sonny Boy Williamson are released on LP, in Spain.

1983 June Dreja, McCarty and Samwell-Smith reunite for gigs at the Marquee. The trio, augmented by John Fiddler (vocals) and Mark Feltham (harmonica) forms new band, Box of Frogs, and signs to Epic Records.

1984 June Box of Frogs' *Back Where I Started* is released.

YAZOO

Alison Moyet (vocals)
Vince Clarke (keyboards)

1982 Jan Keyboard/synthesizer whizz Clarke, having left Depeche Mode° after writing three hit singles and much of the group's first LP, is looking for a singer to work with when he answers an ad placed by "Alf" Moyet° for a "rootsy blues band". Moyet has been a vocalist with UK Southend R&B acts like The Vicars and The Screaming Abdabs.

May *Only You*, on independent Mute label, which also handles Depeche Mode°, hits UK #2.

July Follow-up *Don't Go* hits UK #3.

Sept Yazoo tours UK to promote debut LP *Upstairs At Eric's*, which hits UK #2 in its week of entry. Moyet° begins to write for the duo, which launches itself in US with a New York performance.

Oct *Situation* (UK B-side of *Only You*) reaches US #73. The duo has to go under the name Yaz in US where a small record company has already registered the name Yazoo.

Nov *Upstairs At Eric's* reaches US #92.

Dec *The Other Side Of Love* makes UK #13.

1983 Mar *Only You* reaches US #67.

June *Nobody's Diary* hits UK #3. It is announced that Yazoo will break up after completion of a second LP, currently being recorded.

July LP *You And Me Both* enters the UK chart at #2 (behind Wham's° *Fantastic*), but rises to hit #1.

Sept *You And Me Both* peaks at US #69. (Both will go on to be successful: Moyet° as a solo performer and Clarke as the instrumental half of two more Mute Records duos, Assembly and Erasure°.)

YES

Jon Anderson (vocals)
Steve Howe (guitar)
Tony Kaye (keyboards)
Chris Squire (bass)
Bill Bruford (drums)

1968 June Anderson (b. Oct.25, 1944, Lancs., UK) meets Squire (b. Mar.4, 1948, London, UK) in a club in Soho, London. Anderson has worked in beat group The Warriors, who released one single for UK Decca in 1964, and has cut two solo singles for Parlophone in 1967. Squire has been in The Syn, which has recorded for Deram. They are joined by ex-Federals Kaye, ex-Savoy Brown Bruford (b. May 17, 1948, London) and guitarist Peter Banks (also ex-The Syn) to form Yes.

Nov [26] They open Cream's° farewell concert at London's Royal Albert Hall (which leads to a residency at London's Marquee).

1969 June Signed to Atlantic, first release *Sweetness* makes little impact.

Nov Debut LP *Yes* features re-workings of The Beatles'° *Every Little Thing* and The Byrds'° *I See You*.

1970 Mar Banks is replaced by guitarist Steve Howe, who has played with The Syndicats, The In Crowd, Tomorrow and Bodast. (Banks will later form Flash.)

Aug LP *Time And A Word* makes UK #45.

1971 Apr LP *The Yes Album*, produced by Eddy Offord, hits UK #7 and is US chart debut at #40.

Aug Kaye leaves to form Badger and is replaced by Rick Wakeman (b. May 18, 1949), ex-Strawbs, to give more flamboyant keyboard style.

Dec *Your Move* makes US #40 as LP *Fragile* hits UK #7 and US #4. It is the group's first LP to feature the artwork of Roger Dean, who creates The Yes logo and the distinctive sci-fi fantasy style of future sleeves.

1972 Apr *Roundabout* reaches US #13.

Aug Bruford quits to join King Crimson°, and is replaced by ex-Plastic Ono Band and Happy Magazine drummer Alan White.

Sept A revival of Paul Simon's° *America* reaches US #46, as LP *Close To The Edge* hits UK #4 and US #3.

Dec *And You And I (Part II)* makes US #42.

1973 Feb Wakeman releases solo LP *The Six Wives Of Henry VIII*, which hits UK #7 and US #30.

May Three LP set, *Yessongs*, of live shows from the previous year, hits UK #7 and US #12. (A movie is later released with the same name.)

1974 Jan Double LP set *Tales From Topographic Oceans*, based on the Shastric scriptures, tops the UK chart for 2 weeks and hits US #6.

Feb [18] Yes plays the first of two nights at New York's Madison Square Garden.

May Wakeman's solo LP *Journey To The Centre Of The Earth* tops the UK chart and hits US #3.

June [8] Wakeman leaves the band.

Aug [18] Ex-Refugee member Patrick Moraz joins on keyboards.

Nov LP *Relayer* hits UK #4 and US #5. Side one features *The Gates Of Delirium*, based on Leo Tolstoy's *War and Peace*. Movie *Yessongs* is released.

1975 The band take a rest for most of the year.

Mar LP *Yesterdays*, including tracks from the first two LPs, reaches UK

P431 DEMAND FACTOR

Electrical Systems in Buildings

ELECTRICAL SYSTEMS in Buildings

S. DAVID HUGHES
British Columbia Institute of Technology

Delmar Publishers Inc.®

NOTICE TO THE READER

Publisher does not warrant or guarantee any of the products described herein or perform any independent analysis in connection with any of the product information contained herein. Publisher does not assume, and expressly disclaims, any obligation to obtain and include information other than that provided to it by the manufacturer.

The reader is expressly warned to consider and adopt all safety precautions that might be indicated by the activities described herein and to avoid all potential hazards. By following the instructions contained herein, the reader willingly assumes all risks in connection with such instructions.

The publisher makes no representation or warranties of any kind, including but not limited to, the warranties of fitness for particular purpose or merchantability, nor are any such representations implied with respect to the material set forth herein, and the publisher takes no responsibility with respect to such material. The publisher shall not be liable for any special, consequential or exemplary damages resulting, in whole or in part, from the readers' use of, or reliance upon, this material.

For information, address Delmar Publishers Inc.,
2 Computer Drive West, Box 15-015
Albany, New York 12212

Printed in the United States of America
Published simultaneously in Canada
by Nelson Canada
A Division of The Thomson Corporation

10 9 8 7 6 5 4 3 2 1

ISBN 0-8273-3876-7

Acknowledgments: Figures and tables not credited in text are reprinted courtesy of the following firms and associations. Figures 2.12, 2.13(b), 2.18, 9.7, and 9.8: *Canadian General Electric Company Limited.* Figures 2.5(b) and 9.5: *General Electric Company.* Figures 3.1, 4.1, 4.2, 4.3, 4.4, 4.5, 4.6, 4.10, 4.13, 4.16, 4.17, 5.6, and 5.14(a): *North American Philips Lighting Corp.* Figure 4.11: *Osram Corp.* Figures 4.14, 4.18, 5.4, and 5.5: *Illuminating Engineering Society of North America.* Figures 7.2 and 10.13: *Institute of Electrical and Electronic Engineers.* Figures 7.5, 7.6, 7.8, 7.9, 7.10, and 7.11: *Bussman Division, Cooper Industries, Inc.* Figures 7.12(a) and 14.1: *Square D Company Canada.* Figures 7.12(b), 8.10, 8.11, 8.12, 8.15(b), 10.17, and 12.3: *Federal Pioneer Limited.* Figures 7.14, 7.15, 7.16, 7.17, 15.5, and 15.6; Table 7.4: *S & C Electric Company.* Figures 8.4, 8.5, 8.6, 8.7, 8.8, 8.9, 8.13, 8.15(a), 8.17, 8.19, 8.20, 9.2, 9.4, 11.14(a), 11.15, and 15.7: *Westinghouse Electric Corporation and Westinghouse Canada, Inc.* Figures 11.5, 11.6, and 11.7: *Canada Wire and Cable Limited.* Figure 11.13: *Pilgrim Technical Products, Ltd.* Figures 12.1(b), 12.11: *Hubbell Canada, Inc.* Figure 12.13: *Electrical Construction and Maintenance.* Figures 14.3, 14.7, 14.9, 14.10, and 16.5; Table 16.2: *Allen-Bradley Canada Limited.* Figure 11.2: *Okonite Company.* Figures 5.15 and 5.16: *Holophane Division of Manville Canada, Inc.*

Preface

This text covers all aspects of the design of electrical power systems as they apply to buildings: industrial and commercial.

The term *commercial building,* as used in this textbook, covers office buildings, schools, stores, institutions, and so forth that are primarily people and public oriented. The term *industrial plant* covers buildings and complexes that are primarily machine and production oriented. The intent of this book is to help the reader understand electrical power systems as they apply to these types of buildings and to appreciate the methods followed by the system designer in selecting the lighting, wiring and devices to be used.

The forms of energy required in a building are thermal (heat), light, and kinetic (mechanical). Why then is energy delivered to a building (or generated within) in the electrical form? The answer is that electrical energy can be transmitted so easily throughout the building to the exact point where the energy is required and then converted to a useful form by the heating unit, light source, or electric motor. This end-use apparatus constitutes the utilization equipment, or system load, of electrical power systems.

The design of an electrical system must begin with a complete listing of the utilization equipment that is to be supplied by the system. Chapters 2–4 of this text deal with two major types of equipment: electric motors and light sources. The material on motors is an overview of the major motor types, including advantages, disadvantages, and principal applications of each type. The material on lighting is an introduction to the major types of light sources, including the application of these sources to illuminate indoor areas to recommended minimum lighting levels.

The design of an electrical system must next focus on two different requirements:

1. The adequacy of the system to deliver sufficient electrical energy of the correct frequency, phase relationships, and voltages to each piece of utilization equipment. That is, under normal continuous load conditions, the system must operate in a safe and efficient manner.

2. The protection of the system to minimize power outages and damage in the event of prolonged overloading or insulation breakdowns. That is, under abnormal conditions, the potential for damage (both thermal and mechanical) from overcurrents must be minimized.

Chapters 6–10 cover system protection requirements, since the heart of any electrical system consists of those devices that protect and control the flow of power through the feeders and circuits to the utilization points within the system; that is, switches, fuses, circuit breakers, and so on. Also, the very important topic of system and equipment grounding is covered in Chapter 10.

Chapters 11–16 deal with the fundamentals of the design of the electrical system: branch circuits, panelboards, feeders, motor control centers, unit substations, and system protection coordination.

Throughout the text, all related electrical system devices are described and illustrated. In addition, examples show the selection and incorporation of these devices into an overall system. The theory and examples presented are at a level that should be readily understood by students not majoring in electrical technology and yet thorough enough to satisfy those who are.

Chapter 1 covers the basic electrical relationships and standards, which should allow students to understand the balance of the technical material presented in the text. However, the background gained from a basic course in ac circuits, including three-phase wye and delta systems, would be to the student's advantage. For a student on a program of self-study, there are many excellent textbooks that can be used as references in order to gain a better understanding of electrical fundamentals. Some of these books are listed in the bibliography.

Throughout the text, frequent reference is made to the *National Electrical Code*® 1987 (*NEC*®). The titles *National Electrical Code* and *NEC* are registered trademarks of the National Fire Protection Association, Batterymarch Park, Quincy, Massachusetts. In order to better understand the electrical code requirements as they are discussed in this textbook, it is recommended that the reader obtain a copy of the *National Electrical Code* for reference. The *NEC* is the nationally accepted guide in the United States for the safe installation of electrical conductors and equipment. For the Canadian reader, the electrical code requirements are cross-referenced in Appendix A to the *Canadian Electrical Code,* Part 1, which is published by the Canadian Standards Association, Rexdale, Ontario.

Wherever possible throughout this textbook, the International System of Units has been used. This system, given the designation SI, incorporates the metric system of units (meter, kilogram, second). However, for quantities involving physical measurements, the units of feet and inches is also recognized. For example, in lighting, the illuminance level is designated by the number of lumens per unit of area. The unit predominantly used in the United States up to the present time is the lumen per square foot or footcandle. Therefore, the examples involving lighting calculations in Chapter 5 use primarily English units; a few examples using SI units are also included. The tables of recommended illuminance values, prepared by the Illuminating Engineering Society of North America, show the values in both the SI unit (lumens per square meter or Lux) and the English unit (footcandle). Also, the calculations for minimum power demands covered in Chapter 12 are based on unit loadings of volt-amperes per square foot as listed in the *National Electrical Code*.

Another area where English units are used in the United States is the designation of wire and conduit sizes, equipment measurements, and sizes of motors. Wire sizes are based on the unit of the mil (1/1000th of an inch) and conduit sizes are based on inches. Also, table values used for calculating voltage drops and impedances of feeders are based on the distance in feet. Section 90–8, in the introduction to the *National Electrical Code,* states that *values of measurement in the code text will be followed by an approximate equivalent value in SI units. Tables will have a footnote for SI conversion units used in the table.* However, Section 90–8 also states that *conduit size, wire size, horsepower designation for motors, and trade sizes that do not reflect actual measurements; e.g., box sizes, will not be assigned dual designation SI units.* Therefore, all references in this textbook in this regard use the English units.

At the time of writing this textbook, there are many ongoing research projects, which no doubt will have a profound effect on power distribution systems of the future. For example, research work is currently underway on replacing separate wiring systems for electric power, telephones, cable television, security systems, heating controls, and so forth with a single system to service all applications from a common outlet. Article 780, entitled ''Closed-Loop and Programmed Power Distribution'' has been added to the 1987 edition of the *National Electrical Code* not because there are any working systems of this type available but rather to provide a set of objectives for the guidance of those working to develop this new technology. While applications for this system are directed mainly toward residential installations, there will no doubt be spin-offs that will influence the future installation of systems for office and institutional applications.

The requirements of fire alarm systems, communication systems, public address systems, surveillance systems, and so forth, which may fall within the overall *electrical work* of a building, are beyond the intent of this textbook. These systems are very important but size constraints preclude their being included.

The discussion of code regulations that specifically detail the methods of installing wiring and equipment, which are the concern of the electrical contractor, are generally not within the intent of this textbook. The role of electrical contractors in the successful completion of the electrical system is very important and their expertise is relied upon to properly install the wiring and equipment.

The information and data contained in this textbook is presented solely for the purpose of following the examples, solving the problems at the ends of the chapters, and preparing classroom-related projects. While every attempt has been made to have the data reflect current standards in industry, the manufacturers of the equipment types discussed within this text should be contacted for confirmation of all data and ratings before using any equipment type in actual design specifications. The author and DELMAR Publishers can assume no responsibility for damages that might result from the use of the information presented in this textbook.

ACKNOWLEDGMENTS

I wish to thank Mr. Robert Forst for his invaluable assistance in proofreading my preliminary manuscript. I also wish to thank Mr. Roy F. Hughes, P.E., (no relation) for the many hours spent checking the technical accuracy of the manuscript and for his comments, which were appreciated. Finally, I want to acknowledge the associations and manufacturers who generously supplied photographs, drawings, and data.

I am indebted to the following reviewers for their suggestions and comments: Robert I. Eversoll, Western Kentucky University; Robert Spinti, University of Wisconsin–Stout; Walter Coffer, University of Houston—University Park; Ray Fisher, Cleveland Technical College.

Contents

CHAPTER 2 Electric Motors 48

CHAPTER 3 Lighting Fundamentals 86

CHAPTER 4 Light Sources 105

CHAPTER 5 Lighting System Layouts for Interior Spaces 143

CHAPTER 10 Grounding and Ground-Fault Protection 299

CHAPTER 11 Design of Feeders 338

CHAPTER 14 Motor Starters and Motor-Control Centers 436

CHAPTER 15 Secondary Unit Substations 468

CHAPTER 16 Fault Calculations and System Coordination 493

1 Review of Electric Power Fundamentals

OBJECTIVES

After studying this chapter, you will be able to:

- Describe the basic electrical units for current, voltage, resistance, power, and energy.
- Explain the characteristics of series and parallel circuits.
- Describe the additional relationships for alternating currents.
- Recognize the use of phasor diagrams.
- Discuss the effects of inductance and capacitance in alternating current circuits.
- Calculate the impedance and power factor of alternating current circuits.
- Describe the single-phase, three-wire system.
- Describe the relationships of three-phase systems.
- Explain the characteristics of the wye and delta configurations.
- Calculate the line currents and the power of three-phase systems.
- Recognize the problems associated with third harmonics.
- Describe the basic relationships for a transformer and calculate its rated currents.
- Define and properly use the terms nominal voltage, rated voltage, and voltage class.
- Recognize the preferred standard voltages.

INTRODUCTION

The purpose of this chapter is to cover the fundamentals of electricity that will enable the reader to understand the material presented in the balance of this book. Of necessity, the coverage can only be an overview of the basic electrical relationships. For the reader who has had no prior formal training in electrical circuit theory, it is to be hoped that the material presented here will encourage him or her to do further study, using any one of the many textbooks entirely devoted to circuit theory. To this end, a few of the available books are listed in the bibliography. For the reader who has had prior formal training in electrical circuits, it is to be hoped that the material presented here will serve as a good review of the fundamentals of electricity.

As mentioned in the preface, the electrical system is used to transmit energy throughout the building to an exact point, where the energy is then converted to other forms, that is, heat, light, and kinetic. The flow of electrical energy through the feeders and circuits that radiate out from the power source to the utilization points must be understood in order to properly select the components of the system.

1.1 BASIC ELECTRICAL UNITS

The flow of electricity through a circuit is often equated to the flow of liquid through a pipe. For the latter, there is a rate of flow of the liquid, a pressure to force the liquid through the pipe, and a resistance to the flow of the liquid. Similarly, in an electrical circuit there is a rate of flow of electricity (the current), a pressure to force the current through the circuit (the voltage), and a resistance to the flow of current. The basic electric circuit is shown in Figure 1.1. Let us examine these basic relationships in more detail.

1.1.1 Current

All matter is made up of atoms. Each atom has a nucleus around which electrons orbit in a manner similar to the planets revolving around the sun. Depending on the structure of the atom, some electrons are able to move freely from one atom to an adjacent atom. Normally, the movement of electrons within the matter is random; that is, there is no net movement in a specific direction. However, when a force is applied to the ends of the matter, there is a net drift

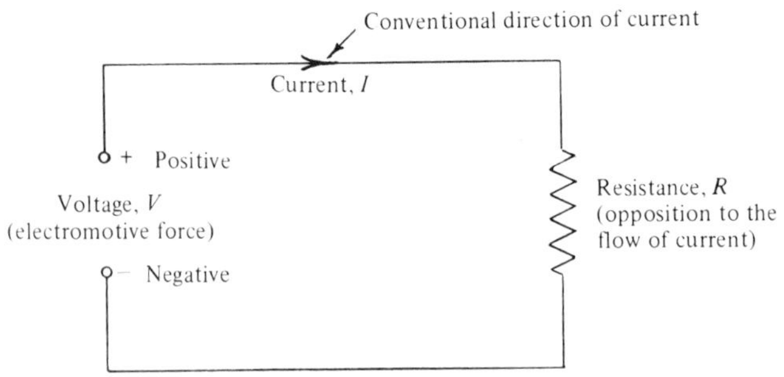

FIGURE 1.1

Basic electric circuit

There must be a complete loop before any current can flow.

of electrons in one direction. This net drift of electrons constitutes an electrical current.

The atomic structure of metals is such that there are electrons in the outer orbit that are relatively free to move from one atom to another. Metals are therefore classified as conductors, with silver having the highest conductivity, copper 95% relative conductivity, and aluminum about 60% relative conductivity. On the other hand, the atomic structure of insulators is such that relatively few free electrons are available; therefore, for all practical purposes, insulators are unable to carry any current.

Before any current can flow, an electric circuit must form a complete loop, as shown in Figure 1.1. Current is a quantity since it is a measure of the net drift of electrons through a conductor, that is, the rate of flow of the electric medium per unit of time. The symbol for current is I (from intensity of electron flow) and the unit of measure is the ampere (A). It has been calculated that 1 ampere is equal to 1 coulomb (6.25×10^{18} electrons) passing a given point in 1 second. If you are wondering why such an awkward number, it must be remembered that the electrical units were established before the electron theory for matter was formulated. Since the precise measurement of the rate of flow of electrons is difficult, the SI definition of the *ampere is the constant current that, if maintained in two straight parallel conductors of infinite length of negligible circular cross section and placed 1 meter apart in vacuum, would produce between these conductors a force equal to* 2×10^{-7} *newton per meter of length.*

1.1.2 Voltage

As we have already mentioned, for current to flow in a conductor, a force must be applied to the ends of the conductor. This force is called the *electromotive force* (electron moving force). The electromotive force (emf) can be produced by chemical means (for example, a battery) or by electromechanical means (a generator). The voltage is then a measure of the electromotive force produced by the source. The general symbol for voltage is V, and the unit of measurement is the volt, also symbol V. *One volt is the potential difference between two points in an electrical circuit when the energy involved in moving 1 coulomb of electrons from the one point to the other is 1 joule*. Thus, the volt is equated to the SI unit of energy, the joule, which is defined in Section 1.1.4. Note that the term voltage may also be applied to the potential difference across an element within a circuit, as is explained in the next section.

The direction of current flow within a circuit is determined by the polarity of the source voltage. The polarity in turn is designated by positive and negative terminals. The conventional current direction is such that current flows through the circuit from the positive terminal to the negative terminal of the source, as shown in Figure 1.1. Unfortunately, this is opposite to the direction of flow of the electrons through the circuit. Again, the discrepancy arises from the fact that the laws governing electricity were established long before the electron theory was formulated. Readers who refer to other books for additional reading on electrical circuits should always check whether the author is using the conventional current direction or is in fact using the direction of electron flow. If the latter, then relationships such as the right-hand rule are referred to as the left-hand rule.

1.1.3 Resistance and Ohm's Law

The resistance of a circuit is a measure of the opposition to the flow of the current through the circuit. For a circuit with a constant resistance, there is a direct relationship between the current that flows and the voltage that is applied. If the voltage is doubled, then the current will double; if the voltage is tripled, then the current will triple. In other words, for a given circuit, the ratio of the applied voltage to the current is a constant. This relationship can be expressed in equation form thus:

$$R = \frac{V}{I} \tag{1.1}$$

where V = voltage
I = current
R = resistance

This basic relationship is known as Ohm's law. Note that the resistance is a measure of the voltage required per ampere of current that flows and, as such, a unit of volts per ampere could have been adopted. However, the ohm was selected as the unit of electrical resistance with the symbol Ω (capital Greek letter omega). *One ohm is the electrical resistance that allows exactly 1 ampere to flow when exactly 1 volt is applied.*

Note that resistance is a quality of the conducting material. The term *resistor* then applies to a device designed to have a specific resistance. Ohm's law can be used in many ways to solve electrical circuit problems, as shown in the following examples.

EXAMPLE 1.1

If 120 V is applied to a circuit and the current is measured at 10 A, calculate the resistance of the circuit.

Solution

From Ohm's law,

$$R = \frac{V}{I} = \frac{120}{10} = 12\ \Omega$$

EXAMPLE 1.2

If 120 V is applied to a circuit that has 15 Ω of resistance, calculate the current that will flow.

Solution

Rearranging Ohm's law,

$$I = \frac{V}{R} = \frac{120}{15} = 8 \text{ A}$$

EXAMPLE 1.3

The current flowing through a 5 Ω resistor is 20 A. Calculate the potential difference across the resistor.

Solution

Rearranging Ohm's law again,

$$V = IR = 20 \times 5 = 100 \text{ V}$$

Note the use of the term potential difference in Example 1.3. Previously, voltage was described as a measure of the electromotive force applied to a circuit. However, voltage can also represent a difference in potential across a circuit element. This potential difference is more commonly referred to as *voltage drop*.

Refer to Figure 1.2. Voltmeter V_1 measures the voltage of the source and voltmeter V_2 measures the voltage across the resistance R. When the switch is closed, both voltmeters read the same since the voltage drop across the resistance must match the emf of the source. Next, the switch is opened. V_1 will still show a reading as the emf of the source is still present. However, voltmeter V_2 now reads zero, as there can be no voltage drop across the resistance when there is no current flowing through it. In fact, the voltage drop across a circuit element is often called the *IR drop*.

In a circuit where it is important to differentiate between the source voltage and the voltage drops, the symbol E is used to designate the source voltage and the symbol V is used to designate the voltage drop. When the switch is closed and current is flowing, the circuit is referred to as a *closed* or *energized* circuit, and when the switch is opened, the circuit is referred to as an *open* or *de-energized* circuit.

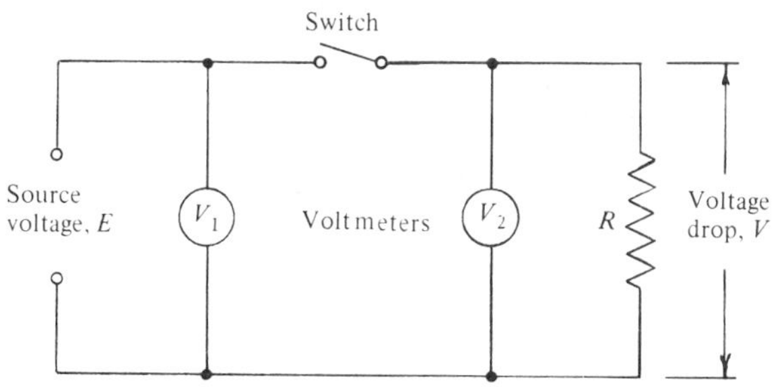

FIGURE 1.2

Difference between source voltage and voltage drop

1.1.4 Power and Energy

We return again to the basic function of an electric circuit and that is to transmit energy. Thus, there must be a point where energy is put into the circuit (the source) and a point where energy is taken out of the circuit (the load). Energy can most easily be defined as the ability to do work. Work, in turn, can be thought of as the process of transforming energy from one form into another. An electric motor converts electrical energy into kinetic (mechanical) energy, an electric heater converts electrical energy into thermal energy (heat), and a light bulb converts electric energy into light. Energy and work are numerically equal, and the same unit of measurement is used for both. The SI unit for energy is the joule (J). *One joule is the energy required to move an object 1 meter against a force of 1 newton.* Note that the joule is defined in mechanical terms. It is desirable that the same unit of energy be used for both mechanical and electrical systems so that calculations can be readily related from one system to the other. Therefore, the equivalent amount of electrical energy is also called a joule.

Power is the rate at which energy is converted or in other words the rate of doing work. The symbol for power is P, and the SI unit of measurement is the watt (W). *One watt is the rate of doing work when 1 joule of energy is expended in 1 second.* For large units of power, the kilowatt (kW), which equals 1000 watts, is used.

By combining the definitions for the volt and the ampere and rationalizing their units, the following relationship is derived:

$$P = VI \tag{1.2}$$

where P is the power in watts. This is one of the most useful equations in electrical technology; that is, the power in watts is the product of the volts times the amperes. Substituting $V = IR$ from Ohm's law into Equation 1.2 gives the following:

$$P = I^2R \tag{1.3}$$

The following examples illustrate the use of these power relationships.

EXAMPLE 1.4

If 120 V is applied to a circuit and the resulting current is measured at 10 A, calculate the power.

Solution

From Equation 1.2,

$$P = VI = 120 \times 10 = 1200 \text{ W}$$

■ EXAMPLE 1.5

The current flowing through a 15 Ω resistor is 20 A. Calculate the power.

Solution

From Equation 1.3,

$$P = I^2R = (20)^2 \times 15 = 6000 \text{ W}$$
$$= 6.0 \text{ kW}$$

■ EXAMPLE 1.6

Calculate the current drawn by a 120 V, 100 W light bulb when it is energized.

Solution

Rearranging Equation 1.2,

$$I = \frac{P}{V} = \frac{100}{120} = 0.833 \text{ A}$$

It is important that the reader not only follow the mathematical calculations in the previous examples but also realize the information being provided. In Example 1.4, the values given apply to a circuit and therefore the watts calculated not only indicate the power being supplied but also represent the total power being dissipated throughout the circuit (that is, turned into another form). In Example 1.5, the values given apply to a resistor (an element in the circuit), and therefore the watts calculated indicate the power being dissipated by the resistor (that is, turned into heat). This resistor could be just one of several elements connected into the circuit. Note that the power dissipated through a resistance is directly proportional to the square of the current. If the current is doubled, the heat generated is increased four times. This is important to remember with regard to feeders and circuits supplying utilization equipment. The heat given off due to the resistance of the conductors is power that for all practical purposes is a loss to the system. This loss is often referred to as the *I^2R loss*. In Example 1.6, the values given also apply to a single device (the light bulb), and Equation 1.2 is used to determine the current requirements of the device.

Remembering again that a watt is 1 joule per second, then 1 joule of electrical energy is equal to 1 watt-second. However, the unit of watt-second is very small, so a more practical unit is the kilowatt-hour (kWh). The kilowatt is 1000 watts and 1 hour is 3600 seconds. Therefore, 1 kilowatt-hour is equal to 1000 × 3600 or 3,600,000 watt-seconds or joules.

■ EXAMPLE 1.7

A 100 W light bulb burns for 24 h. The rate for electrical energy is 5 cents/kWh. Calculate the cost of operating the light bulb.

Solution

$$\text{Energy consumed} = \frac{100}{1000} \times 24 = 2.4 \text{ kWh}$$

$$\text{Cost of energy} = 2.4 \times 5 = 12 \text{ cents} = \$0.12$$

All the foregoing has been based on the SI system of units. Fortunately, both the English and the SI units for electrical measurements are the same. However, the units of mechanical power are different. The English system is based on the unit of the horsepower (hp), which is equal to doing work at the rate of 550 foot-pounds per second. The conversion factor between the horsepower and the watt is then:

$$1 \text{ hp} = 746 \text{ W} = 0.746 \text{ kW} \tag{1.4}$$

EXAMPLE 1.8

Determine the rating in kilowatts of a 10 hp motor.

Solution

$$10 \text{ hp} = 10 \times 0.746 = 7.46 \text{ kW}$$

1.2 CIRCUIT ARRANGEMENTS

Section 1.1 dealt with the basic electrical relationships of a simple circuit. Practical circuits can consist of more than one circuit element. The configuration in which these elements are connected into the circuit determines whether it is a series circuit, a parallel circuit, or a combination of the two.

1.2.1 Series Circuit

A *series circuit* is one in which all the elements are connected end to end so that there is only one complete path for the current. Figure 1.3 shows a circuit with three elements connected in series. The

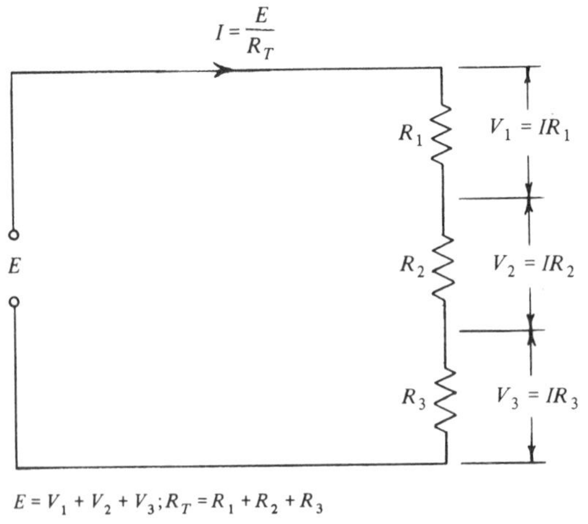

FIGURE 1.3

Series circuit with three elements

characteristics of a series circuit are that the current through each element is the same, but the voltage across each element can be different. The voltage across each element (V_1, V_2, and V_3), from Ohm's law, is the product of the current times the specific resistance of the element. The applied voltage E must equal the sum of the individual voltage drops across the circuit elements. The following example illustrates the relationships for a series circuit.

EXAMPLE 1.9

The values of the circuit elements in Figure 1.3 are $R_1 = 10\ \Omega$, $R_2 = 20\ \Omega$, and $R_3 = 30\ \Omega$. The source voltage E is 120 V. Calculate (a) the current flowing in the circuit and (b) the voltage drop across each element.

Solution

(a) Total resistance $R_T = 10 + 20 + 30 = 60\ \Omega$

$$I = \frac{E}{R_T} = \frac{120}{60} = 2\ \text{A}$$

(b)

$$V_1 = IR_1 = 2 \times 10 = 20\ \text{V}$$

$$V_2 = IR_2 = 2 \times 20 = 40\ \text{V}$$

$$V_3 = IR_3 = 2 \times 30 = \underline{60}\ \text{V}$$

Total voltage drop = 120 V (same as voltage E)

The connection of load elements in series is not commonly found in circuits used in building electrical systems. First, any change in any one of the circuit elements affects the current through all elements. In the extreme, if one element fails (for example, a light bulb), then all the other circuit elements are also turned off. Second, the voltage across each element depends on its relationship with the total circuit resistance. Note that in Example 1.9 the ratio of the voltage drops is the same as the ratio of the resistances. If any of the circuit elements are changed or the number of elements altered, then the voltage across a particular element changes. Thus, it would be impossible to have the circuit elements designed for one specific rated voltage as the required operating voltage would depend on the circuit configuration.

While not normally thought of as a series circuit, one common circuit configuration nevertheless operates on the principle of a series circuit. All circuits have wiring connecting the load to the source. The resistance of the circuit wires is then in series with the load, as shown in Figure 1.4. The resistance of the circuit wires must be kept low enough so that the voltage across the load is within a few percentage points of the source voltage, as illustrated in the following example.

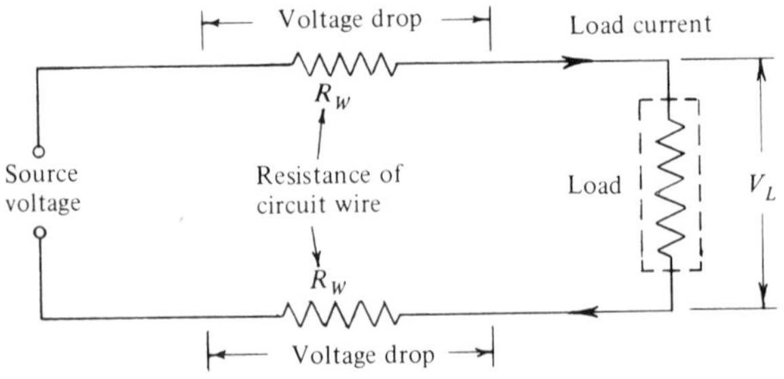

FIGURE 1.4

Practical circuit showing voltage drops in the circuit wires

■ EXAMPLE 1.10

The load in Figure 1.4 will draw a current of 10 A. The source voltage is 120 V. Calculate the maximum resistance R_W of each of the conductors if the voltage across the load V_L is to be within 2.0% of the source voltage.

Solution

The maximum voltage drop permitted is $0.02 \times 120 = 2.4$ V. Therefore, the maximum voltage drop per conductor is 1.2 V. From Equation 1.1,

$$R_W = \frac{V}{I} = \frac{1.2}{10} = 0.12\ \Omega \text{ maximum}$$

While the previous calculation could also be used for small alternating current circuits (for example, 15 amperes), it should be noted that the voltage drop calculation for large feeders is more complicated because of the inductive reactance of the feeder. This is discussed in detail in Section 11.3.

1.2.2 Parallel Circuit

A *parallel circuit* is one in which all the elements are connected between two common points so that there are multiple paths for the current. Figure 1.5 shows a circuit with three elements connected in parallel. The characteristics of a parallel circuit are that the voltage across each element is the same, but that the current through each element can be different. Note that these characteristics are the exact opposite to those for a series circuit. The currents through each element (I_1, I_2, and I_3), from Ohm's law, are inversely proportional to the resistance of each element. The total current I_T is the

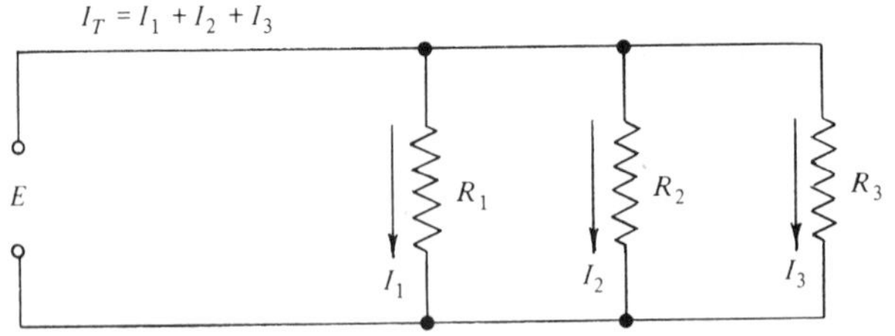

FIGURE 1.5

Parallel circuit with three elements

sum of the individual currents through each element. Finally, the total circuit power is the sum of the individual power requirements of the elements. The following example illustrates the relationships for a parallel circuit.

EXAMPLE 1.11

The values of the circuit elements in Figure 1.5 are $R_1 = 10\ \Omega$, $R_2 = 20\ \Omega$, and $R_3 = 30\ \Omega$. The source voltage E is 120 V. Calculate (a) the current through each element, (b) the total circuit current, and (c) the power requirements of each element and the total circuit power.

Solution

(a)

$$I_1 = \frac{E}{R_1} = \frac{120}{10} = 12\text{ A}; \quad I_2 = \frac{E}{R_2} = \frac{120}{20} = 6\text{ A}$$

$$I_3 = \frac{E}{R_3} = \frac{120}{30} = 4\text{ A}$$

(b)

$$I_T = I_1 + I_2 + I_3 = 12 + 6 + 4 = 22\text{ A}$$

(c)

$$P_1 = I_1^2 R_1 = (12)^2 \times 10 = 1440\text{ W}$$

$$P_2 = I_2^2 R_2 = (6)^2 \times 20 = 720\text{ W}$$

$$P_3 = I_3^2 R_3 = (4)^2 \times 30 = \underline{480}\text{ W}$$

Total power of elements = 2640 W

Total power input to circuit = EI = 120 × 22 = 2640 W

These two power values must be equal.

Note that, even though the resistances of the three elements in the parallel circuit are the same as for the three elements in the series circuit in Example 1.9 and the source voltages are equal, the results are entirely different.

The parallel arrangement is the only practical way of connecting the load elements in a power circuit. In this way, other than the very minor voltage drops in the circuit wiring, the voltage applied across each element is independent of the other elements in the circuit. This is very important, for instance, in lighting systems where individual lights are continually being switched on and off.

With the parallel arrangement, as elements are added the total current increases and hence the total power increases. This power requirement is referred to as the load on the circuit. In subsequent chapters that deal with circuits, you will find very little reference to the resistance (or impedance in alternating current circuits) of the individual circuit elements, but rather the emphasis is on the load that each element adds to the circuit. However, do not lose sight of the fact that as the load increases (that is, as elements are added in parallel) the total equivalent resistance of the circuit is decreasing. Therefore, do not think of the load on a circuit in terms of resistance (or impedance), but rather in terms of power requirements. With a fixed voltage, the power is directly proportional to the current (overlooking the power factor, which is discussed later with regard to alternating current circuits).

1.3 ALTERNATING CURRENT RELATIONSHIPS

Although not specifically mentioned, all the discussions to this point have been based on direct currents. With direct current (dc), the voltage is constant in magnitude and polarity and the current flows constantly in one direction. With alternating current (ac), as the term implies, the voltage is continuously varying in magnitude and polarity, and the current is continuously changing direction. With steady dc circuits, only the resistance need be of concern. With ac circuits, the additional parameters of inductance, capacitance, and power factor must be considered. This, in turn, requires an understanding of sine waves, frequency, rms values, impedance, and phase relationships.

If the use of alternating currents causes extra problems, the first question must then be: Why use ac systems? There are two very important reasons. First, the voltage levels can be easily raised or lowered by means of a transformer, as described in Section 1.7. Second, ac systems allow the use of the squirrel-cage induction motor, which is very simple in construction, requiring no commutator bars and brushes, and the like, as discussed in Section 2.5.

1.3.1 Sine Waves, Cycles, and Frequency

The voltages and currents of ac systems vary in a sinusoidal manner; that is, their waveforms vary according to the sine function of an angle over a linear period of time. Other waveforms could be used (for example, square or sawtooth), but the sine wave is the only waveform with a rate of change that in itself is also sinusoidal. This is shown in Sections 1.4.1 and 1.4.2 with respect to inductance and capacitance.

The shape of the sine wave is obtained from the trigonometric relationship of the sine of each angle throughout the 360° of a complete circle or revolution, as shown in Figure 1.6. In the diagram, the circle is shown divided into 12 equal segments of 30° each. The vertical distance from the zero axis of each 30° segment (that is, the sine of the angle) is projected to outline the waveform. One cycle is the complete change of the varying quantity from zero through a positive peak, through a negative peak, and back to zero, as indicated.

The horizontal axis of the waveform is marked in degrees from 0 to 360. However, the horizontal axis also represents time. The time to complete one cycle is called the *period*. The *frequency* is the

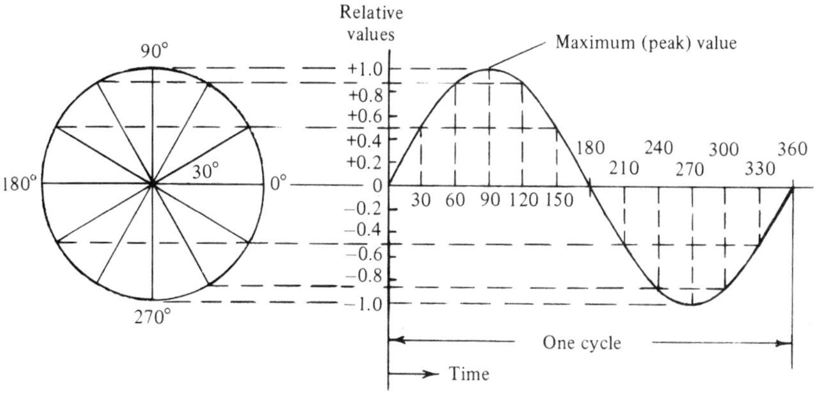

FIGURE 1.6

Development of the sine wave

number of cycles completed in 1 second. The unit for frequency is the hertz (Hz). One hertz equals one cycle per second. The standard frequency for the United States and Canada is 60 hertz. Europe and much of the rest of the world have standardized on 50 hertz. A 60 hertz system is one in which the voltage and current alternate through 60 cycles each second. The period for each cycle is therefore $\frac{1}{60}$ or 0.0167 second.

Since the magnitude of a sine wave voltage or current is continuously varying with time, the magnitude at one specific instant of time is referred to as the *instantaneous value*. For example, at 0°, 180°, and 360°, the instantaneous value, as per Figure 1.6, is zero. At 90°, the instantaneous value has reached its maximum positive value, which is therefore referred to as the *maximum* or *peak* value of the quantity.

1.3.2 Root-Mean-Square Values

Since the use of sine wave alternating voltages and currents is so common, it is desirable to have a method by which their magnitudes can be easily specified. However, in doing so, the fundamental relationships of the volt, the ampere, and the watt as they apply to dc circuits must not be altered.

Referring to the shape of the sine wave, we can see that the average value of an ac current is zero since the negative half cycle exactly matches the positive half cycle. Therefore, the average value cannot be used as a means of specifying the magnitude of the current. The rational method then is to establish an effective value that represents the magnitude of ac current that in terms of power is equivalent to a steady dc current of the same magnitude. The power dissipated by a resistor is expressed in Equation 1.3 as $P = I^2R$. With ac systems, the instantaneous power is also varying, as shown in Figure 1.14(a). The equivalent constant power over one cycle is the average or mean value of the varying power. To obtain the average power using Equation 1.3, the instantaneous values of the current over one complete cycle must be squared, and the average or mean of these values calculated. The effective value of the current is then the square root of this mean value. (Note that the value of the resistance is a constant throughout all these calculations.) A similar set of calculations can also be done for the ac voltage.

The effective value of the ac current and voltage is also known as the *root-mean-square* (rms) *value,* which describes the operation to obtain the value, that is, taking the square root of the mean value of the current or voltage squared. These calculations result in the following relationships:

$$E = \frac{E_{max}}{\sqrt{2}} = 0.7071E_{max} \tag{1.5}$$

$$I = \frac{I_{max}}{\sqrt{2}} = 0.7071I_{max} \tag{1.6}$$

where E and I = rms values
E_{max} and I_{max} = maximum or peak values

Note that no subscript is applied to the rms value as it is understood that, unless otherwise indicated, any reference to an ac voltage or current is to the rms value. The meters installed in ac systems record the rms values of the voltage and current.

EXAMPLE 1.12

Calculate the maximum or peak voltage of a 120 V ac system (the 120 V being the rms value).

Solution

Rearranging Equation 1.5,

$$E_{max} = \sqrt{2} \times 120 = 170 \text{ V}$$

These voltages are shown graphically in Figure 1.7.

With the adoption of the rms values for ac circuits, the relationships developed for dc circuits are still valid. For example, a 120 volt, 100 watt light bulb has the same light output, whether it is connected to a 120 volt ac circuit or a 120 volt dc circuit. All the calculations shown in Examples 1.1 to 1.11 are still valid for ac circuits, providing that the circuits consist only of resistive elements. The effects of inductance and capacitance are discussed in Section 1.4.

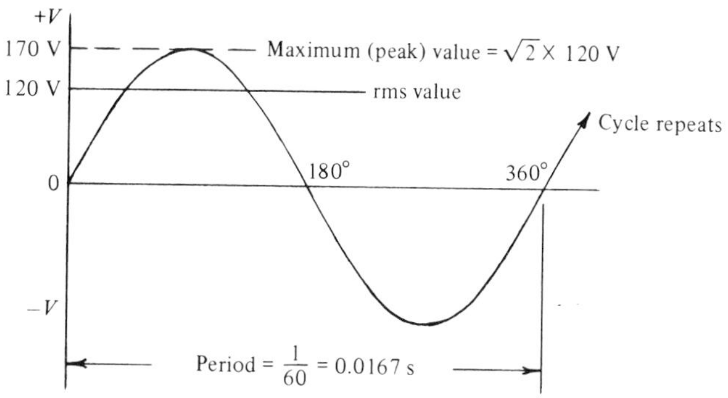

FIGURE 1.7

Voltage waveform for 120 V, 60 Hz system

1.3.3 Phasor Diagrams

With dc circuits, since both the voltage and the current are steady, there is no need to worry about any time relationship between the two quantities. However, with ac circuits, the voltage and current, as previously discussed, are time-varying quantities, that is, a quantity whose magnitude is continually changing with respect to time. Therefore, the time relationship between the voltage and the current is important. This time relationship is referred to as the *phase relationship*. With reference to Figure 1.6, the time scale for the sine wave is also marked with respect to the degrees of revolution around the circle. Therefore, this time or phase relationship can be expressed in terms of a *phase angle*.

When an ac voltage is applied to a circuit that has only resistance, the resulting current has the same time relationship; that is, as the voltage changes, the current changes proportionally at the same instant of time. Thus, the two quantities vary together and are said to be *in phase* with each other, as shown in Figure 1.8(a).

Not all circuits, however, are purely resistive in nature. Many circuits have characteristics (to be discussed in Section 1.4) that result in the voltage and current being out of phase with each other; that is, they do not both pass through the zero axis and reach their maximum values at the same instant of time. Figure 1.8(b) shows the case where the current passes through the zero axis after the voltage does and reaches its maximum value after the voltage does. In other words, the current is lagging in time with respect to the voltage and is said to be a *lagging current*. Since each point on the current sine wave is 45° behind the equivalent point on the voltage sine wave, the phase angle is −45°.

Figure 1.8(c) shows the case where the current passes through the zero axis before the voltage and reaches its maximum value before the voltage. In other words, the current is leading in time with respect to the voltage and is said to be a *leading current*. Since each point on the current sine wave is 30° ahead of the equivalent point on the voltage sine wave, the phase angle is +30°. Note that a lagging

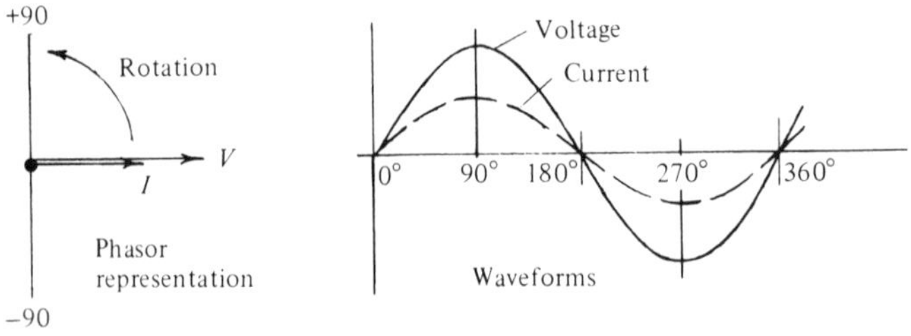

(a) Voltage and current in phase

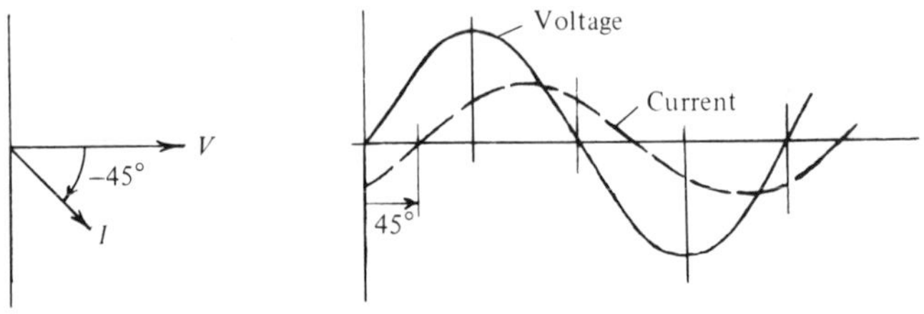

(b) Current lagging the voltage by 45°

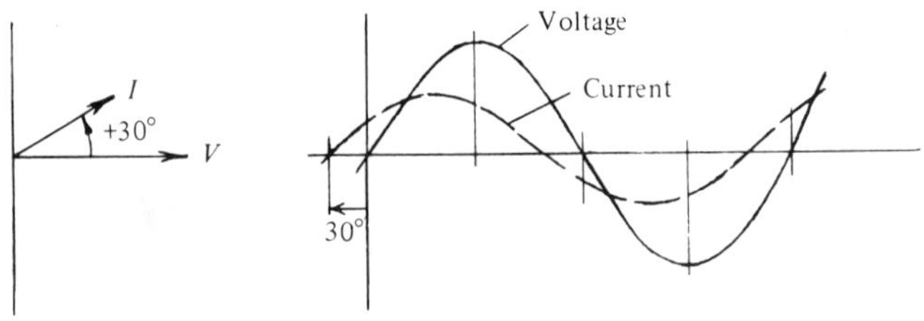

(c) Current leading the voltage by 30°

FIGURE 1.8

Phase relationships and phasor diagrams for ac voltages and currents

phase angle is regarded as negative and a leading phase angle as positive.

Up to this point, we have represented ac quantities by means of sine waves. However, a much simpler method is to use the phasor diagram such as shown to the left of each set of sine waves in Figure 1.8. Each quantity is represented by a straight line drawn from a common point, with its length scaled for the magnitude and its direction indicating the phase relationship. It is normal to show the voltage phasor horizontally from left to right as the reference. Where it is necessary to designate the phase relationship of a voltage or current, the polar notation $V\underline{/\theta}$ or $I\underline{/\theta}$ is used. V or I represents the scalor magnitude of the quantity (usually the rms value), and θ represents the phase angle of the quantity with respect to a reference. For example, a 10 ampere current that lags the voltage by 30° is shown as 10 A $\underline{/-30°}$.

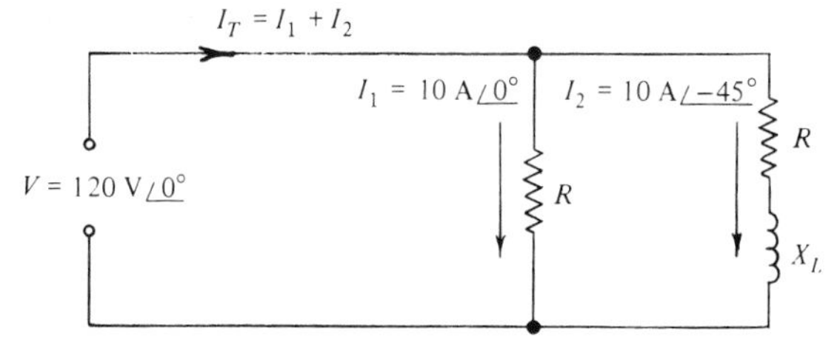

(a) Parallel circuit with branch currents not in phase

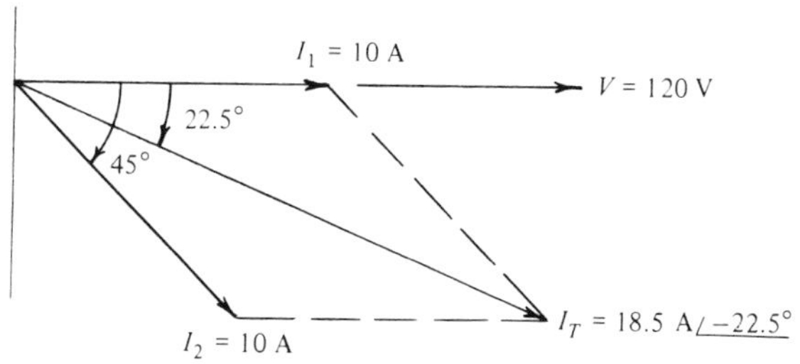

(b) Phasor diagram for the currents

FIGURE 1.9

Addition of two currents that are not in phase

With a parallel circuit, it is possible to have currents in the branches that are not in phase with each other, such as shown in Figure 1.9(a). The method of adding these branch currents to obtain the total current is shown graphically in Figure 1.9(b). Calculations using phasor quantities can also be done using phasor arithmetic. The reader is referred to the books on circuits listed in the bibliography for the methods employed in phasor arithmetic.

1.4 ALTERNATING CURRENT CIRCUITS

When a current flows through a resistor, regardless of whether the current is steady or continually changing in magnitude, all the electrical energy is converted to heat and is therefore lost to the circuit. Such is not the case with ac circuits, which have components with inductance or capacitance. Energy is stored in these components for part of the cycle and then returned to the circuit. As a result, the current is no longer in phase with the voltage, and circuit calculations must be based on the impedance and power factor of the circuit.

1.4.1 Effect of Inductance

When a current flows in a conductor, it creates a magnetic field that completely surrounds the conductor, as shown in Figure 1.10(a). The effect of this field is referred to as *electromagnetism*. The direction of the field, which is at right angles to the direction of the

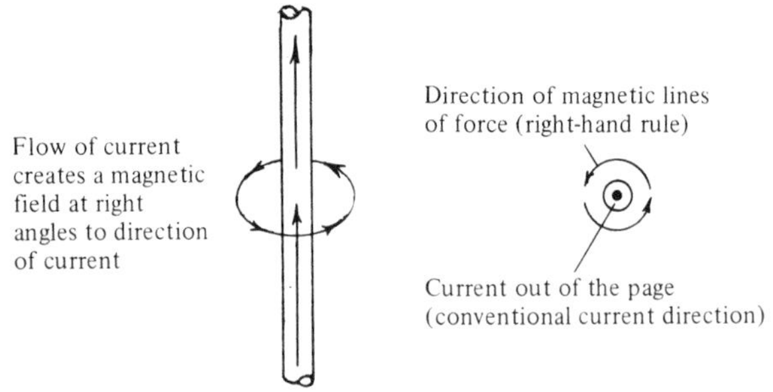

(a) Single conductor

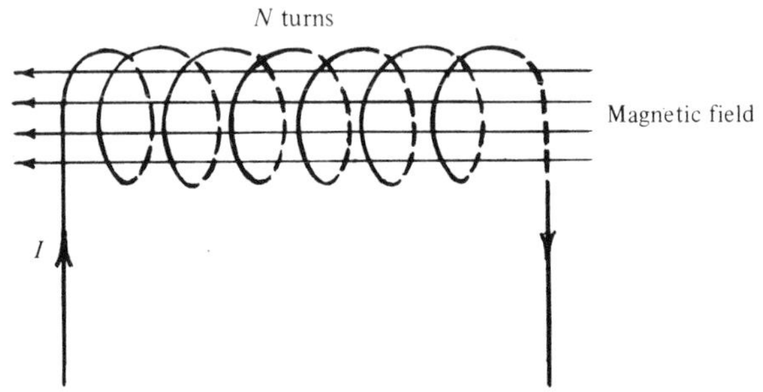

(b) Conductor arranged in form of a coil

FIGURE 1.10

Magnetic field around a current-carrying conductor

The strength of the magnetic field is directly proportional to the current I and the number of turns N in the coil (i.e., to the ampere-turns)

current, is determined by the right-hand rule; that is, with the thumb of the right hand pointing in the conventional direction of the current, the fingers then point in the direction of the magnetic lines of force. When the conductor is wound in the form of a coil, as shown in Figure 1.10(b), the magnetic field is concentrated into a smaller area and becomes much stronger; its strength is a function of the magnitude of the current and the number of turns in the coil (the ampere-turns). With a fixed number of turns, the field strength is proportional to the current.

With direct current, once the current has reached its steady state, the magnetic field remains constant and it has no further effect on the current. In contrast, alternating current is continuously changing, and therefore the magnetic field that it creates is also continuously changing. This changing field induces a voltage that opposes the change of current, a process referred to as *self-inductance* or, for short, *inductance*.

Faraday's law of electromagnetic induction states that the magnitude of an induced emf is proportional to the rate of change of the magnetic flux linkage. One example of this relationship is the electric generator in which a conductor is moved through a magnetic field, as discussed in Section 2.1. Another example is the transformer, as discussed in Section 1.7.

With self-inductance, the induced emf in the conductor is proportional to the rate of change of the magnetic field, which in turn means that the induced emf is proportional to the rate of change of current in the conductor. Figure 1.11(a) shows a theoretical circuit that has only inductance and no resistance. Figure 1.11(b) shows the

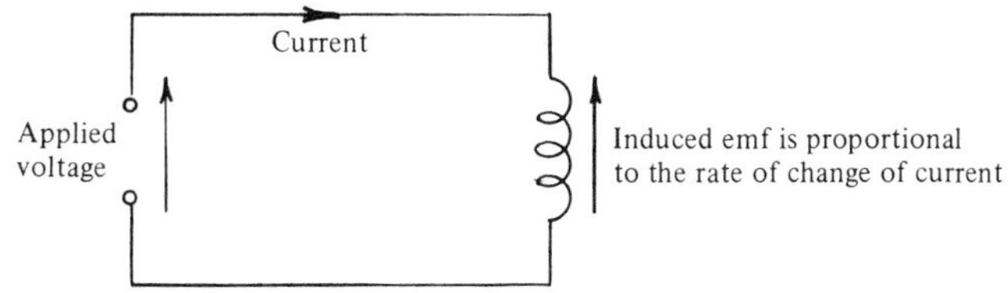

(a) Theoretical circuit with pure inductance

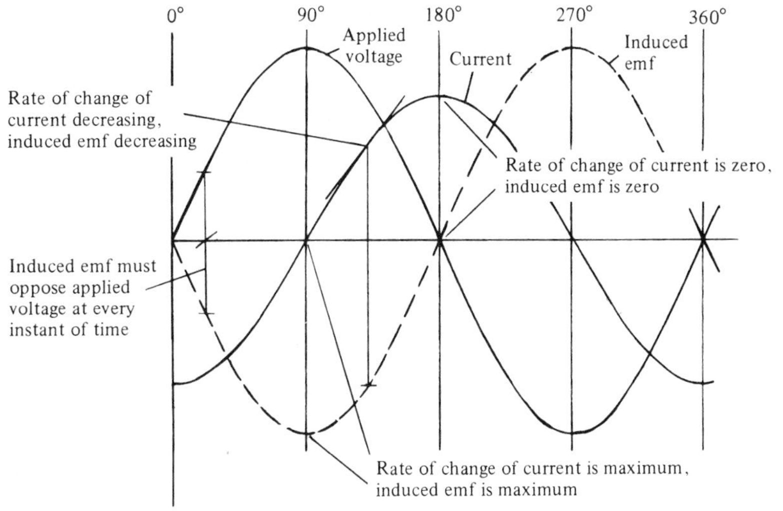

(b) Relationship of sine waves

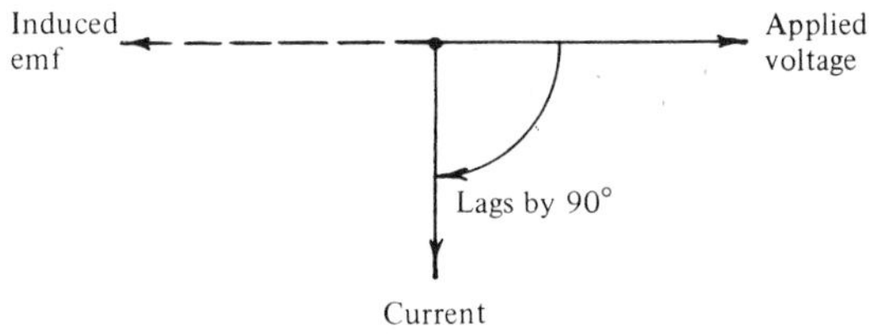

(c) Phasor diagram

FIGURE 1.11

Phase relationship between voltage and current in a purely inductive circuit relationship between the sine waves of the applied voltage, the induced emf, and the current. Note that the induced emf must oppose the applied voltage at every instant of time. The relationships over part of the cycle are detailed on the diagram. Following similar reasoning over the balance of the cycle, we can conclude that the current in a purely inductive circuit is also sinusoidal, but that it lags the applied voltage by 90°. The phasor diagram for this relationship is shown in Figure 1.11(c).

Rather than consider the opposition of the induced voltage to the flow of current in terms of volts, it can instead be considered as another circuit property that uses ohms as the unit of measurement of the opposition. This property is then referred to as *inductive reactance*, X_L (the subscript L denotes inductance). Inductive reactance is directly proportional to frequency, but with the fixed frequency of power systems it becomes a constant. In a practical circuit, which has resistance as well as inductive reactance, the combined effect of the two is referred to as the *impedance*. The calculation of the impedance of a circuit is covered in Section 1.4.3.

Many items normally encountered in electric power systems affect the inductive reactance of circuits, for example, motor windings, transformer windings, and lighting ballast windings. On large feeders carrying heavy currents, the inductive reactance of the feeder itself must be considered.

1.4.2 Effect of Capacitance

When a voltage is applied across two adjacent parallel plates separated by an insulator, an electric field is set up between the plates. This electric field is a form of energy. *Capacitance* is a measure of the ability to store energy in the electric field. The device that stores the energy is called a *capacitor*.

Figure 1.12(a) shows a diagrammatic representation of a capacitor. Current flows into and out of the capacitor as first the capacitor is charged by applying a voltage to it and then as it is discharged. When the voltage is reversed, the charging current is in the opposite direction.

Figure 1.12(c) shows the standard symbol used for capacitance in a circuit diagram. If a steady dc voltage is applied to the capacitor circuit, there can be no more current flow once the capacitor is charged because of the insulation between the plates. However, when an ac voltage is applied, the capacitor acts like a conductor, because the varying voltage causes the capacitor to be continuously charged and discharged. The circuit current (the charging current of the capacitor) is proportional to the rate of change of the applied voltage.

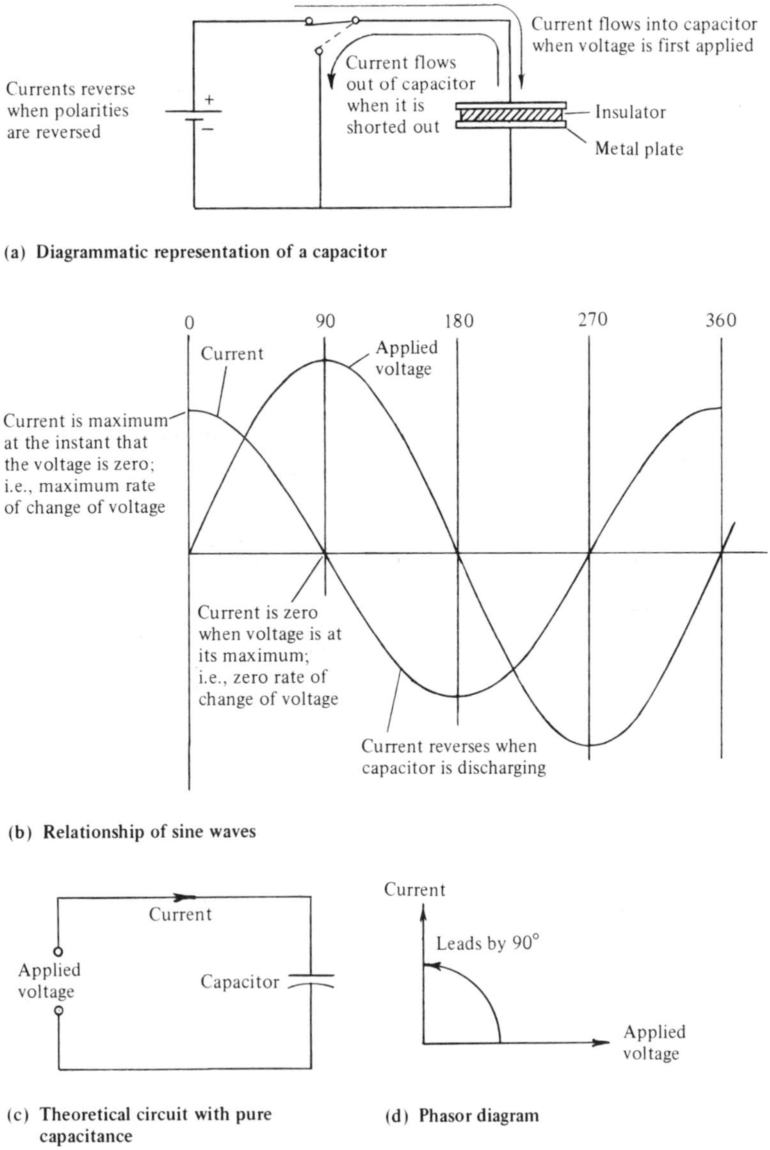

(a) Diagrammatic representation of a capacitor

(b) Relationship of sine waves

(c) Theoretical circuit with pure capacitance

(d) Phasor diagram

FIGURE 1.12

Phase relationship between voltage and current in a purely capacitive circuit

Figure 1.12(b) shows the relationship between the sine waves of the applied voltage and the resulting current. The relationship over the first part of the cycle is detailed on the diagram. Following similar reasoning for the balance of the cycle, we can conclude that the current in a purely capacitive circuit is also sinusoidal, but that it leads the voltage by 90°. The phasor diagram for this relationship is shown in Figure 1.12(d).

Similar to the approach taken with inductive reactance, the opposition to the flow of current through a capacitor can be considered as another circuit property that is measured in ohms. This property is then referred to as *capacitive reactance,* X_C (the subscript C denotes capacitance). Capacitive reactance is inversely proportional to frequency, but with the fixed frequency of power systems it becomes a constant.

The capacitive reactance also affects the total impedance of a circuit. However, in power systems encountered in buildings, the effect of capacitive reactance within the system itself is negligible. Capacitors themselves are used mainly for power factor correction, in which case they are connected in parallel with the system at specific points (see Section 1.4.4). The following section on impedance is therefore limited to the effect of resistance and inductive reactance in a circuit.

1.4.3 Impedance

The property that combines the effect of the circuit resistance and reactance is referred to as *impedance, Z.* Impedance is the total opposition to the flow of current in an ac circuit. The Ohm's law for ac circuits then becomes:

$$Z = \frac{E}{I} \tag{1.7}$$

where E and I = rms values of voltage and current
Z = impedance in ohms

In determining the value of the impedance of a circuit, the ohmic values of the resistances and reactances cannot just be added arithmetically to get the total because of their phase relationships.

Figure 1.13(a) shows a circuit that has resistance R and inductive reactance X_L in series. From Ohm's law, the voltage drop across the resistance is IR and that across the inductive reactance is IX_L. The IR drop is in phase with the current, but the IX_L drop leads the current by 90° (Figure 1.11; the current lags the voltage, and therefore the voltage leads the current). Figure 1.13(b) shows the phase relationship of these voltage drops and how they must add together to equal the applied voltage. Since the current is the common factor, the resistance R, the inductive reactance X_L, and the impedance can be represented by a right angle triangle, as shown in Figure 1.13(c). This diagram is referred to as the *impedance triangle*.

To facilitate the designation of the components of the impedance triangle, the j operator is introduced. The j operator is used to indicate that an electrical quantity is rotated through 90°, with a positive sign (+) indicating that rotation is counterclockwise and the

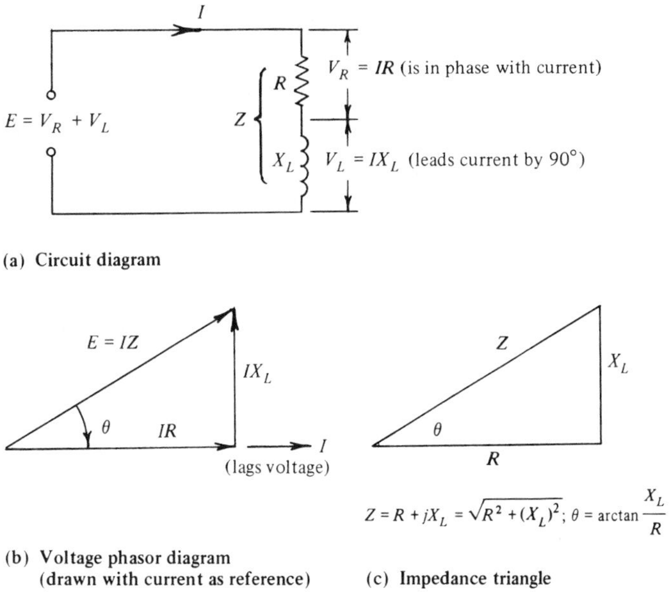

FIGURE 1.13

Impedance triangle for a circuit with resistance and inductance

negative sign (−) indicating that rotation is clockwise. Therefore, the impedance for the *RL* circuit of Figure 1.13, using rectangular notation, is $R + jX_L$. The impedance Z is represented by the hypotenuse of the right angle triangle and:

$$Z = R + jX_L = \sqrt{R^2 + (X_L)^2} \tag{1.8}$$

■ EXAMPLE 1.13

Refer to Figure 1.13. Assume that $R = 8\ \Omega$, $X_L = 6\ \Omega$, and $E = 120$ V. Calculate the magnitude of the current I and its phase relationship with the voltage.

Solution

From Equation 1.8,

$$Z = 8 + j6 = \sqrt{8^2 + 6^2} = 10\ \Omega$$

From Equation 1.7,

$$I = \frac{120}{10} = 12 \text{ A}$$

From the impedance triangle,

$$\theta = \arctan \frac{X_L}{R} = \arctan \frac{6}{8} = 36.9°$$

Using polar notation,

$$I = 12 \text{ A} \angle{-36.9°} \quad \text{(current lags the voltage)}$$

1.4.4 Power Factor

In a dc circuit, the power involved is the product of the voltage and current (Equation 1.2). For ac circuits, the calculation of the power is more involved, requiring the power factor of the circuit to be taken into account.

The power at any instant of time in an ac circuit is the product of the voltage and current at that same instant of time. First, let us consider a circuit that has only resistance, and therefore the current is in phase with the voltage. Figure 1.14(a) shows the instantaneous power plotted over one cycle for this case. Note that the power is always positive (that is, above the zero line). This results from the fact that, for every instant that the voltage is positive, the current is also positive, and for every instant that the voltage is negative, the current is also negative. Thus, even for the second half of the cycle, the power is still positive, since the product of two negative quanti-

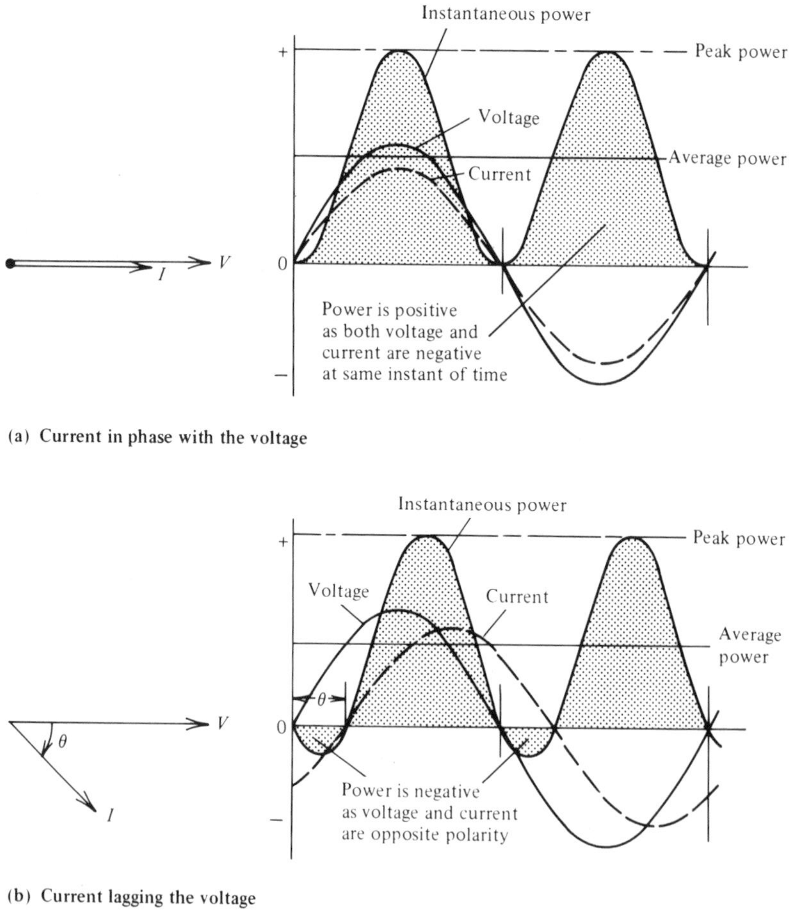

FIGURE 1.14

Plots of instantaneous power over one cycle

ties is a positive quantity. In a practical sense, this means that, regardless of the direction of current through the resistance, the electrical energy is being converted to heat. Positive power, which is electric power converted to another form and therefore lost to the circuit, is referred to as *active* power.

The average power over the complete cycle, as shown in Figure 1.14(a), is one-half of the peak power. This average power was used in Section 1.3.2 to establish the effective or rms values for the voltage and current. Therefore, the power for this circuit is equal to the product of the rms values of the voltage and current. As we will see, the power factor for this circuit is 100% or unity.

Next, we will consider the circuit shown in Figure 1.13(a), which has resistance and inductive reactance in series, with the result that the current lags the voltage. Figure 1.14(b) shows the instantaneous power plotted over one cycle for this circuit. Note that there are now two periods of time during the cycle where the power is negative. The negative power occurs over those periods of time, first when the voltage is positive and the current is negative and next when the voltage is negative and the current is positive. Negative power represents power that is being returned to the circuit as a result of the collapse of the magnetic field associated with the inductance (energy is stored during the positive portions of the cycle). Negative power is referred to as *reactive* power. Because of the reactive power, the average power over the cycle is less than that shown in part (a) for the same values of voltage and current. Therefore, the product of the rms voltage times the rms current no longer represents the positive or active power in the circuit. The product of the voltage and current is instead called the *apparent* power, since, if the voltage and current only are considered, it appears that the circuit uses this much power. The unit for apparent power is the volt-ampere (VA) or the kilovolt-ampere (kVA), which is equal to 1000 volt-amperes.

Refer to Figure 1.15(a), which shows the phasor relationship between the voltage and current as per Figure 1.14(b). The lagging current can be considered as being made up of two components, a component that is in phase with the voltage and a component that lags the voltage by 90°. The in-phase component is termed the active component since it is associated with the active (positive) power of the circuit. The 90° component is termed the reactive component since it is associated with the reactive (negative) power of the circuit.

Figure 1.15(b) shows the resulting power triangle obtained by multiplying each current component by the voltage. The horizontal side represents the active power in watts, the vertical side represents the reactive power in vars (volt-amperes reactive), and the

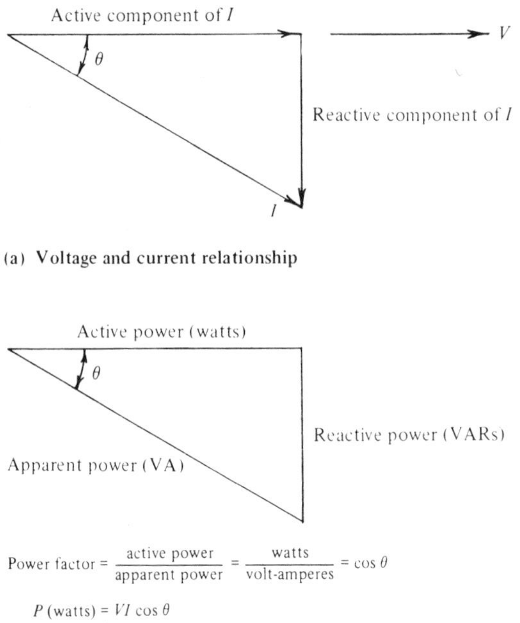

(a) Voltage and current relationship

(b) Power triangle

FIGURE 1.15

Power triangle for circuit with lagging power factor

hypotenuse represents the apparent power in volt-amperes. The term *power factor* is used to express the ratio between the active power and the apparent power. Therefore:

$$\text{Power factor} = \frac{\text{active power}}{\text{apparent power}} = \frac{\text{W}}{\text{VA}}$$

From the power triangle, we can see that the power factor is also equal to the cosine of the angle θ, which is also the phase angle between the current and voltage. This then leads to the power relationship for ac circuits:

$$P\ (\text{watts}) = VI \cos\theta \quad \textbf{(1.9)}$$

where $\cos\theta$ is the power factor. Power factor can be expressed as a decimal (for example, 0.80) or as a percentage (80%). Since the current in a circuit with inductive reactance lags the voltage, the power factor is a lagging power factor. For the case where the current leads the voltage, the power factor is a leading power factor. A power factor of 1.0 or 100% is referred to as *unity* power factor. Meters designed to read power in ac systems measure the active power and are therefore wattmeters or kilowattmeters.

■ **EXAMPLE 1.14**

For a 120 V, two-wire ac circuit, the wattmeter reads 1920 W and the ammeter reads 20 A. Calculate the power factor.

Solution

$$\text{Apparent power} = VI = 120 \times 20 = 2400 \text{ VA}$$

$$\text{Power factor} = \frac{1920}{2400} = 0.80 \quad (80\%)$$

Note that the meter readings in themselves do not indicate whether the power factor is leading or lagging. However, if any item in the circuit is inductive in nature (for example, a motor), then the power factor is lagging.

■ **EXAMPLE 1.15**

The load on a 240 V, two-wire ac circuit draws 15 A at a lagging power factor of 90%. Calculate the power.

Solution

From Equation 1.9,

$$P = 240 \times 15 \times 0.9 = 3240 \text{ W}$$

Note that the decimal form for the power factor is used.

■ **EXAMPLE 1.16**

The load on a 240 V, two-wire ac circuit is rated at 5.0 kW, 80% power factor. Calculate the current.

Solution

Rearranging Equation 1.9,

$$I = \frac{P}{V \cos \theta} = \frac{5 \times 1000}{240 \times 0.8} = 26 \text{ A}$$

When designing the circuits and feeders for loads which are rated in watts or kilowatts, it is imperative that the power factor of the load be known. Otherwise, the conductor size chosen may be too small for the actual current that will flow.

As previously mentioned, the reactive power of a system is the power that is alternately being stored in and returned from the magnetic fields associated with the inductive reactance. This power is surging back and forth in the system between the source and the load. The electric utility's meter that records the energy consumed on a customer's premises measures this energy on the basis of active power. However, the reactive power, as we have seen, requires that more current flow in the system than that required for the active power alone. Therefore, the utility assesses a penalty to customers whose systems operate at too low a power factor (for example, less than 90 percent).

For a system with an unsatisfactory power factor, power factor correction should be considered. Refer to Figure 1.12, which shows that a capacitor draws a current that leads the voltage by 90°. Capacitors can therefore be used to improve the power factor since the current they draw is 180° out of phase with the 90° lagging reactive current component of the system [Figure 1.15(a)]. By reducing the reactive component of the power, the load current drawn by the system is reduced. Capacitors can be individually connected to the terminals of equipment that has a poor power factor, such as induction motors (see Section 2.5.1 and Figure 2.15) and ballasts for lighting (see Section 4.2), or one central capacitor bank can be installed at the main service entrance. Synchronous motors can also be used for power factor correction. Section 2.4 and Figure 2.11(c) show that a synchronous motor, when the field is overexcited, operates with a leading power factor.

1.5 SINGLE-PHASE, THREE-WIRE SYSTEMS

The 120/240 volt, single-phase, three-wire system is the common arrangement used to supply power to individual residences and small commercial buildings. The three-wire configuration is shown in Figure 1.16(a). The diagram indicates that a single-phase transformer with two 120 volt secondary windings is the source. Note that the center connection between the two windings is grounded and that the conductor connected to that point is called the *neutral* since it operates at ground potential. The grounding of systems is fully discussed in Chapter 10.

The instantaneous direction of the line currents I_1 and I_2 are such that the neutral conductor only has to carry the difference between currents I_1 and I_2. When the two line currents are equal, the neutral current I_N is zero. Therefore, one advantage of this system is that the total of loads 1 and 2 can be supplied using only three wires. The second advantage is that two voltage levels are available.

The arrangement of circuits for a panelboard supplied from a single-phase, three-wire system is shown in Figure 1.16(b). For 120 volt equipment, the circuit is connected to one of the lines and the neutral. Two circuits connected to opposite lines can be connected to the same neutral conductor. For 240 volt equipment, the circuit is connected to the two lines through a two-pole breaker and there is no connection to the neutral. Panelboards and branch circuits are discussed in detail in Chapter 12.

1.6 THREE-PHASE SYSTEMS

Three-phase systems are universally used today to generate and transmit large amounts of electrical energy because of their many inherent technical and economic advantages. Initially, the easiest

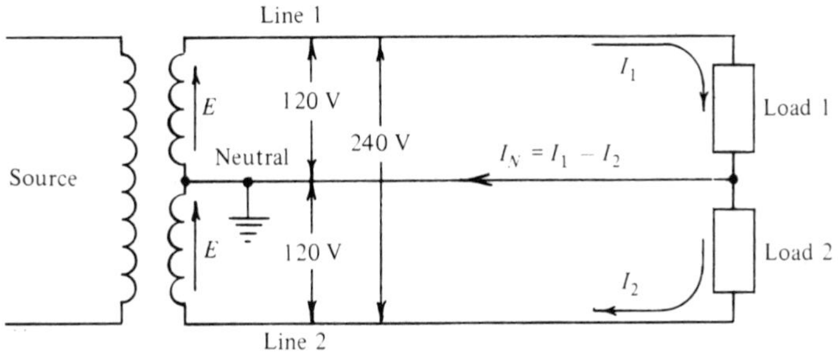

(a) System configuration

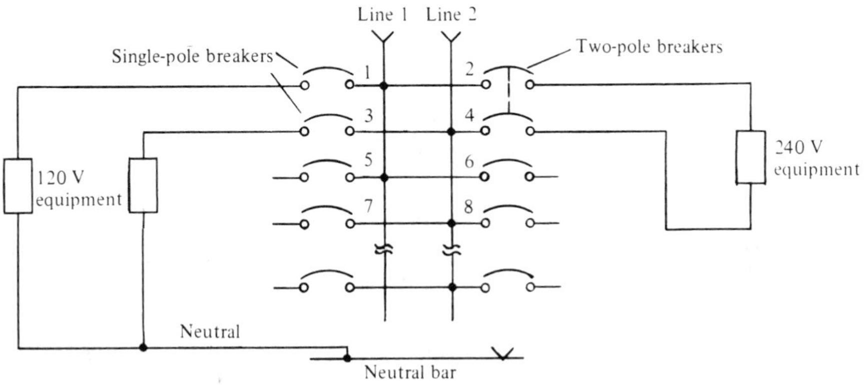

(b) Typical circuit arrangement in a panel

FIGURE 1.16

Single-phase, three-wire system

way to approach the concept of a three-phase system is to assume that three separate sources of emf are used, with each source generating a sine wave voltage that is identical in magnitude but, when compared on a time basis, is 120° out of phase with respect to the others. When combined into one system, each of these sources is then referred to as a phase: phase A, phase B, and phase C.

The sine waves for the three phase voltages are shown in Figure 1.17(a). Phase A is taken as the reference voltage, so it is shown passing through the zero voltage axis at 0° and reaching its maximum positive value at 90°. Each equivalent value of phase B then follows behind in intervals of time equivalent to 120° (one-third of a cycle). Similarly, each equivalent value of phase C follows behind phase A in intervals of time equivalent to 240° (two-thirds of a cycle). The resulting phasor diagram is shown in Figure 1.17(b).

In practice, three-phase power is produced using one generator. The phase emfs are generated by three separate sets of windings, which are mounted around the generator so that they are physically

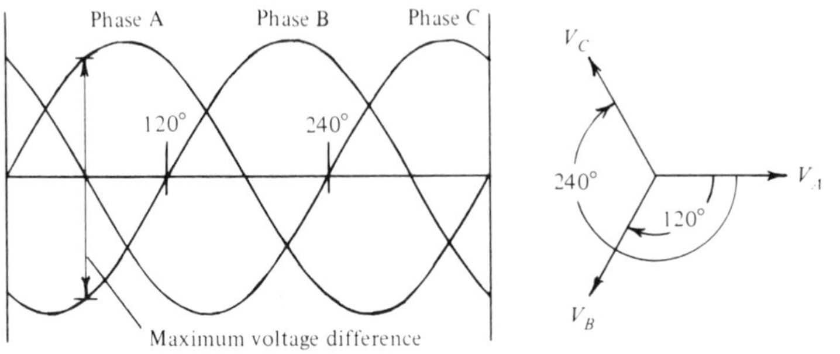

(a) Waveforms of the three-phase voltages

(b) Phasor diagram

FIGURE 1.17

Voltage relationships for three-phase systems

displaced 120 electrical degrees from each other. These windings can then be electrically connected in either a wye (Y) configuration or a delta (Δ) configuration.

1.6.1 Wye Configuration

With the wye configuration, one end of each winding is connected to a common point, as shown in Figure 1.18(a). The common point (n) is called the *neutral* and the opposite ends of the windings are called the *line terminals* (points a, b, and c). The voltage between each line terminal and the neutral is the line-to-neutral voltage (commonly referred to as the *phase voltage*), and the voltage between two line terminals is the line-to-line voltage (commonly referred to as the *line voltage*).

The line voltage is not the arithmetical sum of two phase voltages because of the 120° phase relationship. If we refer back to

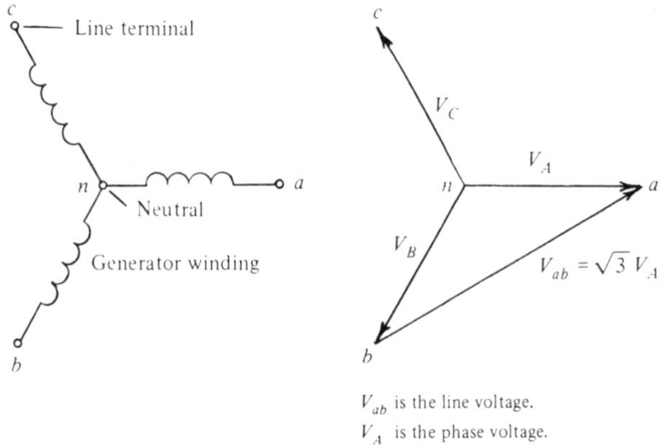

(a) Wye configuration

(b) Phasor diagram of voltages

FIGURE 1.18

Wye-connected, three-phase generator

Figure 1.17(a), the maximum voltage difference between two phase voltages does not occur when either one is at its maximum. In the case of phases A and B, the first maximum difference occurs at 60°, where each phase voltage has an instantaneous value that is less than its maximum. The exact relationship between the voltages can be determined by reference to the phasor diagram of Figure 1.18(b). By drawing the phasor V_{ab} between points b and a, it can be determined graphically and proved by phasor arithmetic that the line voltage is $\sqrt{3}$ or 1.732 times the phase voltage. Therefore, in a balanced wye system:

$$V_L = \sqrt{3}\ V_P = 1.732\ V_p \tag{1.10}$$

where V_L = line voltage (line to line)
V_P = phase voltage (line to neutral)

Since the neutral point of the wye configuration is also available in addition to the three line terminals, four wires can be used for connection to the loads in the system, as shown in Figure 1.19(a). The system is referred to as three-phase, four-wire. The neutral is grounded as described in Section 10.2. One common three-phase, four-wire system is designated 208Y/120 volts. In this case, the standard 120 volts is used for the line-to-neutral voltage, with the line-to-line voltage then becoming 1.732 times 120, or 208 volts. Another common system is designated 480Y/277 volts. In this case the standard 480 volts is used for the line-to-line voltage, with the line-to-neutral voltage then becoming 480 divided by 1.732, or 277 volts. It is a significant advantage for each system to have the two voltage levels available. For example, the 208Y/120 volt system provides 120 volts for single-phase loads, such as lighting and small appliances, and 208 volts for single-phase loads, such as electric heaters, and three-phase loads, such as motors.

Figure 1.19(a) shows a wye-connected load supplied from a three-phase, four-wire source. In a balanced system (that is, with identical loads connected to each phase), since the phase voltages are 120° out of phase with each other, the phase currents I_A, I_B, and I_C are also 120° out of phase with each other. The phase current through each load is also the line current that flows through the connecting wiring. The waveforms for the three phase currents are shown in Figure 1.19(b), and the phasor diagram is shown in Figure 1.19(c). The neutral current I_N is the sum of the three phase (line) currents. If the instantaneous values of each phase currents are measured, we can establish the fact that these currents always sum to zero. For example, the instantaneous relative values of the currents at 90° are $I_A = +1.0$, $I_B = -0.5$, and $I_C = -0.5$, which adds up

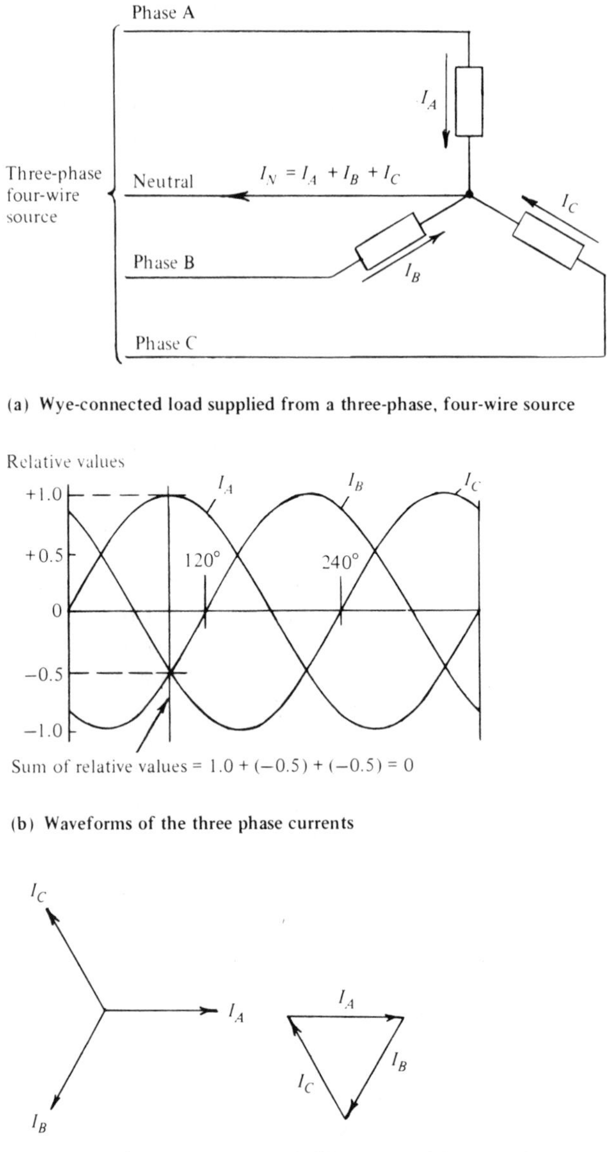

(a) Wye-connected load supplied from a three-phase, four-wire source

(b) Waveforms of the three phase currents

(c) Phasor diagram

(d) Phasor sum of three equal phase currents

FIGURE 1.19

Current relationships for a three-phase, four-wire system

to zero. This can also be verified by adding the phasors for each current end to end, as shown in Figure 1.19(d). The resulting triangle closes, indicating that the three currents sum to zero and therefore the neutral current is zero.

Even if the the load on one phase is disconnected (for example, the phase C load), the neutral current, which is the sum of the other two phase currents (I_A and I_B), is only the same magnitude as each of the phase currents themselves. Therefore, the neutral conductor of the system can be the same size as the phase (line) conductors. Another significant advantage of the three-phase, four-wire system is that three single-phase loads can be supplied using only four wires as compared to the six wires required if three separate two-wire circuits are used. This can result in substantial savings in the cost of the wiring throughout a building. The connection of single-phase branch circuit loads to three-phase, four-wire panelboards is discussed in detail in Section 12.5 and shown in Figure 12.5.

1.6.2 Delta Configuration

With the delta configuration, one end of each phase winding is connected to the end of the adjacent phase winding, as shown in Figure 1.20(a). This configuration is shown electrically in the form of a triangle designated by the Greek letter delta (Δ). The line connec-

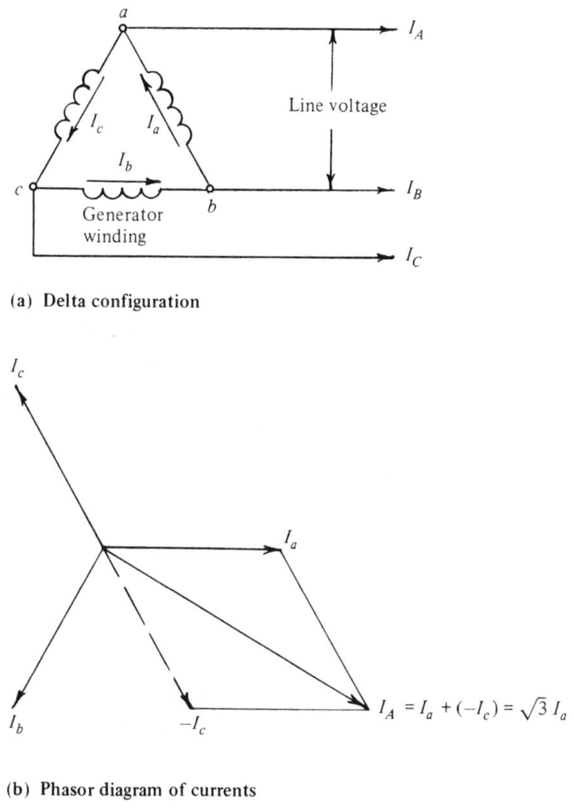

(b) Phasor diagram of currents

I_A is the line current.
I_a is the phase current.

FIGURE 1.20

Delta-connected, three-phase generator

tions are then made at the common connection between the phases. The line voltage is the same as the voltage across each winding (that is, the phase voltage). However, the line currents are not the same as the winding or phase currents. For example, as shown in Figure 1.20(b), the line current I_A is the vector sum of the phase current I_a (since it flows toward point a) plus the negative of phase current I_c (since it flows away from point a). It can be determined graphically and proved by phasor arithmetic that the line current is $\sqrt{3}$, or 1.732, times the phase current. Therefore, in a balanced delta system:

$$I_L = \sqrt{3} I_P = 1.732 I_P \tag{1.11}$$

where I_L = line current

I_P = phase current

Note that the same relationship holds with regard to a delta-connected load.

All delta systems are designated as being three-wire since there can be only three wires connected to this configuration. Common delta systems are 240 volt, three-phase, three-wire; 480 volt, three-phase, three-wire; and 600 volt, three-phase, three-wire. Delta systems are not normally used in buildings for supplying single-phase loads such as lighting because the system cannot be easily grounded. Where a load is primarily motors, such as in industrial plants, the delta system is commonly used. The advantages and disadvantages of the delta and wye systems are discussed in detail in Chapter 10.

1.6.3 Power Relationships

From the relationship developed for a single-phase circuit (Equation 1.9), the power associated with each individual phase, whether the wye or delta configuration, is $P_P = V_P I_P \cos\theta$, where all parameters are expressed in terms of phase values. Therefore, the total power for a balanced three-phase system is three times the phase power or $P = 3V_P I_p \cos\theta$. In a wye system, $I_P = I_L$, and from Equation 1.10, $V_P = V_L/\sqrt{3}$. Substituting these values in the foregoing gives:

$$P = 3\left(\frac{V_L}{\sqrt{3}}\right) I_L \cos\theta = \sqrt{3}\, V_L I_L \cos\theta$$

In a delta system, $V_P = V_L$ and, from Equation 1.11, $I = I_L/\sqrt{3}$. Substituting this in the foregoing gives:

$$P = 3V_L\left(\frac{I_L}{\sqrt{3}}\right) \cos\theta = \sqrt{3}\, V_L I_L \cos\theta$$

Therefore, the same expression can be used, regardless of whether the system is wye or delta:

$$P = \sqrt{3}\, V_L I_L \cos\theta = 1.732 V_L I_L \cos\theta \qquad \textbf{(1.12)}$$

where P = total three-phase power

V_L = line-to-line voltage

I_L = line current

$\cos\theta$ = power factor of the system

■ EXAMPLE 1.17

A three-phase load with an 80% power factor is supplied by a 208Y/120 system. The line current is 40 A. Calculate the power.

Solution

From Equation 1.12

$$P = 1.732 \times 208 \times 40 \times 0.80 = 11{,}528 \text{ W}$$
$$= 11.528 \text{ kW}$$

■ EXAMPLE 1.18

A 50 kW load with a 90% power factor is supplied from a 480 V delta system. Calculate the line current.

Solution

Rearranging Equation 1.12,

$$I_L = \frac{P}{1.732 V_L \cos\theta}$$
$$= \frac{50 \times 1000}{1.732 \times 480 \times 0.9} = 66.8 \text{ A}$$

If we refer back to Figure 1.14, it shows that, for a single-phase circuit, the power is pulsating, peaking twice in each cycle. If we were to plot the instantaneous power of a three-phase system, it would be a straight line. Even though the instantaneous power of each phase is pulsating, the peaks are spread out over the cycle, and the sum of these instantaneous powers is always the same value. Therefore, a further advantage of three-phase systems is that the power is constant. This results in very smooth operation with three-phase motors because they produce a constant torque at the shaft. In addition, three-phase motors are self-starting. In contrast, single-phase motors produce a pulsating torque that causes vibrations and noise, and they require a special winding and centrifugal switch to start. Therefore, three-phase motors are recommended for all but the very small fractional horsepower motors. Motors are discussed in detail in Chapter 2.

1.6.4 Third Harmonics

In the previous discussions on ac circuits and systems, it was assumed that the currents that flowed were always sinusoidal. However, that is not always the case. Nonsinusoidal currents result when the iron cores of transformers, motors, and the like, saturate during peak periods of the cycle. This periodic saturation causes the inductance of the associated winding to momentarily decrease, thus permitting a sudden increase in the instantaneous current. A typical waveform of the resulting current is shown in Figure 1.21(a). This distorted waveshape of the current can be reduced to a fundamental sine wave component plus a number of sine wave components at higher frequencies, which are referred to as *harmonics*. The most prominent is usually the third harmonic, which is a sine wave component that has a frequency three times the system frequency (that is, 180 hertz for the 60 hertz system). The fundamental and third-harmonic components are also shown in Figure 1.21(a).

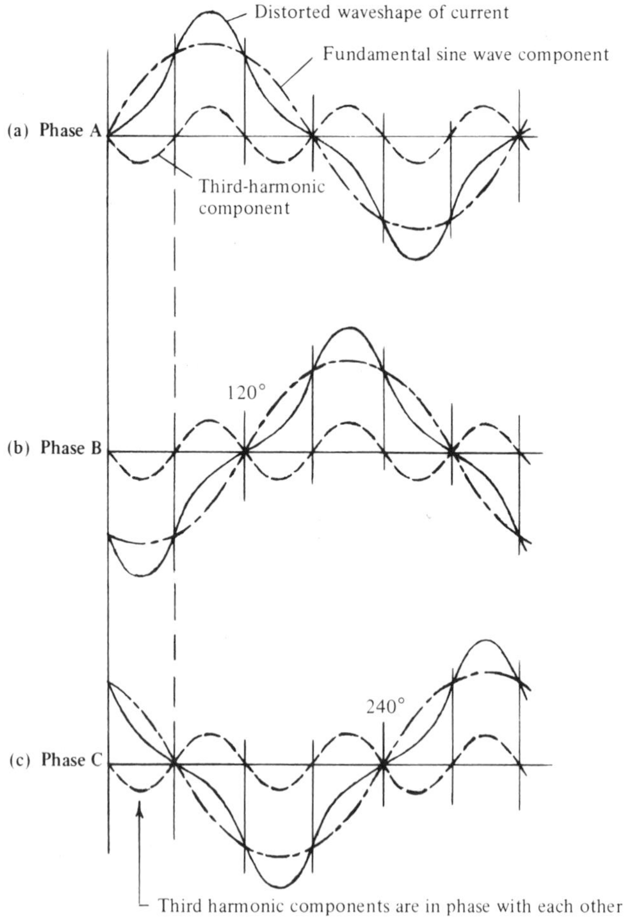

FIGURE 1.21

Third harmonic components on three-phase system

With three-phase, four-wire systems, the third harmonics can cause a problem. Figure 1.21 shows the third harmonics with respect to the currents of each of the three phases. Note that, even though the fundamental components are 120° out of phase with each other, the third harmonics of each phase are in phase with each other. The fundamental current components add up to zero (see Figure 1.19), but the third harmonics do not. They instead add together, and the only path for this current is back through the neutral to the source.

In the design of feeders for many loads, it is assumed that under balanced conditions there will be no current flowing in the neutral conductor. However, for feeders supplying loads that produce third harmonics, such as lighting units equipped with magnetic-core ballasts, the neutral conductor does carry current even under balanced load conditions. This problem is discussed in Section 11.1.5.

1.7 TRANSFORMERS

In the introduction to Section 1.3, one reason given for the universal use of alternating current to transmit power is the ease with which voltage levels can be raised or lowered as desired. The device used to change voltage levels is the *transformer*. Transformers are used at generating stations to raise the transmission voltages to high levels. This results in much lower line currents and therefore much lower line (I^2R) losses in the transmission lines. At the load end, transformers lower the voltages, first to levels that suit the distribution of power to the customer's premises and, finally, if required, to levels to suit the utilization equipment. Only the basic operation of the transformer is discussed in this section. See Chapter 15 for further details on types of transformers.

The basic single-phase transformer consists of two windings, as shown in Figure 1.22(a). The winding connected to the source of power is referred to as the *primary*, and the winding connected to the load is referred to as the *secondary*. There are no electrical connections between the primary and secondary windings. Energy is transferred through mutual inductance. Transformers work only on alternating current, because a continuously changing current is required in the primary to produce a magnetic flux in the iron core that is also continuously changing. This flux then links with the secondary winding, inducing a voltage that is proportional to the rate of change of the flux. Since the flux varies sinusoidally, the induced voltage also varies sinusoidally.

1.7.1 Voltage, Current, and Power Relationships

The primary and secondary voltages are directly related to the respective number of turns in the windings. For example, in Figure 1.22(a), if the primary winding has 1000 turns and the secondary winding has 100 turns, then the primary voltage is 10 times the

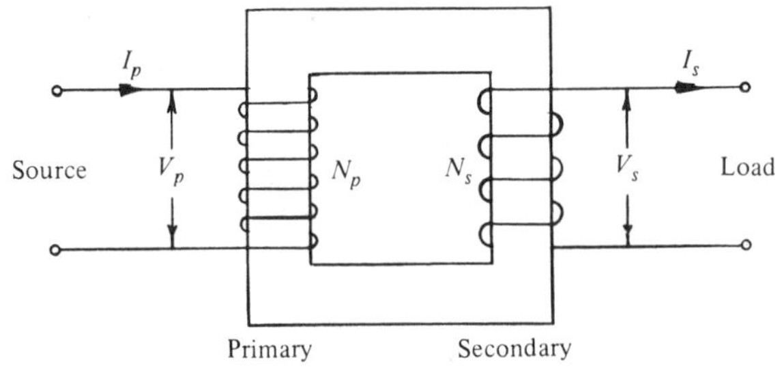

(a) Diagrammatic representation of a single-phase transformer

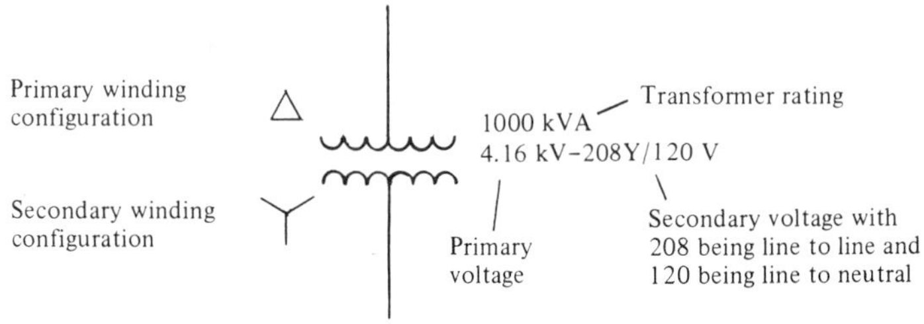

(b) Method of designating a three-phase transformer on a one-line diagram

FIGURE 1.22

Transformers

secondary voltage. This leads to the following relationship:

$$\frac{V_p}{V_s} = \frac{N_p}{N_s} = \alpha \qquad \textbf{(1.13)}$$

where V_p = primary voltage
V_s = secondary voltage
N_p = number of turns on the primary
N_s = number of turns on the secondary
α = turns ratio

Note that the turns ratio can be determined from the voltages without knowing the actual number of turns on the windings.

The amount of power that a transformer can continuously carry is largely dependent on the load current. The I^2R losses in the windings create heat, and the load current is restricted by the ability of the transformer to dissipate this heat. Therefore, transformers are rated by their volt-ampere capacity. Large transformers have a kilovolt-ampere or kVA rating. For a single-phase transformer, the rated current is obtained by dividing the volt-ampere rating by the rated voltage of the winding.

Single-phase transformers can be electrically connected to form three-phase transformer banks. However, the growing trend is to combine the individual phase coils into one overall three-phase transformer unit. The primary and secondary windings can be connected in either the wye or delta configuration. The most common arrangement for transformers used in unit substations for buildings is the delta-connected primary and the wye-connected secondary. Figure 1.22(b) shows the method of designating a three-phase transformer on an electrical system diagram.

The power relationships of three-phase transformers must include the $\sqrt{3}$ (1.732) factor as developed for Equation 1.12. Since transformer ratings are in volt-amperes, the power factor does not have to be included and therefore:

$$\text{kVA of three-phase transformer} = \frac{1.732\ V_s I_s}{1000}$$

from which

$$I_s = \frac{\text{kVA} \times 1000}{1.732 V_s} \qquad \textbf{(1.14)}$$

where I_s = rated secondary line current

V_s = rated secondary line-to-line voltage

The kilovolt-ampere rating of a transformer is based on the rated output from the secondary. Transformers are very efficient, normally having losses (that is, heat) as low as 1% to 2%. Therefore, the input power at rated loading can be assumed to equal the rated kVA, and the rated primary current can be obtained by using the rated primary voltage V_p in place of V_s in Equation 1.14. Note that as the voltage is stepped down through the transformer the current is stepped up, and vice versa.

EXAMPLE 1.19

A single-phase transformer has a 600 V primary and a 120 V secondary. The primary winding has 800 turns. Calculate (a) the number of turns on the secondary and (b) the turns ratio.

Solution

(a) From Equation 1.13,

$$N_s = N_p \times \frac{V_s}{V_p} = 800 \times \frac{120}{600} = 160 \text{ turns}$$

(b) The turns ratio is

$$\alpha = \frac{V_p}{V_s} = \frac{600}{120} = 5$$

Note that the ratio $N_p/N_s = 800/160 = 5$ also.

EXAMPLE 1.20

A 100 kVA, three-phase transformer is rated for 480-208Y/120 V. Calculate the rated primary and secondary currents.

Solution

From Equation 1.14,

$$I_p = \frac{100 \times 1000}{1.732 \times 480} = 120.3 \text{ A}$$

$$I_s = \frac{100 \times 1000}{1.732 \times 208} = 277.6 \text{ A}$$

Note that the line-to-line voltage (208 V) must be used to calculate the secondary current. Note also that the ratio of the currents is equal to the inverse of the ratio of the voltages (that is, to the turns ratio).

1.7.2 Equivalent Impedance

So far we have treated the transformer as an ideal device that has no losses. However, as with any device carrying current, the windings of the transformer have resistance, which results in some degree of I^2R losses under load conditions. Also, not all the magnetic flux created by the primary winding links with the secondary winding, and vice versa. The small amount of flux that does not link properly is referred to as the *leakage flux,* which causes an inductive reactance in each of the windings (referred to as *leakage reactance*). Figure 1.23(a) shows the equivalent circuit diagram for a transformer that includes the resistance R and leakage reactance X of each winding. Note that this is a simplified diagram in that the magnetizing component of the primary current is neglected.

To further simplify the transformer circuit diagram for the purposes of performing system calculations, the total effects of the resistance and leakage reactance can be transferred to either the primary or secondary side of the transformer. Figure 1.23(b) shows the effects transferred to the secondary side. Note that, in transferring the effect of the primary resistance and leakage reactance to the secondary, their value in ohms is divided by the square of the turns ratio (α^2). The reader can refer to one of the electrical machinery and transformer textbooks listed in the bibliography for an explanation of this operation. The combined effect is referred to as the equivalent resistance, leakage reactance, and impedance, respectively. Example 6.3 shows how these equivalent values in ohms can be converted to per unit values for the purpose of calculating fault currents on systems (see Section 6.4).

The equivalent impedance of the transformer results in a voltage drop when the transformer is under load. However, the change in the secondary terminal voltage from full-load to no-load on the transformer, referred to as the voltage regulation, is normally less than 5%.

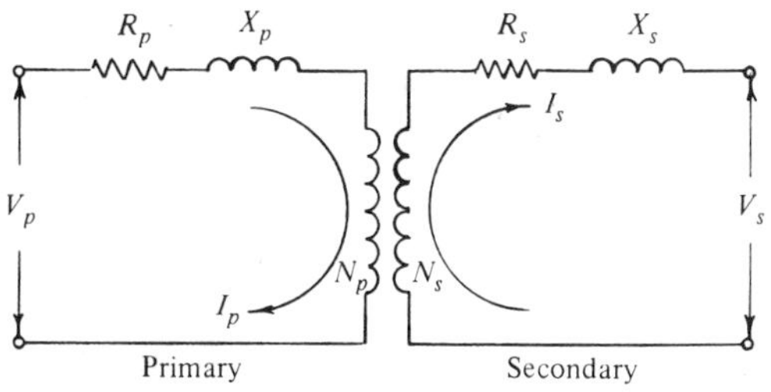

Note: The magnetizing component of the primary current is neglected.

(a) Simplified circuit diagram of transformer

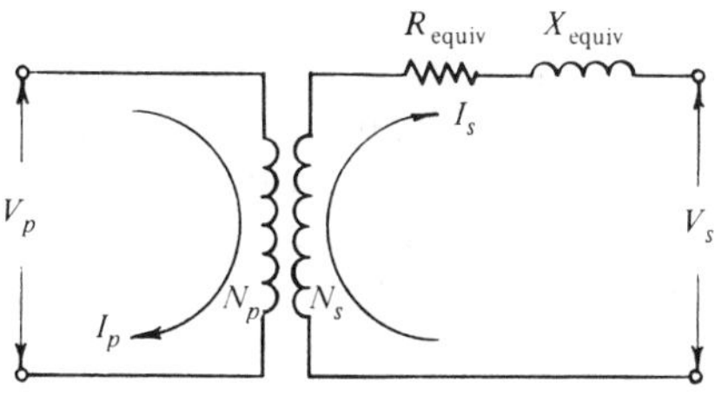

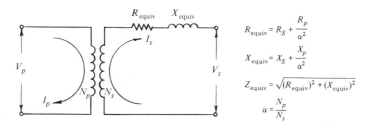

$$R_{equiv} = R_S + \frac{R_p}{\alpha^2}$$

$$X_{equiv} = X_S + \frac{X_p}{\alpha^2}$$

$$Z_{equiv} = \sqrt{(R_{equiv})^2 + (X_{equiv})^2}$$

$$\alpha = \frac{N_p}{N_s}$$

FIGURE 1.23

Equivalent circuit diagram of transformer

(b) Equivalent circuit diagram with effects transferred to secondary side

1.8 VOLTAGE TERMINOLOGY AND STANDARDS

There have been many different voltage levels used over the 100 years since electric power became universally available, not only around the world but within North America. We still hear references to system voltages such as 110, 115, 220, and 230 volts. Much confusion results from not understanding the terminology that applies to voltages. The following three terms will therefore be defined before we discuss the voltage standards themselves:

1. *Nominal voltage* *The value assigned to a system or part of a system for the purpose of identifying the system.* This term can be applied only to systems, not to equipment. It indicates the desired level of the supply voltage for the system, but the actual voltage at any given point on the system may vary slightly from this nominal voltage within a range that still permits satisfactory operation of the utilization equipment.

2. *Rated voltage* *The value to which all the operating characteristics of a type of equipment are referred.* This term can be applied only to equipment, not to systems. Most equipment can operate satisfactorily within a specified range of voltage variations from the rated value, although there may be some change to the listed design ratings. Motors, for example, have an allowable range of plus or minus 10% from their rated voltage (see Section 2.9).

3. *Voltage class* *This value indicates the maximum voltage level at which the insulation of wiring and equipment is designed to operate continuously* (that is, for years). This term can be applied only to wiring and equipment, not to systems.

In the early development of electrical power distribution systems, the loads were small and the distances short. Therefore, the supply voltage was the same as the equipment voltage, that is, 110 volts. As alternating current systems came into use, higher voltage levels based on multiples of 110 volts became common (220, 440, 550, and so on). However, as systems grew in size, the supply voltages were raised to help overcome the problems of voltage drop, first to 115 volts and multiples thereof (230, 460, 575, and so on). Finally, the 208Y/120 volt, three-phase, four-wire system was developed, which enabled lighting loads and three-phase motors to both be fed from the same system. As a result of the wide adoption of this system, supply voltages were raised again to 120 volts and multiples thereof (240, 480, 600, and so on).

Voltage-sensitive equipment such as lighting was redesigned so that its rated voltage generally matched the increases in the supply voltages. However, for many years, motors, which can tolerate a greater voltage variation, were still designed with rated voltages of 110, 220, 440, 550 volts, and so on, on the basis that the voltage drops inherent in most systems brought the voltage at the motor terminals down close to these values. In the 1960s, a survey of industrial and commercial premises was conducted, which showed that this was not the case; in fact, motors were generally operating on overvoltages. As a result, since the late 1960s, motors have been designed with rated voltages of 115, 230, 460, 575 volts, and so on. Also, since 230 volt motors were no longer suitable for operation on 208 volt systems (as were the 220 volt rated motors), 200 volt ($\sqrt{3} \times$ 115V) rated motors are now available.

The following classifications have been adopted with regard to voltage levels:

— Low voltage: 0 to 1000 V
— Medium voltage: 1001 to 72,500 V
— High voltage: above 72.5 kV up to 242 kV
— Extra-high voltage: above 242 kV

For electrical systems in buildings, only the low and medium voltages (up to 34.5 kilovolts) are used. It should be noted that the *National Electrical Code* (*NEC*)* classifies *low voltage* as ranging

* *National Electrical Code*® and *NEC*® are Registered Trademarks of the National Fire Protection Association, Inc., Quincy, MA.

TABLE 1.1 Voltage Standards for Building Electrical Systems up to 15 Kilovolts

	Standard Nominal System Voltages	Rated Voltages for Motors	Voltage Class
	Single-phase systems:		
	120/240 V, three-wire	115 and 230 V	125 and 250 V[a]
	Three-phase systems:		
Low voltage	208Y/120 V, four-wire	200 V	125 and 250 V[a]
	(240 V, three-wire)	230 V	250 V[a]
	480Y/277 V, four-wire	460 V	600 V
	480 V, three-wire	460 V	600 V
	(600 V, three-wire)	575 V	600 V
Medium voltage	(2400 V, three-wire)	2300 V	5 kV
	(4160Y/2400 V, four-wire)	4000 V	5 kV
	4160 V, three-wire	4000 V	5 kV
	(4800 V, three-wire)	4600 V	5 kV
	(6900 V, three-wire)	6600 V	15 kV
	(13,800Y/7970 V, four-wire)	13,200 V	15 kV
	13,800 V, three-wire	13,200 V	15 kV

[a] Most low-voltage cables and equipment are insulated for a maximum of 600 volts.

System voltages shown without parentheses are preferred.

For a complete listing of standard system voltages, see ANSI C84.1-1982.

up to 600 volts nominal, with higher levels being designated *above 600 volts nominal.*

To minimize the number of different operating voltages used throughout the United States, the American National Standards Institute (ANSI) has issued a list of preferred standard nominal system voltages. These nominal voltages, together with the standard rated voltages for motors and the voltage classes, up to 15 kilovolts are shown in Table 1.1.

SUMMARY

- Current I is the flow of electrons in a circuit, and its unit of measurement is the ampere.
- Voltage V is the electromotive force applied to a circuit, and its unit of measurement is the volt. Voltage can also represent a potential drop across a circuit element.
- Resistance R is the measure of opposition to the flow of current in a circuit, and its unit is the ohm.
- Ohm's law states that $R = V/I$.

- Energy is the ability to do work, and its unit is the joule. Power is the rate of doing work and its unit is the watt.
- Electrical power in watts = volts × amperes.
- The power dissipated by resistance is I^2R.
- Electrical energy is measured in kilowatt-hours:

$$1 \text{ kWh} = 3.6 \times 10 \text{ wattseconds or joules}$$

- Mechanical power is measured in horsepower:

$$1 \text{ hp} = 746 \text{ watts} = 0.746 \text{ kW}$$

- A series circuit provides only one path for the current. The voltage drop across each circuit element is directly proportional to the resistance of the element.
- A parallel circuit provides multiple paths for the current. There is one common voltage across all circuit elements and the current through each element is inversely proportional to the resistance of the element.
- Alternating current systems have currents and voltages that alternate in a sinsusoidal manner.
- Frequency is the number of cycles per second, designated hertz.
- Ac voltages and currents are designated by their rms values where:

$$E = 0.7071\ E_{max}$$

$$I = 0.7071\ I_{max}$$

- The time relationship between an ac voltage and current is designated by a phase angle.
- In a purely inductive ac circuit, the current lags the voltage by 90°.
- In a purely capacitive ac circuit, the current leads the voltage by 90°.
- Inductive reactance X_L is a measure of the opposition to the flow of ac current due to self-inductance, and its unit is the ohm.
- Capacitive reactance X_C is a measure of the opposition to the flow of ac current due to capacitance, and its unit is the ohm.
- Impedance Z is the circuit property that represents the combined effects of resistance and reactance, and its unit is the ohm.
- Ohm's law for ac circuits is $Z = E/I$, where E and I are rms values.
- For a circuit with resistance and inductive reactance:

$$Z = R + jX_L = \sqrt{R^2 + (X_L)^2}$$

where $+j$ is an operator that indicates that the quantity is rotated 90° counterclockwise.

- Power factor is the ratio of the active power to the apparent power and is expressed as a decimal or a percentage:

$$\text{Power factor} = \cos\theta$$

where θ is the angle between the current and voltage.

- Power in a single-phase ac circuit is P (watts) $= VI\cos\theta$.
- The 120/240 volt, single-phase, three-wire system provides two voltage levels, and two 120 volt loads can be supplied using only three wires.
- In a three-phase, wye-connected system, $V_L = \sqrt{3}V_P$, where L is the line value and P is the phase value.
- The three-phase, four-wire, wye-connected system provides two voltage levels. Three single-phase loads can be supplied using only four wires.
- In a three-phase, delta-connected system, $I_L = \sqrt{3}\, I_P$.
- The power in a balanced three-phase system is

$$P\ (\text{watts}) = \sqrt{3}\, V_L I_L \cos\theta$$

- The third harmonics in a three-phase system add together, and therefore a neutral current flows in a four-wire system, even under balanced conditions.
- Transformers are used to raise and lower voltage levels:

$$\frac{V_p}{V_s} = \frac{N_p}{N_s} = \text{turns ratio } \alpha$$

where p is primary value and s is secondary value.

- For a three-phase transformer,

$$\text{kVA} = \frac{\sqrt{3}\, V_s I_s}{1000}$$

- The equivalent impedance of a transformer represents the total effect of the resistances and leakage reactances of the windings as referred to one side of the transformer.
- Nominal system voltages represent the desired voltage of the power source and are in multiples of 120 volts.
- Rated voltages represent the ideal operating voltages of equipment. Motors are rated in multiples of 115 volts.

- Voltage class represents the level to which wiring and equipment are insulated.
- Low-voltage systems range from 0 to 1000 volts. The maximum standard at the present time is 600 volts nominal.
- Medium-voltage systems range from 1001 to 72,500 volts. The maximum standard voltage normally used within buildings is 34,500 volts nominal.

QUESTIONS

1. Describe in basic terms what the current in an electric circuit represents and state its unit of measurement.
2. State the difference between a conductor and an insulator.
3. What is the electron moving force called and how is it measured?
4. What is the alternative to the ohm for the unit for resistance?
5. Explain the distinction between emf and voltage drop.
6. State the difference between the source and the load in a circuit.
7. What is the alternative to the watt for the unit for power?
8. List the differences between a series circuit and a parallel circuit.
9. For a power circuit, explain why it is normal to have load elements connected in parallel rather than in series.
10. What is the advantage of having ac currents and voltages vary in a sinusoidal manner?
11. State the relationship between frequency, period, and cycles.
12. Why are the rms values of the current and voltage used for circuit calculations?
13. Explain phase relationship.
14. Why are phasor diagrams used?
15. Explain how inductance affects an ac circuit.
16. Explain how capacitance affects an ac circuit.
17. Explain why the impedance of a circuit cannot be calculated by simply adding arithmetically the numerical values of the resistances and reactances.
18. Explain why the power factor must be included when calculating the power in watts for an ac circuit.
19. How can a lagging power factor on an electrical system be improved?
20. What are the advantages of the single-phase, three-wire system as compared to a two-wire system?
21. What are the advantages of the three-phase, four-wire system as compared to a two-wire, single-phase system?
22. State the difference between a wye system and a delta system.
23. For a wye system with a phase voltage of 120 volts, explain why the line voltage is 208 and not 240 volts.
24. Explain why the relationship $P = 1.732 V_L I_L \cos\theta$ applies to both the wye and delta systems.
25. Explain why third harmonics can cause a problem on a four-wire wye system.
26. What is the significance of the turns ratio of a transformer?
27. State what is meant by the equivalent impedance of a transformer.
28. State the differences between nominal voltage, rated voltage, and voltage class.

PROBLEMS

1. If 240 V ac is applied to a two-wire circuit and the current is measured at 16 A, calculate the impedance of the circuit.
2. Calculate the voltage drop across an impedance of 10 Ω when an ac current of 5 A is flowing through it.

3. Calculate the current drawn by a single-phase load that has an impedance of 20 Ω when connected to a 120 V ac source.
4. Calculate the power being supplied to a two-wire, 120 V ac circuit that draws 15 A. The load on the circuit is purely resistive.
5. Calculate the resistance of a circuit element if the power being dissipated is 800 W when 10 A ac current is flowing through it.
6. Calculate the cost of operating a 500 W heater for 10 h if energy costs 6 cents/kWh.
7. Refer to Figure 1.3. The values of R_1, R_2, and R_3 are 5, 8, and 12 Ω, respectively. Calculate the applied voltage E when 8 A is flowing in the circuit.
8. Refer to Figure 1.5. The values of R_1, R_2, and R_3 are 15, 20, and 24 Ω, respectively. The current through R_1 is 8 A. Calculate (a) the applied voltage E and (b) the total circuit current I_T.
9. The peak value of an ac sinusoidal voltage is 679 V. Calculate its rms value.
10. Refer to Figure 1.9(a). Assume that current I_1 is 15 A $\angle 0°$ and I_2 is 20 A $\angle -30°$. Determine the total circuit current I_T.
11. A 240 V, single-phase load has a resistance of 10 Ω and an inductive reactance of 5 Ω. Calculate (a) the impedance of the load, (b) the power factor of the load, and (c) the power consumed by the load.
12. Calculate the current drawn by a 120 V, single-phase load, rated at 2.0 kW, 90% power factor.
13. Refer to Figure 1.16(a). Assume that load 1 is rated at 3.0 kW, 100% power factor, and load 2 is rated at 2.4 kW, 100% power factor. Calculate the neutral current.
14. A three-phase, 90% power factor load draws a line current of 30 A from a 480Y/277 V system. Calculate the power drawn from the system.
15. Calculate the line current drawn by a 10.0 kW, unity power factor load supplied from a 208Y/120 V, three-phase system.
16. Calculate the line current drawn by a 25.0 kW, 80% power factor load supplied from a 480Y/277 V, three-phase system.
17. Calculate the turns ratio of a 10 kVA, 2400-120 V, single-phase transformer.
18. Calculate the rated primary and secondary currents of a 500 kVA, three-phase transformer rated at 4160-480Y/277 V.

2 Electric Motors

OBJECTIVES

After studying this chapter, you will be able to:

- Identify the factors involved in electromagnetic energy conversion.
- Recognize the different types of motors.
- Explain how each type basically functions.
- Identify typical applications for each type.
- Identify the advantages of each type.
- Identify the disadvantages of each type.

INTRODUCTION

The electric motor is an energy converter. Energy is initially delivered to a building (or generated within) in the electrical form because of the ease with which the electrical energy can be transmitted throughout the building to the exact point where the energy is ultimately required. The electric motor then converts this electrical energy to mechanical energy. The motor is connected to a driven machine for the purpose of moving air (supply and exhaust fans), moving liquids (pumps), moving objects (elevators, conveyors), compressing gases (air compressors, refrigerators), forming materials (production equipment), and so on. In large industrial plants, motors can account for upward of 90% of the total electrical load. In large commercial buildings, motors can still account for more than 50% of the total electrical load.

The selection of the type of motor for a particular application depends first on the form in which the electrical energy is delivered to the motor: direct current (dc), alternating current (ac), single or three phase. Next the selection depends on the requirements of the driven equipment: constant or variable speed, load cycles, starting and acceleration of the load, and so on. Finally, the selection depends on the environment in which the motor is to operate: normal, where an open-type ventilated enclosure is acceptable; hostile, where a totally enclosed motor must be used to prevent the free exchange of air between the inside and outside of the motor; or hazardous, where an explosion-proof enclosure must be used to prevent fires and explosions.

The main classifications of motors are as follows:

— DC motors
  - Shunt
  - Series
  - Compound

— AC motors
  - Three phase: synchronous or induction
  - Single-phase induction: split phase or capacitor start

Each type is first discussed as to its method of operation and characteristics. The summary at the end of the chapter then lists the general applications and the advantages and disadvantages of each type.

The transmission of electrical energy using alternating current is now universal. As a result, ac motors account for the majority of the motors used in buildings and industry. Therefore, the discussions in this chapter will focus primarily on the ac motors, with dc motors being discussed only to introduce motor principles and to show their good speed control characteristics.

2.1 ELECTRO-MECHANICAL ENERGY CONVERSION

To study the conversion of electrical energy to mechanical energy, or vice versa, we must look at the relationships between the electromotive force induced in a conductor, the current flow through the conductor, the magnetic field surrounding the conductor, the motion of the conductor, and the mechanical force on the conductor.

Let us first consider the conversion of mechanical energy to electrical energy (that is, generator action). Figure 2.1 shows a conductor moving through a magnetic field. From Faraday's law of induction, the voltage induced in the conductor is directly proportional to the strength of the magnetic field and the velocity of the conductor. A practical application of this is the dc generator, as shown in Figure 2.2. The generated voltage E can be expressed as:

$$E = K\phi S \tag{2.1}$$

where K = a machine constant
ϕ = strength of the magnetic field
S = rotational speed of the machine

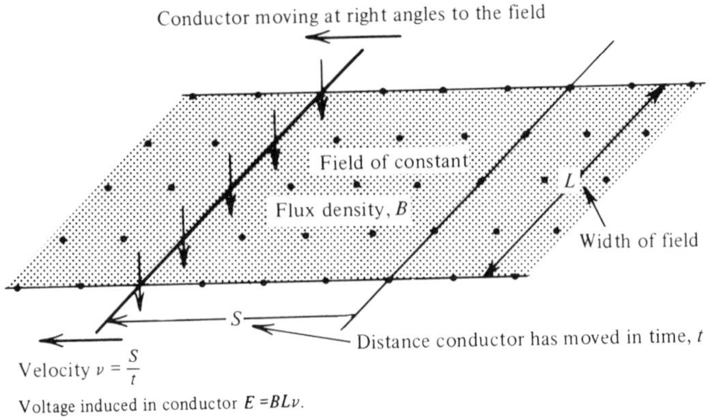

FIGURE 2.1

Conductor moving through a magnetic field

This relationship is equally applicable to a motor, because a motor also has conductors moving in a magnetic field and therefore has an internal generated voltage.

Next consider the conversion of electrical energy to mechanical energy (that is, motor action). Figure 2.3 shows a conductor in a magnetic field. The mechanical force produced on the conductor is proportional to the strength of the magnetic field and to the current in the conductor. If the conductor is placed on the rotor of a motor in the form of a loop, as shown in Figure 2.4, then the force on the conductor produces rotating motion. The important factor now becomes the turning effort or the *torque*. Torque is the product of the force F and its radial distance from the center of rotation R. The torque T produced by a motor is expressed as:

$$T = C\phi I \tag{2.2}$$

where C = machine constant
ϕ = strength of the magnetic field
I = current through the conductors

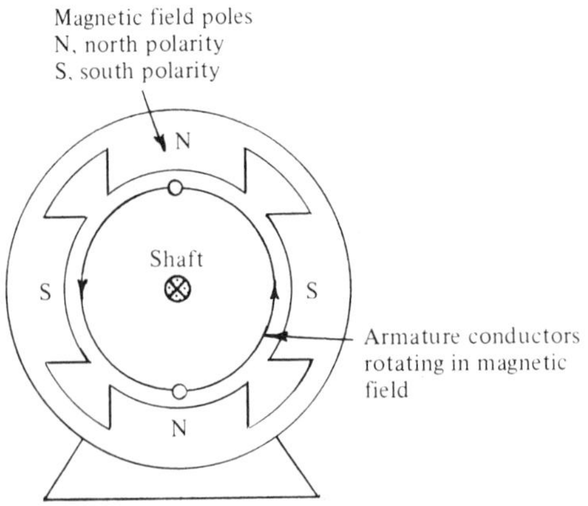

FIGURE 2.2

Elementary four-pole dc generator or motor

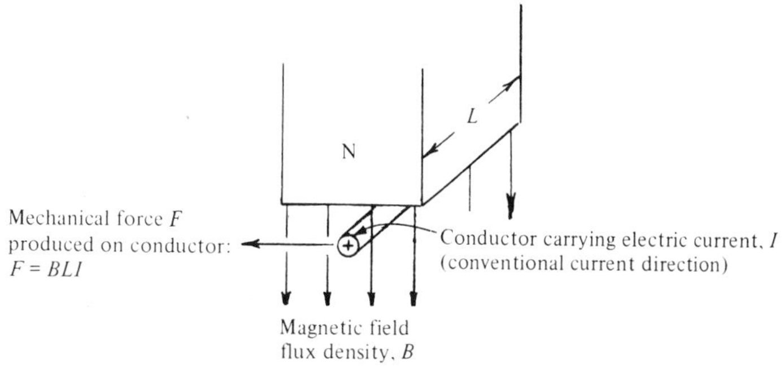

FIGURE 2.3

Force produced on a conductor in a magnetic field

Power is the rate of doing work (see Section 1.1.4). In the Systeme International (SI), the mechanical power output of the motor is expressed as:

$$P = T\omega \tag{2.3}$$

where P = power in watts
T = torque in newton-meters (N · m)
ω = angular velocity in radians per second (rad/s)

Remember that the watt is equally a measure of mechanical power (1 horsepower = 746 watts; Equation 1.4).

In the English system, the mechanical output of the motor is expressed as:

$$\text{Horsepower} = \frac{TS}{5252} \tag{2.4}$$

where T = torque in pound-feet (lb-ft)
S = speed in revolutions per minute (rpm)
5252 = necessary conversion factor

The following examples illustrate these relationships.

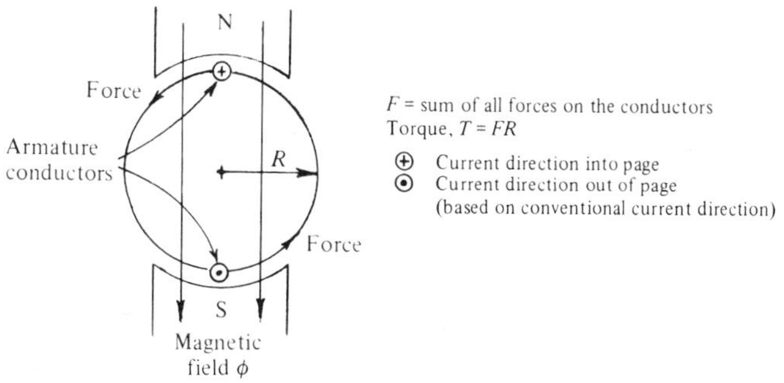

FIGURE 2.4

Torque produced by motor

■ EXAMPLE 2.1

A motor is developing a torque of 10.5 N · m at a speed of 180 rad/s. Calculate the power output of the motor using SI units.

Solution

From Equation 2.3,

$$P = T\omega = 10.5 \times 180 = 1890 \text{ W}$$
$$= 1.89 \text{ kW}$$

■ EXAMPLE 2.2

A motor is rated at 10.0 hp with a full load speed of 1750 rpm. Calculate the full load torque of the motor using English units.

Solution

Rearranging Equation 2.4 gives

$$T = \frac{\text{horsepower} \times 5252}{S} = \frac{10.0 \times 5252}{1750} = 30.0 \text{ lb-ft}$$

2.2 DIRECT CURRENT MOTORS

The direct current (dc) motor has two sets of windings: (1) the field winding, which is mounted on the frame, and (2) the armature winding, which is mounted on the rotor. Figure 2.5(a) shows a simplified connection diagram for the two sets of windings, and Figure 2.5(b) shows a cutaway view of the motor. The field current controls the strength of the magnetic field (see Figure 1.10). The armature winding carries the load current of the motor. The armature conductors rotate alternately under a north pole and then under a south pole. The commutator acts like a switch to reverse the individual conductor currents so that the torque is constant in the one direction.

Direct current motors are classified according to the mode of connection of the field winding with respect to the armature winding, that is, shunt, series, or compound.

2.2.1 Shunt Motor

The field winding of the shunt motor is designed for connection across the source voltage to the motor. The winding consists of many turns of light wire, which then requires only a relatively small field current to produce the required magnetic flux. The equivalent circuit diagram of a separately excited shunt motor is shown in Figure 2.6. This mode of connection is preferred so that the field of the motor can be controlled completely independent of any adjustments being made to the armature voltage.

When the motor is running, the armature conductors are cutting the magnetic lines of force and therefore a voltage is generated. This voltage opposes the flow of the current through the armature and is

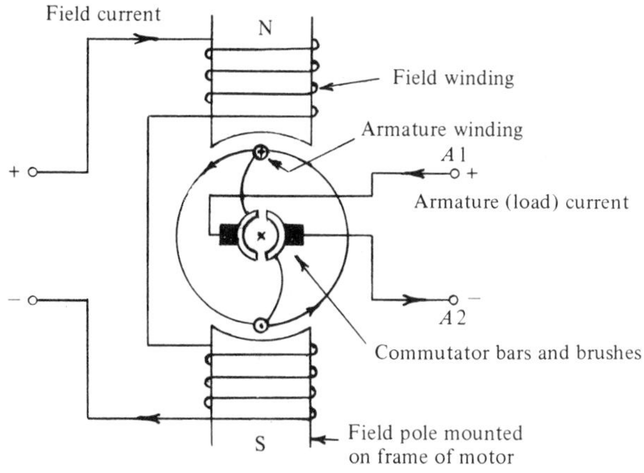

(a) Simplified connection diagram

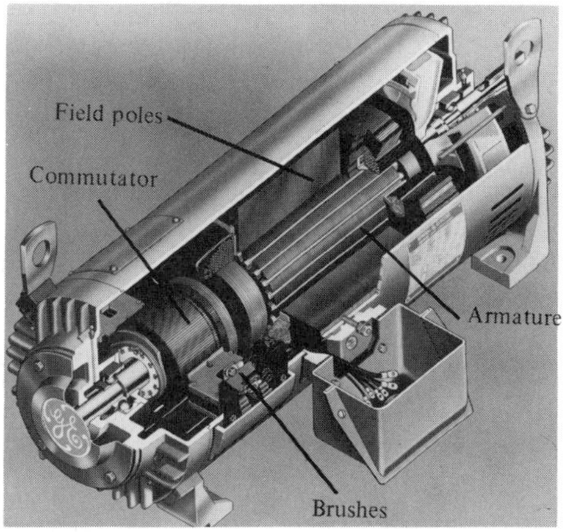

(b) Cutaway view

FIGURE 2.5

Direct current motor

referred to as the *counter* emf, shown on the diagram as E_c. Using the circuit laws as outlined in Chapter 1, the equation for the armature circuit becomes:

$$V_a = I_aR_a + E_c \tag{2.5}$$

Solving for the armature current gives:

$$I_a = \frac{V_a - E_c}{R_a} \tag{2.6}$$

Assume that the motor is operating with a constant magnetic field (that is, the field current is constant). From Equation 2.1, the counter emf E_c is then directly proportional to the speed. From

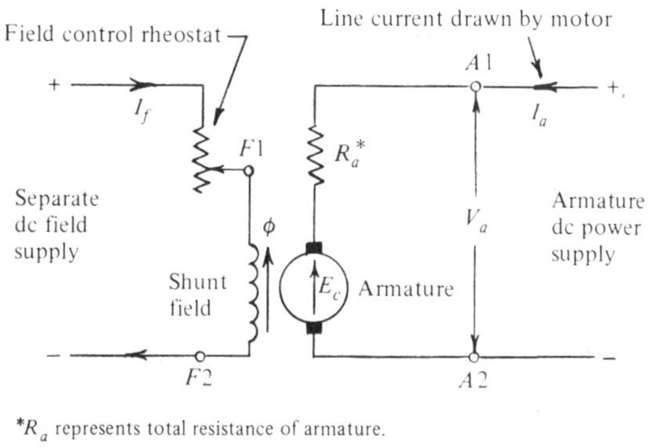

FIGURE 2.6

Equivalent circuit diagram of a dc shunt motor separately excited

Equation 2.2, the torque is then directly proportional to the motor current. For the motor to pick up load (for the torque to increase), the current drawn by the motor must increase. From Equation 2.6, for the current to increase, the counter emf E_c must decrease, which in turn requires that the motor slow down. The speed has to drop only slightly for there to be a significant increase in the current. The speed of a dc shunt motor operating from a fixed supply voltage decreases no more than 5% from no load to full load.

The previous description is the basic way any motor picks up load. As the load changes, the motor adjusts its speed (even if only momentarily) so that the motor current can reach the value necessary to develop the required torque. When the field of the motor and the applied voltage are held constant, the amount of current drawn by the motor is dictated solely by the load that it is driving. This is discussed further in Section 2.9.

2.2.2 Speed Control of Shunt Motors

The dc shunt motor is most often used where a variable-speed drive is required. From Equation 2.1, $E_c = K\phi S$. Substituting for E_c in Equation 2.5 and solving for the speed gives:

$$S = \frac{V_a - I_a R_a}{K\phi} \tag{2.7}$$

This relationship shows that there are three ways to control the speed of the shunt motor:

1. *Increase the armature circuit resistance, R_a.* This is done by connecting resistance into the circuit external to the motor. As resistance is added, the speed of the motor decreases, the exact amount being dependent on the load current I_a of the motor. This method has two major disadvantages: (1) It is inefficient because of the heat loss in the added resistors, and (2) the speed of the motor varies as the load on the motor varies.

2. *Vary the supply voltage, V_a.* With the development of relatively inexpensive solid-state variable-voltage power sources, this method has now become the accepted way to control the speed of dc motors, especially when large speed changes are required. Neglecting the effect of the voltage drop across the armature I_aR_a, which is negligible, and assuming the field ϕ is constant, the speed is directly proportional to the voltage.

3. *Vary the shunt field current.* The amount of flux ϕ is controlled by the field current. The speed is inversely proportional to the flux. Therefore, decreasing the field current causes the motor to speed up and, conversely, increasing the field current causes the

motor to slow down. The field current can easily be controlled by an external rheostat, as shown in Figure 2.6. Since the field current is relatively very small, the heat loss in the rheostat is not significant. Solid-state devices are also used for field control.

Variable-speed drive systems generally incorporate both methods 2 and 3. Large changes of speed are made by varying the armature voltage, and very precise speed settings are made by controlling the field current. Most applications of dc motors today are for variable-speed drives because of their superior characteristics.

2.2.3 Series and Compound Motors

The series motor has the field winding connected in series with the armature, as shown in Figure 2.7. Since the field winding carries the full motor load current, the winding consists of a few turns of heavy wire. The magnetic flux is now dependent on the load current, with the result that the torque and speed characteristics are quite different from those of the shunt motor. Refer to Equation 2.2. With the flux ϕ also dependent on I_a, the torque is directly proportional to the square of the load current. Refer to Equation 2.7. With the flux ϕ in the denominator, the speed is inversely proportional to the load current when V_a is held constant. This gives the motor a very high torque at low speeds and high currents, and a low torque at high speeds and low currents. These characteristics are very desirable for the traction motors used to drive trains and electric buses and for other applications requiring high starting torques. The starter motor on your car is a series motor. However, the use of series motors in buildings is very rare other than in battery-operated mobile equipment.

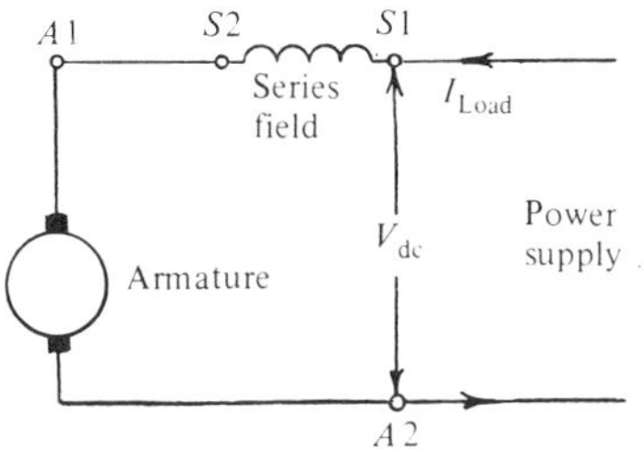

FIGURE 2.7

Direct current series motor

The compound motor uses a combination of the shunt and series windings, giving it higher starting torques than a comparable shunt motor and greater speed drops under load. However, ac motors are available with similar characteristics, so the use of compound motors in buildings or for industrial applications is rare.

2.3 POLYPHASE ALTERNATING CURRENT MOTORS

Polyphase alternating current (ac) motors have many characteristics that are similar to those for dc shunt motors, but there are several major differences. Electrically, commutation is not required with alternating current. Mechanically, the armature winding is mounted on the frame and the field winding is mounted on the rotor, which is the reverse of the arrangement for the dc motor. It makes no difference whether the field is stationary and the armature conductors rotate, or vice versa, as long as there is relative motion between the two. Since no commutation is required for ac motors, it makes sense to place the higher voltage, higher current armature windings on the frame (stator), where fixed connections can be made. The field winding, on the other hand, requires only a fraction of the power. In the case of the synchronous motor, the collector ring and brush assembly required for the electrical connections to the rotor can be relatively much smaller.

2.3.1 Rotating Magnetic Field

Before the operation of polyphase motors can be explained, it is necessary to understand the phenomenon of the rotating magnetic field. It is hard to imagine that pulsating currents flowing through fixed coils produce a field that is constant in strength and that rotates around the frame. For the explanation, refer to Figure 2.8, which shows a simplified arrangement of three armature coils mounted on the stator. Each coil is located 120° from the other around the stator, as shown in part (c). The coils are connected to the three-phase power supply as shown in part (a) so that their currents are 120° out of phase with each other (see Section 1.6.1 and Figure 1.19). The relative instantaneous values of the currents over one full electrical cycle are similarly shown in Figure 2.8(b). The positive sign indicates that the current is flowing toward the neutral at that instant of time, and the negative sign indicates that the current is flowing away from the neutral at a later instant of time. ϕ_A, ϕ_B, and ϕ_C represent the components of flux set up by each phase winding. Their magnitude is directly proportional to the current through their respective windings, and their direction is determined by the right-hand rule (see Section 1.4.1 and Figure 1.10).

The directions and relative magnitudes of the phase currents and of the magnetic flux components are shown for four different instants of time Figure 2.8(c), (d), (e), and (f). The single resulting magnetic field ϕ_{RES} is the vector sum of the individual phase components. Note that in each case the relative magnitude of ϕ_{RES} remains constant at a value of 1.5, but that the position of this field moves. The rotation of the field in mechanical degrees is the same as the electrical degrees covered in the cycle. The time span covered is 90° or one-quarter of a cycle, and the field has moved 90° or one-quarter of a revolution in a clockwise direction. The constant field is very desirable as it results in a constant torque being developed by three-phase motors, giving them very smooth running and quiet operation.

With the two-pole configuration (that is, there is one resulting north pole and one resulting south pole) shown in Figure 2.8, the field will complete one full revolution around the stator for every one cycle of the electrical system. If we were to analyze the performance of a motor wound to produce a resulting field having two north poles and two south poles (a four-pole motor), then the field

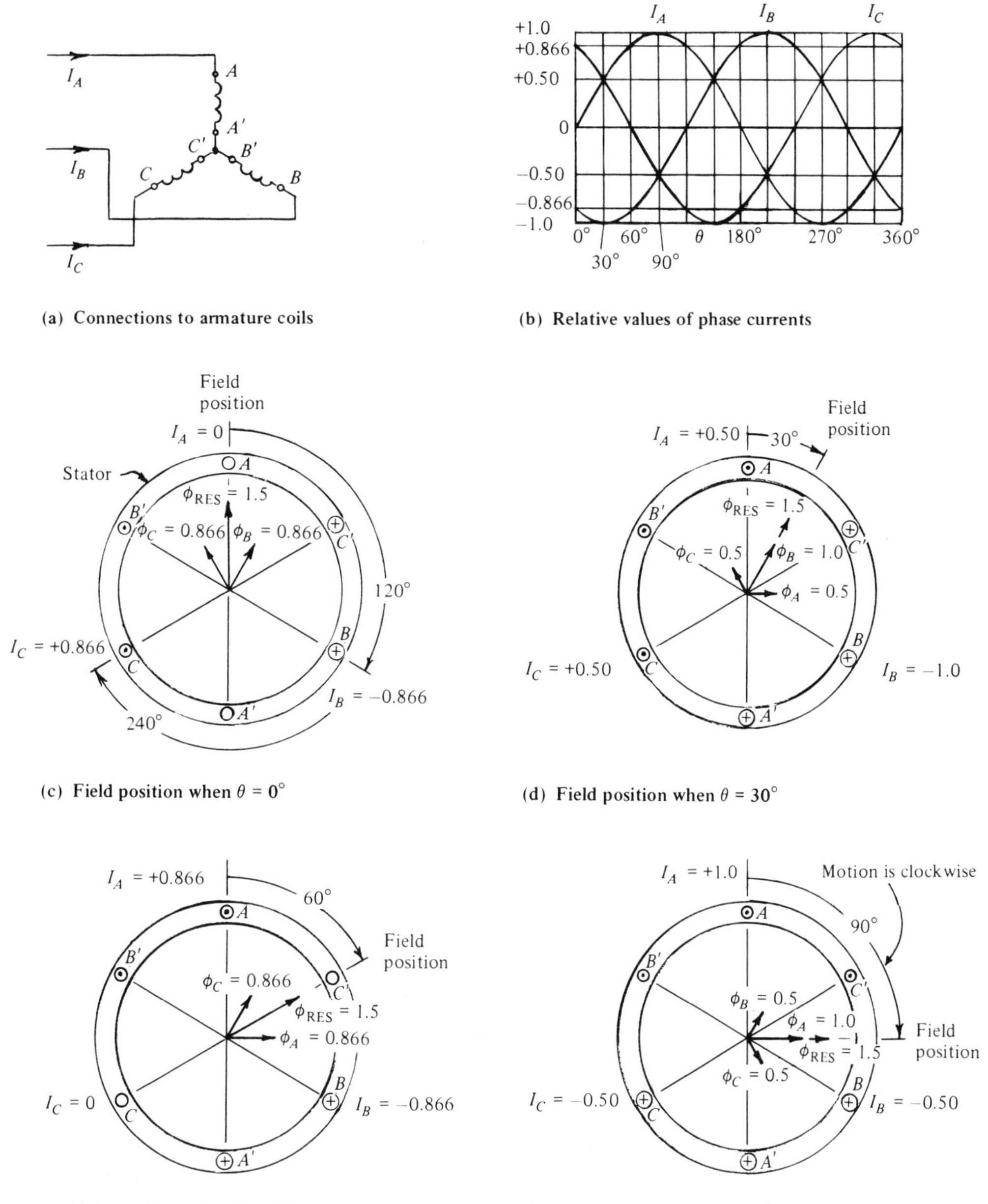

(a) Connections to armature coils

(b) Relative values of phase currents

(c) Field position when $\theta = 0°$

(d) Field position when $\theta = 30°$

(e) Field position when $\theta = 60°$

(f) Field position when $\theta = 90°$

FIGURE 2.8

Rotating magnetic field of a three-phase ac motor

would rotate only one-half of a revolution for each complete electrical cycle. Similarly, for a six-pole motor, the field would rotate only one-third of a revolution for each complete electrical cycle. Thus, a relationship for the English system is established as follows:

$$N_s = \frac{120f}{P} \text{ rpm} \tag{2.8}$$

where N_s = synchronous speed of a motor (the speed of rotation of the field)
f = frequency of the electrical system
P = number of poles

The relationship for SI is as follows:

$$\omega_s = 4\pi \frac{f}{P} \text{ rad/s} \tag{2.9}$$

These relationships are used to analyze the operation of ac motors in Sections 2.4 and 2.5.

Refer again to the two-pole winding configuration shown in Figure 2.8. Note that the physical arrangement of the windings with reference to phase A is that phase B is at 120° and phase C is at 240°, both in a clockwise direction around the stator. With this arrangement, the field rotates in a clockwise direction. Let us reverse the electrical connections to two of the phase windings, as shown in Figure 2.9(a). Now phase B is 120° and phase C is 240° in a counterclockwise direction from phase A. The directions and relative magnitudes of the phase currents and of the flux components are shown for two instants of time in parts (b) and (c). Note that the resulting field ϕ_{RES} is now rotating in the counterclockwise direction. Thus, the direction of rotation of the magnetic field (and that of a three-phase motor) can be reversed by simply interchanging any two of the three lines to the motor.

2.4 THREE-PHASE SYNCHRONOUS MOTORS

The synchronous motor, as the name implies, synchronizes its speed with that of the rotating magnetic field. Since this speed of rotation is a function of the frequency (Equations 2.8 and 2.9), a particular synchronous motor with a fixed number of poles and connected to a fixed frequency will operate at an absolutely constant speed regardless of the load. This characteristic can be a very desirable feature for certain types of loads.

The following examples show the speeds of operation of two motors having different numbers of poles and operating on different frequencies.

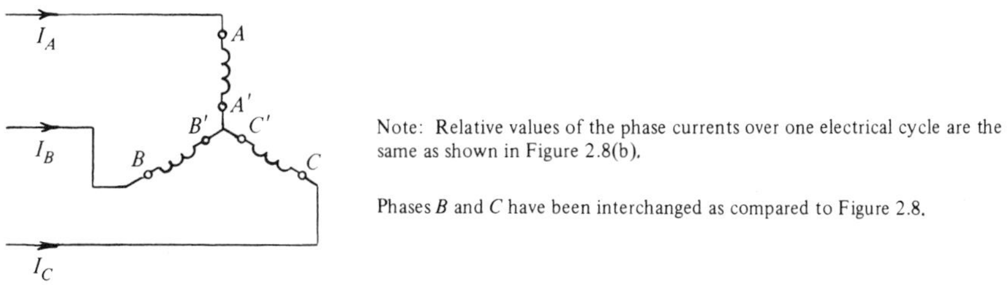

(a) Connections to armature coils

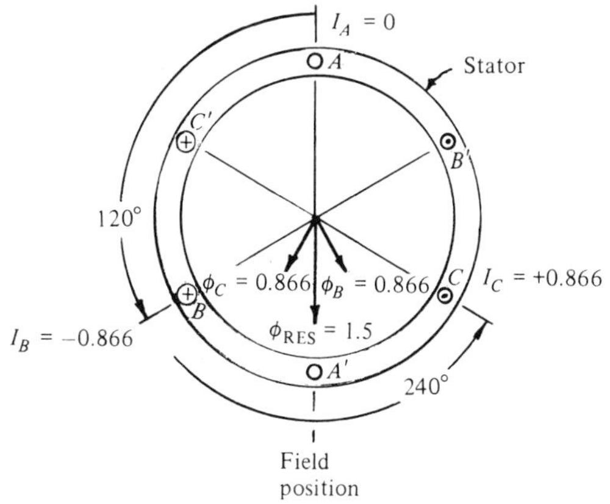

(b) Field position when $\theta = 0°$

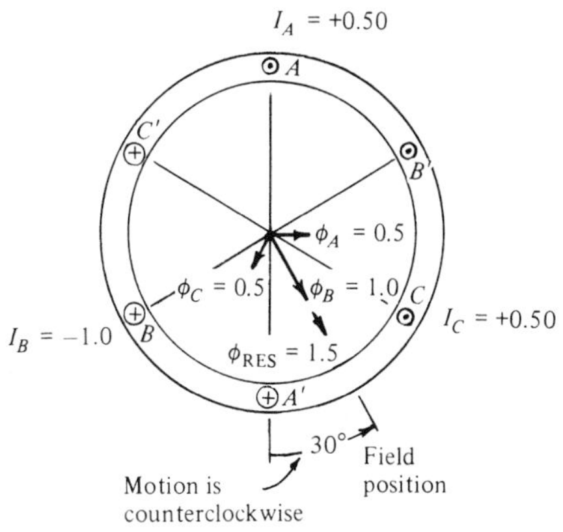

(c) Field position when $\theta = 30°$

FIGURE 2.9

Direction of rotation of field compared to Figure 2.8

■ EXAMPLE 2.3

A synchronous motor has four poles and is operated from a 60 Hz, three-phase supply. Calculate the speed in rpm.

Solution

Using Equation 2.8,

$$N_s = \frac{120 \times 60}{4} = 1800 \text{ rpm}$$

■ EXAMPLE 2.4

A synchronous motor has six poles and is operated from a 50 Hz, three-phase supply. Calculate the speed in rad/s.

Solution

Using Equation 2.9,

$$\omega_s = 4\pi \frac{50}{6} = 104.7 \text{ rad/s}$$

See Table 2.1 for the synchronous speeds of 50 and 60 hertz motors for the number of poles as listed. Note that with a fixed frequency, motors are restricted to operating at certain specific speeds.

For the reasons outlined in Section 2.3, the synchronous motor is constructed with the armature windings mounted on the stator (frame) and the field winding mounted on the rotor. This is shown schematically in Figure 2.10(a). Ignore for the moment the problem of starting a synchronous motor. Assume that the armature has been energized from the three-phase source and that the motor is running. The magnetic field created by the armature is rotating at synchronous speed around the stator. The winding on the rotor is next energized from its dc source, creating a second strong magnetic field, which then locks onto the rotating armature field. Thus the motor continues to rotate at the constant synchronous speed except for very momentary adjustments as the load on the motor changes.

The operation of the synchronous motor is similar to that of the dc shunt motor (see Section 2.2 and Equation 2.5) in that there is an internal voltage drop across the armature and a counter emf generated within the motor. However, the armature winding not only has a resistance R_a, but also a synchronous reactance X_s. The equivalent circuit diagram (on a per phase basis) is shown in Figure 2.10(b). The phasor diagram indicating the current and voltage relationship is shown in Figure 2.11(a). See Section 1.3.3 for the explanation of phasor diagrams. The phasor sum of the voltage drops across the armature (I_aR_a and I_aX_s) plus the counter emf E_c must be equal to the voltage applied to the armature V_a.

Similar to the dc shunt motor, as the load on the motor increases the armature current must increase in order to produce the required

TABLE 2.1 Synchronous Speeds of Alternating-Current Motors

Number of Poles	Synchronous Speeds 50 Hz rpm	50 Hz rad/s	60 Hz rpm	60 Hz rad/s
2	3000	314.2	3600	377.0
4	1500	157.1	1800	188.5
6	1000	104.7	1200	125.7
8	750	78.5	900	94.2
10	600	62.8	720	75.4
12	500	52.4	600	62.8
16	375	39.3	450	47.1
20	300	31.4	360	37.7

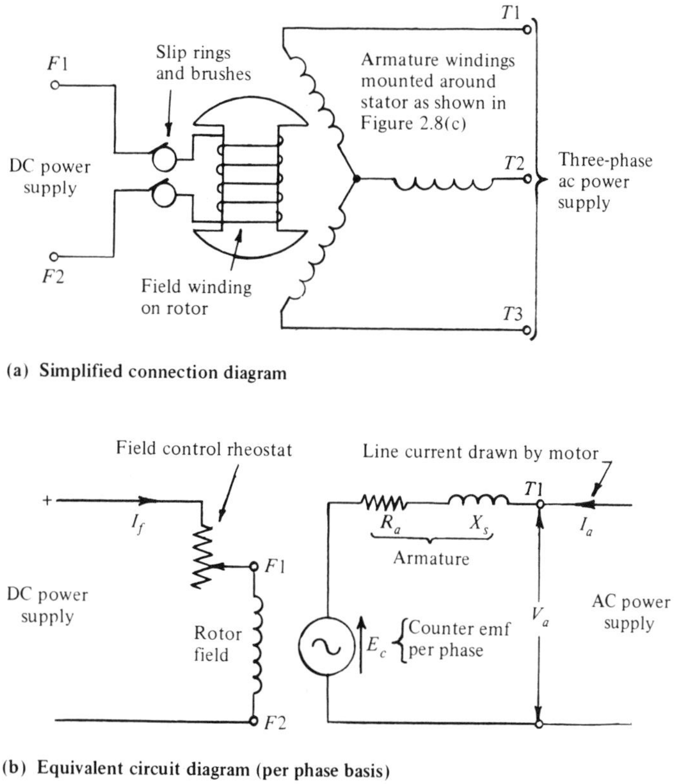

FIGURE 2.10

Three-phase synchronous motor

torque. This requires that the counter emf E_c must change. However, unlike the dc motor, the synchronous motor cannot permanently change speed. It only slows down momentarily, which changes the position of the rotor with respect to the rotating magnetic field. This change in the phase relationship between V_a and E_c allows the current to increase. Once the motor has adjusted to its new load, it then resumes rotating at its synchronous speed. Thus, like all motors, the synchronous motor adjusts to the load demands of the driven equipment by drawing more or less current from the power supply. However, unlike other motors, it does not vary its speed with load. If the motor is overloaded beyond its ability to maintain the speed, it pulls out of synchronism and must be immediately shut down.

There is a second major characteristic of the operation of the synchronous motor. Refer again to Figure 2.11(a). This phasor diagram shows the condition when the armature current I_a is in phase with the applied voltage V_a; that is, the motor is operating at unity (100%) power factor (refer to Section 1.4.4). Parts (b) and (c) show

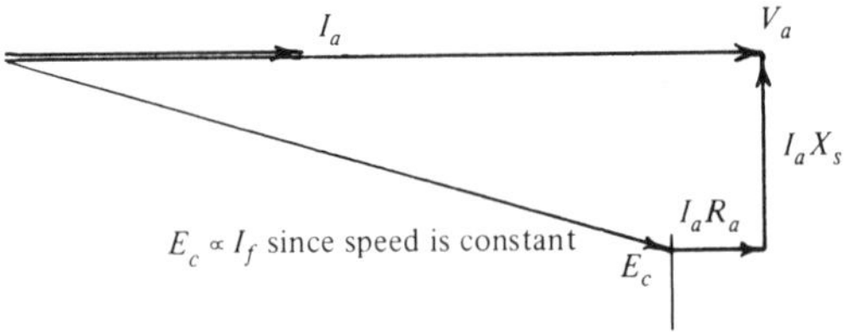

(a) **Field current set for unity power factor operation**

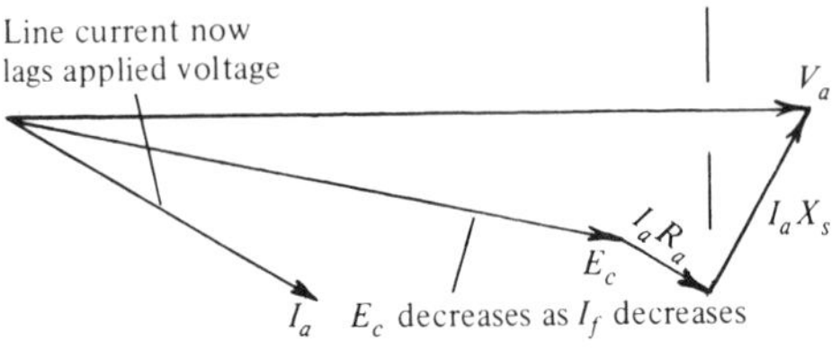

(b) **Field current decreased, lagging power factor operation (i.e., underexcitation of field)**

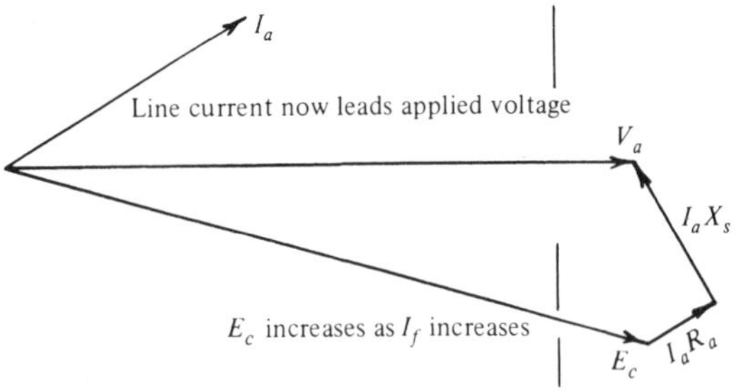

(c) **Field current increased, leading power factor operation (i.e., overexcitation of field)**

FIGURE 2.11

Operation of synchronous motor with constant load, but with varying field current

what happens when the dc rotor field current is varied with a constant load on the motor. When the field current is decreased, the motor operates at a lagging power factor, and when it is increased, the motor operates at a leading power factor. Thus the power factor at which the motor operates can very simply be controlled by adjusting the relatively small dc field current. This is a tremendous advantage where large motors are operating on a system. A synchronous motor not only drives the load, but it can be used for power-factor correction on the system.

The synchronous motor is not inherently self-starting. The usual method of overcoming this problem is to superimpose a degree of squirrel-cage winding onto the rotor [see Figure 2.13(a)]. Thus the motor is started as a squirrel-cage motor, and when the rotor is almost up to speed, the dc field is applied and the motor then runs as a synchronous motor.

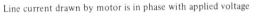

2.5 THREE-PHASE INDUCTION MOTORS

There are two types of three-phase induction motors: squirrel cage and wound rotor. The squirrel-cage type will be discussed first.

The three-phase, squirrel-cage induction motor is very simple in construction, as shown in Figure 2.12. There are no commutator bars, slip rings, brushes, and the like. This simple construction results in a much lower cost motor with less maintenance problems. The squirrel-cage motor is by far the most common electric motor in use today.

The dc motor and the ac synchronous motor previously discussed are both doubly excited motors; that is, they have separate windings for the armature and for the field. The induction motor requires only one source of power and that is to the armature windings on the stator. Excitation of the rotor is achieved by induction, hence the name for the motor.

Motor action as in Figure 2.3 requires that a conductor carrying an electric current be acted on by a magnetic field. In the induction motor, the magnetic field is provided by the armature windings on the stator. The conductors on which the field acts are bars that are mounted on the rotor. These bars run the length of the rotor and are joined at the ends by conducting rings. A typical rotor winding is shown in Figure 2.13(a). At the time that this type of motor first appeared toward the end of the nineteenth century, it was very common for people to have a squirrel as a pet. To provide these pets with exercise, they had rotating cages. The rotor winding construction resembled these cages. Hence the term squirrel cage was selected for this type of motor to differentiate it from the wound-rotor induction motor (see Section 2.5.4).

For small- and medium-sized squirrel-cage motors, the rotor bars and end rings can be cast in one piece using aluminum. This results in much lower production costs in comparison to motors

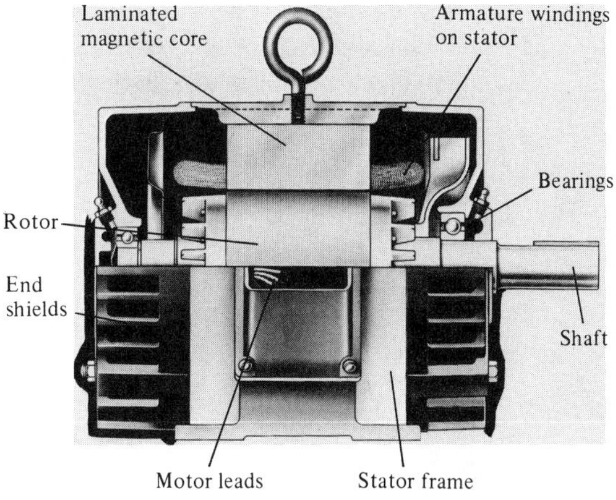

FIGURE 2.12

Cutaway view of squirrel-cage induction motor

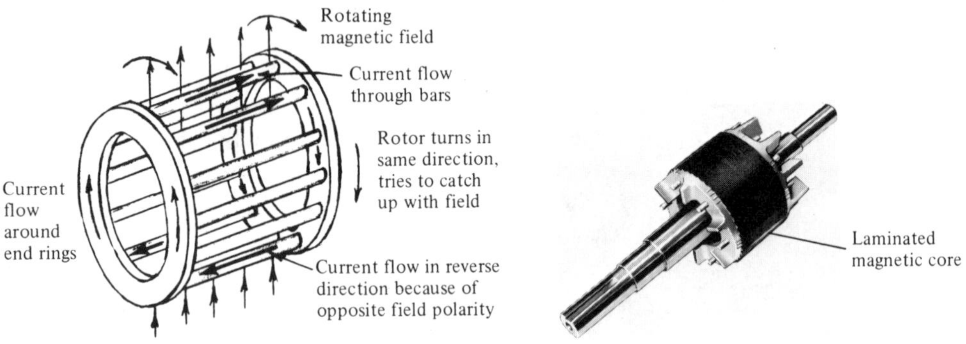

(a) Squirrel-cage rotor winding

(b) Fully assembled rotor mounted on shaft

FIGURE 2.13

Rotor for squirrel-cage induction motor

requiring wound rotors. To have as strong a magnetic field as possible, the rotor bars must be surrounded by a laminated magnetic core. Figure 2.13(b) shows the complete rotor assembly mounted on the shaft. The rotor bars themselves are not visible as they are just beneath the surface of the laminated magnetic core, but the end rings are visible. The protrusions on the end rings act like a fan to circulate air through the motor for cooling.

2.5.1 Running Characteristics of Squirrel-Cage Motors

To begin to understand how the three-phase induction motor operates, we must return to the rotating magnetic field as described in Section 2.3.1. The armature windings on the stator are arranged as shown in Figure 2.8(c). The instant that the motor is energized from its three-phase source, the currents through the windings establish the rotating magnetic field. With the rotor standing still, this rotating field sweeps past the rotor bars. This action induces a voltage, which in turn causes current to flow in the bars. See Figure 2.13(a) for the paths of the rotor current. The interaction of the rotor current with the field produces a torque, which starts the rotor turning in the same direction as the rotating field. As the rotor comes up to speed (that is, as it tries to catch up with the rotating field), the relative speed between the field and the rotor decreases. To differentiate between the two speeds, the speed of rotation of the field is referred to as the *synchronous speed* N_s. As per Equation 2.8, N_s is constant for a given motor with a fixed number of poles when operated from a constant frequency (60 Hz). The difference between N_s and the actual speed of the rotor S_R is the *slip*. The relative speed of the rotor with respect to the field is then expressed as:

$$\% \text{ Slip } (S) = \frac{N_s - S_R}{N_s} \times 100 \qquad \textbf{(2.10)}$$

The speed of the rotor can never exactly reach the synchronous speed. There must always be some slip in order to produce the necessary current in the rotor bars to keep the motor turning.

The simplified connection diagram for the squirrel-cage induction motor is shown in Figure 2.14(a), and the equivalent circuit diagram (on a per phase basis) is shown in Figure 2.14(b). The induced voltage in the rotor E_R is a function of the slip, which in turn means that the rotor current I_R is a function of the slip. As the load on the motor increases, the torque produced by the motor must also increase. From Equation 2.2, the rotor current must increase, which then means that the slip must increase. Thus, the motor has to slow down to the point where the increase in torque is sufficient to match the new load demand. The change in speed is slight, as shown by the following examples.

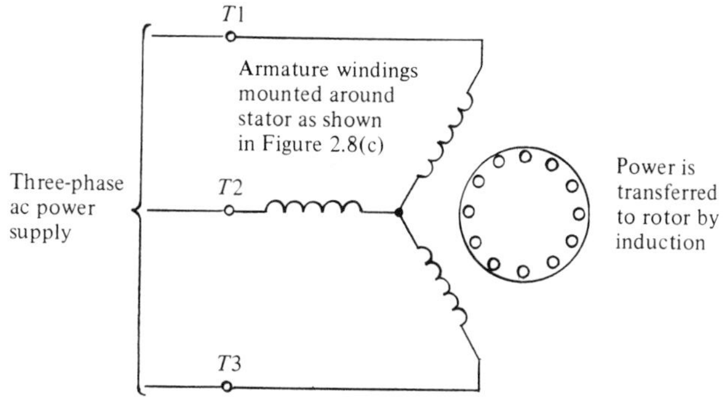

(a) Simplified connection diagram

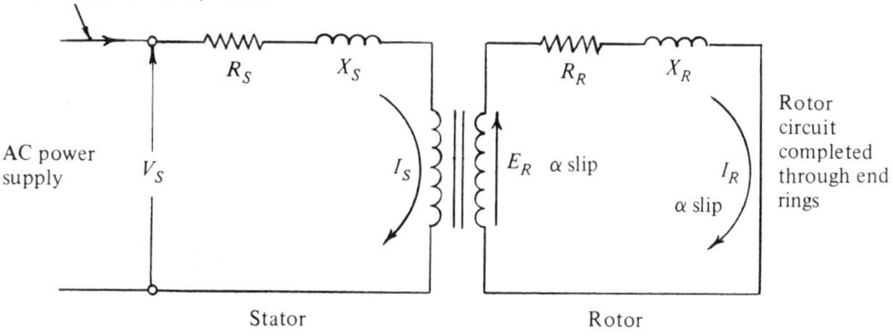

(b) Equivalent circuit diagram (per phase basis)

FIGURE 2.14

Three-phase, squirrel-cage induction motor

■ **EXAMPLE 2.5**

A four-pole, 60 Hz induction motor is operating with a slip of 2.0%. Calculate the actual speed of the motor.

Solution

From Equation 2.8,

$$N_s = \frac{120 \times 60}{4} = 1800 \text{ rpm}$$

Rearranging Equation 2.10,

$$S_R = 1800 - \frac{2.0 \times 1800}{100} = 1764 \text{ rpm}$$

■ **EXAMPLE 2.6**

The load on the motor in Example 2.5 is now doubled. Calculate the new speed of motor.

Solution

The slip was 1800 − 1764 = 36 rpm. This must increase to 2 × 36 = 72 rpm. The new speed is 1800 − 72 = 1728 rpm.

Thus the decrease in speed in the previous examples is only on the order of 2%. The slip at full load should not exceed 5% for the typical squirrel-cage motor.

Let us next examine the current that the induction motor draws from the line. Refer to Figure 2.14(b). By transformer action, any current flow in the rotor must be reflected into the stator (primary) winding. As the load on the motor increases, the rotor current increases and therefore the stator current increases. However, this reflected current from the rotor is only one component of the stator or line current. Since there is no separate field winding for an induction motor, the line current must also have a component to provide the magnetizing current to produce the field. Refer to Figure 2.15, which shows the components of the line current both at no load (motor spinning free of any load) and at full load (motor producing full load). The magnetizing component of current lags the applied voltage by 90 electrical degrees (see Section 1.4.1). This component is relatively very large because of the air gaps in the magnetic circuit between the stator and the rotor. Therefore, the line current of the motor at no load can be as high as 50% of the full-load current, resulting in a very low power factor. At full load, the motor still operates with a lagging power factor. Small motors may have full-load power factors of less than 80%. Large motors are better, having full-load power factors of at least 90%. This lagging power factor operation is one of the major disadvantages of the induction motor.

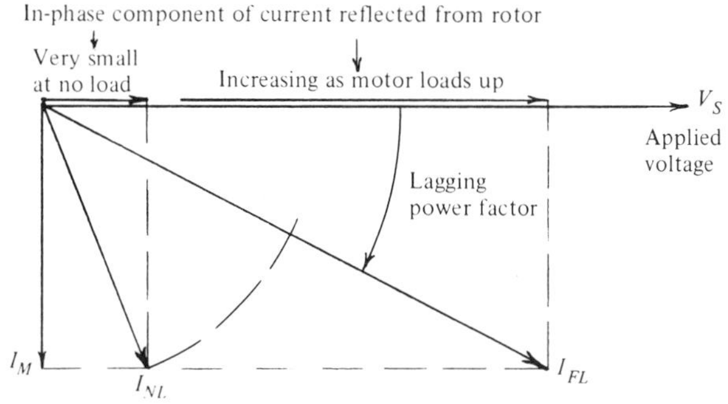

FIGURE 2.15

Running currents of induction motor

I_M, magnetizing component of current, very large because of air gaps in motor. Constant regardless of load.
I_{NL}, no-load line current of motor, up to 50% of I_{FL}.
I_{FL}, full-load line current of motor.

It is usually the major cause of power factor problems on electrical systems in buildings (see Section 1.4.4 for power factor).

2.5.2 Starting Characteristics of Squirrel-Cage Motors

The starting characteristics of a motor are equally as important as their running characteristics. Mechanically, the motor must be able to break the driven load free to start it turning and then be able to rapidly accelerate up to full speed within 15 seconds. Electrically, the motor must not draw excessive currents from the power system when starting.

The squirrel-cage induction motor inherently has good starting and accelerating torque characteristics. Its starting torque is generally greater than its full-load running torque. As the motor accelerates, its developed torque increases, reaching a maximum at approximately 80% of the synchronous speed. The maximum torque is also known as the *breakdown torque*. A motor, once it is up to speed, can successfully withstand a temporary mechanical overload up to its maximum torque before it will break down and stall.

The squirrel-cage induction motor has a starting current that is low enough to usually permit starting directly across the line (that is, with full voltage). Typically, the starting current is 600% of the full-load running current of the motor. The motor itself is designed to withstand this inrush current during a normal starting cycle. However, a problem can arise when a particular motor accounts for a good part of the total load on an electrical system. The 600% starting current may cause unacceptable voltage drops on the system. For methods of starting induction motors, see Sections 14.2 and 14.4.

The starting torque and current of a motor are often referred to as the *locked-rotor* torque and current since, at the instant of start-

TABLE 2.2 Characteristics of Design Classes for Squirrel-Cage Induction Motors

NEMA Design Class	Torque[a] Starting	Torque[a] Breakdown	Maximum Full-Load Slip	Starting Current[b]	Name/ Characteristic
B	150%	200%	5%	600%	General purpose
C	225%	200%	5%	600%	High torque
D	275%	At stand-still	15%	600%	High torque, High slip
F	125%	160%	5%	400%	Low starting current, Low torque

[a] Average value expressed as a percentage of full-load running torque.

[b] Maximum value expressed as a percentage of full-load running current.

Starting values apply for motors started full voltage.

Note: Exact values vary for each design class depending on horsepower rating and number of poles.

ing, the rotor is in effect locked into position. These values are measured by actually locking the rotor so that it cannot turn.

The exact values of the starting torque, the maximum torque, and the starting current of a squirrel-cage induction motor can be controlled by the design of the rotor bars. For example, if the resistance of the rotor bars is increased, the starting torque increases and the starting current decreases. However, offsetting these gains are the disadvantages of high full-load slip and lower efficiency because of the extra heat produced in the rotor bars. Another approach is to install two sets of bars on the rotor (a double squirrel-cage design). One set comes into action during starting, giving a higher starting torque and a lower starting current. The other set comes into action when the motor is up to speed, giving a normal full-load slip and efficiency. However, this type of construction increases the cost of the motor considerably.

Squirrel-cage induction motors are classed according to their starting torque, breakdown torque, full-load running slip, and starting current. These classes are designated as design classes B, C, D, and F. Design class A was assigned to the original squirrel-cage motor. The class B design has a slightly modified rotor, which results in a lower starting current while still providing the normal running characteristics. Therefore, the class A motor is no longer in general use, and the class B motor has been designated as the general-purpose motor. The class C design uses the double squirrel-cage rotor. The class D design uses rotor bars with higher than normal resistance. The class F design gives the lowest starting current, but this results in a low starting torque. Class F motors are only available above 30 horsepower. Table 2.2 outlines the general characteristics of each design class.

2.5.3 Speed Control of Squirrel-Cage Motors

Speed control of the squirrel-cage induction motor is not practical when operated from a fixed frequency source. The running speed of the motor is basically set by its synchronous speed, which in turn is set by the frequency (Equation 2.8). If the voltage applied to the motor is reduced below the rated value, the motor will start to slip a little more, but the drop in the actual speed will be slight. On the other hand, the motor current will increase significantly with the possibility that the motor will overheat. Also, there is no possibility of controlling the speed through field control, as the induction motor has no separate field winding.

The speed of an induction motor can be changed by changing the number of poles (Equation 2.8). However, this results in large step changes. For example, if a motor is connected for four-pole operation on 60 hertz, it will run just below its synchronous speed of 1800 rpm. If the electrical connections to the stator windings are now changed by external switching so that eight-pole operation is obtained, then the motor will operate at half the speed. The synchronous speed of the motor has been changed to 900 rpm. Two-speed motors are often used to drive such loads as fans so that two different levels of air movement can be selected. Four-speed motors are also available that have additional combinations of winding connections, but these all add to the cost of the motor and the switching becomes quite complicated.

The only method of obtaining satisfactory stepless speed control of the squirrel-cage induction motor is by varying the frequency of the power source. The adjustable frequency controller used for this purpose rectifies the ac power to dc and then inverts the dc to a variable frequency and voltage output. While the inexpensive, standard squirrel-cage motor can be used, the adjustable frequency controller is costly. However, present development work is lowering the cost of controllers. Adjustable frequency controller and squirrel-cage motor packages are now becoming cost effective compared with other systems, such as variable dc voltage controller and dc motor packages. The adjustable frequency controller is complex and requires highly trained personnel to maintain. At the present time, due to limitations in technology, applications are restricted to 500 horsepower and below.

2.5.4 Wound-Rotor Motor

The wound-rotor induction motor differs from the squirrel-cage motor in that the rotor windings are not shorted out internally in the rotor. The electrical connections to the rotor windings are instead brought out via slip rings and brushes to terminals on the frame of the motor. Thus, the rotor circuit is accessible, and external resistance can be added to each phase as desired in order to change the starting torque and starting current or the full-load running speed of the motor.

For example, resistance can be added so that the maximum torque is developed at the instant of starting, thereby at least doubling the starting torque. At the same time, the starting current of the motor is considerably reduced. Then, as the motor comes up to speed, the added resistance can progressively be reduced so that maximum torque output is maintained during acceleration. Once up to speed and with all the resistance shorted out, the motor runs as a normal squirrel-cage motor.

On the other hand, once the motor is running, external resistance can be added to the rotor circuit for the purpose of controlling the speed of the motor. When the resistance of the rotor is increased with a constant load on the motor, the slip increases in direct proportion to the resistance. Thus, the motor slows down. The speed can therefore be controlled by varying the resistance. However, there are two major disadvantages to this method of speed control. First, the speed regulation is very poor. As the load on the motor decreases, the motor speeds up toward its synchronous speed, and it will only slow down again as load is added. Second, the efficiency of the motor is drastically reduced as the motor slows down because of the amount of heat that is dissipated in the resistors. For example, if sufficient resistance is added to slow the motor down to half speed, then approximately 50% of the total power input to the motor is wasted in heat from the resistors.

The wound-rotor motor is much more expensive than the squirrel-cage motor. The construction of the wound type of rotor is much more complicated than the cast type for the squirrel cage. The added ring and brush assembly also adds to the maintenance of the motor. The use of the wound-rotor motor for speed control has declined in recent years because of the development of dc and ac variable-speed drive systems. However, the wound-rotor motor continues to be used for applications involving high inertia loads, where high starting and accelerating torques combined with low starting currents are required.

Very recently, there has been some revival of interest in the use of the wound-rotor induction motor for speed control with the development of the slip energy-recovery system. With this system, the previously wasted rotor energy is regenerated and fed back into the supply lines, thus increasing the overall efficiency of the drive system. The solid-state circuitry required for the regeneration is quite complex, but further development work may make this an acceptable means of speed control in the future.

2.6 SINGLE-PHASE ALTERNATING CURRENT MOTORS

Single-phase motors are normally made in sizes up to 10 horsepower at 230 volts. However, the full-load current for a motor this size is 50 amperes. It could have a starting current of up to 300 amperes, and the problems that this would cause on most single-phase systems would be extreme. Therefore, single-phase motors should only be considered where three-phase power is not available or for very small fractional horsepower loads where it is not convenient to provide three-phase power.

The most commonly used type of single-phase motor is the induction motor. Unfortunately, single-phase induction motors are not inherently self-starting as are three-phase induction motors. Also, they are not as smooth running nor generally as efficient as three-phase motors.

To understand why single phase motors are not inherently self-starting, refer to Figure 2.8. If we look at the magnetic field that is set up by a single winding only (winding $A - A'$), the flux created by this winding, ϕ_A, does not rotate but remains on a fixed line (that is, horizontal). The flux increases in one direction for the first part of the cycle as shown in parts (c) to (f). If the analysis of the behavior of the flux were carried on for a full cycle, ϕ_A would then decrease back to zero and reverse its direction for the last half of the cycle. Thus the flux created by a single winding only pulses back and forth on a fixed line. This would not create a torque in the rotor of the motor to start it. Instead, there would be a loud vibration as the rotor is buffeted back and forth by the reversing field. If the rotor were to be mechanically spun, then the motor would continue to run. There would be a pulsating torque created each half-cycle in the same direction. The momentum of the rotor would carry it through the zero torque points that occur each time the current reverses. Therefore, a single-phase motor runs satisfactorily once it has started turning.

The pulsating torque causes the single-phase motor to run much noisier than is the case with three-phase motors. Other than this, single-phase induction motors run in a very similar manner and display similar torque and speed characteristics as for three-phase, squirrel-cage induction motors. The synchronous speeds are as shown in Table 2.1, and the speed control characteristics and comments in Section 2.5.3 also apply.

Before a single-phase motor will start on its own, there must be some component of rotating flux created in order to produce a starting torque. The two requirements for creating a rotating field as per Section 2.3.1 are (1) that there be windings physically displaced from each other around the stator and (2) that the currents through the windings be out of phase with each other. The standard single-phase induction motor therefore has a second winding called the start winding placed at 90° to the main winding. There are two different methods of then obtaining the phase difference in the currents.

2.6.1 Resistance Split-Phase Starting

The resistance split-phase method of starting obtains the phase difference in the currents by designing the two windings to have different resistances and inductive reactances. Refer to Figure 2.16. The main winding has low resistance and high inductive reactance, whereas the start winding has the opposite. Thus, the current through the main winding I_M lags the applied voltage by a greater angle than does the current through the start winding I_S, as shown in part (b). The phase difference of some 25° between the two currents is sufficient to create a starting torque of at least 150% of the full-load running torque. The motor employing this type of starting has become known simply as the *split-phase* motor.

Once the motor is up to 75% of its synchronous speed, a centrifugal switch on the shaft opens a contact, disconnecting the start winding from the circuit. The start winding is not rated for continuous service. The motor then continues to run on the main winding. The centrifugal starting switch can be a source of trouble over the life of the motor. If the switch fails to open at the end of the starting

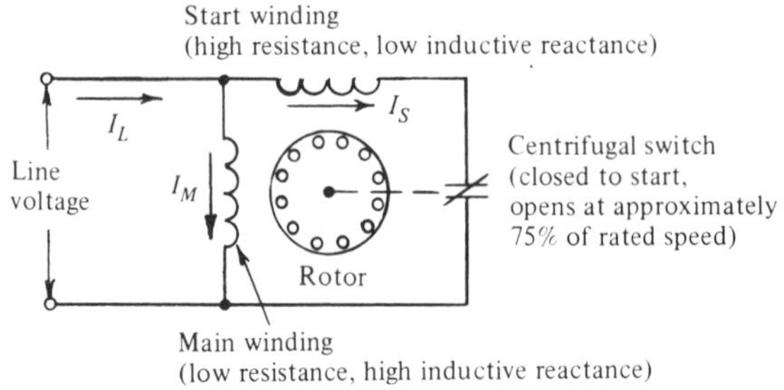

(a) Simplified connection diagram

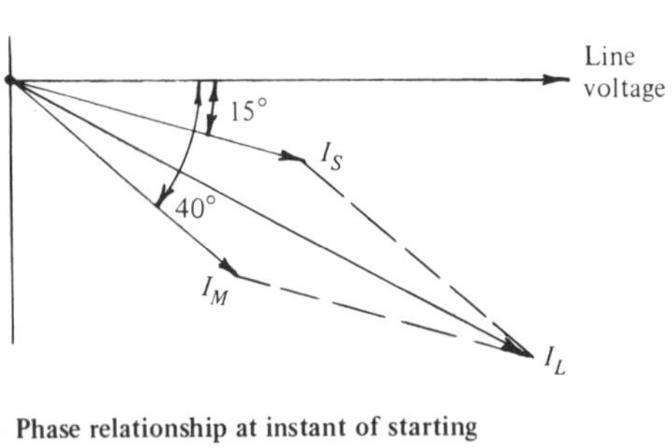

(b) Phase relationship at instant of starting

FIGURE 2.16

Resistance split-phase induction motor starting (motor is referred to as a *split-phase* motor) cycle, the start winding will burn out. If the switch does not close properly when the motor comes to a stop, the motor will not start the next time it is energized.

In addition to its relatively lower starting torque, the other disadvantage of this type of motor is its high starting current. The current I_L [Figure 2.16(b)] drawn by the motor during the starting cycle is the phasor sum of the two winding currents, which as shown is large.

The single-phase induction motor cannot be reversed by simply reversing the two line connections to the motor. The direction of current through the start winding only must be reversed. The leads from the start winding have to be connected to a reversing switch.

2.6.2 Capacitance Split-Phase Starting

The capacitance split-phase method of starting uses a capacitor to obtain the phase difference between the two currents. Refer to Figure 2.17. The main winding is still highly inductive and its current lags the applied voltage, similar to the split-phase motor. With a capacitor in the start winding circuit, I_S is shifted so that it leads the applied voltage as shown in part (b). The phase difference between

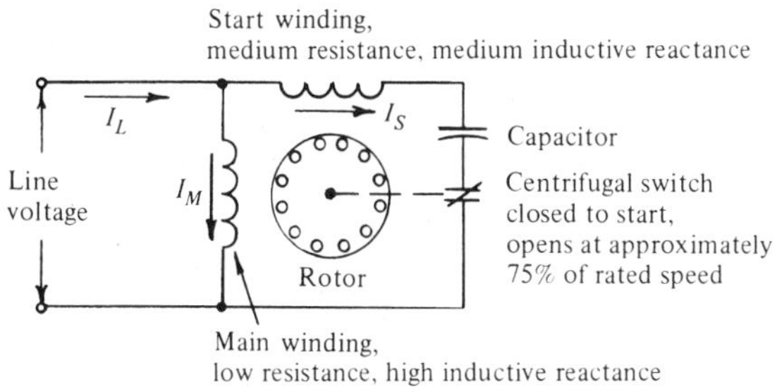

(a) Simplified connection diagram

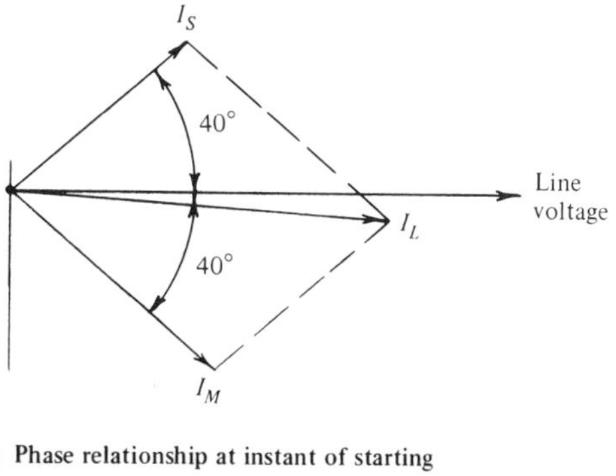

(b) Phase relationship at instant of starting

FIGURE 2.17

Capacitance split-phase induction motor starting (motor is referred to as a *capacitor-start* motor) the two currents now approaches 90°, thus creating a much higher starting torque, up to 450% of the full-load running torque. In addition, the starting current is lower. As shown in part (b), the phasor sum I_L of the two winding currents is much lower than is the case with the resistance split-phase method of starting. The motor employing the capacitance split-phase method of starting has become known simply as the *capacitor-start* motor.

The capacitor-start motor also employs a centrifugal switch to disconnect the start winding and the capacitor at the end of the starting cycle. Therefore, the split-phase and capacitor-start motors perform exactly the same once they are running. The capacitor-start motor costs more because of the capacitor. It is selected for applications where a high starting torque and low starting current are required.

2.6.3 Other Types of Single-Phase Motors

The shaded-pole motor and the reluctance-start motor are two types of single-phase motors that use means other than phase splitting to produce some degree of rotating magnetic flux in order to start.

The *shaded-pole motor* has only the one main winding. Each stator pole is physically divided into a large and small section. The small section is surrounded by a short-circuited coil. The result is a flux that is distorted and moves across the face of the pole when the motor is energized. This produces enough torque to start the motor turning. The starting torque is low and the efficiency of the motor when running is poor. Also, the motor cannot be reversed electrically. Shaded-pole motors are restricted to very small ratings, up to $\frac{1}{4}$ horsepower. However, because of their low cost, they are widely used on very small drives.

The *reluctance-start motor* also has only the one main winding. The stator pole tips are modified so that the flux in the air gaps is distorted, thereby creating some degree of rotating flux. The motor has a low starting torque and poor running efficiency. The reluctance-start motor is becoming obsolete.

The reluctance motor and the hysteresis motor are single-phase motors that operate at synchronous speed. They are used for constant-speed applications such as recording instruments and timing devices.

The *reluctance motor* has a rotor that is physically modified so that poles are formed. As the rotor approaches synchronous speed after being started, it locks onto the rotating magnetic field. The motor then runs exactly at the synchronous speed. The reluctance motor operates with a poor power factor and at a low efficiency. It is restricted to very small horsepower ratings.

The *hysteresis motor* uses a permanent magnet for the rotor, which locks the rotor into its synchronous speed. It is restricted to very small horsepower ratings. This is the common synchronous motor used in clocks.

Finally, the last type of single-phase motor to be discussed, the *universal motor,* does not use the induction principle. It is in fact the series motor. Refer to Figure 2.7, which is the circuit diagram for the dc series motor. This type of motor will also work on alternating current. Since the armature current and the field current are one and the same, they both reverse at the same time. The reversal of the armature current is canceled by the reversal of the field, and therefore the developed torque is constant in the one direction. Because of its ability to operate on both dc and ac, this motor is called the universal motor. The major problem with ac operation is the much higher hysteresis and eddy-current losses in the magnetic core. The universal motor must be especially designed to handle these losses so that the motor will not overheat. It is generally restricted to smaller ratings.

The most common use for this type of motor is for portable tools, such as drills and skillsaws, and portable household appliances, such as vacuum cleaners. The universal motor is used because a high output can be obtained from a relatively small frame operating at high speeds for short periods. This motor is not restricted to operating at synchronous speeds and can be designed for speeds as high as 20,000 rpm. The speed can be controlled over a wide range using variable series resistors or more recently by solid-state silicon-controlled units. The direction of rotation of the motor can be reversed by interchanging the electrical connections to the series field winding. The universal motor has the disadvantage of requiring maintenance of the commutator bars and brushes.

2.7 EFFICIENCY OF MOTORS

The efficiency of any type of equipment is the ratio of the useful output power as compared to the total input power. In the case of electric motors, the useful output is the mechanical power developed at the shaft, and the input is the total electrical power delivered to the motor. Power that is converted to heat within the motor and power that is consumed just to turn the motor itself are considered losses. Heat losses result from the current flowing through the windings (I^2R losses, Equation 1.3) and from the hysteresis and eddy-current losses in the magnetic core of the motor. Mechanical power losses result from friction at the bearings and brush contacts, if used, and from windage losses (it takes power just to spin the rotor in air).

The efficiency of a motor is expressed as:

$$\%\ \text{Efficiency} = \frac{\text{mechanical power output}}{\text{electrical power input}} \times 100 \qquad \textbf{(2.11)}$$

Electric motors can be very efficient, with large motors having efficiencies as high as 95%. However, the trend in the design of electric motors, especially the smaller horsepower, squirrel-cage induction motors, was to provide as much horsepower rating for a given physical size of motor as possible. Competitive factors in the marketplace require manufacturers to keep their costs as low as possible. This is done in part by keeping the amount of magnetic material in the motor to a minimum and by using the smallest conductors possible for the windings. Unfortunately, this all increases the heat losses and lowers the efficiency of the motor. The increased operating temperature of the motor is made possible by better insulating materials. In the past with power costs low, the lower price for the motor was traded off against the increase in power consumption.

Energy shortages in the 1970s, however, resulted in considerable increases to the cost of electrical energy. Using a motor with a higher efficiency (lower losses), even though it costs more, can be beneficial. Manufacturers are now offering energy-efficient electric motors. The lower losses are the result of using more and better steels in the magnetic core and larger diameter copper (rather than aluminum) wire in the windings. The following example shows the advantage of using energy-efficient motors.

EXAMPLE 2.7

A 20 hp motor is to operate 4000 h/yr at 100% load. An energy-efficient motor has an efficiency of 91.5% as compared to 89.1% for the standard motor. Assume that the energy-efficient motor costs $770, the standard motor costs $630, and energy costs 5.0 cents per kWh. Calculate the payback period for the energy-efficient motor.

Solution

From Equation 1.4,

$$20 \text{ hp} = 20 \times 0.746 = 14.92 \text{ kW output}$$

From Equation 2.11, the input power to the two motors is:

$$\text{Std. motor} = \frac{14.92 \times 100}{89.1} = 16.75 \text{ kW}$$

$$\text{EE motor} = \frac{14.92 \times 100}{91.5} = 16.31 \text{ kW}$$

The cost of energy consumed (see Section 1.1.4) is:

$$\text{Std. motor} = 16.75 \times 4000 \times \$0.05 = \$3350$$

$$\text{EE motor} = 16.31 \times 4000 \times \$0.05 = \underline{\$3262}$$

$$\text{Energy savings for EE motor} = \$88$$

$$\text{Difference in cost of motors} = \$770 - \$630 = \$140$$

Time to pay back extra cost of energy efficient motor is

$$\frac{140}{88} = 1.6 \text{ years}$$

With a payback period as short as 1.6 years, it makes sense to purchase the higher cost motor. The assumed cost of 5.0 cents per kilowatt-hour is very conservative. The example also assumed a cost premium of 22% for the energy-efficient motor. No doubt competition will lower this premium in the future.

In evaluating an electric motor for purchase, the efficiency quoted by the manufacturer should be one of the most important factors that is considered.

2.8 FRAME SIZES AND ENCLOSURES

The frame size indicates the main physical dimensions of a motor. The National Electrical Manufacturers Association (NEMA) has established frame sizes in an attempt to standardize the dimensions of motors. Thus, motors of different manufacturers, but with the same frame size, can be readily interchanged. The frame size is designated by up to three numbers followed in some cases by a letter. The first two numbers indicate the height of the shaft above the motor mounting plate. Since this also sets the overall width of the motor, the space crosswise between the bolt holes on the mounting plate is fixed. The third number is a code for the length of the motor, which in turn sets the space lengthwise between the bolt holes.

The original frame sizes, beginning in 1928, also set the shaft diameters. However, with the development of new types of insulation and with improved designs over a period of time, it was possible to provide higher horsepower ratings in a given frame size. This increased power required a larger diameter of shaft for a particular frame size, which is indicated by a letter after the frame number. The letter U refers to new ratings initiated in 1953, and the letter T refers to a further rerating of motors initiated in 1964.

An example of a frame size designation is 254T. The height of the center line of the shaft above the mounting plate is 6.25 inches (one-quarter of 25), and the bolt holes for mounting the motor are spaced 10.0 inches across and 8.25 inches lengthwise. The shaft size is in accordance with the 1964 rerate program and is 1.625 inches in diameter. Thus, any other motor with the same frame size can be physically interchanged with this motor.

NEMA frame sizes are at present based on the dimensions being in inches. An attempt is being made to standardize motor frame sizes with the International Standards Organization (ISO) metric-dimensioned sizes, but progress toward this is slow.

Motors must operate in a wide range of environmental conditions from reasonably dry and clean to wet, dusty, or corrosive. A number of different types of motor enclosures are available. Each is designed to provide adequate protection for the motor and a degree of operating safety relative to the particular environment in which the motor is to operate. The two basic types of motor enclosures are the *open* type and the *totally enclosed* type, as shown in Figure 2.18.

In the open-type motor, a free exchange of air is permitted between the surrounding atmosphere and the interior of the motor. The air is circulated by means of fans formed on each end of the rotor assembly. Open-type motors may be further classed as drip proof or splash proof. The ventilating openings of drip-proof motors are constructed so that liquids or solid particles falling on the motor at angles up to 15° from the vertical will not interfere with the successful operation of the motor. Splash-proof motors can handle liquid or solid particles splashed on the motor at angles up to 100° from the vertical.

In the totally enclosed motor, there is no free exchange of air between the surrounding atmosphere and the interior of the motor. Totally enclosed motors may be either nonventilated or fan-cooled, as shown in Figure 2.18. The nonventilated motor is cooled solely by the radiation of heat from the surface of the motor. The fan-cooled motor has a fan that is external to the main enclosure and blows air along cooling fins on the outer surface of the motor housing to increase the rate of heat dissipation. In addition, totally enclosed motors can be classed as explosion proof, for use where hazardous gases or vapors are present, and dust and explosion proof, for use where dust is present. The dust may be either the type that can be ignited or the type that can cause explosions.

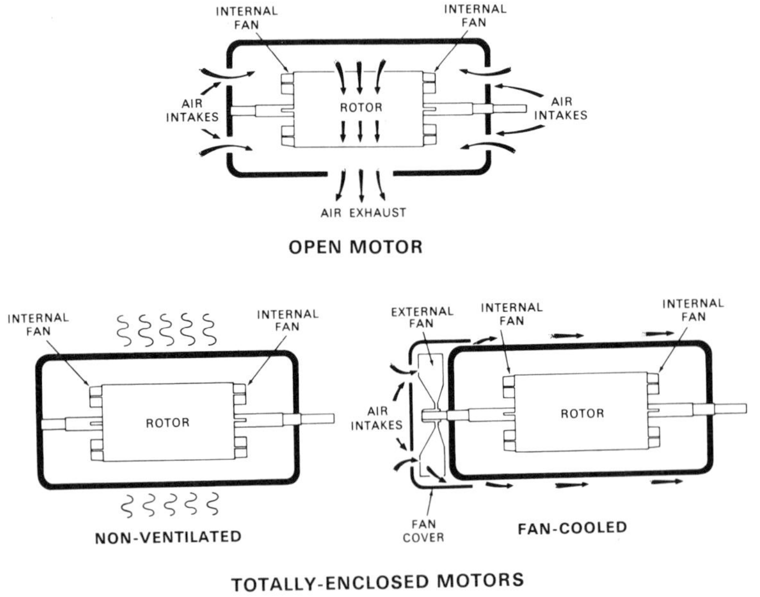

FIGURE 2.18

Basic types of motor enclosures

2.9 RATINGS OF MOTORS

When selecting a motor for a particular application, the most important criterion is the amount of mechanical power that the motor can produce at the shaft. Therefore, motors are rated by their mechanical power output, not by their electrical power input. For many years, the mechanical power has been rated in horsepower. However, the Systeme International (SI) recommends the use of the watt as the unit for mechanical power, in addition to its use for electrical power, which results in motors being rated in kilowatts. This unfortunately can lead to confusion in that the kilowatt rating can mistakenly be taken for the input electrical power to the motor. Because of losses in the motor as discussed in Section 2.7, the input power is higher than the output power. The term horsepower, because of its instant recognition as referring to the mechanical power output, will in all probability be used for many years to come.

It must be clearly understood what the horsepower rating of a motor means. As previously discussed, a motor picks up load by adjusting its speed, even if only momentarily, so that the current can increase to the value necessary to develop the required torque. Therefore, with a constant voltage, the current drawn by a motor from the power source is dictated solely by the load that the motor is driving. As the load and hence the line current increase, more heat is generated within the windings by the I^2R losses. The motor is designed to expel a certain amount of heat by circulating air through the windings. The horsepower rating (the rating stamped on its nameplate) is the amount of power that the motor can deliver continuously without seriously overheating. The motor can easily produce more power than its rated horsepower, but if it does so for more than a short period of time, the temperature within the motor will increase to the point that the insulation will start to deteriorate and eventually fail.

Some motors, however, are designed to take some degree of loading above their nameplate horsepower rating. This is indicated by the *service factor.* When the voltage and frequency are maintained at the nameplate values, the motor may be loaded up to the horsepower obtained by multiplying the rated horsepower by the service factor shown on the nameplate. For example, a 10.0 horsepower, general-purpose, open-type motor with a service factor of 1.15 can be continuously loaded up to 11.5 horsepower. Many other motors (for example, the totally enclosed type) have service factors of 1.0, which means that they cannot be continuously loaded beyond their nameplate horsepower.

Other nameplate ratings are as follows. The rated voltage is the voltage that should be applied to the terminals of the motor in order to get rated output from the motor. See Section 1.8 for definitions of voltages and for voltage standards. For alternating current motors operating on a fixed frequency, if the voltage is varied too far from the rated value, the line current increases, losses within the motor increase, and the motor can overheat. Therefore, the actual voltage applied to the motor must be within plus or minus 10% of the rated value in order to obtain satisfactory operation of the motor. The rated line current is the amperes that the motor will draw from the power system when delivering rated horsepower with rated voltage and frequency applied. This is also referred to as the full-load current of the motor. The rated speed is the speed at which the motor will run when delivering rated horsepower with rated voltage applied. For the alternating current induction motor, this speed is about 3% below the synchronous speed, because the motor must slip in order to produce the required power (see Section 2.5.1).

The allowable temperature rise is the maximum amount by which the internal temperature of the motor can rise above the ambient temperature. The term ambient means the air that immediately surrounds the motor and that is used for cooling the motor. For a general-purpose motor with class B insulation, the maximum rise is 90°C from an ambient temperature of 40°C. An ambient temperature above 40°C affects the ability of the motor to cool itself and therefore reduces its ability to produce the rated horsepower.

In the case of ac motors, the source frequency must exactly match the nameplate frequency of the motor if it is to operate satisfactorily at its rated conditions. The United States and Canada have standardized on 60 hertz, but most other parts of the world use 50 hertz.

Refer to Section 430-7 of the *National Electrical Code* for a complete listing of the information that is required to be shown on the nameplate of a motor.

A motor must be carefully selected to match the electrical characteristics of the power supply and the mechanical requirements of the load that it will be driving. It is especially important to match the horsepower requirements. An undersized motor will either overheat or trip its overload protective devices and shut down. On the other hand, an oversized motor will be operating at only partial load. The efficiency of the typical motor starts to decrease quite rapidly for loads below 80% of rated. This lower efficiency results in wasted energy and increased energy costs. For squirrel-cage induction motors, the partial loading means that the motor will also be operating at a poorer power factor than if fully loaded.

Tables 13.1 and 13.2 list the standard horsepower ratings and full-load currents for single-phase and three-phase ac motors (up to 200 horsepower), respectively. These values are used for the design of branch circuits and feeders for motors.

SUMMARY

The following is a summary of the advantages, disadvantages, and general applications of the types of motors covered in this chapter.

- Direct current motors (general). The transmission of electrical energy using alternating current is now universal, and therefore any dc motor requires rectifying equipment to provide the dc power. This added cost, coupled with the higher cost of the dc motor, precludes their use for general applications where a constant-speed drive is to be used. DC motors are only used for special applications such as those indicated for the specific types.
- Shunt dc motor

  —Advantages

  Very flexible and accurate speed control characteristics.

  Wide range of operating speeds.

  Very precise speed regulation.

  Flexible starting and accelerating torques.

  Competitive prices for complete speed-control package, including motor and rectifier for converting three-phase ac power.

  Very good efficiency for the speed-control package.

  —Disadvantages

  Requires maintenance of brushes and commutators.

  Speed controller complex to maintain.

  —Typical drive applications: where variable-speed drives are required for paper machines, printing presses, rolling mills, elevators, hoists, and machine tools.

- Series dc motor

  —Advantages

  Very high starting torques.

  High torques at low speeds for acceleration.

  Low torques at high constant speeds.

  —Disadvantages

  Requires maintenance of brushes and commutator.

  Motor can run away if disconnected from its load.

  —Typical drive applications: traction motors for trains, electric buses, and mobile battery-operated equipment.

- Compound dc motor. The torque and speed characteristics of the compound motor can be matched by ac induction motors, which are cheaper. Today, compound motors are not normally used.

- Three-phase synchronous motor
  - Advantages
    - Runs exactly at synchronous speed.
    - Power factor can easily be controlled.
    - More efficient than induction motors.
  - Disadvantages
    - Generally more expensive than induction motors.
    - Requires maintenance of brushes and slip rings.
    - Requires separate dc power supply for field.
  - Typical drive applications
    - Where an absolutely constant speed is mandatory.
    - Where using the motor for power-factor correction saves the cost of the capacitor installation otherwise required.
    - For large drives above 1000 hp and below 450 rpm, the synchronous motor can be less expensive.

- Three-phase, squirrel-cage induction motor
  - Advantages
    - Very simple in design, rugged, and reliable.
    - No brushes and commutators to maintain.
    - Generally the least expensive of all motors.
    - Two- and four-speed motors available.
    - Runs at almost constant speed.
    - Can be started directly across the line.
  - Disadvantages
    - Runs at a lagging power factor even at full load.
    - High no-load currents (up to 50% of full load).
    - Very poor power factor at light loads.
    - Stepless speed control by variable frequency can be more expensive than other speed-control methods and equipment is complex to maintain.
  - Typical drive applications
    - General-purpose design class B motors, where normal starting torques and currents are acceptable; fans, centrifugal pumps, rotary compressors.
    - Design class C motors, where high starting torques are required; reciprocating pumps and compressors, crushers.
    - Design class D motors, where high starting torques and high full-load slips are required for high-peak intermittent loads with flywheels; punch presses, shears, bending rolls.

Design class F motors, where lower than normal starting currents are required and the lower starting torques are acceptable; fans, blowers.

- Wound-rotor induction motor

  — Advantages

  Very high starting torques combined with low starting currents can be obtained by varying the rotor circuit resistance when starting.

  Speed can be controlled by varying the external rotor circuit resistance when running under load.

  — Disadvantages

  Cost of motor is high.

  Requires maintenance of brushes and slip rings.

  Very poor speed regulation with added resistance.

  Very poor efficiency with added resistance.

  — Typical drive applications: for high inertia loads where high starting and accelerating torques are required, but where normal starting currents would cause severe problems; large compressors, large cranes, conveyors, ballmills.

- Single-phase ac induction motor

  — Advantages

  Generally inexpensive.

  Has good starting torque.

  More convenient to supply single-phase 120 and 240 V power to small, fractional-horsepower drives.

  — Disadvantages

  Requires maintenance of centrifugal starting switch.

  Pulsating torques, noisy operation.

  Starting currents for the larger ratings can cause problems on most single-phase systems.

  — Typical drive applications

  Machine tools, refrigerators, oil burners, exhaust fans, washing machines, dryer blowers, pumps.

  Split-phase motors are used where normal starting torques are acceptable; up to $\frac{3}{4}$ hp

  Capacitor-start motors are used where high starting torques are required; up to 10 hp

- Other single-phase motors
  - Shaded-pole motors are low cost but inefficient. They are used for low power drives such as record players, portable fans, dishwasher pumps, and typewriters.
  - Synchronous motors (reluctance and hysteresis) operate exactly at synchronous speed and are used for clocks, appliance timers, and recording instruments.
  - Universal motors can operate up to 20,000 rpm, have a high output in a relatively small frame, and can be speed controlled. They are used for portable tools and appliances such as drills, skillsaws, vacuum cleaners, sewing machines, and office machinery. The brushes and commutator require maintenance.

QUESTIONS

1. What is the relationship between the voltage, the magnetic field, and the speed of a generator?
2. What is the relationship between the torque, the magnetic field, and the current of a motor?
3. What is the relationship between the horsepower, the torque, and the speed of a motor?
4. What are the two basic sets of windings associated with the dc motor?
5. What are the three ways to control the speed of a dc motor?
6. How does the connection of the field winding for a series dc motor differ from that of the shunt dc motor?
7. What is the relationship between the synchronous speed, the frequency, and the number of poles for an ac motor?
8. How is the direction of rotation of a polyphase ac motor reversed?
9. With a fixed frequency, why are ac motors restricted to running at certain specific speeds?
10. Explain the significance of the term synchronous speed.
11. Both the dc motor and the ac synchronous motor are doubly excited motors. How does the induction motor differ in this respect?
12. Why is the basic induction motor referred to as a squirrel cage?
13. Why are squirrel-cage motors less costly to produce than motors requiring wound rotors?
14. What is meant by the term slip?
15. Why does the induction motor have a very poor power factor when running lightly loaded?
16. Explain the significance of design classes B, C, D, and F with regard to squirrel-cage induction motors.
17. What is the limitation of the method that changes the speed of an induction motor by changing the number of poles?
18. How is stepless speed control of a squirrel-cage induction motor obtained?
19. What is the major difference in construction between the squirrel-cage and the wound-rotor motor?
20. Why does the single-phase induction motor require a starting winding?
21. What is the difference between the split-phase and the capacitor-start motor with regard to method of starting?
22. What is the difference between the split-phase and the capacitor-start motor with regard to starting characteristics?
23. List the other types of single-phase motors with regard to method of starting and running.
24. Describe the losses associated with electric motors.
25. State what the efficiency of a motor indicates.
26. What does the frame size of a motor indicate?
27. The frame size of a motor is 215T. What is the

height of the center line of the shaft above the mounting plate? What is the significance of the T designation?

28. What is the difference between an open motor and a totally enclosed motor?

29. What does the nameplate horsepower rating of a motor mean?

30. What is the significance of the rated voltage of a motor?

31. What does a service factor of 1.15 indicate?

32. What does the rated line current of a motor indicate?

33. What is meant by the allowable temperature rise?

34. Why are dc motors not used for general constant-speed drive applications?

35. List suitable applications for dc motors?

36. List two major reasons why three-phase synchronous motors are used.

37. What are the two major advantages of squirrel-cage induction motors?

38. What is the major disadvantage of squirrel-cage induction motors?

39. What is the major type of application for the wound-rotor induction motor?

40. When three-phase power is available, why are three-phase induction motors preferable to single-phase motors?

PROBLEMS

1. A 20 hp motor has a full-load speed of 1150 rpm. Calculate its full-load torque.

2. A motor is producing 50 lb-ft of torque at 870 rpm. Calculate the horsepower output of the motor.

3. Calculate the synchronous speed of a 60 Hz, eight-pole motor in (a) rpm and (b) rad/s.

4. Calculate the slip of a 60 Hz, four-pole induction motor with a speed of 1740 rpm in (a) rpm and (b) percent.

5. A 60 Hz, six-pole induction motor has a full-load slip of 3.0%. Calculate its rated speed.

6. Calculate the full-load efficiency of a 50 hp, three-phase, 460 V motor that has a rated line current of 65 A at a power factor of 90%. (Use Equation 1.12 for power input.)

7. Refer to Example 2.7. The 20 hp motor is to operate for 6000 h/yr at an average of 80% of its rated horsepower. The cost of energy is 8.0 cents/kWh. Calculate the payback period for the energy-efficient motor.

8. A 30 hp motor is to operate 5000 h/yr at 100% load. An energy-efficient motor has an efficiency of 92.5%, compared to 90.0% for the standard motor. Assume that the energy-efficient motor costs $1100, the standard motor costs $900, and energy costs 6.0 cents/kWh. Calculate the payback period for the energy-efficient motor.

3 Lighting Fundamentals

OBJECTIVES

After studying this chapter, you will be able to:

- Identify the factors involved in the seeing process.
- Discuss light and how the eye determines color.
- Use the terminology of lighting.
- Calculate lighting quantities.
- Read an intensity distribution curve.

INTRODUCTION

The design of the lighting for an indoor working environment is considered to be more of an art than a science. The fundamental requirement is to provide sufficient light for the performance of visual tasks to enable the person to do these tasks efficiently and accurately, yet at the same time to create a comfortable environment with a minimum of eye strain and fatigue. Since the eye responds to the light reflected from an object, this becomes a very individual response with a great many variables to consider.

However, the primary objective of Chapters 3, 4, and 5 is to cover the *science* of lighting, that is, the use of well-established criteria to determine the *quantity* of light required to provide adequate levels of illumination for the average person under normal conditions. Only brief mention can be made of the equally important but far more nebulous requirement of the *quality* of lighting. This involves the comfort of the seeing environment and is only fully understood by lighting designers after years of experience.

3.1 FACTORS INVOLVED IN SEEING

The study of lighting must begin with a brief discussion of the eye and the seeing process, since the purpose of lighting is to make vision possible. Vision, the sense of sight, perceives the form, size, color, distance, and movement of objects. The eye is a marvelous organ with the ability to react efficiently to a wide variety of conditions. A simple comparison between the eye and a camera is shown in Figure 3.1(a). The characteristics that enable the eye to perform are discussed next.

Accommodation This process enables the eye to focus on an object regardless of the distance. It does this by adjusting the curvature of the lens with the ciliary muscles. For focusing on near objects, the lens must be rounded by the contraction of the muscles; conversely, when focusing on distant objects, the lens must be flattened, as shown in Figure 3.1(b).

Adaptation This process enables the eye to adjust to a wide range of lighting levels, on the order of 1 million to 1. In very dim light the pupil opens wide, while in very bright light the pupil contracts to a much smaller size. Adaptation also involves photochemical changes in the retina. As we all have experienced, the process of adaptation takes time, particularly when going from a bright area to a dark area. The lighting designer must always take this into consideration when lighting adjacent areas.

Spectral luminous response The eye creates the sensation of color by responding to the different wavelengths of light. Unfortunately, the eye is not equally sensitive to the energy of all wavelengths. For the normal eye, the greatest response is in the center of the visible spectrum, which is the yellow-green region, while the least response is at the extremities of the visible spectrum, the red and blue regions. Thus red or blue objects must be lighted to a higher

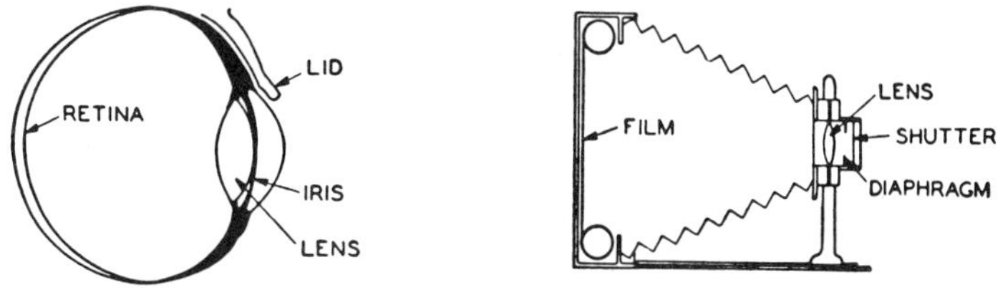

(a) Comparison between the eye and the camera

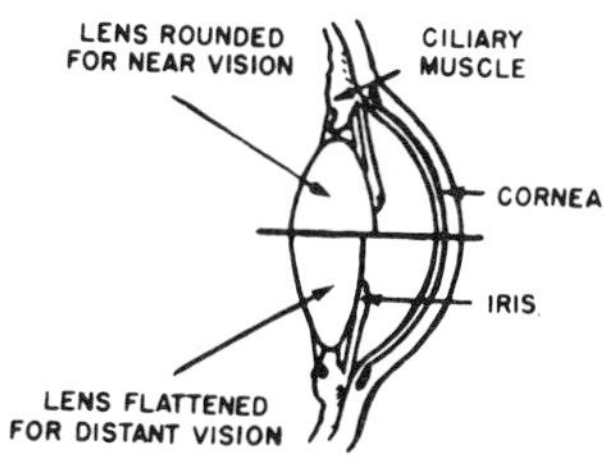

(b) Focusing of the eye

FIGURE 3.1

The human eye

level than yellow or green in order for the eye to respond to them equally.

Since the eyes must continually adjust to the conditions imposed on them, eye fatigue will result if they must do this too often and too quickly. Therefore, poor quality or insufficient quantity of light can seriously affect a person's ability to perform efficiently.

External to the eye are additional factors that affect the seeing process.

Size of object One concept easily accepted is that the larger the object the more easily it can be seen. Visual acuity is a measure of the smallest detail that can easily be seen. It is a function of the visual angle, that is, the angle subtended at the eye by the object. By bringing a small object closer to the eye, a person is increasing the visual angle in order to see it more clearly. Increasing lighting levels will markedly increase visual acuity.

Brightness of object This depends both on the amount of light striking an object and the proportion of the light that is reflected from it in the direction of the eye. Naturally, a dark-colored object reflects less light and is harder to see than a light-colored object with the same lighting levels. Therefore, a dark object requires more lighting for it to be seen as clearly as a light object.

Contrast Equally important in clearly seeing an object is the contrast between it and its immediate background. As an example, the print on this page is dark lettering against a near white background. If the same printing were on dark gray paper, then the printing would be harder to see. Where poor contrast conditions cannot be avoided, higher lighting levels are required to clearly see an object.

Time It requires time for the eye to properly see an object. The longer the time available, the greater the detail that the eye can see. Conversely, more light is required for rapid seeing. In the case of a moving object, the time factor is particularly important. Higher lighting levels make moving objects appear to be moving more slowly.

Our manner of living, especially in the Western World, has changed a great deal over the last 100 years, due in no small part to the development of the electric light source. It has changed from a life of largely working outside, with activities confined to daylight hours, to one of largely working indoors under artificial lighting and often performing difficult visual tasks. Direct sunlight provides a level of lighting of from 5,000 to 10,000 footcandles. An overcast day can provide a level of 500 footcandles. Therefore, the present recommendation of an average of 75 footcandles for office lighting is not that high by comparison.

3.2 LIGHT AND COLOR

In the most basic terms, light is that portion of the electromagnetic spectrum to which the eye responds. This visible energy is an exceedingly small part of the total spectrum, which ranges from cosmic rays with extremely short wavelengths (1×10^{-14} meter) to electric power frequencies with wavelengths in hundreds of kilometers, as shown in Figure 3.2. The visible portion lies between 380 and 770 nanometers (the nanometer, nm, is a unit of wavelength equal to 1×10^{-9} meter or one-billionth of a meter).

The color of light is determined by its wavelength. Visible energy with the shortest wavelengths (380 to 450 nm) produce the sensation of violet and those with the longest wavelengths (630 to 770 nm) produce the sensation of red. In between lie blue (450 to 490 nm), green (490 to 560 nm), yellow (560 to 590 nm), and orange (590 to 630 nm). The region with slightly longer wavelengths immediately adjacent to the red end of the visible spectrum is known as the *infrared,* and the region with slightly shorter wavelengths immediately adjacent to the violet end of the visible spectrum is the *ultravi-*

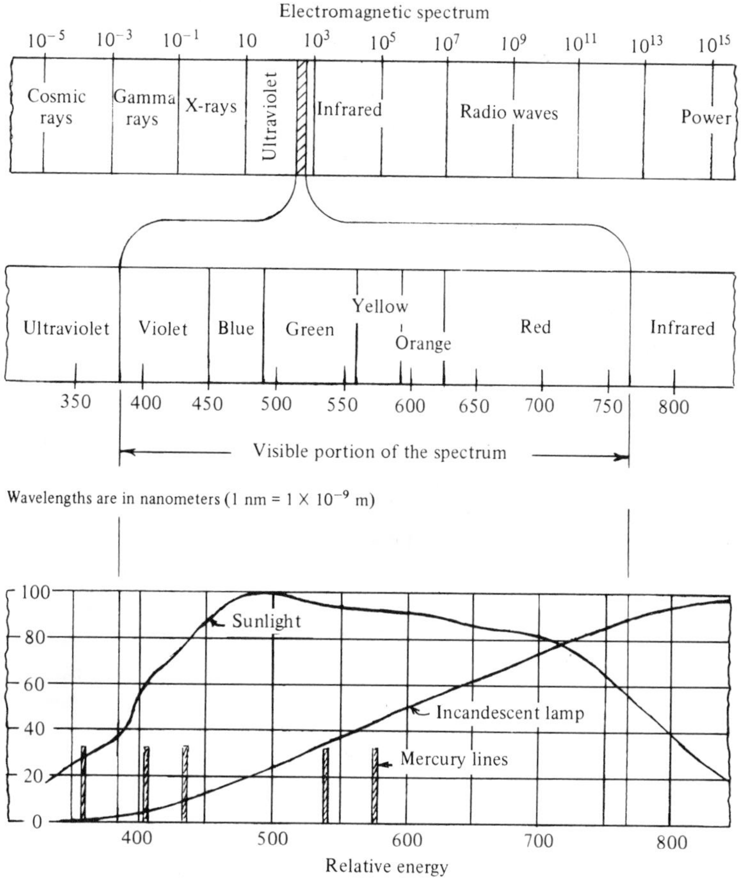

FIGURE 3.2

Electromagnetic spectrum

olet. Neither of these is visible to the human eye; but their effect on humans is very important, and neither can be ignored in lighting applications. For instance, the incandescent light bulb produces a large percentage of infrared energy, which can be very uncomfortable to anyone exposed to it continuously for even a few hours. Conversely, the mercury vapor lamp can produce ultraviolet energy, some of which can be beneficial, but the balance of which can be very harmful.

Light sources can have continuous spectrums; that is, they produce some energy in all wavelengths across the visible spectrum. Or they can have line or band spectrums, in which case energy is produced in only a few separate groups of wavelengths. Also, most light sources do not have equal-energy spectrums, that is, equal quantities of energy in all wavelengths. Refer to Figure 3.2. The incandescent lamp has a continuous spectrum, but it is high at the red end and low at the blue end. The mercury vapor lamp has a line spectrum with its output concentrated in a few specific areas mainly at the blue end of the spectrum. These and other light sources are fully discussed in Chapter 4.

Noon sunlight approximates an equal-energy continuous spectrum that produces the sensation of white light. Since the eye responds to the light reflected from an object, the light source can distort the color of the object as perceived by the eye if the light source does not have an equal-energy continuous spectrum.

3.3 LIGHTING TERMINOLOGY AND BASIC UNITS

Specialized terminology is required for any technology, and to communicate within that technology you must be familiar with the terminology. It is necessary to establish the meaning of all new terms and to define the basic units of measurement. This is done in Table 3.1.

Referring to Table 3.1, the starting point has to be the establishment of the means of measuring the light output or intensity of a source. The definition of the unit *candela* as shown is only approximate, because most people are familiar with the ordinary candle. This was also the obvious starting point when the electric light bulb was first introduced over 100 years ago. However, there must be a very precise definition for the unit candela, as all other units are derived from it. *One candela is defined as the luminous intensity, in a given direction, of a source that emits monochromatic radiation of frequency 540 × 10^{12} hertz and of which the radiant intensity in that direction is 1/683 watt per steradian.* Now you can see why it is easier to relate this unit to the ordinary candle.

The next criterion to establish is a means of measuring the amount of light (that is, luminous flux). Since light is not something that you can measure by weight or volume, another approach has to

TABLE 3.1 Lighting Terminology and Basic Units

Quantity	Quantity Is a Measure of	Symbol	Unit SI	Unit English	Definition of Unit
Luminous intensity (candlepower)	Ability of source to produce light in a given direction	I	Candela (cd)		Approximately equal to the luminous intensity produced by a standard candle
Luminous flux	Total amount of light	ϕ	Lumen (lm)		Luminous flux emitted in a solid angle of 1 steradian by a 1 candela uniform point source
Illuminance (illumination)	Amount of light received on a unit area of surface (density)	E	Lux (1x)	Footcandle (fc)	One lumen equally distributed over one unit area of surface
Luminous exitance	Density of light reflected or transmitted from a surface	M	lm/m^2	lm/ft^{2a}	A surface reflecting or emitting 1 lumen per unit of area
Luminance (brightness)	Intensity of light per unit of area reflected or transmitted from a surface	L	cd/m^2	cd/in.^{2}	A surface reflecting or emitting light at the rate of 1 candela per unit of projected area

1 meter (m) = 3.28 ft; 1 cd/m^2 = 3.14 lm/m^2

1 $m^2 = (3.28)^2 = 10.76$ ft^2; 1 cd/in.^{2} = 452 lm/ft^2

1 fc = 10.76 1x

[a] Formerly "footlambert," which is no longer a preferred term.

be used. The unit for the amount of light, the *lumen,* is defined by equating it to the luminous flux emitted in a specific solid angle from a point source of light, as shown in Figure 3.3. The solid angle is defined as one *steradian* since the angle of projection in both planes is 1 radian. Fortunately, this definition is equally applicable in both the SI and English systems.

Having established the unit for the amount of light, the next step is to establish a measurement for the concentration or density of light, that is, the amount of light falling on each unit of area. This could be likened to having 1 gallon of liquid in a can and then spilling the liquid all over the floor. The amount of liquid in each case is the same, but its concentration may be quite different. Since the eye responds to the density of light, this quantity is most important in the design of a lighting system. The term *illuminance* then refers to the lighting levels that should be or have been obtained for the

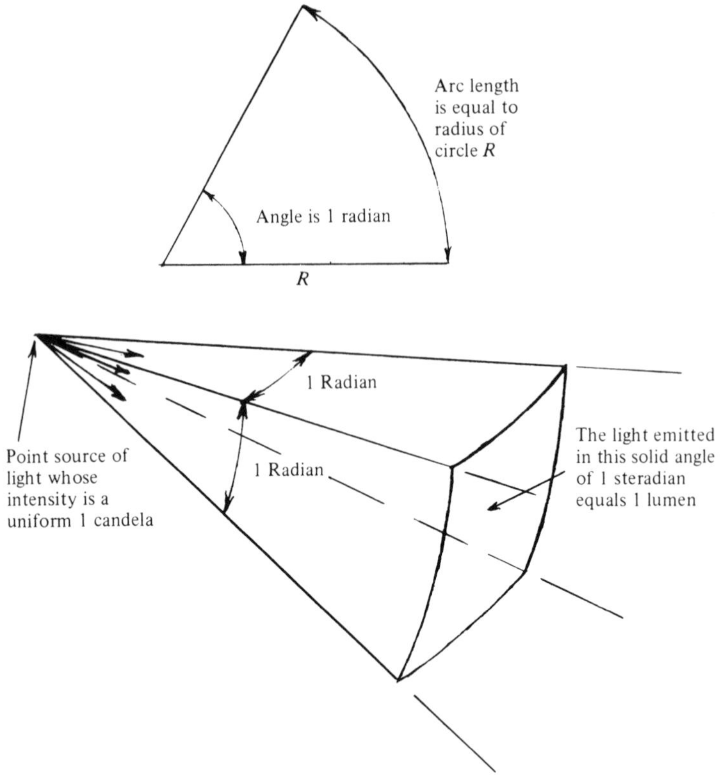
Arc length
is equal to
radius of
circle R
Angle is 1 radian
R
1 Radian
1 Radian
Point source of
light whose
intensity is a
uniform 1 candela
The light emitted
in this solid angle
of 1 steradian
equals 1 lumen

FIGURE 3.3

Definition of the unit lumen

lighting of a particular area. (The term illuminance, which is a more precise term, has replaced the more familiar term *illumination*.)

Unfortunately, since the unit of area depends on the system of measurement, there is a difference between the unit of illuminance for the SI system and that for the English system, as noted in the table. To indicate the same level of illuminance, the numerical value of *lux* (SI) is approximately 10 times the numerical value of *footcandles* (English). As an example, 1000 lux very closely equals 100 footcandles (see Example 3.1).

In Section 3.1, reference was made to the levels of lighting provided by sunlight and to the levels recommended for office lighting. The unit used was the footcandle, because the important criterion to compare is the amount of light per unit of area, and not just the total amount of light.

The final quantity to establish is a measure of the amount of light reflected from or transmitted through a surface, as shown in Figure 3.4. The density of light that leaves the surface is referred to as *luminous exitance* and is also expressed in lumens per unit of area. Since some of the light energy is normally absorbed by the surface material as it is reflected or transmitted, the luminous exitance is

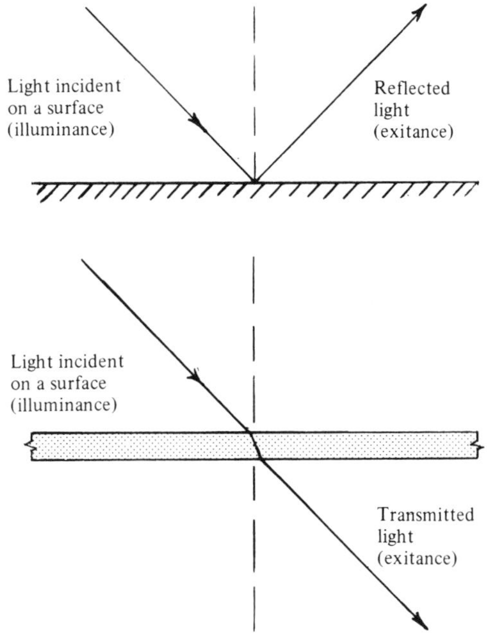

FIGURE 3.4

Reflected and transmitted light

less than the incident light, that is, the light that is received on the surface. The reflectance and transmittance factors, which indicate the ratio of light that is reflected or transmitted, are defined in Section 3.4. In the English system, the unit for luminous exitance was formerly called a footlambert, rather than lumen per square foot, in order to differentiate it from the footcandle, which is also given in lumens per square foot.

The luminous exitance is a measure of the brightness of an object, and it is brightness to which the eye responds. This brightness can also be expressed in a second way: the reflected or transmitted light can be considered as a new source of light, with the unit of measurement expressed as the intensity of light per unit of area. This quantity is then referred to as *luminance*, and it is particularly useful in expressing the brightness of a light source that transmits light energy through a diffusing glass envelope, such as an inside-frosted incandescent lamp.

3.4 RELATIONSHIPS OF QUANTITIES

From the definition of illuminance (E) as shown in Table 3.1, the relationship between E, the total amount of light (luminous flux, ϕ), and the area over which the light is to be spread (A) can be expressed as:

$$E = \frac{\phi}{A} \quad \textbf{(3.1)}$$

EXAMPLE 3.1

In a room 12 by 20 ft, the total light incident on the horizontal workplane is 10,000 lm. Calculate the illuminance on the workplane in (a) English units and (b) SI units.

Solution

(a) $$E = \frac{10{,}000}{12 \times 20} = 41.7 \text{ fc}$$

(b) $$\text{Area of room in metric} = \frac{12 \times 20}{3.28 \times 3.28} = 22.3 \text{ m}^2$$

$$E = \frac{10{,}000}{22.3} = 448.4 \text{ lx}$$

When luminous exitance is concerned with reflected light, the reflectance factor (ρ) is expressed as:

$$\rho = \frac{\text{reflected light}}{\text{incident light}} = \frac{M}{E} \qquad \textbf{(3.2)}$$

EXAMPLE 3.2

A sheet of paper has a reflectance factor of 70%. It is illuminated to 50 fc. Calculate the luminous exitance of the surface of the paper.

Solution

$$M = \rho E = 0.7 \times 50 = 35 \text{ lm/ft}^2 \quad \text{(footlamberts)}$$

When luminous exitance is concerned with transmitted light, the transmittance factor (τ) is expressed as:

$$\tau = \frac{\text{transmitted light}}{\text{incident light}} = \frac{M}{E} \qquad \textbf{(3.3)}$$

EXAMPLE 3.3

A piece of white diffusing glass has a transmittance factor of 50%. The surface nearest to the light source is illuminated to 30 fc. Calculate the luminous exitance on the far side of the glass.

Solution

$$M = \tau E = 0.5 \times 30 = 15 \text{ lm/ft}^2 \quad \text{(footlamberts)}$$

Both the reflectance and the transmittance factors result in a relationship expressed as M/E, but it must be remembered that the first is concerned with reflected light from a surface and the second is concerned with light transmitted through a surface (see Figure 3.4).

3.5 LAWS FOR POINT SOURCES OF LIGHT

In theory, a point source of light should have zero area. In practice, however, light emanating from a source whose dimensions are negligible in comparison with the distance from which it is observed may be considered as coming from a point. A clear incandescent lamp is considered to be a point source. The following are the laws governing point sources of light.

1. *Inverse square law* Consider a surface that is normal to (that is, at right angles to) the incident light as in Figure 3.5(a). Illuminance (*E*) *varies directly with the intensity of the light source.* With the distance fixed, if the intensity is doubled, then the light falling on the surface is doubled, and since the area is the same, the density of the light (*E*) doubles, and so on. Illuminance also *varies*

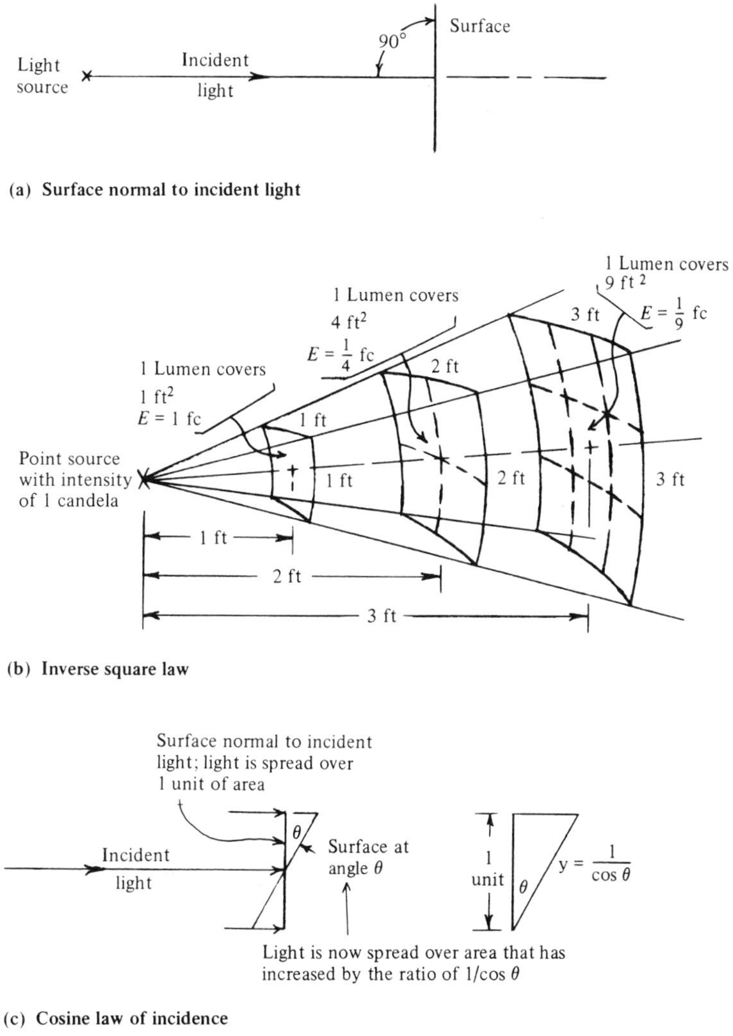

FIGURE 3.5

Laws for point sources of light

inversely with the square of the distance from the light source. Refer to Figure 3.5(b). From the definition of luminous flux (ϕ), the amount of light falling on a surface 1 foot away from a point source of light having 1 candela of intensity is 1 lumen. If we now consider a surface 2 feet away from the source, the same amount of light falls on a surface that is 2 feet on each side, or 4 square feet, because of the diverging light rays. Therefore, the density of light (E) is only $(1/2)^2$ or one-quarter as much as for the 1 foot distance. Similarly, for a distance of 3 feet, the same amount of light would fall on an area of 9 square feet, and the density of light is only one-ninth as much. Thus, there is a relationship that varies inversely as the square of the distance. This applies equally if the distance is considered in meters. Combining the previous two statements yields:

$$E = \frac{I}{D^2} \tag{3.4}$$

2. *Cosine law of incidence* Consider a surface that is other than normal to the incident light, as in Figure 3.5(c). If we first consider the density of light that falls on the surface when normal to the incident light, then the area over which the light is spread is one unit square. If the surface is now rotated an angle θ from the normal, then the same amount of light has to spread over an area that has increased by the ratio of $1/(\cos\theta)$, and therefore the *density of the light* (E) *has decreased by the ratio of* $\cos\theta$.

Combining these two laws gives the following relationship:

$$E = \frac{I\cos\theta}{D^2} \tag{3.5}$$

EXAMPLE 3.4

A surface is at an angle of 30 degrees to the normal and is 10 ft from a light source with an intensity of 1000 cd. Calculate the illuminance on the surface in both (a) English units and (b) SI units.

Solution

(a) $$E = \frac{1000(\cos 30^\circ)}{10^2} = \frac{1000 \times 0.866}{100} = 8.66 \text{ fc}$$

(b) $$10 \text{ ft} = \frac{10}{3.28} = 3.05 \text{ m}$$

$$E = \frac{1000(\cos 30^\circ)}{3.05^2} = \frac{1000 \times 0.866}{9.30} = 93.1 \text{ lx}$$

A practical application for the previous laws is the very common situation of a light mounted in the ceiling of a room, as shown in Figure 3.6. We wish to calculate the illuminance on a horizontal

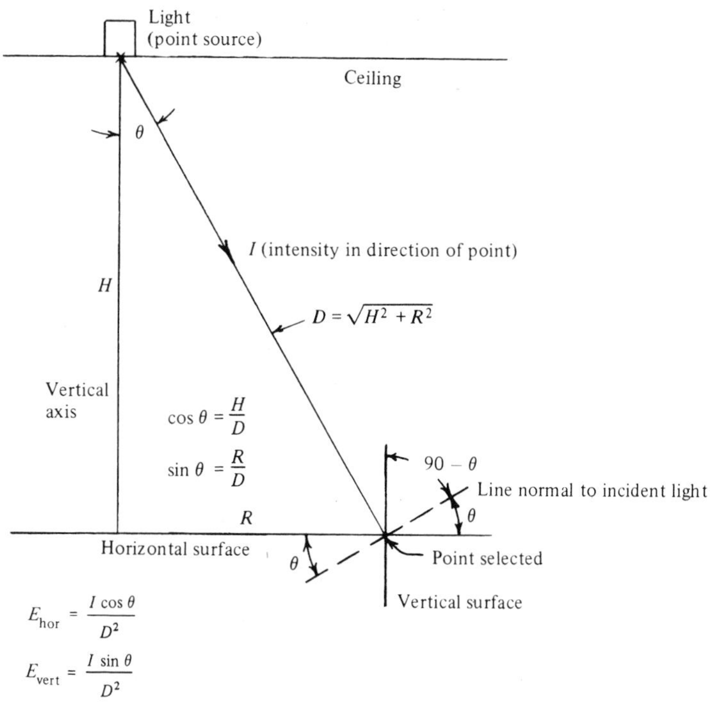

FIGURE 3.6

Calculation of horizontal and vertical illuminance

surface (the top of a desk) at a point that is not directly under the light source. The angle between a line normal to the incident light and the horizontal plane is θ degrees. Note that, by the laws of geometry, the angle between the vertical axis of the light and the direction of the light from the source to the point is also θ degrees. Therefore, the illuminance on the horizontal plane at the point chosen is:

$$E_{\text{hor}} = \frac{I \cos \theta}{D^2} \tag{3.6}$$

where $\cos \theta = H/D$. Also, we may wish to calculate the illuminance on a vertical surface (a blackboard) at this point. The angle between the incident light and the vertical surface is $(90 - \theta)$. But $\cos (90 - \theta)$ is $\sin \theta$. Therefore:

$$E_{\text{vert}} = \frac{I \sin \theta}{D^2} \tag{3.7}$$

where $\sin \theta = R/D$. In both cases, $D = \sqrt{H^2 + R^2}$.

EXAMPLE 3.5

A light has an intensity of 4000 cd in the direction of a point that is 8 ft below and 6 ft horizontally from the vertical axis of the light. Calculate the illuminance at this point on a surface that is (a) horizontal and (b) vertical.

Solution

Refer to Figure 3.6: $H = 8$; $R = 6$; and $D = \sqrt{8^2 + 6^2} = 10$ ft

$$\cos\theta = \frac{8}{10} = 0.8; \qquad \sin\theta = \frac{6}{10} = 0.6$$

(a) $$E_{hor} = \frac{4000 \times 0.8}{10^2} = 32.0 \text{ fc}$$

(b) $$E_{vert} = \frac{4000 \times 0.6}{10^2} = 24.0 \text{ fc}$$

3.6 TOTAL LUMENS EMITTED BY A LIGHT SOURCE

As you will see in the practical lighting layout problems in Chapter 5, it is very useful to know the total lumens emitted by a light source. The relationship between total lumens and the intensity of a source is developed by once again referring to the definition of the unit of the lumen given in Section 3.3 (that is, the light emitted in the solid angle of 1 steradian when the intensity of the light source is 1 candela). Referring to Figure 3.7, the amount of light on the one square unit of area on the surface of the sphere is then 1 lumen. The surface area of a sphere is:

$$\begin{aligned} \text{Area} &= 4\pi R^2 \\ &= 4\pi, \quad \text{when } R \text{ is one unit} \\ &= 12.57 \end{aligned}$$

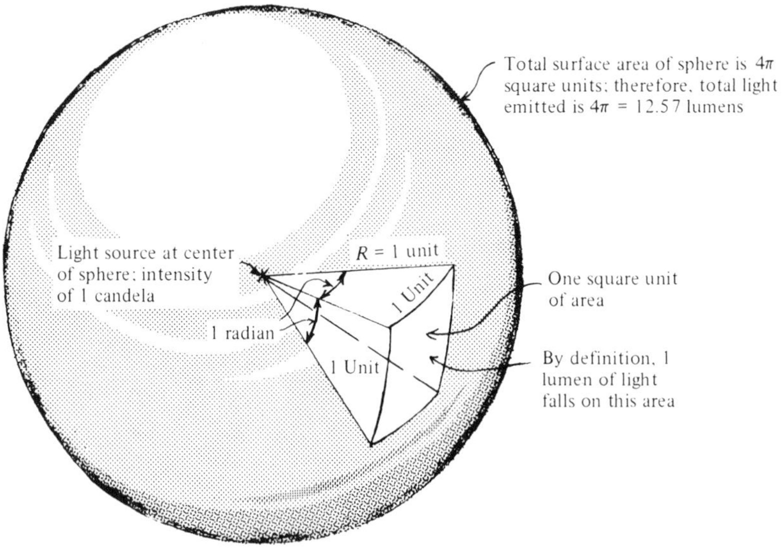
Total surface area of sphere is 4π square units; therefore, total light emitted is 4π = 12.57 lumens
Light source at center of sphere; intensity of 1 candela
R = 1 unit
1 Unit
1 radian
1 Unit
One square unit of area
By definition, 1 lumen of light falls on this area

FIGURE 3.7

Total lumens emitted by a light source

Therefore, the total amount of light emitted in all directions from a 1 candela source is 12.57 lumens.

Expanding this to consider a source with an intensity other than 1 candela and that may not be uniform:

$$\text{Total lumens } (\phi) = \text{MSCP} \times 12.57 \qquad \textbf{(3.8)}$$

where MSCP is the *mean spherical candlepower* (the mean of many intensity measurements taken in all directions from the source).

■ EXAMPLE 3.6

A light source has a mean intensity of 300 cd. Calculate the rating of the source in lumens.

Solution

$$\text{Rating} = 300 \times 12.57 = 3770 \text{ lm}$$

3.7 INTENSITY DISTRIBUTION CURVES

One function of a *luminaire* (this is the preferred term for a lighting fixture) is to project the light produced by the source in a particular pattern. As an example, a luminaire using an incandescent lamp that is flush mounted in a ceiling may have a reflector mounted above the bulb so that as much light as possible is directed downward toward the work area below. However, the beam pattern may be concentrated as shown in Figure 3.8(a), or it may be wide, as shown in Figure 3.8(b). When selecting a luminaire for a lighting system, it is important to know its distribution pattern.

As part of catalogue information, a manufacturer will provide an *intensity distribution curve* for each luminaire. This curve shows the intensity at every angle around the complete 360 degrees, usually in the vertical plane through the axis of the luminaire. However, instead of plotting these values on the standard rectangular graph, they are plotted on a graph using polar coordinates; that is, the angles are arranged in a circle, starting with zero degrees at the bottom representing the center axis of the luminaire, and the values of the intensity at each angle are scaled using concentric circles around the zero point at the center. Figure 3.9 is an example of an intensity distribution curve. This curve represents a luminaire that projects some light upward from the luminaire, very little from the sides, and the majority downward. Since there is an upward component of light, this luminaire would be suspended from the ceiling.

The advantage of using the polar coordinate form of graph is that the pattern of light output from the luminaire is immediately

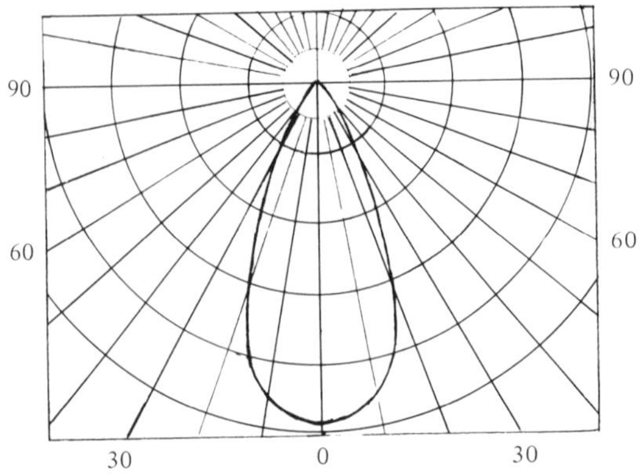

(a) Concentrated beam pattern

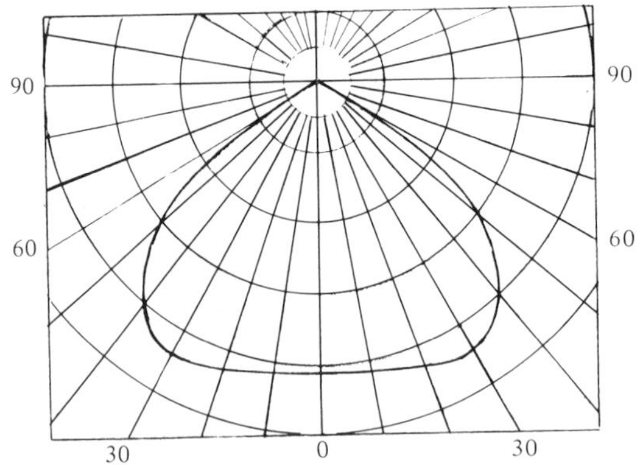

(b) Wide beam pattern

FIGURE 3.8

Comparison of beam patterns for luminaires

apparent. Figure 3.9 also shows an example of a specific value of intensity; for example, at an angle of 21 degrees, the intensity of the projected light is 1400 candelas.

Only one curve is required for a luminaire with a symmetrical distribution pattern, that is, a luminaire with the same pattern in all planes around the vertical axis. A luminaire with a point source of light such as the incandescent lamp would be an example. However, luminaires using the long fluorescent lamp cannot have a symmetrical distribution pattern. It is therefore necessary for the graph to show at least three distribution patterns, one for a plane normal to the lamps, the second for a plane parallel to the lamps, and the third for a plane at 45 degrees to the lamps.

Luminaires are classified on the basis of their distribution patterns, that is, on the relative amount of light projected upward and/or downward from the luminaire. These classifications are discussed in detail in Section 5.4.

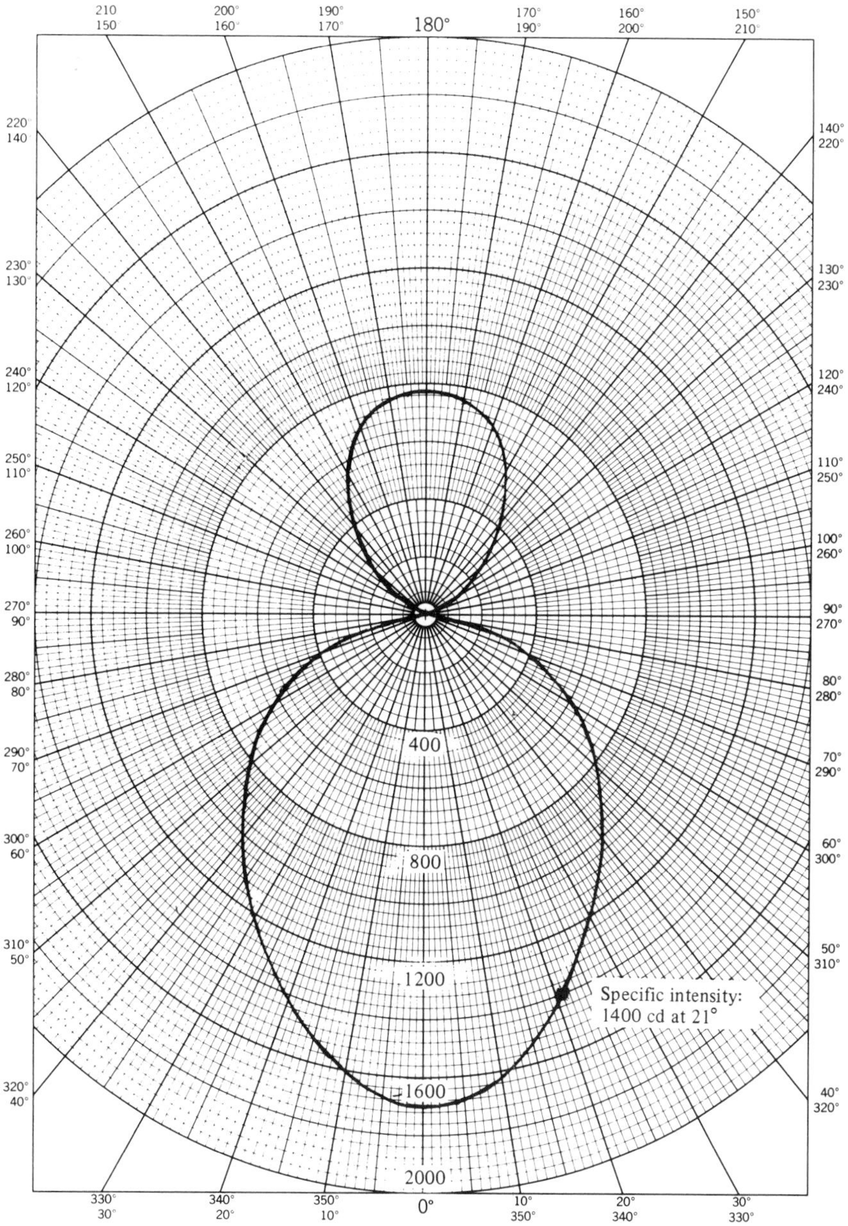

FIGURE 3.9

Example of an intensity distribution curve

Finally, from the intensity distribution curves, the manufacturer can determine the efficiency of a luminaire, which is a very important measure of its performance. The efficiency indicates the proportion of the total lumens emitted by the luminaire as compared to the total lumens produced by the lamps. Thus a luminaire with an efficiency of 90% emits 90% of the total lumens produced by the lamps, the balance being trapped and absorbed within the luminaire. If this is compared to a luminaire with an efficiency of only 60%, then more luminaires of the latter type would be required to give the same level of illumination. This would also result in higher energy costs.

3.8 POINT-BY-POINT METHOD

In Section 3.5, the inverse square and cosine laws, as represented by Equation 3.5, are used to calculate the illuminance at a single point on a plane. Since each calculation gives the value at only one point, a number of calculations are required to determine the illuminance at a series of points over the plane. This method is therefore referred to as the point-by-point method. An intensity distribution curve (Section 3.7) of the luminaire is required to obtain the intensity of the light source at the specific angle θ involved in each calculation.

Besides the multiplicity of calculations required, there are two inherent disadvantages to the point-by-point method; it does not take into account any light reflected from the surfaces of a room, and it is only applicable to point sources of light. Therefore, the lumen method as covered in Chapter 5 is the preferred way to handle lighting calculations for an indoor space. The point-by-point method, however, is widely used for outdoor lighting calculations where there is little or no reflected light and the light source is usually a point source. Computer programs are available for performing the many calculations required by the point-by-point method for such applications as streetlighting, sports field lighting, and floodlighting.

SUMMARY

- Poor lighting can seriously affect your ability to perform efficiently.
- Your response to the seeing environment is very individual.
- Light is that portion of the electromagnetic spectrum to which your eyes respond.
- Color is determined by the response of your eyes to the different wavelengths of light.
- Light sources do not produce energy equally in all regions of the visible spectrum and can therefore distort your response to color.
- The candela is the measure of the luminous intensity of a light source.
- The lumen is the measure of the luminous flux (light).
- Illuminance is the measure of the density of light falling on a surface. It represents the level of illumination.
- The lux is the SI unit for illuminance.

- The footcandle is the English unit for illuminance.
- Exitance is the measure of the density of light reflected from or transmitted through a surface.
- The candela per meter squared is the SI unit for the brightness of an object.
- The candela per inch squared is the English unit for the brightness of an object.
- The reflectance factor is the ratio of the amount of light reflected from a surface.
- The transmittance factor is the ratio of the amount of light transmitted through a surface.
- For a point source of light:

$$E = \frac{I \cos \theta}{D^2}$$

- Light emitted by a source:

$$\text{Total lumens} = \text{MSCP} \times 12.57$$

- The intensity distribution curve displays the pattern of light emitted from a luminaire.
- The point-by-point method using the inverse square and cosine laws is suitable for outdoor lighting calculations for point sources of light.

QUESTIONS

1. Explain the difference between the terms quantity and quality with regard to lighting.
2. Explain the difference between accommodation and adaptation with regard to the functioning of the eye.
3. What four factors affect the seeing process?
4. How does the eye respond to color?
5. What is light?
6. What is infrared energy?
7. What is ultraviolet energy?
8. What is the lighting quantity associated with the ability of the source to produce light in a given direction?
9. Why is the unit lumen the same in both the English and SI systems of measurement?
10. What does the quantity of illuminance indicate?
11. What is the relationship between the units footcandle and lux?
12. Explain the difference between luminous exitance and luminance (brightness).
13. What does the reflectance factor represent?
14. What does the transmittance factor represent?
15. What is the relationship between the mean spherical candlepower and the total lumens emitted by a light source?
16. What is an intensity distribution curve?
17. What does the efficiency of a luminaire indicate?
18. Why is the point-by-point method suitable for the calculations for outdoor lighting?

PROBLEMS

1. A room is 10 m by 16 m and there is a total of 120,000 lm falling on the workplane. Calculate the average illuminance in SI units.
2. A room is 15 ft by 30 ft and has an average illuminance of 50 fc at the workplane. Calculate the total lumens falling on the workplane.
3. The luminous exitance from a surface with a reflectance factor of 80% is 100 lm/ft^2. Calculate the illuminance of the surface.
4. A piece of white diffusing glass has a transmittance factor of 75%. The side opposite the light source has a luminous exitance of 30 lm/ft^2. Calculate the footcandles measured on the side nearest the light source.
5. A surface is at an angle of 20° to the normal and is 6 ft from a light source with an intensity of 3000 cd. Calculate the illuminance on the surface in both (a) English and (b) SI units.
6. The illuminance of a surface normal to and 5 m away from a light source is 360 lx. Calculate the illuminance of the surface if the light source is moved 5 m farther away.
7. An opaque surface has a reflectance factor of 80%. The surface is normal to the light source, which has an intensity of 8000 cd and is 8 ft away. Calculate the luminous exitance of the surface.
8. A light has an intensity of 10,000 cd in the direction of a point that is 12 ft below and 8 ft horizontally from the vertical axis of the light. Calculate the illuminance at this point on a surface that is (a) horizontal and (b) vertical.
9. The illuminance on the horizontal plane at a point 10 ft below and 5 ft from the vertical axis of a light is 10 fc. Calculate the intensity of the light source in the direction of the point.
10. A 500 W lamp is rated at 10,000 lm. Determine the mean spherical candlepower of the lamp.

4 Light Sources

OBJECTIVES

After studying this chapter, you will be able to:

- Recognize the different types of light sources.
- Explain how each type functions.
- Identify the characteristics and ratings of each type.
- Identify the advantages of each type.
- Identify the disadvantages of each type.
- List the general applications for each type.

INTRODUCTION

The primary purpose of the electric light source is to convert electrical energy into light energy. The measure of how well the source performs this function is its *luminous efficacy* expressed in *lumens emitted per watt of power consumed*. If the energy in a light source could be converted without loss into yellow-green light, the efficacy of the source would be 683 lumens per watt. The theoretical maximum efficacy of a practical source that produces some light across all sections of the visible spectrum would be less than 683 lumens per watt.

No light source presently being manufactured comes close to its theoretical maximum efficacy. As an introduction to light sources, the following list gives the approximate efficacies of some of the light sources:

Type	Lumens/watt
Original incandescent lamp (1879)	1.4
200 Watt incandescent lamp (1981)	20
400 Watt mercury lamp	50[a]
40 Watt fluorescent lamp	70[a]
400 Watt metal halide lamp	75[a]
400 Watt high-pressure sodium lamp	110[a]

[a] Assuming an average ballast loss.

The first thing to notice is the tremendous improvement that has been made in the performance of the incandescent lamp since its inception. However, with all this improvement, it is still less than 10% efficient. Even the most efficient source, the high-pressure sodium lamp, converts only some 35% of the input energy to light, the rest of the energy being given off as ultraviolet or infrared (heat energy).

The following is a list of the various types of sources with regard to method of operation:

— Incandescent (passage of an electric current through a filament)
— Electric discharge (passage of an electric current through a vapor)
    Low intensity: (1) fluorescent (mercury vapor) and (2) sodium vapor
    High intensity: (1) mercury vapor, (2) metal halide (multivapor), and (3) sodium vapor

As with any technology, continuous research is being carried on to improve existing light sources and to develop new ones. In the last 10 years, many new lighting products have been brought to market. However, since the purpose of this text is to introduce you to lighting, the scope of the discussions in this chapter is limited primarily to those sources that, by their usage up to the present, have been accepted as standards in the industry. Only brief mention can be made of new developments.

4.1 INCANDESCENT LAMPS

The *incandescent lamp* produces light *by the passage of an electric current through a filament, which heats it to incandescence,* that is, to the point where some of the energy is emitted in the visible region. However, the percentage of input energy emitted as light is relatively low, and the majority of the energy is emitted as heat. In spite of this major disadvantage, the incandescent lamp is still widely used because of inherent advantages, which will be discussed later.

4.1.1 Principal Parts of the Incandescent Lamp

The construction of a general-purpose incandescent lamp is shown in Figure 4.1. The bulb, the base, and the filament are described next.

Bulb. The enclosed glass envelope that seals in the filament is the bulb. The filament, once it reaches incandescence, would rapidly oxidize if it were not sealed in either a vacuum or an atmosphere of inert gas. The various shapes that the bulb can have are shown in

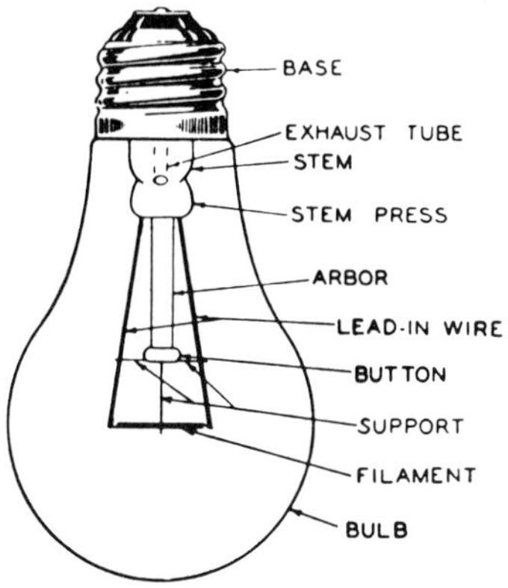

FIGURE 4.1

General-purpose incandescent lamp

Figure 4.2. Some shapes are for practical reasons, such as the R type, which is shaped like a parabola in order to beam the light; others are for decorative purposes, such as the F type. The overall diameter of the bulb is designated by a number given in eighths of an inch. Thus the designation *R40* indicates the R shape with a diameter of 40/8 or 5 inches.

Lamps with clear glass bulbs are used when a point source of light is required for good optical control. However, these types of lamps are extremely bright and require good shielding if they are not to be annoying. For most applications, lamps with the bulb treated to diffuse the light are used. This considerably reduces the brightness. The inside surface of the bulb is either etched with acid (inside frosted) or coated with white silica. Bulbs can also be treated to produce colored lamps for decorative lighting.

Bases. The base provides both the means of making the electrical connections to the filament and the means of supporting the lamp in the socket. The different types used are shown in Figure 4.3. The two most common types for general-purpose lighting are the *medium* base, used on lamps up to 300 watts, and the *mogul* base, used on lamps 300 watts and over.

Filament. The filament is the most critical part of the lamp and must be designed to give the maximum light output at its rated voltage and wattage, and yet still provide a satisfactory life (that is, hours to burn-out). Tungsten, which has the properties of high melting point and low rate of evaporation, is used almost exclusively to make the filaments. The majority of lamps have coiled filaments so that the heat can be concentrated in a smaller space. The larger lamps have double-coiled filaments to increase efficiency and reduce their size.

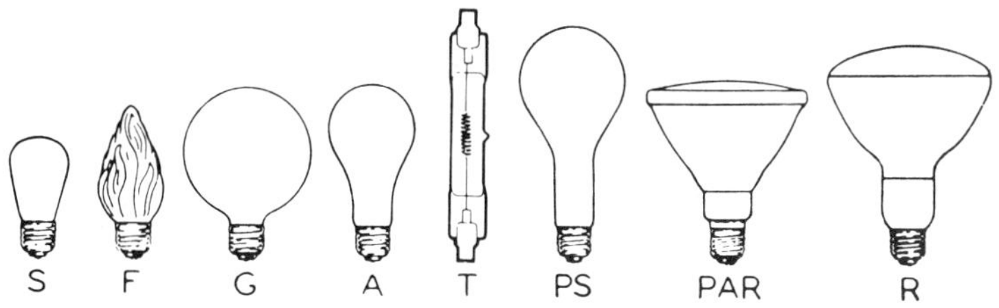

FIGURE 4.2

Bulb shapes for incandescent lamps

4.1.2 Efficacy of Lamps versus Wattage and Voltage

The rated wattage of a lamp is equal to its rated voltage times the current that flows through the filament. For lamps designed to operate on a specific voltage (for example, rated for 120 volts), the higher the wattage rating is the higher the current drawn by the lamp. This

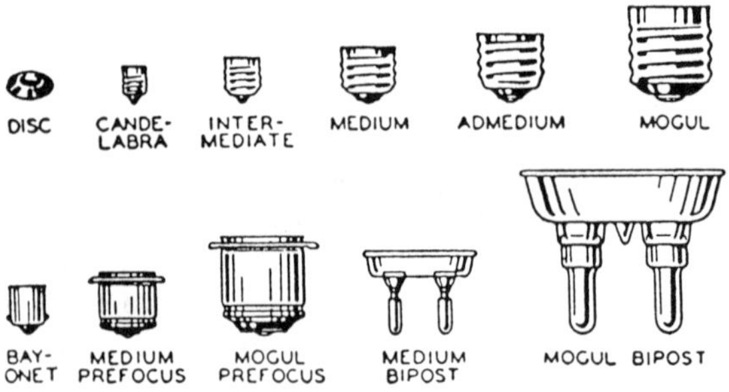

FIGURE 4.3

Bases for incandescent lamps

in turn requires a larger-diameter filament to carry this current. The heavier filament can be operated at a higher temperature without having excessive evaporation, thus maintaining its rated life. This higher temperature results in a greater portion of the energy being emitted as light and less as heat, and therefore the efficacy of the lamp increases. Refer to Table 4.1 and note that the values in the column headed *lumens per watt* increase as the rated wattage increases. This is important to remember when designing a lighting layout using incandescent lamps. The wattage of the lamps selected should be as high as possible, consistent with satisfying all other design criteria. Refer to Example 5.12.

Next consider lamps that have the same rated wattage but are

TABLE 4.1 General-Service Incandescent Lamps for 120 Volts

Watts	Bulb	Finish	Base	Length (inches)	Rated Life (hours)	Initial Lumens	Lumens per Watt	LLD[a] (%)
40	A-19	Inside frosted or white	Medium	$4\frac{1}{4}$	1500	455	11.4	87.5
60	A-19		Medium	$4\frac{7}{16}$	1000	860	14.3	93
75	A-19		Medium	$4\frac{7}{16}$	750	1,180	15.7	92
100	A-19		Medium	$4\frac{7}{16}$	750	1,740	17.4	90.5
150	A-23	Inside frosted or clear	Medium	$6\frac{3}{16}$	750	2,780	18.5	89
200	A-23		Medium	$6\frac{5}{16}$	750	4,000	20.0	89.5
300	PS-25		Medium	$6\frac{15}{16}$	750	6,360	21.2	87.5
300	PS-30		Mogul	$8\frac{5}{8}$	1000	5,960	19.8	89
500	PS-35		Mogul	$9\frac{3}{8}$	1000	10,600	21.2	89
750	PS-52		Mogul	$13\frac{1}{16}$	1000	17,000	22.6	89
1000	PS-52		Mogul	$13\frac{1}{16}$	1000	23,600	23.6	89
1500	PS-52		Mogul	$13\frac{1}{16}$	1000	34,000	22.6	78

[a] Lamp lumen depreciation: percent of initial light output at 70% of rated life.

This table is only a partial listing of general-service lamps. Refer to the *IES Lighting Handbook*, 1984 Reference Volume, for a complete listing.

designed to operate on different voltages. As the rated voltage of the lamp decreases, the current drawn by the lamp increases, since the wattage is the same. This again requires a larger-diameter filament, allowing the lamp to operate with increased efficacy. To take advantage of this increase in efficacy, a line of 6 and 12 volt reflectorized lamps has been developed that incorporate their own step-down transformers to allow operation from the standard 120 volt circuit.

The converse of the foregoing, however, means that the higher the rated voltage of an incandescent lamp is the lower its efficacy. This then becomes a disadvantage for the use of incandescent lamps for general lighting in buildings. To keep the sizes of feeders within the building to a minimum, the system voltages should be as high as possible (for example, many large buildings have 480Y/277 volt systems). This is incompatible with the incandescent lamp. The highest rating for general-service lamps is 230 volts, but 120 volt lamps are normally selected as a compromise because of the higher efficacy. The electric discharge type of light sources can easily be designed to operate from the higher system voltages and therefore do not have this disadvantage.

4.1.3 Rated Life of Incandescent Lamps

As previously discussed, the light output of an incandescent lamp can be increased by raising the operating temperature of the filament. However, this higher temperature results in an increased rate of evaporation of the tungsten, which shortens the life of the lamp. The normal end of life is reached when the filament wire breaks or burns through at its thinnest point. Thus the light output and the life of a lamp are very interdependent. For a specific wattage and voltage rating, a lamp can be designed for a higher light output, but only at the expense of its rated life. Conversely, a lamp can be designed to have a long rated life by reducing the operating temperature of the filament, but this significantly reduces the light output.

The rated life for which a lamp is designed must balance all economic factors. One very important factor is the cost of the energy consumed by the lamp during its life. For general-service lamps, the accepted standard for rated life is 1000 hours. Thus a 100 watt lamp will consume 100 kilowatt-hours of energy over its rated life, which, at a cost of \$0.05 per kilowatt-hour, amounts to \$5.00. The cost of the lamp is only approximately 15% of that amount. To increase life at the expense of light output means that, to provide the same level of lighting, more lamps consuming more energy would be required. This would not be economically justified.

The preceding does not take into account the cost of the labor to replace a burned out lamp. For those cases where the lamp is very difficult to replace (with resulting higher labor charges) and where the lighting level is not critical, long-life lamps (for example, 5000 hours) may be the better selection.

The meaning of the published data on rated lamp life must be understood. The data refer to the average or mean life of a group from a specific type and rating of lamp. This group of lamps is operated under a controlled set of test conditions, and the rated life is determined by the elapsed time to the point when 50% of the total number are still burning (that is, 50% have burned out). The rated life is not intended as a guarantee of the performance of any individual lamp.

4.1.4 Operating Characteristics of Incandescent Lamps

The effects of voltage variations and lamp lumen depreciation are the chief operating characteristics of concern.

Effects of Voltage Variations. The rated values for the lamps as previously discussed are based on operating the lamp exactly at its proper voltage; that is, the actual operating voltage at the lamp socket must be the same as the rated voltage of the lamp. In most electrical systems, the actual voltage will vary from the rated value because of voltage drops within the system and variations in the voltages supplied by the electric utility. Small deviations from the rated lamp voltage cause approximately 3% decrease in lumen output for each 1% decrease in voltage. However, there is an improvement in the expected life of the lamp; a 5% decrease in voltage doubles the life. It is important that correct voltage levels be maintained at the lamps if rated light output is to be obtained. On the other hand, where it is desired that lighting levels be adjustable, incandescent lamps can very easily be dimmed by reducing the applied voltage. This makes them ideal for such applications as stage lighting.

Lamp Lumen Depreciation. As the operating hours of a lamp increase, the filament gradually deteriorates due to the evaporation of the tungsten. (Actually, the tungsten sublimes, as it goes directly from the solid to the vapor state.) The tungsten is then deposited on the inner surface of the bulb, causing a noticeable blackening of the lamp, especially near the base if the lamp is operated in the base up (normal) position. Thus the light output of the lamp decreases with usage, first because of the deterioration of the filament, and second because of the absorption of some of the light by the black tungsten deposits. This loss of light must be taken into account when designing a lighting system. The *lamp lumen depreciation* factor is used in lighting calculations, as discussed in Section 5.3. Typical values of lamp lumen depreciation (LLD) for incandescent lamps are shown in Table 4.1.

4.1.5 Types of Incandescent Lamps

The types of lamps we will discuss are those most often used for general lighting applications in buildings.

General-Service Lamps. This is the most familiar type, as they are used extensively in our homes. They have either the type A or PS shape bulb (Figure 4.2), with inside frosted, white silica, or clear finishes, and screw bases. Wattage ratings range from 10 to 1500 watts. See Table 4.1 for a partial listing of general-service lamps.

Reflectorized Lamps. These lamps combine in one unit the light source and a very efficient sealed-in reflector. There are two types designated PAR and R, as shown in Figure 4.2. The PAR (parabolic aluminized reflector) lamp has a molded reflector to which a separate lens is then attached. The R lamp uses a less expensive, one-piece blown-glass bulb, which can result in a less accurate beam pattern than for the molded type.

Both types can have either spot (narrow) or flood (wide) beams. For outdoor use, the smaller wattage PAR lamps up to 150 watts may be used directly exposed to the elements without breakage, but the larger wattages must be mounted in a protective enclosure. The total lumen output of these lamps is lower than for general-purpose lamps of the same wattage because light is lost in controlling the beam. Nevertheless, they are widely used where compact lighting units with precise beam control are necessary. Wattages for the type R range from 30 to 1000 watts, and for the type PAR they range from 75 to 1000 watts. See Table 4.2 for a partial listing of 120 volt reflectorized lamps.

The type ER lamps are a recent development. They use an elliptical-shaped reflector that focuses the light beam 2 inches in front of the lamp. When type ER lamps are used in deep-recessed downlights, less light is trapped by the baffles in the luminaire, and therefore more light is projected downward to the workplane, making the overall system more efficient. Wattages for the type ER range from 44 to 135 watts.

Tungsten–halogen Lamps. These lamps are often referred to as quartz or iodine lamps. They have a long tubular quartz envelope, as shown in Figure 4.4. Iodine is added inside the envelope to create a chemical cycle with the tungsten that has evaporated from the filament. This effectively reduces the deposits of tungsten on the envelope surface, which in turn increases the maintenance of light over the life of the lamp and allows for a rated life of 2000 hours.

The double-ended type of lamp also has the advantage that it can be easily designed for operation at higher voltages. For the higher voltages, the filament diameter can remain the same, and instead the filament length can be increased (a longer tube) to provide the required higher filament resistance. Thus the

TABLE 4.2 Reflectorized Lamps for 120 Volts

Watts	Bulb	Base	Beam Pattern	Beam Spread (degrees)	Length (inches)	Rated Life (hours)	Total Initial Lumens
50	R-20	Medium	Flood	90	$3\frac{15}{16}$	2000	435
75	R-30	Medium	Spot	50	$5\frac{3}{8}$	2000	850
75	R-30	Medium	Flood	130	$5\frac{3}{8}$	2000	850
150	R-40	Medium	Spot	37	$6\frac{1}{2}$	2000	1,825
150	R-40	Medium	Flood	110	$6\frac{1}{2}$	2000	1,825
300	R-40	Medium	Spot	35	$6\frac{1}{2}$	2000	3,600
300	R-40	Medium	Flood	115	$6\frac{1}{2}$	2000	3,600
500	R-40	Mogul	Spot	60	$7\frac{1}{4}$	2000	6,500
500	R-40	Mogul	Flood	120	$7\frac{1}{4}$	2000	6,500
1000	R-60	Mogul	Spot	32	$10\frac{1}{8}$	3000	18,300
1000	R-60	Mogul	Flood	110	$10\frac{1}{8}$	3000	18,300
75	PAR-38	Medium	Spot	30 × 30	$5\frac{5}{16}$	2000	750
75	PAR-38	Medium	Flood	60 × 60	$5\frac{5}{16}$	2000	750
100	PAR-38	Medium	Spot	30 × 30	$5\frac{5}{16}$	2000	1,250
100	PAR-38	Medium	Flood	60 × 60	$5\frac{5}{16}$	2000	1,250
150	PAR-38	Medium	Spot	30 × 30	$5\frac{5}{16}$	2000	1,735
150	PAR-38	Medium	Flood	60 × 60	$5\frac{5}{16}$	2000	1,735
300	PAR-56	Mogul end prong	Narrow	15 × 20	5	2000	3,750
300	PAR-56	Mogul end prong	Medium flood	20 × 35	5	2000	3,750
300	PAR-56	Mogul end prong	Wide flood	30 × 60	5	2000	3,750
500	PAR-56	Mogul end prong	Narrow	15 × 32	5	4000	7,650
500	PAR-56	Mogul end prong	Medium flood	20 × 42	5	4000	7,650
500	PAR-56	Mogul end prong	Wide flood	34 × 66	5	4000	7,650

This table is only a partial listing of reflectorized lamps. Refer to the *IES Lighting Handbook,* 1984 Reference Volume, for a complete listing.

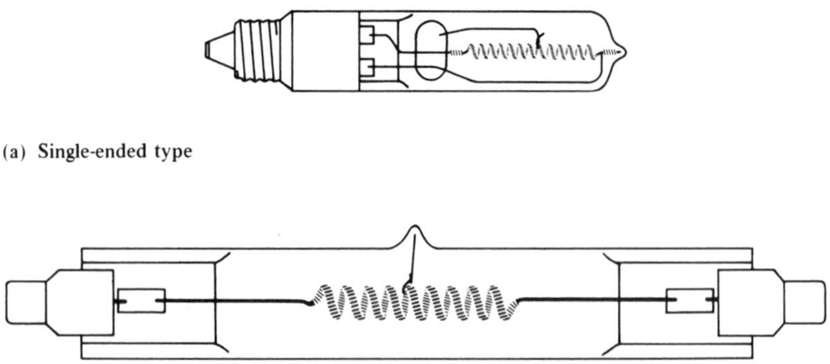

(a) Single-ended type

(b) Double-ended type

FIGURE 4.4

Tungsten–halogen lamps

higher-voltage lamps (available up to 277 volts) have almost the same efficacy as the 120 volt lamps.

The tungsten–halogen lamps are very compact, but they operate with very high socket temperatures and have to be mounted in well-constructed enclosures. A major application for these lamps is floodlighting. For the double-ended type, wattages range from 200 to 1500 watts, and for the single-ended type, they range from 75 to 1000 watts. For a partial listing of tungsten–halogen lamps, see Table 4.3.

PAR and R tungsten–halogen lamps are another recent development. These lamps have a very compact, small-wattage, low-voltage tungsten–halogen source mounted and sealed within a PAR or R bulb. Each unit is complete with a built-in step-down transformer for operation from 120 volts. These lamps combine the higher efficacy and longer life of the low-voltage tungsten–halogen source with the beam control afforded by the PAR and R reflectors. They are being widely used for special accent lighting for display purposes in stores and art galleries.

TABLE 4.3 Tungsten–Halogen Lamps: Clear Bulb Type

Watts	Volts	Bulb	Type	Length (inches)	Rated Life (hours)	Initial Lumens	Lumens per Watt	LLD[a] (%)
200	120	T-3	Double ended	3 1/8	1500	3,460	17.3	96
300	120	T-3		4 11/16	2000	5,950	19.8	96
400	120	T-4		3 1/8	2000	7,750	19.4	96
500	120	T-3		4 11/16	2000	10,950	21.9	96
1000	120	T-6		5 5/8	2000	23,400	23.4	96
1000	240	T-3		10 1/16	2000	21,400	21.4	96
1250	208	T-3		10 1/16	2000	28,000	22.4	96
1500	208	T-3		10 1/16	2000	35,800	23.9	96
1500	240	T-3		10 1/16	2000	35,800	23.9	96
1500	277	T-3		10 1/16	2000	33,700	22.5	96
100	120	T-4	Single ended	2 3/4	1000	1,800	18.0	—
150	120	T-4		2 3/4	1500	2,900	19.3	—
250	120	T-4		3 1/8	2000	4,850	19.4	96
400	120	T-4		3 5/8	2000	8,800	22.0	96
500	120	T-4		3 3/4	2000	11,500	23.0	—
1000	120	T-24		9 1/2	3000	22,400	22.44	93

[a] Lamp lumen depreciation: percent of initial light output at 70% of rated life.

This table is only a partial listing of tungsten–halogen lamps. Refer to the *IES Lighting Handbook,* 1984 Reference Volume, for a complete listing.

4.2 ELECTRIC DISCHARGE LIGHT SOURCES

The *electric discharge* type of source produces light by *the passage of an electric current through a vapor or gas*. When an electrical potential is applied between the electrodes at each end of the lamp tube, the gas is ionized and current (that is, electrons) flows between the electrodes. The electrons travel at tremendous speeds, and when they collide with the atoms of the vapor, they temporarily alter the atomic structure. Energy is given off in the visible and/or ultraviolet region as the disturbed atoms return to their normal state. The electrodes at the ends of the tube are generally made of tungsten and are coated with some form of emission material that, when heated, gives off electrons.

The various types of electric discharge lamps differ mainly in the size of the lamp tube, the operating pressure within the tube, and the metal used for the vapor.

4.2.1 Ballasts

A fundamental characteristic of the electric current through the vapor, called an *arc,* is that it has a negative volt–ampere relationship; as the current increases, the resistance of the arc decreases. If a constant voltage were to be applied to the ends of the lamp, once the arc was struck (that is, electrons started to flow), the lamp current would very quickly increase to a destructive value. Therefore, the lamp circuit must have a device that can limit the current to a constant value that is safely handled by the lamp. This device is referred to as a *ballast*. A ballast can be as simple as a high-inductance coil in series with the lamp.

Most types of electric discharge lamps cannot be started using the standard 120 volts. Either because of the length of the tube or the pressure within the tube, this voltage (even though it peaks at 170 volts) is not high enough to initially ionize the gas in the tube. An autotransformer is required to raise the voltage to a value that will ionize the gas and strike the arc. Thus the lamp circuit is not as simple as it is for the incandescent lamp. With the requirement of inductance coils and transformers, the current drawn by the lamp will lag the voltage, creating lagging power factor problems in the system. To prevent this, a capacitor may be added to the lamp circuit for power factor correction. (See Section 1.4.4 for a discussion of power factor.) The autotransformer, the coil, and, if used, the capacitor are all mounted in one enclosure that constitutes the final form of the ballast.

The input or primary winding of the autotransformer in a ballast can easily be designed for voltages other than 120 volts. This is a considerable advantage over the incandescent lamp. The electric discharge type of lamp through its ballast can be operated directly from higher-voltage systems (up to 600 volts), which permits considerable savings in the distribution system (Examples 11.11 and 11.14).

The conventional ballast has a magnetic core and windings, and losses are associated with its operation. These losses reduce the overall efficiency of converting the electrical energy to light energy. Ballast losses can amount to 15% of the total power input to the system. A recent development is the introduction of electronic ballasts using solid-state technology (Section 4.3.5). One advantage of this new type is the reduction of ballast losses. As the cost of these units comes down and as their reliability improves, they no doubt will start to replace the conventional magnetic-core ballasts.

4.2.2 Lamp Flicker and Stroboscopic Effect

One problem with any light source operating on alternating current systems is lamp flicker. This is caused by the fact that the current passes through zero twice in each cycle (see Section 1.3.1). For the incandescent lamp, this does not cause much of a problem with the 60 hertz systems because the filament does not have time to cool down enough to noticeably affect light output. However, with the electric discharge type of source, the arc current is extinguished at each current zero and it must be restruck. This causes a 120 cycle per second flicker, which fortunately is too fast for the eye to notice because of the persistence of our vision. However, where rotating objects are observed under electric discharge type of lighting, problems can occur. If the frequency of the lamp flicker approaches the speed of rotation, then an object appears to be rotating at a very slow speed. If the frequency and speed exactly match, then the object appears to be stationary. This is referred to as the *stroboscopic effect.* In fact, this is the means by which strobe lights are used to measure the speed of rotating machinery. The stroboscopic effect can create a very dangerous situation with regard to rotating equipment.

There are several ways by which the problem can be minimized. For the fluorescent lamp, which uses phosphors as discussed in Section 4.3, the type of phosphor is selected partly on the basis of its persistence, that is, its ability to continue to fluoresce over the current zero periods. When it is practical to mount lamps in pairs, another method is to operate one lamp with a lagging lamp current and the other with a leading lamp current. The flickers of the lamps are then out of phase with each other, reducing the stroboscopic effect of the complete luminaire. This method is very common with fluorescent lamps, as discussed in Section 4.3.2. When it is not practical to operate lamps in pairs, such as with large-wattage, high-intensity sources, adjacent lamps can be operated from alternate phases of the three-phase system. This makes the flicker of the adjacent lamps 120° out of phase with each other, again reducing the overall stroboscopic effect.

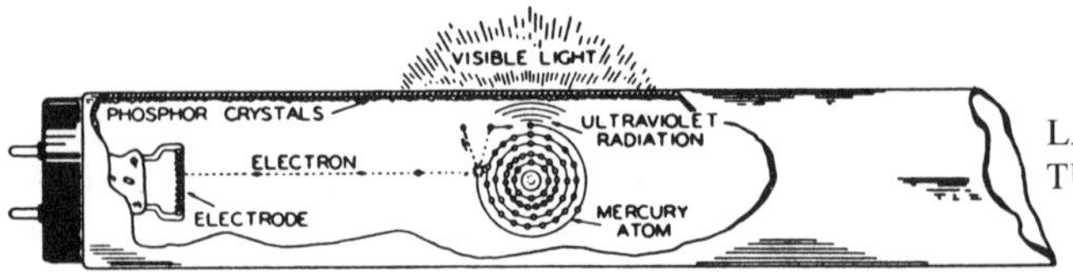

FIGURE 4.5

Operation of the fluorescent lamp

4.3 FLUORESCENT LAMPS

The fluorescent lamp is a low-intensity type of electric discharge lamp using mercury vapor. See Figure 4.5 for the details of the lamp. As discussed in Section 4.2, electrons are propelled at extremely high speeds between the electrodes at each end of the lamp. The energy resulting from the collisions between the electrons and the mercury atoms, because of the very low vapor pressure, is emitted mainly in the ultraviolet region. To convert the ultraviolet into visible energy, the inside of the lamp tube is coated with phosphors. The ultraviolet radiation activates the phosphors, causing them to give off light, or to *fluoresce*; hence the name of the lamp. Approximately 90% of the total light output of the lamp is produced by fluorescence; the remaining 10% is produced directly by the visible lines in the mercury spectrum. A small amount of an inert gas, usually argon, is added to the arc tube to facilitate starting the lamp.

The standard fluorescent lamp has a tubular bulb that varies in diameter from $\frac{5}{8}$ to $2\frac{1}{8}$ inches and in length from 6 to 96 inches. Similar to the incandescent bulb, the overall diameter of the tube is designated by a number that indicates eighths of an inch. The most common size is the nominal 40 watt lamp, which is designated T-12 (tube shape, $1\frac{1}{2}$ inches in diameter) and has a length of 48 inches. There are also special lamps with circular tubes and U-shaped tubes.

The types and shapes of the bases at each end of the lamp are shown in Figure 4.6. As is shown in the circuit diagrams of the lamps in Section 4.3.1, the preheat and rapid-start lamps require bipin bases for the connection of the electrode circuits, whereas the instant-start lamps designated as slimline require only a single pin. The medium and highly loaded lamps, as discussed in Section 4.3.3, require the more rugged, recessed, double-contact bases.

Fluorescent lamps are classified by (1) method of starting, (2) operating currents, and (3) color output. Each characteristic is discussed in the following sections.

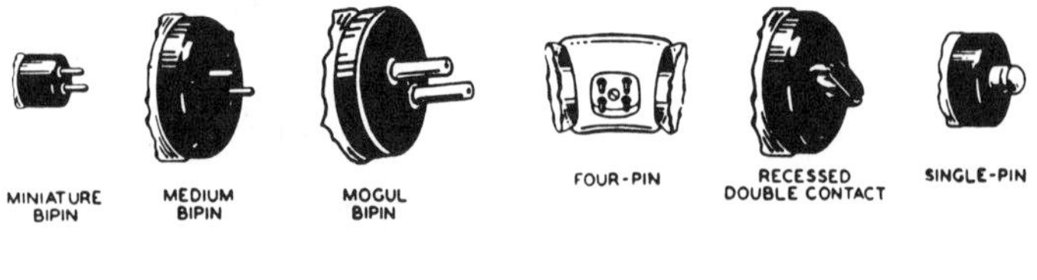

FIGURE 4.6

Bases for fluorescent lamps

4.3.1 Methods of Starting Fluorescent Lamps

The methods of starting fluorescent lamps are presented in the order in which they were developed and used. The preheat method was introduced with the original fluorescent lamp in 1938, followed by the instant-start method introduced in 1944. However, because of the disadvantages listed for these methods, the vast majority of fluorescent lighting installed at the present uses the third method, introduced in 1952, which is the rapid start.

Preheat Method of Starting. Refer to Figure 4.7(a) for the circuit diagram, which shows the connections for the operation of a single lamp. For a source of 120 volts and the standard 48 inch lamp, an

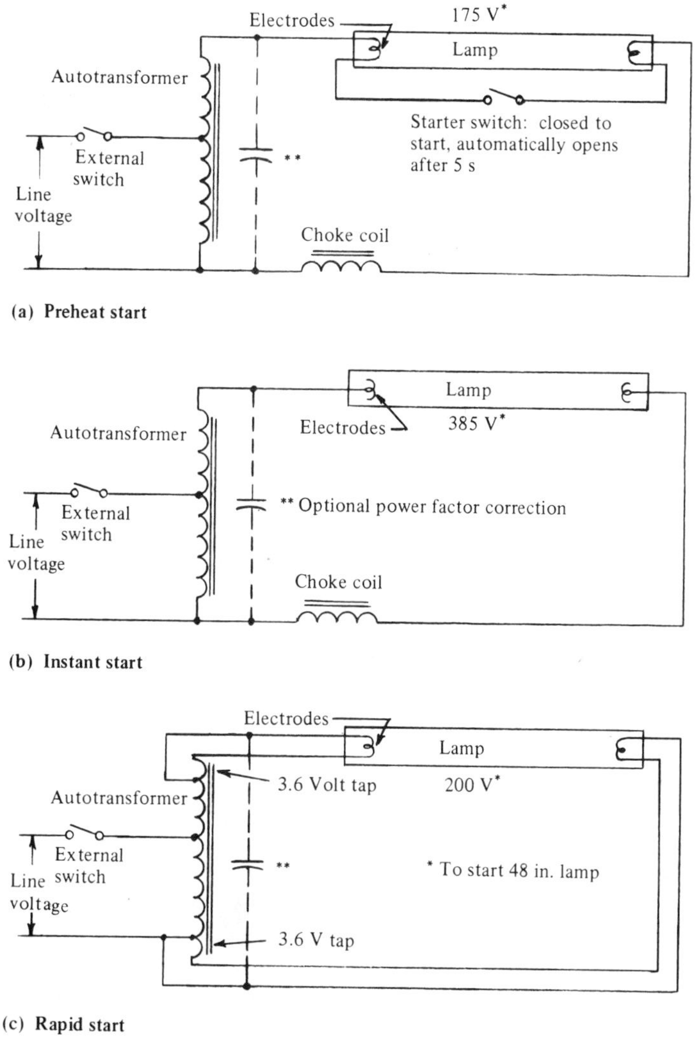

FIGURE 4.7

Methods of starting fluorescent lamps

autotransformer is required to step up the voltage applied across the ends of the lamp in order to strike the arc (that is, start the lamp). To keep this starting voltage as low as possible, the electrodes are preheated for a period of 5 seconds after the external operating switch is first turned on. At the end of 5 seconds, the starting switch automatically opens, applying the full output voltage from the autotransformer across the lamp and striking the arc. The path of the current is then through the lamp. A high-inductance (choke) coil is required to stabilize this current, as previously discussed in Section 4.2.1. The capacitor for power factor correction is optional. Without the capacitor, the ballast is labeled low power factor, and with it, high power factor.

The two major disadvantages with the preheat system are the annoying 5 second delay in the starting of the lamps and the maintenance problems encountered with the automatic starting switch, which often fails after a relatively short period of operation.

Instant-Start Method. Refer to Figure 4.7(b). To eliminate the starter switch, the autotransformer for this method is designed to provide a much higher starting voltage, which directly strikes the arc in the lamp without any preheating of the electrodes. While this eliminates the starter problem, this method results in additional disadvantages:

1. *High unsafe starting voltages* If the power is turned on without the lamps in the sockets, a hazardous voltage exists at these sockets. This voltage can be as high as 565 volts for the 96 inch lamp. Some instant-start systems incorporate a special system to prevent the ballasts from being energized unless the lamps are installed in the sockets.

2. *Shorter lamp life* The severe starting conditions with the electrode cold causes emission material to be torn from the electrodes each time the lamp is started. The end of lamp life comes when there is insufficient material to allow the lamp to start.

3. *Requires a special lamp* Since there is no electrode heating circuit, only one electrical connection is required at each socket. The instant-start lamps referred to as *slimline* have only single-pin bases (see Figure 4.6). The smaller instant-start lamps still use bipin bases, but the pins are shorted together inside the lamp. Neither of these two types is compatible with the other two systems.

Rapid-Start Method. Refer to Figure 4.7(c). This method returns to the principle of electrode heating. The electrodes are heated by drawing current from separate low-voltage taps on the ballast. However, unlike the preheat system, the electrodes are continuously heated during the operation of the lamp by this separate current. Also, to minimize starting time, the starting voltage is slightly higher than for the preheat system, but nowhere near that for the instant start. The delay in starting is only about 1 second, which is acceptable.

The continuous heating of the electrodes causes a small power drain, but this is more than offset by the more efficient operation of the electrodes. Hot spots on the electrodes are eliminated. With the previous two methods, the heating of the electrodes, once the lamp is operating, is provided only by the electron stream bombarding the electrodes. This causes very localized heating or hot spots. Continuous electrode heating with the rapid-start system leads to longer life because the deterioration of the electrode is uniform over its entire length. Thus the advantages of this system are as follows:

1. Starter is eliminated.
2. Starting time is short and acceptable.
3. Lamp life is increased.
4. Lamps are interchangeable with preheat. This is of less importance today, but at the time of their introduction, it was of considerable advantage when existing systems using preheat lamps were expanded.

For these reasons, the rapid-start system is by far the most prevalent method used today.

4.3.2 Two-Lamp, Rapid-Start Operation

As previously mentioned in Section 4.2.2, it is desirable to operate electric discharge lamps in pairs to minimize the stroboscopic effect. This arrangement is particularly suited to the fluorescent lamp, and therefore most fluorescent luminaires have pairs of lamps housed in the one enclosure. Both the preheat and instant-start systems have ballasts for two-lamp operation. However, since these systems have largely been superceded, only the detailed circuit arrangement for the two-lamp, rapid-start ballast will be discussed. Refer to Figure 4.8. This type of circuit diagram is arranged in schematic form; that is, it is arranged in a manner to allow the sequence of operation to be easily understood, and it does not necessarily indicate the relative physical location of the various parts of the system. Note that there are three sets of individual windings for the electrode heating circuits and that the lamps are operated in series with each other. The starting sequence for the lamps is as follows:

1. When the ballast is first energized, the voltages across $C1$ and $C2$ are zero, and the full output voltage from the autotransformer is applied across lamp 1, striking the arc in that lamp.

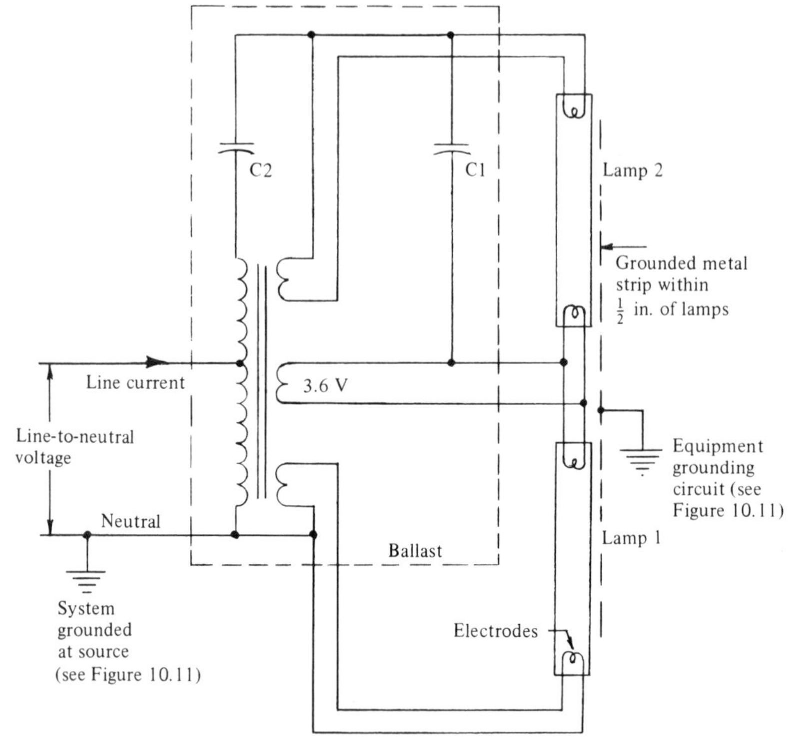

FIGURE 4.8

Diagram for two-lamp, rapid-start operation

2. This lamp current then flows in series through starting capacitor *C*1. This causes the voltage to rapidly build up across this capacitor, which, being in parallel with lamp 2, causes the arc to strike in that lamp.
3. The two lamps now operate in series, and the lamp current increases until stable hot cathode operation at rated current is established.

As discussed in Section 4.2.1, since the arcs in the lamps have negative volt–ampere characteristics, there must be a means of stabilizing their current. This is accomplished by having capacitor *C*2 in series with the lamps and by having the autotransformer designed with a high inductive reactance. Capacitors *C*1 and *C*2 provide power factor correction so that the ballast operates very close to unity (100%) power factor.

Capacitor *C*1 is also required so that the individual lamp currents are out of phase with each other in order to minimize the stroboscopic effect. Since capacitor *C*1 is in parallel with lamp 2, the voltage across this lamp leads the voltage across lamp 1. Therefore, the current through lamp 2 also leads the current through lamp 1.

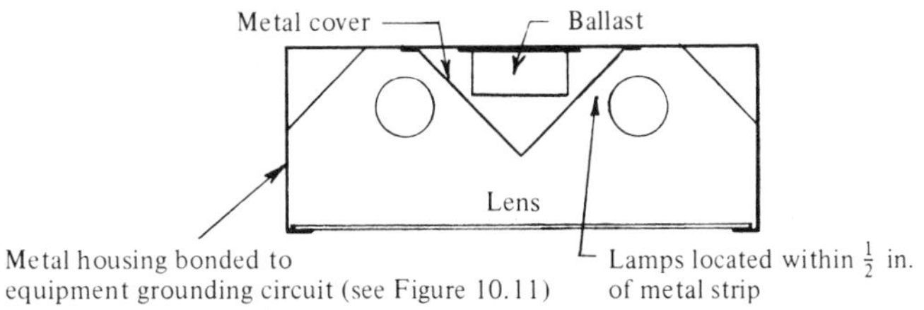

FIGURE 4.9

Cross section of typical fluorescent luminaire

Finally, to ensure reliable starting, there must be a grounded metal strip located within $\frac{1}{2}$ inch of each lamp and running the full length of the lamp. For most luminaires, this is not a problem since the metal housing can serve for this purpose, as shown in Figure 4.9. The ballast must also be operated from a grounded electrical system, that is, one with the neutral grounded. The ballast is then connected to the line-to-neutral voltage. Grounded electrical systems are discussed in Section 10.2.

Refer again to Figure 4.8. There is a maintenance problem with the operation of the lamps in series. If lamp 1 burns out, no lamp current can flow and both lamps are out. This could result in both lamps being replaced when only one is faulty. On the other hand, if lamp 2 burns out, lamp 1 can continue to operate with the current flow through capacitor *C*1, although at a reduced light output.

4.3.3 Operating Currents of Fluorescent Lamps

Fluorescent lamps are further classified by the magnitude of their operating current. Do not confuse this with the line current drawn by the ballast. The classifications of the lamps by currents are as follows:

1. **Lightly loaded lamps.** These lamps operate with a nominal current of 430 milliamperes (mA). An example is the 40 W, T-12, 48 in. lamp with 3150 lm, which is extensively used for office and classroom lighting.
2. **Medium loaded lamps.** These lamps operate with a nominal current of 800 mA. They are referred to as high-output (HO) lamps. An example is the 63 W, T-12, 48 in. lamp with 4300 lm.
3. **Highly loaded lamps.** These lamps operate with a nominal current of 1500 mA. They are variously referred to as very high output (VHO) or power groove (PG). This latter name comes from the construction of the lamp tube, which has a larger than normal diameter (T-17) and has grooves in the glass envelope alternating along the length of the tube. This forces the arc through a longer path. An example of the VHO type is the 116 W, T-12, 48 in. lamp with 6900 lm.

Table 4.4 shows some of the more commonly used rapid-start lamps. The 430 milliampere lamps come in 36 and 48 inch lengths, but the 48 inch lamp is by far the most common, mainly because of its higher lumens per watt rating. The HO and VHO lamps come in various lengths up to 96 inches. However, the standard lengths of

TABLE 4.4 Rapid-Start Fluorescent Lamps

Lamp Current	Bulb Size and Length	Lamp (watts)	Color[a]	Initial Lumens per Lamp	Rated Life (hours)	LLD[b] (%)	Two-lamp Circuit: Input Watts to Ballast	Two-lamp Circuit: Lumens per Watt
Standard Lamps								
Lightly loaded, 430 mA	T-12, 48 in. (1200 mm)	40	CW	3,150	20,000	84	95	66.3
			WW	3,175				66.8
			CWX	2,200				46.3
			WWX	2,165				45.6
Medium loaded, 800 mA (HO)	T-12, 48 in. (1200 mm)	63	CW	4,300	12,000	82	146	65.7
			WW	4,300			146	65.7
	T-12, 96 in. (2400 mm)	113	CW	9,150			252	72.6
			WW	9,200			252	73.0
Highly loaded, 1500 mA (VHO)	T-12, 48 in. (1200 mm)	116	CW	6,900	9,000	69	252	54.8
			WW	6,700		69	252	53.2
	T-12, 96 in. (2400 mm)	215	CW	15,250		72	450	67.8
			WW	14,650		72	450	65.1
Energy-Saving Lamps								
Lightly loaded, 450 mA	T-12, 48 in. (1200 mm)	34	CW	2,770	20,000	84	74[c]	74.9
			WW	2,820				76.2
			CWX	1,925				52.0
			WWX	1,925				52.0
			SSII	3,050				82.4
Medium loaded, 810 mA	T-12, 96 in. (2400 mm)	95	CW	8,500	12,000	82	207[c]	82.1
			WW	8,458				81.7

[a] CW: cool white, WW: warm white; X: deluxe lamp; SSII: super saver II

[b] Lamp lumen depreciation: percent of initial light output at 70% of rated life

[c] Using energy-saving ballast

This table is only a partial listing of rapid-start fluorescent lamps. Refer to the *IES Lighting Handbook*, 1984 Reference Volume, for a complete listing of all fluorescent lamps.

luminaires is either 48 or 96 inches. Table 4.4 lists only the lamps for these two common lengths. Note the following with regard to the cool-white lamps operating in the two-lamp circuit: (1) HO lamps of 48 and 96 inches have lumen per watt ratings of 65.7 and 72.6, respectively, and (2) VHO lamps of 48 and 96 inches have lumen per watt ratings of 54.8 and 67.8, respectively. Therefore, the 96 inch lamps with the higher efficacies should be used wherever possible, unless the length of lamp causes installation problems. In the layout examples shown in Chapter 5, the 96 inch lamps are used when considering the HO and VHO lamps.

When selecting the type of lamp with regard to the lamp operating current for a particular lighting layout, the following should be considered:

1. **Luminance (brightness) of the lamps.** The higher-current lamps, because they produce more light per unit of length, will have a higher luminance. The luminance of the HO lamp is approximately one and one-half times and the VHO lamp is approximately two and one-half times that of the standard 430 mA lamp. Therefore, the HO and VHO lamps could cause problems with glare.
2. **Spacing ratios of luminaires.** The increased light output from the HO and VHO lamps results in fewer lamps and luminaires being required for a given lighting level. This may result in the luminaires being spaced too far apart, creating uneven lighting levels. The spacing ratio of luminaires is fully discussed in Section 5.5.1.
3. **Noise of ballasts.** The HO and VHO lamps, since they have higher wattage ratings, require much larger ballasts. The power input to the ballast for two 96 in. VHO lamps is 450 W. The iron core required for this much power creates considerable hum because of the ac supply, especially when magnified by the metal body of the luminaire.

For these reasons, the HO and VHO lamps are not normally used in low-ceiling areas such as offices or classrooms. The 430 milliampere, 48 inch lamps are generally the choice for these types of areas. The HO and VHO lamps are much more suitable for the higher-ceiling areas of factories and warehouses.

4.3.4 Color Output of Fluorescent Lamps

Fluorescent lamps are also classified as to color output. They are offered in a wide variety of colors. However, the discussion here will be concerned only with lamps producing the so-called *white* light. In this case, the color output of the lamp refers to the type of atmosphere created by the light. A *cool* atmosphere has a connotation of efficiency and neatness, and a *warm* atmosphere that of friendliness or coziness. These lamps then are referred to as cool white or warm white.

From its introduction in 1938, the fluorescent lamp has naturally been compared to the incandescent lamp with which people are familiar. The incandescent lamp inherently creates a warm and friendly atmosphere because of its higher output at the red end of the spectrum (refer to Figure 3.2). This output is also flattering to skin tones. The early fluorescent lamps, because of the mercury spectrum, were high in output at the blue end of the spectrum, which is not flattering to skin tones. This created an unfavorable reaction to these lamps. Extensive research with the phosphors has since created lamps with much more acceptable color outputs.

The spectral distribution curves for the *cool white* and *warm white* lamps are shown on the left in Figure 4.10. They show that the warm white lamp has more output in the yellow-red area and therefore an output that creates a warmer atmosphere. If these two types of lamps are viewed side by side, the difference is quite apparent.

However, these lamps are still relatively low in energy output at the red end of the spectrum. The deluxe lamps were developed for use where a high degree of color rendering is required. Color rendering is a general expression for the effect of a light source on the color of an object. The spectral distribution curves for the *cool white deluxe* and the *warm white deluxe* lamps are shown on the right in Figure 4.10. The warm white deluxe lamp has the highest output at the red end of the spectrum. This is the type that should be used, for

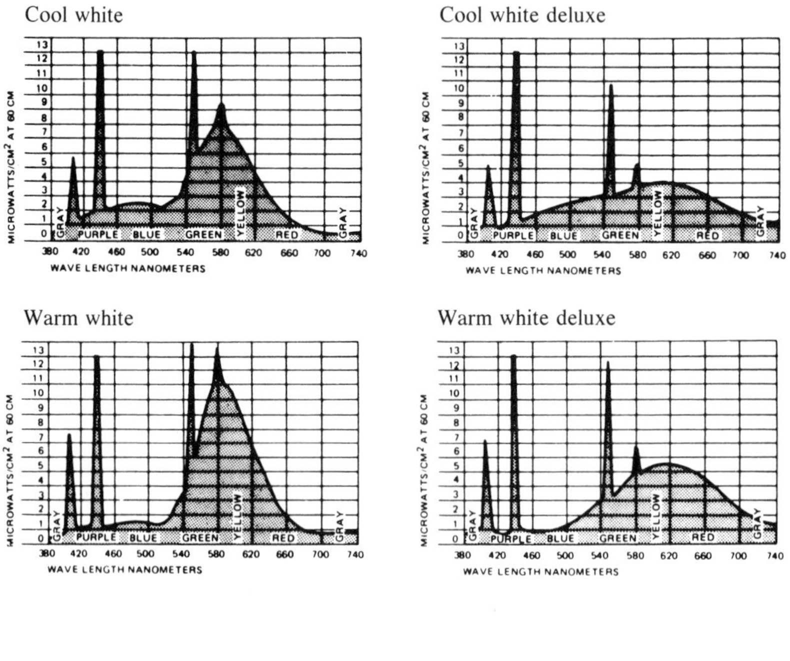

FIGURE 4.10

Spectral distribution curves for fluorescent lamps

example, in residential lighting, because it comes the closest to matching the color output of the incandescent lamp. Unfortunately, this improvement in color output is at the expense of total light output. As shown in Table 4.4, the initial lumen rating of the deluxe lamps is only some 70% of the standard cool white lamp.

Additional advances have recently been made in the development of phosphors that improve both the efficacy and color output of fluorescent lamps. Unfortunately, the new variations of lamps being offered by manufacturers are too numerous to list here. Lamp manufacturers should be consulted for the latest data on their lamps.

4.3.5 Energy-Saving Fluorescent Lamps and Ballasts

As a result of the energy shortage caused by the oil embargo in the early 1970s, much emphasis has been put on saving energy. One area that has received a lot of attention is the lighting of offices and factories.

The first step was the development of lower-wattage lamps that could be used in place of the standard fluorescent lamps. As an example, a new type of lamp with a rating of only 34 watts was produced as a replacement for the standard 40 watt, 430 milliampere, 48 inch lamp. The first versions of this lamp, however, had correspondingly lower lumen outputs. Since then improvements have been made so that there are now types of energy-saving lamps that nearly equal the light output of the standard lamps and therefore have improved lumen per watt ratings.

Some energy-saving lamps are listed in Table 4.4. These lamps are generally more expensive than standard lamps, but their use can be justified on the basis of savings in the cost of the electrical energy to operate the lighting system. Refer to Example 5.17, which shows a good rate of return on investment for relamping with energy-saving lamps for a typical fluorescent lighting layout. In all probability, the new energy-saving lamps will be the standard of the future.

Parallel with these new trends in lamps has been the development of energy-saving ballasts. Table 4.4 shows power inputs to the new energy-saving ballasts when used with the energy-saving lamps. A comparison with the standard cool white 40 watt, 430 milliampere, 48 inch lamps operated on the conventional two-lamp ballast shows the following:

— Conventional lamps and ballasts: 66.3 lm/W
— Energy-saving SSII lamps and ballasts: 82.4 lm/W

With very nearly a 25% increase in efficacy, the energy-saving systems should be given a great deal of consideration, notwithstanding their higher initial cost.

Advancements in solid-state technology have resulted in the recent development of electronic ballasts. This system reduces the ballast losses by substituting integrated circuits and a high-frequency transformer for the conventional magnetic core transformer. In addition, tests have shown that the efficacy of fluorescent lamps is increased on the order of 10% when operated on higher frequencies up to 22,000 hertz. With conventional ballasts, the frequency applied to the lamps can only be the same as that of the power supply (60 hertz). With an electronic ballast, the 60 hertz input can be converted to the higher frequency necessary for optimum operation of the lamps. Also, the ability to dim the fluorescent lamps can easily be incorporated into the solid-state circuitry, resulting in further benefits (see Section 4.3.9).

Unfortunately, some earlier models of electronic ballasts did not live up to expectations, resulting in poor lamp operation and early component failures. However, these problems are gradually being overcome, and electronic ballasts are now gaining a small but increasing share of the market, notwithstanding their higher costs, because of their many potential advantages. To date, no standards have been developed for electronic ballasts. Therefore, there are no criteria against which the performance of a particular manufacturer's ballast can be judged.

4.3.6 Compact Fluorescent Lamps

Recent advances in phosphor technology have led to the development of much smaller single-ended fluorescent lamps. These compact lamps were first introduced as a replacement for incandescent lamps so that the much higher efficacy of the fluorescent lamp could be utilized, and therefore they had to be comparable in physical size. The reduction in size from the standard fluorescent lamp was accomplished by adopting a much smaller diameter tube [T-4 (10 mm) or T-5 (15 mm)] and by using parallel tubes (twin tube or quad tube). The T-4 twin-tube lamps range from 5 to 13 watts, and the T-4 quad-tube lamps range from 10 to 26 watts. Figure 4.11 shows the comparison in size between the 13 watt, T-4, quad-tube, compact fluorescent lamp and a standard 60 watt incandescent lamp, both of which have comparable light outputs. Even when the ballast losses are included, the compact fluorescent lamp has four times the efficacy (lumens per watt rating) as compared to the incandescent lamp. The new lamps also have a rated life of 10,000 hours, compared to the 1000 hours for the standard incandescent lamp.

FIGURE 4.11

Comparison of size between the 13 watt compact quad-tube fluorescent lamp and a standard 60 watt incandescent lamp

For compact fluorescent lamps to be a direct replacement for incandescent lamps, some models are available with built-in ballasts and are mounted on a medium screw base that fits the standard light socket. However, these compact lamps are not a point source of light and therefore cannot provide the optical control of light pattern that is possible with incandescent lamps.

A second generation of longer, twin-tube, compact lamps is now available that has light outputs comparable to the standard T-12, single-tube fluorescent lamps. As an example, the 36 watt, T-5, twin-tube, compact lamp has a rated light output of 3000 lumens and yet is only 16.5 inches long. The standard 40 watt, T-12, 48 inch long lamp has a rated output of 3150 lumens. The compact lamp provides 163 lumens per cubic inch of volume, whereas the standard lamp provides only 35 lumens per cubic inch; a ratio of almost 5 to 1. The T-5, twin-tube lamps range from 18 to 55 watts. The compact size of these new lamps means that the luminaires in turn can be much smaller, allowing for a greater degree of flexibility in the luminaire ceiling arrangement. As the technology of compact fluorescent lamps progresses, and as the necessary ballasts and luminaires to go along with them are developed, these new lamps will have a significant impact on the design of lighting systems.

4.3.7 Rated Life of Fluorescent Lamps

As discussed in Section 4.1.3 with regard to incandescent lamps, the rated life means the average or mean life of a group of lamps. The normal end of life for a fluorescent lamp comes when there is insufficient electron emission material remaining on the electrodes to allow the arc to strike. Some emission material is continuously consumed as the lamp burns, but a considerable amount is removed by the impact of the arc each time the lamp is started. Therefore, the life of the lamp is affected by the number of starts. The standard is to rate fluorescent lamps on the basis of a minimum of 3 hours burning per start. Refer to Table 4.4 for the rated life of the lamps listed. Note that the rated life is many times that for incandescent lamps. For example, the standard 40 watt, rapid-start lamp has a rated life of 20,000 hours, 20 times that of the standard incandescent lamp.

4.3.8 Operating Characteristics of Fluorescent Lamps

The chief operating characteristics of concern are the effects of voltage variation, lamp lumen depreciation, and the effects of ambient temperature.

The Effects of Voltage Variation. A fluorescent lamp is not nearly so sensitive to voltage changes as the incandescent lamp. A 1% variation in line voltage changes the lumen output also by about 1%. However, low voltage will not extend the life of the fluorescent lamp, as is the case with the incandescent lamp, but will instead shorten it. Low voltage can cause starting problems, which can seriously deteriorate the electrodes. Operating voltages above normal cause excessive lamp operating currents, which can cause premature lamp failure and overheating of the ballasts. For these reasons, the supply voltage should be maintained within a small tolerance, generally plus or minus 5% of the rated voltage of the ballast.

A serious voltage dip on the system, even for a few cycles, will cause the fluorescent lamp to go out. For the rapid-start ballasts, if the voltage drops below 80% of rated, the arc becomes unstable and is extinguished. Fortunately, the lamp will restrike almost immediately upon restoration of full voltage. However, this creates a serious problem for the dimming of fluorescent lamps (see Section 4.3.9).

Lamp Lumen Depreciation. As with the incandescent lamp, the light output of a fluorescent lamp depreciates as it burns. This is caused by the deterioration of the phosphor powders and by the blackening of the inside of the tube from deposits of electrode material. Typical lamp lumen (LLD) factors are shown in Table 4.4. These factors are used in the lighting calculations discussed in Section 5.3.

The Effects of Ambient Temperature. The performance of fluorescent lamps is seriously affected by the ambient temperature (the temperature of the air that surrounds the lamp). The temperature of the tube wall controls the amount of ultraviolet energy generated by the arc, which in turn affects the amount of light produced by fluorescence. Because the area of the tube wall is relatively large, the temperature of the air can easily affect the temperature of the tube wall. The rated initial lumens of fluorescent lamps are based on measurements made with the lamp in still air at an ambient temperature of 25°C (77°F). The effects of higher and lower ambient temperatures are shown in Figure 4.12. Note that light output also falls off with temperatures that are too high. This

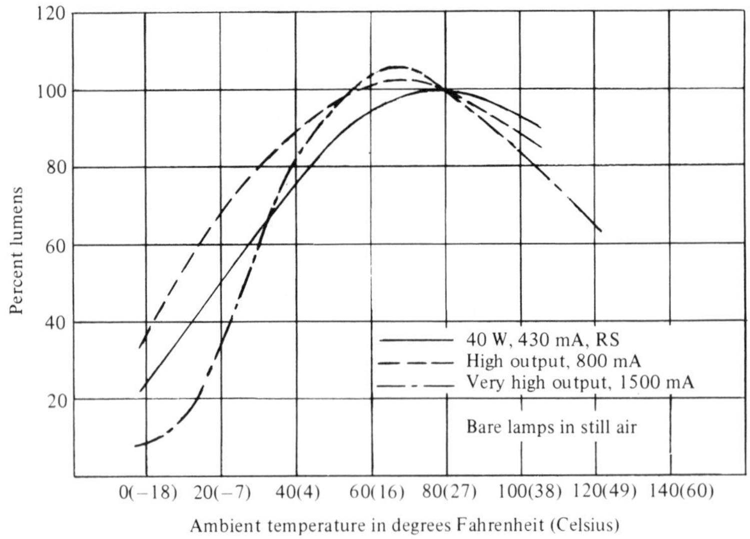

FIGURE 4.12

Effect of ambient temperature on fluorescent lamps

requires that luminaires must be well designed so that the lamps are properly ventilated even when used in a normal environment.

The most serious problem, however, is the use of fluorescent lamps outdoors or in unheated areas in those parts of the country that experience any degree of cold weather. With reference to Figure 4.12, if the ambient temperature falls to −7°C (20°F), the light output of the standard 40 watt lamp is only 50% of the rated output. If the lamps are exposed to any wind, the output is even lower. An equally serious problem is the fact that the starting of the lamps is extremely unreliable. Standard rapid-start ballasts provide reliable starting down to only 10°C (50°F). Special ballasts that provide higher starting voltages are available for cold weather starting down to −29°C (−20°F), but they are more expensive.

The use of fluorescent lighting in areas that can experience low ambient temperatures is therefore not normally recommended. Also, care must be taken in the location of fluorescent lamps for indoor lighting with respect to air-conditioning outlets. If cool air is allowed to blow over the lamps, the light output can be decreased and the color of the light can be noticeably affected.

4.3.9 Dimming of Fluorescent Lamps

The dimming of fluorescent lamps is not nearly as simple as the dimming of incandescent lamps. The voltage to the ballast cannot just be reduced to dim the lamps. As mentioned in Section 4.3.8, if the voltage across a rapid-start lamp decreases below 80% of normal, the arc becomes unstable and the lamp can suddenly turn off. To have a steady controlled decrease of light output, it is required that:

1. Constant voltage be maintained on the electrode heating circuits so that the electrodes remain at their proper temperature.
2. A high-voltage pulse of very short duration be generated after each current zero to restrike the arc for the next half-cycle as the voltage across the ends of the lamp is decreased.

These requirements call for a much more complicated and costly ballast than the conventional one using magnetic cores and coils. However, with the development of the electronic type of ballast discussed in Section 4.3.5, the dimming requirements can be incorporated more readily, and therefore the dimming of fluorescent lamps can be more easily justified on a cost basis. For applications of dimming, see Section 5.9.

4.4 LOW-PRESSURE SODIUM LAMPS

The low-pressure sodium lamp (also referred to as the low-*intensity* sodium lamp) is similar to the fluorescent lamp in that it has a long narrow tube and operates at a very low vapor pressure. Otherwise,

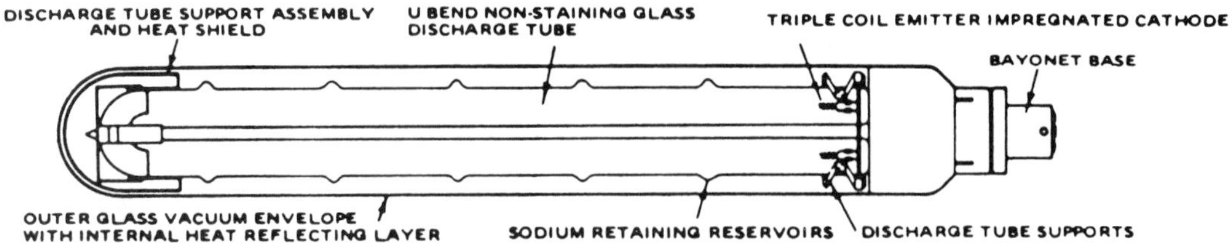

Lamp Wattage	Lamp Lumens	Rated Life Hours	Overall Length (in.)	Maximum Diameter (in.)
18	1,800	12,000	8.50	2.13
35	4,800	18,000	12.19	2.13
55	8,000	18,000	16.75	2.13
90	13,500	18,000	20.79	2.68
135	22,500	18,000	30.50	2.68
180	33,000	18,000	44.13	2.68

(a) Lamp construction and performance data

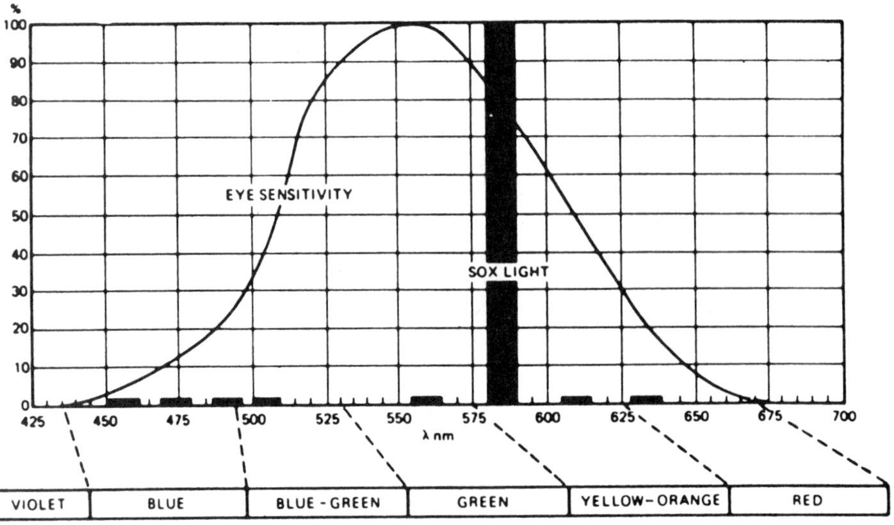

(b) Relative spectral light distribution curve

FIGURE 4.13

Low-pressure sodium lamp

it is very different. The metal used for the vapor is sodium instead of mercury. The arc tube is a U-shape that is enclosed in a separate outer glass envelope, as shown in Figure 4.13(a). Both electrodes are located at the same end of the lamp and there is just one base. The arc then travels twice the length of the lamp.

The collision of the electron stream with the atoms of sodium creates energy directly in the visible region. Unfortunately, over 98% of this energy lies in a very narrow band in the yellow-orange area, and negligible amounts are created in the other color areas, as shown in the relative spectral light distribution curve of Figure 4.13(b). This is the major disadvantage of this type of lamp. The color distortion of objects viewed under this source can be extreme. Why then is it used? As compared to other sources, it has the highest efficacy rating, approximately 165 lumens per watt (assuming a 10% loss in the ballast). Also, the light output is near the peak of the eye sensitivity curve.

Other advantages are long life, good lumen maintenance throughout its life, reliable cold weather starting, and prompt reignition after a temporary power interruption. Another disadvantage is the relatively long warm-up time. The available wattages of lamps with their rated lumen output are listed in Figure 4.13(a).

This type of lamp is used for such outdoor applications as the lighting of roadways and intersections, the lighting of yard areas for factories, railways, and docks, and floodlighting. For these types of applications, the severe color distortion can be overlooked in favor of the efficient operation of the lamp. The long warm-up time is of little consequence if the lighting is turned on as darkness begins to fall.

4.5 HIGH-INTENSITY MERCURY VAPOR LAMPS

The high-intensity mercury vapor lamp is most often referred to as simply the *mercury lamp*. It was the first high-intensity discharge (HID) lamp to be developed. The characteristics that most differentiate the HID sources from the low-intensity type (that is, the fluorescent) are that the arc tubes are much smaller and they operate at much higher vapor pressures, up to 10 atmospheres in extreme cases. The exact spectral distribution of an electric discharge lamp varies greatly with the vapor pressure at which the arc operates.

The basic operation of the electric discharge type of source is discussed in Section 4.2. In the case of the mercury lamp, the higher vapor pressure results in a much larger percentage of the energy from the electron activity being produced directly in the visible region, with only a small percentage being in the ultraviolet region.

The construction of the typical mercury lamp is shown in Figure 4.14. Note that there are two bulbs. The inner bulb is the arc tube and is made of quartz. Because of the intense energy developed in this small arc tube, it must be shielded by an outer bulb. The space between the two is filled with an inert gas. The outer glass envelope also filters out unwanted and harmful ultraviolet energy.

The original mercury lamps had clear glass envelopes. The spectral energy distribution curve for the clear mercury lamp is shown in

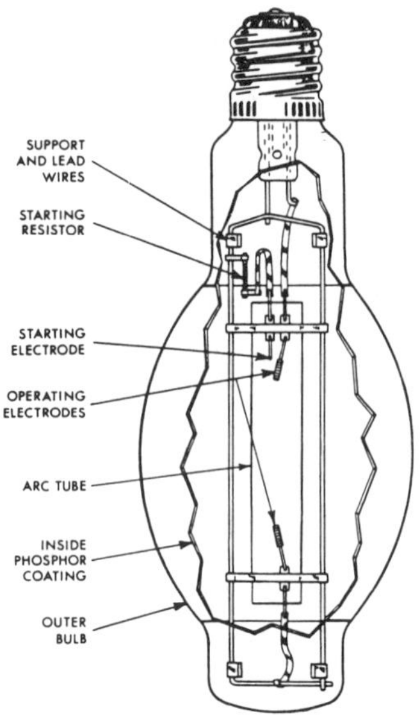

FIGURE 4.14

Construction of the mercury lamp

Figure 4.17(a). Note that relatively large amounts of energy are produced in the blue and green-yellow regions. Hence these lamps are characterized by a very noticeable bluish color of their light. They have the disadvantage of color distortion, especially for the red colors. In spite of this disadvantage, the mercury lamp gained acceptance for such applications as roadway and parking lot lighting and high-bay industrial area lighting. Its efficacy is approximately 250% that of the incandescent lamp, yet it is still essentially a point source of light, which permits good control of the distribution pattern of the luminaire. Also, mercury lamps have a much longer life than the incandescent lamp.

The next development was the introduction of the color-improved mercury lamp. In this type, the inside of the outer bulb is coated with a white phosphor that converts most of the ultraviolet energy radiated by the arc into visible energy. This not only increases the efficacy of the lamp but improves its color output. For example, the 400 watt clear lamp has an initial output of 21,000 lumens, whereas the 400 watt deluxe white lamp has 23,125. However, this higher initial output is partly offset by a higher rate of lumen depreciation. There are various degrees of color improvement: deluxe white, warm deluxe white, and so on. The spectral energy distribution curve for the deluxe white lamp is shown in Figure 4.17(b). Note that there is less output in the blue and yellow-green regions and considerably more output in the red region as compared to the clear lamp. However, in spite of these improvements, the metal halide lamp, which is a further development of the mercury lamp, is now beginning to supercede the mercury lamp (see Section 4.6).

The mercury lamp can continue to operate for many hours in the event that the outer glass bulb is accidentally broken, allowing the harmful ultraviolet energy to escape from the lamp. To prevent this, the lamp can be provided with an internal switch that extinguishes the arc if the outer glass envelope is broken or removed. This is especially important for lamps mounted in open luminaires that are subject to acts of vandalism. Self-extinguishing lamps are mandatory in many jurisdictions.

Lamp wattages for the mercury lamp range from 40 to 1000 watts. For a partial listing of mercury lamps, refer to Table 4.5. Mercury lamps can have a great many variations of characteristics. For instance, a lamp of the same wattage can have different operating voltages and currents. These lamps would not be interchangeable. The American National Standards Institute (ANSI) has established the following nomenclature system for the designation of lamps. As an example, the ANSI designation shown in Table 4.5 for one lamp is H33GL-400/DX. The coding indicates the following:

H identifies lamp as mercury vapor.
33 identifies the electrical characteristics.
GL identifies the physical characteristics.
400 identifies the wattage.
DX identifies the color correction (deluxe white). No designation indicates a clear lamp.

A "T" before the wattage indicates a self-extinguishing lamp.

4.5.1 Ballasts for Mercury Lamps

As discussed in Section 4.2.1, all electric discharge lamps require a ballast. The circuit diagram for a ballast operating a single mercury lamp is shown in Figure 4.15. The windings of the autotransformer are designed to have high inductive reactance, which then provides the necessary current limitation to the lamp. Power factor correction (90% or better) can be provided by a capacitor as shown.

Figure 4.16(a) shows the effect on the operation of the mercury lamp from variations in the line (primary) voltage to the ballast. Since many applications using the mercury lamp involve long runs of feeders (for example, streetlighting), the voltages at the ballast can often vary more than the allowable 5%. To help overcome this, self-regulated (or constant wattage) ballasts are available. These ballasts keep the lamp wattage and hence the light output almost constant over a range of plus or minus 10% of the rated primary volts, as shown in Figure 4.16(b).

With the use of an autotransformer type of ballast, the output (that is, the lamp circuit) cannot be electrically isolated from the power supply. Where it is necessary to be able to electrically isolate the lamp circuit from the power supply, ballasts using separate pri-

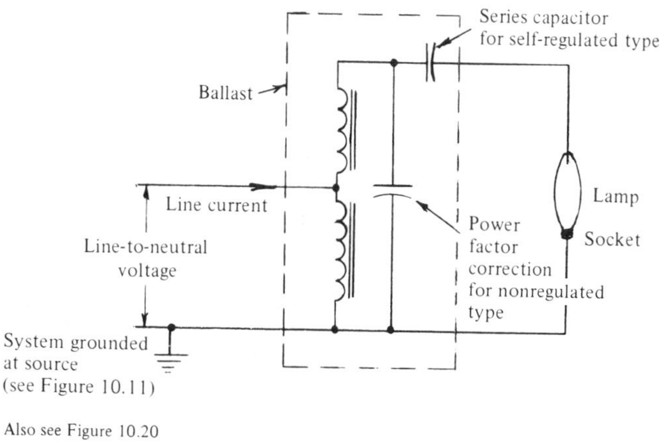

FIGURE 4.15

Autotransformer type of ballast for single mercury lamp

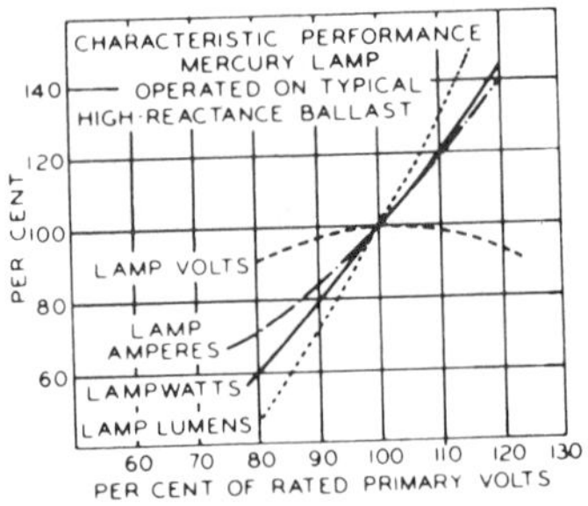

(a) Unregulated ballast

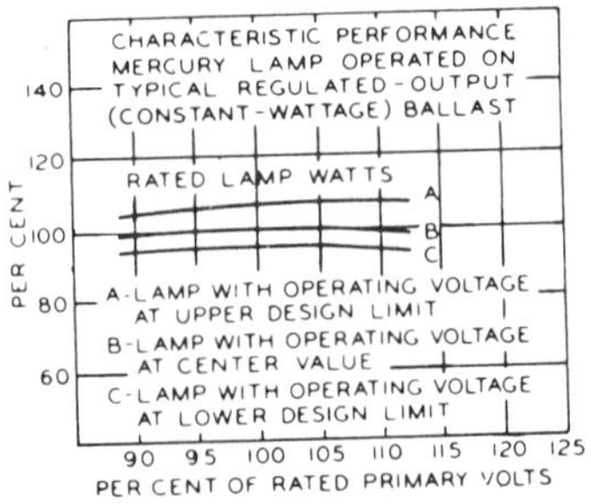

(b) Regulated ballast

FIGURE 4.16

Characteristic operating curves for mercury lamp

mary and secondary windings are required. This is discussed further in Section 10.6 and shown in Figure 10.20.

Two-lamp ballasts are available that operate one lamp on a leading current and the other on a lagging current, as discussed in Section 4.2.2. However, the operation of two mercury lamps from one ballast is not always practical. Since uniform lighting levels are desirable, lamps should be equally spaced from one another. Therefore, two-lamp ballasts would have to be placed midway between two pairs of widely separated lamps, which would increase the cost of the wiring. The present trend is to operate each lamp from its own ballast, which is mounted as an integral part of the luminaire.

4.5.2 Operating Characteristics of Mercury Lamps

There are six major factors to consider with regard to the operation of mercury lamps.

Starting of Lamps. The method of starting the HID mercury lamp differs somewhat from the method discussed in Section 4.3.1 for the low-intensity mercury (fluorescent) lamp. There is no separate electrode heating circuit. Instead, in addition to the two operating electrodes, there is a separate starting electrode, as shown in Figure 4.14. In addition to the mercury, the arc tube contains a small amount of the more readily ionized argon gas. Upon energizing the ballast, the full output voltage is applied between the starting electrode and the adjacent operating electrode, creating an emission of electrons that sets up a local glow. This causes the mercury to slowly vaporize, which then allows the arc to strike between the two operating electrodes. It takes from 3 to 4 minutes for the lamp to reach its full light output and for the lamp current to stabilize.

Lamp Restarting after Power Interruption. Any interruption in the power supply, even a serious voltage dip for a few cycles, will cause the mercury lamp to go out. It then requires a period of up to 4 minutes before the lamp will restart. It is necessary for the lamp to cool and the vapor pressure to decrease to the point where the arc can restrike. Together with the warm-up period, this can mean up to 8 minutes before full light returns. This is a serious problem when mercury lamps are used for indoor lighting in industrial areas with moving equipment. Emergency incandescent lighting to span the blackout period may be required.

Lamp Life. In common with other electric discharge lamps, the mercury lamp has a long life of up to 24,000 hours.

Lamp Lumen Depreciation. The light output of the mercury lamp, especially the color-corrected type, can depreciate up to 50% if allowed to operate to burn-out. It is often more economical to replace the lamp after no more than 18,000 hours. Typical values for lamp lumen depreciation (LLD) are shown in Table 4.5.

TABLE 4.5 High-Intensity Discharge (HID) Lamps

Watts	Outer Bulb Finish	ANSI Designation	Length (inches)	Rated Life (hours)	Initial Lumens[a]	Input Watts to Ballast	Lumens per Watt	LLD[b] (%)
Mercury Lamps								
100	Phos.	H38JA-100/DX	$7\frac{1}{2}$	24,000	4,425	120	33.9	69
175	Phos.	H39KC-175/DX	$8\frac{5}{16}$	24,000	8,600	205	42.0	78
250	Phos.	H37KC-250/DX	$8\frac{5}{16}$	24,000	12,775	285	44.9	76
400	Clear	H33CD-400	$11\frac{1}{2}$	24,000	21,000	450	46.7	80
400	Phos.	H33GL-400/DX	$11\frac{1}{2}$	24,000	23,125	450	51.4	71
1000	Clear	H36GV-1000	$15\frac{3}{8}$	24,000	56,150	1085	51.8	80
1000	Phos.	H36GW-1000/DX	$15\frac{3}{8}$	24,000	63,000	1085	58.1	71
Metal Halide Lamps								
175	Clear	M57PE-175	$8\frac{5}{16}$	7,500	14,000	210	66.7	77
250	Clear	M58PG-250	$8\frac{5}{16}$	10,000	20,500	290	70.7	76
400	Clear	M59PJ-400	$11\frac{1}{2}$	15,000	34,000	455	74.7	70
400	Phos.	M59PK-400	$11\frac{1}{2}$	15,000	34,000	455	74.7	68
1000	Clear	M47PA-1000	$15\frac{3}{8}$	10,000	110,000	1090	100.9	73
1000	Phos.	M47PB-1000	$15\frac{3}{8}$	10,000	105,000	1090	96.4	70
1500	Clear	M48PC-1500	$15\frac{3}{8}$	3,000	155,000	1610	96.3	—
High-Pressure Sodium (HPS) Lamps								
100	Clear	S54SB-100	$7\frac{3}{4}$	24,000	9,500	130	73.1	—
150	Clear	S55SC-150	$7\frac{3}{4}$	24,000	16,000	180	88.9	88
250	Clear	S50VA-250/S	$9\frac{3}{4}$	24,000	30,000	295	101.7	88
400	Clear	S51WA-400	$9\frac{3}{4}$	24,000	50,000	460	108.7	88
1000	Clear	S52XB-1000	$15\frac{1}{16}$	24,000	140,000	1085	129.0	90

[a] Lamps burning in the vertical position.

[b] Lamp lumen depreciation: percent of initial light output at 70% of rated life.

This table is only a partial listing of HID lamps. Refer to the *IES Lighting Handbook*, 1984 Reference Volume, for a complete listing of all HID sources.

Effects of Ambient Temperature. Because of the double-bulb construction, mercury lamps are not significantly affected by the ambient temperature once they are operating at full output. However, the starting of the lamp can be a problem. Since they are often used outdoors, ballasts are normally designed to provide sufficient starting voltage to give reliable starting down to −29°C (−20°F).

Circuit Protection. The starting of some mercury lamps can cause a problem with the overcurrent protection of the circuits feeding the lamps. The unregulated autotransformer type of ballast draws a line current during the starting period that is higher than the normal operating current. This higher current, which lasts for most of the 4 minute warm-up time, may be sufficient to operate the circuit overcurrent protection and shut the lamps off, unless allowance is made for it in the design of the circuit. The self-regulated type of ballast does not cause this type of problem. It draws less than the normal current when starting.

4.6 METAL HALIDE LAMPS

The metal halide lamp is basically a high-intensity mercury lamp with traces of metal halides added to the arc tube. Various combinations of scandium, thallium, indium, dysprosium, and sodium iodides are used. The addition of these trace elements improves the efficacy of the lamp. The efficacies for metal halide lamps average 75 lumens per watt against 50 lumens per watt for mercury lamps,

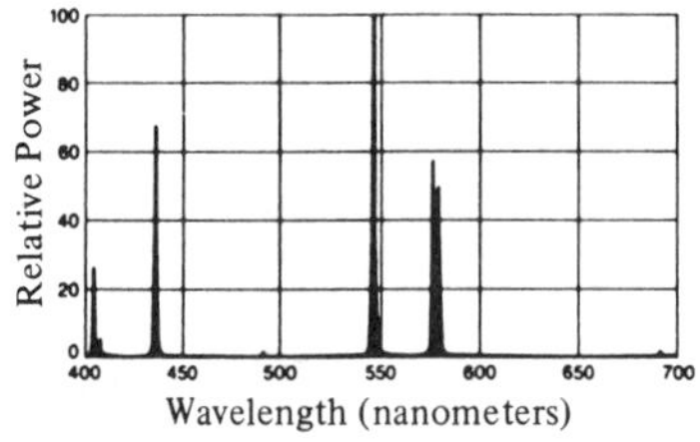

(a) Clear mercury lamp

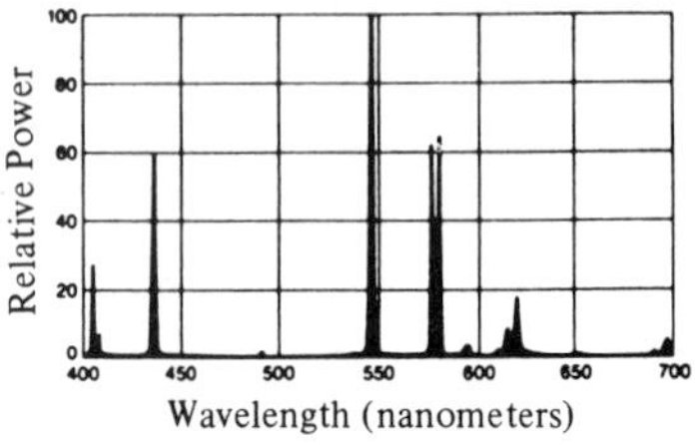

(b) Deluxe white mercury lamp

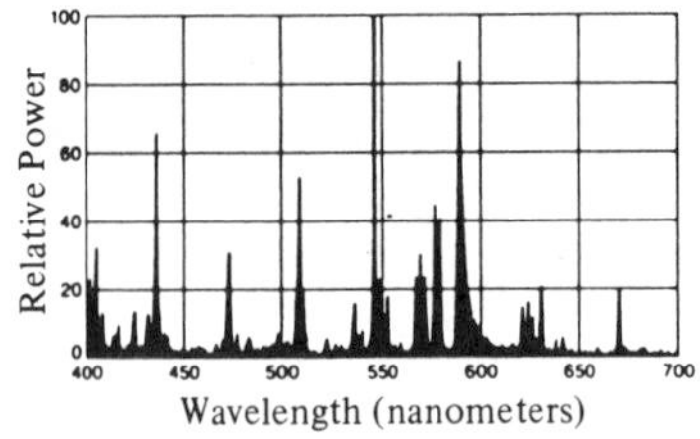

(c) Metal halide lamp

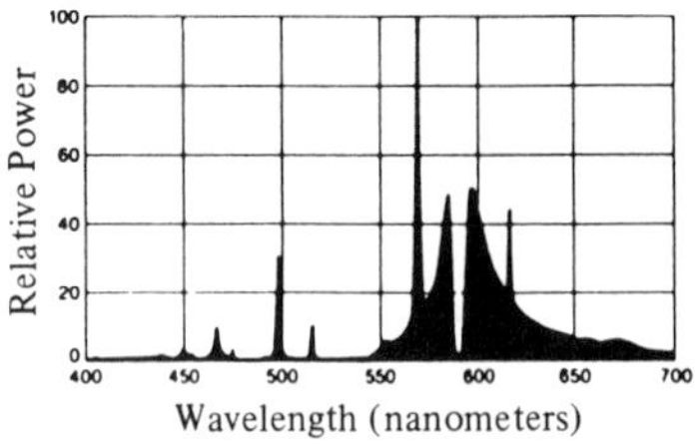

(d) High pressure sodium lamp

FIGURE 4.17

Spectral energy distribution curves for HID lamps

assuming average ballast losses. There is also considerable improvement in the color output. Refer to Figure 4.17(c) and compare the spectral energy distribution curve for the metal halide lamp with that for the clear mercury lamp. Note that the distribution of the outputs across the color spectrum is improved, especially at the red end. Similarly to the mercury lamp, the metal halide lamp is available with a clear outer bulb or it can have the inside of the outer bulb coated with phosphor for additional color improvement. More recently, very compact, low-wattage, metal halide lamps have been developed. These new types now allow for the use of the much more efficient metal halide lamps in low-ceiling interior applications in place of inefficient incandescent lamps.

The metal halide lamp has some disadvantages when compared to the mercury lamp. The rated life is shorter, typically 15,000 hours, and the rate at which the lamp lumens depreciate is somewhat higher. Also, the warm-up and restrike times are even longer, up to 10 minutes. Notwithstanding these disadvantages, the metal halide lamp has largely replaced the mercury lamp, especially on new lighting installations, because of its higher efficacy and better color output.

Ballasts for the metal halide lamp are similar in principle to those for the mercury lamp. However, metal halide lamps, even of the same wattage, are not interchangeable with mercury lamps as they have different operating voltages and currents. The coding of the ANSI lamp designations is similar to that outlined for the mercury lamp in Section 4.5, with the exception that the first letter is an M to designate the metal halide type. Lamp wattages range from 75 to 3500 watts. Refer to Table 4.5 for a partial listing of metal halide lamps.

4.7 HIGH-PRESSURE SODIUM LAMPS

The high-pressure sodium (HPS) lamp, introduced in 1964, is the latest development of the high-intensity discharge (HID) sources. As the name implies, it uses sodium as the main metal in the arc tube. It is the most efficient of all of the light sources which have acceptable color outputs, averaging 110 lumens per watt (assuming normal ballast losses).

To obtain good color output, it is necessary that the arc pass through the sodium vapor at a pressure higher than normal for the other HID sources. The arc tube is constructed from a new type of ceramic material, translucent aluminum oxide, that was developed in the late 1950s. This material can withstand the much higher pressures and temperatures of the arc, and is also resistant to the extremely corrosive effects of the hot sodium and can transmit over 90% of the visible energy generated by the arc.

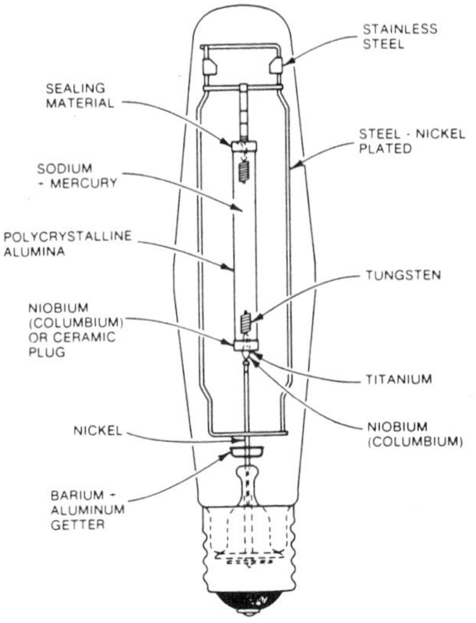

FIGURE 4.18

Construction of the high-pressure sodium lamp

The construction of the lamp is shown in Figure 4.18. It is an extremely compact lamp, considering the amount of light that it produces. In addition to the sodium, the arc tube contains a small amount of xenon as a starting gas. The small diameter of the arc tube does not permit the installation of a separate starting electrode as is used for the mercury lamp. Instead, the ballast contains a special starting circuit that creates a high pulse of voltage each half-cycle, peaking at 2500 volts and lasting 1 microsecond. These high-voltage pulses ionize the xenon gas, allowing the arc to strike between the electrodes. Once the arc has struck, the starting pulses cease.

Similarly to the mercury lamp, the HPS lamp takes 3 to 4 minutes to warm up and reach its full light output and final color. However, unlike the other HID sources, the restrike time of the HPS lamp is short, usually less than 1 minute. This is the result of the high starting pulses that the ballast produces when there is no lamp current.

The spectral energy distribution curve of the HPS lamp is shown in Figure 4.17(d). The output is high in the yellow-orange region, giving the lamp a very distinctive golden color. However, there is some output in all regions across the color spectrum, making the light source acceptable for many general-purpose lighting applications. It is now widely used for outdoor lighting and for indoor, high-bay, industrial lighting because of its high efficacy. Further research has very recently produced an HPS lamp with an enhanced color output that makes it much more acceptable for lighting areas where color rendition is important. This new lamp has a lower efficacy and shorter rated life than the standard HPS lamp, but no doubt further research will improve on these deficiencies. Therefore, in the future the use of the high-efficacy HPS lamp will no doubt increase even further. In addition to its wide use in industrial and outside lighting, its use will extend into the lighting of commercial and merchandising areas.

Lamp wattages range from 35 to 1000 watts. Refer to Table 4.5 for a partial listing of HPS lamps. The rated life of the HPS lamp is very good, up to 24,000 hours. The lumen maintenance over the life of the lamp is excellent. Typical lamp lumen depreciation (LLD) factors as shown in Table 4.5 approach 90%. The coding of the ANSI lamp designations is similar to that outlined for the mercury lamp in Section 4.5, with the exception that the first letter is an S to designate the HPS lamp.

Ballasts for HPS lamps are similar in type to those outlined for the mercury lamp in Section 4.5, with the exception of the addition of the special starting circuit as previously mentioned. HPS lamps, even those with the same wattage, are not interchangeable with mercury lamps because of different voltage and current characteristics.

SUMMARY

The following is a summary of the advantages and disadvantages of the main types of light sources covered in this chapter, together with typical applications.

- Incandescent lamps
  - Advantages
    - Point source of light, easy to control light distribution pattern
    - Low initial cost
    - Simple; no ballasts required, no ballast noise
    - Light output not affected by ambient temperature
    - Small size, compact luminaires
    - Very simple to dim
    - Favorable color output for humans
    - No delay on starting or restarting
    - No stroboscopic problems on 60 hertz
  - Disadvantages
    - Very low efficacy
    - Very high operating temperature
    - High infrared component
    - Seriously affected by voltage variations
    - Extremely bright source
    - Short life
    - Restricted to operating on lower voltages

— Applications

Incandescent lamps, because of their low efficacies and short lives, are not normally a good choice for large-area commercial, industrial, and outdoor lighting. They are a good choice for social areas where good color rendering and a warm, pleasant, low-key effect is desired, for accent and display lighting where good light control is necessary, for localized or supplementary lighting, and for decorative lighting.

- Standard fluorescent lamps
  - — Advantages
    - Good efficacy
    - Very long life
    - Low brightness
    - Low operating temperature
    - Low infrared output
    - Good color rendition
    - Can be operated on higher system voltages
    - Only minor delay on starting and restarting
  - — Disadvantages
    - Not a point source of light, light distribution more difficult to control.
    - Require ballast; extra weight; noise
    - Higher initial cost
    - Seriously affected by ambient temperature
    - Large size; require bulky luminaires
    - Require special ballasts to dim
  - — Applications

    Fluorescent lamps are widely used for large-area general lighting in offices and industrial plants. They provide approximately 70% of all light generated in North America.
- High-intensity discharge lamps (mercury, metal halide, and HPS)
  - — Advantages
    - Very good efficacies
    - Very long life
    - High output in compact size
    - Essentially a point source of light
    - Negligible infrared component
    - Light output not affected by ambient temperature
    - Can be operated on higher system voltages

— Disadvantages

Can cause color-rendition problems

High initial cost

Requires ballast; extra weight; noise

Very bright source

Very difficult and expensive to dim

Long warm-up and restrike times

Stroboscopic effect can be a problem

Cold weather starting problems

— Applications

HID lamps are widely used for high-bay interior industrial applications and many outdoor applications, such as street, parking lot, and security lighting. With the development of the better color-rendering metal halide lamps, they are being used with increasing frequency for indoor commercial applications.

QUESTIONS

1. What is the luminous efficacy of a perfect light source that could convert all the energy into yellow-green light without any losses?
2. List the following lamp types in order of their luminous efficacies from the lowest to the highest: (a) 400 W mercury, (b) 400 W metal halide, (c) 200 W incandescent, (d) 400 W high-pressure sodium, and (e) 40 W fluorescent.
3. State what the designation PS-25 for an incandescent lamp indicates.
4. For a given rated voltage and lamp life, are large-wattage incandescent lamps more or less efficient than small-wattage lamps? Explain your answer.
5. For a given rated wattage and lamp life, are high-voltage incandescent lamps more or less efficient than low-voltage lamps? Explain your answer.
6. Explain what is meant by the rated life of a lamp.
7. If the voltage applied to an incandescent lamp is 5% below rated voltage, approximately how much does its lumen output decrease?
8. List the two causes of lamp lumen depreciation in an incandescent lamp?
9. Where are reflectorized incandescent lamps used?
10. Describe the tungsten–halogen lamp and list its advantages.
11. State the two major reasons why ballasts are required for electric discharge lamps.
12. State the means of minimizing the stroboscopic effect of electric discharge lamps.
13. What are the main differences between the major types of electric discharge lamps?
14. Describe the basic operation of the fluorescent lamp (that is, how electric energy is converted to light).
15. State the three completely separate ways by which fluorescent lamps are classified.
16. State the difference between the preheat and rapid-start methods for fluorescent lamps.
17. State the disadvantages of the instant-start method.
18. What is the lamp operating current of the medium loaded fluorescent lamp and how is the lamp designated?
19. What is the lamp operating current of the highly loaded fluorescent lamp and how is the lamp designated?
20. List the four common types of white fluorescent lamps with regard to color output and indicate which type has the highest output at the red end of the spectrum.

21. Besides the hours of burning, what else affects the life of a fluorescent lamp?
22. State the problems with operating fluorescent lamps in low ambient temperatures.
23. State the problems that must be considered in the application of HO and VHO fluorescent lamps to lighting indoor areas.
24. State the major advantage and disadvantage of the low-pressure sodium lamp.
25. An HID lamp is coded H38JA-100/DX. State the characteristic that each of the numbers or letters designates.
26. Indicate the starting sequence of the mercury lamp.
27. State the effects of low ambient temperature on the operation of the standard mercury lamp.
28. Describe the metal halide lamp.
29. Describe the HPS lamp.
30. Explain why the HPS lamp has a relatively short restrike time.
31. List the advantages and disadvantages of the incandescent lamp.
32. List the advantages and disadvantages of the fluorescent lamp.
33. List the advantages and disadvantages of HID lamps.
34. List four good applications for incandescent lamps.
35. List typical applications for HID lamps.

5 Lighting System Layouts for Interior Spaces

OBJECTIVES

After studying this chapter, you will be able to:

- Determine the lighting level recommended for a specific task.
- Calculate the required number of luminaires.
- Prepare a plan of the actual arrangement of luminaires.
- Do an economic comparison between lighting systems.
- Discuss the factors involved in the quality of light.

INTRODUCTION

The design of a lighting system for an interior space involves many variable factors. These factors include the size and shape of the space; the types of finishes on the ceilings, walls, and floors; the details of the construction; the economic considerations of both the initial and the operating costs; the compatibility of the lighting system with the architectural design; and the type of activities that will be carried out in the space.

As discussed in the introduction to Chapter 3, there are two differing criteria in the design of a lighting system: *quantity* and *quality*. This chapter concentrates on the means by which the quantity of light is determined (that is, how many luminaires are required to properly light the space). The quality of light (the comfort of the seeing environment) is only discussed very briefly, not because it is not important, but only because of the size constraints of this textbook.

The methods outlined in this chapter for designing lighting layouts are based on the recommended procedures of the Illuminating Engineering Society of North America (IES). The examples presented are only meant to be a general overview of these procedures. The reader is referred to the *IES Lighting Handbook (Reference Volume* and *Application Volume)* for all aspects of the design of lighting systems.

5.1 ILLUMINANCE SELECTION

The lighting levels required to efficiently perform specific tasks can vary widely. Many factors involved in the seeing process were discussed in Section 3.1. It has not been easy to establish recommendations for lighting levels. Many research studies have been carried out. On the basis of these studies, the IES has published recommended illuminance values. Until 1979, a single value was recommended for each specific task. However, in that year the IES adopted a more flexible approach that recommends a range of illuminance values for each specific task accompanied by a weighting factor guidance system. These weighting factors take into account

TABLE 5.1 Illuminance Categories: Commercial, Institutional, Residential, and Public Assembly Interiors

Area/Activity	Illuminance Category
Auditoriums	
Assembly	C
Social activity	B
Drafting	
Tracing paper: high contrast	E
low contrast	F
Educational facilities	
Science laboratories	E
Lecture rooms: audience	(see Reading)
demonstration	F
Offices	
General and private offices	(see Reading)
Lobbies, lounges, and reception areas	C
Off-set Printing and Duplicating Areas	D
Reading	
Copied tasks: photocopies	D
Handwritten tasks: carbon copies	E
Residences	
General lighting: conversation, relaxation, and entertainment	B
Reading: books, magazines, and newspapers	D
Service areas	
Stairways and corridors	C
Toilets and washrooms	C

Source: Adapted from *IES Lighting Handbook, 1987 Application Volume* (New York: Illuminating Engineering Society of North America, 1987). Refer to the *1987 Application Volume* for a complete listing of areas and activities.

the object being viewed (the visual display), the age of the observer, the importance of speed and accuracy for visual performance, and the reflectance of the task background against which the details are seen.

Nine illuminance categories designated A through I have been established. Each letter has been assigned a range of illuminance values. Categories A, B, and C range from 20 to 200 lux. At these low levels, it is considered that all the lighting in the area will be provided by general overall lighting and that no specific task or task locations are involved. Such areas include lobbies and hallways. Categories D, E, and F, which range from 200 to 2000 lux, are for the lighting of specific tasks at fixed locations. The lighting may be provided by a combination of general overall lighting and local lighting at the task or by general overall lighting alone. Categories G, H, and I, which range from 2000 to 20,000 lux, are for the lighting of extremely difficult visual tasks requiring high levels of lighting. For practical and economic reasons, lighting systems for these levels should definitely be a combination of general overall lighting and specific lighting at the task area.

Tables 5.1 and 5.2 show the letter categories for a few specific areas and activities. Table 5.3 is a partial listing of the recommended ranges of illuminances for categories E and F. The criteria for the final single-value illuminance selection involves the workers' ages, the demand for speed and/or accuracy, and the task background reflectance. To use these tables, the first step is to determine the type of activity involved. After selecting the letter category from either Table 5.1 or 5.2, next refer to Table 5.3 for the single-value recommendation.

■ EXAMPLE 5.1

An office area is to be lighted. The task is reading handwritten carbon copies with a background (paper) reflectance of 70%. The average age of the workers is 35. Speed and accuracy are important but not critical. Select the recommended illuminance.

Solution

STEP 1 From Table 5.1, for general offices under *Reading, handwritten carbon copies,* category E is listed.

STEP 2 From Table 5.3, for category E, average of workers' ages under 40, demand for speed and/or accuracy important, task background reflectance 30% to 70%, the recommended illuminance is 750 lx.

The recommended values in Table 5.3 are in lux. For the equivalent values in footcandles, it is accepted that the values in the table

TABLE 5.2 Illuminance Categories: Industrial Group Interiors

Area/Activity	Illuminance Category
Assembly	
Simple	D
Moderately difficult	E
Difficult	F
Garages	
Repairs	E
Active traffic areas	C
Inspection	
Simple	D
Difficult	F
Exacting	H
Locker rooms	C
Machine shops	
Rough bench or machine work	D
Medium bench or machine work	E
Fine bench or machine work	G
Service spaces	
Stairways and corridors	B
Toilets and washrooms	C
Storage rooms or warehouses	
Inactive	B
Active: rough bulky items	C
small items	D
Woodworking	
Rough sawing and bench work	D
Fine bench work	E

Source: Adapted from *IES Lighting Handbook, 1987 Application Volume* (New York: Illuminating Engineering Society of North America, 1987). Refer to the *1987 Application Volume* for a complete listing of areas and activities.

be divided by 10 (refer to Table 3.1; 1.0 footcandle equals 10.76 lux). In Example 5.1, the recommended level is 75 footcandles.

The use of selected illuminance values may be influenced by work areas involving many tasks. If general overall lighting only is to be provided, then the selection should be based on the task of prime importance. With general overall lighting, the recommended illuminance values are the average of the lighting levels over the entire area. For good lighting, the individual values should be as uniform as possible.

TABLE 5.3 Recommended Illuminance Values Maintained in Lux for Illuminance on Task for Categories E and F

Weighting Factors			Categories[b]	
Average of Workers' Ages	Demand for Speed and/or Accuracy[a]	Task Background Reflectance (%)	E	F
Under 40	NI	Over 70	500	1000
		30 to 70	500	1000
		Under 30	750	1500
	I	Over 70	500	1000
		30 to 70	750	1500
		Under 30	750	1500
	C	Over 70	750	1500
		30 to 70	750	1500
		Under 30	750	1500

[a] NI, not important; I, important; C, critical.

[b] For footcandles, divide by 10.

Source: Adapted from the *IES Lighting Handbook, 1987 Application Volume* (New York: Illuminating Engineering Society of North America, 1987). Refer to the *IES Lighting Handbook, 1987 Application Volume,* for the complete table on recommended illuminance values for categories A through I and for the full range of ages.

5.2 LUMEN METHOD

The lumen method is used to design the general overall lighting of a room. This method calculates the illuminance that represents the average of the values at all points over the entire workplane of the room. The workplane is an imaginary horizontal plane at the height at which the task will be performed. For example, in an office the workplane is assumed to be 2.5 feet above the floor, as this is the standard height of desk tops. The lumen method is based on the definition of illuminance as covered in Section 3.3 and Table 3.1:

$$\text{Illuminance} = \frac{\text{luminous flux } (\phi)}{\text{area}}$$

Since the illuminance level applies to the workplane, and the workplane for general lighting covers the whole room:

$$E = \frac{\text{total luminous flux falling on the workplane}}{\text{area of room}}$$

Now consider a room in which the lighting has already been installed. By noting the number of luminaires in the room and the number and type of lamps installed in each luminaire, the total lumens generated by the lamps can easily be calculated:

$$\text{TILL} = \text{total lamps} \times \text{initial lumens per lamp}$$

where TILL is the total initial lamp lumens. However, not all these lamp lumens reach the workplane as some are trapped within the luminaire and some are absorbed by the room surfaces. Before the illuminance at the workplane can be calculated, it is necessary to establish a factor that represents the ratio between the lumens reaching the workplane and the total lamp lumens. This factor is known as the *coefficient of utilization* (CU). Thus,

$$\text{CU} = \frac{\text{total lumens falling on the workplane}}{\text{total initial lamp lumens}}$$

Combining the previous relationships gives

$$E = \frac{\text{TILL} \times \text{CU}}{\text{area}} \tag{5.1}$$

where E is the average illuminance at the workplane. To complete this calculation, it is necessary to be able to determine the coefficient of utilization for the particular lighting system.

5.2.1 Coefficient of Utilization

The coefficient of utilization represents the efficiency of the whole lighting system, including the luminaires and the space (room) in which they are installed. [It does not include the efficiency (efficacy) of the light source itself.] The coefficient of utilization depends on a number of factors.

1. *Type of luminaire* Its efficiency and distribution pattern (see Section 3.7).

2. *Reflectance of the room surfaces* The higher the reflectance factors of ceilings, walls, and floors, the greater the percentage of the lamp lumens that will be redirected to the workplane. Also, their effect will vary with the type of distribution pattern of the luminaire. For example, compare the case where the luminaire has an upward light component and is suspended from the ceiling with the case where the luminaire has only a downward light component and is recessed in the ceiling. In the first case, the amount of light reaching the workplane is very dependent on the reflected light from the ceiling. In the latter case, most of the light reaching the workplane comes directly from the luminaire, and the ceiling reflectance has far less effect.

3. *Mounting height of the luminaire* The greater the height, the greater the area of the wall surfaces is, which in turn absorbs more of the lamp lumens.

4. *Area of the room* The larger the room is, the greater the number of luminaires required. The light distributed from each luminaire overlaps one another, helping to increase the overall lighting level. Also, there is less wall surface per unit of area to absorb the light.

5. *Proportions of the room* A room may be long and narrow or square. Figure 5.1 shows the effect of doubling the size of the room, first by increasing its length, and second by increasing its width. In part (a), the additional two lamps have very little effect on the lighting level in the original area, and vice versa. However, in part (b),

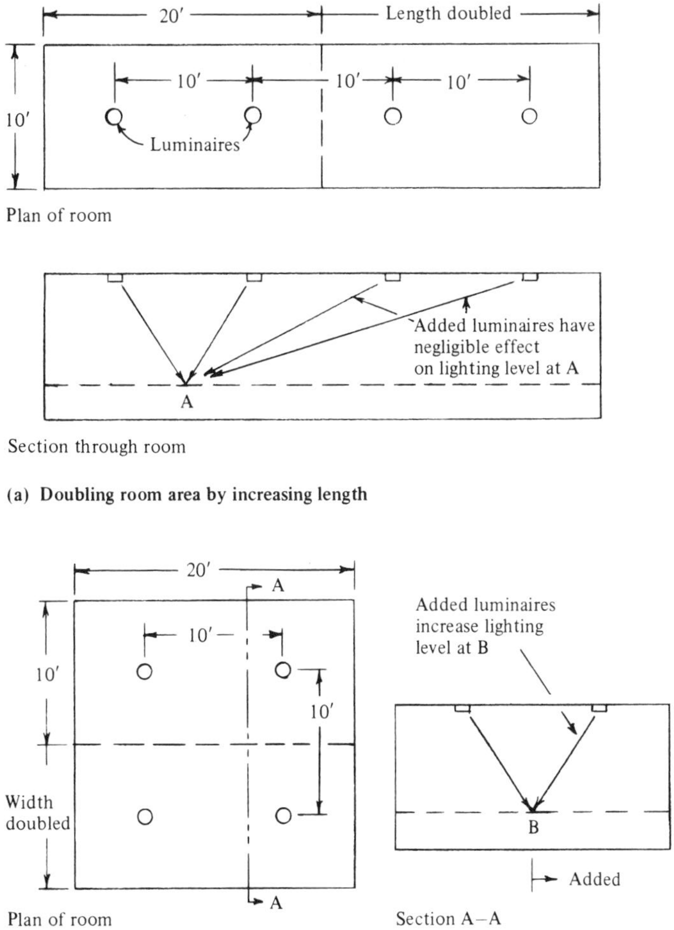

FIGURE 5.1

Effect of room proportions on lighting levels

the additional two lamps do increase the overall lighting level, even though each luminaire still covers an area of 10 feet by 10 feet as before. Also, compare the amount of wall surface enclosing the 10 × 40 foot room with that enclosing the 20 × 20 foot room, both of which have the same floor area. The greater wall surface area of the former will absorb more light. As a result, a square room has a higher coefficient of utilization than a long and narrow room, all other factors being the same.

To take all of the preceding factors into account, tables of coefficient of utilization (CU) factors are required. Refer to Table 5.5. There is a separate set of CU values shown for each type of luminaire. The type is identified by a sketch, together with its distribution pattern and the type of light source used. Across the top of the table, effective ceiling cavity reflectance (ρ_{CC}) factors are listed, (columns 4 to 9), and for each of these there are three different wall reflectance (ρ_W) factors. Finally, in column 3, headed RCR (room cavity ratio), the numbers 0 to 10 are listed. The room cavity ratio takes into account items 3, 4, and 5, which affect the CU. The RCR factor is calculated using the *zonal-cavity* method.

5.2.2 Zonal-Cavity Method

In the zonal-cavity method of computing the coefficient of utilization, the effects of the luminaire mounting height, the room size and proportions, and the height of the workplane are taken into account. As shown in Figure 5.2, the cross section of a room is divided into

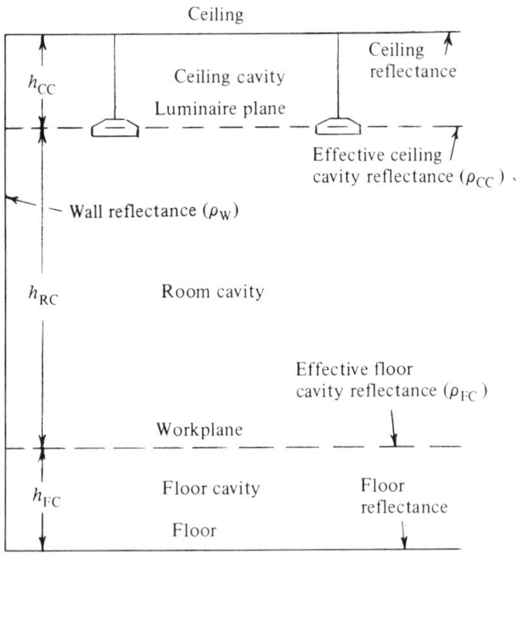

FIGURE 5.2

Zonal-cavity method using three cavities

three separate cavities. The space between the ceiling and the luminaire plane is the ceiling cavity, the space between the luminaire plane and the workplane is the room cavity, and the space between the workplane and the floor is the floor cavity. The cavity ratios (CR) for these three cavities are determined by using the following formula:

$$CR = \frac{5h \times (\text{room width} + \text{room length})}{\text{room width} \times \text{room length}} \tag{5.2}$$

where $h = h_{CC}$ for the ceiling cavity ratio (CCR)
$= h_{RC}$ for the room cavity ratio (RCR)
$= h_{FC}$ for the floor cavity ratio (FCR)

Note that for a given room the cavity ratios are in direct proportion to their respective cavity heights. For the case where the luminaires are mounted on the surface of the ceiling or are recessed into the ceiling, the ceiling cavity ratio is zero. The following are three examples of room cavity ratios.

Note that both rooms in Examples 5.2 and 5.3 have the same area, but the room in Example 5.3 is long and narrow and this is reflected in the higher value of the RCR.

EXAMPLE 5.2

A room is 100 ft by 100 ft (10,000 ft^2 in area). The luminaire is mounted 20 ft above the workplane.

Solution

$$RCR = \frac{5 \times 20 \times (100 + 100)}{100 \times 100} = 2.0$$

EXAMPLE 5.3

A room is 40 ft by 250 ft (10,000 ft^2 in area). The luminaire is mounted 20 ft above the workplane.

Solution

$$RCR = \frac{5 \times 20 \times (40 + 250)}{40 \times 250} = 2.9$$

EXAMPLE 5.4

A room is 12 ft by 12 ft (144 ft^2 in area). The luminaire is mounted 6 ft above the workplane.

Solution

$$RCR = \frac{5 \times 6 \times (12 + 12)}{12 \times 12} = 5.0$$

Note that the rooms in Examples 5.2 and 5.4 are both square, but the room in Example 5.4 is much smaller. This is reflected in a much higher value of RCR. Note also that the room cavity ratio is directly proportional to the height of the room cavity (h_{RC}), which is also the mounting height of the luminaire above the workplane. The greater the mounting height is, the greater the value of the RCR factor (for the same width and length).

Refer to Table 5.5. Note that for any of the luminaires, as the RCR factor increases from 0 toward 10, the coefficient of utilization factor decreases (for the same reflectance factors). This substantiates the points made in Section 5.2.1, items 3, 4, and 5. Note also that the cavity ratios are dimensionless and that the calculated values would be the same if the dimensions were in meters.

Since the coefficient of utilization is based on the room cavity ratio, it is necessary to treat this cavity as if there were a ceiling surface at the luminaire plane and a floor surface at the workplane level as shown in Figure 5.2. Therefore, it is necessary to convert the actual ceiling reflectance into an *effective ceiling cavity reflectance* (ρ_{CC}). Similarly, the actual floor reflectance must be con-

TABLE 5.4 Effective Cavity Reflectances

Base Refl. %	90						
Wall Refl. %	90	80	70	50	30	10	0
Cavity Ratio 0.2	89	88	88	86	85	84	82
0.4	88	87	86	84	81	79	76
0.6	87	86	84	80	77	74	73
0.8	87	85	82	77	73	69	67
1.0	86	83	80	75	69	64	62
1.5	85	80	76	68	61	55	51
2.0	83	77	72	62	53	47	43
2.5	82	75	68	57	47	40	36
3.0	80	72	64	52	42	34	30
3.5	79	70	61	48	37	31	26
4.0	77	69	58	44	33	25	22
5.0	75	59	53	38	28	20	16
6.0	73	61	49	34	24	16	11
8.0	68	55	42	27	18	12	06
10.0	65	51	36	22	15	09	04

Base Refl. %	80						
Wall Refl. %	90	80	70	50	30	10	0
Cavity Ratio 0.2	79	78	78	77	76	74	72
0.4	79	77	76	74	72	70	68
0.6	78	76	75	71	68	65	63
0.8	78	75	73	69	65	61	57
1.0	77	74	72	67	62	57	55
1.5	75	72	68	61	54	49	46
2.0	74	69	64	56	48	41	38
2.5	73	67	61	51	42	35	32
3.0	72	65	58	47	37	30	27
3.5	71	63	55	43	33	26	24
4.0	70	61	53	40	30	22	20
5.0	68	58	48	35	25	18	14
6.0	66	55	44	31	22	15	10
8.0	62	50	38	25	17	11	05
10.0	59	46	33	21	14	08	03

Base Refl. %	70						
Wall Refl. %	90	80	70	50	30	10	0
Cavity Ratio 0.2	70	69	68	67	66	65	64
0.4	69	68	67	65	63	61	58
0.6	69	67	65	63	59	57	54
0.8	68	66	64	60	56	53	50
1.0	68	65	62	58	53	50	47
1.5	67	62	59	54	46	42	40
2.0	66	60	56	49	40	36	33
2.5	65	60	54	45	36	31	29
3.0	64	58	52	42	32	27	24
3.5	63	57	50	38	29	23	21
4.0	63	55	48	36	26	20	17
5.0	61	52	44	31	22	16	12
6.0	60	51	41	28	19	13	09
8.0	57	46	35	23	15	10	05
10.0	55	43	31	19	12	08	03

Base Refl. %	60						
Wall Refl. %	90	80	70	50	30	10	0
Cavity Ratio 0.2	60	59	59	58	56	55	53
0.4	60	59	59	57	54	52	50
0.6	60	58	57	55	51	50	46
0.8	59	57	56	54	48	46	43
1.0	59	57	55	51	45	43	41
1.5	59	55	52	46	40	37	34
2.0	58	54	50	43	35	31	29
2.5	58	53	47	39	30	25	23
3.0	57	52	46	37	28	23	20
3.5	57	50	44	35	25	20	17
4.0	57	49	42	32	23	18	14
5.0	56	48	40	28	20	14	11
6.0	55	45	37	25	17	11	07
8.0	53	42	33	22	14	08	04
10.0	51	39	29	18	11	07	02

Base Refl. %	50						
Wall Refl. %	90	80	70	50	30	10	0
Cavity Ratio 0.2	50	50	49	48	47	46	44
0.4	50	49	48	47	45	44	42
0.6	50	48	47	45	43	41	38
0.8	50	48	47	44	40	38	36
1.0	50	48	46	43	38	36	34
1.5	50	47	45	40	34	31	26
2.0	50	46	43	37	30	26	24
2.5	50	46	41	35	27	22	21
3.0	50	45	40	32	24	19	17
3.5	50	44	39	30	22	17	15
4.0	50	44	38	28	20	15	12
5.0	50	42	35	25	17	12	09
6.0	50	42	34	23	15	10	06
8.0	49	40	30	19	12	07	03
10.0	47	37	27	17	10	06	02

Base Refl. %	40						
Wall Refl. %	90	80	70	50	30	10	0
Cavity Ratio 0.2	40	40	39	39	38	36	36
0.4	41	40	39	38	36	34	34
0.6	41	40	39	37	34	32	31
0.8	41	40	38	36	33	31	29
1.0	42	30	38	34	32	29	27
1.5	42	39	37	32	28	24	22
2.0	42	39	36	31	25	21	19
2.5	43	39	35	29	23	18	15
3.0	43	39	35	27	21	16	13
3.5	44	39	34	26	20	14	12
4.0	44	38	33	25	18	12	10
5.0	45	38	31	22	15	10	07
6.0	44	37	30	20	13	08	05
8.0	44	35	28	18	11	06	03
10.0	43	34	25	15	08	05	02

Base Refl. %	30						
Wall Refl. %	90	80	70	50	30	10	0
Cavity Ratio 0.2	31	31	30	29	29	28	27
0.4	31	31	30	29	28	26	25
0.6	32	31	30	28	26	25	23
0.8	32	31	30	28	25	23	22
1.0	33	32	30	27	24	22	20
1.5	34	33	30	25	22	18	17
2.0	35	33	29	24	20	16	14
2.5	36	32	29	24	18	14	12
3.0	37	33	29	22	17	12	10
3.5	38	33	29	21	15	10	09
4.0	38	33	28	21	14	09	07
5.0	39	33	28	19	13	08	05
6.0	39	33	27	18	11	06	04
8.0	40	33	26	16	09	04	02
10.0	40	32	24	14	08	03	01

Base Refl. %	20						
Wall Refl. %	90	80	70	50	30	10	0
Cavity Ratio 0.2	21	20	20	20	19	19	17
0.4	22	21	20	20	19	18	16
0.6	23	21	21	19	18	17	15
0.8	24	22	21	19	18	16	14
1.0	25	23	22	19	17	15	13
1.5	26	24	22	18	16	13	11
2.0	28	25	23	18	15	11	09
2.5	29	26	23	18	14	10	08
3.0	30	27	23	17	13	09	07
3.5	32	27	23	17	12	08	05
4.0	33	28	23	17	11	07	07
5.0	35	29	24	16	10	06	04
6.0	36	30	24	16	10	05	02
8.0	37	30	23	15	08	03	01
10.0	37	29	22	13	07	03	01

Base Refl. %	10						
Wall Refl. %	90	80	70	50	30	10	0
Cavity Ratio 0.2	11	11	11	10	10	09	09
0.4	12	11	11	11	10	09	08
0.6	13	13	12	11	10	08	08
0.8	15	14	13	11	10	08	07
1.0	16	14	13	12	10	08	07
1.5	18	16	15	12	10	07	06
2.0	20	18	16	13	09	06	05
2.5	22	20	17	13	09	05	04
3.0	24	21	18	13	09	05	03
3.5	26	22	19	13	09	05	03
4.0	27	23	20	14	09	04	02
5.0	30	25	20	14	08	04	02
6.0	31	26	21	14	08	03	01
8.0	33	27	21	13	07	03	01
10.0	34	28	21	12	07	02	01

Base Refl. %	0						
Wall Refl. %	90	80	70	50	30	10	0
Cavity Ratio 0.2	02	02	02	01	01	00	0
0.4	04	03	03	02	01	00	0
0.6	05	05	04	03	02	01	0
0.8	07	06	05	04	02	01	0
1.0	08	07	06	04	02	01	0
1.5	11	10	08	06	03	01	0
2.0	14	12	10	07	04	01	0
2.5	16	14	12	08	05	02	0
3.0	18	16	13	09	05	02	0
3.5	20	17	15	10	05	02	0
4.0	22	18	15	10	05	02	0
5.0	25	21	17	11	06	02	0
6.0	27	23	18	12	06	02	0
8.0	30	25	20	12	06	02	0
10.0	31	25	20	12	06	02	0

Source: Adapted from the *IES Lighting Handbook, 1984 Reference Volume* (New York: Illuminating Engineering Society of North America, 1984). Refer to the *1984 Reference Volume* for the complete table on effective cavity reflectances.

verted to an *effective floor cavity reflectance* (ρ_{FC}). Refer to Table 5.5 and note that it is the effective values of reflectances that are used to obtain the coefficient of utilization.

The values for the effective reflectances are obtained from Table 5.4. The term *base reflectance* refers to the actual reflectance of the cavity surface. For instance, when obtaining the effective reflectance for the ceiling cavity, the base reflectance is the actual reflectance of the ceiling. Similarly, when obtaining the effective reflectance for the floor cavity, the base reflectance is the actual reflectance of the floor. Note that the coefficient of utilization factors in

TABLE 5.5 Coefficients of Utilization

Typical Luminaire	Typical Intensity Distribution and Per Cent Lamp Lumens		ρ_{CC} →	80			70			50			30			10			0
			ρ_W →	50	30	10	50	30	10	50	30	10	50	30	10	50	30	10	0
	Maint. Cat.	SC	RCR ↓	Coefficients of Utilization for 20 Per Cent Effective Floor Cavity Reflectance (ρ_{FC} = 20)															
1	IV	1.3	0	.99	.99	.99	.97	.97	.97	.93	.93	.93	.89	.89	.89	.85	.85	.85	.83
	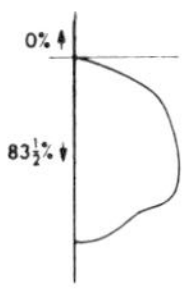		1	.87	.84	.81	.85	.82	.79	.82	.79	.77	.79	.76	.74	.76	.74	.72	.71
			2	.76	.70	.65	.74	.69	.65	.71	.67	.63	.69	.65	.62	.66	.63	.60	.59
			3	.66	.59	.54	.65	.59	.53	.62	.57	.53	.60	.56	.52	.58	.54	.51	.49
			4	.58	.51	.45	.57	.50	.45	.55	.49	.44	.53	.48	.44	.51	.47	.43	.41
			5	.52	.44	.39	.51	.44	.38	.49	.43	.38	.47	.42	.37	.46	.41	.37	.35
			6	.46	.39	.33	.46	.38	.33	.44	.38	.33	.43	.37	.33	.41	.36	.32	.31
			7	.42	.34	.29	.41	.34	.29	.40	.33	.29	.39	.33	.29	.38	.32	.28	.27
			8	.38	.31	.26	.37	.31	.26	.36	.30	.26	.35	.30	.25	.34	.29	.25	.24
Porcelain-enameled ventilated standard dome with incandescent lamp			9	.35	.28	.23	.34	.28	.23	.33	.27	.23	.32	.27	.23	.32	.26	.23	.21
			10	.32	.25	.21	.32	.25	.21	.31	.25	.21	.30	.24	.21	.29	.24	.20	.19
2	V	1.4/1.2	0	.75	.75	.75	.73	.73	.73	.70	.70	.70	.67	.67	.67	.64	.64	.64	.63
	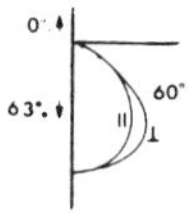		1	.67	.64	.62	.65	.63	.61	.63	.61	.59	.60	.59	.58	.58	.57	.56	.55
			2	.59	.56	.52	.58	.55	.52	.56	.53	.51	.54	.52	.49	.52	.50	.48	.47
			3	.53	.48	.45	.52	.48	.44	.50	.46	.43	.48	.45	.43	.47	.44	.42	.41
			4	.47	.42	.38	.46	.42	.38	.45	.41	.38	.44	.40	.37	.42	.39	.37	.35
			5	.43	.37	.34	.42	.37	.33	.41	.36	.33	.39	.36	.33	.38	.35	.32	.31
			6	.39	.33	.30	.38	.33	.29	.37	.32	.29	.36	.32	.29	.35	.31	.29	.27
			7	.35	.30	.26	.35	.30	.26	.34	.29	.26	.33	.29	.26	.32	.28	.26	.24
			8	.32	.27	.24	.32	.27	.23	.31	.26	.23	.30	.26	.23	.29	.26	.23	.22
Fluorescent unit with flat prismatic lens, 4-lamp 610 mm (2′) wide—see note			9	.30	.25	.21	.29	.24	.21	.28	.24	.21	.28	.24	.21	.27	.24	.21	.20
			10	.27	.22	.19	.27	.22	.19	.26	.22	.19	.26	.22	.19	.25	.22	.19	.18
3	II	1.3	0	.99	.99	.99	.94	.94	.94	.85	.85	.85	.77	.77	.77	.69	.69	.69	.65
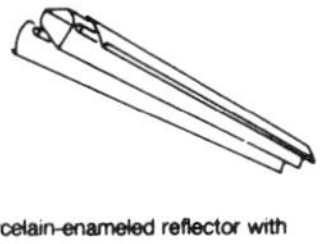	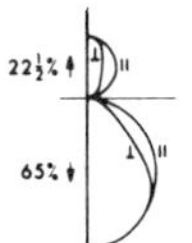		1	.87	.84	.81	.83	.80	.77	.75	.73	.71	.68	.66	.65	.62	.60	.59	.56
			2	.77	.71	.67	.73	.68	.64	.67	.63	.60	.60	.58	.55	.55	.53	.51	.48
			3	.68	.62	.56	.65	.59	.54	.59	.55	.51	.54	.50	.47	.49	.46	.44	.41
			4	.61	.54	.48	.58	.52	.47	.53	.48	.44	.48	.44	.41	.44	.41	.38	.35
			5	.54	.47	.42	.52	.46	.41	.48	.42	.38	.44	.39	.36	.40	.36	.33	.31
			6	.49	.42	.37	.47	.40	.36	.43	.38	.34	.40	.35	.32	.36	.33	.30	.27
			7	.45	.37	.32	.43	.36	.32	.39	.34	.30	.36	.32	.28	.33	.29	.26	.24
			8	.41	.34	.29	.39	.33	.28	.36	.31	.27	.33	.29	.25	.31	.27	.24	.22
Porcelain-enameled reflector with 35°CW shielding			9	.37	.31	.26	.36	.30	.25	.33	.28	.24	.31	.26	.23	.28	.24	.22	.20
			10	.34	.28	.24	.33	.27	.23	.31	.25	.22	.28	.24	.21	.26	.22	.20	.18
4	III	1.5	0	.93	.93	.93	.91	.91	.91	.87	.87	.87	.83	.83	.83	.79	.79	.79	.78
	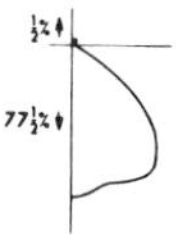		1	.84	.81	.79	.82	.80	.78	.79	.77	.75	.76	.74	.73	.73	.72	.70	.69
			2	.75	.71	.67	.74	.70	.66	.71	.68	.65	.68	.66	.63	.66	.64	.62	.60
			3	.67	.62	.57	.66	.61	.57	.64	.59	.56	.61	.58	.55	.59	.56	.54	.52
			4	.60	.54	.50	.59	.54	.49	.57	.52	.48	.55	.51	.48	.54	.50	.47	.46
			5	.54	.48	.43	.53	.47	.43	.52	.46	.42	.50	.45	.42	.49	.45	.41	.40
			6	.49	.42	.38	.48	.42	.38	.47	.41	.37	.45	.41	.37	.44	.40	.37	.35
			7	.44	.38	.34	.44	.38	.33	.42	.37	.33	.41	.36	.33	.40	.36	.33	.31
			8	.40	.34	.30	.40	.34	.30	.39	.33	.30	.38	.33	.29	.37	.32	.29	.28
"High bay" wide distribution ventilated reflector with clear HID lamp			9	.37	.31	.27	.37	.31	.27	.36	.30	.27	.35	.30	.26	.34	.29	.26	.25
			10	.34	.28	.24	.34	.28	.24	.33	.28	.24	.32	.27	.24	.31	.27	.24	.22

For a luminaire similar to No. 2 except 1 ft (300 mm) wide using two lamps, multiply CU values by 0.9.

Source: Adapted from the *IES Lighting Handbook, 1984 Reference Volume* (New York: Illuminating Engineering Society of North America, 1984). Refer to the *1984 Reference Volume* for a more complete listing of luminaires.

TABLE 5.6 Multiplying Factors for Other Than 20% Effective Floor Cavity Reflectances

% Effective Ceiling Cavity Reflectance, ρ_{CC}	80				70				50			30			10		
% Wall Reflectance, ρ_W	70	50	30	10	70	50	30	10	50	30	10	50	30	10	50	30	10
For 30 Per Cent Effective Floor Cavity Reflectance (20 Per Cent = 1.00)																	
Room Cavity Ratio																	
1	1.092	1.082	1.075	1.068	1.077	1.070	1.064	1.059	1.049	1.044	1.040	1.028	1.026	1.023	1.012	1.010	1.008
2	1.079	1.066	1.055	1.047	1.068	1.057	1.048	1.039	1.041	1.033	1.027	1.026	1.021	1.017	1.013	1.010	1.006
3	1.070	1.054	1.042	1.033	1.061	1.048	1.037	1.028	1.034	1.027	1.020	1.024	1.017	1.012	1.014	1.009	1.005
4	1.062	1.045	1.033	1.024	1.055	1.040	1.029	1.021	1.030	1.022	1.015	1.022	1.015	1.010	1.014	1.009	1.004
5	1.056	1.038	1.026	1.018	1.050	1.034	1.024	1.015	1.027	1.018	1.012	1.020	1.013	1.008	1.014	1.009	1.004
6	1.052	1.033	1.021	1.014	1.047	1.030	1.020	1.012	1.024	1.015	1.009	1.019	1.012	1.006	1.014	1.008	1.003
7	1.047	1.029	1.018	1.011	1.043	1.026	1.017	1.009	1.022	1.013	1.007	1.018	1.010	1.005	1.014	1.008	1.003
8	1.044	1.026	1.015	1.009	1.040	1.024	1.015	1.007	1.020	1.012	1.006	1.017	1.009	1.004	1.013	1.007	1.003
9	1.040	1.024	1.014	1.007	1.037	1.022	1.014	1.006	1.019	1.011	1.005	1.016	1.009	1.004	1.013	1.007	1.002
10	1.037	1.022	1.012	1.006	1.034	1.020	1.012	1.005	1.017	1.010	1.004	1.015	1.009	1.003	1.013	1.007	1.002
For 10 Per Cent Effective Floor Cavity Reflectance (20 Per Cent = 1.00)																	
Room Cavity Ratio																	
1	.923	.929	.935	.940	.933	.939	.943	.948	.956	.960	.963	.973	.976	.979	.989	.991	.993
2	.931	.942	.950	.958	.940	.949	.957	.963	.962	.968	.974	.976	.980	.985	.988	.991	.995
3	.939	.951	.961	.969	.945	.957	.966	.973	.967	.975	.981	.978	.983	.988	.988	.992	.996
4	.944	.958	.969	.978	.950	.963	.973	.980	.972	.980	.986	.980	.986	.991	.987	.992	.996
5	.949	.964	.976	.983	.954	.968	.978	.985	.975	.983	.989	.981	.988	.993	.987	.992	.997
6	.953	.969	.980	.986	.958	.972	.982	.989	.977	.985	.992	.982	.989	.995	.987	.993	.997
7	.957	.973	.983	.991	.961	.975	.985	.991	.979	.987	.994	.983	.990	.996	.987	.993	.998
8	.960	.976	.986	.993	.963	.977	.987	.993	.981	.988	.995	.984	.991	.997	.987	.994	.998
9	.963	.978	.987	.994	.965	.979	.989	.994	.983	.990	.996	.985	.992	.998	.988	.994	.999
10	.965	.980	.989	.995	.967	.981	.990	.995	.984	.991	.997	.986	.993	.998	.988	.994	.999

Source: Adapted from the *IES Lighting Handbook, 1984 Reference Volume* (New York: Illuminating Engineering Society of North America, 1984). Refer to the *1984 Reference Volume* for the complete table.

Table 5.5 are based on an effective floor cavity reflectance (ρ_{FC}) of 20% as indicated at the top of the table. For values other than 20%, the value of the CU obtained from Table 5.5 is corrected by applying the appropriate multiplying factor obtained from Table 5.6. See Example 5.5 for the calculation of the coefficient of utilization for a typical lighting layout.

■ EXAMPLE 5.5

A room is 60 ft by 120 ft in area with a 24 ft high ceiling. The luminaire 1 in Table 5.5 is used, and it is suspended 5 ft below the ceiling. The reflectance factors are ceiling 60%, walls 30%, and floor 10%. The workplane is 3 ft above the floor. Calculate the coefficient of utilization.

Solution

STEP 1 Draw the cross section through the room and determine the cavity heights (see Figure 5.3).

STEP 2 Calculate the cavity ratios using Equation 5.2:

$$\text{CCR} = \frac{5 \times 5 \times (60 + 120)}{60 \times 120} = 0.625 \approx 0.6$$

$$\text{RCR} = \frac{5 \times 16 \times (60 + 120)}{60 \times 120} = 2.0$$

$$\text{FCR} = \frac{5 \times 3 \times (60 + 120)}{60 \times 120} = 0.375 \approx 0.4$$

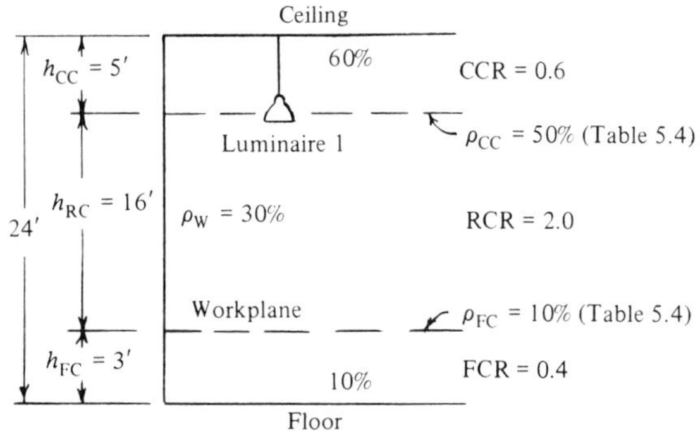

FIGURE 5.3

Cross section diagram for Example 5.5

STEP 3 Determine the effective ceiling cavity reflectance from Table 5.4. For a base reflectance of 60%, wall reflectance of 30%, and cavity ratio of 0.6, $\rho_{CC} = 51$ (use 50%).

STEP 4 Determine the effective floor cavity reflectance from Table 5.4. For a base reflectance of 10%, wall reflectance of 30%, and cavity ratio of 0.4, $\rho_{FC} = 10\%$ (no change).

STEP 5 Determine the coefficient of utilization (CU) from Table 5.5. For luminaire 1, $\rho_{CC} = 50\%$, $\rho_W = 30\%$, and RCR = 2. CU = 0.67 (for 20% floor reflectance).

STEP 6 Determine the correction for 10% floor reflectance from Table 5.6. For $\rho_{CC} = 50\%$, $\rho_W = 30\%$, and RCR = 2, the multiplying factor is 0.968.

$$\text{Final CU} = 0.67 \times 0.968 = 0.648 = 0.65$$

(Two-figure accuracy is acceptable.)

5.3 LIGHT LOSS FACTOR

From the time that a new lighting system is first energized, the lighting level gradually decreases because of aging. The recommended lighting levels as discussed in Section 5.1 are based on minimum values that should be maintained over the operating life of the system. Therefore, it is necessary to provide higher initial illuminance levels to compensate for the loss of light with time. The light loss factor is the ratio of the illuminance when it reaches its lower level just before corrective action is taken as compared to the initial level. The light loss factor is the product of all the individual factors that contribute to the loss of light. These factors are divided into two categories, unrecoverable and recoverable. The unrecoverable factors are those attributed to equipment and site conditions that cannot be changed with normal maintenance. Recoverable factors are those that can be changed by regular scheduled maintenance, such as cleaning and relamping luminaires and cleaning and painting room surfaces. The three chief unrecoverable factors are the temperature factor, line voltage factor, and ballast factor.

Temperature Factor. Variations in ambient temperature above or below those normally encountered in interiors have little effect on the light output of incandescent and HID lamps, but they significantly affect fluorescent lamps (refer to Section 4.3.8, item 3). In the examples presented in this chapter, it is assumed that the ambient temperature will not create a problem.

Line Voltage Factor. As discussed for each light source in Chapter 4, its light output is affected by variations in the supply voltage. In the examples presented in this chapter, it is assumed that voltages will be kept at the proper level to maintain full light output from the lamps.

Ballast Factor. The published initial lumen ratings for fluorescent and HID lamps are based on the use of test quality ballasts. The commercially available ballasts actually installed with the luminaires may not operate the lamps with the same efficacy. The ballast factor (BF) is the ratio of the lamp lumens generated on commercial ballasts to those generated on the test quality ballasts. The ballast factor for good quality fluorescent ballasts is nominally 0.95. There is no published standard for HID source ballasts and therefore a factor of 1.0 is assumed in the examples.

Other unrecoverable factors are the equipment operating factor, the lamp positioning factor, and the luminaire surface depreciating factor. For the sake of simplifying the examples, these factors are not considered.

The recoverable factors that must be considered in calculating the light loss factor are lamp lumen depreciation, luminaire dirt depreciation, and room surface dirt depreciation.

Lamp Lumen Depreciation. This item is discussed in Chapter 4 for each type of light source. The lamp lumen depreciation (LLD) factors are listed in the appropriate tables in that chapter.

Luminaire Dirt Depreciation. With the passage of time, dirt accumulates on the lamps and on the surfaces of the luminaires. This dirt absorbs some of the light. The resulting loss of light is accounted for by the luminaire dirt depreciation (LDD) factor, which is determined by referring to Figure 5.4. Depending on the type of construction, luminaires are divided into six maintenance categories. Each luminaire listed in Table 5.5 has an assigned maintenance category that indicates which of the graphs in Figure 5.4 to use. Also, there are five degrees of operating atmosphere, ranging from very clean to very dirty. In the examples presented in

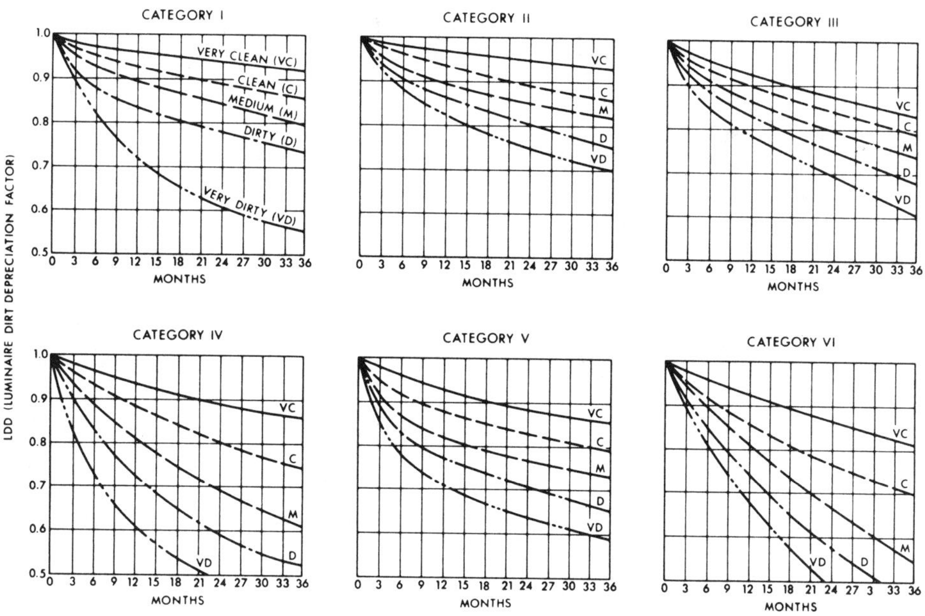

FIGURE 5.4

Luminaire dirt depreciation (LDD) factors

this chapter, the degree of operating atmosphere is given. For information on how to determine the specific degree of an operating atmosphere, consult the *IES Lighting Handbook, 1984 Reference Volume*.

■ EXAMPLE 5.6

Luminaire 3 in Table 5.5 is used for a lighting layout. The atmosphere will be clean and the period between cleanings will be 24 months. Determine the LDD factor.

Solution

From Table 5.5, the assigned maintenance category for luminaire 3 is II. From Figure 5.4, category II graph, for clean atmosphere at 24 months, the LDD factor is 0.89.

Room Surface Dirt Depreciation. With the passage of time, the accumulation of dirt on the surfaces of the room further reduces the amount of light that reaches the workplane. The exact effect of dirt on light loss varies according to the size and proportions of the room (that is, the room cavity ratio), the type of operating atmosphere, and the luminaire distribution type. The resulting loss of light is accounted for by the room surface dirt depreciation (RSDD) factor, which is determined by referring to Table 5.7. First, select the

TABLE 5.7 Room Surface Dirt Depreciation (RSDD) Factors

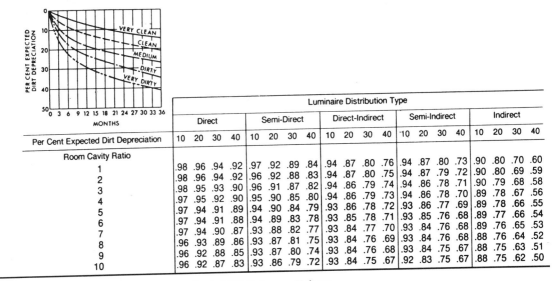

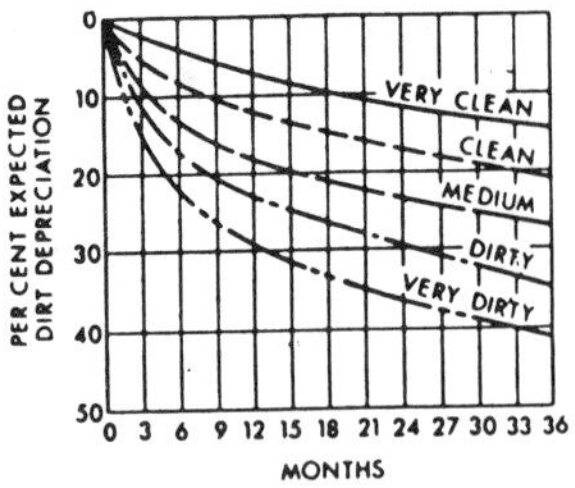

	Luminaire Distribution Type																			
	Direct				Semi-Direct				Direct-Indirect				Semi-Indirect				Indirect			
Per Cent Expected Dirt Depreciation	10	20	30	40	10	20	30	40	10	20	30	40	10	20	30	40	10	20	30	40
Room Cavity Ratio																				
1	.98	.96	.94	.92	.97	.92	.89	.84	.94	.87	.80	.76	.94	.87	.80	.73	.90	.80	.70	.60
2	.98	.96	.94	.92	.96	.92	.88	.83	.94	.87	.80	.75	.94	.87	.79	.72	.90	.80	.69	.59
3	.98	.95	.93	.90	.96	.91	.87	.82	.94	.86	.79	.74	.94	.86	.78	.71	.90	.79	.68	.58
4	.97	.95	.92	.90	.95	.90	.85	.80	.94	.86	.79	.73	.94	.86	.78	.70	.89	.78	.67	.56
5	.97	.94	.91	.89	.94	.90	.84	.79	.93	.86	.78	.72	.93	.86	.77	.69	.89	.78	.66	.55
6	.97	.94	.91	.88	.94	.89	.83	.78	.93	.85	.78	.71	.93	.85	.76	.68	.89	.77	.66	.54
7	.97	.94	.90	.87	.93	.88	.82	.77	.93	.84	.77	.70	.93	.84	.76	.68	.89	.76	.65	.53
8	.96	.93	.89	.86	.93	.87	.81	.75	.93	.84	.76	.69	.93	.84	.76	.68	.88	.76	.64	.52
9	.96	.92	.88	.85	.93	.87	.80	.74	.93	.84	.76	.68	.93	.84	.75	.67	.88	.75	.63	.51
10	.96	.92	.87	.83	.93	.86	.79	.72	.93	.84	.75	.67	.92	.83	.75	.67	.88	.75	.62	.50

Source: Adapted from the *IES Lighting Handbook, 1984 Reference Volume.*

percent of expected dirt depreciation from the graph accompanying Table 5.7, using the appropriate atmosphere curve and the time interval in months between cleaning. Then refer to the table and, depending on the room cavity ratio and the luminaire distribution type, select the RSDD factor. Refer to Section 5.4 and Figure 5.5 for the luminaire distribution types.

■ EXAMPLE 5.7

Luminaire 3 is to be used, the atmosphere will be clean, and the period between cleanings will be 24 months (all the same as in Example 5.6). The room cavity ratio has been calculated to be 2.0. Determine the RSDD factor.

Solution

STEP 1 From Table 5.5, luminaire 3 has a ratio of 22.5% to 65% for upward and downward light components, which translates to 26% upward and 74% downward.

STEP 2 From Figure 5.5, the luminaire is a semidirect type.

STEP 3 From the graph in Table 5.7, for a clean atmosphere at 24 months, the percent of expected dirt depreciation is 17.5%.

STEP 4 From Table 5.7 for a semidirect luminaire and a room cavity ratio of 2, the room surface dirt depreciation (RSDD) factor is 0.93 (interpolate between 0.96 for 10% and 0.92 for 20% expected dirt depreciation).

The light loss factor is then the product of all the individual factors discussed.

■ **EXAMPLE 5.8**

Continue on from Examples 5.6 and 5.7. Luminaire 3 is a fluorescent type, and 800 mA rapid-start lamps are to be used. Calculate the light loss factor.

Solution

STEP 1 From Table 4.4, the lamp lumen depreciation (LLD) factor for 800 mA fluorescent lamps is 82% (use 0.82).

STEP 2 Ballast factor (BF) is 0.95.

STEP 3 The light loss factor is

$$\begin{aligned} \text{LLF} &= \text{BF} \times \text{LLD} \times \text{LDD} \times \text{RSDD} \\ &= 0.95 \times 0.82 \times 0.89 \text{ (Ex. 5.6)} \times 0.93 \text{ (Ex. 5.7)} \\ &= 0.6448 \approx .64 \text{ (two-figure accuracy)} \end{aligned}$$

Thus the lighting level will be reduced to 64% of its initial level just before corrective action is taken.

With reference to Equation 5.1, the illuminance E in that relationship represents the initial value, that is, the lighting level when the system is first turned on. To include the light loss factor, the equation expands to

$$E = \frac{\text{TILL} \times \text{CU} \times \text{LLF}}{\text{area}} \tag{5.3}$$

where E is the minimum average illuminance at the workplane just before corrective action is taken.

5.4 LUMINAIRE DISTRIBUTION TYPES

Luminaires are classified on the basis of their distribution pattern, that is, on the relative amounts of light projected upward and/or downward from the luminaire (see Section 3.7). There are six categories, each of which is assigned a percentage range for the upward and downward components, as shown in Figure 5.5. These percentages are based on the total lumens emitted from the luminaire.

Note that the general-diffuse and the direct–indirect types have the same percentage ranges. However, the general-diffuse type has a fairly uniform light output around the full 360 degrees, such as a suspended type of incandescent luminaire with an enclosing glass globe. In contrast, the direct–indirect type has very little light output in the few degrees above and below the horizontal. Typical of this type is a suspended type of fluorescent luminaire with open top and bottom but with very dense side panels.

Lighting systems using the direct type of luminaire are generally the most efficient since the majority of the light is projected directly down onto the workplane. However, this efficiency can be at the

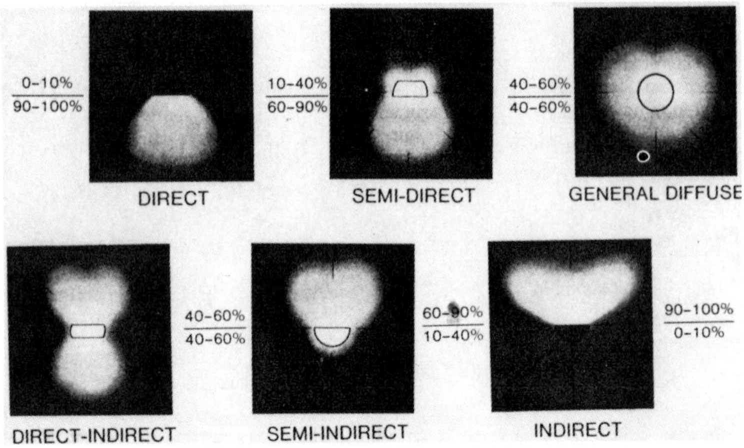

FIGURE 5.5

Luminaire distribution types

expense of the quality of the lighting environment because of possible problems with direct and reflected glare. Lighting systems using the indirect type of luminaire are generally the least efficient, since the majority of the light has to be reflected back down from the ceiling to the workplane. However, this type of system can be the most comfortable, as the lighting is very diffuse with far less glare and annoying shadows. Very often the semidirect type of luminaire is chosen as a compromise.

Any luminaire with an upward component of light must, of course, be suspended from the ceiling. This requires a higher ceiling level to keep the luminaire at an acceptable height above the floor. Many types of building construction preclude high ceilings, and therefore the direct type of luminaire recessed into the ceiling is the only possible choice.

See Section 5.8 for further discussion on the quality of lighting systems.

5.5 CALCULATION OF NUMBER OF LUMINAIRES

In Section 5.2, the assumption made is that the lighting system already exists and Equations 5.1 and 5.3 therefore will give the illuminance level for that lighting system. However, this is not the situation for most lighting layout problems. What is required is a method of calculating the number of luminaires that will be required to provide the recommended minimum levels of illuminance as determined according to Section 5.1.

The relationship of Equation 5.3 can be rearranged as follows:

$$\text{TILL} = \frac{E \times \text{area}}{\text{CU} \times \text{LLF}} \tag{5.4}$$

where TILL = the total initial lamp lumens required
E = recommended minimum illuminance

The number of luminaires can then be calculated:

$$\text{No. of luminaires} = \frac{\text{TILL}}{\begin{pmatrix}\text{no. of lamps}\\ \text{per luminaire}\end{pmatrix} \times \begin{pmatrix}\text{initial lumens}\\ \text{per lamp}\end{pmatrix}} \tag{5.5}$$

The value of E used in Equation 5.4 can only be a target value. The number of luminaires calculated using Equations 5.4 and 5.5 can therefore only be considered as the theoretical number required, as a practical layout may dictate an adjustment to this number. Example 5.9 shows a sample calculation of the theoretical number of luminaires required for a lighting layout.

EXAMPLE 5.9

Refer to Example 5.5. Continue with the same room, for which a CU of 0.65 has been calculated using luminaire 1. A 300 W, mogul base, 1000 hr incandescent lamp is to be installed in the luminaire. The room is to be lighted to an illuminance level of 20 fc. The atmosphere will be clean and the luminaires and room surfaces will be cleaned every 18 months. Calculate the number of luminaires required.

Solution

STEP 1 Determine the lamp lumen depreciation factor. From Table 4.1, LLD is 89% (use 0.89).

STEP 2 Determine the luminaire dirt depreciation factor.
— From Table 5.5, luminaire 1 is category IV.
— From Figure 5.4, for clean and 18 months, LDD is 0.84.

STEP 3 Determine the room surface dirt depreciation factor.
— From the graph in Table 5.7, for clean and 18 months, the percent of expected dirt depreciation is 15%.
— From Table 5.5, for luminaire 1, the light output is all down (direct distribution; see Figure 5.5).
— From Table 5.7, for direct and RCR 2, interpolate between 0.98 for 10% and 0.96 for 20%; RSDD is 0.97.

STEP 4 Calculate the light loss factor:

$$\text{LLF} = 0.89 \times 0.84 \times 0.97 = 0.73 \quad \text{(two-figure accuracy)}$$

STEP 5 Calculate the total initial lamp lumens (Equation 5.4):

$$\text{TILL} = \frac{20 \times (60 \times 120)}{0.65 \times 0.73} = 303{,}500$$

STEP 6 Calculate the required number of luminaires (Equation 5.5). From Table 4.1, for a 300 W, mogul base, 1000 hr lamp, the initial lamp lumens are 5960.

$$\text{No. of luminaires} = \frac{303{,}500}{1 \times 5960} = 50.9$$

See Example 5.10 for the actual number selected.

5.5.1 Practical Layout of Luminaires

An arrangement of luminaires that provides a reasonably uniform lighting level on the workplane over an entire area is known as general lighting. Equations 5.4 and 5.5 were developed from the lumen method and, as such, give the number of luminaires required to provide the recommended average level of illuminance for general lighting. However, if the luminaires are not spaced properly, the actual point-by-point levels throughout the room may not be uniform, and there will be noticeable variations in the levels.

Uniform lighting requires that the spacing between adjacent luminaires must not exceed defined limits. Refer to Figure 5.6. The diagram on the left shows a spacing arrangement that does not give uniform lighting. The diagram on the right shows that with reduced spacing the lighting levels are reasonably uniform.

Spacing limitations between luminaires are a function of their intensity distribution patterns (see Section 3.7) and their mounting heights. The luminaire *spacing criterion* (SC) is a classification relating to its distribution pattern. This classification is done numerically. Refer to Table 5.5. In column 3 under the heading SC, a number is shown for each luminaire. For example, luminaire 1 has a value of 1.3 for SC. This means that the spacing between adjacent luminaires of this type cannot exceed 1.3 times their mounting height above the workplane if reasonably acceptable uniformity of horizontal illuminance is to be obtained.

For luminaires using essentially point sources of light, such as incandescent or HID lamps, the maximum spacing applies equally to both directions in the room. Luminaires using fluorescent lamps, because of their length, do not necessarily fit this pattern. A very common and desirable arrangement is continuous rows of fluorescent luminaires in one direction in the room, usually lengthwise, as shown in Figure 5.7(a). The maximum spacing then applies only between the center lines of each row. Where rows of fluorescent luminaires are not continuous, the maximum spacing along the rows applies as shown in Figure 5.7(b). For 4 foot long luminaires, the maximum spacing is from center line to center line (the same as for

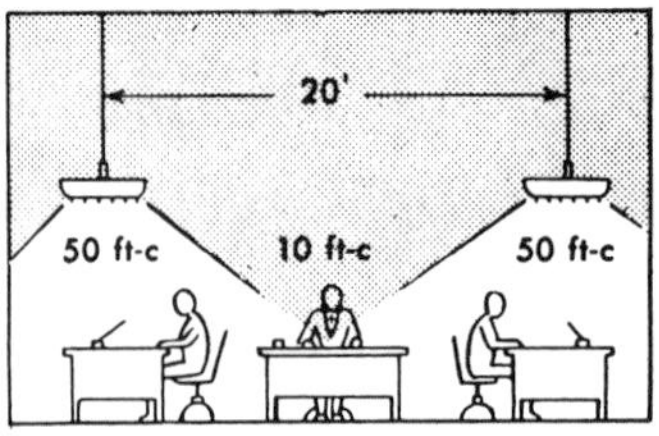

(a) Not acceptable

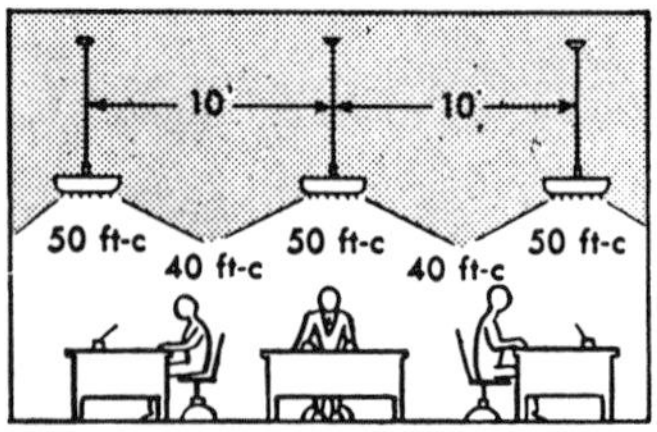

(b) Acceptable

FIGURE 5.6

Spacing requirements for reasonably uniform lighting

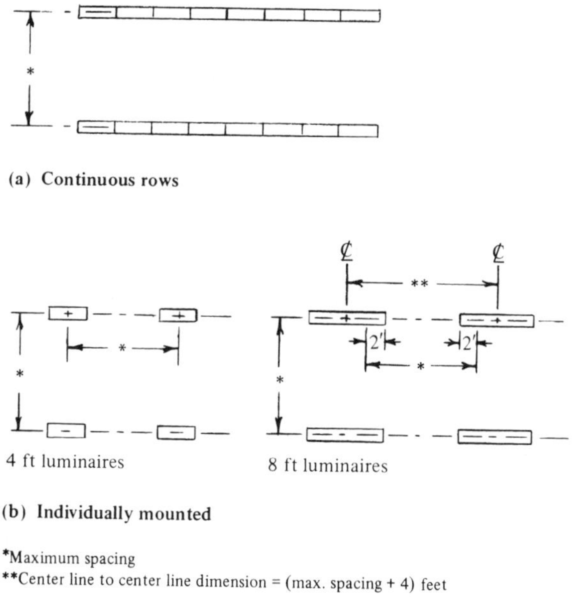

FIGURE 5.7

Maximum spacing dimensions (in feet) for fluorescent luminaires

point sources). For 8 foot long luminaires, the maximum lengthwise spacing applies from a point 2 feet from the end of one luminaire to a point 2 feet from the adjacent end of the next luminaire. These guidelines are based on the fact that the distribution of light from the ends of fluorescent luminaires is not as good as it is from the sides.

In many lighting layouts, the final spacing is less than the maximum permitted by the spacing criterion. After the theoretical number of luminaires required for the layout has been calculated, it is necessary to adjust this number so that it can be evenly divisible by the number of rows.

For point sources of light, the ratio between the number of rows and the number of luminaires per row should be in proportion to the width-to-length ratio of the room. This is required to give symmetrical spacing in both directions in the room for uniform lighting. Refer to Figure 5.8(a). The exact spacing between rows is calculated by dividing the room width by the number of rows, and spacing between luminaires in each row by dividing the room length by the number of luminaires per row. This means that the spacing between the outer luminaires and the adjacent wall is one-half of the luminaire spacing. Refer to Figure 5.6. If the spacing from the wall to the first luminaire was to be greater than one-half, the lighting level adjacent to the wall would noticeably fall off. In fact, if it is known that desks or other work areas are to be located alongside the walls, then the wall-to-luminaire spacing should be reduced to one-third of the luminaire spacing.

For fluorescent luminaires, it is often necessary to first establish the maximum number that can be installed in one row. Refer to Figure 5.8(b). It is necessary to allow some space between the ends of the rows and the walls. Therefore, the maximum number is calculated by subtracting at least 1 foot (0.3 meter) from the room length and then dividing by the length of the luminaire. The spacing between rows of fluorescent luminaires is determined the same as previously indicated for rows of point sources.

The final layout of luminaires in practice is very often influenced by the building structural details. Such things as the location of beams and columns must be considered in locating luminaires. Since

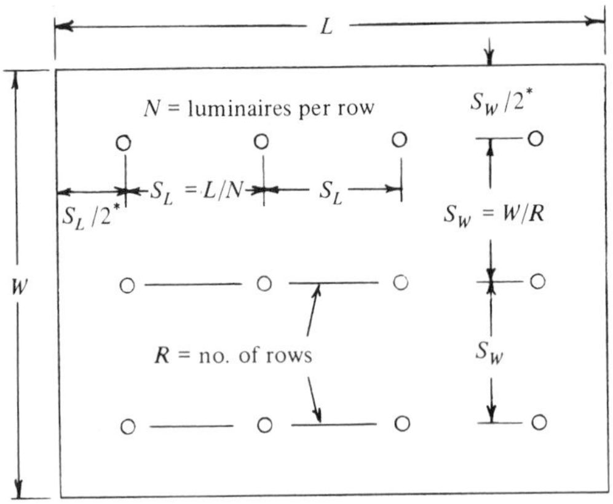

S_L and S_W should be approximately equal.
*Can be reduced to one-third luminaire spacing.

(a) **Incandescent and HID**

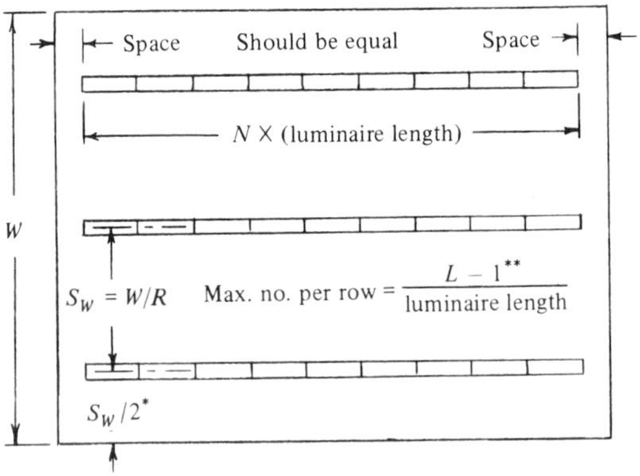

**Minimum 1.0 ft (0.3 m)

(b) **Fluorescent, continuous rows**

FIGURE 5.8

Layout arrangements for luminaires

these details introduce much more complexity into the design of the lighting system, they are not considered in the examples shown in this chapter. However, designers of lighting systems in the real world must be able to read structural, mechanical, and architectural drawings in order to coordinate the lighting systems.

Example 5.10 shows the development of a practical layout using point sources. Incandescent lamps have been used for this layout to simplify the example. However, with today's emphasis on saving energy, one of the more efficient low wattage HID sources would likely be used, even for a lighting level as low as 20 footcandles. Example 5.11 shows a practical layout using fluorescent luminaires.

EXAMPLE 5.10

Refer to Example 5.9. A total of 50.9 incandescent luminaires was calculated as being required to provide an average level of illuminance of 20 fc for a 60 by 120 ft room. Select a practical layout for the lighting in this room.

Solution

STEP 1 Draw a plan, reasonably to scale, of the outline of the room as in Figure 5.9.

STEP 2 Note the ratio between the width and length of the room, which is 60 to 120, or 1 to 2. There should be the same ratio between the number of rows and the number of luminaires per row in order to have a symmetrical arrangement.

STEP 3 Select an arrangement of 5 rows of 10 luminaires for a total of 50. *Note:* Four rows of 13 (= 52) would not give a suitable ratio.

STEP 4 Calculate the luminaire spacing as in Figure 5.8(a):

$$S_W = \frac{60}{5} = 12 \text{ ft}, \qquad S_L = \frac{120}{10} = 12 \text{ ft}$$

Thus the spacing between the luminaires and walls is 12/2, or 6 ft.

STEP 5 Check maximum spacing allowed:

— From Table 5.5 for luminaire 1, SC is 1.3.

— Maximum spacing = 1.3 × 16 = 20.8 ft (h_{RC} = 16 from Figure 5.3).

— 12 ft spacing is well within limit.

STEP 6 Draw the luminaires on a room layout (Figure 5.9) and show dimensions.

STEP 7 Calculate the actual minimum maintained lighting level: If 50.9 luminaires are required to give 20 fc (step 6 in Example 5.9), then 50 luminaires will give

$$E = \frac{50}{50.9} \times 20 = 19.6 \text{ fc}$$

This is within 2% of the desired value.

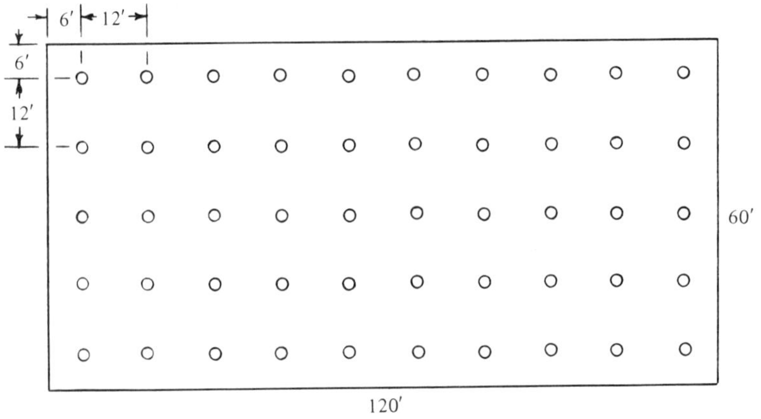

FIGURE 5.9

Plan of room showing luminaires for Example 5.10 (dimensions are in feet)

EXAMPLE 5.11

Refer to Example 5.5. This same 60 by 120 ft room is now to be lighted to a level of 75 fc by installing luminaire 3 (Table 5.5) suspended 5 ft from the ceiling. The luminaire will be 8 ft long and each will have two rapid-start, 800 mA, T-12, 96 in., cool white fluorescent lamps. The atmosphere and cleaning times will be the same as in Examples 5.6 and 5.7. Select a practical lighting layout.

Solution

STEP 1 Since the cross section and room surface reflectances are still the same, the cavity ratios and effective ceiling and floor reflectances as calculated in Example 5.5 still apply.

STEP 2 Determine the coefficient of utilization from Table 5.5:

— For luminaire 3, ρ_{CC} = 50%, ρ_W = 30%, and RCR = 2.0, a value of 0.63 is read (for 20% floor reflectance).

— The multiplying factor for 10% floor reflectance is the same as in Example 5.5.

$$\text{Final CU} = 0.63 \times 0.968 = 0.61$$

STEP 3 Calculate the light loss factor:

— Ballast factor (BF) is 0.95.

— LLD from Table 4.4 is 82% (use 0.82).

— LDD is 0.89 as in Example 5.6.

— RSDD is 0.93 as in Example 5.7.

$$\text{LLF} = 0.95 \times 0.82 \times 0.89 \times 0.93 = 0.645$$

STEP 4 Calculate the total initial lamp lumens (Equation 5.4):

$$\text{TILL} = \frac{75 \times (60 \times 120)}{0.61 \times 0.645} = 1{,}372{,}500$$

STEP 5 Calculate the required number of luminaires (Equation 5.5). From Table 4.4, for an 800 mA, 96 in., CW lamp, the initial lamp lumens are 9150 and there are two per luminaire.

$$\text{No. of luminaires} = \frac{1{,}372{,}500}{2 \times 9150} = 75.0$$

STEP 6 Select a practical layout for the luminaires:

— Assume that continuous rows will be necessary.
— Calculate the maximum number per row lengthwise in the room as in Figure 5.8(b):

$$\text{Max. no. per row} = \frac{120 - 1}{8} \approx 14$$

— Number of rows required using 14 per row = 75.0/14 ≈ 5.
— Select 5 rows of 14 = 70 (most practical arrangement):

$$E\ (\text{maintained}) = \frac{70}{75.0} \times 75 = 70.0\ \text{fc}$$

This is 6.7% below the desired value, but acceptable.

STEP 7 Calculate the luminaire spacing as in Figure 5.8(b):

$$S_W = \frac{60}{5} = 12\ \text{ft}$$

$$\text{Total length of each row} = 14 \times 8 = 112\ \text{ft}$$

$$\text{Space at ends of row} = \frac{120 - 112}{2} = 4\ \text{ft}$$

STEP 8 Check the maximum spacing allowed between rows:

— From Table 5.5 for luminaire 3, SC is 1.3.
— Maximum spacing = 1.3 × 16 = 20.8 ft (h_{RC} = 16 from Figure 5.3).
— 12 ft spacing is well within the limit.

STEP 9 Draw a plan of the room and indicate the luminaires and their locations as shown in Figure 5.10.

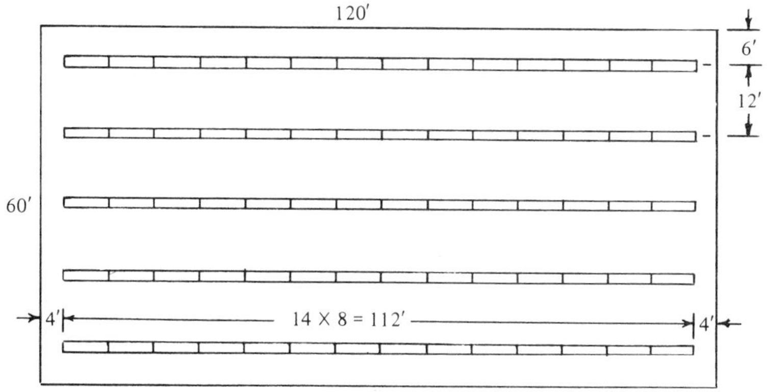

FIGURE 5.10

Plan of room showing luminaires for Example 5.11

5.5.2 Determining Maximum Wattage

When considering incandescent lamps for a lighting system, the fact that the efficacy of the lamps increases as the rated wattage of the lamps increases (Section 4.1.2) should be taken into account. When a luminaire type such as luminaire 1 in Table 5.5 can accommodate any wattage of lamp, it is advantageous to determine the maximum wattage that can be used, consistent with the spacing limitations of the luminaire. There is also the added advantage of lower installation costs with fewer luminaires. Example 5.12 shows how this calculation is done.

■ EXAMPLE 5.12

Refer to Examples 5.5 and 5.9. This same room is to be lighted to the same level (20 fc) again using luminaire 1. The lamp wattage is to be the maximum that can be used consistent with the spacing limitations.

Solution

STEP 1 The CU is 0.65, the same as calculated in Example 5.5.

STEP 2 The LLF is 0.73; assume at this point that it remains the same as calculated in Example 5.9.

STEP 3 The TILL of 303,500 lumens therefore remains the same.

STEP 4 The maximum luminaire spacing is 20.8 ft, the same as calculated in Example 5.10.

STEP 5 Calculate the minimum number of luminaires that can be installed without exceeding 20.8 ft:

$$\text{Min. no. of rows} = \frac{\text{room width}}{\text{max spacing}} = \frac{60}{20.8} \approx 3$$

$$\text{Min. no. per row} = \frac{\text{room length}}{\text{max spacing}} = \frac{120}{20.8} \approx 6$$

$$\text{Min. total} = 3 \times 6 = 18$$

STEP 6 Calculate the maximum lamp lumens that can be used:

$$\text{Max. lamp lumens} = \frac{\text{TILL}}{\text{min. no.}} = \frac{303{,}500}{18} = 16{,}900$$

STEP 7 From Table 4.1, a 750 W lamp with initial lamp lumens of 17,000 can be used.

STEP 8 Recheck the LLF using a 750 W lamp. From Table 4.1, the LLD is 89% (0.89). This is the same factor as used in Example 5.9. Therefore, LLF as assumed in step 2 is correct.

STEP 9 Calculate the actual maintained lighting level (Equation 5.3):

$$\text{TILL} = 18 \times 17{,}000 = 306{,}000 \quad \text{(for eighteen 750 W lamps)}$$

$$E = \frac{306{,}000 \times 0.65 \times 0.73}{60 \times 120} = 20.2 \text{ fc}$$

This is only 1% above target level.

We can compare layouts using 300 W (Example 5.10) and 750 W lamps:

	300 watt	750 watt
Total power (W)	50 × 300 = 15,000	18 × 750 = 13,500
Illuminance (fc)	19.6	20.2

Note that with less total power consumed the layout using the 750 W lamp gives a slightly higher lighting level. However, offsetting this advantage could be the matter of the quality of light (see Section 5.8).

5.6 COMPLETE DESIGN OF LIGHTING SYSTEM

We have now been through many examples, each showing individual steps in the design of a lighting layout. Examples 5.13 and 5.15, which follow, each present a complete design, from the selection of the recommended luminance level to the detailed layout drawing. Example 5.14 is an alternative method of lighting the same room as in Example 5.13. An economic comparison can then be made between the two systems.

■ EXAMPLE 5.13

An industrial area to be lighted is as follows:

Type of building: Industrial
Area/activity: Assembly, moderately difficult
Average age of workers: 35 years
Demand for speed and/or accuracy: Important
Task background reflectance: 40%
Size of room: 60 by 84 ft, 22.5 ft ceiling
Height of workplane: 3 ft
Reflectance factors: Ceiling 70%, walls 50%, and floor 20%
Luminaire type: 3, Table 5.5
Luminaire mounting: Suspended 5.5 ft
Lamps: 1500 mA, 96 in., T-12, CW, rapid-start fluorescent
Atmosphere: Medium
Interval between cleaning: 30 months

Solution

STEP 1 Determine the recommended illuminance level:
— From Table 5.2, the illuminance category is *E*.
— From Table 5.3, the recommended level is 750 lx or 75 fc.

STEP 2 Draw a cross section of the room and determine the cavity heights [see Figure 5.11(a)].

STEP 3 Calculate the cavity ratios using Equation 5.2 [see Figure 5.11(a)].

STEP 4 Determine the effective ceiling (ρ_{CC}) and floor (ρ_{FC}) cavity reflectances from Table 5.4 [see Figure 5.11(a)].

STEP 5 Determine the coefficient of utilization from Table 5.5:
— For luminaire 3, ρ_{CC} = 60%, ρ_W = 50%, and RCR = 2.
— CU = 0.70 (interpolate between ρ_{CC} of 70% and 50%).
— No correction required for 20% floor.

STEP 6 Calculate the light loss factor:
— Ballast factor (BF) = 0.95.
— LLD from Table 4.4 is 72% (use 0.72).
— Luminaire is category II (Table 5.5).
— LDD from Figure 5.4 is 0.83.
— RSDD: From Table 5.5 and Figure 5.5, the luminaire is semi-direct. From Table 5.7, the expected dirt depreciation is 25% and RSDD is 0.90 (interpolate between 20% and 30%).

$$\text{LLF} = 0.95 \times 0.72 \times 0.83 \times 0.90 = 0.51$$

STEP 7 Calculate the total initial lamp lumens using Equation 5.4:

$$\text{TILL} = \frac{75 \times (60 \times 84)}{0.70 \times 0.51} = 1{,}059{,}000$$

STEP 8 Calculate the required number of luminaires using Equation 5.5. From Table 4.4, initial lamp lumens are 15,250 and there are two lamps per luminaire:

$$\text{No. of luminaires} = \frac{1{,}059{,}000}{2 \times 15{,}250} = 34.7$$

STEP 9 Select a practical layout for the luminaires:

— From Table 5.5, for luminaire 3, SC is 1.3.
— Maximum spacing between rows is $1.3 \times 14 = 18.2$ ft.
— Minimum number of rows is $60/18.2 \approx 4$.
— Possible arrangements:

4 rows of 8 = 32 (too low)
4 rows of 9 = 36 (too high)
5 rows of 7 = 35 (select this arrangement)

STEP 10 Calculate the luminaire spacing as in Figure 5.8(a):

$$S_W = \frac{60}{5} = 12 \text{ ft}, \qquad S_L = \frac{84}{7} = 12 \text{ ft}$$

Note: There are not enough luminaires for continuous rows.

STEP 11 Draw a plan of the room and indicate the locations of luminaires [see Figure 5.11(b)].

STEP 12 Calculate the actual minimum maintained lighting level. If 34.7 luminaires will provide 75 fc (see steps 7 and 8), then 35 luminaires will provide

$$E = \frac{35}{34.7} \times 75 = 75.6 \text{ fc} \quad \text{(within 1\% of target value)}$$

STEP 13 Calculate the unit power density (UPD); see Section 5.7. From Table 4.4, the power input to the ballast for each luminaire (two 1500 mA 96 in. lamps) is 450 W.

$$\text{UPD} = \frac{\text{total power}}{\text{area}} = \frac{35 \times 450}{60 \times 84} = 3.125 \text{ W/ft}^2$$

EXAMPLE 5.14

The room to be lighted and the conditions are the same as outlined for Example 5.13 with the following exceptions:

Luminaire type: 4, Table 5.5
Lamp: 250 W HPS

Solution

STEP 1 The recommended illuminance level is the same (75 fc).

STEP 2 The cavity ratios and the effective ceiling and floor cavity reflectances remain the same as in Figure 5.11(a).

STEP 3 Determine the coefficient of utilization from Table 5.5:

— For luminaire 4, $\rho_{CC} = 60\%$, $\rho_W = 50\%$, and RCR = 2.
— CU = 0.725 (interpolate between P_{CC} of 70% and 50%).
— No correction required for 20% floor.

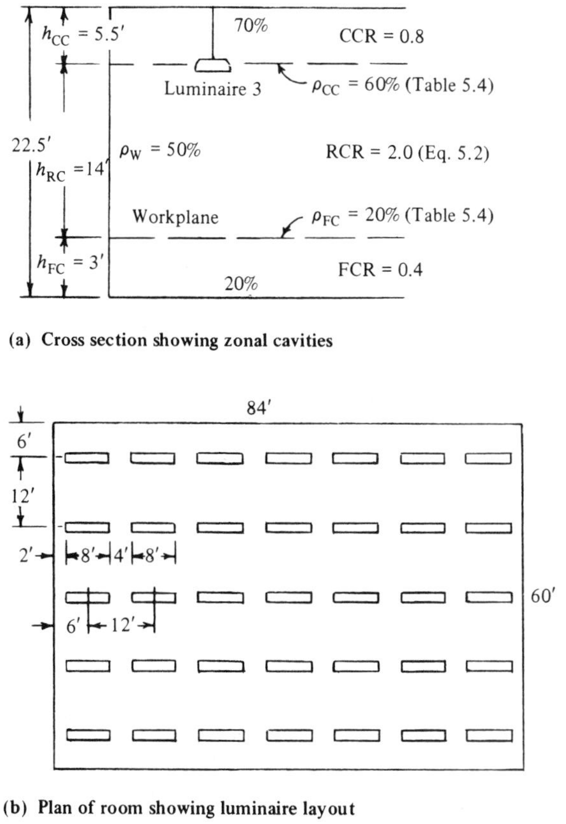

FIGURE 5.11

Diagrams for Example 5.13

STEP 4 Calculate the light loss factor:

— Ballast factor is assumed to be 1.0.
— LLD from Table 4.5 is 88% (use 0.88).
— Luminaire is category III (Table 5.5).
— LDD from Figure 5.4 is 0.77.
— RSDD: From Table 5.5 and Figure 5.5, the luminaire is direct. From Table 5.7, the expected dirt depreciation is 25% and RSDD is 0.95 (interpolate between 20% and 30%).

$$\text{LLF} = 1.0 \times 0.88 \times 0.77 \times 0.95 = 0.64$$

STEP 5 Calculate the total initial lamp lumens using Equation 5.4:

$$\text{TILL} = \frac{75 \times (60 \times 84)}{0.725 \times 0.64} = 814{,}600$$

STEP 6 Calculate the required number of luminaires using Equation 5.5.

From Table 4.5, initial lamp lumens are 30,000.

$$\text{No. of luminaires} = \frac{814{,}600}{30{,}000} = 27.2$$

STEP 7 Select a practical layout for the luminaires:

— From Table 5.5, for luminaire 4, SC is 1.5.
— Maximum spacing between rows is $1.5 \times 14 = 21$ ft.
— Minimum number of rows is $60/21 \approx 3$.
— Minimum number per row is $84/21 = 4$.
— Possible arrangements:

3 rows of 9 = 27 (will give very unequal spacing)
4 rows of 6 = 24 (more symmetrical spacing but too few)
4 rows of 7 = 28 (select this arrangement)

STEP 8 Calculate the luminaire spacing as in Figure 5.8(a):

$$S_W = \frac{60}{4} = 15 \text{ ft}, \qquad S_L = \frac{84}{7} = 12 \text{ ft}$$

This does not give symmetrical spacing, but it is the best that can be obtained.

STEP 9 Draw a plan of the room and indicate the locations of luminaires as shown in Figure 5.12.

STEP 10 Calculate the actual minimum maintained lighting level:

$$E = \frac{28}{27.2} \times 75 = 77.2 \text{ fc} \quad \text{(slightly higher than Ex. 5.13)}$$

STEP 11 Calculate the unit power density (UPD); see Section 5.7. From Table 4.5, the power input to each ballast is 295 watts:

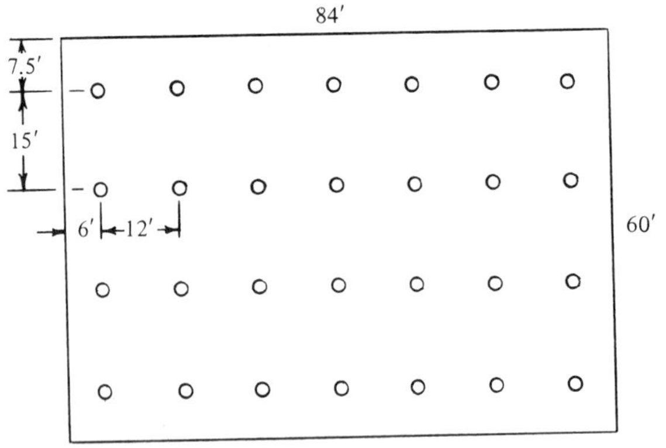

For cross section of room, see Figure 5.11(a)

FIGURE 5.12

Plan of room showing luminaires for Example 5.14

$$\text{UPD} = \frac{\text{total power}}{\text{area}} = \frac{28 \times 295}{60 \times 84} = 1.64 \text{ W/ft}^2$$

Note the much lower watts per square foot for the unit power density as compared with Example 5.13. This is discussed further in Section 5.7 and Example 5.16.

EXAMPLE 5.15

Measurements for this example are in meters. The room to be lighted is as follows:

Type of building: Commercial
Area/activity: Drafting: tracing paper, low contrast
Average age of workers: 35 years
Demand for speed and/or accuracy: Important
Task background reflectance: 75%
Size of room: 10.0 by 13.25 m; 2.91 m ceiling
Height of workplane: 0.91 m
Reflectance factors: Ceiling 80%, walls 50%, and floor 30%
Luminaire type: 2, Table 5.5; 300 mm wide with two lamps
Luminaire mounting: Recessed in ceiling
Lamps: 430 mA, 40 W, 1200 mm, WW, RS standard fluorescent
Atmosphere: Clean
Interval between cleaning: 12 months

Solution

STEP 1 Determine the recommended illuminance level:

— From Table 5.1, the illuminance category is F.
— From Table 5.3, the recommended level is 1000 lx.

STEP 2 Draw a cross section of the room and determine the cavity heights [see Figure 5.13(a)]. Note there is no ceiling cavity.

STEP 3 Calculate the cavity ratios using Equation 5.2 [see Figure 5.13(a)].

STEP 4 Determine the effective floor cavity reflectance (ρ_{FC}) from Table 5.4 [see Figure 5.13(a)]. Note that the effective ceiling cavity reflectance is the same as the actual ceiling reflectance.

STEP 5 Determine the coefficient of utilization:

— It is necessary to interpolate for RCR = 1.75.
— For luminaire 2, ρ_{CC} = 80% and ρ_W = 50%.

RCR	Table 5.5 CU	Table 5.6 Factor for 30% Floor
1.0	0.67	1.082
1.75 (interpolate)	0.61	1.070
2.0	0.59	1.066

— Multiplying factor for effective floor of 28%:

30%	1.070 (from above)
28% (interpolate)	1.056
20%	1.00

— Multiply by factor of 0.9 as per note on Table 5.5 for luminaire 2, 300 mm wide using two lamps.

Final CU = 0.61 × 1.056 × 0.9 = 0.58 (two-figure accuracy)

STEP 6 Calculate the light loss factor:

— Ballast factor = 0.95.
— LLD from Table 4.4 is 84% (use 0.84).
— Luminaire is category V (Table 5.5).
— LDD from Figure 5.4 is 0.88.
— RSDD: From Table 5.5 and Figure 5.5, the luminaire is direct.

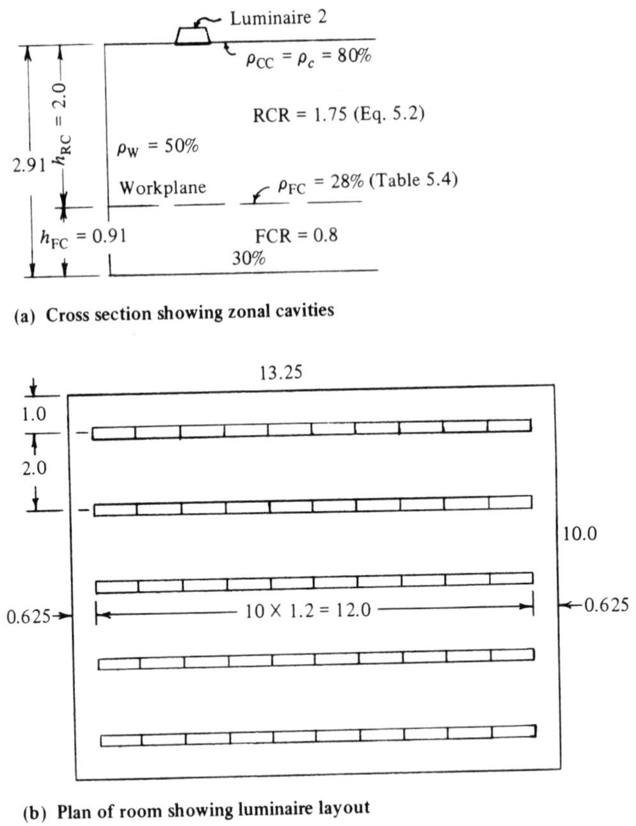

FIGURE 5.13

Diagrams for Example 5.15 (dimensions are in meters)

From Table 5.7, the expected dirt depreciation is 12% (use 10%) and RSDD is 0.98.

$$\text{LLF} = 0.95 \times 0.84 \times 0.88 \times 0.98 = 0.69$$

STEP 7 Calculate the total initial lamp lumens using Equation 5.4:

$$\text{TILL} = \frac{1000 \times (10.0 \times 13.25)}{0.58 \times 0.69} = 331{,}000$$

STEP 8 Calculate the required number of luminaires using Equation 5.5. From Table 4.4, the initial lamp lumens are 3175 and there are two lamps per luminaire.

$$\text{No. of luminaires} = \frac{331{,}000}{2 \times 3175} = 52.1$$

STEP 9 Select a practical layout for the luminaires:

— Assume continuous rows are required.
— Calculate the maximum number per row lengthwise in the room as in Figure 5.8(b) for 1.2 m long luminaires.

$$\text{Max. no. per row} = \frac{13.25 - 0.3}{1.2} \approx 10$$

— Number of rows required is 52/10 ≈ 5.
— Select 5 rows of 10 = 50.

STEP 10 Calculate the luminaire spacing as in Figure 5.8(b):

$$S_W = \frac{10.0}{5} = 2.0 \text{ m}$$

$$\text{Total length of each row} = 10 \times 1.2 = 12.0 \text{ m}$$

$$\text{Space at ends of rows} = \frac{13.25 - 12.0}{2} = 0.625 \text{ m}$$

STEP 11 Check the maximum spacing allowed between rows:

— From Table 5.5, for luminaire 2, SC is 1.4 for crosswise spacing.
— Max. spacing = $1.4 \times h_{RC} = 1.4 \times 2.0 = 2.8$ m.
— 2.0 m spacing is within the limits.

STEP 12 Draw a plan of the room and indicate the locations of luminaires (see Figure 5.13(b)].

STEP 13 Calculate the actual minimum maintained lighting level:

$$E = \frac{50}{52.1} \times 1000 = 960 \text{ lx} \quad \text{(within 4\% of target value)}$$

STEP 14 Calculate the unit power density (UPD); see Section 5.7. From Table 4.4, the power input to the ballast for each luminaire (two 430 mA, 1200 mm lamps) is 95 W.

$$\text{UPD} = \frac{\text{total power}}{\text{area}} = \frac{50 \times 95}{10.0 \times 13.25} = 35.85 \text{ W/m}^2$$

For comparison with other examples,

$35.85/10.76 = 3.33 \text{ W/ft}^2$

The unit power density of 3.33 watts per square foot in Example 5.15 is high. Before the advent of the energy shortage, this value was accepted as normal. Today's practices, however, dictate that the lighting load be kept as low as possible by using energy-saving lamps and ballasts. Example 5.17 shows the economics of using energy-saving lamps. Also, it may be necessary to redesign the layout for the drafting room as in Example 5.15 so that the 1000 lux recommended at the task is provided by a combination of general overall lighting for the room and task lighting at the individual drafting stations.

5.7 ECONOMIC ANALYSIS OF LIGHTING SYSTEMS

Economic analysis of lighting systems enables the designer to make a comparison of alternative methods of providing the required lighting for an area. This analysis should cover both the initial costs and the operating costs. The initial or capital costs cover the purchase and installation of all luminaires, together with the necessary wiring and controls. The operating costs cover the power costs, replacement of lamp and ballast costs, cleaning maintenance costs, and so on. In many instances, the system with the least initial costs may be the most expensive alternative over the life of the system because of higher operating costs.

The concept of energy management for buildings has gained importance since the early 1970s. There is a need to limit the amount of power used for lighting. The Illuminating Engineering Society of North America (IES) has established recommended lighting power limits using the *unit power density* (UPD) procedure. The unit power density is measured in watts per square meter or watts per square foot. The power must include all inputs to the lighting system, including any losses from the use of ballasts. It is beyond the scope of this textbook to present the complete UPD procedure. For information on the procedure and the recommended limitations, refer to the *IES Lighting Handbook, 1987 Application Volume*.

In Examples 5.13, 5.14, and 5.15, the unit power density values are calculated. These values give an immediate comparison between systems as to their relative power requirements. For instance, Examples 5.13 and 5.14 show the design of alternative lighting systems for the same area. The relative UPD values for the two examples are 3.125 and 1.64 watts per square foot, respectively. This shows that the system in Example 5.14 is far more efficient than the system in Example 5.13. Most of the increase in efficiency is due to the much higher efficacy of the high-pressure sodium lamp. Other factors that also contribute, but to a lesser degree, are the higher coefficient of utilization typical for a point source luminaire and the much better lumen maintenance (LLD factor) of the HPS lamp over its life.

Example 5.16, which follows, shows an economic analysis of the two systems as designed in Examples 5.13 and 5.14. This analysis shows that the latter system using the HPS lamps, while initially costing more, is the least costly over the life of the system because of the lower electrical energy costs. The assumed energy rate of \$0.05 per kilowatt-hour (kWh) used in the example is very conservative. Areas with higher rates would show an even better rate of return than that calculated in the example. This analysis shows why the use of the HPS lamp is increasing and that of the highly loaded fluorescent lamp is decreasing. However, there is still the matter of the quality of light, as discussed in Section 5.8.

EXAMPLE 5.16

Prepare an economic analysis of the alternative systems designed in Examples 5.13 and 5.14 for lighting the same area; that is, compare the initial and operating costs of the two alternative systems. Operating costs are to be based on 6000 hr of operation per year and group relamping at 80% of the rated life of the lamps. The basic costs are shown in Table 5.8 (the values shown are estimates reflecting relative costs only).

TABLE 5.8 Cost Data for Example 5.16

	Initial (Capital) Costs	
Ex. 5.13:	Luminaire 3	\$135.00 each
	1500 mA, 96 in. fluorescent lamp	\$8.00 each
	Installation and wiring for luminaire	\$120.00 each
Ex. 5.14:	Luminaire 4	\$300.00 each
	250 W HPS lamp	\$60.00 each
	Installation and wiring for luminaire	\$120.00 each
	Operating Costs	
Energy rate		\$0.05 per kWh
Labor rates for relamping:	1500 mA, 96 in. fluorescent	\$5.00 per lamp
	250 W HPS	\$10.00 per lamp

Solution

The cost analysis for Example 5.16 is as follows.

Initial Costs

Ex. 5.13: Total cost per luminaire installed and wired:

\$135 + (2 × \$8) + \$120 = \$271

Total cost of system = 35 × \$271 = \$9,485

Ex. 5.14: Total cost per luminaire installed and wired:

\$300 + \$60 + \$120 = \$480

Total cost of system = 28 × \$480 = \$13,440

Additional cost for Ex. 5.14 system \$3,955

Annual Operating Costs: 6000 Hours Operation

Ex. 5.13: From Table 4.4, power input to each ballast for two 1500 mA, 96 in. lamps is 450 W:

$$\text{Total power} = 35 \times 450/1000 = 15.75 \text{ kW}$$

See Section 1.1.4 for energy calculations:

$$\text{Energy consumption} = 15.75 \times 6000 = 94{,}500 \text{ kWh}$$

Annual cost of energy = 94,500 × \$0.05 = \$4725

Rated lamp life is 9000 hr (Table 4.4); 80% of rated life = 0.8 × 9000 = 7200 hr; and lamp replacement every 7200/6000 = 1.2 years:

Annual cost of relamping (2 lamps per luminaire at \$8.00 per lamp plus \$5.00 labor) =

35 × 2 × (\$8.00 + \$5.00)/1.2 = \$758

Total annual operating cost for Ex. 5.13 system \$5483

Ex. 5.14: From Table 4.5, power input to each ballast for 250 W HPS lamp is 295 W:

$$\text{Total power} = 28 \times 295/1000 = 8.26 \text{ kW}$$

$$\text{Energy consumption} = 8.26 \times 6000 = 49{,}560 \text{ kWh}$$

Annual cost of energy = 49,560 × \$0.05 = \$2478

Rated lamp life is 24,000 hr (Table 4.5); 80% of rated life = 0.8 × 24,000 = 19,200 hr; and lamp replacement every 19,200/6,000 = 3.2 years:

Annual cost of relamping (at \$60.00 per lamp plus \$10.00 labor) =

28 × (\$60.00 + \$10.00)/3.2 = \$613

Total annual operating cost for Ex. 5.14 system \$3091

Operating cost saving in favor of Ex. 5.14 = \$5483 − \$3091 = \$2392

The system as designed in Example 5.14 using HPS lamps costs \$3955 extra to install but saves \$2392 every year. Therefore, it will take only 3955/2392 = 1.65 years to recover the extra costs. The return on investment is

$$\frac{2392}{3955} \times 100 = 60.5\%$$

There are also savings that can be considered when it is time to relamp an existing lighting system. As discussed in Section 4.3.5, energy-saving lamps have been developed that offer higher efficacies than standard lamps. These new lamps can operate from the same ballasts as used for standard lamps. However, they are more expensive than standard lamps. Example 5.17 shows whether relamping a lighting system with energy-saving lamps is justified.

EXAMPLE 5.17

Refer to Example 5.15, where 50 luminaires with a total of 100 fluorescent lamps (40 W, WW standard) are required for the system. It is now time to relamp the system and a decision as to whether to relamp with energy-saving lamps should be made. The relative costs of the lamps are assumed to be:

Standard 40 W warm white: $2.37 each
Energy-saving, 34 W Super Saver II: $3.40 each

The existing standard ballasts will still be used. The power input to each ballast will be reduced from 95 to 81 W with the energy-saving lamps. Assume 4000 hours operation per year and energy costs of $0.05 per kWh.

Solution

The cost analysis is as follows.

STEP 1 The energy-saving SSII lamps have initial lamp lumens of 3050 as compared with 3175 lumens for the standard WW lamps (Table 4.4). This slight drop should not cause a noticeable problem.

STEP 2 The added cost to relamp with energy-saving lamps is

$$(\$3.40 - \$2.37) \times 2 \times 50 = \$103.00$$

STEP 3 The energy savings per year are

$$\frac{50 \times (95 - 81)}{1000} \times 4000 = 2800 \text{ kWh}$$

STEP 4 The savings in energy costs per year are 2800 × $0.05 = $140.

Therefore, the extra cost of the energy-saving lamps would be recovered in less than 1 year. The rated life of the lamps is 20,000 hours or 5 years. Relamping with energy-saving lamps would be recommended.

5.8 QUALITY OF LIGHT

The quality of light involves the comfort of the visual environment. Previous discussions and examples in this chapter have concentrated on providing a sufficient quantity of light. However, having the correct quantity of light does not necessarily mean that the quality of the lighting will be good. The main factors to consider in analyzing the quality of light are glare, luminance ratios, diffusion, and color.

Glare is any luminance (brightness) that causes discomfort, interference with vision, or eye fatigue. The major cause of glare is usually the light source itself. Point sources of light can be particularly troublesome because of their concentrated light output, which results in extremely high brightness. Fluorescent lamps are lower in brightness because their light output is spread over a larger area, but they too can cause problems because of their size. A large area of low brightness may be as uncomfortable as a smaller area of higher brightness.

The glare from the light source that can cause the most concern is that which enters the eye directly. However, a secondary problem can be caused by light reflected in the direction of the eye. Refer to Figure 5.14(a), which shows the direct and reflected glare zones.

The effect of glare is also dependent on the brightness of the area around the source of the glare. An example of this is car headlights. We have all experienced the discomfort of the glare from oncoming headlights at night on a dark road. Yet those same headlights, if left turned on in daylight, cause virtually no problem. The time that a person is exposed to the glare is a further factor. A condition that can easily be tolerated for a short time may become very uncomfortable and fatiguing to the person who must work under it for an 8 hour day.

A few of the more effective methods of reducing glare are as follows:

1. Use luminaires that shield the light source within the normal field of vision. This reduces the effect of direct glare. Figure 5.14(b) shows how luminaires and reflectors can provide shielding. Note that a fluorescent luminaire, because it is not symmetrical, has crosswise shielding and, if a louver is used, also lengthwise shielding. The two shielding angles may be different. Direct glare can also be minimized by using a lens to control the direction of the light output from the luminaire. Certain fluorescent luminaires, such as the commercial types that are for surface or suspended mounting, do not completely shield the light in the direct glare zone. Instead, they use very dense side panels, which considerably reduce the luminance on the sides of the luminaire but still provide enough light so that there is less contrast between the outside of the luminaire and its bright interior.
2. Finish the ceilings and walls with materials having light colors and high reflectance factors. This reduces the contrast between the luminaires and their background.
3. Use suspended luminaires with some upward component of light wherever the ceiling height permits. This further helps to reduce the contrast between the luminaire and its background by increasing the luminance of the ceiling.
4. Mount the luminaires above the normal field of vision wherever

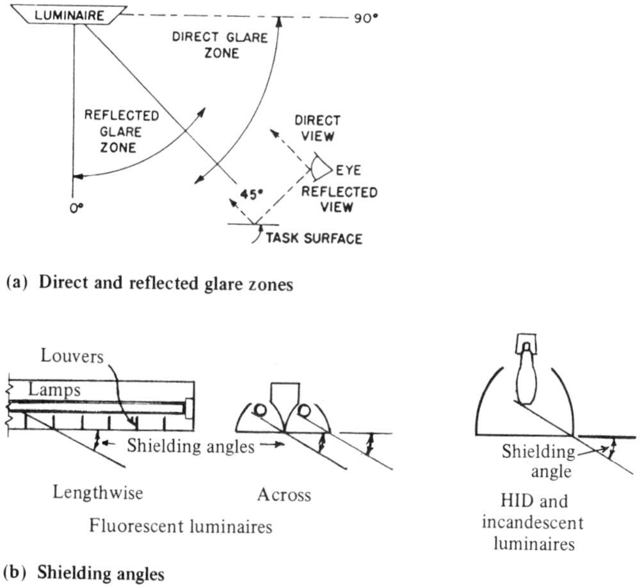

FIGURE 5.14

Glare zones and shielding angles of luminaires

possible. For example, the luminaires in high-bay industrial areas can be mounted at a considerable height. This allows the use of the very bright HID point sources. Those luminaires that fall within the normal field of vision are far enough away so that, with proper shielding, any glare problem is eliminated.

5. Avoid the use of any shiny surfaces within the normal field of vision to minimize reflected glare. As an example, desk tops should have a dull, nonglossy finish that helps to diffuse any reflected light.

Figure 5.15 shows an example of the lighting of an industrial area using high-bay HID luminaires. Note the upward component of light from the luminaire, which helps to light the ceiling. Figure 5.16 shows an example of the lighting of an office area using recessed fluorescent luminaires equipped with flat lens.

The second factor in the quality of light involves luminance ratios or brightness contrast. Consider a task that has a high brightness in contrast to its background. Eye fatigue will result since the eyes are forced to continually adjust from one brightness level to the other. On the other hand, any brightness in the peripheral field that is higher than the task brightness tends to attract the eyes away from the task. The ideal situation is to have the background brightness the same as the task brightness. However, this is difficult to achieve. The recommendations are that the ratio of the task luminance to that of its immediate background should not exceed 3 to 1 and that the

FIGURE 5.15

Example of industrial lighting using high-bay HID luminaires

ratio of task luminance to any luminance in the visual field should not exceed 10 to 1.

An example could be the desk where you study. You generally are working on white paper. If the desk top is dark, the contrast may be too high. Furthermore, if you use only a desk lamp over your work with no other lighting in the room, the contrast between the white paper and the surrounding room background may be excessive. Both condition can cause undue eye fatigue. The top of your desk should be a light color with a nonglossy finish. Also, there should be some general lighting in the room in addition to the desk lamp to brighten up the background.

The third factor in the quality of light concerns diffusion. Diffuse light is light that comes from many directions, as opposed to light that comes from only one direction. The latter creates shadows, which for most lighting applications are not desirable. Perfectly diffuse light that creates no shadows is the ideal for many critical seeing tasks, particularly in school and office areas. Fortunately, lighting layouts with a high level of illuminance require a considerable number of light sources, which in itself provides a fair degree of diffuse light. The degree of diffusion can be further in-

FIGURE 5.16

Example of office lighting using recessed fluorescent luminaires

creased by the use of suspended luminaires with some upward light output. The components of light reflected back from the ceiling increase the directions from which the light reaches the work area.

The fourth factor with regard to the quality of light is color. With equal illumination, the various "white" light sources probably have little effect on the speed of seeing. However, each type of light source, as discussed in Chapter 4, has a different spectral distribution curve. An object viewed separately under these different sources could appear to be a different color. The type of source should be carefully selected where color discrimination is important (see Section 3.2). The color output of the light source can also affect the atmosphere of the space being lighted (see Section 4.3.4). This can be important for areas in which workers remain at their jobs for long periods of time.

An example where the color output of the light source is important is the lighting of merchandising areas that display items for use in our homes. The lighting in our homes is predominantly incandescent, which has a high output in the red end of the spectrum. Therefore, the light source used in the merchandising area should also have a reasonably high output in the red end of the spectrum. If fluorescent lamps are to be used, they should be the warm white deluxe type (see Figure 4.10).

In Example 5.12, a comparison is made between using 300 watt and 750 watt incandescent lamps for the lighting of a room. It is shown that the layout using the 750 watt lamps is more efficient. However, offsetting this advantage is the fact that the larger wattage lamps could cause more glare and that, with fewer lamps, the lighting would be less diffuse and more uneven. Depending on the activities that are planned for the room, the 300 watt lamps may still be the final choice because of overriding requirements with regard to the quality of light.

In Example 5.16, the cost analysis shows that the HPS lamps have a considerable advantage over the highly loaded fluorescent lamps. However, the quality of the lighting must also be considered. The extremely high light output from the point source HPS lamps may cause glare problems. Also, with fewer luminaires, the lighting would be less diffuse and more uneven. The light output of the HPS lamp is very high in the yellow-orange area of the spectral energy distribution curve, as shown in Figure 4.17(d). This may not be compatible with planned color-matching tasks. Therefore, the fluorescent lamps may still be the final choice based on the requirements for the quality of light.

5.9 LIGHTING CONTROLS

Lighting controls can range from simple on–off devices to automatically controlled, continuous dimming systems. The simple switching of lights is discussed in Section 12.8. The basic method used in the past for dimming light sources has been to vary the voltage to the lamp with such devices as variable autotransformers. A newer method uses electronic circuitry to vary the amount of time during each cycle that the lamp current is permitted to flow. Solid-state dimming equipment has now largely taken over the field of dimming equipment because of its versatility and low power losses. Incandescent lamps are very easy to dim. Electric discharge lamps are more difficult to dim because the arc goes unstable as the voltage is decreased. See Section 4.3.9 with regard to the dimming of fluorescent lamps. Recent advances in device technology and circuit design have made it possible to have limited dimming of HID sources. However, it is very expensive.

The original use for dimming was to provide local control of the level of lighting in a particular area to suit the activities being carried out at varying times during the day. With the emphasis on energy conservation in the last few years, another use for the dimming of lighting has developed and that is to maintain constant lighting levels over the life of a system. Refer to Section 5.3 on the light loss factor. In the examples shown in this chapter on lighting layout design, the light loss factor is included in the calculations to account for the decrease in the illuminance level because of aging. Thus, with a system operating on a constant power input, the initial lighting level is much higher than required.

With dimming, however, the required lighting level can initially be set by reducing the power input to the lamps. Then, as the system operates, the power inputs can be slowly increased to compensate for lamp, luminaire, and other light losses (Section 5.3), thus keeping the lighting levels at the workplane constant with time. This type of dimming system is automatically controlled through photoelectric feedback devices that monitor the actual level of lighting. The accumulated savings in power costs can be worthwhile. For example, assume that the lighting system for an office area totaling 10,000 square feet has an average light loss of 25% over a year. Without dimming, the initial lighting level is 100/0.75 = 133.3% or 33.3% higher than required. This also means that the power input is higher by the same amount. Assume that the unit power density for the system is 3.0 watts per square foot for a total connected load of 30.0 kilowatts. With a dimming system, the initial power requirement can be reduced to 75% or 22.5 kilowatts for a saving of 7.5 kilowatts. The power input is then increased gradually with time until the full 30.0 kilowatts is required at the end of the year. Assuming the increase over the year is linear, the average power saving is one-half of the 7.5 kilowatts. If the total hours of operation for the year are 4000 and the energy rate is \$0.08 per kilowatt-hour, then the savings are

$$\frac{7.5}{2} \times 4000 \times \$0.08 = \$1200/\text{yr}$$

Further savings can be realized by incorporating a time programming that automatically adjusts the lighting levels throughout the day to suit task changes, such as from work modes to cleaning and security modes. Many new buildings are being constructed so that advantage can be taken of daylight. The costs of the automatic dimming and programming system can usually be recovered in a very few years from the accumulated savings in energy.

SUMMARY

- The quantity of light involves the generation of the necessary amount of light to provide the recommended lighting level.
- The recommended lighting level is based on the type of area or activity being performed, the average of the workers' ages, the im-

portance of speed and accuracy, and the reflectance of the task background.

- The lumen method is used to calculate the average illuminance for general lighting.
- The coefficient of utilization (CU) represents the efficiency of the lighting system.
- The CU depends on the type of luminaire, the reflectances of the room surfaces, and the size and shape of the room.
- The zonal-cavity method is used to calculate the CU.
- Cavity ratios are calculated as follows:

$$\text{CR} = \frac{5h \times (\text{room width} + \text{room length})}{\text{room width} \times \text{room length}}$$

- The light loss factor (LLF) represents the degree by which the lighting level decreases up to the time corrective action is taken.
- The LLF is the product of lamp lumen depreciation (LLD), luminaire dirt depreciation (LDD), room surface dirt depreciation (RSDD), and where applicable the ballast factor.
- Luminaires are divided into six distribution types ranging from direct to indirect.
- The minimum average maintained illuminance is calculated as follows:

$$E = \frac{\text{TILL} \times \text{CU} \times \text{LLF}}{\text{area}}$$

- The total initial lamp lumens required to provide the recommended lighting level is calculated as follows:

$$\text{TILL} = \frac{E \times \text{area}}{\text{CU} \times \text{LLF}}$$

- The required number of luminaires is calculated as follows:

$$\text{No. of luminaires} = \frac{\text{TILL}}{\begin{pmatrix}\text{no. of lamps}\\ \text{per luminaire}\end{pmatrix} \times \begin{pmatrix}\text{initial lumens}\\ \text{per lamp}\end{pmatrix}}$$

- The luminaire layout and the actual number used is based on selecting a symmetrical arrangement that suits the room proportions.
- The spacing criterion (SC) sets the maximum spacing permitted for the luminaires in order to have reasonably uniform levels for general lighting.

- The economic analysis of a lighting system must consider both the initial (capital) and operating costs.
- Systems having the lowest initial cost may not have the lowest total lifetime costs.
- The quality of light involves the comfort of the seeing environment.
- The factors to consider for quality of light are glare, luminance ratios, diffusion, and color.
- Automatic dimming and time control systems for lighting can offer lifetime economic benefits.

QUESTIONS

1. What weighting factors must be considered when selecting the IES recommended illuminance value?
2. What is the workplane?
3. What does the coefficient of utilization (CU) represent?
4. State the five factors that affect the CU.
5. What does the effective ceiling reflectance represent?
6. When are the effective and actual ceiling reflectances the same?
7. Why is it necessary to include the light loss factor in the calculations for the required number of luminaires?
8. Differentiate between unrecoverable and recoverable light loss factors.
9. Why is it necessary to include luminaire dirt depreciation and room surface dirt depreciation factors?
10. Why is the room surface dirt depreciation factor affected by the luminaire distribution type?
11. List the six classifications of luminaires according to their distribution pattern.
12. Why are systems that use indirect luminaires generally the least efficient?
13. What is the significance of the luminaire spacing criterion?
14. What is the unit power density?
15. What factors are involved in the quality of light?
16. Why is glare a major concern?
17. What is the shielding angle?
18. How does a light-colored ceiling with a high reflectance factor help reduce glare?
19. Why is it recommended that suspended luminaires have some upward component of light?
20. Why do luminance ratios affect the quality of the lighting?
21. What is diffuse light?
22. Why should automatic dimming and programming of lighting systems be considered?

PROBLEMS

1. Select the recommended illuminance value for a science laboratory in a high school. The task background reflectance is 50% and the demand for speed and/or accuracy is not important.
2. Calculate the ceiling, room, and floor cavity ratios for a 17 by 24 ft room with a 13 ft ceiling. The workplane is 3 ft above the floor and the luminaires are suspended 2 ft from the ceiling.
3. The ceiling, walls, and floor reflectance factors for the room in Problem 2 are 90%, 50%, and 30%, respectively. Determine the effective ceiling and effective floor cavity reflectances.
4. Calculate the coefficient of utilization for the room in Problems 2 and 3 using the luminaire 3 in Table 5.5.
5. Determine the luminaire dirt depreciation (LDD) factor for luminaire 3 operating in a dirty atmosphere with cleaning every 2 years.

6. Determine the room surface dirt depreciation (RSDD) factor for Problem 5 if the room cavity ratio is 3.0.
7. Calculate the light loss factor for Problems 5 and 6 if the lamps used are the 40 W, 430 mA standard fluorescent.
8. Calculate the maximum spacing in feet permitted between rows for luminaire 3 mounted in the room as in Problem 2.
9. If the fluorescent luminaires in Problem 8 are to be individually mounted, calculate the maximum center line to center line spacing permitted lengthwise in the rows if the luminaires are (a) 4 ft long; (b) 8 ft long.
10. Calculate the theoretical number of luminaires required to light the following room:

    — Type of building: Industrial
    — Area/activity: Woodworking, fine bench work
    — Average age of workers: 35 years
    — Demand for speed and/or accuracy: Important
    — Task background reflectance: 25%
    — Size of room: 42 by 60 ft; 21 ft ceiling
    — Height of workplane: 3 ft
    — Reflectance factors: Ceiling 80%, walls 50%, and floor 10%
    — Luminaire type: 4, Table 5.5
    — Luminaire mounting: Suspended, 3 ft
    — Lamps: 400 W, clear metal halide
    — Atmosphere: Medium
    — Interval between cleaning: 12 months

11. Select a practical layout for the lighting in Problem 10. Calculate the luminaire spacings crosswise between rows and lengthwise between luminaires in each row. Check that your selected layout conforms to the spacing criterion.
12. Calculate the unit power density of the lighting system selected in Problem 11.
13. Calculate the theoretical number of luminaires required to light the following room:

    — Type of building: Commercial
    — Area/activity: General office, reading handwritten carbon copies
    — Average age of workers: 35 years
    — Demand for speed and/or accuracy: Important
    — Task background reflectance: 75%
    — Size of room: 36 by 54 ft; 9 ft ceiling
    — Height of workplane: 2.5 ft
    — Reflectance factors: Ceiling 80%, walls 50%, and floor 30%
    — Luminaire type: 2, Table 5.5; 2 ft wide with four lamps
    — Luminaire mounting: Recessed in ceiling
    — Lamps: 34 W, 48 in., SS II energy-saving fluorescent
    — Atmosphere: Clean
    — Interval between cleaning: 18 months

14. Select a practical layout for the lighting in Problem 13. Calculate the luminaire spacings crosswise between rows and lengthwise between luminaires in each row. Check that the selected layout conforms to the spacing criterion.
15. Calculate the unit power density of the lighting system selected in Problem 14. Energy-saving ballasts are to be used along with the energy-saving lamps.
16. Two designs for lighting an industrial area show that:

    — Design A requires 60 of luminaire 3 each having two 1500 mA, 96 in. fluorescent lamps.
    — Design B requires 48 of luminaire 4 each having one 250 W HPS lamp.

    Operating costs are to be based on 5000 hr operation per year and group relamping at 75% of rated life of the lamps. The basic costs are as in Example 5.16, except that energy costs are $0.08 per kWh. Calculate the years to recover the extra costs using luminaire 4.
17. An office area has 100 of luminaire 2 each having four 40 W, WW standard fluorescent lamps. Calculate the years to recover the extra costs to relamp with 34 W energy-saving lamps instead of the standard 40 W lamps. The costs of the lamps and the ballast watts are as in Example 5.17. Hours of operation are 3000 h per year and energy costs are $0.06 per kWh.

6 Protection of Electrical Systems

OBJECTIVES

After studying this chapter, you will be able to:

- Realize the objectives of system protection.
- Recognize the difference between an overload and a short circuit.
- Refer to the *National Electrical Code* requirements for overcurrent protection.
- Identify the stresses imposed by fault currents.
- Identify the types of short-circuit faults.
- Do elementary calculations for fault currents.
- Use the per unit method of calculations.
- Explain asymmetrical fault currents.
- Discuss the general ratings of protective devices.
- Identify inverse-time and instantaneous-response characteristics.

INTRODUCTION

All electrical systems have the common purpose of providing electrical energy to the utilization equipment as safely and reliably as is economically feasible. The utilization equipment then converts the electrical energy to other forms, such as mechanical, light, and heat energy. The design of the electrical system to transmit the electrical energy to the utilization equipment must focus on two basic requirements. First, the system must be adequate to deliver to each piece of equipment the necessary energy on a continuous basis under normal conditions. Second, the system must be designed to minimize power outages and damage in the event that abnormal conditions occur on the system. It is this second requirement that will now be addressed. The next five chapters cover the means of protecting electrical systems and the protective devices involved.

Since nothing manufactured can be deemed to be perfect, it must be assumed that equipment will fail. Failure on any part of an electrical system can result in the uncontrolled flow of tremendous amounts of energy that can cause major damage in split seconds. Protective systems cannot prevent the failure of equipment. Their purpose then is to remove the faulted segment of the system as quickly and safely as possible. The protection of electrical systems should be designed with the following order of priorities in mind:

—To prevent injuries to personnel
—To prevent fires
—To minimize the damage to electrical equipment
—To minimize the disturbances to the system

That the protection of people and property is paramount is emphasized in the *National Electrical Code* (*NEC*). This code is the nationally accepted guide for the safe installation of electrical conductors and equipment and is the basis for all electrical codes used in the United States. *NEC* Article 90—Introduction, Section 90-1; Purpose, states the following: (*a*) *Practical Safeguarding—The purpose of this code is the practical safeguarding of persons and property from hazards arising from the use of electricity.* The titles *National Electrical Code*® and *NEC*® are registered trademarks of the National Fire Protection Association.

Next in order of priorities is the desirability of keeping any damage to the electrical equipment to the absolute minimum so that normal operation can resume as quickly as possible. Finally, it makes economic sense, especially with large systems, to restrict any power outages to as small a section as possible so that the balance of the system can continue to operate normally. This requirement for the least amount of shutdown of the system involves coordination of the protective devices, which is a fairly complicated matter. This topic is therefore dealt with at length in Chapter 16 at the end of the book after protective devices and electrical systems themselves have been fully discussed.

6.1 TYPES OF ABNORMAL CONDITIONS

The following is a list of abnormal conditions that can occur on a system and for which corrective action should be taken:

1. Overloads
2. Short circuits
3. Under voltage
4. Single phasing of three-phase systems
5. Overvoltages and transient surges

6. Incorrect synchronizing of frequencies
7. Incorrect phase sequence
8. Reverse power flow

We will deal with these in reverse order. Items 6, 7, and 8 are abnormal conditions that can only arise on a large system that combines two or more sources of power operating in parallel at the same time. This type of system is complex, and the protection against these types of abnormal conditions is beyond the scope of this book. Item 5 is an abnormal condition associated with lightning. The application of lightning or surge arresters is briefly covered in Section 15.2.2. Items 3 and 4 are abnormal conditions that are of major concern where motors are involved. Therefore, these particular conditions are dealt with in Sections 14.2 and 14.2.1 when discussing motor starters. That leaves overloads and short circuits, which are the most common of the abnormal conditions that occur on electrical systems. Even the small systems in our residences must be fully protected against these.

First, let us fully understand the difference between an overload and a short circuit.

Overload This is caused by an excessive demand from the utilization equipment. During an overload, currents continue to flow only in the normal circuit conductors. An overload can be tolerated for a short period of time (minutes) before corrective action has to be taken. An overload is not caused by the failure of any electrical component of the system.

Short circuit This is caused by an electrical failure such as the breakdown of insulation. The resulting fault currents can be very large, in the tens of thousands of amperes, depending on the capacity of the system. These fault currents can flow in abnormal current paths, such as from one phase to ground. Since the damage can be immediate, the faulted part of the system must be disconnected as quickly as possible (within cycles).

An example of an overload is the mechanical overloading of a motor that results in the motor drawing above-normal current. Another example is above-normal demand from a group of utilization equipment that is all supplied through the same system. Overload currents are considered to range up to 600% of the full-load capacity of the section of the system involved. This relates to the fact that a stalled induction motor (the rotor is jammed or locked) can draw up to 600% of its full-load current rating. Any fault currents in excess of 600% are then assumed to be the result of a short circuit.

The *National Electrical Code* uses the term *overcurrent* as follows: *Any current in excess of the rated current of equipment or the ampacity of a conductor. It may result from overload, short circuit, or ground fault.* Article 240 of the *NEC* covers overcurrent protection. Sections 240-20(a) and 240-21 require that a fuse or an overcurrent trip unit of a circuit breaker be connected in series with each ungrounded conductor and that this overcurrent device be connected at the point where the conductor to be protected receives its supply. The term *device* is defined *as a unit of an electrical system that is intended to carry but not utilize electrical energy*. An ungrounded conductor is one that is operating at some potential above ground as opposed to a conductor that is solidly connected to ground (that is, the neutral of a system). Fuses and circuit breakers are discussed in Chapters 7 and 8 of this book. System grounding and ground faults are covered in Chapter 10. Ampacities of conductors and the selection of ratings for overcurrent devices are covered in Chapters 11 to 14.

6.2 STRESSES IMPOSED BY FAULT CURRENTS

Fault currents impose two types of stresses on the electrical system and its components.

Mechanical stresses These stresses are the result of the fault currents flowing in adjacent parallel conductors. The magnetic fields created by the currents produce a strong mechanical force that can either repel or attract the adjacent conductors. This force is proportional to the square of the current. Thus a fault current that is 20 times normal creates a force that is 400 times greater than with normal current flowing. This magnitude of force can bend the conductors and break their supports. Equipment must therefore be braced to withstand the forces created by the maximum possible fault current. This is discussed further in Chapters 14 and 15 with regard to the bracing of bus bars in motor control centers and switchboards.

Thermal stresses These stresses are the result of the heat generated in the conductors by the fault currents. The heat generated is proportional to the product of the square of the current multiplied by the time that the current flows (I^2t). The heat can very quickly raise the temperature of the conductors to the point where the insulation is damaged. In extreme cases, the material may vaporize. With large fault currents, the protective device must operate very rapidly (within cycles) to limit the buildup of heat. This is discussed further in Section 11.2 with regard to the short-circuit rating of conductors.

6.3 TYPES OF SHORT-CIRCUIT FAULTS

There are two types of short-circuit faults, as follows:

Arcing fault This type of fault is usually the result of insulation breakdown. An arc then jumps between two phases of the system or between one phase and an adjacent grounded metal surface. Because of the relatively high resistance of the arc, the resulting fault current tends to be smaller. However, this type of fault can be the most destructive because of the intense energy that is concentrated in the small area of the arc, coupled with the fact that the protective device may be slow in responding to the smaller fault current. The protection of low-voltage systems against arcing ground faults requires special consideration. This is fully discussed in Sections 10.4 and 10.5.

Bolted fault This type of fault results from a solid connection accidentally being made between two phases of the system or between one phase and an adjacent grounded metal surface. Bolted faults can be caused by such mishaps as incorrect connections, a metal tool touching bare conductors, or a loose conductor dropping down and welding itself to a steel enclosure. As a result of the extremely low resistance of the connection, the resulting fault currents can be very large. However, with the proper protection, this type of fault may actually be less destructive because the energy is spread over a large area and the protective devices are activated very rapidly by the large current.

6.4 CALCULATION OF FAULT CURRENTS

It is essential to calculate the maximum fault current that can flow at any given point on the electrical system to ensure the correct selection of equipment. Refer to Sections 110-9 and 110-10 of the *National Electrical Code,* which require that equipment intended to break current at fault levels shall have an interrupting rating sufficient for the system voltage and the current that is available at the line terminals of the equipment. In addition, the overcurrent protective devices, the total impedance, the component short-circuit withstand ratings, and other characteristics of the circuit to be protected shall be selected and coordinated so that the circuit protective devices can clear a fault without the occurrence of extensive damage to the electrical components of the circuit.

The fault current calculations can be very complex, especially on the higher-voltage systems (above 1000 volts). Fortunately, with low-voltage systems, the procedure can be simplified by making a few basic assumptions. As long as these assumptions have the effect of slightly increasing the calculated value of the maximum possible fault current, they err on the side of safety. This ensures that equipment is chosen with sufficient withstand and interrupting capacity. The maximum fault currents on low-voltage systems occur with three-phase, line-to-line bolted faults. Therefore, calculations are done on this basis. With balanced three-phase faults, the calculations can be done on a per phase basis, providing phase-to-neutral values are used. The following examples are simplified so that this initial presentation of the calculations can be more easily understood. Make certain at this point that you are familiar with the circuit theory in Chapter 1.

Let us start off by considering the simple circuit as shown in Figure 6.1(a). The source voltage E is 100 volts and the rated load current I_L of the circuit is 1.0 ampere. The impedance Z_S of the system connecting the load to the source is 5.0 ohms. Thus, with the load current at rated value, the load must have an equivalent impedance Z_L of 95 ohms for a total Z_B of 100 ohms. (These values have been chosen for easy calculation rather than to represent typical circuit values. Also, for the sake of simplicity, the correct vector addition of the resistance and reactance components of the impedance is ignored.) A bolted fault then occurs on the system as shown in Figure 6.1(b), which shorts out all the load impedance. The fault in effect creates a new circuit with a much lower impedance. Now the current that flows (fault current I_{SC}) is restricted only by the 5.0 ohm impedance Z_S, which represents the total impedance of the system between the source and the fault, including the return path. Thus the

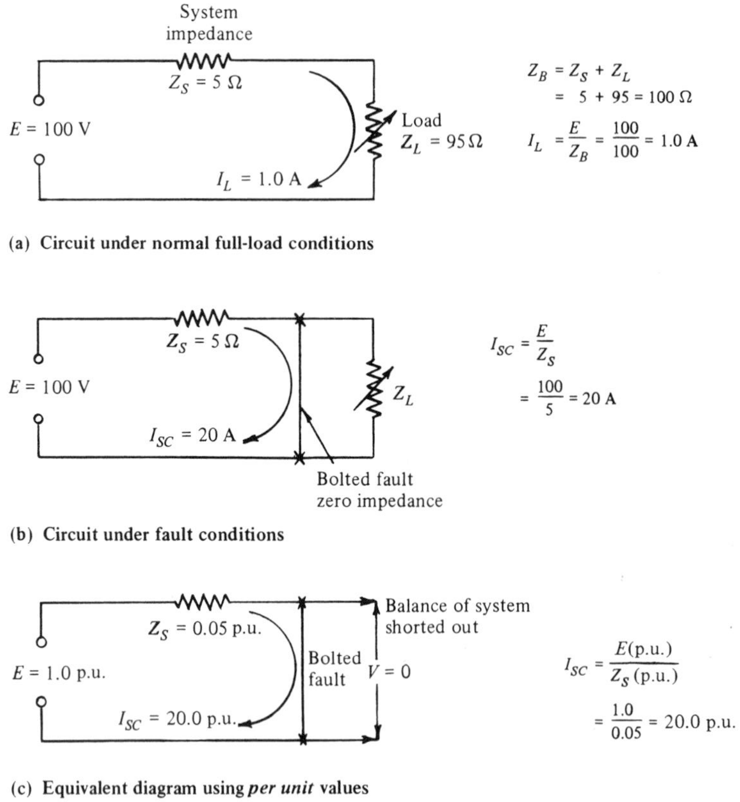

FIGURE 6.1

Calculation of a short-circuit fault current

short-circuit current, by Ohm's law, is 20 amperes or 20 times the rated current of the circuit.

Next let us make this example more universal by designating the source as 100% instead of 100 volts, meaning that the source voltage is at 100% of its rated value, whatever that may be. Next designate the total impedance of the system under full-load conditions as 100% instead of 100 ohms. However, if calculations are done using these percentage values, they do not work out properly. With 100% voltage applied to the system and with 100% impedance, 100% current should flow. But, mathematically, $I = E/Z = 100/100 = 1.0$. This difficulty can easily be overcome by using per unit values instead of percent values. Thus, with 1.0 per unit voltage applied and with 1.0 per unit impedance, the current is 1.0 per unit. The value of the single impedance that, if inserted in the system with rated voltage applied, allows rated current to flow is called the *base impedance*. Therefore,

$$\text{Base impedance } (\Omega) = \frac{\text{rated line-to-neutral volts}}{\text{rated current}} \tag{6.1}$$

If we compare the system impedance of 5.0 ohms with the base impedance of 100 ohms in Figure 6.1(a), then the system impedance is 5/100 or 0.05 per unit. The per unit value of any component in the system can be calculated as follows:

$$\text{Per unit value} = \frac{\text{actual value } (\Omega)}{\text{base impedance } (\Omega)} \tag{6.2}$$

Figure 6.1(c) shows the per unit values applied to the circuit under fault conditions. The short-circuit current from Ohm's law is

$$\text{Per unit } I_{SC} = \frac{E(\text{p.u.})}{Z_S(\text{p.u.})} \tag{6.3}$$

where Z_S is the equivalent system per unit impedance between the source and the point of the fault. The actual fault current in amperes can then be calculated as follows:

$$I_{SC}(\text{A}) = (\text{rated current}) \times (\text{per unit } I_{SC}) \tag{6.4}$$

The short-circuit current in the example is 1.0/0.05, which equals 20.0 per unit. The short-circuit current in amperes is (1.0) × (20.0), which equals 20 amperes. This agrees with our original calculation in part (b).

The complexity of fault calculations comes in determining the equivalent system impedance Z_S between the source and the point of the fault, especially if there is more than one source of power.

Let us apply the per unit system of calculations to some sample systems.

EXAMPLE 6.1

A three-phase, 480 V system has a rated current of 50 A. The feeder has an impedance of 0.15 Ω. Calculate the per unit impedance of the feeder.

Solution

The line-to-neutral voltage is 480/1.732 = 277 V. From Eq. 6.1:

$$\text{Base impedance} = \frac{277}{50} = 5.54\ \Omega$$

From Eq. 6.2:

$$\text{Per unit impedance} = \frac{0.15}{5.54} = 0.027$$

EXAMPLE 6.2

Refer to Figure 6.2(a), which shows the diagram of a typical electrical system. Power is supplied over a primary feeder line to a 500 kVA transformer, which steps the voltage down to a utilization level of 208Y/120 V for distribution to a number of loads. (Refer to Section 1.6.1 for designation of voltages.) The calculated percentage impedance of the primary feeder line is 1.0% (or 0.01 per unit), and the transformer has an impedance of 5.0% (or 0.05 per unit). Calculate the short-circuit current on the secondary of the transformer under three-phase bolted fault conditions.

Solution

Figure 6.2(b) shows the equivalent circuit diagram of the system on a single-phase basis when operating under normal full-load conditions. Note that with the various parameters shown in per unit values there is no need to worry about voltage levels at any point. Figure 6.2(c) shows the system with a bolted fault at the secondary of the transformer. The maximum fault current on the low-voltage part of the system will occur at this point, as the impedance of the low-voltage feeders will not be a factor in limiting the fault current. The remaining impedances that will limit the short-circuit current are those of the primary feeder and the transformer. Since these impedances are in series, the total impedance is

$$Z_S = 0.01 + 0.05 = 0.06 \text{ p.u.}$$

From Eq. 6.3,

$$I_{SC} = \frac{1.0}{0.06} = 16.67 \text{ p.u.}$$

The rated secondary current (on the 208Y/120 side of the transformer) is (from Eq. 1.14)

$$I_S = \frac{500 \times 1000}{1.732 \times 208} = 1388 \text{ A}$$

And, from Eq. 6.4,

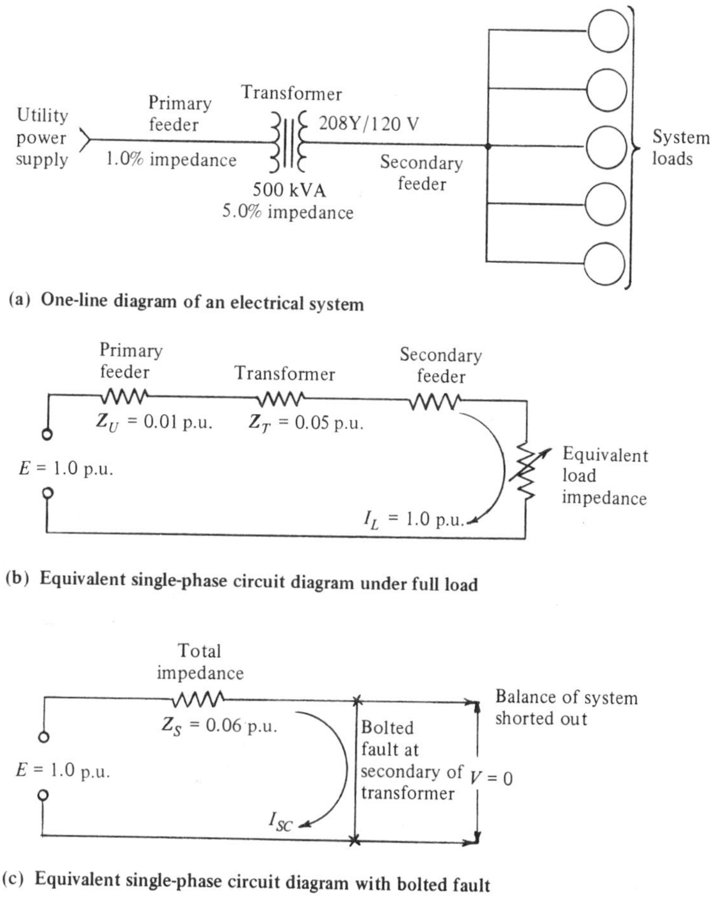

(a) One-line diagram of an electrical system

(b) Equivalent single-phase circuit diagram under full load

(c) Equivalent single-phase circuit diagram with bolted fault

FIGURE 6.2

Diagrams for Example 6.2

Note: Figure 6.2 is in the form known as one-line (see Chapter 11). No switches or protective devices are shown because they have a negligible effect on the magnitude of the maximum possible fault current.

$$I_{SC} = 1389 \times 16.67 = 23{,}150 \text{ A}$$

Note: Since the voltages used in this example are rms values, the calculated value of the current is also the rms value. Note the importance of the transformer impedance in limiting the magnitude of the fault current. This is discussed in more detail in Section 16.2.

These examples are just an introduction to the calculation of fault currents. More detailed examples are presented in Chapter 16.

In Example 6.2, the total impedance Z_S is calculated by simply adding the impedance values without properly taking into account their respective resistance and reactance components. However, the effect of this shortcut is very minor. The following example shows the calculation of the percentage impedance of a transformer, taking into account the resistance and reactance values.

EXAMPLE 6.3

A 100 kVA, three-phase transformer has a secondary voltage of 480Y/277. The equivalent resistance of the transformer is 0.03 Ω and the equivalent leakage reactance is 0.11 Ω when referred to the secondary side (see Section 1.7.2). Calculate the percentage impedance of the transformer.

Solution

The rated secondary current of the transformer is (from Eq. 1.14)

$$I_S = \frac{100 \times 1000}{1.732 \times 480} = 120 \text{ A}$$

From Eq. 6.1,

$$\text{Base impedance} = \frac{277}{120} = 2.31\ \Omega$$

From Eq. 6.2,

$$\text{Per unit resistance} = \frac{0.03}{2.31} = 0.013$$

$$\text{Per unit reactance} = \frac{0.11}{2.31} = 0.048$$

From Eq. 1.8,

$$\text{Per unit impedance} = \sqrt{(0.013)^2 + (0.048)^2} = 0.05 \quad \text{or} \quad 5.0\%$$

Note that the reactance of the transformer is by far the most important parameter of the total impedance. The resistance has a minor effect. However, there are conditions under which the effect of the resistance of the transformer must be included in the fault calculations. These conditions are discussed in Section 16.3.

6.5 ASYMMETRICAL FAULT CURRENTS

The previous calculations on fault currents assumed that the currents would remain symmetrical after the occurrence of a fault on the system. By *symmetrical* it is meant that *the fault current has the same axis as the normal current that was flowing prior to the fault* [see Figure 6.3(b)]. However, this is not always the case. Depending on the exact time at which the fault occurs during the cycle, the resulting fault current can be offset from the normal-current axis; that is, it becomes *asymmetrical*.

For an explanation as to why fault currents become asymmetrical, at least for the first few cycles, refer again to Figure 6.3. Power systems are highly inductive under fault conditions (that is, transformer reactances and the like). Figure 6.3(a) shows a theoretical circuit with a pure inductive reactance component and no resistance. The closing of the switch simulates a fault on the system; that is, the current that flows in this circuit represents the fault current

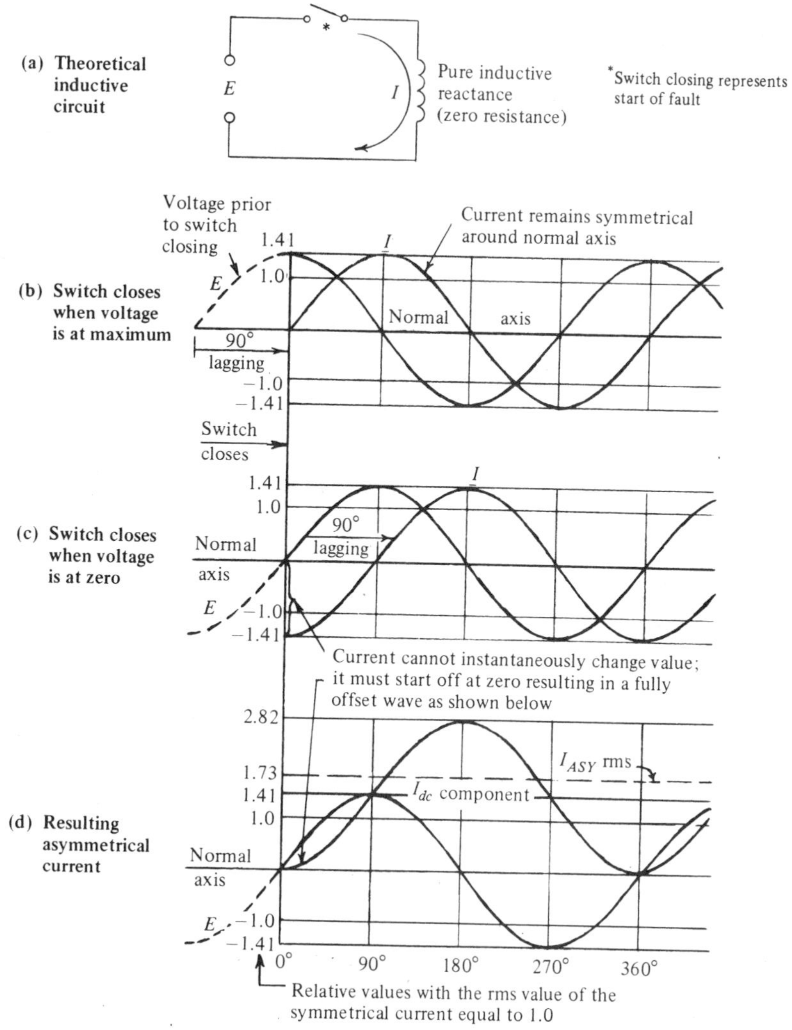

FIGURE 6.3

Theoretical asymmetrical fault currents

that would flow in a shorted power system. The current in a pure inductive circuit must lag the voltage by 90 electrical degrees (see Section 1.4.1). Part (b) shows the voltage and current relationship for the case when the switch closes with the voltage at its maximum positive value. Since the current at that instant of time would normally be at zero, the current that then flows in the circuit remains symmetrical about the normal axis, as shown. Part (c) shows the case when the switch closes with the voltage at zero. If the current is drawn with its normal 90 degree lagging relationship and projected back to the time that the switch closes, it would have to be at its maximum negative value. This cannot happen, as it means that the current would have to instantly change in magnitude, which it cannot do in an inductive circuit. The current must start off at zero. The actual resulting current must therefore be offset from the normal axis as shown in part (d). This offset or asymmetrical current can be thought of as an alternating current component I_{ac} alternating around a new axis that represents a direct current component I_{dc}. This dc component has a relative value of 1.41, which is equal to the peak value of the ac component (the rms value of the ac component being 1.0). The rms value of the asymmetrical current I_{ASY} is calculated as follows:

$$I_{ASY} = \sqrt{(I_{ac})^2 + (I_{dc})^2}$$
$$= \sqrt{(1.0)^2 + (1.41)^2} = \sqrt{3.0} = 1.73$$

This means that the rms value of the asymmetrical current is 1.73 times the rms value of the symmetrical current. As can be imagined, the mechanical and thermal stresses imposed on the electrical system and equipment are much greater. These stresses are directly proportional to the square of the rms value of the current (Section 6.2). With an asymmetrical current of 1.73 times the symmetrical current, these stresses are then $(1.73)^2$, or three times as great.

As indicated, Figure 6.3 is based on the theoretical case where the circuit resistance is zero. Therefore, the relative values are the maximum theoretically possible. In practice, all circuits must have some resistance. As a result, the dc component of the asymmetrical current starts to decrease immediately after the fault occurs, usually decaying away to zero within a few cycles. This is shown in Figure 6.4. The exact rate at which the dc component decays depends on the ratio of the system reactance X and resistance R under fault conditions. This is related to the time constant of the system. The reader is referred to the electrical circuit books listed in the Bibliography for a discussion on time constants. With low-voltage systems, the X/R ratio tends to be lower and the rate of decay is faster. Conversely, with high-voltage systems, the X/R ratio tends to be higher and the rate of decay is slower. Studies have been done on typical power systems and multiplying factors have been recommended to account for asymmetrical fault currents in the design of electrical systems and equipment. Figure 6.4 shows the rate of decay for a system with an X/R ratio of 6.6, which is typical for low-voltage power systems (below 1000 volts). At the end of a half-cycle, the rms value of the asymmetrical current is 1.33 times the rms value of the symmetrical current. On systems above 1000 volts, the recommended multiplying factor is 1.6. The use of the multiplying factor is illustrated in the following example.

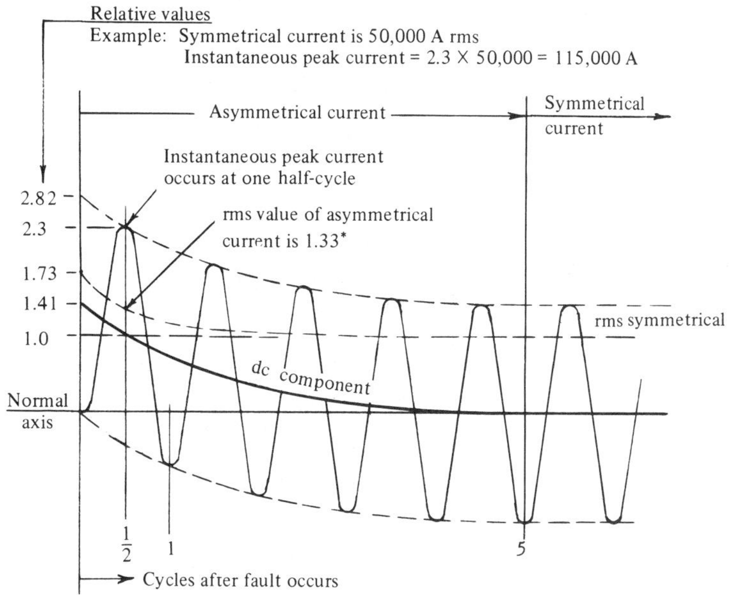

FIGURE 6.4

Asymmetrical fault current for X/R ratio of 6.6

* Value depends on rate at which dc component decays away, which in turn depends on the X/R ratio of system; an X/R ratio of 6.6 is typical for low-voltage systems

■ EXAMPLE 6.4

Calculate the rms value of the asymmetrical fault current at the end of one half-cycle for one phase of the secondary low-voltage system in Example 6.2.

Solution

$$I_{ASY} = 1.33 \times I_{SC} = 1.33 \times 23{,}100 = 30{,}700 \text{ A}$$

The application of these multiplying factors is covered in Chapters 8, 11, and 16.

6.6 FUNCTIONS OF PROTECTIVE DEVICES

The protective device has two major functions: (1) to detect an abnormal condition on that portion of the system that it is protecting, and (2) to automatically and safely disconnect the faulted portion from the balance of the system. Protective devices such as fuses and most low-voltage circuit breakers combine both the detection unit and the disconnecting means in the one unit. Other types of protective devices separate the two functions. For example, medium- and high-voltage circuit breakers normally only perform the disconnecting function. They must be used in conjunction with separate protective relays that detect the abnormal conditions and then initiate the tripping of the circuit breaker. Protective relays are discussed in Chapter 9. It must be emphasized again that protective devices cannot prevent faults from occurring on the system, but can only minimize their effects.

Protective devices are rated for the following:

1. *Maximum continuous voltage:* This is the maximum voltage that can be continuously applied to the device without eventually causing the insulation to fail.
2. *Maximum continuous current:* This is the maximum load current that the device can carry continuously without the contacts or other current-carrying parts overheating.
3. *Interrupting rating:* This is the maximum current that the device can safely interrupt at the specified voltage.
4. *Short-time current ratings:*
   (a) *Momentary:* This is the maximum rms current that the device can withstand with regard to mechanical stressing. As shown in Figure 6.4, the maximum stressing occurs one half-cycle (0.00833 second) after the fault starts. This rating is necessary to ensure that the device is not physically damaged before it can operate to disconnect the faulted part of the system.
   (b) *Specified time:* This is the maximum rms current that the device can withstand for a specified time (0.5 s) with regard to thermal stressing. In the case of breakers, it is sometimes necessary under severe short circuits to delay their opening for a very short period of time in order to coordinate with other devices. This rating is necessary to ensure that the breaker is not damaged by heat before it can operate to disconnect the faulted part of the system.

These ratings apply to the basic protective device mechanism. The point at which the detection unit, which is incorporated into the protective device, starts to respond to an overcurrent is a separate rating. There are many more ratings of detection units than there are ratings of the basic devices. For example, in our residences there are 15, 20, 30, and 40 ampere circuits that need overcurrent protection set at these values. It is not justified to have circuit breaker mechanisms designed for each of these currents. Therefore, there is one breaker mechanism designed to handle up to 100 amperes into which detection units rated for specific currents are installed. Thus a breaker with a rating of 15 amperes stamped on the handle is in reality a 100 ampere breaker with a detection unit that is set to respond to any overcurrent above 15 amperes. Similarly, a 40 ampere fuse is actually a 60 ampere fuse body incorporating a fuse element that responds to any overcurrent above 40 amperes. The specific details of fuses and circuit breakers are covered in Chapters 7 and 8.

6.7 INVERSE-TIME AND INSTANTANEOUS-RESPONSE CHARACTERISTICS

A basic requirement for the detection unit of the protective device is that it have the ability to react very quickly to large fault currents, but to react very slowly to minor overloads. This requirement is known as the *inverse-time characteristic*. It is a desirable characteristic for the protection of most types of equipment (motors, feeder conductors, and so on). These types of equipment are damaged very quickly with large fault currents, but take a relatively long time to overheat with minor overloads.

Figure 6.5 shows the plot of an inverse-time response curve. An ideal arrangement is obtained when the response time of the protective device is always slightly less than the point at which the equip-

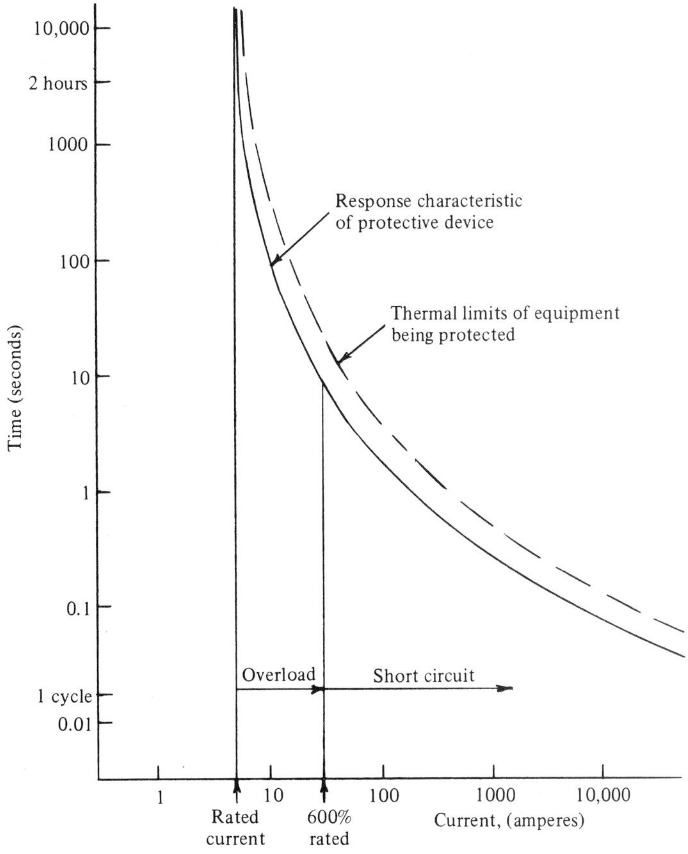

FIGURE 6.5

Inverse-time curves plotted on log–log scales

ment is damaged. In this way, needless shutdowns for harmless short-duration overloads can be avoided. Inverse-time curves are usually plotted using log–log scales for both the current (horizontal) and time (vertical). This is necessary because the currents range from a few amperes under normal conditions up to tens of thousands of amperes under short-circuit fault conditions. Similarly, the response time can range from fractions of a second (cycles) for large currents up to hours for minor overloads. Examples of curves for specific fuses are shown in Chapter 7.

In the case of circuit breakers, it is also desirable that the detection unit have an element that responds immediately at a specific value of fault current to trip open the breaker. This is known as *instantaneous tripping*, which is defined as *tripping with no intentional time delay*. Note that breakers take some finite time to fully open the circuit because of the inertia of their moving parts. Figure 6.6 shows a typical time response curve for a circuit breaker that combines the inverse-time element and the instantaneous element. The point at which the breaker changes from inverse-time tripping to instantaneous tripping is known as the *knee* of the curve. Examples of curves for specific breakers are shown in Chapter 8 and for protective relays in Chapter 9.

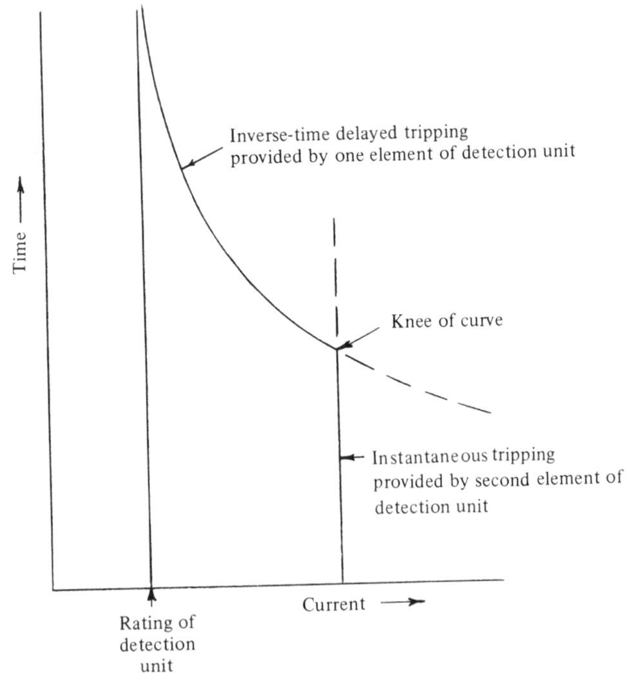

FIGURE 6.6

Typical response curve of dual-element circuit breaker

SUMMARY

- Electrical systems must operate in a safe manner.
- Overloads can be tolerated for short periods of time.
- Short circuits must be disconnected immediately.
- All circuits and equipment must be protected against overcurrents.
- Fault currents impose severe mechanical and thermal stresses on the system and equipment.
- Arcing faults have lower fault currents but can cause extensive damage if not properly detected.
- Bolted faults have higher fault currents but can be quickly detected and removed from the system.
- Calculations of fault currents are necessary to ensure the proper selection of devices and equipment.
- Base impedance is the value of a single impedance that, if inserted in a circuit with rated voltage applied, allows rated current to flow.
- Base impedance (ohms) is

$$\frac{\text{rated line-to-neutral voltage}}{\text{rated current}}$$

- Fault calculations can be simplified by using per unit values for the circuit parameters.
- The per unit value of resistance, reactance, and impedance is

$$\frac{\text{actual value (ohms)}}{\text{base impedance (ohms)}}$$

- The faulted circuit must be reduced to a single equivalent impedance Z_S, which represents the total impedance between the source and the point of the fault.
- The impedance of the power transformer is a very important factor in limiting fault currents.
- The short-circuit current is calculated as follows:

$$\text{Per unit } I_{SC} = \frac{E\text{ (p.u.)}}{Z_S\text{ (p.u.)}}$$

  and I_{SC} (amperes) = (rated current) × (per unit I_{SC}).
- The currents that flow under fault conditions are most likely to be asymmetrical for the first few cycles.
- Asymmetrical fault currents increase the mechanical and thermal stressing on the system and equipment.
- The rate of decay of the dc component of the asymmetrical current depends on the X/R ratio of the system.
- Protective devices are rated for the following:

— Maximum continuous voltage rating
— Maximum continuous current rating
— Interrupting rating
— Short-time ratings: momentary and specified time

- The detection unit of a protective device should have an inverse-time characteristic.
- Circuit breakers can have a combination of inverse-time delayed tripping and instantaneous tripping.

QUESTIONS

1. Explain the difference between an overload and a short circuit.
2. Explain the term overcurrent.
3. Why can an overload be left on the system for a relatively long period of time (minutes)?
4. Why must a short circuit be disconnected from a system within a very short period of time (cycles)?
5. What causes mechanical stressing under fault conditions?
6. What causes thermal stressing under fault conditions?
7. Explain the difference between an arcing fault and a bolted fault.
8. Why is the arcing fault potentially the most destructive type of fault?
9. Why is it necessary to calculate the maximum fault current that can flow at any given point on a system?
10. What is the base impedance of a system?
11. What is an asymmetrical current?
12. What are the two major functions of a protective device?
13. List the four ratings of protective devices.
14. Describe the inverse-time characteristics.
15. Why is it desirable for a protective device to have an inverse-time response characteristic?
16. What is meant by instantaneous tripping?

PROBLEMS

1. Refer to Figure 6.1(a). The voltage $E = 120$ V, the system impedance $Z_S = 0.1\ \Omega$, and the load impedance $Z_L = 1.5\ \Omega$. Calculate (a) the normal load current I_L of the circuit, (b) the fault current I_{SC} as per Figure 6.1(b), and (c) the per unit values for Z_S and I_{SC} as per Figure 6.1(c). Assume the impedances are primarily resistive.
2. Repeat Problem 1, except $E = 277$ V, $Z_S = 0.025\ \Omega$, and $Z_L = 0.529\ \Omega$.
3. A three-phase, 208 V system has a rated current of 100 A. A feeder has an impedance of 0.018 Ω. Calculate the per unit impedance of the feeder.
4. Refer to Figure 6.2(a). The transformer is 1000 kVA, its impedance is 5.75%, the primary feeder impedance is 0.75%, and the secondary voltage is 480Y/277 V. Calculate the short-circuit current on the secondary of the transformer under three-phase bolted fault conditions.
5. Repeat Problem 4, except the transformer is 1500 kVA, its impedance is 5.0%, and the primary feeder impedance is 0.5%.
6. A 200 kVA, three-phase transformer has a secondary voltage of 208Y/120 V. The equivalent resistance of the transformer is 0.002 Ω and the equivalent leakage reactance is 0.009 Ω. Calculate the percentage impedance of the transformer.

7 Fuses

OBJECTIVES

After studying this chapter, you will be able to:

- Interpret time–current characteristic curves of fuses.
- Recognize the categories of low-voltage fuses.
- Explain the term current limiting.
- Explain dual-element fuses.
- Recognize time-delay fuses.
- Recognize the classifications of low-voltage fuses.
- Coordinate low-voltage fuses.
- Recognize the major types of high-voltage fuses.
- Identify the advantages of fuses.
- Identify the disadvantages of fuses.

INTRODUCTION

The protection of electrical systems all started with Thomas Edison, as did so many other aspects of the electrical industry. In 1880, Edison applied for and was granted a patent entitled *Safety Conductor for Electric Lights*. This patent stated in part:

> The safety device consists of a piece of very small conductor . . . [having] such a degree of conductivity as to readily allow the passage of the amount of current designed for its particular branch. If . . . an abnormal amount of current . . . is diverted through a branch, the small safety wire becomes heated and melts away, breaking the overloaded branch circuit. It is desirable, however, that the few drops of hot molten metal resulting therefrom should not be allowed to fall upon carpets and furniture and also that the small safety conductor should be relieved of all tensile strain; hence I enclose the safety wire in a jacket or shell of nonconducting material.

Since Edison had earlier developed the incandescent lamp and was in the process of building electrical systems to supply electrical power to customers installing the new lighting, he naturally was interested in protecting the circuits to these electric lights. The term *electric fuse* came into use some time later.

Edison's description of the fuse is still valid today. The transition from his fuse to the modern fuse has been primarily in the development of special alloys for the fusible element, with the use of fillers surrounding the element and hermetically sealing the element in a strong shell. The *National Electrical Code* defines the *fuse* as an *overcurrent protective device with a circuit opening fusible part that is heated and severed by the passage of current through it*. Thus the fuse combines the current sensing and interrupting functions into the one element.

Many types of fuses are now available for different applications. It is no longer satisfactory to just specify that a fuse shall be, for example, *100 amperes, 250 volts*. Apart from having different ampere and voltage ratings, fuses have widely different interrupting ratings, different response characteristics, and different current-limiting capabilities. Fuses with fast overload response times are used for the protection of solid-state devices, which have low overload capabilities. Fuses with relatively slow overload response times are used on motor circuits where large starting currents must be handled. Fuses are further divided into low voltage (for systems 1000 volts and below) and medium and high voltage (for systems above 1000 volts). Today, the proper application of fuses requires a sound knowledge of the types available. The discussions in this chapter are limited to those fuses used for the feeders and circuits normally encountered in the electrical systems in buildings.

7.1 RESPONSE CHARACTERISTICS OF FUSES

A fuse does not instantly open when the current exceeds its rating, nor should it. The fusible element within the fuse responds to the heat generated by the passage of the current through it. The heat is a function of I^2t; thus the fuse inherently has an inverse time–current response, which is a desirable characteristic (see Section 6.7 and Figure 6.5). The response times of fuses of the same voltage and ampere rating can vary widely. This is controlled by the type of material and construction used for the fusible element. These times are plotted as a function of the current on log–log, time–current graphs. The general form of the graph used by industry is shown in Figure 7.1. The vertical time scale extends from 0.01 to 1000 seconds, and the horizontal current scale extends from 0.5 to 10,000 amperes. However, note that this latter scale is often modified by a factor of 10, 100, or even 1000. Figure 7.1 indicates *current in am-*

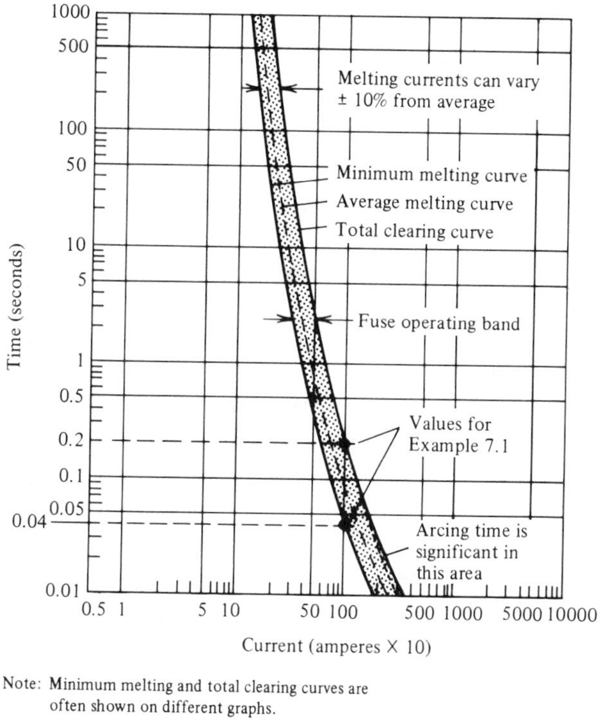

FIGURE 7.1

Typical fuse response curves

peres × 10, which means that all values marked on the scale are multiplied by a factor of 10; for example, 100 on the scale is actually 1000 amperes.

Before attempting to read fuse curves, we should look at some related terminology. In the past, such terms as *opening time* and *blowing time* have been used. However, these terms can be misleading. The operation of the fuse is divided into two time intervals. The first is the time required for the fusible element to heat up to the point where it starts to melt, designated the *melting time*. The second is the time for the severed element to separate and for the resulting arc to be fully extinguished, designated the *arcing time*. The total of the melting plus the arcing time is then properly referred to as the *total clearing time*. For currents in the overload range, the melting times are relatively long and the arcing times are insignificant. However, for high short-circuit currents, the arcing time is significant relative to the melting times (see Figure 7.4).

The precise melting characteristics of the fusible element depend on the purity of the metals and/or the mixture of the ingredients in the alloy used and on its exact thickness and length. No matter how strict the quality control maintained by the manufacturer, there is bound to be some discrepancies between individual fuses for any one of the manufacturer's types. The American National Standards Institute (ANSI) standards allow a maximum tolerance of plus or minus 10% in the melting current for any given time. Since 1972, fuse manufacturers have been issuing two sets of curves for each type of fuse, one labeled *minimum melt time* and the other labeled *total clearing time*. If these two curves for any one type and rating of fuse are traced onto one sheet as shown in Figure 7.1, the area between the two lines then represents the operating band for that type and rating of fuse. An individual fuse will operate within the limits defined by this band.

■ EXAMPLE 7.1

Using Figure 7.1, determine the minimum melt and total clearing times for the fuse at 1000 A.

Solution

— In Fig. 7.1, 1000 A is 100 on the scale (that is, 100×10)
— Intersection of 100 A with minimum melt curve is 0.04 s
— Intersection of 100 A with total clearing curve is 0.2 s

The example indicates that, from a large sampling of this same type of fuse, none will melt in less than 0.04 second and none will take longer than 0.2 second to totally clear the circuit at 1000 amperes. The curves in Figure 7.1 have been purposely shown with an exaggerated tolerance band to emphasize this effect. The spread of operating times for most fuses is nevertheless significant, and the minimum melt and total clearing curves must both be used when coordinating fuses with other types of protective devices (see Sections 16.4 and 16.5). Examples of curves for specific types of fuses are shown in Figures 7.10, 7.11, 7.15, and 7.16.

7.2 CATEGORIES OF LOW-VOLTAGE FUSES

The *NEC* recognizes two principal categories of fuses: the plug fuse and the cartridge fuse. Figure 7.2 shows the various plug and cartridge configurations.

Plug fuses are rated for 125 volts and are available with current ratings up to 30 amperes. Their use is limited to circuits not exceeding 125 volts between conductors or, if the system has a grounded neutral conductor, not exceeding 150 volts to ground. Plug fuses of the Edison-base type can be used only for replacement of existing fuses. The type S plug fuse must be used on new installations. This type of base is constructed so that a fuse of a higher ampere range cannot be inserted into the same fuseholder. Adapters are available to convert Edison-base holders so that they can accept the type S fuse. Plug fuses are mainly used for residential wiring. Their use for

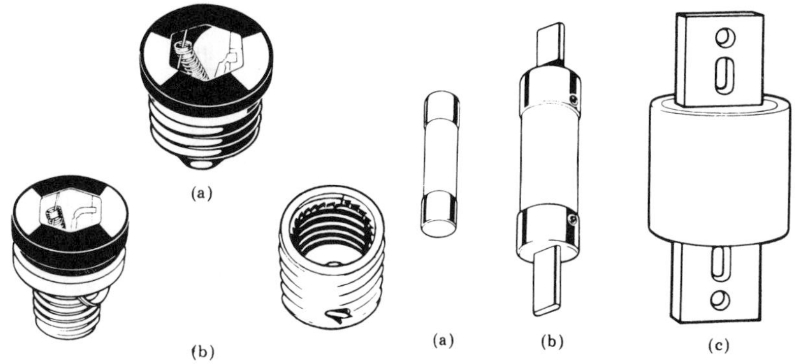

Plug Fuses. (a) Edison Base Fuse
(b) Type S Fuse and Adapter

Cartridge Fuses. (a) Ferrule Type, 0–60 A
(b) Knife-Blade Type, 70–600 A
(c) Bolt Type, 601–6000 A

FIGURE 7.2

Principal low-voltage fuse categories as recognized by the *NEC*

the protection of branch circuits in commercial and industrial buildings is rare.

Cartridge fuses are rated up to 600 volts and are available with current ratings up to 6000 amperes. They have three different physical configurations, as shown in Figure 7.2: ferrule type, from 0 to 60 amperes; knife-blade type, from 70 to 600 amperes; and bolt type, from 601 to 6000 amperes. Fuses up to 600 amperes are rated for either 250 or 600 volts. There are also special fuses from 0 to 60 amperes that are rated for 300 volts. Fuses above 600 amperes are rated for 600 volts only. Fuses rated for 250 volts can be used on 120, 208, and 240 volt systems. Fuses rated for 300 volts can be used on circuits for systems having a grounded neutral and with no conductor operating at more than 300 volts to ground (that is, a 480Y/277 volt system). Fuses rated for 600 volts can be used on any circuit up to 600 volts (120, 208, 240, 480, and 600 volts). The fuses for each voltage rating have different dimensions so that they cannot be interchanged in the fuseholder.

The ampere ratings that are available up to 600 amperes are shown in Table 7.1. These ratings are actually the ratings of the fusible element within the fuse cartridge. The different ratings are grouped into cartridge sizes as shown in the table. For example, the 15, 20, 25, and 30 ampere fuses all have the same cartridge size and therefore, for the same voltage rating, they have the same physical dimensions (see Figure 7.8). Fuses are available with ratings below 15 amperes, but these are used for the protection of special equipment. The 15 ampere rating is normally the smallest size used for the protection of branch circuits in buildings.

There are many classifications of cartridge fuses with regard to operating characteristics and interrupting ratings. These are discussed in Section 7.5.

TABLE 7.1 Ratings and Clearing Time Limits for Low-Voltage Fuses up to 600 Amperes

Fuse Rating (A)	Cartridge Size	UL Maximum Allowable Clearing Times (min)	
		135% Rating	200% Rating
15	30 A	60	2
20			
25			
30			
35	60 A	60	4
40			
45			
50			
60			
70	100 A	120	6
80			
90			
100			
110	200 A	120	8
125			
150			
175			
200			
225	400 A	120	10
250			
300			
350			
400			
450	600 A	120	12
500			
600			

See Figure 7.8 for the dimensions of each size of cartridge.

7.3 CURRENT-LIMITING FUSES

The standard low-voltage code fuses that were available for many years had interrupting ratings of only 10,000 amperes. This became inadequate for many low-voltage systems where the available fault currents were well above this level. Furthermore, the fusible elements were generally made of zinc, a metal that tends to crystallize and deteriorate with age, resulting in unreliable operation. As a result of these problems, for the overcurrent protection of low-voltage circuits, the trend was toward the use of air circuit breakers.

In the late 1940s, the fuse industry developed a new type of fuse. This fuse is very fast acting on high short-circuit currents, so fast in fact that it can actually limit the magnitude of the fault current. Figure 7.3(a) shows the typical construction of this *current-limiting* type of fuse. The major changes from the standard code fuse are that the fusible element is made of silver (a very stable element), it is packed in a quartz filler, and then it is hermetically sealed inside a strong ceramic case. The diagram shows only one element. High-current fuses have two or more elements connected in parallel.

Figure 7.3(b) shows the action of the fuse under large fault currents. As the notched sections of the fusible element vaporize, the resulting arcs melt the surrounding quartz. This absorbs the heat from the arcs, quickly extinguishing the arcs and clearing the circuit. Then the molten quartz rapidly cools and solidifies, forming insulating plugs between the severed ends of the fuse links and preventing the arcs from restriking, as shown in Figure 7.3(c). The heat and

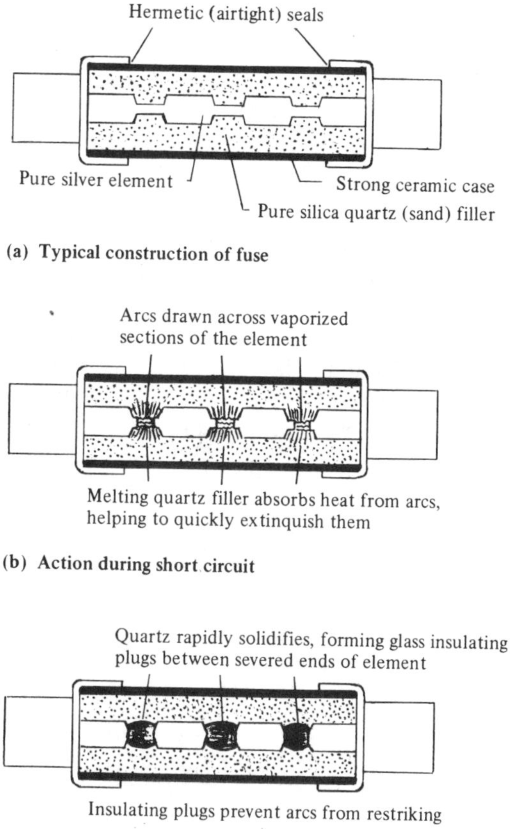
Hermetic (airtight) seals
Pure silver element
Strong ceramic case
Pure silica quartz (sand) filler
Arcs drawn across vaporized sections of the element
Melting quartz filler absorbs heat from arcs, helping to quickly extinquish them
Quartz rapidly solidifies, forming glass insulating plugs between severed ends of element
Insulating plugs prevent arcs from restriking

(a) Typical construction of fuse

(b) Action during short circuit

(c) Immediately after arcs extinguished

FIGURE 7.3

Construction and operation of current-limiting fuses

pressure created by the arcs are safely contained within the strong fuse casing. These high interrupting capacity, current-limiting fuses are a one-time nonrenewable type that is discarded after operation and replaced by a completely new fuse. In contrast, the older, standard code fuses are generally the renewable type with a reusable outer cartridge; only the fuse link is replaced after operation.

Figure 7.4 shows the plot of the fault current against time and the resulting ability of the fuse to limit the magnitude of the let-through current. The current shown in the diagram is the asymmetrical fault current described in Section 6.5 and shown in Figure 6.4. Since the fuse acts so fast, only the first cycle of this prospective fault current need be shown. *NEC* Section 240-11 defines a *current-limiting overcurrent device* as:

> A device which, when interrupting currents in its current limiting range, will reduce the current flowing in the faulted circuit to a magnitude substantially less than that obtainable in the same circuit if the device were replaced with a solid conductor having comparable impedance.

The heat produced as the current rises very rapidly under fault conditions causes the fuse element to melt before the current can reach its instantaneous peak value, as shown in the diagram. It then takes a finite time for the arc quenching process within the fuse to reduce the current to zero and completely open the circuit. The total clearing time is one half-cycle or less. The maximum instantaneous value that the current does reach is known as the *peak let-through current*. The area under the curve represents the total energy that is let through the fuse before the short-circuit current is fully interrupted. This is known as the *thermal energy let-through* and is referred to as the I^2t value (remember, energy also involves time).

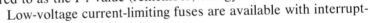

Low-voltage current-limiting fuses are available with interrupt-

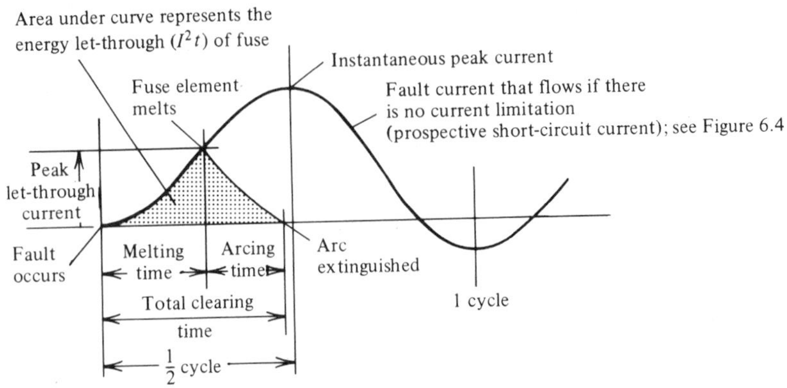

FIGURE 7.4

Typical current limitation on high short-circuit currents

ing ratings as high as 200,000 rms symmetrical amperes. As shown, the fuse does not actually interrupt this magnitude of current. However, this is academic, as a fuse so rated can be placed in a circuit where 200,000 amperes of fault current is available, and it will safely clear the circuit on a fault of this magnitude.

Underwriters Laboratories, Inc. (UL) standards specify the maximum permitted peak let-through currents and thermal energy let-through (I^2t) values for the various classes of fuses. Manufacturers publish peak let-through current curves for their current-limiting fuses. A typical set of curves is shown in Figure 7.5(a). The diagonal line *AB* represents the instantaneous peak value that the current could reach for the associated value of the prospective rms symmetrical short-circuit current if there is no current limitation. For example, if the prospective short-circuit current is 50,000 symmetrical rms amperes as shown in the example in Figure 7.5(b), then the instantaneous peak current is 115,000 amperes. This agrees with the value shown in Figure 6.4 at the end of one half-cycle.

Now assume that the feeder is protected by 250 volt, 100 ampere current-limiting fuses. As shown in the example, the peak let-through current of the fuse is only 20,000 amperes. This translates into an effective rms value of 9000 amperes. Thus the value of the fault current is reduced to less than 20% of what it would be with no current limitation. As previously discussed in Section 6.2, under fault conditions the mechanical stresses imposed on the system and equipment are proportional to the square of the peak current, and the thermal stresses are proportional to the square of the rms current multiplied by the time (I^2t). With a reduction of the fault current to less than 20%, the mechanical stresses are reduced to less than 4% and the thermal stresses are reduced even further because of the shorter duration of the fault current.

This reduction of stresses is a tremendous advantage for low-voltage systems. With the increasing trend to larger-capacity systems, the use of current-limiting fuses can provide an inexpensive solution to the problems of the high levels of available fault current. Standard switches, panelboards, motor controllers, and the like, with their lower short-circuit withstand capabilities, can be used without concern that they could be damaged by the heavy fault currents. The size of the feeder conductors required for short-circuit duty can often be reduced (see Section 11.2 and Example 11.18). In most cases, a feeder whose conductors have been sized for the ampacity requirements will also be properly protected by the current-limiting fuses against damage from short circuits.

Note that these fuses do not current limit for all levels of fault current. The 250 volt, 100 ampere fuse used in our example does not current limit below 2500 amperes. However, current limitation is very seldom required at this low level of fault current.

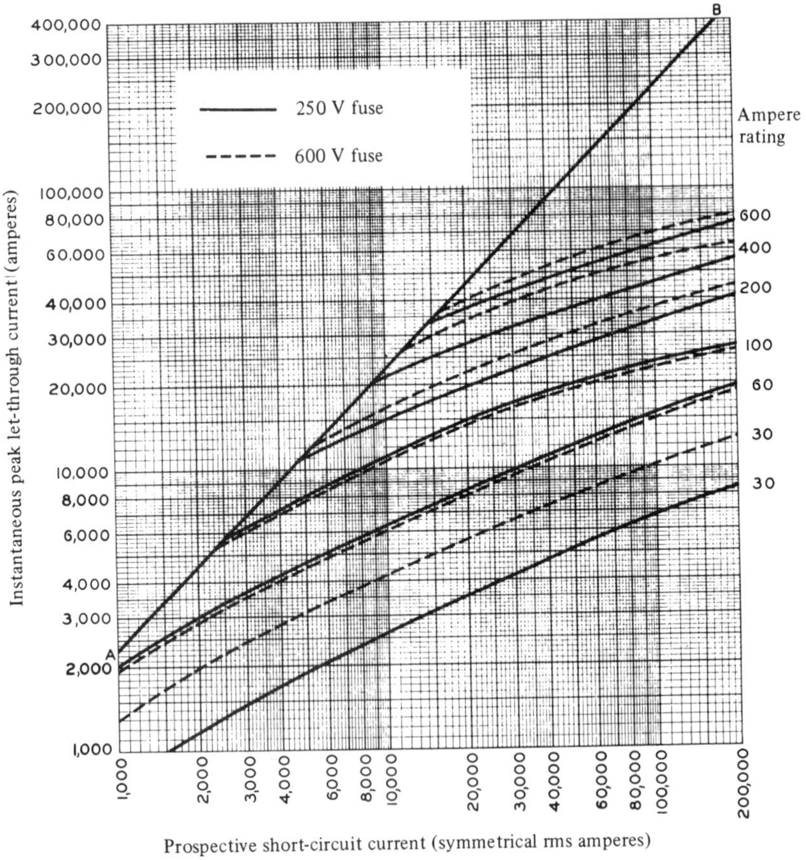

(a) Manufacturer's published curves

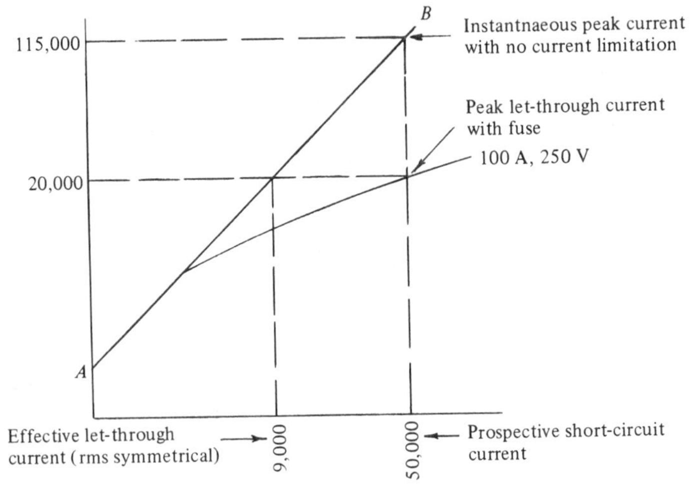

(b) Example of using curves

FIGURE 7.5

Typical current limitation curves for a low-voltage fuse

7.4 DUAL-ELEMENT TIME-DELAY FUSES

The requirements for the fusible element of the fast-acting current-limiting type of fuse just discussed are high conductivity, high but abrupt melting point, and small mass to reduce the heating time. While providing the very desirable current-limiting feature on high currents, these characteristics also mean that the fuse blows too frequently on harmless, low-level overload currents.

The requirements for the fusible element of a fuse that will provide satisfactory time delay on overloads are relatively lower conductivity, lower melting point (because the heat has time to dissipate), and a large mass to provide the time delay. These are the exact opposites to the requirements for high currents. To overcome these conflicts, the dual-element fuse was developed, with one element for overloads and one element (or a pair) for short circuits (see Section 6.1 for the differences between overloads and short circuits). These elements are connected in series within the one cartridge. Figure 7.6 shows an example of the construction of a dual-element fuse. Figure 7.7 shows a typical response curve for the dual-element fuse. The two elements of the fuse are coordinated so that the overload time-delay element melts first on currents up to approximately 500% of the fuse rating, and the short-circuit element(s) then takes over and melts first on currents above this point. Thus the fuse has time delay in the overload region and still has fast current-limiting action on the high fault currents.

For the time delay not to be so excessive that the fuse does not provide proper overload protection, it is necessary to set limits on the total clearing times for specific percentages of the rated current of the fuse. Table 7.1 shows the maximum clearing times acceptable by the Underwriters Laboratories, Inc. for 135 and 200% rated current for fuses up to 600 amperes. Figure 7.7 shows these points plotted on a graph for a 100 ampere fuse.

The response curve for a single-element fuse is also plotted in Figure 7.7 for comparison with the dual-element fuse of the same rating. Both minimum melt curves are compiled from one manufacturer's data. Both meet the UL requirements for maximum overload clearing times. However, at 500 amperes (that is, 500% of the fuse rating), as indicated on the graph, the dual-element fuse does not

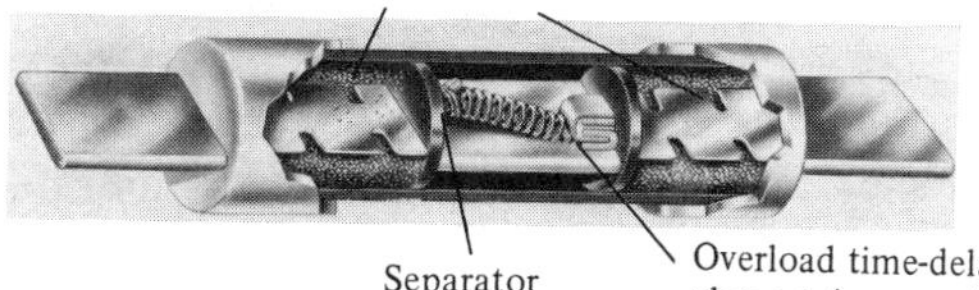

FIGURE 7.6

Construction of a dual-element fuse

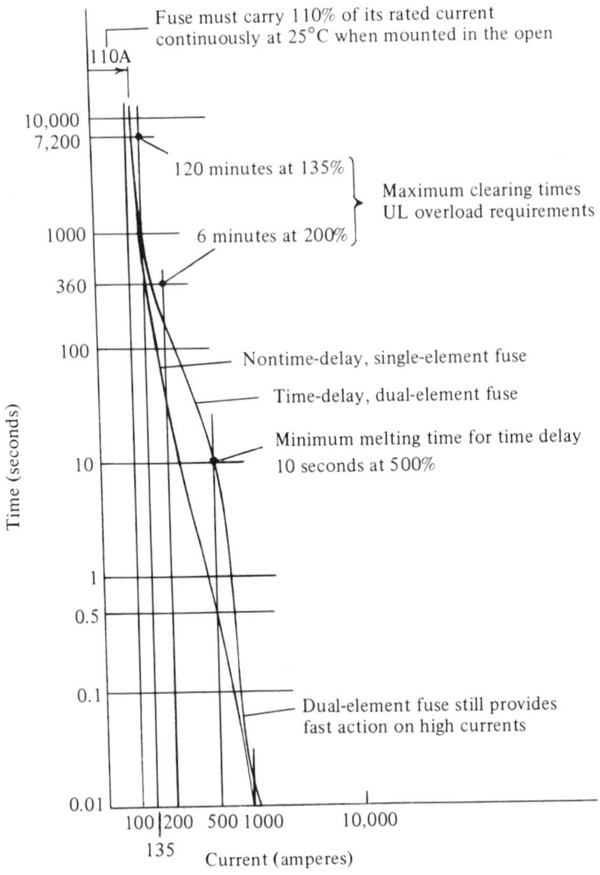

Minimum melt times for 100 ampere fuses

FIGURE 7.7

Comparison of response times for nontime-delay and time-delay fuses

melt until 10 seconds, whereas the single-element fuse melts in only 0.5 second, a difference of 20 to 1. This shows that there can be tremendous differences in the response characteristics of fuses even though they have the same current and voltage ratings.

The increased melting times of the dual-element fuse in the overload region led to the creation of a further category of fuse, the time-delay fuse. To be labeled *time delay*, a fuse must have *a minimum melting time of 10 seconds at 500% of its rating*. Fuses that do not meet the 10 second minimum time are then classified as *nontime delay*. Referring again to the curves in Figure 7.7, the dual-element fuse shown is a time-delay fuse and the single-element fuse is a nontime-delay fuse. A time-delay fuse does not necessarily have to be a dual-element fuse, but for practical purposes most, if not all, time-delay fuses are in fact dual element.

Time-delay fuses are particularly advantageous on motor circuits. This is discussed in Section 13.1.1. Smaller-rated fuses can be used for overcurrent protection, leading to reduced sizes and costs for switches, as shown in Example 13.2 and Figure 13.6(b).

7.5 CLASSIFICATIONS OF LOW-VOLTAGE FUSES

Since there are now many different types of cartridge fuses on the market, the Underwriters Laboratories, Inc., has established letter classifications to identify them. The more commonly used classifications are as follows:

UL Class H Fuses. These are the cartridge fuses that were formerly referred to as *NEC fuses* and that do not meet the standards of any of the other classes. These fuses have only 10,000 ampere interrupting capacity and they are not current limiting. Fuses are rated for 250 or 600 volts with current ratings up to 600 amperes. The standard dimensions for the different cartridge sizes and voltage ratings were adopted in 1904 and still apply today. These fuses can be either the one-time, nonrenewable or the renewable type. The renewable type cannot be labeled as time delay. Because of their low interrupting rating, class H fuses are not normally used nowadays for new systems.

UL Class J Fuses. These are nonrenewable current-limiting fuses with an interrupting rating of 200,000 amperes rms symmetrical. They are only rated for 600 volts with current ratings up to 600 amperes. They must meet standards for the maximum peak let-through currents and the thermal energy let-through (I^2t) values at 50,000, 100,000, and 200,000 rms symmetrical amperes. New standard dimensions were developed for class J fuses, making them smaller than class H, so they are not interchangeable with any other class of fuse. There are no time-delay standards for class J fuses.

UL Class L Fuses. These are basically the same as class J except that their current ratings range from 601 to 6000 amperes and they may be labeled as time delay, although there are no UL standards for time delay above 600 amperes.

UL Class R Fuses. These are nonrenewable current-limiting fuses with an interrupting rating of 200,000 amperes rms symmetrical. They have similar electrical characteristics to the older class K, but they have a rejection feature so that other classes of fuses cannot be inserted into the same fuseholder. They are rated for 250 and 600 volts with current ratings up to 600 amperes. There are two subclasses, RK-1 and RK-5; the main difference between the two is in the degree of current limitation. Class RK-1 fuses have lower peak let-through currents and thermal energy let-through (I^2t) values. They can be either nontime delay or time delay (minimum melt time of 10 seconds at 500% of fuse rating). They have the same 250 and 600 volt dimensions as the class H fuses, so they can be used as replacements for these fuses, thus providing a much higher interrupting capability. Figure 7.8 shows the rejection feature for the class R fuses and includes a table of dimensions for the different cartridge sizes.

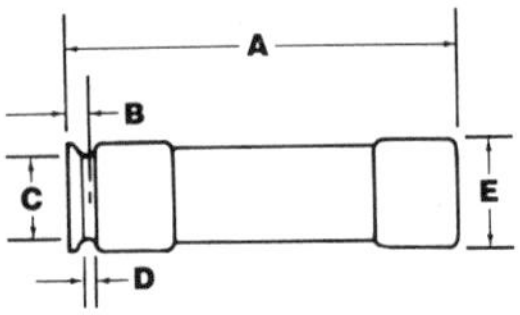

(a) Outline dimension of 0 to 60 ampere fuses

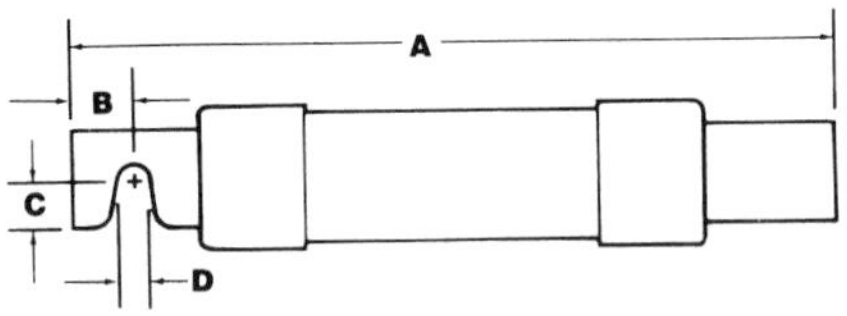

(b) Outline dimension of 70 to 600 ampere fuses

Dimensions

Fig. Ref.	Ampere Ratings	A	B	C	D	E	Wt. (lbs.)
LPN-RK (250V)							
A	**0-30**	2	5/32	3/8	5/64	9/16	—
	35-60	3	3/16	5/8	3/32	13/16	—
B	**70-100**	5 7/8	1/2	23/64	9/32	—	0.30
	110-200	7 1/8	11/16	35/64	9/32	—	0.69
	225-400	8 5/8	15/16	51/64	13/32	—	1.75
	450-600	10 3/8	1 1/8	63/64	17/32	—	3.25
LPS-RK (600V)							
A	**0-30**	5	3/16	5/8	3/32	13/16	—
	35-60	5 1/2	1/4	7/8	3/32	1 1/16	—
B	**70-100**	7 7/8	1/2	23/64	9/32	—	0.80
	110-200	7 5/8	11/16	35/64	9/32	—	2.00
	225-400	11 5/8	15/16	51/64	13/32	—	4.60
	450-600	13 3/8	1 1/8	63/64	17/32	—	5.60

Dimensions (Inches): columns A–E.

FIGURE 7.8

Outline dimensions for UL class R fuses

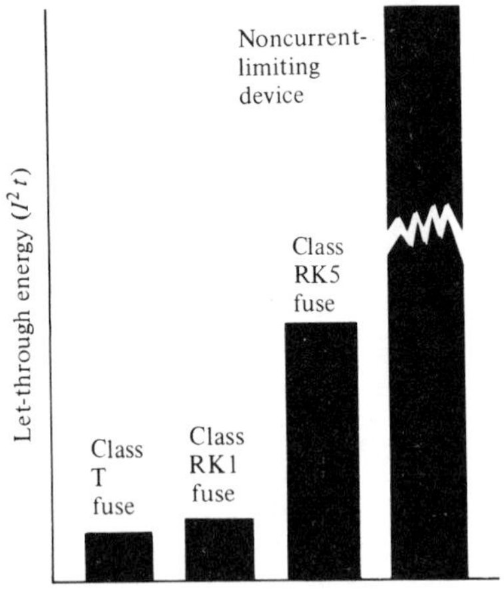

FIGURE 7.9

Relative values of let-through energy for three UL classifications of fuses

The energy (I^2t) let-through during the interval of time required for the fuse to clear the circuit is an important measure of the degree of protection provided by a fuse.

UL Class T Fuses. These are nonrenewable current-limiting fuses with an interrupting rating of 200,000 amperes rms symmetrical and are nontime delay only. They are rated for 250 and 600 volts with current ratings up to 600 amperes. They are very fast acting, with lower peak let-through currents and thermal energy let-through (I^2t) values than the other classes. They have new standard dimensions that make them even smaller than the class J fuses, and therefore they are not interchangeable with any other class of fuse.

Figure 7.9 shows the relative let-through energy values of class T, RK-1, and RK-5 fuses. Figure 7.10 shows a typical set of curves

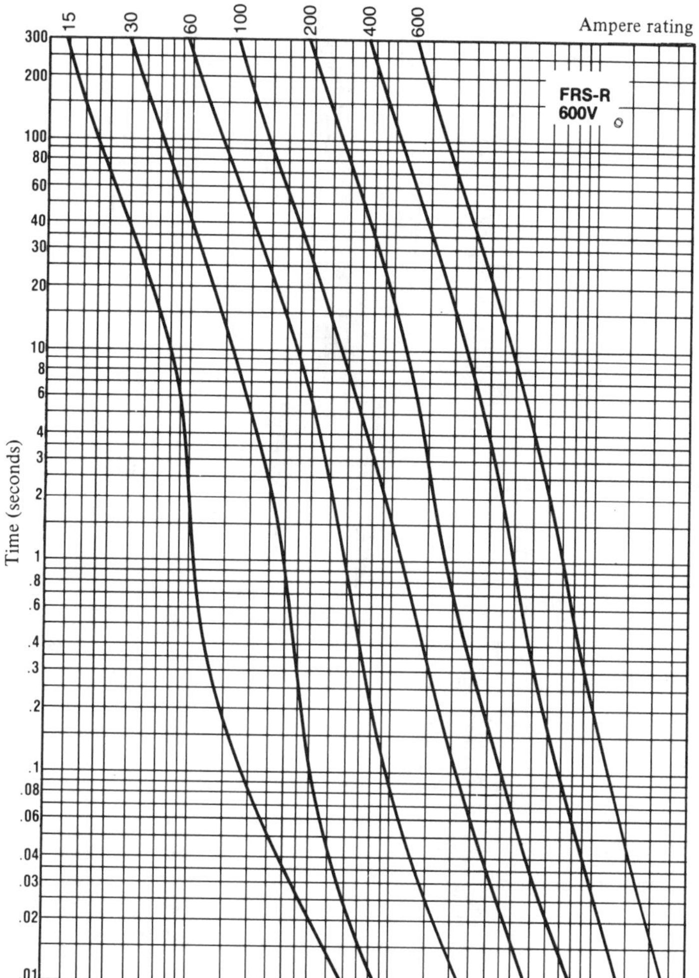

Note: Not all of the available ampere ratings are shown.

FIGURE 7.10

Average melting time–current characteristic curves for UL class RK-5, time-delay, dual-element 600 volt fuses

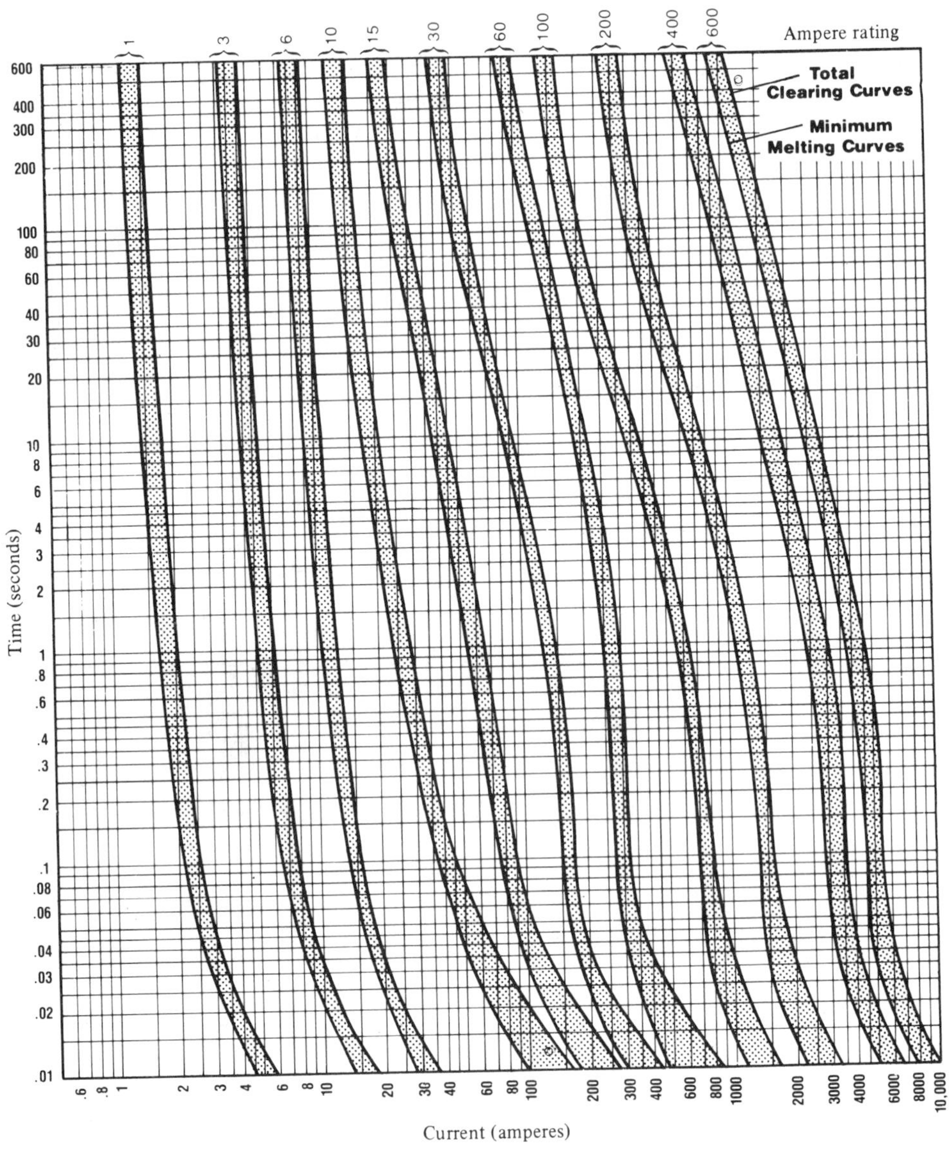

Note: Not all of the available ampere ratings are shown.

FIGURE 7.11

Minimum melting and total clearing time–current characteristic curves for UL class T 600 volt fuses

for class RK-5 dual-element, time-delay fuses. Note that the curves show only the average melting times for each rating, which was the method used prior to 1972. Figure 7.11 shows a typical set of curves for class T fuses. These curves show the new method of indicating both the true minimum melt and the total clearing times for each rating.

Refer to Section 6.6, which lists the required ratings for protective devices. There are no short-time current ratings listed for fuses. Since they operate so fast, the short-time ratings are not necessary.

7.6 FUSIBLE SWITCHES

Section 240-40 of the *National Electrical Code* requires that disconnecting means shall be provided on the supply side of all cartridge fuses so that each individual circuit containing fuses can be independently disconnected from the source of supply. The switch for the disconnecting means and the fuseholders for accommodating the fuses are usually mounted together in one enclosure. A common form of fusible switch, designated general use, is shown in Figure 7.12(a). The standard ratings and enclosure dimensions for general-use switches are shown in Table 7.2. Switches used in motor circuits, designated motor-circuit switches, are required to be horsepower rated as covered in Section 13.2.2. Fused switches mounted in combination with motor starters in one enclosure are shown in Figure 14.3(a). Fusible switches can also be group mounted in a panelboard as shown in Figure 7.12(b). For large-capacity feeders or service entrances, special fusible bolted-pressure switches and power-service protectors rated from 800 to 6000 amperes are available.

Fuses are tested to carry 110% of their rated current continuously at 25°C ambient temperature when mounted in the open. However, fuses respond to heat no matter how it is generated. When

TABLE 7.2 Standard Ratings of General-Use Fusible Switches

Ampere Rating	Approximate Dimensions (in.)		
	Height	Width	Depth
30	15	8	5½
60	15	8	5½
100	20	11	7½
200	28	14	8½
400	40	24	12
600	46	24	12
800	50	32	13
1200	56	38	13

Switches are rated for 250 and 600 volts.

Switches are two and three pole.

See Table 13.4 for horsepower ratings of switches.

Manufacturers should be consulted for exact dimensions.

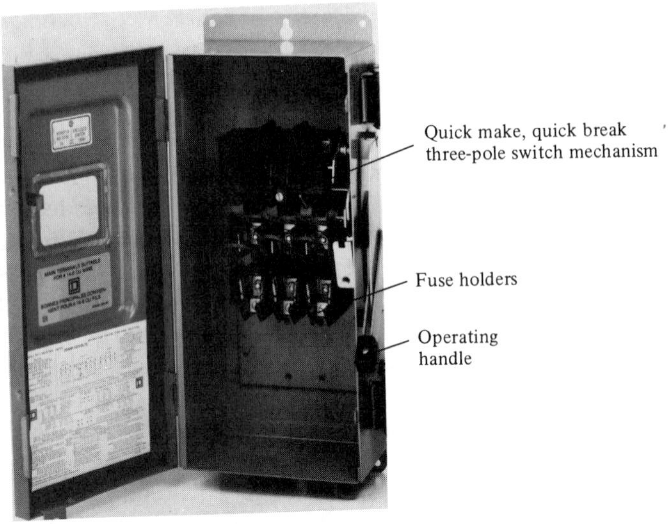

All exposed electrical parts must be dead when door is open

(a) **Individual general-use fusible switch**

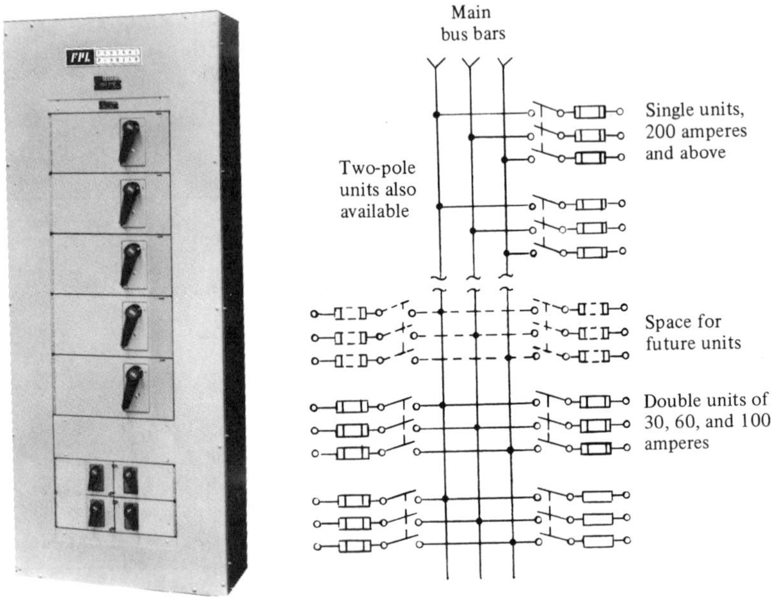

FIGURE 7.12

Low-voltage fusible switches

(b) **Fusible switches group mounted in a panelboard**

fuses are operating within their switch enclosures, heat accumulates due to the load current, with the result that the ambient temperature inside the enclosure is usually well above 25°C. Therefore, the fuses may no longer be able to carry their rated current on a continuous basis. This matter is dealt with at more length in Section 11.8 with regard to applying fuses for overcurrent protection to feeders. The selection of switch sizes and fuses for motor circuits is covered in Sections 13.1.1 and 13.3.

7.7 COORDINATING LOW-VOLTAGE FUSES

Coordination of protective devices in an electrical system, as mentioned in the Introduction to Chapter 6, is very desirable. With proper coordination, a faulted circuit is completely isolated by the protective device nearest to the fault without disturbing any of the other protective devices in the system, thereby preventing further shutdowns of the system. The following is the method of achieving coordination using fuses. At this point, the reader should review Section 6.4 for the concepts of a system under fault conditions.

Refer to Figure 7.13. Part (a) shows the one-line diagram of a simple distribution system. See the Introduction to Chapter 11 for an explanation of the one-line diagram. Fuse A is the overcurrent protection for a feeder, and fuse B is the overcurrent protection for one

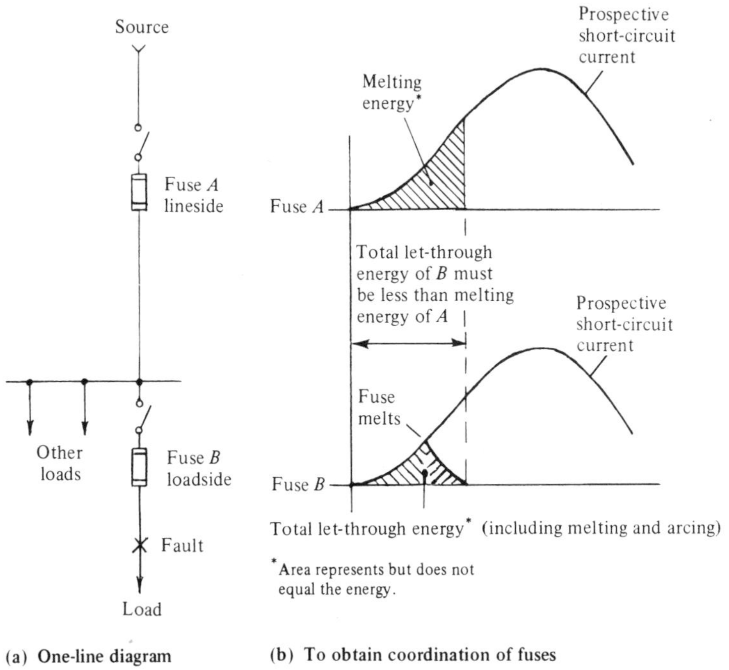

FIGURE 7.13

Coordination of low-voltage current-limiting fuses

of the branch circuits being fed by the feeder. Assume that a short-circuit fault occurs on the branch circuit at the point marked with an × on the diagram. The resulting fault current that flows is instantly *seen* by both fuses. The two fuses are connected in series between the source and the point of the fault and are subjected to exactly the same current. Therefore, coordination can only be achieved if fuse B reacts fast enough to completely open the faulted circuit before fuse A has reached the point where it starts to blow. Figure 7.13(b) shows the general principle for obtaining coordination between fuses. The total let-through energy of fuse B, which includes the energy during both its melting and arcing periods, must be less than the energy required to bring the fusible element of fuse A to its melting point. If this is the case, then the fault current is interrupted before fuse A can operate. The faulted circuit is now isolated, and the balance of the system can continue to operate normally. Note that if fuse A even just reaches its melting point it will end up blowing and shutting down all the other circuits as well.

The coordination of fuses of the same manufacturer is fairly straightforward. Most manufacturers provide a selectivity ratio guide for use with their fuses. Typical ratios are shown in Table 7.3. The term *lineside* means the fuse that is closest to the source (fuse A in Figure 7.13), and *loadside* means the fuse closest to the fault (fuse B).

TABLE 7.3 Selectivity Ratio Guide for Low-Voltage Fuses

	Class and Type of Fuse, Loadside				
Class and Type of Fuse, Lineside	**Class J**	**Class RK-1, Nontime Delay**	**Class RK-1, Time Delay**	**Class RK-5, Time Delay**	**Class T**
Class J	3 : 1	3 : 1	3 : 1	8 : 1	3 : 1
Class RK-1, nontime delay	3 : 1	3 : 1	3 : 1	8 : 1	3 : 1
Class RK-1, time delay	3 : 1	3 : 1	2 : 1	8 : 1	3 : 1
Class RK-5, time delay	1.5 : 1	1.5 : 1	1.5 : 1	2 : 1	1.5 : 1
Class T	3 : 1	3 : 1	3 : 1	8 : 1	3 : 1

These ratios are typical only and apply when the fuses are all from the same manufacturer.

■ EXAMPLE 7.2

In Figure 7.13, both fuses are UL class J and fuse B is 100 A. Determine the smallest rating for fuse A that will coordinate with fuse B.

Solution

— From Table 7.3, the selectivity ratio is 3 : 1.
— Smallest rating for fuse A = 3 × 100 = 300 A.
— From Table 7.1, 300 A is standard rating.

■ EXAMPLE 7.3

In Figure 7.13, fuse A is UL class RK-5 time delay and fuse B is UL class RK-1 time delay. Fuse B is 90 A. Determine the smallest rating for fuse A that will coordinate with fuse B.

Solution

— From Table 7.3, the selectivity ratio is 1.5 : 1.
— Smallest rating for fuse A = 1.5 × 90 = 135 A.
— From Table 7.1, the nearest standard rating above 135 is 150 A.

Note, in Example 7.3, that if the fuse types were reversed (fuse A, class RK-1 and fuse B, class RK-5) then the selectivity ratio would be 8 : 1, which would make coordination virtually impossible. The problem here is that the class RK-1 fuse operates much faster on high fault currents than does the class RK-5 fuse.

The ratios specified by the manufacturer cover all possible levels of fault current up to the interrupting rating of the fuses. For lower levels of fault current, the specified selectivity ratios may be lowered to permit closer fuse sizing. However, the fuse curves compiled by the manufacturer would have to be compared to determine the allowable ratio. Furthermore, the ratios only apply between fuses of the same manufacturer. The coordination between fuses of different manufacturers is much more complex and again requires detailed information from each manufacturer to make comparisons. The coordination of fuses with other types of devices is covered in Sections 16.4 and 16.5.

7.8 MEDIUM-VOLTAGE FUSES

Fuses are available for voltage levels ranging from 2.3 to 161 kilovolts. The higher-voltage fuses are designed for outdoor use only, typically on electric utility systems. Fuses used indoors are limited to systems of 34.5 kilovolts (medium voltages).

Medium-voltage fuses are divided into two general categories, distribution fuse cutouts and power fuses. Distribution fuse cutouts were developed primarily for overhead distribution circuits. Power fuses were developed primarily for substation-type applications and are available with higher-voltage, load-current, and interrupting ratings. They are also available in forms suitable for use within buildings. The following discussion covers only the power-type fuses typically used indoors in switchgear enclosures. Power fuses can be divided into two basic types:

—Solid-material fuses
—Current-limiting fuses

7.8.1 Solid-Material Power Fuses

The solid-material power fuse interrupts fault currents through the combined action of high-speed elongation and deionization of the arc. When an overcurrent melts the fusible element, a spring-driven arcing rod is rapidly driven upward, elongating the arc drawn in the solid-material-lined bore of the interrupting chamber within the fuse. The heat from the confined arc reacts with the solid material, creating gases that deionize and extinguish the arc.

To eliminate the problem of the expulsion of any hot gases from the fuse, an exhaust control device is used to reduce the velocity of the gases to the point that they cannot cause any burning or flashovers within the confined space of a switchgear enclosure. The solid-material power fuse is considered to be a nonexpulsion type with regard to the minimum electrical clearances required for indoor mounted fuses.

A typical solid-material power fuse is shown in Figure 7.14. The exhaust control device, item d, is assembled on the bottom of the replaceable fuse unit, item b. The complete fuse assembly is available with maximum continuous current ratings of 200 and 400 amperes. The ampere rating of the replaceable fuse unit selected then sets the point above which the fuse will respond to an overcurrent. Typical dimensions and interrupting ratings for 5 and 15 kilovolt fuses are shown in Table 7.4. The interrupting ratings are given in both amperes and equivalent three-phase symmetrical MVA (1 million volt–amperes). The three-phase MVA ratings are given to make an easy comparison with circuit breakers, which, in themselves, are three-phase devices.

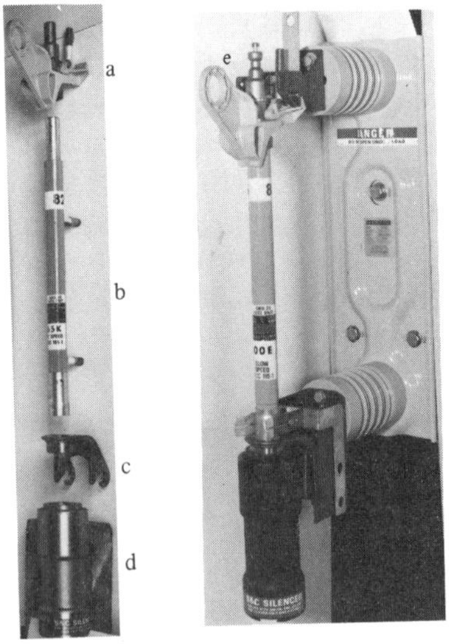

a, Upper end fitting; b, Fuse unit; c, Lower end fitting; d, Exhaust control device; e, Blown-fuse target

FIGURE 7.14

Medium-voltage, solid-material power fuse

As shown on the outline diagram in Table 7.4, the fuse is hinged to allow for easy removal. However, this feature does not allow the fuse to be used as a disconnecting means for the circuit.

Typical minimum melting and total clearing time–current characteristic curves are shown in Figures 7.15 and 7.16, respectively. Minimum melt and total clearing times are discussed in Section 7.1. The ampere ratings of the replaceable fuse units are shown at the top of each curve. The E rating designates that the fuse complies with the National Electrical Manufacturers Association (NEMA) standards for medium- and high-voltage fuses; that is,

TABLE 7.4 Typical Ratings and Dimensions of 5 and 15 Kilovolt Solid-Material Power Fuses for Indoor Use

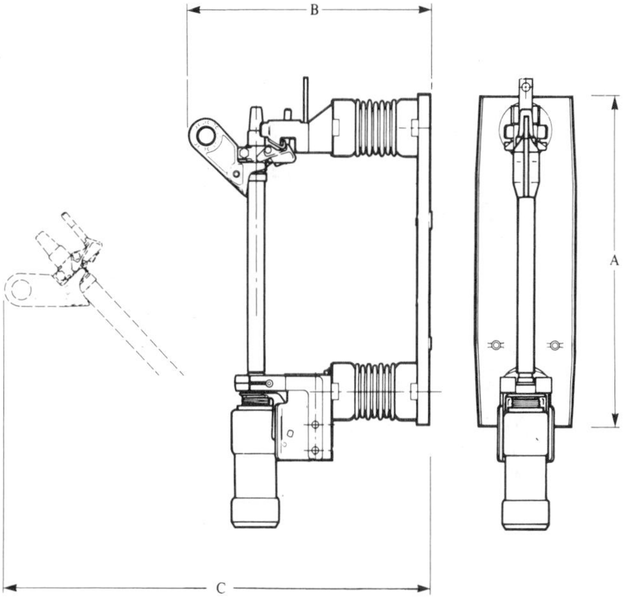

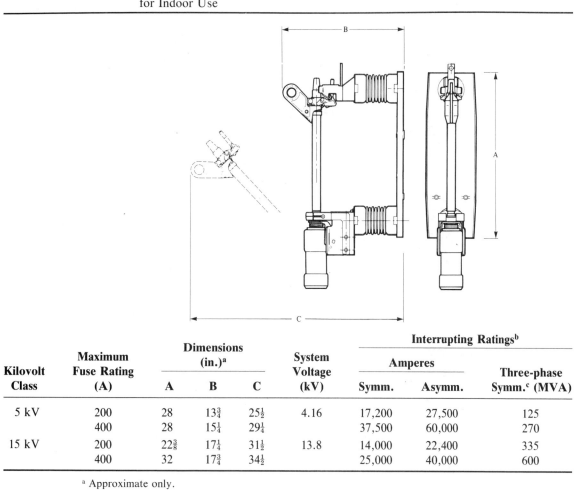

Kilovolt Class	Maximum Fuse Rating (A)	Dimensions (in.)[a]			System Voltage (kV)	Interrupting Ratings[b]		
						Amperes		
		A	B	C		Symm.	Asymm.	Three-phase Symm.[c] (MVA)
5 kV	200	28	$13\frac{3}{4}$	$25\frac{1}{2}$	4.16	17,200	27,500	125
	400	28	$15\frac{1}{4}$	$29\frac{1}{4}$		37,500	60,000	270
15 kV	200	$22\frac{3}{8}$	$17\frac{1}{4}$	$31\frac{1}{2}$	13.8	14,000	22,400	335
	400	32	$17\frac{3}{4}$	$34\frac{1}{2}$		25,000	40,000	600

[a] Approximate only.

[b] With exhaust-control device. Based on X/R ratio of 15.

[c] Equivalent value for 3 fuses (one in each phase of circuit).

Manufacturers should be consulted for confirmed ratings.

Source: Courtesy of S&C Electric Co.

That the fuse shall carry its rated current continuously, that a fuse rated 100 ampere or less shall melt in 300 seconds at an rms current within the range of 200 to 240% of the continuous rating of the fuse element, and that a fuse rated above 100 amperes shall melt in 600 seconds at an rms current within the range of 220 to 264% of the continuous rating of the fuse element.

The ampere ratings of the replaceable fuse units range from 3E up to 200E for the fuse assembly rated for a maximum of 200 amperes continuous and from 3E up to 400E for the fuse assembly rated

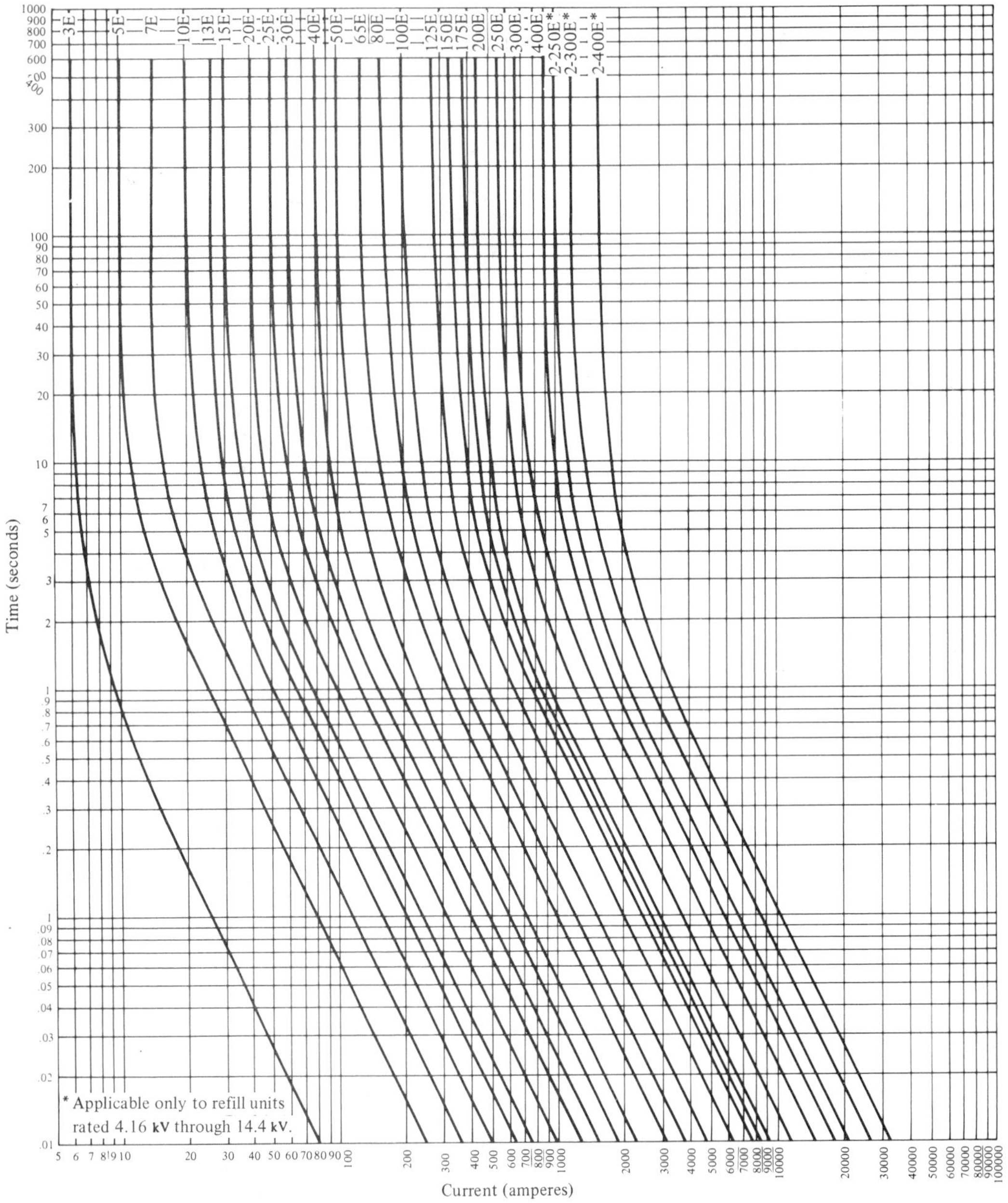

FIGURE 7.15 Typical minimum melting time–current characteristic curves for 5 and 15 kV solid-material power fuses

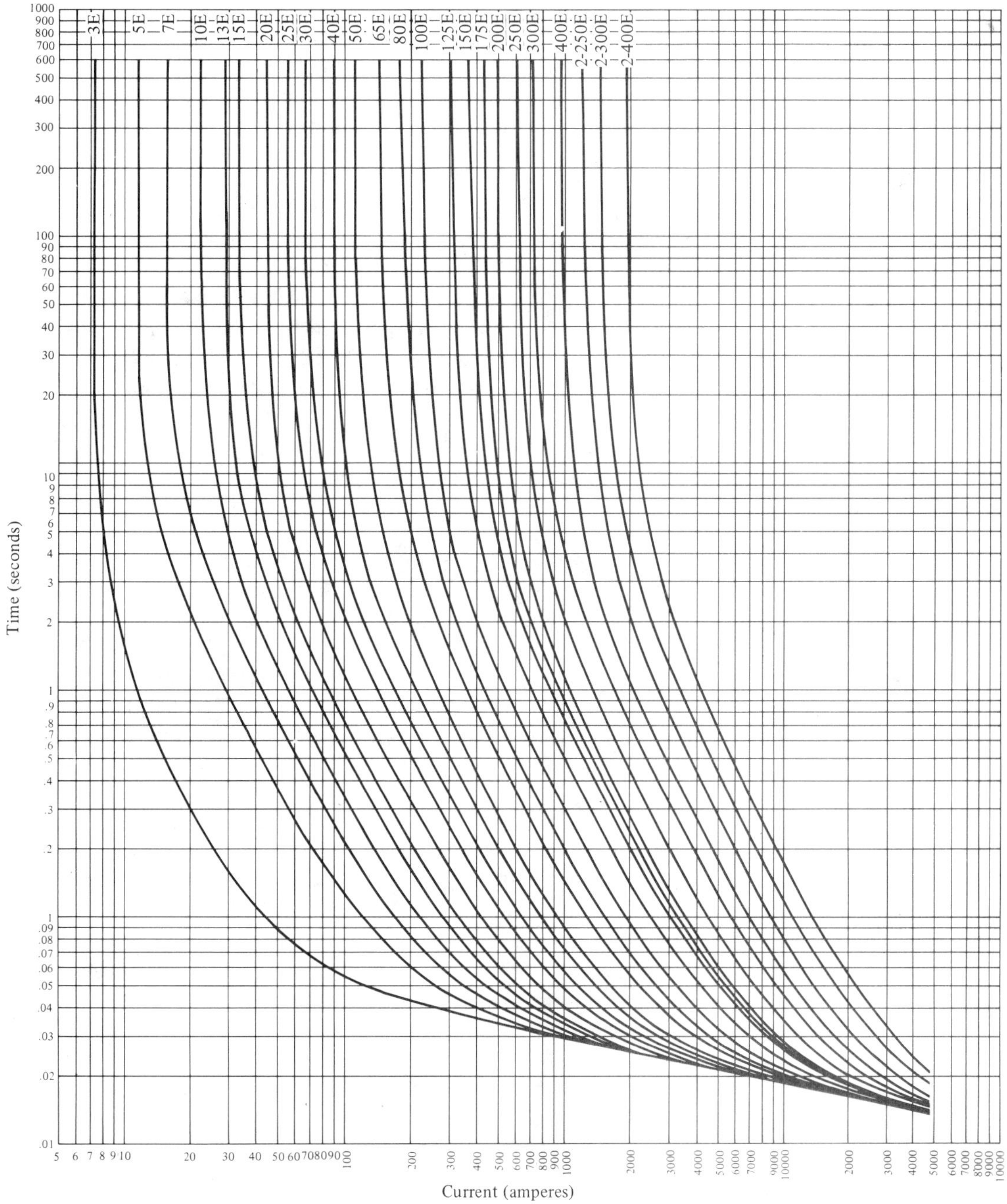

FIGURE 7.16 Typical curves for 5 and 15 kV solid-material power fuses

for a maximum of 400 amperes continuous. The reason for having ratings less than 200 amperes for the 400 ampere assembly is to allow the selection of the larger unit with its higher interrupting rating. For example, on a 4.16 kilovolt circuit, the load requirements may be 100 amperes, but the available fault level may be 200 MVA, which is greater than the interrupting rating of the 200 ampere unit. Therefore, the 400 ampere unit must be used with a 100 ampere replaceable fuse unit. Those ampere ratings listed as 2-250E, and the like, are for special units using two parallel fuse assemblies to give combined ratings of 500 amperes, in this case.

A typical application of solid-material power fuses is for the overcurrent protection of the primary of a power transformer used to step down the voltage for distribution within a building. Assemblies of three fuses (one for each phase) are combined with a gang-operated load-interrupter switch and are mounted in a metal switchgear cabinet as shown in Figure 15.6. The selection of ratings for fuses in this type of application is covered in section 16.5.

7.8.2 Current-Limiting Power Fuses

The medium-voltage, current-limiting power fuses operate on the same principle as discussed for low-voltage fuses in Section 7.3. The extremely fast interruption of the fault currents is accomplished by having the arcing energy absorbed by the quartz (sand) filler. No gases are generated within the fuse, as is the case with the solid-material type of fuse. The current limitation and reduction of the mechanical and thermal stresses are all as discussed in Section 7.3 and shown in Figure 7.4. The current-limiting fuse is a one-time fuse, and the whole fuse case must be replaced after operation, which can become costly. It has maximum continuous current ratings ranging from 100 to 450 amperes, voltage ratings ranging from 2.4 to 34.5 kilovolts, and equivalent three-phase symmetrical interrupting ratings ranging from 155 MVA at 2.4 kilovolts to 2600 MVA at 34.5 kilovolts.

Because of its ability to reduce the let-through currents under fault conditions, the current-limiting fuse is extensively used in combination with magnetic contactors for starters for medium-voltage motors (see Section 14.6). Another application is for overcurrent protection of the primaries of potential transformers (metering and relaying) and capacitor banks. Since the fuses in these applications are for branch circuit protection (that is, they are the last overcurrent device in the circuit), their extremely fast action causes no coordination problems and is very desirable for the protection of the equipment from damage. Current-limiting fuses may be used at other points in the system, but their fast action may cause coordination problems with downstream devices. Also, because of their extreme current chopping action when clearing a fault, they can cause high transient overvoltages on the system, which may break down the insulation. Applications of these fuses must be studied very carefully so that the proper fuse is selected. These studies are beyond the scope of this textbook.

7.8.3 Electronic Fuses

A fault-interrupting electronic fuse has recently been developed that incorporates unique overcurrent sensing, response, and interrupting techniques. This fuse offers a wide selection of time–current characteristic curves, combined with efficient current-limiting action in a compact, self-contained package not requiring external sensing or control power. Improved protection and coordination can be provided for a wide variety of medium-voltage circuit and equipment applications, some of which cannot be properly addressed with previously available devices.

The electronic fuse consists of two separate components: (1) an electronic control module that provides the time–current characteristics and the energy to initiate tripping, and (2) an interrupting module that carries the normal load current and then interrupts the current under fault conditions. The two modules are joined together in a complete package that is compatible in size with standard power fuses, as shown in Figure 7.17(a). The fuse is available in both 5 and 15 kilovolt ratings, with a continuous current rating of 600 amperes and an interrupting rating of 40,000 amperes rms symmetrical. Models rated for 25 and 34.5 kilovolts are under development.

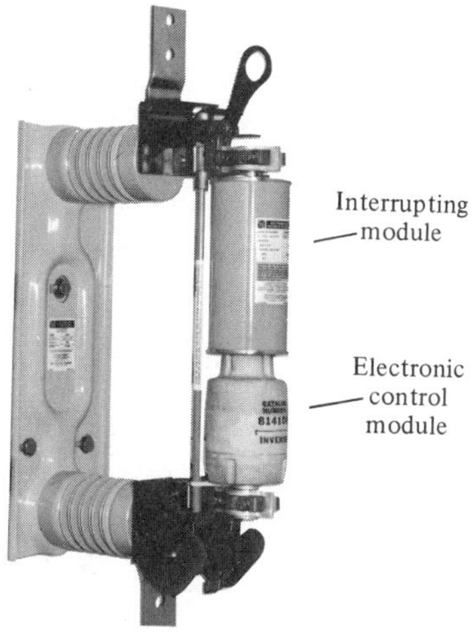

(a) Fuse assembly

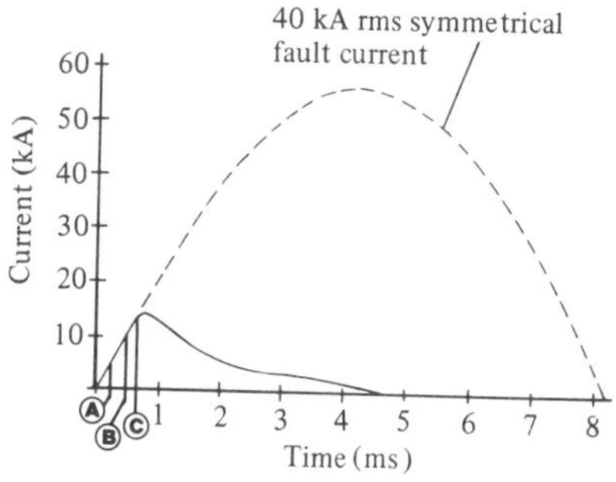

Event	Time
Ⓐ Control module sends trip signal to power cartridge	250 μs
Ⓑ Current transfer to current-limiting element completed	480 μs
Ⓒ Current-limiting element melts; current-limiting action begins	640 μs

(b) Operating sequence with 6 kA trip setting

FIGURE 7.17

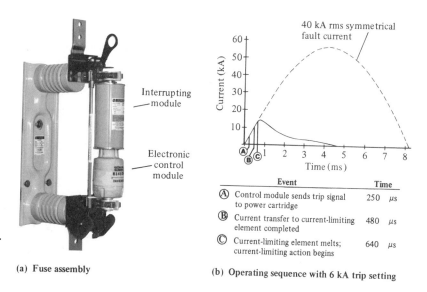

Medium-voltage 5 and 15 kV, 600 A electronic fuse

The electronic control module is a self-powered unit with all the control power and energy to operate the interrupting module being obtained from the current flowing in the lines through a current transformer. The output of the built-in current transformer feeds a full-wave rectifier, which then provides a signal to the logic circuitry that is proportional to the line current and is used by the logic circuitry to determine when to trip. Two types of logic circuits are employed, one with time-delay tripping characteristics and one with instantaneous tripping characteristics. These two circuits can be used alone or in combination to provide a variety of time–current characteristics.

The interrupting module contains two sections: a main current section that carries the current normally and a current-limiting section. The main section, when required to operate on a fault, separates at high speed to transfer the current to the current-limiting section, which then interrupts the current. These two sections are electrically in parallel, with the main section carrying almost all the current during normal operation. When a fault occurs, the control module sends an appropriate signal to a power cartridge, which initiates operation of the interrupting module. The sequence of operation is shown in Figure 7.17(b).

The electronic fuse is suitable for a number of important applications. One application is the protection of power transformers. The availability of the flexible time–current characteristics permits the selection of fuses for the primary protection of the transformer that coordinates extremely well with the secondary-side protective device (a low-voltage power circuit breaker). In addition, the instantaneous tripping logic of the fuse provides current-limiting action in the event of a transformer primary fault. A second important application is one requiring protective devices that can provide a full range of coordination in service entrance and feeder protection, which previously required the use of expensive, relayed, circuit-breaker-type equipment.

The reader is referred to the manufacturer's bulletin entitled "A New Fault-Interrupting Device for Improved Medium-Voltage System and Equipment Protection" as listed in the Bibliography for more detailed application information for this fuse.

SUMMARY

- Modern fuses have many different characteristics, and it is no longer satisfactory to just specify a voltage and current rating for them. Each type must be studied so that the application of fuses is done with full knowledge of their respective characteristics. The following is a summary of the advantages and disadvantages of the modern fuse as compared with other types of overcurrent protection.

- Advantages
  - —Low initial cost
  - —Simple, no parts to maintain
  - —Compact, require little space
  - —High current interrupting capabilities
  - —Provide current limitation, thus materially reducing or eliminating the possibility of the conductors or equipment being damaged by mechanical or thermal stresses under fault conditions
  - —Can provide good selective coordination on electrical faults, thus eliminating unnecessary shutdowns
  - —Inherently fail-safe; that is, if they fail, they open the circuit, thus making it safe
- Disadvantages
  - —Must be replaced after each operation; longer downtime
  - —Can cause single phasing, which is detrimental for motors
  - —Not adjustable; time–current characteristics are fixed
  - —Affected by ambient temperature, which may cause needless blowing of fuses
  - —Can be replaced by another fuse with incorrect ratings or characteristics (unless there is a rejection feature)
  - —Require the stocking of replacement fuses for each type used
  - —Cannot by themselves be used as an isolating means for the circuit; they must be mounted in combination with a switch

QUESTIONS

1. Explain why the basic fuse is a direct-acting, single-element device.
2. Why is the fuse a fail-safe device?
3. Explain the difference between the minimum melting and the total clearing times.
4. What are the two principal *NEC* categories of fuses?
5. Define a current-limiting fuse.
6. What is meant by the peak let-through current?
7. Explain the advantages of designing a fuse with two different types of elements in series (that is, a dual-element fuse).
8. What is the criterion that a fuse must meet in order to be labeled time delay?
9. On what type of circuit are time-delay fuses particularly advantageous? Explain.
10. Why are UL class H fuses no longer recommended for new electrical installations?
11. What is the main difference between UL class K and class R fuses?
12. What is the main difference between class RK-1 and RK-5 fuses?
13. Why is a disconnecting means required on the supply side of all cartridge fuses?
14. What is meant by the selectivity ratio with regards to coordinating fuses?
15. Briefly describe the interrupting action of the medium-voltage, solid-material-type power fuse.
16. Why are equivalent three-phase interrupting ratings given for medium-voltage fuses?
17. What is a typical application for solid-material power fuses?
18. Why is the overcurrent protection of medium-voltage motor circuits a good application for current-limiting power fuses?

PROBLEMS

1. Using Figure 7.10, determine the average melting times at 2000 A of the following fuses: (a) 100 A, (b) 200 A, and (c) 600 A.
2. Using Figure 7.11, determine the minimum melting and total clearing times for (a) 200 A fuse with a current of 1000 A, and (b) 30 A fuse with a current of 100 A.
3. Using Figures 7.15 and 7.16, determine the minimum melting and total clearing times for a 50E fuse with a current of 200 A.
4. Using Figure 7.5, determine the effective let-through symmetrical rms current with a 200 A, 250 V current-limiting fuse if the prospective short-circuit current is 70,000 symmetrical rms amperes.
5. Refer to Figure 7.13. Both fuses are class RK-5, time delay. Fuse B is rated for 60 A. Determine the smallest standard rating for fuse A that will coordinate with fuse B.
6. Repeat Problem 5, except fuse A is class T.

8 Circuit Breakers

OBJECTIVES

After studying this chapter, you will be able to:

- Discuss the means of safely interrupting large currents.
- Explain the operation of circuit breakers.
- Understand the significance of frame sizes and trip ratings.
- Differentiate between the molded-case, the power, and the encased types of low-voltage circuit breakers.
- Explain the operation of thermal–magnetic trip units.
- Interpret time–current characteristic curves of breakers.
- Discuss interrupting and short-time ratings of breakers.
- Discuss the characteristics of solid-state trip units.
- Identify the problems of coordinating molded-case breakers.
- Understand the principle of fused circuit breakers.
- Explain the operation of current-limiting circuit breakers.
- Recognize medium-voltage air circuit breakers.
- Identify the advantages of circuit breakers.
- Identify the disadvantages of circuit breakers.

INTRODUCTION

Within a few years of the introduction of the fuse, the growing electrical industry started looking for an alternative method of providing protection for electric circuits. They wanted a device that would not be destroyed by its operation, that could simply be reset to restore power, and that could also be used as a means of switching for the circuit. Out of this development work came the circuit breaker, which is an electromechanical device. The *National Electrical Code* defines the *circuit breaker* as *a device designed to open and close a circuit by nonautomatic means and to open the circuit automatically on a predetermined overcurrent without injury to itself when properly applied within its rating.*

As with other equipment, circuit breakers are divided into those rated for 1000 volts and less (low voltage) and those rated for more than 1000 volts (medium and high voltage). Low-voltage circuit breakers were also divided into two distinct categories, molded-case and power types. However, in the past few years the distinction between these two types has become less clear-cut as a new type of encased breaker has been introduced that combines the characteristics of each type. Low-voltage breakers are universally operated in air, so it is not necessary to designate them as *air circuit breakers* as this is understood. Medium- and high-voltage breakers, on the other hand, use mediums other than air in which to open the circuit and therefore must be designated as being air, oil, gas, and so on.

Apart from having different voltage and continuous current ratings, breakers have widely different interrupting ratings, response characteristics, and methods of operation. The proper application of circuit breakers requires a good knowledge of all the characteristics and options available for each type. Sections 6.6 and 6.7 discuss the necessary ratings for protective devices and the inverse time and instantaneous tripping of circuit breakers. These are now dealt with in detail. The discussions in this chapter are limited to circuit breakers used for circuits and feeders normally encountered in the electrical systems within buildings.

8.1 INTERRUPTING ACTION OF CIRCUIT BREAKERS

The simplest circuit-opening device is the manually operated knife switch, as shown in Figure 8.1(a). This switch has the basic parts required of any circuit-opening device: a fixed contact, a moving contact, an operating handle, and a base-plate or frame. However, as anyone who has opened a knife switch under load has witnessed, there is a luminous discharge drawn between the separating contacts of the switch. This discharge is called an *arc,* and it consists of a stream of positive and negative ions. The current flowing in a circuit cannot be instantaneously interrupted. As a result, the arc continues until the switch contacts have separated far enough to finally extinguish the arc. The arc can make the opening of the switch very unsafe and unreliable when interrupting a circuit under heavy loads. Also, the arc burns would soon destroy the surfaces of the contacts. A circuit breaker must provide a safer and more reliable interrupting action. The following are the means by which low-voltage circuit breakers can be made to safely interrupt large fault currents with a minimum of contact damage.

1. *Fast speed of operation* The duration and severity of an arc depends in part on the speed with which the contacts can be

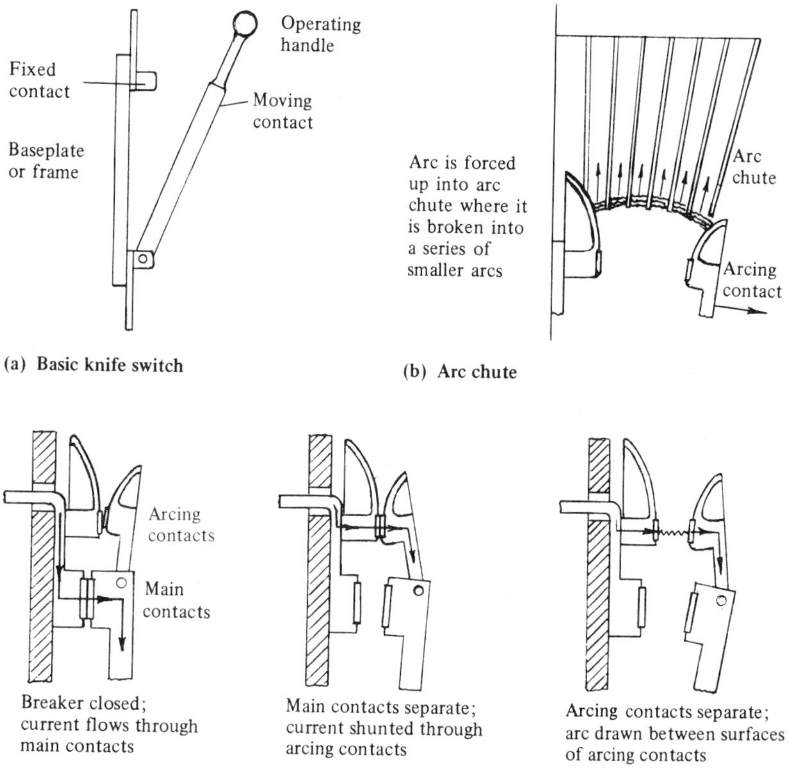
Operating
handle
Fixed
contact
Moving
contact
Baseplate
or frame
Arc is forced
up into arc
chute where it
is broken into
a series of
smaller arcs
Arc
chute
Arcing
contact
Arcing
contacts
Main
contacts
Breaker closed;
current flows through
main contacts
Main contacts separate;
current shunted through
arcing contacts
Arcing contacts separate;
arc drawn between surfaces
of arcing contacts

(a) **Basic knife switch**

(b) **Arc chute**

(c) **Simplified diagram of breaker contact mechanism showing main and arcing contacts**

FIGURE 8.1

Methods of interrupting current

separated. Therefore, powerful springs are used to rapidly force the contacts open. These springs are compressed (charged) during the closing operation. The breaker contacts are then mechanically held closed and are released by a separate trip mechanism. An operator can initiate the opening of the breaker but has no control over the speed with which the contacts separate.

2. *Use of arcing contacts* The arc burn can cause pitting, which eventually affects the ability of the contacts to carry the load current when closed. To offset this, two parallel sets of contacts are used for each pole of the breaker, a main current carrying set and an auxiliary or arcing set, as shown in Figure 8.1(c). When the breaker is tripped open, the main contacts separate first, transferring the current flow to the arcing contacts. The arcing contacts then separate a split second later, drawing the arc between them and leaving the main contacts free of any arcing. This allows the surfaces of the main current carrying contacts to be made of a high-conductivity

metal such as silver. The surfaces of the arcing contacts are then made of a tougher alloy better able to withstand the effects of arcing.

3. *Use of arc chutes* Parallel plates enclosed in the form of a chute are mounted directly above the arcing contacts, as shown in Figure 8.1(b). As the arcing contacts separate, the resulting arc creates a strong magnetic field that forces the arc upward into the plates. The arc stream is then broken into a series of small arcs, which are quickly cooled, deionized, and extinguished. The ionized gases created by the arc stream must be deionized before they are expelled from the arc chute; otherwise, secondary arcing could occur between the lineside terminals of the breaker, which are still energized.

Medium- and high-voltage breakers can also incorporate one of the following methods for current interruption:

1. *Opening the contacts in a vacuum* This would seem to be the ideal way to interrupt the flow of current as an arc cannot exist in an absolute vacuum. However, apart from the difficulty of obtaining an absolute vacuum, the extreme current chopping effect can create very high transient overvoltages on the system, which can lead to insulation failures. Nevertheless, recent advances in the technology of vacuum circuit opening devices have overcome these problems. Vacuum circuit breakers are now available for use on systems up to 15 kilovolts. Medium-voltage motor starters using vacuum contactors are also available (see Section 14.6).

2. *Air blast* A blast of compressed dry air is forced between the separating arcing contacts to further aid in driving the arc into the arc chute and to aid in cooling the arc.

3. *Using a medium other than air* The contacts are enclosed in oil or SF_6 gas, both of which have good dielectric properties and are very effective in quenching the arc and preventing it from restriking.

The air blast, the oil, and the SF_6 gas breakers are relatively expensive. The oil circuit breakers require special fireproof vaults if used indoors. The air blast and SF_6 gas circuit breakers require complicated enclosures and pressure systems. Therefore, these types of breakers are used mainly in large substations and for this reason are not covered in any further detail in this book.

8.2 OPERATION OF CIRCUIT BREAKERS

As well as providing overcurrent protection, a circuit breaker can, and usually does, serve also as the circuit switching device. Therefore, it must incorporate a means of being opened and closed. Breakers are either single pole or multipole. The term *pole* refers to each set of contacts that are connected into a separate line or phase of the circuit. The electrical code requires that each ungrounded line of a circuit must be broken. For example, a three-phase circuit requires a three-pole breaker. Multipole breakers are generally gang operated; that is, each pole is simultaneously closed and opened by one common operating handle or mechanism such as shown in Figure 8.4. Similarly, when the breaker is tripped open, all poles open even if the fault is only on the one phase. Thus circuit breakers cannot cause single phasing, as is the case with fuses.

Figure 8.2 is a diagrammatical representation of the main operating components of the typical breaker. The following is a general outline of the methods of operating breakers. More precise details are given with the description of each type of breaker. Two types of methods are available for the normal opening and closing of breakers: (1) manual for local operation only, and (2) electrical for both local and remote operation. Electrical operation is also desirable when the size of the breaker makes it difficult to close the breaker by manual means. Furthermore, there are two types of mechanical arrangements for closing the breaker, direct action and stored energy. The direct action method is a one-step operation, with the operating handle being directly linked to the contact mechanism. The stored energy method is a two-step operation. First, a spring is compressed either manually or by a small electric gear motor. Then the spring is released, which forces the contacts closed. This permits larger breakers to be safely closed manually or, in the case of electrical operation, it allows a much smaller motor to be used. In either method, during the closing sequence, a separate set of springs is compressed. The contacts are then mechanically latched into the

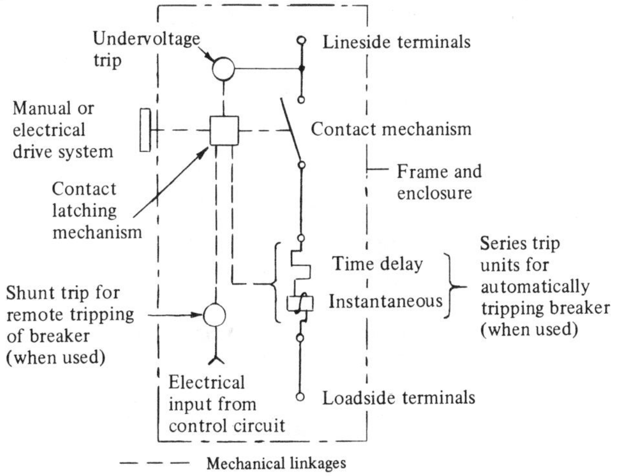

FIGURE 8.2

Diagrammatic representation of the operating parts of a circuit breaker closed position. The breaker is opened by either manually or electrically activating the trip mechanism and releasing the energy stored in the opening springs. The actual speed with which the contacts close and open is controlled by the springs. The quick-make, quick-break action cannot be affected by the operator.

The electrical operation of a breaker requires either a separate source of supply or a control circuit that is tapped off the line side of the breaker. This may also require a small control transformer to step down the voltage to a suitable level for the control system. Remote operation requires control wiring to be run to separate close-trip switches.

All breakers must be *trip free*; that is, *the breaker contacts cannot be held closed by the closing mechanism if the trip mechanism has been activated*. Thus, even if the operating handle is held in the closed position, the breaker contacts will still trip open. This is also a desirable safety feature. If a breaker is manually closed on a short circuit, the instantaneous tripping of the breaker does not kick back the handle, which could injure the operator.

As mentioned in Section 6.6, the two main functions of a protective device are to sense the circuit conditions and then to interrupt the circuit at a predetermined set of time and overcurrent conditions. The means of automatically tripping breakers under these overcurrent conditions are discussed for each type of breaker.

8.3 LOW-VOLTAGE CIRCUIT BREAKERS (GENERAL)

Low-voltage circuit breakers are universally air circuit breakers, meaning that the arc interruption takes place in air. Therefore, in referring to low-voltage breakers, it is not necessary to designate them as "air" circuit breakers, as this is understood. For low-voltage systems, it is desirable to have circuit breakers that are operated in air, which makes them more versatile in their application. The use of oil, even though it offers many advantages as an interrupting medium, presents a severe fire hazard, requiring fireproof vaults.

8.3.1 Frame Size Designations

In terms of applying ratings to automatic circuit breakers (that is, tripped automatically on overcurrents), there are two separate components to consider, the frame and the trip unit. As shown in Figure 8.1(a), a basic part of any circuit-opening device is the frame. This term then is used to designate the characteristics and size of a low-voltage breaker. The Underwriters Laboratories, Inc. defines *frame size* as *a group of circuit breakers of similar physical configuration. Frame size is expressed in amperes and corresponds to the largest ampere rating available in the group*. The frame size of a breaker sets the following electrical characteristics:

—Maximum continuous voltage rating (insulation level)
—Maximum continuous current rating
—Maximum interrupting rating
—Maximum permissible rating of trip unit

The trip rating then sets the value of the current above which the unit will respond and initiate the tripping of the breaker. To be able to provide close overcurrent protection for circuits, there are many more trip ratings available than there are frame sizes. For example, the smallest standard-duty molded-case frame is 100 amperes. However, there are many trip units ranging from 15 up to 100 amperes that can be installed within this frame size.

Very often, confusion is caused by the use of the phrase *rated continuous current* because the term is actually being used to indicate the current that the breaker can carry continuously before being tripped. However, the continuous current rating of the frame itself is set by the ampacity of the current-carrying parts (the contacts, terminals, and connections). It is preferable to use the term *trip rating* for the current above which the breaker will trip and then use the continuous current rating to designate the size of the frame. Many references to circuit breakers just indicate the one current rating, for example 70 amperes. However, this is incomplete because it presumably just refers to the trip rating. The frame size would normally be 100 amperes, but if a higher interrupting capacity is required, then the frame size may be 225 amperes. Therefore, both ratings should be specified. Specific ratings for breakers are covered in the following sections for each type of breaker.

8.3.2 Means of Automatically Tripping Breakers

Low-voltage circuit breakers generally have integrally mounted trip units that both monitor the circuit current and then automatically initiate tripping action based on their built-in time–current characteristics. There are two types of integrally mounted trip units, the series and the solid-state types. The series trips are thermal and/or magnetic units that are connected in series with each line of the circuit, as shown in Figure 8.3(a). They are acted on by the passage of the circuit current through them and, by means of a mechanical linkage, operate directly to trip the breaker.

The solid-state trip unit requires current transformers or sensors in each line of the circuit to reduce the current to a suitable level for input to the sensing circuits, as shown in Figure 8.3(b). The sensing circuits then function to initiate an output to the shunt trip that opens the breaker. The series trips are still generally used in the molded-case breakers, with the solid-state units being available for the larger ratings. The solid-state units have largely replaced the series trips on the power circuit breakers. More details on the trip units are given in the following sections on each type of breaker.

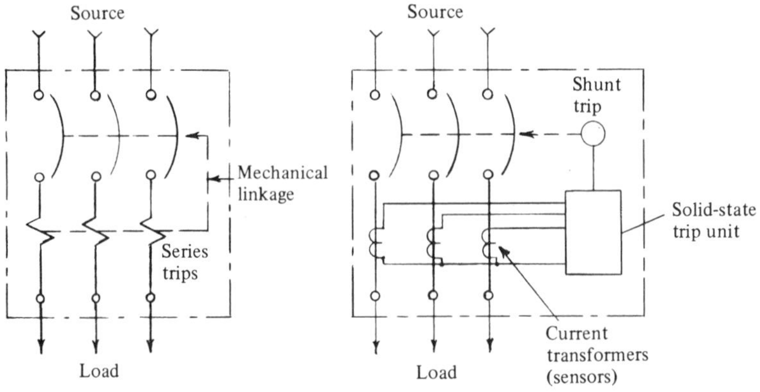

FIGURE 8.3

Methods of tripping automatic low-voltage circuit breakers

(a) **Breaker with series trips** (b) **Breaker with solid-state trips**

Also see Figure 10.16 for addition of ground-fault protection.

An optional feature that can be easily added to circuit breakers is undervoltage protection. This option is not available when fuses are used for circuit protection. A voltage-sensitive coil is connected to the line side of the circuit breaker, as shown in Figure 8.2, which trips the breaker if the supply voltage drops to an unsatisfactory level. Also, it prevents the breaker from being closed until the voltage is restored to 80% or more of its normal value.

8.3.3 Interrupting and Short-Time Ratings

Since the late 1950s, the interrupting ratings for low-voltage circuit breakers have been stated in symmetrical amperes. The ratings are based on the assumption that the X/R ratio of the typical low-voltage system is 6.6. Refer to Section 6.5 and Figure 6.4 for symmetrical and asymmetrical currents and X/R ratios. As indicated, the rms value of the asymmetrical current one half-cycle after the fault occurs is 1.33 times the rms value of the symmetrical fault current on a per phase basis. However, on three-phase circuits, if the fault occurs at the instant of time that causes the maximum offset of current in one phase, then, because of the 120° phase relationship, the other two phases cannot also experience maximum offsets. The average of the asymmetrical currents of the three phases is 1.17 times the symmetrical fault current. Therefore, the asymmetrical rating of a low-voltage breaker is approximately 1.17 times its symmetrical rating. Breakers were originally rated only in asymmetrical amperes and standard values, such as 25,000 or 50,000, were selected. The symmetrical ratings are based on these values and therefore become 22,000 or 42,000 amperes, and so on. Specific interrupting ratings are given in the following sections for each type of circuit breaker.

Refer to Section 6.6 with regard to the short-time current ratings of protective devices. For low-voltage circuit breakers that are tripped instantaneously, no short-time ratings are listed. Since the breaker opens so rapidly (the contacts are starting to separate within one half-cycle), the short-time rating is assumed to be the same as the interrupting rating of the breaker. For circuit breakers with delayed short-time tripping, a short-time current rating is listed. This rating is also stated in symmetrical amperes. Specific short-time ratings are listed in the tables for the power and encased types of breakers as these breakers can be applied with delayed short-time tripping.

8.4 LOW-VOLTAGE, MOLDED-CASE CIRCUIT BREAKERS

In the early 1920s, a small, compact circuit breaker was developed that differed considerably from the standard low-voltage circuit breakers in use at that time, which were large, rugged types designed for high-amperage circuits. The small size and lower cost of this new type of breaker meant that it could economically be used in place of fuses for the protection of small-capacity, low-voltage circuits. The fact that they could be simply reset after a fault and that they were tamper proof were considerable improvements over the fuses. The term *molded case* was ultimately created to classify this type of breaker. The National Electrical Manufacturers Association standards defines the *molded-case circuit breaker* as *one that is assembled as an integral unit in a supporting and enclosing housing of insulating materials.*

Refer to Figure 8.4 for a typical three-pole molded-case circuit breaker. This cutaway view shows the contacts, the arc extinguish-

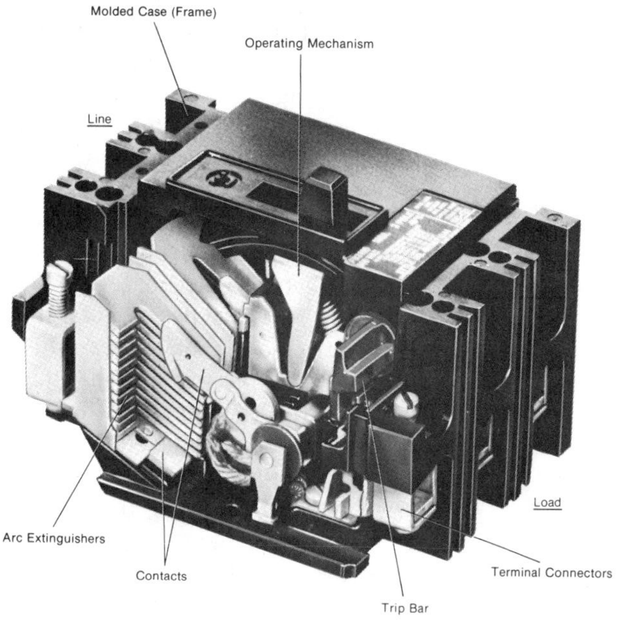

FIGURE 8.4

Cutaway view of a low-voltage, molded-case circuit breaker

ers (arc chutes), the trip bar, and the operating mechanism. The handle of the mechanism operates through a toggle arrangement to snap the contacts open or closed. The action is quick-make, quick-break, meaning that the speed with which the contacts move is independent of how fast the handle is operated. In addition to indicating whether the breaker is on or off, the operating handle indicates when the breaker is automatically tripped by moving to a position midway between the extremes. This distinct trip point is advantageous where breakers are grouped in a panelboard because it clearly indicates the faulty circuit. To restore service after the breaker trips, the handle must first be moved to the fully off position to reset the mechanism and then to the on position.

8.4.1 Thermal–Magnetic Trip Units

The standard molded-case circuit breaker has a thermal–magnetic trip unit with detection elements connected in series with each pole, as shown in Figure 8.3(a). The thermal action provides inverse time-delayed tripping on overloads, and the magnetic action provides instantaneous tripping on short circuits (see Section 6.7 and Figures 6.5 and 6.6).

The thermal time-delayed tripping is achieved through the use of a bimetal element that is heated directly by the passage of the circuit current, as shown in Figure 8.5(a). The bimetal element has two bonded strips of metal with different rates of thermal expansion. The heat from an overload current causes the element to bend, the rate being dependent on the amount of current. Ultimately, the element deflects far enough to physically push the trip bar and unlatch the breaker contacts. Figure 8.5(a) shows a typical inverse time–current response curve indicating that, with an overload current of 135%, the tripping time is on the order of 30 minutes (1800 seconds), whereas with a current of 500% the time is down to 10 seconds. The thermal elements are calibrated in the factory and are not adjustable after the breaker has been assembled. A specific thermal element must be supplied for each trip rating.

The magnetic instantaneous action is achieved through the use of an electromagnet in series with the load current, as shown in Figure 8.5(b). The passage of a short-circuit current through the coil of the electromagnet creates sufficient force to attract the armature, thus moving the trip bar and unlatching the breaker contacts. The only delaying factor is the fraction of time (1 cycle or less) that it takes for the unlatching action to take place. Thus the action is said to be instantaneous. The smaller breakers have fixed magnetic trip elements, as shown in the time–current response curve in Figure 8.5(b). The breaker does not trip until the fault current reaches or exceeds its pickup value, usually 1000% of its rating.

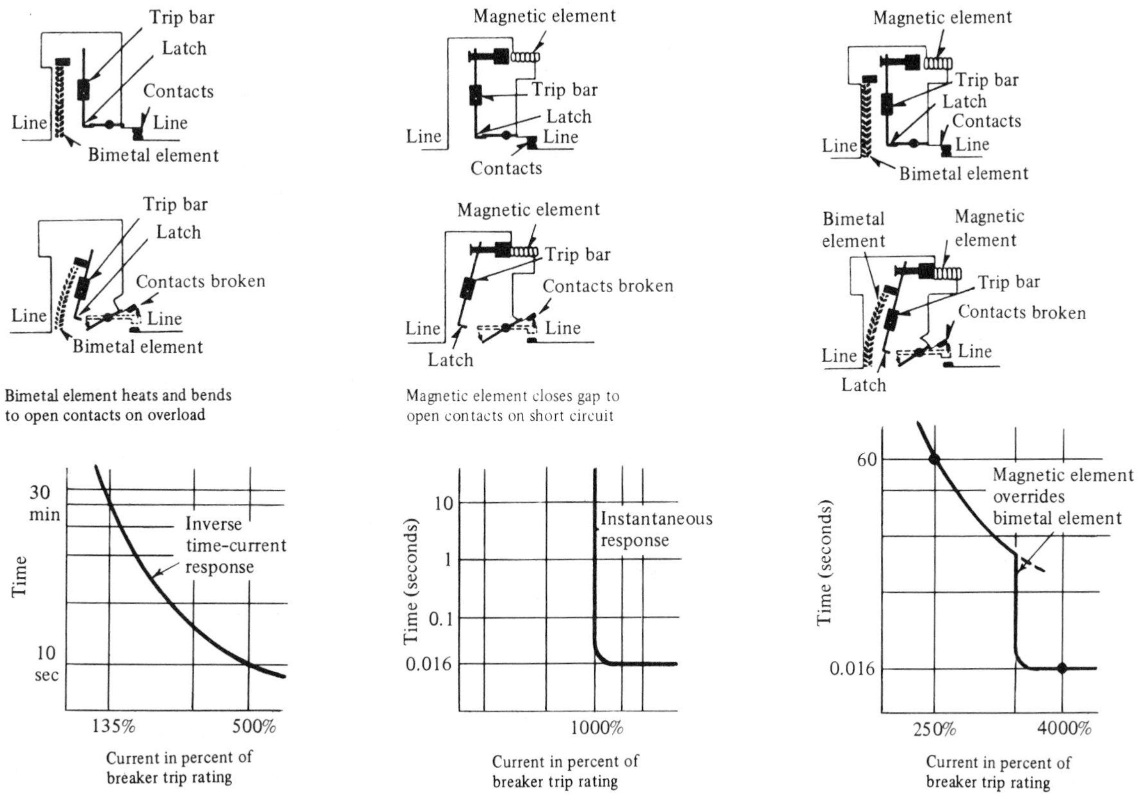

(a) Thermal action (b) Magnetic action (c) Combined thermal-magnetic action

FIGURE 8.5

Thermal–magnetic trip units for molded-case circuit breakers

The combined thermal–magnetic action is shown in Figure 8.5(c), together with the typical time–current response curve. Thermal action with time-delayed tripping occurs up to the point where the current is large enough to activate the magnetic trip. Above this point, the magnetic action trips the breaker instantaneously. For example, a 250% overload current takes 60 seconds to deflect the bimetal element far enough to trip the breaker. On the other hand, a short-circuit current of 4000% (40 times the breaker trip rating) attracts the magnetic armature and trips the breaker instantaneously (0.016 second).

The larger molded-case breakers have adjustable instantaneous trip units. By adjusting the gap in the electromagnet, the actual value of the current required to activate the trip mechanism can be varied. Figure 8.6 shows a thermal–magnetic breaker with adjustable mag-

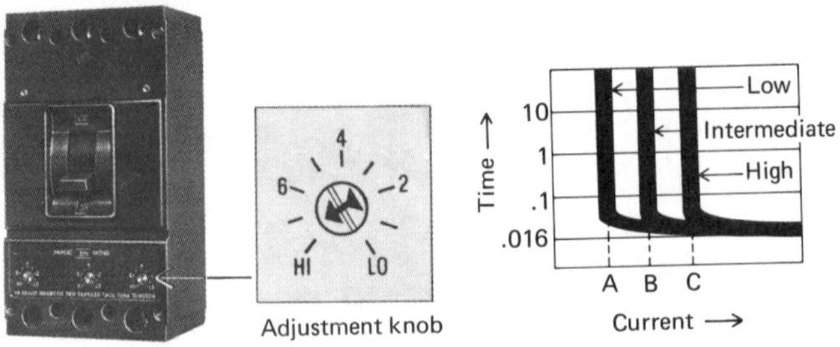

FIGURE 8.6

Thermal–magnetic breaker with adjustable magnetic trip

netic trips. The time–current curve shows the range of adjustments, from a low setting of 500% of the current rating of the trip unit (line A) to a high setting of 1000% (line C).

8.4.2 Time–Current Characteristic Curves

The response characteristic curves for each type of breaker are plotted on standard log–log, time–current graphs. Figure 8.7 shows a typical set of curves for a 150 ampere frame molded-case breaker with thermal time delay and fixed magnetic instantaneous trip units. Note that the horizontal scale is not directly in amperes, but is current in percent of the breaker trip unit rating.

No matter how strict the quality control maintained by the manufacturer, there will be discrepancies between individual breakers of any one type. The graph shows minimum and maximum lines, which represent the tolerance limits for the breaker type, and the area between the lines then represents the operating band. An individual breaker will operate within the limits defined by the band.

■ EXAMPLE 8.1

Using Figure 8.7, for a breaker with a 90 A trip unit, determine the minimum and maximum tripping times for a current of 360 A.

Solution

— 360 A is 360/90 = 4.0 or 400%.
— Intersection of 400% with minimum line is 12 s.
— Intersection of 400% with maximum line is 30 s.

These points are indicated on the graph. This means that, from a large sampling of breakers of this type using a 90 A trip unit, none will trip in less than 12 s and none will take longer than 30 s to totally clear the circuit at 360 A.

The actual time for the breaker to open and fully extinguish the arc once it has been tripped is insignificant in the time-delayed tripping region, but it is the major factor in the instantaneous tripping region. Therefore, the maximum interrupting time becomes virtually constant at 0.016 second for currents above the instantaneous tripping value. Note that the tolerances for the magnetic instantaneous

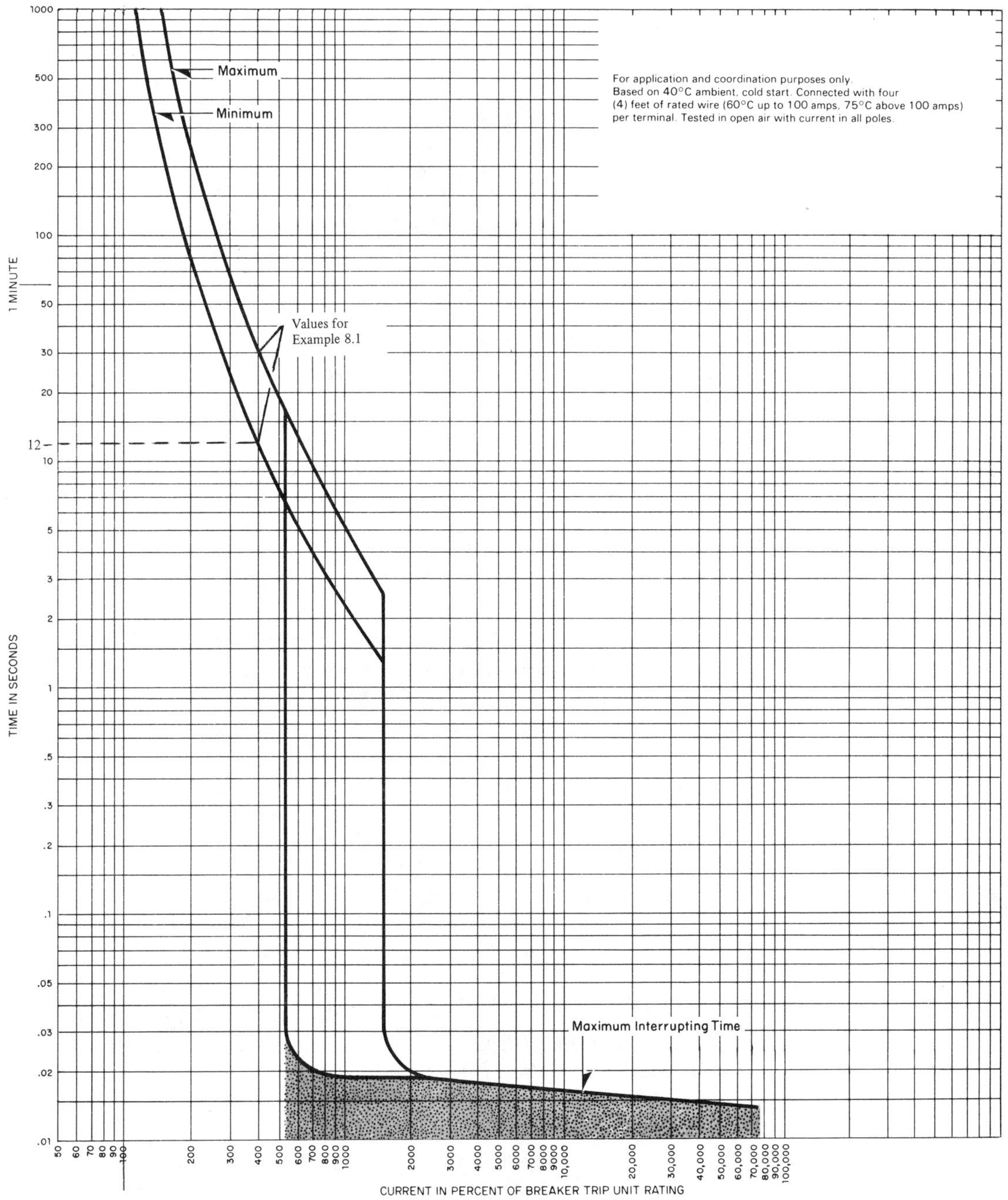

FIGURE 8.7 Typical time–current characteristic curves for molded-case breaker, 150 ampere frame, with thermal time delay and fixed magnetic instantaneous trip unit

element are fairly wide, from a low of 530% to a high of 1600% of the current rating of the trip unit. This becomes significant when coordinating breakers, as discussed in Section 8.6.

Figure 8.8 shows a typical set of time–current curves for a 400 ampere frame molded-case breaker with thermal time delay and adjustable magnetic instantaneous trip units. The curves in the overload region are similar to those discussed for Figure 8.7. However, the vertical minimum and maximum lines for the instantaneous tripping represent the range of adjustments for the magnetic units, that is, from a low of 500% to a high of 1000%. Then, as noted, there are tolerances with regard to these settings: ±25% at the 500% setting and ±10% at the 1000% setting. Therefore, the complete operating band of the breaker can only be determined after the instantaneous tripping point has been selected. This is covered further in Section 8.6.

8.4.3 Frame Sizes and Ratings

Frame sizes and ratings for molded-case circuit breakers were essentially standardized for many years, with letters used to designate a particular frame. For example, an E frame was rated for a maximum of 100 amperes at 240 volts, and a K frame was rated for a maximum of 225 amperes at 600 volts. However, recent advances have brought forth so many variations among manufacturers with regard to frame sizes and ratings that the letter designations are no longer standard throughout the industry. Frame sizes are therefore designated by their ampere rating.

Table 8.1 lists the more common frame sizes, together with their ratings and ranges of trip units for the *industrial* type of circuit breaker. The term industrial is used here to differentiate these standard-duty breakers from the light-duty breakers described at the end of this section, which are used in lighting panels (Section 12.4). The table includes ratings up to 1200 amperes, but it should be noted that some manufacturers now offer molded-case breakers up to 3000 amperes.

The interrupting ratings of the standard-duty breakers are often a limiting factor in their application to large-capacity systems. To help overcome this limitation, some manufacturers have developed high interrupting capacity breakers that have cases made from a high-impact, high-tensile, flame-resistant glass polyester material. As a comparison, the standard 225 ampere breaker has an interrupting rating of 25,000 rms symmetrical amperes at 240 volts, whereas the high interrupting capacity breaker has a rating of 65,000 amperes. Table 8.1 shows the ratings of both types. Note that the increase in ratings for the high interrupting capacity units is not nearly so great at 480 and 600 volts. These special breakers cost roughly 50% more than the standard breakers, but they offer a low-

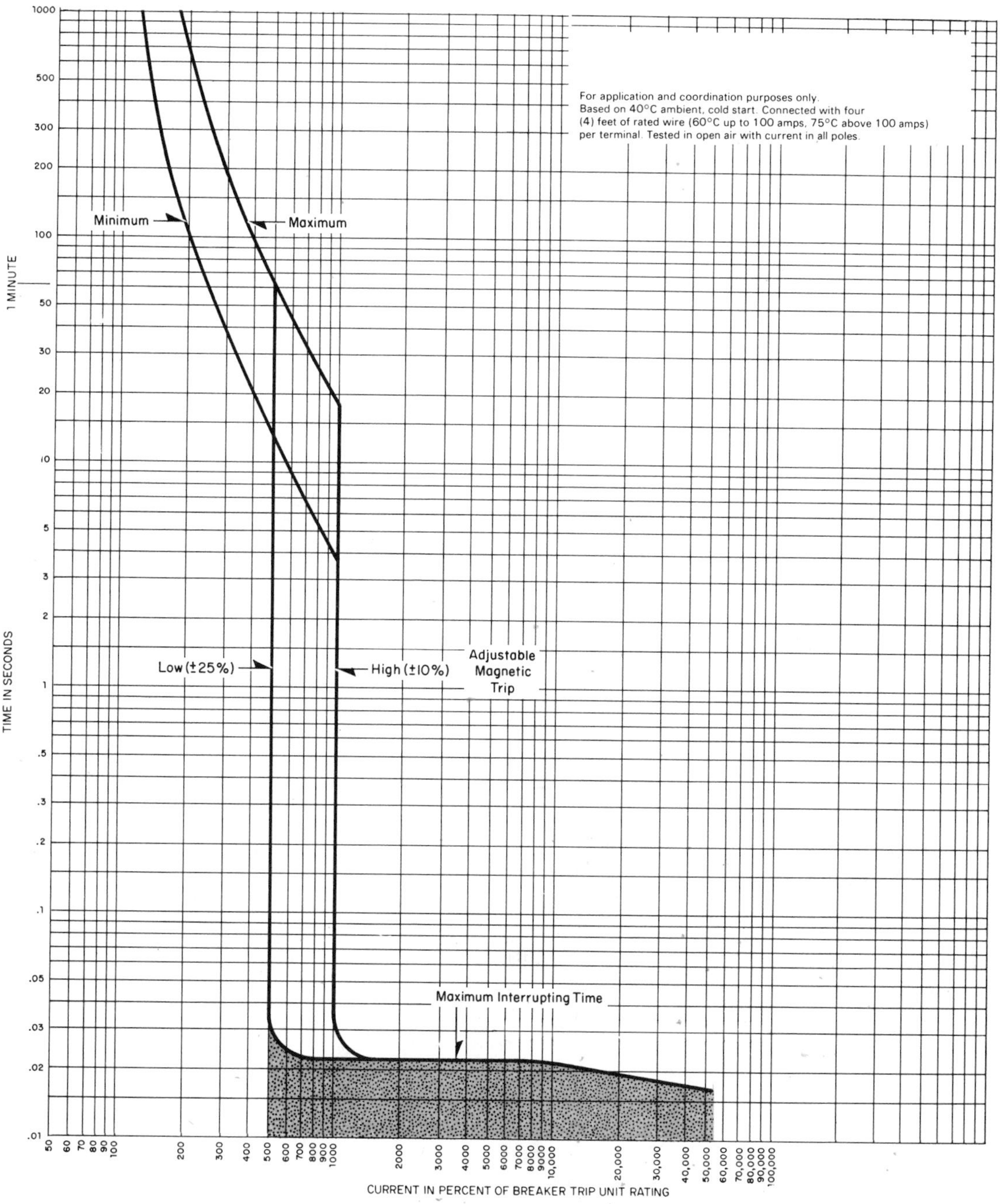

FIGURE 8.8 Typical time–current characteristic curves for molded-case breaker, 400 ampere frame, with thermal time delay and adjustable magnetic instantaneous trip unit

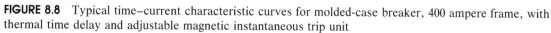

TABLE 8.1 Frame Sizes and Typical Ratings for Industrial-Type Molded-Case Circuit Breakers

Frame Size (A)	Rated Voltage (V)	Range of Trip Ratings (A)	Dimensions (in.)			Interrupting Ratings (rms symmetrical amperes)		
			W	H	D	240 V[a]	480 V[a]	600 V[a]
100 Std 100 HIC	240	15–100	$4\frac{1}{8}$	6	$3\frac{3}{8}$	10,000 65,000	— —	— —
100 Std	480	15–100	$4\frac{1}{8}$	6	$3\frac{3}{8}$	18,000	14,000	—
150 Std 150 HIC	600	15–150	$4\frac{1}{8}$	6	$3\frac{3}{8}$	18,000 65,000	14,000 25,000	14,000 18,000
225 Std 225 HIC	600	70–225	$4\frac{1}{8}$	10	$4\frac{1}{16}$	25,000 65,000	22,000 25,000	18,000 22,000
400 Std 400 HIC	600	125–400	$5\frac{1}{2}$	$10\frac{1}{8}$	$4\frac{1}{16}$	42,000 65,000	30,000 35,000	22,000 25,000
600 Std 600 HIC	600	250–600	$8\frac{1}{4}$	$10\frac{3}{4}$	$4\frac{1}{16}$	42,000 65,000	30,000 35,000	22,000 25,000
800 Std 800 HIC	600	400–800	$8\frac{1}{4}$	16	$4\frac{1}{16}$	42,000 65,000	30,000 50,000	22,000 25,000
1200 Std 1200 HIC	600	600–1200	$8\frac{1}{4}$	16	$5\frac{1}{2}$	42,000 65,000	30,000 50,000	22,000 25,000

[a] System voltage.

Std, standard duty; HIC, high interrupting capacity.

W, width (for three-pole breakers); *H*, height; *D*, depth.

100 ampere breakers are available in single, two, and three poles. Balance of breakers are available in two and three poles.

Standard trip ratings: 15, 20, 25, 30, 35, 40, 50, 60, 70, 80, 90, 100, 125, 150, 175, 200, 225, 250, 300, 350, 400, 450, 500, 600, 800, 1000, and 1200 amperes.

Manufacturers should be consulted for confirmed ratings.

cost solution to the problem of high available fault currents on 208/120 volt systems.

Note that no short-time ratings (see Section 6.6) are listed for molded-case breakers as they must be tripped instantaneously on high fault currents. Note also that the interrupting ratings increase with lower system voltages. For example, a 400 ampere, standard-duty breaker rated for 600 volts has a rating of 22,000 amperes when

FIGURE 8.9

Molded-case circuit breaker with side-mounted motor operator

used on a 600 volt system, but has a rating of 42,000 amperes when used on a 240 or 208 volt system.

The smaller-rated circuit breakers, such as shown in Figure 8.4, are completely sealed in the factory and cannot be altered in the field. Larger breakers (400 amperes and above) have a removable cover and the trip units are interchangeable. Figure 8.9 shows how a breaker can be converted to electrical operation by the addition of a motor operator. Other options, such as shunt trips, undervoltage trips, auxiliary contacts for control, or alarm circuits, can also be added. Molded-case breakers from 600 amperes up to 3000 amperes are now on the market that have solid-state trip units in place of the standard series thermal–magnetic units. The response characteristics of these solid-state units are similar to those discussed for the power circuit breakers in Section 8.5.

Molded-case circuit breakers can be mounted in separate enclosures, such as shown in Figure 8.10(a), or they can be group mounted in a panelboard, as shown in Figure 8.10(b). The panelboard may be installed separately in its own enclosure or it may be installed as part of a switchboard assembly. When these breakers are operating within their enclosures, heat accumulates due to the load currents, with the result that the ambient air temperature within the enclosure can be above normal. This added heat can affect the thermal trip unit, and the breaker may not be able to carry its rated current on a continuous basis. This matter is dealt with at more length in Section 11.8 with regard to applying breakers for overcurrent protection. Molded-case circuit breakers can also be mounted in conjunction with motor starters to form combination units, as shown in Figure 14.3(b). The application of breakers for the overcurrent protection of motor circuits is covered in Section 13.1.1 and Example 13.3.

There is a class of molded-case breakers labeled *light duty,* although this is not an industry recognized term. These small breakers are used in lighting panels and residential-type load centers. They are available in single pole up to 70 amperes at 120 volts, in two- and three-pole up to 100 amperes at 240 volts, and in single pole up to 30 amperes at 277 volts. These breakers normally have interrupting ratings of only 10,000 amperes symmetrical. However, some manufacturers offer this type of breaker with interrupting ratings of 22,000 amperes. The application of these light-duty breakers in lighting panels is covered in Sections 12.4 and 12.5.

8.4.4 UL Test Requirements

The following are a few of the many requirements of the Underwriters Laboratories, Inc., when they test molded-case circuit breakers for approval.

(a) Individually mounted in separate enclosure

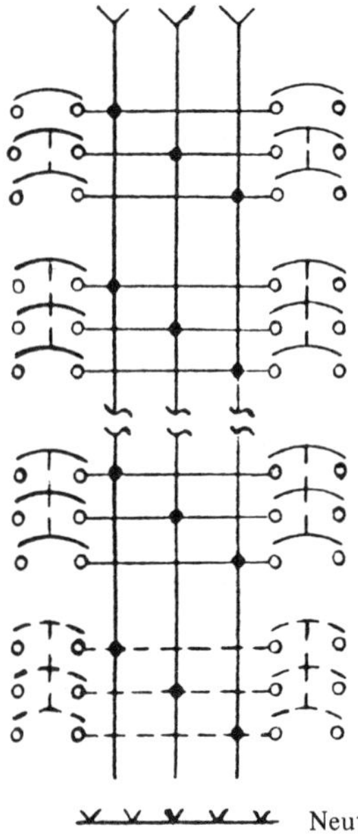

*On three-phase, four-wire systems only (i.e., 208Y/120 volt)

(b) Group mounted in a panelboard

FIGURE 8.10

Mounting of molded-case circuit breakers

Each type of breaker first undergoes a calibration test to ensure that it provides proper overload protection. Maximum clearing times at 135% and 200% of the rated current of the trip unit are checked. These clearing times are similar to those listed in Table 7.1 for fuses. For example, a breaker with a 100 ampere trip unit must clear the circuit in a maximum of 120 minutes at 135% and 6 minutes at 200% of rated current.

To ensure that the breaker is suitable for use as a motor disconnecting means (see Section 13.2.2), it is tested at 600% of its normal current at rated voltage. Depending on the size, it must successfully open the circuit a specified number of times. For example, a 400 ampere breaker must safely interrupt 2400 amperes 50 times. The breaker is continuously loaded at its rated current in an ambient temperature of 25°C and checked for temperature rises, which must not exceed specified limits. An endurance test ensures that the breaker can successfully open and close a minimum number of times. For example, a 225 ampere breaker must operate a minimum of 8000 times at a rate of five operations per minute, with half the operations being made with rated current flowing.

The breaker must pass a short-circuit test to confirm its interrupting rating. With the breaker closed, it must first successfully interrupt its rated fault current. Then, after 2 minutes, the breaker is closed in on this fault current and again must successfully interrupt the current, all at the specified voltages.

The final test is the dielectric withstand test to check the insulation level of the breaker. A 60 hertz voltage equal to twice the rated voltage of the breaker plus 1000 is applied to the breaker for 1 minute. For example, the voltage applied to a 600 volt rated breaker is 2200 volts.

The foregoing is only a brief listing of the test requirements. The complete sequence of tests for molded-case circuit breakers is covered in UL Standard 489.

8.5 LOW-VOLTAGE POWER CIRCUIT BREAKERS

Low-voltage power circuit breakers are more rugged and more flexible and generally have higher ratings than the molded-case circuit breakers. The designation *power circuit breaker* was adopted after the introduction of the molded-case breaker to differentiate between the two types. The term unfortunately does not adequately describe these breakers, as all breakers in reality are power breakers in that they make and break power circuits. The term *power* presumably was chosen since these breakers can be used to handle large blocks of power, up to 4000 amperes at 600 volts, three-phase, whereas the molded-case breakers originally could only handle loads up to 600 amperes. The National Electrical Manufacturers Association defines the *low-voltage power circuit breaker* as *one for use on circuits rated 1000 volts alternating current and below, or 3000 volts direct current and below, but not including molded-case breakers.*

The power circuit breaker has an open-type heavy steel frame upon which the components are mounted, making them more readily accessible. These breakers tend to be heavier, larger, and more costly than molded-case breakers. Fixed breakers are available for mounting in individual enclosures but generally the breakers are of the drawout type for mounting in metal-enclosed switchboards as shown in Figure 8.11. Figure 8.11(a) shows the breaker in its fully engaged position (with the cubicle door open). Figure 8.11(b) shows the breaker in its drawout position. The breaker is moved into and out of its cubicle by means of a crank. Figure 8.12 is a rear view of the breaker itself, showing the disconnecting contacts at the rear by which the breaker is electrically connected or disconnected from the fixed plug-in contacts within the switchboard cubicle. These contacts cannot be used to make or break the load current as the breaker must be in the open position before it can be moved into or out of the cubicle. The drawout feature allows maintenance to be done on the breaker with complete safety, as it is fully disengaged from the live electrical connections in the switchboard. It also allows for the quick replacement of a faulty breaker. Figure 8.11(b) also shows the arc chutes mounted above the breaker contact mechanism [see Figure 8.1(b)]. Section 8.1 outlines the use of arcing contacts and arc chutes.

The breakers are closed using the two-step, stored-energy spring mechanism. Manual operation is accomplished by first compressing a heavy spring using the operating handle as shown in Figure 8.11(b). With the closing spring compressed, the breaker can be closed at any time by pushing the close button mounted on the breaker faceplate, which mechanically releases the spring. Electrical operation uses an electric gear motor to compress the spring.

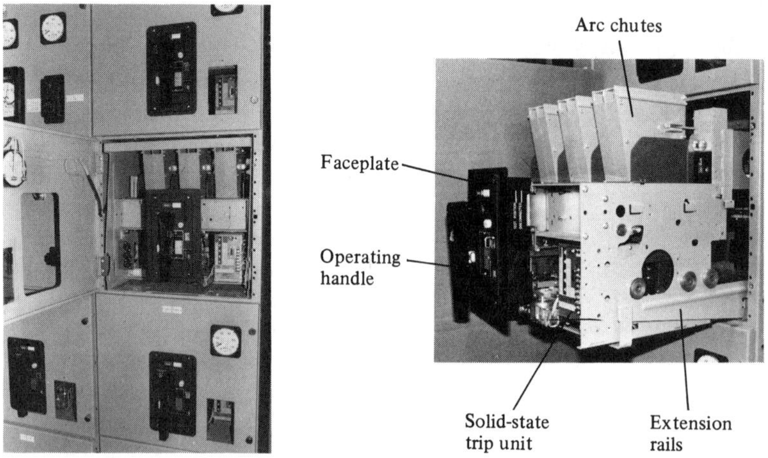

FIGURE 8.11

Drawout-type, low-voltage power circuit breakers

(a) Breaker fully inserted into its enclosure

(b) Breaker in its fully withdrawn position

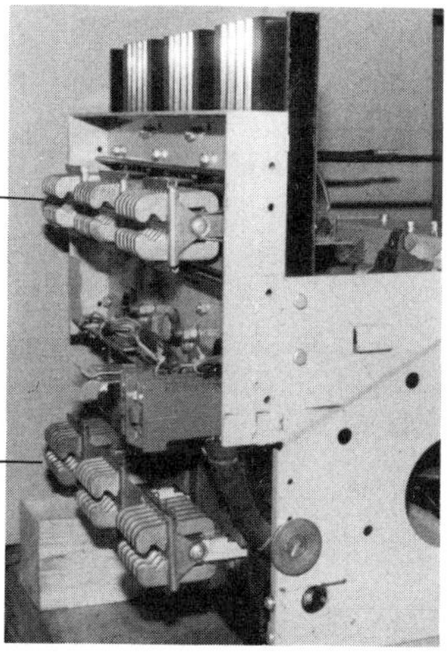

FIGURE 8.12

Rear view of drawout power circuit breaker

The breaker is then closed by electrically activating a small close solenoid, which releases the closing spring. The breakers are opened manually by pressing the separate trip button mounted on the breaker faceplate, which mechanically unlatches the breaker, allowing the opening springs to rapidly force the main contacts apart. The breakers are opened electrically by energizing a shunt trip coil from a remote push button, which then similarly unlatches the breaker contacts. Refer to Section 8.2 for an introductory discussion on the operation of breakers. The breakers can have optional undervoltage trip units and auxiliary control contacts for external alarm circuits and remote indicating lights.

8.5.1 Solid-State Trip Units

The trip units used with power circuit breakers are today almost universally of the solid-state type. These units have replaced the mechanical dual-magnetic trip units that were the standard for many years. The dual-magnetic type provides inverse time delay in the overload region by means of a dashpot mechanism that controls the rate of movement and thus the timing of the mechanism. On large fault currents, the magnetic force becomes great enough to bypass the restraining force of the dashpot and the breaker is tripped instantaneously. Calibration is provided by adjusting the tension of the springs that oppose the movement of the tripping elements. The solid-state trip units can easily duplicate these time–current characteristics, but, in addition, can provide more flexibility in the range of adjustments and more accuracy in their setting.

As shown in Figure 8.3(b), solid-state tripping requires three basic components: (1) the current transformers (or sensors as they are usually called), (2) the solid-state unit itself, and (3) a separate shunt trip mechanism. The sensors are connected into each pole of the breaker on the loadside of the main contacts. The sensors produce an output current that is proportional to the load current. This reduced current is fed into the solid-state detector circuits that monitor the current and, based on the preset response characteristics, initiate an output to the shunt trip to open the breaker. The shunt trip (or actuator) is a special design requiring very little power to activate it and mechanically unlatch the breaker. All necessary tripping energy is derived from the output current from the sensors. Thus the automatic tripping system is self-contained, requiring no separate source of power.

Seven different settings are available on the typical solid-state unit:

1. Long-delay pickup
2. Long delay time
3. Short-delay pickup
4. Short delay time
5. Instantaneous pickup
6. Ground pickup
7. Ground delay time

Figure 8.13 shows the typical time–current characteristic curves, together with the ranges of adjustments available for each setting. The term *pickup means the magnitude of the current at which the detector circuit timing function begins*. Note that the pickup settings on the adjustment dials are in multiples of the sensor rating. Thus the actual pickup points in amperes depends on the ampere rating of the sensors. For example, if the sensors are rated at 800 amperes and the long delay is set at 1.0, then the long-delay pickup point is at a load current of 800 amperes. If the sensors are rated at 1200 amperes and the long delay is set at 0.7, then the long-delay pickup is 1200 times 0.7 or 840 amperes. Many sensor ratings are available for each frame size as shown in Table 8.2, which, together with the adjustments on the dials, gives an almost unlimited range of actual pickup currents.

As with any manufactured device, there must be a tolerance allowance on the operation of the solid-state trip units. As noted in Figure 8.13, this tolerance is ±10 percent with regard to the current pickup values. The resulting band of operation is shown by the hatched area. Note that the minimum calibration band curve shows the response curve with the long-time and short-time adjustments set at their minimum values, and the maximum calibration band curve shows the response curve with these adjustments set at their maximum. The actual operating curve for any particular breaker can

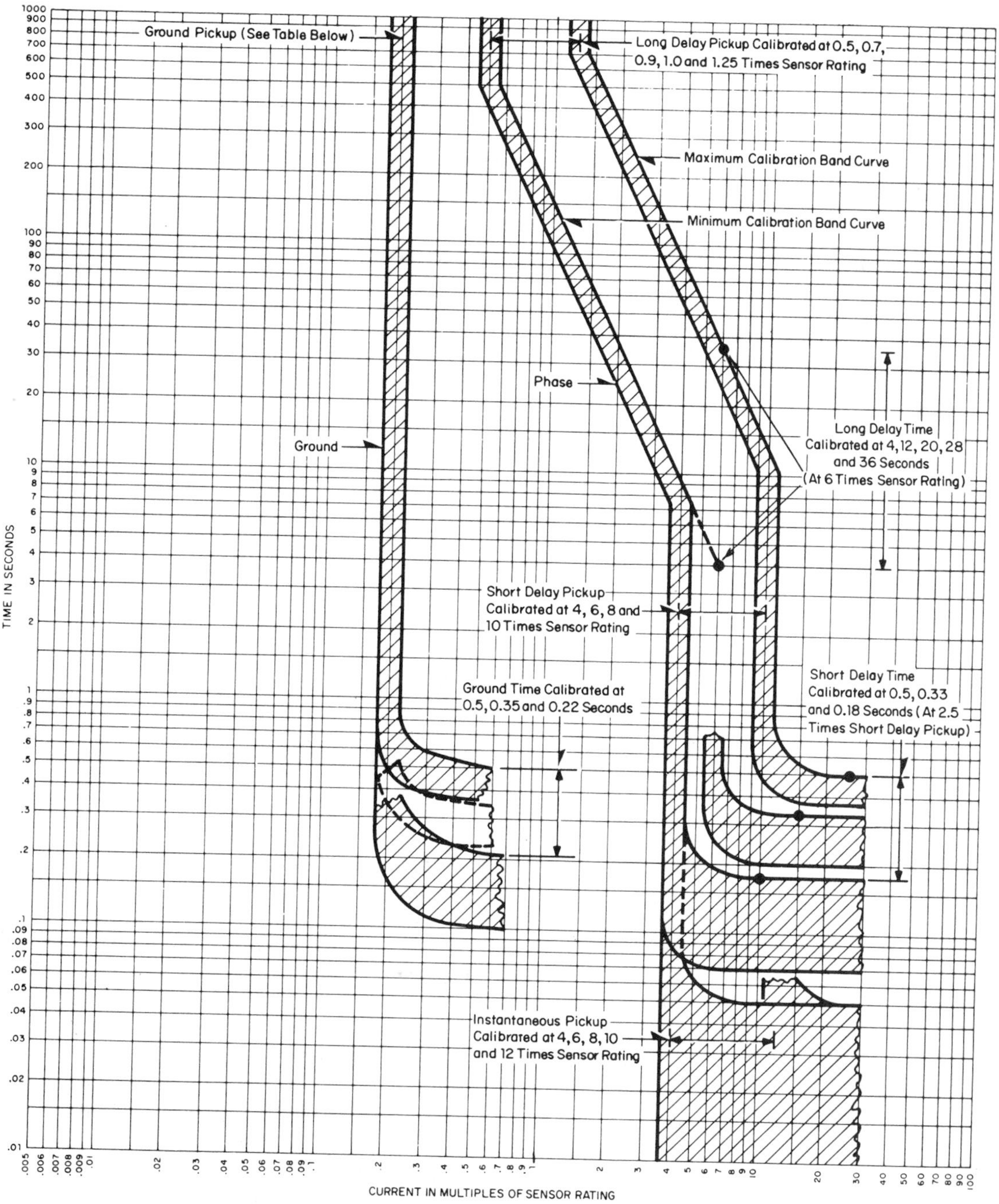

Ground Pick-Up Value—Amperes

Dial Setting	Sensor Rating 50	100	150	200	300	400	600	800	1200	1600	2000	2400	3200	4000
A	13	57	60	65	80	110	145	180	260	330	400	530	640	800
B	18	67	75	85	110	150	205	260	385	505	600	770	1000	1200
C	22	75	85	100	130	185	250	325	480	625	760	960	1200	N.A.
D	33	100	120	145	200	270	385	500	730	970	1200	N.A.	N.A.	N.A.

All pick-up values may vary ±10%

FIGURE 8.13 Typical time–current characteristic curves for power circuit breaker with solid-state trip unit

TABLE 8.2 Frame Sizes and Typical Ratings for Low-Voltage Power Circuit Breakers

Frame Size (A)	Range of Trip Ratings (A)	Interrupting Ratings with Instantaneous Trips (rms symmetrical amperes)			Short-time Ratings, 0.5 Second (30 cycle) Delay (rms symmetrical amperes)		
		208/240 V[a]	480 V[a]	600 V[a]	240 V[a]	480 V[a]	600 V[a]
600[b]	50–600	42,000	30,000	30,000	30,000	30,000	30,000
800	50–800	42,000	30,000	30,000	30,000	30,000	30,000
1600[b]	50–1600	65,000	50,000	42,000	50,000	50,000	42,000
2000	50–2000	65,000	50,000	50,000	50,000	50,000	50,000
3000[c]	1200–3000	85,000	65,000	65,000	65,000	65,000	65,000
4000	1600–4000	130,000	85,000	85,000	85,000	85,000	85,000

[a] System voltage.

[b] The 600 and 1600 ampere frames may not be offered by all manufacturers.

[c] Some manufacturers offer a 3200 ampere frame.

All breakers are rated for 600 volts.

Interrupting ratings are based on an X/R ratio of 6.6 (see Section 8.3.3).

Trip ratings are determined by the rating of the sensors. Typical ratings of sensors are 50, 100, 150, 200, 300, 400, 600, 800, 1200, 1600, 2000, 2400, 3000 (3200), and 4000 amperes.

Manufacturers should be consulted for confirmed ratings.

be set to follow any line between these two extremes. The operation of the ground fault pickup is discussed in Section 10.5 and shown in Figures 10.16(b) and 10.18. A complete example showing the selection of all the settings on a breaker with solid-state trip units is shown in Section 16.5.

8.5.2 Frame Sizes and Ratings

The frame sizes for the low-voltage power circuit breakers were for many years standardized on the following ratings: 225, 600, 1600, 3000, and 4000 amperes. However, these standards have undergone changes in recent years. The 225 ampere frame is no longer offered by manufacturers. Some manufacturers offer an 800 ampere frame, either in addition to or in place of the 600 ampere frame. Similarly, some manufacturers offer a 2000 ampere frame, either in addition to or in place of the 1600 ampere frame. Finally, in place of the 3000 ampere frame, at least one manufacturer offers a 3200 ampere frame. Table 8.2 lists the frame sizes of low-voltage power circuit breakers, together with their ratings and range of trip ratings. All power circuit breakers are rated for 600 volts.

Since power circuit breakers can have short-time delayed tripping (see Section 8.3.3), short-time ratings are also included in the table. The short-time delayed tripping is usually selected for a line-side breaker so that the loadside devices can operate first to clear the faults (see Section 8.6 on coordination). This time delay substantially increases the thermal stressing on the breaker (see Section 6.2). The short-time rating indicates that the breaker can withstand the thermal stresses associated with the listed current for a period of 0.5 second (30 cycles) and then interrupt this current. Note that, with instantaneous tripping, the interrupting ratings increase substantially as the system voltage decreases, whereas the short-time ratings are largely unchanged with the lower system voltages.

The majority of the power circuit breakers are UL listed for application at 100% of their designated current ratings when mounted in suitable enclosures. This eliminates the need for oversizing the breakers and cables for continuous loads (see Section 11.8). Section 15.4 details the selection of low-voltage power breakers with regard to their ratings and their physical arrangement in a switchboard.

8.5.3 Test Requirements

The testing of low-voltage power circuit breakers is done in accordance with the American National Standards Institute requirements. Many of the tests are similar to those covered in Section 8.4.4 for molded-case breakers. The breakers must successfully pass the calibration tests, the temperature rise test, the endurance test, the short-circuit tests, and the dielectric withstand tests. Each breaker is tested while mounted in its normal enclosure. In addition, a power breaker is subjected to the momentary test to confirm its short-time rating. For this test, the overcurrent trips on the breaker are made inactive. The breaker is closed and is then subjected to a current equal to its short-time rating for a period of 0.5 second (30 cycles). This current is stopped for a period of 15 seconds and then repeated for another 0.5 second period. After this duty cycle, the trip units are reactivated and the breaker is subjected to a final interrupting capacity test at 635 volts. The breaker is forced to open at the instant that the power is applied to ensure that the breaker can also interrupt the offset or asymmetrical current that is associated with the first few cycles of a fault (see Figure 6.4). The breaker calibration is again checked, and finally it is subjected to the dielectric withstand test of 2200 volts for 1 minute.

The full sequence of tests for the power circuit breakers is covered by ANSI test standard 37.50. UL test standards, which are expected to follow the ANSI standards, are in the process of being developed.

8.6 COORDINATION OF CIRCUIT BREAKERS

The coordination of protective devices in an electrical system is first mentioned in the Introduction to Chapter 6 and again in Section 7.7 with regard to the application of fuses. Similarly, it is equally important to achieve coordination of the system protection when using circuit breakers.

First, let us look at the application of molded-case circuit breakers to system protection, such as the example shown in Figure 8.14. The breaker protecting the feeder to a group of branch circuits has a 400 ampere frame with a 300 ampere trip unit (designated the lineside breaker since it is closest to the source). The breaker protecting one of the branch circuits has a 150 ampere frame with a 100 ampere trip unit (designated the loadside breaker). With a fault at point *A*, it is desirable that the loadside breaker trip first and completely clear its circuit before the lineside breaker has a chance to trip, and shut down the balance of the circuits. This should ideally happen for all levels of overcurrent up to the maximum short-circuit current available at point *A*.

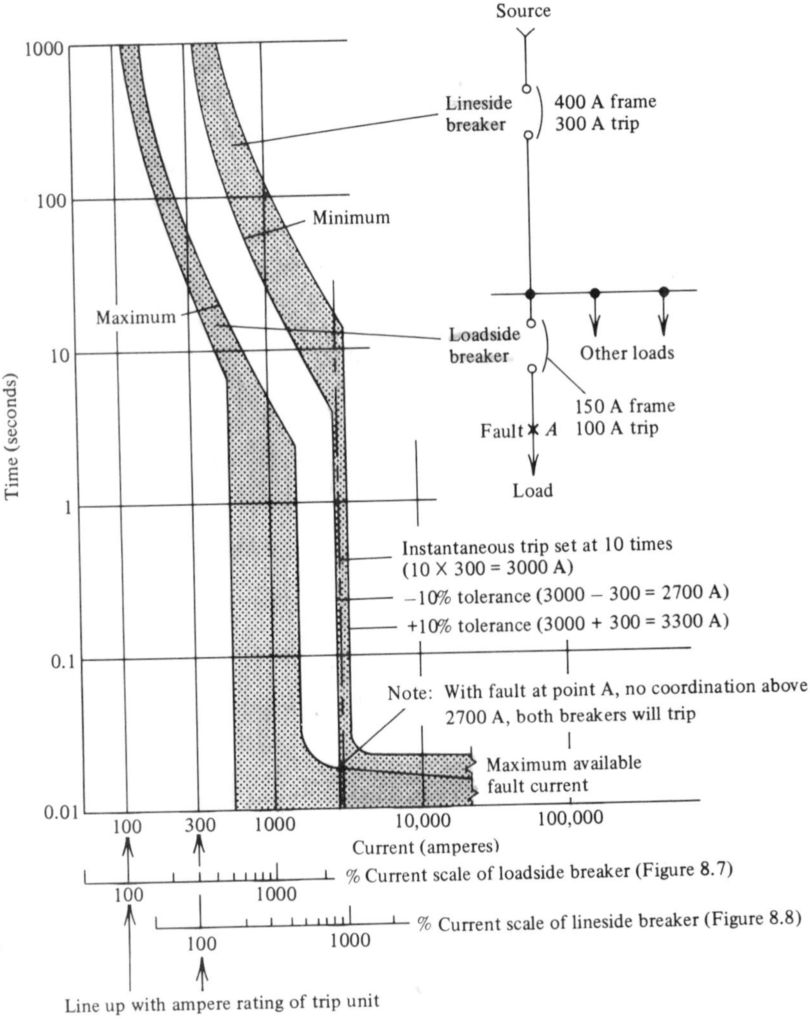

FIGURE 8.14

Coordination study for molded-case breakers

To check the complete coordination between the two breakers, it is necessary to copy the time–current characteristic curves for each onto a common graph referred to as an overlay. The preparation of overlays is discussed in greater detail in Section 16.4. Figure 8.14 shows the overlay for this example. The curves for the loadside breaker are copied from Figure 8.7 and those for the lineside breaker from Figure 8.8. The horizontal scale of the overlay must be in amperes so that the two sets of curves can be directly compared. To properly align the loadside breaker curves, the 100% line of Figure 8.7 must be lined up on the overlay with the 100 ampere line (with the breaker trip rating). Similarly, to align the curves for the lineside breaker, the 100% line of Figure 8.8 must be lined up with the 300 ampere line (with the breaker trip rating). In addition, since the lineside breaker has an adjustable magnetic trip, its setting must be selected and the resulting minimum and maximum instantaneous tripping lines properly drawn. It makes sense here to set the magnetic trip adjustment as high as possible (at 10 times) to obtain as much separation as possible between the two breaker curves. Thus, with a 300 ampere rated trip unit, the instantaneous trip will pick up at 3000 amperes subject to the tolerance allowance, which, as shown in Figure 8.8, is ±10% when the adjustment is set at the maximum. Thus the breaker could be tripped instantaneously on a current as low as 2700 amperes or as high as 3300 amperes. After the overlay of the two breaker curves has been completed, the extent of the coordination between the breakers is evident. With a fault at point A, on any current up to 2700 amperes, the loadside breaker can easily totally clear the circuit (as represented by its maximum line) before the lineside breaker reaches the point at which it could begin to trip (as represented by its minimum line). However, at currents above 2700 amperes, there is the possibility that the lineside breaker will be tripped instantaneously at the same time that the loadside breaker is opening to clear the fault. At currents above 3300 amperes, both breakers will definitely be tripped. Thus coordination is lost, because power is interrupted to all the branch circuit loads and not just the faulted circuit.

The fact that molded-case circuit breakers must be tripped instantaneously means that complete coordination cannot be obtained at the higher levels of fault current. This is a decided disadvantage against the application of these breakers for the overcurrent protection of feeders.

Next, let us consider the application of low-voltage power circuit breakers to system protection. Refer to the time–current characteristic curves for this type of breaker, as shown in Figure 8.13. As indicated on the graph and as discussed in Section 8.5.1, these breakers can be delayed from tripping in the short-time area (that is, with large faults), and coordination over the full range of possible fault currents is obtainable. For example, the loadside breaker can be set to trip instantaneously, and the lineside breaker can be set so that it will not trip for 0.18 second in the short-time region. Thus the loadside breaker has time to fully clear any faults that occur on the circuit that it is protecting before the lineside breaker has reached its tripping point. Refer to Section 16.5, which shows a complete coordination study of a system that in part uses the power circuit breakers for protection.

8.7 COMBINATION FUSED CIRCUIT BREAKERS

As the capacity of low-voltage electrical systems increased over the years, the interrupting capacities of circuit breakers became a limiting factor in their application to system protection. The development of low-voltage, current-limiting fuses that can be applied to systems with up to 200,000 amperes of available fault current offered a low-cost alternative to the use of circuit breakers. In addition, the fuses provide current limitation, which is a decided advantage in protecting systems from damage under fault conditions.

The solution, therefore, lay in combining the advantages of the circuit breaker with those of the current-limiting fuse. Figure 8.15(a) shows an example of a fused molded-case circuit breaker. The fuses are mounted in an extension to the standard molded enclosure and are available through a removable cover. Combination fused power circuit breakers are also available. The fuses are mounted on the lineside terminals at the rear of the breaker as shown in Figure 8.15(b) and are accessible by fully withdrawing the breaker from its enclosure. These breakers are listed with interrupting ratings of 200,000 rms symmetrical amperes.

The rating and characteristics of the fuse are chosen to properly coordinate with the circuit breaker characteristics so that the fuses do not take over and blow until the fault current is in excess of 80% of the interrupting capacity of the breaker. This coordination is shown in Figure 8.16. In this way, the breaker clears the circuit on all overloads and low-level fault currents, and the fuses only blow on the rare occurrence of high-level short circuits. When the fuses do blow, the peak let-through current and the thermal energy let-through (I^2t) are materially reduced, as discussed in Section 7.3 and shown in Figure 7.4. However, it should be noted that this current limitation does not take over until a much higher level of current than if fuses, rated to match the full-load current of the circuit, were used alone. Since the fuses used with the breakers function only to interrupt and current limit at the high current levels and do not themselves operate on overloads, they are often referred to as current *limiters* rather than fuses.

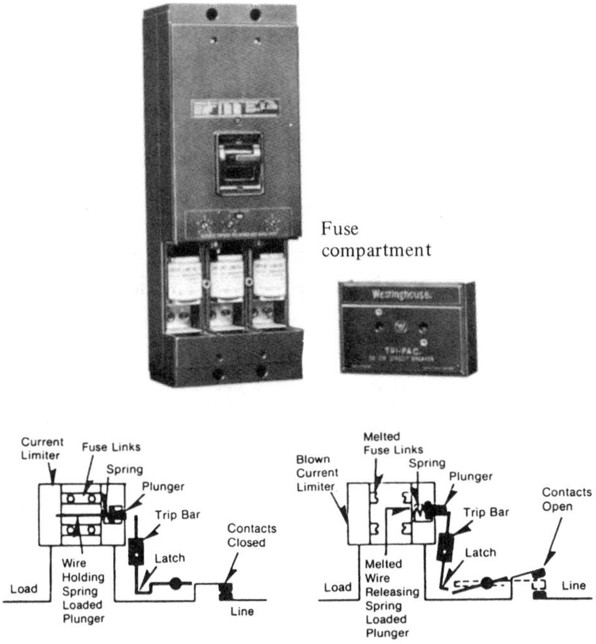

Method of preventing single phasing when one fuse blows.

(a) **Fused molded-case circuit breaker**

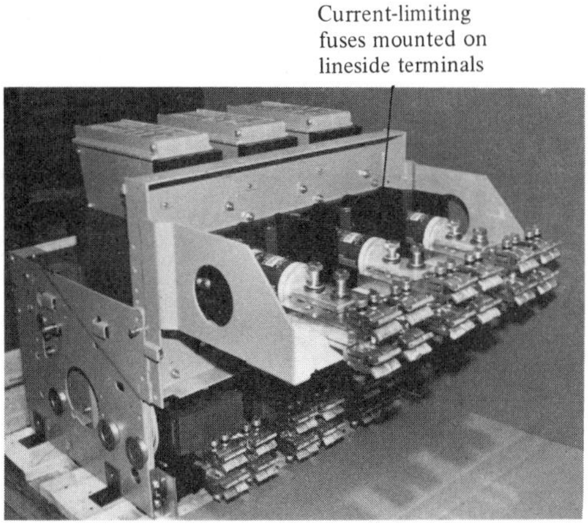

(b) **Fused power circuit breaker**

FIGURE 8.15 Low-voltage combination fused circuit breakers

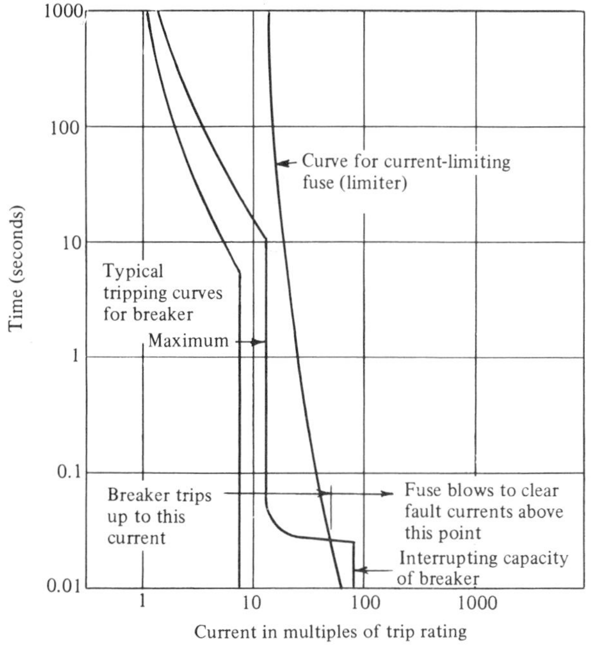

FIGURE 8.16

Curves showing typical coordination between breaker and fuse for combination fusible circuit breaker

To prevent single phasing of the feeder or circuit being protected by the fused breaker in the event that only one fuse blows, the units incorporate a method of automatically tripping the breaker should this occur. For the molded-case breakers, a plunger in the fuse (current limiter) is released when it blows, as shown in Figure 8.15(a). The movement of the plunger hitting the trip bar then opens the breaker. For the power circuit breakers, the primaries of small auxiliary transformers are connected in parallel across the terminals of each fuse. As long as the fuses are intact, no voltage is applied to the transformers. However, when a fuse blows and opens the circuit, the resulting voltage across the fuse terminals energizes the transformer, which picks up a solenoid, which in turn mechanically trips the breaker. The breakers do not have to interrupt currents beyond their rating as the fuse(s) will have cleared any faulted phase of the circuit. The breakers cannot be closed until unblown fuses are properly inserted into each pole of the breaker.

8.8 LOW-VOLTAGE ENCASED CIRCUIT BREAKERS

Not only has the distinction between molded-case and power circuit breakers been lessened by the development of larger frame molded-case breakers with solid-state trip units, but now at least two manufacturers offer a line of circuit breakers that incorporate features of both types. These new breakers are molded-case in that they have outer cases that are molded from strong, glass-reinforced plastic. However, their operating principles and range of options are similar to those of the power circuit breakers. They are variously being referred to as *encased* circuit breakers or even as *hybrid* circuit breakers. An example of this new type of breaker is shown in Figure 8.17.

Table 8.3 shows frame sizes and typical ratings for the encased circuit breakers as offered by one manufacturer. Frame sizes range from 250 up to 5000 amperes. There are three classifications of interrupting capacities: special, standard, and high. Thus this new type of breaker offers a wide range of ratings, with interrupting capacities ranging up to 200,000 rms symmetrical amperes at 240 volts. However, a comparison of the short-time ratings show that those for the encased breaker are generally lower than those for the power circuit breaker with comparable frame sizes. Also, the maximum duration of the delayed tripping can only be 0.3 second (18 cycles), instead of the 0.5 second (30 cycle) delay permitted for the power circuit breakers.

Subject to the lower short-time ratings, the encased breakers can be used in many applications formerly requiring power circuit breakers with savings in both cost and space. The encased breakers are very compact, as indicated by the dimensions shown in Figure

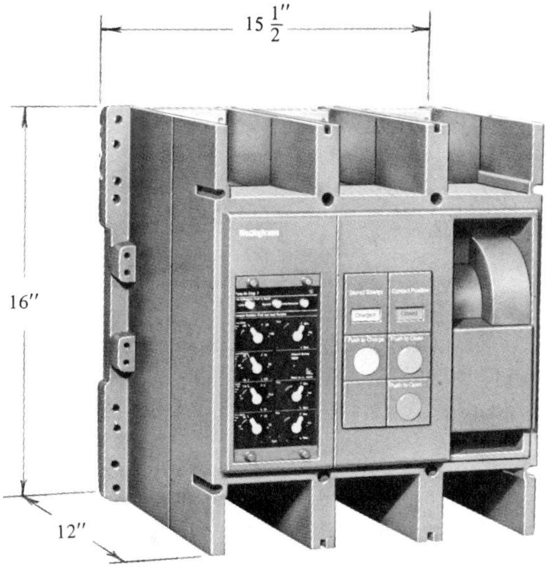

FIGURE 8.17

The new encased type of circuit breaker

TABLE 8.3 Frame Sizes and Typical Ratings for Low-Voltage Encased Circuit Breakers

	Frame Sizes (A)	Interrupting Ratings with Instantaneous Trips (rms symmetrical amperes) 240 V[a]	480 V[a]	600 V[a]	Short-Time Ratings, 0.3 Second Delay (rms symmetrical amperes)
Special interrupting capacity	250, 800	65,000	50,000	42,000	25,000
	1200	85,000	65,000	42,000	35,000
	1600, 2000	85,000	65,000	50,000	35,000
Standard interrupting capacity	250, 800	100,000	100,000	50,000	25,000
	1200	100,000	100,000	50,000	35,000
	1600, 2000, 2500, 3000	100,000	100,000	85,000	35,000
	4000, 5000	100,000	100,000	85,000	65,000
High interrupting capacity	250, 800	200,000	150,000	100,000	25,000
	1200	200,000	150,000	100,000	35,000
	1600, 2000, 2500, 3000	200,000	150,000	100,000	51,000
	4000, 5000	200,000	150,000	100,000	85,000

[a] System voltage.

All breakers are rated for 600 volts.

Interrupting ratings are based on an X/R ratio of 6.6 (see Section 8.3.3).

Trip ratings are similar to those listed in Table 8.2.

Manufacturers should be consulted for confirmed ratings.

8.17 for the 1600 ampere frame. They are available with drawout mechanisms for mounting in switchboards. In a typical 90 inch high switchboard, six 800 ampere drawout breakers can be mounted in one vertical section, or four 1600 ampere breakers or two 3000 ampere breakers, which can mean a reduction in the overall size of the switchboard. For a comparison with a switchboard layout using power circuit breakers, see Sections 15.4 and 15.5.

The encased circuit breakers have built-in, solid-state trip systems similar to those discussed for the power circuit breakers. As a further option, a tripping system incorporating a microprocessor rather than the conventional analog electronic circuitry is available. The use of the microprocessor allows the trip unit to perform a number of functions much better and provides a wider range of adjustments to the breaker response curve with a greater degree of accuracy. It can also indicate the cause of the tripping (overload, short circuit, or ground fault) and provide a digital readout of the magnitude of the fault current that caused the breaker to trip. See Section 16.5 for a coordination study using breakers with the conventional solid-state trip units.

The encased breakers have the two-step, stored-energy closing mechanism with the option of electrical operation, similar to the power circuit breakers. They have a full line of accessories, such as shunt trips for remote operation, undervoltage release, and auxiliary contacts for indicating lights, alarm circuits, and interlocking. They are UL listed for application at 100% of their designated frame ratings when mounted in suitable enclosures, which eliminates the need for oversizing breakers and cables for continuous loads (see Section 11.8).

8.9 CURRENT-LIMITING CIRCUIT BREAKERS

The standard breaker is not able to provide any current limitation when clearing a fault from the system. The inertia of the moving parts of the breaker means that the contacts, when operated just by the force from springs, cannot separate fast enough to extinguish the arc before the fault current has passed through its first instantaneous peak current at one half-cycle (see Figure 6.4). The development of the fused circuit breaker as discussed in Section 8.7 was a partial answer to the problem, but the use of fuses brings the disadvantage of having to replace them after operation, requiring spare fuses to be stocked.

However, two domestic manufacturers and at least one European manufacturer have recently developed true molded-case, current-limiting breakers that do not require fuses. One method of providing the extremely fast contact separation required for current limitation uses the slot motor principle, as shown in Figure 8.18. The

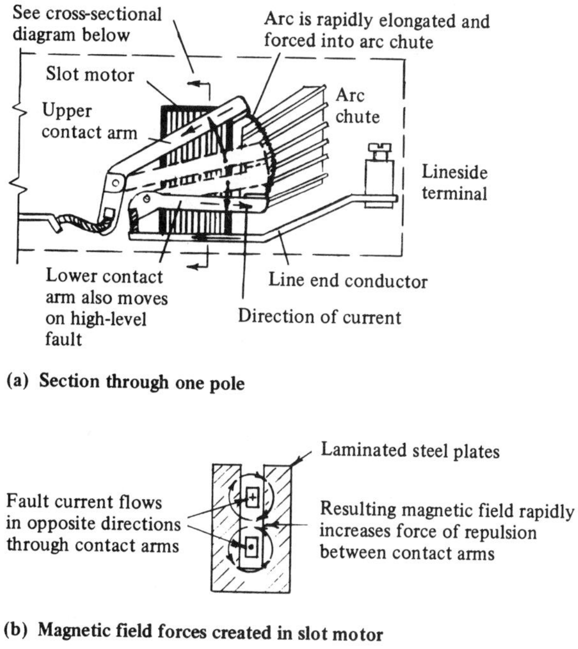
See cross-sectional diagram below
Arc is rapidly elongated and forced into arc chute
Slot motor
Upper contact arm
Arc chute
Lineside terminal
Lower contact arm also moves on high-level fault
Line end conductor
Direction of current
(a) Section through one pole
Laminated steel plates
Fault current flows in opposite directions through contact arms
Resulting magnetic field rapidly increases force of repulsion between contact arms
(b) Magnetic field forces created in slot motor

FIGURE 8.18

Operation of current-limiting circuit breaker

slot motor is a U-shaped block of laminated steel plates. The upper and lower contact arms rest within this slot motor, arranged so that in the closed position they are parallel with each other. On overloads and low-level faults where current limitation is not required, the breaker is tripped normally and the upper contact only moves to open the circuit. However, when a high-level fault occurs, the large current traveling in opposite directions through the contact arms creates a tremendous repulsion force that drives the contacts apart. The slot motor greatly enhances the strength of the magnetic field created by the current flow, which in turn increases this repulsion force. The force increases exponentially with the current. A fault current of 14,000 amperes develops a force some 17 times that produced by a current of 2000 amperes. This increased force is great enough to also move the lower contact, which increases the rate at which the contacts separate. The rapid elongation of the arc increases its resistance, which in itself provides a degree of current limitation. The elongated arc also breaks up faster when driven into the arc chute. On large fault currents, the contacts are driven apart so fast that the arc is extinguished before the first instantaneous peak current has been reached, thus reducing the peak let-through current and the thermal energy let-through values, similar to current-limiting fuses (see Section 7.3 and Figure 7.4). On 240 volt systems, the current-limiting ability of these slot motor breakers approaches that of class RK-1 fuses.

These new molded-case, current-limiting breakers are at present available in frame sizes of 100, 250, and 400 amperes, with interrupting ratings of 150,000 amperes at 480 volts and 200,000 amperes at 240 volts. Future developments are sure to expand the available types and ratings of these current-limiting breakers.

8.10 MEDIUM-VOLTAGE CIRCUIT BREAKERS

Medium-voltage circuit breakers are available in a wide variety of designs. They are primarily identified by the medium in which the main contacts interrupt the circuit: air, air blast, oil, or gas (SF_6). See Section 8.1 for a brief outline of the air blast, oil, and gas breakers. As discussed, these types of circuit breakers are relatively expensive and require extra facilities, such as complicated pressure equipment, fireproof vaults, or gas-tight enclosures. They are therefore primarily used on large power substations.

The air circuit breaker has long been the standard for industrial and commercial installations where power is received and/or distributed at voltages up to 15 kilovolts. Figure 8.19 shows a typical medium-voltage air circuit breaker, together with the type of metal-clad switchgear used to house the breakers. The medium-voltage air circuit breaker is basically an enlargement of the low-voltage power circuit breaker. They are naturally bulkier units, partly because of the larger insulators required for the higher voltages, but mostly because of the very large arc chutes required to handle the tremendous energy in the arcs during circuit interruption. Figure 8.19(a) shows the relative size of the arc chutes, which are the largest components of the breaker. These breakers are often referred to as magnetic air circuit breakers because of the importance of the magnetic field that drives the arc up into the arc chute. A blow-out coil is added to the center of the arc chute. During the circuit interruption, the arc current flows in series through this coil, materially increasing the magnetic field and thus rapidly forcing the arc further into the arc chute. Section 8.1 outlines the use of arcing contacts and arc chutes. Because of the higher inertia of the moving parts and the greater difficulty in extinguishing the arc at the higher voltages, the total time to fully interrupt the circuit can be as much as 5 cycles.

The breakers are mounted on wheels to permit them to be easily moved into and out of their switchgear cubicle [Figure 8.19(b)]. There are disconnecting contacts at the rear of the breaker by which electrical connections are made to the fixed plug-in contacts within the cubicle. The closing mechanism is the two-step, stored-energy, spring-powered type similar to that described for the low-voltage

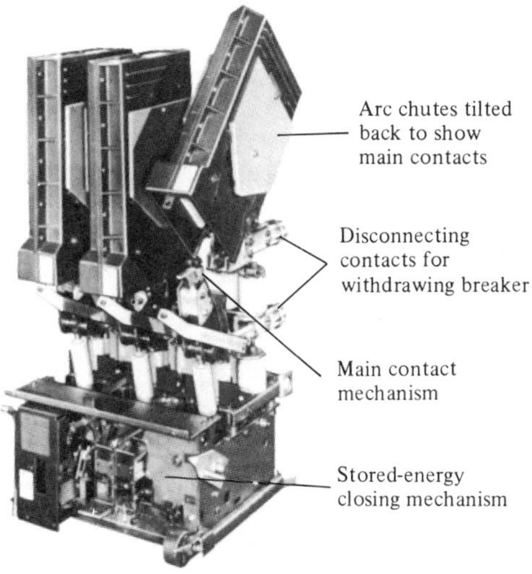

(a) Breaker shown with protective barriers removed

(b) Breaker being withdrawn from its cell

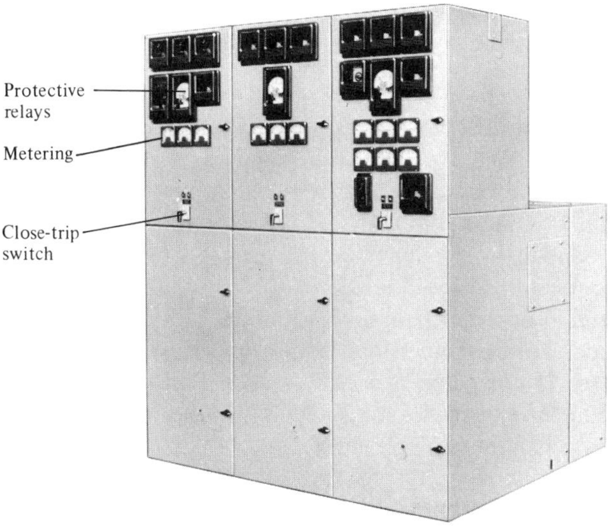

(c) Typical metalclad switchgear

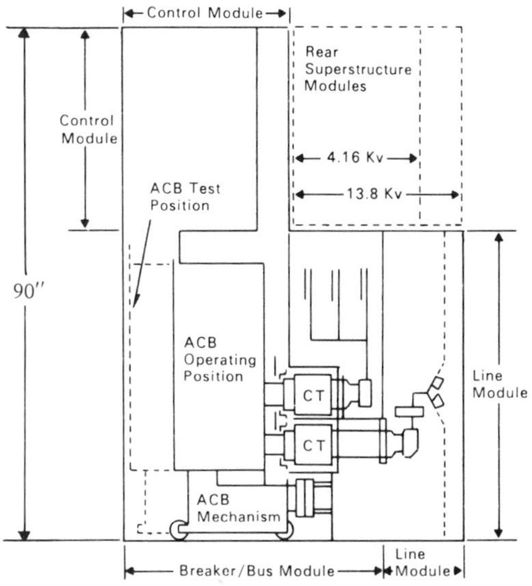

(d) Section through one breaker cell

FIGURE 8.19

Medium-voltage air circuit breaker and switchgear assembly

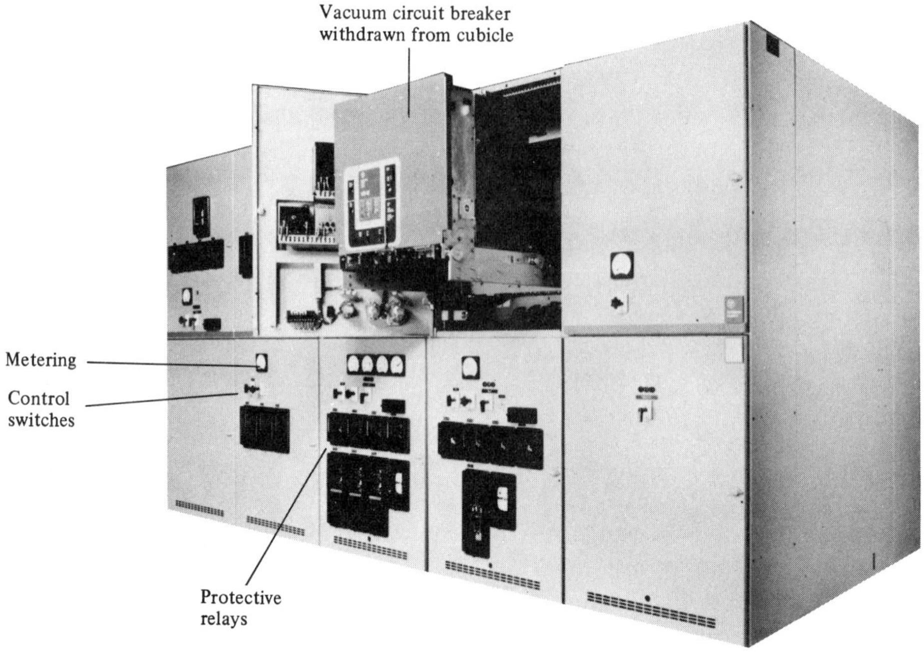

FIGURE 8.20

Medium-voltage switchgear using vacuum circuit breakers

power circuit breaker. The breakers are normally opened and closed by electrical means. A local close-trip switch is mounted on the front panel of the breaker cubicle, as shown in Figure 8.19(c). Additional close-trip switches can be added at remote locations. In an emergency the breakers can be opened and closed manually. Control power for the breaker is usually obtained from a small step-down transformer, connected to the lineside of the breaker through current-limiting fuses. For the critical power required to ensure that the breaker is properly tripped under fault conditions, separate batteries may be installed. If not, then a capacitor is used, which is kept charged during normal operation and which has enough stored energy to activate the shunt trip solenoid.

The conventional air circuit breakers are large, bulky units requiring one vertical cell in the switchgear assembly for each unit, as shown in Figure 8.19. The use of vacuum contactors allows a more compact breaker to be constructed. As mentioned in Section 8.1, there are problems with the interruption of currents in a vacuum. However, recent advances in the technology of vacuum circuit opening devices have overcome these problems. Medium-voltage vacuum circuit breakers up to 15 kilovolts are now available and are rapidly becoming the new standard for industrial and commercial installations in place of the magnetic air circuit breakers. Figure 8.20

shows a typical switchgear assembly using vacuum breakers. Note that two circuit breakers can be mounted in the one vertical section, allowing for more efficient use of space. The total floor space required for the installation of the switchgear can be reduced by as much as 50% compared to that required for conventional switchgear. This can be important in the restricted confines of a building.

Medium-voltage breakers are primarily circuit opening and closing devices. Unlike low-voltage breakers, they do not incorporate built-in automatic trip units. Separate protective relays are used to monitor the circuit conditions and then send an electrical signal to trip the breaker. The protective relays are normally mounted on the front panel of each circuit breaker cubicle, as shown in both Figures 8.19 and 8.20. Chapter 9 details the application of protective relays, together with the use of current and potential transformers.

Table 8.4 lists typical ratings for 5 and 15 kilovolt circuit breakers. Medium-voltage breakers are primarily rated by their nominal three-phase interrupting capacity in millions of volt–amperes (MVA). Because these breakers take 5 cycles to fully clear a fault, they must have a momentary rating that is a factor of 1.6 times their

TABLE 8.4 Typical Ratings for Medium-Voltage Air Circuit Breakers

Kilovolt Class	Nominal Three-Phase (MVA)	Rated Continuous Current (A)	System Voltage (kV)	Maximum Symm. Interrupting Rating (A)[a]	Short-time Rating (3 second) (A)[a]	Momentary Rating (Closing and Latching) (A)[a]
5 kV	75	1200	4.16	12,000	12,000	19,000
	250	1200 2000		36,000	36,000	58,000
	350	1200 2000 3000		49,000	49,000	78,000
15 kV	500	1200 2000 3000	13.8	23,000	23,000	37,000
	750	1200 2000 3000		36,000	36,000	58,000
	1000	1200 2000 3000		48,000	48,000	77,000

[a] rms values.

For a complete listing of all ratings, see ANSI standards.

rated short-circuit current (see Sections 6.5 and 6.6). These breakers have a 3 second short-time current-carrying capability, which allows for the tripping of the breaker on high fault currents to be delayed as necessary to ensure that all downstream devices closer to the fault operate first.

SUMMARY

The application of circuit breakers to system protection requires a detailed knowledge of their ratings, characteristics, and means of operation. Standard molded-case breakers are compact and relatively less expensive, but their generally lower interrupting ratings are a limiting factor in their application to large-capacity systems. Also, the fact that coordination between these breakers at high fault currents is not possible is a decided disadvantage. Power breakers are relatively more expensive and require more space, but they offer higher interrupting ratings and more flexibility in their operating characteristics. Also these breakers can be fully coordinated over the complete range of currents up to their interrupting ratings.

The following is a summary of the advantages and disadvantages of the standard circuit breakers as compared with fuses.

- Advantages

  — Can be safely opened under all load and fault currents up to their interrupting ratings
  — Can serve as both a means of protecting and of switching a circuit
  — Does not cause single phasing
  — Has repetitive operation, nothing to replace, no parts to stock
  — Are relatively tamper proof; operating characteristics cannot inadvertently be changed
  — Can be remotely operated
  — Undervoltage protection can be easily incorporated
  — Ground-fault protection can easily be incorporated

With the exception of the smaller molded-case breakers, further advantages are:

  — Tripping characteristics are not affected by the ambient temperature
  — Wide selection of operating characteristics and adjustments
  — UL listed for application at 100% of their designated current ratings

- Disadvantages

  — Higher initial cost
  — Larger and heavier, require much more space

— More complex, require maintenance
— Not basically a current limiting device; equipment being protected is subjected to higher thermal and mechanical stressing under fault conditions
— Not fail-safe; if the trip mechanism jams or the trip coil burns out, breaker can be left closed, creating a dangerous situation

QUESTIONS

1. Why is the use of a simple knife switch to interrupt large currents unreliable and unsafe?
2. What are three means by which circuit-opening devices can be made to safely interrupt large currents?
3. What is the purpose of an arc chute?
4. What is meant by a three-pole, gang-operated breaker?
5. When is electrical operation of breakers required?
6. Describe the stored-energy method of closing breakers.
7. What is meant by trip-free?
8. What breaker ratings are set by the frame size?
9. What is the significance of the trip rating of a breaker?
10. Describe how the series trip units operate to trip a breaker.
11. What physical characteristic differentiates the molded-case breaker from the standard power breaker?
12. Explain the thermal–magnetic trip unit as used on the standard molded-case breaker.
13. Describe the adjustable instantaneous trip unit as used on the larger molded-case breakers.
14. On breaker time–current characteristic curves such as Figure 8.7, why is it necessary to have a tolerance band as defined by the maximum and minimum lines?
15. How are frame sizes designated?
16. What is the major limitation to the use of standard molded-case breakers on large systems?
17. For a molded-case breaker with a 100 ampere trip unit, what is the maximum clearing time permitted at 200 amperes?
18. Why is a molded-case breaker tested at 600% of its normal current rating?
19. What is the definition of the low-voltage power circuit breaker?
20. What are the advantages of the drawout-type breaker?
21. How does a shunt trip coil operate to trip a breaker?
22. Why have the solid-state trip units largely replaced the mechanical dual-magnetic trip units on power circuit breakers?
23. What is the function of the sensors?
24. What does the pickup current represent?
25. Why does a power circuit breaker have a short-time rating?
26. With reference to Figure 8.14, why is there a lack of coordination between the two breakers above 2700 amperes?
27. Why were combination fused circuit breakers developed?
28. Which features does the encased circuit breaker incorporate from the molded-case and the power circuit breaker?
29. What advantages does the encased circuit breaker have over the power circuit breaker?
30. How does the molded-case current-limiting breaker provide the current-limiting feature?
31. Why are protective relays normally required to be used with medium-voltage breakers?
32. What is the major disadvantage of using oil circuit breakers for indoor installations?

PROBLEMS

1. Using Figure 8.7, for a breaker with a 150 A trip unit, determine the maximum and minimum tripping times for a current of 450 A.
2. Repeat Problem 2, except with a 50 A trip unit at 500 A.
3. Using Figure 8.8, for a breaker with a 300 A trip

unit, determine the maximum and minimum tripping times for a current of 1200 A?

4. Repeat Problem 3, except with a 400 A trip unit.
5. A 400 A frame breaker has a 200 A trip unit. The adjustable instantaneous unit is set at 10 times. Determine the current at which the breaker will be instantaneously tripped (ignoring tolerance allowance).
6. In Problem 5, with a tolerance allowance of $\pm 10\%$, over what range of currents could the breaker actually be tripped instantaneously?
7. A 600 A frame power circuit breaker has a solid-state tripping unit with 400 A sensors. The long delay is set at 0.9 on the dial. Calculate the current at which the long delay timing will pickup.
8. Repeat Problem 7, except the breaker has a 2000 A frame, 1600 A sensors, and the dial is set at 1.0.

9 Instrument Transformers and Protective Relays

OBJECTIVES

After studying this chapter, you will be able to:

- Explain the use of instrument transformers to represent power circuit voltages and currents.
- List the accuracy classifications of instrument transformers.
- Recognize the effect of burden on the accuracy of instrument transformers.
- Outline the special operating features of current transformers.
- Recognize the forms of construction of current transformers.
- Detail the basic operation of the electromagnetic type of overcurrent relay.
- Determine the time delay and instantaneous response of overcurrent relays.
- Detail the sequence of operation of the trip circuit for the circuit breaker.
- Recognize the application of directional relays.
- Recognize the application of differential relays.

INTRODUCTION

Many breakers have no built-in intelligence; that is, they have no ability to directly monitor the system parameters and to initiate action when abnormal or dangerous conditions arise. The function of the protective relay then is to provide this intelligence. Normally, protective relays are required for medium- and high-voltage breakers as these types are usually just circuit opening and closing devices, as discussed in Section 8.10. On the other hand, low-voltage breakers normally have integral trip units, although they too can be used in conjunction with separate protective relays when special requirements must be met.

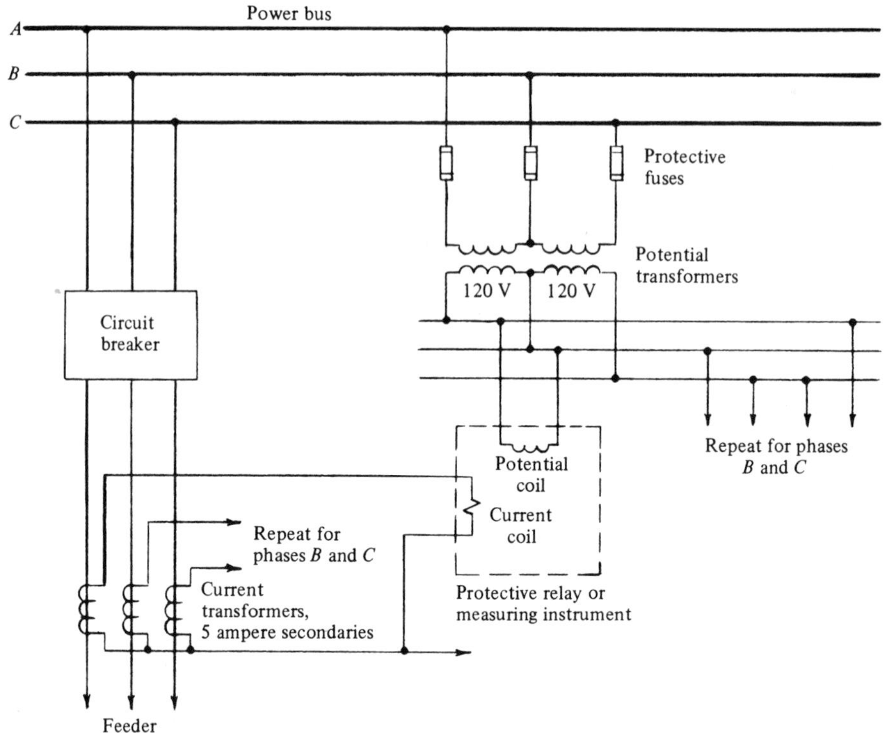

FIGURE 9.1

Typical instrument transformer connections to a power system

The protective relays themselves cannot be directly connected into the electrical power circuits. Separate sensors, in the form of *potential* and *current transformers,* are required to reduce the power circuit voltages and currents to levels that are compatible with the detection units of the protective relays and measuring instruments. Potential transformers (PTs) and current transformers (CTs) are classified as *instrument transformers* to differentiate them from power transformers. Figure 9.1 shows the typical interconnections when both the voltage and current parameters of a system are required for the operation of the protective relays and/or measuring instruments. The instrument transformers are discussed first, followed by the types and applications of protective relays.

There are literally hundreds of different types of protective relays. Some respond to current magnitude only, while others not only respond to the magnitude of the current but also to its direction (to the direction of power flow). Others operate on a differential principle (they compare values), while others operate on an impedance principle (distance to the fault location). Complex systems, which have many sources of power and different voltage levels, require sophisticated protection systems using many special types of relays.

The application of these more complex relays to such systems is beyond the scope of this book. The material presented in this chapter covers only the basic application of relays for the overcurrent protection of feeders, for monitoring the direction of power flow, and for the differential protection of equipment.

9.1 INSTRUMENT TRANSFORMERS

The purpose of instrument transformers is to represent, with acceptable accuracy, the primary (the power) circuit conditions of voltage, current, and phase position in the secondary circuits to the protective relays and measuring instruments. There are two types: potential transformers (PTs) and current transformers (CTs). They have two basic functions. The first is to transform the high voltages or high currents of the power circuit down to a common secondary base, generally 120 volts and 5 amperes. The second is to isolate the operating coils of the protective relays and measuring instruments from the high potentials of the power system. The use of the common base of 120 volts and 5 amperes allows the relays and meters to be standardized.

All transformers operate basically on the same principle as outlined in Section 1.7. The turns ratio of a transformer is the number of turns on the primary winding divided by the number of turns on the secondary winding. If there were no losses in the transformer, then the primary and secondary voltages would be exactly proportional to the turns ratio, and the primary and secondary currents would be exactly inversely proportional to the turns ratio. However, the transformer does have losses. There are heat losses caused by the flow of current through the windings and core losses caused by the alternating magnetic field in the iron core. Also, there is a magnetizing component of the primary current, which is required to create the magnetic flux, and there are voltage drops caused by the impedances of the windings. As a result of all these factors, the secondary voltage and current cannot exactly represent the primary voltage and current; that is, there are errors in the transformation. The amount by which the ratio of the primary voltage or current to the actual secondary voltage or current differs from the turns ratio (the nameplate ratio) is known as the *ratio error*. The amount in minutes (1 degree = 60 minutes) by which the phase angle of the voltage or current differs from its correct position is known as the *phase angle error*. Where instrument transformers are used for metering purposes, the errors must be small, that is, a maximum of 1.2% for the ratio error and a maximum of 60 minutes for the phase angle error. Where instrument transformers are used only for relaying purposes, the accuracy is not so critical. Ratio errors can be as high as 10% under certain conditions. This is discussed in more detail for each type of instrument transformer.

9.2 POTENTIAL TRANSFORMERS

Potential transformers are connected to the power system as shown in Figure 9.1. Their primary windings are normally protected by current-limiting power fuses (Section 7.8.2). The turns ratios are selected so that at rated primary voltage there is 120 volts at the secondary terminals. A typical potential transformer with the primary fuses mounted on the top is shown in Figure 9.2.

The operation of a potential transformer is the same as that of a power transformer except that the currents are much smaller. The secondary current and hence the primary current are set by the amount of load connected to the transformer. The loads are connected in parallel, and the secondary current increases as more load is connected. The primary and secondary voltages are relatively constant and are largely independent of the load. The loads connected to a potential transformer are the potential coils of protective relays and measuring instruments, such as voltmeters and wattmeters. To differentiate this load from that connected to the power circuit being measured, the potential transformer load is known as the *burden*. The burden is expressed in volt–amperes, that is, the voltage (usually 120 volts) times the total secondary current drawn by the relays and instruments. To keep the transformer ratio error to an acceptable value, the volt–ampere burden must be limited. Potential transformers are classified by their accuracy at specified levels of burden. Table 9.1 shows the standard accuracy classifications, together with the allowable burdens. These burdens are designated by letters that indicate the volt–amperes and minimum power factor. For example, a potential transformer classified as 0.3 Y has a maximum of 0.3% ratio error and 15 minute phase angle error with a

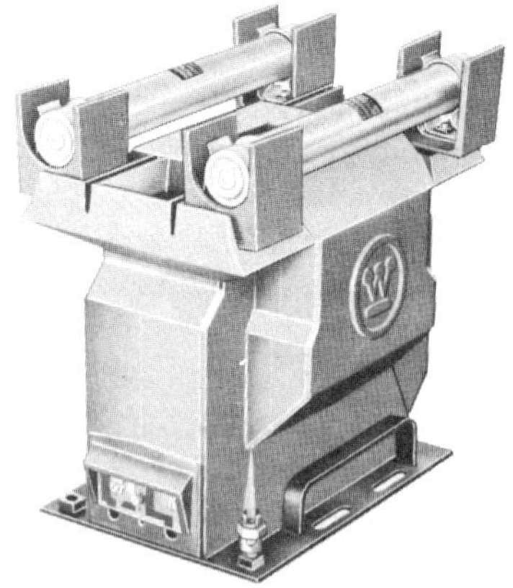

FIGURE 9.2

Potential transformer complete with primary fuses

TABLE 9.1 Standard Accuracy Classifications and Burdens for Potential Transformers

Accuracy Classifications

Maximum Percentage Ratio Errors	Maximum Phase Angle Error (min)
0.3	15
0.6	30
1.2	60

Standard Burdens

Letter Designation	Volt–Amperes at 120 Volts	Minimum Power Factor
W	12.5	0.10
X	25.0	0.70
Y	75.0	0.85
Z	200.0	0.85
ZZ	400.0	0.85

burden of 75 volt–amperes at 120 volts and a power factor of 0.85. The permissible burden for accuracy is much lower than that which the transformer can handle before overheating, which is its thermal rating. For example, this same transformer may have a thermal rating of 750 volts–amperes.

9.3 CURRENT TRANSFORMERS

The primary windings of current transformers (CTs) are connected in series with the circuit to be monitored as shown in Figure 9.1. The primary winding must be insulated for the higher voltage level of this circuit. The rated current of the primary winding should be from 110% to 125% of the full-load current of the circuit to prevent the CT from overheating in the event of minor overloading. The current transformer ratio (the turns ratio) is then selected to give a rated secondary current of 5 amperes. For example, a 1000/5 ampere CT produces a 5 ampere secondary current when the primary current is 1000 amperes. This CT has a turns ratio of 1000/5 or 200. It should be used with a circuit that has a full-load current in the range of 800 to 900 amperes.

A current transformer operates on the same principle as other transformers, that is, with regard to turns ratio, magnetizing current, and so on. However, the manner in which it is connected into the system causes it to display much different operating characteristics.

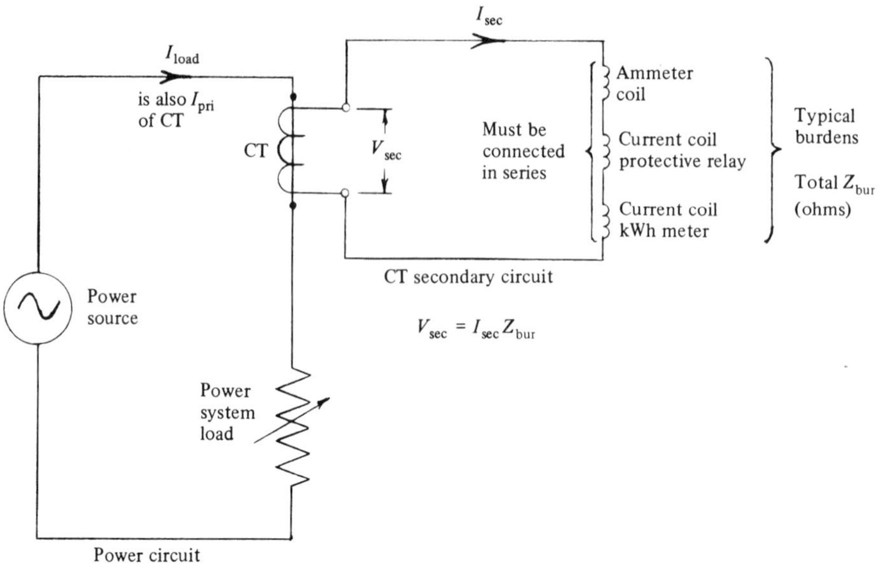

FIGURE 9.3

Simplified single-phase schematic diagram of the circuit connections for a current transformer

Figure 9.3 shows a simplified single-phase schematic diagram of the circuit connections of a CT. The loads connected to a CT are the current coils of protective relays and measuring instruments, such as ammeters, wattmeters, and the like. As shown in the diagram, these loads are connected in series since the same current must flow through each coil. Once again, to differentiate the CT load from that connected to the power circuit being monitored, the CT load is known as the *burden*. However, because of the series connection, the burden is expressed in total ohms of impedance at a specified power factor.

The operating characteristics of a current transformer differ significantly from those of power and potential transformers. First, the primary current of the CT is solely a function of the power circuit load and not of the secondary load (burden) as is normally the case with transformers. The secondary current is the reflected value of the primary current and, therefore, it too is independent of the burden on the secondary of the CT. Second, the CT voltages vary directly with the current, whereas with other transformers the voltages are largely independent of current. As shown in Figure 9.3, the CT secondary voltage is equal to the product of the secondary current and the burden in ohms. If this secondary voltage becomes excessive, the transformer will be driven into saturation, and the ratio error and phase angle error will increase very rapidly. Therefore, to keep these errors to acceptable values, the total burden permitted to be connected to a current transformer must be limited.

Similar to potential transformers, current transformers, when used for metering purposes, are classified by their accuracy at specified values of burden. Table 9.2 shows the standard accuracy classifications (which are the same as for PTs), together with the standard burdens in ohms at a minimum power factor. For example, a current transformer designated 0.3B-2.0 has a maximum of 0.3% ratio error with a burden of 2.0 ohms at 0.5 power factor. Manufacturers list the burdens of the current coils of their protective relays and meters. The total burden of all the current coils of the equipment to be connected in series to the one CT is first calculated. Then the proper classification of CT can be selected. If the total burden is excessive, two sets of CTs are required to split the burdens so that the required degree of accuracy can be obtained.

When a current transformer is used only for protective relaying service, the accuracy is not so critical. However, since the protective relay must respond properly well up into the short-circuit range, the errors with these high currents must not be too excessive. When a fault occurs on the power circuit, the secondary current should be the reflected value of the high primary current. With a fixed burden on the secondary and with this high secondary current, the secondary voltage must rise accordingly. If this high voltage drives the

TABLE 9.2 Standard Accuracy Classifications and Burdens for Current Transformers

Accuracy Classifications

Maximum Percentage Ratio Error	Maximum Phase Angle Error (min)
0.3	15
0.6	30
1.2	60

Standard Burdens

Burden Designation	Impedance (ohms)	Minimum Power Factor
B-0.1	0.1	0.9
B-0.2	0.2	0.9
B-0.5	0.5	0.9
B-0.9	0.9	0.9
B-1.0	1.0	0.5
B-2.0	2.0	0.5
B-4.0	4.0	0.5
B-8.0	8.0	0.5

transformer too far into saturation, the ratio error becomes significant, and the actual CT secondary current no longer reasonably represents the primary (the short circuit) current. Therefore, the measure of the current transformer's ability to perform properly under high fault current conditions is the value of the highest secondary voltage that it can induce without severe saturation and consequent large errors.

There are two ratio accuracy standards, 2.5% and 10%. There are two performance classifications, H and L. For the H classification, the maximum stated voltage can be induced without exceeding the specified error at any secondary current from 5 to 20 times normal (25 to 100 amperes). For the L classification, the maximum stated voltage can be induced without exceeding the specified error at 20 times normal current only. The H classification is more generally used. The standard voltage ratings are 10, 20, 50, 100, 200, 400, and 800 volts.

As an example, a current transformer designated 2.5H100 has a maximum ratio error of 2.5% as long as it does not have to induce more than 100 volts at any secondary current between 5 and 20 times normal. Current transformers that are to be used for relaying applications are physically much larger than those used just for metering, as they must have much larger magnetic cores to prevent saturation at the higher voltages. A current transformer can have both a metering and a relaying classification. For example, a CT may be labeled 0.3B2.0 for metering and 2.5H100 for relaying.

The secondary circuit of a current transformer must never be open circuited when under load conditions. Refer again to Figure 9.3. If the secondary circuit is broken at any point (for example, at the drawout contacts of a protective relay), there can be no secondary current. However, current continues to flow through the primary winding of the CT, as this is the load current of the power circuit. With no secondary current, all the primary current becomes the magnetizing current, which drives the magnetic core of the transformer deep into saturation. This causes the secondary voltage to rise to dangerous values, which can result in flash-overs. This arcing would cause severe damage to the delicate components of the relays and meters. In addition, it creates a hazardous situation for maintenance personnel. Therefore, current transformers are equipped with a shorting bar that must be placed between the secondary terminals before any work is done on the secondary circuit and removed only when the circuit has been fully reconnected. Drawout protective relays have means of automatically shorting their current circuits before they can be withdrawn from their cases (see Section 9.4).

Current transformers have two basic types of construction: the through-type, which is the most common, and the wound primary.

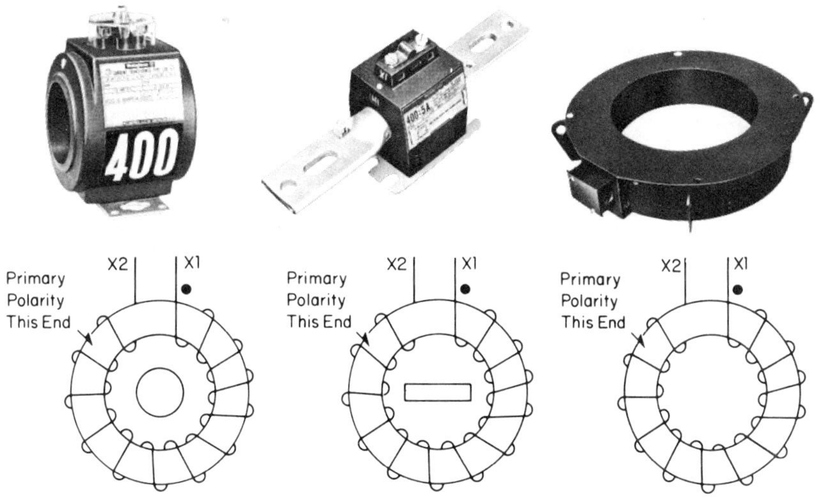

(a) Window type (b) Bar type (c) Bushing type

FIGURE 9.4

Three forms of through-type current transformers

Figure 9.4 shows three forms of through-type construction. The window-type CT has the secondary winding permanently assembled on the transformer core. There is no fixed primary winding. The CT is installed with one phase of the feeder, either a cable or a bus bar, passing straight through the opening in the center of the transformer. This feeder conductor then becomes the primary winding, since it forms one turn by virtue of the complete return loop of the power circuit. The bar-type CT similarly has the secondary winding permanently assembled on the transformer core, but it also has a permanent primary winding in the form of an insulated bar passing directly through the center of the core. The bushing-type CT is similar to the window type, but it is specifically designed to be mounted as part of the insulated bushing used on equipment such as a circuit breaker or transformer. The conductor passing through the center of the bushing forms the primary winding of the CT. The wound primary type of current transformer has a primary winding of two or more turns. Both the primary and secondary windings are insulated and are permanently mounted on the transformer core.

9.4 PROTECTIVE RELAYS (GENERAL)

The *protective relay* is defined as *a device that causes an abrupt change in an electrical control circuit when the measured quantity to which it responds changes in a prescribed manner*. The electrical control circuit is usually the trip circuit of a circuit breaker, and the measured quantity is the power circuit current and/or voltage as represented by the instrument transformers.

Protective relays can be divided into two fundamental types: electromechanical relays and solid-state relays. Electromechanical relays have been the standard for many years and, in spite of the development of the newer solid-state units, are still widely used because of their proven reliability. Solid-state units, since they have no moving parts, have greater accuracy and faster reset times than electromagnetic relays. However, solid-state relays have the drawback that they can initiate false tripping of the circuit breakers because they may improperly react to spurious transient voltage spikes. These transient voltages, which may only last for a few microseconds, can be the result of disruptions on the power system, such as the switching of a power circuit. A solid-state relay must have a filtering system that blocks any chance of these transient conditions from triggering any of its detection circuits. Electromagnetic relays, on the other hand, are inherently immune to transient disturbances. The following discussions refer to electromagnetic relay types. Solid-state relays can offer the same operating characteristics and, in fact, usually use the same type of housing and terminal arrangements, so they are virtually interchangeable with electromagnetic units.

The typical protective relay is housed in a drawout type of case as shown in Figure 9.5. The case is designed for recessed mounting in a panel, such as shown in Figures 8.19 and 8.20. The external wiring from the instrument transformers and the breaker control circuit are connected to terminals on the rear of the relay case. Internal connections to the operating unit of the relay are made through sliding contacts so that the unit can be withdrawn without having to disconnect any wiring. As discussed in Section 9.3, the secondary connections of a current transformer should never be open circuited when they are energized. Therefore, as the relay unit is withdrawn, any CT connections to the relay are automatically shorted together, thus maintaining the CT secondary circuit. The

FIGURE 9.5

Exploded view of a protective relay showing the drawout feature drawout feature allows the relay to be tested without the necessity of having to shut down the power circuit.

9.5 OVERCURRENT RELAYS

The most common protective relay is the overcurrent relay, which is used for the overload and short-circuit protection of feeders and equipment (see Section 6.1). The overcurrent relay normally uses two basic types of operating mechanisms, (1) the electromagnetic induction unit to provide the inverse-time response on overloads, and (2) the electromagnetic attraction unit to provide the instantaneous response on short circuits. Refer to Section 6.7 for inverse-time and instantaneous responses.

The electromagnetic induction unit operates on the same principle as the induction motor. Figure 9.6(a) is a diagrammatic represen-

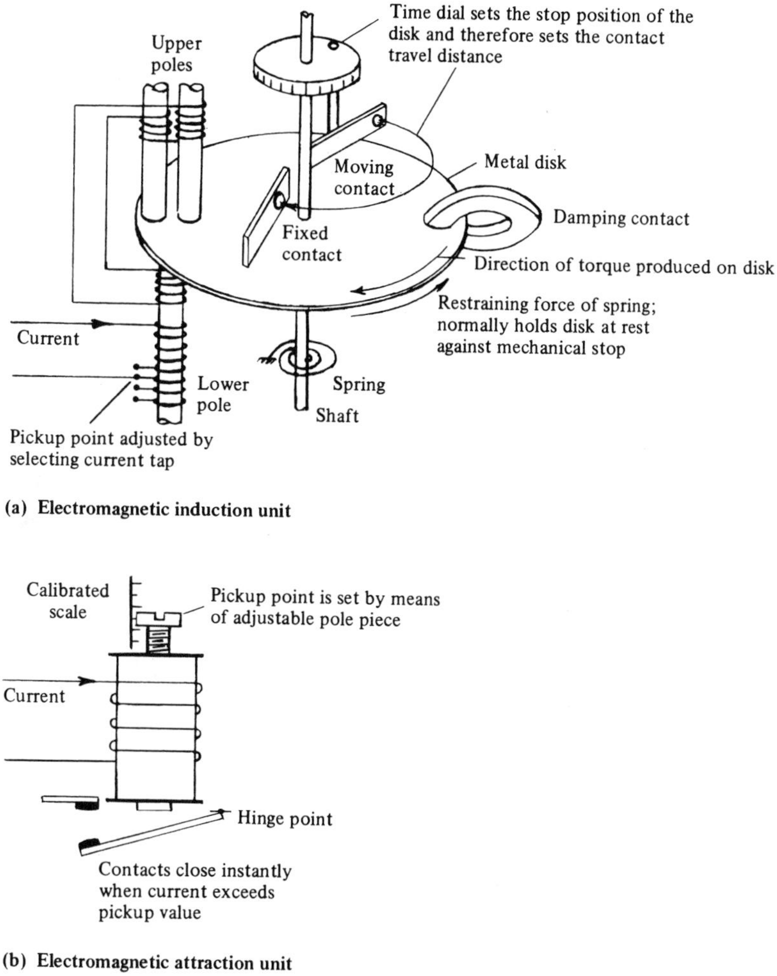

FIGURE 9.6

Diagrammatic representation of the operating units of an overcurrent relay tation of this type of unit. The moving element (the rotor) is simply a metal disk mounted on a vertical shaft. The operating current coils (the stator) create a magnetic field that induces eddy currents in the metal disk. These eddy currents interact with the magnetic field to produce a torque on the disk. The rotation of the disk is initially restrained by a spring until the torque is sufficient to overcome the spring tension. A damping magnet is used to stabilize the rotation of the disk after it starts moving. A contact is attached to the shaft of the disk, and when this contact eventually touches the fixed contact, the tripping sequence of the breaker is initiated (see Section 9.5.2). The timing function of the unit is a combination of the rate at which the disk rotates, which is dependent on the current, and the contact travel distance, which is set by the time dial.

The electromagnetic attraction unit is a simple solenoid that attracts a hinged armature, as shown in Figure 9.6(b). The operation is instantaneous; that is, the armature moves when the current through the operating coil reaches a prescribed value and snaps the trip contacts closed immediately. This is the same principle as used for the instantaneous trip units for the molded-case circuit breaker shown in Figure 8.5(b), with the difference that in the latter case the device acts directly through a mechanical linkage to trip the breaker.

Figure 9.7 shows the typical construction of an overcurrent re-

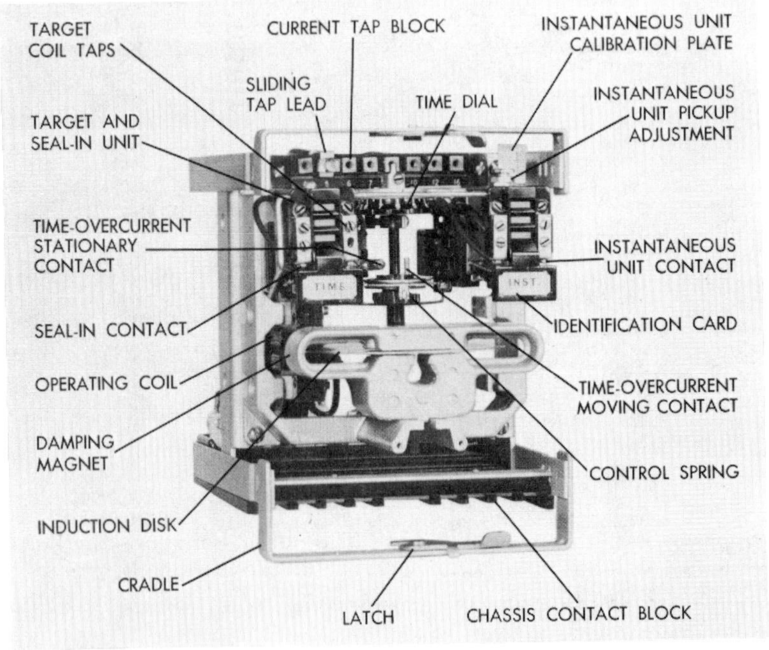

FIGURE 9.7

Induction disk overcurrent relay with instantaneous unit (relay withdrawn from its mounting case) lay. The settings and response characteristics of the relay are outlined in the next section.

9.5.1 Settings and Response Characteristics

The induction disk inverse-time unit of the overcurrent relay has two different adjustments, the current pickup setting and the time dial setting.

The current pickup adjustment is provided by a series of taps on the operating current coil, as shown in Figure 9.6(a). The term *pickup* refers to *the point at which the disk on the unit just starts to move and therefore to start its timing function*. Relays are available with three different ranges of taps: 0.5 to 2.0 amperes, 1.5 to 6.0 amperes, and 4 to 16 amperes. As an example, the 1.5 to 6.0 range has taps for 1.5, 2.0, 2.5, 3.0, 4.0, 5.0, and 6.0 amperes. The current coil of the induction unit is connected to the secondary of the current transformer as shown in Figure 9.9 so that it responds to the magnitude of the power circuit current. The actual pickup current for the power circuit then is a function of both the current transformer ratio (Section 9.3) and the relay current tap setting. This allows for the selection of a wide range of pickup values for the time-delayed tripping of a circuit breaker.

EXAMPLE 9.1

The current transformer is rated 400/5 A. The tap on the relay is set at 4.0 A. Determine the current in the power circuit at which the inverse-time (induction) unit will pick up and begin its timing function.

Solution

— The ratio of the CT is 400/5 = 80.
— The circuit pickup current is $80 \times 4 = 320$ A.

The time dial setting on the induction unit controls the actual time at a specific current to close the trip contact. The adjustment is accomplished by varying the distance that the disk has to rotate from its normal stop position to the point where the contacts close. This is shown in Figure 9.6(a). The distance (and hence the time) is set by rotating the time dial on the shaft of the moving disk. The dial is marked in intervals numbered from 0 to 10. At the 0 setting, the time is zero as the contacts are already closed. The time increases as the dial is turned toward 10. Figure 9.8 shows the family of time–current curves for the typical overcurrent relay. Each curve represents the response of the unit for the indicated setting of the time dial. Note that the horizontal scale is the current in multiples of the relay tap setting.

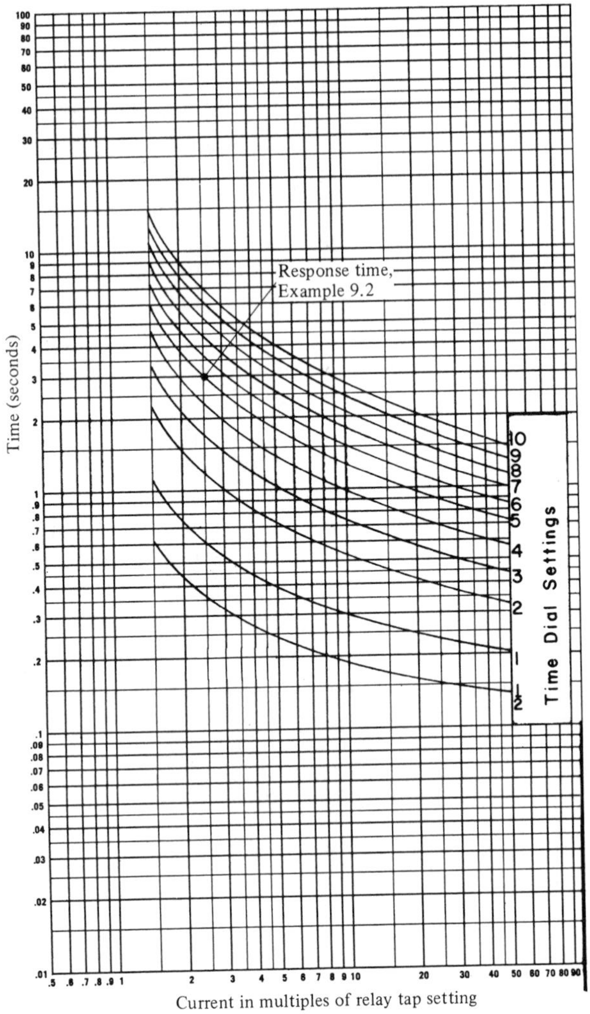

FIGURE 9.8

Overcurrent relay time–current curves (typical inverse characteristics)

■ EXAMPLE 9.2

Continuing with Example 9.1, the time dial on the relay is set at 5. Determine the response time of the inverse-time unit for a power circuit current of 800 A.

Solution

— The CT ratio is 80, as before.
— The CT secondary current is 800/80 = 10 A.
— The 10 A is 10/4 = 2.5 times the relay tap setting.
— From Figure 9.8, the time is 3 s.

Overcurrent relays can be made with different degrees of inverse time–current characteristics. The curves shown in Figure 9.8 are for the standard inverse-time relay. By modifying the design of the induction disk unit, the rate at which the time decreases with increases in current can be altered. For example, relays with very inverse and extremely inverse time–current characteristics have progressively steeper curves than those shown in Figure 9.8. The type of time–current characteristic is selected so that the relay can best coordinate with the other protective devices in the system.

The instantaneous unit of the overcurrent relay has only the one adjustment, that being for the pickup current. The timing function is instantaneous (no intentional time delay). The pickup current is set by adjusting the air gap on the electromagnetic unit as shown in Figure 9.6(b). Two ranges of settings are normally available: 10 to 40 amperes and 20 to 80 amperes. Similar to the induction unit, the actual pickup current for the power circuit is the current transformer ratio times the value of the current setting on the instantaneous unit of the relay.

■ EXAMPLE 9.3

Continuing with Example 9.1, the instantaneous unit is set at 30 A. Determine the current in the power circuit at which the instantaneous unit will pick up and trip the breaker.

Solution

— The CT ratio is 80, as before.
— The circuit pickup current is $80 \times 30 = 2400$ A.

9.5.2 Sequence of Operation for Tripping the Breaker

First, let us refer back to Section 8.2 and Figure 8.2 with regard to the operation of a circuit breaker. The breaker is tripped by energizing the shunt trip coil, which then mechanically releases the contact latching mechanism, allowing the breaker to open and interrupt the power circuit. For breakers controlled by protective relays, there would be no series trips.

Refer to Figure 9.9 for the schematic diagram of the current and trip circuits for the overcurrent relay. One current transformer and one relay are required for each phase of the power circuit being protected. The current coils (ID and IS) for each relay are connected in series with the output of the respective phase CT. Ground-fault protection can also be obtained by connecting the current coils of a fourth relay into the neutral return, as shown in the diagram. See Section 10.5 for ground-fault protection.

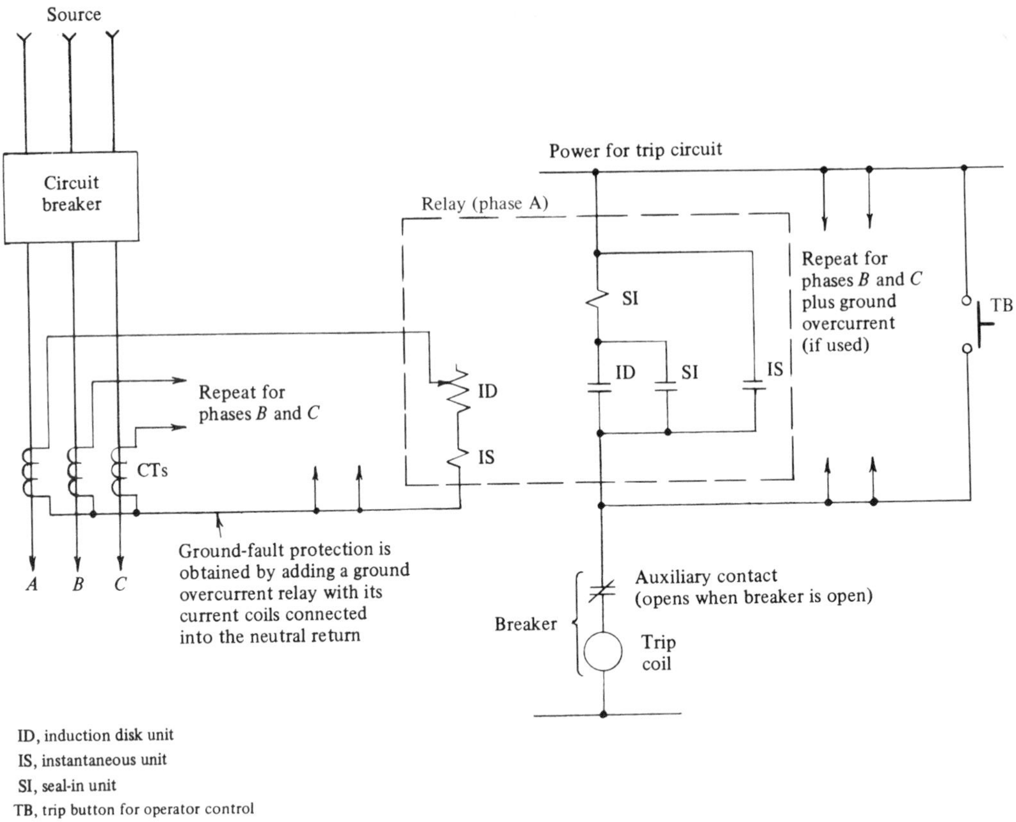

FIGURE 9.9

Schematic diagram of the current and trip circuits for the overcurrent relay

The trip circuit has some special features to ensure that the breaker is properly tripped once any one relay contact closes. As shown in the schematic diagram, each relay includes a seal-in unit, which is required to overcome the possibility of contact bounce on the induction disk unit. Once the current in the operating coil exceeds the pickup value, the induction disk starts to turn. If the overload current continues, as shown in Figure 9.6(a), the moving contact will eventually touch the fixed contact. This is shown as contact ID in the schematic diagram. As soon as contact ID closes, the circuit to the breaker trip coil is completed. The coil for the seal-in unit (SI), which is in series in the trip circuit, is immediately energized, closing contact SI. Contact SI is in parallel with contact ID and, therefore, even if contact ID were to bounce open after its initial contact, the trip circuit is now sealed in and the trip coil can be fully energized and can positively complete the tripping action of the breaker. When the breaker is fully opened, an auxiliary contact on the breaker snaps open, thus de-energizing the trip circuit. Note that the trip contacts of each phase relay, and the ground relay if used, are connected in parallel so that an overcurrent or ground fault on any phase will trip the breaker.

Reviewing the results of Examples 9.1, 9.2, and 9.3, the relays in Figure 9.9 (with the same CT ratios and relay settings) would protect the power circuit as follows. If the circuit current exceeds 320 amperes (there is an overload on the circuit), the induction disk unit picks up and, after the time interval associated with the curve for the time dial setting of 5, closes contact ID. The tripping sequence of the breaker is then completed as previously outlined.

At the same time, the operation of the seal-in unit mechanically releases its target, which then indicates that the breaker has been tripped on an overload. The target is a colored disk located on the front of the seal-in unit, as shown in Figure 9.7. If the circuit current exceeds 2400 amperes (there is a fault on the circuit), then the instantaneous unit picks up, closing contact IS (Figure 9.9), which bypasses the induction unit contact ID and immediately trips the breaker. At the same time, the operation of the instantaneous unit mechanically releases its target, which then indicates that the breaker has been tripped because of a fault on the power circuit.

As shown in Figure 9.9, a separate source of supply is normally used for the trip circuits. On large installations, where an extremely reliable source is desirable to ensure the proper tripping of the breakers regardless of the state of the main power system, batteries are used. On smaller systems, where the cost of separate batteries and associated charging equipment may not be warranted, special ac tripping units can be utilized. When the relay operates on an abnormal condition, this tripping unit transfers the current from the secondary of the current transformer into the trip circuit of the breaker. The CT then provides the momentary energy required to activate the trip coil and release the breaker.

9.6 DIRECTIONAL RELAYS

All the protective devices previously discussed (fuses, low-voltage circuit breakers, overcurrent relays) respond only to the magnitude of the current being monitored; that is, they are nondirectional. The directional relay has the ability to also respond to a change in the direction of the current, that is, to the change in direction of the power flow in a circuit. For this reason, the relays are often referred to as power directional relays.

The reversal of current in an ac system means the reversal of the instantaneous direction of the current with respect to the voltage. Therefore, for the relay to be able to detect the current direction, there must be a voltage reference. First, refer to Figure 9.6(a) for the induction unit. The flux created by both the upper and lower poles is a function of the current (the upper pole by induction). Therefore, the torque produced on the disk is a function of only the magnitude of the current and is always in the same direction, regardless of the direction of the current.

Refer now to Figure 9.10(a). The change for the directional relay is that the flux created by the upper pole is now a function of the system voltage. Through the use of phase shifting circuits within the relay, the torque produced on the induction disk is greatest when the system current is in phase with the system voltage (at unity power factor). By the proper selection of the current and potential transformer polarity connections, the torque is made to be counterclockwise when the power flow is in the desired direction, which then

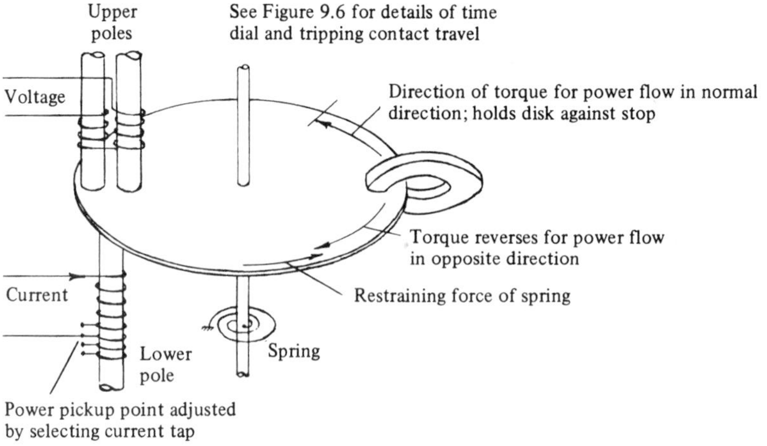

(a) Diagrammatic representation of the operating unit

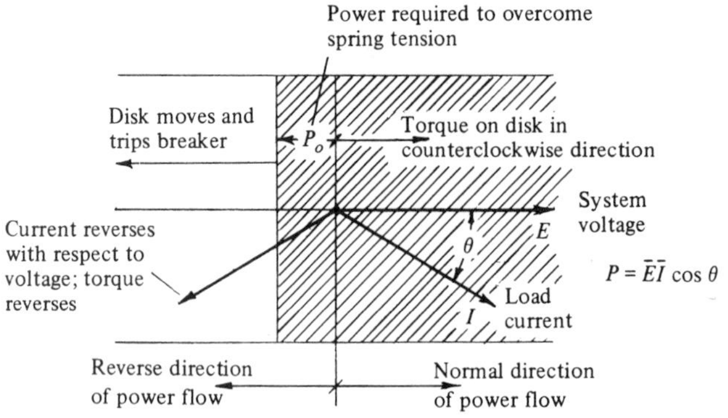

(b) Power vector diagram

FIGURE 9.10

Method of operation of the directional relay

holds the disk against the stop. The relay then ignores any power flow in that direction. However, if the current now reverses with respect to the voltage (that is, the power flow reverses direction), the torque on the disk also reverses and the disk moves in a clockwise direction. The relay then begins its timing function similar to the overcurrent relay. To prevent the relay from responding to very minor reversals of current, which could be the result of power surges on the system, a retarding spring is used. The spring tension prevents the disk from moving until there is a minimum amount of reverse power flow (P_o on diagram). This minimum power is adjusted by means of taps on the relay and is normally set to be a small percentage of the power that flows in the preferred direction. Figure 9.10(b) shows the power vector diagram for the operation of the directional relay.

There are many applications for the power directional relay. One example is an industrial plant that has an in-house generator to supply its own needs. There is also a normally closed feeder to a large electric utility system for the purpose of supplying any excess demand within the plant or to pick up the load if the in-house generator fails. However, if something abnormal happens on the utility system, power may suddenly be flowing out from plant and into the large load on the utility system. This could rapidly overload the in-house generator and shut it down. To prevent this shutdown, power directional relays are used to monitor the feeder connection to the utility. As soon as the set amount of power is detected flowing in the wrong direction (out of the plant), the breaker controlling this feeder is tripped, thus keeping the in-house system intact and operating.

Another example for the use of power directional relays is when there are two service feeders into a plant, each with its own transformer. The secondaries of the transformers are permanently connected in parallel so that failure of one service feeder or transformer does not disrupt any part of the load being fed. Figure 9.11 shows the one-line diagram for this arrangement. This type of connection, however, creates an unusual problem with regard to protecting the system. Assume that a fault occurs on the primary of transformer 2 (point × on the diagram). The primary fuses for transformer 2 would immediately blow, disconnecting feeder 2. However, the fault will be back-fed from the still energized secondary bus through transformer 1. To prevent this back-feed from continuing, the secondary breaker is equipped with directional relays that will immediately trip the breaker as soon as there is any reversal of current. Only then is the fault completely isolated. Both secondary breakers must be similarly equipped to cover faults on either transformer. Separate overcurrent relays are used for the protection of the system for normal power flows.

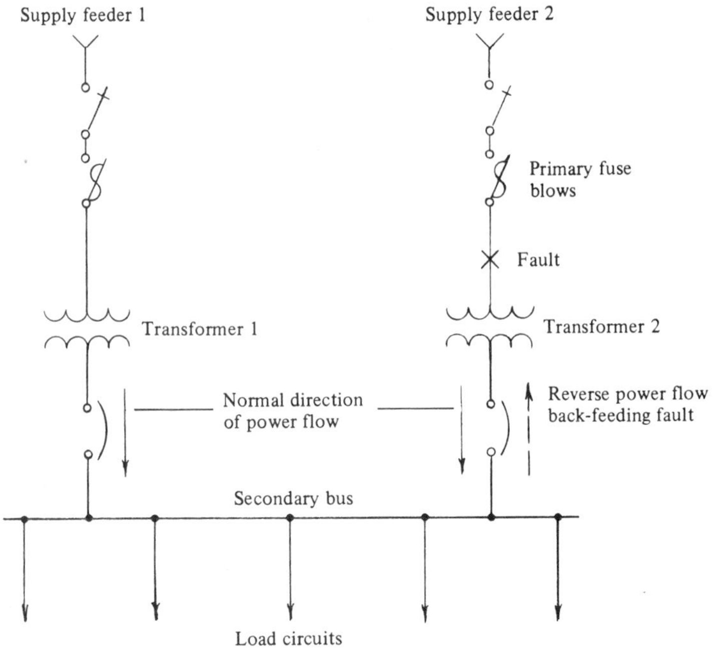

FIGURE 9.11

Parallel operation of two transformers

9.7 DIFFERENTIAL RELAYS

The differential relay responds to the difference between two measured values of current. If conditions are normal, the current flowing into a piece of equipment (a generator or motor) must equal the current leaving the equipment. If the input and output currents are not equal, this can only mean that there is an electrical fault within the equipment. It is the function of differential relays to monitor the two sets of currents. In the event that there is a set percentage difference between them, the relays operate to trip the necessary breakers and isolate the faulted piece of equipment.

Figure 9.12 shows the connections of the differential relays to the system through the current transformers. As long as currents I_1 and I_2 are balanced, there is no current through the operating coil. As soon as there is an unbalance, the difference between the two currents flows through the operating coil, thus causing the relay to operate.

Differential protection of equipment permits the detection of internal arcing faults as low as 10% of the normal load current and yet not cause needless shutdowns on minor overloads. Overcurrent relays are incapable of providing this degree of protection for internal arcing faults. Overcurrent relays are still needed to provide for protection against overloads and faults external to the equipment. Differential protection can also be applied to transformers. However, the difference between the normal primary and secondary cur-

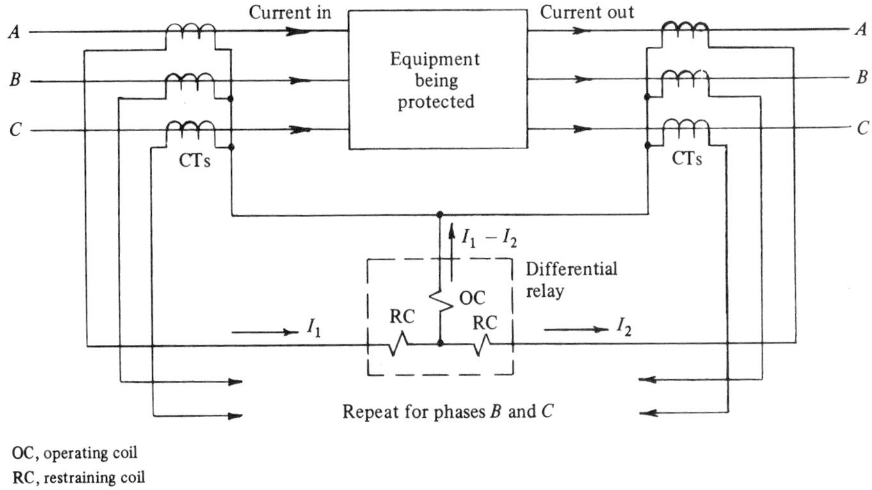

FIGURE 9.12

Schematic diagram of the connections for the differential relay

rents due to the transformer turns ratio must be compensated for by the proper selection of the CT ratios so that their currents I_1 and I_2 are then matched.

SUMMARY

- The function of protective relays is to provide the intelligence for circuit breakers.
- Instrument transformers are required to provide protective relays and measuring instruments with scaled down representative values of the power system voltage and current.
- The accuracy of instrument transformers is dependent on the burden, that is, the amount of load connected to the transformers.
- Protective relays are usually of the drawout type so that they are readily accessible for testing and maintenance without the necessity of shutting down the power system.
- Overcurrent relays are widely used to provide protection to feeders and equipment.
- Overcurrent relays are available with a wide range of response characteristics.
- The pickup values and the timing of relays can be adjusted in the field.
- The trip circuit of the protective relay is arranged to provide positive tripping of the breaker.
- Directional relays can react to the incorrect direction of power flow in a system.
- Differential relays provide very close protection from internal faults in equipment.

QUESTIONS

1. Why are instrument transformers required?
2. What are the two basic functions of instrument transformers?
3. What is the ratio error?
4. What is the phase angle error?
5. Define the term burden.
6. Why are the load elements on the secondary of a PT connected in parallel?
7. How are the burdens for PTs expressed?
8. Explain the designation 1.2-Z for a PT.
9. Why are the load elements on the secondary of a CT connected in series?
10. How are the burdens of CTs expressed?
11. Why must the burden on a CT be limited?
12. Explain the designation 1.2B-4.0 for a CT.
13. Explain the designation 10H400 for a CT.
14. Why are there two separate methods of designating CTs?
15. Why must the secondary of a CT never be open circuited?
16. What adjustments are available on the inverse-time unit of the overcurrent relay?
17. What adjustments are available on the instantaneous unit of the overcurrent relay?
18. What is the purpose of the seal-in unit in the trip circuit of the overcurrent relay?
19. Describe how the directional relay is able to respond to a change in direction of the flow of power?
20. What prevents the directional relay from responding to very minor (transient) reversals of current?
21. Describe one application of the power directional relay.
22. How does the differential relay provide protection?

PROBLEMS

1. The current transformers for a power circuit are rated 1000/5 A. The tap on the inverse-time unit of the overcurrent relay is set at 6.0 A. Determine the current in the power circuit at which the relay will pick up and begin its timing function.
2. The time dial on the relay in Problem 1 is set at 10. Determine the response time of the relay for a power circuit current of 6000 A using Figure 9.8.
3. The instantaneous unit on the relay in Problem 1 is set at 40 A. Determine the current in the power circuit at which the instantaneous unit will pick up.
4. Repeat Problems 1, 2, and 3, except that (a) in Problem 1, the CTs are rated 500/5 A and the tap is set at 5.0 A; (b) in Problem 2, the time dial is set at 2 and power circuit current is 1000 A; and (c) in Problem 3, the instantaneous unit is set at 50 A.

10 Grounding and Ground-Fault Protection

OBJECTIVES

After studying this chapter, you will be able to:

- Discuss the importance of grounding.
- Recognize the difference between system and equipment grounding.
- Identify the advantages and disadvantages of ungrounded systems.
- Identify the advantages and disadvantages of grounded systems.
- Select the points for grounding systems.
- List the purposes of equipment grounding.
- Explain the effect of the equipment grounding circuit impedance.
- Select the size of the system and equipment grounding conductors.
- Identify the characteristics of arcing ground faults.
- Estimate the damage that can result from arcing ground faults.
- Explain the methods used for ground-fault protection.
- Discuss the merits of high-resistance grounding.

INTRODUCTION

The importance of proper grounding for electrical systems in buildings is often underestimated. Under normal conditions, an electrical system can continue to operate satisfactorily (that is, deliver power to the utilization equipment) even without proper grounding. It is not until an abnormal condition has occurred, and after either someone has been injured, equipment has been damaged, or a fire has been started, that it is realized that improper or faulty grounding was the reason. Therefore, a good understanding of the functions of grounding is essential for the proper design, installation, and mainte-

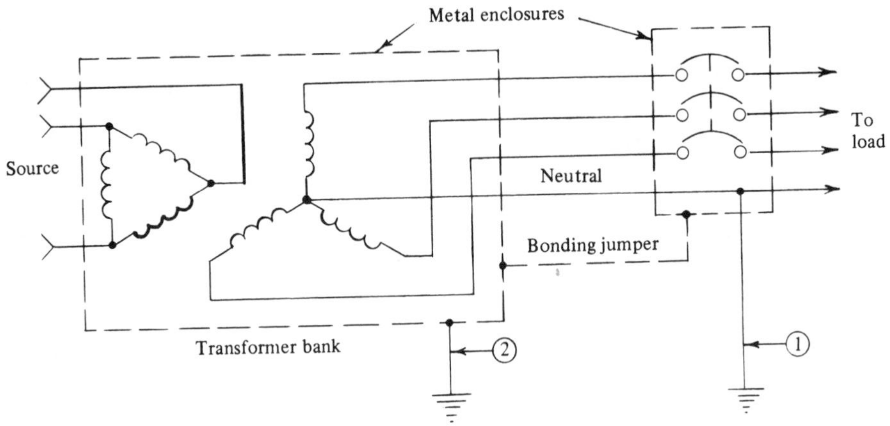

① System grounding: The intentional connection to ground of one of the current-carrying conductors of the system

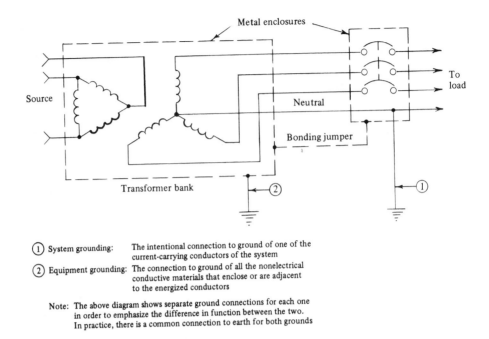

② Equipment grounding: The connection to ground of all the nonelectrical conductive materials that enclose or are adjacent to the energized conductors

Note: The above diagram shows separate ground connections for each one in order to emphasize the difference in function between the two. In practice, there is a common connection to earth for both grounds

FIGURE 10.1

System and equipment grounding

nance of an electrical system. The mandatory requirements for grounding are covered in Article 250 of the *National Electrical Code* and in Section 1910.304(f) of the Occupational, Safety and Health Administration (OSHA) regulations. The *NEC* defines the term *grounded* as *connected to earth or to some conducting body that serves in place of earth*. In most cases, the connection is made by direct metallic contact with earth. The large mass of the earth then serves as a zero potential reference point.

The study of grounding must begin by identifying the different aspects of grounding: system grounding, equipment grouping, lightning protection grounding, and static electricity grounding. The protection of electrical systems and equipment against the effects of lightning and against the unsafe buildup of static electricity is involved and is beyond the scope of this textbook. The discussions in this chapter cover the very important aspects of system and equipment grounding and of ground-fault protection.

Figure 10.1 shows the basic difference between *system* grounding and *equipment* grounding. System grounding *is the intentional electrical connection to ground of one of the current-carrying conductors of the electrical system*. Equipment grounding *is the connection to ground of all the nonelectrical conductive materials that enclose or are adjacent to the energized conductors*. The electrical code requires that all equipment must be properly grounded, except in very rare special cases. However, the application of system grounding is not so universal. Certain types of systems, such as the 120/240 volt, single-phase, three-wire and the 208Y/120 volt, three-phase, four-wire systems used to supply lighting have always been grounded. On the other hand, the 480 and 600 volt, three-phase systems used to supply loads such as motors have until recently usually been operated ungrounded. To better understand the operating advantages of grounded systems, the ungrounded systems are discussed first.

10.1 UNGROUNDED SYSTEMS

An ungrounded system is one in which there is no intentional connection between any of the current-carrying conductors of the system and ground. The term intentional is included because there can always be an unintentional ground on the system due to breakdowns in the insulation or mechanical damage. Both the delta and wye systems (see Section 1.6) can be operated ungrounded, but it is usual that ungrounded systems are the delta configuration, as shown in Figure 10.2(a). Until the 1950s, most power systems in buildings (for motors as opposed to lighting) were operated as ungrounded delta systems. As will be shown, problems can arise with the operation of ungrounded systems, so the first question is why were they popular.

The principal reason for the selection of the ungrounded system is the fact that the first ground fault on the system does not require that any part of the system be shut down. As shown in Figure 10.2(b), this first ground fault merely puts that line of the system at ground potential. No fault current can flow because there is no other connection to ground on the system and hence no return path for the current to flow back to the source of supply. The very small charging current that does flow to ground can easily be tolerated on the system until it is convenient to shut the system down and make repairs.

A further reason for the use of the delta ungrounded system involves the connection of the transformer bank, as shown in Figure 10.3(a). When single-phase transformers are used and one transformer fails, it can be disconnected and the system can continue to operate with the two remaining transformers in open delta. The open-delta configuration can still provide three-phase power as shown in part (b), but at a reduced capacity (57% of normal). This allows the essential loads to be operated until the faulted single-phase transformer is repaired (or a new one obtained) and reconnected to the system.

While these two advantages are attractive when deciding whether to operate a system in the ungrounded mode, the following long-term operating disadvantages cannot be overlooked. In any system, there is a capacitive coupling between the system and

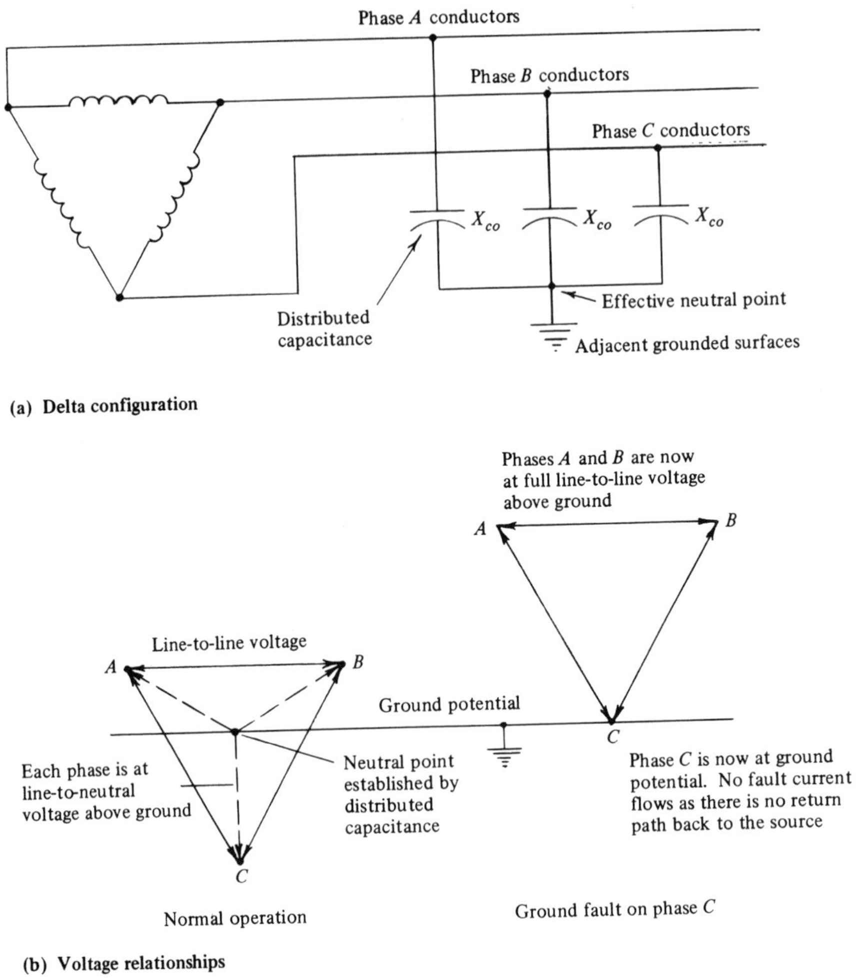

FIGURE 10.2

Ungrounded delta system

ground, as shown in Figure 10.2(a). Each phase of the system is in effect a large capacitor, with the phase conductor forming one plate of the capacitor and the adjacent grounded surfaces forming the other plate (see Section 1.4.2). Because this capacitive coupling is spread over the entire system, it is referred to as *distributed* capacitance. Under normal operating conditions, this distributed capacitance causes no problem and, in fact, is beneficial because it in effect establishes a neutral point for the system, as shown in Figure 10.2(b). Therefore, the phase conductors are stressed at only line-to-neutral voltage above ground. However, it is under abnormal conditions (when a ground fault has occurred) that serious problems can arise on the system, as discussed in the next section.

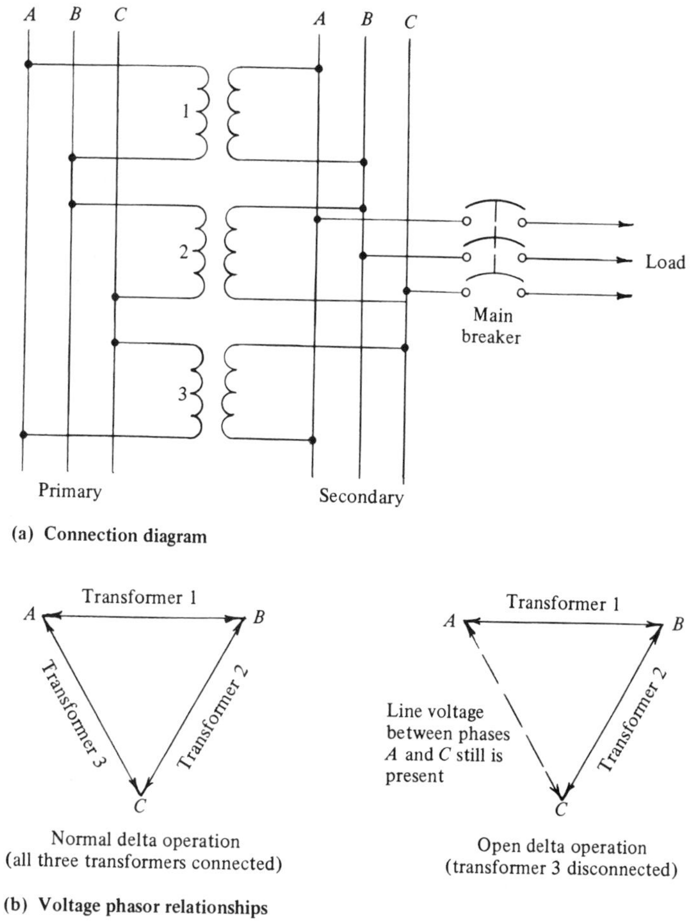

FIGURE 10.3

Bank of three single-phase transformers connected delta–delta.

10.1.1 Overvoltage Problems with Ungrounded Systems

The first ground fault on an ungrounded system, as previously discussed, does not shut the system down. However, the interaction between the faulted system and its distributed capacitance may cause destructive overvoltages to appear on the system. These overvoltages are between the system and ground and do not affect the line-to-line voltages. Therefore, the system can continue to operate and conditions can appear to be normal. The voltmeters, which read line-to-line volts, will not indicate that there is any problem. However, depending on the severity of the overvoltage, breakdowns of conductor and equipment insulation may soon start happening. There is a documented case involving an industrial plant in which upward of 50 motors failed during a 2-hour period before the offending ground fault was located and disconnected. These transient overvoltages can be caused by high inductive reactance ground faults or by intermittent ground faults.

A high inductive reactance ground fault is one in which the fault causes the unintentional connection of one of the phase conductors to ground through a high inductive reactance. This can happen in many ways, such as the grounding of one side of the operating coil of a motor starter. One control wire to a remote push-button station could accidentally be shorted to ground. Another way is the accidental grounding of one side of a transformer winding. In any event, a series *RLC* circuit is created, as shown in Figure 10.4(a). Refer to Section 1.4 for the effects of inductance (*L*) and capacitance (*C*).

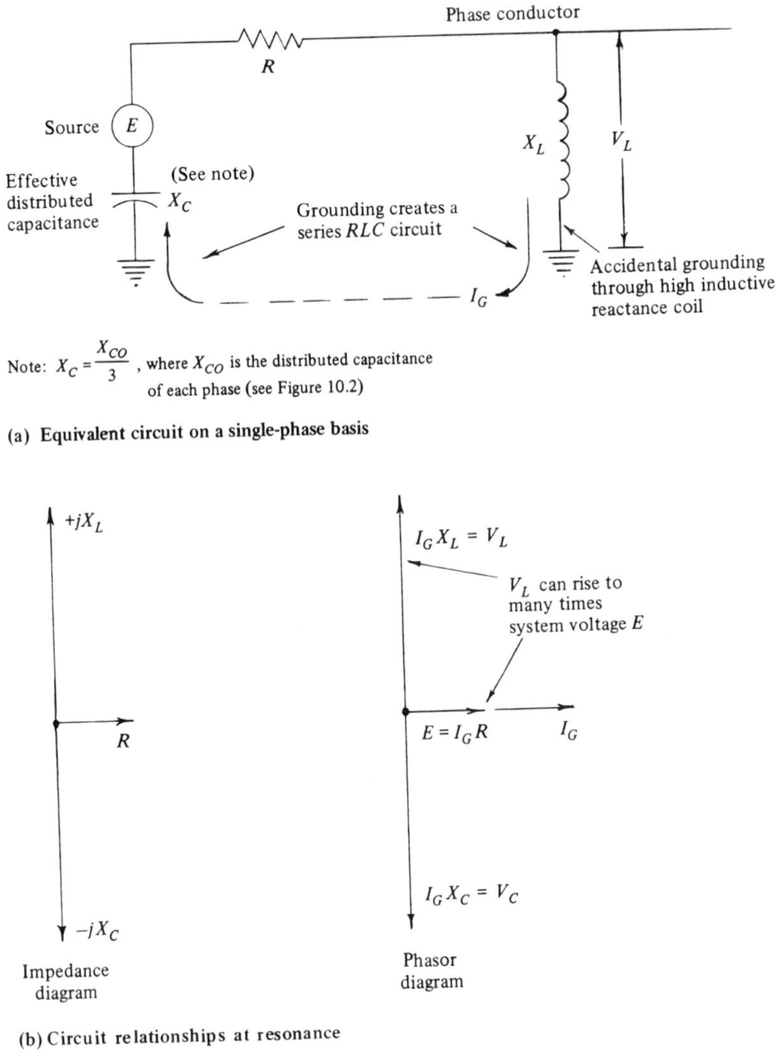

FIGURE 10.4

Unintentional grounding of an ungrounded delta system through a high inductive reactance

The relationships for a series *RLC* circuit at resonance are shown in Figure 10.4(b). A voltage many times the source (that is, the system) voltage can be induced across the inductive reactance. Since this voltage is between the affected phase and ground, the voltage stressing on the insulation is similarly increased, leading to early failures of equipment. The current I_G that flows through the fault is very small, because of the high values of X_L and X_C, and does not activate the overcurrent devices protecting the system. High transient overvoltages can still occur even though the fault does not operate exactly at resonance. The essential element of this type of destructive fault is that the inductive reactance be of a high value, approaching in ohmic value that of the distributed capacitance of the system.

Intermittent ground faults do not involve a solid connection to ground but are rather intermittent in nature, caused by such problems as vibration or arcing. Figure 10.5 shows this type of fault, with a switch representing the intermittent nature of the fault and with a

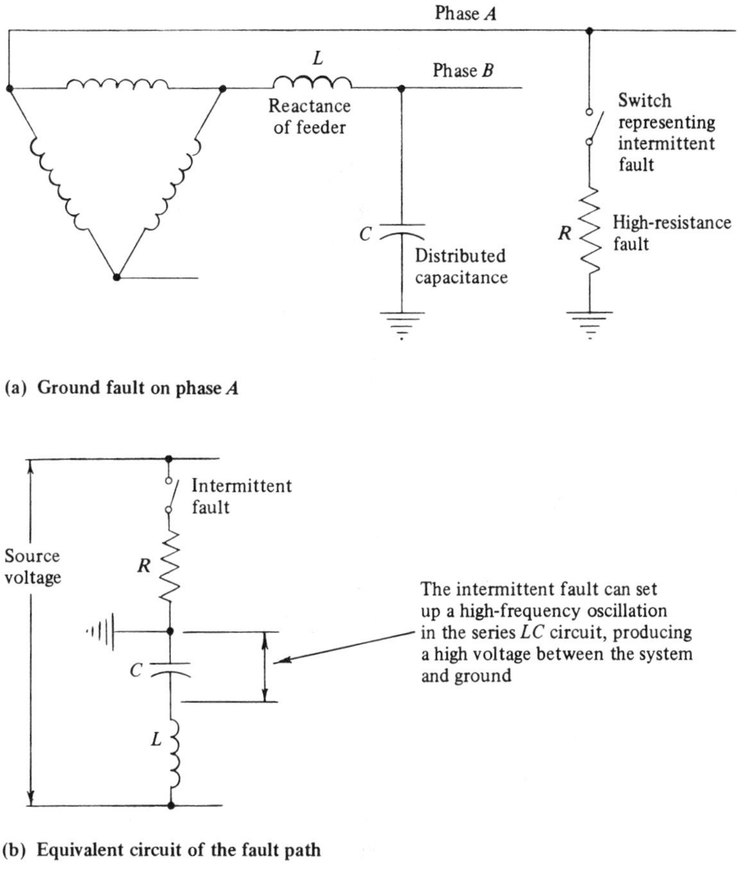

FIGURE 10.5

Intermittent high-resistance ground fault on an ungrounded delta system high resistance for the fault path to ground through an arc. Part (b) shows the equivalent circuit of the fault path, which in effect becomes an oscillator. A peculiar trait of an oscillator is that, regardless of the relative values of L and C, with an intermittent input the circuit will tend to operate at or near its resonant frequency. These high-frequency oscillations can produce a voltage as high as six times the system voltage. This voltage is induced between the system and ground, badly overstressing the insulation, which can lead to early breakdowns of equipment. In spite of the fact that this high voltage is induced, the high resistance of the fault connection means that only a small fault current flows, which does not activate the overcurrent devices protecting the system. The essential element of this type of destructive fault is that it be of an intermittent nature.

Other means of producing excessive line-to-ground voltages on ungrounded systems are more obvious, such as accidental contact with a higher-voltage system. These contacts can be as a result of the breakdown of insulation between the primary and secondary windings of a transformer or of high-voltage overhead wires falling down across lower-voltage circuits.

Notwithstanding that any of the preceding fault conditions occur, the first ground fault on an ungrounded system increases the voltage stressing to ground on the two remaining unfaulted phases by 73%. As shown in Figure 10.2(b), these two phases now operate at the full line-to-line voltage above ground, which is 1.73 times the line-to-neutral voltage experienced under normal conditions. Even though systems are insulated for line-to-line voltages, as systems age the increased stressing can lead to increased frequency of insulation breakdowns. Experience has indicated that, because the first ground fault is often left on a system for long periods of time, ungrounded systems suffer more ground faults than do grounded systems over their operating lifetime.

10.1.2 Operating Problems with Ungrounded Systems

Operating procedures with regard to ground faults are more difficult with ungrounded systems. It is very difficult to locate the first ground fault. Note that it is easy to detect the existence of the ground fault. This is done by using a ground-fault indicator, which consists of three lights connected in a wye configuration, as shown in Figure 10.6. The grounding of the wye point for these lights does not effectively ground the system itself. With the resistors in series with the indicating lights, the lamp currents are very small, less than the charging current of the system. Under normal conditions each light burns at an equal but partial brightness. With a ground on one phase, the light associated with that phase goes out and the other two lights increase to full brightness. However, these lights in no way indicate the location of the fault. Figure 10.6(a) shows a typical radial system that has a ground fault on a remote branch circuit on

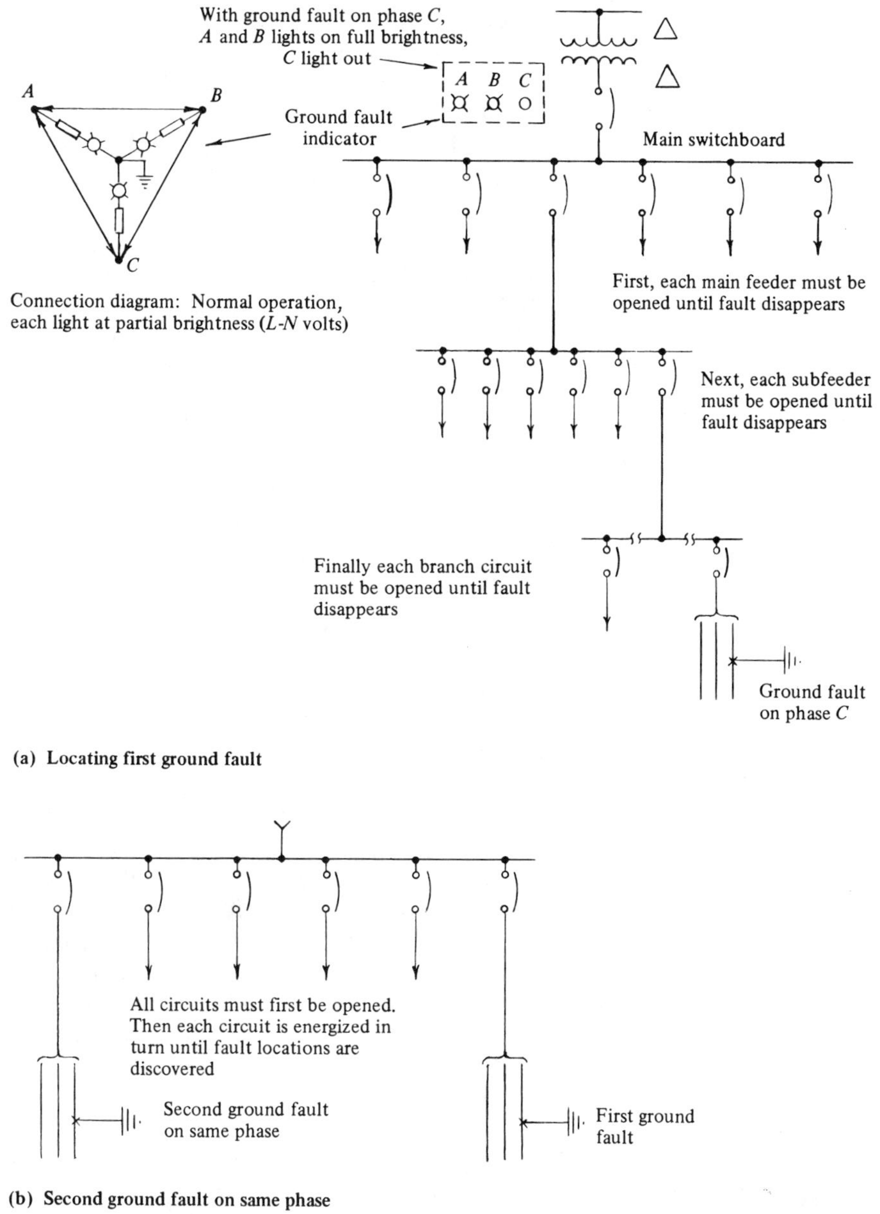
With ground fault on phase C, A and B lights on full brightness, C light out
A B C
Ground fault indicator
Main switchboard
A
B
C
Connection diagram: Normal operation, each light at partial brightness (L-N volts)
First, each main feeder must be opened until fault disappears
Next, each subfeeder must be opened until fault disappears
Finally each branch circuit must be opened until fault disappears
Ground fault on phase C
(a) Locating first ground fault
All circuits must first be opened. Then each circuit is energized in turn until fault locations are discovered
Second ground fault on same phase
First ground fault
(b) Second ground fault on same phase

FIGURE 10.6

Difficulty of locating ground faults on ungrounded systems

one of many panelboards on the system. No matter how many ground-fault indicators there are on the system, every one will show a ground fault on the faulted phase. In the absence of special and costly fault-locating equipment, the procedure involves the opening and closing in turn of each main feeder, each subfeeder on the affected feeder, and finally each branch circuit on the affected panelboard until the faulted circuit is discovered. Obviously, this is very disruptive to the system and generally must be done at a time that least affects production and work schedules. As a result, the first ground fault is often left on the system for long periods of time.

The occurrence of a second ground fault on another circuit, but on the same phase, before the first fault has been cleared makes the locating of the faults even more difficult. First, there is no indication that the second fault exists, as the lights on the ground fault indicators would already be indicating a fault on that phase. As shown in Figure 10.6(b), the ultimate solution requires that all circuits must first be opened and then each circuit energized in turn until both fault locations have been determined. The disruption to the system is even more extensive.

Finally, the occurrence of a second ground fault on another phase and another circuit results in both circuits being shut down simultaneously, as shown in Figure 10.7. The two faults effectively become a line-to-line short circuit. The resulting large fault current must flow over all the interconnecting equipment grounding circuit (conduits, equipment enclosures, and so on), which can result in damage to equipment. Since the faults can occur on widely separated circuits, the relationship between the two outages may not be fully realized. Experience has shown that double faults are very common on ungrounded systems because of the tendency to leave the first ground fault on the system. The 73% rise in the line-to-ground voltage on the unfaulted phases after the first ground fault increases the likelihood of a second breakdown on one of these phases.

As can be seen, the decision to operate a system in the ungrounded mode, while initially offering important advantages, may in the long run prove not to be a good decision. One final disadvantage of the ungrounded delta system is the fact that a separate system has to be used for those single-phase loads such as lighting that must be connected to a grounded circuit. This is discussed further in Section 10.2.

10.2 GROUNDED SYSTEMS

Now that the problems associated with ungrounded systems have been pointed out, the merits of grounded systems can be discussed. First, return to Figure 10.1 and review what constitutes system grounding; that is, the intentional connection to ground of one of the current-carrying conductors of the system. Delta systems can be operated as grounded systems by either grounding one corner of the delta or by grounding the midpoint of one of the phases. However, this is not the usual method. The majority of grounded systems use the wye configuration with the neutral grounded. This is the most

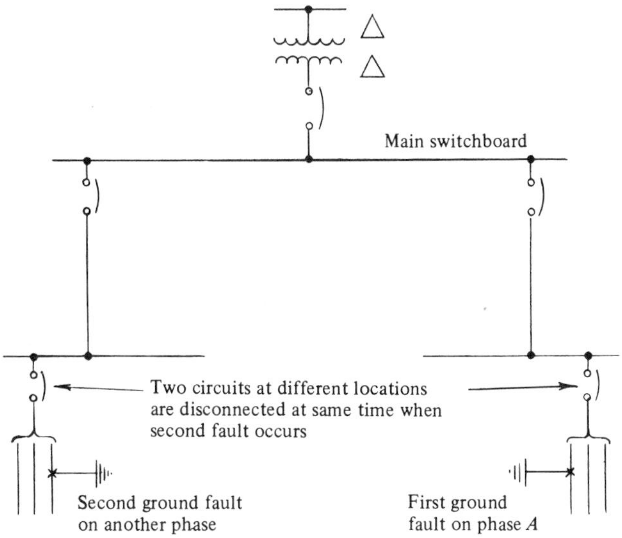

(a) One-line diagram

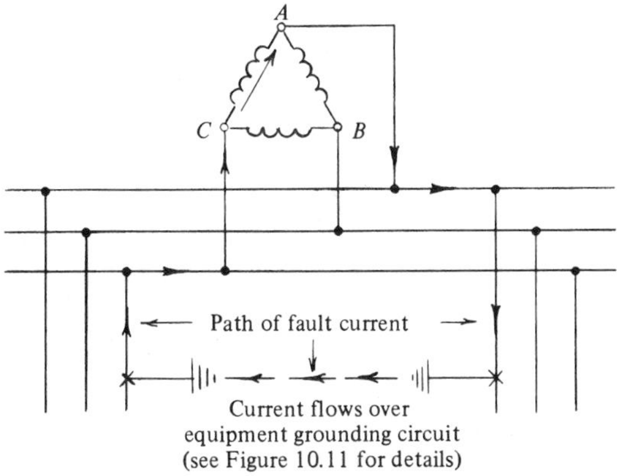

(b) Equivalent three-phase diagram

FIGURE 10.7

Problem with second ground fault on another phase

logical arrangement as it results in each phase of the system being at the same potential above ground. Therefore, the remaining discussions in this chapter are on the basis of wye-connected systems.

The most significant difference in operating characteristics between the grounded and ungrounded systems is what happens when the first ground fault occurs. With the grounded system, there is a path for the fault current to flow when the first ground fault occurs, as shown in Figure 10.8. The overcurrent devices are now activated by the resulting fault current. It must be emphasized that the difference between the two systems involves ground faults only. Line-to-

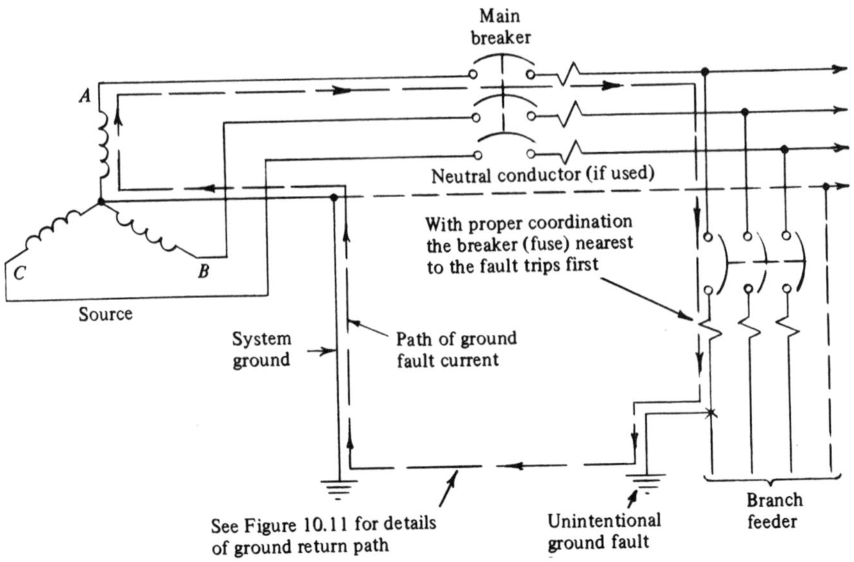

FIGURE 10.8

Ground fault on a grounded wye system

line faults are cleared in the same manner whether a system is grounded or ungrounded. However, there is a much greater likelihood that faults will be between an energized conductor and ground (line to ground) than between two energized conductors (line to line). There is only one layer of insulation between a conductor and its surrounding grounded surfaces, and only one point of breakdown is required for a ground fault. On the other hand, before a line-to-line fault can happen, two simultaneous breakdowns of insulation must occur at the same location before there is a fault path directly between two phases. The exception would be at locations with bare phase conductors, but these only occur at switchboards, panelboards, switches, and the like. Proper design and testing of this equipment should minimize the possibility of line-to-line faults at these locations. Therefore, line-to-ground faults are far more likely to occur on a system than line-to-line faults.

The *National Electrical Code,* Article 250, Parts B and C, covers system grounding. Section 250-5(b) covers alternating current systems, 50 to 1000 volts, that must be grounded, specifically where the system can be so grounded that the maximum voltage to ground on the ungrounded conductors does not exceed 150 volts, and for any system where the neutral is to be used as a circuit conductor. Thus, 120/240 volt single-phase, three-wire, and 208Y/120 volt three-phase, four-wire systems must be grounded. Those 480Y/277 volt three-phase, four-wire systems where the neutral is used as a circuit conductor (that is, for single-phase fluorescent lighting loads) must also be grounded. The 480 and 600 volt three-phase systems where the neutral is not used for load connections may or may not be grounded. The trend over the last few years, however, has been to also ground these systems.

The primary purpose for grounding an electrical system is one of safety, that is, to limit the potential to ground that otherwise could occur from accidental contact with higher-voltage systems or from transient overvoltages. However, there are other important benefits associated with grounded systems, as follows:

1. *Service reliability is improved:* The transient overvoltage conditions that are possible with ungrounded systems (Section 10.1.1) cannot occur. With the elimination of this overvoltage stressing of the insulation, fewer ground faults should occur over the operating life of grounded systems.
2. *Much simpler to locate the first ground fault:* With proper coordination, the overcurrent device (circuit breaker or fuse) nearest to the fault operates to disconnect the faulted circuit, thus leaving the balance of the system operating. This principle is shown in Figure 10.8. The tripped breaker or blown fuse immediately indicates the circuit where the fault has occurred.
3. *Ground-fault protection can be easily added:* Arcing ground faults can be difficult to detect and therefore require special attention. With grounded systems, the protection against ground faults is easily obtained, as discussed in Section 10.5.
4. *Provides two voltage levels on the same system:* Single-phase loads such as lighting can be connected across the line-to-neutral voltage (120 volts on a 208Y/120 volt system). Three-phase loads such as motors can then be connected across the line-to-line voltages (208 volts). See Section 1.6.1 for the voltage relationships of three-phase wye systems.

As is the case with most arrangements, there are some drawbacks to the use of grounded systems, as follows:

1. The first ground fault results in the immediate shutdown of part of the system.
2. There can be very high ground-fault currents on bolted-type faults. These large currents must flow over the equipment grounding circuit (see Section 10.3).

10.2.1 Selection of System Grounding Points

Once the decision has been made to ground an electrical system, the following should govern the selection of the system grounding points. These comments are based on the system being *separately derived,* that is, *a system whose power is derived from generator, transformer or converter windings and that has no direct electrical*

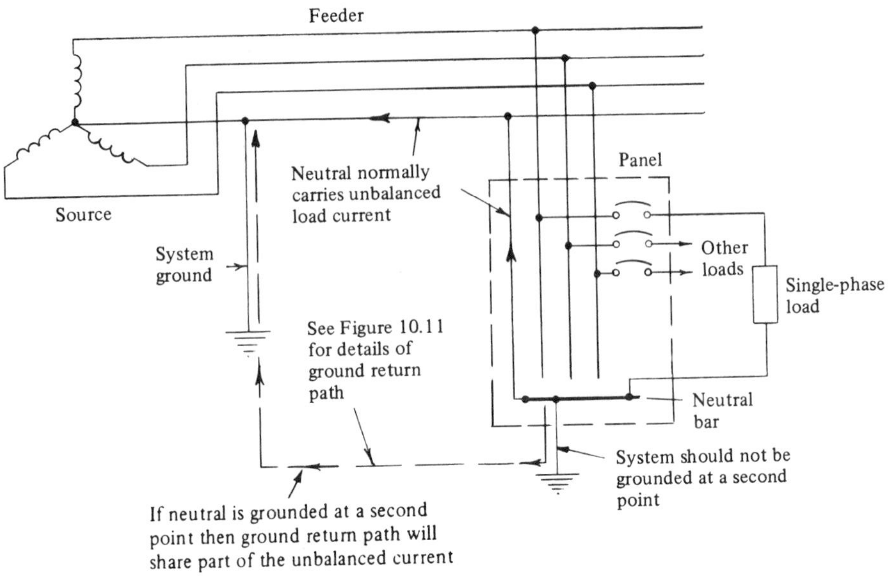

FIGURE 10.9

Each separately derived system should be grounded at one point only

connection, including a solidly connected grounded circuit conductor, to supply conductors originating in another system. In a typical separately derived system, the main transformer is on the customer's premises and is used solely to supply power to those premises. In contrast, a system that is not separately derived is fed from a common utility transformer bank external to the premises and which also supplies other customers in separate premises.

The following points should govern the grounding of separately derived systems:

1. *Ground each system at one point only.* Figure 10.9 shows what would happen if, for instance, the neutral bar of a panel is grounded in addition to the system neutral being grounded at the source. The second ground connection at the panel then puts the ground return path (the equipment grounding circuit) in parallel with the neutral conductor of the feeder. Therefore, the equipment grounding circuit will share part of the unbalanced current that flows when the single-phase loads are not equal over the three phases. Thus, under normal conditions, the equipment grounding circuit is carrying current, which is not a desirable condition. Section 250-21 of the *NEC* states in part that *The grounding of electrical systems . . . and conductive noncurrent-carrying materials and equipment shall be installed and arranged in a manner that will prevent an objectionable flow of current over the grounding conductors or grounding path.* Furthermore, if the neutral conductor were acci-

dently broken or disconnected, then, with the second ground connection, the equipment grounding circuit would carry all the unbalanced neutral current. Finally, the second ground connection would interfere with the proper operation of the ground-fault protection (see Section 10.5). For these reasons, the neutral of the system must be grounded at one point only, and the neutral conductor (including the neutral bars in panels) must be insulated for its entire length to prevent any further unintentional grounds.

2. *The system grounding point must be as close to the source as possible.* Refer to Figure 10.10(a). Suppose the system is grounded at one of the loads (for example, the neutral point of a motor winding). If a ground fault occurs on another branch feeder, the distance of the return path for the fault current is unnecessarily long, creating problems with the proper operation of the overcurrent protective

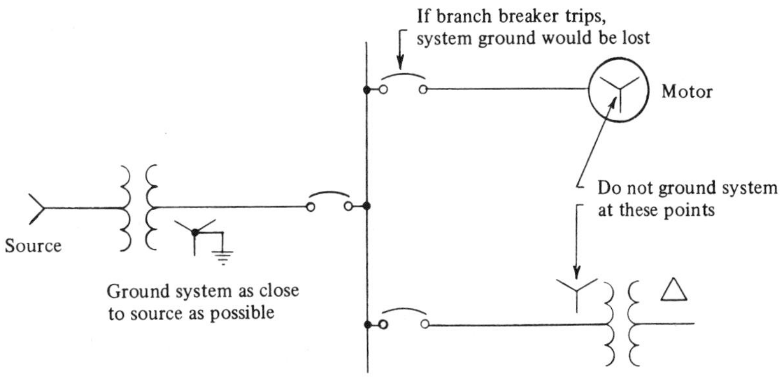

(a) Location of the one ground connection for each separately derived system

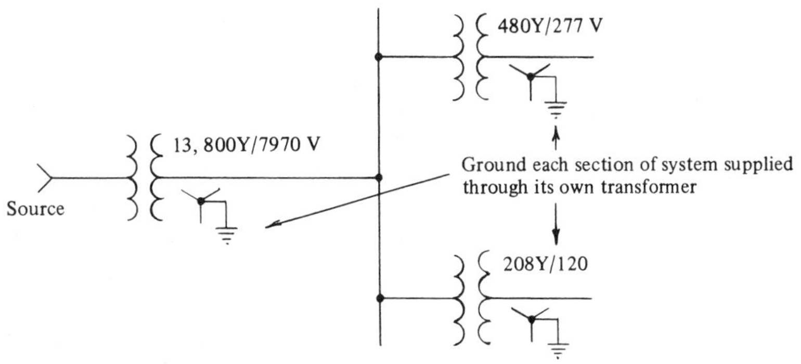

(b) Grounding of system with more than one separately derived section

FIGURE 10.10

Location of system ground connections

devices. Furthermore, if the branch breaker feeding the motor is opened, the system grounding is lost. Therefore, the system ground connection should be made as close to the source as possible, that is, on the line side of the first disconnecting means for the system.

3. *Ground each separately derived section of the system.* It is necessary to reestablish the system ground on the secondary side of each of the power transformers, as shown in Figure 10.10(b).

10.3 EQUIPMENT GROUNDING

Equipment grounding is concerned with the interconnecting of all the nonelectrical conductive materials that enclose or are adjacent to the energized conductors of the system and their connection to ground. The term *nonelectrical* means *those metal parts of the system that do not carry current under normal conditions* (that is, when there are no faults on the system) and are referred to as the *noncurrent-carrying conductors*.

Figure 10.11 shows the equipment grounding arrangement for a typical electrical system. The complete equipment grounding circuit of any system must include the metal enclosures, frames, and/or support structures of the following: service entrance equipment, transformers, switchboards, panels, switches, motor controllers, motors, generators, lighting equipment, outlet boxes, junction boxes, and cabinets. These devices are then all interconnected by means of metal raceways, metal sheaths, and armors of cables, cable trays, metal enclosures of bus ducts, equipment grounding bus, bare copper ground wires, and the green insulated conductor in nonmetallic sheath cables. The equipment grounding circuit path must be permanent and continuous. Where metal raceways, cable armor, cable sheaths, and the like, are terminated at enclosures, approved fittings designed to give positive bonding must be used. Positive electrical contact must be made between the metal parts in spite of any paint or other surface coating on the enclosure.

The primary purpose of equipment grounding is safety, that is, to eliminate any dangerous shock hazard to personnel by limiting the potential between the exposed nonelectrical parts of the system and any adjacent surfaces that are at earth potential, such as the building steel or the mechanical system piping. Accident statistics show that many fatalities have been caused by electric shock that resulted from persons making contact with metallic enclosures that normally should have been at ground potential but, due to faulty grounding, were not.

A further very important objective of the equipment grounding system is to provide adequate current-carrying capability for any ground-fault current that is likely to flow. Figure 10.11 shows the path of the ground-fault current for a fault at the three-phase load.

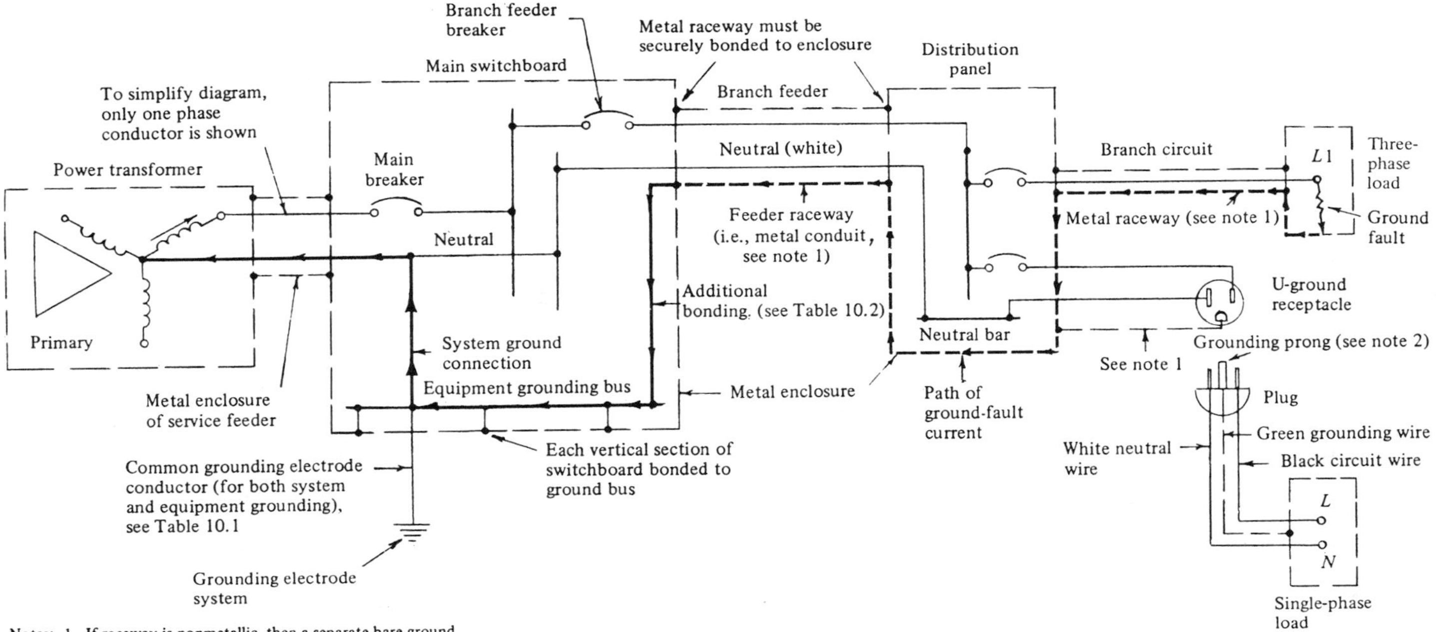

Notes: 1. If raceway is nonmetallic, then a separate bare ground wire must be installed in the raceway (see Table 10.2)

2. If equipment ground connection is broken, there is no return path for the ground fault current. In the event of a ground fault, the metal case of the load will be at line-to-neutral potential above ground

FIGURE 10.11

Typical equipment grounding circuit and ground-fault return path

Any excess heating or sparking caused by inadequate or improper equipment grounding connections could result in a fire or explosion. Finally, the equipment grounding must provide a low-impedance return path for the ground-fault current to ensure that the overcurrent devices respond properly to the fault.

10.3.1 Impedance of Equipment Grounding Circuit

The importance of having a low impedance for the equipment grounding circuit can best be emphasized by showing what happens when the impedance is too high. Figure 10.12(a) shows the equivalent circuit of one phase of a 208Y/120 volt, three-phase system feeding a piece of equipment. The resistance of the feeder conductor is 0.02 ohms, which is typical if the voltage drop is to be approxi-

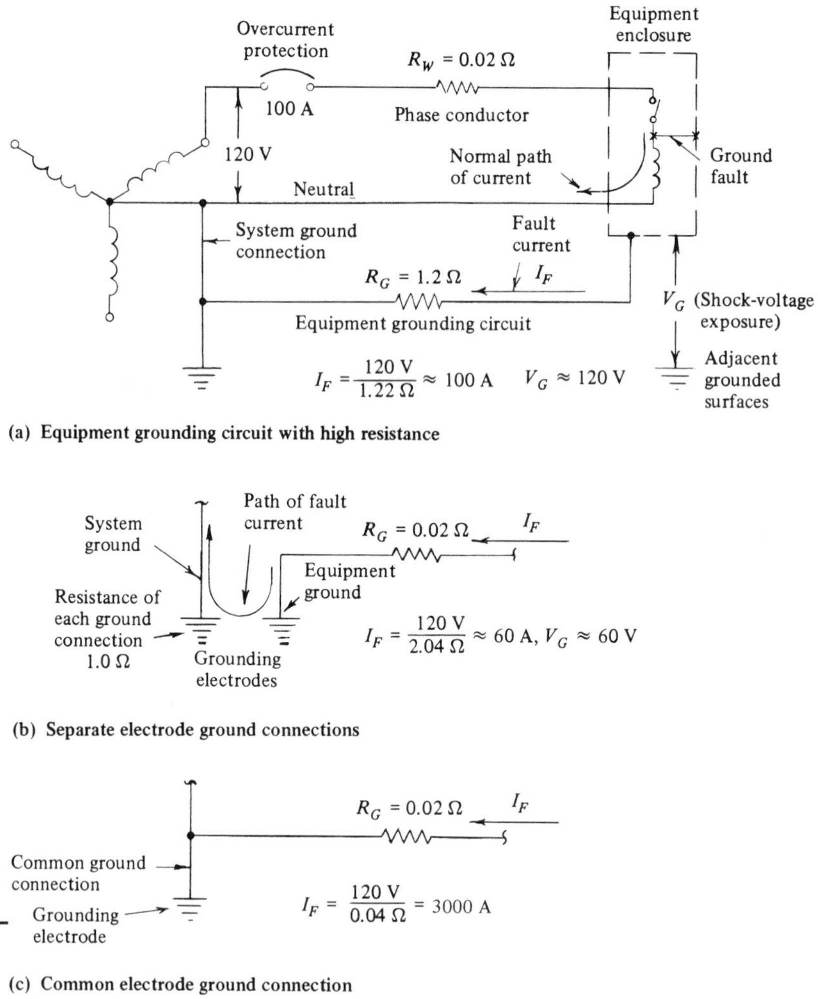

FIGURE 10.12

Effects of impedance in the ground-fault return path

mately 2% under normal load conditions. A ground fault is assumed to have occurred between the energized conductor in the equipment and its grounded enclosure. The resistance of the equipment grounding circuit through which the fault current must flow back to the source is indicated as 1.2 ohms. While this 1.2 ohms in itself seems low, it is nevertheless many times that of the feeder conductor and, in fact, is the major part of the total fault circuit impedance. As indicated, even with a solid ground fault to the equipment enclosure, the maximum ground fault current is only 100 amperes. This is not high enough to positively activate the 100 ampere overcurrent device. The shock-voltage exposure between the metal case of the equipment and any adjacent grounded surface is approximately 120 volts. Clearly, this is an unsafe situation.

Figure 10.12(b) shows the situation where the equipment grounding circuit resistance has been reduced to that of the phase conductor, but there are now separate grounding electrodes for the system and for the equipment. It is very difficult to establish very low resistance connections to the earth, and therefore the 1.0 ohm values shown are very acceptable. However, the ground-fault current must flow through both of these electrode connections in series, with the consequence that they constitute the majority of the total impedance of the fault path (2.0 ohms). As indicated, the maximum ground-fault current that can flow is approximately 60 amperes, which would never activate the overcurrent protective device. The shock-voltage exposure of 60 volts would persist and there would be no indication that anything was wrong. Again, this is an unsafe situation.

Figure 10.12(c) shows the preferred method of making the ground connection, that is, making only one common connection to earth for both the system and the equipment grounding. In this way, the ground-fault current does not have to pass through any earth connections and, together with the low resistance of the equipment grounding circuit, the fault current is now on the order of 3000 amperes (ignoring any impedance of the power source, which will be low). This high value (30 times the full-load current of the feeder) will instantly activate the overcurrent protective device and de-energize the faulted equipment.

In the past, many cases were uncovered where the improper operation of overcurrent devices under ground faults was directly attributable to the practice of using one grounding electrode for the system and a separate grounding electrode for the equipment. Section 250-54 of the *NEC* now makes the use of one common grounding electrode mandatory. Note that two or more grounding electrodes that are effectively bonded together are considered as a single grounding electrode system for the purpose of this requirement.

10.3.2 Inductive Reactance of Equipment Grounding Circuit

The examples shown in Figure 10.12 and discussed in the previous section considered only the resistance of the ground-fault circuit path for simplification. However, on ac systems with feeders rated at more than 50 amperes, the inductive reactance (X_L) of the ground fault return path (the equipment grounding circuit) becomes an important parameter of the total impedance of the circuit ($Z = R + jX_L$; see Section 1.4.3).

Three factors affect the inductive reactance of the equipment grounding circuit: (1) the location of the grounding circuit with respect to the phase conductors, (2) the configuration of the grounding circuit, and (3) the material used (whether magnetic or nonmagnetic). Comprehensive testing has been done to show the effects of these factors. Figure 10.13 shows the arrangements used for the test circuits and lists a few of the test results. For each test the source voltage was adjusted so that the fault current flowing in the circuit was 5500 amperes. In part (a), the equipment grounding circuit consists of a No. 4/0 grounding conductor run parallel to the phase conductor at a fixed spacing for the entire 200 foot length of the feeder. The test results show that the location of the grounding conductor is critical. The inductive reactance is reduced by more than one-half when the spacing is decreased from 30 inches to 2 inches. Therefore, when a conductor is used for equipment grounding, it must be run as close as possible to the phase conductors of the feeder supplying the equipment. The test results also show that the use of the building steel as the return path for ground faults is not a good practice. The remote location of the ground return path through the steel with respect to the phase conductors would create a very high inductive reactance and therefore severely limit the flow of fault current. This could result in unsatisfactory operation of the overcurrent protective devices.

In Figure 10.13(b), the grounding conductor is replaced by an enclosing metal raceway that is connected to form the fault return path. The test results with this arrangement show that the impedance of the return path through the raceway (as measured by the voltage V_G with the same I_F) are even much lower than when using a closely spaced grounding conductor. As shown in the cross section through the raceway, the returning fault current in the shell of the raceway completely surrounds the current flowing outward in the phase conductor. Therefore, there is a complete cancellation of the magnetic flux, and the inductive reactance of the circuit approaches zero. As expected, the higher conductivity of the aluminum raceway provides the lowest impedance of all. Thus metallic raceways as used for the support and mechanical protection of the insulated feeder and circuit conductors (see Section 11.5) also serve very effectively as part of the equipment grounding system when properly installed and solidly connected at all joints.

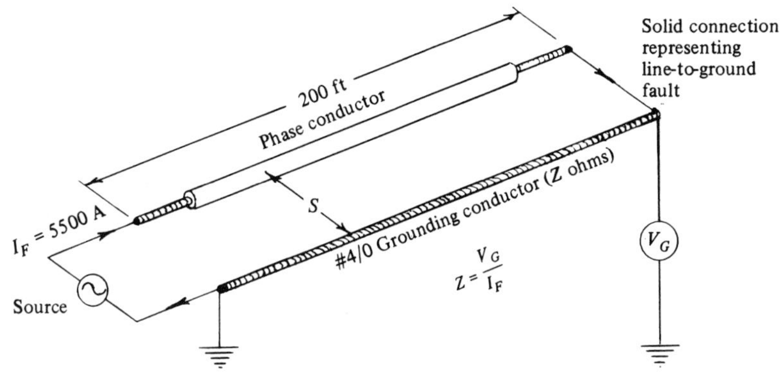

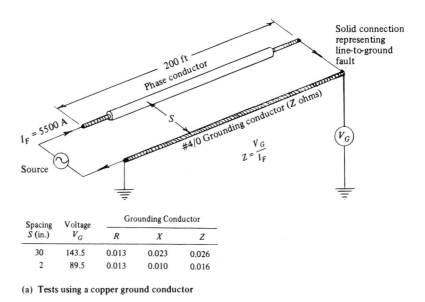

Spacing S (in.)	Voltage V_G	Grounding Conductor R	X	Z
30	143.5	0.013	0.023	0.026
2	89.5	0.013	0.010	0.016

(a) Tests using a copper ground conductor

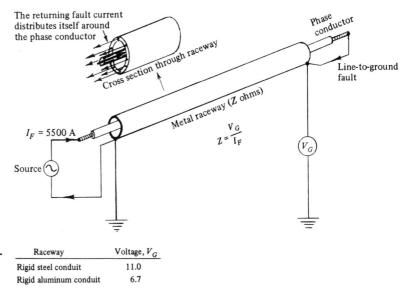

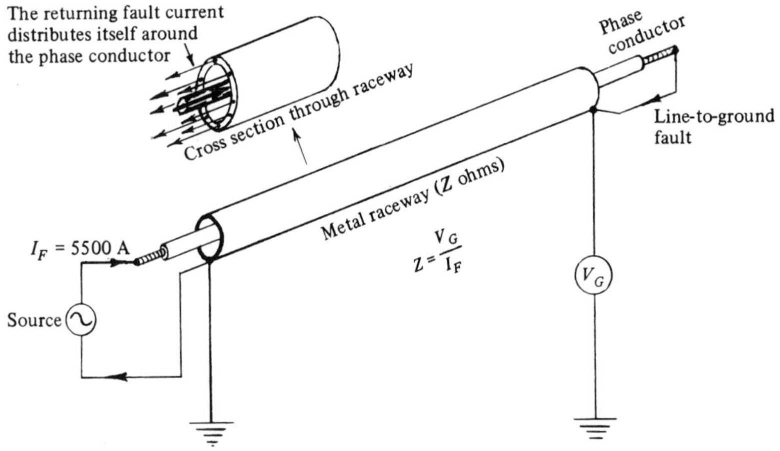

Raceway	Voltage, V_G
Rigid steel conduit	11.0
Rigid aluminum conduit	6.7

(b) Tests using a metal raceway as the ground conductor

FIGURE 10.13

Equipment grounding circuit impedance as a function of its location and configuration

10.3.3 Summary of National Electrical Code Requirements

As shown in the previous examples, a well-planned equipment grounding system must be provided for every electrical system to minimize shock and fire hazards and to ensure proper operation of the protective devices. The total impedance of the equipment grounding circuit must be kept as low as possible. It would be well at this time to reemphasize the difference between a grounded conductor and a grounding conductor. Refer to Figure 10.11. The grounded conductor is the neutral, which is a normal current-carrying conductor of the system. It must be insulated (except in very rare special circumstances) and must be identified by either a white outer finish or a distinctive white mark at its termination (see *NEC* Article 200). The grounding conductor is used to ground the equipment and is a noncurrent-carrying conductor; that is, it carries current only under ground-fault conditions. It usually is bare, but where it is insulated it must be identified by a continuous green color [see *NEC* Section 250-57(b)]. The functions of the two types of conductors are quite different, and there must not be any confusion between them when installing wiring and making connections.

With reference to the *National Electrical Code,* Article 250, Parts D and E, covers the specific requirements for enclosure and equipment grounding. Part F covers methods of grounding, Part G covers bonding, which is the permanent joining of metallic parts to form an electrically conductive path that will assure electrical continuity and the capacity to conduct safely any current likely to be

TABLE 10.1 Minimum Size of Conductors for Grounding AC Systems (from *NEC* Table 250-94)

Size of Largest Service-Entrance Conductor or Equivalent Area for Parallel Conductors		**Size of Grounding Electrode Conductor**	
Copper	**Aluminum or Copper-Clad Aluminum**	**Copper**	**[a]Aluminum or Copper-Clad Aluminum**
2 or smaller	0 or smaller	8	6
1 or 0	2/0 or 3/0	6	4
2/0 or 3/0	4/0 or 250 MCM	4	2
Over 3/0 thru 350 MCM	Over 250 MCM thru 500 MCM	2	0
Over 350 MCM thru 600 MCM	Over 500 MCM thru 900 MCM	0	3/0
Over 600 MCM thru 1100 MCM	Over 900 MCM thru 1750 MCM	2/0	4/0
Over 1100 MCM	Over 1750 MCM	3/0	250 MCM

[a] See installation restrictions in Section 250-92(a).

See Section 250-23(b).

Where there are no service-entrance conductors, the grounding electrode conductor size shall be determined by the equivalent size of the largest service-entrance conductor required for the load to be served.

imposed. Any improper bonding at connections in the equipment grounding circuit could result in dangerous differences of potential under heavy fault conditions. Part H covers the requirements for the grounding electrode system, including the use of metal underground water pipes, metal frames of buildings, and made electrodes (those specifically installed for grounding to the earth). Parts J and K cover the grounding conductors and their connections. Part L covers the special requirements for instrument transformers, relays, and so on. Finally, Part M covers additional requirements for the grounding of systems and circuits of 1 kilovolt and over (medium and high voltage). See Appendix A for Canadian Electrical Code references.

In Figure 10.11, the common grounding electrode conductor as required by *NEC* Section 250-54 is shown connected to the equipment grounding bus. This is permitted by Section 250-23(a), Exception No. 5, and in fact is the preferred arrangement for the application of ground-fault protection as shown in Figure 10.15.

Table 10.1 in this text (*NEC* Table 250-94) shows the minimum size of conductors for grounding ac systems. Table 10.2 (*NEC* Table 250-95) shows the minimum size of equipment grounding conductors for grounding raceways and equipment. The following examples will illustrate the use of these tables.

■ EXAMPLE 10.1

Refer to Figure 10.11. The main secondary feeder from the transformer to the main breaker (the service feeder) consists of two parallel runs of 500 MCM XHHW copper conductors per phase. Determine the size of the common grounding electrode conductor.

Solution

— The equivalent area of the parallel conductors per phase is $2 \times 500 = 1000$ MCM.
— From Table 10.1, the minimum size is No. 2/0 copper.

■ EXAMPLE 10.2

Refer to Figure 10.11. The trip unit for the branch feeder breaker is rated for 350 A, and the branch feeder to the distribution panel is enclosed in a nonmetallic raceway. Determine the size of the bare conductor that has to be run in the raceway for grounding the equipment.

Solution

From Table 10.2, the minimum size is No. 3 copper.

TABLE 10.2 Minimum Size of Equipment Grounding Conductors for Grounding Raceways and Equipment (from *NEC* Table 250-95)

Rating or Setting of Automatic Overcurrent Device in Circuit Ahead of Equipment, Conduit, etc., Not Exceeding (Amperes)	Size	
	Copper Wire No.	Aluminum or Copper-Clad Aluminum Wire No.[a]
15	14	12
20	12	10
30	10	8
40	10	8
60	10	8
100	8	6
200	6	4
300	4	2
400	3	1
500	2	1/0
600	1	2/0
800	0	3/0
1000	2/0	4/0
1200	3/0	250 MCM
1600	4/0	350 MCM
2000	250 MCM	400 MCM
2500	350 MCM	600 MCM
3000	400 MCM	600 MCM
4000	500 MCM	800 MCM
5000	700 MCM	1200 MCM
6000	800 MCM	1200 MCM

[a] See installation restrictions in Section 250-92(a).

10.4 ARCING GROUND FAULTS

As previously discussed in Section 6.3, there are two types of faults: bolted type and arcing type. Bolted-type ground faults are rare. If they do occur, the fault currents are large (with proper equipment grounding), and the overcurrent devices should respond very rapidly, thus minimizing any damage. Ground faults are more likely to be of the arcing types. Because of the relatively higher resistance of the arc and its intermittent nature, the resulting fault currents are much smaller than those for bolted faults and are therefore harder to detect. In recent years, especially as the size of low-voltage systems increased in capacity, in a number of instances extensive damage has been done by arcing faults that were improperly handled. Arcing ground faults have the following characteristics:

1. Arcs have a negative volt–ampere relationship; as the arc current increases, the resistance of the arc decreases. As a result, the voltage drop across an arcing fault is relatively constant (that is, it is independent of the current). Tests have shown that arc voltages fluctuate between 60 and 140 volts, with the average being around 100 volts.
2. Most of the fault energy is concentrated at the arc itself as most of the voltage drop is at the arc. This energy, being confined to a small area, can therefore cause a lot of damage.
3. The arc can travel from its point of origin and can rapidly extend the area of damage.
4. All arcs are extinguished at each current zero point (at each point where the ac current reverses direction) and require a voltage much higher than the arcing voltage drop to restrike. This restrike voltage is approximately 375 volts.
5. Arcs under 200 amperes are unstable and are generally self-extinguishing.

Because of the high restrike voltage, most arcing ground faults extinguish themselves on 208Y/120 volt systems as the peak line-to-ground voltage is only 170 volts (see Figure 1.7). However, on 480Y/277 volt systems (and above), the arcs can be sustained as the peak voltage is 390 volts ($\sqrt{2} \times 277$).

It is difficult to express the amount of damage that can be caused by an arcing fault in absolute terms. After the fact, the amount of damage can of course be indicated in terms of the number of sections of switchgear destroyed, the amount of cable damaged, the number of motors destroyed, and so on. The extent of the damage has some relationship to the amount of electrical energy dissipated in the arc, but equal amounts of energy can cause different amounts of damage in different circumstances. However, notwithstanding these difficulties, Table 10.3 is an attempt to quantify the levels of damage that might be expected. The amount of energy involved in the arc is expressed in kilowatt-cycles (rather than kilowatt-hours) because the elapsed time is relatively short. To demonstrate the amount of damage that can be caused by arcing faults, refer to the two cases shown in Figure 10.14.

In case 1, a 1600 ampere feeder is protected by a low-voltage power circuit breaker that has the older type of electromechanical

TABLE 10.3 Estimated Levels of Damage Caused by Arcing Faults

Fault Energy (kW-cycles)	Estimated Level of Damage
100	Location of fault identifiable only by observation. Some spit and smoke marks.
2,000	Little damage; likely no hardware to replace. Equipment can be restored by cleaning smoke marks and repairing punctured insulation. This is recommended maximum level of let-through fault energy.
10,000	Fault will probably be contained by a metal enclosure.
20,000	Fault will probably burn through a single-thickness enclosure and spread to other sections of the equipment.
Above 20,000	Considerable destruction to equipment in proportion to the let-through fault energy.

series trip units, which respond only to overcurrents (see Section 8.3.2). The typical time–current curve for a breaker with these types of trip units is shown in the diagram. There is inverse time-delayed tripping up to 10 times the rating of the trip unit (that is, its pickup point) and instantaneous tripping above that point (see Section 6.7). Assume that an arcing fault has occurred from one phase of the feeder to ground, which has an rms value of 4000 amperes. This value is only 2.5 times the rating of the trip unit and therefore falls within the range of time-delayed tripping. The breaker with only the series-type trips cannot in fact discriminate between a 4000 ampere overload on the feeder and this arcing fault and therefore takes 80 seconds to disconnect the feeder and extinguish the arc. The 80 seconds amounts to 80 × 60 or 4800 cycles at 60 hertz. Assuming the voltage drop across the arc is 100 volts (the average value), the amount of arcing fault energy is calculated to be 1,920,000 kilowatt-cycles. Reference to Table 10.3 indicates that the amount of damage could be extensive.

On the other hand, if the fault in case 1 is a bolted type with the resulting large current, then the breaker will be tripped instantaneously. Assume a fault current of 32,000 amperes or 20 times the trip rating. The breaker would trip in 0.03 second or approximately 2 cycles, and even though there would be a higher current, the reduction in the elapsed time from 4800 to 2 cycles reduces the amount of fault energy to the point where no permanent damage should be done.

In case 2, a 600 ampere feeder is protected by current-limiting fuses (see Section 7.3). The arcing ground-fault current is assumed

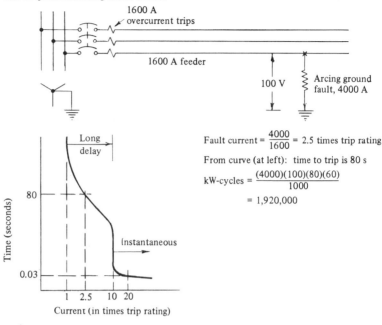

Case 1: protection using circuit breaker

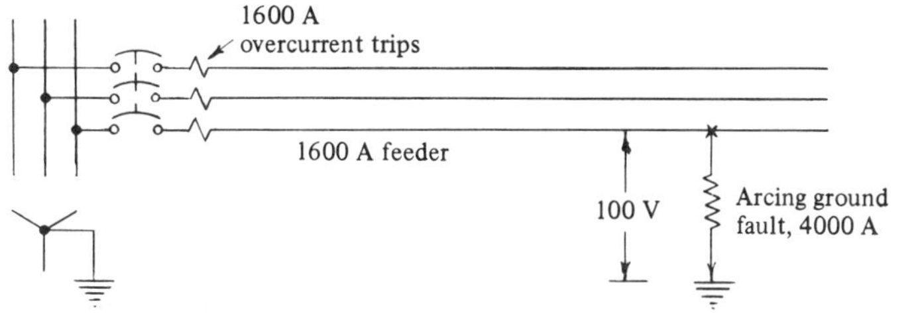

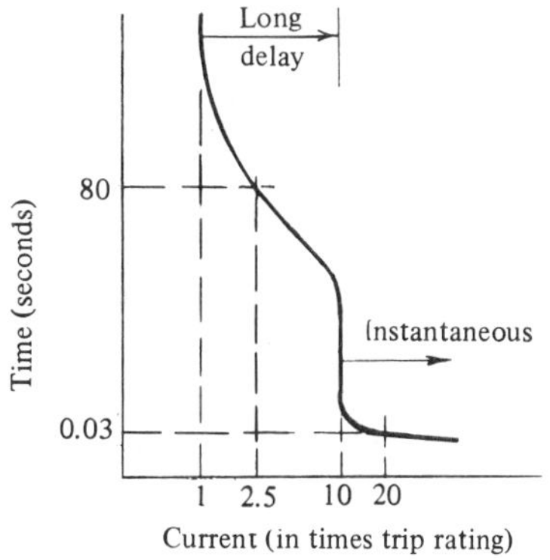

Typical time-current curves for circuit breakers with magnetic trips

$$\text{Fault current} = \frac{4000}{1600} = 2.5 \text{ times trip rating}$$

From curve (at left): time to trip is 80 s

$$\text{kW-cycles} = \frac{(4000)(100)(80)(60)}{1000}$$

$$= 1{,}920{,}000$$

Case 2: protection using fuses

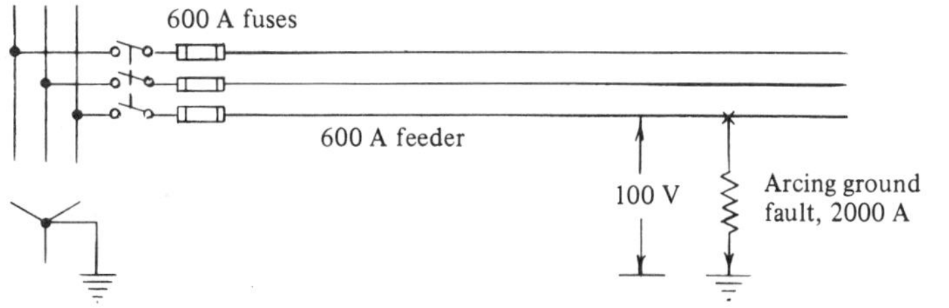

From Figure 7.10, the fuse blows in 70 seconds at 2000 amperes;

$$\text{kW cycles} = \frac{(2000)(100)(70)(60)}{1000} = 840{,}000$$

FIGURE 10.14

Effects of arcing ground faults on feeders with only overcurrent protection

to be 2000 amperes rms. Referring to Figure 7.10, which shows the typical response curves for UL class RK-5 current-limiting fuses, the blowing time for a 600 ampere fuse at 2000 amperes is 70 seconds ($70 \times 60 = 4200$ cycles). Assuming 100 volts across the arc, the fault energy is calculated as 840,000 kilowatt-cycles. Again, at this level of energy, a great deal of damage could be done. Similar to the breaker in case 1, the fuse is incapable of discriminating between an overload current and an arcing fault current. The 2000 ampere fault current is only 3.33 times the fuse rating and therefore well below the level at which the fuse will begin to current limit. If the fault were the bolted type with, for example, a value of 30,000 amperes, then the fuse would blow within one half-cycle and reduce the let-through value of energy to the point where no damage would be done.

10.5 GROUND-FAULT PROTECTION

The two examples presented in Section 10.4 clearly show that the standard type of overcurrent protection, while capable of providing proper protection against overloads and bolted-type faults, cannot at the same time provide adequate protection against arcing-type ground faults, particularly on the larger-capacity feeders. Let us review the parameters against which systems can be protected and which have previously been discussed, that is, overcurrents (Section 6.1), reverse power flow (Section 9.6), and differential protection (Section 9.7). For ground-fault protection, a new parameter must be added; this is the ability to detect the path of the fault current. The protective device must be able to detect whether the current is flowing only in the normal current-carrying conductors of the system or whether the current is flowing partly in the noncurrent-carrying parts of the system. If it is the former, then there may only be a temporary overload on the system, in which case time-delayed operation of the protective device is desirable. If it is the latter, then there must be a ground fault on the system, and the protective device should respond as fast as possible to disconnect the faulted circuit.

The most basic and simplest method of adding ground-fault protection is shown in Figure 10.15. This diagram shows the single-phase representation of a typical three-phase system, such as shown in Figures 10.8 and 10.11. With a ground fault anywhere on the

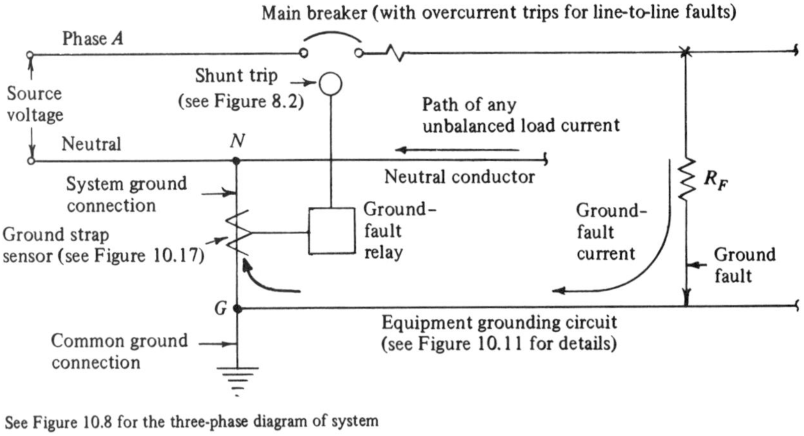

FIGURE 10.15

Basic method of adding ground-fault protection to a system

system, the ground-fault current must flow back through the system ground connection (*G* to *N* on the diagram). Note that any unbalanced load current flows through the neutral conductor directly back to the system neutral point and does not flow through the connection *G–N*. Furthermore, any overloads or line-to-line fault currents will flow only in the phase conductors and will be detected by the standard overcurrent trip units. Therefore, by placing a current sensor in the connection *G–N* as shown, the presence of a ground fault anywhere on the system can immediately be detected. When the ground fault occurs, the resulting fault current through the sensor induces an output to the ground-fault relay, which then energizes the shunt trip on the main breaker to shut the system down.

The pickup point and the timing of the ground-fault relay can be set quite independently from those set for the overcurrent trip units. For example, returning to case 1 in Figure 10.14, assume that ground-fault protection has been added. The ground-fault relay can be set to pick up at a much lower value than 1600 amperes (at 20% of 1600 or 320 amperes) and can be set to instantly trip the breaker. Therefore, the 4000 ampere arcing ground fault will now immediately trip the breaker, thus preventing the arc from doing any permanent damage. On the other hand, a 4000 ampere overload on the feeder will not affect the ground-fault relay, and the breaker will be opened by the series overcurrent trips only if the overload persists for more than 80 seconds.

Figure 10.17 shows a typical current sensor used for this method of ground-fault protection. It is referred to as a ground strap sensor since it is normally installed over the copper bar or strap used to connect the system neutral to the ground bus at the main switchboard. The sensor is essentially a current transformer with the ground strap acting as the primary (see Section 9.3). If a switch and fuse combination is used for the overcurrent protection, the switch must be equipped with an automatic means of opening. The switch must also be able to safely interrupt all currents up to the point where the fuses will take over and clear the fault currents first.

Because of the unusually high number of burn-downs from arcing ground faults that were occurring on 480Y/277 volt systems, the *National Electrical Code,* Section 230-95, now requires that

> Ground-fault protection of equipment shall be provided for solidly grounded wye electrical services of more than 150 volts to ground, but not exceeding 600 volts phase-to-phase for each service disconnecting means rated 1000 amperes or more. The ground-fault protection system shall operate to cause the service disconnecting means to open all ungrounded conductors of the faulted circuit. The maximum setting of the ground-fault protection shall be 1200 amperes and the maximum time delay shall be one second for ground-fault currents equal to or greater than 3000 amperes.

Section 230-95 also carries a note to the effect that *ground-fault protection may be desirable for service disconnecting means rated less than 1000 amperes*. Case 2 in Figure 10.14 shows that ground-fault protection should definitely be considered for services less than 1000 amperes.

The foregoing method of ground-fault protection is relatively inexpensive to add to a system and it fully meets the code requirements. However, it has one major disadvantage: a ground fault anywhere on the system in excess of the pickup point of the ground-fault relay shuts down the entire system. This could prove to be inconvenient and costly in the long run because of the loss of work time and production. To overcome this disadvantage, ground-fault protection with selective coordination can be used.

10.5.1 Selective Coordination of Ground-Fault Protection

Selective coordination requires that only the actual circuit that is faulted be shut down. The desirability of having coordination of the protective devices is discussed in the introduction to Chapter 6. To obtain coordination, each branch feeder must be provided with its own ground-fault protection system.

Circuit breakers that use thermal–magnetic series overcurrent trip units, such as the standard molded-case breakers (Section 8.4.1) and the older type of low-voltage power circuit breakers that use magnetic series trip units, must have ground-fault protection added as shown in Figure 10.16(a). A ground-fault sensor is located on the loadside of the breaker through which all the feeder current-carrying conductors (phase conductors and the neutral when used) must be run. As long as the feeder currents flow only in these conductors, the instantaneous values of all the currents add up to zero, and there is no output from the sensor (see Section 1.6 for the current relationships in three-phase systems). However, when a ground fault occurs on any of the phases, part of the current returns outside the sensor through the equipment grounding circuit, and the currents flowing through the sensor no longer sum to zero. The resulting magnetic field induces an output from the sensor, which activates the ground-fault relay, which in turn energizes the shunt trip to open the breaker. Depending on the type and size of the breaker, an external source of control power may be needed to operate the system. The sensors come in two basic shapes, as shown in Figure 10.17. The toroidal shape is used when the sensor is to enclose cables, and the rectangular shape is used when the sensor is to enclose rigid copper or aluminum bus bars. These sensors are also referred to as *zero-sequence*, or preferably *core balance* current transformers.

The larger frame sizes of molded-case circuit breakers and the newer versions of the low-voltage power circuit breakers with solid-state trip units (Section 8.5.1) have the ground-fault protection in-

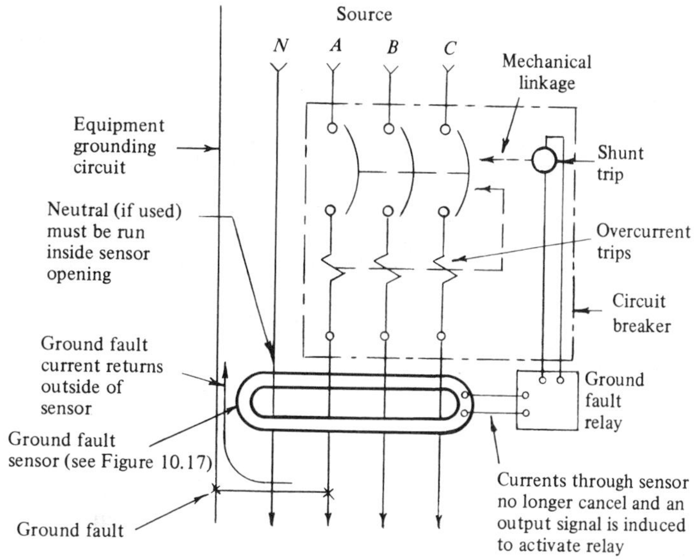

(a) Breakers with thermal and/or magnetic overcurrent trip units

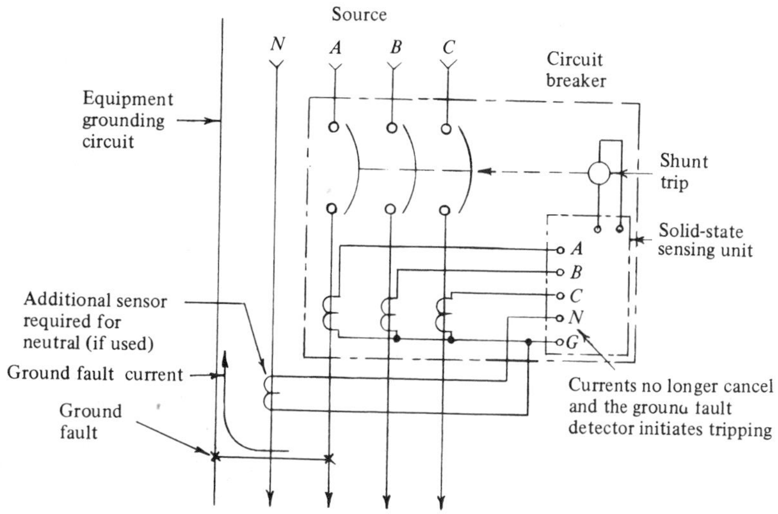

(b) Breakers with solid-state trip units

FIGURE 10.16

Methods of providing ground-fault protection using circuit breakers

corporated directly into the system, as shown in Figure 10.16(b). An additional sensor is required for the neutral conductor when used in the feeder. As long as the current outputs from the sensors sum to zero, the input to the ground-fault detector (N–G) is zero. However, when a ground fault occurs, the current outputs from the sensors no

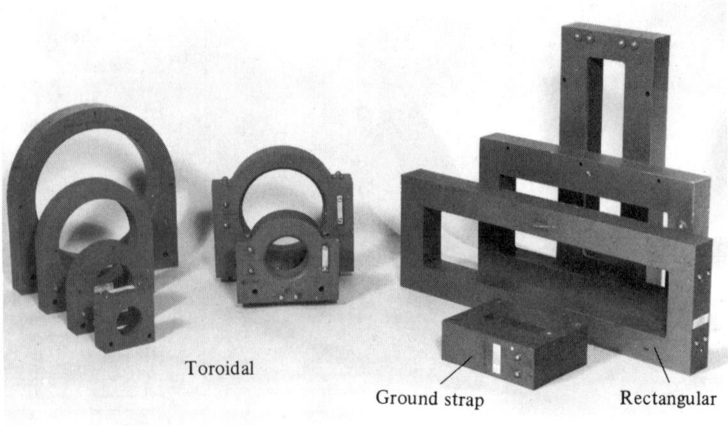

FIGURE 10.17

Ground-fault sensors (core-balance CTs)

longer sum to zero, since part of the current is returning through the equipment grounding circuit. The ground-fault detector is activated and initiates tripping of the breaker.

Selective coordination can be achieved in two ways, the time-coordinated method and the zone-selective interlocking method. Refer to Figure 10.18. The systems shown are in the form of one-line diagrams. For an explanation of this type of diagram, refer to the introduction to Chapter 11. The time-coordinated method, as shown in part (a), obtains coordination by progressively setting longer time delays on the ground-fault protection system for the breakers closer to the source. The tripping times shown on the diagram are obtained from Figure 8.13. If a ground fault occurs on a subfeeder (point *C*), breaker 3 can clear this fault before the main feeder breaker 2 has time to react. Therefore, only the faulted subfeeder is shut down. Similarly, if a ground fault occurs on a main feeder (point *B*), breaker 2 can clear this fault and the main breaker stays closed. The drawback to the time-coordinated method is that the duration of the faults becomes progressively longer with more levels of selectivity. For example, a large fault on the main bus at point *A*, which should be cleared instantly, is instead allowed to persist for 0.50 second (30 cycles) before it is cleared. This considerably increases the probability that damage will occur at a very vital section of the system.

The zone-selective interlocking method overcomes this disadvantage of the time-coordinated method. As shown in Figure 10.18(b), control wiring is run between the breakers at each level of protection. With the addition of special circuitry within the ground-fault relays to provide appropriate restraint signals, each level of breaker is then able to discriminate between a fault in its own zone and one in a zone further downstream. Thus a breaker instantly clears a fault in its own zone. If the fault is in a downstream zone, it

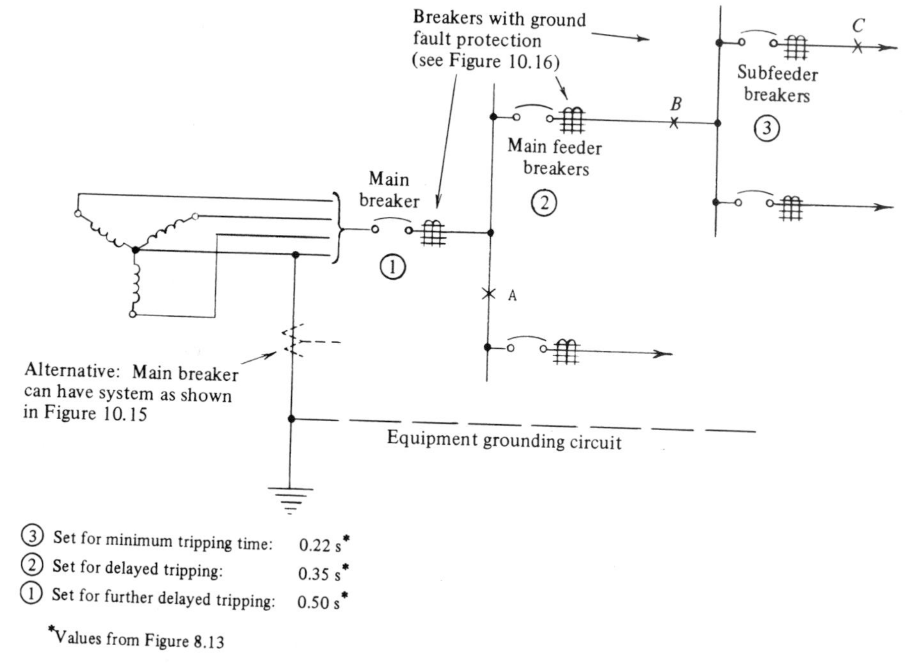

Breakers with ground fault protection (see Figure 10.16)
C
Subfeeder breakers
③
B
Main feeder breakers
②
Main breaker
①
A
Alternative: Main breaker can have system as shown in Figure 10.15
Equipment grounding circuit
③ Set for minimum tripping time: 0.22 s*
② Set for delayed tripping: 0.35 s*
① Set for further delayed tripping: 0.50 s*
*Values from Figure 8.13

(a) Time-coordinated selective method

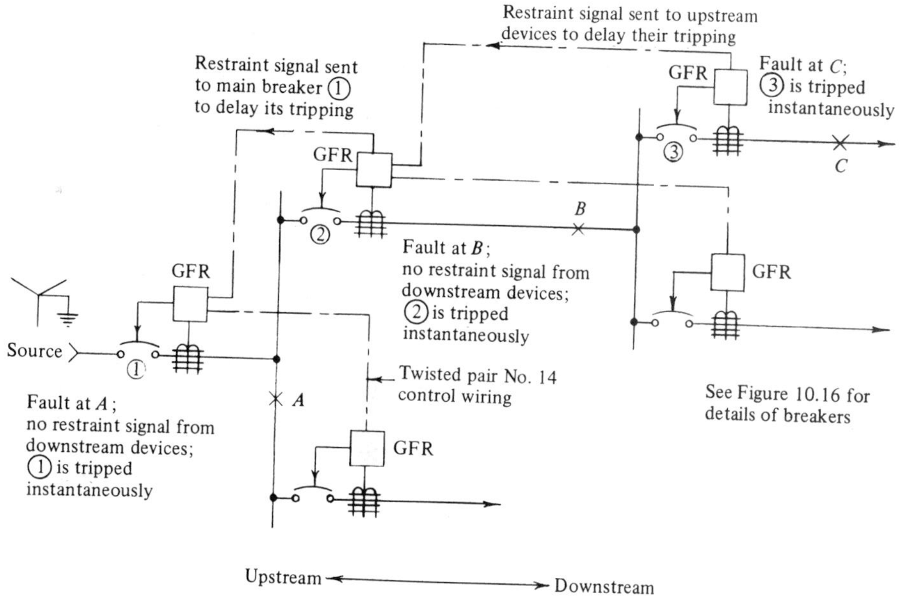

Restraint signal sent to upstream devices to delay their tripping
Restraint signal sent to main breaker ① to delay its tripping
GFR
Fault at C; ③ is tripped instantaneously
③
C
GFR
②
B
Fault at B; no restraint signal from downstream devices; ② is tripped instantaneously
GFR
GFR
Source
①
Twisted pair No. 14 control wiring
Fault at A; no restraint signal from downstream devices; ① is tripped instantaneously
A
See Figure 10.16 for details of breakers
GFR
Upstream
Downstream

(b) Zone-selective interlocking method

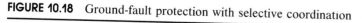

FIGURE 10.18 Ground-fault protection with selective coordination

is put on time delay and will only trip if the appropriate downstream breaker fails to clear the fault. This system then provides the best possible protection to a system, confining the area of shutdown to the faulted circuit and minimizing the possibility of damage from heavy faults at points close to the source. There is, however, the disadvantage of the additional cost of installing the control wiring between the various levels of protection. In the long run, this could turn out to be a wise investment if it prevents costly shutdowns.

Ground-fault protection can also be provided when using protective relays in conjunction with a circuit breaker, as discussed in Section 9.5.2 and shown in Figure 9.9.

The previous discussions have all been concerned with the protection of systems and equipment. Equally important is the protection of personnel from the shock hazards of ground faults. However, this requires a much keener level of response than that required for equipment. A ground-fault circuit interrupter (GFCI), which responds to ground faults at a level of 5.0 milliamperes, is used for the protection of branch circuits where required by the code. The use of GFCIs is covered in Section 12.10.

10.6 HIGH-RESISTANCE GROUNDED SYSTEMS

In previous discussions of grounded systems, it has been assumed that the systems were solidly grounded. A solidly grounded system is one in which there is no intentional impedance in the system ground connection. However, a system can be grounded through a resistor. With resistance grounding, an intentional resistance is inserted in the system ground connection for the purpose of limiting the magnitude of the ground-fault current. There are two levels of resistance grounding, low resistance and high resistance.

With low-resistance grounding, the value of the resistance is sufficient only to limit the magnitude of the ground-fault current so that serious damage does not occur. The system must still be shut down after the first ground fault. This level of resistance grounding is generally used only on medium- and high-voltage systems.

On the other hand, for high-resistance grounding, the value of the resistance is high enough to limit the ground-fault current to a very low value, typically on the order of 5 amperes. This low magnitude of current can be tolerated on the system until the ground fault is located and removed. The major advantage then is the fact that the system does not have to be shut down for the first ground fault that occurs on the system. This is the same advantage enjoyed with the ungrounded system, but it is obtained without many of the disadvantages of the ungrounded system.

Figure 10.19 shows a system with high-resistance grounding. Note the position of the grounding resistor R_N. It must be placed

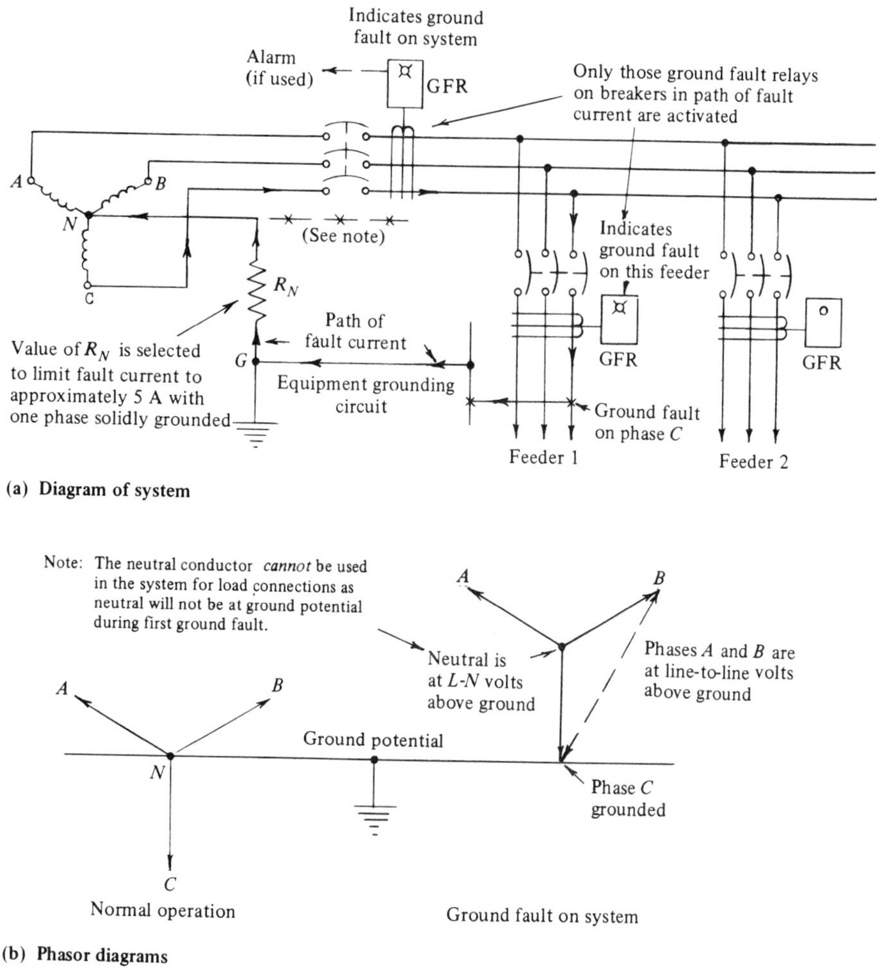

FIGURE 10.19

High-resistance grounded system

between the source neutral point N and point G. It cannot be placed in the common grounding connection (between point G and the earth connection), nor can it be placed in the actual equipment grounding circuit. The value of R_N for a 480Y/277 volt system, if the ground-fault current is going to be limited to the 5 amperes shown, is 277/5 or 55 ohms. The value of R_N cannot be too high. Refer to Figure 10.4(a). The ohmic value of R_N must be less than the ohmic value of the effective distributed capacitance X_C of the system. Otherwise, the transient overvoltage conditions, as is possible with ungrounded systems, can occur. In other words, if the value of R_N is too high, the system will start to behave like an ungrounded system.

With high-resistance grounded systems, in addition to allowing the system to continue operating after the first ground fault without any shutdowns, other advantages can be incorporated into the system. As shown in Figure 10.19, the ground-fault relays do not trip the breakers on a ground fault. They are used instead, first, to indicate that a ground fault has occurred and, second, to indicate the location of the ground fault (that is, which feeder is faulted). This is a tremendous advantage over the ungrounded system, as the location of the fault is indicated without the necessity of shutting down any part of the system. The ground fault can then be removed at the first convenient time. The final advantage of the high-resistance grounded system is that it eliminates any dangerous and destructive flash-overs to ground, such as can occur on solidly grounded systems.

As is the case with most systems, there are some disadvantages. Similar to the ungrounded systems, after the first ground fault on the system, the voltage to ground of the two unfaulted phases rises to the line-to-line voltage, as shown in the phasor diagrams in Figure 10.19. While each phase is insulated for the full line-to-line voltage, the 73% increase in the voltage stressing can increase the likelihood of insulation breakdowns over the expected life of the system. A second disadvantage, again similar to the ungrounded system, is that the occurrence of a second ground fault on another phase before the first ground fault is removed then creates a line-to-line fault. Both faulted parts of the system will be shut down simultaneously. Also, the large fault current must travel over the equipment grounding circuit between the two fault points. Both disadvantages can be minimized by removing the first ground fault as quickly as possible.

The third disadvantage with the high-resistance grounded system is the fact that, with a ground fault on one of the phases, the neutral point of the system rises to line-to-neutral voltage above ground, as shown in Figure 10.19 (b). Therefore, the neutral cannot be used in the system for load connections, as the neutral when used as a circuit conductor must remain at ground potential at all times. This precludes such single-phase loads as fluorescent lighting, which is normally connected line-to-neutral, from being directly connected to the system. Instead, these loads must be fed through separate transformers, with the neutral of the secondaries of these transformers solidly grounded. High-intensity discharge (HID) light sources are an exception to this problem. Two-winding transformers can be used for the ballasts of each lamp, as shown in Figure 10.20. The primary of the ballast can be connected line to line to the high-resistance grounded system and the secondary, which is electrically isolated from the primary, can then be grounded as shown.

In conclusion, the high-resistance grounded system is not a good choice for a commercial building where a significant part of the

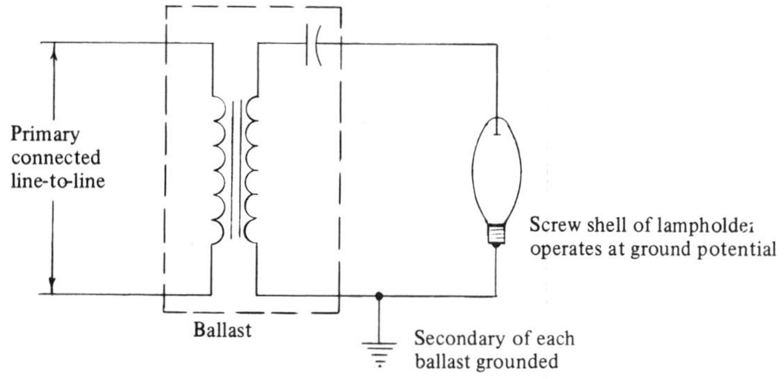

FIGURE 10.20

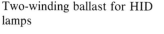

Two-winding ballast for HID lamps

load is likely to be fluorescent lighting. However, for an industrial plant where the majority of the load consists of three-phase motors and where the HID light source (mercury, metal halide, or high-pressure sodium lamp) is usually the best choice for large area lighting, the high-resistance grounded system should be considered. The small amount of power required for office lighting and 120 volt, single-phase loads can easily be supplied through separate transformers with solidly grounded secondaries.

There has been a definite trend in the last few years toward the use of high-resistance grounding for 480Y/277 volt and 600Y/347 volt systems in industrial plants, especially those where continuity of power is vital. Exception 5 has been added to Section 250-5(b) in the 1987 *National Electrical Code*. This exception permits the use of high-resistance grounded neutral systems for three-phase ac systems of 480 to 1000 volts provided that (1) the conditions of maintenance and supervision assure that only qualified persons will service the installation, (2) continuity of power is required, (3) ground detectors are installed on the system, and (4) line-to-neutral loads are not served. Section 250-27 has also been added to cover the requirements for high-impedance grounded neutral system connections.

SUMMARY

- System grounding is the intentional electrical connection to ground of one of the current-carrying conductors of the electrical system.
- Equipment grounding is the connection to ground of all the nonelectrical conductive materials that enclose or are adjacent to the energized conductors.
- Ungrounded delta systems, while offering some advantages, have many operating disadvantages. High transient overvoltages can occur that are not immediately evident. Ground faults are difficult to locate.

- Grounded wye systems, while having the disadvantage of a partial shutdown after the first ground fault, have many important advantages. System potentials to ground are limited to safe values. The location of the ground fault is immediately indicated.
- The neutral of each separately derived system or section of a system should be grounded only once as close to the source as possible.
- The primary purpose of equipment grounding is to eliminate any shock hazards between the exposed enclosures of the system and ground.
- The equipment grounding system must have adequate current-carrying capability to handle any ground-fault current without creating any shock, fire, or explosion hazards.
- The impedance of the equipment grounding circuit must be kept as low as possible to ensure proper operation of protective devices and to minimize any dangerous differences of potential under fault conditions.
- There must be only one common connection to earth for both the system and equipment grounding.
- The metallic raceways used to carry circuit conductors offer a very low impedance return path for ground-fault currents when properly installed as part of the equipment grounding system.
- Arcing ground faults, if not properly handled, can do a great deal of damage on systems that operate at more than 150 volts to ground.
- Ground-fault protection is required by code on all solidly grounded systems that exceed 150 volts to ground and are rated at 1000 amperes or more.
- Selective coordination of the ground-fault protection confines any power shutdown to the faulted circuit.
- High-resistance grounding of systems, where practical, offers some important operating advantages. No part of the system has to be shut down after the first ground fault. The location of the ground fault can easily be determined without disrupting the operation of the system.

QUESTIONS

1. What is the difference between system grounding and equipment grounding?
2. What is an ungrounded system?
3. What is the principal reason for operating a system ungrounded?
4. What is the advantage of using three single-phase transformers connected in delta?
5. List four disadvantages of ungrounded systems.
6. What is the most significant operating characteristic of the grounded system?
7. Which low-voltage systems are required by the electrical code to be grounded?
8. What is the primary purpose for grounding an electrical system?

9. List all other benefits of a grounded system.
10. What are the two disadvantages of grounded systems?
11. What differentiates a separately derived system from one that is not separately derived?
12. List three points governing the grounding of separately derived systems.
13. Explain why the neutral of a separately derived system should be grounded at one location only.
14. What are the noncurrent-carrying conductors of a system?
15. List the components that can form part of the equipment grounding circuit of a system.
16. What are the three objectives of the equipment grounding system?
17. What operating problems arise if the impedance of the equipment grounding circuit is too high?
18. Why does the electrical code call for one common grounding electrode for both the system and equipment grounding?
19. Why is it necessary to keep an equipment grounding circuit conductor as close as possible to the feeder phase conductors?
20. Does a metal raceway used to carry the feeder conductors serve as a good equipment grounding conductor? Explain.
21. Why are arcing ground faults hard to detect with the standard overcurrent devices?
22. Why can arcing ground faults cause a lot of damage?
23. Why do sustained arcing ground faults rarely occur on 208Y/120 volt systems?
24. What is the additional parameter required for ground-fault protection?
25. With reference to Figure 10.15, explain why the ground-fault relay sensor must be located between points N and G.
26. What is the major disadvantage of the method of ground-fault protection as shown in Figure 10.15?
27. Which systems are required by the electrical code to have ground-fault protection?
28. What is the major disadvantage of the time-coordinated method of ground-fault protection?
29. What is the major improvement offered by the zone-selective interlocking method of ground-fault protection?
30. What is the purpose of high resistance as used for grounding a system?
31. What is the major advantage of the high-resistance grounded system?
32. With reference to Figure 10.19, explain why the grounding resistor R_N must be connected between points N and G.
33. For a high-resistance grounded system, why is the neutral not permitted to be used as a circuit conductor to connect to loads?

PROBLEMS

1. The service entrance feeder conductors for a system are 300 MCM THW copper. Determine the minimum size of the common grounding electrode conductor (copper).
2. The service entrance feeder conductors for a system are No. 1 aluminum. Determine the minimum size of the common grounding electrode conductor (aluminum).
3. A feeder is protected by a 1600 A frame breaker with a 1200 A trip unit. Determine the minimum size of the equipment grounding conductor (copper).
4. A feeder is protected by a 600 A fuse. Determine the minimum size of the equipment grounding conductor (copper).
5. Determine the estimated level of damage if a 1000 rms ampere arcing ground fault occurs on a feeder protected by 400 A UL class RK-5 fuses (Figure 7.10).

11 Design of Feeders

OBJECTIVES

After studying this chapter, you will be able to:

- Identify the factors that affect ampacity ratings of conductors.
- Determine the ampacity ratings of conductors.
- Determine the short-circuit rating of conductors.
- Determine the voltage drop of a feeder.
- Identify types of cables.
- Recognize the uses of raceways.
- Select conduit sizes.
- Design feeders.
- Recognize the purpose for using cable trays and busways.

INTRODUCTION

We have now reached the point where we can begin to discuss the actual design of the electrical system itself. All electrical systems have the common purpose of providing electrical energy to the utilization equipment as safely and reliably as economically possible. The system must be adequate to deliver to the location of each piece of equipment the necessary energy on a continuous basis, without any component overheating or causing unacceptable voltage drops.

The initial planning of a system involves the preparation of a one-line diagram showing all the interconnections and basic components, such as shown in Figure 11.1. The one-line format uses simplified symbols and a single line to represent a feeder or circuit, rather than using a line to represent each phase or conductor of the system. For further explanation of the one-line concept, refer to Figure 13.1.

An important part of any electrical system is the electrical wiring that connects all the components. The connecting wiring can be divided into three sections, as shown in Figure 11.1:

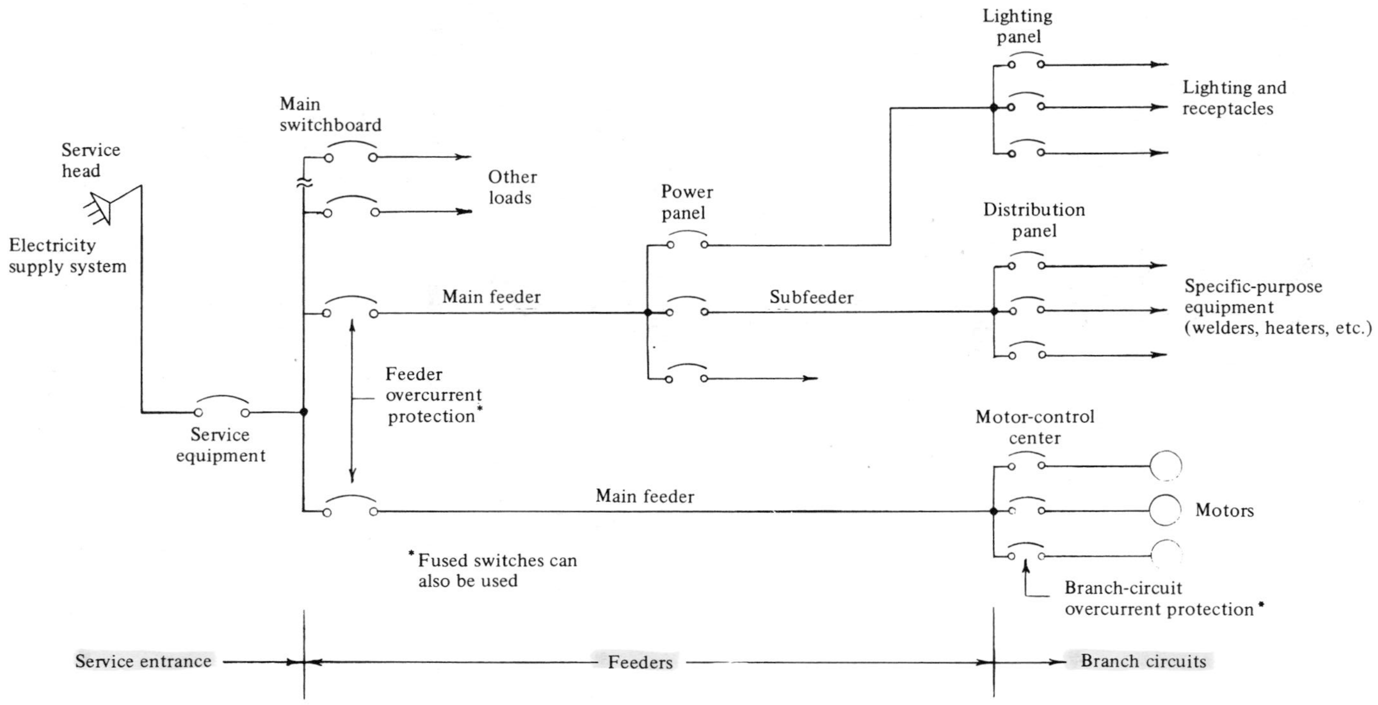

FIGURE 11.1

One-line diagram showing basic system components

1. *Service entrance:* These are the conductors for delivering energy from the electricity supply system to the premises being served. The conductors are terminated near their point of entrance into the building in the service equipment. The service equipment is the main control and means of cutoff for the supply. In the case of a large premise, the electric power is usually supplied by the electric utility at a medium-voltage level, requiring a transformer to step down the voltage to the utilization level. The typical one-line diagram for such an arrangement is shown in Figure 15.1.
2. *Feeders:* These are the conductors for delivering the energy from the service equipment location to the final branch-circuit overcurrent device protecting each piece of utilization equipment. Main feeders originate at the service equipment location, and subfeeders originate at panelboards or distribution centers at other than the service equipment location.
3. *Branch circuits:* These are the conductors for delivering the energy from the point of the final overcurrent device to the utilization equipment.

Each feeder, subfeeder, and branch circuit in turn needs its own overcurrent protection in the form of a circuit breaker or fused switch.

Perhaps at this time we should clear up some basic terminology related to *wires*. The term *conductor* refers properly to the copper or aluminum wire that actually carries the electric current. An insulated conductor is one that is encased within electrical insulation material. The term *cable* then refers to the complete wire assembly including the conductor, the insulation, and any shielding and/or outer protective covering where used. Cables can have just a single conductor or they can have more than one conductor, each separately insulated, but all enclosed in one overall covering. See Figure 11.2 for examples of some commonly used cables. The primary function of the cable is to carry the electrical energy reliably between the source and the utilization equipment.

This chapter deals in general with the proper selection of conductors for feeders and circuits. The reader is also referred to the *National Electrical Code,* Chapter 3, Wiring Methods and Materials. See Appendix A for the Canadian Electrical Code (CEC) requirements. The specific codes relating to branch circuits for lighting and receptacles are covered in Chapter 12 and those for motors are covered in Chapter 13.

The selection of the correct size of the conductors for feeders and branch circuits depends on the following:

1. Continuous current rating

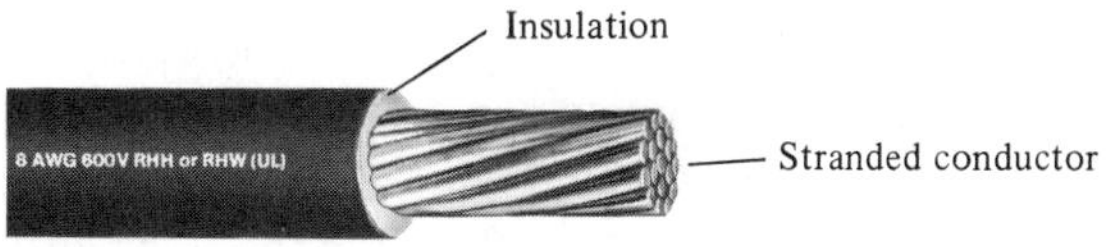

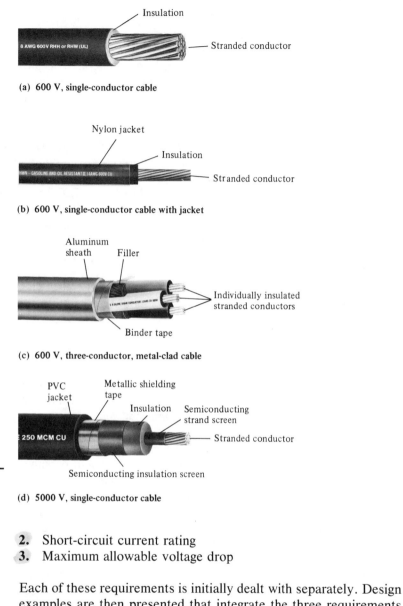

(a) 600 V, single-conductor cable

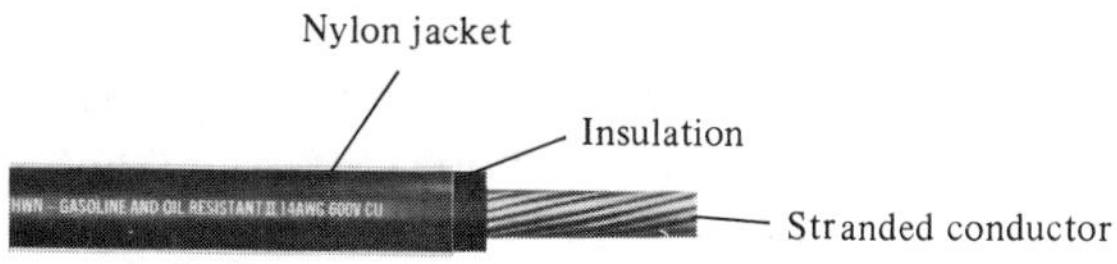

(b) 600 V, single-conductor cable with jacket

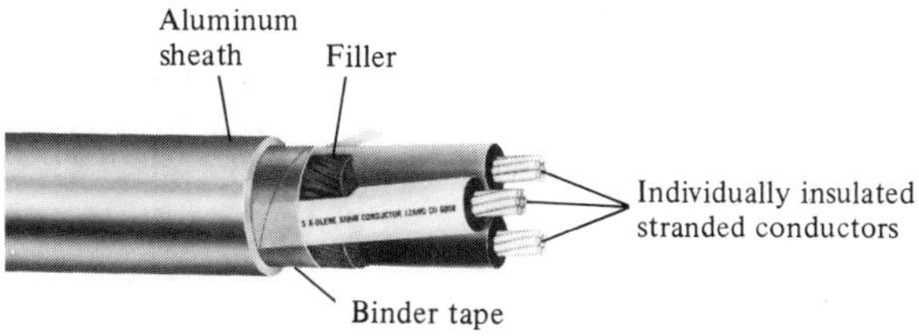

(c) 600 V, three-conductor, metal-clad cable

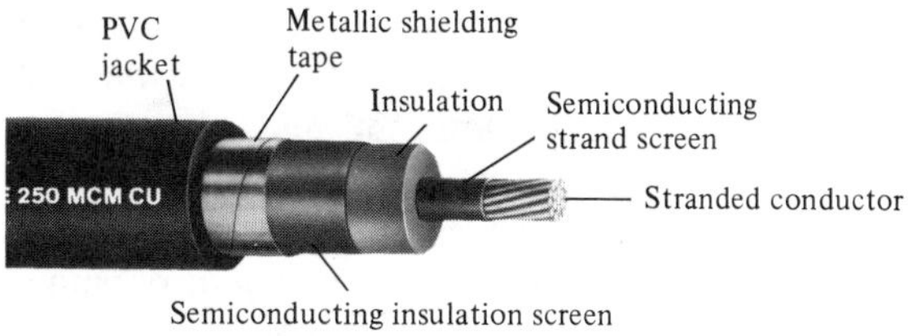

(d) 5000 V, single-conductor cable

FIGURE 11.2

Examples of commonly used cables

2. Short-circuit current rating
3. Maximum allowable voltage drop

Each of these requirements is initially dealt with separately. Design examples are then presented that integrate the three requirements into the selection of the conductor size for a particular feeder.

11.1 CONTINUOUS CURRENT RATING OF CONDUCTORS

The continuous current rating of a conductor is referred to in the *National Electrical Code* as *ampacity* and is defined as *the current in amperes a conductor can carry continuously under the conditions of use without exceeding its temperature rating*. The physical characteristics of a cable obviously play an important part in determining the ampacity rating of the conductor. However, equally important, as indicated in the foregoing definition, are the *conditions of use* under which the cable operates. As current flows in the conductor of the cable, heat is generated because of the resistance of the conductor (the heat is proportional to I^2R as per Section 1.1.4). The rate at which this heat can be dissipated is not only dependent on the insulating material of the cable but also on the environment that surrounds the cable, for example the air temperature. The precise calculations to determine the ampacity of a conductor operating under specific conditions are very complex. Fortunately, tables have been prepared that allow us to obtain this ampacity rating fairly quickly. Section 310-15 of the *NEC* specifically covers the ampacities of conductors. Tables 310-16 through 310-31 apply to conductors rated for 0 to 2000 volts, and Tables 310-69 through 310-84 apply to solid dielectric insulated cables rated for 2001 to 35,000 volts. We will start by analyzing *NEC* Tables 310-16 and 310-27 (reproduced here as Tables 11.1 and 11.2), which are the two most applicable to wiring in and adjacent to buildings. The ampacity rating of a conductor depends on the following characteristics and conditions.

11.1.1 Size of Conductor

The size of a conductor is a measure of its cross-sectional area. There are two methods of indicating conductor sizes. The smaller sizes are designated by the American Wire Gage (AWG) number; the lower the number, the greater the cross-sectional area (thus a No. 12 conductor is larger than a No. 14). For general power wiring in a building, the smallest size of copper conductor that can be used for the low-voltage wiring is No. 14 (rated for a maximum loading of 15 amperes). Unfortunately, when the AWG designation was adopted many years ago, presumably it was not foreseen that conductors larger than No. 1 would be in common use. For the next size larger the designation 0 was adopted. Then in an attempt to carry on with this system the next three larger sizes were designated as 00, 000, and 0000, respectively. However, as shown in Tables 11.1 and 11.2, it is common practice to identify these conductor sizes as 1/0, 2/0, 3/0, and 4/0 (pronounced one-aught, two-aught, and so on).

For conductors larger than 4/0, the cross-sectional area in thousands of circular mils (MCM) is used to designate their size. Thus the next size above 4/0 (211.6 MCM) is 250 MCM. Note that M is used here to designate 1000. This is not consistent with the SI system, which uses k for 1000. Thus MCM should be more properly designated kcmil. A circular mil is the area of a circle that is 1 mil or 1/1000th of an inch in diameter. The circular mil area of a conductor is then equal to its diameter in mils squared. Thus a solid conductor, 1 inch (1000 mils) in diameter, has a circular mil area of 1000 times 1000 or 1,000,000, which is designated 1000 MCM. Its area in square

TABLE 11.1 Ampacities of Not More Than Three Single Insulated Conductors, Rated 0 through 2000 Volts, in Raceway in Free Air (from *NEC* Table 310-16)

Based on Ambient Air Temperature of 30°C (86°F).

Size	Temperature Rating of Conductor. See Table 310-13.								Size
	60°C (140°F)	75°C (167°F)	85°C (185°F)	90°C (194°F)	60°C (140°F)	75°C (167°F)	85°C (185°F)	90°C (194°F)	
AWG MCM	TYPES †TW, †UF	TYPES †FEPW, †RH, †RHW, †THW, †THWN, †XHHW, †USE, †ZW	TYPE V	TYPES TA, TBS, SA, AVB, SIS, †FEP, †FEPB, †RHH, †THHN, †XHHW*	TYPES †TW, †UF	TYPES †RH, †RHW, †THW, †THWN, †XHHW †USE	TYPE V	TYPES TA, TBS, SA, AVB, SIS, †RHH, †THHN, †XHHW*	AWG MCM
	COPPER				ALUMINUM OR COPPER-CLAD ALUMINUM				
18	....	....	....	14	....	....	....	....	....
16	....	....	18	18	....	....	....	....	....
14	20†	20†	25	25†	....	....	....	....	....
12	25†	25†	30	30†	20†	20†	25	25†	12
10	30	35†	40	40†	25	30†	30	35†	10
8	40	50	55	55	30	40	40	45	8
6	55	65	70	75	40	50	55	60	6
4	70	85	95	95	55	65	75	75	4
3	85	100	110	110	65	75	85	85	3
2	95	115	125	130	75	90	100	100	2
1	110	130	145	150	85	100	110	115	1
1/0	125	150	165	170	100	120	130	135	1/0
2/0	145	175	190	195	115	135	145	150	2/0
3/0	165	200	215	225	130	155	170	175	3/0
4/0	195	230	250	260	150	180	195	205	4/0
250	215	255	275	290	170	205	220	230	250
300	240	285	310	320	190	230	250	255	300
350	260	310	340	350	210	250	270	280	350
400	280	335	365	380	225	270	295	305	400
500	320	380	415	430	260	310	335	350	500
600	355	420	460	475	285	340	370	385	600
700	385	460	500	520	310	375	405	420	700
750	400	475	515	535	320	385	420	435	750
800	410	490	535	555	330	395	430	450	800
900	435	520	565	585	355	425	465	480	900
1000	455	545	590	615	375	445	485	500	1000
1250	495	590	640	665	405	485	525	545	1250
1500	520	625	680	705	435	520	565	585	1500
1750	545	650	705	735	455	545	595	615	1750
2000	560	665	725	750	470	560	610	630	2000
	AMPACITY CORRECTION FACTORS								
Ambient Temp. °C	For ambient temperatures other than 30°C (86°F), multiply the ampacities shown above by the appropriate factor shown below.								Ambient Temp. °F
21-25	1.08	1.05	1.04	1.04	1.08	1.05	1.04	1.04	70-77
26-30	1.00	1.00	1.00	1.00	1.00	1.00	1.00	1.00	79-86
31-35	.91	.94	.95	.96	.91	.94	.95	.96	88-95
36-40	.82	.88	.90	.91	.82	.88	.90	.91	97-104
41-45	.71	.82	.85	.87	.71	.82	.85	.87	106-113
46-50	.58	.75	.80	.82	.58	.75	.80	.82	115-122
51-55	.41	.67	.74	.76	.41	.67	74	.76	124-131
56-60	....	.58	.67	.71	....	.58	.67	.71	133-140
61-70	....	.33	.52	.58	....	.33	.52	.58	142-158
71-80	....	....	.30	.41	....	....	.30	.41	160-176

† Unless otherwise specifically permitted elsewhere in this Code, the overcurrent protection for conductor types marked with an obelisk (†) shall not exceed 15 amperes for 14 AWG, 20 amperes for 12 AWG, and 30 amperes for 10 AWG copper; or 15 amperes for 12 AWG and 25 amperes for 10 AWG aluminum and copper-clad aluminum after any correction factors for ambient temperature and number of conductors have been applied.

* For dry and damp locations only. See 75°C column for wet locations.

TABLE 11.2 Ampacities of Three Single Insulated Conductors, Rated 0 through 2000 Volts, in Underground Electrical Ducts (from *NEC* Table 310-27)

Table 310-27. Ampacities of Three Single Insulated Conductors, Rated 0 through 2000 Volts, in Underground Electrical Ducts (Three Conductors per Electrical Duct) Based on Ambient Earth Temperature of 20°C (68°F), Electrical Duct Arrangement per Figure 310-1, 100 Percent Load Factor, Thermal Resistance (RHO) of 90, Conductor Temperature 75°C (167°F)

Size							Size
	1 Electrical Duct (Fig. 310-1 Detail 1)	3 Electrical Ducts (Fig. 310-1 Detail 2)	6 Electrical Ducts (Fig. 310-1 Detail 3)	1 Electrical Duct (Fig. 310-1 Detail 1)	3 Electrical Ducts (Fig. 310-1 Detail 2)	6 Electrical Ducts (Fig. 310-1 Detail 3)	
AWG MCM	TYPES †RHW, †THW, †THWN, †XHHW, †USE	TYPES †RHW, †THW, †THWN, †XHHW, †USE	TYPES †RHW, †THW, †THWN, †XHHW, †USE	TYPES †RHW, †THW, †THWN, †XHHW, †USE	TYPES †RHW, †THW, †THWN, †XHHW, †USE	TYPES †RHW, †THW, †THWN, †XHHW, †USE	AWG MCM
	COPPER			ALUMINUM OR COPPER-CLAD ALUMINUM			
14	24†	22†	16†	....	....	....	14
12	36†	31†	24†	28†	22†	18†	12
10	46†	41†	32†	36†	31†	25†	10
8	58	51	44	45	40	34	8
6	77	67	56	60	52	44	6
4	100	86	73	78	67	57	4
3	116	99	83	91	77	65	3
2	132	112	93	103	87	73	2
1	153	128	106	119	100	83	1
1/0	175	146	121	136	114	94	1/0
2/0	200	166	136	156	130	106	2/0
3/0	228	189	154	178	147	121	3/0
4/0	263	215	175	205	168	137	4/0
250	290	236	192	227	185	150	250
300	321	260	210	252	204	165	300
350	351	283	228	276	222	179	350
400	376	302	243	297	238	191	400
500	427	341	273	338	270	216	500
600	468	371	296	373	296	236	600
700	509	402	319	408	321	255	700
750	529	417	330	425	334	265	750
800	544	428	338	439	344	273	800
900	575	450	355	466	365	288	900
1000	605	472	372	494	385	304	1000

Ambient Temp. °C	For ambient temperatures other than 20°C (68°F) multiply the ampacities shown above by the appropriate factor shown below.						Ambient Temp. °F
6-10	1.09	1.09	1.09	1.09	1.09	1.09	43-50
11-15	1.04	1.04	1.04	1.04	1.04	1.04	52-59
16-20	1.00	1.00	1.00	1.00	1.00	1.00	61-68
21-25	.95	.95	.95	.95	.95	.95	70-77
26-30	.90	.90	.90	.90	.90	.90	79-86

†Unless otherwise specifically permitted elsewhere in this Code, the overcurrent protection for conductor types marked with an obelisk (†) shall not exceed 15 amperes for 14 AWG, 20 amperes for 12 AWG and 30 amperes for 10 AWG copper; or 15 amperes for 12 AWG and 25 amperes for 10 AWG aluminum and copper-clad aluminum.

inches is $\pi D^2/4 = \pi/4 = 0.746$ square inches. It is not practical to use solid conductors for the larger sizes as they would be very difficult to bend. Therefore, smaller strands of wire are twisted together to form one large conductor (see Figure 11.2). The wire size designation then gives the total actual cross-sectional area of all the individual strands added together.

If we refer to Tables 11.1 and 11.2, the conductor sizes in either AWG or MCM are listed in the left column and are repeated for convenience on the right side. Naturally, the larger the cross-sectional area (the size) of the conductor, the greater its ampacity rating. However, the ampacity rating is not a linear function of size. For example, in Table 11.1 the rating of a 250 MCM copper conductor with 60°C insulation (column 2) is 215 amperes, whereas the rating of a 500 MCM copper conductor (twice the size) is 320 amperes, only 1.5 times as much. With alternating current circuits, the current-carrying capacity per circular mil of conductor area decreases with size because of the skin effect, plus the fact that it is harder to dissipate the heat within large conductors. Therefore, it is often preferable to parallel smaller conductors for each phase of a feeder rather than use one large conductor. Paralleling of conductors is discussed in Section 11.6.

11.1.2 Conductor Material

The two conductor materials in common use are copper and aluminum. Copper has historically been used for conductors of insulated cables because of its desirable electrical and mechanical properties. Aluminum has had restricted use but is considered where its ampacity rating to weight ratio and its relative cost are favorable. The use of aluminum requires a larger conductor size in order to have the same ampacity rating as copper. For example, refer to Table 11.1. A No. 1 AWG copper conductor with 90°C temperature rating (column 5) has a rating of 150 amperes. An aluminum conductor with the same temperature rating (column 9) has to be size 2/0 (two sizes larger) to have the same rating of 150 amperes.

Unlike copper, aluminum has a few undesirable properties when used as the conductor material. An oxide film forms on the surface of aluminum. This aluminum oxide is essentially an insulating film, causing poor electrical contact at connections. To help overcome this problem, the aluminum must be cleaned immediately prior to being connected. On the other hand, the oxide film that forms on copper is a relatively good conductor, causing no real problem at connections. Aluminum conductors can break after bending much more readily than copper conductors and therefore aluminum conductors must be handled very carefully during installation. Aluminum deforms at a lower pressure than copper and can become loose at connections after a period of time. The resulting poor electrical contact can cause excessive heat buildup, leading to the ultimate failure of the insulation. The terminals of equipment, unless otherwise marked, are approved for use with copper conductors only.

11.1.3 Maximum Allowable Operating Temperature

The maximum continuous current that a conductor can carry is ultimately determined by the temperature at which it is allowed to operate for prolonged periods of time. This maximum allowable temperature is set by the type of insulating material that surrounds the conductor and is selected so that a reasonable working life (years) is obtained. If this operating temperature is exceeded for long periods of time, the insulation ages much more rapidly, becoming hard and brittle and subject to failure. The temperature rating classifications for building wires are 60°C, 75°C, and 90°C, as shown in Table 11.1 (note that 85°C is also shown, but this classification only applies to one very special type of cable).

A higher allowable operating temperature increases the ampacity rating for a particular conductor size. For example, from Table 11.1, a No. 2 AWG copper conductor, with 60°C insulation (column 2), has an ampacity of 95 amperes, whereas, with 90°C insulation (column 5), its ampacity is increased to 130 amperes. The higher permissible operating temperature means that there is a greater temperature difference between the conductor and the surrounding medium, resulting in a more rapid dissipation of the heat generated in the conductor. The higher temperature rated insulation may cost a bit more, but if its use results in a smaller size conductor being required for a given feeder, then the overall cost may be less (see Examples 11.15 and 11.16). An exception to the foregoing is with regard to conductor sizes Nos. 14, 12, and 10. See the note at the foot of Tables 11.1 and 11.2. The setting of the overcurrent protection for the conductors indicated cannot exceed the values quoted in the note regardless of the temperature classification of the insulation. The application of this restriction is discussed further in Section 12.1. Also refer to Section 11.1.7 for limitations imposed by conductor terminations.

11.1.4 Ambient Temperature

The ambient temperature refers to the temperature of the medium through which the wiring is to be run (air or earth). As the ambient temperature increases, there is less temperature differential between the conductor and the surrounding medium, and the rate at which the heat is dissipated from the conductor decreases. This means that the conductor can carry less current before it reaches its maximum operating temperature.

Table 11.1 is based on an ambient air temperature of 30°C (86°F), as noted in the heading. There can be areas within a building where the ambient temperature exceeds 30°C, such as in enclosed ceiling areas adjacent to heating pipes and in rooms with heating equipment. For wiring installed in areas with ambient temperatures higher than 30°C, the ampacity of the conductors must be reduced. Conversely, if the ambient temperature is lower than 30°C, the ampacity can be increased. Table 11.2 is based on an earth ambient temperature of 20°C. The appropriate correction factors are shown at the bottom of the ampacity tables. For example, from Table 11.1 for a conductor with 90°C insulation (columns 5 and 9) operating in an ambient temperature of 40°C, the correction factor is 0.91. Thus a No. 6 copper conductor, 90°C, has an ampacity rating of 75 amperes at 30°C and only a rating of 0.91 times 75 or 68 amperes at 40°C. Further examples are shown in Section 11.1.6.

11.1.5 Conductors Installed in Raceways

The most common method of installing wiring in a building is to run the conductors in a raceway, as shown in Figure 11.3. The use of raceways is discussed in Section 11.5. Note the heading of Table 11.1, which states *not more than three single insulated conductors, rated 0 to 2000 volts, in raceway*. The raceway enclosure impedes the dissipation of the heat from the conductors. This fact requires the derating of a conductor as compared to its ampacity rating when run by itself in air (its free air rating). As an example, if we refer to Table 310-17 in the *NEC*, the free air rating of a No. 1/0 copper conductor, 90°C, is 260 amperes, whereas when three No. 1/0 copper conductors, 90°C, are installed in a raceway, the ampacity of each conductor is only 170 amperes (Table 11.1).

Note that Table 11.1 applies to conductors in raceways installed in free air. However, this table can also be applied where conduits are installed in walls and structural floor slabs that are above grade level. Where conduits are run adjacent to each other, sufficient spacing must be maintained between them to permit proper cooling. Table 11.2, on the other hand, applies to 75°C rated conductors installed in underground electrical ducts. The ampacities are based

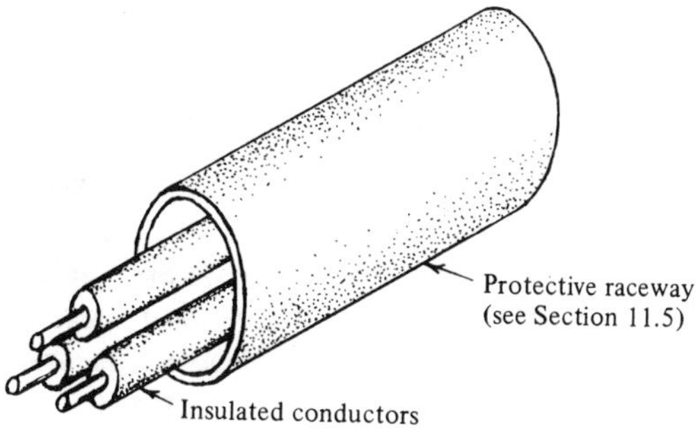

FIGURE 11.3

Conductors installed in a raceway

on an ambient earth temperature of 20°C (68°F). Ratings are shown for arrangements where from 1 to 6 electrical ducts are run in the same duct bank. The duct arrangements and accompanying notes are shown in Table 11.3(a).

The ratings in Tables 11.1 and 11.2 apply when not more than three conductors are installed in the one raceway or electrical duct. When more than three conductors are installed, their ampacity rating must be decreased to compensate for the added conductors. Adjacent conductors have the dual effect of raising the temperature within the raceway and of impeding the heat dissipated from the raceway. Table 11.3(b) shows the percentages that must be applied to the values listed in Tables 11.1 and 11.2. For example, as previously indicated, three No. 1/0 copper conductors, 90°C, installed in a raceway in free air have an ampacity of 170 amperes. If six No. 1/0 copper conductors, 90°C, are installed in one raceway, then the rating of each conductor is reduced to 80% of 170, or 136 amperes. Note that for more than nine conductors in one raceway the percentage values are based on a load diversity of 50% between the circuits involved.

The interpretation of the number of conductors in a raceway for the purpose of establishing their ampacity rating is actually based on the number of current-carrying conductors. In the case of a three-phase, four-wire system employing a neutral conductor (see Section 1.6.1), it must be determined whether the neutral has to be considered as a current-carrying conductor. This is covered in Note No. 10 that accompanies *NEC* Tables 310-16 through 310-31. Normally, the neutral conductor of a three-phase, four-wire system does not have to be counted when applying the percentages listed in Table 11.3(b), as the neutral current is zero under balanced conditions. A major exception to this is the case where the majority (more than 50%) of the load on a feeder or circuit consists of electric discharge type of lighting (see Section 4.2), electronic data processing systems, or other similar types of equipment. The current waveforms characteristic of such loads are very high in third-harmonic components. In the case of electric discharge type of lighting, the third harmonics are the result of the saturation of the magnetic cores of the ballasts during part of each cycle. In the case of electronic data processing and similar types of equipment, the third harmonics are the result of the use of diodes for charging capacitors on the input of the power supplies. As discussed in Section 1.6.4, the third-harmonic components do not cancel at the neutral, but in fact add together to flow back through the neutral conductor. Therefore, even under balanced load conditions, the neutral carries a large current and must be counted as a current-carrying conductor (see example 11.2). Note

TABLE 11.3 Details and Adjustment Factors for Tables 11.1 and 11.2

(a) Electrical duct details for use with Table 11.2 (from *NEC* Figure 310-1 and Notes to Tables 310-25 through 310-27).

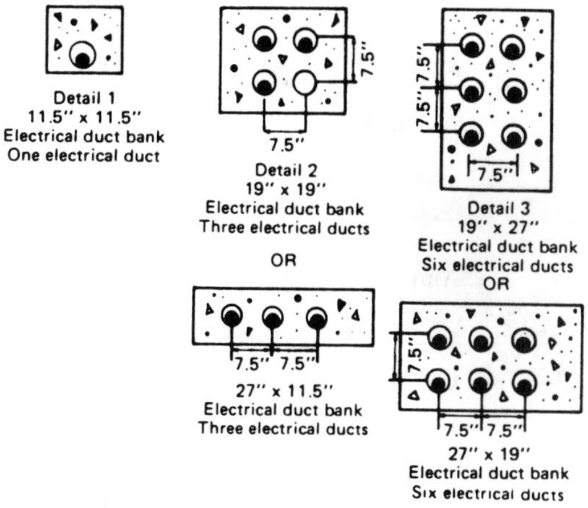

(i) For cables installed in two electrical ducts in one horizontal row, 7.5-inch center-to-center spacing, multiply ampacity shown for 1 electrical duct by 0.88.

(ii) For cables installed in four electrical ducts in one horizontal row, 7.5-inch center-to-center spacing, multiply ampacity shown for 3 electrical ducts by 0.94.

(b) Ampacity adjustment factors for more than three conductors in a raceway or cable [from *NEC* Notes to Tables 310-16 through 310-31, No. 8(a)].

Number of Conductors	Percent of Values in Tables 11.1 and 11.2
4–6	80
7–9	70
10–24[a]	70
25–42[a]	60
43 and above[a]	50

[a] These factors include the effects of a load diversity of 50%.

that grounding or bonding conductors do not have to be counted when applying the percentages listed in Table 11.3(b).

11.1.6 Determining the Ampacity of Conductors

The following examples illustrate the use of the ampacity tables and derating factors as discussed in the previous sections. (See Appendix A for application of CEC rules.)

■ EXAMPLE 11.1

Determine the ampacity of a three-phase, four-wire feeder using 250 MCM copper conductors, 75°C insulation, installed in a raceway in free air, 40°C ambient temperature, and feeding an incandescent lighting load.

Solution

From Table 11.1, column 3, the rating for 250 MCM is 255 A. The correction factor for 40°C is 0.88:

$$\text{Ampacity} = 255 \times 0.88 = 224 \text{ A}$$

There is no need to derate for the neutral (the fourth wire) because there are no third harmonics with incandescent lighting.

■ EXAMPLE 11.2

Determine the ampacity of a three-phase, four-wire feeder using 400 MCM copper conductors, 90°C insulation, installed in a raceway in free air, 30°C ambient temperature, and feeding a fluorescent lighting load.

Solution

From Table 11.1, column 5, the rating for 400 MCM is 380 A. The neutral must be counted as the fourth current-carrying conductor because of the fluorescent lighting (which is an electric discharge type). From Table 11.3(b), the ampacity adjustment factor for four conductors is 0.80:

$$\text{Ampacity} = 380 \times 0.80 = 304 \text{ A}$$

■ EXAMPLE 11.3

Determine the ampacity of No. 6 aluminum conductors, 75°C insulation, eight current-carrying conductors in a raceway in free air, 45°C ambient temperature.

Solution

From Table 11.1, column 7, the rating for No. 6 is 50 A. The correction factor for 45°C is 0.82. From Table 11.3(b), the ampacity adjustment factor for eight conductors is 0.70:

$$\text{Ampacity} = 50 \times 0.82 \times 0.70 = 28.7 \text{ A}$$

■ **EXAMPLE 11.4**

Determine the ampacity of a three-phase, three-wire feeder using 4/0 copper conductors, 75°C insulation, installed in an underground electrical duct, ambient earth temperature of 20°C. There is a second feeder installed in the same duct bank.

Solution

From Table 11.2, column 2, the rating for No. 4/0 is 263 A. From Table 11.3(a), the multiplying factor for two ducts is 0.88:

$$\text{Ampacity} = 263 \times 0.88 = 231 \text{ A}$$

11.1.7 Ampacity Limitations Imposed by Conductor Terminations

The foregoing discussions and examples have not taken into consideration the ampacity limitations imposed by the terminations of the feeder and circuit conductors at equipment terminals. Refer to Figure 11.4. The maximum allowable operating temperature permitted for the terminals is covered by the approvals granted for the equipment. The *National Electrical Code* requires that all equipment required or permitted by the code be approved by a qualified electrical

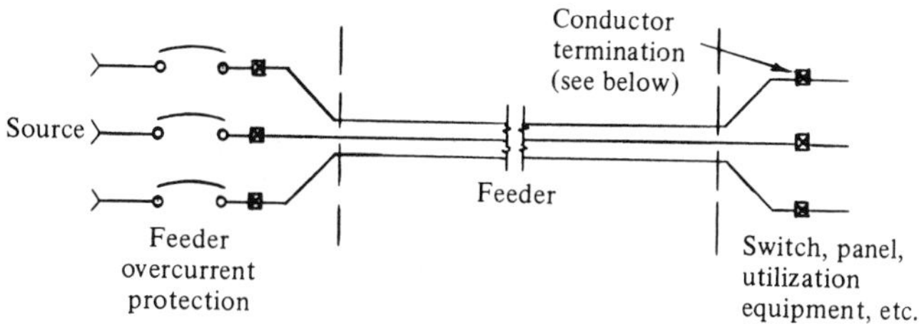

(a) Typical feeder connections

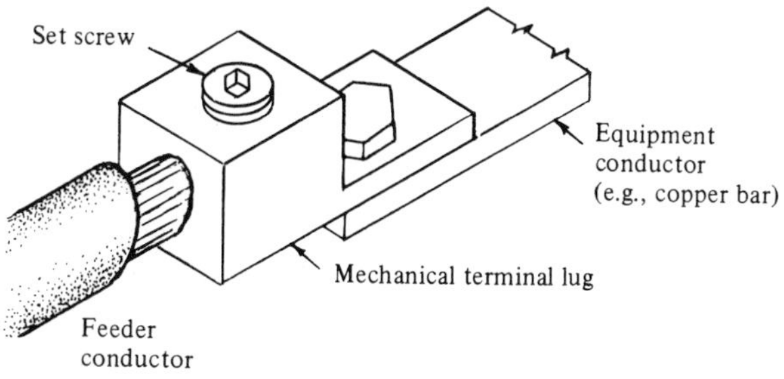

(b) Typical conductor termination

FIGURE 11.4

Feeder terminations

testing laboratory and that this equipment be used or installed in accordance with any instructions included in the testing or labeling of the equipment. A major electrical testing laboratory is the Underwriters Laboratories, Inc. (UL). A basic statement in the *UL Electrical Construction Materials Directory* notes that

> The termination provisions of the approved equipment are based on the use of 60°C insulated conductors in circuits rated 100 amperes or less and the use of 75°C insulated conductors in higher rated circuits. The 60°C ampacities for circuits rated 100 amperes or less and the 75°C ampacities for circuits rated over 100 amperes shall be based on Table 310-16 of the *National Electrical Code* [Table 11.1]. Conductors having a temperature rating higher than specified may be used if the size of the conductor is based on the 60°C ampacity for circuits 100 amperes and less and the 75°C ampacity for circuits over 100 amperes.

These temperature limitations are required to protect electrical equipment. A cable rated for 90°C, when loaded to its full ampacity rating, operates at a temperature of 90°C. If this cable is connected to an equipment terminal rated for 75°C, then the higher conductor temperature can eventually overheat the terminal, even though the load current does not exceed the rated current of the equipment. The excess heat can ultimately damage the equipment.

The foregoing would appear to eliminate the use of the 90°C insulated conductors for the majority of the feeders installed in a building, since most of the feeders and circuits are terminated in UL-approved equipment. However, this is not necessarily the case. The use of 90°C rated cables is justified where derating factors as previously discussed must be applied. To explain this, return to Example 11.2. Since the final ampacity of 304 amperes is less than the listed 75°C ampacity of 335 amperes for 400 MCM, there will be no problem at the terminations of this feeder. If 75°C rated conductors were to be used for this feeder, then one size larger (500 MCM) would have had to be selected to obtain the same ampacity rating of 304 amperes after the 80% derate factor is applied.

11.2 SHORT-CIRCUIT CURRENT RATING OF CONDUCTORS

Short-circuit conditions can impose tremendous stresses on an electrical system (see Sections 6.2 and 6.3). In the case of feeders, the resulting high short-circuit currents can cause the conductor temperature to rise very rapidly. The device protecting the feeder requires some finite time before it can detect and then fully interrupt the fault current. The feeder conductors must be sized large enough to carry the fault current for this time interval without reaching a temperature that will permanently damage the insulation (see Section 6.4). The maximum allowable short-circuit transient temperature rating of a cable is much higher than its maximum allowable operating temperature rating because the short circuit is of such short duration. The maximum short-circuit temperature rating depends on the type of insulation material used for the cable.

At this point we must return to Section 6.5 on asymmetrical fault currents and in particular to Figure 6.4. With an asymmetrical fault current, the heating of the conductors is greater than it would be if the fault current were symmetrical. Therefore, allowance must be made for this increased heating in selecting the correct size of conductor. The ratio between the asymmetrical and the symmetrical current is dependent on the rate of decay of the dc component after the fault occurs. If we let K_0 represent this ratio, then

$$I_{ASY} = K_0 \times I_{SYM} \qquad \textbf{(11.1)}$$

where I_{ASY} = asymmetrical short-circuit current used to size the conductor

I_{SYM} = available short-circuit symmetrical current

The value of K_0 depends on the system voltage and type of overcurrent device used for the feeder, as shown in Table 11.4. This table also shows the total clearing times for the overcurrent devices.

The precise calculation to determine the short-circuit current rating of a cable is very complex. Fortunately, graphs have been prepared that simplify the process. Refer to Figures 11.5, 11.6, and 11.7. These graphs show short-circuit current on the vertical axis and the conductor size on the horizontal axis, with a series of diagonal lines indicating the duration of the fault (the total clearing time of

TABLE 11.4 Clearing Times and K_0 Factors

System Voltage	Feeder Overcurrent Device	Total Clearing Time (cycles)	K_0 Factor
Up to 1000 V	Circuit breaker[a]	2	1.3
	Current-limiting fuse	$\frac{1}{2}$	1.4
Above 1000 V	Air circuit breaker	5	1.15
	Oil circuit breaker	8	1.1
	Power fuse	1	1.6
	Current-limiting fuse	$\frac{1}{2}$	1.6

[a] Noncurrent-limiting type.

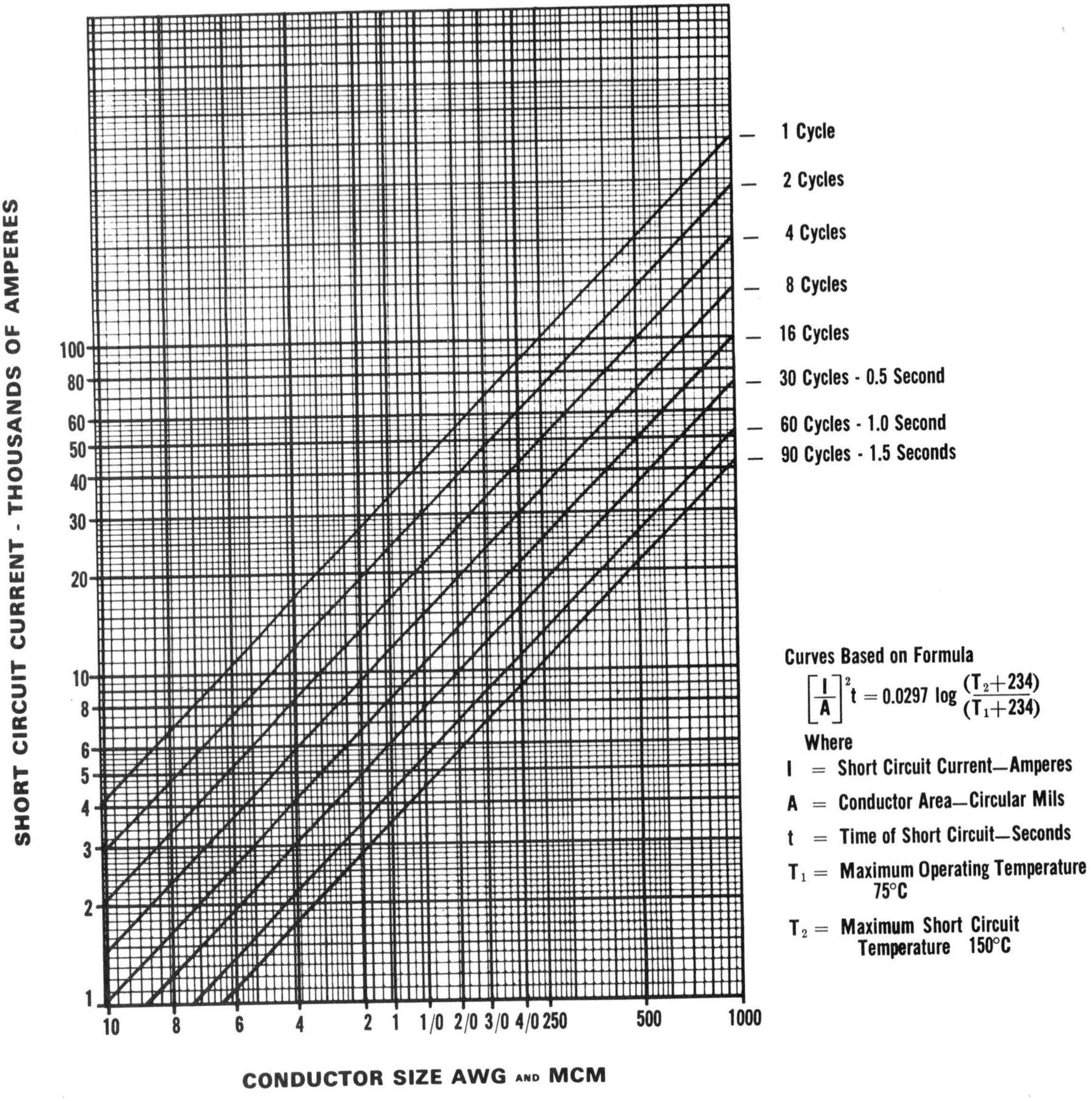

FIGURE 11.5

Allowable short-circuit currents for *copper* conductors with thermoplastic insulation (*NEC* type THW, CSA type TW75)

the overcurrent device protecting the conductors). Note the descriptions for the different graphs. Figure 11.5 applies to copper conductors with thermoplastic insulation, which has a maximum operating temperature of 75°C and a maximum short-circuit temperature of 150°C. Figure 11.6 applies to copper conductors with cross-linked

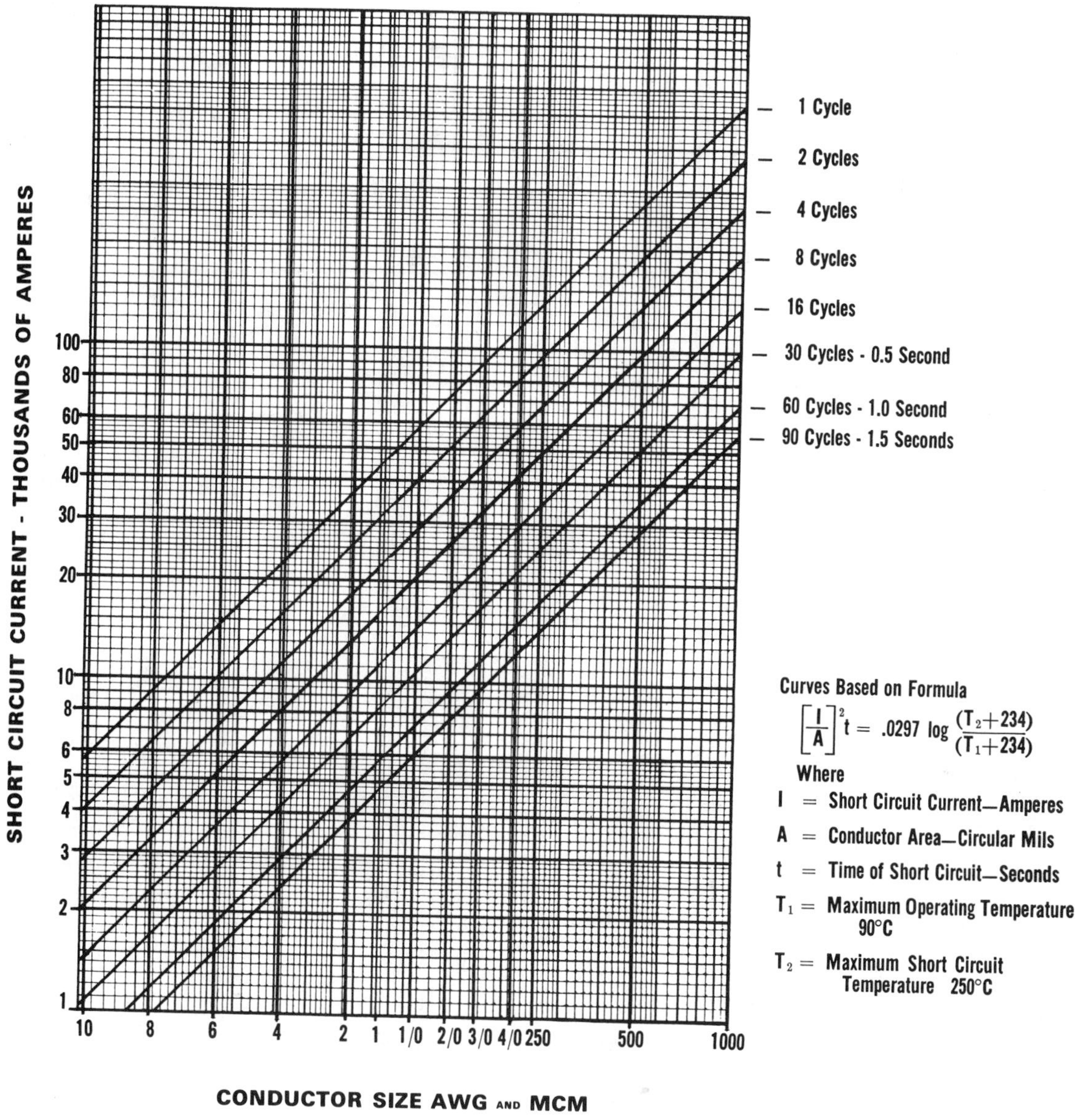

FIGURE 11.6

Allowable short-circuit currents for *copper* conductors with cross-linked synthetic polymer insulation [*NEC* type XHHW, CSA type RW90 (XLPE)]

synthetic polymer insulation, which has a maximum operating temperature of 90°C and a maximum short-circuit temperature of 250°C. Figure 11.7 applies to aluminum conductors with the cross-linked synthetic polymer insulation. Examples 11.5–11.7 will show how to use these graphs.

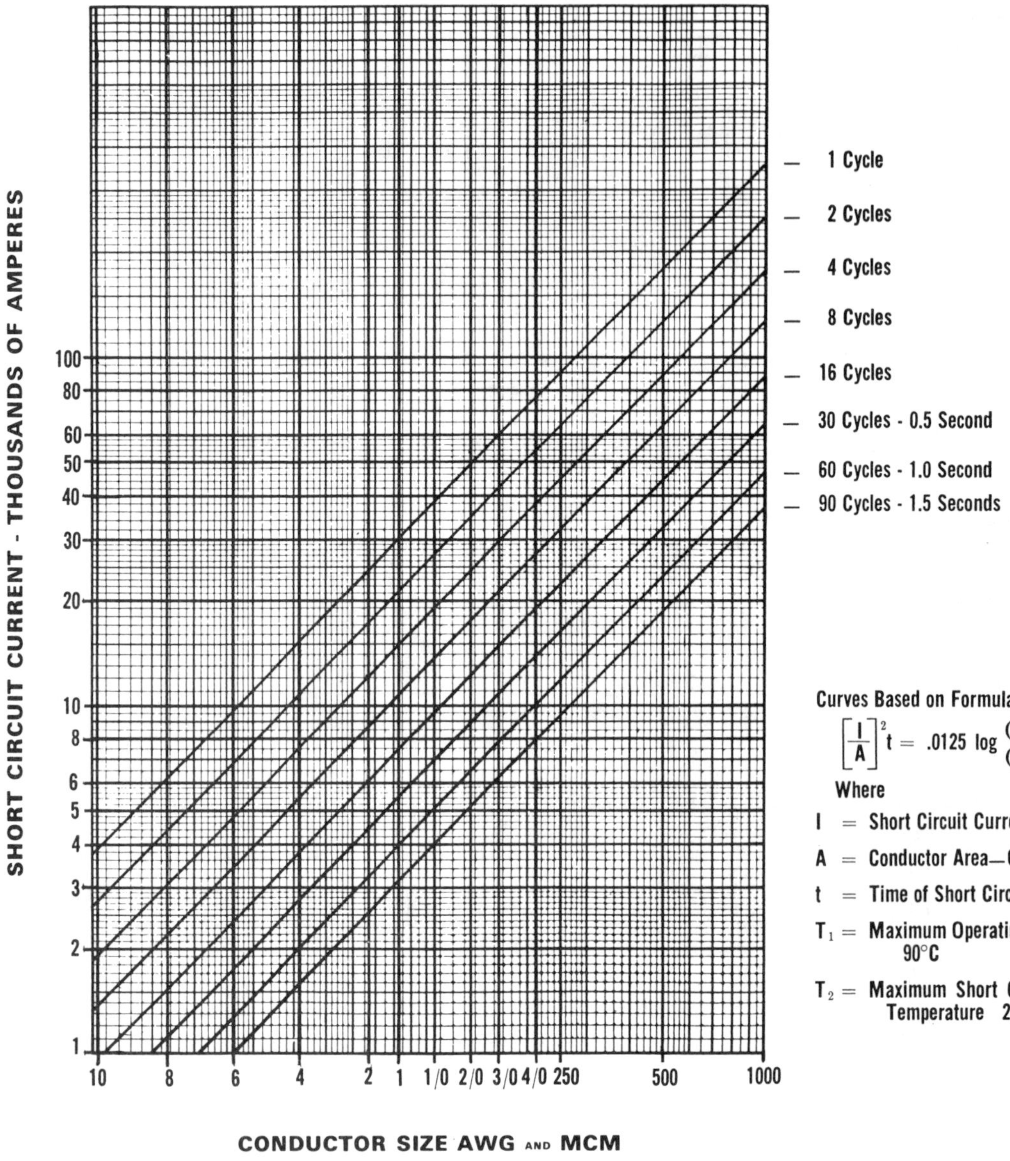

Curves Based on Formula

$$\left[\frac{I}{A}\right]^2 t = .0125 \log \frac{(T_2+228)}{(T_1+228)}$$

Where

I = Short Circuit Current—Amperes

A = Conductor Area—Circular Mils

t = Time of Short Circuit—Seconds

T_1 = Maximum Operating Temperature 90°C

T_2 = Maximum Short Circuit Temperature 250°C

FIGURE 11.7

Allowable short-circuit currents for *aluminium* conductors with cross-linked synthetic polymer insulation [*NEC* type XHHW, CSA type RW90 (XLPE)]

EXAMPLE 11.5

Determine the symmetrical short-circuit current rating of a 250 MCM copper conductor with thermoplastic insulation on a 480 V feeder protected by a circuit breaker.

Solution

From Table 11.4, the clearing time is 2 cycles and K_0 is 1.3. From Figure 11.5, the point of intersection of the vertical line for 250 MCM and the diagonal line for 2 cycles is 72 × 1000 A (I_{ASY}). Using Equation 11.1,

$$I_{SYM} = \frac{72{,}000}{1.3} = 55{,}400 \text{ A}$$

EXAMPLE 11.6

Repeat Example 11.5 except that the insulation is the cross-linked synthetic polymer type.

Solution

From Figure 11.6, using the same values as in Example 11.5, the intersection of the lines gives 95 × 1000 A. Using Equation 11.1,

$$I_{SYM} = \frac{95{,}000}{1.3} = 73{,}100 \text{ A}$$

EXAMPLE 11.7

Determine the symmetrical short-circuit current rating of a No. 1/0 aluminum conductor with cross-linked synthetic polymer insulation on a 4160 V feeder protected by an oil circuit breaker.

Solution

From Table 11.4, the clearing time is 8 cycles and K_0 is 1.1. From Figure 11.7, the point of intersection of the vertical line for No. 1/0 and the diagonal line for 8 cycles is 13.6 × 1000 A (I_{ASY}). Using Equation 11.1,

$$I_{SYM} = \frac{13{,}600}{1.1} = 12{,}400 \text{ A}$$

11.3 MAXIMUM ALLOWABLE VOLTAGE DROP

It is very important to have the correct voltage at the outlet that serves a piece of utilization equipment. Most equipment is voltage sensitive, and an excessive voltage drop impairs the starting and operation of the equipment. See Section 2.9 with regard to motors and their rated voltages. See Chapter 4 with regard to light sources: Section 4.1.4 for incandescent lamps, Section 4.3.8 for fluorescent lamps, and Section 4.5.1 for mercury lamps. The *National Electrical Code* recommends a maximum voltage drop of 3% for any one branch circuit or feeder with a maximum voltage drop from the service entrance to the utilization outlet of 5% [*NEC* Sections 210-19(a) and 215-2(b)].

The voltage drop of a feeder or branch circuit when carrying current (under load conditions) is caused by the resistance and inductive reactance associated with the conductors. Refer to Figure 11.8(a), which shows the equivalent single-phase circuit diagram of a three-phase feeder under balanced load conditions. The resistance *R*

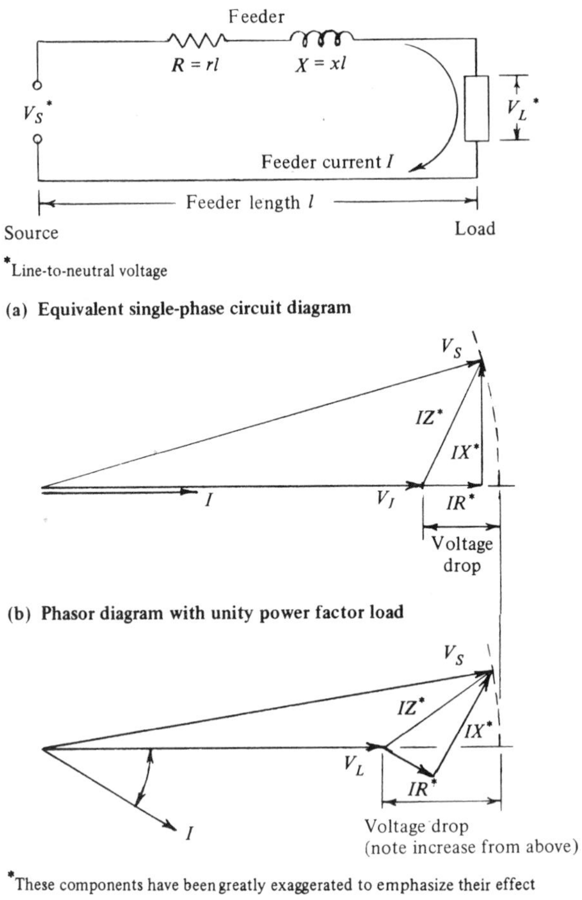

(a) **Equivalent single-phase circuit diagram**

(b) **Phasor diagram with unity power factor load**

(c) **Phasor diagram with lagging power factor load**

FIGURE 11.8

Voltage drop on a feeder

and the inductive reactance X are shown as lumped values that represent the total resistance and inductive reactance actually distributed over the entire circuit. Figure 11.8(b) shows the voltage and current relationships of the circuit when operating with a unity (100%) power factor load (see Section 1.4.4). The voltage drop is the difference between the voltage at the source of the feeder V_S, which is assumed to be constant, and the voltage across the load V_L, which varies with the feeder current I. This voltage drop in volts is then expressed as a percentage of the source voltage. Therefore,

$$\% \text{ voltage drop} = \frac{V_S - V_L}{V_S} \times 100 \qquad \textbf{(11.2)}$$

The voltage drop on the feeder depends on

1. Current I flowing in the feeder
2. Length l of the feeder

3. Resistance per unit of length r
4. Inductive reactance per unit of length x
5. Power factor of the load

The fact that the power factor of the load affects the voltage drop is illustrated in Figure 11.8(c). With a lagging power factor load, the load current lags the voltage, which alters the relationships of the voltage drop components IR and IX with respect to the voltage. This change in relationships increases the difference between V_S and V_L, thus increasing the voltage drop even though the magnitudes (scalor values) of the components have not changed.

The resistance per unit of length depends on

1. Conductor material
2. Cross-sectional area of the conductor (size)
3. Conductor operating temperature

The inductive reactance per unit of length depends on

1. Diameter of the conductor (self-inductance)
2. Spacing between conductors (mutual inductance)
3. Material surrounding the conductors (whether magnetic or non-magnetic)
4. Frequency of the power supply

The precise calculations to determine the voltage drop for a particular feeder are complex. However, once again tables can be used to give fairly accurate values that are satisfactory for most applications. Because of the many factors previously listed, these tables must be prepared for specific conditions. Refer to Table 11.5, which shows voltage drops for 60 hertz systems. Note that this table applies to three single conductors in conduit, which in effect ties down the conductor spacing. Next, note the various columns for either copper or aluminum conductors and for either magnetic (steel) or nonmagnetic (aluminum or plastic) conduit or armor. Finally, values are listed for 80% and 90% lagging and 100% power factor. The values in the table are for conductors operating at temperatures up to 75°C, with the correction factor for 90°C as per footnote 2. For different sets of conditions, such as conductor spacing, other tables or graphs are required.

The two factors previously listed as affecting the voltage drop and that would be hard to accommodate directly into the table are the current flowing in the feeder and the length of the feeder. Therefore, the values listed in the table represent the voltage drops for each 1000 ampere-feet of circuit. The unit ampere-feet is simply the product of the current times the length in feet. The following examples illustrate the use of Table 11.5.

TABLE 11.5 Voltage Drops for 60 Hz Systems*

Size AWG or MCM	COPPER: Magnetic Conduit or Armour 80% P.F.	90% P.F.	100% P.F.	COPPER: Non-Mag. Conduit or Armour 80% P.F.	90% P.F.	100% P.F.	ALUMINUM: Magnetic Conduit or Armour 80% P.F.	90% P.F.	100% P.F.	ALUMINUM: Non-Mag. Conduit or Armour 80% P.F.	90% P.F.	100% P.F.
14	2.540	2.790	3.067	2.535	2.780	3.060						
12	1.570	1.749	1.917	1.565	1.749	1.923	2.460	2.748	3.020	2.448	2.743	3.020
10	.993	1.103	1.200	.987	1.103	1.201	1.553	1.732	1.900	1.547	1.726	1.900
8	.635	.699	.750	.629	.693	.751	.993	1.103	1.195	.981	1.091	1.195
6	.421	.462	.485	.461	.456	.485	.647	.710	.762	.641	.710	.768
4	.277	.300	.306	.271	.294	.306	.421	.456	.491	.410	.450	.479
2	.185	.196	.196	.179	.191	.191	.271	.294	.300	.266	.289	.306
1	.150	.162	.150	.150	.156	.150	.225	.237	.242	.219	.231	.242
1/0	.127	.133	.121	.121	.127	.121	.185	.196	.191	.179	.191	.191
2/0	.109	.110	.098	.098	.104	.092	.150	.156	.150	.144	.150	.150
3/0	.092	.092	.081	.081	.087	.075	.127	.133	.121	.121	.127	.121
4/0	.081	.075	.064	.069	.069	.057	.104	.104	.098	.098	.104	.098
250	.070	.070	.054	.064	.064	.051	.092	.092	.081	.086	.087	.081
300	.064	.064	.045	.056	.055	.042	.081	.081	.069	.075	.075	.069
350	.058	.055	.039	.051	.049	.036	.075	.075	.058	.069	.069	.057
400	.055	.051	.035	.047	.044	.032	.069	.069	.053	.064	.064	.050
500	.049	.045	.029	.042	.039	.026	.058	.057	.043	.053	.051	.040
600	.046	.041	.024	.038	.034	.022	.055	.051	.036	.048	.046	.034
700	.043	.038	.021	.036	.032	.019	.051	.047	.032	.044	.041	.029
750	.042	.037	.020	.034	.031	.017	.049	.046	.030	.042	.039	.028
1000	.038	.032	.016	.029	.025	.013	.044	.040	.024	.039	.036	.024

* Values are per 1000 ampere-feet for three single conductors in conduit.

1. Values are based on three-phase, line-to-neutral voltages. For line-to-line voltage drops, multiply by a factor of 1.73. For single-phase circuits, multiply by a factor of 2.0.

2. Values are for conductor operating temperatures up to 75°C. For conductors operating at 90°C, multiply by a factor of 1.1.

Source: Courtesy of Canada Wire and Cable Limited

EXAMPLE 11.8

Calculate the percentage voltage drop on a 60 Hz, 480 V, three-phase feeder, load current 100 A, power factor of load 100%, length 300 ft, consisting of three No. 2 copper conductors rated for 75°C operation installed in steel conduit.

Solution

From Table 11.5, column 4 (copper, magnetic conduit, 100% P.F.), the voltage drop/1000 ampere-feet for No. 2 is 0.196. From note 2, no correction is needed for 75°C.

Ampere-feet = 100 × 300 = 30,000 = 30 × 1000

Voltage drop (line to neutral) = 30 × 0.196 = 5.88 V

Voltage drop (line to line) = 1.73 × 5.88 = 10.2 V (note 1)

The 10.2 V represents the difference between V_S and V_L. Using Equation 11.2,

$$\% \text{ voltage drop} = \frac{10.2}{480} \times 100 = 2.1\%$$

EXAMPLE 11.9

Calculate the percentage voltage drop on a 60 Hz, 208 V, three-phase feeder, load current 290 A, power factor 90% lagging, length 150 ft, consisting of three 250 MCM copper conductors rated for 90°C operation installed in aluminum conduit.

Solution

From Table 11.5, column 6 (copper, nonmagnetic conduit, 90% P.F.), the voltage drop/1000 ampere-feet for 250 MCM is 0.064. From note 2, the correction for 90°C is 1.1 × 0.064 = 0.070.

Amperere-feet = 290 × 150 = 43,500 = 43.5 × 1000

Voltage drop (line to neutral) = 43.5 × 0.070 = 3.05 V

Voltage drop (line to line) = 1.73 × 3.05 = 5.3 V

Using Equation 11.2,

$$\% \text{ voltage drop} = \frac{5.3}{208} \times 100 = 2.5\%$$

11.4 LETTER DESIGNATION OF CABLES

Letter designations are used to identify types of cables with regard to the type of insulation and their conditions of use. The following lists include the common types used for fixed building wiring systems operating on low voltage (up to 1000 volts).

The following letters identify the insulation.

1. According to the type of insulation material:
A, asbestos
MI, mineral insulation
R, rubber
SA, silicone asbestos (rubber)

T, thermoplastic
V, varnished cambric
X, cross-linked synthetic polymer

2. According to conditions of use:
H, heat resistant up to 75°C
HH, heat resistant up to 90°C (Note: no designation indicates 60°C)
UF, suitable for underground, direct burial
W, moisture resistant, suitable for use in wet locations

The *National Electrical Code* defines a wet location as

> Installations underground or in concrete slabs or masonry in direct contact with the earth, and locations subject to saturation with water or other liquids, such as vehicle washing areas, and locations exposed to weather and unprotected.

Refer to Table 11.1 and note the headings of the columns that show the letter designations of insulated conductors. Some examples are

— THW: thermoplastic insulation, rated for maximum operating temperature of 75°C and suitable for use in wet locations (also dry locations).
— XHHW: cross-linked synthetic polymer insulation, rated for maximum operating temperature of 90°C and suitable for use in wet locations. However, see the asterisk (*) beside this type and the footnote in the table to the effect that the 90°C ampacity applies only in dry and damp locations and that the 75°C ampacity must be used in wet locations.

In addition to the insulation around the conductor, some types of cables have an outer jacket or sheath, either enclosing a single conductor or a group of individually insulated conductors, as shown in Figure 11.2. These outer coverings provide mechanical and/or corrosion protection. The following letters identify some of these types of cables:

— AC, armored cable (flexible metallic interlocked armor sheath)
— L, lead sheath
— MC, metal-clad cable (metallic sheath of interlocking tape or a smooth or corrugated tube)
— NM, nonmetallic sheath cable (moisture resistant, flame retardant)
— N, cables with nylon jacket

Care must be taken in identifying some of the letter combinations. For example, with type MI, the M stands for "mineral," whereas with type MC, the M stands for "metal." For a full description of all types of insulated conductors and their uses, refer to the *National Electrical Code,* Article 310 and Table 310-13.

11.5 RACEWAYS

The function of a raceway is to provide space for, and support and mechanical protection to, the insulated conductors of a feeder or branch circuit. An equal function is to protect people against electrical hazards and to minimize the likelihood of fires being caused by faults in the electrical wiring. As already discussed in Section 11.1.5, the ampacities of conductors are reduced by having them installed in a raceway, but in the interest of safety the *National Electrical Code* requires all wiring must be properly protected (Section 300-4). The final function of metallic-type raceways is to provide for continuity of the equipment grounding system throughout the building (see Section 10.3, this text). Raceways, therefore, are an important part of an electrical system in a building.

The *NEC* defines a *raceway* as *an enclosed channel designed expressly for holding wires, cables, or busbars.* Raceways may be constructed from metal or insulating material. Raceways may be rigid or flexible conduit, tubing, underfloor raceways, cellular floor raceways, wireways, and busways. The most common type of raceway for general wiring is the conduit, which in effect is a pipe or tube through which the insulated conductors are pulled, as shown in Figure 11.3.

11.5.1 Types of Conduit

The various types of electrical conduit are as follows:

1. *Rigid metal conduit* (either steel or aluminum) has the thickest wall of all types and can be threaded so that joints can be made very secure and tight.
2. *Intermediate metal conduit* is a thinner-walled rigid metal conduit and may be used the same as rigid metal conduit.
3. *Electrical metallic tubing* (EMT) is a metal conduit with much thinner walls. In fact it is also referred to as thin-wall conduit. Connections are simplified by using threadless components of the compression, indentation, or set-screw type. The lighter weight of EMT is also a decided advantage during installation. However, its thin-wall construction makes it less able to withstand punishment. The *NEC* therefore restricts the use of EMT to areas where it will not be subjected to severe physical damage during installation or after installation.

4. *Rigid nonmetallic conduit* is made of nonmetallic material such as fiber, asbestos cement, and rigid polyvinyl chloride (PVC). Only PVC, however, is permitted to be used both underground and above ground. Rigid nonmetallic conduit cannot be used where subject to physical damage unless approved for such use.
5. *Electrical nonmetallic tubing* is a pliable corrugated raceway of circular cross section that can be bent by hand with a reasonable force. This type can be concealed within walls, ceilings, and floors where the floor, wall, or ceiling provides a thermal barrier of material that has at least a 15-minute fire rating.
6. *Flexible conduit* is constructed so that it can be readily flexed and therefore is not affected by vibration. A common application is for the final connection to a motor, as shown in Figure 11.9(a). The flexible conduit isolates the rigid conduit distribution system from the vibrations and movement of the motor. Another use is for the final connections to recessed lighting fixtures, as shown in Figure 11.9(b). The flexible conduit can be either metallic or nonmetallic. Liquid-tight flexible metal conduit is a special form that allows it to be used where protection from liquids or vapors is required. The *NEC* restricts the use of flexible metal conduit as an equipment grounding conductor, often requiring that an additional grounding jumper be installed (see *NEC* Sections 350-5 and 351-9).

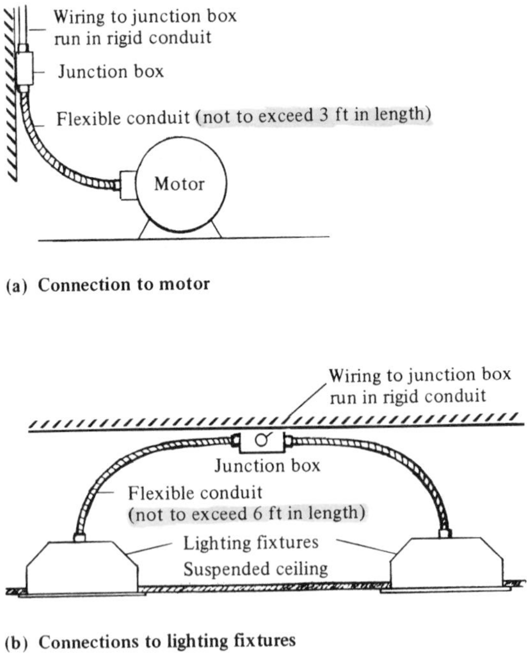

FIGURE 11.9

Common uses of flexible conduit

All runs of conduit and tubing must be properly protected against corrosion both during installation and after installation. Particular care must be taken where conduit runs are installed in concrete and in wet locations. Metal conduit with galvanized and/or plastic-coated finishes is available. Nonmetallic conduit or tubing cannot be used where its use would substantially increase the possible spread of fire or the products of combustion. For example, *NEC* Section 300-22(b) and (c) prohibits the use of nonmetallic conduit or tubing in ducts, plenums, and other spaces used for environmental air. This includes spaces over hung ceilings that are used for environmental air-handling purposes. Nonmetallic conduit and tubing cannot be used where either the ambient temperature or the insulation temperature limitations of the conductors would exceed those for which the conduit or tubing is approved. Also, the *NEC* carries a warning that *extreme cold may cause some nonmetallic conduit to become brittle and therefore more susceptible to physical damage from physical contact.* With nonmetallic conduit and tubing, a separate ground wire must be installed to maintain the equipment grounding circuit (see Section 10.3 of this text).

Some of the means of running conduit are shown in Figure 11.10. Overhead runs must be properly supported along their entire length. Sufficient access points in the form of junction boxes have to be provided on long runs of conduit to facilitate the installation of the conductors. Otherwise, if a run is too long or has too many bends between access points, the conductors could be damaged as they are pulled through the conduit. The reader is referred to *NEC* Articles 331 and 345 through 351 for the complete set of regulations governing the use and installation of conduit and tubing.

Underfloor raceways are used as a common means of distributing wiring in office areas. This type of system is discussed in Section 12.9 of this text.

11.5.2 Number of Conductors Permitted in Conduit

The number of conductors that can be installed in any one run of conduit must be restricted. The total cross-sectional area of the conductors, including the insulation, must not exceed a specified percentage of the cross-sectional area of the inside of the conduit. This is referred to as the *percentage fill.* If the percentage fill is too high, then the cables can be damaged as they are pulled through the run of conduit. Also the heat buildup within the conduit from the conductor currents could become excessive under operation because of overcrowding.

The *National Electrical Code* restricts the percentage fill to 40% for three or more conductors. Refer to Table 11.6, which shows the maximum number of type THW and XHHW conductors permitted in one run of conduit or tubing. Trade sizes of conduit or tubing are

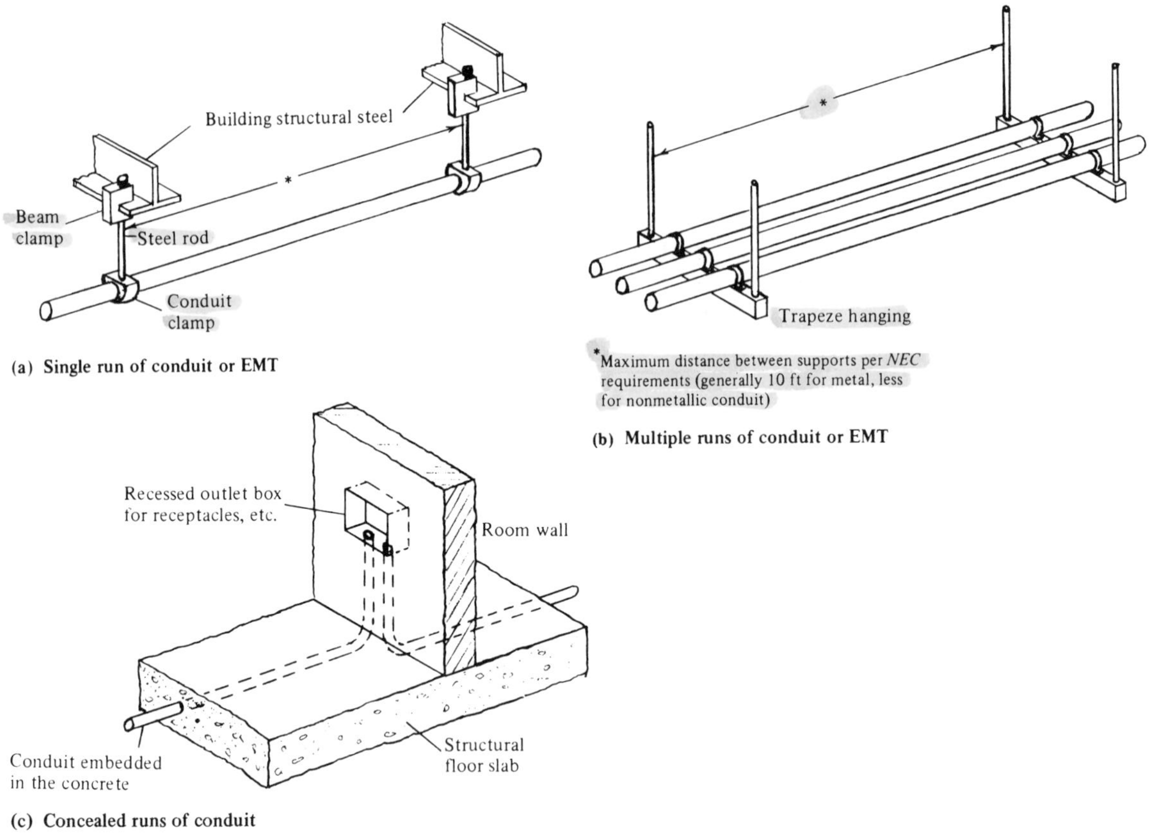

FIGURE 11.10

Common methods of installing rigid conduit

shown from $\frac{1}{2}$ inch to 3 inches and conductor sizes from No. 14 up to 500 MCM. Since each type of insulated conductor has a different insulation thickness, the appropriate type of wire (indicated by letter type) must be selected. This table is based on all conductors in the run of conduit being the same size and type. The trade size of a conduit or tube is actually only its nominal or approximate inside diameter. It is used for the identification of a particular size. For example, the 1 inch trade size conduit has an actual internal diameter of 1.049 inches. The following example illustrates the use of Table 11.6.

■ EXAMPLE 11.10

A three-phase, four-wire feeder requires No. 4/0 type THW conductors. Determine the trade size of conduit required for the feeder.

Solution

Four conductors have to be installed in the conduit (the neutral must be counted). From Table 11.6, for type THW, size 4/0, a 2 in. conduit can only accommodate three conductors; therefore, a $2\frac{1}{2}$ in. conduit (maximum of 5) is required. A common method of indicating the above feeder on a one-line diagram is as follows: $2\frac{1}{2}''$ C, 4 -#4/0, THW

TABLE 11.6 Maximum Number of Conductors in Trade Size of Conduit or Tubing (from *NEC* Chapter 9, Tables 3A and 3B)

Conduit Trade Size (inches)		$\frac{1}{2}$	$\frac{3}{4}$	1	$1\frac{1}{4}$	$1\frac{1}{2}$	2	$2\frac{1}{2}$	3
Type Letters	Conductor Size								
THW	14	6	10	16	29	40	65	93	143
	12	4	8	13	24	32	53	76	117
	10	4	6	11	19	26	43	61	95
	8	1	3	5	10	13	22	32	49
	6	1	2	4	7	10	16	23	36
	4	1	1	3	5	7	12	17	27
	3	1	1	2	4	6	10	15	23
	2	1	1	2	4	5	9	13	20
	1		1	1	3	4	6	9	14
	1/0		1	1	2	3	5	8	12
	2/0		1	1	1	3	5	7	10
	3/0		1	1	1	2	4	6	9
	4/0			1	1	1	3	5	7
	250 MCM			1	1	1	2	4	6
	300 MCM			1	1	1	2	3	5
	350 MCM				1	1	1	3	4
	400 MCM				1	1	1	2	4
	500 MCM				1	1	1	1	3
XHHW	14	9	15	25	44	60	99	142	
	12	7	12	19	35	47	78	111	171
	10	5	9	15	26	36	60	85	131
	8	2	4	7	12	17	28	40	62
	6	1	3	5	9	13	21	30	47
	4	1	2	4	7	9	16	22	35
	3	1	1	3	6	8	13	19	29
	2	1	1	3	5	7	11	16	25
	1		1	1	3	5	8	12	18
	1/0		1	1	3	4	7	10	15
	2/0		1	1	2	3	6	8	13
	3/0		1	1	1	3	5	7	11
	4/0		1	1	1	2	4	6	9
	250 MCM			1	1	1	3	4	7
	300 MCM			1	1	1	3	4	6
	350 MCM			1	1	1	2	3	5
	400 MCM				1	1	1	3	5
	500 MCM				1	1	1	2	4

These values apply only when all conductors in the conduit run are the same type and size.

For a complete listing of all types of cables, for conductor sizes above 500 MCM, and for conduit trade sizes above 3 inches, see *NEC* Chapter 9, Tables 1 to 7.

11.6 CONDUCTORS IN PARALLEL

For larger-rated feeders, it may be desirable to parallel two or more conductors per phase, rather than use one large conductor. Paralleling means that the conductors of each phase are electrically joined at both ends to effectively form a single conductor, as shown in Figure 11.11. As previously illustrated in Section 11.1.1, the ampacity of conductors is not a linear function of their size; that is, the doubling of the cross-sectional area of the conductor does not result in the doubling of its ampacity rating. Another reason to avoid using large conductors is the difficulty of pulling them into the raceway. Also, a large-sized conduit is required, which is cumbersome to handle during installation. The general recommendation for conductors installed in conduit is that, if the required conductor size is computed to be larger than 500 MCM, then paralleling should definitely be considered. In fact, the *National Electrical Code* allows conductors size 1/0 and larger to be paralleled (see Section 310-4).

As an example of the desirability of paralleling, consider the following. A three-wire feeder requires an ampacity of 500 amperes. If one THW conductor per phase is used, the size required is 900 MCM (Table 11.1 rated for 520 A). If two conductors in parallel are used, then the size required for each is only 250 MCM (rated 255 A for a total of 510 amperes). The two 250 MCM conductors have a total of only 55% of the cross-sectional area of the 900 MCM conductor and will therefore cost less. The six 250 MCM conductors can be installed in two runs of $2\frac{1}{2}$ inch conduit, whereas the three 900 MCM conductors require a 4 inch conduit.

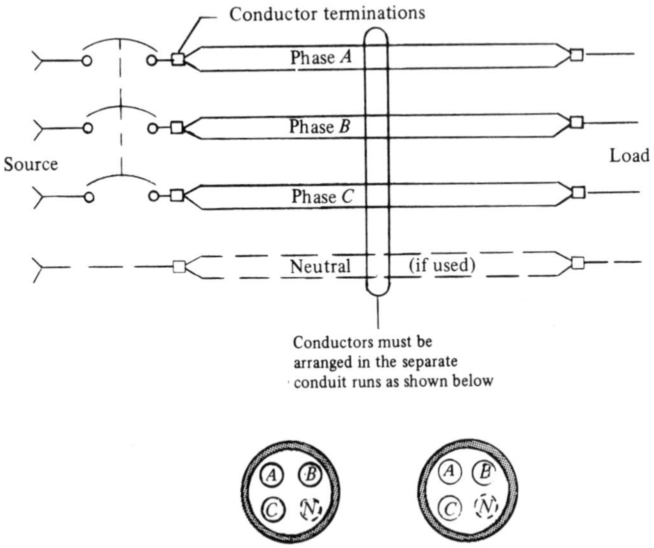

FIGURE 11.11

Conductors run in parallel

In the foregoing example, the six 250 MCM conductors could have been installed in one run of conduit. However, this would mean that the derate factor for more than three conductors in a raceway [Table 11.3(b)] would have to be applied, resulting in larger-sized conductors being required. The recommendation, therefore, is that the parallel conductors be installed in separate runs of conduit. This requires that one of each of the phase conductors and the neutral (if used) must be grouped together in each conduit run, as shown in Figure 11.11. If this is not done, then there is not a complete canceling of the magnetic flux around the conductors, with the result that the parallel conductors do not have the same reactance and therefore do not equally share the total feeder current. In addition, if steel conduits are used, then the residual flux causes severe heating problems in the steel through induced eddy current and hysteresis losses.

The parallel conductors must equally share the total feeder current. Otherwise, one conductor could end up being overloaded, resulting in overheating problems. In addition to the arrangement of the conductors as in Figure 11.11, the parallel conductors in each phase and the neutral must be of the same length, material, and size, have the same insulation, and be terminated in the same manner. The conduits must all be of the same size and type. Refer also to Example 11.14 for the use of parallel conductors where voltage drop is a problem.

11.7 EXAMPLES OF FEEDER DESIGN

In the normal course of the design of a feeder, the unknown factor is the required minimum conductor size that will meet each of the three separate requirements previously outlined: the ampacity rating, the short-circuit current rating, and the maximum allowable voltage drop. However, before proceeding with some design problems, there is one more item to discuss.

Article 220 of the *National Electrical Code* covers Branch-Circuit and Feeder Calculations. Part B of this article is concerned with the ampacity requirements of feeders, and in particular Section 220-10(b) deals with Continuous and Noncontinuous Loads. For a *continuous load,* the maximum current is expected to continue steadily for 3 hours or more. Conversely, a *noncontinuous load* fluctuates and only operates at its maximum current for short periods of time. An example of a continuous load is the general lighting for an office, which usually operates with all the lighting fixtures turned on continuously for 8 hours or more. An example of a noncontinuous load is the lighting in a residential complex, where each lighting fixture is randomly switched on and off, and it is extremely unlikely that all the units would be on at the same time for long periods of time.

Where a feeder supplies any combination of a continuous and/or noncontinuous load, the ampacity of the feeder shall not be less than 125% of the continuous load plus the noncontinuous load. There are two exceptions to this requirement. The first concerns feeders to groups of motors and is covered in Section 13.4 of this text. The second concerns 100% rated overcurrent devices and is covered in Section 11.8. For the method of calculating minimum load requirements for the feeders to panels supplying lighting units and general-purpose receptacles, see Section 12.11.

The following examples show the procedures for the selection of feeder conductors.

EXAMPLE 11.11

Select the size of the conductors and conduit for the feeder required for the following:

- Load is 100 kW at 90% power factor and is noncontinuous.
- Load is less than 50% ballast-type lighting and there are no other loads that cause third harmonics.
- Supply is three-phase, four-wire, 480Y/277 V.
- Length of feeder is 250 ft and it is to be run above grade.
- Available short-circuit current is 17,000 A symmetrical.
- Feeder overcurrent protection is a molded-case breaker.
- Maximum allowable voltage drop is to be 2%.
- Conductors to be copper, type THW in steel conduit.

Solution

Using Equation 1.12,

$$I_L \text{ (of load)} = \frac{100 \times 1000}{(1.73)(480)(0.9)} = 134 \text{ A}$$

(a) Minimum size required for ampacity:

- Minimum ampacity for noncontinuous load is 100%: 134 A.
- Neutral does not count as a fourth current-carrying conductor.
- From Table 11.1, minimum size is No. 1/0 (rated for 150 A).

(b) Minimum size required for short-circuit current:

- From Table 11.4, K_0 factor is 1.3, clearing time is 2 cycles.
- Using Equation 11.1,

$$I_{ASY} = 1.3 \times 17{,}000 = 22{,}100 \text{ A}$$

- From Figure 11.5, minimum size is No. 1 (see Figure 11.12 for method of reading the short-circuit graph).

(c) Minimum size required for voltage drop:

- Maximum allowable = 2% of 277 = 5.54 V (line-to-neutral).
- Ampere-feet = 134 × 250 = 33,500 = 33.5 × 1000.
- Maximum voltage drop/1000 AF = 5.54/33.5 = 0.165.
- From Table 11.5, minimum size is No. 1 with value of 0.162.

(d) Therefore, the ampacity requires the largest size: No. 1/0.

(e) From Table 11.6, the size of conduit is 2 in. for four conductors.

Feeder designation: 2″ C, 4 -#1/0, THW (Cu)

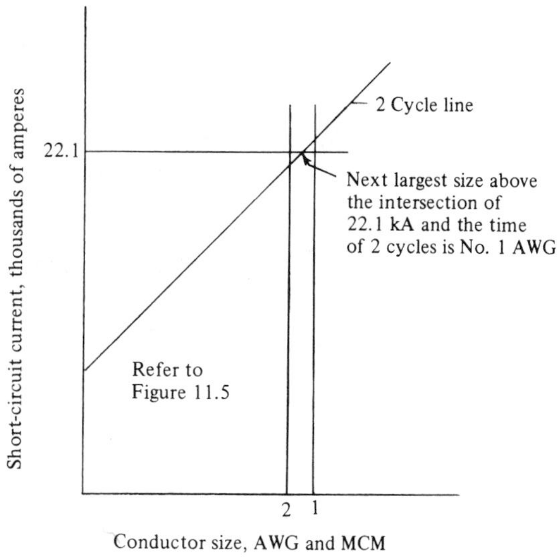

FIGURE 11.12

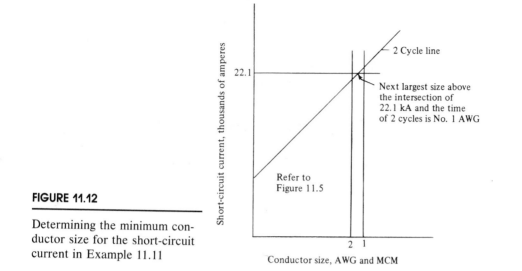

Determining the minimum conductor size for the short-circuit current in Example 11.11

■ EXAMPLE 11.12

Repeat Example 11.11, except the available short-circuit current is 35,000 A symmetrical.

Solution

(a) Minimum size for ampacity same as in Example 11.11: No. 1/0.

(b) Minimum size required for short-circuit current:

— K_0 factor and clearing time same as in Example 11.11.
— Using Equation 11.1,

$$I_{ASY} = 1.3 \times 35{,}000 = 45{,}500 \text{ A}$$

— From Figure 11.5, minimum size is No. 3/0.

(c) Minimum size for voltage drop same as in Example 11.11: No. 1.

(d) Therefore, short-circuit current requires largest size: No. 3/0.

(e) From Table 11.6, the size of conduit is 2 in. for four conductors.

Feeder designation: 2″ C, 4 -#3/0 THW (Cu)

■ EXAMPLE 11.13

Repeat Example 11.11, except the length of the feeder is 330 ft.

Solution

(a) Minimum size for ampacity same as in Example 11.11: No. 1/0.

(b) Minimum size for short-circuit current same as in Example 11.11: No. 1.

(c) Minimum size required for voltage drop:

— Maximum allowable = 2% of 277 = 5.54 V (line-to-neutral).
— Ampere-feet = 134 × 330 = 44,200 = 44.2 × 1000.
— Maximum voltage drop/1000 AF = 5.54/44.2 = 0.125.
— From Table 11.5, minimum size is No. 2/0 with value of 0.110.

(d) Therefore, the voltage drop requires the largest size: No. 2/0.

(e) From Table 11.6, the size of conduit is 2 in. for four conductors.

Feeder designation: 2″ C, 4 -#2/0 THW (Cu)

The foregoing examples show that the final selection of the conductor size for a feeder can be dictated by any one of the three requirements and that each must be checked out before the final decision is made.

■ EXAMPLE 11.14

Repeat Example 11.11, except the supply voltage is 208Y/120V. Determine the size required to meet the 2% voltage drop requirement only for this example.

Solution

$$I_L \text{ (of load)} = \frac{100 \times 1000}{(1.732)(208)(0.9)} = 308 \text{ A}$$

— Maximum voltage drop = 2% of 120 = 2.4 V (line-to-neutral).
— Ampere-feet = 308 × 250 = 77,000 = 77.0 × 1000.
— Maximum voltage drop/1000 AF = 2.4/77.0 = 0.031.
— From Table 11.5, minimum size is in excess of 1000 MCM.
— Since this is a very large size, consider two parallel conductors.
— Each conductor will carry 308/2 = 154 A.
— Ampere-feet = 154 × 250 = 38,500 = 38.5 × 1000.
— Maximum voltage drop/1000 AF = 2.4/38.5 = 0.062 (for each conductor).
— From Table 11.5, minimum size is 350 MCM with a value of 0.055.
— From Table 11.6, the size of conduit is 3 in. for four conductors.

Feeder designation: Two parallel runs, each to be 3″ C, 4-350 MCM, THW (Cu)

Example 11.14 illustrates the problem of feeding large loads from a 208Y/120 volt system, especially if there are long feeder distances to contend with. There is a large increase in the size and cost of the feeders, as compared to loads of the same size that are fed from a 480Y/277 volt system. This emphasizes the importance of selecting the highest possible standard voltage for the electrical distribution system within large buildings (see Section 1.8).

■ EXAMPLE 11.15

Repeat Example 11.11, except that the 100 kW load is continuous and consists of more than 50% electric discharge type of lighting. Consider both types THW and XHHW conductors (dry location).

Solution

The load has same full-load current of 134 A.

(a) Minimum size required for ampacity:

- Minimum ampacity for continuous load = 125% of 134 = 167.5 A.
- Neutral must be counted as fourth current-carrying conductor.
- From Table 11.3(b), the ampacity adjustment factor is 80% (0.80).
- Rating to select from Table 11.1 is 167.5/0.80 = 209 A.
- THW minimum size is No. 4/0 (rating in table of 230 A).
- XHHW minimum size is No. 3/0 (rating in table of 225 A) (satisfactory for equipment terminals; see Section 11.1.7).

(b) Minimum size required for short-circuit current:

- I_{ASY} = 22,000 A, same as in Example 11.11.
- THW from Figure 11.5, minimum size is No. 1, same as in Example 11.11.
- XHHW from figure 11.6, minimum size is No. 2.

(c) Minimum size required for voltage drop (still based on actual load current of 134 A):

- Maximum voltage drop/1000 AF = 0.165, same as in Example 11.11.
- THW minimum size is No. 1, same as in Example 11.11.
- XHHW correction factor for 90°C is 1.1 (note 2, Table 11.5). The value for use in Table 11.5 = 0.165/1.1 = 0.150. The minimum size is No. 1/0 with a value of 0.133.

(d) Summary

	THW	XHHW
Ampacity	4/0	3/0
Short circuit	1	2
Voltage drop	1	1/0

Therefore, the preferred selection is No. 3/0 XHHW.

(e) From Table 11.6, the conduit size is 2 in. for four conductors.

Feeder designation: 2″ C, 4 -#3/0 XHHW (Cu)

■ EXAMPLE 11.16

Repeat Example 11.15, except that the available short-circuit current is 53,000 A.

Solution

(a) Minimum sizes for ampacity and voltage drop same as in Example 11.15.

(b) Minimum size required for short-circuit current:

- Using Equation 11.1,

$$I_{ASY} = 1.3 \times 53{,}000 = 68{,}900 \text{ A}$$

- THW: from Figure 11.5, minimum size is 250 MCM.
- XHHW: from Figure 11.6, minimum size is No. 4/0.

(c) Summary

	THW	XHHW
Ampacity	4/0	3/0
Short circuit	250 MCM	4/0
Voltage drop	1	1/0

Therefore, the preferred selection is No. 4/0 XHHW.

(d) From Table 11.6, the conduit size is 2 in. for four conductors.

Feeder designation: 2″ C, 4 -#4/0 XHHW (Cu)

Examples 11.15 and 11.16 show that the use of 90°C rated conductors (for example, XHHW) often allows a smaller size of conductor and conduit to be used. This more than offsets the slightly higher cost of the 90°C rated conductors (as compared to the same size of 75°C rated conductor).

11.8 OVERCURRENT PROTECTION OF FEEDERS

The *National Electrical Code* defines the term *overcurrent* as *any current in excess of the rated current of equipment or the ampacity of a conductor*. An overcurrent may result from an overload, a short circuit, or a ground fault. The reader should review Section 6.1 with regard to overloads and short circuits and to the reference to *NEC* Sections 240-20(a) and 240-21, which govern the requirements and locations of overcurrent protection (fuses and circuit breakers). In addition, *NEC* Section 240-3 states in part that

> Conductors shall be protected against overcurrent in accordance with their ampacities . . . [except that] where the ampacity of the conductor does not correspond with the standard rating of a fuse or a circuit breaker without overload trip adjustments . . . the next higher standard device rating shall be permitted only if this rating does not exceed 800 amperes . . . .

Underwriters Laboratories, Inc., standards require that a fuse must be able to continuously carry 110% of its rated current at an ambient temperature of 25°C and that a circuit breaker must be able to carry 100% of its rated current at an ambient temperature of 40°C. The acceptance tests for these requirements are carried out with the fuse or circuit breaker mounted in the open. However, in practice, the fuses and circuit breakers are mounted within switch or panel enclosures (see Figures 7.12 and 8.10). Even under normal loading, the heat generated by the fuse or circuit breaker plus that generated by the feeder conductors and terminals may cause the ambient temperature within the enclosure to rise above the ambient temperature values used for the UL tests. Since a fuse or thermally operated circuit breaker responds to heat, no matter how it is generated, the protective device may no longer be able to continuously carry its rated current. Therefore, *NEC* Section 220-10(b) requires that the rating of the overcurrent device for a feeder supplying a continuous load shall not be less than 125% of the continuous load current. Continuous loads are discussed in Section 11.7. This in effect means that the protective device cannot be continuously loaded beyond 80% of its rating. The *NEC* allows an exception to this 80% derating rule:

> That where the assembly, including the overcurrent devices protecting the feeder, are listed [that is, approved] for continuous operation at 100% of their rating, then the feeder can be loaded to 100% of its ampacity rating.

However, to date the only fusible equipment that has UL approval for 100% continuous operation is some large bolted-pressure switches rated above 600 amperes and using class L fuses. Also, only low-voltage power and encased-type circuit breakers (Sections 8.5 and 8.8) have UL approval for 100% continuous operation. This is an area that requires a lot more attention by manufacturers and the standards agencies. The 80% derating causes extra costs for electrical systems in requiring oversized feeders, switches, fuses, circuit breakers, panelboards, and the like, when supplying continuous loads.

The following examples illustrate the method of selecting the overcurrent protection (fuse or circuit breaker) for a feeder or subfeeder (see Figure 11.1). The standard ratings of low-voltage fuses and switches are shown in Tables 7.1 and 7.2, respectively. The standard ratings of low-voltage circuit breakers are shown in Tables 8.1, 8.2, and 8.3. For a complete discussion on fuses and circuit breakers, see Chapters 7 and 8, respectively. For the special requirements of overcurrent protection for motor circuits and feeders, see Sections 13.1.1 and 13.4.

■ EXAMPLE 11.17

Select the molded-case circuit breaker ratings for overcurrent protection of the feeder in Example 11.15. Note that molded-case breakers are not normally UL listed for 100% continuous operation.

Solution

- The minimum trip rating for the breaker is 125% of 134 = 167.5 A.
- From Table 8.1, the next highest standard trip rating is 175 A (the ampacity of the four #3/0 XHHW in conduit is 0.80 × 225 = 180 A).
- The frame size required for the 175 A trip is 225 A, which has an interrupting rating of 22,000 A symmetrical at 480 V (Table 8.1), which is satisfactory for the available short-circuit current of 17,000 A symmetrical (from Example 11.11).

■ EXAMPLE 11.18

Current-limiting fuses (Section 7.3) are to be used for the overcurrent protection of the feeder in Example 11.12 (instead of a circuit breaker).

(a) Select the fuse and switch ratings.

(b) Determine the conductor size for the short-circuit current.

Solution

(a) Load current is 134 A and is noncontinuous (from Example 11.11).

- —From Table 7.1, the next highest standard fuse rating is 150 A.
- —From Table 7.2, the switch rating is 200 A, 600 V.

(b) Prospective short-circuit current is 35,000 A.

- —From Figure 7.5, the effective let-through current for a 150 A, 600 V fuse is estimated to be 10,000 A symmetrical (interpolate between the 100 and 200 A, 600 V fuses).
- —From Table 11.4, K_0 factor is 1.4 and clearing time is $\frac{1}{2}$ cycle.
- —Using Equation 11.1,

$$I_{ASY} = 1.4 \times 10{,}000 = 14{,}000 \text{ A}$$

- —From Figure 11.5, the minimum size is No. 1 (using 1 cycle line).

No. 1/0, which is required for ampacity, can now be used for the feeder, rather than No. 3/0 previously required.

Example 11.18 shows the advantage of using current-limiting fuses for the overcurrent protection of feeders in situations where the available fault currents are at a high level. Current-limiting circuit breakers (Section 8.9) also offer the same advantage but at a considerable increase in cost.

11.9 CABLE TRAYS

A *cable tray* is *an assembly of rigid structural sections that, together with the associated fittings, forms a continuous support system for cables*. Cable tray systems include the ladder type and perforated and solid bottom types. The ladder type, which, as its name implies, resembles a ladder, is generally the type used for feeder runs as it does not impede the dissipation of the heat from the cables. Figure 11.13 shows some typical applications of ladder-type cable trays for spanning open areas. Cable trays are particularly useful where there are a number of cables to be run in the same general direction.

The cables installed in the trays are generally the metal-clad type similar to that shown in Figure 11.2(c). The cable trays must be installed so that they are accessible, except where they pass through a wall or structural floor. There must be sufficient space around the trays to permit access for the installation and maintenance of the cables. Metallic cable trays have to be grounded and can therefore

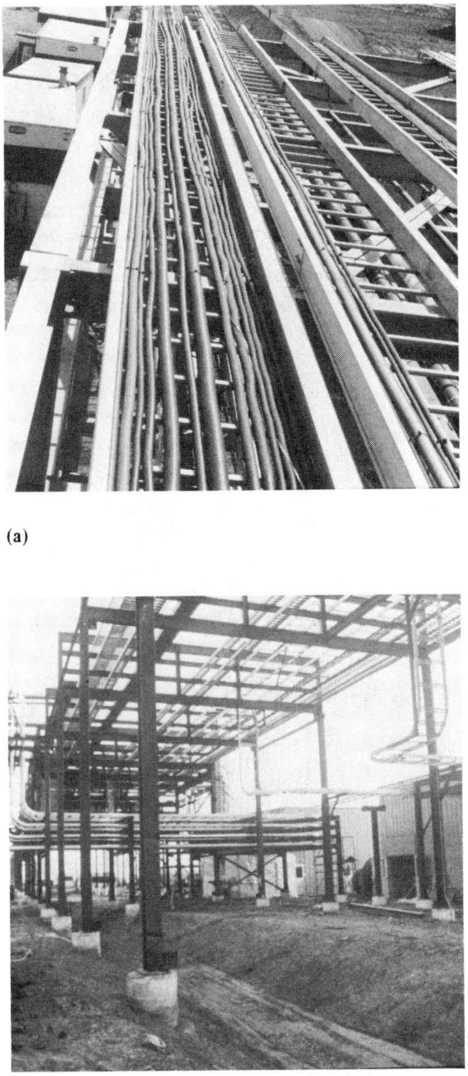

(a)

(b)

FIGURE 11.13

Typical applications of ladder-type cable trays for the support of electric cables across open spaces

serve as part of the equipment grounding circuit (see Chapter 10). The complete requirements for the installation of cable trays are covered in Article 318 of the *National Electrical Code*.

11.10 BUSWAYS

In large commercial and industrial buildings where high-ampacity feeders are required, the use of insulated conductors in conduit becomes cumbersome and expensive because of the number of parallel runs needed to obtain the desired ampacity. An alternative method is the use of busways for the feeders. A *busway* (also called bus duct) is *a metal enclosure containing factory assembled conductors, which are usually copper or aluminum bars or tubes*. An example of a feeder busway is shown in Figure 11.14(a). This shows one typical section of bus duct, which is usually manufactured in 10 foot lengths. These sections together with available elbows and other manufactured fittings are bolted together on the building site to form complete feeders. Some typical applications for high-rise commercial or institutional buildings are shown in Figure 11.14(b). In large

(a) Typical section of low-impedance bus duct

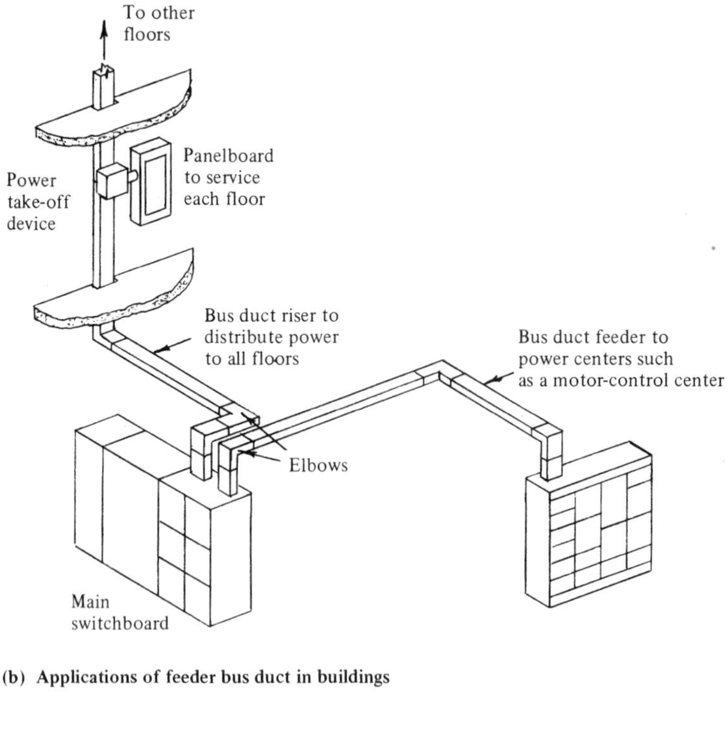

(b) Applications of feeder bus duct in buildings

FIGURE 11.14

Low-voltage feeder-type busways

industrial plants, feeder bus duct is extensively used in horizontal runs from the main switchboards to the major power centers located throughout the plant.

The type of feeder duct shown in Figure 11.14(a) is known as *low-impedance bus duct*. The low impedance is obtained by the close phase-to-phase spacing of the bus bars, which reduces the inductive reactance of the conductors to a minimum. This type is desirable so that the voltage drop on a feeder is kept as low as possible. Ratings for the feeder busways range from 600 up to 5000 amperes at 600 volts based on a temperature rise of 55°C from an ambient temperature of 40°C. Voltage drops range from approximately 2 to 3.5 volts line-to-line per 100 feet of run, where the load is concentrated at the end of the feeder run. Since the bus bars in the busway can be subjected to severe mechanical stressing during short circuits, they must be adequately braced so that the bars are not permanently bent and their supports broken (see Section 6.2). Short-circuit current ratings vary from 15,000 up to 150,000 amperes symmetrical.

Another common type of busway is the plug-in bus duct shown in Figure 11.15. This type is used in industrial plants as an overhead distribution system to supply readily available power to adjacent machine tools and other utilization equipment. In effect, the plug-in busway is an elongated panelboard with the plug-in openings provided at closely spaced intervals along its entire run from which power can be tapped. The plug-in units are usually switch and fuse combinations or circuit breakers that provide overcurrent protection

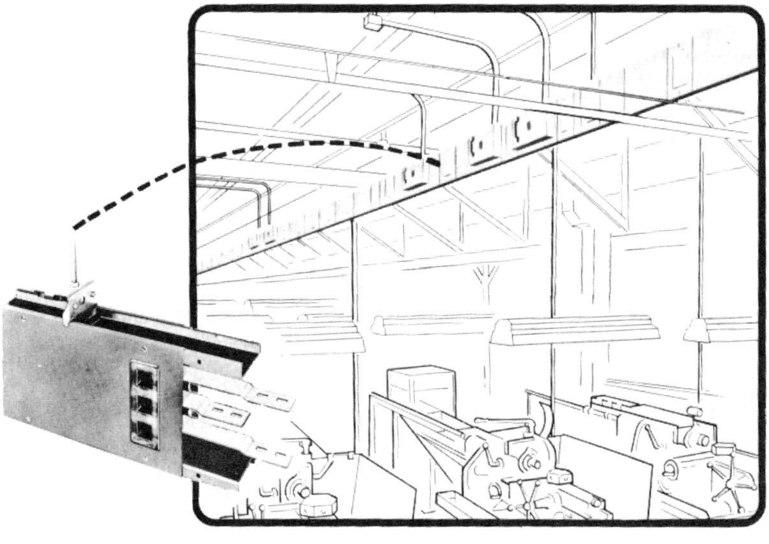

FIGURE 11.15

Typical application of plug-in bus duct in an industrial plant for the branch circuit cable runs to the utilization equipment. Because plug-in busways are used as much for their flexibility as they are to provide feeder capacity, they are available in ratings as low as 100 amperes.

The complete requirements for the installation of busways is covered in Article 364 of the *National Electrical Code*.

SUMMARY

- The connecting wiring within a building is divided into the service entrance, the feeders, and the branch circuits.
- The correct selection of conductors for feeders and circuits must take into account ampacity, short circuit, and voltage drop requirements.
- All conductors installed in a building must be properly protected, usually by installing them in raceways.
- The ampacity rating of conductors in a raceway depends on the conductor material, size, and temperature rating; the number of current-carrying conductors in the raceway; and the ambient temperature.
- The short-circuit current rating of a conductor depends on the conductor material, the temperature limitations of the insulation, and the duration of the short circuit.
- The short-circuit ratings must be based on asymmetrical currents, such that $I_{ASY} = K_0 \times I_{SYM}$, where K_0 depends on the voltage level of the system and the clearing time of the protective device.
- The voltage drop on a 60 hertz feeder installed in a raceway is affected by the load current and power factor; the length of the feeder; the size, type, and operating temperature of the conductors; and the raceway material (magnetic or nonmagnetic).
- The percentage voltage drop is the difference between the source voltage V_S and the load voltage V_L expressed as a percentage of the source voltage. Thus

$$\% \text{ voltage drop} = \frac{V_S - V_L}{V_S} \times 100$$

- The voltage drop of a feeder should not exceed 3%, and the total of the system should not exceed 5%.
- The terminals of UL-approved equipment are limited to the 60°C ampacity rating for circuits 100 amperes and below and to the 75°C ampacity rating for circuits above 100 amperes.
- Letters are used to designate the type of insulation and construction of a cable and its condition of use.

- Raceways provide space, support, and mechanical protection for conductors, and they minimize the hazards from electrical shocks and fires.
- The most common type of raceway used for feeders is conduit, which is available in rigid and flexible, metallic and nonmetallic types.
- Conduit runs must be properly supported and have sufficient access points to facilitate the installation of the conductors.
- Conduits must be large enough to accommodate the number of conductors based generally on a 40% fill ratio.
- Paralleling of conductors should be considered if the use of one conductor per phase requires larger than 500 MCM.
- The load on a feeder must be considered as being continuous if the maximum current is expected to continue steadily for 3 hours or more, in which case the feeder and its overcurrent protection must be rated for a minimum of 125% of the load current, unless the overcurrent protective device is UL approved for continuous operation at 100% of its rating.
- The highest possible standard system voltage should be selected to minimize feeder sizes and costs.
- All feeders must be properly protected against overcurrents.
- Cable trays are used for supporting feeder cables where a number of them are to be run in the same location.
- Low-impedance busways (bus duct) are used in buildings for high-capacity feeders.
- Plug-in busways are used for overhead distribution systems, providing convenient power tap-offs to the utilization equipment.

QUESTIONS

1. State the difference between a feeder and a branch circuit.
2. What are the three separate requirements that can dictate the final selection of the conductor size for a feeder?
3. What is the definition of ampacity?
4. Explain why the conditions of use can affect the ampacity rating of a cable?
5. What does the AWG number designate?
6. What does 500 MCM designate?
7. Explain why the maximum allowable operating temperature of the insulation affects the ampacity of a conductor.
8. Explain why the ambient temperature affects the ampacity of a conductor.
9. Explain why a conductor installed in a raceway has a lower ampacity rating than if it were run in free air.
10. For a three-phase, four-wire feeder supplying an electric discharge type of lighting load (for example, fluorescent lighting), why must the neutral be considered as a fourth current-carrying

conductor in the raceway and how does this affect the ampacity rating of the conductors?

11. What are the ampacity limitations imposed by the termination of conductors at equipment terminals?
12. Explain why it is necessary to check the short-circuit current rating of the conductors in a feeder.
13. Explain why the asymmetrical value of current must be used to determine the short-circuit rating of a conductor.
14. Why is it important to calculate the voltage drop on a feeder or branch circuit?
15. What does the unit of ampere-feet represent and why is it used?
16. Explain the letter designations RHW and THWN.
17. What are the two main functions of raceways?
18. What are the restrictions in the use of nonmetallic (plastic) conduit and tubing?
19. Why must the number of conductors installed in a specific size of conduit be restricted?
20. On large-capacity feeders, why is it advantageous to consider the paralleling of conductors?
21. What is meant by a continuous load and how does a continuous load affect the sizing of a feeder?
22. Explain the significance of an overcurrent.
23. What is a cable tray and why are cable trays used?
24. What is meant by low-impedance bus duct and why is it used?
25. What is meant by plug-in bus duct and why is it used?

PROBLEMS

1. Determine the ampacity of No. 4 XHHW copper conductors, five current-carrying conductors in a raceway in free air, ambient temperature of 40°C.
2. Determine the ampacity of a three-phase, four-wire feeder using No. 1/0 RHW copper conductors installed in a raceway in free air supplying a fluorescent lighting load.
3. Repeat Problem 2, except the feeder is to be installed in a single underground electrical duct with an ambient earth temperature of 20°C.
4. Determine the symmetrical short-circuit current rating of a 300 MCM XHHW copper conductor on a 208 V feeder protected by a circuit breaker.
5. Repeat Problem 4, except the feeder is protected by current-limiting fuses (use 1 cycle line on graph).
6. Calculate the percentage of voltage drop on a 480 V, three-phase feeder supplying a 90 kW, 80% power factor load, length 240 ft, consisting of three No. 1 XHHW copper conductors in an aluminum conduit.
7. Determine the trade size of conduit required for a run of six No. 1/0 XHHW conductors.
8. Select the size of the conductors and conduit for the feeder required for the following:

    — Load is 80 kW at 100% power factor and is noncontinuous.
    — Load is incandescent lighting.
    — Supply is 208Y/120 V, three-phase, four-wire.
    — Length of feeder is 200 ft, to be run above grade.
    — Available short-circuit current is 22,000 A symmetrical.
    — Feeder overcurrent protection is a molded-case breaker.
    — Maximum allowable voltage drop is 3%.
    — Conductors to be type THW, copper in steel conduit.

9. Repeat Problem 8, except the load is fluorescent lighting that will be on continuously for 10 hours.
10. Repeat Problem 8, except the maximum allowable voltage drop is 2%.
11. Repeat Problem 8, except the available fault current is 50,000 A symmetrical.
12. Select the size of conductors and conduit for the feeder required for the following (consider the paralleling of conductors):

    — Load is 268 kW at 90% power factor and is continuous.
    — More than 50% of load has high third-harmonic components.

—Supply is 480Y/277 V, three-phase, four-wire.
—Length of feeder is 235 ft.
—Available fault current is 39,000 A symmetrical.
—Feeder overcurrent protection is a molded-case breaker.
—Maximum allowable voltage drop is 2%.
—Conductors to be type XHHW copper in steel conduit.

13. Select the frame and trip ratings for the circuit breaker protecting the feeder in Problem 8.

14. Select the frame and trip ratings for the circuit breaker protecting the feeder in Problem 9.

15. Select the frame and trip ratings for the circuit breaker protecting the feeder in Problem 11.

16. Select the frame and trip ratings for the circuit breaker protecting the feeder in Problem 12.

17. Repeat Problem 12, except the feeder overcurrent protection will be a power circuit breaker approved for 100% continuous operation.

18. Select the frame and trip ratings for the circuit breaker in Problem 17.

12 Branch Circuits and Computed Loads for Lighting and Receptacles

OBJECTIVES

After studying this chapter, you will be able to:

- Organize the branch circuits for lighting.
- Organize the branch circuits for general-purpose receptacles.
- Lay out the branch circuit wiring on a floor plan.
- Make out a lighting panel schedule.
- Read electrical floor plan drawings.
- Recognize the use of underfloor raceway systems.
- Explain the application of ground-fault circuit-interrupters.
- Compute the loads for the feeders to lighting panels.

INTRODUCTION

A *branch circuit* is *the segment that extends beyond the final automatic overcurrent device in the system to the connection at the utilization equipment.* As discussed in the introduction to Chapter 11, the initial planning of the electrical system involves the preparation of a one-line diagram to establish the general means of distributing the electric power within the building. However, the design of the system cannot be finalized until the requirements of all the branch circuits have been fully determined and their exact loading has been calculated. Thus the final stage in the complete design of an electrical system begins with the preparation of the detailed layouts for all the branch circuits throughout the building.

Refer to Figure 11.1, which shows a typical one-line diagram of an electrical system. Most branch circuits originate at panelboards and/or motor-control centers. There can be branch circuits for lighting and general-use receptacles, for specific-purpose equipment, and for motors. The detailed requirements for specific-purpose equipment, such as electric welders and space-heating equipment, are too broad for the scope of this textbook. The requirements for motors are covered separately in Chapter 13. This chapter then concentrates on the requirements for the branch circuits for lighting and general-use receptacles such as encountered in commercial, institutional, and industrial establishments. The reader is referred to the *National Electrical Code,* Articles 210 and 220, for the general requirements for branch circuits and their computed loads. For reference to the Canadian Electrical Code, see Appendix A.

12.1 BRANCH CIRCUIT CONDUCTORS

The branch circuit conductors must have an ampacity of not less than the maximum load to be served. However, a circuit is not classified by the ampacity rating of the conductors, but rather by the rating of the overcurrent device protecting the circuit. Typical values are 15, 20, 30, 40, and 50 amperes. For example, a circuit may use No. 10 THW copper conductors to compensate for voltage drop. Even though these conductors have an ampacity rating of 35 amperes, if the circuit is protected by a 20 ampere overcurrent device, then the circuit is classified as 20 ampere.

In most areas of large buildings, the branch-circuit wiring is installed in either conduit or electrical metallic tubing (EMT) in order to meet the requirements of the electrical code with regard to the protection of insulated conductors from physical damage. Refer to Sections 11.1 through 11.4 for details of ampacity ratings, temperature ratings, voltage drops, and letter designations of circuit conductors and to Section 11.5 for details of raceways. Refer specifically to Table 11.1 for the ampacities of conductors in raceways and to Table 11.6 for the maximum number of conductors permitted in conduit or EMT.

In Table 11.1, a footnote covering AWG sizes 14, 12, and 10 sets the maximum overcurrent protection for these sizes. For example, the overcurrent protection for No. 12 copper cannot exceed 20 amperes, regardless of the fact that the listed ampacities for this size are higher (for example, THW, 25 A; RHH, 30 A). However, it is advantageous to have these higher ampacity ratings. The ratings as listed in Table 11.1 apply at an ambient temperature of 30°C and with not more than three conductors in a raceway. With higher ambient temperatures and more than three conductors, derating factors must be applied as discussed in Sections 11.1.4 and 11.1.5. A No. 12 AWG conductor may still be satisfactory for a 20 ampere branch circuit, rather than having to go to the next larger size.

■ EXAMPLE 12.1

Six No. 12 RHH copper conductors for a number of 20 A circuits are all to be run in the

Solution

From Table 11.1, the ampacity rating of the conductors is 30 A. The correction factor for 40°C is 0.91. From Table 11.3(b), the adjustment factor for six conductors is 80%.

same conduit. The ambient temperature is 40°C. Determine whether the ampacity rating of the conductors is satisfactory.

$$\text{Ampacity} = 30 \times 0.91 \times 0.80 = 21.8\text{ A} \quad \text{(satisfactory)}$$

Note that No. 12 THW conductors would not be satisfactory for this application. Their ampacity is listed as 25 amperes and, after the application of the derating factors, they would only be good for 17.6 amperes. Number 10 THW copper conductors would have to be used. However, regardless of ampacity ratings, there are specific *NEC* rules with regard to the minimum temperature rating of conductors used to connect to lighting fixtures (*NEC* Section 410-31). Branch-circuit conductors brought within 3 inches of a ballast in a lighting fixture must have a temperature rating not less than 90°C, such as types RHH, THHN, XHHW, and THW (note that THW has a 90°C rating when used in fluorescent fixtures, *NEC* Table 310-13). Otherwise, the temperature rating of the wiring connected to a lighting fixture shall be suitable for the temperature as listed by the Underwriters Laboratories approval for the fixture.

NEC Section 310-5 states that the minimum size of copper conductors that can be used for branch circuits is No. 14 AWG. However, for commercial and industrial establishments, it is good design practice to specify No. 12 copper as the minimum size even for 15 ampere circuits. The larger size helps to keep the voltage drop within the allowable limits over the longer circuit runs encountered.

12.2 BRANCH CIRCUITS FOR LIGHTING

Branch circuits for lighting shall have a maximum rating of 20 amperes unless the lighting units have heavy-duty lampholders. Thus, branch circuits for fluorescent lighting and for the smaller-wattage, medium-base incandescent lamps (up to 300 watts) are restricted to 15 or 20 amperes. Fixed lighting units with heavy-duty lampholders [that is, the larger-wattage, mogul-base incandescent and high-intensity discharge (HID) lamps] can be connected to circuits rated up to 50 amperes when installed in other-than-dwelling units. HID lamps are the mercury, metal-halide, and high-pressure sodium lamps. The reader at this time should review Chapter 4 for the details of light sources, in particular, Figure 4.3 on bases for lamps and Tables 4.1 through 4.5 for listings of lamps.

The lighting involved in the general illumination of such areas as offices, schools, and industrial plants is considered to be a continuous load. The *NEC* restricts the maximum loading on a circuit supplying a continuous load to 80% of the rating of the circuit (*NEC* Section 210-22). Thus, on a 20 ampere lighting circuit, the maximum loading is 0.80 times 20, or 16 amperes. The calculated load for circuits supplying electric discharge lamps that have ballasts must be based on the line current to the ballasts (see Figures 4.8 and 4.15) and not just on the wattage of the lamps alone. The total input to the lighting unit must include the ballast losses. See Tables 4.4 and 4.5 for total input watts to ballasts for fluorescent and HID lamps, respectively.

The voltage limitations of branch circuits are governed by *NEC* Section 210-6. All lighting fixtures in dwelling units, guest rooms of hotels, motels, and similar occupancies are restricted to circuits not exceeding 120 volts nominal between conductors (line-to-neutral of 120/240 volt single phase, three-wire and 208Y/120 volt three-phase, four-wire systems). All lighting units using medium-base, screw-shell, incandescent lampholders, regardless of location, are restricted to circuits not exceeding 120 volts nominal. The ballasts for the electric discharge lamps (fluorescent and HID) and lighting fixtures equipped with mogul-base, screw-shell lampholders or with lampholders other than the screw-shell type applied within their voltage rating can be connected to circuits exceeding 120 volts, but not exceeding 277 volts nominal to ground (480Y/277 volt, three-phase, four-wire grounded system). For the illumination of outdoor areas such as roadways, parking lots, and athletic fields, the ballasts for electric discharge lamps can be connected to circuits not exceeding 600 volts nominal between conductors, providing that the lighting units are mounted on poles or similar structures at a minimum height of 22 feet. This permits these outdoor units to be connected to 480 volt ungrounded systems.

The ballasts for fluorescent lamps should be operated from the line-to-neutral voltage of grounded systems as shown in Figure 4.8. This ensures reliable starting, as discussed in Section 4.3.2. Ballasts for HID lamps may be operated either from line-to-neutral or line-to-line voltages. However, if operated from the line-to-line voltage, two-winding ballasts, as shown in Figure 10.20, should be used to permit the grounding of the shell of the lamp socket.

The general illumination of large office and industrial areas is normally provided by fluorescent or HID lamps because of their much higher efficacies (see Introduction to Chapter 4). The fact that these lighting units can be operated from the 480Y/277 volt, three-phase, four-wire system is of considerable advantage. First, the savings in feeder and branch-circuit wiring can be considerable as illustrated in Example 12.2. Second, the voltage drop is far less of a problem. Every 1 volt drop on a 120 volt circuit results in a 0.83% voltage drop, whereas every 1 volt drop on a 277 volt circuit causes only a 0.36% voltage drop. Thus larger areas of the building can be covered from each lighting panel. Finally, both the three-phase motors and the lighting can be supplied from the same system. The relatively small amount of power required for the 120 volt lighting and general-purpose receptacle loads can be supplied from dry-type step-down transformers located throughout the building. It should be noted that the 480Y/277 volt, three-phase, four-wire system must have the neutral solidly grounded. See Section 10.2 for a full description of grounded systems. If the neutral is not grounded, then the voltage to ground is considered to be 480 volts (see *NEC* definition "voltage to ground") and the indoor lighting units cannot be connected to the system.

EXAMPLE 12.2

Refer to the lighting layout in Example 5.11 and Figure 5.10. A total of 70 luminaires (lighting units) is required for the area to be lighted. Each luminaire has two 800 mA, 96 in., 113 W fluorescent lamps. The ballast for each lighting unit is rated at 252 W (Table 4.4), with a line current of 2.1 A at 120 V and 0.92 A at 277 V. Determine the minimum number of branch circuits required for the lighting load with a system voltage of (a) 208Y/120 V and (b) 480Y/277 V.

Solution

The maximum allowable rating of each circuit is 20 A. The maximum loading of each circuit is $0.80 \times 20 = 16$ A.

(a) 208Y/120 V system (ballasts connected to 120 V):

— Maximum number of units per circuit is $16/2.1 = 7.6 \approx 7$.
— Minimum number of circuits is $70/7 = 10$.

The logical arrangement is two circuits per row. The circuit loading is $7 \times 2.1 = 14.7$ A.

(b) 480Y/277 V system (ballasts connected to 277 V):

— Maximum number of units per circuit is $16/0.92 = 17.4 \approx 17$.
— Minimum number of circuits is $70/17 = 4.1 \approx 5$.

The logical arrangement is one circuit for each row. The circuit loading is $14 \times 0.92 = 12.9$ A.

Note that it takes only one-half the number of circuits to wire the complete lighting system using 277 V.

12.3 BRANCH CIRCUITS FOR RECEPTACLES

A *receptacle* is defined as *a contact device installed at the outlet for the connection of a single attachment plug*. An *outlet* is further defined as *a point on the wiring system at which current is taken to supply utilization equipment*. A *duplex* receptacle has two devices mounted on a common yoke and is installed in one outlet box, and, similarly, a triplex receptacle has three devices mounted on a common yoke and is installed in one outlet box.

A single receptacle installed on an individual branch circuit must have an ampere rating not less than that of the branch circuit. For example, a single receptacle on a 20 ampere circuit must be rated at 20 amperes. The one exception to this requirement is that two or more 15 ampere receptacles are permitted on a 20 ampere circuit. Figure 12.1(a) shows the configuration of a few of the common ratings of receptacles. The configurations are arranged so that the receptacle will not accept an attachment plug of a different ampere or voltage rating from that of the receptacle. The one exception is the 20 ampere T-slot receptacle, which can also accept a 15 ampere attachment plug of the same voltage rating. Receptacles installed on 15 and 20 ampere branch circuits must be of the grounding type. This means that all 120 volt general-purpose plug outlets must be of the three-pole type. The grounding terminal must be properly bonded to the equipment grounding circuit as shown in Figure 10.11. If the branch-circuit wiring is of the nonmetallic type, then a separate equipment grounding conductor must be run with the circuit conductors for this purpose. The 125 volt, 15 ampere, U-ground duplex receptacle shown in Figure 12.1(b) is a very common type of general-purpose receptacle.

The minimum load for an outlet installed for a specific appliance or load is set by the ampere rating of the appliance or load served. The continuous load supplied by the branch circuit must not exceed 80% of the branch-circuit rating. However, the majority of receptacles are installed for general-purpose use and the exact loads are most likely unknown. In this case, a minimum loading of 180 volt–amperes must be allowed for each general-use receptacle. Figure

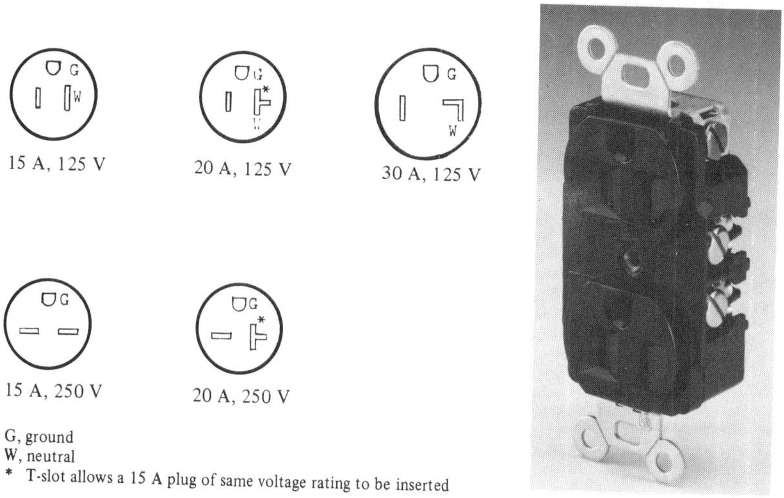

FIGURE 12.1

General-purpose receptacles

(a) Configurations for nonlocking receptacles. (for a complete listing, see ANSI C73 standard and for CSA configurations, see Appendix A)

(b) U-ground duplex receptacle, 125 V, 15 A

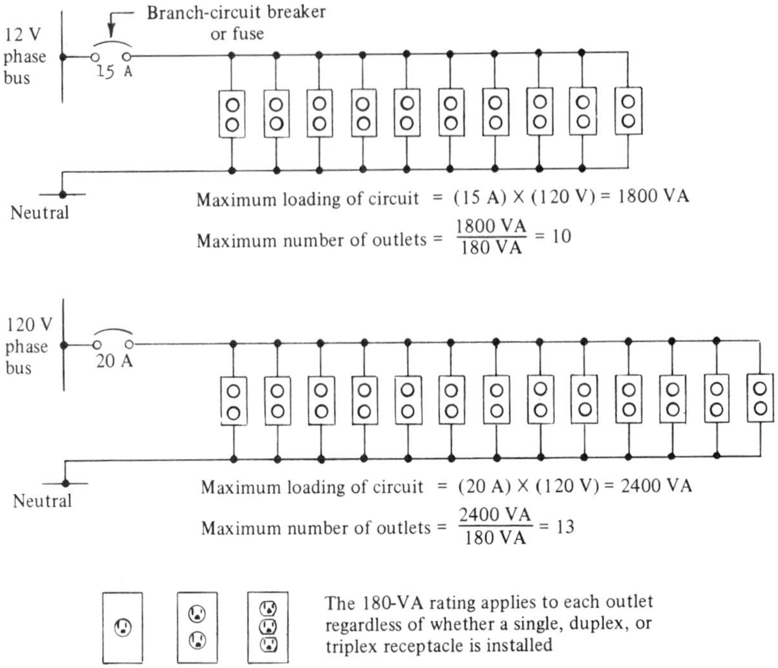

For Canadian Electrical Code regulations, see Appendix A

FIGURE 12.2

Maximum number of general-use receptacles permitted on branch circuits

12.2 shows the maximum number of general-use receptacles that are permitted on 15 and 20 ampere branch circuits. Note that the 180 volt–ampere rating is applied per outlet point, regardless of whether a single, duplex, or triplex receptacle is used at that outlet. For certain office and industrial areas, good design practices may dictate the use of fewer receptacles per circuit then the maximum allowed by the code.

12.4 LIGHTING PANELS

A panelboard is a group of panel units designed for assembly into a single panel, including buses, automatic overcurrent devices, and/or switches, for the control of light, heat, and power circuits. This assembly is suitable for mounting in a cabinet, which can then be placed in or against a wall and which is accessible only from the front. In other words, a panelboard is a convenient method of grouping together those overcurrent devices that are fed from a common source and that provide circuit protection to a number of branch circuits. The *NEC* further defines a *lighting and appliance branch-circuit panelboard as one having more than 10% of its overcurrent devices rated 30 amperes or less for which neutral connections are provided*. Most panels installed for lighting and receptacle branch circuits (often just referred to as lighting panels) fall within this definition and are therefore subject to the special *NEC* requirements with regard to these types of panels (see *NEC* Sections 384-13 to 384-27 inclusive). Section 384-15 restricts any one lighting panel to a maximum of 42 single-pole overcurrent devices or their equivalent (that is, a two-pole device is considered as two single-pole devices and a three-pole device as three single pole devices in determining this number).

A very common form of lighting panel consists of an assembly of light-duty, molded-case circuit breakers. These types of breakers are discussed in Section 8.4.3. A typical lighting panel using the double-row arrangement of breakers is shown in Figure 12.3(a). In commercial or institutional buildings, these panels can either be flush mounted into a wall in finished areas or they can be surface mounted on a wall in unfinished areas. A growing trend in large office buildings is to provide small electrical closets at the same location on each floor (see Figure 12.8). The panels can then be surface mounted on the walls of the closet, and the feeders supplying the panels can be run vertically up through the closet space. In industrial installations, it is frequently impossible to find a suitable wall in an open manufacturing area on which to mount the panels. Column-width panels specifically designed to fit between the flanges

FIGURE 12.3

Lighting and appliance branch-circuit panelboards

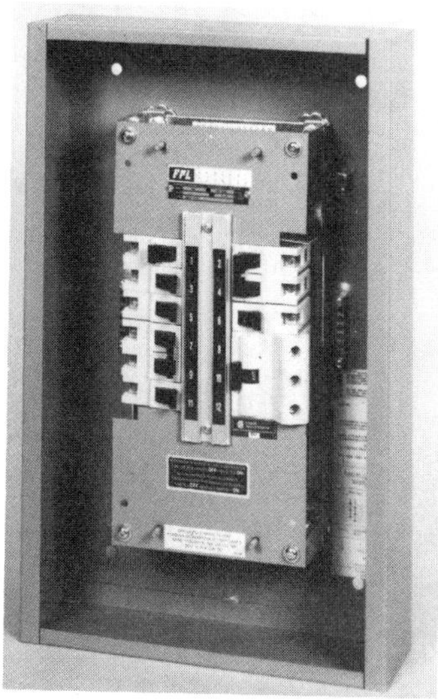

(a) Standard panel with double-row arrangement of branch breakers (shown with cover and door removed)

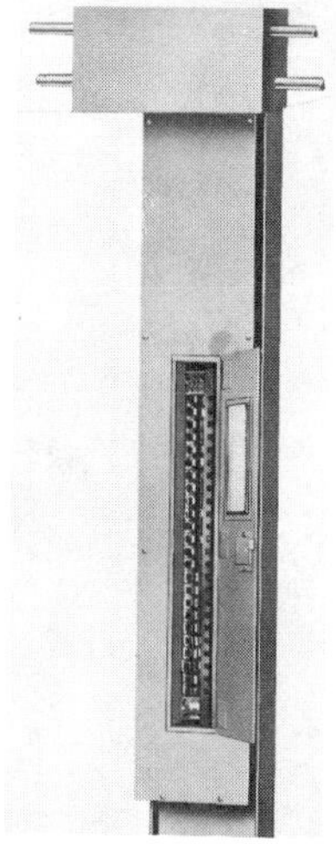

(b) Special column-type panel with single-row arrangement of branch breakers

of the structural steel columns are available for such locations. The circuit breakers are mounted in one vertical row, as shown in Figure 12.3(b). A pull-box containing the neutral connections for all the branch circuits is mounted above the panel, with a continuous wireway provided to connect the panel with the pull-box.

Standard panels are available for 120/240 volt single-phase, three-wire; 208Y/120 volt, three-phase, four-wire; and 480Y/277 volt, three-phase, four-wire systems. The typical arrangement of circuits for a 120/240 volt, single-phase panel is shown in Figure 1.16. The layout of a three-phase, four-wire panel using the conventional double-row arrangement of branch breakers is shown in Figure 12.5. A panel must have an ampacity rating (capacity of the main bus) not less than that required for the total computed load for the panel. See Section 12.11 for the method of computing this load.

Each lighting panel must be individually protected on its supply side by an overcurrent device having a rating not more than that of the lighting panel. If a panel is supplied through its own individual feeder or subfeeder, as shown in Figure 12.4(a), then a main overcurrent device is not required at the panel if the feeder overcurrent protection is not greater than the rating of the panel. A main overcurrent device (main breaker) is required for a lighting panel that is supplied directly from the secondary of its own step-down transformer, as shown in Figure 12.4(b). If the panel is tapped off a feeder that also supplies other panels, as shown in Figure 12.4(c), then a main breaker is required at each panel to provide individual protection to the panel itself and to enable the panel to be shut off without the necessity of affecting the power to the other panels on the feeder. The feeder arrangement shown in Figure 12.4(c) is often used in multistory buildings where panels are located one above the other on each floor. One vertical feeder is used to feed a number of panels. Note the code requirements for the feeder taps from the main feeder to each panel as detailed on the diagram.

12.5 CIRCUIT ARRANGEMENTS FOR LIGHTING PANELS

For large buildings where three-phase power is normally used, the lighting panels are arranged for three-phase, four-wire operation, as shown in Figure 12.5. The individual circuits for the lighting and receptacle circuits are connected from one phase of the panel to the neutral, as shown. One important advantage of using the three-phase, four-wire configuration is that it permits up to three circuits to be connected to the one common neutral. Note that to make use of this arrangement each circuit selected must be on a different phase. The reader should review the basic voltage and current relationships for three-phase systems given in Section 1.6.

As shown in Figure 12.5, when the loads on each of the three circuits connected to the one common neutral are balanced, the

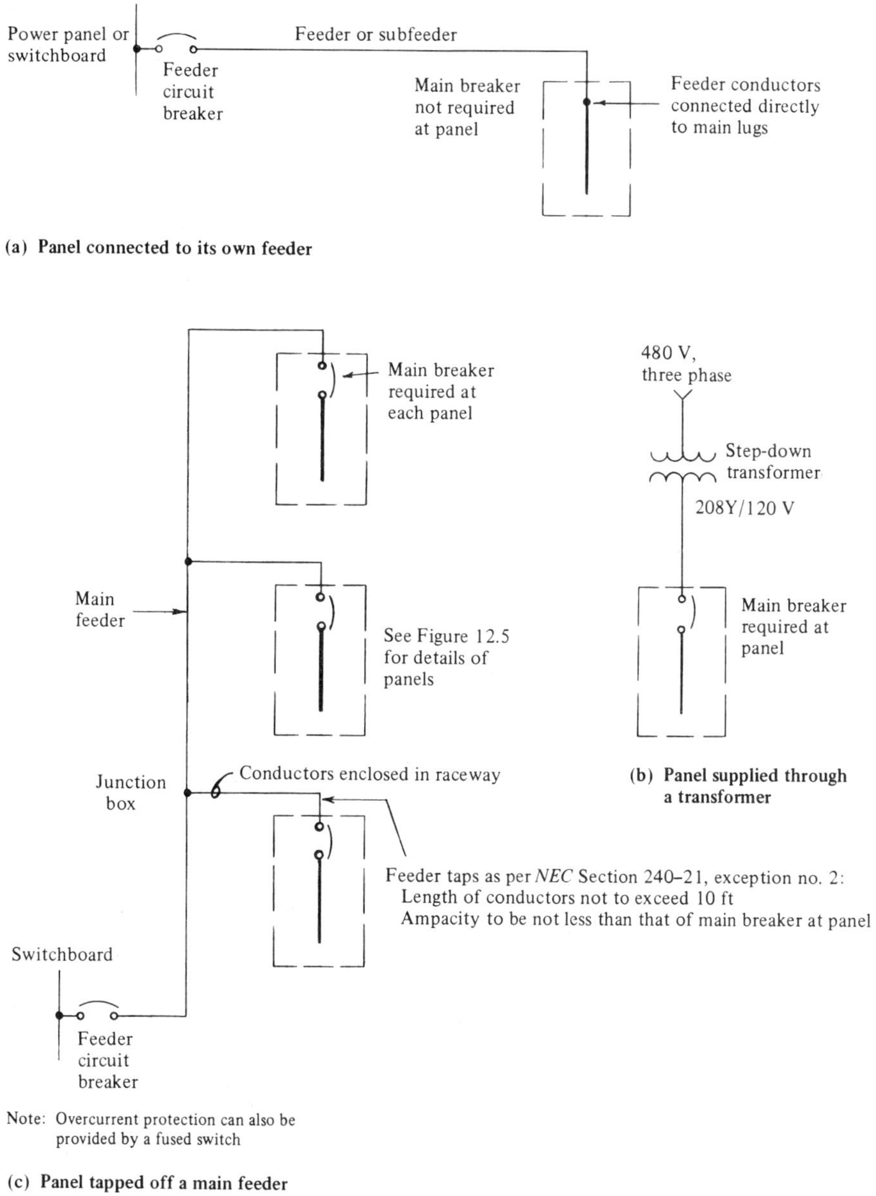

FIGURE 12.4

Requirements for main breakers in lighting and appliance branch-circuit panelboards

neutral current is zero (ignoring any third-harmonic components). Even if the load on one of the circuits is disconnected, the neutral current (the phasor sum of the two remaining circuit currents) still only equals the magnitude of one of the circuit currents. Therefore, the magnitude of the neutral current can never exceed the magnitude allowed for each of the circuit currents and the same size of conduc-

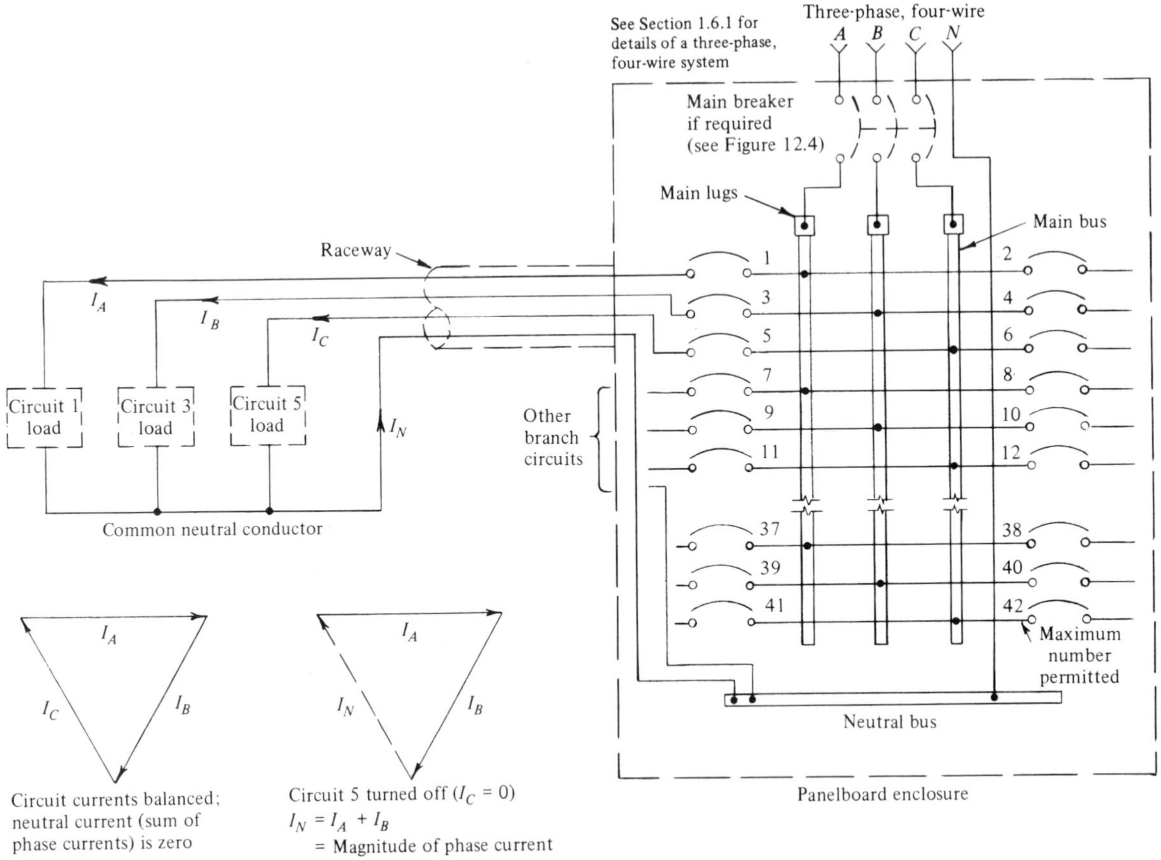

FIGURE 12.5

Lighting and appliance branch-circuit panelboard, three-phase, four-wire.

tor as used for the phases can be used throughout for the neutral. The use of a common neutral conductor for each grouping of three circuits results in considerable savings in the cost of the branch circuit wiring.

Note in Figure 12.5 that the circuit breaker connections to the main bus are arranged so that consecutive breakers on one side are on different phases. For example, circuits 1, 3, and 5 are connected to phases *A*, *B*, and *C*, respectively, and can therefore be grouped together on the one common neutral, as shown. Similarly, circuits 2, 4, and 6 can be grouped together, 7, 9, and 11, and so on. On the other hand, a combination of circuits 1, 2, and 3 would not be acceptable for grouping together as both circuits 1 and 2 are connected to phase *A*. Circuit 2 must be connected to a different neutral circuit conductor than that for circuit 1. See Figure 12.9 for an example of the layout of circuits for a three-phase, four-wire lighting panel. In the case of single-phase, three-wire panels, only two circuits, which must be on different lines, can be grouped together on one common neutral.

12.6 MODIFIED CONNECTION DIAGRAMS FOR FLOOR LAYOUTS

To show how the branch circuits for lighting and receptacles are to be arranged, a floor plan of the area must be prepared. This floor plan must show the location of walls, doorways, stairways, and such other building details that dictate the location of lighting units, switches, and receptacles and that affect the routing of the wiring. In most instances, this information is copied from the architectural and structural drawings for the building. The branch-circuit wiring is then superimposed on these floor plans.

Floor plans are normally drawn to a scale of $\frac{1}{8}''$ = 1′-0″ unless the layout is unusually complicated, in which case the scale may be $\frac{1}{4}''$ = 1′-0″. Note that the scale of $\frac{1}{8}''$ = 1′-0″ is a ratio of 1 : 96. For layouts drawn using SI units, a scale of 1 : 100 (1 cm = 1 m) is normally used. With this scale of drawing, it would be very difficult (and impractical) to attempt to show every individual conductor involved in the branch-circuit wiring. Therefore, a modified method is used to convey the necessary information. The following is an explanation of this method.

Let us start by completely detailing the lighting in three rooms, including the switching. The floor plan for these rooms is shown in Figure 12.7. The schematic diagram of the branch circuit, including the local switching and the necessary connections to the lighting fixtures in each room, is shown in Figure 12.6. Room 3 requires three-way switching because it has two entrances. Note how the three-way switches (which are actually single-pole, double-throw switches) operate so that the lighting may be turned on and off at either entrance in any sequence. The diagram shows the position of the switches such that the lights are turned off. Moving either switch to its other position will complete the circuit and turn the lights on. Then moving either switch to its other location will break the circuit and turn the lights off. Note that there is no fixed on or off position for either switch.

Figure 12.7(a) indicates on the floor plan the complete connection diagram, showing all the runs of individual conductors and their connections that are necessary to complete the system. As can be appreciated, to draw all the branch-circuit wiring throughout the building in this degree of detail would be very time consuming and indeed next to impossible to show clearly on a layout scaled at $\frac{1}{8}''$ = 1′-0″. Therefore, the modified connection diagram as shown in Fig-

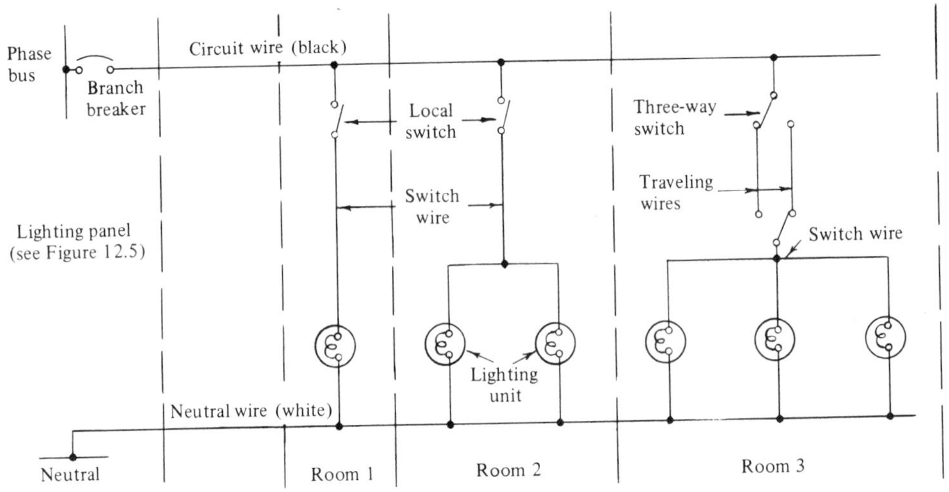

FIGURE 12.6

Schematic diagram for lighting layout as shown in Figure 12.7

ure 12.7(b) is the method adopted to actually show the branch-circuit wiring. In this method, the solid line becomes the routing of the wiring, and the actual number of wires in any one section is indicated by the number of marks. As discussed in Section 12.1, the wiring in large buildings is installed in conduit or EMT. The solid line then indicates the run of conduit or EMT into which the individual insulated conductors are pulled. See Section 11.5 for details of raceways. Note the change of symbols for the modified connection diagram. The symbol is chosen to reflect the function of the device, as there is no need to show the detailed connections to it.

If we refer again to Figure 12.6, there are three classifications of conductors in the complete circuit: the circuit wire (which is at the circuit potential of 120 volts), the neutral wire (which is at ground potential) and the switch wire (which is energized only when the local switch is closed). To differentiate these wires in each run of conduit, the method shown in Figure 12.7(b) has been adopted for the sample layout as shown in Section 12.7. More is stated in this section about the identification of the wires.

The layout shown in Figure 12.7(b) is for the lighting only. Most areas also require branch-circuit wiring for receptacles. In commercial, institutional, and industrial types of buildings, it is normal practice to have circuits dedicated solely to lighting and other circuits dedicated solely to receptacles. Also, for practical reasons, the runs of wiring are usually kept separate, since the wiring for the lighting is run at the ceiling level and the wiring for the receptacles is run at the floor level. To differentiate between these runs on the floor plans, a solid line indicates a run of conduit at ceiling level and a dashed line

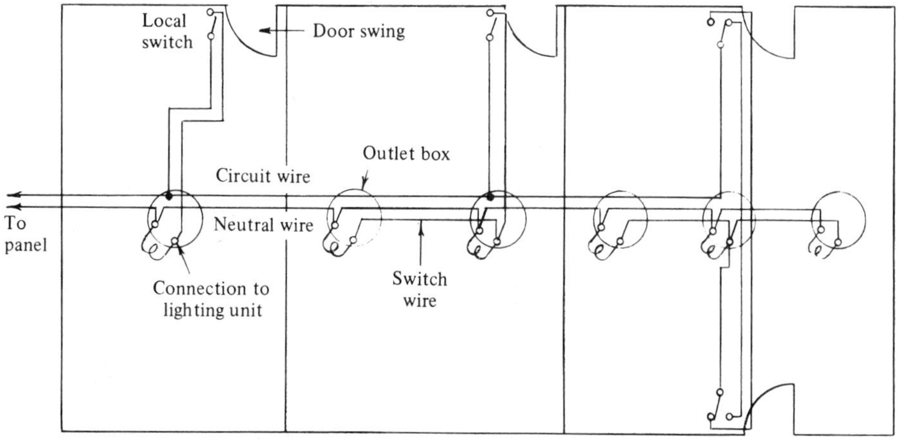

(a) Complete connection diagram for branch circuit

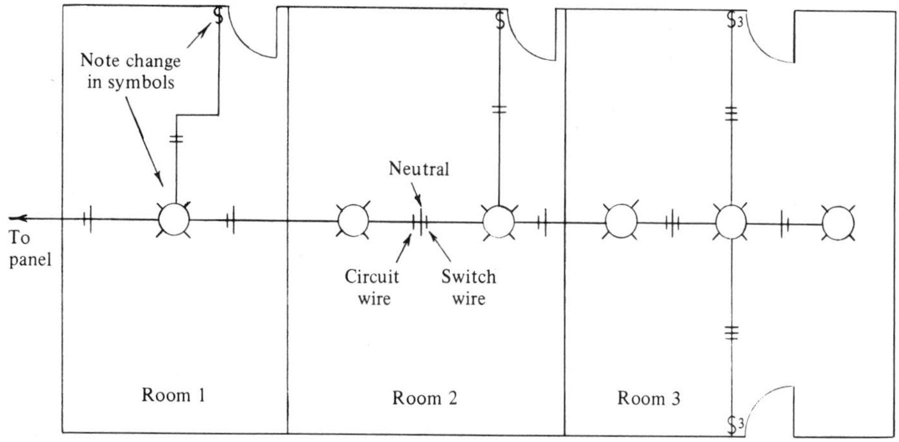

See Figure 12.10 for a complete description of symbols

(b) Modified connection diagram for branch circuit

FIGURE 12.7

Method of showing branch-circuit wiring on floor plan

indicates a run of conduit at floor level (usually concealed in the structural floor member). See the legend of symbols in Figure 12.10 for more details on the method of indicating branch-circuit wiring.

12.7 EXAMPLE FLOOR LAYOUT OF LIGHTING AND RECEPTACLES

Figure 12.8 shows the layout of an area that is part of an office building. The branch circuits for the lighting and for the receptacles are indicated using the modified method just discussed in Section 12.6. The panel schedule is shown in Figure 12.9 and the legend of

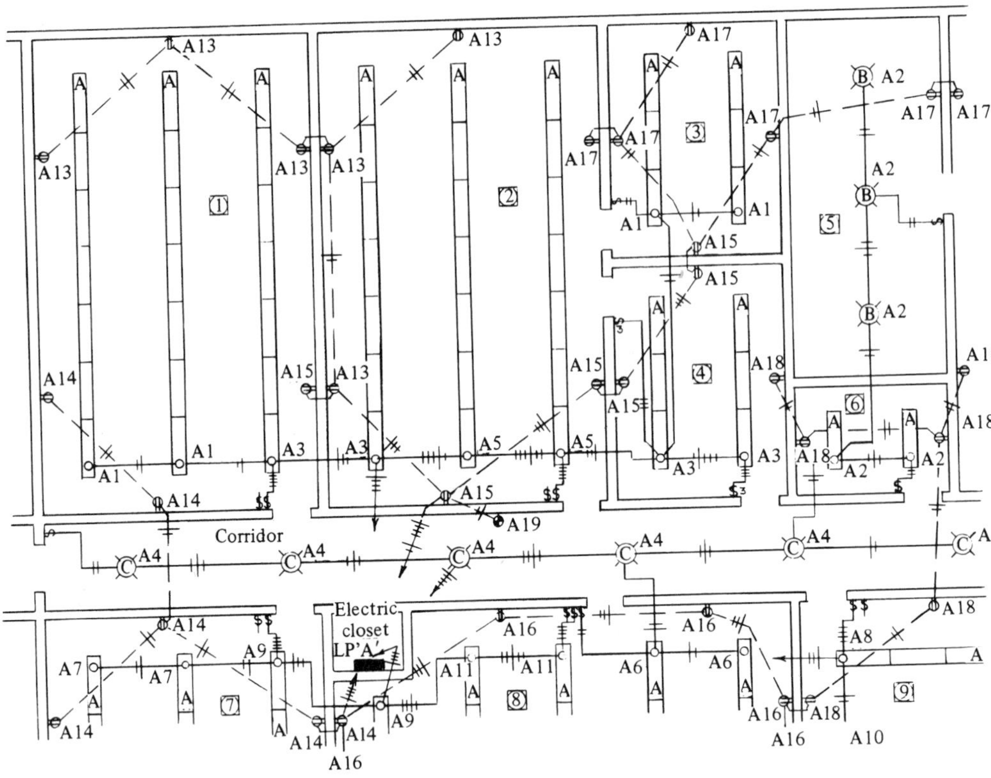

Note: Details such as windows and door swings have been omitted from floor plan

FIGURE 12.8

Layout of branch circuits for an office area

symbols is shown in Figure 12.10. Note that the layout is only meant to cover one section of a much larger overall area. As such, there would be other lighting panels located throughout the area, and in multistory buildings, there would be panels on each floor. Therefore, a means of identifying each panel must be adopted. One method is simply to assign a letter designation to each panel. The letter A has been selected for the panel shown on the layout, and thus the circuits from this panel are identified as A1, A3, A5, and so on (note the A identification has nothing to do with phase *A*). There is local switching of the lights in each room. See Section 12.8 for further discussion on the switching of lighting systems. The power supply to the lighting panel is 208Y/120 volts, three-phase, four-wire.

As noted in the legend, the fluorescent lighting units (designated type A) draw a line current of 0.80 ampere at 120 volts. Following the code rules discussed in Section 12.2 for the branch circuits for lighting, 20 ampere circuits are used, which permits a maximum loading of 16 amperes. This then allows a maximum of 16/0.80 = 20

Lighting panel A

System: 208Y/120 volts, 3-PHASE, 4-WIRE

Description	Load (A) A	Load (A) B	Load (A) C	Bkr. Trip (A)	Ckt.	Ckt.	Bkr. Trip (A)	Load (A) A	Load (A) B	Load (A) C	Description
20 Type A ltg. fixtures Rooms 1 and 3	16.0			20	1	2	20	6.6			3 Type B, 2 Type A ltg. fixtures, Rooms 5 and 6
20 Type A ltg. fixtures Rooms 1, 2, and 4		16.0		20	3	4	20		15.0		6 Type C ltg. fixtures, Corridor
14 Type A ltg. fixtures Room 2			11.2	20	5	6	20			12.8	16 Type A ltg. fixtures Room 8
16 Type A ltg. fixtures Room 7	12.8			20	7	8	20	14.4			18 Type A ltg. fixtures Room 9
15 Type A ltg. fixtures Rooms 7 and 8		12.0		20	9	10	20		9.6		12 Type A ltg. fixtures Room 9
16 Type A ltg. fixtures Room 8			12.8	20	11	12	20			16.0[a]	Spare
6 Duplex receptacles Rooms 1 and 2	12.0[b]			15	13	14	15	12.0			6 Duplex receptacles Rooms 1, 7, and 8
6 Duplex receptacles Rooms 1, 2, 3, and 4		12.0		15	15	16	15		10.0		5 Duplex receptacles Room 8
6 Duplex receptacles Rooms 2, 3, and 5			12.0	15	17	18	15			12.0	6 Duplex receptacles Rooms 4, 5, 6, and 9
1 20 amp. receptacle Corridor	16.0			20	19	20					Spaces only No breakers installed
Spare		12.0[a]		15	21	22					
Spare			12.0[a]	15	23	24					
	56.8	52.0	48.0					33.0	34.6	40.8	

Total load phase A: 89.8 A

Total load phase B: 86.6 A

Total load phase C: 88.8 A

Total load on panel: 31.8 kVA

[a] Allowance for future loads

[b] Allowance for each duplex receptacle, 240 VA

Note: Figure 12.8 does not show the complete layout for all the above circuits See Appendix A for modifications to meet Canadian Electrical Code regulations

FIGURE 12.9

Lighting panel schedule for layout of Figure 12.8

of the type A fixtures to be connected to one circuit. However, the arrangement of the fixtures must also be taken into account so that the wiring and switching are kept as simple as possible. Two basic rules to follow are that (1) the minimum number of circuits should be used for each room, and (2) where possible each continuous row of fixtures should be on the same circuit. Considering room 1, there are 3 rows of 7 for a total of 21 type A fixtures in this room, just one

Legend of Symbols for Layout Shown on Figure 12.8

	Fluorescent fixture, 2 F40CW lamps, 120 V, 0.80 A input to ballast
	Incandescent fixture; 120 V, 200 watt
	Incandescent fixture, 120 V, 300 watt, medium base
O A1	Ceiling mounted outlet box (circuit 1, panel A)
 A14	Duplex receptacle, 125 V, 15 A (circuit 14, panel A)
	Single receptacle, 125 V, 20 A
$	AC general-use snap switch, 120 V, 20 A, single pole
$_3	AC general-use snap switch, 120 V, 20 A, three-way
LP'A' 	Surface-mounted panelboard (lighting panel A)
	Room number
	Wiring concealed in wall or ceiling
	Wiring concealed in floor
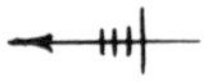	Branch circuit homerun to panelboards } (three circuit wires on common neutral)
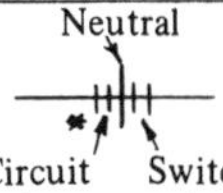	Run of wiring indicating number and type of wires (i.e., two circuit wires, one neutral, and two switch wires) *On side toward direction back to panelboard

Method of Showing Wiring as per ANSI Standards

	Indicates three wires, four marks = four wires, etc.
	Branch circuit homeruns to panelboard, number of arrows = number of circuits, numerals indicate circuit numbers

Refer to American National Standards Institute publication Y32.9 for a complete list of recommended symbols.

FIGURE 12.10

Graphic symbols for electric wiring and layout diagrams

more than can be accommodated on one circuit. It would create an illogical switching and circuiting pattern to put two complete rows plus six units of the third row on one circuit, leaving just one unit for a second circuit. Note that the same problem applies to room 2. Therefore, as shown on the plan, three circuits (A1, A3, and A5) are used for these two rooms, with two complete rows (total of 14 units) put on each of these circuits. This leaves spare capacity on these circuits, so the six type A units in room 3 are also put on circuit A1 and the six type A fixtures in room 4 are also put on circuit A3, which then brings these circuits up to their maximum loading.

The possible extra loading for circuit A5 is not so straightforward. The next adjacent areas are rooms 5 and 6. The loading in room 5 consists of three type B, 200 watt incandescent units with a demand of $(3 \times 200)/120 = 5.0$ amperes. This is too much to add to circuit A5. The two type A units in room 6 could easily be added to circuit A5, but a new circuit must be brought to room 5; so it is decided to put both rooms 5 and 6 on this new circuit (A2). The loading on circuit A5 is left at only 14 type A units or 11.2 amperes. Because of this lighter loading on circuit A5, which is connected to phase *C*, the loadings on subsequent groups of circuits are arranged to offset this unbalance as shown in the panel schedule. The total load on the panel should be balanced between the three phases as closely as possible (within $\pm 10\%$), as per the total loads indicated at the bottom of the panel schedule.

Circuits A1, A3, and A5 were chosen for the first grouping of circuits so that the one common neutral can be used for wiring these circuits and for the homerun (see Figure 12.5). The term *homerun* applies to *that portion of the branch circuit wiring running from the closest outlet point back to the panel.* There are no further connections to the circuits. The homerun is indicated on the floor plan by a line with an arrow pointing in the direction of the panel. Note that, with regard to the local switching in rooms 1 and 2, a minimum of one switch is required for each circuit in the room. If separate switching of each row of fixtures had been desired, then three switches per room would be required and an extra switch wire run to the third row.

It is the usual practice to locate the lighting branch circuits at the top of the panel, with the branch circuits for the receptacles coming next. Therefore, circuits A2, A4, and A6 are chosen for the next grouping of circuits, followed by A7, A9, and A11. The final two lighting circuits required are assigned to A8 and A10, with circuit A12 left as a spare for possible future lighting.

The circuiting for the receptacles in the example layout is done on the basis that 15 ampere branch circuits are used, with a maximum of six duplex receptacles connected to each circuit. This is less than the maximum permitted by the code (see Section 12.3), but it reduces the possibility of overloading the circuit by having too many pieces of office equipment plugged in at the same time on the same circuit. In calculating the load on the lighting panel, a rating of 240 volt–amperes is assumed for each 15 ampere duplex receptacle. Note that the receptacle circuits are also grouped together so that the one common neutral can be used (for example, A13, A15, and

A17). Figure 11.10(c) shows the typical method of running conduit to the outlet boxes for receptacles.

It is a good idea to locate a few 20 ampere receptacles at regular intervals around an office area. These receptacles, each on their own dedicated 20 ampere circuit, are required for cleaning equipment such as floor polishers. If such equipment is plugged into the general 15 ampere circuit, it usually trips the circuit breaker on starting. The example layout includes one 20 ampere receptacle located in the hallway.

The complete circuiting of the area covered by lighting panel A is shown on the lighting panel schedule. Note that the panel layout includes some spare breakers for future use and some spaces. The spaces permit the installation of additional breakers if and as required. As well as serving as a record of the circuits being used during the design and construction of the electrical system, the panel schedule should be posted on the door of the lighting panel as a reference for maintenance purposes.

The method used to identify circuit wires, neutral wires, and, in the case of lighting circuits, switch wires on the sample layout (Figure 12.8) is detailed in the legend of symbols (Figure 12.10). Also shown is the American National Standards Institute (ANSI) recommended method of showing branch circuit wiring and homeruns. The more detailed method used in this textbook has been adopted to help the reader follow the wiring and to better understand the number of wires required for the circuiting and switching. In practice, a complete legend of symbols should be presented with every set of electrical floor plans so that there is no misunderstanding as to the precise intent of each symbol. Refer to ANSI publication Y32.9 for a complete listing of the recommended graphic symbols for electrical wiring and layout diagrams used in architecture and building construction.

The reader is referred to Chapter 3 of the *National Electrical Code* with regard to wiring methods and materials. In particular Article 300 covers wiring methods, Article 310 covers conductors for general wiring, and Article 370 covers outlet, device, pull and junction boxes, and conduit bodies and fittings. The following are a few of the requirements that affect the layout of the branch circuit wiring. A box or fitting must be installed at each conductor splice connection point, outlet, switch point, junction point, or pull point for the connection of conduit, electrical metallic tubing, surface raceway, or other raceways. Junction, pull, and outlet boxes must be so installed that the wiring contained in them can be rendered accessible without removing any part of the building. Boxes must be of sufficient size to provide free space for all conductors plus any device (switch, receptacle) or fitting (fixture stud, cable clamp) that is enclosed in the box. To ensure that standard boxes can be used, the number of wires routed through any one box should be limited to conform with the requirements of *NEC* Section 370-6.

NEC Article 410 covers the installation of lighting fixtures and receptacles. In particular, note that lighting fixtures cannot be used as raceways for circuit conductors unless specifically approved for such. One exception to this requirement is that fixtures designed for end-to-end assembly to form a continuous row are permitted to carry through conductors of a two-wire or multiwire branch circuit supplying the fixtures. Another exception allows one additional two-wire branch circuit to be carried through the fixtures to supply switched night-lighting units.

The partial layout shown in Figure 12.8 is meant only to introduce the method of organizing branch circuits for a typical office area. No attempt is made to show such items as separate night lighting, exit lights, and emergency lighting systems. The requirements for emergency systems and exit lights are covered by municipal, state, federal, and other codes or governmental agencies having jurisdiction. Where emergency systems are required, their installation is covered by *NEC* Article 700.

12.8 SWITCHING OF LIGHTING SYSTEMS

The example layout shown in Figure 12.8 includes local switching of the lighting at the entrance to each room using direct-acting, ac, general-use snap switches of the type shown in Figure 12.11. These switches are available with 15, 20 and 30 ampere ratings and are designed for installation in flush-mounted device boxes. As previously mentioned in Section 12.2, in large buildings it is advantageous to supply fluorescent and HID-type lighting from the 480Y/277 volt systems. If local switching is desired, ac general-use snap switches rated for 277 volts are available. See also *NEC* Article 380.

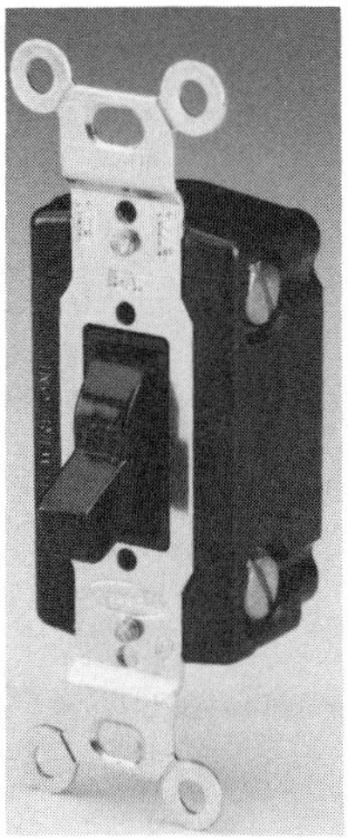

FIGURE 12.11

AC general-use snap switch

In many commercial establishments with wide-open areas, local switching of lights is often not practical. The lighting is instead switched directly from the lighting panel using the branch circuit breakers. The area lighting of large, open industrial areas is also normally switched using the branch circuit breakers at the lighting panel. Where circuit breakers are used to frequently switch the lighting circuits, they should be the type marked SWD. These breakers have been tested and found suitable for the greater frequency of on–off operations required for switching duty, as compared to the infrequent use normally encountered with breakers used only for overcurrent protection and maintenance. A further step in the control of large-area lighting is to have a separate lighting panel feeding only the lighting branch circuits. The panel is then energized through a magnetic contactor, which can either be controlled manually through a remote on–off push button or automatically by a time switch or photoelectric device.

Finally, a more sophisticated and flexible means of switching individual and/or blocks of lighting units involves the use of low-voltage, remote-control switching relays. The basic operation of these relays is shown in Figure 12.12. The relays are operated from a low-voltage source (usually 24 volts) through a step-down control transformer. The contacts of the relays can switch circuits up to 277 volts. The relays can be installed in the outlet boxes for the lighting units if desired so that the branch-circuit wiring goes directly to the lighting unit. The cost of then installing the low-voltage control wiring to the switching points is much less than that for power circuit wiring. The system is flexible in that each relay can be controlled from more than one point, or, conversely, a number of relays can be controlled simultaneously from one point. Programmable lighting controllers specifically designed for use with the low-voltage switching relays are available. These controllers can automatically

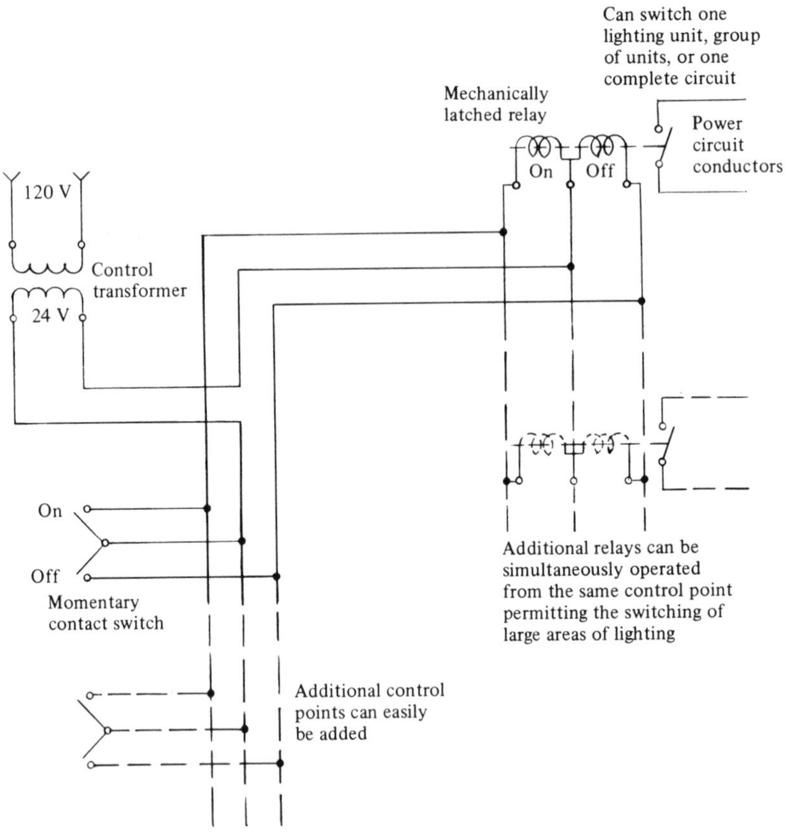

FIGURE 12.12

Low-voltage, remote-control switching for lighting

switch lighting units to control lighting levels as activities in the area change throughout the day (for example, after hours for cleaning purposes). Passive infrared control devices are now available that sense when a person enters or leaves an area and automatically turns the lights on or off. The off function has a 12 minute delay feature to allow the occupant to leave the room momentarily without any unnecessary switching of the lights.

With the advent of the energy crisis in the 1970s and with the subsequent substantial increase in the cost of electrical energy, a great deal more attention is now paid to the switching of the lighting in a building as a means of saving energy. The added cost of the switching controls can often be recovered within a reasonable time from the accumulated savings in energy consumption.

12.9 UNDERFLOOR RACEWAY SYSTEMS

In the example layout shown in Figure 12.8, the general-purpose receptacles for the office areas are installed in the walls at preselected locations. This can be satisfactory if the rooms are small and a detailed layout of the office equipment is available at the time of the design of the electrical system. However, this is often not the case in large office buildings, especially those built for the purposes of renting space to various tenants. At the time of the design of the building, little if anything is known of the detailed layout of the rentable space. Therefore, a flexible system is required that will allow power wiring to be taken at a later time to any area of the floor for connection to receptacles. Such a system is an *underfloor raceway system*.

There are two basic types of such systems: *underfloor duct* and *cellular floor systems*. Underfloor duct is a system of parallel ducts spaced not more than 6 feet apart running just beneath the finished floor level. Normally, the ducts for the power wiring are combined with side-by-side runs of ducts for the telephone system wiring and in some cases for separate in-house communication or signaling system wiring. Junction boxes are located at a maximum spacing of 40 feet along the runs, with cross runs to connect the junction boxes.

Cellular floor systems make use of the cellular floor decks that are installed as part of the structure of the building. Cellular metal floor raceways are the hollow spaces provided by the forming of sheet metal sections that are used as the structural floor members. Cellular concrete floor raceways are the hollow spaces left in the precast concrete floor slabs that are used as the structural floor members. The cells are normally divided into groups of two (power and telephone) or groups of three (power, telephone, and communications), depending on the requirements of the area. Header ducts are installed at right angles to the cells, which provide access to predetermined cells.

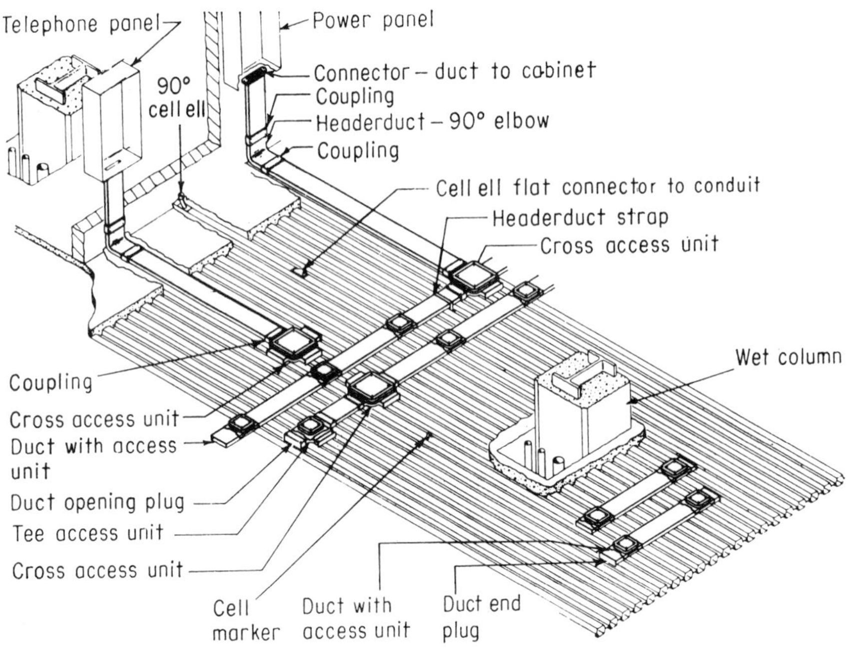

HEADER DUCTS may be installed on top of cellular flooring parallel with or at right angles to structural cell members, with access boxes of various sizes to coincide with local wiring requirements. Diagram shows how power and telephone circuits can be routed longitudinally through floor cells, then shifted laterally via header ducts to bypass such obstructions as structural columns or riser shafts.

FIGURE 12.13

Cellular metal floor raceway system

The complete matrix of ducts or cells in any one area is then connected by header ducts to separate power, telephone, and communication panels. Figure 12.13 shows a typical cellular metal floor system complete with header ducts and connections to a power panel and a telephone panel. The view shows the system just prior to the finished concrete fill being poured over the entire floor.

At the time of the design and layout of the electrical system, an estimated number of branch circuit breakers is specified to be included in the power (that is, lighting) panel for the eventual use for the receptacle circuits. As soon as the layout details of any particular area are known, floor receptacle assemblies can be easily installed at any location on the floor (for example, within the area covered by a desk). Markers are installed in the floor during construction so that the exact location of the nearest power duct or cell can be determined. Access to the floor duct or cell is then obtained by cutting through the concrete floor finish using a properly sized concrete-boring drill. The necessary branch-circuit wiring is pulled through the header duct and cell system from the lighting panel. After the electrical connections are made to the receptacle, the receptacle assembly is firmly attached to the floor.

Metal underfloor duct and cellular metal floor raceway systems must be so constructed that adequate electrical and mechanical continuity of the complete system is maintained to provide proper grounding of the system and of the power receptacles. In the case of the cellular concrete floor raceway systems, separate grounding conductors must be installed in the cells as necessary to maintain the grounding system to the receptacles. *NEC* Articles 354, 356, and 358 cover the requirements with regard to the installation of underfloor duct, cellular metal floor, and cellular concrete floor raceway systems, respectively.

12.10 GROUND-FAULT CIRCUIT-INTERRUPTERS

In Section 10.5, the protection of systems and equipment against ground faults is thoroughly discussed. However, equally important is the protection of personnel from the shock hazards of ground faults, which requires a level of response as low as 5.0 milliamperes. Refer to Figure 10.12(a) which shows the possible shock-voltage exposure with respect to a piece of equipment that has a ground fault. If the equipment grounding circuit to the equipment is not installed properly or, worse still, if it is accidentally broken, anyone touching the faulted equipment is subject to the shock voltage and can then become part of the return path of the ground-fault current. In situations where the person could be grounded, such as working outdoors on wet ground or in areas with grounded water pipes such as bathrooms, the shock could easily be fatal. The protection of a circuit to such an area then requires a ground-fault circuit-interrupter (GFCI), which can automatically disconnect the circuit when the flow of current to ground exceeds 5.0 milliamperes. Protection may be provided either by a GFCI circuit breaker mounted in a panelboard, which protects the entire branch circuit, or by a GFCI-type receptacle that protects anything plugged into the receptacle. Figure 12.14 shows the connection and method of operation of a GFCI circuit breaker.

The *National Electrical Code* requires that all 125 volt, single-phase, 15 and 20 ampere receptacles in the following areas shall have ground-fault protection for personnel: receptacles in the bathrooms of dwelling units and of guest rooms in hotels and motels; receptacles installed in the garages of dwelling units and outdoors where there is direct grade-level access; receptacles in dwelling units within 6 feet of the kitchen sink and located above the counter top; receptacles in wet areas of health-care facilities; receptacles within 20 feet of swimming pools; and receptacles in commercial garages. In addition, all underwater lights in swimming pools operating at more than 15 volts shall have GFCI protection. This list is not meant to cover all the areas requiring GFCI protection, but rather to indicate the type of areas involved. Certainly, GFCI protection

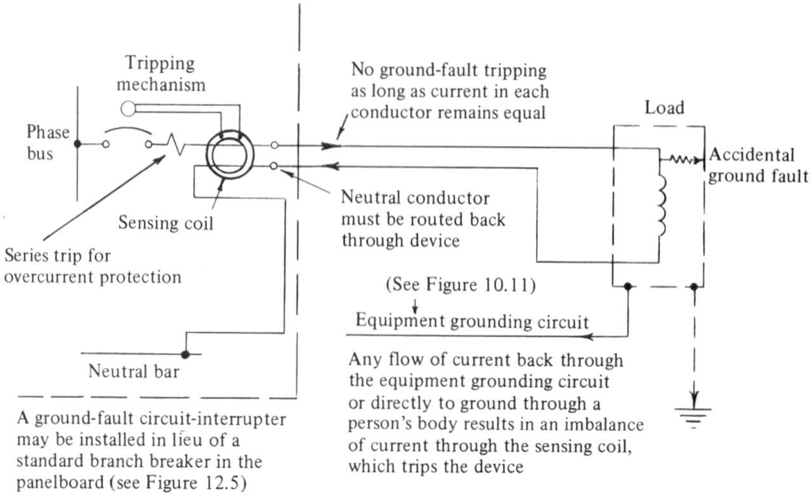

FIGURE 12.14

Connection and method of operation of a ground-fault circuit-interrupter (GFCI)

should be provided for any type of circuit where there is any danger to personnel from ground faults. The *NEC* permits the feeders to panels supplying 15 and 20 ampere receptacle branch circuits to be protected by a GFCI in lieu of providing GFCIs for the individual branch circuits. It may be more economical or convenient to install GFCIs for feeders, but there is the disadvantage that a ground fault on any one circuit will de-energize all the circuits.

12.11 COMPUTED LOADS FOR LIGHTING AND RECEPTACLES

After determining the branch circuit requirements for a lighting and appliance branch-circuit panelboard (lighting panel), the total load has to be calculated for the purpose of selecting the feeder to the panel. Notwithstanding the determination of this load from the actual loads connected to each circuit, the *NEC* regulations require that a unit load, based on volt–amperes per square foot, be used to compute the minimum loading. Refer to Table 12.1 [*NEC* Table 220-3(b)], which shows the type of occupancies for which this requirement applies and the unit loads per square foot associated with each type of occupancy. Note that, for buildings laid out using the SI units, the conversion factor is listed at the foot of the table.

For office buildings, the unit loading for the general lighting is listed as $3\frac{1}{2}$ volt–amperes per square foot. Refer to Example 5.15, which shows the calculations for the lighting of a commercial area to a level 1000 lux (100 footcandles). The unit load for the layout (item 14) is calculated to be 3.33 watts per square foot. Since two lamp high power factor ballasts are normally used for good quality fluorescent lighting fixtures, the loading in volt–amperes would be virtually the same. Refer next to the layout shown in Figure 12.8. Using room 1 as being typical of the lighting load, the total area of the room

TABLE 12.1 Unit Loads for General Lighting (from *NEC* Table 220-3(b)]

Type of Occupancy	Unit Load per Square Foot (volt–amperes)
Armories and auditoriums	1
Banks	$3\frac{1}{2}$[b]
Barber shops and beauty parlors	3
Churches	1
Clubs	2
Court rooms	2
Dwelling units[a]	3
Garages: Commercial (storage)	$\frac{1}{2}$
Hospitals	2
Hotels and motels, including apartment houses without provisions for cooking by tenants[a]	2
Industrial commercial (loft) buildings	2
Lodge rooms	$1\frac{1}{2}$
Office buildings	$3\frac{1}{2}$[b]
Restaurants	2
Schools	3
Stores	3
Warehouses (storage)	$\frac{1}{4}$
In any of the above occupancies except one-family dwellings and individual dwelling units of two-family and multifamily dwellings:	
Assembly halls and auditoriums	1
Halls, corridors, closets, stairways	$\frac{1}{2}$
Storage spaces	$\frac{1}{4}$

For SI units, 1 square foot = 0.093 square meter.

[a] All general-use receptacle outlets of 20-ampere or less rating in one-family, two-family, and multifamily dwellings and in guest rooms of hotels and motels [except those connected to the receptacle circuits specified in Section 220-4(b) and (c)] shall be considered as outlets for general illumination, and no additional load calculations shall be required for such outlets.

[b] In addition, a unit load of 1 volt–ampere per square foot shall be included for general-purpose receptacle outlets when the actual number of general-purpose receptacle outlets is unknown.

is 20 by 30 feet, or 600 square feet. There are 21 fixtures in the room with an input of 96 volt–amperes (120 volts time 0.8 ampere), for a total of 21 times 96 = 2016 volt–amperes. The unit loading is 2016 divided by 600 = 3.36 volt–amperes per square foot. These examples indicate that the minimum value of $3\frac{1}{2}$ volt–amperes per square foot required by the code is very adequate for most office areas, especially with the advent of the more efficient fluorescent and HID lamps and energy-saving ballasts. However, should the actual connected load for the general lighting exceed the load computed using the values in Table 12.1, the actual load must be used for the feeder calculations. The general lighting load for such areas as offices, banks, stores, and schools is considered to be a continuous load, and therefore the computed load for the feeder must be based on 125% of the continuous load (see Section 11.7).

As explained in Section 12.9, the detailed loads for the general-purpose receptacles in office areas are usually not known at the time of designing the electrical system. For this situation, refer to the footnote to Table 12.1, which states that an additional unit load of 1 volt–ampere per square foot be added for the general-purpose receptacle outlets.

The demand factor for a load is the measure of the part of the load that will actually be called for at any given time (averaged over a short period of time). It is therefore the ratio of the maximum demand to be expected as compared to the total connected load for

TABLE 12.2 Lighting Load Feeder Demand Factors (from *NEC* Table 220-11)

Type of Occupancy	Portion of Lighting Load to Which Demand Factor Applies (volt–amperes)	Demand Factor (%)
Dwelling Units	First 3000 or less at	100
	From 3001 to 120,000 at	35
	Remainder over 120,000 at	25
Hospitals[a]	First 50,000 or less at	40
	Remainder over 50,000 at	20
Hotels and motels, including apartment houses without provision for cooking by tenants[a]	First 20,000 or less at	50
	From 20,000 to 100,000 at	40
	Remainder over 100,000 at	30
Warehouses (storage)	First 12,500 or less at	100
	Remainder over 12,500 at	50
All others	Total volt–amperes	100

[a] The demand factors of this table shall not apply to the computed load of feeders to areas in hospitals, hotels, and motels where the entire lighting is likely to be used at one time, as in operating rooms, ballrooms, or dining rooms.

TABLE 12.3 Demand Factors for Nondwelling Receptacle Loads (from *NEC* Table 220-13)

Portion of Receptacle Load to Which Demand Factor Applies (volt–amperes)	Demand Factor (%)
First 10 kVA or less	100
Remainder over 10 kVA at	50

Applies to receptacle loads computed at not more than 180 volt–amperes per outlet.

that part of the system under consideration. Table 12.2 (*NEC* Table 220-11) shows the demand factors that are allowed for general lighting loads according to types of occupancy. These demand factors can only be used in computing the load for the feeders. They cannot be used for determining the number or size of the branch circuits for the general illumination. For receptacle loads in other-than-dwelling units, either the demand factors listed in Table 12.2 or those listed in Table 12.3 (*NEC* Table 220-13) may be used. The receptacle loads for Table 12.3 are based on the minimum of 180 volt–amperes per outlet, as discussed in Section 12.3. For the purposes of computing the minimum ampacity rating of a feeder, the nominal system voltage can be used in the calculations.

EXAMPLE 12.3

A lighting panel supplies the lighting and receptacle load for an office area of 10,000 sq. ft. There are a total of 100 general-use duplex receptacles. The service is 208Y/120 V, three phase, four wire. Calculate the minimum ampacity rating for the feeder conductors to the panel. For these calculations, assume that the entire lighting load is continuous, and the actual lighting load is less than the computed lighting load.

Solution

— General lighting load, from Table 12.1:

$(10{,}000 \text{ ft}^2 \text{ at } 3.5 \text{ VA/ft}^2) \times 1.25 \qquad = 43{,}750 \text{ VA}$

— Receptacle load: $100 \times 180 \text{ VA} = 18{,}000 \text{ VA}$:

From Table 12.3: first 10,000 VA at 100%	= 10,000 VA
Remaining (18,000 − 10,000) VA at 50%	= 4,000 VA
Total computed load	= 57,750 VA

— Minimum ampacity $= \dfrac{57{,}750}{1.732 \times 208} = 160.4 \approx 160 \text{ A}$

■ EXAMPLE 12.4

Refer to Figure 12.4(c). Assume that the feeder shown supplies three lighting panels in a hospital. Each panel supplies the lighting and receptacle load for an area of 12,000 sq. ft., 2000 sq. ft. of which is corridor, closet, and stairway areas. Each panel supplies 120 general-use duplex receptacles. The areas fed by the panels do not include any operating rooms, general office areas, or dining rooms. Assume the actual connected lighting loads are less than the computed lighting loads. The service is 208Y/120 V, three phase, four wire. Determine the minimum ampacity for (a) the taps to each panel and (b) the main feeder supplying the three panels.

Solution

(a) For the feeder taps to each panel:

— General lighting load, from Table 12.1:

2000 ft^2 at 0.5 VA/ft^2	= 1,000 VA
(12,000 − 2000) ft^2 at 2.0 VA/ft^2	= 20,000 VA
— Receptacle load: 120 × 180 VA	= 21,600 VA
Total computed load	= 42,600 VA

— Net computed load using demand factors from Table 12.2:
42,600 VA at 40% (50,000 VA or less) = 17,040 VA

$$\text{— Minimum ampacity} = \frac{17{,}040}{1.732 \times 208} = 47 \text{ A}$$

(b) For the main feeder:

— Total computed load for 3 panels = 3 × 42,600 = 127,800 VA

— Using demand factors from Table 12.2:

First 50,000 VA at 40%	= 20,000 VA
Remainder (127,800 − 50,000) at 20%	= 15,560 VA
Net computed load	= 35,560 VA

$$\text{— Minimum ampacity} = \frac{35{,}560}{1.732 \times 208} = 98.8 \approx 99 \text{ A}$$

Note that, in both Examples 12.3 and 12.4, had the actual lighting loads exceeded the computed lighting loads using Table 12.1, then the actual lighting loads would be used in the calculations. In the case of Example 12.3, the actual lighting load would again be multiplied by the 1.25 factor as required for a continuous load.

Refer to Section 11.7 for complete examples showing the selection of the actual wire sizes and types for feeders, taking into account derating factors, available short-circuit current, and voltage drop. Refer to *NEC* Article 220 for the complete requirements of feeder calculations, and to NEC Chapter 9 for examples of calculations.

SUMMARY

- A branch circuit is that segment of the electrical system between the final overcurrent device and the outlet for the utilization equipment.
- A branch circuit is classified by the rating of the overcurrent device protecting the circuit.
- Branch circuits for lighting are restricted to a maximum of 20 amperes unless supplying heavy-duty lampholders.

- The continuous load on a branch circuit is restricted to a maximum of 80% of the rating of the circuit.
- Branch circuits for the lighting in dwellings and guest rooms are restricted to a maximum of 120 volts.
- Branch circuits for medium-base, screw-shell incandescent lampholders are restricted to a maximum of 120 volts.
- Branch circuits for electric discharge lamp type of lighting fixtures may be 277 volts nominal.
- The minimum load for general-use receptacles is 180 volt–amperes per outlet.
- The maximum number of general-use receptacles allowed on a 15 ampere circuit is 10 and on a 20 ampere circuit is 13.
- A lighting and appliance branch-circuit panelboard (often referred to as simply a lighting panel) is one that has more than 10% of its overcurrent devices rated at 30 amperes or less for which neutral connections are provided.
- A lighting panel is restricted to a maximum of 42 single-pole overcurrent devices.
- A lighting panel must be individually protected on its supply side by its own overcurrent device.
- Branch circuits that are connected to a common neutral must each be on separate lines (120/240 volt, single-phase, three-wire systems) or separate phases (three-phase, four-wire systems).
- The modified connection diagram is used to show the layout of the branch circuits on building floor plans.
- Single-phase loads must be arranged so that the total loading on a panel is reasonably balanced between the phases.
- A junction box or fitting must be installed at each conductor splice connection point, outlet, switch point, junction point, or pull point.
- All boxes and fittings must be accessible.
- A lighting fixture cannot be used as a raceway for circuit conductors unless specifically approved for such.
- Attention should be paid to the switching of the lighting units providing general illumination as a means of reducing the energy consumption of a building.
- Underfloor raceway systems provide a flexible means of distributing power to floor outlets in office and store areas.
- Ground-fault circuit-interrupters provide protection to personnel in areas where they could accidently be exposed to the hazards of ground faults.

- The minimum ampacity for the feeder to a panelboard must be based on the computed loads as per the *National Electrical Code* requirements.

QUESTIONS

1. Define a branch circuit.
2. How is a branch circuit classified?
3. What is the maximum rating permitted for the overcurrent protection of a general-purpose circuit consisting of (a) three No. 14 RHH copper and (b) three No. 10 THW copper.
4. What type of conductors must be used for connecting to a ballast inside a lighting fixture?
5. What is the maximum current rating permitted for a circuit that supplies lighting fixtures with medium-base lampholders?
6. What is the maximum current rating permitted for a circuit that supplies lighting fixtures with mogul-base lampholders?
7. What is the maximum continuous load permitted on a circuit?
8. What is the maximum circuit voltage permitted for medium-base, screw-shell lampholders?
9. What is the maximum circuit voltage permitted for indoor fluorescent lighting fixtures (other than in dwelling units)?
10. What are the advantages of supplying the lighting for large areas from 480Y/277 volt systems?
11. What is the minimum rating permitted for a single receptacle on a 30 ampere circuit?
12. What is the maximum number of general-use 15 ampere duplex receptacles permitted on a 15 ampere circuit? Explain how this is determined.
13. What is the definition of a lighting and appliance branch-circuit panelboard?
14. What is the maximum number of single-pole overcurrent devices permitted in one panelboard?
15. A lighting panel rated for 200 amperes is fed by a feeder that has 200 ampere overcurrent protection. Is a main breaker required at the panel? Explain.
16. A lighting panel is connected to the secondary of a 480-208Y/120 volt, three-phase transformer. Is a main breaker required at the panel?
17. Explain how and why three circuits can be connected to one common neutral on a three-phase, four-wire system.
18. In the layout in Figure 12.8, explain why a maximum of 20 type A fluorescent lighting units can be connected to one 20 ampere circuit.
19. What is a homerun and how is it designated on a layout drawing?
20. What is the significance of the SWD marking on a branch-circuit breaker used in a lighting panel?
21. What is a low-voltage, remote-control switching relay?
22. Why are underfloor raceway systems used?
23. Explain the GFCI circuit breaker.
24. List at least four types of circuits (by location) that require GFCI protection.
25. What is the unit loading for the general lighting and general-use receptacles (number unknown) for office areas?
26. What is a demand factor?

PROBLEMS

1. Nine No. 14 THW copper conductors for a number of 15 A circuits are all run in the same conduit. The ambient temperature is 35°C. Determine whether the ampacity rating of the conductors is satisfactory.
2. Six No. 10 RHH copper conductors for a number of 30 A circuits are all run in the same conduit. The ambient temperature is 35°C. Determine whether the ampacity rating of the conductors is satisfactory.
3. Refer to the lighting layout in Example 5.13 and Figure 5.11(b). A total of 35 lighting fixtures is required. The ballast for each fixture is rated at 450 W (Table 4.4), with a line current of 1.62 A at 277 V. The system is 480Y/277 V, three phase, four wire. Determine (a) the minimum number of

branch circuits required for the lighting and (b) the practical number to use, taking into account the arrangement of the fixtures.

4. Refer to the lighting layout in Example 5.14 and Figure 5.12. A total of 28 lighting fixtures is required. The ballast for each fixture is rated at 295 W (Table 4.5), with a line current of 1.1 A at 277 V. The system is 480Y/277 V, three-phase, four-wire. Determine the minimum number of 30 A branch circuits required for the lighting.
5. It is estimated that an office area requires a total of 115 general-use, 120 V duplex receptacles. Calculate the minimum number of 20 A circuits required.
6. A lighting panel supplies the lighting and receptacle load for an office area of 12,000 sq. ft, of which 1000 sq. ft are corridors and stairwells. There are a total of 150 general-use receptacles. The service is 208Y/120 volt, three-phase, four-wire. Calculate the minimum ampacity rating for the feeder conductors to the panel. Assume that the entire lighting load is continuous and that the actual lighting load is less than the calculated load.
7. Repeat Problem 6, except that the number of general-use receptacles is unknown.
8. Refer to Figure 12.4(c). Assume that the feeder shown supplies three lighting panels in a motel. Each panel supplies the lighting and receptacle load for an area of 14,000 sq. ft, 1500 sq. ft of which is corridor, closet, and stairway areas. Each panel supplies 50 general-use duplex receptacles. The areas fed by the panels do not include any dining rooms or kitchens or any appliances. Assume the actual lighting loads are less than the computed loads. The service is 208Y/120 V, three-phase, four-wire. Determine the minimum ampacity for (a) the taps to each panel and (b) the main feeder supplying the three panels.

13 Branch Circuits and Feeders for Motors

OBJECTIVES

After studying this chapter, you will be able to:

- Define the special problems of motor branch circuits.
- Identify the essential components of a motor branch circuit.
- Select the protective device for a motor branch circuit.
- Select the overload protection for a motor.
- Size the motor branch circuit conductors.
- Select the disconnecting means.
- Select the conductors and size the protective device for a feeder to a group of motors.
- Apply the special rules for a single motor tap.

INTRODUCTION

The design of the branch circuits and feeders for motors requires special considerations. Electric motors have unique starting and running characteristics, as discussed in Chapter 2. Also of great importance is the protection of personnel from the electrical and mechanical hazards of motors and the safeguarding of the equipment from damage.

Motors typically have starting currents that are many times (for example, six times) their full-load running currents. Unless this large transient starting current, which can last for upward of 15 seconds, is allowed for in the design of the circuit feeding the motor, the motor will be unnecessarily shut down. Once the motor is properly started and running, it must then be protected from overheating due to mechanical overloading of the motor. The protective devices must be able to bypass the transient starting currents, yet still be able to react very accurately to any overloads and protect the motor from being damaged. The circuit conductors, switches, and controllers must all be rated to carry the maximum load current that the motor is permitted to carry on a continuous basis. The branch circuit and motor must be protected from damage due to possible short circuits. In addition to these electrical requirements, it is mandatory that the motor and its controller be provided with a safe disconnecting means so that they can be isolated from the electrical supply in order that maintenance of the equipment can be done with no hazard to personnel.

The material presented in this chapter concentrates only on the requirements for alternating current, squirrel-cage induction motors, which are by far the most common motors used in buildings (Section 2.5). There are induction motors used for continuous duty (that is, loaded on a continuous basis), and there are motors used for short-time, intermittent, periodic, or varying duty, such as motors used for positioning and for elevators. Unless otherwise noted, all discussions are with regard to continuous-duty motors that are stationary and permanently connected to the power system.

The reader is referred to the *National Electrical Code* (*NEC*), Article 430, Motors, Motor Circuits, and Controllers, for the complete requirements for all types of motors. The reader should also refer to the Occupational Safety and Health Administration (OSHA) regulations 1910.305(j)4. There are many exceptions to the general code requirements permitted for small fractional horsepower motors that plug into outlets. Again the reader is referred to *NEC* Article 430 for these exceptions. For the Canadian Electrical Code requirements, see Appendix A.

13.1 BRANCH CIRCUIT FOR A SINGLE MOTOR

The branch circuit for a single motor consists of all conductors and electrical equipment between the point of connection of the final overcurrent device protecting the motor and the motor. Figure 13.1 illustrates the essential components of a motor branch circuit, which are:

1. Branch-circuit, short-circuit, and ground-fault protection
2. Branch-circuit conductors
3. Motor controller with overload protection
4. Disconnecting means

The motor controller can be any switch or device used to start and stop the motor by making and breaking the motor current. One of the most common forms of controller for three-phase motors of 1 horsepower and greater is the magnetic type of starter, which is discussed in Chapter 14.

The *National Electrical Code* requires that, where the current rating of a motor is used to determine the ampacity of conductors,

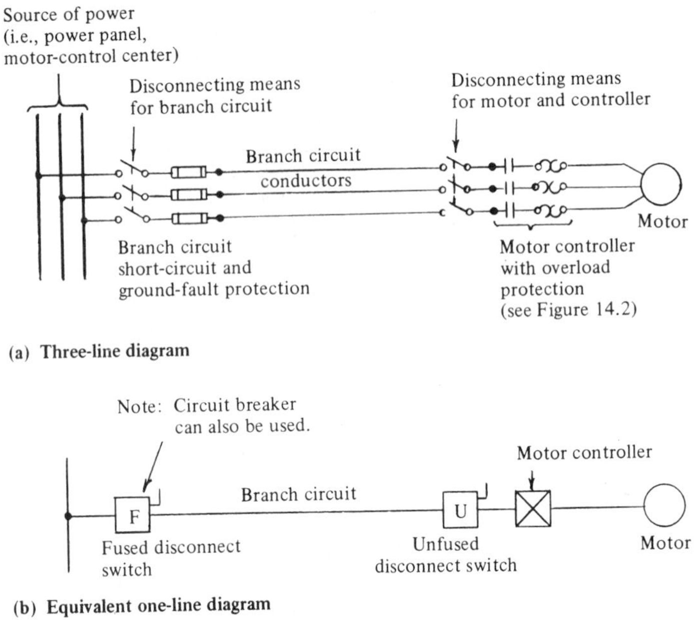

FIGURE 13.1

Typical branch circuit for squirrel-cage induction motor

the ampere rating of switches, branch-circuit protective devices, and so on, the values listed in *NEC* Tables 430-147 to 430-150 including notes be used, instead of the actual current rating marked on the motor nameplate. Tables 13.1 and 13.2 show the *NEC* values for single- and three-phase alternating current motors, respectively.

The rated full-load currents of motors for a given voltage and horsepower rating may vary slightly depending on their rated speed (number of poles) and application. Therefore, the final selection of the motor overload protection, which is very critical, shall be based on the actual motor nameplate current rating. This latter requirement makes certain that the overload protection is then matched to the actual motor being protected.

The requirements for motor branch circuits, which are 600 volts and less, are as outlined in the following articles.

13.1.1 Short-Circuit and Ground-Fault Protection

As required for any feeder, the motor branch circuit must have a protective device located at the point where the circuit conductors receive their supply of current (see Section 6.1). However, the protective device cannot be rated to match the ampacity of the motor branch-circuit conductors because of the high starting current of the motor. Figure 13.2(a) shows the plot of the typical motor current as a function of time from the instant of starting up to the full-load running of the motor. The diagram also shows the typical response

TABLE 13.1 Full-Load Currents for Single-Phase Alternating Current Motors (from *NEC* 430-148)

HP	115 V	230 V
$\frac{1}{6}$	4.4	2.2
$\frac{1}{4}$	5.8	2.9
$\frac{1}{3}$	7.2	3.6
$\frac{1}{2}$	9.8	4.9
$\frac{3}{4}$	13.8	6.9
1	16	8
$1\frac{1}{2}$	20	10
2	24	12
3	34	17
5	56	28
$7\frac{1}{2}$	80	40
10	100	50

The values of full-load currents given are for motors running at usual speeds and motors with normal torque characteristics. Motors built for especially low speeds or high torques may have higher full-load currents, and multispeed motors will have full-load current varying with speed, in which case the nameplate current ratings shall be used.

To obtain full-load currents of 208- and 200-volt motors, increase corresponding 230-volt motor full-load currents by 10% and 15%, respectively.

The voltages listed are rated motor voltages. The currents listed shall be permitted for system voltage ranges of 110 to 120 and 220 to 240.

curve for a nontime-delay fuse, indicating its relationship to the motor current. If the rating of the fuse is too low, then the large starting current of the motor will blow the fuse before the motor can accelerate to its rated speed. Figure 13.2(b) similarly shows the relationship with a time-delay fuse, indicating why it can have a lower rating yet still not blow during starting. Figure 13.3 shows the relationship between a typical circuit breaker with inverse time-delay elements and the motor starting and running currents.

Another approach to motor circuit protection is to use a circuit breaker with adjustable magnetic trip action [see Figure 8.5(b)], thus providing instantaneous tripping only. The trip unit is set to exceed the locked-rotor (that is, starting) current of the motor. Therefore, the breaker will only be tripped if there is a short circuit on the motor branch circuit or within the motor. As such, this device is

TABLE 13.2 Full-Load Currents[a] for Three-Phase Alternating Current Motors (from *NEC* 430-150)

	Induction Type, Squirrel-Cage and Wound-Rotor (A)					Synchronous Type Unity Power Factor[b] (A)			
HP	**115 V**	**230 V**	**460 V**	**575 V**	**2300 V**	**230 V**	**460 V**	**575 V**	**2300 V**
½	4	2	1	.8					
¾	5.6	2.8	1.4	1.1					
1	7.2	3.6	1.8	1.4					
1½	10.4	5.2	2.6	2.1					
2	13.6	6.8	3.4	2.7					
3		9.6	4.8	3.9					
5		15.2	7.6	6.1					
7½		22	11	9					
10		28	14	11					
15		42	21	17					
20		54	27	22					
25		68	34	27		53	26	21	
30		80	40	32		63	32	26	
40		104	52	41		83	41	33	
50		130	65	52		104	52	42	
60		154	77	62	16	123	61	49	12
75		192	96	77	20	155	78	62	15
100		248	124	99	26	202	101	81	20
125		312	156	125	31	253	126	101	25
150		360	180	144	37	302	151	121	30
200		480	240	192	49	400	201	161	40

For full-load currents of 208- and 200-volt motors, increase the corresponding 230-volt motor full-load current by 10% and 15%, respectively.

[a] These values of full-load current are for motors running at speeds usual for belted motors and motors with normal torque characteristics. Motors built for especially low speeds or high torques may require more running current, and multispeed motors will have full-load current varying with speed, in which case the nameplate current rating shall be used.

[b] For 90% and 80% percent power factor, the figures given shall be multiplied by 1.1 and 1.25, respectively.

The voltages listed are rated motor voltages. The currents listed shall be permitted for system voltage ranges of 110 to 120, 220 to 240, 440 to 480, and 550 to 600 volts.

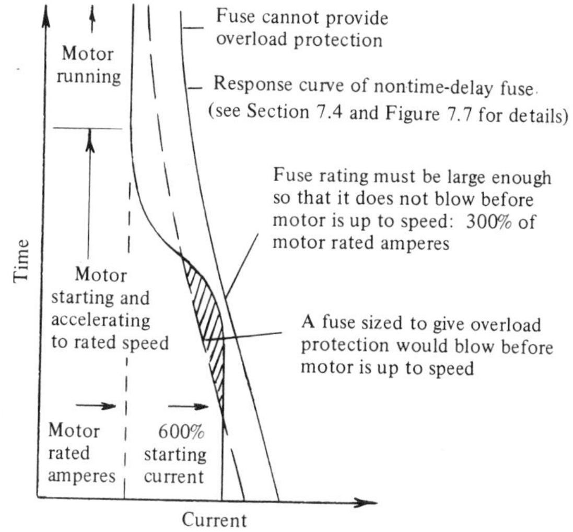

(a) **Motor starting using nontime-delay fuses**

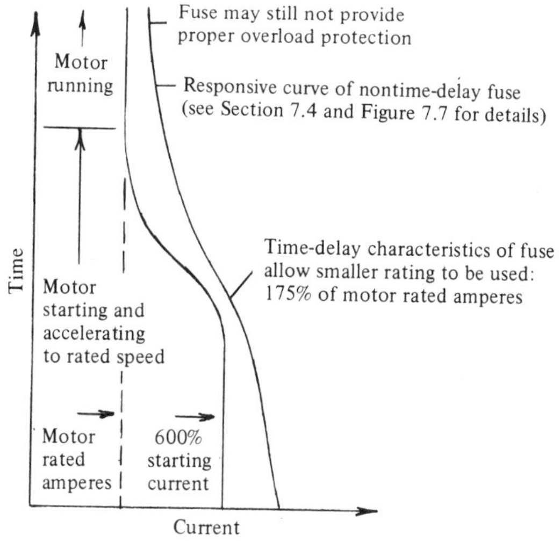

(b) **Motor starting using time-delay fuses**

FIGURE 13.2

Relationship of fuse rating to motor starting current

referred to as a motor short-circuit protector (MSCP). An MSCP can only be used as part of a complete combination starter unit that provides coordinated motor branch-circuit overload and short-circuit and ground-fault protection and that has been approved for such purpose.

From the foregoing, it is evident that the protective device for a motor branch circuit cannot adequately protect the circuit against overloads, but can only provide short-circuit and ground-fault pro-

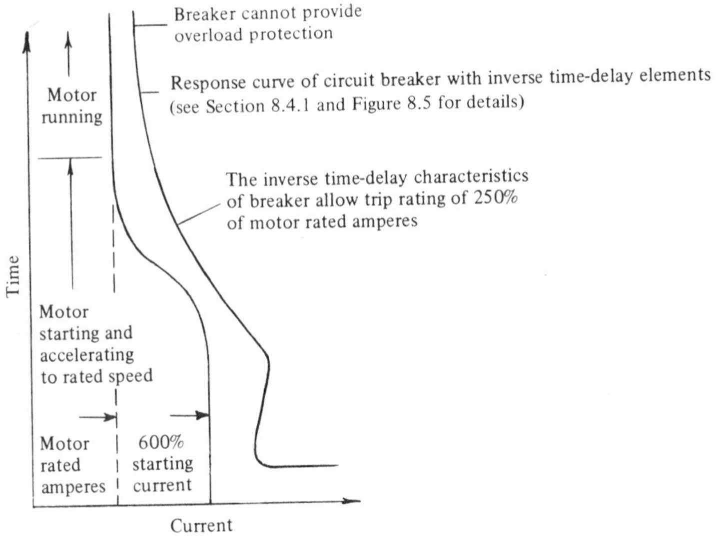

FIGURE 13.3

Relationship of circuit breaker rating to motor starting current

tection. See Section 6.1 for the differences between an overload and a short circuit, and see Section 10.5 for ground-fault protection. The rating or setting of the motor branch-circuit protective device shall not exceed the value calculated using the percentage values shown in Table 13.3 based on the full-load current of the motor. Where the calculated value does not correspond to a standard rating of fuse or circuit breaker trip unit, then the next higher rating is permitted. Refer to *NEC* Section 430-52.

The values obtained by using the percentages as listed in Table 13.3 and adjusted to the next highest standard rating are the maximum permissible. A lower rating of fuse or circuit breaker trip unit may be used if a detailed study of the time–current characteristics of the device indicates that it will not operate to shut down the motor during the normal start-up of the motor (see Section 16.4). The standard ratings of fuses are listed in Table 7.1, and those for circuit breakers are listed in Tables 8.1, 8.2, and 8.3.

13.1.2 Overload Protection

Each motor must be protected against harmful heating due to failure to start or from mechanical overloading of the motor. Since the branch-circuit protective device cannot properly provide this protection, the motor must be separately protected against overloads. Refer to *NEC* Section 430-32. The most common method is to have overload relays mounted integral with a magnetic contactor. These overload relays are responsive to the motor current and operate automatically to open the contactor if a harmful overload occurs.

TABLE 13.3 Maximum Rating or Setting of Motor Branch-Circuit, Short-Circuit, and Ground-fault Protective Devices

Type of Branch Overcurrent Device	Percent of Motor Full-Load Current: Full-Voltage Starting or Reduced Voltage Resistor or Reactor Starting	Percent of Motor Full-Load Current: Reduced Voltage Autotransformer or Wye–Delta Starting
Fuse: Nontime-delay	300	250
Time-delay (dual element)	175	175
Circuit breaker with inverse time-delay element	250	200
Circuit breaker with only instantaneous trip unit	700	700

1. The values given are for single- and three-phase ac squirrel-cage and synchronous motors with locked-rotor (starting) currents of 600% of motor full-load current.
2. For description of fuses, see Sections 7.4 and 7.5.
3. For description of circuit breakers, see Sections 8.4 and 8.5.
4. For description of reduced-voltage starters, see Section 14.4.
5. For a complete set of values for all types of motors, see *NEC* Table 430-152.

The contactor, complete with overload relays, is known as a magnetic motor starter. These starters are fully discussed in Section 14.2.

The overload devices shall be rated or set at a maximum value determined by applying the following percentages to the motor nameplate full-load current:

—Motors with a marked service factor of 1.15: 125%
—Motors with a marked service factor of 1.0: 115%

See Section 2.8 for the explanation of the service factors of motors. The overload device must still be able to pass the normal 600% starting currents of the motor for the time taken for the motor to accelerate up to its rated speed. However, since they do not also have to respond to large short-circuit currents, they can be designed to meet this requirement, as shown in Figure 13.4.

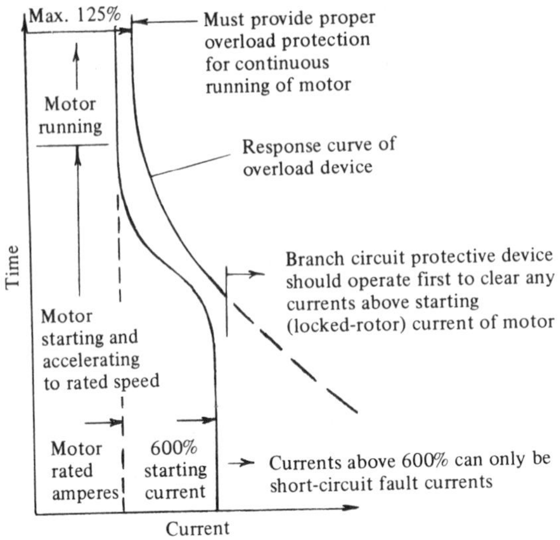
Max. 125%
Must provide proper overload protection for continuous running of motor
Motor running
Response curve of overload device
Time
Branch circuit protective device should operate first to clear any currents above starting (locked-rotor) current of motor
Motor starting and accelerating to rated speed
Motor rated amperes
600% starting current
Currents above 600% can only be short-circuit fault currents
Current

FIGURE 13.4

Relationship of overload device to motor current

13.1.3 Branch-Circuit Conductors

The ampacity of the branch-circuit conductors to the motor must not be less than 125% of the full-load current of the motor (see *NEC* Section 430-22). This, in effect, means that the conductors are loaded to only 80% of their rating under full-load conditions, which is standard for circuits with continuous loads. Note that it is not necessary to size the conductors to match the rating permitted for the branch-circuit protective device, which can be as high as 700% of the motor full-load current. The conductors are adequately protected by the motor overload protection. Any excess load currents can only be the result of motor operation and therefore must pass through the overload devices. Even though these devices are often located at the motor end of the branch circuit, when they operate they will interrupt the flow of current in the complete circuit. Any short circuit on the circuit conductors or within the motor will be cleared by the branch-circuit protective device located at the source end of the circuit, as shown in Figure 13.1.

The selection of conductor sizes to meet the ampacity requirements is detailed in Section 11.1. Where motors are connected to large-capacity systems, the short-circuit current ratings should be investigated as in Section 11.2. On long circuit runs, the conductor sizes must be investigated for excessive voltage drop, as in Section 11.3.

13.2 DISCONNECTING MEANS

Motors and controllers must be provided with a means of safely disconnecting them from their source of supply so that maintenance of the controller, motor, and its driven equipment can be done with no hazard to personnel. Disconnecting means must be provided for each motor, each controller, and each branch circuit. Refer to *NEC* Article 430, part H.

13.2.1 Location

Each disconnecting means shall be located so as to be readily accessible. The *National Electrical Code* defines *readily accessible* as

> Admitting close approach: not guarded by locked doors, elevation, or other effective means and capable of being reached quickly for operation without the necessity of removing obstacles or resorting to portable ladders or chairs.

The disconnecting means for the branch circuit, as for any circuit, shall be located at the source of supply for the circuit. The disconnecting means for the motor shall be located within sight from the motor and its driven equipment. Similarly, the disconnecting means for the controller shall be located within sight from the controller. The *NEC* defines *within sight from* as *the disconnecting means being visible and not more than 50 feet from the equipment being controlled.*

When the source for the motor branch circuit is within sight from the motor, then the same disconnecting means can be used to satisfy all the code requirements, as shown in Figure 13.5(a). Where the source for the motor branch circuit is not within sight from the motor, an additional disconnecting means is required, as shown in Figure 13.5(b). If the source, controller, and motor are all not within sight from each other, three separate disconnecting means are required, as shown in Figure 13.5(c).

Where several motors are controlled from one location, such as a motor-control center, it may not be possible to locate the control center within sight from all the motors. Where any motor and its driven equipment is not within sight from its controller location, it is permissible to delete the disconnecting means at the motor, providing that *the controller disconnecting means is capable of being locked into the open (off) position.* The controller must also be clearly marked as to the equipment being controlled. Motor-control centers are discussed in Section 14.5.

13.2.2 Ratings and Types

The disconnecting means shall have an ampacity rating of at least 115% of the full-load current rating of the motor. The disconnecting means shall open all the ungrounded supply conductors and shall be gang operated so that the one operating mechanism opens all poles simultaneously. There shall be a clear indication as to whether the disconnect is in the open (off) or closed (on) position. The disconnecting means shall be horsepower rated, which means that it is

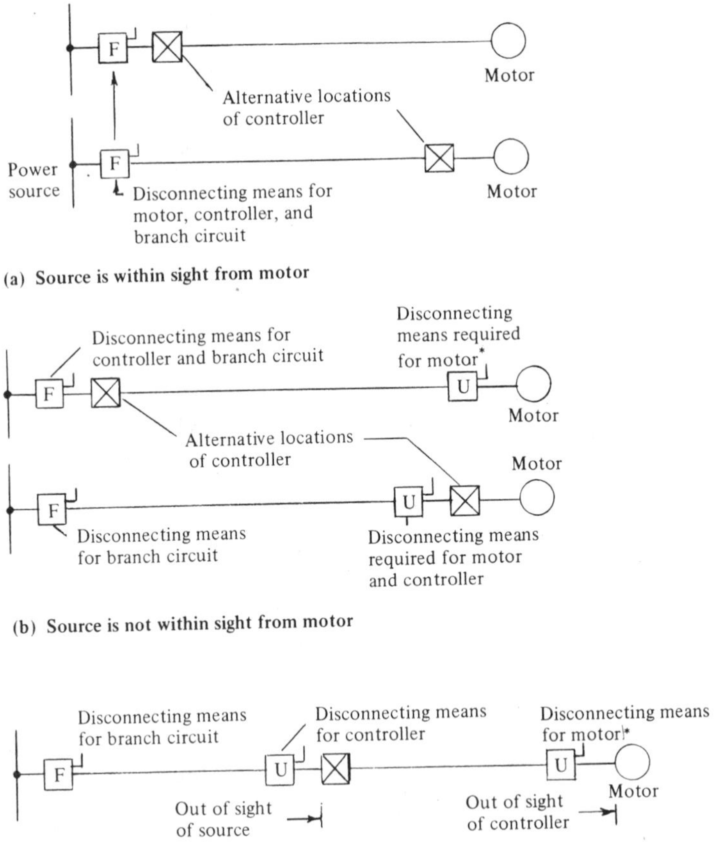

*Can be deleted if controller disconnecting means can be locked into the off position
See Figure 13.1 for meaning of symbols

(c) Source, controller, and motor not within sight of each other

FIGURE 13.5

Disconnecting means required for motor branch circuits

capable of safely interrupting the locked-rotor current of a motor of the same horsepower rating. The horsepower rating is required in the event that a motor stalls and the motor controller fails to properly open the circuit. When the disconnect switch is operated, it then has to interrupt the locked-rotor current of the motor, which is typically 600% of the motor full-load current. Table 13.4 lists the standard sizes and ratings of three-pole motor circuit switches up to 600 amperes. Note that the switches are horsepower rated only up to 100 horsepower. For motors larger than 100 horsepower, a general-use or isolating switch may have to be used, in which case it must be clearly marked "Do not operate under load." Another exemption from the horsepower rating requirement is for stationary motors

TABLE 13.4 Standard Ratings of Three-Pole Motor Circuit Switches (rated 250 and 600 V)

	Maximum Horsepower Rating								
	Fused						Unfused		
	240 VAC[a]		480 VAC[a]		600 VAC[a]				
Ampere Rating	Nontime-Delay Fuses	Time-Delay Fuses	Nontime Delay Fuses	Time-Delay Fuses	Nontime-Delay Fuses	Time-Delay Fuses	240 VAC[a]	480 VAC[a]	600 VAC[a]
30	3	$7\frac{1}{2}$	$7\frac{1}{2}$	15	10	20	$7\frac{1}{2}$	15	20
60	$7\frac{1}{2}$	15	15	30	20	50	15	30	50
100	15	30	25	60	30	75	30	60	75
200	25	60	50	100	50	100	60	100	100
400	50	100	—	100	—	100	100	—	—
600	—	—	—	—	—	—	—	—	—

[a] System voltage. See Table 7.2 for dimensions of switches.

rated at 2 horsepower or less and 300 volts or less. The disconnecting means can then be a general-use switch having an ampere rating not less than 200% of the full-load current rating of the motor.

When fuses are used for the protection of the motor circuit, the fuses and the disconnecting means can be mounted in the same enclosure. Figure 7.12 shows a typical fusible switch. The motor circuit switch must be sized to accommodate the size of fuse as required by Table 13.3. When nontime-delay fuses are used, the switch ampere rating may be more than three times the full-load current of the motor because of the size of fuse required. When time-delay (dual-element) fuses are used, a smaller-sized switch is possible because these fuses are required to be rated at only 175% of the motor full-load current. This can result in considerable savings in the cost and space requirements of the switch. The ratings of switches using each type of fuse are shown in Table 13.4. Example 13.2 illustrates a specific motor branch circuit where the size of the motor circuit switch, when using time-delay fuses, can be reduced.

Circuit breakers can be used as the disconnecting means because they are tested to interrupt a minimum of 600% of their current rating. Automatic circuit breakers (with integral trip units) are used for both the motor branch-circuit overcurrent protection and the disconnecting means. Where only disconnecting means are required, then nonautomatic breakers (with no trip units) are used.

The motor controller and its disconnecting means may also be mounted in the same enclosure. However, the disconnecting means cannot be part of the actual controller itself because it must be possible to isolate the entire controller mechanism from its supply to allow for maintenance. Figure 14.3 shows examples of motor starters together with the branch-circuit overcurrent protection and disconnecting means all mounted in one enclosure. These are referred to as combination starters and are the common arrangement used in motor-control centers (Section 14.5).

13.3 EXAMPLES OF MOTOR BRANCH CIRCUITS

The following examples illustrate the application of the electrical code rules to the design of motor branch circuits.

EXAMPLE 13.1

Design the branch circuit for a 40 hp, 460 V, three-phase squirrel-cage induction motor, service factor 1.15, with nameplate full-load current of 50 A. The motor will be started full voltage. There will be non-time-delay fuses for the circuit protection, motor circuit switches for disconnecting means, and type THW copper conductors. Ambient temperature will be 30°C. The motor controller will be adjacent to the motor, but both will be out of sight from the branch circuit source of supply.

Solution

1. From Table 13.2, the rated current of a 40 hp motor is 52 A (this value must be used except for overload protection).
2. Branch-circuit protective device and disconnecting means:
   From Table 13.3, maximum fuse = 300% of 52 = 156 A
   From Table 7.1, the next largest standard size is 175 A
   From Table 13.4, switch size is 200 A (hp rating of 50)
3. Overload protection:
   From Section 13.1.2, maximum allowed = 125% of 50 = 62.5 A
   (note use of the actual nameplate full-load current)
   See Section 16.5 for selection of actual heater element.
4. Branch-circuit conductors:
   From Section 13.1.3, minimum ampacity = 125% of 52 = 65.0 A
   From Table 11.1, conductor size is No. 6 THW (rated at 65 A)
   From Table 11.6, conduit size is 1 in. (three conductors)
5. Unfused disconnect switch for controller and motor:
   From Table 13.4, switch size is 100 A (hp rating of 60); also exceeds 115% of motor full-load amperes

Figure 13.6(a) shows the one-line diagram for this circuit. Note that the nominal voltage for the power source is 480 V (see Section 1.8).

EXAMPLE 13.2

Repeat Example 13.1, except that time-delay fuses will be used for the circuit protection.

Solution

— From Table 13.3, maximum fuse = 175% of 52 = 91 A
— From Table 7.1, the nearest standard size is 90 A (note that size could be increased to 100 A)
— From Table 13.4, switch size is 100 A (hp rating of 60)

All other aspects of the circuit remain the same [see Figure 13.6(b)]. This example shows the advantages in using time-delay (dual-element) fuses in reducing the size and cost of the fused switch.

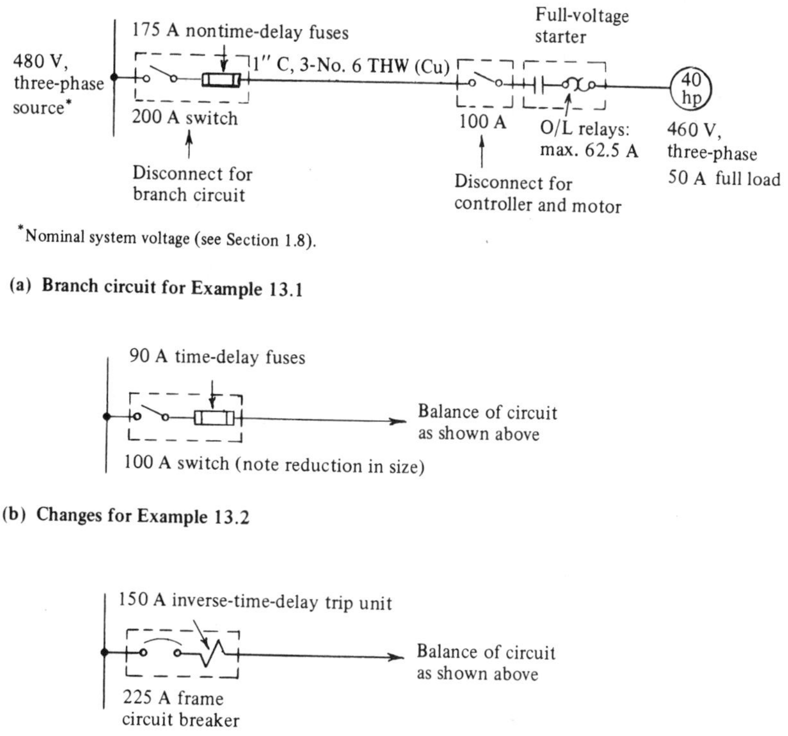

(a) Branch circuit for Example 13.1

(b) Changes for Example 13.2

(c) Changes for Example 13.3

FIGURE 13.6

One-line diagrams for Examples 13.1, 13.2, and 13.3

EXAMPLE 13.3

Repeat Example 13.1, except that a molded-case circuit breaker with time-delay element will be used for the circuit protection.

Solution

- From Table 13.3, maximum breaker = 250% of 52 = 130 A
- From Table 8.1, the next highest standard trip rating is 150 A
- Frame size of breaker is 225 A

All other aspects of the circuit remain the same [see Figure 13.6(c)].

In the foregoing examples, only the ampacity requirement for the branch-circuit conductors is considered. On large-capacity systems, the conductors should also be sized for the available short-circuit current as in Section 11.2. On long branch-circuit runs, the conductors should also be sized to meet the voltage drop requirements as in Section 11.3. The interrupting capacity of the branch-circuit overcurrent device must be suitable for the available short-circuit current.

13.4 FEEDERS FOR TWO OR MORE MOTORS

An example of a feeder supplying a group of two or more motors is shown in Figure 13.7. The ampacity of the feeder shall be equal to the sum of 125% of the rated full-load current of the largest motor, plus the sum of the rated full-load currents of all the remaining motors in the group (*NEC* Section 430-24). It is not necessary to provide for simultaneous overloads on all motors. Where there are two or more motors, all the same rating, that are the largest motors in the group, then only one of the motors need be treated as the largest. If there are other types of loads, such as lighting, being supplied by the feeder in addition to the motors, then these loads shall be computed in accordance with the appropriate *NEC* requirements (see Section 12.11 this text) and added to the motor load as calculated by the foregoing.

The largest current that the feeder to a group of motors will have to handle occurs when the largest motor is started at a time when all the other motors in the group are running and drawing their full-load currents. This is based on the assumption that only one motor will be starting at any one instant. The feeder protective device must be sized to allow for this transient condition and not react to open the circuit before the largest motor has accelerated to its rated speed. Therefore, the feeder protective device shall be rated or set at not greater than the value calculated by taking the largest rating of the branch-circuit short-circuit and ground-fault protective device allowed for any motor of the group, and adding to this value the rated full-load currents of all the remaining motors (*NEC* Section 430-62). If other types of loads are being supplied by the feeder in addition to the motors, then these loads will be added to the calculated value. Note that the code does not allow the next largest standard size of fuse or circuit breaker to be selected, as is permitted for individual motor circuit protection.

Since the rating or setting of the feeder protective device may be higher than the ampacity of the feeder conductors, precise overload protection is not provided to the feeder. However, overloads on the feeder can only occur if too many of the motors are being overloaded at the same time, which is not likely. Also, any excessive

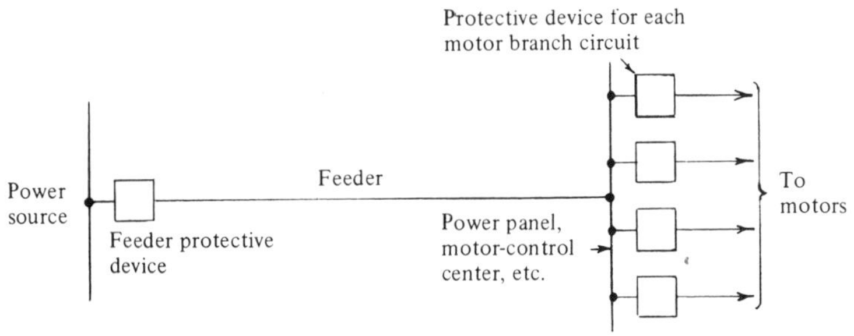

FIGURE 13.7

Feeder for a group of motors

overloads on individual motors are cleared by their own overload protection. The feeder protective device does provide short-circuit and ground-fault protection.

For large industrial plants, the nature of the work being performed may be such that all the motors are unlikely to be running fully loaded simultaneously for any length of time. In this case, demand factors of less than 100% may be used when calculating the minimum ampacity requirements for groups of motors. However, permission to use lower demand factors must be granted by the authority having jurisdiction for the installation (*NEC* Section 430-26).

The following examples illustrate the method of designing a feeder to a group of motors.

EXAMPLE 13.4

Design the feeder for the following group of 200 V, three-phase squirrel-cage induction motors: 1-10 hp, 1-15 hp, 1-20 hp, and 1-40 hp. The individual motors will be protected by dual-element (time-delay) fuses, and they will be started full voltage. The feeder will also be protected using dual-element fuses mounted in a motor circuit switch. Feeder conductors will be type THW copper.

Solution

Motor Horsepower	Motor Full-Load Amperes	Feeder Calculations: Ampacity		Feeder Calculations: Protection	
40	104 × 1.15[a] = 120 A	125% of 120	= 150	175%[b] of 120	= 210
20	54 × 1.15 = 62 A	Plus 100% of remaining	= 142		= 142
15	42 × 1.15 = 48 A				
10	28 × 1.15 = 32 A				
		Min. ampacity	= 292 A	Max. rating	= 352 A

[a] Values from Table 13.2 for 230 V are increased by 15% for 200 V motors from the footnote to the table. *Note:* The 1.15 factor used here is not related to the service factor.

[b] As in Table 13.3, using time-delay fuses.

1. Feeder conductors and conduit:
   From Table 11.1, conductor size = 350 MCM THW (rated 310 A)
   From Table 11.6, conduit size = $2\frac{1}{2}$ in. (three conductors)
2. Feeder protective device:
   From Table 7.1, the nearest standard fuse size is 350 A (<352 A)
   From Table 13.4, the switch size is 400 A

Figure 13.8 shows the one-line diagram of the feeder.

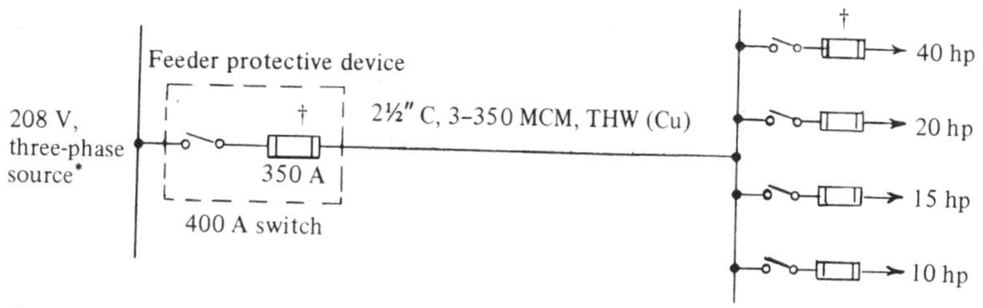

*Nominal system voltage (see Section 1.8)

† Dual-element time-delay fuses

FIGURE 13.8

One-line diagram for Example 13.4

■ **EXAMPLE 13.5**

Repeat Example 13.4, except that the feeder protective device will be a circuit breaker.

Solution

Maximum trip rating of breaker = (250%[a] of 120) + 142
= 300 + 142 = 442 A

From Table 8.1, the nearest standard trip rating that does not exceed 442 A is 400 A. In Figure 13.8, the 400 A fused switch would be replaced with a 400 A frame breaker with 400 A trip unit.

[a] From Table 13.3.

Once again, the foregoing examples considered only the ampacity requirements for the feeder conductors. Short-circuit and voltage drop requirements should also be investigated.

13.5 SINGLE MOTOR TAPS

In an industrial plant, it is often convenient to run a main branch circuit overhead through the building from which motors at different locations are fed. It is then necessary to tap off the main branch circuit conductors with a run down to the motor and its controller at floor level. Rather than require that the tap conductors be the same size as the main conductors, the following is permitted [*NEC* section 430-53(d)]. Refer to Figure 13.9. The size of the tap conductors down to the motor controller may be reduced without requiring additional overcurrent protection at the point of the tap (which would be hard to reach) providing that:

1. The ampacity of the tap conductors to the motor is a minimum of one-third the ampacity of the main branch-circuit conductors.
2. The distance from the tap to the motor controller with overload devices is a maximum of 25 ft.
3. The tap conductors are adequately protected from physical damage.
4. The motor controller and overload devices are each listed for group installation with the size of the branch-circuit overcurrent protection provided.

The tap conductors must also be a minimum of 125% of the full-load current of the motor as required for any motor circuit. The following examples illustrate the application of the foregoing requirements.

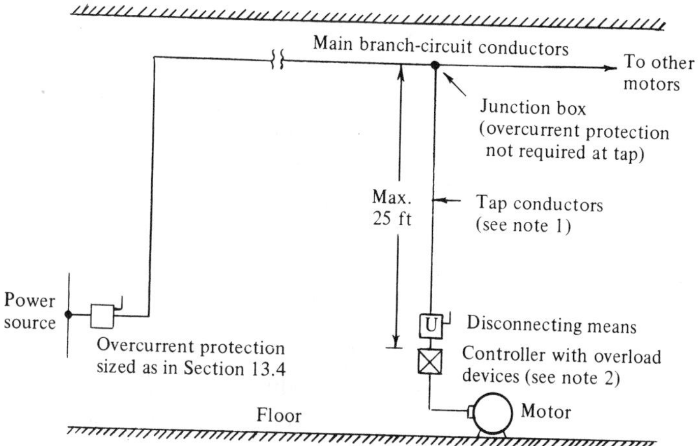

FIGURE 13.9

Tap for single motor from main branch circuit

■ EXAMPLE 13.6

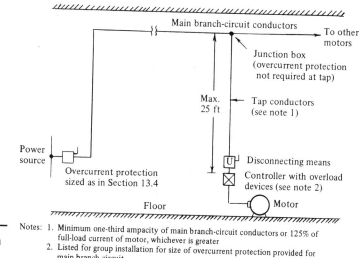

The overhead main branch-circuit conductors are No. 1/0 THW copper. Determine the minimum size of THW conductors permitted for the tap down to the motor controller (maximum distance of 25 ft) for a 10 hp, 460 V, three-phase motor.

Solution

— From Table 11.1, the ampacity of 1/0 THW is 150 A
— Minimum ampacity for tap conductors is one-third of 150 = 50 A
— From Table 11.1, select No. 8 THW (rated at 50 A)
— From Table 13.2, the motor full-load current is 14 A (ampacity rating of No. 8 THW exceeds 125% of 14 A)

■ EXAMPLE 13.7

Repeat Example 13.6, except the motor is 40 hp.

Solution

— From Table 13.2, the motor full-load current is 52 A
— Minimum ampacity of tap conductors is 125% of 52 = 65 A
— No. 8 THW as in Example 13.5 is not large enough
— Tap conductors required are No. 6 THW (rated at 65 A)

SUMMARY

- Motor branch circuits require special consideration.
- The rating of the branch-circuit protective device must be high enough to bypass the motor starting current, the maximum rating permitted depending on the type of device used.

- Since the protective device does not provide proper overload protection, separate overload devices must be used to protect the motor from damage due to overheating.
- The maximum rating or setting permitted for the overload devices depends on the service factor of the motor.
- Branch circuit conductors must have a minimum ampacity rating of 125% of the motor full-load current.
- The motor, controller, and branch circuit must all have means of disconnecting them from the source of supply.
- The disconnecting means must be visible and not more than 50 feet from the equipment being controlled.
- The disconnecting means must be horsepower rated.
- The ampacity of the feeder to a group of motors must be equal to the sum of 125% of the rated full-load current of the largest motor, plus the sum of the rated full-load currents of all the remaining motors.
- The protective device for the feeder to a group of motors shall be rated or set at not greater than the value calculated by taking the largest rating of the branch-circuit short-circuit and ground-fault protective device allowed for any motor of the group and adding to this value the rated full-load currents of all the remaining motors.
- Conductor sizes may be reduced for a tap to a single motor, providing that the tap conductors are not less than one-third the ampacity of the main conductors and do not extend more than 25 feet to the motor overload devices.

QUESTIONS

1. Outline the essential components of a motor branch circuit.
2. What are the special problems with regard to motor branch circuits?
3. Why must the overload protection for a motor be based on the actual motor nameplate current rating, rather than on the values listed by the *NEC* (Tables 13.1 and 13.2)?
4. Explain why the motor branch-circuit protective device (the fused switch or circuit breaker) can provide only short-circuit and ground-fault protection.
5. What is the function of the motor overload protection?
6. Why does the maximum rating or setting permitted for the overload protection depend on the service factor of the motor?
7. Explain why it is not necessary to size the motor branch-circuit conductors to match the rating permitted for the branch-circuit protective device.
8. What is the purpose of the disconnecting means for the motor and its controller?
9. What is meant by readily accessible?
10. What is meant by within sight from?
11. When can the same disconnecting means be used for the motor, its controller, and the motor branch circuit?
12. A motor is controlled from but is out of sight from a motor-control center. What are the requirements for deleting the disconnecting means at the motor?
13. Explain why the motor disconnecting means must be horsepower rated.

14. Explain why the use of time-delay fuses can often result in a smaller rating of disconnect switch being required as compared to using non-time-delay fuses.
15. Does the protective device for a feeder to a group of motors necessarily provide overload protection to the feeder? If not, why not?
16. What is a motor tap?
17. What are the requirements for a single motor tap?

PROBLEMS

Note: The following problems are based on the motors being the squirrel-cage induction type, continuous duty.

1. Determine the minimum size of type THW copper conductors required for the branch circuit to a 10 hp, 200 V, three-phase motor.
2. Determine the maximum standard fuse rating permitted for the short-circuit and ground-fault protection for the branch circuit to a 50 hp, 460 V, three-phase motor that has reduced-voltage autotransformer starting. Fuses are the nontime-delay type.
3. Determine the maximum standard trip rating permitted for the short-circuit and ground-fault protection for the branch circuit to a 30 hp, 200 V, three-phase motor that has reduced-voltage autotransformer starting. The circuit breaker has inverse time-delay elements.
4. Determine the maximum overload setting permitted for a 100 hp, 460 V, three-phase motor, service factor 1.15, whose nameplate current rating is 120 A.
5. Select the rating of the fused disconnect switch required for the branch circuit to a 25 hp, 575 V, three-phase motor. The motor is started full voltage, and the fuses are the nontime-delay type.
6. Repeat Problem 5, except the fuses are time-delay.
7. The motor in Problem 5 is out of sight from its controller. Select the rating of the unfused disconnect switch that must be located adjacent to the motor.
8. Determine the minimum size of THW copper conductors for the feeder to the following group of 200 V, three-phase motors: 1-25 hp, 1-10 hp, 1-5 hp and 1-3 hp.
9. Determine the maximum standard fuse rating permitted for the short-circuit and ground-fault protection of the feeder in Problem 8. The fuses are the nontime-delay type and the motors are to be started full voltage. Also select the rating of the fused disconnect switch.
10. Repeat Problem 9, except fuses are time-delay.
11. Repeat Problem 8, except motors are 460 V, three-phase.
12. Determine the maximum standard fuse rating permitted for the short-circuit and ground-fault protection of the feeder in Problem 11. The fuses are the nontime-delay type, and the motors are started full voltage. Also select the rating of the fused disconnect switch.
13. Repeat Problem 12, except fuses are time-delay.
14. Refer to Figure 13.9. The overhead main branch-circuit conductors are No. 2 THW copper. Determine the minimum size of THW conductors permitted for the tap down to the motor controller (maximum distance of 25 feet) for a 15 hp, 200 V, three-phase motor.

14 Motor Starters and Motor-Control Centers

OBJECTIVES

After studying this chapter, you will be able to:

- Recognize manual and magnetic starters.
- Describe the operation of magnetic starters.
- Identify the NEMA sizes for starters.
- Describe the operation of overload relays.
- Recognize combination starters.
- Read basic schematic motor-control diagrams.
- Explain the characteristics of two- and three-wire control.
- Determine the need for separate control circuit protection.
- Describe the operation of full-voltage reversing starters.
- Recognize the problems of reduced-voltage starting.
- Explain the characteristics of autotransformer and wye–delta starting.
- List the advantages of motor-control centers.
- Recognize the classifications of motor-control centers.
- Lay out a motor-control center.
- Describe the operation of medium-voltage starters.

INTRODUCTION

Motors constitute by far the largest load on the electrical system of a typical industrial plant. Even in a commercial type of building, motors still account for a significant part of the total load. The proper control of these motors is very important. A motor controller is a device or group of devices that serves to govern, in a predetermined manner, the electric power delivered to the motor. The motor controller can incorporate features to start and stop the motor, to reverse the direction of rotation of the motor, to protect the motor against overloads, undervoltage, and single phasing, and to control the operating characteristics of the motor, such as acceleration, speed, torque, and braking. Article 430, Parts F and G of the *National Electrical Code (NEC),* cover the requirements for motor controllers and their associated control circuits. For the Canadian Electrical Code requirements, see Appendix A.

A motor starter is a basic type of controller whose primary function is to start and stop the motor. Starters can be either the manual or the automatic type. The automatic type can in turn be either the magnetic or the solid-state type. Magnetic starters have been the standard for many years and are still in wide use because of their proven reliability. The solid-state starters have only recently come on the market and have had only limited acceptance to date. The discussions in this text are therefore confined to the magnetic type of automatic starter.

This chapter covers the standard motor starters used with ac squirrel-cage induction motors, along with standard features such as overload, undervoltage, and single-phase protection, reversal of direction of rotation, and reduced voltage starting, which are or can be easily incorporated into a starter. Squirrel-cage induction motors account for the large majority of all drives used today. These motors are self-starting, requiring only that power be connected to the stator terminals to start and run. The reader should refer to Sections 2.5 and 2.6 of this textbook for a review of three-phase, squirrel-cage induction motors and single-phase ac motors, respectively. Also included in this chapter are a few basic control circuits for the magnetic starter. The reader is referred to the books listed in the bibliography for a more comprehensive coverage of motor control circuits and their associated control devices.

Where it is convenient to mount a number of starters at one location, the use of motor-control centers is recommended. The general arrangements for the layout of these centers are discussed and a sample layout is presented. The majority of the discussions in this chapter are with regard to low-voltage starters. Starters rated for voltages above 600 volts are discussed briefly at the end of the chapter.

14.1 MANUAL MOTOR STARTERS

Manual motor starters are used where only on–off operation is required for small, single- or three-phase motors and where full-voltage starting is satisfactory. Typical applications include the control of small machine tools, pumps, and fans. A manual starter consists of a hand-operated snap switch combined with an overload mechanism that will automatically release the closed switch in the event of an overload on the motor. Low-voltage protection is not obtainable with a manual starter. This means that in the event of a power

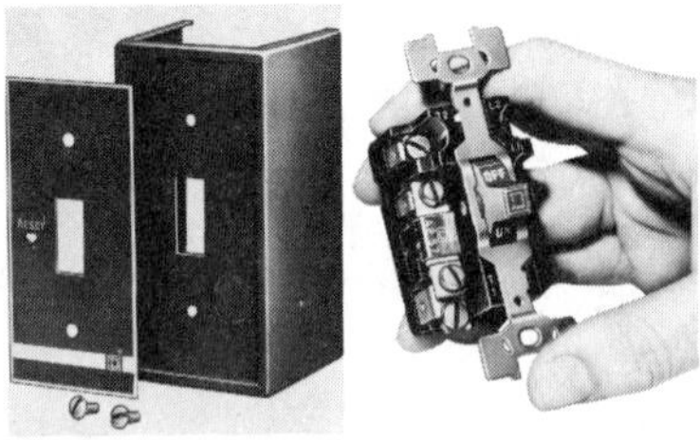

(a) Single-phase manual starter

(b) Three-phase manual starter

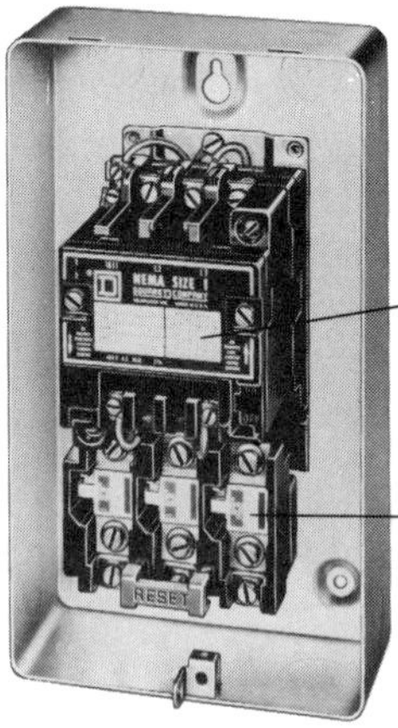

(c) Three-phase magnetic starter (cover removed)

FIGURE 14.1

Full-voltage nonreversing (FVNR) motor starters

interruption all motors controlled by manual starters will instantly restart upon return of the power, a situation that is not always desirable. Remote operation of a manual starter is not possible.

Figure 14.1(a) shows a typical single-phase manual starter. These starters have a maximum rating of 1 horsepower up to 230 volts ac and are available in either single- or two-pole versions. Figure 14.1(b) shows a typical three-phase manual starter. These starters have a maximum rating of 7½ horsepower up to 230 volts and 10 horsepower at 460 and 575 volts ac. The starters are very compact and can either be surface mounted in their own enclosures, as shown, or mounted in a recessed box with a flush face plate.

14.2 FULL-VOLTAGE NONREVERSING MAGNETIC STARTERS

A magnetic starter is required where a three-phase motor is to be remotely controlled by means of a push-button station or an automatic sensing device (for example, a thermostat). A magnetic starter must also be used to control any motor with a horsepower rating beyond that of manual starters (above $7\frac{1}{2}$ horsepower at 200 volts and 10 horsepower at 460 and 575 volts). A major advantage of magnetic starters is that they are very versatile and can accommodate a great many variations in the method of control.

The full-voltage nonreversing (FVNR) starter is used where full-voltage starting is acceptable and where the motor is to start up and run in one direction only. As discussed in Section 2.5.2 and as indicated in Table 2.2, the starting current of a general-purpose squirrel-cage induction motor is 600% of its full-load running current when full voltage is applied at the instant of starting. The motor itself is designed to withstand this inrush current during a normal start-up cycle. The problem then is whether the system supplying the motor can accept this sudden surge of current without encountering unacceptable voltage dips. With most systems of modern design, unless the motor is large enough to be a significant part of the total system load, full-voltage starting is satisfactory.

A starter must be able to continuously carry the full-load current and safely interrupt the locked-rotor current of the motor it is controlling. If the motor stalls, or if it does not start properly (it is jammed and cannot begin to turn), then the current drawn by the motor is referred to as the locked-rotor current. This current is typically 600% of the full-load current of the motor (the same as the starting current), and the starter must be able to safely open the circuit under this condition. Since both the full-load and locked-rotor currents are a function of the horsepower rating of the motor at a specified voltage, starters are rated for the maximum horsepower that they can safely handle at these voltages. The starters are classified by a size number. Table 14.1 shows the maximum horsepower ratings of starters ranging from NEMA (National Electrical Manufacturers Association) size 00 to size 9. Figure 14.1(c) shows a typical size 1, three-phase FVNR magnetic starter mounted in its own enclosure. As the NEMA size classification increases, so does the physical size of the starter, as larger contacts are needed to carry and break the higher motor currents and heavier mechanisms are required to open and close the contacts. Low-voltage magnetic starters are suitable for operation on systems up to a maximum of 600 volts nominal.

The magnetic starter is basically an on–off device operated by electromagnetic means. When the starter coil is energized through a separate control circuit, the resulting magnetic field mechanically forces the main contacts of the starter to close, thus starting the motor. The coil must then be continuously energized to hold the contacts closed and keep the motor running. When the coil is de-energized, the main starter contacts are forced open by either spring pressure or gravity, thus stopping the motor. The coil and contact assembly is called a *magnetic contactor*. With the addition of over-

TABLE 14.1 Horsepower Ratings of Low-Voltage Starters

NEMA Size	Maximum Horsepower			
	Single-Phase (V)		Three-Phase (V)	
	115 V	230 V	200 V	460 and 575 V
00	$\frac{1}{3}$	1	$1\frac{1}{2}$	2
0	1	2	3	5
1	2	3	$7\frac{1}{2}$	10
2	3	$7\frac{1}{2}$	10	25
3	$7\frac{1}{2}$	15	25	50
4	—	—	40	100
5	—	—	75	200
6	—	—	150	400
7	—	—	—	600
8	—	—	—	900
9	—	—	—	1600

load relays, the assembly then constitutes the basic magnetic starter, as shown in Figure 14.1(c).

Figure 14.2(a) shows a representative connection diagram of the standard full-voltage nonreversing magnetic starter, indicating the starter coil, the three main (or power) contacts, one auxiliary contact, which is connected in the control circuit, and the overload relays. Additional auxiliary contacts, either normally open or closed, can be added for use in more advanced control schemes (for example, to operate indicating lights or to provide interlocking with other motors).

The overload relays are connected on the loadside of the magnetic contactor as shown on the connection diagram. Each relay has two major parts. There is the thermal sensing element, often referred to as the heater, which is directly acted on by the line current drawn by the motor. If the motor load current exceeds the rated value of the thermal element for a specified length of time, the relay reacts to open the overload contacts, which in turn breaks the control circuit to the starter coil, thus shutting down the motor. The time–current response characteristics of the overload relay must ensure that the motor is automatically shut down before an overload can persist to the point where the motor becomes overheated and damaged. Section 16.4 describes the common types of thermal-responsive relays, and Figure 16.5 shows typical time–current characteristic curves. Example 16.8 shows the method of selecting the actual overload relay heater elements for a motor starter. Section 13.1.2 of this textbook outlines the *NEC* code requirements for the

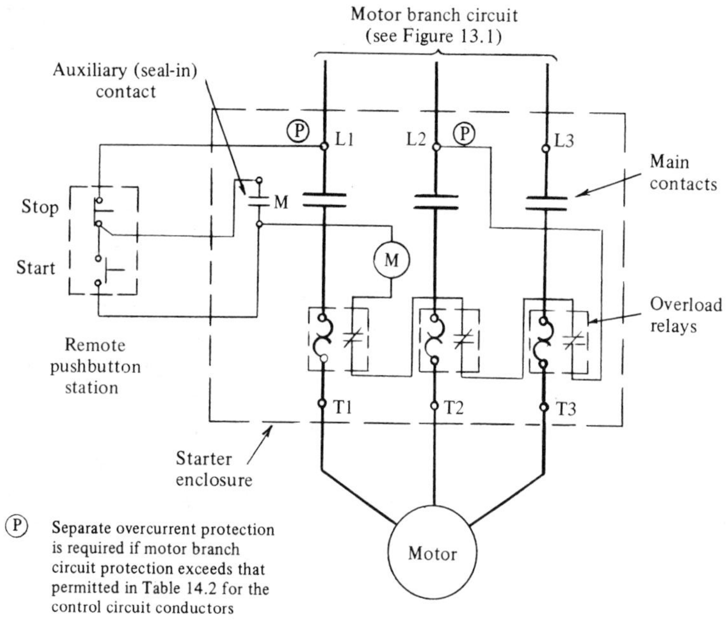

(a) Connection diagram including one remote stop-start push-button station

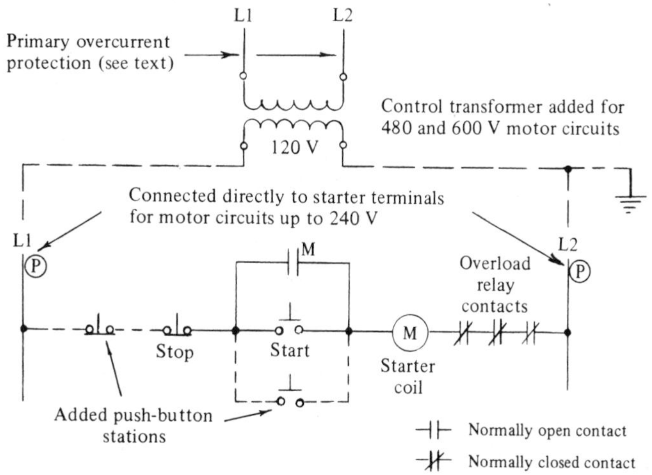

(b) Schematic diagram of three-wire control circuit

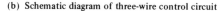

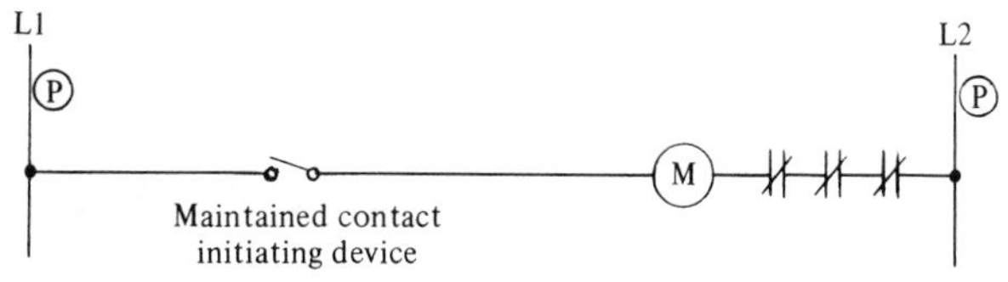

(c) Schematic diagram of two-wire control circuit

FIGURE 14.2

Full-voltage, nonreversing, three-phase magnetic starter

overload protection of a motor, and Section 13.3 includes an example of the calculations for the maximum allowable rating of the overload relays.

It is now standard practice to install three overload relays in a three-phase starter, one for each phase connection to the motor. The reason that three sensing elements are used is to provide complete protection to the motor against single phasing. It is always possible, especially when fuses are used, that one phase of the system will fail, thus leaving a three-phase motor running on one phase. As discussed in Section 2.6, an induction motor, once it is turning, can continue to run on single-phase power even though the torque is a pulsating one, causing the motor to run much noisier. However, the current drawn by the motor from the remaining two lines must increase by 73% to make up for the loss of the third line. This extra current through the motor windings still connected can rapidly overheat the motor. Regardless of the combination of events that cause the single phasing (it could occur on the primary of the supply transformer), a sensing element in each phase ensures that the problem will always be detected and the motor shut down.

Figure 13.5 shows the locations for the disconnecting means and protective devices as required for motor branch circuits. Where the disconnecting means and/or the branch-circuit protective device are at the same location as the controller (motor starter), combination starters that combine all these devices into the one enclosure can be used. Figure 14.3(a) shows a combination starter with a fusible disconnect switch. Figure 14.3(b) shows a combination starter with a molded-case circuit breaker. Where only disconnecting means is required, an unfused disconnect switch is used for the combination starter. Combination starters offer a compact unit that can save space and installation costs, as compared to using a separate switch or circuit breaker and starter enclosures. A combination starter also offers increased safety as the cover of the unit can be interlocked so that it cannot be opened until the disconnecting means is in the off position. Combination starters are used in motor-control centers, as discussed in Section 14.5.

14.2.1 Control for Magnetic Starters

A *motor control circuit* is the *circuit that carries the electric signal directing the performance of the starter but does not carry the main motor current*. Figure 14.2(a) includes the typical control wiring for a full-voltage nonreversing starter with the control circuit tapped off the lineside terminals of the starter. Since the control circuit derives its current supply from the same branch circuit that supplies the power to the motor, it is also disconnected when the disconnecting means ahead of the starter is opened (see Figure 13.1).

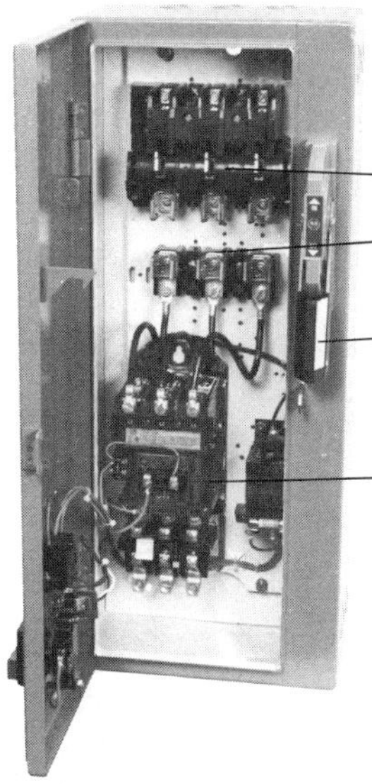

(a) Combination fusible switch type

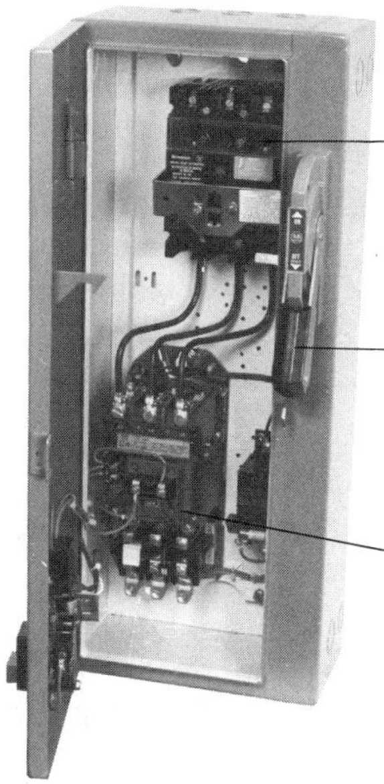

(b) Combination circuit breaker type

FIGURE 14.3

Combination full-voltage, nonreversing magnetic starters

Figure 14.2(b) shows the schematic diagram for the control circuit for the starter in part (a). Note the difference between a connection diagram [part (a)] and a schematic diagram. A connection diagram shows the various electrical components in their relative physical location with the necessary interconnecting wiring. A schematic diagram does not show the components in their proper physical location, but rather arranges them in their logical sequence in the control scheme. Therefore, it is much easier to follow the sequence of operation of a control scheme when using the schematic diagram. Note that wiring diagrams show electrical contacts in their de-energized or nonoperative position. Thus a normally open contact is shown in the open position, and it closes when the device is activated. Conversely, a normally closed contact is shown in the closed position, and it opens when the device is activated.

Figure 14.2(a) shows a control scheme using a remote stop–start push-button station for the control of the motor. Since three wires are required for the connections from the starter to the push-button station, this arrangement is known as *three-wire control*. The push buttons for the three-wire control scheme are the momentary type; that is, they return to their normal position when released. Following the schematic diagram in part (b), when the start button is pushed, the circuit to the starter coil is completed and the main contacts of the starter close to start the motor. At the same instant, the auxiliary contact M closes, completing the circuit around the start button so that when it is released the circuit to the coil is maintained. Contact M is referred to as the *seal-in contact,* as the control circuit is now sealed in until the stop button is operated. The momentary depression of the stop button breaks the control circuit, releasing the starter contacts, which removes the power to the motor. By the time the stop button is released, the M contact of the starter has opened, blocking the circuit to the starter coil. The motor can only be restarted by once again pushing the start button. Note that the closing of the main starter contacts connects the motor directly across the line, hence starting it full voltage.

The three-wire control scheme has two important advantages. First, any number of additional stop–start stations can be easily added to the control circuit, as shown in Figure 14.2(b), without in any way interfering with the operation of any other station. Second, if there is a power failure, the motor will not automatically restart when the power is restored. Since the control contact M opens when the loss of power releases the starter, the return of the power in itself cannot re-energize the starter coil. Once again the start button must be operated before the motor restarts. This is very important when there are many motors on a system. If all the motors were to automatically restart the instant that the power returned, their combined starting currents could easily trip out the main protective device of the system, resulting in the shut down of the system once again. Using the three-wire control scheme for each motor allows for the orderly restarting of the motors by operating personnel.

The system voltage does not have to totally collapse for the motor starter to drop out and stop the motor. The starter coil generally is unable to hold the starter contacts closed if the voltage falls below 50% to 60% of normal. Thus even a prolonged (more than a few cycles) drop of the voltage at the starter terminals will stop the motor. This feature is referred to as undervoltage protection and is desirable to prevent the motor from laboring under prolonged low voltage (see Section 2.9).

A *two-wire control circuit,* as shown in Figure 14.2(c), cannot offer the same advantages as the three-wire control scheme. First, the initiating device must have maintained contacts. Therefore, other on–off devices cannot be added to the control circuit. Second, after a power failure, the motor will automatically restart upon the return of the power, as the maintained initiating contact device remains closed. However, in spite of these disadvantages, the two-wire control scheme has to be used where the motor is controlled by a remote device, such as a thermostat, pressure switch, float switch, or limit switch.

In either the two- or three-wire control schemes, the opening of any one of the overload relay contacts breaks the control circuit to the starter coil, removing the power from the motor. The overload contact normally remains open and requires manual resetting. This allows the motor and its driven equipment to be inspected before any attempt is made to restart the motor.

The arrangement shown in Figure 14.2 uses the motor circuit voltage for the control circuit. This is generally satisfactory up to 240 volts. For motor circuit voltages of 480 and 600 volts, a small step-down control transformer can be used to provide 120 volts for the control circuit for greater operator safety. This transformer is mounted in the starter enclosure, and its primary is tapped from the lineside terminals of the starter, as shown with dashed lines in Figure 14.2(b).

Note that Figure 14.2 shows no separate overcurrent protection for the control circuit. Table 14.2 shows the maximum rating of the overcurrent protective device in amperes allowed for copper conductors when used for control circuit wiring. Note that the rating depends on whether or not the control conductors extend beyond

TABLE 14.2 Overcurrent Protection of Conductors Used for Control Circuit Wiring

Size of Copper Conductor	Maximum Rating of Overcurrent Protective Device (A)	
	Wiring Does Not Extend beyond Starter Enclosure	Wiring Extends beyond Starter Enclosure
14	100	45
12	120	60
10	160	90
Larger than No. 10	Note 1	Note 2

Notes: 1. 400% of value specified in *NEC* Table 310-17 for 60°C rated conductors.

2. 300% percent of value specified in *NEC* Table 310-16 (Table 11.1 this text) for 60°C rated conductors.

The above applies to control circuit conductors tapped from the line side of the motor starter as shown in Figure 14.2 and protected by the motor branch circuit short-circuit and ground-fault protection as shown in Figure 13.1.

For the complete requirements for the protection of motor-control circuits, see *NEC* Article 430, Part F and Table 430-72(b).

the starter enclosure. For example, for the control circuit shown in Figure 14.2, which has control wiring extending beyond the starter enclosure, if No. 14 copper conductors are used, no additional overcurrent protection is required for the control circuit, providing that the rating of the overcurrent protective device for the motor branch circuit (Figure 13.1) does not exceed 45 amperes. If the rating does exceed 45 amperes, either larger control circuit conductors must be used or a separate overcurrent protective device (fuses) rated at 45 amperes or less must be installed at the points marked Ⓟ on the diagram. If a step-down control transformer is used and is mounted within the starter enclosure as previously discussed, then the primary overcurrent protection of the transformer cannot exceed 500% of its rated primary current. This applies if the rated primary current does not exceed 2 amperes, which is the case for all but the largest starters. If separate primary overcurrent protection is required for the control transformer, then fuses are normally used.

14.3 FULL-VOLTAGE REVERSING MAGNETIC STARTERS

The full-voltage reversing (FVR) starter is used where it is necessary to be able to start and run a motor in either direction. The direction of rotation of three-phase induction motors can be easily reversed by simply interchanging any two of the three line connections to the motor (see Section 2.3.1). The reversing starter consists of two magnetic contactors mounted in one enclosure. One contactor is connected to apply the three phases to the motor so that the motor starts up and runs in the forward direction. The other contactor is connected so that when it closes two of the lines to the motor are interchanged, thus reversing the direction of rotation of the motor. The power connections and the control circuit for the reversing starter are shown in Figure 14.4. The two contactors must be interlocked so that it is impossible to close the second contactor if the other contactor is already closed. Otherwise, if both contactors were to be closed at the same time, there would be a dead short-circuit across two of the phases. The standard overload relays are incorporated into the starter as shown. Combination reversing starters similar to those described for nonreversing starters are also available.

The control circuit shown in Figure 14.4(b) is the most basic scheme. With the motor running in the forward direction, the stop button must first be pressed to open the forward contactor before the reverse button can be used to reverse the direction of the motor, and vice versa, when going from reverse to forward. If desired, with the use of double-contact forward and reverse pushbuttons, the scheme can easily be modified so that it is possible to go directly from forward to reverse, and vice versa, without having to first push the stop button.

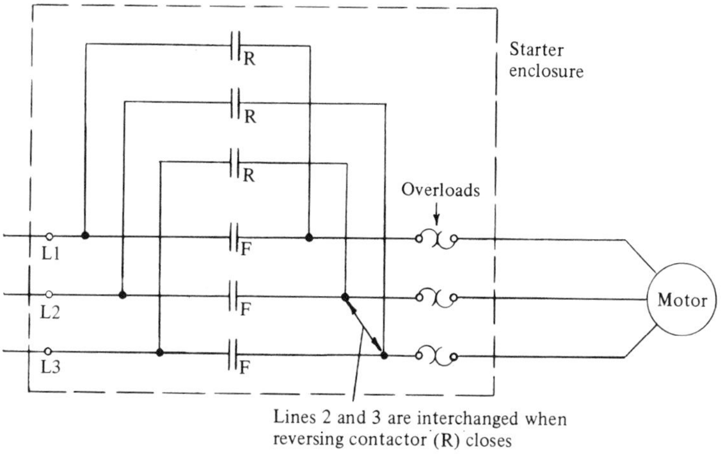

Note: Power connections only are shown

(a) Diagram showing power connections to motor

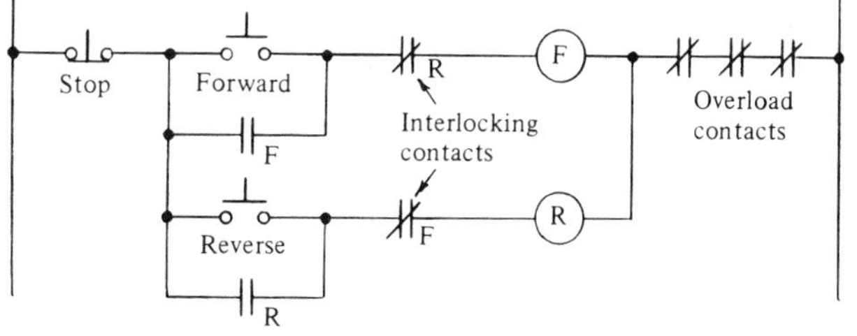

(b) Schematic diagram of basic control scheme

FIGURE 14.4

Full-voltage reversing magnetic starter

Reversing starters can also be applied for motor plugging, which is an operation where the reversal of torque is used to rapidly bring a motor and its driven equipment to a full stop. With this scheme, there is only a start and a stop button. The start button closes the forward contactor the same as for a standard starter. However, when the stop button is pushed, the forward contactor drops out, and the reversing contactor is automatically closed to plug the motor to a stop. A zero speed switch mounted on the motor shaft is used to then open the reversing contactor and finally remove all power before the motor can start up in the reverse direction.

14.4 REDUCED-VOLTAGE NONREVERSING MAGNETIC STARTERS

The reduced-voltage nonreversing (RVNR) starter is used where full voltage starting would cause serious problems. If full-voltage starting were to be used, the 600% starting current could cause unacceptable voltage disturbances on the balance of the system, or the sudden snap of the high starting torque could mechanically overstress the driven equipment. Most power companies have restrictions on the amount of power that can suddenly be taken from their system for a short period of time. These restrictions often dictate whether reduced voltage starting has to be used.

The starting current of a squirrel-cage motor is directly proportional to the voltage applied to the motor terminals at the instant of starting. Thus, if 50% of the full rated voltage is applied to start the motor, then the motor starting current will be reduced to 50% of normal (300% of the full-load motor current rather than 600%). There is, however, a serious disadvantage inherent with the reduced-voltage starting of squirrel-cage induction motors. Refer to Equation 2.2. The torque developed by a motor depends on both the strength of the magnetic field (ϕ) and the current (I) in the rotor bars. As the applied starting voltage is reduced, both the strength of the magnetic field and the rotor current are proportionally reduced. Thus the starting torque is directly proportional to the square of the starting voltage. For example, if the starting voltage is reduced to 50% (0.50 per unit) as just discussed, then the starting torque is reduced to $(0.50)^2$ or 0.25 per unit (25%) of the full-voltage starting torque. This serious reduction in torque could result in the motor not being able to break the load free to start it turning. Also, the torque developed by the motor to accelerate the load up to speed is similarly reduced, and even if the motor does start turning, the acceleration time may be excessive. Therefore, where a motor has to start and accelerate a high-inertia load, the application of reduced voltage starting must be carefully studied.

The easiest means of applying a reduced voltage to the motor terminals at the instant of starting is to insert large power resistors in each line to the motor. Then, as the motor approaches its full speed, the resistors are shorted out and the motor runs normally on full voltage. A major disadvantage with this type of reduced-voltage starting is the bulk of the starting resistors and the problem of mounting them so that the heat can be dissipated. Also, this method suffers from the much higher reduction in starting torque as compared with the reduction in starting current as just outlined. The two preferred methods for reduced-voltage starting of low-voltage motors are the autotransformer and wye–delta types, which overcome these disadvantages.

14.4.1 Autotransformer Starters

The autotransformer starter applies a reduced voltage through taps on the transformer coil. Figure 14.5(a) shows the equivalent single-phase circuit diagram of the connections through the autotransformer to the motor at the instant of starting. The voltage and current relationships are also shown. Assume that the motor is

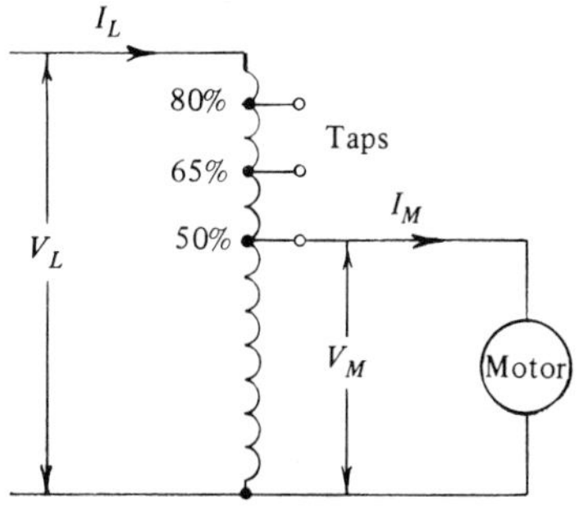

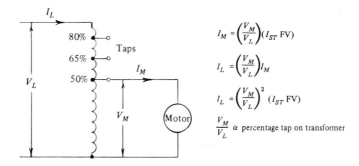

$$I_M = \left(\frac{V_M}{V_L}\right)(I_{ST}\ \mathrm{FV})$$

$$I_L = \left(\frac{V_M}{V_L}\right)I_M$$

$$I_L = \left(\frac{V_M}{V_L}\right)^2 (I_{ST}\ \mathrm{FV})$$

$$\frac{V_M}{V_L}\ \alpha \text{ percentage tap on transformer}$$

(a) Equivalent single-phase circuit

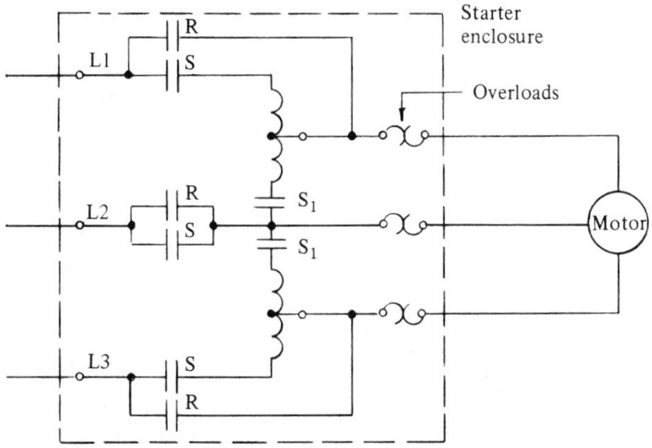

Note: This diagram shows the power connections only

(b) Connection diagram for open-delta type

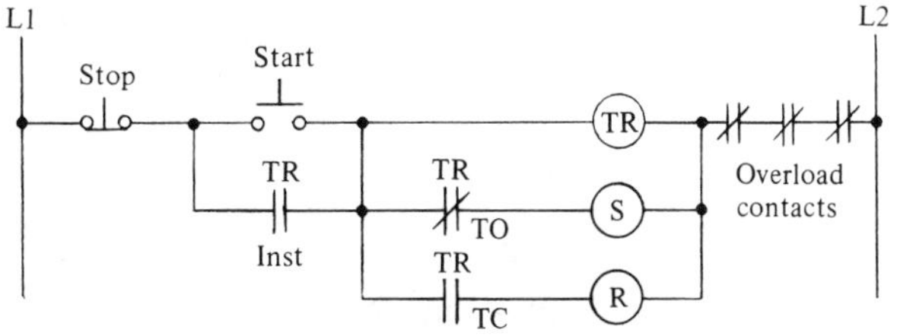

See Figure 14.2 for protection of control circuit and use of control transformer

S, start contactor
R, run contactor
TR, timing relay
Inst, instantaneously closing contact
TO, time opening contact
TC, time closing contact

(c) Schematic diagram of typical control scheme

FIGURE 14.5

Autotransformer reduced-voltage starter

connected to the 50% tap on the transformer coil. This means that 50% of the full voltage is applied to the motor and therefore the current I_M drawn by the motor is 50% of the full-voltage starting current. However, by transformer action, the line current I_L (the primary current of transformer) is only 50% of the motor current (the secondary current of the transformer). Thus the line current drawn from the system is only $(0.50)^2$ or 0.25 (25%) of the full-voltage starting current. The starting torque with 50% voltage applied to the motor is again $(0.50)^2$ or 0.25 (25%) of the full-voltage starting torque. Therefore, the reduction in the starting current drawn from the line is the same as that for the starting torque. However, this analysis neglects the effect of the magnetizing current drawn by the transformer, which can range from 10% to 20% of the full-load current of the motor. In practice, the reduction in the line current does not quite equal the theoretical reduction as just indicated. Nevertheless, the starting torque efficiency is very high. The *starting torque efficiency* is *the ratio of the starting torque developed per ampere of line current when starting at reduced voltage as compared to the starting torque developed per ampere of line current when starting at full voltage*. The high starting torque efficiency combined with the flexibility provided by the various taps available makes the autotransformer starter a very popular choice when reduced-voltage starting is required.

Manual autotransformer starters are available that accomplish the required switching from the reduced-voltage starting mode to the full-voltage starting mode by means of a manually operated lever. However, most autotransformer starters are the automatic type that use magnetic contactors to do the switching and a pneumatic timing relay to control the start and run sequence. Figure 12.5(b) shows the power connections to the motor, including the main contacts of the magnetic contactors. Note that only two autotransformer coils are used, connected in open delta. This arrangement causes a slight unbalance of the voltages applied to each phase of the motor. Where this unbalance is unacceptable (that is, for large motors), three autotransformers connected in a wye configuration are used instead. It is standard to have transformer taps of 50%, 65%, and 80% so that a range of starting currents and torques can be selected. A permanent connection is then made to one set of taps.

Figure 14.5(c) shows the typical control circuit used to automatically control the necessary switching functions. The sequence of starting is as follows. Operating the start button closes contactor S, which then connects each autotransformer to the line [contacts S and S_1 part (b)] and energizes the motor through the taps. At the same instant, the timing relay is energized to begin its preselected timing cycle. As the motor accelerates toward full speed, the timing relay operates to open contactor S, which disconnects the autotransformers and closes contactor R, which connects the motor directly to the lines so that it runs normally on full voltage.

Note that in the foregoing sequence the motor is momentarily disconnected from the power supply during the transition from the starting mode to the running mode (contactor S must open before contactor R closes). This is referred to as *open transition*. This can cause a problem, as there could be a second inrush of current when the motor is reconnected to full voltage. To avoid this problem, the scheme shown in Figure 14.5(b) can be slightly modified. Instead of using one five-pole contactor for S and S_1, two separate contactors are used, one for contacts S and the other for contacts S_1. Then, in the transition sequence, contactor S_1 is opened first, with the motor then being fed through the remaining part of the transformer coils, which are now in series with the motor. Next, contactor R closes to connect the motor to the full voltage, and finally contactor S is opened to fully disconnect the autotransformer coils from the power supply. Since the motor is always connected to the power supply for the complete starting sequence, this is referred to as *closed transition*. Many manufacturers offer closed transition autotransformer starters as standard.

14.4.2 Wye–Delta Starters

The wye–delta starter uses the method of connecting the motor windings into a wye configuration to start and then switching the windings into a delta configuration to run. The reader should at this time review the wye and delta voltage and current relationships given in Section 1.6. Refer next to Figure 14.6(a). First, look at the voltage and current relationships if the motor is started in the delta configuration. This is in effect full-voltage starting, as the voltage applied across each motor winding is the full line voltage. Assume that the current through each phase winding is I_W. Then the line current I_L (FV) drawn by the motor is $\sqrt{3}I_W$. Now let us compare the wye mode of starting. The voltage applied across each motor winding is $1/\sqrt{3}$ or 57% of the line-to-line voltage, thus in effect applying a reduced voltage. This means that the motor winding current is $I_W/\sqrt{3}$, which is also the line current I_L (RV) drawn by the motor. Therefore, if the two line currents drawn by the motor are compared as shown, we see that the line current for the wye starting mode is only one-third that of line current in the delta (full voltage) mode. Also as shown, the starting torque in the wye mode is proportional to the square of the voltage applied across the motor winding and therefore is only one-third that for full-voltage starting. Thus the starting current and torque are both reduced by the same amount.

Figure 14.6(b) shows the power connections for the wye–delta starting. Three contactors are required to complete the start and run

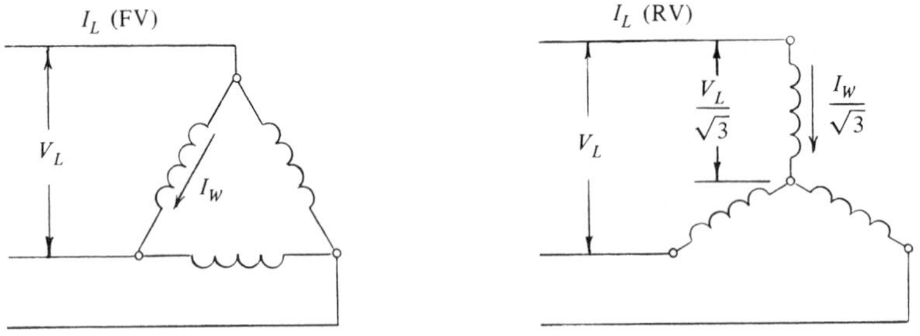

$I_L\ (\text{FV}) = \sqrt{3}\, I_W$

Motor started in the delta configuration
(i.e., full voltage)

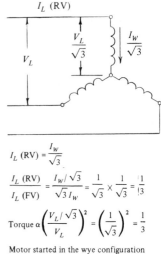

$I_L\ (\text{RV}) = \dfrac{I_W}{\sqrt{3}}$

$$\frac{I_L\ (\text{RV})}{I_L\ (\text{FV})} = \frac{I_W/\sqrt{3}}{\sqrt{3}\, I_W} = \frac{1}{\sqrt{3}} \times \frac{1}{\sqrt{3}} = \frac{1}{3}$$

$$\text{Torque}\ \alpha \left(\frac{V_L/\sqrt{3}}{V_L}\right)^2 = \left(\frac{1}{\sqrt{3}}\right)^2 = \frac{1}{3}$$

Motor started in the wye configuration
(i.e., reduced voltage)

(a) Comparison of starting currents and torques

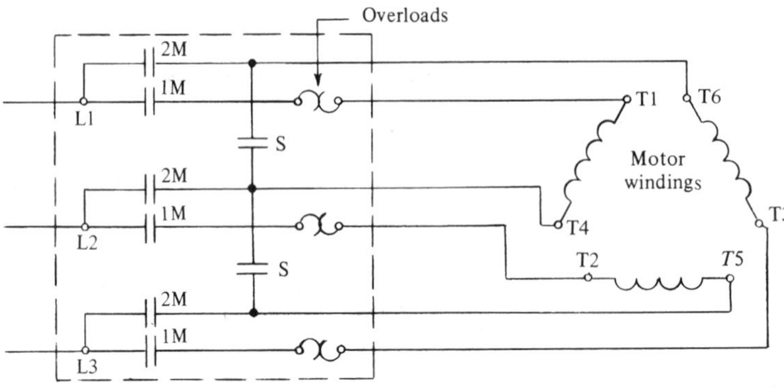

Note: This diagram shows the power connections only

(b) Power connections for starter and motor

FIGURE 14.6

Wye–delta reduced-voltage starting

sequence. The control circuit, which is not shown, is similar to that shown for the autotransformer starter in Figure 14.5(c), in that a timing relay is used to control the switching sequence. When the start button is pushed, contactor S closes to establish the wye point for the motor winding (joins terminals T4, T5, and T6) and contactor 1M closes to connect terminals T1, T2, and T3 to the power source. At the same instant, the timing relay is energized to begin its preselected timing cycle. As the motor accelerates toward full speed, the timing relay operates to open contactor S, breaking the wye point, and close contactor 2M to connect the motor in the delta mode for full-voltage operation.

The wye–delta starting is the only method that has a starting torque efficiency of 100%; that is, it maintains the same starting torque per ampere of current drawn from the line during reduced-voltage starting as compared to full-voltage starting. Also the starter is relatively inexpensive, as no resistors or autotransformers are required. However, offsetting these advantages are a few disadvantages. First, there can be no adjustments to the starting torque. If the one-third normal torque should fail to turn the motor over or should it accelerate the load too slowly, nothing can be done about the problem. Second, a special motor is required, one with all six winding leads brought out to the terminal box, as shown in the diagram. This can considerably increase the cost of the motor as compared to a standard motor. Finally, the starter as shown is open transition, as the motor must be disconnected for the transition from wye to delta. There is a method of converting the starter to a closed transition type, but it requires power resistors and extra contactors, which increase the cost. Nevertheless, this type of starter is often used to start large motors such as are used for air-conditioning units. These motors are generally custom built for the compressor units that they drive, and the units can be started unloaded.

14.5 MOTOR-CONTROL CENTERS

Where it is necessary to control a number of motors from one location, the use of a motor-control center is recommended. *Motor-control center* is a term applied to *a grouping of various motor-control units in a series of steel-clad enclosures bolted together to form a continuous structure,* such as shown in Figure 14.7. The standard 600 volt class motor-control center is made up of vertical sections 20 inches wide by 20 inches deep and 90 inches high. A set of main horizontal bus is run across the complete width of the structure, with vertical bus tapped off at each section to supply power to the individual drawout control units. Vertical wireways run the full height of each section, and horizontal wireways run across the total width, both at the top and bottom. These wireways accommodate all the control wiring between control units and to external control devices and power wiring from the control units to the motors. The motor-control center, when in operation, is completely dead-front; that is, no live parts are exposed to a person on the operating side of the equipment.

Motor-control centers are free standing; that is, they are self-supporting and can be floor mounted, allowing access from both the front and rear of the unit if desired. The complete motor-control

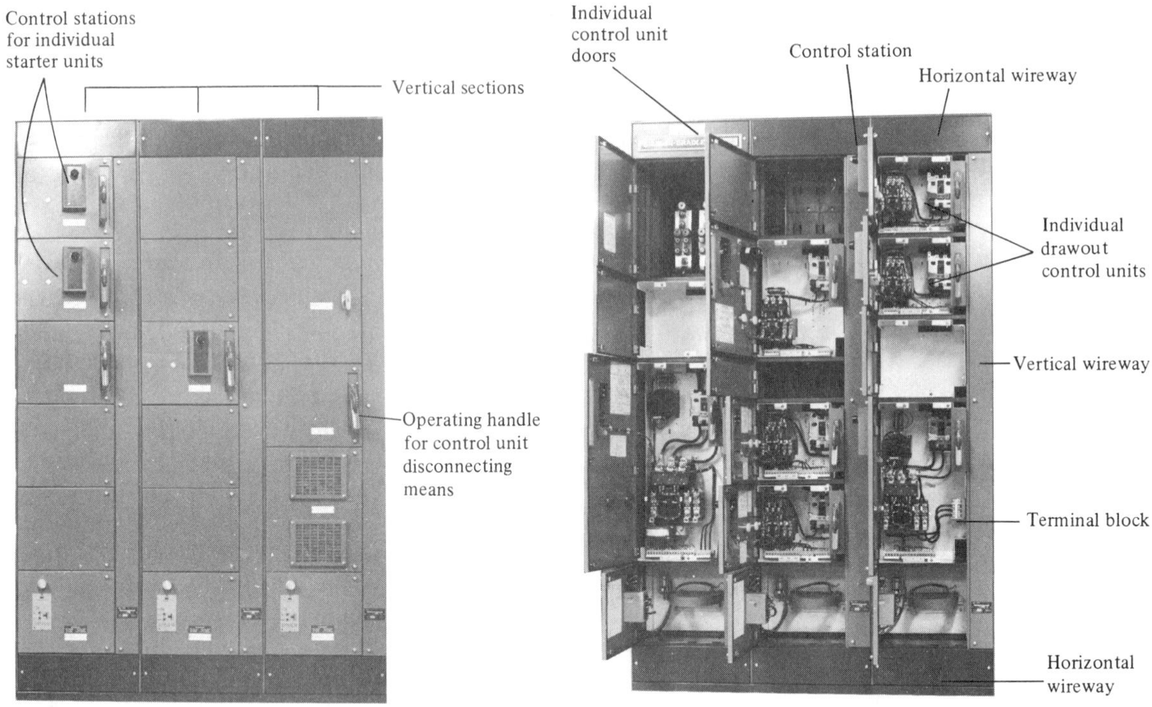

(a) Normal view of motor-control center

(b) View shown with control-unit doors open

FIGURE 14.7

Typical motor-control center, 600 volt class

center assembly is available in a variety of configurations, such as L-shaped and U-shaped, and with control units mounted on both the front and the back. However, the most common arrangement is a straight line, with the individual control units mounted on the front only, as shown in Figure 14.7. Motor-control centers can form part or all of the low-voltage distribution section of a unit substation (Section 15.4).

In industrial plants, the trend is to install complete motor-control centers in separate rooms adjacent to the center of the load, thus isolating them from the environment found in the manufacturing area. In commercial buildings, the motor-control centers are usually located in the various mechanical equipment rooms housing the supply and exhaust fans, pumps, and heating and air-conditioning equipment.

The most common control unit used in the motor-control center is the combination magnetic motor starter. However, a variety of other types of units are available. Feeder tap units that contain only a circuit breaker or a fused disconnect switch are used for feeders to remote equipment, such as heaters or motorized equipment that has its own built-in starter and/or control panel. Lighting panels can also be incorporated into the structure, complete with a step-down transformer where required. Thus the motor-control center can serve as the distribution point for all electrical loads within its area if so desired. Motor-control centers can reduce the total costs of electrical systems by keeping the on-site installation time and labor to a minimum. They offer a compact assembly of motor starters and associated equipment. The centralized location of the control units allows for convenient operation and easier maintenance. The modular arrangement provides for future expansion and/or realignment of the individual drawout units.

Each drawout control unit is assembled in its own enclosure, complete with spring-tempered stab fingers for plugging onto the vertical bus. This allows any unit to be easily withdrawn from its space in the motor-control center either for maintenance purposes or for replacement with a working unit. Typical drawout starter units with the unit doors open are shown in Figure 14.7(b). Each unit is complete with its own disconnecting device and magnetic starter. Short-circuit and ground-fault protection for the starter and motor branch circuit (Section 13.1.1) can be provided by either a fusible disconnect switch or a molded-case circuit breaker. The operating handle for the disconnecting means is interlocked with the unit door so that the door cannot be opened when the handle is in the on position. The handle can be padlocked in the off position to satisfy code requirements with regard to the disconnecting means for the motor (see Section 13.2.1 and Figure 13.5).

Each starter unit can be supplied with stop and start push buttons, selector switches, and/or pilot lights in a door-mounted control station for the individual control of the starter. A control transformer, if required, can be mounted within the drawout structure. The magnetic starter and its basic control scheme are all as previously described in Sections 14.2 and 14.2.1. All motor-starting types are available for installation in motor-control centers, including reversing starters (Section 14.3), autotransformer starters (Section 14.4.1) and wye–delta starters (Section 14.4.2).

The drawout control units are constructed on a modular basis; that is, they have standard incremental dimensions to allow for flexibility and variety of use. The smallest unit is normally 12 inches, with larger units increasing in increments of 6 inches (12, 18, 24, 30 inches, and so on). Typical space requirements for the various types of drawout units are shown in Table 14.3. An example of the layout for a motor-control center is given in Section 14.5.3. Although the table and example in this text use 6 inch increments, other modules based on increments such as $4\frac{3}{8}$, $6\frac{1}{2}$, or 7 inches are not uncommon.

TABLE 14.3 Space Requirements for Motor-Control Centers[a]

	Combination Starter Units			
	Number of Space Factors Required			
Starter Size[b]	**Full Voltage Nonreversing**	**Full Voltage Reversing**	**Reduced Voltage Autotransformer**	**Reduced Voltage Wye–Delta[c]**
Type				
1	2	3	—	—
2	2	3	6	5
3	4	4	9	6
4	4	4	9	7
5	6	10	12	12[d]
6	12	12[d]	12[e]	—
Fusible Switch Type[f]				
1	2	3	—	—
2	2	3	6	5
3	4	5	10	8
4	6	6	10	12
5	7	12[d]	12	12[e]
6	12	12[d]	12[e]	—

Feeder Tap Units			
Circuit Breakers		**Fusible Switches**	
Amperes	**Space Factors**	**Amperes**	**Space Factors**
100	2[g]	30	2[g]
150	2[g]	60	2[g]
225	3	100	2
400	4	200	4
		400	6

[a] Based on one space factor = 6 inches. Space factors based on 4$\frac{3}{8}$, 6$\frac{1}{2}$, and 7 inches are also common. All space requirements should be confirmed by manufacturer.

[b] See Table 14.1 for horsepower ratings.

[c] Horsepower ratings are higher than for other types of starters.

[d] Requires structure 24 inches wide.

[e] Requires structure 28 inches wide.

[f] Using UL class J fuses.

[g] Can be dual mounted (two breakers or switches in one drawout unit).

14.5.1 Classifications of Motor-Control Centers

The control schemes required for the motor starters and other control devices housed in the motor-control center can range from very basic (only stop–start push buttons located at each starter unit) to very complex (extensive electrical interlocking between starters and connections to remote pilot devices such as pressure, level, temperature, and speed sensing switches). Therefore, a range of options is available with regards to the degree of control wiring that is done by the manufacturer before the motor-control center is shipped to the site. The National Electrical Manufacturers Association classifications are defined as class I, types A, B or C, and class II, types B or C. A class I motor-control center is primarily a mechanical grouping of starter units requiring only a minimum degree of control wiring. A class II motor-control center is designed as a complete control system requiring system analysis and engineering, as well as interlocking and interwiring between units and provisions for connections to remote pilot devices. The types A, B, and C subclassifications cover the provision of terminal blocks and wiring. With type A, terminal blocks are not provided. Only the internal wiring within each starter control unit is completed. Any field wiring has to be brought into the individual unit for connection. With type B, terminal blocks are provided for each starter control unit [see Figure 14.7(b)] and all internal unit wiring is then connected to the terminal blocks. With type C, in addition to the terminal blocks at each unit, master terminal blocks are provided for each vertical section, mounted either in the top or the bottom horizontal wireway [Figure 14.7(b)]. All internal wiring is completed up to these master terminal blocks. The field wiring need only to be brought to these terminal blocks. The one exception is the power wiring for starters of size 3 and larger, in which case the feeder conductors from the motor have to be terminated at the starter loadside terminals. In summary, a class I, type A motor-control center incorporates very little control wiring, whereas a class II, type C motor-control center is a completely engineered and wired structure requiring only external field wiring to be connected to the master terminal blocks.

14.5.2 Standard Ratings for Motor-Control Centers

All components of motor-control centers are rated for use on systems up to 600 volts nominal. However, the operating coils of all starters and control relays must be rated for the actual control voltage that is used.

Power is distributed from the main incoming feeder lines throughout the motor-control center by three-phase main horizontal bus and by vertical bus at each section. The standard continuous current rating for the horizontal bus is 600 amperes, with optional ratings of 1000, 1200, 1600, and 2000 amperes being available. The vertical bus is available in ratings of 300, 450, and 600 amperes. The bus must also be braced to withstand the maximum available fault current that can exist at the incoming terminals of the motor-control center (see Section 6.2). The standard bus bracing rating is 22,000 amperes symmetrical, with optional ratings of 42,000 and 65,000 amperes being available. These continuous current and bus bracing ratings are typical, and each manufacturer should be consulted for the exact ratings offered. Examples showing the calculations of the available fault current for the purpose of selecting the bus bracing rating are included in Chapter 16.

The combination starter and feeder tap drawout units must also be able to withstand the stresses of the potential fault currents and to safely interrupt any fault currents caused by a short circuit on the feeder that they control. With the combination fusible disconnect type of control unit, the use of high interrupting capacity current-limiting fuses with interrupting ratings of 200,000 amperes rms symmetrical is recommended. Refer to Section 7.3 with regard to current-limiting fuses and Section 7.5 with regard to the classifications of low-voltage fuses.

The combination circuit breaker type of unit is listed for use where the available fault current at the motor-control center is a maximum of 22,000 amperes symmetrical. Reference to Table 8.1 shows that the interrupting rating of the standard molded-case breaker, 150 amperes or less, is only 14,000 amperes at 480 and 600 volts. This discrepancy is explained as follows. NEMA standards specify that the combination starter be tested with its output terminals shorted with minimum-length conductors. Therefore, the impedance of the breaker, starter contacts, overload relay heater elements, and wiring are in series during this test, all of which combine to lower the actual magnitude of the short-circuit test current. Furthermore, the test specifications require that any damage caused by the fault current be contained within the unit involved. This means that the unit may pass the test even though the starter or breaker may require repair or replacement. As an alternative to using the standard breakers, the more costly high-interrupting breakers can be used (see Table 8.1). A second alternative is to use fused circuit breakers (Section 8.7) to increase the interrupting rating up to 200,000 amperes. This arrangement has the advantage of being able to restore power quickly after clearing a low-level fault—the fuses having to be replaced only after clearing a high-level fault, which should be rare.

14.5.3 Layout of Motor-Control Centers

It is important that, early in the design process, the overall size of each motor-control center required for the electrical system be determined so that adequate space is allocated during the preliminary planning of the building. The following example illustrates the method of determining the overall size required for a motor-control center.

EXAMPLE 14.1

A motor-control center is to control the following motors using the type of starters given in Table 14.4. In addition, two 30kW, three-phase heating loads are to be supplied. The source of supply is 480 V, three-phase, and the motors are rated at 460 V, three-phase. The control units are the fusible switch type. Determine **(a)** the overall size of the motor-control center, and **(b)** the ampacity rating of the main bus.

TABLE 14.4

Number	HP	Type of Starter
4	$7\frac{1}{2}$	Full voltage, nonreversing (FVNR)
5	10	Full voltage, nonreversing (FVNR)
2	20	Full voltage, nonreversing (FVNR)
2	30	
2	40	Full voltage, reversing (FVR)
1	100	Reduced voltage, nonreversing (RVNR; autotransformer type)

Solution

(a) Based on Table 14.3, the space requirements for motor starters are given in Table 14.5.

TABLE 14.5

Motor Starters			No. of Space Factors	
Motor HP	Type of Starting	Starter Size (Table 14.1)	Each Unit	Total
$7\frac{1}{2}$	FVNR	1	2	4 × 2 = 8
10	FVNR	1	2	5 × 2 = 10
20	FVNR	2	2	2 × 2 = 4
30	FVNR	3	4	2 × 4 = 8
40	FVR	3	5	2 × 5 = 10
100	RVNR	4	10	1 × 10 = 10
				Total for starters = 50

Additional space factors are determined.

— Two 30 kW heating loads:

$$\text{load current} = \frac{30 \times 1000}{1.732 \times 480} = 38 \text{ A}$$

which requires two 60 A switches, dual mounted: 2 space factors
— Allowance for main incoming feeder cables: 1 space factor

Total required space factors is found.

$$50 + 2 + 1 = 53$$

— Maximum possible space factors per vertical section = 12
— Minimum number of vertical sections = $53/12 \approx 5$
— Total number of space factors = $5 \times 12 = 60$
Number used = 53
Number of spare space factors = 7

Figure 14.8 shows a suggested layout for the motor-control center. This example is meant to show the procedure only for laying out an MCC. The manufacturers should be consulted for their exact space requirements.

(b) Table 14.6 gives the calculation for ampacity of main bus. Note that it is the same as that required for the feeder to a group of motors (see Section 13.4).

TABLE 14.6

Motor HP	FLMA (A) (Table 13.2)		
100	123	125% of largest	= 1.25 × 124 = 155
$7\frac{1}{2}$	11	Plus 100% of remaining	4 × 11 = 44
10	14		5 × 14 = 70
20	27		2 × 27 = 54
30	40		2 × 40 = 80
40	52		2 × 52 = 104
Two 30 kW heaters			2 × 38 = 76
		Minimum ampacity	= 583 A

Select the standard main bus rating of 600 A.

It is also necessary to determine the available fault current at the mains of the motor-control center in order to specify the bus bracing. See Sections 16.3 and 16.5 for examples of the necessary calculations. See Section 13.3 for examples of the design of the individual motor branch feeders.

The motor-control center in Figure 14.8 can either be mounted free standing or, since the starters are mounted on the front of the unit only, it can be mounted against a wall. In either case, sufficient clear working space must be provided in front of the enclosure to

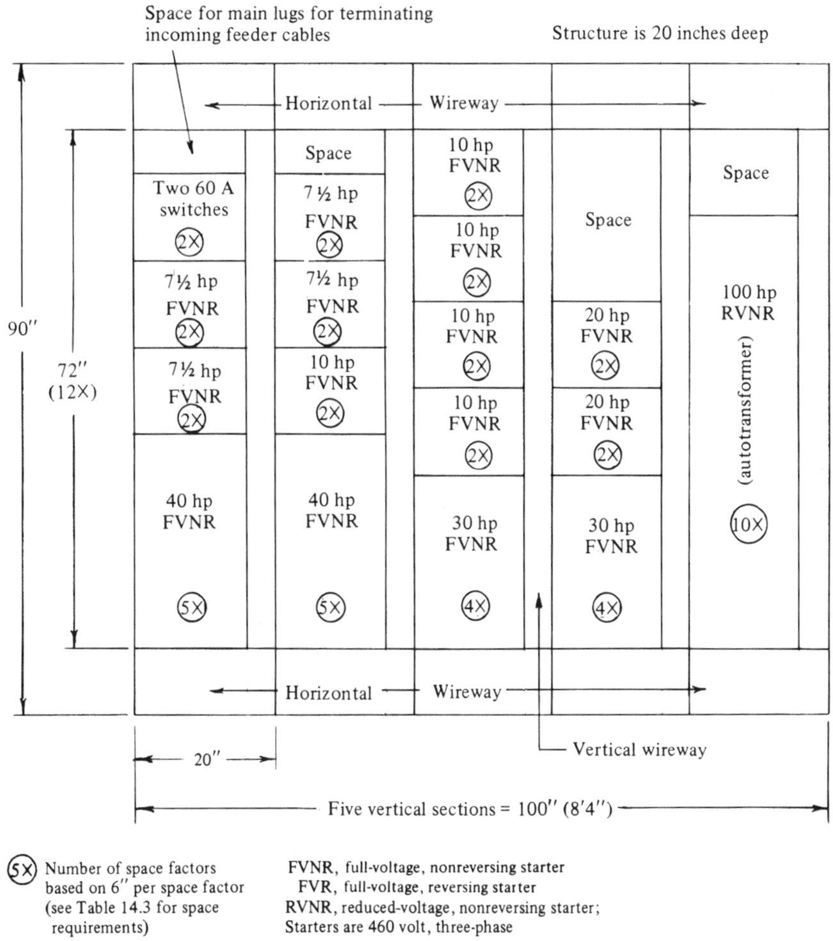

FIGURE 14.8

Layout of motor-control center for Example 14.1

permit ready and safe operation and maintenance of all devices. Section 110-16 of the *National Electrical Code* governs the working space about electrical equipment operating at 600 volts nominal or less. For the motor-control center in the foregoing example operating at 480 volts, there must be a minimum clearance of $3\frac{1}{2}$ feet from the front face of the unit to the nearest grounded surface (concrete, brick, or tile wall). In planning the location of the motor-control center, this working space requirement must be taken into account.

14.6 MEDIUM-VOLTAGE STARTERS

In industrial plants or large commercial buildings that distribute power at voltages above 600 volts, it may be more economical to supply large motors (above 200 hp) directly from the higher-voltage system, rather than step down the power to 480 volts (or even 600 volts). The increased cost of the higher-voltage control equipment can be offset by the reduced transformer and feeder capacities required. Medium-voltage starters rated up to 7.2 kilovolts and 10,000 horsepower are available, although the standard starters are normally rated for 5.0 kilovolts and a maximum of 2500 horsepower.

Medium-voltage starters operate basically the same as low-voltage magnetic starters. Naturally, the starters are much larger and bulkier because of the extra insulation and the need for large arc chutes to interrupt the currents at the higher voltages (see Section 8.1). Full-voltage and reduced-voltage, nonreversing and reversing starters are available to control squirrel-cage induction, wound-rotor induction, and synchronous motors.

A typical medium-voltage starter is made up as a complete assembly of components in a compact drawout unit. Up to three of these units can be mounted vertically in a free standing, 90 inch high, metal-enclosed structure, as shown in Figure 14.9. Each starter unit has electrical and mechanical interlocking to ensure that the starter has to be de-energized and isolated from the main power supply before the door to the unit can be opened. Short-circuit protection is normally provided by current-limiting power fuses (Section 7.8.2) that have a minimum short-circuit interrupting duty of 150,000 kVA at 2500 volts and 250,000 kVA at 5000 volts. Additional vertical sections can be bolted together as required, with the resulting metal-enclosed structure supplied complete with all bus work for distributing power to each individual starter unit, similar to low-voltage motor-control centers.

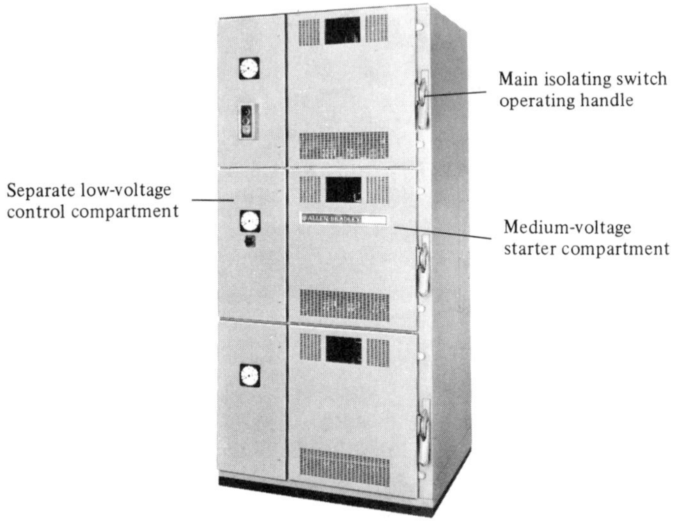

FIGURE 14.9

Typical medium-voltage starter enclosure (three-high construction)

Designation	Device Description
CAP	Capacitor
CPS	Control Power Switch
CPT	Control Power Transformer
CR	Control Relay
CT	Current Transformer
HFU	Fuse for CPT Primary
LB	Late Break
M	Main Line Contactor
MFU	Main Fuse
MIS	Main Isolating Switch
OL	Overload Relay
P1(M)	M Position Interlock
REC	Rectifier
MOV	Suppressor
TSP	Test Source Plug
XFU	Fuse for CPT Secondary
1R, 2R	Resistors

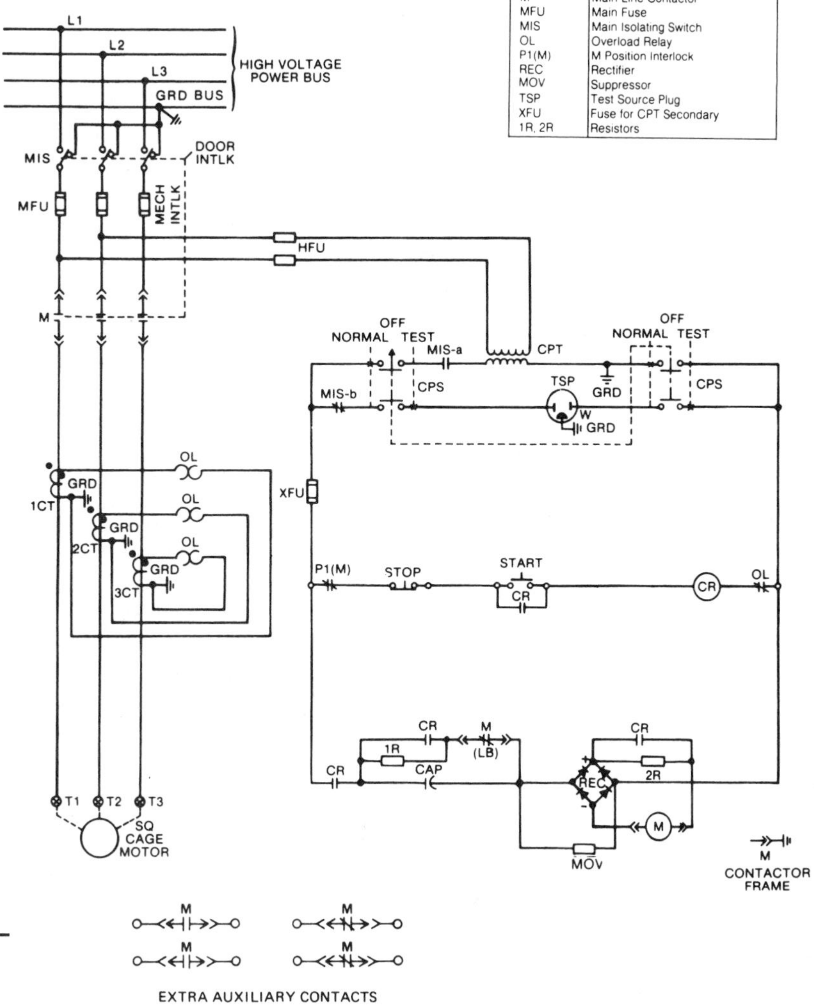

FIGURE 14.10

Typical wiring diagram for a medium-voltage starter

A typical wiring diagram of a medium-voltage starter unit is shown in Figure 14.10. This diagram shows the unit complete with a main isolating switch (MIS). However, the *NEC* permits the drawout feature of the starter unit to be used as the isolating means, providing that the unit can be locked in the drawout position. The control system for the starter has similar features to those described for the low-voltage starters in Section 14.2.1 in that momentary stop–start pushbuttons are used, which provides the advantages of three-wire control with undervoltage protection. The differences are that a control transformer is always used to step down the motor circuit voltage to a safe level and that the thermal elements of the overload relays are connected through current transformers as shown. In addition, the main line contactor coil M is energized through a rectifier (REC). As compared to ac operation, the use of dc to energize the operating coil gives a much more positive action to force the heavy contactor closed. Finally, there is a control power switch (CPS) at the secondary of the control power transformer that allows the control circuit to be transferred to a test source plug (TSP). An external control power source can then be connected to this plug so that the starter can be safely tested in its drawout position, that is, with the starter completely disconnected from the high motor circuit voltage. Ground-fault protection (Section 10.5) can be easily incorporated into the control scheme with the addition of a ground fault sensor similar to that shown in Figures 10.16(a) and 10.17.

The air break contactor has long been the standard for medium-voltage starters. However, the problem with interrupting a current in air is the distance that the moving contact must travel to fully extinguish the arc. As a result, when the contactor is closed, the impact when the contacts meet is severe. If the starter is required to perform repeated operations, the jarring of the mechanism can lead to early maintenance problems. A solution to this problem is the use of vacuum contactors. As previously discussed in Section 8.1 with regard to the opening of contacts in a vacuum, there can be problems with current chopping and the like. However, modern technology has largely overcome these problems, and vacuum contactors are now available for use in medium-voltage starters. One main advantage with interrupting an alternating current in a vacuum is that the arc only continues until the first current zero, at which instant a region of high dielectric strength is established between the contacts, preventing the arc from being reestablished. Since the arcing period does not exceed one half-cycle and the length of the arc is exceedingly small, the energy of the arc is considerably lower as compared to breaking the arc in air. With the short contact travel, the mechanical stressing on the contactor mechanism as it opens and closes is greatly reduced, leading to far less maintenance problems with repeated operations. Also, with the much smaller magnetic operating mechanism required and the absence of large arc chutes, the vacuum starter can be built as a very compact unit.

SUMMARY

- Manual starters can only be used for the starting and stopping of small motors.

- Full-voltage starting can only be used if the motor starting current does not cause serious disturbances on the electrical system.
- Magnetic starters are designated by their NEMA size number, which sets their maximum horsepower rating at a specific voltage.
- The function of the overload relays is to properly protect the motor against overloads and single phasing.
- Combination starters offer a safe, compact unit, combining disconnecting means and overcurrent protection with the magnetic starter.
- Three-wire control of a magnetic starter allows multiple stop and start points and provides undervoltage protection.
- Undervoltage protection prevents motors from all instantly restarting when power is restored.
- Step-down control transformers are normally used when the motor circuit voltage is 480 or 600 volts.
- If the rating of the motor branch-circuit overcurrent protection exceeds that allowed for the motor control circuit, then separate protection must be provided for the control circuit.
- The reversing of three-phase induction motors is accomplished by adding a second contactor to the starter to interchange two of the three motor leads.
- Reversing starters can also be used to plug a motor to a rapid stop.
- Reduced-voltage starters are used where full-voltage starting would otherwise cause unacceptable disturbances on the electrical system.
- The starting torque of a squirrel-cage induction motor varies as the square of the applied voltage. The resulting lower torque with reduced voltage starting could cause problems with the motor starting and accelerating up to speed.
- Starting torque efficiency is the ratio of the starting torque developed per ampere of line current when starting at reduced voltage, as compared to the starting torque developed per ampere of line current when starting at full voltage.
- The autotransformer reduced-voltage starter has the flexibility of the three tap settings and a very high starting torque efficiency and can easily be made closed transition.
- The wye–delta starter has 100% starting torque efficiency and requires no autotransformers or power resistors. However, it has no adjustments, is basically open transition, and requires a special motor.
- Motor-control centers offer a centralized location for the control of a group of motors.

- Motor-control centers are classified as class I, type A, B, or C, and class II, type B or C, which specifies the amount of internal wiring provided by the manufacturer.
- All components of motor-control centers are rated for a maximum of 600 volts nominal. The standard ratings for the main bus is 600 amperes continuous with 22,000 amperes symmetrical bus bracing. Higher ratings are available when required.
- Motor-control centers use modular plug-in units, allowing for flexibility in arrangement and ease of maintenance.
- Standard plug-in units using circuit breakers are rated for 22,000 amperes symmetrical, and those using current-limiting fuses are rated for 200,000 amperes symmetrical.
- Sufficient space for each motor-control center has to be allowed for in the planning of the building.
- Medium-voltage starters are available for controlling large motors where it is more economical to supply them directly from the higher-voltage distribution system.
- Standard medium-voltage starters are rated for a maximum of 5.0 kilovolts and 2500 horsepower.
- Medium-voltage starters using vacuum contactors offer a compact unit allowing many thousands of operations free of mechanical maintenance problems.

QUESTIONS

1. What are the advantages and disadvantages of manual starters?
2. What are the horsepower limitations of single-phase manual starters?
3. What are the horsepower limitations of three-phase manual starters?
4. When are magnetic starters required?
5. What does FVNR signify?
6. What are the limitations on starting a motor at full voltage?
7. Why must starters be horsepower rated?
8. What is the purpose of the overload relays on the starter?
9. Why are three overload relays used on three-phase starters?
10. What are the several advantages of combination starters?
11. What is a motor control circuit?
12. What is a normally open contact?
13. What is meant by a three-wire control scheme?
14. List the advantages of the three-wire control scheme.
15. When does the two-wire control scheme have to be used?
16. What are the disadvantages of the two-wire control scheme?
17. Why must the two contactors for a reversing starter be interlocked so that only one contactor can be closed at any one time?
18. What is meant by plugging a motor?
19. Explain why the starting torque of a squirrel-cage induction motor is directly proportional to the square of the starting voltage.
20. Why are reduced-voltage starters used?
21. What are the advantages of the autotransformer starter?
22. What are the advantages and disadvantages of the wye–delta starter?

23. What is meant by starting torque efficiency?
24. What is meant by closed transition with regard to reduced-voltage starters?
25. What is a motor-control center?
26. How is power distributed to each control unit in an MCC?
27. What is meant by free standing?
28. What are the advantages of motor-control centers?
29. What is a class II, type B motor-control center?
30. Why is the bus bracing rating of an MCC important?
31. Explain why the standard molded-case breaker with an interrupting rating of only 14,000 A can be used in an MCC rated for 22,000 A available fault current.
32. Why are medium-voltage motors and starters used?
33. How is short-circuit protection usually provided on medium-voltage starters?
34. What are the advantages of using vacuum contactors for medium-voltage starters?

PROBLEMS

1. What size of starter is required for the following motors: (a) 10 hp, 230 V, single-phase; (b) 10 hp, 200 V, three-phase; (c) 60 hp, 200 V, three-phase; (d) 60 hp, 460 V, three-phase.
2. A control circuit for a motor starter consisting of No. 14 copper conductors is contained entirely within the starter enclosure. The motor branch circuit is protected by a 100 A fuse. Does the control circuit require its own separate overcurrent protection? Explain your answer.
3. Repeat Problem 2, except that the control circuit extends beyond the starter enclosure.
4. A motor-control center is to control the following motors using the type of starters noted:

Five 10 hp, FVNR	One 30 hp, FVNR
Three 25 hp, FVNR	One 40 hp, FVNR
One 25 hp, FVR	One 75 hp, FVR

The source of supply is 208 V, three-phase, and the motors are rated at 200 V, three-phase. The control units are the circuit breaker type.
(a) Determine the overall size and draw a layout of the motor-control center.
(b) Determine the ampacity rating for the main bus.
5. Repeat Problem 4, except the supply is 480 V, three-phase, and the motors are rated at 460 V, three-phase.

15 Secondary Unit Substations

OBJECTIVES

After studying this chapter, you will be able to:

- Compare the advantages and disadvantages of the radial, secondary selective, and primary selective circuit arrangements.
- Discuss the advantages of the load-center system.
- Explain the operation of a load-interrupter switch.
- Identify primary switchgear using fused load-interrupter switches.
- Estimate the space requirements for dry-type transformers.
- Determine the general arrangement of circuit breakers in the low-voltage distribution section.
- Lay out a unit substation.
- Determine the space requirements for the unit substation.

INTRODUCTION

Secondary unit substations form the heart of all large industrial plant or commercial building electrical distribution systems. They receive the electrical power at the primary level as prescribed by the electrical utility and step it down to the utilization voltage level of 600 volts nominal or less for distribution throughout the building (or portion thereof). Figure 11.1 shows the one-line diagram of a building electrical system that does not include a main step-down transformer. This is the case when the electrical power is purchased from the electrical utility at a low-voltage level and then distributed at this same level throughout the building. This type of arrangement is usually confined to premises with only a few hundred kVA of load or to premises in areas where there is a concentration of loads and the electric utility has an extensive low-voltage secondary network to provide for larger loads (for example, downtown areas of cities). In other cases, the electric power is purchased at higher voltage levels, requiring a substation to be installed on the customer's premises. Many utilities offer billing savings of as much as 5% to customers who own their own transformers and associated switchgear.

A secondary unit substation consists of primary incoming line, transformer, and low-voltage distribution sections, coordinated in design so that when joined together they form one overall continuous and uniform enclosure complete with all interconnecting buswork. The primary and secondary distribution sections can be made up using different types of switchgear (fused switches or circuit breakers) as required to suit the many variations in the system requirements. The switchgear can also be arranged to suit different power distribution methods.

The unit substation is completely enclosed on all sides with sheet metal (except for the required ventilating openings and viewing windows) so that no live parts are exposed to a person on the operating side of the equipment. Access within the enclosure is provided only through interlocked doors or bolted-on removable panels. The unit is factory assembled and tested according to the appropriate American National Standards Institute (ANSI) and National Electrical Manufacturers Association (NEMA) standards and is designed to require a minimum amount of labor for installation at the site. Large units may have to be divided into smaller sections for the purpose of shipping to the site.

Because of the importance of the unit substation in the electrical system, it is necessary to plan the overall layout of each unit. This planning must be done early in the design process so that, for one thing, adequate space can be allocated in the building. This chapter concludes with an example layout for a unit substation, showing the minimum space requirements for its installation.

The circuit diagrams presented in this chapter use the one-line format. The reader should review the comments in the Introduction to Chapter 11 and Figure 13.1 with regard to one-line diagrams.

15.1 TYPES OF CIRCUIT ARRANGEMENTS

Many types of circuit arrangements can be selected for substations, although only three basic types are discussed here: the radial, the secondary selective, and the primary selective. The choice as to which circuit arrangement to use is usually a compromise between cost and service reliability. The degree to which the extra costs can be justified depends on the reliability of the power source and the characteristics of the load being fed. First, the power supply to the building must be very reliable before the extra cost to increase the reliability of the building system can be justified. Second, the characteristics of the load within the building should be such that any major power outage would result in heavy production losses. As an example, for an industrial plant with a continuous process, short outages may result in the spoilage of considerable material, and it may take many hours to fully restore the process. In this case, extra costs can be justified to increase the reliability of the building distribution system to minimize these production losses.

15.1.1 Radial System

The radial system is the simplest of the circuit arrangements in that there is only one primary feeder and one transformer through which the associated secondary bus is served. Figure 15.1(a) shows the one-line diagram of a typical radial system. This system is the least costly as there is no duplication of equipment and it is the easiest and safest to operate, since there is only the one source of power. However, the obvious disadvantage with this system is that the loss of the primary feeder or a fault on the transformer results in the loss of the entire substation load until the trouble has been cleared. A less obvious drawback is that the maintenance of the system is more difficult, as the substation load must be shut down before any work can be done on the primary feeder or transformer. These planned outages for maintenance may be more of a handicap than the infrequent forced outages.

Figure 15.1(b) shows the physical layout of a typical secondary unit substation using the radial system arrangement. This type is also referred to as a single-ended substation, as there is only a primary incoming line section at the one end of the unit. Note that Figure 15.1 shows drawout-type circuit breakers for the low-voltage distribution section. Fixed molded-case breakers or fused switches could also be used.

15.1.2 Load-Center System

In early radial systems, a single substation, located at the point of the primary service entrance, was used to supply the total load of the building complex. For systems covering a large area, this arrangement required long, large-capacity, and costly low-voltage feeders to distribute the power throughout the building or complex. The modern trend is toward the load-center system using the radial-type circuit arrangement shown in Figure 15.2. The load-center concept allows the power to be distributed at the highest economical voltage level (usually 4.16 or 13.8 kilovolts) to areas of concentrated load where the voltage is transformed down to the utilization level (for example, 480Y/277 volts). The utilization equipment can then be supplied using relatively short low-voltage feeders.

The load-center type of distribution has been made possible by the development of dry-type medium-voltage switchgear and transformers that do not require expensive fireproof vaults and by the development of lower-cost medium-voltage feeder cables [Figure 11.2(d)]. The primary distribution switchgear can be the metal-clad

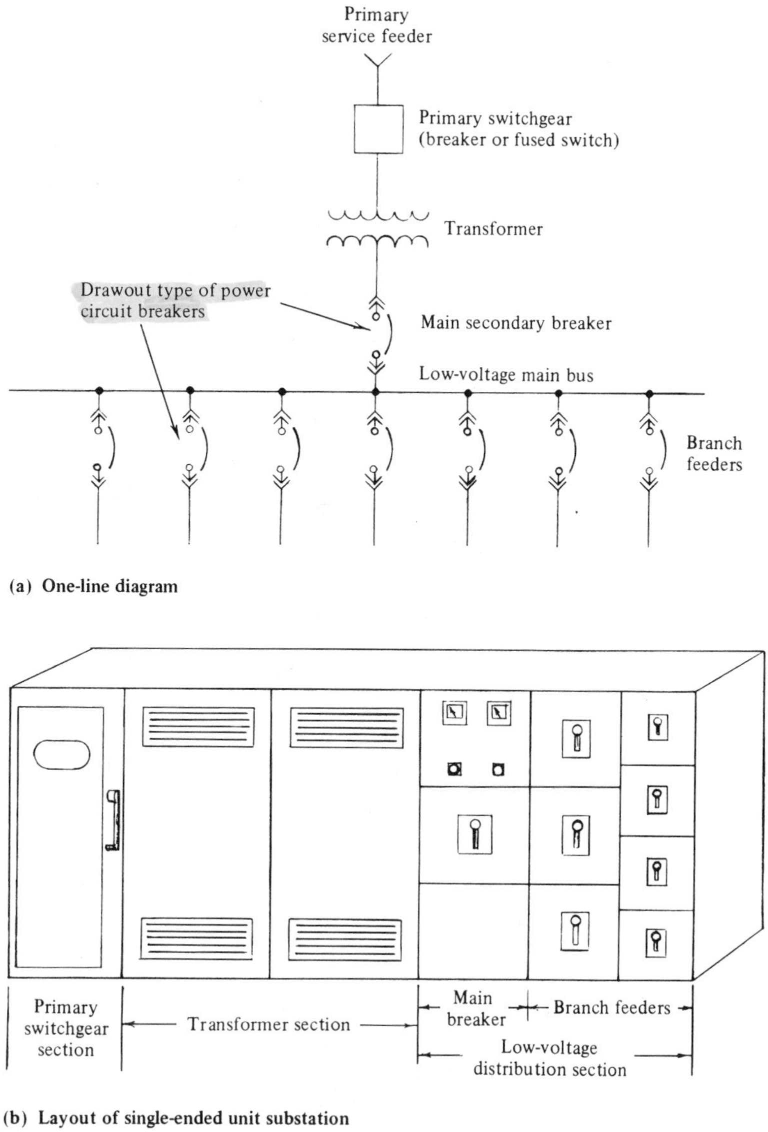

FIGURE 15.1

Typical radial system

type using either medium-voltage air circuit breakers (Section 8.10 and Figures 8.19 and 8.20) or load-interrupter switches (Section 15.2.1 and Figure 15.6). Each load center is in itself a radial type of substation, as shown in Figure 15.1.

The added cost of the load centers can be offset by the savings in the cost of feeders. With the older type of single-substation system, the cost of the long low-voltage feeders for distributing the power

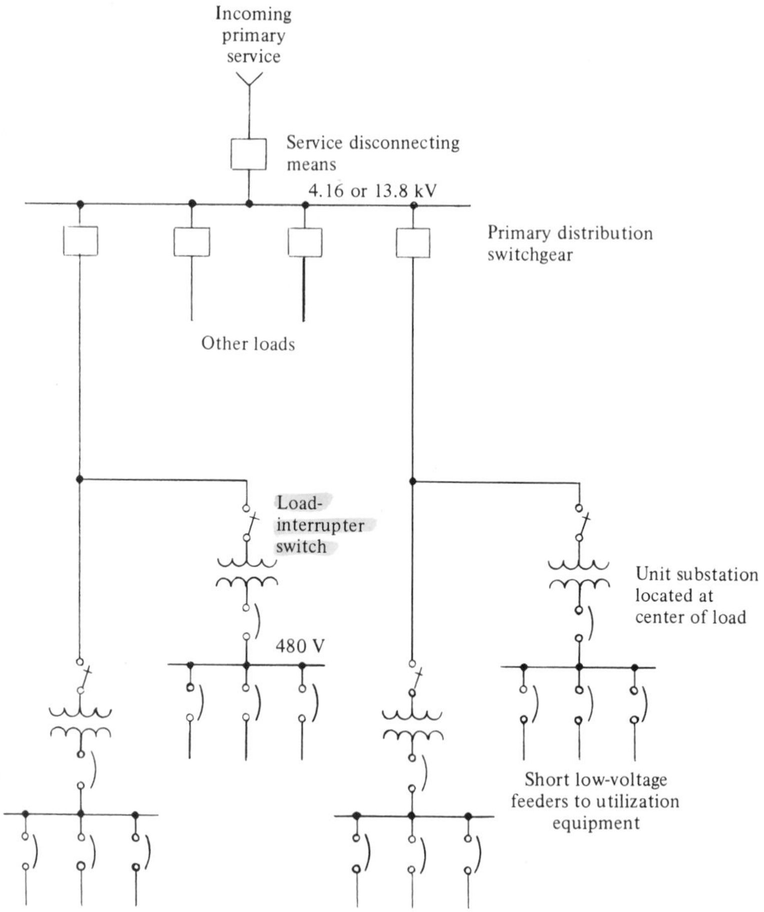

FIGURE 15.2

Load-center system using radial-type circuit arrangement

can be high because of the number of large parallel conductors required to keep the voltage drop within acceptable limits. On the other hand, using higher voltages to distribute power over the longer distances within the building complex substantially reduces the size of the conductors required. Not only are the ampacity requirements per kVA of power transmitted much lower, but also the voltage drop is seldom a problem. Furthermore, the use of a number of smaller substations, rather than one large substation, results in lower available fault current levels at the secondaries of the transformers. Additional savings can be realized because lower interrupting capacity circuit breakers can be used for the protection of the low-voltage feeders. Examples 16.2 and 16.4 show the effect of transformer kVA ratings on the levels of available fault current. The load-center distribution type of radial system should be considered when the total load on a system exceeds 1500 to 2000 kVA, especially if the area to be served is extensive.

15.1.3 Secondary Selective System

The secondary selective system overcomes the major disadvantage of the radial system in that it provides duplicate paths of supply to the secondary bus of each load center. This system has two step-down transformers, each with its own incoming primary feeder, as shown in Figure 15.3(a). The secondary bus associated with each transformer is connected through a tie breaker. Normally, the system is operated with the tie connection open, that is, as two separate radial systems operating independently of each other. However, with the loss of one of the primary feeders and/or transformers, the main secondary breaker for that circuit can be opened and the tie breaker closed, allowing the one remaining primary feeder and transformer to energize all the secondary bus. The service to one-half of the load is momentarily interrupted during this transition period.

The degree to which the total load can be continuously supplied from the one remaining transformer depends on its kVA rating. As a very minimum, each transformer can have just sufficient capacity to handle its own share of the load. Thus, in an emergency only some 50% of the total load can be picked up, the 50% being priority loads, with the less essential loads being dropped. As a maximum, each transformer can be rated to handle the total load. During an emergency, one transformer can then pick up the entire load on the secondary buses with no problem. Naturally, it costs extra to provide this reserve capacity. Usually the kVA rating selected is a compromise between the two extremes; for example, each transformer is sized to handle 75% of the total load. Normally, some loads can be dropped during an emergency.

There are two possible arrangements for the secondary selective system. In the first arrangement, shown in Figure 15.3(a), the total system is enclosed in one complete unit, such as shown in part (c). This arrangement is known as a double-ended unit substation, as there is a primary incoming line section at both ends of the substation. Only one tie breaker, as shown, is required to interconnect the two sections of secondary bus. In the second arrangement, the two sections of the system are actually two single-ended substations located some distance apart and then interconnected through a tie feeder. This arrangement requires a tie breaker at each end of the tie feeder, as shown in part (b).

The tie breaker(s) is normally interlocked with the two main breakers so that the tie connection cannot be made unless one main breaker is open. This prevents the two transformers from being operated in parallel, a condition that would almost double the amount of fault current available at the secondary bus and would materially increase the cost of providing the higher interrupting capacity secondary feeder breakers. Therefore, it is preferable to interlock the system so that the maximum fault current available

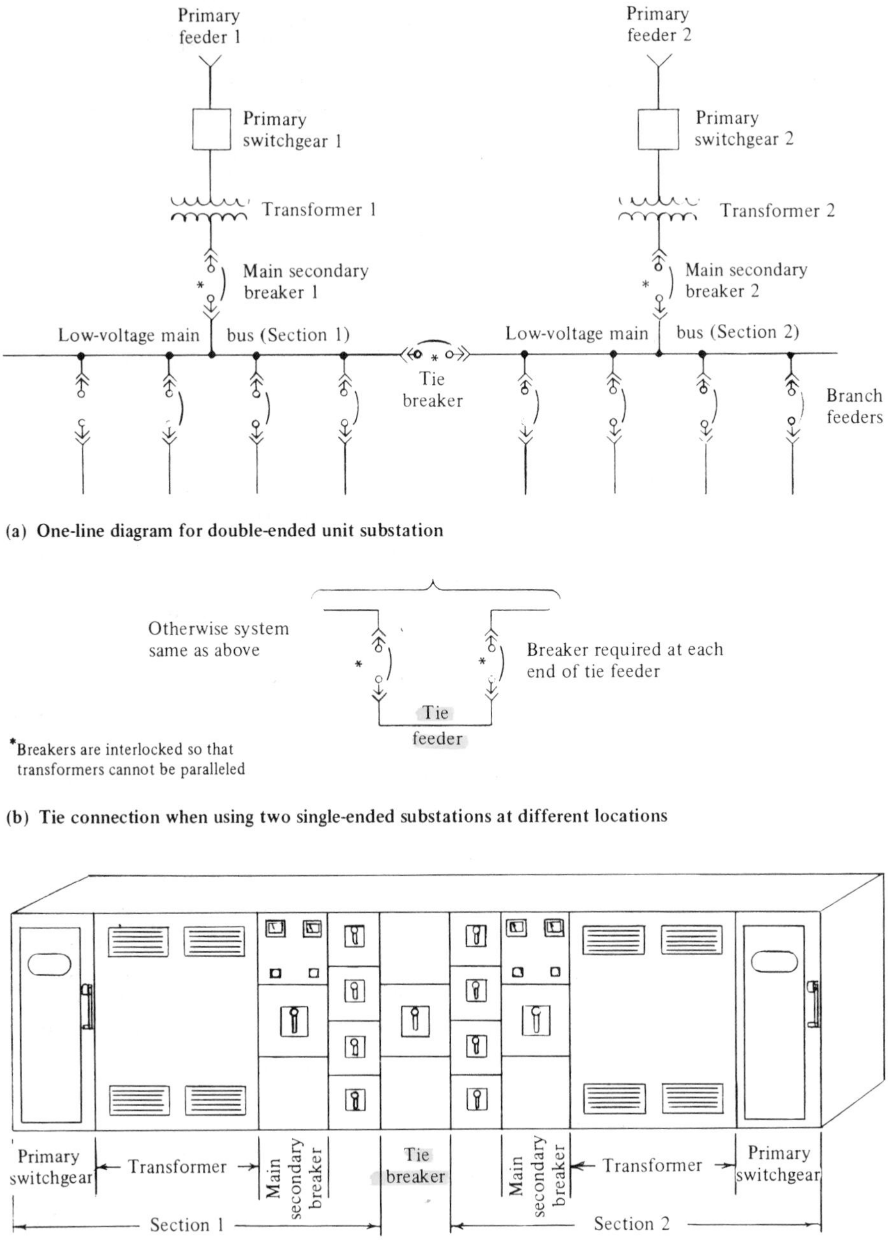

(a) One-line diagram for double-ended unit substation

(b) Tie connection when using two single-ended substations at different locations

(c) Layout of double-ended unit substation

FIGURE 15.3

Typical secondary selective system

under any condition is only the current that can be provided through the one feeder and transformer.

The closing of the tie breaker under emergency conditions can be done either manually or automatically, depending on how urgent it is to pick up the lost load. With automatic operation, voltage sensing relays are connected to each section of the secondary bus. Upon sensing the loss of voltage on one section, these relays initiate the tripping of the associated main secondary breaker, the closing of the tie breaker(s), and, if necessary, the shedding of any nonessential loads. This automatic scheme must, however, have an overriding feature that blocks the transfer of power if one of the main secondary breakers has been tripped due to a fault on its section of the low-voltage bus.

The obvious advantage of the secondary selective system is the increased service reliability provided to the system. A less obvious, but equally important, advantage is the extra flexibility that it allows for maintenance. Work can now be scheduled without the necessity of a prolonged power outage, at least to the essential loads. Naturally, the system costs more than the radial system, especially if reserve capacity is provided in each transformer. Also, the system is more complex to operate because of the possibility of incorrectly interconnecting the two sources of power.

15.1.4 Primary Selective System

The primary selective system also offers duplicate paths of supply, but only as far as providing two primary feeders to each substation, as shown in Figure 15.4. The complete system normally incorporates a number of substations supplied through two primary feeders, with the substations equally distributed between the two. In the event that one feeder is out of service, the system is designed so that the remaining feeder has sufficient capacity to carry the entire load.

As with the secondary selective system, service to one-half of the load is interrupted when a fault occurs on one of the primary feeders. The transformers normally supplied from the faulted feeder then must be switched over to the good feeder to restore service. The use of two circuit breakers at each substation to perform the transfer from one feeder to the other is the safest method. However, the relatively high cost of the breakers often precludes their use unless an automatic transfer scheme is required. The normal practice is to use two load-interrupter switches (Section 15.2.1) interlocked so that only one switch can be closed at any one time.

As with the secondary selective system, the primary selective system offers increased service reliability. It also provides flexibility in allowing scheduled outages for maintenance on the primary feeders. Its major drawback is that the loss of a transformer still means that all the load connected to that substation is shut down until

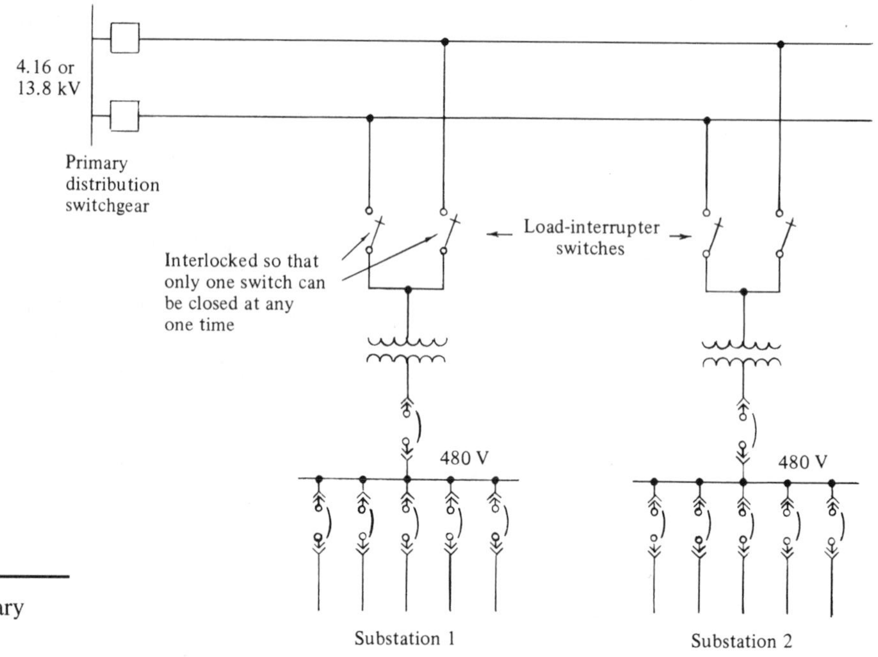

FIGURE 15.4

One-line diagram of primary selective system

temporary connections can be made to an alternative secondary source. However, transformer faults usually happen much less frequently than feeder faults.

The physical layout of a typical unit substation using the primary selective system is similar to that shown in Figure 15.1(b), except there are two primary incoming line sections located side by side at one end of the enclosure.

15.2 PRIMARY INCOMING LINE SECTION

The primary incoming line section incorporates the terminations for the primary feeder cables and the primary switchgear all housed in one metal-clad enclosure. The switchgear used can range from load-interrupter switches, fused or unfused, to drawout circuit breakers. The latter, as described in Section 8.10, provide the ultimate in primary protection and flexibility in operation and maintenance. However, because of the high cost of breakers, the medium-voltage load-interrupter switch offers an acceptable alternative.

15.2.1 Load-Interrupter Switches

A load-interrupter switch (sometimes referred to as a load-break switch) is designed to safely interrupt a current up to the continuous ampere rating of the switch. Figure 15.5 shows one method of providing this load-interrupting capability. Part (a) shows the switch in the closed position, with the load current flowing through the main

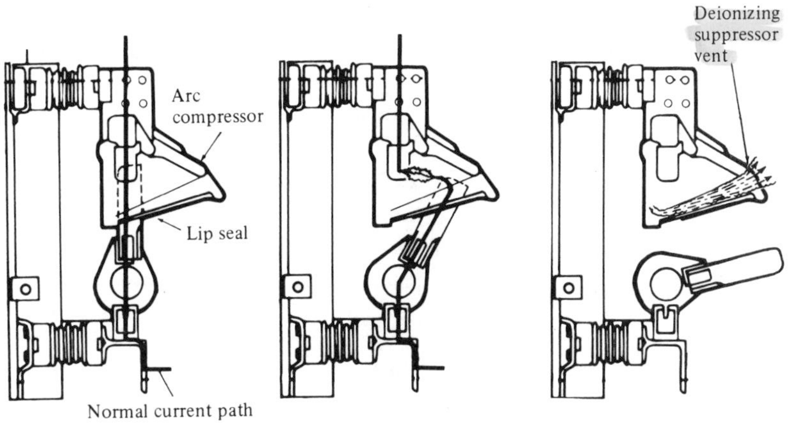

(a) Switch in closed position

(b) Switch blade separates from main contact at high-speed; arc compressor provides controlled circuit interruption without external arc or flame

(c) Unique lip seal wipes blade as blade exits arc compressor, keeps the arc under compression, and directs controlled arc gases through the deionizing suppressor vent

FIGURE 15.5

Opening sequence of medium-voltage load-interrupter switch

contacts and switch blade. Parts (b) and (c) detail the opening sequences. By combining high-speed opening action with arc suppression, the current is interrupted without any external arc or flame. The switches are normally gang operated; that is, all three blades are opened and closed simultaneously. This quick-make, quick-break mechanism uses the stored-energy method, which incorporates springs to rapidly force the switch blades open and closed. The speed of operation of the switch blade is not dependent on the speed with which the operating handle is moved.

It must be emphasized that load-interrupter switches can safely interrupt currents only up to their continuous ampere rating and can therefore be used only for switching under normal load conditions. They cannot be used to interrupt fault currents. However, as part of its switching functions, the switch could inadvertently be closed in on a faulted feeder. The switch mechanism must therefore have the ability to safely withstand the tremendous mechanical forces created by the fault currents as the switch contacts touch to make the circuit. The operating handle must not kick back and endanger the operator. This is known as the *make rating* of the switch. When the load-interrupter switch is combined with fuses to provide for overcurrent protection of a circuit, the switch must also be able to withstand the peak fault current that occurs during the first cycle until the fuse blows to clear the fault. This is known as the *momentary rating* (see Section 6.6). Standard ratings for load-interrupter switches are 600 and 1200 amperes, 5 and 15 kilovolts, although they are also available up to 34.5 kilovolts. The make and momentary ratings are a minimum of 40,000 amperes rms symmetrical.

Load-interrupter switches are also used in applications where only disconnecting means are required at the unit substation. Such an application occurs when the substation forms part of a load-center system, as shown in Figure 15.2. Overcurrent protection for the primary of each substation is provided by the branch feeder device in the primary distribution switchgear. The load-interrupter switch allows each unit substation to be shut down and isolated without interfering with the other loads on the same primary feeder.

In smaller plants or commercial buildings where only one secondary unit substation is required to supply the entire load, the primary switchgear must provide overcurrent protection for the primary of the transformer, as well as serve as the service entrance disconnecting means. In this case, the load-interrupter switch is combined with power fuses. Figure 15.6 shows a typical metal-enclosed switchgear cubicle complete with a three-pole, gang-operated load-interrupter switch and three power fuses. Interlocks are provided so that access to the fuses is only possible when the switch operating handle is in the off position. For details and ratings of power fuses, see Section 7.8.1 and Table 7.4. As an alternative, the new electronic fuses as described in Section 7.8.3 can be used.

Incoming line section cubicles containing fused load-interrupter switches are typically 36 inches wide, 90 inches high, and 54 inches deep to match the adjoining transformer cubicle. When primary metering is required, the necessary potential and current transformers can also be mounted within the cubicle. The cubicle comes complete with all necessary interconnecting bus work, starting from the point of termination for the incoming feeder cables.

15.2.2 Lightning Protection

In many instances, lightning protection is also required at the primary switchgear location. If the premises are supplied from a distribution system, any part of which runs overhead, protection from lightning surges should be provided. Lightning discharges can produce excessive voltages on electrical systems either by direct stroke or by induction. Protection against direct strokes at outdoor substations is provided by overhead ground wires that intercept the lightning strokes and deflect them to ground. However, the majority of lightning surges are caused by induction. A lightning stroke sets up a tremendous electrostatic field. When the field collapses, it induces high voltages into adjacent overhead power lines. These voltage surges then travel at high speeds along the lines away from the point of origin. Service entrance equipment inside buildings should there-

a, Steel enclosure
b, Bulkhead-type door
c, Interior screen
d, Load-interrupter switch
e, Power fuses (see Figure 7.14)
f, Cover for switch operator and controls
g, Stored-energy switch operator
h, Open-phase (single-phasing) detector
i, Voltage sensors (one for each phase)

FIGURE 15.6

Typical metal-enclosed medium-voltage fused load-interrupter switch

fore be protected against these traveling voltage waves, which enter the system through the service entrance cables.

It is characteristic of most insulations that the voltage stressing that they can successfully withstand varies inversely with time. Power distribution equipment is required to withstand two different types of voltage stressing tests. The first is a test at low frequency (60 hertz) with a moderate overvoltage for a duration of 1 minute. The second is an impulse test to prove that the insulation will not break down on voltage surges of high magnitude but extremely short duration (on the order of microseconds). The peak value of the maximum voltage surge that the equipment can successfully withstand establishes the basic impulse level (BIL) for the equipment being tested.

It is the function of the surge arrester (formerly referred to as a lightning arrester) to limit the overvoltage from any induced traveling wave to a value below the BIL rating of the equipment being protected. It does this by providing a low-impedance conducting path to ground. This low-impedance path must not exist before the overvoltage appears, and it must be immediately broken after the voltage returns to normal. This is accompanied in the surge arrester by an enclosed air gap that can withstand the normal operating voltage, but will spark over and become conducting at a higher voltage. In series with the spark gap is a column of material whose resistance varies inversely as some power of the voltage. This column, known as a valve, has a low resistance at high voltages (when the surge arrester is discharging) and a high value at low voltages (when voltage returns to normal). This valve aids in interrupting the arc in the gap, which prevents any power-frequency current from flowing to ground after the surge has passed.

The application of surge arresters requires a thorough knowledge of their characteristics and ratings. The reader should consult the reference listed in the Bibliography for a more detailed discussion of lightning protection. Article 280 of the *National Electrical Code* covers the general requirements for surge arresters installed on premises wiring systems.

15.3 TRANSFORMER SECTION

This section houses the transformer for stepping down the primary voltage to the low-voltage utilization level (see Section 1.7). Ventilated dry-type transformers using air as the insulating and cooling medium are now universally used for secondary unit substations located inside buildings.

Mineral insulating oil, because of its superior dielectric properties, has long been used as an insulating and cooling medium for transformers. However, oil-filled transformers create a severe fire and explosion hazard and as such either have to be mounted outdoors or in expensive fireproof and explosion-proof vaults if installed indoors. To overcome this requirement, askarel-filled transformers were developed some years ago. The synthetic askarel has the same excellent insulating qualities as mineral oil, but it will not burn or explode. However, askarel contains polychlorinated biphenyls and can therefore cause severe environmental problems. Because of great concern in the past few years regarding contamination from polychlorinated biphenyls, this type of transformer has rapidly lost favor. As a result, the dry-type transformer, which does not constitute any fire, explosion, or environmental hazard and which requires little if any maintenance, is the accepted type to use for indoor installations. Dry-type transformers with 80°C rise or higher ratings and of completely enclosed and ventilated-type construction do not have to be installed in a room of fire-resistant construction (*NEC* Section 450-21).

The transformer enclosure where possible is constructed to match the overall dimensions of the primary and secondary switchgear sections. Table 15.1 shows standard kVA ratings and typical cubicle dimensions for 5 and 15 kilovolt ventilated dry-type transformers up to 2500 kVA as used for unit substations. With the continued development of solid-type insulating materials, dry-type transformers are now also available with primaries rated up to 34.5

TABLE 15.1 Ratings and Typical Cubicle Dimensions for Dry-Type Transformers Used with Unit Substations

	Dimensions of Transformer Cubicle (in.)					
	5 kV Class			15 kV Class		
kVA Rating[a]	H	W	D[b]	H	W	D[b]
112½	90	30	54	90	30	54
150	90	30	54	90	30	54
225	90	30	54	90	42	54
300	90	42	54	90	90	54
500	90	42	54	90	90	54
750	90	90	54	90	90	54
1000	90	90	54	90	100	54
1500	90	100	54	90	100	54
2000	90	100	54	100	100	54
2500	90	100	54	100	100	54

[a] Some manufacturers offer additional ratings to those listed.

[b] Depth can be increased to match other sections of unit substation where required.

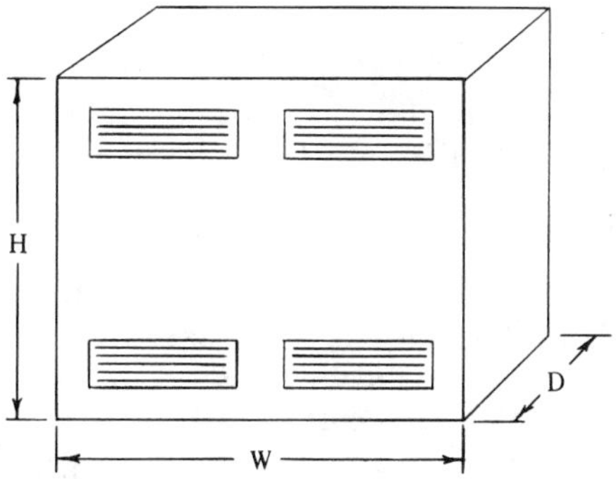

kilovolts and ratings up to 5000 kVA. See Section 16.2 with regard to the effect of the transformer kVA rating on the level of available fault current.

15.4 LOW-VOLTAGE DISTRIBUTION SECTION

The low-voltage distribution section provides the protection and control for the low-voltage feeder circuits. This switchboard section may consist of fusible switches, molded-case circuit breakers, power circuit breakers, or any combination of these devices. Motor-control center assemblies (Section 14.5) can also form part or all of the low-voltage section.

The selection of the type of device to use for a particular application should take into account functional requirements, economic factors, and safety requirements. Refer to Chapters 7 and 8 for a complete discussion and comparison of the use of fuses, molded-case circuit breakers, and low-voltage power circuit breakers, including the combination fused circuit breakers and the new type of encased breaker. Since these low-voltage encased breakers offer most of the same ratings and operating characteristics as the standard type of power circuit breakers, for the purposes of the discussions in this chapter they are assumed to be included with power circuit breakers. From purely economical considerations, fused switches generally have the lowest initial cost, followed by molded-case circuit breakers, with the power circuit breakers having the highest initial cost. All these devices are completely safe when properly applied and maintained.

When fused switches are used for the low-voltage switchboard section, the form of construction usually incorporates the panelboard type of arrangement shown in Figure 7.12(b), with one or more of these vertical panelboard sections being used as required. The standard ratings of general-use fusible switches are listed in Table 7.2. On all but the smallest ratings of unit substations, a power circuit breaker is usually used for the main secondary protection and disconnecting means ahead of the fused switches.

When molded-case breakers are used for the low-voltage switchboard section, the form of construction may incorporate the panelboard type of arrangement shown in Figure 8.10(b), with one or more of these vertical panelboard sections being used as required. As an alternative, the molded-case circuit breakers can be individually mounted in their vertical position, either singularly or in groups, with the operating handles extending through the front panels of the switchboard enclosure. The ratings of standard and high-interrupting capacity molded-case circuit breakers are listed in Table 8.1.

Drawout-type power circuit breakers are normally preferred on large systems, especially in industrial plants, because of the importance of the unit substation in the overall system. Power circuit breakers offer a wide selection of operating characteristics and adjustments, making it possible to obtain excellent coordination with other protective devices in the system. A typical drawout type of power circuit breaker is shown in Figures 8.11 and 8.12. The ratings of power circuit breakers are listed in Table 8.2, and those of the newer encased type of circuit breakers are listed in Table 8.3.

Individual power circuit breakers are installed in separate compartments so that the breakers are isolated from each other and from the bus. The breaker cubicles are designed on a modular basis so that combinations of cubicles and instrument panels can be mounted in 90 inch high vertical sections. These vertical sections are then joined together to form the overall switchboard unit. A typical cross section through a low-voltage switchboard is shown in Figure 15.7, indicating three breakers mounted one above the other and with an instrument panel at the top. Instruments can be ammeters, voltmeters, watt-hour meters, and so on. Also, where protective relays are used to control breakers (Chapter 9), these relays are also mounted in the instrument panel. This cross section shows a breaker in the connected position (compartment B), in the test position (compartment C), and in the disconnected position (compartment D). The test position allows the operation of the breaker to be checked without repeatedly making and breaking the power circuit to the branch circuit load.

Note the separate secondary contacts shown at the top of the breaker. These contacts are included on any electrically operated breaker where the control circuit has to be extended to remotely located control devices. The secondary contacts are still engaged in the test position, even though the main power disconnecting contacts have separated. Refer also to Figure 8.11, which shows a picture of a power circuit breaker in the fully connected position [part (a)] and in the fully withdrawn position [part (b)]. Figure 8.12 shows the disconnecting contacts on the rear of the breaker that engage with the fixed contacts in the breaker cubicle.

Figure 15.7 also shows the bus compartment, which contains the horizontal main bus that electrically ties the vertical sections together and the vertical bus that connects to the lineside of each individual breaker. There is then space at the rear of each section for the outgoing feeder cables. The main bus and tap connections usually consist of bare tin-plated aluminum bars. Copper bus with silver-plated connections, which is more expensive, is available as an option. Standard continuous current ratings for the main horizontal bus are 1600, 2000, 2500, 3000, and 4000 amperes. All the switchgear and bus work is rated for a maximum of 600 volts nominal. The main bus must also be properly braced to withstand the maximum possible fault current (see Section 6.2). The standard bus bracing rating is

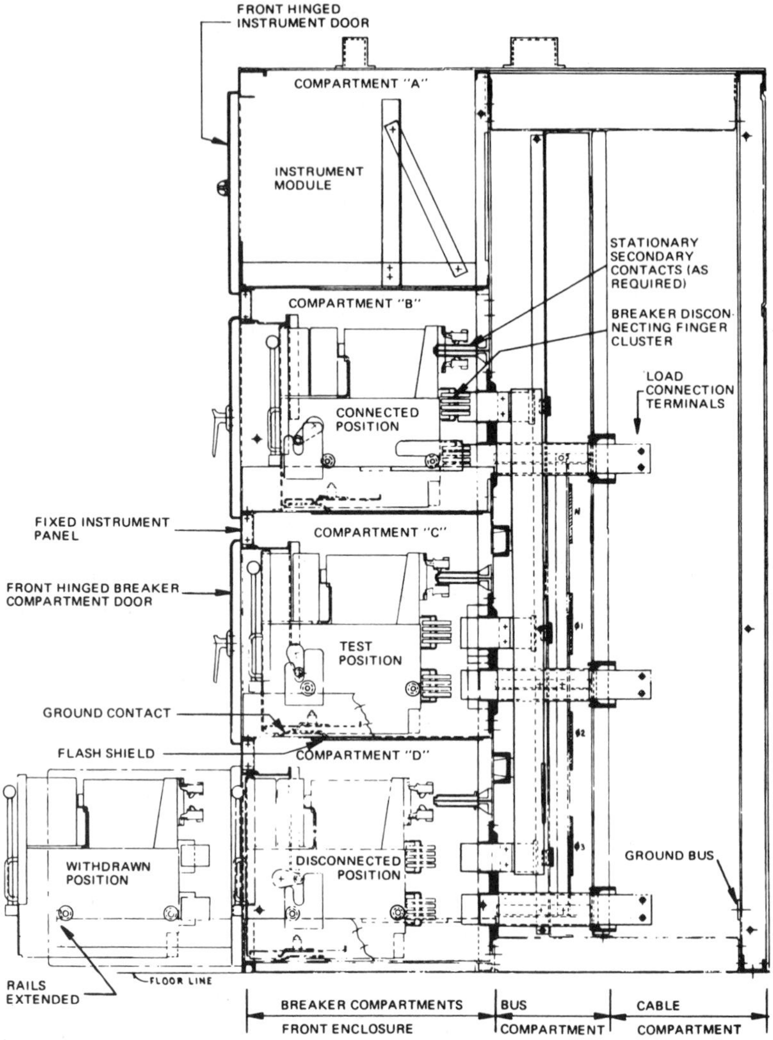

FIGURE 15.7

Cross section through typical low-voltage switchboard (refer also to Figure 8.11)

42,000 amperes symmetrical, with optional ratings of 65,000 and 85,000 amperes symmetrical being available. These continuous current and bus bracing ratings are typical, and each manufacturer should be consulted for the exact ratings that are offered.

A few of the possible modular stacking arrangements for the low-voltage power circuit breakers and associated instrument panels are shown in Figure 15.8. These diagrams are meant only to be representative arrangements, as there are variations in requirements between manufacturers. For example, unit 3 shows the 1600 ampere frame size breakers as being mounted in a three-high vertical ar-

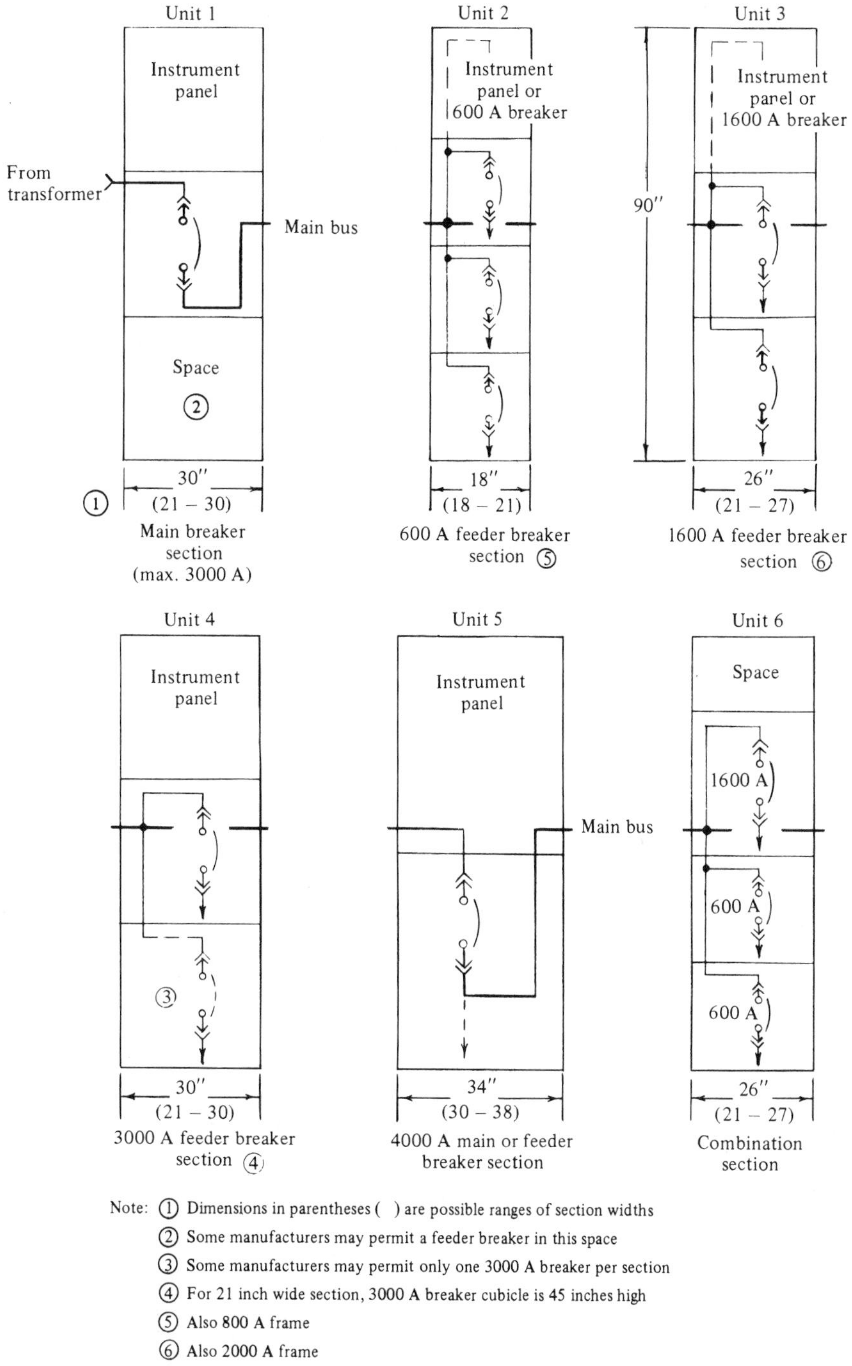

FIGURE 15.8

Modular stacking arrangements for low-voltage circuit breaker switchboards rangement. One manufacturer allows this size of breaker to be mounted four high in one vertical section, providing that their total trip settings do not exceed a specified amount (1800 amperes). This restriction is required because of the accumulated heat produced under load conditions by the breakers when stacked four high. Other possible variations are shown on the diagram. Wherever possible, breakers of the same frame size are mounted in the same vertical section or sections. However, when this is not possible, breakers with different frame sizes can be accommodated in the one vertical section, such as shown for unit 6.

15.5 EXAMPLE LAYOUT OF UNIT SUBSTATION

It is important that, early in the design process, the overall size of each unit substation required for an electrical system be determined so that adequate space is allocated during the preliminary planning of the building. The following example illustrates the method of determining the expected size of a unit substation.

EXAMPLE 15.1

A unit substation is required to step the incoming 13.8 kV, three-phase primary service down to 480Y/277 V for distribution throughout the building. The circuit arrangement will be the basic radial system using a single-ended substation. The primary switchgear will be a fused load-interrupter switch. The transformer will be the dry-type with 5.75% impedance. Preliminary estimates of the total building load indicate that a 1500 kVA transformer is required. The low-voltage switchgear will be the drawout type of power circuit breaker. There will be a main breaker and seven feeder breakers to distribute the power throughout the building. The continuous loading on any one feeder breaker will be a maximum of 500 A. The calculated available fault current at the main secondary bus is 37,000 A symmetrical, which includes the contribu-

Solution

(a) Draw a one-line diagram as shown in Figure 15.9(a).

(b) Calculate the full-load primary current: Using Equation 1.14,

$$I_p = \frac{1500 \times 1000}{1.732 \times 13.8 \text{ kV}} = 63 \text{ A}$$

As in Section 15.2, the standard 15 kV, 600 A fused load-interrupter switch will be satisfactory. The primary switchgear cubicle is 36 in. wide (Figure 15.6).

(c) Refer to Table 15.1. The transformer cubicle for 15 kV, 1500 kVA is 100 in. wide.

(d) Calculate the full-load secondary current:

$$I_s = \frac{1500 \times 1000}{1.732 \times 480 \text{ V}} = 1804 \text{ A}$$

Minimum ampacity = 1.25 × 1804 = 2255 A (See Section 16.5)

Main bus: select standard rating of 2500 A (minimum).
Main breaker: from Table 8.2, select 3000 A frame with interrupting rating of 65,000 A symmetrical.
From Figure 15.8, select unit 1, 30 in. wide.

(e) Branch breakers: Referring to Table 8.2, it is noted that the 600 A frame breakers (as required for the expected continuous loading on each feeder) have an interrupting rating of only 30,000 A symmetrical at 480 V, whereas 37,000 A is available. Therefore, all branch breakers will have to be the 1600 A frame size with an interrupting rating of 50,000 A symmetrical and with trip ratings to suit feeder full-load currents. From tion from the motors. (Section 16.5 shows a complete example of the calculation of the available fault current.) Determine the layout of the unit substation.

Figure 15.8, three vertical units similar to unit 3, each 26 in. wide, are required for the seven 1600 A feeder breakers, leaving two spaces for future breakers.

(f) Draw the overall outline of the unit substation as in Figure 15.9(b). The overall depth of the unit is estimated to be 66 in. This depth is required for the low-voltage section to accommodate the 2500 A main bus and to provide sufficient space at the rear for the outgoing branch feeder cables.

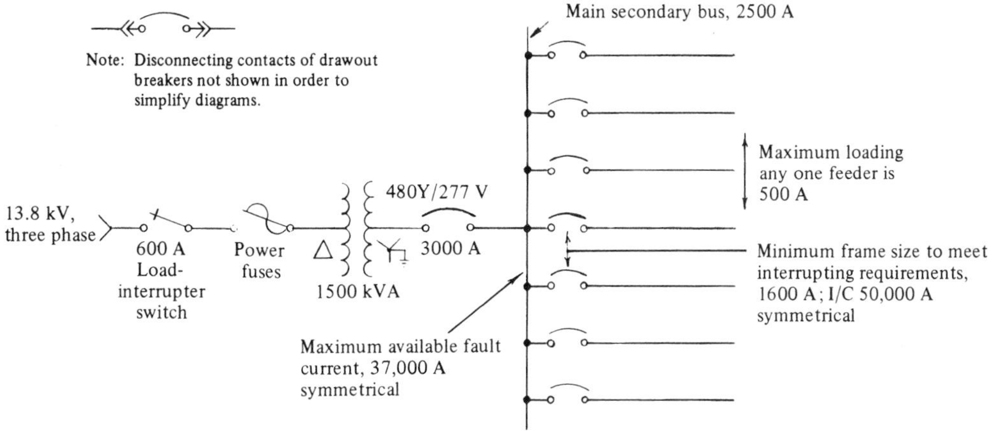

(a) One-line diagram of system

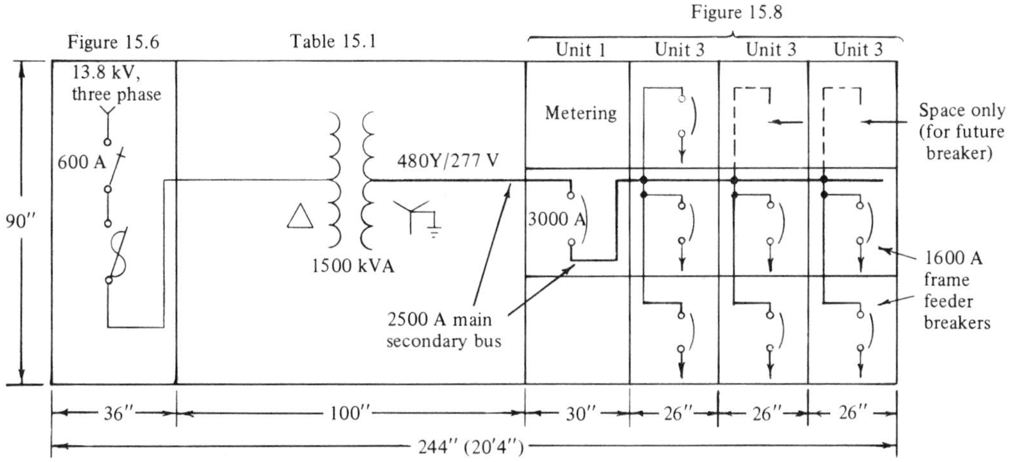

(b) Outline of unit substation

FIGURE 15.9

Layout of unit substation for Example 15.1

In the foregoing example layout of the unit substation, in place of using the 1600 ampere frame standard breakers, the combination fused circuit breakers could be selected. As described in Section 8.7, the addition of the current-limiting fuses increases the interrupting capacity of a breaker unit to 200,000 amperes, thus allowing the 600 ampere frame breakers to be used for the branch feeders. As shown in Figure 8.16, the breaker and fuse are coordinated so that the fuses blow to clear fault currents above approximately 80% of the interrupting rating of the breaker itself. Thus, with the 600 ampere breaker, the fuses will blow on fault currents above 80% of 30,000, or 24,000 amperes. The use of the 600 ampere fused breakers means that only two vertical sections, each similar to unit 2, are required for the seven feeder breakers. Four breakers can be stacked in one vertical section and the remaining three stacked in the second vertical section, leaving one space for a future breaker. With reference to Figure 15.9, this would decrease the space required for the branch feeder breakers from 3 times 26 = 78 inches to 2 times 18 = 36 inches, for a saving of 42 inches. The overall length of the substation would then be 16 feet, 10 inches. The disadvantages of using the fused breakers are the longer downtimes on high-level faults in order to replace the fuses and the necessity of having to stock replacement fuse elements.

The reader should also refer to Chapter 16 and Example 16.5 for a complete design with regard to selecting all the ratings for the devices installed in a unit substation and for the selection of the primary fuses and trip ratings of the circuit breakers for coordination.

15.6 LOCATION OF UNIT SUBSTATIONS

In industrial plants, for systems that require just the one unit substation to step down the incoming primary power to the low-voltage utilization level, the substation is usually located in a separate room near the entrance point of the service. The service entrance feeder is very often run underground from a pole at the edge of the property. In larger industrial plants using the load-center concept as shown in Figure 15.2, the unit substations should be located as close to the center of the load as possible. In production areas where a separate room would take up valuable space, very often a mezzanine area is constructed on which to locate the unit substation. The space below can then be utilized for tool cribs, shop offices, and the like. Access to the mezzanine must be by a permanent set of stairs or by a fixed ladder.

In larger commercial buildings that receive their power at above utilization levels (4.16 or 13.8 kilovolts) the unit substation is normally located in a separate room in the basement near the point of entry of the service feeder. In very tall office buildings, a second unit substation is usually located in the mechanical penthouse at the top of the building; some extremely tall buildings have additional units located at intermediate floors, again in mechanical equipment areas. These unit substations are then fed by medium-voltage feeders (4.16 or 13.8 kilovolts) from the primary switchgear located in the basement.

Sections 110-30 to 110-34 of the *National Electrical Code* govern the installation of electrical equipment over 600 volts. In particular, sufficient access and working space must be provided and maintained about all electrical equipment to permit ready and safe operation and maintenance of such equipment. With dead-front equipment, which is normal with unit substations, the minimum clear working space that must be maintained from the front panel of the unit to any adjacent vertical grounded surface (concrete or brick wall, metal fencing) is 5 feet for equipment operating at 4.16 kilovolts) and 6 feet for equipment operating at 13.8 kilovolts. Since unit substations have removable panels at the rear, the same clear working space must also be maintained at the rear of the unit, as well as at each end to provide access. Note that the clearance is required at both ends so that a person cannot be trapped behind the unit with only one way out should trouble arise, such as the equipment flashing over and arcing to ground. Finally, the working space must permit at least a 90-degree opening of equipment doors or hinged panels. See Appendix A for Canadian Electrical Code requirements.

For switchboards exceeding 6 feet in width, which includes most unit substations, there must be one entrance to the working space around the unit located at each end of the switchboard. An exception to this allows one entrance only to the area, providing the required working space in front of the switchboard is doubled or where the switchboard location permits a continuous and unobstructed way of exit travel.

Figure 15.10 shows the minimum space (size of room) required to accommodate the unit substation detailed in Example 15.1 and Figure 15.9. It would be prudent to increase the final size of the room or area above the minimum size required to allow for flexibility in design and space for future expansion of equipment.

The unit substation should be located in a dry area. Dust or corrosive atmospheres should be avoided. Adequate ventilation of the substation area must be provided to ensure proper cooling of the dry-type transformer. A typical requirement calls for 3 cubic feet of air movement per minute for each kilovolt-ampere of transformer capacity. Thus, for the unit substation in Example 15.1 and Figure 15.10, the minimum air movement for the substation area is three

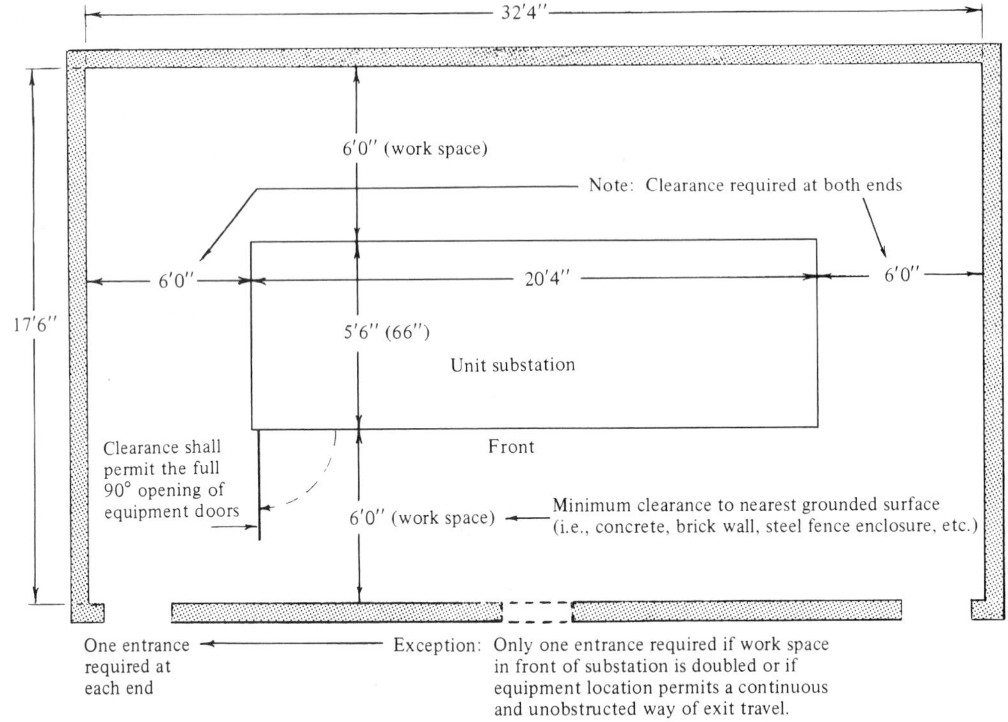

FIGURE 15.10

Space requirements for unit substation in Example 15.1

times 1500, or 4500 cubic feet per minute. Forced ventilation (a fan) is usually required to provide this air movement.

SUMMARY

- Unit substations offer a coordinated and integrated switchgear and transformer package, factory assembled and tested, requiring a minimum amount of labor for installation at the site.
- The radial system is generally the least expensive of the circuit arrangements and the easiest to operate, but it is the least reliable.
- The secondary selective system is more reliable and offers flexibility with regard to scheduled maintenance, but it costs more and is more difficult to operate.
- The primary selective system also is more reliable, but it costs more and a fault on the single substation transformer shuts down all load on that substation.
- The modern trend for large electrical systems is the use of the load-center system, which allows the power to be distributed at the highest economical voltage level.
- The load-interrupter switch and fuse assembly are widely used for the primary switchgear of unit substations.

- The load-interrupter switch can interrupt currents only up to its continuous current rating, normally either 600 or 1200 amperes.
- Lightning protection should be provided if the unit substation is supplied from a distribution system, any part of which runs overhead.
- Dry-type, air-cooled transformers are universally used in unit substations as they do not require any special fireproof vault construction.
- The low-voltage distribution section can utilize fusible switches, molded-case circuit breakers, power circuit breakers, or a combination of these devices.
- The fused switches generally have the lowest initial cost, followed by molded-case circuit breakers, with the power circuit breakers being the most expensive.
- The drawout power circuit breakers are normally preferred on large systems because of their wide range of operating characteristics.
- The overall size of the unit substation should be estimated early in the design stages so that adequate space can be allocated for its installation.
- Adequate working space must be provided around each unit substation to permit ready and safe operation and maintenance of the equipment.
- The substation area should be dry, free of dust and corrosive atmospheres, and adequately ventilated.

QUESTIONS

1. What are the advantages and disadvantages of the radial system?
2. What are the advantages of the load-center system?
3. Describe the secondary selective system.
4. What are the advantages and disadvantages of the secondary selective system?
5. With the secondary selective system, why must the tie breaker(s) be interlocked with the main secondary breakers so that the tie connection cannot be made unless one of the main breakers is open?
6. When is it necessary to block the automatic transfer of power in a secondary selective system?
7. What are the advantages and disadvantages of the primary selective system?
8. How much current can a load-interrupter switch safely interrupt?
9. Why is the load-interrupter switch referred to as being quick make, quick break?
10. Explain the make rating of a load-interrupt switch.
11. Why must the load-break switch have a momentary rating?
12. What is the significance of the BIL rating of equipment?
13. What is the basic function of a surge arrester?
14. Why are dry-type transformers normally used for indoor unit substations?
15. Why is the test position provided for drawout-type low-voltage circuit breakers?
16. What are the standard continuous current ratings and bus bracing ratings for the main bus of

the low-voltage distribution section of a unit substation?

17. What are the basic space requirements with regard to installing a unit substation in a room?

18. What is the requirement with regard to ventilation of the room housing a unit substation?

PROBLEMS

1. A unit substation has a 4.16 kV-480 V, three-phase, 1000 kVA transformer. Available fault current at the main secondary bus is 25,000 A symmetrical. Calculate the rated secondary current of the transformer and select the frame size of the main secondary breaker.
2. For the unit substation in Problem 1, select the frame size of a branch feeder breaker (low-voltage power type) if the continuous load on the feeder is 400 A.
3. A unit substation has a 4.16 kV-208Y/120 V, three-phase, 750 kVA transformer. Available fault current at the main secondary bus is 37,500 A symmetrical. Calculate the rated secondary current of the transformer and select the frame size of the main secondary breaker.
4. For the unit substation in Problem 3, select the frame size of a branch feeder breaker (low-voltage power type) if the continuous load on the feeder is 900 A.
5. Repeat Example 15.1, except that the incoming primary service is 4.16 kV, the secondary voltage is 208Y/120 V, the transformer is 1000 kVA, the number of feeder breakers is 10, the maximum loading on any one feeder is 400 A, and the available fault current is 50,800 amperes symmetrical.
6. Determine the minimum length and width of room required to house the unit substation of Problem 5.
7. Repeat Problems 5 and 6, except that combination fused circuit breakers will be used for the branch feeders.

16 Fault Calculations and System Coordination

OBJECTIVES

After studying this chapter, you will be able to:

- Calculate the per unit impedance of the utility system source.
- List the sources of short-circuit currents.
- Include the motor contribution to available fault currents.
- Calculate the equivalent system fault impedance.
- Calculate the effect of system components on fault currents.
- Calculate the per unit impedance of a feeder.
- Use rules of thumb to simplify fault calculations.
- Calculate fault currents at specific points on the system.
- Select the heater elements for motor starter overload relays.
- Coordinate the motor branch-circuit protective device with the overload relays.
- Follow the design of a complete system.
- Select the necessary settings for circuit breakers.
- Follow the coordination of a complete system.

INTRODUCTION

As discussed in the Preface, the primary function of the electrical system is to provide electrical energy to each piece of utilization equipment at the correct voltage and phase relationship and with sufficient capacity to supply the required current on a continuous basis, without any component overheating or causing unacceptable voltage drops. If only the normal operation of the system had to be considered, then the design of the system would be much simpler. However, since nothing that is manufactured can be deemed to be perfect, the system must also be capable of safely handling any abnormal situation that can arise. Therefore, an equally important aspect of the design of the system is the proper selection, application, and coordination of those devices that operate to protect the system when an abnormal condition does occur. The proper coordination of these protective devices ensures that any power outages due to faults on the system are restricted to as small a section of the system as possible and that any resulting damage is kept to an absolute minimum.

So far in this text, we have generally been looking at individual parts of the electrical system, such as substations, feeder cables, circuit breakers, fused disconnect switches, motor starters, panelboards, and branch circuits. In this last chapter, we will now concentrate on looking at the electrical system as a whole with respect to its ability to continuously handle the normal loads and to properly protect itself when an abnormal condition arises.

The reader should review Chapter 6 with regard to the priorities of system protection, the problems associated with electric faults, and the functions of protective devices in dealing with these faults. The reader should also review Section 7.7 on the coordination of low-voltage fuses and Section 8.6 on the coordination of circuit breakers, as these introduce the reader to the first applications of system coordination. The examples in this chapter expand on the basic methods of calculating fault currents and obtaining coordination between protective devices.

16.1 CALCULATION OF FAULT CURRENTS

The first step in providing adequate protection to a system is to calculate the magnitude of the available fault current at specific locations in the system. Protective devices such as fuses and circuit breakers must have sufficient capacity to safely interrupt the largest possible fault current that can occur at their location in the system. Other parts of the system, such as switches, feeder cables, bus duct, and bus bars, must be capable of withstanding the mechanical and thermal stresses associated with these large fault currents (Section 6.2).

The term *available fault current* means *the maximum current that can flow under the worst possible fault conditions*. Important assumptions in the fault calculations are that the fault itself is *bolted;* that is, it has zero impedance (see Section 6.3) and that it is a three-phase fault. These assumptions not only simplify the calculations but also add a margin of safety, as they result in the maximum possible fault current. Actual fault currents are usually less than the calculated three-phase bolted value. Bolted line-to-line fault currents are approximately 87% of the three-phase values. In industrial and commercial systems, bolted line-to-ground faults rarely exceed the three-phase values. Furthermore, absolutely zero impedance bolted faults seldom happen. Any degree of fault impedance will act to reduce the magnitude of the fault current. In fact, many faults involve arcing, which reduces the magnitude of the fault currents because of the relatively high resistance of the arc. Arcing faults and ground-fault protection are discussed in detail in Sections 10.4 and 10.5.

The reader is first introduced to fault current calculations in Chapter 6 and in particular in Section 6.4, where the concept of per unit values is developed. We will now expand on the examples in Section 6.4 to show how more complete fault calculations are done.

In Example 6.2, the primary utility feeder to the transformer is assumed to have an impedance of 1.0% (0.01 per unit). This value is obtained by comparing the system kVA with the maximum three-phase short-circuit kVA that the utility system can produce at the service entrance location. The equivalent per unit impedance of the utility system connection can then be obtained as follows:

$$Z_U = \frac{\text{base kVA}}{\text{short-circuit kVA}} \quad \textbf{(16.1)}$$

where Z_U = per unit impedance of the utility system.
base kVA = chosen system three-phase kVA (usually the transformer kVA)
short-circuit kVA = utility system three-phase symmetrical short-circuit capability

The short-circuit kVA value is provided by the local electric utility company.

■ EXAMPLE 16.1

Refer to Example 6.2 and Figure 6.2. The kVA rating of the transformer is 500 kVA. Assume that the utility system short-circuit capability is 50,000 kVA. Calculate the per unit impedance of the utility system.

Solution

The base kVA = 500 (the transformer rating). From Equation 16.1,

$$Z_U = \frac{500}{50{,}000} = 0.01 \text{ p.u.}$$

which agrees with the value used in Example 6.2.

16.1.1 Sources of Short-Circuit Currents

In the example calculations for the available fault current previously presented in Chapter 6, the only source considered was the electric utility system. However, other sources must also be considered, for example, in-house generators and all motors, both synchronous and induction types. As indicated in Figure 16.1, the available fault cur-

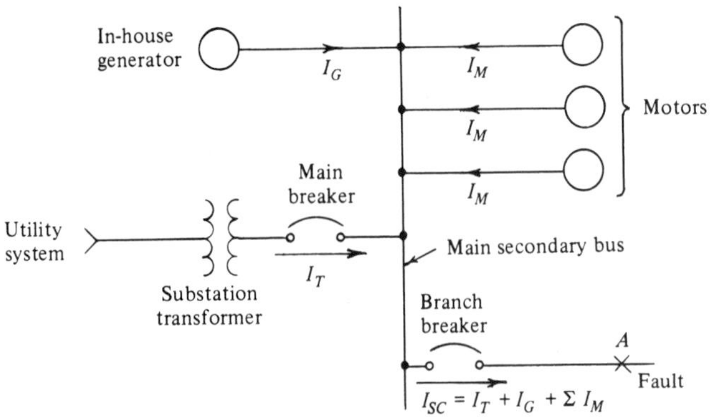

FIGURE 16.1

Sources of short-circuit currents

rent at point A is the total of the current I_T supplied from the utility system through the substation transformer, the current I_G supplied by the in-house generator (or generators), and the sum of all currents ΣI_M supplied by the motors. The feeder breaker protecting the faulted feeder must be able to safely interrupt the total current I_{SC}.

Large in-house generators are usually found only on very complex industrial systems. Their inclusion into the fault calculations is beyond the scope of this text. Small emergency standby generators are often included in building electrical systems. However, these generators usually serve only as a power source during power outages on the utility system connection. Then they only pick up emergency lighting and other such essential loads through throw-over switches. As such, they are never run in parallel with the substation transformer and therefore do not contribute to fault currents.

It would be easy to overlook motors as a source of power during fault conditions. The motor is normally thought of as a power user, not as a power source. At the instant that a bolted fault occurs on a system, the system voltage at that point collapses. Thus the voltage at the motor terminals also collapses. However, the inertia of the motors and their driven equipment keeps them turning, at least for a short time. In the case of synchronous motors, which have separate dc fields (see Section 2.4), the motor turns into a generator and begins to pump power back into the system. Induction motors do not have a separate dc field, but instead their excitation is provided by the main armature winding (see Section 2.5). However, the magnetic field that existed just prior to the collapse of the voltage cannot decrease to zero instantly, but takes several cycles to do so. Thus an induction motor becomes a generator for these few cycles. In the case of low-voltage systems, the circuit breakers interrupt the current within two cycles, and therefore the contributions from the induction motors must be included.

The precise calculations necessary to include the contribution from each motor are complex. Studies on typical low-voltage systems have indicated that the following rule-of-thumb method is satisfactory for most system fault calculations, probably erring on the side of safety. This method assumes that *the motor contribution to the fault current will be four times the full-load running current of each motor*. It is further assumed that, in the case of 480 and 600 volt systems, the connected motor load equals 100% of the system kVA. In effect, this means that the sum of the full-load running currents of all the motors equals the rated secondary current of the system transformer. In the case of 208Y/120 volt systems, it is not logical to assume a 100% motor load. This system is normally selected because a substantial part of the load is lighting and other nonmotor loads requiring 120 volt circuits. Therefore, for a 208Y/120 volt system, it is assumed that the motor load is 50% of the system kVA, meaning that the sum of the full-load running currents of all the motors is equal to 50% of the rated secondary current of the system transformer.

The following examples illustrate the application of these rule-of-thumb methods to calculating the available fault current. Because these calculations are based on assumptions, the results need not be taken to too many significant figures. All calculated values of fault current used in the examples in this chapter are rounded out to the nearest 100 amperes.

EXAMPLE 16.2

Power is supplied over a primary utility feeder to a 1000 kVA, 5.75% impedance transformer that steps down the voltage to 480Y/277 V for distribution throughout the building, as shown in Figure 16.2(a). The utility system short-circuit kVA capability is 250,000. Feeder 1 has a continuous load of 400 A. Determine the available short-circuit current at the main secondary bus and select the frame size for the feeder breaker (power type).

Solution

The base kVA = 1000 (rating of substation transformer). The rated voltage = 480 V (line-to-line), 277 V (line-to-neutral). Using Equation 1.14,

$$\text{rated secondary current} = \frac{1000 \times 1000}{1.732 \times 480 \text{ V}} = 1203 \text{ A}$$

Draw the equivalent single-phase fault circuit diagram [Fig. 16.2(b)]. From Equation 16.1,

$$Z_U = \frac{1000}{250{,}000} = 0.004 \text{ p.u.}$$

The total impedance of the source through the substation is:

$$Z_{UT} = Z_U + Z_T = 0.004 + 0.0575 = 0.0615 \text{ p.u.}$$

The current I_T through the transformer is

Using Equation 16.3, $I_T = \dfrac{E}{Z_{UT}} = \dfrac{1.0}{0.0615} = 16.26$ p.u.

Using Equation 16.4, $I_T = 1203 \times 16.26 = 19{,}600$ A

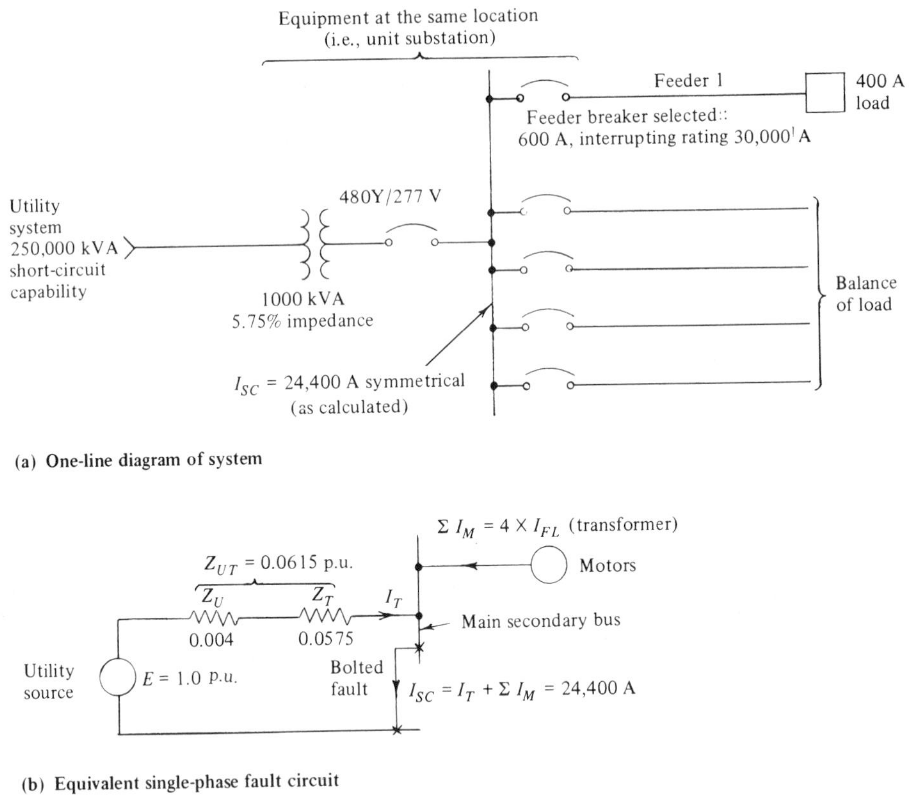

FIGURE 16.2

Diagrams for Example 16.2

The motor load is assumed to be 100%. The sum of all motor contributions is:

$$\Sigma I_M = 4 \times \text{rated current} = 4 \times 1203 = 4800 \text{ A}$$

Therefore, the total fault current is:

$$I_{SC} = I_T + \Sigma I_M = 19{,}600 + 4800 = 24{,}400 \text{ A symmetrical}$$

Refer to Table 8.2 for the ratings of the power type of circuit breaker. Select a 600 A frame size for the branch breaker since it can carry the 400 A continuous load on the feeder, and it has an interrupting rating of 30,000 A symmetrical at 480 V.

With respect to the foregoing example, assume that one of the branch feeders requires a 225 ampere rating for the continuous load, and molded-case circuit breakers are to be used. Refer to Table 8.1. for the ratings of molded-case breakers. The interrupting rating of the standard 225 ampere frame breaker is only 22,000 amperes symmetrical and would not be satisfactory on the basis of the preceding calculations. Had the motor contribution not been included, the standard 225 ampere breaker would appear to be satisfactory. As it is, either the 225 ampere high-interrupting capacity breaker (interrupting rating 25,000 A) or the 400 ampere standard breaker (interrupting rating 30,000 A) has to be used, both of which cost more.

■ EXAMPLE 16.3

Repeat Example 16.2 except that the secondary voltage is 208Y/120 V.

Solution

The per unit current supplied through the transformer is the same as previously calculated: I_T = 16.26 P.U.

$$\text{Rated secondary current} = \frac{1000 \times 1000}{1.732 \times 208\ \text{V}} = 2780\ \text{A}$$

$$I_T = 2780 \times 16.26 = 45{,}200\ \text{A}$$

The motor load is assumed to be 50%:

$$\Sigma\, I_M = 4 \times (0.5 \times 2780) = 5600\ \text{A}$$

$$I_{SC} = 45{,}200 + 5600 = 50{,}800\ \text{A symmetrical}$$

From Table 8.2, the smallest frame size that can be used is 1600 A, which has an interrupting rating of 65,000 A symmetrical at 208 V (if instantaneous tripping of the breaker is used).

Note the significant increase in the available fault current in Example 16.3 as compared to Example 16.2. Another characteristic of 208Y/120 volt systems is the problem with high available fault currents, indicating again the desirability of keeping the voltage level at which power is distributed throughout a building as high as possible. Where 208Y/120 volts is required for utilization equipment, substations should be kept down to a reasonable size.

16.2 EFFECT OF SYSTEM COMPONENTS ON FAULT CURRENTS

The kVA rating of the substation transformer has a significant effect on the magnitude of the available fault current on the low-voltage system. This can best be illustrated by the following example.

■ EXAMPLE 16.4

Repeat Example 16.2, except that the transformer rating is 2000 kVA.

Solution

$$\text{Base kVA} = 2000$$

$$\text{Rated secondary current} = \frac{2000 \times 1000}{1.732 \times 480\ \text{V}} = 2405\ \text{A}$$

$$Z_U = \frac{2000}{250{,}000} = 0.008 \text{ p.u.}$$

$$Z_{UT} = 0.008 + 0.0575 = 0.0655 \text{ p.u.}$$

$$I_T = \frac{1.0}{0.0655} = 15.27 \text{ p.u.}$$

$$I_T = 2405 \times 15.27 = 36{,}700 \text{ A}$$

$$\Sigma I_M = 4 \times 2405 = 9600 \text{ A}$$

$$I_{SC} = 36{,}700 + 9600 = 46{,}300 \text{ A symmetrical}$$

Note that the available fault current has nearly doubled as compared to that calculated in Example 16.2. This means that the 600 ampere frame size for the feeder breaker is no longer satisfactory, as it does not have sufficient interrupting capacity. A 1600 ampere frame breaker with an interrupting rating of 50,000 amperes has to be used, even though the load on the breaker remains at 400 amperes. A minimum frame size of 1600 amperes must be used for all branch breakers in the substation at a considerable increase in cost. Once again the alternative is to consider the use of the combination fused circuit breakers with current-limiting fuses (Section 8.7).

The selection of circuit breakers involves two ratings, the frame size and the trip rating. Refer to Section 8.3.1 for an explanation of these ratings. The frame size of the breaker is selected to satisfy both the continuous (load) current and the fault interrupting requirements, as shown in the previous examples. On the other hand, the trip rating of the breaker is selected to provide proper overcurrent protection for the feeder, and it remains the same regardless of the change in frame size. See Section 11.8 on the overcurrent protection of feeders.

Examples 16.2 and 16.4 show the significant effect that the substation transformer kVA *rating* has on the available fault current on the low-voltage system. Note that the magnitude of the load on feeder 1 has no effect on the magnitude of the available fault current at the location of the feeder circuit breaker. Conversely, the size of the transformer has no effect on the feeder load. It will draw 400 amperes regardless of whether it is fed through a 1000 or 2000 kVA transformer. Indirectly, the load on each feeder does of course have an effect in that these loads in total dictate the size of the transformer required.

The selection of kVA ratings of substation transformers is very critical in establishing the levels of available fault current on the secondary side of the substation. In large systems, it may be advantageous to split up the loads between several smaller substations to reduce the available fault current levels (see Section 15.1.2 on load-center systems).

Referring again to the previous examples of fault current calculations, note that the impedance of the transformer is the main factor in limiting the magnitude of the fault current available on the low-voltage section of the system, especially at points close to the substation. If the impedance of the transformer is materially reduced, the level of available fault current rises accordingly, as shown in the following example.

■ EXAMPLE 16.5

Repeat Example 16.2, with the exception that the impedance of the transformer is 3.0%.

Solution

$$Z_{UT} = 0.004 + 0.030 = 0.034 \text{ p.u.}$$

$$I_T = \frac{1.0}{0.034} = 29.4 \text{ p.u.}$$

$$I_T = 1203 \times 29.4 = 35{,}400 \text{ A}$$

$$\Sigma I_M = 4800 \text{ A} \quad \text{(no change)}$$

$$I_{SC} = 35{,}400 + 4800 = 40{,}200 \text{ A symmetrical}$$

Note the significant increase in the available fault current as compared to Example 16.2. This means that the interrupting capacity of the 600 A frame breaker is insufficient, and the 1600 A frame has to be used, considerably increasing the cost of the breakers.

Because of the importance of the transformer impedance in limiting the available fault current, substation transformers are designed on purpose to have impedances of at least 5.0%, with a typical value being 5.75%. This high impedance is obtained by increasing the leakage reactance of the transformer windings, rather than their resistance. Higher-resistance windings would increase the heat losses in the transformer, which is not desirable. Refer to Example 6.3, which shows the typical ratio of the reactance to the resistance of transformer windings. Note that the reactance is by far the more important parameter of the total impedance of the transformer. The impedance of the transformer, however, cannot be made too high; otherwise, its secondary voltage would vary excessively under normal loading conditions because of internal voltage drop. The expected percentage impedance of each substation transformer to be installed on a system should always be specified as part of the ordering information.

16.3 EFFECT OF FEEDER IMPEDANCES ON FAULT CURRENTS

The previous examples calculated the available fault current immediately adjacent to the secondary terminals of the substation transformer. At that location, the only limiting factors for the fault current are the impedance of the primary feeder and the substation transformer. It is necessary to also calculate available fault currents at other locations on the system that are some distance from the substation, such as at power panels and motor-control centers. The impedance of the feeder cables acts to further limit the available fault current at these locations and therefore must be included in calculating the total impedance up to the point of the fault.

Table 16.1 lists the ac resistance and inductive reactance of three-phase feeders consisting of three single 600 volt copper conductors installed in one run of conduit. As with the impedances of other system components previously included in the fault calculations, the resistance and reactance of the conductors must be converted into per unit values. The reader at this time should review

TABLE 16.1 AC Resistance and Inductive Reactance of 600 V Cables, Three-Phase, 60 Hz, 75°C, Three Single *Copper* Conductors in Conduit

Wire Size, AWG or MCM	Ohms per 1000 Feet, Line to Neutral			
	AC Resistance (R_{ac})		Inductive Reactance (X_L)	
	Aluminum Conduit	Steel Conduit	Aluminum Conduit	Steel Conduit
2	0.20	0.20	0.045	0.057
1	0.16	0.16	0.046	0.057
1/0	0.13	0.12	0.044	0.055
2/0	0.10	0.10	0.043	0.054
3/0	0.082	0.079	0.042	0.052
4/0	0.067	0.063	0.041	0.051
250 MCM	0.057	0.054	0.041	0.052
300 MCM	0.049	0.045	0.041	0.051
350 MCM	0.043	0.039	0.040	0.050
400 MCM	0.038	0.035	0.040	0.049
500 MCM	0.032	0.029	0.039	0.048

For a complete set of values, including those for aluminum conductors, see *NEC* Table 9, Chapter 9.

Section 6.4 with particular reference to the term *base impedance*. Equation 6.1 shows how the base impedance of a system is calculated. Note that the rated line-to-neutral voltage of the system must be used in this calculation. This is necessary as the fault calculations for a three-phase system are simplified by equating it to a single-phase system and using phase-to-neutral values. Note that in Table 16.1 the heading indicates that the values of the resistances and reactances are *line to neutral*. Equation 6.2 shows how the actual value in ohms is changed to a per unit value. Using these equations, the following example shows how to calculate the per unit values for a feeder.

■ EXAMPLE 16.6

A three-phase feeder consisting of three 250 MCM copper conductors in a steel conduit is 100 ft in length. The capacity of the transformer supplying the feeder is 1000 kVA and the system is 480 V. Calculate the per unit resistance and reactance of the feeder.

Solution

Base kVA = 1000 kVA

Rated voltage = 480 V (line to line), 277 V (line to neutral)

Rated secondary current = 1203 A (see Example 16.2)

From Table 16.1, the resistance and reactance of 250 MCM copper conductors in steel (magnetic) conduit are:

$$R_{ac} = 0.054\ \Omega/1000\text{ ft},\qquad X_L = 0.052\ \Omega/1000\text{ ft}$$

The resistance and reactance for 100 ft are then:

$$R_{ac} = \frac{0.054 \times 100}{1000} = 0.0054\ \Omega,\qquad X_L = \frac{0.052 \times 100}{1000} = 0.0052\ \Omega$$

Using Equation 6.1,

$$\text{Base impedance} = \frac{277}{1203} = 0.23\ \Omega$$

The per unit values of the feeder are, using Equation 6.2,

$$R_F = \frac{0.0054}{0.23} = 0.0235\text{ p.u.}\quad (2.35\%)$$

$$X_F = \frac{0.0052}{0.23} = 0.0226\text{ p.u.}\quad (2.26\%)$$

Note in this example that the resistance of the feeder is slightly greater than the reactance. This is contrary to the situation with the primary feeder and substation transformer, in which case the reactance is many times that of the resistance. In previous examples, the total system impedance was calculated by simply adding the numerical value of each impedance. While this is not strictly correct, the error introduced is small. Now, however, if the impedance of the feeder, with its high component of resistance, is simply added arithmetically to the system impedance, which is largely reactive, a significant error will occur, unfortunately in the wrong direction. It would give a larger value of overall impedance than is actually the case, resulting in a calculated value of available fault current that is low. Therefore, account must now be taken of the resistance of the system up to the source of the feeder. The following rule of thumb is adopted as a satisfactory means of adjusting to this problem. This rule assumes *that the resistance of the system is 25% that of the reactance of the system.*

An equivalent impedance of the system has to be determined so that it can be broken down into its respective resistance and reactance components. Refer to Figure 16.3. Part (a) shows the typical equivalent single-phase circuit as previously used to solve for the fault current at the main secondary bus of the substation. The path for the current I_T and the path for the current ΣI_M can be considered to be in parallel, as shown in part (b). This then permits the two parallel paths to be combined into one equivalent system impedance

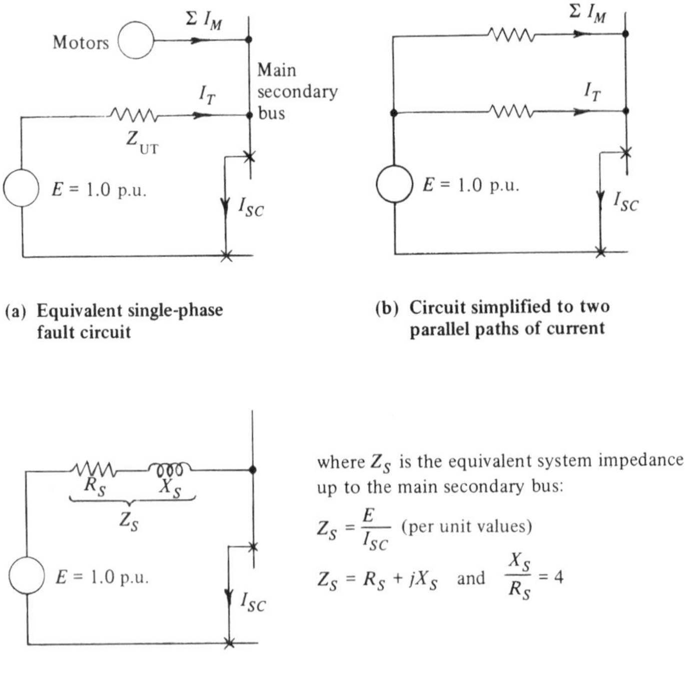

(a) Equivalent single-phase fault circuit

(b) Circuit simplified to two parallel paths of current

(c) Circuit further simplified to one current path

FIGURE 16.3

Reducing system to one equivalent fault impedance

Z_S, as shown in part (c), such that:

$$\text{per unit } Z_S = \frac{\text{E(p.u.)}}{I_{SC}\text{(p.u.)}} \qquad \textbf{(16.2)}$$

From the previously stated rule-of-thumb:

$$Z_S = R_S + jX_S, \qquad \text{where } X_S/R_S = 4 \qquad (16.3)$$

(The reader should review Section 1.4.3).

The following example illustrates the method of including the effect of a feeder in the calculations for the available fault current.

■ EXAMPLE 16.7

Combine Example 16.2 with Example 16.6 as shown in Figure 16.4. Determine the available fault current at the power panel being supplied by the feeder.

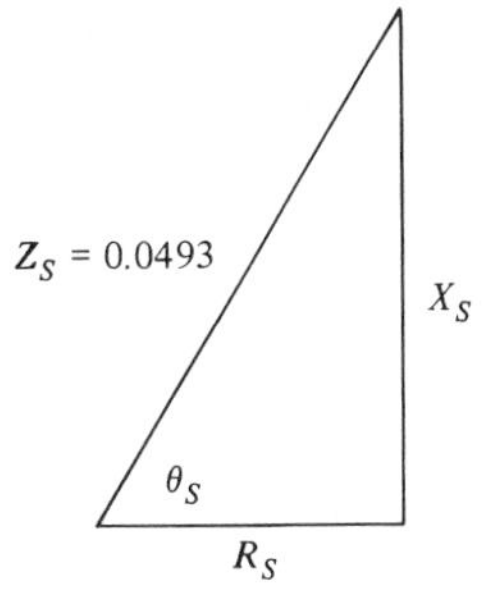

Solution

From previous calculations in Example 16.2, the available fault current at the main secondary bus is 24,400 A and the rated current is 1203 A. Therefore, the per unit fault current is:

$$I_{SC} = \frac{24{,}400}{1203} = 20.3 \text{ p.u. (at main secondary bus)}$$

Using Equation 16.2,

$$Z_S = \frac{1.0}{20.3} = 0.0493 \text{ p.u.}$$

From Equation 16.3,

$$R_S + jX_S = 0.0493 \quad \text{and} \quad X_S/R_S = 4$$

$$\text{Tan } \theta_S = 4/1, \quad \theta_S = 76°$$

$$R_S = 0.0493 \times \cos 76° = 0.0119 \text{ p.u.}$$

$$X_S = 0.0493 \times \sin 76° = 0.0478 \text{ p.u.}$$

From Example 16.6, the values for the feeder are:

$$R_F = 0.0235 \text{ p.u.} \quad \text{and} \quad X_F = 0.0226 \text{ p.u.}$$

$$\begin{aligned} Z \text{ (total)} &= (R_S + R_F) + j(X_S + X_F) \\ &= (0.0119 + 0.0235) + j(0.0478 + 0.0226) \\ &= 0.0354 + j0.0704 = 0.0788 \text{ p.u.} \end{aligned}$$

$$I_{SC} = \frac{1.0}{0.0788} = 12.7 \text{ p.u.}$$

$$= 1203 \times 12.7 = 15{,}300 \text{ A symmetrical} \quad \text{(at power panel)}$$

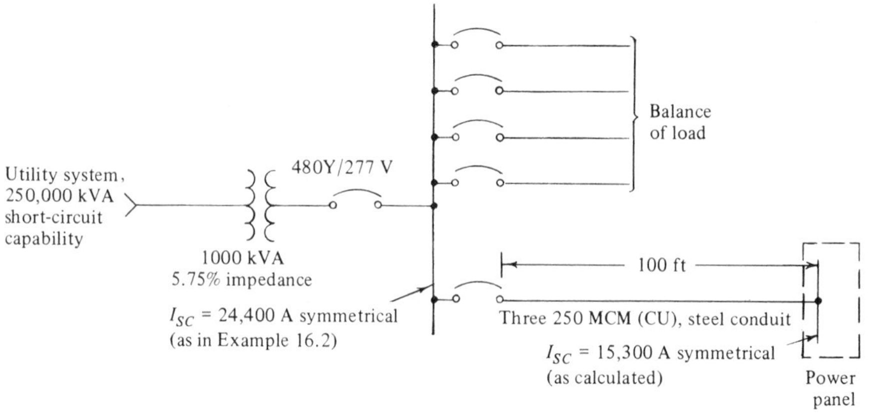

(a) One-line diagram

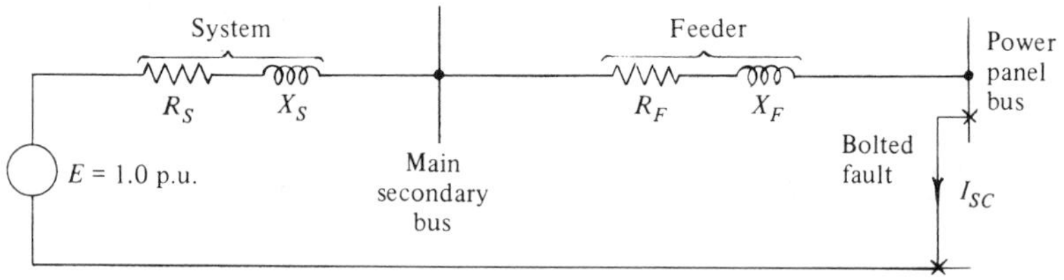

(b) Equivalent single-phase fault circuit

FIGURE 16.4

Diagrams for Example 16.7

Note that the 100 feet of feeder has a significant effect on further limiting the magnitude of the available fault current. Therefore, the short-circuit duty requirements for equipment decrease as the distance from the substation increases. However, it must also be remembered that the greater the feeder impedance, the greater the voltage drop under normal load conditions. This means that there is always a compromise between the normal operating requirements and the desire to limit the available fault currents.

16.4 SELECTION AND COORDINATION OF MOTOR PROTECTION

The purpose of this section is to outline the method of selecting the proper rating of the thermal sensing (heater) elements of the overload relays for a motor starter and then to show how the motor branch circuit protective device (fuse or breaker) is coordinated with this overload protection. The operation of magnetic starters is described in Section 14.2. Figure 14.2(a) shows the connection diagram for a three-phase full-voltage starter, including the three overload relays. Figures 14.2(b) and (c) show how the relay contacts are connected in series with the starter coil such that the release of any overload contact de-energizes the coil and opens the starter to stop the motor.

The most common thermal-responsive relays are the bimetallic and the eutectic-solder types. The bimetallic relay has a bimetal strip that is heated by the passage of the motor current through the heater element. If the current is excessive, the heat eventually deflects the bimetal strip to the point where it releases the normally closed relay contact. The eutectic-solder relay uses an alloy that melts at a specific temperature. The alloy is heated by the passage of the motor current through the heater element. When the alloy melts, because of an excessive motor current, it allows a ratchet to turn, thus releasing the normally closed relay contact.

Both types of relays have an inverse time–current characteristic (Section 6.7). Industry standards designate an overload relay by a class number indicating the maximum time in seconds at which it will trip when carrying 600% of its rated current. A class 10 relay will trip in 10 seconds or less, a class 20 in 20 seconds or less, and a class 30 in 30 seconds or less. The class 20 relay is used for general applications where the accelerating time of the motor is normal. Figure 16.5 shows the typical time–current curves of class 20 and class 30 overload relays. The curves are plotted with the time in seconds on a log scale against the percentage of current of the relay on a linear scale.

Table 16.2 lists typical ratings for overload relay heater elements. The heater type number is selected using the full-load amperes nearest to the actual full-load current shown on the nameplate of the motor. The rated current of the relay in amperes at 40°C is 115% of the full-load amperes listed for the heater type number. Note that the heater type numbers shown in the left column are the manufacturer's designation. Each manufacturer has his own form of heater designation and ranges of heater ratings. The precise current ratings of the heater elements depend on many factors, such as the number of heater elements in a starter, type of starter enclosure, and whether the starter is a combination type using circuit breakers or fuses. It is necessary to follow the manufacturer's complete set of recommendations before the final heater selection is made.

The following example illustrates the method recommended by the manufacturer for the selection of the correct heater element from Table 16.2 for the situation where the ambient temperature is the same for both the starter and the motor.

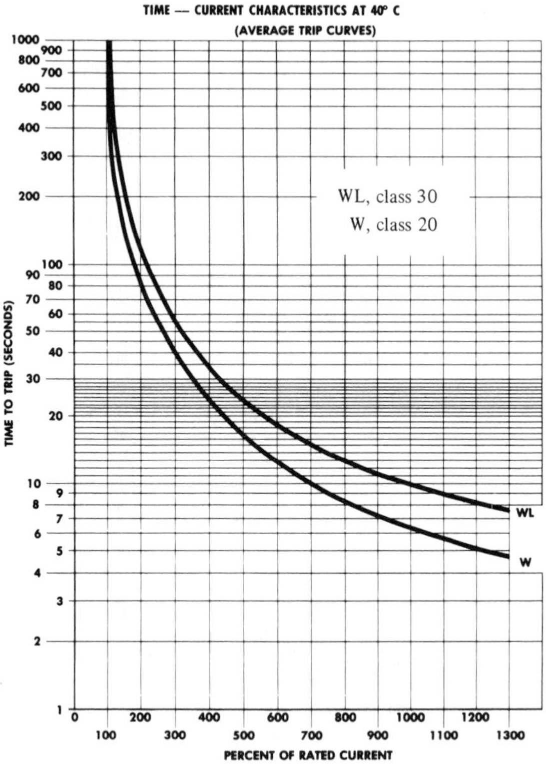

FIGURE 16.5

Typical time–current characteristic curves for motor overload relays

■ EXAMPLE 16.8

Refer to Example 13.1, which shows the design of a motor branch circuit for a 40 hp, 460 V, three-phase motor, service factor 1.15, and with a nameplate full-load current of 50 A. Select the heater type number and calculate its rated current.

Solution

From Table 14.1, a size 3 starter is required. From Table 16.2, select the manufacturer's heater type No. W69, listed for full-load amperes of 52.0 (nearest to 50 A). The rated current of overload relay is $1.15 \times 52.0 = 59.8 \approx 60$ A. Note that this is less than the maximum allowed by code as calculated in part (3) of Example 13.1.

We will next show how the motor branch-circuit protective device should coordinate with the overload relay just selected. Previous examples of coordination between protective devices have been for devices with similar characteristics (see Section 7.7 for fuses and Section 8.6 for circuit breakers). The following is then an example of coordination between devices with different response characteristics.

First, however, review Section 13.1.1 with regard to the func-

TABLE 16.2 Typical Ratings of Overload Heater Elements for Three-Phase Magnetic Motor Starters

Heater Type Number	Full Load Amps.				
	Size 0	Size 1	Size 2	Size 3	Size 4
W40	3.04	3.04	....	....	....
W41	3.34	3.34	....	....	....
W42	3.68	3.68	....	....	....
W43	4.04	4.04	....	....	....
W44	4.46	4.46	....	....	....
W45	4.94	4.94	5.13	....	....
W46	5.46	5.46	5.64	....	....
W47	6.03	6.03	6.22	....	....
W48	6.65	6.65	6.85	....	....
W49	7.33	7.33	7.56	....	....
W50	8.13	8.13	8.45	....	....
W51	8.95	8.95	9.32	....	....
W52	9.90	9.90	10.3	10.4	....
W53	10.7	10.7	11.3	11.4	....
W54	11.7	11.7	12.3	12.5	....
W55	12.8	12.8	13.4	13.7	....
W56	14.0	14.0	14.5	15.1	....
W57	15.3	15.3	15.8	16.7	....
W58	16.2	16.2	16.7	18.4	19.0
W59	17.5	17.5	18.0	20.3	21.0
W60	19.4	19.4	19.9	22.5	23.1
W61	....	21.3	21.9	24.8	25.5
W62	....	23.3	24.2	27.2	28.0
W63	....	25.5	26.8	30.0	31.0
W64	....	27.2	28.7	33.0	34.0
W65	....	....	31.0	36.0	37.0
W66	....	....	33.5	39.5	40.0
W67	....	....	36.0	43.5	44.0
W68	....	....	38.5	47.5	48.5
W69	....	....	41.5	52.0	53.0
W70	....	....	45.0	56.0	57.0
W71	....	....	....	60.0	62.0
W72	....	....	....	65.0	67.0
W73	....	....	....	69.0	72.0
W74	....	....	....	74.0	77.0
W75	....	....	....	79.0	82.0
W76	....	....	....	85.0	87.0
W77	....	....	....	91.0	93.0
W78	....	....	....	....	99.0
W79	....	....	....	....	105
W80	....	....	....	....	112
W81	....	....	....	....	117
W82	....	....	....	....	123
W83	....	....	....	....	129
W84	....	....	....	....	135
W85	....	....	....	....	....

Heater Type Number	Full Load Amps.				
	Size 5	Size 6	Size 7	Size 8	Size 9
W29	74	144	240	360	600
W30	81	157	261	390	650
W31	88	171	285	430	710
W32	97	186	310	465	780
W33	106	209	340	510	850
W34	115	222	370	555	920
W35	126	242	405	610	1020
W36	138	268	445	670	1120
W37	151	294	490	740	1220
W38	165	325	540	810	1350
W39	180	355	590	890	1480
W40	197	390	650	970	1620
W41	215	430	710	1070	1780
W42	235	470	780	1170	1960
W43	256	515	860	1290	2150
W44	281	560	....	....	2360

Ratings from 0.18 A to 2.76 A for size 1 and 2 starters are not shown.

Ratings apply to starters mounted in standard enclosures.

For size 5 starters and above, overload relays are connected through current transformers.

Consult manufacturer for complete listing of heater ratings and for complete set of recommendations with regard to selection of heater type number.

tion of motor branch-circuit short-circuit and ground-fault protection and Section 13.1.2 with regard to motor overload protection. In particular, Figure 13.4 shows the relationship between the overload device and the motor starting and running currents. The overload relay in the motor starter should operate first to shut down the motor for any excess currents up to the locked-rotor (starting) current of motor. This locked-rotor current is typically 600% of the full-load running current of the motor. Any current in the motor circuit that exceeds 600% can only be as the result of a fault in the motor windings or the circuit itself, in which case the circuit should be interrupted as soon as possible. Thus, the response of the circuit protective device should be such that it operates first to clear any current in excess of the 600%.

For a coordination study, the response curves of the various devices must be copied on one common graph so that they may be compared at all current and time points. The best way to do this is to use the industry standard log–log graph paper, such as shown in Figure 16.6 (which is reduced to approximately 60% of its actual size). A typical log–log graph sheet is K and E No. 48-5258, which is available in drafting supply outlets. The vertical axis represents time and consists of a five-decade scale ranging from 0.01 to 1000 seconds. The horizontal axis represents current and consists of a four-and-a-half-decade scale ranging from 0.5 to 10,000 amperes. The current scale can be shifted for a particular graph by modifying the current scale by a factor of times 10, 100 (×10, ×100), and so on. Time–current characteristic curves of fuses and circuit breakers, prepared on full-size transparencies, are available from most manufacturers of the devices. An overlay can then be made by tracing the manufacturer's curves onto one single sheet, making sure that both the time and current scales are lined up properly. The following example shows the method of plotting various devices on the one graph to check their coordination.

■ EXAMPLE 16.9

Select the minimum rating for the following overcurrent devices when used for the motor branch circuit as in Examples 13.1 and 16.8:

(a) Nontime-delay fuses

(b) Time-delay dual-element fuses

(c) Circuit breaker with inverse time-delay element

Solution

The characteristic curve for the overload relay as selected in Example 16.8 must first be plotted on the standard log–log graph paper using the curve shown in Figure 16.5. Since this particular set of curves is not drawn on the industry standard form of graph, points must be selected from this graph for plotting on the standard log–log graph. Also, since the horizontal scale is in percent of rated current, the actual current for each point must be calculated on the basis that the 100% rating of the W69 heater element in Example 16.8 is 60 A. The following table shows the points selected from the curve for the type W (Class 20) heater element:

Percent of Rated Current	Actual Current (A)	Time (s)
100	60	Infinity
200	120	85
300	180	40
400	240	24.5
500	300	16.8
600	360	12.8
800	480	8.3

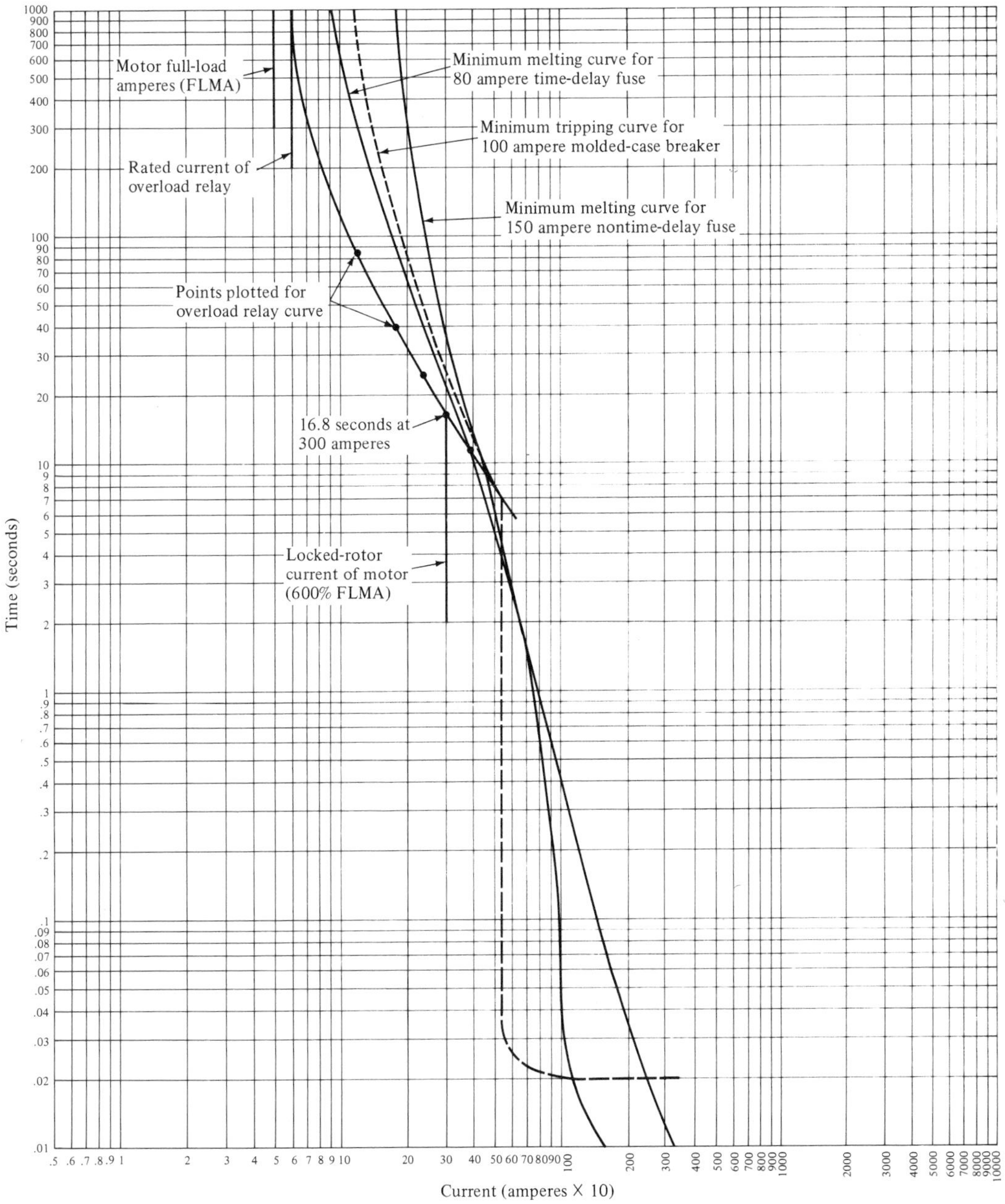

FIGURE 16.6

Time–current curves for motor branch-circuit protection as outlined in Example 16.9

These points are shown plotted on Figure 16.6, with the resulting curve drawn in. This overload relay curve crosses the locked-rotor current of the motor (300 A) at 16.8 s. Thus, if the motor fails to start (is jammed so that it cannot turn), the starter will automatically open in 16.8 seconds and disconnect the power.

(a) Selection of nontime delay fuses: The curves for typical nontime-delay fuses are shown in Figure 7.11. The graph of these curves is lined up with the graph in Figure 16.6. Note that the current scale in Figure 16.6 is ($\times$10). The rating of the fuse selected has to have a minimum melting curve that just clears (stays to the right of) the point of intersection of the overload relay curve and the locked-rotor current of the motor (16.8 s at 300 A). A quick inspection shows that the 100 A fuse is too small and the 200 A fuse is larger than need be. The final selection of the 150 A fuse is made by interpolating between the 100 and 200 A curves. (Standard ratings of fuses are listed in Table 7.1.) The minimum melting curve of the 150 A fuse is shown in Figure 16.6. Reference to Example 13.1 indicates that the maximum fuse rating allowed by code as per part (2) is 175 A. The actual 300% calculated value is 156 A. The selection of the 150 A fuse for Figure 16.6 shows that the next smallest standard rating can be used instead of the next larger standard size as allowed by the code.

(b) Selection of time-delay, dual-element fuses: The curves for typical time-delay dual-element fuses are shown in Figure 7.10. By lining up the graph of these curves with Figure 16.6, it is evident that the 60 A fuse is too small and the 100 A fuse is larger than need be. The 80 A fuse (as interpolated) is then selected, as shown. Reference to Example 13.2 indicates that the maximum rating allowed by code is 90 A. Once again the actual rating selected can be less than this maximum. The 80 A rating as compared to the 150 A rating required for the nontime-delay fuse shows once again the advantage of using time-delay fuses for motor circuits.

(c) Selection of circuit breaker: The curve for a typical molded-case circuit breaker with an inverse time-delay element is shown in Figure 8.7. Note that the horizontal scale is in percent of the breaker trip unit. Therefore, the trip rating of the breaker first has to be determined. Once again, the point that the breaker curve has to clear is 16.8 s at 300 A. By looking at the minimum curve of the breaker at 16.8 s, the percent of trip rating is approximately 340%. Equating the 340% to 300 A means that the trip rating cannot be less than:

$$\frac{300}{3.4} = 88 \text{ A}$$

From Table 8.1, the next highest trip rating is 90 A, but to be on the safe side a rating of 100 A is selected, as reference to Example 13.3 indicates that the maximum rating permitted by code is 150 A. The method of plotting breaker curves on a current basis is shown in Section 8.6 and

Figure 8.14. For Figure 16.6, the 100% line of Figure 8.7 is lined up with the 100 A line (the trip rating of the breaker). The resulting minimum curve of the breaker is shown.

16.5 DESIGN OF AN ELECTRICAL SYSTEM

The example now presented covers the design and coordination of a system starting from the branch circuit of a motor and working back through the system to the primary switchgear at the source. The system is shown in Figure 16.7. The branch circuit supplies a 150-horsepower, three-phase, 460 volt squirrel-cage induction motor, which is the largest motor fed from the motor-control center (MCC). The sum of the full-load currents from the balance of the motors connected to the MCC has been calculated at 425 amperes. With all motors running, the power factor of the MCC motor load is estimated to be 85%. The MCC is supplied over a 200 foot feeder from the main unit substation which has a 1500 kVA, 5.75% impedance, 13,800-480Y/277 volt transformer (see Chapter 15). The balance of the feeders connected to the unit substation has a combined demand of 1000 kVA. The utility system short-circuit kVA capability is 500,000. The primary switchgear is a fused load-interrupter switch (Section 15.2.1). The low-voltage main and feeder breakers at the unit substation are the power circuit breaker type (Section 8.5). The branch breaker for the motor circuit is the molded-case type (Section 8.4). The feeder conductors are to be type THW copper installed in steel conduit above grade.

The design procedures for most of the individual parts of the system are covered in preceding sections and examples in the text. Reference to the relevant section or example is made at each step so that the reader can review the necessary procedures.

16.5.1 Calculations

This part of the design involves the selection of the feeder to the MCC, the selection of the ratings of the devices required in the system, and the calculations for the maximum values of overload and overcurrent protection as permitted by the *National Electrical Code*. The results are summarized in Figure 16.7. The following steps outline the method of selecting the system components and ratings.

Step 1. Calculate the available fault current at the secondary main bus of the unit substation (references: Section 16.1.1 and Example 16.2):

Base kVA = 1500

Rated voltage
= 480 V (line to line), 277 V (line to neutral)

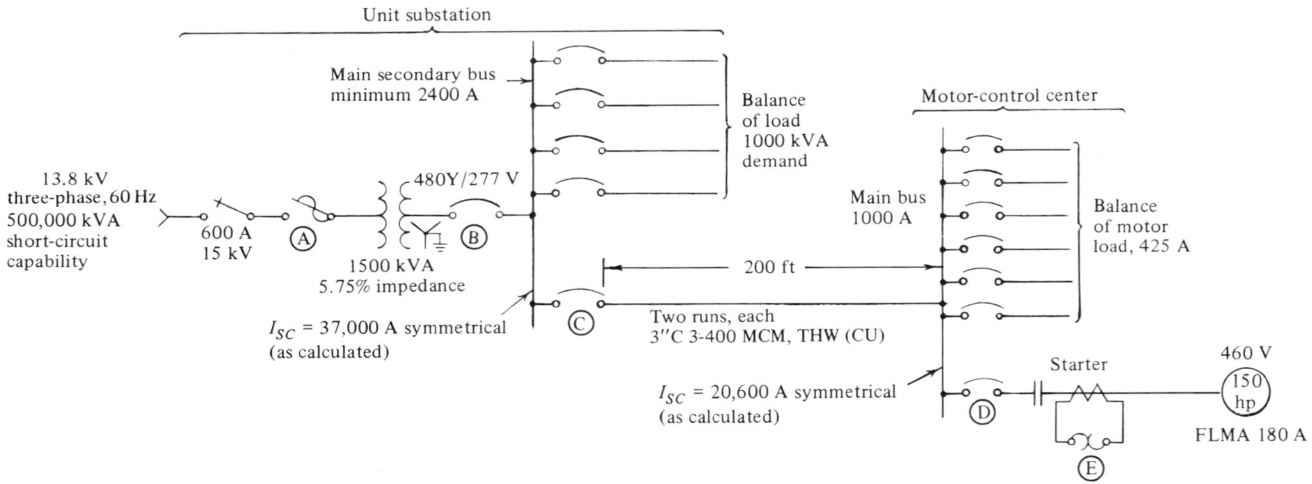

Ⓐ Power fuses
Fuse assembly, 400 A
I/C, 600,000 kVA*
Fuse unit, 150E A

Ⓑ Power circuit breaker
Frame, 3000 A
I/C, 65,000 A
Sensor, 2400 A
LDPU, 2160 A

Ⓒ Power circuit breaker
Frame, 1600 A
I/C, 50,000 A
Sensor, 1200 A
LDPU, 840 A

Ⓓ Molded-case breaker
Frame, 400 A
I/C, 30,000 A
Trip, 350 A

Ⓔ Overload relay
Rated 207 A
(motor amperes)

*Equivalent three phase
I/C, interrupting capacity, symmetrical
LDPU, long delay pickup

FIGURE 16.7

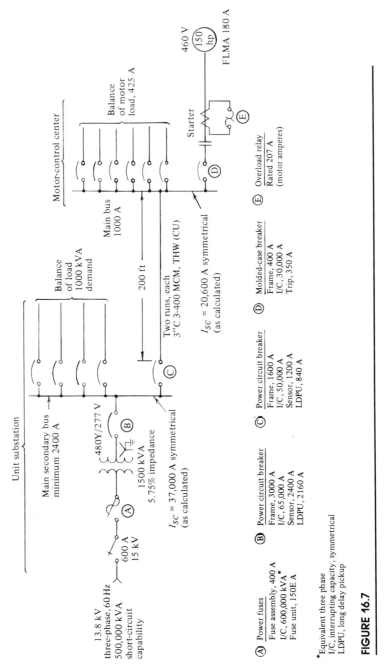

One-line diagram for system as outlined in Section 16.5

$$\text{Rated secondary current} = \frac{1500 \times 1000}{1.732 \times 480\ \text{V}} = 1804\ \text{A}$$

$$Z_U = \frac{1500}{500{,}000} = 0.003\ \text{p.u.}$$

$$Z_{UT} = 0.003 + 0.0575 = 0.0605\ \text{p.u.}$$

$$I_T = \frac{1.0}{0.0605} = 16.53\ \text{p.u.}$$

$$I_T = 1804 \times 16.53 = 29{,}800\ \text{A}$$

$$\Sigma\, I_M = 4 \times 1804 = 7200\ \text{A}$$

$$I_{SC} = 29{,}800 + 7200 = 37{,}000\ \text{A symmetrical}$$

Step 2. Select the feeder to the motor-control center (references: Section 11.7 and Examples 11.11 to 11.16; Section 13.4 and Example 13.4):

a. Minimum size required for ampacity. From Table 13.2, the full-load motor amperes (FLMA) of a 150 hp, 460 V motor is 180 A.

Sum of FLMA of remaining motors (as given) = 425 A

Minimum ampacity = 125% of largest + 100% of remainder
= (1.25 × 180) + 425 = 650 A

From Table 11.1, minimum size is 1750 MCM, THW. This is too large a size; recommend paralleling (Section 11.6).

Minimum ampacity per conductor = 650/2 = 325 A

Minimum size of each conductor = 400 MCM, THW (rated 335 A based on two runs of conduit)

b. Minimum size required for short-circuit current. From step 1, I_{SC} = 37,000 A symmetrical. From Table 11.4, K_0 is 1.3 and clearing time is 2 cycles.

$$I_{ASY} = 1.3 \times 37{,}000 = 48{,}100\ \text{A}$$

From Figure 11.5, the minimum size is No. 3/0.

c. Minimum size required for voltage drop.

Current per conductor = 325 A

Ampere-feet = 325 × 200 = 65,000 = 65 × 1000

$$\text{Maximum allowable volts drop} = 2\% \text{ of } 277 = 5.54 \text{ V}$$

$$\text{Maximum volts drop/1000 AF} = 5.54/65 = 0.085$$

From Table 11.5, the minimum size is No. 4/0 THW for each conductor (interpolate between 80% and 90% power factor).

Final selection of feeder (as dictated by ampacity) is

two runs, <u>each 3″ C, 3-400 MCM, THW (CU)</u>

(conduit size from Table 11.6).

Step 3. Calculate the available fault current at MCC (references: Section 16.3 and Examples 16.6 and 16.7):

a. Per unit resistance and reactance of system up to main secondary bus:

From step 1, $I_{SC} = 37{,}000$ A, rated current = 1804 A

$$\text{per unit } I_{SC} = \frac{37{,}000}{1804} = 20.5 \text{ p.u.}$$

$$Z_S = \frac{1.0}{20.5} = 0.049 = R_S + jX_S$$

$$\text{where } \frac{X_S}{R_S} = 4 \text{ and } \theta_S = 76°$$

$$R_S = 0.049 \cos 76° = 0.012 \text{ p.u.}$$

$$X_S = 0.049 \sin 76° = 0.048 \text{ p.u.}$$

b. Per unit resistance and reactance of feeder. From Table 16.1, for 400 MCM copper in steel conduit:

$$R_{ac} = 0.035\ \Omega/1000 \text{ ft}, \qquad X_L = 0.049\ \Omega/1000 \text{ ft}$$

For 200 ft:

$$R_{ac} = \frac{0.035 \times 200}{1000} = 0.070\ \Omega$$

$$X_L = \frac{0.049 \times 200}{1000} = 0.0098\ \Omega$$

$$\text{Base impedance} = \frac{277}{1804} = 0.1535\ \Omega$$

$$R_F = \frac{0.0070}{0.1535} = 0.046 \text{ p.u.}, \qquad X_F = \frac{0.0098}{0.1535} = 0.064 \text{ p.u.}$$

The foregoing are the values for each conductor. For two conductors in parallel:

$$R_F = \frac{0.046}{2} = 0.023 \text{ p.u.}, \qquad X_F = \frac{0.064}{2} = 0.032 \text{ p.u.}$$

c. Total impedance up to MCC:

$$\begin{aligned} Z\text{ (total)} &= (0.012 + 0.023) + j(0.048 + 0.032) \\ &= 0.035 + j(0.080) = 0.087 \text{ p.u.} \end{aligned}$$

d. $$I_{SC} = \frac{1.0}{0.087} = 11.5 \text{ P.U.} = 1804 \times 11.5$$

$$= 20{,}700 \text{ A symmetrical}$$

e. Ratings of MCC main bus (Section 14.5.2):
Bus bracing: standard 22,000 A symmetrical
Continuous current: 1000 A (minimum 650 A, step 1)

Step 4. Select overload protection Ⓔ for motor (references: Section 16.4 and Example 16.8). From Table 13.2, FLMA = 180 (assume nameplate amperes are the same). From Table 14.1, a size 5 starter is required. From Table 16.2, select the manufacturer's heater type W39 listed for 180 amperes (the 180 amperes is the equivalent rating as the heater is connected through a current transformer):

$$\text{Rated current of overload relay} = 1.15 \times 180 = 207 \text{ A}$$

Step 5. Select the motor branch breaker Ⓓ (references: Section 13.1.1 and Example 13.3).

$$\text{Maximum rating of trip unit} = 250\% \text{ of } 180 = 450 \text{ A}$$

From Table 8.1, the nearest standard trip rating is 450 amperes. From step 3, the available fault current is 20,700 amperes symmetrical. From Table 8.1, both 400 and 600 ampere standard frames have interrupting ratings of 30,000 amperes symmetrical at 480 volts. (*Note:* See step 11, Section 16.5.2, for final selection of breaker ratings as required for coordination.

Step 6. Select the feeder breaker Ⓒ (references: Section 13.4 and Example 13.5). From step 1, the available fault current is 37,000 amperes symmetrical.

$$\begin{aligned} \text{Maximum setting of trip unit} &= (250\% \text{ of } 180) + 425 \\ &= 875 \text{ A} \end{aligned}$$

From step 2, the minimum ampacity is 650 amperes. From Table 8.2, select 1600 ampere frame with interrupting rating of 50,000 amperes symmetrical at 480 volts (note that the 800 ampere frame does not have sufficient interrupting capacity). Select a 1200 ampere sensor (next rating above 875 amperes). See step 12 for trip unit settings for coordination.

Step 7. Select the main secondary breaker Ⓑ and main bus.

Transformers are capable of sustaining from 15% to 25% overloads. Section 450-3 of *NEC* limits the maximum setting of the secondary overcurrent device to 125% of rated current.

Rated secondary current (from step 1) = 1804 A

Maximum setting of trip unit = 1.25 × 1804 = 2255 A

From Table 8.2, select a 3000 ampere frame with interrupting rating of 65,000 amperes symmetrical at 480 V. Select a 2400 ampere sensor. See step 13 for trip unit settings for coordination.

Ratings of substation main secondary bus (Section 15.4) are

—Bus bracing: standard 42,000 A symmetrical
—Continuous current: 2400 A (minimum)

Step 8. Select the primary fuse Ⓐ.

$$\text{Rated primary current} = \frac{1500 \times 1000}{1.732 \times 13{,}800} = 63 \text{ A}$$

Section 450-3 of *NEC* limits primary fusing to a maximum of 300% of rated current of transformer.

Maximum rating of fuse unit = 3 × 63 = 189 A

Short-circuit kVA capability (as given)
= 500,000 (500 MVA)

From Table 7.4, select a 400 ampere fuse assembly with equivalent three-phase symmetrical interrupting capacity of 600 MVA. Note that the 200 ampere fuse assembly has insufficient interrupting capacity even though it is large enough for the fuse unit. See step 10 for the final selection of the rating of the fusible element as required for coordination.

16.5.2 Coordination

This part of the design involves the selection of the time–current characteristics of the breakers and the rating of the primary fuse element to provide coordination of the system protection. The curves of devices Ⓐ through Ⓔ are plotted on an overlay as in Figure 16.8 (see Section 16.4 for the method of making overlays). Note that the current scale on the overlay is times 100 (that is, 1 on scale = 100 A) and that it is with reference to the secondary currents (at the 480 volt level).

Step 9. Plot the overload relay curves Ⓔ (reference: Example 16.9).

Rated current of overload relay (from step 4) = 207 A

Therefore, in applying Figure 16.5, the 100% line is equal to 207 amperes. Using the same procedure as in Example 16.9 (200% = 414 A, time is 85 seconds, and so on), points are plotted and the curve for the overload relay is established in Figure 16.8. The full-load and 600% locked-rotor (starting) currents of a 150 horsepower motor are also marked on the graph.

Note: The overload relay curve is plotted first, as it is set by the motor full-load amperes and cannot be adjusted. It therefore establishes the low current (downstream) boundary of the curves for the five overcurrent protective devices that are in series.

Step 10. Plot the primary fuse curves Ⓐ. The primary fuse curves are plotted next as they set the high current (upstream) boundary of the set of curves. The main purpose of the primary fuses is to provide short-circuit protection to the transformer. The fuse must operate in response to a fault before the magnitude and duration of the fault current exceed the short-time limits recommended by the transformer manufacturer. A typical transformer through-fault protection curve is first drawn on Figure 16.8. This curve is based on the requirement that transformers must be designed to withstand the stresses caused by short circuits on their external terminals within the following limitations;

— 25 times rated current for 2 s
— 20 times rated current for 3 s
— 16.6 times rated current for 4 s
— 14.3 times rated current for 5 s

The reader is referred to Chapter 10 of ANSI/IEEE Std 242-1986 (see Bibliography) for a more detailed discussion on the protection of transformers and the application of transformer through-fault protection curves.

The fuse also must be able to carry the inrush current that occurs when the transformer is energized. This current, which is assumed to be 12 times the rated current of the transformer with a

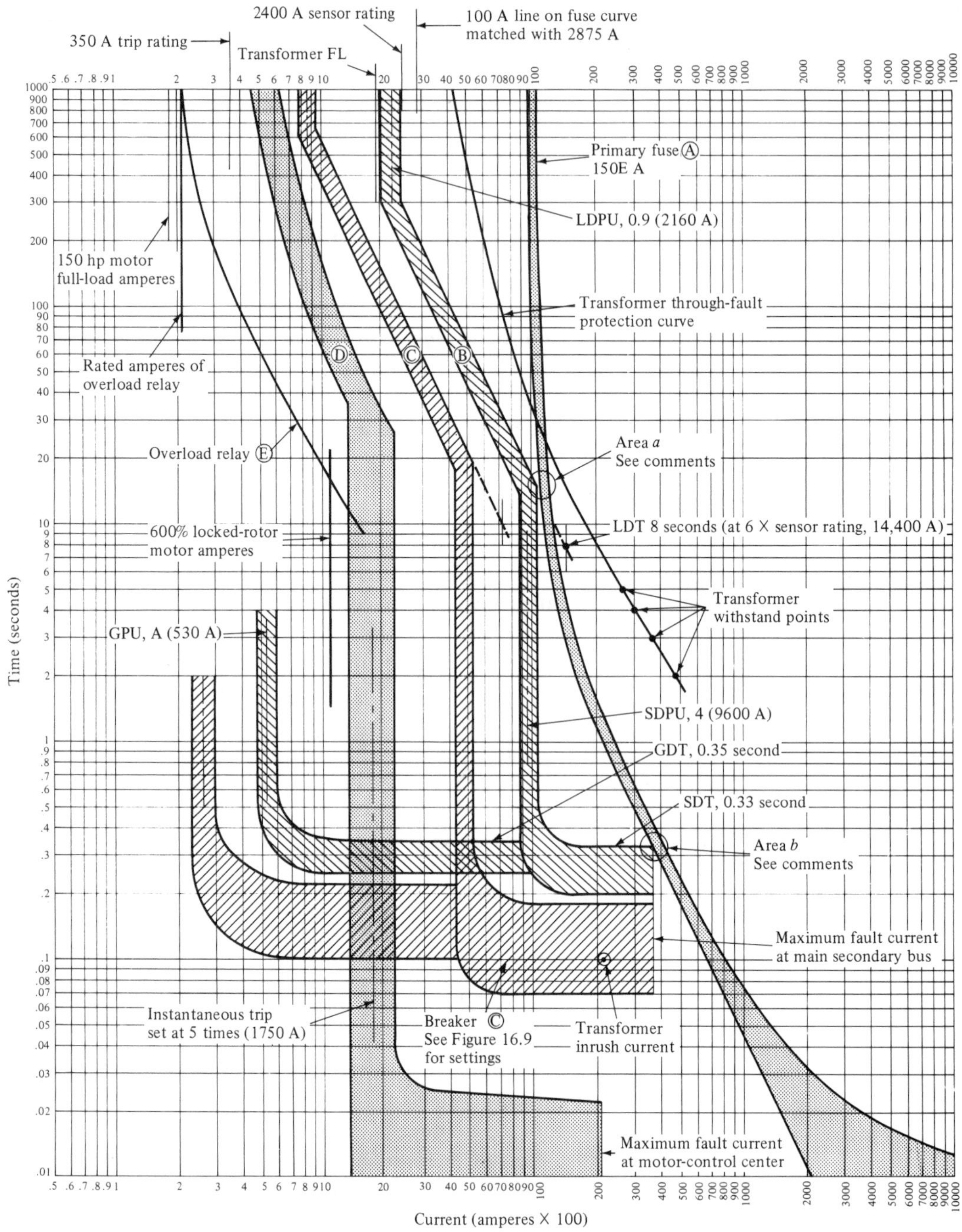

FIGURE 16.8

Time–current curves for devices in system as shown in Figure 16.7

duration of 0.1 seconds, must not blow the fuse. This point is plotted on Figure 16.8.

The transformer through-fault protection curve, the current inrush point, and the primary fuse curves are plotted with reference to the rated secondary current of the transformer. Otherwise, these points and curves would not have the correct relationship with the curves drawn for the other four devices that are on the secondary side of the transformer. The fuse curves used are shown in Figures 7.15 (minimum melting) and 7.16 (total clearing). See Section 7.1 and Figure 7.1 with regard to the meaning of minimum melting and total clearing times of fuses. The fuse curves are copied onto the overlay (Figure 16.8) by matching a particular current on the fuse curve with its equivalent secondary current, taking into account the turns ratio of the transformer. The turns ratio of a transformer is the ratio of the rated primary to secondary voltages.

$$\text{Turns ratio} = \frac{13{,}800}{480} = 28.75$$

The fuse curves are traced by matching the 100 ampere line on the fuse curves with the (100 × 28.75) = 2875 ampere line on the overlay. The rating of the fuse unit selected is 150 E amperes. This is below the maximum of 189 amperes as permitted by the *NEC* code (see step 8). Note that the minimum melting line of the fuse is well clear of (to the right of) the transformer inrush current point. The total clearing time curve of the fuse crosses the transformer through-fault protection curve at approximately 12,000 amperes or 660% of the rated current of the transformer. Therefore, the fuse provides protection against short circuits, but not against overloads on the transformer. More is stated about this in the conclusions in Section 16.5.3.

Step 11. Plot the motor branch circuit breaker curves Ⓓ [reference: Example 16.9, part (c)]. As previously determined in step 5, both a 400 and 600 ampere frame breaker can be used. The breaker curve for a 400 ampere frame molded-case circuit breaker is shown in Figure 8.8. By matching up the 100% line on the breaker curve with the possible trip ratings (400, 350 amperes, and so on) on the overlay, a trip rating of 350 amperes is selected, since the minimum line for this trip rating stays clear of the curve for the motor overload relay Ⓔ up to the locked-rotor motor amperes.

The 400 ampere frame molded-case breaker also has a magnetic (instantaneous) trip that is adjustable from 500% to 1000% (see Sections 8.4.2 and 8.6). The 500% setting is chosen (5 × 350 = 1750 A). The ±25% tolerance lines (1750 − 25% = 1315 A and 1750 + 25% = 2185 A) are also plotted, as the actual instantaneous pickup can occur anywhere between these extremes. The low limit of the pickup still clears the locked-rotor current of the motor (1080 A). Since the 350 ampere trip unit is satisfactory, the 400 ampere frame can be used. Note that the 350 ampere trip rating is below the maximum of 450 amperes as permitted by the *NEC* code (step 5).

Step 12. Plot the curves for the feeder breaker Ⓒ. The type of device specified for this and the main breaker have solid-state trip units. The reader should review Section 8.5.1 and Figure 8.13, which outline all of the adjustments that can be made to the breaker time–current characteristics. Note that the adjustments are continuous, with calibration points marked on the dial as indicated. The ranges of adjustments and the final selection of each setting with the resulting time–current curve for breaker Ⓒ are shown in Figure 16.9. The selection of these settings is summarized below:

— Long delay pickup (LDPU). From step 6, the sensor rating is 1200 A and the maximum setting of the trip unit is 875 A. The setting selected is 0.7 ($0.7 \times 1200 = 840$ A).
— Long delay time (LDT). By inspection of breaker curves, a setting of 10 seconds is selected so that the minimum line clears the maximum line of breaker Ⓓ. Note that the dial setting of 10 represents the time in seconds for the breaker to operate at six times the sensor rating (even though this point ultimately falls outside the selected breaker curve).
— Short delay pickup (SDPU). The minimum setting of 4 is selected, as it clears breaker Ⓓ and allows space for breaker Ⓑ.
— Short delay time (SDT). The minimum setting of 0.18 s is chosen, as this clears the instantaneous tripping time of breaker Ⓓ.
— Instantaneous pickup. Not used.
— Ground pickup (GPU). Since this is the first device with ground-fault protection in the upstream direction, it is set to the lowest point: dial setting A, pickup of 260 A for a 1200 A sensor (see table at the bottom of Figure 8.13).
— Ground delay time (GDT). Set to lowest setting: 0.22 s.

Figure 16.9 shows the center line only of the resulting breaker response curve. In Figure 16.8, breaker Ⓒ is shown with the tolerance allowances included.

Step 13. Plot the curves for main secondary breaker Ⓑ.

— Long delay pick-up (LDPU). From step 7, the sensor rating is 2400 A and the maximum setting of the trip unit is 2255 A. The setting selected is 0.9 ($0.9 \times 2400 = 2160$ A).

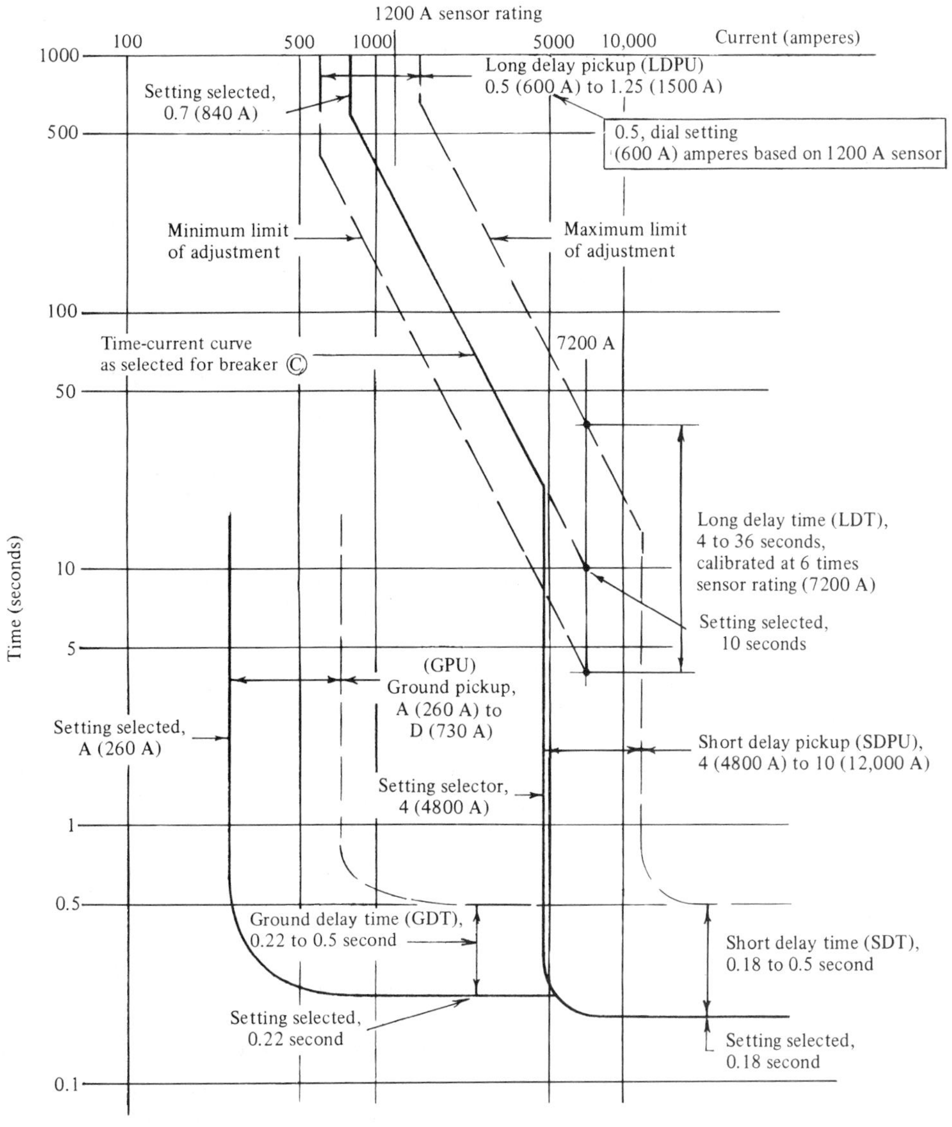

Note: Tolerance limits not shown on this diagram. Refer to Figure 8.13.

FIGURE 16.9

Summary of settings and resulting time–current curve for breaker ©

—Long delay time (LDT). By inspection of breaker curves, a setting of 8 s is selected so that the minimum line clears the maximum line of breaker © and so that the maximum line is below the transformer through-fault protection curve.

—Short delay pickup (SDPU). The minimum setting of 4 is selected so that the maximum line is clear of the minimum melting line of the primary fuse.

— Short delay time (SDT). The calibrated time of 0.33 s is selected so that it clears the maximum short-time tripping of breaker Ⓒ.
— Instantaneous pickup: Not used.
— Ground pickup (GPU). Dial setting A selected, pickup of 530 A for 2400 A sensor, which clears the maximum ground pickup of breaker Ⓒ. (*Note:* The maximum setting allowed by *NEC* code is 1200 A.)
— Ground delay time (GDT). The calibrated time of 0.35 s is selected so that it clears the maximum ground fault tripping time of breaker Ⓒ.

16.5.3 Conclusions of Coordination Study

Once the overlay of all the time–current characteristic curves for devices Ⓐ to Ⓔ has been completed as in Figure 16.8, the coordination or lack of coordination can be assessed. The following are a few selected examples to illustrate where proper coordination is obtained. Figure 16.10 shows the location of the faults as analyzed.

1. A 10,000 A fault on the 150 hp motor branch circuit at point Z will be cleared by breaker Ⓓ in a maximum of 0.024 s (approximately $1\frac{1}{2}$ cycles), which is well below the minimum of 0.07 s (approximately 4 cycles) required to initiate tripping of feeder breaker Ⓒ. Thus, only the 150 hp motor will be shut down, and the balance of the load on the motor-control center can continue to operate.
2. A 20,000 A fault on the feeder to the motor-control center at point Y will be cleared by breaker Ⓒ in a maximum of 0.18 s, which is less than the minimum of 0.20 s required to initiate tripping of main breaker Ⓑ. Thus only this feeder will be shut down, and the balance of the loads on the unit substation can continue to operate.
3. A 30,000 A fault on the main secondary bus at point X will be cleared by main breaker Ⓑ in a maximum of 0.33 s, which is less than the minimum of 0.5 s required to initiate the blowing of primary fuse Ⓐ. Even though all the load on the substation is shut down, it is preferable to be able to restore power by closing the breaker, rather than having to replace fuse units in the primary fuse assembly.
4. An overload of 3000 A on the feeder to the motor-control center will trip breaker Ⓒ in a maximum of 60 s, which is less than the minimum of 120 s required to initiate tripping of main breaker Ⓑ.

There is, however, one case where proper coordination is not obtained. A line-to-ground fault of 1200 amperes on the 150 horsepower motor branch circuit at point Z will trip breaker Ⓒ in a maximum of 0.22 second, which is well before the minimum time of

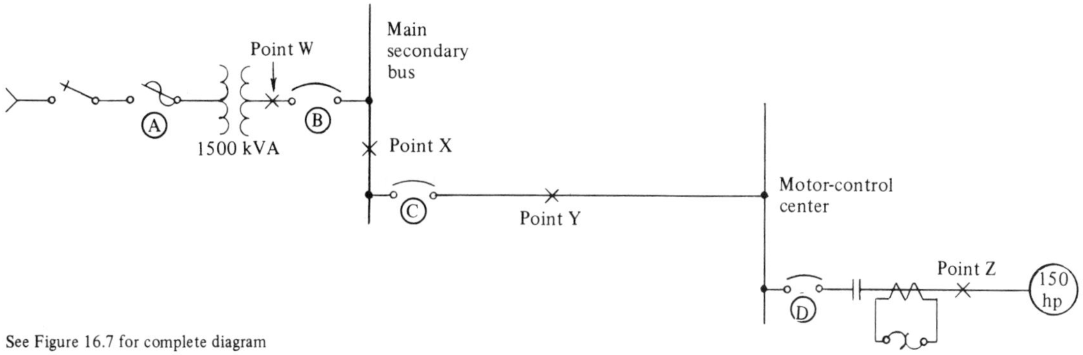

See Figure 16.7 for complete diagram

FIGURE 16.10

Location of faults as analyzed in Section 16.5.3

43 seconds required to initiate tripping of the branch breaker Ⓓ. Thus, the complete motor-control center is shut down even though the fault is only on the one motor branch circuit. This happens because breaker Ⓓ is not equipped with ground-fault protection, whereas breaker Ⓒ does have ground-fault protection and can therefore discriminate between a line-to-line fault and a line-to-ground fault, as explained in Section 10.5.1 and shown in Figure 10.16(b). A 1200 ampere line-to-line current (an overload), for example, would take 240 seconds to trip breaker Ⓒ, and there would be no coordination problem with breaker Ⓓ. This problem on line-to-ground faults on the motor branch feeder, ranging from approximately 230 up to 1300 amperes (a high resistance arcing type fault) can only be overcome by equipping the motor branch breaker with ground-fault protection. This is an economic decision, as the cost of adding ground-fault protection to the many motor branch circuits throughout the system could be substantial.

There are also two fault areas where coordination could possibly be lost. The first area of concern is designated area *a* in Figure 16.8. The minimum melting line of the primary fuse Ⓐ comes very close to the maximum line of the main breaker Ⓑ at the *knee* of the curve. Any shifting of the fuse curve to the left (which can occur with preloading of fuse) could result in both the fuse blowing and the main breaker tripping for faults at point X (Figure 16.10) in the 10,000 ampere range. The short time pickup of breaker Ⓑ is set at its minimum value of four times (9600 amperes) and cannot be decreased. However, some models of circuit breakers permit the short time pickup to be set as low as two times the sensor rating, rather than the four times shown in Figure 8.13. If this model of breaker is used, then the short time pickup of breaker Ⓑ could be set down to a lower value, for example, three times or 7200 amperes, which would eliminate the possibility of lack of coordination with the primary fuse.

The other area of concern is designated area *b* in Figure 16.8. Again, the minimum melting line of the primary fuse Ⓐ comes very close to the maximum line of breaker Ⓑ. For a maximum bolted fault of 37,000 amperes at point X, the primary fuse could possibly blow, in addition to the main breaker tripping. This possibility can be overcome by using the instantaneous trip on breaker Ⓑ and setting it to pick up at 12 times or (12 × 2400) = 28,800 amperes. However, to maintain coordination between breakers Ⓑ and Ⓒ, the instantaneous trip on breaker Ⓒ would also have to be set at 12 times or (12 × 1200) = 14,400 amperes. This, unfortunately, would result in loss of coordination between breakers Ⓒ and Ⓓ in the 14,400 to 20,600 ampere range.

Finally, a comparison of the primary fuse curve Ⓐ with the transformer through-fault protection curve shows that the fuse only properly protects the transformer from internal faults from a point above approximately (12,000/1804) or 6.6 times its full-load rating. Any low-current arcing faults of less than this magnitude that occur ahead of the main breaker (point W in Figure 16.10) or internally within the transformer will not initially be detected by the fuse. The fault will persist until the current builds up to the point where the fuse will eventually blow, thus increasing the damage. It should be noted that the 150 ampere rating of the fuse is below the maximum of 300% permitted by the *NEC* code. This situation can be improved somewhat by selecting a lower rating for the fuse unit (for example, 125 amperes). But then coordination with breaker Ⓑ could only be maintained if the short delay pickup of the breaker can be set below 4 times and the instantaneous trip is set at 12 times, as previously discussed. Improved coordination may be possible through the use of the new electronic fuses discussed in Section 7.8.3.

The foregoing discussion is presented primarily to show that complete coordination is not always possible, at least not at a reasonable cost. It also shows that many options are available to the system designer and it takes experience to determine which set of options is best for a particular system, balancing the economics of the system costs against the costs of unnecessary shutdowns. Simply complying with the provisions of the *National Electrical Code* does not necessarily mean that the system will be properly coordinated. The primary function of the *NEC* is to ensure safety, which must always have a higher priority than coordination.

With regard to the calculations shown for the fault currents, the method employed assumed the rules of thumb as outlined. Also, the impedances of such system devices as switches, circuit breakers, and substation bus have not been included, as they have a very minor effect, and, in any event, would act to further decrease the available fault current. In step 3, the calculations for the available fault current at the mains of the motor-control center were made using the assumption that all the motor contributions occurred at the main switchboard when, in fact, those motors connected to the MCC would contribute directly at the mains of the MCC. This would tend to make the actual fault current slightly higher than the calculated value. However, for motor-control centers the standard bus bracing and interrupting rating for the motor circuit breakers is 22,000 amperes. The calculated value of 20,700 amperes for the available fault current is some 6% below the 22,000 amperes, and it is highly unlikely that the degree of error in the simplified calculations would approach this amount. In the event that a calculated value is very close to the standard ratings for equipment, a more precise set of calculations would be in order.

The one example design shown is not meant to show all the problems inherent in designing an electrical system nor all the possible solutions to obtaining a good design. However, it is hoped that the example has introduced the reader to the fundamentals of system design and that it can act as an introduction to further study on the principles of system design and coordination.

There is now a growing use of computers in the design and study of electric power systems. There are programs that can materially aid in the calculations of available fault currents. Also, computer graphic routines allow the user to construct time–current curves quickly and systematically to arrive at a final set of coordinated curves. However, it should always be remembered that the computer is just another tool. The designer should first have a thorough understanding of the principles involved before applying the computer to solve the various problems.

SUMMARY

- The magnitude of available fault currents must be calculated for each section of a system to ensure the proper selection of feeders and protective devices.
- On low-voltage systems, calculations are done on the basis of three-phase bolted faults, as these generally result in the maximum possible fault current.
- The per unit impedance of the utility system is calculated as follows:

$$Z_U = \frac{\text{base kVA}}{\text{short-circuit kVA}}$$

- All motors on the system contribute to the available fault current. The contribution is assumed to be four times the full-load current of each motor.

- With 480 and 600 volt systems, it is assumed that the motor load is 100% of the system kVA.
- With 208Y/120 volt systems, it is assumed that the motor load is 50% of the system kVA.
- The kVA rating and the percentage impedance of the substation transformer have a significant effect on the magnitude of the available fault current.
- When the impedance of a feeder is to be included in the fault calculations, the equivalent system impedance up to the source of the feeder is assumed to have an inductive reactance to resistance ratio of 4.
- There are three classes of motor overload relays: classes 10, 20, and 30. The number specifies the maximum time in seconds for the relay to operate at 600% of its rating.
- Proper coordination on motor circuits is obtained when the overload relay opens the starter on all excess currents up to 600% and the overcurrent device clears all currents above 600% of the motor rated current.
- The rating of the primary protection of a transformer operating at more than 600 volts should not exceed 300% of the transformer rated primary current.
- The rating of the secondary protection of a transformer operating at more than 600 volts should not exceed 125% of the transformer rated secondary current.
- The coordination of a system is studied by preparing an overlay of the time–current characteristic curves of the protective devices, with all curves properly lined up on a common current scale.

QUESTIONS

1. Why is it necessary to calculate the available fault current at specific locations in an electrical system?
2. What does the term available fault current mean?
3. In calculating the available fault current on a low-voltage system, why is the fault assumed to be a three-phase bolted type?
4. List the possible sources of fault current in a building electrical system.
5. Explain why induction motors are a source of fault current for the first few cycles after a fault occurs.
6. What is the assumption with regard to the motor contribution to the available fault current for 208Y/120 V systems?
7. What are the two types of ratings with regard to circuit breakers that must be specified when applying them to protect a feeder?
8. Explain why it is desirable to select power transformers with impedances of at least 5.0%.
9. Explain why the short-circuit duty requirements for equipment decrease as the distance from the substation increases.
10. Why is it undesirable to increase the system impedance to a high value to keep fault currents to a low value?

11. Describe the two most common types of thermal-response motor overload relays.
12. What does class 20 designate with regard to overload relays?
13. What factors affect the precise current rating of a motor overload heater element?
14. Why should the motor circuit protective device (fuse or circuit breaker) operate first to clear any current above 600% of the full-load current of motor?
15. In the design procedure covered in Section 16.5.1, why is the calculation of the available fault current at the secondary main bus the first step?
16. Why is it necessary to calculate the available fault current at the motor-control center as in step 3, Section 16.5.1?
17. The minimum ampacity required for the feeder to the motor-control center is 650 A. Explain why an 800 A frame breaker cannot be used for breaker Ⓒ.
18. Explain why the primary fuse Ⓐ (Figure 16.7) does not adequately protect the substation transformer for fault currents less than approximately 660% of the full-load current of the transformer.

PROBLEMS

1. The utility short-circuit capability is 100,000 kVA. The transformer rating is 750 kVA. Calculate the per unit impedance of the utility system connection.
2. Power is supplied over a primary feeder to a 13,800-208Y/120 V, 500 kVA unit substation. The impedance of the transformer is 5.0%. The utility system short-circuit capability is 150,000 kVA. Assume 50% of the load is motors. Calculate the available short-circuit current at the main secondary bus of the substation.
3. Repeat Problem 2, except the secondary voltage is 480Y/277 V and motor load is 100%.
4. A three-phase feeder consists of three No. 4/0 copper conductors in a steel conduit and is 150 ft in length. The feeder is connected to a 750 kVA unit substation, and the system voltage is 208Y/120 V. Calculate the per unit resistance and reactance of the feeder.
5. In Problem 4, the utility short-circuit capability is 250,000 kVA and the transformer impedance is 5.75%. Assume a 50% motor load on the substation. The feeder is connected to a power panel. Calculate the available fault current at the mains of the power panel.
6. Repeat Problem 4, except the system voltage is 480Y/277 V.
7. Repeat Problem 5, except the system voltage is 480Y/277 V and motor load is 100%.
8. Select the overload heater elements from Table 16.2 for the magnetic starters for the following three-phase squirrel-cage induction motors with service factors of 1.15: (a) 10 hp, 200 V; (b) 10 hp, 460 V; (c) 25 hp, 460 V; and (d) 60 hp, 460 V. Assume that the nameplate full-load current ratings of the motors are the same as the values listed in Table 13.2.
9. Calculate the rated current of each overload heater element selected in Problem 8.
10. Express the rated current of each overload relay selected in Problem 8 as a percentage of the full-load current of the motor it is protecting. Does your selection satisfy the code requirements with regard to overload protection of motors (see Section 13.1.2 of this text).
11. Determine the response time for each overload heater element selected in Problem 8 at 600% of the motor full-load amperes (at locked-rotor amperes). Use the curve for class 20 relays in Figure 16.5.
12. A motor-control center controls the following 460 V, three-phase squirrel-cage induction motors: five 5 hp, two $7\frac{1}{2}$ hp, two 10 hp, two 15 hp, two 25 hp, and one 60 hp. The motor-control center is supplied over a 300 ft feeder from a 13,800-480Y/277 V, 2000 kVA unit substation. The transformer impedance is 5.75%. The utility system short-circuit kVA capability is 150,000. The feeder conductors are to be type THW copper installed in steel conduit above grade. The voltage drop on the feeder is not to exceed 3%. Assume the power factor of the motor load is

85%. Select the feeder to the motor-control center.

13. Select the feeder breaker for the feeder to the motor-control center in Problem 12, including the sensor rating and the setting on the long delay pickup (based on the maximum permitted by the code). The breaker will be the low-voltage power type as in Section 8.5 in this text.

14. Select the main secondary breaker for the substation in Problem 12, including the sensor rating and the setting of the long delay pickup.

15. The primary switchgear for the substation in Problem 12 is a fused load-interrupter switch. Select the primary fuse and indicate the maximum rating of the fuse unit permitted by the code.

Appendix A

REFERENCES TO 1986 CANADIAN ELECTRICAL CODE

General

The *Canadian Electrical Code* (CEC) is published by the Canadian Standards Association (CSA), 178 Rexdale Boulevard, Rexdale, Ontario. The code is divided into two parts: Part I, CSA Standard C22.1-1986, covers safety standards for electrical *installations,* and Part II covers safety standards for electrical *equipment.* The list of Part II standards is shown in Appendix A of the Canadian Electrical Code, Part I.

The general arrangement of the Canadian Electrical Code, Part I, is shown on page 30 of the 1986 edition of the code. It is divided into numbered sections, with each section further divided into numbered rules. Rules applicable to a specific subject are grouped together under 100, 200, and so on, numbered series. As an example, Rules 10-100, 10-102, 10-104, and so on, are in Section 10, Grounding and Bonding, and are grouped under the heading *System and Circuit Grounding.* The tables and diagrams are shown separately after the sections and are numbered 1, 2, and so on.

The objective of the Canadian Electrical Code, as stated in Section 0, Object, Scope, and Definitions, is *to establish safety standards for the installation and maintenance of electrical equipment and for the prevention of fire and shock hazards.* The CEC requirements are generally consistent with the *National Electrical Code* requirements. The following is a list of those rules in the 1986 Canadian Electrical Code that are applicable in place of the National Electrical Code rules mentioned in the main text of this book. The related comments indicate any differences between the two codes.

Chapter 1

1.8 Voltage Terminology and Standards

- Table 1.1, Voltage standards for building electrical systems.
- Reference: CSA Standard CAN3-C235-82, Preferred voltage levels for ac systems, 0 to 50,000 volts

Comments: The CSA method of designating three-phase, four-wire wye systems differ slightly from that shown in Table 1.1. For example, CSA designates a system as 120/208Y, rather than 208Y/120.

The major difference in CSA voltage standards less than 750 volts is that the 277/480Y system is not a preferred standard, whereas the 347/600Y system is a preferred standard. The 240/416Y system is an additional preferred standard.

Chapter 6

- Introduction
- Reference: Section 0, Object

6.1 Types of Abnormal Conditions

- Reference: Section 14 and Rule 14-100

Chapter 7

7.2 Categories of Low-Voltage Fuses

- Reference: 14-000 series of rules and CSA Standard C22.2 No. 59-M1984; Fuses (both plug and cartridge-enclosed types)

7.5 Classifications of Low-Voltage Fuses

- Reference: CSA Standard C22.2 No. 106-M1985; HRC Fuses

Comments: The CSA has the additional classifications of form I and form II fuses. Form I fuses must meet the 135% and 200% maximum allowable clearing times as required for standard code fuses (see Table 7.1). Form II fuses must meet specified clearing times at only 160% of their rating, and these times are similar to those specified at 135% for the standard code fuses. For example, a 100 A form II fuse has a maximum clearing time of 120 minutes at 160% of its rating, as compared to 120 minutes at 135% for a standard fuse. Therefore, form II fuses applied at their rated current provide only short-circuit protection and must be used in conjunction with other means of providing overload protection. A typical application is to use form II fuses for motor branch circuit protection, with the overload protection being provided by the overload relays in the motor starter. An example of a CSA designation is HRCI-J, which signifies that the fuse is a high rupturing capacity type, form I, class J.

Rule 14-212 governs the use of form I and form II high rupturing capacity (HRC) fuses.

7.6 Fusible Switches

- Reference: Rule 14-402

Chapter 10

- Reference: Section 10, Grounding and bonding

Comments: The 1986 edition of the CEC clearly differentiates between grounding and bonding (see definitions in Section 0). Grounding means a permanent and continuous conductive path to earth. Bonding means a low-impedance path obtained by permanently joining all noncurrent-carrying metal parts to assure electrical continuity of the equipment grounding circuit.

10.2 Grounded Systems

- Reference: 10-100 and 10-200 series of rules

  Comment: Rule 10-106(b) does not specify a voltage and therefore both the 240/416Y and the 347/600Y volt, three-phase, four-wire systems in which the neutral is used for a circuit conductor are included in the system grounding requirements.

10.2.1 Selection of System Grounding Points

- Reference: Rule 10-206, Grounding connections for isolated systems

  Comment: The CEC uses the term *isolated* system rather than *separately derived* system, but the intent is the same.
- Reference: Rule 10-200, Current over grounding and bonding conductors

10.3.1 Impedance of Equipment Grounding Circuit

- Reference: Rule 10-504, Common grounding electrode

  Comment: This rule states that the same electrode *may* be used, rather than making it mandatory (which it should be).

10.3.3 Summary of *National Electrical Code* requirements

- References with regard to Canadian Electrical Code:

  — Rules 4-028 and 030, Identification of insulated neutral conductors
  — Rule 4-036(1), Identification of insulated grounding conductor
  — 10-300 series, Conductor enclosure bonding
  — 10-400 series, Equipment bonding
  — 10-500 series, Methods of grounding
  — 10-600 series, Bonding methods
  — 10-700 series, Grounding electrodes
  — 10-800 series, Grounding and bonding conductors
  — 10-900 series, Grounding and bonding conductor connections
  — 36-300 series, High voltage installations, grounding
  — Table 16, Minimum size of conductors, metal conduit, or electrical metallic tubing for bonding raceways and equipment
  — Table 17, Minimum size of grounding conductor for ac systems or common grounding conductor
  — Table 18, Minimum size of grounding conductor for service raceway and service equipment

  Comments: Table 17 is based on ampacity of largest service conductor rather than on size. Table 18 covers grounding of raceways and equipment where the ac system is not grounded at the premises. Note that aluminum conductors are not approved for use as grounding conductors.
- *Example 10.1* RW90(XLPE) is CSA equivalent of type XHHW. Ampacity of conductors from CEC Table 2 = 395 amperes. Two parallel runs (separate conduit) = 2 × 395 = 890 amperes. From CEC Table 17, No. 3/0 (000) copper ground wire is required.

- *Example 10.2* CEC Table 17 also requires No. 3 copper as indicated.

10.5 Ground-Fault Protection

- Reference: Rule 14-102

Comment: This rule also requires ground-fault protection for systems of 150 volts or less to ground (120/208Y) and 2000 A or more.

10.6 High-Resistance Grounded Systems

- There is no reference in the CEC to this type of system.

Chapter 11

- References: Section 4, Conductors; Section 12, Wiring methods

11.1 Continuous Current Rating of Conductors

- References: Rule 4-004, Tables 2 (copper) and 4 (aluminum).

Comment: Tables 2 and 4 are used in lieu of Table 11.1 (*NEC* Table 310-16) as shown in this text. The CEC and *NEC* tables are for the most part compatible with the following major exceptions:

— AWG sizes 14, 12, and 10 copper and 12, 10, and 8 aluminum have the same ampacities for 60°, 75°, and 90°C rated conductors.
— CEC ampacities for 90°C rated conductors tend to be lower.
— kcmil instead of MCM and 0, 00, etc. instead of 1/0, 2/0, etc.

There is no CEC equivalent for Table 11.2 (*NEC* Table 310-27). Tables 2 and 4 are also used for conductors run in underground raceways.

11.1.4 Ambient Temperature

- Reference: Table 5A, Ampacity correction factors for ambient temperatures above 30°C

Comment: There are no correction factors listed for ambient temperatures below 30°C and values for 90°C conductors are not the same.

11.1.5 Conductors Installed in Raceways

- Reference: Rule 4-004

Comment: There is no mention in the CEC that the neutral of a three-phase, four-wire circuit, where the majority of the load consists of electric-discharge lighting, data-processing, or similar equipment, must be considered as a current-carrying conductor. However, at least one provincial inspection authority (British Columbia) requires that the neutral for such loads shall be considered as a fourth current-carrying conductor (Bulletin 4-1-0).

11.1.6 Determining the Ampacities of Conductors

- *Example 11.1* From CEC Tables 2 and 5A, ampacity same as shown.

- *Example 11.2* From CEC Table 2 and Rule 4-004(1)(c), ampacity = 345 × 0.80 = 276 amperes.
- *Example 11.3* From CEC Tables 4 and 5A and Rule 4-004(2)(d), ampacity same as shown.
- *Example 11.4* CEC Table 2 is used and no allowance is made for 20°C ambient earth temperature nor any correction for two ducts. Ampacity = 230 amperes.

11.3 Maximum Allowable Voltage Drop

- Reference: Rule 8-102

11.4 Letter Designation of Cables

- Differences in CSA designations (see Table D1):

  — Separate designation XLPE used to indicate cross-linked synthetic polymer (polyethylene) insulation.
  — Temperature ratings above 60°C designated by 75 or 90.

Examples: TW75 is equivalent of *NEC* type THW. RW90(XLPE) is equivalent of *NEC* type XHHW.

11.5 Raceways

- Reference: Section 0, Definition of raceways

11.5.1 Types of Conduit

- References: 12-1000 to 12-5000 series, Use and installation of conduit and tubing; Rule 12-010, Wiring in ducts and plenum chambers; Rule 10-510(3), Separate grounding conductor for liquid-tight flexible metal conduit

  Comment: Intermediate conduit and electrical nonmetallic tubing is not mentioned.

11.5.2 Number of Conductors Permitted in Conduit

- Reference: Rule 12-1116 and Table 6
- *Example 11.10* The CSA equivalent for THW is TW75. From CEC Table 6, 2½ inch conduit required (no change).

11.6 Conductors in Parallel

- References: Rules 12-108 and 12-1004(1)

11.7 Examples of Feeder Design

- References: Section 8, Circuit loading and demand factors; Rule 8-104(3), Continuous and noncontinuous loads

Comment: For loads of 225 amperes or less, the time is reduced to 1 hour.

- Reference: Rule 8-104(5) and Appendix B

  Comment: Unless the fusible switch or circuit breaker is marked as being suitable for 100% operation, a feeder can only be continuously loaded to 80% of its ampacity rating, which is the same as saying that its ampacity rating must be 125% of the continuous load.

- *Example 11.11* Equivalent CSA conductor type is TW75. **(a)** Minimum size required for ampacity; From CEC Table 2, ampacity of No. 1/0 TW75 is 150 amperes. **(e)** From CEC Table 6, conduit size required is 2 inch. Therefore, there is no change to solution as shown.
- *Example 11.15* Equivalent CSA conductor types are TW75 and RW90(X-LPE). **(a)** Minimum size required for ampacity: Derating factor of 80%, see Rule 4-004(1)(c). From CEC Table 2, No. 4/0 TW75 rated at 230 amperes; No. 3/0 RW90 rated at 210 amperes. **(e)** From CEC Table 6, four No. 3/0 RW90(XLPE) requires 2 inch conduit. Therefore, there is no change to solution as shown.
- *Example 11.16* **(d)** From CEC Table 6, four No. 4/0 RW90(XLPE) requires $2\frac{1}{2}$ inch conduit.

11.8 Overcurrent Protection of Feeders

- References: 14-000 series and Rules 14-100 and 104, Requirements and locations of overcurrent protection; Rule 8-104 for continuous loading of devices
- *Example 11.17* From CEC Table 2, ampacity of No. 3/0 RW90 is 210 amperes. Ampacity of four No. 3/0 in conduit = $0.80 \times 210 = 168$ amperes, which is satisfactory (see CEC Table 13).

11.9 Cable Trays

- References: Section 0, Definition of cabletrough; 12-2200 series, Installation of cabletroughs

  Comment: CEC uses term cabletrough for cable tray.

11.10 Busways

- References: Section 0, Definition of busyway; 12-2000 series, Installation of busways

Chapter 12

- References: Section 8, Circuit loading and demand factors; Section 12, Wiring methods; Section 14, Protection and control; Section 30, Installation of lighting equipment

12.1 Branch Circuit Conductors See comments for Sections 11.1 through 11.5.2 in this appendix

- *Example 12.1* Ampacity of No. 12 R90 copper from CEC Table 2 is 20 amperes. Temperature correction factor from CEC Table 5A is 0.90. Derating factor from Rule 4-004(1)(c) is 80% for six conductors. Ampacity = 20 × 0.90 × 0.80 = 14.4 amperes. Therefore, ampacity is not sufficient and No. 10 R90 copper (rated for 30 amperes) has to be used.

- References: Rule 30-312, Temperature rating of conductors for ballasts in lighting fixtures

  Comment: RW75 is not approved for 90°C use in fixtures. Rule 4-002, Minimum size of conductors

12.2 Branch Circuits for Lighting

- References: Section 30, Installation of lighting equipment; Rule 30-104, Protection of lighting circuits

  Comments: The CEC requirements are summarized as follows:

  — Branch circuits for incandescent medium-base luminaires shall have a maximum rating of 15 A.
  — Branch circuits for incandescent mogul-base luminaires shall have a maximum rating of 40 A.
  — Branch circuits for metal-enclosed fluorescent and medium-base HID luminaires shall have a maximum rating of 20 A.
  — Branch circuits for mogul-base HID luminaires shall have maximum ratings of (i) 40 A at 120 V, (ii) 20 amperes up to 277 volts, and (iii) 15 A above 277 V.

- Reference: Rule 30-102, Voltage

  Comments: The CEC requirements are as follows:

  — Circuit voltages shall not exceed 150 volts-to-ground in any dwelling unit.
  — In industrial and commercial establishments where a trained and qualified maintenance staff is available, the voltage-to-ground shall not exceed that of a nominal 347/600Y system.

  The fact that 347 volt (line-to-ground) branch circuits are permitted means further savings in branch circuit and feeder wiring as compared to 277 volt circuits. The ballasts necessary for operating fluorescent and HID luminaires on 347 volts are CSA approved.

- *Example 12.2* Add the following: **(c)** 347/600Y volts. Ballast has a line current of 0.75 amperes at 347 volts.
- *Solution:* Maximum loading of each circuit is again 16 amperes. **(c)** 347/600Y volt system (ballasts connected to 347 volts)

  — Maximum number of units per circuit = 16.0/0.75 = 21.3 ≈ 21.
  — Minimum number of circuits = 70/21 = 3.3 ≈ 4.

  Therefore, it is possible to wire the lighting layout as in Example 5.11 using only four circuits, as compared to ten required using 120 volt circuits.

12.3 Branch Circuits for Receptacles

- Reference: Rule 14-600, Protection of receptacles

  Comment: Two or more 15 ampere receptacles *cannot* be connected to a 20 ampere circuit.
- Reference: Diagram 1, CSA configurations for nonlocking receptacles

  Comment: The 20 ampere receptacle does not have a T-slot and therefore *cannot* accept 15 ampere attachment plugs.
- Reference: Rule 12-3000, Maximum number of outlets per circuit

  Comment: There shall not be more than 12 general-purpose receptacle outlets on any two-wire branch circuit. Each outlet shall be rated at not less than 1 ampere.
- Reference: Rule 26-700, Installation of receptacles

12.4 Lighting Panels

- Reference: CSA Standard C22.2 No. 29-M1983, Panelboard and panelboard enclosures

  Comments: Standard panels are available for 347/600Y, three-phase, four-wire systems.
- Reference: Rule 14-606, Panelboard overcurrent protection

  Comments: Individual overcurrent protection is required for panelboards supplied by conductors having overcurrent protection *greater than 100 amperes*.
- Reference: Rule 14-100(b), Requirements for feeder taps, same as shown in Figure 12.4(c)

12.7 Example Floor Layout of Lighting and Receptacles

- In Figures 12.8 and 12.9, the following modifications are required:

  — Circuit A2, since it supplies medium-base incandescent fixtures, must be protected by a 15 A breaker.
  — Circuit A4 must similarly be protected by a 15 A breaker. Only *four* type C, 300 W, medium-base incandescent fixtures can be connected to this circuit, giving a load of 10 A (maximum permitted is 80% of 15 = 12 A). The two other type C fixtures shown in the corridor have to be combined with two or more units and connected to an additional 15 A circuit.

- References: The following are applicable to branch circuits:

  — 12-100 series; Conductors in general
  — 12-3000 series; Installation of boxes, cabinets, outlets, and terminal fittings
  — Rule 12-3040; Maximum number of conductors in a box
  — Rule 30-312; Luminaire as a raceway
  — Section 46; Emergency Systems, Unit Equipment, and Exit Signs

12.8 Switching of Lighting Systems

Comments: Local switches rated for 347 volts, 15 and 20 amperes, and low-voltage remote-control switching relays with contacts rated for 347 volts are available.

12.9 Underfloor Raceway Systems

- References: 12-1700 series, Underfloor raceways; 12-1800 series, Cellular floors

12.10 Ground-Fault Circuit Interrupters

- References: Rule 26-702, Receptacles in residential occupancies; Section 68, Swimming pools (includes therapeutic pools and hydromassage bath tubs)

12.11 Computed Loads for Lighting and Receptacles

- References: Section 8, Circuit loading and demand factors; Table 14, Watts per square meter and demand factors for various types of occupancies
- *Example 12.3*

$$10{,}000\ \text{ft}^2 = 10{,}000 \times 0.093 = 930\ \text{m}^2$$

Unit loading from CEC Table 14 is 50 watts per square meter (this includes allowance for general-use receptacles).

$$\text{Total computed load} = 930 \times 50 = 46{,}500\ \text{W}$$

$$\text{Load current} = \frac{46{,}500}{1.732 \times 208 \times 1.0^{a}} = 129.2\ \text{A}$$

[a] Assume 100% power factor.
This continuous load cannot exceed 80% of feeder ampacity.

$$\text{Minimum ampacity} = \frac{129.2}{0.80} = 161.5\ \text{A}$$

- *Example 12.4*

$$12{,}000\ \text{ft}^2 = 12{,}000 \times 0.093 = 1116\ \text{m}^2$$

(a) For feeder taps to each panel:

— From Rule 8-206, basic load is 20 W/m^2
— Demand for first 900 m^2 is 80% of (20 × 900) = 14,400 W
— Demand for remaining area:

$$(1116 - 900) = 216\ \text{m}^2 = 65\%\ \text{of}\ (20 \times 216) = \underline{2{,}808\ \text{W}}$$

$$\text{Total computed load} = 17{,}208\ \text{W}$$

$$\text{Load current} = \frac{17{,}208}{1.732 \times 208 \times 1.0} = 47.8 \text{ A}$$

Since the load as calculated by Rule 8-206 is not specifically excluded from being considered as a continuous load:

$$\text{Minimum ampacity} = \frac{47.8}{0.80} = 59.75 \approx 60 \text{ A}$$

(b) For the main feeder:

— Total area is $3 \times 1116 = 3348 \text{ m}^2$
— Demand for first 900 m^2 is 80% of $(20 \times 900) = 14{,}400$ W
— Demand for remaining area:

$$(3348 - 900) = 2448 \text{ m}^2 = 65\% \text{ of } (20 \times 2448) = \underline{31{,}824 \text{ W}}$$

$$\text{Total computed load} = 46{,}224 \text{ W}$$

$$\text{Load current} = \frac{46{,}224}{1.732 \times 208 \times 1.0} = 128.4 \text{ A}$$

$$\text{Minimum ampacity} = \frac{128.4}{0.80} = 160.5 \quad (160 \text{ A})$$

Chapter 13

- References: Section 28, Motors and generators; Table 26

  Comment: Table 26 lists specific values for the minimum ampacity of the motor circuit conductors and the maximum rating permitted for overload and overcurrent protection for motor full-load currents up to 500 amperes.

13.1 Branch Circuit for a Single Motor

- References: Tables 44 and 45

  Comments: The values listed in Table 13.1 of this text for single-phase motors are consistent with the values listed in CEC Table 45. The values listed in Table 13.2 of this text for three-phase induction type motors are consistent with the values listed in CEC Table 44.

13.1.1 Short-Circuit and Ground-Fault Protection

- References: Rules 28-200 and 28-210; Table 26 or 29 (whichever is applicable)

  Comments: The CEC uses the term overcurrent protection. However, for the reasons stated in this text, the motor branch circuit protective device cannot adequately protect the circuit from overloads and in reality provides only short-circuit and ground-fault protection.

  The values listed in CEC Table 29 are consistent with the values shown in Table 13.3 of this text except that for reduced-voltage autotransformer starting of more than 30 amperes the maximum value permitted for non-time-delay fuses is 200%.

13.1.2 Overload Protection

- References: 28-300 series

  Comments: The values of the setting of overload devices as listed in CEC Table 26 are also based on being a maximum of 125% of the full-load current of motor with a service factor of 1.15.

  Separate overheating protection is required under the conditions as specified in Rule 28-302.

13.1.3 Branch-Circuit Conductors

- References: Rules 28-104 and 28-106

  Comment: Rule 28-104 requires that, even if the temperature rating of the insulation is 90°C, the ampacity of the conductors connected to the motor shall be based on the 75°C rating.

13.2 Disconnecting Means

- Reference: 28-600 series

13.2.1 Location

Comments: The disconnecting means must be located within sight of and within *9 meters* (approximately 30 ft) of the motor or controller.

A disconnecting means, capable of being locked in the open position, may be installed out of sight or more than 9 meters from a motor or controller only if *a trained and qualified electrical maintenance staff is available.*

13.2.2 Ratings and Types

Comments: A manually operated, general-purpose ac switch can only be used as a disconnecting means for a *single-phase* motor. The ac switch shall have a rating *not less than 125%* of the rated motor current.

13.3 Examples of Motor Branch Circuits

- *Example 13.1* Conductor type will be TW75. Using CEC Tables 2, 6, and 26, all ratings and conductor and conduit sizes as selected remain the same.
- *Example 13.2* CEC Table 26 permits a maximum of *100 ampere* time-delay fuses to be used for a full-load motor current of 52 amperes.
- *Example 13.3* CEC Table 26 permits a maximum of only *125 ampere* trip rating for the breaker. See Figure 16.6 of this text, which shows that a trip rating as low as 100 amperes would still be satisfactory.

13.4 Feeders for Two or More Motors

- References: Rules 28-108, 28-110, and 28-204
- *Example 13.4* Conductor type will be TW75. Calculations for feeder protection: from CEC Table 26, the maximum time-delay fuse permitted for a 40 horsepower motor with full-load current of 120 amperes is *225 amperes*.

The maximum rating of feeder protection is 225 + 142 = 367 amperes. A 350 ampere fuse will still be selected. Otherwise, all calculations, ratings, and sizes of conductors and conduit as selected remain the same.

- *Example 13.5* CEC Table 26 permits a 300 ampere circuit breaker for the 40 horsepower motor, full-load current of 120 amperes. Therefore, all calculations and ratings selected remain the same.

13.5 Single Motor Taps

- Reference: Rule 28-106(4)

  Comment: Maximum distance for tap is 7.5 meters (approximately 25 feet).
- *Example 13.6* Conductor type will be TW75. From CEC Table 2, 1/0 copper is also rated for 150 amperes but No. 8 copper is rated for *only 45 amperes*. Therefore, tap conductors will have to be No. 6 TW75.
- *Example 13.7* From CEC Table 2, the ampacity of No. 6 TW75 copper is also 65 amperes; therefore, no change to selection.

Chapter 14

- Reference: 28-500 series, Control

14.2.1 Control for Magnetic Starters

- Reference: Rule 14-100(d), Protection of control circuits

  Comment: This rule covers only control circuits that extend beyond the starter enclosure. The maximum rating of the overcurrent device cannot be more than 300% of the ampacity of control circuit conductors. This agrees with the values shown in Table 14.2 of this text. For example, No. 14 copper conductors (60°, 75°, and 90°C) are rated for 15 amperes (CEC Table 2). The maximum rating of overcurrent protective devices is (3 × 45) = 45 amperes.

14.5.3 Layout of Motor-Control Centers

- Reference: Rule 2-308, Working space about electrical equipment

  Comment: Minimum working space of *1 meter* is required.

Chapter 15

15.2.2 Lightning Protection

- Reference: 26-500 series

  Comment: The term *lightning* arrester is used rather than surge arrester.

15.3 Transformer Section

- Reference: Rule 26-248, Installation of dry-core, open-ventilated type transformers

15.6 Location of Unit Substations

- References: Rule 2-308, Working space about electrical equipment; Rule 2-310, Entrance to and exit from working space

Comment: A minimum working space of 1 meter is required about a switchboard. This space is in addition to the space required for the drawout circuit breakers (see Figure 15.7, this text).

- *Figure 15.10* Clearance required by the CEC is a minimum of 1 meter at the rear and ends of the unit substation. The minimum clearance in front of the unit is 1 meter plus the space required to withdraw the largest circuit breaker.

Chapter 16

16.5 Design of an Electrical System

- The feeder conductors are to be type TW75. The 480Y/277 volt system is not a preferred voltage in Canada. A 347/600Y volt system would normally be used. However, the presentation serves as an example of the methods used to design a system.
- *Step 2* The ampacities of type TW75 copper conductors as per CEC Table 2 and the conduit size as per CEC Table 6 agree with the values as shown.
- *Step 5* The maximum rating for the trip unit of the motor branch breaker from CEC Table 26 (FLMA = 180 amperes) is 400 amperes (a 350 ampere trip rating is eventually selected in Step 11).
- *Step 6* The maximum setting of the trip unit for the feeder breaker is 400 + 425 = 825 amperes. The final setting selected in Step 12 is 840 amperes, which is satisfactory.
- *Steps 7 and 8*

  Reference: Rule 26-252 and Table 50, Overcurrent protection for power and distribution transformers rated over 600 V

  Comment: The values as selected for the primary fuse and the secondary breaker comply with the CEC requirements with regard to the overcurrent protection of the transformer.

Appendix B

ASSOCIATIONS THAT ISSUE ELECTRICAL STANDARDS

Standards are extensively used throughout the design and installation of the electrical system for a building. Standards establish specific requirements, such as the ratings and dimensions of equipment, performance requirements, methods of measurement and test procedures, and definition of electrical terms. The following associations issue standards documents that relate to electrical equipment and recommended practices for the installation of electrical systems.

United States

1. *American National Standards Institute* (ANSI): This association does not write standards. It promotes and coordinates the development of standards and approves as American National Standards those documents that are prepared in accordance with ANSI regulations.
2. *Institute of Electrical and Electronic Engineers* (IEEE): This association issues several hundred standards documents covering most fields of electrical engineering. Those that specifically relate to building electrical systems are listed in the Bibliography.
3. *National Electrical Manufacturers Association* (NEMA): This association prepares standards that establish dimensions, ratings, and performance requirements for electrical equipment among manufacturers.
4. *National Fire Protection Association* (NFPA): This association publishes standards documents specifying requirements for fire protection and safety. One of its publications is NFPA 70, *National Electrical Code* (*NEC*).
5. *Occupational Safety and Health Administration* (OSHA): This administration of the U.S. Department of Labor is responsible for the Occupational Safety and Health Act. OSHA's electrical safety standards cover all electrical equipment and installations used to provide electric power and light for employee workplaces.
6. *Underwriters Laboratories, Inc.* (UL): Underwriters Laboratories, Inc., prepares safety standards for electrical equipment, including appliances, and tests equipment for compliance with these standards. Manufacturers whose products are approved by UL are authorized to use the UL label on the equipment.

Canada

1. *Canadian Standards Association* (CSA): This association prepares and publishes the *Canadian Electrical Code* (CEC). It also tests equipment for compliance with CSA standards. Manufacturers whose products are approved by CSA are authorized to use the CSA label on the equipment.
2. *Electrical and Electronic Manufacturers of Canada* (EEMAC): This association develops product standards for the electrical and electronic industry to encourage uniformity in equipment nomenclature, performance, rating, dimensions, and test methods and to assure users that the equipment complies with established performance, safety, rating, and capacity requirements. These standards are developed in cooperation with inspection authorities, utilities, user groups, consultants, CSA, and Canadian Government agencies.

Bibliography

General References

Constructing Electrical Systems. Published by Electrical Construction and Maintenance, a McGraw-Hill publication, New York.

The National Electrical Code 1987 Handbook. Quincy, Ma: National Fire Protection Association.

Recommended Practice for Electric Power Distribution for Industrial Plants, ANSI/IEEE Std 141-1986. New York: The Institute of Electrical and Electronics Engineers, Inc.

Recommended Practice for Electric Systems in Commercial Buildings, ANSI/IEEE Std 241-1983. New York: The Institute of Electrical and Electronics Engineers, Inc.

Recommended Practice for Emergency and Standby Power for Industrial and Commercial Applications, ANSI/IEEE Std 446-1987. New York: The Institute of Electrical and Electronics Engineers, Inc.

Recommended Practice for Industrial and Commercial Power System Analysis, ANSI/IEEE Std 399-1980. New York: The Institute of Electrical and Electronics Engineers, Inc.

Recommended Practice for Protection and Coordination of Industrial and Commercial Power Systems, ANSI/IEEE Std 242-1986. New York: The Institute of Electrical and Electronics Engineers, Inc.

Chapter 1: Review of Electric Power Fundamentals

Angerbauer, G. J. *Principles of DC and AC Circuits,* 2nd ed. Boston: PWS–KENT Publishers.

Jackson, H. W. *Introduction to Electric Circuits,* 6th ed. Englewood Cliffs, N.J.: Prentice-Hall, Inc.

Ridsdale, R. E. *Electric Circuits for Engineering Technology,* 2nd ed. New York: McGraw-Hill Book Company.

Chapter 2: Electric Motors

Kosow, I. L. *Electric Machinery and Transformers*. Englewood Cliffs, N.J.: Prentice-Hall, Inc.

Richardson, D. V. *Rotating Electric Machinery and Transformer Technology,* 3rd ed. Reston, Va.: Reston Publishing Company, Inc.

Siskind, C. S., *Electrical Machines, Direct and Alternating Current,* 2nd ed. New York: McGraw-Hill Book Company.

Chapters 3, 4, and 5: Lighting

Lighting Handbook. Somerset, N.J.: North American Philips Lighting Corporation.

Chapter 7: Fuses

Electrical Protection Handbook. St. Louis, Mo.: Bussmann Division, McGraw-Edison Company.

A New Fault-Interrupting Device for Improved Medium-Voltage System and Equipment Protection. Chicago: S & C Electric Co.

Reichenstein, H. W. *Applying Low-voltage Fuses.* Published by Electrical Construction and Maintenance, a McGraw-Hill Publication, New York.

Chapter 8: Circuit Breakers

Breaker Basics. Beaver, Pa.: Westinghouse Electric Corporation, Low-Voltage Breaker Division.

Chapter 10: Grounding

Recommended Practice for Grounding of Industrial and Commercial Power Systems, ANSI/IEEE Std 142-1982. New York: The Institute of Electrical and Electronics Engineers, Inc.

Chapter 14: Motor Starters and Motor-Control Centers

Humphries, J. T., and L. P. Sheets. *Industrial Electronics,* 2nd ed. Boston: PWS–KENT Publishers.

Kosow, I. L. *Control of Electric Machines.* Englewood Cliffs, N.J.: Prentice-Hall, Inc.

Siskind, C. S. *Electrical Control Systems in Industry.* New York: McGraw-Hill, Inc.

Chapter 15: Secondary Unit Substations

Guide for the Application of Valve-Type Surge Arresters for Alternating-Current Systems, ANSI C62.2-1981. New York: American National Standards Institute.

Answers to Selected Problems

Chapter 1

1. 15 Ω
3. 6 A
5. 8 Ω
7. 200 V
9. 480 V
11. (a) 11.18 Ω (b) 0.894 [89.4%] (c) 4606 W
13. 5 A
15. 27.8 A
17. 20

Chapter 2

1. 91.3 lb. ft
3. (a) 900 rpm (b) 94.2 rad/s
5. 1164 rpm
7. 0.83 yr

Chapter 3

1. 750 lx
3. 125 fc
5. (a) 78.3 fc (b) 842 lx
7. 100 lm/ft^2
9. 1398 cd

Chapter 5

1. 500 lx (50 fc)
3. $\rho_{CC} = 75\%$; $\rho_{FC} = 25\%$
5. 0.80
7. 0.56
9. (a) 10.4 ft (b) 14.4 ft
11. 3 rows of 5; $S_W = 14.0$ ft, $S_L = 12.0$ ft
13. 27.0 luminaires
15. 2.13 W/ft^2
17. 0.82 yr

Chapter 6

1. (a) 75 A (b) 1200 A (c) $Z_S = 0.0625$ pu: $I_{SC} = 16.0$ pu
3. 0.015 pu
5. 32,800 A symmetrical

Chapter 7

1. (a) 0.12 s (b) 0.7 s (c) 70 s
3. 1.5 and 2.0 s
5. 125 A

Chapter 8

1. 65 and 24 s
3. 95 and 20 s
5. 2000 A
7. 360 A

Chapter 9

1. 1200 A
3. 8000 A

Chapter 10

1. No. 2 copper
3. No. 3/0 copper
5. 690,000 kW-cycles; extensive damage

Chapter 11

1. 69 A
3. 140 A
5. 118,000 A
7. 2″ C
9. 3½″C, 4-500 MCM, TWH (CU)
11. 2½″C, 4-250 MCM, TWH (CU)
13. 225 A frame, 225 A trip
15. 225 A, high interrupting capacity
17. two parallel runs, each 2″ C, 4-#3/0, XHHW (cu)

Chapter 12

1. Ampacity is 13.2 A; not satisfactory
3. (a) 4 circuits (b) 5 circuits
5. 9 circuits
7. 169 A

Chapter 13

1. No. 8 THW
3. 200 A
5. 100 A, 600 V
7. 60 A, 600 V
9. 250 A fuse; 250 V, 400 A switch
11. No. 4 THW
13. 80 A fuse; 600 V, 100 A switch

Chapter 14

1. (a) Size 3 (b) Size 2 (c) Size 5 (d) Size 4
3. Yes. Maximum protection allowed is 45 A
5. (a) Three vertical sections; 31 space factors used leaving 5 spare
   (b) Standard 600 A bus

Chapter 15

1. I_S = 1203 A; frame size is 1600 A
3. I_S = 2080 A; frame size is 3000 A
5. (b) I_P = 139 A; load-interrupter switch is 5 kV, 600 A
   (c) Transformer cubicle is 90″ wide
   (d) I_S = 2780 A; main bus is 4000 A and main breaker is 4000 A frame; use Unit 5, 34″ wide
   (e) Branch breakers, minimum 1600 A frame with interrupting capacity of 65,000 A sym at 208 V. Four vertical sections, similar to Unit 3, 26″ wide, for 10 branch breakers leaving 2 spaces.
   (f) Overall length of unit substation is 22′0″. Assume 66″ depth.
7. Branch breakers are 600 A frame (combination fused type). Three vertical sections, similar to Unit 2, 18″ wide, for 10 branch breakers leaving 2 spaces. Overall length of unit substation is 17′10″. Minimum room size is 27′10″ by 16′2″.

Chapter 16

1. Z_U = 0.0075 pu
3. I_{SC} = 13,700 A symmetrical
5. I_{SC} = 8130 A symmetrical
7. I_{SC} = 10.700 A symmetrical
9. (a) 35.6 A (b) 16.1 A (c) 38.5 A
   (d) 88.5 A
11. (a) 14.5 s (b) 15.5 s (c) 15 s (d) 15.5 s
13. 1600 A frame, 400 A sensor with LDPU set at 0.9
15. 200 A fuse assembly with 200 A fuse unit. Maximum permitted by code is 250 A.

Modifications to answers to suit Canadian Electrical Code

Chapter 10

1. No. 1/0 copper (service entrance feeders, CSA type TW75)

Chapter 11

1. 61 A (CSA type RW90 conductors)
3. 120 A (CSA type RW75 conductors and CEC Table 2)
7. 2½″ C [CSA type RW90(XLPE) conductors]
9. 3½″ C, 4-300 kcmil, TW75 (Cu)
11. 2½″ C, 4-250 kcmil, TW75 (Cu)
17. Two parallel runs, each 2½″ C, 4-#4/0 RW90(XLPE) Cu

Chapter 12

1. Ampacity is 9.24 A (CSA type TW75 conductors); not satisfactory
5. 10–15 A circuits
7. 190 A

Chapter 13

1. No. 8 TW75
3. 175 A
9. 300 A fuse; 250 V, 400 A switch
11. No. 4 TW75

Chapter 15

7. Minimum room size is 7.44 m by 4.68 m (use 0.80 m allowance for space required for the drawout circuit breakers).

Index